42ND EDITION

KOVELS' Antiques & Collectibles PRICE GUIDE 2010

Black Dog
& Leventhal
Publishers
New York

Published by
Black Dog & Leventhal Publishers, Inc.
151 W. 19th Street
New York, NY 10011

Distributed by
Workman Publishing Company
225 Varick Street
New York, NY 10014

Designed by Sheila Hart Design, Inc.
Manufactured in the United States of America

ISBN-13: 978-1-57912-816-6
Library of Congress Cataloging-in-Publication Data is available on file at
the offices of the publisher.

Paperback
b d f h g e c a

Front cover photographs, from top to bottom:
Roseville Baneda vase, Empire drop leaf table, and merry-go-round toy.
On the spine: German silver bowl.
Back cover photographs, from top to bottom:
Pairpoint puffy lamp with Stratford hummingbird shade,
Chintz Orient stacking teapot set,
and Diamond Dyes cabinet with Evolution of Women panel.

BOOKS BY RALPH AND TERRY KOVEL

American Country Furniture, 1780–1875

A Directory of American Silver, Pewter, and Silver Plate

Kovels' Advertising Collectibles Price List

Kovels' American Antiques 1750–1900

Kovels' American Art Pottery

Kovels' American Collectibles 1900–2000

Kovels' American Silver Marks, 1650 to the Present

Kovels' Antiques & Collectibles Fix-It Source Book

Kovels' Antiques & Collectibles Price Guide

Kovels' Bid, Buy, and Sell Online

Kovels' Book of Antique Labels

Kovels' Bottles Price List

Kovels' Collector's Guide to American Art Pottery

Kovels' Collectors' Guide to Limited Editions

Kovels' Collectors' Source Book

Kovels' Depression Glass & Dinnerware Price List

Kovels' Dictionary of Marks—Pottery and Porcelain, 1650 to 1850

Kovels' Guide to Selling, Buying, and Fixing Your Antiques and Collectibles

Kovels' Guide to Selling Your Antiques & Collectibles

Kovels' Illustrated Price Guide to Royal Doulton

Kovels' Know Your Antiques

Kovels' Know Your Collectibles

Kovels' New Dictionary of Marks—Pottery and Porcelain, 1850 to the Present

Kovels' Organizer for Collectors

Kovels' Price Guide for Collector Plates, Figurines, Paperweights, and Other Limited Edition Items

Kovels' Quick Tips: 799 Helpful Hints on How to Care for Your Collectibles

Kovels' Yellow Pages: A Resource Guide for Collectors

The Label Made Me Buy It: From Aunt Jemima to Zonkers—The Best-Dressed Boxes, Bottles, and Cans from the Past

To Ralph Kovel

Who never knew his work would be acclaimed
as a major reason the "average guy" would start to
collect extraordinary things from the everyday past.
The world of collecting misses him.
His family and friends miss him. So do I.

Terry Kovel

INTRODUCTION

This is the forty-second year *Kovels' Antiques & Collectibles Price Guide* has been published. Many things have changed over the past year. The worldwide recession and the U.S. stock market crash in September 2008 have affected the value of stocks, real estate—and antiques. The absence of eBay as a live online auction as of January 1, 2009, meant that some sales by both auction galleries and shop owners were repositioned. Most large auctions are now held online and on land in real time, so anyone in any country in the world can bid. Prices for items offered by individuals on eBay have dropped; it is said only one-third of the collectibles offered for bids are actually sold. Prices have gone up for some things that have international appeal and down for other things, like World's Fair collectibles, that are not as rare as once thought. Through it all, the malls, shows, and shops have seen a slower economy and lower prices than they could get three years ago. But we have talked to collectors and dealers, and most agree that "good stuff sells" and that well-run shows, shops, and sales are doing "okay." It also means that auction prices are closer to retail than they were before because of the large, new, worldwide pool of bidders.

There is another change. This edition of *Kovels' Antiques & Collectibles Price Guide* is written by its original authors, Ralph and Terry Kovel, but also by their daughter, Kim, who joined the family business after Ralph's death late in 2008. It still has the same reliable content plus the added advantage of having two generations of collectors choosing the content. The format introduced in 2008, with 2,500 color photographs, 44,000 prices, and dozens of added tips about care and facts of interest, was a welcome improvement. This book has the same features. Each photograph is shown with a complete caption that includes the price. The book has color tabs and color-coded paragraphs that make it easy to find the listings you want. And it has a modern, readable typestyle. There are about 775 categories with introductory paragraphs. There have been many changes in corporate ownership over the past year, and we have indicated new owners or new distributors in the paragraphs describing each category. These include Frankoma, Goebel, Hummel, Hutschenreuther, Lenox, Minton, Royal Doulton, Wedgwood, and the Steuben and Waterford glassworks. And, as always, all of the antiques and collectibles priced here were offered for sale during the past year, most of them in the American market.

READ THIS FIRST

This is a book for the collector. We check prices, visit shops, shows, and flea markets, read hundreds of publications and catalogs, check Internet sales and other online services, and decide which antiques and collectibles are of most interest to most collectors. We concentrate on the average pieces in any category. Sometimes high-priced items are included so you will realize that rarities are very valuable.

Examples of furniture, silver, Tiffany, art pottery, and some other items may sell for more than $40,000; we list a few. Most listed pieces cost less than $10,000. The highest price in this book is $301,000 for an illusminated teak library table with glass and metal parts, designed by Pierre Jeanneret about 1966. Another high-priced item is a carved walnut Chippendale wing chair made in Philadelphia in 1770 that sold for $374,500. The lowest price is 25 cents for a small advertising label for Laxal, a medication called "the baby's friend." The smallest item in the book is a 5/8-inch art nouveau sterling silver button picturing Ophelia with long hair and a garland of flowers, $15. The biggest is an architectural gazebo made of cast iron with a dome top and six figural columns, 156 x 118 in., $8,813.

We also include the weird and the wonderful. This year you can find leg irons owned by Houdini and engraved with his name, $8,400. In clothing prices, we list a silk screen-on-paper dress picturing the faces of Universal Studios movie stars, c.1968, 37 ½ in., $1,200. Two guillotines are listed under tool prices. A full-sized hardwood and metal guillotine with 40-pound blade weights, c.1920, 101 x 47 x 40 inches, sold for $26,290. A miniature wood and metal guillotine, an example of prisoner's art made on Devil's Island, 1928, 14 in., brought $598. Another strange item is a patent model of an artificial leg, $880. Sports memorabilia is always popular and often unique. A full-size bicycle ice cream cart for the Good Humor man brought $22,000. A horsehair bridle with Indian designs made by Montana

Correctional prisoners was $588, and a mahogany pool cue cabinet auctioned for $8,050. The strangest piece of furniture is a wooden chair with a carved skeleton back, open rib cage, carved skull, and bone feet. Made in the 1900s, it is 53 x 24 in. and brought $3,068. The history of the chair is a mystery, but we have seen several of these handmade skeleton chairs; they probably were part of a fraternal ritual.

Collecting is alive and well. Although the national economic outlook is gloomy, the prices of antiques and collectibles are "behaving" normally. The high end of the art market has not been as lucky, although even there the very best pieces are bringing record prices. Over the years, we have seen the rise and fall (or sometimes the fall and rise) of Victorian, oak, mid-century modern and shabby country furniture, bottles, trivets, collector plates, plastic, majolica, Royal Doulton, pressed glass, and Depression glass. But through it all, clever collectors and dealers made good buys and profitable sales

When we started collecting, we were young, and antiques dealers and buyers were "old" (in their late fifties and sixties). By 1967, the year our first price book was published, there was a new group of dealers—free-spirited independent entrepreneurs who were willing to gamble on their own talent and taste. Books that explained or priced antiques were not readily available, so collectors depended on dealers. Today the older dealers have retired, younger (under forty years old) dealers are appearing at shows and online, and everyone has access to information on the Internet and in price guides like this one.

There are still bargains to be had, but most are in newer categories like modernist jewelry and twentieth-century studio pottery from England and France. Big is "big." Small sets of figurines or plates are out. But large-scale accent pieces with colors and lines that blend in with modern furnishings—pieces like huge crocks, floor vases, centerpieces, and garden statuary—attract decorators and those with large homes. Anything from clothes and glass to ceramics and furniture that was in the newest style in the 1950s to 1990s is hot. Pieces representing a theme (American Indian, African, Asian, Western, or rustic) all have special buyers. And some old standbys, like toy cars, mechanical banks, war and political memorabilia, and art pottery, are going up in price because they are attracting new buyers. Quality sells high and although the economy is uncertain, it retains its value.

This book seems to have gotten younger over the past forty years. Most items in our original book were made before 1860. Today we list pieces made as recently as 2000, and there is great interest in furniture, glass, and ceramics made since 1950.

The book is about 800 pages long, and crammed full of prices and photographs. We try to have a balanced format—not too many glass, pottery, or collectible items; furniture from the eighteenth through the twentieth centuries; and not too many items that sell for over $5,000. We list a few very expensive pieces so you can realize that a great paperweight may cost $9,000 and an average one only $25. Nearly all the prices are from the American market for the American market. Few European sales are reported. We take the editorial privilege of not including prices we think result from "auction fever." There is a computer-generated index. Use it often. It includes categories and much more. For example, there is a category for Celluloid. Most celluloid will be there, but a toy made of celluloid will be listed under Toy and also indexed under Celluloid. There are also cross-references in the listings and in the paragraphs. But some searching must be done. For example, Barbie dolls are in the Doll category; there is no Barbie category. And when you look at "doll, Barbie," you see a note that Barbie is under "doll, Mattel, Barbie" because most dolls are listed by maker. Where possible, we list the maker at the beginning of an entry, and the size and age at the end.

All photographs and prices are new. Antiques and collectibles pictured are items that were offered for sale or sold for the amount listed in 2008-09. Prices include the buyer's premium. Wherever we had extra space on a page, we filled it with new tips about care of collections and other useful information. Don't discard this book. Old Kovels' price guides should be saved for future reference and for tax and appraisal information.

The prices in this book are reports of the general antiques market. Every price in the book is new. We do not estimate or "update" prices. Prices are either realized prices from auctions or completed sales or they're asking prices; a buyer may have negotiated an asking price to a lower selling price. But no price is an estimate. We do not pay dealers, collectors, or experts to estimate prices. Experience has shown us that estimated prices are usually high or low, but rarely an accurate report. If a price range is given, at least two identical items were offered for sale at different prices. Price ranges are found only in categories like Pressed Glass, where identical items can be identified. If the price is from an auction, it includes the buyer's premium; but like all the prices, it does not include sales tax. Some prices in *Kovels' Antiques & Collectibles Price Guide* may seem high and some may seem low because of regional variations, but each price is one you could have paid for the object somewhere in the United States. Some Internet prices, carefully edited, are included, but we find prices there can be misleading. Because so many non-collectors sell online but know little about the objects they are describing, there are often inaccuracies in the descriptions.

If you are selling your collection, do not expect to get retail value unless you are a dealer. Wholesale prices for antiques are usually 50 percent of retail prices. The antiques dealer must make a profit or go out of business. Internet auction prices are less predictable—because of an international audience and "auction fever," prices can be higher or lower than retail.

RECORD PRICES

ADVERTISING

A.L. Hall shell box: $8,294 for an A.L. Hall (Seattle, Wash.) shell box, with contents, featuring hunter in field, setter with quail in its mouth.

American advertising poster/baseball-related advertising poster: $188,000 for an 1889 Anson-Ewing Beer poster, featuring the two 19th-century baseball stars endorsing "Burke Ale," mounted and framed, 26 x 32 in.

American Ammunition empty shell box: $6,859 for an American Ammunition Co. Smokeless 12-gauge empty shell box, featuring the American flag in the center, surrounded by American shields and red and blue banners, end panel reads "Long Brass, Smokeless Powder, 3 ⅛ Drams – 1 ¼ Oz. No. 7 ½ Chilled."

Winchester 3-panel triangle mobile-style die-cut poster: $13,080 for a Winchester mobile-style die-cut poster, with 3 triangle-shaped panels, one panel each for shotgun shells picturing a quail; .22 ammunition picturing a rabbit; and big game cartridges picturing a big-horned sheep, patented February 9, 1909, by John Ingelstroem Co., 15 x 21 ½ in.

CLOCKS & WATCHES

George Reed pocket watch: $55,000 for a George Reed pivoted detent chronometer pocket watch in 18K gold hunting case, Serial No. 13, c.1865, 54 mm.

Howard clock: $165,900 for a No. 67 regulator oak wall clock by E. Howard & Co., Boston, c.1890, surmounted with a carved steer's head, engraved presentation inscription on brass plate, "Presented by D.W. Hitchcock to the People's National Bank, Marlboro, Mass., November 14, 1892," 104 in. h.

Howard No. 1 banjo clock: $22,000 for an E. Howard & Co. No. 1 eight-day banjo wall clock, fruitwood case, rosewood graining and factory label, c.1890, 50 in.

Howard No. 12 regulator clock: $61,600 for a No. 12 regulator wall clock by E. Howard & Co., c.1875, with special-order base that allows the clock to stand as a floor clock, original hanger still in place, main clock 60 in. h., overall with base 87 in. h.

DECOYS

Enoch Reindahl decoy: $92,000 for a preening mallard drake by Enoch Reindahl.

North Carolina decoy: $269,000 for a ruddy duck decoy by Lee Dudley.

FURNITURE

Duncan Phyfe side chairs: $236,500 for a pair of Duncan Phyfe classical carved and figured mahogany harp-back side chairs, New York, c.1815, 32 ½ in.

Seating furniture: $5,234,500 for a carved walnut Queen Anne compass-seat stool, Philadelphia, c.1750, 15 ⅝ in.

MISCELLANEOUS

Louis Sullivan item at auction: $602,500 for a Chicago Stock Exchange elevator surround by Louis Sullivan, c.1893, cast and wrought iron, manufactured by Winslow Brothers Co., 116 ¾ x 165 x 6 in.

Native American item: $2,185,000 for an 18th-century Northwest Coast Tlingit warrior's helmet mask made from burled spruce, carved in a stylized bear form and painted. The helmet was worn on the top of the head in battle.

Sachem Bitters bottle in pure green: $26,880 for an Old Sachem Bitters and Wigwam Tonic bottle in pure green.

Tennessee sampler: $28,125 for a Tennessee sampler signed "Mary Elizabeth Collins' work, Franklin Tennessee April 1836," featuring 9 different stitching techniques as well as a floral border, vase, basket of flowers, alphabets, and verse, framed, 19 ⅞ in. h. x 19 ⅜ in. w.

Vampire-killing kit: $14,850 for a vampire killing kit complete with stakes, mirrors, gun with silver bullets, crosses, Bible, holy water, candles, and garlic, in an American walnut case with carved cross, c.1800.

POTTERY & PORCELAIN

Occupational shaving mug: $45,000 for an occupational shaving mug titled "Aeronaut" with original newspaper article, mug picturing a man flying through the air hanging from a parachute, HCL mark on bottom. Earlier, at the same auction, an ambulance occupational shaving mug picturing a horse-drawn wagon and driver set the record at $29,000, but was surpassed when the "Aeronaut" shaving mug sold.

Spatterware: $39,780 for a five-color rainbow spatterware platter, red, blue, black, yellow, and green, 13 x 15 ½ in.

Stoneware water cooler: $103,500 for a keg-form stoneware 2-gallon water cooler made by Boyton Pottery, Albany, New York, decorated in cobalt blue with incised figures of birds and fish, 12 ¾ in.

Tennessee pottery: $63,000 for a Tennessee pottery copper-colored redware storage jar, with extruded handles, incised decoration at the handle attachments and stamped name, created by J.A. (John Alexander) Lowe, c.1860, 13 ⅝ in.

Western Pennsylvania stoneware: $65,550 for a Western Pennsylvania stoneware cylindrical wax sealer jar with flared base, painted cobalt blue design of a baseball player's face, side profile shows curled mustache, short sideburn, eye and eyelashes, and baseball cap, c.1875, 8 ¼ in.

SILVER & OTHER METALS

American pewter coffeepot: $315,000 for a William Will pewter coffeepot, c.1764-98, stamped maker's mark, scroll tree handle, gadrooned edges and 5-knuckle hinge, 15 ¾ in. h. x 4 ⅜ in. diam.

American pewter communion service: $269,000 for a 3-piece communion service, each piece inscribed, consisting of flagon, chalice, and paten, by William Will of Philadelphia, 1765, 12-in. flagon with flame finial and domed lid, 7 ½-in. chalice with swelled knop and stepped base, 9-in. salver-shape paten with gadrooned border and zigzag engraving.

SPORTS

1915 Philadelphia Phillies press pin: $15,275 for a 1915 Philadelphia Phillies press pin, a medallion suspended from a red ribbon lettered "Press" and attached to the pin, issued for the 1915 World Series against the Boston Red Sox, manufactured by J.E. Caldwell & Co., 4 ¾ in. h.

1950s non-Hall of Famer uniform: $22,325 for a complete St. Louis Cardinals home uniform (jersey, pants, and socks) worn by Ken Boyer during his 1955 rookie season.

Babe Ruth Butter Cream Confectionery card: $111,625 for the 1933 R306 Butter Cream Confectionery card of Babe Ruth saved in the same family since 1933.

Babe Ruth rookie baseball card: $517,000 for the 1914 Baltimore News Babe Ruth rookie card in very good condition.

Baseball photograph from the 1860s: $58,750 for an 1862 Knickerbockers baseball team photograph.

Casey Stengel Old Mill Tobacco card: $41,125 for a 1911 T210 Old Mill Tobacco card of Casey Stengel.

Fishing creel: $23,444 for a potbellied fishing creel made of heavily stitched leather, with white painted interior, brass hinged leather lid embossed with a sunburst pattern, brass hasp, brass plaque engraved with name and address, and fitted with 5 brass plaques dated 1890-94 with details of trout and grayling caught.

Jim Brown Cleveland Browns jersey: $70,500 for a Cleveland Browns football jersey worn by Jim Brown, 1962-65.

Jim Thorpe Sporting News No. 176 baseball card: $44,062 for the No. 176 Jim Thorpe baseball card from the 1916 M101-5 Sporting News set.

Nineteenth-century baseball card: $141,000 for the 1887 Kalamazoo Bats tobacco card of John Ward.

Signed Hall of Fame postcard for any player: $44,062 for a sepia Hall of Fame postcard signed by Babe Ruth, issued between 1939 and 1943.

TOYS, DOLLS & GAMES

Lehmann Anxious Bride toy: $7,200 for a Lehmann Anxious Bride toy, driver of a 3-wheeled vehicle pulling, in attached cart, a distressed fiancée, who raises her arm with a tissue in her hand, original box, French label, 8 ½ in.

Lehmann Autobus toy: $14,400 for a lithographed double-decker red bus marked "Lehmann's Autobus 590," spoke wheels, curved stairway, original box, patented 1903, 8 ¼ x 5 in.

Lehmann Duo toy: $6,325 for a Lehmann Duo windup toy, whimsical rabbit standing on an egg on wheels being pulled by a rooster, original box has blue and white lithographed paper label, 7 in.

Lehmann Lila toy: $7,200 for a Lehmann Lila tin windup toy of a hansom cab driver with 2 women passengers, one woman with umbrella hits dog over the head, painted, original box, 5 x 5 ½ in.

Lehmann Zulu toy: $5,750 for a Lehmann Zulu windup toy, lithographed black driver of ostrich-pulled cart, head swings back and forth, toy is also a bank with slot in back, original box, label, 7 ½ in.

Marklin "Fidelitas" Clown Car Train toy: $103,500 for a 1909 Marklin "Fidelitas" clown-car train, features four seated clowns in separate 3-wheeled cars with different props in their hands, a hoop, flowers, and a sign that reads "Fidelitas," hand painted, Germany, 37 ½ in. (from the Donald Kaufman collection).

Marx play set: $15,255 for a Wagon Train play set with original box (based on the television show) made by Marx Toys, Series 5000, Stock No. 4888, c.1960.

Schoenhut milk wagon toy: $10,925 for a St. Clair Dairy Co. milk wagon, by Schoenhut Toy Co., with driver, milk crates and brown horse, c.1925, 23 in. l.

A NOTE TO COLLECTORS

You already know this is a great overall price guide for antiques and collectibles. Each entry is current, every photograph is new, and all prices are accurate.

There is also another Kovel publication designed to keep you up-to-the-minute in the world of collecting. Things change quickly. Important sales produce new record prices. Fakes appear. Rarities are discovered. To keep up with developments, you can read *Kovels on Antiques and Collectibles*, our monthly newsletter. It is now available by subscription in two forms, a print edition that is mailed and an electronic format that is included in the searchable archives on our website, www.Kovels.com. Both have the identical current information on collecting. They are filled with color photographs, about forty per issue. The newsletter reports prices, trends, auction results, Internet sales, and other news for collectors as it happens. Join the community of collectors at www.Kovels.com to keep up on the buy-sell world of antiques. Register; there is no charge for most of the information on the site, including our directory of services for collectors and dealers. Other information, including a database of pottery and porcelain marks, is available for a fee.

HOW TO USE THIS BOOK

There are a few rules for using this book. Each listing is arranged in the following manner: CATEGORY (such as Pressed Glass), OBJECT (such as vase), DESCRIPTION (as much information as possible about size, age, color, and pattern). Some types of glass, pottery, and silver are exceptions to this rule. These are listed CATEGORY, PATTERN, OBJECT, DESCRIPTION. All items are presumed to be in good condition and undamaged, unless otherwise noted. In most sections, if a maker's name is easily recognized, like Gustav Stickley, we include it near the beginning of the entry. If the maker is obscure, the name may be at the end.

Many of the general glass entries are in special categories: Glass-Art, Glass-Blown, Glass-Bohemian, Glass-Contemporary, Glass-Midcentury, and Glass-Venetian. Major glass factories are listed under factory names. Well-known types of glass, such as Cut, Pressed, Depression, Carnival, etc., can be found in their own categories. You will find silver flatware in either Silver Flatware Plated or Silver Flatware Sterling. There is also a section for Silver Plate, which includes coffeepots, trays, and other plated pieces. Most solid or sterling silver is listed by country, so look for Silver-American, Silver-Danish, Silver-English, etc. Silver jewelry is listed under Jewelry. Most pottery and porcelain is listed by factory name, such as Weller; by item, such as Calendar Plate; in sections like Dinnerware or Kitchen; or in a special section, such as Pottery-Art, Pottery-Contemporary, Pottery-Midcentury, etc.

Sometimes we make arbitrary decisions. Fishing has its own category, but hunting is part of the larger category called Sports. We have omitted all guns except toys. It is not legal to sell weapons without a special license, so guns are not part of the general antiques market. Airguns, BB guns, rocket guns, and others are listed in the Toy section. Everything is listed according to the computer alphabetizing system. This means words such as "Mt." are alphabetized as "M-T," not as "M-O-U-N-T." All numerals are before all letters; thus "2" comes before "A."

We made several editorial decisions. A butter dish is a "butter." A salt dish is called a "salt" to differentiate it from a saltshaker. It is always "sugar and creamer," never "creamer and sugar." Political collectors often refer to "pinbacks," the round celluloid or tin pins decorated with candidates' names and faces. We use the word "button" instead of "pinback." The word "button" is also used when referring to fasteners on clothing. Where one dimension is given, it is the height; or if the object is round, the dimension is the diameter. The height of a picture is listed before width. Glass is clear unless a color is indicated.

Entries are listed alphabetically, but idiosyncrasies of language remain. There is some confusion caused by words with more than one meaning, like iron (the metal) and iron (the pressing tool) or enamel (granite ware) and enamel (painted decoration on glass) and enamel (ground glass heated on metal to make an ashtray or piece of jewelry). We have indexed these so the appropriate pieces are listed together.

Some antiques terms, such as "Sheffield" or "Pratt," have two meanings. Read the paragraph headings to know the meaning used. All category headings are based on the language of the average person, and we use terms like "mud figures" even if not technically correct.

This book does not include price listings for fine art paintings, antiquities, stamps, coins, or most types of books. Big Little Books and similar children's books are included. Comic books are listed only in special categories like Superman, but original comic art and cels are listed in Animation Art.

Prices for items pictured can be found in the appropriate category. Look for the matching entry with the abbreviation "Illus." The picture will be nearby.

Because of the computer, the book can be produced quickly. The last entries are added in June; the book is available in September. But human help finds prices and checks accuracy. We read everything at least three times, sometimes more. We edit more than 55,000 entries down to the approximately 47,000 entries found here. We correct spelling, remove incorrect data, write category paragraphs, and decide on new categories. We proofread copy and prices many times, but there will always be some misspelled words and other errors. Information in the paragraphs is updated each year and this year more than forty updates and additions were made.

Prices are reported from all parts of the United States, Canada, and Europe, converted to U.S. dollars at the time of the sale. The average rate of exchange between June 2008 and June 2009 was $1 U.S. to about $1.16 Canadian, .73 (Euro), and £.62 (British Pound). Prices are from auctions, shops, Internet sales, and shows. Every price is checked for accuracy, but we are not responsible for errors.

We cannot answer your letters asking for price information, but please write if you have any requests for categories to be included in future editions or any corrections to the paragraphs or prices.

When you see us at shows and flea markets, stop and say hello. Don't be surprised if we ask for your suggestions. You can write to us at P.O. Box 22200-K, Beachwood, Ohio 44122, or visit us on our website, www.Kovels.com.

TERRY KOVEL & KIM KOVEL
July 2009

ACKNOWLEDGMENTS

The world of antiques and collectibles is filled with people who have answered our every request for help. Dealers, auction houses and shops have given advice and opinions, sent pictures and prices, and made suggestions for changes. Special thanks to all of them: Alderfer Auction Co., Auction Team Koln, Belhorn Auction Services, Bertoia Auctions, Brunk Auctions, Cincinnati Art Galleries, Conestoga Auction Co., Copake Auction, Cowan's Auctions, DuMouchelles, Early Auction Co., Eastbourne Auction, Garth's Auctions, Glass Works Auctions, Green Valley Auctions & Jeffrey S. Evans, Hake's Americana & Collectibles, Heritage Auction Galleries, Jackson's International Auctioneers, James D. Julia Auctioneers, Lang's Sporting Collectables, Leland Little Auctions, McMasters Harris Auction Co., Monsen & Baer, Morphy Auctions, Neal Auction Co., Noel Barrett Antiques & Auctions, Richard Opfer Auctioneering, Pook & Pook, Rago Arts & Auction Center, Rich Penn Auctions, RSL Auction Co., Ruby Lane, Showtime Auction Services, Skinner, Sollo Rago Modern Auctions, Sotheby's, Stein Auction Co., Strawser Auctions, Tom Harris Auctions, Treadway Gallery and Woody Auction Co.

To the others who knowingly or unknowingly contributed to this book we say "thank you": Aberdeen Auctions, Aleph-Bet Books, Alex Cooper Auctioneers, Alistair Crawford, Allard Auctions, American Bottle Auctions, American Cut Glass Association, Anderson Auctions, Antique Bottle & Glass Collector, Antique Fan Collectors Association, Auction Gallery of the Palm Beaches, Austin Auction Co., BBR Auctions, Be-hold, Bill Hood & Sons Auctions, Bob Courtney Auctions, Bonhams & Butterfields, B.S. Slosberg Auctioneers, Burley Auction Group, Cairns Antiques, Case Antiques Auctions, Carlton Antique Toys, Charles Gilbert Toys, Christie's, Circle M Auctions, Clars Auction Gallery, Cottone Auctions, Crosstie Glass, Crown Jewels of the Wire, Cyr Auction Gallery, Dan Ripley's Antique Helper, Dennis Auction Service, Depew Auction Gallery, Dirk Soulis Auctions, Doyle New York, Early American History Auctions, Eldred's Auction, Faganarms, Bottles & Extras, Fenton Art Glass Collectors, Fontaine's Auction Gallery, Frank & Grace Zuest, Freeman's Auctioneers, Glass Cupboard, Grey Flannel Auctions, Guernsey's, Halls Fine Art, Harlowe-Powell Auction Gallery, Heisey Collectors of America, Hollywood Poster Auction, Homestead Auctions, Ivey-Selkirk Auctioneers, J. Greenstein & Co., JK Galleries, John Toomey Gallery, Joy Luke Auctioneers, Just Art Pottery, Kaminski Auctions, Ken Farmer Auctions, Keystone Toy Trader, L.H. Selman, Last Moving Picture Co., Leonard Auction, Leslie Hindman Auctioneers, Live Free or Die Antique Tool Auctions, Lloyd Ralston Gallery, Los Angeles Modern Auctions, Love's Auctioneers, Manion's International Auction House, Mastro Auctions, Matthews Auctions, McCoy Lovers' NMXpress, McCulloh's Antiques & Collectibles, McMurray Antiques & Auctions, Mechantiques, Michael Ivankovich Antiques & Auction Co., National Association of Aladdin Lamp Collectors, National Association of Breweriana Advertising, National Association of Milk Bottle Collectors, National Toothpick Holder Collector's Society, New Orleans Auction Galleries, Norman C. Heckler & Co., Northeast Auctions, O'Gallerie, O.J. Club, Old Barn Auction, Old Toy Shop, Old Toy Soldier Auction, Page Button Auctions, Paper & Advertising Collectors' Marketplace, Past Tyme Pleasures, PBA Galleries, Pewter Collectors Club of America, Philip Weiss Auctions, Phoebus Auction Gallery, American Political Items Collectors, Potteries Specialists Auctions, Quinn & Waverly Auction Galleries, Rachel Davis Fine Arts, Randy Inman Auctions, Red Wing Collectors Society, Richard D. Hatch & Associates, Robert Edward Auctions, Russ Cochran's Comic Art Auction, San Rafael Auction Gallery, Savoia's Auction, R.O. Schmitt Fine Arts, Seeck Auctions, Serious Toyz, Showplace Antique Center, Silver Magazine, Simmons & Co. Auctioneers, Sloans & Kenyon, Smith House Toys & Auction Co., Southern Folk Pottery Collectors Society, Stanton's Auctioneers, Stephen Bennett Auctions, Steve Butler, Swann Auction Galleries, Tea Leaf Club International, Team's Tiffany Treasures, Ted Kromer, Theriault's, Thomaston Place Auction Galleries, The Internet Antique Shop, Toy Shop, Treasures of Yesterday, Trocadero, Vicki & Bruce Waasdorp, Victorian Casino Antique Auction, Vintage Jewelry, Vintage Treasures, W. Yoder Auction, William J. Jenack Auctioneers, William Morford Auctions, Willis Henry Auctions and Yankee Toys.

Our publisher, Black Dog & Leventhal, and its president, J.P. Leventhal, have continued to suggest and implement improvements to this book. There are added improvements in design and technology that add to the speed of production and the ease of use. Thanks to J.P. Leventhal; Camille March, our editor; and their staff: True Sims, production director; Judy Courtade and Maureen Winter, sales; and Liz Hartman, publicity. Mary Flower, Georgia Maas, and Robin Perlow did the job of copyediting and proofreading the entire book and found the tiniest of errors.

Thanks to Sheila Hart and her assistant, Mike Levay, who put all the prices, photographs, and paragraphs together and solved creative problems to create the look and content of *Kovels' Antiques & Collectibles Price Guide 2010.*

The details and hard work required to record prices, assemble photos and information, check accuracy and spelling, and solve many other problems are all done by our Kovel staff. We thank Carmie Amata, Lisa Bell, Grace DeFrancisco, Marcia Goldberg, Katie Karrick, Kim Kovel, Liz Lillis, Mary Ellen Malone, Tina McBean, Renee McRitchie, Nancy Saada, Brooke Seaman, Julie Seaman, Nikki Seaman, June Smith, and Cherrie Smrekar. Pictures come from many sources and they were all sized and digitally enhanced by Karen Kneisley, our photo editor. Gay Hunter, our book editor, always worries the most about the book. She kept our records and made sure all of us were on track and on schedule. She read and reviewed pages of prices, corrected our spelling errors, and handled computer problems. Together we solved problems like changing paragraph information when a company closed or was purchased. Thanks to all of them. We have what we are sure is our best book ever. We know that the book is possible only because of the group effort, even though it is our names that appear on the cover.

A. WALTER watchmade pate-de-verre glass under contract at the Daum glassworks from 1908 to 1914. He decorated pottery during his early years in his studio in Sevres, where he also developed his formula for pale, translucent pate-de-verre. He started his own firm in Nancy, France, in 1919. Pieces made before 1914 are signed *Daum, Nancy* with a cross. After 1919 the signature is *A. Walter Nancy*.

Figurine, Bird, Mottled Blue, Signed, c.1926, 4 In. . . . *illus* 1420.00
Figurine, Frog, Lily Pad, Green, A. Walter Nancy & Berge, 1920, 4 In. . . . 5500.00
Inkwell, Lizard, Bee, Orange To Mustard Ground, Signed, 4 In. . . . *illus* 10200.00
Paperweight, Duck Swimming In Stream, Green, Impressed, 3 ¼ In. . . . 800.00
Pendant, Triangle, Iguana, Yellow, Berry Branch, Orange Tassel Cord, Signed AW, 3 In. . . . 1150.00
Sculpture, Woman, Yellow Nude, Long Red Hair, c.1920, 10 In. . . . 5192.00
Tray, Leaf, Lizard, Green, Marked, A. Walter Nancy, 2 x 8 ½ x 2 In. . . . 3100.00

ABC plates, or children's alphabet plates, were most popular from 1780 to 1860, but are still being made. The letters on the plate were meant as teaching aids for children learning to read. The plates were made of pottery, porcelain, metal, or glass. Mugs and other items were also made with alphabet decorations.

Plate, 2 Boys, Hitting Sleeping Man With Stick, Transfer, Marked, Elsmore & Son, 7 ⅛ In. . . . 40.00
Plate, 4 Women, Soared In The Swing Half Pleased, Blue Transfer, Green Border, 5 ⅛ In. . . . 140.00
Plate, American Sports, Base Ball, Black Transfer, Soft Paste, Staffordshire, c.1850, 8 In. . . . 500.00
Plate, Boy & Girl, Embossed, Tin, 5 ½ In. . . . 40.00
Plate, Cat's Learning Alphabet, Embossed, Gold Line, 7 ¼ In. . . . 50.00
Plate, Clock, School, Dinner-To-Bed, Red Rim, Flow Blue, Marked, LS, 8 In. . . . 125.00
Plate, Clockface Center, Brown Transfer, Alphabet, Months & Dates, 7 ⅜ In. . . . 275.00
Plate, Cock Robin, Tin, 8 In. . . . *illus* 50.00
Plate, Eagle & Shield, Centennial, Embossed, Tin, 6 ¼ In. . . . 150.00
Plate, Elephant & Riders, Man Holding U.S. Flag, Clear . . . 30.00
Plate, Family Scene, Outdoors, Lake, Boat, Mulberry Transfer, 6 ¾ In. . . . 55.00
Plate, Geo. McClellan, Union General, Troops, Black Transfer, 7 In. . . . 358.00
Plate, Hay Wagon, Red Rope Border, Transfer, Staffordshire, 6 In. . . . 30.00
Plate, Independence Hall, Philadelphia, Brown, Green Transfer, 7 In. . . . 25.00
Plate, Juvenile Companions, Jump Tom Jump, Red Transfer, Pearlware, c.1840 . . . 90.00
Plate, Landscape Scene, Mulberry Transfer, 6 ¾ In. . . . 55.00
Plate, Lincoln Portrait, Multicolored, 1860s, 6 In. . . . 1554.00
Plate, Tin, Profile Ulysses S. Grant, 5 ½ In. . . . 155.00
Plate, Ulysses S. Grant, Military Attire, Black Transfer, 1860s, 5 In. . . . 287.00
Plate, Who Killed Cock Robin, I Killed Cock Robin, Tin, Raised Letters, 19th Century, 7 ¾ In. 65.00

ABINGDON POTTERY was established in 1908 by Raymond E. Bidwell as the Abingdon Sanitary Manufacturing Company. The company started making art pottery in 1934. The factory ceased production of art pottery in 1950.

ABINGDON MADE IN U.S.A.

Bookends, Horse Heads, Black, 6 ½ x 6 x 3 ½ In. . . . 100.00
Bookends, Sea Gulls, White, 6 In. . . . 150.00
Bowl, Blue Gray, Shell, Ribbed, Scalloped, 12 x 7 ¾ In. . . . 35.00
Candleholder, Pink, Leaf Shape, 3 ½ x 4 In., Pair . . . 18.00
Console, Pink, Scroll Handles, 14 ¼ x 4 ⅛ In. . . . 23.00
Cookie Jar, Hippo, No. 549, Paper Tag, c.1942, 8 ½ x 7 ½ In. . . . 185.00
Cookie Jar, Humpty Dumpty, 11 In. . . . 258.00
Flowerpot, Saucer, Peach, Flared, Ribs, 5 ¼ x 5 ¾ In. . . . 22.00
Planter, Pink, 9 ¾ x 7 x 1 ¾ In. . . . 22.00
Planter, Window Box, Aqua, 10 x 3 x 3 ¾ In. . . . 36.00
Vase, Beige, Scrolls, Marked, 8 In. . . . 75.00
Vase, Beige High Glaze, Vertical Scrolls On Neck, 8 In. . . . 83.00
Vase, Blue Wave, Original Foil Label, 10 ¾ x 11 ½ In. . . . 28.00
Vase, Cornucopia, Pink, Raised White Star Flower, 1947-48, 4 ½ In., 4 ¼ x 3-In. Base . . . 36.00
Vase, Double Cornucopia, White, Ribbed, Scalloped Top, 11 In. . . . 35.00
Vase, Pink, Raised White Flowers, Scalloped Top, 8 ¾ In. . . . 40.00
Vase, Raised Egret, Grasses, White, Scalloped Top, Trumpet Shape, 13 ⅞ In. . . . 195.00
Vase, Sailing Ship On Both Sides, Blue, 7 In. . . . 40.00
Vase, Sailing Ship On Both Sides, Green, 7 In. . . . 25.00
Vase, Scroll, Beige High Glaze, Marked, 8 In. . . . *illus* 33.00
Wall Pocket, Fern Leaf, Green, Stamped, 9 In. . . . 80.00

ADAMS china was made by William Adams and Sons of Staffordshire, England. The firm was founded in 1769 and became part of the Wedgwood Group in 1966. The name *Adams* appeared on various items through 1998. All types of tablewares and useful wares were made. Other pieces of Adams may be found listed under Flow Blue and Tea Leaf Ironstone.

Bowl, Dessert, Blue Calyx Ware, Pink & Green, 6 In. . . . 8.00

A. Walter, Figurine, Bird, Mottled Blue, Signed, c.1926, 4 In.
$1420.00

A. Walter, Inkwell, Lizard, Bee, Orange To Mustard Ground, Signed, 4 In.
$10200.00

ABC, Plate, Cock Robin, Tin, 8 In.
$50.00

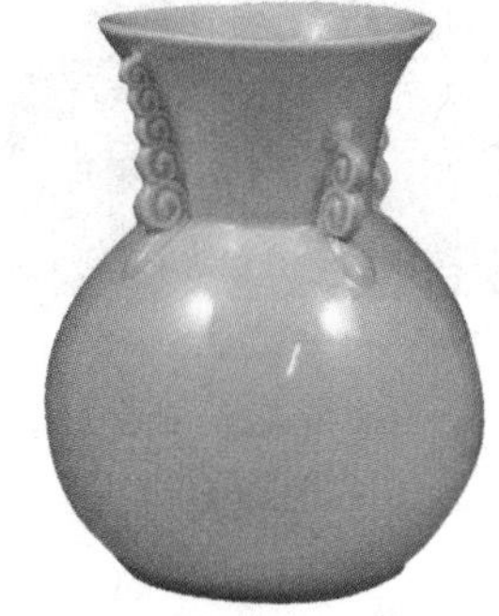

Abingdon, Vase, Scroll, Beige High Glaze, Marked, 8 In.
$33.00

As always, the edited listings in *Kovels' Antiques & Collectibles Price Guide 2010* aren't available on any website, but readers should visit Kovels.com for information on trends, tips, reproductions, marks, old prices, and more!

Adams, Jardiniere, Figures, Dark Blue Ground, Jasperware, Marked, J.C., 1890s, 8 ⅝ In.
$100.00

Adams, Plate, Kyber, Flow Blue, 8 ⅞ In.
$125.00

Advertising, Apron, B H Hershey Coal, Manheim, Pa.
$30.00

Bowl, Fairy Villas, Flow Blue, c.1891, 10 ¼ In., 2 Piece 11.80
Bowl, Vegetable, Bologna, Man Serenading Woman, Brown Transfer, Oval, 10 x 8 In., Pair... 207.00
Bowl, Vegetable, Cover, Kyber, 19th Century, 7 x 11 In. 168.00
Bowl, Vegetable, Oval, Vermont, 9 ¾ x 7 ¼ x 2 ¼ In. 18.00
Butter, Cover, Ironstone, White, Ribbed Cover, Tab Handles, c.1865, 9 x 2 ½ In. 95.00
Candlestick, King Henry VI, Roses Of York & Lancaster, 8 In., Pair 25.00
Flowerpot, Undertray, Adams' Rose, Red, Blue Spatter, 5 ½ In. 761.00
Humidor, Macbeth, 6 ¼ In. 28.00
Jardiniere, Figures, Dark Blue Ground, Jasperware, Marked, J.C., 1890s, 8 ⅝ In. .... *illus* 100.00
Jardiniere, Women, Trees, Birds, Jasperware, Blue & White, 8 ½ x 8 In. 250.00
Jug & Basin, Blue Spatter, Scalloped Edge, Ribbed Sides, Landscape, c.1850, 11 & 13 In. 374.00
Mug, Coffee, Baltic, Blue & White, 3 In. 6.00
Pitcher, Aurora On Clouds, Grape Border, Black, Basalt, c.1780, 4 In. 170.00
Pitcher, Persia, Blue Transferware, 10 ½ In. 350.00
Plate, Adams' Rose, Red Flower, Green Leaves, Blue, Spatter, Paneled, 8 ⅛ In. 66.00
Plate, Adams' Rose, Ironstone, 9 ⅞ x 14 In. 121.00
Plate, Bread & Butter, Vermont, 6 In. 4.00
Plate, Dessert, Blue Calyx Ware, Center Flower, Pink & Green, 5 ⅞ In. 6.00
Plate, Dinner, Claudette, Oriental Scene, 10 ⅛ In. 5.25
Plate, Dinner, White, Ribbed Inner Border, 10 In. 5.00
Plate, Fairy Villas, Flow Blue, 9 In. 75.00
Plate, Fountain, Purple & Black, 7 In. 85.00
Plate, Jeddo, Flow Blue Transferware, 14-Sided, 10 In. 49.00
Plate, Kyber, Flow Blue, 8 ⅞ In. .... *illus* 125.00
Plate, Luncheon, Baltic, Blue & White, 8 In. 5.50
Plate, Red, Blue, Green, Spatter, Scalloped Edge, Impressed, 8 In. 143.00
Plate, Salad, Regent, 7 ⅞ In. 15.00
Plate, Seasons, Brown Transferware, Beaded Scalloped Edge, 10 ½ In. 75.00
Plate, Soup, Fountain, Purple & Black, 10 ½ In. 200.00
Plate, Soup, Isola Bella, Blue Transferware, 14-Sided, 10 ½ In. 125.00
Plate, Temple Warriors, Green & Red, Scalloped Border, 9 ¼ In. 200.00
Plate, Temple Warriors, Red Transferware, 8 In. 125.00
Plate, Temple Warriors, Red Transferware, 9 In. 125.00
Plate, Tonquin, Flow Blue, Paneled, 14-Sided, c.1845, 8 ½ In. 100.00
Plate, View Near Conway, New Hampshire, Red Transferware, 9 In. 175.00
Platter, Claudette, Oriental Scene, 2 Women, River, Black & White Border, 11 ¾ In. 12.00
Platter, Country Manor, Cattle In Foreground, Blue Transfer, 9 ¾ x 7 ¾ In. 345.00
Platter, Palestine, Blue Transferware, 15 ½ x 12 ½ In. 335.00
Slop Bowl, The Sower, Red & White, 3 ½ x 6 ¼ In. 85.00
Teapot, Ironstone, White, Hexagonal Shape, 1950s, 7 ½ In. 65.00
Teapot, The Sower, Horses, Flower Finial, Red & White, 8 ½ In. 200.00
Tobacco Jar, Lid, Winged Dragons, Blue, White, 5 ½ In. 235.00
Toddy Plate, Red Transferware, 5 In. 65.00
Tureen, Cover, Berlin Groups, Flow Blue, 8-Sided, c.1860, 9 In. 83.00
Tureen, Sauce, Cover, White, Loops & Bud, Ironstone, Bud Finial, 8 x 7 In. 175.00

ADVERTISING containers and products sold in the old country store are now all collectibles. These stores, with the crackers in a barrel and a potbellied stove, are a symbol of an earlier, less hectic time. Listed here are many of the advertising items. Other similar pieces may be found under the product name, such as Planters Peanuts. We have tried to list items in the logical places, so large store fixtures will be found under the Architectural category, enameled tin dishes under Graniteware, paper items in the Paper category, etc. Store fixtures, cases, signs, and other items that have no advertising as part of the decoration are listed in the Store category. The early Dr Pepper logo included a period after "Dr," but it was dropped in 1950. We list all Dr Pepper items without a period so they alphabetize together. For more prices, go to Kovels.com.

Ad, Flip, Hammondsport Wine Co., New York, 3 Pages, Cardboard, 1892, 3 ½ x 6 In. 55.00
Apron, B H Hershey Coal, Manheim, Pa. .... *illus* 30.00
Apron, J.H. Reitz & Sons Building Supplies, Millway, Pa. 20.00
Ashtray, Be Alumite Wise, Figural, Owl, Bisque, Glass Eyes, 1930s, 8 ½ In. 115.00
Ashtray, Davis The Barber-Durant, Partially Dressed Woman, Phone, Yellow, Tin 60.00
Ashtray, Dr Pepper, Green, Red, Marked, Sample 580, ½ x 3 ¾ x 6 In. 20.00
Ashtray, Lemp Beer, Original Lager, Dark Purple, Gold Trim, Tin, 5 ¼ In. 60.00
Ashtray, Noxzema, Blue Glass, 1920s, 5 In. 110.00
Ashtray, Smokey The Bear, Tin Lithograph, Smokey On Both Sides, 1950s, 4 x 4 In. 45.00
Automaton, Wilson Whiskey, Soldier, Bends, Eyes Light Up, Wood, Composition, 48 In. 1900.00
Awning, Dr Pepper, Porcelain, c.1935, 46 x 42 In. 3025.00

Bag, Flour, Bob White Milling Co., 12 Lb. 40.00
Bag Holder, Wood Goodard Peck Grocery, Stenciled Country Leaves, Bags, 16 x 15 In. 780.00
Banner, Brown's Mule Chewing Tobacco, Kicking For, Cloth, 1920s, 36 x 48 In. 260.00
Banner, Cetacolor Soap, Glass, Frame, c.1910, 24 x 36 In. 144.00
Banner, Frank's Mentholated White Pine Cough Syrup, Canvas, c.1900, 29 x 85 In. 558.00
Banner, Lee Riders, Authentic Cowboy Pants, Rider On Horse, 36 x 48 In. 350.00
Banner, Town Talk Bread, 4th Of July, 35 In. 20.00
Banner, Town Talk Bread, Golden Harvest, 35 ½ In. 20.00
Banner, Town Talk Bread, Vacation, 35 ½ In. 40.00
Banner, Try Frank's Rheumatic Capsules, Canvas, Black Paint, c.1900, 29 x 85 In. 264.00
Barrel, Heinz, Mince Meat, Wood, Paper Label, Handle, 11 x 8 ¼ In. 385.00
Barrel, Washburn Gold Metal Flour, Wood, Paper Label, 28 In. 193.00
Belt Buckle, Coors Beer, Cast Brass, Recycle Logos On Back, 3 ¾ x 12 ¼ In. 36.00
Bench, Poll-Parrot Shoes, Animal Seat Dividers, Painted, 1950s, 35 x 96 In. .... *illus* 4400.00
Bench, Red Goose School Shoes, 3-Seat, 62 x 36 In. 275.00
Bin, A&P, Bulk Store, Hinged Lid, Red, Greek Key, Logo, Wood Floor, 18 x 30 In. 115.00
Bin, Coffee, A&P, Wood, Nailed Construction, Red, Black, Yellow Ground, 30 x 18 In. 330.00
Bin, Evans Coffee, Fresh Roasted, Orange, Red, White, 19 x 13 x 19 In. .... 350.00 to 403.00
Bin, Huyler's Soda Cocoa, Tin, 19 In. 77.00
Bin, Johnson's Peacemaker Coffee, Cabin, Tin Lithograph, c.1900, 28 x 24 In. 2475.00
Bin, Lipton's Tea, Hinged Lid, Wood, Stenciling, Slant Top, 31 x 23 In. 225.00
Bin, Nectar Coffee, Fresh Roasted, Blue, Yellow, 20 In. 345.00
Book Ledger Marker, Aetna Insurance Co., Hartford, Conn., Tin Lithograph, 12 ¼ In. 400.00
Book Ledger Marker, American Line, Red Star Line, Tin Lithograph, 1821, 12 In. 600.00
Book Ledger Marker, American Writing Machine Co., Calligraphy, Tin, 12 ¼ In. 900.00
Book Ledger Marker, Guardian Assurance Co. Of London, Tin Lithograph, 1821, 12 ¼ In. 150.00
Book Ledger Marker, State Mutual Life Assurance Co., Tin Lithograph, 1844, 12 ½ In. 450.00
Book Ledger Marker, Western Assurance Co., Toronto, Tin Lithograph, 1851, 12 ¼ In. 100.00
Booklet, Warner's Log Cabin Sarsaparilla, Remedies, 5 ½ x 5 In., 32 Pages 33.00
Booklet, Warner's Safe Cure, Woman Sitting On Safe, 8 ½ x 5 ¾ In., 32 Pages 292.00
Books may be included in the Paper category.
Bootjack, Use Musselman's Plug Tobacco, Cast Iron, 1910, 9 ¾ In. .... 176.00 to 220.00
Bottle Carrier, 7Up, You Like It, It Likes You, White, Metal, Handle, 1940s, 4 x 11 x 9 In. 40.00
Bottle Carrier, Donald Duck Cola, 6 Bottles, Cardboard, c.1950, 7 x 8 In. 230.00
Bottle Carrier, Ma's Old Fashion Root Beer, Wood, 1941, 11 x 16 x 8 In. 88.00
Bottle Openers are listed in their own category.
Bottle Topper, Ma's Old Fashion Root Beer, Die Cut Cardboard, 1950s, 11 x 6 ½ In. 115.00
Bottles are listed in their own category.
Box, Adams' Tutti Frutti Brand, Gum, Little Boy With Gum, Cardboard, 4 x 8 In. 175.00
Box, Ball Wax Sealing Fruit Jar Rings, 1 Dozen, Contents, c.1900, 3 ½ In. 275.00
Box, Barker's Special Poultry Remedy, Chicken, Contents, Sealed, 8 x 4 ¾ In. 60.00
Box, Colorado Rocky Mountain Cough & Catarrh Root, Wrapper, Sealed, 3 x 3 ½ In. 22.00
Box, Crosman Seed Co., Red, White, Marked, E E Kready, 1925, 12 ¼ In. 50.00
Box, Diehl's Condition Powders, For Horses, Cattle, Swine, Contents, 6 ½ x 3 ½ In. 176.00
Box, Display, Bubblegum, Spins & Needles, Singers, 5 Cent, Empty, 1960, 8 x 4 In. 480.00
Box, Dr. Matchette's Nerviti For The Heart, Blood, Nerves, Yellow, Contents, 3 x 4 In. 49.00
Box, Dr Pepper, Pony Pack, Wood, 1930-40, 7 ¾ x 8 ½ x 5 ½ In. 150.00
Box, Dr Pepper, Wood, 6-Pack, 1930-40, 9 ½ x 8 x 5 ½ In. 175.00
Box, Dr. Haines' Golden Remedy For The Liquor Habit, 3, 3 x 4 In. 88.00
Box, Dr. LeGear's Poultry Worm Powder, 50 Cents, Contents, 1 ½ Lb., 7 x 4 ½ In. 165.00
Box, Dr. Lesure's Lice & Flea Powder, Paper Label, Dovetailed, 10 ½ x 8 x 6 In. 232.00
Box, Drover's Hog Cure, Prevents Hog Cholera & Kindred Diseases, 7 x 5 x 3 In. 121.00
Box, El Bubble, Children's Gum Cigars, Indian, 8 ¼ In. 20.00
Box, Ferry's Seed Sales, 10 Cents Per Pack, Wood, 19th Century, 3 x 24 x 16 In. 50.00
Box, Flyswatter, Flies Spread Germs, Wire, Gatch Wire Goods, 23 ½ In. 40.00
Box, Franklin Sugar, Standard Of Purity, 13 ¾ In. 50.00
Box, Fun-To-Wash, 25 Cents, Mammy Graphic, 5 x 7 In. 56.00
Box, Garbage Pail Kids, Topps Stickers, 1st Series, 48 Packs, 1985 .... 780.00
Box, Gold Dust Scouring Cleanser, Cardboard, Unopened, Contents, 4 ¾ In. 70.00
Box, Gold Dust Twins, Let Them Do Your Work, Wood, 12 ½ x 27 x 19 ½ In. 44.00
Box, Heide's Licorice, Black Children, Cardboard Lithograph, 5 Lb., 2 ⅞ x 10 x 7 In. 330.00
Box, Hershey's Chocolate, Chocolate That Is Pure, Wood, Silkaleens, 2 ½ In. 210.00
Box, Holloway's Vegetable Vermifuge Confections, Paper Label, Lift Top, 2 x 3 In. 33.00
Box, Honey-Fruit Pepsin Gum, Dovetailed, Wood, Va., 1915, 6 x 12 x 5 In. .... *illus* 144.00
Box, Ivins Famous Spice Wafers, 3 Lb., 10 ½ In. 50.00
Box, Jones, Douglas & Co. Crackers, Wood, Paper Labels, 13 x 20 ½ In. 50.00

Advertising, Bench, Poll-Parrot Shoes, Animal Seat Dividers, Painted, 1950s, 35 x 96 In.
$4400.00

Advertising, Box, Honey-Fruit Pepsin Gum, Dovetailed, Wood, Va., 1915, 6 x 12 x 5 In.
$144.00

TIP

Never wash a "flannel" (also called a "blanket" or "felt"), the small pieces of fabric packed in cigar or cigarette packs about 1914. Some valuable flannels picture baseball players. Washing the small fabric pieces will fade them. Put dry flannels and a clean, dry towel in the clothes drier set on the cool setting. A few tumbles will remove dust.

Advertising, Box, Lutted's S.P. Cough Drop, Log Cabin, Slag Glass, 7 x 8 x 5 ½ In.
$457.00

Advertising, Cabinet, Diamond Dyes, Evolution Of Women, Tin, Wood, 1890s, 30 ½ In.
$1100.00

Advertising, Cabinet, Putnam Fadeless Dyes-Tints, Tin Lithograph, 1940-50, 15 x 19 x 7 In.
$125.00

Advertising, Cabinet, Spool, Richardson Silk Co., Oak, 14 Drawers, With Thread, 23 x 35 In.
$944.00

Box, Lid, St. Louis Cracker, Leather Straps, Manewall-Lange, c.1900, 13 x 22 x 13 In. ... 95.00
Box, Lititiz Springs, Handles, Stenciled, Wood, Dovetailed, 10 x 18 ½ In. ... 120.00
Box, Log Cabin Brownies, Cabin Shape, Cloth Bale, Cardboard, Uneeda Bakers, 4 x 3 In. ... 236.00
Box, Lutted's S.P. Cough Drop, Log Cabin, Slag Glass, 7 x 8 x 5 ½ In. ... *illus* 457.00
Box, Mandeville & King Flower Seeds, Wood, Paper Label, 8 ½ In. ... 110.00
Box, Mouse De-Stroy, 39 Cents, 1930s, 7 In. ... 10.00
Box, Nabisco Assorted Biscuit, Yellow, 1 Lb., 11 In. ... 20.00
Box, Oneida Clown Cookies, 3 ¼ In. ... 120.00
Box, Pastime Tobacco, Hunting Scene, Red, Black, 4 x 12 ½ In. ... 88.00
Box, Recipe, Robin Hood Flour, Red, Plastic, 1950s ... 12.50
Box, Rinehart's Vegetable Cathartic Liver Pills, Pillbox, Wood, Oval, 2 In. ... 27.00
Box, Rinso Blue, Unopened, Paladin Trading Card, F373, 1959, 6 x 9 In. ... 2040.00
Box, Sealed Iroquois Famous Herb Tea, Indian, Canister, Cardboard, Label, 3 ½ x 2 In. ... 60.00
Box, see also Box category.
Box, Seed Display, Hirschy Bros., Walnut, Dovetailed, Fruit, Vegetables, 5 x 24 In. ... 201.00
Box, Slide Top, Glover's Imperial Worm Capsules, For Dog, Puppies, Foxes, 2 x 2 In. ... 71.00
Box, Soap, Toboggan, Teddy Bears, Castile, Paperboard, 1930s, 8 In. ... 95.00
Box, Starin's Renovating Powder, Mortar & Pestle, Horse, Steer, Sealed, 5 x 3 ½ In. ... 143.00
Box, Sunshine Biscuits, Hinged Lid, Wood, Paper Label, 12 ½ x 21 In. ... 50.00
Box, Tide Laundry Soap, Yellow, Orange, Blue, 16 Lb. 1 Oz., 17 ¼ In. ... 100.00
Box, W.J. Sands & Sons, Biscuits & Crackers, Wood, Paper Label, 10 x 19 ½ In. ... 248.00
Box, Wacker Brewery, Handles, Wood, Metal Rim, Early 1900s, 12 ½ x 19 In. ... 40.00
Box, Wrigley's Doublemint, Green, 25 Cent, 35 ½ In. ... 70.00
Box, Wrigley's Doublemint Chewing Gum, Chain, c.1950, 10 x 36 x 8 In. ... 90.00
Box, Wrigley's Spearmint, White, 10 Cent, 36 ½ In. ... 40.00
Broadside, Hollis' Compound Boneset & Wild Cherry Cough Candy, 10 x 8 In. ... 121.00
Broadside, Hollis' Original & Genuine Liquid Opodeldoc, Liniment, 10 x 8 In. ... 49.00
Broadside, Hollis' Vegetable Pectoral Syrup, Cough, Colds, Influenza, 7 x 8 In. ... 27.00
Broom Holder, Garland Stove, Whisk, Tin Lithograph, 3 In. ... 220.00
Broom Holder, Wilbur's Cocoa, Tin Lithograph, 3 ¾ In. ... 350.00
Broom Rack, Bond Bread, Porcelain, 4 Brooms, c.1920, 60 x 19 In. ... 173.00
Cabinet, Crowley's Needles, Ash, 12 Drawers, 9 x 19 In. ... 518.00
Cabinet, Crowley's Needles, Oak, Drawer, 1890s, 14 In. ... 250.00
Cabinet, Diamond Dyes, Children With Balloon, Tin, Oak, 24 x 15 x 9 In. ... 515.00 to 805.00
Cabinet, Diamond Dyes, Evolution Of Women, Tin, Wood, 1890s, 30 ½ In. ... *illus* 1100.00
Cabinet, Diamond Dyes, Governess, Children, Embossed Tin, Oak, 20 x 30 In. ... 826.00
Cabinet, Diamond Dyes, Governess, Tin Front, Oak Frame, 23 x 30 In. ... 550.00
Cabinet, Diamond Dyes, Mansion, Children, Tin Panel, c.1912, 15 x 25 In. ... 805.00
Cabinet, Diamond Dyes, Washer Woman, Tin Panel, Blue Ground, c.1910, 22 x 30 In. ... 1380.00
Cabinet, Dr. Scholl's Foot Remedies, Shelf, 2 Drawers, Painted, Tin, c.1920, 18 In. ... 144.00
Cabinet, Humphreys' Specifics, Tin, Oak, 34 Interior Drawers, 28 x 22 x 10 In. ... 350.00 to 605.00
Cabinet, Humphreys' Veterinary Specifics, Oak, Composition Panel, 21 x 33 In. ... 7188.00
Cabinet, New York Bakery, Oak, Original Stencil, 26 x 37 In. ... 531.00
Cabinet, Pratt's Veterinary, Walnut, Tin Panel, Horse Head, Product List, 18 x 32 In. ... 3450.00
Cabinet, Putnam Dye, Woman With Dyed Clothes, Tin Lithograph, Hinged Lid, 12 x 16 In. ... 173.00
Cabinet, Putnam Fadeless Dyes-Tints, Tin Lithograph, 1940-50, 15 x 19 x 7 In. ... *illus* 125.00
Cabinet, Rit Dye, Cake Or Flake, 10 Cent, Never Say Dye, Say Rit, Tin, 16 x 13 ¾ x 12 In. ... 99.00
Cabinet, Shults Bread, 2 Piece, 28 x 67 In. ... 708.00
Cabinet, Spool, Belding Bros., Oak, 9 Drawers, Glass, c.1900, 23 x 21 In. ... 935.00
Cabinet, Spool, Brainerd & Armstrong, Oak, Drawer, c.1900, 15 ½ x 17 ½ In. ... 263.00
Cabinet, Spool, Clark's Mile End, Oak, 6 Drawers, Lift Top, Late 1800s, 15 x 33 x 24 In. ... 175.00
Cabinet, Spool, Clark's O.N.T., Ash, 4 Drawers, Drop Pulls, 24 ½ x 15 x 19 In. ... 58.00
Cabinet, Spool, Clark's O.N.T., Oak, 4 Drawers, 14 x 21 In. ... 200.00
Cabinet, Spool, Clark's O.N.T., Oak, Tambour Doors, 30 x 21 In. ... 805.00
Cabinet, Spool, Corticelli, No. 61, Braid, Oak, 3 Drawers, 12 In. ... 225.00
Cabinet, Spool, Corticelli Curved Glass Front, 2 Drawers, 22 x 18 In. ... 1430.00
Cabinet, Spool, Crowley's Needles, Victorian, Oak, c.1900, 10 ½ x 18 ½ In. ... 439.00
Cabinet, Spool, J. & P. Coats', Ash, 6 Drawers, 24 ½ x 20 ½ x 17 ½ In. ... 690.00
Cabinet, Spool, J. & P. Coats', Best Six Cord, Walnut, 2 Drawers, 7 x 18 ½ x 15 In. ... 175.00
Cabinet, Spool, J. & P. Coats', Fruitwood, Drawers, 24 ½ x 18 ½ x 16 ½ In. ... 575.00
Cabinet, Spool, J. & P. Coats', Oak, 4 Drawers, Counter, 18 x 19 x 14 In. ... 259.00
Cabinet, Spool, J. & P. Coats', Oak, Drawers, Anchor Pulls, Shelf, Glass, 21 x 24 In. ... 330.00
Cabinet, Spool, Richardson Silk Co., Oak, 14 Drawers, With Thread, 23 x 35 In. ... *illus* 944.00
Cabinet, Spool, Richardson's, Oak, 3 Drawers, c.1910, 19 x 18 x 9 In. ... 115.00
Cabinet, Spool, Spool Cotton Co., Ash, 2 Drawers, c.1900, 8 x 20 In. ... 468.00
Cabinet, Spool, Star Twist, Metal, Glass, 4 Drawer, 14 x 16 x 8 In. ... 173.00

Cabinet, Spool, Willimantic, Wood, 2 Drawers, 15 x 24 In. 144.00
Cabinet, Spool, Willimantic Spool Cotton, 6 Drawers, 20 x 25 ½ x 19 In. 405.00
Cabinet, Storage, Syracuse Drill Bits, Stepback, 72 Drawers, 29 x 27 In. 660.00
Calendars are listed in their own category.
Canisters, see introductory paragraph to Tins in this category.
Cards are listed in the Card category.
Carrier, Star Egg Carriers & Trays, John G. Elbs, Wood, 1906, 2 ¾ In. 143.00
Cart, Good Humor Ice Cream, Painted Graphics, Chrome Trim, 35 x 48 In. 25300.00
Carton, Borden's Ice Cream, Elsie The Cow On Front, 1957, Pt. 15.00
Carton, Tobias American Poultry, Uncle Sam In Barnyard, 8 ½ x 5 In. 330.00
Case, Arrow Collars, Glass, Wood, Metal, 1900-15, 12 x 50 In. 690.00
Case, Display, E.J. Kruce & Co. Cracker Bakers, Wood, Glass, Detroit, 24 x 32 In. 385.00
Case, Display, Waterman's Fountain, Ideal Pens, Oak, Glass, N.Y., 17 x 18 In. 885.00
Case, Freihofer's Quality Cakes, Display, Glass, Tin, 15 x 28 In. 531.00
Case, Hickory Elastic, Wood, Glass, 7 ½ x 18 ½ In. 173.00
Case, Sauer's Extracts, Oak, House, Richmond, Va., 25 x 11 In. 413.00
Catalog, John P. Levell Arms Co., Tennis Supplies, 1896, 8 x 6 ½ In., 8 Pages 70.00
Catalog, L.L. Bean, General Store Cover, P.E. Parson, c.1949, 7 ½ x 9 In., 90 Pages 45.00
Catalog, Matchbook, Salesman's, 50 Graphic Images, 1953, 9 x 11 In., 172 Pages 410.00
Ceiling Fixture, Hires Root Beer, Glass, Barrel Shape, 26 x 11 In. 715.00
Chair, Piedmont Cigarettes, Folding, Wood, c.1915-20 .... *illus* 288.00
Chalkboard, Cloverdale Beverages, Special Today, Celluloid, Easel Back, 17 x 9 In. 140.00
Chalkboard, Slim Jim Pretzels, To-Day's Specials, Snappy-Kracky, 21 x 12 In. 70.00
Change Receiver, Moxie Our Idol, Cutout Pointing Man, Photo In Bowl, Tin, 6 x 12 In. 826.00
Change Receiver, Muriel Cigar, Reverse Painted Glass, Brunhoff Mfg., 2 x 7 In. 110.00
Change Receiver, see also Tip Tray in this category.
Charger, Buffalo Brewing Co., Gold Gesso Frame, Sacramento, Calif., Tin, 21 ¼ In. 57500.00
Charger, Prince Albert Tobacco, Tin, Black Ground, Prince Smoking, 1930s, 24 In. 2875.00
Cigar Box, Al Simmons, Home Run Brand, Simmons At Bat, c.1930 .... 180.00
Cigar Box, Green, Round Head Nails, Arched Back, Hanging, 9 ¼ x 5 ½ x 2 ¾ In. 330.00
Cigar Box, La Flor De Generall Arthur Cigars 60.00
Cigar Box, Wood, Aurelia Sports, c.1935, 8 ½ x 4 ¾ In. 20.00
Cigar Box, Wood, Oval Photo, Al Simmons, Erlinda Cigar Co., 1930s, 5 ½ x 9 x 2 ¾ In. 180.00
Cigar Cutter, Bond Value Cigars, Donkey, Cast Iron, 7 ½ x 6 ½ In. 330.00
Cigar Cutter, Cuckoo Cigar, 5 Cent, White, Red, Blue, 6 x 7 ½ x 6 ¼ In. 330.00
Cigar Cutter, Enterprise, Large Plug, Champion Improved, Iron, 1870, 18 ½ In. 60.00
Cigar Cutter, Enterprise, Medium Plug, Champion Improved, Iron, 1871, 17 ½ In. 120.00
Cigar Cutter, Griswold, Gold Accents, Cast Iron, 1870, 18 ½ In. 225.00
Cigar Cutter, Josada 10 Cent Cigar, Cast Iron, 14 In. .... *illus* 1540.00
Cigar Cutter, La Fendrich Havana Cigar, Suits Most Exacting Taste, 5 Cent, 5 x 8 x 6 In. 250.00
Cigar Cutter, Lighter, Barnes Smith & Co., Knight, Horse, N.Y., c.1890, 17 x 6 In. 1955.00
Cigar Cutter, Lighter, Spanish Maid, Globe, Key Wind, Iron, New York, 6 x 18 In. 3835.00
Cigar Cutter, New Currency Tobacco, 5 Cent, Peter Hauptmann Co., 4 x 8 x 6 In. 275.00
Cigar Cutter, Peter Schuyler, Odd Moments, Key Wind, Cast Iron, 5 x 34 In. 330.00
Cigar Cutter, Rob Roy, Quality Cigar, 5 Cent, Marked, Brunhoff Mfg., 3 x 7 x 7 In. 440.00
Cigar Cutter, Smoke Moss Agate, For Quality, Painted, Marked, 1092, 6 ½ x 8 x 6 In. 550.00
Cigar Cutter, Smoke Pony H.P.B. Cigars, 5 Cent, Tin, Erie Specialty Co., 3 x 6 In. 330.00
Clocks are listed in their own category.
Coaster, Drink Regal Beer, American Brewing Co., Red, White, Miami. 5.00
Coaster, Knickerbocker Beer, Metal, Logo 3 ¾ In., 5 Piece 25.00
Coaster, Regal Light Lager Beer, Musketeer, Glass, Red, Green, American Brewing Co. 17.00
Coaster, Tropical Ale-Beer, Orange, Green, Tampa Florida Brewery, Tampa 10.00
Cooler, Dr Pepper, Light Green, White, 1950s, 18 ½ x 17 ¾ x 13 In. 30.00
Cooler, Drink Squirt, Yellow, Red, Metal, Progress Refrigerator Co., 20 x 18 x 13 In. 40.00
Cooler, Hi-Brow Ginger Ale, Pine, Zinc Lining, Hinged Top, Stenciled, 38 x 38 In. 575.00
Cooler, Moxie, Man, Girl, Footed, Wood, Metal Liner, 28 x 24 x 18 In. 330.00
Crock, Colonial Mince Meat, Original Label, 1940, 9 In. 60.00
Crock, Copenhagen Snuff, Weyman & Bro, Painted, Tin Lid, c.1900, 9 x 6 In. 66.00
Crock, Heinz, Apple Butter, White, Paper Label, 36 Oz. .... *illus* 385.00
Cuspidor, Bulldog Cut Plug, Brass, Raised Logo, 10 ½ In. 44.00
Cuspidor, Golden Novelty, Turtle, Metal Shell, Head Opens, c.1890, 15 x 11 In. 248.00
Dish, Sander's Mt. Olive, Ill., Dry Goods, Melrose, Harker, 6 x 4 ½ In. 6.00
Dispenser, Admiration Ice Tea, Crock, Brown, No Lid, Marked, U.S.A., 9 x 10 In. 30.00
Dispenser, Alka-Seltzer, Be Wise Alkalize, 14 ½ x 5 x 6 ½ In. 145.00
Dispenser, Alka-Seltzer, Get Well & Keep Well, Be Wise, Alkalize, Blue, Tin, 15 In. 253.00
Dispenser, Birchola Root Beer Syrup, Ceramic, Globular, Boughs, 13 ½ In. 1680.00

Advertising, Chair, Piedmont Cigarettes, Folding, Wood, c.1915-20
$288.00

Advertising, Cigar Cutter, Josada 10 Cent Cigar, Cast Iron, 14 In.
$1540.00

Advertising, Crock, Heinz, Apple Butter, White, Paper Label, 36 Oz.
$385.00

A

Advertising, Dispenser,
Dr. Swett's Root Beer, Wood, Brass,
Barrel Shape, 23 In.
$690.00

Advertising, Dispenser,
Marrowfood Syrup,
Makes Rich Red Blood, c.1920, 15 In.
$1500.00

Dispenser, Birchola Syrup, Drink, 5 Cent, Leaves, Ceramic, Marked, 14 x 9 In. 3000.00
Dispenser, Bowey's Root Beer, Barrel Form, Ceramic, Pump, 1920s, 14 ½ In. 748.00
Dispenser, Buckeye Root Beer, Black, Inverted Teardrop Dispenser, 15 In. 1092.00
Dispenser, Buckeye Root Beer, Black, Metal, 1925, 20 x 24 x 12 In. 350.00
Dispenser, Buckeye Root Beer, White, Inverted Teardrop Dispenser, c.1920 .... 920.00
Dispenser, Buckeye Root Beer Syrup, Ceramic, Goat Imps, 5 Cents, 13 ¾ In. 1208.00
Dispenser, Buckeye Root Beer Syrup, Urn Shape, 14 ½ In. 575.00
Dispenser, Cherry Julep Syrup, Ceramic, Red, Plunger Pump, c.1910, 14 In. 575.00
Dispenser, Cherry Smash, Glass Marked 5 Cents, 3 Leaves, Ceramic, 15 In. 3737.00
Dispenser, Cherry Smash Syrup, Ceramic, Always Drink Cherry Smash, 15 In. 1150.00
Dispenser, Copenhagen Chew, Best Chew Ever Made, Tin, 2 Shelves, Tray, 9 x 11 In. 440.00
Dispenser, Crawford Cherry-Fizz Syrup, It's Jake-A-Loo, Pump, 9 x 15 In. 5500.00
Dispenser, Dr Pepper, Upside Down Label, Square Marble Base, 1900s 26000.00
Dispenser, Dr. Swett's Root Beer, Wood, Brass, Barrel Shape, 23 In. .... *illus* 690.00
Dispenser, Drink My-Co, Wood, Cast Iron Base, Glass Ball Feet, 14 x 30 In. 165.00
Dispenser, Drink Smile, Blue Frosted Glass, Embossed, Metal Spigot, 15 In. 140.00
Dispenser, Emerald Isle, 3-Leaf Clover, Green, White, Smith Jr. Co., 13 ½ In. 88.00
Dispenser, Fowler's Cherry Smash, Always Drink, Cherries, Ceramic, 14 ½ x 9 ½ In. 1500.00 to 3100.00
Dispenser, Fowler's Cherry Smash, White, Original Pump, 16 In. 3163.00
Dispenser, Fowler's Root Beer, 5 Cent, The Best, Red, White, Pump, 14 x 9 ½ In. 900.00
Dispenser, Grape Crush, Barrel, Amethyst Glass, 13 ¾ x 6 ½ In. 550.00
Dispenser, Grape Julep, Ceramic, Pump, Hall China, 13 ½ In. 12800.00
Dispenser, Grape Julep Syrup, Pump, 10 x 15 In. 1770.00
Dispenser, Hires, Hour Glass, Plunger Button, 14 In. 1045.00
Dispenser, Hires Munimaker Marble Syrup, Nickel, Glass, 1900, 35 x 17 In. 2990.00
Dispenser, Hires Root Beer, Barrel Shape, Chrome Bands, Claw Feet, 1940s, 31 In. 58.00
Dispenser, Hires Root Beer, Barrel Shape, Oak, Brass Bands, Onyx Knob Tap, 23 In. 360.00
Dispenser, Hires Root Beer, Drink Hires, It Is Pure, Ceramic, 11 x 7 ¾ In. 286.00
Dispenser, Hires Root Beer, Drink Hires, It Is Pure, Hourglass Shape, Red, White, Spigot, 14 In. 600.00
Dispenser, Hires Root Beer, Wood, Brass, Barrel Shape, Spigot, Claw Feet, 23 x 13 In. 460.00
Dispenser, Hires Root Beer Syrup, It Is Pure, Ceramic, Hourglass Shape, Spigot, 13 In. 633.00
Dispenser, Howel's Orange-Julep, Metal Base, Spigot, Frosted Glass, 17 In. 138.00
Dispenser, Imperial Ginger Ale, Green Bands, Barrel Shape, Porcelain, 14 In. 121.00
Dispenser, Indian Rock Ginger Ale, Gold Base Trim, Ball Style Pump, 16 In. 7700.00
Dispenser, Indian Rock Ginger Ale 5, Ceramic, Bulbous, Indian At Brook, 15 In. 5750.00
Dispenser, Jersey-Creme Perfect, Porcelain, 17 In. 795.00
Dispenser, Jersey-Creme Syrup, Ceramic, Embossed, Fleur-De-Lis, Pump, 15 In. 1150.00
Dispenser, Knut Kola, Gilt Bands, Ceramic, Marked, Hall, Dur Bur Co., Liverpool 715.00
Dispenser, Liberty Loganberry, Drink A Loganberry, Richardson Corp., 31 In. 230.00
Dispenser, Liberty Orange Drink, Drink An Orange, Richardson Corp., 31 In. 210.00
Dispenser, Lid, Armour, Vigoral, Ceramic, 4 Cups, 21 In. 230.00
Dispenser, Malted Grape-Nuts, Chocolate Flavor, Tin, Metal, 15 In. 660.00
Dispenser, Marrowfood Syrup, Makes Rich Red Blood, c.1920, 15 In. .... *illus* 1500.00
Dispenser, Mission Orange, Pink & Black Glass, Embossed, Rubber, 13 ¾ In. 350.00
Dispenser, Old Highland Whiskey, John Walker & Sons, 24 In. 2251.00
Dispenser, Orange Crush, Frosted Glass, Black Base, Perfection Cooler Co., 16 In. 440.00
Dispenser, Orange Crush Syrup, Pump, 9 x 13 In. 531.00
Dispenser, Puritan Paper Cup, Glass Cylinder, Wall Mount, 21 x 5 x 5 In. 150.00
Dispenser, Rosary Root Beer, White, Barrel Shape, Ceramic, Pump, c.1920 .... 1840.00
Dispenser, Rum, Ceramic, Painted English Puppet, Punch, Toasting, 10 ½ In. 345.00
Dispenser, Schuster's Root Beer, Barrel, Ceramic, Red, Blue Bands, Gold, 1920s 690.00
Dispenser, Snuff, Fresh Copenhagen, It's A Pleasure, Metal, Hanging, 1949, 15 In. 66.00
Dispenser, Special Scotch, Straight Whiskey Pure Malt Pot, Scotland, 27 In. 3600.00
Dispenser, Straws, Hires Root Beer, Fees 5 Cents A Glass, Metal, 1912, 4 x 10 In. 633.00
Dispenser, Vernor's Ginger Ale, Nickel Plated, Porcelain, 2 Taps, 16 x 17 x 22 In. 518.00
Dispenser, Ward's Lemon Crush, Lemon Shape, Bally Style Pump, c.1920, 13 In. 1870.00
Dispenser, Ward's Orange Crush, Orange, 14 x 9 In. 900.00
Dispenser, Ward's Orange Crush Syrup, Orange Shape, Ceramic, 15 ¼ In. 863.00
Display, Adams Tutti-Frutti Gum, Oak, Glass Shelves, c.1900s, 18 x 12 In. 715.00
Display, American Girl, C.I. Hood & Co., Mass, 1898, 8 ¼ In. 30.00
Display, Bakers Soda Fountain, Glass, Metal, 41 x 21 x 26 In. 4670.00
Display, Beech-Nut Peppermint Flavored Chewing Gum, Little Girl, Gum, Box, Tin, 6 x 4 In. . 2495.00
Display, Bickmore Easy-Shave Cream, Die Cut, Cardboard, Easel, 31 x 21 In. 303.00
Display, Bickmore Gall Salve, Be Sure & Work The Horse, Cardboard, 34 x 22 In. 168.00
Display, Bishop-Conklin Paints Co., Figural Elf With Paintbrush & Can, 1930s, 8 In. 300.00
Display, Black Diamond Strings, World's Best, Tin, 24 x 14 ½ x 10 ½ In. 275.00

Display, Bulldog Suspenders, Papier-Mache, Tin Plate, Box, 24 x 17 In. 3520.00
Display, Buster Brown Shoes, Lithographed Die Cut Tin, Buster & Tige, 12 x 8 In. 2310.00
Display, C. Howard Hunt Pen Co., Wood, 12 Compartments, 11 x 4 x 1 ½ In. 134.00
Display, Candy Store, Schrafft's, 5 Cents, 4 Shelves, Tin, 8 x 12 x 16 In.. .... 173.00
Display, Champion Light Bulb, Tin Lithograph, 17 ½ In. 330.00
Display, Chico's Spanish Peanuts, Glass, Tin, 3-Sided Base, 12 x 8 In. 645.00
Display, Clark's Teaberry Gum, Stand, Vaseline Glass, 6 x 7 In. 248.00
Display, Clark's Teaberry Gum, Take Your Change, Green Glass, 2 x 9 x 6 In. 275.00
Display, Columbian Rope, 3-D, Die Cut Cardboard, Ships, c.1920, 40 x 40 x 18 In. 330.00
Display, Curtiss Penny Candies, Use Your Cents, 3 Sections, Tin, 7 ½ x 10 x 8 In. 440.00
Display, Daisy BB Gun, Die Cut Cardboard, Boy, Gun, c.1920, 33 x 28 x 9 In. 3250.00
Display, Edison Mazda Lamp, 2 Cavaliers, Light Bulb Form, Bulbs, Yellow, Parrish 2500.00
Display, Fashion Hour Brassiere, Figural, Size 10C, 1920s, 9 x 20 In.. .... 245.00
Display, Ferry's Seeds, 5 Cent & 10 Cent, Wood, 5 ½ x 24 x 11 ½ In. 65.00
Display, Flexible Flyer, Die Cut Cardboard, Girl Riding Sled, c.1915, 19 x 51 In. 440.00
Display, Golden Arches, McDonald's Over 15 Million Sold, 15 Cents, Neon, 36 x 68 In. 339.00
Display, Green River Whiskey, Man, Horse, 1930-40, 12 x 14 x 4 In. .... *illus* 201.00
Display, Grippo's Buttered Pretzels, 3-Sided, Hinged Lid, Glass, 14 x 12 In. 90.00
Display, Hand Painted Masterpieces, Plastic, Cardboard Panels, Labels, 8 x 15 x 22 In. 474.00
Display, Hunt's Pens, Oak, Sloped Front, Glass, Hinged Lid, 8 ¼ x 17 ⅛ x 13 In.. .... 308.00
Display, Jacob's Biscuits, New Air Tight Cartons, Wood, Stencil, 35 x 23 x 12 ½ In. 330.00
Display, Jockey Menswear, Figural, Metal, Wood Base, Counter, 1950s, 6 x 14 In. 65.00
Display, Lamb Knit Sweaters, Pure Wool, Composition, Old King Cole, 16 x 16 In. 364.00
Display, Lash's Orangeade, From Sun Ripened Fruit, Porcelain, 24 x 16 In. 410.00
Display, Learbury Clothiers, Tiger, Crouching, Papier-Mache, 76 x 30 x 29 In. 3738.00
Display, Life Savers, Metal, Glass Dividers, H.D. Beech Co., 9 x 12 ½ In.. .... 115.00
Display, Little Boy Blue Bluing, Red, White, Blue, Tin Lithograph, Bottle, 18 x 4 In.. .... 219.00
Display, Lone Star Beer, 2 Cans, 2 Monkeys, Paul Stanley, 1960s, 57 In. 1980.00
Display, Lyons' Pola Maid Ice Cream Cone, Iron Holder, 48 x 18 In. 1320.00
Display, Mackintosh Candy, Tin, Faux Wood Grain, 4 Sections, 1930, 18 x 13 x 8 In. 92.00
Display, National Mazda Lamps, 11 Different Bulbs, Tin, 19 x 28 x 6 In.. .... 905.00
Display, Neuweiler Beer Ale, Waiter In Yellow Jacket, Molded Plastic, 1960s, 12 In. 173.00
Display, Ohio Brand Matches, Pocket Size, 14 ½ x 9 ¼ In. 30.00
Display, Our Standard Remedy, 4 Boxes, Contents, 1, 5 ¼ x 2 ½ In.. .... 55.00
Display, Owl, Book Of Knowledge, Composition, 22 In. 795.00
Display, Pabst Blue Ribbon Beer, Popular Prices, Metal, 1955, 15 x 10 In. .... *illus* 288.00
Display, Parke-Davis, Medicated Throat Discs, Cardboard, 1940, 42 x 28 In. .... *illus* 173.00
Display, Pensupreme Ice Cream, Flavors, Red, White, Tin, 20 ¼ In.. .... 60.00
Display, Philip Morris, Little Johnny Cutout, Bell Hop, Slogans, c.1925, 15 x 6 In. 230.00
Display, Phillip Morris Cigarette, Lucy & Desi Holding Carton, Cardboard, 10 x 9 In. 96.00
Display, Rack, Curtiss Candy, Plastic, Metal, c.1960, 10 x 15 x 6 In.. .... 144.00
Display, Ram, Wool Is Best By Every Test, Woolen Corp., Papier-Mache, 18 x 16 In. 1210.00
Display, Razor, Cattaraugus Cutlery Co., c.1890, 17 x 18 In.. .... 1650.00
Display, Red Lodge Brewery, Cardboard, Die Cut, 7 x 11 ¼ In. 700.00
Display, Rexall Pens, Oak, Compartments, Pen Tips, Hinged Glass Lid, 14 x 14 In. 308.00
Display, Robin Hood Shoes, Figural, Plaster, 15 x 6 x 5 In. 275.00
Display, Sanford's Ink, Oak, 2 Glass Shelves, Door, 16 x 12 ½ x 11 In. 476.00
Display, Sanford's Ink, Oak, 2 Glass Shelves, Sliding Door, 18 x 12 x 10 In. 840.00
Display, Sanford's Ink, Oak, 5 Shelves, 36 ¼ x 20 ¼ x 9 ¼ In. 504.00
Display, Sen-Sen Chewing Gum, Die Cut Cardboard, c.1920s, 7 x 5 In. 44.00
Display, Shumate Razor, Oak, Slanted Glass Top, Specialty Case Co., 5 x 36 In. 330.00
Display, Smile Soda Pop, Embossed Glass Bottle, Patent July 11, 1922, Gal., 19 In. 193.00
Display, Smith Bros. Cough Drops, Tin, Samples, 9 ¾ x 4 x 4 In. 495.00
Display, Steiff, Noah's Ark, Trees & House Removable, 1950s, 18 x 34 x 12 In. 525.00
Display, Sunbeam Shavemaster, Bakelite, Glass, Mirror, Electric, 11 x 12 In. 55.00
Display, Sunbeam Shavemaster, Light, Plastic, Wood, 21 In. 140.00
Display, Sweet Cuba Chewing Tobacco, Yellow, Red, Tin, 18 x 12 In. 236.00
Display, Topps Gum, 1 Cent, Cardboard, 2 ½ In. 5.00
Display, Twenty Grand Razor Blades, Horse, Jockey, 20 Boxes, 1940s 93.00
Display, Venida Hair Net, Wood, 7 ½ x 22 x 13 In. 110.00
Display, Waterman's Fountain Pen, Oak, Hinged Door, Drawer, 12 x 21 x 18 ½ In. 616.00
Display, Watta Pop, 1 Cent, Dog, Chalkware, 1930-40, 5 x 7 In. .... *illus* 173.00
Display, Welch's Grape Juice, Girl, Die Cut, Cardboard, 24 ¾ x 14 ½ In. .... *illus* 460.00
Display, West Hair Net, Tin, 4 Nets, c.1918, 7 x 20 x 6 In. .... *illus* 460.00
Display, Whistle Soda, Hand Holding Bottle, Metal, Glass, 1930s, 14 In. 517.00
Display, Woman's Corset, Mannequin, Clothes, Chas. DeBevoise Co., 19 x 8 In. 610.00

Advertising, Display,
Green River Whiskey, Man, Horse,
1930-40, 12 x 14 x 4 In.
$201.00

Advertising, Display,
Pabst Blue Ribbon Beer, Popular Prices,
Metal, 1955, 15 x 10 In.
$288.00

Advertising, Display, Parke-Davis,
Medicated Throat Discs, Cardboard,
1940, 42 x 28 In.
$173.00

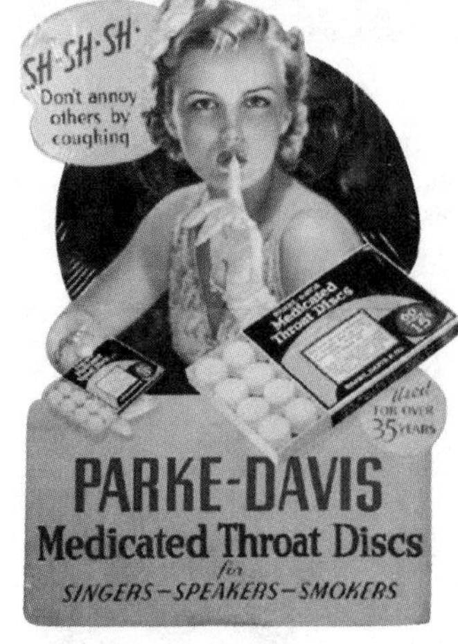

Advertising, Display, Watta Pop, 1 Cent, Dog, Chalkware, 1930-40, 5 x 7 In.
$173.00

Advertising, Display, Welch's Grape Juice, Girl, Die Cut, Cardboard, 24 ¾ x 14 ½ In.
$460.00

Advertising, Display, West Hair Net, Tin, 4 Nets, c.1918, 7 x 20 x 6 In.
$460.00

Display, Wrigley's Chewing Gum, Cardboard, Girl, Cash Register, 5 Cent Price, c.1930 .... 1430.00
Display, Wrigley's Gum, 5-Sided, Revolving, Metal, 16 In.............................. 345.00
Dolls are listed in their own category.
Door Pull, Dr Pepper, Bottle Form, White, Red, 1940s, 9 ¾ x 3 ¾ In..................... 275.00
Door Pull, Dr Pepper, Red, White, Marked, Ad-Nov. Co., 1930-40, 12 x 3 ½ In............. 175.00
Door Push, Kirk's Soap, Red, White Letters, 8 ½ x 3 ¾ In.............................. 55.00
Door Push, Salada Tea, Brass Grommets, 1930s, 3 x 31 ½ In........................... 144.00
Door Push, Sunbeam Bread, Enameled Metal, Loaf Shape, 21 x 18 In. 310.00
Door Push, Sunbeam Bread, Girl Eating Bread, Tin, Metal, 1940s, 9 x 34 In.............. 500.00
Drink Token, A. Scholz, Palm Garden, San Antonio, Tex., Spelter, 12 ½ Cent............. 80.00
Envelope, Merchant's Gargling Oil Liniment, For Man & Beast, 3 ½ x 6 ½ In............. 22.00
Fan Pull, Dr Pepper, Madalon Mason, Drink A Bite To Eat, 1930-40, 6 ½ x 5 In. 125.00
Fan Pull, Dr Pepper, Woman, Squirrel, Drink A Bite To Eat, 1930-40, 7 x 4 ¾ In............ 100.00
Fan Pull, J.P. Alley's Hambone, 5 Cent, Black Man In Plane, Gold Leaf, 7 In. Diam.......... 110.00
Fans are listed in their own category.
Festoon, Hires Root Beer, Woman, Fold-Out Display, Wall Pockets, Cardboard, 5 Piece 518.00
Figure, Alka-Seltzer, Speedy, Painted, Rubber, Miles Lab, 8 In........................... 220.00
Figure, American Lady Corsets, Silk & Broadcloth Over Wood, Base, c.1880, 29 In. 4125.00
Figure, Big Boy, Holding Hamburger Tray, Fiberglass, Checkered Overalls, 41 x 54 x 29 In.... 6325.00
Figure, Bryant Furnace, Bulldog, Black, White, Reclining, Papier-Mache, 1935, 11 x 19 In. .. 495.00
Figure, California Raisin, Hardee's Kid Meal Premium, 1967, Set Of 5 .... 9.00
Figure, Dog, RCA Nipper, Composition, White, Collar, 9 x 41 In.......................... 690.00
Figure, Dog, RCA Nipper, Half-Bodied, Plastic, 21 ½ In. 140.00
Figure, Dog, RCA Nipper, Papier-Mache, Old King Cole, 11 In........................... 90.00
Figure, Dog, RCA Nipper, Papier-Mache, Red Studded Collar, 18 In...................... 40.00
Figure, Dog, RCA Nipper, Plaster, Glass Eyes, Brown Ears, Marked Victor Records, 13 In...... 100.00
Figure, Dog, RCA Nipper, RCA Victor, Papier-Mache, Black, White, c.1900, 35 In. 450.00
Figure, Dutch Boy, Boy With Metal Pail, Composition, 12 ½ In........................... 403.00
Figure, General Electric, Drum Major, Red Coat, Wood, Posable, c.1927, 18 In. 1200.00
Figure, Ice Cream Cone, Tan, Concrete, 25 x 10 In.................................... 770.00
Figure, Jack Daniels, Standing, White, Plastic, Mold, Base, 76 x 20 x 20 In. 350.00
Figure, Lowenbrau Beer, Tiger Holding Beer Mug, Composite, 12 x 30 In.................. 55.00
Figure, McDonald's Hamburgler, Head, Fiberglass 22 x 28 In. 59.00
Figure, Mountain Dew, Willy The Hillbilly, Vinyl, Plush Body, 1965, 20 In. 185.00
Figure, National Tailoring, Man In Tuxedo, Top Hat, Papier-Mache, 31 x 9 x 7 In............ 585.00
Figure, Ohio Matches, Indian, Reclining, Holding Pipe, Painted, Plaster, 12 x 24 In......... 176.00
Figure, Philip Morris, Johnny Goes Places, Bell Cap With Case.......................... 400.00
Figure, Pilgrim Rum, Pilgrim, Chalkware, 16 ½ In. .... *illus* 345.00
Figure, RCA, Radiotron Boy, Jointed, Red, Blue, Yellow, Silver, Wood, 16 In. 863.00
Figure, Red Goose Shoes, Red Goose, Chalk, 12 In.................................... 120.00
Figure, Red Top Rye, Confederate Man, Flag, Old Rye Jug, Wood, Paint, c.1900, 47 In. 660.00
Figure, Ronald McDonald, Fiberglass, 1980s, 84 In..................................... 339.00
Figure, Squirt, With Bottle, Just Call Me Squirt, Painted, Plaster, 1947, 13 ½ In. 220.00
Figure, White Eagle Gas Co., Eagle, Brown, White, Blue Iron, Mobil, Kansas, 33 In.......... 1800.00
Figure, Williams & Humberts Sherry, Woman, Holding Tray With Bottle, Chalkware........ 99.00
Flyer, Hollis' Celebrated Eye Water For Sore, Weak & Inflamed Eyes, 7 ¾ x 5 In............ 33.00
Flyer, Kickapoo Indian Prairie Plane, Indian Woman, Remedy, 8 ½ x 6 ½ In. 38.00
Foam Scraper, Anheuser-Busch, World's Largest Brewery, Plastic, 10 ¼ x 1 In............. 27.00
Foam Scraper, Goetz Country Club Beer, Red, Plastic, 8 ¾ x 1 In........................ 38.00
Footrest, Thom McAn, Wood, c.1920, 12 x 15 In. .... *illus* 29.00
Furance, Stamford, Aluminum, Potbelly, Case, Salesman's Sample, 12 x 9 In.............. 345.00
Furnace, Lennox, Pressed Steel, Aluminum, Torrid Zone, Salesman's Sample, 14 x 10 In. ... 1725.00
Furnace, National Cycloidal, Aluminum, Excelsior, Salesman's Sample, 12 x 9 In.......... 460.00
Furnace, National Horizontal, Aluminum, Salesman's Sample, 16 x 8 x 17 In............. 920.00
Furnace, Red Cross, Sheet Metal, Cylindrical, Salesman's Sample, 1924, 19 x 9 ½ In........ 115.00
Furnace, Round Oak Mistair, Tin, Aluminum, Salesman's Sample, 12 x 9 In. 1840.00
Furnace, Sunbeam, Aluminum, No. 1044C, Salesman's Sample, 13 x 11 In. 575.00
Furnace, Williamson, Aluminum, Potbelly, Case, Salesman's Sample, 13 x 10 In........... 575.00
Game Counter, Dr. Kendall's Pectoral Balsam, F. Penn Prop, Vt., 1 ½ x 3 ½ In............. 60.00
Hand Scrubber, Crystal White Family Soap, Billion Bubble, Tin Lithograph, 4 ½ x 6 ½ In... 78.00
Ice Cream Scoop, Cupid Cream Cakes, Rectangular Bowl, Nickel Plated Brass, 8 In........ 1045.00
Ice Shaver, Swan, Cast Iron, 14 x 27 x 14 In.. 770.00
Indian, Bust, Arapaho Cigar, 21 x 13 In... 220.00
Indian, Bust, Brave, Black Hawk, Mohawk, Chalk, 11 x 6 In............................ 880.00
Ink Blotter, Kemp's Balsam, For Coughs Colds & Throat, c.1910, 6 x 3 ¼ In............... 28.00
Jar, Adams Chewing Gum, Glass, Etched, Ground Neck & Stopper, 11 ½ In. 201.00

Jar, Bunte Candy, Ground Lip, Stopper, 12 x 5 ½ In. 71.00
Jar, Carnation Malted Milk, Red, Green, Milk Glass, Aluminum Lid, 8 ¼ In. 130.00
Jar, Chico's Peanuts, Metal Base, Lid, c.1920, 12 In. 303.00
Jar, Deco Candies, Necco, Glass, Metal Lid. 49.00
Jar, Dr. King's New Life Pills, Ground Neck, Label Under Glass, Lid, 12 x 5 In. 523.00
Jar, Kis-Me Chewing Gum, Glass, Embossed, Square, Angled Corners, 11 In. 81.00
Jar, Kis-Me Chewing Gum, Original Label, Girl Receiving Kiss, Glass, Lid, 5 x 11 In. 330.00
Jar, Lance, Blue Crossed Swords, Red Lid, 12 In. 150.00
Jar, National Biscuit Company, Embossed, Round 85.00
Jar, Plains County Peanut Butter, White Glass, c.1900 25.00
Jar, Sealtest Dairy, Sour Cream, c.1951, ½ Pt. 40.00
Jar, Simon Bros. Dairy, Sour Cream, Orange Lettering, c.1948, Pt. 40.00
Jar, Tom's Peanut Butter, Glass, Red Top, Stenciled, 10 In. 40.00
Jar, Walla Walla Pepsin Gum, Lid, c.1900, 13 In. 144.00
Jigsaw Puzzle, Hood's Sarsaparilla Rainy Day, 2-Sided, C.I. Hood & Co., 10 x 15 In. 44.00
Jug, Ed Hattinger's Liquor Store, Lancaster, O., Stoneware, Brown Glaze Neck, c.1885, 3 In. 115.00
Jug, Griel Bros. Co., Wholesale Grocers, Bristol Glaze, White, Flat Handle, 11 ¼ In. 330.00
Jug, Picnic, Red Hat, Man Walking, Green, Handle, Poloron Products, 9 ¾ In. 44.00
Jug, Whiskey, Rist's Special, 4 Quarts $3.00, Tan Glaze, Blue Stenciled Letters, 3 In. 259.00
Kickplate, Polo Club Ginger Ale, Pale Dry, Green, Red, Porcelain, 1920s, 9 x 24 In. 230.00
Kickplate, Star Tobacco, Sold Here, Yellow, Blue, Brown, Porcelain, c.1920, 12 x 24 In. 173.00
Kickplate, Sweet-Orr Overalls, Yellow, Blue, Porcelain, c.1940, 8 x 30 In. 340.00
Label, Beer, Friars Ale, Smiling Friar's Face, 10 Piece 2.00
Label, Beer, SB Beer, Southern Brewing, Pirates, Palm Trees, Ships, Red, Green, Tampa 7.00
Label, Beer, Silver Bar, Premium Lager, Black Ground, Gold Panel, Southern Brewing, Tampa 17.00
Label, Beer, Spearman Ale, Ace High English Type, Card, Green, Red 10.00
Label, Beer, Spearman Draft, Keg, Text, Blue, Red, Cream, Spearman Brewing, Pensacola 6.00
Label, Beer, Spearman Draft, Stein, Glass, Overflowing Suds, Spearman Brewing, Pensacola 5.00
Label, Cigar Box, 5th Ave. Club, Woman Golfer, Links, Inner, 8 x 7 In. 665.00
Label, Cigar Box, American Mascot, Bald Eagle Perched On Columbia, Inner, 7 x 7 In. 358.00
Label, Cigar Box, Bachelor, Young Man Smokes Cigar Thinking, Inner, 10 x 7 In. 418.00
Label, Cigar Box, Brown Beauties, Palm Trees & Teepees, Inner, 8 x 7 In. 262.00
Label, Cigar Box, Century Club, Stone Building, Traffic, Cars & Carriage, Inner, 10 x 7 In. 286.00
Label, Cigar Box, Colonial Girl, Woman Seated At Spinning Wheel, Inner, 1899, 8 x 7 In. 292.00
Label, Cigar Box, Cuban Spy, Buckskinned Ranger, Plantation, Inner, 7 x 7 In. 239.00
Label, Cigar Box, Dan De Ace, Spanish Gentleman, Dice, Inner, 12 x 8 In. 10.00
Label, Cigar Box, Don Alasco, Inner, 10 x 7 In. 89.00
Label, Cigar Box, E Arabe, White Arabian Mount, Inner, 7 x 7 In. 179.00
Label, Cigar Box, Exposition, Pan-American Exposition, Inner, 10 x 7 In. 388.00
Label, Cigar Box, Fluffy Ruffles, Woman Holding Umbrella, Inner, 10 x 7 In. 119.00
Label, Cigar Box, Green Belle, Green Woman, Gold Hat, Dress, Inner, 10 x 7 In. 71.00
Label, Cigar Box, Hazel-Kirke, Woman Lighting Thin Cigar, Inner, 10 x 7 In. 203.00
Label, Cigar Box, Woman Dressed As Santa, Inner, 1898, 10 x 7 In. 262.00
Label, Cigar Box, Yankee Bird, Tom Turkey, Inner, 1898, 10 x 7 In. 657.00
Label, Cosmetic, Columbia Greaseless Hair Cream, Redheaded Woman, 4 x 1 ½ In. .75
Label, Cosmetic, Rose Toilet Water, Red Rose, 1 ½ x 3 ¾ In. .50
Label, Food, Dixie Boy, Black Child Eating Grapefruit, 9 x 9 In. 3.00
Label, Food, Full O' Juice, Peeled Orange, Lavender Ground. 2.00
Label, Food, Santa, St. Nick With Bag Of Goodies, 1928. 8.00
Label, Medical, Epsom Salt, Topless Woman, Roses, 2 ½ x 6 ½ In. .50
Label, Medical, Laxal, The Baby's Friend, 1 ¼ x 4 In. .25
Label, Tobacco, America's Emblem, Eagle, On Shield, Trees, Frame, 7 x 14 In. 295.00
Label, Tobacco, Dixie Kid, Cut Plug, Yellow, Red, Black, Nall & Williams, 9 ½ In. 5.00
Label, Tobacco, General George Custer, c.1880-90, 7 ½ x 6 ½ In. 50.00
Label, Tobacco, Gentlemen Of Quality, 3 Men, Woman, 6 ¼ x 9 ½ In. 140.00
Label, Tobacco, King Coal 100, King On Throne, Gold Highlights, V.E. Richardi 1.00
Label, Tobacco, Majestic, Luxury Liner, 6 ½ x 10 In. 50.00
Label, Tobacco, Memory, Man Seated By Fireplace, Gold Highlights, 6 x 10 In. 50.00
Label, Tobacco, Scotch Piper, Man Playing Bagpipes, Wm. Steiner, 6 x 10 In. 110.00
Label, Tobacco, Smoke Chief Joseph, Indian, Embossed, 6 x 9 In. 50.00
Label, Tobacco, Welcome Nugget, Paper, Frame, c.1900, 7 x 15 In. 58.00
Label, Tobacco, William Tell, Aims At Apple, Gold Highlights, 6 x 9 ½ In. 50.00
Label, Whiskey, Old Sport, Bourbon, Jockey, Jumping Horse, 10 Piece 3.00
Label, Whiskey, Red Man, Indian Holding Tomahawk, White Grape Wine 2.00
Lamps are listed in the Lamp category.
Letter Opener, U-Needa Biscuit, Boy, Raincoat, Carrying Biscuits, 1920s, 8 In. 33.00

Advertising, Figure, Pilgrim Rum, Pilgrim, Chalkware, 16 ½ In.
$345.00

Advertising, Footrest, Thom McAn, Wood, c.1920, 12 x 15 In.
$29.00

TIP

Never store old paper collectibles in ordinary cardboard boxes or plastic bags. Buy the acid-free boxes and Mylar wrapping film that are approved for long-term storage. Many picture-framing and supply stores will have these items.

Advertising, Menu Board, Borden's Ice Cream, Tin, 1950s, 11 x 26 In.
$288.00

Advertising, Nodder, Big Boy, Red, White Check Overalls, Composite, 8 In.
$295.00

Advertising, Pot Scraper, King Midas Flour, c.1910, 2 ¼ x 3 In.
$230.00

License Plate Topper, Drink Zesto, Safety Pays, Porcelain, Die Cut, 6 ½ x 5 ½ In. 123.00
Lorillard Tobacco, Cabinet, Walnut, Etched Glass, Carved Top, 33 x 36 In. 2475.00
Lunch Box, Red Crown Chewing Tobacco, John J. Bagley & Co., 4 ½ x 6 ½ x 5 In. 86.00
Lunch Boxes are also listed in their own category.
Lunch Pail, Boy Blue Toffee, Handle, Tin Lithograph, 8 In. 77.00
Lunch Pail, Tiger Chewing Tobacco, Red, Basket Weave, Tin, 2 Handles, 10 x 8 In. 44.00
Lunch Pail, Union Leader Cut Plug, Milk Can Shape, Top, Handle, 9 In. 110.00
Mask, Babe Ruth Feen-A-Mint Laxative Gum, c.1933, 9 ½ x 6 ½ In. 940.00
Matchbook, Budweiser, St. Louis, Mo., 1939 .... 5.00
Matchbook, La Tropical Florida's Famous Beer, Taste Tells, Tampa Brewery 11.00
Menu Board, 7Up, Fresh Up, Tin, Stout Sign Co., 1961, 30 x 19 ½ In. 45.00
Menu Board, Borden's Ice Cream, Tin, 1950s, 11 x 26 In. .... *illus* 288.00
Menu Board, Camel Cigarettes, So Mild, So Good, Reverse Glass, c.1950, 13 x 28 In. 275.00
Menu Board, Dr Pepper, Green, Red, White, Marked, Grace Sign Co., 1950s, 28 x 20 In. 80.00
Menu Board, Hires Root Beer, Refreshes, Glass, Cardboard, Metal, 1950s, 13 x 28 In. 144.00
Menu Board, Kayo Soda, Tin, Enameled, Blackboard, Rolled Edge, 1950s, 14 x 27 ½ In. 280.00
Menu Board, Moxie, Try Our Soda Syrups, 12 Flavors, Embossed, Tin, 1905, 19 x 13 In. 1093.00
Menu Board, Orange Crush, Tin Lithograph, Embossed, c.1950, 23 x 35 In. 275.00
Milk Carton, Meadow Sweet All Star Dairies, Eire, Kan., Mickey Mantle, c.1957, Qt. 2350.00

Advertising mirrors of all sizes with advertising are listed here. Pocket mirrors range in size from 1 ½ to 5 inches in diameter. Most of these mirrors were given away as advertising promotions and include the name of the company in the design.

Mirror, Chicago Hats, Kindly Remember Me, Portrait, Pocket, 1 ¾ In. Diam 33.00
Mirror, Chicago Tailoring, Woman, Green Dress, Celluloid, Oval, 2 ½ x 1 ¾ In. 50.00
Mirror, Coney Island, Bathing Beauty, Park, Celluloid, 1950s, 3 In. 125.00
Mirror, Corina Cigar, Reverse Paint, 9 ¾ In. 55.00
Mirror, Cow-Ease, Farmer, Cow, Carpenter-Morton Co., Boston, Blue, White, Oval, 3 In. 440.00
Mirror, Dr Pepper, 2 Bottles, Stamped, 40051, 1938, 16 x 8 In. 200.00
Mirror, Dr Pepper, Lion, Vim, Vigor & Vitality, Oval, Plastic Frame, 18 ¼ x 26 In. 50.00
Mirror, Englehart, Woman In Hat, St. Joseph, Missouri, Celluloid, Oval, 2 ¾ x 2 In. 60.00
Mirror, Enjoy Grapette Soda, Thirsty Or Not, Navy Blue, 8 x 12 In. 67.00
Mirror, Equitable Loan Society, Phil. Athletics Players, Celluloid, Pocket, 1910, 2 In. 2938.00
Mirror, Furrier, Tiger On Front, Blue Ground, Yost Furrier, Detroit, Pocket, 3 x 2 In. 120.00
Mirror, Geo. Wm. Hoffman Co., Bar-Keepers Friend, Nude Woman, Celluloid, 2 In. 275.00
Mirror, H.W. Holl's Wrapped Bread, Every Bit Just Rite, Mother Goose, Pocket, 2 x 3 In. 44.00
Mirror, Horlick's Malted Milk, Girl With Cow, Celluloid, Pocket, 2 In. Diam. 72.00
Mirror, KC Breweries, Talk Of The Town, 2 Dutch Women, Celluloid, 2 ¾ x 1 ¾ In. 330.00
Mirror, Knox Hats Clothing Store, Embossed Wood Frame, 12 x 15 In. 275.00
Mirror, Lawecki The Druggist, Portrait, Pittsburgh, Round, Celluloid, Pocket, 2 ¼ In. 175.00
Mirror, Lowenbach Bros. Wakefield Rye, Nude Woman, Celluloid, 2 ½ x 1 ¾ In. 176.00
Mirror, Lucky Tiger, Cures Dandruff, Red, White, Celluloid, 2 In. 165.00
Mirror, McCoy's Funeral Home & Invalid Coach, Middletown, c.1915, 3 ½ x 2 In. 195.00
Mirror, Mennen's, Violet Talcum Toilet Powder, Celluloid, Pocket, 2 x 1 ¾ In. 67.00
Mirror, Mennen's Talcum, Pink Powder Not A Rouge, Celluloid, 2 x 2 ¾ In. 45.00
Mirror, Ohio Blue Tip Matches, Kurtz & Mayers, Celluloid, 3 ½ In. Diam. 140.00
Mirror, Pabst's, Okay Special, Price $3.99, Johnson's Pharmacy, Frame, 11 ½ x 9 In. 44.00
Mirror, Schenley Whiskies Co., Be Bright Go Light, Dated 1940, 18 x 24 In. 80.00
Mirror, Thoroughbred Hats, 3 Horses Image, Celluloid, S.J. Miller, Lithograph, 2 ¼ In. 134.00
Mirror, Traveler's Insurance, Railroad Men's Alliance, Celluloid, Oval, 1 ½ x 2 In. 66.00
Mixer, Sifter, Jones Excelsior Drug & Baking Powder, Metal, Pat. 1887 .... 1500.00
Mold, Hershey's, No. 1 Premium Chocolates, Lancaster, Pa., 1 Lb., 6 ½ In. 225.00
Mug, Esso Tiger, Milk Glass, Fire-King, 9 Oz., 3 ½ In. 12.00
Mug, Fleischmann's Vienna Cafe & Rathskeller, Stoneware, Tan, Red, c.1900, 4 In. 34.00
Mug, Hires Root Beer, Ugly Kid, Holding Mug, Flared Rim, Marked, Cauldon, 3 ¾ In. 33.00
Mug, Ovaltine House, White Porcelain, Image Of Uncle Wiggily, 1924, 4 In. 60.00
Nodder, Big Boy, Red, White Check Overalls, Composite, 8 In. .... *illus* 295.00
Nodder, Red Goose Shoes, Goose, Red, Yellow, Black, c.1960, 6 In. 230.00
Page Turner, American Line, Red Star Line, Fleet, Locations, Tin Lithograph, 12 x 3 In. 622.00
Pail, Armour's Peanut Butter, Bail Handle, Tin, 1 Lb., 3 ¾ x 3 ½ In. 55.00
Pail, Big Sister Peanut Butter, Witches Flying, Moon, Bail Handle, Tin, 3 x 3 ¾ In. 330.00
Pail, Derby's Peter Pan Peanut Butter, 2 x 1 ½ In. 154.00
Pail, Hoody's Famous Peanut Butter, Peanut Seesaw, Bail Handle, 4 x 4 In. 480.00
Pail, Peter Rabbit Peanut Butter, Bail Handle, Tin, 4 x 3 ½ In. .... 135.00 to 220.00
Pail, Pickaninny Brand Peanut Butter, Mammy On Front, 1 Lb. 45.00
Pail, Pickaninny Brand Peanut Butter, Tin, Gold Ground, Bail Handle, 3 ½ x 3 ½ In. 60.00

Pail, Purity Ice Cream, Bail, Lid, Tin, 8 In. 360.00
Pail, Sultana Peanut Butter, Children, Handle 95.00
Pail, Toyland Peanut Butter, Marching Band, Indian, Woman, Horses, Bail Handle, 3 ½ x 4 In. 170.00
Pail, Toyland Peanut Butter, Tin Lithograph, Blue, Wire Bail Handle, 4 In. 110.00
Pail, Uncle Wiggily's Peanut Butter, At Seashore, Bail Handle, 1923, 3 ½ x 4 In. 550.00
Pails are also listed in the Lunch Box category.
Pin, Althouse Wheeler Co., Windmill Apparatus, Early 1900s, 2 ¼ In. 612.00
Pin, Aunt Fanny's Bread, Fran Allison, Kukla Fran & Ollie, 1950s, 1 ⅛ In. 52.00
Pin, Avery, Steam Engine, Tin, Die Cut, Embossed, 1 x 1 ⅞ In. 253.00
Pin, Clerk's, Quaker Cereals, Photo Of Babe Ruth, Ask Me, 1937, 3 In. 515.00
Pin, Dr. A.C. Daniels Horse Medicines, Wild Eyed Horse, Early 1900s, 1 3/16 In. 388.00
Pin, Frog In Your Throat?, For Coughs & Colds, 10 Cents, Celluloid, 1 ¼ In. 27.00
Pin, General Electric Clocks, Peter Max Design, Celluloid, c.1968, 3 In. 207.00
Pin, Indian Motorcycle, Celluloid, Handee Mfg., Lithograph, Whitehead & Hoag, ⅞ In. 56.00
Pin, Moxie, Die Cut, Pretty Woman Serving Up Soda, 1908, 1 ¾ x 2 In. 89.00
Pin, Tony The Tiger, Astronaut Breakfast Game, c.1960, 1 In. 8.00
Pin, U.N.C.L.E. Bubble Gum, Illya Kuryakin Picture, Pink Ground, 1960s, ⅞ In. 86.00
Pincushion, Detmer Woolen Co., Nickel Finish Brass, Top Hat Shape, 2 ¼ x 2 ¾ In. 86.00
Plaque, Dealer, Goodyear, Cast, Zeppelin, Airplane, Medal Art Co., 17 ½ In. 288.00
Plaque, Match Holder, Genesee Plating Works, N.Y, Face, Cast Iron, Red Paint, 4 x 8 In. 367.00
Plaque, Michigan Stove Co., Iron, High Relief Casting, 7 ¼ x 11 ¼ In. 66.00
Plate, Clear Heads Choose Calvert, Owl, Taylor Smith & Taylor, 10 In. 45.00
Plate, Dr Pepper King Of Beverages, Free From Caffeine, Roses, Tin, 1900s, 10 In. 300.00
Plate, Moxie, Moxie Girl, Porcelain, 1915-20, 6 ¼ In. 65.00
Plate, Perkins-Huffman Co., Pansies, Orange Rim, c.1910, 7 ¼ In. 19.00
Plate, Trader's Bank Of Toronto, Flow Blue, 10 ½ In. 115.00
Playing Cards, Eagle White Lead Co., Cincinnati, Spread Wing Eagle On Mountain 28.00
Pot Scraper, American-Maid, Die Cut Tin, Loaf Of Bread, Red, White, Blue, 1 x 3 In. 270.00
Pot Scraper, King Midas Flour, c.1910, 2 ¼ x 3 In. . . . . . *illus* 230.00
Pouch, Victory Smoking Tobacco, Indian On Horseback, Unopened, c.1912, 2 ½ In. 275.00
Prize Machine, Red Goose Shoes, Goose, Lays Egg, Wood, Papier-Mache, 31 x 23 In. 405.00
Rack, Blu-J Brooms, Metal, Tin, Embossed, 1920-30, 35 x 23 In. 350.00
Rack, Chore Boy & Chore Girl, Metal, 1930-40, 14 x 10 x 7 In. 200.00
Rack, Curity Medical Tapes, Tin, Spins, Red, White 20.00
Rack, Lifesaver's, Wire, Tin, 36 ¾ In. 90.00
Rack, Snow King Baking Powder, Bag, 2-Sided, Tin, Metal, 1915-20, 17 x 9 In. . . . . . *illus* 173.00
Rack, Sunshine Biscuits, Always Ask For, Metal, Yellow, Red, 52 x 20 x 17 In. 225.00
Ring, Premium, Robin Hood Shoes, Plastic, 1950s 225.00
Rolling Pin, Blazier & Kimble, Stoneware, Brown Bands, 8 In. 413.00
Rolling Pin, Complements Of C.J. Buckley, Blue, White, Stoneware, Wood, 15 ½ In. 275.00
Ruler, Fry's Cocoa, No Better Food, Tin, Folds, 4 Sections, 12 x ¾ In. 385.00
Salt & Pepper Shakers are listed in their own category.
Sample, Luzianne Coffee, Free Sample, Black Mammy Pouring Coffee, 3 x 2 ½ In. 150.00
Scales are listed in their own category.
Screen Door, Rainbo Bread, Push Bar, 98 x 32 In. 288.00
Shelf, Tetley Tea, Lithograph On Metal, Hanging Chains, 4 x 37 In. 303.00
Shoehorn, Shinola, Wonderful Shoe Polish, Tin Lithograph, 4 x 1 ½ In. 72.00
Shot Glass, Whiskey, Drink Ol Kentucky Home Club O.P.S., Red, White, Blue Enamel, 1 ¾ x 2 In. 375.00
Shot Glass, Whiskey, Rohrer's Liquor Store, Clear, Tapered Sides, 2 ⅜ x 2 In. 22.00
Sign, 2-Joes Co., Bohemic Nude Woman, Green Sofa, Paper, Frame, 15 ½ x 10 In. 150.00
Sign, 5 Cent To 5 Dollars, 3-D, Mounted To Strip, Red, Porcelain, 17 x 72 In. 330.00
Sign, 7Up, Enjoy A 7Up Float, Bottles, Cardboard, 1956, 21 x 33 ¼ In. 50.00
Sign, 7Up, Fresh Up, Embossed, Tin, 1959, 43 x 13 In. . . . . . *illus* 260.00
Sign, 7Up, Fresh Up, Hand Holding Bottle, Green, White, Red, Tin, 30 ¼ In. 60.00
Sign, 7Up, Fresh Up, Red, Green, White, Tin, Enamel, 12 x 30 In. 80.00
Sign, 7Up, Light-Up Motion, Ohio Advertising Display Co., 16 In. 385.00
Sign, 7Up, Sold Here, Red, White, Green, Flange, 2-Sided, 18 In. 80.00
Sign, 7Up, We Proudly Serve, It Likes You, Green, Red, Embossed, Tin, 1944, 11 x 31 In. 230.00
Sign, 10 Cent Men's Size Handkerchief, Porcelain, Red & White, 6 ½ x 13 In. 300.00
Sign, 394 Office W.H. Grahm Undertaker, Tombstone Shape, Reverse Painted Glass, 24 x 30 In. 173.00
Sign, A & W Ice Cold Root Beer, Red, Black & White, 1950s, 4 In. 139.00
Sign, A.J. Cripe, Hobo Bread, Man With, Hat, Banjo, Enameled, 2-Sided, 1940s, 20 x 30 In. 588.00
Sign, AA Motorcycle, Porcelain, 30 x 24 In. 675.00
Sign, Abbott's Ice Cream, Red, White, Blue, Porcelain, Flange, Oval, Bracket, 15 x 22 In. 420.00
Sign, Adams' Pepsin Gum, Girl, Curly Hair, Die Cut, Cardboard, Embossed, 13 x 10 In. 944.00
Sign, Agfa Camera Film, Boy Taking Picture, Red, White, Blue, Porcelain, 46 x 26 In. 475.00

Advertising, Rack,
Snow King Baking Powder, Bag, 2-Sided, Tin, Metal, 1915-20, 17 x 9 In.
$173.00

Advertising, Sign, 7Up, Fresh Up, Embossed, Tin, 1959, 43 x 13 In.
$260.00

TIP

Any lithographed can with a picture is of more value than a lithographed can with just names. Any paper-labeled can that can be dated before 1875 is rare. Any ad that pictures an American flag or a black person has added value.

Advertising, Sign, Alfa-Laval, Paper, France, 1910-15, 25 x 16 In.
$87.00

Advertising, Sign, Bobby Lou Lemon Drink, Woman, Frame, 1920s, 19 x 14 ½ In.
$144.00

Advertising, Sign, Brown's Jumbo Bread, Elephant, Die Cut, 15 x 13 In.
$316.00

Advertising, Sign, Centlivre Brewing Co., Plant, Paper, Frame, c.1890, 24 x 37 In.
$316.00

Sign, Akron Brewing, Co., Plant View, Wood, Meyerord Co., 36 x 24 In. 590.00
Sign, Akron Brewing Co., Wood, Image Of Factory, Akron, 1905, 36 x 24 In. 425.00
Sign, Albers Pearl Barley, 1 Lb. Container, Cardboard, 2-Sided, c.1927, 3 ½ x 5 In. 134.00
Sign, Albis Barber Shop, Wood, 1890-1910, 35 ½ x 9 ½ In. 296.00
Sign, Alfa-Laval, Paper, France, 1910-15, 25 x 16 In. .... *illus* 87.00
Sign, Allied Mills, Feed Bag Shape, Red, White, Black, Porcelain, 32 x 24 ½ In. 140.00
Sign, All-In-One Kennel Meal, Used In Bulk Bins, Rolled Edge, Dog On Top, 7 x 13 In. 88.00
Sign, American Beauty Massage Cream, Reverse Glass, Frame, 10 ¾ x 13 In. 190.00
Sign, American Gas, American Marches Ahead, Drummer, Cloth, Rockwell, 36 x 76 In. 225.00
Sign, American Insurance Co., Newark, N.J., Reverse Painted, Frame, 1890s, 14 x 23 In. 220.00
Sign, Anheuser-Busch, On Draught, Reverse Painted, Copper Flashed, Metal, 30 x 17 In. 3430.00
Sign, Apothecary, Mortar & Pestle, Oak, 19th Century, 15 In. 450.00
Sign, Arcadia Table Waters, Lemon Tree, Boy, Arched, Porcelain, 40 ½ x 61 In. 165.00
Sign, Arden Ice Cream, Red, White, Die Cut, Porcelain, 2-Sided, 1940s, 42 x 28 In. 2850.00
Sign, Arm & Hammer Baking Soda, Woodpecker, M.E. Eaton, 1915, 14 ⅜ x 11 In. 50.00
Sign, Arrow Collars & Shirts, Image On Canvas, Sailboat, 27 x 20 In. 210.00
Sign, Astrologer, Open Book Shape, Symbols, c.1905, 21 x 23 In. 5036.00
Sign, Authorized Dealer Agency, Blue, White, 9 x 40 In. 450.00
Sign, Ayer's Cathartic Pills, Country Doctor, Black Man, Children, Frame, 15 x 10 In. 880.00
Sign, Ayer's Cherry Pectoral, St. Nick, Sleigh, Die Cut, Cardboard, 1884, 13 x 7 In. 529.00
Sign, Ayer's Sarsaparilla, Deacon, Die Cut, Cardboard, 13 x 7 In. 232.00
Sign, Ayer's Sarsaparilla, Old Folks At Home, Die Cut, Cardboard, 1884, 11 x 8 In. 210.00
Sign, B.B. Poultry Feed, Yellow, Red, Black, Tin, 12 x 24 In. 82.00
Sign, B.R. Cobb Stable, Hack & Boarding, Erected 1888, Gold Letters, 20 Ft. x 40 In. 9200.00
Sign, Baby Beef, Our Specialty, Cow, Porcelain, 1951, 26 x 34 In. 373.00
Sign, Badger Brand Farm Seed, Authorized Dealer, Red, Yellow, Green, Tin, 14 x 20 In. 55.00
Sign, Ball Mason Jar, Now Is The Time To Can, Lithograph, 1947, 43 ¼ In. 130.00
Sign, Band Leader, Major Appliances Basement, Wood, Painted, Blue, White, Yellow, 73 In. 175.00
Sign, Banner Milk, It Tastes Better, Red, White, Porcelain, 21 x 36 In. 250.00
Sign, Bates Market, Large Painted Cod, Yellow Field, Black Letters, 14 x 30 In. 863.00
Sign, Beauty Shop, Blue, White, 2-Sided, Porcelain, Flange, No. 1223, 22 ½ In. 60.00
Sign, Beech-Nut Chewing Tobacco, Pack, Red, White, Blue, Porcelain, 1930s, 10 x 22 In. 173.00
Sign, Beeman's, Enamel, Tin Lithograph, c.1935, 17 ½ x 2 ½ In. 179.00
Sign, Beeman's Pepsin Gum, Tin, Beveled, Embossed, Mr. Beeman Image, 13 x 9 In. 150.00
Sign, Benny's Bat 'Em Down, 1 Cent, 4 Black Faces, c.1905, 10 x 26 In. 889.00
Sign, Berec Batteries, Sun, Porcelain, Belgium, 48 ¾ In. 80.00
Sign, Beringer Jewelry Store, Man, Woman, Flowers, Moving Swing, Electric, 25 x 13 In. 4425.00
Sign, Berliner Caramel, Enamel On Metal, 12 ¼ x 16 ½ In. 207.00
Sign, Big Dandy Bread, Tin, Flange, Red, White, Blue, Yellow, 1930s, 6 x 12 In. 633.00
Sign, Black Bass Navy Chew, Fish, Figural, 2-Sided, Die Cut, Tin Lithograph, 12 x 19 In. 270.00
Sign, Black Cat Virginia Cigarette, Porcelain, 20 x 14 In. 245.00
Sign, Black Man, Word To The Wise, Molded, Tin, 1890-1910, 33 ¾ x 27 In. 2252.00
Sign, Bobby Lou Lemon Drink, Woman, Frame, 1920s, 19 x 14 ½ In. .... *illus* 144.00
Sign, Bond Bread, Fresh, Enamel, Red, Beige, White, 19 x 14 In. 90.00
Sign, Bond Bread, Home-Like, Yellow, Blue, Porcelain, 14 x 19 In. 60.00
Sign, Bond Street Pipe Tobacco, Cardboard, 33 x 24 In. 50.00
Sign, Booth's Crescent Brand, Broiled Mackerel, Die Cut, Cardboard, 13 x 8 In. 67.00
Sign, Borden's Dairy, Meadow Brands, Cow, Fiberglass, Painted, Wood, 40 x 48 In. 975.00
Sign, Borden's Ice Cream, Candy, Sodas, Blue, Red, White, Porcelain, Frame, 47 x 59 In. 1250.00
Sign, Botl'o Grape, Other Flavors, Blue, Green, Enamel, 2-Sided, Flange, 22 In. 300.00
Sign, Boyce Moto Meter, Woman Pointing To Gauge, 2-Sided, Tin Flange, 22 x 19 In. 18700.00
Sign, Breinig Oil Paint, Man Painting Cupola, Embossed, Tin, 28 x 19 ½ In. 425.00
Sign, Breyers Ice Cream, Leaf, Mirror, 2-Sided, 34 ½ x 22 In. 350.00
Sign, Breyers Ice Cream, Leaf, Red, Green, White, Oval, Tin, 31 ½ x 51 In. 100.00
Sign, Brotherhood Tobacco Chewing & Smoking, Laborer, Millionaire, 22 x 30 In. 1920.00
Sign, Brown Shoe Co., Star-Five-Star Shoes, Blue, White, Tin, 14 x 20 In. 35.00
Sign, Brown's Jumbo Bread, Elephant, Die Cut, 15 x 13 In. .... *illus* 316.00
Sign, Bruton's Snuff, Keep Right On Using, Black, White, Tin Lithograph, 4 x 21 In. 80.00
Sign, Buckeye Beer, On Draught Here, Man With Hat & Sign, Embossed, Tin, 1940s, 3 x 13 In. 114.00
Sign, Budweiser, All Aboard, Red, White, Tin, 20 x 30 In. 15.00
Sign, Budweiser, King Of Bottled Beer, Painted, Copper Flashed, Metal, 30 x 17 In. 3300.00
Sign, Budweiser Beer, Embossed Metal Lithograph, Wood Back, 24 x 72 In. 468.00
Sign, Budweiser Girl, Pink Dress, Holding Bottle, Frame, 1904, 39 x 24 In. 2300.00
Sign, Bull Durham Smoking Tobacco, 17 x 12 In. 110.00
Sign, Bull Woods Quality Tobacco, Yellow, Black, Tin Lithograph, 20 x 14 In. 275.00
Sign, Bunny Bread, That's What Ah Said, Bunny, Bread, Tin, 19 x 54 In. 340.00

Sign, Bus Stop, Red, White, Embossed, Cast Iron, Stand, c.1930, 28 In. 300.00
Sign, Buster Brown Children's Clothing, Buster & Dog, 9 ½ x 7 In. 40.00
Sign, Buster Brown Shoes, Buster, Tige, Teeter-Totter, 35 x 14 In. 12000.00
Sign, Butterick & Co., Men's Fashion, Paper Lithograph, Frame, c.1900, 23 x 29 In. 58.00
Sign, Butter-Nut Bread, 2 Girls Holding Bread, Cardboard, Schulze Baking, 11 x 20 In. 44.00
Sign, C.C. Martin's Forge, Wood, Blue & White Paint, 2-Sided, c.1900, 18 x 96 In. 650.00
Sign, C.C.C. Certain Chill Cure, No Cure, No Pay, Girl, Paper, Frame, 20 x 10 In. 1430.00
Sign, Calumet Chief, Superior Colorado Coal, Red, White, Pressed Board, 12 x 12 In. 65.00
Sign, Camel Cigarettes, Porcelain, 15 x 15 In. 475.00
Sign, Campbell's, Tomato Soup, Can, Porcelain, 22 ½ x 13 In. 130.00
Sign, Canoe Rental, Canoe, Wood, Painted, 18 x 23 In. 175.00
Sign, Cardboard, Boston Garter, 2 Baseball Players, Sock Garters, 1912, 22 x 11 In. 15275.00
Sign, Cargill Seed, Yellow, Black, White, Tin, 33 x 57 In. 30.00
Sign, Carhartt's Overalls, Blue, Yellow, Porcelain, 10 x 27 ½ In. 253.00
Sign, Carhartt's Pants, Overalls, Gloves, Die Cut, Heart, Tin, 2-Sided, Flange, 18 x 18 In. 2500.00
Sign, Carstairs Whiskey, John L. Sullivan, c.1950 .... 120.00
Sign, Cash Or Credit, Chipped Reverse Glass, Frame, 9 ¾ x 33 In. 715.00
Sign, Cataract Brewing Co., Pilsner Beer, Cream Ale, 13 ¾ In. Diam. 55.00
Sign, Caterpillar Implement, Porcelain, 2-Sided, Bulldozer, Iron Frame, 30 In. 4950.00
Sign, Cat-Tex Rubber Heels & Soles, Glass, Metal, 8-Sided, c.1940, 15 x 19 In. 300.00
Sign, Centlivre Beer, Vitrolite, 16 x 22 ½ x 7 In. 8050.00
Sign, Centlivre Brewing Co., Plant, Paper, Frame, c.1890, 24 x 37 In. .... *illus* 316.00
Sign, Centlivre Tonic, Builds Up The System, Nurse, Cardboard, Frame, 1910, 10 x 20 In. 115.00
Sign, Chamberlain's Cough Remedy, Pleasant & Safe To Take, 20 x 28 In., Pair 187.00
Sign, Chancellor Cigar, Cardboard, Elegant Woman, With Fan, Frame, 24 x 41 In. 2875.00
Sign, Charles Denby Cigar, Cardboard Cutout, Frame, c.1940, 13 x 35 In. 345.00
Sign, Chase & Sanborn's Coffees, Cardboard, Frame, 31 x 26 In. .... *illus* 345.00
Sign, Chase's Chocolates, Taste The Difference, Reverse Painted, Frame, 11 ½ x 15 In. 110.00
Sign, Chateau D'Ambroise, French Railroad, Linen Backed, 1900s. 330.00
Sign, Checker Cab Co., Taxi, Dial 2-3434, Car, Green, Black, White, Cardboard, 7 x 11 In. 260.00
Sign, Cheer Up, Drink, Delightful, Red, White, Blue, Tin, Flange, 1940, 10 x 12 In. 275.00
Sign, Cherry Blossoms, Boy, Girl, Drinking, Die Cut, Tin, 2-Sided, 1921, 7 x 11 ½ In. 575.00
Sign, Cherry Blossoms, Ice Cold, Sold Here, Bottle, 2-Sided, Enamel, Flange, 16 In. 350.00
Sign, Cherry's Ice Cream, We Serve, Red, White, Porcelain, Flange, 1930s, 12 x 16 In. 305.00
Sign, Chesterfield Cigarettes, 21 & 20, Red, White, Paper, 24 x 17 ¾ In. 20.00
Sign, Chesterfield Cigarettes, Joe Louis, c.1940 .... 156.00
Sign, Chesterfield Cigarettes, Nothing Stops 'Em, Football Players, Color, 17 x 27 In. 1680.00
Sign, Chew Yucatan Gum, Mother, Girl, On Horseback, Die Cut Cardboard, 10 x 14 In. 2478.00
Sign, Chief Paints, Indian, Headdress, Black, Yellow, Red, Tin, 2-Sided, 24 x 18 In. 363.00
Sign, Chin Laundry, Wood, 2-Sided, Painted, Red, White Lettering, Molded Frame, 13 ¾ x 43 In. 187.00
Sign, Citizens Ice Company, Blue, White, Porcelain, 24 x 24 In. 420.00
Sign, Clabber Girl Baking Powder, Yellow, Red, Black, Tin, 12 x 34 In. 55.00
Sign, Clark's Teaberry Chewing Gum, Mountain Tea Flavor, Tin Lithograph, 11 ½ x 8 ½ In. 364.00
Sign, Clark's Teaberry Gum, A Happy Thought, Tin, 1920s, 8 ¾ x 11 ¾ In. 60.00
Sign, Cleo Cola, Genuine, 12 Oz. For 5 Cents, Cleopatra, Tin, Frame, 12 x 26 In. 330.00
Sign, Clock, Chapman, Watches, Clocks, Jewelry, Painted, Wood, Metal, Iron Stand, 37 x 24 In. 1100.00
Sign, Cloverdale Soft Drinks, Red, White, Green, 2-Sided, Flange, 22 In. 120.00
Sign, Cognac Jacquet, Peacock, Camille Bouchet, Frame, France, c.1905, 43 x 60 In. 3000.00
Sign, Coles Peruvian Bark & Wild Cherry Bitters, Blue, White, Porcelain, 6 x 16 In. 1210.00
Sign, Colonial Club Cigars, 5 Cent, Blue, Red, White, 2-Sided, Metal, Flange, 8 ¾ x 18 In. 167.00
Sign, Colt's Fire Arms Cowgirl, Variation No. 2, Lithograph, 1910, 18 x 29 In. 14000.00
Sign, Columbia Grafonola, Chas. W. Norton, Tin, 1920-30, 18 x 24 In. .... *illus* 460.00
Sign, Columbia Records, Record, Black, Yellow, 28 In. Diam. 900.00
Sign, Community State Bank, Glue Chip, Reverse Painted Glass, c.1900, 34 x 28 In. 825.00
Sign, Continental Insurance Co., Paper, American Indians, Forest Fire, c.1895, 32 x 27 In. 690.00
Sign, Coon's Ice Cream, Cardboard, Outer Metal Frame, c.1920, 21 x 60 In. 58.00
Sign, Coors Beer, De Boss Sho Likes His Coors, Tin Cardboard, Maid, Butler, 21 x 13 In. 440.00
Sign, Copenhagen, More Satisfying, Best Chew Ever Made, Red, Porcelain, 6 x 23 In. 180.00
Sign, Copper Goose Bourbon, Bottle Form, Silk Screen Print, 2-Sided, 40 In. 45.00
Sign, Country Club Ginger Ale, Orange, White, Black, Porcelain, 1930s, 12 x 36 In. 260.00
Sign, Cream Pure Rye, Cardboard, c.1900, 20 x 25 In. 345.00
Sign, Crown Quality Ice Cream, Embossed, Tin, 1935, 28 x 20 In. .... *illus* 58.00
Sign, Custom House, Shield, Painted, Cast Iron, 1890-1910, 11 ¾ x 18 In. 1126.00
Sign, Dairy Made Ice Cream, Child, Embossed, Tin, Frame, 30 x 21 ½ In. 305.00
Sign, Dawn Donuts, There's A Difference, Celluloid Over Cardboard, 6 x 11 In. 252.00
Sign, Dekalb, Weather Vane Sign, Corn, Tin Lithograph, 2-Sided, Pole, 8 ½ x 18 In. 180.00

Advertising, Sign,
Chase & Sanborn's Coffees,
Cardboard, Frame, 31 x 26 In.
$345.00

Advertising, Sign,
Columbia Grafonola, Chas. W. Norton,
Tin, 1920-30, 18 x 24 In.
$460.00

Advertising, Sign,
Crown Quality Ice Cream, Embossed,
Tin, 1935, 28 x 20 In.
$58.00

Advertising, Sign, DeLaval, Milker, Embossed, Tin, 1940s, 16 x 12 In. $403.00

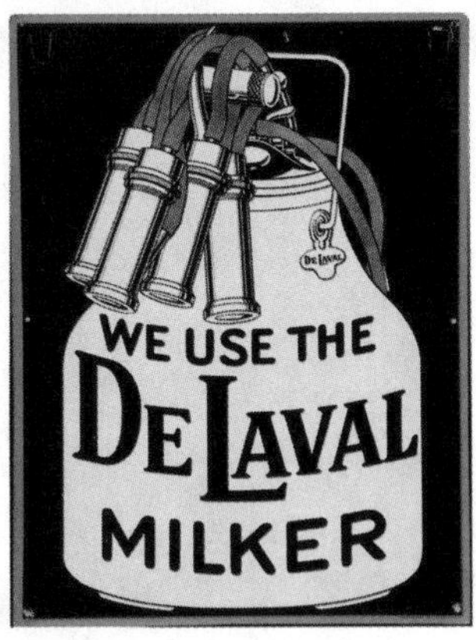

Advertising, Sign, Dr Pepper, Drink A Bite To Eat, Celluloid, Envelope, 1940s, 9 In. $403.00

Advertising, Sign, Escabana Beer, Reverse On Glass, c.1890, 18 In. $863.00

Sign, Dekalb Feed, Rooster Head, Red, White, Yellow, Porcelain, 5 x 42 In. 1050.00
Sign, DeLaval, Cream Separators, Tin, Gesso Frame, 1907, 30 x 40 In. 2588.00
Sign, DeLaval, Cream Separators & Milkers, Painted, Tin, Wood Frame, 26 x 96 In. 550.00
Sign, DeLaval, Dairy Equipment, Yellow, Blue, Tin, 12 x 18 In. 35.00
Sign, DeLaval, Milker, Embossed, Tin, 1940s, 16 x 12 In. . . . . . *illus* 403.00
Sign, DeLaval, Milkmaid, Tin Lithograph, Red Ground, Gold Wood Frame, 38 x 27 In. 1320.00
Sign, DeVilbiss Atomizers, George Petty, Stand-Up, 1926, 28 x 39 In. 2400.00
Sign, Devilish Good Cigar, None Better, 5 Cent, Painted, Tin, c.1900, 10 x 14 In. 250.00
Sign, Devoe Paint, Devoe & Raynolds Co., Sioux City, Iowa, Tin, 29 x 19 In. 180.00
Sign, Dewey Cement, Mt. Horeb Lumber Co., Red, White, Blue, Porcelain, 17 x 47 In. 95.00
Sign, Dexter's Mother's Bread, Porcelain, Blackboard, c.1930, 18 x 24 In. 58.00
Sign, Doc Jones Germ Killer, Wood Mallet, 1950s, 20 x 36 In. 391.00
Sign, Douglas Corn, Cow, 1930s-40s, 2 x 3 In. 345.00
Sign, Dr Pepper, Bottle Cap, 10, 2, 4, Red, White, Yellow, Flange, 17 ¼ x 22 In. 400.00
Sign, Dr Pepper, Bottle Cap, Red, White, 10, 2, 4, Tin, 35 ½ In. Diam. 275.00
Sign, Dr Pepper, Diet Dr Pepper, Bottle Cap, Stripes, White, Red, 1980s, 27 In. Diam. 10.00
Sign, Dr Pepper, Drink, Red, Black, White, Porcelain, 1930s, 10 ½ x 26 ¼ In. 200.00
Sign, Dr Pepper, Drink A Bite To Eat, Celluloid, Envelope, 1940s, 9 In. . . . . . *illus* 403.00
Sign, Dr Pepper, Good For Life, Celluloid Over Tin, Beveled, 6 x 7 ½ In. 224.00
Sign, Dr Pepper, Hance Grocery Service Station, 2-Sided, 1930s, 9 x 84 In. 500.00
Sign, Dr Pepper, Join Me, Woman, Hamburger In Car, Frame, 15 x 23 ½ In. 300.00
Sign, Dr Pepper, Thank You Call Again, Black, Yellow, Celluloid, 1940s, 11 x 8 In. 400.00
Sign, Dr. D. Davis Eye Water, Sore, Weak Or Inflamed Eyes, Paper, Frame, 6 x 9 ¾ In. 132.00
Sign, Dr. Drake's For Croupy Coughs, Children, Goose, Die Cut, Cardboard, 4 x 2 ½ In. 88.00
Sign, Dr. LeGear, Horse, Tin Lithograph, 14 ¼ x 17 ⅝ In. 141.00
Sign, Dr. Physician & Surgeon, Black, Gold Paint, Wood, 16 In. 352.00
Sign, Dr. R. Wien, Dentist, 2-Sided, Raised Gilt Letters, Late 19th Century, 22 x 36 In. 244.00
Sign, Dr. Shoop's, Nerve Pills, Best Cure, Blue, White, Reverse Paint On Glass, 6 x 18 In. 630.00
Sign, Dr. Siegert's Angostura Bitters, Black, White, Tin, 1830, 14 x 10 In. 50.00
Sign, Dr. Walker's California Vinegar Bitters, Triangular, 12 x 12 In. 1870.00
Sign, Dr. Wells, Bottle, 5 Cent, Tin, 27 x 9 ¾ In. 200.00
Sign, Draper & Maynard Gloves, Al Simmons, Cardboard, 1930s, 9 x 12 In. 570.00
Sign, Drink Barq's, It's Good, Cardboard, Black & White, 28 x 11 In. 44.00
Sign, Drink Barq's, It's Good, Red, Black, White, Enamel, 2-Sided, Flange, 21 ½ In. 300.00
Sign, Drink Moxie, Red, Yellow, Black, 2-Sided, Flange, 18 In. 450.00
Sign, Drink Orange Crush, Tin, Navy Round, Girl Drinking Pop, 1938, 6 x 10 In. 780.00
Sign, Drink Popeye, 5 Cents, Tin, Embossed, 9 x 16 In. 200.00
Sign, Drink Pop's Root Beer, Tin, Embossed, 1948, 18 x 24 In. 245.00
Sign, Drink Red Seal Beverages, Tin, Embossed, 12 x 24 In. 135.00
Sign, Drink Smile Soda, Orange Smiling, Blue, Orange, Tin, Flange, 1940s, 10 x 20 In. 460.00
Sign, Drug Store Prescriptions, Neon In Metal Box, c.1920, 8 x 30 In. 468.00
Sign, Drugs, Nature's Remedy, Chipped Reverse Glass, 24 x 17 ½ In. 645.00
Sign, DuPont Ballistite Gun Powder, Ducks Taking Flight, Copyright 1913, 20 x 30 In. 1668.00
Sign, Durkee's Flavor Bar, Red, Green, White, Tin, 6 ¼ x 30 ¼ In. 20.00
Sign, Dyer's Pork & Beans, Hand Holding Can, Tin Over Cardboard, 1930s, 11 x 8 In. 195.00
Sign, E.M. Lyman & Son, Flower & Vegetable Seeds, Tin, 20 In. 495.00
Sign, Eagle Stamps, Extra Savings, Red, Green, White, Embossed, Tin, 1950s, 30 x 54 In. 150.00
Sign, Economy Ice Cream, Enjoy, Best For Less, Aluminum, 2-Sided, Flange, 15 In. 100.00
Sign, Edison Mazda Lamps, Sun's Only Rival, Light Bulb, Sun, Frame, 1930, 11 ½ x 9 In. 110.00
Sign, Eggs, Burgundy, Green, Wood, Early 20th Century, 12 x 31 ½ In. 35.00
Sign, Egret Cigar, Bird Graphic, Blue, Green, Red, Yellow, 48 x 31 In. 3450.00
Sign, Egyptienne Luxury Cigarettes, Woman, Pink Dress, Frame, 1910, 22 x 17 In. 144.00
Sign, Eichler's Beer On Draught, Tin, Under Glass, Grain Paint, 19 In. Diam. 85.00
Sign, Eisenlohrs Cinco Cigar, Red, Yellow, Porcelain, 46 In. 325.00
Sign, Electric Furnace Man, Authorized Dealer, 2-Sided, Tin, Flange, 8 x 18 In. 50.00
Sign, Ellicott Hydraulic Dredge, Dragon Model, Red, White, Blue, Porcelain, 24 x 36 In. 200.00
Sign, Erie City Iron Works, Embossed, Cast Iron, 6 x 43 In. 190.00
Sign, Escabana Beer, Reverse On Glass, c.1890, 18 In. . . . . . *illus* 863.00
Sign, Eveready Battery, Black Bellhop With Flashlight, Porcelain, 34 x 18 In. 550.00
Sign, Eveready Flashlights, Batteries & Bulbs, 2-Sided Flange, Porcelain, 12 x 18 In. 403.00
Sign, Eveready Flashlights & Batteries, Man, Green, Red, White, Porcelain, 34 x 18 In. 1060.00
Sign, Evermore Cigars, Red, White, Porcelain, 10 x 28 In. 180.00
Sign, Everybody Likes Popsicle, Easy To Eat, Boy, Cardboard, Easel Back, 1932, 16 x 24 In. 235.00
Sign, Expert Watch Repairing, Reverse Glass, Silver Foil Lettering, c.1920, 10 x 2 In. 90.00
Sign, F.H. Preston Jeweler, Glo-Dial, Metal, Frosted White Neon, 26 In. 266.00
Sign, Fahy's Watch Cases, Factory Scene, Sag Harbor, Long Island, c.1890, 31 x 27 In. 345.00

Sign, Fairbanks Morse & Howe Scales, Porcelain, 9 x 50 In. 259.00
Sign, Fairmont's Ice Cream, Porcelain, 2-Sided, 36 x 20 In. 275.00
Sign, Falstaff Beer, Lemp, St. Louis, Gold Reverse On Glass, Mirror, c.1915, 9 x 10 In. 7950.00
Sign, Fatima Cigarettes, Jack Webb, Die Cut, Cardboard, 1950s, 15 ½ x 16 In. *illus* 403.00
Sign, Faygo Cola, Refresh-Ability, Bottle, Painted, Metal, 20th Century, 18 x 54 In. 40.00
Sign, Federal Express Money Order, Embossed, Tin, c.1950s, 26 x 35 In. 58.00
Sign, Ferguson System, Tractor, Blue, White, Porcelain, 34 ½ x 60 In. 1650.00
Sign, Ferris Waists, Embossed, Children Wearing Corsets, Tin, 16 x 22 In. 784.00
Sign, Firestone, Bridgestone, Porcelain, 2-Sided, 12 x 48 In. 115.00
Sign, Fishing Tackle For Sale, Fish Shape, Hollow Metal, Green Scales, Applied Fins, 38 In. 978.00
Sign, Fitger's Beer, Duluth, Minn., 18 In. 610.00
Sign, Foley's Kidney Cure, Good Results Guaranteed, Blue, Yellow, Canvas, 12 x 48 In. 143.00
Sign, Folgers Coffee, Yellow, Cowboy, Girl, Out On Range Drinking Coffee, Painted, 1940 2045.00
Sign, Ford V8, Neon, Multicolor, Porcelain, 75 x 80 x 12 In. 18400.00
Sign, Fortschendorf Bavaria, Enameled On Metal, 18 ½ x 12 In. 219.00
Sign, Four Roses Whiskey, Hunting Lodge, Signed, A.W. Woelfle, Frame, 46 x 32 In. 325.00
Sign, Fowler's Cherry Smash, Celluloid Over Tin, 12 ½ x 9 ½ In., 5 Piece 484.00
Sign, Frank's Orange Nectar, 6 Bottles, Embossed, Tin, 1950s, 13 ½ x 39 In. 173.00
Sign, Freeman's Milk, Elsie The Cow, Tin, Enamel, c.1930s, 23 x 16 In. 120.00
Sign, Fremont Quality Suspenders, Guarantee With Every Pair, Paper, 8 x 6 In. 75.00
Sign, Frigidaire, Cow, We Cool Our Milk, Blue, White, Porcelain, 1930-40, 14 x 20 In. 1100.00
Sign, Frog In Your Throat, For Coughs & Colds, Porcelain, 10 ½ x 8 In. 179.00
Sign, Frontenac White Cap Ale, Relief, Chalk, 1940s, 27 x 23 x 3 ½ In. *illus* 87.00
Sign, Frostie Root Beer, Bottle Cap, Embossed, Metal, 32 In. 303.00
Sign, Frostie Root Beer, Molded Plastic, Frostie Riding Snowmobile, 1960s, 10 x 15 In. 215.00
Sign, Funk's G Hoffmans Seeds, Landisville, Red, White, Tin, 22 In. 40.00
Sign, G.W. Prior, Undertaker, Furniture, Wood, 1850s, 9 In. 3600.00
Sign, Garland Stoves & Ranges, Yellow, Black, Porcelain, 38 In. 440.00
Sign, GE Radio Television Appliances, Neon, 2-Sided, 55 x 72 x 16 In. 2750.00
Sign, Geo. Kelley Co., Dargai Cigar, 2-Sided, Tin, 6 ¾ x 9 ½ In. 143.00
Sign, Ghiradelli's Chocolate & Cocoa, Girl, Doll, Cocoa Party, Painted, Tin, 23 x 17 In. 9000.00
Sign, Gold Bond Stamps, Yellow, Black, White, Tin, 48 x 42 In. 30.00
Sign, Golden Arrow, Robin Hood Shooting Arrow, Green, Black, Porcelain, 29 x 30 In. 420.00
Sign, Golden Orangeade, Delicious, 5 Cents, Black, Red, Gold, Rolled Edge, 6 x 10 In. 605.00
Sign, Golden Rule Hybrids, Grown By Phillip Grau, Graymont, Ill., Corn, Tin, 24 x 18 In. 35.00
Sign, Gordon Collar, Paper, Hand, Man's Collar, Whitehead & Hoag, 7 x 9 In. 220.00
Sign, Grace Bros. G & B Beer, Light-Up, 17 In. 975.00
Sign, Gramophone Co. Ltd., Wood, 28 ¾ x 21 ½ In. 200.00
Sign, Grandin's Feeds, Poultry, Dairy Stock, Blue, White, Red, Porcelain, 18 x 30 In. 100.00
Sign, Gran'pa Graf's Root Beer, Die Cut, Cardboard, 36 x 20 In. *illus* 385.00
Sign, Grape-Nuts, Girl, St. Bernard, There's A Reason, Self-Framed, 30 ¼ x 20 In. 1542.00
Sign, Grapette Soda, Girl In Flower Garden, Cardboard, 20 x 31 In. 66.00
Sign, Green Marked Coal, A Glance Identifies, Flame, Porcelain, 24 ½ In. 90.00
Sign, Green River, Neon, Oval, Light-Up, Reverse Paint On Glass, Metal Frame, 6 x 11 In. 1540.00
Sign, Greyhound Bus Lines, Greyhound Dog, 1940-60, 9 Ft. 500.00
Sign, Greyhound Lines, Greyhound, Blue, Yellow, 2-Sided, Porcelain, Oval, 20 x 36 In. 650.00
Sign, Gum Drops, Cardboard, Licorice Gun, Boy In Wagon, 8 ⅜ x 8 ⅜ In. 1135.00
Sign, H.R. Finney & Son, Contractors & Builders, Phone, Painted, Wood, 1920s, 16 x 69 In. 1250.00
Sign, Haberle Brewing Co., Porcelain, 14 x 20 In. 510.00
Sign, Halt, Drink Chocolate Soldier, Cannon, Soldier, Multicolored, 19 x 12 In. 20.00
Sign, Handy Box Matches, 3 For 10 Cents, Red, White, Paper, 15 ½ x 9 ½ In. 300.00
Sign, Hanger, A & W The Burger Family, Light-Up, Chain Hanger, 1950s, 14 x 23 In. 316.00
Sign, Hanger, Griesidieck Beer, Easel Back, Hanging, 22 x 39 In. 66.00
Sign, Hanger, Winchester Warranted Gunsmith, 2-Sided, Tin Lithograph, 38 In. 990.00
Sign, Hart Canned Fruits, 2 Cans, Tin Over Cardboard, 1930s, 9 x 13 In. 165.00
Sign, Harvard Brewing Co., Light-Up, 17 ½ x 13 x 6 In. 1659.00
Sign, Harvest Horse Feed, Lower Your Feed Cost, Yellow, Red, Black, Tin, 16 x 11 In. 200.00
Sign, Hazard Powder Sign, Rifles, Hunter, Indians, Buffalo, Deer, Tin, 39 x 30 In. 3850.00
Sign, Headlight Overalls, Union Made, Red, White, Blue, Porcelain, 1930-40, 15 x 48 In. 440.00
Sign, Hecker Pancake Flour, Package To Griddle, Paper, Frame, 10 x 20 In. 27.00
Sign, Helmar Turkish Cigarettes, Woman, Large Hat, Paper, Frame, 1907, 30 x 22 In. 1500.00
Sign, Helmbold's Buchu Fluid Extract, Reverse Paint On Glass, Frame, 7 ½ x 13 In. 1265.00
Sign, Hendler's Ice Cream, Pay When Served, Reverse Painted Glass, 11 In. Diam. 225.00
Sign, Hendler's Ice Cream, Velvet Kind, Blue, Yellow, Embossed, Tin, 28 x 20 In. 132.00
Sign, Hep, Get Hep For Yourself, Bottle, Enamel, 2-Sided, Flange, 17 ½ In. 160.00
Sign, Hereford Farms Cattle, Cow, Green, Brown, White, 2-Sided, 47 x 60 ½ In. 464.00

Advertising, Sign,
Fatima Cigarettes, Jack Webb, Die Cut,
Cardboard, 1950s, 15 ½ x 16 In.
$403.00

Advertising, Sign,
Frontenac White Cap Ale, Relief,
Chalk, 1940s, 27 x 23 x 3 ½ In.
$87.00

Advertising, Sign,
Gran'pa Graf's Root Beer, Die Cut,
Cardboard, 36 x 20 In.
$385.00

A

Advertising, Sign,
Hires Ginger Ale, None So Good,
Embossed, Tin, 1900-10, 5 ½ x 6 ½ In.
$173.00

Sign, Ice Cream Cone, Pin, Tan,
Milk Glass, Light-Up, George Jones Co.,
12 x 5 ½ In.
$990.00

Advertising, Sign, Kern's Bread,
Take Home, Tin, 1952, 20 x 28 In.
$317.00

Advertising, Sign,
Lambertville Snag-Proof Boots,
Brownies, Tin, Frame, 18 ½ x 22 ½ In.
$288.00

Sign, Hickman-Ebbert Wagon Co., Shade Of The Old Apple Tree, Tin, 35 ½ x 37 In. 355.00
Sign, Hill, Evan's & Co., Pure Malt Vinegar, Shield Form, Painted, Tin, 11 ½ x 9 ½ In. 70.00
Sign, Hires Ginger Ale, None So Good, Embossed, Tin, 1900-10, 5 ½ x 6 ½ In. . . . . *illus* 173.00
Sign, Hires Root Beer, Bottle, Tin, Embossed, 1950s, 13 ½ x 42 In. 230.00
Sign, Hires Root Beer, Bottle Cap, Drink Hires In Bottles, Blue Stripes, 35 In. Diam. 170.00
Sign, Hires Root Beer, Drink Hires, Ugly Kid, Cardboard, Frame, 1900-05, 10 x 14 In. 1840.00
Sign, Hires Root Beer, Girl, Drink Hires, Celluloid On Tin, Haskell Coffin, 1920, 10 x 7 In. 316.00
Sign, Hires Root Beer, Josh Slinger, Holding Bottle, Tin Lithograph, 1914, 17 ¾ x 9 In. 575.00
Sign, Hires Root Beer, Navy, Red & White, Rolled Edge, Tin, Embossed, 27 x 19 In. 90.00
Sign, Hires Root Beer, R-J, So Good, Ice Cold, Embossed, Tin, 1930s, 13 x 39 In. 230.00
Sign, Hires Root Beer, So Refreshing, Green, Yellow, Red, Black, Tin, 24 x 28 In. 330.00
Sign, Hires Root Beer, So Refreshing, Roots, Barks, Herbs, Enamel, 2-Sided, 13 ¾ In. 225.00
Sign, Hires Root Beer, Woman, Blue Dress, Die Cut, Cardboard, Easel Back, 14 x 9 In. 115.00
Sign, Hires Root Beer, Woman, Holding Glass, Cardboard, 14 ¾ x 20 ¾ In. 600.00
Sign, Hoblit Hybrids Corn Seed, Red, Yellow, Blue, Tin Lithograph, 10 x 14 In. 40.00
Sign, Hoefler Ice Cream, The Cream Supreme, Woman, Tin, Self-Framed, Oval 230.00
Sign, Holyoke Toilet Paper, Paper Broadside, Frame, O'Connell-Quirk, 24 x 14 In. 288.00
Sign, Home Insurance Company, New York, Blue, White, Porcelain, 14 x 20 In. 350.00
Sign, Home Run Cigarettes, Lithograph, Paper Stock, Frame, c.1910, 19 x 13 In. 11163.00
Sign, Honest Scrap Tobacco, Dog, Cat, Tobacco Box, Window, Translucent, 11 x 8 In. 1200.00
Sign, Hood's Ice Cream, Cow, Tin Flange, 22 x 19 In. 385.00
Sign, Hood's Ice Cream, Red, Yellow, White, Blue, Tin, 28 ½ x 50 In. 82.00
Sign, Hopsburger The Golden Beer, Embossed, Self-Framed, 12 x 6 In. 350.00
Sign, Horse Shoe Tobacco, Blue, Orange, White, Porcelain, Flange, 8 x 18 In. 300.00
Sign, Horse Shoe Tobacco, We Sell, Orange, Blue, Porcelain, 2-Sided, 8 x 19 ½ In. 330.00
Sign, Hotel MacArthur, Wood, Red, Yellow, Black, Painted, 1890-1910, 36 x 14 In. 207.00
Sign, Houston Ice & Brewing Co., Lithograph, 16 x 22 In. 5000.00
Sign, Howel's Root Beer, Round, Embossed Metal, American Art Works, 24 In. 138.00
Sign, Hump Hair Pin, Camel, Die Cut, Tin, 14 ½ x 16 In. 132.00
Sign, I.W. Harper Whiskey, Here's Happy Days, Milk Glass Panel, 1909, 24 x 18 In. 625.00
Sign, Ice Cream Cone, 5 Cent, Red Paint, Copper, 13 In. 550.00
Sign, Ice Cream Cone, Pin, Tan, Milk Glass, Light-Up, George Jones Co., 12 x 5 ½ In. . . . *illus* 990.00
Sign, Ice Cream Cone, Tin, Enameled, Embossed, Die Cut, 21 x 48 In. 168.00
Sign, Icy Pi, Ice Cream Sandwich, 5 Cent, Paper, 21 ½ x 39 ½ In. 70.00
Sign, Illinois Polled Hereford Assoc., Member, Yellow, Brown, Tin, 2-Sided, 28 x 22 In. 65.00
Sign, Imperial Granum Food, For Nursing Mother, Baby, Paper, Frame, 19 x 15 In. 92.00
Sign, Imperical Club Cigars, Best For The Money, 5 Cent, Embossed, Tin, 10 x 14 In. 165.00
Sign, Invincible Motor Insurance, Car, Ship, Spotlight, Tin, Britain, 1930, 9 x 20 In. 228.00
Sign, Iso Glass Boats, Dorsett Authorized Dealer, Red, Green, White, Tin, 20 x 30 In. 160.00
Sign, J. Trinka, Tailor, Painted, Wood, Early 20th Century, 17 ½ x 31 In. 468.00
Sign, J.A. Tuell, Provisions, Cigars, Wood, Painted, Norway, Maine, 16 x 125 In. 2300.00
Sign, J.C. Logan Hardware, Padlock, Tin, Painted, Late 19th Century, 37 x 25 In. 881.00
Sign, Jack Frost Fontaine, French Fondant Co., Paper, Frame, 13 x 10 In. 72.00
Sign, Jack Frost Sugar, Hockey Players On Pond, Cardboard, c.1929, 21 x 30 In. 358.00
Sign, Jacob Ruppert's New York Beer, Glass, Metal Frame, Oval, 13 x 18 ¼ In. 55.00
Sign, Jell-O, Die Cut Cardboard, Woman With Packages, c.1930, 31 x 21 In. 165.00
Sign, Jewel Stoves, Ranges, Detroit Stove, Curved, Blue, Yellow, Porcelain, 18 x 19 In. 875.00
Sign, John Deere, Tractors Sold Here, Burn Low Cost Fuel, Yellow, Green, Tin, 11 x 15 In. 140.00
Sign, John Deere Farm Implements, Black, Red, Yellow, Porcelain, 24 x 72 In. 660.00
Sign, Johnson & Johnson Baby Department, Blue, White, Red, Glass, Frame, 7 x 29 In. 580.00
Sign, Julius Saul, Grand Opening, Woman With Fan, Cardboard, Embossed, 1889, 7 x 13 In. . 90.00
Sign, Kayo Chocolate, Demand Kayo, Real Chocolate, Porcelain, 17 x 8 In. 15.00
Sign, Kayo Chocolate, It's Real Chocolate, Man Holding Bottle, Porcelain, 17 x 8 In. 40.00
Sign, Kayo Chocolate Drink, It's Real Chocolate, Tin Lithograph, 29 x 13 In. 50.00
Sign, Keen Kutter Tools, W.M. Bennett Hardware, Tin, 9 ¾ x 27 ¾ In. 66.00
Sign, Kent Feeds, Guaranteed, Red, Yellow, Black, Tin, 22 ½ x 46 ½ In. 70.00
Sign, Kern's Bread, Take Home, Tin, 1952, 20 x 28 In. . . . . *illus* 317.00
Sign, King Kard Overalls, Look For Trademark, Red, White, Blue, Porcelain, 10 x 32 In. 1150.00
Sign, Kingfisher Silk Fishing Lies, Frame, Horton Mfg. Co., Conn., 18 x 28 In. 8800.00
Sign, Kis-Me Gum, 2 Doves, Die Cut, Cardboard, Embossed, 15 ½ x 12 In. 464.00
Sign, Kis-Me Gum, Victorian Woman, Die Cut, Cardboard, Embossed, 15 x 13 In. 396.00
Sign, Kis-Me Gum, Woman, Hydrangeas, Die Cut, Cardboard, Embossed, 17 x 12 In. 330.00
Sign, Klein's Apex Cocoa, Elizabethtown, Pa., 11 In. 120.00
Sign, Knickerbocker Portland Cement Co., Goss Supply Co., 36 x 36 In. 80.00
Sign, Knowlton's Milk-Ice Cream, Red, White, Porcelain, 2-Sided, Marked, 30 x 60 In. 800.00
Sign, Knox Sparkling Gelatin, Die Cut, Cardboard, 11 x 11 In. 99.00

Sign, Kositos Cooked Maize, Horse, Cow, Porcelain, 50 x 30 In. 187.00
Sign, Kresge's, Red, Black, White, Glass, Frame, 7 x 34 ½ In. 232.00
Sign, L & M Tobacco, Get Lots More, Hand With Cigarette Pack, Tin, 1950s, 22 x 18 In. 65.00
Sign, L.N. Thurne Coal Co., 505 Central Ave., Blue, White, Porcelain, 18 x 24 In. 50.00
Sign, L.W. Marston, Merchant Tailor, Tin, Painted, Late 19th Century, 15 x 20 ½ In. 497.00
Sign, La Palina Cigar, Easel, Military Man Smoking, Die Cut, Cardboard, 28 x 28 In. 193.00
Sign, Lambertville Snag-Proof Boots, Brownies, Tin, Frame, 18 ½ x 22 ½ In. . . . . *illus* 288.00
Sign, Lampertus Brau, Enameled On Metal, 20 x 14 In. 242.00
Sign, L'Aperitif, Nuxy, Bird, Bottle, Funnel, Gabrielle Favre, Frame, c.1930, 60 x 40 In. 1800.00
Sign, Lassy Feeds, Red, White, Tin, Schreiber Mills Inc., 43 x 43 In. 100.00
Sign, Lehnert's Beer & Porter, Beer Of Merit, Tin, Black Paint, Frame, 27 x 17 In. 2300.00
Sign, Lehnert's Beer & Porter, Catasauqua, Pa., Tin, 17 x 27 In. 2300.00
Sign, Levi's, We Put A Little Blue Jean In Everything We Make, Wood, 26 x 33 In. 265.00
Sign, Life Guard Dog Feed, Let Your Dog Wake Up & Live, Red, Gold, Blue, Tin, 13 x 9 In. 320.00
Sign, Life Savers, Candy Mint With The Hole, Frame, 10 ½ x 20 ½ In. 143.00
Sign, Lincoln Paints, Abe Lincoln, 2-Sided, Enamel, Porcelain, 20 In. . . . . *illus* 400.00
Sign, Lins' Sausage, What Shall I Serve, Black Boy Eating Sausage, Tin, Paper, 13 x 9 In. 275.00
Sign, Lipton's Instant Cocoa, Woman Holding Cup, Tin On Cardboard, 1930, 13 x 9 In. 605.00
Sign, Locksmith Trade, Key Shape, Wood, Gold Paint, c.1890, 36 In. 646.00
Sign, London Life Cigarettes, People Outdoors, Tin, Self-Framed, c.1910, 39 x 28 In. 1300.00
Sign, Lone Star Portland Cement, Lyon Gray Lumber Co., Porcelain, 24 x 30 In. 400.00
Sign, Los Angeles Brewing Co., Victorian Woman, Car, Gold Wood Frame, 35 x 25 In. 2475.00
Sign, Louis Fishing Tackle, Fish Shape, Gray Ground, White, Black, Gold Letters, 49 In. 1840.00
Sign, Lowney's Chocolates, Candy Box, Die Cut, Tin, Chains, 15 ½ x 17 In., 3 Piece 725.00
Sign, Lucky Strike, Cardboard, Die Cut, Display, Stand-Up, 15 ½ x 28 ½ In. 474.00
Sign, Lucky Strike, Woman In Fur Coat, Boarding Airline, Lindbergh Line, 1940, 14 x 22 In. . 75.00
Sign, Lucky Strike, Woman Wearing Fur Coat Smoking As She Boards Train, 1940, 14 x 22 In. 75.00
Sign, Lucky Strike Cigarette, Paul Waner, Batting, Trolley Car, Frame, 1928, 26 x 16 In. 4113.00
Sign, Lucky Strike Cigarettes, Red, Green, Black, Tin Lithograph, 12 ¾ x 9 ¾ In. 110.00
Sign, Luden Cough Drops, Embossed, Tin Lithograph 330.00
Sign, Lunch, White, Black, Painted, 2-Sided, Early 20th Century, 20 x 41 In. 1500.00
Sign, Luxury Cigarette, Convincingly Mild, Woman, Paper, Frame, 24 x 16 In. 100.00
Sign, Lycoming Rubber Boots & Shoes, Hamilton Brown Shoe Co., Paper, 24 x 16 In. 275.00
Sign, Lyons Superbread, Red, White, Blue, 2-Sided, Porcelain, Flange, 10 x 12 In. 100.00
Sign, Macon Hybrids, Cardinal, Red, White, Tin Lithograph, 6 x 20 In. 25.00
Sign, Made-Rite Flour, Orange, Blue, Tin, 9 x 19 ½ In. 50.00
Sign, Magnus Root Beer, It's Fine In The Bottle, Embossed, Tin, 1940, 8 ½ x 19 In. 115.00
Sign, Mail Pouch, Chew & Smoke, Quality, Blue, Yellow, Porcelain, 1930s, 11 x 36 In. 245.00
Sign, Mallard Seed Corn Dealers, Red, White, Green, Tin, 17 ¾ x 24 In. 160.00
Sign, Martin-Senour Paints, Man Pouring Paint, Die Cut, Cardboard, 40 x 24 In. . . . . . *illus* 385.00
Sign, Masse Pere & Sons Champagne, France, c.1920, 31 x 46 ½ In. 425.00
Sign, Mavis Chocolate Drink, It's Real Chocolate, Cardboard, 36 In. 40.00
Sign, Maxwell House Coffee, Flange, Tin, 2-Sided, Turquoise, Orange, 14 x 27 In. 1265.00
Sign, Meats, White, Green Ground, Porcelain, 18 x 30 In. 40.00
Sign, Melox Dog Foods, Foods That Nourish, Red, White, Blue, Porcelain, 26 x 18 In. 420.00
Sign, Member Farm Bureau, Lorenze Warneke, Corn, Yellow, Black, Tin, 10 x 14 In. 40.00
Sign, Memory Lane Dairy, Milk Truck Form, White, Red, Black, 18 x 35 In. 100.00
Sign, Mercedes Duurt Typewriter, Locomotive, Art Deco, Signed, 26 ½ x 42 In. 720.00
Sign, MFA Feeds, Red, White, Blue, Shield, Porcelain, 24 x 66 In. 232.00
Sign, Milk Association, Horse, Milk Carriage, People, Black, White, Paper, 1927, 34 In. 30.00
Sign, Miller High Life Beer, Fisherman, Tin, 26 ½ x 18 ½ In. 440.00
Sign, Mission Orange, Cardboard Lithograph, Frame, 16 x 20 In. 55.00
Sign, Model Range & Stoves, Reverse Glass, Inlay Letters, Boston, 1892, 28 x 18 In. 1650.00
Sign, Moore's Candy Ice Cream Karmel Korn, Yellow, Black, Wood, Corner, 17 x 25 In. 2100.00
Sign, Moran's Ginger Ale, Board, 23 ¾ x 16 In. 70.00
Sign, Morse's, Dutchess Filled Candies, Fruit, Can, Candy, Paper, 24 ½ x 18 In. 145.00
Sign, Mountain States Tel. & Tel. Co., Porcelain, Navy & White, 19 x 5 ½ In. 258.00
Sign, Mouse House Tavern, Tavern, Mouse, Carved, Wood, Multicolored, 12 ¼ x 24 In. 2200.00
Sign, Moxie, Bottle, Ted Williams The Kid, 1950s, 2 ½ x 6 ½ In. 305.00
Sign, Moxie, Distinctively Different, Red, Blue, Embossed, Tin Lithograph, 27 x 18 In. 225.00
Sign, Mozart Cigar, Wood, Marked, Mevercord Co., 17 ½ x 15 ½ In. 165.00
Sign, Mule-Hide Roofing, Metal, Embossed, Mule Graphic, 27 x 21 In. 165.00
Sign, Muncy Chief Hybrids, Muncy Pa., Indian Chief, Corn, Tin, 20 x 27 In. 230.00
Sign, Murad Turkish Cigarette, 15 Cent, Woman, 2-Sided, Flange, 20 x 12 In. 550.00
Sign, Murray's Warrior Plug Tobacco, Sign, Pirate, Ship, Cardboard, 1920, 15 x 10 In. 288.00
Sign, Mutoscope Penny Arcade, 1 Cent, New York, Wood Slats, 24 x 15 In. 58.00

Advertising, Sign,
Lincoln Paints, Abe Lincoln,
2-Sided, Enamel, Porcelain, 20 In.
$400.00

Advertising, Sign,
Martin-Senour Paints,
Man Pouring Paint, Die Cut,
Cardboard, 40 x 24 In.
$385.00

Research Help

When doing research into the history of your antiques and collectibles, avoid depending on old books. Company materials, like original catalogs, are fine. New scientific methods, archaeological digs, and years of research have turned up many errors and myths found in early information. This year we made minor additions or corrections to over 40 paragraphs in this book.

Advertising, Sign,
NuGrape, A Flavor You Can't Forget,
Bottle, Embossed, Tin, 1940s, 12 x 16 In.
$306.00

Advertising, Sign,
Pabst Blue Ribbon Beer,
Girl Holding Glass, Tin, 24 x 20 In.
$748.00

Advertising, Sign,
Perfection Cigarettes, Cardboard,
Frame, 1910, 27 x 20 In.
$230.00

Sign, My Pop's Root Beer, It's Tops, Embossed, Tin, Multicolored, 1948, 18 x 24 In. 173.00
Sign, My-T-Fine Pudding, Woman, Paper, Frame, 22 ½ x 20 ½ In. 44.00
Sign, National Brewing Co., San Francisco, Ca., Lithograph, 1894, 19 x 26 In. 6250.00
Sign, Nature's Best Milk, Boy Holding Bottle In Ring, Painted, Carved, Wood, 19 ½ In. 700.00
Sign, Neal's Carriage Paint, Wood, Miniature Wagon Wheel, Wood, Label, 14 x 18 In. 632.00
Sign, Nebo Cigarettes, Die Cut, Tin Lithograph, 15 x 13 ½ In. 160.00
Sign, Necco, Maple Sugar Cream & Cocoanut, Frame, 10 ½ x 20 ½ In. 50.00
Sign, Necco Candies, Tin, Embossed, 1920s-30s, 9 x 27 In. 201.00
Sign, Necco English Fruit Tablet, Candy Jars, Wafers, Paper, Frame, 17 x 11 In. 250.00
Sign, Needraw Boston Garter, Leg, Cool, Easy, Clinging, Paper, Frame, 6 x 8 In. 350.00
Sign, Nehi, Drink Nehi, Bottle, Yellow, Red, Black, Die Cut, Tin, Flange, 1930-40 499.00
Sign, Nehi Cola, Bottle, Woman's Legs, Paper Lithograph, Frame, 13 x 20 In. 33.00
Sign, Neon, Here Comes The Judge, Double Stroke Lettering, 67 x 24 x 9 In. 5175.00
Sign, Nestor Cigarettes, Exquisite Egyptians, Man, Camel, Paper, 9 ½ x 7 ½ In. 150.00
Sign, New England Coke, Blue, White, Porcelain, Shield Form, 48 x 48 In. 410.00
Sign, New Yorker Beverages, Bottle, Couple, Tin, Embossed, 56 In. 375.00
Sign, Niagara Shoes, Tin Over Cardboard, Black Ground, 19 x 9 In. 345.00
Sign, Nichol Kola, Tin, Brown, Red & White, 1936, 29 ½ x 12 In. 98.00
Sign, Nil Brand Cigarette Papers, Joseph Bardou & Sons, 63 x 46 ½ In. 720.00
Sign, Nipper, His Master's Voice, On Canvas, Frame, Lithograph, c.1920, 26 x 32 In. 1422.00
Sign, Norka Root Beer, Tin, Norka Is Akron Spelled Backwards, 1950s, 12 x 24 In. 115.00
Sign, North Dakota Highway 58, Indian Silhouette, Black, White, Tin, 24 x 24 In. 190.00
Sign, NuGrape, A Flavor You Can't Forget, Bottle, Embossed, Tin, 1940s, 12 x 16 In. *illus* 306.00
Sign, NuGrape Soda, Bottle Cap, Tin, Enameled, Robertson Sign Co., 1950s, 36 In. 308.00
Sign, NuGrape Soda, Flavor You Can't Forget, Bottle, Embossed, Tin, 1940s, 11 x 23 In. 517.00
Sign, NuGrape Soda, Flavor You Can't Forget, Hand, Bottle, Tin, Die Cut, Flange, 1940, 13 x 20 In. 627.00
Sign, Occident Flour, Makes Better Bread, Blue, White, Wood, 47 In. 450.00
Sign, Occident Flour, Wood, Smaltz, Black, White Lettering, c.1900, 5 ½ x 47 In. 173.00
Sign, Odin Cigars, 5 Cent, Man, Smoking Cigar, Embossed, Tin Lithograph, 27 ½ In. 180.00
Sign, Ogilvie's Royal Household Flour, Blue, Red, White, Porcelain, 48 x 30 In. 132.00
Sign, O'Keefe's Dry Ginger Ale, Bottle, Yellow, Red, Embossed, Tin, 39 ¼ In. 70.00
Sign, Old Colony Club Pale, Be Ale Wise, Bottle Form, Tin, 24 In. 175.00
Sign, Old Dutch Cleanser, Tin Over Cardboard, 1930s, 10 x 8 In. 518.00
Sign, Old Gold Cigarettes, Not A Cough In A Carload, Yellow, Red, Porcelain, 12 x 36 In. 150.00
Sign, Olivetti, Lettora 22, Raymond Sarignac, c.1953, 23 ½ x 26 ½ In. 1080.00
Sign, Omar Cigarettes, 2 Men Smoking, Joy Of Life, Frame, 24 ½ x 18 In. 143.00
Sign, Open Book Trade, Open Book, School Supplies, Metal, Gilt, c.1878, 19 x 28 In. 823.00
Sign, Orange Crush, Flavor Sealed In Brown Bottle, White, Orange, Tin, 1940s, 18 x 48 In. 316.00
Sign, Oranges, Vitamins A, B, C, Kendric Ruker, 18 ⅛ x 22 ½ In. 960.00
Sign, Orient Coal, Davis Elevator, Lenox, Tin Lithograph, 14 x 19 ½ In. 90.00
Sign, Pabst, Okay Special, Blue, Yellow, Embossed, Tin, 8 ½ x 6 In. 44.00
Sign, Pabst Blue Ribbon, Six Pack, Tin, 17 x 22 ½ In. 10.00
Sign, Pabst Blue Ribbon, Wilbur Stock Food, Co., Beer Wagon, Horses, Paper, 35 x 16 In. 138.00
Sign, Pabst Blue Ribbon Beer, Girl Holding Glass, Tin, 24 x 20 In. *illus* 748.00
Sign, Pabst Blue Ribbon Beer, Mirror, This Is The Place, Frame, 14 ½ x 20 ½ In. 5.00
Sign, Padlock, De Long & Son, Sheet Metal, Wood, Gold, Black, c.1890, 36 x 26 In. 1410.00
Sign, Page Evaporated Milk, Flashing, Lithograph On Cardboard, 11 ½ x 17 ½ In. 193.00
Sign, Pall Mall, Mildness Is A Pleasure, Woman, Easel Back, 21 x 15 In. 40.00
Sign, Palm Beach Suits, As Stylish As Grownups, Cardboard, Frame, 11 x 20 In. 50.00
Sign, Parkway Hotel, In Reno A Good Place To Stop, Metal, Enamel, 1940s, 28 x 28 In. 415.00
Sign, Paul Jones & Co., Temptation Of St. Anthony, Black Couple, Tin, 13 ½ x 19 In. 1430.00
Sign, Paul Jones Whiskey, Cabin, Dead Game, Rifles, Tin Lithograph, 1915, 50 x 36 In. 1210.00
Sign, Peacock Valley Farm, Geo. A. Avery, Wood, Painted, c.1900, 14 x 53 ½ In. 351.00
Sign, Peats Wallpaper, Porcelain, c.1910, 14 x 17 In. 58.00
Sign, Pepper's Hygrade Ginger Ale, Celluloid, Parisian Novelty Co., Chicago, 7 x 5 In. 144.00
Sign, Perfection Cigarettes, Cardboard, Frame, 1910, 27 x 20 In. *illus* 230.00
Sign, Perrier, Henry Le Monnier, Lithograph, c.1931, 47 x 62 ½ In. 420.00
Sign, Peter Lorillard Plug Tobacco, Splendid, 5 Women, 14 x 9 In. 531.00
Sign, Peters Shotgun Shells, Paper, Metal Band, Peter's Cartridge Co., 15 x 23 In. 1265.00
Sign, Pfluger Fishing Tackle, Enjoy Life, Man Fishing, Cardstock, 1938, 25 x 20 In. 230.00
Sign, Philip Morris, Bellhop, If You Inhale, Die Cut, Cardboard, 41 In. 121.00
Sign, Philip Morris, Call For, America's Finest Cigarette, Brown, Board, 3 x 34 In. 50.00
Sign, Philip Morris, Call For, Man, Cigarette, Red, Yellow, Tin, Marked, 10 x 28 In. 88.00
Sign, Philip Morris Cigarettes, Stand-Up, Die Cut, Frame, 1940s, 15 x 44 In. 288.00
Sign, Piccadilly Little Cigars, Couple, Hugging, 10 For 10 Cent, Frame, 21 x 12 In. 250.00
Sign, Piedmont, Virginia Cigarette, Blue, White, Porcelain, 9 x 17 ¾ In. 403.00

Sign, Piedmont Cigarette, Lithograph On Paper, Oak Frame, 23 x 16 In.. . . . . 358.00
Sign, Pine Cone Ice Cream, Die Cut, Cardboard, Easel Back, 13 x 20 ½ In. 55.00
Sign, Pioneer Corn, Corncob, Yellow, Black, Tin, 96 x 22 In. 875.00
Sign, Pioneer Hybrids, Leon Albert Love, Corn, Tin, 2-Sided, 24 x 20 In. 100.00
Sign, Player's Please, Tobacco, Yellow, Red, Porcelain, Flange, c.1920, 16 x 16 ½ In. 403.00
Sign, Player's Tobacco, Shield Shape, Yellow Ground, Red, c.1920, 16 x 16 ½ In. 403.00
Sign, Pocket Watch, Geo. H. Wood, Painted Metal, c.1875, 20 In. 1410.00
Sign, Pocket Watch, Zinc, Ingersoll Dollar Watch, Late 1800s, 24 ½ In. 764.00
Sign, Poll-Parrot Shoes, 2-Sided, Wood, Parrot, 46 x 22 In. 4950.00
Sign, Polly Stamps, Ask For, Premiums-Trade-Cash, Red, White, Tin, 2-Sided, 28 x 20 In. 175.00
Sign, Polly Stamps, More Cash Value, Red, Yellow, White, Tin, 1950-60, 18 x 36 In. 100.00
Sign, Pop Kola, American's Finest Kola, Tin, Navy & White, 35 x 35 In. 134.00
Sign, Popsicle, Everybody Likes, Red, Black, Yellow, Embossed, Tin, 12 x 35 In. 110.00
Sign, Portland Cement, Blue Circle, Porcelain, 15 In. Diam. 95.00
Sign, Portland Cement & Lime Co., Dragon Brand, Porcelain, 41 x 36 In.. . . . . 352.00
Sign, Post Toasties, Die Cut Cardboard, 3-D, Boy, Dog, Cereal Bowl, c.1930, 31 x 18 In. 460.00
Sign, Premier Coffee, Mill Behind A Good Cup Of Coffee, Yellow, White, Black, 18 In.. . . . . 90.00
Sign, Private Closets 5 Cents, Directions, Porcelain, Iron, 12 x 3 In.. . . . . 259.00
Sign, Pub, Charrington & Co., Lock, Keys, Red, Black, Green, Gold Paint, 1900s, 43 x 58 In. . . 374.00
Sign, Purity White Loaf Baking Powder, Wise Women Use, Tin, 9 ⅞ x 13 ⅝ In. 175.00
Sign, Quaker Oats, Porcelain, Convex, For Health & Energy, Germany, 12 x 24 In.. . . . . 288.00
Sign, Quaker Tea, Agent, Blue, White, Porcelain, Flange, c.1915-20, 9 x 18 In. 315.00
Sign, R.I.A.C. Hotel, Officially Appointed, Porcelain, 2-Sided, 1950s, 28 x 28 In. 259.00
Sign, Raleigh Cigarettes, Pride Of The Regiment, Girl, Cardboard, 1940s, 30 x 20 In. 86.00
Sign, Raspberry Charms, Fruit Tablets, Frame, 10 x 20 In. 33.00
Sign, Rawlings, Basketball Player, c.1955 . . . . 270.00
Sign, RC Cola, Bottle, Tin, Die Cut, Embossed, Frame, 1940s, 60 In.. . . . . *illus* 201.00
Sign, RC Cola, RC Tastes Best, Joan Crawford, Cardboard, Frame, 1940s, 11 x 28 In. 173.00
Sign, RC Cola, Take Home A Carton, 6 Pack, 2-Sided, Tin, Bracket, 1941, 16 x 24 In. 3162.00
Sign, RCA, His Master's Voice, Dog, Gramophone, Painted, Porcelain, 8 ½ x 10 In.. . . . . 250.00
Sign, RCA, His Master's Voice, Dog, Phonograph, Enamel, 8 x 11 In. 195.00
Sign, RCA Radio, Electric, Light-Up, 2-Sided, 12 x 22 In.. . . . . 468.00
Sign, RCA Victor Electric Tuning, Light-Up, 8 ¼ x 16 x 6 ½ In. 400.00
Sign, Reading Brewing Co., Factory Scene, Tin Lithograph, Frame, 1890s, 36 x 48 In.. . . . . 3250.00
Sign, Reading Brewing Co., Men In Pub, Paper, Frame, 1890s, 22 x 29 In. 750.00
Sign, Red Coon Chewing Tobacco, Sun Cured, 18 x 12 In. 100.00
Sign, Red Goose Shoes, Beasley's Store, Red, Yellow, Black, Tin, 13 x 18 In.. . . . . 220.00
Sign, Red Goose Shoes, Red, Yellow, Black, Tin, Embossed, Rolled Edge, 19 x 13 In.. . . . . 134.00
Sign, Red Man Tobacco, Cardboard, 2-Sided, 1930s, 11 x 16 In.. . . . . 316.00
Sign, Red Rock Cola, Easel Back, Cardboard, Frame, Girl Fishing, c.1940, 15 x 24 In. 230.00
Sign, Red Top Beer, Embossed Die Cut Metal, 21 x 14 In. 220.00
Sign, Reddy Kilowatt, Another Home Heated Electrically, Cardboard, 1950, 21 x 32 In. 115.00
Sign, Reddy Kilowatt, Cardboard, Black Ground, Reddy In Corner, 1950s, 21 x 32 In. 205.00
Sign, Regalos Cigars, 5 Cent, Brown, Yellow, Tin, Flange, 12 x 18 ¼ In.. . . . . 140.00
Sign, Reinhard A. Spol, Enameled On Metal, 12 ½ x 10 In.. . . . . 339.00
Sign, Reinkens Havana Plantation Cigars, Woman, Embossed, Tin, 14 In. Diam.. . . . . 325.00
Sign, Rexall, Raised Letters, Border, Black Sand Paint, Gilt, 80 x 28 x 2 ½ In. . . . . *illus* 660.00
Sign, Rexall Pharmacy, Porcelain, Cobalt Blue On Orange, 3 Sections, 34 x 68 In.. . . . . 77.00
Sign, Richardson's Root Beer, Man Holding Mug, Die Cut, Cardboard, 11 ½ x 13 In. 86.00
Sign, Richmond Straight Cut No. 1 Cigarettes, Boy Holding Ball, c.1890, 27 x 16 In. 2115.00
Sign, Riley Bros. That's Oil, 5 x 12 In.. . . . . 95.00
Sign, Rocky Ford Cigar, Delicious Flavor, Indian, 5 Cent, Paper, Frame, 1920, 20 x 26 In. 1035.00
Sign, Roessle Brewery Lager Beer, Boston, Silver & Gold Foil, Round, 27 In. 920.00
Sign, Roma Wines, Figure With Mustache, Apron, Chalkware. 88.00
Sign, Rose Bud Tobacco, Have A Chew, Mild Burley, Blue, Yellow, Tin, 18 x 12 In. 95.00
Sign, Royal Crown Cola, Best By Taste Test, Enamel, 2-Sided, Flange, 18 In. 250.00
Sign, Royal Crown Cola, Drink, Red, White, Enamel, 2-Sided, Flange, 17 ¾ In. 225.00
Sign, Royal Crown Cola, Metal, Embossed, Bottle Graphics, Wood Frame, 19 x 54 In. 275.00
Sign, Royal Crown Cola, Red, White, Tin, 18 x 54 In.. . . . . 110.00
Sign, Royal Crown Cola, Tin, Embossed, c.1940, 22 x 34 In. 275.00
Sign, Royal Liver Friendly Society, Brass, 10 x 13 In. 30.00
Sign, Royal Tailors, Chicago, New York, Tiger, Die Cut, Tin Lithograph, Flange, 9 x 19 In.. . . . 1750.00
Sign, Rubberset Paintbrush, Sold Here, Embossed, Tin, 19 ¾ In. 90.00
Sign, Salada Tea Served Here, Teapot Shape, Orange, Black, Enamel, 42 In.. . . . . 660.00
Sign, Salada Tea Served Here, Teapot Shape, Yellow, Black, Porcelain, 24 x 34 In. 88.00
Sign, Salt Take A Bag Or Barrel Home, Enamel, 19 ¾ x 50 In. 4994.00

Advertising, Sign, RC Cola, Bottle, Tin, Die Cut, Embossed, Frame, 1940s, 60 In.
$201.00

Advertising, Sign, Rexall, Raised Letters, Border, Black Sand Paint, Gilt, 80 x 28 x 2 ½ In.
$660.00

TIP

Never bid at an auction if you have not previewed the items.

Advertising, Sign,
Squire's Arlington Hams, Bacon, Sausage, Embossed, Tin, 1915, 24 x 20 In.
$460.00

Advertising, Sign,
Telonette Cigars, Elephant, Cigar Box, Paper, 1950s, 22 x 17 In.
$403.00

Advertising, Sign,
Tuxedo Tobacco, Geo. M. Cohan, Cardboard, 24 In.
$316.00

Sign, Salvation Army, Lithograph On Die Cut Cardboard, c.1900, Frame, 30 x 21 In. 110.00
Sign, Santa Fe The Scout, Cowboy Riding Horse, Porcelain, 20 ¼ x 40 ½ In. 5000.00
Sign, Sapolin Stove Pipe Enamel, Tin Lithograph, 24 ½ In. 475.00
Sign, Satin Skin Powder & Cream, Woman, Japanese Dress, Paper, 28 x 42 In. 112.00
Sign, Save 2 Cents Gallon, Red, White, 30 In. Diam. 300.00
Sign, Saxoleine, Jules Cheret, Lithograph, c.1900, 49 x 34 ½ In.. . . . . 660.00
Sign, Say Hires, Smiling Child, Mug, Hires Root Beer, Tin, 20 x 24 In. 2712.00
Sign, Schaefer Beer, Brooklyn Dodgers, Woman, Cap, Glass, c.1955, 16 x 13 In. 1080.00
Sign, Schlitz Brewing Co., Milwaukee, Wis, Lithograph, Paper, Frame, 35 x 23 ½ In. 3000.00
Sign, Selz Shoes, Make Your Feet Glad, Blue, White, Porcelain, 1930-40, 6 x 60 In. 145.00
Sign, Seneca Cameras & Supplies, Indian Maiden, Die Cut, Tin, Flange, 18 ½ x 14 In. 6000.00
Sign, Serve It & You Please All, Ice Cream Slice, Porcelain, Mulholland, 18 In. Diam. 250.00
Sign, Shakespeare, Fine Fishing Tackle, Glass, Reverse Painted, c.1940, 19 In. 431.00
Sign, Shakespeare, Fine Fishing Tackle, Leaping Bass, Composite, c.1955, 8 x 11 In. 374.00
Sign, Shapleigh Hardware Co., Lithograph On Tin, c.1931, 6 ¼ x 9 ¼ In. 138.00
Sign, Shears Shape, Wood, Painted Silver & Black, Late 1800s, 30 In. 1763.00
Sign, Shell, 2-Sided, Porcelain, 2 Parts, Orange, Red Letters, 36 x 15 In. 300.00
Sign, Sherwin-Williams Paints, Porcelain, Cover The Earth, Embossed, 18 x 35 In.. . . . . 690.00
Sign, Shoe Shape, Laminated Pine, Gilt, Wood Base, Late 1800s, 8 x 18 In.. . . . . 1058.00
Sign, Silver King Golf Ball, Metal, Slogan, Board, Hooks, Chain, c.1920s, 27 x 60 In. 2520.00
Sign, Simpson Springs Beverages, Best Of All, Red, Green, Embossed, Tin, 19 x 14 In. 265.00
Sign, Sinclair Aircraft, Red, White, Porcelain, 2-Sided, Frame, Late 1920s, 48 In. Diam. 8000.00
Sign, Singer Sewing Machines, Porcelain, Victorian Woman, c.1915, 37 x 24 In. 385.00
Sign, Skinner's Satin Paint, Metal, Lithograph, Indian, Headdress, c.1910, 20 x 16 In. 3750.00
Sign, Skippy Peanut Butter, Peanut Wearing Football Helmet, 1966, 9 x 12 In.. . . . . 10.00
Sign, Smith Bros Cough Drops, Health Sake, White, Black, Embossed, Tin, 19 x 41 In. 500.00
Sign, Smoke Garryowen Plug, It Satisfies, Dog, Porcelain, Canada, 17 x 24 In.. . . . . 144.00
Sign, Snider's Catsup, 6-Sided, Painted, Embossed, Tin, 17 x 11 In. 144.00
Sign, Soft Drinks, Red, White, Painted, Wood, Signed, A.E. Beney, Early 1900s, 18 x 36 ½ In. . 1170.00
Sign, Solo Soda, Airplane, Red, White, Blue, Tin, 30 x 15 In.. . . . . 550.00
Sign, Sorge's Ice Cream, Porcelain, 2-Sided, 26 In. 330.00
Sign, Spa Soda Water, Bottle, Bruxelles, Porcelain, 18 ½ In. 143.00
Sign, Spaten Brau Muchen, Enameled On Metal, 15 ½ x 11 ½ In. 265.00
Sign, Spear Head Tobacco, Tin Lithograph, 1910s 600.00
Sign, Squeeze, Drink All The Flavors, Red, Black, White, Embossed, Tin, 10 x 28 In. 200.00
Sign, Squeeze, Satisfying Orange Drink, Flange, Round, 12 x 13 In. 403.00
Sign, Squeeze, That Distinctive Orange Drink, Bottle, Kids, Tin Lithograph, 19 x 27 In. 1200.00
Sign, Squire's Arlington Hams, Bacon, Sausage, Embossed, Tin, 1915, 24 x 20 In. . . . . . *illus* 460.00
Sign, Squirrel Brand Salted Peanuts, Gray, Red, Yellow, White, Die Cut, Pair. 135.00
Sign, Squirt, Drink Squirt, Bottle, Yellow, Green, Red, Blue, Embossed, Tin,1941 . . . . 125.00
Sign, Squirt, Switch To Squirt, Never An Alter-Thirst, Boy, Bottle, 1958, 10 x 28 In.. . . . . 316.00
Sign, Standard Air Lines, Tri Motor Plane, Tin, Embossed, 2 In. 425.00
Sign, Standard Tobacco, Cardboard, Lithograph, Frame, 1920-30s, 14 x 19 In. 403.00
Sign, Star Tobacco, 10 Cent, Yellow, Blue, Tin, Embossed, 1930-40, 12 x 24 In.. . . . . 150.00
Sign, Star Tobacco, Best For 70 Years, 10 Cent, Yellow, Red, Tin, Embossed, 12 x 24 In. 175.00
Sign, Star Tobacco, We Sell, Blue, White, 2-Sided, Porcelain, 8 x 18 In. 110.00
Sign, Stoneware, Best Food Container, Boy, Dog, Tin On Cardboard, 1930s, 19 x 13 In. 1000.00
Sign, Storz Beer, 70 Years Of Quality, Red, Yellow, Black, White, 43 x 96 In. 375.00
Sign, Stull Hybrids, Man Smoking, Yellow, White Corn, Tin, Press Sign Co., 25 x 20 In. 80.00
Sign, Sugar Lake Hotel, Arrow, Die Cut Metal, Embossed, 4 ½ x 24 In.. . . . . 880.00
Sign, Sun Crest Soda, Bottle, Orange, Blue, White, Aluminum, 1949, 22 x 8 In. 472.00
Sign, Sunbeam Bread, Miss Sunbeam, Embossed Metal, 47 x 47 In. 374.00
Sign, Sunbeam Rolls, Tin, Embossed, We Serve The Best Made With, c.1953, 19 x 55 In. 1725.00
Sign, Sweet Caporal Cigarettes, Woman, Tin, Frame, Canada, 61 x 17 In. 550.00
Sign, Sweet-Orr, Clothes To Work In, Overalls, Pants, Shirts, Yellow, Porcelain, 29 x 8 In. 504.00
Sign, Sweet-Orr, Pants, Shirts, Overalls, Yellow, Blue, Red, Porcelain, 10 x 23 ½ In. 360.00
Sign, Teeters Packing, General Offices, Green, Red, Reverse Painted, Frame, 18 x 28 In. 45.00
Sign, Tellings Ice Cream, Blue, White, 2-Sided, Porcelain, 28 x 20 In. 290.00
Sign, Telonette Cigars, Elephant, Cigar Box, Paper, 1950s, 22 x 17 In. . . . . *illus* 403.00
Sign, The Grist Mill, Barrel Form, Painted, Mid 20th Century, 36 x 22 In. 29.00
Sign, Thompson's Double Malted, Man Walking, 23 x 7 In. 70.00
Sign, Three Queens Hose Of Distinction, Cardboard, 23 x 29 In.. . . . . 220.00
Sign, Tiger Chewing Tobacco, Tiger In Grass, Tin Lithograph, Frame, 32 ¾ x 27 In. 475.00
Sign, Tobacco, Bull Of The Woods, Snorting Bull, Tin, Lithograph, Black, Yellow, 20 x 14 In. . 303.00
Sign, Todco Door, Parts, Sales, Service, Man, Red, White, Black, 18 x 36 In. 55.00
Sign, Triple AAA Root Beer, Bottle, Die Cut, Enamel, Tin, 44 ¼ In. 200.00

Sign, Trojan, Northern Bred Corn Seed, Red, White, Tin, 13 ½ x 27 ½ In. 95.00
Sign, Trojan Corn Co., Stanley Ness, Blue, White, Red, Tin Lithograph, 4 x 22 In. 15.00
Sign, Tuxedo Tobacco, Geo. M. Cohan, Cardboard, 24 In. . . . . . *illus* 316.00
Sign, TWA, New York Fly TWA, David Klein, 40 x 24 ⅞ In. 3360.00
Sign, U.S. Coast Guard, Reservation, No Trespassing, Blue, Porcelain, 8 ½ x 13 ½ In. 90.00
Sign, U.S. Hosp. Corp Undertaker, D.H. Lawson, 1890, 9 ¼ x 24 x ¾ In. 295.00
Sign, Uncle Wabash Cupcakes, Cardboard, Schulze Baking, 1924, 10 ½ x 13 In. 50.00
Sign, Uneeda Bakers, Almona, Red, Brown, Frame, 7 ½ x 22 In. 70.00
Sign, Uneeda Biscuit, National Biscuit Co., Boy, In Raincoat, Paper, Frame, 23 x 16 In. 175.00
Sign, United States Post Office, Vermont, Painted, Wood, 25 ½ x 57 ½ In. 225.00
Sign, Valley Forge Special In Bottles, Red, Yellow, Tin, 5 In. 60.00
Sign, Valley Of Repose, Hand, Wood, White, Yellow Letters, Black Ground, 11 x 23 In. 550.00
Sign, Valvoline, Tin, Embossed, Wood Frame, 1930s, 3 x 6 Ft. 650.00
Sign, Van Dam Cigars, Java Wrapped, Red, White, Black, 10 Cent, Tin, c.1930, 14 x 28 In. 75.00 to 225.00
Sign, Velvet & Piedmont, Tin, Flange, 1920s, 13 ½ x 18 In. 1093.00
Sign, Velvet Ice Cream, Red, White, Neon, Light-Up, 2-Sided, 13 x 27 In. 154.00
Sign, Vernis Paint, Reputes Les Meilleurs, Red, Black, White, Tin, Belgium, 19 x 13 In. 50.00
Sign, Viceroy Cigarettes, We Are Open, Store Hours, Tin, Red, Yellow 60.00
Sign, Voigt's Snow Drift Flour, Porcelain, Flange, c.1910, 14 x 18 In. . . . . . *illus* 345.00
Sign, W.L. Brubaker & Bros., Taps & Dyes, Woman, Paper, Frame, 21 ½ x 17 In. 300.00
Sign, W.L. Douglas Shoes, In Every Walk Of Life, D.M. Brosey & Son, 21 In. 40.00
Sign, Walgreens, There Is A Drug Store In E. St. Louis, Blue, Porcelain, 30 x 40 In. 75.00
Sign, Ward's Orange Crush, Drink Bottle, Embossed, Tin, 9 x 20 In. 473.00
Sign, Warner's Safe Cure, Jungle Expedition, Slaves, Paper, Frame, 15 x 11 In. 1870.00
Sign, Warner's Safe Cure Palmistry, Hand, Wood Frame, 13 ¼ x 16 In. 235.00
Sign, Waterman's Fountain Pen, 2 Boys, Tin Lithograph, 13 x 19 In. 600.00
Sign, Watts Matthieu Co. Druggist, Little Girl, Embossed, Die Cut Cardboard, 6 x 9 In. 55.00
Sign, We Recommend Squires, Pork, J.P. Squire & Co., Boston, Oval, Tin, 20 x 24 In. 1062.00
Sign, Webster Cigars, Agency For Special Selection, Reverse Painted, Frame, 17 x 13 In. 300.00
Sign, Wellsboro Cigar Factory, Ballet Dancer Tying Shoe, 1904, 14 x 11 In. 350.00
Sign, Western Union, Light-Up, 2-Sided, Metal Stand, Glass Inserts, 22 x 15 In. 1320.00
Sign, Westinghouse, Easy To Operate, Embossed, Tin, 1920s, 24 x 22 In. . . . . . *illus* 345.00
Sign, Westward Ho, Smoking Mixture, Enameled Steel, 36 x 18 In. 265.00
Sign, Whishands Corn Feed, Arcola, Illinois, Tin Lithograph, 14 x 20 In. 45.00
Sign, Whistle Soda, Thirsty?, Just Whistle, Bottle, Cardboard, Frame, 1940, 16 x 12 In. 173.00
Sign, Whitbread's London Stout & Ales, Blue, Yellow, Porcelain On Metal, 24 x 96 In. 165.00
Sign, White Label Cigars, Embossed, Tin, c.1900, 10 x 14 In. . . . . . *illus* 58.00
Sign, White Mountain, In A Million Homes, Man, Kids, Die Cut, Cardboard, 17 x 19 In. 242.00
Sign, Wilcox Bro's & Co Cigar, Cardboard, Embossed, c.1900, 7 x 13 In. 308.00
Sign, Wilcox Jewelers, Pocket Watch, Painted, Cast Iron, Tin, 23 x 16 In. 990.00
Sign, Wild Woodbine Cigarettes, Blue, White, Porcelain, 36 x 24 In. 165.00
Sign, Wild Woodbine Cigarettes, Imperial Tobacco, Porcelain, 36 x 18 In. 400.00
Sign, Willys Jeeps-Trucks, Painted Sheet Metal, Wood, c.1950, 95 x 45 In. 711.00
Sign, Winchester, Grouse, 1909, 30 ½ x 15 ⅛ In. 6175.00
Sign, Winchester, Winning Combination For Field, Fowl, Shooting, 1907, 15 x 29 In. 4035.00
Sign, Wm. J. Lemp Brewing Co., Tin, St. Louis, Mo., Self-Framed, 31 x 23 In. 8500.00
Sign, Wm. Sparks Holsteins, Cow, Red, White, Black, Die Cut, 2-Sided, Tin, 24 x 24 In. 380.00
Sign, Wonder Bread, Leatherhead Football Player, 1939, 44 x 32 In. 115.00
Sign, Won-Up Grapefruit Juice, Health's Sake, 5 Cent, Woman, Tin, Cardboard, Easel, 9 x 13 In. 153.00
Sign, Worden's Ice Cream, Bricks, Qts., Pts., Red, White, Porcelain, 30 x 20 In. 250.00
Sign, Wright's Inn, White, Black, Wood, Late 19th Century, 16 ¾ x 35 ½ In. 350.00
Sign, Wrigley's Gum, Delicious Flavors, Tin On Cardboard, 1920-30, 7 x 11 In. . . . . . *illus* 575.00
Sign, Wrigley's Spearmint Gum, Cardboard, Tin Lithograph 228.00
Sign, Wunder Brewing Co., Woman, Tin, Self-Framed, 1890s, 22 x 16 In. . . . . . *illus* 4025.00
Sign, Yale Brewing Co., Lager Beer, Reverse On Glass, 1890s, 29 x 37 In. . . . . . *illus* 2530.00
Sign, Yankee Doodle Root Beer, Tin, Embossed, 1950s, 19 x 27 In. 115.00
Sign, Yankee Girl Chewing Tobacco, Shield, Red, White, Black, Tin, 13 ½ x 9 ½ In. 160.00
Sign, Yellow Cab 5 Cent Cigar, Takes The Right Of Way, Porcelain, 6 x 18 In. 100.00
Sign, Yellowstone Bourbon Whiskey, Hand Tinted Photo, Woman & Bottle, 15 x 19 In. 345.00
Soap, Wrigley's Mineral Bar, Red, Wrapper, 4 In. 50.00
Soap Holder, Garland Stoves & Ranges, Tin, 4 x 5 In. 276.00
Spatula, Hygeia Ice Cream Co., Elmira, N.Y. 18.00
Stand, Philip Morris, Little Johnny, Painted, Wood, 41 In. 135.00
Straw Hat, Elis, Salesman's Sample, c.1915, 7 x 2 In. 288.00
Stickpin, McCormick, Man On Horse Drawn Thresher, Embossed, 1 ¼ x 2 In. 143.00
Stoplight, Pickwick Night Coach, Bus, Red, Marked, Pickwick SS, Bracket, 6 In. 58.00

Advertising, Sign, Voigt's Snow Drift Flour, Porcelain, Flange, c.1910, 14 x 18 In. $345.00

Advertising, Sign, Westinghouse, Easy To Operate, Embossed, Tin, 1920s, 24 x 22 In. $345.00

Advertising, Sign, White Label Cigars, Embossed, Tin, c.1900, 10 x 14 In. $58.00

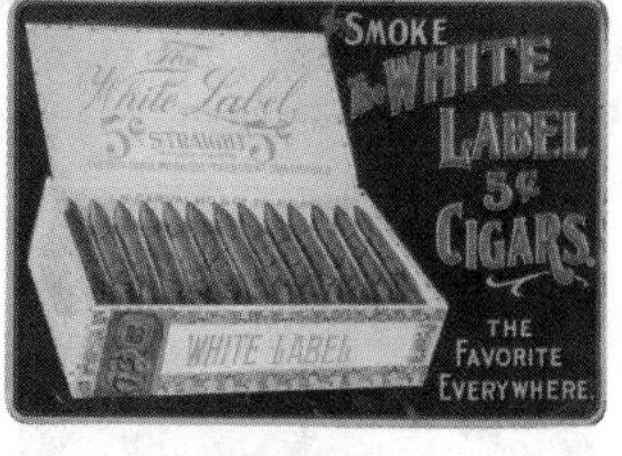

Advertising, Sign, Wrigley's Gum, Delicious Flavors, Tin On Cardboard, 1920-30, 7 x 11 In. $575.00

Advertising, Sign,
Wunder Brewing Co., Woman, Tin,
Self-Framed, 1890s, 22 x 16 In.
$4025.00

Advertising, Sign,
Yale Brewing Co., Lager Beer,
Reverse On Glass, 1890s, 29 x 37 In.
$2530.00

Advertising, Tin, Apache Trail Cigars,
Indian On Horse, Oval, 5 ¾ In.
$1610.00

Stove, Parlor, Friedland, Black, Cast Nickel, Salesman's Sample, 8 In. 1725.00
Stringholder, Bean Hole Beans, Tin, Die Cut, 12 x 14 In. 961.00
Stringholder, Dutch Boy Paints, Tin, Phoenix Eckstein White Lead, 14 x 30 In. 2860.00
Stringholder, Heinz, Pickle Shape, Metal Lithograph, 2-Sided, c.1900s, 24 x 17 In. 8250.00
Sucker Holder, Chief Watta Pop, Chalkware, 9 ½ In. 385.00
Syrup Dispenser, Fan-Taz, Drink Of The Fans, Baseball Shape, c.1910, 15 In. 16450.00
Tablecloth, Shakespeare Fine Fishing Tackle, Blue Felt, Embroidered, c.1935, 70 x 45 In. 403.00
Thermometers, are listed in their own category.
Tie Bar, Deming Pumps, 75 Years, Goldtone, Signed, Hickok, c.1955 12.50

Advertising tin cans or canisters were first used commercially in the United States in 1819 and were called tins. Today the word tin is used by most collectors to describe many types of containers, including food tins, biscuit boxes, roly poly tobacco containers, gunpowder cans, talcum powder sprinkle-top cans, cigarette flat-fifty tins, and more. Beer Cans are listed in their own category. Things made of undecorated tin are listed under Tinware.

Tin, 3 Little Pigs Candy, Paper Label, Handle, 3 In. 66.00
Tin, 400 Blend Coffee, Paper Label, Githens, Rexsamer & Co., Philadelphia, Lb. 177.00
Tin, Acme Pellets, National Licorice Co., Glass Window Display, Hinged Lid, 5 Lb. 33.00
Tin, Adams Chiclets, 1 Cent, Canister, 3 ½ In. 130.00
Tin, Allen's Royal Remedy Foot Powder, Red, Green Yellow, Cylindrical, 4 ⅛ In. 66.00
Tin, Allen's Sanitary Tooth-Ease, Allen S. Olmsted Image, Paper Label, Cylindrical, 4 In. 232.00
Tin, Anheuser-Busch, A Logo, Eagle, Red, Green, Strap Handles, 1890s, 13 x 17 ½ In. 550.00
Tin, ANTM Selected Dainties Toffees, Green, Black, Gold, 15 x 11 x 7 In. 110.00
Tin, Apache Trail Cigars, Indian On Horse, Oval, 5 ¾ In. *illus* 1610.00
Tin, Areca Nut Tooth Soap, Contents, Embossed, Hinged Lid, 2 x 3 In. 242.00
Tin, Aromatic Tooth Soap, Red, Frederick Stearns & Co., Hinged Lid, 2 x 3 In. 132.00
Tin, Bagdad Tobacco, Vertical Pocket, 4 x 3 x 1 In. 86.00
Tin, Beech-Nut Chewing Gum, Peppermint Flavour, 4 x 5 x 3 ½ In. 55.00
Tin, Billhook, Breakfast Cheer Coffee, Woman, Bell, Green, Red, Celluloid, Metal, 7 In. 187.00
Tin, Biscuit, Carr's Carlisle, Trunk Form, Tan, Brown, Gold, 2 ½ x 3 ½ x 2 ½ In. 30.00
Tin, Biscuit, Chad Valley, Delivery Van, Tin Lithograph, Removable Roof, 9 ½ In. 978.00
Tin, Biscuit, Huntley & Palmers, 7 Books, Bookends, 4 x 9 x 4 In. 275.00
Tin, Biscuit, Huntley & Palmers, Basket, Flowers, Handle, 7 ¼ x 5 x 3 In. 90.00
Tin, Biscuit, Huntley & Palmers, Bell, Silver, When Ye Doe Ring, 6 ¾ x 6 In. 22.00
Tin, Biscuit, Huntley & Palmers, Bookcase, Embossed, 6 ½ x 4 ½ x 3 ¾ In. 105.00
Tin, Biscuit, Huntley & Palmers, Canister, Embossed Trees, Handles, 8 x 5 In. 605.00
Tin, Biscuit, Huntley & Palmers, Egyptian Design, Urn, Ring Handles, 8 ¾ x 3 ¾ In. 22.00
Tin, Biscuit, Huntley & Palmers, Farmhouse, Farm Animals, 4 x 6 x 3 ½ In. 625.00
Tin, Biscuit, Huntley & Palmers, Grandfather Clock, Black, Gold, 1928, 11 ½ x 2 x 3 In. 605.00
Tin, Biscuit, Huntley & Palmers, Lost Cause, Flight Of King James II, 3 x 4 x 7 In. 11.00
Tin, Biscuit, Huntley & Palmers, Pen Box, Fox Hunt, Hinged Lid, 2 ½ x 3 x 9 ½ In. 22.00
Tin, Biscuit, Huntley & Palmers, Post Office, Red, Black, Embossed, ER, 6 ½ x 6 In. 165.00
Tin, Biscuit, Huntley & Palmers, Purse, Alligator, Silver, Handle, 5 x 8 x 3 In. 33.00
Tin, Biscuit, Huntley & Palmers, Suitcase Form, Gray, 8 x 8 ½ x 4 In. 17.00
Tin, Biscuit, Huntley & Palmers, Sylvan, Handles, Trees, Landscape, 7 ½ In. 150.00
Tin, Biscuit, Marsh & Co., Purse Form, Alligator Skin, Brown, Gold, Handle, 2 x 5 x 5 In. 245.00
Tin, Biscuit, Will Crawford, Bicky House, Lucie Attwell Kiddibics, 7 x 8 x 4 In. 88.00
Tin, Bouquet Mocha Java Coffee, Red, Tin Lithograph, 2 Lb., 7 x 6 x 3 ¾ In. 100.00
Tin, Boy Blue Licorice Nougat, George W. Horner & Co., 9 ¼ x 6 In. 44.00
Tin, Buchanan's J.B.B. Mints, Animals, 8-Sided, Tin, Glass Front, 7 In. 110.00
Tin, Bunnies Salted Peanuts, Red, Blue, Yellow, 10 Lb., 11 ¼ x 8 In. 584.00
Tin, Bunte Marshmallows, Boy, Est. 1876, 9 ½ x 12 ¾ In. 72.00
Tin, Burkholder's Potato Chips, Red, White, 10 ½ In. 15.00
Tin, Camel Cigar, American Can Co., Arabian On Camel, 5 ½ x 4 ½ x 2 ½ In. 201.00
Tin, Campfire Marshmallows, 6 x 10 In. 25.00
Tin, Capital City Asthma Cure, Walace E. Bartlett, Yellow, Black, 3 x 4 ½ In. 66.00
Tin, Cardinal Tobacco, Meyers Cox & Co., Vertical Pocket, 4 ½ x 3 x 1 In. 518.00
Tin, Carlton Club, Beige Round, Blue Letters, Pocket, 4 ½ x 3 x ⅞ In. 160.00
Tin, Carnation Malted Milk, Red, White, Blue, Canister, Aluminum, 9 x 6 In. 299.00
Tin, Cheney's Listerated Tooth Powder, 25 Cents, Cylindrical, 4 ½ In. 209.00
Tin, Chewing Tobacco, Sure Shot, It Touches The Spot, Display Bin, Indian, Bow, 15 x 8 In. 708.00
Tin, Chicago Cubs Chewing Tobacco, Eagle & Flag, Hinged Lid, 3 Lb., 4 x 6 ½ In. 143.00
Tin, Chicago Cubs Chewing Tobacco, Rock City Tobacco Co., Quebec, 1936, 6 x 3 ½ In. 255.00
Tin, Clover Farm Coffee, Image Of Red Rose On Front, 1 Lb. 66.00
Tin, Coffee, Star Mills, Courting Scene, Geometric Design, Flint, 27 x 14 In. 605.00
Tin, College Town Spice, Cinnamon, Pictures College, Cream & Brown, 4 Oz. 270.00
Tin, Condoms, Image Of 3 Male Lifeguards, Cream Color, 1930s, 1 ½ x ½ In. 1100.00

Tin, Consolidated Dental, Red & Black, 3 ½ x 3 ½ In. 99.00
Tin, Convention Hall Coffee, Red Ground, Blue Lettering, Ridenour-Baker, Kansas City, Lb. 118.00
Tin, Co-Re-Ga Denture Powder, Holds Dental Plates In Mouth, 2 ¼ x 1 ¼ x ½ In. 44.00
Tin, Crane's Tobacco, Cream & Green, Pocket, 4 ½ In. 330.00
Tin, Cummings Solid Comfort Foot Powder, Man Kicking Heels, Contents, 4 ½ In. 105.00
Tin, CW Coffee, Wildar Co., 5 ¾ x 4 ¼ In. 5.00
Tin, Dairymen's League Member, Embossed, Tin, Navy & Blue, 10 x 8 ½ In. 66.00
Tin, Dark Hill Coffee, House, Hill Label, E.C. Hall Company, Brockton, Mass., Lb. 148.00
Tin, DeLite's Cocoa, Black Boy, Embossed, Pepper Lid, Paper Label, 3 ¾ In. 80.00
Tin, Dill's Best Tobacco, Yellow, Mild, Cool, Fragrant, 1 ½ x 3 x 1 In. 27.00
Tin, Dining Car Coffee, Image Of People Drinking Coffee On Train, Blue Ground, 5 In. 490.00
Tin, Dixie Jumbo Salted Peanuts, Red, Yellow, 10 Lb., 11 ½ x 8 ½ In. 526.00
Tin, Dr. Charles Foot Relief, Flesh Food, 3 ½ x 2 ¼ In. 60.00
Tin, Dr. Constan's Nerve Pills, Fred'k F. Ingram Co., Hinged Lid, 4 x 5 In. 580.00
Tin, Dr. E.L. Graves Tooth Powder, Cylindrical, 4 In. 60.00
Tin, Dr. Flormaneck's Eye-Lash-Ine, For Blepharitis, Lovely Woman, Round, 1 ½ x 1 In. 95.00
Tin, Dr. Foote's White Lily Sanitary Tampons, Cylindrical, 3 ⅛ In. 154.00
Tin, Dr. Lyon's Perfect Tooth Powder, Woman, Blue, Cylindrical, Box, 4 In. 88.00
Tin, Dr. Schiffmann's Asthma Cure, Free Sample, Red, Black, 1 ¼ x 2 In. 60.00
Tin, Dr. White's Celebrated Cough Drops, Yellow, Red, Hinged Lid, 2 x 3 ½ In. 33.00
Tin, Elephant Salted Peanuts, Red, Gold, 10 Lb., 11 ½ x 7 ½ In. 121.00
Tin, Ethiopian Black Enamel, Paper Label, 1/16 Gal., 3 ¼ In. 80.00
Tin, Falstaff, Woman In Red Dress & Hat Sitting On Tobacco Tin, Pocket, 4 x 2 ½ In. 210.00
Tin, Fast Mail Tobacco, Sommers Bros., Pocket, 2 ¼ x 3 ¾ In. *illus* 345.00
Tin, Fawn Tobacco, American Eagle Brand, Orange Ground, Black Fawn, 4 ¼ In. 440.00
Tin, Fisher's Indian Remedy, Indian, Teepee, Red, White, Hinged Lid, 2 ¾ x 2 ½ In. 132.00
Tin, Fisher's Peanuts, Salted In The Shell, Yellow, Red, 25 Lb., 20 ½ x 12 ¼ In. 110.00
Tin, Flor De Franklin Cigars, Man Flying Kite, From Factory, 5 ¼ In. 180.00
Tin, Fo-Po Foot Powder, For Refreshing Feet, Pink, Black, 50 Cents, Contents, 4 In. 49.00
Tin, Forbes Tea & Spice, Allspice, Red Plastic Slide, 2 ½ x 2 ¼ In. 4.50
Tin, Forbes Tea & Spice, Cloves, Cardboard, Pull-Off Metal Lid, 3 ¼ x 2 ¼ In. 6.00
Tin, Forbes Tea & Spice, Curry, Cardboard, Pull-Off Metal Lid, 3 ¼ x 2 ¼ In. 8.00
Tin, Forbes Tea & Spice, Marjoram, Cardboard, Pull-Off Metal Lid, 3 ¼ x 2 ¼ In. 8.00
Tin, Forbes Tea & Spice, Oregano, Cardboard, Pull-Off Metal Lid, 3 ¼ x 2 ¼ In. 8.00
Tin, Forbes Tea & Spice, Poultry Seasoning, Red Plastic Slide, 2 ½ x 2 ¼ In. 4.50
Tin, Forbes Tea & Spice, Red Pepper, Red Plastic Slide, 2 ½ x 2 ¼ In. 4.50
Tin, Forbes Tea & Spice, Sage, Ground, Metal Slide, 2 ½ x 2 ¼ In. 4.50
Tin, Fountain Tobacco, Water Fountain, Red, Green, Gold, 6 ½ x 5 ¼ In. 440.00
Tin, Game Fine Cut, 48 5-Cent Packages, Canister, 7 ½ x 11 ½ In. 330.00
Tin, Game Fine Cut, Jn. J. Bagley & Co., Lithograph, 11 ½ In. 633.00
Tin, Gloria Swanson Face Powder, Canco, 1951, 4 x 1 ½ In. 67.00
Tin, Golden Brown Salted Peanuts, Brown, Gold, 10 Lb., 9 ¾ In. 60.00
Tin, Golden Brown Salted Peanuts, Brown, Gold, 5 ¼ In. 60.00
Tin, Golden West Coffee, Red, Black, Cowgirl, 7 In. 259.00
Tin, Hand Made Tobacco, Blue, White, Globe Tobacco Co., 6 ½ In. *illus* 259.00
Tin, Handbag Cut Plug Tobacco, Handbag Shape, Bail Handle, Yellow, 6 x 7 x 4 In. 55.00
Tin, Havana Cadet Cigars, Imported Sumatra Wrapper, 50, Lb., 5 x 5 In. 320.00
Tin, Hershey's Chocolate & Cocoa, 5 x 12 In. 16.00
Tin, Hershey's Chocolatier Hot Chocolate Drink, Yellow, Red, 7 In. 60.00
Tin, Hillaby's, Best Pontefract Cakes, Yellow, Red, Hinged Lid, 4 Lb., 8 ¾ In. 40.00
Tin, Hindoo Smoking Tobacco, Granulated Plug, Man Smoking, 3 In. 275.00
Tin, Hirsutine, Only Infallible Hair & Beard Grower, 1, Hinged Lid, 1 ½ x 3 In. 110.00
Tin, Honey Moon Tobacco, Rum Flavored, Image Of Man On Moon, Contents, 4 ½ In. 635.00
Tin, International Louse Killer, Child, Chickens, Canister, Sealed, 7 x 3 In. 99.00
Tin, Jack Sprat Peanut Butter, Western Grocer Mills, Iowa, 25 Lb., 10 x 9 In. 235.00
Tin, Jackie Coogan Peanut Butter, The Kid Eating Sandwich, Kelly Co., 1920s, 4 In. 310.00
Tin, Kipling Cut Plug, Man, Harry Weissinger Tobacco Co., 4 ½ x 2 ¾ In. 55.00
Tin, Laflin Gunpowder, Supplied Gunpowder To U.S. Troops In Revolutionary War, 5 In. 2750.00
Tin, Lenox Tobacco, L. Warnick Brown & Co., Vertical Pocket, 4 ½ x 3 ½ x ¾ In. 1840.00
Tin, Liberty Toffee, Airplane Graphics, Orange, Inserts, 8 ½ x 9 ½ In. 144.00
Tin, Lucky Strike, Christmas, American Tobacco Co., Green, Red, Holly, 5 ¾ x 4 ¼ In. 67.00
Tin, Luxor Antiseptic Tooth Powder, Brown, Beige, Gold Wash Top, 4 ¼ In. 165.00
Tin, Mackintosh's Extra Cream Toffee, English Sweetmeat, Green, 5 ½ x 6 ½ In. 11.00
Tin, Macmahan's Handicap Tooth Powder, Embossed, Metal Cap, Box, 4 ½ In. 253.00
Tin, Matoaka Blue Ribbon Smoking Tobacco, 1910, 4 ¼ In. 1980.00
Tin, Mayflower Coffee, Flavor Fresh, Green, Handle, Gerhart Co., Lancaster, 25 Lb., 15 In. 170.00
Tin, Mei Lan Fan Dental Powder, Japanese Actor, Hinged Lid, 3 x 1 ½ x 1 ¾ In. 187.00

Advertising, Tin,
Fast Mail Tobacco, Sommers Bros.,
Pocket, 2 ¼ x 3 ¾ In.
$345.00

Advertising, Tin,
Handmade Tobacco, Blue, White,
Globe Tobacco Co., 6 ½ In.
$259.00

TIP

Don't use old home-canning jars to preserve food. The jars with wire bails, glass caps, zinc porcelain-lined caps, or metal caps with rubber rings do not seal as well as the new two-piece vacuum-cap jars.

Advertising, Tin, Moses Cough Drops, 5 Lb., 8 ½ x 6 x 4 In.
$87.00

Advertising, Tin, Orange Flower Cigars, 5 Cent, Liberty Can Co., 6 x 5 ½ In.
$115.00

Advertising, Tin, Pippins Cigars, 5 Cent, 5 ½ x 3 x 3 In.
$288.00

Tin, Mellomints, Red, Blue, Sample, Brandle Smith Co., 1 ¼ x 2 In. 27.00
Tin, Mennen's Borated Talcum Powder, Baby On Front, 4 Oz. 45.00
Tin, Monarch Peanut Butter, Picture Of Lion, By Reid Murdoch Co., 55 Lb., 13 x 14 In. 110.00
Tin, Monte Christo Superior Tobacco, 3 King Mixture, 1888, 2 x 8 ½ x 1 In. 66.00
Tin, Moses Cough Drops, 5 Lb., 8 ½ x 6 x 4 In. . . . . . *illus* 87.00
Tin, Moss Bros. Peanuts, 5 Cent, 10 Lb., 12 ½ In. 60.00
Tin, National Licorice Co., N.L. Co. Lozenges, Tin, Glass Front, Orange, Black, Silver, 5 Lb. 120.00
Tin, New Era Potato Chips, 11 ½ x 7 ½ In. 15.00
Tin, Nigger Hair Tobacco, Woman, Hoop Earrings, Handle, c.1910, 6 ½ In. 110.00
Tin, Old Dutch Cleanser, Chases Dirt, Paper Label, Contents, 1930s, 14 Oz., 5 In. 35.00
Tin, Orange Flower Cigars, 5 Cent, Liberty Can Co., 6 x 5 ½ In. . . . . . *illus* 115.00
Tin, Oriental Tea, Black, Gold, Stamped, Empire Hardware Co., 27 ½ x 15 x 18 In. 330.00
Tin, Orinco Five Cent Cigar, 6 x 6 x 4 In. 550.00
Tin, Osgood's Fragrant Tooth Powder, Woman Holding Toothbrush, Cylindrical, 4 In. 143.00
Tin, P.D.C. Guaranteed Cure For Dyspepsia In Any Form, Parker Chemical Co., 3 In. 242.00
Tin, Paiestleys Baby Powder, Stork & Baby, Paper Label, 4 ½ x 2 In. 33.00
Tin, Patterson's Tuxedo Tobacco, 4 ¾ x 4 x 6 In. 173.00
Tin, Paul Jones, Continental Tobacco Co., Vertical Pocket, 4 ½ x 3 x 1 In. 748.00
Tin, Peachy Tobacco, Double Cut, Peach, Leaves, Yellow, Orange, Green, 4 ⅛ x 2 ½ In. 193.00
Tin, Pep Boys Handy Bulb Kit, Red, Black, 2 ¼ In. . . . . . 20.00 to 50.00
Tin, Pipe Tobacco, Autobacco, Male Driver, Smoking, Red, S.S. Pierce Co., Boston, 5 x 5 In. . . 177.00
Tin, Pippins Cigars, 5 Cent, 5 ½ x 3 x 3 In. . . . . . *illus* 288.00
Tin, Piso's Antiseptic Tooth Powder, 25 Cents, Green, Yellow, 4 ½ In. 143.00
Tin, Polar Bear Tobacco, Always Fresh, Blue, Gold, Tin, 12 x 18 x 14 In. 220.00
Tin, Pow Wow Brand Salted Peanuts, Green, Red, 10 Lb., 9 ¾ x 8 ½ In. 523.00
Tin, Prof. Dyke's Hair & Beard Elixir, Blue, 25 Cents, Hinged Lid, 1 ½ x 2 ½ In. 105.00
Tin, Puck Canadian Cigarette, Hockey Players, Canister 173.00
Tin, Puck Virginia Cigarette Tobacco, Yellow, Red, Round, Canada, 3 ½ x 4 In. 50.00
Tin, Puritan Tobacco, Phillip Morris Tobacco Co., Vertical Pocket, 4 ½ x 3 x 1 In. 200.00
Tin, Puritan Tobacco, Pilgrim, Crushed Plug Mixture, Gray, Black, White, 4 ⅜ x 3 In. 160.00
Tin, Quaker Oats, Quaker Man On Front, Red, White & Black, 10 Oz. 120.00
Tin, Queen Quality Salted Nuts, Black, Yellow, Red, 5 ¼ In. 100.00
Tin, Quinlan's Pretzels, Tin, Glass Top, 13 ⅓ x 12 ¼ In. 20.00
Tin, Reed's Butter Scotch Wafers, Pure As Gold, 20 Lb., 8 x 10 In. 22.00
Tin, Regennas Hard Candies, Green, Red, Blue, 7 In. 90.00
Tin, Regulation Paint, Paper Label, Gal., 7 ¾ In. 20.00
Tin, Rexall Tooth Powder, Girl, Green, Gold, Contents, Sample, 1 ⅞ In. 209.00
Tin, Robertson Bros. Chocolates, Golf Bag Form, Man, Woman, 11 x 3 ½ In. 625.00
Tin, Roly Poly, Mayo's Cut, Man With Pipe, 7 ½ In. 195.00
Tin, Roly Poly, Mayo's Tobacco, Dutchman, Figural, Yellow Shirt, Red Scarf, 7 In. 316.00
Tin, Roly Poly, Mayo's Tobacco Cut Plug, Mammy, Corncob Pipe, 6 ½ x 5 ½ In. 410.00
Tin, Scholl's Fixo Foot Powder, Applying Powder To Foot, Yellow, Red, Contents, 4 In. 305.00
Tin, Seal Of North Carolina Plug Cut, 2 Women By Field, Shore, Small Top 177.00
Tin, Severa's Foot Powder, Blue, Beige, Gold, 25 Cents, Cylindrical, Contents, 4 ¼ In. 60.00
Tin, Shenandoah Valley Apple Candy, Yellow Apple, 3 ¼ x 3 ¼ In. 33.00
Tin, Shogun Mixture, Man, Flowers, For Pipe & Tobacco Smokers, Red, Yellow, White 11650.00
Tin, Smoke Or Chew Nigger Hair Tobacco, Yellow, Black, Wire Handle, 6 ⅝ In. 187.00
Tin, Squirrel Brand Salted Peanuts, Yellow, 10 Lb., 10 x 8 In. 360.00
Tin, Star Razor, Image Of Man Shaving, Black & White, Kampfe Bros., 1880, 2 x 1 In. 110.00
Tin, Sterling Tobacco, Green, Gold, Yellow, 11 ½ In. 77.00
Tin, Sterling Tobacco, Green, White, 11 ½ x 8 ¼ In. 132.00
Tin, Sweet Burley Tobacco, Yellow, Red, 11 ¼ x 8 ¼ In. 90.00
Tin, Sweet Cuba Tobacco Fine Cut, 5 Cent, Yellow, Red, 7 ⅜ x 8 x 9 ½ In. 200.00
Tin, Sweet-Heart Sugar Cones, Light Blue, Red, White, 300 Count, 15 In. 120.00
Tin, Temple Bar Tobacco, Double Concave, Vertical, 4 x 3 x 1 In. 201.00
Tin, Texaco Home Lubricant, 6 ½ In. 30.00
Tin, Thermo Anti-Freeze, Snowman, Salesman's Sample, 2 ¾ In. 15.00
Tin, Thompson's Malted Milk, Yellow, Granite Enamel, Canister, Nickel Lid, 10 x 6 In. 405.00
Tin, Three Cadets, Condoms, Black, Red & Yellow, 1 ⅝ x ⅝ In. 170.00
Tin, Tiger Chewing Tobacco, 5 Cent, Cardboard, Tin Top, Base, 11 In. 33.00
Tin, Tiger Chewing Tobacco, Red, Hinged Lid, Handles, 10 x 10 In. 55.00
Tin, Toffee, Riley's, Royal Princesses, Elizabeth, Margaret Rose, Round, 1930s, 5 In. 45.00
Tin, Tooth Powder For Cleansing, Preserving & Beautifying Teeth, Woman, 3 In. 297.00
Tin, Tooth Powder For Cleansing & Beautifying The Teeth, Cylindrical, 4 ⅛ In. 176.00
Tin, Trout Line Tobacco, Vertical Pocket, 3 ½ x 2 ½ x 1 In. 316.00
Tin, Tuxedo, Green & Gold, Distinguished Man, Pocket 28.00
Tin, Two Orphans Cigars, Image Of Orphans, 50 Ct., 5 x 5 In. 165.00

Tin, Union Leader Redi Cut Tobacco, Uncle Sam Image, Pocket, c.1917, 3 x 4 ½ In. 56.00
Tin, Unity Tobacco, Vertical Pocket 2 ¾ x 3 ½ x 1 In.. .... 460.00
Tin, Veterinary Cascarin Tonic Powder, Horse, Steer, Canister, Contents, Sealed, 5 x 3 ½ In. .. 17.00
Tin, Victory V Gums, Mantel Clock, Brown, Tan, Gold, Fryer & Co., 6 x 8 In. 220.00
Tin, Victory Vapor Balm, Orange, Black, Oval, 50 Cents, Contents, 2 ½ x 2 In.. .... 11.00
Tin, Wagon Paint, Yellow & Implement, Paper Label, 1 Pt., 4 In. 30.00
Tin, Watkins' Tooth Powder, Image Of Dr. Watkins, 25 Cents, 4 ½ In.. .... 305.00
Tin, Weideman Popcorn, Kid On Front, Image Of Cannon Shooting Corn, 2 x 4 In. 242.00
Tin, Western Grocer Mills, Chocolate Cream Coffee, Yellow, Blue, 3 Lb., 9 ½ In. 44.00
Tin, White Villa Coffee, House, Car, Fence, Label, Key Wind, Lb. 300.00
Tin, Will Crawford & Sons Ltd., Stagecoach Shape, Red, Black, Yellow, 6 ¼ x 8 x 3 In. 70.00
Tin, Y & S Old Fashioned Licorice Lozenges, Black, Orange, Glass Front, 8 x 6 x 4 In. 38.00
Tin, Yacht Club Tobacco, P. Lorelord, Vertical Pocket, c., 4 ½ x 3 x 1 In.. .... 518.00
Tin, Yankee Boy Tobacco, Lithographed, Red Pennant, Batter, 1910. .... 472.00
Tin, Yellow Cigar, American Can Co., Canister, 5 ½ x 5 ½ In. 2300.00
Tin, Zatek Cocoa, Building Form, 13 In. 330.00

Tip tray Advertising tip trays are decorated metal trays less than 5 inches in diameter. They were placed on the table or counter to hold either the bill or the coins that were left as a tip. Change receivers could be made of glass, plastic, or metal. They were kept on the counter near the cash register and held the money passed back and forth by the cashier. Related items may be listed in the Advertising category under Change Receiver.

Tip Tray, Antikamnia Tablets, Woman, Seated, St. Louis World's Fair, 1904. .... 33.00
Tip Tray, Beck's Bottled Beer, Metal Lithograph, 4 ¼ In. 248.00
Tip Tray, Cigar, Andrew D. White, Mild & Satisfying, Harkert Cigar Co., 4 In. 112.00
Tip Tray, Cracker Jack, Bears, Verse, 1906, 5 x 3 ¼ In.. .... 121.00
Tip Tray, Dr Pepper, Dog, At All Soda Fountains, 5 Cent, Scalloped Rim, 1900s, 3 x 2 In. 500.00
Tip Tray, Dr Pepper, Kittens, At All Soda Fountains, 5 Cent, Scalloped Rim, 2 ½ In. 350.00
Tip Tray, Fairy Soap, Lithograph, Girl Sitting On Soap Bar, Shonk, 4 ¼ In.. .... 56.00
Tip Tray, Ginger Ale, Woman In Large Hat, Black & Yellow, 4 ¼ In. 380.00
Tip Tray, Heptol Splits Laxative, For Health's Sake, Bronco Rider, 4 ¼ In. 900.00
Tip Tray, Highland Evaporated Cream, Lithograph, Milk Can, 1904, 3 ½ In. 115.00
Tip Tray, I.P. Thomas & Son, High Grade Fertilizers, Lithograph, Early 1900s, 4 In. 115.00
Tip Tray, Jingo, Hunting Dog, Tin Lithograph, Scalloped Edge, 3 ½ In. 110.00
Tip Tray, Krueger's Beer & Ales, Image Of Ales & Food, 1930s, 4 ¼ In. 115.00
Tip Tray, Liberty Beer, In Bottles Only, Indian, American Brew Co., 4 ¼ In.. .... 363.00
Tip Tray, Moxie, Girl, I Just Love Moxie, Don't You, c.1910, 6 In. 132.00
Tip Tray, National Brewing Co., San Francisco, Calif., 4 ½ In. 650.00
Tip Tray, Quick Meal Ranges, Chicks In Field, Oval, 3 ¼ x 4 ½ In.. .... 44.00
Tip Tray, Red Raven Aperient Water, For Headache, Indigestion, Tin, 6 x 4 In. 121.00
Tip Tray, Rockford High Grade Watches, Woman, Green, Oval, 4 ½ x 3 ½ In. 66.00
Tobacco Cutter, Star Tobacco, Save The Tags, Cast Iron, 6 ¾ x 18 ¾ In. 66.00
Tobacco Cutter, Sylvester Bros. Co., Wholesale Grocers, Pat. 1914, 8 ¼ x 15 ¼ In. 120.00
Token, Force Cereal, Sunny Jim, Good Luck, Good Health, Metal, 1930s, 1 ¼ In. 7.50
Trash Can, Chief Metal Ware, Trash Can Form, Steel, Salesman's Sample, 1940, 3 ⅔ In. 125.00
Trash Can, Dr Pepper, Bullet Form, Push Lid, Marked, United, 1930s, 36 x 15 In. 175.00
Trash Can, Drive A Buick, Keep Our Streets Clean, Blue, White, Steel, 1930s, 3 ½ In.. .... 165.00
Tray, Anheuser-Busch, Factory Scene, 18 ¾ x 15 ½ In. 900.00
Tray, Balloon Yeast, Never Done Rising, Ceramic, c.1900, 15 x 12 x 1 In. .... *illus* 202.00
Tray, Benham's Ice Cream, Brownies, Tin Lithograph, 13 ½ x 10 ⅜ In. 140.00
Tray, Blue Wing Whiskey, 2 Dead Ducks, Blue, Yellow, Tin, 16 ½ x 13 ½ In.. .... 700.00
Tray, Buffalo Brewing Co., Indian Maiden, Riding Buffalo, Tin, 12 In.. .... 8800.00
Tray, Cameron Bottling Works, 3 Dogs, Tin Lithograph, 14 x 17 In. 143.00
Tray, Carta Blanca Beer, Tin Lithograph, 1930-40, 13 In. Diam. .... *illus* 144.00
Tray, Compliments Of Lortig's Grocery, DePere, Wis., Rose, Black Ground, 12 ¾ In. 36.00
Tray, Costa's Ice-Cream, Ice-Cream I Want, Girl, Brown, Yellow, Tin, 13 x 10 ½ In. 143.00
Tray, Dairy Made Ice-Cream, You're Sure, It's Pure, Girl, Tin, 13 x 10 ½ In. .... 66.00 to 77.00
Tray, Dr Pepper, Drink, King Of Beverages, Yellow, Red, Tin, Oval, 1900s, 14 x 17 In. 2000.00
Tray, Dr Pepper, Woman Holding 2 Bottles, 1940s, 13 ¼ x 10 ½ In. 300.00
Tray, Drink Orange Julep, Woman With Drink, 1920s, 10 x 13 ½ In. 169.00
Tray, Drink Zipp's 5 Cent Cheeri-O, Bird Drinking Lithograph, Beach, Round, 12 In. .... *illus* 700.00
Tray, Dubl-Ex Ice Cream, Sundae, Buy Ice Cream With Confidence, Tin 30.00
Tray, East Greenwich Dairy Ice Cream, Woman, Eating Ice Cream, Parker Brawner Co. 110.00
Tray, Fitger's Beer, Since 1881, Duluth, Minn., 13 In.. .... 350.00
Tray, Germania Brewing Co., Philadelphia, Penn., 11 x 16 ½ In. 1300.00
Tray, Gottfried Krueger Brewing Co., Beer, Marked, American Art Works, 13 In. Diam. 66.00
Tray, H.L. Griesedieck Distilling Co., 2 Dogs, Old Scenter Rye, Tin, 10 ½ x 13 In. 355.00

Advertising, Tray, Balloon Yeast, Never Done Rising, Ceramic, c.1900, 15 x 12 x 1 In. $202.00

Advertising, Tray, Carta Blanca Beer, Tin Lithograph, 1930-40, 13 In. Diam. $144.00

Advertising, Tray, Drink Zipp's 5 Cent Cheeri-O, Bird Drinking Lithograph, Beach, Round, 12 In. $700.00

As always, the edited listings in *Kovels' Antiques & Collectibles Price Guide 2010* aren't available on any website, but readers should visit Kovels.com for information on trends, tips, reproductions, marks, old prices, and more!

TIP
The best time to buy an antique is when you see it.

Advertising, Tray, Miller Beer, Woman On Half Moon, Tin, c.1920, 13 In. Diam. $345.00

Advertising, Tray, Rainier Beer, Woman, Tin Lithograph, 1905-10, 13 In. Diam. $1495.00

Advertising, Tray, Velvet Ice Cream, Girl Eating, 17 ½ x 11 ½ In. $193.00

Tray, Haefner Bros. Dry Goods, Notions, Furnishings, Flower Vase, Tin, 16 ½ x 13 In. 55.00
Tray, Hampden Brewing Co., Waiter Holding Tray Of Beer, Metal, 1934, 13 In. Diam. 90.00
Tray, Henry Weinhard City Brewery, Factory, Columbia Export, Oval, Tin, 13 ½ x 16 In. 279.00
Tray, Hires Root Beer, Josh Slinger At Soda Fountain, Round, Tin, c.1915, 13 In. 403.00
Tray, Hires Root Beer, Ugly Kid, Blue, Yellow, Tin, c.1900, 12 In. Diam. 115.00
Tray, Hyan Dry Ginger Ale, Boy Riding Bottle, 10 ½ x 13 In. 60.00
Tray, Kuebler's Famous Beer, Boy With Lantern, Tin, American Artworks, 13 x 10 In. 15.00
Tray, Lakeside Grape Juice, Tin, 13 ½ In. 220.00
Tray, Lykens Brewing Co., Girl, Horse, Oval, Tin, 17 x 14 In. 650.00
Tray, Miller Beer, Woman On Half Moon, Tin, c.1920, 13 In. Diam. .... *illus* 345.00
Tray, Narragansett Lager & Ale, Indian, Dr. Seuss, 12 In. Diam. 300.00
Tray, National Brewing Co., San Francisco, Calif., 13 x 16 In. 1800.00
Tray, NuGrape Soda, Hand With Bottle, 13 x 10 ½ In. 60.00
Tray, Orange Crush, 6 Bottles, Orange, Black, 12 In. Diam. 157.00
Tray, Orange Crush, Crushy Man, Tin Lithograph, 13 x 10 ½ In. 170.00
Tray, Parfait, Drink, At Founts & Bottles, Girl, Holding Cup, 13 x 10 In. 176.00
Tray, Peerless Ice Cream, 3 Girls, White Mountain Creamery, Tin, 1915, 10 x 13 In. 130.00
Tray, Rainier Beer, Woman, Tin Lithograph, 1905-10, 13 In. Diam. .... *illus* 1495.00
Tray, Red Raven, Ask The Man, Nude Child Reaching For Bottle, Tin, 1905, 12 In. Diam. 403.00
Tray, Royal Pilsner Beer, Kansas City, Elk, Black, Gold, 12 In. Diam. 198.00
Tray, Scheidt's Beer Ale, Valley Forge, Washington With Troops, Oval, 11 ¼ In., Pair 25.00
Tray, Spatz-Barrett Ice Cream, Boy, Girl, Eating Ice Cream, 13 ½ In. Diam. 220.00
Tray, Tip, see Tip Trays in this category.
Tray, Utah Brau Beer, Woman, Holding Bottle, Standard Brewery, Tin, 12 In. Diam. 400.00
Tray, Valley Forge Special Beer, Maid, Holding Tray, Tin Lithograph, 13 x 10 ½ In. 140.00
Tray, Van Nostrand Beer, Bulldog, 12 In. Diam. 165.00
Tray, Velvet Ice Cream, Girl Eating, 17 ½ x 11 ½ In. .... *illus* 193.00
Tray, Wagner's Ice Cream, Woman In Ice Cream Shop, Oval, 12 ½ In. 184.00
Tray, West End Brewing Co., Girl, Stars & Stripes Dress, Tin, 13 In. Diam. 800.00
Trophy, Dr Pepper, Perky Sales Award, Man, 2 Bottles, Silver, Wood Base, 8 x 4 x 4 In. 350.00
Wall Hanging, A & W Root Beer, Dennis The Menace, Cloth, 1960s, 3 x 7 Ft. 305.00
Window Display, Hanes Merrichild Sleepers, Sleepy Child, Puppy, 1950s, 12 x 22 In. 336.00
Window Display, Snow King Baking Powder, Cardboard, Die Cut, c.1930s, 30 x 17 In. 173.00
Wrapper, Babe Ruth Candy Bar, c.1928, 5 x 7 ½ In. 1175.00

AKRO AGATE glass was founded in Akron, Ohio, in 1911, and moved to Clarksburg, West Virginia, in 1914. The company made marbles and toys. In the 1930s it began making other products, including vases, lamps, flowerpots, candlesticks, and children's dishes, Most of the glass is marked with a crow flying through the letter *A*. The company was sold to Clarksburg Glass Co. in 1951. Akro Agate marbles are listed in this book in the Marble category.

Ashtray, Ivory Brown, Marbleized, Square, 2 ⅞ x 2 ⅞ In. 15.00
Ashtray, Pink, Red Swirls, 4 In. 18.00
Bowl, Cereal, Interior Panel, Canary Yellow, 3 ⅜ In. 30.00
Bowl, Cereal, Interior Panel, Transparent Green, 3 ⅜ In. 25.00
Bowl, Cereal, Octagonal, Green, 3 ⅜ In. 18.00
Creamer, Interior Panel, Transparent Green, 1 ⅜ In. 20.00
Creamer, Octagonal, Light Blue, 1 ½ In. 20.00
Creamer, Octagonal, White, 1 ½ In. 20.00
Creamer, Stacked Disc, Chalaine, 1 5/16 In. 20.00
Creamer, Stacked Disc, Interior Panel, Transparent Blue 65.00
Creamer, Stacked Disc, Jadite, 1 5/16 In. 15.00
Creamer, Stacked Disc, Yellow, 1 5/16 In. 15.00
Creamer, Stippled Band, Transparent Topaz, 1 ½ In. 28.00
Cup, Concentric Ring, Chalaine, Opaque, 2 In. 15.00
Cup, Concentric Ring, Dark Blue, Opaque, 2 In. 10.00
Cup, Concentric Ring, Delphite, Translucent, 2 In. 12.00
Cup, Concentric Ring, Green, Transparent, 2 In. 15.00
Cup, Concentric Ring, Jadite, Opaque, 2 In. 7.00
Cup, Concentric Ring, Transparent Cobalt Blue, 2 In. 65.00
Cup, Interior Panel, Jadite, 1 ½ In. 20.00
Cup, Interior Panel, Pink Luster, 1 5/16 In. 35.00
Cup, Interior Panel, Transparent Green, 1 ⅜ In. 15.00
Cup, Octagonal, Jadite, Open Handle, 1 ¼ In. 30.00
Cup, Octagonal, Pumpkin, Open Handle, 1 ¼ In. 30.00
Cup, Raised Daisy, Jadite, 1 5/16 In. 30.00
Cup, Stacked Disc, Interior Panel, Transparent Green, 1 ⅜ In. 40.00

Cup, Stippled Band, Transparent Topaz, 1 ¼ In. .... 18.00 to 20.00
Cup & Saucer, Transparent Green, Small Stippled Band 30.00
Dish Set, Octagonal, Green & White, 8 Piece 84.00
Flowerpot, Blue .... *illus* 8.00
Flowerpot, Translucent White Opalescent, Jade Green, Marbleized, Smooth Top, 3 In. 16.00
Lamp, Electric, Brown, 3-Footed, 1930s, 13 In. 85.00
Pitcher, Concentric Ring, Blue, Opaque, 2 ⅞ In. 40.00
Pitcher, Octagonal, Medium Blue, Open Handle, 2 ⅞ In. 45.00
Pitcher, Stacked Disc, Delphite, 2 ⅝ In. 25.00
Pitcher, Stacked Disc, Interior Panel, Transparent Blue, 2 ⅞ In. 75.00
Pitcher, Stacked Disc, Jadite, 2 ⅞ In. 35.00
Pitcher, Stippled Band, Transparent Green, 2 ⅞ In. 40.00
Pitcher, Stippled Band, Transparent Topaz, 2 ⅞ In. 42.00
Planter, Blue, Marbleized, Rectangular, 8 In. 40.00
Planter, Jade Green, Oval, Scalloped Edge, 6 In. 35.00
Plate, Concentric Ring, Blue, Opaque, 3 ¼ In. .... 9.00 to 10.00
Plate, Concentric Ring, Blue, Transparent, 3 ¼ In. 35.00
Plate, Concentric Ring, Dark Blue, Opaque, 3 ¼ In. 9.00
Plate, Concentric Ring, Jadite, Opaque, 3 ¼ In. 4.00
Plate, Concentric Ring, Medium Green, Opaque, 3 ¼ In. 6.00
Plate, Interior Panel, Pink Luster, 3 5/16 In. 15.00
Plate, Interior Panel, Transparent Topaz, 4 ¼ In. 12.00
Plate, Interior Panel, Transparent Topaz, 4 ¾ In. 18.00
Plate, Octagonal, Dark Blue, 4 ¼ In. 18.00
Plate, Octagonal, Green, 4 ¼ In. 8.00
Plate, Stippled Band, Transparent Green, 3 ¼ In. 12.00
Plate, Stippled Band, Transparent Topaz, 4 ¼ In. 10.00
Powder Jar, Colonial Lady, Light Blue Opaque, 6 ½ In. 150.00
Saucer, Interior Panel, Blue Luster, 2 ¾ In. 18.00
Saucer, Interior Panel, Canary Yellow, 2 ¾ In. 20.00
Saucer, Interior Panel, Pink Luster, 2 ¾ In. 20.00
Saucer, Octagonal, Canary Yellow, 2 ¾ In. 12.00
Saucer, Octagonal, Pink, 3 ⅜ In. 4.25
Saucer, Stippled Band, Transparent Green, 2 ¾ In. 8.00
Saucer, Stippled Band, Transparent Topaz, 3 ¼ In. 8.00
Sugar, Cover, Octagonal, White, 2 ½ In. 15.00
Sugar, Cover Only, Interior Panel, Transparent Topaz, 2 ⅝ In. 20.00
Sugar, Stacked Disc, Interior Panel, Light Blue Opaque, 1 ⅜ In. 25.00
Sugar, Stacked Disc, Yellow, 1 5/16 In. 15.00
Sugar, Stippled Band, Transparent Topaz, 1 ½ In. 28.00
Tea Set, Interior Panel, Transparent Topaz, Box, Child's, 21 Piece 525.00
Teapot, Cover, Interior Panel, 2 ½ In. 45.00
Teapot, Cover, Stippled Band, Transparent Green, 2 ⅜ In. .... 50.00 to 115.00
Teapot, Cover Only, Octagonal, Green, 2 ⅝ In. 20.00
Teapot, Cover Only, Stacked Disc, Pink, 2 5/16 In. 15.00
Teapot, Interior Panel, Blue Luster, 2 ½ In. 50.00
Teapot, Interior Panel, Jadite, 2 ½ In. 25.00
Teapot, Octagonal, Medium Blue, Open Handle, 2 ⅜ In. 40.00
Teapot, Stacked Disc, Chalaine, 2 ⅜ In. 25.00
Teapot, Stacked Disc, Interior Panel, Transparent Green, 2 ¾ In. 50.00
Teapot, Stacked Disc, Jadite, 2 ⅝ In. 18.00
Teapot, Stippled Band, Transparent Green, 2 ⅜ In. 30.00
Teapot, Stippled Band, Transparent Topaz, 2 ⅜ In. 25.00
Toothpick, Cornucopia, Green, Marbleized, 3 ¼ In. .... *illus* 12.00
Tumbler, Octagonal, Canary Yellow, 2 In. 20.00
Tumbler, Stacked Disc, Beige, 2 In. 10.00
Tumbler, Stacked Disc, White, 2 In. 8.00
Tumbler, Stippled Band, Transparent Green, 1 ¾ In. 15.00
Urn, Beaded Top, Square Foot, Orange, Marbleized, c.1949, 3 ¼ In. 12.00
Vase, Yellow, Orange, Marbleized, Flowers, 4 ¾ x 2 ⅞ In. 30.00
Water Set, Stippled Band, Transparent Green, 7 Piece 145.00

ALABASTER is a very soft form of gypsum, a stone that resembles marble. It was often carved into vases or statues in Victorian times. There are alabaster carvings being made even today.

Box, Enameled Cameo, Gilt Metal Decoration, 3 x 5 ⅜ x 4 ½ In. 775.00

Akro Agate, Flowerpot, Blue
$8.00

Akro Agate, Toothpick, Cornucopia, Green, Marbleized, 3 ¼ In.
$12.00

Alabaster, Cassolette, Ormolu Mounted, Covered Bowl, Tripod Base, 1800s, 9 ¼ In., Pair
$2133.00

TIP

Never clean alabaster with water. Test a small spot before you use anything. First use turpentine applied with a soft cloth. If the stain is stubborn, try alcohol.

Alabaster, Figurine, Nude, Seated In Chair, Bronze, 16 In.
$1840.00

Aluminum, Candleholder, 4-Light, Sculptural, Signed, D. Drumm, 1970s, 30 x 25 x 5 In.
$1400.00

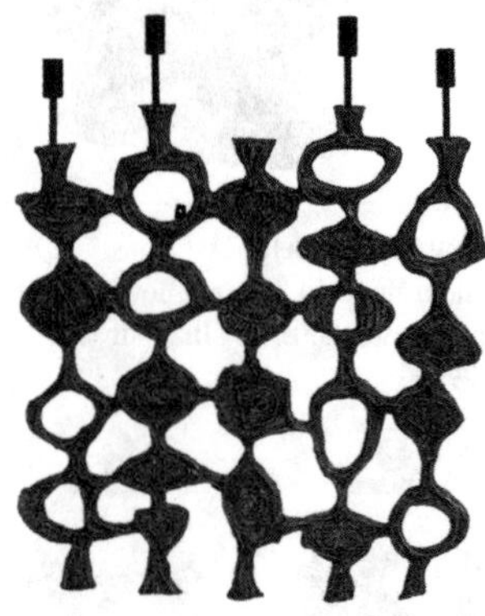

Aluminum, Ice Bucket, Lid, Hammered, Insulated, Marked Made In Italy, 1950s, 7 ½ In.
$23.00

Box, Figural, Carved, Demilune, Adonis & Venus, Italy, 19th Century, 13 x 14 In. 761.00
Bust, Child, Square Marble Base, P. Bellunny, Italy, Early 1900s, 16 ½ In. 1020.00
Bust, Girl, Crying, With Shawl, Carved, 14 In. 275.00
Bust, Woman, Braided Hair, Holding Flower, Carved, 22 ½ In. 702.00
Bust, Woman, Hand Carved, Marble Plinth, 5 In.. .... 87.00
Candlestick, Gypsy Woman, Seated, Veined, Base, Italy, 22 ½ In.. .... 1430.00
Cassolette, Ormolu Mounted, Covered Bowl, Tripod Base, 1800s, 9 ¼ In., Pair. .... *illus* 2133.00
Column, White, 3-Step Base, Twisted Shaft, Acanthus Carving, 40 ½ In.. .... 75.00
Figurine, Nude, Seated In Chair, Bronze, 16 In. .... *illus* 1840.00
Jewelry Box, Shell Shape, Brass Rim, Feet, Blue, White, Italy, 4 x 6 In. 263.00
Lamp, Carved, Column Support, Putti, Bell-Form Shade, Italy, Malavoli, c.1900, 70 In.. .... 8225.00
Lamp, Electric, Bare Chested Woman Holding Up Globe, 56 In. 2650.00
Lamp, Electric, Carved, Boy, Girl, Half Domed Shade, Italy, 19 ½ In. 118.00
Lamp, Electric, Leaning Tower Of Pisa, Carved, 15 In.. .... 350.00
Lamp, Electric, Woman Picking Flowers, Lighted Pond, 2 Birds, c.1920, 17 x 13 x 11 In.. .... 1955.00
Obelisk, Black, White, 24 x 5 In. 263.00
Obelisk, Diamonds, Ovals, Inset, 20 ¼ x 4 In. 495.00
Pedestal, Circular Top On Standard, Vine-Carved Collar, Italy, 19th Century, 39 ½ In. 470.00
Pedestal, Garland & Urn Carving, Fluted, Square Top, 42 ¾ x 12 In.. .... 325.00
Plaque, Virgin, Child, 2 Angels, 1800s, 8 In.. .... 1770.00
Sconce, Iron, Folded Geometric Shapes, Pierre Chareau, Paris, c.1924, 11 In., Pair. 17500.00
Statue, Woman, Long Robe, Belt, Fringed Necklace, Italy, 25 ⅜ In. 2468.00

ALUMINUM was more expensive than gold or silver until the 1850s. Chemists learned how to refine bauxite to get aluminum. Jewelry and other small objects were made of the valuable metal until 1914, when an inexpensive smelting process was invented. The aluminum collected today dates from the 1930s through the 1950s. Hand-hammered pieces are the most popular.

Bowl, Flowers, Flared, Ruffled Edge, 11 ½ x 3 ½ In. 68.00
Bowl, Roses, Embossed, Flat Rim, 11 ½ In.. .... 10.00
Bowl, Scalloped, Incised Floral & Scroll Pattern, 8 ¼ x 13 In. 18.00
Bowl, Vegetable, Cover, Hammered, Handles, Relief Pattern, Italy, 9 x 4 In.. .... 25.00
Bread Box, Slide Door, 17 x 16 ½ In. 50.00
Cake Set, Glass Plate, Aluminum Cover, Black Trim, Kromex, c.1950, 12 ½-In. Plate 65.00
Candleholder, 4-Light, Sculptural, Signed, D. Drumm, 1970s, 30 x 25 x 5 In. .... *illus* 1400.00
Coffee Server, Mayfair No, 7200, Wood Handle, Kensington, 1940, 10 In.. .... 70.00
Crumb Catcher & Brush, Pan, Tulip Series By Rodney Kent, 8 ¾ x 5 ½ In.. .... 25.00
Dish, Poinsettia, Fluted Edge, Coiled Handle, Farber & Shlevin, 7 ½ In. 14.50
Dutch Oven, Lid, Bail Handle, Hammered Club Aluminum, Hammercraft, 4 ½ Qt.. .... 35.00
Frame, Holds 2 Small Photos, British Registry Mark, 1905, 3 ½ x 3 ⅜ In.. .... 38.00
Ice Bucket, Lid, Hammered, Insulated, Marked Made In Italy, 1950s, 7 ½ In. .... *illus* 23.00
Ice Bucket, Lid, Harbor Scene, Forman, Brooklyn, N.Y., With Aluminum Ice Tongs, 7 ½ In... 25.00
Ice Bucket, Sea Lion Form, Arched Back, Cast, Arthur Court, 1982, 16 x 20 x 10 In. 950.00
Milk Can, A Leyse Product, Made In USA, 2 Qt. 17.00
Pitcher, Ice Lip, Marked Everlast Forged Aluminum, 9 In. 25.00
Pitcher, Ice Lip, Wood Handle, BW Buenilum, 1930s-50s, 11 x 3 ½ In. 32.00
Silent Butler, Lid, Bamboo Design, Everlast Forged Aluminum, 1940s, 2 ½ x 10 x 5 ⅝ In.... 40.00
Teapot, Black Plastic Handle, Lid Knob, Mirro, 5 Cup 13.00
Tidbit, 2 Tiers, 8 x 11 ¼ In. 10.00
Tidbit, Dogwood, Hammered, Stamped Design, Aluminum, Handles, 5 ¾ In. 12.00
Tidbit, Embossed Dogwood Blossoms, Hammered, Handle, 6 x 5 In. 15.00
Tray, Engraved, Flowers, Fruit, Handwrought, Handles, Cromwell, 14 ½ In. 20.00
Tray, Etched Designs, Fluted Edges, 13 ½ In. 12.00
Tray, Fruit Design, Hammered Measures, 21 ½ x 12 In. 85.00
Tray, Leaf Pattern, Twisted Coil Handles, Hammered, c.1930-50, 5 ½ x 15 In.. .... 13.00
Tray, Square, Marked Everlast Forged Aluminum, 11 ½ In. 37.50
Wastebasket, Embossed With World Map, Gold Tint, Oval, Arthur Armour, 10 In. 310.00

AMBER, *see Jewelry category.*

AMBER GLASS is the name of any glassware with the proper yellow-brown shading. It was a popular color just after the Civil War and many pressed glass pieces were made of amber glass. Depression glass of the 1930s–50s was also made in shades of amber glass. Other pieces may be found in the Depression Glass, Pressed Glass, and other glass categories. All types are being reproduced.

Bowl, Moon & Star, Ruffled Rim, 4 ¼ x 7 ½ In. 35.00

Dresser Set, No. 18, New Martinsville, 1930s, 3 Piece ... 150.00
Jug, Wine, France, Early 20th Century, 20 x 13 In. ... 150.00

AMBERETTE *pieces are listed in the Pressed Glass category under the pattern name Amberette.*

AMBERINA, a two-toned glassware, was originally made from 1883 to about 1900. It was patented by Joseph Locke of the New England Glass Company, but was also made by other companies and is still being made. The glass shades from red to amber. Similar pieces of glass may be found in the Baccarat, Libbey, Plated Amberina, and other categories. Glass shaded from blue to amber is called Blue Amberina or Bluerina.

Basket, Coin Spot, Ruffled Rim, Rigaree Feet, Applied Handle, 9 In. ... 144.00
Basket, Swirled Ribs, Rigaree Rim, Thorny Handles, 7 In. ... 518.00
Bottle, Barber, Thumbprint, Metal, Cork Stopper, 9 In. ... 345.00
Celery Vase, Optic Ribs, Crimped Top, Mt. Washington, 6 ½ In. ... 575.00
Compote, Diamond Optic, Footed, Scalloped Rim, 7 In. ... 259.00
Condiment Set, Coin Spot, 2 Shakers, Mustard, Cruet, Faceted Stopper, Caddy, 5 & 8 In. ... 863.00
Cruet, Diamond Faceted Stopper, Pontil, 1880s, 5 ¾ x 4 In. ... 275.00
Cruet, Optic Swirl, Tricornered Rim, Pontil, 5 ⅝ In. ... 500.00
Decanter, Bulbous, Rigaree Collar, 9 In. ... 173.00
Lemonade Set, Ribbed, Applied Scalloped Handle, 1880s, 12-In. Pitcher, 5 Piece ... 450.00
Pickle Castor, Cover, Ribbed, Silver Tray, 4-Footed, 7 & 6 ⅝ In. ... 196.00
Pitcher, Dewdrop, 6 ¾ In. ... 125.00
Spooner, Diamond-Quilted, Scalloped Rim, 4 ¾ x 3 ⅜ In. ... 385.00
Syrup, Coin Spot, Egg Shape, Embossed Metal Flip Lid, 5 ½ In. ... 805.00
Syrup, Inverted Coin Spot, Pewter Mounts, 5 ½ In. ... 920.00
Syrup, Oval, Coin Spot, Embossed Flip Lid, Silver Plated Tray, 6 In. ... 1610.00
Toothpick, Diamond-Quilted, 6-Sided, 2 ⅛ In. ... 175.00 to 250.00
Toothpick, Diamond-Quilted, Mt.Washington, 2 ⅝ In. ... 489.00
Vase, Coin Spot, Oval, 5-Leaf Applied Amber Foot, 5 ½ In., Pair ... *illus* 142.00
Vase, Diamond-Quilted, Flared Rim, Gilt Metal Stand, 10 ½ In. ... 115.00
Vase, Double Gourd, Flared Ruffled Rim, 12 ¾ x 5 ½ In. ... 950.00
Vase, Enameled, Stork, c.1870, 6 ⅛ In. ... 351.00
Vase, Thumbprint, Scalloped Rim, c.1804, 7 In. ... 205.00
Water Set, Inverted Thumbprint, Clear Reeded Handle, 7-In. Pitcher, 6 Piece ... *illus* 405.00
Water Set, Optic Rib, Female Handle, Metal Frame, Tankard, 5 Tumblers, 17-In. Pitcher ... 863.00

AMERICAN DINNERWARE, *see Dinnerware.*

AMERICAN ENCAUSTIC TILING COMPANY was founded in Zanesville, Ohio, in 1875. The company planned to make a variety of tiles to compete with the English tiles that were selling in the United States for use in fireplaces and other architectural designs. The first glazed tiles were made in 1880, embossed tiles in 1881, faience tiles in the 1920s. The firm closed in 1935 and reopened in 1937 as the Shawnee Pottery.

Tile, Egyptian Woman, Roman Man, Green Glaze, 18 x 6 In., 2 Piece ... 711.00
Tile, Female Standing On Dragon With Fangs, Frame, 29 x 6 In. ... 345.00
Tile, L'Automne, Female Profile, Grapes, Green Glaze, 10 In. ... 360.00
Tile, Man, Woman, Brown, Marked, 18 x 6 In., 2 Piece ... *illus* 275.00
Tile, Parrot, Blue Ground, Limited Works, 5 ⅞ x 11 ¾ In. ... 190.00
Tile, Victorian Woman, Blue High Glaze, Frame, 6 In., 3 Piece ... 259.00
Tile, Woman, 3 Children, Brown Glaze, Marked, 18 In. ... 498.00
Tile, Woman Wearing Hat & Gown, Brown Glaze, Frame, 7 In. ... 184.00
Vase, Bat Shape, Tan, Brown Glaze, Marked, 6 x 4 ½ In. ... 420.00

AMETHYST GLASS is any of the many glasswares made in the dark purple color of the gemstone amethyst. Included in this category are many pieces made in the nineteenth and twentieth centuries. Very dark pieces are called black amethyst and are listed under that heading.

Bowl, Flowers, Ruffled Rim, Bubble Base, 3 ½ x 7 In. ... 45.00
Candlestick, 7 In., Pair ... 46.00
Vase, Crackle, 5 In. ... 85.00
Vase, Gold Enameled Flowers, Scrolls, Ribs, Pontil, 5 In. ... *illus* 22.00
Vase, Hyacinth, Squat, 7 In. ... 225.00
Vase, Rippled, Bubble Prunts, Clear Base, 11 x 2 In. ... 150.00
Vase, White Enamel Bird, Tree, Gold Trim, Flared Rim, 9 In. ... 120.00

Amberina, Vase, Coin Spot, Oval, 5-Leaf Applied Amber Foot, 5 ½ In., Pair
$142.00

Amberina, Water Set, Inverted Thumbprint, Clear Reeded Handle, 7-In. Pitcher, 6 Piece
$405.00

American Encaustic, Tile, Man, Woman, Brown, Marked, 18 x 6 In., 2 Piece
$275.00

Amethyst Glass, Vase, Gold Enameled Flowers, Scrolls, Ribs, Pontil, 5 In.
$22.00

Animal Trophy, African Impala Antelope, Head, Mounted, 32 x 10 In. $410.00

Animal Trophy, Brook Trout, Skin Mount, Resin Head, Wood Backboard, David Footer, Maine, 21 In. $690.00

Anna Pottery, Bottle, Pig, Brown, Albany Slip Glaze, 1880s, 3 ¼ x 6 ¼ In. $2640.00

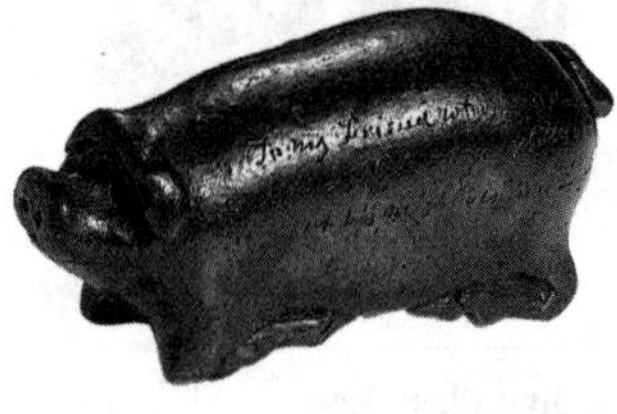

TIP

Remove traces of gum, adhesive tape, and other sticky tape by rubbing the glue with lemon juice.

AMPHORA *pieces are listed in the Teplitz category*

ANDIRONS *and related fireplace items are included in the Fireplace category.*

ANIMAL TROPHIES, such as stuffed animals, rugs made of animal skins, and other similar collectibles made from animal, fish, or bird parts are listed in this category. Collectors should be aware of the endangered species laws that make it illegal to buy and sell some of these items. Any eagle feathers, many types of pelts or rugs (such as leopard), ivory, and many forms of tortoiseshell can be confiscated by the government. Related trophies may be found in the Fishing category. Ivory items may be found in the Scrimshaw or Ivory categories.

African Cape Buffalo, Horns, Mounted, 18 x 34 In. ... 322.00
African Impala Antelope, Head, Mounted, 32 x 10 In. ... *illus* 410.00
Bird, Glass Dome, Victorian, 9 ½ In. ... 47.00
Bird, Taxidermy, Cylindrical Glass Dome, Victorian, 8 In. ... 270.00
Birds, Glass Dome, Victorian, 10 ½ In. ... 59.00
Brook Trout, Skin Mount, Resin Head, Wood Backboard, David Footer, Maine, 21 In. ... *illus* 690.00
Caribou, Antlers, Mounted, 47 x 42 In. ... 176.00
Musky, Skin Mount, 50 In. ... 86.00
Nubian Ibex Goat, Head, Mounted, Africa, 58 x 20 In. ... 439.00
Rug, Black Bear, Felted ... 675.00
Skull, Woodland Caribou, Mounted ... 475.00
Trout, Skin Mount, Oval Rustic Plaque, Signed, Nash, Maine, 1903, 18 In. ... 518.00

ANIMATION ART collectibles include cels that are painted drawings on celluloid needed to make animated cartoons shown in movie theaters or on TV. Hundreds of cels were made, then photographed in sequence to make a cartoon showing moving figures. Early examples made by the Walt Disney Studios are popular with collectors today. Original sketches used by the artists are also listed here. Modern animated cartoons are made using computer-generated pictures. Some of these are being produced as cels to be sold to collectors. Other cartoon art is listed in Comic Art and Disneyana.

Cel, Bugs Bunny, c.1970 ... 248.00
Cel, Cheshire Cat, Frame, 6 ½ x 9 In. ... 2400.00
Cel, Dumbo, Storks Flying To Deliver Babies, Frame ... 1150.00
Cel, Fat Albert, Original, Hand Painted, Royal Animation Art Inc., 8 x 11 In. ... 190.00
Cel, Lady & The Tramp, Acetate, Tramp In Night Colors, c.1955, 9 ½ x 12 In. ... 690.00
Cel, Pinocchio, Geppetto Sleeping With Figaro, Frame, 7 ½ In. ... 1500.00
Cel, Pinocchio, Jiminy Cricket In Bottle, Sea Gulls, Frame ... 1850.00
Cel, Snow White & Seven Dwarfs, Grumpy On Barrel, Wood Veneer Ground, Frame ... 1600.00
Drawing, Mickey Mouse, Alphabet Letters, 13 x 11 In., 26 Piece ... 978.00
Drawing, Mother Goose, Graphite, Red & Green Pencil, 1937, 12 x 10 In. ... 633.00
Drawing, Puppy Love, Mickey & Minnie Mouse, c.1933, 4 x 5 In. ... 176.00
Drawing, Puppy Love, Mickey Gives Minnie Candy, Graphite, Disney, 1933, 12 x 10 In. ... 418.00
Drawing, Red Hot Riding Hood, 1943, 7 ½ x 3 In. ... 193.00
Drawing, Steeplechase, 1933 ... 2200.00

ANNA POTTERY was started in Anna, Illinois, in 1859 by Cornwall and Wallace Kirkpatrick. They made many types of utilitarian wares, bricks, drain tiles, and giftware. The most collectible pieces made by the pottery are the pig-shaped bottles and jugs with special inscriptions, applied animals, and figures. The pottery closed in 1894.

Anna Pottery

Bottle, Pig, Brown, Albany Slip Glaze, 1880s, 3 ¼ x 6 ¼ In. ... *illus* 2640.00
Bottle, Pig, Inscribed, Good Ole Rye, Salt Glaze, Kirkpatrick, 1880, 3 ¼ x 7 ¼ In. ... 1320.00
Bottle, Pig, Railroad, Inscribed, Albany Slip Glaze, Kirkpatrick, 1880, 3 ¼ x 7 ¼ In. ... 8000.00
Bottle, Pig, Slip Glazed, Molded, Incised Map, Verse Inscription, Illinois, 1880, 3 x 6 In. ... 2644.00

APPLE PEELERS *are listed in the Kitchen category under Peeler, Apple.*

ARABIA began producing ceramics in 1874. The pottery was established in Helsinki, Finland, by Rörstrand, a Swedish pottery that wanted to export porcelain, earthenware, and other pottery from Finland to Russia. Most of the early workers at Arabia were Swedish. Arabia started producing its own models of tiled stoves, vases, and tableware c.1900. Rörstrand sold its interest in Arabia in 1916. By the late 1930s, Arabia was the largest producer of porcelain in Europe. Most of its products were exported. A line of stoneware was introduced in the 1960s. Arabia worked in cooperation with Rörstrand from 1975 to 1977. Arabia was bought by Hackman Group in 1990 and Hackman was bought by Iittala Group in 2004. Arabia is now a brand owned by Iittala Group.

ARABIA FINLAND

Bowl, Black & Blue Matte Glaze, Annikki Hovisarri, 3 ½ x 7 ½ In. ... 485.00

Bowl, Cereal, Paratiisi, Birger Kaipiainen, 6 ¾ In. . . . 45.00
Bowl, Gray Matte Haresfur Glaze, Incised, Lisa Larsen, 5 x 7 In. . . . 1450.00
Candle Sconce, Black Metal, 5 Glazed Iridescent Tiles, Konrad Galaaen, Late 1960s, 12 x 6 In. 165.00
Cup & Saucer, Continental, Paratiisi, Birger Kaipiainen, ⅓ Qt. . . . 45.00
Cup & Saucer, Kaira, Gray, Blue Brown & Black Bands, Jaatinen-Winqvist, 2 ¼ x 2 ¼ In. . . . 25.00
Dish, Oak Leaf, Sung Glaze, Shallow, Incised, Toini Muona, 9 x 10 In. . . . 1200.00
Dish, Porcelain, Red Purple Glossy Glaze, Incised Decoration, Toini Muona, c.1958, 14 In. . . 2800.00
Gravy Boat, Koralli, 3 ⅛ x 5 ½ In. . . . 85.00
Mug, Haarikka, Valencia, Cobalt Blue & Green, 2 ⅛ x 2 In. . . . 65.00
Plate, Koralli, 7 ¾ In. . . . 25.00
Teapot, Dark Brown, Bamboo Handle, Whisk, Kaj Franck, 4 ¼ x 6 In. . . . 360.00
Tray, Tab, Square, Flower Design, Blue, Yellow, Juurikkala & Grandlund, 9 x 9 ½ In. . . . 175.00
Trivet, Fish Shape, Dark Green Gloss Glaze, Mark, 12 ¼ In. . . . 25.00
Vase, Charcoal Matte Glaze, Incised, Annikki Hovisarri, 4 x 2 ¼ In. . . . 245.00
Vase, Light Green Matte Glaze, Incised, Richard Lindh, 9 ¾ x 2 ¼ In. . . . 565.00
Vase, Red Brown Matte Glaze, Green Turquoise & Purple Drip Glaze Inside, 8 ¼ x 9 ¼ In. . . . 1600.00
Vase, Squat, Oval Mouth, Oatmeal Matte & Iron Spot Glaze, Mascitti Lindh, c.1960, 5 x 7 In. . 850.00
Wall Pocket, White Glaze, Orange Hearts, Flowers, Wood Lid, c.1964, 5 x 3 x 6 ¾ In. . . . 72.00

ARC-EN-CIEL is the French word for rainbow. A pottery factory named Arc-en-ciel was founded in Zanesville, Ohio, in 1903. The company made art pottery for a short time, then became the Brighton Pottery in 1905.

Ewer, Iridescent Gold Luster, No. 506, John Lessell, Marked, 1904, 10 ⅞ In. . . . 130.00
Ewer, Yellow & Red Flambe, Marked, 6 ⅜ In. . . . 150.00
Vase, 4 Vignettes, Raised Figures, Gray, Green Matte Glaze, 4 ½ In. . . . 179.00
Vase, Oak Leaves & Acorns, Art Nouveau, Gray High Glaze, Marked, 6 ½ In. . . . 175.00
Vase, Poppy, Art Nouveau, Gold Luster Glaze, Pinched Waist, Marked, 10 ¼ In. . . . 120.00

ARCHITECTURAL antiques include a variety of collectibles, usually very large, that have been removed from buildings. Hardware, backbars, doors, paneling, and even old bathtubs are now wanted by collectors. Pieces of the Victorian, Art Nouveau, and Art Deco styles are in greatest demand.

Backbar, Oak, Sliding Doors, Marble Top, Columns, 9-Ft. Mirror, Jos. Middleby Jr., Victorian . 1150.00
Basin, Wall Mount, Iron, 1930s, 16 x 10 In. . . . 400.00
Bathtub, Claw Foot, Faucet, 4-Footed, 22 x 30 x 48 In. . . . 950.00
Bathtub, Iron, Claw Foot, White, 28 x 64 In. . . . 130.00
Bracket, Carved Oak, Winged Dolphins, Cattails, Mounted As Lamp, 18 x 23 In., Pair . . . 748.00
Bracket, George III, Walnut, Scroll, Carved Leaves, 13 x 9 ½ x 10 ½ In., Pair . . . 2350.00
Bracket, Iron, Scrolling Leaves, 26 x 40 In. . . . 70.00
Bracket, Wall, Rococo, Gilt Composition, Hoho Bird, Shaped, 1900s, 16 x 13 In., Pair . . . 777.00
Bracket, Walnut, Egg & Dart, Dragons, Putti, Renaissance Revival, 1890s, 24 ½ x 36 ½ x 9 In. *illus* 1320.00
Bracket, Wood, Painted, Carved, Gilt, Scrolling Leaf Apron, Putti, Italy, 16 x 29 In. . . . 717.00
Capital, Ionic, Gesso, Carved, Scrolled, 3 ½ x 8 ¼ In. . . . 145.00
Carving, Flowers, Ribbons, Federal, Pink, Blue, Green Paint, c.1845, 21 x 35 In. . . . 3450.00
Chimney Pot, Terra-Cotta, Crown Crest, Round, Square Base, England, 27 x 13 In. . . . 173.00
Chimney Pot, Yellowware, Crenellated Top, Square Column, England, 29 In., Pair . . . 316.00
Chimney Pot, Yellowware, Octagonal, England, 25 ½ In. . . . 46.00
Chimney Pot, Yellowware, Stepped Round Diffusers, England, 38 In. . . . 69.00
Colonnade, Quartersawn Oak, Wood Capitals, Egg & Dart Detail, c.1890, 112 x 39 In. . . . 8000.00
Column, Corinthian Capital, Spiral Twist Turned, Square Plinth, 84 x 12 In., Pair . . . 575.00
Column, Marble, Round Top, Stepped Octagonal Plinth, 46 ½ x 13 ¼ In. . . . 156.00
Column, Neoclassical, Marble, Mask Frieze, Carved Shaft, Lotus Band, 44 ½ x 16 In. . . . 3055.00
Column, Oak, 57 In., Pair . . . 85.00
Column, Terra-Cotta, Doric, Fluted, Separate Urn Top, Stamped, 414 Italy, 1900s, 67 In., Pair 1762.00
Corbel, Copper, Classical, Acanthus, Verdigris Patina, 1800s, 12 x 10 In., 4 Piece . . . 518.00
Corbel, Sandstone, Flower Medallion, Carved, 12 x 15 In. . . . 60.00
Cornice, Building, Indian, Headdress, Openwork, Orange Paint, 13 x 22 In. . . . *illus* 385.00
Cupboard, Built-In, Carved Shell, Shelf, Wood, c.1800, 42 x 31 ½ In. . . . 4950.00
Cupola, Church, 8-Sided, Wide Molding, Shingle Roof, Maine, 1830s, 24 x 13 Ft. . . . 1150.00
Door, Chrome, Etched Glass, Maiden, Art Deco, G.M. Ketchem, 67 x 26 In. . . . 1175.00
Door, Indian, Mahogany, Carved, 20th Century, 70 x 31 ½ In. . . . 540.00
Door, Louis XV, Gilt, Cream Paint, Bronze Locks, Shells, Leaves, 94 x 28 In., Pair . . . 2585.00
Door, Oak, Turned & Carved Stiles, Crockets, Trefoils, Gothic Revival, 100 x 31 In. . . . *illus* 3173.00
Door, Painted Wood, Green, Milk Glass Panels, Blossoms, Leaves, 85 x 17 In. . . . 2400.00
Door, Pine, Stained Glass, c.1900, 87 ½ x 34 ½ In. . . . 2400.00

TIP

Need a quick measurement at an antiques show? A penny is ¾ inch in diameter; a dollar bill is almost 6 inches long.

Architectural, Bracket, Walnut, Egg & Dart, Dragons, Putti, Renaissance Revival, 1890s, 24 ½ x 36 ½ x 9 In.
$1320.00

Architectural, Cornice, Building, Indian, Headdress, Openwork, Orange Paint, 13 x 22 In.
$385.00

Architectural, Door, Oak, Turned & Carved Stiles, Crockets, Trefoils, Gothic Revival, 100 x 31 In.
$3173.00

Architectural, Door Handle, Wrought Iron, Pineapple, Thumb Latch, 9 ⅛ x 2 ½ In.
$30.00

Architectural, Door Handle, Wrought Iron, Tulip, 10 x 5 ½ In.
$523.00

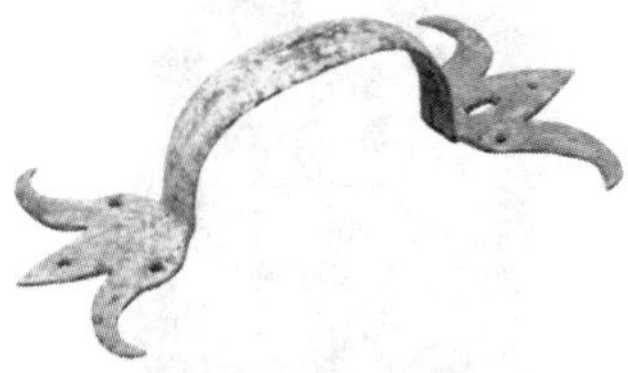

TIP

If you clean brass-plated hardware too well and remove some of the plating, try this first aid suggestion. Get a gold or brass wax at a craft shop. Rub a little on the bad spot. Then seal with clear lacquer. Don't use brass-colored spray paint

Door, Pocket, Leaded Stained Glass, Flower, Butterfly Design, 35 x 67 In., Pair . . . 780.00
Door, Pocket, Quartersawn Oak, Recessed Horizontal Panels, 1900s, 89 x 54 In. . . . 995.00
Door, Royal, New Testament Scenes, Carved, High Relief, Giltwood, Russia, 1700s, 71 In. . . . 8260.00
Door, Screen, Ornate Design, Wood, Salesman's Sample, 21 ½ In. . . . 330.00
Door Handle, Bronze, Erotic Mythological Figure, Asia, 10 In. . . . 80.00
Door Handle, Keyhole, Bronze, Scrolling, Flares, France, 19th Century, 10 In. . . . 165.00
Door Handle, Latch, Iron, Rounded, Teardrop Terminals, 1700s, 11 x 2 In. . . . 22.00
Door Handle, Wrought Iron, Pineapple, Thumb Latch, 9 ⅛ x 2 ½ In. . . . *illus* 30.00
Door Handle, Wrought Iron, Tulip, 10 x 5 ½ In. . . . *illus* 523.00
Door Icon, Pierced Carved Wood, Crowned Eagle, Dragons, Persia, 5 x 19 In. . . . 144.00
Door Latch, Iron, Forged, Thumb Latch, 18th Century, 6 ¼ x 1 ¼ In. . . . 145.00
Door Lock, Wrought Iron, 2 Lever Handles, Slide Lock, 19th Century, 3 ¼ x 6 ½ In. . . . 206.00
Door Panel, Leaded Glass, Mirrored, Etched Hunt Scene . . . 1725.00
Door Surround, Iron, Painted Red, Broken Scroll, Pilasters, 1800s, 105 x 59 In. . . . 3335.00
Doorknob, Bronze, Red, Holly, c.1890 . . . 52.00
Doorknocker, Brass, Anchor On Shield, 8 x 6 In. . . . 195.00
Doorknocker, Brass, Bell Shape, Scrolled Ringed Swing Arm, France, c.1900, 7 ½ In., Pair . . . 440.00
Doorknocker, Brass, Lion's Head, 8 x 4 ½ In. . . . 75.00
Doorknocker, Bronze, Stylized Lion's Mask, Beaded Ring In Mouth, 7 ½ x 5 In. . . . 100.00
Doorknocker, Bronze, Stylized Lion's Mask & Face, Leaves, Patina, 10 ½ x 7 In. . . . 225.00
Doorknocker, Centurian, Iron, Black, 4 ½ x 2 ¼ In. . . . 145.00
Doorknocker, Iron, Elephant Head, Red Paint, 6 In. . . . 374.00
Doorknocker, Iron, Flowers, Basket, 3 ⅝ x 3 In. . . . 230.00
Doorknocker, Iron, Flowers, Urn, 4 x 2 ½ In. . . . 259.00
Doorknocker, Iron, Flowers In Vase, Painted, 3 ¾ x 2 ¼ In. . . . *illus* 220.00
Doorknocker, Iron, Girl, Knocking, Painted, G.R., Hubley, 1921, 3 ⅝ x 2 In. . . . *illus* 495.00
Doorknocker, Iron, Lady With Bonnet, Embossed Hair, 4 ¾ In. . . . 230.00
Doorknocker, Iron, Pear, Mixed Flowers, 3 ⅞ x 3 In. . . . 345.00
Doorknocker, Iron, Rabbit Eating Cabbage, Painted, Albany, 5 In. . . . *illus* 880.00
Doorknocker, Iron, Scholar Seated, Reading Book, 4 ¼ x 2 ⅜ In. . . . 230.00
Doorknocker, Iron, Totem Pole, Stacked Style, 4 In. . . . 431.00
Doorknocker, Iron, Woodpecker, Multicolored, Hubley, 3 ¾ x 2 ¾ In. . . . 413.00
Doorknocker, Iron, Woodpecker, On Tree, Painted, Hubley, No. 251, 3 ¾ x 3 In. . . . 375.00
Doorway, Fretwork, Stick & Ball, 2 Sections, Victorian, 78 ½ x 118 In. . . . 650.00
Downspout, Copper, Figural, Dog Head, Verdigris, 10 x 9 In. . . . 403.00
Downspout, Koi Fish Shape, Chinese, 1920s, 11 x 9 In. . . . 150.00
Drawer Pull, Glass, Cobalt Blue, Blown, Bronze Collar, 2 ⅛ x 1 ½ In., Pair . . . 275.00
Drawerknob, Glass, Amber, c.1930, 1 x 1 ¼ In. . . . 28.00
Drawerknob, Glass, Chalaine Blue, c.1930, 1 x 1 ¼ In. . . . 32.00
Drawerknob, Glass, Green, c.1930, 1 x 1 In. . . . 28.00
Eagle, Pine, Carved, Spread Wings, Gilt Talons, Beak, c.1820, 52 x 45 In. . . . 14900.00
Fan, Over Door, Mixed Woods, Louvered, Keystone, Red Paint, c.1820, 26 x 84 ½ In. . . . 2115.00
Fan Light, Pine, Starburst, Old Paint, 19th Century, 23 x 44 In., Pair . . . 173.00
Finial, Balustrade, Beechwood, Winged Female Sphinx Torsos, 23 x 18 In., Pair . . . 1560.00
Finial, Flag Pole, Bronze, Eagle, Silver Leaf, 19th Century, 7 ½ x 5 ½ In. . . . 475.00
Finial, Pineapple, Giltwood, Carved, Square Pickled Wood Base, 11 ½ x 4 ½ In., Pair . . . 660.00
Finial, Rooftop, Spire, Zinc, 36 x 6 In. . . . 700.00
Finial, Terra-Cotta, Red Surface, Fleur-De-Lis Form, c.1885, 9 In. . . . 118.00
Fireplace, Marble, Rectangular, Carved Leaves, Louis XV Style, 48 x 78 In. . . . 1920.00
Fireplace Surround, 3 Mirrors, Columns, Lion's Head, c.1800, 65 x 80 ½ x 9 In. . . . 12500.00
Fireplace Surround, Oak, Mixed Wood, Dog, Waterfowl, Shelf, 73 x 59 x 11 In. . . . 2607.00
Fragment, Baluster, Chicago Stock Exchange, Iron, c.1893, 21 x 11 In. . . . 1560.00
Fretwork, Wood, Victorian, Stick & Ball, c.1890, 18 ½ x 60 In. . . . 330.00
Gate, Iron, Ornamental, Latticework, Leaf & Flower Panel, 114 x 157 In., Pair . . . 4112.00
Gate, Iron, Square Frame, Spread Eagle Top, White, 1890, 43 x 34 In. . . . 1770.00
Gate, Wood, Iron, Eagle Shape, Cutout, Iron Straps, 24 x 27 In. . . . 3055.00
Gate Weight, Iron, 4-Pointed Star, Red Paint, Ring Top, Marked, 5 Lb., 9 x 7 ¼ In. . . . 250.00
Gazebo, Iron, 6 Figural Columns, Dome Top, White Paint, 156 x 118 In. . . . 8813.00
Hinge, Iron, Scrolls, 3 x 8 In. . . . 11.00
Hinge, Iron, Scrolls, 6 x 7 ½ In. . . . 22.00
Hinge, Iron, Stylized Ends, 21 ¾ In., Pair . . . 358.00
Hinge, Y Form, Iron, 40 In., Pair . . . 293.00
Holy Water Font, Our Lady Of Perpetual Help, Bronze, Burl, Silver, Gilt Relief, 13 In. . . . 531.00
Hook, Ceiling, Figural, Dolphin, Iron, 9 ¼ In. . . . 125.00
Keystone, Carrara Marble, Carved, 11 ¾ x 9 ⅝ In. . . . 550.00
Latch, Iron, Heart Shape Terminal, Pa., 11 ¾ In. . . . 234.00
Letter Box, Iron, Steel, U.S. Mail, Cutler Mail Chute Co., Rochester, N.Y., 21 x 36 In. . . . 1770.00

Lintel, Temple, Clay, Carved, Lion Doors, Chinese, Early Qing, 11 x 24 In. 418.00
Mailbox, Brass, 30 Slots, c.1920, 26 x 23 x 14 In. 175.00
Mailbox, Metal, Clear, Embossed, U.S. Mail, Liberty, 12 In. 50.00
Mantel, Black Walnut, Arts & Crafts, c.1895, 47 x 62 x 11 In. 650.00
Mantel, Black Walnut, Attached Molding, Shelf, 1800s, 77 x 39 In. 4250.00
Mantel, Carrara Marble, Louis XV, Shell, Leaf Carvings, White, France, 42 x 63 In. 2990.00
Mantel, Cherry, Classical, Carved Roundels, Raised Panels, Shelves, 82 ½ x 60 In. 1575.00
Mantel, French Walnut, Molded Serpentine Shelf, Conforming Opening, 61 x 44 In. 59.00
Mantel, Limestone, Louis XVI, Asymmetrical, Cartouche, Shields, 41 x 40 In. 2205.00
Mantel, Louis XVI Style, Carrara Figures, Marble, Hand Sculpted, 55 x 72 In. 1980.00
Mantel, Marble, Arched Gadrooned Opening, Sprays, Flower Brackets, c.1800, 48 x 75 In. 8812.00
Mantel, Marble, Violet Jura Brocatelle, Louis XV, 1700s, 44 x 68 In. 4116.00
Mantel, Oak, Carved, White, 19th Century, 50 x 60 x 12 ½ In. 100.00
Mantel, Oak, Carved Inset Panels, Columns, Shelf, 90 x 60 In. 3500.00
Mantel, Oak, Carved Lion's Head Support, Acanthus Leaf, c.1880, 84 x 60 x 13 In. 2760.00
Mantel, Oak, Seated Lion, Red Paint, Late 19th Century, 30 x 60 x 15 In. 250.00
Mantel, Pine, Federal, Molded Cornice, Fluted Pilasters, Painted, c.1810, 40 x 51 In. 936.00
Mantel, Pine, Federal, Reeded Pilasters, Yellow Paint, c.1800, 32 x 26 ½ In. 702.00
Mantel, Pine, Federal, Stepped Cornice, Fluted Pilasters, Painted, c.1800, 57 x 71 In. 761.00
Mantel, Rouge Marble, Louis XV Style, Center Shell, Shaped Apron, 50 In. 1800.00
Mantel, Sandstone, Marble, Louis XV, Fan & Scroll Center, Fluted Corners, 46 x 60 In. 960.00
Mantel, Softwood, Olive Green Paint, Applied Molding, 50 x 72 x 6 ¼ In. 70.00
Mantel, Softwood, Painted Olive Green, Applied Molding, 50 x 72 In. 77.00
Mantel, Stone, Scroll, Acanthus Corbels, William Jackson Cretan, c.1930, 68 x 82 In. 3950.00
Mantel, Yellow Pine, Arched Firebox Opening, 1700s, 67 x 76 In. 1725.00
Medallion, Plaster, Round, Tiers Of Acanthus, 18 In. 295.00
Newel Post, Oak, Winged Griffin, Carved, Bronze, Twisted Columns, 1880, 78 In., Pair 12500.00
Niche, Wood, Carved, Lacquered, Blue, Gold Highlights, Italy, c.1820, 48 x 24 In. 3600.00
Overmantel Mirror, Aesthetic, Reticulated Crest, Flower Panels, 79 x 63 In. 3408.00
Overmantel Mirror, Beechwood, Carved, Painted, Restauration, 54 x 39 ½ In. 1800.00
Overmantel Mirror, Beechwood, Giltwood, Matte Gris-De-Trianon, 67 ½ x 42 In. 4800.00
Overmantel Mirror, Ebony Frame, 3 Plates, Cut Star Design, Early 1700s, 20 x 51 In. 4680.00
Overmantel Mirror, Eglomise, Gesso, Giltwood, Urn, Bellflower, Adam, 42 x 52 In. 1380.00
Overmantel Mirror, Georgian Style, Mahogany, Parcel Gilt, 49 ½ x 55 ½ x 1 ½ In. 717.00
Overmantel Mirror, Giltwood, 3 Panels, Turnings, Rosettes, Leaves, c.1910, 63 x 28 In. 235.00
Overmantel Mirror, Giltwood, Carved, Arched Molded Frame, Fan Corners, 60 x 46 In. 1058.00
Overmantel Mirror, Giltwood, Carved, Flower & Urn Crest, c.1860, Pair 13800.00
Overmantel Mirror, Giltwood, Carved, Latticework, 3 Panels, 1800s, 25 x 62 In. 633.00
Overmantel Mirror, Giltwood, Classical Scenes, 3 Panels, England, 1800s, 36 x 72 In. 1093.00
Overmantel Mirror, Giltwood, Federal, 3 Sections, 19th Century, 25 ½ x 61 In. 146.00
Overmantel Mirror, Giltwood, Federal, Garland, Fluted Columns, 27 x 60 In. 2990.00
Overmantel Mirror, Giltwood, Rococo, Scrolled Reticulated Crest, c.1860, 69 x 37 In. 940.00
Overmantel Mirror, Mahogany, Tortoiseshell Veneer, England, 1800s, 21 x 56 In. 3438.00
Overmantel Mirror, Molded Frame, Divided Plates, Giltwood, 19th Century, 25 x 49 In. 1057.00
Overmantel Mirror, Neoclassical Figures, Gilt Gesso, Black Paint, c.1812, 33 x 73 In. 3437.00
Overmantel Mirror, Pine, Rococo, Carved, Scalloped Pieced Frame, 61 x 63 In. 3819.00
Overmantel Mirror, Split Baluster, Marble, Gilt Gesso, E. Lothrop, c.1835, 58 x 24 In. 2133.00
Overmantel Mirror, Wood, Classical, Turned & Carved, 3 Sections, c.1835, 24 x 59 In. 235.00
Overmantel Mirror, Wood, White Painted, Carved, Scandinavia, 67 ¼ x 33 In. 1440.00
Panel, B & O Railroad, Iron, Rosette, Laurel Border, Late 1800s, 47 x 25 In., 4 Piece 2714.00
Panel, Beechwood, Carved, Parcel Gilt, Leaf Scrolls, 1900s, 21 x 11 ¾ In., Pair 1320.00
Panel, Oak, Carved, Woman, Child, Renaissance Revival, 1600s, 13 x 10 In. 148.00
Panel, Walnut, Renaissance Style, Carved, Putto, Figures, 1800s, 58 x 22 In., Pair 1150.00
Panel, Walnut, Satyr Mask, Flowers, Scrolls, 23 x 15 In. 1062.00
Panel, Wood, Carved, Wall, Trees, Chinese, 1800s, 9 x 24 In. 293.00
Pedestal, Cast Iron, Stepped Top, Tapered Column, Relief Leaf Cluster, Square Base, 44 x 21 In. 1116.00
Pedestal, Marble, Turquin, Fluted, Round Top, Ormolu Rim, 34 x 19 In., Pair 37500.00
Pediment, Brownstone, Corbels, Early 19th Century, 48 x 72 In. 2950.00
Plinth, Carved Griffins, Dragons, Scrolls, Vines, Inset Lion, Wood, Germany, 1800s, 23 x 6 In. 1003.00
Post, Wood, Turned, Painted, Ball Finial, Early 20th Century, 9 ½ x 47 In. 235.00
Roof Crest, Terra-Cotta, Glazed Black, France, 19th Century, 34 x 33 In. 259.00
Roof Finial, Wood, Carved, Ocher Painted, Stepped Steel Stand, Black Matte, India, 19 x 11 ½ In. 780.00
Roof Tile, Ceramic, Figure, On Mythical Animal, Glazed, Chinese, 11 x 10 In. 130.00
Roof Tile, Earthenware, Fish, Painted, Glazed, Resin Figure, Chinese, 9 ¾ In. 190.00
Roof Tile, Molded Fish, 3-Color Glaze, Chinese, 9 ½ In. 540.00
Roof Tile, Pottery, Molded Winged Horse, 3-Color Glaze, Chinese, 11 ¼ In. 570.00
Sconce, Federal, Pine, Eagle, Ebonized, Parcel Gilt, Brass, c.1825, 26 x 17 In. 9375.00

Architectural, Doorknocker, Iron, Flowers In Vase, Painted, 3 ¾ x 2 ¼ In.
$220.00

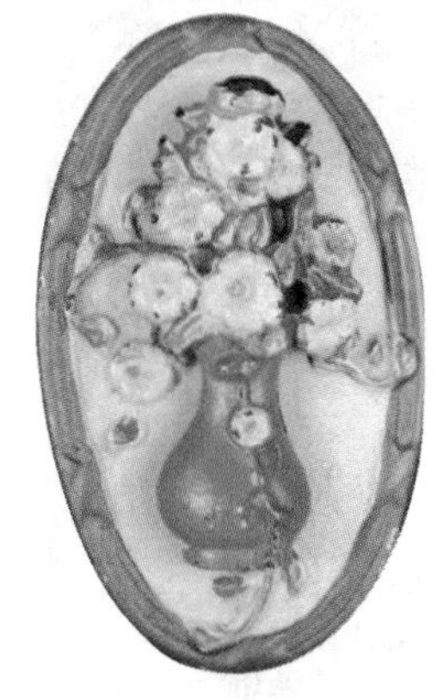

Architectural, Doorknocker, Iron, Girl, Knocking, Painted, G.R., Hubley, 1921, 3 ⅝ x 2 In.
$495.00

Architectural, Doorknocker, Iron, Rabbit Eating Cabbage, Painted, Albany, 5 In.
$880.00

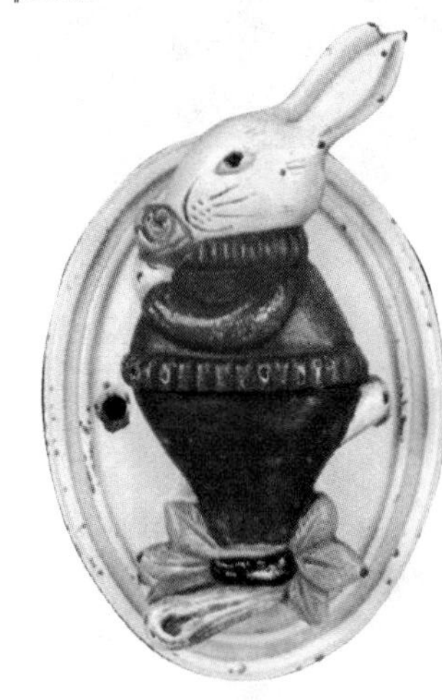

Arequipa, Vase, Leaf Chains, White, Brown, Green Matte Ground, 6 ¼ x 4 In.
$6000.00

Arequipa, Vase, Leaves, Frothy Pale Yellow Glaze, Carved, Incised, Label, 8 x 4 ½ In.
$1440.00

Arequipa, Vase, Peacock Feathers, Turquoise Ground, Stamped, 1912, 2 ¼ x 4 ½ In.
$4500.00

TIP
Put books in the freezer overnight to get rid of many types of insects.

Scroll, Giltwood, Pendant, Leaf, Rococo Style, Italy, 17 x 10 ½ In., Pair 1680.00
Shrine, Walnut, Carved Nativity, Madonna, Leaves, Putti, Scrolls, c.1850, 102 x 64 In. 10030.00
Shutter, Painted Green, c.1910, 80 x 31 In. 165.00
Staircase, Oak, 5 Curved Steps, Carved Handrail, England, 1800s, 77 x 49 x 43 In. 460.00
Star, Iron, Painted, 8 In., 11 Piece 316.00
Thumb Latch, Iron, Pineapple For Plates, 18th Century, 15 ¾ In. 439.00
Thumb Latch, Scalloped Back Plate, Iron, Pa., 11 In. 527.00
Traffic Light, Metal, 3-Color, Yellow Ground, 14 x 17 In. 35.00
Valance, Crowns, Flowers, Leaves, Gilt Gesso Over Wood, 27 x 54 x 14 In. 475.00
Valance, Walnut, 1880s, 29 ½ x 68 ½ In. 1995.00
Wall Bracket, Louis XVI Style, Giltwood, Demilune Shelf, Tassel, 7 ½ x 6 In., Pair 420.00
Well Head, Marble, Iron Arch, Bacchantes, S & C-Scroll Volutes, 121 x 40 In. 8225.00

AREQUIPA POTTERY was produced from 1911 to 1918 by the patients of the Arequipa Sanatorium in Marin County, north of San Francisco. The patients were trained by Frederick Hurten Rhead, who had worked at the Roseville Pottery.

Bowl, Gunmetal Matte Glaze, Designed Rim, 3 x 13 ¼ x 10 In. 400.00
Bowl, Rim Design, Gunmetal Glaze, 10 x 13 ¼ In. 316.00
Bowl, Vine, Green, Pink, Textured Gray Ground, Squeezebag, Ink Mark, 5 x 9 ½ In. 3400.00
Plate, Amber Flowers, Painted, Carved Flowers & Leaves, Mustard Ground, Marked, 9 In. 1080.00
Vase, Blue Ivory Glaze, Bulbous, Impressed Mark, 4 x 3 In. 540.00
Vase, Carved Leaves, Pale Yellow Glaze, Bulbous, Paper Label, Marked, 8 x 4 ½ In. 1440.00
Vase, Geometric Band, Blue, Green, Pale Green Ground, Bulbous, Incised, 3 ¾ x 4 In. 1700.00
Vase, Green Flower, Leaves, Brown, Green Ground, Oval, 8 x 3 In. 3000.00
Vase, Green Matte Glaze, Iris Carving, Egg Shape, Stamped, 7 ¾ x 3 ¼ In. 1320.00
Vase, Hand Thrown, California, Mark, c.1915, 4 x 3 In. 650.00
Vase, Iris, Green Matte Glaze, Oval, Stamp Mark, 7 ¾ x 3 ¼ In. 1100.00
Vase, Leaf Band, Brown, White, Yellow, Frothy Green Ground, Squeezebag, Mark, 7 ½ In. 2400.00
Vase, Leaf Chains, White, Brown, Green Matte Ground, 6 ¼ x 4 In. .... *illus* 6000.00
Vase, Leaves, Frothy Pale Yellow Glaze, Carved, Incised, Label, 8 x 4 ½ In. .... *illus* 1440.00
Vase, Peacock Feathers, Turquoise Ground, Stamped, 1912, 2 ¼ x 4 ½ In. .... *illus* 4500.00
Vase, Spade Shape Leaf Band, Blue Gray, Purple Ground, Bulbous, Incised, 5 ½ x 4 In. 2400.00
Vase, Spade Shape Leaves, Mottled Eggplant, Brown Ground, Squeezebag, 7 x 3 ½ In. 2400.00
Vase, Tapered, Green Glaze, Squeezebag Decorated Yellow Leaves, Marked, 7 ½ x 3 ¾ In. 3000.00

ARGY-ROUSSEAU, *see G. Argy-Rousseau category.*

ARITA is a port in Japan. Porcelain was made there from about 1616. Many types of decorations were used, including the popular Imari designs, which are listed under Imari in this book.

Charger, Birds, Flowers, Blue, White, Scalloped Edge, Late 19th Century, 16 In. 425.00
Charger, House, Water, Bridge, Trees, Blue, White, c.1870, 12 In. 125.00
Figurine, Bunny, Sniffing Ground, Black, White, Pink, 6 In. 2050.00
Plate, Cranes, Clouds, Blue, White, Basket Weave Border, Scalloped Rim, 13 In. 100.00

ART DECO or Art Moderne, a style started at the Paris Exposition of 1925, is characterized by linear, geometric designs. All types of furniture and decorative arts, jewelry, book bindings, and even games were designed in this style. Additional items may be found in the Furniture category or in various glass and pottery categories, etc.

Bowl, Molded Mermaid, Hair, Tail, Bubbles, Chocolate Stain, Lalique Style, 9 ¼ In. 431.00
Figurine, Dog, Seated, Egyptian Style, Metal, Onyx Plinth, 8 ⅛ x 10 In. .... *illus* 300.00
Tea Set, Hagenauer, Stainless Steel, Wood, Marked, Karl, 4 Piece .... *illus* 720.00
Thermos & Tray, Turquoise, Enamel, Metal, American Thermos Bottle Co. .... *illus* 435.00
Vase, Molded, School Of Fish, Waves, Lalique Style, 7 ⅜ In. 150.00

ART GLASS, *see Glass-Art category.*

ART NOUVEAU is a style of design that was at its most popular from 1895 to 1905. Famous designers, including Rene Lalique and Emile Galle, produced furniture, glass, silver, metal-work, and buildings in the new style. Ladies with long flowing hair and elongated bodies were among the more easily recognized design elements. Copies of this style are being made today. Many modern pieces of jewelry can be found. Additional Art Nouveau pieces may be found in Furniture or in various glass categories.

Ewer, Stopper, Amber, Pewter Spout, Blossom, Vine Tendrils Handle, 10 In. 288.00

Figurine, Nude Woman, With Disc, Blowing Trumpet, 9 ½ x 12 x 3 ½ In. 77.00

ART POTTERY *see Pottery-Art*

ARTHUR OSBORNE *plaques are found in the Ivorex category.*

ARTS & CRAFTS was a design style popular in American decorative arts from 1894 to 1923. In the 1970s collectors began to rediscover Mission furniture, art pottery, metalwork, linens, and light fixtures from this period. The interest has continued. Today everything from this era is collectible, including jewelry, graphics, and silverware. Additional items may be found in the Furniture category and other categories.

Pitcher, Copper, Hammered, Baluster, 17 In. 440.00
Screen, 3-Panel, Wisteria Branches, Pierced Copper, Slag Glass, Frame, 21 x 21 In. 840.00
Vase, Copper, Hammered, Baluster, Handles, 12 In. 235.00

AURENE glass was made by Frederick Carder of New York about 1904. It is an iridescent gold, blue, green, or red glass, usually marked *Aurene* or *Steuben*.

AURENE

Atomizer, Blue, Embossed Collar, 10 In. 460.00
Atomizer, Blue, Footed, Embossed Metal Fittings, Signed, 8 In. 374.00
Atomizer, Blue, Intaglio Band, Lattice, Flowers, DeVilbiss, 8 ½ In. 920.00
Atomizer, Gold, Reverse Trumpet, Embossed Metal Fittings, Signed, 9 In. 403.00
Basket, Gold, Coiled Buttons, Arched Handle, 7 ¾ x 6 ½ In. 346.00
Bowl, Blue, Footed, Signed, 6 x 12 ¼ In. .... *illus* 2760.00
Bowl, Gold, 3-Footed, Signed, 10 In. .... 388.00 to 518.00
Bowl, Gold, Bulbous, Cupped Rim, 6 x 10 In. 2106.00
Bowl, Gold, Calcite, Flared, Footed, 10 x 4 In. 186.00
Bowl, Gold, Green & Purple Highlights, Rolled & Ruffled Edge, 5 ¾ In. 380.00
Bowl, Gold, Ruffled Edge, Polished Pontil, 6 ½ In. 270.00
Bowl, Stand, Gold, Calcite, 4 ⅞ x 11 ¼ In. 1053.00
Candlestick, Blue, Footed, Twist Stem, Signed, Steuben, 8 ½ In. 805.00
Candlestick, Blue, Steuben, 8 In., Pair 1610.00
Candlestick, Gold, Blue Highlights, Twisted, 8 x 3 ½ In., Pair 1560.00
Candlestick, Gold, Calcite Flared Base, 6 In. 374.00
Candlestick, Gold, Twisted Stem, 4 x 8 In., Pair 1440.00
Candlestick, Gold, Twisted Stem, Blue Highlights, Signed, 10 In., Pair 1725.00
Champagne, Gold, 7 In. 690.00
Chandelier, 5-Light, Green, White, Intarsia Shades, Ceiling Cap, Chains, 5-In. Shade 4313.00
Chandelier, Gold Feather, Center Stalactite, 6 Ruffled Trumpet Shades, 9 & 5-In. Shades 3450.00
Cologne, Blue, Footed, Bird Stopper, c.1905, 12 In. 2340.00
Compote, Blue, Calcite, Flared Rim, c.1910, 3 ¼ x 7 ¼ In. 1053.00
Compote, Blue, Cupped, Ladyleg Stem, Signed, 8 In. 800.00
Compote, Blue, Swirled, Baluster Ribbed Stem, Ribbed Foot, 8 In. 1495.00
Compote, Gold, Calcite, Platinum, Pink Highlights, 8 In. 144.00
Compote, Gold, Magenta, Blue Highlights, 2 ⅞ In. 431.00
Compote, Gold, Ruffled & Stretched Rim, 6 ⅛ In. 863.00
Compote, Gold, Ruffled Bowl, Half Twist Stem, 6 ⅛ In. 920.00
Decanter, Blue, Stopper, 12 In. 2875.00
Finger Bowl, Underplate, Gold, Calcite, Purple Highlights, Signed, 6 ¼ x 2 ¾ In. 230.00
Flower Frog, Gold, 2 Tiers, 8 Holes, 2 ¼ In. 403.00
Goblet, Gold, Signed, 5 In. 140.00
Jar, Cover, Gold, Pink & Blue Highlights, 5 ½ In. 1265.00
Lamp, Electric, Gold Shade Bell Shape, Purple & Blue Iridescence, Ribbed, 10 In. 403.00
Lamp, Piano, Gold, Ribbed, S-Scroll Brass Base, 23 In. 374.00
Lampshade, Bell Shape, Gold, White Pulled Feather, Green, 5 x 2 ¼ In., 8 Piece 1438.00
Nappy, Gold, Diamond Quilted, 5 In. 345.00
Nut Dish, Gold, Purple, Blue Highlights, Twisted Stem, Footed, 6 In. 403.00
Perfume Bottle, Blue, Footed, Teardrop Stopper, 8 In. 805.00
Perfume Bottle, Blue, Footed, Teardrop Stopper, Steuben, 10 In. 1265.00
Perfume Bottle, Blue, Pedestal, Stopper, 7 ½ In. 550.00
Perfume Bottle, Gold, Footed, Mirror Black Stopper 6 ½ In. 575.00
Perfume Bottle, Gold, Melon Ribbed, Teardrop Stopper, Steuben, 6 In. 460.00
Pitcher, Tumble Up, Blue, Bulbous, Applied Handle, Steuben, 6 ½ In. 575.00
Ring Tray, Gold, Oval, Ring Handle, 5 In. 690.00
Rose Bowl, Gold, Oval, Opal, Cascading Hooked Feathers, Signed, 4 In. 4600.00
Salt, Gold, Platinum, Blue Highlights, 1 ¾ In. 201.00

Art Deco, Figure, Dog, Seated, Egyptian Style, Metal, Onyx Plinth, 8 ⅛ x 10 In.
$300.00

Art Deco, Tea Set, Hagenauer, Stainless Steel, Wood, Marked, Karl, 4 Piece
$720.00

Art Deco, Thermos & Tray, Turquoise, Enamel, Metal, American Thermos Bottle Co.
$435.00

Aurene, Bowl, Blue, Footed, Signed, 6 x 12 ¼ In.
$2760.00

A

Aurene, Vase, Blue, Trumpet, 10 x 6 In.
$2340.00

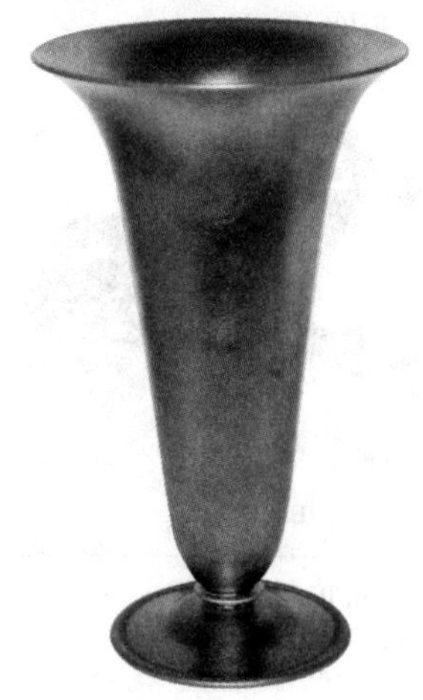

Aurene, Vase, Gold, Millefiori Flowers, Leaves, Vines, Blue & Pink Highlights, Signed, 6 In.
$6325.00

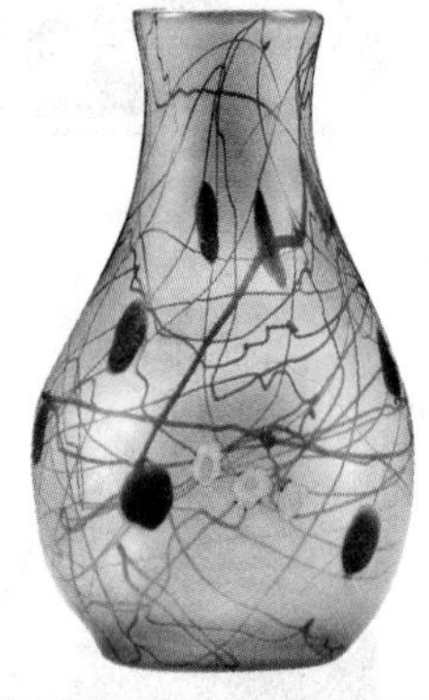

Aurene, Vase, Tree Trunk, 3-Prong, Gold, Blue Highlights, Signed, 6 In..
$700.00

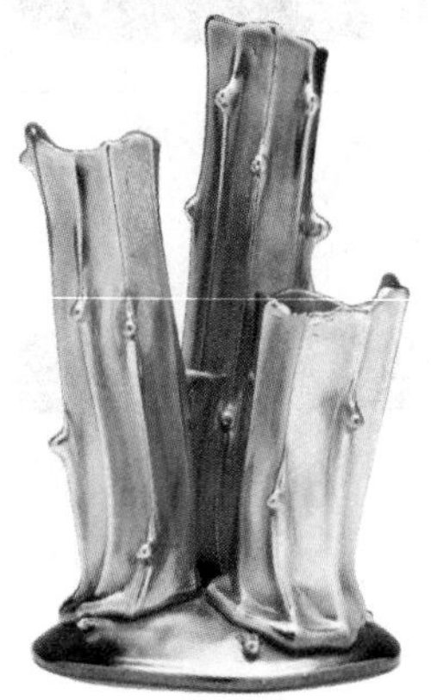

Sconce, Gold Shades, Brass, Flower Wreaths, Bulbous, 8 ½ x 12 x 8 ¾ In.. . . . . 518.00
Shade, Brown, Pulled Feather, Emerald Green Trim, Pinched Waist, 6 x 5 In.. . . . . 403.00
Shade, Gold, Bell, Double Pulled Feathers, Platinum Ground, 5 ½ In. 201.00
Shade, Gold, Bell, Ribbed, 5 ½ In.. . . . . 150.00
Shade, Gold, Calcite, White, Medallion & Garland, Engraved, Signed, 4 ¾ In. 150.00
Shade, Gold, Green Pulled Loops, Ruffled Rim, 4 ¾ x 6 ¼ In., Pair 633.00
Shade, Gold, Ribbed, Flared, Scalloped Rim, Signed, 5 In., 6 Piece 1610.00
Shade, Gold, Ribbed, Flared Lip, Gold, Platinum Blue Lip, 5 In., 3 Piece. 600.00
Shade, Green, Gold Pulled Feather, Gold Interior, 4 ½ x 2 ¼ In., 4 Piece. 690.00
Shade, Red, Gold Heart & Vine, 4 ¾ In. 2400.00
Sherbet, Underplate, Gold, Calcite, c.1910, 4 x 6 ¼ In., 2 Piece 293.00
Sugar & Creamer, Gold, Applied Reeded Handle, Oval, Steuben, 3 ½ In. 863.00
Tumbler, Gold, Flared Rim, 4 In., 6 Piece. 2588.00
Underplate, Blue, Gold Highlights, 6 ½ In. 155.00
Vase, Acid Cutback, Dragon, Gold, 12 In. 1725.00
Vase, Acid Cutback, Hunting, Yellow Jade, Blue, Steuben, 6 Sides, 10 In. 690.00
Vase, Automobile, Blue, Etched, 8 In. 550.00
Vase, Blue, Bulbous, Wide Mouth, Flared Rim, Footed, 11 In. 1062.00
Vase, Blue, Calcite, Flared Rim, Steuben, 4 x 5 ½ In. 250.00
Vase, Blue, Flared, Ruffled Rim, Signed, 5 ¾ x 3 ½ In. 200.00
Vase, Blue, Flared, Ruffled Rim, Signed, 6 In.. . . . . 1100.00
Vase, Blue, Ruffled Rim, Footed, Steuben, 12 ¾ In. 1035.00
Vase, Blue, Shouldered, Flared Rim, 8 In. . . . . . 708.00 to 1320.00
Vase, Blue, Trumpet, 10 x 6 In. . . . . . *illus* 2340.00
Vase, Blue, Trumpet, Purple & Green Highlights, Steuben, 8 In.. . . . . 1524.00
Vase, Blue, Urn Shape, Flared Rim, 4 In. 201.00
Vase, Clear, Trumpet, Gold, Ribbed, 6 In. 267.00
Vase, Fan, Blue, Applied Rigaree Band, 8 ¼ In.. . . . . 3968.00
Vase, Gold, Baluster, 8 ½ x 4 ½ In. 660.00
Vase, Gold, Calcite, Footed, Flared Rim, 7 x 6 ¼ In. 995.00
Vase, Gold, Cone Shape, Swirled Body, 12 ¼ In. 1265.00
Vase, Gold, Diamond Quilted, Pulled Feather, 5 ¾ In. 3450.00
Vase, Gold, Footed, Shaped Handles, 10 ¼ x 7 In.. . . . . 4388.00
Vase, Gold, Gourd, Pulled Neck, Blue & Purple Highlights, 6 ¼ In. 575.00
Vase, Gold, Green Leaf, Vine, White Millefiori Flowers, Signed, 5 ½ In.. . . . . 3250.00
Vase, Gold, Millefiori Flowers, Leaves, Vines, Blue & Pink Highlights, Signed, 6 In. . . . . . *illus* 6325.00
Vase, Gold, Pedestal, 3 Applied Handles, Signed, 6 In. 374.00
Vase, Gold, Pink Highlights, Shouldered, 6 ½ In. 403.00
Vase, Gold, Red Highlights, Urn Shape, Scrolled Handles, Steuben, 12 In. 1840.00
Vase, Gold, Shouldered, Handles, Steuben, 10 In.. . . . . 3738.00
Vase, Jack-In-The-Pulpit, Gold, Scalloped Rim, Signed, 6 In. 1150.00
Vase, Peacock, Green & Gold Pulled Feathers, Highlights, 8 ½ In. 7475.00
Vase, Purple, Blue Highlights, Morphic Shape, Ruffled Edge, Applied Foot, Steuben, 6 ⅝ In. . . 1380.00
Vase, Tree Trunk, 3-Prong, Gold, 10 In. 1053.00
Vase, Tree Trunk, 3-Prong, Gold, Blue Highlights, Signed, 6 In. . . . . . *illus* 700.00
Wine, Green, Amber Iridescent, 6 ½ In. 201.00

AUSTRIA *is a collecting term that covers pieces made by a wide variety of factories. They are listed in this book in categories such as Royal Dux or Porcelain.*

AUTO parts and accessories are collectors' items today. Gas pump globes and license plates are part of this specialty. Prices are determined by age, rarity, and condition. Signs and packaging related to automobiles may also be found in the Advertising category. Lalique hood ornaments will be listed in the Lalique category.

Air Meter, ECO, Overhead Lamp, Hose, Red, 85 x 16 ½ In. 2000.00
Air Pump, 2 Chambers, Long Handle, Cleveland Faucet Co.. . . . . 150.00
Air Pump, Balance Inflation, Red, ECOo Tireflator, Mich., 49 ½ In. 870.00
Ashtray, Goodyear Tire, 5 ½ In.. . . . . 5.00
Badge, Shell Oil, Red & Orange, Shell Emblem At Top, 2 ⅛ x 2 ⅛ In. 120.00
Battery Charger, General Electric, Tungar, Porcelain, Metal, Bakelite Switch, Art Deco, 1930 300.00
Bottle, Shell Oil, Clear, Qt., 14 ½ In. 60.00
Bottle, U-Neek Motor Oil, Clear, Ribs, 1920, Tall 25.00
Cabinet, Oil, Mobiloil, Ask For Gargoyle, Painted, Metal, Porcelain Sign. 400.00
Display, Gas Pump, Sunray Gasoline, Wayne Tank & Pump, Indiana, 120 In. 1595.00
Display, Mobiloil, Socony-Vacuum, Oil Bottles, Pullout Holder, 29 x 16 x 11 In. 523.00
Display, Polly Premium Motor Oil, Parrot, Green, Black, Yellow, 48 x 22 x 22 In.. . . . . 600.00
Doorstop, Texaco, Star, T, Lollipop Form, Painted, White, Red, Black, 10 In. 50.00

Figure, Michelin Tires Mascot, Plaster, Painted, 1920, 32 In. 8800.00
Gas Can, Copper, Handle, Ribbed, Pat. 3/21/1921, 25 In., 5 Gal. 65.00
Gas Can, Mobilgas, Pegasus, Red, Metal, Handle, Signed, Ellisco, 5 Gal. 35.00
Gas Can, Sohio, Blue, White Fuel, Handle, Cincinnati, Oh., 1925, 5 Gal. 35.00
Gas Can, Sohio, Diamond Point, Metal, Painted, Red, White, Blue, 3 Caps, Bail Handle, 5 Gal. 25.00
Gas Can, Texaco, Fire-Chief Gasoline, Metal, Red, Handles, Cincinnati, Oh., 1925, 10 Gal. 70.00
Gas Can, Texaco, Milwaukee Tank Works, Metal, Painted, 20th Century, 52 x 23 In. 70.00
Gas Pump, Blue Sunoco, Brass Plaque, Hose, Nozzle, No. 12042N, 10 Ft. 1000.00
Gas Pump, Flying A, Green, 20 x 72 In. 1035.00
Gas Pump, Red Crown, Crown Globe, Gilbert & Barker, 10 Ft. 1600.00
Gas Pump, Sun Ray, Ripple Body Globe, Yellow, Red, 10 Gal., 120 In. 3750.00
Gas Pump, Texaco, Mae West, Fry Visible, Model 17, White, Red, Glass Globe, 5 Gal., 118 In. .. 2250.00
Gas Pump, Texaco, Star, Milk Glass Globe, Red, Green, White, 8 Ft. 1000.00
Gas Pump Globe, Goodrich Gasoline, 1930-40, 19 In., 3 Piece .... *illus* 460.00
Gas Pump Globe, Oriental Ethyl Gasoline, Plastic, 18 x 17 In. 165.00
Gas Pump Globe, Richfield Hi-Octane, 1940s, 16 ½ In., 3 Piece .... *illus* 403.00
Gas Pump Globe, Shell, Figural, Embossed, White, Red, 21 In. 450.00
Gas Pump Globe, Shell, Milk Glass, Stenciled, 18 x 18 In. 373.00
Gas Pump Globe, Shell, Milk Glass, White, Red Lettering, 1930s-40s, 18 x 18 In. 518.00
Hood Ornament, Art Deco, Nickel Plated, Reclining Nude Woman, 1920s, 6 x 15 In. 205.00
Hood Ornament, Flying Lady, Mounted On Plaque 60.00
Hood Ornament, Policeman, Whirligig, Painted, Cast Aluminum, Bakelite Cap, 9 ½ In. 110.00
Hood Ornament, Red Goose Shoes, Goose, Red, Cast Iron, Arcade, 4 ½ In. 72.00
Hood Ornament, Texas Longhorn, 4 x 9 In. 30.00
License Plate, Maine, Dealer, DL284, 1934 .... 95.00
License Plate Attachment, Texsun, Rio Grande Valley Citrus Exchange, White Ground, 10 In. 45.00
Lighter, Standard Oil, Enamel Emblem, Silver, Idealine, Japan 30.00
Lubester, Dixie Motor Oil, Flags, Red, White, Blue, 53 x 23 x 11 ½ In. 200.00
Lubester, Mobil Oil, Red, White, 53 x 23 x 10 In. 200.00
Lubester, Mohawk, Indian, Red, Black, White Ground, 55 x 22 ½ x 10 In. 400.00
Manual, Buick, Series 90 80 60, 1932 .... 40.00
Measure, Gasoline, Built-In Brass Funnel, Lidded Spout, Copper, Brass Swing Handle, 19 x 12 In. 104.00
Oil Can, Archer Lubricants, Yellow, Red, Black, 10 ½ x 8 ½ x 5 ½ In., 2 Gal. 10.00
Oil Can, Special Automobile Oil For Ford Cars, Sears & Roebuck's, c.1918, 5 Gal. 50.00
Oil Can, Standard Oil, Metal, Red, Bail Handle, Fixed Bottom Handle, 5 Gal. 35.00
Oil Can, Standard Oil Co., Embossed, 5 Gal., 24 In., Pair 176.00
Oil Can, Veedol Tractor Oil, Soldered, Bail Handle, 5 Gal., 14 In. 70.00
Pin, Signal Gasoline, Tarzan Club, Green, Yellow, Celluloid, 1 In. 45.00
Poster, Peugeot, Race Car, Driver Is G. Biollot, Frame, Rene Vincent, c.1919, 74 x 59 In. 13000.00
Pump Plate, Mobilgas Special, Porcelain, Red Winged Horse, 1940s, 13 x 12 In. 325.00
Rack, Tidewater Motor Oil, Quality Oil, Red, White 600.00
Radiator, Ford Model T, Polished Brass, 25 x 20 In. 242.00
Radiator Cap, Buick, 1928, 3 ½ In. .... *illus* 770.00
Radiator Cap, Doc Yak, No. 348, Red, Yellow, Painted, Cast Iron, Wood Base, Arcade, 4 ¾ In. .. 512.00
Radiator Cap, Eagle, Art Deco, Chrome Plated, c.1930, 7 x 7 In. 176.00
Radiator Mascot, Daughter, Art Deco, Frosted Glass, c.1930, 4 ¾ In. 275.00
Radio, Champion Spark Plugs, Figural, Spark Plug, No. 5770, AM, 14 x 8 x 5 In. 300.00
Sign, 76, Neon, Red, White, 38 x 28 x 7 In. 900.00
Sign, Buick, Authorized Service, Porcelain, 41 ½ In. Diam. 2300.00
Sign, Champion Gasoline, Eagle, Flying, Red, White, Blue, Porcelain, 2-Sided, 36 x 60 In. 675.00
Sign, Champion Spark Plugs, More Power, More Speed, Blue, White, Yellow, Red, 14 x 30 In. .. 2300.00
Sign, Champlin Hi-V-I Motor Oil, Yellow, Red, Black, Porcelain, 2-Sided, 20 x 32 In. 389.00
Sign, Chrysler, Approved Service, Red, Blue, Yellow, Die Cut, Porcelain, 2-Sided, 32 x 30 In. ... 1210.00
Sign, Cooper Tires, American Made & Owned, Red, White, Blue, Tin, 12 x 47 ½ In. 25.00
Sign, Dynafuel, Porcelain, Yellow Diamond Shape, Blue, Red, 8 x 12 In. 144.00
Sign, Esso Blue, We Sell, Red, White, Blue, Porcelain, 2-Sided, Flange, 18 x 18 In. 200.00
Sign, Esso Gasoline, Black Man, Bass, Swing Along With Power, Paper, Frame, 41 x 27 In. 425.00
Sign, Esso Motor Oil, Porcelain, 2-Sided, 10 x 18 In. 85.00
Sign, Firestone Batteries, Orange, White, Black, Flange, 16 x 24 In. 700.00
Sign, Fisk Tires, Civilize Savage Trails, Indians, Car, Paper, N.C. Wyeth, 1919, 21 x 13 In. 825.00
Sign, FoMoCo, Genuine Ford Parts, Red, White, Hanging Bracket, 24 ½ x 25 In. 900.00
Sign, Ford, Black, White, Porcelain, Oval, 22 ½ x 33 In. 197.00
Sign, Frontier Gasoline, Rarin'-To-Go, Man On Horse, Red, White, Black, 72 In. Diam. 2750.00
Sign, Fuelman, Robot Holding Gas Hose, Red, White, Black, 2-Sided, Bracket, 16 x 24 In. 35.00
Sign, Gargoyle Mobiloil, Ask For, Vacuum Oil Co., Red, Black, White, 24 x 20 In. 1700.00
Sign, Genuine Ford Parts, Blue Neon, Oval, 17 x 24 ½ In. 650.00
Sign, Genuine Ford Parts, Ford In Neon, Blue, White, Art Deco, 21 ½ x 33 x 7 In. 600.00
Sign, Genuine Ford V8 Parts, Multicolored Neon, 25 ½ In. Diam. 850.00

Auto, Gas Pump Globe, Goodrich Gasoline, 1930-40, 19 In., 3 Piece
$460.00

Auto, Gas Pump Globe, Richfield Hi-Octane, 1940s, 16 ½ In., 3 Piece
$403.00

Auto, Radiator Cap, Buick, 1928, 3 ½ In.
$770.00

Auto, Sign, Globe, Tourists, Rooms, 4-Sided, 1920-30, 11 x 9 ½ x 9 ½ In.
$1093.00

Auto, Sign, Mobilgas, Pegasus, Porcelain, 12 x 12 In. $230.00

Auto, Sign, Oilzum, America's Finest Oil, 2-Sided, Porcelain, 1930-40, 28 x 20 In. $5750.00

Auto, Sign, Phillips 66, Shield, Porcelain, 2-Sided, 1950s, 29 x 30 In. $690.00

Auto, Sign, Shell Gasoline, Red, Yellow, Die Cut, 2-Sided, Porcelain, 1930-40, 24 x 25 In. $633.00

Sign, Globe, Tourists, Rooms, 4-Sided, 1920-30, 11 x 9 ½ x 9 ½ In. . . . . *illus* 1093.00
Sign, Good Year Tyres, Blue, Yellow, Winged Foot, Porcelain, 1930-40, 21 x 60 In. 460.00
Sign, Goodrich Tires, Silvertown, Red, Blue, Black, Porcelain, 26 ½ x 19 In. 500.00
Sign, Goodrich Tires, White, Red, Green, Blue Ground, Porcelain, 20 x 60 In. 475.00
Sign, Goodyear, Winged Foot, Die Cut Porcelain, White, Black, 16 x 46 In. 173.00
Sign, Greyhound Bus Lines, Porcelain, 2-Sided, Blue, Orange, White, c.1940, 20 x 36 In. 690.00
Sign, Gulf Gasoline, That Good Gasoline, Orange, Blue, White, Porcelain, Flange, 22 x 18 In. 325.00
Sign, Hudson Regular Hi-Octane Gas, Truck, Red, White, Black, Porcelain, 25 ½ In. 363.00
Sign, Humble Oil Company, Oval Center, Red, White, Porcelain, 26 x 52 In. 575.00
Sign, Indian Gasoline, Porcelain, Curved, Marked, 14855, 18 x 10 ¼ In. 300.00
Sign, Lion Oil, Red, White, Black, Tin, 42 In. Diam. 220.00
Sign, Marine Gasoline, Positive Octane, Boat, Blue, White, Porcelain, 8-Sided, 48 x 30 In. . . . 3654.00
Sign, Michelin, Michelin Man & Tire, Blue, White, Yellow, Black, Porcelain, Europe, 1970, 33 x 14 In. 125.00
Sign, Mobil, Pegasus, Red, Cutout, Porcelain, 35 x 48 In. 2300.00
Sign, Mobileoil, Enamel, Die Cut, 2-Sided, Oilcan Shape, 18 In. 1521.00
Sign, Mobilgas, Pegasus, Neon, Red Pegasus, Blue, 20 In. Diam. 600.00
Sign, Mobilgas, Pegasus, Porcelain, 12 x 12 In. . . . . *illus* 230.00
Sign, Mobilgas, Pegasus, Red, White, Blue, Porcelain, Marked, I.R. 47, 12 x 12 ¼ In. 154.00
Sign, Mobilgas, Shield Shape, Porcelain, White Ground, Red Horse, Blue, 12 x 12 In. 230.00
Sign, Mobilgas Special, Metal Band, Pegasus, Red, White, 15 In. 220.00
Sign, Mobiloil, Flying Horse, Drive Safely, Red, Black, Gray, Tin Lithograph, 5 ⅜ x 6 ½ In. . . . 130.00
Sign, Mobiloil Gargoyle, Porcelain, 2-Sided, 24 In. 325.00
Sign, Morgan & Wright Tire Co., Driver, Yellow Coat, Paper, Frame, 1906, 24 x 19 In. 1790.00
Sign, Motorola, Auto Radio, Neon, 11 ½ x 25 ½ x 6 In. 2500.00
Sign, Oak Motor Oil, Tree, Red, Green, White, Porcelain, 2-Sided, 16 ¾ x 26 In. 460.00
Sign, Official AAA Emergency Service, Chambersburg Motor Club, 22 x 24 In., 2 Piece 1300.00
Sign, Oilzum, America's Finest Oil, 2-Sided, Porcelain, 1930-40, 28 x 20 In. . . . . *illus* 5750.00
Sign, Pan-Am Gasoline, Motor Oils, Green, Red, White, 42 In. Diam. 750.00
Sign, Pennzoil, Sound Horn, We'll Open, White, Red, Yellow, Black, Tin, A-M7-71, 15 x 32 In.. 40.00
Sign, Perfect Circle Piston Rings, Red, White, Light-Up, 2-Sided. 105.00
Sign, Phillips 66, Orange, Black, Shield Form, 2-Sided, Marked, 28 ½ x 30 In. 1650.00
Sign, Phillips 66, Shield, Porcelain, 2-Sided, 1950s, 29 x 30 In. . . . . *illus* 690.00
Sign, Phillips 66 Motor Oil, Shield, Orange, Black, White, 2-Sided, Tin, 11 x 21 ¾ In. 187.00
Sign, Pontiac Parts, Indian, Red, Yellow, Black, Die Cut, Steel, 2-Sided, 1946, 18 x 23 ½ In. . . 1205.00
Sign, Pontiac Service, Indian, Red, White, Blue, 2-Sided, Porcelain, 42 In. Diam. 3850.00
Sign, Pontiac Service, Indian Brave Profile, Porcelain, Walter & Co., Detroit, 42 In. 1650.00
Sign, Price's Motor Oils, Red, White, Blue, Porcelain, Flange, 2-Sided, 18 x 24 In. 290.00
Sign, Quaker State Motor Oil, Green, White, Porcelain, 2-Sided, 29 x 26 ½ In. 453.00
Sign, Red Crown Gasoline, Crown, Red, White, Blue, Tin, 30 In. 1250.00
Sign, Red Hat Motor Oil, Tin Flanged, 18 x 17 ½ In. 3124.00
Sign, Red Indian Motor Oils, Indian Chief, Red, White, Black, Porcelain, 24 x 17 In. 4000.00
Sign, Richfield, Bird Flying, Blue, Yellow, White, 60 In. Diam. 2100.00
Sign, Robot Aligning & Axel Strengthening, Blue, White, Porcelain, 2-Sided, 36 x 60 In. 3100.00
Sign, Shell Gasoline, Red, Yellow, Die Cut, 2-Sided, Porcelain, 1930-40, 24 x 25 In. . . . . *illus* 633.00
Sign, Shell Motor Oil, Clamshell Form, Yellow, Red, 25 x 25 In. 250.00
Sign, Sico Gas, Wood, Painted, Tongue & Groove, 2-Sided, 79 x 35 x 2 ½ In. 190.00
Sign, Sinclair Diesel, Porcelain, White Ground, Green, Red, 12 x 13 ½ In. 316.00
Sign, Sinclair Opaline Motor Oil, Red, White, Green, Porcelain, 60 In. 225.00
Sign, Speed Limit 20 Miles, Battery Operated, 24 x 18 In. 250.00
Sign, Standard Oil, Division Of American Oil Co., Red, White, Blue, 28 x 96 In. 150.00
Sign, Star Cars Authorized Service, Durant Motors, Green, Porcelain, 2-Sided, 24 x 36 In. . . . 1320.00
Sign, Sterling Gasoline, Ethyl, Yellow, Black, Red, Porcelain, Oval, 8 ¾ x 11 ¼ In. 387.00
Sign, Stop & Sound Horn, Red, White, Porcelain, 1950s, 14 x 20 In. 173.00
Sign, Studebaker Authorized Sales & Service, 2-Sided, 1930-40, 4 In. . . . . *illus* 805.00
Sign, Texaco, Gasoline, Motor Oil, Star, Red, White, 42 In. Diam. 550.00
Sign, Texaco, Sky Chief Su-Preme Gasoline, Red, Green, White, 18 x 12 In. 90.00
Sign, Texaco Certified Lubrication, 2 Stars, Red, White, Porcelain, 8 ¾ x 38 ¾ In. 725.00
Sign, Texaco Fire Chief Gasoline, Hat, Red, White, Black, 1940, 18 x 12 In. 300.00
Sign, Texaco Fire Chief Gasoline, Star, Hat, Porcelain, 1960s, 18 x 12 In. 200.00
Sign, Texaco Motor Oil, Clean, Clear, Golden, 8-Sided, Porcelain, 30 x 30 In. 775.00
Sign, Texaco Sky Chief, Petrox, Porcelain, 1962, 12 x 8 In. . . . . *illus* 345.00
Sign, Texaco Sky Chief Gasoline, Porcelain, Red, Green, White, Black, c.1954, 12 x 18 In. 115.00
Sign, The Jordan Auto Co., Gold Letter, Wood, Stepped, 19 x 19 In. 600.00
Sign, Touring Club Of America, Original Frame, Brass Medallion, 25 x 32 In. 345.00
Sign, Tydol, Ethyl, Red, White, Porcelain, 10 In. Diam. 288.00
Sign, Tydol Gasoline, Porcelain, 2-Sided, Hanging, 1930, 48 In. 695.00

Sign, Weed Chains Gasoline, Price Dial, Din Over Wood, Rotating Dial, c.1920, 24 x 17 In.... 2121.00
Sign, Whippet & Willey-Knight Genuine Parts, Brown, White, 2-Sided, Porcelain, 27 x 35 In.. 165.00
Sign, White Star Gasoline, Blue, White, 2-Sided, Porcelain, 30 In. Diam.. 380.00
Steering Wheel, Ferrari 365 GTB4, Momo, Wood Rimmed, 1960s, 15 ¾ In.. 6386.00
Tin, Havoline Oil, It Makes A Difference, Black, Gold, Indian Refining Co., Gal., 10 ¾ In. 40.00
Tin, Marvel Mystery Oil, Red, Black, 5 Gal., 14 In. 50.00
Tin, Phillips 66, Grease, Orange, Black, 5 Lb., 7 ½ x 5 ½ In. 60.00
Tin, Texaco, Water Pump Grease, Green, White, Red 20.00
Tin, Texaco Home Lubricant, Red, Green, Blue, 6 ½ In.. 30.00
Tin, Thermo Anti-Freeze, Snowman, 1936, 5 Gal., 13 ½ In. 20.00
Tin, Veedol Tractor Oil, Bail Handle, 5 Gal., 14 In. 70.00
Trunk, Packard Motor Car Co., Chrome Trim, 36 x 20 x 18 In. 1035.00
Tumbler, All-American Soap Box Derby, Shell Oil, Akron, Ohio, 40038, 1950, 5 In. 5.00
Vehicle Plate, Vigilante Cattle Country, Embossed, 14 x 6 In.. 90.00
Whiskbroom, Motorist's, Celluloid, 5 x 2 ¼ In. 129.00

AUTUMN LEAF pattern china was made for the Jewel Tea Company beginning in 1933. Hall China Company of East Liverpool, Ohio, Crooksville China Company of Crooksville, Ohio, Harker Potteries of Chester, West Virginia, and Paden City Pottery, Paden City, West Virginia, made dishes with this design. Autumn Leaf has remained popular and was made by Hall China Company until 1978. Some other pieces in the Autumn Leaf pattern are still being made. For more prices, go to Kovels.com.

Baker, French, 3 Pt. 25.00
Bean Pot, Handle, Lid, 20th Century Shape, 2 Qt. 224.00
Bowl, 7 ½ In.. 55.00
Bowl, Cereal, 6 ½ In. 8.00
Bowl, Gold Rim, 9 x 5 In.. 35.00
Bowl, Vegetable, 1940s, 8 ½ x 4 ⅝ In. 10.00
Butter, Cover, ¼ Lb. 165.00
Butter, Cover, Lb. 500.00
Butter, Wings, ¼ Lb.. 1600.00
Cake Plate, 9 ½ In. 19.00
Cake Taker, Metal, 1950s. 65.00
Candy Dish, Cover, Pedestal, 5 ½ x 1 ½ In. 95.00
Canister, Tin, Plastic Lid, 6 x 5 In. 25.00
Canister, Tin, Round, Short. 28.00
Casserole, Cover, 6 In. 25.00
Casserole, Cover, 8 ¾ In. 33.00
Cookie Jar, Big Ear Handles, Eva Zeisel 325.00
Cup & Saucer 6.99
Mixing Bowl, 6 x 3 ½ In.. 45.00
Mug, 10 Oz. 45.00
Pitcher, 5 ½ In. 68.00
Pitcher, Ball, 7 In. 60.00
Plate, Salad, 7 In. 10.00
Stack Set, Cover, 4 Piece 95.00
Syrup, 6 In.. 115.00
Teapot, 8 ½ In. 95.00
Teapot, Aladdin 75.00
Teapot, Boston, 5 x 6 In. 140.00
Teapot, Newport, Gold Mark, 7 ⅜ In. *illus* 11.00
Thimble 25.00
Tidbit, 3 Tiers 125.00
Tin, Fruit Cake, 7 In.. 22.00
Tumbler, Iced Tea, Anchor Hocking, 16 Oz. 6.00
Tumbler, Water, Banded, 5 ½ In.. 45.00
Tumbler, Water, Frosted, 5 ½ In. 22.00
Vase, Bud, 5 ¼ In. 275.00

AVON *bottles are listed in the Bottle category under Avon.*

AZALEA dinnerware was made for Larkin Company customers from 1918 to 1941. Larkin, the soap company, was in Buffalo, New York. The dishes were made by Noritake China Company of Japan. Each piece of the white china was decorated with pink azaleas.

Bowl, Dessert, 5 ¼ In.. 8.50

Auto, Sign, Studebaker Authorized Sales & Service, 2-Sided, 1930-40, 4 In.
$805.00

Auto, Sign, Texaco Sky Chief, Petrox, Porcelain, 1962, 12 x 8 In.
$345.00

Road Maps
The first automobile road maps were printed in 1914.

Autumn Leaf, Teapot, Newport, Gold Mark, 7 ⅜ In.
$11.00

TIP
To get a mirror finish on patent leather, rub the shoes with a raw onion, then buff with a dry cloth.

Baccarat, Fairy Lamp, Rose Teinte, Saucer Base, Scalloped Edge, 4 In.
$170.00

Baccarat, Paperweight, Butterfly, Amber, c.1920, 4 x 3 In.
$70.00

Baccarat, Paperweight, Millefiori, Star, Canes, Pink, Blue, Green, 1848, 1 ⅛ x 2 ½ In.
$250.00

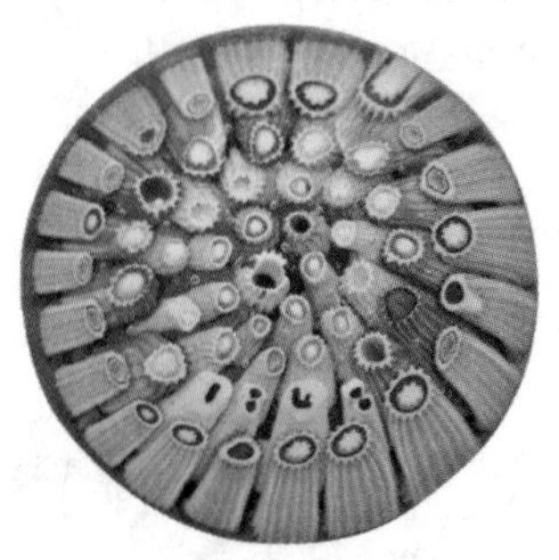

Baccarat, Ring Tree, Rose Teinte, Swirl, 3 ¾ In.
$40.00

Candy Jar, Cover 600.00
Creamer, Underplate 25.00
Gravy Boat, Attached Underplate 40.00
Plate, Luncheon, 8 In. 12.00
Plate, Salad, 7 ⅝ In. 12.00
Relish, Divided, 8 ½ x 5 In. 65.00
Salt & Pepper 25.00
Sugar, Cover, 2 Handles 25.00
Teapot, Cover, 5 ½ In. 160.00

BACCARAT glass was made in France by La Compagnie des Cristalleries de Baccarat, located 150 miles from Paris. The factory was started in 1765. The firm went bankrupt and began operating again about 1822. Cane and millefiori paperweights were made during the 1845 to 1880 period. The firm is still working near Paris making paperweights and glasswares.

Ashtray, Clear, Applied Frog, Green, Signed, 6 ¾ In. 90.00
Ashtray, Concentric Ring, Ruffled Rim, 2 ⅜ x 7 ¾ In.. . . . . 72.00
Atomizer, Rose Teinte, Swirl, 4 ¾ In. 150.00
Bowl, Engraved, Rose, Geometric, 8 In. 323.00
Bowl, Rose Teinte, Swirl Rolled Rim, Signed, 6 ½ In. 270.00
Box, Rose Teinte, Swirl, Round, Hinged, 3 ½ In.. . . . . 40.00
Candlestick, Amberina, Swirl, Bobeches, Signed, 8 In., Pair. 475.00
Candlestick, Clear, 6 ½ In., Pair 468.00
Candlestick, Clear, Rope Twist, 1880s, 7 ¼ x 3 ⅜ In.. . . . . 150.00
Candlestick, Rose Teinte, Swirl, Signed, 7 In. 170.00
Compote, Aqua Green, Swirl, 5 In. 35.00
Compote, Aqua Green, Swirl, Pedestal, Base Signed, 3 ¼ x 7 In. 110.00
Compote, Engraved Strawberries, Faceted Knop, Petticoat Base, 8 ½ x 6 In. 440.00
Compote, Rose Teinte, Swirl, Pedestal Base, 3 ½ x 7 ¾ In. 225.00
Compote, Rose Teinte, Swirl, Pedestal Base, Signed, 6 ½ In.. . . . . 150.00
Cordial, Zurich Cutting, 6-Sided Stem, 4 ¾ x 2 ¼ In. 45.00
Decanter, Engraved, Scrolls, Flat Stopper, Signed, 8 ¼ x 4 ¼ In. 130.00
Decanter, Hennessy Cognac, Signed, 10 In. 100.00
Decanter, Remy Martin, 10 In. 88.00
Decanter, Rose Teinte, Swirl, Ball Stopper, 8 ¼ In. 100.00
Dresser Box, Triangular, Gold Band, Signed, 5 ½ In. 224.00
Epergne, Engraved Flowers, Leaves, Frosted Dolphin Stem, 22 ½ In.. . . . . 1500.00
Fairy Lamp, Rose Teinte, Saucer Base, Scalloped Edge, 4 In. . . . . *illus* 170.00
Figurine, Bird, Blue, 3 In. 75.00
Figurine, Bird, Clear, 7 In.. . . . . 55.00
Figurine, Camel, Reclining, Clear, 3 ½ x 7 x 2 In. . . . . 50.00 to 70.00
Figurine, Cat, Arched Back, Clear, 4 ¼ x 5 In. 110.00
Figurine, Cat, Seated, 6 ¼ x 3 ½ In., Pair. 322.00
Figurine, Cat, Seated, Clear, 6 In. 135.00
Figurine, Elephant, Clear, 3 14 x 5 ½ In. 82.00
Figurine, Elephant, Hand Cooler, Clear, Stopper, 9 In. 70.00
Figurine, Elephant, Trunk Raised, Clear, 6 x 7 ½ In.. . . . . 85.00
Figurine, Frog, Clear, 2 ½ x 4 In. 82.00
Figurine, Golfer, Man Putting, Clear, 8 ¾ In. 135.00
Figurine, Golfer, Woman Putting, Clear, 9 In. 55.00
Figurine, Hippopotamus, Clear, 2 ½ x 5 ½ In. 110.00
Figurine, Horse, Clear, 3 x 4 ½ In. 82.00
Figurine, Owl, Clear, 4 In. 99.00
Figurine, Pelican, Clear, 6 ⅜ In. 55.00
Figurine, Pig, Clear, 4 x 6 ½ In. 82.00
Figurine, Polar Bear, Neck Out, 4 x 6 ½ In. 135.00
Figurine, Porcupine, Clear, 5 In.. . . . . 147.00
Figurine, Rabbit, Clear, 2 ½ x 4 In. . . . . 44.00 to 55.00
Figurine, Rabbit, Clear, 5 x 5 ½ In.. . . . . 110.00
Figurine, Rearing Horse, Clear, Signed, 8 ½ In.. . . . . 120.00
Figurine, Seal, Clear, 3 ½ x 3 ½ In.. . . . . 55.00
Figurine, Tennis Player, Clear, 11 ½ In. 292.00
Goblet, Aquarelle, Ribbed, 7 x 3 ½ In., 10 Piece 1100.00
Goblet, Biarritz Cutting, Signed, 6 x 3 ½ In.. . . . . 65.00
Goblet, Jewel Tone Flashed Bowl, Clear Base, 5 In., 6 Piece. 410.00

Ice Bucket, Clear, Brass Handles, Bottle Holder, 9 x 8 In. 500.00
Lamp, Ecru Ball Globe, Silvered Metal Base, J. Adnet, 1930s, 7 In., Pair 11250.00
Lamp, Kerosene, Rose Teinte, Swirl, Square Shape, Signed, 8 In. 1300.00
Lamp, Oil, Rose Teinte, Embossed Cherubs, Ruffled Rim Shade, 15 In. 266.00
Lamp, Perfume, Rose Teinte, Swirl, Cover, 6 ½ In. 100.00
Obelisk, Prismatic Cutting, Signed, 15 In. 200.00
Paperweight, Butterfly, Amber, c.1920, 4 x 3 In. .... *illus* 70.00
Paperweight, Clematis, 5-Petal Pink Flower, Leaves, Stem, 1 ¾ In. 840.00
Paperweight, Concentric Millefiori, Green, White, Amethyst, Red, Clear Ground, 2 ½ In. 201.00
Paperweight, Macedoine, Twists, Filigree, Canes, 3 In. 403.00
Paperweight, Millefiori, Cinque Foil Garland, 6 Millefiori Cane Clusters, 3 x 2 In. 460.00
Paperweight, Millefiori, Interlaced Trefoils, Pink, White, Green, Green Ground, 3 x 2 In. 900.00
Paperweight, Millefiori, Magnum, Spaced, Signed, 1848, 3 ¾ In. 3600.00
Paperweight, Millefiori, Scramble, Multicolored Twist, Filigree, 2 In. 230.00
Paperweight, Millefiori, Star, Canes, Pink, Blue, Green, 1848, 1 ⅛ x 2 ½ In. .... *illus* 250.00
Paperweight, Primrose, Blue & White, Green Leaves, Stem, Clear Ground, Star Base, 2 ⅜ In. 460.00
Paperweight, Rose Teinte, Swirl, Pinwheel Ribs, 2 x 2 ¼ In. 140.00
Paperweight, Sulphide, George Washington, Clear Ground, 2 ½ In. 360.00
Paperweight, Sulphide, Joan Of Arc, Wreath, Clear Ground, 3 ¼ In. 690.00
Paperweight, Sulphide, Massillon Bust, c.1800s, 2 ½ x 4 ¾ In. 468.00
Paperweight, Sulphide, Woman Bust, Footed, c.1840, 3 In. 488.00
Perfume Bottle, Guerlain, Rolled Shoulder, Inverted Heart Stopper, 4 ¾ In. 29.00
Perfume Bottle, Rose Teinte, Swirl, Pinched Waist, 7 In. 58.00
Pitcher, Clear, Squat, C-Scroll Handle, 5 x 6 ½ In. 88.00
Ring Tree, Rose Teinte, Swirl, 3 ¾ In. .... *illus* 40.00
Scent Bottle, Stopper, Crystal, Swirling Ribs, 4 ¼ x 2 ¾ In. 120.00
Sherry Set, Bell Shape Goblets, Scrolling Vines, 12 ¾ In., 7 Piece 625.00
Tumbler, Diamond Cutting, Gold Plate Rim, Ram's Head Ormolu, 2 ¾ x 1 ¾ In. 114.00
Tumbler, Empire Cutting, Fired Gold, 3 ¾ In, 12 Piece 1170.00
Vase, Clear, Flared Lip, 10 In. 380.00
Vase, Clear, Twisted, Ribbed, 9 x 9 In. 1287.00
Vase, Clear Flowers, Violet Grasshopper, Frosted, 4 Gilt Brass Feet, 9 In., Pair 948.00
Vase, Fan Shape, Gingko, 12 x 21 x 5 In. 3159.00
Vase, Opalescent, Enameled Snake, Metal Beetle Mounts, Blown Bamboo Stem, 9 In. 2013.00
Vase, Trumpet, Ornate Stepped Stem, Cut Foot, 1900, 18 x 5 In. 900.00

BADGES have been used since before the Civil War. Collectors search for examples of all types, including law enforcement and company identification badges. Well-known prison or law enforcement badges are most desirable. Most are made of nickel or brass. Many recent reproductions have been made.

AAA Safety Patrol, Massapequa, N.Y., Silver Color, C-Clasp, 1960s, ¾ In. 12.00
Award, National Marble Tournament 1935, Fabric, Brass Hanger, Eagle, Boys, Marbles, 1 ½ In. 115.00
Chauffeur, New York, Brass, Green & Black Enamel, Louis Markowitz, 1920, 1 ½ x 1 In. 49.00
Deputy Sheriff, Kern County, Ca., Eagle, Shield, Gold Plated, Blue, 1915-25, 2 In. .... *illus* 100.00
Employee ID Badge, General Time Instrument, Brass, Photo 30.00
Fireman, Chief, Brass, Hanger, Cello Insert, Embossed, Eagle Over Flames, Helmet, 3 ½ In. 78.00
Fireman, Chief, Brass, Hanger, Phoenix Rising From Flames, Crossed Trumpets, 3 ½ In. 78.00
Fireman, Chief, Reliance Fire Co., No. 1, West York, Pa., Brass, Enamel, Eagle, 3 In. 65.00
Fireman, Citizen Steam Fire Engine Co. No. 3, Spelter, Harrisburg, Pa., York, 1911, 4 In. 76.00
Fireman, Foreman, No. 14 Clinton, New Jersey, Wood, c.1850, 20 x 23 .... 4520.00
Fireman, J. Rooney, Hook & Ladder, No. 10, Copper, Wood, Stencil, 1882, 15 x 18 In. 5368.00
Fireman, Springfield Fire Dept., Patented In 1938 .... 32.00
Fireman, Visitation, Spelter, Brass Luster, Harrisburg, Pa., 1911, 4 In. 76.00
Greyhound Line, Embossed Greyhound, Blue & Gray Ground, 2 ½ x 2 In. 88.00
Pennsylvania Licensed Driver, Nickel Coated Brass, 1919, 2 ¼ x 1 ½ In. 55.00
Pilot, Alcatraz Prison Officer, Shield Shape, Eagle Form Top, 2 ⅛ In. 200.00
Police, Detroit Police Lieutenant, Retired 60.00
Police, FDR Inauguration, Silver, Eagle, Capital Building, 1937, 2 x 3 In. 3120.00
Police, New York City Shield, Acanthus Leaves, Shells, Nickeled Silver, 1852, 2 ¾ In. 1380.00
Police, Orange, California, Brass, Enamel, 3 In. .... *illus* 290.00
Police, Pyramid Lake, Nevada, Lake Seal Center, 7-Point Star, Enamel, 2 ½ In. 130.00
Police, Tom's River, New Jersey, State Seal Center, Embossed 50.00
Presentation, Alderman John P. Douglass, 11th Ward, Brooklyn, 18K Gold, 1872, 1 In. .... *illus* 1708.00
Press, International Live Stock Exposition, Buildings, Brass, Green Enamel, 1927 .... 65.00
Prison Guard, Sing Sing, New York, State Seal, Blue Enamel Ground, 2 ¼ In. 50.00

Badge, Deputy Sheriff, Kern County, Ca., Eagle, Shield, Gold Plated, Blue, 1915-25, 2 In.
$100.00

Badge, Police, Orange, California, Brass, Enamel, 3 In.
$290.00

Badge, Presentation, Alderman John P. Douglass, 11th Ward, Brooklyn, 18K Gold, 1872, 1 In.
$1708.00

TIP

Don't put your name on your mailbox, front door mat, or screen door. It helps burglars find your phone number, then find out when you are away.

Bank, Bank Building, Globe Savings Fund, Cast Iron, Painted, Kyser & Rex, 1890 $2640.00

Bank, Bird, Long Beak, Painted, Spelter, Germany, 1920-35 $1045.00

Bank, Frog, Singing, Painted, Lead, Germany, 3 ¼ In. $363.00

BANKS of metal have been made since 1868. There are still banks, mechanical banks, and registering banks (those that show the total money deposited on the face of the bank). Many old iron or tin banks have been reproduced since the 1950s in iron or plastic. Some old reproductions marked *Book of Knowledge, John Wright*, or *Capron* are listed. Pottery, glass, and plastic banks are also listed here. Mickey Mouse and other Disneyana banks are listed in Disneyana. We have added the M numbers based on *The Penny Bank Book: Collecting Still Banks* by Andy and Susan Moore and the R numbers based on *Coin Banks by Banthrico* by James L. Redwine.

Apollo Moon, Cast Resin, Royal Design Of Florida, 6 ½ In. 99.00
Apple, Leaves, Cast Iron, Kyser & Rex, c.1882, M 1621, 3 x 5 ¼ In. . . . . 632.00 to 920.00
Aunt Jemima, Cast Iron, A.C. Williams, c.1905, M 168, 5 ⅞ In. 150.00
Baby In Cradle, Bird, Cast Iron, Tin Base, 1890s, 3 ¼ x 4 In.. . . . . 115.00
Baby In Cradle, Nickeled Cast Iron, Steel Bed, 1890s, M 51, 3 ¼ x 4 In.. . . . . 355.00 to 1035.00
Bank Building, Bureaux Caisse, Cupola, Flag, Embossed, Iron, Japanned, M 1137, 6 ½ x 4 ¾ In. 287.00
Bank Building, Cast Iron, Japanned Finish, Bronze, Gold Highlights, Kenton, 6 In. 230.00
Bank Building, Cast Iron, Red, Green, Yellow, Kyser & Rex, M 1633, 5 ¾ In. 863.00
Bank Building, Crown Bank, Iron, White, Red, Blue, Green Trim, J. & E. Stevens, M 1225, 3 1⁄4 In. 374.00
Bank Building, Cupola, Cast Iron, Brown, J. & E. Stevens, M 1146, 4 ⅛ x 3 ⅜ In. 110.00
Bank Building, Cupola, Cast Iron, Brown, Mica Roof, J. & E. Stevens, M 1145, 5 ½ x 4 ½ In.. 175.00
Bank Building, Cupola, Cast Iron, Red, White, Blue Paint, J. & E. Stevens, M 1145, 5 ½ In. . . 546.00
Bank Building, Cupola, Cream, Blue Windows, Red Sills, J. & E. Stevens, M 1145, 5 ½ x 3 In. 119.00
Bank Building, Cupola, Iron, Brown, White, Red Trim, Gray Roof, J. & E. Stevens, M 1445, 5 ½ In. 230.00
Bank Building, Eagle Bank, Cast Iron, U.S., M 1134, 10 In.. . . . . 900.00
Bank Building, Globe Savings Fund, Cast Iron, Painted, Kyser & Rex, 1890 . . . . . *illus* 2640.00
Bank Building, Home, Crown Molded Roof, Iron, Red, White, Blue, J. & E. Stevens, M 1232, 6 In. 1035.00
Bank Building, Home Savings, Animal Head Finial, Cast Iron, Shimer Toys, M 1126, 6 x 4 ½ In. 195.00
Bank Building, Home Savings, Dog Head Finial, Cast Iron, J. & E. Stevens, 1891, M 1126 . . . 220.00
Baseball, On 3 Bats, Cast Iron, Silver, Red Paint, Hubley, M 1608, 5 ¼ In.. . . . . 1380.00
Baseball Player, Bat, Red Cap, Cast Iron, A.C. Williams, c.1900, M 20, 5 ¾ In.. . . . . 1100.00
Baseball Player, Cast Iron, Gold Paint, Red Cap, Socks, A.C. Williams, M 18, 5 ¾ In. 518.00
Beach Wagon, Spoke Wheels, Cabana, Flow Blue Colors, Delftware, c.1920, 4 ¾ In. 86.00
Bear, Stealing Honey, Beehive, Cast Iron, Sydenham & McOustra, M 1308, 7 In.. . . . . 748.00
Belsnickle, Cast Iron, Ives, 7 ½ In. 225.00
Billy Bounce, Give Billy A Penny, Cast Iron, Silver Paint, Hubley, M 154 ¾ In.. . . . . 518.00
Bird, Long Beak, Painted, Spelter, Germany, 1920-35 . . . . . *illus* 1045.00
Birdhouse, Perched Bird, Silvered Lead, Germany, M 653, 4 ¼ In. 115.00
Bishop Bust, Miter Hat, Embossed, Cast Iron, Silver, 4 ⅝ In. 431.00
Black Boy, 2 Faces, A.C. Williams, c.1901, M 84, 3 x 2 ½ In. 125.00
Black Child, Nodding, On Ball, Hand Painted, Tin Box, Germany, 4 ½ In. 805.00
Black Girl, Seated, White Dress, Lead, Hand Painted, Germany, 4 ½ In. 1610.00
Boat, Battleship Iowa, Lifeboats, Masts, Cast Iron, J. & E. Stevens, c.1902, M 1439, 6 x 10 ¼ In. 1455.00
Boat, Battleship Maine, Cast Iron, Gold Trim, Grey Iron Casting, M 1440, 4 ⅝ x 4 ½ In. 374.00
Bottle, Bear Shape, Snow Crest, Screw Cap, 7 In.. . . . . 35.00
Bottle, Fox, 2 Faces, Screw Cap, 8 ¾ In. 35.00
Brown Cab, Mesh Windows, Cast Iron, White, Arcade, 7 ¾ In. 518.00
Buffalo, Cast Iron, U.S. 1970, M 557, 5 x 8 In. 60.00
Building, 2 Story, 6-Sided, Cast Iron, Silver, Gold Roof, M 1008, 3 ¾ In. 86.00
Building, Administration, Nickeled Cast Iron, Embossed, Magic Intro., M 1063, 5 ¼ In. 115.00
Building, Blackpool Tower, Iron, Japanned, Chamberlain & Hill, England, M 954, 7 ⅜ x 4 ⅜ In. 230.00
Building, Castle, 2 Towers, Cast Iron, Japanned Finish, John Harper, M 114, 7 In. 636.00
Building, Eiffel Tower, Embossed, Cast Iron, Black Paint, England, M 1075, 11 In. 1495.00 to 1725.00
Building, Flat Iron, Cast Iron, Kenton, M 1161, 5 ½ In. 201.00
Building, Flat Iron, Cast Iron, Painted, Kenton, M 1159, 8 ¼ In. 1870.00
Building, Gingerbread, Embossed, Silver Plated, Denmark, c.1930s, M 1033, 4 x 4 x 3 In. . . . 144.00
Building, Independence Hall, 3 Slots, Bell, Cast Iron, Enterprise, 1875, 15 ½ In. 593.00
Building, Independence Hall, Cast Iron, Enterprise, M 1242, 10 x 9 ¾ x 9 ⅜ In.. . . . . 690.00
Building, Independence Hall, Copper, Enterprise Mfg., Co., 9 ¾ In. 360.00
Building, Independence Hall, Embossed, Cast Iron, Gold Paint, Enterprise, 11 ½ In.. . . . . 1380.00
Building, Independence Hall Tower, Painted, Cast Iron, M 1205, 9 ½ In. 250.00
Building, Litchfield Cathedral, Iron, Japanned Finish, Chamberlain & Hill, c.1908, M 968, 6 ½ In. 374.00
Building, New England Church, Cast Iron, Aluminum, U.S., M 986, 4 x 7 x 7 ½ In.. . . . . 546.00
Building, Pagoda, Cast Iron, Green, Gold, Silver, England, M 1153, 5 In. 632.00
Building, Palace, Cast Iron, Green Base, Ives, c.1885, M 1116, 7 ½ x 8 In. 1035.00
Building, Tower, Cast Iron, Eagles Finials, John Harper, 9 ½ In.. . . . . 86.00
Building, Tower, Cast Iron, Japanned Finish, Eagle Finials, John Harper, M 1208, 9 ½ In.. . . . 259.00
Building, Villa, Cast Iron, Japanned, Gold Trim, Red Finial, Kyser & Rex, c.1882, M 959, 4 x 3 ⅜ In. 316.00 to 515.00

Building, Westwood Memorial Building, Embossed, Cast Iron, 5 ½ x 3 ½ In. 115.00
Camel, Cast Iron, A.C. Williams, M 767, 7 ¼ x 6 ¼ In. . . . . 200.00 to 250.00
Camel, Kneeling, Backpack, Cast Iron, Kyser & Rex, M 770, 2 ½ x 4 ¾ In. 259.00
Captain Kidd, Cast Iron, Painted, M 38, 6 In. 248.00
Car, Mercury, Die Cast, Maroon, Wood Wheels, Straights Mfg., 1939-40, 5 In. 115.00
Cash Register, Junior Cash, Cast Iron, Gold, J. & E. Stevens, M 931, 5 ¼ x 4 ½ x 4 In. 125.00
Choirboy, Holding Sheet Music, Lead, Hand Painted, Germany, c.1915, M 294, 4 In. 1610.00
Clown, Cast Iron, c.1950, 5 ½ In. 65.00
Clown, Crooked Hat, Cast Iron, Gold Paint, M 210, 6 ¾ In. 287.00
Cope's Dried Sweet Corn, Red, Green, White, Tin, Paper Label, 1950, 6 ½ In. 15.00
Dog, Nipper, Flocked Metal, 6 In. 35.00
Dog, On Tub, Cast Iron, A.C. Williams, M 359, 4 x 2 In. . . . . 200.00 to 230.00
Dog, Pup With Bee, Cast Iron, Black, White, Hubley, 5 ½ In. . . . . 55.00 to 143.00
Duck, Cast Iron, A.C. Williams, M 615, 4 ⅞ In. 100.00
Elephant, Cast Iron, Art Deco, G.O.P., M 450, 4 ⅜ In. 287.00
Elephant, Chariot, Cast Iron, Gray, Green, Yellow, Gold Ears, Hubley, M 479, 12 In. 1725.00
Elephant, Circus, Clown Outfit, Seated, Cast Iron, Hubley, M 462, 4 In. 403.00
Elephant, Gray, Red Blanket, Cast Iron, Kenton, M 487, 5 In. 4025.00
Elephant, On Wheels, A.C. Williams, c.1920, M 446, 4 ⅛ x 4 ⅜ In. 450.00
Fish, Carved Coconut, Scrolled Legend, Souvenir From Ulua, Mexico, 1850, 4 ½ x 3 ½ In. . . . 375.00
Flintstones, Fred Loves Wilma, Apco Manufacturer 180.00
Florida, Orange Bird, Plastic, c.1970, 5 In. 14.00
Football Player, Football Under Arm, Cast Iron, Gold Paint, A.C. Williams, M 11, 5 ⅞ In. 517.00
Frog, Singing, Painted, Lead, Germany, 3 ¼ In. . . . . *illus* 363.00
Gas Stove, Save Your Money & Buy A Gas Stove, c.1901, 5 ¼ x 4 In. 200.00
General Pershing, Cast Iron, Painted, Grey Iron Casting, 1918, M 151, 7 ¾ In. 110.00
Girl On Bed, Painted, Germany, c.1910, 2 ¾ In. 86.00
Golliwog, Cast Iron, Red Pants, Blue Jacket, John Harper, M 85, 6 In. 115.00
Good Luck, Horse, Gold Horseshoe, Cast Iron, Arcade, M 508, 4 ½ x 4 In. 345.00
Hat, Lincoln High Hat, Pass Around The Hat, Cast Iron, Black, M 1380, 3 x 2 ½ In. 50.00
Heart, Engraved Flowers, Footed, Wood, Pa., c.1820-40 . . . . 165.00
Honey Bear, Cast Iron, Gold Paint, M 696, 2 ⅝ In. 489.00
Honey Bear, Licking Paws, Cast Iron, Brown Paint, M 696, 2 ½ x 2 ⅝ In. 115.00
Horse, On Tub, Cast Iron, A.C. Williams, M 509, 5 ½ In. 110.00
Horse, On Wheels, Cast Iron, Gold, Red, M 512, 5 In. . . . . 77.00 to 175.00
Horse, Prancing, On Base, Cast Iron, A.C. Williams, M 520, 7 In. 90.00
Indian Chief, Glass, Green, Wheaton, 6 In. 35.00
Indian Chief, Lanape State Bank, Glass, Ruby Red, Raised Slot, 6 In. 95.00
Indian With Tomahawk, Cast Iron, Brown, Gold Pants, Red Headdress, Hubley, M 228, 5 In. 115.00
Kittens, On Money Bag, Silvered Lead, Germany, 3 ¾ In. 230.00
Kitty, Cast Iron, White, Hubley, M 349, 4 ¾ In. 125.00
Liberty Bell, Sesquicentennial, Cast Iron, Grey Iron Casting, 1926, M 782, 4 In. 75.00
Lincoln Foods, Bottle, Figural, Screw Top, 8 ½ In. 35.00
Lion, On Tub, Cast Iron, A.C. Williams, M 746, 5 ½ In. 90.00
Lion, On Wheels, Cast Iron, Green, A.C. Williams, c.1920, M 760, 4 ½ x 4 ⅝ In. 350.00
Log Cabin Syrup, Figural, Tin, Cabin Shape, Towle's Brand, 3 x 3 ½ In. 230.00
Mammy, Hands On Hips, Cast Iron, Hubley, M 176, 5 ¼ In. 460.00

Mechanical banks were first made about 1870. Any bank with moving parts is considered mechanical. The metal banks made before World War I are the most desirable. Copies and new designs of mechanical banks have been made in metal or plastic since the 1920s. The condition of the paint on the old banks is important. Worn paint can lower a price by 90 percent.

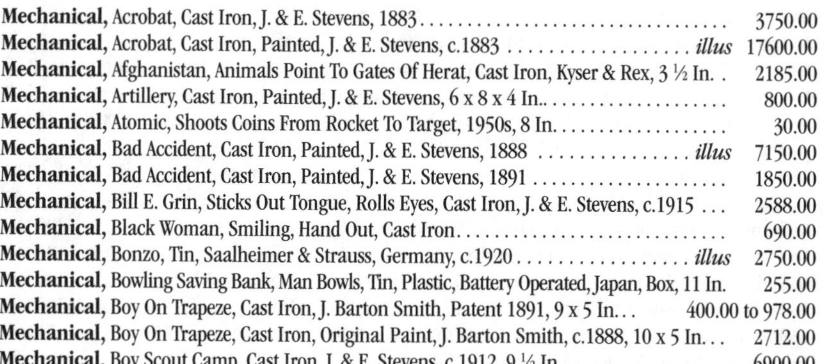

Mechanical, Acrobat, Cast Iron, J. & E. Stevens, 1883 . . . . 3750.00
Mechanical, Acrobat, Cast Iron, Painted, J. & E. Stevens, c.1883 . . . . *illus* 17600.00
Mechanical, Afghanistan, Animals Point To Gates Of Herat, Cast Iron, Kyser & Rex, 3 ½ In. . 2185.00
Mechanical, Artillery, Cast Iron, Painted, J. & E. Stevens, 6 x 8 x 4 In. 800.00
Mechanical, Atomic, Shoots Coins From Rocket To Target, 1950s, 8 In. 30.00
Mechanical, Bad Accident, Cast Iron, Painted, J. & E. Stevens, 1888 . . . . *illus* 7150.00
Mechanical, Bad Accident, Cast Iron, Painted, J. & E. Stevens, 1891 . . . . 1850.00
Mechanical, Bill E. Grin, Sticks Out Tongue, Rolls Eyes, Cast Iron, J. & E. Stevens, c.1915 . . . 2588.00
Mechanical, Black Woman, Smiling, Hand Out, Cast Iron 690.00
Mechanical, Bonzo, Tin, Saalheimer & Strauss, Germany, c.1920 . . . . *illus* 2750.00
Mechanical, Bowling Saving Bank, Man Bowls, Tin, Plastic, Battery Operated, Japan, Box, 11 In. 255.00
Mechanical, Boy On Trapeze, Cast Iron, J. Barton Smith, Patent 1891, 9 x 5 In. . . 400.00 to 978.00
Mechanical, Boy On Trapeze, Cast Iron, Original Paint, J. Barton Smith, c.1888, 10 x 5 In. . . 2712.00
Mechanical, Boy Scout Camp, Cast Iron, J. & E. Stevens, c.1912, 9 ½ In. 6900.00

Bank, Mechanical, Acrobat,
Cast Iron, Painted, J. & E. Stevens, c.1883
$17600.00

Bank, Mechanical, Bad Accident,
Cast Iron, Painted, J. & E. Stevens, 1888
$7150.00

Bank, Mechanical, Bonzo,
Tin, Saalheimer & Strauss,
Germany, c.1920
$2750.00

Bank, Mechanical, Cabin, Cast Iron, Painted, J. & E. Stevens, c.1885
$2200.00

Bank, Mechanical, Calamity, 3 Football Players, Cast Iron, Painted, J. & E. Stevens, 1905
$33000.00

Bank, Mechanical, Clown On Globe, Cast Iron, Painted, J. & E. Stevens, 5/20/1890
$11500.00

Bank, Mechanical, Mama Katzenjammer, Eyes Roll, Cast Iron, Painted, Kenton, c.1905
$10450.00

Mechanical, Boy Stealing Watermelons, Cast Iron, Kyser & Rex, c.1894 .... 1725.00
Mechanical, Bulldog, Seated, Cast Iron, J. & E. Stevens, c.1880, 7 ½ x 7 ¾ x 3 In. 440.00 to 990.00
Mechanical, Bulldog, Standing, Pull Tail, Coin Flies From Nose To Mouth, J. & E. Stevens, c.1880 1495.00
Mechanical, Butting Buffalo, Boy, Tree, Cast Iron, Painted, Pat'd Mar. 20, 1888, Kyser & Rex 1100.00
Mechanical, Cabin, Black Man, Cast Iron, Painted, J. & E. Stevens, 1885 .... 518.00 to 1725.00
Mechanical, Cabin, Black Man, Red Shirt, Blue Trousers, J. & E. Stevens, c.1885, 4 In. 533.00
Mechanical, Cabin, Cast Iron, Painted, J. & E. Stevens, c.1885 .... *illus* 2200.00
Mechanical, Calamity, 3 Football Players, Cast Iron, Painted, J. & E. Stevens, 1905 .... *illus* 33000.00
Mechanical, Cat & Mouse, Press Lever, Kitten Turns Somersault, Cast Iron, J. & E. Stevens, c.1891 1725.00
Mechanical, Chief Big Moon, Cast Iron, J. & E. Stevens, 6 x 10 In. .... 1045.00 to 3450.00
Mechanical, Chief Big Moon, Cast Iron, Red Base, J. & E. Stevens, c.1899 .... 1320.00
Mechanical, Clown, Signed, Gene Bosch, Chein 215.00
Mechanical, Clown On Globe, Cast Iron, Painted, J. & E. Stevens, 5/20/1890 .... *illus* 11500.00
Mechanical, Confectionary, Girl At Counter, Cast Iron, Kyser & Rex, c.1891 .... 9560.00
Mechanical, Cupid At Piano, Musical, Spelter, Windup, c.1890s 8050.00
Mechanical, Darktown Battery, Baseball, Cast Iron, Painted, J. & E. Stevens, 9 ¾ In. 1210.00 to 9200.00
Mechanical, Darktown Battery, Cast Iron, Painted, Wood Box, c.1888, 9 ¾ x 7 In. 14100.00
Mechanical, Destination Moon, Moon Landing, Duro, 1962, 10 ½ In. 73.00
Mechanical, Dinah Bust, Yellow Sleeve, Cast Iron, John Harper, England, 1911 .... 840.00
Mechanical, Dog, On Turntable, Cast Iron, Copper Finish, H.L. Judd, 5 x 4 In. 518.00
Mechanical, Dog, On Turntable, Cast Iron, H.L. Judd, 1895 .... 1870.00
Mechanical, Dog, On Turntable, Dog Deposits Penny, Gold Base, H.L. Judd, 1870s 374.00
Mechanical, Eagle & Eaglets, Cast Iron, Painted, J. & E. Stevens, Patent 1883, 6 x 8 In. 316.00 to 700.00
Mechanical, Elephant, 3 Clowns, Cast Iron, Painted, J. & E. Stevens, c.1882 ..... 2185.00 to 2200.00
Mechanical, Elephant, Howdah, Cast Iron, Enterprise, 1884, 6 x 6 ½ In. .... 193.00 to 250.00
Mechanical, Elephant, Howdah, Man Pops Out, Cast Iron, Enterprise, 1884 .... 650.00
Mechanical, Elephant, Howdah, Pull Tail, Trunk Swings, Iron, White, Hubley, c.1930 99.00 to 201.00
Mechanical, Frog On Lattice, Cast Iron, Painted, J. & E. Stevens, Patent 1872, 4 x 4 In. 495.00 to 1320.00
Mechanical, Frogs, Cast Iron, J. & E. Stevens, c.1882, 4 ¼ x 9 x 3 ½ In. .... 600.00 to 990.00
Mechanical, General Butler, Caricature, Frog's Body, Cast Iron, J. & E. Stevens, 6 ½ In. 1495.00
Mechanical, Giant, Standing, Cast Iron, H.L. Judd 6000.00
Mechanical, Girl Skipping Rope, Cast Iron, J. & E. Stevens 10670.00
Mechanical, Hall's Excelsior, Cashier Receives Deposit, Iron, Red, J. & E. Stevens, c.1869 142.00 to 711.00
Mechanical, Hall's Liliput, Cast Iron, Painted, J. & E. Stevens, 1877, 4 ¼ x 3 ¼ In. 600.00 to 1100.00
Mechanical, Hall's Liliput Bank, Green, Cupola, Coin Return Door, Teller, J. & E. Stevens, 3 In. 504.00
Mechanical, Hen & Chick, Chick Pecks Coin, Iron, White, J. & E. Stevens, 1901, 5 In. 895.00 to 2300.00
Mechanical, Hold The Fort, 7 Holes In Fort, Cast Iron 5500.00
Mechanical, Home Bank, Dormers, Roof, Cashier, Cast Iron, J. & E. Stevens, 1872, 3 ¾ In. ... 3851.00
Mechanical, Horse Race, Cast Iron, Sheet Metal, 5 ½ In. 2070.00
Mechanical, Humpty Dumpty, Clown Head, Cast Iron, Shepard Hardware, 1882, 7 ½ In. 316.00 to 1200.00
Mechanical, I Always Did 'Spise A Mule, Boy On Bench, J. & E. Stevens, 1879, 10 In. 1035.00 to 1126.00
Mechanical, Indian Shooting Bear, Cast Iron, Brown, J. & E. Stevens, c.1900 .... 1000.00 to 1610.00
Mechanical, Indian Squaw Cooking, Frog In Pond, Cast Iron, J. & E. Stevens, c.1899, 5 ¾ In. 1075.00
Mechanical, Jolly Nigger, Bust, Butterfly Tie, Cast Iron, John Harper, England, 1880s, 6 In. .. 720.00
Mechanical, Jonah & The Whale, Shepard Hardware, Patent 1890, 10 ¼ In. .... 1220.00 to 1540.00
Mechanical, Jumbo Savings, On Wheels, Elephant Head Nods, Cast Iron, c.1883 .... 230.00
Mechanical, Leap Frog, Cast Iron, Painted, Shepard Hardware, 1891 .... 644.00 to 2700.00
Mechanical, Lighthouse, Cast Iron, Painted, c.1890, 10 ¼ In. .... 2015.00 to 9460.00
Mechanical, Lion & 2 Monkeys, Cast Iron, Kyser & Rex, 8 ½ In. .... 1070.00 to 1422.00
Mechanical, Lion Hunter, Teddy Roosevelt, Cast Iron, J. & E. Stevens, 7 ½ In. .... 2760.00 to 7810.00
Mechanical, Magic, Door Opens, Cashier Puts Money In Vault, Yellow, J. & E. Stevens, c.1886 316.00
Mechanical, Mama Katzenjammer, Eyes Roll, Cast Iron, Painted, Kenton, c.1905 ..... *illus* 10450.00
Mechanical, Mammy & Child, Cast Iron, Kyser & Rex, c.1884 .... 1955.00
Mechanical, Merry-Go-Round, Cast Iron, Painted, Kyser & Rex, c.1888 .... 8140.00
Mechanical, Milking Cow, Cow Kicking Man, Cast Iron, Painted, J. & E. Stevens, c.1888 431.00 to 1650.00
Mechanical, Monkey & Coconut, Coin In Monkey's Hand, Cast Iron, J. & E. Stevens, Dated 3-2-1886 1155.00
Mechanical, Monkey With Tray, Press Tail, Monkey's Arm Rises, Head Tilts, Tin Lithograph, c.1900 230.00
Mechanical, Mule, Boy, Cast Iron, Painted J. & E. Stevens, Conn., c.1897, 6 In. 1304.00
Mechanical, Mule Entering Barn, Cast Iron, Gray, J. & E. Stevens, Patent 1/6/1880 .... 2300.00
Mechanical, Mule Entering Barn, Cast Iron, J. & E. Stevens, 1880, 8 ½ In. .... 504.00 to 700.00
Mechanical, Mule Entering Barn, Cast Iron, Painted, Kyser & Rex, 1880 .... 2090.00
Mechanical, National Cash Register, Cast Iron, 6 ½ x 5 ¼ In. 230.00
Mechanical, Novelty Bank, Swing-Out Cashier, Cast Iron, J. & E. Stevens, c.1873, 7 In. 1007.00
Mechanical, Old Woman In Shoe, Cast Iron, Painted, W.S. Reed, c.1884 .... *illus* 230000.00
Mechanical, Organ, Boy & Girl, Monkey, Cast Iron, Kyser & Rex, 1882, 5 ⅜ In. 711.00
Mechanical, Organ, Cast Iron, Kyser & Rex, 1890s 650.00

Mechanical, Organ, Cat & Dog, With Monkey, Cast Iron, Kyser & Rex, 1882 ..... 750.00 to 1180.00
Mechanical, Organ, Monkey, Cast Iron, Brown, Yellow, Kyser & Rex, 4 In. 385.00
Mechanical, Organ Grinder & Bear, Cast Iron, Painted, Kyser & Rex, 1890s, 6 ¾ x 5 x 5 ½ In. 2420.00
Mechanical, Organ Grinder & Monkey, Cast Iron, Hubley, c.1925 .... 2300.00
Mechanical, Owl, Cast Iron, Original Paint, J. & E. Stevens, c.1880, 7 In. 472.00
Mechanical, Owl Turns Head, Cast Iron, J. & E. Stevens, 1880, 7 ¾ x 4 In.. ...... 245.00 to 889.00
Mechanical, Paddy & The Pig, Cast Iron, Painted, J. & E. Stevens, c.1886 .... 1200.00
Mechanical, Pay Phone, Ball Rings, Cast Iron, Painted, c.1926 .... 660.00
Mechanical, Peg-Leg Beggar, Cast Iron, H.L. Judd, c.1880 .... 1265.00
Mechanical, Penny Pineapple, Commemorates Hawaii As 50th State, Cast Iron, John Wright, 9 In. 517.00
Mechanical, Piano, Musical, Cast Iron, Nickel Finish, Keywind, Roche Novelty Co. 374.00
Mechanical, Pig In High Chair, Cast Iron, J. & E. Stevens, 5 ¾ x 3 In. .... 533.00 to 875.00
Mechanical, Presto, Pull Drawer, Cast Iron, Painted, Kyser & Rex, c.1894 .... 115.00
Mechanical, Punch & Judy, Cast Iron, Shepard Hardware, 1884. .... 633.00 to 1175.00
Mechanical, Rabbit, Standing, Cast Iron, Lockwood, 1882 .... *illus* 2200.00
Mechanical, Rabbit In Cabbage, Cast Iron, Painted, Kilgore. .... 350.00 to 825.00
Mechanical, Reclining Chinaman, Cast Iron, J. & E. Stevens, Patent 1885, 5 x 8 In. 1100.00
Mechanical, Red Riding Hood, Cast Iron, W.S. Reed 28600.00
Mechanical, Rocket, Shoots Coin Into Nose, Astro Mfg., 1957, 13 ¼ In. 114.00
Mechanical, Royal Trick Elephant, Tin, Germany, c.1912, 4 ½ In. 978.00
Mechanical, Saluting Sailor, Tin, Saalheimer & Strauss, Germany 1090.00
Mechanical, Saluting Sailor, Tin Lithograph, Saalheimer & Strauss, Germany, c.1915 .. *illus* 770.00
Mechanical, Santa Claus, At Chimney, Cast Iron, Red, Shepard Hardware, 1889, 5 ¾ x 3 In. 660.00 to 1540.00
Mechanical, Satellite, Rocket Ship, Key, Die Cast, Duro Mold & Mfg., 10 ½ In.. .... 124.00
Mechanical, Satellite, Shoots Coins Into Rocket Nose, 1950s, 8 In. 148.00
Mechanical, Sewing Machine, Cast Iron, American Sewing Machine Co., c.1880. .... 15400.00
Mechanical, Shoot That Hat, Boy Lowers Hat On Seated Boy's Head, Cast Iron, c.1882 ...... 2875.00
Mechanical, Snake & Frog, In Pond, Tin, Germany 3738.00
Mechanical, Snap It, Building, Turn Pin, Cast Iron, Black, H.L. Judd, 4 In. 431.00
Mechanical, Spaceship, Shoots Coin In Globe, River Oaks State Bank, Houston, 1960, 3 x 9 In. 60.00
Mechanical, Speaking Dog, Cast Iron, John Harper, 1902 .... 1150.00
Mechanical, Speaking Dog, Girl In Blue Dress, Cast Iron, J. & E. Stevens, c.1885. .... 1380.00
Mechanical, Speaking Dog, Girl In Red Dress, Cast Iron, J. & E. Stevens, 7 ¼ In. 356.00
Mechanical, Speaking Dog, Girl In Red Dress, Cast Iron, Shepard Hardware, Pat. 1885, 7 x 7 In. 413.00
Mechanical, Springing Cat, Chase The Mouse, Lead, Wood, Charles A. Bailey 13200.00
Mechanical, Strato, Rocket Ship, Key, Duro Mold & Mfg., Box, 10 ½ In. 181.00
Mechanical, Strato, Shoots Coins From Rocket To Moon, Duro, 1950s, 8 In. 65.00
Mechanical, Stump Speaker, Black Man, Top Hat, Shepard Hardware, 1886..... 1850.00 to 4025.00
Mechanical, Sweet Thrift, Tin, Beverly Novelty, c.1928 .... 144.00
Mechanical, Symphonion Musical Savings, Wood, Windup, Germany, c.1900 .... 6900.00
Mechanical, Tabby Cat On Egg, Cast Iron 201.00
Mechanical, Tammany, Blue Jacket, Cast Iron, J. & E. Stevens, c.1873 .... 259.00
Mechanical, Tammany, Cast Iron, Painted, J. & E. Stevens, 1873 .... 205.00 to 469.00
Mechanical, Tank & Cannon, Cast Iron, Starkie .... 633.00 to 1320.00
Mechanical, Teddy & The Bear, Cast Iron, Blue, Brown, J. & E. Stevens, 9 ¾ In. .. 1195.00 to 1659.00
Mechanical, Tommy Bank, Cast Iron, John Harper, England. 3300.00
Mechanical, Trick Dog, Yellow Clown, Solid Base, Cast Iron, Hubley, c.1930 .... *illus* 3850.00
Mechanical, Trick Pony, Cast Iron, Shepard Hardware, Pat. 1885, 8 x 7 ½ In.. ... 402.00 to 1150.00
Mechanical, Try Your Weight Scale, Tin, Germany, c.1907 .... 1495.00
Mechanical, Uncle Sam, Jaw Opens, Coin Goes Into Satchel, Shepard Hardware, 1886 1380.00 to 6500.00
Mechanical, Vending, Chocolat Menier, Kiosk, 6-Sided, Tin, 9 ½ In. 237.00
Mechanical, Vending, Star & 3 Clowns, Stollwerck, Germany 288.00
Mechanical, Vending, Tit-Bits, Tin, Lehmann, Germany, c.1889 .... 2875.00
Mechanical, Vending, Victoria, Spar Automat, Chocolate, Tin Lithograph, Stollwerck, Germany, 11 In. 978.00
Mechanical, Vending, Victoria, Tin, Stollwerck, Germany 460.00
Mechanical, Watchdog Safe, Dog Opens Mouth, Cast Iron, J. & E. Stevens, c.1880. .... 374.00
Mechanical, Weeden's Plantation Darky Savings, Tin, Windup, Weeden Mfg., c.1888... 1035.00 to 8050.00
Mechanical, William Tell, Cast Iron, Painted, J. & E. Stevens, 1886, 10 x 6 In. ... 431.00 to 770.00
Mechanical, Zoo, Monkey, Lion, Bear, Cast Iron, Kyser & Rex, 1890, 4 x 4 In. 750.00
Merry-Go-Round, Cast Iron, Grey Iron Casting Co., M 1614, 4 ½ In. 431.00
Merry-Go-Round, Cast Iron, Painted, Kenton, c.1900 .... *illus* 1100.00
Metro Van, First Gear, Roberts Dairy Graphics 50.00
Mill House, Water Wheel, Trees, Porcelain, 3 ½ In. 230.00
Minuteman, Soldier, Holding Rifle, Cast Iron, Hubley, M 44, 6 In.. .... 431.00
Monkey, Smoking Cigarette, Red Fez, Hinged Head, Lead, Hand Painted, Germany, M 739, 4 ½ In. 805.00
Mulligan, None So Good, Billy Club, Embossed Lettering, Cast Iron, 5 ¾ In. 460.00

Bank, Mechanical, Old Woman In Shoe, Cast Iron, Painted, W.S. Reed, c.1884
$230000.00

Bank, Mechanical, Rabbit, Standing, Cast Iron, Lockwood, 1882
$2200.00

Bank, Mechanical, Saluting Sailor, Tin Lithograph, Saalheimer & Strauss, Germany, c.1915
$770.00

B

Bank, Mechanical, Trick Dog, Yellow Clown, Solid Base, Cast Iron, Hubley, c.1930
$3850.00

Bank, Merry-Go-Round, Cast Iron, Painted, Kenton, c.1900
$1100.00

Bank, Register, Building, Cast Iron, Painted, Kyser & Rex, c.1890, M 1200
$9350.00

Mutt & Jeff, Cast Iron, Painted, A.C. Williams, M 157, 5 In. 70.00 to 77.00
National Bank, Medallion & Leaves, 3 Glass Sides, Cast Iron, Hinged Lid, 6 x 6 ¾ In. 90.00
National Safe Deposit, Cast Iron, Sheet Metal, M 986 325.00
Owl, Be Wise & Save, Cast Iron, A.C. Williams, M 598, 5 In. 80.00 to 90.00
Owl, Cast Iron, Brown, White, Vindex, M 597, 4 ¼ In. 275.00
Pelican, Cast Iron, White, Green Oval Base, Hubley, M 679, 4 ¾ In. 690.00
Pickaninny, Cast Iron, Red Shirt, White Collar, Blue Bowtie, M 171, England, 5 ⅛ In. 259.00
Pig, I Made Chicago Famous, Cast Iron, John Harper, c.1902, M 631, 5 ½ In. 86.00
Piggy, Glass, Amber, Hobnail, Mold, 3 ⅛ In. 35.00
Piggy, Glass, Carnival, Marigold Iridescent, Anchor Hocking, 4 In. 12.50
Piggy, Glass, Ruby Red, Raised Slot, 3 In. 18.00
Pittsburgh Paints, Smooth As Glass, Paper Label, 3 x 2 ¾ In. 134.00
Plan-It, Solar System, Sun, Planets, Die Cast, Astro, 1950s, 9 In. 55.00 to 173.00
Polish Rooster, Cast Iron, Black, White Plumes, Red Wattle, M 1646, 5 ½ In. 1725.00
Possum, Cast Iron, Gold Paint, Arcade, 1910-13, M 561, 2 ⅜ x 4 ⅜ In. 500.00 to 747.00
Potbelly Stove, Glass, Blue, Raised Slot, Wheaton, 6 In. 45.00
Potbelly Stove, Glass, Green, Raised Slot, Wheaton, 6 In. 45.00
Rabbit, On Base, Cast Iron, Japanned Finish, 1884, M 569, 3 In. 546.00
Radio, Cast Iron, Sheet Metal, Kenton, M 831, 3 ⅜ x 4 ½ x 3 ¼ In. 250.00
Radio, Green, Combination Door, Cast Iron, Sheet Metal, Kenton, M 833 80.00
Recruit, Cutie, Cast Iron, White, Blue, Full Figure, John Harper, England, c.1918, 6 In. 115.00
Red Goose School Shoes, Goose, Cast Iron, Red, 3 ¾ x 2 ½ x 1 ½ In. 88.00
Red Goose Shoes, Goose, Cast Iron, Arcade, c.1920, M 610, 3 ¾ x 2 ½ x 1 ½ In. 300.00
Red Goose Shoes, Goose, Cast Iron, Red Paint, 4 ½ In. 70.00 to 275.00
Register, Building, Cast Iron, Painted, Kyser & Rex, c.1890, M 1200 *illus* 9350.00
Register, Kettle, Cast Iron, Nickel, 3 x 4 In. 193.00
Register, National Recording, Dime, Cast Iron, Marked, Pat'd. Apl. 7, 91, 6 ¾ In. 187.00
Register, Uncle Sam's, 3 Coin, Tin, Black Paint, Durable Toy & Novelty, Mich., 6 ¼ In. 20.00
Rhino, Cast Iron, Arcade, M 721, 2 ⅝ In. 400.00
Rhino, Cast Iron, Black, Gold Horn, Arcade, 2 ⅝ x 5 In. 431.00
Rocking Chair, Cast Iron, Manning, c.1898, M 1375, 6 ¾ In. 230.00
Rooster, Cast Iron, Black, Red Wattle & Comb, Decal, Arcade, M 547, 4 In. 288.00
Safe, Diamond, Cast Iron, 7 ½ x 6 ½ x 5 ½ In. 200.00
Safe, Junior Safe Deposit, Cast Iron, M 898, 4 ½ x 3 ¼ x 2 In. 60.00
Safe, Little Red Riding Hood, Cast Iron, Harper, c.1907, M 25, 5 In. 4313.00
Santa Claus, With Sack, Cast Iron, Red, Silver, Harper, c.1907, M 63, 4 ⅛ In. 4313.00
Security Peoples Trust Co., Ceramic, Brown, 3 x 3 ½ x 4 ½ In. 65.00
Silo, Marietta, Cast Iron, Gray, Silver Roof, M 1246, 5 ½ In 575.00 to 862.00
Soldier, Doughboy, Cast Iron, Yellow, Grey Iron Casting, c.1919, M 48, 7 x 2 ½ x 2 ¼ In. 250.00
Space Heater, Cupid, Cast Iron, England, c.1895, M 1090, 6 ½ In. 115.00
Statue Of Liberty, Cast Iron, Green Paint, Kenton, M 1166, 10 In. 862.00
Steamboat, Cast Iron, A.C. Williams, M 1459, 2 x 8 In. 425.00
Steamboat, Cast Iron, Gold Paint, Arcade, M 1460, 7 ½ In. 201.00
Stove, Parlor, Reliable, Cast Iron, Red Inserts, Schneider & Trenkamp, M 1356, 6 ¼ In. 345.00
Street Clock, Cast Iron, Red, Gold Face, Pressed Steel Back, A.C. Williams, M 1548, 6 In. 403.00
Teddy Bear, Cast Iron, Black, Arcade, M 694, 2 ½ x 3 ⅞ In. 225.00
Thermos Anti-Freeze, Snowman, Tin, 2 ¾ In. 30.00
Three Wise Monkeys, Cast Iron, A.C. Williams, M 743, 3 ¼ x 3 ½ In. 250.00
Transvaal Money Box, Man, Smoking, Movable Pipe, Cast Iron, Painted, 6 x 4 In. 175.00
Trolley, Floor Rolls, Cast Iron, Silver, Kenton, 5 ¼ In. 259.00
Trolley, Main Street, People In Windows, A.C. Williams, c.1920, M 1471, 3 x 7 x 2 In. 259.00 to 325.00
Trolley, Marquee On Roof, Embossed, Cast Iron, c.1889, M 1468, 4 x 4 ½ In. 201.00
Uncle Sam, Glass, Blue, Wheaton, 6 In. 45.00
Vegetable Man, Vinyl, Kraft, 1960s, 7 In. 65.00
Washington Monument, Cast Iron, Gold Over Black, A.C. Williams, M 1049, 8 In. 345.00
Water Wheel, Nickeled Cast Iron, Tin Base, M 1606, 4 ½ In. 1495.00
Windmill, Spins, Cast Iron, Japanned, Base, 5 ¼ x 4 ¼ x 7 ½ In. 201.00
Windmill, Spins, Nickeled Cast Iron, England, 4 ½ In. 4313.00
Wise Pig, Thrifty, Cast Iron, White, Pink, Red, Hubley, 6 ⅝ x 2 ⅞ In. 99.00
Yellow Cab, Cast Iron, Orange, Black, Arcade, 8 In. 633.00
Yellow Cab, Steel Wheels, Cast Iron, 4 ¼ x 7 ⅞ In. 403.00

BANKO is a group of rustic Japanese wares made in the nineteenth and twentieth centuries. Some pieces are made of mosaics of colored clay; some are fanciful teapots. Redware and other materials were also used.

Humidor, Elephant In Barrel, Green, White, Red, 8 x 5 ½ In. 270.00

Humidor, Sailor 7, Lucky God Daikoku, Green Hat, 1930s, 6 ¼ x 5 In. 325.00
Nodder, Geisha, Seated, Holding Flowers, Blue Dress, 1930s, 4 x 4 In. 130.00
Nodder, Geisha, Seated, Wearing Hat, Floral Kimono, Japan, 1930s, 4 x 4 In. 143.00
Nodder, Geisha, Seated, Wearing Hat, Yellow, Blue Flowers, 1930s, 4 x 3 ⅔ In. 130.00
Nodder, Geisha, Seated, Wrapping Arms Around Herself, 1930s, 4 ⅛ x 3 ½ In. 150.00
Nodder, Samurai, 1930s, 4 ½ x 4 In. 110.00
Nodder, Samurai, Seated, Holding Fan, 1920s, 3 ¾ x 2 ¾ In. 100.00
Teapot, Double Tanuki Badger, Flying Cranes, Figural, 4 ½ x 7 ¼ In. 50.00
Teapot, Phoenix Form, Blue, Green, Red, Yellow, Orange, Marked, 5 ½ x 7 In. 150.00
Wall Pocket, Monkey With Peach, Figural, 4 ¾ x 5 In. 310.00

BARBER collectibles range from the popular red and white striped pole that used to be found in front of every shop to the small scissors and tools of the trade. Barber chairs are wanted, especially the older models with elaborate iron trim.

Chair, Brown, Reclining, Rolling Stool, Narda, 44 x 49 x 40 In. 1200.00
Chair, Cast Iron, Plated Metal, Enamel, Vinyl Upholstery, Theo. A. Kochs Co., 1920s, 41 In.... 10575.00
Chair, Chrome, Enamel, Red Leather, Koken 925.00
Chair, Hat & Coat Rack, Porcelain, Wood Pole, Nickel Rack, Koken, 82 In. 4012.00
Chair, Horse Head On Seat, Dark Green, Porcelain, Child's, 18 x 44 In. 1100.00
Chair, Oak, Burgundy Velvet, Diamond Tuck, Koken, 47 x 44 x 26 In. .... *illus* 1000.00
Chair, Oak, Leather, Figural Animal Head Armrests, Upholstered, 45 In. 1550.00
Chair, Oak, Red Velvet, Hydraulic Pedestal, Label, Collins, Koken Barber's Supply Co. 1840.00
Chair, Porcelain, Black Vinyl, Chrome Footrest, Koken, 48 x 28 x 38 In. 3500.00
Chair, Salesman's Sample, Leather Upholstery, c.1900, 16 x 10 x 16 In. 34800.00
Chair, Salesman's Sample, St. Louis, Koken, 16 x 14 In. 11000.00
Chair, Wood, Plank Seat, Stool Form Base, Child's, 19th Century, 35 ½ In. 205.00
Pole, Cast Iron, Tin, Pieced Baluster Body, Red, White, Blue, c.1909, 80 In. 1210.00
Pole, Pine, Red, White, Blue, Gold, Brackets, Late 19th Century, 41 In. .... *illus* 500.00
Pole, Red, White, Blue, Electric, Dome Metal Top & Bottom, 23 ½ In. 175.00
Pole, Red, White, Blue, Rotates, Light-Up, 40 x 12 In. 2600.00
Pole, Red, White, Blue, Wm. Marley Co., 48 In. 59.00
Pole, Wood, Eagle Finial, Turned, Iron Bracket, 45 In. 1980.00
Pole, Wood, Red, White, Blue, Carved, Gold Ball, 20th Century, 34 ½ In. 275.00
Pole, Wood, Red, White, Blue, Gold Ball, Iron Hangers, 41 In. 170.00
Pole, Wood, Red, White, Blue, Gold Ball, Stepped Base, c.1900, 86 ½ In. 2340.00
Pole, Wood, Red, White, Blue, Stars & Stripes, Gold Acorn Terminals, Turned, 35 ½ In. 9000.00
Pole, Wood, Red, White, Blue, Turned Acorn Ends, c.1885, 35 In. 588.00
Pole, Wood, Red, White, Carved, Globe Finial 4 Bracket Holes, c.1910, 35 In. 353.00
Pole, Wood, Red & White, Stripes, Blue Band, Globe Finial, 20th Century, 58 In. 881.00
Rack, Hat, Coat, Wood, Nickel, Porcelain Base, Koken, 74 In. 550.00
Shaving Paper Vase, Horizontal Bands, 6-Sided Indents, Ground Lip, Blue, c.1885, 7 In. 316.00
Sign, Barber Shop, Pole, Die Cut, Enamel Over Metal, 2-Sided, 1920, 36 x 24 In. 187.00
Sign, Barber Shop, Red, White, Blue Stripes, Curved, Porcelain, Steel Brackets, 24 x 16 In.... 200.00
Sign, Barber Shop, Red, White & Blue Stripes, Curved, Porcelain, c.1940, 15 x 24 In. 230.00
Sign, Barber Shop, Red, White Blue, Enamel, 2-Sided, c.1940, 12 x 26 In. 25.00
Sign, Bergeron's Barber Shop, Shield Form, Black, White, Red, 22 x 28 In. 300.00
Sign, Pole, Modern Service, Red, White, Blue, Porcelain, 48 x 8 In. 185.00
Sign, Striped Pole, Half Round, Red, White, Blue, Enameled, Bob White Sign Co., c.1950, 48 In. 3055.00
Vase, Waste, Dutch Windmill Scene, Pink Ground, 14 In. 472.00

BAROMETERS are used to forecast the weather. Antique barometers with elaborate wooden cases and brass trim are the most desirable. Mercury column barometers are also popular with collectors. It is difficult to find someone to repair a broken one, so be sure your barometer is in working condition.

Aneroid, Lizars, Carved, 1870, 39 ⅝ x 12 In. 1750.00
Aneroid, Marble, Round Dial, Tapered Turned Foot, Early 20th Century, 10 ¾ In. 533.00
Aneroid, Thermometer, Brass, Exposed Movement, England, c.1900 .... 485.00
Angelus, Brass, Ship's Wheel Shape, Pedestal, 11 ¼ In. 144.00
Banjo, A. Vigano, Regency, Mahogany, Flower & Shell Inlay, Signed, 39 ½ In. 936.00
Banjo, Cetti & Co., Regency, Mahogany, Inlay, Inscribed, 38 In. 819.00
Banjo, Gally, Regency, Mahogany, Inlaid Flowers, Shells, Signed, London, 38 In. 400.00
Banjo, J. Della Torre, Regency, Mahogany, Inscribed, Perth, 1800s, 39 ¼ In. .... *illus* 468.00
Banjo, John Schalfino Tauntan, Regency, Mahogany, Shell Inlay, Signed, c.1835, 38 In. 610.00
Banjo, L. Braham & Co., English Oak, Carved, London, c.1860 .... 3500.00
Banjo, Mahogany, Shell & Floral Inlay, Silvered Dial, Inscribed, Salop, 38 ¼ In. 178.00

Barber, Chair, Oak, Burgundy Velvet, Diamond Tuck, Koken, 47 x 44 x 26 In
$1000.00

Barber, Pole, Pine, Red, White, Blue, Gold, Brackets, Late 19th Century, 41 In.
$500.00

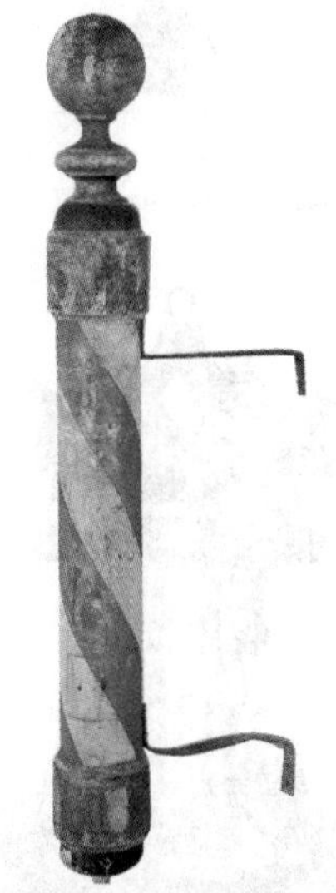

TIP

Don't burn red, green, black, or dark blue candles where they might drip on a wooden surface. The color may bleed into the wood. Put a dish or aluminum foil under the candle holder. Be careful of votive candles too. If burned too low, they can heat the glass holder and scorch the wood.

BAROMETER

Barometer, Banjo, P. Salomon Guisbro, Regency, Mahogany, Signed, 19th Century, 38 ¼ In.
$468.00

Barometer, Foranderligt, Leaves, Twigs, Wood, Carved, Signed, 17 ¼ In.
$117.00

TIP
Stains can be removed from woven baskets with a diluted solution of hydrogen peroxide.

Banjo, Mattoni Sheffield, Regency, Mahogany, Signed, 19th Century, 38 ½ In. 878.00
Banjo, Oreggia, George III, Mahogany, Inlay, 4 Gauge, Broken Scrolling Arch Pediment. 418.00
Banjo, P. Salomon Guisbro, Regency, Mahogany, Signed, 19th Century, 38 ¼ In. .... *illus* 468.00
Banjo, Rosewood Veneer, Abalone Inlay, 19th Century, 36 ¼ In. 497.00
Foranderligt, Leaves, Twigs, Wood, Carved, Signed, 17 ¼ In. .... *illus* 117.00
Round, Wood Molded Back, Heavy Glass Bezel, Brass Ring, 9 In. 58.00
Sharman D Neill, Oak, Carved, Marked, Belfast, 26 In. 500.00
Stick, A. Donegan, Mahogany, Inlay, Inscribed, Edinburgh, Scotland, 38 In. 1800.00
Stick, A. Donegan, Mahogany, Inscribed, Edinburgh, Scotland, 19th Century, 38 In. 2106.00
Stick, Acanthus Leaf Crest, Flowers, Wood, Carved, Gilt, England, c.1780, 42 In. 850.00
Stick, J. Jenkins, Mahogany, Ivory Face, Knob, Swansea, 19th Century, 36 x 4 x 3 In. 650.00
Stick, J. Walker, Mahogany, Curved Molded Pediment, 2 Silver Dials, England, c.1800, 37 In. . 2133.00
Stick, J. Williams, Rosewood, Signed, Londonderry, 19th Century, 35 ½ In. 761.00
Stick, Mahogany, Arch Pediment, 2 Columns, Mercury Tube, Label, 1780s, 38 In. 353.00
Stick, Mahogany Veneer, Glass Mercury Tube, Broken Arch, Urn Finial, c.1830, 39 In. 1762.00
Stick, Marine, Brass, Weighted Stem, Portugal, Signed, J.J.B.L.M., Lisbon, 1880, 37 ½ In. 400.00
Stick, Simmons & Son, Rosewood, Engraved, Thermometer Scale, 37 ½ In. 474.00
Stick, Watkins & Hill, Rosewood, Bowfront, London, Silvered Scale, Engraved, 38 In. 5333.00
Thermometer, Admiral Fitzroys, Cottage Style, Oak, Marked, Britain, 1881, 42 x 8 x 2 In. 350.00
Thermometer, Air Guide, Fruitwood, Case, c.1960, 20 In. 45.00
Thermometer, Banjo, Cheron Opticien, 83 Rue Grand-Pont, 19th Century, 36 x 10 In. 275.00
Thermometer, Fatima Cigarettes, Yellow, Red, White, Porcelain, 1920-30, 27 x 7 In. 600.00
Thermometer, Federal, Mahogany, Shell Inlay, Broken Pediment, 39 x 10 In. 495.00
Thermometer, Martin & Co., Oak, Barley Twist, Flower, Leaves, Marked, Antwerp, 27 In. 105.00
Thermometer, Oak, Carved, Art Nouveau, Brass, c.1905, 19 ½ x 8 In. 75.00
Thermometer, R & J Beck, Victorian, Verniers, Wood Knobs, Spiral Reservoir, 45 In. 1896.00
Thermometer, Rohrer Funeral Homes, c.1930, 36 x 12 In. 316.00
Thermometer, Wheel, J. Grafst, Dry-Damp Indicator, Vial, Mahogany Trunk, England, 43 In. 711.00
Wheel, Mahogany, Broken Arch Pediment, String Inlaid Edge, 38 In. 294.00
Wheel, Martinelli, Boxwood, Ebony Strung Mahogany Case, Flame Veneer, 5 Dials, 38 x 10 In. 518.00
Wheel, Scrolled Arch Top, Brass Finial, Veneer Case, Ivory Knob, c.1700, 38 x 10 In. 800.00

BASALT is a special type of ceramic invented by Josiah Wedgwood in the eighteenth century. It is a fine-grained, unglazed stoneware. Some pieces are listed in that section. The most common type is black, but many other colors were made. It was made by many factories. Some pieces are listed in the Wedgwood section.

Bowl, Maidens, Cornucopia, Instruments, Flowers, Black, Signed, L.F.F. Pottery, 3 x 6 ½ In. . . 110.00
Creamer, Lower Ribs, Black, E. Mayer, 1786-1813, 3 ¾ In. 120.00
Creamer, Lower Ribs, Leaf & Ribbed Handle, Black, E. Mayer, 1786-1813, 4 ⅝ In. 140.00
Sugar, Cover, Engine Turned Ribs, Maiden Finial, Black, Mackwood, c.1780, 4 ½ x 4 ½ In. . . 100.00
Sugar, Cover, Flowers, Ribs, 4-Sided, c.1822-30, 4 ½ x 5 ½ In. 50.00
Sugar, Cover, Pot Form, Ribs, Maiden Finial, c.1800, 3 x 3 ¼ In. 85.00
Vase, Chrysanthemums, Incised, Black Matte, Bulbous, Flared, c.1840, 9 ½ x 3 In. 75.00
Vase, Trumpet Form, Scalloped Rim, 11 In. 80.00

BASEBALL *collectibles are in the Sports category, except for baseball cards, which are listed under Baseball in the Card category.*

BASKETS of all types are popular with collectors. American Indian, Japanese, African, Shaker, and many other kinds of baskets can be found. Of course, baskets are still being made, so the collector must learn to tell the age and style of the basket to determine the value.

Apache, Large Geometric Design, Black, Brown, 4 ½ x 8 ½ In. 780.00
Arschbacke, Woven, Oak Splint, Handle, Penn., 19th Century, 10 x 11 ¼ In. 385.00
Buttocks, Splint, Ash, Flat Bentwood Handle, Rim, Ribs, Lobed Sides, 11 ¾ x 17 x 13 In. 55.00
Buttocks, Splint, Cane Woven, Handle, 4 ½ x 5 x 4 In. .... *illus* 700.00
Buttocks, Splint, Oak, Bentwood Handle, Rim, Rib Type, 7 ½ x 9 ¾ x 8 ¾ In. 187.00
Buttocks, Splint, Oak, Bentwood Handle, Rim, Wire Attachment, Rib, 9 ½ x 12 x 12 In. 120.00
Buttocks, Splint, Oak, Blue, Round Ribs, Bentwood Handle, 7 x 7 ½ In. 1650.00
Buttocks, Splint, Oak, Rib Type, Bentwood Handle, Rim, Vertical Weave, 6 x 8 ½ x 7 ¾ In. ... 880.00
Buttocks, Splint, Oak, Ribs, Bentwood Handle, Decorative Rim, Aged Patina, 8 x 8 In. 88.00
Buttocks, Splint, Oak, Ribs, Bentwood Handle, Rim, 10 x 15 x 13 ½ In. 110.00
Carrying, Bentwood Handle, Brown Paint, North Carolina, 1800s, 7 x 7 ¼ In. 535.00
Cutlery, Rye Straw, Oval, Late 19th Century, 8 x 14 ½ In. .... *illus* 1287.00
Dog Carrier, Wicker, Wirework Door, Arched Shape, 21 x 17 x 24 In. 345.00
Egg, Hexagonal, Handle, 19th Century, 3 ½ x 3 ¼ In. 55.00

Feather, Splint, Oak, Woven Cover, New England, 19th Century, 30 x 16 In. 165.00
Field, Round, Oak Splints, Carved & Bentwood Handles, Rim, Yellow, 14 ½ x 19 In. 440.00
Field, Splint, Ash, Yellow, Bentwood Handles, Rim, Round, Flat Bottom, 11 x 18 ½ In. 1210.00
Field, Splint, Oak, 2 Handles, Oval, Double Wrap Rim, Penn., 1800s, 9 x 17 In. 143.00
Field, Splint, Oak, Straight-Sided, Carved Bentwood Handle, Rim, 14 x 14 ½ In. 121.00
Flower, Splint, Oak, Pine, Bentwood Handle, Rim, Rectangular, 12 ¼ x 18 ½ x 8 ½ In. 248.00
Fruit, Splint, Oak, Flared, Wood Bottom, Marked, Mason, 1858, Penn., 5 x 9 ½ In. 660.00
Gathering, Split, Oak, Split Handle, Lattice Style, Double Banded Rim, 13 x 11 In. 110.00
Hickory Splint Staves, Rattan Weaver, Fixed Handles, Wrap Rim, c.1880, 6 x 5 ¼ In. 2090.00
Key, Leather, Tooled, Heart & Star Design, Early 19th Century, 8 ½ x 8 In. 6435.00
Key, Leather, Tooled Design, Boat Form, Early 19th Century, 7 ¼ x 10 x 5 ½ In. 3500.00
Laundry, Hotel, Wicker, Wood Slat Bottom, France, c.1900, 26 ½ x 31 ½ In. 390.00
Laundry, Hotel, Woven Wicker, Pierced Handles, Wood Slat Bottom, 26 x 32 In. 660.00
Leather, Rolled Leather Handle, Black, Scalloped Edge, c.1800, 7 ½ x 2 ½ In. 3055.00
Market, Splint, Oak, Bentwood Handle, Rim, Oval, Round Bottom, 11 ¼ x 14 x 10 ½ In. 143.00
Market, Splint, Oak, Bentwood Handle, Rim, Stained Splits, Elongated, 10 ½ x 17 x 8 In. 44.00
Market, Splint, Oak, Bentwood Handle, Stained, 11 x 14 ½ x 11 In. 100.00
Market, Splint, Oak, Square Bottom, Round Rim, Decorative Weave, 12 ⅜ x 12 ½ x 11 In. 44.00
Market, Splint, Oak, Tapered, Bentwood Handle, Rim, Flat Base, Side Struts, 15 x 15 x 12 In. 110.00
Market, Splint, Round, Handle, 15 x 14 x 14 In. 35.00
Matterson, Swing Handle, Nut Brown Patina, Rhode Island, 1880-90, 4 x 6 In. . . . . *illus* 750.00
Nantucket, Nesting Set, Carved Oak Bail Handle, Jose F. Reyes, c.1970, 15 x 14 In., 10 Piece . . 30810.00
Nantucket, Oval, Oak Bentwood Handles, Woven, Mahogany Bottom, 12 ¾ x 28 x 25 ½ In. . . 4830.00
Nantucket, Purse, Splint, Cane, Cover, Hinges, Wood Panel, Whale, 6 ½ x 9 ½ x 6 ¼ In. 935.00
Nantucket, Swing Handle, Mahogany Bottom, Wrap Rim, Oak Staves, c.1870, 10 x 15 In. . . . 2860.00
Nantucket, Swing Handle, Wood Bottom, Mitchell Ray, 11 ½ x 9 In. 448.00
Nantucket, Swing Handle, Wrap Rim, Oak Staves, Brass Ears, c.1880, 12 x 10 ½ In. 1320.00
Nantucket, Tray, Round, 2 Oak Heart Handles, Mahogany Base, Jose F. Reyes, c.1970, 5 x 25 In. 8888.00
Nantucket, Woven, Bentwood Swing Handle, Copper & Brass Rivets, 5 ½ x 4 In. 323.00
Nantucket, Woven Cane, Turned Wood Base, Bentwood Swing Handle, 4 ½ x 5 ½ In. 440.00
Picnic, Cover, Rectangular, Splint Oak Weave, Hickory Frame, Bentwood Handle, 8 ½ x 18 In. 935.00
Picnic, Splint, Oak, Hickory, Bentwood Handle, J.T. Hill, N.C., 1925, 8 x 18 x 11 In. . . . . *illus* 935.00
Poplar, Sycamore Slats, Carved Handles, Rim, c.1880, 12 x 21 In. . . . . *illus* 1400.00
Potato Stamp, Swing Handle, 6 x 8 x 4 In. 173.00
Rhode Island, Rowse Matterson, Oak Staves, Cane Weaves, c.1900, 4 x 6 ½ In. 187.00
Rice Straw, Cover, Rounded Sides, Footed, 4 ½ x 9 ½ x 5 In. 11.00
Rice Straw, Footed, Oval, Braided Handle, Decorative Weave, 4 ¾ x 8 x 4 ½ In. 44.00
Round, Coiled Body, Fitted Rim, Bundled Straw, Binding, Lid, c.1782, 10 ½ x 12 In. 805.00
Rush, Twig Woven, Handle, Oval, Holds 6 Champagne Bottles, Early 1900s, 19 ½ x 18 In. . . . 360.00
Rye Straw, Coiled Berry, Round, Tapered, Straw Handle Across Top, 6 ¾ x 8 ½ In. 121.00
Rye Straw, Red, Yellow, Green, Purple Design, Pa., c.1900s, 4 ¾ x 11 ½ In. . . . . *illus* 150.00
Rye Straw, Table, Coiled, Footed, Tapered, Open Weave Handles, 3 ½ x 8 ¾ In. 154.00
Seed, Ribbed, Oak Splint, Painted Green, Bentwood Rim, 5 ½ x 16 ½ In. 55.00
Splint, Ash, Bentwood Handles, Round, Ribbed, Carved, Rim, 12 ½ x 14 ½ In. 44.00
Splint, Ash, Carved Bentwood Handle, Rim, Aged Patina, Round, 12 x 8 ½ In. 66.00
Splint, Ash, Cover, Bentwood Handle, Attached, Square Bottom, 13 x 9 x 11 ½ In. 44.00
Splint, Ash, Purse, Oval Top, Multicolored Splints, Rope Handles, 9 x 11 ¾ x 8 In. 55.00
Splint, Ash, Splint Cover, Swing Handle, 19th Century, 4 ½ x 6 ½ In. 187.00
Splint, Ash, Sweetzer, Wood Rim, Handles, New Hampshire, c.1800s, 6 ½ x 6 In. . . . . *illus* 250.00
Splint, Ash, Swing Handle, Double Wrap Rim, Raised Bottom, 1800s, 8 ½ x 12 ½ In. 1100.00
Splint, Ash, Table, Bentwood Handles, Square Bottom, Round Rim, 4 x 9 ¼ x 7 ¼ In. 55.00
Splint, Bentwood, Woven Handle, Ribs, Oval, Shallow, 8 ¾ x 13 ¾ x 13 ½ In. 22.00
Splint, Collecting, Bentwood Handles, Rim, Kidney Bean Shape, 11 ½ x 18 x 11 In. 209.00
Splint, Field, Hardwood, Ribbed Field, Dome Form, 9 ½ x 11 In. 523.00
Splint, Flower, Hardwood, Bentwood Handle, Slatted Ribs, 10 ½ x 19 x 9 ½ In. 55.00
Splint, Gathering, God's-Eye Handle, Sweetgrass Bands, 7 x 9 In. 176.00
Splint, Oak, Bentwood Handle, Ribbed, Aged Patina, 6 x 6 ¾ In. 77.00
Splint, Oak, Bentwood Handle, Ribs, Rim, 4 ½ x 6 ¼ In. 468.00
Splint, Oak, Bentwood Handle, Rim, Convex Cone, 11 ¼ x 11 ½ In. 110.00
Splint, Oak, Bentwood Handle, Rim, Ribbed, Round, Dark Patina, 6 ½ x 7 ½ In. 88.00
Splint, Oak, Carved, Bentwood Handle, Ribs, Dome Shape, Rim, 11 x 13 ½ In. 44.00
Splint, Oak, Cheese, Bentwood Handle, Rim, Open Weave, 14 x 19 ½ In. 176.00
Splint, Oak, Cheese, Carved Rim, New England, 3 ¾ x 13 In. 110.00
Splint, Oak, Double Swing Handle, Belfont, Penn., c.1910, 11 ½ x 13 In. 330.00
Splint, Oak, Flat Ribs, Bentwood Handle, Rim, 6 ½ x 8 ¼ In. 99.00
Splint, Oak, God's-Eye Weave, Bentwood Handle, Rim, Flat Ribs, 8 ½ x 8 ½ In. 209.00
Splint, Oak, God's-Eye Weave, Ribbed, Bentwood Handle, Rim, 6 ¾ x 8 In. 110.00

Basket, Buttocks, Splint, Cane Woven, Handle, 4 ½ x 5 x 4 In.
$700.00

Basket, Cutlery, Rye Straw, Oval, Late 19th Century, 8 x 14 ½ In.
$1287.00

Basket, Matterson, Swing Handle, Nut Brown Patina, Rhode Island, 1880-90, 4 x 6 In.
$750.00

Basket, Picnic, Splint, Oak, Hickory, Bentwood Handle, J.T. Hill, N.C., 1925, 8 x 18 x 11 In.
$935.00

As always, the edited listings in *Kovels' Antiques & Collectibles Price Guide 2010* aren't available on any website, but readers should visit Kovels.com for information on trends, tips, reproductions, marks, old prices, and more!

B

Basket, Poplar, Sycamore Slats, Carved Handles, Rim, c.1880, 12 x 21 In. $1400.00

Basket, Rye Straw, Red, Yellow, Green, Purple Design, Pa., c.1900s, 4 ¾ x 11 ½ In. $150.00

Basket, Splint, Ash, Sweetzer, Wood Rim, Handles, New Hampshire, c.1800s, 6 ½ x 6 In. $250.00

Basket, Splint, Pigeon Carrier, 2 Compartments, Handle, Maine, c.1830-50, 19 x 11 x 6 In. $600.00

Splint, Oak, Market, Bentwood Handle, Rim, Bulbous, Round, 12 x 12 In. 132.00
Splint, Oak, Nesting, Bentwood, Woven Handle, Flat Ribs, 4 Piece, 14 ¼ x 15 ½ In. 358.00
Splint, Oak, Oval, Wood Bottom, Penn., 1870-90, 9 x 12 ¼ In. 330.00
Splint, Oak, Round, Tapered, Open Weave Handles, Bentwood Rim, 8 x 13 ¾ In. 33.00
Splint, Oak, Sweetzer, 2 Handles, Wood Rim, 19th Century, 5 x 6 ¾ In. 330.00
Splint, Oak, Swing Handle, Double Wrapped Rim, Raised Ring Bottom, c.1870, 9 x 10 ¾ In. . . 2310.00
Splint, Oak, Swing Handle, Wood Ears, Wrapped Rim, Raised Ring, 1800s, 10 x 14 ½ In. 523.00
Splint, Oak, Wood Runners, Double Wrapped Rim, 12 ¾ x 14 ¼ In. 176.00
Splint, Oak, Woven God's-Eye Rim, Handle, Melon Shape, 1800s, Penn., 4 ¼ x 11 ¼ In. 605.00
Splint, Painted, Pumpkin, Blue, Green, 13 x 10 In. 690.00
Splint, Pigeon Carrier, 2 Compartments, Handle, Maine, c.1830-50, 19 x 11 x 6 In. . . . . *illus* 600.00
Splint, Purse, Ash, Oval, Bulbous Form, Handles, Loop Banding, 14 ½ x 13 x 7 ½ In. 11.00
Splint, Purse, Bent Cane Handles, Red, Green Stain, Flat Wood Base, 15 x 16 ½ x 8 In. 11.00
Splint, Sewing, Yarn Holder, Ash, Paper, String Woven, Multicolored Stain, 6 x 9 In. 33.00
Splint, Swing Handle, Oak, Double Wrapped Rim, 1850-60, 10 x 13 ½ In. 2640.00
Splint, Table, Ash, Bentwood Handles, Square, Tapered, 7 ¼ x 13 ½ x 13 In. 220.00
Splint, Wall, Woven, Half Melon Shape, 7 ½ x 7 ½ In. 575.00
Splint, Wall Pocket, Ash, Hanger Loop, Banding, 9 x 9 ¾ x 4 In. 55.00
Splint, Wood, Scalloped, Bentwood Handle, Ribs, Decorative Rim, 12 x 11 ½ In. 77.00
Splint, Wood, Straight, Flat Bottom, Bentwood Handle, Rectangular, 12 x 17 x 10 ½ In. 110.00
Straw, Red Cover, String Wrapped, Painted, 4 ½ x 11 ½ In. 250.00
Sweetgrass, Palmetto, Rush Plant, Spiraling, 3 ¾ x 12 In. 193.00
Taghkanic, Notched Handles, Double Wrapped Rim, Kicked Up Bottom, Patina, 7 ¾ In. 300.00
Wall, Painted, Yellow Over Black, Long Wood Handle, Maine, 1800s, 16 ½ x 7 In. 165.00
Wicker, Handle, Scenes In Panes, 3 Tiers, Black, Brown, Chinese, 22 x 16 x 19 In. 239.00
Winnowing, Straw, Coiled, Bundled, Overlapping Oak Split Banding, 1700s, 20 In. 805.00

BATCHELDER products are made from California clay. Ernest Batchelder established a tile studio in Pasadena, California, in 1909 and expanded until 1916. Then he built a larger factory with a new partner. The Batchelder-Wilson Company made all types of architectural tiles, garden pots, and bookends. The plant closed in 1932. In 1936 Batchelder opened Batchelder Ceramics, also in Pasadena, and made bowls, vases, and earthenware pots. He retired in 1951 and died in 1957. Pieces are marked *Batchelder Pasadena* or *Batchelder Los Angeles*.

BATCHELDER
LOS ANGELES

Tile, 2 Peacocks, Flower Border, Blue Engobe, Stamped, 5 ¾ In. 240.00
Tile, Bird, Blue, Yellow, Green, White, 3 ¾ In. . . . . *illus* 88.00
Tile, Birds, In Leaves, Blue, Gray, Cream, Carved, Marked 425.00
Tile, Birds, Nest With Eggs, Brown, Blue Ground, Impressed Mark, 5 ¾ In. 350.00
Tile, Boy & Girl, Dog Drawn Carriage, 5 ½ x 17 ¾ In. 720.00
Tile, Medieval Scene, Knight, On Horse, Castle, Blue Brown Engobe, Stamped, 7 ½ In. 880.00
Tile, Village, By Bend In Road, Blue & Beige Matte Glaze, Stamped, Frame, 8 In. 480.00

BATMAN and Robin are characters from a comic strip by Bob Kane that started in 1939. In 1966, the characters became part of a popular television series. There have been radio and movie serials that featured the pair. The first full-length movie was made in 1989.

Batmobile, BZ Official, Slot Car, Box, 1966, 8 In. 335.00
Batmobile, Husky Model, Gray Wheels, Moving Flame, Corgi, 1968, 3 In. 201.00
Batmobile, Rocket Firing, No. 267, Die Cast, Plastic, Instructions, Corgi, Box, c.1972, 5 In. . . 497.00
Batphone, Hard Wired, Battery Operated, Italy, 1960 . . . . 270.00
Batphone, Hot-Line, Red, Marx, 1966, 8 In. 435.00
Bicycle Ornament, Batman, With Cape, 1966, 8 ½ In. 30.00
Boots, Clipper, Batgirl, White Vinyl, Image Of Batgirl, WOW Along Side, 7 ¾ In. 402.00
Boots, Robin, Pixie, Green Suede, R Monogram, Graphic Box, 1966, Size 10M 917.00
Bottle, Soaky, Batman & Robin, Plastic, Colgate, Neck Tags, 10 ¼ In. & 9 ¾ In., Pair 352.00
Card, Contest, Scratch-Off, Promotion For Big D's Supermarket In New York, 1966 . . . . 95.00
Comic Book, No. 15, February 3, 1945 . . . . 291.00
Costume, Helmet & Cape, Plastic, Vinyl, Instructions, Box, 1960 . . . . *illus* 421.00
Display, Batman, Arms Move, Black, Yellow, Electric, 66 In. 385.00
Display, Countertop, Unbreakable Pocket Combs, Slots, Vinyl Sleeves, 12 x 5 In. 557.00
Display, Joker, Arms Move, Purple, Yellow, Composition Head, Electric, 66 In. 150.00
Figure, Batgirl, Bend N' Flex, Mego, 1973, 5 In. 73.00
Figure, Batman, Bend N' Flex, Chinese, 1960s, 5 ½ In. 31.00
Figure, Batman, Climbing, Original Box, Remco, 1980, 9 In. 95.00
Figure, Batman, Towering Above City, Plastic, Crafthouse, Taiwan, 1984, 5 In. 158.00
Figure, Batman, Walker, Swings Arms, Cloth Cape, Tin, Windup, Billiken, 1989, 9 In. 141.00
Figure, Batmouse, Stuffed, Vinyl, Japan, 1960, 9-In. Earspan, 6 In. 25.00

Figure, Joker, Bend N' Flex, Mego, 1974, 5 In. 99.00
Figure, Joker, Holding Skull, Hat, Porcelain, Box, 12 ½ In. 288.00
Figure, Joker, Price Imports, Japan, 1978, 7 ½ In. 55.00
Figure, Penguin, Bend N' Flex, Mego, 1974, 4 In. 99.00
Figure, Riddler, Bend N' Flex, Mego, 1974, 5 In. 99.00
Figure, Robin, Mego, 1975, 3 ¾ In. 37.00
Flashlight, Batman, Nasta Industries, 1974, 3 ½ In. 77.00
Game, Batman & Robin, Hasbro, 1965, 8 x 16 In. 40.00
Game, Horseshoe, Batman & Robin 4 Batarangs, 2 Dowels, 10 x 15 x 1 ½ In. 431.00
Game, Pinball, Bagatelle, Marble, Marx, 1966, 10 x 22 In. 117.00
Game, Target, Batman & Robin Plastic Dart Gun, Darts, Cardboard, 11 ¼ x 14 ¾ In. 863.00
Hand Puppet, Batman, Ideal, 1965, 10 ¾ In. 65.00
Jar, Peanut Butter, Batman On Cover, Dominion Foods, 1987, 5 ½ In. 25.00
Model Kit, Robin, The Boy Wonder, Aurora, 1966, 13 x 5 In. 141.00
Night-Light, Batman, Cale Electric Products, 1966, 2 ¾ In. 40.00
Night-Light, Batman, Figural, Plastic, 1966, 7 In. 10.00
Night-Light, Penguin, Price Imports, Japan, 1978, 7 In. 50.00
Play Set, Shaker Maker Batman, Makes Bobbleheads, Ideal, 1974. 160.00
Puppet, Washcloth, Robin, Terry Cloth, Hang Tab, 1966, 7 ½ In. 634.00
Puzzle, Tray, Batman & Robin, Watkins-Strathmore, 1966, 14 ½ x 11 ½ In. 66.00
Radio, Plastic, AM, Batman Figure On Front, Vanity Fair, 1978, 6 x 5 In. 175.00
Radio, Wrist, Buzz, Click Signals, Remco, 4 ½ In. 40.00
Sign, All Star Milk, Batman Punching Word Burst, Paper, 24 x 44 In. 345.00
Stringholder, Figural, Batman Head, Plaster, Painted, Hole In Mouth, c.1966, 6 x 9 In. 1529.00
Toy, Batmobile, 2-Speed Antenna Shifts Gear, Tin, Friction, Alps, 1966, 8 ½ In. 375.00
Toy, Batmobile, Blue, Tin, Plastic, Battery Operated, Bump-N-Go, Lights, Japan, 1972, 12 In. 775.00
Toy, Batmobile, Die Cast, Tony Piccione, 9 ½ In. 77.00
Toy, Batmobile, Ride-On, Marx, 24 In., 1966 150.00
Toy, Figure, Riddler, Mego Superheroes, Box *illus* 518.00
Toy, Play Set, Batman Action Heroes, Exploding Bridge, Batmobile, Mego, 1979 195.00
Toy, Top, With Rip Cord, Japan, 1977, 4 ½ In. 15.00
Tumbler, Batgirl, Pepsi-Cola Premium, 1976, 6 ¼ In. 15.00
Tumbler, Batman, Sound Effects, Graphics, 1960s, 5 In. 31.00
Tumbler, Robin, Sound Effects, Graphics, 1960s, 5 In. 31.00
Wallet, Batman & Robin, Yellow Vinyl, Standard Plastic Products, 1966, 3 ½ x 4 In. 93.00

BATTERSEA enamels, which are enamels painted on copper, were made in the Battersea district of London from about 1750 to 1756. Many similar enamels are mistakenly called Battersea.

Box, Egg, Figural Landscape, Painted, Gilt Trim, Hinged Lid, England, 18th Century, 3 In. 556.00
Snuffbox, Benjamin Franklin, Oval, 2 In. 239.00
Snuffbox, Figures In Park, Brass Mounts, Rectangular, Hinged Lid, 3 ¼ In. 819.00
Tea Caddy, Turquoise, Cartouches, Landscapes, Figures, Gilt Scrolls, Lid, 4 ½ In. 605.00

BAUER pottery is a California-made ware. J.A. Bauer bought Paducah Pottery in Paducah, Kentucky, in 1885. He moved the pottery to Los Angeles, California, in 1909. The company made art pottery after 1912 and dinnerwares marked *Bauer* in 1930. The factory went out of business in 1962. See also the Russel Wright category.

Bowl, Flecked Green Matte, Marked, 2 ¼ x 8 ½ In. 75.00
Bowl, Salad, Leaf Form, Pink Flecked, 11 ¼ x 4 ¾ In. 75.00
Candleholder, Pink Matte Glaze, Cal-Art 45.00
Canister Set, Farm Scene, Wood Lids, Metal Handles, 8 In., 6 In., 4 In., 3 Piece 200.00
Cookie Jar, Speckle Twist, Blue 50.00
Creamer, Light Brown, Marked, 3 ½ In. 45.00
Figurine, Duck, Head Up, White, Cal-Art, 4 ⅝ In. 45.00
Flowerpot, Yellow, Incised, 5 In. *illus* 32.00
Gravy Boat, Dusty Rose, Handle, 6 In. 60.00
Gloss Pastel Kitchenware, Pitcher, Ray Murray, 1941, 6 x 8 ½ In. 100.00
Mixing Bowl, Pumpkin, 8 ½ x 4 ⅛ In. 50.00
Monterey, Cup, Magenta, Plain Bowl & Handle, Marked, 2 ½ In. 35.00
Monterey, Pitcher, Ice Lip, Burgundy 250.00
Monterey, Saucer, Red Brown, 6 ¼ In. 9.00
Monterey Moderne, Grill Plate, Gray, 10 ¾ In. 40.00
Monterey Moderne, Platter, Burgundy, 10 x 7 In. 45.00
Monterey Moderne, Salt & Pepper, Brown, Handles, 3 ⅛ In. 12.50

Batchelder, Tile, Bird, Blue, Yellow, Green, White, 3 ¾ In.
$88.00

Batman, Costume, Helmet & Cape, Plastic, Vinyl, Instructions, Box, 1960
$421.00

Batman, Toy, Figure, Riddler, Mego Superheroes, Box
$518.00

Bauer, Flowerpot, Yellow, Incised, 5 In.
$32.00

Bauer, Plain, Carafe, Orange, Wood Handle, Marked, 9 ¼ In.
$85.00

Bavaria, Plate, Empress Dresden Flowers, Scalloped, Embossed, Schumann, 7 ¾ In.
$40.00

TIP
Don't put pottery or porcelain with crazed glaze in the dishwasher. It will crack even more.

Pitcher, Batter, Green Speckled, Marked, Qt. 60.00
Plain, Bean Pot, Cover, Gloss Brown, Handle, 2 Qt. 65.00
Plain, Bowl, Pudding, Yellow, 5 ¼ In. 50.00
Plain, Carafe, Orange, Wood Handle, Marked, 9 ¼ In. *illus* 85.00
Plain, Creamer, Orange, Individual, 1 ⅞ In.. 200.00
Plain, Grill Plate, Cobalt Blue, 10 ⅜ In. 75.00
Plain, Grill Plate, Orange, 10 ½ In.. 85.00
Plain, Mixing Bowl, Dusty Rose, 8 ¼ In.. 150.00
Ring, Baking Dish, Cover, Orange, 4 ½ In. 65.00
Ring, Bowl, Batter, Jade, 10 ½ In. 17.50
Ring, Bowl, Cereal, Gray, 5 In. 75.00
Ring, Bowl, Fruit, Gray, 5 ⅝ In. 75.00
Ring, Bowl, Vegetable, Burgundy, 10 ½ In. 148.00
Ring, Casserole, Cover, Copper & Wood Rack, Yellow, 6 ¾ In. 175.00
Ring, Chop Plate, Burgundy, 12 In. 95.00
Ring, Chop Plate, Yellow, Marked, 15 In.. 239.00
Ring, Coffee Carafe, Jade, Wood Handle 150.00
Ring, Creamer, Black, 2 ⅔ In. 75.00
Ring, Cup, Papaya 100.00
Ring, Cup & Saucer, Burgundy 55.00
Ring, Cup & Saucer, Jade 50.00
Ring, Custard Cup, Cobalt Blue 35.00
Ring, Flowerpot, Light Blue, 6 ¼ In. 75.00
Ring, Flowerpot, Turquoise, 6 ¼ In. 75.00
Ring, Jardiniere, Yellow, 5 ⅝ x 7 In. 65.00
Ring, Mixing Bowl, Royal Blue, 7 ¼ In. 25.00
Ring, Nappy, Chinese Yellow, Marked 100.00
Ring, Nappy, Light Blue, 5 ¾ In. 100.00
Ring, Pitcher, Ball, Ice Lip, Jade. 200.00
Ring, Pitcher, Buttermilk, Light Blue, 5 In.. 20.00
Ring, Pitcher, Light Mauve, 5 ½ In.. 75.00
Ring, Plate, Bread & Butter, Burgundy, 6 In. 40.00
Ring, Plate, Bread & Butter, Yellow, Marked, 6 ⅛ In. 25.00
Ring, Plate, Dinner, Orange, 9 ⅜ In. 50.00
Ring, Plate, Orange, 5 ⅛ In. 85.00
Ring, Plate, Salad, Burgundy, 7 ¾ In. 35.00 to 40.00
Ring, Plate, Salad, Gray, 7 ¾ In. 49.95
Ring, Plate, Salad, Jade, 7 ¾ In. 35.00
Ring, Saltshaker, Cobalt Blue, 5 Hole 20.00
Ring, Saucer, Burgundy 15.00
Ring, Sugar, Cover, Orange, Handles 12.50
Ring, Sugar & Creamer, Light Blue 75.00
Ring, Vase, Bud, Yellow, Tapered, 5 ½ In. 100.00
Salt & Pepper, Glossy Yellow, Cork Stoppers, 3 In.. 18.00
Vase, Cornucopia Horn, Yellow, 6 ¼ In.. 32.00
Vase, Tan, Satin, Flared Rim, Cal-Art, 10 In.. 75.00

BAVARIA is a region in Europe where many types of porcelain were made. In the nineteenth century, the mark often included the word *Bavaria*. After 1871, the words *Bavaria, Germany*, were used. Listed here are pieces that include the name *Bavaria* in some form, but major porcelain makers, such as Rosenthal are listed in their own categories.

Candlestick, Owls, Black, Tapered, Gold Cup Rim, Round Base, c.1950, 9 In., Pair 148.00
Plate, Empress Dresden Flowers, Scalloped, Embossed, Schumann, 6 ¼ In. 34.00
Plate, Empress Dresden Flowers, Scalloped, Embossed, Schumann, 7 ¾ In. *illus* 40.00
Plate, Flowers, 2 Women, Cobalt Blue, Gold Rim, Transfer, Marked, PIN, 12 ¾ In. 90.00
Plate, Soup, Flower Relief, Gilt Border, Rose Reserve, Faience, Nymphenburg, 10 In., 6 Piece. 1880.00

BEADED BAGS *are included in the Purse category.*

BEATLES collectors search for any items picturing the four members of the famous music group or any of their recordings. Because these items are so new, the condition is very important and top prices are paid only for items in mint condition. The Beatles first appeared on American network television in 1964. The group disbanded in 1971. Ringo Starr and Paul McCartney are still performing. John Lennon died in 1980. George Harrison died in 2001

Advertisement, Beatles, Shea Stadium, Sunday Eve., Aug. 15, 8 P.M., 1965, 9 ½ x 12 In. 1050.00

Bank, Yellow Submarine, Ceramic, Pride Creations, King Feature Synd. Films, 1968, Set Of 4, 8 In. 2800.00
Button, Cartoon Image Of The Beatles, Set Of 4, 1960s. 55.00
Cap, Ringo, Black, Wool, United Hatters Cap & Millinery Workers, Size M, 7 ½ x 10 In. 115.00
Card, Window, Yellow Submarine, c.1968, 15 x 23 ¼ In. 403.00
Case, Overnight, Facsimile Signatures, Vinyl, Zipper, Air Flite, 1964, 12 ¾ x 5 ⅛ In. 672.00
Costumes, Halloween, Beatles, Ben Cooper, Box, 1964, 4 Piece 3380.00
Cup, Beatles Photos, Signatures, Washington Pottery, England, 1964, 4 In. 157.00
Display Box, Topps, New Series, 5 Cent Bubble Gum Card, 24, Black, White, 1964, 8 x 4 In. 360.00
Doll, Inflatable, Cartoon, Nestles Quick Premium, Sealed, 1964, 4 Piece. 112.00
Doll Set, George, Paul, John, Ringo, Remco, Sears, 1964, 4 ½ In., 4 Piece. 1232.00
Doll Set, Vinyl, Inflatable, Cartoon Images, Facsimile Signature, Lux Soap, 15 In., 4 Piece. 115.00
Drum Set, Ringo Starr, New Beat, Beatles Faces, Orange & Burgundy, Plastic, 1964, 14 In. 3000.00
Float Pen, Yellow Submarine, Moves When Tilted, 1996. 9.00
Hair Bow, Facsimile Signatures, Photos, 1964, 5 ½ In. 254.00
Hairbrush, Embossed Portraits, Picture Card, Plastic, 1964, 3 ¾ In. 82.00
Handbag, 4 Beatles, Signatures, Orange, Vinyl, Metal Handle, Zipper, 1964 340.00
Lunch Box, George, Paul, John, Ringo, Blue, Metal, Aladdin, 1966, 8 x 7 ½ x 4 In. 495.00
Lunch Box, John, Paul, George, Ringo, Embossed Metal, Thermos, 1965, NEMS Ltd. *illus* 518.00
Music Box, Ceramic, Figures Spin, Music Plays Imagine, 1980 81.00
Nodder, Ringo Starr, Playing Drum, Blue Suit, 1960s, 7 ½ In. 94.00
Nodder Set, John, Paul, George, Ringo, Playing Instruments, Car Mascot Inc., 4 Piece. *illus* 350.00
Ornament, Beatle Playing Brown Plastic Guitar, Blue Glass, Italy, 1964, 7 In. 196.00
Pennant, Beatles, Red, Felt, John, Paul, Ringo, George, Hollywood Bowl. 120.00
Pillow, Portrait, Image In Blue Suit, Red Tie, Nordic House, 1964, 12 x 12 In. 168.00
Poster, Help, United Artists, 1965, 81 x 40 In. 748.00
Poster, Let It Be, c.1970, 41 x 27 In. 345.00
Poster, Let It Be, United Artists, 1970, 81 x 40 In. 748.00
Poster, Philadelphia Convention Center, Black & White, c.1964, 14 x 22 In. 4780.00
Record, Sgt. Pepper's Lonely Hearts Club Band, Sealed, 33 RPM, c.1967. 1135.00
Scarf, Facsimile Signatures, Ulster, 1964, 31 In. 280.00
Squirt Gun, Yellow Submarine, Taiwan, 1968, 6 In. 41.00
Switch Plate Cover, Yellow Submarine, Cardboard, c.1968, 7 ¾ x 6 ¼ In. 115.00
Thermos, George, Paul, John, Ringo, Blue, Aladdin, 1966 330.00
Ticket, Busch Stadium Concert, August 21, 1966, Admission $5.50, Unused 360.00
Ticket, New York, Shea Stadium, Sid Bernstein Presents, 8/23/66 1450.00
Ticket, San Francisco Concert, KYA Radio 1260, Candlestick Park, 8/29/66. 1400.00
Toy, Yellow Submarine, Revolving Periscope, Hatch Opens, Die Cast, Corgi, c.1969, 5 ¼ In. 158.00
Tumbler Set, George, Paul, John, Ringo, Photos, Gold Rim, Dairy Queen, 1964, 4 ¾ In. 549.00
Vase, Lucy In The Sky With Diamonds, Psychedelic Colors, Butler Designs, 16 ½ In. 840.00
Wall Plaques, 4 Heads, Ceramic, Kelsboro Ware, England, 1964, 5 x 3 ½ In., 4 Piece 2464.00
Wristwatch, Woman's, Faces At 3, 6, 9 & 12, Blue Band, Box, Bradley, 1970s 519.00

BEEHIVE , Austria, or Beehive, Vienna, are terms used in English-speaking countries to refer to the many types of decorated porcelain bearing a mark that looks like a beehive. The mark is actually a shield, viewed upside down. It was first used in 1744 by the Royal Porcelain Manufactory of Vienna. The firm made what collectors call Royal Vienna porcelains until it closed in 1864. Many other German, Austrian, and Japanese factories have reproduced Royal Vienna wares, complete with the original shield or beehive mark. This listing includes the expensive, original Royal Vienna porcelains and many other types of beehive porcelain. The Royal Vienna pieces include that name in the description.

Charger, Scenic, Apollo, Returning To Parnassus, Muses, Vienna, Late 1800s, 16 In. 6250.00
Charger, Scenic, Shepherd Musicians, Signed, Wagner, Vienna, Late 1800s, 14 In. 6250.00
Cup & Saucer, 2 People In Forest, Burgundy, Enamel Beads, Gold Scrolls, Signed, A. Kert 400.00
Cup & Saucer, Belvedere Castle, c.1817 800.00
Cup & Saucer, Demitasse, Man Holding Woman's Hand, Gold & Blue Dot, Royal Vienna 125.00
Cup & Saucer, Garden Of Prince Sikwartzenberg, Green Ground, c.1808. 1000.00
Cup & Saucer, Man Playing Violin, Woman Sings, Roses, Gold & Blue Dots, Royal Vienna. 125.00
Cup & Saucer, Vienna, Green Ground, c.1818. 900.00
Cup & Saucer, Woman, Portrait, Cobalt Blue, Gilt, Signed, Richter. 175.00
Dresser Box, Courting Couple, Scenic, White, Rectangular, R. Coulory, 11 In. 230.00
Group, 4 Women, 4 Children, Serving Tea, Boy Playing With Dog, 8 In. 825.00
Loving Cup, Alexander & Abeles, Gilt, 3 Handles, 3-Footed, Signed, Kauffman, 8 In. *illus* 850.00
Plate, 3 Women Holding Rubies, Red, Blue, Gilt, Carl Larson, Austria, 12 In. *illus* 99.00
Plate, Children At Play, Murillo, Royal Vienna, 10 In. 53.00
Plate, Dog, Gilt Border, Bronze Ground, Royal Vienna, 19th Century, 9 ½ In. 960.00
Plate, Louis XVI, Hand Painted, Royal Vienna 575.00
Plate, Man, Woman, Gilt, Pierced Scalloped Border, Royal Vienna, 9 In., Pair 925.00

Beatles, Lunch Box, John, Paul, George, Ringo, Embossed Metal, Thermos, 1965, NEMS Ltd.
$518.00

Beatles, Nodder Set, John, Paul, George, Ringo, Playing Instruments, Car Mascot Inc.,
$350.00

Beehive, Loving Cup, Alexander & Abeles, Gilt, 3 Handles, 3-Footed, Signed, Kauffman, 8 In.
$850.00

Beehive, Plate, 3 Women Holding Rubies, Red, Blue, Gilt, Carl Larson, Austria, 12 In.
$99.00

Bell, Bronze, Pig, Windup Snout, Tail, c.1890, 6 ½ In.
$950.00

Bell, School, Iron, Montana, No. 26, 24 x 25 In.
$560.00

Bell, Sleigh, 3 Brass Bells, Eagle Finial, 19th Century, 10 ½ In.
$236.00

Bell, Wagon, Wrought Iron, Cast Brass, Oval Bracket, Spikes, 3 Bells, 16 In.
$90.00

Plate, Woman, Marie De Medicis Depose, Signed, Wagner, 9 ½ In. 1400.00
Plate, Woman, Pink Flower In Hair, Blue Under Glaze, 9 ⅜ In. 690.00
Plate, Woman, Pompadour, Gilt Frame, Royal Vienna, C. Wagner, 10 In. 1920.00
Plate, Woman, Sleeping Child, Royal Vienna, Marked, Blue Beehive, 9 ¾ In. 575.00
Plate, Woman, Wearing Aqua Scarf, Red Dress, 9 ½ In. 1495.00
Stein, Bacchus, Vines, Mythical Mask Heads, Silver Gilt, Multicolored, Enamel, 7 In. 2370.00
Urn, Woman, Blue, Gilt, Royal Vienna, Marked, Blue Beehive, 11 In. 700.00
Urn, Woman, Wooded Landscape, Lid, Wagner, Signed, 17 In. 2880.00
Vase, Allegorical Scenes, Footed, Royal Vienna, Loffler, Signed, 8 In. 1920.00
Vase, Art Nouveau, Maidens, Floral Garlands, Copper Luster Ground, 22 x 11 In. 12925.00
Vase, Demure Maiden, Rose Garlands, Royal Vienna, 5 ⅝ In. 1150.00
Vase, Marie Antoinette Portrait, Burgundy Luster, Raised Gold Bouquet, Handles, 9 ½ In. 2415.00
Vase, Ophelia, Girl, Flowers In Hair, Gilt Bronze Rim, c.1910, 6 ¾ In. 468.00
Vase, Stick, Cobalt Blue, Flowers, Butterfly Highlights, Royal Vienna, 10 In. 160.00
Vase, Woman, Gold Flowers, Reverse Gold Flower Sprigs, Royal Vienna, 3 ⅞ In. 546.00
Vase, Woman With Hands On Face, Pastel Luster, Handles, Royal Vienna, 5 ¾ In. 1840.00

BEER BOTTLES *are listed in the Bottle category under Beer.*

BEER CANS are a twentieth-century idea. Beer was sold in kegs or returnable bottles until 1934.The first patent for a can was issued to the American Can Company in September of that year; and Gotfried Kruger Brewing Company, Newark, New Jersey, was the first to use the can. The cone-top can was first made in 1935, the aluminum pop-top in 1962. Collectors should look for cans in good condition, with no dents or rust. Serious collectors prefer cans that have been opened from the bottom.

Anheuser-Busch Natural Light, Pull Tab, Pitch In!, St. Louis Mo., 12 Oz. 10.00
Big Cat Malt Liquor, Pull Tab, Pabst Brewing Company, 12 Oz. 13.00
Cerveza Tecate, Push Tab, Cerveceria Cuauhtemoc, Mexico, 12 Oz. 11.00
Champagne Velvet Brand Premium Pilsner, Cone Top, Terre Haute Brewing Co. 45.00
Colt 45 Malt Liquor, Pull Tab, Pabst, Please Don't Litter, 12 Oz. 9.00
Coors Banquet Waterfall, Push Tab, 12 Oz. 10.00
John Courage Ale, Pull Tab, London, England, 12 Oz. 10.00
JR Ewing's Private Stock, Push Tab, Pearl Brewing Co., San Antonio, Texas, 11.6 Oz. 9.00
Leinenkugel's Beer, White Ground, Blue Letters & Indian Logo, Crown Style, 5 ⅛ In. 130.00
Light Beer, Beer, Generic, Florida Brewery, Yellow, Black, Auburndale, Pair 15.00
National Bohemian Light Beer, Flat Top, National Brewing, Red, White, Black, Miami 47.00
Old Falstaff, America's Premium Quality Beer, Fort Wayne, Indiana. 25.00
Olde Frothingslosh Fatima Yechburgh, Pittsburgh Brewing Co., Pull Tab, 12 Oz. 5.00
Regal Light Lager Beer, Flat Top, Regal, White, Gold, Red, Miami 45.00
Regal Premium, Flat Top, Regal Brewery, White Ground, Gold, Red Label, Miami 45.00
Regal Premium, Regal Brewery, Green, White, Gold, Aluminum, Tab Top, Miami 10.00
Schlitz, Flat Top, Schlitz Brewing, Brown, White, Tampa, 12 Oz. 10.00
Tropical Ale, Cone Top, Tampa Florida Brewery, Green Metal, White Label, Tampa 405.00
Whales White Ale, National Brewing Co., Whale, Black Can, White Text, Tab Top, Miami 4.00

BELL collectors collect all types of bells. Favorites include glass bells, figural bells, school bells, and cowbells. Bells have been made of porcelain, china, or metal through the centuries.

Brass, Buddhist, Japan, 5 ½ In. 177.00
Brass, Church, Lititz Moravian, 1957, 4 ⅛ In. 200.00
Brass, Desk, Abalone, 3 Oval Shells, Bird Finial, Victorian, Late 19th Century, 5 ½ x 9 In. 90.00
Brass, Hotel, Embossed Base & Finial, 5 ¼ In. 90.00
Brass, Hotel, Embossed Leaf Design On Base & Finial, 6 In. 50.00
Brass, Hotel, Open Leaf Design On Base, 6 In. 275.00
Brass, Ornate Designs, Bust On Handle, 4-Cornered Crown Finial, 6 x 3 In. 145.00
Brass, Sacristy, Wall Mount, Ornate, Spain, 18 In. 47.00
Brass, Teakwood Frame, Chinese, 15 x 8 In. 176.00
Brass Base, Bell Metal Dome, Repousse Base & Finial, 1880s, 4 x 2 ¾ In. 135.00
Bronze, Iron Mount, Clapper, Buckeye Bell Foundry, c.1850, 13 x 11 In. 822.00
Bronze, Liberty Bell Shape, Troy Bell Co., N.Y., 51 x 34 In. 4950.00
Bronze, Oval, Bosses, Mythical Animal Finial, Korea, 12 In. 3776.00
Bronze, Pig, Windup Snout, Tail, c.1890, 6 ½ In. *illus* 950.00
Bronze, Plantation, Leaf Collar, Iron Clapper, Buckeye Bell Foundry, c.1875, 22 x 20 In. 2350.00
Bronze, Taotie Mask, Chinese, 15 In. 384.00
Cast Bronze, Oval, Bosses, Mythical Animal Shape Finial, Korea, Choson Dynasty, 12 In. 448.00
Cast Metal, Hotel, Nickel Plated, Figural Of Lady In Flowing Wrap, 3 ½ x 3 ½ In. 336.00

Cranberry Glass, Etched Flowers, Gold Bands, Crystal Clapper, Hungary, 5 ½ In. 45.00
Glass, Cabbage Leaf, Purple, Viking Glass, 5 ¾ x 3 ¾ In. 25.00
Glass, Clear, Frosted Angel On Top, Clapper On Chain, 4 ½ In. 30.00
Iron, Hexagonal, 3-Footed, Loop 2 Holes, Buddha Emblems, Chinese, 5 ½ In. 330.00
Iron, Hotel, Turtle, Nickel Plated, Windup, Germany, c.1880, 6 ¾ In. 456.00
Iron, Hotel, Turtle, Nickel Plated, Windup, Push Head Or Tail To Ring, Germany, 2 x 5 In. 248.00
Metal, Gold Colored, Daisy, Molded, Painted Leatherette Strap, Salzburg, 10 x 3 ¾ In. 22.00
Nickel, Plantation, Iron Yoke & Wheel, Buckeye Foundry, c.1850, 29 x 19 ½ In. 4406.00
Porcelain, Blue, Red Flowers, Wheelbarrow, Price Products, Bellmawr, N.J., Taiwan, 5 ½ In. . 12.00
Porcelain, Girl, Red Nightgown, Striped Cap, Holding Candle, Merri-Bells Tag, 4 ¼ In. 19.00
Pottery, Elf, Red Suit & Hat, Green Base, 1950s-60s, 4 In. 15.00
Pottery, Girl, Kites, Basket, Doves, Hand Painted, Black Cord, De Grazia, 5 ¼ In. 95.00
School, Brass, Turned Wood Handle, 11 In. 30.00
School, Iron, Marked, CS Bell Hillsboro, No Clapper, 29 x 26 In. 110.00
School, Iron, Montana, No. 26, 24 x 25 In. .... *illus* 560.00
Silver, Dinner, 3-Rattle, Twisted Handle, Ball Finial, 3 Applied Bees, Mexico, c.1960, 5 In. 2390.00
Silver, Dinner, G. Albertus, Cactus Pattern, Copenhagen, G. Jensen, c.1930, 3 In. 263.00
Silver, Table, Georg Jensen, Flared, Hammered Surface, Leaf Handle, 4 In. 590.00
Silver, Woman Carrying Water Jug Handle, Coin, 4 ¼ In. 140.00
Sleigh, 3 Brass Bells, Eagle Finial, 19th Century, 10 ½ In. .... *illus* 236.00
Sleigh, 12 Brass Bells, Leather Strap, 19th Century 75.00
Sleigh, 12 Brass Bells, Leather Strap, 83 In. 175.00
Sleigh, 14 Brass Bells, Leather Strap, Buckle, 1 ¼ In. 55.00
Sleigh, 14 Brass Bells, Leather Strap, 81 In. 75.00
Sleigh, 36 Bells, Leather Strap 92.00
Sterling Silver, Dinner, Chantilly, Gorham, 5 ¼ In. 30.00
Sterling Silver, Figural Dog On Top, Begging, Concord Silversmiths, Boston, 3 x 2 In. 85.00
Trolley, Brass, EW Departure, Bristol, Conn., Pat. 1892 .... 105.00
Wagon, Wrought Iron, Cast Brass, Oval Bracket, Spikes, 3 Bells, 16 In. .... *illus* 90.00

BELLEEK china was made in Ireland, other European countries, and the United States. The glaze is creamy yellow and appears wet. The first Belleek was made in 1857. All pieces listed here are Irish Belleek. The mark changed through the years. The first mark, black, dates from 1863 to 1890. The second mark, black, dates from 1891 to 1926 and includes the words *Co. Fermanagh, Ireland.* The third mark, black, dates from 1926 to 1946 and has the words *Deanta in Eirinn.* The fourth mark, same as the third mark but green, dates from 1946 to 1955. The fifth mark (second green mark) dates from 1955 to 1965 and has an R in a circle added in the upper right. The sixth mark (third green mark) dates from 1965 to 1981 and the words *Co. Fermanagh* have been omitted. The seventh mark, gold, was used from 1981 to 1992 and omits the words *Deanta in Eirinn.* The eighth mark, used from 1993 to 1996, is similar to the second mark but is printed in blue. The ninth mark, blue, includes the words *Est. 1857* and the words *Co. Fermanagh Ireland* are omitted. The tenth mark, black, is similar to the ninth mark but includes the words *Millennium 2000* and *Ireland.* It was used only in 2000. The eleventh mark, similar to the millennium mark but green, was introduced in 2001 and will be used until 2010, according to the company. The word *Belleek* is now used only on the pieces made in Ireland even though earlier pieces from other countries were sometimes marked *Belleek.* These early pieces are listed by manufacturer, such as Ceramic Art Co., Haviland, Lenox, Ott & Brewer, and Willets.

Basket, Heart Shape, Lace Weave, Flower Rim, 2 x 5 In. 205.00
Basket, Round, Embossed Flora, Weave, 4th Mark, Green, 1946-55, 3 x 6 In. 176.00
Bowl, Latticework, Pierced Rim, Red, Yellow, Purple Flowers, Twist Handles, Oval, Marked, 9 In. 288.00
Bowl, Shell, White, Black, 1st Mark, 1863-90, 9 ¼ In. 176.00
Bust, Sorrow, 6th Mark, Green, 1965-81, 10 In. 220.00
Butter, Dish, Cottage Shape, 4 ¼ x 6 ½ In. 105.00
Ewer, Aberdeen Rose, Green Mark, 9 ½ In. .... *illus* 100.00
Honey Pot, Beehive, 5 ¾ x 5 In. 88.00
Sandwich Server, Reticulated, Cream, 10 In. 146.00
Statue, Affection, 6th Mark, Green, 1965-81, 14 In. 255.00
Sugar & Creamer, Dragonfly, Signed, Ireland 45.00
Tankard Set, Scenic, Hunting Dogs, Dragon Handle, 5 Steins, c.1907, 15 & 5 ¼ In., 6 Piece . 920.00
Tea Set, Nautilus, Teapot, Creamer, Cup & Saucer, 3rd Mark, Black, 1926-46, 11 Piece 293.00
Vase, Fish Shape, White, Black Mark, 7 In. 210.00
Vase, Iris, Cylindrical, c.1900, 11 x 3 ¾ In. 146.00
Vase, Parrot, Cylindrical, 1910, 15 ½ x 5 ¼ In. 275.00
Vase, Reeded, Scalloped, Trumpet, Flower Encrusted Base, 2nd Mark, Black, 12 In. .... *illus* 400.00
Vase, Rose Isle, Painted, Handles, 2nd Mark, Green, 1955-65, 14 In. 110.00

Belleek, Ewer, Aberdeen Rose, Green Mark, 9 ½ In.
$100.00

Belleek, Vase, Reeded, Scalloped, Trumpet, Flower Encrusted Base, 2nd Mark, Black, 12 In.
$400.00

TIP

If you want to use a valuable porcelain punch bowl at a party, try this: Buy a piece of lightweight clear plastic hose at a hardware store. Slit the hose and use it to protect the rim of the bowl from the punch ladle.

Bennington, Crock, Stag, Cobalt Blue, J. Norton & Co., 1859-61, 4 Gal., 11 ½ In.
$23700.00

Bennington, Figurine, Lion, Coleslaw Mane, Flint Enamel, Lyman Fenton, 1850, 9 x 11 In.
$9945.00

Bennington, Pitcher, Hound Handle, Tan Rockingham Glaze, 3 Qt., 10 ¼ In.
$575.00

TIP

Rearrange lamps, figurines, vases, and other knickknacks on tabletops. If you don't, sunlight will fade the exposed wood, which will become lighter than the covered sections.

BENNINGTON ware was the product of two factories working in Bennington, Vermont. Both the Norton Company and the Lyman Fenton Company were out of business by 1896. The wares include brown and yellow mottled pottery, Parian, scroddled ware, stoneware, graniteware, yellowware, and Staffordshire-type vases. The name is also a generic term for mottled brownware of the type made in Bennington.

Bank, Bulldog, Standing, Rockingham Glaze, 5 In. 80.00
Bank, House, Brown, 4 ½ x 3 x 2 ⅝ In. 45.00
Bottle, Book, Rockingham Glaze, 4 ⅞ In. 200.00
Bottle, Coachman, 1849, 10 In. 875.00
Bottle, Coachman, Albany Slip Glaze, 8 ½ In. 198.00
Bottle, Coachman, Rockingham Glaze, c.1850, 10 In. 115.00
Bottle, Coachman, With Mug, Mottled Brown, Flint Enamel, Fenton 1849, 10 ½ In. 170.00
Bottle, Flask, Book, Bennington Battle, Flint Enamel, 6 x 3 ¾ x 2 In. 578.00
Crock, Bird, Cobalt Blue, E. & L.P. Norton, 3 Gal. 518.00
Crock, Cover, Flowers, Cobalt Blue, Lug Handles, J. & E. Norton, c.1855, 2 Gal., 12 In. 1659.00
Crock, Flowers, Cobalt Blue, Applied Handle, J. Norton & Co., c.1850, 10 In. 411.00
Crock, Stag, Cobalt Blue, J. Norton & Co., 1859-61, 4 Gal., 11 ½ In. . . . . *illus* 23700.00
Crock, Stag, Tree, Cobalt Blue, Stoneware, J. Norton, Vermont, 4 Gal., c.1840, 12 In. 23700.00
Figurine, Lion, Coleslaw Mane, Flint Enamel, Lyman Fenton, 1850, 9 x 11 In. . . . . *illus* 9945.00
Figurine, Spaniel, Coleslaw Hair, Brown Glaze, 19th Century, 8 ¼ In., Pair 2574.00
Figurine, Spaniel, Seated, Mottled Brown Glaze, Base, 10 ½ x 7 ½ In. 99.00
Flask, Book, Bennington Companion, Green, Tan, Ocher, Brown, 10 ¾ x 8 ¼ In. 3105.00
Flask, Book, Scroddled, Cream, Green, Gray, c.1849, 5 ½ x 4 ½ In. 1495.00
Flask, Pint Book, Bead Spout, Departed Spirit, Brown Flint Enamel, c.1852, Pt., 6 x 4 In. 345.00
Frame, Picture, Flint Enamel, Scalloped Edge, Green, Orange, Ocher, 11 x 10 In. 920.00
Frame, Scalloped Edges, Green, Orange, Ocher Flint Enamel, c.1855, 7 x 6 In. 2300.00
Mold, Cake, Mottled, Rockingham Glaze, Miniature, 1 ½ x 3 ¾ In., 3 Piece 210.00
Paperweight, Spaniel, Mottled Brown, Flint Enamel, Marked, Fenton, 1849, 3 x 4 In. 120.00
Pitcher, Alternate Ribs, Mottled Brown, Flint Enamel, 6 In. 50.00
Pitcher, Hound Handle, Dogs, Grapes, Trees, c.1860, 6 Qt., 12 In. 633.00
Pitcher, Hound Handle, Dogs, Grapes Trees, Tan Glaze, c.1860, 3 Qt., 11 In. 575.00
Pitcher, Hound Handle, Dogs, Grapevines, c.1860, 2 Qt., 9 ½ In. 1610.00
Pitcher, Hound Handle, Tan Rockingham Glaze, 3 Qt., 10 ¼ In. . . . . *illus* 575.00
Pitcher, Panels, Mottled Brown, Blue Highlights, Flint Enamel, 10 ¾ x 10 In. 350.00
Plaque, Owl, Green, Oval, 8 In. 50.00
Plate, Escargot, Blue, White Interior, 6 Sections, 5-Sided 35.00
Plate, Lion, Green Glaze Face & Tail, Stoneware, Oval, 8 ½ In. 65.00
Slop Jar, Scalloped Rib, Applied Handles, Flint Enamel, c.1858, 14 x 10 In. 3450.00
Teapot, Alternate Rib, Green Mottled Lid, Flint Enamel, c.1858, 6 ½ In. 288.00
Tobacco Jar, Cover, Alternate Rib, Applied Handles, Marked, c.1849, 8 x 6 In. 403.00
Toby Jug, Pirate, Crossed Arms, c.1850, 6 In. 47.00
Washbowl, Pitcher, Scalloped Rib, Brown, Blue, Orange Glaze, Flint Enamel, c.1858 . . . . . 920.00

BERLIN, a German porcelain factory, was started in 1751 by Wilhelm Kaspar Wegely. In 1763, the factory was taken over by Frederick the Great and became the Royal Berlin Porcelain Manufactory. It is still in operation today. Pieces have been marked in a variety of ways.

Plaque, Girl & Horse, Oval, Mat, Frame, 8 ½ x 6 In. 900.00
Plaque, Vestal Virgin, After Angelica Kauffman, Champleve Enamel, Gilt Metal Frame, 5 In. 504.00
Plate, Gypsy Woman, Reading Tea Leaves, Cobalt Blue Rim, Gilt Scrolls, 9 ¼ In. 474.00
Urn, Roman Revival Scenes, Masks, Swags, Hand Painted, 10 In. 475.00
Vase, Poppies, Daisies, Multicolored, Gilt, Footed, 19th Century, 8 In. 200.00

BESWICK started making earthenware in Staffordshire, England, in 1936. The company is now part of Royal Doulton Tableware, Ltd. Figurines of animals, especially dogs and horses, Beatrix Potter animals, and other wares are still being made.

Figurine, A Good Read, No. 2529, 1975-83, 2 ½ In. . . . . 53.00 to 96.00
Figurine, Aberdeen Angus Calf, No.1406A, 1956-75, 3 In. 240.00
Figurine, All I Do Is Think Of You, No. 2589, 1976-83, 2 ½ In. 340.00
Figurine, American Blue Jay, No. 925, 1941-65, 5 In. 53.00
Figurine, Amiable Guinea Pig, BP 3B, 1967-83, 3 ½ In. . . . . 60.00 to 72.00
Figurine, Anna Maria, BP 3A, 1963-83, 3 In. 96.00
Figurine, Arab Xayal, Brown Matte, Wood Plinth, No. 1265, 1952, 6 ¼ In. 118.00
Figurine, Ayrshire Cow, No. 1350, 1985-89, 5 In. 168.00
Figurine, Black Beauty Foal, No. 2536, 1976-89, 3 ½ In. 36.00
Figurine, Boar, Wall Champion Boy 53rd, 1987-89, 2 ¾ In. 74.00

Figurine, Bulldog, Gloss, No. 965, 1987-89, 5 ½ In. 513.00
Figurine, Cairn Terrier, With Ball, No. 1055A, 1946-69, 4 In. 74.00
Figurine, Canadian Mountie, Black, No. 1375, 1955-76, 8 ¼ In. 1008.00
Figurine, Cantering Shire, Gray, No. 975, 1961-89, 8 ¾ In. 96.00
Figurine, Cantering Shire, Palomino, No. 975, 1961-70, 8 ¾ In. 336.00
Figurine, Charalois Calf, No. 1827B, 1987-89, 3 In. 96.00
Figurine, Chihuahua, Seated On Cushion, No. 2454, 1984-89, 2 ⅔ In. . . . . *illus* 48.00
Figurine, Christopher Robin, No. 2395, 1971-90, 4 ¾ In. 108.00
Figurine, Clydesdale, Harness, No. 2465, 1974-82, 10 ¾ In. 275.00
Figurine, Cockatoo, No. 1180, 1949-75, 8 ½ In. 149.00
Figurine, Connoisseur Model Of Lester Piggot On Nijinsky, No. 2352, 1971-82, 12 ½ In. 596.00
Figurine, Connoisseur Model Of Pat Taaffe On Arkle, No. 2084, 1970-82, 12 ½ In. 443.00
Figurine, Cuckoo, No. 2315, 1970-82, 5 In. 156.00
Figurine, Dales Pony, No. 1671, 1961-82, 6 ½ In. 202.00
Figurine, Dog, Golden Retriever, Matte, No. 2287, 1987-94, 5 ½ In. 39.00
Figurine, Dog, Seated, Blue, No. 286, 1934-54, 7 In. 85.00
Figurine, Dog, Seated, Ladybird On Nose, No. 804, 1940-69, 4 In. 39.00
Figurine, Duchess With Pie, BP 3B, 1979-82, 4 In. . . . . 228.00 to 404.00
Figurine, Emperor Butterfly, Purple, No. 1487, 1957-63, 6 ¼ In. 962.00
Figurine, Fawn, Tail Up, No. 1000A, 1943-55, 3 ½ In. 88.00
Figurine, Foal, Opaque, No. 815, 1961-73, 3 ¼ In. 170.00
Figurine, Galloway Bull, Black, No. 1746A, 1962-69, 4 ½ In. 3512.00
Figurine, Ginger, BP 3B, 1976-82, 3 ¾ In. 228.00
Figurine, Girl On Skewbald Pony, No. 1499, 1957-65, 5 ½ In. . . . . *illus* 264.00
Figurine, Gouldian Finch, No. 1178, 1949-59, 4 In. 456.00
Figurine, Gray Palomino, No. 1261, 1970, 6 ¾ In. 48.00
Figurine, Grouse Pair, No. 2063, 1966-75, 5 ½ In. 480.00
Figurine, Guernsey Cow, No. 1248A, 1952-53, 4 ¼ In. 319.00
Figurine, Hereford Bull, No. 1363A, 1955, 4 ½ In. 120.00
Figurine, Hereford Cow, No. 948, 1941-57, 5 In. 553.00
Figurine, Highland Pony, No. 1644, 1961-89, 7 ¼ In. 113.00
Figurine, Huntsman's Horse, Palomino, No. 1484, 1957-82, 6 ¾ In. 77.00
Figurine, Jemima Puddleduck, BP 2A, 1948-2002 . . . . . 60.00
Figurine, Jeremy Fisher, Digging, BP 4 . . . . . 64.00
Figurine, Jersey Bull, No. 1422, 1985-89, 4 ½ In. 144.00
Figurine, Jersey Cow, No. 1345, 1985-89, 4 ½ In. 156.00
Figurine, Lady Mouse, BP 2, 1950-2000, 4 In. . . . . 64.00 to 132.00
Figurine, Miss Moppet, BP 2, 1954-78, 3 In. 24.00
Figurine, Mittens & Moppet, BP 6A, 1990-94, 3 ¾ In. 108.00
Figurine, Mr. Benjamin Bunny, BP 4, 1975-2000, 4 ¼ In. 80.00
Figurine, Mr. Benjamin Bunny & Peter Rabbit, BP 3B, 1975-95, 4 In. 129.00
Figurine, Mr. Jeremy Fisher, Digging, BP 6A, 1988-94, 3 ¾ In. 84.00
Figurine, Mrs. Flopsy Bunny, BP 2A, 1965-98, 4 In. 120.00
Figurine, Mrs. Rabbit, BP 3B, 1951-74, 4 ¼ In. 360.00
Figurine, Mrs. Tiggy Winkle & Lucie, Box, No. 3867, 1999, 4 In. 98.00
Figurine, New Forest Pony, No. 1646, 7 In. 77.00
Figurine, Old Mother Hubbard, Dog, Bone, DNR 3, 1999, 7 ½ In. 32.00
Figurine, Old Mr. Pricklepin BP 6A, 1983-89, 2 ½ In. 840.00
Figurine, Peter Rabbit, BP 1A, 1948-80, 4 ½ In. 250.00
Figurine, Pheasant Pair, No. 2078, 1966-75, 6 ¾ In. 432.00
Figurine, Pickles, BP 3B, 1971-82, 4 ½ In. 211.00
Figurine, Pinto Pony, Palomino, No. 1373, 1961-70, 6 ½ In. 1277.00
Figurine, Pinto Pony, Skewbald, No. 1373, 1955, 6 ½ In. 127.00
Figurine, Puma, Rock, No. 1702, 1970-73, 8 ½ In. 85.00
Figurine, Samuel Whiskers, BP 2A, 1948-95, 3 ¼ In. . . . . *illus* 225.00
Figurine, Sea Gull On Rock, No. 768, 1939-54, 8 ½ In. 1680.00
Figurine, Shire Mare, Brown, No. 818, 1979-89, 8 ½ In. 53.00
Figurine, Shire Mare, Gray, No. 818, 1961-89, 8 ½ In. 638.00
Figurine, Shire Mare, No. 818, 1940-89, 8 ½ In. 1532.00
Figurine, Simpkin, BP 3B, 1975-83, 4 In. . . . . 192.00 to 228.00
Figurine, Sir Isaac Newton, BP 3A, 1973-84, 3 ¾ In. 211.00
Figurine, Sir Isaac Newton, BP 3B, 1973-84, 3 ¾ In. 149.00
Figurine, Spaniel, White, No. 967, 1970-94, 5 ½ In. 110.00
Figurine, Steeplechaser, No. 2505, 1975-81, 8 ¾ In. 596.00
Figurine, Swandale Ewe, No. 3071-1765, 4 ½ In. 138.00
Figurine, Swish Tail Horse, Palomino, No. 1182, 1970-82, 8 ¾ In. 96.00

Beswick, Figurine, Chihuahua, Seated On Cushion, No. 2454, 1984-89, 2 ⅔ In.
$48.00

Beswick, Figurine, Girl On Skewbald Pony, No. 1499, 1957-65, 5 ½ In.
$264.00

Beswick, Figurine, Samuel Whiskers, BP 2A, 1948-95, 3 ¼ In.
$225.00

Beswick, Toby Jug, Tony Weller, No. 281, 6 ½ In.
$48.00

Betty Boop, Figurine, Betty Boop, Dog, Painted, Plaster, c.1930-35, 6 x 5 In. $2087.00

Betty Boop, Stringholder, Painted, Plaster, 10 x 9 x 2 ½ In. $518.00

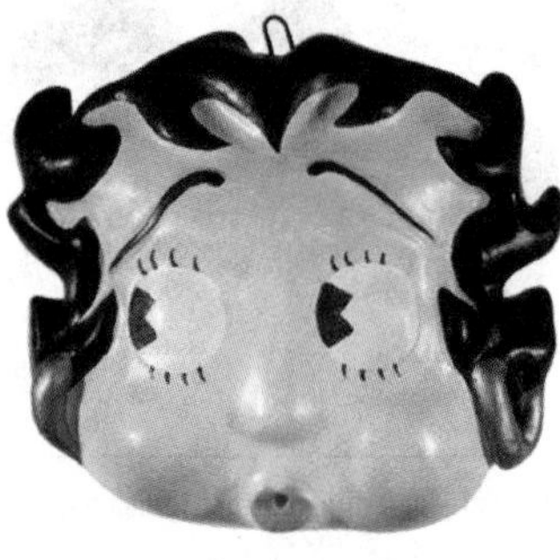

Bicycle, Tricycle, Boneshaker, Wood Spokes, Iron Frame, 1800s, 26-In. Front, 45-In. Rear $11825.00

Schreckengost

Viktor Schreckengost, best known to collectors for his ceramic designs, including the famous Cowan Pottery Jazz Bowl, also did industrial designing. He designed pedal cars and bicycles for Murray Ohio Company of Cleveland.

Figurine, Tailor Of Gloucester, BP 3B, 1949-2002, 3 ½ In. 53.00
Figurine, The Christmas Stocking, BP 6A, 1991-94, 3 ¼ In. 228.00
Figurine, Timmy Willie, BP 2A, 1949-93, 2 ½ In. 120.00
Figurine, Welsh Cobb, Gray No. 1793, 1962-75, 7 ½ In. 341.00
Figurine, White Poodle, No. 2339, 1971-83, 5 ¾ In. 24.00
Figurine, Yellow Budgie, No. 1216B, 1970-72, 7 In. 1277.00
Tankard, Christmas Carolers, 1972, 5 ¼ In. 11.00
Teapot, Peggotty, No. 1116, 1948-1973, 6 In. 135.00
Toby Jug, Tony Weller, No. 281, 6 ½ In. .... *illus* 48.00

BETTY BOOP, the cartoon figure, first appeared on the screen in 1931. Her face was modeled after the famous singer Helen Kane and her body after Mae West. In 1935, a comic strip was started. Her dog was named Bimbo. Although the Betty Boop cartoons ended by 1938, there was a revival of interest in the Betty Boop image in the 1980s and new pieces are being made.

Doll, Ceramic, Jointed, Marie Shay, 1986, 10 ½ In. 195.00
Doll, Composition, Wood, Green Dress, 12 In. 460.00
Doll, Wood, Composition, Jointed, Black Outfit, 13 In. 400.00
Doll, Wood, Composition, Jointed, Black Version, Fleischer Studios, 1930s, 12 In. 690.00
Figure, Celluloid, Movable Arms, Painted, c.1930, 5 ¾ In. 172.00
Figurine, Betty Boop, Dog, Painted, Plaster, c.1930-35, 6 x 5 In. .... *illus* 2087.00
Mask, Paper, Die Cut, Metal Fasteners, Fleischer Studios, 1930s, 8 ¼ x 8 ¾ In. 115.00
Nodder, Celluloid, Windup, 1920s, 7 In. 1450.00
Stringholder, Painted, Plaster, 10 x 9 x 2 ½ In. .... *illus* 518.00

BICYCLES were invented in 1839. The first manufactured bicycle was made in 1861. Special ladies' bicycles were made after 1874. The modern safety bicycle was not produced until 1885. Collectors search for all types of bicycles and tricycles. Bicycle-related items are also listed here.

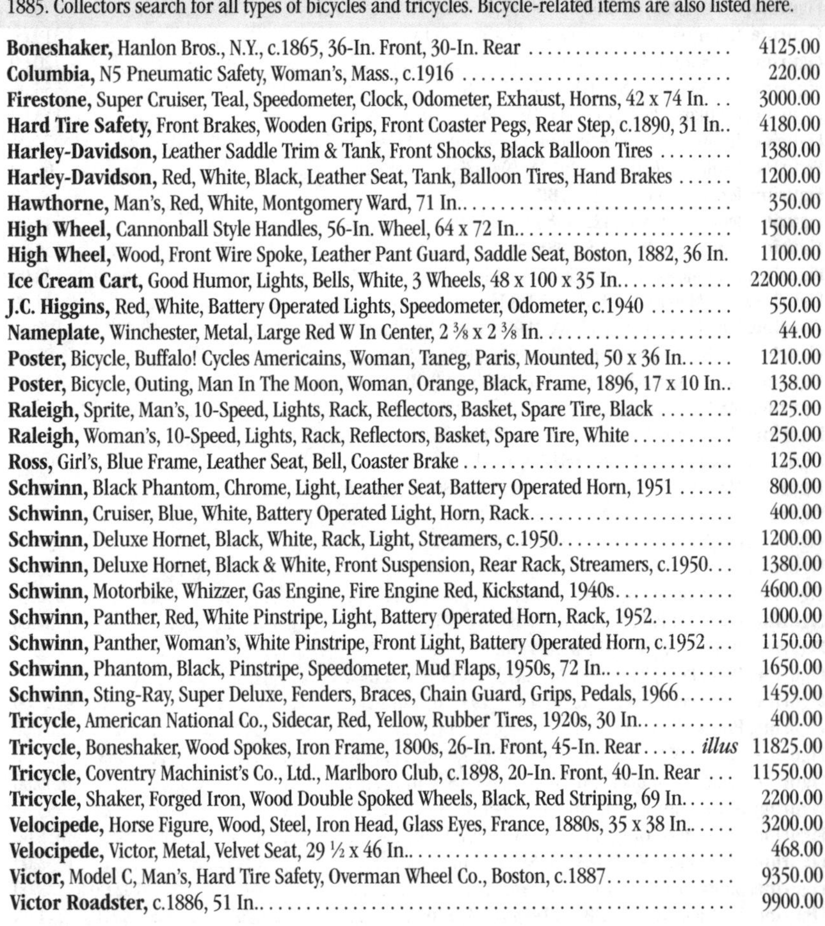

Boneshaker, Hanlon Bros., N.Y., c.1865, 36-In. Front, 30-In. Rear 4125.00
Columbia, N5 Pneumatic Safety, Woman's, Mass., c.1916 .... 220.00
Firestone, Super Cruiser, Teal, Speedometer, Clock, Odometer, Exhaust, Horns, 42 x 74 In. ... 3000.00
Hard Tire Safety, Front Brakes, Wooden Grips, Front Coaster Pegs, Rear Step, c.1890, 31 In. . 4180.00
Harley-Davidson, Leather Saddle Trim & Tank, Front Shocks, Black Balloon Tires 1380.00
Harley-Davidson, Red, White, Black, Leather Seat, Tank, Balloon Tires, Hand Brakes 1200.00
Hawthorne, Man's, Red, White, Montgomery Ward, 71 In. 350.00
High Wheel, Cannonball Style Handles, 56-In. Wheel, 64 x 72 In. 1500.00
High Wheel, Wood, Front Wire Spoke, Leather Pant Guard, Saddle Seat, Boston, 1882, 36 In. 1100.00
Ice Cream Cart, Good Humor, Lights, Bells, White, 3 Wheels, 48 x 100 x 35 In. 22000.00
J.C. Higgins, Red, White, Battery Operated Lights, Speedometer, Odometer, c.1940 .... 550.00
Nameplate, Winchester, Metal, Large Red W In Center, 2 ⅜ x 2 ⅜ In. 44.00
Poster, Bicycle, Buffalo! Cycles Americains, Woman, Taneg, Paris, Mounted, 50 x 36 In. 1210.00
Poster, Bicycle, Outing, Man In The Moon, Woman, Orange, Black, Frame, 1896, 17 x 10 In. . 138.00
Raleigh, Sprite, Man's, 10-Speed, Lights, Rack, Reflectors, Basket, Spare Tire, Black 225.00
Raleigh, Woman's, 10-Speed, Lights, Rack, Reflectors, Basket, Spare Tire, White 250.00
Ross, Girl's, Blue Frame, Leather Seat, Bell, Coaster Brake 125.00
Schwinn, Black Phantom, Chrome, Light, Leather Seat, Battery Operated Horn, 1951 .... 800.00
Schwinn, Cruiser, Blue, White, Battery Operated Light, Horn, Rack 400.00
Schwinn, Deluxe Hornet, Black, White, Rack, Light, Streamers, c.1950 .... 1200.00
Schwinn, Deluxe Hornet, Black & White, Front Suspension, Rear Rack, Streamers, c.1950 ... 1380.00
Schwinn, Motorbike, Whizzer, Gas Engine, Fire Engine Red, Kickstand, 1940s 4600.00
Schwinn, Panther, Red, White Pinstripe, Light, Battery Operated Horn, Rack, 1952 .... 1000.00
Schwinn, Panther, Woman's, White Pinstripe, Front Light, Battery Operated Horn, c.1952 ... 1150.00
Schwinn, Phantom, Black, Pinstripe, Speedometer, Mud Flaps, 1950s, 72 In. 1650.00
Schwinn, Sting-Ray, Super Deluxe, Fenders, Braces, Chain Guard, Grips, Pedals, 1966 .... 1459.00
Tricycle, American National Co., Sidecar, Red, Yellow, Rubber Tires, 1920s, 30 In. 400.00
Tricycle, Boneshaker, Wood Spokes, Iron Frame, 1800s, 26-In. Front, 45-In. Rear ...... *illus* 11825.00
Tricycle, Coventry Machinist's Co., Ltd., Marlboro Club, c.1898, 20-In. Front, 40-In. Rear ... 11550.00
Tricycle, Shaker, Forged Iron, Wood Double Spoked Wheels, Black, Red Striping, 69 In. 2200.00
Velocipede, Horse Figure, Wood, Steel, Iron Head, Glass Eyes, France, 1880s, 35 x 38 In. 3200.00
Velocipede, Victor, Metal, Velvet Seat, 29 ½ x 46 In. 468.00
Victor, Model C, Man's, Hard Tire Safety, Overman Wheel Co., Boston, c.1887 .... 9350.00
Victor Roadster, c.1886, 51 In. 9900.00

BING & GRONDAHL is a famous Danish factory making fine porcelains from 1853 to the present. Underglaze blue decoration was started in 1886. The annual Christmas plate series was introduced in 1895. Dinnerwares, stoneware, and figurines are still being made today. The firm has used the initials B & G and a stylized castle as part of the mark since 1898. The company became part of Royal Copenhagen in 1987.

Figurine, Boy, Fixing Shorts, Marked, 6 ½ x 2 In. 50.00
Figurine, Boy, Kissing Girl, No. 2162, 7 ½ In. 50.00
Figurine, Boy, With Fishing Net, 8 x 2 In. 50.00
Figurine, Boy, With Umbrellas, No. 2055, 7 In. 50.00
Figurine, Cat, Gray & White, Seated, No. 1876, 4 ½ In. 50.00
Figurine, Dickie, Crouching, No. 1636, 3 ½ In. 60.00
Figurine, Girl, Feeding Cat, No. 1745, 5 ½ In. .... 90.00 to 100.00
Figurine, Girl, Holding Doll, No. 1721, 7 ½ In. 90.00
Figurine, Grethe, Girl Knitting, No. 1656, 6 ¾ In. 66.00
Figurine, Love Refused, Boy & Girl, No. 1614, 6 ¾ In. 44.00
Figurine, Man Playing Accordion, Seated, 8 ¾ In. 53.00
Figurine, Milkmaid, Cow, No. 2017, Signed, AxH Locher, 7 ¼ x 8 In. .... *illus* 395.00
Figurine, Parrot, No. 2019, Marked, 5 ½ In. 85.00
Figurine, Polar Bear, No. 1857, 14 In. 300.00
Figurine, Water Mother, Nursing 2 Children, White, K Nielsen, 1925, 11 x 19 In. . 1800.00 to 2133.00
Plate, Boat Of The King Of Denmark, 1953 .... 99.00
Plate, Christmas, 1895, Behind The Frozen Window 6799.00
Plate, Christmas, 1914, Royal Castle Of Amalienborg 89.00
Plate, Christmas, 1920, Hare In The Snow 78.00
Plate, Christmas, 1942, Danish Farm On Christmas Night 245.00
Plate, Christmas, 1974, Christmas In The Village 15.00
Tureen, Cover, Blue & White, Dolphin Shape, 7 ½ x 11 In. 176.00

Bing & Grondahl
When Bing & Grondahl became part of Royal Copenhagen in 1987, some Bing & Grondahl dinnerware, figurines, and vases were discontinued; some remained in production but were marked with the Royal Copenhagen mark. The Bing & Grondahl name was used only on commemorative and annual pieces and a few overglaze-decorated figurines.

BINOCULARS of all types are wanted by collectors. Those made in the eighteenth and nineteenth centuries are favored by serious collectors. The small, attractive binoculars called opera glasses are listed in their own category.

C.F. Foth & Co., Black Leather, 8x, Danzig, Germany, 4 ½ x 5 ¼ In. 100.00
P. Roulot, Optician, Black Leather Case, Paris, 1878, 2 ½ x 4 In. 45.00
Vendome, Leather Covered, Paris, 6 In. .... 45.00 to 95.00

BIRDCAGES are collected for use as homes for pet birds and as decorative objects of folk art. Elaborate wooden cages of the past centuries can still be found. The brass or wicker cages of the 1930s are popular with bird owners.

Brass, House Shape, Surrounding Fence, Wire, Painted, Gray, Wood Base, 15 x 22 In. 440.00
Georgian Style, Stenciled, Arched Crested Roof, Shell Applique, Stand, 83 x 37 In. 325.00
Iron, Glass Feeder, Floor Stand, 66 In. 15.00
Iron, Scrolled Cylindrical Hood, Arched Legs, 67 x 43 In. 1645.00
Tin, 8-Sided, Bird Finials, Painted, Late 1800s, 19 x 15 In. .... *illus* 700.00
Tin, Bird Finials, Enclosed In Glass Globe, 8-Sided, Painted, c.1900, 19 x 15 In. 823.00
Tin, Blue, White, Stevens & Brown, 18 x 17 In. 1092.00
Tin, Painted, Oval, Round Hanger, Mid 19th Century, 19 In. 234.00
Tin, Punched, White Paint, 16 x 11 ¾ In. 200.00
Wood, House Shape, Chip Carved, Dowel Fence, Green & Red Paint, 1900s, 18 x 11 x 24 In. .. 646.00
Wood, Round Aviary Top, Wire Bars, Pull Out Drawers, Late 19th Century, 28 x 25 In. 895.00

BISQUE is an unglazed baked porcelain. Finished bisque has a slightly sandy texture with a dull finish. Some of it may be decorated with various colors. Bisque gained favor during the late Victorian era when thousands of bisque figurines were made. It is still being made. Additional bisque items may be listed under the factory name.

Bust, Classical Woman, Continental, c.1900, 11 x 8 In. .... 234.00 to 298.00
Bust, Marie Antoinette, Cobalt Blue, Gilt Decorated Plinth Base, France, c.1915, 15 x 6 In. 118.00
Bust, Woman, Upswept Hair, Socle Base, 19th Century, 17 ¼ In. 705.00
Figurine, Andy Gump, Painted, Germany, 7 ½ x 3 ½ x 2 In. 33.00
Figurine, Cupid Peeking Through Keyhole, Yellow Wings, Shoes, Boots, Germany, 1912, 5 In. 680.00
Figurine, Flautist With Dog, c.1800, 7 ½ In. 411.00
Figurine, Gentleman, Fine Dress, Gold Decoration, Rocaille Base, Marked, 11 In. 36.00
Figurine, Kneeling Woman, Wood Base, 11 ½ In. 35.00
Figurine, Ladder Backed Woodpecker, Kazmar, 9 x 5 In. 94.00
Figurine, Lady In Chair, Early 20th Century, 12 In. 175.00
Figurine, Polar Bear Cubs, Kazmar, 6 x 7 In. 70.00
Flower, Lily Harlequin, Burgues, 10 x 9 In. 70.00
Flower, Magnolia, Audrey Billings, 5 x 11 In. 59.00
Planter, Figural, Draped Woman, Reclining Amidst Lilies, Austria, c.1900, 11 x 16 In. 644.00

Bing & Grondahl, Figurine, Milkmaid, Cow, No. 2017, Signed, AxH Locher, 7 ¼ x 8 In.
$395.00

Birdcage, Tin, 8-Sided, Bird Finials, Painted, Late 1800s, 19 x 15 In.
$700.00

TIP
To remove the remains of sticky glue and tape from antiques, try rubbing peanut butter on the sticky area until the glue is gone. Don't use this method on porous materials; the oil from the peanut butter could leave a stain.

Bisque, Urn, Grape Clusters, Vine Leaves, Gilt, Handles, Marked, c.1860-70, 10 ½ In.
$420.00

Black, Lamp, Electric, Mammy, Opaque, Black Base, Painted, Early 1900s, 6 ¾ x 4 ¾ In.
$423.00

Planter, Uncle Willie & Emmy, Painted, 5 In.. 195.00
Salt Dip, Figural, Child In Bonnet Near Bird Nest, 3 ½ In. 150.00
Stein, Devil Head, Painted, Marked, Ernst Bohne Sohne, c.1900, ¼ Liter. 450.00
Urn, Grape Clusters, Vine Leaves, Gilt, Handles, Marked, c.1860-70, 10 ½ In. *illus* 420.00

BLACK memorabilia has become an important area of collecting since the 1970s. The best material dates from past centuries, but many recent items are also of interest. F & F is the mark used on plastic made by Fiedler & Fiedler Mold & Die Works, Inc. in the 1930s and 1940s. Objects that picture a black person may also be listed in this book under Advertising, Sign; Bank; Bottle Opener; Cookie Jar; Doll; Salt & Pepper; Sheet Music; Toy; etc.

Andirons, Man, Formal Attire, Hands On Knee, Cast Half Round, Black Paint, c.1910, 17 In.. 575.00
Ashtray, Amos 'n' Andy, Barrel, Painted, Chalk, 7 ½ In. 220.00
Ashtray, Waiter, Red Jacket, Long Black Legs, Cast Iron, 33 In.. 354.00
Box, Black Musicians, Lacquer, Hand Painted, Multicolored, 1800s, 3 ¼ In. 1062.00
Box, Pop-Up, Composition, Lithograph, 6 ½ In. 184.00
Broom Holder, Black Boy, Cast Iron, c.1894, 1 ½ In. 230.00
Broom Holder, Boy, Red Jacket, Figural, Painted, Cast Iron, Signed, 1894, 4 ½ x 1 ⅝ In. 230.00
Bust, Man, Terra-Cotta, Signed, James Wilds, 1980, 12 x 11 In. 330.00
Candleholder, Black Clown Bust, Milk Glass, 3 ¼ x 2 ⅞ In.. 80.00
Cigar Lighter, Bust, Cast Iron, Eagle Claw Feet, Cotton Wick, c.1880s, 5 x 9 In. 708.00
Doll, Babyland Rag, Girl, Cloth, Printed Features, Black Wool Hair, 1900, 15 In. 345.00
Doll, Bisque, Boy, Black Glass Eyes, Curly Mohair, 5-Piece Body, 3 ¼ In. 563.00
Doll, Bisque, Open Mouth, Glass Eyes, Domed Head, Cloth, Composition Hands, 9 ¾ In. 296.00
Doll, Bottle, Mammy, Stockinet, Button Eyes, Stitched Features, Sand Filled, 1920, 13 In. 29.00
Doll, Cloth, Aunt Jemima, Tag, Saalfield Publishing, 1910, 23 In. 90.00
Doll, Cloth, Bisque, Glass Eyes, Domed Head, Composition Hands, Baby, 9 ¾ In. 296.00
Doll, Cloth, Stitched Features, Bead Eyes, Tag, Oneida, July 25, 1899, 14 In. 690.00
Doll, Flip Dress, Stuffed, Needlework Facial Features, 16 x 7 In. 50.00
Doll, Mammy, Blue Print Dress, White Collar, Scarf, Red Lips, 17 In. 275.00
Doll, Rag, Golliwog, Black Jacket, Red Pants, Velvet, England, 1930s, 18 In. 633.00
Doll, Rag, Golliwog, Button Eyes, Sewn Mouth, Fuzzy Hair, Cloth, Velvet, 25 ½ x 7 In. 60.00
Doll, Rag, Golliwog, Sewn Facial Features, Fuzzy Hair, Sailor Suit, Cloth, Velvet, 16 ½ x 5 In.. 30.00
Figurine, Cigar Smoker, Habana, Man, Top Hat, Seated On Orange, Box, Composition, c.1900, 8 In. 263.00
Figurine, Cigar Smoker, Man, White Top Hat, Seated Near Match Basket, Pot Metal, 8 In.. 293.00
Figurine, Egg, Embossed Face Emerging From Egg, U Bet, Milk Glass, 2 ½ In.. 145.00
Figurine, Egg, Young Man's Face, More Chicken, Milk Glass, 4 ¼ In. 285.00
Figurine, Golly Band, Flute Player, Trumpet Player, Name Stand, Carlton Ware, 3 Piece. 96.00
Figurine, Jungle Imps, Ceramic, Winsor McCay Jr., Cannibal Chef, Water Tester, 3 ⅝ In., 3 Piece 345.00
Figurine, Mammy, Tin Lithograph, Windup, Lindstrom, 8 In. 196.00
Figurine, Man, Calling Card Holder, Hammered Dish, Tiered Stand, Cast Iron, c.1880, 9 In.. 1500.00
Figurine, Man, Country Attire, Basket, Crab, Net, Cloth, Vargas Mark, New Orleans, 7 x 7 In., 3 Piece 403.00
Figurine, Man, Holding Accordion, Smoking Cigar, Baskets, Bisque, c.1900, 8 In. 117.00
Figurine, Man, Red Jacket, Metal Ashtray, Matchbox Holder, Cast Iron, 34 In. 1180.00
Figurine, Man, Smoking Cigar, Barrel, Composition, Austria, c.1900, 9 In.. 410.00
Game, Bowling, Pickaninny, 5 Open Mouth Faces, 5 Balls, Box, 15 x 11 In. 485.00
Game, Dexterity Puzzle, Baby On Pillow, Eating Watermelon, 1 ¾ In. 125.00
Game, Pitch Toss, Black Man, Watermelon, Die Cut Cardboard, c.1900, 7 ½ In. 201.00
Game, Puzzle, Man Smiling, Mirror, 2-Sided, Embossed, Tin, Marked, D.R.G.M., 1 ¾ In.. 50.00
Humidor, Man's Head, Mustache, 1920s Cap, Smoking Cigarette, 6 ⅜ x 5 ⅜ In.. 695.00
Jar, Pomade, Milk Glass, 1885, 2 ½ x 2 ½ In. 100.00
Lamp, Electric, Mammy, Opaque, Black Base, Painted, Early 1900s, 6 ¾ x 4 ¾ In. *illus* 423.00
Lamp Shade, Smiling Black Man, Milk Glass, 3 x 3 x 2 In. 80.00
Letter Opener, Johnny Griffin, Figural Handle, Cast Bronze, Multicolored, 13 ¼ In. 495.00
Nodder, Metal, Wood, Chalk, Composition, Cloth, Windup, Key, c.1897, 22 ½ In. 575.00
Notepad, Aunt Jemima, Red Dress, Yellow Bandanna, F & F Mold & Die Works, 10 In.. 100.00
Nutcracker, Sambo, Painted, Wood, Carved, Black Forest, 8 In.. 550.00
Pie Bird, Aunt Jemima, Bisque, Porcelain, Painted, New Orleans, Souvenir, 2 ½ In. 20.00
Pillow, Minstrel, Appliqued Figures In Black Face, 10 x 16 In. 121.00
Plaque, Boy Chasing Chicken, Milk Glass, Embossed, 1940s, 6 x 7 In.. 735.00
Plaque, Men Eating Watermelon, Milk Glass, 1930s, 6 x 7 In. 535.00
Postcard, Children, At Beach. 35.00
Postcard, Children, Gambling, 1900-10. 55.00
Poster, H. Rap Brown, Wanted, Interstate Flight, Arson, c.1970, 8 x 8 In.. 115.00
Poster, Military, Colored Man Is No Slacker, Soldier, Woman Holding Hands, Troop, 14 x 20 In. 275.00
Slave Shackles, Iron, Half-Moon, Connecting Links, Missile Shape Lock, Child's, 3 x 2 ¾ In. 1416.00
Slave Tag, Diamond Shape, Copper, Charleston, c.1838 1770.00

Sprinkler, Lawn, Sambo, Firestone Tire & Rubber Co., Black Americana, Hose, 34 In. 173.00
Stereo Card, Sharecroppers Grinding Sugar Cane, c.1890. ...... 65.00
Stringholder, Black Man, Red Cap, Frederick Factory Art Pottery, 6 ¾ In. 77.00
Stringholder, Butler Figure, Ceramic, Japan, 6 In. 104.00
Tobacco Jar, Page Boy, Painted, Pottery, Germany, 5 ½ In. 250.00
Tobacco Jar, Pappy, Milk Glass, 1930s, 5 ¼ x 4 ¼ In. 565.00
Toothpick, Clown Bust, Raised On Ribbed Base, Milk Glass, 4 x 3 In. 80.00
Toy, Dancing Man, Carved Wood, Long Coat, Boots, Articulated Limbs, 1800s, 10 ½ In. 352.00
Tray, Mammoth Shoe & Clothing, Black Boy With Watermelon, Scalloped Rim, 3 ¼ x 2 In. ... 60.00

BLACK AMETHYST glass appears black until it is held to the light, then a dark purple can be seen. It has been made in many factories from 1860 to the present.

Candlestick, 3-Toed, Pair 21.00
Ivy Ball, Golf Ball, Bryce Brothers, 4 In. 93.00
Vase, 12 Panels, Oval Reserve, Gold Enameled, Depicting Balcony Scene, 6 ½ In. 270.00
Vase, Trophy Cup, Silver Enameled Flowers, Ruffled Rim, L.E. Smith, 8 In. 18.00

BLENKO GLASS COMPANY is the 1930s successor to several glassworks founded by William John Blenko in Milton, West Virginia. In 1933, his son, William H. Blenko Sr., took charge. They made tablewares and vases in classical shapes. In the late 1940s the company hired talented designers and made innovative pieces. The company made a line of reproductions for Colonial Williamsburg. It is still in business and is best known today for its decorative wares and stained glass.

Bottle, Green, Double Spout, 8 ¼ x 6 ½ In. 12.00
Bottle, Ruby Red, Crackle, Pinched, Cut Clear Stopper, 10 In. 58.00
Bowl, Amber, Free-Form, 4 x 15 In. 23.00
Bowl, Amberina, 11 ¼ x 4 ⅜ In. 86.00
Bowl, Amethyst, Deep Lobed Rim, 3 x 5 In. 6.00
Bowl, Centerpiece, Yellow Green, Flattened Oval, 5 x 19 In. 265.00
Compote, Amethyst Bowl, Fluted Edge, Label, 13 ¾ x 6 In. 52.00
Goblet, Sea Green, Air Twist Stem, 13 x 5 ¼ In. 100.00
Pitcher, Double Spout, Blue To Clear, Triangular, Pinched Grip, 8 ½ In. 35.00
Vase, Amberina, Bubble Wrap, No. 6041, Signed, c.1960, 9 ¼ x 5 ½ In. ...... *illus* 155.00
Vase, Amberina, Bulbous, 5 x 6 ½ In. 23.00
Vase, Amberina, Square Base To Round Top, 8 x 9 In. 120.00
Vase, Avocado Green, Shouldered, Flared Rim, 20 ¼ In. 63.00
Vase, Clear Crackle, Applied Green Rosettes, 7 ½ x 6 ½ In. 175.00
Vase, Cobalt Blue, Amphora Shape, 13 ½ In. 18.00
Vase, Fan, Yellow, Cobalt Blue Foot, 11 ¾ x 10 In. 115.00
Vase, Green, Clear Applied Handles, Straight-Sided, Husted, 16 ¾ In. 115.00
Vase, Shaded Blue, Cone Shape, Flared Rim, Clear Foot, 11 ¼ x 8 In. 35.00
Vase, Yellow, Purple, Orange, Flared Rim, 25 x 9 In. 92.00

BLOWN GLASS, *see Glass-Blown category.*

BLUE GLASS, *see Cobalt Blue category.*

BLUE ONION, *see Onion category.*

BLUE WILLOW, *see Willow category.*

BOCH FRERES factory was founded in 1841 in La Louviere in eastern Belgium. The wares resemble the work of Villeroy & Boch. The factory is still in business.

Box, Blue Geometrics, Craquelure Ground, Bronze Mounts, c.1915, 5 ½ x 4 x 2 ½ In. 225.00
Box, Cover, Art Deco, Green, Black, Maroon, Orange, Yellow, 2 ⅞ x 4 ⅝ In. 295.00
Charger, Smiling Bacchus, Crackled Enamel Glaze, Marked, Keramis, 14 ½ In. ...... *illus* 2300.00
Tile, Heraldic Eagles, Blue, Yellow, Brown, Green, Cuerda Seca, 8 In., Pair 120.00
Vase, 2 Geishas, Landscape, 2 Fishermen, Flat Sided, 10 ½ In. 1150.00
Vase, Alternating Panels, Vertical Grooves, White, Squat, Art Deco, 7 In. 104.00
Vase, Art Deco Flowers, Multicolored, Matte Enamel, 19 ½ In. 6613.00
Vase, Band Of Birds, Repeating, Matte Enamel, 10 In. 2530.00
Vase, Birds, Flowers, Antelope, Crackled White Ground, 13 ½ In. 1725.00
Vase, Birds On Branches, Matte Enamel, Blue Slip, Gold Bands, Ch. Catteau, 7 In. 1180.00
Vase, Deer, Turquoise, Blue, White Ground, Cuerda Seca, Pillow, Art Deco, 9 x 8 ½ In. 768.00

Blenko, Vase, Amberina, Bubble Wrap, No. 6041, Signed, c.1960, 9 ¼ x 5 ½ In.
$155.00

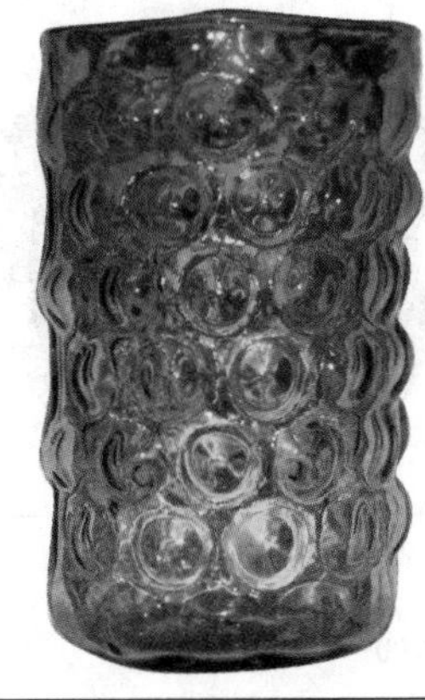

Boch Freres, Charger, Smiling Bacchus, Crackled Enamel Glaze, Marked, Keramis, 14 ½ In.
$2300.00

TIP

Think about security when you landscape your house. Cut bushes low under windows. Don't plant trees or bushes near doors where prowlers could hide. Place decorative lights in the yard to illuminate windows and doors. You might try the nineteenth-century style of landscaping used in Midwest farm areas—no shrubbery plantings, but flowers near the house.

Boch Freres, Vase, Flowers, Black Ink Stamp, 6 ½ x 6 ¾ In. $143.00

Vase, Wooly Mammoth, Pebbly, Flat, 9 ⅛ In. $2300.00

TIP

If you live in an earthquake area, a few precautions may help limit damage. Be sure there is a lip on the edge of a shelf that holds dishes and glassware. String a fishing line across the front of a shelf holding baskets or other very light objects to help keep them from falling. Use dental wax to stick the objects to the shelf. Keep cabinet doors locked shut so pieces will not fall out. Magnetic "childproof" locks help some also.

Vase, Feeding Deer, Crackled, Charles Catteau, 9 ⅛ In. 805.00
Vase, Flowers, Black Ink Stamp, 6 ½ x 6 ¾ In. *illus* 143.00
Vase, Flowers, Orange, Blue, Yellow, Long Neck, Art Deco, 8 ⅜ In. 236.00
Vase, Peonies, Yellow, Blue Ground, Enamel, Oval, 9 ½ In. 275.00
Vase, Peonies, Yellow, Turquoise Bands, Blue Ground, Enamel, Oval, 9 ½ In. 275.00
Vase, Roosters, Globular, Keramis, 6 ⅞ In. 345.00
Vase, Sailboats, Sea Gulls, Multicolored, Crackled Enamel, 12 ⅜ In. 1725.00
Vase, Stylized Flowers, Blue, Amber, White, Round, Catteau, 5 ½ x 5 ½ In. 1920.00
Vase, Tulips, Blue, Multicolored Enamel, Oval, 9 ½ In. 275.00
Vase, Tulips, Leaves, Enamel, Oval, 9 ½ In. 330.00
Vase, Tulips, Yellow, Blue Flowers, Green Leaves, Enamel, Oval, 9 ½ In. 275.00
Vase, Wooly Mammoth, Pebbly, Flat, 9 ⅛ In. *illus* 2300.00

BOEHM is the collector's name for the porcelains of Edward Marshall Boehm. In 1953 the Osso China Company was reorganized as Edward Marshall Boehm, Inc. The company is still working in England and New Jersey. In the early days of the factory, dishes were made, but the elaborate and lifelike bird figurines are the best-known ware. Edward Marshall Boehm, the founder, died in 1969, but the firm has continued to design and produce porcelain. Today, the firm makes both limited and unlimited editions of figurines and plates.

Boehm MADE IN USA

African Elephant, Bisque, 8 x 10 In. 294.00
American Bald Eagle, 1994, 12 x 9 In. 585.00
American Bald Eagle, 40th Presidential Inauguration, No. 224, Box, 1981, 8 ½ In. 350.00
American Wild Turkey, No. 37, Signed, 17 In. 475.00
Baby Buntings, No. 400-20, 2 x 3 ½ In. 100.00
Black Capped Chickadee, No. 401-95, 8 In. 110.00
Black Headed Grosbeak, 10 In. 175.00 to 400.00
Blue Jays, Chameleon, 13 ¾ x 10 x 8 ½ In. 1300.00
Bluebird, Spread Wings, No. 106, 1977, 14 In. 140.00
Bobolink, On Cornstalk, No. 475, 12 x 7 In. 322.00
Brown Pelican, Shore Life, 25 x 16 In. 1900.00
Canadian Goose, Male & Female, 7 ⅜ x 4 ⅞ In., Pair 585.00
Cardinal, Grape Plant, No 419, 10 In. 140.00
Cardinal, Spread Wings, No. 415, 15 In. 250.00
Cat, 2 Kittens, Green Mark, 5 In. 130.00 to 175.00
Cedar Waxwing, Eating Berries, No. 188, 8 In. 135.00
Cheetah Head, Gold, Blue, Black, No. 723, 7 x 4 ½ In. 527.00
Colt, Reclining, 24K Gold, 1978, 4 x 5 In. 264.00
Cygnet, No. 400-27, 6 ½ In. 60.00
Fledgling Blue Jay, No. 400-77, 5 In. 70.00
Fledgling Chickadee, No. 400-08, 4 ¼ In. 88.00
Fledgling Kingfisher, On Log, No. 404-42, 6 In. 35.00
Fledgling Owl, Great Horn, Marked, 7 In. 132.00
Flower, Camellia, White, 11 ¼ x 13 ½ x 6 ½ In. 80.00
Flower, Paphiopedilum, No. 400-08, 5 x 9 In. 130.00
Flower, Poinsettia, Red, 7 In. 50.00
Giant Panda Cub, Eating Leaf, No. 400-47, c.1974, 6 x 8 In. 130.00
Glory Falcon, Sweeping Down, No. 61, Marked, c.1990, 34 x 32 In. 1430.00
God Anubis, Black, Gold, Bisque, 9 ½ In. 760.00
Goldfinch, No. 403-26, 5 ⅞ In. 110.00
Golden Crown Kinglets, Poppies, No. 419, 1958, 11 In. 575.00
Green Lizard, 3 ⅜ In. 117.00
Horned Lark, Grapevines, No. 400-25, Signed, 19 ¼ In. 2100.00
Jenny Wren, On Rocks, 6 x 4 In. 117.00
Junco, Bittersweet, Snow, No. 400-12H, Limited Edition, Marked, 11 ½ In. 640.00
Lady's Slipper, No. 26-001, 7 ½ In. 160.00
Lion Cub, Seated, Signed, 5 In. 60.00
Mearns' Quails, No. 467R, 15 ¼ In. 375.00
Mourning Doves, No. 443, 15 x 9 In. 176.00
Nativity Set, White, Bisque, 13 Piece 995.00
Northern Water Thrush, No. 490, 10 ¾ In. 325.00
Oven Bird, No. 400-04, 10 In. 325.00
Panda, No. 400-47, 9 In. 135.00
Peregrine Falcon, Spread Wings, Signed, 21 In. 600.00
Presidential Eagle, For Ronald Reagan, No. 65 Of 500, 1985, 12 x 11 In. 440.00
Rabbit, Seated, No. 400-86, 4 ½ In. 60.00
Raccoons, On Tree, Limited Edition, 12 In. 310.00

Racquet-Tailed Hummingbird With Hibiscus, No. 185/1053, 1985, 13 ½ In. 420.00
Robin, No. 55, c.1977, 8 ¾ In. .... *illus* 275.00
Royal Tern, Signed, Helen Boehm, 19 x 19 In. 234.00
Snowy Owl, On Books, 9 ½ In., Pair 240.00
Tree Sparrow, No. 468, 8 x 6 In. 176.00
Tumbler Pigeons, No. 416, 9 x 10 In., Pair 146.00
Varied Buntings, No. 481, 23 In. 1053.00
Western Meadowlark, No. 400-15, 11 In. 80.00
Western Meadowlark, No. 400-95, 13 In. .... 350.00 to 375.00
White Throated Sparrow, No. 430, 9 In. 146.00
Wood Thrush, 15 ½ x 11 x 7 In. 400.00
Woodcock, No. 413, 10 ½ In. 644.00
Yellow Bellied Sapsucker, No. 400-18, 13 x 9 In. .... 350.00 to 380.00
Yellow Throated Warbler, No. 431, 9 ½ In. 585.00
Young & Free, Fawns, No. 146, 1980, 13 In. .... *illus* 175.00
Young & Spirited, Edward Marshall, 1976, 12 x 10 In. 450.00
Young & Spirited Eagles, No. 400-49, 1976, 9 ½ In. .... 250.00 to 450.00

BONE includes those articles made of bone not listed elsewhere in this book.

Boar Tusk, Fetish, Knotted Strings, Black Steel Mount, Indonesia, 9 ½ In. 180.00
Figurine, Bear, Begging, Seated, Carved, Painted Eyes, 1800s, 3 ⅝ In. 120.00
Figurine, White Owl, On Snow, Whalebone, Carved, Cape Dorset, c.1955, 12 In. 125.00
Knitting Needle, Ivory & Wood Inlay, 15 In., Pair 385.00
Pie Crimper, Unicorn Form, Whalebone 125.00
Scoop, Joint Terminal, Carved Scoop, 4 ¾ In. 55.00
Spoon, Cutout On Handle, 19th Century, 15 In. 175.00

BOOKENDS have probably been used since books became inexpensive. Early libraries kept books in cupboards, not on open shelves. By the 1870s bookends appeared, especially homemade fret-carved wooden examples. Most bookends listed in this book date from the twentieth century. Bookends are also listed in other categories by manufacturer or material. All bookends listed here are pairs.

Art Deco, Nude, Patinated Metal, Pedestal, Max Le Verrier, 7 ¼ x 8 ½ In. 690.00
Bald Eagle, Marked, Pennsbury, 8 x 6 In. 297.00
Black Stallions, Half Horse Head, Fit Together, Virginia Metalcrafters, 1954, 9 In. 68.00
Boy & Girl, Seated, Reading Book, Painted, Cast Iron, 5 ½ In. 110.00
Bucking Bronco, Bronze, Signed, c.1905, 8 In. 1265.00
Cabin In Woods, Trees, Moon, Painted, Cast Iron, 5 ¾ x 5 In. .... *illus* 58.00
Camel, Man, Walking, Bronze Color, Cast Iron, c.1920s, 5 ⅜ x 5 ¾ x 5 ¼ In. 165.00
Cane, Brass, Carl Aubock, Austria, c.1955, 4 x 3 x 4 In. 600.00
Cat, Seated, Gold Paint, Spelter, Art Deco, c.1930, 8 In. 150.00
Cello, Brass, 20th Century, 7 x 4 x 5 In. 65.00
Child's Bust, Milk Glass, Frosted, Hollow, 7 ¼ In. 120.00
Clown, Red, White, Cast Iron, Hubley, 6 ¼ x 3 In. .... *illus* 460.00
Cottage, Edgar Allen Poe, Cast Iron, Bradley & Hubbard, 4 x 4 ½ In. 144.00
Dog, Beagle, Seated, Pottery, Nubian Black Glaze, c.1927 .... 575.00
Dog, Boston Terrier, Cast Iron, Creations Co., 5 ½ x 5 ⅝ In. 144.00
Dog, Dachshund, Chewing Edges Of Books, Brass, 5 In. 45.00
Dog, English Bulldog, Puppy, In Barrel, Cast Iron, 5 x 5 ⅜ In. 288.00
Dog, German Shepherd, Patinated Metal, Green Onyx Base, Mid 1900s, 7 x 6 ¾ In. 80.00
Dog, Pointer, Cast Iron, 4 ⅝ x 5 ⅝ In. 144.00
Dog, Scottie, Hubley, Cast Iron, 5 x 6 In. .... 173.00 to 201.00
Dog, Wirehaired Terrier, Painted, Cast Iron, Hubley, 5 ⅝ x 5 ½ In. .... *illus* 259.00
Dog, Wirehaired Terrier & Scottie, Cast Iron, 4 ¾ x 5 ⅜ In. 633.00
Duck Head, Full Figure, Cast Iron, 5 ½ x 3 In. 58.00
Dutch Boy & Girl, Painted, Composition, Signed, M. Marron, France, 8 In. 40.00
Dutch Couple, Kissing, Hubley, Cast Iron, 4 ¾ In. 58.00
Eagle, On Rock, Bronze, Signed, M. Peinlich, 7 ½ In. 350.00
Elephant, Patinated Metal, c.1900, 6 x 6 In. 53.00
Elephant, Standing, On Stack Of Books, Metal, 4 x 4 ¼ x 3 In. 40.00
Flower, Tooled, Bronze, Impressed, 6 x 4 ½ In. 270.00
Frog, Playing Banjo, Painted, Pottery, 4 ½ x 3 ½ In. 25.00
Gear Cog Form, Industrial, Bronze, 2 ½ x 6 x 3 In. 200.00
Geometrics, Stepped, Red, Blue, Gold, Black, Cast Iron, Art Deco, c.1920, 6 x 4 ⅜ x 3 In. 195.00

Boehm, Robin, No. 55, c.1977, 8 ¾ In.
$275.00

Boehm, Young & Free, Fawns, No. 146, 1980, 13 In.
$175.00

Bookends, Cabin In Woods, Trees, Moon, Painted, Cast Iron, 5 ¾ x 5 In.
$58.00

Bookends, Clown, Red, White, Cast Iron, Hubley, 6 ¼ x 3 In.
$460.00

B

Bookends, Dog, Wirehaired Terrier, Painted, Cast Iron, Hubley, 5 ⅝ x 5 ½ In.
$259.00

Bookends, Girl, Holding Dress, Painted, Cast Iron, Albany Foundry, 5 x 4 ¾ In.
$87.00

Bookends, Quail, Painted, Cast Iron, Hubley, 5 ½ x 5 ¾ In.
$460.00

Bookends, Snowy Owl, On Branch, Embossed, Cast Iron, CJO, 5 ½ x 3 ½ In.
$317.00

Girl, Holding Dress, Painted, Cast Iron, Albany Foundry, 5 x 4 ¾ In. ... *illus* 87.00
Greco-Roman Soldier, Dore Bronze, Black Base, Signed J.P., 9 In. ... 300.00
Horse, Rearing, Brass, 7 ½ x 7 In. ... 20.00
Horse, Variegated Brown Matte Glaze, Plinth, Auburn Pottery, 9 ½ x 11 In. ... 805.00
Horse Heads, Carved, Signed, Watty Chiltosky, 4 ¼ In. ... 316.00 to 345.00
Horse Heads, Cast Metal, USA Lite, 6 ½ In. ... 15.00
House, Shakespeare's, Cast Iron, Signed, No. 262, 4 ⅝ x 5 ¾ In. ... 29.00
Iceberg, Crystal, 9 x 9 In. ... 25.00
James Whitcomb Riley, Cast Iron, Bronze Finish, Bradley & Hubbard, 5 ⅝ In. ... 35.00
Knight, Armor, Gothic Arch, Travelers Insurance, Bronze, Gorham Mark, 1931, 8 In. ... 590.00
Letters, A, Z, Wood, Signed, Curtis Jere, c.1969, 5 x 6 In. ... 840.00
Liberty Bell, Pressed Wood, 6 x 6 x 2 ½ In. ... 75.00
Lincoln Memorial, Bronze, Jennings Bros., Conn., 1920s, 7 In. ... 240.00
Lion, Cast Iron, Spelter, 7 ½ x 7 ½ In. ... 100.00
Man, Seated In Armchair, Reading, Painted, Gilt, Metal, Marked, J.B.H. Co., 5 x 4 In. ... 110.00
Mask, Theatrical, Book Shape Base, Brown Patina, Bronze, Early 1900s, 6 In. ... 1896.00
Owl Family, On Branch, Castle, Iron, Weidlich Bros., 1929, 5 ½ x 4 ¼ x 2 ⅜ In. ... 85.00
Owls, Sterling Silver, Arts & Crafts, Signed, Pearce, 5 x 6 x 5 In. ... 1725.00
Parrots, Painted, Bronze, Art Deco, Marked, Armor Bronze Corp., 6 In. ... 150.00
Parrots, Reticulated, Chrome, c.1927, 7 In. ... 3565.00
Penguins, 2, Cast Iron, Creations Co., c.1930, 3 x 3 ¼ In. ... 230.00
Pilgrim, Mayflower Ship, Cast Iron, Bradley & Hubbard, 6 x 4 ⅜ In. ... 173.00
Pirates, Man & Woman, Metal, Bronze Tone, Painted Accents, K & O Co., 1932, 10 In. ... 195.00
Puppy, Kitten On Fence, Cast Iron, 5 ¾ x 4 ⅝ In. ... 144.00
Quail, Painted, Cast Iron, Hubley, 5 ½ x 5 ¾ In. ... *illus* 460.00
Quotes, Bacon & Johnsoniana, Bradley & Hubbard, 6 ½ In. ... 99.00
Ram's Head, Bronze Finish, Marble Base, 6 x 4 x 5 In. ... 30.00
Roses & Petunias, Hubley, 6 ¾ x 4 ¾ In. ... 172.00
Sailfish, Syroco Wood, 4 ½ x 6 ½ x 1 In. ... 50.00
Scales, Brass, Black Striated Marble Base, 5 ¾ x 4 In. ... 90.00
Shakespeare Bust, Electroplated, Armor Bronze, 7 x 4 ¼ x 3 In. ... 175.00
Ship, Cast Iron, Japanned Brass Patina, Bradley & Hubbard, 6 ¼ In. ... 125.00
Ship, Sailing, Cast Iron, Flying Cloud, Marked, 6 x 6 In. ... 240.00
Ship, Sailing, Painted, Cast Iron, Marked, Early 1900s, 5 ⅜ x 4 ¾ In. ... 425.00
Snowy Owl, On Branch, Embossed, Cast Iron, CJO, 5 ½ x 3 ½ In. ... *illus* 317.00
Sphinx, Dark Blue Matte Glaze, c.1919, 7 In. ... 805.00
Squirrel, Brasstown, Walnut, Carved, Painted Eyes, 7 ½ In. ... 431.00
Stack Of 4 Books, Leather Bindings, Drawer At Base, Maitland Smith, 9 x 10 ½ In. ... 325.00
Stylized Flowers, Copper, Hammered, Arts & Crafts, 6 x 7 In. ... 180.00
Swordfish, Metal, Philadelphia Hand Cast Mfg., 8 ¼ In. ... 30.00
Thinker, Copper, Composition, 7 ½ In. ... 50.00
Wagner & Liszt, Cast Iron, Bradley & Hubbard, 4 ¾ x 6 x 2 ¾ In. ... 275.00
Walnut Veneer, Expandable, Folding Ends, 14 ½ In. ... 90.00
Windmill, Cutout, Copper, Hammered, Arts & Crafts, 4 x 6 In. ... 90.00
Woman's Head, Expandable, Brass, Art Nouveau, 6 In. ... 100.00

BOOKMARKS were originally made of parchment, cloth, or leather. Soon woven silk ribbon, thin cardboard, celluloid, wood, silver, tortoiseshell, and metals were used. Examples made before 1850 are scarce, but there are many to be found dating before 1920.

Bone, Carved, Elephant Finial, 2 ½ In. ... 21.00
Celluloid, Green, Daffodil Drawing On Top, 1920s, 4 ⅜ x 1 ⅛ In. ... 29.00
Leather, Embossed, Flower, Leaves, Attached Copper Page Turner, c.1910 ... 125.00
Mennen's Talcum Powder, Embossed, Advertiserment, Child, 2-Sided, 5 ½ x 2 In. ... 10.00
Niagara Falls, Prospect Point, Shield Form Top, Engraved View, Metal, 5 In. ... 20.00
Nubian Head, Marble Hat, 4 In. ... 175.00
Psychedelic Design, Antioch Bookplate Co., Yellow Springs, O., 1972, 5 ¾ x 1 ⅜ In. ... 2.50
Star Spangled Banner, Silk, Woven, Warner Mfg. Co., Patterson, N.J., 10 ½ x 2 ½ In. ... 60.00
Sterling Silver, Dragonfly, 2 ¼ x 1 ¼ In. ... 30.00
Sterling Silver, Guilloche Enamel Yellow Flower At Top, Silky Tassel, Edwardian Era, 2 x ⅝ In. 24.00
Sterling Silver, Tulip, Cutout, 2 ¼ x ¾ In. ... 30.00

BOSSONS character wall masks (heads), plaques, figurines, and other decorative pieces are made by W.H. Bossons, Ltd., of Congleton, England. The company was founded in 1946 and closed in 1996. Dates shown are the date the item was introduced.

BOSSONS

Shelf Ornament, Himalayan, 1963, 6 In. ... 100.00
Wall Figure, Buccaneer, 7 ½ In. ... 105.00

Wall Figure, Desert Hunters, Man & Dog, 9 In. 28.00
Wall Figure, Drummer Man, 9 ½ In. 70.00
Wall Figure, Peon, 1963, 15 ½ In. 275.00
Wall Figure, Sherpa, 15 ¾ In. 36.00
Wall Mask, Abdhul, c.1960, 8 In. 76.00
Wall Mask, Bretonne Woman, c.1982, 5 ½ In. 185.00
Wall Mask, Caspian Man, c.1959, 6 In. 125.00
Wall Mask, Eskimo, c.1970, 8 In. 175.00
Wall Mask, Saracen, 1960, 8 In. 165.00
Wall Plaque, Market Day, 14 In. 20.00
Wall Plaque, The Arrival, 14 In. 11.00

BOSTON & SANDWICH CO. *pieces may be found in the Lutz and Sandwich Glass categories.*

BOTTLE collecting has become a major American hobby. There are several general categories of bottles, such as historic flasks, bitters, household, and figural. ABM means the bottle was made by an automatic bottle machine after 1903. Pyro is the shortened form of the word *pyroglaze*, an enameled lettering used on bottles after the mid-1930s. This form of decoration is also called ACL or applied color label. For more bottle prices, see the book *Kovels' Bottles Price List* by Ralph and Terry Kovel.

AVON, Avon started in 1886 as the California Perfume Company. It was not until 1929 that the name Avon was used. In 1939, it became Avon Products, Inc. Avon has made many figural bottles filled with cosmetic products. Ceramic, plastic, and glass bottles were made in limited editions.

Avon, Decanter, Marine Binoculars, Tribut Cologne, 1973, 4 Oz. 15.00
Avon, Decanter, Victorian Lady, Milk Glass, 1970, 8 ½ In. 15.00
Barber, Bay Rum, Opalescent, John N. Semiller, Bird On Branch, Metal Stopper, 1890, 10 In. 300.00
Barber, Beehive, Aqua, Swirled Ribs, Applied Mouth, Pontil, c.1815, 9 ⅜ In. 173.00
Barber, Cherubs, Hand Painted Milk Glass, 7 In. 28.00
Barber, Coin Spot Optic, Yellow Amber, Enamel Flowers, Tooled Mouth, Pontil, 11 ⅜ In. *illus* 150.00
Barber, Cranberry, White Spatter, Spiraled Ribs, 3 Graduated Sections, 10 In. 125.00
Barber, Cranberry Opalescent Splotches, Tooled Mouth, Pontil, c.1885, 8 ⅛ In. 92.00
Barber, Cut Glass, Cranberry Cut To Clear, Block Cut Base, 8 In. 28.00
Barber, Figural, Boy On Barrel, Our Boy Fine Hair Oil, Label, Ground Lip, c.1890, 4 ⅞ In. 115.00
Barber, Green, Ribbed, Rolled Lip, Pontil, Art Nouveau Style, c.1885, 8 ⅛ In. 92.00
Barber, Green Opalescent Thumbprint, Melon Ribs, Outward Rolled Lip, 7 ⅜ In. 174.00
Barber, Hobnail, Rolled Lip, Pontil, c.1885, 6 ⅞ In. 92.00
Barber, Milk Glass, Green Enamel Clover Leaves, Black Letters, Tooled Lip, 9 In. 120.00
Barber, Peppermint, Enamel, Bulbous, Ribs, Pour Top, 9 In. 193.00
Barber, Purple Amethyst, Ribbed, White Enamel Boy, Rolled Lip, Pontil, c.1885, 7 ⅞ In. 150.00
Barber, St. Claire's Hair Lotion, Blue, Tooled Top, 8 In. 78.00
Barber, Teal Green, Ribbed, White Enamel, Girl, Rolled Lip, Pontil, c.1885, 7 ¾ In. 196.00
Barber, Witch Hazel, Milk Glass, Porcelain & Cork Stopper, 7 ¾ In. 20.00
Beer, Anchor Glass, Not To Be Refilled, No Deposit No Return, Crown Top, Ruby, c.1949, 8 In. 78.00
Beer, C.C. Haley & Co., Celebrated California, Tobacco Amber, Double Collar, Qt. 245.00
Beer, Celebrated HoXie, W. Stewart, Amber, Fat, Qt. 85.00
Beer, Cone Top, White Cap 300.00
Beer, Florida Brewing Co., Embossed, Round Panel, Light Green, Tampa 31.00
Beer, Fred Heim's Brewing Co., Kansas City, Mo., Brown, Embossed, Cork Top, 12 In. 88.00 to 110.00
Beer, Henry Elias Brewing Co., New York, Lager Beer, Honey Amber, Pt. 155.00
Beer, J. Gahm & Son, Charlestown, Mass., Citron, Pt. 120.00
Beer, Nebraska Brewing Co., Tobacco Amber, Teepee, ½ Pt. 135.00
Beer, Reno Brewing Co., Amber, Blob Top, Reno, Nev., Pt. 50.00
Beer, Shelby Street Brewery, Louisville, Ky., Golden Amber, Stopper, Qt. 55.00
Beer, Swan Brewery Co., XXX Ale, Applied Top, Amber, c.1870 .... 2240.00
Beer, Trenton Brewing Co., Red Amber, Stopper, Pt. 40.00
Beer, Weiss Beer Brewing Co., St. Louis, Brown, Embossed, Cork Top, 9 ¼ In. 55.00
Beer, White Bear Brewery, Strong, Bear With Can, Blob Top 750.00
Beer, Yankee Premium Beer, Sailing Ship 175.00
Bininger, Clock, Regulator, 19 Broad St. New York, Amber, Pontil, c.1855, 6 In. 489.00
Bitters, Alpine, Bulbous, Yellow Green, Ribs, Tooled Lip, Handle, Qt. 295.00
Bitters, Baker's Orange Grove, Amber, Smooth Base, Applied Sloping Collar, c.1865, 9 In. 460.00
Bitters, Baker's Orange Grove, Apricot, Roped Corners, Applied Collar, 9 In. 728.00
Bitters, Baker's Orange Grove, Yellow Olive Amber, 1860-75, 9 ¾ In. .... *illus* 2000.00
Bitters, Barrel, Blue, Rings, Applied Top, 9 ¾ In. 3584.00

Bottle, Barber, Coin Spot Optic, Yellow Amber, Enamel Flowers, Tooled Mouth, Pontil, 11 ⅜ In. $150.00

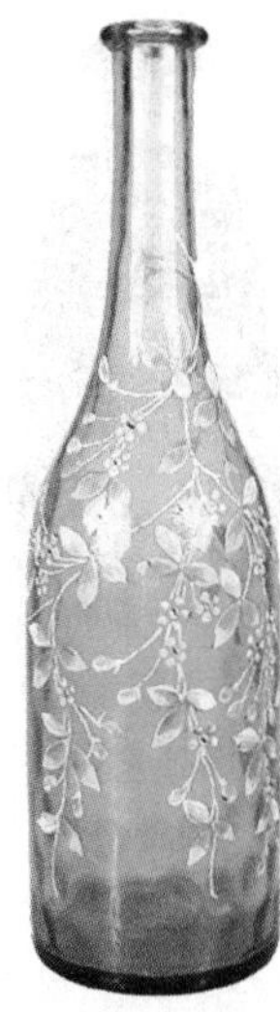

Bottle, Bitters, Baker's Orange Grove, Yellow Olive Amber, 1860-75, 9 ¾ In. $2000.00

What's a Slug Plate?
The "slug plate," used to put letters into a bottle mold, was invented in the late nineteenth century. It meant that a new mold did not have to be made for each customer's name. The bottle mold had a depression that held a slug plate that could be changed. The finished bottle had a round or oval line around the raised letters.

Bitters, Bourbon Whiskey, Barrel, Deep Cherry Puce, Applied Mouth, 1860-70, 9 3/8 In. $560.00

Bottle, Bitters, Dr L.G. Bertram's, Long Life, Aromatic Stomach, Amber, c.1870-80, 9 1/2 In. $315.00

TIP

To make a quick "photo" of your old bottle, try using a photocopying machine. Put the bottle on the machine, then cover it with white paper or cloth to block out any extra light. Lower the cover gently and take the picture.

Bitters, Bell's Cocktail, Jas. M. Bell & Co., Lady's Leg, Amber, 10 In. 952.00
Bitters, Bell's Cocktail, Jas. M. Bell & Co., Light Amber, 10 1/4 In. 896.00
Bitters, Big Bill Best, Amber, Tooled Top, 11 1/2 In. 392.00
Bitters, Bininger, A.M. & Co., Barrel, Glass Screw Stopper, Applied Top, Pontil, 8 In. 336.00
Bitters, Bourbon Whiskey, Barrel, Deep Cherry Puce, Applied Mouth, 1860-70, 9 3/8 In. .. *illus* 560.00
Bitters, Bourbon Whiskey, Pinkish Puce Barrel, Smooth Base, Applied Mouth, c.1865, 9 3/8 In. 1093.00
Bitters, Brown's Celebrated Indian Herb, Indian Queen, Amber, 12 1/4 In. .... 784.00 to 1008.00
Bitters, Brown's Celebrated Indian Herb, Indian Queen, Yellow Amber, 12 1/4 In. 1456.00
Bitters, Brown's Celebrated Indian Herb, Indian Queen, Yellow Amber, Ground Lip, c.1868, 12 1/4 In. 1035.00
Bitters, Brown's Celebrated Indian Herb, Pat. Feb 1868, Amber Shaded To Yellow Amber, 12 In. 1540.00
Bitters, Brown's Celebrated Indian Herb, Pat. Feb 1868, Yellow Amber, Rolled Lip, 12 In. 890.00
Bitters, Brown's Celebrated Indian Herb, Pat. Feb 1868, Yellow Green, Sheared Lip, 12 In. 7280.00
Bitters, Brown's Iron, O.K. Plantation Brown Chemical Co., Yellow, Applied Mouth, c.1880, 8 5/8 In. 288.00
Bitters, Caldwell's Herb, 3-Sided, Amber, Applied Mouth, Iron Pontil, c.1865, 12 In. 288.00
Bitters, Catawba Wine, Embossed Grapes, Square, Olive, Applied Mouth, c.1860, 9 1/2 In. 2240.00
Bitters, Doctor Fisch's, W.H. Ware, Fish, Yellow Amber, Rolled Lip, c.1866, 11 3/4 In. 431.00
Bitters, Doyles Hop, 1872, Semi-Cabin, Amber, 9 In. 35.00
Bitters, Dr A.H. Smith's Old Style, O.S., 2781, Golden Amber, Sloping Collar, 8 3/4 In. 310.00
Bitters, Dr L.G. Bertram's, Long Life, Aromatic Stomach, Amber, c.1870-80, 9 1/2 In. ..... *illus* 315.00
Bitters, Dr. B.F. Sherman's Compound, Prickly Ash, Yellow Olive, Sloping Collar, 9 1/4 In. 1270.00
Bitters, Dr. Baxter's Mandrake, Aqua, 12-Sided, 6 1/2 In. 48.00
Bitters, Dr. Birmingham's Antibilious Blood Purifying, Blue Green, Cylindrical, 8 3/4 In. 840.00
Bitters, Dr. C.W. Roback's Stomach, Barrel, Amber, Applied Sloping Collar, 1865-75, 9 1/4 In. .. 510.00
Bitters, Dr. C.W. Roback's Stomach, Barrel, Orange Amber, Sloping Collar, Pontil, 9 7/8 In. ... 200.00
Bitters, Dr. C.W. Roback's Stomach, Barrel, Yellow Amber, Applied Collar, 1865-75, 9 3/4 In. 180.00 to 425.00
Bitters, Dr. C.W. Roback's Stomach, Barrel, Yellow Olive, Sloping Collar, 1865-75, 9 3/8 In. ... 1010.00
Bitters, Dr. Caldwell's Herb, Medium Amber, Triangular, Applied Mouth, 12 1/2 In. 364.00
Bitters, Dr. De Andries Sarsaparilla, Yellow Olive Amber, Applied Mouth, 9 7/8 In. .. 1792.00 to 11456.00
Bitters, Dr. Dimock's Compound, Tamarac, Orange Amber, Applied Mouth, 8 3/4 In. 2016.00
Bitters, Dr. Geo Pierce's Indian Restorative, Lowell, Mass., Aqua, Pontil, c.1850, 7 5/8 In. . *illus* 275.00
Bitters, Dr. H.A. Jackson's, Blue Aqua, Applied Sloping Collar, Pontil, 7 3/8 In. 160.00
Bitters, Dr. J. Hostetter's Stomach, Square, Golden Amber, Applied Sloping Collar, 9 In. 140.00
Bitters, Dr. J. Hostetter's Stomach, Square, Yellow Olive, Applied Mouth, 8 3/4 In. 250.00
Bitters, Dr. J.L. Fleece's Female, Lebanon, Ky., Aqua, Applied Mouth, 8 7/8 In. 4802.00
Bitters, Dr. Jacob's, Aqua Blue, Applied Sloping Collar, Open Pontil, 8 1/2 In. 300.00
Bitters, Dr. John Bull's Compound Cedron, Yellow Amber, Applied Sloping Mouth, 9 3/8 In. 575.00
Bitters, Dr. Owen's European Life, Blue Aqua, Applied Mouth, Open Pontil, 1840-60, 7 In. 495.00
Bitters, Dr. Skinner's Celebrated, 25 Cent, Aqua, Double Collar Mouth, Open Pontil, 8 5/8 In. . 250.00
Bitters, Dr. Soule's, Hop 1872, Semi-Cabin, Olive Green, Applied Mouth, 9 1/2 In. 2016.00
Bitters, Dr. Soule's Hop Bitterine, 1872, Semi-Cabin, Pink Puce, Sloping Collar, 9 5/8 In. 2010.00
Bitters, Dr. Sperry's Female Strengthening, Clear, Tooled Lip, Label, 9 1/4 In. 728.00
Bitters, Dr. Taylor's Female, Blue Aqua, Applied Sloping Collar, Open Pontil, 1850, 6 1/8 In. ... 1380.00
Bitters, Dr. Tompkins' Vegetable, Teal Blue, Sloping Collar Mouth, c.1870, 8 7/8 In. 1690.00
Bitters, Dr. Varena's Japan, Yellow Amber, Tooled Mouth, 1885-95, 9 In. 205.00
Bitters, Dr. Wonser's U.S.A. Indian Root, Amber, Applied Mouth, c.1870, 11 In. 9520.00
Bitters, Dr. Wood's Sarsaparilla & Wild Cherry, Aqua, Sloping Double Collar, OP, 8 1/2 In. 230.00
Bitters, Dr. Young's Wild Cherry, Brooklyn, N.Y., Amber, Tooled Mouth, 8 1/4 In. 308.00
Bitters, Drake's Plantation, 4 Log, Amber, Applied Sloping Collar Mouth, 10 1/8 In. 140.00 to 200.00
Bitters, Drake's Plantation, 4 Log, Orange Amber, Applied Sloping Collar Mouth, 10 3/8 In. ... 40.00
Bitters, Drake's Plantation, 6 Log, Amber, Applied Mouth, 1860, 10 1/8 In. 210.00
Bitters, Drake's Plantation, 6 Log, Cabin, Strawberry Puce, 10 In. 195.00
Bitters, Drake's Plantation, 6 Log, Copper Puce, Applied Mouth, 10 1/8 In. 269.00
Bitters, Drake's Plantation, 6 Log, Deep Strawberry Puce, Applied Mouth, 10 In. 269.00
Bitters, Drake's Plantation, 6 Log, Medium Puce, Applied Mouth, 10 In. 896.00
Bitters, Drake's Plantation, 6 Log, Yellow, Applied Sloping Collar, c.1862, 10 In. ... 139.00 to 403.00
Bitters, Drake's Plantation, S.T. Drake's, 4 Log, Yellow, Patented 1862, 10 1/2 In. 1800.00
Bitters, E. Dexter Loveridge's, Wahoo, Yellow Amber, Paneled, Sloping Collar, 10 1/4 In. 1840.00
Bitters, Edw. Wilder's Stomach, 5-Story House, Hobnail Corners, Tooled Mouth, 10 In. 290.00 to 680.00
Bitters, Eureka, Granger & Co., Square, Yellow Amber, Indented Panels, 9 3/8 In. 1035.00
Bitters, Fish, W.H. Ware, Patented 1866, Amber, Applied Lip, 11 5/8 In. 616.00
Bitters, Fish, W.H. Ware, Patented 1866, Olive Yellow, Amber, Applied Lip, 11 5/8 In. 308.00
Bitters, Frazier's Root, For The Blood, Blue Aqua, Long Neck, Applied Mouth, 7 3/4 In. 157.00
Bitters, Geo. Benz & Sons, Appetine, Amber, Tooled Lip, St. Paul, Minn. 280.00
Bitters, German Balsam, W.M. Watson & Co., Milk Glass, Applied Top, 1880s, 9 In. 1008.00
Bitters, Globe Tonic, Amber, Applied Sloping Collar, 9 1/2 In. 336.00
Bitters, Greeley's Bourbon Whiskey, Barrel, Deep Plum, Applied Square Collar, 9 3/8 In. 1700.00

Bitters, Hall's, Barrel, Amber, Applied Rolled Lip 258.00
Bitters, Hall's, Barrel, Orange Amber, Applied Mouth, 9 ¼ In. 315.00
Bitters, Hall's, Barrel, Red Amber, Puce, Square Collar, 9 ½ In. 1955.00
Bitters, Hartwig Kantorowicz, Posen, Hamburg, Germany, Milk Glass, 9 In. 39.00
Bitters, Herkules, Globular, Green, 2 Flattened Sides, Tooled Mouth, c.1890, 7 ½ In., Qt. 1380.00
Bitters, Holtzermann's Stomach, Cabin, Amber, Tooled Mouth, c.1880, 10 In. 207.00
Bitters, Johnson's Calisaya, Square, Peach Puce, Beveled Corners, Applied Collar, 10 In. 3100.00
Bitters, Koehler & Hinrichs, Red Star Stomach, Deep Tobacco Amber, Fluted, 11 ½ In. 616.00
Bitters, Lash's Kidney & Liver, Square, Red Amber, Applied Top, 9 In. 123.00
Bitters, Lediard's St. Louis, Applied Top, 6-Sided, Ringed Neck, 11 In. 560.00
Bitters, Moulton's Oloroso, Pineapple Trademark, Blue Aqua, Fluted Base 202.00
Bitters, National, Ear Of Corn, Amber, Applied Mouth, 1867, 12 ⅜ In. 495.00
Bitters, National, Ear Of Corn, Amber To Yellow Amber, Applied Mouth, 1867, 12 ½ In. 575.00
Bitters, National, Ear Of Corn, Blue Aqua, Applied Mouth, 1867, 12 ⅝ In. 16800.00
Bitters, National, Ear Of Corn, Patent 1867, Light Amber, 12 ½ In. 6160.00
Bitters, National, Square, Red Amber, Fluted Neck, 9 ¼ In. 504.00
Bitters, Old Dr. Solomon's, Great Indian, Aqua, Tooled Lip, 8 ½ In. 95.00
Bitters, Old Dr. Warren's, Herb & Root, Rectangular, Aqua, Applied Mouth, Labels, 9 ⅞ In. 672.00
Bitters, Old Sachem & Wigwam, Deep Cherry Tonic, Barrel, Puce, Ribbed, 9 ¼ In. 896.00
Bitters, Old Sachem & Wigwam Tonic, Barrel, Amber, 9 ¼ In. 560.00
Bitters, Old Sachem & Wigwam Tonic, Barrel, Copper Puce, Applied Square Collar, 9 ⅜ In. 625.00
Bitters, Old Sachem & Wigwam Tonic, Barrel, Medium Copper, Applied Square Collar, 9 In. 375.00
Bitters, Old Sachem & Wigwam Tonic, Barrel, Topaz, 9 ¼ In. 1840.00
Bitters, Old Sachem & Wigwam Tonic, Barrel, Topaz, Square Collar, 9 ⅛ In. 3738.00
Bitters, Original Pocahontas, Barrel, Blue Aqua, Applied Square Collar, 9 ⅜ In. 5200.00
Bitters, Peoples Favorite, Powell & Stutenroth, Amber, Swirled Ribs, Applied Mouth, 10 ½ In. 25760.00
Bitters, Peruvian, Red Amber, Applied Top, 1871-91, 9 In. 728.00
Bitters, Pineapple, Amber, 9 In. 525.00
Bitters, Pineapple, W & Co., N.Y., Diamond Diaper, Applied Lip, Open Pontil 896.00
Bitters, Pineapple, Yellow Amber, Applied Lip, 9 In. 235.00
Bitters, Pond's Kidney & Liver, Amber, Square, 9 ½ In. 39.00
Bitters, Professor Geo. J. Byrne Stomach, Golden Amber, Arched Panels, Roped Corners, 10 In. 1150.00
Bitters, Royce's Sherry Wine, Tombstone Panel, Aqua, Applied Mouth, 8 In. 134.00
Bitters, Russ' St. Domingo, New York, Puce, Applied Sloping Collar, 1865-75, 10 In. 485.00 to 910.00
Bitters, S.O. Richardson's, South Reading, Mass., Aqua, Flared Lip, Pontil, 6 ¼ In. 40.00
Bitters, Sanborn's Kidney & Liver, Rectangular, Amber, Tooled Lip, 10 In. 168.00
Bitters, Sazerac Aromatic, Milk Glass, Lady's Leg, Applied Mouth, c.1870, 12 In. 374.00
Bitters, Simon's Centennial, Bust Of George Washington, c.1876, 9 ¾ In. 748.00
Bitters, Suffolk, Philbrook & Tucker, Boston, Pig, Yellow Amber, Square Collar, 10 ⅛ In. 845.00
Bitters, Tippecanoe, H.H. Warner & Co., Log, Yellow Amber, Mushroom Top, 9 In. 720.00
Bitters, Warner's Safe Tonic, Rochester, N.Y., Safe, Red Amber, Double Collar, 9 ½ In. 1370.00
Bitters, Warner's Safe Tonic, Rochester, N.Y., Safe, Yellow Amber, Applied Mouth, 7 ⅜ In. 955.00
Bitters, West India Stomach, St. Louis, Mo., Golden Amber, Applied Mouth, c.1875, 8 ¾ In. 345.00
Bitters, Witch Horseshoe, Amber, Applied Double Collar, 8 In. 532.00
Bitters, Yerba Buena, Amber, Strap Side Flask, Sloping Double Collar, 8 ⅜ In. 110.00
Bitters, Yerba Buena S.F. Cal., Amber To Red, Applied Mouth, 9 ½ In. 123.00
Bitters, Zingari, F. Rahter, Lady's Leg, Amber, Applied Ring Mouth, 11 ¾ In. 235.00
Black Glass, Dutch Mallet, Olive Yellow, String Lip, Pontil, 1820-40, 6 ⅝ In. .... *illus* 270.00
Black Glass, Dutch Onion, Threaded Neck, Handle, 7 In. 4914.00
Black Glass, Mallet, Olive Amber, String Lip, Pontil, England, 1740-50, 8 x 4 ⅞ In. ..... *illus* 385.00
Black Glass, Mallet, Wine, Dark Olive Green, Applied String Lip, Gold Metallic, 7 ⅜ In. 202.00
Black Glass, Onion, Horsehoof, Olive Green, Dip Mold, Applied Mouth, Pontil, England, 9 In. 90.00
Black Glass, Onion, Olive Green, Applied String Lip, Pontil, Germany, 7 x 5 ½ In. 100.00
Black Glass, Onion, Olive Green, Dip Mold, Applied String Lip, Pontil, Germany, 12 In. 300.00
Black Glass, Onion, Wine, Olive Green, Applied String Lip, Gold Metallic, 6 ⅞ In. 235.00
Black Glass, Storage, Olive Amber, Sheared, Applied String Lip, Pontil, 12 ⅛ In. 120.00
Blown, Globular, Aqua, High Kick Up, Early 19th Century, 11 ¾ In. 316.00
Blown, Globular, Chocolate Amber, Sheared Mouth, Applied Ring Lip, Pontil, 8 ⅞ In. 448.00
Blown, Globular, Olive Amber, Applied Lip, Pontil, 3 ¼ In. .... 1150.00 to 3450.00
Blown, Jar, Yellow Olive, Cylindrical, Sheared & Flared Mouth, Pontil, 5 ¾ In. 978.00
Blown, Mallet, Olive, High Kick Up, Early 18th Century, 7 ½ In. 230.00
Blown, Mallet, Olive Green, High Kick Up, Applied Lip, 8 ¼ In. 316.00
Cherub Holding Medallion, Milk Glass, Blue, Pontil, Glass Pinwheel Stopper, c.1885, 11 In. 392.00
Coca-Cola bottles are listed in the Coca-Cola category.
Cologne, Ball Shape, Crosscut Diamond, Strawberry Diamond, Hobstar, 5 In., Pair. 225.00
Cologne, Ball Shape, Harvard Pattern, Hobstar Base, Libbey, 7 In. 150.00

Bottle, Bitters,
Dr. Geo Pierce's Indian Restorative,
Lowell, Mass., Aqua, Pontil,
c.1850, 7 ⅝ In.
$275.00

Bottle, Black Glass, Dutch Mallet,
Olive Yellow, String Lip, Pontil,
1820-40, 6 ⅝ In.
$270.00

Bottle, Black Glass, Mallet,
Olive Amber, String Lip, Pontil,
England, 1740-50, 8 x 4 ⅞ In.
$385.00

Bottle, Figural, 3 Busts, Milk Glass, Amber Cased, Tooled Mouth, 1900s, 13 ⅝ In.
$85.00

Bottle, Figural, Book, Coming Thro The Rye, Cobalt Blue, 1860-80, 4 ¾ In.
$575.00

Bottle, Figural, Coachman, Milk Glass, Sheared Lip, 10 ⅜ In.
$82.00

Cologne, Blue Cut To Clear, Cane Pattern, Pattern Cut Stopper, 5 ½ In. 300.00
Cologne, Bulbous, DeVilbiss, Atomizer, 4 ¾ In. 45.00
Cologne, Crosscut & Strawberry Diamond, Star, Facet Cut Stopper, 5 ½ In., Pair 250.00
Cologne, Crosscut Diamond Body, Ball Shape, 6 In., Pair 150.00
Cologne, Stopper, Squat Base, 7 x 4 ½ In., Pair 146.00
Cordial, Cloud's, Straw Yellow, Olive, Applied Sloping Collar Mouth, 1870-80, 10 ½ In. 364.00
Cordial, T.J. Dunbar & Co., Schnapps Schiedam, Green, 10 In. 300.00
Cordial, Wishart's Pine Tree Tar, Embossed Tree, Aqua, 8 In. 75.00
Cordial, Zollickoffer's Antirheumatic, Deep Olive Green, Applied Mouth, Pontil, 6 ¼ In. 3360.00
Cosmetic, Ayer's Hair Invigorator, Cobalt Blue, Stopper, ABM, Contents, Box, 7 In. 232.00
Cosmetic, Ayer's Hair Vigor, Sapphire Blue, Tooled Mouth, Glass Stopper, 6 ⅝ In. 80.00
Cosmetic, Blue Bell Antiseptic Tooth Powder, Paper Label, Metal Cap, 4 ½ x 2 ¾ In. 220.00
Cosmetic, Buckingham Whisker Dye, Amber, Label, ½ Pt. 35.00
Cosmetic, Florentine Hair Promoter, Contents, Wrapper, 7 ½ In. 104.00
Cosmetic, Glyceroil For The Hair, Recessed, Panels, Aqua, Cork Stopper, Box, 6 ½ In. 143.00
Cosmetic, Hair Tonic, LeVarn's Rose, Mettowee Toilet Specialty, Label Under Glass, 7 ½ In. 275.00
Cosmetic, LeVarn's Golden Wash, Mettowee Toilet Specialty, Label Under Glass, 7 ½ In. 187.00
Cure, Dr. L.E. Keeley's Gold Cure For Drunkenness, Dwight, Ill., 5 ½ In. 688.00
Cure, Humphreys' Medicine Co., Horse's Head, Coil, Embossed, 4 ½ x 2 ¾ In. 187.00
Cure, Kendall's Spavin, For Human Flesh, Enosburgh Falls, Vt., Amber, Paper Label, 5 ½ In. 253.00
Cure, Sanford's Radical, Cobalt Blue, Labels, ½ Pt., 7 ¼ In. 69.00 to 100.00
Cure, Warner's Safe, London, Toronto, Rochester, Amber, 40 Oz., 11 ¼ In. 1080.00
Cure, Warner's Safe, Olive Green, Applied Blob Top, Germany, 9 ¼ In. 308.00
Cure, Wm. Radam's Microbe Killer, Amber, Tooled Lip, 3-Sided Label, 10 ½ In. 728.00
Decanter, Bitters, Silver Overlay, Faceted Stopper, 7 In. 29.00
Decanter, Blown, Sapphire Blue, Tooled Flared Lip, Pontil, Stopper, 1820-40, Qt. 2875.00
Decanter, Blue, 3-Piece Mold, Flared Mouth, Pontil, 6 ⅞ In. 1456.00
Decanter, Olive Green, 3-Piece Mold, Tooled Lip, 9 ⅛ In. 840.00
Decanter, Olive Yellow, 3-Piece Mold, Cylindrical, Tapered, Sheared Mouth, Pontil, Qt. 1790.00
Decanter, Olive Yellow, Cylindrical, Tapered, Sheared Mouth, Pontil, 1820-40, Qt. 2185.00
Decanter, Pillar Mold, Cobalt Blue, 8 Pillars, Pontil, 11 ½ In. 2128.00
Decanter, Pillar Mold, Lavender, Stopper, Pontil, c.1850, 14 In. 1904.00
Decanter, Yellow, Ribs, Swirled To Left, Tapered, Flared Lip, Pontil, 7 In. 495.00
Decanter, Yellow Olive, Dark Gray Tint, 3-Piece Mold, Flared Mouth, Pontil. 2016.00
Demijohn, Bread Loaf Shape, Applied Sloping Collar, Gal. 728.00
Demijohn, Deep Olive Green, Applied Lip, 1800s, 16 ½ In. 180.00
Demijohn, Kidney Shape, Blue Aqua, Open Pontil, 2 ⅞ In. 69.00
Demijohn, Red Amber, Applied Mouth, Pontil, 16 ⅝ In. 308.00
Demijohn, Yellow Amber, Applied Mouth, Pontil, 13 ¾ In. 134.00
Demijohn, Yellow Green, Gal., 15 In. 55.00
Figural, 3 Busts, Milk Glass, Amber Cased, Tooled Mouth, 1900s, 13 ⅝ In. *illus* 85.00
Figural, Bear, Kummel, Milk Glass, Applied Mouth, c.1885-1900, 10 ¾ In. 60.00
Figural, Bear On Pole, Frosted, Milk Glass, Tooled Mouth, Depose Embossed, c.1890, 11 ¼ In. 374.00
Figural, Book, Coming Thro The Rye, Cobalt Blue, 1860-80, 4 ¾ In. *illus* 575.00
Figural, Cannon, Olive Amber, Frosted, Tooled Lip, 4-Piece Mold, 9 ¾ In. 202.00
Figural, Child's Head, Milk Glass, Sheared Lip, 1880-1900, 2 ½ In. 70.00
Figural, Clown, Milk Glass, Gold & Red Paint, Pontil, Tooled Mouth, c.1890, 15 ½ In. 280.00
Figural, Coachman, Milk Glass, Sheared Lip, 10 ⅜ In. *illus* 82.00
Figural, Fish, Citron, Rolled Lip, Pontil, c.1890-1910, 6 ¼ In. 120.00
Figural, Frog, Aqua, Deponiert, Embossed, Polished Lip, Germany, 5 ¼ In. *illus* 245.00
Figural, Grant's Tomb, Milk Glass, Sheared Lip, c.1893-1900, 8 ¼ In. 90.00
Figural, Grover Cleveland, Frosted, Embossed Name, Pontil, 9 ¾ In. 227.00
Figural, Hand, Milk Glass, Turquoise Glass Ring, Ground Lip, c.1890, 5 ½ In. 104.00
Figural, Hand, Ring On Finger, Milk Glass, Sheared Lip, 1885-1910, 4 In. 50.00
Figural, Hand Holding Bottle, Yellow Topaz, Tooled Lip, Pontil, c.1890-1910, 9 ½ In. 30.00
Figural, Life Preserver, Lime Green, Frosted, Black Enamel Letters, 1890-1910, 7 ⅛ In. 50.00
Figural, Matador, Milk Glass, Tooled Lip, c.1880-1910, 12 ¾ In. 70.00
Figural, Monkey-On-Barrel, Milk Glass, Tooled Lip, Geschutz, Europe, c.1890, 9 ⅝ In. 560.00
Figural, Pig, Pottery, Straw Glaze, 12 ½ In. 1265.00
Figural, Pig, Yellow Orange, Philbrook & Tucker, Boston, 10 In. 1195.00
Figural, Pretzel, Salted, Porcelain, Germany, 5 ½ In. 160.00
Figural, Revolver, Amber, Checkered Handle, Metal Cap, 8 In. 79.00
Figural, Seated Chinese Man, Milk Glass, Smooth Base, Patent No. 39603, Shaker Lid, c.1890, 4 In. 179.00
Figural, Statue Of Liberty, Milk Glass, Pewter Statue Stopper, Ground Lip, c.1892, 9 ¼ In. 184.00
Figural, Violin, Milk Glass, Opalescent, Embossed Strings & Notes, America, c.1890, 10 In. 2352.00
Fish, Footed, Flattened Rim, Pontil, American, c.1800, 11 ¼ In. 424.00

Fish Bowl, Globe Over Tapered Lower Portion, 1800s, 18 x 8 In. 275.00
Flask, 2 Men Talking, Grotesque Head, Cobalt Blue, Sheared Mouth, Pontil, 1850-70, ½ Pt. 620.00
Flask, 10 Diamond, Golden Amber, Chestnut, c.1830, 4 ¾ In. 3978.00
Flask, 13 Swirled Ribs, Cobalt Blue, 1800s, 7 ½ In. 118.00
Flask, 16 Ribs, Amethyst, Flattened, Teardrop, Sheared Mouth, Pontil, 1763-75, 5 ⅞ In. 1500.00
Flask, 20 Ribs, Amber, c.1840, 8 ¼ In. 59.00
Flask, 20 Swirled Ribs, Amber, c.1840, 6 ½ In. 59.00
Flask, 25 Ribs, Light Green, Elongated Neck, c.1825, 6 ½ In. 264.00
Flask, Amber, Ribbed, c.1800, 5 In. 529.00
Flask, Amber, Swirled Ribs, Zanesville Glass Works, Tooled Mouth, Pontil, c.1815, 5 ¼ In. 288.00
Flask, Aqua, Flattened, Sheared Lip, Open Pontil, c.1800-30, Qt., 8 In. 48.00
Flask, Bellows, White Ribbing, Applied Leaves, Serrated Edges, 9 ½ x 4 ½ In. 143.00
Flask, Blue Green, Sheared Mouth, Pontil, 1830-40, Pt. 3395.00
Flask, Chestnut, Aqua, Open Pontil, c.1815-35, 4 In. 299.00
Flask, Chestnut, Quilted Shoulder & Neck, c.1825, 5 In. 1528.00
Flask, Chestnut, Red Amber, White Herringbone, Tooled Lip, Pontil, 5 ⅛ In. 476.00
Flask, Chestnut, Yellow Olive, Amber, Flattened, Applied Mouth, Open Pontil, 7 ½ In. 364.00
Flask, Cornflower Blue, Leaf & Rope Decoration, Applied Handle, Pontil, Stopper, 8 In. 99.00
Flask, Cornucopia, Olive Green, Sheared Lip, Open Pontil, Pt. 364.00
Flask, Cornucopia, Urn, Olive, ½ Pt., 5 ½ In. 431.00
Flask, Cornucopia & Urn, Aqua, Lancaster Glass Works, Sheared Lip, Tubular Pontil, Pt. 896.00
Flask, Cornucopia & Urn, Olive Amber, 6 ½ In. 112.00
Flask, Cornucopia & Urn, Olive Green, Sheared & Tooled Mouth, Pontil, 1830, Pt. *illus* 105.00
Flask, Cornucopia & Urn, Sapphire Blue, Sheared Mouth, Pontil, 1840-60, Pt. 4090.00
Flask, Cornucopia & Urn, Yellow Amber, Pontil, Pt. 198.00
Flask, Cornucopia & Urn, Yellow Olive Amber, Tooled Lip, Pontil, ½ Pt. 110.00
Flask, Double Eagle, Amber, Bubbles, Stoddard, Sheared Lip, Pontil, Pt. 280.00
Flask, Double Eagle, Aqua, Applied Ring Mouth, ½ Pt. 70.00
Flask, Double Eagle, Aqua, Sheared, Tooled Lip, Open Pontil, ½ Pt. 448.00
Flask, Double Eagle, Blue Aqua, Applied Mouth, Pt. 60.00
Flask, Double Eagle, Light Blue Green, Sheared Mouth, Pontil, 1840-60, Pt. 1385.00
Flask, Double Eagle, Light To Medium Yellow Green, Sheared Mouth, Pontil, 1850-55, Pt. 3600.00
Flask, Double Eagle, Root Beer Amber, Vertical Ribs, Raised Oval Panel, Applied Mouth, ½ Pt. 2415.00
Flask, Double Eagle, Root Beer Amber, Vertical Ribs, Ring, Applied Mouth, ½ Pt. 3600.00
Flask, Eagle & Agriculture, Green Aqua, Sheared Mouth, Pontil, 1830s, Pt. 1580.00
Flask, Eagle & Anchor, Green, Sheared Mouth, Pontil, New London Glass Works, ½ Pt. 4025.00
Flask, Eagle & Anchor, Olive Yellow, Applied Double Collar, Iron Pontil, 1856-60, Pt. 4100.00
Flask, Eagle & Cornucopia, Aquamarine, Sheared Mouth, Pontil, 1820-40, ½ Pt. 840.00
Flask, Eagle & Cornucopia, Deep Red Amber, Sheared Mouth, Pontil, 1830-40, ½ Pt. 2100.00
Flask, Eagle & Cornucopia, Medium Yellow Amber, Olive Tint, Sheared Lip, Pontil, Pt. 150.00
Flask, Eagle & Cornucopia, Yellow Green, Sheared Lip, Open Pontil, c.1830, Pt. *illus* 175.00
Flask, Eagle & Medallion, Blue Green, Tooled Mouth, Pontil, c.1850-55, Pt. 2800.00
Flask, Eagle & Oak Tree, Aqua, Sheared Mouth, Pontil, 1820-40, ½ Pt. 795.00
Flask, Eagle & Sunburst, Vaseline Tint, Sheared Mouth, Pontil, 1820-40, Pt. 6085.00
Flask, Figural, Octopus-On-Coin, Eagle, Head Of Liberty, Milk Glass, Ground Lip, c.1901, 4 In. 253.00
Flask, Girl Riding Bicycle, Not For Joe, Red Amber, Puce Tint, Applied Mouth, Pt. 5175.00
Flask, Hard Cider, Cabin, Aqua, Sheared Mouth, Pontil, 1820-40, Pt. 15900.00
Flask, Henry Clay & Eagle, Aqua, Sheared Mouth, Pontil, 1820-40, Pt. 8050.00
Flask, Here's To You, Long Life & Prosperity, Clear, Embossed, 6 ½ In. 43.00
Flask, Hip, Stainless Steel, Enameled Crest, Russia, 4 Oz., 4 x 3 x ¾ In. 58.00
Flask, Horseman & Hound, Aqua, Sheared, Tooled Lip, Pontil, Pt. 170.00
Flask, Hunter & Fisherman, Amber, Calabash, Iron Pontil 475.00
Flask, Hunter & Fisherman, Orange Amber, Calabash, Iron Pontil 459.00
Flask, Hunter's, Clusters Of Grapes, Cobalt Blue, Tool Flared Mouth, Pontil, c.1850, 6 ½ In. 184.00
Flask, Jas. Tharp's Sons Wines & Liquors, Orange Amber, Strap Side, ½ Pt. 48.00
Flask, Jenny Lind & Glasshouse, Calabash, Cornflower Blue, Purple Tint, Sloping Collar, Qt. 4400.00
Flask, John Sullivan, Boston, Amber, Strap Side, Embossed, Large 75.00
Flask, Kossuth & Frigate, Calabash, Golden Amber, Sloping Collar, Pontil, Qt. 4495.00
Flask, Lafayette & Clinton, Yellow Amber, Olive Tint, Pontil, ½ Pt. 1232.00
Flask, Lafayette & Eagle, Blue Aqua, Tooled Mouth, Pontil, 1825, Pt. 672.00
Flask, Lafayette & Liberty, Aqua, Bubbles, Sheared Mouth, Pontil, 1824-25, ½ Pt. 5250.00
Flask, Lafayette & Liberty, Olive Yellow, Green, Sheared Mouth, Pontil, Pt. 3163.00
Flask, Lafayette & Masonic, Light Yellow Olive, Sheared Mouth, Pontil, 1824-25, ½ Pt. 10000.00
Flask, Man With Staff, House, Trees, Clear, Embossed, Pontil, c.1850, ½ Pt. 69.00
Flask, Masonic & Eagle, Calabash, Aqua, Open Pontil, Qt. 109.00
Flask, Masonic & Eagle, Green, Sheared Mouth, Pontil, Pt. 1093.00

Bottle, Figural, Frog, Aqua, Deponiert, Embossed, Polished Lip, Germany, 5 ¼ In.
$245.00

Bottle, Flask, Cornucopia & Urn, Olive Green, Sheared & Tooled Mouth, Pontil, 1830, Pt.
$105.00

Bottle, Flask, Eagle & Cornucopia, Yellow Green, Sheared Lip, Open Pontil, c.1830, Pt.
$175.00

B

Bottle, Flask, Scroll, Ice Blue, Sheared Lip, Pontil, c.1850-60, Pt. $55.00

Bottle, Flask, Washington & Taylor, Blue Green, Sheared & Tooled Lip, Open Pontil, 1852, Qt. $275.00

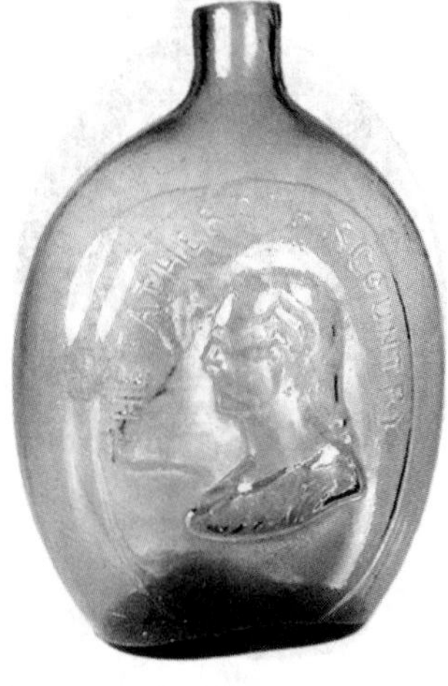

Bottle, Food, Dorlon & Schaffer Pickled Oysters, Fulton Market, Aqua, c.1890, Pt. $410.00

Flask, Masonic & Eagle, Medium To Deep Blue Green, Sheared Lip, Pontil, 1820-30, Pt. 8900.00
Flask, Masonic & Eagle, Olive Amber, Embossed KCCNC, Pt. 375.00
Flask, Masonic & Eagle, Sheaf Of Wheat, Green Aqua, Pt. 308.00
Flask, Masonic Arch, Olive Amber, Sheared & Tooled Lip, Pontil, c.1815, ½ Pt. 345.00
Flask, Murdock & Cassel, Light Blue Green, Amber Splotches, Sheared Mouth, Pontil, Pt. 2610.00
Flask, Pitkin Type, 16 Ribs, Pink Amethyst, Sheared & Tooled Lip, Open Pontil, 6 ¾ In. 1792.00
Flask, Pitkin Type, 24 Ribs, Sapphire Blue, Sheared Mouth, Pontil, 7 ¼ In. 2875.00
Flask, Pitkin Type, 36 Ribs, Amethyst, Sheared Mouth, Pontil, 1780-1830, 4 ¼ In. 1120.00
Flask, Pitkin Type, 36 Ribs, Swirled To Left, Root Beer Amber, Sheared Mouth, Pontil, 5 ¾ In. 1120.00
Flask, Pitkin Type, 36 Ribs, Swirled To Right, Light Yellow Olive, Sheared Mouth, Pontil, 6 In. 675.00
Flask, Pitkin Type, 36 Ribs, Swirled To Right, Olive Yellow, Tooled Mouth, Pontil, c.1790, 5 ⅜ In. 518.00
Flask, Pitkin Type, Broken Ribs, Swirled To Left, Deep Amber, Sheared & Tooled Lip, 6 ½ In. . 952.00
Flask, Pitkin Type, Broken Ribs, Swirled To Left, Olive Green, Tooled, Mouth, 5 ⅛ In. 728.00
Flask, Richardson & Tullidge, Coffin, Clear, Tooled Lip, Labels, Qt. 112.00
Flask, Scroll, Aqua, Sheared & Tooled Lip, Pontil, Pt. 60.00
Flask, Scroll, Blue Aqua, Sheared & Tooled Lip, Pontil, Pt. 50.00
Flask, Scroll, Green, Pear Shape, Sheared Lip, Iron Pontil, c.1845, Qt. 150.00
Flask, Scroll, Green, Sheared Lip, Iron Pontil, ½ Pt. 4256.00
Flask, Scroll, Green Aqua, Corset Shape, Sheared Mouth, Pontil, 1830-40, Pt. 900.00
Flask, Scroll, Ice Blue, Corset Shape, Sheared Mouth, Pontil, J.R. & Son, 1830-40, Pt. 1490.00
Flask, Scroll, Ice Blue, Sheared Lip, Pontil, c.1850-60, Pt. . . . . . *illus* 55.00
Flask, Scroll, Light To Medium Blue Green, Sheared Mouth, Pontil, 1845-60, Qt. 1590.00
Flask, Scroll, Medium Cobalt Blue, Sheared Mouth, Tubular Pontil, 1845-60, Pt. 5100.00
Flask, Scroll, Moonstone, Lavender Tint, Sheared Mouth, Pontil, Qt. 1618.00
Flask, Scroll, Pale Blue Green, Hearts, Flowers, Sheared Mouth, Pontil, 1830-50, Qt. 7200.00
Flask, Scroll, Sapphire Blue, Sheared Lip, Red Iron Pontil, Qt. 1120.00
Flask, Scroll, Sapphire Blue, Sheared Mouth, Pontil, 1845-60, Pt. 2995.00
Flask, Scroll, Yellow Green, Applied Collar, Ring, Iron Pontil, 1845-60, Pt. 2375.00
Flask, Scroll, Yellow Green, Sheared Mouth, Pontil, 1845-60, Pt. 1390.00
Flask, Scroll, Yellow Olive Amber, Inward Rolled Mouth, Pontil, c.1850, Pt. 1800.00
Flask, Sheaf Of Grain, Calabash, Sapphire Blue, Double Collar, Tubular Pontil, Qt. 3163.00
Flask, Sloop, Light To Medium Yellow Green, Sheared Mouth, Pontil, ½ Pt. 2685.00
Flask, Sloop & Star, Blue Aqua, Sheared & Tooled Lip, Pontil, ½ Pt. 240.00
Flask, Soldier & Hound, Amber, Sheared Mouth, Tubular Pontil, Qt. 1380.00
Flask, Soldier & Star, Calabash, Blue Aqua, Applied Mouth, Iron Pontil 190.00
Flask, Strap Side, Sapphire Blue, Applied Neck Ring, Seed Bubbles, Sheared Lip, c.1860, Pt. . . 69.00
Flask, Success To The Railroad, Aqua, Sheared Mouth, Pontil, 1830-50, Pt. . . . . . 1490.00 to 1800.00
Flask, Success To The Railroad, Aqua, Sheared Mouth, Pontil, Pt. 863.00
Flask, Success To The Railroad, Forest Green, Sheared Mouth, Pontil, 1830-50, Pt. 940.00
Flask, Success To The Railroad, Horse Drawn Cart, Deep Olive Amber, Open Pontil, Pt. 476.00
Flask, Success To The Railroad, Olive Green, Sheared Lip, Open Pontil, Pt. 728.00
Flask, Success To The Railroad, Olive Green, Sheared Mouth, Pontil, 1830-50, Pt. 5250.00
Flask, Success To The Railroad, Olive Green, Yellow Tone, Applied Collar Mouth, 1860-70, Pt. 1490.00
Flask, Success To The Railroad, Olive Yellow, Sheared Mouth, Pontil, Pt. 7480.00
Flask, Success To The Railroad, Yellow Olive, Sheared Mouth, Pontil, 1830-50, Pt. 1080.00
Flask, Sunburst, Deep Blue Aqua, Green Tint, Rolled Lip, Pontil, ½ Pt. 476.00
Flask, Sunburst, Forest Green, Sheared Mouth, Pontil, 1815-30, ½ Pt. 2495.00
Flask, Sunburst, Golden Amber, Olive, Sheared Mouth, Pontil, 1820-30, ½ Pt. 1480.00
Flask, Sunburst, Green, Sheared & Tooled Mouth, Pontil, c.1815, Pt. 575.00
Flask, Sunburst, Light Blue, Sheared Lip, Pontil, 1 Pt. 476.00
Flask, Sunburst, Light Olive Yellow, Sheared Mouth, Pontil, 1813-30, ½ Pt. 1700.00
Flask, Sunburst, Light Olive Yellow, Sheared Mouth, Pontil, 1813-30, Pt. 945.00
Flask, Sunburst, Light To Medium Yellow Green, Ribs, Applied Collar, Pontil, ½ Pt. 2600.00
Flask, Sunburst, Light Yellow Olive To Dark, Sheared Mouth, Pontil, 1820-30, Pt. 1120.00
Flask, Sunburst, Medium To Deep Amber, Sheared, Mouth, Pontil, ½ Pt. 1232.00
Flask, Sunburst, Medium To Deep Golden Amber, Sheared Mouth, Pontil, 1820-30, Pt. 3395.00
Flask, Sunburst, Olive Yellow, Sheared Mouth, Pontil, ½ Pt. 1093.00
Flask, Sunburst, Pale Vaseline, Sheared Mouth, Pontil, 1820-30, Pt. 965.00
Flask, Sunburst, Sea Green, Applied Sloping Collar, Pontil, 1815-30, ½ Pt. 8900.00
Flask, Sunburst, Sea Green, Sloping Collar, Pontil, ½ Pt. 3163.00
Flask, Sunburst, Yellow Amber, Olive Tint, Sheared Mouth, Pontil, 1813-30, Pt. 975.00
Flask, Sunburst, Yellow Emerald Green, Sheared Mouth, Pontil, 1815-30, Pt. 8950.00
Flask, Sunburst, Yellow Olive, Amber Neck, Sheared Mouth, Pontil, ½ Pt. 9450.00
Flask, Sunburst, Yellow Olive, Sheared Mouth, Pontil, 1813-30, Pt. 3000.00
Flask, Union, Clasped Hands, Blue Aqua, Applied Mouth, 1860-1870, Qt. 140.00
Flask, Union, Clasped Hands, Orange Amber, Blob Top, Pt. 379.00

Flask, Union, Clasped Hands & Eagle, Olive Yellow, Applied Ring, Qt. 1792.00
Flask, Union, Clasped Hands & Eagle, Orange Amber, Applied Collar, 1860-70, Pt. 575.00
Flask, Washington & Eagle, Medium Green, Sheared Mouth, Tubular Pontil, 1825-30, Pt. 9400.00
Flask, Washington & Sailing Ship, Green, Golden Amber Striations, Double Collar, Pontil, Pt. 4888.00
Flask, Washington & Taylor, Aqua, Tooled Lip, Pontil, Qt. 40.00
Flask, Washington & Taylor, Aqua, Tooled Mouth, Pontil, ½ Pt. 90.00
Flask, Washington & Taylor, Blue Aqua, Open Pontil, Qt. 119.00
Flask, Washington & Taylor, Blue Green, Sheared & Tooled Lip, Open Pontil, 1852, Qt. . *illus* 275.00
Flask, Washington & Taylor, Yellow Topaz, Double Collar Mouth, Pontil, 1840-60, Pt. 3000.00
Flask, Zanesville, 24 Swirled Ribs, Golden Amber, 9 In. 7638.00
Flask, Zanesville, 30 Swirled Ribs, Amber, Globular, 12 In. 10869.00
Food, Blueberry Preserves, Golden Amber, Cylindrical, Fluted, Double Collar, 11 ¼ In. 1490.00
Food, Dorlon & Schaffer Pickled Oysters, Fulton Market, Aqua, c.1890, Pt. .... *illus* 410.00
Food, Empire, Aqua, Ground Lip, Metal Clamp, Pat. Feb. 13, 1866, Qt. .... *illus* 275.00
Food, F. & J. Heinz's Grape Jelly, Paper Label, Glass Lid 100.00
Food, F.C.G. Co., Cobalt Blue, Groove Ring Wax Sealer, c.1875-90, Qt. .... *illus* 2840.00
Food, Globe, Medium Yellow Olive, 33, Ground Lip, Patented May 25th 1886, Qt. ...... *illus* 1750.00
Food, Globe, Straw Yellow, Ground Lip, Patented May 25, 1886, ½ Gal. 650.00
Food, Hartell's, Light Apple Green, Embossed, Ground Lip, Oct. 19, 1858, Pt. .... *illus* 110.00
Food, Heinz's Dusseldorf Mustard, Handle, Paper Label, Metal Lid 175.00
Food, Heinz's Keystone Chow Chow, Paper Label 85.00
Food, Heinz's Manzanilla Olives, Paper Label, Cork Stopper 100.00
Food, Heinz's Piquant Dressing, Paper Label, Flat 50.00
Food, Heinz's Queen Olives, 8-Sided, Paper Label, Snow Globe 100.00
Food, Heinz's Standard Catsup, Paper Label 200.00
Food, Heinz's Strawberry Preserves, Square, Paper Label, Snow Globe, 11 In. 200.00
Food, Heinz's Stuffed Olives, Glass Stopper, Footed, Paper Label 175.00
Food, Horlick's Original Malted Milk, Blue Enamel, Ribbed Lid, 9 ¼ In. .... *illus* 10.00
Food, Mustard, Yellow Kid, Milk Glass, Yellow Coat, Frosted Head, 6 ¾ In. 600.00
Food Jar, 3-Piece Mold, Olive Yellow, Cylindrical, Wide Mouth, Applied Collar, Pontil, 8 In. ... 920.00
Fruit Jar, Ball Perfect Mason, Yellow Olive, ABM Lip, 1925-35, Qt. .... *illus* 85.00
Fruit Jar, Baltimore Glass Works, Aqua, Applied Mouth, Stopper, c.1855, Qt. 489.00
Fruit Jar, Barrel, Blue Aqua, Sheared Mouth, Applied Wax Seal Groove, Lid, Iron Pontil, c.1850, Qt. 633.00
Fruit Jar, Beaver, Amber, Insert, Ground Lip, Screw Band, Canada, c.1880, Qt. 1035.00
Fruit Jar, Bee, Aqua, Ground Lip, Iron Screw Clamp, c.1870, ½ Gal. 127.00
Fruit Jar, Belle, Pat. Dec. 14 1869, Aqua, Domed Lid, Wire Bail, 3 Feet, Qt. 1904.00
Fruit Jar, Best, Amber, Zinc Ground Lip, Screw Lid, Canada, 1885-90, Qt. .... *illus* 252.00
Fruit Jar, Burlington B.G. Co. R'd 1876, ½ Gal. 70.00
Fruit Jar, Carter's, Butter & Fruit Preserving, Pat. Sep 28 1897, Clear, Wire Handle, c.1905... 127.00
Fruit Jar, Cohansey Glass Mfg. Co., 2, Pat. Feb. 12 1867, Aqua, Ground Lip, Pt. .... *illus* 72.00
Fruit Jar, Cunningham & Co. Pittsburgh, Blue Green, Applied Lip, Pontil, c.1855, Qt. 242.00
Fruit Jar, Dodge Sweeney & Co's California Butter, Mason's, Aqua, 1870, ½ Gal. ...... *illus* 495.00
Fruit Jar, Eagle, Blue Aqua, Applied Mouth, Lid, Iron Clamp, ½ Gal. 180.00
Fruti Jar, Empress, Aqua, Ground Lip, Insert, Canada, c.1883, Qt. .... *illus* 295.00
Fruit Jar, Gilberds, Star, Aqua, Embossed, Wire Closure, c.1883-90, Qt. .... *illus* 209.00
Fruit Jar, Gilberds, Star, Pat'd 1883, Glass Lid, Wire Closure, Qt. 209.00
Fruit Jar, Gilberds, Trade Mark Dandy, Medium Amber, Pat. Oct. 13th, 1885, ½ Gal. .... *illus* 92.00
Fruit Jar, Glass Lid, Metal Yoke Clamp, Lever Closure, c.1866, Qt. 275.00
Fruit Jar, Glass Lid, Spring Wire Clamp, Wooden Roller Closure, c.1875, Qt. 360.00
Fruit Jar, Globe, Amber, Qt. 99.00
Fruit Jar, Gregory's, Common Sense Jar, Pat Aug 17th 1869, Aqua, Applied Mouth, Qt. .. *illus* 390.00
Fruit Jar, Ground Lip, Glass Lid, Metal Clamp Closure, c.1886, Qt. 1750.00
Fruit Jar, Hemingray, Forest Green, 3-Piece Mold, Sheared Lip, Lid, c.1860, 6 ½ In. 690.00
Fruit Jar, J.C. Lefferts, Cast Iron, Thumb Screw Closure, c.1859, Qt. 840.00
Fruit Jar, Lafayette, Script, Cylindrical, Aqua, Metal & Glass Stopper, Qt. 978.00
Fruit Jar, Mason Vacuum, Knowlton Patent June 9th 1908, Cornflower, Glass Lid, Wire Closure, Qt. 80.00
Fruit Jar, Mason's, Snowflake, Tudor Rose, Honey Amber, Porcelain Lined Cap, ½ Gal. 3808.00
Fruit Jar, Mason's, Yellow Amber, Ground Lip, Milk Glass Insert, Zinc Screw Band, ½ Gal. ... 160.00
Fruit Jar, Mason's Patent, 1870, Ground Lip, Glass Insert, Screw Lid, ½ Gal. 495.00
Fruit Jar, Mason's Patent, Nov 30th 1858, Dupont, K, Blue Aqua, Zinc Lid, Qt. .... *illus* 365.00
Fruit Jar, Mason's Patent, Nov 30th 1858, Golden Yellow Amber, Zinc Lid, Qt. .... *illus* 1080.00
Fruit Jar, Mason's Patent, Nov 30th 1858, Olive Green, Amber Striations, ½ Gal. ...... *illus* 575.00
Fruit Jar, Mason's Patent, Nov 30th 1858, Sky Blue, Tudor Rose, Qt. .... *illus* 1440.00
Fruit Jar, Mason's Patent, Nov 30th 1858, Teal Blue, 70, Ground Lip, Zinc Lid, Qt. ..... *illus* 8950.00
Fruit Jar, Mason's Patent, Nov. 30th 1858, Teal Blue, Lid, Qt. 8090.00
Fruit Jar, Mason's Patent, Nov. 30th 1858, Yellow Amber, Lid, Qt. 1080.00

Bottle, Food, Empire, Aqua, Ground Lip, Metal Clamp, Pat. Feb. 13, 1866, Qt.
$275.00

Bottle, Food, F.C.G. Co., Cobalt Blue, Groove Ring Wax Sealer, c.1875-90, Qt.
$2840.00

Bottle, Food, Globe, Medium Yellow Olive, 33, Ground Lip, Patented May 25th 1886, Qt.
$1750.00

Bottle, Food, Globe, Straw Yellow, Ground Lip, Patented May 25, 1886, ½ Gal.
$650.00

Bottle, Food, Horlick's Original Malted Milk, Blue Enamel, Ribbed Lid, 9 ¼ In.
$10.00

Bottle, Fruit Jar, Ball Perfect Mason, Yellow Olive, ABM Lip, 1925-35, Qt.
$85.00

Fruit Jar, Mason's Patent, Nov. 30th 1858, Yellow Olive, Lid, Qt. 890.00
Fruit Jar, Mason's Patent Nov 30th, 1858, Blue Aqua, Ground Lip, Zinc Lid, Qt. . . . . *illus* 445.00
Fruit Jar, Mason's Patent Nov 30th, Orange Amber, Ground Lip, Zinc Screw Lid, ½ Gal. 80.00
Fruit Jar, Mason's Patent Nov 30th 1858, Blue Aqua, Ground Lip, Zinc Screw Lid 325.00
Fruit Jar, Mason's Patent Nov. 30th 1858, HGCo., 10, Dark Olive Amber, Qt. . . . . *illus* 11500.00
Fruit Jar, Mason's Union Shield, Aqua, Ground Lip, 1870-85, Qt. 90.00
Fruit Jar, Peerless, Aqua, Metal Yoke Clamp, c.1863-70, Qt. . . . . *illus* 197.00
Fruit Jar, Petal, Olive Green, 10 Panels, Applied Mouth, Iron Pontil, c.1845, 8 ½ In. 2185.00
Fruit Jar, Potter & Bodine's Air-Tight, Patented April 13th 1858, Barrel, Aqua, Pontil, Qt. . *illus* 175.00
Fruit Jar, Puritan Trade Mark, Ship, LSCo, Blue Aqua, Ground Lip, Iron Ring, Qt. . . . . . *illus* 320.00
Fruit Jar, Quong Hop & Co., Clear, Wire Bail, Lid, ½ Pt. 30.00
Fruit Jar, R.M. Dalbey's, Pat Nov 16 1858, Metal Lid & Collar, Qt., 8 ½ x 4 ¼ In. 17360.00
Fruit Jar, Royal Of 1876, Pale Apple Green, Berries & Leaf, Ground Lip, Qt. . . . . *illus* 360.00
Fruit Jar, S.B. Dewey Jr., No. 65, Buffalo St., Rochester, Aqua, c.1860, Qt. . . . . *illus* 295.00
Fruit Jar, Safety Valve Patd May 21 1895, HC, Emerald Green, Bail Handle, ½ Gal. . . . . . *illus* 480.00
Fruit Jar, Scranton, Blue Aqua, Ground Lip, Wood Roller, Wire Clamp, c.1880, Qt. . . . . . *illus* 360.00
Fruit Jar, Star, Aqua, Ground Lip, Zinc Insert, Haller's Patent Feb 5 67, Qt. . . . . *illus* 415.00
Fruit Jar, Stone Mason, Union Stoneware Co., Red Wing, Minn., Jan. 24, 1899, Zinc Lid, 8 x 6 In. 160.00
Fruit Jar, Thomas Patent, July 12 1892, Aqua, Metal Clamp, Qt. 1265.00
Fruit Jar, Trademark Lightening, Amber, Glass Lid, Qt. 134.00
Fruit Jar, Valve Jar Co., Philadelphia, Blue Aqua, Patd Mar 10th 1868, Qt. . . . . *illus* 435.00
Fruit Jar, Victory, Aqua, Ground Lip, No Closure, c.1870-80, Qt. . . . . *illus* 515.00
Fruit Jar, Webster's, Patent Feb. 16. 1864, Deep Blue Aqua, Ground Lip, Qt. . . . . *illus* 1015.00
Fruit Jar, Wide Mouth, Adjustable, Olive, Seal, Canada, c.1915, Pt. 115.00
Fruit Jar, Yeoman's Fruit Bottle, Aqua, Applied Mouth, ½ Gal. 100.00
Gin, Cased, Olive Green, Dip Mold, Open Pontil, Dutch, 1770-1810, 10 ⅞ In. . . . . *illus* 155.00
Gin, Hoffschlaeger Co., Monogram, Deep Amber, Tooled Top, Fifth 224.00
Ink, 12-Sided, Amber, Inward Rolled Lip, Open Pontil, 1 In. 259.00
Ink, Baker's Carmine, Clear, Domed, Stopper, 1 In. 39.00
Ink, Barrel, Tooled Disc Mouth, Pontil, c.1835, 2 x 1 ¾ In. 224.00
Ink, Beehive, Apple Green, Sheared Mouth, 2 In. 532.00
Ink, Bertinguiot, Cylindrical, Yellow Olive, Embossed, Open Pontil, 2 In. 259.00
Ink, Blown, Cylindrical, Diamond Crosshatch, Amber, Coventry, 1 ¾ x 2 ⅝ In. 115.00
Ink, Blown, Olive Amber, Geometric, Open Pontil, Coventry, 2 ¾ In. 150.00
Ink, Butler's, Cincinnati, 12-Sided, Sheared Lip, Open Pontil, c.1840, 3 x 2 In. 392.00
Ink, Cabin, Clear, 2 x 2 In. 119.00
Ink, Carter's, Cathedral, 6-Sided, Cobalt Blue, ABM Lip, 9 ¾ In. . . . . *illus* 70.00
Ink, Carter's, Cathedral, 6-Sided, Cobalt Blue, Labels, 8 In. 258.00
Ink, Carter's, Cathedral, Blue Green, 3-Piece Mold, Crimped Spout, 9 ¾ In. 50.00
Ink, Carter's, Cathedral, Cobalt Blue, ABM, Screw Cap, Labels, 7 In. 469.00
Ink, Carter's, Cathedral, Cobalt Blue, ABM, Screw Cap, Labels, 9 In. 300.00
Ink, Carter's, Cathedral, Cobalt Blue, ABM, Screw Cap, Labels, 10 ¾ In. 300.00
Ink, Carter's French Railroad Copying, Embossed, Label, Pour Spout, Cork Top, 8 ½ In. 440.00
Ink, Cobalt Blue, 6-Sided, Rolled & Flared Lip, Open Pontil, c.1830, 2 ⅝ In. 299.00
Ink, Cobalt Blue, Cathedral, 6 ½ In. 165.00
Ink, Cone, Golden Amber, Pontil, 2 In. 299.00
Ink, Cone, Yellow Olive Green, Inward Rolled Lip, Pontil, c.1840, 2 ⅜ In. 242.00
Ink, Cottage, Milk Glass, Tooled Mouth, c.1865, 4 ⅞ In. 805.00
Ink, Davids' Electro Chemical Writing Fluid, Cobalt Blue, Box, 32 Oz., 10 In. 209.00
Ink, Deep Cobalt Blue, 12 Ribs, Tooled Lip, Pontil, 2 ¼ In. . . . . *illus* 110.00
Ink, Drum, Light Green, Pontil, c.1850, 2 x 1 ¾ In. 179.00
Ink, Emerald Green, Umbrella, 8-Sided, Tooled Mouth, 2 ⅜ In. 364.00
Ink, Farley's, 8-Sided, Yellow Amber, Pontil, Flared Out Lip, c.1840, 3 ⅝ In. 3450.00
Ink, Funnel, Aqua, 9 Horizontal Rings, Pontil, c.1850, 2 ⅛ In. 181.00
Ink, Geometric, Diamond Diaper, Amber, 3-Piece Mold, Open Pontil, 2 ¼ In. 202.00
Ink, Geometric, Medium Yellow Amber, Tooled Disc Mouth, Pontil, 1815-25, 1 ⅞ In. . . . *illus* 120.00
Ink, Geometric, Olive Amber, Tooled Disc Mouth, Pontil, Coventry Glass Works, 1 ¾ In. 150.00
Ink, Geometric, Olive Amber, Tooled Disc Mouth, Pontil, Mt. Vernon Glass Works, 1 ¾ In. 275.00
Ink, Harrison's Columbian, 8-Sided, Blue Aqua, Rolled Lip, Pontil, 2 ⅛ In. 60.00
Ink, Harrison's Columbian, 12-Sided, Teal Green, Sloping Collar, Pontil, 6 ¼ In. 5463.00
Ink, Harrison's Columbian, Cobalt Blue, Applied Mouth, Pontil, c.1840, 5 ½ In. 1955.00
Ink, Harrison's Columbian, Cobalt Blue, Round, Inward Rolled Lip, Pontil, c.1840, 2 In. 633.00
Ink, Hohental Bros. & Co., Olive, Striations, Cylindrical, Applied Mouth, Pour Spout, 7 ¼ In. . 2645.00
Ink, Igloo, Cobalt Blue, Ground Mouth, 1860-80, 2 In. 1265.00
Ink, J. & I.E. M, Igloo, Teal, Panels, Tooled Mouth, c.1875, 1 ¾ In. 920.00
Ink, Jones Empire, 12-Sided, Emerald Green, Applied Collar, Iron Pontil, 7 ⅜ In. 2415.00

Bottle, Fruit Jar, Best, Amber, Zinc Ground Lip, Screw Lid, Canada, 1885-90, Qt.
$252.00

Bottle, Fruit Jar, Cohansey Glass Mfg. Co., 2, Pat. Feb. 12 1867, Aqua, Ground Lip, Pt.
$72.00

Bottle, Fruit Jar, Dodge Sweeney & Co's California Butter, Mason's, Aqua, 1870, ½ Gal.
$495.00

Bottle, Fruti Jar, Empress, Aqua, Ground Lip, Insert, Canada, c.1883, Qt.
$295.00

Bottle, Fruit Jar, Gilberds, Star, Aqua, Embossed, Wire Closure, c.1883-90, Qt.
$209.00

Bottle, Fruit Jar, Gilberds, Trade Mark Dandy, Medium Amber, Pat. Oct. 13th, 1885, ½ Gal.
$92.00

TIP

If you want to clean a bottle that has a paper label, try to protect the label. Wrap the bottle tightly in thin plastic wrap. Seal the wrap with tape and rubber bands. Clean the inside carefully, using a mixture of water, automatic dishwasher detergent and slightly abrasive kitty litter. Fill the bottle part way and shake.

Bottle, Fruit Jar, Gregory's, Common Sense Jar, Pat Aug 17th 1869, Aqua, Applied Mouth, Qt.
$390.00

Bottle, Fruit Jar, Mason's Patent, Nov 30th 1858, Dupont, K, Blue Aqua, Zinc Lid, Qt.
$365.00

Bottle, Fruit Jar, Mason's Patent, Nov 30th 1858, Golden Yellow Amber, Zinc Lid, Qt.
$1080.00

Bottle, Fruit Jar, Mason's Patent, Nov 30th 1858, Olive Green, Amber Striations, ½ Gal.
$575.00

Bottle, Fruit Jar, Mason's Patent, Nov 30th 1858, Sky Blue, Tudor Rose, Qt.
$1440.00

Bottle, Fruit Jar, Mason's Patent, Nov 30th 1858, Teal Blue, 70, Ground Lip, Zinc Lid, Qt.
$8950.00

Bottle, Fruit Jar, Mason's Patent Nov 30th, 1858, Blue Aqua, Ground Lip, Zinc Lid, Qt.
$445.00

Bottle, Fruit Jar, Mason's Patent Nov. 30th 1858, HGCo., 10, Dark Olive Amber, Qt.
$11500.00

Bottle, Fruit Jar, Peerless, Aqua, Metal Yoke Clamp, c.1863-70, Qt.
$197.00

Bottle, Fruit Jar, Potter & Bodine's Air-Tight, Patented April 13th 1858, Barrel, Aqua, Pontil, Qt.
$175.00

Bottle, Fruit Jar, Puritan Trade Mark, Ship, LSCo, Blue Aqua, Ground Lip, Iron Ring, Qt.
$320.00

Bottle, Fruit Jar, Royal Of 1876, Pale Apple Green, Berries & Leaf, Ground Lip, Qt.
$360.00

Ink, Locomotive, Lochman's, Clear, Sheared & Ground Lip, c.1875, 2 x 2 In. 1093.00
Ink, Ma & Pa Carter, Bisque, Multicolored, Carter's Inx, Germany, 3 ⅝ In., Pair *illus* 108.00
Ink, Master, Cover, Straight Sides, Yellow Bands, Wavy Lines, Redware, c.1824, 7 In. 1185.00
Ink, S.I. Comp, Barrel, Milk Glass, Embossed, 2 ⅛ In. 395.00
Ink, Stafford's, Blue, Green, Pour Spout, Pt. 69.00
Ink, Stafford's, Teal, Applied Top, Master, 9 ½ In. 112.00
Ink, Stafford's, Teal Blue, Applied Mouth, Crimped Spout, 7 ¾ In. 110.00
Ink, Teakettle, 6-Sided, Cobalt, Painted Decoration, Sheared Mouth, c.1875, 1 ⅞ In. 748.00
Ink, Teakettle, 6-Sided, Deep Teal Green, 2 ⅛ In. 560.00
Ink, Teakettle, 8-Sided, Amethyst, Metal Neck Ring, Hinged Lid, 2 In. 476.00
Ink, Teakettle, 8-Sided, Cobalt Blue, 2 ⅛ In. 350.00
Ink, Teakettle, 8-Sided, Cobalt Blue, Sheared Mouth, 2 In. 420.00
Ink, Teakettle, 8-Sided, Milk Glass, Opalescent, Blue, Gold Enamel, 2 In. 235.00
Ink, Teakettle, Amethyst, Ground Lip, Smooth Base, 2 x 2 In. 532.00
Ink, Teakettle, Amethyst, Sheared Ground Lip, Brass Neck Ring, c.1875, 2 ¼ In. 1150.00
Ink, Teakettle, Aquamarine, Ribbed, Applied Spouts, Swan Top, Pontil, 6 ¼ In. 215.00
Ink, Teakettle, Barrel, Turquoise, Gold Paint, Brass Cap 1560.00
Ink, Teakettle, Beehive, Aqua, Ground Lip, c.1880, 1 ⅛ In. 295.00
Ink, Teakettle, Clambroth, Blue, 2 ½ In. 476.00
Ink, Teakettle, Cobalt Blue, Ground Lip, Brass Neck Ring, Hinged Lid, 2 ¼ In. *illus* 160.00
Ink, Teakettle, Melon Ribbed, Cobalt Blue, Ground Lip, Brass Collar, Cap, 1 ½ x 3 ¾ In. 1290.00
Ink, Teakettle, Milk Glass, Opalescent, Enamel Flowers, Brass Neck Ring, Hinged Lid, 2 ½ In. 364.00
Ink, Umbrella, 8-Sided, Amber, Galleried Mouth, Pontil, c.1850, 2 ⅜ In. 226.00
Ink, Umbrella, 8-Sided, Apricot Puce, Open Pontil, Inward Rolled Lip, 2 ⅝ In. 1904.00
Ink, Umbrella, 8-Sided, Blue Green, Open Pontil, Inward Rolled Lip, 2 ½ In. 672.00
Ink, Umbrella, 8-Sided, Cobalt Blue, Applied Mouth, 2 ⅝ In. 840.00
Ink, Umbrella, 8-Sided, Cobalt Blue, Rolled Lip, Pontil, c.1840, 2 ⅜ In. 2645.00
Ink, Umbrella, 8-Sided, Cobalt Blue, Tooled Mouth, Pontil, 2 ⅜ In. 1904.00
Ink, Umbrella, 8-Sided, Golden Yellow, Amber, Inward Rolled Lip, Open Pontil, 2 ⅝ In. 616.00
Ink, Umbrella, 8-Sided, Olive Yellow, Inward Rolled Lip, 2 ⅜ In. 476.00
Ink, Umbrella, 8-Sided, Tobacco, Amber, 2 In. 339.00
Ink, Umbrella, 8-Sided, Yellow Amber, Inward Rolled Lip, Open Pontil, 2 ½ In. 448.00
Ink, Umbrella, 12-Sided, Blue Green, Rolled Lip, 2 ⅛ In. 40.00
Ink, Umbrella, Rolled Lip, Open Pontil, 2 ⅛ In. 364.00
Ink, Umbrella, Rolled Lip, Open Pontil, 2 ⅜ In. 392.00
Ink, Umbrella, Teal, Rolled Lip, Pontil, 2 ½ In. 235.00
Ink, W.E. Bonney, Barrel, Blue Aqua, Applied Sloping Collar, c.1860-70, 6 In. 200.00
Ink, Ward's, Olive Green, Applied Sloping Collar, Crimped Spout, 6 In. *illus* 100.00
Jar, Globe Tobacco Company, Detroit, Barrel, Golden Amber, 7 ⅛ In. *illus* 112.00
Jar, Palm Fruit Brazil, Swirl Top, Footed, Paper Label, Columbia, 13 In. 220.00
Jar, Royal Ispahan Hair Dye, Cobalt Blue, 8-Sided, Ground Lip, Metal Lid, 1870s, 2 ⅜ In. 1290.00
Jar, Salt, Saratoga, N.Y., Olive Green, High Shoulder, 3-Piece Mold, Wide Mouth, c.1855, Qt. 5463.00
Jar, Snuff, Olive Amber, Yellow, Flared Mouth, Pontil, c.1770-1810, 6 ⅛ In. 672.00
Jar, Storage, Blue, Slug Plate, San Francisco Glassworks, Qt. 224.00
Jar, Utility, 8-Sided, Olive Green, Yellow, Applied String Lip, c.1770-1800, 6 ⅜ In. 840.00
Jar, Utility, Beehive, Deep Olive Yellow, Amber, Applied Mouth, Pontil, 6 ⅝ In. 728.00
Jar, Utility, Black Glass, Square, Olive Yellow, Turned Down Lip, Wide Mouth, 5 x 2 ⅝ In. 896.00
Jar, Utility, Deep Olive Amber, Wide Mouth, Sheared Mouth, Applied Lip, Pontil, 6 ⅛ In. 448.00
Jar, Van Vliet Of 1881, Aqua, Ground Lip, Embossed Lid, Pt. *illus* 725.00
Medical, Poison, Parke Davis, Amber, Ribbed, Embossed, 2 ½ In. 38.00
Medicine, A.J. White, New York, Laxol, Teal Blue, 6 In. 39.00
Medicine, Allan's Anti-Fat Botanic Medicine Co., Buffalo, N.Y., Blue, Applied Top, 7 ½ In. 532.00
Medicine, Allan's Anti-Fat Botanic Medicine Co., Cobalt Blue, 7 In. 199.00
Medicine, Apothecary, Clear, Applied Foot, Tooled Lip, Stopper, 10 ⅛ In. 224.00
Medicine, Apothecary, Clear, Cobalt Blue Bands, Folded Rim, Stopper, 7 ⅛ In. 280.00
Medicine, Apothecary, Clear, Cobalt Blue Bands, Knob, Stopper, 14 ¼ In. 504.00
Medicine, Apothecary, Engraved Flower, Pedestal, Stopper, 20 In. 75.00
Medicine, Apothecary, J.G. Gooding & Co., Cobalt Blue, 6-Sided, 6 ¼ In. 202.00
Medicine, Apothecary, Opium, Label Under Glass, c.1890, 12 ½ In. *illus* 100.00
Medicine, Apothecary, Syr. Pruni V., Recessed Gold Label, Pat'd Dec. 10 '95, 10 In. 300.00
Medicine, Apothecary, Tr. Cinch Co., Recessed Gold Label, Pat'd Dec. 10 '95, 10 In. 415.00
Medicine, Armstrong's Reliable Worm Syrup, Paper Label, Contents, Box, 6 ¼ In. 207.00
Medicine, Baby Cough Syrup, Girl, Chapin Chemical Co., Paper Label, Contents, Box, 6 In. 232.00
Medicine, Bartine's Lotion, Yellow Green, Olive Tone, Applied Sloping Collar Mouth, 6 In. 2530.00
Medicine, C. Brinckerhoff's, Health Restorative, Olive Yellow, Green, 7 ⅜ In. 1344.00
Medicine, C. Ellis & Co., Philada, Druggist, Cylindrical, Aqua, Open Pontil, 6 In. 69.00

Bottle, Fruit Jar, S.B. Dewey Jr., No. 65, Buffalo St., Rochester, Aqua, c.1860, Qt.
$295.00

Bottle, Fruit Jar,
Safety Valve Patd May 21 1895, HC, Emerald Green, Bail Handle, ½ Gal.
$480.00

Bottle, Fruit Jar, Scranton, Blue Aqua, Ground Lip, Wood Roller, Wire Clamp, c.1880, Qt.
$360.00

As always, the edited listings in *Kovels' Antiques & Collectibles Price Guide 2010* aren't available on any website, but readers should visit Kovels.com for information on trends, tips, reproductions, marks, old prices, and more!

Bottle, Fruit Jar, Star, Aqua, Ground Lip, Zinc Insert, Haller's Patent Feb 5 67, Qt.
$415.00

Bottle, Fruit Jar, Valve Jar Co., Philadelphia, Blue Aqua, Patd Mar 10th 1868, Qt.
$435.00

Bottle, Fruit Jar, Victory, Aqua, Ground Lip, No Closure, c.1870-80, Qt.
$515.00

Medicine, Caswell, Mack & Co., Omnia Vincit Labor, Cobalt Blue, 1890, 7 In. *illus* 82.00
Medicine, Citrate Of Magnesia, G.A. Morehead, Cobalt Blue, Tooled Top, Wire Bail, 7 ¾ In. 3136.00
Medicine, Clement Handly & Co., Aurogentine, Rectangular, Cobalt, Beveled Corners, 4 In. 60.00
Medicine, Columbia Liniment, Horse, F.C. Sturtevant Co., Label, Aqua, Contents, Box, 6 ½ In. 298.00
Medicine, Crisp's Hot Shot Treatment, For Running Fits, Contents, Label, Box, 7 ⅛ In. 121.00
Medicine, Dickey, Pioneer Chemist, Sky Blue, Embossed Mortar & Pestle, c.1850, 5 ½ In. 175.00
Medicine, Dr. Beard's Alterative Tonic, Oval, Blue Aqua, Tooled Mouth, 8 ½ In. 80.00
Medicine, Dr. Bull's Cough Syrup, Baltimore, Md., Aqua, Label, ½ Pt. 12.00
Medicine, Dr. Gun's Cough Remedy, Cannon, Aqua, Label, Contents, Box, 5 ½ In. 88.00
Medicine, Dr. Harshorn's, Oval, Olive Yellow Amber, Square Collar, 6 ⅛ In. 2070.00
Medicine, Dr. Haynes' Arabian Balsam, 12-Sided, Blue Aqua, 7 In. 48.00
Medicine, Dr. Hoofland's German Tonic, Square, Blue Aqua, Embossed, 9 In. 79.00
Medicine, Dr. J. Kauffman's Angeline, Angel, Jos. Schumaker & Co., Contents, Box, 8 In. 200.00
Medicine, Dr. J.N. Keeler's Vegetable Panacea, Blue Aqua, Applied Mouth, Pontil, 7 ⅜ In. 1680.00
Medicine, Dr. J.W. Bull's Vegetable Baby Syrup, Corkscrew, Aqua, Contents, Box, 5 In. 230.00
Medicine, Dr. Kilmer's Swamp Root, Label, Contents, Wrapper, 4 ¼ In. 49.00
Medicine, Dr. Langley's Root & Herb, Aqua, 6 ¾ In. 75.00
Medicine, Dr. M.M. Fenner Peoples Remedies, 1872-1898, Label, Contents, Box, 6 In. 33.00
Medicine, Dr. Ordway's Celebrated Pain Destroyer, 12-Sided, Aqua, Rolled Lip, Pontil, Cork 65.00
Medicine, Dr. Townsend's Expectorant, Light Blue Green, Applied Mouth, Pontil, 7 ½ In. 2352.00
Medicine, Dr. W. Burton's Syrup, Blue Green, Cylindrical, Applied Mouth, Pontil, 7 ½ In. 3640.00
Medicine, Dr. W.B. Caldwell's Syrup Pepsin, Pepsi Syrup Co., Label, Contents, Box, 8 ⅞ In. 49.00
Medicine, Druggist, Cobalt Blue, Applied Double Collar, Citrate Type, 7 In. 39.00
Medicine, Duff Gordon Sherry, Olive Green, Cylindrical, Applied Mouth, 10 In. 532.00
Medicine, E.A. Buckhout's Dutch Liniment, Blue Aqua, Inward Rolled Lip, Open Pontil, 4 ⅝ In. 840.00
Medicine, Enameled Flowers, 1870s, 3 In. 100.00
Medicine, Fluid Extract Of Valerian, Cylindrical, Olive Green, Flared Lip, Label, 3 In. 224.00
Medicine, Gargling Oil, 7Up Green, 5 In. 89.00
Medicine, Gargling Oil, Lockport, N.Y., Green, ½ Pt. 70.00
Medicine, Gargling Oil, Merchant's, Liniment, Cobalt Blue, ABM, Label, Contents, Box, 5 In. 77.00
Medicine, H. Lake's Indian Specific, Blue Aqua, Applied Ring, Pontil, 8 ⅜ In. 560.00
Medicine, H.H. Hay Druggist, Tombstone Shape, Blue Aqua, Strap Side, Pontil, 8 ½ In. 308.00
Medicine, H.T. Helmbold, Genuine Fluid Extracts, Phila., Aqua, Open Pontil, 6 In. 69.00
Medicine, Hall's Balsam For The Lungs, Rectangular Panels, Blue Green, 7 In. 39.00 to 59.00
Medicine, Hankins Specific, Borden Town, N.J., Embossed, Rectangular, 6 ½ In. 25.00
Medicine, Hill's Humane Oil, For Man, Beast, Des Moines, Ia., Label, Contents, Box, 4 ¾ In. 176.00
Medicine, Hoykendorf Pharmacy, 636 Park Ave., Cor 66th St., N.Y., Blue, Tooled Lip, 5 In. 146.00
Medicine, Improved Colic Remedy For Baby, Paper Label, Contents, Box, 5 ⅞ In. 72.00
Medicine, J.H.K., Deep Olive Amber, Applied Mouth, Pontil, 1840-60, 6 ⅞ In. 6720.00
Medicine, J.J. Peter's Trademark, Embossed Rooster, On Bicycle, Amber, Applied Top, 8 In. 364.00
Medicine, J.M. Maris & Co., No. 9 S 3rd St., Philada, Open Pontil, 5 In. 69.00
Medicine, John Wyeth & Bro., Cobalt Blue, Dose Cap, Label, Physicians Sample, 5 ½ In. 132.00
Medicine, Leeches, Porcelain, Applied Knobs, Perforated Lid, 9 ½ In. 4950.00
Medicine, Lyman Brown, Seven Barks, Contents, Box, 3 ½ In. 88.00
Medicine, Lyon's Powder, B & P, N.Y., Dark Amethyst, Rolled Lip, Open Pontil, 4 ⅜ In. 898.00
Medicine, Lyon's Powder, B & P, N.Y., Olive Green, Rolled Lip, Open Pontil, 4 ¼ In. 835.00
Medicine, McMunn's Elixir Of Opium, Aqua, Cylindrical, Paper Wrapper, 4 ½ In. 71.00
Medicine, Noah's Fever Remedy, For Horses & Mules, 50 Cents, Box, 5 In. 523.00
Medicine, Owl Drug, Rectangular, Cobalt Blue, Embossed, 6 ¼ In. 224.00
Medicine, Owl Drug Co., Embossed Owl, Amber, 11 ½ In. 448.00
Medicine, Pacific Congress Water, Running Deer, Tooled Top, c.1869 78.00
Medicine, Paine Drug Co., Rochester, N.Y., 6-Sided, Grass Green, 3 ⅜ In. 308.00 to 358.00
Medicine, Pettit's Worm Honey, Hints To Mothers, Contents, Label, 7 In. 22.00
Medicine, Phillip's Milk Of Magnesia, Phillips, Cobalt Blue, Embossed, 9 x 4 In. 8.00
Medicine, Phillips' Palatable Cod Liver Oil, Dark Amber, 7 ¼ In. 20.00
Medicine, Pike & Osgood Alternative Syrup, Olive Yellow, Sloping Collar, Pontil, 8 ⅝ In. 9775.00
Medicine, Ramon's Pills, Enamel, Lid, 11 x 5 In. 210.00
Medicine, Rohrer's Expectoral Wild Cherry Tonic, Red Amber, Roped Corners, 10 ½ In. 280.00
Medicine, Smith's Green Mountain Renovator, Olive Amber, Double Collar, Pontil, 6 ⅞ In. 4025.00
Medicine, Sniteman's X-Ray Liniment, Horse, Contents, Paper Label, Box, 12 In. 66.00
Medicine, Swaim's Panacea, Philada, Green, Applied Sloping Collar, 8 In. 336.00
Medicine, Swaim's Tonic, St. Louis, Mo., Cylindrical, Cork, Contents, Wrapper, 8 In. 405.00
Medicine, Trial, Watkins, Mark, Aqua, Paper Labels, 8 ½ In. 132.00
Medicine, Trout Oil Liniment Remedy No. 2, Embossed Fish & Star, Aqua, Square Collar, 6 In. 896.00
Medicine, U.S.A. Hosp. Dept., Cobalt Blue, Applied Top, Embossed, Flared Lip, 7 ¼ In. 1064.00
Medicine, U.S.A. Hosp. Dept., Green, Applied Square Collar, Clear Stopper, c.1861, 6 ¾ In. 1568.00

Medicine, U.S.A. Hosp. Dept., Lime Green, Bubbles, Applied Top, c.1865 . . . . 2240.00
Medicine, U.S.A. Hosp. Dept., Olive Amber, Glass Stopper, Applied Top, 9 ¼ In. 1568.00
Medicine, U.S.A. Hosp. Dept., Red, Applied Double Collar, Kick-Up, c.1861, 9 In. 11760.00
Medicine, U.S.A. Hosp. Dept., Strawberry Puce, Bubbles, Applied Top, 9 ⅛ In. 3808.00
Medicine, Vaughn's Vegetable Lithontriptic Mixture, Ice Blue, Applied Mouth, Iron Pontil, 8 In. 1792.00
Medicine, W. Sawen's Med. Co., Celebrated Oil Liniment, Utica, N.Y., Aqua, Contents, 6 In. . . . 72.00
Medicine, Yamara Female Remedy, Chicago, Ill., Square, Contents, Label, Box, 4 ½ In. 88.00
Milk, A.W. Spangler, Myerstown, Pa., Round, Embossed, Qt. 350.00
Milk, Acme Dairy, Fargo, N.D., Embossed, Qt. 38.00
Milk, Allen's Pasteurized Milk, Vicksburg, Miss., Round, ACL, Qt. 60.00
Milk, Asgaard Dairy, Rockwell Kent, Child With Cow, Green ACL, ABM Lip, Qt. . . . . *illus* 112.00
Milk, Beechmont Dairy, Round, Embossed, 5 Cent Store 15.00
Milk, Beechmont Dairy, Square, ACL, Pt. 10.00
Milk, Benson Co-Op Creamery, Benson, Minn., Snow White, 2 Dwarfs, ACL, Pt. 170.00
Milk, Betsy Ross Dairy, Shamokin, Pa., Embossed, Round, Qt. 610.00
Milk, Blais Dairy Farm, Jersey Milk, Cow's Head, Orange & Black 45.00
Milk, Boellner Bros. Goat's Milk, Maumee, Ohio, Round, Embossed, Qt. 175.00
Milk, Borden's, Elsie, Orange ACL, Square, Qt. 15.00
Milk, Bushnell Dairy, Centerbrook, Conn., Red ACL, Round, Qt. 311.00
Milk, C.D. Youngman, Clear, Tooled Lip, Tin Cap, Wire Closure, Pt., 6 ⅞ In. 70.00
Milk, Central Dairy, Albany, N.Y., Embossed, ½ Pt. 10.00
Milk, Chinquapin Dairy Farm, Green, Guernsey Milk Watch Our Creamline, ACL, Qt. 75.00
Milk, Chipola Dairy, Marianna, Fla., Red ACL, Script & Block Letters, Qt. 25.00
Milk, Clark Dairy, Drink Clark's Milk Everyday, Round, Embossed, ACL, Qt. 40.00
Milk, Clover Dairy, 3-Leaf Clover, Embossed, ½ Pt. 16.00
Milk, Clover Farms, Cow, Milkman, Barn, Silo, 3-Color ACL, Square, Qt. 20.00
Milk, Cloverleaf Dairy, Manheim, Pa., Flared, Lid, 6 ¾ In. 80.00
Milk, Cloverleaf Dairy, Springfield, Mo., 3-Leaf Clover, Soldiers, Guns, Green ACL, Qt. 105.00
Milk, Cloverleaf Dairy, Springfield, Mo., Red & Green ACL, Squat, Qt. 15.00
Milk, Cream Top Dairy, Lancaster Pa., Red, ½ Pt. 5.00
Milk, Dairy Dale, Meyersdale, Pa., Multicolored, Qt. 26.00
Milk, Dairy Fresh, Orange ACL, Square, Qt. 6.00
Milk, Devon Farm Products, Round, Embossed, Qt. 48.00
Milk, Edgewood's, Square, 3-Color ACL, Qt. 14.00
Milk, Fredrick's Farm Dairy, Conyngham, Pa., Ayrshire Cow, Square, ½ Pt. 25.00
Milk, Greenfield Dairy Co., Red ACL, Script & Block Letters 20.00
Milk, Harrisburg Dairies, ½ Gal. 2.00
Milk, Hertzler's Dairy, Elizabethtown, Pa., Cow, 2-Color ACL, Round, Qt. 340.00
Milk, Hillside Dairy, Silo, Barn, Orange, ACL, Qt. 45.00
Milk, Hilo Dairyman's Center, Grade A Raw, Mickey, Minnie, Pluto, School, Black, Pt. 50.00
Milk, Home Of Better Milk, Milking Shed, Cow Head, Orange, ACL, Qt. 35.00
Milk, Kruger's Dairy Products, Amber, Square, ACL, Qt. 20.00
Milk, Laneland Farm, Milford, N.J., Guernsey Milk, Red ACL, Pt. 30.00
Milk, Meadow Ridge Goat Milk, Derby, N.Y, Goat, Blue, ACL, Pt. 22.00
Milk, Meadowlark Dairy, Cooperstown, N.Y., Bird, Lake, Baseball Bat, Red ACL, Square, Qt. . . . 45.00
Milk, Mountain Dairy, 125th Anniversary, Trucks, Wagon, Square, ACL, Qt. 14.00
Milk, New Era Dairy, Old Lady In Shoe, Red & Black ACL, Qt. 123.00
Milk, New Haven Dairy, Round, Embossed, Patent Number On Bottom, Qt. 16.00
Milk, Nickledale Farm, Baby & Bottle, Cow Face, Round, 2-Color ACL, Qt. 40.00
Milk, Ohleen's Milk, Minneapolis, Minn., Barn, Silo, House, Red & Green ACL, Qt. 35.00
Milk, Orchard Grove Dairy, Green, Eaton Rapids., Mich., ACL, Qt. 4200.00
Milk, Osborndale Farm, Derby, Conn., Embossed, Round, Qt. 45.00
Milk, P.H. Sanger, Lebanon, Pa., Embossed, Round, Pt. 450.00
Milk, Parkers Dairy, Red ACL, ½ Pt. 35.00
Milk, People's Milk Co., 70-78 East Ferry St., Amber, Round, Embossed 45.00
Milk, Quinby's Milk, Tomatoes, Lettuce, Vitamin A, Red & Green ACL, Qt. 15.00
Milk, Raw Milk Producer Distributor Assn., Barn Silo, Truck, Maroon, ACL, Qt. 59.00
Milk, Richard B. Jones Goat's Milk, Youngstown, Ohio, Round, Embossed, Qt. 175.00
Milk, Robert S. Moon & Son, Boy Swimming, Lantern, Looking For Daylight, Round, ACL, Qt. 40.00
Milk, Saint Paul Milk Company, Puritan Brand, Pilgrims, Cabin, ACL, Qt. 50.00
Milk, Schuchardt's Dairy, Sheboygan, Wis., Little Jack Horner, Cow, Red ACL, Qt. 32.00
Milk, Sealtest, Chestnut Farms, Chevy Chase, Md., Red ACL, Longneck, Square, Qt. 20.00
Milk, Skyline Farms, Lincoln, Neb., Red Letters 40.00
Milk, Snider's Grade A Milk, Medford, Ore., Black ACL, Qt. 30.00
Milk, Spickler's Dairy, Elizabethtown, Pa., Embossed, 5 ½ In. 20.00
Milk, Spinney Run Farms, Round, Embossed, ½ Pt. 38.00

Bottle, Fruit Jar, Webster's, Patent Feb. 16. 1864, Deep Blue Aqua, Ground Lip, Qt.
$1015.00

Bottle, Gin, Cased, Olive Green, Dip Mold, Open Pontil, Dutch, 1770-1810, 10 ⅞ In.
$155.00

Bottle, Ink, Carter's, Cathedral, 6-Sided, Cobalt Blue, ABM Lip, 9 ¾ In.
$70.00

Bottle, Ink, Deep Cobalt Blue, 12 Ribs, Tooled Lip, Pontil, 2 ¼ In. $110.00

Bottle, Ink, Geometric, Medium Yellow Amber, Tooled Disc Mouth, Pontil, 1815-25, 1 ⅞ In. $120.00

Bottle, Ink, Ma & Pa Carter, Bisque, Multicolored, Carter's Inx, Germany, 3 ⅝ In., Pair $108.00

Bottle, Ink, Teakettle, Cobalt Blue, Ground Lip, Brass Neck Ring, Hinged Lid, 2 ¼ In. $160.00

Milk, Sunset Farm, Tyringham, Mass., Cow, Etched, ½ Pt 12.00
Milk, Sunshine Goat Milk Dairy, Standing Goat, ACL, Pt. 26.00
Milk, Town Farms Dairy, Simsbury, Ct., Red ACL, ½ Gal. 60.00
Milk, Turner Falls Dairy, Baby's Face, Round, ACL, Squat, Qt. 10.00
Milk, Willowdale Dairy, Jordan, N.Y., Embossed, ½ Pt. 5.00
Mineral Water, A.D. Schnackenberg, Golden Amber, Applied Sloping Collar, Pt. 275.00
Mineral Water, Albert Crook, Paradise Spring, Saratoga, Olive Green, Applied Mouth, Qt. . . . 6160.00
Mineral Water, Alburgh A Springs, Golden Amber, Sloping Double Collar, Qt. 375.00
Mineral Water, Ashton Mineral Water, Co., Green, ½ Pt. 10.00
Mineral Water, Beard's Boston, Blob Top, c. 1860. . . . . . 224.00
Mineral Water, Boyd & Beard, Green, Tapered Lip 200.00
Mineral Water, Buffalo Lithia Water, Nature's Materia Medica, Amber, c.1900, 10 In. 2.00
Mineral Water, C. & K., Orange Amber, Etched, Sloping Double Collar, Pt. 80.00
Mineral Water, Cayuga Water, S.O.I.M., Orange Amber, Square Collar, 1874, Qt. . . . . . *illus* 395.00
Mineral Water, Chalybeate Water, Blue Aqua, Blob Top, c.1870-80, Pt. . . . . . *illus* 480.00
Mineral Water, Cherry Valley, Phosphate, Golden Amber, Applied Sloping Collar, Qt. 80.00
Mineral Water, Congress & Empire Spring Co., N.Y., Emerald Green, Sloping Collar, Qt. 100.00
Mineral Water, Congress & Empire Spring Co., N.Y., Saratoga, Green, Double Tapered Collar, Pt. 90.00
Mineral Water, Congress & Empire Spring Co., Olive Green, Applied Sloping Double Collar, 1 ¼ In. 50.00
Mineral Water, Congress Spring, Co., Congress Water, Emerald Green, Pt. 65.00
Mineral Water, Congress Spring Co., Emerald Green, Sloping Collar, Qt. 70.00
Mineral Water, Cooper's Well Water, Miss., Orange Amber, Sloping Double Collar, Qt. 60.00
Mineral Water, E. Roussell, Philada., Blue, Green, Applied Blob Mouth, Iron Pontil, 7 ½ In. . 50.00
Mineral Water, Emerald Green, Sloping Double Collar, Qt. 60.00
Mineral Water, Empire Spring Co., Saratoga, N.Y., Emerald Green, Sloping Shoulder, Qt. . . . 70.00
Mineral Water, Excelsior Rock Spring, Saratoga, N.Y., Olive Yellow, Applied Mouth 2240.00
Mineral Water, Excelsior Spring, Amber, Sloping Double Collar, Pt. 210.00
Mineral Water, Excelsior Spring, Saratoga, N.Y., Green, Pt. 100.00
Mineral Water, G.W. Weston & Co., Saratoga, N.Y., Emerald Green, Qt. 179.00
Mineral Water, Geo. Eagle, Aqua, Ribs, Applied Mouth, Pontil, 6 ⅞ In. 476.00
Mineral Water, Gettysburg Katalysine Water, Blue, Double Collar, Qt. 179.00
Mineral Water, Gettysburg Katalysine Water, Green, Qt. 75.00
Mineral Water, Highrock Congress Spring, C & W, Saratoga, N.Y., Amber, Qt. 336.00
Mineral Water, Highrock Congress Spring, C & W, Saratoga, N.Y., Emerald Green, Pt. 150.00
Mineral Water, Highrock Congress Spring, C & W, Saratoga, N.Y., Teal Blue, Pt. . . . . . *illus* 295.00
Mineral Water, Hopkins Chalybeate, Baltimore, Teal Blue, Pt. 125.00
Mineral Water, Iodine Spring Water, South Hero, Vt., Golden Amber, 1860-80, Qt. 1495.00
Mineral Water, J. Boardman & Co., Cobalt Blue, Blob Top, 8-Sided, Iron Pontil, 7 ¼ In. 190.00
Mineral Water, John Clarke, New York, Olive Green, Double Collar, c.1855, Qt. 316.00
Mineral Water, John Clarke, New York, Olive Yellow Green, 3-Part Mold, 1855-65, Qt. . . *illus* 232.00
Mineral Water, Kissingen Water, Emerald Green, Applied Sloping Collar, ½ Pt. 100.00
Mineral Water, Kissingen Water, Hanbury Smith, Olive Green, Pt. 125.00
Mineral Water, Kissingen Water, W.H. Read, Baltimore, Strawberry Puce Amber, Sloping Collar, Pt. 633.00
Mineral Water, Middletown Healing Springs, Golden Amber, Applied Double Collar, Qt. 100.00
Mineral Water, Middletown Healing Springs, Grays & Clark, Middletown, Vt., Amber, 9 ½ In. 113.00
Mineral Water, Napa Soda, Natural, Cobalt Blue, Blob Top 224.00
Mineral Water, Oak Orchard Acid Springs, Green, Qt. 150.00
Mineral Water, Oak Orchard Acid Springs, H.W. Bostwick, Olive Yellow, Qt. . . . . . *illus* 1080.00
Mineral Water, Oak Orchard Acid Springs, Yellow Amber, Applied Sloping Collar, Qt. 70.00
Mineral Water, O'Rourke & Hurley Druggists, Little Falls, N.Y. Cobalt Blue, ½ Pt. 100.00
Mineral Water, Pacific Congress Springs, Cobalt Blue, Sloping Double Collar, c.1860. . . . . . 7840.00
Mineral Water, Pacific Congress Springs, Double Rolled Collar, c.1860 . . . . . . 896.00
Mineral Water, R.C. Wortendyke, Agent Superior, Blue, 8 Sided, Applied Top 448.00
Mineral Water, Saratoga A Spring Co., N.Y., Emerald Green, Sloping Double Collar, Pt. 100.00
Mineral Water, Saratoga Springs Co., Olive Green, Qt. 180.00
Mineral Water, Saratoga Vichy Spouting Spring, V, Saratoga, N.Y., Slug Plate, Aqua, ½ Pt. . . 200.00
Mineral Water, Saratoga Vichy Water, Aqua, Sloping Double Collar, Qt. 110.00
Mineral Water, Seitz & Bro., Easton, Pa., S, Olive Yellow Green, Wire Closure, 7 In. . . . . *illus* 360.00
Mineral Water, Star Spring Co., Red Amber, Sloping Double Collar, Pt. 50.00
Mineral Water, Stirlings Magnetic, Eaton Rapids Mich., Orange Amber, 1870-80, Qt. . . . *illus* 185.00
Mineral Water, Teller's, Detroit, Blue Aqua, Applied Sloping Collar, Iron Pontil, 7 ¼ In. 130.00
Mineral Water, Torpedo, Olive Amber, Applied Mouth, Silver Plated Stand, 8 In. 120.00
Mineral Water, Veronica, Square, Amber, Tooled Top, Qt. 65.00
Mineral Water, Vichy Water, Emerald Green, Applied Sloping Collar, ½ Pt. 100.00
Mineral Water, Vichy Water, Hanbury Smith, Amber, ½ Pt. 125.00
Mineral Water, Washington Lithia Well, Bullston Spa, N.Y., Aqua, Applied Mouth, Pt. 50.00

Bottle, Ink, Ward's, Olive Green, Applied Sloping Collar, Crimped Spout, 6 In.
$100.00

Bottle, Jar, Globe Tobacco Company, Detroit, Barrel, Golden Amber, 7 ⅛ In.
$112.00

Bottle, Jar, Van Vliet Of 1881, Aqua, Ground Lip, Embossed Lid, Pt.
$725.00

Bottle, Medicine, Apothecary, Opium, Label Under Glass, c.1890, 12 ½ In.
$100.00

Bottle, Medicine, Caswell, Mack & Co., Omnia Vincit Labor, Cobalt Blue, 1890, 7 In.
$82.00

Bottle, Milk, Asgaard Dairy, Rockwell Kent, Child With Cow, Green ACL, ABM Lip, Qt.
$112.00

Bottle, Mineral Water, Cayuga Water, S.O.I.M., Orange Amber, Square Collar, 1874, Qt.
$395.00

Bottle, Mineral Water, Chalybeate Water, Blue Aqua, Blob Top, c.1870-80, Pt.
$480.00

Bottle, Mineral Water, Highrock Congress Spring, C & W, Saratoga, N.Y., Teal Blue, Pt.
$295.00

Bottle, Mineral Water, John Clarke, New York, Olive Yellow Green, 3-Part Mold, 1855-65, Qt.
$232.00

Bottle, Mineral Water, Oak Orchard Acid Springs, H.W. Bostwick, Olive Yellow, Qt.
$1080.00

Bottle, Mineral Water, Seitz & Bro., Easton, Pa., S, Olive Yellow Green, Wire Closure, 7 In.
$360.00

Bottle, Mineral Water, Stirlings Magnetic, Eaton Rapids Mich., Orange Amber, 1870-80, Qt.
$185.00

Bottles

After 1860, cast-iron molds were used to make inexpensive bottles and wooden molds were discontinued. But iron molds were made with the help of a wooden pattern.

Bottle, Poison, G.L.G. & Co., 5-Sided, Medium Olive Green, c.1890-1910, 5 ½ In.
$185.00

Bottle, Poison, Lattice & Diamond, Cobalt Blue, Tooled Lip, Stopper, 1890-1910, 7 In.
$95.00

Bottle, Seal, A.S.C.R., Black Glass, Olive Green, String Lip, Pontil, 1790-1810, 10 ⅝ In.
$242.00

Mineral Water, Washington Spring, Saratoga, N.Y., Emerald Green, Pt. 550.00
Mineral Water, Welden Spring, St. Albans, Vt., Cylindrical, Emerald Green, Sloping Collar, Qt. 4025.00
Mineral Water, Wm Pond & Co., Blue Green, Blob Top, Squat, Iron Pontil, 6 ⅝ In. 200.00
Nursing, Paper Sleeve, Narrow Neck, Pyrex, 8 Oz. 25.00
Nursing, Royal Glass, Flattened, Embossed, 8 Oz., 6 ¼ In. 70.00
Pepper Sauce, Cathedral, 6-Sided, Aqua, Double Collar, Pontil, c.1840, 10 In. 127.00
Pepper Sauce, Cathedral, 6-Sided, Blue Aqua, Double Collar, Pontil, 9 In. 110.00
Pepper Sauce, Cathedral, 6-Sided, Teal, Double Collar, Pontil, c.1845, 8 In. 276.00
Pepper Sauce, Cathedral, Applied Lip, Open Pontil, 11 In. 1232.00
Pepper Sauce, Cathedral, Blue Aqua, Windows, IMAL, c.1855, 8 In. 69.00
Pepper Sauce, Cathedral, Blue Green, Double Collar, c.1860-70, 8 ¾ In. 130.00
Pepper Sauce, Cathedral, Cleveland, Aqua, Double Collar Mouth, c.1855, 8 ½ In. 288.00
Pepper Sauce, Cathedral, Collet & Son, St. Louis, Square, Aqua, Inward Rolled Lip, c.1840, 8 In. 863.00
Pepper Sauce, Cathedral, Embossed, Stippled, Iron Pontil, 10 ¼ In. 840.00
Pepper Sauce, Cathedral, Square, Aqua, Double Collar, Iron Pontil, c.1845, 9 In. 207.00
Pepper Sauce, Cathedral, Square, Green Aqua, Double Collar, 10 ⅛ In. 40.00
Pepper Sauce, Cathedral, W.K. Lewis & Co., Applied Sloping Collar, Pontil, 10 In. 672.00
Pepper Sauce, Green, Tapered, Flared Lip, Pontil, 7 In. 139.00
Perfume bottles are listed in their own category
Pickle, 6-Sided, Embossed Design, Applied Lip, c.1870, 13 In. 224.00
Pickle, Cathedral, 4-Sided, Green, Beveled Corners, Tooled Collar, 9 ⅛ In. 1380.00
Pickle, Cathedral, 6-Sided, Shaded Emerald Green, Outward Rolled Lip, 12 ½ In. 2795.00
Pickle, Cathedral, 6-Sided, Teal Green, Outward Rolled Lip, 1860-70, 13 ¼ In. 1333.00
Pickle, Cathedral, Blue Aqua, Outward Rolled Lip, 8 In. 224.00
Pickle, Cathedral, Blue Green, Outward Rolled Lip, 11 ½ In. 448.00
Pickle, Cathedral, Green, Outward Rolled Lip, 1860-70, 13 ¾ x 4 In. 1598.00
Pickle, Cathedral, Light Teal, Applied Lip, 11 ½ In. 1232.00
Pickle, Cathedral, Light To Medium Blue Green, Rolled Lip, 11 ⅞ In. 1232.00
Pickle, Cathedral, Square, Aqua, Arches, Lattice, Wide Mouth, c.1850, 13 ¾ In. 201.00
Pickle, Cathedral, Teal Blue, Outward Rolled Lip, 11 ½ In. 1344.00
Pickle, Clover Leaf, Octofoil, Square, Ribs, Yellow Green, Rolled Mouth, Pontil, 7 ¾ In. 839.00
Pickle, H.J. Heinz Sweet Mixed, 3 Paper Labels. 100.00
Pickle, H.J. Heinz's Mixed, 6-Sided, Paper Label, Show Globe, 12 In. 200.00
Pickle, Wm. Underwood & Co., Boston, Blue Green, 2 Oz., 8 In. 129.00
Poison, Coffin, Cobalt Blue, Tooled Lip, c.1890, 7 ¾ In. 1093.00
Poison, Coffin, Sapphire Blue, 3 ½ In. 65.00
Poison, Embalming Fluid, National Casket Co., Embossed Square, Aqua 125.00
Poison, G.L.G. & Co., 5-Sided, Medium Olive Green, c.1890-1910, 5 ½ In. .... *illus* 185.00
Poison, H.K. Mulford Co., Skull & Crossbones, Yellow Amber, Tooled Lip, 3 ¼ In. 420.00
Poison, Lattice & Diamond, Cobalt Blue, Tooled Lip, Stopper, 1890-1910, 7 In. .... *illus* 95.00
Poison, Martin, Ice Blue, Tooled Lip, 3 Oz., 5 ⅜ In. 560.00
Poison, N.B. & Co., 6-Sided, Amber, Irregular, 11 Rows Of 5 Stars, 8 ¼ In. 616.00
Poison, Not To Be Taken, Caution, Triangular, Lime Green, Finger Grip Corners, c.1899, 3 In. 219.00
Poison, Owl Drug Co., 1-Wing Owl, Embossed Poison, 7 ¾ In. 350.00
Poison, Owl Drug Co., Triangular, Cobalt Blue, 8 In. 800.00
Poison, Poison Tinct Iodine, Skull, Crossbones, Cobalt Blue, 2 ⅛ In. 69.00
Poison, Skull, 3-Sided, Cobalt Blue, 3 ⅝ In. 4256.00
Poison, Skull, Clear, Tooled Mouth, c.1880, 4 ⅛ In. 7480.00
Poison, Skull & Crossbones, 2 Stars, Embossed, Lattice, Amber, c.1890, 4 In. 633.00
Poison, Square, Ribbed Corners, Amber, Tooled Lip, c.1890, 10 ½ In. 184.00
Poison, Submarine, Cobalt Blue, Registry Numbers, 3 x 1 ½ In. 1555.00
Poison, Triangular, Clear, Tooled Mouth, c.1890, 5 ⅛ In. 431.00
Poison, Yellow Amber, Smooth Base, Tooled Lip, c.1890, 4 ⅞ In. 127.00
Rye, U.S. Mailbox Rye, Figural Mailbox, Clear, Label, Tooled Lip, c.1891, 8 ¾ In. 184.00
Sarsaparilla, Crescent Drug Co., Blue Aqua, Tooled Lip, 9 In. 280.00
Sarsaparilla, Dalton's Sarsaparilla & Nerve Tonic, Belfast, Maine, Aqua, 9 ¼ In. 30.00
Sarsaparilla, Dr. Marshall's, Extract Of Sarsaparilla, Dandelion, Rectangular, Aqua 90.00
Sarsaparilla, Dr. Townsends', Teal, Applied Top 168.00
Sarsaparilla, John Bull Extract, Louisville, Ky., Ice Blue, 9 In. 199.00
Sarsaparilla, Radway's Sarsaparillian Resolvent, R.R.R., Aqua, Contents, Box, 7 ½ In. 104.00
Sarsaparilla, Shaker's, Blue Aqua, Applied Mouth, 5 ¼ In. 616.00
Scent, Bunker Hill Monument, Milk Glass, Tooled Lip, 12 In. 80.00
Scent, Champleve Enamel, Multicolored, Hinged Lid, Russia, 1800s, 3 In. 1062.00
Scent, Nephrite, Rubies, Nephrite Collar, Hinged Lid, France, 4 ⅛ In. 2760.00
Scent, Oval, Clear Glass, Engraved, Heart, Arrows, Ferns, Tapered, Fluted, Monogram, VC. ... 118.00
Scent, Porcelain, Flowers, Stopper, Jacob Petit, France, c.1840, 4 ¼ x 2 ¼ x 3 ¼ In. 510.00

Bottle, Seal, L.G. Co., Medium Amber, Applied Wax Groove Ring, c.1875-90, Qt.
$260.00

Bottle, Snuff, J.M. Venabbe & Co., Petersburg, Va., Amber To Yellow Amber, 1860, 4 ¼ In.
$350.00

TIP
There are dozens of kinds of felt, cork, plastic, and glass products made to protect tables from heavy lamps, carpets from sofa-leg marks, or mirrors from bumping walls. If you think an object is making a mark or scratch on another piece or the wall or floor, check at the store for the correct protector.

Bottle, Snuff, Lapis Lazuli, Carved Birds, Flowering Trees, 2 ¼ In.
$593.00

Bottle, Snuff, Mother-Of-Pearl, Goldfish, c.1900, 2 ½ In.
$119.00

Bottle, Snuff, Peking Glass, Flowers, Leaves, Green Overlay, Chinese, 19th Century, 3 ⅛ In.
$121.00

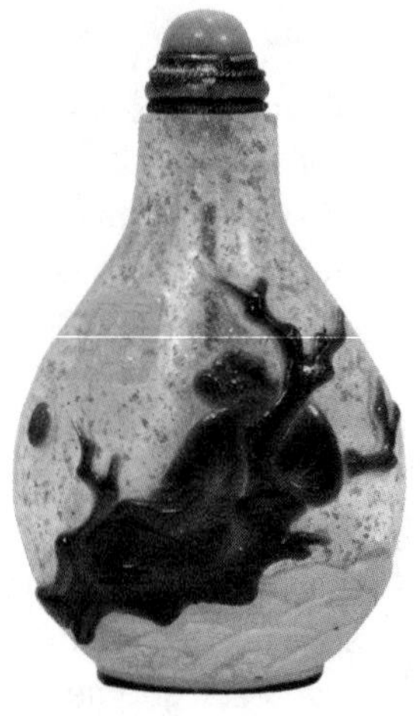

Scent, Sunburst, Teardrop Shape, Amethyst, Beaded Edges, Sheared Mouth, Pontil, 2 ¾ In. . . . 2100.00
Seal, A.S.C.R., Black Glass, Olive Green, String Lip, Pontil, 1790-1810, 10 ⅝ In. . . . . *illus* 242.00
Seal, L.G. Co., Medium Amber, Applied Wax Groove Ring, c.1875-90, Qt. . . . . *illus* 260.00
Seal, Parker Barn, Boston, Black Glass, Deep Olive Yellow, Applied Ring Collar, Pontil, Qt. . . . 910.00
Seltzer, Bubbling Water, Bisbee Bottling Works Reg. Ariz., Spout, Qt., 11 ¾ In. 504.00
Seltzer, Dr Pepper, Comal Bottling Works, R.C. Feltner, New Braunsfels, Tex., Austria, 11 In.. . 200.00
Seltzer, Dr Pepper, Green, Shreveport, La., C In Square, H 9, 805 . . . . 125.00
Seltzer, Dr Pepper, New Braunfels, Tex., C In Square, 11 In. 200.00
Seltzer, Mill's Seltzer Springs, Green, Applied Top, c.1874 . . . . 280.00
Seltzer, National Soda Works, Hawaii, Green, Pewter Top, Pinched Waist, 12-Sided 364.00
Seltzer, Orange Crush, Blue, George J. Lanmi, 12 ½ In. 80.00
Seltzer, Varennes, Round Bottom, c.1870, 8 ¾ In. 784.00
Snuff, A. Delpit, No. 16, St. Louis St., New Orleans, Yellow, Flared Mouth, Pontil, c.1835, 4 In. 1150.00
Snuff, Agate, Carved, Flattened, Mask & Ring Handles, Coral Stopper, 2 ⅕ In. 1200.00
Snuff, Agate, Horse, Tethered, Chinese, 19th Century, 2 ½ In.. . . . . 474.00
Snuff, Agate, Lion Mask Handles, Pear Shape, Chinese, 2 ¼ In. 178.00
Snuff, Agate, Lion Mask Handles, Rose Quartz Stopper, Chinese, 2 In.. . . . . 294.00
Snuff, Agate, Monkey, Horse, Bee, 19th Century, 2 In. 889.00
Snuff, Agate, Yellow, Man Under Tree, Carved, Flattened Oval, Chinese 236.00
Snuff, Amber, Foo Dogs, Thunder Meander Borders, Coral Stopper, Chinese, 2 ½ In.. . . . . 770.00
Snuff, Amethyst, Flowering Tree, 19th Century, 2 In.. . . . . 267.00
Snuff, Black Slate, Relief Scenes, Man On Mythical Beast, Coral, Metal Stopper, 3 ⅝ In. 59.00
Snuff, Bone, Carved, Jackrabbits, Desert Scene, Spoon Attached To Cap, 2 ⅝ In. 55.00
Snuff, Brass, Dragons, Square Sides, Oval Bosses, Red Gemstone Stopper, Chinese, 2 ¼ In. . . . 444.00
Snuff, Cinnabar, Lacquer, Melons, Grapes, Squirrel Reserves, Buddhist Borders, 2 ½ In. 948.00
Snuff, Cinnabar, Man, On Horseback, Woman In Cart, Green Stone Stopper, Chinese, 2 ¾ In. 470.00
Snuff, Cinnabar, Relief Carved, 8 Immortals, Black Lacquer, Green Stone Stopper, 3 In. 323.00
Snuff, Cinnabar, Sage, Attendant, Landscape, 2 Colors, Jade Stopper, Chinese, 2 ½ In.. . . . . . . 2844.00
Snuff, Cloisonne, Flowers, Blue Ground, Chinese, 20th Century, 3 In. 33.00
Snuff, Coral, Figural, Buddha, Stopper, Chinese, 2 ⅞ In.. . . . . 118.00
Snuff, Coral, Leaves, Butterflies, Carved, Double Gourd Shape, Chinese, 2 In.. . . . . 1185.00
Snuff, Enamel, Women, Blue Ground, Gilt Copper Stopper, Chinese, 2 ¼ In. 1422.00
Snuff, Forest Green, Lion's Mask Handles, Coral Stopper, 19th Century, 2 ¾ In. 385.00
Snuff, Glass, Enamel, Figures On Horses, Buffaloes, Landscape, Chinese, 2 ¾ In.. . . . . 1304.00
Snuff, Glass, Olive Yellow, Tooled Lip, Open Pontil, 1835-60, 4 ¼ In. 1064.00
Snuff, Glass, Yellow Olive, Rectangular, Tooled Lip, Pontil, 4 ¼ In. 100.00
Snuff, Gourd, Carved, Riverscape, Oval, Chinese, 2 ½ In. 1673.00
Snuff, Hornbill, Carved, 3 ½ In. 702.00
Snuff, Ivory, 2 Figures, Fans, Multicolored, Chinese, 3 x 2 In.. . . . . 70.00
Snuff, Ivory, 8 Immortals, Calligraphy, Double Gourd Shape, 20th Century, 2 ¼ In. 148.00
Snuff, Ivory, Figural, Geisha, Removable Head, Spoon, Painted, Multicolored, 3 ¾ In. 55.00
Snuff, Ivory, Figures In Landscape, Carved, Chinese, 3 In. 1126.00
Snuff, Ivory, Melon, Leaves, Insects, Carved, Chinese, 3 In.. . . . . 1659.00
Snuff, J.M. Venabbe & Co., Petersburg, Va., Amber To Yellow Amber, 1860, 4 ¼ In. . . . . . *illus* 350.00
Snuff, jade, Celadon, Immortals, Rectangular, Relief Carved, Chinese 1180.00
Snuff, Jade, Celadon, Rooster, Cockscomb Plant, 19th Century, 2 ¼ In.. . . . . 2370.00
Snuff, Jade, Scrolls, Green Stopper, 2 ¼ In. 356.00
Snuff, Jade, Silver, Orange, Carved, Chinese, 3 In. 146.00
Snuff, Jade, White, Incised Egrets, Flowers, Bats, Silver Lid, Red Stone, Chinese, c.1900, 2 In.. 3776.00
Snuff, Lapis Lazuli, Carved Birds, Flowering Trees, 2 ¼ In.. . . . . *illus* 593.00
Snuff, Lapis Lazuli, Chinese, Late 19th Century, 3 ½ In. 100.00
Snuff, Milk Glass, Animal Figures, Raised, Multicolored, 1890, 4 ½ x 3 ½ In. 590.00
Snuff, Moss Agate, Coral & Turquoise Cabochons, Gilt Wirework, 3 ½ In.. . . . . 72.00
Snuff, Mother-Of-Pearl, Goldfish, c.1900, 2 ½ In. . . . . *illus* 119.00
Snuff, Olive Amber, Beveled Panels, Wavy Glass Threads, Tooled Lip, 8 ¼ In. 120.00
Snuff, Opal, Triangular, Onyx Stopper, 2 ½ x 2 In. 375.00
Snuff, Peking Glass, Brown, Green Top, Chinese, Late 18th Century, 2 ½ In.. . . . . 33.00
Snuff, Peking Glass, Flowers, Leaves, Green Overlay, Chinese, 19th Century, 3 ⅛ In. . . . . *illus* 121.00
Snuff, Peking Glass, Horse & Rider, Red Cut To Clear, Green Glass Stopper, Chinese, 2 ⅞ In.. . 176.00
Snuff, Peking Glass, Morning Glories, Mustard Yellow Overlay, Carved, Chinese, 1800s, 3 ⅛ In. 88.00
Snuff, Porcelain, 2 Oriental Men, Molded, Carnelian Glass Stoppers, 1900, 4 ⅜ In. . . . . *illus* 325.00
Snuff, Porcelain, Brown, Green, Glazed, Carved, c.1920-30, 2 ¾ In., Pair 35.00
Snuff, Porcelain, Buddhist Saints, Relief, Enamel, Chinese, 2 ¾ In.. . . . . 385.00
Snuff, Porcelain, Enamel, Man In Boat, Trees, Red 4 Character Mark, Chinese, 2 ⅝ In. 216.00
Snuff, Porcelain, Famille, Peach, Rose, Chinese, 19th Century, 2 ¼ In. 178.00
Snuff, Porcelain, Multicolored Enamel Relief, Flattened Oval, Gold Trim, Chinese, 3 ¼ In. . . 353.00

Snuff, Quartz, Amethyst, Carved, Birds, Flowers, Bird Stopper, 3 ¼ In. 411.00
Snuff, Quartz, Pine Tree, 20th Century, 2 ¼ In. 148.00
Snuff, Rock Crystal, Carved, Lotus Plants, Jade Stopper, 2 ¼ In. 356.00
Snuff, Rock Crystal, Green Skin, Carved, Melon Shape, Pebble, Bat, Leaf, Chinese, 2 In. 1422.00
Snuff, Rock Crystal, Spanish Coin, Stopper, Chinese, 2 In. 8888.00
Snuff, Rose Quartz, Carved, Pine Tree, 20th Century, 2 ¼ In. 148.00
Snuff, Rose Quartz, Immortals In Garden, Silver Mount, Green Glass Stopper, 3 ¼ In. 415.00
Snuff, Rosewood, Lady's Shoe, 1 x 3 x 1 In. 88.00
Snuff, Shadow Agate, Man Fishing, Willow Trees, Globular, 2 ½ In. 119.00
Snuff, Silver, Jade, Coral, Turquoise Inlay, Chinese, 3 In. 267.00
Snuff, Smoky Quartz, Eggplant Shape, 19th Century, 2 In. 770.00
Snuff, Smoky Quartz, Immortal, Crane, Flowering Tree, 19th Century, 2 ½ In. 356.00
Snuff, Smoky Quartz, Tourmaline Stopper, Chinese, 2 ¼ In. 176.00
Snuff, Soapstone, Child, Ram, Plants, Butterscotch, Elongated, Flattened, 2 ¼ In. 444.00
Snuff, Stone, Off-White Mottled & Green, Carved, Pink Stone Stopper, Chinese, 2 ½ In. 118.00
Snuff, Tigers Eye, Chinese, Early 20th Century, 2 ½ In. 100.00
Snuff, Toby Jug, Removable Hat, 1849, 4 ½ In. 1495.00
Snuff, Turquoise, Horse, Relief, 3 x 1 ½ x 1 In. 225.00
Snuff, Turquoise, Pebble Shape, Carved Foot & Neck, 2 ¼ In. 178.00
Snuff, Yellow, Amber, Tooled Lip, Iron Pontil, c.1835-60, 4 ⅝ In. 1120.00
Soda, 7Up, Star Beverage Co., San Diego, Painted Label, Crown Top, 7 Oz. 448.00
Soda, Albuquerque Bottling Works, Light Blue Aqua, Tooled Top 448.00
Soda, Anaconda Bottling Co., Montana, Tooled Top 179.00
Soda, Azule Seltzer Springs, Walking Bear, Aqua, Blob Top, 1885-90 224.00
Soda, Benicia Steam Soda Works, Pontil, c.1850 672.00
Soda, C.W. Rider, Watertown, N.Y., Applied Top, Emerald Green 784.00
Soda, Cherry Smash, Fowler's, 5 Cents, Aluminum Cap, Label Under Glass 392.00
Soda, Cledon's Limel, Lo, Clear, Yellow, White, Gold Label Under Glass, 12 In. 174.00
Soda, Concord Bottling Co., Concord N.H., Applied Top, 6 ¾ In. 235.00
Soda, Daisy Root Beer, C.W. Campbell, Lancaster, Pa., Woman, Paper Label, Contents 40.00
Soda, Diamond A Ginger Beer Co., Stoneware, Black Transfer, 1870-1900, 6 ¾ In. *illus* 55.00
Soda, E. Roussel Philada, Blue Green, Iron Pontil, 7 ½ In. 69.00
Soda, Eagle, Shield, Crossed Flags, Cobalt Blue, Cylindrical, Sloping Collar, ½ Pt. 1610.00
Soda, Escambia Pepsi-Cola Bottling Co., Pensacola, Fla., Hutchinson 75.00
Soda, Excelsior Soda Works, Cobalt Blue, Blob Top, 7 ¼ In. 70.00 to 110.00
Soda, Geo Schmuck's Ginger Ale, Cleveland O., 12-Sided, Amber, Blob Top, 7 ¾ In. 269.00
Soda, H.W. Hall, Batavia, N.Y., Blue Green, Squat, Blob Top 59.00
Soda, Haddock & Sons, Torpedo, Olive Yellow, Applied Collar, 6 ½ In. 3738.00
Soda, J.T. Brown, Chemist, Boston Torpedo, Double, Green, Blob Top 448.00
Soda, John Ryan, Savannah, Ga., 1859, Cobalt Blue, Squat, 7 In. 119.00
Soda, Lynch Bros., Plymouth, Pa., Olive Yellow, Metal Cap, c.1885-95, 9 ¼ In. *illus* 165.00
Soda, N. Richardson & Son, Trenton, N.J., Applied Top, Aqua 202.00
Soda, Owen Casey, Eagle Soda Works, Sac. City, Cobalt Blue, 1867-1871 364.00
Soda, Seitz Bros., Easton, Pa., Olive Yellow Green, Squat, Applied Mouth, 7 In. *illus* 130.00
Soda, Silver State, Mule & Miner, Clear, Embossed, Scallops 50.00
Soda, Taylor's Soda Water Mfg. Co., Boise, Ida., Tooled Top, 12-Panel, Base, 6 ½ In. 101.00
Soda, W. Eagle's Superior, Cobalt Blue, Swirls, Applied Top, Graphite Pontil 212.00
Soda, W.P. Knickerbocker, Blue, Blob Top, Iron Pontil, 1850s 504.00
Soda, William Sugden Tonic Root Beer, Ballston Spa, N.Y., Applied Top, Wire Bail 728.00
Soda, Wm. Aylmer, Fargo, Dakota Territory, Ice Blue, Applied Top 2016.00
Stoneware, Jar, Jas. Hamilton & Co., Gray, Cobalt Blue, Salt Glaze, Wax Seal, 10 In. *illus* 44.00
Storage, Dark Amber, Dip Mold, Wide Mouth, Applied String Lip, 13 ¼ In. 392.00
Storage, Globular, Olive Green, Applied Double Collar, Pontil, 12 In. 728.00
Storage, Olive Yellow, Sheared & Tooled Lip, Pontil, Dutch, 9 ⅜ In. 90.00
Syrup, Lemon Life, Soda, Label Under Glass, Metal Cap, 12 In. 303.00
Syrup, Soda, Logan Johnson, Ambrosia Punch, Label Under Glass, 12 ½ In. *illus* 900.00
Target Ball, Amber, 3-Piece Mold, 6 Dots, Sheared Lip 308.00
Target Ball, Amethyst, Diamond, Ground Mouth, 1 ¾ In. 364.00
Target Ball, Amethystine, Embossed Shooter, Purple Streaks, 2.7 Oz., 2 ⅞ In. 448.00
Target Ball, Blue, Pat'd Sept 25th 1877, Sand Ball, 3-Piece Mold, 2 ⅞ In. 3136.00
Target Ball, Boers & Co. Delft Fleschenfabriek, Lattice, Green, Ground Lip, 2 ¾ In. 2912.00
Target Ball, Bogardus, Pat'd Apr 10 1877, Hobnail, Amber, 3 ¼ In. 1344.00
Target Ball, Bogardus, Pat'd April 10 1877, Smoky Yellow, 3 In. 1456.00
Target Ball, C. Newman, Burst Lip, 3 In. 3808.00
Target Ball, C.G. Purdy's, Star, Bull's-Eye, Pat'd App For, Flattened Circle Design, Amber, 3 In. 8960.00
Target Ball, C.T.H. Graphite, Sept 9 1879, Pat. Feb March 9 1880, 2-Piece Mold, 3 In. 134.00

Bottle, Snuff, Porcelain, 2 Oriental Men, Molded, Carnelian Glass Stoppers, 1900, 4 ⅜ In.
$325.00

Bottle, Soda, Diamond A Ginger Beer Co., Stoneware, Black Transfer, 1870-1900, 6 ¾ In.
$55.00

Bottle, Soda, Lynch Bros., Plymouth, Pa., Olive Yellow, Metal Cap, c.1885-95, 9 ¼ In.
$165.00

Bottle, Soda, Seitz Bros., Easton, Pa., Olive Yellow Green, Squat, Applied Mouth, 7 In. $130.00

Bottle, Stoneware, Jar, Jas. Hamilton & Co., Gray, Cobalt Blue, Salt Glaze, Wax Seal, 10 In. $44.00

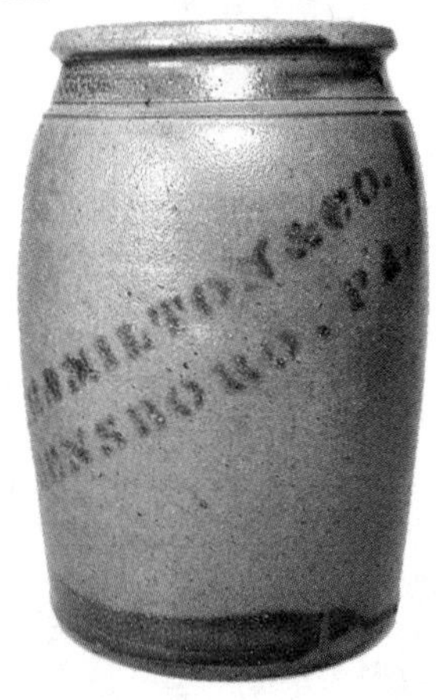

TIP

You can date an old bottle from the spelling of the word "Pittsburgh." From 1891 to 1911 the "h" was removed by the U.S. Board of Geographic Names. The old spelling was resumed because of complaints from those who lived in the city.

Target Ball, Charlottenburg Glasshutten, Dr. A. Frank, Diamond, Olive Yellow, 2 ⅝ In. 476.00
Target Ball, Chocolate Amber, 7 Horizontal Bands, 3 In. 3360.00
Target Ball, Clay, 2 Embossed Pigeons, 3 In. 2464.00
Target Ball, Clay, Embossed Pigeons, 3 ¼ In. 2016.00
Target Ball, Clay, Embossed Pigeons, 3 In. 2200.00
Target Ball, Cobalt Blue, 3-Piece Mold, 3 In. 235.00
Target Ball, Cobalt Blue, 3-Piece Mold, Bubbles, 3 In. 4928.00
Target Ball, Cobalt Blue, Burst Lip, 2 In. 246.00
Target Ball, Composite Pitch, Hollow, 3 ½ Oz., 2 ½ In. 134.00
Target Ball, E. Jones Gunmaker, Blue, Lattice, Sheared Lip, 3 In. 280.00
Target Ball, E.E. Eaton Guns, Cobalt Blue, 3-Piece Mold, 3 In. 4928.00
Target Ball, Emerald Green, Lattice, Unembossed Band, Ground Lip, 2 ¾ In. 896.00
Target Ball, For Hockey's Patent Trap, 8-Legged Whirligig Design, Green, Embossed, 2 ½ In. . 1568.00
Target Ball, G.H. Henry, Aqua, Trap, 2 ¾ In. 784.00
Target Ball, Gurd & Son, Embossed Center Band, Tobacco Amber, 2 ¾ In. 1008.00
Target Ball, H. Robinson, Shooting Gallery, Deep Blue, 2 ¼ In. 784.00
Target Ball, H. Robinson Birm, Green, Striations, 2 ½ In. 728.00
Target Ball, Horizontal Ring, Blue, 3 In. 308.00
Target Ball, Ira Paine's, Embossed A, Light Amber, c.1877, 3 In. 616.00
Target Ball, J. Palmer O'Neil & Co., Olive Amber, 3-Piece Mold, 2 ⅞ In. 8960.00
Target Ball, J. Palmer O'Neil & Co., Pittsburgh, Yellow Green, 3-Piece Mold, 3 In. 5152.00
Target Ball, J. Yandell Bristol, Range, Light Blue, 2 In. 784.00
Target Ball, J.H. Johnston, Great Western Gun Works, Yellow Amber, Sheared Lip, 2 ⅝ In. . . . 9520.00
Target Ball, Lattice, Blue, Burst Lip, 2 ⅞ In. 280.00
Target Ball, Lime Green, Burst Lip, 3 In. 476.00
Target Ball, Man, Shooting, Blue, Cobalt Blue Streaks, 3 In. 392.00
Target Ball, Man, Shooting, Green, 3 In. 672.00
Target Ball, Man, Shooting, Light Cobalt Blue, 3 In. 616.00
Target Ball, N.B. Glassworks, Perth, Clear, Burst Lip, 3 In. 364.00
Target Ball, N.B. Glassworks, Perth, Cobalt Blue, Backward Letters, 3 In. 224.00
Target Ball, N.B. Glassworks, Perth, Cobalt Blue, Slug Plate, 3 In. 224.00
Target Ball, Purple, 3-Piece Mold, Unembossed, Whittle, 3 In. 392.00
Target Ball, Range, Light To Medium Blue, Stars, 2 In. 213.00
Target Ball, Sheared Lip, c.1885, 2 In. 50.00
Target Ball, Shooting Gallery, Blue Green, Misshapen, London, 2 ½ In. 224.00
Target Ball, Shooting Gallery, Lattice, 2 ⅜ In. 246.00
Target Ball, Teal, Embossed Marksman, Diamond, 2 ⅞ In. 784.00
Target Ball, Thrower, Bogardus, Felt Cup Liner, 32 ⅜ x 11 ½ In. 448.00
Target Ball, Thrower, Chamberlin Cartridge & Target, Holds Small Ball, c.1905, 21 x 3 In. . . 448.00
Target Ball, Tobacco Amber, Lattice, Ground Lip, 2 ¾ In. 364.00
Target Ball, Van Cutsem, A St Quentin, Lattice, Burst Lip, France, ⅛ Oz., 3 ¼ In. 269.00
Target Ball, Van Cutsem, A St Quentin, Lattice, Light Blue, Burst Lip, 3 ¼ In. 269.00
Target Ball, W.W. Greener's, Lattice, Medium Blue, 2.2 Oz., 3 In. 280.00
Target Ball, W.W. Greener's, St. Mary's Works, London, Amethyst, 3 In. 672.00
Target Ball, W.W. Greener's, St. Mary's Works, London, Blue, 3 In. . . . . . . 280.00 to 504.00
Target Ball, W.W. Greener's, St. Mary's Works, London, Diamond, Light Pink Amethyst, 3 In. . 784.00
Target Ball, W.W. Greener's, St. Mary's Works, London, Lattice, Amethyst, 3 In. 560.00
Target Ball, Whithall, Tatum & Co., Pat'd Aug 13 1878, Light Aqua, Inverted Dot, 2-Piece Mold, 3 In. 3136.00
Whiskey, Backbar, Cut Glass, 12 Panels, Fluted Shoulders, Qt. 112.00
Whiskey, Backbar, Paul Jones, Man Pouring, Enamel, 5 Colors, Clear, 8 x 4 In. 70.00
Whiskey, Backbar, Puritan Rye, Swirled, c.1900, 11 In. 308.00
Whiskey, Barrel, Golden Yellow Amber, Tooled Mouth, 9 ⅜ In. 60.00
Whiskey, Brown & Forman, Enamel Label, Ground Glass Stopper, 10 ½ In. 118.00
Whiskey, Campus, Gossler Bros., Columbus Ave. & 104th St., N.Y., Amber, Handle, c.1870, 3 In. 616.00
Whiskey, Case, Palm Boom, G. Meyer & C., Schiedam On Seal, Embossed Palm Tree, 11 In. . . 190.00
Whiskey, Chesley's, Jockey Club, SF, Green, Applied Mouth, c.1873. . . . . . . 4032.00
Whiskey, Chestnut Grove, C.W., Amber, Applied Mouth, Handle, Pontil, 1855-75, 9 In. . . *illus* 252.00
Whiskey, Chestnut Grove, C.W., Seal, Orange Amber, Applied Handle, Open Pontil 246.00
Whiskey, Dewar's Perth Whisky, Gold Letters, Dispenser, c.1890, 26 x 9 x 11 In. 495.00
Whiskey, Dip Mold, Emerald Green, Applied Mouth, Open Pontil, c.1770-1800, 11 ⅞ In. 302.00
Whiskey, Distillery Pepper, Hand Made Sour Mash, Yellow, Applied Top, 11 ¾ In. 364.00
Whiskey, Dog At Point, Clear, Oval Medallion, Cylindrical, Fluted Shoulder, Neck, 11 In. 2645.00
Whiskey, Dyottville Glassworks, Phila., Olive Yellow, Cylindrical, Sloping Collar, Pontil, 11 ¼ In. 60.00
Whiskey, E.G. Booz's Old Cabin, Medium Yellow Amber, Applied Mouth, 7 ¾ In. 1064.00
Whiskey, Eye Opener, Figural, Milk Glass, Painted, Screw Cap, Nip, 1895, 5 In. . . . . . . *illus* 195.00
Whiskey, Gold Dust Kentucky Bourbon, Aqua, Glob Top 1120.00

Whiskey, Gourd Shape, Deep Green, Applied Top, Graphite Pontil, Eagle, Qt. 308.00
Whiskey, H.F. & B., N.Y., Melon Shape, Yellow Green, Embossed, Applied Ring Collar, 9 In. ... 3100.00
Whiskey, Hiram Walker & Sons, Jug, c.1910, 2 Gal., 16 In. 205.00
Whiskey, J.H. Cutter Old Bourbon, Olive Green, Whittle, 11 ¾ In.. .... 2464.00
Whiskey, Kentucky Reserve, Enamel Label, Ground Glass Stopper, 8 In. 59.00
Whiskey, My Choice Bourbon, McKinley For President, Metal Cap, 6 In. 896.00
Whiskey, Pride Of Kentucky, Sour Mash, Applied Handle, 8 In.. .... 280.00
Whiskey, Saml. Hart & Co., Clear, Metal Neck Band, Ground Lip, Screw Cap, Flask, 6 In.. .... 70.00
Whiskey, Sour Mash Old Fashion, Hand Made, Star, Milk Glass, Tooled Lip, 6 ⅞ In.. .... 40.00
Whiskey, Swallow Bros., Norristown, Pa., Rectangular, Amber, Applied Top, Qt. 39.00
Whiskey, Teakettle Old Bourbon, Amber, 12 In. 1064.00
Whiskey, Udolpho Wolfe's Shiedam, Aromatic Schnapps, Citron, Applied Top, Pt. 35.00
Whiskey, Van Brunt's Aromatic Schnapps, Schiedam, Green, Applied Top, 9 In. 476.00
Whiskey, W. McC & Co., Cylindrical, Olive Yellow, Embossed, Applied Neck Ring, 12 In.. ...... 48.00
Whiskey, W.C. Peacock & Co., Red Amber, Applied Top, 11 In.. .... 364.00
Whiskey, Whitney Glass Works, Amber, Embossed, Qt.. .... 38.00
Wine, 8-Sided, Deep Olive Amber, Beveled Corner Panels, England, c.1740-45, 8 ¼ In. 2128.00
Wine, 8-Sided, Olive Yellow, 9 ⅛ x 4 ¼ In. 2016.00
Wine, Black Glass, H.C. On Seal, Applied Mouth, Pontil, c.1780, 8 ⅝ In. 460.00
Wine, Black Glass, Onion, Olive Amber, Sheared Mouth, Applied String Lip, 5 ¼ In.. .... 784.00
Wine, Black Glass, Pancake Onion, Applied String Lip, 5 ⅞ x 6 ¼ In. 672.00
Wine, Black Glass, Pancake Onion, Applied String Lip, Pontil, c.1690, 5 ⅜ x 6 ⅛ In. 575.00
Wine, Mallet, Black Glass, Amber, Applied String Rim, England, c.1749, 9 ¼ In.. .... 2760.00
Wine, Mallet, Black Glass, Olive Amber, Seal, Sheared Mouth, String Rim, Pontil, 11 ¼ In.. .. 2645.00
Wine, Mallet, Black Glass, Olive Green, Sheared Mouth, 5 ¾ In.. .... 9775.00
Wine, W. Fitzhugh, Mallet, Black Glass, Olive Yellow, Seal, Sloping Collar, Pontil, 9 ½ In. 978.00
Wine, W. Major, Black Glass, Applied Tapered Collar & Seal, 1800, 9 In. 1380.00
Wm. Russell, Torpedo, Lime Green, Applied Tapered Collar 1232.00

BOTTLE CAPS for milk bottles are the printed cardboard caps used since the 1920s. Crown caps, used after 1892 on soda bottles, are also popular collectibles. Unusual mottoes, graphics, and caps from bottlers that are out of business bring the highest prices.

Crown, Ballantine Pale Ale, Twist Off, Red, Gold Ground, Black. 4.00
Crown, Ritz Orange Pineapple Soda, Yellow & Black, Metal, Cork Lining 1.00
Crown, Yoo Hoo, Me For Yoo Hoo, New York Yankees, c.1960, 8 Piece 405.00
Maple View Farm Dairy, Moscow, Pa., Pasteurized Whipping Cream. 10.00
Whatley's Dairy, Griffin, Georgia, Milk, Cardboard, 2 In.. .... 6.00

BOTTLE OPENERS are needed to open many bottles. As soon as the commercial bottle was invented, the opener to be used with the new types of closures became a necessity. Many types of bottle openers can be found, most dating from the twentieth century. Collectors prize advertising and comic openers.

7UP, You Like It, It Likes You, Embossed, Wall Mount, Starr X, Brown Co. 2.00
Alligator, Cast Iron, Wilton, 1 ¼ x 6 In. 138.00
Bakelite Handle, Butterscotch, Carved, 4 In.. .... 25.00
Bakelite Handle, Caramel, Chrome Can Opener, 7 ¾ In.. .... 7.00
Ballantine Ale & Beer, Metal, Marked, Handy Walden U.S.A. 62, 3 ½ In. 5.00
Bottle Shape, Brass, Brazil, 5 ¼ x 1 ⅜ In. 8.00
Boy, Red Shirt, Black Pants, Hat, Cast Iron, c.1935, 4 In.. .... 193.00
Can Piercer, Amber & Brown Bakelite Handle, 7 ½ x 2 In.. .... 9.00
Canadian Goose, Cast Iron, 1 x 3 ⅝ In.. .... 84.00
Cathy Coed, Girl With Books, Cast Iron, 4 ½ In. 336.00
Cold Spring Lager, Sunbury, Pa., 4 In. 18.00
Corkscrew, Marble Base, Asprey, 5 ½ x 3 In. 165.00
Cowboy, Strumming Guitar, Cast Metal, Painted, 4 ¾ In.. .... 30.00
Dog's Head, Metal, Black, White, Barnard Stamp & Stencil Ltd., Ontario, 3 ¾ In. 15.00
Drunk At Street Sign Post, Fond Du Lac, Wis., Cast Iron, Painted. 25.00
Duck, Standing, Cast Iron, Painted, 2 ¾ x 3 x 1 ¼ In.. .... 80.00
Freckle Faced Kid, Cast Iron, Painted, Wall Mount, Box 748.00
Freckle Faced Kid, Winking, Cast Iron, Painted, Wall Mount, Box 650.00
Goat, Brass, Cast, Horn Opener, Stamped Made In Canada, 4 x 2 ½ In. 54.00
Golf, Cast Iron, Nickel, 5 ¼ x 2 In.. .... 115.00
Golf Caddy, Nickel Over Cast Iron, Marked, 1932, 5 $^{3}/_{16}$ x 1 ⅞ In. 115.00
Man, Stick Figure, Green Hat, Holding Guitar Opener, Magnetic, Japan, 1950, 6 In.. .... 20.00
Pabst Blue Ribbon Beer Bottle, Metal, 4 x 1 ⅛ In.. .... 24.00

Bottle, Syrup, Soda, Logan Johnson, Ambrosia Punch, Label Under Glass, 12 ½ In.
$900.00

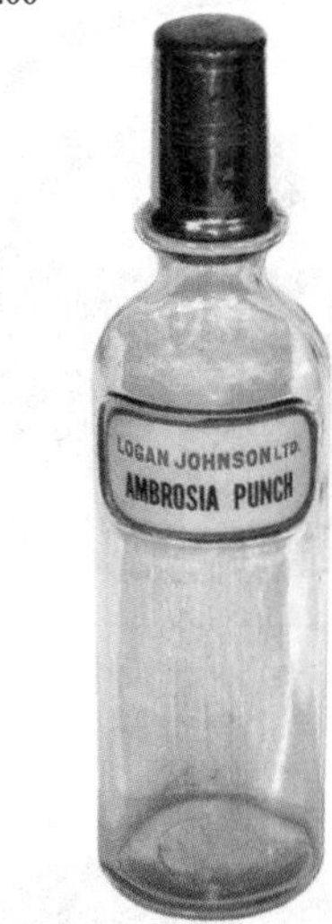

Bottle, Whiskey, Chestnut Grove, C.W., Amber, Applied Mouth, Handle, Pontil, 1855-75, 9 In.
$252.00

Bottle, Whiskey, Eye Opener, Figural, Milk Glass, Painted, Screw Cap, Nip, 1895, 5 In.
$195.00

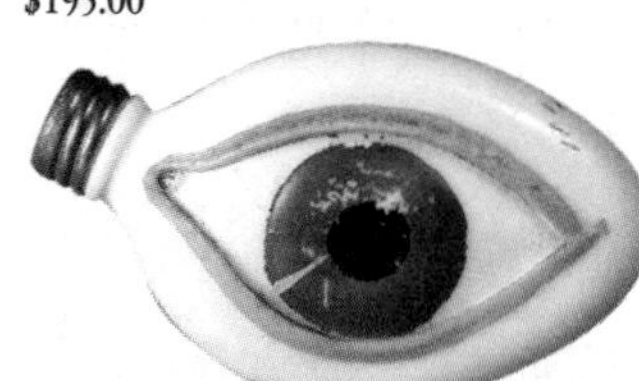

Box, Band, Bentwood, Lap Joints, Handle, Red Paint, 7 x 11 ½ In.
$275.00

Box, Band, Bentwood, Wallpaper, Salmon Flowers, Blue Ground, 1850s, 13 x 19 In.
$936.00

Box, Band, Wallpaper, Flowers, Geometrics, Blue, Brown Ground, 4 ¾ x 8 In.
$275.00

Box, Band, Wallpaper, Paper Board, Flowers, Geometrics, Green, Blue, Red, 5 ½ x 8 In.
$220.00

Parrot, Figural, Brass, 4 ¾ In. 26.00
Parrot, Large Open Mouth, Cast Iron, Art Deco 20.00
Parrot, On Perch, Beak Opener, Cast Iron, Painted, Shenandoah Caverns, Virg., 1920s, 5 In. . . 60.00
Ruppert Old Knickerbocker Beer, Metal, 1940s, 3 ¼ In. 15.00
Ryan's Pure Beers, Syracuse, N.Y, Metal 50.00
Stainless Steel, Sterling Silver Handle, Bird Mark, Brodrene Mylius, Norway 45.00
Watt & Shand, Milk, Lancaster & Columbia, Pa., Celluloid, 2 ½ In. 40.00

BOXES of all kinds are collected. They were made of thin strips of inlaid wood, metal, tortoiseshell, embroidery, or other material. Additional boxes may be listed in other sections, such as Advertising, Battersea, Ivory, Shaker, Tinware, and various Porcelain categories. Tea Caddies are listed in their own category.

4 Season Views, Lunette Lid, Academy Painted, Inscribed, Mass., c.1800, 5 x 12 In. 1422.00
Amethyst Cut To Clear, Round, Hobstar & Diamond, Lid, 2 ¾ In. 130.00
Apothecary, Burl, Drawers, Top Handle, Metal Strapwork Hinges, c.1825, 6 x 6 In. 444.00
Ballot, Bird's-Eye Maple, Walnut, Dovetailed, Slide Lid, Finger Pull, 2 ¾ x 12 ½ x 5 ¾ In. 1045.00
Ballot, Walnut, Dovetailed, Slide Lid, Slot, Lock, Keyhole On Side, c.1850, 11 x 6 x 6 In. 205.00
Band, Bentwood, Lap Joints, Green Paint, 4 ⅜ x 8 ⅞ In. 248.00
Band, Bentwood, Lap Joints, Handle, Red Paint, 7 x 11 ½ In. . . . . . *illus* 275.00
Band, Bentwood, Wallpaper, Salmon Flowers, Blue Ground, 1850s, 13 x 19 In. . . . . . *illus* 936.00
Band, Chickens, Trailing Vines, Yellow Ground, Late 19th Century, 4 ½ In. 8190.00
Band, Cloth, Flowers, Hand Stitched, c.1835, 9 x 18 In. 264.00
Band, Mixed Wood, Red Paint, Tacked Lap Joints, Bentwood Handle, 7 x 11 ½ In. 303.00
Band, Oval, Softwood, Stylized Tulips, House, Tree, Black Ground, 5 ¼ x 13 ¾ x 8 ¾ In. 2750.00
Band, Oval, Softwood, Tacked Lap Joints, Green Paint, 1 ½ x 4 ⅛ x 3 In. 660.00
Band, Oval, Wallpaper, Paper Board, Village Scene, 9 ½ x 11 x 13 ½ In. 791.00
Band, Stylized Flowers, Softwood, Multicolored, Tacked Lap Joints, 3 ⅛ x 7 ¼ In. 77.00
Band, Wallpaper, 2 Women, Square, Blue, Brown Geometric, Flower, 3 ¾ x 12 ½ x 13 In. 44.00
Band, Wallpaper, Birds, 1797 Printed Legislative Publication, 1800s, 5 12 x 9 ¼ In. 881.00
Band, Wallpaper, Birds, Flowers, 1833 Vermont Newspaper, Hannah Davis, 12 ½ x 9 ½ In. . . . 646.00
Band, Wallpaper, Black & White Flowers, Blue Ground, N.E., 1890s, 3 x 4 ¾ In. 1980.00
Band, Wallpaper, Blue, Orange, White, Round, 5 x 3 In. 690.00
Band, Wallpaper, Blue Flowers, Yellow Ground, Mid 19th Century, 6 ½ x 10 ¼ In. 2100.00
Band, Wallpaper, Faux Birch Bark, Round, 4 x 3 In. 230.00
Band, Wallpaper, Flower, Geometrics, Multicolored, c.1850s, 5 ½ x 11 ¼ x 7 ¼ In. 154.00
Band, Wallpaper, Flower, Red, White, Signed, Ephraim Huver, 1850s, 2 x 2 ¾ In. 1320.00
Band, Wallpaper, Flowers, Geometrics, Blue, Brown Ground, 4 ¾ x 8 In. . . . . . *illus* 275.00
Band, Wallpaper, Flowers, Red, Yellow, Blue, Green Ground, Pa., 1890s, 2 ¼ x 3 ½ In. 3100.00
Band, Wallpaper, Grand Canal Scene, Mid 19th Century, 12 x 19 x 15 ½ In. 1404.00
Band, Wallpaper, Green, Orange & Burgundy Leaves, Early 1800s, 8 ¾ x 10 ¼ In. 575.00
Band, Wallpaper, Hat Shape, Block Printed, Leaf Scrolls, Phila., c.1853, 14 ½ x 8 ½ In. 575.00
Band, Wallpaper, Hat Shape, Yellow Flowers, Blue Ground, Cornith, Phila., 1850s, 9 ½ x 13 In. 3300.00
Band, Wallpaper, Hunters, Horses, Dogs, New York City Hall, 11 ¾ x 17 x 13 ¼ In. 715.00
Band, Wallpaper, Newspaper, Blue, Brown Geometric, Flower, 3 x 10 x 11 ¾ In. 143.00
Band, Wallpaper, Paper Board, Flowers, Geometrics, Green, Blue, Red, 5 ½ x 8 In. . . . . . *illus* 220.00
Band, Wallpaper, Red & Green Print, Yellow Paper Label, c.1851, 12 x 7 In. 316.00
Band, Wallpaper, Sapphire, Yellow Bird, Swing, Flowers, Oblong, New England, 1800s, 17 In. . 3125.00
Band, Wallpaper, Stylized Flower, Black, White, Salmon Ground, 1890s, 4 ¾ x 9 In. 2100.00
Band, Wallpaper, Tulips, White, Purple Ground, Blue Lid, Pa., 1850s, 2 ¾ x 5 ¼ In. 1320.00
Band, Wallpaper, Woman, Children, Multicolored, Geometric, 3 x 5 ⅜ x 8 ½ In. 77.00
Band, Wallpaper, Wood, Rose Ground, Blue & Black Geometric, Flowers, 4 ¾ x 10 In. 440.00
Basswood, Orange Grain Design, Yellow Ground, Lock, N.E., Early 19th Century, 8 x 27 In. . . 497.00
Bentwood, 2 Yellow Birds On Branch, Black Ground, 19th Century, 2 ¼ x 5 ½ In. 117.00
Bentwood, Red Stain, 19th Century, 9 x 19 In. 59.00
Bible, Charles II, Oak, Fan Carved Case, Lift Lid, Late 17th Century, 7 ½ x 23 x 15 ¾ In. 585.00
Bible, Oak, Arcaded Lid, Scalloped Apron, Bracket Feet, Late 18th Century, 7 ½ x 17 ¾ In. . . . 351.00
Bible, Oak, Carved, Iron Decorative Hinges, Hasp, Stand, England, 19th Century, 30 x 25 ½ In. 460.00
Blackballing, Pine, Painted, Drawers, Inscribed, Fortuna Club Organ, May 24, 1869, 11 x 8 In. 761.00
Bone Veneer, Inlay, Flower Head Finial, Ribs, Pincushion, 5 ½ x 7 ⅜ x 5 ½ In. 2880.00
Book Shape, Wood, Puzzle Lock, Slide Lid, 4 ⅝ x 4 ⅝ In. 77.00
Brass, Arts & Crafts, Embossed, Craquelure Raised Design, Patina, 13 x 20 x 12 In. 430.00
Brass Mounted, Lacquered, Parquetry, Mother-Of-Pearl, Hinged Lid, 12 x 6 In. 620.00
Bride's, Bentwood, Bride, Tulips, c.1800, 6 x 18 In. 995.00
Bride's, Bentwood, Orange, Red, Green Roses, Marked, G &DL 1810, 12 x 22 x 13 In. . . . *illus* 375.00
Bride's, Bentwood, Pine, Flower Basket, Multicolored, Tin Clasp, 1800s, 6 x 14 In. 646.00
Bride's, Bentwood, Tulips In Urn, Multicolored, Stitched, 8 ½ x 12 ½ In. 382.00

Bride's, Bentwood, Woman, Tulips, Multicolored, Stitched, Pegged, 5 x 10 ¾ In. 823.00
Bride's, Bride & Tulip, Bentwood, Oval, c.1800, 6 x 18 In.............................. 995.00
Bride's, Flowers On Sides, Couple On Lid, Painted, Oval, 19th Century, 5 ¼ x 17 x 11 In. 644.00
Bride's, Flowers On Sides, Couple On Lid, Painted, Oval, 19th Century, 7 ¾ x 18 x 11 ½ In. .. 761.00
Bride's, Pine, Flowers, Woman, Laced Lap Joint, Black Ground, 7 x 16 x 10 In. .... *illus* 500.00
Bride's, Pine, Man, Trees, Flowers, Painted, Continental, Early 19th Century, 7 x 17 ¾ x 11 In. 556.00
Bride's, Wood, Flowers, Hand Painted, Gold Trim, 9 x 11 In. 234.00
Burl, Mother-Of-Pearl Inlay, Marquetry, Escutcheon, Dome Lid, 1800s, 4 x 10 x 7 In. 176.00
Burl, Turned Lid, c.1830, 7 ¾ x 10 In.. 41475.00
Burl Hufa Wood, Bone Lovebirds Finial, Art Deco, 5 ½ x 4 In. 750.00
Candle, Cherry, Slide Lid, Carved Tulip, Pa., 19th Century, 3 ¼ x 4 ½ x 10 ¼ In. 720.00
Candle, Mahogany, Dovetailed Slide Lid, Wall Mount, 18 In. 86.00
Candle, Pine, Slide Lid, Flower, Blue, White, Salmon Ground, 1800s, 5 x 14 x 10 In. .... *illus* 995.00
Candle, Pine, Slide Lid, Flower, Ivory, Red Ground, Johannes Stauffer Anno, 1797, 3 x 9 x 5 In. 49140.00
Candle, Pine, Slide Lid, Iron Handle, 2 ⅔ x 24 x 6 In................................ 250.00
Candle, Pine, Slide Lid, Tulips, Ocher Ground, Comb Design, Early 1800s, 4 x 11 In......... 7605.00
Candle, Poplar, Slide Lid, Carved Heart, Pennsylvania, 7 x 10 ½ x 7 ½ In. 325.00
Candle, Softwood, Red Paint, Dovetailed, Shaped Crest, Hanging, 1800s, 12 x 5 In.......... 431.00
Candle, Softwood, Slide Lid, Tiger Maple, Dovetailed, Gouged Finger Pulls, 5 ¾ x 11 ½ In.... 132.00
Candle, Walnut, Slide Lid, Reeded Panel To Crest, 1800s, 18 In.......................... 235.00
Card, Rosewood, Brass Mounts, Brass & Ivory Corner, Dome Lid, Mid 1800s, 3 x 9 In........ 570.00
Cellarette, Mahogany, Brass Corners, Milk Glass Liner, Stand, Drawer, c.1900, 38 x 25 In.... 354.00
Cherry, Poplar, Dovetailed, Divided Interior, Slide Lid, 1800s, 3 x 9 x 6 ¼ In. 235.00
Chest, Softwood, Dovetailed, Brass Hinges, False Key Escutcheon, 5 ½ x 8 ¾ x 4 ¾ In....... 3575.00
Cigarette, Terrier, Mold Ruff, 2 ¼ x 3 ¼ In.. 15.00
Coffer, Oak, Incised Design, Jacobean, 17th Century, 8 ½ x 19 x 13 ½ In................. 351.00
Collar, Maiden, Cherubs, Scrolls, Smoke, Papier-Mache, Lacquer, Gilt, Cylindrical, 4 ½ x 6 In.. 50.00
Conestoga Wagon, Softwood, Prussian Blue, Iron Hinges, Nails, 11 x 16 x 7 In........... 880.00
Cutlery, Cherry, Wedding, 2 Lovebirds On Heart Handle, Pa., 19th Century, 7 ½ In......... 1112.00
Cutlery, George III, Mahogany, Serpentine Front, Hinged Lid, Inlaid Shell, Slots, c.1780, 15 In. 1198.00
Cutlery, Pine, Gray Paint, Cutout Heart Handle, New England, c.1830, 7 x 9 In............ 2133.00
Cutlery, Pine, Hanging, 2 Tiers, c.1790, 21 x 14 In..................................... 230.00
Cutlery, Red Stain, Cutout Handle, Wainscot Bottom, 6 x 15 ½ x 9 ½ In. 33.00
Cutlery, Tiger Maple, Divided, Carved Handle, 13 ½ In. 275.00
Deed, Elm, Satinwood Crossband, Velvet Liner, Hinged Lid, Mahogany Stand, 21 x 17 x 17 In. 1673.00
Desk, Caddy, Regency, Rosewood, Inlay, 3 Inkwells, Pen Trays, Brass Handle, 8 x 15 x 11 ¾ In. 403.00
Desk, Wood, Brass, Leather, Linen, Book Form, Marked, Journal, France, 3 ½ x 16 x 11 In.... 450.00
Ditty, 2-Finger, White Paint, Inlaid 1836, 4 ½ In. Diam................................. 990.00
Ditty, 4-Finger, Sailor's, Pine, Maple, Pewter Tacks, Openwork, Heart, Compass, 9 In. 748.00
Ditty, Parquetry, 19th Century, 5 ¼ x 9 ½ In.. 322.00
Ditty, Walnut, Heart Form, Oval Inset Mirror, Pa., 19th Century, 1 ½ x 2 ¾ In............. 1755.00
Document, Molded Top, Iron Strap Hinges, Turned Feet, 18th Century, 8 ¾ x 19 ½ In....... 431.00
Document, Moroccan Leather, Red, Brass Inset, Hinged Lid, England, 5 x 15 ½ x 10 ½ In.... 250.00
Document, Oak, Iron Hinges, Lock, Carved, Slant Lid, England, 1748, 20 x 15 x 11 In........ 646.00
Document, Poplar, Dovetailed, Red Over Yellow, Wallpaper, 7 x 17 ¾ x 9 ¾ In. 1410.00
Document, Poplar, Lions, Hearts, Cornucopia, Multicolored, Black Ground, N.Y., 1800s, 6 x 11 In. 646.00
Document, Walnut, Beveled Lid, American Shield, Shield Shape Keyhole, 1900s, 14 x 10 x 4 In. 176.00
Document, Walnut, Dovetailed, Applied Molding, Bracket Feet, 14 ½ x 8 In. 734.00
Document, Wood, Painted, Swag & Nut Design, Grain Paint, Metal Handle, Clasp, N.H. 1800.00
Dome Lid, Balsa, Staple Hinges, Wire Bail Handle, 19th Century, 9 ¼ x 5 ¼ In............ 489.00
Dome Lid, Basswood, Black Over Red Paint, Dovetailed, New England, 10 x 24 In. 558.00
Dome Lid, Basswood, Yellow Flowers, Green Vines, Blue Ground, Early 1800s, 14 x 27 ½ In. . 5616.00
Dome Lid, Hinged, Rock Crystal, Foil Back Gemstones, Gold, 19th Century, 1 ½ x 2 In....... 2880.00
Dome Lid, Leaf Scrolls, Multicolored, Red Ground, Blue Trim, Pine Interior, 6 x 5 ½ In..... 230.00
Dome Lid, Multicolored Stencils, Black Ground, Cincinnati Newspaper Interior, c.1815, 14 x 28 In. 499.00
Dome Lid, Pine, Dovetailed, Floral Sprigs, Peacock Feathers, Painted, Putty, 12 x 28 In...... 176.00
Dome Lid, Pine, Polka Dot Tulips, Black Ground, Pa., 1763, 5 ¼ x 11 ¾ In............... 3978.00
Dome Lid, Poplar, Brown-Red Over Yellow-Green Sponging, Pegged, Tin Hinges, Hasp, 4 1/2 x 8 In. 176.00
Dome Lid, Poplar, Stylized Flowers, Red, White, Blue Ground, Compass, 1800, 10 x 17 In. 17550.00
Dome Lid, Wood, Painted, House, Church, Trees, Square Nails, 19th Century, 9 x 18 x 10 In. . 2500.00
Donation, Wood, Painted, Man, In Suit, Holding Red Cross Box, Figural, c.1800, 30 ½ In.... 761.00
Dovetailed, Grain Paint, Interior Tray, Wood Pull, Bone Escutcheon, 8 ⅝ x 12 In.......... 187.00
Dresser, Cherry, Line, Berry Inlays, Bracket Feet, Lift Lid, c.1760, 7 ½ x 10 In............ 9945.00
Dresser, Giltwood, Mirror, Grisaille Cut Paper Flowers, 3 Sections, 3 ¼ x 20 In............ 360.00
Dresser, Glass, Ruby, Enamel, Black, White, Gold, 6-Sided, 3 ½ x 5 x 3 In. 225.00
Dresser, Glass, Turquoise, Boy With Net, Girl With Basket, 2 ⅛ x 8 ¼ x 2 ⅝ In. 118.00
Dresser, Oak, Carved, Shield, Flowers, Vines, Pen, Forget-Me-Not, Gilt, England, 7 x 13 x 8 In. 230.00

Box, Bride's, Bentwood, Orange, Red, Green Roses, Marked, G &DL 1810, 12 x 22 x 13 In. $375.00

Box, Bride's, Pine, Flowers, Woman, Laced Lap Joint, Black Ground, 7 x 16 x 10 In. $500.00

TIP

Be very careful if you're trying to clean a cigar box or other paper-labeled wooden box. First glue any loose spots on the label with diluted white glue, but be sure no glue seeps from under the paper to show on the wood. Never use liquid cleaners, not even water. A Pink Pearl eraser may be used on the wood and an art gum eraser on the paper. Always erase with the wood grain. Avoid any lettering.

Box, Candle, Pine, Slide Lid, Flower, Blue, White, Salmon Ground, 1800s, 5 x 14 x 10 In.
$995.00

Box, Exotic Wood, Brass, Gothic Revival, Merchi & Bazin, London, 1890s, 7 x 10 x 6 In.
$575.00

Box, Glove, Napoleon III, Sarcophagus, Thuya Burl, Marquetry Medallion, Inlay, 9 x 3 In.
$1120.00

Box, Hen On Nest, Composition, Wallpaper, 19th Century, 6 ¼ In.
$1287.00

Dresser, Pine, 2 Birds, On Scrolled Garland, Red Grain Ground, 19th Century, 7 x 11 ½ In. . . 439.00
Dresser, Pine, Burl Heart, Black Corners, Green Ground, N.E., 19th Century, 6 x 10 In. 819.00
Dresser, Pine, Red & White Flowers, Black Ground, I.C.H., Late 18th Century, 3 x 10 x 9 In. . . 4680.00
Dresser, Pine, Tulips, Red Ground, Trees & Lawn, Lift Lid, Fivepointville, Pa., 1850, 2 x 3 ½ In. 21060.00
Dresser, Poplar, Red Grain Ground, Drawer, Mid 19th Century, 7 ½ x 13 In. 117.00
Dresser, Poplar, White Stylized Flowers, Red, Blue, Dome Lid, Compass Artist, 1820s, 7 x 10 In. 64350.00
Dresser, Stylized Flowers, House, Lawn, Yellow Ground, Jonas Weber, Pa., 3 ¼ x 5 In. 12100.00
Dresser, Tulips, Trees, House, Painted, Jacob Weber, 1850, 3 x 4 ¾ In. 1053.00
Ebonized, Mother-Of-Pearl Inlay, Diamond Pattern, Scrolled Bracket Feet, 18 x 23 In. 1410.00
Exotic Wood, Brass, Gothic Revival, Merchi & Bazin, London, 1890s, 7 x 10 x 6 In. . . . . *illus* 575.00
Flowers, Grain Paint, 12 x 8 x 4 ½ In. 374.00
Fruitwood, Classical Scene, Mirror, Jasper, Steel Mounted, England, 4 In. 415.00
Glass, Brass Lock, French Cut, 5 ¾ x 4 ½ x 6 ¾ In. 936.00
Glove, Napoleon III, Sarcophagus, Thuya Burl, Marquetry Medallion, Inlay, 9 x 3 In. . . *illus* 1120.00
Glove, Opal Glass, Leaves, Rectangular, Pairpoint, c.1890, 10 In. 354.00
Hat, Cardboard, Fitted, Blue, Hat Cases By William Warren Baltimore, c.1841, 14 x 9 In. 587.00
Hat, Leather, Steamer Stickers, Handle, Hinges, Square, 15 In. 90.00
Hat, Pulp, Old Blue Paint, 1930s, 8 x 15 x 13 In. 20.00
Hat, Walnut, Tricornered, Lift Lid, Iron Strap Hinges, c.1770, 8 ½ x 20 In. 7605.00
Heart Shape, Quillwork Sides, New England, 19th Century, 5 x 8 x 9 In. 205.00
Hen On Nest, Composition, Wallpaper, 19th Century, 6 ¼ In. . . . . *illus* 1287.00
Jacobean, Oak, Carved, Flowers, Lock, Late 17th Century, 11 x 23 In. 750.00
Japanned, Portrait, Willem De Tweede, King Of The Netherlands, Dutch, 1800s, 5 x 3 In. 390.00
Jewel Encrusted, Mirrored, Jade, Coral, Ivory, Late 19th Century, 10 ½ x 13 ½ x 8 ¼ In. 780.00
Jewelry, 23 Panels, Nudes, Cherub Finial, Drawers, Ebony, Enamel, Metal, France, 14 x 12 In. 7000.00
Jewelry, Bronze, Embossed, Relief, 4-Footed, Germany, 1930s, 5 x 7 In. 450.00
Jewelry, Burl Walnut, Dome Lid, 18th Century, 6 ¼ x 9 ¾ In. 643.00
Jewelry, Casket, Aesthetic Revival, Brass, Mixed Metals, Pedestal, Silk Lining, 13 ½ x 17 ½ In. 5100.00
Jewelry, Casket, Anglo-Colonial, Gilt Brass Mount, Penwork, Paw Feet, 4 ¼ x 11 ½ In. 780.00
Jewelry, Casket, Porcelain Plaques, Sevres Style, Brass Mount, 4 x 5 ¼ x 5 ¼ In. 480.00
Jewelry, Inlaid, Hispano-Moresque, Octagonal, 7 x 17 In. 2572.00
Jewelry, Ivory & Boulle Marquetry, Hinged Lid, France, Late 1800s, 3 ¾ x 5 ½ In. 227.00
Jewelry, Lacquer, Black Abalone Shell Inlay, 2 Doors, 3 Inside Drawers, c.1910, 8 x 11 x 7 In. 205.00
Jewelry, Rosewood, Ivory Inlay 863.00
Jewelry, Rosewood, Musical Trophee, Marquetry, Melon Ribs, Italy, 5 x 17 x 9 ½ In. 900.00
Jewelry, Satinwood Inlay, Lunette Banding, Federal, Seymour, Boston, c.1800, 4 x 10 In. 11258.00
Jewelry, Scenic Panels, Columns, Ebony, Gilt, Griffin Feet, Cherub Finial, Urn Lid, Drawers, 14 In. 7000.00
Jewelry, Tole Painted, Gilt, Multicolored & Gesso Figure Scene, Chinese, 4 x 10 In. 900.00
Jewelry, Tortoiseshell, Bone, Edwardian, Dome Lid, Velvet Basal Interior, Bun Feet, 2 x 7 x 4 In. 900.00
Jewelry, Walnut, Drawers, Red Velvet Lining, Bun Feet, Italy, 20th Century, 12 x 16 x 6 In. . . . 354.00
Jewelry, Wood, Relief Carved, Scholars In Court Garden, Chinese, 4 ½ In. 478.00
Jewelry Cabinet, Lift Lid, Wood, Ivory Painted, 2 Doors, 3 Drawers, Figures, 12 x 12 x 9 In. . . 1800.00
Knife, Dovetailed, Wire Nail Construction, Turned Handle, Gray Paint, c.1885, 8 x 13 x 5 In. . 205.00
Knife, Edwardian, Mahogany, Bands, Shell Center, 14 x 9 In. 385.00
Knife, Federal, Mahogany, Serpentine Front, Dividers, c.1810, 14 In. 600.00
Knife, Georgian, Mahogany, Burl, Serpentine, Inlay, Star, Britain, Late 1700s, 15 In. 780.00
Knife, Georgian, Mahogany, Line Inlay, Slant Lid, Late 18th Century, 14 ¾ In. 725.00
Knife, Georgian, Mahogany, Marquetry, Slant Front, Cutlery Grilles, 14 x 8 ¾ x 10 In., Pair . . 5040.00
Knife, Georgian, Mahogany, Serpentine, Early 19th Century, 13 ¾ x 8 ¼ x 10 In. 275.00
Knife, Hepplewhite, Mahogany, Inlay, Shell, Herringbone, Britain, 14 ½ In. 975.00
Knife, Mahogany, Inlay, Oak Interior, Compass Star, England, c.1790, 15 x 9 In. 382.00
Knife, Mahogany, Tapered, Inlaid Stringing, Ball Feet, George III, 15 x 10 In., Pair 2040.00
Knife, Mahogany, Urn Shape, Lift Lid, Fitted Interior, England, c.1950, 26 x 10 In., Pair 1998.00
Knife, Mahogany Inlay, Serpentine Front, 15 x 10 ½ In., Pair 3585.00
Knife, Pine, Grain Painted Over Red, 2 Lift Lids, Central Divider, Cutout Handle, 13 x 8 In. . . . 646.00
Knife, Shagreen, Tapered Lid, Fabric & Metallic Thread Lined Interior, 1800s, 12 x 4 In. 345.00
Knife, Walnut, Inlaid, Teardrop Escutcheon, Federal, 1900s, 11 ¾ x 8 ¼ In., Pair 2415.00
Komei-Style, Dragons, Clouds, Plants, Iron Body, Inlaid Gold, Silver, 6 x 4 ½ x 2 ¼ In. 326.00
Lacquer, Emblems, Gold, 8-Sided, Japan, 19th Century, 5 In. 652.00
Lacquer, Flowers, Gold Flecked Ground, 2 Sections, Japan, 19th Century, 4 ½ x 3 x 2 In. 889.00
Lacquer, Gold, Pavilions, Mountain Landscape, Tray, Japan, 1868-1911, 6 ½ x 5 x 3 In. 1067.00
Lacquer, Gold Flowers, Inkstone, Water Dropper, Japan, 19th Century, 4 ¾ x 3 ¾ In. 1422.00
Lacquer, Pine Trees, Dandelions, Black, Gold, Silver, Japan, 19th Century, 11 ¼ x 9 x 9 In. . . . 836.00
Lacquer, Satsuma Crest, Leaves, Black, Gold, Japan, 19th Century, 3 In. 770.00
Lacquer, Scholars, Landscape, Mother-Of-Pearl Inlay, Tiered, 6-Sided, Japan, 20 In. 4148.00
Lacquer, Stylized Flowers, Silver, Abalone Shell, Nashiji Surface Inlay, Japan, 3 ¼ In. Diam. . 889.00
Lacquer, Tin, Black, Horsemen Playing Polo, Hinged Lid, 1 x 3 ¼ x 2 In. 22.00

Leather, Brass Tack Design, 19th Century, 6 ¾ x 18 x 8 In. . . . 183.00
Leather, Over Pine, Brass Mounted, Ebonized Wood Stand, 19th Century, 32 x 19 In. . . . 460.00
Lock, Yew, Concentric Circles, Pinwheels, Inlay, England, Early 1700s, 6 ¾ In. . . . 497.00
Log, Walnut, Copper, Hammered, France, c.1900, 15 ¾ x 26 x 15 In. . . . 875.00
Mahogany, Dovetailed, Brass Handle, Openwork Escutcheon, Early 1800s, 5 ½ x 10 In. . . . 173.00
Mahogany, Hepplewhite, Fan Patera, Barber Pole Canted Corners, 5 x 9 In. . . . 460.00
Mahogany, Ivory Crescent Escutcheon Inlay, 5 x 12 In. . . . 104.00
Maple, Turned, Red Paint, Threaded Lid, c.1900, 2 x 4 ¼ In. . . . 147.00
Memory, Mahogany, Ivory, Crescent Moon, Sword, Hinged Lid, 8 x 11 ¼ x 3 ½ In. . . . 1250.00
Mother-Of-Pearl, Hinges, French Style, 1 ¼ x 3 x 2 ⅛ In. . . . 409.00
Nailed Construction, Painted Orange, Red, Black, Lock, Key, Slide Lid, c.1829, 3 ½ x 5 ½ In. 470.00
On Stand, Georgian Style, Mahogany, Brass, Chamfered Square Legs, 24 x 13 x 13 In. . . . 495.00
Oval, Bentwood, Blue Paint, Laced Seam, Rosemaling, 19th Century, 7 x 3 In. . . . 374.00
Oval, Bentwood, Pine, Maple, Red & Green Flowers, Square Tacks, c.1840, 6 x 4 ½ In. . . . 690.00
Painted, Tan Ground, Dovetailed, Drawer, Wood Pull, Slide Lid, Oval, 10 ¼ x 24 x 15 ½ In. . . 413.00
Pantry, Beechwood, Painted, Sugar Holder, Lid, 1800s, 13 In. . . . 489.00
Pantry, Bentwood, Green Paint, Lapped Seams, Iron Tacks, Round, 1800s, 12 x 7 ¼ In. . . . 115.00
Pantry, Bentwood, Red Paint, Harvard Finger Seams, Copper Tacks, 1800s, 6 ½ x 2 ½ In. . . . 176.00
Pantry, Bentwood, Red Paint, Lapped Seams, Iron Tacks, Late 1800s, 4 x 7 In. . . . 499.00
Pantry, Black Over Green Paint, Round, 6 ¼ In. . . . 115.00
Pantry, Black Paint, Bail Handle, 9 ½ In. . . . 288.00
Pantry, Blue Green Paint, Round, 7 ¾ In. . . . 230.00
Pantry, Gray Blue Paint, Round, 6 ¾ In. . . . 201.00
Pantry, Light Blue Paint, Round, 7 ½ In. . . . 115.00
Pantry, Mixed Wood, Blue Paint, Bentwood Swing Handle, 6 ½ x 13 In. . . . 1430.00
Pantry, Mustard Paint, Bail Handle, 11 ½ In. . . . 288.00
Pantry, Mustard Paint, Round, 6 ¾ In. . . . 288.00
Pantry, Navy Blue Paint, Round, 5 ¾ In. . . . 230.00
Pantry, Putty Paint, Round, 8 ¼ In. . . . 316.00
Pantry, Red Paint, Bail Handle, 12 In. . . . 144.00
Pantry, Red Paint, Round, 6 ½ In. . . . 230.00
Pantry, Salmon Paint, Round, 8 ½ In. . . . 173.00
Pantry, Softwood, Green Paint, Tacked Lap Joints, Oval, 7 ½ x 17 ¾ In. . . . *illus* 935.00
Pantry, Softwood, Prussian Blue, Bentwood Lap Joints, 7 x 15 ½ In. . . . 209.00
Paper Board, Wallpaper, Flower, Geometric, Multicolored, Oval, 1 ½ x 2 ¾ x 1 ¾ In. . . . *illus* 935.00
Paper Board, Wallpaper, Flowers, Multicolored, Oval, 4 ¼ x 8 ¾ x 5 In. . . . 55.00
Paper Board, Wallpaper, Geometric, Multicolored, 5 x 9 ¾ x 8 ½ In. . . . 88.00
Paper Board, Wallpaper, Orange Flower, Leather Hinged Lid, 3 ¾ x 6 ½ In. . . . 275.00
Paper Board, Wallpaper, Poplar, Flower, Vase, Tin Hasp, Wire Hinges, Dome Lid, 6 ¾ x 9 ¼ In. 55.00
Paper Board, Wallpaper, Wood, Grape, Leaf, Oval, 2 x 4 ¾ x 2 ¾ In. . . . 303.00
Paper Board, Wallpaper, Yellow Tiger, Wood Top, Bottom, Oval, c.1790, 4 x 8 x 6 In. . . . 523.00
Pencil, Composition, Black, c.1875, 1 x 7 ⅞ In. . . . 45.00
Pencil, House, Landscape Scenes, Slide Lid, Academy Painted, R. Washburn, c.1825, 6 x 10 In. 38513.00
Pencil, Walnut, Carved, Heart Design, 19th Century, 1 ½ x 7 ½ x 2 In. . . . 380.00
Pencil, Wood, Farm Scene, Airplane, Hot Air Balloon, Spring Action Compartments, 9 x 2 In. 65.00
Pencil, Wooden, Papier-Mache Lid, Children, Bubbles, Compartments, Hinged . . . 59.00
Pine, Brass Tack Design, Red & Black Swirls, Dome Lid, Lock, 19th Century, 4 ¾ x 11 ½ In. . . 146.00
Pine, Dovetailed, Black Over Gray Smoke, Stenciled Bands, Flowers, 8 x 19 In. . . . 588.00
Pine, Dovetailed, Black Over Red, Molded Lid, Decorated, 1800s, 7 ¼ x 13 In. . . . 529.00
Pine, Dovetailed, Crown & Cross Inlay, Dog On Front Panel, c.1880, 12 x 9 x 5 In. . . . 118.00
Pine, Dovetailed, Dome Lid, Square Nails, Original Paint, Initials U.D., 12 ⅝ x 8 x 7 In. . . . 1528.00
Pine, Dovetailed, Hinges, Lock, Handles, c.1830s, 11 x 24 x 11 ¾ In. . . . 588.00
Pine, Dovetailed, Vinegar Design, Green, Yellow, Brown, Divided Tray, 5 ¾ x 10 In. . . . 705.00
Pine, Dovetailed, Red, Brown, Cream Vinegar Decor, 1800s, 7 x 18 In. . . . 588.00
Pine, Grain Paint, White Ground, Lock, Brass Hinges, Applied Molding, 4 ½ x 10 ¾ In. . . . 358.00
Pine, Iron Salmon, Blue, Lock, Dome Lid, Early 1800s, 9 x 18 ½ In. . . . 237.00
Pine, Nailed Construction, Compartments, Slide Lid, c.1800, 5 ¼ x 9 ½ In. . . . 147.00
Pine, Red Ocher, Yellow, Dovetailed Joints, Pegged, Dividers, Slide Lid, c.1750, 3 x 10 In. . . . 495.00
Pine, Wall, Old Red Paint, Scalloped Top, Late 1700s, 20 x 13 In. . . . 702.00
Pipe, Mahogany, Scalloped, Thumb Molded Drawer, Base, 17 x 6 x 4 In. . . . 2300.00
Pipe, Mahogany, Scalloped Crest, Drawer, Fryman Farm, Early 19th Century, 18 In. . . . 11115.00
Pipe, Mahogany, Scalloped Sides, Heart Cutout, Patina, N.E., Late 18th Century, 20 ¾ x 5 In. . 6435.00
Pipe, Maple, Scalloped Back, Drawer, Late 18th Century, 17 ¼ x 5 ⅜ In. . . . 4914.00
Pipe, Painted, Scalloped Back, Drawer, New England, Late 18th Century, 16 ¾ x 5 ¼ In. . . . 995.00
Pipe, Pine, Carved, Human Head Sides, Drawer, 19th Century, 18 ½ In. . . . 380.00
Pipe, Pine, Drawer, Lollipop Hanger, White Paint Trace Over Red, 19 x 6 In. . . . 1410.00
Pipe, White Pine, Scroll Top, Drawer, Multicolored, Gold Stencil Wreath, 1830, 13 x 7 In. . . . 34500.00

Box, Pantry, Softwood, Green Paint, Tacked Lap Joints, Oval, 7 ½ x 17 ¾ In.
$935.00

Box, Paper Board, Wallpaper, Flower, Geometric, Multicolored, Oval, 1 ½ x 2 ¾ x 1 ¾ In.
$935.00

Box, String, Acorn Form, Regency, Lignum Vitae, Carved, c.1810, 8 ½ x 5 In.
$400.00

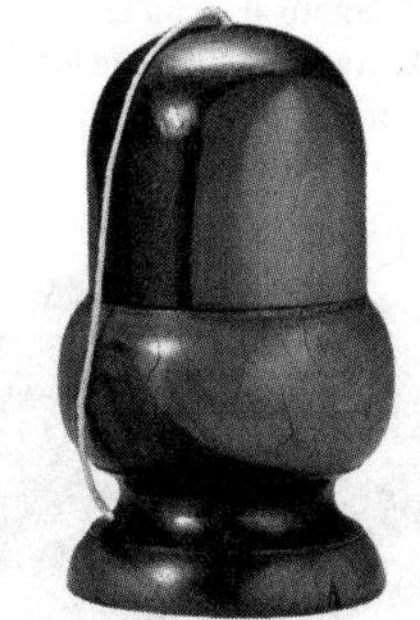

TIP
You'll find the best selection at a weekend show on Friday, the biggest crowd on Saturday, and the best bargains on Sunday. Allow yourself plenty of time. Have a price range in mind. When you see it, buy it. And keep tabs on your wallet and purchases.

Box, Tantalus Style, Oak, 4 Jars, Stoppers, Key, 7 ½ x 10 x 8 In. $430.00

Box, Wall, Poplar, Tulips, Pinwheels, Zigzag Border, 1826, 13 x 10 In. $2574.00

Box, Wall, Softwood, Slant Lid, Stylized Leaves, Red, Black, Yellow Paint, 11 x 17 x 9 ½ In. $935.00

Box, Wall, Spoon Rack, Pine, Arched Top, 20 x 12 x 4 ½ In. $275.00

Poplar, 2 Drawers, Black Paint, Wall, 1800s, 18 x 14 In. 1528.00
Poplar, Painted, Red, Brown, Gilt Letters, Sarah Crawford, c.1830, 8 x 18 In. 470.00
Poplar, Stylized Pinwheels, Blue Ground, Compass Artist, Pa., c.1800, 9 ½ x 13 In. 38000.00
Poplar, Tulips, Yellow, Red, Green Leaves, Blue Ground, Lift Lid, Pa., c.1800, 3 ½ x 7 ½ In. 25740.00
Poplar, Wallpaper, Flowers, Multicolored, Leather Hinges, Tin Hasp, Dome Lid, 3 ¼ x 5 ½ x 4 In. 1430.00
Poplar, Walnut Interior, Grapevines, Leaves, Convex Lid, Base, 5 ⅜ x 18 ¾ x 11 ½ In. 660.00
Porcelain, Louis XVI, Sevres Style, Flowers, Gilt Brass Mount, Oval, 10 x 13 x 6 ½ In. 1080.00
Quill, Anglo Indian, Slide Lid, 8 In. 228.00
Quill, Sarcophagus Shape, Bone Borders, Lift-Out Tray, Compartments, India, c.1890, 10 x 7 In. 1036.00
Salt, Green Glass, Paneled, Round Foot, Hinged Metal Cover, U.S. Glass, 4 ¾ x 3 In. 225.00
Salt, Poplar, Heart Cutout, Scalloped Back, Lift Lid, Drawer, Early 19th Century, 15 x 7 ½ In. 1638.00
Scarf, Gloves, Mahogany, Cedar, Lacquered, Black, Gold, Chinoiserie, 10 ¼ x 4 ⅛ In. 660.00
Shadow, Pine, Blue Paint, Arched Top, 19th Century, 19 x 7 In. 263.00
Shagreen, Queen Anne, Silver Bail, Escutcheon, Ball & Claw Feet, Early 1700s, 10 x 13 In. 863.00
Shell, Victorian, Angled Horseshoe Shape, Metal Inserts, Round, 2 ¾ In. 300.00
Shell, Victorian, Bone Feet, Metal Escutcheon, Dome Lid, 5 In. 275.00
Shirtwaist, G. Stickley, No. 95, Spindle Sides, Panel Lid, 16 x 20 In. 7200.00
Shirtwaist, Wood, Spindled Sides, Tops, Label, G. Stickley, 15 x 30 x 16 In. 5700.00
Shot, Salmon, Black Borders, 4 Compartments, Splayed Sides, Molded Base, 3 ¾ x 20 In. 1870.00
Shrine, Damascene, Flowers, Gold On Iron, Japan, 19th Century, 3 ¼ x 2 ¾ In. 563.00
Softwood, Carved, Incised, Flowers, German Text, Slate Pencils, Slide Lid, c.1832, 1 x 7 ½ In. 660.00
Softwood, Carved, Molded Edges, Green Velvet Lining, Continental, Early 1900s, 8 x 12 ¼ In. 147.00
Softwood, Dovetailed, Metal Key Escutcheon, Slide Lid, 6 ⅛ x 16 x 9 ⅞ In. 385.00
Softwood, Dovetailed, Yellow Ocher, Double Hinged, Turned Feet, 20 ¼ x 61 ½ In. 468.00
Softwood, Leather, Brass Tack Border, Brass Pull, Iron Lock, Swing Cover, 5 x 10 x 7 In. 33.00
Softwood, Red Flower, Painted, 4 Sections, Wood, Slide Lid, Jonas Weber, 2 ½ x 7 x 4 In. 715.00
Stamp, Walnut, Carved Squirrel, Holding Nut, c.1917-28, 4 x 5 In. 1430.00
Stamp, Wood, Embossed Man's Profile, Germany, c.1759, 3 ¾ In. 90.00
Stamp, Wood, Hinge, Rivets, Carved, Painted, 1903, 2 x 3 ½ x 3 ½ In. 1440.00
Storage, Basswood, Green Paint, Stippled Ivory Design, c.1810, 6 ¼ x 12 x 7 ¼ In. 2223.00
Storage, Mahogany, Inlay, Line, Flowers, Tree, Rabbit, Birds, Dome Lid, c.1775, 8 x 13 ½ x 6 In. 7020.00
Storage, Pine, Ash, Green Paint, Inscribed M.N., 1800s, 6 ¼ x 15 ⅞ In. 474.00
Storage, Pine, Gold Over Yellow Paint, Dovetailed, Canted Sides, Turned Feet, c.1850, 19 x 37 In. 440.00
Storage, Pine, Grain Paint, Hinged Lid, c.1830, 17 x 16 In. 237.00
String, Acorn Form, Regency, Lignum Vitae, Carved, c.1810, 8 ½ x 5 In. *illus* 400.00
Sycamore, Dovetailed, Red Diamond, Stars, Pinwheel, Blue Ground, Slide Lid, 3 ¾ x 4 ¾ In. 1116.00
Tantalus, Edwardian, Metal Mounted, Oak, 3 Decanters, c.1890, 12 ½ x 16 ¼ In. 288.00
Tantalus Style, Oak, 4 Jars, Stoppers, Key, 7 ½ x 10 x 8 In. *illus* 430.00
Tiger Maple, Dovetailed, c.1880, 14 x 7 ¼ x 7 ¼ In. 525.00
Tiger Maple, Removable Lid, Brass Pin, Bracket Feet, 3 ½ x 7 ¼ x 4 ½ In. 121.00
Tin, 4 Seasonal Landscapes, Lew Hudnall, c.1975, 12 ¼ x 11 x 6 ½ In. 264.00
Tobacco, Brass, Copper, Embossed, Portrait, George III, Hebrew Writing, Germany, 1790s, 6 In. 1112.00
Tortoiseshell, Rectangular, Silvered Plaque, Ivory Bun Feet, 4 ½ x 11 In. 4800.00
Tortoiseshell Veneer, Flowers, Pierced Carved Bone Overlay, Paw Feet, Ink Designs, 6 x 5 In. 558.00
Trinket, Crystal, Byrdes, Hofbauer, West Germany, 3 ¾ x 2 ¾ In. 23.00
Trinket, Heart Shape, Star & Heart Inlays, c.1830, 4 x 10 In. 410.00
Trinket, Pine, Leaves, Green Paint, Dovetailed, Compass Stars, Stenciled, 3 ¾ x 7 ¼ In. 1045.00
Trinket, Poplar, Theorem Painting, Flowers, Paper Covered, Vermont, 4 x 10 In. 764.00
Trinket, Softwood, Dovetailed, Molded Lid, Base, Wire Hinges, Paper, 1 ¾ x 5 ½ x 3 ¼ In. 385.00
Trinket, Wallpaper, Softwood, Stylized Leaves, Tin Hasp, Hinges, Dome Lid, 3 x 4 ¼ x 2 ¾ In. 55.00
Trunk Shape, Pottery, Dome Lid, Blue & Iron Red Designs, 6 x 7 x 4 In. 71.00
Utility, Softwood, Dovetailed, Raised Handle, Oval Cutout Handle, Slant Lid, 11 x 19 x 13 In. 550.00
Vinaigrette, Agate Inlay, Engraved Silver Mount, Oval, Flattened, Hinged Lid, 1 ½ In. 761.00
Vinaigrette, Bloodstone, Gold Bezel Mount, Pierced Grill, Birds, c.1850, 1 ¼ x 1 In. 1943.00
Vinaigrette, Gold, Book Shape, Enameled Flowers, Black Ground, Scrolled Corners, 1 ¼ In. 1208.00
Vinaigrette, Gold, Enameled Flower Plaques, Engraved, Hinged Lid, c.1860, ¾ x ½ In. 709.00
Vinaigrette, Gold, Oval, Engraved, Cobalt Blue Enamel Top, Flower Rim, Pierced Grill, 1840, 1 ½ In. 1523.00
Vinaigrette, Sterling Silver, 6 Lobes With Agate Stones, Scrolled Grill, Birmingham, 1 ¼ In. 998.00
Wagon, Conestoga, Green Paint, Iron Hardware, Late 18th Century, 16 x 15 In. 819.00
Wagon, Tool, Rosehead Nails, Pine Lid, Hinges, Iron, 9 ¾ In. 358.00
Wall, Pine, Dovetailed, Blue Paint, Shaped Back, Late 1800s 176.00
Wall, Pine, Green Paint, Moon & Stars Cutouts, Drawer, Door, 1800s, 19 x 14 In. 1170.00
Wall, Poplar, Shaped Crest, 2 Tiers Of Shelves, New England, 1800s, 13 ¾ x 19 In. 353.00
Wall, Poplar, Tulips, Pinwheels, Zigzag Border, 1826, 13 x 10 In. *illus* 2574.00
Wall, Red Paint, Heart Cutout, Lift Lid, Drawer, 8 x 8 x 13 In. 1035.00
Wall, Softwood, Blue Green, Iron Hinged Door, Knob, Shelf, 23 x 14 x 7 ¾ In. 1210.00
Wall, Softwood, Slant Lid, Stylized Leaves, Red, Black, Yellow Paint, 11 x 17 x 9 ½ In. *illus* 935.00
Wall, Softwood, Teal Paint, Broken Arch Crest, Hinged Lid, Shaped Bottom, 15 x 10 In. 385.00

Wall, Spoon Rack, Pine, Arched Top, 20 x 12 x 4 ½ In. . . . . *illus* 275.00
Wall, Walnut, Wood Hinged Lid, Divider, 13 ¼ x 12 x 7 ¼ In. 303.00
Walnut, Cove, Stepped Molded Lid, Drawer, Ogee Feet, c.1770, 10 x 12 In. 529.00
Walnut, Ebony, Ivory Inlay, 19th Century, 5 x 8 x 13 In. 643.00
Walnut, Lift Lid, Compartment, Drawer, Carved Urn, Flowers, France, c.1870, 16 x 8 In. 1020.00
Walnut, Mother-Of-Pearl Inlay, Fold-Out Compartment, Tray, England, 6 x 12 x 9 In. 316.00
Wood, Applied Cone Feet, Ball Finial, Round, 6 x 6 ½ In. 440.00
Wood, Blue Paint, Flower Design, Wire Nail Construction, c.1875, 9 ½ x 5 x 5 ½ In. 764.00
Wood, Dovetailed, Grain Paint, Eagle Head Brass, 15 ½ x 11 ½ In. 264.00
Wood, Florentine, Hinged, c.1950, 7 x 17 x 11 In. 117.00
Wood, Stylized Flower, Painted, Laced Lap Joints, 3 x 10 ½ x 5 In. 605.00
Writing, Continental, Parquetry, Slant Lid, Interior Fitted Compartments, 1800s, 13 x 15 In. . 359.00
Writing, Hinged Lid, Hepplewhite, Mahogany, Inlay, Nautilus Shell, Drawers, 7 x 16 x 10 In. . 805.00
Writing, Napoleon III, Inlaid, Brass, Mother-Of-Pearl, 8 x 12 In. 120.00
Writing, Oak, Iron, Tin Mounted, Slant Lift Lid, Molded Edge, Bun Feet, Denmark, 1700s, 9 x 11 In. 104.00
Writing, Regency, Sloping Lid, Hardwoods, Inlay, Compartments, Brass Handles, 8 x 15 ½ In. 1080.00
Zitan, Dragon Relief Decoration, Chinese, 20th Century, 3 ¼ x 12 In. 1135.00

BOY SCOUT collectibles include any material related to scouting, including patches, manuals, and uniforms. The Boy Scout movement in the United States started in 1910. The first Jamboree was held in 1937. Girl Scout items are listed under their own heading.

Badge, National Scout Jamboree, Adventure Begins Shuttle, Flies Round World, 1989, 3 x 4 In. 9.00
Bank, Boy Scout, Holding Pole, Painted, Cast Iron, 6 In. 50.00
Belt, Leather, Hand Tooled, Brass Buckle, National Scout Jamboree, 1977. . . . . 85.00
Book, Wolf Cub Scout, 1967. . . . . 14.00
Bookends, Logo & Motto, A Scout Is Trustworthy, Resin, Maryland, 1940s, 5 ⅜ x 5 ¼ In. 50.00
Booklet, Merit Badge, Public Speaking, 1964. . . . . 6.00
Compass, Aluminum, Plastic, National Council, New York City Seal, Silva, 2 x 3 In. 32.00
Cookware Set, Aluminum, Dish, Lidded Kettle, Skillet, Foldover Handle, 3 Piece. 18.00
Doll, Skippy, Composition Head, Arms, Legs, Cloth Body, Uniform, Effanbee, 1930, 14 In. 3738.00
Drum, Scouts Having Rifle Practice, Buglers, Drummer, Flag Raising, Drumsticks, 3 ⅜ x 6 In. 225.00
First Aid Kit, Tin, Leather Pouch, 1928 . . . . . 55.00
Flashlight, Scout Logo, 90-Degree Head, Belt Clip, Bridgeport Metal Mfg. Co., 7 x 2 In. 68.00
Game, Boy Scouts, McLoughlin Bros., April 7, 1914, 10 ¾ x 21 In. 295.00
Game, Game Of Boy Scouts, Milton Bradley, Board, Box, 22 x 10 ½ In. 330.00
Handbook, 1965 . . . . . 10.00
Hatchet, Leather Guard, Bridgeport, Conn., Signed. 15.00
Hatchet, Plum, Leather Guard, Signed. 15.00
Kerchief Slide, Brass, Trylon & Perisphere, World's Fair, Wire, Orange, Blue, 1939 . . . . . 131.00
Marionette, Cub Scout, 14 In. 200.00
Mug, Ceramic, White, Green Boy Scout Logo, c.1991 . . . . . 29.50
Neckerchief, Turquoise, Badge, Pelham Manor, N.Y., 38 x 18 In. 7.00
Neckerchief Slide, Sailor's Knot, Eagle, Adjustable Back, Metal, 1 ¾ x 1 ½ In. . . . 7.50 to 15.00
Patch, Delhi India Jamboree Patch, 1937, 2 ¾ x 2 In. 185.00
Patch, Jubilee Express, 1952, 2 ½ In. 7.00
Pin, Bobcat, Brass, C-Clasp Back, c.1949. . . . . 20.00
Pin, Strengthen The Arm Of Liberty, Gold Tone, ¾ x ½ In. 28.50
Poster, Scouts Today, Leaders Tomorrow, Kellogg's, Paper, c.1925, 30 ½ x 23 In. . . . . *illus* 1500.00
Poster, World War I, U.S.A. Bonds, Heyendecker, 30 x 20 In. . . . . *illus* 225.00
Suspender Clasps, Sterling Silver, Wanless & Co., England, 1 ½ x 1 ⅛ In. 200.00
Totem Pole, Carved, Multicolored, 6-Sided, Relief Carved Squares, Symbols, 23 In. 500.00
Uniform, Badges, Camp Chickagami, c.1950. . . . . 112.00
View-Master Reels, Boy Scout Jamboree, View-Master, 1955 . . . . . 75.00
Whistle, Brass, Chrome Plated, Emblem 23.00

BRADLEY & HUBBARD is a name found on many metal objects. Walter Hubbard and his brother-in-law, Nathaniel Lyman Bradley, started making cast iron clocks, tables, frames, andirons, lamps, chandeliers, sconces, and sewing birds in 1854 in Meriden, Connecticut. The company became Bradley & Hubbard Manufacturing Company in 1875. Charles Parker Company bought the firm in 1940. Their lamps are especially prized by collectors.

Clock, Lion, Blinking Eye, Painted, Cast Iron, Signed, 8 x 10 ¼ In. 4500.00
Cuspidor, Dragon, 11 In. 259.00
Cuspidor, Dragon, Cast Iron, Lift Lid, Metal Bowl, Marked, 6 x 12 In. 325.00
Inkstand, Art Nouveau, 3 ½ x 9 ½ x 6 ¾ In. 85.00
Lamp, 3-Light, Geometric Metal Over Green Slag Glass, c.1920, 15 x 22 In. 1067.00
Lamp, 3-Light, Gilt Metal Base, 8-Sided Shade, Green Striated Panels, 22 In. 400.00
Lamp, 3-Light, Leaded Glass, Tulips, Leaves, Hanging, 36 x 26 In. . . . . *illus* 2880.00

TIP
Be sure that any restorer, refinisher, or upholsterer working on your antique is insured.

Boy Scout, Poster, Scouts Today, Leaders Tomorrow, Kellogg's, Paper, c.1925, 30 ½ x 23 In.
$1500.00

Boy Scout, Poster, World War I, U.S.A. Bonds, Heyendecker, 30 x 20 In.
$225.00

TIP
Do not hide a key outside the house, not even in a key-holding stone. Burglars are smart.

Bradley & Hubbard, Lamp, 3-Light, Leaded Glass, Tulips, Leaves, Hanging, 36 x 26 In. $2880.00

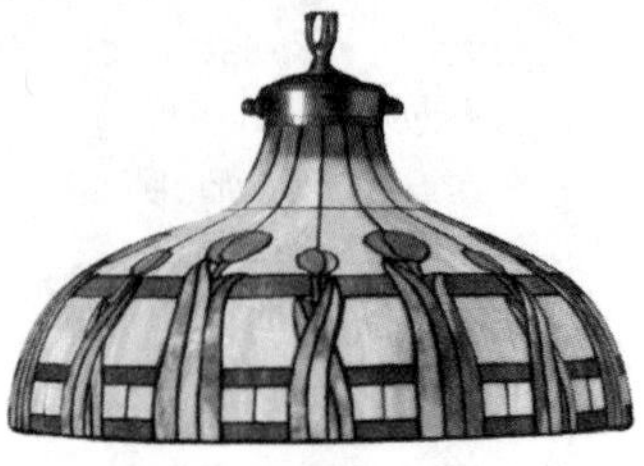

TIP
Brass that has been lacquered should be cleaned only with a solution of liquid dishwashing detergent and warm sudsy water, then rinsed in warm water and dried. Polish will harm the lacquer.

Bradley & Hubbard, Sconce, Copper, Slag Glass, Patina, 13 ¼ x 6 In., Pair $1200.00

TIP
Brass tarnishes more quickly in direct sunlight.

Lamp, 3-Light, Yellow Slag Shade, Green Metal Design Overlay, c.1910, 20 x 14 In. 1541.00
Lamp, 3-Owl Base, Domed Shade, 6-Sided Green Slag Glass, Leaves, 11 x 6 In. . . . 805.00 to 1100.00
Lamp, Electric, Frosted Globe, Etched, 31 x 7 ½ In. 280.00
Lamp, Electric, Hexagonal Shade, Slag Panels, Berry, Leaves, 24 In. 2415.00
Lamp, Telescoping Body, Caramel Curved Glass Shade, Floor. 115.00
Letter Holder, 2 Sections, Pierced, Scroll Feet, Cast Metal, Marked, 1920, 8 In. 55.00
Letter Holder, Brass, Reticulated Design, 12 In. 200.00
Sconce, Copper, Slag Glass, Patina, 13 ¼ x 6 In., Pair . . . . *illus* 1200.00
Sconce, Figural, Beveled Mirror, Cast Iron, 17 x 10 In. 80.00
Thermometer, Rampant Lion, Gilt, Metal, 6 ½ x 6 ½ In. 44.00

BRASS has been used for decorative pieces and useful tablewares since ancient times. It is an alloy of copper, zinc, and other metals. Additional brass items may be found under Bell, Candlestick, Tool, or Trivet.

Ashtray, Empire State Wine Co., State Seal, Art Nouveau Woman, Grapes, Holder, 5 x 7 x 4 In. 330.00
Basket, Hammered, Cast Iron Handle, Italy, 12 x 15 In. 88.00
Bed Warmer, Copper, Baluster Shape Wood Handle, Incised, Stamped, 41 x 12 In. 44.00
Bed Warmer, Floral Tooled Pan, Turned Wood Handle, 1800s, 45 In. 235.00
Bed Warmer, Flowers, Wood Handle, 47 x 12 In.. . . . . 55.00
Bed Warmer, Rooster, Flowers, Wood Handle, Incised, Stamped, Cherry Handle, 44 In. 66.00
Bed Warmer, Scrolls, Grain Painted Applewood Handle, Round Pan, 44 x 12 In.. . . . . 109.00
Bed Warmer, Spirals, Medallions, Maple Handle, 19th Century, 44 ½ In. 289.00
Bed Warmer, Swan, Engraved, Hinged, Copper Ring, Maple Handle, 42 x 11 x 3 In. 252.00
Bed Warmer, Wriggle Work, Iron Handle, Pierced Lid, 18th Century, 34 In. 50.00
Bedstead, White Variegated Onyx Stone Inserts, c.1890s, 66 x 84 x 57 In.. . . . . 374.00
Belt Buckle, University Of Alabama, Spread Wing Eagle, c.1930-40, 3 ¼ x 2 In. 12.00
Book, Horn, Cast, St. Paul's, A.D. 1729, Raised Alphabet, 5 ⅝ x 2 ½ In. 889.00
Bookrack, Romanov Eagle, Hinged, Arts & Crafts, 5 ¼ x 20 In.. . . . . 230.00
Brazier, Footed, Tripod, Punched Brass Base, Turned Wood Handle, 18th Century, 4 ¾ x 14 In. 374.00
Bucket, Coal, Riveted Construction, Handle, England, c.1720, 12 In.. . . . . 250.00
Candleholder, Abstract, 20th Century, 4 ¾ x 4 ⅛ x 4 ¼ In. 750.00
Candleholder, Frying Pan Shape, Copper Riveted Handle, 1 ¾ x 11 ¾ In. 77.00
Candlesnuffer, Cone Form, Handle, c.1770. . . . . 365.00
Candlesnuffer, Tray, Hourglass Form, Marked, IB, c.1720, 7 ¾ In. 427.00
Candlestand, Drip Tray, Flared Base, 4 ⅜ x 4 ⅜ In.. . . . . 715.00
Cannon, Signal, Iron Base, England, 18 In.. . . . . 600.00
Cigar Cutter, Bull, Lift Tail To Cut, 3 In. 460.00
Cigar Cutter, Frog, On Rock, 4 x 3 In. 748.00
Cigar Cutter, Mechanical Wheel, Wood, 7 In. 316.00
Cigar Cutter, Poodle, Bends At Waist, 2 In.. . . . . 173.00
Cigar Cutter, Singing Man, Holding Book, 8 In. 633.00
Cigar Cutter, Skull, On Books, Austria, 2 x 1 ½ In. 403.00
Cigar Cutter, Snake, Coiled, Albacore Shell, 6 x 4 In. 863.00
Cigar Holder, Putti Finial, Victorian, 10 In.. . . . . 295.00
Coffeepot, Espresso, Imperial Eagle Hallmark, Russia, c.1890, 10 In.. . . . . 234.00
Coffeepot, Imperial Eagle Hallmark, Russia, c.1890, 8 x 11 In.. . . . . 322.00
Crumber, Georgian, Mahogany, Shell Inlay, 9 In. 144.00
Easel, Flowers, Leaves, Vines, 20th Century, 69 In.. . . . . 549.00
Ewer, Hammered, Italy, 20th Century, 29 x 15 In. 29.00
Figure, Pheasant, 13 ½ In., Pair 18.00
Figure, Woman, Turkish Dress, Ivory, Onyx Base, White Enamel Jewels, Art Deco, 14 In. 5875.00
Foot Warmer, Wood, Copper, 5 x 12 x 10 In., Pair. 47.00
Garment Rack, Round Top, Finial, Sliding Hooks, Cast Iron Base, 1900s, 74 x 19 In. 167.00
Gong, Dinner, Stag's Head, Round, Oval Plaque Mount, Oak, Late 1800s, 22 x 12 In.. . . . . 518.00
Hand Warmer, Cranes, Deer, Ling Chih, Pierced, Chinese, 19th Century, 6 ½ In.. . . . . 415.00
Hat, Coat Rack, Salesman's Sample, 16 In.. . . . . 165.00
Jar, Silver & Patinated Brass, Ivory Finial, Paul Haustein, Cover, c.1929, 10 x 8 In. 8750.00
Kettle, Iron Bail Handle, Hudson's Bay Fur Trade Co., c.1875, 5 ¾ x 9 In.. . . . . 127.00
Kettle, Oval, Curved Spout, Dome Lid, Acorn Finial, c.1880, 9 ½ In. 380.00
Lavabo, Repousse Tank, Old Slavic Text, Shepherd, Shepherdess, Russia, 1800s, 11 In.. . . . . . 1180.00
Luggage Rack, Railroad, Wire Back & Shelf, Polished, 28 In. 259.00
Pomander, Egg Shape, Cut Decoration, c.1770, 1 ½ x 1 In. 100.00
Print Plate, Old Reading Beer, Reverse Print, Curved, 12 In., 2 Piece 58.00
Rattle, Whistle End, 18th Century. 350.00
Samovar, 2-Headed Eagle, Russia, Late 19th Century, 17 In. 266.00
Samovar, Russia, Late 19th Century, 15 ½ In. 472.00
Samovar, Wood Handles, Russia, c.1900, 28 In. . . . . *illus* 110.00

Sconce, Lozenges & Grapes, Repousse, Heart On Reflector, Sweden, 18th Century, 22 ½ In. . . 1872.00
Sconce, Tooled Arts & Crafts, Signed, Jarvie, 13 ½ x 6 x 2 ½ In. . . . 5100.00
Sculpture, Bengal Tiger, Paw Raised, c.1920, 8 x 11 x 5 In. . . . 176.00
Sculpture, Female Golfer, Hagenauer, Impressed Mark, 1 ½ x 4 In. . . . 450.00
Sculpture, Lotus Leaf, Polished, Oskar J.W. Hansen, 4 ½ x 15 In.. . . . 115.00
Sleigh, Bells, Strap, Eagle Finial, 10 ½ In. . . . 236.00
Stand, Pedestal, Flat Top, Raised Heart, Leaf, Geometric Cutwork, Scalloped, 9 ¾ x 8 x 8 In. . 44.00
Stirrups, Stylized Plumes, Flower, Leaves, Traditional Form, Patina, 19th Century, 5 x 9 In.. . 50.00
Stool, Barrel Shape, 6 Panels, Embossed, Chinese, 16 ¼ x 15 x 13 In. . . . 41.00
Tankard, Quart Measure, Scroll Handle, Tin Interior, England, c.1800, 6 In. . . . 88.00
Teakettle, Hinged Flat Handle, Domed, Goose Neck Spout, 9 ½ x 7 In. . . . 44.00
Teapot, Bail Handle, Louis & Co., Lexington, Ky., 19th Century, 7 ½ In.. . . . 2415.00
Tieback, Curtain, Ruby Glass Flower, Gilt Leaves, 10 ½ x 5 In., Pair . . . 140.00
Torchere, Baluster, Pierced, Oriental, 39 ½ In. . . . 75.00
Umbrella Stand, 2 Scenes, Woman, Seated, Fireplace, 20 x 9 In. . . . 55.00
Vase, Satyr Mask, Ring Handles, Baluster, 19 ¾ In. . . . 192.00
Watch Hutch, Courting Couple, Rooster Finial, Waltham Pocket Watch, Late 1800s, 14 In. . . 995.00
Watering Can, Spout, Loop Handles, Footed, Mid 19th Century, 26 x 23 In. . . . 110.00
Weight Set, 2 Ounces To 7 Pounds, Hallmarks, 1 ½ To 7 ⅛ In., 7 Piece . . . 288.00

BRASTOFF, *see Sascha Brastoff category.*

BREAD PLATE, *see various silver categories, porcelain factories, and pressed glass patterns.*

BRIDE'S BOWLS OR BASKETS were usually one-of-a-kind novelties made in American and European glass factories. They were especially popular about 1880 when the decorated basket was often given as a wedding gift. Cut glass baskets were popular after 1890. All bride's bowls lost favor about 1905. Bride's bowls and baskets may also be found in other glass sections. Check the index at the back of the book.

Amethyst, Amber Free-Form Handle, 1890s, 7 ⅝ x 6 ¾ In. . . . 125.00
Amethyst, Flat Panel Border, White Interior, Ruffled Rim, 3 ¼ x 10 In.. . . . 46.00
Blue, Diamond Quilted, White Cased, Ruffled Rim, Enameled Flowers, 5 ¼ x 12 ¾ In. . . . 1528.00
Blue Cased, Melon Ribbed, Frosted Ruffled Rim, Oval, 13 x 5 In. . . . 176.00
Blue Satin, Multicolored Coralene Stemmed Flowers, Leaves, 4-Footed, Handle, 11 In.. . . . 413.00
Blue Satin, Ruffled Edge, Shell Shape, Enameled Blossom, Webb, 12 x 3 ¼ In. . . . 225.00
Butterscotch, White, Enameled Flowers, Silver Plated Frame, Handle, 12 In. . . . *illus* 175.00
Butterscotch Interior, White, Orange Enameled Flowers, Silver Plated Frame, 12 x 12 In. . . 259.00
Cream, Enameled Flowers, Ruffled Edges, Metal Frame, Flowers, Scrolling, 10 ½ x 12 In. . . . 94.00
Green, White, Ruffled Rim, Silver Plated Frame, Pierced Handle, 1890, 17 In. . . . *illus* 384.00
Green Ruffled Rim, 4-Footed, Silver Plated Frame, Pierced Handles, 17 In. . . . 384.00
Iridescent, Green, Red Border, Fluted, Silver Plated Frame, Aurora, 10 ½ In.. . . . 259.00
Opal, Leaves, Robin, Fruit, Leaf Embossed, 13 In. . . . 354.00
Opal To Rose, Ruffled Rim, Multicolored Flowers, Figural Frame, 14 In. . . . 384.00
Opalescent, Cranberry Border, Thistle, Silver Plated Frame, Rockford, 11 ½ In. . . . 207.00
Pink, Enameled Decoration, Ruffled Edge, Silver Plated Frame, Handle, 1800s, 14 In. . . . 205.00
Pink, Ruffled Edge, Silver Plated Frame, Handle, 11 x 10 In. . . . 100.00
Pink, White, Griffin, Flower, Cameo, Silver Plated Frame, Handle, 10 ½ x 10 In. . . . 450.00
Pink, White Cased, Amber Ruffled Rim, 3 ⅜ x 9 ⅜ In.. . . . 47.00
Pink, White Cased, Amber Ruffled Rim, Silver Plated Frame, Rogers Smith, 9 ½ x 13 In. . . . 118.00
Pink, White Cased, Scalloped Rim, Floral Silver Plated Frame, Meriden, 12 ¾ In. . . . 206.00
Pink, Yellow Enameled Flowers, Ruffled, Embossed Meriden Frame, Handle, 10 In.. . . . 413.00
Pink & White Satin Cased, Frosted Twist Handle, Blue Flowers, 9 x 7 In. . . . 70.00
Pink Cased, Leaf Mold, Square Bowl, Silver Plated Frame, Handle, 10 x 9 In. . . . 150.00
Pink Cased, Satin, Melon Ribbed, Frosted Grass Ruffled Rim, Oval, 13 x 5 In. . . . 53.00
Pink Interior, Ruffled Edges, Gold Enameled Leaf Decoration, Metal Frame, 9 x 10 ½ In. . . . 235.00
Pink Satin, Clear Ruffled Rim, Pinched Corners, Enameled Flowers, 4 ½ x 8 In.. . . . 353.00
Pink Satin, Ribbed, Crimped, Frosted Glass Edge, 3 ¾ x 10 ¾ In. . . . 104.00
Pink Satin, Ribbed, Ruffled Rim, Crimped Border, 3 ¾ x 10 ¾ In. . . . 90.00
Purple, Yellow Enameled Flowers, Figural Frame, 1800s, 13 In. . . . 502.00
Rainbow Swirl, Oval, Metal Base, Blossom Branch, 5 ½ x 7 In. . . . 130.00
Ruffled, Green Opalescent, Pink, 6 ½ x 8 ½ In. . . . 70.00
White, Blue Windmill Scene, Square, Silver Plated Frame, Flowers, Masks, 8 x 8 ½ In. . . . 288.00
White, Pink Interior, Vaseline, Ruffled Rim, Silver Plated Frame, Handle, 12 ½ x 10 In. . . . 225.00
White Cased, Amber Ruffled Rim, Yellow Enameled Flowers, 4 x 10 x 10 In. . . . 104.00
White Ribbed, Pink Cased Lining, Applied Clear Fruit, Loop Handle, 12 In. . . . 230.00
Yellow, Orange Swirl, Melon Ribbed, Twisted Thorn Handle, 8 In. . . . 100.00

Brass, Samovar, Wood Handles, Russia, c.1900, 28 In.
$110.00

Bride's Bowl, Butterscotch, White, Enameled Flowers, Silver Plated Frame, Handle, 12 In.
$175.00

Bride's Bowl, Green, White, Ruffled Rim, Silver Plated Frame, Pierced Handle, 1890, 17 In.
$384.00

Bristol, Biscuit Jar, Opalescent, Flowers, Enameled, Silver Plated Cover, Handle, 6 ¾ In.
$77.00

Bronze, Brushpot, 4-Claw Dragon, Flaming Pearl, Relief, Cylindrical, Asia, 3 ½ x 2 ¼ In
$88.00

Bronze, Bust, Selenes, Horse, 30 x 38 In.
$3525.00

Bronze, Censer, Foo Dog, Brocade Ball, Chinese, 15 In.
$9480.00

BRISTOL glass was made in Bristol, England, after the 1700s. The Bristol glass most often seen today is a Victorian, lightweight opaque glass that is often blue. Some of the glass was decorated with enamels.

Biscuit Jar, Opalescent, Flowers, Enameled, Silver Plated Cover, Handle, 6 ¾ In. . . . . . . *illus* 77.00
Mug, American Eagle, White, Black, Red, White, Blue, Gold Trim, c.1825, 3 In. 1793.00
Vase, 2 Medallions, Birds, Dogwood Branch, Urn Shape, 14 In. 144.00
Vase, Birds, Flowers, Pink, Gold Trim, White Enameled Beaded Bands, 1800s, 13 In. 237.00
Vase, Blue, Coralene Roses, Shouldered, 7 ¾ In. 40.00
Vase, Blue, Enameled Flowers, Ruffled Rim, Handle, 8 ¼ In., Pair 55.00
Vase, Bud, Blue, Enameled Flowers, 5 In., Pair. 205.00
Vase, Capital Of The U.S. Washington, Buildings, White, Gold, Black, Early 1800s, 9 In. 1075.00
Vase, Classical Figures Scene, White Ground, Red Base, Footed, c.1860, 17 x 6 In., Pair. 293.00
Vase, Opal, Enameled Flowers, Gold Band, 19th Century, 13 ¼ x 5 ½ In., Pair 100.00

BRITANNIA, *see Pewter category*

BRONZE is an alloy of copper, tin, and other metals. It is used to make figurines, lamps, and other decorative objects. Bronze lamps are listed in the Lamp category. Pieces listed here date from the eighteenth, nineteenth, and twentieth centuries.

Ashtray, Elephant, Onyx Base, c.1920, 2 x 7 In. 64.00
Ashtray, Hermes, Horseshoe, Leather, c.1920, 6 ¼ x 6 ½ In. 1100.00
Bas Relief, Itasse, A., Mother Of God, Gilt, Inscribed, Paris, c.1870, 6 In.. . . . . 502.00
Basin, Animal Shape Feet, 12 ½ In.. . . . . 1528.00
Basket, Bird, Oval, Handles, Japan, c.1875, 5 In. 201.00
Blotter, Parrot Shape, Marked, Austria, 7 In. 400.00
Bowl, 2 Handles, Chinese, 4 ¼ x 7 ¼ In. 3510.00
Bowl, Lily Pad, Frog On Rim, Stem & Pad Foot, 4 ½ In. 50.00
Box, Liquor, Pagoda Shape, 3 Gilt Bottles, Stoppers, 4 Glasses, France, c.1905, 17 x 17 In.. . . . 9375.00
Brushpot, 4-Claw Dragon, Flaming Pearl, Relief, Cylindrical, Asia, 3 ½ x 2 ¼ In. . . . . . . *illus* 88.00
Bust, Athena, Upswept Hair, Corinthian Helmet, Engraved Eyes, Breast Plate, 4 ¼ In. 4025.00
Bust, Berthous, P.F., Woman, Patinated, Gilt, c.1900, 14 ¾ In. 5000.00
Bust, Boyle, John, Woman, Looking Up, Column Base, 25 ½ In.. . . . . 1793.00
Bust, Czar Nicholas II, Military Attire, Brown Patina, Russia, 19 In. 17700.00
Bust, Diana Of Versailles, 10 x 17 In. 863.00
Bust, George Washington, 24 In.. . . . . 5938.00
Bust, Gerhardt, Karl, U.S. Grant, Signed, 1885, 9 In. 1600.00
Bust, Jupiter, Turned Head, Cloak, Wavy Beard, Festoon, 5 x 4 ¼ In. 4715.00
Bust, Minerva, Upswept Hair, Corinthian Helmet, Engraved Crest, 4 ½ In. 1320.00
Bust, Peter The Great, In Armor, Wood Base, 12 ½ In.. . . . . 660.00
Bust, Selenes, Horse, 30 x 38 In. . . . . *illus* 3525.00
Bust, Tauregs, Man & Woman, Wood Plinth, Vienna, Geschutzt, Bergman, 5 In., Pair 3163.00
Bust, Van Der Straten, Georges, Woman, Smiling, Red Marble Base, Signed, 8 ¼ In. 345.00
Bust, Voltaire, Variegated Marble Socle, France, c.1900, 22 In.. . . . . 5625.00
Bust, Woman, Wavy Hair, Ruffled Neckline, c.1930, 19 ½ x 14 ½ In. 439.00
Candleholder, Gilt, Pierre Forsell, 1960s, 5 ¼ In., Pair. 938.00
Candleholder, Patinated, Jens Quistgaard, 1960s, 9 ¼ In., Pair. 4375.00
Cannon, Signal, Wood Base, 15 ½ In.. . . . . 325.00
Cannon, Signal, Wood Cradle, 27 ½ x 2 In. 990.00
Cannon, Wood Base, Wheels, France, 18th Century, 6 ¼ x 15 In.. . . . . 1870.00
Censer, Bombe Shape, Handles, Chinese, 4 ½ In.. . . . . 354.00
Censer, Dragon Shape Finial, Handle, Chinese, 12 x 10 ½ In.. . . . . 4425.00
Censer, Duck Shape, C-Form Neck, Open Beak, Almond Shaped Eyes, Japan, 13 ½ In.. . . . . 1180.00
Censer, Foo Dog, Brocade Ball, Chinese, 15 In. . . . . *illus* 9480.00
Censer, Foo Dog, Glass Eyes, Chinese, 18th Century, 9 ½ In.. . . . . 3851.00
Censer, Foo Dog Finial, Flared Handles, 3 Legs, Upturned Feet, Chinese, 21 In. 510.00
Censer, Gilt, Dragon Shape Lid, Handle, Chinese, 1800s, 8 ½ In. 179.00
Censer, Lotus Plant Shape, Japan, 19th Century, 9 ½ In.. . . . . 504.00
Censer, Pierced Egret Lid, Bail Handle, c.1775, 5 ½ x 7 In.. . . . . 173.00
Censer, Stylized Leaf, Lotus Flower Base, 4 ½ x 6 ½ In.. . . . . 6518.00
Censer, Taotie Masks, Fish, Waves, Chinese, 10 ½ x 10 ½ In. 472.00
Censer, Taotie Masks, Ring Handles, Hexagonal, Chinese, 7 In.. . . . . 502.00
Centerpiece, Bacchante, Silver, Gilt, Ram's Head Handles, Round, Paris, c.1875, 15 In. 7188.00
Centerpiece, Classical Woman, Symbols, Scroll Handles, Porcelain, France, c.1890, 14 x 19 In. 5750.00
Crane, Chinese, 19th Century, 65 In., Pair 4740.00
Cricket Box, Copper, Relief Design, Signed, Chinese, 8 ½ x 9 In.. . . . . 644.00
Cup, Ram's Head, Marble Base, Grand Tour, 19th Century, 7 In.. . . . . 650.00

Desk Clip, Hound Head, Cold Painted, Late 19th Century, 6 ½ x 2 ¾ In. 1778.00
Desk Set, Marble, 2 Bronze Dore Inkstands, Brass Feet, France, Late 1800s, 4 ½ x 12 In. 316.00
Desk Set, Marble, Gallery, Pineapple Finials, Urn, Cupids, 2 Wells, Bun Feet, 6 ½ x 14 In. 288.00
Ding, Stylized Dragon, Foo Dog Finials, Upright Handles, 3-Footed, Chinese, 9 ½ In. 5378.00
Ewer, Double Gourd, Bamboo Molded Handle, Korea, 10 In. 504.00
Ewer, Stupa Finial, Engraved Handle, Korea, 10 In. 2252.00
Garniture Set, Champleve Enamel, Classical Scenes, Blue, Clock, 2 Urns, 1899, 15 ½ In. 538.00
Garniture Set, Clock, Classical, Gilt Marble, 2 Maidens, Satyr, Urns, France, 1800s, 33 In. 14750.00
Garniture Set, Clock, Gilt Metal Putti, Swags, Porcelain Panels, 5-Light Candelabra, 24 In., Pair 1265.00
Garniture Set, Clock, Gothic Revival, Bronze Dore, Pendulum, 5-Cup Candelabra, c.1875, 20 In. 1265.00
Garniture Set, Clock, Porcelain Dial, Mask, 5-Light Candelabra, France, c.1900, 18 In. 1528.00
Garniture Set, Lily, Faience, Hand Painted, Clock, 5-Light Candelabra, c.1900, 28 In. 2124.00
Garniture Set, Vase, 2 Urns, Flowers, Cobalt Blue Ground, Gilt, Enamel, France, c.1890, 12 In. 5625.00
Hook, Baldaquin, Khmer, 8 In. 239.00
Incense Burner, Carved Lid, Ivory Finial, 3 Mask Legs, Handles, 10 ½ x 8 ¼ In. 5400.00
Incense Burner, Foo Dog Finial, Signed, Chinese, c.1890, 10 x 9 In. 760.00
Incense Burner, Foo Dogs, Cast, Heads Hinged At Neck, Wood Base, Oriental, 14 x 19 In., Pair 558.00
Incense Burner, Mythical Animal, Standing, Chinese, 15 In. 3200.00
Jardiniere, Applied Birds, Japan, 19th Century, 11 x 15 In. 643.00
Jardiniere, Bail Handle, Claw Feet, 10 x 31 x 23 In., Pair 4406.00
Letter Holder, Eagle, Spread Wings, Flowers, Glass Eye, Holder, 4 ½ x 7 ⅜ x 2 In. 355.00
Mirror Plateau, Louis XV, Children, Dog, Duck Mounts, Silver Wash, c.1880, 41 In. 12500.00
Pen Wipe, Boar Shape, Bristles, Early 20th Century, 1 ¾ In. 385.00
Phurba, Stand, 3 Transitional Faces Of Joy, Peace, Wrath, Skulls, Finial, Tibet, 1800s, 15 In. 270.00
Pitcher, Neoclassical, Putti, Mermaids, Figural Sculpted Handles, Patina, c.1850, 17 In., Pair 1003.00
Planter, Napoleon III, Brass, Blackamoors, Carrying Barrow, 7 x 4 x 12 ¼ In. 7500.00
Planter, Round Bowl, Ram's Heads, Claw Feet, Base, 43 ½ x 16 In. 1440.00
Plaque, 10 Buddhas, Seated, Rectangular, Korea, 18th Century, 16 x 13 In. 1541.00
Plaque, A. Lincoln, Relief Profile, Walnut, Oval, Stand, c.1905, 24 x 19 In. 546.00
Plaque, Banishment From The Garden, France, Early 20th Century, 9 ¾ In. 236.00
Plaque, Bazor, Lucien, Le Doute, Classical Male Nude, Lyre, Sculpted, 1925, 8 x 12 In. 780.00
Plaque, Christopher Columbus, 15 ½ x 25 In. 1380.00
Plaque, Clodion, Napoleon III, Putti, Hunting Dog, Frolicking Goat, 11 x 18 In., Pair 1320.00
Plaque, Fraser, James Earle, Roosevelt, Bas Relief, Brown Patina, c.1920, 12 ¾ x 10 In. 443.00
Plaque, Judas Kissing Jesus, High Relief, Germany, 1800s, 6 x 9 In. 590.00
Plaque, Male Athlete, Holding Laurel, Winged Trophy, Wood Mount, 14 x 6 ⅝ In. 220.00
Plaque, Surya, Holding Sword, Shield, India, 18th Century, 10 In. 237.00
Plaque, Villanis, E., 3 Nudes, Painted, Signed, 17 In. 1500.00
Pocket Watch Holder, Woman Holding Scroll, 5 ½ In. 70.00
Reliquary, Cathedral Shape, Fish Scale Roof, Crucifix Finial, 1880, 18 x 14 x 6 In. 1045.00
Reliquary, Flanking Angels, Red Exposition Window, Gilt, Italy, 1800s, 19 In. *illus* 1770.00
Salver, 6 Bacchus Masks, Rosette Center Raised Rim, Silver, Gilt, 1800s, 16 In. 561.00
Samovar, Tula Tray, Brass, Handles, Russia, Mid 19th Century, 16 x 23 In. 388.00
Sconce, Dore, Mirror Back, 2 Paired Socket Arms, Ornate, France, c.1900, 15 x 18 In., Pair 1485.00
Sculpture, Angel, Gilt, Kneeling, Wood Stand, France, 1800s, 18 In., Pair 7080.00
Sculpture, Barye, Antoine Louis, Stag, Standing, Suisse Fres, c.1850, 20 In. 4012.00
Sculpture, Barye, Tigre Terrassant Une Biche, Patina, Signed, 11 x 18 x 6 In. *illus* 2500.00
Sculpture, Bathing Beauty, Woman, In Swim Attire, Red Marble Plinth, 15 ¾ In. 374.00
Sculpture, Bauchod, Woman, Flowers, Art Nouveau, Round Marble Base, Signed, 24 ¾ In. 440.00
Sculpture, Bear, Prowling, Russia, c.1950, 8 x 15 In. 708.00
Sculpture, Bengal Tiger, c.1920, 8 x 11 x 5 In. 176.00
Sculpture, Bergman, African Trader, Kneeling On Mat, c.1900, 8 ⅛ In. 2868.00
Sculpture, Bergman, Servant Girl, Draping Woman In Towel, Namgreb, Vienna, 11 ½ In. 12650.00
Sculpture, Bird, On Branch, Green-Brown Patina, Signed, 19th Century, 4 ½ In. 489.00
Sculpture, Bird, On Branch, Acorns, Basket, Geschutzt, Vienna, 4 x 5 ¾ In. 575.00
Sculpture, Bodhisattva, 4-Heads, Arms Standing, Lotus Throne, Halo, Java, 13 In. 1304.00
Sculpture, Bodhisattva, Seated On Lotus Throne, Tibet, 18 In. 837.00
Sculpture, Boisseau, Emile-Andre, Figaro, Title On Base, 19 ½ In. 3055.00
Sculpture, Bonheur, Isidore, Lioness, 12 x 5 ¼ In. 2070.00
Sculpture, Bonheur, Lionne A L'Affut, Patina, Signed, Early 1900s, 7 ¾ x 18 ½ In. 1725.00
Sculpture, Boschetti, Benedetto, Nude Woman, Reclining, Italy, 23 x 23 x 9 ½ In. 2400.00
Sculpture, Bouraine, M., Penthesilia, Queen Of The Amazons, Silver, c.1925, 21 x 31 In. 15000.00
Sculpture, Bouraine, Marcel-Andre, Master Of The Beast, Cold Painted, Ivory, 1920s, 24 ¼ In. 37500.00
Sculpture, Bouval, Maurice, Flamenco Dancer, Draped Attire, Signed, France, 15 ¾ In. 1500.00
Sculpture, Buddha, Gilt, Seated In Dhyanasana, Lotus Throne, Tibetan-Chinese, 14 ½ In. 359.00
Sculpture, Buddha, Head, Arched Eyebrows, Incised Eyes, Aquiline Nose, 12 ½ In. 203.00
Sculpture, Buddha, Seated, Flame Halo, Gilt, Chinese, 18th Century, 8 ¼ In. 5925.00

George Washington's Hatchet

A cast bronze hatchet labeled "Washington Inaugurated President of the U.S. Apr. 30, 1789" is one of the most misunderstood antiques. It certainly isn't the hatchet used to chop the mythological cherry tree (the story of the cherry tree first appeared in 1809, a decade after Washington died). The hatchet was distributed in 1899 to commemorate the 100th anniversary of Washington's inauguration.

Bronze, Reliquary, Flanking Angels, Red Exposition Window, Gilt, Italy, 1800s, 19 In.
$1770.00

Bronze, Sculpture, Barye, Tigre Terrassant Une Biche, Patina, Signed, 11 x 18 x 6 In.
$2500.00

As always, the edited listings in *Kovels' Antiques & Collectibles Price Guide 2010* aren't available on any website, but readers should visit Kovels.com for information on trends, tips, reproductions, marks, old prices, and more!

Bronze, Sculpture, Buddha, Standing, Gilt, Thailand, 1700s, 44 In.
$2048.00

Bronze, Sculpture, Dog, Whippet, Seated, Octagonal Socle, Marble Base, 41 ½ In., Pair
$7110.00

Bronze, Sculpture, Esherick, Wharton, Horse Race, 1926, 4 x 7 x 2 ½ In.
$4800.00

Bronze, Sculpture, Girl, Kneeling, Lamb, Art Deco, Marked, 8 ¼ x 17 ½ In.
$2820.00

Sculpture, Buddha, Seated In Dhyanasana, Lotus Throne, 1800s, Thailand, 20 ½ In. 388.00
Sculpture, Buddha, Seated On Throne, Gilt, Chinese, 18th Century, 8 ¼ In. 5629.00
Sculpture, Buddha, Standing, Gilt, Thailand, 1700s, 44 In. . . . . *illus* 2048.00
Sculpture, Bull, Walking, Head Lowered, Oval, Green Marble Plinth, 14 ½ In. 1067.00
Sculpture, Caesar, Doris, Nude Woman, Standing, Arms Behind Back, 9 ¾ In. 1195.00
Sculpture, Cain, A., Rooster, Crowing, Brown Patina, France, c.1890, 19 In. 3540.00
Sculpture, Cansonni, Ambrogio, Justice, Patina, Signed, Italy, 1900s, 19 ¼ In. 345.00
Sculpture, Carie, Warrior, Griffins, Marked, 12 ¼ In. 413.00
Sculpture, Cartier, T., Tiger, Saber Tooth, Marble Plinth, Signed, 17 ¾ In. 330.00
Sculpture, Cat, Seated, Chinese, 18th Century, 8 ¼ In. 2370.00
Sculpture, Chariot, Horses, Sepia & Black Marble Base, c.1850, 5 x 11 In. 587.00
Sculpture, Chiparus, D.H., Boy, Little Clown, Ivory, Marble Base, France, 7 ¾ In. 3120.00
Sculpture, Chiparus, D.H., Children Sledding, Ivory, Marble Base, France, 11 x 6 x 9 In. 4500.00
Sculpture, Chiparus, D.H., Friends Forever, Cold Painted, Ivory, c.1928, 24 ¾ In. 43750.00
Sculpture, Classical Nude, Holding A Star, Plinth, France, 1800s, 36 In. 1062.00
Sculpture, Clodion, Bacchanal Satyr, Children, Inscribed, France, c.1810, 18 In. 1770.00
Sculpture, Colinet, C., Theban Dancer, Gilt, Cold Painted, Ivory, 10 ¼ In. 35000.00
Sculpture, Colinet, C., Woman Snake Dancer, Ivory, Marble Base, 12 ½ x 13 x 5 ¾ In. 7200.00
Sculpture, Coulon, J., Aegina & Zeus, Brown Patina, France, c.1900, 25 In. 5428.00
Sculpture, Cupid & Psyche, Gilt, Porphyry Base, France, Late 19th Century, 17 x 6 ¾ In., Pair 7500.00
Sculpture, Dallin, Cyrus, Appeal To The Great Spirit, Signed, c.1944, 11 x 16 x 18 In. 1200.00
Sculpture, Dancing Flapper, Brown Patina, Black Marble Socle, 20th Century, 14 In. 413.00
Sculpture, D'Aste, J., Kissing Putti, Green, Brown Patina, 26 x 15 In. 2242.00
Sculpture, Deer, Backward Curving Antlers, Cold Painted, Austria, 3 ¾ In. 207.00
Sculpture, Deity, Gilt, Stepped Base, Mandala, Sino-Tibetan, 17 In. 2714.00
Sculpture, Deity, Seated, Crossed Arms, Weapon, Scrolled Headdress, Chinese, 15 x 6 In. 3600.00
Sculpture, Dervish, Standing, Geschutzt, Vienna, 7 ⅞ & 6 ½ In., 2 Piece 2588.00
Sculpture, Descamps, J.B., Lion, Green Patina, 5 x 18 x 12 In. 1093.00
Sculpture, Diana The Huntress, Seated, Dog, Bow, Quiver Of Arrows, 26 x 12 x 10 In. 2880.00
Sculpture, Dog, Dachshund, Sleeping Hat, Pillow, Cold Painted, Black, Green, Austria, 2 In. . 205.00
Sculpture, Dog, Setter, Green Marble Dish, Cold Painted, Austria, 4 ¾ x 15 ⅜ In. 201.00
Sculpture, Dog, Whippet, Reclining, Marble Base, France, 6 ¾ x 8 ¾ x 4 ¾ In., Pair. 1680.00
Sculpture, Dog, Whippet, Seated, Octagonal Socle, Marble Base, 41 ½ In., Pair. . . . . *illus* 7110.00
Sculpture, Doriot, J., Joan Of Arc, Brown Patina, France, c.1900, 25 In. 1534.00
Sculpture, D'Orleans, M., Joan Of Arc, Maid, Armor, Bowed Head, France, c.1890, 20 In. 2596.00
Sculpture, Dubois, P., Chanteur Florentin, Signed, France, 1865, 19 In. 1888.00
Sculpture, Dubois, P., Woman, Praying, Signed, 25 ½ In. 2640.00
Sculpture, Duboy, P., Allegory Of Music, Woman, Musical Instruments, Gilt, c.1878, 14 In. . . 3776.00
Sculpture, Eagle, Raised Wings, Claws Extended, Patina, c.1800, 12 In. 999.00
Sculpture, Elephant, Brown Patina, 4-Character Mark, Mid 20th Century, 5 ½ x 7 ¾ In. 460.00
Sculpture, Elephant, Ivory Tusks, Fight 3 Tigers, Japan, 19th Century, 20 ½ x 15 x 6 In. 2880.00
Sculpture, Epstein, Jacob, Woman, Nude, Standing, 1951, 14 ½ In. 3068.00
Sculpture, Esherick, Wharton, Horse Race, 1926, 4 x 7 x 2 ½ In. . . . . *illus* 4800.00
Sculpture, Finelli, Woman, Nude, Standing, Right Hand On Hip, Touching Hair, 36 In. 797.00
Sculpture, Foo Dog, Seated, Plinth Base, Chinese, 5 ¾ In., Pair. 300.00
Sculpture, Foo Dog, Seated, Raised Platform, Oriental, 16 x 8 ¼ In., Pair 702.00
Sculpture, Fox, Hunting Rabbit, Rabbit Head Tucked In Base, Marble, 9 x 5 ¼ In. 978.00
Sculpture, Fratin, Racing Greyhounds, Patinated, Signed, 19th Century, 5 x 12 ¼ In. 3450.00
Sculpture, Fremiet, E., Knight, Suit Of Mail, Credo Banner, Brown Patina, France, c.1900 . . . 6136.00
Sculpture, Gallo, I., Woman With Greyhound, Patina, Green Marble Base, Signed, 25 ¾ In. . 1430.00
Sculpture, Gaudez, Adrien Etienne, Man Drawing Sword, Patina, 19 ½ In. 1150.00
Sculpture, Gaudez, Esmerelda, Brown Patina, c.1890, 28 In. 3540.00
Sculpture, Gechter, T., Unwanted Visitor, Horse & Lizard, France, c.1840, 16 In. 1298.00
Sculpture, Girl, Kneeling, Lamb, Art Deco, Marked, 8 ¼ x 17 ½ In. . . . . *illus* 2820.00
Sculpture, Goor, Ilana, Birds, On Line, Signed, 20th Century, 72 In. 1434.00
Sculpture, Gossin, L., Young Girl At Fountain, France, c.1900, 21 In. 2124.00
Sculpture, Graham, R., Female Torso, Free-Form Base, c.1975, 20 In. 3600.00
Sculpture, Graham, R., Nude, Armless Male, Mounded Gold, Cone, Black, 1986, 15 In. 24000.00
Sculpture, Grass, Philippe, Icarus, Brown Patina, France, c.1750, 21 In. 3068.00
Sculpture, Gregoire, L., Girl With Braids, Brown Patina, 1872, 19 In. 1180.00
Sculpture, Greyhounds, 19th Century, 18 ½ x 39 ½ In., Pair. 2938.00
Sculpture, Griffin, On Demi Dome, Plinth Base, 15 ½ x 7 In., Pair. 2233.00
Sculpture, Guanyin, Ivory, Standing, On Clouds, Japan, 16 In. 660.00
Sculpture, Guanyin, On Elephant, With Lotus, Leaf, Pearl Of Wisdom, Gilt, Chinese, 12 x 10 In. 960.00
Sculpture, Guanyin, Seated, Double Lotus Throne, Wearing Diadem, Chinese, 10 In. 502.00
Sculpture, Guilbert, E., Napoleon On Horseback, 16 x 14 In. 1800.00
Sculpture, Guittet, Georges Henri, Water Carrier, Brown Patina, Signed, 21 In. 6250.00

Sculpture, Hercules, Battling Serpent, Marble Base, 23 x 10 In. 460.00
Sculpture, Hermes, Fortuna, Brown Patina, After Jean De Bologne, Late 1800s, 32 In., Pair. . 5000.00
Sculpture, Hoffman, M., Gaelic Dancer, Scottish Attire, Arm Raised, On Hip, 13 ¾ In.. ...... 2629.00
Sculpture, Homage To Sir Isaac Newton, Falling Apple, Marble Base, 15 ¼ In. 2640.00
Sculpture, Humphriss, Indian Chief, Wounded Warrior, Bowl Of Water, 20 In.. .... 3585.00
Sculpture, Huntington, Anna, Alligator, Signed, 1968, 5 ⅝ x 12 ¾ In. 6210.00
Sculpture, Indian Tiger Hunt, Elephant, Hunters, Attacking Tiger, Painted, 9 x 10 In. 12650.00
Sculpture, Korschann, C., Woman, Among Flowers, In Vase, Gilt, Czechoslovakia, c.1900, 6 In. 649.00
Sculpture, Kowarzik, J., Blacksmith, Children, Germany, c.1900, 13 In.. .... 885.00
Sculpture, LaLanne, Claude, Surmulot, Mouse, Tail Ending In Leaf, No. 2, 1987, 5 In....... 12500.00
Sculpture, Laurent, E., Psyche, Slate Plinth, France, c.1880, 8 In.. .... 1121.00
Sculpture, Lenordez, P., Horse, Dog, Fox Hunting Accessories, France, Signed, 14 x 10 ¾ In. . 3600.00
Sculpture, Leroux, G., Jeune Fille Arabe, Woman, Water Jug On Head, c.1930, 18 In. 2360.00
Sculpture, Les Feuilles D'Automne, Wood Base, After Hippolyte Francois Moreau, 31 ½ In. . . 2360.00
Sculpture, Levasseur, H., Angel, Children Asleep On Wing, 30 x 15 x 14 ½ In. 5750.00
Sculpture, Maiden, Pouring Water, Basin, Urns, c.1900, 7 x 4 x 3 In. 9775.00
Sculpture, Man, On Horseback, After Heinz Mueller, Austria, c.1900, 12 ¼ x 11 ¼ In.. ...... 690.00
Sculpture, Margulies, Isidore, Nude Woman Torso, 24 x 12 ½ In.. .... 3640.00
Sculpture, Marioton, E., Vainqueur, Archer, Laurel Branch, France, c.1900, 28 In. 3304.00
Sculpture, McAriotonse, Man, Playing Mandolin, Signed, 30 ½ In.. .... 1210.00
Sculpture, McCain, Buck, American Indian On Horseback, Invocation & Requiem, 10 In.... 440.00
Sculpture, Men, Carrying Wide Rim Bowl On Shoulders, Art Deco, 13 ¼ In. 3851.00
Sculpture, Mene, P.J., Dog, Irish Setter, Patina, Inscribed, 1800s, 8 ½ x 13 x 5 In. ..... *illus* 1980.00
Sculpture, Mercury, Resting, Nude, Winged Sandals, Marble, Early 1900s, 20 In. 1778.00
Sculpture, Moigniez, Jules, Bird Feeding Chicks, Oval Base, Signed, 12 ¾ x 8 ¼ In.. .... 1778.00
Sculpture, Moigniez, Jules, Dog, Seated, Raised Black Plinth, Signed 5 ½ In.. .... 960.00
Sculpture, Moigniez, Jules, Dog, Setter, Pheasant In Mouth, Marble Plinth, 17 In. ..... *illus* 948.00
Sculpture, Moigniez, Jules, Horse, Saddle, Grassy Plinth, Signed, 10 ½ x 14 ¼ In.. .... 863.00
Sculpture, Monk, 2 Robes Flowing, Arm Raised, Gilt, Sino-Tibetan, 5 ½ In.. .... 1652.00
Sculpture, Moreau Lecourtier, H.& P., Le Piqueux Sonnant De La Trompe, Signed, 31 ½ In. . 3042.00
Sculpture, Moses, Seated, Tablet, Dark Patina, France, 1800s, 20 In. 1534.00
Sculpture, Muller, H., Sportsman, Gun Under Cloak, Brown Patina, Signed, 9 ½ In.. .... 1093.00
Sculpture, Napoleon, Standing, Military Dress, Cannonballs, Oval Base, 10 ⅛ In.. .... 356.00
Sculpture, Naps, Cossack, On Horseback, Signed, Russia, Early 1900s, 12 x 9 ¼ In. 5520.00
Sculpture, Nestor, Emile Joseph, Woman, In Flowing Flowered Dress, Art Nouveau, Patina, 9 In. 411.00
Sculpture, Nude, Wearing Feathered Hat, Marble Base, Art Deco, Signed, 12 ½ In. 822.00
Sculpture, Nude Woman, Holding Garland, Roses, Cylinder Stand, Ivory, Priess, c.1920, 11 In. 5900.00
Sculpture, Oge, Pierre, Mephistopheles, Dark Brown Patina, 32 In. 4740.00
Sculpture, Oge, Pierre, Renaissance Woman, Holding Stem, Oval Base, Signed, 30 In., Pair. . 1059.00
Sculpture, Parvati, Standing, Round Lotus Plinth, India, 20 ½ In.. .... 299.00
Sculpture, Peaucelle, Joan Of Arc, Marble Base, French, 20th Century, 17 ¼ In. 558.00
Sculpture, Penshansky-Glasser, N., Woman, Seated, 11 x 11 In. 705.00
Sculpture, Pompon, F., Coq, Patina, c.1913, 10 x 7 In.. .... 37500.00
Sculpture, Pompon, F., Panthere Noire, Patina, Valsuani Mark, c.1925, 6 x 15 In.. .... 80500.00
Sculpture, Prawn, Inset Mother-Of-Pearl Shell, Early 20th Century, 10 In. 411.00
Sculpture, Presard, Woman, Seated, Arranging Necklace, Porcelain, Red Marble Base, Signed, 13 In. 2013.00
Sculpture, Prost, Maurice, Panther, Black, Patina, Marble Base, 7 ⅜ x 14 In. 6875.00
Sculpture, Putti, Cornucopia, Patinated, Marble & Ormolu Pedestal, Signed, 8 x 2 In., Pair . 1293.00
Sculpture, Rancoulet, Ernest, Spaniard, Round Base, 15 x 50 In.. .... 3105.00
Sculpture, Rattlesnake, After Frederic Remington, Patinated, Green Marble Stand, 22 ¼ In. . 1495.00
Sculpture, Rebecca At The Well, Signed, 20th Century, 27 In. 588.00
Sculpture, Robus, Hugo, Girl Washing Hair, Wood Base, 1939, 8 x 14 In.. .... 2875.00
Sculpture, Russell, Assiniboine Warrior, Signed, c.1913, 10 ½ In.. .... 2185.00
Sculpture, Salmones, Victor, Boy With Folded Arms, Signed, 9 ½ In.. .... 1770.00
Sculpture, Schmidt, O., Man Wrestling Snake, Marble Base, 13 x 25 In.. .... 2400.00
Sculpture, Seated Goddess Tara, Lotus Base, Tibet, c.1900, 8 In.. .... 1180.00
Sculpture, Shiva, Dancing Apasmara Purusha, India, c.1800, 9 In. 1534.00
Sculpture, Shiva, Dancing On Lotus, With Instrument, India, c.1900, 6 In.. .... 177.00
Sculpture, Spring, Winged Child, Rouge De Fer Marble Base, France, 19th Century, 18 In.... 418.00
Sculpture, Stag, After Charles Paillet, Patinated, Signed, France, 20th Century, 24 x 18 In. . . 1293.00
Sculpture, Steiner, L., Cupid, Psyche, Brown, Germany, c.1880, 28 In. 7500.00
Sculpture, Stork, Frog In Beak, Cold Painted, Early 20th Century, 2 ½ In.. .... 267.00
Sculpture, Turner, Avis, Altar Sticks, Angel Shape, Nude, c.1988, 30 In., 3 Piece Set. 2151.00
Sculpture, Turolt, E., Nude Boy On Horseback, Black Pedestal Base, 46 In. 5378.00
Sculpture, Turtle, Champleve Shell, Lift Top, Patina, Cartouche, Japan, 1900s, 1 ¾ x 6 ¾ In. 575.00
Sculpture, Ulrich, J., Woman Reclining On Chair, Skirt Hides Drawer, Marble, Ivory, 6 ½ x 9 In. 4800.00
Sculpture, Van Der Kant, Wim, Suspensus, Brown Patina, Signed, 25 ½ In.. .... 2006.00

Bronze, Sculpture, Mene, P.J., Dog, Irish Setter, Patina, Inscribed, 1800s, 8 ½ x 13 x 5 In.
$1980.00

Bronze, Sculpture, Moigniez, Jules, Dog, Setter, Pheasant In Mouth, Marble Plinth, 17 In.
$948.00

TIP

Removing stickers from collectibles can be a problem. Try these on glass or ceramics, not paper. First, try to remove a paper sticker with water. Then try to rub off the glue or try to dissolve the glue with paint thinner (look for toluene or xylene products). Don't use very much and use it quickly. Alcohol and lacquer thinner can be used on ceramics or glass, but not on wood or paint because it will damage the finish. Transparent tape or adhesive tape is harder. You have to try to get the solvent under the tape. The last resort is to scrape off the tape, which may damage the finish.

Bronze, Sculpture, Wagner, C., No Foolin', Grizzly Bear, Standing, 2/35, Signed, 78, 16 x 16 x 12 In.
$825.00

Brownies, Andirons, Male, Female, Legs Spread, Hands On Hips, Cast Iron, Late 1800s, 16 x 8 In.
$300.00

Brownies, Humidor, Sailor Bust, Defender On Rim, Figural, Majolica, Continental, Palmer Cox, 6 In.
$140.00

Brush, Bank, Brownie, Green Hat
$30.00

Sculpture, Venus, In The Shell, Brown, Green Base, Inscribed, A.M., France, c.1935, 7 In. 236.00
Sculpture, Villanis, E., Woman, With Harp, Sappho, 36 x 12 ½ x 9 ½ In. 8050.00
Sculpture, Wager, Industry, Man Holding Tool, Signed, 24 In. 460.00
Sculpture, Wagner, C., No Foolin', Grizzly Bear, Standing, Signed, 78, 16 x 16 x 12 In. .... *illus* 825.00
Sculpture, Warner, Carl, Grizzly Bear, Inscribed, 20th Century, 16 x 17 In. 863.00
Sculpture, Warrior, Standing With Spear, Chinese, 20th Century, 32 x 14 ½ x 14 In. 468.00
Sculpture, William Tell, Standard, Crossbow, Son Holding Apple, Signed, 14 x 12 In. 1380.00
Sculpture, Winans, Walter, Buffalo Bill, On His Horse Charlie, 1890, 15 ¾ In. 6168.00
Sculpture, Woman, Wings, Wreath, Horn, Gilt, Marble Base, France, c.1890, 26 In. 8750.00
Sculpture, Yarnan, A., Nude Woman, Standing, 20th Century, 15 In. 323.00
Tazza, Greek Revival, Center Medallion, Anthemion, Mask Handles, 1890s, 11 x 16 In. 450.00
Tazza, Hache, E., Cavalier, Castle, Lion Handles, Signed, France, 1900s, 17 In. 443.00
Tazza, Head In Relief, Laurel Wreath, Strapwork, Cupid, Swag & Tassel, Dore, 5 ¾ In. 288.00
Tazza, Renaissance Revival, Fluted, Leaf Tip Trumpet Foot, Leaf Scrolls, 10 x 3 ¼ In. 356.00
Tray, 2 Male Profiles, Headdresses, Garland, Latin Text, A. Stone, c.1917, 7 x 5 In. 3318.00
Tray, Nude, Reclining, Swirling Flower Patch, Owl, Art Nouveau, 10 ½ x 7 ½ In. 345.00
Umbrella Stand, Art Nouveau, Multicolored Design, 23 ½ x 9 In. 440.00
Umbrella Stand, Brown Bear, Standing, Holding Branch Form Ring, 28 In. 425.00
Umbrella Stand, Landscape, Gilt, Japan, 23 ½ In. 267.00
Urn, Bird & Cherry Blossom, Relief Design, Japan, Late 19th Century, 10 ½ x 13 In. 322.00
Urn, Charles X, Gilt, Patina, Marble Base, Bronze Wreath Mount, 9 In., Pair 2185.00
Urn, Cover, Cherub, Holding Cornucopia, 19th Century, 15 ¾ In. 3588.00
Urn, Eagle, Cherry Blossom Branches, Dark Brown Patina, Japan, c.1885, 22 x 17 In. 1045.00
Urn, Empire Style, Garniture, Applied Medallions, Marble Base, France, Late 1800s, 15 In., Pair 224.00
Urn, Figures, Leaves, Blue, Enamel, Raised Field, c.1850s, 12 x 16 In. 234.00
Urn, Serpents, Cherub, Green Patina, Marked, Depose, 6 ¾ In. 300.00
Vase, Birds, Flowers, Baluster, 3-Footed, Round Base, Japan, 18 In., Pair 780.00
Vase, Delbaux, A., Flower, Pink, Cloisonne, Pillow, Signed, France, 4 In. 81.00
Vase, Dragon, Red Drips, Bulbous, Brown Patina, Japan, 1900s, 11 In. 413.00
Vase, Flattened Oval, Dragon Handles, Red Patina, Ming Dynasty, Chinese, 8 ½ In. 448.00
Vase, Flower, Ho Ho Twins, Holding Flared Rim, Cast, Cloud Feet, Chinese, 5 ¾ In. 120.00
Vase, Flowers, Blue Ground Champleve, Gilt Mask Handles, Paris, c.1890, 15 In., Pair 6250.00
Vase, Geometrics, Patina, Cylindrical, Japan, 19th Century, 9 ¼ In. 540.00
Vase, Gold, Silver Damascene, Patina, Handles, Late 1800s, 12 x 7 In., Pair 5938.00
Vase, Landscape, Shou Figures, Silver, Copper, Foo Dog Handles, 12 In., Pair 178.00
Vase, Lid, Courting Couple, Porcelain, Painted Cobalt Blue Ground, France, 1885, 14 x 19 In. 5750.00
Vase, Mt. Fuji, Cranes, Tied Brocade Bag Shape, Gilt, Japan, 19 In. 1007.00
Wall, Sconce, Figural, Opposing Arms, Holding Torch, 9 x 5 x 15 In., Pair 1175.00

BROWNIES were first drawn in 1883 by Palmer Cox. They are characterized by large round eyes, downturned mouths, and skinny legs. Toys, books, dinnerware, and other objects were made with the Brownies as part of the design.

Andirons, Male, Female, Legs Spread, Hands On Hips, Iron, Late 1800s, 16 x 8 In. .... *illus* 300.00
Game, Bowling, Ball, Wood, Paper Label, Palmer Cox, c.1892, 13 In. 805.00
Humidor, Sailor Bust, Defender On Rim, Majolica, Palmer Cox, 6 In. .... *illus* 140.00
Ornament, Hand Formed Legs, Blown Glass, Painted, Palmer Cox, 4 ¾ In. 325.00
Ornament, Hand Formed Legs Protruding From Head, Blown Glass, Palmer Cox, 5 In. 1500.00
Paperweight, 3 Brownies, Standing On Hill, Stars In Sky, Millville, 3 ⅛ In. 50.00
Rattle, Brownie, Standing On Ring, Painted, Celluloid, Palmer Cox, Japan, 6 x 1 ¾ In. 27.00
Stein, Brownies In Forest, Blue Salt Glaze, Relief, Inlaid Lid, Marked, 131, Gerz, ½ Liter 518.00
Toy, Drummer, Paper Lithograph, Wood, Palmer Cox, 8 x 3 In. 22.00
Tray, Brownies, Ice Cream, Eating, Singing, Palmer Cox, 13 x 10 ½ In. 99.00

BRUSH Pottery was started in 1925. George Brush first worked in 1901 in Zanesville, Ohio. He started his own pottery in 1907, but it burned to the ground soon after. In 1909 he became manager of the J.W. McCoy Pottery. In 1911, Brush and J.W. McCoy formed the Brush-McCoy Pottery Co. After a series of name changes, the company became The Brush Pottery in 1925.It closed in 1982. Old Brush was marked with impressed letters or a palette-shaped mark. Some new pieces are being marked in raised letters or with a raised mark. Collectors favor the figural cookie jars made by this company. Because there was a company named Brush-McCoy, there is great confusion between Brush and Nelson McCoy pieces. See McCoy category for more information.

BRUSH WARE
MARK

Bank, Brownie, Green Hat .... *illus* 30.00
Candleholder, Cleo, Art Nouveau, 12 ½ In., Pair 215.00
Cookie Jar, Bunny Chef, 13 ½ In. 83.00
Cookie Jar, Treasure Chest 17.00
Vase, Princess, Angle Handles, Yellow, Green, Flower, 1960s, 12 x 7 In. 115.00

Vase, Princess, Art Deco, 1960s, 12 ¼ x 7 In. 115.00
Vase, Sylvan II, Double Handles, No. 787, 1935, 5 x 8 In. 145.00

BRUSH-MCCOY, *see Brush category and related pieces in McCoy category.*

BUCK ROGERS was the first American science fiction comic strip. It started in 1929 and continued until 1967. Buck has also appeared in comic books, movies, and, in the 1980s, a television series. Any memorabilia connected with the character Buck Rogers is collectible.

Badge, Commander, Solar Scouts Space Ship, Silvered Brass, 1936-42, 1 ¾ In. 141.00
Badge, Member, Solar Scouts, Cream Of Wheat Premium, 1936-42, Pair 113.00
Flashlight, Sonic Ray, Light Beam, Buzz, Code Book, Plastic, Box, c.1955, 7 ½ In. 237.00
Jigsaw Puzzle, Atomic Bomber, Dick Calkins, Puzzle Craft, Box, c.1945, 8 ½ x 11 In. 633.00
Kite, Aero-Kite Company, Die Cut, Paper, Strato, c.1946, 18 ½ x 18 ¾ In. 115.00
Magazine, Amazing Stories, Air Lords Of Han, Vol. 3, No. 12, 1929, 38 Pages 230.00
Magazine, Amazing Stories, Armageddon 2419 A.D., Vol. 3, No. 5, August, 1928. . . . . . 367.00
Pencil Box, 25th Century, Cardboard, Snap Closure, John F. Dille, c.1936, 4 ½ x 8 In. 173.00
Pocket Watch, Buck & Wilma, Lightning Bolt Hands, Ingraham, Box, c.1935 . . . . . . 1808.00
Poster, Tragedy On Saturn, Chapter 2, Mat, Frame, 47 ½ x 33 In. 1051.00
Puzzle, Buck Rogers, Original Sleeve, Rick Yager, Milton Bradley, c.1952, 10 x 14 In. 113.00
Toy, Disintegrator Gun, 25th Century, Sparks, Daisy Mfg., 6 x 9 ½ In. 160.00
Toy, Helmet, 1936 . . . . . . 510.00
Toy, Rocket Ship, 25th Century, Boing Noise, Sparks, Tin, 12 In. 254.00
Toy, Rocket Ship, 25th Century, Boing Noise, Tin Lithograph, Box, c.1934, 12 In. 2383.00
Toy, Rocket Ship, Flash Blast Attack, White, Red, No. 1033, Tootsietoy, Box 550.00
Toy, Space Rocket, Tin, Marx, 12 In. 100.00
Toy, Squirt Gun, Steel, XZ-44, Yellow, Red Flames, Daisy Mfg., 1936 . . . . . . 480.00
Toy, Water Pistol, Liquid Helium, Painted, Steel, Popsicle Premium, Daisy, c.1936, 7 In. 351.00

BUFFALO POTTERY was made in Buffalo, New York, after 1902. The company was established by the Larkin Company, famous manufacturers of soap. The wares are marked with a picture of a buffalo and the date of manufacture. Deldare ware is the most famous pottery made at the factory. It has either a khaki-colored or green background with hand-painted transfer designs.

BUFFALO POTTERY

Butter Chip, Plymouth, Green Transfer, White Ground, 1927, 3 ⅛ In. 12.00
Pitcher, Roosevelt Bears, Brown Transfer, Marked, c.1907, 7 ¾ In. . . . . . *illus* 1350.00
Plate, Teddy B, Teddy G, Quote, 5 Scenes, Gold Sponge Rim, No. 1249, 10 ½ In. 556.00
Platter, Abraham Lincoln, Grand Review Of The Army, Blue, White, 1910, 14 In. 1016.00

BUFFALO POTTERY DELDARE

Calendar Plate, Woodland Pixies, A. Wade, 1910, 9 ½ In. . . . . . *illus* 420.00
Candlestick, Colonial Scenes, 1909, 9 In., Pair 649.00
Candlestick, Village Life, Arch Back Holder, Matchbox, 1909, 5 x 4 In. 2767.00
Chamberstick, Flowers, Back Shield, Emerald, 6 ¼ x 6 ¾ In. 3450.00
Chamberstick, Flowers, Emerald, Signed, M.B., 1911, 7 x 6 In. . . . . . *illus* 3600.00
Chop Plate, At Ye Lion Inn, Signed, W. Foster, 1908, 13 ¾ In. 275.00
Mug, Ye Lion Inn, Signed, c.1908, 5 ¼ x 4 ¼ In. 345.00
Pitcher, Noble Hunting Party, Emerald, 1911, 10 In. 161.00
Plate, An Evening At Ye Lion Inn, 1909, 14 In. 253.00
Plate, Daughter Of The Revolution, Emerald, Marked, 9 ¼ In. 825.00
Plate, Dr. Syntax Presenting A Floral Offering, 6 ¼ In. 205.00
Plate, Fallowfield Hunt, The Death, Signed, L. Streissel, 1908, 8 In. 90.00
Plate, John Alden & Priscilla, Emerald, Marked, 8 ½ In. 1650.00
Plate, Yankee Doodle, 10 In. 2310.00
Plate, Ye Lion Inn, Signed, L. Anna, 1909, 12 In. 250.00
Tankard, Great Controversy, Teach The Dutchman English, 1908, 12 ⅜ In. 475.00
Vase, Stylized Designs, Flared, Emerald, Signed, 6 ½ x 8 ½ In. 3680.00

BUNNYKINS, *see Royal Doulton category.*

BURMESE GLASS was developed by Frederick Shirley at the Mt. Washington Glass Works in New Bedford, Massachusetts, in 1885. It is a two-toned glass, shading from peach to yellow. Some pieces have a pattern mold design. A few Burmese pieces were decorated with pictures or applied glass flowers of colored Burmese glass. Other factories made similar glass also called Burmese. Related items may be listed in the Fenton category, the Gundersen category, and under Webb Burmese.

Biscuit Jar, Enameled White & Yellow Blossoms, Cover, 5 x 4 In. 863.00

Buffalo Pottery, Pitcher, Roosevelt Bears, Brown Transfer, Marked, c.1907, 7 ¾ In.
$1350.00

Buffalo Pottery Deldare, Calendar Plate, Woodland Pixies, A. Wade, 1910, 9 ½ In.
$420.00

Buffalo Pottery Deldare, Chamberstick, Flowers, Emerald, Signed, M.B., 1911, 7 x 6 In.
$3600.00

TIP

Old Burmese glass will fluoresce yellow-green under a black light. Recent reproductions will not.

Burmese Glass, Fairy Lamp, Etched, Ruffled Rim, 3-Piece Pedestal Base, Clarke, 11 ¾ In.
$1093.00

Burmese Glass, Pitcher, Oval, Enameled, Roses, Verse, Cowslip Is A Country Lass, T. Hood, 4 ½ In.
$1150.00

Burmese Glass, Vase, Egyptian Bottle Form, Scroll Handles, 10 ½ In.
$1560.00

Bowl, Tricornered Rim, 2 ½ x 5 In. 200.00
Bride's Bowl, Daisies, Ruffled Rim, Pairpoint Base, Handles, 11 In. 489.00
Condiment Set, 2 Shakers, Ribbed Pillar, Silver Plated Caddy, Birds, 5 ½ In. 518.00
Creamer, Footed, Urn Shape, 4 In. 403.00
Cup & Saucer, 6 In., 3 Sets 230.00
Cup & Saucer, Applied Amber Handle, Pink, Yellow, 5 In. 144.00
Epergne, 2 Fairy Lamps, Brass Frame, Cut Glass Base, 18 x 15 In. 518.00
Epergne, 4 Fairy Lamps, 3 Bud Vases, Brass Frame, Pedestal Base, 16 In. 1438.00
Ewer, Queens Lace Pattern, Gold Handle, Highlights, 10 In. 9200.00
Fairy Lamp, Epergne, Etched, Mounted, Brass Framework, Clarke, 16 In. 1438.00
Fairy Lamp, Etched, Clarke, 5 ¼ In. 633.00
Fairy Lamp, Etched, Clear, Piecrust Rim, Clarke, 5 ½ x 5 ¾ In. 633.00
Fairy Lamp, Etched, Marked, Clarke, 5 ¼ In. 575.00
Fairy Lamp, Etched, Pyramid, Reversible Base, Piecrust Rim, 4 ¾ In. 863.00
Fairy Lamp, Etched, Pyramid Dome, Crystal Cup, 3 ¾ In., Pair 201.00
Fairy Lamp, Etched, Pyramid Dome, Prunus, Clarke, 4 ⅛ In. 690.00
Fairy Lamp, Etched, Pyramid Dome, Ruffled Edge, Clarke, 4 ¾ In. 805.00
Fairy Lamp, Etched, Ruffled Rim, 3-Piece Pedestal Base, Clarke, 11 ¾ In. *illus* 1093.00
Fairy Lamp, Etched, Tricornered Bowl, Clarke, 6 ¼ x 5 ¼ In. 173.00
Fairy Lamp, Etched, Upturned Ruffled Bowl, Pyramid Dome, Clarke, 6 ¼ x 5 In. 300.00
Fairy Lamp, Ivy Dome, Ruffled Edge Base, 2 Clear Glass Cups, 6 x 7 In., 3 Piece 173.00
Fairy Lamp, Pyramid Dome, Gold, White Creamware Base, Signed, 5 x 8 In. 403.00
Figurine, Rooster, Dollop Stand, 6 ¾ In. 201.00
Marmalade, Grape, Silver Plated Cover, Bail Handle, 6 x 5 In. 1250.00
Mustard, Ribbed Pillar, Blue, White Daisies, Metal Hinged Cover, Spoon, 4 In. 460.00
Pitcher, Amber Handle, Oval, 7 In. 288.00
Pitcher, Milk, Amber Handle, Egg Shape, 4 ½ In. 316.00
Pitcher, Milk, Oval, Applied Handle, 4 ½ In. 144.00
Pitcher, Oval, Enameled, Roses, Verse, Cowslip Is A Country Lass, T. Hood, 4 ½ In. *illus* 1150.00
Plate, Dinner, Satin, 10 In. 86.00
Plate, Luncheon, Glossy, 8 In., 4 Piece 253.00
Potpourri Jar, Cover, Squat, Oval, Metal Insert, 4 ½ In. 518.00
Rose Bowl, Crimped Ruffled Rim, 2 ¼ In. 115.00
Rose Bowl, Prunus Blossom, Enameled Crimped Rim, 2 ½ x 2 ¾ In. 595.00
Salt & Pepper, Fig, White, Enameled Flowers 110.00
Spooner, Stovepipe Shape, Crimped Rim, 4 ½ In. 115.00
Sugar Shaker, Egg Shape, Forget-Me-Not, 4 ½ x 3 ½ In. 750.00
Sugar Shaker, Enameled Pansies, Oval, 4 ¼ In. 100.00
Syrup, Enameled Daisies, 7 In. 2875.00
Toothpick, Diamond-Quilted, White, Yellow Chrysanthemums, Tricornered, 2 ¼ x 2 In. 895.00
Toothpick, Enameled Chrysanthemum, Tricornered Rim, 2 x 2 ½ In. 895.00
Toothpick, Enameled Forget-Me-Not, Urn Shape, 2 ¾ x 2 ¼ In. 750.00
Toothpick, Fig, Enameled Blossoms, Tendrils, 2 x 2 ½ In. 985.00
Toothpick, Lobe, Footed, 2 ½ x 2 ¾ In. 895.00
Tumbler, Lemonade, Diamond-Quilted, 5 In. 431.00
Vase, Bulbous, Green, Red, Gingko, Scroll Handles, 11 In. 460.00
Vase, Double Gourd, 6 ¾ In. 400.00
Vase, Egyptian Bottle Form, Scroll Handles, 10 ½ In. *illus* 1560.00
Vase, Enameled Cascading Oak Leaves, Gourd Shape, 9 In. 403.00
Vase, Enameled Flowers, 9 ¾ In. 805.00
Vase, Gold Flowers, Bulbous Stick Shape, Amber, Rose, 12 In. 1380.00
Vase, Gourd Shape, 12 In. 374.00
Vase, Guba Ducks, Sun, Cattails, Lily Pads, Flask Shape, Scroll Handles, 11 In. 3450.00
Vase, Hawthorn Pattern, Egyptian Urn Shape, Handles, 8 In. 1035.00
Vase, Jack-In-The-Pulpit, 9 ½ In. 173.00
Vase, Jack-In-The-Pulpit, Crimped Ruffled Edge, 10 In., Pair 805.00
Vase, Jack-In-The-Pulpit, Lily, Footed, 7 In. 173.00
Vase, Lily, Glossy, 5 ¾ In. 225.00
Vase, Pouch, Flared Rim, 8 Pulled Points, 5 x 5 In. 374.00
Vase, Queen's Pattern, 8 In. 2070.00
Vase, Star Crimped Rim, 3 ½ In. 125.00
Vase, Stick, Green Ivy, Bulbous Base, 7 ½ x 3 In. 1850.00
Vase, Trumpet, Flared Scalloped Rim, Footed, 10 In. 173.00
Vase, Trumpet, Tricornered Rim, Applied Foot, 7 ½ In. 120.00
Whimsy, Mouse, Glossy, 3 In. 575.00
Whiskey, Diamond-Quilted, 2 ⅝ In. 259.00

BUSTER BROWN, the comic strip, first appeared in color in 1902. Buster and his dog, Tige, remained a popular comic and soon became even more famous as the emblem for a shoe company, a textile firm, and other companies. The strip was discontinued in 1920. Buster Brown sponsored a radio show from 1943 to 1955 and a TV show from 1950 to 1956. The Buster Brown characters are still used by Brown Shoe Company, Buster Brown Apparel, Inc., and Gateway Hosiery.

Ad, More Kids Will Go To Grandma's In Buster Brown Shoes, 1957, 10 x 14 In. 10.00
Bank, Buster Brown & Tige, Cast Iron, A.C Williams, 6 In. 201.00
Bank, Buster Brown & Tige, Cast Iron, A.C. Williams, No. 241 125.00
Bank, Buster Brown & Tige, Cast Iron, Gold Paint, A.C. Williams, No. 241, c.1910, 5 ¼ In. 113.00
Bank, Buster Brown & Tige, Good Luck Horseshoe, Cast Iron, 4 ½ x 5 x 2 In. 66.00
Bank, Buster Brown & Tige, Horseshoe, Cast Iron, 4 ¼ x 4 ¾ In. 150.00
Bank, Buster Brown & Tige, Cast Iron, Painted, 5 In. 50.00
Banner, Cloth, Headquarters For Buster Brown, Children's Wear, 1900s, 36 x 58 In. 100.00
Button, You Can't Buster Brown Hose Supporter, Buster, Tige, Celluloid, 1 In. 34.00
Display, Buster Brown Holding Treat, Tige Jumping, Die Cut, Tin, 39-In. Buster, 32-In. Tige 9000.00
Doll, Tige, Mohair, Jointed, Shoebutton Eyes, Stitched Nose, Steiff, 1910, 9 In. 575.00
Figurine, Buster Brown, Buster Brown Shoes, Red Suit & Hat, Bisque, Marked, 1920s, 3 In. 45.00
Hook, Buster Brown, Tige, Vacation Days Carnival, Celluloid, 6 ½ x 2 In. 22.00
Match Holder, Buster Brown Bread, Striker On Bottom, Die Cut, Tin, 2 x 6 ¾ In. 875.00
Match Holder, Buster Brown Serving Bread, Tin Lithograph, 6 ¾ In. 360.00
Mirror, Buster Brown Vacation Days Carnival, 1946 16.00
Postcard, Buster Brown & Tige, Leather, Postmarked 1907 25.00
Shoes, Brown, 3 Side Buttons, Leather, Blue-Ribbon, Child's, Size 5, c.1910 35.00
Shoetree, Buster Brown Head, Figural Plastic, Green, Package, 5 x 9 ¼ In., 2 Piece 65.00
Sign, Buster Brown & Tige, Tin, 39 x 32 In. *illus* 7500.00
Sign, Buster Brown & Tige On Teeter-Totter, Tin, 35 x 14 In. 10000.00
Sign, Buster Brown Shoes, Buster & Tige, Porcelain, Neon, Electric, 54 x 54 In. 4200.00
Sign, Buster Brown Shoes For Boys & Girls, Tige, Cast Iron, 17 ½ In. *illus* 4889.00
Sign, Golden Sheaf Bakery, Buster, Tige, Embossed, Tin, 1920s, 20 x 28 In. *illus* 345.00
Statue, Buster Brown Shoes, Buster & Tige, Painted, Rubber, Flex-O-Moulds, 13 In. 165.00
Tin, Cream Of Tartar, Buster Brown, Tige, Steinwinder-Stoffgren Co., 4 ½ x 2 In. 92.00
Toy, Rocker, Buster Brown, Tige, Ball Rolls, Tin, Windup, Germany, 10 In. *illus* 2100.00
Tray, B.B. Lion Taming Done While You Wait, Buster, Lion, Rockford Quadruple Silver Plate, 8 In. 52.00
Wonder Horse, Rocking, Springs, Wood, Red, Advertising, 1950s, 28 x 36 In. 550.00

BUTTER MOLDS *are listed in the Kitchen category under Mold, Butter.*

BUTTON collecting has been popular since the nineteenth century. Buttons have been known throughout the centuries, and there are millions of styles. Gold, silver, or precious stones were used for the best buttons, but most were made of natural materials, like bone or shell, or from inexpensive metals. Only a few types are listed for comparison.

Bakelite, Anchor, Embossed, Black, 1940s, 1 ¼ In. 20.00
Bakelite, Cherry Red, 2 Holes, 1 ¼ In., Pair 6.00
Bakelite, Dog, Scottie, Butterscotch, 2 Holes, 1 ⅜ In. 10.00
Bakelite, Red, 2 Hole, 1 ¼ In., Pair 6.00
Brass, Cut Steel, Braided, Faceted & Stamped Design, Loop Brass Shank, c.1870, 1 ¼ In. 17.50
Brass, Police, City Of Camden, New Jersey 6.00
Celluloid, Glass Floral Center, Extra Large 146.00
Enamel, Flower Center, Paste Border 785.00
Enamel On Brass, 3 Pink Rosebuds, Long Stems, ¾ In. 30.00
Gibson Girl, Picture, Silver Plate, 1 ¼ In. 59.00
Jade, White, Green, Bat On Edge, Carved, Engraved Symbols, Chinese, 1 ⅛ In. 30.00
Metal, Embossed Pansy, Loop Shank, Victorian, 1 ⅛ In. 10.00
Metal, Silver Color, Mother-Of-Pearl Flower Center, Cut Steel Beads, Loop Shank, ⅝ In. 10.00
Mother-Of Pearl, Fish, Figural, Carved, Shank, ¾ x ½ In. 10.00
Papier-Mache, Mother-Of-Pearl Flowers Inlay, Cornucopia, Shank, France, ¾ x ½ In. 18.00
Silver, Art Nouveau, Edward VII, Round, Woman, Flowing Hair, Flowers, c.1902, 1 ¼ In. 230.00
Sterling Silver, Ophelia, Long Hair, Garland Of Flowers, Art Nouveau, ⅝ In. 15.00

BUTTONHOOKS have been a popular collectible in England for many years but are now gaining the attention of American collectors. The buttonhooks were made to help fasten the many buttons of the old-fashioned high-button shoes and other items of apparel.

Metal, Walk-Over Shoes For Men & Women, Fancy Design On Reverse, 3 ½ In. 22.00
Plastic Handle, Marbleized, 2 ⅜ In. 22.00

Buster Brown, Sign,
Buster Brown & Tige, Tin, 39 x 32 In.
$7500.00

Buster Brown, Sign,
Buster Brown Shoes For Boys & Girls,
Tige, Cast Iron, 17 ½ In.
$4889.00

Buster Brown, Sign,
Golden Sheaf Bakery, Buster, Tige,
Embossed, Tin, 1920s, 20 x 28 In.
$345.00

Buster Brown, Toy, Rocker,
Buster Brown, Tige, Ball Rolls,
Tin, Windup, Germany, 10 In.
$2100.00

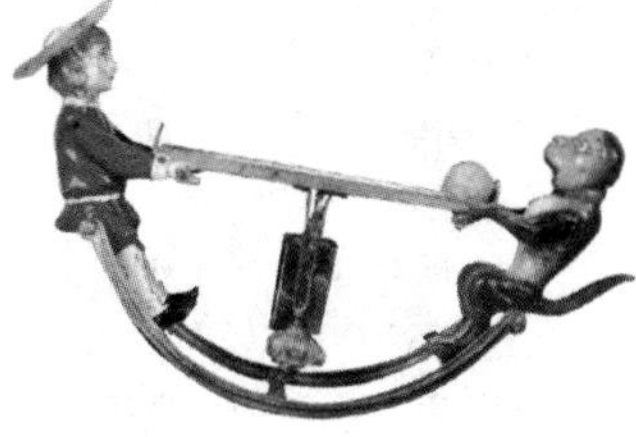

Calendar, 1909, Dupont Explosive, Dog, September Page, 30 x 20 In.
$1000.00

Calendar, 1912, Winchester, 2 Men, Bear, N.C. Wyeth, Full Pad, Frame, 31 x 15 In.
$4100.00

TIP

Try to keep your paper collectibles out of the light. If you frame and display some pieces, keep them on the dark side of the room, away from sunlight and direct lamp light.

Sterling Silver, Angels, Steel Shank, Victorian, Marked, JD WD, 6 ⅝ In. 100.00
Sterling Silver, Repousse, Shoehorn, Birmingham, England, Case, 2 Piece 175.00
Sterling Silver, Repousse Tulip Design, Hallmarked, 7 ½ In. 20.00

BYBEE POTTERY of Bybee, Kentucky, was started by Webster Cornelison. The company claims it started in 1809, although sales records were not kept until 1845. The pottery is still operated by members of the sixth generation of the Cornelison family. The handmade stoneware pottery is sold at the factory. Various marks were used, including the name Bybee, the name Cornelison, or the initials BB. Not all pieces are marked. A mark shaped like the state of Kentucky with the words "Genuine Bybee" and similar marks were used by a different company, Bybee Pottery Company of Lexington, Kentucky. It was a distributor of various pottery lines from 1922 to 1929.

Bank, Pig, Standing, Glossy Gray, 5 ⅝ In. 16.00
Bowl, Blue, 4 x 10 In. 38.00
Bowl, Handles, Marked BB, 2 ¼ x 9 In. 15.00
Jar, Cover, Light Green Glaze, No. 55, Marked, Bybee Ky, 8 ½ In. 44.00
Mug, Blue Speckle, 4 ½ In. 35.00
Mug, Cornelison, Mottled Green Glaze, 3 ½ In. 5.50
Pitcher, Blue, Wheel Thrown, 8 In. 65.00
Pitcher, Rebecca, Blue, Handles, 15 ½ x 9 In. 50.00
Vase, Blue Speckle, Handles, 6 ½ x 5 ½ In. 70.00
Vase, Bulbous, Green Over Mauve, 3 Handles, Marked, 1927, 7 ¼ In. 132.00
Vase, Flared, Green, 6 In. 60.00
Vase, Molded Grass Design, Mauve Matte Glaze, No. 512, Marked, 10 ½ x 4 In. .... 250.00 to 270.00
Vase, Multi-Green, Bulbous, 3 Handles, No. 905, Signed, 1927, 5 x 7 ½ In. 44.00

CALENDARS made to hang on the wall or to be displayed on a desk top have been popular since the last quarter of the nineteenth century. Many were printed with advertising as part of the artwork and were given away as premiums. Calendars with guns, gunpowder, or Coca-Cola advertising are most prized.

1888, Scott's Emulsion, Little Girl, 4 ½ x 8 In. 50.00
1892, Union Metallic Cartridge Co., Boy, Shotgun, Cartridge Belt, 14 x 29 In. 2200.00
1898, Union Metallic Cartridge Co., Molly Pitcher At Monmouth, G. Gull, 13 ½ x 26 In. 2016.00
1899, Homer B Summy Shoe Store, Village Scene, 14 In. 30.00
1900, Laflin & Rand Powder Co., Full Pad, New York City, 3 ¾ x 5 ¾ In. 588.00
1901, B.H. Hershey Coal, Girl Sleeping On Dog, Manheim, Pa., 13 ¾ In. 50.00
1901, Central Hotel, Dog Chasing Bird, Elizabethtown, Pa., 14 ¼ In. 50.00
1902, Coal Dealer, Woonsocket, Cardboard, Die Cut, Lithograph, Children, 22 x 15 In. 187.00
1902, Dr. A.C. Daniels, 3 Women, October To December, Pad, 5 ¼ x 3 ⅜ In. 155.00
1902, Fold-Out, Pretty Girl, Letter, Die Cut, Embossed, Youth Companion, Boston, 24 x 11 In. 89.00
1903, Metropolitan Life, All Aboard, Trunk, Children, Dog, Cardboard, 9 ½ x 13 In. 115.00
1903, Seattle Brewing & Malting Co., Seattle, Washington, Paper, 22 x 28 In. 4500.00
1904, Kelle & Dillard Monuments, Washington, In., Boy & Girl On Teeter-Totter, 21 x 17 In. . 248.00
1904, Marlin Firearms, Repeating Rifles, Man Hunting, 6 x 3 In. 1225.00
1906, Columbia Stove Company, Eleanor Robson, 11 x 17 In. 38.00
1906, Victorian, Die Cut, Baby Girl In Swing, Flowers, Mat, Frame, 35 x 17 In. 193.00
1907, Schwenk & Caldwell, Girl Holding 2 Cats, Die Cut, Embossed, 17 In. 170.00
1908, Big Black Foot Milling Co., Fatima, 11 x 15 In. 224.00
1908, Compliments Of Joseph Earley, Girl, Cat, Embossed, Die Cut, Frame, 23 x 11 In. 180.00
1908, Frank Ruhstaller Brewery, Lorelei, Sacramento, Ca., Paper, 15 x 20 In. 5750.00
1909, Dupont Explosive, Dog, September Page, 30 x 20 In. .... *illus* 1000.00
1910, Boston Red Sox, Schedule, Player Portraits, Black & White, 10 x 14 In. 1057.00
1910, DeLaval Separator Co., Cream Separators, Pretty Girl, Flower, 12 x 20 In. 1540.00
1911, Compliments Of Oscar Florence, Woman, Roses, Die Cut, Embossed, Pad, 19 x 11 In. ... 150.00
1912, Bristol Fishing Rod, Couple Camping, Oliver Kemp, Horton Mfg. Co., 17 x 31 In. 1375.00
1912, Winchester, 2 Men, Bear, N.C. Wyeth, Full Pad, Frame, 31 x 15 In. .... *illus* 4100.00
1913, National Lead Dutch Boy, Barn Wood Frame, 42 x 18 ½ In. 330.00
1914, Emil Cermak Apothecary, Mat, Frame, 23 x 18 In. 55.00
1917, Wrigley's, 3 Packs Of Gum, Black, Tin Lithograph, 17 ¼ In. 425.00
1919, Peter Cartridge Co., Hurrah You Got Him, Men Hunting, 27 x 13 In. 4050.00
1920, Shaples Separators, Boy, Head In Milk Bucket, W.T. Hamilton, Michigan, 12 x 23 In. ... 660.00
1921, Mother, Child, Lattice, Flowers, Birds, Die Cut, Mat, Frame, Germany, 18 x 18 In. 44.00
1922, Manheim Milling Co., Mother & Daughter Baking, 14 In. 40.00
1922, Manheim Sentinel, Country Scene, Embossed, 11 ¾ In. 30.00
1924, Wrigley's, P.K. Chewing Gum, Mother Reading To Girls, 5 ½ In. 60.00
1926, Cassels Clothing Store, Christy Girl, 37 In. 375.00

1926, Lydia Pinkham's Vegetable Compound, Girl & Dog, Feb. To Dec., Frame, 15 x 8 In. 253.00
1926, Robin Hood Shoes, Indian Woman Looking Over Falls, 9 ½ x 17 In. ... 100.00
1926, Round Oak Stoves, Thomsen Hardware Co., Full Pad, Frame, 20 ½ x 10 In. ... *illus* 425.00
1928, J. Harvey Spahr, Flying Cloud, Ship, Manheim, Pa., 48 In. ... 160.00
1928, Lancaster County Farm Sales, 41 ½ In. ... 40.00
1929, Cassels Clothing Store, Woman Looking In Mirror, Earl Chambecks, 37 In. ... 275.00
1929, Indian Maiden, Wood Frame, May, 24 x 17 In. ... 77.00
1931, Litzenberger Hardware, Water Scene, Landscape, Painted, 15 ½ In. ... 25.00
1932, Boy Scouts, Norman Rockwell, Insurance Co. Of North America, 7 ½ x 14 In. ... 86.00
1934, Binkley Bros. & Ober, Camp Scene, 16 ½ In. ... 30.00
1935, R R Graybill Dodge-Plymouth, Landscape Scene, 47 In. ... 60.00
1938, Hy Hintermeister, Wolves Chased Deer Off Ledge Into River, 14 x 24 In. ... 101.00
1946, Consumers Feed Co., Fisherman, Waterfall, Sioux City, Frank Stick, 9 x 15 In. ... 235.00
1951, Season's Greetings, Sneedville Electric Co., Sneedville, Tenn. ... 50.00
1954, Norco Liquors, Marilyn Monroe Nude, Full Pad, 12 x 19 In. ... 67.00
1956, His Master's Voice, RCA Victor Television, Sun TV, California, Frame ... 25.00
1957, Marilyn Monroe, Golden Dreams, Peek-A-Boo, Wintersville, Ohio, 16 x 9 In. ... 70.00

CALENDAR PLATES a few were popular in the United States as advertising giveaways from 1906 to 1929. Since then, plates have been made every year. A calendar and the name of a store, a picture of flowers, a girl, or a scene were featured on the plate.

1909, Mountain Lake Scene, Multicolored, Scalloped Border, E.E.C. Co., 9 In. ... 15.00
1910, Horseshoe, Woman & Dog In Center, H.H. Wiefel, Home Bakery, Scalloped ... 65.00
1910, Pioneer Flour, San Antonio Tex., Marked, Carnation McNicol, 8 ½ In. ... 255.00
1911, Flowers, Andrews Jewelry Co., Gold Line Border, Dresden, 8 ¼ In. ... 75.00
1911, Woman, Compliments R.A. Shimer & Co., Signed, Archie Gunn, 9 In. ... 20.00
1911, Woman, Purple Bow, Compliments R.A. Shimer & Co., McNicol, 9 In. ... 22.00
1912, Farmers State Bank, Ashland, Ill., 10 In. ... 20.00
1912, Hunting Scene, Bird, Hunter, Compliments Of J.R. Dietrich & Co., W.S. George, 8 ¼ In.. 20.00
1912, Pointer Dog, Tottenville Ferry Hotel, Multicolored, McNicol Pottery, 7 ½ In. ... 35.00
1912, Woman In Sailor Dress At Ship's Wheel, Art Nouveau Border, Carnation McNicol, 8 ¼ In. 85.00
1912, Wright Aeroplane, What Made Dayton Famous, Marked, 8 ½ In. ... 2.00
1914, Alternating Currents, Gibson Girl, Man, Pink Roses Encircling Months, 8 ¼ In. ... 75.00
1918, Pioneer Flour, San Antonio Tex., Marked, D.E. McNicol, 9 In. ... 110.00
1920, Globe, Flags, Peace, Great World War, Muskegon Heights Furn. Co., 8 ¼ In. ... 35.00
1952, Ivory, Black Design, Windmill, 10 In. ... 25.00
1955, Ivory, Black, Floral Border, Gold, Simplicity, Canonsburg, 10 In. ... 22.00
1961, Calendar In Center, Floral Border, Gold, On Ivory, 10 In. ... 20.00
1961, Ivory, Hourglass, Scythe, Gold Trim, Flowers, 10 ⅝ In. ... 9.00
1967, Dog, Springer Spaniel Center, Walter's Auction Gallery, Pa., Sabina Line ... 24.00
1967, Eagle, Zodiac, Worked Gold, Fluted Border, Gold Rim, 10 In. ... 18.00
1967, Sun, Turquoise, Floral Border, 10 In. ... 15.00
1969, Fox Hunt, Horses, Dogs, Compliments Of Walter's Auction Gallery, Pa., 9 ¼ In. ... 4.75
1970, Gold Bless Our House, Farm Scene, Alfred Meakin, Staffordshire, 9 In. ... 15.00
1970, Ivory, Avocado Green Border, 10 In. ... 18.00
1972, Ivory, Maroon Transfer, Farm Scene, Alfred Meakin, Staffordshire, 8 ½ In. ... 19.00
1973, God Bless Our House, Zodiac, Brown Transferware, Meakin, 9 In. ... 9.00
1977, God Bless America, Red White & Blue, Spencer Gifts, 9 In. ... 15.00
1979, Alpine Boy & Girl, Lamb, Flowers, Multicolored, Chadwick Miller, 9 In. ... 15.00
1979, White, Blue, Zodiac, God Bless Our House, Alfred Meakin, Staffordshire, 9 In. ... 15.00
1980, Red Transfer, God Bless Our Home, Astrological Scenes, Myott, 9 In. ... 10.00

CAMARK POTTERY started in 1924 in Camden, Arkansas. Jack Carnes founded the firm and made many types of glazes and wares. The company was bought by Mary Daniel. Production was halted in 1983.

Bowl, Molded Flowers & Leaves, Pink, White Highlights, 11 x 8 ½ In. ... 49.00
Figurine, Nude, Flower Holder, Maroon Glaze, 8 ¾ In. ... 82.00
Flower Frog, 2 ¾ x 4 In. ... 10.00
Jug, Ball, Mirror Black, Impressed Mark, 7 ½ x 6 ¼ In. ... *illus* 33.00
Pitcher, Ball, Sea Green Matte Over Lavender, 6 ½ In. ... 55.00
Planter, Double Swan, Black, 7 x 7 ¼ In. ... 34.00
Vase, Blue Matte Glaze, Yellow Drip, Tapered, Label, 6 ½ x 3 ½ In. ... *illus* 360.00
Vase, Crackle Glaze, Forest Green, 9 ⅜ In. ... 385.00
Vase, Fan, Ruffled Rim, Green Matte, Label, 6 x 10 In. ... 65.00
Vase, Green Matte Glaze, 6 x 4 In. ... 115.00

Calendar, 1926, Round Oak Stoves, Thomsen Hardware Co., Full Pad, Frame, 20 ½ x 10 In.
$425.00

Camark, Jug, Ball, Mirror Black, Impressed Mark, 7 ½ x 6 ¼ In.
$33.00

Camark, Vase, Blue Matte Glaze, Yellow Drip, Tapered, Label, 6 ½ x 3 ½ In.
$360.00

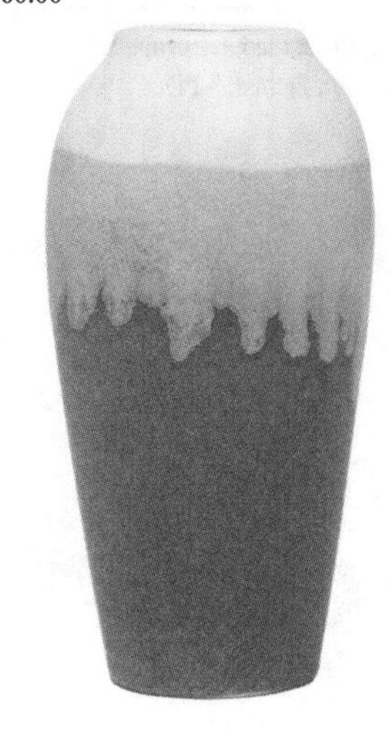

Cambridge, Apple Blossom, Tray, Silver Encrusted, Keyhole Handles, 13 In.
$115.00

Cambridge, Baroque, Vanity Set, Peach-Blo, 4 ½ x 8 ½ In.
$135.00

Cambridge, Caprice, Wine, Moonlight Blue, 2 ½ Oz., 4 In.
$85.00

Cambridge, Cleo, Beverage Set, Peach-Blo, Etched, 5 Piece
$85.00

Vase, Iris, Blue & Yellow, Ernst Anton Lechner, 1940s, 6 ¼ x 9 ¼ In. 85.00
Vase, Iris Basket, Blue, Green Glaze, 10 x 10 In. 85.00
Vase, Iris Basket, Pink, Green, Glaze, 10 x 10 In. 75.00
Vase, Ivory Crackle, Semi-Iridescent, 8 ⅜ x 4 In. 265.00
Vase, Mottled Blue, 2 Handles, 5 In. .... 16.50 to 27.50

CAMBRIDGE GLASS Company was founded in 1901 in Cambridge, Ohio. The company closed in 1954, reopened briefly, and closed again in 1958. The firm made all types of glass. It's early wares included heavy pressed glass with the mark *Near Cut*. Later wares included Crown Tuscan, etched stemware, and clear and colored glass. The firm used a C in a triangle mark after 1920.

Adonis, Bowl, Footed, 12 In. 190.00
Adonis, Dish, Mayonnaise, Underplate, Sections 80.00
Allegro, Cordial, Paisley Etching 75.00
Apple Blossom, Ashtray, Gold Krystol, 3 In. 20.00
Apple Blossom, Candelabrum, 3-Light, Keyhole, 6 In. 40.00
Apple Blossom, Tray, Silver Encrusted, Keyhole Handles, 13 In. .... *illus* 115.00
Arcadia, Candlestick, 2-Light, 5 ¾ In., Pair 90.00
Arcadia, Console, Footed, 4 x 12 In. 60.00
Azurite, Candlestick, Square Base, 10 In., Pair 35.00
Azurite, Compote, Gold Trim, 10 ½ In. 125.00
Ball, Pitcher, Royal Blue, Ice Lip, 80 Oz. 95.00
Baroque, Vanity Set, Peach-Blo, 4 ½ x 8 ½ In. .... *illus* 135.00
Bluebell, Atomizer, 7 In. 525.00
Buzz Saw, Bowl, Footed, 3 x 5 ½ In. 25.00
Caprice, Bowl, Oval, Handles, 4-Footed, 11 In. 36.00
Caprice, Candlestick, 3-Light, Cascading, 6 ½ x 6 ½ In., Pair 55.00
Caprice, Celery Dish, Oval, 9 In. 15.00
Caprice, Cigarette Box, Dolphin, Mandarin Gold, Footed, 4 ½ x 3 ½ In. 145.00
Caprice, Goblet, Cordial, Moonlight Blue, Blown, Oz. 150.00
Caprice, Plate, Bread & Butter, Moonlight Blue, 6 In. 24.00
Caprice, Plate, Luncheon, 8 ½ In. 12.00
Caprice, Platter, Round, 3-Footed, 13 ¾ In. 30.00
Caprice, Relish, 3 Sections, 8 In. 18.00
Caprice, Rose Bowl, Moonlight Blue, Footed, 6 In. 175.00
Caprice, Sugar, Individual 12.00
Caprice, Wine, Moonlight Blue, 2 ½ Oz., 4 In. .... *illus* 85.00
Cascade, Goblet, 8 Oz., 5 ½ In. 15.00
Chantilly, Bowl, Ruffled Edge, 4-Footed, 13 ½ In. 85.00
Chantilly, Creamer 21.00
Chantilly, Sugar & Creamer 20.00
Chrysanthemum, Tumbler, Amber, 12 Oz., 5 ⅛ In. 20.00
Cleo, Beverage Set, Peach-Blo, Etched, 5 Piece .... *illus* 85.00
Cleo, Bowl, Emerald Green, 9 ¼ In. 25.00
Cleo, Candlestick, Moonlight Blue, 3 ¾ In. 150.00
Cleo, Candy Dish, Cover, Pink, 3-Footed 214.00
Cleo, Cracker Plate, Peach-Blo, 10 ½ In. 40.00
Crown Tuscan, Candlestick, Dolphin 60.00
Crown Tuscan, Compote, Keyhole Stem, 10 ½ In., Pair .... *illus* 110.00
Crown Tuscan, Vase, Pink Flowers, Scroll On Foot, Flared Rim, 12 In. .... 20.00 to 50.00
Decagon, Bonbon, Pistachio, Etched, Keyhole Handle, 6 ¼ In. 10.00
Decagon, Ice Bucket, Peach-Blo, 5 ½ In. 100.00
Decagon, Sugar, Moonlight Blue, Etched, Gold Trim, Footed, Handles 35.00
Decagon, Tray, Pink, Gold Trim, Etched, Handles, 14 ½ In. 30.00
Diane, Epergne 40.00
Diane, Jam Jar, Cover, Etched, 8 Oz. 55.00
Diane, Platter, Handles, 16 x 11 In. 52.00
Ebony, Bottle, Etched Bath Salts, Gold Encrusted 295.00
Ebony, Compote, Decagon, Sterling Silver Overlay, 7 In. 85.00
Flower Frog, Draped Lady, Light Emerald Green, 8 ½ In. 140.00
Georgian, Tumbler, Willow Blue, 9 Oz. 10.00
Gloria, Tumbler, Gold Krystol, Footed, 5 Oz. 36.00
Heron, Flower Frog, 8 ¾ In. 75.00
Horn Of Plenty, Wall Pocket 15.00
Inverted Strawberry, Berry Set, Child's, 4 Piece 102.00
Ladle, Mayonnaise, Gold Trim, Gold 3-Petal Handle, 5 ½ In. 20.00

Lorna, Sandwich Server, Gold Krystol, Center Handle 62.00
Majestic, Tray, Amber, Handles 20.00
Martha Washington, Compote, Carmen, Footed, Rockwell Sterling Silver Base, 5 In. 310.00
Mayflower, Candlestick, Flame, 4 ¼ x 4 ⅛ In., Pair 70.00
No. 3020, Sherbet, Peach-Blo, 6 Oz., 4 In., Pair 5.00
Portia, Ice Bucket, Chrome Handle, 5 ¾ In. 105.00
Portia, Vase, Crown Tuscan, Gold Encrusted, Bulbous, Flared Rim, Stamped, Pair. 140.00
Rose Lady, Flower Frog, Amber, 9 ¾ In. . . . . *illus* 395.00
Rose Point, Bowl, Open Handles, Low Footed, 8 In. 30.00
Rose Point, Candlestick, Keyhole Stem, 5 In., Pair 70.00
Rose Point, Champagne, Pressed, Blue Bowl, Cone Shape, 4 ¾ In. 125.00
Rose Point, Cocktail, 3 Oz., 6 In. . . . . 20.00 to 25.00
Rose Point, Cordial, Oz., 5 In. . . . . 45.00 to 60.00
Rose Point, Cruet, Oil, Stopper, 6 Oz. 75.00
Rose Point, Cup & Saucer 35.00
Rose Point, Goblet, 10 Oz., 8 ¼ In. . . . . 35.00 to 38.00
Rose Point, Ladle, Condiment, 5 ½ In. 20.00
Rose Point, Mayonnaise Set, 3 Piece 55.00
Rose Point, Oyster Cocktail, 4 ½ Oz., 4 ¾ In. . . . . 25.00 to 30.00
Rose Point, Parfait, Handle, 6 ½ Oz., 6 ¼ In. 55.00
Rose Point, Relish, 2 Sections, Open Handles, 6 In. 35.00
Rose Point, Relish, 3 Sections, 2 Open Handles, 10 In. 60.00
Rose Point, Relish, 3 Sections, 4-Footed, 9 In. 49.00
Rose Point, Relish, 3 Sections, Handle, 6 ½ In. 61.00
Rose Point, Relish, 4 Sections, Handles, 7 ½ In. 78.00
Rose Point, Salt & Pepper 60.00
Rose Point, Sherbet, 6 Oz., 6 ½ In. . . . . 18.00 to 22.00
Rose Point, Sherbet, 7 Oz., 6 ½ In. 24.00
Rose Point, Sugar & Creamer, Ruffled Edge 30.00
Rose Point, Torte Plate, Rolled Edge, 3-Footed, 13 In. 55.00
Rose Point, Tumbler, 10 Oz., 6 ½ In. 27.00
Rose Point, Tumbler, Iced Tea, 12 Oz., 7 ⅝ In. 35.00
Rose Point, Tumbler, Juice, Footed, 5 Oz., 5 ¼ In. 27.00
Rose Point, Tumbler, Juice, Gold Encrusted, 5 Oz., 5 ¾ In. 28.00
Rose Point, Tumbler, Whiskey, 2 ½ Oz., 4 ½ In. 85.00
Rose Point, Vase, Bud, Footed, 10 In. 63.00
Rose Point, Vase, Crown Tuscan, 8 ½ In. . . . . *illus* 165.00
Rose Point, Vase, Trumpet, Flared, Footed, 6 In. 70.00
Rose Point, Wine, 2 ½ Oz., 6 ⅝ In. 45.00
Rose Point, Wine, Gold Encrusted, 3 ½ Oz., 18 In. 40.00
Swan, Dish, 8 In. 109.00
Swan, Salt, Green 25.00
Two Kids, Flower Frog, Peach-Blo, 9 ¼ In. 210.00

CAMBRIDGE POTTERY was made in Cambridge, Ohio, from about 1895 until World War I. The factory made brown glazed decorated artwares with a variety of marks, including an acorn, the name *Cambridge*, the name *Oakwood*, or the name *Terrhea*.

Vase, Flowers, Black Ground, Pinched Neck, 5 ¼ In. 230.00
Vase, Lilies, Brown, Yellow, Green, Marked, c.1904, 14 In. . . . . *illus* 225.00

CAMEO GLASS was made in much the same manner as a cameo in jewelry. Parts of the top layer of glass were cut away to reveal a different colored glass beneath. The most famous cameo glass was made during the nineteenth century. Signed cameo glass pieces are listed under the glasswork's name, such as Daum or Galle.

Biscuit Jar, Frosted Red, White Flowers, Leaves, Butterfly, Flower Finial, 6 In. . . . . *illus* 1320.00
Biscuit Jar, Opal, Floral Scrolling, Stippling, Oval, Pinched Sides, 6 In. 920.00
Biscuit Jar, Red Decorated, Cascading Dogwood, Oval, 7 In. 920.00
Fairy Lamp, Flowers, Light Blue, Cylindrical, Bulge, Ruffled, Flared Rim, France, 6 ½ In. . . . 950.00
Lamp, Art Deco Leaves On Shade, Blue Opaline Base, France, 19 In. 259.00
Lamp, Dragonflies, Bronze, Peacock, Iridescent Inset Jewels, Mt. Joye 6325.00
Lamp, Kerosene, Blue Cameo, Carved Flowers & Butterflies, 3-Footed, 4 In. 550.00
Lamp, Kerosene, Griffins, Flower, White, Yellow Base, Milk Glass Shade, Metal Foot, 31 In. . . . 345.00
Lamp, Mushroom Shade, Amber, Art Deco Flowers, Lemaire, 20 In. 1495.00
Magnifying Glass, Prussian Blue Handle, Stemmed Flowers, Oval Metal Frame, 7 In. 690.00
Perfume Bottle, Citron, Flower Branch, Butterfly, Twist Silver Lid, England, 3 ½ In. 690.00

Cambridge, Crown Tuscan, Compote, Keyhole Stem, 10 ½ In., Pair
$110.00

Cambridge, Rose Lady, Flower Frog, Amber, 9 ¾ In.
$395.00

Cambridge, Rose Point, Vase, Crown Tuscan, 8 ½ In.
$165.00

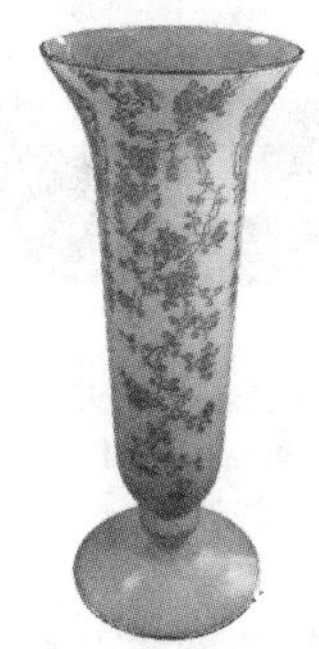

Cambridge Pottery, Vase, Lilies, Brown, Yellow, Green, Marked, c.1904, 14 In.
$225.00

Cameo Glass, Biscuit Jar, Frosted Red, White Flowers, Leaves, Butterfly, Flower Finial, 6 In.
$1320.00

Cameo Glass, Vase, Pink, Green Flowers, Purple, Frosted, Burgur, Schverer, 1900s, 4 In.
$3850.00

Cameo Glass, Vase, Poppies, Hammered, Streaks, Gold Trim, Verre D'Art De Lorraine, 7 In.
$4200.00

Perfume Bottle, Primrose, Citron, Oval, Crisscross Collar, Silver Twist Lid, 6 In. 920.00
Perfume Bottle, Red, Stemmed Leafy Flowers, Teardrop, Stalactite, England, 4 In. 1955.00
Perfume Bottle, Turquoise, White Flower, Round, Vine Overlay, Silver, England, c.1908, 3 In. 652.00
Plate, Rainbow Leaves, Ruffled White Rim, Rigaree Feet, Metal Handle, England, 6 In. 403.00
Vase, Amethyst, White Mottled Ground, Flowers, Leaves, 4 ¾ In. 120.00
Vase, Amethyst Thistles, Vessiere, 10 In. 480.00
Vase, Banjo, Purple Leaves, Stems, Yellow Ground, Blue Flower, Cameo, 6 ½ In. 1495.00
Vase, Citron, Stick, Banded Waist, Leafy Roses, Honeysuckle, Bulbous Base, 12 In. 920.00
Vase, Crimson, Green Leafy Stemmed Fuchsia, Signed, Arsall, 12 ¼ In. 690.00
Vase, Enameled, Aspen Trees, Pond, Mottled Pink, Lamartine, 8 ½ In. 2300.00
Vase, Enameled, Scenic, Stream, Rocks, Trees, White Ground, Lamartine, 8 ½ In. 3738.00
Vase, Flowers, Metal Base, G. Falkenberg, 3 ⅝ In. 250.00
Vase, Green Stems & Berries Band, Art Deco, Paul Nicholas, 10 In. 2300.00
Vase, Landscape Scene, Frogs, Green, Yellow, Signed, 8 In. 146.00
Vase, Lavender To Clear, Daffodils, Pinched Waist, 12 In. 90.00
Vase, Mottled Orange, Yellow, Long Stem Bouquets, Tulip Shape, 14 ⅛ In. 2868.00
Vase, Pink, Green Flowers, Purple, Frosted, Burgur, Schverer, 1900s, 4 In. . . . . *illus* 3850.00
Vase, Poppies, Hammered, Streaks, Gold Trim, Verre D'Art De Lorraine, 7 In. . . . . *illus* 4200.00
Vase, Prussian Blue, Shouldered, Leaves, Primroses, Triple Carved Border, 6 In. 1093.00
Vase, Purple, Pink, Green Flowers, Gold Trim, Bulbous, Bergun & Schverer, c.1900, 4 In. 4148.00
Vase, Purple Scene, Rocky Cliff Shrine, Biarritz, Shouldered, Flared Rim, Frosted, 9 In. 518.00
Vase, Stick, Blue, Cascading Flower, Bulbous Base, Footed, England, 6 In. 920.00
Vase, Stick, Frosted, Red Flowers, Green Leafy Stems, Bulbous Base, c.1900, 7 ¼ In. 3450.00
Vase, Stick, Frosted, Ruby Thistle, Bulbous, Pantin, 5 ½ In. 303.00
Vase, Yellow Spider Mums, Clear To Amethyst, Optic Ribbed, Ruffled Edge, St. Louis, 12 In. . . 235.00

CAMPAIGN *memorabilia are listed in the Political category.*

CAMPBELL KIDS were first used as part of an advertisement for the Campbell Soup Company in 1904. The kids were created by Grace Drayton, a popular illustrator of the day. The kids were used in magazine and newspaper ads until about 1951. They were presented again in 1966; and in 1983, they were redesigned with a slimmer, more contemporary appearance.

Bank, Boy & Girl Walking, Cast Iron, Gold Paint, 3 ¼ x 4 ¼ In. 180.00
Bank, Cast Iron, A.C. Williams, M 163, 3 ½ x 4 In. . . . . 66.00 to 90.00
Dish, Child's, Boy Holding Girl Doll, Alphabet Around Rim, 7 ½ In. 100.00
Dish, Child's, Girl Holding Boy Doll, Buffalo Pottery, c.1917, 7 ½ x 1 ⅜ In. 96.00
Doll, Girl, Hat, Composition, 6 Piece Body, Organdy Dress, Teddy, 13 In. . . . . *illus* 400.00
Figurine, Boy & Girl Walking, Gold Paint, Cast Iron, 3 ½ x 4 In. 55.00
Mug, Plastic, Boy & Girl, M'm! M'm! Good!, Anchor Hocking, 1992 . . . . 8.00
Paper Doll, Girl, 2 Outfits, Nurse Uniform & Hat, Dress, Dolly In Her Arms, Cut, 1930s. 22.00
Salt & Pepper, Plastic, F & F Mold & Die Works, Dayton, Ohio, 4 ¼ In. 42.00
Sign, Menu, Have You Had Your Soup Today, 15 Flavors, Tin, 1940s, 18 x 19 In. 288.00
Spoon, Silver Plate, International Silver Co., 1950-60s, 5 ½ In. 22.00
Tea Set, Tray, Pots, Pitcher, Creamer, Sugar, Utensils, Plates, Saucers, Cups, Chilton Toys 125.00

CAMPHOR GLASS is a cloudy white glass that has been blown or pressed. It was made by many factories in the Midwest during the mid-nineteenth century.

Decanter, Stopper, Hand Painted, Forget-Me-Nots, 1880s, 9 ½ x 6 In. 155.00
Lavaliere, Art Deco, Filigree, Sterling Silver, 19 ½ In. 116.00
Necklace, Filigree Setting, Sunburst Design, Emerald, Linked Chain, ⅞ x 1 ⅝ In. 150.00
Pendant, Art Deco, Sterling Silver, Filigree, Rhinestone, 1 ½ x ¾ In. 50.00

CANDELABRUM refers to a candleholder with more than one arm to hold many candles; a candlestick is designed to hold one candle. The eccentricity of the English language makes the plural of candelabrum into candelabra.

2-Light, Art Deco, Scrolled & Paneled Arms, Oval Base, Early 1900s, 5 ½ x 10 In., Pair 115.00
2-Light, Brass, George III, Cut Glass, c.1775, Pair 13750.00
2-Light, Brass, Marble, Draped Chains Of Cut Glass Beads, Sweden, c.1880, 15 In., Pair 2880.00
2-Light, Bronze, Art Nouveau, Nude Woman Emerging From Tree, 1903, 13 In., Pair 2640.00
2-Light, Bronze, Dog, Sleeping Children, Marble Base, 16 ½ In., Pair . . . . *illus* 1650.00
2-Light, Bronze, Dogs, Children On Marble Base, 16 ½ In., Pair 1725.00
2-Light, Bronze, Infant Satyr, Ormolu Mounts, White Marble Base, c.1780, 19 In., Pair 37500.00
2-Light, Bronze, Louis XVI, Cherub, Rouge Marble Plinth Base, 10 x 14 In., Pair. 1896.00
2-Light, Cased, Amethyst, Cut To Clear, Czechoslovakia, Early 1900s, 24 In., Pair 474.00
2-Light, Crystal, Central Spire, Scrolling Arms, Suspended Lustres, c.1900, 19 In., Pair. 568.00

2-Light, Cut Glass, Scroll Arm, Gilt Mounted, Prisms, Paw Feet, 15 In., Pair . . . 2300.00
2-Light, Gilt Bronze, Figural Elk, Wooded Landscape, Late 1800s, 13 In. . . . 299.00
2-Light, Gilt Bronze, Rococo Revival, Dolphin Standard, Scroll Arms, c.1855, 9 ½ In. . . . 940.00
2-Light, Gilt Metal, Cut Glass, Scrolling Arms, Diamond Cut Stem, 16 In., Pair . . . 600.00
2-Light, Iron, Arts & Crafts, 3-Footed, 13 In., Pair . . . 30.00
2-Light, Ormolu, 7-Candle, Fluted Column, Louis-Philippe, c.1840, 41 x 14 In., Pair . . . 15000.00
2-Light, Pewter, Arts & Crafts, Raised Leaves, Vines, 10 x 11 In. . . . 1800.00
2-Light, Porcelain, Cup, Lid, Flowers, Putti, Gold Mounts, Meissen, c.1750, 10 x 11 In. . . . 13750.00
2-Light, Sheffield Silver, Regency, Removable Bobeche, 1900s, 20 ½ In., Pair . . . 823.00
2-Light, Sheffield Silver, Scrolls, 16 In., Pair . . . 220.00
2-Light, Sterling Silver, Art Deco, Durham Art, Signed, 8 ½ x 10 In., Pair . . . 1100.00
2-Light, Sterling Silver, Signed, Mexico, 5 ½ x 7 ½ In., Pair . . . 300.00
3-Light, Brass, Scrolling, 15 x 8 ¼ In., Pair . . . 293.00
3-Light, Bronze, Art Nouveau, Pierced, Marble Base, 18 In., Pair . . . 225.00
3-Light, Bronze, Empire, Claw Feet, Marble Base, France, 1860s, 31 ½ x 12 In., Pair . . . 990.00
3-Light, Bronze, Scrolls, Putti, Applied Green Patina, 1890s, 19 x 12 In., Pair . . . *illus* 880.00
3-Light, Bronze, Shield Shape, Ed. Hurley, c.1918, 15 x 10 In., Pair . . . 819.00
3-Light, Bronze, Thistle, France, 19th Century, 20 In. . . . 468.00
3-Light, Chantilly Pattern, Scroll Arms, Weighted Base, Gorham, 13 ¼ x 11 ¼ In., Pair . . . 403.00
3-Light, Gilt Bronze, Tulips, Leaves, Marble Base, Paris, c.1915, 18 In., Pair . . . 5750.00
3-Light, Porcelain, Man In 1700s Clothes, Flowers, 17 ¼ x 10 In., Pair . . . 192.00
3-Light, Porcelain, Owl, Marked, E. Bohne & Sohne, 15 x 12 In. . . . 1438.00
3-Light, Silver, Baluster, Scrolling Arms, Gorham, 13 In., Pair . . . 300.00
3-Light, Silver, Baluster Shape, 2 Arms, Japan, c.1950, 9 ⅝ In., Pair . . . 900.00
3-Light, Silver, Chantilly Pattern, Gorham, 1895, 12 x 12 In., Pair . . . 448.00
3-Light, Silver, Circular Foot, Bead Trim, Flared Shaft, c.1970, Mexico, 12 ¾ In., Pair . . . 944.00
3-Light, Silver Plate, Convertible, Round Foot, Baluster, Scrolling Arms, 20 In., Pair . . . 227.00
3-Light, Silvered Bronze, Empire, Classical Woman, Urn, Gilt, France, c.1875, 37 In., Pair . . . 2360.00
3-Light, Sterling Silver, Buccellati, Domed Foot, Scrolled Arms, 16 x 12 ½ In., Pair . . . 2280.00
3-Light, Sterling Silver, Convertible, Birks, 13 x 11 In., Pair . . . 585.00
3-Light, Sterling Silver, Hunt Silver Co., Weighted, 8 In., Pair . . . 120.00
3-Light, Sterling Silver, Urn Form, Gadroon Edge, Mueck-Cary Co., 1950, 13 In., Pair . . . 425.00
3-Light, Sterling Silver, Weighted, Gorham, Late 1900s, 13 x 11 ¾ In., Pair . . . 468.00
3-Light, Urn Shape, Ormolu Scrolls, Goat Mounts, France, c.1795, 24 x 10 In., Pair . . . 10625.00
3-Light, Urn Sockets, Coil & Bead Finials, Shaped Posts, Denmark, 13 ¼ In., Pair . . . 3910.00
4-Light, Brass, Flowers, Patina, Edward Spencer, 1912, 17 x 13 In. . . . *illus* 5300.00
4-Light, Brass, Gothic Revival Style, Late 19th Century, 16 In., Pair . . . 100.00
4-Light, Bronze, Patina, Figural Bird Center, Hoofed Feet, Signed, Barbedienne, 24 In. . . . 500.00
4-Light, Bronze Dore, Rococo Style, 14 ¼ In. . . . 374.00
4-Light, Cut Glass, Suspended Prisms, 18 In. . . . 826.00
4-Light, Gilt Bronze, Champleve Enamel, Late 1800s, 20 In., Pair . . . 6250.00
4-Light, Gilt Bronze, Palm Tree, Dragon, Grapevine, Louis XV, 26 ½ x 17 In., Pair . . . 5000.00
4-Light, Gilt Metal, Applied Gilt Metal Swags, France, 21 In., Pair . . . 502.00
4-Light, Ormolu, Painted Chinese Men, Curved Branches, Base, c.1730, 11 x 12 In., Pair . . . 13750.00
4-Light, Porcelain, Figural Base, Flowers, Von Schierholtz, Dresden, c.1920, 15 In. . . . 146.00
4-Light, Scrolled, Handled Urn, Polished Slate Base, Napoleon III, c.1900, 26 In., Pair . . . 265.00
5-Light, Brass, Banquet, Multiple Tiers, Suspending Lustres, Victorian, 27 In., Pair . . . 269.00
5-Light, Bronze, Empire, Carved Marble Urns, Swan Handles, c.1975, 28 In., Pair . . . 2006.00
5-Light, Bronze, Empire Style, Woman, Candle Branches, Marble Plinth Base, 27 In. . . . 2015.00
5-Light, Bronze, Figural, Empire Style, Gilt, Patinated Scrolled, Malachite, 19 x 9 In. . . . 823.00
5-Light, Bronze, French Empire, Winged Woman, Globe, Gilt, 1800s, 29 In. . . . 4830.00
5-Light, Bronze, Tree Shape, Just Anderson, Denmark, c.1930, 19 x 18 In, Pair . . . 15600.00
5-Light, Bronze, Victory, Holding Lights, Orb, Ormolu Mounts, c.1805, 26 x 6 In., Pair . . . 18750.00
5-Light, Bronze Dore, Putti, Branches, Porcelain Flowers, Louis XV, c.1875, 23 ½ In. . . . 1912.00
5-Light, Empire Revival, Gilt Bronze, Marble, Swan Handles, 27 ½ In., Pair . . . *illus* 1870.00
5-Light, Gadrooned Candlecups, Flowered Drip Pans & Arms, c.1850, 13 In. . . . 1057.00
5-Light, Iron, Leaf Design, Scrolled Legs, 19th Century, 62 x 19 In. . . . 1020.00
5-Light, Iron, Rococo, c.1900, 20 x 10 In., Pair . . . 117.00
5-Light, Ormolu Spirals, Patinated Bronze Stem, Marble Base, c.1810, 20 x 8 In., Pair . . . 12500.00
5-Light, Silver, 4 Arms, Michael Boulton, Old Sheffield, England, 1800s, 22 In., Pair . . . 978.00
5-Light, Silver, Baluster Shape, 4 Scrolling Arms, Fluted, Germany, c.1887, 8 ½ In. . . . 216.00
5-Light, Silver, England, c.1901, 18 ½ In., Pair . . . 6435.00
5-Light, Silver, Scrolled Leaves, Mexico, 14 ½ In., Pair . . . 3450.00
5-Light, Silver, Vase Shape Standard, Female Bust Handles, 25 x 13 In., Pair . . . 1140.00
5-Light, Silver Gilt, Ivory, Carved Children Stem, Tripod Base, Italy, c.1910, 17 In. . . . 6875.00
5-Light, Silver Plate, Center Flame Finial, Rounded Base, Scroll Border, 29 In., Pair . . . 2300.00

Campbell Kids, Doll, Girl, Hat, Composition, 6 Piece Body, Organdy Dress, Teddy, 13 In.
$400.00

Candelabrum, 2-Light, Bronze, Dog, Sleeping Children, Marble Base, 16 ½ In., Pair
$1650.00

Candelabrum, 3-Light, Bronze, Scrolls, Putti, Applied Green Patina, 1890s, 19 x 12 In., Pair
$880.00

Candelabrum, 4-Light, Brass, Flowers, Patina, Edward Spencer, 1912, 17 x 13 In.
$5300.00

Candelabrum, 5-Light, Empire Revival, Gilt Bronze, Marble, Swan Handles, 27 ½ In., Pair
$1870.00

Candelabrum, 6-Light, Brass, Louis XVI Style, Satyr, Branches, Late 1800s, 24 ½ In., Pair
$3107.00

Candlestick, Brass, Chinoiserie, Tapered Slate Shaft, Bells, 19th Century, 10 In., Pair
$1760.00

Candlestick, Brass, Flared, Snuffer, Push-Up, 5 ¾ x 7 x 6 ½ In.
$200.00

5-Light, Silver Plate, Urn Socket, Scroll, Shell, Late 19th Century, 21 ¼ In., Pair 275.00
6-Light, Brass, Double Swivel Arms, Ribbed Shaft, Flared Base, 16 x 27 ¼ In.. .... 3000.00
6-Light, Brass, Louis XIV, Reticulated, Continental, Early 1900s, 22 ½ In., Pair 600.00
6-Light, Brass, Louis XVI Style, Satyr, Branches, Late 1800s, 24 ½ In., Pair .... *illus* 3107.00
6-Light, Bronze Dore, Marble, Louis XV Style, 19th Century, 26 ½ In., Pair................ 2360.00
6-Light, Gilt Bronze, Marble, Putti Holding Cornucopia, Paris, c.1890, 38 In.. .... 11500.00
6-Light, Silver, Ceres, Bacchus Stem, Mask Feet, Austria, c.1890, 26 In., Pair 12500.00
7-Light, Bronze, Putti Figures, France, 19th Century, 21 In.............................. 995.00
7-Light, Bronze, Woman, Faces, Art Nouveau, 31 x 20 In., Pair 305.00
7-Light, Bronze Dore, Scrolled Base, Garland, Louis XV Style, 29 ½ In., Pair 1475.00
7-Light, Gilt Bronze, Cut Glass, Rock Crystal, Louis XIV, c.1900, 31 In., Pair............... 6250.00
7-Light, Gilt Bronze, Ormolu, Opaline Glass, Tall Lily Sprays, Victorian, 35 x 14 In., Pair.... 353.00
7-Light, Silver, Flowers, Putti, Scroll Arms, Germany, c.1895, 28 In., Pair 8625.00
9-Light, Bronze, Women, Dolphins, Masks, Ormolu Mounts, c.1810, 49 x 12 In., Pair....... 98500.00
Silver, Mid 20th Century, Signed, RJ, Mexico, 12 ¾ In. 410.00
Spelter, Statue, Figure Holding Candelabra, Gold Paint, Blackamoor, c.1880, 60 In......... 2115.00

CANDLESTICKS were made of brass, pewter, glass, sterling silver, plated silver, and all types of pottery and porcelain. The earliest candlesticks, dating from the sixteenth century, held the candle on a pricket (sharp pointed spike). These lost favor because in times of strife the large church candlesticks with prickets became formidable weapons, so the socket was mandated. Candlesticks changed in style through the centuries, and designs range from Classical to Rococo to Art Nouveau to Art Deco.

Amethyst Glass, Etched Grapes, Leaves, Footed, Twist Stem, Sinclair, 10 In., Pair 230.00
Beechwood, Parcel Gilt, Gray Painted, Louis XVI Style, Lamp Mounted, 61 In.. .... 1440.00
Brass, 3-Ring Stem, Octagonal Base, Spain, Late 17th Century, 5 ¾ In.. .... 259.00
Brass, Alpha Shape, Original Bobeche, Jarvie, 11 x 5 In., Pair 840.00
Brass, Baluster Shape, Octagonal Base, England, 12 In., Pair 153.00
Brass, Banded Shaft, Flared Base, 10 In.. .... 44.00
Brass, Beehive, Push-Up, 8 ¾ In., Pair 95.00
Brass, Bells, Dish Base, England, 1850-1900, 11 ¼ In. 207.00
Brass, Black, Gilt Lacquer, 3 Paw Feet, Louis Philippe Style, 19 ¼ In., Pair 2880.00
Brass, Bulbous Top, Jarvie, 14 x 7 In. 4200.00
Brass, Cast, Canted Corners, Baluster Posts, Cylindrical Sockets, 1800s, 12 In., Pair 460.00
Brass, Chinoiserie, Tapered Slate Shaft, Bells, 19th Century, 10 In., Pair .... *illus* 1760.00
Brass, Flared, Snuffer, Push-Up, 5 ¾ x 7 x 6 ½ In. .... *illus* 200.00
Brass, Fluted Columns, Scalloped Base, France, 18th Century, 9 In., Pair 380.00
Brass, George II, Faceted Cup, Tapering 3-Part Shaft, Scalloped Base, 9 ½ In., Pair......... 588.00
Brass, George III, Turned & Faceted, Scalloped Foot, c.1800, 9 ¾ In., Pair 612.00
Brass, Glass Shade, Red Rim, Cut Glass Prisms, Russia, c.1885, 19 In., Pair............... 175.00
Brass, Hammered, Flowers, Insects, Square Base, 6 ½ In., Pair 99.00
Brass, Hog Scraper, Black, Wedding Band, Early 19th Century, 10 In., Pair................ 1170.00
Brass, King Of Diamonds, England, c.1880, 12 ½ In., Pair 375.00
Brass, Knopped Shaft, Scalloped Base, England, Late 18th Century, 9 In., Pair............. 380.00
Brass, Lota, Marked, Jarvie, 14 ¼ In.. .... 3000.00
Brass, Louis XVI, Reed Posts, Flowers, Leaves, Thistles, France, c.1780, 11 In., Pair 575.00
Brass, Onyx, Continental Style, 28 In., Pair 468.00
Brass, Pricket, Mid-Drip, Dutch, 17th Century, 8 ¼ In., Pair............................. 936.00
Brass, Queen Anne, Petal Base, Mid 18th Century, 9 In., Pair 468.00
Brass, Queen Anne, Scalloped Base, c.1750, 7 ½ In., Pair 556.00
Brass, Queen Anne, Shell Embossed Base, Mid 18th Century, 9 In., Pair 1900.00
Brass, Queen Anne, Square Base, Mid 18th Century, 6 ½ In., Pair 322.00
Brass, Rose Colored, Engraved, Bell Metal, France, 9 ⅞ x 5 ¼ In., Pair 1200.00
Brass, Short Stem, Octagonal Base, Spain, Late 17th Century, 3 ½ In.. .... 206.00
Brass, Square Base, Cut Corners, Signed, Rostand, 8 ½ In., Pair 30.00
Brass, Tapered, Reeded Column, Flowers, Leaves On Base, France, c.1795, 10 In., Pair 575.00
Brass, Tavern, Working Bells, Bradley & Hubbard, 11 In. 1285.00
Brass, Trumpet Base, Sausage Turned Shaft, England, 17th Century, 5 ½ In. 1404.00
Brass, Trumpet Base, Sausage Turned Shaft, England, 17th Century, 5 ¾ In. 3276.00
Brass, Wax Jack, Urn Shape, Drip Tray, Handle, 6 x 3 ⅛ In. .... *illus* 355.00
Bronze, Alpha Shape, Jarvie, 11 ½ x 5 In., Pair 480.00
Bronze, Baluster Form, Masque-Head Terminals, 3 Hoof Feet, Continental, 1800s, 17 In., Pair. 191.00
Bronze, Comic Opera Figures, Italy, 9 ½ In.. .... 144.00
Bronze, Figure, Napoleon III, Winged Victory, Red Marble Pedestal, 1800s, 29 In. 944.00
Bronze, Flared Torchere, Seated Griffins, Upright Wings, Square Base, Ring, 1800s, 55 In., Pair 3068.00
Bronze, Flowers, Scrolls, Gilt, Marked, France, 1800s, 17 ½ In., Pair..................... 345.00

Bronze, Gilt King, Queen, Glass Prisms, White Marble Base, 1800s, 15 In., Pair 230.00
Bronze, Gold Dore, Gothic, Gargoyle, Jewels, 3-Footed, c.1870, 20 ½ x 9 x 9 In., Pair........ 2200.00
Bronze, Gourd, Lion's Head Feet, Handles, Pricket, Drip Pan, Dragon, Japan, 10 In., Pair.... 150.00
Bronze, Lotus Capitals, Fluted, Acanthus Socles, Tripod Leaf & Claw Feet, 19 In., Pair....... 1762.00
Bronze, Louis XV, Scrolls, Leaves, France, 1700s, 10 In., Pair 1093.00
Bronze, Oil Lamp Shape, Classical Female Reading, Ormolu, c.1785, 15 x 14 In., Pair 31250.00
Bronze, Organic Form, Patina, No. 1, Signed, J. Preston, Chicago, 15 In. 7700.00
Bronze, Ornate Cup, Base, Oval Blue Porcelain Stem, Flower Cameo, Sevres, 9 In., Pair..... 129.00
Bronze, Pierced Design Over Green Glass Cup, Long Stem, Round Base, 1900s, 15 In., Pair .. 3200.00
Bronze, Seahorse, Sculpted, Patina, Signed, E.T. Hurley, 1916, 13 x 5 In. 1820.00
Bronze, Seahorse, Signed E.T. Hurley, 1905, 7 x 5 In. 960.00
Bronze, Swirl, Hexagonal Base, Button Feet, 23 ½ In., Pair 780.00
Bronze & Brass, Oak Branches, Leaves, Acorns, Removable Inserts, c.1900, 10 In., Pair..... 352.00
Cassolette, Ormolu, Beau Bleu Porcelain, Louis XVI Sevres Style, 12 x 4 ½ In., Pair 1140.00
Cast Iron, Figural, Colonial Lady, Painted, Judd Co., 10 ¼ x 5 ¾ In. .... *illus* 575.00
Chamber, Silver, Cone Snuffer, Drip Pan, Engraved, England, George II, c.1750, 6 In........ 540.00
Chamber, Silver, Leaf Base, Flower Form Ring Handle, Flower Nozzle, Russia, 3 ½ In. 1062.00
Chamber, Silver, Lobed, Paris, c.1768, 1 ½ x 8 ½ In.................................. 1170.00
Chamber, Silver, Wide Rim, Column Shape, Lobed Ribbed Base, Gyllenberg, c.1910, 4 In. ... 474.00
Cut Crystal, Scalloped Foot, Baluster Shape Stem, Petal Rimmed Nozzle, 9 ¾ In., Pair 191.00
Cut Glass, Rayed Sockets, Prisms, Waffle Cut Base, Early 1800s, 6 ¼ In., Pair 646.00
Enamel, Cobalt, Allover Gilt, Flowers, Birds, 9 In., Pair................................ 1035.00
Enamel, Copper, Battersea Stick, Cobalt Blue, Multicolor, Late 1700s, 9 ¼ In., Pair 1410.00
English Oak, Open Barley Twist, Metal Top, 10 ½ In., Pair............................ 325.00
English Oak, Open Barley Twist, Metal Top, 12 In., Pair............................... 350.00
Figural, Country Boy & Maid, Porcelain, Gilt Bronze, 13 In., Pair 1680.00
Gilt Brass, Kneeling Putti, Napoleon III, 6 ¾ x 3 In., Pair 210.00
Gilt Brass, Rococo, Baluster Standards, Medallions, Christ, Crown Of Thorns, 12 In., Pair... 823.00
Gilt Bronze, Figural, Stork On Turtle, Serpents, 19th Century, 14 In. 1175.00
Gilt Bronze, Louis XV, Henry Dasson, c.1881, 11 ¼ In., Pair........................... 5313.00
Gilt Lacquer, Bronze, Flower & Lotus Cup, Restauration, 9 ¾ x 4 In., Pair................ 1140.00
Giltwood, Figural, Carved, Kneeling Angel Holding Candlestick, Continental, 1800s, 22 In. .. 593.00
Giltwood, Pricket, Neoclassical, Fluted Standard, Rosettes, Draped Rows, 36 In., Pair....... 1560.00
Glass, Amberina, Moon & Star, 6 In., Pair 48.00
Glass, Bulbous Socket, Pewter Insert, Pyriform Stem, Pontil, c.1810, 9 ½ In. 847.00
Glass, Chippendale, 6-Sided Base, Central & Jefferson Glass, 7 x 4 ¾ In.................. 25.00
Glass, Dolphin, Step Base, Shells, Boston & Sandwich, c.1870, 9 ½ In., Pair................ 588.00
Glass, Emerald Green, Loop Base, Hexagonal Socket, Boston & Sandwich, 7 In............. 2115.00
Glass, Viking Pink, Square, 1 ¾ x 2 x 2 In... 25.00
Glass, White Opalescent, Fry Style Turquoise Diagonal Threading, Italy, 10 ¼ In. 115.00
Hexagonal, Purple, Lipped Socket, Flared Base, c.1840, 7 ¼ In.......................... 508.00
Hexagonal Socket, Dolphins, Shells, Stepped Base, c.1845, 9 ½ In. 158.00
Iron, Adjustable, Spiraling Stem, Handle, Wood Base, 7 ½ x 3 ¾ In. 468.00
Iron, Figural, Man & Woman Silhouette, American, 6 In., Pair 295.00
Iron, Hog Scraper, Flared Top, Tube Stem, Push-Up, Pat. 1853, Pa., 5 x 3 ⅞ In., Pair........ 350.00
Oak, Copper Bobeche, Base, Splayed, Charles Rohlfs, 14 ½ x 7 x 7 In.................... 6000.00
Oak, Turned, Silk Lined Wicker Shade, Hammered Copper Cap, Stickley, No. 55, 15 x 10 In... 2000.00
Onyx, Ormolu, Lion, Feather, Watch Hook, Brass Eagle, Pink Marble Column, 7 In., Pair.... 115.00
Ormolu, Fluted Shaft, Flower Mounts, 3 Female Caryatids, c.1820, 13 In., Pair 8750.00
Ormolu, Neoclassical, Palm Leaves, Egyptian Masks, Round Base, c.1800, 12 In., Pair 8125.00
Pewter, Bullet Form, 3 Fins, Swirl Base, Tudric, No. 0223, c.1905, 9 ¼ In................. 400.00
Pewter, Dome Base, Pear Stem, Hollow, Netherlands, Late 17th Century, 6 In., Pair......... 470.00
Pewter, Vase Form Stem, Octagon Base, Push-Up, 8 ½ In. 99.00
Porcelain, Flower Sprays, Jacob Petit, Paris, 10 ¾ x 5 ¾ In., Pair 900.00
Porcelain, Gilt Brass, Putti, Holding Cornucopia, Sevres Style, 23 x 11 x 6 In., Pair 1680.00
Porcelain, Hummingbird, Flowers, Bow, 18th Century, 8 ¾ In., Pair .... *illus* 385.00
Pressed Glass, Gallery Rim Socket, Quatrefoil Base, c.1835, 8 ½ In...................... 113.00
Rock Crystal, Classical, Tapered Standard, Stepped Base, 8 ½ x 3 In., 4 Piece 2233.00
Sandwich Glass, Cobalt Blue, 6-Sided Base, 9 In., Pair 250.00
Silver, Bobeche, Stippled, Chased Leaves, Flowers, Scrolls, Russia, 12 In., Pair 518.00
Silver, Columnar, Corinthian Capitals, Masks At Base, Sheffield, England, 11 ¼ In., Pair 588.00
Silver, Fluted Column, J.E. Caldwell, Gorham Hallmarks, 7 ½ In., Pair.................... 450.00
Silver, Fluted Shaft, Shell Base, Scroll Border, Geo. Happe, England, c.1899, 10 In. 1673.00
Silver, Leaf Decoration, Stepped Foot, Russia, 11 ½ In., Pair 1440.00
Silver, Leaf Scroll Border, Diamond Pattern Handle, France, 2 ½ x 10 ⅝ In................ 1527.00
Silver, Louis XVI Style, Towle, c.1920, 10 ½ In., Pair 405.00

Candlestick, Brass, Wax Jack, Urn Shape, Drip Tray, Handle, 6 x 3 ⅛ In.
$355.00

Candlestick, Cast Iron, Figural, Colonial Lady, Painted, Judd Co., 10 ¼ x 5 ¾ In.
$575.00

Candlestick, Porcelain, Hummingbird, Flowers, Bow, 18th Century, 8 ¾ In., Pair
$385.00

Candlestick, Tin, Sconce, Mirrored, Mosaic, Round, Crimped Drip Tray, 9 ½ In., Pair
$470.00

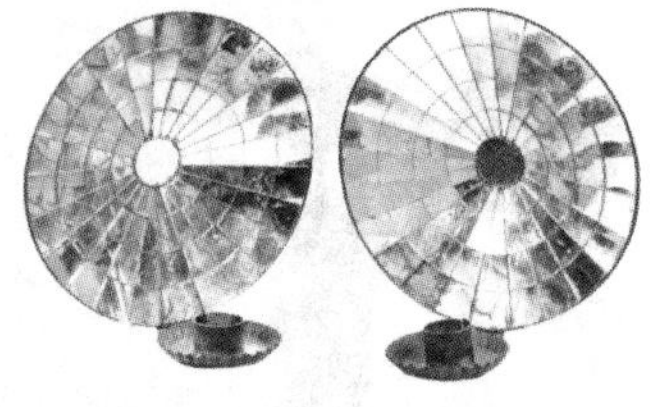

Candlestick, Tin, Wiggle Work, Tulips, Initialed, UT, GT, Pa., 1930s, 9 ¾ In., Pair
$266.00

Candy Container, Dog, Seated, White, Brown, Composition, Glass Eyes, Germany, 4 ¼ In.
$275.00

Candy Container, Peep In Suit, Painted, Composition, 4 ½ x 2 ¼ In.
$187.00

Silver, Neoclassical Style, London Hallmark, Monogram, 1891, 10 ¾ In., Pair 822.00
Silver, Square Base, Marked, Black Star & Frost, 13 In., Pair 900.00
Silver, Tapering Shape, 9 ¼ In., Pair. 96.00
Silver, Weighted, Bulbous Nozzles, Tapered Stem, Splayed Foot, 8 ½ In., Pair. 510.00
Silver Base, Round Green Quartz Stem, Paul Belvoir, 1997, 5 In. 2500.00
Silver Plate, Baluster Shape, 12 ⅜ x 5 ⅜ In., Pair 234.00
Silver Plate, Column, Urn Socket, Swags, Fluted Posts, Ram's Heads, 12 x 5 ½ In., Pair. 575.00
Silver Plate, Georgian, Paneled Stems, Electrified, Elkington & Co., 9 ¾ In., Pair. 121.00
Silver Plate, Owl, Branches, Gilt, No. 136166, Pairpoint, 7 ¼ In., Pair 60.00
Silver Plate, Ribbed Columns, Bulbous Center, 39 ¾ In. 33.00
Silver Plate, Sheffield, Corinthian Column, 19th Century, 11 In. 173.00
Silver Plate, Stepped Base, Capital, Ivory Fluted Column, Rodgers, c.1880, 12 In., Pair 885.00
Silver Washed Brass, Baroque, Italy, 19th Century, 21 ½ In., Pair. 745.00
Sticking Tommy, Wrought Iron, Scroll Decorated, Hanger Hook, Penn., 7 ½ x 5 ¼ In.. . . . . . 248.00
Tin, Adjustable, Green Paint, Brass Ring Finial, Holder, c.1820, 20 In.. . . . . 889.00
Tin, Brass, Hog Scraper, Wedding Band, Push-Up, Brass Ring, 1800s, 7 ¾ In., Pair. 646.00
Tin, Cone Shape Base, Prince Of Wales Feather Push-Up, Black Paint, 1800s, 9 ¼ In., Pair. . . 411.00
Tin, Hog Scraper, Flared Drip Pans, Wedding Ring Bands, Push-Up, 6 ¾ In., Pair 440.00
Tin, Hog Scraper, Wedding Band, Push-Up, 1800s, 6 ¾ & 5 ¾ & 5 ⅜ In., 3 Piece 441.00
Tin, Sconce, Mirrored, Mosaic, Round, Crimped Drip Tray, 9 ½ In., Pair . . . . *illus* 470.00
Tin, Wiggle Work, Tulips, Initialed, UT, GT, Pa., 1930s, 9 ¾ In., Pair. . . . . *illus* 266.00
Wood, Black Paint, Gilt, Round Base, 10 ¾ In., Pair 550.00
Wood, Reverse Painted Glass Shade, Leaves, Berries, Yellow, Pairpoint, 21 x 6 In., Pair 1080.00
Wood, Spiraling Shafts, Molded Base, Varnished, 12 In., Pair. 44.00

CANDLEWICK *items may be listed in the Imperial Glass and Pressed Glass categories.*

CANDY CONTAINERS have been popular since the late Victorian era. Collectors have long favored the glass containers, but now all types, including tin and papier-mache, are collected. Probably the earliest glass container sold commercially was the Liberty Bell made in 1876 for sale at the Centennial Exposition. Thousands of designs were made until the cost became too high in the 1960s. By the late 1970s, reproductions were being made and sold without the candy. Containers listed here are glass unless otherwise described. A Belsnickle is a nineteenth-century figure of Father Christmas. Some candy containers may be listed in Toy or in other categories.

Acrobats, 2 Seated, Supports Partners, Handstand, Bisque, Papier-Mache, 24 ½ In. 3081.00
Airplane, Spirit Of St. Louis, Glass, Tin, 6 ½ In.. . . . . 330.00
Amos 'N' Andy, Taxi Cab, Glass, 1 ½ x 5 x 2 ½ In.. . . . . 316.00
Barney Google, Painted, Glass, Tin Cap, Round Base, Marked, 1923, 3 ¾ In.. . . . . 11.00
Baseball, Graphics Of Stitches, Dresden, 3 In. 201.00
Belsnickle, Crepe Paper Robe, Fur Trim, Dresden Buttons, Germany, 12 In.. . . . . 1380.00
Belsnickle, Red Jacket, Blue Pants, Germany, 11 ½ In.. . . . . 450.00
Black Cat, Red Bow, Celluloid, 4 x 1 ½ In. 250.00
Bonzo, Glass, Brown Paint, Tin Lid, 3 ½ In. 201.00
Boot, Fashion, Mid Calf, Silver Ground, Gold Trim, Dresden, 4 ¼ In.. . . . . 1840.00
Camera On Tripod, Glass, Tin, Black, Red, Wood, 5 ¼ x 2 ½ In.. . . . . 11.00
Candlestick Phone, Glass, Wood, Wire, 5 In. 11.00
Cat, In Shoe, Composition, Applied Glass Eyes, Germany, 7 In.. . . . . 374.00
Chick, Papier-Mache, Brown Jacket, Striped Pants, Bowtie, Top Hat, 4 ½ In.. . . . . 220.00
Chick, Papier-Mache, Yellow Head, Blue Hat, Oval Body, 6 ¼ In. 88.00
Chicken, On Tree Stump, Papier-Mache, 3 ¼ x 1 ½ In.. . . . . 44.00
Child, Large Snowball, Composition, Tree Sprig, Spun Cotton Outfit, 4 ½ In.. . . . . 345.00
Clown Face, Red Hat, Painted, Composition, 3 ¼ In. 195.00
Crown, Jeweled, Orange Silk, Dresden, 2 ¾ In.. . . . . 518.00
Dog, Seated, White, Brown, Composition, Glass Eyes, Germany, 4 ¼ In. . . . . *illus* 275.00
Donkey Cart, Crystal, L.E. Smith, 4 ¾ x 2 ¼ In. 20.00
Don't Park Here, Glass, Painted, Embossed, Tin Lid, 4 ½ In.. . . . . 187.00
Easter Egg, Paper Lithograph Cover, Alligator, Natives, Ostrich, Boy, 5 ¼ In. 345.00
Felix The Cat, Roly Poly, Composition, Painted, 5 ½ In.. . . . . 220.00
George Washington, Composition, Cherry Tree Stump, Germany, 1920s, 6 In.. . . . . 115.00
George Washington, On Horseback, Bisque Head, Mohair, 8 ¼ In.. . . . . 1541.00
Glass, Metal, Red, Green, Handle, 3 ½ In.. . . . . 5.00
Kiddie Kar Horse Cart, Running Dog, Glass, Black, Red, Tin, Avor, 3 x 4 ½ In.. . . . . 121.00
Lantern, Glass, Red, Gold, Cardboard, Wire Handle, 4 ½ In.. . . . . 11.00
Lantern, Glass, Red & Green Lid, Handle, 3 ½ In.. . . . . 5.00
Liberty Bell, Shaker Top Closure 61.00
Locomotive, Silver, Gold, Pierced Wheels, Dresden, 3 ⅛ In.. . . . . 1150.00

Locomotive, Small, Plain, Screw Cap, Friction Type Closure 61.00
Mailbox, Glass, Green Paint 286.00
Monkey, Top Hat, Painted Face, Outstretched Arms, Silk Bag, Dresden, 2 ¾ In. 1610.00
Moon Face, Lithography, Fry's Chocolate, Dresden, 4 In. 575.00
Opera Glasses, Glass, Ribs, Metal, Wood, 4 x 3 ½ In. 55.00
Padlock, Attached Key, Dresden, 2 ¾ In.. .... 1035.00
Pail, Cover, Fleur-De-Lis, 3 Little Pigs, Tin, Bail Handle, 4 Oz., 3 x 3 x 2 In. 56.00
Peep, Applied Hat, Removable Head, Composition, Multicolored, 6 ¼ x 4 x 4 In. 110.00
Peep In Suit, Painted, Composition, 4 ½ x 2 ¼ In. .... *illus* 187.00
PEZ, Bullwinkle, Yellow Antlers, Copyright Ward Productions, 4 In. 145.00
PEZ, Creature From The Black Lagoon, Green, Austria, 1960s 253.00
PEZ, Frankenstein, White Face, Red Scar On Forehead, Black Base, 1960s, 5 In. 175.00
Piano, Milk Glass, Gilt Trim, 2 ¾ In.. .... 67.00
Pipe, Glass, Germany, 4 In. 55.00
Pumpkin Head Man, Band Uniform, Marked, Germany, 5 In. 330.00
Rabbit, Painted, Brown, White Belly, Cloth Bow, Dresden, 2 ½ In. 489.00
Rabbit, Peasant Outfit, Basket, Papier-Mache, c.1900, 15 ¾ In. .... *illus* 2440.00
Rabbit, Seated, Composition, Painted, Flocked, Glass Eyes, 12 In. 275.00
Rabbit, Seated, Wicker Basket, Composition, Painted, Glass Eyes, 16 In. 520.00
Rabbit & Chick, Papier-Mache, Cloth, Metal Wheels, 7 In. .... *illus* 460.00
Rabbit Family, Papier-Mache, Red Jackets, 7 ⅝ & 9 ¾ In., 3 Piece 1430.00
Ram's Head, Blue Silk Bag, Silver, Dresden, Germany, 4 In.. .... 3450.00
Red Goose Shoes, Football Form, Tin Lithograph, 1 ½ x 2 ¼ In. 11.00
Reindeer, Belsnickle Rider, Red Jacket, Blue Pants, 6 x 5 In. 950.00
Reindeer, Belsnickle Rider, Red Jacket, Blue Pants, Langer, 7 x 8 In. 1400.00
Rooster, Composition, Painted, Lead Feet, 9 ½ In.. .... 305.00
Rooster, Head Lifts, Hand Painted, Lead Feet, 8 ¼ In. .... *illus* 240.00
Santa Claus, At Chimney, Glass, Painted, 5 In. 230.00
Santa Claus, Boot, Santa Figure On Side, Pressed Cardboard, 5 In. 30.00
Santa Claus, Composition, Cloth, Rabbit Fur Beard, Tree, Germany, 13 ½ In. 550.00
Santa Claus, Composition, Germany, 13 ¾ In. 862.00
Santa Claus, Composition, Head & Hands, Painted, Rabbit Fur Beard, Hair, 15 In. 690.00
Santa Claus, Composition, Painted, Cardboard, Rabbit Fur Beard, 6 In. 86.00
Santa Claus, Composition, Rabbit Fur Beard, Germany, 5 In. 115.00
Santa Claus, Composition, Red Coat, White Trim, 6 ½ In. 523.00
Santa Claus, Composition Face, Cotton Beard, Red Suit, 1930s, 10 In. 190.00
Santa Claus, Feather Tree, Cloth, Fur, Germany, Early 1900s, 23 In.. .... 2310.00
Santa Claus, Glass, Plastic Head, Screw Cap, 6 In. 11.00
Santa Claus, Going Down Chimney, Glass, Painted, Marked, Avor, 5 In. 165.00
Santa Claus, Holding Tree, Pressed Cardboard, West Germany, 13 In.. .... 11.00
Santa Claus, In Sleigh, Composition, Cardboard, Painted, Glitter, Germany, 4 In.. .... 66.00
Santa Claus, Molded Head, Rabbit Fur Beard, Blue Coat, Tan Pants, Feather Sprig, 10 In. 978.00
Santa Claus, On Roof, Snow Covered, Cardboard, Cotton, Japan, 4 ½ In. 66.00
Santa Claus, On Sled, Painted, Rabbit Fur Beard, Felt Clothes, Germany, 5 ¼ In. 201.00
Santa Claus, On Sled With Barrel, Composition, Rabbit Fur Beard, 8 ¼ In. 172.00
Santa Claus, Red Jacket, Gray Pants, Brown Sack, 7 ½ In.. .... 500.00
Santa Claus, Rocker, Pipe In Mouth, Composition, Painted, Germany, 7 In. 1150.00
Santa Claus, Roly Poly, Composition, Cloth Covered, 10 ½ In. 1265.00
Santa Claus, Sack On Back, Cardboard, Wheels, Pull, c.1930, 2 x 7 In.. .... 173.00
Santa Claus, Seated On Log Stump, Crepe Paper Robe, Rabbit Fur Beard, Bag, 8 ½ In. 2300.00
Snowman, Cotton, Black Top Hat, Branch Cigar, 6 In. 173.00
Snowman, Pipe Cleaner Covering, Germany, 9 ½ x 4 ½ In. 40.00
Snowman, Red Top Hat, Bell, Musical, Cardboard, U.S. Zone Germany, 9 In. 30.00
Sphinx Head, Egyptian Style, Dresden, 4 ¼ In. 1035.00
Stagecoach, Opaque White, Painted, Gilt, Tin Closure, 1900s, 3 ¼ x 3 ¼ In. .... *illus* 205.00
Straw Hat, Germany, 1 ½ x 4 ½ In. 22.00
Suffragette, Metal Glasses, Green Hat, Plaid Jacket, Composition, Painted, 5 In. 165.00
Suitcase, Glass, Wire Handle, 3 x 3 ½ In. 33.00
Telephone, Plastic Mouthpiece, Wooden Earpiece, Contents, 3 ½ In.. .... 175.00
Trumpet, Milk Glass, Bear Decal, Germania Souvenir, Original Closure 90.00
Turkey, Composition, Lead Feet, Germany, 8 In. 920.00
Turkey, Composition, Painted, Metal Legs, 12 ½ x 7 ½ In. 1400.00
Wagon Car, Glass, Slide, 3 x 3 ¼ In. 121.00
Wedding Slipper, Painted, Crepe Paper Bag, Embossed, Dresden, 3 ¾ In. 201.00
Witch, Broom, Hat, Red Cape, Papier-Mache, Painted, Germany, 1900s, 12 In. 1600.00
Witch, Pumpkin Head, Broom, Papier-Mache, Painted, Germany, 1920, 8 In.. .... 350.00
Witch, Straw Broom, Paper Hat, Cape, 12 In. 1840.00

Candy Container, Rabbit, Peasant Outfit, Basket, Papier-Mache, c.1900, 15 ¾ In.
$2440.00

Candy Container, Rabbit & Chick, Papier-Mache, Cloth, Metal Wheels, 7 In.
$460.00

Candy Container, Rooster, Head Lifts, Hand Painted, Lead Feet, 8 ¼ In.
$240.00

Candy Container, Stagecoach, Opaque White, Painted, Gilt, Tin Closure, 1900s, 3 ¼ x 3 ¼ In.
$205.00

Cane, Telescope, Brass, Ebonized Shaft, Ivory Ferrule, 36 In.
$600.00

Cane, Walking Stick, Chased Sterling Knob, Beechwood Shaft, c.1890s, 36 ¾ In.
$300.00

CANES and walking sticks were used by every well-dressed man in the nineteenth century, but by World War I the style had changed. Today canes are used by few but the infirm. Collectors prize old canes made with special features, like hidden swords, whiskey flasks, or risqué pictures seen through peepholes. Examples with solid gold heads or made from exotic materials are among the higher-priced canes. See also Scrimshaw.

2-Piece Horn Knob, Carved, Engraved, Presidential Campaign Symbols, Maple, 1896, 38 In. 1080.00
Campaign, Grover Cleveland, Noisemaker, Wood Shaft, 35 In. 219.00
Dog, Mouth Operated With Lever, 31 ¾ In. 240.00
Glass, Twist, 33 ½ In. 130.00
Glass, Twist Handle & Point, 39 In. 60.00
Hardwood, Entwined Snakes, Crosshatched Metal Tip, Wire Chain Loop, 38 In. 143.00
Hardwood, Man's Head, Crosshatched Shaft, Stylized Snakes, 35 ¾ In. 187.00
Ivory, Bone, Curved Handle, Etched, 33 ⅜ In. 295.00
Ivory, Eagle Head, Wood Shaft, Silver Ferrule, Sterling Collar, 34 In. 2250.00
Ivory, Globe, Scrimshaw, Ebony Shaft, 36 In. 1062.00
Ivory, Hippopotamus, Glass Eyes, Ball In Mouth, 36 In. 590.00
Ivory, Horse Head, Macasser Ebony, Brass Ferrule, 35 In. 2750.00
Ivory, Hunter, Knotty Wood, Bone Ferrule, 19th Century, 34 In. 356.00
Ivory, Phrenology, Man's Head, Sterling Ferrule, Ebony, Monogram, 35 ½ In. 3422.00
Leather, Bearded Man, Meerschaum, 39 In. 50.00
Malacca, Ivory, Queen, Bust, Vertical Ribbed Knop, 36 ⅝ In. 652.00
Oak, Whimsy, Ball, Enclosed In Shaft, 1900s, 39 In. 147.00
Parade, Green Glass, Blown, c.1920, 37 ½ In. 88.00
Political, Abraham Lincoln, Bust, Pine, Metal Tip, 34 In. 55.00
Political, Cleveland & Hendricks Campaign, Wood Eagle, Flag, Heart, Leaves, c.1884, 33 In. 1265.00
Political, Harrison, Tyler, Corwin Campaign, Eagle Head Handle, Slogans, 1840, 37 In. 1320.00
Political, James Polk, Slogan, Profile, Glass, Whale Ivory Knob, Bone Shaft, 1844, 34 In. 6000.00
Presentation, Coin Silver, Flat Knob, Engraved, Alabama, c.1853, 36 In. 518.00
Quartz, Owl Head, Pink, Glass Eyes, Gold Collar, c.1975 944.00
Stagecoach, Wood, Malacca Shaft, Ferrule, Brass Fittings, c.1790, 58 In. 500.00
Stagecoach, Wood, Malacca Shaft, Ferrule, Brass Fittings, c.1820, 49 ¾ In. 250.00
Stagecoach, Wood, Snarling Dog Head, 37 In. 250.00
Telescope, Brass, Ebonized Shaft, Ivory Ferrule, 36 In. *illus* 600.00
Telescope Compass, Brass Lens Cap, 4-Draw, Spotter, Ebony Shaft, J.H. Steward, 16 ¾ In. 1093.00
Walking Stick, Benjamin Harrison Bust Handle, Black, 35 In. 837.00
Walking Stick, Blackthorn, Boar's Tusk, Ivory, Iron Ferrule, 37 ¾ In. 480.00
Walking Stick, Chased Sterling Knob, Beechwood Shaft, c.1890s, 36 ¾ In. *illus* 300.00
Walking Stick, Dog Head, Glass Eyes, Bamboo Shaft, c.1930, 34 In. 440.00
Walking Stick, Dog Head Grip, Star Chain Collar, Horses, Eagle, 1800s, 38 In. 854.00
Walking Stick, Ebony, Gold, Iron, Dragons, Phoenixes, Flowers, Japan, 19th Century 1185.00
Walking Stick, Ebony, Gold Filigree, Robert Hopkin, c.1895, 35 ½ In. 1872.00
Walking Stick, G. Cleveland, Under Glass Portrait On Top, Sterling Ring, 35 In. 657.00
Walking Stick, Grover Cleveland, Bust, Silver Top, 35 ¾ In. 1075.00
Walking Stick, Grover Cleveland, Bust, St. Louis, Brass Top, 37 In. 777.00
Walking Stick, Harrison, Morton Handle, Spelter, Wood, 1888, 34 In. 1135.00
Walking Stick, Ivory, Dog, Seated, Glass Eyes, Wood, 37 In. 110.00
Walking Stick, Ivory, Ebony, Multiple Faces, Japan, c.1900, 36 In. 410.00
Walking Stick, Jockey Riding Horse, Carved, Ebonized Shaft, c.1890, 37 In. 110.00
Walking Stick, Lincoln Fence Rail, Engraved, 1860 Quarter Top, 25 ¼ In. 10755.00
Walking Stick, Roosevelt, Knob Portrait, Bronze Plate, Wood, 1904, 34 In. 2270.00
Walking Stick, Teddy Roosevelt, Knob Portrait, Rebus Rose & Velvet Ribbon, 35 In. 1195.00
Walking Stick, William McKinley, Knob Portrait, Silver, 1896, 34 In. 448.00
Walking Stick, Wm. H. Taft, Knob Portrait, Slogan, 1908 Campaign, 36 In. 1554.00
Walking Stick, Wm. McKinley, Knob Portrait, Pot Metal, Our Next President, 36 In. 598.00
Walking Stick, Young Byran Figural Head, Slogans, Pot Metal, 1896, 35 In. 538.00
Watch, Cloisonne Case, Key Wind, Painted, Lakeside Scene, 36 ½ In. 690.00
Wood, Ball Above 4 Snakes, Multicolored, New England, c.1880, 36 In. 1645.00
Wood, Duck Head, Knob Top, c.1910, 34 In. 59.00
Wood, Fish, Bird, Alligator, Horse Head Handle, 1930, 37 In. 770.00
Wood, Hound's Head, Rooster & Sawtooth Band, Schtockschnitzler, 33 In. 1100.00
Wood, Man & Dog Head, Maple, Tools, Horses, Animals, c.1880, 34 In. 470.00
Wood, Man's Head, 1800s, 30 ¼ In. 119.00
Wood, Monkey Head, Glove Holder, 35 In. 322.00
Wood, Russian Wolfhound Head, 35 ½ In. 70.00
Wood, Sea Gull Head, Cast Iron, 32 In. 57.00
Wood, Snake, Eagle Head Around Mermaid, Whale, Anchor, U.S. Flag, 40 In. 460.00
Wood, Twisted, Multicolored, Thailand, c.1900, 37 In. 478.00

CANTON CHINA is blue-and-white ware made near the city of Canton, in China, from about 1785 to 1895. It is hand decorated with Chinese scenes. Canton is part of the group of porcelains known today as Chinese Export Porcelain.

Basket, Reticulated, 4 ¼ x 10 In. 247.00
Basket, Tray, Landscape, Reticulated, Oval, Flared Lip, 4 x 10 ½ In. 518.00
Bowl, Harbor Scene, Fishing Boats, Scalloped Rim, 10 & 8 & 7 In., 3 Piece 1035.00
Bowl, Vegetable, Cover, Boar's Head Handles, 19th Century, 10 x 12 In. 700.00
Bowl, Vegetable, Cover, Fruit Form Finial, Rectangular, 4 ¾ x 8 ¼ x 7 In. 99.00
Bowl, Vegetable, Cover, Shell Finial, Rectangular, 5 ½ x 9 ½ x 8 ¼ In. 132.00
Dish, Landscape, Rain & Cloud Border, Leaf Shape, c.1800, 8 In., Pair 205.00
Dish, Square, Blue Border, 8 ¾ In. 472.00
Ewer, Leaf Design, c.1850, 12 ¼ In. 2013.00
Ginger Jar, Lid, Fishermen, Net, Landscapes, 19th Century, 9 x 8 In., Pair 403.00
Ginger Jar, Underglaze Blue Lake, Architectural, Landscape Scenes, 1800s, 9 In., 5 Piece 489.00
Jardiniere, Chinese, c.1970, 5 x 11 In. 35.00
Platter, Houses, Water, Boats, 8-Sided, 19th Century, 15 x 18 ½ In. 644.00
Platter, Landscape, Cut Corner, Chinese, Mid 1800s, 12 x 9 ½ In., Pair 575.00
Platter, Landscape, Octagonal, 14 x 11 In. 330.00
Platter, Landscape, Oval, 10 ¼ x 13 ¼ In. .... *illus* 275.00
Platter, Water Scene, 8-Sided, 15 x 18 ⅜ In. 275.00
Platter, Well & Tree, Chinese, 19th Century, 12 ¾ x 9 ¼ In. 236.00
Sauce, Cover, Fruit Form Finial, 3 x 8 ¼ x 6 ½ In. 77.00
Sugar, Footed, Strap Handles, Dome Lid, Crab Finial, 5 x 4 In. 150.00
Teapot, Landscape, Spherical Finial, 5 ½ In. 55.00
Tureen, Cover, Houses, Landscape, Rabbit Handles, 8 x 13 x 9 In. 495.00
Tureen, Cover, Underplate, Boar's Head Handles, 7 ½ x 13 x 8 In. .... *illus* 489.00
Tureen, Soup, Oriental Scenes, Oval, Berry Finial, Strap Handles, c.1850, 8 ½ x 12 ¼ In. 288.00
Vase, Cover, 20th Century, 13 ½ x 8 ¾ In. 345.00

CAPO-DI-MONTE porcelain was first made in Naples, Italy, from 1743 to 1759. The factory moved near Madrid, Spain, reopened in 1771, and worked to 1821. Since that time, the Doccia factory of Italy acquired the molds and is using the crown and N mark. Societa Ceramica Richard is a modern-day firm often referred to as Ginori or Capo-di-Monte. This company also uses the crown and N mark.

Box, 2 Puttis, Lyre, Music, Lobed Front, 3 ½ In. .... *illus* 168.00
Box, Lid, Brass Mounted, Putti, Goats, Pink, Blue Purple, Oval, 4 x 6 In. 575.00
Box, Lid, Gilt Metal Mounting, Relief Cherubs, 3 ¼ x 6 x 3 In. 173.00
Bust, Napoleon, Stand, 15 ½ In. 225.00
Bust, Woman, Green Dress, Flowers In Hat, Gilt, 25 x 13 x 10 In. 605.00
Figurine, Cherub, On Ice Skates, Fur Trimmed Green Drape, Blue Mark, Ginori, 5 In. 75.00
Group, Couple, With Dog, Hare, Duck, Round Base, 7 ½ x 8 ¼ In. 144.00
Group, Courting Couple, On Canape, Painted Clothes, Features, 7 ¾ In. 90.00
Group, Man, Woman, Cello, Violin, 1700s Attire, 12 x 11 In. 489.00
Pedestal, Landscape, Figural, Multicolored Glaze, 20th Century, 37 In. 224.00
Plaque, Venus, Gold, Black Frame, c.1890, 6 x 7 In. 760.00
Plate, Center Crests, Pleasure Seeking Figures On Raised Borders, 9 In., 12 Piece 748.00
Statue, Jesus Taken Off Cross, c.1880, 19 x 13 ½ x 8 ½ In. 990.00
Stein, Bacchanalian Scene, Lion On Handle, Finial, Blue Crest Mark, 9 In. .... *illus* 207.00
Stein, Figures, Cherub Finial, Tree Branch Handle, c.1880, 10 ½ x 7 x 4 ¼ In. 400.00
Stein, Figures In Garden Landscape, Cherub Finial, Caryatid Handle, 2 Liters, 13 In. 2015.00
Stein, Inlaid Lid, Hand Painted Relief, Marked, N With Crown, ½ Liter 288.00
Stein, Noblemen Hunting Lion, Lion Finial, Gilt Metal Hinge, Eagle, 10 ¾ In. 889.00
Stein, Roman Soldiers In Battle, Helmet Finial, Gilt Metal Hinge, Eagle, 9 ½ In., Pair 1007.00
Urn, Cover, Medallions, Herculean Scenes, Early 20th Century, 18 In. 472.00

CAPTAIN MARVEL was introduced in February 1940 in Whiz comic books. An orphan named Billy Batson met the wizard, Shazam, and whenever he said the magic word, he was transformed into a superhero. A movie serial was released in 1940. The comic was discontinued in 1954. A second Captain Marvel appeared in 1966, a third in 1967. Only the original was transformed by shouting "Shazam."

Bank, Magic Dime Saver, Opens At $5.00, 8-Sided, Tin, 2 ⅝ In. 360.00
Blotter, Adventures Of Captain Marvel, Ruler, 1941, 3 x 7 In. 85.00
Comic Book, No. 20, Small Comic Attached, Fawcett, 1943 .... 2200.00
Magic Flute, On Die Cut Card, Lee-Tex Rubber Products Corp, 1946, 4 x 7 In. 173.00
Membership Card, Magic, Secret Code 47.00
Ring, Compass, Rocket Raider, Red, Black, Brass, Japan, c.1946 .... 330.00

Canton China, Platter, Landscape, Oval, 10 ¼ x 13 ¼ In.
$275.00

Canton China, Tureen, Cover, Underplate, Boar's Head Handles, 7 ½ x 13 x 8 In.
$489.00

Capo-Di-Monte, Box, 2 Puttis, Lyre, Music, Lobed Front, 3 ½ In.
$168.00

Capo-Di-Monte, Stein, Bacchanalian Scene, Lion On Handle, Finial, Blue Crest Mark, 9 In.
$207.00

Captain Midnight, Ring, Mystic Sun God, Brass, Plastic, Ovaltine Premium, 1946
$460.00

Card, Advertising, Trick Pony, Mechanical Bank
$518.00

Card, Advertising, Uncle Sam, Mechanical Bank
$863.00

Card, Baseball, John J. Evers, Piedmont Cigarettes, Factory 25, T-205
$390.00

Toy, Car, Racing, Windup, 1947, 4 In. 175.00

Toy, Car Set, Racers, Tin, Windup, Rubber, Automatic Toy Co., Box, 1947, 4 In., 4 Piece 990.00

Toy, Racer, Tin Lithograph, Green, Windup, Automatic Toy Co., 1947, 4 In. 376.00

Wristwatch, Captain Marvel Image, Fighter Jet, Green Band, Chromed Metal, Box, 1948 .... 878.00

Wristwatch, Metal Case, Vinyl, Leather Strap, Captain Marvel Jr. 403.00

Wristwatch, Shock Protected, Leather Band, Fawcett Pub. Co., 1948 .... 88.00

CAPTAIN MIDNIGHT began as a network radio show in September 1940. The first comic book appeared in July 1941. Captain Midnight was really the aviator Captain Albright, who was to defeat the Nazis. A movie serial was made in 1942 and a comic strip was published for a short time. The comic book version of Captain Midnight ended his career in 1948. Radio premiums are the prized collector memorabilia today.

Badge, Photomatic Decoder, Brass, Secret Squadron, Photo, 1942, 2 In. 45.00

Comic Book, No. 15, Fawcett, 1943 .... 550.00

Decoder, Brass, Aluminum Knob, Red Plastic Cover, 1948, 2 In. 158.00

Decoder, Mirro-Magic, Brass, Plastic, c.1948, 2 In. 125.00

Decoder, Mystery Dial Code-O-Graph, 1941 .... 29.00

Decoder, Whistling Code-O-Graph, Plastic, Radio Series, c.1947 .... 29.00

Ring, Mystic Sun God, Brass, Plastic, Ovaltine Premium, 1946 .... *illus* 460.00

Spinner, Flight Patrol, Burnished Bronze, Skelly Oil Logo, 1940, 1 ½ In. 12.00

Transfer, Iron-On, Captain Midnight's Secret Squadron, Ovaltine, 1949, 4 ¼ In. 115.00

Wings, Flight Patrol, Mysto-Magic, Skelly Oil Logo, c.1939, 3 In. 13.50

CARAMEL SLAG, *see Imperial Glass category.*

CARDS listed here include advertising cards (often called trade cards), baseball cards, playing cards, and others. Color photographs were rare in the nineteenth century, so companies gave away colorful cards with pictures of children, flowers, products, or related scenes that promoted the company name. These were often collected and stored in albums. Baseball cards also date from the nineteenth century when they were used by tobacco companies as giveaways. Gum cards were started in 1933, but it was not until after World War II that the bubble gum cards favored today were produced. Today over 1,000 cards are issued each year by the gum companies. Related items may be found in the Christmas, Halloween, Movie, Paper, and Postcard categories.

Advertising, C.H. Bean, Wine & Liquor, Ales & Beers, Clam Shell, Foldout, 3 x 4 In. 336.00

Advertising, Daimler Test First Auto, Topps Scoop, No. 116, 1954 .... 203.00

Advertising, Darktown Battery Baseball Bank, c.1888, 3 ¼ x 5 ½ In. 4700.00

Advertising, Dirigible Hindenberg Burns, Topps Scoop, No. 20, 1954 .... 478.00

Advertising, Dr. O. Fitzgerald, Dr. Image, Secret Of Health, 8-Sided, 4 ½ x 4 ½ In. 27.00

Advertising, Garrigues' Vegetable Worm Confections, White Ground, Red, Green, 5 x 6 ⅝ In. 80.00

Advertising, Great Atlantic & Pacific Tea Co., Couple On High Wheeler, c.1883, 7 x 10 In. 308.00

Advertising, Little Orphans Cigar, Best On Earth For 5 Cents, Image Of Orphans, 7 x 4 In. 55.00

Advertising, May Coal & Grain Co., Family Around Stove, Coal Bucket Form, 3 ½ x 3 ½ In. 5.00

Advertising, Morse's Yellow Dock, Horse, Root Syrup, Providence, R.I. 22.00

Advertising, Myers Pumps & Haying Tools, Girl, Dog, 2-Sided, Lithograph, 5 ¾ In. 110.00

Advertising, Trick Pony, Mechanical Bank .... *illus* 518.00

Advertising, Uncle Sam, Mechanical Bank .... *illus* 863.00

Advertising, Wilbur & Sons, Woman, With Children, 1889, 8 ¼ In. 80.00

Advertising, WM Deering & Co., Dogs In Field, 2-Sided, Lithograph, 6 In. 200.00

Baseball, Admiral Schlei, Batting, Lenox, 1909 .... 1500.00

Baseball, Arthur Hofman, Cracker Jack, No. 9, 1915 .... 600.00

Baseball, Babe Ruth, Butter Cream Confectionery, R306, 1933 .... 111625.00

Baseball, Babe Ruth, Maple Crispette, 1923 .... 1900.00

Baseball, Babe Ruth, Sets Record, Topps Scoop, No. 41, 1954 .... 1673.00

Baseball, Bob Clemente, Autographed, Topps, No. 478, 1959 .... 2280.00

Baseball, Branch Rickey, Cracker Jack, No. 133, 1915 .... 1175.00

Baseball, Cap Anson, Mayo's Cut Plug, N300, Chicago, 1895 .... 14100.00

Baseball, Christy Mathewson, Post Cereal, Hand Cut, 1930 .... 800.00

Baseball, Ed Rousch, Cracker Jack, No. 161, 1915 .... 1680.00

Baseball, F.W. Boyd, Just So Tobacco, 1893 .... 3525.00

Baseball, Geo. Buck Weaver, Broad Leaf Cigarettes, T207, Chicago Amer., 1912 .... 1800.00

Baseball, Honus Wagner, American Tobacco Co., T206, 1909 .... 188000.00

Baseball, Honus Wagner, Croft Candy, E92, 1909 .... 2000.00 to 2938.00

Baseball, Ike Boone, Zee-Nut, Old Pacific Coast League, 1 ⅞ x 2 ⅝ In. 145.00

Baseball, Jackie Robinson, Autographed, Exhibit Arcade, 1947 .... 400.00

Baseball, Jim Bottomley, Rookie, Maple Crispette, 1923 .... 1300.00

Baseball, Jim Mooney, Goudey, No. 83, 1934 .... 510.00
Baseball, Joe Jackson, American Caramel, E90-1, c.1910 .... 19975.00
Baseball, Joe Jackson, Cleveland Americans, Fatima Tobacco, T200, 1913 .... 823.00
Baseball, Joe Jackson, National Game, 1913 .... 1330.00
Baseball, John Clarkson, Allen & Ginter, N28, 1888 .... 1175.00
Baseball, John J. Evers, Piedmont Cigarettes, Factory 25, T-205 .... *illus* 390.00
Baseball, John Ward, Giants, Old Judge Cabinet, N173, 1888 .... 8813.00
Baseball, John Ward, Kalamazoo Bats, N.Y., N690, 1887 .... 141000.00
Baseball, Leo Durocher, Topps, 1952 .... 1500.00
Baseball, Lou Brissie, Leaf, No. 31, 1948 .... 228.00
Baseball, Lou Gehrig, Goudey, 1934 .... 1000.00
Baseball, Lou Gehrig, Goudey, No, 37, Signed, 1934 .... 5676.00
Baseball, Luke Appling, Leaf, 1948 .... 300.00
Baseball, Mel Harder, Goudey, No. 66, 1934 .... 450.00
Baseball, Mickey Mantle, Topps, No. 311, 1952 .... 7638.00
Baseball, Mike King Kelly, Old Judge Cabinet, N173, 1888 .... 9988.00
Baseball, Oscar Robinson, Negro League, Aquilitas Cigars, Cuba, No. 969, 1924 .... 5288.00
Baseball, Ray Demmitt, Polar Bear, 1910 .... 1200.00
Baseball, Roderick J. Wallace, Hassan Cigarettes, T-205 .... *illus* 720.00
Baseball, Roger Bresnahan, Gold Border, T205, 1911 .... 1528.00
Baseball, Satchel Paige, Autographed, Topps, No. 220, 1953 .... 1175.00
Baseball, Sherry Magie, Misspelled Magee, Piedmont Cigarettes, White Border, T 296, 1909.. 10200.00
Baseball, Stan Musial, 1952 .... 600.00
Baseball, Ted Williams, Topps, 1956 .... 900.00
Baseball, Ted Williams, Topps, No. 250, 1954 .... 2500.00
Baseball, Tom McLaughlin, Mets, Kalamazoo Bats, N690, 1887 .... 38188.00
Baseball, Topps, Unopened Wax Case, 1985, 20 Boxes 950.00
Baseball, Ty Cobb, Batting, American Caramel, 1922 .... 650.00
Baseball, Ty Cobb, Ty Cobb Card Co., T206, c.1910 .... 64625.00
Baseball, Walter Johnson, Ramly Tobacco, T204, 1909 .... 9988.00
Baseball, Walter Johnson, Washington National Player, 1909-11 .... 1302.00
Baseball, Willie Mays, Topps, No. 90, 1954 .... 1175.00
Basketball, Bob Pettit, 1961 .... 1680.00
Basketball, Michael Jordan, Rookie, Fleer, 1986 .... 1075.00
Basketball, Wilt Chamberlain, Rookie, 1961 .... 2040.00
Boxing, Ad Wolgast, Turkey Red, No. 53, 1911 .... 155.00
Boxing, Battling Nelson, Turkey Red, No. 57, 1911 .... 143.00
Boxing, Evan Lewis, S.F. Hess, 1888 .... 1314.00
Boxing, Harry Woodson, Lorillard's, No. 26, 1887 .... 508.00
Boxing, Jack Johnson, American Caramel, 1909 .... 836.00
Boxing, Jack McAuliffe, Old Judge Cigarettes, 1886 .... 2629.00
Boxing, James J. Corbett, Comics Novelty & Candy, c.1950 .... 777.00
Boxing, Jimmy Elliot, Lorillard's, No. 31, 1887 .... 418.00
Boxing, John Sullivan, Kinney Brothers, 1889 .... 956.00
Boxing, Johnny Marto, Turkey Red, No. 61, 1911 .... *illus* 263.00
Boxing, Paddy Carney & Austin Mitchell, Red Cross, N266, 1893 .... *illus* 287.00
Boxing, Paddy Ryan, Lorillard's, No. 16, 1887 .... 896.00
Boxing, Willie Lewis, Turkey Red, No. 74, 1911 .... 263.00
Boxing, Young Corbett, Robertson Candy Co., 1910 .... 358.00
Buffalo Bill, S.F. Hess, 1888 .... 1016.00
Fire Sweeps Chicago, Topps Scoop, No. 2, 1954 .... 478.00
Football, Bob Waterfield, Rookie, Leaf, No. 26, 1948 .... 3346.00
Football, Ed Beecher, Yale, Very First Football Card, Goodwin Champions, 1888 .... 3600.00
Football, George Connor, Leaf, No. 37, 1948 .... 1016.00
Football, Herb Adderly, Philadelphia, No. 71, 1964 .... 1673.00
Football, Knute Rockne, National Chicle, 1935 .... 1300.00
Football, Notre Dame's 4 Horsemen, Topps Scoop, No. 110, 1954 .... 448.00
Football, Sammy Baugh, Bowman, No. 30, 1952 .... *illus* 202.00
Football, Terry Bradshaw, Rookie, Topps, No. 156, 1971 .... 2868.00
Football, Tom Fears, Bowman, No. 51, 1950 .... *illus* 658.00
Greeting, New Year's Greeting, Roosevelt Portrait, Flag Pin, Mounted, 4 ½ x 3 In. 263.00
Greeting, Valentine, Boy & Girls, Heart Shape, 1920s, 3 ¼ x 3 ½ In. 12.00
Greeting, Valentine, Children, Ship, Crepe Paper Sails, 3-D Box, 14 x 13 In. 1200.00
Greeting, Valentine, Girl, To My Valentine, Jointed, Embossed, Die Cut, 12 x 6 ¼ In. 132.00
Greeting, Valentine, Penguin, Eyes Move With Fin, Easel Back, 1920s, 6 ¼ x 3 ½ In. 20.00
Greeting, Valentine, Sweetheart, 6 Blades, Tuck, c.1900, 9 x 12 In. 436.00

Card, Baseball, Roderick J. Wallace, Hassan Cigarettes, T-205
$720.00

Card, Boxing, Johnny Marto, Turkey Red, No. 61, 1911
$263.00

Card, Boxing, Paddy Carney & Austin Mitchell, Red Cross, N266, 1893
$287.00

Card, Football, Sammy Baugh, Bowman, No. 30, 1952
$202.00

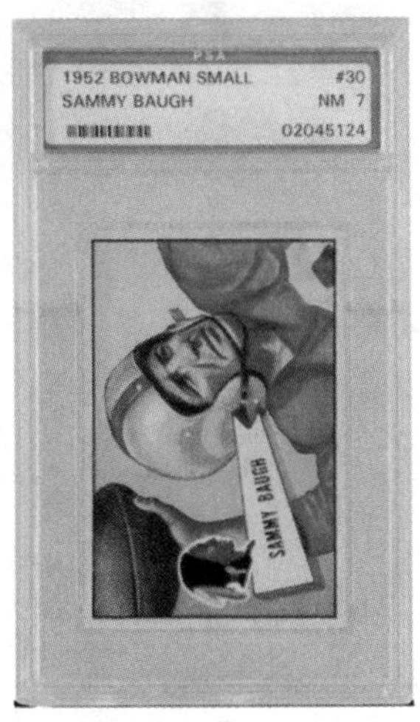

Card, Football, Tom Fears, Bowman, No. 51, 1950
$658.00

Top Ten Carnival Glass Patterns
Hundreds of thousands of users visit our website, Kovels.com, each month. The ten Carnival Glass patterns that are the most popular among our visitors are:

1. Grape & Cable
2. Acanthus
3. Imperial Grape
4. Dragon & Lotus
5. Holly Sprig
6. Peacock & Urn
7. Basket
8. Grape
9. Grape Leaves
10. Luster Rose

Hockey, Bobby Hull, Rookie, Topps, 1958 .... 2270.00
Hockey, Glenn Hall, Rookie, Topps, 1957 .... 777.00
Hockey, Gordie Howe, Topps, No. 89, 1964 .... 956.00
Hockey, Henri Richard, Parkhurst, 1957 .... 1673.00
Hockey, Leo Boivin, Topps, 1958 .... 299.00
Hockey, Topps, Complete Set, 1964-65 .... 2760.00
Playing, Harlequin, C.E. Carryl, Tiffany & Co., 1879, 3 ¾ x 2 ⅝ In., 52 Cards 1000.00

CARDER, *see Aurene and Steuben categories.*

CARLSBAD is a mark found on china made by several factories in Germany, Austria, and Bavaria. Many pieces were exported to the United States. Most of the pieces available today were made after 1891.

Oyster Plate, 6 Wells, 4-Sided, Scalloped Rim, Burgundy, Gilt, Flower Border, 8 ¾ In. 99.00
Plate, Woman In Garden, Pink, Carl Knoll, Fischern, Frame, c.1900, 10 ½ In. 380.00

CARLTON WARE was made at the Carlton Works of Stoke-on-Trent, England, beginning about 1890. The firm traded as Wiltshaw & Robinson until 1957. It was renamed Carlton Ware Ltd. in 1958. The company went bankrupt in 1995, but the name is still in use.

Ashtray, Bird, Tree, Green Ground, 4 x 4 In. 60.00
Biscuit Jar, Flowers, Cream Ground, Sheffield Silver Plated Lid, Handle, 10 In. 82.00
Bowl, Leaf Form, Flowers, Green, Branch Handle, No. 1681, Stamped, 3 ½ x 10 In. 50.00
Cup & Saucer, Rouge, Heron, Flowers, Gold, Demitasse 110.00
Ginger Jar, Lid, Multicolored Chinese Pagoda Scene, Blue Ground, 11 In. 170.00
Jug, Rouge Royale, Insects, Spider Web, Gilt, Marked, 7 ¼ In. 110.00
Pitcher, Flowers, Green, Branch Handle, 10 ½ x 6 ¼ In. .... 110.00 to 150.00
Teapot, Figural, British Bulldog Car, Dog In Driver's Seat, Flag Painted Auto Body 36.00
Teapot, Figural, London Bobby 35.00
Vase, Blue Royale, Spider Web, Flowers, Insects, Gilt, Enamel, 4 ¾ In. 300.00
Vase, Dragonfly, Hand Painted, Marie Graves, 5 ½ In. 180.00
Vase, Dragonfly, Hand Painted, Marie Graves, 7 In. 156.00
Vase, Ribbed, Pagoda, Yellow Ground, 7 ¼ In. 157.00

CARNIVAL GLASS was an inexpensive, iridescent, pressed glass made from about 1907 to about 1925. More than 1,000 different patterns are known. Carnival glass is currently being reproduced. Additional pieces may be found in the Northwood category.

Acorn, Bowl, Blue, 6 In. 67.50
Acorn, Bowl, Marigold, 7 ½ In. 77.50
Acorn, Bowl, Ruffled Edge, Blue, 7 ½ In. 95.00
Acorn Burrs, Berry Bowl, Green, 8 In. 115.00
Acorn Burrs, Berry Set, Amethyst, 7 Piece 475.00
Acorn Burrs, Punch Cup, Green 67.50
Acorn Burrs, Water Set, Amethyst, 7 Piece .... *illus* 500.00
Acorn Burrs & Bark pattern is listed here as Acorn Burrs.
Amaryllis pattern is listed here as Tiger Lily.
American Beauty Roses pattern is listed here as Wreath Of Roses.
Apple Blossom Twigs, Bowl, Ruffled Edge, Amethyst 65.00
Apple Blossom Twigs, Bowl, Ruffled Edge, Peach Opalescent 85.00
April Showers, Vase, Amethyst, Peacock Tail Feathers Interior, 11 In. 90.00
April Showers, Vase, Blue, 10 ½ In. 35.00
April Showers, Vase, Cobalt Blue, 6 ¾ In. 135.00
April Showers, Vase, Green, Squatty, 7 ¼ In. 135.00
April Showers, Vase, Marigold, 10 ½ In. 67.50
April Showers, Vase, White, 7 In. 1435.00
Argonaut Shell pattern is listed here as Nautilus.
Asters, Bowl, Marigold, 9 In. 25.00
Australian Butterfly Bower, Bowl, Dome Foot, Amethyst, 6 In. 85.00
Autumn pattern is listed here as Wild Berry.
Banded Medallion & Teardrop pattern is listed here as Beaded Bull's-Eye.
Basketweave, Basket, Open Edge, Blue .... *illus* 30.00
Basketweave, Basket, Open Edge, Green 70.00
Basketweave, Basket, Open Edge, Ruffled, Ice Blue 125.00
Battenburg Lace No. 1 pattern is listed here as Hearts & Flowers.
Battenburg Lace No. 2 pattern is listed here as Captive Rose.
Battenburg Lace No. 3 pattern is listed here as Fanciful.

Beaded Bull's-Eye, Vase, Amethyst, Squat, 6 ½ In. 200.00
Beaded Bull's-Eye, Vase, Marigold, 10 In. 86.00
Beaded Cable, Rose Bowl, Amethyst 30.00
Beaded Cable, Rose Bowl, Blue Opalescent 135.00
Beaded Cable, Rose Bowl, Marigold 30.00
Beaded Medallion & Teardrop pattern is listed here as Beaded Bull's-Eye.
Beaded Star & Snail pattern is listed here as Constellation.
Bells & Beads, Bowl, Ruffled Edge, Amethyst, 7 In. 85.00
Big Basketweave, Vase, Blue, 10 In. 105.00
Big Basketweave, Vase, Lavender, 10 In. 275.00
Big Basketweave, Vase, Marigold, 10 In. 145.00
Birds & Cherries, Bonbon, Blue 50.00
Birds & Cherries, Bonbon, Marigold 15.00
Birds & Cherries, Compote, Ruffled Edge, Blue 50.00
Birds On Bough pattern is listed here as Birds & Cherries.
Blackberry, Basket, Marigold, 7 x 5 ¾ In. 87.50
Blackberry, Basket, Open Edge, Amethyst 165.00
Blackberry, Compote, Amethyst 90.00
Blackberry A pattern is listed here as Blackberry.
Blackberry & Checkerboard pattern is listed here as Blackberry Block.
Blackberry B pattern is listed here as Blackberry Spray.
Blackberry Block, Tumbler, Blue 87.50
Blackberry Bramble, Compote, Green 95.00
Blackberry Bramble, Compote, Ruffled Edge, Amethyst 10.00
Blackberry Spray, Hat, Ruffled Edge, Aqua 30.00
Blackberry Spray, Hat, Ruffled Edge, Marigold 52.50
Blackberry Spray, Hat, Ruffled Edge, Red 395.00
Blossomtime, Compote, Ruffled Edge, Amethyst 205.00
Brooklyn Bridge, Bowl, Ruffled Edge, Marigold 125.00
Butterfly, Bonbon, Ribbed Back, Amethyst 275.00
Butterfly & Stippled Rays pattern is listed here as Butterfly.
Butterfly & Tulip, Bowl, Ruffled Edge, Footed, Amethyst 875.00
Buzz Saw, Cruet, Green 180.00
Cactus Leaf Rays pattern is listed here as Leaf Rays.
Captive Rose, Bonbon, Cobalt Blue, 7 ¼ In. 65.00
Captive Rose, Bowl, Ruffled Edge, Amethyst 75.00
Captive Rose, Bowl, Ruffled Edge, Green, 6 In. .... *illus* 85.00
Captive Rose, Plate, Blue, 9 In. 325.00
Carolina Dogwood, Bowl, Ruffled Edge, Milk Glass 33.00
Caroline, Basket, Peach Opalescent, Handle 55.00
Caroline, Plate, Handgrip, Crimped Edge, Peach Opalescent 15.00
Cattails & Fish pattern is listed here as Fisherman's Mug.
Cattails & Water Lily pattern is listed here as Water Lily & Cattails.
Checkerboard, Goblet, Marigold 205.00
Cherries, Bowl, Ruffled Edge, Footed, Amethyst, 7 In. 105.00
Cherries, Bowl, Ruffled Edge, Peach Opalescent, 9 In. 75.00
Cherries, Bowl, Scalloped Rim, 4 x 12 In. 35.00
Cherries, Plate, Amethyst, 6 In. 200.00
Cherries & Mums pattern is listed here as Mikado.
Cherry Chain, Plate, Marigold, 6 ¼ In. 30.00
Cherry Wreathed pattern is listed here as Wreathed Cherry.
Christmas, Compote, Amethyst 1800.00
Christmas, Compote, Red 175.00
Christmas Cactus pattern is listed here as Thistle.
Christmas Rose & Poppy pattern is listed here as Six Petals.
Chrysanthemum, Bowl, Crimped Edge, Footed, Blue 125.00
Circle Scroll, Pitcher, Marigold 210.00
Cobblestone, Bowl, Ruffled Edge, Amethyst 405.00
Cobblestone, Bowl, Ruffled Edge, Marigold 375.00
Coin Dot, Bowl, Deep, Red, 7 In. 825.00
Concave Diamonds, Tumbler, Vaseline 175.00
Concave Flute, Vase, Peach Opalescent, 10 In. 115.00
Concord, Bowl, Ruffled Edge, Amethyst 225.00
Constellation, Compote, Ruffled Edge, White 50.00
Corn, Vase, Olive Green, 6 ½ In. .... *illus* 440.00
Cosmos & Cane, Tumbler, Marigold 15.00
Cosmos Variant, Bowl, Marigold, 10 In. 45.00

Carnival Glass, Acorn Burrs, Water Set, Amethyst, 7 Piece
$500.00

Carnival Glass, Basketweave, Basket, Open Edge, Blue
$30.00

Carnival Glass, Captive Rose, Bowl, Ruffled Edge, Green, 6 In.
$85.00

Carnival Glass, Corn, Vase, Olive Green, 6 ½ In.
$440.00

C

Carnival Glass, Fine Cut & Roses, Candy Dish, Amethyst
$45.00

Carnival Glass, Fisherman's Mug, Amethyst
$35.00

Carnival Glass, Four Seventy Four, Pitcher, Milk, Marigold
$125.00

TIP
Don't put glass with an iridescent finish in the dishwasher. The hot water and soap will remove the finish.

Dahlia, Berry Bowl, Footed, White. 75.00
Daisy & Drape, Vase, Flared, Aqua Opalescent. 375.00
Daisy & Little Flower, Water Set, Enameled, Blue, 5 Piece. 155.00
Daisy Band & Drape pattern is listed here as Daisy & Drape.
Daisy Dear, Bowl, Marigold, Ruffled Edge, c.1915, 2 ½ x 7 ¼ In.. . . . . 60.00
Daisy Wreath, Bowl, Ruffled Edge, Blue Opalescent 350.00
Diamond Point, Vase, Lime Green, 9 ½ In. 300.00
Diamond Point & Daisy pattern is listed here as Cosmos & Cane.
Diamond Point, Vase, Amethyst, 10 In. 225.00
Diamond Point, Vase, Blue, 10 In. 300.00
Diamond Point, Vase, Emerald Green, 10 In. 500.00
Diamond Point, Vase, Marigold, 9 In. 25.00
Diamond Point, Vase, White, 9 In. 25.00
Dogwood & Marsh Lily pattern is listed here as Two Flowers.
Dogwood Sprays, Bowl, Ruffled Edge, Dome Foot, Amethyst. 165.00
Dogwood Sprays, Bowl, Ruffled Edge, Dome Foot, Peach Opalescent. 85.00
Double Star, Tumbler, Green 10.00
Double Stem Rose, Bowl, Dome Foot, Marigold. 40.00
Dragon & Lotus, Bowl, Ruffled Edge, Marigold, 9 In.. . . . . 10.00
Drapery, Candy Dish, Ice Blue . . . . . 45.00 to 75.00
Drapery, Rose Bowl, Aqua Opalescent 150.00
Drapery, Vase, Ice Green, 8 In. 125.00
Drapery, Vase, White, 8 In.. . . . . 45.00
Egyptian Band pattern is listed here as Round-Up.
Embroidered Mums, Bonbon, White. 900.00
Embroidered Mums, Bowl, Ruffled Edge, Ribbed Back, Amethyst 325.00
Fan & Arch pattern is listed here as Persian Garden.
Fanciful, Bowl, Ruffled Edge, Amethyst, 8 ½ In. 195.00
Fantasy pattern is listed here as Question Marks.
Fenton's Butterfly pattern is listed here as Butterfly.
Fern, Compote, Ruffled Edge, Green 45.00
Field Flower, Water Set, Amethyst, 5 Piece. 700.00
Field Thistle, Plate, Marigold, 6 In. 115.00
Fine Cut & Roses, Candy Dish, Amethyst. . . . . *illus* 45.00
Fine Cut & Roses, Candy Dish, Green 35.00
Fine Cut & Roses, Candy Dish, White 30.00
Fine Cut & Roses, Candy Dish, White, Footed 100.00
Fine Rib, Vase, Marigold, 10 In.. . . . . 38.00
Fisherman's Mug, Amethyst. . . . . *illus* 35.00
Fisherman's Mug, Marigold. 20.00
Fisherman's Mug, Peach Opalescent. 1200.00
Fisherman's Net pattern is listed here as Tree Bark.
Fishscale & Beads, Banana Boat, Peach Opalescent 25.00
Fishscale & Beads, Plate, Marigold, 6 In. 85.00
Floral & Diamond Point pattern is listed here as Fine Cut & Roses.
Floral & Grape, Pitcher, Amethyst 60.00
Floral & Grape, Water Set, Marigold, 7 Piece 35.00
Floral & Grapevine pattern is listed here as Floral & Grape.
Flour Flowers, Berry Set, Ruffled Edge, Peach Opalescent, 7 Piece 165.00
Flower Pot pattern is listed here as Butterfly & Tulip.
Flowering Almonds pattern is listed here as Peacock Tail.
Fluffy Bird pattern is listed here as Peacock.
Fluffy Peacock, Water Set, Marigold, 7 Piece 500.00
Four Flowers, Banana Boat, Peach Opalescent, 10 In.. . . . . 125.00
Four Flowers, Sauce, Peach Opalescent. 30.00
Four Seventy Four, Pitcher, Milk, Green 400.00
Four Seventy Four, Pitcher, Milk, Marigold . . . . . *illus* 125.00
Fruits & Flowers, Bonbon, Amethyst 65.00
Fruits & Flowers, Bonbon, Green. 50.00
Garden Mums, Plate, Amethyst, 6 In.. . . . . 105.00
Garden Path, Plate, Peach Opalescent, 6 In.. . . . . 105.00
Garland, Compote, Blue, 7 ¾ x 8 ½ In. 30.00
Good Luck, Bowl, Ribbed Back, Marigold, 8 ½ In.. . . . . 110.00
Graceful, Vase, Marigold 24.00
Grape & Cable, Berry Bowl, Amethyst, 9 In.. . . . . 99.00
Grape & Cable, Bonbon, Basketweave Back, Handles, Green, 7 In. 44.00
Grape & Cable, Bowl, Ruffled Edge, Aqua Opalescent, 7 In. 3250.00

Grape & Cable, Butter, Cover, Amethyst . . . 215.00
Grape & Cable, Candlelamp, Marigold . . . 575.00
Grape & Cable, Creamer, Amethyst, 4 ½ In. . . . 55.00
Grape & Cable, Dish, Sweetmeat, Amethyst . . . 95.00
Grape & Cable, Plate, Stippled, Green, 9 ⅛ In. . . . 176.00
Grape & Cable, Spooner, Amethyst, 4 In. . . . 55.00
Grape & Cable, Table Set, Amethyst, 4 Piece . . . 85.00
Grape & Cable, Tray, Dresser, Amethyst . . . 145.00
Grape Arbor, Tumbler, White . . . 25.00
Grape Delight pattern is listed here as Vintage.
Grapevine Diamonds pattern is listed here as Grapevine Lattice.
Grapevine Lattice, Plate, Marigold, 6 In. . . . 180.00
Grapevine Lattice, Tumbler, White . . . 110.00
Greek Key, Bowl, Basketweave Back, Scalloped Rim, Amethyst, 8 ¾ In. . . . 140.00
Hattie, Chop Plate, Green . . . 135.00
Heart & Vine, Bowl, Ruffled Edge, Amethyst . . . 55.00
Hearts & Flowers, Bowl, Ruffled Edge, Ice Blue . . . 205.00
Hearts & Flowers, Bowl, Ruffled Edge, Ribbed Back, Amethyst . . . *illus* 425.00
Hearts & Flowers, Bowl, Ruffled Edge, Ribbed Back, Aqua, 8 ½ In. . . . 1800.00
Hearts & Flowers, Bowl, Ruffled Edge, Ribbed Back, Ice Blue . . . 105.00
Heavy Vine, Powder Jar, Marigold . . . 155.00
Hobnail pattern is listed in this book as its own category.
Hobstar & Torch pattern is listed here as Double Star.
Holly, Compote, Ruffled Edge, Green . . . 25.00
Holly, Compote, Ruffled Edge, Marigold . . . *illus* 20.00
Holly, Plate, Marigold, 9 In. . . . 650.00
Holly, Plate, White, 9 In. . . . 300.00
Holly & Berry, Bowl, Ruffled Edge, Amethyst . . . 40.00
Homestead, Plate, Amethyst, 10 ¼ In. . . . *illus* 1540.00
Honeycomb, Rose Bowl, Peach Opalescent . . . 85.00
Honeycomb Collar pattern is listed here as Fishscale & Beads.
Horse Medallions pattern is listed here as Horses' Heads.
Horses' Heads, Plate, Marigold, 7 In. . . . *illus* 105.00
Illinois Soldiers & Sailor Home, Plate, Marigold, 7 In. . . . 25.00
Imperial Grape, Plate, Marigold, 6 In. . . . 45.00
Imperial Grape, Wine Set, Green, 6 Piece . . . 35.00
Interior Of Cherries & Mums pattern is listed here as Mikado.
Inverted Strawberry, Bowl, Green, 6 In. . . . 20.00
Inverted Strawberry, Candlestick, Marigold . . . 220.00
Inverted Thistle, Pitcher, Amethyst . . . 130.00
Iris, Compote, Ruffled Edge, Blue . . . 95.00
Iris, Goblet, Amethyst . . . 70.00
Iris, Goblet, Buttermilk, Marigold . . . 30.00 to 55.00
Irish Lace pattern is listed here as Louisa.
Kimberly pattern is listed here as Concave Diamonds.
Kittens, Cup, Marigold . . . 45.00 to 75.00
Kittens, Dish, 2 Sides Up, Marigold . . . 75.00
Knotted Beads, Vase, Marigold, 10 ½ In. . . . 55.00
Kokomo, Rose Bowl, Marigold . . . 13.00
Kulor, Vase, Blue, 6 In. . . . 525.00
Labelle Poppy pattern is listed here as Poppy Show.
Labelle Rose pattern is listed here as Rose Show.
Lattice & Grape, Pitcher, Tankard, Marigold . . . 45.00
Lattice & Grapevine pattern is listed here as Lattice & Grape.
Lattice & Points, Vase, White, Squat, 4 ½ In. . . . 85.00
Leaf, Bowl, Blue, 5 ¾ x 1 ½ In., Pair . . . 115.00
Leaf & Beads, Rose Bowl, Amethyst . . . 55.00
Leaf Rays, Nappy, White . . . 15.00
Leaf Tiers, Tumbler, Marigold . . . 60.00
Lily Of The Valley, Candy Dish, Cover, Amethyst . . . 45.00
Lily Of The Valley, Pitcher, Tankard, Blue . . . 1600.00
Lined Lattice, Vase, Squat, Peach Opalescent, 6 In. . . . 125.00
Lined Lattice, Vase, White, 10 ½ In. . . . 55.00
Little Barrel, Tumbler, Marigold . . . 75.00
Little Flowers, Sauce, Amethyst . . . 12.50
Loganberry, Vase, Amethyst . . . 200.00
Loop & Column pattern is listed here as Pulled Loop.

Carnival Glass, Hearts & Flowers, Bowl, Ruffled Edge, Ribbed Back, Amethyst
$425.00

Carnival Glass, Holly, Compote, Ruffled Edge, Marigold
$20.00

Carnival Glass, Homestead, Plate, Amethyst, 10 ¼ In.
$1540.00

Carnival Glass, Horses' Heads, Plate, Marigold, 7 In.
$105.00

Carnival Glass, Mikado, Compote, Marigold, 8 In.
$77.00

Carnival Glass, Open Edge, Vase, Hat, Red, 6 In.
$143.00

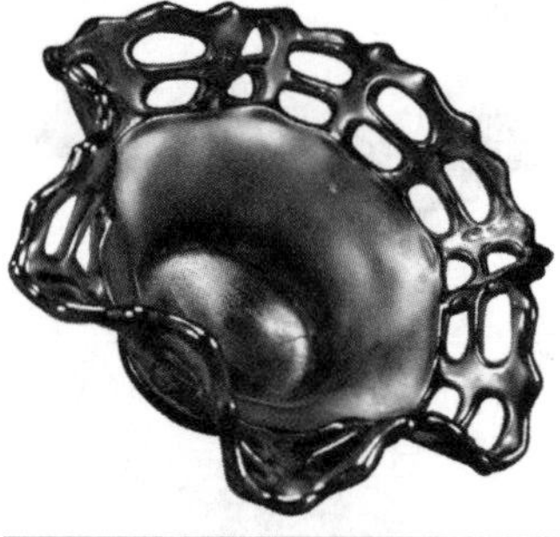

Carnival Glass, Orange Tree, Hatpin Holder, Blue, 7 In.
$213.00

Lotus & Grape, Bonbon, Blue . . . 55.00
Louisa, Rose Bowl, Green . . . 25.00
Luster Rose, Fernery, Blue . . . 42.00
Magnolia & Drape, Water Set, Marigold, Enameled, 7 Piece . . . 95.00
Magnolia & Poinsettia pattern is listed here as Water Lily.
Many Fruits, Punch Set, Amethyst, 7 Piece . . . 500.00
Maple Leaf, Berry Set, Amethyst, 8 Piece . . . 105.00
Mary Ann, Vase, Amethyst . . . 225.00
Mary Ann, Vase, Marigold . . . 10.00 to 30.00
Maryland pattern is listed here as Rustic.
Mayflower, Shade, Marigold . . . 10.00
Melind pattern is listed here as Wishbone.
Memphis, Punch Cup, Amethyst, 2 ¾ x 4 ¼ In. . . . 30.00
Memphis, Punch Set, Scalloped Rim, Amethyst, Bowl Base, 6 Cups . . . 445.00
Mikado, Compote, Marigold, 8 In. . . . *illus* 77.00
Mikado, Compote, Ruffled Edge, Blue . . . 225.00
Mirrored Lotus, Bowl, Ruffled Edge, Blue, 7 In. . . . 75.00
Morning Glory, Vase, Marigold, 9 In. . . . 55.00
Multi Fruit & Flowers pattern is listed here as Many Fruits.
Mums & Greek Key pattern is listed here as Embroidered Mums.
Nautilus, Creamer, Whimsy, Peach Opalescent . . . 145.00
Nautilus, Sugar, Whimsy, Peach Opalescent . . . 205.00
Oak Leaf & Acorn pattern is listed here as Acorn.
Old Fashion Flag pattern is listed here as Iris.
Open Edge, Vase, Hat, Red, 6 In. . . . *illus* 143.00
Open Rose, Bowl, Marigold, 7 In. . . . 45.00
Open Rose, Plate, Amber, 9 In. . . . 115.00
Open Rose, Plate, Pastel Marigold, 9 In. . . . 65.00
Orange Tree, Bowl, Ruffled Rim, Cobalt Blue, 9 In. . . . 25.00
Orange Tree, Dish, Amber, 9 In. . . . 330.00
Orange Tree, Hatpin Holder, Blue, 7 In. . . . *illus* 213.00
Orange Tree, Hatpin Holder, Marigold . . . 500.00
Orange Tree, Hatpin Holder, Marigold, 4-Footed, 6 ½ x 2 ½ In. . . . 77.00
Orange Tree, Loving Cup, Blue . . . 50.00
Orange Tree, Loving Cup, Marigold . . . 125.00
Orange Tree, Mug, Blue . . . 50.00
Orange Tree, Plate, Tree Trunk Center, White, 9 In. . . . 155.00
Panther, Sauce, Ruffled Edge, Footed, Marigold . . . 15.00
Peach, Tumbler, Blue . . . 50.00
Peacock, Bowl, Ruffled Edge, Ribbed Back, Amethyst . . . 375.00
Peacock, Plate, Marigold, 9 In. . . . *illus* 250.00
Peacock, Plate, Stippled, Ribbed Back, Amethyst, 9 In. . . . 4900.00
Peacock, Plate, Stippled, Ribbed Back, Marigold, 9 In. . . . 325.00
Peacock & Grape, Bowl, Ruffled Edge, Footed, Amethyst . . . 55.00
Peacock & Grape, Bowl, Ruffled Edge, Footed, Green . . . 55.00
Peacock & Urn, Bowl, Ruffled Edge, Blue . . . 95.00
Peacock & Urn, Bowl, Ruffled Edge, Persian Blue . . . 875.00
Peacock & Urn, Compote, Cover, Marigold, Clear Foot, 5 ½ x 4 ½ In. . . . 38.00
Peacock & Urn, Dish, Ice Cream, Scalloped, Amethyst, 10 In. . . . 130.00
Peacock At The Fountain, Table Set, Marigold, 4 Piece . . . 220.00
Peacock Tail, Compote, Ruffled Edge, Amethyst . . . 35.00
Peacock Tail, Compote, Ruffled Edge, Marigold . . . 25.00
Persian Garden, Bowl, Fruit, Marigold . . . 130.00
Persian Garden, Bowl, Peach Opalescent, 11 In. . . . 300.00
Persian Garden, Bowl, White, 11 In. . . . 155.00
Persian Garden, Plate, Marigold, 6 In. . . . 50.00 to 75.00
Persian Garden, Plate, Peach Opalescent, 6 In. . . . 125.00
Persian Garden, Plate, Pearl Of Pearls Back, White, 6 In. . . . 35.00
Persian Medallion, Card Tray, Sides Up, Blue . . . 35.00
Persian Medallion, Chop Plate, Blue . . . 250.00
Persian Medallion, Rose Bowl, Marigold . . . 85.00
Persian Medallion, Rose Bowl, White . . . 55.00
Petal & Fan, Plate, Crimped Rim, Amethyst, 6 In. . . . 145.00
Petal & Fan, Sauce, Crimped Rim, Amethyst . . . 125.00
Peter Rabbit, Plate, Blue, 9 In. . . . 6500.00
Peter Rabbit, Plate, Green, 9 In. . . . 2500.00
Pinched Swirl, Rose Bowl, Peach Opalescent . . . 50.00

Pine Cone, Plate, Green, 6 In. 55.00
Pine Cone Wreath pattern is listed here as Pine Cone.
Pineapple & Fan, Wine Set, Marigold, 8 Piece 265.00
Poinsettia & Lattice, Bowl, Amethyst, 7 ½ In. 1485.00
Pond Lily, Card Tray, Sides Up, White 40.00
Pony, Bowl, Marigold, 8 ½ In. *illus* 176.00
Pony, Bowl, Ruffled Edge, Amethyst, 8 ½ In. 65.00
Pony, Bowl, Ruffled Edge, Marigold, 8 ½ In. 45.00
Pony Rosette pattern is listed here as Pony.
Poppy, Compote, Amethyst, 7 In. *illus* 443.00
Poppy, Dish, Pickle, Blue 175.00
Poppy Scroll pattern is listed here as Poppy.
Poppy Show, Plate, Marigold, 9 In. 1500.00
Pulled Loop, Vase, Amethyst, 10 In. 25.00
Question Marks, Bonbon, Amethyst 25.00
Question Marks, Bonbon, Black Amethyst, Handles, 7 x 4 In. 90.00
Question Marks, Compote, Crimped & Ruffled Edge, Marigold 10.00
Question Marks, Plate, Crimped Edge, Peach Opalescent 40.00
Ragged Robin, Bowl, Ruffled Edge, Blue 95.00
Raspberry, Gravy Boat, Amethyst 45.00 to 50.00
Raspberry, Pitcher, Milk, Marigold 75.00
Ripple, Vase, Amethyst, 17 In. 1300.00
Ripple, Vase, Marigold, 3 ⅞ In. 70.00
Rose & Ruffles pattern is listed here as Open Rose.
Rose Paneled Dandelion, Pitcher, Tankard, Blue 300.00
Rose Show, Bowl, Blue 1650.00
Rose Show, Bowl, Ruffled Edge, Amethyst 300.00
Rose Show, Bowl, Ruffled Edge, Aqua Opalescent 550.00
Roses & Loops pattern is listed here as Double Stem Rose.
Rosette, Bowl, Ruffled Edge, Footed, Amethyst 40.00
Rosette & Prisms pattern is listed here as Rosette.
Round Up, Plate, Blue, 9 In. 250.00
Ruffles & Rings, Bowl, Blue, 3-Footed, 8 In. 65.00
Rustic, Vase, Amethyst, 10 ½ In. 35.00
Sailboat & Windmill pattern is listed here as Sailboats.
Sailboats, Plate, Marigold, 6 In. 65.00
Scotch Thistle, Compote, Ruffled Edge, Blue 30.00
Shell & Wild Rose pattern is listed here as Wild Rose.
Singing Birds, Berry Bowl, Amethyst, 8 ¾ In. 201.00
Singing Birds, Mug, Amethyst 40.00 to 70.00
Singing Birds, Pitcher, Amethyst, 8 ¾ In. 355.00
Singing Birds, Water Set, Amethyst, 7 Piece 550.00
Single Flower, Bowl, Enameled, Peach Opalescent 35.00
Six Petals, Bowl, Tricornered Rim, Crimped Edge, Peach Opalescent 30.00
Ski Star, Bowl, Ruffled Edge, Peach Opalescent 50.00 to 105.00
Ski Star, Plate, Crimped Edge, Peach Opalescent, 6 In. 40.00
Smooth Rays, Bowl, Ruffled Edge, Peach Opalescent 15.00
Stag & Holly, Bowl, Footed, Blue, 10 In. 175.00 to 225.00
Stag & Holly, Dish, Marigold, 9 In. 429.00
Stag & Holly, Plate, Ruffled Edge, Marigold, 9 ½ In. 25.00
Star & Fan, Cordial Set, Tray, Marigold, 8 Piece 185.00
Star Medallion, Pitcher, Milk, Smoke 15.00 to 35.00
Star Of David, Bowl, Ruffled Edge, Amethyst 55.00
Starfish, Bonbon, Peach Opalescent 55.00
Starfish, Compote, Peach Opalescent 50.00
Stippled Diamond & Flower pattern is listed here as Little Flowers.
Stippled Estate, Vase, Peach Opalescent 425.00
Stippled Leaf pattern is listed here as Leaf Tiers.
Stippled Leaf & Beads pattern is listed here as Leaf & Beads.
Stippled Posy & Pods pattern is listed here as Four Flowers.
Stippled Rays, Bowl, Amethyst, c.1920, 10 ½ x 3 In. 85.00
Stippled Rays, Bowl, White, 10 In. 85.00
Stippled Rays, Plate, Marigold, 6 In. 10.00
Stippled Rays, Plate, Pink, 6 In. 30.00
Strawberry, Bowl, Ruffled Edge, Amethyst, 8 ½ In. *illus* 154.00
Sunflower, Bowl, Footed, Amethyst 575.00
Sunflower & Wheat pattern is listed here as Field Flower.

Carnival Glass, Peacock, Plate, Marigold, 9 In.
$250.00

Carnival Glass, Pony, Bowl, Marigold, 8 ½ In.
$176.00

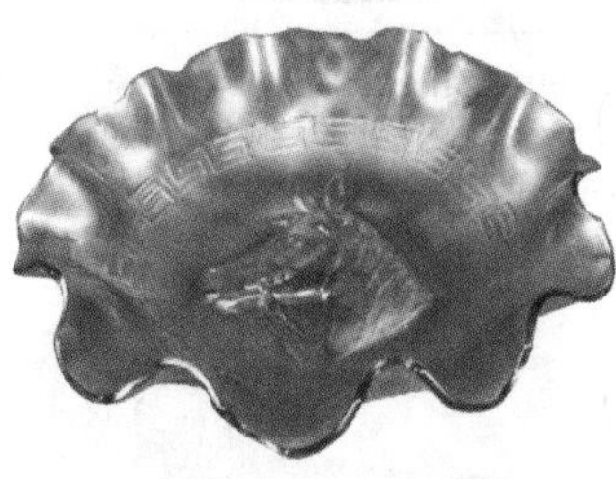

Carnival Glass, Poppy, Compote, Amethyst, 7 In.
$443.00

Carnival Glass, Strawberry, Bowl, Ruffled Edge, Amethyst, 8 ½ In.
$154.00

Carnival Glass, Town Pump, Vase, Amethyst, 6 ¼ In.
$475.00

Carousel, Horse, Painted, Wood, Dentzel, 58 x 70 In.
$4025.00

Carriage, Stroller, Wicker, Quatrefoil Panels, Simmons Hardware, c.1900, 35 In.
$525.00

Target, Vase, Peach Opalescent, 11 In. 25.00
Target, Vase, Squat, Peach Opalescent, 6 ½ In. 65.00
Thin Panel, Vase, Peach Opalescent, 7 ½ In. 85.00
Thistle, Banana Boat, 4-Footed, Green, 4 x 10 ¾ In. 150.00
Three Fruits, Bowl, Blue Ruffled Edge, 2 ½ x 8 ½ In. 175.00
Three Fruits, Bowl, Medallion, Green, Spatula Footed 115.00
Three Fruits, Bowl, Stippled, Ruffled Edge, Ribbed Back, Ice Blue 2700.00
Three Fruits, Plate, Amethyst, 9 In. 155.00
Three Fruits, Plate, Marigold, 9 ¼ In. 150.00
Tiger Lily, Pitcher, Marigold, 8 ½ In. 225.00
Tiger Lily, Water Set, Green, 6 Piece 175.00
Tornado, Vase, Amethyst. . . . . 300.00 to 400.00
Tornado, Vase, Marigold 400.00
Town Pump, Vase, Amethyst, 6 ¼ In. . . . . *illus* 475.00
Tree Bark, Pitcher, Marigold, Straight Sides, 8 ¾ In. 75.00
Tree Trunk, Vase, Amethyst, 9 ½ In. 260.00
Tree Trunk, Vase, Amethyst, 10 In. 55.00
Tree Trunk, Vase, Aqua Opalescent, 11 In. 1000.00
Tree Trunk, Vase, Blue, 10 ½ In. 375.00
Tree Trunk, Vase, Green, 10 In. 65.00
Tree Trunk, Vase, Ice Blue, 10 ½ In. 650.00
Two Flowers, Bowl, Marigold, 3 ½ x 6 In. 85.00
Vintage, Compote, Ruffled Edge, Green 45.00
Vintage, Rose Bowl, Amethyst 25.00
Water Lily, Berry Bowl, Ruffled Edge, Marigold, 8 In. 40.00
Water Lily, Pitcher, Marigold. 250.00
Water Lily & Cattails, Tumbler, Marigold, 4 x 3 In. 25.00
Wild Berry, Powder Jar, Marigold 65.00
Wild Blackberry, Bowl, Amethyst. 65.00
Wild Blackberry, Bowl, Ruffled & Crimped Edge, Green 65.00
Wild Bouquet, Creamer, Aqua Opalescent. 75.00
Wild Rose, Bowl, Green, 5 ¾ In. 75.00
Wild Strawberry, Bowl, Ruffled Edge, Amethyst 375.00
Wild Strawberry, Plate, Amethyst, Handgrip, 8 In. . . . . 85.00 to 100.00
Wild Strawberry, Plate, Green, Handgrip, 8 In. 265.00
Windmill, Pitcher, Milk, Green 80.00
Windmill, Pitcher, Milk, Marigold. 40.00
Windmill Medallion pattern is listed here as Windmill.
Wishbone, Bowl, Marigold, 9 ½ In. 275.00
Wishbone, Plate, Footed, Amethyst, 9 In. 250.00
Wishbone, Plate, Ruffled Edge, Footed, Green, 9 In. 1300.00
Wishbone, Plate, Ruffled Edge, White 225.00
Wishbone & Spades, Bowl, Ruffled Edge, Amethyst 200.00
Wishbone & Spades, Bowl, Ruffled Edge, Peach Opalescent 40.00
Wishbone & Spades, Chop Plate, Amethyst. 950.00
Wishbone & Spades, Plate, Amethyst, 6 In. 145.00
Wreath Of Roses, Bonbon, Amethyst . . . . . 30.00 to 35.00
Wreath Of Roses, Bonbon, Blue. 45.00
Wreath Of Roses, Bonbon, Green 30.00
Wreath Of Roses, Bonbon, Marigold. 10.00
Wreath Of Roses, Compote, Ruffled Edge, Green 30.00
Wreathed Cherry, Berry Set, Amethyst, 7 Piece. 55.00

CAROUSEL or merry-go-round figures were first carved in the United States in 1867 by Gustav Dentzel. Collectors discovered the charm of the hand-carved figures in the 1970s, and they were soon classed as folk art. Most desirable are the figures other than horses, such as pigs, camels, lions, or dogs. A jumper is a figure that was made to move up and down on a pole; a stander was placed in a stationary position.

Camel, Leather, Wool Saddle, Iron Stirrups, Rope Tail, Painted, c.1890, 34 x 48 In. 3555.00
Horse, Carved Mane, Saddle, Blankets, Rosettes, Criss Cross, Glass Eyes, 64 x 65 In. 863.00
Horse, Galloping, Jewels, Horsehair Tail, Glass Eyes, c.1915, 54 x 52 x 12 In. 3190.00
Horse, Galloping, Multicolored, Glass Eyes, Spillman, N.Y., c.1925, 46 x 39 In. 881.00
Horse, Jumper, Carved Saddle, Blanket, Fringe, Horseshoes, Glass Eyes, Parker, 59 x 51 In. 1380.00
Horse, Original Brown, Blue, Yellow Paint, Coca-Cola Lollipop Base, Aluminum, 46 x 68 In. 165.00
Horse, Painted, Wood, Dentzel, 58 x 70 In. . . . . *illus* 4025.00
Horse, Prancer, Wood, Carved, Painted, Glass Eyes, Gustav Dentzel, c.1905, 61 x 59 In. 17550.00
Horse, Scale Armor, Carved Saddle, Face Shield, Family Crests, 68 x 60 In. 633.00

Horse, Standing, Carved, Painted, Late 19th Century, 50 x 41 In. 690.00
Horse, Standing, Pine, Painted, Horsehair Mane & Tail, Metal Base, c.1875, 29 x 36 In. 705.00
Horse, Wood, Carved, Glowing Mane, Saddle, Glass Eyes, 60 x 60 In. 4600.00
Pig, Flying, Carved, Painted, Flowered Blanket, Saddle, Glass Eyes, 1800s, 62 x 24 In. 1495.00
Zebra, Wood, Carved, Red, White, Blue, Chas. I.D. Looff, New York, c.1875, 46 x 47 In. 22500.00

CARRIAGE means several things, so this category lists baby carriages, buggies for adults, horse-drawn sleighs, and even strollers. Doll-sized carriages are listed in the Toy category.

Baby Buggy, Wicker, JC Penney's Tag, 1940s 180.00
Baby Buggy, Wicker, Lloyd Loom, Menominee, Mich., c.1917, 24 x 17 In. 1000.00
Baby Buggy, Wicker, Scrollwork, Velvet Seat, Heywood-Wakefield, c.1880, 50 x 24 x 35 In. 345.00
Baby Buggy, Wicker, Stick & Ball, Wood Wheels, Stenciling On Base 120.00
Baby Buggy, Wicker, White, Rubber Wheels, Metal Handle, 16 x 34 x 40 In. 27.00
Horse Drawn, Wood, Wheel Under Horse, Horsehair Mane, Child's, c.1875, 63 x 33 In. 999.00
Sleigh, Portland Cutter, Wood, Painted, Red, Black, Red Metal Runners, Jackson Sleigh Co... 2271.00
Stroller, Wicker, Quatrefoil Panels, Simmons Hardware, c.1900, 35 In. .... *illus* 525.00

CASH REGISTERS were invented in 1884 because an eye on the cash was a necessity in stores of the nineteenth century, too. John and James Ritty invented a large model that resembled a clock and kept a record of the dollars and cents exchanged in the store. John Patterson improved the cash register with a paper roll to record the money. By the early 1900s, elaborate brass registers were made. About World War I, the fancy case was exchanged for the more modern types.

Hopkins & Robinson, Ky., Pat. Nov. 20, 1883, 14 x 19 In. 720.00
Kolter & Seitz, Walnut, Scrolls, Flowers Inlay, Plaque, 1888, 18 ½ x 16 x 19 In. 3500.00
McCaskey, 4 Drawers, 18 Ledger Slots, 43 x 27 ½ x 21 In. 173.00
Michigan, Brass, 9-Key 519.00
National, Brass, Wood Base, Numbered Keys Up To $3.00, c.1900, 16 x 17 In. 655.00
National, Model 46, Cast Brass, Marble Shelf, John Kolbe Co., 17 x 19 ½ In. 900.00
National, Model 49, Wood Crate, Candy Store Size, 1915 .... 718.00
National, Model 130, Painted, Wood Drawer, 15 In. 66.00
National, Model 313, Brass, 15-Key 439.00
National, Model 313, Brass, Marble Shelf, c.1912, 10 x 20 x 16 In. 948.00
National, Model 313, Brass, Nickel Plated, 21 x 9 ½ x 15 In. 495.00
National, Model 313, Bronze, Nickel Plated, Marble Shelf 385.00
National, Model 313, Candy Store, No Top Sign 500.00
National, Model 313, Cast Brass Alloy, Wood Shelf, 17 x 15 ½ x 10 In. 600.00
National, Model 313, Embossed, Polished Brass, 21 x 10 ½ In. 770.00
National, Model 313, Milk Glass Shelf, Oak Trim Base, c.1910, 17 x 10 ½ x 16 In. 1195.00
National, Model 332, Brass, 17 ½ In. .... 650.00 to 748.00
National, Model 349, Brass, Marquee Top, 24 x 17 x 16 In. .... *illus* 345.00
National, Model 349-2-2, Saloon, Brass, Marble, 2 Drawers, 34-Key .... 485.00 to 1570.00
National, Model 441, Brass, 21 x 19 x 15 ¼ In. 450.00
National, Model 442, Brass, 21 x 19 x 15 In. 90.00
National, Model 442, Nickel Plated, 1914 .... 275.00
National, Model 448, Nickel Plated, Wood Base, Prints, 1911, 24 x 18 x 15 In. .... *illus* 922.00
National, Model 717, Wood Grain, Steel Case, 17 x 10 In. 44.00
Offenbaker Manufacturers, Brass, Oak Drawer, 17 x 11 ½ In. 3600.00
Royal, Model 313, Fleur-De-Lis, 21 x 10 x 16 In. 600.00
St. Louis, Model 45, Brass, Copper, Mahogany 590.00

CASTOR JARS for pickles are glass jars about six inches in height, held in special metal holders. They became a popular dinner table accessory about 1890. Each jar had a top that was usually silver or silver plate. The frame, also of a silver metal, had a handle that arched above the jar and a hook that held a pair of tongs. By 1900, the pickle castor was out of fashion. Many examples found today have reproduced glass jars in old holders. Additional pickle castors may be found in the various Glass categories.

Pickle, 2 Clear Inserts, Meriden Silver Plated Holder, 10 ¾ x 8 In. 110.00
Pickle, 2 Jars, Flowers, c.1875, Lidded, 11 ¼ In. 47.00
Pickle, Amber, Silver Plate, 19th Century, 11 In. 88.00
Pickle, Blue, Victorian Quadruple, Plated Frame, Late 19th Century, 11 In. .... *illus* 275.00
Pickle, Bristol Glass, Silver Plate, 19th Century, 11 In. 70.00
Pickle, Clear, Embossed Swan, Aurora Silver Plated Frame, 10 ½ In. 100.00
Pickle, Clear, Engraved Insert, Silver Plated Base, 11 ¼ In. 110.00
Pickle, Cranberry, Coin Spot, Enameled Flowers, Palm Leaf, Meriden, Silver Plated Frame, 12 In. 600.00

Cash Register, National, Model 349, Brass, Marquee Top, 24 x 17 x 16 In.
$345.00

TIP

The best burglary protection is a dog. Inmates from three Ohio prisons were surveyed and said timed lights, deadbolt locks, and alarms are deterrents; but the thing most avoided by a professional thief is a noisy dog.

Cash Register, National, Model 448, Nickel Plated, Wood Base, Prints, 1911, 24 x 18 x 15 In.
$922.00

As always, the edited listings in *Kovels' Antiques & Collectibles Price Guide 2010* aren't available on any website, but readers should visit Kovels.com for information on trends, tips, reproductions, marks, old prices, and more!

Castor Jar, Pickle, Blue, Victorian Quadruple, Plated Frame, Late 19th Century, 11 In.
$275.00

Castor Jar, Pickle, Cranberry, Silver Plated Frame, 12 ½ In.
$225.00

Castor Set, 2 Bottles, Cranberry, Grapes, Shakers, Silver Plated Stand, 11 ½ x 9 In.
$250.00

Castor Jar, Pickle, Cranberry, Optic Rib, Bird Embossed Pierced Frame, c.1900, 12 In.
$590.00

Castor Jar, Pickle, Frosted, Birds, Embossed Caddy, Reed & Barton, 1900s, 13 In.
$472.00

Castor Set, 6 Bottles, Daisy & Button, Vaseline, Birds, Silver Plated Stand, 19-In. Stand
$550.00

Castor Jar, Pickle, Cranberry, Ribs, Bulbous, Miller, Silver Plated Frame, Tongs, c.1890, 12 In.
$100.00

Castor Jar, Pickle, Satin, Reed & Barton, c.1890, 9 In.
$425.00

Castor Set, 7 Bottles, Cruets, Shakers, Mustard, Lazy Susan Caddy, Late 1800s, 17 In.
$413.00

Pickle, Cranberry, Coin Spot, Silver Plated Frame, 10 ½ In. 50.00
Pickle, Cranberry, Opalescent, Hobnail, Silver Plated Stand, 10 In. 259.00
Pickle, Cranberry, Optic Rib, Bird Embossed Pierced Frame, c.1900, 12 In. .... *illus* 590.00
Pickle, Cranberry, Ribs, Bulbous, Miller, Silver Plated Frame, Tongs, c.1890, 12 In. .... *illus* 100.00
Pickle, Cranberry, Silver Plated Frame, 12 ½ In. .... *illus* 225.00
Pickle, Cranberry, Thumbprint, Silver Plated Frame 400.00
Pickle, Cranberry, Thumbprint, Silver Plated Frame, Hartford, 8 In. 176.00
Pickle, Cranberry, Silver Plate, Tongs, 19th Century, 11 In. 117.00
Pickle, Frosted, Birds, Embossed Caddy, Reed & Barton, 1900s, 13 In. .... *illus* 472.00
Pickle, Pink Glass Insert, Tongs, Frame, Rockford Silver Co., c.1890, 11 In. 138.00
Pickle, Pressed Glass, Victorian, Silver Plated Frame, 11 In. 38.00
Pickle, Ruby, Ornate, Silver Plated Frame, Victorian, 12 In. 292.00
Pickle, Satin, Blue, Footed, Tongs, Reed & Barton, Plated Frame, c.1890, 11 In. 275.00
Pickle, Satin, Reed & Barton, c.1890, 9 In. .... *illus* 425.00
Pickle, Silver & Blue, Silver Plate, 19th Century, 12 In. 88.00
Pickle, Victorian, Cranberry, Thumbprint, Silver Plated Frame, 10 ½ In. 88.00

CASTOR SETS holding just salt and pepper castors were used in the seventeenth century. The sugar castor, mustard pot, spice dredger (shaker), bottles for vinegar and oil, and other spice holders became popular by the eighteenth century. These sets were usually made of sterling silver. The American Victorian castor set, the type most collected today, was made of silver plated Britannia metal. Colored glass bottles were introduced after the Civil War. The sets were out of fashion by World War I. Be careful when buying sets with colored bottles; many are reproductions. Other castor sets may be listed in various porcelain and glass categories in this book.

2 Bottles, Cranberry, Grapes, Shakers, Silver Plated Stand, 11 ½ x 9 In. .... *illus* 250.00
2 Bottles, Silver Lids, Lobbed Stand, Shell Salt, 2 Spoons, London, 1875, 5 x 5 In. 805.00
3 Bottles, Crystal, English Sheffield Plate, 11 x 10 In. 146.00
5 Bottles, Scroll Etched Cut Glass, George III Silver Stand, Tops, London, 1756, 8 In. 805.00
6 Bottles, Daisy & Button, Vaseline, Birds, Silver Plated Stand, 19-In. Stand .... *illus* 550.00
6 Bottles, Elk Heads, Relief Design, Silver Plated Stand, Meridan Britainia, 18 In. 225.00
6 Bottles, Engraved, Gadrooned Holder, Silver Handles, Tops, 10 ½ In. 540.00
6 Bottles, Nickle Plate, Embossed Gothic Style, E. Gleason, c.1857, 17 x 7 In. 1150.00
7 Bottles, Cruets, Shakers, Mustard, Lazy Susan Caddy, Late 1800s, 17 In. .... *illus* 413.00

CATALOGS *are listed in the Paper category.*

CAUGHLEY porcelain was made in England from 1772 to 1814. Caughley porcelains are very similar in appearance to those made at the Worcester factory. See the Salopian category for related items.

Bowl, Cover, Flowers & Butterfly, Flower Finial, Blue, White, c.1780, 5 x 4 In. 125.00
Bowl, Fence & House, Fitzhugh Border, Blue, White, Label, c.1780, 6 ¼ In. 180.00
Bowl, Fisherman, Blue, White, c.1780, 2 ½ x 6 In. 80.00
Bowl, Garland Border, Ribs, Gilt, c.1790, 3 x 6 In. 75.00
Creamer, Fisherman, Sparrow Beak, Blue, White, c.1774-1800, 3 ¾ x 3 In. 125.00
Cup, Bird On Branch, Blue, White, c.1770, 2 ¼ In. 85.00
Cup & Saucer, House & Fence, Blue, White, c.1780 .... 110.00
Cup & Saucer, Temple, Gilt, Ribs, Scalloped Rim, Blue, White 60.00
Dish, Asparagus, Fisherman, Blue, White, c.1785-90, 3 x 3 In. 80.00
Dish, Dessert, Weir, Kidney Form, Blue, White, 1785-90, 10 In. 280.00
Dish, Pleasure Boat, Scallop Shell Form, Blue, White, c.1780, 6 ½ In. 140.00
Dish, Trailing Vine, Leaf Form, Blue, White, c.1880, 3 In. 25.00
Jug, Milk, 3 Flowers, Butterfly, Baluster, Blue, White, Marked, c.1780, 5 ½ In. 460.00
Pitcher, Cover, Pagoda & Temple, Blue, White, c.1775, 2 ½ x 6 In. 225.00
Plate, Flowers & Cone, Blue, White, Scalloped Rim, c.1780, 9 ¾ In. 125.00
Spoon Tray, Rose Sprays, Gilt, Blue, White, Cell Diaper Border, c.1780, 6 ¼ In. 340.00
Teapot, Fence Pattern, Flower Finial, Blue, White, c.1780, 5 ½ x 6 ½ In. 100.00

CAULDON Limited worked in Staffordshire, Great Britain, and went through many name changes. John Ridgway made porcelain at Cauldon Place, Hanley, until 1855. The firm of John Ridgway, Bates and Co. of Cauldon Place worked from 1856 to 1859. It became Bates, Brown-Westhead, Moore and Co. from 1859 to 1862. Brown-Westhead, Moore and Co. worked from 1862 to 1904. About 1890, this firm started using the words *Cauldon* or *Cauldon Ware* as part of the mark. Cauldon Ltd. worked from 1905 to 1920, Cauldon Potteries from 1920 to 1962. Related items may be found in the Indian Tree category.

Cauldon, Cuspidor, Blue Willow, Stamped, Plymouth, England, 7 ½ x 8 In. **$550.00**

Cauldon, Platter, Byzantium, Blue Transfer, Oval, 10 ⅜ x 13 In. **$10.00**

TIP

Don't wear vintage clothes to a flea market. You don't want dealers to realize you know the vintage market and may have spotted a bargain. And leave your expensive jewelry, old or new, at home. Expensive jewelry signals that you can afford what you like. In either case, you have given dealers a reason not to budge on price.

Celadon, Figurine, Karashishi, Pouncing, Pale Green, Japan, 1800s, 2 ½ In.
$225.00

Celluloid, Album, Photo, Painted, Cowgirl On Horse, Red Shirt, Jeans, 9 x 11 ½ x 3 In.
$540.00

Celluloid, Cigarette Holder, Indian Chief, 7 ½ In.
$87.00

Celluloid, Dresser Set, Ivory, France, Box, c.1900, 7 Piece
$71.00

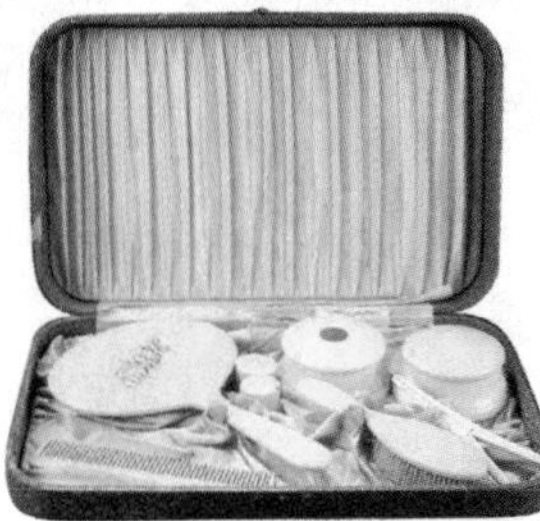

Cuspidor, Blue Willow, Stamped, Plymouth, England, 7 ½ x 8 In. . . . . *illus* 550.00
Plate, Dessert, Green Border, Center Flower Spray, Gilt, Early 1900s, 8 Piece 165.00
Plate, Fruit, Flowers, Butterfly, Flow Blue, c.1891, 10 ½ In. 15.00
Platter, Byzantium, Blue Transfer, Oval, 10 ⅜ x 13 In. . . . . *illus* 10.00
Platter, Flowers, Blue Transfer, Oval, 10 ¼ x 12 ½ In. 44.00
Platter, Siam Pattern, Blue, White, Late 19th Century, 13 In. 50.00

CELADON is the name of a velvet-textured green-gray glaze used by Chinese, Japanese, Korean, and other factories. The name refers both to the glaze and to pieces covered with the glaze. It is still being made.

Bowl, 2 Pink Fish, 10 In. . . . . 200.00 to 325.00
Bowl, Blue Shading, Flower Center, Japan, 4 x 11 In., Pair 585.00
Bowl, Carved Thunder Meander, Sea Green, Chinese, 18th Century, 10 ¼ In. 237.00
Bowl, Enamel, Flower Designs, Square, Chinese, 19th Century, 3 ½ x 7 In. 88.00
Bowl, Fitted Stand, Korea, 5 ½ In. 120.00
Bowl, Mt. Fuji, Green, White, Signed, 5 x 12 In. 40.00
Bowl, Shallow, Glazed, Incised, Dragon Chasing Flaming Pearl Of Wisdom, 16 In. 7768.00
Box, Cover, Jade, Carved, Pomegranate, Chinese, 1 ½ In. 3705.00
Box, Jade, Phoenix & Dragon, Chinese, 2 ½ In. 418.00
Box, Jade, Quail Shape, Chinese, 2 ¼ x 4 In. 1912.00
Brushpot, Flowers, Landscape, Chinese, 19th Century, 6 ¾ x 7 ¾ In. 652.00
Cachepot, Square, Bird, Flower, Relief, Footed, Chinese, 9 ½ x 1 In. 179.00
Censer, Animal Form Feet, Sea Green, Engraved Trigrams, Chinese, 10 In. 207.00
Censer, Peonies, Leaves, Cylindrical, Hardwood Stand, 7 x 8 ½ In. 504.00
Figurine, Bird, Mythical 2-Headed Creature, White, Wood Stand, Korea, 5 x 5 In. 117.00
Figurine, Elephant, Reclining, Pale Green, Chinese, 4 ½ x 9 ½ x 5 ½ In. 7200.00
Figurine, Karashishi, Pouncing, Pale Green, Japan, 1800s, 2 ½ In. . . . . *illus* 225.00
Flask, Moon, Molded, Dragon Design, Qianlong, Blue Seal Mark, 8 In. 2868.00
Incense Burner, Foo Dog, Chinese, 1800s, 7 ½ x 4 In. 936.00
Jar, 3-Footed, Wide Rim, 3 x 3 ½ In. 200.00
Jar, Lid, Blue Underglaze, Peonies, Peacock, On Tree Stump, 12 ¼ In. 144.00
Jar, Lid, Cranes, Flowering Plants, Peonies, Blue, White, Rose Glaze, Chinese, 15 In. 173.00
Jar, Lid, Ribbed Body, Footed, Porcelain Ming Design, Chinese, 9 ½ In. 239.00
Mask, Mythical Beast, 3 Skulls On Headdress, Ring In Tongue, Stand, Chinese, c.1875, 7 ½ In. 359.00
Platter, Blue, Green Flowers, Pottery, c.1900, 11 x 14 In. 117.00
Screen, Table, 4 Panels, Birds, Flowers, Carved Wood, Chinese, 10 x 17 In. 598.00
Teapot, Crackle Glaze, Underglaze Blue Design, Flowers, Trees, 2-Dog Handle, Ball, 8 In. 81.00
Teapot, Song Dynasty, Globular Ribbed Body, 2 ¾ In. 478.00
Urn, Dragon Handles, Chinese, 13 ½ x 6 In. 421.00
Vase, 2 Applied Handles, Neck, Base Black Relief Design, Signed, Chinese, 18 x 9 In., Pair 1870.00
Vase, 8-Sided, Handles, Embossed Geometric Design, Chinese, 9 ½ In., Pair 239.00
Vase, Copper Red, Blue, Cloud & Bat, 15 ½ In. 239.00
Vase, Cranes, Crackle Glaze, Lappet Borders, Cylindrical, Korean, 11 ½ In. 78.00
Vase, Double Gourd, Loop Handles, 8 ⅛ In. 150.00
Vase, Dragon Rising From Waves, 6 Characters, Sea Green, 13 ¼ In. 356.00
Vase, Flowers, Leaves, Crackle Glaze, Marked, 13 In. 100.00
Vase, Flowers, Multicolored, 23 In. 413.00
Vase, Green, Amethyst, Prunus, 10 x 5 In. 35.00
Vase, Incised Leaf Decoration, Chinese, 15 ¼ In. 413.00
Vase, Leaf Shape Handles, Military Scene, Gold Luster, Chinese, 17 ½ x 26 In., Pair 863.00
Vase, Molded Prunus Branch Handles, Chinese, 8 ½ In. 568.00
Vase, Molded Taotie Mask, Lappet, 14 ½ In. 944.00
Vase, Painted Flowers, Ormolu Mounted Twisted Snake Handles, Rims, c.1790, 8 x 15 In. 17500.00
Vase, Prunus Branches On Neck, Shoulder, Molded Incised, Ming Dynasty, Chinese, 15 In. . . . 3346.00
Vase, Relief Design, Blue Leaves, Vines, Pastel Berries, 11 In. 81.00

CELLULOID is a trademark for a plastic developed in 1868 by John W. Hyatt. Celluloid Manufacturing Company, the Celluloid Novelty Company, Celluloid Fancy Goods Company, and American Xylonite Company all used celluloid to make jewelry, games, sewing equipment, false teeth, and piano keys. The name *celluloid* was often used to identify any similar plastic. Celluloid toys are listed under Toy.

Album, Photo, Painted, Cowgirl On Horse, Red Shirt, Jeans, 9 x 11 ½ x 3 In. . . . . *illus* 540.00
Baseball Score Counter, Diamond, Players, 5 Number Windows, Babe Ruth Photo, 2 In. . . . 99.00
Box, Glove, Embossed Flowers, Scrolls, Printed Cloth On Ends, 1870s, 10 In. 22.00
Bust, Chopin, 2 ¾ In. 5.00

Charm, Baseball Catcher's Mitt Holding Ball, 1940s, 1 In. 11.00
Cigarette Holder, Indian Chief, 7 ½ In. .... *illus* 87.00
Comb, Hair, Amber, Fan Form, 13 ½ x 12 In. 154.00
Dresser Box, Tray, Black Urns, Swags, Flowers, Scalloped Edges, Art Deco, 11-In. Tray 28.00
Dresser Box, Yellow Flowers, Blue Scrolls, Stepped, Rolled Edges, Victorian, 6 x 12 x 8 In. 39.00
Dresser Set, Ivory, France, Box, c.1900, 7 Piece .... *illus* 71.00
Dresser Set, Mirror, Brush, Comb, Boxes, France, c.1900, 18-In. Fitted Case, 8 Piece 66.00
Fan, Painted, 18th Century People In Landscape, Frame, 14 x 21 In., Pair 330.00
Figurine, Sailor & Girl Dancing, Windup, Japan, 8 In. 33.00
Hair Clip, Flowers, Blue Trim, Box, 2 ¾ x 1 ½ In. 11.00
Hair Comb, Brown, Marbleized, Openwork, 6 Prongs, Victorian, 9 x 11 In. 275.00
Mask, Wolf Head, Painted, Early 20th Century, France, 14 x 9 x 9 In. 83.00
Mirror, Fencing Scenes, Painted, 2 Panels, Pierced Brass Folding Frame, 8 In. 358.00
Pepper Mill, Sterling Silver, 3 Bands, England, c.1960, 2 ½ x 1 In. .... *illus* 153.00
Teething Ring, Blue Ring, Sterling Silver Bell, Engraved Birth Record, 3 ¼ In. 48.00

CELS *are listed in this book in the Animation Art category.*

CERAMIC ARTS STUDIO was founded about 1940 in Madison, Wisconsin, by Lawrence Rabbett and Ruben Sand. Their most popular products were expensive molded figurines. The pottery closed in 1955. Do not confuse these products with those of the Ceramic Art Co. of Trenton, New Jersey.

Figurine, Boy, Green Outfit, Looking Over Back Of Chair, 2 In. 60.00
Figurine, Little Bo Peep, Yellow Dress, c.1955, 5 ¼ In. 56.00
Head Vase, Barbie, 7 ¼ In. 23.00
Salt & Pepper, Dutch Boy & Girl, 3 In., Pair .... *illus* 38.00
Salt & Pepper, Nested, Brown Bear & Cub 75.00
Salt & Pepper, Nested, Gorilla & Baby 95.00
Salt & Pepper, Oriental Boy & Girl, 3 In., Pair 45.00
Salt & Pepper, Whimsical Wee Elephant, 3 ½ x 4 ¼ In. 83.00
Shelf Sitter, Collie, 5 ⅛ In. 65.00
Shelf Sitter, Parrots, Blue, Pete & Polly, 7 ¾ In. .... 235.00 to 265.00
Shelf Sitter, Persian Cat, 5 ½ In. 65.00

CHALKWARE is really plaster of Paris decorated with watercolors. One type was molded from Staffordshire and other porcelain models and painted and sold as inexpensive decorations in the nineteenth century. This type is very valuable today. Figures of plaster, made from about 1910 to 1940 for use as prizes at carnivals, are also known as chalkware. Kewpie dolls made of chalkware will be found in their own category.

Bank, Apple Shape, Painted, Late 19th Century, 3 In. 176.00
Bank, Black Boy, Seated, Watermelon On Lap, Painted, 12 ½ In. 66.00
Bank, Bulldog, Red, Yellow, Black, White, 7 ¼ x 5 ½ In. .... *illus* 88.00
Bank, Chicken, Painted, Red Wings, Late 19th Century, 6 ¼ In. 176.00
Bank, Deer, Lying Down, Antlers, Brown, Hand Painted, Late 1940s, 12 x 10 x 6 In. 90.00
Bank, Dove, Cherry Branch, Penn., Late 1800s, 11 In. 235.00
Bank, Dove, On Branch, White, Slate Blue, c.1875, 11 In. 382.00
Bank, Hen, Mustard, Red Paint, 7 x 8 ½ x 6 In. 2860.00
Bust, Admiral Perry, Multicolored, 19th Century, 13 In. 1872.00
Bust, Woman, Fan In Hair, Pearl Necklace, Corset Top, 30 ½ In. 519.00
Figurine, Angel, Kneeling, Painted Yellow, Green, 7 ½ In. 382.00
Figurine, Bird, On Nest, White, Red, Yellow Green, 19th Century, 4 ¾ In. 234.00
Figurine, Bird, On Nest, Yellow, Red Songbird, On Basket, Late 19th Century, 3 ⅞ In. 345.00
Figurine, Bird, Orange Wings, Plinth, Late 19th Century, 6 ½ In. 118.00
Figurine, Bird, Painted, Late 19th Century, 4 In. 294.00
Figurine, Cat, Nodding, Pink, Red Collar, Ears, Late 19th Century, 4 ½ In. 588.00
Figurine, Cat, Reclining, Cream, Black Stripes, Red Nose, Hollow, 5 ¾ x 10 x 7 ¼ In. 225.00
Figurine, Cat, Seated, Bell, Black Paint, Penn., c.1850, 6 In. 353.00
Figurine, Cat, Seated, Brown Spots, Late 19th Century, 5 ¼ In. 235.00
Figurine, Cat, Seated, Brown Spots, Tail, Late 19th Century, 5 ⅝ In. 323.00
Figurine, Cat, Seated, Brown Stripes, Collar, Pink Ears, Late 19th Century, 10 ½ In. 633.00
Figurine, Cat, Seated, Multicolored, Green Collar, 20th Century, 5 In. 235.00
Figurine, Cat, Seated, Painted, Late 1800s, 6 ½ In. 676.00
Figurine, Cat, Seated, Painted, Late 1800s, 10 In. 823.00
Figurine, Cat, Seated, Painted Spots, Penn., Late 19th Century, 9 ½ In. 1058.00
Figurine, Cat, Seated, Red, Green, 4 ⅞ In. 206.00

Celluloid, Pepper Mill, Sterling Silver, 3 Bands, England, c.1960, 2 ½ x 1 In.
$153.00

TIP
Try cleaning 1920s celluloid with a paste of vinegar and flour. Rub, wait a few minutes, then rinse and dry. If this doesn't work, try dishwasher detergent and warm water.

Ceramic Arts Studio, Salt & Pepper, Dutch Boy & Girl, 3 In., Pair
$38.00

Chalkware, Bank, Bulldog, Red, Yellow, Black, White, 7 ¼ x 5 ½ In.
$88.00

Chalkware or Plaster
Many chalk or plaster figures were made by the Universal Statuary Corporation in the late 1930s and 1940s. The company was started by Jack and Leo Luecchesi. It also made piggy banks, wall plaques, and statues, including a life-sized Indian statue used in western-style restaurants. The date on the chalkware is the patent date, not the year it was made.

C

Chalkware, Figurine, Dog, Spaniel, Seated, Painted, 19th Century, 8 ¼ In.
$75.00

Chalkware, Figurine, Drum Majorette, Painted, 24 In.
$330.00

Chalkware, Fruit Basket, Hollow, Multicolored, New England, 6 x 8 ½ In.
$198.00

Figurine, Cat, Seated, Tabby, Black Smoke, 7 ⅜ In. 3525.00
Figurine, Cat, Seated, Tabby, Smoke Black Markings, Penciled Eyes, 5 ½ In. 345.00
Figurine, Child, Seated, Hair Ringlets, 9 ½ In. 1058.00
Figurine, Deer, Lying Down, Dappled Gray Paint, Late 19th Century, 10 ¾ In. 323.00
Figurine, Deer, Lying Down, Oval Base, Original Paint, c.1875, 4 ¼ x 5 ¼ In. 440.00
Figurine, Deer, Lying Down, Yellow Ocher, Black, Hollow, 7 ¼ x 8 ½ x 3 ½ In., Pair 165.00
Figurine, Deer, Reclining, Hollow, Yellow Ocher, Black, 7 ¼ x 8 ½ x 3 ½ In., Pair 165.00
Figurine, Deer, Reclining, White, Red, Green, Black, Yellow, Hollow, 10 ½ x 10 In. 225.00
Figurine, Dog, Poodle, Dimpled Chest, White, Black, Green, 7 x 6 In. 132.00
Figurine, Dog, Poodle, Seated, Free Standing Front Legs, Holding Basket, Late 1800s, 5 ¾ In. 470.00
Figurine, Dog, Poodle, Standing, Brown Paint, Late 19th Century, 5 ½ In. 59.00
Figurine, Dog, Poodle, Standing, Painted Multicolored, Late 19th Century, 8 In. 382.00
Figurine, Dog, Poodle, Standing, Painted Tan, Late 19th Century, 6 ½ In. 264.00
Figurine, Dog, Spaniel, Painted, Late 1800s, 9 ½ In. 323.00
Figurine, Dog, Spaniel, Seated, Black Spots, Gold Painted Chain, Late 1800s, 10 In. 173.00
Figurine, Dog, Spaniel, Seated, Original Paint, c.1875, 8 ¾ In. 176.00
Figurine, Dog, Spaniel, Seated, Painted, 19th Century, 8 ¼ In. *illus* 75.00
Figurine, Dog, Spaniel, Seated, Painted, Late 19th Century, 7 In. 264.00
Figurine, Dog, Spaniel, Seated, White, Yellow, Hollow, 6 x 5 In. 60.00
Figurine, Dove, On Perch, Red, Yellow, Ocher, White Base, 19th Century, 5 ½ In. 995.00
Figurine, Dove, Painted White, On Cherry Branch Base, 10 ½ In., Pair 999.00
Figurine, Dove, White, Red, Brown, Green, Hollow, 9 ½ x 7 ½ In., Pair 180.00
Figurine, Drum Majorette, Painted, 24 In. *illus* 330.00
Figurine, Dutch Woman, Holding Basket, Water Jug, Beige, Green, Black, 27 x 14 In. 130.00
Figurine, Girl, Full-Length, Pantaloons, Red Paint, Late 19th Century, 9 ¾ In. 470.00
Figurine, Girl, In Pantaloons, Carrying Flower, 9 In. 823.00
Figurine, Goat, Standing, Brown Horns, 8 In. 734.00
Figurine, Indian, Bust, Hiawatha, 20 In. 330.00
Figurine, Lovebirds, Red, Yellow Paint, Pa., c.1850s, 5 In. 1057.00
Figurine, Lovebirds, Red & Black Highlights, Late 19th Century, 3 ¾ In. 588.00
Figurine, Parrot, Dark Green, Yellow, Red Accents, Painted, Late 19th Century, 6 ½ In. 86.00
Figurine, Parrot, Green Wings, Stump Shaped Plinth, Late 1800s, 9 In. 470.00
Figurine, Parrot, On Tree Trunk, Brown & Red Paint, Late 19th Century, 8 ½ In. 86.00
Figurine, Parrot, Red, Yellow, Ball Base, c.1870, 8 In. 323.00
Figurine, Parrot, Yellow, Brown Paint, Gray Tone Wash, Molded Flowers, Late 1800s, 10 ½ In. 575.00
Figurine, Parrot, Yellow Head, Red Beak, Ocher Body, Striped Base, 19th Century, 9 ½ In. 5616.00
Figurine, Pig, Painted Black & Brown, Penn., Late 19th Century, 17 ½ In. 764.00
Figurine, Rabbit, Seated, Black Spots, Pink Accents, Late 19th Century, 5 ¼ In. 288.00
Figurine, Rabbit, Seated, Hollow, Pedestal, Black, Red, Yellow Highlights, 5 ¼ x 4 In. 303.00
Figurine, Rabbit, Seated, On Pedestal, Black, Red & Yellow Highlights, Pa., 1800s, 5 x 4 x 3 In. 275.00
Figurine, Rabbit, Seated, White, Red, Yellow, Hollow, 5 ¼ x 4 ½ In. 100.00
Figurine, Rabbit, Yellow, Black, Brown, 5 ½ In. 294.00
Figurine, Ram, Red, Black Highlights, Late 19th Century, 7 ½ In. 705.00
Figurine, Ram, Red, Black Paint, c.1865, 8 In. 411.00
Figurine, Rooster, Painted, Late 19th Century, 6 ½ In. 999.00
Figurine, Sheep, Lamb, Gold Paint, Multicolor Circles, Mid 19th Century, 9 ½ In. 633.00
Figurine, Sheep, Lamb, Lying Down, 9 x 7 ½ In. 646.00
Figurine, Sheep, Lamb, Reclining, Red & Black, Late 19th Century, 8 In. 470.00
Figurine, Squirrel, Eating Nut, Paint Trace, Penn., Late 1800s, 5 ¾ In. 118.00
Figurine, Squirrel, Eating Nut, Red, Yellow, Blue, Green Design, 19th Century, 6 ¾ In. 1170.00
Figurine, Squirrel, Eating Nut, Yellow Base, 19th Century, 5 In. 3800.00
Figurine, Squirrel, Seated, Eating Nut, Red, Brown, 6 ½ In. 323.00
Figurine, Squirrel, Seated, Multicolored, Late 19th Century, 6 ¼ In. 499.00
Figurine, Squirrel, Seated, Oval Base, Original Paint, Red Tail, c.1850, 5 ½ In. 118.00
Figurine, Squirrel, With Nut, White, Green, Black Red, Hollow, 6 ½ x 5 In. 375.00
Figurine, Stag, Reclining, Red Ear, Neckband, Striped Base, 19th Century, 10 In. 1053.00
Figurine, Stag, Reclining, Yellow Ground, Stripes, Late 19th Century, 10 ½ In. 1293.00
Fruit Basket, Hollow, Multicolored, New England, 6 x 8 ½ In. *illus* 198.00
Garniture, Fruit, In Urn, Multicolored, Penn., Late 1800s, 14 In., Pair 2350.00
Garniture, Mantel, Fruit & Leaves, Green Plinth, 19th Century, 12 ¾ In., Pair 3276.00
Garniture, Pinecone, Painted, Penn., Late 19th Century, 8 ¾ In., Pair 764.00
Garniture, Red, Yellow Fruit, Leaves, White Flower Base, Pa., 11 In., Pair 4113.00
Nodder, Cat, Yellow & Red Design, 19th Century, 4 ¼ x 8 ¼ In. 3300.00
Nodder, Rabbit, Pink Ears, 19th Century, 3 ¼ x 5 ½ In. 1320.00
Potholder Hanger, Comical Vegetable Shape, Miller Studios, Box, Pair 25.00
Statue, James Madison, Constitution In Hand, White, 1800s, 24 In. 896.00

Stringholder, Little Red Riding Hood Face, String Comes From Mouth, c.1940, 9 ½ In. 195.00
Wall Hanging, Bird & Cherries, c.1950, 7 ½ x 6 In.. . . . . 8.00

CHARLIE CHAPLIN the famous comedian, actor, and filmmaker, lived from 1889 to 1977. He made his first movie in 1913. He did the movie *The Tramp* in 1915. The character of the Tramp has remained famous, and in the 1980s appeared in a series of television commercials for computers. Dolls, candy containers, and all sorts of memorabilia with the image of Charlie's Tramp are collected. Pieces are being made even today.

Doll, Ball Jointed, Painted, Composition, Cloth, Bucherer, 7 ½ In. 275.00
Doll, Dean's Rag Book Co., England, c.1930, 12 ½ In.. . . . . 144.00
Figure, Jointed Arms, Holds Cane, Celluloid, Painted, 9 ½ In.. . . . . 200.00
Greeting Card, Valentine, Rocking Easel, Merrimack Pub., 1986 . . . . 12.00
Mask, Cardboard, Wood Stick Handle, Masquer-Aids, c.1970, 16 x 7 In.. . . . . 39.00
Mutoscope, Boob Dentist, 1 Cent, Marked, C.S.5, 71 x 8 In. 3800.00
Ornament, Charlie's Head, Blown Glass, Hand Painted, 3 ¼ In. 250.00
Pencil Box, Tin Lithograph, Signed, Henry Cline, 7 ¾ x 2 ¼ x ¾ In.. . . . . 75.00
Radiator Mascot, The Tramp, Bronze, 1920s, 4 ¼ In. 125.00
Toy, Bicycle Rider, Tin Lithograph, 1920s, 8 In. 465.00
Toy, Dances, Cane Spins, Felt Clothing & Hair, Windup, Schuco, Germany, 6 ½ In.. . . . . 750.00
Toy, Jack-In-The-Box, Musical, Enesco, 1989, 9 x 8 In. 149.00
Toy, Plays Cymbals, Tin, Windup, Distler, 6 In. . . . . *illus* 518.00
Toy, Slate Dancer, Cane, Tin, Windup, Germany KW, 7 In. . . . . 550.00 to 575.00
Toy, Soldier, Walker, Composition, Metal, Cloth, Windup, 1915, 12 In. . . . . 225.00 to 260.00
Toy, Tramp, Tin Lithograph, Windup, Germany, c.1925, 5 ¾ In.. . . . . 2100.00
Toy, Walker, Tin Lithograph, Cast Iron Shoes, Windup, B&R, U.S.A., 8 ½ In. 700.00
Tumbler, Gold Rush, Smoke Colored Glass, Arby's Series No. 1, 1979, 5 ½ In.. . . . . 8.00
Whistle, Movie Prop, Lead, Used In City Lights, Signed Label, 1931, 1 ¾ In.. . . . . 2500.00

CHARLIE MCCARTHY was the ventriloquist's dummy used by Edgar Bergen from the 1930s. He was famous for his work in radio, movies, and television. The act was retired in the 1970s.

Doll, Dinner Jacket, Cloth, Composition, Painted, Effanbee, 19 In.. . . . . 110.00
Doll, Tuxedo, Top Hat, Cloth, Composition, Painted, Effanbee, 19 In.. 220.00
Dummy, Ventriloquist, Booklet, Composition, Hands, Feet, Muslin Body, 19 ½ In. 415.00
Dummy, Ventriloquist, Composition, Cloth Body, Tuxedo, Marked, 18 In.. . . . . 88.00
Puppet, Die Cut, Cardboard Lithograph, c.1930 . . . . 25.00
Radio, Majestic, Cream, 6 x 7 In.. . . . . *illus* 1400.00
Spoon, 6 In. 14.00
Toy, Benzine Buggy, Tin, Windup, Marx, c.1930, 7 ½ In. . . . . *illus* 660.00
Toy, Charlie McCarthy, Driving Car, Tin Lithograph, Windup, Marx. 375.00
Toy, Charlie McCarthy, Mouth, Chin Move, Celluloid, Windup, Japan, Box, 1930s, 7 In.. . . . . . . 550.00
Toy, Charlie McCarthy, Walker, Mouth Moves, Tin Lithograph, Windup, Marx, 8 ½ In. 245.00 to 440.00
Toy, Charlie McCarthy Drummer Boy, Tin, Windup, Marx, Box . . . . 880.00 to 1995.00
Toy, Mortimer Snerd, Crazy Car, Head Spins, Tin, Windup, Marx, 7 In. 735.00
Toy, Mortimer Snerd, Flex Doll, Swivel Neck, Composition Head, 12 ½ In.. . . . . 230.00
Toy, Mortimer Snerd, Shakes, Hat Flips Up, Tin, Windup, Marx, 8 ½ In.. . . . . 412.00
Toy, Whoopee Car, Black, White, Tin Lithograph, Windup, 8 In.. . . . . 180.00

CHELSEA porcelain was made in the Chelsea area of London from about 1745 to 1769. Some pieces made from 1770 to 1784 are called Chelsea Derby and may include the letter *I D* for *Derby* in the mark. Ceramic designs were borrowed from the Meissen models of the day. Pieces were made of soft paste. The gold anchor was used as the mark, but it has been copied by many other factories. Recent copies of Chelsea have been made from the original molds. Do not confuse Chelsea porcelain with Chelsea Grape, a white pottery with luster grape decoration.

Bowl, Reticulated, c.1770, 3 x 8 In.. . . . . 450.00
Dish, Flower, Insect, 3 ½ In.. . . . . 49.00
Dish, Leaf Shaped, Puce Veins, Ruffled Edge, Painted, Figs, Turnip, Butterflies, 11 ½ In.. . . . . . 4375.00
Figurine, Italian Beggar, c.1754, 8 ⅛ In.. . . . . 11974.00
Figurine, Woman, With Flowers & Dog, Man, Pipes & Sheep, Mark, 7 ¼ In., Pair 230.00
Plate, Painted, Flowering Cactus, Feather Molded Border, c.1760, 8 ⅜ In., 3 Piece. 8750.00
Tureen, Cover, Cauliflower, Ribbed Leaves, Painted, c.1755, 4 ½ In. 7500.00
Tureen, Cover, Overlapping Leaves, Green, Puce, Finch Knop, c.1755, 6 ¼ In., Pair. 40625.00
Urn, Crane, Flowers, Pink, Gilt, Griffin Base, Handles, Cover, Marked, 1790s, 18 In.. . . . . 2700.00

Charlie Chaplin, Toy, Plays Cymbals, Tin, Windup, Distler, 6 In.
$518.00

Charlie McCarthy, Radio, Majestic, Cream, 6 x 7 In.
$1400.00

Charlie McCarthy, Toy, Benzine Buggy, Tin, Windup, Marx, c.1930, 7 ½ In.
$660.00

TIP

Use a blow dryer to heat and soften tape on boxes that once held toys. If you see some of the colored parts of the box coming up when you pull the tope, stop removing the tape.

C

Chinese Export, Candlestick, Famille Rose, Molded Band Top, 1800s, 9 ½ In., Pair
$575.00

Chinese Export, Chamberstick, Dragon Handle, 18th Century, 5 ½ x 4 ½ In.
$2100.00

How Old Is Your *Famille Rose*?

Famille Rose (rose family) porcelain is a five-color Chinese porcelain. Collectors have named three patterns of Famille Rose: Rose Medallion, Rose Mandarin, and Rose Canton.

Age can be told by color and glaze. Early pieces had a thick, opaque, muddy mauve pink glaze. By the 1730s, the glaze was opaque rose pink, often mixed with white. By 1800 the rose glaze was thin and almost translucent. Late-eighteenth-century pieces are more valuable than later brilliantly colored and carelessly painted late-nineteenth century pieces.

CHELSEA GRAPE pattern was made before 1840. A small bunch of grapes in a raised design, colored with purple or blue luster, is on the border of the white plate. Most of the pieces are unmarked. The pattern is sometimes called Aynsley or Grandmother. Chelsea Sprig is similar but has a sprig of flowers instead of the bunch of grapes. Chelsea Thistle has a raised thistle pattern. Do not confuse these Chelsea patterns with Chelsea Keramic Art Works, which can be found in the Dedham category, or with Chelsea porcelain, the preceding category.

Creamer, 2 ¾ x 3 ½ In. 25.00
Cup & Saucer, Raised Grapes, Handleless 58.00
Pitcher, Raised Grapes, c.1840 . . . . . 100.00
Plate, 7 In. 30.00
Plate, Bread & Butter, 6 ⅛ In. 13.00
Plate, Cake, Handles, 10 In. 40.00
Plate, Salad, 7 ¾ In. . . . . 10.00 to 12.00
Saucer, 5 ⅝ In. 22.00
Sugar, Master, Cover, 7 x 7 In. 45.00

CHINESE EXPORT porcelain comprises all the many kinds of porcelain made in China for export to America and Europe in the eighteenth, nineteenth, and twentieth centuries. Other pieces may be listed in this book under Canton, Celadon, Nanking, and Rose Medallion.

Basket, Chestnut, Reticulated, Oval, Flared Rim, Leaf Handles, c.1830, 5 x 10 In. 1725.00
Bottle, Scrolling Leaves, Knots, Blue & White, c.1600, 10 ½ In. 1673.00
Bough Pot, Famille Rose, Paneled, Phoenix, Flowers, Gilt Rope Twist Handles, 9 In. 978.00
Bowl, Alternating Panel, Figures, Flowers, 10 ¼ In. 840.00
Bowl, Armorial, Banner, Primus E Stirpe, Blue, White, 18th Century, 6 ¼ In. 110.00
Bowl, Armorial, Shield With Boar, 3 Crowns, Motto, Flowers, Octagonal, 1700s, 8 In., Pair . . . 1840.00
Bowl, Barber, Famille Rose, Flowers, Chinese, 10 ¾ In. 2478.00
Bowl, Court Scene, Down Turned Rim, Foot Rings, Iron Red, Gilt, 1700s, 4 x 10 In. 259.00
Bowl, Famille Jaune, Floral Decoration, 4 ¼ In. 239.00
Bowl, Famille Rose, Bat, Flowers, Blue Ground, Iron Red Seal Mark, c.1800, 5 In., Pair 418.00
Bowl, Famille Rose, Birds, Flowers, Butterflies, 4 ½ x 10 ½ In. 429.00
Bowl, Famille Rose, Buddhist Symbols, Dragon, Phoenix, Flower Heads, 7 In. 224.00
Bowl, Famille Rose, Figural, 20th Century, 8 In. 2124.00
Bowl, Famille Rose, Floral & Butterfly, Turquoise Ground, 4 ½ In. 239.00
Bowl, Famille Rose, Flowers, Birds, Blue Mark, c.1890, 8 In. 717.00
Bowl, Famille Rose, Flowers On Ruby Ground, Iron Red Mark, c.1800, 3 ½ In. 863.00
Bowl, Famille Rose, Footed, Early 19th Century, 4 ¼ x 10 ¼ In. 235.00
Bowl, Famille Rose, Hundred Boys, Dragons, Toys, Multicolored, 1900s, 4 x 9 In. 748.00
Bowl, Famille Rose, Painted, Hunting Scene, 6 In. 717.00
Bowl, Famille Rose, Phoenixes, Birds, Scalloped Rim Designs, Yellow Ground, 5 x 16 In. 863.00
Bowl, Famille Verte, Bird & Flowers, 7 In. 236.00
Bowl, Famille Verte, Flowers, c.1670, 6 ¾ In. 316.00
Bowl, Footed, Scalloped Rim, S. Breck Monogram, White, Gold, Blue, c.1800, 5 x 10 In. 3450.00
Bowl, Gray Biscuit, Rose Diapering, Blue & Pink Flowers, Mid 1800s, 11 In. 235.00
Bowl, Green Fitzhugh, Gilt Rim, 19th Century, 7 ½ In., 8 Piece 1495.00
Bowl, Leaf Form, Eagle, Red, White, Blue Shield, Sun, Fitzhugh, 1700s, 8 ½ x 6 In. 660.00
Bowl, Lotus Design, White Glaze, Northern Song Dynasty, 6 ½ In. 239.00
Bowl, Scalloped Rims, Flowers, Multicolored, 1700s, 9 In., 4 Piece 978.00
Box, Blue & White, Rabbit, Horse, 5 In. 531.00
Box, Cover, Dragons Chasing Pearl Of Wisdom, Ingot Shaped, Lid, 10 x 6 In. 5900.00
Brush Box, Famille Rose, Birds, Butterflies, Lid, Divider, c.1860, 2 ¾ x 7 ¼ In. 518.00
Brush Holder, Applied Bone Immortals, 7 x 5 ¼ In. 354.00
Brush Washer, Famille Rose, Dragon, Bat On Rim, Flowers, 1900s, 3 ½ x 5 ½ In. 443.00
Brushpot, Copper Red, Qing Dynasty, 6 x 7 In. 508.00
Brushpot, Famille Rose, Boys, Carrying Toys, Emblems, Cylindrical, Chinese, 7 In. 780.00
Brushpot, Yellow Glaze Biscuit, Molded Bamboo Branches, Wood Stand, 5 ⅛ In. 354.00
Butter, Cover, Underplate, Blue & Gilt Leaves, Peach Finial, c.1800, 6 ½ In. 275.00
Cachepot, Dragons, High Relief, Turquoise, Qing Dynasty, 7 In. 1673.00
Candlestick, Famille Rose, Molded Band Top, 1800s, 9 ½ In., Pair . . . . . *illus* 575.00
Censer, Blue & White, Calligraphy Design, 1800s, 7 ½ In. 546.00
Chamberstick, Dragon Handle, 18th Century, 5 ½ x 4 ½ In. . . . . *illus* 2100.00
Charger, Famille Rose, Figures, Houses, Landscape, Turquoise Ground, 1900s, 3 x 19 In. 2185.00
Charger, Famille Rose, Flower, Lime Green, 15 In. 4740.00
Charger, Tree & Rooster Center, Blue, White, Scalloped Rim, 16 In. 122.00
Chocolate Pot, Famille Rose, 2 Birds On Flowering Tree, 8 ½ In. 561.00
Cider Jug, Blue, White, Cover, c.1800, 12 In. 117.00

Creamer, Armorial, Banner, Primus E Stirpe, Blue, White, 18th Century, 5 ½ In. 275.00
Cuspidor, Famille Rose, Dome Lid, 100 Boys Scenes, White Ground, c.1950, 5 x 10 In. 3105.00
Dish, Famille Rose, Floral Border, Chinese, 18th Century, 9 In., Pair 657.00
Dish, Famille Verte, Piecrust Rim, Octagonal, Multicolor, Gilt, 13 ¾ In., Pair 1058.00
Dish, Famille Verte, Round, Scalloped, Mandarin, Peonies, 2 x 9 ¼ In., 2 Piece 1495.00
Dish, Green Fitzhugh, Leaf Shape, c.1850, 8 In. 1652.00
Famille Noir, Multicolored Enamels, Figures, Courtyard, Black, 1800s, 18 In. 385.00
Famille Rose, Tureen, Lid, Rabbit Head Handles, Flowers, Prunus, 1800s, 7 ¾ In. 518.00
Figurine, Famille Rose, Bearded Man Wearing Robe, Base, 24 In. 1592.00
Figurine, Famille Rose, Phoenix, Standing, Head Turned, 18 ¾ In., Pair 1320.00
Figurine, Foo Dog, Blue Glaze, 12 In., Pair 70.00
Figurine, Man Riding Foo Dog, Green, Yellow, Red Glaze, 12 x 12 In. 117.00
Figurine, Parrot, Glaze, 5 Colors, Pierced Base, 7 In., Pair 649.00
Figurine, Parrot, Green, Blue, Openwork Rock, Bronze Base, 1800s, 9 In. .... *illus* 978.00
Figurine, Taoist Dignitary, Famille Rose, 9 ½ In. 177.00
Incense Burner, Ball Shape, Pheasant On Top, 10 x 6 In. 292.00
Jar, Blue & White, Quatrefoil Medallions, Prunus Head, Crackled Ice Ground, 8 In., Pair 1180.00
Jar, Cover, Blue & White, Bird, Flowers, Hexagonal, 8 ½ In. 384.00
Jar, Cover, Fitzhugh, Iron Oxide, Painted Overglaze, 13 In. 403.00
Jar, Famille Rose, Cartouches, Crane, Flowering Branches, c.1910, 11 ½ In. 502.00
Jar, Famille Rose, Cover, c.1840, 8 x 8 In. 585.00
Jar, Famille Rose, Enameled, Boys Playing, Trees, Bats, Carved Wood Base, 8 ¾ In., Pair 403.00
Jar, Famille Rose, Oval, Painted, Dragon Chasing Flaming Pearl Of Wisdom, Carp, 9 In. 266.00
Jar, Famille Verte, Enamel, Figural Cartouches, Birds, Flowers, Handles, 29 In., Pair 125.00
Jar, Tea, Blue, White, c.1800, 7 x 4 In. 468.00
Jardiniere, Famille Rose, Peonies, Exotic Birds, Rock Formation, 1900s, 8 ½ In. 460.00
Jardiniere, Stone, Cloud, Wave Design, White, 1900s, 14 x 29 x 17 In. 598.00
Kendi, Famille Rose, Flowers, Yellow & Black Ground, 1800s, 7 In. 354.00
Marriage, Famille Verte, 2 Parts, 14 x 9 In. 1521.00
Mug, Eagle, Shield, 1790-1810, 3 ⅜ In. 1007.00
Mug, Flower Sprays On Urn, Flower Rim, Intertwined Reed Strap, 1736-95, 6 In. 1000.00
Mug, Multicolored Flowers, Raised Pearling Bands, Intertwined Handles, c.1700, 6 In. 411.00
Mug, Ship, England, Flag, Late 1700s, 4 ¼ In. 1541.00
Mug, Strap Handle, Blue & White, Oriental Design, Mid 1800s, 4 ¾ In. 690.00
Panels, Flowers, Birds, Kesi Silk, Frame, Qing Dynasty, 36 x 8 In., Pair 418.00
Pillow, Blue & White, Flowers, 5 ¾ x 6 ¾ x 14 ½ In. 468.00
Planter, Blue & White, 7 x 16 In. 176.00
Planter, Saucer, Famille Rose, Dragon, Flowers, Enamel, Hexagonal, 8 x 11 In. 60.00
Plaque, Famille Rose, Birds On Flowering Tree, Calligraphy, 11 ½ x 8 In. 266.00
Plaque, Famille Rose, Flower Filled Vase, Floral & Dragon Decor, 15 ¼ In. 508.00
Plaque, Famille Rose, Painted, Dragon, Man & Tiger Back, 15 x 10 In. 568.00
Plaque, Famille Rose, Riverscape, 9 ½ x 15 In. 4130.00
Plate, Armorial, Crest, Lion, 3 Birds, Multicolored, Octagon, 1700s, 9 In., Pair 575.00
Plate, Armorial, Pink Floral Scroll Border, Gierson Crest, c.1785, 9 ½ In., Pair. 235.00
Plate, Breck, Star, Cobalt Blue, Monogram, SJB, 1800s, 9 ¾ In., 4 Piece .... *illus* 2320.00
Plate, Butterfly Border, Green Fitzhugh, 1800s, 8 In., 8 Piece 646.00
Plate, Coastal Village Scenes, Sepia, Grisaille, Gilt Plume, 7 ¾ In., Pair 1438.00
Plate, Court Scene, Blue & White, c.1725, 9 In., Pair 538.00
Plate, Famille Rose, Rockefeller Pattern, Figural, 18th Century, 9 ¾ In., Pair 657.00
Plate, Famille Verte, Floral, 9 In. 598.00
Plate, Gilt Metal, Buildings, Landscape, Double Handles, Square Foot, 8 ½ In. 270.00
Plate, Judgment Of Paris, c.1850, 9 In. 761.00
Plate, Urn, Shield, Willow, Profile, Louis XVI & Consort, Green, Brown, 10 In. 3680.00
Plate, Washington Memorial, Early 19th Century, 9 ½ In. 7020.00
Plate, Wavy Rim, Famille Rose, Parrot, Flower Border, Late 1700s, 9 In. 1020.00
Platter, Armorial, Cobalt Blue, Scalloped Rim, Gilt Stars, 11 ¾ x 14 ½ In. 353.00
Platter, Famille Rose, 8 Women, Musical Instruments, Flowers, 1800s, 2 x 20 In. 920.00
Platter, Green Dragon, Oval, Gilt Rim, Detail, Trellis Border, 14 ½ x 11 ¼ In. .... *illus* 978.00
Platter, Pseudo Tobacco Leaf, Fruit, Leaves, Flowers, Oblong, 1700s, 13 x 11 In. 2530.00
Pot, Famille Rose, Geometric Design, 3 Gilt Bands, Turquoise Interior, 3 ¾ In. 90.00
Pot, Lid, Famille Rose, Flowers, Ormolu Mounts, Brown Ground, c.1730, 7 In., Pair 8125.00
Punch Bowl, Armorial, Lion, Ribbon Crest, Motto, Garlands, 1700s, 5 x 12 In. 1380.00
Punch Bowl, Blue Enameled, Gilt Landscapes, Fleur-De-Lis Banding, 5 x 12 ¾ In. 270.00
Punch Bowl, European Hunting Scene, Multicolored, c.1890, 4 ½ x 10 In. 411.00
Punch Bowl, Famille Rose, Late 1800s, 5 ¾ x 14 ½ In. 1093.00
Punch Bowl, Tobacco Leaf, Famille Rose Border, Butterflies, 6 ¼ x 14 ¾ In. 1725.00

China Mark
A mark with the words "Made in the People's Republic of China" was used starting in 1949. The mark appears on baskets, pottery, and other objects. "Made in China" was used from 1891 to 1949 and again staring in 1978.

Chinese Export, Figurine, Parrot, Green, Blue, Openwork Rock, Bronze Base, 1800s, 9 In.
$978.00

Chinese Export, Plate, Breck, Star, Cobalt Blue, Monogram, SJB, 1800s, 9 ¾ In., 4 Piece
$2320.00

Chinese Export, Platter, Green Dragon, Oval, Gilt Rim, Detail, Trellis Border, 14 ½ x 11 ¼ In.
$978.00

Chinese Export, Tureen, Cover, Famille Rose, Rabbit Head Handles, 19th Century, 7 ¾ In.
$495.00

Chinese Export, Urn, 4 Horned Animals, Turquoise, Glazed, 8 x 6 ½ In.
$877.00

Chinese Export, Vase, Famille Rose, Inscribed Trumpet Neck, Flowers, Lion's Head Flanges, 23 In.
$345.00

C

Saucer, Famille Verte, Chrysanthemum, Kakiemon Style, Prunus, 5 ¼ In. 191.00
Sugar, Cover, Armorial, Banner, Primus E Stirpe, Blue, White, 18th Century, 6 x 7 In. 220.00
Tea Service, Iron Red Peonies, Fish Roe Borders, Gilt Monograms, 1800s, 30 In. 546.00
Teapot, Armorial, Banner, Primus, E. Stirpe, Blue, White, 18th Century, 5 ½ x 8 In. 330.00
Teapot, Bird, On Handle, Lid, Flowers, Blue, White, c.1900, 7 ½ In. 1872.00
Teapot, Blue & White, Straight-Sided, Twisted Handle, Strawberry Finial, 1700s, 5 In. 270.00
Teapot, British Frigate, 2-Sided, 18th Century, 5 ½ In. 878.00
Teapot, Cylindrical, Double Strap Handles, Iron Red Overglaze, Vine Border, 6 In. 330.00
Teapot, Famille Verte, Square, Kakiemon Style, Prunus, Birds, 6 ¾ In. 1416.00
Teapot, Flower Sprays, Butterflies, Insects, Off-White Ground, 5 In. 690.00
Teapot, River Scene, c.1800, 5 ½ In. 176.00
Tureen, Cover, Armorial Shields, Flowers, 2 Handles, Porcelain, Oval, c.1770, 14 In. 2188.00
Tureen, Cover, Dragon & Garden Scene, 8-Sided, 19th Century, 9 x 12 ½ In. 585.00
Tureen, Cover, Famille Rose, Rabbit Head Handles, 19th Century, 7 ¾ In. *illus* 495.00
Tureen, Liner, Lid Flower Knop, Rabbit Handles, Garlands, Flowers, 9 x 15 x 11 In. 3680.00
Tureen, Soup, Underplate, Famille Verte, Oval, Double Strap Handles, 11 x 15 In. 2818.00
Tureen Stand, Famille Rose, Terrace Scene, Late 1800s, 5 ¼ x 8 In. 600.00
Umbrella Stand, Famille Rose, Figural Decoration, 19th Century, 25 In. 2714.00
Urn, 4 Horned Animals, Turquoise, Glazed, 8 x 6 ½ In. *illus* 877.00
Urn, Cover, Blossom Finial, Famille Rose, 19 ½ In. 59.00
Urn, Palace, Famille Rose, Jaune, Raised Dragons, Chinese, 42 x 20 In. 293.00
Vase, Blue & White, 17 x 7 In. 235.00
Vase, Blue & White, Bulbous, Flowers, 26 ½ In., Pair. 936.00
Vase, Blue & White, Bulbous, Serpents, 22 In. 819.00
Vase, Blue & White, Cylindrical, 7 x 8 In. 375.00
Vase, Blue & White, Figural Handles, Hexagonal, 25 x 15 In. 351.00
Vase, Blue & White, Figures, Landscape, 23 x 13 In. 351.00
Vase, Blue & White, Flowers, Precious Object, Gu Form, 11 In. 5900.00
Vase, Blue & White, Flowers, Scrolling Waves, 12 In., Pair. 266.00
Vase, Blue & White, Sea Animal, Seascape, 25 x 12 In. 351.00
Vase, Bottle Shape, Famille Rose, Figural & Bird & Flower Panels, 14 ½ In. 390.00
Vase, Double Gourd Shape, Pinched Neck, Footed, People On Bridge, 23 In. 819.00
Vase, Famille Rose, Baluster, Flared Rim, Foo Dog Ring Handles, 23 In., Pair. 4994.00
Vase, Famille Rose, Bat, Calligraphy, Scrolling Flowers, 1800s, 17 ½ In. 472.00
Vase, Famille Rose, Birds, Flowers, Turquoise Ground, 19th Century, 14 In. 295.00
Vase, Famille Rose, Bottle Shape, Elephant Head Handles, Mid 1800s, 24 In., Pair 3565.00
Vase, Famille Rose, Butterfly & Bird Decoration, 19th Century, 8 ¾ In., Pair. 717.00
Vase, Famille Rose, Calligraphy, Flowers, Scrolling Leaves, Turquoise Interior, 17 ½ In. 472.00
Vase, Famille Rose, Dignitaries, Children Playing, 4 Character Red Mark, 8 ½ In. 460.00
Vase, Famille Rose, Dragon, Blossom, Blue Field, 2 Handles, c.1900, 11 In., Pair 805.00
Vase, Famille Rose, Dragons, Gods, Iron Red Seal Mark, c.1800, 22 In. 358.00
Vase, Famille Rose, Faux Bamboo Handles, 19 In. 1840.00
Vase, Famille Rose, Figural Decoration, 19th Century, 16 ¾ In., Pair. 384.00
Vase, Famille Rose, Flattened, Rectangular Rim, Foot, Gilt Lion Mask Flanges, 1900s, 8 ¾ In. 575.00
Vase, Famille Rose, Floral, Iron Red & Gilt Ground, 6 ½ In. 227.00
Vase, Famille Rose, Flowers, c.1862-74, 9 ½ In. 413.00
Vase, Famille Rose, Flowers, Pomegranate Design, 6 Character Red Mark, 1900s, 16 In. 805.00
Vase, Famille Rose, Immortals, Salamander Handles, 19th Century, 10 In. 69.00
Vase, Famille Rose, Inscribed Trumpet Neck, Flowers, Lion's Head Flanges, 23 In. *illus* 345.00
Vase, Famille Rose, Medallion, Cylindrical, Applied Flower Medallions, 1800s, 10 In., Pair 2530.00
Vase, Famille Rose, Oval, Painted, Figures Drinking Wine, Garden, Foo Dog Handles, 8 In. 359.00
Vase, Famille Rose, Painted, 9 Peaches, Bats, 13 In. 598.00
Vase, Famille Rose, Stretched Neck, Iron Red Mark, 1875-1908, 12 In. 561.00
Vase, Famille Verte, Dignitaries In Pavilion & Landscape, 16 In., Pair 805.00
Vase, Famille Verte, Flowering Prunus, Chinese, 19th Century, 8 ¾ In. 236.00
Vase, Famille Verte, Globular, Raised Floral & Crane, 19th Century, 9 In. 598.00
Vase, Famille Verte, Gu Form, Flowers, 19th Century, 13 ½ In. 708.00
Vase, Figures, Desk, Characters, Multicolored, 1800s, 13 In. 657.00
Vase, Figures, Multicolored, c.1900, 18 In. 598.00
Vase, Flowers, Geometric Design, Red, White, Green, Wood Stand, 7 ½ In. 47.00
Vase, Flowers, Leaves, Blue, White, 6-Sided, Baluster, Metal Base, 21 ½ x 11 In. 8540.00
Vase, Gu Shape, Thousand Butterflies, Floral Panels, Gilt, 15 ½ In. 316.00
Vase, Handles, Scrolling Flowers, Leaves, Blue & White, Porcelain, Mark, c.1750, 8 ½ In. 418.00
Vase, Mallet Shape, Molded Flowers, Leaves, Aubergine, Song Dynasty, 7 ½ In. 1434.00
Vase, Oval, Waisted Neck, Dragon Handles, Mocha Brown Glaze, 16 In. 359.00
Vase, Peacocks, Blossoms, Blue, White, Gourd Form, 18 ½ x 13 ½ In. 2440.00
Vase, Red Ground, Landscape Insert, c.1910, 12 In. 585.00

Vase, Stick, Vines, Flowers, 24 ½ In. 1872.00
Vase, Yellow Ground, Snake Wrapped Around Neck, 7 x 5 ½ In. 643.00
Warming Dish, Blue Underglaze Design, Fitzhugh 173.00
Washbasin, Flat Rim, Figures, Natural Reserve Panels, Flower Ground, 16 In. 600.00
Wine Pot, Famille Rose, c.1900, 8 x 7 In. 176.00

CHINTZ is the name of a group of china patterns featuring an overall design of flowers and leaves. The design became popular with English makers about 1928. A few pieces are still being made. The best known are designs by Royal Winton, James Kent Ltd., Crown Ducal, and Shelley. Crown Ducal and Shelley are listed in their own sections.

Anemone, Cheese Keep, Cover, Lord Nelson 125.00
Balmoral, Bowl, Mayonnaise, Saville, Royal Winton 95.00
Bedale, Creamer, Dutch Shape, Royal Winton, 3 ¾ In. 435.00
Bedale, Sauceboat, Stand, Era, Green Edge, Royal Winton 135.00
Beeston, Creamer, Countess Shape, Royal Winton, 3 In. 265.00
Beeston, Mustard Jar, Ascot Shape, Royal Winton, 2 ⅜ In. 245.00
Cheadle, Dish, White, Oval, Cutout Handles, Royal Winton, 8 ½ x 5 ½ In. 95.00
Cheadle, Dish, White, Oval, Royal Winton, 5 x 5 ½ In. 60.00
Cheadle, Honey Pot, Cover, White, Chelsea, Royal Winton 145.00
Crocus, Sauceboat, Stand, White, Era 115.00
Du Barry, Creamer, Granville, James Kent, 3 ¼ In. 75.00
Eleanor, Cake Plate, Ascot, Cutout Handles, Royal Winton, 10 ¾ x 9 ¼ In. 175.00
Eleanor, Dish, 3-Lobed, Handles, Royal Winton, 9 ½ x 9 In. 115.00
English Rose, Sauceboat, Stand, Era, Royal Winton 195.00
Evesham, Creamer, Globe Shape, Royal Winton, 3 ¾ In. 295.00
Fireglow, Jug, White, Globe Shape, Royal Winton, 4 In. 95.00
Floral Feast, Creamer, Dutch Shape, Royal Winton, 3 ¾ In. 375.00
Florita, Dish, Chelsea, Square, Tab Handles, James Kent, 5 ⅜ x 4 In. 65.00
Hazel, Eggcup Set, Tray, Saville Shape, Royal Winton, 5 Piece 750.00
Hazel, Jug, Hot Water, Cover, Sexta, Royal Winton, 7 In. 995.00
Hazel, Nut Scoop, Royal Winton, 5 In. 285.00
Hazel, Shaker, Underplate, Fife, Royal Winton, 4 ⅛ In. 695.00
Hydrangea, Creamer, Granville, James Kent, 3 ⅛ In. 65.00
Julia, Butter Chip, Trefu, Royal Winton, 4 ¾ x 4 In. 85.00
Julia, Compote, Lily, Royal Winton, 2 ½ In. 375.00
Julia, Dish, Art Deco, Royal Winton, 10 x 6 ½ In. 175.00
Julia, Plate, Sandwich, Ascot, Royal Winton, 5 ¼ In. 65.00
Julia, Relish, 2 Sections, Royal Winton, 9 x 5 ¼ In. 525.00
Julia, Sugar, Albans, Royal Winton, 4 ½ In. 125.00
Kew, Cup & Saucer, Demitasse, Albans, Royal Winton 95.00
Kew, Toast Rack, 2-Slice, Queen, Royal Winton 135.00
Majestic, Nut Dish, Heart Shape Cutout Handles, Royal Winton, 6 ⅝ x 5 ¼ In. 335.00
Majestic, Plate, Athena, Royal Winton, 6 In. 65.00
Majestic, Serving Dish, Marina Shape, Royal Winton, 12 x 10 ¾ In. 295.00
Marguerite, Cheese Keep, Cover, Blue Trim, Royal Winton, 7 ½ x 6 ¼ In. 750.00
Marguerite, Jug, Globe Shape, Royal Winton, 4 ½ In. 295.00
Marigold, Jug, York, James Kent, 3 ⅞ In. 40.00
Marigold, Jug, York, James Kent, 4 ⅜ In. 60.00
Marina, Teapot Set, Stacking, Lord Nelson Ware 750.00
Marion, Dish, Humber, Royal Winton, 9 ½ x 7 ¼ In. 175.00
Mauve, Bowl, Green Trim, Wintertonware, 3 ⅝ In. 45.00
Nantwich, Creamer, Stacking, Royal Winton 125.00
Nantwich, Mustard Jar, Royal Winton, 2 ⅜ In. 225.00
Old Cottage, Bowl, Bone China, Silver Plate, Royal Winton, 4 x 9 In. .... *illus* 47.00
Old Cottage, Jug, Globe Shape, Royal Winton, 4 ½ In. 275.00
Old Cottage, Mustard Jar, Cover, Royal Winton, 2 ¼ In. 185.00
Orient, Teapot Set, Stacking, Royal Winton .... *illus* 550.00
Queen Anne, Compote, Royal Winton, 7 x 5 ¾ x 2 ½ In. 145.00
Queen Anne, Dish, Triple, Gem Shape, Royal Winton 150.00
Queen Anne, Jam Jar, Cover, Ascot, Royal Winton 195.00
Queen Anne, Plate, Round, Royal Winton, 9 In. 45.00
Queen Anne, Sugar, Ascot Shape, Royal Winton 45.00
Rosalynde, Toast Rack, 4-Slice, James Kent 550.00
Royalty, Jug, Milk, Globe Shape, Royal Winton, 4 In. 325.00
Royalty, Jug, Water, Cover, Countess, Royal Winton, 7 In. 795.00
Shrewsbury, Jug, Milk, Countess, Royal Winton, 2 ½ In. 165.00
Somerset, Cup & Saucer, Ascot, Royal Winton 125.00

TIP
Don't soak dishes in chlorine bleach to remove a stain. It damages the glaze. This treatment was recommended years ago, but more is known today. And never use other bathroom cleaners. They, too, ruin the glaze.

Chintz, Old Cottage, Bowl, Bone China, Silver Plate, Royal Winton, 4 x 9 In.
$47.00

Chintz, Orient, Teapot Set, Stacking, Royal Winton
$550.00

Chocolate Glass, Cactus, Pitcher, Greentown, 8 x 5 ½ In.
$165.00

TIP
Never burn Christmas greens in the fireplace. The wood will send sparks up the chimney and some evergreens burn so hot they could cause a fire in the flue or a buildup of creosote in the chimney.

C

Christmas, Doll, Santa Claus, Painted, Fur, Cloth, 24 In.
$88.00

Christmas, Figure, Angel, Wax, Spun Glass Wings, Lace Trim Outfit, Painted Eyes, Germany 10 In.
$230.00

Somerset, Jug, Blue Trim, Globe Shape, Royal Winton, 5 In. 595.00
Somerset, Plate, Ascot, Royal Winton, 6 ⅛ In. 65.00
Somerset, Plate, Octagonal, Royal Winton, 5 ⅛ In.. .... 65.00
Spring, Plate, Ascot, Royal Winton, 5 ¼ In. 60.00
Summertime, Jug, Creamer, Dutch Shape, Royal Winton, 4 ½ In. 375.00
Summertime, Jug, Dutch Shape, Royal Winton, 3 ¾ In. 265.00
Summertime, Nut Dish, Royal Winton, Pair 95.00
Sunshine, Compote, Interior & Exterior Pattern, Lily Shape, Royal Winton, 6 x 3 In. 395.00
Sunshine, Sauceboat, Stand, Era, Royal Winton 125.00
Sweetpea, Mustard Jar, Ascot Shape, Royal Winton, 2 ⅛ In. 265.00
Sweetpea, Plate, Saville, Royal Winton, 4 ¼ In.. .... 65.00
Triumph, Mustard Jar, Royal Winton, 2 ⅜ In. 225.00
Victorian Rose, Nut Dish, Royal Winton 110.00
Welbeck, Jam Jar, Cover, Rosebud Shape, Royal Winton 245.00
Welbeck, Plate, Ascot, Royal Winton, 8 In. 175.00
Welbeck, Plate, Saville, Royal Winton, 4 ¼ In.. .... 75.00
Welbeck, Sugar, Grecian, Royal Winton 95.00
Welbeck, Toast Rack, 4-Slice, Queen, Royal Winton 295.00

CHOCOLATE GLASS , sometimes mistakenly called caramel slag, was made by the Indiana Tumbler and Goblet Company of Greentown, Indiana, from 1900 to 1903. It was also made at other National Glass Company factories. Fenton Art Glass Co. made chocolate glass from about 1907 to 1915. More recent pieces have been made by Imperial and others.

Cactus, Jar, Greentown, 6 In. 29.00
Cactus, Mustard, Silver Plated Rim, Hinged Cover, Twisted Bail, 3 ⅝ In. 361.00
Cactus, Pitcher, Greentown, 8 x 5 ½ In. .... *illus* 165.00
Cactus, Tumbler, Greentown, Pair. 23.00
Dolphin, Dish, Cover, Smooth Rim, Greentown 115.00
Honeycomb, Dish, Rectangular, Royal Glass, 1 ¾ x 4 In. 150.00
Nut, Dish, Figural, Footed, Nut Finial, Signed, 5 ¾ x 5 ½ In., Pair 44.00
Wild Rose & Bowknot, Creamer, McKee & Bros., 4 ¼ x 3 ¼ In.. .... 134.00

CHRISTMAS collectibles include not only Christmas trees and ornaments listed below, but also Santa Claus figures, special dishes, and even games and wrapping paper. A Belsnickle is a nineteenth-century figure of Father Christmas. A kugel is an early, heavy ornament made of thick blown glass, lined with zinc or lead, and often covered with colored wax. Christmas collectibles may also be listed in the Candy Container category. Christmas trees are listed in the section that follows.

Bell, Santa Claus, Josef Originals, 4 ¾ x 3 ½ In.. .... 28.00
Bells, Mickey & Minnie Mouse, Donald, Pluto, Clarabelle, Plastic, Box, Noma, 5 x 9 ½ x 2 In. 209.00
Belsnickle, Green, Gold Speckles, Tree, 7 In. 355.00
Belsnickle, Papier-Mache, Blue Coat, Feather Tree, c.1900, 8 ¼ In. 550.00
Belsnickle, Papier-Mache, Blue Coat, Red Hood Trim, Feather Tree, c.1900, 8 ¼ In. 880.00
Belsnickle, Papier-Mache, Green Feather Tree On Back, Fur Trim, c.1900, 9 ¾ In. 475.00
Belsnickle, Papier-Mache, Red Coat, Hat, Fur Trim, Tree, Holding Tree, c.1900, 9 ¾ In. 556.00 to 761.00
Belsnickle, Papier-Mache, Red Coat, Marked Germany, 7 ½ In. 1430.00
Belsnickle, Papier-Mache, Red Coat, Stamped Germany, 7 ¾ In. 275.00
Belsnickle, Papier-Mache, Red Coat, White Trim, 8 ½ In.. .... 275.00
Belsnickle, Papier-Mache, Stands On Snow Mound, Gold Robe, 9 ¾ In. 316.00
Belsnickle, Papier-Mache, Yellow Coat, 6 ¼ In. 248.00
Belsnickle, Papier-Mache, Yellow Coat, Drilled Hole In Hat, 6 ¼ In. 88.00
Belsnickle, Papier-Mache, Yellow Coat, Feather Tree, c.1900, 17 In. 3520.00
Belsnickle, Red Jacket, Blue Pants, Round Belly, Brown Sack, Germany, 10 In. 950.00
Calendar, Fan, Paper Lithograph, Children Images, Holly Leaf Trim, 14 ½ In.. .... 345.00
Candleholder, Child's Head, Clip-On, Blown & Molded Glass, Pastel, 3 ½ In. 863.00
Candleholder, Monkey Clown, Blown & Molded Glass, Clip-On, Painted, 3 ¼ In.. .... 518.00
Candleholder, Monkey Head, Blown Glass, Clip-On, Painted Face, Molded Detail, 2 ¼ In. ... 748.00
Candy Containers are listed in the Candy Container category.
Coin Purse, Santa Claus, 2-Sided, Celluloid 22.00
Creche, Painted, Composition Animals, Box, France, 19th Century, 13 ½ In. 316.00
Display, Santa Claus, Double Action, Cloth, Composition, 63 In. 546.00
Display, Santa Claus Workshop, Mechanical, 84 x 36 In. 990.00
Doll, Santa Claus, Painted, Fur, Cloth, 24 In. .... *illus* 88.00
Figure, Angel, Wax, Spun Glass Wings, Lace Trim Outfit, Painted Eyes, Germany 10 In. .... *illus* 230.00
Figure, Angel, Wax, Spun Glass Wings, Trimmed Clothing, Horn, Germany, 12 In. 863.00

Figure, Angel, Wax, Spun Glass Wings, Varied Outfits, 2 ¾ To 3 ½ In., 3 Piece 345.00
Figure, Elf, Wood Head, Black Hat, Red & White Jacket, Green Shoes, Wool, Silk, 18 In....... 170.00
Figure, Elf, Wood Head, Red Hat, Pants, Green & White Jacket, Wool, Silk, 18 In........... 95.00
Figure, Father Christmas, Tree, Bisque, Cardboard, Papier-Mache, Germany, c.1875, 30 In... 17500.00
Figure, Kris Kringle, Duncan Royale, 12 ¾ In.. 108.00
Figure, Reindeer, 5-Point Buck, Painted, Celluloid, 10 x 11 In. 11.00
Figure, Santa Claus, Child On Back, Multicolored, Chalkware, Late 1800s, 9 ¼ In. 8190.00
Figure, Santa Claus, Composition, Painted Face, Rabbit Fur Beard, Felt Robe, 11 In. 86.00
Figure, Santa Claus, Elf Like, Kloster Ettal, Back Pack, Label, Plush Outfit, c.1930, 9 In...... 58.00
Figure, Santa Claus, Holding Bag, Fruit Box, Celluloid, Viscoloid, 5 x 1 ¾ In.............. 33.00
Figure, Santa Claus, Holding Tree, Composition Face, Hands, Felt, Cardboard, Japan, 10 x 3 In. 77.00
Figure, Santa Claus, Painted, Composition, Cloth, 18 In.............................. 154.00
Figure, Santa Claus, Red Hat, Suit, White Beard, Pigeon Forge Pottery, Tenn., 5 ¼ In........ 250.00
Figure, Santa Claus, Waving, Holding Lantern, Painted, Celluloid, Japan, 4 ½ x 1 ¾ In...... 22.00
Figure, Santa Claus, Wood Head, Wool & Silk Clothes, 18 In........................... 120.00
Figure, Santa Claus In Sleigh, 3 Reindeer, Painted, Celluloid, 13 x 13 In................. 33.00
Lamp, Fairy, Christmas Tree, Embossed, Jewels, Saucer Base, Clarke, 4 ¼ In. .... *illus* 460.00
Lamp, Fairy, Tree, Jeweled Ornaments, Bisque, Painted, Clarke Base, Austria, 5 In. 275.00
Lamp, Oil, Santa Claus, Milk Glass, Red Coat, Blue Eyes, Flush Face, 9 ½ In. 460.00
Lamp, Santa Claus, Milk Glass, Electric, 7 ¾ In. 242.00
Lamp, Santa Claus, White Milk Glass, Red Painted Coat, Hat, Black Boots, Acorn Burner, 10 In. 4313.00
Mask, Santa Claus, Mesh, Animal Hair Beard, 17 In.................................. 38.00
Mold, Cake, Santa Claus, Embossed, Hello Kiddies, Cast Iron, Griswold, No. 898, 12 In....... 413.00
Mold, Chocolate, Father Christmas, Standing, Clips, 9 ½ x 4 ½ In., 2 Piece................ 120.00
Mold, Chocolate, Santa Claus, 12 ½ In. 200.00
Pail, Merry Christmas & Happy New Year, Ice Skaters, Sled Riders, Tin, Handle, 3 x 3 In. 132.00
Pail, Tin Lithograph, Children Playing In Snow, Compliments Of Schaack Bros., 3 ¼ In..... 345.00
Pail, Tin Lithograph, Children Playing Under Tree, Compliments Of O.R. Marcks, 3 ¼ In. ... 287.00
Pail, Tin Lithograph, Santa Claus Riding Sleigh, Compliments Of O.L. Pashby, 3 ¼ In....... 287.00
Plates that are limited edition are listed in the Collector Plate category or in the correct factory listing.
Platter, Christmas Tree, Multicolored, Gold Accents, Plate Hanger, 12 In................. 20.00
Rolling Pin, Xmas, Elmer W. Rosenberger, Pa., Blue, White, Stoneware, Wood, 15 ¼ In...... 400.00
Santa Claus, Composition, Rabbit Beard, German, Prewar, Windup, 6 In................ 275.00
Santa Claus, Enchanted Holiday, Fitz & Floyd, 21 ½ x 12 x 12 In....................... 80.00
Santa Claus, Pig Sled, Feast Meats, Chalk, 21 In. 345.00
Santa Claus, Plastic, Electric, c.1950, 16 In....................................... 28.00
Santa Claus, Sleigh, Plastic, Friction, Elmar, c.1960.................................. 30.00
Santa Claus, Walking, Tin Lithograph, Graphics, Windup, Chein, 5 ½ In. 460.00
Snow Globe, Full Of Water & Snow, Hong Kong, 5 In.................................. 18.00
Snow Globe, Santa Coming Down Chimney, Plastic, c.1960, 6 In......................... 12.00
Toy, Christmas Tree, Roly Poly, Celluloid, Viscoloid, 3 ½ x 2 In. 176.00
Toy, Santa Claus, On Globe, Battery Operated, Japan, Box, 15 In........................ 144.00
Toy, Santa Claus, On Globe, Spins, Arms, Head Move, Bell, Battery Operated, Japan, Box..... 420.00
Toy, Santa Claus, On Handcar, Battery Operated, T.M. Japan, Box........................ 121.00
Toy, Santa Claus, On Sled, Celluloid, Tin, Windup, Occupied Japan, Box, 8 In..... 165.00 to 175.00
Toy, Santa Claus, On Sled, Windup, Bell On Back Rings, Japan, 1940s, 4 In............... 153.00
Toy, Santa Claus, Playing Drums, Tin, Plastic, Cloth, Windup, Battery Operated, Japan, 9 In.. 10.00
Toy, Santa Claus, Roly Poly, Composition, 1910, 8 In................................ 495.00
Toy, Santa Claus, Roly Poly, Partial Box, 1910, 4 ¼ In. 275.00
Toy, Santa Claus, Skier, Cloth, Fur, Windup, Azuma, Box.............................. 40.00
Toy, Santa Claus, Sleigh, 2 Reindeer, Painted, Cast Iron, Hubley, 7 x 16 ½ In.............. 660.00
Toy, Santa Claus, Sleigh, Reindeer, Blue, White, Red, Painted, Cast Iron, Hubley, 15 In....... 1210.00
Toy, Santa Claus, Sleigh, Reindeer, Red, Green, Yellow, Bell, Plastic, Tin, Windup........... 60.00
Toy, Santa Claus, Sleigh, Reindeer, Tin, Windup, Japan, 3 ¼ x 7 In...................... 110.00
Toy, Santa Claus, Sleigh, White Reindeer, Cast Iron, Hubley, 14 ½ In. 1955.00
Toy, Santa Claus, Tin Lithograph, Mechanical, J. Chein, 6 In. .... *illus* 200.00
Toy, Santa Claus, Umbrella Spins, Plastic, Windup, Japan, 6 ½ x 4 In..................... 33.00
Toy, Santee Claus, Tin Lithograph, Windup, Oct. 18, 1921, 11 ½ In. .... *illus* 950.00
Toy, Stable, 2 Story, Wood, Straw Roof, Flat Wagon, 14 Carved Animals, Composition, 16 In.. 345.00
Trade Stimulator, Santa Claus, Riding Donkey, Windup, Red Outfit, Painted Face, 23 In.... 9200.00

CHRISTMAS TREES made of feathers and Christmas tree decorations of all types are popular with collectors. The first decorated Christmas tree in America is claimed by many states, including Pennsylvania (1747), Massachusetts (1832), Illinois (1833), Ohio (1838), and Iowa (1845). The first glass ornaments were imported from Germany about 1860. Dresden ornaments were made about 135 years ago of paper and tinsel. Manufacturers in the

Christmas, Lamp, Fairy, Christmas Tree, Embossed, Jewels, Saucer Base, Clarke, 4 ¼ In.
$460.00

Christmas, Toy, Santa Claus, Tin Lithograph, Mechanical, J. Chein, 6 In.
$200.00

Christmas, Toy, Santee Claus, Tin Lithograph, Windup, Oct. 18, 1921, 11 ½ In.
$950.00

TIP

Never plug more than 1500 watts into any one circuit. You probably have several plugs on one circuit. This is an easy mistake to make when decorating for the holidays. Don't encourage fires.

TIP

Don't try to restore old ornaments. A little damage and wear adds to the charm of old Christmas ornaments. It indicates an antique that has seen many holidays of use. Restoration lowers value.

United States were making ornaments in the early 1870s. Electric lights were first used on a Christmas tree in 1882. Character light bulbs became popular in the 1920s, bubble lights in the 1940s, twinkle bulbs in the 1950s, plastic bulbs by 1955. In this book a Christmas light is a holder for a candle used on the tree. Other forms of lighting include light bulbs. Other Christmas collectibles are listed in the preceding section.

Aluminum, 95 Branches, Revolving Color Projector, Evergleam Make, Box, 72 In. 860.00
Aluminum, Green & Silver, 158 Branches, 2-Piece Pole, 5 ½ Ft. 150.00
Aluminum, Metal Trunk, Colored Glass Balls, Wood Base, Japan, 12 In. 45.00
Aluminum, Rows Of Feathered Aluminum Branches, Colored Glass Balls, Stand, Japan, 12 In. 45.00
Bottle Brush, Green, Spots Of White Paint Depicting Snow, Red Bow, Flat Back, 3 In. 6.00
Bottle Brush, Round Wood Base, Flocking, c.1955, 2 In. 3.50
Bottle Brush, Round Wood Base, Flocking, c.1955, 4 In. 4.50
Bottle Brush, Sprinkled With Snow, In Red Wooden Pot, c.1920s, 16 In. 25.00
Feather, Red Berries, Wood Base, 1900s, 39 In. 280.00
Feather, Red Tinsel, Wired Branches, Colored Mercury Glass Beads, Japan, 20 In. 100.00
Feather, Tin Candleholders, Turned Wood Base, Germany, c.1900, 36 In. .... *illus* 220.00
Fence, Cast Iron, Painted Green, Gold, Openwork Design, 20 Sections, 22 Posts, 9 In. 1093.00
Fence, For Feather Tree, Green Feathers, Red Composition Berries, Wood Frame, 1920s 295.00
Garland, Blue Lead Tinsel Wrapped Around Cloth, Wire Reinforced Cord, Germany, 18 Ft. 65.00
Ornament, Abalone Shell, Mary & Jesus, Religious Themes, 2 To 3 ¾ In., 5 Piece 115.00
Ornament, Airplane, Red & Gold, Wire Wrapped, 7 In. 172.00
Ornament, Airplane, Wire Wrapped, Santa Claus, Blown Glass, Paper Scrap Face, 7 In. 489.00
Ornament, Ali Baba, In Barrel, Blown Glass, 4 In. 518.00
Ornament, Alligator, Pink, Blue, Red, White, Clip-On, Czechoslovakia, 7 ½ In. 460.00
Ornament, Alligator, Wire Wrapped, Molded, Annealed Legs, 6 ¼ In. 546.00
Ornament, Angel Star, Plastic, Blue Nylon Mesh Wired Dress, c.1950, 6 In. 15.00
Ornament, Angelic Procession, Glass Ball, Hummel, Schmid, 1982, 4 ½ In. 16.00
Ornament, Baby, Milk Bottle, Scrap Faced, Cotton Body, Paper Dress, Bonnet, 4 ¼ In. 173.00
Ornament, Baby In Cradle, Wire Wrapped, Crepe Paper, Spun Cotton, Blown Glass, 6 ¼ In. .. 978.00
Ornament, Baby In Tulip, Blown Glass, 4 In. 259.00
Ornament, Baby's 1st Christmas, Hallmark Keepsake, Box, 1984, 3 In. 35.00
Ornament, Ball, Cobalt Blue Hook, Opal, Green, Gold Swags, Daniel Lotton, 4 In. 58.00
Ornament, Ball, Gold Iridescent Swags, Opal, Daniel Lotton, 4 In. 86.00
Ornament, Ball, Pink, Blue Swags, Oval, Daniel Lotton, 4 In. 58.00
Ornament, Beetle, Wire Wrapped, Legs, Antennas, 5 In. .... *illus* 1265.00
Ornament, Bell, Plastic, Painted Blue, 3 White Stripes, No Clapper, 3 x 2 ½ In. 5.00
Ornament, Bell On Bell, Clackers, Wire Wrapped, 8 ¼ In. 259.00
Ornament, Bird, Red, Gold Glitter, Clip-On, Original Paper Tag On Tail, 6 x 4 In. 19.00
Ornament, Bird, White, Papier-Mache, Glitter, 9 x 3 x 5 In. 70.00
Ornament, Black Boy, Sitting, Derby Hat, Exaggerated Face, Germany, 3 ¼ In. 173.00
Ornament, Boot, Popper Bag, Dresden, Lace Trim, Painted, 6 ½ In. 862.00
Ornament, Candle, Blown Glass, Hollow, Clip-On Holder, 4 ½ In. 28.00
Ornament, Car, Red Flowers, Pierced Trim, Running Boards, Dresden, 3 ½ In. 920.00
Ornament, Carriage, Embossed, Gold Paint, Dresden, 4 In. 495.00
Ornament, Cat, Dresden, Embossed, Whiskers, Oversized Ears, 4 In. 863.00
Ornament, Cat, Green Coat, Pressed Cotton, Crepe Paper Tuxedo Jacket, Painted, 4 ¾ In. 431.00
Ornament, Cat Face, Candleholder, Clip-On, 3 In. 690.00
Ornament, Cat In The Hat, Blown Glass, Pink, White Top Hat, Molded Detail, 3 ½ In. 230.00
Ornament, Child, On Sled, Bisque Head, Glass Eyes, Wood Arms, Legs, Cloth Outfit, 4 ¼ In. .. 259.00
Ornament, Christmas Child, Glass Ball, Hummel, 1975 .... 20.00
Ornament, Christmas Tree, Presents Around Bottom, Mercury Glass, 7 In. 25.00
Ornament, Circus Bear, With Walking Stick, Dresden, Chain Collar, 3 In. 1035.00
Ornament, Clown, Paper Clown, Wire Wrapped, 7 In. 230.00
Ornament, Clown Head, Frosted, Glass, Black & White Polka Dot Hat, Collar, 3 ½ In. 201.00
Ornament, Cockatiel, Multicolored, 5 ½ In. 805.00
Ornament, Cowboy Boot, Dresden, 3-D, Silver, Gold Spur, Furth DePose, 5 ½ In. 58.00
Ornament, Cupid, In Sleigh, Dresden, Leaping Reindeer, Embossed, Sprigs, Flowers, 4 In. 4600.00
Ornament, Dr Pepper, Ball, White, Red, Green, Season's Greetings, Box, 12 Piece 60.00
Ornament, Elephant, Walking, Embossed, Silver Paint, Dresden, 3 In. 195.00
Ornament, Elf, Riding Reindeer, Carrying Cloth Sack, Sprig, 3 ½ In. .... *illus* 978.00
Ornament, Fish, Silver, Dorsal Fins, Dresden, 5 ¾ In. 517.00
Ornament, Free-Form, Wire Wrapped, Sphere Shape, Flute Base, Painted, 9 In. 489.00
Ornament, Frog, Embossed, Silver Paint, Dresden, Germany, 2 In. 330.00
Ornament, Girl, Bell Body, Blown Glass, Annealed Arms, Germany, 3 In. 431.00
Ornament, Girl, Skipping Rope, Spun Cotton, Wire Wrapped Rope, Paper Scrap Face, 5 ¾ In. 316.00

Christmas Tree, Feather, Tin Candleholders, Turned Wood Base, Germany, c.1900, 36 In. $220.00

Christmas Tree, Ornament, Beetle, Wire Wrapped, Legs, Antennas, 5 In. $1265.00

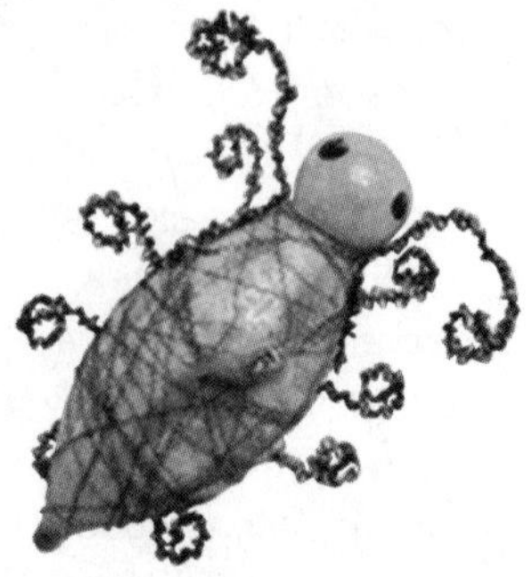

Ornament, Girl On Wheelbarrow, Flowers, Wire Wrapped, 7 In. 575.00
Ornament, Goose, Dresden, White, Orange Beak, Feet, 2 ¾ In. 546.00
Ornament, Graf Zeppelin, Wire Wrapped, Embossed, Germany, 5 In. 489.00
Ornament, Grandma Moses, 2 Scenes, Hallmark, 1977 .... 22.00
Ornament, Grizzly Bear, Dresden, Painted, Black, Red Mouth, 3 In. 431.00
Ornament, Horned Owl, Molded, Glass Eyes, 3 ¾ In. 920.00
Ornament, John Ball, Chenille Legs, Blown Glass, Composition Boots, German, 4 ¼ In.. .... 259.00
Ornament, Judy Twofaced, Glass, Painted, 5 In. 86.00
Ornament, Kangaroo, Standing, Dresden, Full-Body, Germany, 2 ½ In. 518.00
Ornament, Kate Greenaway, Blond Curly Hair, Clip-On, 4 In. 431.00
Ornament, Kitten, Ball In Paws, Cotton, 3 In. 316.00
Ornament, Kitten, Dresden, Embossed, Playful Pose, Red Paint Trace, Bow, 3 ¼ In. 920.00
Ornament, Kugel, Teardrop, Mercury Glass, 6 In. 55.00
Ornament, Mary Pickford, Annealed Legs, Blown Glass, Molding, Painted Shoes, 4 ¼ In.. .... 489.00
Ornament, Merry Carousel, Santa Claus, 2 Reindeer, Motion, Hallmark Keepsake, 1980, 3 In. 105.00
Ornament, Noel, Peasant Man, Woman, Green Velvet Ribbon, Quimper, 1982, 3 In. 55.00
Ornament, Oriental Woman, Dresden, Posed On Lotus Flower, 4 ½ In.. .... 748.00
Ornament, Owl Head, Blown Glass, Teal Eyes, Black Beak, 3 ¼ In. 259.00
Ornament, Parachutist, Molded Glass, Light Green, Flocked, 4 ¼ In. 86.00
Ornament, Peace On Earth, Village Scene, Hallmark Keepsake, 1976, 3 ¼ In. 77.00
Ornament, Pewter, For Unto You A Child Is Born, Skip Winn, c.1989, 2 ½ In. 35.00
Ornament, Pig, Green, Dresden, Germany, 2 ½ In. 201.00
Ornament, Pig, With Horseshoe, Dresden, Embossed, Tan, 4 In. 575.00
Ornament, Popcorn Head, Blown & Molded Glass, Painted, Yellow, Orange, Clip-On, 2 ¾ In.. 518.00
Ornament, Prince, Crown, Painted, Glass, Chenille Arms, Legs, 5 ½ In. 259.00
Ornament, Quarter-Moon Face, Gold Paint, 2-Sided, Dresden, Germany, 3 In. .... *illus* 330.00
Ornament, Quarter-Moon Face, Silver Paint, 2-Sided, Dresden, Germany, 3 In.. .... 330.00
Ornament, Rabbit, Emerging From Egg, 4 ¾ In. 431.00
Ornament, Rifle, Embossed, Painted, Paper Composition, Dresden, 6 ¼ In.. .... 165.00
Ornament, Rooster, Dresden, Germany, 3 ¾ In. 517.00
Ornament, Santa Claus, Cotton Scrap Face, Feather Tree Sprig, Dresden Stars, Germany, 6 In. 316.00
Ornament, Santa Claus, Fur Coat & Beard, Composition Face, Sprig, Wreath, 14 In. 201.00
Ornament, Santa Claus, Holding Tree, Glass, Clip-On, 4 ½ In. 57.00
Ornament, Santa Claus, On Skis, Wooden, Fabric, c.1930, 6 ½ In. 172.00
Ornament, Santa Claus, Pewter, Avon, 2 x 3 ¼ In. 15.00
Ornament, Santa Claus, Pulling Wood Sleigh, Composition, Rabbit Fur Beard, 8 ¾ In. 374.00
Ornament, Santa Claus & Nipper, Dated 1902 .... 25.00
Ornament, Santa Claus's Head, Glass, Poland, 4 ½ x 3 ½ In.. .... 25.00
Ornament, Shamrock Sailboat, Dresden, Pressed Paper, Silvered Sails, 5 In. 460.00
Ornament, Shell Boat, Pulled By Swan, Scalloped Edge, Gold Paint, 4 ½ In. 1495.00
Ornament, Shiny Brite, Bell Shape, Glass, Magenta, Wire Hanger, 1963, 1 In., Box Of 10 .... 24.00
Ornament, Soccer Player, Ball At Feet, Red, White & Blue, 3 In. 374.00
Ornament, Steamship, Dresden, Embossed, Portholes, Railing, 4 In. 460.00
Ornament, Strawberry, Red, 4 Windows, 1 ¾ In.. .... 24.00
Ornament, Suited Fox, Spun Cotton, Crepe Paper Jacket, Dresden Buttons, Germany, 5 In. .. 633.00
Ornament, Swan, Embossed, Gold Paint, 2-Sided, Dresden, Germany, 3 In. 330.00
Ornament, Torpedo Boat, Blown Glass, Wire Wrapped, German Cross, Cotton Smoke, 4 ½ In. 1150.00
Ornament, Tree Topper, Angel Star, Blue Nylon Mesh Dress, 1950s, 6 In. .... *illus* 15.00
Ornament, Tree Topper, Composition Head, White Feather Skirt, Japan, 1950s, 5 In. 34.00
Ornament, Tree Topper, Green & Silver Tinsel, Germany, 9 x 11 ½ In. 45.00
Ornament, Tree Topper, Santa Claus, Curly Cap, Silvered, Painted, 10 In. 259.00
Ornament, Tree Topper, Santa Claus, Glolite, Plastic, c.1950 .... 9.00
Ornament, Uncle Sam, Blown Glass, 7 ¾ In.. .... 431.00
Ornament, Wheat Sheave, Dresden, Painted Gold, Germany, 6 In. 259.00
Ornament, Woman's Head, Hair In Bun, Clip-On, 3 In. 1380.00
Ornament, Yellow Kid, Extended Legs, Molded Glass, Yellow, Black Shoes, 4 ¾ In.. .... 1610.00
Ornament, Zebra, Spun Cotton, Striping, 3 ¼ In. 460.00
Pompon, Silver Tinsel, With Stand, With Box, 1960s, 4 Ft. 133.00
Stand, Angels, Stars, Houses, Cast Iron, Musler-Schott, Germany, 9 x 13 In. 143.00
Stand, Cast Iron, Santa Claus At Center, Red Robe, 12 x 12 In.. .... 345.00
Stand, Musical, 3 Screws, Lador, Switzerland, 8 ½ x 14 In. 225.00
Stand, Rotating, Electric, Metal, Painted White, Multicolored Confetti Sparkles, 10 In. Diam.. 45.00
Stand, Santa Claus, Basket, Cast Iron, Marked, Deutschland, 33, 7 ⅜ x 10 In. .... *illus* 201.00
Stand, Santa Claus, Chimney, Reindeer, Sled, Tin Lithograph, 1935, 8 x 14 In.. .... 110.00
Stand, Santa Claus, Painted, Cast Iron, Stamped, 1919, 18 In. 200.00
Tinsel, Silver, Multicolored Pin Dot Accents, Built-In Stand, 1950s, 24 In.. .... 24.00

Christmas Tree, Ornament, Elf, Riding Reindeer, Carrying Cloth Sack, Sprig, 3 ½ In.
$978.00

Christmas Tree, Ornament, Quarter-Moon Face, Gold Paint, 2-Sided, Dresden, Germany, 3 In.
$330.00

Christmas Tree, Ornament, Tree Topper, Angel Star, Blue Nylon Mesh Dress, 1950s, 6 In.
$15.00

Christmas Tree, Stand, Santa Claus, Basket, Cast Iron, Marked, Deutschland, 33, 7 ⅜ x 10 In.
$201.00

TIP
Clean chrome with a commercial chrome cleaner or an acidic cleaner. Rinse, then rub it shiny with a dry cloth.

Chrome, Coffee Urn, Electric, Art Deco, Bakelite, Manning Bowman, c.1935, 13 In.
$71.00

Chrome, Smoking Stand, Onyx, Art Deco, 29 In.
$71.00

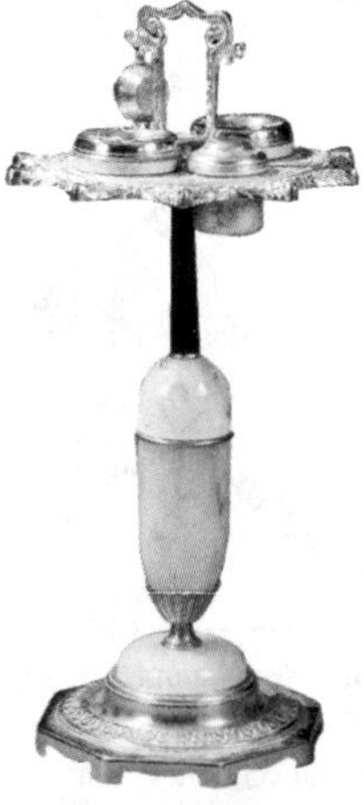

TIP
Old newspapers can be used to polish water spots off chrome.

CHROME items in the Art Deco style became popular in the 1930s. Collectors are most interested in high-style pieces made by the Connecticut firms of Chase Brass & Copper Co. and Manning-Bowman & Co.

Cake Stand, 2 Tiers, Art Deco, Nude Holding Top Tier, Scalloped, Pierced, 1930s, 8 ½ In. 150.00
Cocktail Shaker, Art Deco, Chrome & Stainless Steel, Black Bakelite Handles, 13 ¼ In. 195.00
Cocktail Shaker, Bottom, Strainer, Lid, 8 ½ In., 3 Piece. 16.00
Coffee Set, Coffeepot, Sugar, Creamer, Plated, Plastic Handles, Keystoneware, 1940s-50s 48.00
Coffee Urn, Electric, Art Deco, Bakelite, Manning Bowman, c.1935, 13 In. .... *illus* 71.00
Ice Crusher, Harry Laylon, Chase Logo, 1940, 5 ¾ In. 38.00
Lamp, Dog, Stylized, Jointed Legs, Lucite Ears, Bulb In Top Of Head, 1960s. 600.00
Server, Penguin, Lid, Brown Bakelite Handles & Knob, West Bend, 1940s, 8 x 9 ½ In. 85.00
Shaker, Zeppelin Form, Art Deco, Germany, Case, 9 In.. .... 950.00
Smoking Stand, Onyx, Art Deco, 29 In. .... *illus* 71.00
Tidbit, 2 Tiers, Embossed Design, Irvin, USA, Bottom Plate 12 In., Top Plate 8 In. 15.00
Tray, Art Deco, Red Bakelite Handles, 7 ¼ x 8 In.. .... 135.00
Vase, Butterscotch Bakelite Ribbed Section, Ribbed Panels, Minerva, Chase, 1941, 6 ⅜ In. 42.00

CIGAR STORE FIGURES of carved wood or cast iron were used as advertisements in front of the Victorian cigar store. The carved figures are now collected as folk art. They range in size from counter type, about three feet, to over eight feet high.

Christopher Columbus, Segars, Painted, Zinc, W. Demuth & Co., 1880s, 67 In. 5000.00
Indian, Carved, Holding Knife & Feathers, Early 1900s, 67 In. 519.00
Indian, Chief, Feather Headdress, Mountain Lion, Painted, Zinc, 1890s, 71 In.. .... 5000.00
Indian, Cutout Multicolored, 2-Sided, Initialed E.H., c.1900, 80 In. 16500.00
Indian, Feather Headdress, Skin Cape, Panel, Stand, Paint, St. Louis, c.1890, 69 In. 31995.00
Indian, Full Headdress, Hand On Head, Holding Hatchet, 74 In. 4500.00
Indian, Full Headdress, Holding Cup, Wood, Original Paint, 74 In. 440.00
Indian, Headdress, Holding Items, Red, Gold, Blanket Draped, 76 In. 8625.00
Indian, Maiden, Feather Headdress, Arm Raised, Carved, Painted, c.1900, 69 In. 24500.00
Indian, Maiden, Headdress, Wood, 74 In. 10925.00
Indian, Maiden, Painted, Cast Lead, Early 1900s, 31 In. 2800.00
Indian, Maiden, Wood, 3 Feather Headdress, Cigar Box, Painted, c.1890, 78 In. 22000.00
Indian, Maiden, Wood, Carved, Painted, c.1900, 69 In. .... *illus* 25740.00
Indian, Maiden, Wood, White Attire, Headdress, Holding Cigars, c.1890, Base, 73 In. 5775.00
Indian, Painted, Multicolored, Carved, Stars & Stripes On Skirt, 1900s, 72 In. 472.00
Indian, Princess, Pine, Carved, Painted, Late 19th Century, 39 In.. .... 14950.00
Indian, Stylized Headdress, Red Attire, Rifle, Wood, 70 In. 440.00
Indian, Tobaccos & Pipes, Painted, Metal, Wood Plinth, Early 1900s, 62 In. 2000.00
Indian, Tomahawk, Cast Metal, Miller Dubrul & Peters, 1885, 75 ½ In. .... *illus* 38500.00
Punch, Painted, Solid Wood Construction, c.1940, 57 In. 805.00
Punch, Red Hat, Outfit, White Ruffle Collar, Painted, Wood, c.1940, 57 In. 700.00

CINNABAR is a vermilion or red lacquer. Pieces are made with tens to hundreds of thicknesses of the lacquer that is later carved. Most cinnabar was made in the Orient.

Bowl, Pumpkin Cover, 3 ½ x 6 x 6 In. 30.00
Box, Clouds, Flower Scrolls, Jade Bats, Shou Character Inset, Chinese, 13 In. 1304.00
Box, Figural, Chinese, 19th Century, 9 In.. .... 1075.00
Box, Figures, Clips On 2 Corners, 2 x 5 ⅝ x 3 ¾ In. 33.00
Box, Figures, Landscape, Red Qing Dynasty, 8 In.. .... 1434.00
Box, Hinged Lid, Phoenix, Peonies, Diaper Ground, Chinese, 1910, 6 In.. .... 80.00
Frame, 3 Figures, Rocks, Tree, Flowers, 15 ¼ x 11 ¾ In. 132.00
Ginger Jar, Over Bronze Form, Marked China, 5 ½ In. 294.00
Ink Stick, Siniuos Chilong, Gilt, Inscribed, Zhen Bao Mo, Box, 5 ¼ In. 250.00
Jar, Gourd Shape, Lid, 6 In. 175.00
Lamp, Baluster, Fringe Shade, Electrified, Early 20th Century 300.00
Table, Scholars, Attendants, Garden, Peonies, 1800s, 4 x 16 x 11 In. 1025.00
Tray, Figures, Pavilions, Palace Garden, Square, 19th Century, Japan, 15 In. 1126.00
Vase, Cover, Figures, Scrolls, Stand, Chinese, 19th Century, 14 In. 1050.00
Vase, Figures In Mountain Landscape, Chinese, Late 19th Century, 12 In.. .... 413.00
Vase, Mountainous Landscape, Chinese, 9 ½ In. 354.00
Vase, Riverscape, Chinese, 1900s, 11 ½ In. 598.00
Vase, Swollen Middle, Flared Base & Rim, c.1900, 10 x 5 ½ In.. .... 205.00

CIVIL WAR mementos are important collectors' items. Most of the pieces are military items used from 1861 to 1865. Be sure to avoid any explosive munitions.

Autograph Book, 75th Grand Reunion, Gettysburg Battlefield, Calfskin Cover, c.1938 ..... 130.00
Badge, Confederate, CSA, Tin, 3 x 1 ¾ In. 450.00
Binoculars, Ivory, Brass, E. Pluribus Unum, Eagles, Engraved, Capt. D.A. Taft, 1861 .... 600.00
Booklet, Union Volunteer Refreshment Saloon, Lithographs, 2 ½ x 3 ¾ In., 5 Pages 115.00
Breast Plate, Eagle, Holding Arrows & Branch, Union, 2 ½ In. 150.00
Bucket, Artillery, Grease, Hand Wrought, Riveted, Chain, Handle, 8 ½ x 8 In. .... *illus* 325.00
Bucket, Grease, Civil War Artillery, Iron, Hinged Handle, Flexible Chain, 8 ¼ In. 410.00
Buckle, US, Oval, Union, 3 ¼ In. 210.00
Button, Confederate, Initials CSA, General Service 6776.00
Button, Lamar Mounted Rifles, Georgia 9240.00
Button, Union Officer's Staff, Eagle, Stars, Arrows, R & W Robinson, Attleboro, Mass. 65.00
Canteen, Cedar, Iron Rim, Pewter Spout Insert, c.1860, 7 ⅜ x 2 ⅜ In. 475.00
Canteen, Drum Style, Wood, Iron Bands, Wood Plug 500.00
Chest, Wood, Composition, Tin, W.T. Weeden, 1860s, 18 x 11 In. 630.00
Crutches, Japanned Pine, Lafayette Sykes, 5th Connecticut, c.1862, 52 x 9 In. 403.00
Discharge Paper, Michael Hoover, Company F, 207th Reg., Pa., Vol. Infantry, Frame 153.00
Dog Tag, Brass, Die Engraved, Robert Lovett, c.1860 .... 245.00
Drum, Infantry, Eagle, Banner, Shield, Drumsticks, Holder, Rogers Mfg., 15 ½ x 16 In. 7100.00
Drum, Mahogany, Red Hoops, Star, Wm. L. Tompkins & Sons, N.Y., 1861, 15 x 18 In. 995.00
Drum, Wood, Leather Strap, Tension Rope, Top Skin, 16 ½ x 8 ½ In. 403.00
Field Surgical Kit, Mahogany Case, 3 Tiers, H. Hernstein & Sons, New York 5818.00
Flag, Regimental, New York State Volunteers, Silk, Embroidered, 12 x 22 In. 2478.00
Flag Pike, Bullet Shape, Valley Forge, Incised, Iron Mount, 23 In. 150.00
Flag Pike, Iron, Triangular Tip, Base Mount, Late 19th Century, 91 In. 650.00
Frock Coat, Wool, Navy Blue, 14 Buttons, Vented, Lieutenant Colonel Shoulder Straps 5000.00
Jacket, Confederate, Wool, Uniform Buttons, Napped Gray Blue, Black Braid, 21 In. 999.00
Jacket, Union, Cavalry Shell, Blue, Wool, 12 Buttons, Stamped, Eaves .... *illus* 2200.00
Jacket, Volunteer Militia, Red, 3 Piece Brass Button, Scoville Co., 1850-60 .... 385.00
Jacket, Zouave, Wool Lace, Blue, Twilled Wool, Tan Cotton, 19th Century, 19 In. 646.00
Kepi, Blue, Leather Visor, Brass Wreath, U.S. Emblem, Label, Marked 350.00
Kepi, Federal Navy, Red & Blue Oilcloth, Black Brim, Brass Buttons, 10 ¼ In. 529.00
Knife, Bowie, Confederate, 2 Piece Bone Grip, Iron, Leather, 17 ½ In. .... *illus* 2420.00
Knife, Pocket, Stag Handle, Silver Escutcheon, Inscribed, Marked Blades, 4 In. Closed 425.00
Mug, Union Forever, Constitution, Pressed Glass, Flint, Pontil, 1875, 4 x 2 ¾ In. .... *illus* 523.00
Poster, Recruitment, Union, Stout, Able-Bodied Men, N.Y. Station, 23 x 32 In. 1438.00
Reunion Ribbon, Hagood's Brigade UCV, Stars & Bars, Charleston, Apr. 1896, 2 x 7 ½ In. 460.00
Sign, Johnsons Military, Regimental Record, Company B, Maine, 1862, 26 x 20 In. .... *illus* 143.00
Spoon, General B.N. Forrest, Union & Confederate Flag Handle, Thayer, 1865 .... 175.00
Sword, Black Leather & Brass Scabbard, Horstmann, Philadelphia, 35 In. 1295.00
Trunk, Grain Painted, Major B.B. Hammond, Paymaster, U.S.A., 33 ½ x 19 x 19 In. 400.00
Tumbler, Cannon, Trench Mortar, Flag, Eagle, Pressed Glass, Flint, 1875, 4 ¾ x 3 ¼ In. .. *illus* 150.00

CKAW, *see Dedham category.*

CLAMBROTH glass, popular in the Victorian era, is a grayish color and is somewhat opaque, like clam broth. It was made by several factories in the United States and England.

Candlestick, Dolphin, Pair 1900.00
Vase, Gold Trim, 9 ⅞ In. 48.00

CLARICE CLIFF was a designer who worked in several English factories, including A.J. Wilkinson Ltd., Wilkinson's Royal Staffordshire Pottery, Newport Pottery, and Foley Pottery after the 1920s. She is best known for her brightly colored Art Deco designs, including the Bizarre line. She died in 1972. Reproductions have been made by Wedgwood.

Aurea, Bowl, Flowers, Green Band, c.1935, 8 ½ In. 550.00
Aurea, Teapot, Lynton Shape, Bent Finial, c.1935, 6 In. 250.00
Bizarre, Preserve Pot, Autumn Crocus, Multicolored, Signed, 3 ½ x 3 In. 360.00
Bizarre, Vase, Landscape, Stepped Form, Marked 7 ½ In. 805.00
Bowl, Flowers, Leaves, Orange, Blue Rim, Art Deco, c.1920, 9 In. 275.00
Celtic Harvest, Jar, Metal Lid, Factory Mark, 4 In. .... *illus* 52.00
Crocus, Cup & Saucer, Autumn, Devon Shape Cup, 1930s 245.00

Cigar Store Figure, Indian, Maiden, Wood, Carved, Painted, c.1900, 69 In.
$25740.00

Cigar Store Figure, Indian, Tomahawk, Cast Metal, Miller Dubrul & Peters, 1885, 75 ½ In.
$38500.00

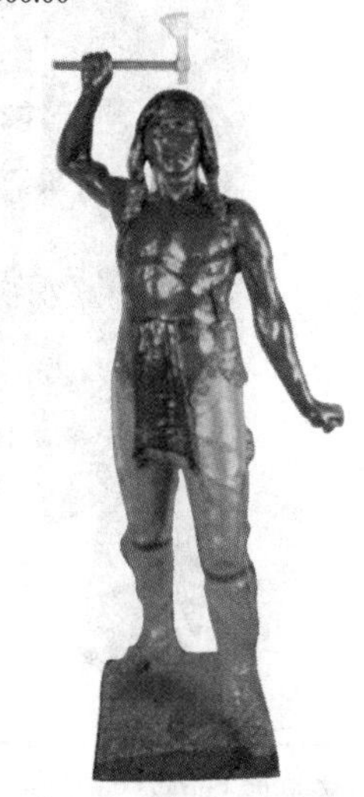

TIP

Smoke stains can be removed from a stone fireplace with an art gum eraser. Soot on the carpet in front of the fireplace can be removed with salt. Sprinkle dry salt on the soot, wait 30 minutes, then vacuum.

Civil War, Bucket, Artillery, Grease, Hand Wrought, Riveted, Chain, Handle, 8 ½ x 8 In.
$325.00

Civil War, Mug, Union Forever, Constitution, Pressed Glass, Flint, Pontil, 1875, 4 x 2 ¾ In.
$523.00

Civil War, Jacket, Union, Cavalry Shell, Blue, Wool, 12 Buttons, Stamped, Eaves
$2200.00

Civil War, Sign, Johnsons Military, Regimental Record, Company B, Maine, 1862, 26 x 20 In.
$143.00

Civil War, Knife, Bowie, Confederate, 2 Piece Bone Grip, Iron, Leather, 17 ½ In.
$2420.00

Civil War, Tumbler, Cannon, Trench Mortar, Flag, Eagle, Pressed Glass, Flint, 1875, 4 ¾ x 3 ¼ In.
$150.00

Crocus, Trio, Spring, 1930s, 6 ½-In. Plate 150.00
Delecia Pansy, Jug, Flowers, Drip Glaze, Horizontal Bands, 1930s, 7 In. 1025.00
Flower Holder, Rockwork, Angular, Flower Holes, Ivory Glaze, 1930s, 3 ¾ In. 135.00
Havre, Bowl, Pink, Blue, Green, Lilac Bands, Marked, c.1928-30, 8 ½ In. 180.00
Honeydew, Trio, c.1935, 6 ⅝-In. Plate 175.00
Honeyglaze, Trio, 3 Flowers, Blue, Pink, Yellow, c.1930, 6 ½-In. Plate 175.00
Jug, Seated Grinning Man, Period Dress, Mug, Wilkinsons Large Toby, 10 ½ In. 240.00
Melon, Bowl, c.1930, 3 ¼ x 7 ¼ In. 485.00
Melon, Cup & Saucer, Athens Shape, 1930s 345.00
Pitcher, Geometrics, Blue, Orange, Red, White, 11 ¼ x 8 ¼ In. 1650.00
Plaque, No. 28, Designed By Frank Brangwyn, Burslem, 17 ½ In. 3450.00
Plate, Cream, Beige Border, Green, Red, Blue Leaves, Black Dots, c.1920, 10 In. 100.00
Rudyard, Cup & Saucer, Fantasque, Daffodil Shape Cup, c.1933 . . . . 500.00
Secrets, Cup & Saucer, c.1935 . . . . 345.00
Teapot, Flowers, Pink, Green, Green Bands, Lynton Shape, Button Finial, 1930s, 5 ¼ In. 250.00
Tonquin, Gravy Boat, Black Transfer, Footed, 1940s, 3 x 5 ½ In. 25.00
Tonquin, Plate, Dinner, Brown Transfer, House In Woods, c.1945, 10 In. 22.00
Tureen, Lid, Round Tan Bowl, 4 Geometric Feet, Multicolored Abstract Accents, c.1930, 7 In. . 325.00
Tureen, Lid, White, Orange, Red, Yellow, Geometrics, Pottery, 1928-36, 6 ¾ In. . . . . *illus* 295.00
Vase, Morning Glory, Incised Bands, Branch Handle, Footed, 1940s, 8 ¾ In. 285.00

CLEWELL ware was made in limited quantities by Charles Walter Clewell of Canton, Ohio, from 1902 to 1955. Pottery was covered with a thin coating of bronze, then treated to make the bronze turn different colors. Pieces covered with copper, brass, or silver were also made. Mr. Clewell's secret formula for blue patinated bronze was burned when he died in 1965.

Vase, Copper Clad, Bulbous, Patina, 12 x 6 In. . . . . *illus* 960.00
Vase, Copper Clad, Flared, Green, Red, Footed, 3 x 8 In. 420.00
Vase, Copper Clad, Patina, Marked, 8 x 4 In. 360.00
Vase, Copper Clad, Shouldered, Blue, Green, Brown Patina, 4 x 6 In. 840.00
Vase, Copper Clad, Shouldered, Incised Flowers, Covering Owens Form, 5 x 12 In. 900.00
Vase, Hourglass Column, Flower, Leaf, Fowl Relief, Mark, 9 In. 652.00

CLIFTON POTTERY was founded by William Long in Newark, New Jersey, in 1905. He worked there until 1909 making lines including Crystal Patina and Clifton Indian Ware. Clifton Pottery made art pottery until 1911 and then concentrated on wall and floor tile. By 1914 the name had been changed to Clifton Porcelain and Tile Company. Another firm, Chesapeake Pottery, sold majolica marked *Clifton Ware*.

Humidor, Indian Ware, Mark, c.1910, 6 x 6 In. 195.00
Vase, Daffodils, Brown Bisque Ground, Squat, Signed, 4 ⅞ x 7 ¾ In. 143.00

CLOCKS of all types have always been popular with collectors. The eighteenth-century tall case, or grandfather's, clock was designed to house a works with a long pendulum. In 1816, Eli Terry patented a new, smaller works for a clock, and the case became smaller. The clock could be kept on a shelf instead of on the floor. By 1840, coiled springs were used and even smaller clocks were made. Battery-powered electric clocks were made in the 1870s. A garniture set can include a clock and other objects displayed on a mantel.

Advertising, 7Up, Get Real Action, Reverse Painted, Metal, Light-Up, 16 In. 110.00
Advertising, Alka-Seltzer, Boy, Pron Tito, Indigestion Acida Dolor De Cabeza, 13 x 13 In. 190.00
Advertising, Baird, Perfection Leather Oil, Pendulum, 18 x 31 ½ In. 2031.00
Advertising, Ballantine Beer, Light-Up, Plastic, 1950s, 12 x 3 ½ In. 115.00
Advertising, Beer, Monk, Straddling Clock, Drinking From Mug, Electric, Automated, 17 x 24 In. 715.00
Advertising, Borden's Dairy Products, Round, Electric, Light-Up, Marked Pam, 15 In. 402.00
Advertising, Buick, Metal, Patina, Round, 19 x 5 In. 700.00
Advertising, Camel & Century Cigarettes, Plastic, Metal, 23 x 66 ¾ In. 20.00
Advertising, Carvel, Beige, Green, Yellow, 20 In. 198.00
Advertising, Cheer-Up Soda, Bottle, Glass, Metal, Light-Up, Telechron, 15 In. 300.00
Advertising, Clappertons, Six Cord Spool Cotton, Baird Clock Co., c.1890, 18 ¾ x 31 In. 345.00
Advertising, Clicquot Club Beverages, Eskimo Holding Bottle, Light-Up, c.1940, 15 In. 350.00
Advertising, Clicquot Club Ginger Ale, Eskimo Holding Bottle, Glass, Metal, 15 In. 180.00
Advertising, Croft Ale, Boston, Mass., 18 x 27 In. 694.00
Advertising, Crosley Radios, Time For Crosley, 8-Sided, Blue & Pink Neon, 22 x 7 In. 2500.00
Advertising, Dad's Root Beer, Bottle Cap, Aluminum, Light-Up, Screen Print Products, 16 In. 140.00
Advertising, Dad's Root Beer, Yellow Ground, Light-Up, Pam Clock Co., 1950, 14 x 4 In. 445.00
Advertising, Dr Pepper, Chevron, Pam Clock Co., 1960s, 15 In. 175.00
Advertising, Dr Pepper, Red Neon, 8-Sided, 1930s, 18 In. 90.00

Clarice Cliff, Celtic Harvest, Jar, Metal Lid, Factory Mark, 4 In.
$52.00

Clarice Cliff, Tureen, Lid, White, Orange, Red, Yellow, Geometrics, Pottery, 1928-36, 6 ¾ In.
$295.00

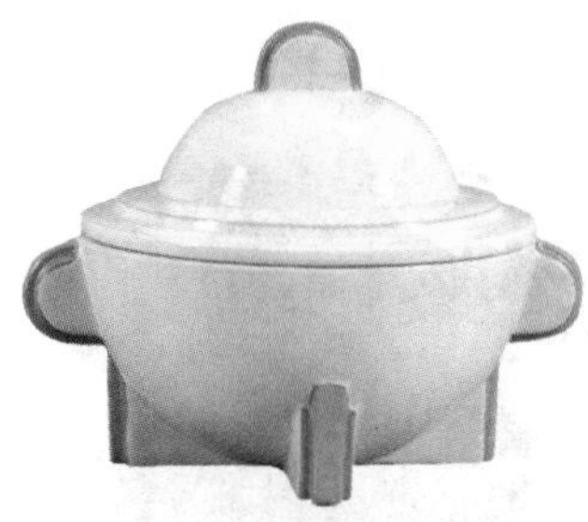

Clewell, Vase, Copper Clad, Bulbous, Patina, 12 x 6 In.
$960.00

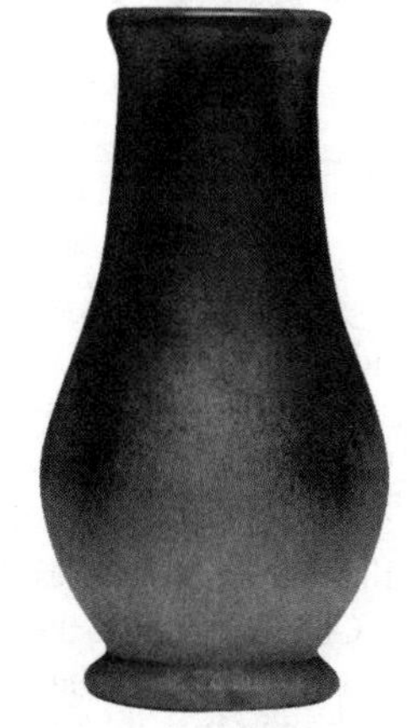

TIP
Clarice Cliff pieces marked in black are worth two to three times as much as pieces marked in any other color.

Clock, Ansonia, Victorian, Cast Iron, Open Escarpment, Late 19th Century, 12 ½ In.
$210.00

Clock, Black Forest, Cuckoo, Buck, 3-Train Steel Movement, c.1890, 25 ½ x 17 x 13 In.
$525.00

Grandmother Clock

A grandmother clock is a smaller version of a grandfather clock. It should be less than six feet six inches high. Grandmother clocks were first popular from about 1750 to 1850. Modern versions are still made.

Advertising, Duke Sessions, Dog, Light-Up Eyes Tell Time, Sirocco Wood, 1920s, 4 ¼ x 5 In. . 1610.00
Advertising, Four Roses Whiskey, Light-Up, 13 x 12 x 5 In. 110.00
Advertising, Gallikers, Johnstown, Pa., Red, White, Blue, Black, Square 125.00
Advertising, Goulding's Manures, Baird, Black, Gold Letterings, 18 ½ x 30 In.. . . . . 2300.00
Advertising, Guerin-Boutron Chocolat, Metal, Embossed, Modele Depose, 19 In.. . . . . 413.00
Advertising, Hecker's Flour, Boy On Stool, Blue, Purple, Red, Light-Up, Pam, 15 In. 225.00
Advertising, J.I. Case Co., Round Plastic Case, Curved Lens, Eagle, General Electric, 15 In.. . . 358.00
Advertising, KFC, Y'all Take Home Extra, Melt In Your Mouth Biscuits, Light-Up, Pam, 15 In. 450.00
Advertising, Kist Beverages, Enjoy, Square, 1930s, 15 ¾ In. 105.00
Advertising, L.O. Grothe & Co. Boston Cigar, Peg-Top Cigar, 2 Gentlemen, 15 x 11 In. 690.00
Advertising, Longines, Store, Light-Up, Electric Time Co., 1950s, 15 In. 173.00
Advertising, Mason's Root Beer, Gold Ground, Light-Up, Pam Clock Corp, 1950, 15 In.. . . . . 316.00
Advertising, Mishler's Herb Bitters, Glass, Silver Letters, Pendulum, Key, 30 ½ In. 5040.00
Advertising, Mobilgas, Multicolored Neon, Round, 26 x 5 In. 600.00
Advertising, Monarch Finer Foods, Lion, Light-Up, 15 In. 250.00
Advertising, Norge Appliances, It's Time To Buy, Red, White, Light-Up, c.1940, 15 In. 450.00
Advertising, Normandie Watch Repair Service, Blue, White, 2-Sided, 15 In. 200.00
Advertising, Norton Door Closers, Pam Clock Co., 15 ½ x 15 ½ In. 77.00
Advertising, Old Drum Whiskey, Drum Form, Wood, Tin, MacLaren Action Sign, 12 In. 150.00
Advertising, Old Mr. Boston Fine Liquors, Flask Form, Painted, Tin, 22 x 10 x 5 In.. . . . . 250.00
Advertising, Old Reading Beer, Reverse Painted Glass, Gilco, 20 In. 11500.00
Advertising, Pabst Blue Ribbon, What'll You Have, Light-Up, White, Blue Letters, Metal, Plastic 225.00
Advertising, Pearl Beer, Bottle Cap Form, White, Red, Marked G10, Box, 14 In. 150.00
Advertising, Quaker State Motor Oil, Light-Up, 16 x 16 In. 175.00
Advertising, Raytheon TV & Radio, Light-Up, Marked, Electric Time Company, 15 In. 275.00
Advertising, RCA Victor 45, The Finest In Recorded Music, Light-Up. 250.00
Advertising, Rexall Druggist, Products Of Tomorrow, Image Of Druggist, Electric, 1950s, 12 In. 101.00
Advertising, Simmons Liver Regulator, Brass, Horseshoe Frame, Paper Dial, Alarm, c.1900, 6 x 5 In. 385.00
Advertising, Skelly Oil & Gasoline, Brown, Black, Red, White, Electric, Pam Mfg., 15 ½ In. . . 100.00
Advertising, Skibiski Insurance, 16 x 16 In. 50.00
Advertising, St. Charles Evaporated Milk, Cast Iron, 8 ¾ In. 420.00
Advertising, St. Joseph Aspirin, Neon Pharmacy, 1940s, 15 x 15 x 5 In.. . . . . 570.00
Advertising, St. Joseph Aspirin, Red, White, Black, Electric, 14 In. 77.00
Advertising, St. Joseph Aspirin, Red, White, Black, Light-Up, 1940-50, 15 In. 450.00
Advertising, Sun Crest Soda, Orange, Green, Yellow, Glass, Metal, Lanshire, 9 In. 70.00
Advertising, Tetley Tea Time, Embossed, Tin, Wood, Waterbury, 1930-40, 20 x 14 In. 350.00
Advertising, Texaco, Star, Light-Up, Black, Red, White, 20 ½ x 2 ½ In. 400.00
Advertising, Vanner & Prests, Stable Supplies, Pendulum Bob, Baird, c.1890, 18 x 31 In. 316.00
Advertising, Weather-Bird Shoes, Rooster On Weather Vane, Light-Up, 15 In. 275.00
Advertising, Weinfurter's, Royal Street, New Orleans, Golden Oak, Octagonal, 1900, 27 x 18 In. 353.00
Advertising, Wurlitzer Music, Yellow & Green Neon, 28 In. 1200.00
Advertising, Yoo-Hoo Chocolate Drink, Yogi Berra, Slogan, Electric, c.1960, 12 x 29 In. 2400.00
Advertising, Yoo-Hoo Chocolate Drink, Yogi Berra Autograph, c.1960 . . . . . 325.00
Ansonia, Cast Iron, Ormolu, Waisted Form, Scrolled Legs, Late 19th Century, 13 ½ In. 148.00
Ansonia, Miranda, Open Escapement, No. 1008, 17 x 11 In.. . . . . 325.00
Ansonia, Olympia, Bacchante Figurine, Footed, 24 In. 800.00
Ansonia, Ophelia, Art Deco, Nude, 16 x 11 In. 300.00
Ansonia, Regulator, Wall, Mixed Wood, Octagonal, Hinged Glass Door, 32 x 17 ½ In. 176.00
Ansonia, Shelf, Aviation, Male Angel, Outstretched Arms, France, 32 In. 8625.00
Ansonia, Shelf, Cygnet, Metal, 13 In. 150.00
Ansonia, Shelf, Parisian, Lady's Head Medallion At Crest, 23 ½ x 13 x 4 ½ In. 154.00
Ansonia, Sybil & Melody, Cast, 8-Day, c.1904, 25 In. 2035.00
Ansonia, Victorian, Cast Iron, Open Escarpment, Late 19th Century, 12 ½ In. . . . . *illus* 210.00
Ansonia, Walnut, Winged Cupids, Reverse Painted, 24 In. 320.00
Ansonia, Woman Playing Harp, Spelter, Patina, Late 1800s, 22 x 19 In. 750.00
Arts & Crafts, Hammered Copper, Trees, Twisted Iron Columns, 11 x 6 ½ In.. . . . . 570.00
Atkins & Downs, Burl, Inlay, Leaf Columns, Scroll Top, Mt. Vernon On Door, 30 In. 1320.00
Atkins Co., Shelf, Rosewood, Black, Gold Painted Upper Door, Mirror Lower Door, 18 In. 2015.00
Atmos, Chrome & Copper, Perpetual Pendulum, Copper Numbers, c.1930, 8 In. 9000.00
Banjo, A. Willard, Mahogany, Brass Bezel, Reverse Painted Eagle, Yellow Ground, c.1825, 38 In. 3200.00
Banjo, A. Willard, Mahogany, Brass Bezel, Reverse Painted Washington, Mt. Vernon, c.1825, 40 In. 3081.00
Banjo, A. Willard, Mahogany, Carved Eagle Finial, Oak Leaves, Reverse Painted Banner, c.1815, 35 In. 2370.00
Banjo, Aaron Willard, Mahogany, Signed, Boston, 1820, 38 In. 4740.00
Banjo, B. Morrill, Boscawen, New Hampshire, c.1820, 29 x 10 In. 936.00
Banjo, Charles Babbitt, Shelf, Mahogany, Bird's-Eye Maple, Glazed, Bezel, Dart Inlay, c.1850, 36 In. 6518.00

Banjo, E. Howard, No. 5, Cherry, Gold Leaf, 8-Day, c.1920, 29 In. 2420.00
Banjo, E. Howard & Co., Rosewood, Weight Driven, 29 In. 1680.00
Banjo, E. Howard & Co., Wall, Cherry, 8-Day, Weight Driven, c.1880, 38 In. 1210.00
Banjo, Eli Holden, Wall, No. 5, Fruitwood, 1-Weight, 8-Day, c.1850, 29 In. 1210.00
Banjo, Eli Terry, Wall, Mahogany, Flat Frames, Painted, Greek Revival Homes, c.1832, 35 In.. 2607.00
Banjo, Ernst Reuschel, Colonial Revival, Oak, Eagle Finial, Reverse Painted Tree, 1912, 42 In. 9480.00
Banjo, Federal, Eglomise Panels, Flowers, Charioteer Base, Acorn Finial, 40 In.. . . . . 990.00
Banjo, Federal, Mahogany, Acorn Finial, Painted Face, c.1820, 33 In. 556.00
Banjo, Federal, Mahogany, Brass Eagle Finial, Man In Boat, Key, Pendulum, Weight, 32 In. . . 940.00
Banjo, Federal, Mahogany, Pine, Reverse Painted Tablets, Lower Drop Finial, 35 ½ In. 235.00
Banjo, Federal Style, Mahogany, Reverse Painted, 42 In.. . . . . 143.00
Banjo, Sawin & Dyar, Federal, Mahogany, Pine, Brass Side Arms, Reverse Painted, 33 In. 881.00
Banjo, Wall, Gold Front, Bay Scene, Carved Gilt Eagle, c.1830, 34 In. 3025.00
Banjo, William Cummens, Federal, Mahogany, Brass Supports, Inset Panel, 33 x 10 In. 1475.00
Banjo, Wood, Gold Paint, Hinged Throat, Boston, c.1840, 29 In. 1375.00
Bates, Classical, Arched Pediment, Openwork, Figures, Cupid, 46 x 18 In.. . . . . 4600.00
Bigelow & Kennard, Bracket, Regency, Mahogany, Architectural, Pitched Roof, 21 x 14 In.. . 3600.00
Birge, Mallory & Co., Shelf, Empire, Mahogany, 19th Century, 32 In. 234.00
Birge, Peck & Co., Shelf, Empire, Mahogany, 19th Century, 32 ½ In.. 336.00
Birge & Fuller, Double Steeple, Wagon Spring, Mahogany, 2 Doors, Painted Tablets, c.1845, 25 In. 2015.00
Birge & Fuller, Shelf, Double Steeple, Wagon Spring, Mahogany, Painted Tablets, c.1840, 28 In. 1659.00
Black, J., Bracket, Mahogany, Brass Finial, Scroll Inlay, 3-Fusee, London, c.1880, 25 In. 2200.00
Black Forest, Cuckoo, Buck, 3-Train Steel Movement, c.1890, 25 ½ x 17 x 13 In. . . . . . *illus* 525.00
Black Forest, Cuckoo, Carved, 42 In. 4888.00
Black Forest, Cuckoo, Elk Head, Pinecone Weights, Walnut, 1900s 131.00
Black Forest, Dog & Stag, Carved Linden Wood, Brienz, Switzerland, c.1900, 22 In. 4025.00
Black Paint, Gilt Copper Dial, Architectural, France, 1890s, 75 In. 1600.00
Boardman, C., Ogee, Mahogany, Frosted Flower Basket Tablet, c.1850, 18 In. 474.00
Bracket, Burl, Ormolu, Alabaster, Urn Finial, Paw Feet, Signed, Germany, 20 ¼ x 12 In.. . . . . 1800.00
Bracket, Burl Walnut Veneer Case, Quarter Chime, Gothic Door, 8-Day, Victorian, 22 ¾ In. . . 2963.00
Bracket, Federal, Mahogany, Figured, Inscribed Wm. Thompson, Ma., 1790, 17 x 11 In.. . . . . 21250.00
Bracket, George III Style, Silver Face, Music, 19th Century, 27 x 15 In.. . . . . 3510.00
Bracket, Inlaid, 3-Fusee, 9 Bells, W. Goodwyn, Maidtone, Signed, France, 39 In. 4600.00
Bradley & Hubbard, Blinking Eye, Lion, Cast Iron, 8 x 10 ¼ In.. . . . . *illus* 5175.00
Bradley & Hubbard, Blinking Eye, Town Crier, Cast Iron, 15 ¾ In. 748.00
Brass, Open Works, Stand, Glass Dome, England, 1920, 11 x 5 In.. . . . . 995.00
Brass, Wood, Time & Strike, Key, Pendulum, 15 In.. . . . . 144.00
Brewster & Ingrahams, Sharp Gothic, Mahogany, Silver Leaf Transfer Glass, Conn., c.1850, 20 In. 237.00
Brewster & Ingrahams, Shelf, Rosewood, Ripple Front, Pitched Pediment, Conn., c.1850, 11 In. 1659.00
Brewster & Ingrahams, Steeple, Mahogany, 19th Century, 20 In. . . . . *illus* 127.00
Bronze, Roman Children, Key, Pendulum, Signed, Waterbury N.Y., 20 x 14 In.. . . . . 259.00
Bronze, Wood, Putti, Hunter, Scrolling Flowers, Garlands, Green, France, c.1900, 38 In.. . . . . 1638.00
Brown, J.C., Beehive, Rosewood, Transfer, Painted Flowers, Miniature, 16 In.. . . . . 3081.00
Brown, J.C., Shelf, Beehive, Ripple Front Glass, Baltimore Cemetery Scene, Conn., 19 In. 1541.00
Burleigh, T.E., Girandole, Carved Eagle Finial, Convex Reverse Painted Wedding, c.1975, 47 In. 8295.00
Caldwell, J.E., Art Deco, Painted Numbers, Enamel, Nickel, 8 x 8 In.. 750.00
Caldwell, J.E., Shelf, Rococo Style, Cloisonne, Cherubs, Fountain, Brass Works, France, 17 In. 4700.00
Calendar, Chrome, Domed Bell, Hinged, Rotary, Alarm, 80-Hour, c.1930, 5 ¼ In. 390.00
Camerer Cuss, Wall, Iron Dial, Beveled Glass, 8-Day, 17 In.. . . . . 237.00
Campos, Foster, Lyre, Mahogany, Carved Finial, Case, Reverse Painted, Woman, Mass., 42 In. 2252.00
Campos, Foster, Wood Shelf, Carved Fret Top, Brass Finials, Inlaid Door, 35 In. 3200.00
Candlestick, Ceramic, Wood Base, Paper Dial, Dome, Union Labor Co., c.1860, 11 In. 715.00
Carriage, Alarm, Bronze, Keys, c.1920, 6 In. 322.00
Carriage, Boudoir, Georgian, Painted Red, Arch Top, Lift Handle, Angel Mask, Spandrels, 8 In. 178.00
Carriage, Brass, 8-Day, Alarm, Cornice Case, Porcelain Dial, France, c.1900 . . . . 880.00
Carriage, Brass, Crystal Studded, Painted Face, Filigree Gryphon Grill, 6 In. 160.00
Carriage, Brass, Handle, France, 5 ½ x 3 In. 150.00
Carriage, Brass, Scroll Pattern, Time, Strike, Repeat, Swiss, c.1870, 7 In.. . . . . 660.00
Carriage, Cloisonne, Painted Porcelain Dial, Woman's Portrait, Brass, Chinese, 11 ¾ In.. . . . 325.00
Cartier, Listening Stag, Bronzed, Marble Plinth, Rocky Base, 33 In.. . . . . *illus* 1045.00
Charles Frodshame & Co., Carriage, Silver, Glass Case, Silver Jubilee, 1977, England, 4 ½ In. 944.00
Chelsea Clock Co., Wall, Regulator, Mahogany, Pendulum, c.1922, 33 ¼ x 16 ¼ In.. . . . . 2000.00
Cherub, Brass Plate, Metal Gold Gilt, Marble, 28 In.. . . . . 995.00
Christofle, Woman, Seated In Chair, Bronze, Malachite, Gilt, France, 31 x 23 x 9 In.. . . . . 12000.00
Crosby & Vosburgh, Cast Iron Front, Woman & Peacock, 30-Hour, Signed Muller, c.1885, 17 In. 61.00

Clock, Bradley & Hubbard, Blinking Eye, Lion, Cast Iron, 8 x 10 ¼ In.
$5175.00

Clock, Brewster & Ingrahams, Steeple, Mahogany, 19th Century, 20 In.
$127.00

Clock, Cartier, Listening Stag, Bronzed, Marble Plinth, Rocky Base, 33 In.
$1045.00

As always, the edited listings in *Kovels' Antiques & Collectibles Price Guide 2010* aren't available on any website, but readers should visit Kovels.com for information on trends, tips, reproductions, marks, old prices, and more!

C

Clock, Eli Terry, Shelf, Fruit Basket, Stenciled, Reverse Painted, Gilt, 1890s, 30 x 17 x 5 In.
$825.00

Clock, French, Empire, Man, Carrying Boy, Sword, Wreath, Gilt, Bronze,1850s, 17 ½ In.
$2650.00

Clock, Gingerbread, Oak, Painted Design, 22 ½ In.
$66.00

Cuckoo, Maple Leaf Pattern, 5 Leaves, Bird, 30-Hour Time, Strike, Germany, c.1920, 17 In. . . 121.00
Deniere, Shelf, Rouge Marble, France, 15 In. . . . 2875.00
Desk, Boulle, Round Dial, France, 9 ½ In. . . . 510.00
Desk, Digital, Chrome & Wood Case, Curved Sides, c.1930, 4 ¼ x 10 In. . . . 720.00
Duminil, A. Bronze, Gilt Brass, Black, Roman Flutist, Tree, 8-Day, c.1850, Paris, 16 In. . . . 2640.00
Dunhill, Alfred, Skeleton, Brass, London, 14 x 10 x 10 In. . . . 440.00
Dunning, J.N., Shelf, Tavern, Mahogany, Ogee Door, Bezel, Vermont, c.1835, 33 In. . . . 7110.00
Elbogen, Johann Andreas Schmidt, Shelf, Wood, Brass, Scrollwork, Paw Feet, 19 x 12 In. . . . 1652.00
Eli Terry, Shelf, Fruit Basket, Stenciled, Reverse Painted, Gilt, 1890s, 30 x 17 x 5 In. . . . *illus* 825.00
Eli Terry, Shelf, Mahogany, Stencils, Flags, Flowers, House, Basket, Conn., 1800s, 30 x 17 In. . 863.00
Empire, Gilt, Patinated Bronze, Orbital, Astrological Signs, c.1880, 18 In. . . . 5000.00
Empire, Pine, Gilded Frame, Turned Columns, Reverse Painted Tablet, Mass., c.1835, 30 In. . 2133.00
Empire, Sphinx Top, Black Marble, Bronze, Winged Feet, Marked, c.1880, 15 x 14 In. . . . 360.00
Figural, Classical Woman, Urn On Pedestal, Spelter, Black Marble, c.1900, 17 x 12 ½ In. . . . 380.00
Figural, Father Time, With Scythe, Round Face, France, 19th Century, 28 x 14 x 7 ½ In. . . . 702.00
Figural, Lighthouse, Barometer, Copper, 7 ⅛ In. . . . 295.00
Figural, Madonna & Child, Gilt, France, 16 x 17 In. . . . 350.00
Figural, Man, Candle In Hat, Match In Hand, Alarm Triggers Strike, Bronze, Metal, France, 5 x 10 In. 715.00
Figural, Man Holding Woman On Lap, Ormolu, France, c.1870, 15 In. . . . 770.00
Figural, Reclining Shepherd, Cast Metal, Marble, Black Marble, 24 ½ In. . . . 4560.00
Forestville Mfg. Co., Acorn, Mahogany, Lyre Shape, Reverse Painted Brown House, c.1845, 24 In. 5925.00
Forestville Mfg. Co., Acorn, Rosewood, Unconventional Design, Painted Flower Tablet, 25 In. 1067.00
Forestville Mfg. Co., Acorn, Rosewood, Veneers, Reverse Painted Flowers, Footed, 1850, 20 In. 11850.00
Forestville Mfg. Co., Shelf, Mahogany, Ogee, 2-Tier Case, 8-Day Time, Conn., c.1850, 31 In. . 563.00
Forestville Mfg. Co., Wall, Acorn, Mahogany, Reverse Painted Landscape, Buildings, c.1845, 28 In. 1778.00
French, Bell Shape, Gothic, Tabernacle, Bronze, Musicians, Grapes, Scrolls, 1825-75, 25 ½ x 12 In. 1920.00
French, Empire, Boat, Bronze, Cylindrical Clock Works, Gilt Bronze Case, 18 In. . . . 5546.00
French, Empire, Man, Carrying Boy, Sword, Wreath, Gilt, Bronze, 1850s, 17 ½ In. . . . *illus* 2650.00
French, Figural, Frederick The Great, Horse, Ormolu, Bronze, Thread Movement, c.1840, 17 In. 4450.00
French, Mahogany, Gilt Bronze, Mother-Of-Pearl Inlay, 1900, 19 ¼ x 9 ¾ x 5 ¾ In. . . . 5000.00
French, Mechanical, Figural, Man's Hands Swing Up & Strike Match, 9 x 5 In. . . . 1650.00
Fuller & Kroeber, Shelf, Walnut, Dome Top, Rope Carving, Shield Cartouche, c.1868, 18 x 16 In. 796.00
Fyler, Orsamus, Shelf, Mahogany, Mirror, Painted Birds, Carvings, Conn., c.1835, 40 In. . . . 1896.00
Geddes, Chas., Shelf, Chippendale, Mahogany, Ormolu Mounts, c.1795, 22 x 13 In. . . . 5938.00
German, Gilded Bird Cage, Stand, Alarm, 8 In. . . . 110.00
German, Secessionist, Mahogany, Pewter, 23 ½ x 14 In. . . . 1850.00
German, Secessionist, Pressed Glass, Cane Columns, Base Metal, 15 ½ x 8 ¾ In. . . . 225.00
Gilbert Clock Co., Regulator, Time, Strike & Calendar Movement, Oak Case, 38 x 16 In. . . . 115.00
Gingerbread, Oak, Painted Design, 22 ½ In. . . . *illus* 66.00
Glo-Dial, Chrome, Neon, 1930s, 10 ¾ In. . . . 720.00
Glo-Dial, Pink Neon, Round, 1960s, 17 In. . . . 403.00
Goodrich, Chauncey, Shelf, Mahogany, Transfer, Painted Rose Tablet, Conn., 14 In. . . . 1007.00
Goodwin, E.O., Shelf, Mahogany, Sleigh Front, Painted Building Tablet, Column, 21 In. . . . 444.00
Goodwin, E.O., Shelf, Rosewood, Glazed Upper Door, Flower Panel, Conn., 15 In. . . . 356.00
Gostl, Anton, Wall, Traditional Case, 3 Carved Finials, Grande Sonnerie, Austria, c.1850, 53 In. 3300.00
Gustav Becker, Regulator, Teardrop, Mahogany, Brass Weights, Pendulum, c.1890, 47 x 15 In. 600.00
Gustav Becker, Regulator, Vienna, 2-Weight, Walnut, Altdeutsch Style, 38 In. . . . 236.00
Gustav Becker, Regulator, Vienna, 2-Weight, Walnut, Altdeutsch Style, 49 In. . . . 590.00 to 649.00
Gustav Becker, Regulator, Vienna, 2-Weight, Walnut, Altdeutsch Style, 51 In. . . . 708.00
Gustav Becker, Regulator, Vienna, 3-Weight, Walnut, Altdeutsch Style, 50 In. . . . 885.00
Gustav Becker, Regulator, Vienna, 3-Weight, Walnut, Altdeutsch Style, 54 In. . . . 885.00
Gustav Becker, Regulator, Vienna, Rosewood, Carved Crest, Finials, Brass Weight, 44 In. . . . 593.00
Hansen, Peter, Original Movement, L. & J.G. Stickley, No. 85, 22 x 16 x 8 In. . . . *illus* 16800.00
Harvard Clock Co., Wall, Walnut Case, Weight Driven, 8-Day, Boston, c.1880, 29 In. . . . 2750.00
Herman Miller, Alarm, Art Deco, Chrome, White, Black Face, Gilbert Rohde, 7 In. . . . 960.00
Herman Miller, Alarm, Chrome, White, Black Dots, Gilbert Rohde, 1934, 6 ½ In. . . . 2040.00
Herman Miller, Desk, Art Deco, c.1934, In. . . . 960.00
Herman Miller, Desk, Dot Face, Chrome, c.1934, 6 ½ In. . . . 2040.00
Hermle, Franz, Bracket, Louis XV Style, Gilded, Germany, 22 x 12 In. . . . 585.00
Herschede Clock Co., Shelf, Mahogany, ¼-Hour Chime, 10 Chimes, c.1920 . . . 468.00
Hills, George, Mirror, Rosewood, Black, Gilt Reverse Painted, Frame, c.1850, 36 In. . . . 889.00
Hilton, Jas. F., Oak, Carved, St. Helens, 19th Century, 42 x 17 In. . . . 644.00
Hotchkiss & Benedict, Shelf, Column & Carved Splat, 2-Deck, 8-Day, c.1835, 38 In. . . . 1100.00
Howard, E., Regulator, No. 10, 8-Day, Weight Driven, Boston, c.1976, 33 In. . . . 2420.00
Howard, E., Regulator, No. 59-8, Vienna Model, Oak, 8-Day, c.1880, 46 In. . . . 5500.00
Howard, E., Regulator, No. 70-16, Oak, 8-Day, Damascene Pendulum, c.1900, 41 In. . . . 8250.00

Howard, E., Regulator, No. 72, Black Walnut, Scroll, Shells, Finials, 8-Day, c.1880, 64 In..... 12100.00
Howard, E., Regulator, No. 89, Walnut, Watchman, Wood & Brass Pendulum, c.1898, 78 x 27 In. 8100.00
Howard, E., Regulator, Wall, No. 1, 50 In. 60.00
Howard, E., Steel Case, Glazed Door, 12-In. Zinc Dial, 8-Day, Iron Weight, 58 In.. .... 889.00
Howard, E., Wall, No. 28, Marble Front, c.1875, 28 In. 1210.00
Howard, E., Wall, Regulator, No. 5, Grain Painted Case, Black, Gold Maroon Tablets, Boston, 29 In. 1659.00
Howard, E., Wall, Regulator, No. 70, Mahogany, Black, Gold, Red Painted Tablet, 35 In...... 3081.00
Howard, E., Wall, Walnut Case, Glazed Door, 8-Day, Weight Driven, 63 In. 4148.00
Howard & Davis, Pine, Zinc Dial, 8-Day, Brass Pendulum Bob, Iron Weight, 73 In. 593.00
Howard Miller, Wall, 12 Balls, Radiating Spokes, No. 4755, G. Nelson, c.1947, 13 In. 420.00
Howard Miller, Wall, Round, Birch, Ebony, Black Metal, G. Nelson, c.1890, 14 In.. .... 570.00
Ingraham, E., Calendar, Round, Drop, c.1880, 24 x 16 In. 293.00
Ingraham, E., Shelf, Mahogany, Doric, Half Columns, Painted Horse, Rider Tablet, 17 In. ... 148.00
Ingraham, E., Wall, Mahogany, Ionic, Black, Gold Transfer Tablet, Bezel, Conn., c.1875, 22 In. 178.00
Iron, Black Face, Gilt Roman Numerals & Hands, Architectural, Late 1800s, 56 In. Diam. ... 3335.00
Ithaca, Calendar Clock Co., Eastlake Style, 2 Dials, Roman Numerals, c.1866, 27 In. 1800.00
Ithaca, Calendar Clock Co., Walnut, Double Dial, 28 In.. .... 715.00
Ithaca Calendar Clock Co., Shelf, Library, Walnut, Burl, Ebony, Calendar, Time Dials, No. 8, 26 In. 5036.00
Ithaca Calendar Clock Co., Walnut, Applied Carvings, Ebony Trim, 2 Dials, c.1880, 21 In... 4148.00
Ithaca Calendar Clock Co., Walnut, Ebony Trim, Standard Box Skeleton, c.1880, 23 In. ... 23700.00
Ives, J., Shelf, Mahogany, Lever Spring, Pewter, Reverse Painted House, Pond, c.1825, 28 In.. 20145.00
Ives, J., Shelf, Rosewood, Double Steeple, Lever Spring, 2 Reverse Painted Doors, c.1845, 27 In. 1067.00
Ives, J., Wall, Mirror, Mahogany, Scrolls, Brass Urn Finials, Painted Tablet, c.1820, 57 In. 3437.00
Jaeger-LeCoultre, Atmos Marina, Sailing Ships, Brass, Lucite, Swiss, 9 x 7 x 5 ½ In.. .... 1350.00
Japy Freres, Blue, Turquoise Enamel, Gilt, Mercury Pendulum, 4-Panel, c.1890, 11 x 7 In... 598.00
Japy Freres, Shelf, Bell, Gilt Metal, Festoons, Urn Finial, Electrified, France, 16 x 11 In...... 472.00
Japy Freres, Shelf, Joan Of Arc On Top, Black Marble, 8-Day, Time, Strike, c.1900, 19 In. 165.00
Jefferson, Atomic Age, Chrome, c.1963, 6 In. 120.00
Jerome & Co., Shelf, Mahogany, Flowers, Blue Border, c.1810, 26 x 15 In. 235.00
Jerome Chauncy, Shelf, Cottage, 11 ½ x 8 In.. .... 30.00
Johnson, William, Ogee, Reverse Painted Glass, Ballston Springs, 26 x 15 ½ In. 25.00
Junghans, Regulator, Vienna, 3-Weight, Embossed Brass, c.1900, 46 x 17 In.. .... 900.00
Junghans, Regulator, Walnut, Mounts, Finials, Scrolls, 1800s, 43 In. 266.00
Junghans, Wall, Mahogany, Germany, c.1900, 28 x 13 In. 117.00
Kroeber, F., Cast Iron, Frogs, Birds, Owls, Enamel Dial, 12 x 14 In. 173.00
Lackner, Desk, Neon Glo, Butterscotch, Catalin, 1930s, 6 ½ In. 780.00
Lackner, Neon Glo, Catalin Face, Brown Bakelite Iris, Keyhole, c.1938, 10 ¼ In. 670.00
Lackner, Pedestal, Neon Dial, Catalin Faceplate, c.1938, 10 ¼ In. 570.00
L'Aine, Gille, Shelf, Louis XVI, Bronze, Woman, Cupid, Doves, Marble Base, Paris, c.1800 .... 3200.00
Lawson Time, Desk, Digital, Art Deco, Chrome, Wood, Telescoping Sides, 1930s, 4 ¼ x 10 In. 720.00
LeCoultre, Atmos, Brass, Glass, Perpetual Movement, Swiss, 9 x 8 x 7 In. 450.00
LeCoultre, Wood, Curved Frame, 8 x 6 In. 550.00
LeCoultre, Wood, Leather, 4 ½ x 4 In.. .... 660.00
Liberty & Co., The Magnus, Silver, Enamel, No. 5024, Archibald Knox, c.1903, 5 In. 37500.00
Liberty & Co., Tudric Pewter, Abalone, No. 96, Archibald Knox, c.1903, 12 In. 10000.00
Luneville, Foo Dog, Floating Ball, Waves, Cloisonne Face, Late 19th Century, 13 ½ In. 4375.00
Mager-Wecker, Shadowbox, Ebonized, Ripple Molded Gilt Picture Frame, Painted, 15 x 13 In. 588.00
Manross, Elisha, Double Steeple, Mahogany, Transfer, Painted Tablets, Label, c.1845, 24 In. . 889.00
Marsh, George, Shelf, Mahogany, Beveled Case, Wooden Works, c.1835. .... 770.00
Mastercrafters, Church, White, Motion, 1940s, 12 In. 25.00
Mayer, Novelty, Dog, Works In Body, Black & White, Germany, c.1890, 7 In. 1018.00
McAllister Humburch & Birk, Bracket, Mahogany, Gilt Bronze, 1800s, 26 x 15 ½ In. 7200.00
Morrill, B., Federal, Mahogany Case, Gilt Turned, Rosette Block Columns, 8-Day, 29 x 14 In.. 1840.00
Muller, Baseball Players, Sportswriters, Fans, Cast Iron Face, Painted, 1876, 16 x 13 In. 11163.00
Mystery, Bronze, Napoleon Bonaparte, First Empire, Bicolor, c.1805 .... 1750.00
Napoleon III, Gilt Metal, Porcelain, Hand Painted, Pink Flowers, Stamped RC, c.1895, 14 In. 568.00
Napoleon III, Rococo, Bronze Dore, Hunter, Dogs, Horns, Brass Works, 1855, 22 x 24 x 8 In.. 2415.00
New Haven, Cherubs, Satin Finish, Draped Cherub On Sides, Milk Glass, 5 ½ In. 45.00
New Haven, Cut Glass, Butterflies, Flowers, Corset Shape, 8 In. 110.00
New Haven, Mahogany, Ogee, Painted Roses, Transfers, 21 In. 207.00
New Haven, Oak, 16 ½ In. Diam. .... *illus* 176.00
New Haven, Rococo, Spelter, Early 20th Century, 11 x 6 ½ In. 70.00
New Haven, Shelf, Little Red Riding Hood, Mahogany, 8-Day, Ogee, 26 In. 177.00
New Haven, Shelf, Wood, Iron, Spires, Black, Gold Highlights, c.1900, 20 x 12 In. 322.00
Olmstead & Barnes, Shelf, Mahogany, Free-Standing Columns, 1829, 27 In. 21330.00
Pearce, Simon, Shelf, Rosewood, Dome Top, Mother-Of-Pearl Inlay, Marked, 19 ⅜ In. 920.00

TIP
Clocks should be cleaned and lubricated every five years.

C

Clock, Hansen, Peter, Original Movement, L. & J.G. Stickley, No. 85, 22 x 16 x 8 In.
$16800.00

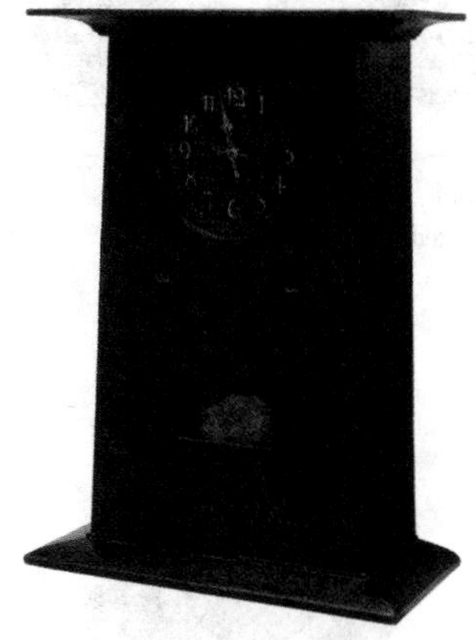

Clock, New Haven, Oak, 16 ½ In. Diam.
$176.00

TIP
Clocks that are wound from the back should be wound counterclockwise because that is really clockwise from the front of the clock. Never wind an old clock counterclockwise.

Clock, Shelf, Napoleon III, Woman, Chariot, Gilt Bronze, Polished Slate, 18 In.
$1100.00

Clock, Shelf, Ormolu, Brass Works, Marked EM, Late 19th Century, 17 ½ x 17 x 7 In.
$365.00

Clock, Shelf, Ormolu, Cloisonne Flower Panels, Enameled, France, c.1900, 16 In.
$940.00

Phelps & Perry, Blue Enamel, Flowers, Gilt, Bronze, Beveled Stone Base, 5 x 3 ⅝ In. 295.00
Poole Mfg. Co., Melrose, No. 20, Bakelite, Electro-Magnetic, N.Y., c.1927, 10 In. 220.00
Pratt, W., Wall, Carved Lyre, Mahogany, Wood Bezel, Reverse Painted Eagle, c.1830, 36 In.... 3318.00
Regulator, Gilt Bronze, Crystal Columns, Porcelain Dial, Waterbury, c.1900, 13 x 8 In. 429.00
Regulator, Jeweler's Pinwheel, Walnut Case, Carved, 92 In. 7475.00
Regulator, Mahogany, Carved, Applied Gilt Metal Crest, Dial, Pendulum, 53 In. 1440.00
Regulator, Mahogany, Round Enameled Dial, Roman Numerals, 43 In. 360.00
Regulator, Victorian, Astronomical, Walnut, Carved, Shield Crest, 1880, 90 x 30 x 16 In..... 15900.00
Regulator, Vienna, 1-Weight, Carved, Germany, c.1860, 40 In. 750.00
Regulator, Vienna, 1-Weight, Walnut, Dachluhr Style, Remember Movement, 47 ½ In. 325.00
Regulator, Vienna, Wall, c.1920, 46 x 15 In. 293.00
Regulator, Vienna, Walnut, c.1870, 53 x 19 In. 702.00
Regulator, Vienna, Walnut, Carved, Finials, Swags, Pillars, 3-Weight, c.1880, 52 In. 1180.00
Regulator, Vienna, Walnut, Carved, Northwind Mask, Pillars, Scrolls, Bronze, c.1885, 53 In.. 2832.00
Regulator, Walnut, 2-Weight, Carved, Altdeutsch Style, 1800s, 43 In. 265.00
Regulator, Walnut, 2-Weight, Carved, Altdeutsch Style, 1800s, 51 In. 324.00
Regulator, Walnut, Enameled Face, Shell Carved Pediment, Spindle Columns, 78 x 27 In.... 690.00
Resch Brothers, Regulator, Vienna, 1-Weight, Austria, c.1880, 45 In.. .... 770.00
Resch Brothers, Regulator, Vienna, 2-Weight, Walnut, Altdeutsch Style, Remember Movement, 50 In. 384.00
Rogers, Wall, Mahogany, London, 8-Day, c.1840, 14 In. 880.00
Rose, Daniel, Bracket, Mahogany, Carved Scrolls, Finials, Feet, Painted Iron, Pa., 1776, 28 In. 5925.00
Savory & Sons, Bracket, Rosewood, 2 Gothic Finials, Beading, 8-Day, London, c.1860, 21 In. 1210.00
Schatz, Brass, Open Case, 20th Century, 10 x 6 x 10 In. 234.00
Servant, G., Shelf, Napoleon III, Bronze, Marble, Griffin Mounts, c.1867, 15 x 23 In. 531.00
Sessions, Gingerbread, Oak, 23 x 15 x 4 In. 55.00
Sessions, Regulator, Oak, c.1900, 19 x 12 In.. .... 82.00
Sessions, Shelf, Oak, Brass Ormolu, 11 x 10 In.. .... 70.00
Sessions, Wood, Painted, c.1920, 12 x 6 x 14 ½ In. 70.00
Seth Thomas, Bracket, Walnut Burl, Scrolls, Figures, Brass Inlay, No. 48R, c.1920, 13 In. ... 207.00
Seth Thomas, Calendar, Double Dial 770.00
Seth Thomas, Calendar, No. 4, 8-Day, Brass Movement, c.1875, 32 x 16 In. 1920.00
Seth Thomas, Calendar, No. 5, Walnut, 19th Century, 20 ½ In. 649.00
Seth Thomas, Carriage, Brass Frame, Beveled Glass, Flower Swags, 12 x 10 x 6 In.. .... 360.00
Seth Thomas, Cottage, Top Illuminated Alarm, Movement Strikes Match, Lights Wick, c.1875, 12 In. 2015.00
Seth Thomas, Duchess, Brass Case, Lion On Top, 13 x 9 In.. .... 275.00
Seth Thomas, Empire, Mahogany, Ogee, Mid 19th Century, 32 ½ x 18 ¾ In. 410.00
Seth Thomas, Oak, Beehive Shape, 16 x 10 In. 234.00
Seth Thomas, Pillar, Off-Center Scroll, Painted House, Yard Tablet, Brass Finials, c.1818, 30 In. 3555.00
Seth Thomas, Regulator, No. 2, Mahogany, 8-Day, c.1890, 36 In. 1870.00
Seth Thomas, Regulator, No. 2, Oak, 1-Weight, 8-Day, No. 2806, c.1976, 36 In. 385.00
Seth Thomas, Regulator, No. 6, Walnut, Finial, 8-Day, Weight Driven, c.1880, 45 In. 1375.00
Seth Thomas, Shelf, Bellflower, Mahogany, Reverse Painted, c.1840, 26 In. 177.00
Seth Thomas, Shelf, Dore Metal, Onion Dome, c.1900, 10 ½ In. 148.00
Seth Thomas, Shelf, Kingsbury, Mahogany, Pillar & Scroll, Mt. Vernon, 8-Day, c.1932, 17 In. 660.00
Seth Thomas, Shelf, Mahogany, Pillar, 8-Day, Painted Elk, 25 In. 130.00
Seth Thomas, Shelf, Mahogany, Pillar, Splat, Short Drop, 30-Hour, c.1830, 28 In.. .... 523.00
Seth Thomas, Shelf, Mahogany, Pillar & Scroll, 30-Hour, Wood Movement, c.1830, Conn., 28 In. 1430.00
Seth Thomas, Shelf, Pillar & Scroll, Reverse Glass Geo. Washington, Conn., c.1820, 32 In. .. 5925.00
Seth Thomas, Shelf, Rosewood, 8-Day, c.1835, 14 ½ In.. .... 118.00
Seth Thomas, Wall, Office, Calendar, No. 1, Rosewood Veneer, 8-Day, Weight Driven, 40 In... 3555.00
Shelf, Abbey Cathedral, Monk Ringing Bell, Germany, 14 In. 200.00
Shelf, Admiral Dewey, Gingerbread Detail, Ship, Patriotic Symbols, 23 In. 568.00
Shelf, Art Nouveau, Brass, Flowers, Beveled Glass, Mercury Pendulum, 7 ¼ x 17 ½ In. 345.00
Shelf, Black Forest, Walnut, Carved, Pronghorn, Edelweiss, Wildflowers, 11 In. 385.00
Shelf, Black Marble, France, 19th Century, 16 x 11 In. 265.00
Shelf, Black Marble, France, c.1878, 12 x 12 In.. .... 117.00
Shelf, Bronze, 2 Women Holding Clock, France, c.1900, 12 x 10 ¼ x 5 ½ In. 3750.00
Shelf, Bronze, Bird Of Paradise, Finial, Classical Figures, Panthers, Satyrs, France, 18 x 15 In. 1560.00
Shelf, Bronze, Porcelain Dial, Lion Masks, Floral Swags, Greek Philosopher, Paw Feet, 21 In.. 1960.00
Shelf, Bronze Putti, White Marble, Dove Ormolu Mounts, Coteau, c.1780, 18 x 25 In. 20000.00
Shelf, Ceramic, Gilt Bronze, Scroll Mounts, Lion's Heads, Urn Finial, Pendulum, Germany, 15 In. 460.00
Shelf, Charles X, Apollo Bust, Ormolu Mounts, Rectangle, France, c.1820, 17 In. 5000.00
Shelf, Classical Revival, Cast Brass, Winged Boy, Seated On Plinth, 22 x 11 ½ x 6 In.. .... 920.00
Shelf, Cupids Holding Clock, Bronze, Dore, Marble, Garlands, France 1265.00
Shelf, Cut Crystal, Bronze, Winged Eagle Feet, 19th Century, 16 x 9 x 6 In. 1057.00
Shelf, Cut Crystal, Engine Turned Dial, 8-Day, c.1880, 22 In. 16800.00

Shelf, Draped Woman, Classical, Locket, Art Nouveau, Plinth, 21 ½ x 16 In.. 450.00
Shelf, Dresden, Figural, Woman Leaning On Pillared Clock, Adorned With Flowers, 30 In. 8625.00
Shelf, Empire, 4 Columns, Black, Gilt Mounts, Dome, Base, France, c.1870, 24 In.. 825.00
Shelf, Empire, Cannon, Officer, Wheel Dial, Panel Base, Ormolu, Bronze, France, c.1810, 17 x 20 In. 8750.00
Shelf, Empire, Woman, Sheaf Of Wheat, Scythe, Gilt Bronze, 2-Train Movement, 15 ⅝ In. 5333.00
Shelf, Federal, Triple Glass, Carved Eagle, 39 In. 1150.00
Shelf, Figural, Pirate, Dagger, Gilded Blue, Porcelain Base, Pendulum, c.1850, 16 ½ In.. 1920.00
Shelf, French Aesthetic, Multicolored Porcelain, Gilt, c.1880, 12 ¼ x 6 x 4 ½ In. 1998.00
Shelf, George III, Walnut, Gilt, Dome Top, Finials, Acanthus Leaves, Beveled Glass, c.1900, 20 In. 705.00
Shelf, Gilt Bronze, Porcelain, Sevres Style, Hand Painted, Putto, Garland, Engraved, 11 ¾ x 9 In. 1725.00
Shelf, Gilt Metal, Marble, Urn Finial, Enamel Dial, 6 Columns, Plinth, 17 In.. 360.00
Shelf, Gothic Style, Dragonslayer, Dragon, Cannon, Flames, Bronze, 21 x 16 x 6 In. 1100.00
Shelf, Louis Philippe, Brass Mounts, Rosewood Inlay, 27 x 12 ¼ x 8 ½ In. 780.00
Shelf, Louis Philippe, Bronze, Woman Leaning On Table, Acanthus Leaves, c.1875, 16 x 12 In. 978.00
Shelf, Louis Philippe, Walnut, Brass Inlay, Pinwheel Escapement, c.1840, 27 x 17 x 11 In. 3408.00
Shelf, Louis XV, Ceramic, Flowers, Multicolored, Pink Field, Brass Works, c.1890, 21 In. 633.00
Shelf, Louis XVI, Gilt Bronze, Porcelain, Sevres Style, Amorous Couple, c.1895, 24 x 21 In. 6875.00
Shelf, Louis XVI, Sienna Marble, Bronze, 2 Atlas Figures, Marble Base, 18 x 8 In.. 8295.00
Shelf, Louis XVI, Venus, Chariot, Doves, Cupid, Putti Plaque, Ormolu, c.1775, 16 x 15 In. 43750.00
Shelf, Louis XVI Style, Bronze, Porcelain, Woman Putting Flowers In Hair, 12 ¾ In. 770.00
Shelf, Lyre, Dome, Brass Movement, Ormolu, Ebonized Wood, c.1880, 18 ½ In. 780.00
Shelf, Lyre, Mahogany, Brass Bezel, Carved Capitals, Harp, New England, 1830, 30 In. 10073.00
Shelf, Mahogany, Carved, France, 24 In.. 1541.00
Shelf, Mahogany, Gilt Metal, Cast Brass Handle, 8-Day, 15 ½ x 11 x 7 ¾ In. 3105.00
Shelf, Man, Woman, Medieval Dress, Plinth, Bronze, Gilt, France, c.1890, 17 x 13 In. 1200.00
Shelf, Marble, Ormolu Mounted Face, Swag Mounts, French, c.1850, 17 ½ x 17 ¼ x 6 ¾ In.. 374.00
Shelf, Meissen, Enamel Dial, Flowers, Putti, 3 Scrolling Feet, 13 In.. 4080.00
Shelf, Napoleon III, Putti, Leaves, Masks, Gilt Bronze, Red Marble, Paris, c.1875, 24 In. 11500.00
Shelf, Napoleon III, Woman, Chariot, Gilt Bronze, Polished Slate, 18 In. *illus* 1100.00
Shelf, Napoleon III, Woman, Horse, Chariot, Gilt Dome, Bronze, Slate, 1800s, 18 In.. 1180.00
Shelf, Neoclassical, Cast Bronze, Ormolu, Robed Youths, Enamel Dial, 18 ½ x 21 ½ In. 1560.00
Shelf, Oak, Brass Dial, Silvered Chapters, 3-Train Movement, England, 22 ¾ In. 4199.00
Shelf, Ormolu, Brass Works, Marked EM, Late 19th Century, 17 ½ x 17 x 7 In. *illus* 365.00
Shelf, Ormolu, Cloisonne Flower Panels, Enameled, France, c.1900, 16 In. *illus* 940.00
Shelf, Porcelain, Applied Flowers, Painted, Gilt, Paris, Late 1800s, 13 ¾ x 9 ½ In. 368.00
Shelf, Porcelain, Gothic Church Shape, Belfry, Maple Plinth, c.1820, 26 ½ x 15 In. 9694.00
Shelf, Portico, Gilt Bronze, Ebonized Wood, Striking Bell, Columns, Flowers, Birds, 1800s, 17 In. 470.00
Shelf, Renaissance Revival, Walnut, Brass, Marked DRP, 1875, 22 ½ In. 525.00
Shelf, Rococo Style, Faux Boule, Ormolu, Roman Numerals, Key, Pendulum, 22 In. 235.00
Shelf, Roman Figure, Gilt Bronze, c.1800. 1980.00
Shelf, Roman Soldier, Urn, Flame Finials, Ebonized Corinthian Columns, 34 x 18 In.. 4288.00
Shelf, Rosewood, Gilt Column, Lower Rose Transfer, Conn., 1870, 17 In.. 415.00
Shelf, Rosewood, Painted Tin Face, Brass Works, 30-Hour, Weight Driven, Key Wind, 26 x 16 In. 690.00
Shelf, Rotary, Louis XVI, Gilt Bronze, Breche Violette Marble, Cupid, Arrows, c.1880s, 24 x 9 In. 9375.00
Shelf, Rotary, Louis XVI, Gilt Bronze, Tole, Alabaster, 3 Graces, Holding Sphere, c.1885, 18 In. 8750.00
Shelf, Slate, Open Escapement, Pendulum, Key, c.1850, 11 x 10 ¼ x 6 ½ In.. 259.00
Shelf, Swinging Arm, Jester, Brass Spelter, Circus Figure On Face, Dog On Base, France, c.1895, 14 In. 4125.00
Shelf, Swinging Baby, Brass Movement, White Enamel Dial, c.1887, 13 ½ x 13 In.. 1200.00
Shelf, Tudrice Pewter, Enameled Face, 4 ¼ x 8 ¼ In.. 1200.00
Shelf, U.S. Grant Bust, Brass, Black Metal, c.1875, 14 In. 1793.00
Shelf, Victorian, Porcelain, Flower Sprays, Scrolled Border, 10 x 11 ½ x 4 ¾ In.. 180.00
Shelf, Victorian, Slate, Open Escapement, Urn Pediment, Late 1800s, 21 In. *illus* 550.00
Shelf, Winged Cherub Holding Stick, Blanket Form Ground, c.1900, 15 In. 2360.00
Shelf, Woman In Automobile, Bronze, Marble, France 3450.00
Shreve, Crump & Low, Black Marble, Gilt, 8-Day, 19 x 11 x 9 ¼ In. 1100.00
Skeleton, Brass, Marble Base, c.1900, 15 x 11 ½ In. 410.00
Skeleton, Silver Plated, Lyle Fretted Pedestal, Glass Dome, c.1870, 18 In. 3555.00
Smith & Brother, Shelf, Beehive, Mahogany, Reverse Painted Tablet, Philadelphia, 21 In. 1304.00
Smith & Goodrich, Cottage, Rosewood, Reverse Painted Glass, Conn., 13 In. 2259.00
Smith & Sons, Skeleton, Brass Plates, Dial, Pendulum Bob, Wood Base, Glass Case, 17 ¾ In. 2489.00
Southern Clock Co., Shelf, Rosewood Veneer, Tin Face, 30-Hour, 25 ½ x 15 ½ In. *illus* 660.00
Sperry, Shelf, Walnut, Ogee, Reverse Painted Landscape, River, 27 ½ In.. 77.00
Sperry, T.S., Cottage, Gutta-Percha Transfer Decorated Tablet, 30-Hour, New York, 12 In. 593.00
Steeple, Gothic, Carved, Germany, c.1890, 39 In.. 263.00
Stennes, Elmer O., Pillar & Scroll, Swan Neck Pediment, Inlaid Tympanum, 30 x 17 In. 1180.00
Stowell, Abel, Marble, Gilt Bronze, Victorious Archer, 8-Day, France, c.1890, 15 In. 1705.00

Clock, Shelf, Victorian, Slate, Open Escapement, Urn Pediment, Late 1800s, 21 In.
$550.00

Clock, Southern Clock Co., Shelf, Rosewood Veneer, Tin Face, 30-Hour, 25 ½ x 15 ½ In.
$660.00

TIP
The inside of an electric clock is warm and dark—the perfect home for a roach, especially if the clock is in the kitchen. Spray for the insects on the outside of the clock case. Be careful when you open the clock to see if repairs are needed.

Clock, Tall Case, Conry A. Louhans, Morbier, Inscribed, France, 19th Century, 92 ½ In.
$772.00

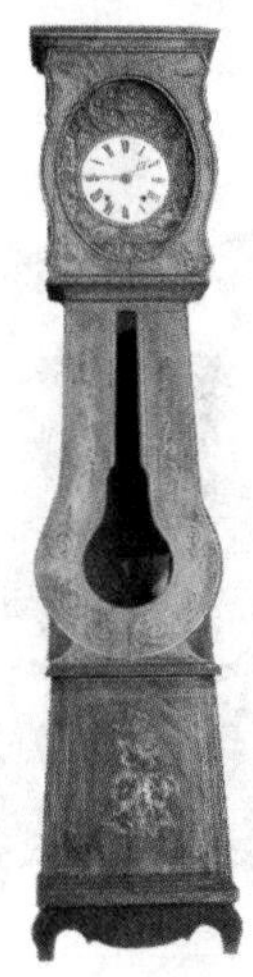

Clock, Tall Case, L. & J.G. Stickley, Copper Face, No. 91, 72 x 18 x 12 ¼ In.
$7200.00

Clock, Tall Case, Tiffany & Co., R.J. Horner, Flemish Style, Carved Oak, Tavern Scene, 102 In.
$25875.00

Taber, E., Shelf, Federal, Mahogany, Dart Inlay, Glazed Dial Door, Mass., c.1800, 29 In. 29625.00
Tall Case, 3 Finials, Pierced Decoration, Columns, Painted Dial, Inlay, Early 1900s, 85 In. 6000.00
Tall Case, A. Frazier, Federal, Mahogany, Scrolled, Pierced Top, Pa., c.1805, 99 x 20 In. 11875.00
Tall Case, Alex Anderson Perth, Sheraton, Mahogany, Broken Arch, 1800s, 87 x 20 In. 2100.00
Tall Case, Arts & Crafts, Ash, Cutout Spindle Door, Original Face, 78 x 23 In. 1140.00
Tall Case, Arts & Crafts, Peak Top, 3 Shelves, Dauler Close & Johns Furniture Label, 31 x 74 In. 960.00
Tall Case, Benjamin Willard, Federal, Rooster In Arch, 8-Day Movement, c.1800, 87 In. 14220.00
Tall Case, Cherry, Scroll Top, Carved Fan, 8-Day, Pa., c.1820, 97 In. 3792.00
Tall Case, Chinoiserie, Stepped Hook, Tempus Fugit, Brass Dial, Landscape, Dragon, 83 x 18 In. 5280.00
Tall Case, Chippendale, Mahogany, 2-Train Movement, Lunar Arch, Swan's Neck Crest, 97 In. 1778.00
Tall Case, Chippendale, Walnut, Fruitwood, Rocking Ship, Broken Arch Pediment, 91 x 23 In. 4600.00
Tall Case, Chippendale Transitional, Walnut, Broken Arch Pediment, Lancaster, 94 x 23 In. . 3466.00
Tall Case, Conry A. Louhans, Morbier, Inscribed, France, 19th Century, 92 ½ In. ...... *illus* 772.00
Tall Case, Country Hepplewhite, Cherry, Broken Arch Pediment, Scroll Cut Door, 91 x 20 In. . 3643.00
Tall Case, Country Sheraton, Cherry, Swan's Neck Pediment, c.1850, 95 x 20 In. 920.00
Tall Case, Dwarf, J. Taber, Birch, Mahogany, Reed Columns, Full-Length Door, Maine, c.1825, 40 In. 5036.00
Tall Case, E. Howard, Master Clock, 2-Vial Mercury Pendulum, c.1920, 60 In. 2750.00
Tall Case, Elmer O. Stennes, Pierced Fretwork, Roxbury, Mass., 60 x 12 In. 1770.00
Tall Case, Federal, Cherry, Arched Painted Dial, Flower Spandrels, Arch Hood, 91 x 19 In. 1495.00
Tall Case, Federal, Cherry, Arched Top, Tombstone Door, 8-Day Movement, Pa., c.1815, 93 In. 4212.00
Tall Case, Federal, Cherry Case, Musical, Waisted, Engaged Columns, c.1820, 99 x 18 In. 2875.00
Tall Case, Federal, Mahogany, Swan's Neck Cresting, Finials, Pa., c.1810, 97 In. 7110.00
Tall Case, Federal, Mahogany Inlay, Molded Hood, Scrolled Crest, c.1815, 90 x 14 In. 6038.00
Tall Case, Federal, Pine, Arched, Painted Dial, Engraved Brass Medallion, 88 x 19 In. 11000.00
Tall Case, Federal, Walnut Inlay, Broken Arch Bonnet, Finials, Weights, Moon Phase, 99 In. . 16450.00
Tall Case, G. Stickley, Beveled Top, Carved, Copper & Brass Face, 71 x 22 x 13 In. 15600.00
Tall Case, Geo. Long, Federal, Mahogany, Eagle, Finials, Musical, Pa., c.1800, 103 x 22 In. ... 98500.00
Tall Case, George II, Walnut, Column Mounted, Rectangular Door, Bracket Feet, Signed, 91 In. 2844.00
Tall Case, George III, Chinoiserie, Faux Bois, Pedimented Bonnet Top, Gilt, 97 x 20 In. 5160.00
Tall Case, George III, Mahogany, Arched Pediment, Fluted Columns, 1700s, 90 x 17 In. 5175.00
Tall Case, George III, Mahogany, Rocking Ship, Bracket Feet, 8-Day Movement, 1800s, 89 In. 2808.00
Tall Case, George III, Oak, Bird, Shell Inlay Door, Signed, 82 x 19 ½ x 10 In. 3840.00
Tall Case, George III, Oak, Japanned, Pagoda Hood, Arched Door, 1790s, 94 x 14 In. 1035.00
Tall Case, George III, Oak Inlay, Painted Face, Second Hand, Moon Phase Dial, 96 x 24 In. .. 6600.00
Tall Case, Georgian, Oak, Mahogany, Inlay, Bird, Cornucopia, Britain, 1890s, 77 x 20 In. 850.00
Tall Case, Harry G. Button, Federal, Wood Dial, 30-Hour Time & Strike, c.1810, 85 x 17 In. .. 920.00
Tall Case, Hawkes Walfall, Georgian, Oak, Arched, Painted Dial, Gothic Door, 59 x 19 In. 1840.00
Tall Case, Isaac Blasdel, Pine, Arched Bonnet, Chester, N.H., Mid 18th Century, 89 In. 10530.00
Tall Case, J. Cole, Federal, Mahogany, Brass, Figured, New Hamp., c.1815, 42 x 12 In. 16250.00
Tall Case, Jeweler's Regulator, Walnut, Nickeled Bezel, 8-Day, Carved Top, c.1890, 95 In. 3850.00
Tall Case, John Lemude Charde, Green, Gold, Japanned, Figures, Landscape, Marked, 1700s . 2200.00
Tall Case, John Watt, Chippendale, Red, Gold Chinoiserie, Irvine, c.1800, 93 x 19 In. 6600.00
Tall Case, L. & J.G. Stickley, Copper Face, No. 91, 72 x 18 x 12 ¼ In. .... *illus* 7200.00
Tall Case, Lawson & Millar, Mahogany, Fluted, Arched Door, 80 x 19 x 9 In. 990.00
Tall Case, Lenzkirch Time, Symphonion Hall, Oak, Strike, 2 Piece, Germany, c.1898, 93 In. .. 9350.00
Tall Case, Louis XVI, Provincial, Walnut, Carved, Molded Crest, Shaped Door, 3 Bell, c.1790. . 1763.00
Tall Case, Mahogany, 8-Day, Strike Movement, Fluted Columns, Shell Inlay, England, 80 In. . 3000.00
Tall Case, Mahogany, Brass Works, New Jersey, 91 In. 3738.00
Tall Case, Mahogany, Flat Top, Fluted Quarter Columns, Bracket Feet, c.1801, 93 x 17 In. ... 5288.00
Tall Case, Martin Schreiner, Chippendale, Walnut, Broken Arch, Rosettes, 1795, 96 In. 35100.00
Tall Case, Parquetry, Mixed Woods, Rounded Hood, Applied Carving, Brass Movement, 93 x 20 In. 1116.00
Tall Case, Pieter Gurns, Wood, Brass Dial, Amsterdam, 18th Century, 92 In. 4650.00
Tall Case, Pine, Flat Top, Tombstone Door, Red Stain, c.1825, 86 x 17 x 9 ½ In. 823.00
Tall Case, Pine, Scrolled Pediment, Red, Black Grain Painting, 30-Hour, 84 x 17 In. 1880.00
Tall Case, Poplar, Broken Arch Pediment, Cutout Feet, Urns, Vines, Flowers, c.1825, 90 In. ... 4994.00
Tall Case, Regency, 8-Day, Finials, c.1811, 88 In. 2300.00
Tall Case, Regency, Mahogany, Pine, Figured Veneer, Inlay, Arched Pediment, 83 In. 1998.00
Tall Case, Renaissance Revival, Oak, Carved, Lunar Arch, Brass, Steel, c.1897, 93 In. 7110.00
Tall Case, Satinwood Veneer, Columns, Bonnet Face, Tombstone Crest, 1800s, 14 ⅜ In. 173.00
Tall Case, Simon Willard, Federal, Mahogany, Pierced Fret Top, Arch Hood, c.1800, 94 In. ... 16590.00
Tall Case, Thomas Crow, Chippendale, Mahogany, 8-Day, Wilmington, 1790, 103 In. 8540.00
Tall Case, Tiffany & Co., R.J. Horner, Flemish Style, Carved Oak, Tavern Scene, 102 In. ..... *illus* 25875.00
Tall Case, Walnut, Pine, Broken Arch Pediment, Shell Carved, Pa., c.1813, 98 x 20 In. 6900.00
Tall Case, Z. Ferris, Cherry, Fruit, Leaves, Ship, White Face, Carvings, Del., c.1810, 94 x 10 In. 41400.00
Terry, S., Pillar & Scroll, Mahogany, Whale's Tail, House, Pond, c.1825, 32 In. .... *illus* 2252.00
Terry, S.B., Shelf, Torsion, Iron Case, Flowers, Painted, c.1852, 8 ½ In. 1018.00

Terry & Son, Shelf, Splat, Stenciled Column, Painted Building Scene Tablet, Label, c.1830, 30 In. 830.00
Terry Clock Co., Self 8-Day, Mantel Spring, 8-Sided Case, Flower Panel, Conn., 1875, 19 In. 1007.00 to 1304.00
Thieme, Carl, Shelf, Saxonian, Porcelain, Dresden, Early 20th Century, 25 x 10 In.......... 936.00
Thwaites & Reed, Bracket, Black Case, Ormolu, Brass Handle, London, c.1850s, 31 x 19 In. . 5880.00
Tiffany clocks that are part of desk sets made by Louis Comfort Tiffany are listed in the Tiffany category. Clocks sold by the store Tiffany & Co. are listed here.
Tiffany & Co., Brass, Glass, Pendulum, Faux Mercury, Key, Early 1900s, 11 ¼ In. 920.00
Tiffany & Co., Carriage, Brass, Glass, Deco Numbers, Chelsea, c.1909, 5 ½ In.............. 248.00
Tiffany & Co., Carriage, Grapevine Pattern, France, 5 In.. .... 6900.00
Tiffany & Co., Desk, Alarm, Gilt Metal, 5 x 6 In. 176.00
Tiffany & Co., Shelf, Bow Front, Columns, 4-Glass Panel, Gilt, Ormolu, Marked, 10 x 7 x 5 In. 475.00
Tiffany & Co., Shelf, Brass Case, Beveled Glass Panels, Faux Mercury Pendulum, 1930s, 11 In. 431.00
Tiffany & Co., Shelf, Bronze, Marble, Pagoda Form, Figures, Animals, Character Dial, c.1890, 18 In. 1016.00
Tiffany & Co., Shelf, Bronze, Paste Set, Portrait Miniature, France, c.1900, 13 In........... 1287.00
Tiffany & Co., Shelf, Louis XV, Gilt Metal, Scrolling, Urn Finial, Musical Trophy, 20 In.. ..... 2880.00
Toyo, Fish Cylinder, Swimming Fish, Etched Glass, 1920, 5 ½ In.. .... 510.00
Train Station, Face, France, 54 In.. .... 1035.00
Travel, Octagonal Gilt Embossed Leather Case, 8-Day, 15 Jewels, Swiss, c.1900, 4 x 2 ¼ In.... 147.00
Travel, Silver, Pocket Style, Hinged Case, Easel, Handle, London, c.1905, 5 ¼ x 4 In......... 403.00
Vincenti & Cie, Regulator, Empire, Mahogany, 8-Day, Brass Crystal, France, c.1900, 17 In. .. 880.00
Vincenti & Cie, Shelf, Brass & Enamel, Columns, Mercury Pendulum, Cloisonne, 14 ½ In. .. 6462.00
Volkstedt, Porcelain, Allegorical Scene, Woman, Putto, Karl Ens, c.1900, 16 In. .... *illus* 220.00
Vuillaume, Louis XV, Garland Gilt Bronze Mounts, Round Onyx Plinth, 1800s, 11 In......... 531.00
Wag-On-Wall, Multicolored, Wood Dial, Rose Spandrels, Dial Arch, 12 ¼ x 9 In.. .... 201.00
Wall, Biedermeier, Wood, Platinum, Half-Hour Strike, Columns, Flowers, 10 x 7 In. 240.00
Wall, Cartel, Louis XV Style, Gilt, Bronze Dore, 17 In. 920.00
Wall, Cartel, Louis XVI, Gilt Bronze, Ribboned Flamed Finial, Female Mask, c.1790, 28 x 14 In. 8225.00
Wall, Cartier, Gothic, Arched Shape, Leather, Early 1900s 990.00
Wall, Dutch Empire, Notary Stoeltjesklok, Bonnet Hood, Scroll Brackets, c.1820, 50 x 16 In. . 767.00
Wall, Hooded, Moon Dial, Brass, Square, Stained Case, c.1870, 20 ½ x 14 ¼ In............. 600.00
Wall, Louis XV, Scrolls, Birds, Figure Ormolu Mounts, Red, Paris, c.1730, 39 x 15 In......... 10000.00
Wall, Mahogany, Pillar & Scroll, Painted Face, Brass Finials, Reverse Painted Panel, 30 x 17 In. 705.00
Wall, Mirror, Mahogany, Striking, Turned, Painted, Gilt Columns, New Hampshire, c.1830, 41 In. 2844.00
Wall, Oak, Chime, 34 x 15 In. 88.00
Wall, Painted Wood, Arched Top, Brass Pendulum, Scrolled Columns, Mid 1900s, 40 x 14 In.. 117.00
Wall, Tavern, Mahogany, 2-Weight, 8-Day, England, c.1810, 47 In. 2090.00
Waltham, Acanthus Columns, EDM Monogram, Silver, Reed & Barton, 8 ¾ x 9 In. .... *illus* 374.00
Waterbury, Beehive, Mahogany, Chime, 16 ½ x 12 ½ In............................. 225.00
Waterbury, Regulator, Oak, Late 19th Century, 33 x 18 In.. .... 146.00
Waterbury, Wall, Leeds, Walnut, 8-Day, Gong Strike, Finial, Bead Border, c.1893, 40 In...... 2970.00
Waterbury, Wall, Walnut Case, Carved Pediment, 8-Day Time & Strike, Labels, c.1893, 42 In. 1127.00
Welsh, Spring & Co., Miniature Italian, Rosewood, Round Top, Painted Rose, Columns, c.1875, 14 In. 119.00
Whiting, Riley, Shelf, Federal, 30 In.. .... 403.00
Willard, A., Tavern, Mahogany, Turned, Glazed Bezel, Solid Waist Door, c.1825, 30 In. 10665.00
Willard, S., Wall, Mahogany, Brass, Figured, Crest, Grafton, Mass., c.1805, 25 x 9 In.......... 170500.00
Windmill, Silver, Dutch Hallmarks, 19th Century, 14 In. 3000.00

CLOISONNE enamel was developed during the tenth century. A glass enamel was applied between small ribbons of metal on a metal base. Most cloisonne is Chinese or Japanese. Pieces marked *China* are twentieth-century examples.

Beaker, Textured Ground, Scroll Floral Overlay, Silver Gilt, Mishukov, Russia, c.1890, 2 x 2 In. 956.00
Bowl, Bronze, Shou Symbol, Buddhist Symbols, Lotus, Turquoise Ground, Gilt, 3 ½ x 7 In. .. 3335.00
Bowl, Buddhist Symbols, Lotuses, Turquoise, Bronze, Gilt, 1800s, 3 ½ x 7 In. .... *illus* 1760.00
Bowl, Butterflies, Flowers, Blue Ground, Late 19th Century, 15 ¼ x 7 In. .... *illus* 510.00
Bowl, Butterflies, Flowers, Turquoise Ground, Chinese, 19th Century, 8 ¼ In.. .... 415.00
Bowl, On Brass, Brown Ground, Wood Stand, Early 20th Century, 3 ½ x 10 In.. .... 150.00
Bowl, Pink, Yellow Flowers, White Scalloped Rim, Blue Background, 4 x 12 In. 117.00
Box, Butterfly Form, 4 ½ x 14 ¾ In. 75.00
Box, Calligraphy, Flower Head, Scrolling Leaves, Blue Ground, Chinese, 5 In.. .... 885.00
Box, Stylized Chrysanthemum, Leaves, Green Ground, Peach Form, 5 x 9 x 8 ½ In.. .... 1500.00
Box, Vermeil, Japan, 2 x 6 x 4 ¾ In.. .... 177.00
Cachepot, Gilt Metal, Lobed Outline, Birds, Flowers, Shi Shi Handles, Japan, 12 x 16 In.. .... 900.00
Candleholder, Phoenix Bird, Standing, 6-Sided Pedestal, Chinese, 42 In., Pair 7500.00
Censer, Foo Dog Finial, Handles, Chinese, 5 ¾ In. 1673.00
Censer, Gray, Tan, Lavender, Armor, Flowers, Japan, 1868-1911, 4 ½ In. 889.00
Charger, Bird, Blue, Fan, Flowers, Bronze, c.1880, 17 ¾ In. Diam.. .... 880.00

Clock, Terry, S., Pillar & Scroll, Mahogany, Whale's Tail, House, Pond, c.1825, 32 In.
$2252.00

Clock, Volkstedt, Porcelain, Allegorical Scene, Woman, Putto, Karl Ens, c.1900, 16 In.
$220.00

Clock, Waltham, Acanthus Columns, EDM Monogram, Silver, Reed & Barton, 8 ¾ x 9 In.
$374.00

Cloisonne, Bowl, Buddhist Symbols, Lotuses, Turquoise, Bronze, Gilt, 1800s, 3 ½ x 7 In.
$1760.00

Cloisonne, Bowl, Butterflies, Flowers, Blue Ground, Late 19th Century, 15 ¼ x 7 In.
$510.00

Cloisonne, Cigarette Case, Swan, Flowers, Enamels, Silver, Moscow, 3 ¾ In.
$5500.00

TIP
The less you handle an antique or collectible the better. Always pick up an antique with two hands.

Charger, Bird, Flowers, Multicolored, Chinese, c.1900, 18 In. 322.00
Charger, Blue Ground, Flowering Shrubs, Bird, Japan, Late 1800s, 18 In. 538.00
Charger, Cranes In Flight, Sky Blue Ground, Geometric Border, Chinese, 18 In. 1654.00
Charger, Multicolored, 19th Century, Japan, 11 ¾ In. 264.00
Charger, Multicolored Dragons, Phoenix, Center Dragon, 12 In. 206.00
Cigarette Case, Silver Gilt, Scrolls Flowers, Black, Red, Blue, White, Moscow, c.1900, 4 In. 1652.00
Cigarette Case, Swan, Flowers, Enamels, Silver, Moscow, 3 ¾ In. .... *illus* 5500.00
Cigarette Case, Turquoise, Filigree Overlay, White, Red, Silver Gilt, Russia, c.1890, 4 x 3 In. 1195.00
Creamer, S-Shape Handle, Flower Blue Overlay, Silver Gilt, Russia, c.1890, 3 x 5 In. 2390.00
Cup, Cover, Butterfly, Flower, Stem, 3 ½ In. 1062.00
Ewer, Engraved Gilt Handle, Spout, Turquoise, Dragons, Chinese, 10 In. 2726.00
Figurine, Pheasant, Multicolored, Base, Chinese, 30 In. 819.00
Figurine, Ram, Standing, Scrolling Blossoms, Turquoise Ground, Copper, 26 x 32 In., Pair 900.00
Incense Burner, Hexagonal, Lid, Chinese, 10 ½ x 6 ⅜ In. 526.00
Inkwell, Tray, Silver Gilt, Crystal, 3 Bun Feet, White, Blue, Moscow, c.1890, 9 In. 5900.00
Jar, Cover, Bird Perched On Bamboo, Red Foil Ground, 20th Century, 7 ¼ In. 175.00
Jar, Cover, Oval Panels, Flowers, Butterflies, Bird, Globular, 1900s, 4 ⅝ In. 125.00
Planter, Stylized Lotus Meanders, Turquoise Ground, Japan, 19th Century, 11 In. 178.00
Plate, Bird On Flowering Branch, Turquoise Ground, On Brass, Chinese, 9 ½ In. 30.00
Punch Bowl, Flowers, Birds, Gilt, Yellow Ground, 20th Century, 7 x 15 ½ In. 450.00
Salt, 3-Ball Feet, Textured Ground, Flower Overlay, Blue Dot Border, Russia, 1896, 1 x 2 In. 598.00
Scoop, Sugar, Silver Gilt, Blue, Green, White, Red, Moscow, c.1910, 5 In. 1003.00
Scoop, Twist Stem, Textured Flower Overlay, Silver Gilt Bowl, Klingert, Russia, c.1894, 4 In. 1016.00
Screen, 4 Panels, Chrysanthemum, Black Ground, Gilt Metal Frame, Japan, 12 x 7 ½ In. 563.00
Spoon, Salt, Partial Twist Stem, Scrolls, Flowers, Multicolored, Klingert, Russia, c.1895, 4 In. 448.00
Spoon, Sugar, Twist Stem, Crown Finial, Dot Bowl Border, Russia, c.1910, 6 In. 478.00
Spoon, Sugar, Twist Stem, Crown Finial, Textured, Flower Overlay, Klingert, Russia, 1896, 6 In. 478.00
Stand, Gilt Bronze, Lotus Flowers, Cobalt Blue, Chinese, 5 ½ x 8 In., Pair 1896.00
Strainer, Fiddle Terminal, Flowers, Dots, Silver Gilt Pierced Bowl, Klingert, Russia, 1895, 5 In. 598.00
Teapot, Brass, Convex Panels, Multicolored Dragons, 20th Century, 7 In. 176.00
Teapot, Cover, Lotus Finial, 3-Footed, Swing Handle, 3 ¾ In. 316.00
Teapot, Duck Shape, Brass, Blue Ground, Animals, Chinese, Early 1900s, 8 ¾ In. 940.00
Teapot, Flowers, Upright Handle, c.1900, 13 In. 690.00
Tongs, Sugar, Textured Ground, Scrolled Filigree Overlay, Flower Pattern, Russia, c.1890, 6 In. 717.00
Tureen, Cover, Blue Ground, Red, Pink Flowers, Green Leaves, Chinese, 10 ½ x 15 In. 410.00
Tureen, Cover, Blue Ground, Wood Stand, Chinese, 16 In. 354.00
Urn, Blue Ground, Painted Vases, Flowers, Leaves, Gold Rim, Chinese, 15 In., Pair 205.00
Urn, Lid, Dragon, 5-Fingered Claws, Footed, 8 ¼ In., Pair 220.00
Urn, Mounted As Lamp, Yellow Ground, Orange Green Leaves, 35 In., Pair 263.00
Vase, Bamboo, Prunus, Midnight Blue Ground, Japan, 19th Century, 6 ½ In. 267.00
Vase, Bird & Flowers, Japan, 12 ¼ In. 224.00
Vase, Birds, Butterflies, Flowering Vines, Medallions, Scrolls, Flowers, 9 ¼ In., Pair 127.00
Vase, Birds, Flowers, Flared Mouth, Silver Wire, Square, Japan, 1868-1911, 6 In. 2252.00
Vase, Birds, Flowers, Hexagonal, Baluster Shape, Mounted, Chinese, 22 ½ In., Pair 1560.00
Vase, Birds, Grapevine, Flower, Pink Ground, Phoenix, Turquoise, 18 In. 920.00
Vase, Birds On Branches, Ivory Ground, 19th Century, 12 In. 643.00
Vase, Bud, Underwater Scene, Silver Overlay, Red Glaze, 6 x 3 In. 819.00
Vase, Chrysanthemum Spray, Bulbous, Teal Ground, Applied Silver Rim, 10 ½ In. 822.00
Vase, Chrysanthemums, Brocade Mouth, Foot, Elongated Oval, Japan, 1868-1911, 12 In. 415.00
Vase, Dark Orange, Flowers, Bulbous, Chinese, 8 In. 234.00
Vase, Dragons, Aqua, Green, Gilt, Footed, Handles, 7 x 7 ½ In. 90.00
Vase, Flower Panels, Brown Ground, Octagonal, 20th Century, Japan, 9 ½ In. 150.00
Vase, Flowers, Black, Blue, Pink, White, Chinese, 7 x 12 In., Pair 234.00
Vase, Flowers, Blue Ground, Duck Shape, 7 ¾ In. 1180.00
Vase, Flowers, Fret Work, Square, Bronze Mounted, Lion Ring Handles, 12 ½ In., Pair 1080.00
Vase, Flowers, Leaves, Turquoise Ground, On Brass, Chinese, 1900s, 8 ¾ In., Pair 58.00
Vase, Flowers, Navy Ground, Silver Wire, Cone Shape, Wood Box, 3 ¾ x 7 ¾ In., Pair 1265.00
Vase, Flowers, Red Ground, Japan, c.1950, 10 x 5 In. 146.00
Vase, Flowers, Red, Turquoise, 9 In. 117.00
Vase, Foo Dogs, Gu Form, 19th Century, 11 ½ In. 690.00
Vase, Grapes, Vines, White Ground, 6 ¼ In. 58.00
Vase, Leaves, Fruits, White Ground, Silver Base & Rim, c.1897, 14 ⅝ In. 101200.00
Vase, Morning Glories, Blue Ground, 7 ⅛ In. 130.00
Vase, Prunus Trees, Flowers, Birds, Navy Ground, Marked, c.1900, 6 ⅛ In., Pair 1495.00
Vase, Quail, Brass Birds, Blue Body, Removable Vase, Chinese, 20th Century, 10 In., Pair 705.00
Vase, Roses, White Shaded, Light Gray Ground, Silvered, Japan, 9 ½ In. 767.00

Vase, Royal Blue, Brown, Tan Snake Design, Long Neck, 30 x 11 In. 410.00
Vase, Scrolling Flowers, Raised, Carved Wood Bases, Chinese, c.1900, 7 In., Pair 201.00
Vase, Wisteria, Midnight Blue Ground, Hexagonal, Japan, 19th Century, 7 ¾ In. 1304.00

CLOTHING of all types is listed in this category. Dresses, hats, shoes, underwear, and more are found here. Other textiles are to be found in the Coverlet, Movie, Quilt, Textile, and World War I and II categories.

Air Force Academy Cadet Uniform, Hat, Jacket, Trousers, 1970s, Size Medium 80.00
Apron, Aqua Checked, Smocked, Lace Trim, c.1960, 21 ½ In. 8.00
Apron, Bib, Tulip, Wrap Around, c.1960, 33 In. 5.60
Apron, Black Checked, Smocked, Pocket, c.1960, 21 In. 8.00
Apron, Blue & Green Flowers, 3 Pockets, c.1965, 19 In. 8.00
Apron, Blue Polka Dot, Flowers, Pocket, c.1965, 18 In. 8.00
Bathing Cap, Flower, Rubber, Purple, Hot Pink, Pastel Pink, Sunwear Tag, Germany, 1950s . 30.00
Belt, Gold Filled, 5 Chains, 5 Coin Frames, Ancient Coins 59.00
Belt, Leather, Burgundy, Goldtone H-Closure Signed, Pouch, Hermes, 35 In. 533.00
Belt, Officer's, Louisiana, Embroidered, Metallic Fabric, Leather, Brass Plate, 38 In. 575.00
Belt, Rhinestone, Woven Silvertone Metal, Round Black Plastic Clasp, Chanel, 28 ½ In. 296.00
Boa, Black Ostrich Feather, Black Satin Tie, Victorian, 44 In. 145.00
Cape, Fox Fur, Dark Brown, Art Deco, 2 Front Fasteners, 1930s, 26 ½ In. 365.00
Cape, Long, Collared, Lace, Satin Ribbon, Black, Isabel Canovas, Woman's, 1980 .... 329.00
Chaps, Brown Leather, Edge Stitching, Marked Belt, S.C. Gallup-Saddle Co., Pueblo 1410.00
Coat, Coopchik Forrest Fox, Knee Length, Woman's, 1970s 90.00
Coat, Lunaraine Mink, Brown Satin Lining, Rosendorf Evans, ¾ Length, Woman's 2006.00
Coat, Mink, Satin Lined, Somper, Beverly Hills Label, Ankle Length 896.00
Coat, Raccoon, Black Satin Lining, ¾ Length, Woman's 1003.00
Coat, Sheared Mink, Brown Silk Lining, Andriana Furs, Full Length, Woman's 4248.00
Coat, Silk, Flowers, Green Damask, Black, Intaglio Stitched, Chinese, c.1925, 26 In. .... *illus* 300.00
Coat, Stroller, Sable, Golden, Cape Collar, Scalloped Sleeve Ends, Edge, ¾ Length, Size 14 ... 2070.00
Coat, Trousers, U.S. Army, Blue, Gold Trim, c.1889 .... 489.00
Coat, White Fox, Wool, Signatures, Cream Color, Interwoven Leather, Ankle Length, 1970s... 143.00
Coat, Woman's, Mink, Monogram DMB, ¾ Length 131.00
Coat, Wool, Black, Fox Collar, Double Breasted, Calf Length, Bromley, Petite 72.00
Coat, Wool, Blue, Magenta, Nubby, Applied Yellow Patch, Koos Van Den Akker, 1980s, Size 6.. 24.00
Coat, Wool, Sheared Fur, Knee Length, Woman's, 1980s 71.00
Dress, Evening, Chemise, Spaghetti Straps, Gold Embroidery, Chiffon, Velvet, Lace, Black, c.1920 179.00
Dress, Evening, Edwardian, 2 Parts, Full Skirt, Taffeta, Silk, Lace, Velvet, Jennings & Co. 143.00
Dress, Evening, Glass Beads, Chantilly Lace, 3-Layer Bottom, 1912, Size 9 .... 2250.00
Dress, Evening, Silk, Aqua, Silver Bugle Beads, Faux Pearls, Size 10 .... 177.00
Dress, Leather, Black, Cutaway Waist & Back, V-Neck Line, Zipper, Size 5-6. .... 220.00
Dress, Long, Matching Wrap, Empire Waist, Yellow Chiffon, Pink Green Chiffon Overlay, 1980s. 108.00
Dress, Mini, Yellow, Pink, Orange, Printed Silk, Signed Emilio Pucci, Italy, 1960s 167.00
Dress, Red, Puffy Shoulders, Crimped Seams, 14 Back Buttons, Girl's, 43 In. .... *illus* 55.00
Dress, Silkscreen On Paper, Universal Studio Stars, c.1968, 37 ½ In. .... *illus* 1200.00
Earmuffs, Mink, Dark Blond, Headband Is Encased In Dark Brown Velvet 40.00
Gloves, Black Leather, Glass Beads, Abstract Design, 1930s, Size 7 .... 75.00
Gloves, Lilac, Cotton Poly, Wrist Length, Woman's, Size 8 .... 4.50
Gloves, Off-White, Cotton, Wrist Length, Woman's, Size 8 .... 4.80
Gloves, White Kidskin, Cutout Flowers, Cream Color, 1930s, Size 6 ½ In. 100.00
Gloves, Woman's, Fingerless, White, Ruffled At Wrist, 1940s 75.00
Handkerchief, Blue Flower, Pink Leaf Pattern, Cotton, c.1955, 11 x 11 In. 2.80
Handkerchief, White, Blue Daisy, c.1955, 11 ½ x 11 ½ In. 3.50
Handkerchief, White, Blue Tulips, Red Border, c.1955, 11 x 11 In. 4.50
Handkerchief, White, Flower Border, c.1955, 14 x 14 In. 3.50
Handkerchief, White, Flowers, Leaves, Rose, Teal, Gold, c.1955, 13 x 13 In. 3.60
Hat, Band, Aqua, Velvet, Netting, c.1950 .... 10.00
Hat, Beanie, Bottle Caps, Premium, Marked, Dutchess Hat Works, Wool, 1930s. 30.00
Hat, Boater, Straw, Woven, 1920, Size 7, 3 ½ x 11 ½ In. 110.00
Hat, Checker Taxi Co. 125.00
Hat, Corona, Black, Rhinestones, Italy, c.1960, 7 In. 28.00
Hat, Court, First Rank Official, Summer, Basketry, Brocade, Chinese, 19th Century 2370.00
Hat, Court, Third Rank Official, Summer, Basketry, Brocade, Chinese, 19th Century 1422.00
Hat, Felt, Black & White, Black & White Straw Ruffle, Golden Globe Label, 1940s. 220.00
Hat, Man's, Felt, 18 In. 138.00
Hat, Mink, Felt, Reddish Brown, 1940s 155.00
Hat, Red, Wool, Feather, Adelle Claire, New York, Late 1940s, 22 In. Diam. .... *illus* 58.00

Clothing, Coat, Silk, Flowers, Green Damask, Black, Intaglio Stitched, Chinese, c.1925, 26 In.
$300.00

Clothing, Dress, Red, Puffy Shoulders, Crimped Seams, 14 Back Buttons, Girl's, 43 In
$55.00

Clothing, Dress, Silkscreen On Paper, Universal Studio Stars, c.1968, 37 ½ In.
$1200.00

C

Clothing, Hat, Red, Wool, Feather, Adelle Claire, New York, Late 1940s, 22 In. Diam.
$58.00

Clothing, Hat, Shrimp Silk, Mini Pleats, Ribbon Bow, Ties, Stern Bros. Importers, Child's
$350.00

Clothing, Necktie, Navy, Stripes, Geometrics, Rayon, Exclusive Design, Late 1950s, 53 x 3 In.
$22.00

Clothing, Shirt, Tartan, Victorian, Green, Navy, Red, White, 16 x 30 In.
$65.00

Hat, Shrimp Silk, Mini Pleats, Ribbon Bow, Ties, Stern Bros. Importers, Child's .... *illus* 350.00
Hat, Straw, Blue, Blue Striped Band, Quality, Man's, c.1960, Size 7 .... 15.00
Hat, Straw, Red, 2-In. Black Ribbon Running Around Band, 17 In. Diam. 140.00
Hat, Yellow Cab 90.00
Helmet, Guard, Military Shako, Leather, Brass Visor, Front Crest, Sunburst, Connecticut, c.1812 889.00
Helmet, Medieval-Style, Ribbed Rounded Crown, Morion-Style Rim, Steel, 16 ¾ In. 1126.00
Jacket, Bear Fur, Bomber Style, Reversible, Leather Lined, 1980s 448.00
Jacket, Bomber, Ranch Mink, Zipper, Black Satin Lining, Mary McFadden Furs, Man's 1416.00
Jacket Apron, Blue Striped, White Trim, 2 Pockets, c.1960, 26 ½ In. 6.80
Mittens, Green, Purple, Knitted, Amish, Connecting String, 10 x 5 ¼ In. 11.00
Mittens, Hooked, Flowers, Green Vine, Red Buds, 15 In., Pair 690.00
Muff, White Rabbit Fur, Black Lucite Handles, Lined In Black Satin, 1920s 90.00
Necktie, Navy, Stripes, Geometrics, Rayon, Exclusive Design, Late 1950s, 53 x 3 In. .... *illus* 22.00
Petticoat, White Cotton, Embroidered With White Daisies, Victorian, 26-In. Waist 160.00
Robe, Dragon, Cobalt Blue Ground, Chinese, Late 19th Century 1304.00
Robe, Dragon, Embroidered Gauze, Gold Thread, Chinese, 50 In. 3186.00
Robe, Embroidered Flowers, Blue, Green, Yellow, 19th Century, Chinese, 54 In. 720.00
Robe, Embroidered Flowers, Butterfly, Dark Blue Ground, Beige Cuffs, Chinese, 42 In. 600.00
Robe, Embroidered Flowers, Foo Dog Rondels, Pink Ground, Woman's, Chinese 652.00
Robe, Gauze, Embroidered, 9 Couched Gold Metallic Dragons, Blue Ground, Chinese, 51 In. . 3680.00
Robe, Priest, Kesa Of Brocade, Dark Blue Ground, Japan, 19th Century, 75 x 42 In. 770.00
Robe, Silk, Embroidered, Beige, Flower Filled Vases, 38 In. 2390.00
Robe, Silk, Embroidered, Flowers, Peach, Bat, Silk Cuffs, Applique Ribbons, Chinese 598.00
Robe, Silk, Embroidered Dragons, Foo Dogs, Emblems, Gold, Chinese, 19th Century 948.00
Robe, Summer, Gauze Weave, 9 Embroidered Dragons, Dark Blue Ground, Chinese 4444.00
Scarf, Clips, Silk, Pink, Yellow, Ivory Earclips, Hermes, Box, 34 In. 119.00
Scarf, Silk, Dachshunds, Hermes, Signed, 35 In. 380.00
Scarf, Silk, Horses, Performing, Multicolored, Moorish Tile Border, Red Ground, Hermes 296.00
Scarf, Silk, Perfume Bottles, Hermes, 1980s, 35 In. 210.00
Shirt, Evening, Gold Beaded, Sleeveless, Cashmere, British Crown Colony, c.1940, Size 40 ... 60.00
Shirt, Tartan, Victorian, Green, Navy, Red, White, 16 x 30 In. .... *illus* 65.00
Skirt, Red Flowers, Black Ground, Green Cotton, Linen, Lace, Victorian 60.00
Stole, Silvertip Fox Fur, Hook & Eye Front Closure, 1930s 235.00
Swimsuit, Iridescent Gold, Block & Line Pattern, 1 Piece, Deuxun 21, Japan, Size 5-6. ...... 100.00
Top Hat, Stovepipe, Beaver Skin 40.00
Undergarment, Quilted, Multicolored Plaid, Milk Glass Button, 36 In. .... *illus* 88.00
Winter Outfit, Hat, Coat, Mittens, Boots, Seal, Buffalo Furs, Hide, Sheepskin, Thread Sewn, c.1870 1058.00

CLUTHRA glass is a two-layered glass with small bubbles and powdered glass trapped between the layers. The Steuben Glass Works of Corning, New York, first made it in 1920. Victor Durand of Kimball Glass Company in Vineland, New Jersey, made a similar glass from about 1925. Durand's pieces are listed in the Durand category. Related items are listed in the Steuben category.

Vase, Black, White, Flared Rim, Steuben, 7 In. .... *illus* 593.00
Vase, Blue, 9 ¾ x 8 In. 293.00
Vase, Green, Raindrop Optic, Steuben, c.1900, 8 In. 774.00
Vase, Lime Green, Flared Rim, Steuben, 7 ½ In. 460.00
Vase, Pink, Raindrop, Steuben, c.1920, 11 ½ In. 1920.00
Vase, Pink, Steuben, c.1925, 10 ½ x 9 ½ In. 4095.00
Vase, Rose Pink, Mottled, Bubbles, Classic Form, Marked, 6 In. 1150.00
Vase, Trumpet, Green, Applied Foot, Steuben, 10 In. 180.00
Vase, White, Green, Pink, Yellow, 5 In. 295.00
Vase, White, Steuben, 6 ½ x 6 In. 2633.00
Vase, White, White Opalescent Handles, Steuben, 10 In. 1208.00

COALBROOKDALE was made by the Coalport porcelain factory of England during the Victorian period. Pieces are decorated with floral encrustations.

Bowl, Flower Heads, Cavetto Center, Pheasant, 4 x 14 ½ x 11 In. 2160.00

COALPORT ware has been made by the Coalport Porcelain Works of England from 1795 to the present time. Early pieces were unmarked. About 1810–25 the pieces were marked with the name *Coalport* in various forms. Later pieces also had the name *John Rose* in the mark. The crown mark has been used with variations since 1881. The date 1750 is printed in some marks, but it is not the date the factory started. Some pieces are listed in Indian Tree.

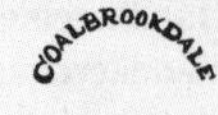

Basket, Creamer, Sugar, Nestled, Strawberries, Leaves, 3 Piece 211.00
Bowl, Silver Jubilee, Queen's Profile, Initials E.R., Crown, Leaves, Gold, 8 In. 96.00
Bowl, Vegetable, Arcadia, Oval, 8 ¾ x 6 ¾ In. 45.00

Creamer, Samarkand, 4 ¾ x 2 ⅝ In. 28.00
Cup, Demitasse, Kings Ware, Canton, Flowers, Multicolored, 1891-1920, 2 x 2 In. 15.00
Cup & Saucer, Demitasse, Blue Flower, Gold Trim, Crown Mark 65.00
Cup & Saucer, Demitasse, Blue Leaves, White Ground, Gold Trim 125.00
Cup & Saucer, Demitasse, Kings Ware, Canton, Flowers, Multicolored, 1891-1920, 2 x 4 In. 27.50 to 35.00
Cup & Saucer, Flowers, Red Border, c.1815 .... 90.00
Cup & Saucer, Salmon, Gold Overlay, Ivory Ground, Raised Flowers, Scrolls 125.00
Figurine, Chelsea Derby, Richard Quinn, Mistress Robinson, 8 ½ In., Pair 47.00
Figurine, Helen, Ladies Of Fashion Series, Woman, Green Dress, 7 ⅝ In. 40.00
Figurine, Stella, Ladies Of Fashion, Factory Mark, 7 ¾ In. .... *illus* 54.00
Figurine, Tinker, 7 ¼ In. 110.00
Mug, Landscape, Black, White, Gilt Leaves, Borders, c.1805, 2 ½ In. 120.00
Plate, Bread & Butter, Glastonbury, 6 ¼ In. 15.00
Plate, Feldspar, Roses, Gilt Grapevine Border, Marked, c.1820-30, 8 ½ In. 60.00
Plate, Passenger Pigeon, On Branch, Yellow, White, Gilt Border, 1756, 9 In. 105.00
Plate, Salad, Geneva, Athens Shape, Gold Trim, 8 In. 26.00
Plate, Soup, Flower Rim, Gold Trim, c.1891, 9 ½ In., 12 Piece 143.00
Saucer, Soup, Cream, Pembroke, 6 ¼ In. 10.00
Shoe, Picture Medallion, Blue, Flowers, Gilt, 6 In. 850.00
Tea Set, Red Oriental Pattern, Teapot, Sugar, Creamer, 3 ¼-In. Teapot 40.00
Vase, Cover, Encrusted Fruit, Flower, Yellow Ground, Blue Bands, Scrolling Gilt, 26 In. 4063.00
Vase, Cream Body, Gilt Banding, Landscape Panel, Turquoise Jewels, Gilt Handles, 6 In. 480.00
Vase, Encrusted Flowers, Hand Painted Flowers, Gilt Trim, Green Ground, c.1840, 10 In., Pair 299.00
Vase, Gold, Turquoise Enamel Jewels, Ivory Ground, Handles, Marked, 5 ¾ In. .... *illus* 925.00
Vase, Jeweled, Cobalt Blue Ground, Short Handles, Raised Turquoise Jewels, 7 In., Pair 1007.00

COBALT BLUE glass was made using oxide of cobalt. The characteristic bright dark blue identifies it for the collector. Most cobalt glass found today was made after the Civil War. There was renewed interest in the dark blue glass in the late 1930s and dinnerwares were made.

Candlestick, Sandwich Glass, Hexagonal, Wafer At Socket, c.1860, 8 ¾ In., Pair 920.00
Compote, Blown Molded, Vertical Ribs, Applied White Rim, 3 x 5 In. 316.00
Pitcher, Molded, 12 Ribs, Applied Ear Handle, Kick-Up Base, c.1840, 5 In. 546.00

COCA-COLA was first served in 1886 in Atlanta, Georgia. It was advertised through signs, newspaper ads, coupons, bottles, trays, calendars, and even lamps and clocks. Collectors want anything with the word *Coca-Cola*, including a few rare products, like gum wrappers and cigar bands. The famous trademark was patented in 1893, the *Coke* mark in 1945. Many modern items and reproductions are being made.

Ashtray, Bottle Center, Drink Coca-Cola Cap, 1950 .... 225.00
Bank, Boy, Bottle Cap On Forehead, Multicolored, Cast Iron, 8 x 4 ½ In. 99.00
Bank, Cast Iron, Coca-Cola Boy's Head, 7 ¾ x 5 ½ In. 70.00
Bank, Put Coin In, Get Drink, Battery Operated, Linemar, Box, 10 In. .... *illus* 518.00
Barrel, Syrup, Wood, Label, 1930-40, 21 In. 260.00
Bingo Set, Compliments Of Coca-Cola, c.1930, 14 x 8 In. 115.00
Bottle, Coca-Cola Bottling Co., Rocky Mount, N.C., Tenpin Shape, 7 Oz. 420.00
Bottle, Royal Palm Seltzer, 1940s .... *illus* 173.00
Bottle, Seltzer, Fullmer's Re-Pete-Er, Red Writing, 11 In. 122.00
Bottle, Seltzer, Green, Club Seltzer, 12 ¼ In. 110.00
Bottle, Seltzer, Green, Indiana, J.K. Beer Dist., 12 In. 132.00
Bottle, Seltzer, Sparkling Club Soda, Blue Writing, 11 In. 110.00
Bottle Opener, Corkscrew, Drink Coca-Cola, Newport News, Va., No. 7, c.1900, 5 In. 30.00
Calendar, 1914, Betty, November & December, 32 ¼ x 13 In. 300.00
Calendar, 1915, Elaine, 33 x 13 In. 2000.00
Calendar, 1917, Constance, 31 ½ x 12 ¾ In. 3250.00
Calendar, 1921, Autumn Girl, Frame, 12 x 31 In. 805.00
Calendar, 1929, Girl With Long String Of Pearls, 24 ½ x 12 In. 935.00
Calendar, 1993, Cap, Drink Coca-Cola In Bottles, Red, Yellow, Tin, 19 In. 225.00
Carrier, Bottle, Yellow, Wood, Red Handle, 1941, 9 x 8 x 5 ½ In. 95.00
Carrier, Coke, Aluminum, 6-Pack 40.00
Cash Register, National, Fountain Service, Pressed Steel, Red, 17 x 15 ½ x 10 In. 550.00
Cash Register, National, Model 726, Red Enamel, 19 x 16 x 14 In. 200.00
Checker Set, Red, White, Bottle Caps, Metal Box, 2 ½ x 7 ¾ In. 20.00
Clock, 2 Bottles, Leafy Branches, Walnut Face, Cast Concrete, c.1940, 21 x 30 x 4 In. 977.00
Clock, Coca-Cola Ice Cold, Metal, Plastic, Electric, 2-Sided, 19 x 31 x 12 In. 1600.00
Clock, Drink Coca-Cola, Pam, Light-Up, Red, White, Late 1958, 16 In. 275.00
Clock, Drink Coca-Cola, Please Pay When Served, Light-Up, Painted, Metal, 9 x 20 In. 660.00

Clothing, Undergarment, Quilted, Multicolored Plaid, Milk Glass Button, 36 In.
$88.00

Cluthra, Vase, Black, White, Flared Rim, Steuben, 7 In.
$593.00

Coalport, Figurine, Stella, Ladies Of Fashion, Factory Mark, 7 ¾ In.
$54.00

Coalport, Vase, Gold, Turquoise Enamel Jewels, Ivory Ground, Handles, Marked, 5 ¾ In.
$925.00

Coca-Cola, Bank, Put Coin In, Get Drink, Battery Operated, Linemar, Box, 10 In.
$518.00

Coca-Cola, Bottle, Royal Palm Seltzer, 1940s
$173.00

Coca-Cola, Dispenser, Ice Cold, Red, Countertop, Dole, 1940s, Box, 14 In.
$2070.00

Coca-Cola, Display, Drink Coca-Cola, Refreshing Custom, 3 Women, Cardboard, 1939
$575.00

Clock, Drink Coca-Cola, Red Center, White, 1950s, 18 In. Diam. 154.00
Clock, Drink Coca-Cola In Bottles, Light-Up, 19 In. 850.00
Clock, Drink Coca-Cola In Bottles, Red, White, Black, Selecto Devices, 1945, 16 x 16 In. 200.00
Clock, Electric, Light-Up, Glass Face & Dome, Aluminum Case, 15 In. 330.00
Clock, Fishtail, Drink Coca-Cola, Pam, Green, Red, Reverse Painted, Light-Up, 1948, 16 In. . . 190.00
Clock, Regulator, Burl, Key, 18 ¼ x 9 x 4 ¼ In. 465.00
Clock, Rocking Bottle, Electric, Aluminum, c.1940s-50s, 20 In. 2185.00
Clock, Things Go Better With Coke, Plastic, Electric, 12 x 12 In. 30.00
Cooler, Airline, Drink Coca-Cola, Red, Metal, c.1950, 12 x 17 x 6 In. 150.00
Cooler, Airline, Original Box, 19 x 14 In. 660.00
Cooler, Double Lid, Red, Embossed, Wheels, Bottle Openers, 34 ½ x 66 ½ In. 150.00
Cooler, Drink Coca-Cola, Red, White, Westinghouse, Model WH5T, 34 x 27 x 27 In. 285.00
Cooler, Drink Coca-Cola In Bottles, Red, Handle, No. 501, Action Mfg. Co., 18 x 17 In. 66.00
Cooler, Drink Coca-Cola In Bottles, Round, Textured Aluminum, Box, 4 Gal., 14 In. 518.00
Cooler, Picnic, Red, White, Metal, Handle, 1950s, 19 In. 403.00
Cooler, Westinghouse, Embossed, Built-In Bottle Opener, 28 x 36 In. 2185.00
Dispenser, Ice Cold, Red, Countertop, Dole, 1940s, Box, 14 In. . . . . . *illus* 2070.00
Dispenser, Syrup, Urn, No. 5/500 Version, Lid, 23 In., 3 Piece. 303.00
Dispenser Base, Syrup, Ceramic, White, Red & Gold, Wheeling Pottery, c.1900, 9 In. 460.00
Display, Bottle, Styrofoam, Painted, 42 In. 110.00
Display, Drink Coca-Cola, Refreshing Custom, 3 Women, Cardboard, 1939 . . . . . . *illus* 575.00
Doll, Buddy Lee, Striped Uniform, Bowtie, 1940s, 12 ½ In. 500.00
Doll, Santa Claus, Black, Rushton, 1960s 90.00
Door Pull, Bottle Form, Have A Coke, Plastic, 7 ½ In. 121.00
Door Pull, Plastic Handle, c.1930s, 3 ¼ x 11 In. 3737.00
Door Push, Have A Coca-Cola, Yellow, Red, White, Porcelain, Canada, 1940s, 3 ½ x 6 ½ In. . . 425.00
Door Push Set, Push, Pull, Be Really Refreshed, Metal Plate, c.1960, 4 x 8 In., Pair 1610.00
Fountain Dispenser, 6-Sided, 5 Cents, Drink Coca-Cola, c.1930, 23 In. 1980.00
Gum, Hand Fan, Richmond, Virginia, Images, 2-Sided, c.1913, 8 x 14 In. 345.00
Keg, Wood, Spout, Paper Label, 10 Gal., 12 x 21 In. 100.00
Kite, Bottle, Red, White, Paper, Wood Stretcher, 1930s, 23 x 23 In. . . . . . *illus* 230.00
Lamp Shade, Leaded Glass, Coca-Cola, Red, Green, White, 12 x 16 In. 402.00
Menu Board, Drink Coca-Cola, Specials Today, Tin Lithograph, 27 x 19 In. 66.00
Menu Board, Painted, Wood Masonite & Metal, 1940s, 14 ½ x 53 In. 1380.00
Mirror, Girl, Glass Poclet, 1914 . . . . . . 800.00
Playing Cards, Girl Holding Bowling Ball, Coke Refreshes You Best, 1961 . . . . . . 38.00
Radio, Cooler Shape, c.1950, 10 x 12 In. 633.00
Radio, Cooler Shape, Model 5A410A, Bakelite, Red, Embossed, 1949, 9 ½ x 12 x 8 In. 400.00
Sandwich Toaster, 1930s, 8 ½ 1150.00
Sheet Music, My Coca-Cola Belle, Train, Honeymoon Express, Fannie Brice, 1910-20. . . . . . 29.00
Sign, 50th Anniversary, 1886-1936, 2 Girls, Cardboard, Frame, 1936, 50 x 30 In. 2070.00
Sign, 6-Pack, Die Cut, Tin, 1954, 13 x 11 In. 230.00
Sign, Add Zest To The Holiday, Take Home Today, 36 Cents, 6-Pack, Paper, 9 x 24 In. 88.00
Sign, Bottle, Coca-Cola, Brown, White, Die Cut, Tin, 1954, 6 In. 345.00
Sign, Bottle, Coca-Cola, Red, Green, Yellow Neon, 46 ½ In. Diam. 2500.00
Sign, Boy, Girl, Accepted Home Refreshment, Frame, 1942, 27 x 56 In. 385.00
Sign, Cap, Bottle, Coca-Cola, Red, Porcelain, 36 In. Diam. 275.00
Sign, Cap, Bottle, White, 1950s, 24 In. Diam. 275.00
Sign, Cap, Buvez Coca-Cola, 48 In. 173.00
Sign, Cap, Drink Coca-Cola, Sign Of Good Taste, Red, White, 24 In. Diam. 484.00
Sign, Cap, Drink Coca-Cola In Bottles, Red, White, Enamel, c.1950, 36 In. 475.00
Sign, Cardboard, Coke For Me Too, Couple Drinking Coke, Black Ground, 1946, 27 x 56 In. . . 690.00
Sign, Cardboard, Girl Ice Skater, Clown, Gold Wood Frame, c.1950, 57 x 35 In. 660.00
Sign, Cardboard, Santa With Coke Bottle, Gold Wood Frame, c.1955, 28 x 20 In. 193.00
Sign, Coca-Cola, Red, White, Porcelain, Arched Bottom, 23 x 36 In. 170.00
Sign, Coca-Cola Belongs, Couple At Cookout, Cardboard, 1942, 27 x 56 In. 115.00
Sign, Coke Belongs, Soldier Enjoying Coke With Girlfriend, 1945, 36 x 20 In. 645.00
Sign, Delicious & Refreshing, Girl, Black Hair, Tin, 54 x 18 In. 500.00
Sign, Delicious & Refreshing, Girl In Boat, Eloyron, 1953, 27 ¾ x 56 ½ In. 1000.00
Sign, Drink, In Bottles, Bottle, 5 Cent, Tin, 1908, 12 x 36 In. 330.00
Sign, Drink Carbonated Coca-Cola, Paper On Linen, Girl, Ormolu Screen, 1902, 15 x 19 In. . . 9200.00
Sign, Drink Coca-Cola, Restaurant, Die Cut, Tin, Iron, 2-Sided, 1930s, 43 x 70 In. . . . . . *illus* 885.00
Sign, Drink Coca-Cola, Serve Yourself, Light-Up, Art Deco, 1910, 9 ½ x 19 ½ x 3 In. 715.00
Sign, Drink Coca-Cola Delicious & Refreshing, Porcelain, 94 x 46 In. 880.00
Sign, Drink Coca-Cola Fountain Service, Porcelain, 2 Soda Taps, c.1938, 27 x 14 In. 360.00
Sign, Eddie Fisher, Cardboard, Die Cut, c.1954, 12 x 20 In. 115.00
Sign, Embossed, Tin, In Bottles 5 Cents, Red, White, Green, Bottle, 1910-15, 12 x 35 In. 460.00
Sign, Enjoy 12 Oz. King Size, Ice Cold Here, Tin, 1960s, 20 x 28 In. 403.00

Sign, Enjoy Coca-Cola In Bottles, Tin, 2-Sided, 17 ½ x 19 ½ In. 484.00
Sign, Fountain Service, Red, Green, Shield, 2-Sided, Enamel, Bracket, 1934, 22 x 25 In. 1650.00
Sign, Glass, Hanging, Please Pay When Served, 1940, 19 x 12 In. 600.00
Sign, Have A Coke, Die Cut, Cardboard, c.1930, 31 x 27 In. 550.00
Sign, Hello Refreshment, Bathing Girl Exiting Pool, Frame, 1942, 50 x 30 In. 632.00
Sign, Here's To Our G.I. Joes, Coca-Cola Girls, Frame, 1944, 20 x 36 In. 1420.00
Sign, Hospitality, Gold Frame, c.1950, 16 x 27 In. 345.00
Sign, It's The Refreshing Thing To Do, Silk Screen Plywood, c.1936, 29 x 17 In. 1725.00
Sign, Man Drinking From Bottle, That Taste Good Feeling, Frame, 1939, 27 x 56 In. 460.00
Sign, Military Girl, Die Cut, Cardboard, Stand-Up, 1940s, 64 x 24 In. 289.00
Sign, Pause That Refreshes At Home, Girl In Garden, Cardboard, 1940, 27 x 56 In. 403.00
Sign, Picnic Grill, Coca-Cola Belongs, Couple, Cardboard, Frame, 1942, 27 x 57 In. 400.00
Sign, Please Pay Cashier, Hanging, Glass, c.1940s, 19 x 10 In. 862.00
Sign, Policeman, Slow School Zone, Base, Die Cut, c.1957, 30 x 67 In. 2588.00
Sign, Santa Claus, Die Cut, Cardboard, 48 x 27 In. 50.00
Sign, Shop Refreshed, Take Enough Home, Yellow Base, Light-Up, 2-Sided, 22 In. 975.00
Sign, Shopping Girl, Stand-Up, Cardboard, 1944, 17 In. 1093.00
Sign, Sign Of Good Taste, Red, Fishtail, Metal, 25 x 68 In. 286.00
Sign, So Delicious, Skiers, Cardboard, 1954, 27 x 56 In. 747.00
Sign, Social Gathering, Cardboard, Frame, Canada, 1920s, 22 x 28 In. *illus* 5463.00
Sign, Sold Here Ice Cold, Bottle, Red Ground, Yellow, Tin, c.1941, 17 x 53 In. 288.00
Sign, Sprite Boy, Tin, c.1940-50s, 12 ¾ In. 633.00
Sign, Sprite Boy, Welcome Friend Have A Coke, Cardboard, 30 In. 250.00
Sign, Take Home Enough, c.1956, 20 x 36 In. 77.00
Sign, Thirst Asks Nothing More, Silk Screen, Plywood, Aluminum, 1938, 38 x 9 ¾ In. 920.00
Sign, Topper, 5 Cent Pay When Served, Brunhoff Mfg. Co., 1947, 12 x 14 In. 4130.00
Sign, WAC Holding Bottle, Stand-Up, Cardboard, 1944, 17 ½ In. 345.00
Sign, Wherever You Are, Kicking Footballer, Large Football, Die Cut Store, 1940s 160.00
Sign, Whirligig, Base, 8-Sided, Spinning, c.1950s, 13 In. 1956.00
Syrup Pump, Black, Porcelain, Metal, Marked, 14 In. 100.00
Thermometer, Be Really Refreshed, Pam, White, Red, Round, 1950s, 12 In. 805.00
Thermometer, Drink Coca-Cola, Be Refreshed, Pam, 1950s, 12 In. *illus* 805.00
Thermometer, Girl Drinking From Bottle, Red, Green, White, 1940, 16 x 6 ½ In. 173.00
Thermometer, Quality Refreshment, Tin, White, Red Disc Logo, 1950s, 9 In. 288.00
Thermometer, Refresh Yourself, Tin, c.1950, 17 x 3 ¼ In. 2875.00
Thermometer, Thirst Knows No Season, Green Version, Porcelain, 1942, 18 x 6 In. 2360.00
Tip Tray, 1906, Juanita, Delicious, Refreshing, White Dress, 4 In. Diam. 275.00
Tip Tray, 1907, Relieves Fatigue, Victorian Girl, Glass Of Coke, 6 x 4 ¼ In. 316.00
Tip Tray, 1909, Exhibition Girl, Oval, 6 ¼ x 4 ½ In. 250.00
Tip Tray, 1914, Betty, Drink Coca-Cola, Oval, 6 x 4 ¼ In. 110.00 to 235.00
Tip Tray, 1916, Elaine, Yellow Dress, Oval, 6 x 4 ¼ In. 130.00 to 170.00
Tip Tray, 1920, Golfer Girl, Yellow Dress, Oval, 6 ¼ x 4 ½ In. 105.00 to 138.00
Toy, Car, Ford, 4-Door, Coke Logo, Bottle On Roof, Friction, Tin, 1960s, 10 ½ In. 215.00
Toy, Truck, Bottle, Metalcraft, Decals, 10 Bottles 1350.00
Toy, Truck, Coca-Cola, Hauler, Matchbox, 12 In. 10.00
Toy, Truck, Delivery, Trailer, Buddy L, Box, 9 ½ In. 65.00
Toy, Truck, Stake, Yellow, Decals, Marx, 1940, 21 In. 250.00
Toy, Truck, Yellow, White, Tin, Battery Operated, 1950s, 12 ¼ In. 286.00
Toy, Van, Delivery, Yellow, Red, Friction, Tin Lithograph, 4 ¼ In. 10.00
Tray, 1901, Hilda Clark, Wooden Frame, Round, 9 ½ In., Diam 1200.00
Tray, 1903, Hilda Clark, Drink Delicious, Refreshing, 19 x 15 In. 10800.00
Tray, 1903, Hilda Clark, Raised Rim, Round, 9 ¾ In. Diam. 3565.00
Tray, 1908, Topless Girl, Coca-Cola Is Better, Try It, 12 In. 16100.00
Tray, 1916, Elaine, Basket Of Flowers, 19 x 8 ½ In. 400.00
Tray, 1922, Summer Girl, 13 ¼ x 10 ½ In. 459.00
Tray, 1925, Party Girl, 13 x 10 ½ In. 220.00 to 350.00
Tray, 1926, Golfers, Man Golfer Pouring Coke For Girl In White Mink, 13 ¼ x 10 ½ In. 700.00
Tray, 1927, Curb Service, Couple In Car, Car Hop, Tin, 13 ½ x 10 ½ In. 1176.00
Tray, 1927, Soda Jerk, 13 ¼ x 10 ½ In. 440.00 to 568.00
Tray, 1930, Bather Girl, 13 ¼ x 10 ¼ In. 325.00
Tray, 1930, Telephone Girl, American Art Works, 13 ¼ x 10 ½ In. 154.00
Tray, 1931, Barefoot Boy, Norman Rockwell, American Art Works, 13 ¼ x 10 ½ In. 550.00
Tray, 1933, Francis Dee, Paramount Player, 13 ¼ x 10 ¼ In. 389.00
Tray, 1934, Tarzan, Maureen O'Sullivan & Johnny Weissmuller, 10 ¼ x 13 ¼ In. 454.00 to 750.00
Tray, 1935, Madge Evans, American Art Works, 13 ¼ x 10 ½ In. 154.00 to 259.00
Tray, 1936, Hostess, American Art Works, 13 ¼ x 10 ½ In. 220.00 to 225.00
Tray, 1937, Running Girl, American Art Works, 13 ¼ x 10 ½ In. 176.00
Tray, 1938, Girl, Yellow Hat, American Art Works, 13 x 10 ½ In. 132.00 to 200.00

Coca-Cola, Kite, Bottle, Red, White, Paper, Wood Stretcher, 1930s, 23 x 23 In.
$230.00

Coca-Cola, Sign, Drink Coca-Cola, Restaurant, Die Cut, Tin, Iron, 2-Sided, 1930s, 43 x 70 In.
$885.00

Coca-Cola, Sign, Social Gathering, Cardboard, Frame, Canada, 1920s, 22 x 28 In.
$5463.00

Coca-Cola, Thermometer, Drink Coca-Cola, Be Refreshed, Pam, 1950s, 12 In.
$805.00

Coffee Mill, C. Parker & Co., No. 370, Cast Iron, Wood, Wall, 8 ¼ In.
$60.00

Coffee Mill, Elgin National, No. 40, Original Paint, Decals, Cast Iron, 30 In.
$750.00

Coffee Mill, Enterprise, No. 12, 2 Wheels, Cast Iron, Original Paint, 29 In.
$550.00

Coffee Mill, Lane Brothers, No. 15, Cast Iron, Tin Drawer, 19 ½-In. Wheel
$600.00

Tray, 1939, Springboard Girl, 13 ¼ x 10 ½ In. .... 110.00 to 300.00
Tray, 1940, Sailor Girl, American Art Works, 10 ½ x 13 ¼ In. .... 110.00 to 300.00
Tray, 1941, Skater Girl, Seated On Log, 13 ¼ x 10 ½ In. .... 100.00 to 220.00
Tray, 1942, 2 Girls At Car, 13 ¼ x 10 ½ In. .... 176.00 to 250.00
Tray, 1950, Menu Girl, Outdoor Activities Border, 13 ¼ x 10 ½ In. 72.00
Tumbler, King Kong, Subway, Skull Island, c.1976, 5 ½ In., Pair 26.00
Vending Machine, 10 Cent, 1950s, 58 x 27 x 20 In. 1150.00
Vending Machine, 10 Cent, Red, Metal, Vendo Co., c.1940, 58 x 27 ¼ x 20 In. 605.00
Vending Machine, 44 Soda, 8-Ounce Bottles, 1956-59, 57 ½ x 16 x 15 ½ In. 4153.00
Vending Machine, Drink Coca-Cola, White, Glass Door, No. CS72A, 57 ½ In. 700.00
Vending Machine, Soda Cooler, Hinged Lid, Bottle Cap Catcher, 1930s, 25 x 34 x 18 In. 805.00
Vending Machine, Vendo 39, 6 Cent, Red, Vendo Co., Kansas City, Mo., 59 x 27 x 21 In. 1100.00
Vending Machine, Vendo C-81, 1950s, 27 x 59 ½ x 22 ½ In. 2645.00
Vendorlator, Model 27, Coca-Cola, Red, White, 10 Cent, Bottles 650.00
Vendorlator, Model 27, Wood Case, 9 Bottles, 58 x 18 ½ In. 2000.00

COFFEE MILLS are also called coffee grinders, although there is a difference in the way each grinds the coffee. Large floor-standing or counter-model coffee mills were used in the nineteenth-century country store. Small home mills were first made about 1894. They lost favor by the 1930s. The renewed interest in fresh-ground coffee has produced many modern electric mills and hand mills and grinders. Reproductions of the old styles are being made.

Arcade, No. 5, Cast Iron, Wall Mount, Wood Back, 6 In. 44.00
Arcade, No. 25, Glass, Cast Iron, Wall Mount, Hand Crank, 15 ½ In. .... 20.00 to 40.00
C. Parker & Co., No. 370, Cast Iron, Wood, Wall, 8 ¼ In. .... *illus* 60.00
C. Parker & Co., No. 3000, 2 Wheels, 11-In. Wheel 935.00
Citizens Wholesale Supply Co., Golden Rule Blend, Wall Mount, Cast Iron, 5 ½ x 19 In. 160.00
Coles Mfg. Co., No. 8, 2 Wheels, Cast Iron, Black, Red, 31 In. 385.00
Elgin National, No. 18, 2 Wheels, Cast Iron, Red, Eagle Finial, 28-In. Wheel 413.00
Elgin National, No. 40, Original Paint, Decals, Cast Iron, 30 In. .... *illus* 750.00
Elgin National, No. 47, 2 Wheels, Iron, Nickel-Plated Hopper, Finial, 27 In. 303.00
Enterprise, No. 2, 2 Wheels, Cast Iron, Drawer, Salmon & Blue Paint, 31 In. 770.00
Enterprise, No. 3, 2 Wheels, Drawer, Cast Iron Hopper, 10-In. Wheel 708.00
Enterprise, No. 4, 2 Wheels, Nickel Plated Hopper, 10-In. Wheel 2750.00
Enterprise, No. 5, 2 Wheels, Cast Iron, Red Paint, Drawer, Wood Base, 17 In. 330.00
Enterprise, No. 7, 2 Wheels, Cast Iron, Drawer, Black, 15-In. Wheel .... 358.00 to 725.00
Enterprise, No. 8, 2 Wheels, Cast Iron, Red, 20 In. 322.00
Enterprise, No. 12, 2 Wheels, Cast Iron, Original Paint, 29 In. .... *illus* 550.00
Enterprise, No. 16, 2 Wheels, Iron Hopper, 30 ½-In. Wheel 2200.00
Enterprise, No. 209, 2 Wheels, Cast Iron, Hinged Cover, Drawer, 25-In. Wheel 1650.00
Enterprise, No. 212, 2 Wheels, Cast Iron, Red, Black, Yellow, Eagle Finial, 31-In. Wheel 605.00
Enterprise, No. 512, 2 Wheels, Iron Hopper, Cast Iron, Brass Eagle, Salmon, Blue Paint, 31 In. 990.00
Enterprise, No. 750, Single Wheel, Cast Iron, Black, 19-In. Wheel 220.00
Golden Rule Blend, Cast Iron, Wall Mount, Glass Window & Receiver, 15 x 19 In. 160.00
Goles Mfg., Red, Cast Iron, Wood Base, Tin Drawer, 13 ½-In. Wheel 220.00
Landers, Frary & Clark, No. 20, 2 Wheels, Cast Iron, Black, Drawer, 12 ½ In. 195.00
Landers, Frary & Clark, No. 24, Universal, Wall Mount, Glass, 1905, 16 ½ In. 20.00
Lane Brothers, No. 15, 2 Wheels, Cast Iron, Tin Drawer, 30 In. 660.00
Lane Brothers, No. 15, Cast Iron, Tin Drawer, 19 ½-In. Wheel .... *illus* 600.00
Lane Brothers, No. 26, 2 Wheels, Stand, Cast Iron, Red, Gold, Eagle Finial, 66 In. 990.00
Peck Stowe & Wilcox, No. 3600, International, Cast Iron, Wall Mount, 7 ⅛ In. 99.00
Peugeot Freres, Lyon, France, c.1900, 14 x 14 In. 259.00
Simmons, No. 19, Keen Kutter, 2 Wheels, Pat. Oct.1, 1901, 19 ½-In. Wheel 2530.00
Star, No. 7, 2 Wheels, Cast Iron, Red, Eagle Finial, 15-In. Wheel 330.00
Star, No. 10, 2 Wheels, Cast Iron, Red & Blue Paint, Pat. Date May 26, 1885, 23-In. Wheel 385.00 to 575.00
Star, No. 18, 2 Wheels, Stand, Black, Nickel Plated Hopper, Eagle Finial, 36-In. Wheel 660.00
Star, No. 20, 2 Wheels, Nickel Plated Hopper, Eagle Finial, Pat. 1885, 42-In. Wheel 1800.00
Sun, No. 1088, Drawer, Hand Crank, Paper Label, 6 x 6 x 3 ¾ In. 55.00

COIN-OPERATED MACHINES of all types are collected. The vending machine is an ancient invention dating back to 200 B.C., when holy water was dispensed in a coin-operated vase. Smokers in seventeenth-century England could buy tobacco from a coin-operated box. It was not until after the Civil War that the technology made modern coin-operated games and vending machines plentiful. Slot machines, arcade games, and dispensers are all collected.

Arcade, Foot Massager, Vibr-O, 1 Cent, Light-Up, Glass, Metal, 1930s, 62 x 16 In. 385.00
Arcade, Football, Chester Pollard, 1920-30, 44 x 18 x 72 In. 2588.00

Arcade, Goalie, Soccer, 46 x 36 x 64 In. 575.00
Arcade, Jumping Jack, Gottlieb, 69 x 54 x 29 In. 330.00
Arcade, Palm Reader, Gypsy Palmist, 1 Cent, Wood Case, 63 In. 4025.00
Arcade, Rifle Gallery, 20 Shots, Model No. 449, 30 x 45 x 91 In. 576.00
Arcade, Rifle Game, Shoot The Bear, Coin Entry Stand, 74 x 44 x 25 In. 3630.00
Arcade, Shocker, Electricity Is Life, Midland Mfg., Chicago, 1 Cent, Key, 22 x 24 In. 4130.00
Arcade, Whirly Bird, Fly Helicopter, 1960s, 66 x 34 x 34 In. 1399.00
Band Box, Jukebox, Curtain Opens, Band Plays, 33 x 48 x 24 In. 2257.00
Baseball, Field, Players, 68 ½ x 63 ½ x 24 ¾ In. 7800.00
Baseball, Game, Rock-Ola, 1933 World Series, 5 Cent. 1562.00
Baseball, Hit A Homer, Wood Backboard, c.1940s, 17 x 22 x 11 In. 486.00
Baseball, Line Drive, 2 Players, Animated, Runners, Sound, 72 x 27 x 61 In. 2520.00
Coin Sorter, Mechanical, Oak Case, Dovetailed Corners, c.1920, 15 x 18 x 10 In. 1650.00
Crane, Holly Crane, 10 Cent, Wood, Glass, Cosmo Mfg, 36 x 48 x 24 In. 295.00
Fortune Teller, Ask Madame X, Napkin Dispenser, 1 Cent, 8 x 8 x 5 In. 522.00
Fortune Teller, Horoscope, Gypsy Madame, Jenko, 1950s, 66 In. 4312.00
Fortune Teller, Puss 'n Boots, Roover Brothers, 1 Cent. 20700.00
Fortune Teller, Zoltan, Phone Receiver, Hear Fortune, c.1950, 72 In. 4313.00
Fortune Teller, Zoltan Wizard, In Window, Fiberglass 3432.00
Gambling, Cards, Cast Iron, Reliance Novelty Co., 13 x 10 x 15 In. 4800.00
Gambling, Dice Popper, Cigar Cutter, Copper, Cast Iron, J.J. Oaks & Son, 7 x 16 In. 7590.00
Gambling, Josephine Baker, No. 196, 3 Coin Slot, Oak Case 1038.00
Gambling, Lukat, The Lucky Cat, 10 Cent, Ticket & Gumball, 1930s, 14 In. 22425.00
Gambling, Poker, Cast Iron, Samuel Nafew, 1890s, 11 x 8 In. 4312.00
Graphophone, Columbia Type N, Oak Case, Lift-Off Lid, Slot, 14 In. 5333.00
Gum, 8 Horses, Official Sweepstakes, Aluminum, Wood, 11 In. 2489.00
Gum, Cardinal, Yellow, Black, Cherries, Bells, Die Cast *illus* 550.00
Gum, Chiclet Chewing Gum, 1 Cent, 16 x 10 x 6 In. 600.00
Gum, Chiclets, Dentyne, Confections, L-Shaped, Porcelain, Wood, 32 x 10 In. 3850.00
Gum, Colgan's Taffy Tolu Chewing Gum, 1 Cent, Aluminum, Glass, Steel, 15 In. 5500.00
Gum, Happy Jap, Yellow Paint, c.1902, 10 x 14 In. 39000.00
Gum, Northwestern Rotary, Model 49, 5 Cent, Red, 1954, 20 x 8 In. 187.00
Gum, Reel Spot, Aluminum Case, Key, 13 x 12 In. 358.00
Gumball, Acorn, 1 Cent, Key, c.1920s 100.00
Gumball, Ad-Lee, Ne An Ez Winner, 5 Cent, Glass, Cast Iron, 24 In. 925.00
Gumball, Blue Bird, 18 In. 460.00
Gumball, Columbus, 1 Cent, 16 In. *illus* 575.00
Gumball, Ford, 1 Cent, Gray & Black Base 85.00
Gumball, Master, Black, Red, Gooseneck Receiver, 16 x 8 x 8 ½ In. 390.00
Gumball, Master, Penny Or Nickel, White, 4-Sided 250.00
Gumball, Simpson, 1 Cent, Red, Metal, Glass, 8 x 15 In. 1180.00
Gumball, Topper, 1 Cent, 4-Sided, Stand, 48 x 7 ½ In. 80.00
Gumball, Topper, Red, Black, 45 ½ x 6 ½ x 6 ½ In. 40.00
Gumball, Victor, 5 Cent, Yellow, Red, Black, 18 x 9 x 9 In. 60.00
Mutoscope, Anti-Aircraft, Gun Sky Fighter, 1944, 24 x 36 x 96 In. 3775.00
Mutoscope, Babe Ruth Reel, Steel, 5 Cent, Stand, 51 x 8 x 16 In. 4834.00
Mutoscope, Cail-O-Scope, 1 Cent, Marquee, Oak, 74 In. 3100.00
Mutoscope, Cail-O-Scope, 5 Cent, Penny Aracade, 72 In. 1035.00
Mutoscope, Cail-O-Scope, 5 Cent, Wood, Cast Iron Legs, 66 x 70 In. 1093.00
Mutoscope, Clamshell, Cast Iron, Yellow, Harold Lloyd Reel, 19 x 17 In. 7425.00
Mutoscope, Indian Head, Style E, No. 13188, American Mutoscope Co., 1906, 75 In. 6518.00
Mutoscope, Voice-O-Graph Recording Booth, 1957, 81 x 33 x 45 In. 5500.00
Peep Show, Cail-O-Scope, Tiger Oak, Carved, c.1890, 72 x 22 x 18 In. 4400.00
Peep Show, Rosenfield, Drop Card, Oak Cabinet, Cash Box, 18 x 75 In. 3025.00
Pinball, Captain Fantastic, Bally, 1976, 70 x 30 In. 990.00
Pinball, Chicago Golden Gloves, 1950s, 55 x 68 ½ x 26 ½ In. 1100.00
Pinball, Circus, Bally, 1948, 65 x 54 x 24 In. 440.00
Pinball, Eight Ball, Bally, 1977, 52 x 71 x 30 ½ In. 1100.00
Pinball, Shuffle Ball, 1 Cent, Wood, c.1932, 38 x 41 x 21 In. 700.00
Pinball, Winner, No. 115001, Williams Electronics, 1972 295.00
Recording Booth, 50 Cents, 45 Or 78 RPM, 1940s, 30 x 42 x 84 In. 5317.00
Ride, Big Bronco, Horse, Black, White, Fiberglass, Saddle, 51 x 66 x 30 In. 4500.00
Ride, Horse, Galloping, Plays Song, Painted, Cast Iron, 42 x 49 x 27 In. 4000.00
Skill, Kicker & Catcher, Oak, 1933, 17 x 14 In. 635.00
Skill, Mills, Flip Skill, Wood, Gingerbread, 1938, 34 x 16 x 15 In. 748.00
Skill, New Frontier, 10 Cent, 28 x 66 x 14 In. *illus* 978.00

Coin-Operated Machine, Gum, Cardinal, Yellow, Black, Cherries, Bells, Die Cast
$550.00

Coin-Operated Machine, Gumball, Columbus, 1 Cent, 16 In.
$575.00

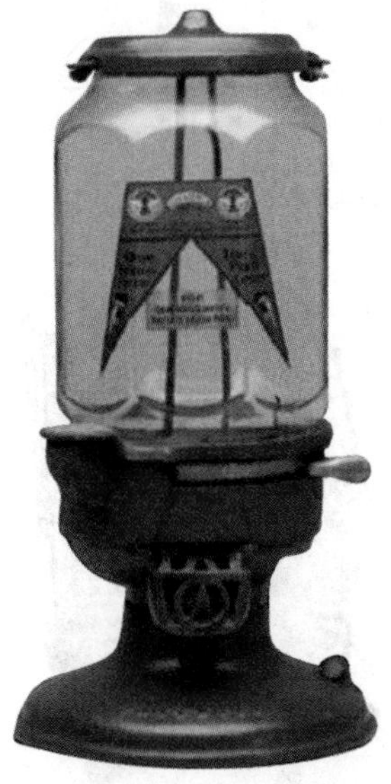

TIP

Coins must be stored properly. Do not put them in a sealed plastic or wooden container or loose in a box or envelope. Plastic, paper, cardboard, and wood give off chemical vapors that speed corrosion. Loose coins may be scratched. Buy archival coin holders, easily found at any coin shop.

C

C

Coin-Operated Machine, Skill, New Frontier, 10 Cent, 28 x 66 x 14 In. $978.00

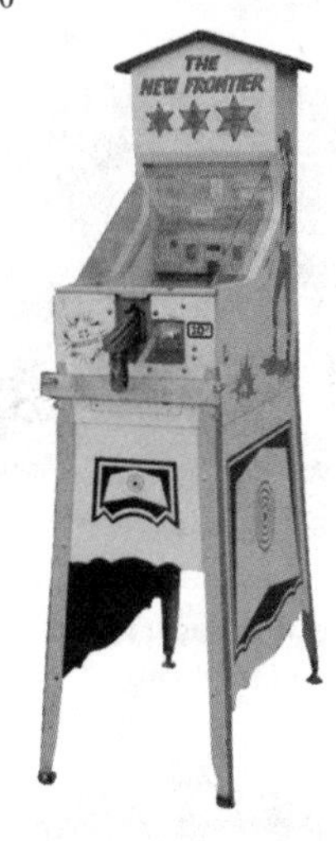

Coin-Operated Machine, Slot, Mills, War Eagle, 25 Cent, c.1931 $1430.00

Coin-Operated Machine, Vending, Matches, Northwestern, 1 Cent, Nickel Plated Cast Iron, 14 In. $770.00

Skill, Play A Hand, 21 Holes, 10 Cent, Wood, Tin, Glass, 8 ½ x 31 x 18 In. . . . 66.00
Skill, Play Football, 5 Cent, 1926, 71 x 46 x 21 In. . . . 2070.00
Skill, Poker, Redeemable Cards For Cigars, Cast Iron, c.1890, 57 ½ x 16 In. . . . 4400.00
Skill, Shooter, Gun Shoots Ball Bearings, 10 Balls, 1 Cent, 15 x 10 x 24 In. . . . 486.00
Skill, Whiz Ball, 1 Cent, 18 x 8 In. . . . 633.00
Slot, Aladdin II, 32 x 19 x 14 In. . . . 100.00
Slot, Bally, 777, 5 Cent, Wood Stand, Key, 46 x 21 x 17 In. . . . 250.00
Slot, Bally, 809, Wood Base, 1968, 34 x 18 x 19 In. . . . 1500.00
Slot, Bally, Triple Bell, 5, 10, 25 Cent, 40 x 58 x 23 In. . . . 1200.00
Slot, Bell-O-Matic, 5 Cent, Base, 37 x 16 ½ x 18 In. . . . 2300.00
Slot, Bird Of Paradise, Rol-A-Top, 1930s, 16 x 16 x 23 In. . . . 4888.00
Slot, Caille, Cast Aluminum, 25 Cent, 1930s, 15 x 15 x 24 In. . . . 1150.00
Slot, Castle Front, 5 Cent, Wood Base, 1936, 26 x 19 ½ x 15 In. . . . 2500.00
Slot, Castle Front, Blue, Red, Yellow, 5 Cent, Cast Iron Stand . . . 1150.00
Slot, Columbia, 5 Cent, Blue, Red, Yellow, Key, 16 x 18 In. . . . 605.00
Slot, Columbia, 5 Cent, Blue, Wood Base, Stamped, C2C713, 18 x 15 In. . . . 480.00
Slot, Columbia, 5 Cent, Metal, Wood, 19 ½ x 14 ¾ x 11 ¾ In. . . . 275.00
Slot, Compulsory Skill, Pinball Action, Wood, 45 x 29 x 23 In. . . . 1500.00
Slot, Golden Nugget, Die Cast Steel, White, 25 x 16 x 15 In. . . . 660.00
Slot, Jennings, Dutch Boy, Dutch Girl, 25 Cent, 15 x 15 x 22 In. . . . 1150.00
Slot, Jennings, Golf Ball Vender, 25 Cent . . . 7788.00
Slot, Jennings, Hunt Scene, Bronze Indian, Oak Stand, 16 x 16 x 26 In. . . . 1610.00
Slot, Jennings, Standard Chief, Chrome, Wood, 1946, 27 x 16 x 15 In. . . . 2250.00
Slot, Jennings, Sun Chief, 5 Cent, Chrome, c.1949, 27 x 15 x 17 In. . . . 2900.00
Slot, Jennings, Super Deluxe Club Chief, Chrome, Wood, 1946, 27 x 16 In. . . . 2500.00
Slot, Jubilee, Tic-Tac-Toe, Electron, 1970, 32 x 16 x 21 In. . . . 1000.00
Slot, Liberty Bell, 25 Cent, Cast Iron Stand, 65 x 22 x 12 In. . . . 1210.00
Slot, Mills, Baseball Front, 5 Cent, 1920-30, 16 x 16 x 23 In. . . . 7475.00 to 9200.00
Slot, Mills, Black Cherry, Raised Cherries, Base, 1946, 26 x 16 In. . . . 2300.00
Slot, Mills, Blue Bell, High Top, Blue, Chrome, c.1948, 16 ½ x 26 In. . . . 4025.00
Slot, Mills, Bursting Cherry, Oak Stand, 1930s, 16 x 16 x 23 In. . . . 2070.00
Slot, Mills, Extraordinary, 5 Cent, c.1933 . . . 1430.00
Slot, Mills, Golden Nugget, The Doll, Oak, 25 Cent, c.1949 . . . 1000.00
Slot, Mills, Golf, Clubs, Balls, 25 Cent, 16 x 16 x 25 In. . . . 2530.00
Slot, Mills, Gum, Countertop, Cast Iron, 1912, 17 x 16 x 25 In. . . . 6038.00
Slot, Mills, High Top, Chrome, Wood, 1948, 26 x 16 x 15 In. . . . 2000.00
Slot, Mills, High Top, Cowboy, 1-Arm, Carved, 72 x 24 x 24 In. . . . 16415.00
Slot, Mills, Horsehead Bonus, 5 Cent, 1930s, 16 x 16 x 25 In. . . . 1847.00
Slot, Mills, Liberty Bell, 5 Cent, Painted, Wood Base, 24 ½ x 16 x 15 In. . . . 1500.00
Slot, Mills, Operator Bell, 1916, 24 x 16 x 15 In. . . . 2250.00
Slot, Mills, Operator Bell, Patina, Wood Base, 25 x 16 x 15 In. . . . 1600.00
Slot, Mills, Owl, Oak, Color Dial, 65 x 22 x 12 In. . . . 7300.00
Slot, Mills, Q.T. Firebird, 1 Cent, Metal, Wood, 19 In. . . . 1200.00
Slot, Mills, Silent Gooseneck, 10 Cent, Metal, Wood, 25 In. . . . 950.00
Slot, Mills, Vest Pocket, Fruit Reels, Key, c.1930s, 8 ½ x 7 In. . . . 242.00
Slot, Mills, War Eagle, 1933, 26 x 16 x 15 In. . . . 2500.00
Slot, Mills, War Eagle, 25 Cent, c.1931 . . . *illus* 1430.00
Slot, Mills, War Eagle, Indian, 25 Cent, Dick Delong, 1940s, 6 In. . . . 3220.00
Slot, Pace, 3 Bars Wins Jackpot, 25 Cent, Cast Metal, Wood, 25 In. . . . 700.00
Slot, Pace, Geometrics, Red, Chrome, Wood Display Base, 1936, 24 x 16 In. . . . 2100.00
Slot, Watling, American, Rol-A-Top, 50 Cent, 1930s, 16 x 16 x 24 In. . . . 4025.00
Stamp, U.S. Postage, 1 Cent, Oak, Aluminum, 10 x 21 In. . . . 5310.00
Strength Tester, 1 Cent, Red, Blue, Cast Iron, 61 x 28 x 17 In. . . . 1540.00
Strength Tester, Test Quest, Question, Answer, Grunig Mfg., 10 x 12 In. . . . 480.00
Strength Tester, Uncle Sam, Caille, c.1950s, 64 In. . . . 25875.00
Trade Stimulator, Caille, 5 Cent, Cast Iron, Wood Base, 8 x 7 x 10 In. . . . 5865.00
Trade Stimulator, Caille, Good Luck, 1 Cent, 5 Reel Cigar, 11 x 15 In. . . . 2520.00
Trade Stimulator, The Ace, Charles Fey, 10 x 8 In. . . . 9660.00
Trade Stimulator, Uncle Sam, Wood Carving, Painted, Early 20th Century, 71 In. . . . 1380.00
Trade Stimulator, Watling Cupid, Gum Vendor, Cast Iron, 15 x 18 In. . . . 44250.00
Vending, Candy, 8 Pulls, 6 x 30 x 14 In. . . . 1981.00
Vending, Candy, DuGrenier, Red, White, 62 ½ x 29 x 16 In. . . . 1000.00
Vending, Candy, Stoner Theater Candy, Mirror, 61 x 29 x 14 In. . . . 3250.00
Vending, Candy, Univendor, Burgundy, Silver Pinstripe, 71 x 29 x 12 In. . . . 2750.00
Vending, Cards, Whom You Should Marry, 1 Cent, 1924, 72 x 25 In. . . . 4154.00

Vending, Cigar, National, Art Deco Style, Chrome Trim, Graphics, 23 x 67 In. 5175.00
Vending, Cigarette, 1 Cent, Mirror, 1940s, 36 x 17 ½ x 9 In. 484.00
Vending, Cigarette, Rowe, Illuminated Clockface, Mirror, 28 x 70 In. 4945.00
Vending, Gum, Hunter Ball, 3 Duck Targets, Pistol, National, 19 ½ In. 474.00
Vending, Gum, Manfield's Automatic Clerk, Glass, Steel Base, 16 In. 1210.00
Vending, Hershey Candy Bar, 5 Cent, Key, 28 x 9 x 8 In. 170.00
Vending, Little Nut Vendor, House Shape, Blue, Cast Iron, 8 x 8 In. 4290.00
Vending, Matches, 1 Cent, Painted, Metal, Wood, 14 x 10 ¾ x 8 In. 275.00
Vending, Matches, Northwestern, 1 Cent, Nickel Plated Cast Iron, 14 In. .... *illus* 770.00
Vending, National, Mints, Chewing Gum, 5 Cents, Tabletop, 8 x 15 x 6 In. 173.00
Vending, Peanut, Double Kay Salted Nuts, Porcelain Base, 3 Globes, c.1920, 18 In. 468.00
Vending, Peanut Dispenser, Peanut Shape, Bakelite Base, England, c.1930. .... 633.00
Vending, Peanuts, Columbus Vendors, Porcelain, Octagonal Glass Globe, 14 In. 420.00
Vending, Perfume, Crown Crab Apple Blossoms, c.1895, 14 x 15 In. 3163.00
Vending, Popcorn Dispenser, Gold Medal Model, 10 Cent, 60 x 24 x 24 In. 710.00
Vending, Pulver Gum, Woody Woodpecker, c.1910, 21 In. 413.00
Vending, Rosebud Matches, 1 Cent, Painted, Metal, 13 x 6 x 5 In. 275.00
Vending, Select-O-Vend, 1 Cent, Red, No. 18163, 18 x 7 ¼ x 8 In. 360.00
Vending, Smilin' Sam From Alabam, Peanuts, Red, Cast Iron, 13 x 10 In. 3198.00
Vending, Tom's Toasted Peanuts, 10 Cent, Red, White, Blue 220.00
Weigh Scale, Beveled Mirror, Watling Scale Co., 1950s, 17 x 61 In. 1265.00

COMIC ART, or cartoon art, is a relatively new field of collecting. Original comic strips, magazine covers, and even printed strips are collected. The first daily comic strip was printed in 1907. The paintings on celluloid used for movie cartoons are listed in this book under Animation Art.

Cover Art, Confession Illustrated, No. 2, 1956, I Destroyed My Marriage, Joe Orlando, 22 x 16 In. 1980.00
Cover Art, Mad Magazine, No. 2, Tales To Drive You Mad, Marie Severin, 1970s, 13 x 8 ½ In. . 484.00
Cover Art, Tales Of Terror, No. 3, Reed Crandall, 1956, 15 x 15 In. 6600.00
Cover Art, Walt Disney's Donald Duck, No. 101 Carl Barks, 1965, 15 x 10 ½ In. 3300.00
Page, Weird Science, No. 7, 4th Dimension Monster, Al Feldstein, 1951, 18 x 13 In. 4840.00
Panel, Conan The Barbarian, Revenge Of Son Of Yara, Thomas Yeates, 1981, 9 ½ x 21 In. ... 121.00
Panel, Dennis The Menace, Only Dog Who Takes Cat Nap, Hank Ketcham, 1971, 8 x 6 ½ In. . 352.00
Strip, Dennis The Menace, Unless It's Got An Ice Cream Bar, Hank Ketcham, c.1972, 8 x 6 ½ In. 375.00
Strip, Dick Tracy, Miss Deal Brings The Cops, Chester Gould, Oct. 23 1966, 23 ½ x 20 In. 1650.00
Strip, Dick Tracy, Oct. 23 1944, Chester Gould, 6 x 20 In. 1100.00
Strip, Dick Tracy, Up The River, Chester Gould, July 4 1943, 6 x 20 In. 528.00
Strip, Family Circus, Tough Bein' An Only Child, Bil Keane, August 4, 1982, 9 ½ x 8 In. 176.00
Strip, Ferris & Misfits, Wally Wood, c.1970, 5 x 8 In. 176.00
Strip, Nancy, Ears To The Ground, Ernie Bushmiller, Jan. 10, 1943, 5 x 19 In. 150.00
Strip, Pogo, What's The Cat Staring At, Walt Kelly, October 16, 1963, 5 x 18 ½ In. 605.00
Strip, Puck, 2 Irishman, C.J. Taylor, July 1887, 6 ½ x 6 ½ In. 99.00
Strip, Rip Kirby, Mysterious Temples Rise In The Rain Forest, John Prentice, 1961, 5 x 17 In.. 275.00
Strip, Sunday, Captain & The Kids, Rudolph Dirks, Feb. 11, 1968, 15 x 22 ½ In. 154.00
Strip, Sunday, Peanuts, Charlie Brown & Snoopy Dancing, July 14, 1963 .... 61020.00
Strip, Terry & The Pirates, Profiteer, Milton Caniff, Oct. 25 1934, 6 x 20 In. 4620.00

COMMEMORATIVE items have been made to honor members of royalty and those of great national fame. World's Fairs and important historical events are also remembered with commemorative pieces. Related collectibles are listed in the Coronation and World's Fair categories.

Compote, Mayflower, 350th Anniversary, c.1970, 5 ⅛ x 2 ½ In. 23.00
Creamer, Admiral Dewey, Eagle Spout, Knotted Rope Handle, Ironstone, 4 In. 187.00
Jug, 250th Anniversary, Rhode Island, Roger Williams, c.1886, 7 ⅜ In. .... *illus* 123.00
Medallion, Charles Lee, He Died For Freedom & Honor, Bronze, 4 ¾ In. 55.00
Mug, Malvern Fire Company, Frosted Glass, Sept. 18, 1982, 5 ⅛ x 3 In. 8.00
Plate, Prince Charles Edward, Basketweave Border, Stoneware, c.1850, 9 ¼ In. .... *illus* 2817.00
Plate, C.D. Kenny Tea Co., Star Spangled Banner, Tin, 1914, 10 In. 95.00
Plate, King George VI & Queen Elizabeth, America Visit, 1939, 9 x 9 In. 75.00
Plate, Patrick Henry, Give Me Liberty, White & Black, Royal Crownford, c.1976 .... 24.00
Snuffbox, Admiral Vernon, Hinged Lid, Brass, England, 18th Century, 1 ⅞ In. 350.00
Stein, Calgary Winter Olympics, Anheuser Busch, Gerz, c.1988 .... 35.00
Tin, KLM, European Flight, Airplane, West Indies, 1934, 7 In. 175.00
Tobacco Jar, Cover, Queen Elizabeth II, French Blue, 1953, 4 x 3 ¾ In. 35.00
Vase, Mardi Gras, Rex, Black Glass, Silver Overlay, New Orleans, 1917, 6 In. 71.00

Commemorative, Jug,
250th Anniversary, Rhode Island, Roger Williams, c.1886, 7 ⅜ In.
$123.00

Commemorative, Plate,
Prince Charles Edward, Basketweave Border, Stoneware, c.1850, 9 ¼ In.
$2817.00

Memory Reminders

Commemorative items have been made to honor members of royalty and others of great national fame. Coronation and royal souvenirs have been made since the 1780s. Pottery, glass, tin, silver, and paper objects with a picture of monarchs and the date have been sold at many coronations. The pieces that mention King Edward VIII, the king who was never crowned, are not rare; check values before buying them. World's Fairs and important historical events are also remembered with commemorative pieces, including directories, buttons, jewelry, postcards, fabrics, ribbons, and ceramics.

Compact, Estee Lauder, Chick, Yellow Crystals, Goldtone Dangling Feet, Mirror, 2 ¾ In.
$375.00

Consolidated, Bonbon, Ruba Rombic, Smoky Topaz, Handles, 3-Part, 8 In.
$550.00

Consolidated, Jug, Catalonian, Jade Green, Stopper, 6 ½ In.
$285.00

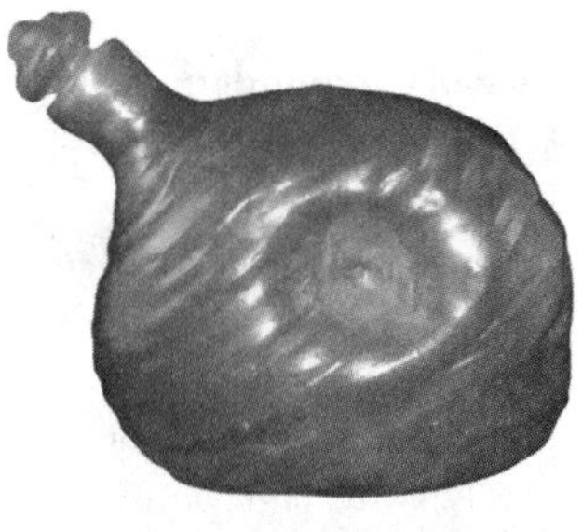

Consolidated, Perfume Bottle, Ruba Rombic, Topaz, Stopper, 7 ¾ In., Pair
$1100.00

COMPACTS hold face powder. A woman did not powder her face in public until after World War I. By 1920, the beauty parlor, permanent waves, and cosmetics had become acceptable. A few companies sold cake face powder in a box with a mirror and a pad or puff. Soon the compact was designed by jewelers and made of gold, silver, and precious materials. Cosmetic companies began to sell powder in attractive compacts of less valuable metal or plastic. Collectors today search for Art Deco designs, commemorative compacts from World's Fairs or political events, and unusual examples. Many were made with companion lipsticks and other fittings.

Aluminum, Green Enamel, Embossed, Pug, Mirror, 1 ½ In. 34.00
Black Enamel, Diamond, Ribbed Case, 18K Gold, 3 ⅜ x 1 ⅞ In. 3437.00
Blue Guilloche Enamel, Silvertone, Flower Garland, Chain, 2 ⅝ In. 206.00
Brushed Copper, Bill Clip, Photo Slot, Cache, 3 x 4 In. 28.00
Chrome, 2-Tone, Applied Enamel Floral Disk, Engraved VY, Lipstick, Puffs, Chain, 3 In. 225.00
Coty, Goldtone Mesh, Envelope Style, Mirror, Puff, 3 ½ x 2 ¾ In. 66.00
Du Barry, Goldtone, Radiating Lines, Mirror, c.1960s, 1 ½ In. 19.00
Elgin American, Box, 4 ½ In. 75.00
Elgin American, Goldtone, Checkerboard Mother-Of-Pearl Lid, Puff, 2 ¾ x 2 ¼ In. 71.00
Elgin American, Goldtone, Rhinestone, Multicolored, Puff, Mirror, 2 ¾ x 2 ¼ In. 54.00
Elgin American Beauty, Clamshell, Ruffled Edges, 3 x 2 ¾ In. 45.00
Elizabeth Arden, Goldtone, Basket Weave, Mirror, 2 ¼ In. 30.00
Enamel, Courting Couple, Pastoral Landscape, Hinged, Continental, 2 ⅜ In. 200.00
Enamel, Silvertone, Scenic Lid, Women In Garden, Marked, Italy, 3 ¼ x 3 ½ In. 529.00
Estee Lauder, Chick, Yellow Crystals, Goldtone Dangling Feet, Mirror, 2 ¾ In. .... *illus* 375.00
Estee Lauder, Silver Plate, Empress Victoria, Perfume, Round, c.1979 .... 90.00
Evans, Chrome, Enamel, Mirror, Powder Pot, Premier, Austria, 3 x 2 ¼ In. 23.00
Evans, Goldtone, Enamel, Faux Pearls, Green Cabochon Stones, 2 ½ x 2 ¾ In. 107.00
Evans, Goldtone, Rhinestone, Purple, Pink, Yellow, Blue, Green, Mirror, Sifter, 3 x ¾ In. 78.00
Georg Jensen, Sterling Silver, 4 Squares, Ram's Head, Tulip, Daisy, Bird, Signed, 2 ½ In. 150.00
Goldtone, Grapes, Puff, Mirror, c.1950, 3 In. 35.00
Guilloche Enamel, Sterling Silver, Bird, 2 ½ x 1 ½ In. 1058.00
Hingeco, Tropical Scene, Rouge, Mirror, c.1920, 3 x 2 ⅛ In. 75.00
Houbigant, Flower Basket, Goldtone, 6-Sided, Marked Paris, New York, Mirror, 2 In. 42.00
Jade & Black Enamel, 14K Yellow Gold, Diamond, Filigree Center, Hinged, 2 ½ In. 748.00
Limoges, Porcelain, Flowers, Goldtone, Mesh, Screen, Puff, 3 In. 135.00
Max Factor, Goldtone, White Enamel Band, Scroll Design, Puff, 2 ¾ In. 38.00
Schuco, Monkey, Red, Head Fits Onto Lipstick Top, Mirror, Powder, 3 ½ In. 425.00
Silver, Enamel, Lovers, Pastoral Scene, Fluted Edges, Florence, c.1960, 4 In. 263.00
Silver, Engraved, Stripes, Monogram, Money Clip, Coin Holders, Mirror, 3 ¾ x 2 ½ In. 59.00
Silvertone, Enamel, Blue, Boat With Red Sails, Bird, Trees, Mirror, 2 Puffs, 2 ¼ In. 224.00
Sterling Silver, Engraved Swirl Design, 2 In. 40.00
Volupte, Mosaic Front & Back, Turquoise, Red, Gold, Mirror, Puff, 4 In. 35.00

CONSOLIDATED LAMP AND GLASS COMPANY of Coraopolis, Pennsylvania, was founded in 1894. The company made lamps, tablewares, and art glass. Collectors are particularly interested in the wares made after 1925, including black satin glass, Cosmos (listed in its own category in this book), Martele (which resembled Lalique), Ruba Rombic (1928–32 Art Deco line), and colored glasswares. Some Consolidated pieces are very similar to those made by the Phoenix Glass Company. The colors are sometimes different. Consolidated made Martele glass in blue, crystal, green, pink, white, or custard glass with added fired-on color or a satin finish. The company closed for the final time in 1967.

Berry Bowl, Dancing Nymph, French Crystal, 4 ½ In. 100.00
Bonbon, Ruba Rombic, Smoky Topaz, Handles, 3-Part, 8 In. .... *illus* 550.00
Bowl, Catalonian, Green, 8 ½ In. 40.00
Bowl, Swallows, Green Ceramic Wash, Martele, 9 In. 295.00
Candlestick, Catalonian, Jade Green 75.00
Creamer, Catalonian, Honey Yellow 65.00
Jug, Catalonian, Emerald Green, 6 ½ In. 150.00
Jug, Catalonian, Jade Green, Stopper, 6 ½ In. .... *illus* 285.00
Lamp, Parrot, Orange, Green, Brown Log, Threaded Black Base, 13 In. 300.00
Perfume Bottle, Ruba Rombic, Topaz, Stopper, 7 ¾ In., Pair .... *illus* 1100.00
Plate, Bread & Butter, Martele, Blue Ceramic Wash, 6 In. 110.00
Plate, Dancing Nymph, White Ceramic Wash, Polished Figures, 8 In. 165.00
Powder Box, Hummingbird, Roses, Leaves, 4 x 7 In. .... *illus* 300.00
Sherbet, Martele, Honey Ceramic Wash 135.00
Sugar, Catalonian, Jade Green 65.00
Tumbler, Catalonian, Jade Green, Footed, 10 Oz. 48.00

Tumbler, Dancing Nymph, Pink Satin, 5 ½ In. 265.00
Tumbler, Juice, Catalonian, Emerald Green, 7 Oz. 38.00
Vase, Catalonian, Green, Flared, 5 ½ In. 45.00
Vase, Catalonian, Jade Green, Fan Shape, 7 ½ In. 130.00
Vase, Catalonian, Jade Green, Pillow Shape, 6 In. 110.00
Vase, Dancing Nymph, White Ground, Flesh & Blue Trim, 11 ¾ In. 210.00
Vase, Fan, Martele, Jade Ceramic Wash, 6 ½ In. 245.00
Vase, Goldfish, Frosted Opalescent, Light Blue, Signed, 9 x 8 ½ x 4 In. 330.00
Vase, Katydid, White Ground, Brown & Blue Trim, 7 ¼ In. 100.00
Vase, Lovebird, Branches, Gold Trim, 11 In. . . . . *illus* 403.00
Vase, Lovebirds, Parakeets, French Crystal, 10 x 10 In. 225.00
Vase, Martele, Olives, French Crystal, 8 x 3 ½ In. 275.00
Vase, Martele, Pinecone, Blue Satin, 6 ½ In. 350.00
Vase, Sea Gull, Gold Trim, Custard Ground, 11 In. 130.00

CONTEMPORARY GLASS, *see Glass-Contemporary.*

COOKBOOKS are collected for various reasons. Some are wanted for the recipes, some for investment, and some as examples of advertising. Cookbooks and recipe pamphlets are included in this category.

Betty Crocker, Picture Cookbook, 5-Ring Notebook, 1st Edition, 1950, 463 Pages 135.00
Calumet, Happy Times Recipe Book, 1934, 23 Pages 5.00
Marshall Field, Taste Of Tradition, Soft Cover, Spiral Bound, 1985, 40 Pages 185.00
Pillsbury 2nd Grand National 100 Prize Winning Recipes, 1951 . . . . . 55.00
Royal Baking Powder Cookbook Recipes, 100 Recipes, 1932, 31 Pages 8.00

COOKIE JARS with brightly painted designs or amusing figural shapes became popular in the mid-1930s. Many companies made them and collectors search for cookie jars either by design or by maker's name. Listed here are examples by the less common makers. Major factories are listed under their own names in other categories of the book, such as Abingdon, Brush, Hull, McCoy, Metlox, Red Wing, and Shawnee. See also the Disneyana category.

Aunt Jemima, White Dress, Apron, 12 In. 351.00
Big Bird, Seated, Holding Cookie Jar, Marked, California Original 45.00
Black Chef, Dripping White Attire, NSCO, 10 In. 201.00
Christmas Tree, Marked, California Originals, 12 In. 150.00
Cooky, Black Chef, 22K Gold Trim, Pearl China Co., 10 In. 230.00
Cooky, Black Chef, Marked, Pearl Co., 11 In. 30.00
Dutch Girl, Blue, Pottery Guild, 11 ½ In. 70.00
Elf Head, Pointed Hat Cover, California Originals 132.00
Elsie The Cow, Pottery Guild, 12 In. 350.00
Flintstones, The Rubbles, Marked, American Bisque, c.1960, 9 ½ In. 225.00
Friar Tuck, Thou Shalt Not Steal, Twin Winton, 12 In. 23.00
Goldilocks, Regal China, 12 In. 99.00
Granny, Yellow Shawl, Embossed Flowers, Brayton Laguna 187.00
Keebler Elf, F & F, 9 In. 145.00
Little Red Riding Hood, Pottery Guild, 12 ¾ In. . . . . 62.00 to 117.00
Locomotive, Cookie R.R., American Bisque, 7 ¼ x 11 ¾ In. 33.75
Mammy, Brayton Laguna, 14 In. 275.00
Ms. Mouse, Pink & White Dress, Holding Teddy Bear, House Of Lloyd, 1990, 13 In. 18.00
Oscar, Green Hat, Robinson-Ransbottom Pottery, RRP, 10 In. 65.00
Pig, Pig Finial, Japan, 1979 . . . . . 20.00
Pot O' Cookies, Twin Winton, 1975 . . . . . 45.00
Spaceship, American Bisque, 12 ½ In. 127.00
Turtle, Sitting, Tan Glaze, California Originals, 12 In. 11.00
Walrus, Brown Glaze, Doranne Of California 23.00
Zero, Man's Head, Yellow & Red Hat, Peter Max, 1989, 8 ½ x 8 ½ x 4 In. 495.00

COORS ware was made by the Coors Porcelain Company of Golden, Colorado, a company founded with the help of the Coors Brewing Company. Its founder, John Herold, started the Herold China and Pottery Company in 1910. The company name was changed in 1920, when Herold left. Dishes were made from the turn of the century. Coors stopped making nonessential wares at the start of World War II. After the war, the pottery made ovenware, teapots, vases, and a general line of pottery, but no dinnerware—except for special orders. The company is still in business making industrial porcelain. For more prices, go to Kovels.com.

COORS
U.S.A.

Baker, Rosebud, Blue, 10 ⅞ x 7 ¼ In. 135.00

TIP
"Cold-painted" items like some glass and porcelain, especially cookie jars, should never be put in a dishwasher. Just wipe them with a damp cloth.

Consolidated, Powder Box, Hummingbird, Roses, Leaves, 4 x 7 In.
$300.00

Consolidated, Vase, Lovebird, Branches, Gold Trim, 11 In.
$403.00

TIP
If the cat or dog stains an antique rug, immediately use soda water to wipe it up. If urine penetrates the rug, it can cause permanent damage.

Copeland, Ewer,
Winged Woman Under Spout,
Vine Handle, Majolica, 14 In.
$348.00

Copper, Bowl, Water Lilies, Embossed, Flared, Verdigris Patina, Stamped, Jauchens, 3 x 12 In.
$960.00

Copper, Candle Mold, Pour Spouts, 12 x 12 In.
$250.00

Copper, Chafing Dish, Silver, Wood, Boar's Heads, Patina, Arts & Crafts, 12 x 16 In.
$600.00

Baker, Rosebud, Blue, Ink Mark, 11 ¼ In. 95.00
Batter Bowl, Rosebud, Blue, Handle, 8 In. .... 110.00 to 115.00
Batter Bowl, Rosebud, Orange, Handle, Ink Mark, 12 ¼ In. 165.00
Bowl, Pudding, Thermo-Porcelain, Open Window, 5 x 8 ½ In. 95.00
Cake Plate, Tulip, Thermo-Porcelain, Ink Mark, 11 In. 85.00
Casserole, Cover, Rosebud, Red, Triple, 2 Pt. 90.00
Casserole, Cover, Tulip Pattern, Triple Service, Thermo-Porcelain Ink Mark 95.00
Cookie Jar, Dusty Rose, White & Pink Flowers, Green Leaves, Stain Glaze, 10 In. 125.00
Cookie Jar, Rosebud, Red, 2 Handles, Die Marked 75.00
Eggcup, Rosebud, Orange, Ink Mark, 2 ⅞ In. 250.00
Loaf Pan, Rosebud, Red, 5 x 9 In. 50.00
Mixing Bowl, Rosebud, Yellow, 9 ¼ In. 100.00
Mug, Thermo-Porcelain, Ivory, High Gloss, White Interior, Ink Mark, 3 ¾ In. 25.00
Pitcher, Thermo-Porcelain, Cover, Tulip, Ink Mark, 8 In. 135.00
Plate, Rosebud, Red, Ink Mark, 6 In. 25.00
Plate, Rosebud, Red, Ink Mark, 7 In. 20.00
Platter, Rosebud, Yellow, Ink Mark, 13 ⅛ In. 70.00
Ramekin, Rosebud, Orange, Handle 75.00
Salt & Pepper, Thermo-Porcelain, Ivory, 4 ¾ In. 25.00
Serving Dish, Brown & White, Chefsware, High Gloss Glaze, Individual, 4 ¼ In. 23.00
Utility Jar, Cover, Rosebud, Yellow, Incised Mark 90.00
Vase, Blue & White, Art Deco Shape, Golden Colorado Ink Mark, 5 In. 90.00
Vase, Bud, Brown, Chefsware, Marked, 6 ⅝ In. 20.00
Vase, Light Turquoise Matte Glaze, Bulbous, 1930s, 8 x 7 In. 80.00
Vase, Yellow Matte Glaze, Bulbous, 1930s, 8 x 7 In. 80.00

COPELAND pieces listed here are those that have a mark including the word *Copeland* used between 1847 and 1976. Marks include *Copeland Spode* and *Copeland & Garrett*. See also Copeland Spode and Royal Worcester.

Bust, Mother, R. Monti, Waisted Round Socle, Pedestal Base, Parian, c.1871, 14 In. 1304.00
Butter Chip, Pansy, Yellow & Cobalt Blue, Majolica 104.00
Butter Chip, Pansy, Yellow & Purple, Majolica 92.00
Candelabrum, 4-Light, Figural, Scrolling Arms, Columnar Base, 3 Seated Putti, 18 In., Pair. 840.00
Cup & Saucer, Paneled, Flowers, Green Reserve, Gilt, England, 5 ½ In. 48.00
Ewer, Winged Woman Under Spout, Vine Handle, Majolica, 14 In. .... *illus* 348.00
Figurine, Girl, Playing Cymbals, c.1890, 7 In. 25.00
Jug, Lady In Shell Riding Dolphins, Lady In Clouds, Grapevines, Footed, Majolica, 10 In. 345.00
Plate, Center Boar, Latin Motto Banner, Beige, Gilt, Blue Mark, England, c.1890, 9 In., 6 Piece. 345.00
Platter, Well & Tree, Blue Transfer, 19th Century, 17 x 20 ¾ In. 80.00
Wall Shelf, Leaves, Vines, Yellow Border, Fan Shape, Majolica, 7 x 8 ½ In. 518.00

COPELAND SPODE appears on some pieces of nineteenth-century English porcelain. Josiah Spode established a pottery at Stoke-on-Trent, England, in 1770. In 1833, the firm was purchased by William Copeland and Thomas Garrett and the mark was changed. In 1847, Copeland became the sole owner and the mark changed again. W.T. Copeland & Sons continued until a 1976 merger when it became Royal Worcester Spode. Pieces are listed in this book under the name that appears in the mark. Copeland Spode, Copeland, and Royal Worcester have separate listings.

COPELAND SPODE ENGLAND

Pitcher, Raised Hunt Scene, Blue, 7 In. 110.00
Pitcher, Windsor Ship, Built 1857, 7 In. 22.00
Pitcher & Bowl, Green Flowers, Basket, 8-Sided Bowl, 8 ½-In. Pitcher 33.00
Plate, Dinner, Yellow Ground, Flower Bouquet & Border, 10 ¾ In., 12 Piece 561.00
Plate, Gilt Lattice Band, Floret Border, Powder Blue Ground, Mark, 1900s, 9 In., 6 Piece. 178.00
Plate, White, Basket Weave, Scalloped Edge, 10 ½ In. 160.00
Platter, Bridge, Water, Landscape, Blue, White, Signed, 19th Century, 7 x 13 ½ In. 200.00
Platter, Camilla, Pink Transfer, 16 ½ x 12 ¾ In. 350.00
Platter, Fish On Riverbed, Green, Beige, Oval, 18 In. 22.00
Saucer, Italian, Blue Transfer, 6 ½ In. 25.00
Soup, Dish, Tudor, Fruit & Flower Center, Scalloped Edge, Basket Weave, 9 In. 36.00

COPPER has been used to make utilitarian items, such as teakettles and cooking pans, since the days of the early American colonists. Copper became a popular metal with the Arts & Crafts makers of the early 1900s, and decorative pieces, like desk sets, were made. Other pieces of copper may be found in Arts & Crafts, Bradley & Hubbard, Kitchen, Roycroft, and other categories.

Ale Warmer, 4 ½ x 10 ½ x 3 ⅞ In. 85.00
Ash Box, Brass, Form Fitting Lid, Urn Finial, Brass Feet, Brass Tongs, 1700s, 16 & 12 In. 230.00

Ashtray, Cowboy Hat, Polished, 1950s, 3 x 6 In. . . . 12.00
Bowl, Geometric, Footed, 3 ¾ x 11 In. . . . 1440.00
Bowl, Hammered, Handle, 10 x 20 In. . . . 2760.00
Bowl, Hammered, Patina, Signed, Kalo, 2 x 7 In. . . . 290.00
Bowl, Hammered, Square, Crimped Corners, Rolled Edge, Craftsman, Anvil Mark, 1910, 8 In. 40.00
Bowl, Patina, F. Novick, 2 ¾ x 7 ½ In. . . . 465.00
Bowl, Water Lilies, Embossed, Flared, Verdigris Patina, Stamped, Jauchens, 3 x 12 In. . . *illus* 960.00
Box, Hammered, Brass Footed, Applied Gilt Metal Wreaths, Birds, Cherubs, 4 ½ x 7 ½ In. . . . 325.00
Bucket, Apple Butter, Dovetailed, Handle, 16 x 25 In. . . . 260.00
Bucket, Bail Handle, 18 In. . . . 40.00
Bucket, Swing Handle, 14 x 18 In. . . . 292.00
Candle Box, Pierced, Hanging, Round, 19th Century . . . 495.00
Candle Mold, Pour Spouts, 12 x 12 In. . . . *illus* 250.00
Chafing Dish, Silver, Wood, Boar's Heads, Patina, Arts & Crafts, 12 x 16 In. . . . *illus* 600.00
Cigarette Box, Hammered, 5 x 7 ½ x 5 ½ In. . . . 2400.00
Coffeepot, Dovetailed, England, c.1750 . . . 185.00
Coffeepot, Stopper, Saracenic Shape, Silver Repousse Flower Band, Gorham, 1881, 13 In. . . . 2032.00
Coffeepot, Turkish Style, Silver Sunflowers Band, Gorham, c.1875, 13 ¼ In. . . . 1320.00
Cooking Pot, Double Handle, 12 In. . . . 47.00
Desk Set, Gilt, Semiprecious Stones, Chinese, 19th Century, 13 ¼ In. . . . 1422.00
Dessert Mold, Steel Suspension Ring, France, 20th Century, 4 ½ x 11 ¼ In. . . . 360.00
Dipper, Stamped, J.S. Cropley, 19th Century, 4 ¾ x 12 ¾ In. . . . 146.00
Ewer, Flowers, 3 Figures, Pine, Bamboo, Prunus, Heraldic Emblems, Japan, 21 In. . . . 474.00
Figure, Buddha, Seated, India, 10 ¾ In. . . . 152.00
Figure, Egg, Cigar Caddy, Cloven Brass Feet, Finial Mount On Lid, 6 x 9 In. . . . 193.00
Figurine, Dog's Head, Signed, E. Kemeys, 6 ½ x 6 In. . . . 850.00
Fire Starter, Hammered, Iron Handle, Old Mission, Kopperkraft, 8 ¾ x 8 ¼ In. . . . 120.00
Jardiniere, Hammered, 2 Handles, Embossed, Stickley Bros., 5 x 11 ½ In. . . . 960.00
Jardiniere, Hammered, Embossed Trees, Flowers, Stickley Bros., 11 x 17 In. . . . 2640.00
Kettle, Apple Butter, Hammered, Handle, 19th Century, 20 x 28 In. . . . 150.00
Kettle, Apple Butter, Handle, 19th Century, 14 ½ x 20 In. . . . 205.00
Kettle, Apple Butter, Handle, 19th Century, 18 x 29 In. . . . 234.00
Kettle, Apple Butter, Iron Bail Handle, c.1850, 15 x 23 In. . . . 205.00
Kettle, Apple Butter, Iron Stand . . . *illus* 502.00
Kettle, Hot Water, Brass, Gooseneck Spout, Riveted Handle, Dovetail Seams, England, 12 In. . 230.00
Kettle, Iron Bail Handle, 19th Century, 12 x 18 ½ In. . . . 234.00
Kettle, Square Handles, 7 ¾ x 10 In. . . . 85.00
Kettle, Stand, WMF, Cutout Base, Brass Frame, 13 x 16 In. . . . 270.00
Kettle, Steel Bail Handle, 24 ½ In. . . . 468.00
Kettle, Water, 13 x 14 In. . . . 70.00
Ladle, Lip, Wood Side Handle, 4 Aperture, 8 x 13 ½ In. . . . 210.00
Mixing Bowl, Brass Handle, Tripod Iron Stand, Early 20th Century, 17 ½ x 18 ½ In. . . . 1020.00
Molds are listed in the Kitchen category.
Pail, Slanted Sides, Bail Handle, 11 x 12 In. . . . 47.00
Pan, Brewery, c.1880, 7 x 31 x 21 ½ In. . . . 275.00
Pan, Lid, Iron Handle, Marked, L.F.D. & H., 10 In. . . . 117.00
Panel, Mask Ritual, Hand Hammered Relief, Signed, G. Ridley, 30 x 78 In. . . . 4600.00
Pedestal, Neoclassical Style, Wood, Late 19th Century, 31 ⅝ In. . . . 956.00
Pitcher, Delft Bail Handle, 21 x 11 In. . . . 47.00
Pitcher, Lobed Embossed Flowers, Brass Applied Feet, Mexico, 2 In. . . . 47.00
Pitcher, Pressed Design, Loop Handle, 20 x 11 In. . . . 59.00
Planter, Circles, Lobes, Lion Ring Handles, 13 ¼ x 15 In. . . . 110.00
Plate, Red, Leaf Shape, Chinese, 19th Century, 6 ¾ In. . . . 1007.00
Pot, Cylindrical, Cover, Handles, 24 x 23 In. . . . 176.00
Pot, Dovetail Construction, Graduated Sizes, 4 ½ To 10 In., 6 Piece . . . 374.00
Pot, Fish Cooker, Lid, Dovetailed, Iron Handle, 19th Century, 7 x 12 ½ In. . . . *illus* 359.00
Rack, Pot, 12 x 42 x 18 In. . . . 40.00
Saucepan, 6 ½ x 8 ¾ In. . . . 10.00
Sconce, Hammered, Bobeches Lotus Flowers, 12 ½ x 3 ½ In., Pair . . . 1320.00
Scuttle, Brass Paw Feet, Tripod, Lion's Head Rings, Engraved Flowers, 19th Century, 18 In. . . 545.00
Sprayer, Exterminator, 1920-40 . . . 20.00
Stein, Scene From Kiev, Khemelnitsky On Horse, Boat Scene On Back, Verse, Russia, ½ Liter. . 920.00
Tea Urn, Brass, Steel, Ebonized Wood Mounted, England, Early 20th Century, 22 x 12 ½ In. . 201.00
Tea Urn, Steel, Brass, Ebonized Wood Mounted, Early 20th Century, 18 x 14 ½ In. . . . 259.00
Teakettle, Dovetailed, Acorn Finial, Stamped, Signed, C. Wampler, 13 x 14 In. . . . 1300.00
Teakettle, Dovetailed, Swing Handle, Brass Finial, W. Heyser, Chambersburg, 6 ½ In. . . . *illus* 3408.00

Copper, Kettle,
Apple Butter, Iron Stand
$502.00

Copper, Pot, Fish Cooker, Lid,
Dovetailed, Iron Handle,
19th Century, 7 x 12 ½ In.
$359.00

Copper, Teakettle, Dovetailed, Swing
Handle, Brass Finial, W. Heyser,
Chambersburg, 6 1/2 In.
$3408.00

TIP
Try the old-time recipe for cleaning copper. Mix lemon juice or vinegar with salt and use as a metal polish.

Coralene, Pitcher, Pink Satin, Yellow Seaweed, White Handle, 9 ½ In. $630.00

Coralene, Vase, Raspberry To White, White Cased Interior, Applied Seaweed, 7 ½ In. $224.00

TIP
To remove a glass stopper stuck in a narrow-necked perfume bottle or decanter, put the bottle in warm water, then gradually add hot water and gently try to loosen the stopper.

Teakettle, Gooseneck, Bail Handle, Richardson Winchester, 8 Qt. 4675.00
Teakettle, Gooseneck, Dome Lid, Dovetailed, Signed, North Drefs 13, 9 ½ x 11 In. 55.00
Teakettle, Gooseneck, Dome Lid, Drum Form, Swing Handle, 11 ½ In. 575.00
Teakettle, Iron Trivet, 3-Footed, 8 & 9 ¾ x 4 In. 470.00
Teakettle, Ship Board, Dovetailed, Sailcloth Cover, 9 ½ In. 575.00
Teakettle, Star Design On Handle, 19th Century, 6 ¾ In. 2223.00
Teapot, Gooseneck, Dovetailed Bottom, W. Heyser, Pa., c.1820, 10 x 11 In. 1215.00
Tray, Cutout Handles, Gustav Stickley, c.1905, 20 ½ In. 9375.00
Tray, Hammered, G. Stickley, Patina, 13 In. Diam. 1070.00
Tray, Hammered, Oval, Handles, Patina, Marked, G. Stickley, 23 In. 1470.00 to 1970.00
Tray, Hammered, Raised Spade, 15 In. 4800.00
Tray, Impressed, Gustav Stickley, c.1905, 20 ¾ In. 9375.00
Umbrella Stand, Hammered, Arts & Crafts, G. Stickley, 16 ¾ x 10 ½ In. 630.00
Umbrella Stand, Hammered, Square, Footed, c.1900, 28 In. 234.00
Urn, Romanov Imperial Crest, Handles, Weighted Base, 21 x 15 x 13 In. 100.00
Vase, 2 Applied Handles, Original Patina, Stickley Bros., 12 x 8 In. 390.00
Vase, Iron, 2 Handles, Gustav Stickley, c.1905, 7 ⅝ x 10 ⅝ In. 3750.00
Vase, Ruffled Rim, Applied Metal Birds, Plants, Gorham, c.1880, 3 ½ x 4 In. 657.00
Warming Tray, Scalloped Cover, Galleried Base, 3 Lamps, 24 x 9 ½ In. 47.00
Washer, Salesman's Sample, Paramount Steam Washer Co., Pat. Aug.11, 1825, 8 x 8 In. 385.00
Washing Machine, Steam, Crank Style, Paramount, Pat. 1916, 20 In. 175.00
Water Tank, Arts & Crafts, Porcelain Spout 100.00

COPPER LUSTER *items are listed in the Luster category.*

CORALENE glass was made by firing many small colored beads on the outside of glassware. It was made in many patterns in the United States and Europe in the 1880s. Reproductions are made today. Coralene-decorated Japanese pottery is listed in the Japanese Coralene category.

Atomizer, Blue Satin Ground, Gold Swirl Design, 2 ¾ x 6 In. 300.00
Atomizer, White Satin, Cased, Dots, Ball Shape, DeVilbiss, 5 ½ In. 100.00
Basket, White Satin Ground, Enameled Daisies, Ruffled Edge, 8 ¼ x 4 ⅜ In. 55.00
Compote, Pansy, Lavender Luster Ground, Gold Accents, Cutout Edge, Footed, 5 x 8 In. 48.00
Cruet, Shaded To Pink, Yellow Beads, Applied Handle, Stopper, 7 ¾ In. 750.00
Pitcher, Pink Satin, Yellow Seaweed, White Handle, 9 ½ In. *illus* 630.00
Tumbler, Clear, Cranberry Glass Rim, Satin, Gold Leaves, Blue Dots, 4 In. 75.00
Tumbler, Cranberry Glass, Thumbprint, Bird, Flowers, c.1900, 2 ¾ In. 145.00
Tumbler, Whiskey, Cranberry, Green & White Enameled Leaves, Flowers, 2 ¾ x 2 In. 55.00
Vase, Beaded Chrysanthemums, Melon Ribbed, Satin, Handles, 10 In. 2300.00
Vase, Blue Satin, Diamond Quilted, Yellow Beading, Fleur-De-Lis, c.1900, 5 x 3 In. 375.00
Vase, Blue Satin, Seaweed, Coral, Yellow Flowers, c.1900, 9 x 5 In. 975.00
Vase, Bulbous, Turquoise Satin, Clear Handles, 6 ¾ x 6 ½ In. 1100.00
Vase, Raspberry To White, White Cased Interior, Applied Seaweed, 7 ½ In. *illus* 224.00
Vase, Rose, Blue Bristol, 7 ¾ In. 40.00
Vase, White To Pink Satin, Bulbous, Flared Straight Neck, c.1870, 4 x 5 In. 295.00
Vase, White To Pink Satin, Gold Flowers, Leaves, Bulbous Base, 2 ½ x 6 In. 275.00
Wall Pocket, Butterfly, Milk Glass, Deep Blue, Coral, c.1900, 5 In. 295.00

CORKSCREWS have been needed since the first bottle was sealed with a cork, probably in the seventeenth century. Today collectors search for the early, unusual patented examples or the figural corkscrews of recent years.

Butterscotch Bakelite Wood Handle, 1950s, 3 ⅝ In. 10.00
Chef, Bone, Carved, 5 In. 55.00
Dog, Scottie, Wood, Googly Eyes, Art Deco, 4 ½ In. 17.00
Lady's Leg, Yellow, Green Stripes, Celluloid, Folding, Germany, 2 ¾ In. Closed 330.00
Marbled Brown & Amber, Bakelite Handle, 1950s, 5 x 3 ½ In. 12.00
Rosewood Handle, Ivory Ends, Iron, 19th Century 55.00

CORONATION souvenirs have been made since the 1800s. Pottery, glass, tin, silver, and paper objects with a picture of the monarchs and date have been sold at many coronations. The pieces that mention King Edward VIII, the king who was never crowned, are not rare; collectors should be sure to check values before buying. Related pieces are found in the Commemorative category.

Bank, King George V & Queen Mary, Flags, Iron, Sydenham & McOustra, c.1911, 7 In. 425.00
Beaker, Emperor Nicholas II, Alexandra Fedorovna, Portraits, Crown, Arms, 1896, 5 In. 800.00
Beaker, Queen Elizabeth II, Portrait, Flags, Belt Logo, June 2nd, 1953, 4 ⅛ In. 70.00

Beaker, Tsar Nicholas II, Enameled, Russia, c.1896, 4 In. . . . . *illus* 472.00
Biscuit Tin, H.R.H. Queen Elizabeth, Gray Dunn, Hinged Lid, 8-Sided, 1953, 5 x 5 ½ In.. . . . . 20.00
Biscuit Tin, King George VI & Queen Elizabeth, 1937, 5 ¼ In. 75.00
Bowl, King Edward VIII, Profile Portrait In Center, Wedgwood, 1937, 4 ¼ x 10 In. 125.00
Compact, King George IV, 1937. . . . . 65.00
Cup & Saucer, Queen Elizabeth II, Flowers, Blue Letters, Aynsley 99.00
Doll, Queen Elizabeth II, Her Majesty In State Robes, Peggy Nisbet, 8 In. . . . . *illus* 32.00
Horse Brass, King George V & Queen Mary, 1911, 4 x 3 In. 28.00
Mug, King Edward VII, Crowning Of King & Queen, Flag, Flowers, 1902 . . . . 145.00
Mug, King Edward VII & Queen Alexandra, 1802, 3 In. 165.00
Mug, King George V & Queen Mary, Late Foley, Shelley China, England, 1911, 2 ¾ In.. . . . . . . 128.00
Mug, King George VI & Queen Elizabeth, May 12 1937, Aynsley China, 3 In. 16.50
Perpetual Calendar, Queen Elizabeth II, 1953. . . . . 45.00
Plate, Edward VII, Portrait Center, 1902, 8 ½ In. 125.00
Plate, Elizabeth II, Clarice Cliff, Confederation Series, Canada, 1953, 10 ⅝ In.. . . . . 90.00
Plate, George V & Queen Mary, Ox Roasted At Idle, Green, White, 1911, 7 ¾ In. 145.00
Plate, H.R.H. Queen Elizabeth II, Portland, c.1953, 10 In. 23.00
Plate, King Edward VII & Queen Alex, 1902 . . . . 100.00
Plate, King Edward VIII, May 12th, 1937, Chelsea, 5 In. 22.00
Plate, King George V & Queen Mary, Ox Roasting On Spit, White, Blue Letters, 10 In. 65.00
Plate, King George V & Queen Mary, Portraits, 1911 . . . . 95.00
Plate, King George VI, Queen Elizabeth, Portraits, c.1930, 10 In. 175.00
Plate, King George VI & Queen Elizabeth, Image In Center, 1939, 4 ½ In.. . . . . 45.00
Plate, Queen Elizabeth II, Sepia Transfer, Clarice Cliff, 1953, 10 ⅝ In. 148.00
Salt & Pepper, Queen Elizabeth, Milk Glass, Triangular, Metal Screw-Off Lids, 1953, 3 In. . . . 35.00
Spoon, Anointing, Queen Elizabeth II, Silver, Portrait, Hallmark, 1953, 4 ½ In.. . . . . 110.00
Teapot, King Edward VII, Portraits, Flags, 6 ¼ In. 22.00
Tin, George V & Queen Mary, City Of Bristol, L.S. Fry & Sons, 6 x 3 ¾ In. 198.00
Tin, George VI & Queen Elizabeth, Portraits, Orange, Silver, 6 x 3 ½ In. 98.00
Tin, King Edward VII, Queen Alexandra, June 26, 1902, Rowntree Co. 17.00
Vase, Queen Mary, White, Portrait, Porcelain, 2 Handles, 2 In. 12.00

COSMOS is a pressed milk glass pattern with colored flowers made from 1894 to 1915 by the Consolidated Lamp and Glass Company. Tablewares and lamps were made in this pattern. A few pieces were also made of clear glass with painted decorations. Other glass patterns are listed under Consolidated Lamp and also in various glass categories. In later years, Cosmos was also made by the Westmoreland Glass Company.

Butter, Cover, 1890s 35.00
Condiment Set, 3 Jars, Stand, 1890s 85.00
Lamp, Oil, Yellow Cased Glass, 7 ½ In. . . . . *illus* 250.00

COVERLETS were made of linen or wool during the nineteenth century. Most of the coverlets date from 1800 to the 1880s. There was a revival of hand weaving in the 1920s and new coverlets, especially geometric patterns, were made. The earliest coverlets were made on narrow looms, so two woven strips were joined together and a seam can be found. The weave structures of coverlets can include summer and winter, double weave, overshot, and others. Jacquard coverlets have elaborate pictorial patterns that are made on a special loom or with the use of a special attachment. Quilts are listed in this book in their own category.

Cotton, Homespun Checked Blue & White Plaid, Buttons, 70 x 58 In. 187.00
Homespun, Brown & White Plaid, 74 x 60 In. 2530.00
Jacquard, Bird & Swag Border, Fringe, Wool, Cotton, Mathias Klein, 82 x 97 In. 940.00
Jacquard, Blue, Green, White, Michael Umbarger, Middle Paxton Twp., 1841, 83 x 73 In.. . . . 410.00
Jacquard, Blue & Red, D. Cosley Xenia, Greene Co., Ohio, 1851, 87 x 82 In. . . . . *illus* 527.00
Jacquard, Blue & White, 4 Blocks, Birds, Animals, Catherine Terheum Retan, c.1833, 71 x 93 In. 978.00
Jacquard, Blue & White, Flower Urns, Birds, Cityscape Border, 86 x 72 In. 44.00
Jacquard, Blue & White, Geometric, Flowers, Fringe, 90 x 82 In. 330.00
Jacquard, Blue Wood, Natural Cotton, L. Baker, c.1851, 74 x 90 In.. . . . . 288.00
Jacquard, Brown, White, Pagoda Border, c.1840, 68 x 74 In. 351.00
Jacquard, Double Weave, Wool, Cotton, Eagle Corner, Samuel Graham, c.1850, 82 x 92 In. . . 588.00
Jacquard, Double Weave, Wool, Cotton, Flower Cornucopias, Courthouse Logo, 1852, 84 x 92 In. 176.00
Jacquard, Double Weave, Wool, Cotton, Heart Design, Eagle Border, Lydia Spier 1836, 83 x 96 In. 235.00
Jacquard, Gray, Cream, Squares, Pine Tree Border, Late 1800s, 96 x 73 In.. . . . . 275.00
Jacquard, Green, Black, White, Wool, Cotton, Fringe, Signed, J.G. Weaver, 1837, 86 x 82 In. . . 470.00
Jacquard, Red, Blue, Green, Burgundy, Capitol, Flags, Wool, Cotton, 1876, 83 x 75 In. 708.00
Jacquard, Red, Blue, Green, Geometric, Wool, Natural Cotton, 80 x 102 In. 288.00

Coronation, Beaker, Tsar Nicholas II, Enameled, Russia, c.1896, 4 In.
$472.00

Coronation, Doll, Queen Elizabeth II, Her Majesty In State Robes, Peggy Nisbet, 8 In.
$32.00

Cosmos, Lamp, Oil, Yellow Cased Glass, 7 ½ In.
$250.00

TIP

Coverlets made before the 1830s were done on a loom that was no more than 40 inches wide. Old coverlets are made of two panels joined at the center seam.

Coverlet, Jacquard, Blue & Red, D. Cosley Xenia, Greene Co., Ohio, 1851, 87 x 82 In.
$527.00

Coverlet, Jacquard, Red, Blue, Green, Tulips, Roses, J. Brosey, F. Kenney, 1841, 104 x 88 In.
$1650.00

Coverlet, Jacquard, Red, Yellow, Green, Geometrics, Wm. Ney, Myerstown, Pa., 82 x 84 In.
$275.00

Jacquard, Red, Blue, Green, Tulips, Roses, J. Brosey, F. Kenney, 1841, 104 x 88 In. . . . . . *illus* 1650.00
Jacquard, Red, Blue, Green, White, Henry Brehm Womelsdorf, E. Knol, 1836, 92 x 82 In. 585.00
Jacquard, Red, Blue, Green, Wool, Natural Cotton, John Sutherland, 74 x 92 In. 201.00
Jacquard, Red, Green, Beige, U.S. Presidents Border, c.1840, 86 x 87 In. 2106.00
Jacquard, Red, Green, Blue, Geometric, Flowers, Birds, Fringe, 1834, 90 x 82 In. 440.00
Jacquard, Red, Peacocks On Grapevines, Wool, Cotton, 4 Corner Blocks, 1840, 86 x 93 In. . . . 206.00
Jacquard, Red, White, Blue, Black, Washington Busts, American Eagles, 1871, 71 x 84 In. . . . 183.00
Jacquard, Red, White, Blue, Green, Black, 4 Geo. Washington Busts, 1871, 71 x 84 In. 502.00
Jacquard, Red, Yellow, Green, Geometrics, Wm. Ney, Myerstown, Pa., 82 x 84 In. . . . . . . *illus* 275.00
Jacquard, Red & Blue, Tulip, Wool, Natural Cotton, Sarah Bowman, c.1860, 71 x 93 In. 201.00
Jacquard, Red & Green, Center Sun, Leaves, Wool, c.1850, 84 x 91 In. 118.00
Overshot, Olive, Blue, Maroon, Geometric, Fringe, Early 19th Century, 97 x 84 In. 880.00
Overshot, Red, Blue, Green, Wool, Natural Cotton, 2 Panel, Mid 1800s, 80 x 84 In. 147.00
Summer & Winter, Blue & White, Geometric Tree Borders, Wool, Cotton, c.1800, 94 x 76 In. 295.00
Trapunto, Center Diamond, Feather Pattern, Fringe, Cotton, Linen, 102 x 62 In. 748.00
Wool, Cotton, Peacock, Allover Flowers, Red, Blue, Green, 83 x 81 In. 469.00
Yellow, Red, Green, 3 Fringed Sides, Star, Geometric, Leaf, Grape, Names, 94 x 88 In. 154.00

COWAN POTTERY made art pottery and wares for florists. Guy Cowan made pottery in Rocky River, Ohio, a suburb of Cleveland, from 1913 to 1931. A stylized mark with the word *Cowan* was used on most pieces. A commercial, mass-produced line was marked *Lakeware*. Collectors today search for the Art Deco pieces by Guy Cowan, Viktor Schreckengost, Waylande Gregory, or Thelma Frazier Winter.

Bookend, Elephant, Semigloss Black Glaze, Margaret Postgate, 7 ¼ In. 805.00
Bookend, Pelican, Children Kneeling, Semigloss, Crackle Glaze, 5 ¼ In. 1150.00
Bowl, Marigold, Handles, Impressed Logo, 11 ½ In. 33.00
Bowl, Pterodactyl, Lapis Blue, Green Interior, 17 In. 121.00
Box, Cover, Parrot Finial, Mother-Of-Pearl Glaze, 5 In. 460.00
Bust, African Head, Black, Bronze Glaze, Waylande Gregory, 14 ¾ In. 4485.00
Candelabrum, Angel, Egyptian Blue Glaze, 9 In. 403.00
Candleholder, 4-Footed, Ivory, 2 x 3 In., Pair 55.00
Candleholder, Seahorse Stem, Ivory, 4 x 4 In., Pair 65.00
Decanter, Stopper, Plum Glaze, 10 ⅜ In. 219.00
Figurine, Bird, Egyptian Blue Glaze, 8 ¼ In. 690.00
Figurine, Woman, Standing, Ivory Glaze, 8 ⅛ In. 489.00
Flower Frog, Dancer, Original Ivory, Scarf, 7 In. 230.00
Flower Frog, Duet, 2 Woman Dancing, Ivory Glaze, 8 In. 259.00
Flower Frog, Female Figure, Dancing, White, Marked, 12 In. 465.00
Flower Frog, Heavenward, Woman, Reaching Up, Ivory Glaze, 8 In. 431.00
Flower Frog, Nude Woman, Kneeling, 6 ¼ In. 484.00
Flower Frog, Steer, Terra-Cotta Glaze, Waylande Gregory, 8 ½ In. 431.00
Flower Frog, Swirl, Ivory Glaze, 9 ⅞ In. 460.00
Humidor, Oriental Red, Impressed, 6 In. 205.00
Jar, Cover, Feu Rouge Glaze, Handles, Impressed Mark, 1930, 8 ½ x 8 In. . . . . *illus* 385.00
Jar, Leaves, Parchment Green, Impressed Logo, 6 ¾ x 5 In. 187.00
Mustard Pot, Sterling Silver Lid, Ivory Finial, Spoon, Marked, France, RGC, 1909, 4 x 3 In. . . 3300.00
Tile, Fish Tea, Multicolored, Thelma Frazier, 6 ⅜ In. 345.00
Vase, Apple Blossom Pink, 7 x 4 In. 125.00
Vase, Black Matte Glaze, Semigloss, Silver Panels, Waylande Gregory, 7 ¾ In. 489.00
Vase, Chinese Dragon, Melon Green Glaze, Impressed Mark, 11 ⅜ x 7 ¾ In. . . . . *illus* 220.00
Vase, Melon Green Over Black Engobe, Whitney Atchley, 6 ⅛ In. 805.00
Vase, Seahorse, Apple Blossom Pink, Fan, Footed, 7 In. 44.00

CRACKER JACK, the molasses-flavored popcorn mixture, was first made in 1896 in Chicago, Illinois. A prize was added to each box in 1912. Collectors search for the old boxes, toys, and advertising materials. Many of the toys are unmarked.

Book, Ben Grows Up, Ben Franklin, As Boy, Flying Kite 7.00
Charm, Dog, Scottie, Black Paint, White, Celluloid, Japan, 1930s, ¾ x ⅞ In. 10.00
Charm, Donkey, Celluloid, Metal Ring For Hanging, Japan, 1 In. 10.00
Charm, Kewpie, Pink, Celluloid, Metal Hanging Ring At Top, Japan, ⅞ x ⅝ In. 20.00
Charm, Roller Skate, High Top Shoe On Skate, Wheelsware, Copper, Japan, 1920-30. . . . . 15.00
Mug, Sailor Jack & Bingo, Marked U.S.A., 1950-60, 3 ⅝ In. 45.00
Tin, Cocoanut Corn Crisp, 8 ½ x 5 ½ In. 10.00
Toy, Buffalo, Standing, Plastic, Red, 1940s, 1 ⅝ In. 10.00
Toy, Cart, Yellow, Green, Tin, 2-Wheels, 1 ½ x 1 ½ x 1 ¼ In. 20.00

Toy, Goat, Standing, Plastic, Marbleized Orange, 1940s, 1 ⅜ In. . . . 7.00
Toy, Harmonica, Light Blue, Logo, 1950s, ½ x 1 x 5⁄16 In. . . . 12.00
Toy, Man Shooting Basketball Through Hoop, Cardboard, 2 Metal Balls, 1 ¼ In. . . . 15.00
Toy, Oriental Man, With Basket, Hollow Back, 1950s, 2 In. . . . 8.00
Toy, Pinball Game, Money Tree, Purple Tree Green Background. . . . 15.00
Toy, Pinball Game, Road Runner . . . 12.00
Toy, Pocket Watch, Cracker Jack Face, Tin, Metal Tab, 1920-30, 1 ⅞ In. . . . 29.00
Toy, Prize Card, Boy Eats Cracker Jacks, Mechanical, Cardboard, 2 x 3 In. . . . 135.00
Toy, Rain Car, Cast Metal, 1920s, 1 In. . . . 45.00
Toy, Sports Car, 2-Seater, Tin, Light Blue, 1930s, 2 In. . . . 45.00
Toy, Sulky, Doll's, Metal, Wood Handle, 1930s, 4 ½ x 1 ½ In. . . . 45.00
Toy, Tiny Tattoos, Stars, Purple Ground . . . 9.00
Toy, Toonerville Trolley, Tin Lithograph, Germany, 1 ¾ In. . . . 200.00
Toy, Top, Always On Top, World's Famous Confection, Metal, Red, White, Blue, Box . . . 25.00
Toy, Truck, Cracker Jack Box, Green, Yellow, Mid 1930s, 8 In. . . . 345.00

CRACKLE GLASS was originally made by the Venetians, but most of the ware found today dates from the 1800s. The glass was heated, cooled, and refired so that many small lines appeared inside the glass. It was made in many factories in the United States and Europe.

Basket, Green, Kanawha, 4 x 4 x 3 ¼ In. . . . 25.00
Candy Jar, Iridescent Body, Smoky Blue Finial & Base, 8 ¼ x 4 In. . . . 70.00
Decanter, Clear, 9 x 6 ¼ In. . . . 65.00
Pitcher, Clear, Applied Coiled Cranberry Glass Snake, Gold Enameled, 1895, 12 ½ In. . . . 695.00
Pitcher, Clear Applied Handle, Pilgrim Glass Co., 4 In. . . . 28.00
Vase, Chartreuse, Goblet Shape, Tapered Sides, 1930s, 13 In. . . . 125.00

CRANBERRY GLASS is an almost transparent yellow-red glass. It resembles the color of cranberry juice. The glass has been made in Europe and America since the Civil War. It is still being made, and reproductions can fool the unwary. Related glass items may be listed in other categories, such as Northwood, Rubina Verde, etc.

Basket, Swirled Ribs, Gold Enameled, Handle, Rim, 6 In. . . . 403.00
Bowl, Centerpiece, Honey, Daisy & Button, Oval, 8 x 10 In. . . . 234.00
Bowl, Oval, Flowers, Footed, Marked, 4 x 6 ½ In. . . . 125.00
Bowl, White Opalescent Ribs, Ruffled Rim, 4 ¼ x 10 ⅝ In. . . . 88.00
Candlestick, Brass Sockets, Bases, 8 ½ In., Pair . . . 403.00
Cordial Set, Flowers, Etched, 8-In. Decanter, 5 Piece . . . 94.00
Decanter, Dimple, Flowers, Rosettes, Footed, 3-Sided, Stopper, 10 ¼ In. . . . 120.00
Dresser Box, Cover, Gold & White Enameled, Metal Holder, 4-Footed, 1890, 4 In. . . . 285.00
Epergne, 3-Lily, Ruffled Rim, Clear Arms, Hanging Baskets, 24 In. . . . 489.00
Lamp, Enameled Flowers, Prisms, Electrified, 29 ½ In., Pair . . . 2714.00
Lamp, Peg, Gilt Bronze, Enameled, 1880s, 17 ½ In. . . . 708.00
Lamp, White Enamel, 9 ¾ In. . . . 173.00
Match Holder, Ruffled Edge, Brass, Handle, 1880s, 3 x 1 ¾ In. . . . 411.00
Perfumer Burner, Scalloped Bowl, 2 Clear Beakers, Brass Frame, Base, 10 x 10 In. . . . 2970.00
Pitcher, Hobnail, Oval, Square Mouth, Applied Clear Handle, Hobbs, Brockunier, 8 In. . . . 201.00
Pitcher, Swirl, Clear Handle, c.1880, 7 ½ x 6 In. . . . 146.00
Shade, 2 Gold Enameled Dragons, 16 Panels, Round, 7 ⅛ In. . . . 270.00
Strawholder, Cover, Thumbprint, Bulbous Base, 13 In. . . . 1100.00
Tumble-Up, Coin Spot, 7 ¾ In., 2 Piece . . . *illus* 40.00
Water Set, Enameled Iris, Ribbed, Multicolored, 12-In. Pitcher, 4 Piece . . . 154.00
Water Set, Rib Optic, Gold Enameled Flowers, 1890s, 9 ¾ In., 5 Piece . . . *illus* 90.00
Wine Rinser, Ribbed, 2 Spouts, Pontil, c.1850, 3 ½ In. . . . 192.00

CREAMWARE , or queensware, was developed by Josiah Wedgwood about 1765. It is a cream-colored earthenware that has been copied by many factories. Similar wares may be listed under Pearlware and Wedgwood.

Basin, Blue Feather Edge, 12 x 3 In. . . . 125.00
Bowl, East Indian Man Sailing From The Downs, 19th Century, 9 In. . . . 200.00
Jug, Mandarin Pattern, c.1871, 7 In. . . . 47.00
Jug, Morse Family Crest, Entwined Vine, Black Transfer, 1800-20, 11 ¼ In. . . . 1100.00
Jug, Portraits, Sam Adams, John Hancock, George Washington Tomb, 8 ½ In. . . . 2530.00
Pitcher, Edmund Gwatking Castle, Flowers, 1776, 10 ½ In. . . . 605.00
Plate, Bird, Perched In Tree, Yellow, Blue Wings, Green Leaves, Brown Banding, 9 In. . . . 22.00
Plate, Eagle, Crown, Yellow, Flower & Dot Border, Early 19th Century, 9 ¼ In. . . . 439.00
Plate, Lead Glaze, Scalloped Rim, Leaf Molded, 9 ⅜ In., Pair . . . 5333.00

Cowan, Jar, Cover, Feu Rouge Glaze, Handles, Impressed Mark, 1930, 8 ½ x 8 In.
$385.00

Cowan, Vase, Chinese Dragon, Melon Green Glaze, Impressed Mark, 11 ⅜ x 7 ¾ In.
$220.00

Cranberry Glass, Tumble-Up, Coin Spot, 7 ¾ In., 2 Piece
$40.00

Cranberry Glass, Water Set, Rib Optic, Gold Enameled Flowers, 1890s, 9 ¾ In., 5 Piece
$90.00

Creamware, Teapot, Flowers, Flower Finial, Late 18th Century, 4 ¼ In.
$200.00

TIP
Don't scrub gilding and gold edges on porcelains.

Crown Milano, Dish, Sweetmeat, Red, Amethyst Flowers, Melon Ribbed, 5 In.
$820.00

Crown Milano, Vase, Twist Neck, Medallion, Gold Stems, Leaves, 8 In.
$1500.00

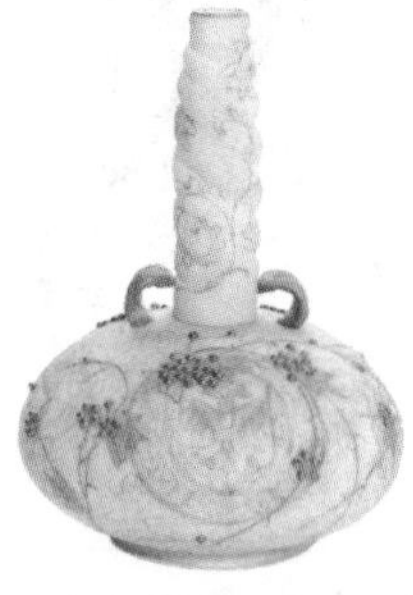

Cup Plate, Staffordshire, Cadmus, Shell Border, Blue, Enoch Wood & Sons, 3 ¾ In.
$358.00

Plate, Spatter Glaze, Molded Basket Weave, Dot, Diaper Border, 1770, 9 In.. 474.00
Plate, Thoroughbred Stallion, Highflyer, Enamels, c.1784, 9 ½ In. 1265.00
Platter, Blue Feather Edge, Scalloped Rim, 17 ½ x 14 ¼ In. 225.00
Platter, Cobalt Blue Feather Edge, Shell Edge, 14 ½ x 11 ½ In. 350.00
Teapot, Cover, Lead Glaze, Hexagonal, Leaf Molded Body, c.1760, 5 ¼ In. 593.00
Teapot, Cover, Lead Glaze, Paneled, Chinese Figures, c.1795, 6 In.. 711.00
Teapot, Flowers, Flower Finial, Late 18th Century, 4 ¼ In. *illus* 200.00
Teapot, Trumpeting Collar, 9 x 5 ½ In.. 125.00
Tureen, Purple Flower Finial, Swag Design, Purple, Green, 7 ½ x 13 In. 819.00

CREDIT CARDS, credit tokens, metal charge plates, phone cards, and other similar collectibles that replace money are now part of the numismatic collecting hobby.

American Express, Admirals Club, Signed, Mickey Mantle, Plastic, c.1986, 3 x 2 In., 2 Piece. 8225.00
Gulf Refining Company, Metal, Leather Holder, 1930s 13.00

CROWN MILANO glass was made by the Mt. Washington Glass Works about 1890. It had a plain biscuit color with a satin finish. It was decorated with flowers and often had large gold scrolls.

Biscuit Jar, Brown, Mauve Ferns, Crown Finial Cover, 8 In. 316.00
Biscuit Jar, Metal Cover, Opal, Gold, Pink Flowers, Signed, 7 In. 978.00
Biscuit Jar, Silver Plated Cover, Pansies, Gold Scrolls, White Ground, Handle, 7 x 6 In. 300.00
Dish, Sweetmeat, Cover, Cream, Jeweled Star Fish, Oval, 6 In.. 472.00
Dish, Sweetmeat, Embossed Cover, Beaded, 5 In. 403.00
Dish, Sweetmeat, Embossed Cover, Melon Ribbed, Opal, Red, Amethyst Flowers, Mauve, 5 In.. 805.00
Dish, Sweetmeat, Embossed Cover, Mold Blown Stars, Jeweled Starfish, 4 ½ In. 920.00
Dish, Sweetmeat, Embossed Cover, Molded Panels, Multicolored Flowers, 5 In.. 690.00
Dish, Sweetmeat, Red, Amethyst Flowers, Melon Ribbed, 5 In. *illus* 820.00
Dish, Sweetmeat, Swirled Ribs, Gold Medallions, Jewels, Oval, 5 In. 345.00
Dresser Box, Crimson Scrolling Flowers, Gold, 6 In.. 295.00
Dresser Box, Red Roses, Lion Mask, Oval, 6 In.. 259.00
Fernery, Squat, Swirl Ribs, Gold Trim, Quatrefoil Rim, Gold Wash, 5 x 4 ½ In. 750.00
Jardiniere, Gold Spider Mums, Leaves, Rust Ground, 11 x 8 In.. 420.00
Pitcher, Raised Panels, Cream, Leaves, Medallions, Jeweled Berries, 8 ¼ In. 2990.00
Rose Bowl, Brown, Leaves, Ruby Jewel, 3 ½ x 4 In. 475.00
Sugar & Creamer, Cover, Grapes, Beige Scrolling, Reeded Handle, 4 ⅜ x 4 ½ In. 3495.00
Syrup, Melon Ribbed, Opal Green, Red Flowers, 5 ½ In. 489.00
Syrup, Metal Cover, Ribbed Opal, Gold Flowers, Blue Ground, 6 In.. 920.00
Toothpick, Little Lobe 81.00
Vase, Ball Shape, Yellow, White, Fern Ground, Gold Trim, Marked, 8 In. 600.00
Vase, Chrysanthemums, Yellow, Gold Trim, 14 ½ x 6 ½ In. 2250.00
Vase, Guba Ducks, In Flight, Snipped & Rolled Rim, 15 ¼ In.. 4600.00
Vase, Salmon Wash, Flowers, Swirled Ribs, Quatrefoil, 5 ¼ x 4 ½ In.. 1050.00
Vase, Slender Neck, Flowers, Gold Trim, Signed, 15 In. 900.00
Vase, Stick, Gold Jeweled Leaves, Green, Cream, Bulbous Base, Leaf Handles, 8 In.. 1495.00
Vase, Thistles, Flowers, Applied Handles, Gold Trim, 14 In. 575.00
Vase, Twist Neck, Medallion, Gold Stems, Leaves, 8 In. *illus* 1500.00
Vase, Wild Rose, Swirl, Beige Ground, Scrolling, Gold Trim, 8 x 7 In.. 1750.00

CROWN TUSCAN *pattern is included in the Cambridge glass category.*

CRUETS of glass or porcelain were made to hold vinegar, oil, and other condiments. They were especially popular during Victorian times and have been made in a variety of styles since the eighteenth century. Additional cruets may be found in the Castor Set category and also in various glass categories.

Aqua Glass, Ribbed, Pontil, Flared Mouth, Zanesville Glass Works, c.1815, 7 In. 253.00
Blue Satin Glass, Clear Handle, Victorian, 7 ¾ In., Pair 99.00
Cobalt Blue Glass, Sheffield Silver Plated Base, Side Handle, c.1910, 7 In, Pair. 205.00
Cut Glass, Hobstar & Prism, Double Bulge Neck, 7 ¾ In. 77.00
Green Cut To Clear, Fluted, Diamond & Pillar Panels, Flower Medallion, Stopper, 5 ½ In.. 700.00

CT GERMANY was first part of a mark used by a company in Altwasser, Germany, in 1845. The initials stand for C. Tielsch, a partner in the firm. The Hutschenreuther firm took over the company in 1918 and continued to use the *CT*.

Pink Flowers, Green Shaded To White Ground, C.T. Altwasser Germany, 10 In. 85.00
Plate, Pink Flower Blossoms, Gold Luster Rim, C.T. Altwasser Germany, 8 ½ In.. 55.00

CUP PLATES are small glass or china plates that held the cup while a diner of the mid-nineteenth century drank coffee or tea from the saucer. The most famous cup plates were made of glass at the Boston and Sandwich factory located in Sandwich, Massachusetts. There have been many new glass cup plates made in recent years for sale to gift shops or collectors of limited edition. These are similar to the old plates but can be recognized as new.

Bull's-Eye, Rings, Arches, 44 Even Scallops, Deep Blue, c.1840, 3 In. ... 124.00
Bull's-Eye, Running Vine, 18 Scallops, Smaller Scallop & 2 Points, c.1840, 3 ½ In. ... 68.00
Cottage In The Woods, Dark Blue Transfer, Enoch Woods, Staffordshire, 3 ⅝ In. ... 70.00
Dahlia, Stippled Band, 28 Scallops, Single Point Between, Blue, c.1840, 2 ¾ In. ... 68.00
Diamond Waffle, New York Battery & Castle Garden, Trefoil Border, Blue, 3 ¾ In. ... 110.00
Diamond Waffle, Plain Rope Rim, Cloudy, c.1835, 3 ⅜ In. ... 180.00
Domestic, Black Transfer, Staffordshire, 4 In. ... 65.00
Dot Center, Running Vine, 9 Pairs Large Scallops, 4 Smaller, c.1840, 3 7/16 In. ... 113.00
Flowers, 17 Even Scallops, Stippled Border, c.1835, 3 ¼ In. ... 124.00
Liberty Torch, 34 Bull's-Eye Scallops, c.1840, 3 9/16 In. ... 68.00
New York Battery, Flag, Spread Winged Eagle, Blue, Staffordshire, 3 ¾ In. ... 250.00
Staffordshire, Cadmus, Shell Border, Blue, Enoch Wood & Sons, 3 ¾ In. ... *illus* 358.00
Staffordshire, Cadmus, Trefoil Border, Blue, Enoch Wood & Sons, 3 ¾ In. ... 110.00
Staffordshire, Landing Of Lafayette, Flower Border, Blue, Clews, 4 ⅜ In. ... 132.00

CURRIER & IVES made the famous American lithographs marked with their name from 1857 to 1907. The mark used on the print included the street address in New York City, and it is possible to date the year of the original issue from this information. Earlier prints were made by N. Currier and use that name from 1835 to 1847. Many reprints of the Currier or Currier & Ives prints have been made. Some collectors buy the insurance calendars that were based on the old prints. The words *large*, *small*, or *medium folio* refer to size. The original print sizes were very small (up to about 7 x 9 in.), small (8.8 x 12.8 in.), medium (9 x 14 in. to 14 x 20 in.), large (larger than 14 x 20 in.). Other sizes are probably later copies. Other prints by Currier & Ives may be listed in the Card category under Advertising and in the Sheet Music category. Currier & Ives dinnerware patterns may be found in the Adams or Dinnerware categories.

American Country Life, October Afternoon, Colored, N. Currier, Frame, 17 x 24 In. ... 956.00
American Country Life, Pleasures Of Winter, Colored, N. Currier, Frame, 17 x 24 In. ... 1673.00
American Country Life, Summer's Evening, Colored, N. Currier, Frame, 16 x 24 In. ... 1195.00
American Winter Scene, Colored, Frame, Oval, 5 ¼ x 7 ¼ In. ... 3107.00
Capturing The Whale, N. Currier, 1850, 10 ¾ x 14 ½ In. ... 1126.00
Celebrated Trotting Horse Hopeful, G. Patchen, 1881, 18 x 28 In. ... 948.00
Central Park, Winter, Skating Carnival, Colored, Frame, 8 x 12 In. ... 1434.00
Central Park, Winter, The Skating Pond, 1862, 18 x 26 In. ... 10073.00
Express Train, 1870, 8 x 12 In. ... 2252.00
Frozen Up, 1892, 9 x 12 In. ... 1659.00
Gen. Andrew Jackson, Hero Of New Orleans, Frame, N. Currier, 22 x 18 In. ... 143.00
Great Fire At Chicago, Octr. 8th, 1871, Frame, 20 ½ x 27 In. ... 18400.00
Holidays In The Country, Frame, 1868, 20 x 25 In. ... 1541.00
Home On The Mississippi, 1871, 8 x 12 In. ... 770.00
Hyde Park, On The Hudson River, 9 ½ x 13 ½ In. ... 239.00
Jay Eye See, Frame, 1883, 23 ¾ x 31 ¾ In. ... 650.00
Life Of A Fireman, Frame, 1866, 29 x 37 In. ... 1020.00
Life Of A Fireman, Metropolitan System, Frame, 1866, 20 x 28 In. ... 2252.00
Life Of A Fireman, The Night Alarm, N. Currier, 1854, 17 x 26 In. ... 1404.00
Low Water In The Mississippi, 1868, 18 x 28 In. ... 288.00
Maple Sugaring, Early Spring In The North Woods, Frame, 1872, 12 x 15 In. ... 1304.00
Morning Ride, Frame, 1849, 21 x 28 In. ... 605.00
New England Winter Scene, 1861, 20 x 26 In. ... 8295.00
New York Winter Street Scene, 1800s, 23 x 34 In. ... 474.00
Old Farm House, 1872, 12 x 16 In. ... 1067.00
Phallas, 1883, Frame, 20 ½ x 28 In. ... 650.00
Pilot Boat In A Storm, Frame, 8 x 12 In. ... 359.00
Regatta Of The New York Yacht Club, N. Currier, Frame, 1854, 20 x 31 In. ... 1304.00
Rising Family, After Arthur Fitzwilliam Tait, Frame, 18 x 24 In. ... 1195.00
Ship Of The Line Pennsylvania, N. Currier, Frame, 16 ½ x 20 ½ In. ... 1035.00
Summer Shades, Gilt Frame, 26 ½ x 32 In. ... 575.00
Tenny, Rayon D'Or, Dam Belle Of Maywood, Frame, 1891, 22 x 29 In. ... *illus* 480.00
Tomb Of Washington, Frame, 20 x 26 ½ In. ... 230.00
Tree Of Life, N. Currier, Frame, 16 ½ x 14 ½ In. ... *illus* 209.00
Trotting Gelding Frank With J.O. Nay, c.1883, 25 ½ x 36 In. ... 240.00

TIP

Bright sunlight will damage antiques by fading colors or drying wood. There are several brands of film that can be applied to your windows to cut UV rays, heat, and glare.

Currier & Ives, Tenny, Rayon D'Or, Dam Belle Of Maywood, Frame, 1891, 22 x 29 In.
$480.00

Currier & Ives, Tree Of Life, N. Currier, Frame, 16 ½ x 14 ½ In.
$209.00

As always, the edited listings in *Kovels' Antiques & Collectibles Price Guide 2010* aren't available on any website, but readers should visit Kovels.com for information on trends, tips, reproductions, marks, old prices, and more!

Currier & Ives, Winter In The Country, A Cold Morning, Wood, Gilt Frame, 1864, 23 ⅜ x 31 In.
$6518.00

Custard Glass, Chrysanthemum Sprig, Cruet, Gold Trim, 6 ½ x 3 ½ In.
$121.00

Custard Glass, Intaglio, Butter, Cover, Blue Stain, Gold Trim, Footed, 7 ½ In.
$79.00

TIP
Custard glass and milk glass can now be repaired by black light-proof methods. Be very careful when buying antiques.

Watchers, Frame, 17 x 13 In. 55.00
Whale Fishery, In A Flurry, N. Currier, Frame, 1852, 9 x 13 In. 1500.00
Wild Duck Shooting, N. Currier, Frame, 1852, 12 ⅞ x 19 ⅞ In. 1300.00
Wild Turkey Shooting, Frame, 1871, 10 ¾ x 14 ¾ In. 593.00
Winter In The Country, A Cold Morning, Wood, Gilt Frame, 1864, 23 ⅜ x 31 In. ...... *illus* 6518.00
Wm. Penn's Treaty With The Indians, N. Currier, Frame, 12 ¾ x 9 In. 288.00

CUSTARD GLASS is a slightly yellow opaque glass. It was made in England in the 1880s and was first made in the United States in the 1890s. It has been reproduced. Additional pieces may be found in the Cambridge, Fenton, Heisey, and Northwood categories. Custard glass is called Ivorina Verde by Heisey and other companies.

Argonaut Shell, Vase, Footed, 7 x 6 ½ In. 175.00
Chrysanthemum Sprig, Berry Set, 9 Piece 259.00
Chrysanthemum Sprig, Cruet, Gold Trim, 6 ½ x 3 ½ In. .... *illus* 121.00
Intaglio, Butter, Cover, Blue Stain, Gold Trim, Footed, 7 ½ In. .... *illus* 79.00
Maize is its own category in this book.

CUT GLASS has been made since ancient times, but the large majority of the pieces now for sale date from the American brilliant period of glass design, 1880 to 1905. These pieces have elaborate geometric designs with a deep miter cut. Modern cut glass with a similar appearance is being made in England, Ireland, Poland, and the Czech and Slovak republics. Chips and scratches are often difficult to notice but lower the value dramatically. A signature on the glass adds significantly to the value. Other cut glass pieces are listed under factory names, like Hawkes, Libbey, and Sinclaire.

Banana Boat, Hobstar, Cane, Strawberry Diamond & Fan, 4 ½ x 11 ½ In. 450.00
Banana Boat, Hobstar, Nailhead Diamond, Strawberry Diamond & Fan, 4 ¼ x 11 ½ In. 100.00
Basket, Green To Rose Flower, Sterling Rim, Handle, Signed, J.E. Caldwell, 2 ½ x 4 ½ In. 700.00
Basket, Hobstar, Strawberry Diamond, Fern & Fan, Notched Handle, Hobstar Base, 11 ¼ In. 300.00
Basket, Hobstar, Strawberry Diamond, Star Blocks, Fans, American Brilliant, 13 x 10 In. 440.00
Basket, Hobstar & Fan, Triple Notched Handle, Hobstar Handle, 8 ½ In. 250.00
Basket, Hobstar, Diamond Field, Arched Bull's-Eye Handle, 17 In. 1495.00
Basket, Intaglio Flowers, Double Notched Handle, 17 In. 200.00
Basket, Shirley, Meriden, 11 x 8 In. 193.00
Bell, Hobstar & Fan, 5 ½ In. 175.00
Bell, Hobstar & Fan, American Brilliant, 4 ½ In. 193.00
Bell, Hobstar & Strawberry, 5 ½ In. 225.00
Bell, Pinwheel, Hobstar & Fan, 4 ½ In. 110.00
Bonbon, Hobstar, Prism & Fan, American Brilliant, 6 In. 303.00
Bottle, Hobstar, Prism, Bull's-Eye, Pinched Waist, Hobstar Base, 11 ¾ In. 225.00
Bottle, Ketchup, Triple Notch Handle, 11 ½ In. 175.00
Bottle, Tabasco Sauce, Hobstar, Crosscut Diamond, Fan & Prism, 5 ¼ In. 175.00
Bottle, Whiskey, Strawberry Diamond, Block & Fan, Sterling Silver Stopper, 11 ½ In. 125.00
Bottle, Worcestershire Sauce, Hobstar & Fan, 8 ½ In. 100.00
Bowl, Amazon Pattern, Oval, 4-Sided Lobed Edge, Bergen, American Brilliant, 8 ¾ In. 110.00
Bowl, Amber, Intaglio Flowers, Thistles, Diagonal Panels, 1890s, 2 ½ x 11 In. 230.00
Bowl, Bread, Vintage, Intaglio Pear & Apple, Oval, American Brilliant, 11 ¾ In. 250.00
Bowl, Bull's-Eye Petal Center, Sharp Hobstar, Strawberry Diamond & Star, 3 ¼ x 8 In. 75.00
Bowl, Centerpiece, Diamonds & Stars, Shaped Rim, 9 x 3 ¾ In. 83.00
Bowl, Cluster Pattern, Egginton, 2 ¼ x 9 In. 250.00
Bowl, Cranberry To Clear, Vesica, Strawberry Diamond, Star & Fan, American Brilliant, 10 In. ... *illus* 140.00
Bowl, Crosscut Diamond & Fan, Napoleon Hat Shape, American Brilliant, 4 ½ x 12 In. 50.00
Bowl, Diamond & Star, Folded Rim, 8 ½ x 4 In. 59.00
Bowl, Diamond & Window, Bakewell, 11 ½ In. 25.00
Bowl, Eleanor Pattern, J. Hoare, 9 In. 325.00
Bowl, Encore Pattern, 3 Lobes, Straus, 3 ¾ x 10 In. 209.00
Bowl, Expanding Star, 4 Sections, Handles, 8 In. 100.00
Bowl, Flashed Thistle, Russian Banners, American Brilliant, 10 In. 275.00
Bowl, Fruit, Leaves, 3 ⅜ x 8 In. 59.00
Bowl, Fruit, Panels Of Stars, Scalloped Rim, 11 ½ x 4 In. 118.00
Bowl, Fruit, Star Diamond & Fan, Pedestal, 9 x 10 In. 70.00
Bowl, Harvard & Daisy, Handles, 8 In. 44.00
Bowl, Harvard Border, Intaglio Flowers, 3-Footed, American Brilliant, 8 In. 44.00
Bowl, Harvard Pattern, Vesica Center, Rolled Rim, 4 x 7 ½ In. 70.00
Bowl, Hobstar, Cane, Strawberry Diamond & Fan, 4 ¼ x 9 In. 60.00
Bowl, Hobstar, Flashed Starburst, Vesica, Strawberry Diamond & Fan, American Brilliant, 9 In. .. *illus* 82.00

Bowl, Hobstar, Intaglio Flower, Cane & File, American Brilliant, 3 ½ x 9 In. 25.00
Bowl, Hobstar, Nailhead Diamond, Star & Hobstar Border, Notched Handles, 4 x 12 In. 22.00
Bowl, Hobstar, Nailhead Diamond, Star & Tusk, American Brilliant, 5 x 9 In. 175.00
Bowl, Hobstar, Nailhead Diamond, Strawberry Diamond & Fan, 4 x 8 ¾ In. 1500.00
Bowl, Hobstar, Nailhead Diamond & Claw, 7 In. 150.00
Bowl, Hobstar, Notched Fan, Strawberry Diamond, 3-Footed, 3 x 8 In. 50.00
Bowl, Hobstar, Pillar & Prism Cut Design, Sterling Silver Rim, 3 ½ x 8 ¼ In. 550.00
Bowl, Hobstar, Russian Vesica, Cane & Prism, Brilliant, 5 x 10 In. 375.00
Bowl, Hobstar, Strawberry Diamond, Flared, American Brilliant, 4 x 9 In. 110.00
Bowl, Hobstar, Strawberry Diamond, Step Cut, 3 ½ x 8 In. 70.00
Bowl, Hobstar, Strawberry Diamond & Zipper, Oval, American Brilliant, 10 ½ In. 20.00
Bowl, Hobstar, Strawberry Diamond, Vesica, Zipper, Oval, 9 ½ In. 90.00
Bowl, Hobstar, Tricornered Rim, 5 x 9 ¼ In. 200.00
Bowl, Hobstar, Vesica & Cane Circles, American Brilliant, 10 In. 250.00
Bowl, Hobstar Center, Cut Star Buttons, Clear Blank, 3 ½ x 8 In. 125.00
Bowl, Hobstar Center, Strawberry Diamond & Fan Border, American Brilliant, 2 ½ x 9 In. 70.00
Bowl, Hobstar Cluster Arches, Center, American Brilliant, 3 ½ In. 100.00
Bowl, Intaglio, Pear, Apples, Plums, 12 Panels, Scalloped Rim, 4 ½ x 11 ¼ In. 173.00
Bowl, Intaglio Flowers, Silver Rim, Gorham, 1913, 4 x 8 In. 299.00
Bowl, Lotus, Meriden, 2 ¼ x 8 ¾ In. 358.00
Bowl, Louis XVI, Oval, 2 Figural Putti Handles, Gilt Bronze Base, c.1850, 18 In. 944.00
Bowl, Mayflower Variant, 3 ½ x 9 In. 70.00
Bowl, Nailhead Diamond & Floral Wreath, American Brilliant, 4 ¼ x 9 In. 22.00
Bowl, No. 51, Elmira, 5 x 10 In. 350.00
Bowl, Pinetree, American Brilliant, 3 ½ x 8 In. 125.00
Bowl, Pinwheel, 3-Point Geometric Center, 4 x 8 In. 60.00
Bowl, Pinwheel Center, Prisms, Sunburst, Stars, American Brilliant, 4 x 9 In. 121.00
Bowl, Pluto, American Brilliant, 4 x 9 In. *illus* 410.00
Bowl, Prima Donna, Clark, 7 In. 110.00
Bowl, Russian, Star Cut Buttons, Square, 4 ¾ x 9 In. 300.00
Bowl, Saturn, Clark, 3 ¼ x 8 In. 44.00
Bowl, Shield, Hobstar, Zipper, Nailhead Diamond, American Brilliant, 4 ¼ x 9 In. 600.00
Bowl, Star Cut Block, 2 ½ x 10 In. 75.00
Bowl, Sterling, American Brilliant, 5 x 13 In. *illus* 880.00
Bowl, Strawberry & Fan, Sawtooth Rim, Star Cut Foot, c.1800, 7 x 9 ½ In. *illus* 646.00
Bowl, Trellis, Hobstar, Scalloped Edge, 1 ¾ x 8 ¾ In. 1150.00
Bowl, Trellis, Signed, Egginton, 2 ½ x 8 In. 1700.00
Bowl, Underplate, Rectangular, Crimped Edge, Ireland, 11 x 7 In. 1675.00
Bowl, Vintage, Intaglio Pear, Apple, Plum, Scalloped Rim, Pedestal, 8 x 9 In. 880.00
Bowl, Wheat, American Brilliant, 5 ½ x 11 In. 150.00
Bowl, Yellow To Clear, Intaglio Cherry, Embossed Sterling Silver Rim, 1 x 8 In. 650.00
Bowl, Yellow To Clear, Intaglio Cherry, Gold Wash Sterling Silver Rim, 3 ½ x 12 In. 300.00
Box, Casket Shape, Blue, Allover Caning, Hinged, 3 ½ x 5 ¼ In. 275.00
Box, Cover, Green To Clear, Gold Wash, Sterling Silver, Cover, Garland, Geometric, 4 x 5 ½ In. 700.00
Box, Thumbprint, Engraved Floral Hinged Cover, 3 x 5 In. 225.00
Bread Tray, Oasis, Anderson, 13 ¾ In. 248.00
Bridge Set, Hobstar, Cane & Star, American Brilliant, 4 Piece *illus* 250.00
Butter, Cover, Hobstar, Shield, 6 x 8 ½ In. 150.00
Butter, Cover, Hobstar, Strawberry Diamond & Fan, American Brilliant, 7 x 9 ½ In. 200.00
Butter, Cover, Pinwheel, Strawberry Diamond, Fan, 5 ¾ x 8 In. 275.00
Butter, Cover, Strawberry Diamond & Fan, Pedestal, American Brilliant, 8 ½ x 8 In. *illus* 220.00
Butter Chip, Cane, American Brilliant, 3 ½ In., 6 Piece 220.00
Butter Dome, Harvard, Daisy, 6 In. 60.00
Cake Stand, Alhambra, Greek Key, Teardrop Stem, American Brilliant, 7 ½ x 9 ¼ In. 500.00
Candelabrum, 5-Light, Harvard Pattern, Silver Plated Top, American Brilliant, 21 In., Pair 990.00
Candlestick, Green Cut To Clear, Vintage Pattern, 10 ½ In., Pair 495.00
Candy Dish, Star, Flower, 5 ¼ x 3 In. 35.00
Carafe, Cranberry To Clear, Diamond & Fan, 8 ½ In. 550.00
Carafe, Green To Clear, Hobstar, Block, Star, Crosshatch, Bull's-Eye, American Brilliant, 8 In. *illus* 1100.00
Carafe, Hobstar, Block & Fan, Hobstar Base, 8 In. 110.00
Carafe, Hobstar, Cane, Vesica, Strawberry Diamond & Fan, 10 In. 50.00
Carafe, Hobstar, Crosscut Diamond, Prism & Fan, 7 ½ In. 50.00
Celery Dish, Russian, Crosshatch Buttons, Boat Shape, 12 In. 110.00
Celery Dish, Star Block, Canoe Shape, American Brilliant, 12 ½ In. 77.00
Celery Tray, Engraved Flower & Hobstar, Oval, Silver Thread, 9 ¾ In. 175.00
Celery Tray, Folded, Hobstar, Prism, Cane & Nailhead Diamond, 12 In. 30.00
Celery Tray, Folded, Hobstar, Strawberry Diamond, Zipper & Cane, American Brilliant, 11 ¾ In. 75.00

TIP
The best cleaner for your cut glass is a perfume-free, softener-free dishwasher detergent. Ammonia is too strong, and scented softeners sometimes leave an oily film.

Cut Glass, Bowl, Cranberry To Clear, Vesica, Strawberry Diamond, Star & Fan, American Brilliant, 10 In.
$140.00

Cut Glass, Bowl, Hobstar, Flashed Starburst, Vesica, Strawberry Diamond & Fan, American Brilliant, 9 In.
$82.00

Cut Glass, Bowl, Pluto, American Brilliant, 4 x 9 In.
$410.00

Cut Glass, Bowl, Sterling, American Brilliant, 5 x 13 In.
$880.00

Cut Glass, Bowl, Strawberry & Fan, Sawtooth Rim, Star Cut Foot, c.1800, 7 x 9 ½ In.
$646.00

Cut Glass, Bridge Set, Hobstar, Cane & Star, American Brilliant, 4 Piece
$250.00

Cut Glass, Butter, Cover, Strawberry Diamond & Fan, Pedestal, American Brilliant, 8 ½ x 8 In.
$220.00

Cut Glass, Carafe, Green To Clear, Hobstar, Block, Star, Crosshatch, Bull's-Eye, American Brilliant, 8 In.
$1100.00

Cut Glass, Cheese & Cracker Plate, Intaglio Fruits, Tuthill, 9 In.
$360.00

Cut Glass, Cheese Dish, Cover, Hobstar, Strawberry Diamond & Fan, American Brilliant, 7 x 10 In.
$305.00

Cut Glass, Coaster, Wine Bottle, Hobstar, Strawberry Diamond & Fan, American Brilliant, 6 ½ In.
$82.00

Cut Glass, Compote, Carolyn, Petticoat Base, American Brilliant, 7 ½ x 8 ½ In.
$220.00

Celery Tray, Vesica, Nailhead, Strawberry & Diamond, Cane, Fan, American Brilliant, 12 In. . 150.00
Centerpiece, Pluto, J. Hoare, 5 ½ x 8 In. 330.00
Chalice, Punties, Intaglio Birds, Daisies, Grapes, c.1825, 7 ¼ In. 450.00
Chalice, Twist Stem, Intaglio Flower, American Brilliant, 17 ½ In. 325.00
Champagne, Crosscut Diamond & Fan, 4 ½ In., 6 Piece 100.00
Champagne, Flute, Crosscut Diamond & Fan, Notched Stem & Ray Base, American Brilliant, 7 In. 150.00
Champagne, Green To Clear, Diamond & Flower, 10 In., Pair 450.00
Champagne, Imperial, Straus, 4 ⅝ In., Pair 77.00
Champagne, Intaglio Grapes, Leaves, 3 ½ x 3 In. 39.00
Champagne, Notch Stem, 3 ½ x 5 In., 8 Piece 650.00
Champagne, Prisms, Hobstar & Strawberry Diamond Border, Rayed Base, 6 ½ In., Pair 440.00
Champagne, Swirl Panels, Strawberry Diamond, Hobstar & Star, Fan, American Brilliant, 4 ¾ In. 40.00
Cheese & Cracker Plate, File & Fan, Sterling Cover, American Brilliant, 4 ½ x 10 In. 130.00
Cheese & Cracker Plate, Intaglio Fruits, Tuthill, 9 In. *illus* 360.00
Cheese Dish, Cover, Hobstar, Strawberry Diamond & Fan, American Brilliant, 7 x 10 In. *illus* 305.00
Cheese Dish, Cover, Underplate, Rearing & Running Horses, 6 ½ x 8 ¼ In. 300.00
Cheese Dish, Dome Cover, Honeycomb, Faceted Finial, 5 ½ x 7 In. 85.00
Cigarette Jar, Marlboro, Dorflinger, 7 ½ In. 495.00
Coaster, Farm Scene, Diamond Border, American Brilliant, 5 In. 250.00
Coaster, Wine Bottle, Hobstar, Strawberry Diamond & Fan, American Brilliant, 6 ½ In. *illus* 82.00
Compote, Carolyn, Petticoat Base, American Brilliant, 7 ½ x 8 ½ In. *illus* 220.00
Compote, Corn Flower, 1960s, 7 ¾ x 5 ¾ In. 25.00
Compote, Diamond Point, Monogram, Hollow Apple Core Stem, American Brilliant, 8 ½ x 8 In. 150.00
Compote, Florence Star, 32-Point Hobstar Scalloped Base, Meriden, 8 x 9 In. *illus* 140.00
Compote, Gravic Strawberry & Pellum, Faceted Knob Stem, 8 ½ x 7 In. 450.00
Compote, Hobstar, Cane, Strawberry Diamond & Fan, Scalloped Base, 9 x 9 In. 350.00
Compote, Hobstar, Cane, Strawberry Diamond & Prism, J. Hoare, 6 ¼ x 7 In. 88.00
Compote, Hobstar, Strawberry Diamond, Prism & Cane, Spread Foot, J. Hoare, 7 x 8 In. 110.00
Compote, Hobstar & Strawberry Diamond, Teardrop & Notched Stem, 10 ¼ x 6 In. 100.00
Compote, Intaglio Orchids, Rolled Rim, Rayed Base, American Brilliant, 7 ½ x 6 In. 83.00
Compote, Jelly, Hobstar & Fan, Solid Stem, Rayed Base, 10 In. 80.00
Compote, Jelly, Hobstar & Star, Hollow Stem, Scalloped Hobstar Base, 10 x 6 In. 200.00
Compote, On Stand, White To Clear, Moorish Windows, Beveled Scalloped Edge, c.1850, 11 x 11 In. 300.00
Compote, Russian, Square Base, Continental, 7 x 14 In. 480.00
Compote, Sawtooth Rim, Alternating Panels, Octagonal, Footed, 9 x 7 ¾ In. 35.00
Compote, Scalloped Fluted Edge, Scalloped Base, Flint, Ireland, 7 ½ In. 1095.00
Compote, Teardrop Stem, American Brilliant, 11 ½ x 6 ½ In. 200.00
Compote, Trefoil, Oblong Windows, New England Glass Co., 8 x 9 ¼ In. 200.00
Condiment Set, Amber, Diamond, Cruet, Shakers, Mustard, Caddy, 9 In. *illus* 115.00
Cookie Jar, Cover, Swirl Pillar, Diamond Border, Cut Finial, Pedestal, Scalloped, 8 In. 300.00
Cordial, Bell Shape, Engraved, Diamond, Long Stem, 4 ½ x 1 ½ In., 6 Piece 150.00
Cordial, Starburst, Arches, Petal Cut Base, Signed, St. Louis, 4 ¼ x 1 ½ In., 6 Piece 295.00
Cruet, Alhambra, Greek Key, Pyramid Shaped, Notched Handle, American Brilliant, 9 ¼ In. 3700.00
Cruet, Butterfly, Flower, Zipper Neck, Sphere Stopper, Handle, Cone Shape, 12 In. 33.00
Cruet, Engraved Iris, Pinched Waist, American Brilliant, 8 ½ In. 100.00
Cruet, Greek Key, Pyramid Shape, Triple Notched Handle, Rayed Base, Meriden, 9 ½ In. 440.00
Cruet, Hobstar & Fan, Pedestal, Hobstar Base, 8 ½ In. 125.00
Cruet, Hobstar & Fan, Tricornered Spout, Triple Notched Handle, 6 ¼ In. 40.00
Cup & Saucer, Crosscut Diamond & Fan, American Brilliant 28.00
Cup & Saucer, Punch, Hobstar, Strawberry Diamond & Fan 375.00
Decanter, Alhambra, Greek Key, Cut Stopper, Hobstar Base, American Brilliant, 12 In. 2400.00
Decanter, Bull's-Eye, Notched Neck & Handle, Star Base, 11 ½ In. 165.00
Decanter, Buzz Star, Zipper, Ball Stopper, 12 In. 22.00
Decanter, Canary Yellow, Engraved, Coat Of Arms, Knight's Head, Stopper, 12 In. 395.00
Decanter, Croesus, Gold Wash Sterling Silver Flip Cap, Chain, American Brilliant, 10 ½ In. 1700.00
Decanter, Diamond, Music Box Base, After Rain Sunshine Follows, c.1955, 10 ¾ x 5 ½ In. 150.00
Decanter, Diamond Point, St. Louis Diamond Neck, Pattern Cut Stopper, 14 ½ In. 100.00
Decanter, DuBarry, Lady's Leg Neck, Ruffled Rim, Quaker City, 12 In. 330.00
Decanter, Engraved Fern, 11 ½ x 5 ½ In. 47.00
Decanter, Engraved Wheat, Handle, Silver Stopper, American Brilliant, 8 ½ In. 83.00
Decanter, Flute, Greek Key Border, American Brilliant, 12 In. 75.00
Decanter, Flute, Ray Base, Stopper, 14 ½ In. 100.00
Decanter, Footed, Applied Faceted Rings On Neck, Greek Key Band, Hollow Stopper, 13 In. 83.00
Decanter, Green To Clear, Sterling Overlay, Bull's-Eye & Prism, Stopper, American Brilliant, 11 In. 325.00
Decanter, Hobstar, Strawberry Diamond, Vesica, Nailhead Diamond, Gooseneck, 13 In. 350.00
Decanter, Hobstar, Strawberry Diamond & Bar, Hobstar Base, 11 In. 75.00

Cut Glass, Condiment Set, Amber, Diamond, Cruet, Shakers, Mustard, Caddy, 9 In.
$115.00

Cut Glass, Lamp, Florence Star, Meriden, American Brilliant, 23 x 12 In.
$4510.00

TIP

Be careful when burning candles in glass candlesticks. If the candle burns too low, the hot wax and flame may break the glass.

Cut Glass, Pitcher, Basket Weave, Triple Notched Handle, American Brilliant, 10 ¾ In. $440.00

Cut Glass, Pitcher, Butterfly & Blossom, Triple Notched Handle, American Brilliant, 10 In. $110.00

TIP

If you are the victim of a theft, be sure to give the police complete information about your antiques. You should have a good description, a photograph, and any known identifying marks. You might want to send information about the stolen antiques to the antiques papers.

Decanter, Middlesex, Snake Handle, Hobstar Stopper, Dorflinger, 10 ½ In., Pair 1540.00
Decanter, Panel & Diamond, Paneled & Ring Neck, Stopper, Anglo-Irish, 10 In., Pair....... 316.00
Decanter, Pinwheel, Strawberry Diamond & Fan, Double Gooseneck, 12 In. 200.00
Decanter, Quatrefoil & Rosettes, Hobstar Base, American Brilliant, 11 In. 1485.00
Decanter, Russian, Buttons, Teardrop Handle, American Brilliant, 10 ½ In.. .... 220.00
Decanter, Swirl Flower Panels, Stopper, Footed, Handle, American Brilliant, 12 ½ In........ 3100.00
Decanter, Vintage, Embossed Sterling Stopper, Squat Shape, American Brilliant, 8 In........ 350.00
Decanter, Westminster, Snake Handle, American Brilliant, 12 ½ In..................... 175.00
Decanter Set, Rogaska, Gorham Silver Plated Labels, 10 ½ x 3 ¾ In., 3 Piece............. 146.00
Dish, Bread, Intaglio Fruit, Pears & Grapes, Tuthill, 3 x 11 ¾ In........................ 303.00
Dish, Crosscut Diamond, Fan & Clear, Block Diamond, Leaf Shape, American Brilliant, 8 ¼ In. 100.00
Dish, Hobstar, Cane, Button, 7 In.. 100.00
Dish, Hobstar, Star, Fan Border, Strawberry Diamond, Oval, 2 ¾ x 13 ½ In. 250.00
Dish, Hobstar & Cane, Butterfly Shape, American Brilliant, 5 ½ In...................... 83.00
Dish, Ice Cream, Bellview Pattern Variant, 6 In.. .... 250.00
Dish, Pedestal, Hobstar & Fan, Scalloped Ray Base, 4 x 5 ½ In. 40.00
Dish, Prism, Strawberry Diamond & Star, Hobstar Base, Footed, 3 x 5 ½ In................ 40.00
Dish, Strawberry Diamond & Star, Folded, American Brilliant, 10 In. 170.00
Epergne, Sweetmeat, Empire Style, 3 Plates, Ormolu Putti Base, 24 x 10 In. 6250.00
Ewer, Intaglio Flowers, Pedestal, Handle, Silver Plated Base, Spout, 11 In., Pair............ 275.00
Ewer, Star Cut Diamond & Pillar Cut, Spout, Ray Base, American Brilliant, 13 ½ In.. .... 350.00
Ferner, Aberdeen, 3-Footed, 4 x 7 ¼ In. 375.00
Ferner, Russian, Hobstar & File, 4 x 7 ½ In.. .... 75.00
Finger Bowl, Hobstar, Cane, File, Fan & Prism, American Brilliant, 3 x 4 In. 550.00
Flower Frog, Feathered Star Base, Hobstar, File, Star, Bull's-Eye & Fan, 4 ½ x 6 In.. .... 300.00
Flowerpot, Star Diamond Body, Hobstar & Fan Border, American Brilliant, 6 x 6 In.. .... 385.00
Goblet, Crosscut Diamond & Fan, Signed, Hawkes, 6 In., 6 Piece....................... 350.00
Goblet, Cut To Clear, Cranberry, Ruby, Amethyst, 8 In., 14 Piece 660.00
Goblet, Kalana Lily, Dorflinger, 5 ¾ In.. .... 193.00
Goblet, Leaf & Spear, Faceted Stem, Versailles, Stuart, 6 ½ x 3 ½ In. 325.00
Goblet, Sharp Diamond, File Band, Notched Stem, American Brilliant, 4 ½ In. 325.00
Goblet, Wine, Rhine, Ruby Over Apple Green, Intaglio, Clear Teardrop Stem, 7 ¾ In. 150.00
Hair Receiver, Flower, Hobstar Base, Sections, American Brilliant, 3 ¼ x 4 ½ In. 20.00
Hair Receiver, Hobstar & Fan, Birks Sterling Silver Cover, American Brilliant, 3 In......... 33.00
Humidor, Marlboro, 9 In. 525.00
Ice Bucket, Fancy Pinwheel, Notch & Fan, Tab Handle, 5 ½ x 7 In.. .... 125.00
Ice Bucket, Hindoo Variant, Tab Handles, J. Hoare, 5 ½ x 6 In. 193.00
Ice Bucket, Intaglio, Sunburst, Pineapple, Flowers, 11 x 7 In.......................... 94.00
Ice Tub, Crosscut Diamond, Strawberry Diamond, Star & Fan, American Brilliant, 5 In.. .... 40.00
Ice Tub, Florence, Silver Plated Insert, Meriden, 6 x 6 ½ In.. .... 80.00
Ice Tub, Sterling Silver Rim, Wilcox, c.1910, 5 x 8 In.. .... 173.00
Jam Jar, Cover, Intaglio Strawberries, 3 Handles, Pink Enamel Finial, 4 ½ x 6 In. 100.00
Jardiniere, Hobstar, Vesica, File & Fan, Ray Base, 8 ¾ x 9 In.. .... 450.00
Jewelry Box, 5-Point Star Center, Intaglio Flowers, Round, 6 In.. .... 450.00
Jewelry Box, Hinged, Flashed Hobstar Cover, 2 Punty Border, American Brilliant, 2 ¾ x 5 In. 225.00
Jewelry Box, Russian, Ray Base, Oval, Hinged Cover, 3 ¼ x 5 In.. .... 175.00
Jug, Whiskey, Cranberry To Clear, Geometric, Engraved, Handle, Stopper, 10 In.. .... 350.00
Keg On Stand, Russian, Barrel Shape, Spigot, 8 ½ x 9 In. 275.00
Lamp, 2-Light, Strawberry Dome Shades, Harvard, Button Vesica, Intaglio Flowers, 28 x 12 In. 1400.00
Lamp, Banquet, Hobstar, Cane, Strawberry Diamond & Zipper, Hobstar Base, 18 In. 3000.00
Lamp, Florence Star, Meriden, American Brilliant, 23 x 12 In.. .... *illus* 4510.00
Lamp, Harvard & Daisy, 13 ¾ x 6 In. 200.00
Lamp, Harvard & Daisy, Flat Prisms, 18 ½ x 10 In. 375.00
Lamp, Mushroom Shade, Hobstar, Vesica, Nailhead, Harvard, Fan, American Brilliant, 17 ½ x 10 In. 800.00
Lamp, Mushroom Shade, Pinched Waist Base, 17 In. 153.00
Lamp, Mushroom Shade, Pinched Waist Base, 20 In. 236.00
Lamp, Strawberry Dome Shade, Harvard & Daisy, 22 x 10 In.. .... 1000.00
Lampshade, Mushroom, Intaglio Tiger Lily, Honeycomb, American Brilliant, 21 ½ x 12 In.. . 450.00
Lampshade, Rainbow To Clear, Crosscut Diamond, Zipper & Fan, American Brilliant, 5 ½ In. 750.00
Lampshade Globe, 8-Sided Hobstars, Miter & Fan, American Brilliant, 6 ½ x 7 ½ In.. .... 600.00
Lampshade Globe, Pedestal, Violet, Hobstar & Long Thumbprint, Solid Stem, Ray Base, 7 In. 200.00
Lampshade Globe, Pedestal, Violet, Pinwheel, Strawberry Diamond & Fan, American Brilliant, 6 In. 150.00
Nappy, Alhambra, Greek Key, Handle, Roden, 6 In. 220.00
Nappy, Butterfly & Star, American Brilliant, 6 In. 413.00
Nappy, Buzz Saw, Triangle Center, Loop Handle, 6 In.. .... 11.00
Nappy, Hobstar, 3-Footed, 5 ¼ In. 40.00

Nappy, Hobstar, Silver Thread, Medallions & Star, Handle, American Brilliant, 6 In. 100.00
Nappy, Hobstar Vesica, Cobalt Blue Handle, Splash Spot Center, American Brilliant, 6 In. 125.00
Nappy, Marlboro, Green To Clear, Handle, Dorflinger, 6 In.. . . . . 1430.00
Pedestal, Crosscut Diamond & Fan, Solid Stem, Ray Base, Signed, Clark, 6 ¾ In., Pair 75.00
Pitcher, Basket Weave, Triple Notched Handle, American Brilliant, 10 ¾ In. . . . . *illus* 440.00
Pitcher, Butterfly & Blossom, Triple Notched Handle, American Brilliant, 10 In. . . . . . . *illus* 110.00
Pitcher, Buzz Star, Zipper, 7 In. 99.00
Pitcher, Cider, Baker's Gothic, Pattern Cut Handle, Clark, 7 In. 450.00
Pitcher, Cider, Drape, Notched Handle, Hobstar Base, American Brilliant, 7 ½ In. 250.00
Pitcher, Cider, Harvard, Triple Notched Handle, Hobstar Base, 6 ½ In. 250.00
Pitcher, Cider, Triple Notched Handle, Hobstar Base, 7 In. 175.00
Pitcher, Cranberry To Clear, Punty & Geometric, 9 In. 350.00
Pitcher, Crosscut & Strawberry Diamond, Fan, Bowling Pin Shape, Notch Handle, 9 ¼ In.. . . 110.00
Pitcher, Dahlia, c.1900, 6 ½ x 9 In.. . . . . 117.00
Pitcher, Encore, Straus, 5 In. . . . . *illus* 140.00
Pitcher, Feather & Fan, Nailhead Diamond, Vesica, Hobstar, American Brilliant, 8 In.. . . . . . . 550.00
Pitcher, Green To Clear, Silver Spout, Engraved, Rococo Swirl, 10 ½ In.. . . . . 650.00
Pitcher, Hobstar, Nailhead Diamond, Vesica, Prisms, Notched Handle, Squat, 6 ½ In.. . . . . 110.00
Pitcher, Hobstar, Strawberry Diamond & Fan, Notched Handle, 8 ¾ In. 50.00
Pitcher, Hobstar & Hobstar Cluster, Notched Handle, 8 In.. . . . . 200.00
Pitcher, Hobstar & Vesica, American Brilliant, 7 2¾ In. 132.00
Pitcher, Hobstar Cluster & Herringbone, Notched Handle, Hobstar Base, 11 In.. . . . . 250.00
Pitcher, Hobstar, Intaglio Fruit Vesica, American Brilliant, 9 In. 138.00
Pitcher, Intaglio Flower, Embossed Sterling Spout, Handle, Pedestal, American Brilliant, 11 ½ In. 1100.00
Pitcher, Lotus, Triple Notched Handle, Egginton, 8 In.. . . . . 193.00
Pitcher, Mandarin, Hobstar Base, Button Cut Handle, Squat, American Brilliant, 8 ½ In. 1900.00
Pitcher, Marlboro, Dorflinger, 9 In. 440.00
Pitcher, Quatrefoil & Rosettes, Hobstar Base, Clark, 9 In.. . . . . 413.00
Pitcher, Russian, Buttons, Notched Handle, Ball Shaped, American Brilliant, 8 ¼ In.. . . . . 175.00
Pitcher, Snow Flake, Buzz Star, Handle, Dots, 9 ¼ In.. . . . . 11.00
Plate, Croesus, J. Hoare, 6 ¾ In. 50.00
Plate, Fan, Daisy, 8 ½ In. 117.00
Plate, Hobstar, Vesica, Strawberry Diamond, 7 In.. . . . . 10.00
Plate, Hobstar, Wreath, Strawberry Diamond, Vesica, Fan, 7 In.. . . . . 70.00
Plate, Hobstar Center, Prism Border, 10 In. 225.00
Plate, Prima Donna, Full Teeth Edge, Signed, Clark, 7 ¼ In. 260.00
Plate, Square, Hobstar, Strawberry Diamond, Nailhead Diamond, 7 In. 80.00
Plate, Turquoise To Clear, Swirl Cane & Zipper, American Brilliant, 7 In. 4000.00
Powder Box, Hobstar, Prism & Fan, Lion & Crest Embossed, Sterling Silver Cover, 4 ½ In.. . . . 120.00
Powder Jar, Engraved Flowers, Butterfly, 3 ¼ x 4 ½ In. 125.00
Powder Jar, Hobstar, Crosscut Diamond & Fan, Sterling Rim, Bail Handle, American Brilliant, 6 In. 300.00
Punch Bowl, Base, Hobstar, Sawtooth Edge, American Brilliant, 14 x 13 ¼ In. 1950.00
Punch Bowl, Base, Hobstar, Strawberry Diamond & Fan, American Brilliant, 8 x 9 In.. . . . . . . 633.00
Punch Bowl, Base, Hobstar & Ray, 9 ¼ x 10 In. 69.00
Punch Bowl, Base, Hobstars, Zipper, File, Clear Tusk Fans, American Brilliant, 9 ½ x 19 In.. . 1500.00
Punch Bowl, Diamond & Fan, Knopped Stem, Stuart, 13 ½ x 10 ¾ In.. 502.00
Punch Bowl, Hobstar, Fans, 11 In. 649.00
Punch Bowl, Vintage, Ladle, American Brilliant, 9 ¼ x 9 ¼ In., 2 Piece 100.00
Punch Cup, Vendome, Pedestal, Egginton, 3 In., 6 Piece 275.00
Punch Set, Heart, Hobstar, Cane, Strawberry Diamond, Fan, 14-In. Bowl, 9 Piece. 3410.00
Relish, Folded, Hobstar, Split Vesica & Fan, Rolled Rim, 7 ½ In.. . . . . 40.00
Relish, Star Medallion Center, Oval, 8 In.. . . . . 11.00
Rose Bowl, Emerald Green To Clear, Bull's-Eye & File, 4 In.. . . . . 880.00
Rose Bowl, Encore, Straus, 5 ½ In.. . . . . 165.00
Rose Bowl, Green To Clear, Leaf & Geometric Design, 5 ¼ x 6 In. 80.00
Rose Bowl, Mistletoe, c.1902, 10 ¼ x 7 ½ In.. . . . . 840.00
Rose Bowl, Punty, Hexagonal, 6 ½ x 7 In. 120.00
Salt, Hobstar & Fan, 3 In.. . . . . 90.00
Salt & Pepper, Green To Clear, Star & Vertical Cut, American Brilliant . . . . *illus* 385.00
Salt & Pepper, Hobstar & Prism, Silver Plated Covers, 4 ½ In.. . . . . 28.00
Salt & Pepper, Prism, Embossed Sterling Silver Covers, American Brilliant, 2 ¼ In. 28.00
Salt & Pepper, Prism Cut Body, Embossed Sterling Silver Covers, 3 In., Pair 225.00
Sandwich Server, Crosscut Diamond, Vertical Notch, Center Handle, Round, 7 x 10 In.. . . . . 90.00
Sandwich Server, Dahlia & Starburst, c.1900, 12 In.. . . . . 351.00
Sandwich Server, Greek Key, Meriden, 10 In. 990.00
Sandwich Server, Hobstar, Cane, Strawberry Diamond & Fan, Wafer Base, American Brilliant, 10 In. 100.00

Cut Glass, Pitcher, Encore, Straus, 5 In.
$140.00

Cut Glass, Salt & Pepper, Green To Clear, Star & Vertical Cut, American Brilliant
$385.00

TIP
Having trouble with a stain in a glass bottle or vase? Sometimes this type of stain can be removed. Fill the bottle with water, drop in an Alka-Seltzer, and let it soak for about 24 hours. Then rub the ring with a brush or a cloth. If the deposit is a chemical deposit, this treatment should remove it. If the ring is actually caused by etching of the glass, it cannot be removed unless the bottle is professionally polished.

Cut Glass, Tankard, Cranberry To Clear, Hobstar Base, Signed, Dorflinger, Tiffany & Co., 14 ½ In.
$53900.00

Cut Glass, Tray, Flashed Hobstar, Strawberry Diamond, Fan & Hobstar, American Brilliant, 12 In.
$110.00

Cut Glass, Tray, Hobstar, Prism, Strawberry Diamond, 8-Sided, American Brilliant, 11 In.
$495.00

Sandwich Server, Shirley, Center Handle, Meriden, 10 In. 66.00
Shade, Hurricane, Intaglio, Grapes, Vines, Rolled Rim, 1800s, 22 ¾ In., Pair 2990.00
Spooner, Hobstar, Star, Prism & Fan, Pinched Waist, American Brilliant, 4 ¼ In. 220.00
Sugar, Dome Cover, Strawberry Diamond, Cut Finial, Drum Shape, 6 ¾ x 4 ¾ In. 420.00
Sugar, Strawberry Diamond, Crosshatch, Anglo-Irish, 7 ¼ x 4 ½ In. 390.00
Sugar & Creamer, Buzz Star, Bulbous, 2 ¼ & 3 In. 11.00
Sugar & Creamer, Byrns, Footed, American Brilliant 165.00
Sugar & Creamer, Easter, Bulbous, 3 ¼ & 2 ⅞ In. 11.00
Sugar & Creamer, Hobstar, Pinwheel Ends, 6 ¾ & 5 ¼ In. 315.00
Sugar & Creamer, Hobstar, Split Strawberry Diamond & Cane, Notched Handles 110.00
Sugar & Creamer, Hobstar & Fan, Notched Handles, Rayed Base, American Brilliant 77.00
Sugar Shaker, Electra, Embossed Sterling Silver Cover, American Brilliant, 4 ½ In. 350.00
Sugar Shaker, Intaglio Flowers, Wilcox Sterling Silver Cover, 4 ¾ In. 40.00
Syrup, Hobstar, Strawberry Diamond & Fan, Silver Plated Spout, 6 In. 175.00
Syrup, Prism Cut Body, Strawberry Diamond & Hobstar, Triple Notched Handle, 5 ¼ In. 100.00
Tankard, Buttons, Cane, Crosshatch, Double Notched Handle, Rayed Star Base, 14 In. 288.00
Tankard, Cranberry To Clear, Hobstar Base, Signed, Dorflinger, Tiffany & Co., 14 ½ In. *illus* 53900.00
Tankard, Grapevine, Triple Notched Handle, Fluted Spout, 10 ¼ x 6 ¼ In. 115.00
Tankard, Hobstar, Strawberry Diamond, Cane, Vesica, Star & Notch, Pinched Waist, 12 ¾ In. 650.00
Tankard, Hobstar, Triple Notched Handle, 11 In. 225.00
Tankard, Hobstar Vesica, Strawberry Diamond, Notch & Fan, American Brilliant, 13 In. 303.00
Tankard, Lotus Variant, Egginton, Triple Notched Handle, 14 ¾ In. 660.00
Tankard, Notched Prism Swirled, Tiffany & Co., Sterling Silver Spout, Mark, c.1907, 11 In. 323.00
Tankard, Strawberry Diamond, Hobstar & Fan, Notched Handle, American Brilliant, 13 ¼ In. 750.00
Tazza, Elmira, Hobstar Base, 9 In. 550.00
Tazza, Rolled Rim, Harvard, Hobstar Base, 7 ¾ In. 200.00
Tip Tray, Sterling Rim, Hobstar, Block, Vesica & Strawberry Diamond, American Brilliant, 6 In. 350.00
Toothpick, Crosscut Diamond, Egg Shape, Signed, Alfred, 4 In. 175.00
Toothpick, Pedestal, Hobstar, Diamond, Pair 80.00
Tray, Atlantic, Round, Empire, 12 In. 275.00
Tray, Baker's Gothic, Heart Shape, Clark, 7 ½ In. 138.00
Tray, Cane, Round, American Brilliant, 10 ¼ In. 44.00
Tray, Crosscut Diamond & Fan, Hobstar Center, Rectangular, American Brilliant, 11 x 7 In. 40.00
Tray, Diamond Band, Castle & Forest Scene, Round, American Brilliant, 9 ¾ In. 500.00
Tray, Fish Tail, Flashed Hobstar Center, Cane, Hobstar & Fan, 13 ½ In. 900.00
Tray, Flashed Hobstar, Strawberry Diamond, Fan & Hobstar, American Brilliant, 12 In. *illus* 110.00
Tray, Hobstar, Fans, Round, 11 ⅞ In. 115.00
Tray, Hobstar, Prism, Strawberry Diamond, 8-Sided, American Brilliant, 11 In. *illus* 495.00
Tray, Hobstar, Strawberry Diamond Button & Fan, Tab Handles, 13 x 5 ½ In. 90.00
Tray, Hobstar Center, Hobstar & Fan Border, American Brilliant, 12 In. *illus* 440.00
Tray, Ice Cream, Hobstar, Pinwheel, Nailhead Diamond & Fan, American Brilliant, 14 x 7 ½ In. 200.00
Tray, Ice Cream, Hobstar, Strawberry Diamond, Vesica, Nailhead Diamond, 14 x 7 ½ In. 300.00
Tray, Ice Cream, Hobstar Center, Fan & Hobstar Border, Tab Handle, 13 ¼ x 8 ½ In. 250.00
Tray, Ice Cream, Hobstar Cluster, Strawberry Diamond, Star & Fan, American Brilliant, 12 In. 350.00
Tray, Ice Cream, Star, Hobstar, Cane, Notch & Fan, Scalloped Side, 18 x 10 ½ In. 715.00
Tray, Ice Cream, Victoria Pattern, Tab Handle, American Brilliant, 13 ½ x 8 ¾ In. 400.00
Tray, Intaglio 3 Fruits, American Brilliant, 11 ½ In. 193.00
Tray, Intaglio Strawberry & Vine, Round, 11 ¼ In. 125.00
Tray, Owl Face, Hobstars, Crosshatch, Button Cut Hobstar Ends, Oblong, 12 ½ x 5 In. 115.00
Tray, Russian, Cut Buttons, Ray Center, Square, 11 In. 25.00
Tray, Russian, Star Cut Buttons, Pedestal, Round, 3 ¼ x 9 In. 250.00 to 325.00
Tray, Thistle, Harvard Bands, 6 Panels, American Brilliant, 12 ¼ In. 130.00
Tray, Vaseline, Cluster, Bull's-Eye, Arch & Hobstar, 9 ½ In. 275.00
Tray, Wild Rose, 5 Lobes, Tuthill, 14 In. 4290.00
Tumbler, Iced Tea, Alhambra, Greek Key, Meriden, 4 ¾ In. 300.00
Tumbler, Primrose, Tuthill, 3 ¾ In., 6 Piece 385.00
Tumbler, Whiskey, Carolyn, J. Hoare, 3 In. 165.00
Tumbler, Whiskey, Hobstar, Prism & Fan, American Brilliant, 2 ½ In., Pair 20.00
Urn, Napoleon III Style, Gilt Bronze Flared Rim, Handles, Mask Mounts, Base, c.1875, 22 In. 590.00
Urn, Shannon, Intaglio Flowers, 12 x 8 In. 125.00
Vase, Alhambra, Greek Key, Pinched Waist, Hobstar Base, 15 ¾ In. 2700.00
Vase, Amethyst To Clear, Engraved, Minstrel Scene, Gondola, Birds, Signed, 8 ½ In. 500.00
Vase, Bull's-Eye, Hobstar Border, Feather & Step Cut Neck, Bowling Pin Shape, 10 In. 495.00
Vase, Chalice Shape, Strawberry With Gold Scrolls & Leaves, Signed, Hutte, 12 In. 345.00
Vase, Cobalt Blue, Ribbed, Baluster Stem, Footed, c.1875, 9 ¾ x 4 In. 1469.00
Vase, Cranberry To Clear, Hobstar & Nailhead Diamond, Bowling Pin Shape, 11 ¾ In. 4200.00

Vase, Creswick, Scalloped Rim, Pinched Neck, Egginton, 7 ¼ In. . . . 489.00
Vase, Crosscut Diamond Vesica, Engraved Flower, Flared Top, American Brilliant, 7 In. . . . 125.00
Vase, Fans, Crisscrosses, Triangles, Flared, Footed, 6 ½ x 5 ½ In. . . . 35.00
Vase, Florence Hobstar, Sunburst, Pedestal, Pinched Waist, 8 ¼ In. . . . 60.00
Vase, Flower & Fern, Hobstar Base, Pedestal, 10 In. . . . 50.00
Vase, Flower Shape, Diamond & Star, 17 ¼ In. . . . 914.00
Vase, Harvard, Pinched Waist, 12 In. . . . 210.00
Vase, Hindoo, Bowling Pin Shape, J. Hoare, 11 ¾ In. . . . 275.00
Vase, Hobstar, Crosscut Diamond, Strawberry Diamond & Fan, Bowling Pin Shape, 10 In. . . . 225.00
Vase, Hobstar, Feather, Button & Fan, Hobstar Base, 13 ¾ In. . . . 400.00
Vase, Hobstar, Pinwheel, Cane, Strawberry Diamond & Fan, 10 In. . . . 90.00
Vase, Hobstar, Prism, Strawberry Diamond, Pinwheel, Fan, Pinched Waist, 18 ¼ In. . . . 650.00
Vase, Hobstar, Prism & Fan, 3-Footed, 4 In. . . . 140.00
Vase, Hobstar, Strawberry Diamond & Fan, Bowling Pin Shape, 9 ½ In. . . . 275.00
Vase, Hobstar, Zipper, Crosscut Diamond, Fan, Bowling Pin Shape, 7 ¾ In. . . . 300.00
Vase, Hobstar & File, Pinched Waist, Sterling Silver Rim, American Brilliant, 7 ¼ In. . . . 130.00
Vase, Hobstar & Strawberry Diamond, Pinched Waist, American Brilliant, 4 x 5 In. . . . 225.00
Vase, Hobstar Bands, Thistle Band, Honeycomb Windows, Pinched Waist, 11 ¾ In. . . . 250.00
Vase, Hobstar Columns, Prism Columns, Pinwheel, Diamond Bands, Clark, 13 ½ In. . . . 450.00
Vase, Hobstar In Square Blocks, Rolled Rim, American Brilliant, 5 ½ In. . . . 121.00
Vase, Hobstars, Thumbprint, Cane, Fan, Sawtooth Rim, Hexagonal, 14 x 8 In. . . . 230.00
Vase, Intaglio, Thistles, Sunflowers, Flared, Scalloped Rim, 17 ¾ In. . . . 127.00
Vase, Intaglio Thistle, Butterfly, Flared Rim, 10 In. . . . 822.00
Vase, Intaglio, Iris, Flared, c.1910, 14 x 7 ¼ In. . . . 205.00
Vase, Pedestal, Hobstar, Vesica, Strawberry Diamond & Fan, Pinched Waist, 11 ¾ In. . . . 400.00
Vase, Pinwheel, Prism & Fan, Pedestal Base, Maple City, 11 In. . . . 99.00
Vase, Primrose, Pinched Waist, 10 In. . . . 150.00
Vase, Shannon, Diamond, Godinger, 10 x 6 ½ In. . . . 75.00
Vase, Shannon, Frosted, Flowers, Godinger, 12 x 8 In. . . . 125.00
Vase, Stars, Geometric, Sawtooth Rim, Tapered, American Brilliant, 16 In. . . . 206.00
Vase, Sweet Pea, Creswick, Hobstar Base, Egginton, 4 ¾ x 8 ¾ In. . . . 175.00
Vase, Swirled Pillar & Diamond Pillar, Hobstar, Sterling Silver Rim, American Brilliant, 11 ½ In. 450.00
Vase, Swirled Pillars, Flowers, Ray Cut Base, Pedestal, 6 ¾ In. . . . 450.00
Vase, Trumpet, Crosscut Diamond, Notch, Star & Fan, 15 ½ In. . . . 80.00
Vase, Trumpet, Emerald Green To Clear, Strawberry Diamond, Star & Fan, Ray Base, 12 In. . . . 500.00
Vase, Trumpet, Flute & Vertical Cane, Ray Base, 8 In. . . . 300.00
Vase, Trumpet, Zipper, Dot, 12 In. . . . 22.00
Vase, Tulip Shape, Hobstar & Hobstar Cluster, Scalloped Base, 12 In., Pair . . . 500.00
Vase, Vertical Hobstar & Bull's-Eye, Footed, American Brilliant, 15 In. . . . 193.00
Vase, Violet, Star, Strawberry Diamond & Fan, 3 ¾ In. . . . 60.00
Vase, White Rose, Tricornered, Flared, American Brilliant, 4 ¾ x 7 In. . . . 66.00
Water Set, Harvard, Flower, & Gothic Windows, Notched Handle, 10 ½ In., 6 Piece . . . 125.00
Water Set, Hobstar, File Border, Star Button Body, Triple Notched Handle, 10 ½ In., 7 Piece . . 30.00
Water Set, Intaglio Poppy, Crosshatch, Star Obelisk, Dot Handle, 7 Piece . . . 33.00
Wine, Cranberry To Clear, Cane & Pillar Arches, Clear Stem, 4 ¾ In. . . . 500.00
Wine, Cranberry To Clear, Crosscut Diamond, Strawberry Diamond & Fan, 4 ¾ In. . . . 475.00
Wine, Cranberry To Clear, Intaglio Vintage, Faceted Teardrop Stem, American Brilliant, 4 ¾ In. 125.00
Wine, Cranberry To Clear, No. 50, Dorflinger, 4 ⅝ In., Pair . . . 1210.00
Wine, Cranberry To Clear, Parisian, Hobstar Base, American Brilliant, 4 ¾ In. . . . 575.00
Wine, Cranberry To Clear, Russian, Star Buttons, Clear Stem, American Brilliant, 4 ½ In. . . . 25.00
Wine, Cranberry To Clear, Star, 4 ¾ In., 6 Piece . . . 900.00
Wine, Cranberry To Clear, Strawberry Diamond, Block & Fan, 6-Sided Stem, 4 ½ In. . . . 275.00
Wine, Cranberry To Vaseline, Strawberry Diamond, Star & Fan, Notched Stem, 4 ¾ In. . . . 950.00
Wine, Green, Clear Stem & Base, Picket Fence, 4 ½ In., Pair . . . 99.00
Wine, Green, Diamond & Fan, Clear Stem, Ray Base, American Brilliant, 4 ¾ In. . . . 325.00
Wine, Monarch, Scalloped Hobstar Base, J. Hoare, 4 In. . . . 100.00
Wine, Rhine, Cranberry To Clear, Intaglio Flower Swirl, Bow Border, 7 ½ In. . . . 3900.00
Wine, Russian, Apple Green, American Brilliant, 4 ⅞ In., Pair . . . *illus* 880.00
Wine, Vaseline, 6 Panels, 2 3-Petal Tulips, Medial Knop Stem, c.1875, 4 ½ In. . . . 60.00
Wine, Yellow, Diamonds & Punty, Clear Stem, Ray Base, American Brilliant, 5 ¼ In. . . . 375.00
Wine Cooler, Diamond Lozenge Panels, Silver Plated Rim & Handles, 8 ½ In. . . . 71.00

CUT VELVET is a special type of art glass, made with two layers of blown glass, that shows a raised pattern. It usually had an acid finish or a texture like velvet. It was made by many glass factories during the late Victorian years.

Vase, Mustard Yellow, Diamond Quilted, 8 In. . . . *illus* 225.00

Cut Glass, Tray, Hobstar Center, Hobstar & Fan Border, American Brilliant, 12 In. $440.00

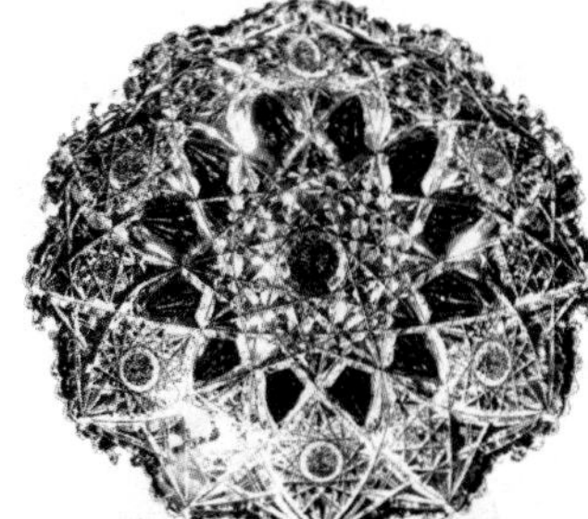

Cut Glass, Wine, Russian, Apple Green, American Brilliant, 4 ⅞ In., Pair $880.00

Cut Velvet, Vase, Mustard Yellow, Diamond Quilted, 8 In. $225.00

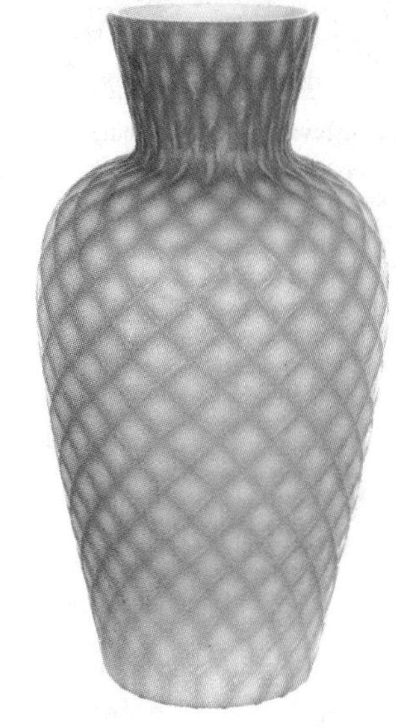

C

Czechoslavakia, Perfume Bottle, Art Deco Woman, Turquoise Glass, 6-Sided, Stopper, 6 In.
$1840.00

Czechoslavakia, Perfume Bottle, Cut Glass, Frosted Bear Stopper, Dabber, Signed, 5 ¾ In.
$5175.00

Czechoslavakia, Perfume Bottle, Cut Glass, Frosted Man & Woman, Dabber, 5 ¾ In.
$230.00

CYBIS porcelain is a twentieth-century product. Boleslaw Cybis came to the United States from Poland in 1939. He started making porcelains in Long Island, New York, in 1940. He moved to Trenton, New Jersey, in 1942 as one of the founders of Cordey China Co. and started his own Cybis Porcelains about 1950. The firm is still working.

CYBIS

Bust, Clown, Funny Face, Ruffled Collar, Light Blue Bow, Stand, 9 ½ In. . . . 110.00
Bust, Indian Boy, Little Eagle, Feathered Headband, Signed, 12 In. . . . 100.00 to 130.00
Bust, Indian Girl, Feathers In Hair, 9 ½ In. . . . 200.00
Bust, Indian Girl, Running Deer, Feather Headband, Signed, 10 In. . . . 100.00 to 200.00
Figurine, Apollo II, Eagle Has Landed, July 20 1969, 17 x 6 In. . . . 585.00
Figurine, Baby Owl, On Branch, White, 4 ½ In. . . . 25.00
Figurine, Bird, Striped Tail, White Flowers, Green Vines, Wood Base, 13 In. . . . 120.00
Figurine, Clown, Rumples, Hands On Chin, Seated, 6 ½ In. . . . 80.00
Figurine, Court Jester, 15 In. . . . 300.00
Figurine, Dakota Laughing Water, Minnehaha, Limited Edition, 9 ½ x 8 ½ In. . . . 290.00
Figurine, High Rise, 3 Squirrels Looking Out Of Tree, Leaves, 8 In. . . . 70.00
Figurine, Hippocampus, Sea King's Steed, 14 x 12 In. . . . 400.00
Figurine, Horse, Poppy, Performing Pony, Light Blue, Pink & Gilt Harness, 6 x 9 In. . . . 225.00
Figurine, Little Blue Heron, 9 ⅛ In. . . . 351.00
Figurine, Onondaga Hiawatha, Limited Edition, 11 In. . . . 50.00
Figurine, Sandpiper, 5 x 8 In. . . . 47.00
Figurine, Turtle Doves, c.1957, 13 x 11 In. . . . 293.00
Figurine, Windflower, 8 In. . . . 50.00
Flower, Magnolia, 6 x 11 In. . . . 128.00

CZECHOSLOVAKIA is a popular term with collectors. The name, first used as a mark after the country was formed in 1918, appears on glass and porcelain and other decorative items. Although Czechoslovakia split into Slovakia and the Czech Republic on January 1, 1993, the name continues to be used in some trademarks.

Bookends, Embossed, Wave, Frosted, Art Deco, 5 In. . . . 30.00
Charger, Clear, Engraved, Thistle & Thorn, 14 ½ In. . . . 125.00
Charger, Engraved, Thistle & Thorn, 14 ½ In. . . . 125.00
Cordial, Clear, Frosted, Black Enameled Geometric, 7 Piece . . . 837.00
Perfume Bottle, Amber, Intaglio Stopper, Draped Nude Woman, 6 ½ In. . . . 2875.00
Perfume Bottle, Art Deco Woman, Turquoise Glass, 6-Sided, Stopper, 6 In. . . . *illus* 1840.00
Perfume Bottle, Black, Clear Intaglio Stopper, Cleopatra With Attendants, 4 ¾ In. . . . 518.00
Perfume Bottle, Black, Clear Intaglio Stopper, Ship, Dabber, 6 In. . . . 489.00
Perfume Bottle, Black, Cone Shape, Jeweled Metal Stopper, 5 ½ In. . . . 127.00
Perfume Bottle, Blue, Clear Tiara Stopper, Flowers, 7 ¾ In. . . . 374.00
Perfume Bottle, Charcoal, Metal Cap, Framework, Enameled, 4 ¾ In. . . . 920.00
Perfume Bottle, Cherub, Cupid, Frosted, Atomizer, Hoffman, 10 In. . . . 2400.00
Perfume Bottle, Clear, 2 Hearts, Cut Allover, 2-Sided Cut Stopper, 7 ¾ In. . . . 518.00
Perfume Bottle, Clear, Blue, Stopper, Dabber, 1 ¾ In. . . . 403.00
Perfume Bottle, Clear, Figural Stopper, Shoe, Allover Cutting, Dabber, 5 ¼ In. . . . 1380.00
Perfume Bottle, Clear, Frosted, Violet Intaglio Stopper, Rose, Dabber, 4 ¼ In. . . . 299.00
Perfume Bottle, Clear, Frosted Intaglio Stopper, Bear On Ball, Dabber, 5 ¾ In. . . . 5175.00
Perfume Bottle, Clear, Intaglio Stopper, Flowers, 6 In. . . . 58.00
Perfume Bottle, Clear, Intaglio Stopper, Flowers, Red Jewels, Dabber, 7 In. . . . 805.00
Perfume Bottle, Clear, Intaglio Stopper, Frosted, Man Caressing Woman's Hand, 8 In. . . . 230.00
Perfume Bottle, Clear, Intaglio Stopper, Woman, Cupid Blowing Bubbles, 7 In. . . . 242.00
Perfume Bottle, Clear, Pink Intaglio Stopper, Cupids About To Kiss, Dabber, 5 ½ In. . . . 58.00
Perfume Bottle, Clear, Ruby Intaglio Stopper, Art Deco Flowers, Dabber, 6 In. . . . 431.00
Perfume Bottle, Clear, Screw Cap, Amber, Green Jewels, Chains, 2 ¼ In., Pair . . . 184.00
Perfume Bottle, Clear, Screw Stopper, Metal Frieze, Stones, Dabber, 2 ½ In. . . . 92.00
Perfume Bottle, Clear, Tiara Intaglio Stopper, Flowers, Dabber, 6 ¼ In. . . . 104.00
Perfume Bottle, Clear, Violet Stopper, Violet Jewel, Dabber, 3 In. . . . 173.00
Perfume Bottle, Clear, Yellow Intaglio Stopper, Flowers, 5 In. . . . 81.00
Perfume Bottle, Cut Glass, Frosted Bear Stopper, Dabber, Signed, 5 ¾ In. . . . *illus* 5175.00
Perfume Bottle, Cut Glass, Frosted Man & Woman, Dabber, 5 ¾ In. . . . *illus* 230.00
Perfume Bottle, Enameled Stopper, Gold Trim, 3 x 2 In. . . . 30.00
Perfume Bottle, Figural, Seated Cat, Purple, Flower Stopper, 1920, 3 ¾ In. . . . 1800.00
Perfume Bottle, Flowers, Black, Intaglio Stopper, Nude Woman, 1930s, 5 In. . . . 250.00
Perfume Bottle, Jeurelle, Clear, Stopper, 1 ½ In. . . . 345.00
Perfume Bottle, Lapis Lazuli, Bluebells, Molded, Dabber, Signed, 9 In. . . . *illus* 2875.00
Perfume Bottle, Le Clairac, Forbidden Love, Pink, 1930s, 7 ¼ In. . . . 360.00

Perfume Bottle, Malachite, Cupids, Flower Garlands, Stopper, 6 ½ In. 110.00
Perfume Bottle, Opalescent, Blossom Shape, Dabber, Stopper, 3 ¼ In. 374.00
Perfume Bottle, Peach, Stopper, Dabber, 2 In. 150.00
Perfume Bottle, Red, Pleated Stopper, Dabber, 5 In. 633.00
Perfume Bottle, Tiara, Clear, Blue Frosted Stopper, 6 ⅝ In. 1800.00
Perfume Bottle, Turquoise, 6-Sided, Art Deco Woman, Stopper, 5 ¾ In. 1840.00
Perfume Bottle, Turquoise, Intaglio Stopper, Nude Woman, Branches, Leaves, 5 ½ In. 1610.00
Perfume Bottle, Turquoise, White Art Deco Woman, Hexagonal, 5 ¾ In. 1840.00
Perfume Bottle, Violet, Clear Flower Stopper, Dabber, 6 ½ In. 299.00
Perfume Bottle, Violet, Stopper, Allover Cutting, Dabber, 6 ½ In. 311.00
Sculpture, Fighting Stags, Wooded Landscape, 8 ½ In. 1195.00
Sugar, Cover, Clear, Pinwheel Cutting, 6 x 3 ½ In. 34.00
Tantalus, Flowers, Birds, Pink, Gilt, Painted, 9 ½ In. 88.00
Vase, Clear, Engraved, Thistle & Thorn, 12 In. 125.00
Vase, Clear, Frosted, Geometric, Red, Black, Art Deco, 9 In. 944.00
Vase, Clear, Frosted, Geometric, Red, Black, Rectangular, 1930, 10 ½ In. 590.00
Vase, Clear, Frosted, Geometric, Yellow, Black, 3-Sided, Art Deco, 10 ¼ In. 826.00
Vase, Clear, Frosted, Red Geometric, c.1930, 11 In. 568.00
Vase, Clear Pinwheel Cutting, 8 ¼ x 5 In. 55.00
Vase, Enameled, Frosted, Yellow & Black Geometric, 8 In. 1062.00
Vase, End Of Day, Red Body, White, Blue Spatter, 8 In. 65.00
Vase, End Of Day, Yellow, Brown, Spatter, 7 In. 35.00
Vase, Geometric Etch, Frosted, Enameled, Rectangular, Art Deco, 10 ¾ In. 598.00
Vase, Gold Mercury, Cuspidor Shape, 7 In. 50.00
Vase, Intaglio, Nudes, 6 Fluted Panels, Josef Drahonovsky, 9 In. 2588.00
Vase, Opaque Orange, 3 Cobalt Blue Handles, Pontil, 5 In. *illus* 150.00
Vase, Poppies, Translucent Green, Art Nouveau, 4 ½ In. 443.00
Vase, Red, Black Geometric, Art Deco, Enameled, Etched, Frosted, 9 In. 1416.00
Vase, Trumpet, Gold Iridescent, Rolled Rim, Signed, 12 In. 350.00

CZECHOSLOVAKIA POTTERY

Dish, Cover, Cobalt Blue Border, Peasant, Children, 4 x 9 In. 59.00
Dresser Set, Figures, Green, 24K Gold, Porcelain, 4 Piece 205.00
Pitcher, Rooster, Black, Orange, Art Deco, Ditmar-Urbach, 7 ½ In. 180.00
Pitcher, Toucan, Yellow, Black Red, Art Deco, Ditmar-Urbach, 9 In. 235.00
Planter, Girl, Boy, Garlands, Marked, Amphora, 9 ½ In., Pair *illus* 250.00
Plate, Dinner, Blue & Cream Border, Gold & Flower Highlights, 2 Girls, 9 In. 90.00

DANIEL BOONE, a pre–Revolutionary War folk hero, was a surveyor, trapper, and frontiersman. A television series, which ran from 1964 to 1970, was based on his life and starred Fess Parker. All types of Daniel Boone memorabilia are collected.

Lunch Box, Fess Parker, Lunch Kit, Metal, 1965 95.00
Lunch Box, Fighting Indians, Bear, Yellow, Red, Metal, Thermos, 1955. 44.00
Toy, Frontier Attack Play Set, Fess Parker As Daniel Boone, Box, 1964, 16 x 24 In. *illus* 87.00

D'ARGENTAL is a mark used in France by the Compagnie des Cristalleries de St. Louis. The firm made multilayered, acid-cut cameo glass in the late nineteenth and twentieth centuries. D'Argental is the French name for the city of Munzthal, home of the glassworks. Later the company made enameled etched glass.

Candy Dish, Cover, Flowers, Yellow, Maroon, Cameo, Signed, 6 ¼ In. 700.00
Vase, Brown Leaves, Cone Shape, Signed, 4 ½ In. 300.00
Vase, Brown Thistle, Frosted Amber Ground, 3 ½ In. 403.00
Vase, Castle Scene, Chateau D'alleuze, Amber Leaves, Tapered Oval, Cameo, 5 In. 1035.00
Vase, Citron, 5 Crimson Roses, Squat, Egg Shape, Signed, 5 ½ In. 719.00
Vase, Clematis, Leafy Vine, Purple On Sky Blue, Signed, 5 In. 605.00
Vase, Clematis, Leafy Vines, Mulberry On Periwinkle Ground, Squat, 5 ¾ x 9 In. 825.00
Vase, Red Cherries, Frosted Yellow Ground, 4 In. 575.00
Vase, Yellow Ground, Red Flowers, Red Foot, 12 In. 920.00

DAUM, a glassworks in Nancy, France, was started by Jean Daum in 1875. The company, now called *Cristalleries de Nancy*, is still working. The *Daum Nancy* mark has been used in many variations. The name of the city and the artist are usually both included. The term *martele* is used to describe applied decorations that are carved or etched in the cameo process.

Basket, Flowers, Leaves, Red, Purple, Spider Web, Blue Ground, Enameled, Cameo, 7 ¼ In. 9775.00
Bottle, Clear, Art Deco, Stopper, Engraved, 8 ½ In. 920.00

Czechoslavakia Glass, Perfume Bottle, Lapis Lazuli, Bluebells, Molded, Dabber, Signed, 9 In.
$2875.00

Czechoslavakia Glass, Vase, Opaque Orange, 3 Cobalt Blue Handles, Pontil, 5 In.
$150.00

Czechoslavakia Pottery, Planter, Girl, Boy, Garlands, Marked, Amphora, 9 ½ In., Pair
$250.00

Daniel Boone, Toy, Frontier Attack Play Set, Fess Parker As Daniel Boone, Box, 1964, 16 x 24 In.
$87.00

Daum, Figurine, Horse Head, Blue, Amber, Pate-De-Verre, c.1980, 9 In. $885.00

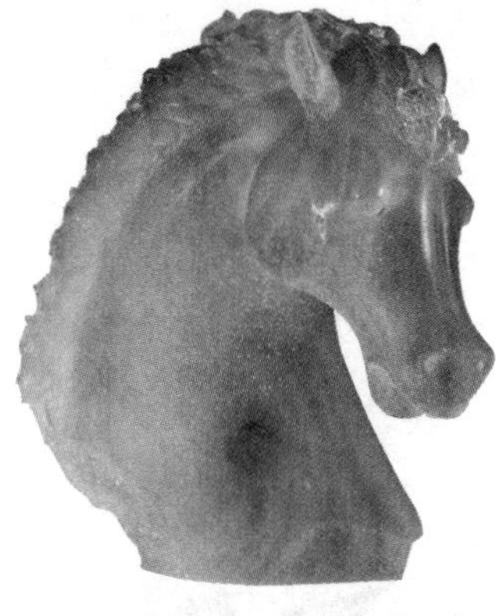

Daum, Paperweight, Squirrel, Mauve, Green, Pate-De-Verre, Signed, 4 ½ In. $3900.00

Daum, Vase, Black Berries, Amber Leaves, Cameo, Footed, Signed, 10 x 5 In. $3600.00

Bottle, Poppies, Red, 3-Sided, Frosted, Striped Ground, 4 ¾ x 4 ½ In. 2520.00
Bowl, Citron, Textured, Frosted, Amber Mottled Ground, Branches, Seed Pods, Cameo, 9 In. 2300.00
Bowl, Flowers, Red, Green Stems, Frosted, Amber Mottled Ground, Bulbous, Cameo, 3 ½ In. 1093.00
Bowl, Flowers, Yellow, Mottled, Brown, Pink, Yellow, White, Enameled, Cameo, 7 ¾ In. 4600.00
Bowl, Landscape, Lake Scene, Gold Enameled Leaves, Signed, 4 In. 225.00
Bowl, Thistle, Textured Amber, Gold Highlights, Quatrefoil Rim, 7 In. 1610.00
Bowl, Trees, Lake, Mottled Blue, Wavy Quatrefoil Rim, Oval, Cameo, 8 In. 5175.00
Box, Cover, Applied Green, Orange, Foil Back, Mottled Orange, Brown Ground, 3 x 3 ½ In. 600.00
Box, Cover, Bumblebees, Stylized Flowers, Enameled, Cameo, 3 ½ In. 7475.00
Box, Cover, Flowers, Butterfly, Insects, Amber Ground, Beaded Trim, Enameled, 5 ¼ x 5 In. 4025.00
Box, Cover, Mistletoe Sprigs, Enameled Berries, Gold Rim, 1 ⅞ In. 1725.00
Champagne Flute, Rose, Pate-De-Verre, Green, Pink, 12 In., 8 Piece 3802.00
Chandelier, Mottled Amber, c.1910, 17 In. 8750.00
Clock, Clear, Iceberg Shape, Black Face, White Numerals, Battery Operated, 5 ½ x 8 In. 86.00
Cologne Bottle, Mistletoe, White Green Textured, Gold Trim, Stopper, 3 In. 805.00
Creamer, Sun Rising Over Water, Applied Camphor Handle, 3 In. 550.00
Cruet, Thistles, Ribbed, Crisscross Stopper, Reeded Handle, Gold Trim, 5 In. 518.00
Cruet, Winter Landscape, Cameo, Signed, 3 In. 3220.00
Decanter, Clear, Square, Pineapple Stopper, 9 ½ x 3 ½ In. 205.00
Decanter, Enameled, Green, Gold, Silver Neck, Cameo, c.1920, 9 ½ In. 1050.00
Decanter, Green, Gold Fleur-De-Lis, Stylized Stopper, c.1900, 9 ½ x 5 In. 3819.00
Decanter, Ruby, Gold Intaglio, Gold Enameled Cross Of Lorraine, Stylized Stopper, c.1900, 13 ¼ In. 2520.00
Dish, Cover, Winter Scene, Enameled, Cameo, c.1920s, 6 In. 4688.00
Figurine, Camel, Clear Box, 10 In. 660.00
Figurine, Cat, Orange, Butterscotch, 2 ½ x 3 In. 117.00
Figurine, Dragon, Pate-De-Verre, Crystal, Orange, 8 x 8 In. 205.00
Figurine, Horse Head, Blue, Amber, Pate-De-Verre, c.1980, 9 In. .... *illus* 885.00
Figurine, Pelican, On Rock, Clear, Signed, 9 x 8 In. 403.00
Figurine, Sailing Boat, Above Wave, Clear, 7 x 15 ⅜ In. 345.00
Ice Bucket, Clear, Rounded Overlapping Design, 5 ¼ x 5 ½ In. 265.00
Jar, Cover, Green, Gold Applied Leaf, Insect, Brown Maple Leaves, Cameo, Signed, 5 In. 9200.00
Lamp, Mottled Red, Yellow, Flowers, Stems, 3-Arm, Greek Key, Bronze Base, Cameo, 6 ½ In. 3450.00
Lamp, Wooded Winter Scene, Vase Shape, Footed, Cameo, Signed, 10 ⅛ In. 355.00
Night-Light, Grapes, Leaves, Yellow Ground, Cameo, Iron Base, Signed 6000.00
Paperweight, Squirrel, Mauve, Green, Pate-De-Verre, Signed, 4 ½ In. .... *illus* 3900.00
Perfume Bottle, Dragonfly, Cameo, Wheel Carved, Stopper, 1910, 6 ⅛ In. 7500.00
Plaque, Venus Draped, Frosted, Amber, Pate-De-Verre, Signed, Oliver Brice, 12 In. 1287.00
Plate, Autumn, Nude Woman & Cherub, Brown, Pate-De-Verre, Signed, Corbin, SC, 1970, 10 ½ In. 175.00
Plate, Grapes, Leaves, Leaf Shape, Signed, 3 ½ x 17 x 12 ½ In. 1760.00
Rose Bowl, Winter Scene, White, Brown, Black, Cameo, Signed, 4 x 5 In. 8625.00
Salt, Fall Trees, Green Meadow, Blue, Handles, Bucket Shape, 2 In. 1495.00
Salt, Mountain, Lake Scene, Pink, Enameled, Oval, 1 In. 345.00
Sculpture, Lovers Sitting On Rock, Blue, Pate-De-Vere, Signed, SCS, 15 In. 1000.00
Sculpture, Wavy Abstract Flower, Purple Center, White, Pate-De-Verre, Signed, Dali, 18 In. 4500.00
Vase, 3 Mermaids, Pate-De-Verre, Signed, 5 ¼ x 4 ½ In. 330.00
Vase, Amethyst, Green, White, Forest Scene, Pillow Shape, Cameo, 6 In. 2070.00
Vase, Apple Blossom, Enameled, White, Green, Brown, Yellow Mottled Ground, Cameo, 7 In. 6613.00
Vase, Applied Plum, Oak Leaves, Cabochon Beetles, Foil Backed, Cameo, 17 ¾ In. 2530.00
Vase, Banjo, Winter Scene, Brown, White, Black, Cameo, Signed, 12 In. 10350.00
Vase, Bellflowers, Amber, Opalescent, Green, Gold Enameled, Martele Ground, Cameo, 6 In. 2040.00
Vase, Bird, Perched On Branch, Etched, Handles, 11 In. 8750.00
Vase, Black Berries, Amber Leaves, Cameo, Footed, Signed, 10 x 5 In. .... *illus* 3600.00
Vase, Black To Pink, Bulb Top, Flared Rectangular Rim, Footed, 24 ¾ In. 1725.00
Vase, Blue Berries, Amber, Green Mottled Ground, Bulbous, Cameo, Signed, 5 In. 1380.00
Vase, Blue Cornflowers, Green Stems, Frost Rose Ground, Blue Base, Enameled, Cameo, 4 x 4 In. 4255.00
Vase, Branches, Fruit, Multicolored, Mottled Ground, Footed, Pulled Rim, 9 ½ x 5 ½ In. 2640.00
Vase, Branches, Leaves, Brown, Yellow, Orange Mottled Ground, Coupe Shape, 11 ½ x 7 In. 3120.00
Vase, Bud, Lilies Of The Valley, Cranberry, Cameo, c.1900, 7 ½ In. 1855.00
Vase, Crocuses, Purple, White, Martele Ground, Footed, 14 x 3 ¾ In. 3120.00
Vase, Crocuses, Red, Frosted Martele Ground, Footed, 5 ½ x 3 ¾ In. 2760.00
Vase, Daffodils, Green, Frosted Ground, Opalescent Interior, Cameo, Signed, 8 In. 6000.00
Vase, Earth Tone Leaves, Applied Jewels, Diamond Shape, Cameo, 6 In. 2820.00
Vase, Etched Linear Bands, Amber, Bulbous, c.1940, 10 x 12 In. 1755.00
Vase, Fisherman Scene, Frame, Green, Textured, Gold, Gingko, Enameled, Cameo, 6 In. 2300.00
Vase, Flower, Pink, Burgundy, Cameo, 11 ¼ In. 6875.00
Vase, Flower, Yellow, Green, Martele Ground, Cameo, 13 In. 6000.00

Vase, Flower Blossoms, Leaves, Russet Over Yellow, Cameo, 9 In. . . . 2040.00
Vase, Flowers, Amethyst To Green Foot, Textured, Oval, Cameo, 3 ½ In. . . . 920.00
Vase, Flowers, Blue, Purple, Green Ground, Square, Enameled, Cameo, Signed, 5 In. . . . 2400.00
Vase, Flowers, Leaves, Red Tobacco, Orange Ground, 10 ¾ x 2 ¾ In. . . . 2280.00
Vase, Flowers, Opalescent Purple, Coupe Shape, Cameo, 4 In. . . . 1438.00
Vase, Flowers, Pink, Pate-De-Verre, Crystal, Green, Pink, 11 x 11 In. . . . 878.00
Vase, Flowers, Red Tobacco, Mottled Orange, Amber Ground, Footed, 8 x 3 In. . . . 2280.00
Vase, Flowers, Stems, Etched, Red Flowers, Orange, Mottled, Enameled, Cameo, 8 In. . . . 3335.00
Vase, Flowers, Stems, Leaves, Opalescent Ground, Cameo, 5 ¾ In. . . . 5175.00
Vase, Forest Scene, White Mottled Ground, Frosted, Enameled, Footed, 15 ¼ x 4 ½ In. . . . 1560.00
Vase, Fuchsia, Yellow, Red, Green Stems, Bulbous, Flared, Cameo, Signed, 3 ¼ In. . . . 1265.00
Vase, Fuchsia Flower, Red, Blue, Blue Textured Ground, Enameled, Cameo, 4 ¾ In. . . . 4200.00
Vase, Geometric Leaves, Berries, Peach, Cameo, Signed, 6 ¼ x 7 ¾ In. . . . *illus* 605.00
Vase, Grapes, Leaves, Yellow, Tan Ground, Applied Snails, Cameo, Signed, 9 In. . . . 10925.00
Vase, Green & Brown Mottled, Orange, Blue, Art Deco, 9 ½ In. . . . 575.00
Vase, Green Body, Mottled Blue & White, Maroon Spiral Band, Applied Handles, 6 In. . . . 480.00
Vase, Green Flowers, Blue Ground, Dark Foot, Cameo, Signed, 12 In. . . . 8400.00
Vase, Green Leaves, Stems, Red Berries, Applied Cabochon Berries, Cameo, 12 In. . . . 8625.00
Vase, Haystacks, Trees, Yellow, Frosted, Amber, Cranberry, Blue, Handles, Signed, 6 ¼ In. . . . *illus* 3304.00
Vase, Iris, Brown, Lavender, Padded, Purple Leaves, Cameo, Signed, 12 In. . . . 7200.00
Vase, Iris, Mottled Ground, Green & Yellow Shaded To Blue, 3 ¾ In. . . . 748.00
Vase, Iris, Purple, Clear Ground, Diamond Shape, Cameo, 7 ¼ In. . . . 711.00
Vase, Iris, Purple Frosted, Clear Ground, 8 ⅜ In. . . . 695.00
Vase, Ivy Vines, Berries, Enameled, Mustard, Amethyst, Cameo, 4 ¾ In. . . . 1093.00
Vase, Lakeland Scene, Autumn Tones, Signed, 21 ½ x 10 ½ In. . . . 5100.00
Vase, Landscape, Amethyst, White, Spring Scene, Enameled, Cameo, 5 ¼ In. . . . 3600.00
Vase, Leaves, Blue Mottled To White Ground, Cameo, 10 ½ In. . . . 7475.00
Vase, Leaves, Mottled, Yellow, Purple, Brown, Green, Cameo, Signed, 12 x 4 ¼ In. . . . 1440.00
Vase, Lotus Flowers, Leaves, Green, Green To Pink Martele Ground, 8 x 4 ¼ In. . . . 2040.00
Vase, Monkeys, Clear, Engraved, c.1930, 5 ½ In. . . . 5625.00
Vase, Monkeys, Clear, Engraved, Handles, c.1925, 4 ¾ In. . . . 2000.00
Vase, Orange, Brown Flowers, Leaves, Yellow To Red Ground, Bulbous, Long Neck, 5 x 10 In. . . . 1200.00
Vase, Orange Poppies, Orange Shaded To Yellow, Square, Enameled, Cameo, 3 ¾ In. . . . 3600.00
Vase, Parrot Tulip, Purple Ground, Cameo, Signed, 6 In. . . . 6000.00
Vase, Patches Of Gold Foil Inclusions, Scarlet & Brown, Footed, 14 In. . . . 805.00
Vase, Peacock Feather, Green, Purple Mottled Shading, Blue Ground, Cameo, 3 ½ In. . . . 4600.00
Vase, Pillow, Brown, Green Leaves, Yellow Ground, Orange, Mushrooms, Nancy, 5 x 5 In. . . . 1560.00
Vase, Pillow, Mottled Green & Blue, Signed, 4 ½ x 7 x 2 ¼ In. . . . 550.00
Vase, Pillow, Red Berries, Green Leaves, Mottled Ground, Enameled, Cameo, 5 In. . . . 5175.00
Vase, Pillow, Violets, Purple, Frosted, Yellow Ground, Enameled, Cameo, Signed, 5 x 5 In. . . . 4313.00
Vase, Pink, Textured Leafy Branch, Red Flowers, Gold Rim & Foot, Cameo, 7 ¾ In. . . . 2415.00
Vase, Poppies, Leaves, Yellow, Orange, Gold Line Base, Square, Enameled, Cameo, Signed, 5 In. 4200.00
Vase, Poppies, Orange, Padded, Green, Yellow Stems, Frosted Ground, 8 ½ x 2 ¾ In. . . . 2880.00
Vase, Poppies, Orange, Padded, Martele Ground, Brown Intaglio Foot, Cameo, 16 In. . . . 9200.00
Vase, Rain Scene, Silver, Green, Black, Textured, Square, Enameled, Signed, 4 In. . . . 8625.00
Vase, Red Berries, Green Leaves, Yellow Ground, Enameled, Cameo, 15 In. . . . 8050.00
Vase, Sailboats, Leafy Trees, Shoreline, Squared, Footed, 9 In. . . . 863.00
Vase, Scenic, Islands, Shoreline, Amber Ground, Enameled, Cameo, 8 ¼ In. . . . 1955.00
Vase, Shaded Plum, Opalescent Ground, Cameo, c.1900, 5 ¾ In. . . . 3300.00
Vase, Ships In Harbor, Brown Trees, Yellow & Orange Ground, Cameo, 4 ½ In. . . . 920.00
Vase, Silver, Amber Flowers, Green Stems, Leaves, Cameo, Signed, 7 ¼ In. . . . 9775.00
Vase, Spanish Green, Vert D'Espagne, Pate-De-Verre, Salvador Dali, 13 x 11 In. . . . 1521.00
Vase, Spring Scene, Etched, Enameled Trees, Cinched Base, Cameo, Signed, 11 In. . . . 6325.00
Vase, Spring Scene, Trees Along River, Yellow, Rust, Gray, Enameled, 9 In. . . . 9200.00
Vase, Stylized Berries, Leaves, Orange, Signed, c.1910, 8 x 5 In. . . . *illus* 1640.00
Vase, Swan, Trees, Leaves, Blue Mottled Ground, Enameled, Cameo, 4 ½ In. . . . 5175.00
Vase, Swans, Birds, Enameled Landscape, Cameo, Signed, 25 In. . . . 18400.00
Vase, Teal, Mottled Yellow, Frosted, Oval, Rectangular Rim, 1920s, 4 ½ x 7 x 2 ½ In. . . . 198.00
Vase, Thistle, Flowers, Etched Yellow Ground, Flower Lip Band, Cinched Mouth, Enameled, 8 In. 5750.00
Vase, Tree Scene, Red, Black, Yellow, Shouldered, Cameo, Signed, 8 In. . . . 1725.00
Vase, Trees, Forest, Lake, Bamboo Shoots On Base, Blue, Footed, Signed, 10 In. . . . 1500.00
Vase, Trumpet, Flowers, Cross Of Lorraine, Round Foot, Cameo, c.1821, 9 ½ In. . . . 9000.00
Vase, Tulips, Red, Etched, c.1920, 9 ½ In. . . . 3750.00
Vase, Vines, Pink, Opalescent Martele Ground, Bulbous, 8 ¾ x 5 ¾ In. . . . 2520.00
Vase, Violets, Frosted To Purple, Enameled, Cameo, 5 ½ In. . . . 431.00
Vase, Violets, Purple, Padded, Pastel Ground, Cameo, Footed, 8 ¼ x 2 ¼ In. . . . 1440.00
Vase, Waves, Carved, White, Blue, Flared, Signed, 9 x 8 In. . . . 660.00

Daum, Vase, Geometric Leaves, Berries, Peach, Cameo, Signed, 6 ¼ x 7 ¾ In.
$605.00

Daum, Vase, Haystacks, Trees, Yellow, Frosted, Amber, Cranberry, Blue, Handles, Signed, 6 ¼ In.
$3304.00

Daum, Vase, Stylized Berries, Leaves, Orange, Signed, c.1910, 8 x 5 In.
$1640.00

TIP

Remove stains from old ceramic vases by scrubbing with salt.

Davenport, Pitcher, Washbowl, Columbine, Gaudy, Multicolored Enamel, 10 In. Pitcher
$518.00

Davy Crockett , Mug, Hazel Atlas, 1950s, 3 ¼ In.
$20.00

De Vez, Vase, Fishing Boat, Opalescent, Blue, Cranberry Overlay, Signed, 1910, 4 In.
$385.00

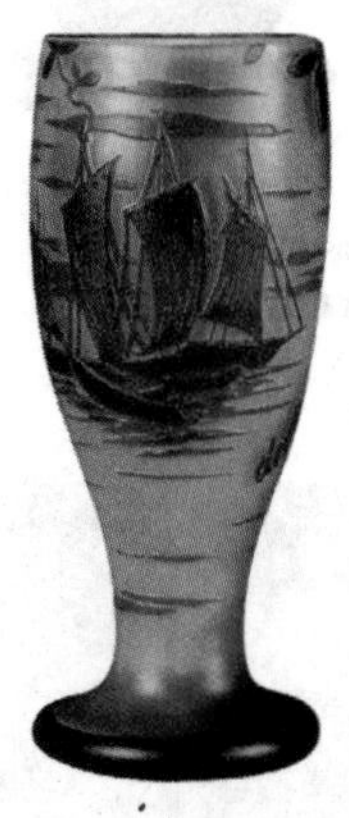

TIP

Floodlights facing toward the house are better protection than floodlights facing away from the house. Moving figures and shadows can be seen more easily.

Vase, Wild Daisies, Frosted Ground, Multicolored, Baluster, Cameo, c.1905, 18 In. 6431.00
Vase, Wildflowers, Enameled, Multicolored, Gold Trim, Frosted Ground, 3 ½ In. 1680.00
Vase, Winter Landscape, Brown, Yellow, Cameo, Signed, 4 In. 6325.00
Vase, Winter Scene, Etched, Brown, White, Black, Canoe Shape, Cameo, Signed, 7 In. 6325.00
Vase, Yellow, Disc Base, Fluted Rim, Ball Shape, 11 In. 345.00

DAVENPORT pottery and porcelain were made at the Davenport factory in Longport, Staffordshire, England, from 1793 to 1887. Earthenwares, creamwares, porcelains, ironstone, and other ceramics were made. Most of the pieces are marked with a form of the word *Davenport*.

Pitcher, Washbowl, Columbine, Gaudy, Multicolored Enamel, 10 In. Pitcher .... *illus* 518.00
Plate, Chinese Pastime, Purple, 9 In. 125.00
Plate, Fig Cousin, White, Ironstone, 12-Sided Crabstock Band Rim, 9 ½ In. 75.00
Plate, Fig Cousin, White, Ironstone, 9 ½ In. 95.00
Plate, Florentine Fountain, Pink Transfer, 9 In. 135.00
Plate, Florentine Fountain, Purple Transfer, 5 ½ In. 85.00
Plate, High Bridge, Blue Transfer, 9 ¾ In. 175.00
Plate, Muleteer, Blue, Black, Green, 10 ¼ In. 225.00
Plate, Soup, Tyrol Hunters, Blue Transfer, 10 ½ In. 125.00
Plate, Swiss Lake & Village, Blue Transfer, 10 ½ In. 145.00
Platter, Fisherman, By Lake, Blue, White, Transfer, 8-Sided, Marked, 21 In. 100.00
Soup, Underplate, Scalloped Decagon, White, Ironstone, Staffordshire, 14 ¼ x 10 ½ In. 125.00
Toothbrush Holder, View In Geneva, Blue Transfer, 1 ¾ x 7 ⅞ x 3 In. 220.00
Tureen, Cover, Amoy, Flow Blue, 8-Sided, c.1844, 9 ¼ In. 153.00
Tureen, Cover, Corn & Oats, White, Ironstone, 9 x 6 ½ In. 100.00
Tureen, Vegetable, Cover, Gothic Octagonal, White, Ironstone, 10 x 7 ½ In. 250.00
Tureen, Vegetable, Scalloped Decagon, White, Staffordshire, 12 ½ x 8 In. 275.00

DAVY CROCKETT, the American frontiersman, was born in 1786 and died in 1836. The historical character gained new fame in 1954 when the Walt Disney television show ran a series of episodes featuring Fess Parker as Davy Crockett. Coonskin caps and buckskins became popular and hundreds of different Davy Crockett items were made.

Banjo, Pressed Wood, Jefferson, Philadelphia, Box, 24 ½ x 11 In. 173.00
Boots, Frontiersman, Rubber, Fringe Trim, Yorktown, Box, Child's, Size 9, 9 x 11 In. 173.00
Clock, Pendulum, Davy With Rifle, Decal, Pressed Wood, Box, c.1955, 8 ½ x 8 ½ In. 173.00
Display Box, 1 Cent, Topps, 1956 .... 550.00
Doll, Cloth, Coonskin Hat, Laced Moccasins, Hallmark, c.1979 .... 16.00
Guitar, Wood, Peter Puppet Playthings, 1950s, 24 In. 95.00
Handkerchief, Embroidered, 10 x 10 In. 15.00
Knife, Fess Parker, Yellow, Can Opener, Screwdriver, Imperial, 3 ½ In. 30.00
Label, Cigar, Woodsman, Inner Label, 8 x 7 In. 507.00
Moccasins, Frontier Moc, Suede, Sure Step Rubber Soles, Box, c.1950s, 4 ½ x 9 ½ In. 115.00
Mug, Hazel Atlas, 1950s, 3 ¼ In. .... *illus* 20.00
Mug, Red, Fire-King 30.00
Mug, White, Brown Graphics, Fire-King, D Handle, 1950s, 8 Oz. 30.00
Pitcher, 48 Oz., 7 In. 10.00
Poster, Paper Lithograph, Mat, Glass, Frame, c.1900, 20 x 28 In. 518.00
Rifle, Davy Crockett Image, Double Barrel, Tin Cork, Japan, c.1950s, 20 In. 109.00
Toy, Indian Dart Game, Original Plastic Packaging, 1950s, 8-In. Tin Targets 115.00
Tumbler, Holiday Freeze, 6 ½ In. 25.00
Tumbler, Indian Fighter, Hero Of Alamo 1786-1836, Yellow, Brown, Orange, 5 ¼ In. 10.00
Tumbler, Morristown Centennial, 1955, 4 ¾ In. 30.00
Tumbler, Snowflake Bakeries, Frosted, Honolulu, T.H., 1950s, 4 ¾ In. 25.00

DE VEZ was a signature used on cameo glass after 1910. E. S. Monot founded the glass company near Paris in 1851. The company changed names many times. Mt. Joye, another glass by this factory, is listed in its own category.

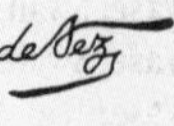

Atomizer, Dark Sunflowers, Butterfly Overlay, Teal Ground, Signed, 6 In. 90.00
Bowl, Red Lake, Trees, Citron, Ground, Squat, Oval, Signed, 6 In. 978.00
Dresser Box, 2 Deer, Water Scene, Blue, Frosted, Enameled, c.1930, 2 ⅛ x 4 ½ In. 125.00
Lamp, Blue Mountains, Lakes, Flowers, Amber, Electrified, France, 12 In. 316.00
Lamp, Mushroom Shade, Green Trees, Red Mountains, Citron Base, Signed, 13 In. 1035.00
Vase, Amber Trees, Castle, Frosted Lake, Blue Mountains, Blue, Signed, 8 In. 1093.00
Vase, Fishing Boat, Opalescent, Blue, Cranberry Overlay, Signed, 1910, 4 In. .... *illus* 385.00
Vase, Fruit Trees, Water, Town, Baluster, Bulbous, c.1920, 8 ⅛ In. 400.00

Vase, Green Over Yellow Over Cream, Scenic, Trees, Birds, 12 In. 1020.00
Vase, Mountain, Lake, Trees, Light Blue Ground, Ruffled Rim, Flared, Signed, 3 ¼ x 4 ¼ In. .. 750.00
Vase, Pines, Amber Mountains, Birds, Iridescent, Bottle Shape, Signed, 7 In. 1150.00
Vase, Scenic, Blue Over Pink & Yellow Ground, 6 In. 863.00
Vase, Tapered, Flared Lip, Mountains, Trees, Purple, Red, c.1900, 6 In. 385.00
Vase, Village & River Scene, Signed, c.1920, 7 In. 600.00

DECORATED TUMBLERS have been made by Anchor Hocking, Federal, Hazel Atlas, Libbey, and other companies since the 1930s, when the pyroglaze process of printing was introduced. The barware and other glasses feature drinking jokes, characters, or decorative geometric patterns. Swankyswigs are listed in their own category. Decorated tumblers may also be listed in Advertising, Coca-Cola, Pepsi-Cola, and many other categories.

Apollo 13, Red White & Blue, Capsule, Moon, Astronauts, c.1970 .... 6.00
Arkansas, Satin Glass, Orange Map, Hazel Atlas, 5 x 2 ⅝ In. 10.00
Atlantic City, Cobalt Blue, 10 Oz., 4 ¾ In. 32.00
Gas Buggy, Iced Tea, Forest Green, 6 ½ In. 10.00
Hi-Di-Ho, Tumbler, Federal, 12 Oz., 6 In. 14.00
Hires Root Beer, Etched, Flared Rim, c.1915-20, 4 In. 258.00
Howard Johnson, Anchor Hocking, 4 x 2 ½ In. 20.00
Kentucky, Teal Ground, Gold Lettering, State Outline, Hazel Atlas, 2 ⅝ x 5 In. 10.00
Kentucky Derby, Churchill Downs, May 2, 1987 .... 8.00
Mug, B & B Restaurant, Nappanee, Indiana, White Ground, Red & Black, 3 ½ In. 10.00
Pizza Hut, Libbey, 5 ¾ In. 8.00
South Dakota, Badlands, Mount Rushmore, Blue & White, 2 ⅝ x 5 In. 9.00
Tomato & Sun, Juice, Red, Yellow, 3 ½ In. 7.00
Wisconsin, Frosted Panel, Red Lettering, State Outline, Hazel Atlas, 4 ¾ In. 9.00
York Peanut Butter, Phil Goyette, Montreal Canadiens, 1961 .... 17925.00

DECOYS are carved or turned wooden copies of birds, fish, or animals. The decoy was placed in the water or propped on the shore to lure flying birds to the pond for hunters. Some decoys are handmade; some are commercial products. Today there is a group of artists making modern decoys for display, not for use in a pond.

Black Duck, Carved Wings, Eyes, Augustus Wilson, 18 In. 1560.00
Black Duck, Ralph Rengi, Mich., 17 In. 58.00
Blue Goose, C.C. Roberts & J.J. Rheinschmidt, 1930s, 21 ½ In. 58.00
Bluebill, Carved, Painted, Applied Head, 6 ¾ x 13 x 6 ½ In. .... *illus* 605.00
Bufflehead, White Pine, Glass Eyes, Long Island Sound, 1950s, 8 ½ In., Pair 440.00
Canada Goose, Painted, Canvas, Wire Frame Body, Wood Head, Ron Vick, 23 ½ In. 118.00
Canada Goose, Pine, Black & White Neck, Head, Glass Eyes, H. McChesney, 14 x 27 In. 201.00
Canada Goose, Pine, Folksy, Stylized, Painted, Glass Eyes, 14 ¾ x 22 In. 176.00
Canada Goose, R. Madison Mitchell, Solid Body, Painted Eyes, 11 ¼ x 24 In. 288.00
Canada Goose, Wood, Carved, Glass Eyes, Rodgers, Port Austin, 24 ½ In. 2990.00
Canada Goose, Wood, Carved, Original Paint, Glass Eyes, Branded BJ, 1900s, 24 x 13 In. 176.00
Canada Goose, Wood, Carved, Original Paint, Glass Eyes, Michigan, 1900s, 26 x 11 In. 147.00
Canada Goose, Wood, Repainted, Shot Scars, 1900s, 10 ½ x 22 ¼ In. 88.00
Canvasback, Pine, Hollow Body, Gray & Black Paint, Brandt, 1900s, 6 x 19 In. 205.00
Canvasback Drake, Carved, Painted, Flat Bottom, Wood Peg Eyes, 16 ½ In. 118.00
Canvasback Drake, St. Clair Flats, Carved, Painted, Glass Eyes, Mount Clemens, 17 In. 295.00
Coot, Pratt Decoy Factory, Joliet, Ill., 1920s 58.00
Crow, Glass Eye, Raised Wing Tip, Hook, Black, 19 In. 144.00
Duck, Carved, Black, Gray, White, Attributed To H.H. Ackerman, 14 x 18 In. 234.00
Duck, Hollow, Carved, Painted, c.1920, 16 In. 1250.00
Duck, Mason Standard, Glass Eyes, Black, 16 In. 259.00
Duck, Painted, Black, Hollow, Applied Head, Multicolored, Glass Eyes, 5 ½ x 14 ½ In. 88.00
Duck, Wood, Carved, Painted, c.1930, 6 x 6 x 15 In. 70.00
Duck Drake, Wood, Carved, Painted, Applied Head, Glass Eyes, 5 x 10 ½ In. 330.00
Duck Drake, Wood, Carved, Painted, On Driftwood, Cape Cod, Mid 1900s, 18 ½ In. 1659.00
Duck Drake, Wood, Charles Perdew, Miniature 3163.00
Eider Drake, Solid Body, Inletted Neck, White, Early 20th Century 920.00
Fish, Carved, Painted, John Linblom, Minnesota, c.1950, 8 In. 12.00
Fish, Fire Gill Head, Leroy Howell, 1930s 115.00
Fish, Ice Fishing, Wood, Yellow, Red, Silver, Metal Fins, Tack Eyes, Chautauqua, 10 In. 403.00
Fish, Ocean Sunfish, Painted, Inch Worm Tie Line, 1940s, 4 In. 58.00
Fish, Pike, Carved, Brass Tack Eyes, Red, Black, Gold, Oscar Peterson, Michigan, 7 In. 920.00
Fish, Pike, John Fairfield, 1989, 10 ½ In. 173.00

TIP

Never put hot glass in cold water, or cold glass in hot water. The temperature change can crack the glass.

D

Decoys, Bluebill, Carved, Painted, Applied Head, 6 ¾ x 13 x 6 ½ In.
$605.00

Decoys, Green-Winged Teal, Softwood, Glass Eyes, Carved, Painted, Stamped, K, 4 ½ x 11 In.
$303.00

Decoy, Redhead Duck, Frank Combs, Alexandria Bay, N.Y., c.1900
$230.00

Decoy, Turtle, Green, Brown, Wood, Metal Feet, 9 In.
$144.00

Chelsea and Dedham Marks

The monogram for Chelsea Keramic Art Works or the name Chelsea Keramic Art Works, Robertson & Sons was used from about 1875 to 1889.

A cloverleaf with the initials CPUS was used from 1891 to 1895.

Dedham Pottery mark (1895–1932)

Dedham Pottery mark (1896–1943)

Dedham, Azalea, Pitcher, 4 ½ In.
$207.00

Dedham, Elephant Baby, Plate, 8 ½ In.
$805.00

Fish, Rainbow Trout, Red, Green, Yellow, Wood, 11 In. 61.00
Fish, Red, Black, Beige, Painted, Tin Fins, Wood, Glass Eyes, 7 ½ x 2 ½ In. 100.00
Fish, Softwood, Tin Fins, Painted White, Early 20th Century, 7 In. 59.00
Fish, Trout, Jim Nelson, Cadillac, Mich., Red & White, Tack Eyes, Metal Fins, c.1950, 7 In. 86.00
Fish, Whitefish, Ken Bruning, Michigan, 7 ½ In. 1265.00
Fish, Wood, Black, Red Paint, Tin Fins, Bead Eyes, c.1940, 21 ½ In. 206.00
Fish On Fish, Carved, Frank Mizra, Black, Yellow, Orange, White Belly, 9 In. 1164.00
Frog, Jointed, Wood, Leather Tail, 2 Snag Hooks, Folk Art, 11 In. 184.00
Goldeneye, Willie Ross, 16 In. 201.00
Goldeneye Drake, Painted, Roy Tilton, c.1946, 13 ¾ In. 173.00
Green-Winged Teal, Softwood, Glass Eyes, Carved, Painted, Stamped, K, 4 ½ x 11 In. *illus* 303.00
Mallard Drake, Frank Schmidt, Detroit, Mich., 1940s 115.00
Mallard Drake, Hays Decoy Factory, Jefferson City, Mo., c.1920. 92.00
Mallard Drake, Mason, Glass Eye Standard Grade, 16 ½ In. 460.00
Merganser, Applied Head, Glass Eyes, Multicolored, 6 ½ x 20 ½ x 5 ¾ In. 198.00
Merganser, Carved, Painted, Early 20th Century, 16 In. 345.00
Merganser, Wood, Applied Head, Crest, Black, White, Metal Tack Eyes, 6 ¾ x 17 x 4 ¾ In. 413.00
Old Squaw, Canvas Covered, Wooden Head, Feather Tail, Early 20th Century, 11 ¾ In. 705.00
Pigeon, Wood, Tin, Early 1900s, 3 ½ x 14 ¾ In. 1007.00
Pintail Drake, A. Elmer Crowell, c.1930, 5 In. 2875.00
Pintail Drake & Hen, Ward Brothers, Signed, 1962, Quarter Size, Pair 2013.00
Pintail Hen, Ward Brothers, 1962, Half Size 1265.00
Red-Breasted Merganser, Carved, Painted, Applied Head, Glass Eyes, Pa., 5 ¾ x 17 ¾ In. 900.00
Red-Breasted Merganser, Head Angled To Left, George Huey, 18 ½ In. 3600.00
Redhead Duck, Frank Combs, Alexandria Bay, N.Y., c.1900 *illus* 230.00
Redhead Duck, Wood, Carved, Painted, 9 x 18 In. 41.00
Scaup Drake, Carved, Painted, Black & White, Applied Head, Glass Eyes, 6 ½ x 13 In. 77.00
Shorebird, Snipe, Painted, Glass Eyes, Nail Beak, 20th Century, 15 x 18 ¾ In. 259.00
Sink Box, Layers Of White Paint, Cast Iron, c.1900, 16 In. 235.00
Sink Box, Worn Original Black & White Paint, Cast Iron, c.1900, 14 In. 705.00
Swan, White, Wood, Carved, 23 x 24 x 11 In. 120.00
Turtle, Green, Brown, Wood, Metal Feet, 9 In. *illus* 144.00

DEDHAM Pottery was started in 1895. Chelsea Keramic Art Works was established in 1872 in Chelsea, Massachusetts, by members of the Robertson family. The factory closed in 1889 and was reorganized as the Chelsea Pottery U.S. in 1891. The firm used the marks CKAW and CPUS. It became the Dedham Pottery of Dedham, Massachusetts. The factory closed in 1943. It was famous for its crackleware dishes, which picture blue outlines of animals, flowers, and other natural motifs. Pottery by Chelsea Keramic Art Works and Dedham Pottery are listed here.

Azalea, Pitcher, 4 ½ In. *illus* 207.00
Bird In Potted Orange Tree, Plate, 6 ⅛ In. 240.00
Duck, Plate, 8 ½ In. 230.00
Duck, Plate, 9 ⅞ In. 121.00
Elephant, Plate, Baby Breakfast, 8 ¼ In. 889.00
Elephant, Sugar, Cover, 3 ½ x 4 ¼ In. 1380.00
Elephant Baby, Bowl, 5 ¼ In. 690.00
Elephant Baby, Plate, 8 ½ In. *illus* 805.00
Grape, Plate, 8 ½ In. 99.00
Grape, Plate, 10 In. 55.00
Iris, Plate, 8 ¼ In. 110.00
Iris, Plate, 9 ⅝ In. 88.00 to 121.00
Lobster, Plate, 8 ½ In. *illus* 495.00
Magnolia, Plate, 10 In. *illus* 132.00
Mushroom, Plate, Breakfast, Rabbit, 8 ½ In. 237.00
Owl, Pitcher, Day & Night, Mark, c.1930, 5 In. 237.00
Pitcher, Berries, Leaves, Vines, Hammered, Green Glaze, CKAW, 7 ½ x 6 In. *illus* 2760.00
Pond Lily, Plate, 8 ⅜ In. 99.00
Poppy, Plate, Rabbit Mark, 8 ½ In. 711.00
Rabbit, Bowl, 11 ½ In. 1422.00
Rabbit, Bowl, Square, 8 In. 267.00
Rabbit, Bowl, Underplate, 2 x 5 ¼ In. 110.00
Rabbit, Creamer, 2 ¼ x 4 ¼ In. *illus* 55.00
Rabbit, Cup & Saucer *illus* 77.00
Rabbit, Jar, Lid, Bulbous, Marked, 3 x 3 In. 270.00
Rabbit, Plate, 8 ½ In. 66.00 to 88.00
Rabbit, Plate, 9 In. 210.00

Dedham, Lobster, Plate, 8 ½ In.
$495.00

Dedham, Magnolia, Plate, 10 In.
$132.00

Dedham, Pitcher, Berries, Leaves, Vines, Hammered, Green Glaze, CKAW, 7 ½ x 6 In.
$2760.00

Dedham, Rabbit, Creamer, 2 ¼ x 4 ¼ In.
$55.00

Dedham, Rabbit, Cup & Saucer
$77.00

Dedham, Rabbit, Plate, Marked, 9 ¾ In.
$121.00

Dedham, Snowtree, Tray, 12 In.
$295.00

Dedham, Vase, Oxblood, Green Mottled Glaze, Volcanic Spot, Experimental, Robertson, 7 In.
$1680.00

Dedham, Vase, Prunus Branches, Crackleware, Signed, CFD, DPR, 6 ½ x 3 ½ In.
$1560.00

TIP

Fishing line is strong and almost invisible and can be used to tie fragile items to a base or wall. This will prevent damage from earthquakes, two-year-olds, and dogs with wagging tails.

Degehart, Figurine, Owl On Books, Milk Blue, Marked, 3 ½ In.
$20.00

Delatte, Vase, Trees, Landscape, Raspberry Silhouettes, Almond, Pink Sky, Footed, 8 In.
$633.00

TIP

Modern bleach can damage eighteenth-century and some nineteenth-century dishes. To clean old dishes, try hydrogen peroxide or bicarbonate of soda. Each removes a different type of stain.

Rabbit, Plate, Marked, 9 ¾ In. . . . *illus* 121.00
Rabbit, Salt & Pepper, 3 ⅜ In. . . . 178.00
Rabbit, Serving Dish, Marked, c.1925, 6 x 10 In. . . . 326.00
Rabbit, Tray, 12 In. Diam. . . . 225.00
Rabbit, Trivet, 4 ¾ In. . . . 207.00
Scottie Dogs, Plate, c.1931, 8 ½ In. . . . 2760.00
Snowtree, Tray, 12 In. . . . *illus* 295.00
Tapestry Lion, Plate, 9 ¾ In. . . . 1080.00
Tapestry Lion, Plate, Rabbit Mark, 8 ⅜ In. . . . 889.00
Turkey, Plate, 8 ½ In. . . . 121.00
Turkey, Plate, 10 In. . . . 385.00
Vase, 2-Tone Oxblood Glaze, Luster, Bulbous, Experimental, 271, HCR, 8 ½ x 5 In. . . . 2200.00
Vase, Cherry Blossoms, Cylindrical, c.1931, 7 In. . . . 2460.00
Vase, Clover Leaves, Blossoms, Bottle Shape, Vellum, Footed, 8 ¼ In. . . . 2400.00
Vase, Forest Green Drip Glaze, Celadon & Brown Flambe Glaze, Bulbous, 7 x 7 In. . . . 2160.00
Vase, Green Drip, Brown Flambe Glaze, Bulbous, Experimental, Hugh Robertson, 7 In. . . . 1800.00
Vase, Green Drip, Brown Volcanic Glaze, Experimental, Hugh Robertson, 11 x 4 ½ In. . . . 1600.00
Vase, Oxblood, Green Mottled Glaze, Volcanic Spot, Experimental, Robertson, 7 In. . . . *illus* 1680.00
Vase, Prunus Branches, Crackleware, Signed, CFD, DPR, 6 ½ x 3 ½ In. . . . *illus* 1560.00
Vase, Red, Green, Blue Mottled Glaze, Bulbous, Experimental, No. 5, H. Robertson, 5 ½ In. . . . 1500.00
Vase, Red, Oxblood Flambe Glaze, Cylindrical, Experimental, Incised, Robertson, 7 x 3 In. . . . 2800.00
Vase, Red & Celadon Oxblood Flambe Glaze, Cylindrical, 7 x 3 In. . . . 3360.00
Vase, Teal Luster & Purple Glaze, Bottle Shape, Hugh Robertson, 9 In. . . . 1200.00
Vase, Yellow, Green Ground, 4-Sided, Embossed Bird Handles, Bee, 6 ¾ x 2 ½ In. . . . 960.00
Wall Pocket, Swallow's Nest, Yellow Glaze, 8 ½ x 6 In. . . . 1080.00
Wild Rose, Butter Chip, 3 ½ In. . . . 237.00

DEGENHART is the name used by collectors for the products of the Crystal Art Glass Company of Cambridge, Ohio. John and Elizabeth Degenhart started the glassworks in 1947. Quality paperweights and other glass objects were made. John died in 1964 and his wife took over management and production ideas. Over 145 colors of glass were made. In 1978, after the death of Mrs. Degenhart, the molds were sold. The D in a heart trademark was removed, so collectors can easily recognize the true Degenhart pieces.

Figurine, Owl On Books, Amethyst Carnival Glass, Marked, 3 ½ In., Pair . . . 20.00
Figurine, Owl On Books, Beige, Marked, 3 ½ In., Pair. . . . 20.00
Figurine, Owl On Books, Cobalt Blue, Marked, 3 ½ In., Pair . . . 15.00
Figurine, Owl On Books, Lime Green, Marked, 3 ½ In., Pair . . . 15.00
Figurine, Owl On Books, Milk Blue, Marked, 3 ½ In. . . . *illus* 20.00
Figurine, Owl On Books, Milk White, Marked, 3 ½ In., Pair . . . 18.00
Figurine, Roller Skate Boot, Amethyst . . . 5.00
Figurine, Roller Skate Boot, Light Blue . . . 5.00
Figurine, Roller Skate Boot, Yellow. . . . 5.00
Toothpick, Sweetheart, Toffee Slag. . . . 45.00

DEGUE is a signature acid-etched on pieces of French glass made in the early 1900s. Cameo, mold blown, and smooth glass with contrasting colored rims are the types most often found.

Chandelier, 4-Light, Cone Shape Base, Bell Shades, Blue & Gray, Brass Chains, 30 ½ In. . . . 1638.00
Compote, Blue, Orange & Yellow Mottled, Black Pedestal, 6 ½ x 5 In. . . . 536.00
Lamp, Bell Shade, Lavender, Orange, Green & Brown Mottled, Gilt Metal Base, 12 ¾ In. . . . 476.00
Lamp, Electric, Frosted, Carved Cameo, Pyramid Shade, Signed, France, c.1920, 15 x 8 In. . . . 1170.00
Lamp, Molded Flowers, Frosted, Pierced Black Metal Dome Base, 31 x 18 ¾ In. . . . 1495.00
Vase, Art Deco, Geometric, Mottled, White & Purple, Wrought Iron Mount, 13 ½ x 16 In. . . . 2000.00
Vase, Fishbowl Shape, Bittersweet Flowers, Satin Yellow, Purple Base, 10 x 13 In. . . . 2300.00
Vase, Frosted Orange Ground, Orange & Blue Flowers, Signed, 8 ½ In. . . . 805.00
Vase, Mottled Green, 14 x 8 ½ In. . . . 224.00
Vase, Opalescent & Pink Ground, Stylized Green Trees, Flowers, 15 ½ In. . . . 1955.00
Vase, Orange Flowers, Leaves, Textured Yellow Ground, Purple Base, Signed, 10 x 13 In. . . . 2000.00

DELATTE glass is a French cameo glass made by Andre Delatte. It was first made in Nancy, France, in 1921. Lighting fixtures and opaque glassware in imitation of Bohemian opaline were made. There were many French cameo glassmakers, so be sure to look in other appropriate categories.

Jar, Cover, Red Leaves, Orange Ground, Pinched Waist, Signed, 4 In. . . . 546.00
Vase, Mottled Iridescent, Blown Into Iron Frame, 4 Curled Feet, France, c.1930, 7 x 10 In. . . . 900.00
Vase, Trees, Landscape, Raspberry Silhouettes, Almond, Pink Sky, Footed, 8 In. . . . *illus* 633.00

DELDARE, *see Buffalo Pottery Deldare.*

DELFT is a tin-glazed pottery that has been made since the seventeenth century. Delft was made in England in the eighteenth century. It is decorated with blue on white or with colored decorations. Most of the pieces sold today were made after 1891, and the name *Holland* usually appears with the Delft factory marks. The word *Delft* appears alone on some inexpensive twentieth- and twenty-first-century pottery from Asia and Germany that is also listed here.

Bowl, Building, Blue, White, Scalloped Rim, 18th Century, 11 ½ In. 468.00
Bowl, Center Flower, Multicolored, Swag & Tassel Border, Dutch, 18th Century, 13 In. 518.00
Bowl, Center Medallion, Flowers, Fence, Blue & Yellow Flower Border, 1700s, 14 ¼ In. 575.00
Bowl, Flower Bouquet, Multicolored, Flower & Vine Border, Dutch, 18th Century, 13 ¼ In. 633.00
Bowl, Flowers, Blue, White, Scalloped Rim, Footed, Marked, 3 ¼ x 11 ¼ In. 45.00
Bowl, Flowers, Vines, Blue, White, Stonewall Glaze, England, c.1740, 9 ⅛ In. 1521.00
Box, Fireplace Shape, Coat Of Arms, Blue & White, Signed, W.K., 18th Century, 15 x 8 In. 702.00
Caddy, Chinoiserie Design, Blue, White, Mid 18th Century, 3 ½ In. .... *illus* 3744.00
Cake Plate, Lambrequins, Flowers, Blue & Red, Signed, APK, c.1700, 10 ¼ In. 840.00
Charger, Chinoiserie Design, Blue, White, 18th Century, 13 ¾ In., Pair 1638.00
Charger, Flowers, Blue & White, England, Mid 1800s, 12 ¼ In. 356.00
Charger, Garden Scene, Peacock, Blue, White, c.1730, 3 ¾ In. 1989.00
Charger, Parrot, Butterflies, Diapered Border, Dutch, Mid 18th Century, 13 ¾ In. 2340.00
Charger, Stylized Flowers, Multicolored, c.1800, 12 In. 178.00
Charger, Stylized Tree, Blue, White, Enamel, Shaped Rim, Late 19th Century, 13 ⅝ In. 178.00
Charger, Sunflower, Green, Red, Yellow, Dutch, c.1735, 13 ¾ In. 1755.00
Cup, Fuddling, 3 Sections, Running Fowl, Blue, Intertwined Handles, Late 17th Century, 3 In. 11700.00
Cup, Fuddling, Blue, White, Continental, Mid 18th Century, 2 ¼ x 6 ¾ In. 936.00
Dish, Fish, Multicolored, Late 18th Century, 8 ¼ In. 3510.00
Ewer, Angel Heads, Medallions, Blue, Raised Panels, Mounts, Continental, 15 ¼ In. 460.00
Fireplace Surround, 20 Tiles, Various Scenes, 18th Century, 35 ¾ x 40 ½ In. 1112.00
Font, Wall Mount, Angel, Blue & White, 1700s, 8 ½ In. 518.00
Jardiniere, Figures, Rope Twist Handles, 19th Century, 10 ½ x 21 ½ In. .... *illus* 1430.00
Jardiniere, Scenic, Brown, Blue, Rope Twist Handle, Chinese, c.1700, 10 ½ x 21 ½ In. 3450.00
Jug, Powdered Manganese Ground, Pewter Lid, 18th Century, 9 ½ In. 497.00
Plaque, Scenic, Blue & White, Keyser & Pynaker, 18th Century, 8 ½ x 11 In. 527.00
Plate, Center Circle, Radiating Fronds, Blue, White, WEL, 1738, 8 ⅞ In. 32760.00
Plate, Fisherman Scene, Blue, White, Incised, P. Ubera 1589, Dutch, 10 ⅛ In. 351.00
Plate, Flowers, Fruit, Blue, Yellow, Brown, Green, Late 18th Century, 9 In. 585.00
Plate, Flowers, Vase, Multicolored, Leaf Border, 18th Century, 6 ⅜ In. 295.00
Plate, Peacock Design, Blue, White, Claw Mark, 2 x 12 ½ In. 480.00
Plate, Portrait Of Prince Of Orange, William V, c.1775 .... 1600.00
Plate, Woman, Landscape, Blue, White, Mid 18th Century, 8 ¾ In. 351.00
Posset Pot, Cover, Blue Cartouche, 2 Handles, Marked, A.S., 1653 .... *illus* 42120.00
Punch Bowl, Chinoiserie, Blue, White, England, c.1735, 4 ¾ x 12 In. 1404.00
Salt, Urn Form, Pedestal Base, White, Mid 18th Century, 2 ½ x 3 ¾ In. 405.00
Strainer, Figures, Landscape, Blue, White, Scalloped Rim, Inscribed, Early 18th Century, 2 In. 878.00
Tankard, Blue, White, Pewter Lid, Early 18th Century, 10 In. 702.00
Tankard, Flowers, Blue & Yellow, Green Leaves, Pewter Lid, Mid 18th Century, 9 ½ In. 878.00
Tazza, Building, Landscape, Blue, White, Continental, c.1700, 2 x 11 In. 117.00
Tile, Lute Player, After Frans Hals, 17 ½ x 10 ½ In. 59.00
Tile, Rembrandt, Sepia, Porcreleyne Fles Factory, 1884, 18 In. 1210.00
Tobacco Jar, Gold, Man, Jar, Tobacco Plants, Lid, Dutch, 1800s, 9 x 7 In. 380.00
Tobacco Jar, Stokius, Blue, White, Brass Lid, 8 ½ In. 450.00
Tobacco Jar, Tabacq De La Matinique, 2 Women, Cartouche, Blue, Brown, 1700s, 11 ½ In. 1150.00
Urn, Cover, Flowers, Landscape Scenes, Blue & White, 25 x 14 In., Pair 702.00
Urn, Cover, Reticulated, Blue & White, Converted To Lamp, 15 x 8 ¾ In. 410.00
Vase, Flowers, Blue, White, Baluster, 8-Sided Base, Dutch, c.1740, 9 ½ In. 878.00
Vase, Flowers, Gourd Shape, Electrified As Lamp, 1800s, 16 ½ In. 235.00
Vase, Harbor Scene, Windmills, Ruffled Rim, Blue, Handles, Marked, Late 19th Century, 14 In. 270.00
Vase, Scenic, Blue & White, 15 ¾ x 7 x 8 ½ In. 117.00
Vase, Ship, Flowers, Baluster, 13 ½ In. 117.00

DENTAL cabinets, chairs, equipment, and other related items are listed here. Other objects may be found in the Medical category.

Cabinet, Ash, Marble Base, 22 Drawers, Milk Glass Countertop, J.H. Rosberg Mfg., Chicago 708.00
Cabinet, Burl Walnut, Marble Top, 12 Drawers, Cash & Sons, 1880s, 60 x 32 x 17 In. 1430.00
Cabinet, Mahogany, Case-On-Case, Drawers, Beveled Glass Door, Tools, 44 x 46 In. 652.00

Delft, Caddy, Chinoiserie Design, Blue, White, Mid 18th Century, 3 ½ In.
$3744.00

Delft, Jardiniere, Figures, Rope Twist Handles, 19th Century, 10 ½ x 21 ½ In.
$1430.00

Delft, Posset Pot, Cover, Blue Cartouche, 2 Handles, Marked, A.S., 1653
$42120.00

TIP

Glass becomes cloudy if not kept completely dry when not in use. That is why decanters and vases often discolor.

D

Cabinet, Mahogany, Marble Base, 21 Drawers, Door, Glass Pulls, 46 x 35 x 12 In. 440.00
Cabinet, Oak, Turned Legs, Lower Shelf, Drawers, Lazy Susan, Sliding Door, 27 x 62 In. 593.00
Chair, Portable, Folding, Leather Seat & Back, Green Paint, Crank, McConnell, N.Y. 119.00
Lamp, Telescoping, Adjustable, Ribbed Shades, 4 Fixtures, 18 x 60 In. 3300.00
Mortar & Pestle, Camphor Glass, 1940s, 1 ¾ x 4 ¾ In., Pair 65.00
Travel Case, Walnut, Dovetailed, Tools, Molds, Vials, 10 x 13 x 9 In. 523.00

Top Ten Depression Glass Patterns

Depression glass has been a bargain this year. Prices are down. Hundreds of thousands of users visit our website, Kovels.com, each month. The ten Depression Glass patterns that are the most popular among our visitors are:

1. Early American Prescut
2. Floragold
3. Moderntone
4. Platonite
5. American Sweetheart
6. Petalware
7. Cherry Blossom
8. Wexford
9. Old Colony
10. Mayfair Open Rose

DEPRESSION GLASS is an inexpensive glass that was manufactured in large quantities during the 1920s and early 1930s. It was made in many colors and patterns by dozens of factories in the United States. Most patterns were also made in clear glass, which the factories called *crystal*. If no color is listed here, it is clear. The name *Depression Glass* is a modern one and also refers to machine-made glass of the 1940s through 1970s. For more prices, go to Kovels.com. Sets missing a few pieces can be completed through the help of one of the many matching services listed on our website, Kovels.com.

1700 Line, Cup, Ransom, Ivory, 9 Oz. 10.00
1700 Line, Cup & Saucer, St. Denis, Jade-Ite 8.00
1700 Line, Plate, Dinner, Ivory, 9 ⅛ In. 12.50
1700 Line, Plate, Pennsylvania Dutch Folk Art, Ivory, 9 In. .... 12.00 to 15.00
Adam, Berry Bowl, Green, 4 ¾ In. 29.00
Adam, Bowl, Cereal, Green, 5 ¾ In. 65.00
Adam, Bowl, Dessert, Pink, 4 ¾ In. 25.00
Adam, Bowl, Pink, 8 In. 40.00
Adam, Bowl, Pink, 9 In. 80.00
Adam, Bowl, Vegetable, Pink, Oval, 10 In. 25.00
Adam, Butter, Cover, Green 350.00
Adam, Butter, Cover, Pink 100.00
Adam, Butter, Cover Only, Pink 60.00
Adam, Cake Plate, Pink, Footed, 9 ¾ In. 38.00
Adam, Candy Dish, Cover, Pink 119.00
Adam, Grill Plate, Green, 9 In. 28.00
Adam, Plate, Pink, 6 In. 10.00
Adam, Saucer, Pink, 6 In. 8.00
Adam, Vase, Green, 7 ½ In. 150.00
Adam's Rib, Compote, Pink, Oval, 8 In. 18.00
Adam's Rib, Cup & Saucer, Green 9.00
Adam's Rib, Sandwich Server, Center Handle, Green, 11 In. 36.00
Alice, Cup & Saucer, Jade-Ite 14.00
Alice, Cup & Saucer, White 25.00
Alice, Cup & Saucer, White, Blue Trim, 3 ¾ x 2 ½ In. 23.00
Alice, Plate, Dinner, Jade-Ite, 9 ½ In. 35.00
American Pioneer, Plate, Luncheon, Pink, 8 In. 12.00
American Sweetheart, Berry Bowl, Monax, 9 In. 75.00
American Sweetheart, Berry Bowl, Pink, 9 In. .... 52.00 to 65.00
American Sweetheart, Bowl, Cereal, Pink, 6 In. .... 15.00 to 18.00
American Sweetheart, Bowl, Vegetable, Oval, Monax, 10 ½ In. 80.00
American Sweetheart, Creamer, Monax .... 10.00 to 11.00
American Sweetheart, Cup, Pink 15.00
American Sweetheart, Cup & Saucer, Monax 10.00
American Sweetheart, Cup & Saucer, Pink 18.00
American Sweetheart, Plate, Dessert, Pink, 6 In. 8.00
American Sweetheart, Plate, Dinner, Monax, 10 In. .... 24.00 to 28.00
American Sweetheart, Plate, Dinner, Pink, 9 ¾ In. .... 30.00 to 40.00
American Sweetheart, Plate, Luncheon, Monax, 9 In. 12.00
American Sweetheart, Plate, Salad, Pink, 8 In. 15.00
American Sweetheart, Platter, Monax, Oval, 13 In. 68.00
American Sweetheart, Platter, Pink, Oval, 13 In. .... 40.00 to 55.00
American Sweetheart, Salver, Monax, 12 In. 25.00
American Sweetheart, Salver, Pink, 12 In. 22.00
American Sweetheart, Saucer, Monax 3.00
American Sweetheart, Saucer, Pink 8.00
American Sweetheart, Sherbet, Monax, ... *illus* 25.00
American Sweetheart, Sherbet, Pink, 4 ½ In. .... 20.00 to 22.00
American Sweetheart, Soup, Cream, Monax, 4 ½ In. .... 100.00 to 145.00
American Sweetheart, Soup, Dish, Pink, 9 ¾ x 1 ¼ In. 75.00
American Sweetheart, Sugar, Monax 8.00
American Sweetheart, Sugar, Pink 22.00

Depression Glass, American Sweetheart, Sherbet, Monax
$25.00

Depression Glass, Anniversary, Wine, Pink, 20 Oz., 4 ⅛ In.
$15.00

Anniversary, Bowl, 3-Footed, 2 ½ x 6 ½ In. . . . 12.00
Anniversary, Cake Plate, 3-Footed, 11 ⅜ In. . . . 15.00
Anniversary, Plate, Soup, Clear, 7 ¼ x 1 ½ In. . . . 9.00
Anniversary, Plate, Soup, Iridescent, 7 ¼ x 1 ½ In. . . . 9.00
Anniversary, Sugar & Creamer, Pink . . . 24.00
Anniversary, Vase, Ruffled Edge, 6 ½ x 5 In. . . . 20.00
Anniversary, Wine, Pink, 20 Oz., 4 ⅛ In. . . . *illus* 15.00
Anniversary Rose, Bowl, Dessert, 4 ⅝ In. . . . 8.00
Anniversary Rose, Creamer . . . 20.00
Anniversary Rose, Plate, Soup, 6 ⅝ In. . . . *illus* 15.00
Anniversary Rose, Sugar & Creamer, Cover . . . 35.00
Apple Blossom pattern is listed here as Dogwood.
Aunt Polly, Berry Bowl, Blue, 4 In. . . . 12.00
Aunt Polly, Bowl, Fruit, Blue, 8 In. . . . *illus* 40.00
Aunt Polly, Dish, Pickle, Handles, Blue, 7 ¼ In. . . . 45.00
Aunt Polly, Dish, Pickle, Handles, Green, 7 ¼ In. . . . 20.00
Aurora, Bowl, Cereal, Pink, 5 ⅜ In. . . . 10.00
Aurora, Tumbler, Ritz Blue, 9 Oz., 4 ¾ In. . . . 20.00
Avocado, Bowl, Handles, Oval, 8 In. . . . 11.00
Avocado, Sugar, Cover, Shell Pink . . . 30.00
Avocado, Sugar, Pink, 3 In. . . . *illus* 37.00
Balda, Plate, Blue, 7 ¼ In. . . . 20.00
Ballerina pattern is listed here as Cameo.
Bambi, Powder Jar, Cover, Iridescent Marigold . . . 44.00
Bamboo Optic, Console, Pink, Rolled Edge, 13 ½ In. . . . 95.00
Bamboo Optic, Creamer, Green . . . 10.00
Bamboo Optic, Plate, Luncheon, Pink, 8 In. . . . 8.00
Bamboo Optic, Plate, Salad, Pink, Octagonal, 7 In. . . . 6.00
Banded Rib pattern is listed here as Coronation.
Banded Rings pattern is listed here as Ring.
Basket pattern is listed here as No. 615.
Beehive, Berry Bowl, Handles, 8 ½ In. . . . 12.00
Beehive, Berry Bowl, Pink, Handles, 8 ½ In. . . . 20.00
Beehive, Bowl, Cereal, 10 Oz., 5 ¼ In. . . . 10.00
Beehive, Butter, Cover . . . 15.00
Beehive, Creamer . . . 6.00
Beehive, Sugar, Cover, Pink . . . 20.00
Block pattern is listed here as Block Optic.
Block Optic, Berry Bowl, Green, 8 In. . . . 36.00
Block Optic, Bowl, Cereal, Green, 5 ½ In. . . . 12.00
Block Optic, Butter, Cover . . . 80.00
Block Optic, Candlestick, Pink, 1 ¾ In., Pair . . . 100.00
Block Optic, Creamer, Green . . . 14.00
Block Optic, Cup, Pink . . . 8.00 to 9.00
Block Optic, Cup, Yellow . . . 5.00 to 8.00
Block Optic, Cup & Saucer, Green . . . 10.00
Block Optic, Cup & Saucer, Yellow . . . 12.00
Block Optic, Goblet, 9 Oz., 5 ¾ In. . . . 15.00
Block Optic, Ice Bucket, Metal Handle, 6 In. . . . 25.00
Block Optic, Knife, Fruit, 8 ⅛ In. . . . 15.00
Block Optic, Pitcher, Green, 54 Oz., 8 ½ In. . . . 65.00
Block Optic, Pitcher, Green, 80 Oz., 9 In. . . . *illus* 22.00
Block Optic, Plate, Dessert, Green, 6 In. . . . 7.00
Block Optic, Plate, Dinner, Green, Snowflake Center, 9 In. . . . 29.00
Block Optic, Plate, Dinner, Yellow, 9 In. . . . 45.00
Block Optic, Plate, Luncheon, Green, 8 In. . . . 7.00
Block Optic, Plate, Luncheon, Pink, 8 In. . . . 8.00
Block Optic, Plate, Luncheon, Yellow, 8 In. . . . 8.00
Block Optic, Plate, Sherbet, Green, 6 In. . . . 4.00 to 8.00
Block Optic, Plate, Sherbet, Pink, 6 In. . . . 3.00 to 4.00
Block Optic, Plate, Sherbet, Yellow, 6 In. . . . 3.50
Block Optic, Salt & Pepper, Pink, Footed, 4 In. . . . 100.00
Block Optic, Sandwich Server, 10 ¼ In. . . . 10.00 to 12.00
Block Optic, Saucer, Green . . . 9.00
Block Optic, Sherbet, 5 ½ Oz., 3 ¼ In. . . . 10.00
Block Optic, Sherbet, 6 Oz., 4 ¾ In. . . . 10.00
Block Optic, Sherbet, Cone Shape, Green, 3 ¾ In. . . . 7.00

Depression Glass, Anniversary Rose, Plate, Soup, 6 ⅝ In.
$15.00

Depression Glass, Aunt Polly, Bowl, Fruit, Blue, 8 In.
$40.00

Depression Glass, Avocado, Sugar, Pink, 3 In.
$37.00

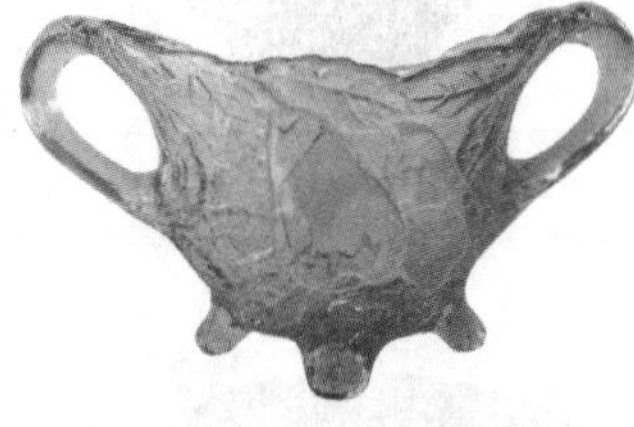

Depression Glass, Block Optic, Pitcher, Green, 80 Oz., 9 In.
$22.00

TIP

Trim shrubs near the house so they don't hide burglars trying to break in basement or first-floor windows.

Depression Glass, Bubble, Sherbet, Forest Green, 6 Oz., 4 In. $16.00

Depression Glass, Bubble, Tumbler, Juice, Royal Ruby, 5 Oz., 3 ¾ In. $7.00

Depression Glass, By Cracky, Pitcher, 9 x 5 In. $39.00

Depression Glass, Cameo, Sugar & Creamer, Yellow $34.00

Block Optic, Sherbet, Yellow, 3 ½ In. 8.00
Block Optic, Sherbet, Yellow, Square, Low Foot, 3 ½ In. 25.00
Block Optic, Sugar, Green 14.00
Block Optic, Sugar, Pink, Footed 13.00
Block Optic, Sugar, Yellow, Short, Footed 16.00
Block Optic, Sugar & Creamer, Green, Footed 28.00
Block Optic, Sugar & Creamer, Green, Footed, Handles 40.00
Block Optic, Sugar & Creamer, Pink 33.00
Block Optic, Tumbler, Iced Tea, Pink, 12 Oz., 6 ⅛ In., 8 Piece 55.00
Block Optic, Tumbler, Juice, Green, 5 Oz., 3 ½ In. 25.00
Block Optic, Tumbler, Juice, Pink, 5 Oz., 3 ½ In. 30.00
Block Optic, Tumbler, Whiskey, Footed, 3 ½ Oz., 3 ¾ In., 5 Piece 15.00
Block Optic, Tumbler, Yellow, Footed, 4 ¾ x 3 ½ In. 28.00
Block Optic, Wine, Pink, 4 ½ In. 40.00
Blue & Gold Leaf, Batter Bowl, Handle, 4 x 8 In. 35.00
Blue & Gold Leaf, Cake Pan, Round, 8 In. 12.00
Blue & Gold Leaf, Loaf Pan, Qt., 5 x 9 In. 15.00
Blue & Gold Leaf, Refrigerator Jar, 4 x 8 In. 19.00
Blue Wheat, Tumbler, Juice 8.00
Bonnie Blue, Cup & Saucer 5.50
Bouquet & Lattice pattern is listed here as Normandie.
Bowknot, Cup, Green 10.00
Bubble, Berry Bowl, 3-Footed, 8 ½ In. 8.00
Bubble, Berry Bowl, Forest Green, 3-Footed, 4 ⅝ In. 7.00
Bubble, Berry Bowl, Forest Green, 3-Footed, 8 ½ In. .... 15.00 to 20.00
Bubble, Berry Bowl, Milk White, 8 ⅜ In. 8.00
Bubble, Berry Bowl, Royal Ruby, 3-Footed, 8 ½ In. 50.00
Bubble, Berry Bowl, Sapphire, 8 ⅜ In. 20.00
Bubble, Bowl, Cereal, 5 ¼ In. 9.00
Bubble, Bowl, Cereal, Sapphire Blue, 5 ¼ In. 15.00
Bubble, Bowl, Fruit, Iridescent, 4 ½ In. 10.00
Bubble, Bowl, Fruit, Royal Red, 4 ½ In. 11.00
Bubble, Bowl, Fruit, Sapphire Blue, 4 ½ In. 10.00
Bubble, Bowl, Vegetable, Pink, 8 ½ In. 12.00
Bubble, Creamer 12.00
Bubble, Creamer, Sapphire Blue 35.00
Bubble, Cup, Royal Ruby, 6 Oz. 8.00
Bubble, Goblet, Desert Gold, 4 Oz., 4 ½ In. 5.00
Bubble, Goblet, Royal Ruby, 5 ¼ In. 12.50
Bubble, Goblet, Royal Ruby, 9 Oz., 5 ½ In. 25.00
Bubble, Plate, Bread & Butter, Sapphire Blue, 6 ¾ In. 4.00
Bubble, Plate, Dinner, Royal Ruby, 9 ⅜ In. 25.00
Bubble, Plate, Dinner, Sapphire Blue, 9 ⅜ In. .... 8.00 to 9.00
Bubble, Platter, Sapphire Blue, Oval, 13 In. 16.00
Bubble, Saucer 1.00
Bubble, Sherbet, Forest Green, 6 Oz., 4 In. .... *illus* 16.00
Bubble, Sherbet, Forest Green, Clear Stem, 6 Oz., 4 ¼ In. 12.00
Bubble, Sherbet, Ruby Red, 4 In. 7.50
Bubble, Soup, Dish, Sapphire Blue, 7 ¾ In. 15.00
Bubble, Sugar, Sapphire Blue 25.00
Bubble, Sugar & Creamer 20.00
Bubble, Tumbler, Iced Tea, 12 Oz., 4 ½ In. 15.00
Bubble, Tumbler, Iced Tea, Footed, 7 In. 16.00
Bubble, Tumbler, Iced Tea, Forest Green, Clear Foot, 14 Oz., 7 In. 15.00
Bubble, Tumbler, Juice, Desert Gold, 3 ½ In. 12.00
Bubble, Tumbler, Juice, Royal Ruby, 5 Oz., 3 ¾ In. .... *illus* 7.00
Bubble, Tumbler, Juice, Ruby Red, Clear Foot, 4 In. 18.00
Bubble, Tumbler, Old Fashioned, Royal Ruby, 8 Oz., 3 ¼ In. .... 12.00 to 18.00
Bubble, Tumbler, Royal Ruby, 16 Oz., 5 ⅞ In. 18.00
Bubble, Tumbler, Ruby Red, 9 Oz., 4 ½ In. 10.00
Bullseye pattern is listed here as Bubble.
Butterflies & Roses pattern is listed here as Flower Garden With Butterflies.
Buttons & Bows pattern is listed here as Holiday.
By Cracky, Pitcher, 9 x 5 In. .... *illus* 39.00
By Cracky, Plate, Canary Yellow, 8 In. 16.00
Cabbage Rose pattern is listed here as Sharon.
Cameo, Berry Bowl, 4 ½ In. 7.00

Cameo, Berry Bowl, Green, 8 ¼ In. 20.00
Cameo, Bowl, Cereal, Green, 5 ½ In. 25.00
Cameo, Bowl, Salad, Green, 7 ¼ In. 70.00
Cameo, Bowl, Vegetable, Green, 8 ½ In. 35.00
Cameo, Bowl, Vegetable, Oval, Green, 10 In. 30.00
Cameo, Bowl, Vegetable, Oval, Yellow, 7 x 10 In. 50.00
Cameo, Butter, Cover, Green 195.00 to 275.00
Cameo, Cake Plate, Green, 3-Footed, 10 In. 40.00
Cameo, Candlestick, Green, 4 In., Pair 110.00
Cameo, Compote, Green, 5 In. 45.00
Cameo, Console, Green, 3-Footed, 11 In. 85.00
Cameo, Console, Pink, 3-Footed, 11 In. 75.00
Cameo, Cookie Jar, Cover, Green 50.00 to 60.00
Cameo, Creamer, Yellow 25.00
Cameo, Cup 7.00
Cameo, Decanter, Green, Stopper, 10 In. 180.00
Cameo, Goblet, Green, 6 In. 65.00 to 70.00
Cameo, Pitcher, Green, 56 Oz., 8 ½ In. 85.00
Cameo, Pitcher, Juice, Green, 36 Oz., 6 In. 75.00
Cameo, Plate, Dinner, Green, 8 In. 14.00
Cameo, Plate, Dinner, Yellow, 9 ⅛ In. 15.00
Cameo, Plate, Salad, 7 In. 5.00
Cameo, Plate, Sherbet, Green, 6 In. 6.00
Cameo, Relish, Green, 3 Sections, 3-Footed, 7 ½ In. 30.00 to 33.00
Cameo, Saltshaker, Green, Footed 40.00
Cameo, Sandwich Server, Pink, 10 In. 75.00
Cameo, Sherbet, Green, 3 ¼ In. 15.00 to 17.00
Cameo, Sherbet, Green, 5 In. 32.00 to 35.00
Cameo, Soup, Cream, Green 175.00
Cameo, Sugar, Green 18.00 to 22.00
Cameo, Sugar & Creamer, Yellow *illus* 34.00
Cameo, Syrup, Green, 5 ¾ In. 425.00
Cameo, Tumbler, Green, 9 Oz., 5 In. 30.00
Cameo, Tumbler, Green, 10 Oz., 4 ⅞ In. 35.00
Cameo, Tumbler, Iced Tea, Green, Footed, 11 Oz., 5 ¾ In. 71.00
Cameo, Tumbler, Juice, Green, 5 Oz., 3 ¾ In. 35.00
Cameo, Tumbler, Juice, Green, Footed, 3 Oz., 3 ½ In. 80.00
Cameo, Vase, Green, 8 In. 65.00
Cameo, Water Bottle, Green 25.00
Cameo, Wine, Green, 4 In. 70.00 to 80.00
Candlewick pattern is listed in the Imperial Glass category.
Candy Stripe, Bowl, Cereal, Hazel Atlas, 5 In. 8.50
Candy Stripe, Tumbler, 10 Oz., 5 x 2 ¾ In. 15.00
Cane, Bowl, Pink, Handles, Lancaster, 10 In. 23.00
Cape Cod pattern is listed in the Imperial Glass category.
Capri Blue, Bowl, Dots, Round, 4 ⅞ In. 6.00
Capri Blue, Candy Jar, Cover, Footed, 7 ½ In. 32.00
Capri Blue, Cup & Saucer, Dots, 3 ½ x 5 ¼ In. 7.00
Capri Blue, Relish, Colony, 7 ¾ In. 15.00
Capri Blue, Sherbet, Dots, 2 ¾ x 3 ¾ In. 8.00
Capri Blue, Snack Set, Seashell, 10-In. Plate, 2 Piece 12.00
Capri Blue, Tumbler, Dots, 5 ¼ In. 6.00
Capri Blue, Tumbler, Juice, Dots, 3 ⅝ In. *illus* 5.00
Capri Blue, Tumbler, Old Fashioned, Dots, 3 ¼ In. 8.00
Caprice pattern is included in the Cambridge Glass category.
Charm, Berry Bowl, Forest Green, 4 ½ In. 10.00
Charm, Bowl, Salad, Azurite, 7 ⅜ x 7 ⅜ In. 38.00
Charm, Bowl, Salad, Royal Ruby, 7 ¼ In. 25.00
Charm, Creamer, Forest Green 10.00 to 12.00
Charm, Cup & Saucer, Azurite 10.00
Charm, Cup & Saucer, Forest Green, 3 ⅝ x 5 ⅜ In. 3.00 to 9.00
Charm, Plate, Azurite, Square, 9 ¼ In. 35.00
Charm, Plate, Dinner, Azurite, 9 ¼ In. 40.00
Charm, Plate, Forest Green, 8 ⅜ In. 10.00 to 12.00
Charm, Plate, Forest Green, Handle, 9 ¼ In. 35.00
Charm, Plate, Luncheon, Forest Green, 8 ⅜ In. 8.00
Charm, Plate, Salad, Azurite, 6 ⅞ In. 18.00

The Birthday of Briefs

January 19, 1935, was the day that Marshall Field and Company, the premier Chicago department store, unveiled a window display featuring a new brief manufactured by Cooper's Underwear Company (originally Samuel T. Cooper & Sons). Until then, all men's underwear had legs, so the Y-front brief, inspired by bathing suits worn by men on the French Riviera, was revolutionary. Even though Chicago experienced blizzard conditions that day, more than 600 briefs were sold before noon, at 50 cents apiece. In 1971, Cooper's changed its name to Jockey. It's still privately owned, headquartered in Kenosha, Wisconsin, and employs over 5,000 people around the world.

Depression Glass, Capri Blue, Tumbler, Juice, Dots, 3 ⅝ In.
$5.00

As always, the edited listings in *Kovels' Antiques & Collectibles Price Guide 2010* aren't available on any website, but readers should visit Kovels.com for information on trends, tips, reproductions, marks, old prices, and more!

Depression Glass, Cherry Blossom, Cup, Green
$21.00

Depression Glass, Chevron, Pitcher, Milk, Ritz Blue, 4 ¼ In.
$24.00

D

Cherry Blossom

Cherry Blossom is one of the most popular Depression glass patterns. The pattern was made by the Jeannette Glass Company, Jeannette, Pennsylvania, from 1930 to 1939. Full dinner sets, serving pieces, and a child's set were made in a wide range of colors. Pieces were made in Crystal, Delphite (opaque blue), Green, Jadite, Pink, and Red. Molds were changed a number of times, resulting in several shapes and styles for some pieces. Reproductions have been made.

Charm, Saucer, Forest Green . . . 4.00
Charm, Soup, Dish, Azurite, 6 In. . . . 28.00
Charm, Sugar, Forest Green . . . 6.00
Cherry Blossom, Berry Bowl, Green, 4 ¾ In. . . . 23.00
Cherry Blossom, Berry Bowl, Green, 8 ½ In. . . . 50.00
Cherry Blossom, Berry Bowl, Pink, 4 ¾ In. . . . 19.00
Cherry Blossom, Berry Bowl, Pink, 8 ½ In. . . . 44.00
Cherry Blossom, Bowl, 8 ½ In. . . . 44.00
Cherry Blossom, Bowl, Cereal, Pink, 5 ¾ In. . . . 50.00
Cherry Blossom, Bowl, Delphite, Handles, 9 ½ In. . . . 25.00
Cherry Blossom, Butter, Cover, Pink . . . 100.00
Cherry Blossom, Butter, Cover Only, Green, 4 ⅝ In. . . . 98.00
Cherry Blossom, Cake Plate, Pink, 3-Footed . . . 30.00
Cherry Blossom, Creamer, Green . . . 22.00
Cherry Blossom, Cup, Delphite . . . 18.00
Cherry Blossom, Cup, Green . . . *illus* 21.00
Cherry Blossom, Cup & Saucer . . . 19.00 to 29.00
Cherry Blossom, Cup & Saucer, Green . . . 14.00
Cherry Blossom, Cup & Saucer, Pink . . . 19.00 to 22.00
Cherry Blossom, Grill Plate, Pink, 9 In. . . . 35.00
Cherry Blossom, Pitcher, Green, Scalloped Base, 36 Oz., 6 ¾ In. . . . 75.00
Cherry Blossom, Pitcher, Pink, Scalloped Base, 36 Oz., 6 ¾ In. . . . 62.00 to 65.00
Cherry Blossom, Plate, Dinner, Pink, 9 In. . . . 28.00
Cherry Blossom, Plate, Salad, Green, 7 In. . . . 22.00 to 25.00
Cherry Blossom, Platter, Pink, 11 In. . . . 70.00
Cherry Blossom, Platter, Pink, 13 In. . . . 75.00
Cherry Blossom, Sandwich Server, Green, 10 ¼ In. . . . 35.00
Cherry Blossom, Saucer, Green . . . 4.00
Cherry Blossom, Saucer, Pink . . . 2.00
Cherry Blossom, Sherbet, Green, 4 In. . . . 20.00
Cherry Blossom, Sherbet, Pink, Scalloped Foot . . . 17.00
Cherry Blossom, Sugar, Cover, Green . . . 35.00
Cherry Blossom, Sugar, Pink . . . 18.00
Cherry Blossom, Sugar & Creamer, Cover, Pink . . . 60.00
Cherry Blossom, Tray, Pink, Handles, Round, 10 ½ In. . . . 32.00
Cherry Blossom, Tumbler, Delphite, Footed, 4 Oz., 3 ¾ In. . . . 24.00
Cherry Blossom, Tumbler, Pink, 9 Oz., 4 ½ In. . . . 25.00 to 30.00
Cherryberry, Butter, Cover, Green . . . 195.00
Cherryberry, Butter, Cover, Iridescent . . . 40.00
Cherryberry, Plate, Sherbet, Green, 6 In. . . . 10.00
Cherryberry, Sherbet, Green . . . 10.00
Chevron, Pitcher, Milk, Ritz Blue, 4 ¼ In. . . . *illus* 24.00
Chinex Classic, Plate, Castle Decal, 9 ¾ In. . . . *illus* 25.00
Christmas Candy, Creamer, Footed . . . 9.00
Christmas Candy, Cup & Saucer, Ultramarine . . . 35.00
Christmas Candy, Saucer, Ultramarine . . . 10.00
Christmas Candy, Sugar, Footed . . . 9.00
Circle, Creamer, Pink . . . 15.00
Circle, Cup, Green, 6 In. . . . 6.00
Circle, Sugar, Pink . . . 15.00
Circus, Child's Set, Mug, Grill Plate, Fired-On Blue, 7 ¼ In. . . . 55.00
Clover Blossom, Plate, Salad, Milk Glass, 7 ⅝ In. . . . 4.00
Clover Blossom, Soup, Dish, 8 In., 8 Piece . . . 50.00
Clover Blossom, Sugar & Creamer, Cover . . . 20.00
Cloverleaf, Creamer, Green . . . 20.00
Cloverleaf, Cup & Saucer, Pink . . . 12.00
Cloverleaf, Grill Plate, Green . . . 30.00
Cloverleaf, Plate, Luncheon, Pink, 8 In. . . . 10.00 to 11.00
Cloverleaf, Sherbet, Black, 3 In. . . . 20.00
Cloverleaf, Sherbet, Green, 3 In. . . . 10.00
Cloverleaf, Sherbet, Pink, 3 In. . . . 10.00
Colonial, Berry Bowl, Green, 4 ½ In. . . . 20.00
Colonial, Berry Bowl, Green, 9 In. . . . 32.00
Colonial, Butter, Cover, Green . . . 60.00
Colonial, Butter, Cover Only . . . 12.00
Colonial, Creamer . . . 16.00
Colonial, Cup . . . 4.00

Colonial, Cup, Green 14.00
Colonial, Pitcher, 68 Oz., 7 ¾ In. 35.00
Colonial, Plate, Luncheon, Pink, 8 ½ In. 12.00
Colonial, Sherbet, Pink, 3 ⅞ In. 12.00
Colonial, Sugar, Cover, Green 45.00
Colonial, Sugar Cover 10.00
Colonial, Tumbler, Whiskey, Green, 1 ½ Oz., 2 ½ In. 14.00
Colonial, Tumbler, Whiskey, Pink, 1 ½ Oz., 2 ½ In. 18.00
Colonial, Wine, Green, 2 ½ Oz., 4 ½ In. 22.00
Colonial Block, Berry Bowl, Green, 4 In. 16.00
Colonial Block, Candy Dish, Green, 8 ½ In. 42.00
Colonial Block, Creamer, Pink 15.00
Colonial Block, Powder Jar, Cover, Green, Footed 40.00
Colonial Block, Sugar, Cover, Pink 25.00
Colonial Block, Sugar, Cover, White 15.00
Colonial Block, Sugar, Green 15.00
Colonial Fluted, Berry Bowl, Green, 7 ½ In. 20.00
Colonial Fluted, Bowl, Cereal, Green, 6 In. 18.00
Colonial Fluted, Cup & Saucer, Green 10.00
Colonial Fluted, Plate, Luncheon, Green, 8 In. 9.00
Colony Swirl, Bowl, Capri Blue, Round, 5 ⅝ x 1 ¹¹⁄₁₆ In. 7.00
Colony Swirl, Cup & Saucer, Moroccan Amethyst, Square 10.00
Colony Swirl, Plate, Dinner, Moroccan Amethyst, Square, 8 In. 12.00
Colony Swirl, Tumbler, Moroccan Amethyst, 6 Oz. 9.00
Colony Swirl, Tumbler, Moroccan Amethyst, Square, 9 Oz. 9.00
Colored Spirals, Pitcher, Blue, Ice Lip, 82 Oz. 65.00
Colored Spirals, Tumbler, 9 Oz., 4 ¾ In. 18.00
Colored Spirals, Tumbler, Blue, 5 Oz., 3 ¾ In. 12.00
Colored Spirals, Tumbler, Blue, 9 Oz., 4 In. 16.00
Columbia, Bowl, Cereal, 5 In. 18.00
Columbia, Plate, Bread & Butter, 6 In. 3.00
Columbia, Soup, Dish, 8 In. 25.00
Coronation, Berry Bowl, Royal Ruby, 4 ½ In. .... 7.00 to 8.00
Coronation, Berry Bowl, Royal Ruby, 8 In. 20.00
Coronation, Bowl, Royal Ruby, 6 ½ In. 20.00
Cremax, Cup & Saucer, Bluebell 12.00
Cremax, Sugar, Bluebell 10.00
Crisscross, Creamer, Clear 29.00
Cube pattern is listed here as Cubist.
Cubist, Bowl, 4 ½ In. 2.00
Cubist, Bowl, Pink, 4 ½ In. 10.00
Cubist, Bowl, Salad, Green, 8 In. 24.00
Cubist, Bowl, Underplate, Gold Trim, 4 ½ x 6 In. 8.00
Cubist, Butter, Cover, Pink 85.00
Cubist, Candy Jar, Cover, Pink 38.00
Cubist, Candy Jar, No Cover, Green 15.00
Cubist, Creamer, 3 In. 8.00
Cubist, Creamer, Crystal, 2 ⅝ In. 2.00
Cubist, Creamer, Green, 3 In. 15.00
Cubist, Creamer, Pink, 2 ⅝ In. 8.00
Cubist, Cup, Green 12.00
Cubist, Cup, Pink 10.00
Cubist, Plate, Luncheon, Green, 8 In. 12.00
Cubist, Plate, Pink, 6 In. 4.00
Cubist, Powder Jar, Cover, Pink, 3-Footed 28.00
Cubist, Salt & Pepper, Green 45.00
Cubist, Saucer, Green 3.00
Cubist, Saucer, Pink 3.00
Cubist, Sugar, Green, 3 In. 12.00
Cubist, Sugar, Pink, 2 ⅝ In. 6.00
Cubist, Sugar & Creamer 10.00
Daisy pattern is listed here as No. 620.
Dancing Girl pattern is listed here as Cameo.
Dewdrop, Creamer 7.00
Dewdrop, Pitcher, ½ Gal. .... *illus* 45.00
Diamond pattern is listed here as Miss America.
Diamond Arches, Berry Bowl, Green, 4 ¼ In. 8.00

TIP

Put a rubber collar on the faucet spout over the sink. This may save you from breaking a piece of glass or china you are washing.

D

Depression Glass, Chinex Classic, Plate, Castle Decal, 9 ¾ In.
$25.00

Depression Glass, Dewdrop, Pitcher, ½ Gal.
$45.00

Colonial Block

A small set of dishes, mostly serving pieces, was made in Colonial Block pattern by Hazel Atlas Glass Company, a firm with factories in Ohio, Pennsylvania, and West Virginia. The dishes were made in the 1930s in Black, Crystal, Green, and Pink, and in the 1950s in White.

TIP
If you collect the decorated glasses from fast-food restaurants, never wash them in the dishwasher. The heat and detergent will change the coloring and lower the value.

D

Depression Glass, Doric, Berry Bowl, Green, 8 ¼ In.
$35.00

Early American Prescut
Early American Prescut was made by Anchor Hocking Glass Corporation, Lancaster, Ohio, from 1960 to 1998. The pieces have an imitation cut glass design and were made in Crystal, Honey Gold, Laser Blue, Royal Ruby, and with tints (Amber, Avocado, Blue, and Ruby). There are other imitation cut glass patterns that are easily confused with Early American Prescut. All of the pieces in Anchor Hocking's pattern have ten-point stars except the punch cups and Lazy Susan inserts.

Diamond Arches, Berry Bowl, Pink, 8 ½ In. 18.00
Diamond Arches, Berry Set, Ritz Blue, 7 Piece 80.00
Diamond Line, Pitcher, Pink, 60 Oz. 48.00
Diamond Line, Tumbler, Pink, 9 Oz., 4 In. 12.00
Diamond Point, Bowl, Amber, 3-Footed, 3 ⅛ x 5 In. 10.00
Diamond Point, Bowl, Ruby Flashed Rim, 13 ½ x 3 ½ In. 40.00
Diamond Point, Compote, 7 ¼ x 5 ¾ In. 15.00
Diamond Point, Salt & Pepper, 4 In. 10.00
Diamond Point, Tray, Round, 12 ½ In. 15.00
Diana, Bowl, Console, Flared, Scalloped, 12 In. 16.00
Diana, Cup, After Dinner 7.00
Diana, Cup, Pink 20.00
Diana, Cup & Saucer 12.00
Diana, Sherbet, Amber 12.00
Dogwood, Berry Bowl, Pink, 8 ½ In. 50.00
Dogwood, Bowl, Vegetable, 3 ¼ x 9 ⅛ In. 10.00
Dogwood, Cup, Pink 15.00
Dogwood, Cup & Saucer, Pink 18.00
Dogwood, Grill Plate, Pink, 10 ½ In. 25.00
Dogwood, Plate, Dinner, Pink, 9 ¼ In. 30.00
Dogwood, Plate, Luncheon, Pink, 8 In. 12.00
Dogwood, Saucer, Pink 7.00
Dogwood, Sugar, Pink, 3 ¼ In. 18.00
Dogwood, Tumbler, Pink, 10 Oz., 4 ¾ In. 25.00
Doric, Berry Bowl, Green, 8 ¼ In. .... *illus* 35.00
Doric, Berry Bowl, Pink, 4 ½ In. 12.00
Doric, Berry Set, Pink, 7 Piece 109.00
Doric, Bowl, Vegetable, Pink, Oval, 9 x 7 ⅜ In. 45.00
Doric, Candy Dish, Pink, 3 Sections 12.00
Doric, Cup, Pink 12.00
Doric, Cup & Saucer, Pink 17.00
Doric, Plate, Dinner, Pink, 9 In. 18.00
Doric, Plate, Sherbet, Green, 6 In. 8.00
Doric, Relish, Pink, 4 x 8 In. 30.00
Doric, Saucer, Pink 4.00
Doric, Sugar, Cover, Green 30.00
Doric, Sugar, Pink 18.00
Doric & Pansy, Plate, Sherbet, Pink, 6 In. 8.00
Double Shield pattern is listed here as Mt. Pleasant.
Driftwood, Bowl, c.1973, 5 In. 15.00
Driftwood, Bowl, Peacock Blue, 5 In. 15.00
Driftwood, Tumbler, Ruby, 6 In. 35.00
Dutch Rose pattern is listed here as Rosemary.
Early American Prescut, Ashtray, 5 In. 15.00
Early American Prescut, Ashtray, Royal Ruby, 7 ¾ In. 22.00
Early American Prescut, Bowl, 3-Toed, 6 ¾ In. 6.00
Early American Prescut, Bowl, Salad, 10 ¾ In. 10.00
Early American Prescut, Butter, Cover, ¼ Lb. 10.00
Early American Prescut, Candlestick, 5 ⅝ x 6 ¾ In. 20.00
Early American Prescut, Candy Dish, Cover, 7 ¼ In. .... 12.00 to 17.00
Early American Prescut, Cruet, 7 ¾ In. 6.00
Early American Prescut, Egg Plate, 11 ½ In. 35.00
Early American Prescut, Goblet, Forest Green, 10 Oz., 5 ½ In. 16.00
Early American Prescut, Goblet, Royal Ruby, 10 Oz., 5 ¼ In. 20.00
Early American Prescut, Goblet, Wine, Royal Ruby, 4 ½ Oz., 4 ¼ In. 18.00
Early American Prescut, Pitcher, 18 Oz., 8 In. .... 12.00 to 17.00
Early American Prescut, Pitcher, Milk, 5 x 3 ¼ In. 10.00
Early American Prescut, Plate, Dinner, 11 In. 12.50
Early American Prescut, Punch Bowl 20.00
Early American Prescut, Relish, 5 Sections, 13 ⅜ In. 30.00
Early American Prescut, Relish, Sections, Oval, 8 ½ In. 10.00
Early American Prescut, Salver, 13 ½ In. 15.00
Early American Prescut, Sugar, Pineapple, 3 x 5 ¾ In. 5.00
Early American Prescut, Tumbler, Juice, 5 Oz., 4 In. 7.00
Early American Prescut, Vase, 8 ½ In. 10.00
Early American Prescut, Vase, 10 In. 15.00
Early American Rock Crystal pattern is listed here as Rock Crystal.

Epic, Bird, Short Tail, Avocado Green, 10 ¼ x 2 ¾ In. 34.00
Epic, Bowl, Amber, Folded Rim, 3 ¼ x 7 ¼ In. 23.00
Epic, Bowl, Avocado Green, 3-Fold, 6 In. . . . . . *illus* 30.00
Epic, Cake Plate, Footed, 3 ¾ x 14 In. 35.00
Epic, Candlestick, 2-Light, Avocado Green, 3 ⅛ x 6 ¼ In. 16.00
Epic, Candlestick, Ruby Red, 4 ½ In. 28.00
Epic, Candy Dish, Persimmon, Drapery, 4 ⅝ x 7 ⅜ In. 35.00
Epic, Compote, Blue, Drapery, Ruffled Edge, Footed, 3-Toed, 4 ¾ x 7 ¼ In. 30.00
Epic, Duck, Persimmon, 5 In. 34.00
Feather, Punch Cup 5.00
Feather, Tray, Venetian, 6 Sections, 16 ½ In. 35.00
Feather, Vase, Green, 14 x 4 In. 40.00
Fine Rib pattern is listed here as Homespun.
Fire-King, Baking Pan, Fruits, Gay Fad, 6 ½ x 11 ½ In. 28.00
Fire-King, Baking Pan, Ivory, 6 ⅝ x 10 ⅝ In. 22.00
Fire-King, Bowl, Blue Heaven, 2 Qt. 28.00
Fire-King, Bowl, Cereal, Green Diamond Band, Milk White, 4 ¼ In. 8.50
Fire-King, Bowl, Cereal, Happy Birthday, Child, White, 5 In. 45.00
Fire-King, Bowl, Cereal, Peach Blossom, Gay Fad, 5 In. 14.50
Fire-King, Bowl, Cereal, Philbe, Sapphire Blue, 5 ⅜ In. 18.00
Fire-King, Bowl, Cereal, Restaurant Ware, White, 15 Oz. 35.00
Fire-King, Bowl, Chili, Jade-Ite, 5 In. 22.00
Fire-King, Bowl, Fired-On Yellow, 5 ¼ In. 12.00
Fire-King, Bowl, Fruits, Gay Fad, 7 $^{3}/_{16}$ In. 18.00
Fire-King, Bowl, Gingham Flowers, Spout Handles, 1 ½ Qt., 7 ½ In. 9.00
Fire-King, Bowl, Leaf & Blossom, Jade-Ite 24.00
Fire-King, Bowl, Maple Leaf, Jade-Ite, Tab Handle, 6 ½ In. 25.00
Fire-King, Bowl, Peach Blossom, Gay Fad, 5 ½ x 6 In. 12.50
Fire-King, Bowl, Restaurant Ware, Jade-Ite, 15 Oz. 38.00
Fire-King, Bowl, Turquoise Blue, Splashproof, Qt. 45.00
Fire-King, Bowl, Utility, Milk White, 6 x 3 In. 5.00
Fire-King, Butter, Cover, Pebbled Texture, Jade-Ite 95.00
Fire-King, Cake Pan, Candleglow, 8 x 8 In. 10.00
Fire-King, Cake Pan, Nature's Bounty, Round, 8 In. 16.00
Fire-King, Candy Dish, Cover, White, Ribbed Sides, Finial, 6 ¾ In. 16.00
Fire-King, Casserole, Blue Cornflower, 5 x 9 In. 8.50
Fire-King, Casserole, Cover, Blue Cornflower, Au Gratin, Oval, 1 ½ Qt. 12.50
Fire-King, Casserole, Cover, Fruits, Gay Fad, 1 ½ Qt. 24.00
Fire-King, Casserole, Cover, Fruits, Gay Fad, Round, 8 In. 25.00
Fire-King, Casserole, Cover, Nature's Bounty, Oval, 1 ½ Qt. . . . . . 15.00 to 18.00
Fire-King, Casserole, Gingham Flowers, Round, 1 ½ In., 8 ¾ In. 9.00
Fire-King, Casserole, Loaf Pan, Blue Cornflower, 5 x 9 In. 8.50
Fire-King, Casserole, Peach Blossom, Gay Fad, Pt. 14.00
Fire-King, Creamer, Turquoise Blue 25.00
Fire-King, Cup, Laurel, Milk Glass 4.00
Fire-King, Cup & Saucer, Ransom, Ivory 16.50
Fire-King, Cup & Saucer, Red Rose 9.50
Fire-King, Cup & Saucer, Restaurant Ware, Jade-Ite . . . . . . 30.00 to 35.00
Fire-King, Cup & Saucer, St. Denis, Jade-Ite 30.00
Fire-King, Cup & Saucer, Tulip 12.50
Fire-King, Custard Cup, Currier & Ives 3.50
Fire-King, Custard Cup, Fruits, Gay Fad 8.50
Fire-King, Custard Cup, Ivory, Flared, 5 Oz. 6.50
Fire-King, Custard Cup, Philbe, Sapphire Blue, Flared 6.50
Fire-King, Custard Cup, Sapphire Blue, Thick, 6 Oz., 3 ¼ In. 7.00
Fire-King, Custard Cup, Sapphire Blue, Thin, Flared, 7 Oz., 4 In. 8.00
Fire-King, French Casserole, Apples, Fruits, Gay Fad, 12 Oz. 16.50
Fire-King, Grease Jar, Tulip Cover, Ivory 40.00
Fire-King, Grease Jar, Tulip Cover, Jade-Ite 85.00
Fire-King, Hot Plate, Ivory, Philbe, Handles 20.00
Fire-King, Hot Plate, Sapphire Blue, Handles 22.00
Fire-King, Jardinere, Hobnail, Milk Glass, 5 ½ In. 6.00
Fire-King, Jardinere, Hobnail, Pink, 4 ½ In. 18.00
Fire-King, Jewelry Box, Rose Pink, Vitrock Cover 35.00
Fire-King, Jug, Ball, Fired-On Tangerine, 2 Qt. 40.00
Fire-King, Jug, Ball, Fired-On Tangerine, Qt. 35.00
Fire-King, Loaf Pan, Blue Flowers, 5 x 9 In. 13.00

Depression Glass, Epic, Bowl, Avocado Green, 3-Fold, 6 In.
$30.00

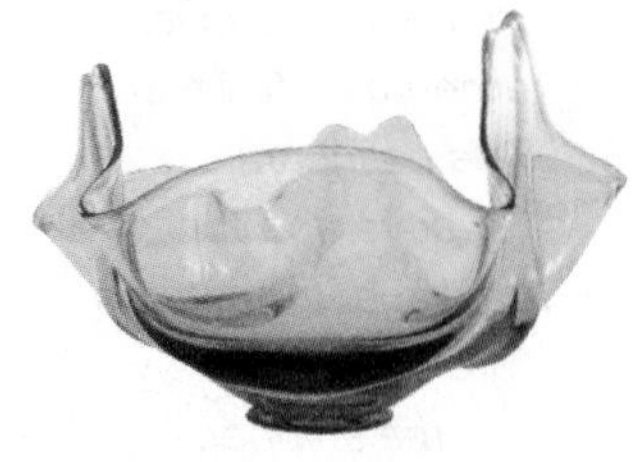

Depression Glass, Fire-King, Mixing Bowl, Splashproof, Modern Tulip, Blue, 9 ½ In.
$75.00

Depression Glass, Fire-King, Mug, Kimberly, Lime Green, 4 In.
$7.00

Depression Glass, Fire-King, Refrigerator Dish, Fruits, Gay Fad, 4 x 8 In.
$16.00

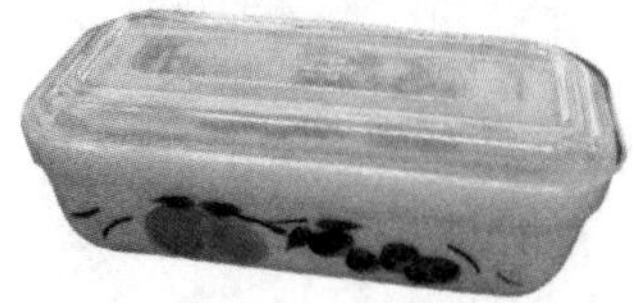

TIP
Clean dirty postcards with a piece of white bread. Be sure to cut the crust off first.

D

TIP

When you move, remember that there is no insurance coverage for breakage if the items are not packed by the shipper.

Depression Glass, Fire-King, Relish, 3 Sections, Turquoise Blue, 11 x 7 ¾ In.
$9.00

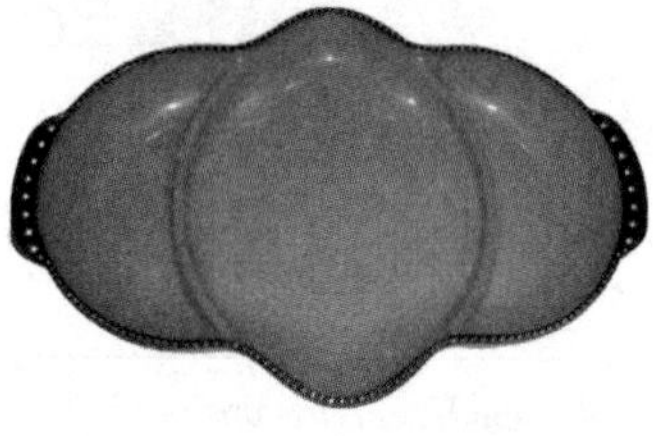

Depression Glass, Fire-King, Sugar & Creamer, Homestead, Stacking
$24.00

Depression Glass, Floragold, Candy Jar, Cover, 6 ¾ In.
$65.00

Fire-King, Loaf Pan, Blue Yellow & Red Fruit, Qt., 5 ¼ x 9 ¼ In. 12.00
Fire-King, Loaf Pan, Fruits, Gay Fad, 5 x 9 In. 18.00
Fire-King, Loaf Pan, Poppy, Gay Fad, Ivory, 5 x 9 In. 48.00
Fire-King, Loaf Pan, Vegetables, Gay Fad, 5 x 7 In. 10.00
Fire-King, Measuring Cup, Sapphire Blue, 3 ½ In. 25.00
Fire-King, Measuring Cup, Sapphire Blue, 8 Oz. 28.00
Fire-King, Mixing Bowl, Beaded Rim, Ivory, 7 ½ In. 19.00
Fire-King, Mixing Bowl, Beaded Rim, Jade-Ite, 4 ⅞ In. 28.00
Fire-King, Mixing Bowl, Chanticleer, White, Spout Handles, 10 In. 30.00
Fire-King, Mixing Bowl, Fruits, Gay Fad, 6 In. 13.00
Fire-King, Mixing Bowl, Gazelles, Turquoise Blue, 9 ½ x 6 In. 45.00
Fire-King, Mixing Bowl, Modern Tulip, Red & Black, 6 ½ In. 33.00
Fire-King, Mixing Bowl, Splashproof, 8 ½ In. 45.00
Fire-King, Mixing Bowl, Splashproof, Apples, 9 ½ In. 65.00
Fire-King, Mixing Bowl, Splashproof, Modern Tulip, Blue, 9 ½ In. .... *illus* 75.00
Fire-King, Mixing Bowl, Swirl, Ivory, 6 In. 18.00
Fire-King, Mixing Bowl, White, Teardrop, Swedish Modern, 5 In. 38.00
Fire-King, Mug, Kimberly, Fired-On Orange, Red, 8 Oz. 4.50
Fire-King, Mug, Kimberly, Lime Green, 4 In. .... *illus* 7.00
Fire-King, Mug, Restaurant Ware, Jade-Ite. 40.00
Fire-King, Mug, Standard, Jade-Ite, 8 Oz. 15.00
Fire-King, Mug, Standard, Turquoise, 8 Oz. 18.00
Fire-King, Pie Plate, Copper Tint, 9 In. 6.00
Fire-King, Pie Plate, Ivory, 9 In. 15.00
Fire-King, Pie Plate, Sapphire Blue, Oven Glass, 9 ¾ In. 15.00
Fire-King, Plate, Dinner, Gray Laurel, 9 ⅛ In. 10.00
Fire-King, Plate, Dinner, Gray Laurel, White, 9 In. 7.50
Fire-King, Plate, Dinner, Turquoise Blue, 9 In. 20.00
Fire-King, Plate, Leaf, Jade-Ite 27.00
Fire-King, Plate, Lexington, 9 In. 7.00
Fire-King, Platter, Oval, Copper Filigree, 12 ½ In. 12.00
Fire-King, Punch Set, Leaf, Milk White, 27 Piece 44.00
Fire-King, Refrigerator Dish, Cover, Jade-Ite, 4 x 4 In. 25.00
Fire-King, Refrigerator Dish, Cover, Milk White, 4 x 4 In. 6.50
Fire-King, Refrigerator Dish, Cover, Sapphire Blue, 4 ½ x 5 In. 25.00
Fire-King, Refrigerator Dish, Cover, Sapphire Blue, 5 x 9 In. 40.00
Fire-King, Refrigerator Dish, Fruits, Gay Fad, 4 x 8 In. .... *illus* 16.00
Fire-King, Relish, 3 Sections, Turquoise Blue, 11 x 7 ¾ In. .... *illus* 9.00
Fire-King, Salt & Pepper, Black Dots, Milk White. 43.00
Fire-King, Salt & Pepper, Jade-Ite, Tulip Lid. 119.00
Fire-King, Salver, Gray Laurel, 11 In. 20.00
Fire-King, Saucer, St. Denis, Milk White 8.00
Fire-King, Saucer, Turquoise Blue 7.50
Fire-King, Soup, Dish, Apples, Fruit, Gay Fad, Handle, 12 Oz. 16.50
Fire-King, Soup, Dish, Restaurant Ware, Milk White, Blue Trim, Flat Rim, 9 In. 12.50
Fire-King, Soup, Dish, Shell, Milk White, 7 ⅝ In. 6.50
Fire-King, Sugar & Creamer, Homestead, Stacking .... *illus* 24.00
Fire-King, Sugar & Creamer, White Charm, Gold Trim 29.00
Fire-King, Sugar Shaker, Black Dots, Milk White. 34.00
Fire-King, Vase, Deco, Jade-Ite, 5 ¼ In. 23.00
Fire-King, Vase, Pineapple, Forest Green, 9 In. 16.00
Fire-King, Vase, Pineapple, Pink, Ruffled Edge, 9 In. .... 14.50 to 30.00
Fire-King, Water Bottle, Fired-On Tangerine, Ribbed, Clear Lid, 3 Pt. 45.00
Fire-King, Water Set, Fired-On Colors, 2-Qt. Ball Jug, Tumblers, 7 Piece 150.00
Fleurette, Creamer 7.00
Fleurette, Plate, Dinner, 9 ⅛ In. .... 5.00 to 6.00
Fleurette, Platter, Oval, 9 x 12 In. 14.00
Fleurette, Soup, Dish, 6 ⅝ In. 6.00
Fleurette, Sugar 6.00
Floradora, Sherbet, Amber, 6 Oz., 3 ¼ In. 6.00
Floradora, Tumbler, Cordial, Footed, Oz., 1 ⅝ In. 8.00
Floragold, Bowl, Salad, 9 ½ In. 32.00
Floragold, Bowl, Square, 8 ½ In. .... 15.00 to 20.00
Floragold, Butter, Cover, 3 ½ x 6 $^{3}/_{16}$ In. 45.00
Floragold, Candlestick, 5 ¼ In., Pair 50.00
Floragold, Candy Dish, 4-Footed, 5 ¼ In. 10.00

Floragold, Candy Jar, Cover, 6 ¾ In. ... *illus* 65.00
Floragold, Cup ... 6.00
Floragold, Cup & Saucer ... 16.00
Floragold, Pitcher, Ice Lip, 64 Oz. ... 45.00
Floragold, Platter, Oval, 11 ¼ In. ... 25.00 to 35.00
Floragold, Saucer ... 10.00
Floragold, Sherbet, 2 ½ In. ... 16.00
Floragold, Sugar, Cover ... 28.00
Floragold, Tumbler, 10 Oz., 5 In. ... 18.00 to 20.00
Floral, Bowl, Vegetable, Cover, 8 In. ... 20.00 to 55.00
Floral, Butter, Cover, Green ... 119.00
Floral, Butter, Cover, Pink ... 110.00
Floral, Butter, No Cover ... 25.00
Floral, Candlestick, Green, 4 In., Pair ... 45.00
Floral, Candy Jar, Cover, Pink, 6 ⅛ x 4 ⅜ In. ... 45.00
Floral, Coaster, Pink, 3 ¼ In. ... 12.00
Floral, Cup ... 14.00
Floral, Cup, Green ... 15.00
Floral, Cup & Saucer, Pink ... 25.00
Floral, Plate, Bread & Butter, Green, 6 In. ... 12.00
Floral, Plate, Dinner, Pink, 9 In. ... 20.00
Floral, Plate, Salad, Pink, 8 In. ... 13.50
Floral, Plate, Sherbet, 6 In. ... 8.00
Floral, Platter, Oval, 10 ¾ In. ... 20.00 to 25.00
Floral, Platter, Pink, Oval, 10 ¾ In. ... 20.00
Floral, Salt & Pepper, Green, 4 In. ... 60.00
Floral, Saucer, Ring ... 12.00
Floral, Sherbet, Green ... 12.00 to 22.00
Floral, Sugar, Cover, Green ... *illus* 48.00
Floral, Sugar, Cover, Pink, 4 ¾ x 3 ½ In. ... 30.00
Floral, Sugar & Creamer, Cover, Pink ... 35.00
Floral, Tray, Square, Pink, 6 ½ In. ... 33.00
Floral, Tumbler, Juice, Pink, 4 In. ... 28.00
Floral & Diamond Band, Berry Bowl, 8 In. ... 20.00
Floral & Diamond Band, Butter, Cover Only, Green ... 75.00
Floral & Diamond Band, Sherbet, Green ... 8.00
Floral & Diamond Band, Sugar, Green, 5 ¼ In. ... 20.00
Floral & Diamond Band, Tumbler, Green, 4 In. ... 25.00
Florentine No. 1, Coaster, Green, 3 ¾ In. ... 65.00
Florentine No. 1, Creamer, Green ... 10.00
Florentine No. 1, Cup, Green ... 10.00
Florentine No. 1, Grill Plate, Pink ... 27.00
Florentine No. 1, Nut Dish, Pink, Ruffled Edge, 5 In. ... 20.00
Florentine No. 1, Pitcher, Yellow, 48 Oz., 7 ½ In. ... 225.00
Florentine No. 1, Pitcher, Yellow, Footed, 36 Oz., 6 ½ In. ... 50.00
Florentine No. 1, Salt & Pepper, Green, 4 In. ... 50.00
Florentine No. 1, Sherbet, Pink ... 10.00
Florentine No. 1, Sugar, Green ... 10.00
Florentine No. 2, Ashtray, Yellow, 5 ½ In. ... 35.00
Florentine No. 2, Berry Bowl, Green, 4 ½ In. ... 17.50
Florentine No. 2, Berry Bowl, Green, 8 In. ... 34.00
Florentine No. 2, Butter, Cover, Yellow ... 150.00
Florentine No. 2, Butter, No Cover, Yellow ... 68.00
Florentine No. 2, Candlestick, Yellow, 2 ½ In. ... 39.00
Florentine No. 2, Candy Dish, Cover, Yellow, 6 In. ... *illus* 185.00
Florentine No. 2, Coaster, Green, 3 ⅜ In. ... 17.50
Florentine No. 2, Creamer, Yellow ... 13.50
Florentine No. 2, Cup, Green ... 8.00 to 10.00
Florentine No. 2, Cup, Yellow ... 9.50
Florentine No. 2, Cup & Saucer, Green ... 13.50
Florentine No. 2, Cup & Saucer, Yellow ... 14.00
Florentine No. 2, Gravy Boat, Underplate, Yellow, 11 ½ In. ... 100.00
Florentine No. 2, Grill Plate, Yellow ... 20.00
Florentine No. 2, Pitcher, Footed, Yellow, 28 Oz., 7 ½ In. ... 38.00
Florentine No. 2, Plate, Dinner, Yellow, 10 In. ... 15.00
Florentine No. 2, Plate, Salad, Yellow, 8 ¼ In. ... 10.00
Florentine No. 2, Plate, Sherbet, Green, 6 In. ... 3.50

Depression Glass, Floral, Sugar, Cover, Green
$48.00

Depression Glass, Florentine No. 2, Candy Dish, Cover, Yellow, 6 In.
$185.00

Florentine

Florentine No. 1, also called Poppy No. 1, is neither Florentine in appearance nor decorated with recognizable poppies. The plates are hexagonal and have scalloped edges. The pattern was made by the Hazel Atlas Glass Company from 1932 to 1935 in Cobalt Blue, Crystal, Green, Pink, and Yellow.

Florentine No. 2, sometimes called Poppy No. 2 or Oriental Poppy, was made by Hazel Atlas Glass Company from 1934 to 1937. It has round plates instead of hexagonal plates, and larger and more prominent flowers than Florentine No. 1. It was made in Amber, Cobalt Blue, Crystal, Green, Ice Blue, Pink, and Yellow. Reproductions of Florentine No. 1 and No. 2 have been made.

TIP

Put pads between stacked plates. Don't stack too many in one pile.

D

Depression Glass, Forest Green, Vase, Pineapple, 9 In.
$24.00

Depression Glass, Game Birds, Mug, Pheasant, 9 Oz.
$9.00

Game Bird
Game Bird, sometimes called Wild Bird, was made by Anchor Hocking Glass Corporation, Lancaster, Ohio, from 1959 to 1962. The opaque white glass was decorated with a decal of a Canada goose, mallard duck, ring-necked pheasant, or ruffled grouse.

Florentine No. 2, Plate, Sherbet, Yellow, 6 In. 5.00
Florentine No. 2, Platter, Oval, Yellow, 11 x 8 In. 25.00
Florentine No. 2, Relish, Oval, Pink, 3 Sections, 10 In. 30.00
Florentine No. 2, Salt & Pepper, Yellow 55.00
Florentine No. 2, Sherbet, Green 10.00
Florentine No. 2, Soup, Cream, Green 17.00
Florentine No. 2, Soup, Cream, Yellow 22.00
Florentine No. 2, Sugar, Green 13.50
Florentine No. 2, Tumbler, Footed, Green, 9 Oz., 5 In. 32.00
Florentine No. 2, Tumbler, Footed, Yellow, 9 Oz., 5 In. 32.00
Florentine No. 2, Tumbler, Iced Tea, Green, 12 Oz., 5 In. 60.00
Florentine No. 2, Tumbler, Juice, Footed, Green, 5 Oz., 3 ¼ In. .... 14.00 to 20.00
Florentine No. 2, Tumbler, Juice, Footed, Yellow, 5 Oz., 4 In. .... 15.00 to 18.00
Florentine No. 2, Tumbler, Juice, Green, 5 Oz., 3 ⅜ In. 12.00
Florentine No. 2, Tumbler, Yellow, 9 Oz., 4 In. 18.50
Flower & Leaf Band pattern is listed here as Indiana Custard.
Flower Garden With Butterflies, Plate, 8 ¼ In. 45.00
Flower Rim pattern is listed here as Vitrock.
Forest Green, Ashtray, Square, 4 ⅝ In. .... 8.00 to 10.00
Forest Green, Bonbon 6.50
Forest Green, Bowl, Dessert, Maple Leaf, 5 ½ In. 12.00
Forest Green, Bowl, Scalloped, 6 ½ In. 10.00
Forest Green, Cocktail Shaker, Grapes & Leaves, 32 Oz., 7 In. 35.00
Forest Green, Pitcher, Polka Dots, Ice Lip, 86 Oz. 45.00
Forest Green, Pitcher, Water, Crinkle, 80 Oz., 8 In. 30.00
Forest Green, Platter, 8 x 11 In. 25.00
Forest Green, Punch Bowl, 10 In. 25.00
Forest Green, Punch Cup 2.50
Forest Green, Salt & Pepper, Windowpane, Diagonal Rib, 4 In., Pair 28.00
Forest Green, Tumbler, Iced Tea, 15 Oz., 6 In. 15.00
Forest Green, Tumbler, Iced Tea, Bicycle Built For Two, 6 ½ In. 10.00
Forest Green, Tumbler, Iced Tea, Square Dance, Swing Her High, 12 Oz. 9.00
Forest Green, Tumbler, Juice, 5 Oz., 3 ⅜ In. 7.00
Forest Green, Tumbler, Juice, Banded, 5 Oz. 5.00
Forest Green, Tumbler, Roly Poly, 9 Oz., 4 ½ In. 10.00
Forest Green, Tumbler, Whirly-Twirly, 18 Oz., 6 ½ In. 20.00
Forest Green, Vaporizer, Prak-T-Kal, Radio Star Series, 7 ⅝ In. 30.00
Forest Green, Vase, Coolidge, 6 ⅜ In. 4.00
Forest Green, Vase, Pineapple, 9 In. .... *illus* 24.00
Forest Green, Vase, Rectangular, Napco, 4 x 5 In. 10.00
Forest Green, Vase, Ruffled Pansy, 3 ½ In. 5.00
Forest Green, Water Bottle, Cover, Horizontal Ribbed 99.00
Forest Green, Water Bottle, Penguin, Qt. 68.00
Fortune, Candy Dish, Cover, Pink 30.00
Frances, Bowl, Amber, 3-Footed, 10 In. 52.00
Fruits, Berry Bowl, Green, 8 In. 115.00
Fruits, Cup, Pink 12.00
Fruits, Cup & Saucer, Green 15.00
Fruits, Plate, Luncheon, Green, 8 In. 14.00
Game Birds, Mug, Pheasant, 9 Oz. .... *illus* 9.00
Game Birds, Tumbler, Iced Tea, 11 Oz., 5 In. 14.00
Georgian, Berry Bowl, Green, 4 ½ In. 10.00
Georgian, Butter, Cover, Green 90.00
Georgian, Butter, No Cover, Green 45.00
Georgian, Creamer, Footed, Green, 4 In. 18.00
Georgian, Plate, Luncheon, Green, 8 ½ In. 12.00
Georgian, Sugar, Footed, Green, 4 In. 18.00
Golden Shell, Bowl, Dessert, 4 ¾ In. 4.00
Golden Shell, Plate, Dinner, 10 In. 6.00
Golden Shell, Plate, Dinner, 1964-65 World's Fair, 10 In. 35.00
Golden Shell, Saucer 1.00
Gothic, Plate, Big Top Peanut Butter, 8 In. 8.00
Gothic, Sherbet, Big Top Peanut Butter, 3 ¾ In. 5.00
Gothic, Tumbler, Iced Tea, Big Top Peanut Butter, 5 ⅝ In. 8.00
Hairpin pattern is listed here as Newport.
Harp, Cake Stand, Gold Trim, 9 In. 30.00
Harp, Cake Stand, Ice Blue, 9 In. 45.00

Harp, Plate, Dessert, Gold Trim, 7 In. 16.00
Harp, Tray, Handles, Rectangular 40.00
Harpo, Pitcher, Cobalt Blue, Clear Handle, 76 Oz., 9 In. 75.00 to 95.00
Harpo, Tumbler, Blue, 3 Oz., 3 ⅛ In. 12.00
Harpo, Tumbler, Blue, 6 Oz., 3 ⅝ In. 15.00
Harpo, Tumbler, Blue, 10 Oz., 4 ⅛ In. 15.00
Harpo, Tumbler, Blue, 13 Oz., 5 ⅛ In. 21.00
Heritage, Basket, 8 ½ x 7 In. 45.00
Heritage, Cup & Saucer 5.00
Heritage, Plate, Luncheon, 8 In. 5.00
Hex Optic pattern is listed here as Hexagon Optic.
Hexagon Optic, Ice Bucket, Green 30.00
Hexagon Optic, Mixing Bowl, Green, Ruffled, 6 ½ In. 20.00
Hexagon Optic, Mixing Bowl, Green, Ruffled, 7 ½ In. 25.00
Hexagon Optic, Pitcher, Ice Lip, 64 Oz., 9 ½ In. 18.00
Hexagon Optic, Saltshaker, Pink 25.00
Hexagon Optic, Tumbler, 15 Oz., 6 ½ In. 4.00
Hexagon Optic, Tumbler, Flared, Pink, 11 Oz., 5 In. 10.00
Hexagon Optic, Tumbler, Flared, Ultramarine, 11 Oz., 5 In. 24.00
Hexagon Optic, Tumbler, Footed, Pink, 8 Oz., 5 ¾ In. 12.00
Hexagon Optic, Tumbler, Footed, Pink, 11 Oz., 7 In. 12.00
Hexagon Optic, Tumbler, Iridized, 12 Oz., 5 In. 4.00
Hexagon Optic, Tumbler, Juice, Iridized, 6 Oz., 3 ¾ In. 3.00
Hexagon Optic, Tumbler, Pink, 12 Oz., 5 In. 10.00
Holiday, Butter, No Cover, Pink 12.00
Holiday, Candlestick, Pink, 3 In., Pair 140.00
Holiday, Console, Pink, 10 ¾ In. 166.00
Holiday, Creamer, Pink *illus* 12.00
Holiday, Cup, Pink 7.50
Holiday, Cup & Saucer, Pink 12.00 to 18.00
Holiday, Pitcher, Milk, Pink, 4 ¾ In. 70.00
Holiday, Pitcher, Pink, 52 Oz. 40.00
Holiday, Plate, Pink, 6 In. 10.00
Holiday, Soup, Dish, Pink, 7 ¾ In. 51.00
Holiday, Tumbler, Footed, Pink, 4 In. 55.00
Holiday, Tumbler, Iridescent, 5 Oz., 4 In. 10.00
Homespun, Berry Bowl, Pink, 8 ¼ In. 31.00
Homespun, Berry Set, Pink, 7 Piece 120.00
Homespun, Cup & Saucer, Child's 35.00
Homespun, Cup & Saucer, Pink, Child's 30.00 to 36.00
Homespun, Plate, Child's, 4 ½ In. 10.00
Homespun, Platter, Pink, Oval 20.00
Homespun, Saucer, Pink, Child's, 3 ¼ In. 10.00
Homespun, Sherbet, Pink, 3 ½ In. 20.00
Homespun, Sugar, Pink 15.00
Homespun, Sugar & Creamer, Pink 40.00
Homespun, Tumbler, Juice, Footed, Pink, 6 Oz., 4 In. 9.00
Homespun, Tumbler, Pink, 9 Oz., 4 ¼ In. *illus* 25.00
Homespun Lookalike, Pitcher, Ritz Blue, Tilted Ball, 80 Oz. 125.00
Homespun Lookalike, Tumbler, 9 Oz., 4 In. 6.00
Homespun Lookalike, Tumbler, Amethyst, 9 Oz., 4 In. 12.00
Homespun Lookalike, Tumbler, Juice, Ritz Blue, 5 Oz., 3 ¼ In. 12.00
Homespun Lookalike, Tumbler, Ritz Blue, 9 Oz., 4 In. 12.00
Homestead, Snack Set, Tray, Cup, Box, 4 Sets 40.00
Honeycomb pattern is listed here as Hexagon Optic.
Horizontal Ribbed pattern is listed here as Manhattan.
Horseshoe pattern is listed here as No. 612.
Indiana Custard, Berry Bowl, 5 ½ In. 15.00
Indiana Custard, Bowl, Cereal, 6 ½ In. 24.00
Indiana Custard, Creamer 16.00
Indiana Custard, Plate, Dinner, 9 ¾ In. 36.00
Indiana Custard, Saucer 10.00 to 15.00
Indiana Custard, Sugar, Cover Only 30.00
Iris, Berry Bowl, Beaded Edge, Iridescent, 8 In. 40.00
Iris, Bowl, Iridescent, 9 ½ In. 20.00
Iris, Butter, Cover, Iridescent 45.00
Iris, Butter, Cover Only 36.00

Depression Glass, Holiday, Creamer, Pink
$12.00

Depression Glass, Homespun, Tumbler, Pink, 9 Oz., 4 ¼ In.
$25.00

Iris

The design of Iris is unusually bold for Depression glass. Molded representations of stalks of iris fill the center of a ribbed plate. Other pieces in the pattern show fewer irises, but the flower is predominant. Edges of pieces may be ruffled or beaded. It was made by Jeannette Glass Company, Jeannette, Pennsylvania, from 1928 to 1932 and then again in the 1950s and 1970s. Early pieces were made in Crystal, Green, Iridescent, and Pink. Later, Crystal and White pieces were decorated with Blue-Green and Red-Yellow two-tone stains. Solid Red-stained after-dinner cups and saucers can be found. The pattern is also called Iris & Herringbone. Reproduction candy vases and coasters have been made in a variety of colors since 1977.

Depression Glass, Iris, Vase, 9 x 5 ½ In. $30.00

Depression Glass, Jadite, Range Set, Salt, Pepper, Flour, Sugar, 4 Piece $225.00

Depression Glass, Jane-Ray, Cup & Saucer, Jade-Ite $10.00

Jane-Ray

Jane-Ray is a plain dinnerware with ribbed edge made mostly in Jade-Ite from 1945 to 1963 by Anchor Hocking Glass Corporation, Lancaster, Ohio. Crystal, Ivory, Peach Lustre, and Vitrock pieces were also made.

Iris, Candlestick, 2-Light ... 25.00
Iris, Cup ... 16.00
Iris, Cup & Saucer, Iridescent ... 23.00
Iris, Goblet, 8 Oz., 5 ⅝ In. ... 25.00
Iris, Pitcher, Footed, 9 ½ In. ... 40.00 to 45.00
Iris, Plate, Dinner, 9 In. ... 46.00
Iris, Plate, Dinner, Iridescent, 9 In. ... 40.00
Iris, Plate, Luncheon, Frosted, 8 In. ... 35.00
Iris, Plate, Sherbet, Iridescent, 5 ½ In. ... 10.00 to 15.00
Iris, Sandwich Server, Frosted, 11 ¾ In. ... 20.00
Iris, Sandwich Server, Iridescent, 11 ¾ In. ... 35.00
Iris, Sauce, Ruffled Edge, 5 In. ... 10.00
Iris, Sauce, Ruffled Edge, Iridescent, 5 In. ... 19.50
Iris, Saucer ... 12.00
Iris, Sherbet ... 25.00
Iris, Soup, Dish, Iridescent, 7 ½ In. ... 65.00
Iris, Sugar, Cover ... 15.00
Iris, Tumbler, Design On Foot, 6 In. ... 50.00
Iris, Tumbler, Iridescent, Footed, 6 In. ... 12.00
Iris, Vase, 9 x 5 ½ In. ... *illus* 30.00
Iris, Wine, 3 ½ Oz., 4 ¼ In. ... 18.00
Iris, Wine, Iridescent, 3 ½ Oz., 4 ¼ In. ... 25.00
Iris & Herringbone pattern is listed here as Iris.
Jadite, Beater Bowl, 11 ½ In. ... 50.00
Jadite, Canister, Coffee, 28 Oz. ... 210.00
Jadite, Canister, Coffee, Square, 48 In. ... 65.00
Jadite, Canister, Spice, 3 In. ... 49.00
Jadite, Canister, Sugar, 48 Oz. ... 65.00
Jadite, Mixing Bowl, Ribbed, 7 In. ... 40.00
Jadite, Range Set, Salt, Pepper, Flour, Sugar, 4 Piece ... *illus* 225.00
Jadite, Salt & Pepper, 4 ¼ In. ... 30.00
Jadite, Shaker, Horizontal Ribbed, 6 Oz. ... 30.00
Jadite, Shaker, Ribbed, Round, 4 ¾ In. ... 60.00 to 65.00
Jane-Ray, Bowl, Dessert, Jade-Ite, 4 ⅞ In. ... 12.00
Jane-Ray, Bowl, Oatmeal, Jade-Ite, 5 ⅞ In. ... 25.00
Jane-Ray, Bowl, Vegetable, Jade-Ite, 8 ¼ In. ... 32.00
Jane-Ray, Creamer, Jade-Ite ... 20.00
Jane-Ray, Cup & Saucer, Jade-Ite ... *illus* 10.00
Jane-Ray, Plate, Dinner, 9 ⅛ In. ... 12.50
Jane-Ray, Plate, Dinner, Jade-Ite, 9 In. ... 12.50 to 16.00
Jane-Ray, Plate, Salad, Jade-Ite, 7 ¾ In. ... 12.00 to 14.50
Jane-Ray, Soup, Dish, Flat Rim, Jade-Ite, 7 ⅝ In. ... 22.00
Jane-Ray, Soup, Dish, Jade-Ite, 7 ½ In. ... 18.00 to 25.00
Jane-Ray, Sugar & Creamer, Cover, Jade-Ite ... 60.00
Jubilee, Cake Tray, Yellow ... 30.00
Jubilee, Sandwich Tray, Center Handle, Yellow, 11 In. ... 30.00
Kings Crown, Bowl, Cereal, Green, 4 ⅛ x 2 ¼ In. ... 10.00
Kings Crown, Compote, Amber, 5 ¼ x 5 In. ... 15.00
Kings Crown, Compote, Gold Trim, 5 ¼ x 5 In. ... 23.00
Kings Crown, Sugar & Creamer, Green, 3 In. ... 15.00
Knife & Fork pattern is listed here as Colonial.
Lace Edge pattern is listed here as Old Colony.
Landrum, Bowl, Pink, Cupped, 3-Footed, 6 ½ x 4 In. ... 75.00
Landrum, Bowl, Yellow, Crimped, 3-Footed, 8 x 3 ¾ In. ... 55.00
Laurel, Berry Bowl, French Ivory, 4 ¾ In. ... 8.00
Laurel, Bowl, Cereal, Jade-Ite, 6 In. ... 28.00
Laurel, Bowl, Vegetable, Oval, French Ivory, 9 ¾ In. ... 27.00
Laurel, Candlestick, French Ivory, 4 In. ... 24.00
Laurel, Cheese Dish, French Ivory, McKee ... 40.00
Laurel, Cup & Saucer, French Ivory ... 10.00
Laurel, Plate, Ivory, Red Trim, Child's, 6 In. ... 16.00
Laurel, Plate, Sherbet, French Ivory, 6 In. ... 5.00
Laurel, Platter, Oval, French Ivory, 10 ¾ In. ... 25.00
Laurel, Sugar, French Ivory ... 12.00 to 15.00
Laurel, Sugar, Jade-Ite ... 35.00
Laurel, Tea Set, Child's, 14 Piece ... 575.00
Laurel Wreath, Relish, 5 Sections, 13 ½ In. ... 20.00

Liberty, Water Set, Gold Eagles, 86-Oz. Pitcher, 7 Piece . . . 30.00
Lido, Salad Set, Avocado Green, Box, c.1970, 11 ⅜ In., 9 Piece . . . 45.00
Line 300 pattern is listed in the Paden City category as Peacock & Wild Rose.
Lorain pattern is listed here as No. 615.
Lorna pattern is included in the Cambridge Glass category.
Louis pattern is listed here as Floragold.
Lovebirds pattern is listed here as Georgian.
Madrid, Bowl, Salad, 8 In. . . . 14.00
Madrid, Cake Plate, Pink, Round, 11 ⅜ In. . . . 30.00
Madrid, Candlestick, Amber, 2 ½ In. . . . *illus* 12.00
Madrid, Candlestick, Iridescent, 2 ½ In. . . . 12.00
Madrid, Console, Iridescent, 11 In. . . . 15.00
Madrid, Cookie Jar, Cover . . . 65.00
Madrid, Cookie Jar, Cover, Pink . . . 38.00 to 45.00
Madrid, Creamer, Footed, Amber . . . 12.00
Madrid, Cup & Saucer, Amber . . . 15.00
Madrid, Grill Plate, Green, 10 ½ In. . . . 18.00
Madrid, Plate, Dinner, Amber, 10 ½ In. . . . 50.00
Madrid, Plate, Luncheon, Amber, 8 ⅞ In. . . . 12.00 to 14.00
Madrid, Plate, Sherbet, Amber, 6 In. . . . 7.00
Madrid, Platter, Amber . . . 18.00
Madrid, Saltshaker, Footed, Green . . . 50.00
Madrid, Saucer, Amber . . . 4.00
Madrid, Sugar, Amber . . . 12.00
Madrid, Sugar, Cover, Amber . . . 70.00
Madrid, Sugar, Cover Only, Green . . . 68.00
Madrid, Tumbler, Iced Tea, Amber, 12 Oz, 5 ½ In. . . . 23.00 to 25.00
Manhattan, Berry Bowl, Handles, 8 In. . . . 10.00
Manhattan, Berry Bowl, Pink, Handles, 5 ¼ In. . . . 25.00
Manhattan, Berry Bowl, Pink, Handles, 8 In. . . . 8.00
Manhattan, Bowl, Candy Dish, Pink, 3-Footed, 6 In. . . . 12.00
Manhattan, Candlestick, 4 ½ In., Pair . . . 15.00
Manhattan, Compote, Pink, 5 ¾ In. . . . 43.00
Manhattan, Creamer, Pink, Oval . . . *illus* 15.00
Manhattan, Plate, Luncheon, Fruits, Green, 8 In. . . . 12.00
Manhattan, Relish Set, Clear Tray, Royal Ruby Inserts, 7 Piece . . . 150.00
Manhattan, Relish Tray Insert . . . 5.00
Manhattan, Saltshaker, Pink . . . 25.00
Many Windows pattern is listed here as Roulette.
Martha Washington pattern is included in the Cambridge Glass category.
Mayfair Open Rose, Bowl, Blue, 11 ¾ In. . . . 95.00
Mayfair Open Rose, Bowl, Blue, Oval, 9 ½ In. . . . 67.00
Mayfair Open Rose, Bowl, Fruit, Scalloped, Green, 12 In. . . . 48.00
Mayfair Open Rose, Bowl, Fruit, Scalloped, Pink, 12 In. . . . 75.00
Mayfair Open Rose, Bowl, Green, 11 ¾ In. . . . 45.00
Mayfair Open Rose, Bowl, Vegetable, Cover, Handles, Pink, 10 In. . . . 125.00
Mayfair Open Rose, Bowl, Vegetable, Handles, Pink, 7 In. . . . 28.00
Mayfair Open Rose, Bowl, Vegetable, Handles, Pink, 10 In. . . . 35.00
Mayfair Open Rose, Cake Plate, Blue, 10 In. . . . 57.00
Mayfair Open Rose, Celery Dish, Blue, Sections, 10 In. . . . 65.00
Mayfair Open Rose, Cocktail, 3 Oz., 4 In. . . . 100.00
Mayfair Open Rose, Cookie Jar, Cover, Pink, 6 In. . . . *illus* 47.00
Mayfair Open Rose, Cup, Pink . . . 18.00
Mayfair Open Rose, Cup & Saucer, Blue . . . 70.00
Mayfair Open Rose, Decanter, Stopper, Pink, 32 Oz. . . . 204.00
Mayfair Open Rose, Pitcher, Blue, 80 Oz., 8 ½ In. . . . 225.00
Mayfair Open Rose, Pitcher, Pink, 80 Oz., 8 ½ In. . . . 95.00
Mayfair Open Rose, Plate, Dinner, Blue, 9 ½ In. . . . 60.00
Mayfair Open Rose, Plate, Dinner, Pink, 9 ½ In. . . . 55.00
Mayfair Open Rose, Platter, Oval, Open Handles, Blue, 12 In. . . . 62.00
Mayfair Open Rose, Sandwich Server, Green, Center Handle . . . 35.00
Mayfair Open Rose, Sandwich Server, Pink, Center Handle . . . 50.00
Mayfair Open Rose, Saucer, Pink . . . 35.00
Mayfair Open Rose, Sherbet, 4 ¾ In. . . . 100.00
Mayfair Open Rose, Soup, Cream, Pink, 5 In. . . . 65.00
Mayfair Open Rose, Sugar, Pink . . . 30.00
Mayfair Open Rose, Tumbler, Iced Tea, Footed, Pink . . . 35.00

Depression Glass, Madrid, Candlestick, Amber, 2 ½ In.
$12.00

Depression Glass, Manhattan, Creamer, Pink, Oval
$15.00

Depression Glass, Mayfair Open Rose, Cookie Jar, Cover, Pink, 6 In.
$47.00

Mayfair Open Rose

Mayfair Open Rose was made by Hocking Glass Company from 1931 to 1937. It was made primarily in Light Blue and Pink, with a few Green and Yellow pieces. Crystal examples are rare. The cookie jar and the whiskey glass have been reproduced since 1982.

Depression Glass, Milano, Pitcher, Avocado Green, 96 Oz.
$12.00

Moderntone
Moderntone, or Wedding Band, was made by Hazel Atlas Glass Company from 1935 to 1942. The simple pattern is popular today with Art Deco enthusiasts. It was made of Amethyst, Cobalt Blue, Crystal, and Pink glass. Green tumblers can be found, too. It was also made of an opaque, almost white glass called Platonite.

Depression Glass, Moderntone, Creamer, Cobalt Blue
$10.00

Depression Glass, Moderntone, Cup, Amethyst
$12.00

Mayfair Open Rose, Tumbler, Pink, 9 Oz., 4 ¼ In. . . . 50.00
Mayfair Open Rose, Tumbler, Whiskey, Pink, 1 ½ Oz., 2 ¼ In. . . . 95.00
Mayfair Open Rose, Wine, Pink, 3 Oz., 4 ½ In. . . . 85.00
Meadow Green, Casserole, Cover, 1 ½ Qt. . . . 15.00
Meadow Green, French Casserole . . . 6.50
Meadow Green, Mixing Bowl, 2 ½ Qt., 8 ¾ In. . . . 11.00
Meadow Green, Utility Pan, 1 ½ Qt., 12 x 6 In. . . . 19.00
Melba, Plate, Pink, Octagonal, 8 In. . . . 8.00
Milano, Pitcher, Avocado Green, 96 Oz. . . . *illus* 12.00
Milano, Pitcher, Forest Green, 96 Oz. . . . 45.00
Miss America, Bowl, Cereal, Pink, 6 ¼ In. . . . 30.00
Miss America, Bowl, Vegetable, Oval, Pink, 10 In. . . . 52.00
Miss America, Celery Dish, Oval, 10 ½ In. . . . 38.00
Miss America, Celery Dish, Oval, Pink, 10 ½ In. . . . 42.00
Miss America, Compote, 5 In. . . . 14.00
Miss America, Compote, Pink, 5 In. . . . 28.00
Miss America, Creamer . . . 10.00
Miss America, Cup . . . 20.00
Miss America, Cup & Saucer, Pink . . . 30.00
Miss America, Grill Plate, Pink, 10 ¼ In. . . . 35.00
Miss America, Plate, Dinner, Pink, 10 ¼ In. . . . 45.00
Miss America, Plate, Sherbet, Pink, 5 ¾ In. . . . 18.00
Miss America, Platter, Oval, 12 ¼ In. . . . 18.00
Miss America, Platter, Oval, Pink, 12 ¼ In. . . . 55.00
Miss America, Saucer, Pink . . . 8.00
Miss America, Sugar & Creamer, Pink . . . 55.00
Miss America, Tumbler, 10 Oz., 4 ½ In. . . . 18.00
Moderntone, Berry Bowl, Cobalt Blue, 5 In. . . . 29.00
Moderntone, Berry Bowl, Cobalt Blue, 8 ¾ In. . . . 55.00
Moderntone, Creamer, Cobalt Blue . . . *illus* 10.00
Moderntone, Creamer, Platonite . . . 3.75
Moderntone, Creamer, Platonite, Fired-On Blue . . . 4.50
Moderntone, Creamer, Platonite, Fired-On Yellow . . . 4.50 to 6.50
Moderntone, Cup, Amethyst . . . *illus* 12.00
Moderntone, Cup, Cobalt Blue . . . 10.00
Moderntone, Cup, Platonite, Blue Stripe . . . 2.50
Moderntone, Cup & Saucer, Platonite, Fired-On Green . . . 8.00
Moderntone, Custard Cup, Amethyst . . . 22.00
Moderntone, Custard Cup, Cobalt Blue . . . 20.00
Moderntone, Plate, Dinner, Amethyst, 8 ⅞ In. . . . 15.00
Moderntone, Plate, Dinner, Cobalt Blue, 8 ⅞ In. . . . 18.00 to 20.00
Moderntone, Plate, Luncheon, Cobalt Blue, 7 ¾ In. . . . 14.00
Moderntone, Plate, Luncheon, Platonite, Blue Stripe, 7 ¾ In. . . . 4.00
Moderntone, Plate, Salad, Cobalt Blue, 6 ¾ In. . . . 12.00
Moderntone, Plate, Salad, Platonite, Fired-On Blue, 6 ¾ In. . . . 4.25 to 6.00
Moderntone, Plate, Salad, Platonite, Fired-On Green, 6 ¾ In. . . . 4.25
Moderntone, Plate, Sherbet, Amethyst, 5 ⅞ In. . . . 7.00
Moderntone, Plate, Sherbet, Cobalt Blue, 5 ⅞ In. . . . 6.00
Moderntone, Plate, Sherbet, Platonite, Fired-On Yellow, 5 ⅞ In. . . . 4.00
Moderntone, Platter, Platonite, Fired-On Yellow, 12 In. . . . 11.50
Moderntone, Saltshaker, Platonite, Fired-On Blue . . . 8.00
Moderntone, Sherbet, Platonite, Fired-On Blue . . . 4.00 to 10.00
Moderntone, Sherbet, Platonite, Fired-On Pink . . . 5.00
Moderntone, Soup, Cream, Cobalt Blue, Ruffled Edge, 5 In. . . . 65.00
Moderntone, Soup, Cream, Handles, Amethyst, 4 ¾ In. . . . 20.00
Moderntone, Soup, Cream, Handles, Cobalt Blue, 4 ¾ In. . . . 23.00
Moderntone, Soup, Cream, Platonite, Blue Stripe, 4 ¾ In. . . . 4.00
Moderntone, Soup, Cream, Platonite, Fired-On Green . . . 6.75
Moderntone, Sugar, Platonite, Fired-On Green . . . 4.50 to 6.50
Moderntone, Sugar & Creamer, Cover, Platonite, Cobalt Blue . . . 65.00
Moderntone, Tumbler, Juice, Platonite, Cobalt Blue, 5 Oz. . . . 75.00
Moderntone, Tumbler, Platonite, Fired-On Orange . . . 9.00 to 11.00
Moderntone Little Hostess Party, Tea Set, 14 Piece . . . 325.00
Moderntone Little Hostess Party, Teapot, Fired-On Maroon, 5 x 3 In. . . . 85.00
Monticello, Basket, Milk Glass, 9 x 11 In. . . . 35.00
Moondrops pattern is listed in the New Martinsville category.
Moonstone, Berry Bowl, 5 ½ In. . . . 22.00

Moonstone, Bowl, Cloverleaf, 3 Sections, 7 In. 16.00
Moonstone, Bowl, Crimped Edge, 7 ¾ In. 15.00 to 18.00
Moonstone, Bowl, Crimped Edge, 9 ½ In. 25.00
Moonstone, Bowl, Dessert, Crimped Edge, 5 ½ In. 18.00
Moonstone, Bowl, Handles, Crimped Edge, 6 ½ In. 22.00
Moonstone, Bowl, Sections, 7 ¾ In. *illus* 14.00
Moonstone, Goblet, 10 Oz. 17.25
Moonstone, Plate, Bread & Butter, 5 ¼ In. 5.00
Moonstone, Sherbet 15.00
Moonstone, Sugar & Creamer 25.00
Moroccan Amethyst, Bowl, Center Handle, Oval, 7 ¾ In. 15.00
Moroccan Amethyst, Bowl, Cereal, 6 In. 10.00
Moroccan Amethyst, Bowl, Fruit, 11 In. 45.00
Moroccan Amethyst, Bowl, Rectangular, 7 ¾ In. 12.50
Moroccan Amethyst, Cup & Saucer 14.00
Moroccan Amethyst, Goblet, 9 Oz., 5 ½ In. 8.00
Moroccan Amethyst, Tumbler, 11 Oz., 4 ¾ In. 9.50
Moroccan Amethyst, Tumbler, Juice, Swirl, 4 Oz., 2 ½ In. 8.00
Moroccan Amethyst, Tumbler, Old Fashioned, Swirl, 8 Oz., 3 ½ In. 12.00
Mt. Pleasant, Bowl, Black Amethyst, Square, Handles, 6 In. 22.00
Mt. Pleasant, Candlestick, 2-Light, Black Amethyst, Pair 48.00
Mt. Pleasant, Cup, Black Amethyst 12.00
Mt. Pleasant, Cup, Cobalt Blue 12.00
Mt. Pleasant, Dish, Mayonnaise, Cobalt Blue, Platinum, 3-Toed, 5 ½ In. 20.00
Mt. Pleasant, Plate, Serving, Black Amethyst, Scalloped, 2 Handles, 9 In. 15.00
Mt. Pleasant, Sandwich Server, Center Handle, Black Amethyst, 9 In. 40.00
Mt. Pleasant, Sugar, Black Amethyst *illus* 10.00
Mt. Pleasant, Tumbler, Footed, Blue, 6 In. 25.00
Mt. Pleasant, Tumbler, Footed, Cobalt Blue, 7 ¼ In. 28.00
National, Pitcher, Ice Lip, 8 ½ x 8 In. 25.00
New Century, Pitcher 35.00
New Century, Tumbler, Amethyst, 9 Oz., 4 In. 14.50
New Century, Tumbler, Juice, Amethyst, 5 Oz., 3 ½ In. 12.50
Newport, Berry Bowl, Amethyst, 4 ¾ In. 20.00
Newport, Bowl, Cereal, Amethyst, 5 ¼ In. 30.00 to 35.00
Newport, Cup & Saucer, Amethyst 17.00
Newport, Plate, Dinner, Amethyst, 8 13/16 In. 17.50
Newport, Plate, Luncheon, Amethyst, 8 ½ In. 15.00
Newport, Plate, Luncheon, Platonite, Fired-On Green, 8 ½ In. 8.00
Newport, Plate, Luncheon, Platonite, Fired-On Yellow, 8 ½ In. 8.00
Newport, Plate, Sherbet, Amethyst, 5 ⅞ In. 7.00
Newport, Platter, Oval, Amethyst, 11 ¾ In. 25.00
Newport, Saltshaker, Platonite, Footed 10.00 to 15.00
Newport, Sherbet, Amethyst 12.50
Newport, Sherbet, Cobalt Blue 15.00
Newport, Soup, Cream, Blue, 4 ¾ In. 20.00
Newport, Soup, Cream, Cobalt Blue, Handles, 4 ¾ In. 25.00
Newport, Sugar, Amethyst 14.00 to 18.00
Newport, Tumbler, Amethyst, 9 Oz., 4 ½ In. 35.00
No. 601 pattern is listed here as Avocado.
No. 612, Bowl, Cereal, Yellow, 6 In. 25.00
No. 612, Butter, Cover, Green 1000.00
No. 612, Creamer, Yellow 15.00
No. 612, Cup & Saucer, Green 18.00
No. 612, Grill Plate, Green 125.00
No. 612, Relish, Footed, Yellow, 3 Sections 25.00
No. 612, Sherbet, Green 16.00
No. 612, Sugar, Green 18.00
No. 612, Tumbler, Footed, Green, 9 Oz., 4 ½ In. 27.00
No. 612, Tumbler, Green, 12 Oz. 225.00
No. 615, Bowl, Salad, Yellow, 7 ¼ In. 100.00
No. 615, Bowl, Vegetable, Oval, Yellow, 9 ¾ In. 70.00
No. 615, Creamer, Yellow 25.00
No. 615, Cup & Saucer, Yellow 19.50
No. 615, Plate, Dinner, Yellow, 10 ¼ In. 88.00
No. 615, Plate, Luncheon, Yellow, 8 ¾ In. 25.00 to 29.00
No. 615, Plate, Salad, 7 ¾ In. 12.50

Moroccan Amethyst
Moroccan Amethyst is the name of a color, not a shape. The smoky-purple glass was made by Hazel Ware, a division of Continental Can Company, Clarksburg, West Virginia, in the 1960s. The modern-looking dishes were made in several shapes, including Apple, Moderne, Seashell, Simplicity, Square, Starlite, Swirl, Swirl Colonial, and Vanity.

Depression Glass, Moonstone, Bowl, Sections, 7 ¾ In.
$14.00

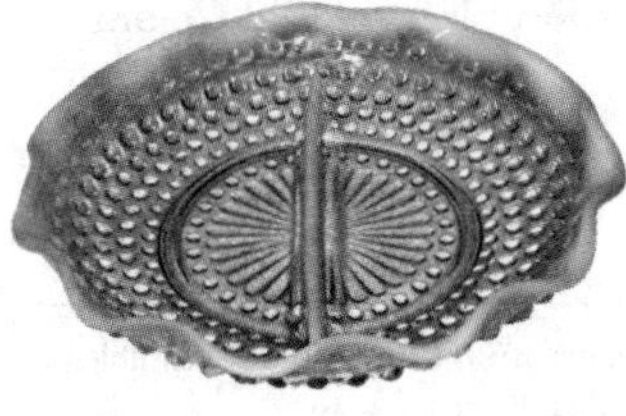

Depression Glass, Mt. Pleasant, Sugar, Black Amethyst
$10.00

TIP
Rubber cement solvent, available at art and office supply stores, has many uses. Put a few drops on a paper towel and rub off ink smudges, adhesive tape glue, or label glue from glass or porcelain.

Old Colony
This pattern, which was advertised as Old Colony, has also been called Colony, Lace Edge, Loop, Open Lace, or Open Scallop. In addition, the pattern is often confused with other similar patterns, such as Imperial's Laced Edge. Cups or tumblers may also be mixed up with Queen Mary or Coronation. The pattern listed here, made by Hocking Glass Company, Lancaster, Ohio, from 1935 to 1938, can usually be identified by the familiar sunburst base common to many of Hocking's designs. Most pieces of Old Colony are Pink, although Crystal is also found.

Depression Glass, No. 615, Tumbler, Yellow, Footed, 4 ¾ In.
$38.00

Depression Glass, Normandie, Grill Plate, Iridescent, 11 In.
$10.00

No. 615, Plate, Salad, Yellow, 7 ¾ In. 15.00
No. 615, Plate, Sherbet, 5 ½ In. 11.50
No. 615, Relish, Yellow, Square, 4 Sections 40.00
No. 615, Saucer, Basket, Yellow 4.50
No. 615, Sherbet, Yellow, Footed, 3 ⅛ x 3 ½ In. 30.00
No. 615, Sugar 18.00
No. 615, Tumbler, Yellow, Footed, 4 ¾ In. .... *illus* 38.00
No. 616, Cup & Saucer 14.00
No. 616, Plate, Luncheon, 8 In. 6.00
No. 618, Bowl, Vegetable, Amber, Oval, 10 In. 18.00
No. 618, Luncheon Set, Amber, 15 Piece 120.00
No. 618, Plate, Dinner, 9 ¼ In. 20.00
No. 620, Candleholder, 4 ½ In. 6.00
No. 620, Cup & Saucer, Amber 6.50
No. 620, Platter, Amber, 10 ¾ In. 16.00
No. 620, Sherbet 8.50
No. 620, Soup, Cream, Amber, Handles .... 5.75 to 10.00
No. 620, Tumbler, Amber, 9 Oz. 20.00
No. 622 pattern is listed here as Pretzel.
Normandie, Berry Bowl, 5 In. 6.50
Normandie, Bowl, Cereal, Iridescent, 6 ½ In. 9.00
Normandie, Creamer, Amber, Footed 9.00
Normandie, Cup, Amber 8.00
Normandie, Cup & Saucer, Pink 12.50
Normandie, Grill Plate, Iridescent, 11 In. .... *illus* 10.00
Normandie, Plate, Luncheon, Amber, 9 ¼ In. 10.00
Normandie, Saucer, Iridescent 3.00
Old Cafe, Berry Bowl, Tab Handles, Pink, 3 ¾ In. 14.00
Old Cafe, Bowl, Cereal, Royal Ruby, 5 ½ In. 30.00
Old Cafe, Butter, No Cover, Pink 45.00
Old Cafe, Candy Dish, Clear, Royal Ruby Cover, 5 ½ In. 25.00
Old Cafe, Candy Dish, Tab Handles, 8 In. 8.00
Old Cafe, Candy Dish, Tab Handles, Pink, 8 In. 20.00
Old Cafe, Candy Dish, Tab Handles, Royal Ruby, 8 In. 12.00
Old Cafe, Cup & Saucer, Pink 18.00
Old Cafe, Sherbet, Pink, 3 ¾ In. 16.00
Old Cafe, Tumbler, Juice, Royal Ruby, 3 In. 22.00
Old Cafe, Tumbler, Pink, 9 Oz., 4 In. 22.00
Old Cafe, Vase, 7 ¼ In. 10.00
Old Colony, Bowl, Cereal, Pink, 6 ⅜ In. 24.00
Old Colony, Bowl, Salad, Pink, 7 ¾ In. 68.00
Old Colony, Bowl, Vegetable, Pink, 9 ½ In. 30.00
Old Colony, Bowl, Vegetable, Ribbed, Pink, 9 ½ In. 27.00
Old Colony, Creamer, Pink 29.00
Old Colony, Plate, Dinner, Pink, 10 ½ In. .... *illus* 30.00
Old Colony, Plate, Luncheon, Pink, 8 ¼ In. 20.00
Old Colony, Platter, Oval, Pink, 12 ¾ In. 42.00
Old Colony, Relish, Pink, 3 Sections, 7 ½ In. 85.00
Old Colony, Saucer, Pink 12.50
Old English, Candlestick, Green, 4 In. 22.00
Old English, Fruit Stand, Green, Footed, 11 In. 30.00
Old English, Tumbler, Footed, Amber, 4 ½ In. 18.00
Old English, Water Set, Fired-On Orange, 7 Piece 150.00
Old Florentine pattern is listed here as Florentine No. 1.
Oleander, Sugar & Creamer, 3 x 3 In. 20.00
Open Lace pattern is listed here as Old Colony.
Open Rose pattern is listed here as Mayfair Open Rose.
Orange Blossom, Plate, Luncheon, 9 ¾ In. 7.50
Ovide, Bowl, Cereal, Black, Red, Gold Bands, 15 Oz., 5 ½ In. 9.00
Ovide, Creamer, Black, Red, Gold Bands 9.00
Ovide, Cup & Saucer, Black, Red, Gold Bands 9.00
Ovide, Cup & Saucer, Platonite, Fired-On Pastel Pink 9.00
Ovide, Cup & Saucer, Platonite, Fired-On Sierra Sunrise 11.00
Ovide, Cup & Saucer, Platonite, Green Band 6.00
Ovide, Plate, Bread & Butter, Black, Red, Gold Bands, 6 In. 5.00
Ovide, Plate, Dinner, Black, Red, Gold Bands, 9 In. 12.00
Ovide, Plate, Dinner, Platonite, 9 In. 9.00

Ovide, Plate, Dinner, Platonite, Fired-On Pastel Yellow, 9 In. 9.00
Ovide, Plate, Luncheon, Platonite, Fired-On Chartreuse, 8 In. 3.00
Ovide, Sherbet, Black, Red, Gold Bands 6.00
Ovide, Sugar, Platonite, Gray & White Trim 6.00
Ovide, Tumbler, Black, Red, Gold Bands, 8 Oz., 3 7/8 In. 12.00
Oyster & Pearl, Relish, Pink, Sections, 10 1/4 In. 20.00
Panelled Aster pattern is listed here as Primo.
Park Avenue, Plate, 8 In. 5.00
Parrot pattern is listed here as Sylvan.
Patrician, Berry Bowl, Amber, 8 1/2 In. 35.00
Patrician, Bowl, Cereal, Amber, 6 In. 20.00
Patrician, Bowl, Vegetable, Oval, 10 In. 18.00
Patrician, Bowl, Vegetable, Oval, Amber, 10 In. 30.00
Patrician, Butter, Cover, Amber 100.00
Patrician, Cookie Jar, Cover 100.00
Patrician, Cookie Jar, Cover, Amber 81.00
Patrician, Creamer, Amber 12.50
Patrician, Creamer, Green 12.00
Patrician, Cup, Amber 9.00
Patrician, Cup, Green 10.00
Patrician, Jam Dish, Amber, 6 3/4 In. 30.00
Patrician, Plate, Dinner, Amber, 11 In. 8.00
Patrician, Plate, Luncheon, Amber, 9 1/4 In. 12.00
Patrician, Plate, Salad, Amber, 7 3/4 In. 13.00
Patrician, Plate, Sherbet, Amber, 6 1/8 In. 9.00
Patrician, Salt & Pepper 65.00
Patrician, Saltshaker, Amber 20.00
Patrician, Sherbet, Amber 10.00
Patrician, Sherbet, Green 9.00
Patrician, Soup, Cream, Amber, 2 Handles .... *illus* 17.50
Patrician, Sugar, Amber, 3 1/2 In. .... 9.50 to 14.00
Patrician, Tumbler, Iced Tea, 14 Oz., 5 1/2 In. 50.00
Patrician, Tumbler, Iced Tea, Amber, 14 Oz., 5 1/2 In. 50.00
Patrician, Tumbler, Water, Amber, 9 Oz., 4 3/8 In. 20.00
Peach Lustre, Bowl, Chili, 5 In. 8.00
Peach Lustre, Bowl, Scalloped, Leaf 14.50
Peach Lustre, Casserole, 6 1/2 x 10 1/2 In. 14.50
Peach Lustre, Custard Cup, Swirl 4.00
Peach Lustre, Dessert Cup, Ruffled Edge 8.00
Peach Lustre, French Casserole, Handle 6.50
Peach Lustre, Pie Plate, 9 In. 8.50
Peacock & Wild Rose pattern is listed in the Paden City category.
Petalware, Bowl, Cereal, Monax, 5 3/4 In. 9.50
Petalware, Bowl, Vegetable, Monax, 8 3/4 x 3 In. 20.00
Petalware, Bowl, Vegetable, Pink, 8 1/2 In. 24.00
Petalware, Cup & Saucer, Florette 12.00
Petalware, Cup & Saucer, Monax .... 6.00 to 9.00
Petalware, Cup & Saucer, Regency, Cremax, Gold Trim 12.00
Petalware, Lampshade, Monax, 6 3/8 In. 20.00
Petalware, Plate, Bread & Butter, Monax, 6 1/2 In. 2.50
Petalware, Plate, Dinner, Cremax, 9 In. 14.00
Petalware, Plate, Dinner, Monax, 9 In. .... 11.50 to 15.00
Petalware, Plate, Salad, Cremax, 8 In. .... 7.50 to 9.00
Petalware, Plate, Salad, Cremax, Pastel Bands, 8 In. 10.00
Petalware, Plate, Salad, Florette, 8 In. 12.00
Petalware, Plate, Salad, Monax, 8 In. 6.00
Petalware, Plate, Salad, Monax, Fruits, 8 In. 15.00
Petalware, Plate, Salad, Pink, 8 In. 10.00
Petalware, Plate, Salad, Regency, Cremax, Gold Trim, 8 In. 10.00
Petalware, Salver, Cremax, Pastel Banded, 11 In. 29.00
Petalware, Salver, Florette, 11 In. 25.00
Petalware, Salver, Monax, 11 In. 15.00
Petalware, Salver, Pink, 11 In. 18.00
Petalware, Saucer, Cremax 2.00
Petalware, Sherbet, Monax 10.00
Petalware, Soup, Cream, Monax 12.50
Petalware, Sugar, Monax .... 6.00 to 7.00

Depression Glass, Old Colony, Plate, Dinner, Pink, 10 1/2 In.
$30.00

Depression Glass, Patrician, Soup, Cream, Amber, 2 Handles
$17.50

Petalware

Macbeth-Evans Glass Company made Petalware from 1930 to 1940. It was first made in Crystal and Pink. In 1932 the dinnerware was made in Monax, and in 1933 in Cremax. The pattern remained popular, and in 1936 Cobalt Blue and several other variations were made. Some pieces were hand-painted with pastel bands of green, ivory, and pink. Some pieces were decorated with gold or red trim. Flower or fruit designs in bright colors were used on others. Bright bands of fired-on blue, green, red, and yellow were used to decorate some wares. Collectors have given some of these patterns their own names, including Banded Petalware, Daisy Petals, Diamond Point, Petal, Shell, and Vivid Bands.

Depression Glass, Petalware, Sugar, Regency, Cremax, Gold Trim
$5.00

Depression Glass, Primrose, Sugar
$5.00

Depression Glass, Princess, Cup & Saucer, Green
$26.00

TIP

When rewiring an old lamp, put a dimmer on the cord to turn the lamp on and off. This will protect the original switch and pull chains. If you must replace any of the parts, save them for the next owner, who may want to restore the lamp.

Petalware, Sugar, Pink 12.00
Petalware, Sugar, Regency, Cremax, Gold Trim . . . . . *illus* 5.00
Petalware, Sugar & Creamer, Regency, Cremax, Gold Trim 14.00
Pillar Optic, Bowl, Centerpiece, Underplate, Pink, 11 ½ & 13 ½ In. 75.00
Pillar Optic, Cup & Saucer, Green 18.00
Pillar Optic, Pitcher, Pink, 60 Oz., 8 In. 45.00
Pillar Optic, Plate, Luncheon, Green, 8 In. 15.00
Pillar Optic, Plate, Sherbet, Green, 6 ½ In. 15.00
Pillar Optic, Pretzel Jar, Cover, Pink, 10 ½ x 6 ½ In. 150.00
Pillar Optic, Refrigerator Dish, Green, Oval, 6 In. 45.00
Pillar Optic, Refrigerator Dish, Green, Oval, 8 In. 85.00
Pillar Optic, Refrigerator Set, Stacking, Green, 3 Piece 140.00
Pillar Optic, Sherbet, Green 9.00
Pillar Optic, Tumbler, Green, 9 Oz., 4 In. 20.00
Pillar Optic, Tumbler, Pink, 9 Oz., 4 In. 20.00
Pineapple & Floral pattern is listed here as No. 618.
Pinwheel pattern is listed here as Sierra.
Poinsettia pattern is listed here as Floral.
Poppy No. 1 pattern is listed here as Florentine No. 1.
Poppy No. 2 pattern is listed here as Florentine No. 2.
Pretty Polly Party Dishes, see the related pattern Doric & Pansy.
Pretzel, Bowl, 7 ⅜ In. 10.00
Pretzel, Celery Dish, 10 ¼ In. 5.00
Pretzel, Creamer 7.00
Pretzel, Cup 7.00
Primo, Cup, Green 12.00
Primo, Plate, Salad, Green, 7 ½ In. 15.00
Primrose, Platter, Oval, 9 x 12 In. 15.00
Primrose, Sugar . . . . . *illus* 5.00
Princess, Bowl, Hat Shape, Green, 9 ½ In. 50.00
Princess, Bowl, Salad, Octagonal, Pink, 9 In. 55.00
Princess, Bowl, Vegetable, Pink, Oval, 9 In. 45.00
Princess, Butter, Cover, Green 75.00
Princess, Butter, No Cover, Pink 35.00
Princess, Candy Dish, Cover, Green 55.00
Princess, Cookie Jar, Green, 7 ½ In. 20.00
Princess, Cup, Pink. . . . . . 12.00 to 15.00
Princess, Cup & Saucer, Green . . . . . *illus* 26.00
Princess, Pitcher, Juice, Green, 37 Oz., 6 In. 70.00
Princess, Plate, Dinner, Topaz, 9 In. 25.00
Princess, Plate, Salad, Topaz, 8 ¼ In. 18.00
Princess, Relish, Pink, 4 Sections, 7 ½ In. 31.00
Princess, Sherbet, Pink 24.00
Princess, Tumbler, Footed, Pink, 12 ½ Oz., 6 ½ In. 114.00
Princess, Tumbler, Iced Tea, Topaz, 13 Oz., 5 ¼ In. 31.00
Princess, Vase, Green, 8 In. 45.00
Princess, Vase, Pink, 8 In. 55.00
Prismatic Line pattern is listed here as Queen Mary.
Provincial pattern is listed here as Bubble.
Queen Mary, Ashtray, 3 ½ In. 2.00
Queen Mary, Ashtray, Forest Green, 3 ½ In. 6.00
Queen Mary, Ashtray, Royal Ruby, 3 ½ In. 10.00
Queen Mary, Berry Bowl, Pink, 8 ½ In. 48.00
Queen Mary, Bowl, Cereal, Pink, 6 In. . . . . . 20.00 to 25.00
Queen Mary, Candlestick, 2-Light, 4 ⅜ In., Pair . . . . . *illus* 25.00
Queen Mary, Candy Dish, Cover, 7 In. 25.00
Queen Mary, Coaster, 3 ½ In. 3.00
Queen Mary, Compote, 5 ½ In. 15.00
Queen Mary, Creamer, Oval 6.00
Queen Mary, Creamer, Pink, Oval, 3 ⅛ In. . . . . . 12.00 to 15.00
Queen Mary, Cup, Pink. 10.00
Queen Mary, Plate, Dinner, Pink, 9 ¾ In. 65.00
Queen Mary, Plate, Pink, 6 ⅝ In. . . . . . 6.00 to 10.00
Queen Mary, Sandwich Server, 12 In. 14.00
Queen Mary, Saucer 3.00
Queen Mary, Soup, Dish, Pink, 7 ¼ In. 38.00
Queen Mary, Sugar, Oval 6.00

Quilted Diamond, Pitcher, Pink, Ice Lip, 48 Oz., 8 In. 40.00
Quilted Diamond, Pitcher, Ritz Blue, Ice Lip, 48 Oz., 8 In. 60.00
Quilted Diamond, Tumbler, Green, 9 Oz., 4 In. 12.00
Quilted Diamond, Tumbler, Iced Tea, Green, 11 Oz., 5 ⅛ In. 14.00
Quilted Diamond, Tumbler, Iced Tea, Ritz Blue, 11 Oz., 5 ⅛ In. 20.00
Quilted Diamond, Tumbler, Juice, Green, 5 Oz., 3 In. 9.00
Quilted Diamond, Tumbler, Juice, Ritz Blue, 5 Oz., 3 In. 10.00
Quilted Diamond, Tumbler, Ritz Blue, 9 Oz., 4 In. 15.00
Quilted Diamond, Tumbler, Whiskey, Green 18.00
Radiance pattern is listed in the New Martinsville category.
Rainbow, Tumbler, Fired-On Green, 10 Oz., 4 ½ In. 12.00
Rainbow, Tumbler, Fired-On Tangerine, 10 Oz., 4 ½ In. 10.00
Rhumba, Pitcher, Ritz Blue, Ice Lip, 86 Oz. 67.00
Rhumba, Tumbler, Ritz Blue, 10 ½ Oz., 4 ¾ In. 15.00
Ribbon, Creamer, Green 15.00
Ribbon, Salt & Pepper, Green 28.00
Ribbon, Sherbet, Green 14.00
Ribbon, Sugar, Green 15.00
Ring, Berry Bowl, Green, Tab Handles, 5 In. 8.00
Ring, Bowl, Black, 3-Footed, 6 In. 15.00
Ring, Cocktail Shaker, 52 Oz., 10 ½ In. 24.00
Ring, Ice Tub, Tab Handles 18.00
Ring, Pitcher, Water, Green, 80 Oz., 8 ½ In. .... 38.00 to 45.00
Ring, Plate, Green, Off-Center Cup Ring, 6 ½ In. 5.00
Ring, Plate, Luncheon, Multicolored Rings, 8 ¼ In. 7.50
Ring, Plate, Sherbet, Multicolored Rings, 6 ⅜ In. 3.00
Ring, Shaker, Platinum Band, Multicolored Rings, 4 ½ In. 12.00
Ring, Tumbler, Multicolored Rings, 9 Oz., 4 ⅛ In. 7.50
Ring, Tumbler, Multicolored Rings, Footed, 10 Oz., 5 ½ In. 7.50
Ring, Tumbler, Pink, 12 Oz., 5 In. 20.00
Ring, Tumbler, Whiskey, Multicolored Rings, 1 ½ Oz., 2 In. 9.50
Rock Crystal, Bowl, Centerpiece, Green, Plain Edge, Footed, 11 ⅜ In. 90.00
Rock Crystal, Bowl, Roll Tray, Red, 13 In. 95.00
Rock Crystal, Candelabrum, 2-Light 12.00
Rock Crystal, Cheese & Cracker Set, Amber, 2 Piece 45.00
Rock Crystal, Compote, Amber, Plain Edge, 4 x 3 In. 20.00
Rock Crystal, Compote, Green, Plain Edge, 4 ½ x 2 ¾ In. 25.00
Rock Crystal, Goblet, 8 Oz. .... 16.00 to 18.00
Rock Crystal, Parfait, Low Footed, Amber, 3 ½ Oz. 16.00
Rock Crystal, Pitcher, Amber, 8 ½ In. .... *illus* 395.00
Rock Crystal, Relish, Sections, 11 ½ In. 27.00
Rock Crystal, Sandwich Server, Green, Black Trim, Center Handle, 10 ¾ In. 35.00
Rock Crystal, Sundae, Low Footed, Pink, 6 Oz. 18.00
Rock Crystal, Tumbler, Whiskey, 2 ½ Oz., 2 ½ In. 25.00
Romanesque, Bowl, Footed, Black, 10 In. 65.00
Romanesque, Plate, Octagonal, Amber, 7 In. 10.00
Romanesque, Plate, Octagonal, Amber, 8 In. 10.00
Romanesque, Plate, Octagonal, Green, 8 In. 15.00
Romanesque, Vase, Fan, Green, 7 ½ In. 70.00
Rope pattern is listed here as Colonial Fluted.
Rose Cameo, Berry Bowl, Green, 4 ½ In. 14.00
Rose Cameo, Bowl, Cereal, Green, 5 In. 25.00
Rose Cameo, Plate, Salad, Green, 7 In. 15.00
Rose Cameo, Sherbet, Green 15.00
Rose Cameo, Tumbler, Cupped Rim, Footed, Green, 5 In. 25.00
Rosemary, Cup & Saucer, Amber 12.50
Rosemary, Plate, Dinner, Amber, 9 In. 10.00
Rosemary, Saucer, Amber 5.00
Roulette, Cup, Green 8.00
Roulette, Saucer, Green 5.00
Roxana, Sherbet, Yellow 10.00
Royal Lace, Bowl, 3-Footed, Ruffled Edge, 10 In. 80.00
Royal Lace, Bowl, 3-Footed, Straight Edge, Pink, 10 In. 65.00
Royal Lace, Bowl, Vegetable, Oval, Cobalt Blue, 11 In. 75.00
Royal Lace, Creamer, Pink 25.00
Royal Lace, Cup & Saucer, Cobalt Blue 50.00
Royal Lace, Grill Plate, Cobalt Blue, 9 ¾ In. .... 34.00 to 45.00

Ring
Hocking Glass Company made Ring from 1927 to 1933. The pattern, also known as Banded Rings, sometimes has colored rings added to the Crystal, Green, Mayfair Blue, Pink, or Red glass. The colored rings were made in various combinations of black, blue, orange, pink, platinum, red, and yellow. Platinum trim is on some pieces. Some solid red pieces also were made. The design is characterized by several sets of rings, each composed of four rings. Circle, a similar Hocking pattern, has only one group of rings.

Depression Glass, Queen Mary, Candlestick, 2-Light, 4 ⅜ In., Pair
$25.00

Depression Glass, Rock Crystal, Pitcher, Amber, 8 ½ In.
$395.00

Depression Glass, Royal Lace, Water Set, Cobalt Blue, 7 Piece
$295.00

Depression Glass, Sandwich Anchor Hocking, Tumbler, Juice, Forest Green, 3 ½ In.
$4.00

Depression Glass, Sharon, Cup & Saucer, Pink
$27.00

TIP

Lock your doors and windows. In 65 percent to 82 percent of all home burglaries, the burglar enters through a door. Most often the doors were unlocked.

Royal Lace, Plate, Bread & Butter, Cobalt Blue, 6 In. 16.50
Royal Lace, Plate, Dinner, 9 ⅞ In. 49.00
Royal Lace, Plate, Dinner, Cobalt Blue, 9 ⅞ In. 29.00 to 49.00
Royal Lace, Plate, Dinner, Green, 9 ⅞ In. 35.00
Royal Lace, Plate, Dinner, Pink, 9 ⅞ In. 24.00
Royal Lace, Plate, Luncheon, Cobalt Blue, 8 ½ In. 48.00
Royal Lace, Platter, Oval, Cobalt Blue, 13 In. 80.00
Royal Lace, Salt & Pepper, Cobalt Blue 300.00
Royal Lace, Salt & Pepper, Pink 60.00
Royal Lace, Soup, Cream, Cobalt Blue, 4 ¾ In. 48.00
Royal Lace, Soup, Cream, Green, 4 ¾ In. 32.00
Royal Lace, Sugar, Green 22.00
Royal Lace, Sugar, Pink 25.00
Royal Lace, Tumbler, Cobalt Blue, 9 Oz., 4 ⅛ In. 38.00 to 45.00
Royal Lace, Tumbler, Cobalt Blue, 12 Oz., 5 ⅜ In. 115.00
Royal Lace, Tumbler, Juice, Cobalt Blue, 5 Oz., 3 ½ In. 55.00
Royal Lace, Water Set, Cobalt Blue, 7 Piece *illus* 295.00
Royal Ruby, Bowl, Popcorn, 5 ¼ In. 20.00
Royal Ruby, Candleholder, Cape Cod 14.00
Royal Ruby, Cup 2.00
Royal Ruby, Goblet, Ball Stem, 9 Oz., 5 ¼ In. 11.00 to 15.00
Royal Ruby, Goblet, Water, 5 ¼ x 3 ¼ In. 10.00
Royal Ruby, Pitcher, Hobnail 45.00
Royal Ruby, Salt & Pepper, Cape Cod 12.00
Royal Ruby, Tumbler, Banded, 10 Oz., 5 ⅛ In. 50.00
Royal Ruby, Tumbler, Juice, Banded, 5 Oz., 3 ¾ In. 40.00
Royal Ruby, Tumbler, Juice, Roly Poly, 5 Oz., 3 ⅜ In. 4.00 to 7.50
Royal Ruby, Tumbler, Wine, Footed, 3 Oz., 2 ½ In. 12.00
Royal Ruby, Vase, Coolidge, 6 ⅜ In. 10.00
Royal Ruby, Vase, Crimped Top, 3 ¾ In. 5.00
Royal Ruby, Vase, Hoover, Bird Nest, 9 In. 35.00
Royal Ruby, Vase, Pineapple, 9 x 6 In. 25.00
Royal Ruby, Vase, Ruffled Pansy, 4 In. 8.00
Royal Ruby, Vase, Whirly Twirly, 3 ½ In. 30.00
Royal Ruby, Water Bottle, Qt. 36.00
S Pattern, Grill Plate, Platinum Trim, 10 ⅜ In. 9.00
Sailboat pattern is listed here as Sportsman Series.
Sandwich Anchor Hocking, Bowl, Forest Green, 4 ¼ x 1 ⅝ In. 6.00
Sandwich Anchor Hocking, Bowl, Forest Green, 6 ½ x 2 ⅝ In. 55.00
Sandwich Anchor Hocking, Bowl, Forest Green, 7 ½ x 3 ⅛ In. 80.00 to 100.00
Sandwich Anchor Hocking, Bowl, Scalloped Edge, 6 ½ In. 10.00
Sandwich Anchor Hocking, Butter, Cover Only, 4 ¾ In. 18.00
Sandwich Anchor Hocking, Creamer, Forest Green 35.00
Sandwich Anchor Hocking, Cup & Saucer 4.00
Sandwich Anchor Hocking, Cup & Saucer, Forest Green 40.00
Sandwich Anchor Hocking, Custard Cup Liner, Crystal, 4 ⅜ In. 23.00
Sandwich Anchor Hocking, Plate, 8 In. 7.00
Sandwich Anchor Hocking, Plate, Dinner, 9 In. 15.00
Sandwich Anchor Hocking, Plate, Dinner, Forest Green, 9 In. 120.00 to 140.00
Sandwich Anchor Hocking, Punch Set, Box, 7 Piece 55.00
Sandwich Anchor Hocking, Saucer 3.50
Sandwich Anchor Hocking, Saucer, Forest Green 15.00
Sandwich Anchor Hocking, Sugar 8.50
Sandwich Anchor Hocking, Sugar, Forest Green 35.00
Sandwich Anchor Hocking, Tumbler, Juice, 4 x 3 In. 8.00
Sandwich Anchor Hocking, Tumbler, Juice, Forest Green, 3 ½ In. *illus* 4.00
Sandwich Indiana, Goblet, Teal Blue, 5 ¼ In. 9.00
Sandwich Indiana, Snack Set, 8-In. Plate, 2 Piece 8.00
Saxon pattern is listed here as Coronation.
Scottie, Powder Jar, Marigold Iridescent 44.00
Shamrock, Bowl, Ruby Flashed Rim, 1 ¾ x 5 In. 23.00
Sharon, Butter, Cover, Amber 45.00
Sharon, Butter, Cover, Green 90.00
Sharon, Butter, Cover, Pink 25.00 to 40.00
Sharon, Creamer, Pink 15.00
Sharon, Cup, Green 18.00
Sharon, Cup & Saucer, Pink *illus* 27.00

Sharon, Plate, Bread & Butter, Green, 6 In. 10.00
Sharon, Plate, Bread & Butter, Pink, 6 In. . . . . 8.00 to 10.00
Sharon, Plate, Dinner, Pink 22.00
Sharon, Platter, Pink, Oval, 12 ½ In. 32.00
Sharon, Saucer, Amber 5.00
Sharon, Saucer, Pink 7.00
Sharon, Sherbet, Green 27.00
Sharon, Sherbet, Pink 12.00
Sharon, Soup, Cream, Pink, 5 In. 44.00
Sharon, Soup, Dish, Pink, 7 ¾ In. . . . . 45.00 to 50.00
Sharon, Sugar, Cover, Pink 45.00
Sharon, Sugar, Pink 15.00
Sharon, Tumbler, Footed, Pink, 15 Oz., 6 ½ In. . . . . 35.00 to 55.00
Sharon, Tumbler, Thin, Amber, 9 Oz., 4 ⅛ In. 24.00
Sharon, Tumbler, Thin, Pink, 12 Oz., 5 ¼ In. 40.00
Shell, Bowl, Cereal, Jade-Ite, 6 ⅜ In. 28.00
Shell, Bowl, Vegetable, Peach Lustre, 8 ½ In. 30.00
Shell, Cup & Saucer 7.00
Shell, Cup & Saucer, After Dinner, Peach Lustre, 3 ¼ x 4 ¾ In. 12.00
Shell, Cup & Saucer, Jade-Ite 20.00
Shell Pink, Bowl, Florentine, Footed, 10 In. 22.00
Shell Pink, Bowl, 3 Pheasants, Footed, 8 x 2 ¾ In. 55.00
Shell Pink, Candleholder, Eagle, 3-Footed 45.00
Shell Pink, Candy Jar, Cover, Square, 6 ½ In. . . . . *illus* 28.00
Shell Pink, Compote, Windsor, 6 In. 20.00
Shell Pink, Powder Jar, Cover, 4 ¾ In. 40.00
Shell Pink, Punch Cup, Feather 5.00
Shell Pink, Sugar & Creamer, Cover 40.00
Shell Pink, Tray, Venetian, 6 Sections, 16 ½ In. 35.00
Shell Pink, Vase, 7 x 5 ½ In. 35.00
Shell Pink, Vase, Crosshatch, Napco, 7 In. 35.00
Shell Pink, Wedding Bowl, Cover, 8 In. 24.00
Sierra, Butter, Cover Only, Green 50.00
Sierra, Butter, Cover Only, Pink 50.00
Sierra, Plate, Dinner, Green, 9 In. 25.00
Sierra, Plate, Dinner, Pink, 9 In. 22.00
Sierra, Salt & Pepper, Green 45.00
Sierra, Saucer, Pink 10.00
Soreno, Soup, Dish, Avocado Green, 1 ¾ x 6 In. 5.00
Soreno, Tumbler, Aquamarine, 6 Oz., 3 In. 5.00
Spiral, Candy Dish, Cover, Green 35.00
Spiral, Cup & Saucer, Green 8.00
Spoke pattern is listed here as Patrician.
Sportsman Series, Cocktail Mixer, Cobalt Blue, Windmill . . . . *illus* 25.00
Sportsman Series, Cocktail Set, Shaker, Tumblers, Cobalt Blue, Windmill, 5 Piece 85.00
Sportsman Series, Cocktail Shaker, Angel Fish 52.00
Sportsman Series, Cocktail Shaker, Cobalt Blue, Fox Hunt, 8 ¼ In. 75.00
Sportsman Series, Ice Tub, Cobalt Blue, Ships 100.00
Sportsman Series, Pitcher, Cobalt Blue, Ships, Ice Lip, 86 Oz. 80.00
Sportsman Series, Pitcher, Cobalt Blue, Spanish Dancers, 82 Oz. 85.00
Sportsman Series, Pitcher, Ice Lip, Angel Fish, 86 Oz. 67.00
Sportsman Series, Tumbler, Blue, Angel Fish, 9 Oz., 4 ½ In. 14.00
Sportsman Series, Tumbler, Cobalt Blue, Ships, 9 Oz., 4 ⅝ In. . . . . 15.00 to 25.00
Sportsman Series, Tumbler, Hunting Dogs, 4 ½ In. 27.00
Sportsman Series, Tumbler, Iced Tea, Cobalt Blue, Sailboats, 10 Oz., 4 ⅞ In. 15.00
Sportsman Series, Tumbler, Red Ship, 9 Oz., 4 ⅞ In. 15.00
Sportsman Series, Tumbler, Roly Poly, Cobalt Blue, Windmill, 6 Oz. 10.00
Sportsman Series, Tumbler, Sailboat, Red, Wire Rack, 5 In., 9 Piece 95.00
Star, Candleholder, Tea Light, Hazel Ware, 4 ½ x 1 ⅜ In. 5.00
Stars & Stripes, Plate, Salad, 8 In. 25.00
Stippled Rose Band pattern is listed here as S Pattern.
Sunburst, Plate, Dessert, 5 ½ In. 10.00
Sunflower, Ashtray, Green, 5 In. 12.00
Sunflower, Cake Plate, Footed, Pink, 10 In. 22.00
Sunflower, Cup, Pink 15.00
Sunflower, Plate, Dinner, Pink, 9 In. 24.00
Swan, Bowl, Centerpiece, Viking, 8 x 9 ⅜ In. 45.00

Depression Glass, Shell Pink, Candy Jar, Cover, Square, 6 ½ In. $28.00

Depression Glass, Sportsman Series, Cocktail Mixer, Cobalt Blue, Windmill $25.00

Sportsman Series
Hazel Atlas Glass Company made this unusual pattern in the 1940s. It was made in Amethyst, Cobalt Blue, or Crystal with fired-on decoration. Although the name of the series was Sportsman, designs included not only golf, sailboats, hunting, and angelfish, but a few odd choices like windmills. White Ship and Windmill are sometimes considered part of this pattern.

TIP
When moving, stuff glasses and cups with crumpled paper, then wrap in bubble wrap.

D

Depression Glass, Swirl Fire-King, Mixing Bowl Set, Jade-Ite, 6, 7, 8 & 9 In., 4 Piece
$180.00

Depression Glass, Tea Room, Sugar, Pink.
$35.00

Vitrock
Vitrock is both a kitchenware and a dinnerware pattern. It has a raised flowered rim and is often called Floral Rim or Flower Rim by collectors. It was made by Hocking Glass Company from 1934 to 1937 and resembles embossed china. It was made in White, sometimes with fired-on colors, in solid Red or Green, and with decal-decorated centers.

Swan, Powder Jar, Marigold Iridescent 35.00
Swirl Fire-King, Bowl, Cereal, Sunrise, 5 ⅞ In. 20.00
Swirl Fire-King, Bowl, Fruit, Azurite, 4 ⅞ In. 9.00
Swirl Fire-King, Bowl, Vegetable, Milk White, 8 ¼ In. 14.00
Swirl Fire-King, Bowl, Vegetable, Sunrise, 8 ¼ In. 22.00
Swirl Fire-King, Creamer, Azurite 20.00
Swirl Fire-King, Cup, Azurite 6.00
Swirl Fire-King, Cup, Pink 12.00
Swirl Fire-King, Cup & Saucer, Azurite 26.00
Swirl Fire-King, Mixing Bowl, Ivory, 9 In. 20.00
Swirl Fire-King, Mixing Bowl, Milk White, 9 In. 20.00
Swirl Fire-King, Mixing Bowl Set, Jade-Ite, 6, 7, 8 & 9 In., 4 Piece .... *illus* 180.00
Swirl Fire-King, Plate, Dinner, Azurite, 9 ⅛ In. 14.00
Swirl Fire-King, Plate, Dinner, Golden Anniversary, 9 ⅛ In. 4.00
Swirl Fire-King, Platter, Ivory, 12 In. 22.00
Swirl Fire-King, Saucer, Azurite, 5 ¾ In. 3.00
Swirl Fire-King, Saucer, Ivory 3.50
Swirl Fire-King, Saucer, Sunrise 4.00
Swirl Fire-King, Saucer, Sunrise, Ivory 6.00
Swirl Fire-King, Sugar, Cover, Azurite 30.00
Swirl Fire-King, Sugar, Pink 12.00
Swirl Jeannette, Berry Bowl, Pink, 5 ¼ In. 9.00
Swirl Jeannette, Bowl, Salad, Pink, Rimmed, 9 In. 32.00
Swirl Jeannette, Bowl, Salad, Ultramarine, 9 In. 28.00
Swirl Jeannette, Candy Dish, Cover, Pink 95.00
Swirl Jeannette, Candy Dish, Ultramarine, 3-Footed, 6 x 2 ¾ In. 20.00
Swirl Jeannette, Coaster, Pink, 3 ¼ In. 16.00
Swirl Jeannette, Creamer, Ultramarine 12.00
Swirl Jeannette, Cup & Saucer, Ultramarine 19.00
Swirl Jeannette, Plate, Dinner, Pink, 9 ¼ In. 16.00
Swirl Jeannette, Plate, Dinner, Ultramarine, 9 ¼ In. 24.00
Swirl Jeannette, Plate, Sherbet, Pink, 6 ½ In. 7.00
Swirl Jeannette, Plate, Sherbet, Ultramarine, 6 ½ In. 8.00
Swirl Jeannette, Sandwich Server, Ultramarine, 12 ½ In. 30.00
Swirl Jeannette, Sherbet, Pink 12.00
Swirl Jeannette, Sherbet, Ultramarine 18.00
Swirl Jeannette, Sugar, Cover, Pink 9.00
Swirl Jeannette, Sugar, Ultramarine 15.00
Swirl Jeannette, Tumbler, Ultramarine, 9 Oz. 14.00
Swirl Jeannette, Vase, Footed, Ultramarine, 8 ½ In. 26.00
Sylvan, Berry Bowl, Green, 5 In. 35.00
Sylvan, Butter, Green 450.00
Sylvan, Tumbler, Green, 10 Oz. 245.00
Sylvan, Tumbler, Green, Footed, 5 ¾ In. 200.00
Tea Room, Bowl, Green, Handles, 8 ½ In. 95.00
Tea Room, Plate, Pink, Handles, 10 ½ In. 60.00
Tea Room, Sugar, Pink .... *illus* 35.00
Tea Room, Tumbler, Footed, Green, 8 Oz., 5 ¼ In. 35.00
Tendril, Creamer, Green 8.00
Tendril, Plate, Luncheon, Green, 8 ⅜ In. 10.00
Tendril, Sandwich Server, Green, Handles, 9 ¾ In. 15.00
Tendril, Sugar, Green 8.00
Threading pattern is listed here as Old English.
Tulip, Ice Tub, Green, 4 ⅞ x 3 In. 50.00
Tulip, Plate, Bread & Butter, Amethyst, 6 In. 10.00
Vernon pattern is listed here as No. 616.
Vertical Ribbed pattern is listed here as Queen Mary.
Victory, Bowl, Cereal, Pink, 6 ½ In. 12.00
Vitrock, Bonbon, Dusty Rose, 6 ½ In. 8.00
Vitrock, Grease Jar, Black Circle 20.00
Vitrock, Range Set, Red Circle, 5 Piece 195.00
Vitrock, Range Set, Red Flowerpot, 5 Piece 180.00
Vitrock, Saltshaker, Ribbed 18.00
Vitrock, Shaker, Pepper, Ribbed 18.00
Vitrock, Tray, Flower Garden, 10 ½ x 7 ¾ In. 16.00
Vitrock, Vase, 5 In. 16.00

Vitrock, Vase, Blue Bird & Leaf, 9 In. 32.50
Vitrock, Vase, Hoover, Springtime, 9 In. 32.00
Waffle pattern is listed here as Waterford.
Waterford, Coaster 4.00
Waterford, Creamer, Oval 5.00
Waterford, Plate, Dinner, Pink, 9 ⅝ In. 35.00
Waterford, Plate, Salad, Pink, 7 ⅛ In. 15.00
Waterford, Sandwich Server, Forest Green, 13 ¾ In. 45.00
Waterford, Sandwich Server, Pink, 13 ¾ In. 40.00
Wexford, Bowl, Centerpiece, Footed, 8 In. 15.00
Wexford, Bowl, Fruit, 5 ⅜ In. 3.50
Wexford, Cup, Footed 3.00
Wexford, Cup & Saucer 8.00
Wexford, Goblet 5.00
Wexford, Mug .... 10.00 to 12.50
Wexford, Pitcher, 64 Oz., 9 ¾ In. 17.00
Wexford, Plate, 6-Sided, 6 ¾ In. 7.00
Wexford, Plate, 6-Sided, 7 ¾ In. 9.00
Wexford, Saucer, 6 In. 4.00
Wexford, Sherbet 5.00
Wexford, Storage Jar, 34 Oz. 7.50
Wexford, Tumbler, Iced Tea, 12 Oz. 7.00
Wheat, Custard Cup, 6 Oz. 4.00
Wheat, Saucer, 5 ¾ In. 1.00
White Ship pattern is listed here as Sportsman Series.
Wig-Wam, Console Set, Ritz Blue, 3 Piece 225.00
Wild Rose pattern is listed here as Dogwood.
Windmill pattern is listed here as Sportsman Series.
Windsor, Ashtray, Match Holder, Pink, 5 ¾ In. 55.00
Windsor, Berry Bowl, Pink, 4 ¾ In. 11.00
Windsor, Berry Bowl, Pink, 8 ½ In. .... 25.00 to 30.00
Windsor, Bowl, Boat Shape, Green, 11 ¾ In. 45.00
Windsor, Bowl, Boat Shape, Pink, 11 ¾ In. 45.00
Windsor, Bowl, Cereal, Green, 20 Oz., 5 ½ In. 35.00
Windsor, Bowl, Cereal, Pink, 20 Oz., 5 ½ In. 35.00
Windsor, Bowl, Pink, Handles, 8 In. 25.00
Windsor, Butter, Cover, Pink 65.00
Windsor, Cake Plate, Pink, Footed, 10 ¾ In. 25.00
Windsor, Creamer, Pink 12.00
Windsor, Cup & Saucer 6.00
Windsor, Cup & Saucer, Pink 16.00
Windsor, Pitcher, 16 Oz., 4 ½ In. 18.00
Windsor, Pitcher, 52 Oz., 6 ¾ In. 13.00
Windsor, Pitcher, Pink, 52 Oz., 6 ¾ In. .... *illus* 35.00
Windsor, Plate, Dinner, 9 In. 8.00
Windsor, Plate, Dinner, Pink, 9 In. 25.00
Windsor, Plate, Sherbet, Green, 6 In. 8.00
Windsor, Plate, Sherbet, Pink, 6 In. 7.00
Windsor, Platter, Oval, 11 ½ In. 8.00
Windsor, Platter, Oval, Pink, 11 ½ In. 25.00
Windsor, Powder Jar, Cover 15.00
Windsor, Salt & Pepper, Green 60.00
Windsor, Saltshaker 10.00
Windsor, Saucer, Green 5.00
Windsor, Sherbet, Pink 8.00
Windsor, Sugar, Cover, Pink .... 29.00 to 32.00
Windsor, Tumbler, Footed, 7 Oz., 4 ¾ In. 20.00
Windsor, Tumbler, Footed, 11 Oz., 5 In. 10.00
Windsor, Tumbler, Green, 9 Oz., 4 In. 30.00
Windsor Diamond pattern is listed here as Windsor.

DERBY has been marked on porcelain made in the city of Derby, England, since about 1748. The original Derby factory closed in 1848, but others opened there and continued to produce quality porcelain. The Crown Derby mark began appearing on Derby wares in the 1770s.

Cup & Saucer, Multicolored Flowers, Gilt, Green Medallion Mark, c.1820, 5 ¾ In. 55.00
Figurine, Man, Holding Document, Dog, 7 ⅝ In. .... *illus* 385.00

Wexford
Wexord is an imitation cut glass pattern made by Anchor Hocking Glass Corporation, Lancaster, Ohio, from 1967 to 1998. Pieces were made in Crystal, Green, Pewter Mist, and with fired-on decorations. Other related patterns are listed in the Fire-King category in this book.

Depression Glass, Windsor, Pitcher, Pink, 52 Oz., 6 ¾ In.
$35.00

Derby, Figurine, Man, Holding Document, Dog, 7 ⅝ In.
$385.00

D

Dick Tracy, Bank, Sparkle Plenty, Baby On Scale, Painted, Plaster, 12 ½ x 9 x 5 ½ In.
$250.00

Dick Tracy, Wristwatch, Silver Luster, Leather Band, 1948, 1 ¼ x 1 In.
$173.00

Dinnerware, Aristocrat, Creamer, Red Trim, Salem China, 1 ⅞ In.
$28.00

Plate, Imari Pattern, c.1840, 9 In. 23.00
Platter, Orange, Blue, Gilt Accents, Mid 19th Century, 13 ½ In. 415.00

DICK TRACY, the comic strip, started in 1931. Tracy was also the hero of movies from 1937 to 1947 and again in 1990, and starred in a radio series in the 1940s and a television series in the 1950s. Memorabilia from all these activities are collected.

Bank, Sparkle Plenty, Baby On Scale, Painted, Plaster, 12 ½ x 9 x 5 ½ In. . . . . . *illus* 250.00
Book, Big Little Book, Dick Tracy Encounters Facey, Hardback, Whitman, 1967 . . . . . . 15.00
Book, Pop-Up, Capture Of Boris Arson, Chester Gould, Pleasure Books, c.1935, 8 x 9 ¼ In. . . . 209.00
Crime Stoppers Lab, Microscope, Fingerprint Book, Accessories, Box, 1950s, 13 In. 345.00 to 900.00
Doll, Little Honeymoon, She Cries, Moon Hair, Ideal, 1965, 19 ½ In. 310.00
Doll, Prune Face, Movie Character, Maroon Suit, Stand, Disney Applause, 9 ½ In. 15.00
Game, Dick Tracy Playing Card Game, Dick Tracy, Thug & Jewel Cards, 1934. . . . . . 35.00
Game, Master Detective, Selchow & Righter Co., Board, 1961, 9 ½ x 19 In. 158.00
Jigsaw Puzzle, Box, Jaymar, c.1946, 14 x 22 In. 73.00
Mug, Dick Tracy, Breathless Mahoney, Big Boy Caprice, Squad Car, Applause, 5 In. 86.00
Pin, Secret Service Patrol, Lithograph, Quaker Cereals, c.1938, 1 ⅜ In. . . . . . 48.00 to 75.00
Toy, B.O. Plenty, Waddles, Baby Sparkles, Tin, Windup, Marx, 9 In. . . . . . 175.00 to 226.00
Toy, B.O. Plenty, Waddles, Baby Sparkles, Tin, Windup, Marx, Box, c.1940, 9 In. . . 220.00 to 495.00
Toy, B.O. Plenty, Walker, Hat Goes Up & Down, Windup, Marx, 1930s 175.00
Toy, Police Station, Riot Car, Tin Lithograph, Pressed Steel Friction, 9 x 6 & 7 ¼ In. 175.00
Toy, Squad Car, Advances With Spark, Tin, Marxc.1949, 7 ¾ In. 124.00
Toy, Squad Car, Blue, Rear License No. 305, Friction, Marx, 1950s, 6 ½ In. 313.00
Toy, Squad Car, Friction, Battery Operated Light, Marx, 1940, 20 In. 725.00
Toy, Squad Car, Green, Tin Lithograph, Windup, Light, Marx, 11 In. . . . . . 143.00 to 322.00
Wristwatch, Dick Tracy On Dial, Red & Gold Hands, Red Leather Band, Marked, Disney, 1980s 129.00
Wristwatch, Silver Luster, Leather Band, 1948, 1 ¼ x 1 In. . . . . . *illus* 173.00

DICKENS WARE *pieces are listed in the Royal Doulton and Weller categories.*

DINNERWARE used in the United States from the 1930s through the 1950s is listed here. Most was made in potteries in southern Ohio, West Virginia, and California. A few patterns were made in Japan, England, and other countries. Dishes were sold in gift shops and department stores, or were given away as premiums. Many of these patterns are listed in this book in their own categories, such as Autumn Leaf, Azalea, Coors, Fiesta, Franciscan, Hall, Harker, Harlequin, Red Wing, Riviera, Russel Wright, Vernon Kilns, Watt, and Willow. For more prices, go to Kovels.com. Sets missing a few pieces can be completed through the help of one of the many matching services listed on our website, Kovels.com.

Amberstone, Bowl, Fruit, Homer Laughlin, 5 ½ In. 3.00
Amberstone, Cup & Saucer, Homer Laughlin 7.50
Amberstone, Plate, Bread & Butter, Homer Laughlin, 6 In. 2.00
Amberstone, Plate, Dinner, Homer Laughlin, 10 In. 6.00
Amberstone, Soup, Dish 7.50
American Beauty, Saucer, Demitasse, Paden City. 4.00
American Rose, Bowl, Fruit, Paden City, 5 In. 6.50
American Rose, Creamer, Paden City, 5 ½ In. 10.50
American Rose, Plate, Dinner, Paden City, 9 ¾ In. 9.95
American Rose, Plate, Luncheon, Paden City, 8 In. 10.00
American Rose, Platter, Square, Paden City, 10 ⅛ In. 14.00
American Rose, Soup, Dish, Square, Paden City, 8 In. 10.00
Apple Blossom, Bowl, Cereal, Steubenville, 7 ¼ In. 8.00
Apple Blossom, Cup & Saucer, Knowles 9.00
Apple Blossom, Pie Baker, Crooksville, 10 In. 35.00
Apple Blossom, Plate, Bread & Butter, Steubenville, 6 ¼ In. 6.00
Apple Blossom, Plate, Dinner, Knowles, 10 ¼ In. 7.50
Apple Blossom, Plate, Dinner, Steubenville, 10 ⅜ In. 12.00
Apple Blossom, Plate, Salad, Crooksville, 8 In. 7.50
Apple Blossom, Platter, Steubenville, 13 ½ In. 25.00
Apple Harvest, Plate, Johnson Brothers, 5 ½ In. 6.00
Aristocrat, Creamer, Red Trim, Salem China, 1 ⅞ In. . . . . . *illus* 28.00
Aristocrat, Cup & Saucer, Demitasse, Salem China. 10.00
Athena, Creamer, Johnson Brothers 9.00
Athena, Cup & Saucer, Johnson Brothers 4.00
Athena, Plate, Bread & Butter, Johnson Brothers, 6 ¼ In. 4.00
Autumn Apple, Plate, Dinner, Blue Ridge, 10 In. 26.00

Autumn Gold, Cup & Saucer, Homer Laughlin 9.99
Autumn Gold, Plate, Salad, Homer Laughlin, 7 ¼ In. 8.99
Autumn Leaves, Plate, Salad, Salem China, 7 ¼ In. 5.00
Autumn Mist, Bowl, Cereal, Royal China, 6 ⅜ In. 4.20
Autumn Mist, Plate, Dinner, Royal China 9.00
Autumn Mist, Saucer, Royal China, 6 ⅜ In. 4.50
Azalea, Cake Plate, Crooksville, 12 In. 35.00
Azalea, Plate, Dinner, Crooksville, 10 In. 12.00
Ballerina, Plate, Dinner, Iris, Universal Potteries, 10 In. 15.00
Ballerina Mist, Pitcher, Pastel Green, Platinum Trim, Universal Potteries, 1950s, 40 Oz. 28.00
Basketweave, Bowl, Cereal, Royal China, 6 ⅜ In. 7.50
Beige Rose, Bowl, Cereal, Ben Seibel, Iroquois, 6 In. 5.99
Beige Rose, Creamer, Ben Seibel, Iroquois, 5 ¾ In. 18.00
Beige Rose, Plate, Bread & Butter, Ben Seibel, Iroquois, 6 ¼ In. 3.99
Beige Rose, Plate, Dinner, Ben Seibel, Iroquois, 10 ½ In. 8.99
Beige Rose, Platter, Ben Seibel, Iroquois, 16 ¼ x 11 ½ In. 39.95
Bells Of Ireland, Bowl, Vegetable, Harmony House, 9 ½ In. 15.00
Bells Of Ireland, Plate, Dinner, Harmony House, 10 ½ In. 10.00
Biscayne, Creamer, Salem China, 3 x 4 In. 9.00
Biscayne, Cup & Saucer, Paden City 10.00
Biscayne, Plate, Bread & Butter, Paden City, 6 ⅛ In. 2.00
Biscayne, Plate, Bread & Butter, Salem China, 6 ⅛ In. 2.00
Biscayne, Plate, Luncheon, Salem China, 9 ⅛ In. 6.00
Blossom Time, Plate, Salad, Knowles, 9 ¼ In. 4.00
Blue Bonnet, Platter, Blue & White Flowers, Harmony House, 12 In. 15.99
Blue Bonnet, Saucer, Harmony House, 6 In. 4.25
Blue Heaven, Gravy Boat, Underplate, Royal China 25.00
Blue Heaven, Plate, Bread & Butter, Royal China, 6 ⅜ In. 5.00
Blue Heaven, Plate, Dinner, Royal China, 10 In. 6.50
Blue Heaven, Platter, Turquoise, Gray, Royal China, 11 ½ x 10 ½ In. . . . . . *illus* 9.00
Blue Heaven, Salt & Pepper, Royal China 13.50
Blue Heaven, Sugar & Creamer, Royal China 17.50
Blue Iris, Plate, Bread & Butter, Homer Laughlin, 6 ¼ In. 3.00
Blue Lace, Creamer, Teal Inside, Taylor, Smith & Taylor, 4 x 6 In. 11.00
Bluebells, Berry Bowl, Knowles 5.00
Bluebells, Plate, Bread & Butter, Knowles, 6 ¼ In. 3.00
Bluebells, Plate, Dinner, Knowles, 10 ¼ In. 5.00
Bouquet, Bowl, Dessert, Johnson Brothers, 5 In. 4.99
Bouquet, Cup & Saucer, Johnson Brothers 6.00
Boutonniere, Berry Bowl, Ever Yours, Taylor, Smith & Taylor, 5 ½ In. 6.00
Bowl, Priscilla, Oval, Homer Laughlin, 9 ¼ In. 19.00
Briar Rose, Bowl, Fruit, Salem China, 6 In. 6.00
Briar Rose, Plate, Dinner, Salem China, 9 In. 10.00
Briar Rose, Platter, Salem China, 11 ½ In. 25.00
Briar Rose, Sugar, Open, Double Handles, Salem China 10.00
Bridal Bouquet, Cup & Saucer, Salem China 8.00
Brides Bouquet, Bowl, Cereal, 1935-1981, 8 In. 6.50
Brides Bouquet, Bowl, Dessert, Taylor, Smith & Taylor, 1935-1981, 5 ⅜ In. 6.00
Brides Bouquet, Creamer, Taylor, Smith & Taylor, 3 x 6 In. 6.50
Brides Bouquet, Saucer, Taylor, Smith & Taylor, 1935-1981, 6 In. 4.00
Bristol, Cup & Saucer, Homer Laughlin 14.99
Bristol, Plate, Bread & Butter, Homer Laughlin, 6 ¼ In. 5.99
Brittany, Sugar, Cover, Maroon, Flowers, Homer Laughlin 30.00
Brocatelle, Plate, Dinner, Taylor, Smith & Taylor, 10 In. . . . . . *illus* 9.00
Bucks County, Cup & Saucer, Royal China 10.00
Bucks County, Soup, Dish, Rim, Landscape, Royal China, 1950s, 8 ⅜ In. 10.00
Calico Fruit, Refrigerator Bowl, Lid, Universal Potteries, 4 ½ In. 5.00
Cambridge, Plate, Bread & Butter, Homer Laughlin, 6 ¼ In. 3.00
Cameo Rose, Chop Plate, Blue & White, Harmony House, 12 In. 15.00
Cameo Rose, Plate, Salad, Blue & White, Harmony House, 7 ½ In. 5.00
Cameo Rose, Spoon, Salad, Blue, Harker 16.00
Can Can, Bowl, Cereal, Royal China, 6 ⅜ In. 4.20
Can Can, Plate, Bread & Butter, Royal China, 6 ⅜ In. 5.60
Candleglow, Cup & Saucer, Harmony House 6.00
Candleglow, Plate, Harmony House, 7 ½ In. 6.00
Carlton, Plate, Bread & Butter, Knowles, 6 In. 3.00
Carnival, Bowl, Cereal, Harlequin Yellow, Homer Laughlin, 6 ⅛ In. 10.00

Recent Marks
Modern inventions have made new marks needed on dishes. "Cooking ware" was first used about 1923, "craze proof" about 1960, "dishwasher proof" after 1955, "freezer-oven-table" in the 1960s, "microwave safe" after 1970, "oven proof" in 1934, and "oven-to-table" in 1978.

D

Dinnerware, Blue Heaven, Platter, Turquoise, Gray, Royal China, 11 ½ x 10 ½ In.
$9.00

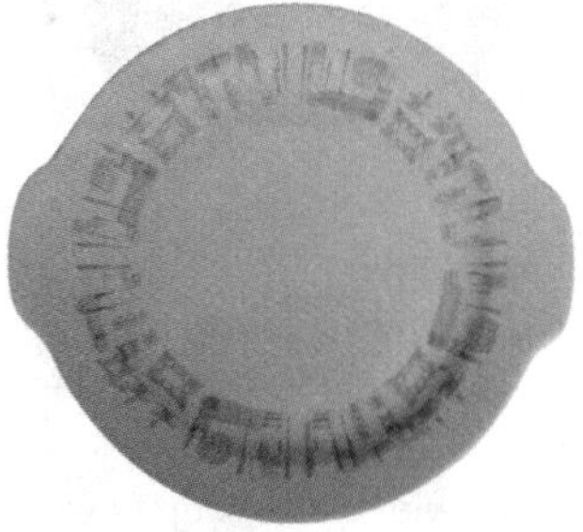

Dinnerware, Brocatelle, Plate, Dinner, Taylor, Smith & Taylor, 10 In.
$9.00

TIP
Dishes that can be used in a microwave or conventional oven can be used in a convection oven.

Dinnerware, Colonial Homestead, Bowl, Vegetable, Royal China, 9 In.
$15.00

Dinnerware, Currier & Ives, Casserole, Cover, Royal China, 3 x 7 ½ In.
$50.00

Soup Servers

Do you own a "cream soup"? From the 1920s to the 1950s, sets of dishes were often made with cream soup bowls and/or other soup bowls. A cream soup looks like a large cup, 5 to 6 inches in diameter, with two handles. It was used to serve cream soup, like clam chowder. Then it was served on a small plate so there was a place to put the spoon. Similar but smaller bowls were for bouillon. Noodle soup was served in a large bowl, usually with a rim, almost the size of a dinner plate. Porcelain and glass sets of dishes included these soup bowls. After the 1950s, some sets used large mugs for soup.

Carnival, Chop Plate, Blue & Chartreuse, Harmony House, 12 In. 40.00
Carnival, Sugar & Creamer, Cover, Harmony House 30.00
Carousel, Plate, Dinner, Royal China, 10 In. 6.00
Cattail, Cup & Saucer, Universal 10.50
Cattail, Mixing Bowl, Universal Potteries, 6 In. 15.50
Cattail, Mixing Bowl, Universal Potteries, 10 ½ In. 30.00
Cattail, Platter, Universal Potteries, 14 ¾ In. 8.00
Cavalier, Plate, Dinner, Homer Laughlin, 10 In. 8.00
Cavalier, Plate, Salad, Homer Laughlin, 7 In. 6.00
Century, Plate, Dinner, Salem China, 11 In. 10.00
Century, Plate, Salad, Salem China, 7 In. 5.00
Century, Platter, Ivory, Homer Laughlin, 15 ¼ In. 15.00
Chalet, Plate, Dinner, Knowles, 10 In. 9.00
Chalet, Platter, Knowles, 10 x 12 ½ In. 25.00
Chalet, Saucer, Knowles 4.00
Chanticleer, Duraprint, Cup & Saucer, Brown Rooster, Homer Laughlin, 1958 15.00
Chanticleer, Duraprint, Platter, Brown Rooster On Tree, Homer Laughlin, 11 ¾ In. 30.00
Chateau Buffet, Cookie Jar, Brown, Turquoise, Taylor, Smith & Taylor, 7 ¼ x 8 In. 25.00
Chateau Buffet, Sugar & Creamer, Lid, Cinnamon Brown, Blue, Taylor, Smith & Taylor 15.00
Cock O' The Walk, Bowl, Vegetable, Blue Ridge, 9 In. 40.00
Cock O' The Walk, Platter, Lug Handles, Round, Salem China, 11 In. 8.00
Colonial Homestead, Berry Bowl, Royal China, 5 ½ In. 5.00
Colonial Homestead, Bowl, Vegetable, Rim, Royal China, 10 In. 12.50
Colonial Homestead, Bowl, Vegetable, Royal China, 9 In. *illus* 15.00
Colonial Homestead, Cake Plate, Handles, Royal China, 11 ½ In. 12.50
Colonial Homestead, Cup & Saucer, Green 2.50
Colonial Homestead, Plate, Bread & Butter, Royal China, 6 ¼ In. 2.75 to 4.00
Colonial Homestead, Plate, Dinner, Royal China, 9 In. 6.50
Colonial Homestead, Sugar, Cover, Royal China 10.00
Colonial Homestead, Sugar & Creamer, Royal China 12.50
Country Fair, Plate, Luncheon, Pears, Blue Ridge, 8 In. 25.00
Country Fair, Plate, Luncheon, Pomegranate & Cherries, Blue Ridge, 8 In. 25.00
Country Sage, Platter, Round, Homer Laughlin, 12 In. 18.00
Country Strawberry, Plate, Dinner, Homer Laughlin, 10 ¼ In. 7.50
Countryside, Bowl, Fruit, Harmony House, 1950s, 6 In. 7.50
Courting Couple, Bowl, Cereal, Liberty Shape, Homer Laughlin, 5 ¾ In. 6.00
Currier & Ives, Casserole, Cover, Royal China, 3 x 7 ½ In. *illus* 50.00
Currier & Ives, Chop Plate, Round, Royal China, 12 In. 20.00
Currier & Ives, Gravy Boat, Cobalt Blue Design, Royal China, 6 In. 25.00
Currier & Ives, Salt & Pepper, Blue & White, Royal China 40.00
Currier & Ives, Sugar, Cover, Royal China 28.00
Daffodil, Creamer, Paden City 8.00
Daffodil, Plate, Dinner, Paden City, 10 In. 7.00
Daybreak, Bowl, Fruit, Harmony House, 5 ½ In. 5.00
Delmar Begonia, Bowl, Fruit, Crooksville, 5 ¼ In. 6.50
Delmar Begonia, Creamer, Crooksville 19.50
Delmar Begonia, Cup & Saucer, Crooksville 12.50
Delmar Begonia, Plate, Luncheon, Crooksville, 9 ¼ In. 7.50
Delmar Begonia, Platter, Oval, Crooksville, 11 ½ In. 32.00
Delmar Begonia, Sugar, Cover, Crooksville 26.50
Dogwood, Pitcher, Universal Potteries, Qt., 6 In. 18.00
Dogwood, Pitcher, Water, Universal Potteries, 2 Qt., 6 In. 30.00
Dogwood, Plate, Luncheon, Ruffled Edge, Gold Trim, Homer Laughlin, 9 ¼ In. 7.99
Double Dutch, Cake Plate, Blue Ridge, 11 x 12 In. 46.00
Dresden, Cup & Saucer, Imperial Blue, Homer Laughlin 8.75
Dresden, Soup, Dish, Rim, Imperial Blue, Homer Laughlin, 8 ½ In. 10.00
Duchess, Bowl, Vegetable, Oval, Harmony House, 11 x 8 In. 17.50
Duchess, Plate, Bread & Butter, Paden City, 6 ⅜ In. 3.00
Duchess, Sugar, Cover, Paden City 13.50
Eggshell Cavalier, Cup & Saucer, Homer Laughlin 5.00
Eggshell Georgian, Baker, Oval, White Flower, Homer Laughlin, 9 ½ In. 9.00
Eggshell Georgian, Berry Bowl, Homer Laughlin, 5 ½ In. 6.00
Eggshell Georgian, Cup & Saucer, Homer Laughlin 20.00
Eggshell Georgian, Platter, Rose, Homer Laughlin, 12 x 9 ⅛ In. 10.00
Eggshell Nautilus, Sugar, Cover, Homer Laughlin, 4 ¾ In. 24.00
Elaine, Gravy Boat, Underplate, Homer Laughlin 70.00

English Chippendale, Bowl, Vegetable, Johnson Brothers, 8 ¾ In. 189.00
English Chippendale, Cup & Saucer, Johnson Brothers. 18.00
English Chippendale, Sugar, Open, Handles, Johnson Brothers, 2 ½ In. 28.00
English Village, Bowl, Vegetable, Salem China, 8 ½ In. 29.00
Evening Song, Plate, Dinner, Knowles, 10 ¼ In. 7.50
Fair Oaks, Cup & Saucer, Royal China 6.75
Fair Oaks, Plate, Bread & Butter, Royal China, 6 ½ In. 2.10
Fair Winds, Platter, USS Delaware, Oval, Brown, Alfred Meakin, 12 ½ x 9 ½ In. 45.00
Fairlane, Bowl, Vegetable, Steubenville, 8 ¾ In. 15.00
Fairlane, Butter, Cover, Steubenville 30.00
Fairlane, Creamer, Steubenville, 4 ½ In. 6.99
Fairlane, Cup & Saucer, Steubenville 3.99
Fairlane, Gravy Boat, Underplate, 8 ½ x 3 In. 20.00
Fairlane, Plate, Salad, Steubenville, 7 ¼ In. 2.50
Fairlane, Platter, Steubenville, 11 ½ In. 12.50
Fairlane, Salt & Pepper, Steubenville 10.00
Fairlane, Sugar, Cover, Steubenville, 4 In. 6.99
Fantasy, Plate, Bread & Butter, Knowles, 6 ¼ In. 3.00
Fantasy, Plate, Dinner, Knowles, 10 ¼ In. 7.50
Ferndale, Bowl, Vegetable, Harmony House, 9 In. 10.00
Floral Pink Rose, Bowl, Vegetable, Paden City, 7 x 8 In. 14.00
Floral Pink Rose, Sugar, Cover, Paden City, 4 x 5 In. 12.00
Forget-Me-Not, Plate, Blue Flowers, Scalloped Edge, Myott, Staffordshire, 10 In. 14.00
Forget-Me-Not, Plate, Myott, Staffordshire, 10 In. 14.00
Forsythia, Creamer, Knowles. 14.00
Forsythia, Plate, Bread & Butter, Knowles, 6 ¼ In. 5.00
Forsythia, Plate, Dinner, Knowles, 10 ¼ In. 25.00
Forsythia, Sugar, Cover, Knowles 9.50
Friendly Village, Cup & Saucer, Johnson Brothers 7.50
Friendly Village, Gravy Boat, Underplate, Johnson Brothers 39.99
Friendly Village, Plate, Bread & Butter, Johnson Brothers, 6 In. 10.00
Friendly Village, Plate, Dinner, Johnson Brothers, 10 In. 12.00
Friendly Village, Platter, Johnson Brothers, 11 ½ In. 20.00
Friendly Village, Sugar & Creamer, Cover, Johnson Brothers. 20.00
Fruits, Jug, Water, Ice Lip, Knowles, 54 Oz., 7 ½ In. 24.00
Game Birds, Mug, Partridge, Johnson Brothers. 19.50
Game Birds, Platter, Pheasant, Johnson Brothers, 11 In. 35.00
Game Birds, Platter, Quail, Johnson Brothers, 11 In. 39.00
Godey Ladies, Charger, Salem China Co., 11 In. *illus* 29.00
Gold Crest, Berry Bowl, Harmony House, 5 ½ In. 8.00
Gold Crest, Cup & Saucer, Harmony House 8.00
Gold Crest, Plate, Dinner, Harmony House, 10 ¼ In. 8.00
Gold Crest, Sugar, Cover, Harmony House, 1960s 25.00
Gold Crown, Plate, Dinner, Homer Laughlin, 10 ⅛ In. 8.00
Gold Crown, Plate, Salad, Homer Laughlin, 7 ¼ In. 5.00
Gold Glade, Plate, Salad, Homer Laughlin, 7 ¼ In. 4.00
Gold Laurel, Bowl, Round, Gold Trim, Taylor, Smith & Taylor, 8 ¾ x 2 ¾ In. 7.00
Gold Laurel, Bowl, Vegetable, Oval, Gold Trim, Taylor, Smith & Taylor, 9 ⅛ x 6 ¾ In. 7.00
Gold Laurel, Cup, Decal, Taylor, Smith & Taylor, 3 ⅜ x 2 ¾ In. 3.00
Gold Laurel, Soup, Dish, Flowers, Taylor, Smith & Taylor, 7 ¾ In. 4.50
Golden Gate, Plate, Dinner, Homer Laughlin, 9 ¾ In. 9.50
Golden Gate, Soup, Dish, Homer Laughlin, 7 ½ In. 7.50
Golden Scepter, Tidbit, Center Handle, Paden City, 10 In. 20.00
Golden Stardrift, Coffeepot, Gold Trim, Royal China, 7 ½ In. 34.00
Golden Wheat, Berry Bowl, Homer Laughlin 4.49
Golden Wheat, Cup & Saucer, Homer Laughlin 5.39
Golden Wheat, Plate, Luncheon, Homer Laughlin, 9 ¼ In. 4.49
Golden Wheat, Soup, Dish, Homer Laughlin, 8 ¼ In. 8.99
Good Morning, Plate, Bread & Butter, Royal China, 6 ⅜ In. 4.00
Good Morning, Plate, Dinner, Royal China, 10 In. *illus* 15.00
Good Morning, Platter, Oval, Royal China, 10 x 13 In. 12.00
Grace, Pitcher, Dark Green, Blue Ridge, 6 ¼ In. *illus* 125.00
Granada, Plate, Bread & Butter, Homer Laughlin, 6 ¼ In. 3.00
Granada, Plate, Dinner, Homer Laughlin, 10 In. 6.00
Grapes, Bowl, Fruit, Pedestal, Ben Seibel, Iroquois 7.00
Grapes, Cup & Saucer, Ben Seibel, Iroquois 8.00

Dinnerware, Godey Ladies, Charger, Salem China Co., 11 In.
$29.00

Dinnerware, Good Morning, Plate, Dinner, Royal China, 10 In.
$15.00

Dinnerware, Grace, Pitcher, Dark Green, Blue Ridge, 6 ¼ In.
$125.00

TIP

Most burglaries take place between 9 a.m. and 3 p.m., when houses are empty. Don't go out during the day without locking your doors and windows.

TIP
To remove coffee stains, try wiping the cup with a damp cloth and baking soda.

Dinnerware, Green Eyes, Cup & Saucer, Blue Ridge Potteries
$12.00

Dinnerware, Harvest Time, Platter, Oval, Ben Seibel, Iroquois, 15 x 10 ½ In.
$65.00

Dinnerware, Liberty Blue, Soup, Dish, Rimmed, Old North Church, 8 ¾ In.
$18.00

Dating the Symbols
The symbol © was first used on dishes in 1914. The symbol ® wasn't used until 1949.

Grapevine, Creamer, Knowles 15.00
Gray-Lure, Plate, Salad, Crooksville, 7 In. 3.00
Green Eyes, Cup & Saucer, Blue Ridge Potteries .... *illus* 12.00
Greendawn, Saucer, Celadon, Scalloped, Johnson Bros., 6 ¼ In. 4.00
Greendawn, Saucer, Johnson Bros., 6 ¼ In. 4.00
Greenfield, Bowl, Cereal, 8-Sided, Johnson Brothers, 6 ⅞ In. 7.00
Hampshire, Plate, Dinner, Brown, Royal China 15.99
Harvest, Pie Baker, Universal Potteries, 10 In. 15.00
Harvest Time, Cup, Tea, Johnson Brothers 5.00
Harvest Time, Platter, Oval, Ben Seibel, Iroquois, 15 x 10 ½ In. .... *illus* 65.00
Heirloom, Creamer, Harmony House, 3 ½ In. 10.00
Heritage Hall, Bowl, Vegetable, Pennsylvania, Field Stone, Johnson Brothers, 8 ¼ In. 18.00
Hibiscus, Bowl, Fruit, Crooksville, 5 ½ In. 5.00
Hibiscus, Plate, Bread & Butter, Crooksville, 6 In. 3.00
Highland Plaid, Platter, Dura-Print, Homer Laughlin, 11 ½ In. 19.50
Hollyhock, Plate, Bread & Butter, Paden City, 6 ½ In. 10.00
Hop Scotch, Cup & Saucer, Footed, Viktor Schreckengost, Salem China 38.00
Hop Scotch, Plate, Bread & Butter, Viktor Schreckengost, Salem China, 1955, 6 ¼ In. 15.00
Hop Scotch, Plate, Dinner, Viktor Schreckengost, Salem China, 10 ⅛ In. 22.00
Hostess, Sugar & Creamer, Pink Daisy, Edwin M. Knowles 17.00
Indian Tree, Cake Plate, Green, Royal China, 12 ½ In. 13.00
Indian Tree, Plate, Salad, Johnson Brothers, 8 In. 9.99
Iris, Plate, Bread & Butter, Universal Potteries, 6 ¼ In. 5.00
Iris, Plate, Salad, Universal Potteries, 7 ¼ In. 5.00
Iva-Lure, Bowl, Cereal, Tab Handles, Crooksville, 7 In. 12.00
Iva-Lure, Bowl, Dessert, Crooksville, 5 ⅜ In. 7.00
Iva-Lure, Bowl, Vegetable, Tab Handles, Crooksville, 9 ½ In. 27.00
Iva-Lure, Creamer, Crooksville 18.00
Iva-Lure, Cup & Saucer, Blossom, Crooksville 15.00
Iva-Lure, Plate, Bread & Butter, Crooksville, 6 In. 15.00
Iva-Lure, Plate, Dinner, Crooksville, 10 ¼ In. 15.00
Iva-Lure, Sugar, Cover, Blossom, Handles, Crooksville 20.00
Ivora, Berry Bowl, Crooksville, 5 ⅛ In. 5.50
Ivora, Cup & Saucer, Crooksville 10.00
Ivora, Plate, Luncheon, 9 In. 7.50
Ivora, Platter, Oval, Crooksville, 11 ½ In. 25.00
Ivy, Celery Dish, Oval, Paden City, 9 ¼ x 5 ⅝ In. 8.00
Ivy, Plate, Bread & Butter, Paden City, 6 ⅜ In. 5.00
Ivy, Plate, Dinner, Paden City, 10 In. 7.50
Ivy, Platter, Oval, Homer Laughlin, 12 In. 10.00
James Riviere, Plate, Dinner, Crooksville, 10 ½ In. 8.50
James Riviere, Platter, Crooksville, 13 ½ In. 25.00
Jamestown, Saucer, Johnson Brothers 5.00
Jennifer, Bowl, Vegetable, Harmony House, 9 ¼ In. 7.50
Jonquil, Creamer, Paden City, 2 ½ In. 10.00
Jonquil, Cup & Saucer, Paden City 7.50
Jonquil, Plate, Dinner, Paden City, 9 ¼ In. 8.50
Jonquil, Sugar, Cover, Paden City, 4 ¼ In. 12.00
Jubilee, Plate, Dinner, Homer Laughlin, 10 In. 5.00
Jubilee, Plate, Salad, Homer Laughlin, 7 ¼ In. 5.00
Kensington, Plate, Dinner, Johnson Brothers, 10 In. 7.00
La Grande, Plate, Bread & Butter, Crooksville 4.00
La Grande, Platter, Oval, Crooksville, 15 ½ In. 12.00
Lace Bouquet, Berry Bowl, Salem China, 5 ⅝ In. 2.80
Lace Bouquet, Cup & Saucer, Salem China 7.00
Lace Bouquet, Plate, Dinner, Salem China, 10 ¼ In. 7.50
Lady Empire, Cake Plate, Ballerina, Universal Potteries, 10 In. 18.00
Lady Empire, Plate, Bread & Butter, Ballerina, Universal Potteries, 6 ¼ In. 4.00
Largo, Pitcher, Water, Universal Potteries, 2 Qt., 6 In. 29.00
Lazy Daisy, Plate, Dinner, Ben Seibel, Iroquois, 10 ½ In. 8.00
Lazy Daisy, Platter, Oval, Ben Seibel, Iroquois, 15 ¼ In. 20.00
Leaf Dance, Bowl, Cereal, Knowles, 6 In. 6.00
Leaf Dance, Bowl, Fruit, Knowles, 5 ¼ In. 5.00
Leaf Dance, Creamer, Knowles 16.50
Leaf Dance, Plate, Bread & Butter, Knowles, 6 In. 4.50
Lemon Tree, Chop Plate, Johnson Brothers, 12 ¼ In. 38.95

Liberty Blue, Berry Bowl, Betsy Ross, 5 ½ In. 11.00
Liberty Blue, Cup, Ride Of Paul Revere 5.50
Liberty Blue, Plate, Bread & Butter, Monticello, 6 In. .... 5.50 to 7.00
Liberty Blue, Plate, Independence Hall, 10 In. 18.00
Liberty Blue, Plate, Salad, Bicentennial, Washington Leaving Christ Church, 7 In. 12.50
Liberty Blue, Platter, Meat, Governors House At Williamsburg, 12 In. 52.00
Liberty Blue, Platter, Washington Crossing Delaware, Box, 14 In. 98.00
Liberty Blue, Saucer, Old North Church 1.50
Liberty Blue, Soup, Dish, Rimmed, Old North Church, 8 ¾ In. .... *illus* 18.00
Liberty Blue, Tureen, Staffordshire 275.00
Love Birds, Bowl, Cereal, Crooksville, 6 In. 7.00
Love Birds, Cup & Saucer, Crooksville 8.00
Love Birds, Plate, Dinner, Crooksville, 9 ¼ In. 10.00
Lu-Ray, Platter, Pink, Taylor, Smith & Taylor, 12 In. .... *illus* 19.00
Lyrica, Plate, Dinner, Homer Laughlin, 10 ⅝ In. 7.49
Maple Leaf, Bowl, Cereal, Salem China, 5 ¼ In. 1.00
Maple Leaf, Platter, Oval, Salem China, 13 In. 20.00
Marlborough, Platter, Johnson Brothers, 11 ½ In. 80.00
Marlene Lace, Plate, Bread & Butter, Paden City, 6 ½ In. 3.50
Mayflower, Bowl, Vegetable, Gold Border, 8 ½ In. 9.00
Mayflower, Cup, Tea, Blue Ridge 4.00
Mayflower, Cup & Saucer, Blue Ridge 8.00
Mayflower, Plate, Blue Ridge, 9 ⅝ In. 8.00
Mayflower, Plate, Bread & Butter, Blue Ridge, 6 ¼ In. 4.00
Melody Lane, Sugar & Creamer, Salem China 15.00
Mexi-Lido, Soup, Dish, W.S. George, 1950s, 8 In. 6.00
Minuet, Plate, Bread & Butter, Johnson Brothers, 6 ⅜ In. 4.00
Minuet, Plate, Dinner, Harmony House, 10 ½ In. 10.00
Minuet, Plate, Dinner, Johnson Brothers, 10 In. 7.00
Minuet, Sugar, Cover, Harmony House 8.00
Modern Orchid, Berry Bowl, Gold Trim, Paden City, 5 ⅜ In. 5.99
Modern Orchid, Platter, Paden City, 9 In. 10.00
Monticello, Place Setting, Harmony House, 6 Piece 55.00
Morning Glory, Platter, Shenandoah Ware, Paden City, 16 x 13 In. 40.00
Mosaic, Serving Bowl, Harmony House, 9 In. 12.00
Mount Vernon, Plate, Bread & Butter, Harmony House, 6 ¼ In. 7.00
Mountain Nosegay, Plate, Square, Blue Ridge, 7 In. 30.00
Nautical, Plate, Dinner, Salem China, 10 In. .... *illus* 5.00
Needlepoint, Bowl, Cereal, Homer Laughlin, 6 ¼ In. 5.00
Needlepoint, Plate, Dinner, Blue & Green, Homer Laughlin, 10 In. 7.50
Needlepoint, Plate, Dinner, Brown & Tan, Homer Laughlin, 10 ¼ In. 6.00
Needlepoint, Plate, Salad, Brown & Tan, Homer Laughlin, 7 ¼ In. 5.00
Neville, Plate, Dinner, Homer Laughlin, 9 ¾ In. 20.00
Noel, Dinner Set, Don Schreckengost, 18 Piece 120.00
Nora, Plate, Bread & Butter, Harmony House, 6 ½ In. 3.00
Nora, Sugar, Cover, Harmony House 18.00
North Star, Cup & Saucer, Salem China 8.00
North Star, Plate, Salad, Salem China, 7 ¼ In. 5.00
North Star, Sugar & Creamer, Salem China 35.00
Old Britain Castles, Plate, Johnson Brothers, 8 In. 7.00
Old Britain Castles, Teapot, Pink Transfer, Johnson Brothers, 6 In. 128.00
Old Curiosity Shop, Bowl, Dessert, Royal China, 5 ⅝ In. 4.00
Old Curiosity Shop, Bowl, Vegetable, Royal China, 9 ⅛ In. 10.50
Old Curiosity Shop, Bowl, Vegetable, Trunk & Jug, Royal China, 10 ¼ In. 24.00
Old Curiosity Shop, Creamer, Royal China 6.25
Old Curiosity Shop, Cup & Saucer, Royal China 5.50
Old Curiosity Shop, Plate, Bread & Butter, Royal China, 6 ½ In. 4.00
Old Curiosity Shop, Plate, Dinner, Royal China, 10 In. .... 5.25 to 7.95
Old Curiosity Shop, Platter, Oval, Royal China, 13 ⅝ x 10 ⅞ In. 75.00
Old English Countryside, Plate, Dinner, Johnson Brothers, 10 In. 30.00
Old Granite, Cup & Saucer, Fruit, Johnson Brothers 12.00
Old Granite, Cup & Saucer, Hearts & Flowers, Johnson Brothers 10.00
Old Granite, Plate, Bread & Butter, Hearts & Flowers, Johnson Brothers, 6 ⅜ In. 9.00
Old Homestead, Pie Plate, Royal China, 10 In. 12.00
Old Rose, Plate, Dinner, Paden City, 9 ¼ In. 9.00
Old Willow, Tureen, Blue & White, Empire, 9 ½ x 9 In. 60.00

TIP

The best way to store plates is vertically in a rack.

D

Dinnerware, Lu-Ray, Platter, Pink, Taylor, Smith & Taylor, 12 In. $19.00

Dinnerware, Nautical, Plate, Dinner, Salem China, 10 In. $5.00

Top Ten American Dinnerware Patterns

Hundreds of thousands of users visit our website, Kovels.com, each month. The dinnerware patterns that are the most popular among our visitors are:

1. Old Curiosity Shop
2. Colonial Homestead
3. Eggshell Nautilus
4. Virginia Rose
5. Briar Rose
6. Iva-lure
7. Vistosa
8. Lu-ray
9. Memory Lane
10. Monticello

TIP

Don't sticky-tape a top on a teapot. The decoration may come off with the tape. Secure a top with dental wax or earthquake wax.

Dinnerware, Pink Petal, Bowl, Vegetable, Homer Laughlin, 9 ¼ x 6 ¾ In.
$22.50

Dinnerware, Priscilla, Gravy Boat, Underplate, Homer Laughlin, 3 ½ x 8 & 9 ¼ In.
$20.00

Dinnerware, Rhythm Rose, Pitcher, Kitchen Kraft, Homer Laughlin, 48 Oz.
$45.00

Orbit, Casserole, Blue, Homer Laughlin, 5 In. 6.00
Patchwork Flower, Casserole, Mount Vernon Shape, Green Trim, Universal, 5 ½ x 8 ¼ In. 20.00
Petal Point, Platter, Gold Trim, Salem China, 11 In. 25.00
Petit Point, Basket, Plate, Salad, Salem China, 7 In. 6.00
Petit Point, Plate, Bread & Butter, Eggshell Nautilus, Homer Laughlin. 3.50
Petit Point, Plate, Dinner, Harmony House, 10 ½ In. 13.00
Petit Point, Platter, Gold Trim, Homer Laughlin, 13 ½ x 11 In. 32.00
Petit Point House, Bowl, Bak-In, Crooksville, 11 In. 59.00
Petit Point House, Pitcher, Cover, Bak-In, Crooksville, 6 In. 79.00
Petit Point House, Plate, Crooksville, 12 ¼ In. 37.50
Petit Point House, Platter, Oval, Crooksville, 13 ¼ In. 40.00
Pine Cone, Plate, Bread & Butter, Paden City, 6 ⅜ In. 3.00
Pine Cone, Plate, Dinner, Paden City, 10 In. 9.50
Pink Dogwood, Bowl, Dessert, Knowles, 5 In. 4.00
Pink Dogwood, Plate, Dinner, Knowles, 10 ¼ In. 12.00
Pink Dogwood, Saucer, Knowles 3.00
Pink Petal, Bowl, Vegetable, Homer Laughlin, 9 ¼ x 6 ¾ In. *illus* 22.50
Pink Petal, Soup, Dish, Flat, Homer Laughlin, 8 ¼ In. 6.00
Pink Poppy, Bowl, Cereal, Ballerina, Universal Potteries, 8 In. 9.95
Pink Poppy, Creamer, Ballerina, Universal Potteries, 3 ⅜ In. 12.00
Pink Poppy, Cup & Saucer, Ballerina, Universal Potteries 12.95
Pink Poppy, Plate, Bread & Butter, Ballerina, Universal Potteries, 6 ⅜ In. 6.50
Pink Poppy, Plate, Dinner, Ballerina, Universal Potteries, 10 In. 12.95
Pink Poppy, Sugar, Cover, Ballerina, Universal Potteries, 2 ¼ x 3 ¾ In. 15.00
Platinum Garland, Bowl, Fruit, Harmony House, 5 ½ In. 18.00
Platinum Garland, Creamer, Harmony House, 3 ½ In. 30.00
Platinum Garland, Plate, Salad, Harmony House, 7 ¾ In. 27.00
Poppy, Berry Bowl, Camwood Ivory Shape, Universal Potteries, 5 In. 3.00
Poppy, Pie Baker, Silver Trim, Universal Potteries, 8 ½ In. 15.00
Poppy, Plate, Camwood Ivory Shape, Universal Potteries, 6 In. 3.00
Poppy, Platter, Oval, Red Trim, Universal Potteries, 13 ½ x 10 ⅜ In. 15.00
Poppy, Spoon, Yellow, Orange, Edwin M. Knowles 12.00
Poppy Duet, Plate, Bread & Butter, Candlewick Shape, Blue Ridge, 6 In. 20.00
Primrose, Gravy Boat, Salem China, 5 In. 32.00
Priscilla, Bowl, Dessert, Eggshell Nautilus, Homer Laughlin, 5 In. 3.00
Priscilla, Cake Plate, Household Institute Ovenware, Homer Laughlin, 11 In. 15.00
Priscilla, Casserole Cover, Ovenware, Homer Laughlin, 8 ½ In. 6.00
Priscilla, Cup & Saucer, Eggshell Nautilus, Homer Laughlin 10.00
Priscilla, Gravy Boat, Underplate, Homer Laughlin, 3 ½ x 8 & 9 ¼ In. *illus* 20.00
Priscilla, Mixing Bowl, Homer Laughlin, 6 In. 24.00
Priscilla, Plate, Eggshell Nautilus, Homer Laughlin, 6 In. 6.00
Priscilla, Plate, Eggshell Nautilus, Homer Laughlin, 8 In. 7.00
Priscilla, Plate, Eggshell Nautilus, Homer Laughlin, 9 In. 8.00
Priscilla, Soup, Dish, Eggshell Nautilus, Homer Laughlin 9.00
Provincial, Plate, Dinner, Johnson Brothers, 9 ¾ In. 9.00
Pyramid, Bowl, Dessert, Pedestal Base, Ben Seibel, Iroquois, 5 ¼ In. 10.80
Pyramid, Bowl, Vegetable, Ben Seibel, Iroquois, 11 ½ x 9 ¾ In. 50.00
Pyramid, Cup & Saucer, Ben Seibel, Iroquois 9.00
Pyramid, Plate, Dinner, Ben Seibel, Iroquois, 10 ¼ In. 17.00
Pyramid, Saucer, Ben Seibel, Iroquois 4.32
Queen Anne's Lace, Cup & Saucer, Knowles 13.50
Ravenna, Plate, Dinner, Knowles, 10 In. 7.50
Ravenna, Platter, Knowles, 12 ½ In. 20.00
Ravenna, Sugar, Cover, Knowles 7.50
Red Flowers, Bowl, Lid, Green 3-Lobed Leaves, Red Trim, Universal Potteries, 4 ½ In. 14.00
Red Rose, Creamer, Paden City 20.00
Red Rose, Cup & Saucer, Paden City 16.00
Red Rose, Plate, Bread & Butter, Paden City 4.00
Red Rose, Platter, Oval, Paden City, 9 ¼ x 5 ¾ In. 15.00
Regency, Bowl, Vegetable, Cover, White, Johnson Brothers, 9 In. 49.99
Regency, Plate, Bread & Butter, White, Johnson Brothers, 6 ¼ In. 3.00
Regency, Sugar, Cover, White, Johnson Brothers 14.00
Restaurant Ware, Plate, Bread, Oval, Gray Trim, Homer Laughlin, 8 x 5 ¾ In. 8.50
Rhythm, Bowl, Fruit, Yellow, Homer Laughlin 8.00
Rhythm, Bowl, Vegetable, Homer Laughlin, 9 In. 4.00
Rhythm, Bowl, Vegetable, Rose, Ovenware, Homer Laughlin, 9 In. 15.00
Rhythm, Gravy Boat, Gray, Homer Laughlin, 8 ¾ x 3 ¼ In. 10.00 to 20.00

Rhythm, Grill Plate, Chartreuse, Eames, Homer Laughlin 30.00
Rhythm, Grill Plate, Forest Green, Eames, Homer Laughlin. 30.00
Rhythm, Grill Plate, Gray, Eames, Homer Laughlin 30.00
Rhythm, Grill Plate, Yellow, Eames, Homer Laughlin 30.00
Rhythm, Nappy, Gray, Homer Laughlin 15.00
Rhythm, Plate, Bread & Butter, Yellow, Homer Laughlin, 6 In. . . . . . 5.00 to 8.00
Rhythm, Plate, Dinner, Chartreuse, Homer Laughlin, 10 In.. . . . . 10.00 to 12.00
Rhythm, Plate, Dinner, Yellow, Homer Laughlin, 10 In. 10.00
Rhythm, Plate, Salad, Homer Laughlin, 7 ½ In. 3.25
Rhythm, Platter, Oval, Chartreuse, Homer Laughlin, 11 ½ In. . . . . . 12.50 to 21.50
Rhythm, Sauceboat, Gray 12.50
Rhythm Rose, Bowl, Vegetable, Homer Laughlin, 9 In. 15.00
Rhythm Rose, Pitcher, Kitchen Kraft, Homer Laughlin, 48 oz. . . . . . *illus* 45.00
Rialto, Bowl, Vegetable, Cover, Maroon, Myott, Staffordshire, 8 In.. . . . . 25.00
Rialto, Bowl, Vegetable, Cover, Maroon, Myott, Staffordshire, 9 In.. . . . . 65.00
Riviera, Creamer, Yellow, Homer Laughlin. 18.00
Riviera, Plate, Bread & Butter, Red, Homer Laughlin, 6 ¼ In. 15.00
Riviera, Saltshaker, Blue, Homer Laughlin 8.00
Rock Rose, Bowl, Vegetable, Blue Ridge, 9 ½ In. . . . . . *illus* 29.00
Romance, Cup & Saucer, Homer Laughlin 12.00
Romance, Plate, Dinner, Homer Laughlin, 10 In. 7.50
Romance, Plate, Dinner, Snowhite, Johnson Brothers, 10 In.. . . . . 7.00
Rooster, Bowl, Oval, Blue Ridge, 9 ½ In. 8.00
Rose, Bowl, Vegetable, Tab Handles, Salem China, 9 ½ In. 22.00
Rose Band, Plate, Bread & Butter, Crooksville, 6 In. 3.50
Rose Band, Plate, Luncheon, Crooksville, 9 In. 6.00
Rose Path, Platter, Knowles, 13 In.. . . . . 31.50
Rose Path, Soup, Dish, Knowles, 8 In. 6.00
Rose Point, Gravy Boat, Attached Underplate, Steubenville, 7 In. 25.00
Rose Point, Plate, Salad, Steubenville, 7 ½ In. 6.99
Rose Point, Saucer, Steubenville 1.99
Rose Point, Sugar, Cover, Steubenville. 9.99
Rosebud, Bowl, Vegetable, Harmony House, 10 ⅜ In. 14.00
Rosedale, Platter, Harmony House, 12 ½ x 9 ⅜ In. . . . . . *illus* 35.00
Rosedawn, Cup & Saucer, Johnson Brothers 18.00
Rosedawn, Plate, Dinner, Johnson Brothers, 10 In.. . . . . 14.00
Rosedawn, Plate, Salad, Square, Johnson Brothers, 7 In. 10.00
Sally, Berry Bowl, Paden City, 5 ⅛ In. 3.00
Sally, Cup & Saucer, Paden City. 8.00
Sally, Plate, Bread & Butter, Paden City, 6 ¼ In.. . . . . 3.00
Sally, Plate, Dessert, Paden City, 7 ½ In. 5.00
Santa Monica, Plate, Dinner, Yellow & Brown Plaid, Knowles, 10 ¼ In. 7.50
Seashell, Plate, Salad, Homer Laughlin, 8 In. 5.00
Serenade, Bowl, Kaysons, 5 ¾ In. 3.00
Serenade, Cake Plate, Tab Handles, Salem China, 1950s, 10 ⅝ In. 20.00
Shakespeare Country, Chop Plate, Homer Laughlin, 12 In. 19.50
Shakespeare Country, Plate, Homer Laughlin, 10 In.. . . . . *illus* 8.00
Shakespeare Country, Sugar & Creamer, Cover, Homer Laughlin 23.00
Sheraton, Bowl, Cereal, Square, Johnson Brothers, 6 ¼ In. 10.00
Simone, Platter, Oval, White, Silver Trim, Harmony House, 12 ¼ In.. . . . . 28.00
Simplicity, Plate, Dinner, Turquoise, Salem China, 10 In. 5.00
Simplicity, Plate, Salad, Turquoise, Salem China, 7 ¼ In., 6 Piece 13.00
Simplicity, Sugar, Cover, Handles, Turquoise, Salem China 6.00
Skytone, Cup & Saucer, Homer Laughlin. 8.00
Skytone, Plate, Dessert, Homer Laughlin, 6 In. 5.00
Skytone, Plate, Dinner, Homer Laughlin, 10 In. 6.00
Skytone, Saucer, Homer Laughlin 6.00
Springtime, Cup & Saucer, Homer Laughlin. 9.00
Springtime, Plate, Bread & Butter, Homer Laughlin, 6 ¼ In.. . . . . 3.00
Springtime, Salt & Pepper, Cavalier Shape, Homer Laughlin. 18.00
Springtime, Sugar, Cover, Cavalier Shape, Homer Laughlin 18.00
Star Glow, Bowl, Dessert, Royal China, 5 ½ In. 4.00
Star Glow, Pie Baker, Royal China, 9 ¾ In. 18.00
Starlite, Creamer, Regal China, 5 ½ In. 15.00
Starlite, Cup & Saucer, Regal China. 17.00
Starlite, Plate, Bread & Butter, Regal China, 6 ⅜ In.. . . . . 8.50
Starlite, Saucer, Regal China, 6 In.. . . . . 8.50

Dinnerware, Rock Rose, Bowl, Vegetable, Blue Ridge, 9 ½ In. $29.00

Dinnerware, Rosedale, Platter, Harmony House, 12 ½ x 9 ⅜ In. $35.00

Dinnerware, Shakespeare Country, Plate, Dinner, Homer Laughlin,10 In. $8.00

TIP

Don't heat food on a cracked plate in either an oven or a microwave. The crack may widen.

As always, the edited listings in *Kovels' Antiques & Collectibles Price Guide 2010* aren't available on any website, but readers should visit Kovels.com for information on trends, tips, reproductions, marks, old prices, and more!

Dinnerware, Virginia Rose, Sugar, Cover, Homer Laughlin, 5 In.
$30.00

Dinnerware, Wheat, Creamer, Cover, Ovenproof, Salem China, 2 ⅝ In.
$8.00

Tokens
If you find a box of old coins and coin-like items or "tokens," don't throw any away. Sometimes the things that are not real money have more value than coins. Streetcar tokens, political tokens, medallions commemorating special events, and even lodge tokens have value.

Dionne Quintuplets, Dolls, Quintuplets In Basket, Madame Alexander, 8 In.
$850.00

Starlite, Sugar, Cover, Regal China, 6 ½ In. . . . 18.00
Sun Light, Berry Bowl, Knowles, 5 ½ In. . . . 6.00
Sunglow, Cup & Saucer, Knowles . . . 15.50
Sunglow, Plate, Bread & Butter, Knowles, 6 ¼ In. . . . 4.00
Symphony, Cup, Chartreuse, Harmony House . . . 3.50
Symphony, Cup & Saucer, Blue, Harmony House . . . 9.50
Symphony, Plate, Bread & Butter, Harmony House, 6 ¼ In. . . . 4.00
Symphony, Plate, Bread & Butter, Pink, Harmony House, 6 ¼ In. . . . 3.00
Symphony, Plate, Dinner, Chartreuse, Harmony House, 10 In. . . . 12.00
Symphony, Plate, Luncheon, Blue, Harmony House, 9 ¼ In. . . . 7.50
Symphony, Saucer, Pink, Harmony House, 6 ¼ In. . . . 3.50
Tea Rose, Plate, Dinner, Knowles, 10 ¼ In. . . . 9.00
Tea Rose, Plate, Salad, Knowles, 8 In. . . . 5.00
Tom & Jerry, Cup, Ivory, Gold Letters, Homer Laughlin, 3 In. . . . 10.00
Triumph, Soup, Dish, Empire Shape, Taylor, Smith & Taylor . . . 12.00
Tulip, Plate, Bread & Butter, Homer Laughlin, 6 ⅛ In. . . . 5.00
Tulip, Plate, Dinner, Homer Laughlin, 9 ⅞ In. . . . 8.00
Tulip & Rose, Saltshaker, Universal Potteries, 5 ¼ In. . . . 6.00
Tulip Time, Bowl, Vegetable, Cover, Salem China, 9 ¼ In. . . . 69.00
Vermillion Rose, Cup & Saucer, Paden City . . . 8.00
Vermillion Rose, Plate, Bread & Butter, Paden City, 6 ¼ In. . . . 3.00
Verna, Plate, Leaf Shape, Blue Ridge, 10 In. . . . 48.00
Vintage, Chop Plate, Lug Handles, Johnson Brothers, 10 ¾ x 11 ½ In. . . . 15.00
Virginia Rose, Bowl, Dessert, Homer Laughlin, 5 In. . . . 6.00
Virginia Rose, Creamer, Homer Laughlin, 3 ½ In. . . . 12.00 to 16.00
Virginia Rose, Gravy Boat, Homer Laughlin . . . 18.50
Virginia Rose, Plate, Bread & Butter, Homer Laughlin, 6 In. . . . 3.50
Virginia Rose, Plate, Salad, Homer Laughlin, 8 ¾ In. . . . 6.00 to 10.00
Virginia Rose, Sugar, Cover, Homer Laughlin, 5 In. . . . *illus* 30.00
Wheat, Creamer, Cover, Ovenproof, Salem China, 2 ⅝ In. . . . *illus* 8.00
Whimsical Christmas, Butter, Cover, Salem China, ¼ Lb. . . . 23.00
Whimsical Christmas, Chop Plate, Salem China, 12 In. . . . 42.00
Whimsical Christmas, Napkin Holder, Salem China . . . 30.00
Whimsical Christmas, Plate, Dinner, Salem China, 10 In. . . . 14.00
Whimsical Christmas, Salt & Pepper, Salem China . . . 20.00
Wild Rose, Cup & Saucer, Paden City . . . 9.00
Wild Rose, Platter, Paden City, 11 ¾ In. . . . 11.70
Wildflower, Bowl, Cereal, Knowles, 6 ¼ In. . . . 8.00
Wildflower, Cup & Saucer, Knowles . . . 9.00
Willow, Plate, Dinner, Paden City, 10 In. . . . 9.00
Willow, Platter, Round, Tab Handles, Paden City, 12 In. . . . 12.50
Windblown, Plate, Dinner, Crooksville, 10 ¼ In. . . . 12.00
Windblown, Soup, Dish, Lug Handle, Crooksville, 6 In. . . . 8.00
Windblown, Sugar, Cover, Crooksville . . . 27.50
Winter Scene, Dish, Royal China, 1953, 6 ¼ In. . . . 6.00
Woodfield, Cup & Saucer, Golden Fawn, Steubenville . . . 9.00
Woodfield, Plate, Dinner, Dove Gray, Steubenville, 10 ⅜ In. . . . 17.00
Woodfield, Snack Set, Chartreuse, Steubenville, 9-In. Plate . . . 28.00
Woodhue, Berry Bowl, Harmony House, 5 ½ In. . . . 18.00
Woodhue, Berry Bowl, Salem China, 5 In. . . . 6.00
Woodhue, Creamer, Harmony House, 4 In. . . . 30.00
Woodhue, Cup & Saucer, Salem China. . . . 7.00
Woodhue, Plate, Bread & Butter, Salem China, 6 ⅜ In. . . . 4.00
Woodhue, Sugar, Cover, Harmony House, 3 ½ In. . . . 30.00
Woodvine, Cup & Saucer, Universal Potteries . . . 10.99
Woodvine, Plate, Bread & Butter, Universal Potteries, 6 ¼ In. . . . 6.99
Woodvine, Plate, Dinner, Universal Potteries, 10 In. . . . 9.99
Woodvine, Plate, Luncheon, Universal Potteries, 9 ⅜ In. . . . 9.99
Yellow Daisy, Bowl, Dessert, Homer Laughlin, 6 ¼ In. . . . 4.00
Yellow Daisy, Bowl, Vegetable, Homer Laughlin, 9 In. . . . 10.00
Yellow Daisy, Cup & Saucer, Homer Laughlin . . . 6.00
Yellow Rose, Plate, Dinner, Paden City, 9 ¼ In. . . . 9.25

DIONNE QUINTUPLETS were born in Canada on May 28, 1934. The publicity about their birth and their special status as wards of the Canadian government made them famous throughout the world. Visitors could watch the girls play; reporters interviewed the girls and the staff. Thousands of special dolls and souvenirs were made picturing the quints at different ages. Emilie died in 1954, Marie in 1970, Yvonne in 2001. Annette and Cecile still live in Canada.

Box, Dionne Quint's Cookie, Image Of Quints In Cookies, Cardboard, 3 x 5 In. . . . 55.00
Calendar, 1947, Everybody Helps, Lipkin Furniture Store, Easton & Bethlehem, Pa., Frame . . 30.00
Card, Quintuplets Born, Topps Scoop, No. 64, 1954 . . . 478.00
Doll, Dr. Dafoe, Composition, Jointed, Madame Alexander, 1930s, 14 In. . . . 995.00
Doll, Toddler, Composition, Jointed, Sleep Eyes, Dress, Bonnet, Madame Alexander, 14 In. . . . 100.00
Doll, Yvonne, Composition, Jointed, Side-Glancing Eyes, Romper, 1936, 7 ½ In. . . . 299.00
Dolls, Bisque, Original Clothes, Embroidered Names, Flannel Pouch, Japan, 5 ½ In. . . . 425.00
Dolls, Composition, Highchair, Names On Bibs, c.1935, 7 In. . . . 748.00
Dolls, Doctor, Nurse, Composition, Bed, Madame Alexander, c.1935, 7 In., 8 Piece . . . 2588.00
Dolls, Quintuplets In Basket, Madame Alexander, 8 In. . . . *illus* 850.00
Dolls, Quintuplets, Composition, Jointed, Rocker, Madame Alexander, 1935 . . . 1495.00
Dolls, We're 2 Years Old, Dressed, Painted Features, Picture & Book, 1935, 12 In. . . . 475.00
Fan, Advertising, Family Circle, Photo Of Babies In Highchairs, 1934, 8 ¼ x 8 ⅝ In. . . . *illus* 30.00
Handkerchief, Quints Climbing Stairs, Names On Stairs, Cotton, Tom Lamb, 8 ¼ x 8 ½ In. 35.00 to 55.00
Paper Dolls, Let's Play House With The Dionne Quints, 5 Books, 1940 . . . 100.00
Postcard, Dionne Quintuplets At Callander, Ontario, Canada, 1938, Unused . . . 8.00
Soap, Pure Castile Soap, Figural, Painted, Foil Label, Austria, 3 In., 5 Piece . . . 20.00
Spoon, Cecile, Girl On Top, Name On Handle, Palmolive Premium, Carlton Silverplate . . . 30.00

DIRK VAN ERP was born in 1860 and died in 1933. He opened his own studio in 1908 in Oakland, California. He moved his studio to San Francisco in 1909 and the studio remained under the direction of his son until 1977. Van Erp made hammered copper accessories, including vases, desk sets, bookends, candlesticks, jardinieres, and trays, but he is best known for his lamps. The hammered copper lamps often had shades with mica panels.

Ashtray Stand, Copper, Hammered, Riveted Bands, 30 ½ In. . . . 660.00
Basket, Copper, Hammered, Canoe Form, Cutout & Riveted Handle, Patina, 8 x 11 In. . . . 2000.00
Bowl, Copper, Hammered, Scalloped Lip, Bronze Foot, Patina, Marked, 2 ½ x 7 In. . . . 410.00
Box, Copper, Wood, Strapwork Hinges, Pierced Plate, Brown Patina, 3 x 9 ⅞ In. . . . 2607.00
Desk Stand, Copper, Hammered, 2 Inkwell Liners, 2 ¾ x 13 ½ x 7 In. . . . 1440.00
Lamp, Copper, Hammered, 3-Panel Mica Shade, Bean Pot Form, Patina, Marked, 10 x 11 In. . 9600.00
Lamp, Copper, Hammered, 4-Panel Mica Shade, 13 x 11 ½ In. . . . 6600.00
Lamp, Copper, Hammered, 4-Panel Mica Shade, 2-Light, Impressed, 16 x 16 In. . . . 18000.00
Lamp, Copper, Hammered, 4-Panel Mica Shade, Flared, 4-Light, Patina, 21 x 19 In. . . . 1560.00
Lamp, Copper, Hammered, Mica & Copper Shade, 3-Light, Signed, 17 x 18 In. . . . 9000.00
Lamp, Copper, Hammered, Paper, 4-Panel Mica Shade, 17 ½ x 16 ¾ In. . . . *illus* 12000.00
Pitcher, Copper, Hammered, Bulbous, Dark Patina, Impressed Windmill Mark, 8 In. . . . 1304.00
Tray, Copper, Hammered, Riveted, Flat Band Handles, 11 x 22 ¼ In. . . . 1320.00
Tray, Copper, Hammered, Twisted Rope Handles, Windmill Stamp, 14 x 23 In. . . . *illus* 1880.00
Vase, Copper, Hammered, Bulbous, Flared Rim, 11 ¾ x 8 ½ In. . . . 3000.00
Vase, Copper, Hammered, Bulbous, Patina, 8 x 6 ½ In. . . . 3600.00
Vase, Copper, Hammered, Globular, Windmill Mark, 7 ¾ x 10 ½ In. . . . 3000.00
Vase, Copper, Hammered, Wide Mouth, 4 In. . . . 2040.00

DISNEYANA is a collector's term. Walt Disney and his company introduced many comic characters to the world. Collectors search for examples of the work of the Disney Studios and the many commercial products modeled after his characters, including Mickey Mouse and Donald Duck, and recent films, like *Beauty and the Beast* and *The Little Mermaid*.

Bank, Donald Duck, Dime Register, Lookie What I Saved, 1939, 2 ½ x 5 x 7 ½ In. . . . 445.00
Bank, Mickey Mouse, Beehive, Bees, Flowers, Tin, Germany, 3 In. . . . *illus* 275.00
Bank, Mickey Mouse, Book Shape, Oilcloth Over Brass, Zell, c.1930, 4 ¼ In. . . . 386.00
Bank, Mickey Mouse, Brown Shorts, White Top, Red Stockings, Aluminum, 8 ½ In. . . . 690.00
Bank, Mickey Mouse, Post Office, Minnie Holding Letter, 1930s, 6 In. . . . 464.00
Bistro Set, Mickey Mouse, Iron, Glass, Table, 2 Chairs, 24 In. Diam. . . . 104.00
Book, Mickey Mouse, Waddle, Disney Enterprise, 1934 . . . 185.00
Book, Snow White & Seven Dwarfs, Dust Jacket, 1937, 80 Pages . . . 315.00
Book Rack, Mickey & Minnie Mouse, Wood, 42 x 25 In. . . . 345.00
Bottle, Donald Duck Beverages, Contents, Walt Disney Productions, 1940s, 7 Fl. Oz. . . . 95.00
Bowl, Fantasia, Sprite, Pink Glaze, Vernon Kilns, 1940, 10 ½ x 3 In. . . . 115.00
Bulb, Donald Duck, Mickey Mouse Decal, Glass Tube, 4 In. . . . 354.00
Cabinet, Curio, Mickey Mouse, Silhouette, Silk Screen, Cut Glass, Light-Up, 81 x 23 x 14 In. . 1210.00
Camera, Mickey Mouse, Ensign Ltd., England, Box, 3 ½ In. . . . 288.00
Candy Wrapper, Mickey Mouse, Offering Premiums, 1930s . . . 75.00
Card, Mickey Mouse, Soup Tonight?, Cannibal, Overland, R162, 1930s, 5 x 7 In. . . . 2160.00
Carousel Figure, Mickey Mouse, Wood, Painted, 42 In. . . . 520.00
Carousel Figure, Pluto, Wood, Painted, Signed, Paris. W. Disney, c.1930, 30 ½ x 41 x 8 In. . . 4950.00

Dionne Quintuplets, Fan, Advertising, Family Circle, Photo Of Babies In Highchairs, 1934, 8 ¼ x 8 ⅝ In.
$30.00

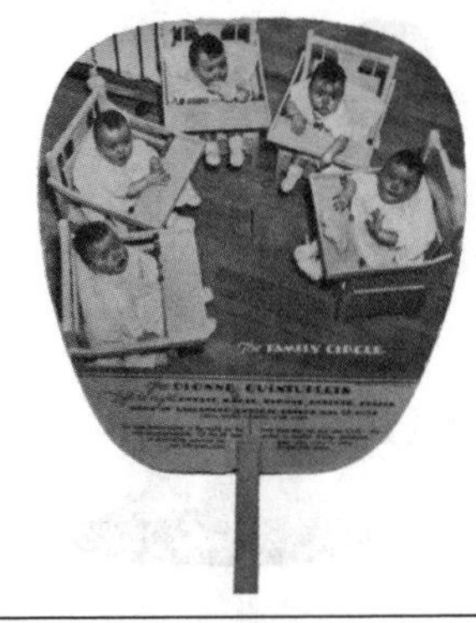

Dirk Van Erp, Lamp, Copper, Hammered, Paper, 4-Panel Mica Shade, 17 ½ x 16 ¾ In.
$12000.00

Dirk Van Erp, Tray, Copper, Hammered, Twisted Rope Handles, Windmill Stamp, 14 x 23 In.
$1880.00

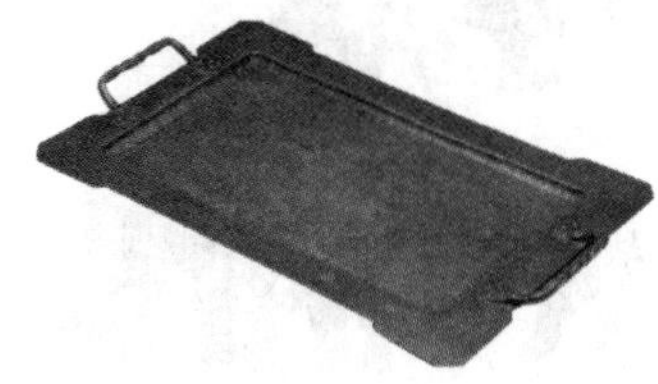

Disneyana, Bank, Mickey Mouse, Beehive, Bees, Flowers, Tin, Germany, 3 In.
$275.00

D

Disneyana, Doorstop, Donald Duck, Stop & Enter Sign, Painted, Cast Iron, Marked, 1971, 8 In.
$115.00

Disneyana, Figurine, Fantasia, Unicorn, Vernon Kilns, 6 In.
$320.00

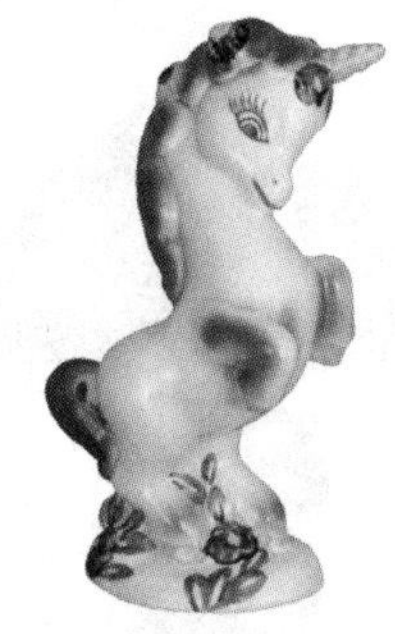

Disneyana, Marionettes, Snow White & Seven Dwarfs, Composition, Cloth, M. Alexander
$2900.00

Snow White
Many Snow White dolls, books, and figures are not based on the Disney movie. The story of Snow White and the Seven Dwarfs first appeared in *Grimm's Fairy Tales* about 1815. The Disney cartoon was released in 1937.

Cel, See Animation Art category.
Clock, Alarm, Brave Little Tailor, Minnie Kissing Mickey, Book Form, c.1938, 3 ½ x 4 In.. . . . . 12.50
Clock, Alarm, Mickey Mouse, White, US Time. 105.00
Colorforms, Mickey Mouse Club Printer Set, No. 5005, c.1962, 16 x 20 In.. . . . . 173.00
Cookie Jar, Snow White & Seven Dwarfs, Wadeheath Ware, 9 In. 118.00
Cookie Jar, Winnie The Pooh, Seated, Blue Honey Jar, California Originals 100.00
Cup & Bowl Set, Mickey & Minnie Mouse, White, Black, Box, Child's, 3 Piece 115.00
Cup & Saucer, Mickey Mouse, 2 ½ In. 31.00
Dish Set, Mickey Mouse, Red, Plastic, Safetyware, Set By Bryant Electric Co., 1930s, 3 Piece. . 575.00
Display Box, Zorro, 5 Cent, Topps, 1958. . . . . 375.00
Doll, Donald Duck, 3 Caballeros, Posable, Composition, Wood, Mexico, 12 ½ In. 1695.00
Doll, Donald Duck, Cloth, Stuffed, 1940s, 12 In. 145.00
Doll, Donald Duck, Cowboy Outfit, Cloth, Stuffed, Knickerbocker, 1940, 13 In.. . . . . 550.00
Doll, Donald Duck, Hat, Stuffed, Knickerbocker, 12 In. 270.00
Doll, Goofy, Cloth, Applied Felt Eyes, Clark, 25 In. 660.00
Doll, Jiminy Cricket, Composition, Jointed, Head, Arms, Knickerbocker, 1940, 10 In. 259.00
Doll, Joe Carioca, 3 Caballeros, Posable, Composition, Wood, Mexico, 11 In.. . . . . 1695.00
Doll, Matador, From Ferdinand The Bull, Tags, Knickerbocker, 23 In. 1600.00
Doll, Mickey & Minnie Mouse, Cloth, Applied Eyes, Clark, 17 In., Pair 1870.00
Doll, Mickey Mouse, Cowboy, Chaps, 2 Guns, Hat, Bandanna, Knickerbocker, 15 ½ In. 4888.00
Doll, Mickey Mouse, Cowboy, Pie Eyes, Stuffed, Cloth, Knickerbocker Toy Co., 16 ½ In. 863.00
Doll, Mickey Mouse, Cowboy Outfit, Cloth, Stuffed, 1930, 12 In.. . . . . 880.00
Doll, Mickey Mouse, Felt, Velveteen, Wire Inserts, Metal Eyes, Buttons, 5 ½ In. 230.00
Doll, Mickey Mouse, Pie Eyes, Composition, 10 In.. . . . . 95.00
Doll, Mickey Mouse, Silky, Metal Eyes, 6 In. 288.00
Doll, Mickey Mouse, Stuffed Velveteen, Oilcloth Eyes, Buttons, 8 In.. . . . . 344.00
Doll, Minnie Mouse, Movable Head, Arms, Legs, Felt, Plush, Franc, c.1940e, 14 In.. . . . . 664.00
Doll, Pinocchio, Composition, Wood Jointed, Painted, Molded, Felt Hat, Ideal, 1940, 11 In.. . . 403.00
Doll, Pinocchio, Wood, Jointed, Composition, Painted, Ideal, 8 ½ In.. . . . . 105.00
Doll, Pinocchio, Wood, Jointed, Painted, Composition, Oilcloth, Felt, Ideal, 7 ½ x 5 ¾ In. 55.00
Doll, Pinocchio, Wood, Red Outfit, Green Bow, Wood, Jointed, 20 In. 385.00
Doll, Snow White, Porcelain Head, Arms, Legs, Box, c.1987, 8 x 20 In.. . . . . 115.00
Doll, Snow White & Seven Dwarfs, Painted, Composition, Cloth, Knickerbocker, 8 Piece 440.00
Doll, Winnie The Pooh, Stuffed, Steiff, Signed, Dick Frantz. 250.00
Doorstop, Donald Duck, Stop & Enter Sign, Painted, Cast Iron, Marked, 1971, 8 In.. . . . *illus* 115.00
Doorstop, March Hare, Alice In Wonderland, Painted, Cast Iron, 8 ½ In. 59.00
Figurine, Big Bad Wolf, Three Little Pigs, Tin Hopper, Linemar, 1960, 4 ½ In. 201.00
Figurine, Donald Duck, Bisque, 1 ¾ In. 65.00
Figurine, Fantasia, Baby Pegasus, Frolicking In Flowers, Vernon Kilns, c.1940, 5 ¾ In.. . . . . 288.00
Figurine, Fantasia, Baby Unicorn, Sitting In Flowers, Vernon Kilns, c.1940, 4 ½ In. 115.00
Figurine, Fantasia, Centaur, Holding Grapes, Vernon Kilns, c.1940, 10 In. 696.00
Figurine, Fantasia, Centaurette, Zebra Body, Vernon Kilns, 7 ½ In. 775.00
Figurine, Fantasia, Hippo Ballerina, Hands On Hips, Vernon Kilns, c.1940, 5 ¼ In. 115.00
Figurine, Fantasia, Hippo Ballerina, Pirouette, Raised Hands, Vernon Kilns, 5 ⅜ In. 348.00
Figurine, Fantasia, Nubian Centaurette, Holding Flowers, Vernon Kilns, c.1940, 8 In. 696.00
Figurine, Fantasia, Satyr, Holding Pan Flute, Vernon Kilns, c.1940, 4 ⅝ In. 139.00
Figurine, Fantasia, Satyr, Hugging Tree Trunk Vase, Glazed Ceramic, c.1940, 5 ½ In. 115.00
Figurine, Fantasia, Satyr, Vernon Kilns, c.1940, 4 ½ In. 175.00
Figurine, Fantasia, Sprite, Sitting On Flowers, Glazed, Vernon Kilns, c.1940, 3 ¾ In. 139.00
Figurine, Fantasia, Unicorn, Vernon Kilns, 6 In. . . . . *illus* 320.00
Figurine, Ferdinand The Bull, Ceramic, Brayton Laguna, 4 x 8 x 7 In. 345.00
Figurine, Ferdinand's Ma, Brayton Laguna, c.1938, 4 x 9 ½ x 5 ¾ In.. . . . . 466.00
Figurine, Matador, Ceramic, Brayton Laguna, 8 ½ In. 1265.00
Figurine, Mickey Mouse, Painted, Composition, 1930s, 12 In. 190.00
Figurine, Mickey Mouse, Playing Violin, Bisque, Japan, c.1930, 4 In. 275.00
Figurine, Mickey Mouse, Riding Pluto, Bisque, 1930s . . . . 75.00 to 95.00
Figurine, Snow White, No. 332A, Beswick, 1954-55, 5 ½ In. 894.00
Figurine Set, Bambi, American Pottery Co., c.1947, 3 ¾ To 8 In., 5 Piece. 201.00
Figurine Set, Seven Dwarfs, Latex, Sieberling, 7 Piece 300.00
Game, Mickey Mouse, Hoop-La, Target, 3 Wood Rings, Die Cut Cardboard, 1930s, 18 ½ In.. . . 615.00
Game, Snow White & Seven Dwarfs, Milton Bradley, c.1937, 9 ½ x 19 In. 58.00
Glass Set, Snow White & Seven Dwarfs, Metal Stand, 8 Piece 110.00
Gumball Machine, Mickey Mouse, 60 Years, Stand, 47 In.. . . . . 55.00
Handkerchief, Snow White & Seven Dwarfs, Dancing, Blue, Red, Maroon, c.1938, 20 x 20 ½ In. 86.00
Hat, Donald Duck, White Mesh, Blue Trim, Signed, Clarence Nash, 1970s, 6 x 9 In. 115.00
Honey Pot, Cover, Happy, Wade Heath 127.00

Jar, Mickey Mouse, Hands On Belly, Bulbous, Brad Elser, 1930s, 3 ½ In. 403.00
Knife, Pocket, Mickey Mouse, Single Blade, Pearlized Grip, c.1930. .... 126.00
Lamp, Dopey, Snow White, Animals On Shade, c.1938, 14 In. 177.00
Lamp, Mickey Mouse, In Green Arm Chair, Plaster, 1936, 6 ½ In. 5750.00
Lamp Base, Mickey Mouse, Enamel, Pressed Steel, Painted, Soreng-Manegold, 6 ¾ In. 58.00
Lobby Card, Dumbo, Performing Elephants, 1941, 11 x 14 In. 337.00
Lunch Box, Disney Characters, Firefighters, Truck, Metal, Thermos, Plastic, 1969. .... 177.00
Lunch Box, Disney Characters, School Bus, Dome Lid, Yellow, Metal, Thermos 44.00
Lunch Box, Mary Poppins, Blue, Embossed, Metal, Thermos, Aladdin, 1964. .... 201.00
Lunch Box, Winnie The Pooh, Thermos, Aladdin, 1967 .... 75.00
Marionette, Goofy, Display, Stand, Pelham Puppets, England, 1950s, 40 In. 175.00
Marionette, Pinocchio, Wood, Painted, Ideal, 10 ½ In. 145.00
Marionette, Pluto, Display, Stand, Pelham Puppets, England, 1950s, 24 In. 167.00
Marionettes, Snow White & Seven Dwarfs, Composition, Cloth, M. Alexander .... *illus* 2900.00
Movie Projector, Mickey Mouse, Green, Keystone Mfg. Co., 11 x 7 In. 230.00
Night-Light, Dopey, Tin Lithograph, Cardboard, Battery Operated, 1938, 3 ¾ In. 209.00
Nodder, Donald Duck, Celluloid, Lead Pendulum, Metal, Windup, 1930s, 6 In. 885.00
Nodder, Donald Duck, Long Billed, Sailor Suit, Celluloid, Japan, 5 ¾ In. 230.00
Nodder, Mickey Mouse, Celluloid, Tin, Windup, 6 ½ In. 835.00
Nodder, Mickey Mouse, Guitar, Celluloid, Windup, 1930s, 6 In. 1250.00
Pail, Beach Scene, Embossed, Tin Lithograph, Ohio Art, 1930s, 5 ¾ In. 1898.00
Pail, Donald Duck, Captain, Mickey Mouse, Castaway, Tin Lithograph, Ohio Art, 1930s, 4 ¼ In. 3163.00
Pail, Mickey Mouse & Friends, Tin Lithograph, Happynak, England, 4 In. 29.00
Pencil Box, Mickey Mouse, Figural, Composition, Marked, Dixon Product, 8 ½ x 5 In. 253.00
Pillow, Mickey & Minnie Mouse, On Beach, Rat Face, 14 In. 10.00
Pitcher, Lid, Seven Dwarfs, Squirrel Finial, Ceramic, Wadeheath Ware, 8 In. 55.00
Pitcher, Snow White, Musical, Wadeheath Ware, London, 9 In. 118.00
Pitcher, Three Little Pigs, Musical, Wolf On Handle, 10 In. .... *illus* 236.00
Poster, Fantasia, Sorcerer's Apprentice, With Stokowski, Style B, 1940, 41 x 27 In. 16500.00
Poster, Goofy, How To Fish, 13 ¼ x 30 In. 230.00
Poster, Mickey Mouse, An Avalanche Of Laughter, Linen Mount, 30 x 39 ¾ In. 6900.00
Poster, Pluto, T-Bone For 2, 13 x 30 In. 379.00
Poster, Snow White & Seven Dwarfs, Dopey, 1951, 27 x 41 In. 345.00
Purse, Mickey Mouse, Leatherette, Silk Screen, Chain, Snap Closure, 4 ½ x 6 ½ In. 115.00
Purse, Mickey Mouse, Oilcloth, Strap, Metal Clasp, 4 ½ In. 115.00
Radio, Mickey Mouse, Black, Disney Characters, Die Cut, Emerson, c.1934, 7 ½ x 7 In. 863.00
Radio, Mickey Mouse, Cream, Green, Emerson, 1930s, 5 ½ x 7 ½ In. 5050.00
Radio, Mickey Mouse, Playing Cello, Emerson, 1930s, 7 x 7 In. .... *illus* 605.00
Ring, Mickey Mouse, Zuni Inlay, Red Coral Shoes, Black Ears, Legs, Turquoise Shorts, Size 2 . 690.00
Rug, Bambi, Pluto, Thumper, Flower, Multicolored, c.1950, 37 x 22 In. 100.00
Rug, Donald Duck, Nephews, Hooked, 1940s, 28 ½ x 44 ½ In. 40.00
Salt & Pepper, Fantasia, Hop Low Mushroom, Vernon Kilns, 3 ¼ In. 138.00
Salt & Pepper, Fantasia, Hop Low Mushrooms, Amber Glaze, Vernon Kilns, 1941, 4 In. 138.00
Sewing Kit, Mickey Mouse, Round, Bakelite, Soreng-Manegold, 1930s 400.00
Sheet Music, Pinocchio, 1930s. 45.00
Sheet Music, Wedding Of Mister Mickey Mouse, 9 ¾ x 12 ½ In., 8 Pages 139.00
Sign, Donald Duck Cola, Die Cut, Cardboard, Easel Back, 1950s, 22 x 26 In. .... *illus* 260.00
Sign, Mickey Mouse, Suitcase, Globe Trotters, Linen, 1930s, 17 x 21 In. 791.00
Sign, Mickey Mouse Recipe Scrapbook, Die Cut, Cardboard, c.1930, 6 x 9 ¾ In. 788.00
Sled, Mickey & Minnie Mouse, Decal, Wood, Metal Runners, 1930s, Child's. 320.00
Stringholder, Pinocchio, Plaster, Painted, WDP, 1940s, 7 x 7 In. 2114.00
Tea Set, Mickey & Minnie Mouse, Japan, Box, 1930s 320.00
Telephone, Mickey Mouse, Red, Pressed Steel, Cardboard, N.N. Hill Brass Co., 1934 .... 265.00
Toothbrush Holder, 3 Little Pigs, Ceramic, 4 ¼ In., 3 Piece 96.00
Toothbrush Holder, Donald Duck, Bisque, Japan, 1930s, 5 In. 325.00
Toothbrush Holder, Jiminy Cricket, Painted, Maw Of London, c.1940, 3 ¼ In. 345.00
Toothbrush Holder, Mickey & Minnie Mouse, Bisque, Japan, c.1930 .... 275.00
Toothbrush Holder, Mickey Mouse, Figural, Bisque, 6 In. 245.00
Toy, Bambi, Rocking Horse, Gong Bell, Painted, Wood, 18 ½ x 28 ½ In. 75.00
Toy, Cinderella, Cleaning Set, Dustpan, Broom, Sweeper, Mop, Apron, Box, Norstar, c.1947 ... 170.00
Toy, Cinderella & Prince, Dancing, Plastic, Windup, Irwin Corp., 1950s, 5 In. 115.00
Toy, Daisy Duck, Elmer Elephant, Dancing, Celluloid, Windup, Japan, 5 ¼ In. 1017.00
Toy, Disneyland, Melody Player, 4 Player Rolls, Chein, 1950s 55.00
Toy, Disneyland Express, Train, Marx, 13 x 21 In. 230.00
Toy, Doc, Dopey, Drum, Mallets, Metal, Wood, Pull Toy, Fisher-Price, No. 770, 12 In. 575.00
Toy, Donald Duck, Beak Opens, Closes, Windup, Box, Germany 550.00

Disneyana, Pitcher, Three Little Pigs, Musical, Wolf On Handle, 10 In.
$236.00

Disneyana, Radio, Mickey Mouse, Playing Cello, Emerson, 1930s, 7 x 7 In.
$605.00

Disneyana, Sign, Donald Duck Cola, Die Cut, Cardboard, Easel Back, 1950s, 22 x 26 In.
$260.00

TIP

When you go away on a driving trip, be sure to cover the window in your garage door so the missing car won't be noticed. New garage doors usually have no window at all, for security reasons.

Disneyana, Toy, Donald Duck, Walker, Tin, Windup, Lewis & Scott, Box, 11 ½ In.
$440.00

Disneyana, Toy, Mickey Mouse, Ferris Wheel, Tin, Windup, Chein, Box, 16 ½ In.
$400.00

Disneyana, Toy, Mickey Mouse, Magician, Tin, Battery Operated, Linemar, Box, 10 In.
$1650.00

Toy, Donald Duck, Dapper Donald Duck, Wood, Pull Toy, Fisher-Price, No. 460, 1936, 9 In. . . . 350.00
Toy, Donald Duck, Delivery Wagon, Tin Lithograph, Celluloid, Friction, 6 x 4 ¼ In. 575.00
Toy, Donald Duck, Dipsy Car, Nodder, Tin, Windup, Marx. 385.00 to 450.00
Toy, Donald Duck, Drummer, Tin, Windup, Marx, Box, 5 ½ In.. . . . . 465.00
Toy, Donald Duck, Duet, Windup, Marx, Box, 1940s. 890.00
Toy, Donald Duck, Fireman, Climbing, Tin, Windup, Linemar, 13 In.. 748.00
Toy, Donald Duck, Goofy, Duet, Tin, Windup, Marx 380.00
Toy, Donald Duck, Goofy, Duet, Tin Lithograph, Windup, Box, 10 ½ In.. . . . . 440.00
Toy, Donald Duck, Jack-In-The-Box, Long Bill, Paperboard, Celluloid, 1930 . . . . 425.00
Toy, Donald Duck, On Trapeze, Celluloid, George Borgfeldt, 8 ½ In.. . . . . 259.00
Toy, Donald Duck, Pluto, Handcar, No. 1107, Lionel, c.1934 . . . . 210.00
Toy, Donald Duck, Squeak, Sun Rubber Toy, Marked, 10 ½ In.. . . . . 55.00
Toy, Donald Duck, Waddles, Celluloid, Windup, Borgfeldt, 1934, 2 In. 790.00
Toy, Donald Duck, Walker, Tin, Windup, Lewis & Scott, Box, 11 ½ In. . . . . *illus* 440.00
Toy, Donald Duck, Whirligig, Windup, Platform, 1930s, 10 In.. . . . . 1450.00
Toy, Donald Duck & Minnie Mouse, Carpet Sweeper, Marked, 1940, 27 In. 185.00
Toy, Donald Duck & Pluto, Dogcart, Wood, Pull Toy, Fisher-Price, 15 In.. . . . . 791.00
Toy, Donald Duck & Pluto, Handcar, Lionel, Box, 1930s 1150.00
Toy, Dumbo, Acrobat, Tin, Windup, Marx, Box, 4 In.. . . . . 330.00
Toy, Dumbo, Carousel, Musical, Tin, Windup, Linemar, 6 In. 1265.00
Toy, Dumbo, Seated, Jumps, Flips, Tin, Windup, Marx, Box, 4 ¼ In. . . . . 350.00 to 403.00
Toy, Ferris Wheel, Tin, Windup, Chein, 1950s, 16 In.. . . . . 450.00
Toy, Goofy, Bicycle, High Wheel, Tin Lithograph, Linemar, Japan, 6 In. 1495.00
Toy, Goofy, Turns In Circle, Tail Spins, Windup, Linemar 350.00
Toy, Goofy, Walker, Tin, Windup, Linemar, Japan, 5 ¼ In.. . . . . 115.00
Toy, Jiminy Cricket, Walker, Rubber Umbrella, Tin, Windup, Linemar, 5 ½ In. 259.00
Toy, Mickey & Minnie Mouse, Celluloid, Jointed, Movable Arms, Heads, 5 ½ In. 431.00
Toy, Mickey & Minnie Mouse, Handcar, Maroon Base, No. 1100, Lionel, 1930s 200.00
Toy, Mickey & Minnie Mouse, Seated On Swings, Bisque, Wood, Painted, Folk Art. 5937.00
Toy, Mickey Mouse, 2 Mickey Dancers, Steam Engine Powered, 7 In.. 3300.00
Toy, Mickey Mouse, Acrobat, Trapeze, Celluloid, Windup, Geo. Borgfeldt Co., 9 In. 402.00
Toy, Mickey Mouse, Binoculars, Donald Duck, Pluto, Red, Yellow, Plastic, 6 x 5 In.. . . . . 35.00
Toy, Mickey Mouse, Bowling Set, 2 Extra Mice Pins, 3 Balls, Plastic, Hong Kong, 4 ½ In. 66.00
Toy, Mickey Mouse, Car, Driving, Blue, Spare Tire, Pull Toy, Fun-E-Flex, 11 & 2 ½ In. 3823.00
Toy, Mickey Mouse, Carousel, Umbrella Spins, Tin, Celluloid, Windup, Japan, 7 In. 909.00
Toy, Mickey Mouse, Circus, Mickey Ringmaster, Minnie Ballerina, Nifty, 11 In.. . . . . 2185.00
Toy, Mickey Mouse, Conductor, Minnie Mouse, Fiddle, Stand, 38 In., Pair 1210.00
Toy, Mickey Mouse, Dipsy Car, Tin, Plastic, Windup, Marx, Box, 6 In.. 435.00
Toy, Mickey Mouse, Dipsy Car, Tin, Windup, Linemar, Box, 5 ½ In.. . . . . 460.00 to 650.00
Toy, Mickey Mouse, Driver, Tin, Plastic, Windup, Marx, Box 650.00
Toy, Mickey Mouse, Drummer, Battery Operated, Linemar, Box, 11 In.. 531.00
Toy, Mickey Mouse, Drummer, Pull Toy, Fisher Price, Marked, 7 ½ In.. 288.00
Toy, Mickey Mouse, Drummer, Tin, Battery Operated, Remote Control, 10 ½ In.. . . . . 748.00
Toy, Mickey Mouse, Express Train, Circles Track, Tin, Windup, Marx, Box, 9 ¼ In.. . . . . 549.00
Toy, Mickey Mouse, Ferris Wheel, Tin, Windup, Chein, Box, 16 ½ In. . . . . *illus* 400.00
Toy, Mickey Mouse, House, Cutout, 17 x 14 In.. . . . . 115.00
Toy, Mickey Mouse, Hurdy-Gurdy, Tin Cutout, Windup, Germany, 1930, 3 x 6 x 8 In.. . . . . 9740.00
Toy, Mickey Mouse, Jazz Drummer, Plunger Operated, Germany, 6 In.. 690.00
Toy, Mickey Mouse, Magician, Tin, Battery Operated, Linemar, Box, 10 In. . . . . *illus* 1650.00
Toy, Mickey Mouse, Organ Grinder, Minnie Dances, Tin, Windup, Distler, c.1930, 6 In.. . . . . . . 5175.00
Toy, Mickey Mouse, Rattle, Clown, Celluloid, Wood, Cloth Suit, 7 ½ In. 173.00
Toy, Mickey Mouse, Riding Pluto, Tin, Windup, Linemar, 6 In. . . . . *illus* 605.00
Toy, Mickey Mouse, Robot, See Through Gears, Plastic, Windup, Gabriel. 50.00
Toy, Mickey Mouse, Roller Skater, Cloth Pants, Windup, Linemar, Japan, 6 ½ In. 374.00
Toy, Mickey Mouse, Rowboat, Removable, Green, Wood, Fun-E-Flex, 11 In. 863.00
Toy, Mickey Mouse, Santa Claus, Handcar, Tree, No. 1105, Lionel, 1930s 320.00
Toy, Mickey Mouse, Saxophone Player, Arms, Legs Move, c.1930, 6 In.. . . . . 575.00
Toy, Mickey Mouse, Tail Spins, Tin, Windup, Linemar, 5 ½ In. 127.00
Toy, Mickey Mouse, Train, Circus, Tent, Tin, Windup, Lionel, 17 x 11 In.. . . . . 4400.00
Toy, Mickey Mouse, Train Set, No. 1549, Bells, Tender, Windup, Lionel, 9 x 13 In.. . . . . 1430.00
Toy, Mickey Mouse, Tricycle, Tin, Celluloid, Windup, Linemar, 3 ¾ In.. 390.00
Toy, Mickey Mouse, Tricycle, Tin, Windup, 4 In.. . . . . 230.00
Toy, Mickey Mouse, Twirling Tail, Tin, Windup, Linemar, Box, 5 ½ In.. 525.00
Toy, Mickey Mouse, Unicyclist, Tin, Windup, Linemar, Box, 6 In. . . . . *illus* 805.00
Toy, Mickey Mouse, Walker, Tin, Windup, Johann Distler, 8 In.. . . . . 9488.00

Toy, Mickey Mouse, Washing Machine, Tin Lithograph, Electric, 10 In. 450.00
Toy, Mickey Mouse, Weather Forecaster, Mickey & Donald Duck Rotate, Plastic, 6 In.. .... 97.00
Toy, Mickey Mouse, Xylophone Player, Plastic, Tin, Windup, 6 ½ In. 190.00
Toy, Mickey Mouse & Donald Duck, Boat, Celluloid, 1930s 1250.00
Toy, Mickey Mouse & Donald Duck, Handcar, Tin, Composition, Windup, Wells, 7 In. 531.00
Toy, Minnie Mouse, Acrobat, Trapeze, Celluloid, Wire, Windup, Japan, Borgfeldt, 6 ½ In...... 230.00
Toy, Minnie Mouse, Rocking Chair, Knitting, Tin, Windup, Linemar, Box, 6 ½ In. . 489.00 to 675.00
Toy, Panchito, 3 Caballeros, Posable, Composition, Wood, Mexico, 13 In. 1695.00
Toy, Parade Roadster, Plastic Figures, Tin Lithograph, Windup, 1950s, 11 In. 518.00
Toy, Piano, Grand, Mickey & Minnie Mouse, Plastic, Lacquer, Box, Japan, 12 x 12 x 7 ½ In. . . 144.00
Toy, Pinocchio, Acrobat, Tin Lithograph, Windup, Marx 270.00
Toy, Pinocchio, No. 494, Pull Toy, Fisher-Price, 1939 .... 395.00
Toy, Pinocchio, Pushing Trunk, Plastic, Marx, 3 ½ In. 226.00
Toy, Pinocchio, Walker, Arms Move, Rubber Nose, Windup, Linemar, Box, 5 ½ In. 403.00
Toy, Pinocchio, Walker, Carrying Buckets, Windup, Marx, c.1939, 8 ½ In. .... 259.00 to 350.00
Toy, Pinocchio, Walker, Tin, Windup, Marx, Box 250.00
Toy, Pluto, Acrobat, Linemar, Box, 12 In. 165.00
Toy, Pluto, Acrobat, Plastic, Windup, Gem Toys, Linemar, Box, 9 In.. .... 450.00
Toy, Pluto, Disney Kart, Tin, Friction, Marked, Marx, Box, 7 x 6 In. 135.00
Toy, Pluto, Drum Major, Rings Bell, Waves, Horn, Tin, Windup, Marx, 6 ½ In. 258.00
Toy, Pluto, Head Bobs, Tail Spins, Tin, Windup, Linemar. 350.00
Toy, Pluto, Head Bobs, Tail Spins, Tin, Windup, Linemar, Box. 450.00
Toy, Pluto, Holding Cane, Bell, Rubber Tail, Tin Lithograph, Windup, 6 x 3 In.. .... 33.00
Toy, Pluto, Jaguar Car, Tin, Celluloid, Friction, Linemar, Japan, 5 ½ In.. .... 575.00
Toy, Pluto, Jumper, Squeeze Controller, Tin Lithograph, Linemar, Box, 5 In. 345.00
Toy, Pluto, Lantern, Battery Operated, Linemar, Box 385.00
Toy, Pluto, Mysterious, Tail Lever, Tin Lithograph, Friction, Marx, Box, 9 In.. .... 330.00
Toy, Pluto, Playful, Tin, Windup, Linemar, Box, 6 In. .... *illus* 230.00
Toy, Pluto, Pulling Cart, Rubber Tires, Tin, Friction, Linemar, 1950s, 8 ½ In. 245.00
Toy, Pluto, Pulls Donald Duck In Cart, Wood, Paper Lithograph, Pull Toy, Fisher-Price, 15 In. 791.00
Toy, Pluto, Slinky, Tin, Windup, Linemar, 7 In.. .... 690.00
Toy, Pluto, Stretchy, Tin, Rubber, Windup, Marked, Linemar, Box, 7 In. 550.00
Toy, Pluto, Tail Spins, Tin, Windup, Linemar, 4 ½ In. .... 403.00 to 650.00
Toy, Pluto, Tin Ears, Collar, Rubber Tail, Nose, Metal Tongue, Windup, Linemar, Japan, 7 In. . 403.00
Toy, Pluto, Top Hat, Horn, Bells, Windup, Plastic, Built-In Key, 1950s, 10 In.. .... 173.00
Toy, Pluto, Tricycle, Bell Ringer, Tin, Celluloid, Windup, Box, Linemar, 3 ¼ In. ... 450.00 to 595.00
Toy, Pluto, Tricycle, Tin, Celluloid, Windup, Linemar, Box, 4 In. 450.00
Toy, Pluto, Tricycle, Tin, Windup, Marx, Box, 3 ¾ In.. .... 220.00
Toy, Pluto, Wise Pluto, Tin, Rubber, Windup, Marx, Box, 8 ¼ In. 275.00
Toy, Pluto, Wood, Painted, Fun-E-Flex, 3 ½ In.. .... 40.00
Toy, Professor Von Drake, Fake Fur Hair, Tin Lithograph, Linemar, Box, 6 In. 345.00
Toy, Snow White, Rattle, Dopey, Pink Bow, 2-Sided, Celluloid, 6 ¾ x 3 ½ In. 40.00
Toy, Snow White, Truck, Van, Trailer, Friction, Linemar, 12 In. 1035.00
Toy, Snow White & Seven Dwarfs, Carpet Sweeper, Marked, 1938, 27 In. 185.00
Toy, Thumper, Marx, Hong Kong, 1950s, 15 In. 10.00
Tricycle, Mickey Mouse, Pressed Steel, Colson Plate, 22 In.. .... 1035.00
Trivet, Tile, Mickey & Minnie Mouse, Cooking, 6 x 4 In. 19.00
Tumbler, Mickey Mouse, Safari, McDonald's Millennium, c.2000, 4 ½ In.. .... 10.00
Walking Stick, Mickey Mouse's Head, Wood, Hand Painted, 34 ½ In. 100.00
Wall Sconce, Mickey & Minnie Mouse, Amber, 1930s, 5 In. 115.00
Watch, Pocket, Mickey Mouse, Fob, Ingersoll, 1930s 575.00
Watch Fob, Mickey Mouse, Silvered Brass, Leather, Ingersoll, 1 ⅜ In. 153.00
Watering Can, Snow White & Seven Dwarfs, Tin Lithograph, Ohio Art, 1938, 6 ½ In. 556.00
Wrapper, Gum, Snow White, 1 Cent, Dietz Gum Co., 1938, 2 ⅝ In. 5.00
Wrapping Paper, Disney Characters, Blue, White, 1930s, 1 Sheet 100.00
Wristwatch, Bambi, Chrome Case, Animated Ears, Ingersoll, Box, c.1949 .... 277.00
Wristwatch, Cinderella, Chrome Case, Plastic Slipper, Box, c.1950 .... 124.00
Wristwatch, Daisy Duck, Animated Arms, Chrome Case, Instructions, c.1949 .... 300.00
Wristwatch, Daisy Duck, Pink Face, c.1940. .... 131.00
Wristwatch, Mickey Mouse, Black Leather Band, Ingersoll, Box, 1934 .... 150.00 to 200.00
Wristwatch, Mickey Mouse, Link Band, Charms, Girls, Ingersoll, Box, 1937. .... 3056.00
Wristwatch, Mickey Mouse, Metal Link Band, Deluxe, Ingersoll, c.1937 .... 2530.00
Wristwatch, Mickey Mouse, Metal Link Band, Ingersoll, c.1933. .... 1228.00
Wristwatch, Mickey Mouse, Red Vinyl Band, Ingersoll, Box 140.00
Wristwatch, Mickey Mouse, Silver, Ingersoll, c.1930. .... 66.00
Wristwatch, Snow White, Red Cloth Band, Magic Mirror Stand, Ingersoll 150.00

Disneyana, Toy, Mickey Mouse, Riding Pluto, Tin, Windup, Linemar, 6 In.
$605.00

D

Disneyana, Toy, Mickey Mouse, Unicyclist, Tin, Windup, Linemar, Box, 6 In.
$805.00

Disneyana, Toy, Pluto, Playful, Tin, Windup, Linemar, Box, 6 In.
$230.00

Doll, Automaton, Harpist, Harp, Cylinder Movement, Plays Mignon Gavotte, 14 In. $504.00

Doll, Effanbee, Patsy, Composition, Wardrobe, 14 In. $440.00

Top Ten Dolls

Hundreds of thousands of users visit our website, Kovels.com, each month. The makers of dolls that are the most popular among our visitors are:

1. Madame Alexander
2. Effanbee
3. Mattel
4. Simon Halbig
5. Heubach Koppelsdorf
6. Ideal
7. Norah Wellings
8. Buddy lee
9. Horsman
10. Schoenau Hoffmeister

DOCTOR, *see Dental and Medical categories.*

DOLL entries are listed by marks printed or incised on the doll, if possible. If there are no marks, the doll is listed by the name of the subject or country or maker. Notice that Barbie is listed under Mattel. G.I. Joe figures are listed in the Toy section. Eskimo dolls are listed in the Eskimo section and Indian dolls are listed in the Indian section. Doll clothes and accessories are listed at the end of this section. The twentieth-century clothes listed here are in mint condition.

A.M., 231, Fany, Bisque, Large Ears, Eyebrows, Glass Sleep Eyes, Composition, 18 In. 9200.00
A.M., 233, Nobbi Kid, Bisque Socket Head, Sleep Eyes, 5-Piece Composition Body, Box, 7 In. . . 730.00
A.M., 253, Googly Eyes, Watermelon Slice Mouth, Painted Lashes, Composition, 6 ½ In. 900.00
A.M., 253, Watermelon Slice Mouth, Googly, Sleep Eyes, Blond Wig, 12 In. 2475.00
A.M., 323, Bisque Socket Head, Googly Eyes, 5-Piece Body, 1920, 11 In. 1290.00
A.M., Baby Gloria, Bisque Head, Jointed, Cloth Body, Bonnet, 12 ½ In. 316.00
A.M., Bisque, Closed Mouth, Dome Head, Blue Eyes, 5-Piece Composition Body, Boy, 8 ⅜ In. . . 178.00
A.M., Bisque Shoulder Head, Glass Eyes, Brown Wig, Kid Body, Bisque Hands, 23 In. 119.00
A.M., Darling, Bisque Shoulder Head, Glass Eyes, Red Mohair, Kid Body, Cloth Legs, 21 ¼ In. . 119.00
A.M., Dream Baby, Black Bisque, Closed Mouth, Sleep Eyes, Painted Hair, Clenched Fist, 15 In. 460.00
A.M., Florodora, Stick Body, 11 In. 150.00
A.M., Googly Fixed Brown Glass Eyes, Closed Mouth, Composition, 11 ½ In. 863.00
Aboriginals, Wednesday, Addams Family, Cloth, Yarn Hair, FAO Schwarz, c.1962, 19 In. 403.00
Advertising, Buddy Lee, Cowboy, Composition, Original Outfit, Outdoor Clothier, Idaho, 12 ½ In. 98.00
Advertising, Cox's Gelatine, Cloth, Feed Sack, Boy Wearing Kilt, 14 x 6 ½ In. 100.00
Advertising, Kellogg's, Goldilocks & The 3 Bears, Premium, Printed Cloth, 9 ¾ To 12 ¾ In. . . 356.00
Advertising, Miss Korn-Krisp, Cloth, Feed Sack, Brown Hair, White Outfit, 1900, 23 In. 176.00
Advertising, Taco Bell Chihuahua, Talking, 1990, 6 In. 15.00
Alexander dolls are listed in this category under Madame Alexander.
Alt Beck & Gottschalck, 1361-59, Open Mouth, Blue Sleep Eyes, 25 In. 431.00
Alt Beck & Gottschalck, Bisque Head, Straight Hair, Bow, Ball-Jointed, 23 In. 144.00
American Character, Betsy McCall, Little Cook, Dress, Apron, Socks, Shoes, Pots & Cake Pans, 1962 170.00
American Character, Sweet Sue, Hard Plastic, 23 In. 63.00
Armand Marseille dolls are listed in this category under A.M.
Automaton, Barber, Parted Hair, 28 x 14 x 14 In. 198.00
Automaton, Bebe Poudreuse, Woman, Puff, Mirror, Melody, Keywind, France, c.1890, 21 In. . 3873.00
Automaton, Clown, Balances Bird On Nose, 28 x 12 x 8 In. 330.00
Automaton, Clown, Circus, Expands, Deflates, Electric, 27 x 27 x 18 In. 1200.00
Automaton, Clown, Circus, Performs Magic Act, Musical, 36 x 19 x 13 In. 2520.00
Automaton, Clown, Circus, Plays Accordion, 26 In. 1020.00
Automaton, Clown Band, Horn, Fiddler, Violinist, Drummer, Accordionist, 96 x 56 x 34 In. . . 5850.00
Automaton, Cow, Gray, White, Collar, Bell, 28 x 10 x 10 In. 300.00
Automaton, Dairy Cow, Maid Milks, Moves Ears, Head, Tail, Sleep Eyes, 67 x 38 x 36 In. 3053.00
Automaton, Doctor, Man, Mustache, Tie, 39 x 12 x 10 In. 198.00
Automaton, Farmer, Dancing, Accordion, Papier-Mache Head, Roullet & Decamps, 21 ½ In. . 5629.00
Automaton, Fiddler, Bisque Head, Holding Violin, Pull Toy, Germany, 12 ½ In. 1541.00
Automaton, Girl, Standing At Piano, 2 Tunes, Roullet & Decamps, 16 ½ In. 10665.00
Automaton, Harpist, Harp, Cylinder Movement, Plays Mignon Gavotte, 14 In. . . . . *illus* 504.00
Automaton, Laughing Sal, Jiggles, Laughs, Speakers, Amusement Park, 80 x 36 x 36 In. 7079.00
Automaton, Loom Worker, Glass & Wood Case, c.1880, 11 x 8 In. 518.00
Automaton, Man, Smoking Cigar, Raises Leg, Wood Lithograph, 1800s, 14 ½ x 8 In. 1650.00
Automaton, Monkeys, Trying To Open Crate, 18 x 27 x 12 In. 1150.00
Automaton, Parrot, Nods, 34 x 12 x 12 In. 218.00
Automaton, Pizza Man, Makes Pizza, Kneads, Rolls Dough, Throws Pizza, 24 x 20 x 14 In. . . 300.00
Automaton, Poodle, Stands On Hind Legs, Pirouettes, 29 x 12 x 12 In. 300.00
Automaton, Professor, Vest, Bowtie, Animal, 20 x 15 x 10 In. 330.00
Automaton, Rabbit, In Cabbage, Ears Twitch, Chomps, Austria, 9 In. 2875.00
Automaton, Skiing Snowman, Carrot Nose, Red Gloves, Blue Hat, 24 x 22 x 26 In. 300.00
Automaton, The Magician, Gypsy Shell Game, c.1880, 8 ½ x 8 ½ x 17 In. 840.00
Automaton, Woman, Man, Baton, Papier-Mache, Pianoforte, Rosewood Platform, 13 x 7 In. . 6500.00
Averill, Bonnie Babe, Bisque, 2 Teeth, Glass Eyes, Jointed Limbs, 1925, 4 ½ In. 863.00
Barbie dolls are listed in this category under Mattel.
Bartenstein, 2 Faces, Wax Over Papier-Mache, Cap, Laughs, Cries, Glass Eyes, 15 In. 115.00
Bergmann dolls are also in this category under Simon & Halbig.
Bergmann, China Head, Composition Body, Jointed, Hat, Parasol, Pearl Inlay, 28 In. 316.00
Bild Lilli, Blond Ponytail, Painted Earrings, Shoes, Black Dress, Brass Stand, 7 In. 1045.00
Bisque, Open Mouth, Weighted Eyes, Blond Mohair, Composition, Jointed, Child, 21 In. 326.00
Bisque, Paperweight Eyes, Painted Features, Straight Wrist, 9 ½ In. 5750.00
Bisque Socket Head, Blue Glass Eyes, Composition, Jointed, Boy, 13 In. 178.00

Bisque Socket Head, Brown Complexion, Sleep Eyes, Mohair, Bent Limb, Baby, Germany, 18 In. 3000.00
Bisque Socket Head, Sleep Eyes, Mohair, Composition, Wood, Jointed Limbs, On Swing, 11 In. 650.00
Borgfeldt, German, Bisque Head, Jointed Body, Short Dress, G.B. Mark, Germany, 22 In. 69.00
Boy, Molded Head, Cloth Body, Wispy Hair, Painted, Germany, 1850, 23 In. 920.00
Bruckner, Topsyturvy, Betty & Topsy, Cloth, Black & White, Molded Mask Face, 12 In.. .... 225.00
Bye-Lo, Bisque, Painted, Molded, Blue Sleep Eyes, Mohair Wig, Jointed Limbs, 1925, 4 ½ In. . 978.00
Bye-Lo, Bisque Flange Head, Blue Glass Sleep Eyes, Cloth Body, 12 In. .... 69.00 to 77.00
Bye-Lo, Bisque Swivel Head, Sleep Eyes, Jointed, 5 In. 500.00
Bye-Lo, Flange Neck, Blue Glass Sleep Eyes, Cloth Body, Celluloid Hands, K&K Pin, 13 ½ In. . 173.00
China Head, Wavy Hair, Cloth Body, Leather Forearms, Pleated Pants, Boy, 1860s, 20 In. 1265.00
China Shoulder Head, Dolley Madison, Molded Hair & Bow, Painted Eyes, Cloth Body, 25 In. 390.00
Cloth, 1-Piece Gusseted Head & Torso, Oil Painted, Homespun Dress, 34 In.. .... 441.00
Cloth, Amish, 3-Piece Head, Band Neck & Torso, Attached Limbs, 16 In. 59.00
Cloth, Amish, Penciled Features, Black Velvet Bonnet, Dress, Apron, Mid 1900s, 26 In.. ...... 345.00
Cloth, Brown Complexion, Painted Features, Button Eyes, Bandanna, c.1940, 19 In.. .... 700.00
Cloth, Feed Sack, Blond Hair, White Outfit, 1900, 24 x 10 In. 66.00
Cloth, Muslin, Painted, Stitch-Jointed, c.1893, 30 In. 2128.00
Cloth, Oil Painted, Jointed, Clothes, c.1900, 13 In.. .... 8800.00
Cloth, Oil Painted Stockinet Head, Muslin Body, Painted Lower Limbs, 14 In.. .... 2252.00
Cloth, Painted Features, Stitch-Jointed Body, c.1910, 24 In. 2576.00
Cloth, Stockinet Face, Oil Painted, Blue Eyes, Stitch-Jointed, 17 In. 178.00
Cloth, Uncle Wiggily Longears, Painted Linen Face, Movable Head, c.1943, 22 In. 288.00
Cloth, Yellow Kid, Composition Head, Big Ears, Open Mouth, 2 Teeth, 13 In. 1670.00
Cowgirl, Hard Plastic, 19 In. 173.00
Demalcol, Googly Blue Glass Eyes, Looking Left, Smiling Mouth, Composition Body, 9 In. ... 489.00
Door Of Hope, Amah, Child On Back, Carved Braid, 2-Piece Gray Blue Costume, 10 ½ In.. .. 2645.00
Door Of Hope, Amah, Painted Hair, Carved Bun, White Tunic, Slippers, 11 In. 690.00
Door Of Hope, Boy, Pearwood Head, Hands, Cloth Body, Silk Outfit, 1910, 6 ½ In. 1610.00
Door Of Hope, Bride & Groom, Elaborate Costumes, 11 ½ In., Pair 2013.00
Door Of Hope, Bride & Groom, Pearwood Head, Cloth Body, Outfit, 1910, 12 In., Pair 3162.00
Door Of Hope, Groom, Wood, Carved, China, c.1930, 12 In. 1150.00
Door Of Hope, Rice Farmer, Carved Hair, Wooden Legs, Bamboo Skirt & Shawl, 12 ½ In. ... 1140.00
Dressel, Admiral Dewey, Bisque Socket Head, Painted, Composition, 5-Piece Body, 14 In. 2100.00
Dressel, Character, Open Mouth, Blue Glass Eyes, Mohair Wig, c.1920, 20 In. 288.00
Dressel, Papier-Mache, Blue Glass Eyes, Curly Mohair Wig, Muslin Body, Marked Holz-Masse, 26 In. 431.00
Effanbee, American Child, Composition, Painted Eyes, Hair Wig, Dewees Cochran, 1936-39, 20 In. 2070.00
Effanbee, American Child, Composition, Sleep Eyes, Hair Wig, Dewees Cochran, 1940, 17 In. 1035.00
Effanbee, American Child, Composition, Sleep Eyes, Hair Wig, Dewees Cochran, 1940, 20 In. 990.00
Effanbee, Little Lady, Composition, Sleep Eyes, Blond Wig, Jointed, 17 ½ In. 119.00
Effanbee, Patsy, Composition, Wardrobe, 14 In. .... *illus* 440.00
Effanbee, Patsy Ann, Composition, Green Sleep Eyes, Brown Molded Hair, 1930, 19 In.. ..... 115.00
Effanbee, Patsy Ann, Composition, Jointed, Green Sleep Eyes, Blond Wig, 1935, 19 ½ In. 575.00
Effanbee, Patsy Jr., Composition, Painted Eyes, Molded Hair, Checked Dress, Box, 1930, 11 In. 345.00
Effanbee, Skippy Aviator, Composition, Original Outfit, Goggles, 14 In. 690.00
Effanbee, Skippy Baseball Player, Composition Head, Arms, Painted, Cloth Body, 1930, 14 In. 1840.00
Effanbee, Skippy Fireman, Composition Head, Arms, Legs, Painted, Cloth Body, 1930, 14 In.. 1035.00
Emma Clear, Bride & Groom, Molded Hair, Cloth Body, Parian, 1940s, 2 Piece .... *illus* 500.00
Fashion, Bisque Head, Shoulder Plate, Kid Body, 15 In. 173.00
Fashion, Bisque Shoulder Head, Blue Glass Eyes, Leather Body, Barrois Style, 1870s, 18 In. .. 2588.00
Fashion, Papier-Mache, Pauline, Shoulder Head, Glass Eyes, Human Hair Wig, 20 In. 748.00
Fashion, Swivel Cup & Saucer Neck, Blue Glass Eyes, Wool Wig, Leather Body, 1870s, 21 In. . 2185.00
Faultier, Bisque, Paperweight Eyes, Gusseted Kid, Parasol, Fashion, 29 In. 2300.00
Freundlich, General Douglas MacArthur, Composition, Holding Flag, 19 In. .... *illus* 50.00
Frozen Charlotte, Black Hair, Original Clothes, Shoes, 4 ½ In. 125.00
G.I. Joe figures are listed In the Toy category.
Gebruder Heubach, dolls may also be listed in this category under Heubach.
Gebruder Heubach, 8723, Einco, Bisque Socket Head, Googly Eyes, Composition, 1912, 11 In. 5680.00
Gebruder Heubach, 8759, Bisque, Sculpted Hair, Pin-Jointed Body, Baby, c.1910, 15 In. 3136.00
Gebruder Heubach, Bisque, Aged Woman, Brown Complexion, White Mohair, 13 In. 5250.00
Gebruder Heubach, Black Bisque, Intaglio Eyes, Molded Hair, Bent Limb, Baby, 10 In. 1380.00
Gebruder Heubach, Blue Glass Sleep Eyes, Pouty, Jointed Wood, Composition, 14 ½ In. 1035.00
Gebruder Heubach, Blue Glass Sleep Eyes, Pouty Mouth, Bent-Limb Body, 9 ½ In. 230.00
Gebruder Heubach, Brown Glass Eyes, Jointed Wood, Composition Body, 10 ¾ In.. .... 1265.00
Gebruder Heubach, Pouty, Blue Glass Sleep Eyes, Mohair Wig, Jointed, 11 ½ In. 518.00
Gebruder Heubach, Whistling Boy, Bisque Head, Molded, Painted, Pursed Mouth, 13 ½ In. . 978.00
Gebruder Heubach, Wood & Composition, Molded & Painted Features, 15 In. 230.00

Doll, Emma Clear, Bride & Groom, Molded Hair, Cloth Body, Parian, 1940s, 2 Piece
$500.00

Doll, Freundlich, General Douglas MacArthur, Composition, Holding Flag, 19 In.
$50.00

TIP

If your doll's body leaks sawdust, try patching the hole by putting a few drops of clear glue in the hole. If the hole is too large, patch it with a piece of muslin or kid cut from an old glove. Cut a circular patch, glue in place.

D

Doll, Ideal, Gabby, Composition, Posable, Ideal, 1939, 10 In.
$220.00

Doll, Ideal, King Little, Gulliver's Travels, Composition, Wood, Jointed, Paramount, 1939, 12 In.
$330.00

Doll, Ideal, Toni, Plastic Head, Sleep Eyes, Brunette, Hairpins, No. P-19, Box, 19 In.
$660.00

Gebruder Kuhnlenz, Bisque, Blue Glass Eyes, Mohair, Composition, Jointed, 17 ¾ In. 178.00
German, American Schoolboy, Bisque Shoulder Head, Glass Eyes, Painted Hair, Cloth Body, 15 In. 230.00
German, Bisque Head, Ball-Jointed, Dressed, B.4 Mark, 22 In. 126.00
German, Bisque Head, Glass Sleep Eyes, Muslin, Celluloid Hands, c.1923, 18 In. 3024.00
German, Bisque Shoulder Head, Glass Eyes, Pierced Ears, Mohair, Jointed Kid Body, 15 In. .. 504.00
German, Bisque Shoulder Head, Glass Eyes, Pierced Ears, Mohair, Jointed Kid Body, 23 In. .. 148.00
German, Bisque Socket Head, Glass Sleep Eyes, Human Hair Wig, Composition, c.1918, 28 In. 1064.00
German, Bisque Swivel Head, Glass Eyes, Mohair Wig, Leather Body, Incised 154, 18 In. 660.00
German, Lappifats, Boy & Girl, Bisque, Painted, Molded Clothes, 1920, 4 In., Pair 230.00
German, Porcelain, Painted Hair, Spiral Thread Detailing, c.1880, 15 In. 616.00
German, Porcelain Flat Head, Sculpted Curly Hair, Cloth Body, Leather Arms, Dress, 21 In. .. 52.00
German, Porcelain Head, Curly Hair, Cloth Body, Calf-Length Dress, Black Shoes, 26 In. 115.00
German, Porcelain Head, Sculpted, Curly Hair, Cloth Body, Jointed, Bisque Hands, 29 In. 403.00
German, Porcelain Head, Sculpted Curly Hair, Cloth Body, Corset, 23 In. 23.00
Gilber & Toys, Honey West, TV Private Eye-Full, Box, 11 ½ In. 275.00
Half Dolls are listed in the Pincushion Doll category.
Handwerck, 79, Bisque Head, Compositon Jointed Body, 15 ½ In. 800.00
Handwerck, Bisque, Open Mouth, Glass Eyes, Curly Mohair, Composition, Jointed, 27 In. ... 830.00
Handwerck, Bisque, Open Mouth, Weighted Eyes, Mohair, Composition, Jointed, 7 ½ In. 444.00
Hartmann, 283HC, Blue Glass Sleep Eyes, Wood, Composition, Head Incised, Child, 22 In. .. 230.00
Herman Toys, Pee Wee Herman, Plush Body, Vinyl Head, Hands & Shoes, Gray Suit, 1989, 40 In. 255.00
Hertel Schwab, 172, Bisque Socket Head, Googly Eyes, Composition, Jointed, Jubilee, 16 In. . 8900.00
Hertel Schwab, Bisque Head, Open Mouth, Glass Eyes, Jointed Wood, Composition, Child, 26 ½ In. 259.00
Hertwig, Bertha, Porcelain Head, Sculpted, Curly Hair, Cloth Body, Formal Dress, Germany, 29 In. 92.00
Heubach, Bisque, Open Mouth, Weighted Glass Eyes, Composition, Bent Limbs, 11 In. 148.00
Heubach, See Also Gebruder Heubach.
Hol-Le Toy Co., Daisy Mae, Cloth, Polka-Dot Blouse, Copyright UFS Hol-Le Toy Co., 1950, 21 In. 195.00
Horsman, Baby Brother, Composition, Metal Eyes, Molded, Painted Hair, Cloth Limbs, 22 In. 59.00
Horsman, Babyland Rag, Cloth, Painted Features, Blond Wig, Brown Eyes, 1900, 20 In. 230.00
Horsman, Babyland Rag, Cloth, Painted Features, Blond Wig, Brown Eyes, Shoes, 1900, 30 In. 690.00
Horsman, Patty Duke, With Telephone, Facsimile Signature, United Artists Television, 1965, 7 In. 350.00
Ideal, Deanna Durbin, Green Eyes, Open Mouth, Upper Teeth, Brown Hair, 1950, 21 In. 805.00
Ideal, Gabby, Composition, Posable, Ideal, 1939, 10 In. ...... *illus* 220.00
Ideal, Judy Garland, As Dorothy, Composition, Hair Wig, Costume, Marked, 18, 1939, 18 In. .. 2070.00
Ideal, King Little, Gulliver's Travels, Composition, Wood, Jointed, Paramount, 1939, 12 In. ..... *illus* 330.00
Ideal, Little Honeymoon, Dick Tracy Jr.'s Daughter, Cries, Hair Can Be Washed, 1965, 19 In. .. 310.00
Ideal, Mr. Magoo, Green Coat, Red, Hat, Scarf, Stuffed, 1962, 14 In. 35.00
Ideal, Pebbles, Flintstones, Box, 14 ½ x 8 In. 75.00
Ideal, Toni, Plastic Head, Sleep Eyes, Brunette, Hairpins, No. P-19, Box, 19 In. ...... *illus* 660.00
Indian dolls are listed In the Indian category.
Ives, Baby, Composition, Cloth, Creeping, Mechanical, c.1890, 11 In. ...... *illus* 173.00
J.D.K. dolls are also listed in this category under Kestner.
Jumeau, Bisque, Cork Pate, Paperweight Eyes, Blond Hair, Composition, Jointed, 18 ¼ In. ... 5333.00
Jumeau, Bisque, Paperweight Eyes, Blond Mohair, Papier-Mache, Voice Box, 16 ½ In. 5629.00
Jumeau, Bisque Head, Closed Mouth, Brown Paperweight Eyes, Painted Face, Brown Wig, 25 In. 1495.00
Jumeau, Bisque Head, Composition Jointed Body, Bebe, Printemps, 25 In. 1900.00
Jumeau, Bisque Head, Open Mouth, Teeth, Composition, Black, Gypsy, 14 In. 3300.00
Jumeau, Bisque Head, Pressed, Paperweight Eyes, Mohair, Papier-Mache, Ball-Jointed, 24 In. 8295.00
K * R, 114, Gretchen, Bisque, Pouty Mouth, Eyes, Mohair, Composition, Ball-Jointed, 18 ½ In. 3200.00
K * R, 115, Bisque, Domed Socket Head, Composition, Wood Ball-Jointed, Toddler, Boy, 14 In. 3300.00
K * R, 116A, Bisque Socket Head, Sleep Eyes, Wood, Composition, Mohair Wig, Toddler, 18 In. 1840.00
K * R, 131, Googly, Blue Glass Eyes, Jointed, Wood, Composition, Human Wig, Toddler, 15 ½ In. 5750.00
K * R, 34, Flapper, Sleep Eyes, Papier-Mache Body, Suitcase, Accessories, 14 In. ...... *illus* 800.00
K * R, Bisque, Brown Glass Sleep Eyes, Mohair Bobbed Wig, Baby, 15 In. 173.00
K * R, Bisque, Composition, Flirty Eye, 25 In. 295.00
K * R, Bisque, Jointed Body, Clothes, Floral Print Presentation Box 1380.00
K * R, Bisque, Molded Painted Hair, Brown Glass Sleep Eyes, Baby, 19 ½ In. 863.00
K * R, Bisque, Painted Eyes, Mohair, Composition, 5-Piece Jointed, Child, 8 ¾ In. 2607.00
K * R, Blue Glass Sleep Eyes, Open Mouth, Jointed Body, Toddler, 15 In. 633.00
Kathe Kruse, Cloth, Painted Features, Muslin Body, Jointed Arms, Disc-Jointed Hips, 16 In. .. 5250.00
Kathe Kruse, Cloth Head, Painted Features, Jointed Hips, Shoulders, Sculpted Hands, Feet, 16 In. 3300.00
Kathe Kruse, Socket Head, Painted Features, Human Hair, Cloth, Jointed Shoulders, Hips, 18 In. 1100.00
Kathe Kruse, Weighted Head, Auburn Hair, Intaglio Eyes, c.1914, 16 ½ In. 1645.00
Kathe Kruse, Weighted Head, Painted Features, Cloth, Stitched Hands, Separate Thumb, 17 In. 5925.00
Kestner, 143, Bisque Head, Sleep Eyes, Teeth, Wig, Jointed Composition Body, 1900, 9 In. 920.00
Kestner, 150, Bisque, Sleep Eyes, Open Mouth, 9 In. 550.00

Kestner, 171, Bisque Socket Head, Sleep Eyes, Mohair, Composition, Wood, Child, 15 In. 1064.00
Kestner, 221, Bisque Socket Head, Googly Eyes, Mohair, Composition, Wood, Ball-Jointed, 11 In. 5600.00
Kestner, 221, Bisque Socket Head, Googly Eyes, Mohair, Composition, Wood, Jointed, 17 In... 12300.00
Kestner, 257, Bisque, Composition, 16 In. 1121.00
Kestner, 257, Bisque Head, Open Mouth, Teeth, Wobble Tongue, Baby 1000.00
Kestner, Bisque, Open Mouth, Glass Eyes, Mohair, Composition, Jointed, Child, 31 ¾ In. 593.00
Kestner, Bisque, Open Mouth, Teeth, Tongue, Glass Eyes, Mohair, Composition, Bent Limbs, 11 In. 178.00
Kestner, Bisque, Square Teeth, Glass Eyes, Blond Mohair, 5-Piece Jointed Body, 9 In.. .... 2963.00
Kestner, Bisque Head, Brown Eyes, Mohair Wig, Composition, 14 ½ In. 700.00
Kestner, Bisque Head, Composition, Ball-Jointed, 19 In.. .... 119.00
Kestner, Bisque Head, Sleep Eyes, Mohair Wig, Jointed Composition Body, 1895, 10 In....... 1495.00
Kestner, Bisque Shoulder Head, Glass Eyes, Blond Hair, Jointed Kid Body, Bisque Hands, 17 ¼ In.. 119.00
Kestner, Bisque Socket Head, Painted Hair, Glass Sleep Eyes, Bent Limb Body, c.1914, 12 In. . 1680.00
Kestner, Bisque Socket Head, Sleep Eyes, Mohair, Composition, Wood-Jointed, Boy, 19 In. ... 3900.00
Kestner, Blue Glass Sleep Eyes, Open Mouth, Mohair Wig, Child, 17 In. 431.00
Kestner, Gibson Girl, Bisque Shoulder Head, Mohair, Plaster Pate, Jointed Kid Body, 18 ½ In. 1659.00
Kestner, Open Mouth, 2 Upper Teeth, Blue Glass Sleep Eyes, Jointed Body, 16 In. 431.00
Kestner, Plaster Pate, Brown Glass Sleep Eyes, Open Mouth, Child, 23 ½ In.. .... 201.00
Kewpie dolls are listed in the Kewpie category.
Kley & Hahn, 18, Walkure, Blue Glass Sleep Eyes, Open Mouth, Human Hair Wig, 34 In..... 1150.00
Kley & Hahn, 549, Bisque Head, Sleep Eyes, Mohair, Composition, 18 ½ In.. .... 2607.00
Kley & Hahn, Bisque, Weighted Glass Eyes, Mohair, Composition, Jointed, 18 ⅝ In. 296.00
Knickerbocker, Little Lulu, Cloth, Red Dress, Premium, 1930, 13 In. 805.00
Lenci, Boy, Felt Swivel Head, Googly Eyes, Mohair, Felt Body, Jointed, Costume, c.1935, 22 In.. 1600.00
Lenci, Golfer, Sport Series, Mohair Wig, No. 1002, 1929-30, 17 ½ In. .... *illus* 1540.00
Lenci Type, Venus Mask, Painted Eyes, Blond Mohair Wig, 1930s, 18 In. .... *illus* 605.00
Libby, I Dream Of Jeannie, Hollow Hard Plastic, Vinyl Arms, Outfit, Headpiece With Veil, 1966, 20 In. 310.00
Lucy Peck, Poured Wax Shoulder Head, Inset Blue Glass Eyes, Cloth Body, 26 In. 1265.00
Madame Alexander, Amy, Plastic, Blond, Curler Box, Dress Tag, Box, 14 In. 675.00
Madame Alexander, Brenda Starr, Titian Hair, Green Dress, Jointed Knees, Booklet, Box.... 77.00
Madame Alexander, Bride, Red Wig, Taffeta Gown, Tulle, No. 1552, Box, 14 In. .... *illus* 330.00
Madame Alexander, Drum Majorette, Walker, Sleep Eyes, No. 482, 1955, 8 In. 1064.00
Madame Alexander, Groom, Walker, Red Wig, No. 181, Box, 18 In. .... *illus* 255.00
Madame Alexander, Jacqueline, Vinyl, Socket Head, Brown Eyes, Coral Lips, 1961, 21 In.... 1800.00
Madame Alexander, Jo, Little Women, Hard Plastic, Original Outfit, c.1949, 14 In. 165.00
Madame Alexander, Little Victoria, Walker, Sleep Eyes, No. 323, 1954, 8 In. 616.00
Madame Alexander, On The Way To The Beach, Walker, Sleep Eyes, No. 427, 1955, 8 In..... 616.00
Madame Alexander, Queen In Court Gown, Walker, Sleep Eyes, No. 499, 1955, 8 In. 448.00
Madame Alexander, Rosamund Bridesmaid, No. 1551, 1953, Box, 15 In. .... *illus* 440.00
Madame Alexander, Scarlett O'Hara, Composition, Green Sleep Eyes, Mohair Wig, 1937, 14 In. 518.00
Madame Alexander, Sculpted Hair, Sleep Eyes, Cloth Body, Compostition Limbs, c.1935, 10 In. 448.00
Madame Alexander, Sonja Henie, Composition, Clothes, Trunk, 15 In. 750.00
Madame Alexander, Sonja Henie, Plastic, Sleep Eyes, Blond Mohair, Original Outfit, 14 In. . 225.00
Madame Alexander, Tommy Bangs, Hard Plastic, Original Outfit, c.1952, 14 In. 330.00
Madame Alexander, Wendy, Alexander-Kins, Bent-Knee Walker, Cerise Gown, 1956-64, 8 In... *illus* 355.00
Madame Alexander, Wendy, Goes To Garden Party, Walker, Sleep Eyes, No. 620, 1956, 8 In.. 2576.00
Madame Alexander, Wendy, Helps Cutting Flowers, Walker, Sleep Eyes, No. 448, 1955, 8 In. . 896.00
Madame Alexander, Wendy, Plays In The Garden, Walker, Sleep Eyes, No. 440, 1955, 8 In. .. 280.00
Marionette, Cisco Kid, Composition Head, Hands, Boots, Straw Hat, 15 In. 152.00
Marlene Dietrich, Black Tuxedo, Top Hat, Blond Hair, Morocco, 1930, 27 In. 315.00
Martha Chase, Boy, Cloth, Blond Painted Hair, Brown Eyes, Sateen Body, R.I., 1910, 12 In... 518.00
Martha Chase, Boy, Cloth, Painted Features, Cotton Sateen Body, Painted Lower Limbs, 26 In. 830.00
Martha Chase, Hospital, Baby, Oil-Painted Stockinet Head, Applied Ears, Weighted, 30 In. .. 474.00
Martha Chase, Little Neil, Painted Face & Long Hair, Blue Eyes, Oilcloth Limbs, 1900, 15 In. 1100.00
Mary Hoyer, Angel, Composition, Blond, Sleep Eyes, Box 250.00
Mary Hoyer, Bride, Composition, Red Hair, Sleep Eyes, 1940, 14 In. 405.00
Mary Hoyer, Bride, Vickie, Vinyl, Brown Hair, Sleep Eyes, Box, 1957, 10 ½ In. 300.00
Mary Hoyer, Daniel Boone, Hard Plastic, Caracul Wig, Coonskin Cap, Sleep Eyes, 14 In. 275.00
Mary Hoyer, Gigi, Red Hair, Sleep Eyes, 1954, 18 In.. .... 660.00
Mary Hoyer, Hard Plastic, Nun, Box, 14 In. .... *illus* 360.00
Mattel, Allan, Painted Red Hair, Bendable Legs, Jacket, Trunks, Accessories, Booklet, Box.... 275.00
Mattel, Allan, Painted Red Hair, Straight Legs, Striped Jacket, Booklet, Stand, Box 110.00
Mattel, Barbie, American Girl, No. 1070, Brunette, Side Part, Bendable Legs, Striped Top, Box 1980.00
Mattel, Barbie, Brunette, Rooted Lashes, 2-Piece Suit, Cover-Up, Trade-In Program, Box 275.00
Mattel, Barbie, Bubble Cut, Blond, Red Swimsuit, Earrings, Booklet, Stand, Box 195.00
Mattel, Barbie, Bubble Cut, Platinum Blond, Red Swimsuit, Shoes, Booklet, Box 245.00

Doll, Ives, Baby, Composition, Cloth, Creeping, Mechanical, c.1890, 11 In.
$173.00

Doll, K * R, 34, Flapper, Sleep Eyes, Papier-Mache Body, Suitcase, Accessories, 14 In.
$800.00

Doll, Lenci, Golfer, Sport Series, Mohair Wig, No. 1002, 1929-30, 17 ½ In.
$1540.00

TIP
Do not wash or restyle the hair on an old doll. It lowers the value.

Doll, Lenci Type, Venus Mask, Painted Eyes, Blond Mohair Wig, 1930s, 18 In.
$605.00

TIP

To clean sleep eyes on a doll, fill an eye dropper with isopropyl alcohol diluted by half with water. Put the doll on its back and hold the eyes open. Drop the solution into each eye, adding liquid until the eyeball is covered. Open and close the eyelid several times. Turn the doll face down and let the fluid drain out. Then stand the doll upright, hold a clean cloth against the eyes, and tip the doll until the last of the liquid drains out.

Doll, Madame Alexander, Bride, Red Wig, Taffeta Gown, Tulle, No. 1552, Box, 14 In.
$330.00

Doll, Madame Alexander, Groom, Walker, Red Wig, No. 181, Box, 18 In.
$255.00

Doll, Madame Alexander, Rosamund Bridesmaid, No. 1551, 1953, Box, 15 In.
$440.00

Doll, Madame Alexander, Wendy, Alexander-Kins, Bent-Knee Walker, Cerise Gown, 1956-64, 8 In.
$355.00

Doll, Mary Hoyer, Hard Plastic, Nun, Box, 14 In.
$360.00

Doll, Mattel, Skipper, Blond, Red & White Swimsuit, Accessories, Booklet, Box
$135.00

Mattel, Barbie, Growin' Pretty Hair, Blond, 2 Hair Pieces, Pink Dress, Box, c.1970 .... 255.00
Mattel, Barbie, Happy Holiday, Black, Black Gown, Rhinestones, Pink Shawl, Silver Tiara, 1998 90.00
Mattel, Barbie, Light Brown Hair, Pink & Green Swimsuit, Wrist Tag, Booklet, Box, c.1969 ... 275.00
Mattel, Barbie, Miss America, Quick Curl, Blond, Accessories, Box 110.00
Mattel, Barbie, No. 2, Blond, Evening Splendor Dress, Pearl Earrings, Purse, Shoes 2750.00
Mattel, Barbie, No. 3, Blond, Black & White Swimsuit, Blue Eyes, Red Lips 250.00
Mattel, Barbie, No. 4, Black Hair, Ponytail, Black & White Swimsuit, Booklet, Accessories, Box 195.00
Mattel, Barbie, No. 4, Blond, Black & White Swimsuit, Accessories, Box 415.00
Mattel, Barbie, No. 4, Blond, Ponytail, Black & White Swimsuit 195.00
Mattel, Barbie, No. 4, Brunette Ponytail, Pierced Ears, Solo In Spotlight Outfit 360.00
Mattel, Barbie, No. 5, Blond Ponytail, American Airlines Stewardess Outfit 245.00
Mattel, Barbie, No. 5, Dark Brown Ponytail, Red Swimsuit, Booklet, Box 275.00
Mattel, Barbie, No. 850, Bubble Cut, Black Hair, Red Swimsuit, Stand, Booklet, Box 77.00
Mattel, Barbie, Ponytail, Brunette Swirl, Red Swimsuit, Accessories, Booklet, Box 440.00
Mattel, Barbie, Ponytail, Platinum Blond Swirl, White Lips, Red Swimsuit, Accessories, Box .. 365.00
Mattel, Barbie, Talking, Brunette, Rooted Lashes, Bendable Legs, Swimsuit, Cover Up, Box ... 250.00
Mattel, Barbie, Twist 'n' Turn, Light Brown Hair, Bendable Legs, No. 1162, Booklet, Box 415.00
Mattel, Barbie, Twist 'n' Turn, No. 8587, Blond, Yellow Outfit, 1975, Box 140.00
Mattel, Christie, Talking, Red Hair, Bendable Legs, Orange Vinyl Swimsuit, Cover Up, Box ... 275.00
Mattel, Christie, Twist 'n' Turn, Brunette, Rooted Lashes, Yellow, Pink, Orange Swimsuit, Box 330.00
Mattel, Dr. Dolittle, Talking, Pull String, Looks Like Rex Harrison, 1967, 23 In. 105.00
Mattel, Francie, Brunette, 2-Piece Swimsuit, Red, White, Accessories, Booklet, Box 415.00
Mattel, Francie, Brunette, Brown Eyes, Lashes, Green, Pink, White Swimsuit, Booklet, Box ... 275.00
Mattel, Ken, Blond, Flocked Hair, Straight Legs, Red Trunks, Accessories, Booklet, Box 275.00
Mattel, Ken, Blond, Flocked Hair, Towel, Sandals, Wrist Tag, Stand, No. 750, Box 140.00
Mattel, Ken, Brown Flocked Hair, Red Trunks, Towel, Sandals, Booklet, Box 245.00
Mattel, Ken, Painted Blond Hair, Striped Jacket, Red Trunks, Sandals, Stand, Box 55.00
Mattel, Ken, Prince, Green Cape, Fake Diamond Buttons, Tights, 1964 .... 510.00
Mattel, Ken, Red Trunks, Blue Jacket, Bendable Legs, Accessories, Booklet, Box 175.00
Mattel, Kiddle, Lucky Locket, Liz, On Card 77.00
Mattel, Kiddle, Lucky Locket, Lorna, On Card 22.00
Mattel, Kiddle, Lucky Locket, Luana, On Card 22.00
Mattel, Kiddle, Tea Party, Lady Lavender, Case 66.00
Mattel, Midge, Blond, Bendable Legs, Multicolored Striped Swimsuit, Shoes, Booklet, Box ... 330.00
Mattel, Rainbow Brite, Starlite, Gift Set, Box 70.00
Mattel, Skipper, Blond, Blue, Red, White Striped Swimsuit, Bendable Legs, Accessories, Booklet, Box 275.00
Mattel, Skipper, Blond, Red & White Swimsuit, Accessories, Booklet, Box .... *illus* 135.00
Mattel, Skipper, No. 950, Barbie's Little Sister, Box-Liner Stand, Booklet 195.00
Mattel, Skipper, Quick Curl, Blond, Box, 1962 .... 77.00
Mattel, Skooter, Blond Pigtails, School Girl Outfit, Accessories 110.00
Mattel, Skooter, Brunette Pigtails, Red & White Swimsuit, Accessories, Booklet, Box .... *illus* 175.00
Mattel, Skooter, Titian Hair, Bendable Legs, Red & White Top, Blue Shorts, Accessories, Booklet, Box 165.00
Mattel, Stacey, Twist 'n' Turn, Copper Penny, Rooted Lashes, Bendable Legs, Swimsuit, Box, c.1967 330.00
Mattel, Steffie, No. 3421, Brown Hair, Bendable Legs, Bubbles & Boots Outfit, 1967 .... 195.00
Mego, Diana Ross, Cutout Accessories, Motown Record Corp., Box, c.1977, 14 In. .... *illus* 115.00
Mego, Farrah Fawcett, Fully Posable, Accessories, Skis, Tennis Racquet, Skateboard, 1977, 8 In. 85.00
Mengersgereuth, 950, Bisque Socket Head, Googly Eyes, Composition Body, c.1925, 7 In. ... 1590.00
Milliner's Model, Long Black Curls, Leather Body, Wood Limbs, Painted Shoes, 1840s, 12 ½ In. 805.00
Nancy Ann Storybook, Plastic, Spring, Mohair, Jointed, Sleep Eyes, No. 90, c.1950, 5 ½ In.. . 29.00
Norah Wellings, Bullfighter, Swivel Head, Mohair, Side Glancing Eyes, England, c.1935, 25 In. 1150.00
Orsini, Mimi, Bisque Head, Torso, Glass Eyes, Mohair Wig, Jointed Limbs, Germany, 1920, 5 In. 1495.00
Paper Dolls are listed in their own category.
Papier-Mache, Shoulder Head, Elongated Throat, Topknot, Braids, Wood Limbs, 10 In...... 750.00
Parian, Shoulder Head, Painted Face, Curly Hair, Hair Ribbon, Pierced Earrings, 1870s, 24 In. 259.00
Pierrette, Composition, Red Molded Hair, Painted, France, Box, 1940, 8 In. .... *illus* 403.00
Pincushion dolls are listed in their own category.
Porcelain, Set Eyes, Open Mouth, Wig, Composition, Jointed, Nippon, 24 In. 224.00
Pumpkin Head, Wax Over Papier-Mache, Glass Eyes, Molded Hair Ribbon, Cloth Body, 13 In. 546.00
Puppet, Boxer, Hit & Miss, Push-Up, Kohner, 1960s, 4 In. 20.00
Puppet, Bronco Bill, Push-Up, Wood, 1940s, 6 In. 20.00
Puppet, Clown, Felt, Rubber, Painted, Steiff, Early 1900s, 10 In. 250.00
Puppet, Clown, Tin Lithograph, Hand Lever, Controls Face, Squeaker Hat, 6 ¾ In.. .... 115.00
Puppet, Grandpa Munster, Vinyl Head, Cloth Body, Ideal, 1964, 10 ½ In. 56.00
Puppet, Happy The Wonder Dog, Push-Up, Wood, Leather Ears, Kohner Bros., Box, 1940, 6 In. 28.00
Puppet, Herman Munster, Mattel, 13 In. .... *illus* 60.00
Puppet, Lily Munster, Screen-Printed Fabric, Soft Vinyl Head, Ideal, c.1964, 10 ¼ In. 115.00

Doll, Mattel, Skooter, Brunette Pigtails, Red & White Swimsuit, Accessories, Booklet, Box
$175.00

Doll, Mego, Diana Ross, Cutout Accessories, Motown Record Corp., Box, c.1977, 14 In.
$115.00

Doll, Pierrette, Composition, Red Molded Hair, Painted, France, Box, 1940, 8 In.
$403.00

Doll, Puppet, Herman Munster, Mattel, 13 In.
$60.00

Doll, Raggedy Ann & Andy, Cloth, Button Eyes, Printed, Georgene Novelties, 1940, 19 In., Pair
$633.00

Schoenhut, 300, Brown Mohair, Jointed, 16 In.
$2318.00

TIP
Small nicks and scratches in iron can be covered with black crayon. Wipe off the excess with paper.

Puppet, Lily Munster, Vinyl Head, Cloth Body, 1964, Ideal, 10 ½ In. . . . 44.00
Queen Elizabeth II, Coronation, Sculpted, Painted Features, Mohair, Robe, Ermine Trim, 14 In. 1300.00
Rabery & Delphieu, Bisque Socket Head, Human Hair, Wood, Composition, Bebe, c.1980 . . . 3100.00
Raggedy Ann, Cloth, Printed Facial Features, Red Yarn Hair, Georgene Novelties, 1935, 19 In. 650.00
Raggedy Ann, Cloth, Printed Features, Yarn Hair, Wrist Tag, 21 In. . . . 1100.00
Raggedy Ann & Andy, Cloth, Button Eyes, Printed, Georgene Novelties, 1940, 19 In., Pair. . . . *illus* 633.00
Raggedy Ann & Andy, Printed Face, Shoebutton Eyes, Cotton Clothes, Volland, 1920, 16 In., Pair 2040.00
S.F.B.J., Bisque, Glass Eyes, Blond Mohair, Composition, Jointed, 6 ¼ In. . . . 173.00
S.F.B.J., Bisque Socket Head, Dome, Composition, Wood, Fully Jointed, Boy, 15 In. . . . 3000.00
S.F.B.J., Bisque Socket Head, Dome, Composition, Wood, Jointed, Toddler, Boy, 13 In. . . . 7500.00
S.F.B.J., Bisque Socket Head, Dome, Open Mouth, Composition, Wood, Jointed, Nursing Bottle, 14 In. 1700.00
S.F.B.J., Bisque Socket Head, Dome, Painted, Composition, Wood, Ball-Jointed, Box, 16 In. . . . 1950.00
S.F.B.J., Blue Glass Jewel Eyes, Molded Upper Teeth, Painted Hair, 15 In. . . . 978.00
Sasha, Harlequin, Guitar, Straw Hat, No. 1932, Box, 1984 . . . 55.00
Sasha, Keltie, Red Hair, No. 183A, Box, 1983 . . . 150.00
Sasha, Light Brown Hair, Velvet Dress, No. 4025, Box, 1981 . . . 165.00
Schoenau & Hoffmeister, My Girlie III, Blue Sleep Eyes, Open Mouth, Composition, 24 ½ In. 173.00
Schoenhut, 100, Wood Socket Head, Carved, Bobbed Hair, Bangs, Spring-Jointed, 16 In. . . . 8000.00
Schoenhut, 105, Wood Socket Head, Carved Hair, Bobbed Style, Bangs, Spring-Jointed, 21 In. 1600.00
Schoenhut, 207, Wood Socket Head, Carved Hair, Spring-Jointed, Foot Holes, 14 In. . . . 4000.00
Schoenhut, 300, Brown Mohair, Jointed, 16 In. . . . *illus* 2318.00
Schoenhut, 405, Twins, Boy & Girl, Blond Wig, Girl In White Dress, Boy In White Suit, 15 In. 1210.00
Schoenhut, Papier-Mache Head, Sculpted Hair, Dutch Cap, Wood, Jointed, 11 In. . . . 750.00
Schoenhut, Pouty, Spring-Jointed, Mohair Wig, Wood, Union Suit . . . 173.00
Schoenhut, Spark Plug, Oilcloth, Brown Body, White Face, 1930s, 12 x 8 ½ In. . . . 100.00
Shirley Temple dolls are included in the Shirley Temple category.
Simon & Halbig dolls are also listed here under Bergmann
Simon & Halbig, 739, Bisque Socket Head, Brown Complexion, Mohair, Composition, Wood, 20 In. 2500.00
Simon & Halbig, Bisque, Oriental, Brown Glass Eyes, Mohair, Jointed, Composition, 11 In. . . 356.00
Simon & Halbig, Eleanor, Blue Wool Nun's Habit, Rosary, Blue Glass Sleep Eyes, 24 In. . . . 400.00
Simon & Halbig, Solid Dome Head, Mohair Wig, Glass Eyes, 11 ½ In. . . . 240.00
Simon & Halbig, Swivel Head, Paperweight Eyes, Wood, Twill Covered, Jointed, 13 In. . . . 7110.00
Sonneberg, Black Bisque, Open Mouth, Black Caracul Wig, Striped Cotton Dress, 14 In. . . . 1955.00
Steiff, Black Coachman, Googly Glass Eyes, 16 In. . . . 6900.00
Steiff, Blacksmith, Shoebutton Eyes, Steiff Button, 20 In. . . . 4025.00
Steiff, Coachman, Glass Eyes, Steiff Button, 21 In. . . . 6325.00
Steiner, Bisque Socket Head, Glass Paperweight Eyes, Mohair, Composition, Jointed, 20 In. . . 2588.00
Stern Toy, Pinky Lee, Molded Vinyl, Squeezed Head Pops Off, 9 In. . . . 12.00
Tammy, Brunette, Red Pants, Print Shirt, Blue Eyes, Stand, Box . . . 55.00
Ventriloquist Dummy, Groucho Marx, Goldberger, Box, 23 In. . . . 58.00
Vogue, Dora Lee, Composition, Blue Sleep Eyes, Blond Braids, Jointed, 1939, 11 In. . . . 95.00
Wax Shoulder Head, Glass Eyes, Mohair, Cloth Body, Wax Limbs, Costume, 1910, 27 In. . . . 2585.00
Wax Shoulder Head, Glass Inset Eyes, Cloth Body, Jointed, 1860s, 26 In. . . . 1495.00
Wax Shoulder Head, Mohair, Glass Inset Eyes, Wax Limbs, England, c.1850, 27 In. . . . 2585.00
Wood, Carved, Blond, Jointed, Metal Hands & Boots, c.1880, 11 In. . . . 510.00

DOLL CLOTHES

Barbie, All That Jazz, No. 1848 . . . 54.00
Barbie, American Airlines Stewardess, No. 984, 1961-64. . . . 85.00
Barbie, Arabian Nights, No. 0874 . . . 100.00
Barbie, Ballerina Barbie, Tutu, Shoes, Pink Satin Bag, No. 989 . . . 25.00
Barbie, Beautiful Blues, No. 3303, 1967 . . . 770.00
Barbie, Bride's Dream, Box . . . 330.00
Barbie, Fab Fur, No. 1493, 1969-70. . . . 385.00
Barbie, Fashion Queen Head, Molded Midge Head, Accessories, On Card . . . 275.00
Barbie, Floating Gardens, No. 1696, 1967 . . . 220.00
Barbie, Floor Length Dress, Black, Red Rose, Long Black Gloves, Shoes, Crystal Bead Necklace 120.00
Barbie, Flying Colors, No. 3492, 1972. . . . 385.00
Barbie, Glimmer Glamour, No. 1547, 1968 . . . 770.00
Barbie, Hostess Set, Barbie Learns To Cook, Accessories, Box, c.1965. . . . 3600.00
Barbie, In Japan, Red Kimono, Socks, Box. . . . 275.00
Barbie, It's Cold Outside, Coat, Red Felt, Simulated Fur Color, Hat, Hanger, No. 0819, c.1965 . 65.00
Barbie, Junior Pro, Accessories, No. 1614, 1965 . . . 63.00
Barbie, Lace Caper, Box, c.1969. . . . 55.00
Barbie, Let's Dance, Accessories, No. 978 . . . 25.00
Barbie, Magnificent Midi, No. 3418, 1971 . . . 193.00
Barbie, Masquerade Outfit, Pantyhose, Mask, Hat, Box. . . . 220.00
Barbie, Mittens, White Cloth . . . 2.50

Barbie, Pajama Pow, No. 1806, 1967-68 .... 138.00
Barbie, Plush Pony, No. 1873 .... 10.00
Barbie, Poodle Parade, Box 475.00
Barbie, Red Trench Coat, Suitcase With Souvenir Stickers, Binoculars, 1971 .... 42.00
Barbie, Shimmering Magic, No. 1664, 1966-67 .... 440.00
Barbie, Skirt, Red, White Flowers, For Free Moving Barbie, 1976 .... 5.00
Barbie, Slumber Party, No. 1642, 1965 .... 68.00
Barbie, Solo In Spotlight, No. 982, Box, 1960-64 .... 330.00 to 527.00
Barbie, Student Teacher, Box 375.00
Barbie, Sundress, Blue, Pink & Orange Flowers, Pink Earrings & Hair Accessory 10.00
Barbie, Sunflower, No. 1683 .... 68.00
Barbie, Theatre Date, Box 275.00
Barbie, Winter Wedding, Box 165.00
Francie, Satin Supper, Blue Gown, Green Dress, Shoes, Booklet, Box 275.00
Hat, Ribbon, Ruffled Lace Edge, Box, For 20 In. Doll 444.00
Hat, Taffeta, Cream, Aqua Ribbon Rosette, For 14-18 In. Doll 563.00
Ken, Cheerful Chef Pack, Apron, Bandanna, Chef Hat, Utensils, Card 99.00
Ken, Dreamboat, No. 785, Box .... 88.00 to 145.00
Ken, Fountain Boy, Box 135.00
Ken, Masquerade, Box 110.00
Ken, Mr. Astronaut, Box 395.00
Ken, Yachtsman, No.789 .... *illus* 125.00
Parasol, Bone Handle, Black Lace, Net Over Silk Shade, 8 In. 148.00
Purse, Green Velvet, Engraved Metal Clasp, France, 2 ⅜ In. 2489.00
Skipper, Country Picnic, Box 770.00
Skipper, Fashion Avenue Teen, Long Slit Skirt, Yellow, Multicolored Flowers, Slipper Shoes .. 10.00
Skipper, Fitted Red Velvet Coat, White Satin Lining, Gold Buttons, 1963 .... 20.00
Skipper, Learning To Ride, Box 195.00
Skipper, Let's Play House, Box 330.00
Skipper, Masquerade, Box 99.00
Skipper, On Wheels, Coat, Hat, Goggles, Scooter, Accessories, Box, c.1964 .... 330.00
Skipper, Pink Princess, Box, c.1969 .... 99.00
Skipper, Platter Party, Long Red Plaid Skirt, Blue Velvet Top, Shoes, Record Player, 1965 .... 49.00
Skipper, School Girl, Box 175.00
Skipper, Tea Party, Yellow Dress, Shoes, Teapot, Booklet, Box 195.00

DONALD DUCK *items are included in the Disneyana category.*

DOORSTOPS have been made in all types of designs. The vast majority of the doorstops sold today are cast iron and were made from about 1890 to 1930. Most of them are shaped like people, animals, flowers, or ships. Reproductions and newly designed examples are sold in gift shops.

Accordion Player, Cast Iron, Hubley, 6 In. 66.00
Baby Camel, Running, Marked, 6 ½ x 7 ½ In. 86.00
Banjo Player, Cast Iron, 6 ¼ In. 920.00
Bear, Honey In Paws, Brown, Black Paint, Cast Iron, 15 In. 4600.00
Bellhop, Black Man In Uniform, Cast Iron, CJO, 9 x 4 ⅝ In. 374.00
Bellhop, Cast Iron, 9 In. 345.00
Black Man, On Cotton Bale, Cast Iron, Pot Metal, 9 ⅛ x 7 In. .... 750.00 to 863.00
Bobby Blake, Holding Teddy Bear, Cast Iron, Hubley, 1930s 375.00
Boy, Girl, Kittens, Grassy Base, Painted, Cast Iron, 5 ¼ x 7 ½ In. 248.00
Boy, Holding Flower Basket, Cast Iron, 9 ¼ x 3 ⅞ In. 633.00
Cat, Black, Full Figure, Cast Iron, 7 x 3 ½ In. 173.00
Cat, Black, Red Eyes, Paws, Cast Iron, 12 ½ x 7 ½ In. 198.00
Cat, Fireside, Bell On Collar, Pink Bow, Hubley, 6 x 10 ½ In. 201.00
Cat, Persian, Seated, Green Eye, Facing Left, Fluffy Tail, Cast Iron, 9 x 6 ½ In. 287.00
Cat, Seated, Amber Glass Eyes, Collar, Cast Iron, England, 15 x 8 In. 300.00
Cat, Seated, Black, Cast Iron, 9 ½ In. 80.00
Cat, Seated, Black, Ribbon, Figural, Cast Iron, 14 x 8 In. 330.00
Cat, Seated, Flat Back, Painted Eyes, Cast Iron, 6 ⅜ In. 316.00
Cat, Seated, Painted, Cast Iron, 10 In. 265.00
Cat, Seated, Side-Glancing, Greenslatt Studio, 1927, 9 x 7 In. 632.00
Cat, Seated, White, Yellow Eyes, Cast Iron, Creations Company, 8 x 5 In. 345.00
Cat, Seated On Rug, Multicolored, Cast Iron, 8 ¾ In. 353.00
Cat, Sleeping, Black, Hollow Body, Hubley, 8 x 5 ½ In. 431.00
Cat, Sleeping, Black, Paint, White Blaze On Face, c.1930, 4 x 13 In. 1175.00

Doll Clothes, Ken, Yachtsman, No.789
$125.00

Doorstop, Cats, 2, Ball, Black, White, Red, Painted, Cast Iron, 7 ½ In.
$60.00

Doorstop, Dog, Boston Terrier, Black, White, Painted, Cast Iron, 6 ½ x 7 ½ In.
$395.00

Composition—A Mixture
The word "composition," when used to describe dolls, refers to a combination of materials that is used to make molded bodies and heads. It is usually sawdust or wood pulp mixed with glue.

Doorstop, Flower Basket, Multicolored Flowers, Blue Bow, Cast Iron, 8 ½ x 6 In.
$220.00

Doorstop, Grapes, Leaves, Painted, Cast Iron, Albany Foundry, 7 ⅞ x 6 ½ In.
$440.00

Doorstop, House, Nathanael Green, Embossed, Painted, Cast Iron, 4 ¾ x 7 ⅞ In.
$465.00

TIP
Rub soap on noisy door hinges.

Cat, Sleeping, Black, White, Cast Iron, 1930s, 4 ¾ x 13 x 10 ½ In. 1100.00
Cat, Tail Curling Under, Black, Elongated Body, Hubley, 10 x 3 ¾ In. 460.00
Cat, White, Black, Cast Iron, 10 ⅜ In., Pair. 259.00
Cat, White, Black, Full Figure, Cast Iron, Hubley, 10 x 5 In. 230.00
Cat, White, Black, Green Eyes, Pink Nose, Cast Iron, c.1900, 10 In. 110.00
Cats, 2, Ball, Black, White, Red, Painted, Cast Iron, 7 ½ In. .... *illus* 60.00
Cats, Side-Glancing, Cast Iron, Hubley, No. 73, Drayton Design, 5 x 7 In. 546.00
Child, With Dog, 2-Piece Casting, Cast Iron, Signed, Russwin, 9 x 10 In. 978.00
Child, Yawning, Full Figure, Cast Iron, Signed, c.1926, 8 ¾ x 5 In. 115.00
Cigar Store Indian, Girl Holding Box, Painted, Cast Iron, 7 In. 200.00
Clown, Outstretched Arms, Cast Iron, 6 ½ x 9 ⅜ In. 748.00
Cockatoo In Ring, Cast Iron, 13 ½ x 7 ¼ In. 201.00
Colonial Doorway, Ornate Pediment, Steps With Flowers, Cast Iron, 6 ½ x 5 In. 546.00
Colonial Lawyer, Purple Jacket, Yellow Knickers, Cast Iron, 9 ¾ x 5 ½ In. 350.00
Colonial Woman, Pink Shawl, Bouquet, Cast Iron, 8 x 4 In. 230.00
Colonial Woman, Yellow Gown, Hat, Purse In Hand, Cast Iron, 10 ½ x 6 In. 318.00
Cottage, Angled Roof, Flowers, Birdhouse, Wedge Back, Cast Iron, 8 x 7 In. 172.00
Cottage, Cape Cod, Climbing Flowers, Hubley, 5 ½ x 7 ¾ In. 230.00
Cottage, Cape Cod, Flowers, Black Roof, Pastel Colors, Cast Iron, 5 ¾ x 8 ¾ In. 115.00
Cottage, Chimney Smoke, Trees, Flowers, Cast Iron, 7 ¼ x 8 ¼ In. 345.00
Cottage, Climbing Flowers, Pastel Colors, Hubley, 5 ⅝ x 7 ⅞ In. 201.00
Cottage, Red Roof, Climbing Flowers, Stone-Like Walkway, Cast Iron, 13 x 8 ¾ In. 201.00
Covered Bridge, Running Stream, Red, Cast Iron, 8 ¼ x 4 ¾ In. 288.00
Cow, Gold Paint, Cast Iron, Holland Foundry, Pa., 9 In. 470.00
Dog, 2 Scotties, Seated, Cast Iron, 5 ¾ x 8 ¾ In. 35.00
Dog, Beagle, Seated, Cream, Black, Brown, Green Collar, Cast Iron, 1930s, 8 x 7 In. 805.00
Dog, Beagle, Seated, Painted, Cast Iron, c.1930, 8 x 7 In. 900.00
Dog, Begging, Newspaper In Mouth, Painted, Cast Iron, 7 ¾ x 6 ¼ x 2 In. 160.00
Dog, Bird Dog, Black, Left Paw Up, Full Figure, Cast Aluminum, 9 x 15 ½ In. 25.00
Dog, Bloodhound, Art Deco Style, Wedge Back, Cast Iron, Spencer, 15 ¼ In. 288.00
Dog, Bloodhound, Wrinkled Face, Hubley, 7 x 6 ½ In. 1072.00
Dog, Boston Terrier, Black, White, Painted, Cast Iron, 6 ½ x 7 ½ In. .... *illus* 395.00
Dog, Boston Terrier, Painted, Cast Iron, 9 ½ x 9 x 4 In. 85.00
Dog, Boston Terrier, Seated, Black, White, Ear Down, Cast Iron, Hubley, 7 x 8 ½ In. 100.00
Dog, Bulldog, Black, White, Cast Iron, 10 x 11 In. 117.00
Dog, Bulldog, Black, White, Head Turned Left, Cast Iron, 8 x 9 In. 30.00
Dog, Bulldog, Black, White, Head Turned Left, Cast Iron, 9 x 10 In. 40.00
Dog, Bulldog, Brown, Head Turned Left, Cast Iron, 9 x 10 In. 40.00
Dog, Bulldog, Brown, White, Head Turned Right, Cast Iron, 9 x 10 In. 40.00
Dog, Bulldog, Full Figure, Cast Aluminum, 8 x 9 In. 25.00
Dog, Bulldog, Seated, Black, White, Head Turned Right, Cast Iron, 8 x 8 In. 50.00
Dog, Bulldog, Seated, Brown, Beige, Cast Iron, 6 x 4 ½ In. 85.00
Dog, Bulldog, Seated, Brown, Head Turned Right, Cast Iron, 6 ½ x 7 ½ In. 50.00
Dog, Bulldog, White, Cast Iron, 5 x 4 ¾ In. 20.00
Dog, Cairn Terrier, Black Toenails, Exposed Tooth, Bradley & Hubbard, 9 x 6 In. 316.00
Dog, Dachshund, Full Figure, 2 Piece, Hubley, 6 x 9 In. 747.00
Dog, Doberman, Figural, Painted, Cast Iron, Hubley, 8 x 8 ½ In. 450.00
Dog, English Bulldog, Black, Head Turned Right, Cast Iron, 8 ½ x 5 ¾ In. 45.00
Dog, English Bulldog, Brown, Head Turned Right, Cast Iron, 8 ½ x 6 ½ In. 30.00
Dog, English Bulldog, Brown, White, Cast Iron, 8 ½ x 6 ½ In. 90.00
Dog, German Shepherd, Brown, Black, Cast Iron, 14 ½ x 10 In. 70.00
Dog, German Shepherd, Cast Iron, 9 x 10 ¾ In. 144.00
Dog, German Shepherd, Head Turned Left, Cast Iron, 8 x 9 In. 50.00
Dog, Greyhound, Cast Iron, 1930s, 6 ½ In. 115.00
Dog, Japanese Spaniel, Black, White, Standing On Hind Legs, Cast Iron, CJO, 9 x 4 ½ In. 316.00
Dog, Pointer, Black, White, Cast Iron, 15 x 8 ½ In. 40.00
Dog, Pointer, Brown, Cast Iron, 7 ½ x 14 In. 44.00
Dog, Scottie, Black, Cast Aluminum, 10 x 8 ½ In. 30.00
Dog, Scottie, Cast Iron, Hubley, 11 ¾ x 16 In. 1840.00
Dog, Scottie, Seated, Cast Iron, 10 ⅞ x 6 In. 345.00
Dog, Scottie, Standing, Cast Iron, 8 ¾ x 10 ⅝ In. 86.00
Dog, Scottie, White, Cast Iron, 9 x 11 In. 88.00
Dog, Sealyham Terrier, Full Figure, Cast Iron, Hubley, 9 ½ x 14 In. 2185.00
Dog, Sealyham Terrier, Painted, Cast Iron, c.1930, 4 x 7 In. 881.00
Dog, Springer Spaniel, Black, White, Ceramic, Iron, 9 x 8 In. 75.00
Dog, St. Bernard, Standing, Brown, White, Painted, Cast Iron, Marked, 7 ⅛ x 9 In. 3500.00

Dog, Terrier, Painted, Beige, Brown, 9 x 8 ½ In. . . . 112.00
Dog, Terrier, Seated, c.1920, 5 In. . . . 351.00
Dog, Terrier, Seated, Green Base, Cast Iron, Hubley, 6 ¼ x 7 In. . . . 288.00
Dog, Walking, Black, Yellow, Blue, Cast Iron, Art Deco, Signed, Taylor Cook, 1930, 7 x 8 In. . . 1600.00
Dog, Wirehaired Fox Terrier, Brown, White, Cast Iron, 8 x 8 ½ In. . . . 30.00
Dog, Wirehaired Fox Terrier, Painted Cast Iron, Hubley, No. 279, c.1930, 9 In. . . . 360.00
Dolly Dingle, Painted, Cast Iron, 7 ⅝ x 4 ½ In. . . . 165.00
Edgar Allen Poe House, Cast Iron, Bradley & Hubbard, 5 ⅞ x 7 ⅞ In. . . . 403.00
Elephant, Trunk Up, Gray, White Tusks, Full Figure, Cast Iron, Hubley, 8 ¼ x 11 ½ In. . . . 345.00
Elephant, Walking, Cast Iron, Signed, 6 ½ x 9 In. . . . 115.00
Elf, Digging For Gold, Cast Iron, 2-Sided, Spencer, 13 ⅜ x 3 ¼ In. . . . 288.00
Fisherman, In Boat, Standing At Bow, Cast Iron, Cap'n Eri, 6 ¾ x 4 In. . . . 115.00
Flapper Girl, Layered Dress, Umbrella, Cast Iron, Marked, 8, 9 ½ In. . . . 690.00
Flower Basket, Multicolored Flowers, Blue Bow, Cast Iron, 8 ½ x 6 In. . . . *illus* 220.00
Flower Basket, Nasturtiums, Buds, Striped Basket, Marked, 8 x 7 In. . . . 144.00
Flower Basket, Painted, Cast Iron, Albany Foundry, 1924, 9 ½ x 8 x 2 In. . . . 110.00
Flower Vase, Roses, Lilacs, White, Painted, Cast Iron, No. 479, 5 ⅝ In. . . . 30.00
Foot Shape, Bronze, Maitland Smith, Thailand, 11 In. . . . 410.00
Footmen, 2, Standing, Multicolored, Cast Iron, Hubley, 12 x 8 ¼ In. . . . 413.00 to 710.00
Franklin Pierce, Bust, Profile, Raised Letters, Cast Iron, 6 ¾ In. . . . 776.00
Frog, Painted, Cast Iron, 7 In. . . . 132.00
Fruit Bowl, Birds, Cast Iron, 6 ½ x 5 ⅝ In. . . . 403.00
Geese, 3, Stepping In Unison, Hubley, 8 x 8 In. . . . 316.00
Geese, Painted, Cast Iron, c.1900, 8 In. . . . 353.00
Geisha, With Mandolin, Full Figure, Cast Iron, Hubley, 7 ½ x 6 ¼ In. . . . 201.00
George Bernard Shaw, Face, Brass, 8 x 4 ½ In. . . . 230.00
Girl, Holding Flower Basket, Cast Iron, 9 x 3 ¾ In. . . . 460.00
Girl, In Canoe, Wide Brimmed Hat, Cast Iron, 10 x 4 In. . . . 1380.00
Gnome, Cast Iron, 13 ⅝ x 6 ¼ In. . . . 403.00
Gnome, With Keys, Red Hat, Blue Shirt, Brown Apron, Cast Iron, 10 x 5 In. . . . 425.00
Grapes, Cast Iron, 7 x 6 In. . . . 144.00
Grapes, Leaves, Painted, Cast Iron, Albany Foundry, 7 ⅞ x 6 ½ In. . . . *illus* 440.00
Halloween Girl, Cast Iron, 13 ¾ x 9 ¾ In. . . . 633.00
Heron, Multicolored, Albany Foundry, 7 ½ x 5 In. . . . 172.00 to 345.00
Heron, Painted, Cast Iron, Bradley & Hubbard, 14 x 9 ⅞ In. . . . 325.00
Honey Bear, Holding Honey, Brown, Black, Full Figure, Cast Iron, 15 ¼ x 6 In. . . 3163.00 to 4600.00
Horse, Cast Iron, Hubley, 8 x 8 ½ In. . . . 402.00
Horse, Cast Iron, Hubley, 11 x 12 ¼ In. . . . 460.00
House, George Washington, Brown, Green, Cast Iron, 1925, 10 ½ x 8 ½ In. . . . 575.00
House, Nathanael Green, Embossed, Painted, Cast Iron, 4 ¾ x 7 ⅞ In. . . . *illus* 465.00
Humpty Dumpty, On Wall, Painted, Cast Iron, 4 ½ x 3 ⅜ In. . . . *illus* 173.00
Humpty Dumpty, Seated, Cast Iron, 9 ¼ In. . . . 881.00
Jayhawk, University Of Kansas, Red, Yellow, Blue, 8 ¼ x 6 ¼ In. . . . 345.00
Jonquils, Painted, Cast Iron, Hubley, 7 ½ x 8 In. . . . 230.00
King Tut, Painted, Cast Iron, 10 ⅝ In. . . . 2300.00
Lighthouse, Highland, Cape Cod, Cast Iron, 9 x 7 ¾ In. . . . 1265.00
Lion, Leaning On Post, Tongue Out, Cast Iron, 14 ½ x 9 In. . . . 30.00
Lion, Shield, Brass, 15 x 10 In. . . . 263.00
Lion & Serpent, Cast Iron, England, 14 ¼ In. . . . 30.00
Little Red Riding Hood, Painted, Cast Iron, Hubley, 9 ½ x 5 In. . . . *illus* 750.00
Little Red Riding Hood, Wolf, Albany Foundry, Cast Iron, 7 ⅜ x 9 ⅝ In. . . . 863.00 to 1495.00
Little Red Riding Hood, Wolf, Painted, Cast Iron, Embossed, Nuydea, 7 ½ x 9 In. . . . *illus* 1760.00
Mad Hatter, Nose In Air, Top Hat, Red Jacket, Full Figure, Cast Iron, 3 x 6 ⅝ In. . . . 173.00
Mail Coach, London, 2 Horses, Driver, Man Blowing Horn, Cast Iron, 7 x 12 x 2 In. . . . 25.00
Mallard Duck, Swimming, Painted, Cast Iron, 6 ⅜ x 12 In. . . . 4313.00
Mammy, Hands On Hips, Blue Dress, Polka Dot Head Wrap, Hubley, 8 ¾ In. . . . 345.00
Mammy, Red Dress, Polka Dot Head Wrap, Hubley, 9 x 5 ½ In. . . . 431.00
Man, Smoking Pipe, Holding Ax, Leaning On Tree, Dog, Brass, England, 12 ¾ x 8 ½ In. . . . 75.00
Messenger Boy, Painted, Cast Iron, Signed, Fish, No. 249, Hubley, 9 ¼ x 3 ½ In. . . . 1725.00
Monkey, On Barrel, Green, Yellow, Cast Iron, Taylor Cook, 1930, 8 ½ In. . . . *illus* 633.00
Monkey, Seated, Full Figure, 6 ½ x 5 In. . . . 258.00
Nasturtiums, Black & White Striped Pot, Embossed, Cast Iron, Hubley, 6 ½ x 7 ½ In. . . . 115.00
Old Salt, Fisherman, Yellow Slicker, Full Figure, Cast Iron, 11 x 4 In. . . . 316.00
Old Tom Magician, Don't You Tell, Jester, Doing Magic Tricks, 17 ¼ x 11 ⅛ In. . . . 863.00
Organ Grinder, Monkey, Holding Cup, 9 ⅞ x 5 ¾ In. . . . 287.00
Oriental Girl, Standing, Painted, Red Coat, Green Pants, Full Figure, Cast Iron, 7 ¾ In. . . . 316.00

TIP
Gummed tags can be removed by heating the tag with a hair dryer, then loosening it with a flat knife.

Doorstop, Humpty Dumpty, On Wall, Painted, Cast Iron, 4 ½ x 3 ⅜ In.
$173.00

Doorstop, Little Red Riding Hood, Painted, Cast Iron, Hubley, 9 ½ x 5 In.
$750.00

Doorstop, Little Red Riding Hood, Wolf, Painted, Cast Iron, Embossed, Nuydea, 7 ½ x 9 In.
$1760.00

Doorstop, Monkey, On Barrel, Green, Yellow, Cast Iron, Taylor Cook, 1930, 8 ½ In.
$633.00

Doorstop, Penguin, Painted, Cast Iron, Signed, Taylor Cook, 1930, 9 ½ x 5 ⅜ In.
$9200.00

Doorstop, Police Boy, Boston Terrier, Painted, Cast Iron, 10 ½ x 7 ¼ In.
$1035.00

Parlor Maid, Painted, Cast Iron, Hubley, Signed, Fish, 9 ¼ x 3 ½ In. 1495.00
Parrot, Cast Iron, Signed, Taylor Cook, c.1930, 10 ½ x 4 ¼ In. 633.00
Parrot, Multicolored, Cast Iron, 10 ¾ In. 575.00
Parrot In Ring, Full Figure, Bradley & Hubbard, 8 x 7 In. 132.00
Peacock, By Urn, Hubley, 7 ½ x 4 ¼ In. 230.00
Penguin, Painted, Cast Iron, Signed, Taylor Cook, 1930, 9 ½ x 5 ⅜ In. .... *illus* 9200.00
Penguin, Top Hat, Bowtie, Painted, Cast Iron, 10 ¼ In. 295.00
Penguins, Pair, Wing To Wing, Turned Heads, 7 ½ x 8 In. 287.00
Pheasant, Standing In Grassy Patch, Head Cocked, Cast Iron, 8 ½ x 7 ½ In. 287.00
Pied Piper, On Mushroom, Children At Base, Cast Iron, 7 ¼ x 5 In. 2300.00
Pilgrim, With Sack, Full Figure, Cast Iron, 12 x 4 ½ In. 805.00
Pirate, With Sack Over Shoulder, Cast Iron, 12 x 9 ¾ In. 863.00
Pirate Girl, Red Shirt, Blue Skirt, Yellow Belt, Cast Iron, 13 In. 575.00
Police Boy, Boston Terrier, Painted, Cast Iron, 10 ½ x 7 ¼ In. .... *illus* 1035.00
Poppies, In Vase, Painted, Cast Iron, Hubley, 10 ⅝ x 7 ⅞ In. .... *illus* 115.00
Puppy, Seated, Painted, Cast Iron, Hubley, 8 ½ x 7 x 5 In. 260.00
Quails, Cast Iron, Hubley, Everett, 7 ¼ In. 575.00
Sailboat, High Seas, 17 In. 1955.00
Sailboat, Under Arch, Embossed, Red Roof Church, Water, 11 ½ x 10 ¾ In. 287.00
Sailor, Bell Bottom Pants, Cap, Cast Iron, 11 ⅝ x 5 In. 1840.00
Saltbox House, Gray, White Rim, Cast Iron, 5 x 7 ⅜ In. 632.00
Ship, Clipper, Painted, Cast Iron, c.1900, 11 x 5 In. 1955.00
Ship, Galleon, Cast Iron, Creations Co., c.1930, 11 ¼ x 11 ⅜ In. 115.00
Ship, U.S. Constitution, Cast Iron, 1974, 12 x 8 In. 88.00
Soldier, Trees, Albany Foundry, 9 ½ x 5 In. 86.00
Spanish Dancer, Open Fan, Waverly Studios, 9 ½ x 5 ¼ In. .... 115.00 to 201.00
Stagecoach, Green, Cast Iron, 1930, 7 ¼ In. 75.00
Stagecoach, Horse Drawn, Cast Iron, Marked, B & H., 5 ¼ x 7 ¼ In. 373.00
Sulgrave Manor, Home Of George Washington, Greenblatt Studios, 1925, 9 x 11 In. 488.00
Swallows, 2 Birds Perched On Berry Tree, Hubley, 8 ½ x 7 ½ In. 747.00
Swan, Cast Iron, Spencer, 13 ½ x 8 In. 2358.00
Tiger, Man, Boots, Top Hat, Cast Iron, Hubley, 9 In. 805.00
Tulips, Multicolored, Cast Iron, New York, c.1925, 8 x 7 In. 385.00
Uncle Sam, For The Open Door, Painted, Cast Iron, 12 x 5 ¼ In. 16000.00
Windmill, Painted, Cast Iron, Pat, Dec. 15, 1925, 6 ⅞ x 7 ½ In. .... *illus* 345.00
Wine Merchant, Bottles In Hand, Cast Iron, 9 x 7 In. 2300.00
Woman, Carrying Flowers, Parasol, Green, Yellow, Bradley & Hubbard, 11 x 7 In. 1610.00
Woman, Spinning Wheel, By Fireplace, Eastern Specialty Co, 8 x 6 In. 402.00
Woman, Victorian, Blue Bonnet, Painted, Cast Iron, 5 In. 30.00
Woman, With Fan, Green, Gold Dress, Hoop Skirt, Waverly Studios, 9 x 6 In. 230.00
Women, Bathing, Holding Umbrella, Cast Iron, c.1920, 11 x 5 x 2 In. 990.00
Zinnias, Blue, Cream, Embossed, Cast Iron, Hubley, 9 ¾ x 8 ½ In. 230.00

DORCHESTER POTTERY was founded by George Henderson in 1895 in Dorchester, Massachusetts. At first, the firm made utilitarian stoneware, but collectors are most interested in the line of decorated blue and white pottery that Dorchester made from 1940 until it went out of business in 1979.

DORCHESTER POTTERY WORKS BOSTON, MASS.

Biscuit Jar, Lid, Incised Design, Green Glaze, Dark Green Band, Squat, Marked. 50.00
Bowl, Scallop Shell Shape, Rust, Brown Glaze, 8 x 6 In. 50.00
Foot Warmer, Henderson Stoneware, Bottle Shape, Metal Spout, 10 ⅝ In. 86.00
Plate, Blue Center, Blueberry Rim, Stamped, 10 ½ In. 85.00
Plate, Light Blue Interior, Blue Scrolled Exterior, Stamped, 5 ½ x 2 ¼ In. 75.00
Plate, Pussy Willow, Blue Swirl Ground, 1950s, 12 ¾ In. 275.00
Pot, Cover, Lily Of The Valley, Blue Ground, Handles, c.1979, 4 ½ x 7 In. 195.00
Vase, White Glaze, Oval Melon Shape, 3 ½ In. 29.00

DOULTON pottery and porcelain were made by Doulton and Co. of Burslem, England, after 1882. The name *Royal Doulton* appeared on the company's wares after 1902. Other pottery by Doulton is listed under Royal Doulton.

DOULTON BURSLEM ENGLAND

Ale Jug, Silver Rim, Disraeli Cameo, Lambeth, c.1910, 8 ¾ In. 146.00
Candlestick, Majolica, Brass Mounted, Multicolored Enamel, Lambeth, c.1895, 9 ⅝ In., Pair 711.00
Candlestick, Stoneware, Metal Mounted, Enameled Leaves, Lambeth, 8 ⅛ In., Pair 444.00
Candlestick, Stoneware, Multicolored Enamel, Raised Flowers, Leaves, Lambeth, 8 In., Pair. 237.00
Chamber Pot, Cover, Flowers, Gilt, Handles, 9 ½ x 10 In. 80.00
Cheese Dish, Cover, Flowers, Yellow, Red, Green Leaves, Gilt, Burslem, Late 1800s, 10 In. 50.00
Dispenser, Barrel Form, Lambeth, 19th Century, 14 In. 75.00

Figurine, Cymbal Player, Merry Musicians, George Tinworth, Lambeth, c.1900, 5 ½ In. 720.00
Jardiniere, Pedestal, Autumn Leaf Pattern, Lambeth, 30 x 13 In. 300.00
Jug, Galleon, Sailing Ships, Blue, White, Burslem, 6 ¼ In. 80.00
Jug, Isthmian Games, Chariot Scene, Gold Glaze, Marked, Burslem, 8 ½ In. 80.00
Jug, Windmill, Boats, Delft Style, Blue, White, Crown, Cogwheel Mark, Burslem, 6 ⅜ In. 50.00
Pitcher, Hannah Barlow, Gray, Blue Enamel, Buff Ground, Landscape, Lambeth, c.1879, 10 In. 1659.00
Pitcher, Verse, Good World, Brown, Yellow, Embossed, Stamped, Lambeth, 8 ½ In. 90.00
Pitcher, Verse, Landlord's Invitation Here Stop, Embossed, Yellow Interior, Lambeth, 8 In. 225.00
Plate, Madras, Flow Blue, c.1902, 10 In. 30.00
Platter, Madras, Flow Blue, 14 x 17 ½ In. 200.00
Punch Bowl, Riders, Hounds, Countryside, Footed, Burslem, 7 ⅞ x 14 ⅜ In. ..... *illus* 564.00
Teapot, River Scene, Boat, Tree, Brown Glaze, Blue Willow Relief, Lambeth, 4 ¾ In. 121.00
Urn, Cover, Art Union Of London, Incised, Slip Decoration, Stoneware, Lambeth, 11 ½ In. 780.00
Vase, Castle, Guys Clift, Oblong Body, Waisted Neck, L. Bentley, Burslem, c.1920, 7 ½ In. 150.00
Vase, Dragon Chasing Beetle, Flowers, Marked, Lambeth, c.1890, 17 In. ..... *illus* 16590.00
Vase, Landscape, Cattle, Dot Border, Wide Band, Hannah Barlow, Lambeth, 9 In. 652.00
Vase, Leaves, Edith Lupton, Lambeth, 4 In. 84.00
Vase, Slip Decorated, Double Gourd Shape, Woman's Portrait, c.1900, 5 ½ In. 326.00
Wall Bracket, Stoneware, Bird On Swag, Pierced, Scrolled, Monogram, Lambeth, 10 In. 2489.00

DRESDEN china is any china made in the town of Dresden, Germany. The most famous factory in Dresden is the Meissen factory. Figurines of eighteenth-century ladies and gentlemen, animal groups, or cherubs and other mythological subjects were popular. One special type of figurine was made with skirts of porcelain-dipped lace. Do not make the mistake of thinking that all pieces marked *Dresden* are from the Meissen factory. The Meissen pieces usually have crossed swords marks, and are listed under Meissen. Some recent porcelain from Ireland, called Irish Dresden, is not included in this book.

DRESDEN S GERMANY

Candelabrum, 2-Light, Flowers, 13 In., Pair 250.00
Centerpiece, 3 Angel Supports, Rose Design, Pierced, Marked, 7 ¾ x 15 In. 140.00
Centerpiece, 3 Cherubs On Base, Oval, Reticulated Bowl, 18 x 12 x 10 In. 900.00
Centerpiece, Leafy, Bowl, Sculpted Fruit & Flowers, Late 1800s, 11 In. 1876.00
Compote, 2 Sections, Octagonal Bowl, Rocaille Footed Base, Flowers, 13 ¾ In. 460.00
Compote, Figural, 4 Children As Feet, 6 ½ x 11 In. 263.00
Compote, Figural, Oval, Florets & Leaves, Tree Form Base, Man & Woman, Vines, 1800s, 18 In. 533.00
Compote, Man, Woman, 18th Century Dress, Flowers, Multicolored, 12 x 18 In. 351.00
Compote, Painted, Fired Gold, c.1940, 4 ½ x 7 ½ In. 176.00
Compote, Reticulated, Hand Painted, Schumann, 6 x 7 ½ In. 70.00
Compote, Woman, Seated, Cherubs, Applied Flower Garlands, Footed, 1890s, 19 In. ..... *illus* 267.00
Cup & Saucer, Demitasse, 3 Putti Circling Cup, Green Ground, Gilt 175.00
Figurine, 3 Women, Holding Flowers, White, Gold Green, 13 x 14 In. 702.00
Figurine, Ballerina, Pink, 7 In. 117.00
Figurine, Butcher, Animal Head, 3 ¾ In. 250.00
Figurine, Mother, Children, 18th Century Attire, Multicolored, c.1900, 10 x 10 In. 322.00
Figurine, Pied Piper, 7 In. 25.00
Figurine, Rooster, Brown, Gray, Red, Green, 4 ½ x 4 In. 55.00
Figurine, Rooster, Long Tail, Multicolored, 20th Century, 8 x 15 In. 200.00
Figurine, Sheep, Ireland, 2 ½ x 2 ½ In., Pair 75.00
Figurine, Woman, Looking Upwards, Wearing Hat, Enameled Flowers, 9 In. 192.00
Figurine, Woman, On Green Sofa, White Ruffled Dress, 5 x 6 In. 117.00
Figurine, Woman, White Gown With Flowers, c.1930, 6 x 5 x 4 In. 125.00
Frame, Angels, 20th Century, 11 In. 570.00
Group, Boy & Girl, Sitting In Field, Birdcage, Lamb, 2 Birds, 20th Century, 5 ¼ In. 175.00
Group, Chess Players, c.1930, 6 x 10 In. 263.00
Group, Children, Pets, Fruits, Flowers, Blue Mark, 8 ½ x 9 ½ In. 495.00
Group, Couple At Piano, 7 x 6 In. 234.00
Group, Die Werbung, Young Lovers In Parlor, Marked, 20th Century, 8 ¼ In. 225.00
Group, Lace, Marie Antoinette, Children, c.1900, 12 ½ In. 570.00
Group, Musicians, 4 Figures, Flute, Piano, Germany, 1899s, 12 x 13 In. 819.00
Group, Woman, 3 Attendants, Putti, Square Plinth, 4 Peg Feet, 15 x 8 ½ In. 1265.00
Placecard Holders, Flowers, 3 In., 8 Piece 76.00
Plate, Christmas 1972, 8 ½ In. 18.00
Plate, Young Woman, Amour Verfolgt Die Nymphen, Signed, A. Heer, 9 ½ In. 460.00
Sauceboat, Flowers, Molded Ozier Rim, Flat Leaf Handles, Enamel, Gilt, 10 In. 178.00
Tazza, Flowers, Gilt, Reticulated Rim, 3 ⅞ x 10 ⅛ In. 170.00
Tea Caddy, Flowers, Hand Painted, 4 In. 60.00
Urn, Cover, Flowers, 10 Children, Hand Painted, Base, Marked, 28 In. 770.00
Urn, Cover, Flowers, Multicolored, Handles, 1800s, 10 In., Pair 351.00

Doorstop, Poppies, In Vase, Painted, Cast Iron, Hubley, 10 ⅝ x 7 ⅞ In.
$115.00

Doorstop, Windmill, Painted, Cast Iron, Pat, Dec. 15, 1925, 6 ⅞ x 7 ½ In.
$345.00

Doulton, Punch Bowl, Riders, Hounds, Countryside, Footed, Burslem, 7 ⅞ x 14 ⅜ In.
$564.00

Doulton, Vase, Dragon Chasing Beetle, Flowers, Marked, Lambeth, c.1890, 17 In.
$16590.00

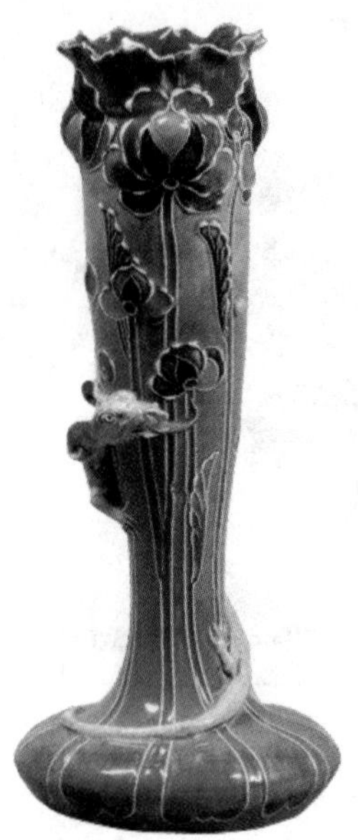

Dresden, Compote, Woman, Seated, Cherubs, Applied Flower Garlands, Footed, 1890s, 19 In.
$267.00

TIP

Stains on crystal stemware can sometimes be removed by rubbing the stain with a cut lemon or a cloth dipped in turpentine.

Urn, Cover, Landscape Scenes, Blue, Red, Gold, Angel Handles, Footed, 15 In. . . . 100.00
Urn, Figural, Applied Flowers, Seated Woman Handles, Base, 20th Century, 20 In. . . . 704.00
Urn, Lakeside Scene, Purple, Green, Gilt, Angel Handles, Marked, V.E.B., 16 ½ In. . . . *illus* 325.00
Vase, Colonial Man & Woman Dancing, Gold Ground, Handles, 8 In. . . . 382.00
Vase, Courting Scene, Pink, White, Gold Ormolu, Handles, Footed, Signed, 10 ½ In. . . . 225.00
Vase, Courting Scene, Pink & White, Gold Ormolu Fittings, Signed, 10 ½ In. . . . 225.00
Vase, Woman, Portrait, Gilt, Art Nouveau, Handles, Signed, c.1890, 11 ½ x 4 In. . . . 1320.00

DUNCAN & MILLER is a term used by collectors when referring to glass made by the George A. Duncan and Sons Company or the Duncan and Miller Glass Company. These companies worked from 1893 to 1955, when the use of the name Duncan was discontinued and the firm became part of the United States Glass Company. Early patterns may be listed under Pressed Glass.

Beehive, Plate, Amber . . . 10.00
Canterbury, Basket, Blue Opalescent, 9 ½ x 6 In. . . . 85.00
Canterbury, Sugar, 2 ½ In. . . . 9.00
Canterbury, Sugar & Creamer, 3 ¼ x 3 ¾ In. . . . 17.00
Canterbury, Tumbler, Cape Cod Blue, 5 ½ In. . . . 45.00
Caribbean, Wine, Ball Stem, Footed, 3 ½ In. . . . 15.00
Chanticleer, Cocktail Shaker, 6 x 3 ¾ In. . . . *illus* 325.00
Diamond Ridge, Cake Stand, 5 x 9 ⅛ In. . . . 57.00
First Love, Bowl, Fitted Flat Rim, 12 In. . . . 120.00
First Love, Candlestick, Flame, 6 In., Pair . . . 58.00
First Love, Compote, 4 ¾ In. . . . 31.00
First Love, Goblet, Terrace, 7 In. . . . 32.00
First Love, Relish, 2 Sections, 6 ½ In. . . . 38.00
First Love, Relish, Tab Handles, Sections, 6 In. . . . 29.00
First Love, Torte Plate, Terrace, 13 In. . . . 58.00
Hobnail, Powder Jar, Pink . . . 85.00
Hobnail, Rose Bowl, Pink . . . *illus* 78.00
Hobnail, Sugar & Creamer, Blue Opalescent, 8-Sided . . . 25.00
Sail Fish, Tumbler, Blue, 4 Piece . . . 25.00
Sandwich, Bowl, Flower, Ruffled Edge, 11 ½ In. . . . 85.00
Sandwich, Candlestick, 8 In., Pair . . . 22.00
Sandwich, Cocktail, 3 Oz., 4 ¼ In. . . . 10.00
Sandwich, Cruet, Oil, 5 In. . . . 45.00
Sandwich, Cup & Saucer, Crystal, 2 ¼ x 6 In. . . . 11.00
Sandwich, Plate, Salad, Crystal, Sawtooth Edge, 7 ⅛ In. . . . 8.00
Sandwich, Sugar & Creamer, Tray . . . 48.00
Sanibel, Bowl, Fruit, Pink Opalescent, 12 x 13 ¼ In. . . . *illus* 165.00
Starlight, Goblet, 10 Oz., 7 In. . . . 150.00
Sun Flower Patch, Bowl, Scalloped Edge, 3 x 9 In. . . . 35.00
Sylvan, Candy Box, Light Green, 3 ¾ x 6 ½ x 7 ¼ In. . . . *illus* 60.00
Tear Drop, Relish, Oval, Handles, 6 In. . . . 12.00
Tear Drop, Relish, Sections, Handles, 7 In. . . . 18.00
Venetian, Vase, Green, 6 ½ x 7 ½ In. . . . *illus* 55.00

DURAND art glass was made from 1924 to 1931. The Vineland Flint Glass Works was established by Victor Durand and Victor Durand Jr. in 1897. In 1924 Martin Bach Jr. and other artisans from the Quezal glassworks joined them at the Vineland, New Jersey, plant to make Durand art glass. They called their gold iridescent glass Gold Luster.

Bottle, White Hearts & Vines, Lustered Blue Ground, Signed, 12 ¾ In. . . . 2885.00
Candlestick, Blue Translucent Stem, Foot, Bobeche, Ambergris Stem, White Scalloped Rim, 4 In. 259.00
Candlestick, Gold Luster, Baluster Shape, Signed, 10 In., Pair . . . 1035.00
Candlestick, Translucent Blue On Ambergris, White Pulled Feathers, Disk Foot, 5 In., Pair . . 575.00
Cocktail Shaker, Green Cut To Clear, Nickel Plated Lid, 12 In. . . . 1438.00
Compote, Ribbed Blue Bowl Foot, Ambergris Stem, White Scalloped Rim, 6 In. . . . 518.00
Ginger Jar, Cover, Heart & Vine, Iridescent Blue, White Heart, Applied Amber Finial, 9 In. . . . 4255.00
Goblet, Cranberry To Clear Rim, Pulled Feather, Diamond Border, Yellow Stem, 6 ½ In. . . . 550.00
Jar, Cover, King Tut, Temple, Gold Iridescent, Green, 16 ½ In. . . . 7800.00
Lamp, Gold Iridescent Shade, Gold Threads, Metal Base, Electric, 11 ¾ In. . . . 403.00
Lamp, Gold Shade, Opal Pulled Feathers, Green, Gold Threads, 7 In. . . . 431.00
Lamp Base, Lady Gay Rose, Gold Iridescent Hooked & Pulled Feather, 25 ½ In. . . . 4600.00
Shade, Green Optic Ribs, Elongated Trumpet, Gold Interior, Blue, Pink Highlights, 10 x 3 In. 1093.00
Vase, Ambergris, Heart Shape Leaves, Hanging Vines, Signed, 12 In. . . . 460.00
Vase, Black, Blue Iridescent, Silvery Blue, Heart & Vine, Signed, 9 ½ In. . . . 2185.00

Dresden, Urn, Lakeside Scene, Purple, Green, Gilt, Angel Handles, Marked, V.E.B., 16 ½ In.
$325.00

Duncan & Miller, Chanticleer, Cocktail Shaker, 6 x 3 ¾ In.
$325.00

Duncan & Miller, Hobnail, Rose Bowl, Pink
$78.00

Duncan & Miller, Sanibel, Bowl, Fruit, Pink Opalescent, 12 x 13 ¼ In.
$165.00

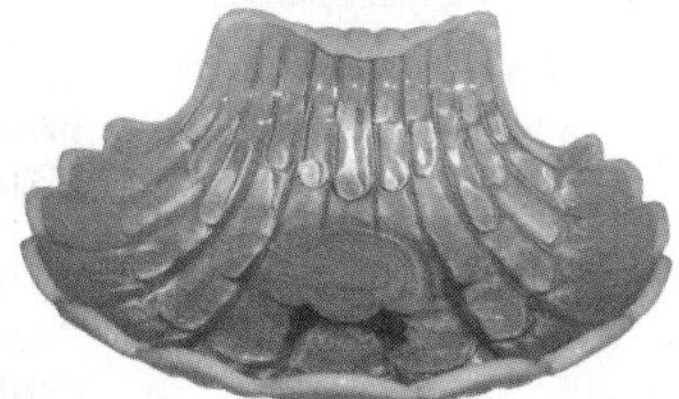

Duncan & Miller, Sylvan, Candy Box, Light Green, 3 ¾ x 6 ½ x 7 ¼ In.
$60.00

Duncan & Miller, Venetian, Vase, Green, 6 ½ x 7 ½ In.
$55.00

Durand, Vase, Cranberry Cut To Clear, Flowers, Signed, Durand 4231, 9 3⁄4 In.
$761.00

TIP

Invert your old glass cake-stand and use it for chips and dip. The pedestal must be hollow to hold the dip; the top plate is fine for the chips.

Durand, Vase, Blue Iridescent, White Heart & Vines, Shouldered, Paper Label, 8 ½ In.
$2100.00

TIP

Products that are used to remove lime buildup in showers will also work on glass vases.

Durand, Vase, Gold Iridescent, Pulled Feather, Pink Ground, Baluster, 9 ½ In.
$4800.00

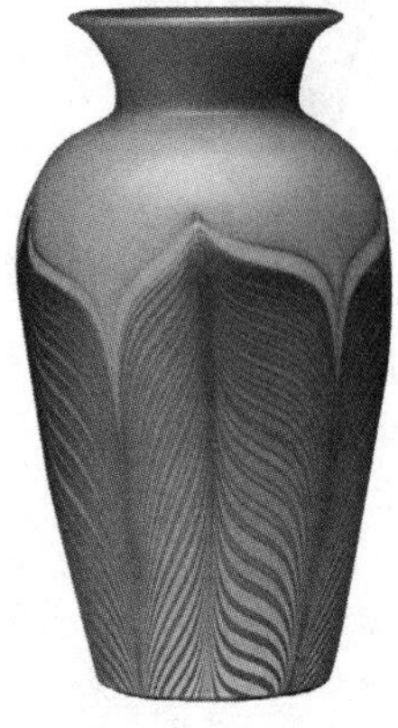

Durand, Vase, Marigold Iridescent, White Feathers, Blue Gray Tip, Gold Threads, 10 ½ In.
$805.00

TIP

Be sure ladders, trash cans, sheds, and cars are not too close to the house. A burglar can use them to climb up to a second-story window.

Vase, Blue, Gold, Shouldered, 5 ¾ In. 489.00
Vase, Blue Cut To Clear, Window Panes, Diamonds, Bulbous, Shouldered, Signed, 6 ¼ In. 633.00
Vase, Blue Iridescent, Baluster, 10 ¼ x 5 In. 700.00
Vase, Blue Iridescent, Gold, Magenta, 14 ⅞ In. 1955.00
Vase, Blue Iridescent, Gold Overtones, Genie Bottle Shape, Signed, 15 In. 1000.00
Vase, Blue Iridescent, Green, Blue Threading, Wide, Signed, 6 In. 575.00
Vase, Blue Iridescent, White Drizzled Vines, Tapered, Ambergris Knob Footed, 5 In. 1285.00
Vase, Blue Iridescent, White Hearts & Vines, Shouldered, Paper Label, 8 ½ In. *illus* 2100.00
Vase, Blue Iridescent, White Hearts & Vines, Tapered, 10 In. 1920.00
Vase, Blue Iridescent, White Hearts & Vines, Gold Iridescent Foot, Flared Rim, 8 ¼ In. 750.00
Vase, Blue Iridescent Luster, Beehive, 7 Rings, Oval, Signed, 6 ¾ In. 575.00
Vase, Blue Luster, Cylinder Shape, Signed, 13 In. 1495.00
Vase, Blue Luster, Gold Threading, Egg Shape, Signed, 5 In. 575.00
Vase, Blue Luster, Pulled Swirls, Flared, Signed, 8 In. 1380.00
Vase, Burnt Orange Iridescent, Black Pulled Heart & Vines, 10 In. 900.00
Vase, Cranberry Cut To Clear, Flowers, Signed, Durand 4231, 9 ¾ In. *illus* 761.00
Vase, Enameled, Purple Branches, Brown Leaves, Lavender Flowers, Pink Ground, 5 ¾ In. 69.00
Vase, Gold, Blue, Lavender, Iridescent Swirl, Baluster, Signed, 10 ½ In. 1380.00
Vase, Gold, Green Pulled Heart & Vines, 10 ¾ In. 1750.00
Vase, Gold Iridescent, Baluster, 14 ½ In., Pair 3120.00
Vase, Gold Iridescent, Gold Luster, Iridescent Blue Coil, Flared Rim, 10 ½ In. 2415.00
Vase, Gold Iridescent, Green Heart & Vine, Gold Interior, 10 x 6 In. 1150.00
Vase, Gold Iridescent, Green Leaf & Vine, Flared Rim, Signed, 8 ¼ In. 920.00
Vase, Gold Iridescent, Pulled Feather, Pink Ground, Baluster, 9 ½ In. *illus* 4800.00
Vase, Gold Iridescent Random Threading, Gold & Orange Ground, 6 In. 230.00
Vase, Gold Iridiscent, Round, Signed, c.1910, 6 In. 206.00
Vase, Gold Luster Iridescent, Red Overtones, Urn Shape, Signed, 9 In. 690.00
Vase, King Tut, Blue Iridescent, Red Coil, White Interior, 4 ½ In. 3335.00
Vase, King Tut, Gold, Apple Green, Footed, Signed, 12 In., Pair 1600.00
Vase, King Tut, Gold, Green Ground, 6 ½ In. 1380.00
Vase, King Tut, Green, Gold, Frosted Marigold, Flared, 6 In. 1380.00
Vase, King Tut, Green, Gold Waves, Glossy Yellow Interior, Signed, 8 x 6 In. 1700.00
Vase, King Tut, Green, Iridescent Marigold, Metal Stand, Signed, 12 In. 1955.00
Vase, King Tut, Platinum & Blue Iridescent, Green Ground, Signed, 4 In. 460.00
Vase, King Tut, Silver & Blue Iridescent, Flared, 7 In. 1093.00
Vase, King Tut, Silvery Blue, Footed, 12 In., Pair 3900.00
Vase, King Tut, Silvery Blue, Footed, 14 In., Pair 4500.00
Vase, Marigold Iridescent, White Feathers, Blue Gray Tip, Gold Threads, 10 ½ In. *illus* 805.00
Vase, Moorish Crackle, Ambergris, Blue Spatter, Cylindrical, 10 In. 748.00
Vase, Moorish Crackle, Ambergris, Iridescent Blue, White, Navy Blue, 13 In. *illus* 2645.00
Vase, Moorish Crackle, Emerald Green, Swirled Amber, Gold Highlights, Ball Shape, 7 ½ In. 748.00
Vase, Moorish Crackle, Iridescent Gold, Royal Blue, White, 8 ½ In. 690.00
Vase, Moorish Crackle, White, Royal Blue Patterns, Ball Shape, c.1928, 11 In. 4485.00
Vase, Moorish Crackle, White & Royal Blue Over Amber, c.1928, 10 x 11 In. 4485.00
Vase, Mottled Orange, Black Handles, Cluthra Glass, Urn Shape, 11 In. 1140.00
Vase, Mottled Orange, Clear Applied Design, 2 Handles, 12 ¼ In., Pair 900.00
Vase, Opal, Blue Pulled Feather, Gold Iridescent Tip, Threading, Shouldered, 9 In. 1380.00
Vase, Opal, Gold, Blue Heart, Vines, Threading, Iridescent Gold Foot, Signed, 12 In. 1380.00
Vase, Opal, Green, Gold Coil, 10 In. 1898.00
Vase, Opal, Iridescent Gold Clinging Vines, Pinched Waist, 11 In. 805.00
Vase, Translucent Red, Platinum White Pulled Feather, Shouldered, 9 In. 604.00
Vase, Translucent Yellow Luster, Cut Flowers Band, Footed, Urn, 12 In. 880.00
Vase, Trumpet, White & Green Pulled Feather, Ambergris & Green Ground, 10 In. 920.00
Vase, Trumpet, White Pulled Feather, Yellow, Green Ground, Cone Shape Foot, 10 In. 805.00
Vase, Turquoise Iridescent, Stovepipe Shape, 10 In. 575.00
Vase, White Pulled Feather, Clear, Flashed Green Top, 13 ¾ In., Pair 1920.00

DURANT KILNS was founded by Jean Durant Rice in 1910 in Bedford Village, New York. He hired Leon Volkmar to oversee production. The pottery made both tableware and artware. Rice died in 1919, leaving Leon Volkmar to run the business. After 1930 the name Durant Kilns was changed and only the Volkmar mark was used.

DuranT

Bowl, Flared, Ridged, Persian Blue Volcanic Glaze, c.1915, 6 x 15 ½ In. 500.00
Bowl, Flora Form, Light Turquoise Glaze, Inscribed, c.1919, 3 x 13 ½ In. 173.00
Bowl, Low, Turquoise Glaze, c.1917, 14 ½ x 4 In. 600.00
Bowl, Persian Blue Glazed Interior, Aubergine Exterior, c.1922, 7 ¼ In. 173.00
Bowl, Turquoise Blue, Crackle Glaze, Unfinished Base, Incised, c.1915, 14 ¾ In. 92.00
Bowl, Turquoise Glaze, Flat Rim, 1917, 4 x 14 ½ In. 650.00

Platter, Persian Blue Crackle Glaze, Signed, 15 ¼ x 7 ¾ In. . . . 95.00
Tray, Blue Egyptian Glaze, 6-Sided, Low Foot, Leon Volkmar, c.1923, 11 ¾ In. . . . 250.00

ELFINWARE is a mark found on Dresden-like porcelain that was sold in dime stores and gift shops. Many pieces were decorated with raised flowers. The mark was registered by Breslauer-Underberg, Inc., of New York City in 1947. Pieces marked Elfinware Made in Germany had been sold since 1945 by this importer.

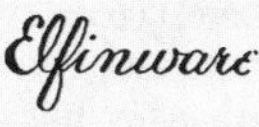

Boot, Flowers, Scalloped Top, Gold Trim, 5 In. . . . 16.00
Dish, Leaf Shape, 3 ½ In. . . . 5.00
Watering Can, Spinach, Flowers, c.1920, 2 ¼ In. . . . 65.00

ELVIS PRESLEY, the well-known singer, lived from 1935 to 1977. He became famous by 1956. Elvis appeared on television, starred in twenty-seven movies, and performed in Las Vegas. Memorabilia from any of the Presley shows, his records, and even memorials made after his death are collected.

Calendar, 1978, 17 Pictures Of Elvis Performing, 9 x 6 In. . . . 10.00
Decanter, Aloha Elvis, First In Series, McCormick, Box, 17 x 7 x 6 In. . . . 25.00
Decanter, Elvis, Guitar, Silver Anniversary, Red Velvet Box, McCormick, 16 x 9 In. . . . 40.00
Decanter, Elvis, Karate, McCormick, Box, 15 ½ x 14 x 5 ¼ In. . . . 20.00
Decanter, Elvis, Singing, Gold, McCormick, Blue Velvet Box, 16 ½ x 7 x 6 In. . . . 40.00
Decanter, Elvis 55, Pink Jacket, Guitar, 2nd In Series, McCormick, Box, 16 ½ x 8 In. . . . 20.00
Decanter, Elvis 68, McCormick, Box, 16 ½ x 7 x 6 ¾ In. . . . 30.00
Head Vase, Elvis, In Blue Shirt, 5 ½ In. . . . 45.00
Mug, Singing Hound Dog, Nostalgia Collectibles, Japan, 1985, 3 ½ In. . . . 45.00
Perfume Bottle, Teddy Bear, Elvis Presley Enterprises, Screw-On Top, Label, 1957, 3 In. . . . 77.00
Record, 33 ⅓ RPM, Elvis, Aloha From Hawaii Via Satellite, 2 Records, RCA, 1973 . . . 24.00
Record, 33 ⅓ RPM, Elvis, Playing Guitar On Cover, Long Playing, RCA Victor, 1956 . . . 45.00
Record, 33 ⅓ RPM, Kissin' Cousins, Soundtrack, 1964 . . . 210.00
Record, 45 RPM, One Night, I Got Stung!, Black Label, 1958 . . . 40.00
Record, 78 RPM, Christmas, Sealed, 1970 . . . 15.00
Sheet Music, Love Me Tender, 1956 . . . 27.00

ENAMELS listed here are made of glass particles and other materials heated and fused to metal. In the eighteenth and nineteenth centuries, workmen from Russia, France, England, and other countries made small boxes and table pieces of enamel on metal. One form of English enamel is called *Battersea* and is listed under that name. There was a revival of interest in enameling in the 1930s and a new style evolved. There is now renewed interest in the artistic enameled plaques, vases, ashtrays, and jewelry. Enamels made since the 1930s are usually on copper or steel, although silver was often used for jewelry. Graniteware is a separate category, and enameled metal kitchen pieces may be included in the Kitchen category.

Ashtray, Blue Green, Black Linear Pattern, Sticker, Bovano . . . 55.00
Bell Push, Silver Gilt Bird, Head Mounts, c.1975, 3 In. . . . 944.00
Bonbonniere, Gold, Crowned Incuse, Round Box, Bleu-De-Roi, Swiss, c.1785, 3 In. . . . 12338.00
Bowl, Blue Green, Shallow, Geometrics, 8 ½ x 6 In. . . . 100.00
Bowl, Indigo Patina, Copper, Footed, Marie Zimmerman, 7 ¼ x 10 ¾ In. . . . 1680.00
Bowl, Rounded Triangle, Turquoise & Orange Design, Green Ground, Kareka, 6 ½ In. . . . 45.00
Bowl, Teal, Copper, Scalloped Rim, Marked, Stavre Gregor Panis, 6 ½ In. . . . *illus* 220.00
Box, Cover, Precious Objects, Foo Dog Finial, Chinese, 20th Century, 4 x 5 ½ In. . . . 944.00
Box, Domed Cover, Copper, Hammered, Green Trees, Sunset, Fruit, Mass., c.1910, 3 x 6 In. . . . 948.00
Box, Heart Shape, Silver Gilt, Flowers, Scrolls, Stippled Ground, Moscow, c.1912, 3 In. . . . 4720.00
Box, Hinged Cover, Heart Shape, Silver, Gems, Flowers, Scrolls, Gilt Interior, Moscow, c.1895 . 3220.00
Box, Peacock Shape, Silver Gilt, Vienna, Late 19th Century, 11 ¼ In. . . . 18750.00
Card Holder, Flower, Copper, Patina, Arts Crafts Shop, 3 ¾ x 2 ¾ In. . . . *illus* 385.00
Cigarette Case, Flower Vines, Multicolored, Gilt, Stratton, 4 ¾ x 3 ⅜ x ⅛ In. . . . 35.00
Cigarette Case, Geometrics, Multiolored, Center Cipher, Crown, Silver Ground, Russia, c.1910, 3 In. 2360.00
Cigarette Case, Silver, Gilt, Flowers, Peacock, Bird Of Paradise, Moscow, c.1900, 4 In. . . . 4248.00
Cigarette Case, Silver, Photo, Nobleman, Gems, Multicolored, Moscow, c.1910, 4 In. . . . 16520.00
Cigarette Case, Silver, Swan, Flowers, Butterfly, V. Andreev, Moscow, c.1902, 4 In. . . . 5900.00
Coaster, Cocktail, Wine Glass Image, Bovano Of Cheshire Sticker, 3 ½ In., 8 Piece . . . 120.00
Coin Purse, Silver Gilt, Flowers, Scrolls, Interior Pouches, Moscow, c.1905, 3 In. . . . 3776.00
Dish, Flower Design, Deep Blue, Signed, Edward Winter, 6 ½ In. . . . 125.00
Egg, Stylized Lotus Flowers, Multicolored, Gilt, Wood Stand, 17 In. . . . 80.00
Fork, Hors D'Oeuvres, Stylized Leaf, Blue, Green, Silver, American, Box, 5 In. . . . 2040.00
Kovsh, Flowers, Leaves, Geometrics, Silver Gilt, Moscow, 1908-17, 4 ½ In. . . . *illus* 8800.00
Kovsh, Ovchinnikov, Silver, Flowers, Scrolls, Blue, Green, Gilt Interior, 2 x 5 x 3 In. . . . 5750.00

Durand, Vase, Moorish Crackle, Ambergris, Iridescent Blue, White, Navy Blue, 13 In.
$2645.00

Enamel, Bowl, Teal, Copper, Scalloped Rim, Marked, Stavre Gregor Panis, 6 ½ In.
$220.00

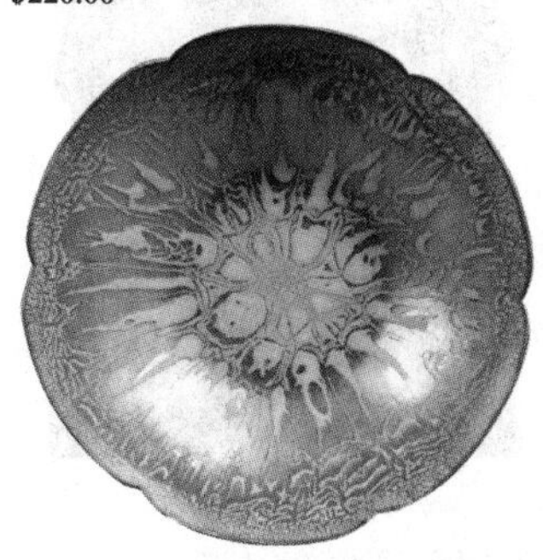

Enamel, Card Holder, Flower, Copper, Patina, Arts Crafts Shop, 3 ¾ x 2 ¾ In.
$385.00

D

TIP

Don't stop your mail and newspapers when you go away if you can get a friend to pick them up. A stop-order may alert a burglar.

Enamel, Kovsh, Flowers, Leaves, Geometrics, Silver Gilt, Moscow, 1908-17, 4 ½ In.
$8800.00

Enamel, Plaque, Spanish Galleon, Copper Frame, Signed, J.H., 1907, 9 ½ x 7 ¼ In.
$1320.00

Erickson, Compote, Clear, Smoke, 4 ⅜ x 6 ¾ In.
$69.00

ES Germany, Ewer, Man, 2 Women, Instruments, Prov Saxe, Green Mark, 10 In.
$275.00

Kovsh, Silver Gilt, Flowers, Scrolls, Geometric Designs, Ring Foot, Moscow, c.1910, 5 In. 9440.00

Panel Set, Bronze, Pewter, Asian Scenes, Figures, P. & K. Laverne, 1960s, 29 x 16 In., 4. 7500.00

Plaque, Spanish Galleon, Copper Frame, Signed, J.H., 1907, 9 ½ x 7 ¼ In. *illus* 1320.00

Plate, Copper, 2 Giraffes, Gold Flecks, 7 ¾ In. 45.00

Plate, Red, Abstract Designs, White Signature On Back, Edward Winter, 7 In. 150.00

Salt, Silver, Gilt, Pan Slavic Designs, Green, Purple, Blue, Moscow, c.1910, 2 In. 826.00

Spoon, Berry, Silver Gilt, Scrolled Bowl, Blue, Green, Red, Moscow, 1912, 7 In. 3304.00

Spoon, Flowers, Multicolored, White Ground, Sterling Silver, Moscow, 1892, 7 In. 600.00

Spoon, Kokoshnik, Paneled Handle, Scroll Bowl Back, Blue, Green, White, Russia, 5 In., 12 Piece 5290.00

Tea Glass Holder, Flowers, Song Birds, Silver Gilt Highlights, Ovchinnikov, c.1980, 5 In. 2360.00

Tray, Green Finish, Zigzag Pattern, Marked Olden, Norway, 18 ½ In. 75.00

Tray, Turquoise, Teal & Orange Design, Gold Green Ground, Square, Bovano, 8 ½ In. 40.00

Vase, Quadrilateral, Copper, Scrolling Lotus, Turquoise Ground, Wooden Stand, Chinese, 7 ⅝ In. 144.00

Vase, Red Orange, Cylinder, Line Designs, Vallenti, Italy, 10 x 2 ⅜ In. 195.00

Vinaigrette, 19th Century Women, Gold Mount, Push Button Top, Scent Bottle Inside, 2 ½ In. 998.00

Vinaigrette, Apple Shape, Gold Mount, Engraved Leaves, Applied Fly, Swiss, 1860, 1 ¼ In. 1418.00

Vinaigrette, Apple Shape, Yellow, Cherubs, Cat, Applied Stem, Austria, c.1870, 1 x ¾ In. 394.00

Vinaigrette, Art Nouveau Flower, Purple, Green Leaves, Silver Mount, Swing-Away Lid, 1 In. 115.00

Vinaigrette, Art Nouveau Woman In Cartouche, Blue Ground, Round, Vienna, 1 ¼ In. 525.00

Vinaigrette, Bird, Flowers, Black Ground, Gold, Book Shape, Cut Grille Inside, 1 x ¾ In. 761.00

Vinaigrette, Blue, Painted Sheet Music, Ball Shape, Push Button Stem, c.1850, 1 ¾ In. 971.00

Vinaigrette, Blue Guilloche, Acorn Shape, Pendant Bail Screws Off, ¾ In. 189.00

Vinaigrette, Cherub, 14K Gold, Tureen Shape, Hinged Lid, Applied Handles, ¾ x 1 ¼ In. 788.00

Vinaigrette, Cobalt Blue, Flowers, Gold Tracery, Egg Shape, Hinged, Lift-Out Grille, Vienna, 2 In. 814.00

Vinaigrette, Courting Couples, Landscape, Silver Mount, Watering Can Shape, Vienna, 1 In. 630.00

Vinaigrette, Figures In Landscape, Ball Shape, Flattened Base, Seaweed Grille, 1 ½ In. 394.00

Vinaigrette, Geometric Design, Silver Mount, Quatrefoil, Center Square Door Opens, 2 In. 168.00

Vinaigrette, Old Master, Bacchanalia Scene, Watch Case Shape, Vienna, 1 ¾ In. 420.00

Vinaigrette, Raised Flowers, 16K Gold, Basket Shape, Hinged Lid, Loop Handle, c.1870, 1 In. 761.00

Vinaigrette, Scent Bottle, Classical Scenes, Quiver Shape, 2 Hinged Lids, Vienna, 4 In. 630.00

Vinaigrette, Strawberries, Flowers, Blue Ground, Engine Turned, Egg Shape, Vienna, 2 In. 289.00

Vinaigrette, Strawberry Shape, Red Guilloche, Rose Gold Leaves, Hinged Stem Lid, ¾ In. 289.00

Vinaigrette, Watering Can, Courting Scene, Engraved Lid, Marked, LP, Austria, 1 ¼ In. 550.00

ERICKSON glass was made in Bremen, Ohio, from 1943 to 1961. Carl and Steven Erickson designed and made free-blown and mold-blown glass. Best known are pieces with heavy ball bases filled with controlled bubbles.

Compote, Clear, Smoke, 4 ⅜ x 6 ¾ In. *illus* 69.00

ERPHILA is a mark found on Czechoslovakian and other pottery and porcelain made after 1920. This mark was used on items imported by Ebeling & Reuss, Philadelphia, a giftware firm that is still operating in Pennsylvania. The mark is a combination of the letters E and R (Ebeling & Reuss) and the first letters of the city, Phila(delphia). Many whimsical figural pitchers and creamers, figurines, platters, and other giftwares carry this mark.

Bowl, Cherry Chintz, Open Weave, Oval, 10 x 6 ⅝ x 2 ¾ In. 55.00

Cigarette Holder, Cat, Black, Orange, Germany, 6 In. 110.00

Figurine, Dog, Dachshund, Germany, Signed, 7 In. 55.00

Figurine, Dog, Terrier, Seated, Smoky Gray Glaze, Germany, Green Stamp, 5 ½ x 3 ½ In. 15.00

Jug, Toucan, Red & Black, Ditmar Urbach, Czechoslovakia, 9 x 7 ½ In. 529.00

Pitcher, Billy Goat, Yellow, Black Red, Art Deco, Czechoslovakia, 8 ¾ In. 390.00

Pitcher, Cat, Yellow, Black, Red, Ring Tail Handle, Czechoslovakia, 8 ¼ In. 390.00

Pitcher, Dog, Yellow, Black Red, Art Deco, Czechoslovakia, 6 ¼ In. 420.00

Pitcher, Ram, Yellow, Black Red, Art Deco, Czechoslovakia, 8 ¾ In. 440.00

ES GERMANY porcelain was made at the factory of Erdmann Schlegelmilch from 1861 to 1937 in Suhl, Germany. The porcelain, marked ES Germany or ES Suhl, was sold decorated or undecorated. Other pieces were made at a factory in Saxony, Prussia, and are marked ES Prussia. Reinhold Schlegelmilch made the famous wares marked RS Germany.

Ewer, Man, 2 Women, Instruments, Prov Saxe, Green Mark, 10 In. *illus* 275.00

ESKIMO artifacts of all types are collected. Carvings of whale or walrus teeth are listed under Scrimshaw. Baskets are in the Basket category. All other types of Eskimo art are listed here. In Canada and some other areas, the term Inuit is used instead of Eskimo.

Basket, Cover, Sinew & Baleen, Carved Ivory Walrus Finial, 3 ½ In. 176.00

Basket, Lid, Cup'it, Hooper Bay Area, Alaska, Pre 1940, 8 ¾ x 9 In. 225.00

Basket, Lid, Dyed Seal Gut Designs, Hooper Bay Area, 6 x 5 In. 175.00
Doll, Cloth, Hand Stitched Felt Face, Fur Coat, Hood, Leggings, Bib, Beaded, Pre 1945, 11 In. .. 125.00
Doll, Hand Painted Leather Face, Fur Trimmed Shift With Hood, Leather Boots, 1945, 8 In. .. 72.00
Doll, Sealskin, Ivory Face, c.1900, 6 In. 705.00
Figure, Eskimo, Man, Wearing Parka, Stone, Late 20th Century, 9 In. 60.00
Figure, Eskimo, Standing, Holding Weapon, On Base, Soapstone, Signed, DMU, 3 In. 20.00
Figure, Eskimo On One Knee, Soapstone, Luke Anowtalik, 7 In. 425.00
Figure, Hunter, With Seal, Artist Signed, 8 ½ In. 175.00
Figure, Inuit Lying On Ice, Soapstone, Carved, 11 In. 519.00
Figure, Man, Wrestling Seal, Soapstone, Marked, c.1975, 8 ⅕ In. 940.00
Figure, Mother & Child, Soapstone, Marked, 1978, 11 ¼ In. 1175.00
Figure, Stylized Bird On Horn, Primitive Elk Horn, Alaska, 9 x 7 ¾ In. 25.00
Figure, Young Seal, Basking, Soapstone, Charlie Eyaituq, Belcher Island, 5 ½ x 2 ¼ In. 295.00
Knife, Scrimshaw Sheath, Inuit, Sinew, Bone Handle, Reindeer, Sleds, c.1886, 12 ½ In. 345.00
Letter Opener, Figural Handle, Seal, Ivory, Carved, 9 ½ x 1 ¼ In. 110.00
Parka, Caribou Fur, Hide Lining, Walrus Tusk Design, Leather Bands, 44 x 54 In. 374.00
Parka, Caribou Fur, Sinew Sewn, Lined With Hide, Walrus Tusk Design At Chest, 44 In. 325.00
Postcard, Eskimo Sunday School, Cape Prince Of Wales, Real Photo 90.00
Rug, Animal Skin & Leather, Russia, 42 x 43 In. 240.00

ETLING glass pieces are very similar in design to those made by Lalique and Phoenix. They were made in France for Etling, a retail shop. They date from the 1920s and 1930s.

ETLING
FRANCE

Bowl, Sunflower, Opalescent, Signed, 12 In. 358.00
Vase, Opaline, 3 Entwined Fish, Footed, 1920s, 8 ½ x 5 In. .... 425.00 to 800.00

FABERGE was a firm of jewelers and goldsmiths founded in St. Petersburg, Russia, in 1842, by Gustav Faberge. Peter Carl Faberge, his son, was jeweler to the Russian Imperial Court from about 1870 to 1914. The rare Imperial Easter eggs, jewelry, and decorative items are very expensive today.

ФАБЕРЖЕ
КФ

Bell Push, Laurels, Silver, Gilt, Enamel, Guilloche, Cabochon, Marked, 1 ½ x 2 In. .... *illus* 11000.00
Bell Push, Silver, Translucent Enamel, Sapphire, Diamond Border, H.W., c.1900, 2 ½ In. 2000.00
Bookmark, Silver, Sword Shape, Sapphire, 6 Rose Cut Diamonds, c.1890. .... 14500.00
Box, Enamel, Gold Vermeil, Tree, 1 ½ In. 2925.00
Box, Ruby, Silver, Egg Shape, Finial, Stand, 4 ¾ In. 2574.00
Case, Repousse Silver, Matte Painted Maid, Goat, Enamel, c.1912, 5 In. 14160.00
Case, Sunburst Design, Center Rose Cut Diamond, Gilt, Yellow Enamel, H. Wigstrom, 4 In. .. 47200.00
Cigarette Case, Enamel, Guilloche, Gold, Silver, Ruby Cabochon, Marked, 3 ¼ In. .... *illus* 27500.00
Cigarette Case, Nephrite, Gold, Diamonds, Engraved, Oblong, Michael Perchin, 4 x 3 In. 17625.00
Compote, Nephrite Jade, Encrusted Diamonds, Silver Mounts, Footed, 3 ⅛ x 4 ⅜ In. 7700.00
Cup, Silver, Griffins Holding Wreath, Gilt Interior, Mark, 3 x 2 In. 5750.00
Dresser Jar, Embossed Flowers, Scroll Lid, Cut Glass, Cylinder Shape, c.1960, 3 x 3 In. 1659.00
Jug, Cut Glass, Claret, Chased Silver Mount Collar, Base, c.1880, 8 In. 11800.00
Kovsh, Flowers, Blue, Pink, Enamel, Silver, Gold Wash Marked, 6 x 5 x 9 In. 4000.00
Spoon, Double Eagle, Enamel, Sterling Silver, Case, 5 ⅜ In., 6 Piece 2350.00
Teaspoon, Silver, Husk Wreath, Reeded Stem, Oak Case, Moscow, c.1910, 6 In., 12 Piece. 9480.00

FAIENCE refers to tin-glazed earthenware, especially the wares made in France, Germany, and Scandinavia. It is also correct to say that faience is the same as majolica or Delft, although usually the term refers only to the tin-glazed pottery of the three regions mentioned.

Basket, Magisterial Painting, Iris, Joseph Hannong, 1760s, 3 x 13 In. 3525.00
Bowl, Men In Tree, Cupid On Throne, c.1750, 3 ½ x 12 ½ In. 881.00
Dish, Leaf, Galle, 3 Sections, Painted, Water Flowers, In Lake, Early 1900s, 10 ¾ In. 770.00
Dish, Lobed Quatrefoil Shape, Grotesque Interior, French Blue & White, 10 ¾ x 8 ½ In. 720.00
Figurine, Lion, Naturalistic, Painted, France, Mid 1700s, 6 ¼ x 5 ¼ In. 1645.00
Figurine, Monk, Drinking, Seated, Basket Of Food, 19th Century, 13 In. 587.00
Figurine, St. Barbara, Crowned, Standing, Holding Tower, France, 12 In. 296.00
Group, Night Watchman, Dutch, Signed, B.P., 12 x 8 ½ In. 351.00
Obelisk, Delft, Flowers, Rinceaux, Chinoiserie Landscapes, Blue, Green, Black, 9 ½ In. 4113.00
Pitcher, Hound Handle, Vance, Brown Glaze, Amber, Tan, c.1902, 10 ½ x 10 ¾ In. 259.00
Plate, Birds, In Landscape, Flower & Bird Border Vignettes, Early 1800s, 9 ¾ In. 588.00
Platter, Flowers, Vignettes, c.1740, 16 ½ x 13 In. 147.00
Punch Bowl, Yellow Ground, Vertical Stripes, Burgundy, Poppies, France, 14 ½ x 7 ⅜ In. 237.00
Sauceboat, Dotted Handles, Chinoiserie Scene, Blue, White Ground, c.1700, 7 ¾ x 1 In. 612.00
Tureen, Chinese Figural & Landscape Scenes, 18th Century, 12 ¼ In. 470.00
Tureen, Cover, Undertray, Birds, Branch Handles, c.1775, 5 ¾ In. .... *illus* 2300.00

Faberge, Bell Push, Laurels, Silver, Gilt, Enamel, Guilloche, Cabochon, Marked, 1 ½ x 2 In.
$11000.00

Faberge, Cigarette Case, Enamel, Guilloche, Gold, Silver, Ruby Cabochon, Marked, 3 ¼ In.
$27500.00

TIP

Bed-and-bath stores stock many of the supplies needed to care for antiques and collectibles. Storage units, cloth hanging bags, repair supplies, gadgets that help in moving furniture, and humidifiers are just a few.

Faience, Tureen, Cover, Undertray, Birds, Branch Handles, c.1775, 5 ¾ In.
$2300.00

Faience, Vase, Aesthetic, Baluster, Eagle, Attacking Dragon, Enameled, Gilt, 15 ⅜ In.
$770.00

Fan, Electric, Westinghouse, Whirlwind, 12 x 9 In.
$350.00

Tureen, Multicolored Sprays, Handles, Finial, Cover, c.1775, 15 ¾ x 10 ¼ In. 587.00
Urn, Landscape, Multicolored, Boat, Serpent Handles, Pear Finial, 22 ½ In., Pair 1200.00
Vase, Aesthetic, Baluster, Eagle, Attacking Dragon, Enameled, Gilt, 15 ⅜ In. . . . . . *illus* 770.00
Vase, Baluster, Ribbed, Blue Lambrequins & Flowers, 18th Century, 9 ½ In. 206.00
Vase, Bleu Persan, Opaque White On Translucent Cobalt Blue Ground, c.1640, 10 ¼ In. 1528.00
Vase, Bottle Shape, Spherical, Scroll Shape Handles, Multicolored Flowers, 12 ¼ x 8 ½ In. . . . 470.00
Vase, Cascading Leaves, Multicolored, Scrolling Handles, 12 ½ In. 130.00
Wine Rinser, Figural & Animal Caricatures, Grotesques, Young, Green, Aqua, 4 x 5 In. 1593.00

FAIRINGS are small souvenir boxes and figurines that were sold at country fairs during the nineteenth century. Most were made in Germany. Reproductions of fairings are being made, especially of the famous Twelve Months after Marriage series.

Figurine, Girl In Cape, Standing, 4 ¾ In. 130.00
Figurine, Highland Lass & Lassie, Holding Spaniels, 5 ¾ In., Pair 72.00
Striker, Shoes, Flower Buckles, 2 ¼ x 2 In. 90.00
Trinket Box, Walnut, Carved, Shaped Panels, Maltese Cross Decoration, 5 ¼ x 8 ¾ In. 209.00

FAIRYLAND LUSTER *pieces are included in the Wedgwood category.*

FAMILLE ROSE, *see Chinese Export category.*

FANS have been used for cooling since the days of the ancients. By the eighteenth century, the fan was an accessory for the lady of fashion and very elaborate and expensive fans were made. Sticks were made of ivory or wood, set with jewels or carved. The fans were made of painted silk or paper. Inexpensive paper fans printed with advertising were giveaways in the late nineteenth and early twentieth centuries. Electric fans were introduced in 1882.

Advertising, C.M. Hunsicker Photographer, Woman, Paddle, Kutztown, Pa., 14 In. 30.00
Advertising, Carhart's Choice Tobacco, Sweet Scotch Snuff, Landscape Scene, Wood Handle . 20.00
Advertising, Dr Pepper, Bottle, Drink A Bite To Eat, Green, c.1930, 11 ½ x 8 In. 80.00
Advertising, Dr Pepper, Dr Pepper Bottling Co., Miss-Eudora, Ark., Frame, 12 ½ x 9 In. 80.00
Advertising, Dr Pepper, Woman In Yellow Dress, c.1930, 14 ¼ x 8 ¼ In. . . . . 50.00 to 70.00
Advertising, Dromoc Cure-All, Windsor Drugs, 7 x 9 In. 123.00
Advertising, Hires Root Beer, Cough Cure, Cardboard Lithograph, 1895, 8 x 14 In. 173.00
Advertising, Woman's Suffrage & Baseball, Votes For Women, Sepia, 7 In. 385.00
Electric, Bankers, 4 Blades, Globe Cage, Cast Iron Base, Variable Speed, c.1930, 19 In. 605.00
Electric, Emerson, 6 Brass Blades, 3-Speed, 1910s-20s, 19 ½ x 16 ¾ In. 252.00
Electric, Emerson, Ceiling, 6 Blades, Light Adapter 150.00
Electric, Emerson, No. 1520, Ornate Base, Yoke Mount, 16 In. 625.00
Electric, Emerson, No. 12648, Oscillator, Levers, 1-Speed, 16 In. 625.00
Electric, Emerson, No. 27668, Oscillator, 3-Speed, 16 In. 225.00
Electric, Emerson, No. 71666, 3-Speed 150.00
Electric, General Electric, Brass Blades, Cage, Side Gear Oscillator, 3-Speed, 12 In. 875.00
Electric, General Electric, Swivel Mount, 5-Speed, 1902, 12 In. 550.00
Electric, Heater, Super Lectric, AC, Bakelite Handle, Superior Elect. Prod. Corp., 10 x 10 In. . . 10.00
Electric, Western Electric, Vane Oscillator, 12 In. 550.00
Electric, Westinghouse, Brass Cage, Blades, 1905, 19 ½ x 16 In. 177.00
Electric, Westinghouse, Vane Oscillator, Brass, 12 In. 725.00
Electric, Westinghouse, Whirlwind, 12 x 9 In. . . . . *illus* 350.00
Ivory, 23 Staves, Landscapes, Figures, Dwellings, 19th Century, 8 ¼ In. 1680.00
Ivory, Carved Flowers, Chinese, 10 In. 3600.00
Ivory Sticks, Flowers, Central Shield, Painted, Chinese, 18th Century, 10 In. 1896.00
Jade, Wood, Carved Figures, Rosettes, Openwork, Chinese, 19 In. 717.00
Lacquer, Figures In Rooms, Hand Painted, Chinese Export, Frame, 19th Century, 9 x 18 In. . 900.00
Mother-Of-Pearl, Lace, Sequins, Gilt Frame, 13 x 21 In. 40.00
Ostrich Plume, Giltwood Sticks, Black, Gold, Frame, France, c.1910 . . . . 84.00
Silk, Women, Grape Arbor, Lubin, Paris, Paper, Signed, G. Barbier, c.1912, 9 ¾ In. . . . . *illus* 1840.00

FAST FOOD COLLECTIBLES *may be included in several categories, such as Advertising, Coca-Cola, Toy, etc.*

FEDERZEICHNUNG, *see Loetz category.*

FENTON Art Glass Company, founded in Martins Ferry, Ohio, by Frank L. Fenton, is now located in Williamstown, West Virginia. It is noted for early carnival glass produced between 1907 and 1920. Some of these pieces are listed in the Carnival Glass category. Many other types of glass were also made. Spanish Lace in this section refers to the pattern made by Fenton. The pottery closed in 2007.

Aqua Crest, Basket, 7 In. 50.00
Aqua Crest, Plate, 8 ¼ In. 35.00
Aqua Crest, Vase, 4 x 4 ⅛ In. 28.00
Aqua Crest, Vase, Ruffled Edge, 8 In. 65.00
Aqua Crest, Vase, Ruffled Edge, 10 x 6 In. 135.00
Baby Polka Dot, Bowl, Cranberry Opalescent, 7 In. 45.00
Baby Thumbprints, Vase, Cranberry Glass, Flared, Ruffled Edge, 9 ½ In. *illus* 44.00
Basket Weave, Bowl, Blue Opalescent, 6 ½ In. 26.00
Basket Weave, Bowl, Lavender Satin, Ruffled Eyelet Edge, 3 ¼ x 5 In. 55.00
Basket Weave, Plate, Blue Opalescent, 7 ½ In. 26.00
Beaded Melon, Ewer, Green, Ruffled Edge, 4 ½ In. 15.00
Beaded Melon, Ewer, Mulberry, Ruffled Edge, 4 ½ In. 15.00
Beaded Melon, Jug, Green Overlay, Squat, 4 In. 55.00
Beaded Melon, Vase, Mulberry, Ruffled Edge, 5 ½ In. 20.00
Beaded Melon, Vase, Mulberry, Ruffled Edge, 8 In. 45.00
Beaded Stars, Rose, Bowl, Pumpkin Marigold 65.00
Bicentennial, Bell, West Virginia, Amber, 6 ¾ x 3 In. 23.00
Bicentennial, Dish, Hen On Nest Cover, Chocolate Glass, 9 In. 45.00
Bicentennial, Paperweight, Eagle, Ruby Slag, 1976, 4 x 3 ¾ In. 45.00
Bicentennial, Patriot's Bell, Red Slag, Eagle Handle, 1976. 15.00
Blue Burmese, Bell, Ruffled Edge, 7 In. 45.00
Blue Burmese, Tumble-Up, 2 Piece 40.00
Blue Burmese, Tumble-Up, Flowers, 7 In., 2 Piece 80.00
Blue Crest, Candlestick, 6 In., Pair 275.00
Blue Crest, Vase, Ruffled Edge, 5 ½ In. 38.00
Blue Marble, Vase, Handkerchief, Blue, Footed, 6 ½ In. 40.00
Blue Satin, Bell, Roses, 7 In. 23.00
Blue Satin, Rose Bowl, Crimped Rim, 3-Toed, 5 x 4 ¼ In. 85.00
Blueberry, Tumbler, Marigold 67.50
Boggy Bayou, Vase, White Opalescent, 11 ½ In. 50.00
Burmese, Basket, Beaded Melon, Ruffled Edge, 8 In. 75.00
Burmese, Ginger Jar, Daisies, 8 ½ In. 225.00
Burmese, Lamp, Dragonfly & Fern Leaves, 16 In. 1250.00
Burmese, Rose Bowl, Yellow, Pink Glossy Ruffled Rim, 4 In. 20.00
Burmese, Vase, Jack-In-The-Pulpit, Glossy, 10 ½ x 5 ¾ In. 100.00
Burmese, Vase, Roses, Ruffled Edge, 11 In. *illus* 225.00
Burmese, Vase, Roses, Ruffled Edge, Squat 175.00
Burmese, Vase, Violets, Crimped Top, 3 ¾ In. 95.00
Butterfly, Ring Holder, Amethyst. 45.00
Butterfly & Berry, Basket, Pink, Handle 35.00
Butterfly & Berry, Tumbler, Blue 77.50
Cactus, Butter, Cover, Topaz, Opalescent, 7 ½ In. 190.00
Cactus, Salt & Pepper, Topaz, Opalescent, 3 In. 50.00
Cactus, Sugar & Creamer, Topaz, Opalescent 60.00
Cameo Opalescent, Bell, 7 In. 35.00
Cameo Opalescent, Bowl, 11 In. 45.00
Cameo Opalescent, Bowl, Flared, Footed, 11 In. 65.00
Cameo Opalescent, Pitcher 75.00
Candlestick, Celeste Blue, 8 ½ In., Pair 145.00
Coin Dot, Basket, Blue Opalescent, Ruffled Edge, Clear Handle, 6 ½ x 4 ¾ In. 80.00
Coin Dot, Bowl, Cranberry Opalescent, 10 In. 135.00
Coin Dot, Candlestick, Cranberry Opalescent, 6 In., Pair 120.00
Coin Dot, Hat, Cranberry Opalescent, Ruffled Edge, 5 In. 115.00
Coin Dot, Hat, French Opalescent, 3 x 3 ¼ In. 38.00
Coin Dot, Top Hat, Green, 4 In. 65.00
Coin Dot, Vase, Cranberry Opalescent, 8 ½ In. 55.00
Coin Dot, Vase, Cranberry Opalescent, Ruffled Edge, 6 In. 125.00
Coin Dot, Vase, French Opalescent, Ruffled Edge, 8 ¾ x 3 ¾ In. 65.00
Coin Dot, Vase, Green, Ruffled Edge, 9 In. 110.00
Coin Dot, Water Set, Cranberry Opalescent, 8 ½-In. Pitcher, 4-In. Tumblers, 7 Piece 395.00
Custard Satin, Bell, Church Scene, Signed, M. Trembly, 6 ⅛ In. 45.00
Custard Satin, Compote, Daisies, Ruffled Edge, 4 x 5 In. 45.00
Daisy & Button, Ashtray, Fan Shape, Plum Opalescent, 5 ¼ In. 25.00
Daisy & Button, Basket, Colonial Blue, Split Handle, 4 x 6 In. 30.00
Daisy & Button, Basket, Milk Glass, Split Handle, Oval, 4 x 6 In. 30.00
Daisy & Button, Bell, Ruffled Edge, Logo, 5 ⅜ x 3 ⅝ In. 28.00
Daisy & Button, Boot, Colonial Amber, 4 ¼ x 4 ¼ In. *illus* 20.00

Fan, Silk, Women, Grape Arbor, Lubin, Paris, Paper, Signed, G. Barbier, c.1912, 9 ¾ In.
$1840.00

Fenton, Baby Thumbprints, Vase, Cranberry Glass, Flared, Ruffled Edge, 9 ½ In.
$44.00

Top Ten Fenton Patterns
Hundreds of thousands of users visit our website, Kovels.com, each month. The Fenton patterns that are the most popular among our visitors are:

1. Coin Dot
2. Hobnail
3. Daisy Fern
4. Silver Crest
5. Burmese
6. Spanish Lace
7. Moonstone
8. Rose Crest
9. Water Lily
10. Aqua Crest

Fenton, Burmese, Vase, Roses, Ruffled Edge, 11 In.
$225.00

Fenton, Daisy & Button, Boot, Colonial Amber, 4 ¼ x 4 ¼ In.
$20.00

TIP
You and your antiques may have different ideas about ideal temperature and humidity. Bronzes and photographs like 40 percent humidity, stone carvings and oil paintings like 50 percent, wooden pieces and paper prefer 55 percent. The level, whatever you choose, should be constant. It can be measured by a hygrometer you will be able to find at a hardware store.

Daisy & Button, Boot, Colonial Orange, 4 ¼ x 4 ¼ In. . . . 20.00
Daisy & Button, Bowl, Colonial Amber, Scalloped Edge, 8 x 6 In. . . . 35.00
Daisy & Button, Bowl, Fruit, Topaz Opalescent, Footed, 10 ¼ In. . . . 30.00
Daisy & Button, Spooner, Amberina, 5 x 3 In. . . . 45.00
Daisy & Button, Sugar & Creamer, 2 ¾ & 3 ⅛ In. . . . 23.00
Daisy & Button, Top Hat, Milk Glass, 3 ¼ x 4 ½ In. . . . 15.00
Diamond Lace, Epergne, 3-Lily, Blue Opalescent, 9 x 10 In. . . . *illus* 66.00
Diamond Optic, Compote, Ruby Overlay, Dolphin Handles, Ruffled Edge, Footed, 4 ½ x 7 ¼ In. 50.00
Diamond Optic, Top Hat, Mulberry, 4 ½ In. . . . 150.00
Diamond Optic, Tray, Jade, 6 x 8 ¾ In. . . . 90.00
Diamond Optic, Vase, Ruby Overlay, Ruffled Edge, 8 In. . . . 65.00
Dianthus, Bell, Custard, Pink & Blue Corn Flowers, 4 ½ x 2 ¼ In. . . . 35.00
Dolphin, Bonbon, Cobalt Blue Satin, 5 ¼ x 2 ½ In. . . . 60.00
Dolphin, Bowl, Ebony, 6 x 9 In. . . . 250.00
Dolphin, Candlestick, Ruby, Pair . . . 40.00
Dolphin, Candy Jar, Cover, Velva Rose, 9 In. . . . 55.00
Dolphin, Compote, Ruby, Ruffled Edge, 4 ½ x 6 In. . . . 90.00
Dolphin, Plate, Jade Green, Handles, 6 ¼ In. . . . 30.00
Dot Optic, Pitcher, French Opalescent, Black Handle, 9 ⅝ In. . . . 150.00
Ebony Crest, Plate, 8 ½ In. . . . 45.00
Ebony Crest, Vase, Ruffled Edge, 7 In. . . . 100.00
Elizabeth, Jug, Jade Green, 48 Oz., 6 ⅜ In. . . . 125.00
Emerald Crest, Compote, Footed, Ruffled Edge, 4 x 7 In. . . . 38.00
Emerald Crest, Finger Bowl, Ruffled Edge, 5 In., Pair . . . 55.00
Empire, Pitcher, Cranberry Glass, Pitcher, 9 In. . . . 125.00
Empress, Vase, Periwinkle Blue. . . . 125.00
Favrene, Vase, Seasons, 8 In. . . . 175.00
Fern, Basket, Ocean Blue Opalescent, Cobalt Blue Crest & Handle, 9 In. . . . 95.00
Fern, Pitcher, Ocean Blue Opalescent, Cobalt Blue Crest & Handle, 5 ½ In. . . . 65.00
Figurine, Bear Cub, Pink, 3 ½ x 2 ¼ In. . . . 30.00
Figurine, Butterfly, On Stand, Blue Green Satin, 4 ½ In. . . . 45.00
Figurine, Butterfly, On Stand, Crystal Satin, 4 ¾ x 3 ¾ In. . . . 35.00
Figurine, Butterfly, On Stand, Fuchsia Satin, 4 ½ In. . . . 45.00
Figurine, Butterfly, On Stand, Orange Satin, 4 ½ In. . . . 45.00
Figurine, Donkey, Plum Opalescent . . . 50.00
Figurine, Fawn, Blue Satin . . . 75.00
Figurine, Happiness Bird, Custard, Painted Holly, 6 In. . . . 55.00
Figurine, Happy Cat, Painted Orange, Black, White, 6 ¼ In. . . . 140.00
Figurine, Happy Cat, Painted Star Nose, Whiskers, Heart Stars & Stripes Collar, 6 ¼ In. . . . 80.00
Figurine, Happy Cat, Rosalene, 6 ¼ In. . . . 80.00
Figurine, Happy Cat, White, Gray, 6 ¼ In. . . . 80.00
Figurine, Panther, Black, Gold Eyes . . . 45.00
Figurine, Turtle, Taverne, Satin . . . 45.00
Figurine, Whale, Blue Satin . . . 75.00
Fine Cut & Block, Basket, Amberina, 7 ½ x 5 ½ In. . . . 45.00
Fine Cut & Block, Vase, Colonial Orange, Swung, 15 In. . . . 35.00
Georgian, Candlestick, Ruby Red, 4 ¼ In. . . . 50.00
Georgian, Claret, Ruby, 4 In. . . . 17.00
Georgian, Cup, Ruby, Footed. . . . 10.00
Georgian, Cup & Saucer, Ruby. . . . 11.50 to 18.00
Georgian, Goblet, Ruby, 10 Oz., 5 ½ In. . . . 24.00
Georgian, Nut Cup, Ruby, 2 x 2 ½ In. . . . 13.50
Georgian, Plate, Salad, Ruby, 8 In. . . . 8.00
Georgian, Sherbet, High, Ruby, 6 Oz., 4 ⅜ In. . . . 18.00
Georgian, Sherbet, Ruby, Footed, 2 ¾ x 4 In. . . . 10.00
Georgian, Sugar & Creamer, Ruby . . . 55.00
Georgian, Tumbler, Juice, Ruby, 3 ⅛ x 2 ⅜ In. . . . 7.50
Georgian, Tumbler, Ruby, Footed, 5 ½ In. . . . 14.00
Georgian, Wine, Cobalt Blue, 4 Oz., 4 x 2 $\frac{9}{16}$ In. . . . 17.00
Gold Crest, Hat, Ruffled Edge, 3 ¼ x 4 ½ In. . . . 28.00
Grape, Fernery, Chocolate Glass, Footed, 6 ⅛ In. . . . 35.00
Hand, Vase, Mulberry, Swung, 13 In. . . . 250.00
Hand, Vase, Turquoise, Ruffled Edge, 10 ½ In. . . . 235.00
Hanging Hearts, Vase, Amethyst, Opalescent, Scalloped Rim, 17 x 4 ½ In. . . . 105.00
Hanging Hearts, Vase, Amethyst, White, Flared Rim, 7 ½ In. . . . 140.00
Hobnail, Basket, Blue Opalescent, 10 In. . . . 95.00

Hobnail, Basket, Colonial Blue, 10 x 9 In. ... 48.00
Hobnail, Basket, Cranberry Opalescent, 7 In. ... 40.00
Hobnail, Basket, French Opalescent, 4 ½ In. ... 30.00
Hobnail, Basket, Milk Glass, 6 In. ... 42.00
Hobnail, Basket, Plum Opalescent, Clear Handle, Ruffled Edge, 5 ¾ In. ... 65.00
Hobnail, Basket, Topaz Opalescent, 7 In. ... *illus* 25.00
Hobnail, Bell, Colonial Amber, 5 ¾ x 3 In. ... 20.00
Hobnail, Bowl, Milk Glass, 3-Toed, 8 x 4 In. ... 12.00
Hobnail, Butter, Cover, Blue Opalescent ... 65.00
Hobnail, Butter, Cover, Topaz Opalescent, 8 ¼-In. Underplate ... 120.00
Hobnail, Candlestick, Blue Opalescent, 4 ½ x 3 In. ... 45.00
Hobnail, Candlestick, Cornucopia, Blue Opalescent, 5 ½ In. ... 38.00
Hobnail, Candlestick, Cornucopia, Topaz Opalescent, 3 ½ In. ... 36.00
Hobnail, Candlestick, Milk Glass, 7 In., Pair ... 69.00
Hobnail, Candlestick, Ruby, Pair ... 60.00
Hobnail, Candlestick, Topaz Opalescent, Pair ... 30.00 to 35.00
Hobnail, Candy Box, Cover, Milk Glass, Ruffled Edge, Footed, 7 x 6 In. ... 35.00 to 48.00
Hobnail, Candy Dish, Cover, Milk Glass, 4-Toed, 8 In. ... 45.00
Hobnail, Candy Dish, Cover, Topaz Opalescent, Footed, 7 In. ... 50.00
Hobnail, Candy Dish, Jonquil Yellow, 3 ½ In. ... 55.00
Hobnail, Chip & Dip Bowl, Milk Glass, 8 x 2 ¼ In. ... 25.00
Hobnail, Cologne Bottle, Stopper, French Opalescent ... 24.00
Hobnail, Cologne Bottle, French Opalescent, 4 ¾ In. ... 30.00
Hobnail, Compote, Blue Marble, Ruffled Edge, 6 x 6 In. ... 35.00
Hobnail, Compote, Rose Pastel, Ruffled Edge, 5 ¼ x 8 In. ... 35.00
Hobnail, Compote, Topaz Opalescent, Ruffled Edge, 4 x 8 In. ... 55.00
Hobnail, Compote, Topaz Opalescent, Ruffled Edge, 5 ½ x 6 ½ In. ... 55.00
Hobnail, Condiment Set, Jars, Covers, Spoons, Tray, Milk Glass, 5 Piece ... 75.00
Hobnail, Creamer, Blue Opalescent, 2 x 2 ⅜ In. ... 17.50
Hobnail, Creamer, Cover, Milk Glass, 5 In. ... 15.00
Hobnail, Dish, Mayonnaise, Underplate, Milk Glass, Spoon ... 35.00
Hobnail, Dish, Metal Handle, Ruby, 2 ⅜ x 7 ⅝ In. ... 30.00
Hobnail, Dish, Wisteria, Ruffled Edge, 5 ¾ In. ... 15.00
Hobnail, Epergne, 1-Lily, Black, 6 ¼ x 3 ½ In. ... 25.00
Hobnail, Epergne, 1-Lily, Plum Opalescent, Ruffled Edge, 8 In. ... 35.00
Hobnail, Epergne, 3-Lily, Milk Glass, Ruffled Edge, 6 ½ In. ... 30.00
Hobnail, Epergne, 3-Lily, Plum Opalescent, Ruffled Edge, 6 ½ In. ... 70.00
Hobnail, Ewer, Cranberry Opalescent, 11 In. ... 10.00
Hobnail, Fairy Lamp, Cranberry Opalescent ... 75.00
Hobnail, Hat, French Opalescent, 2 ⅝ x 3 ⅛ In. ... 23.00
Hobnail, Jug, Squat, Plum Opalescent, 5 ¼ In. ... 90.00
Hobnail, Lamp Base, Topaz Opalescent, Decanter Form, 10 ½ In. ... 40.00
Hobnail, Relish, Milk Glass, 3 Sections, 7 In. ... 18.00
Hobnail, Salt & Pepper, Milk Glass, Chrome Top, 4 In. ... 24.00 to 35.00
Hobnail, Salt & Pepper, Topaz, Footed ... 119.00
Hobnail, Shoe, Cat In Slipper, Avocado Green, 3 x 5 In. ... *illus* 8.00
Hobnail, Shoe, Cat In Slipper, Ruby ... 26.00
Hobnail, Shoe, Green Opalescent, Satin Slipper ... 30.00
Hobnail, Sugar & Creamer, Blue Opalescent, 3 ¼ In. ... 38.00
Hobnail, Sugar & Creamer, Cover, Milk Glass ... 38.00
Hobnail, Sugar & Creamer, Topaz Opalescent, 2 x 2 ⅜ In. ... 58.00
Hobnail, Tumbler, Blue Opalescent, Barrel Shape, 12 Oz. ... 37.00
Hobnail, Tumbler, Topaz Opalescent, 4 In. ... 25.00
Hobnail, Vase, Amber, Ruffled Edge, Footed, 4 x 3 ⅝ In. ... 15.00
Hobnail, Vase, Blue Opalescent, 4 In. ... 35.00
Hobnail, Vase, Blue Opalescent, Tricornered Rim, 3 ½ In. ... 24.00
Hobnail, Vase, Bud, Colonial Amber, 7 ¾ In. ... 12.50
Hobnail, Vase, Bud, Colonial Amber, 11 In. ... 17.00
Hobnail, Vase, Bud, Ruby, 9 ½ In. ... 24.00
Hobnail, Vase, Colonial Amber, Ruffled Edge, 3 ⅛ x 4 In. ... 17.95
Hobnail, Vase, Colonial Blue, 4 In. ... 14.00
Hobnail, Vase, Colonial Blue, Swung, Footed, 20 ½ In. ... 75.00
Hobnail, Vase, Fan, Milk Glass, 4 In. ... 14.00
Hobnail, Vase, Fan, Milk Glass, 8 In. ... 38.00
Hobnail, Vase, Green Opalescent, Ruffled Edge, 7 In. ... 25.00
Hobnail, Vase, Green Opalescent, Swung, 10 In. ... 30.00

TIP
To clean wax from glass candlesticks, scrape with a wooden stick, then wash off the remaining wax with rubbing alcohol.

Fenton, Diamond Lace, Epergne, 3-Lily, Blue Opalescent, 9 x 10 In. $66.00

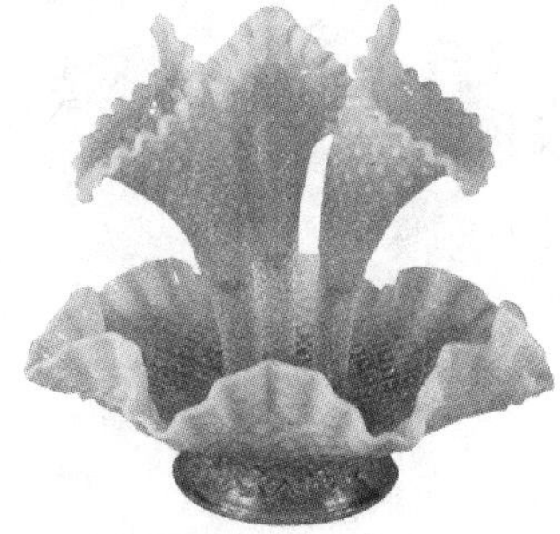

Fenton, Hobnail, Basket, Topaz Opalescent, 7 In. $25.00

TIP
Smoking is bad for the health of your antiques! Smoke causes discoloration and weakens textiles. Another reason to stop smoking!

Fenton, Hobnail, Shoe, Cat In Slipper, Avocado Green, 3 x 5 In. $8.00

Fenton, Peach Crest, Vase, Charleton Roses, Ruffled Edge, 8 In. $95.00

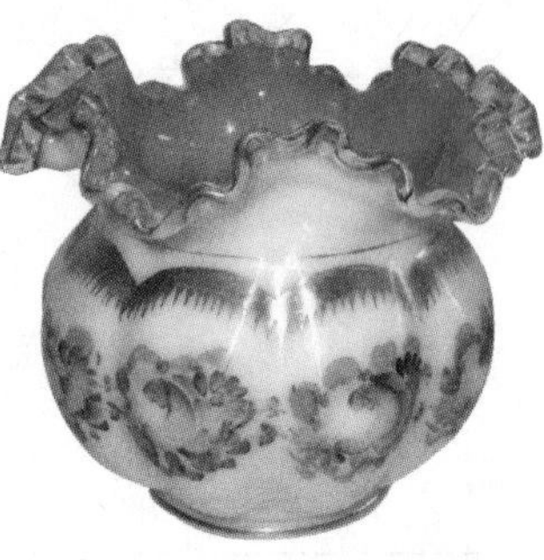

TIP

Don't load your dishwasher with fine crystal, gold-decorated glass or china, dishes with crazed glaze, lacquered metal, wooden wares, bone or ivory or wood handled serving pieces. They should never be cleaned in a dishwasher. The hot water and detergent will damage them.

Hobnail, Vase, Handkerchief, Plum Opalescent, Ruffled Edge, 7 ¼ In. 110.00
Hobnail, Vase, Jonquil Yellow, Ruffled Edge, 11 ½ In. 120.00
Hobnail, Vase, Milk Glass, 4 x 4 ¼ In. 23.00
Hobnail, Vase, Milk Glass, Crimped Edge, 4 In. 14.00
Hobnail, Vase, Ruffled Edge, 7 ½ In. 35.00
Hobnail, Vase, Topaz Opalescent, 4 In. 60.00
Hobnail, Vase, Topaz Opalescent, Crimped Edge, 4 In. 44.00
Hobnail, Vase, Wild Rose, Tricornered Rim, 11 In. 85.00
Ivory Crest, Candlestick, Pair 90.00
Ivory Crest, Hat, Ruffled Edge, 7 In. 75.00
Ivory Crest, Rose Bowl, Cupped Ruffled Edge, 4 In. 45.00
Ivory Crest, Vase, 10 ½ In. 80.00
Jacqueline, Pitcher, Ruby, Clear Handle, 6 ¼ In. 35.00
Jacqueline, Vase, Blue Opalescent, 7 In. 95.00
Jade Green, Ice Bucket 75.00
Jamestown Blue, Vase, Bulbous, Ruffled Edge, 5 ⅜ x 6 In. 80.00
Jamestown Blue, Vase, Tricornered Rim, Ruffled Edge, 7 ⅜ In. 80.00
Jug, Blue Overlay, Clear, Reeded Handle, 4 ¾ In. 45.00
Karnak Red, Vase, Applied Cobalt Blue Foot, Iridescent, 6 In. 1150.00
Karnak Red, Vase, Heart & Vine, Purple, Green & Gold Iridescent, 9 ½ In. 3450.00
Knobby Bull's-Eye, Bell, French Opalescent, 7 In. 35.00
Lavabo, Blue Overlay, Hobnail, Mounted On Board, 3 Piece 225.00
Leaf Tiers, Bowl, Milk Glass, Cupped Rim, 3-Footed, 4 ¼ x 8 ½ In. 60.00
Lotus Mist, Vase, Coastal Waters, 12 In. 75.00
Lotus Mist, Vase, Pillar, Pink Flowers, 9 In. 85.00
Madonna, Vase, Candlelight, Milk Glass, 6 ½ In. 45.00
Magnolia & Berries, Urn, Spruce Green, 13 In. 30.00
Mandarin Red, Basket, Macaroon, 8 ¾ In. 95.00
Ming, Bowl, Cupped, 3-Footed, 5 In. 35.00
Ming, Bowl, Salad, 4 ½ x 10 ½ In. 75.00
Ming, Console Set, Jade Green, 3 Piece 175.00
Ming, Pitcher, Black Handle, Ice Lip, 10 In. 175.00
Mother's Day, Plate, Marigold, 1973, 7 ¾ In. 20.00
Olde Virginia, Basket, Smoke, 7 ¾ x 6 ¾ In. 30.00
Paneled Daisy, Candy Dish, Cover, 9 In. 35.00
Peach Crest, Candlestick, Tall, Pair 40.00
Peach Crest, Vase, Charleton Roses, Ruffled Edge, 8 In. .... *illus* 95.00
Petal, Bowl, Black, 3 ⅛ x 9 In. 30.00
Pineapple, Compote, Ruffled Edge, 5 ½ x 5 ½ In. 30.00
Pineapple, Compote, Satin, Pedestal, 6 ½ In. 35.00
Pineapple, Dish, Olive, Satin, 2 Sections, 10 x 4 ½ In. 35.00
Plymouth, Vase, Ruby, Ruffled Edge, Footed, 6 In. 15.00
Red Cased, Hand Vase, Ruffled Rim, 11 In. 300.00
Rib Optic, Blue Opalescent, Tankard, Cobalt Handle. 160.00
Rib Optic, Tumble-Up, Amber, 7 ½ In., 2 Piece 40.00
Ribbon Tie, Bowl, 2 ¾ x 8 ¼ In. 46.00
Rosalene, Fairy Lamp, Owl, 1976, 2 Piece 45.00
Rose, Compote, Colonial Amber, 7 ½ x 6 In. .... *illus* 26.00
Rose Crest, Epergne Set, 3-Lily, Candlesticks, 6 ½ In., 6 Piece 25.00
Rose Crest, Vase, Beaded Melon, 5 ⅝ x 6 In. 120.00
Roses, Compote, Milk Glass, Ruffled Edge, 5 ¾ x 5 ¾ In. 23.00
Roses, Salt & Pepper, Amber, Chrome Top, 4 ½ In. 28.00
Ruby Crest, Vase, Ruffled Edge, Footed, 8 ½ In. 170.00
Silver Crest, Ashtray, Ruffled Edge, 6 ¾ In. 40.00
Silver Crest, Banana Boat, Square, Footed, 8 ½ x 9 ½ In. 65.00
Silver Crest, Basket, 6 ½ In. 37.00
Silver Crest, Basket, Hat, 7 In. 40.00
Silver Crest, Basket, Violets In The Snow, 7 ½ x 5 ⅜ In. 75.00
Silver Crest, Bonbon, 5 ½ In. 12.00
Silver Crest, Bowl, Double Crimped Edge, 10 In. 53.00
Silver Crest, Bowl, Square, Footed, 8 ¼ x 8 ½ In. 57.00
Silver Crest, Cake Plate, Footed, 1 ¾ x 12 ¼ In. 38.00
Silver Crest, Candlestick, 6 In., Pair .... 45.00 to 62.00
Silver Crest, Candlestick, Flowers, Signed, Louise Piper, 1969, 3 ½ In., Pair 75.00
Silver Crest, Candlestick, Violets In The Snow, 6 In., Pair 45.00
Silver Crest, Candy Bowl, Double Crimped, Ruffled Edge, 7 x 2 ¼ In. 18.00

Silver Crest, Candy Jar, Clear, Cover 90.00
Silver Crest, Cologne, Beaded Melon, Clear Stopper 48.00
Silver Crest, Compote 27.00
Silver Crest, Compote, Violets In The Snow, 8 In. 45.00
Silver Crest, Cornucopia, Candlestick 31.00
Silver Crest, Ivy Ball, Footed 43.00
Silver Crest, Jug, 6 In. 35.00
Silver Crest, Nappy, Heart Shape, Handle, 8 In. 30.00
Silver Crest, Plate, 8 ½ In. 25.00
Silver Crest, Plate, 12 In. 55.00
Silver Crest, Salt & Pepper, 4 In. 25.00
Silver Crest, Sandwich Server 43.00
Silver Crest, Sherbet, 8 Piece 160.00
Silver Crest, Tidbit 29.00
Silver Crest, Top Hat, Ruffled Edge, 6 In. 52.00
Silver Crest, Vase, 5 In. .... 17.00 to 26.00
Silver Crest, Vase, 8 In. 40.00
Silver Crest, Vase, Fan, 12 In. 157.00
Silver Crest, Vase, Flowers, Signed, Louise Piper, 1980, 4 In. 70.00
Silver Crest, Vase, Fluted, Violets In The Snow, 11 In. 65.00
Silver Jamestown, Vase, 6 ½ x 5 In. 50.00
Silver Jamestown, Vase, Jack-In-The-Pulpit, 9 x 5 ¼ In. .... *illus* 95.00
Silver Tone, Pitcher, Iced Tea, Ice Lip, 10 In. 195.00
Silver Tone, Tumbler, Iced Tea, 5 ½ In., 3 Piece 60.00
Snow Crest Emerald, Vase, 4 In. 38.00
Snow Crest Emerald, Vase, 11 In. 185.00
Spanish Lace, Cake Stand, 11 x 5 In. 65.00
Spanish Lace, Vase, Ruffled Edge, 8 In. 55.00
Spiral Optic, Tumbler, Iced Tea, Cranberry Opalescent, 5 In. 10.00
Spiral Optic, Vase, Cranberry, Bottle Shape, 10 In. .... *illus* 65.00
Spiral Optic, Vase, Wisteria, 3-Footed, 7 In. 55.00
Spiral Tulip, Vase, Rosalene 180.00
Starflower, Pitcher, Blue, 8 ¼ In. 440.00
Stretch Glass, Bell, Velva Blue, Ruffled Edge, 6 ¾ In. 35.00
Stretch Glass, Bowl, Fruit, Footed, Tangerine 185.00
Stretch Glass, Plate, Celeste Blue, 9 In., Pair 50.00
Stretch Glass, Vase, Amethyst, 3 ¾ In. 59.00
Stretch Glass, Vase, Blue, 6 In. 52.00
Stretch Glass, Vase, Dolphin-Footed, Fan, Tangerine 125.00
Swirl Optic, Vase, Canberry Opalescent, 9 In. 55.00
Teardrop, Condiment Set, Milk Glass, 1955, 7 x 5 ½ In., 4 Piece 25.00
Thumbprint, Compote, Amberina, Ruffled Edge, Footed, 6 ¼ x 5 ¾ In. 35.00
Thumbprint, Compote, Colonial Amber, 6 x 6 In. 25.00
Thumbprint, Compote, Colonial Amber, Ruffled Edge, 7 ½ x 7 ½ In. 30.00
Thumbprint, Compote, Colonial Green, Ruffled & Crimped Edge, 6 x 6 In. 25.00
Thumbprint, Creamer, Blue Marble, Scalloped Edge, 4 In. 35.00
Thumbprint, Goblet, Colonial Pink, 6 ½ In. 26.00
Thumbprint, Vase, Colonial Green, 16 ½ In. 35.00
Thumbprint, Vase, Colonial Green, Ruffled Edge, Footed, 8 ⅝ In. 30.00
Valencia, Candy Box, Cover, Orange, 6 ½ x 5 ⅜ In. 45.00
Valencia, Cigarette Box, Cover, Amber, 7 ⅜ x 2 ¾ In. 35.00
Valencia, Vase, Bud, Colonial Green, 11 In. 15.00
Valencia, Vase, Colonial Blue, 12 ½ In. 30.00
Vasa Murrhina, Basket, Aventurine Green Blue, 7 In. 75.00
Vasa Murrhina, Vase, Autumn, Orange, Rust, Silver Mica Flecks, Ruffled Edge, 8 x 4 ½ In. ... 75.00
Vasa Murrhina, Vase, Autumn Mist, Melon Ribbed, 8 In. 30.00
Vasa Murrhina, Vase, Aventurine Blue Green, Ruffled Edge, 14 In. 275.00
Velva Rose, Basket, Butterflies & Berry, 7 x 5 ¼ In. 48.00
Velva Rose, Bell, Crimped Rim, 75th Anniversary, 7 In. 45.00
Velva Rose, Vase, Fan, Dolphin Handles, 75th Anniversary, 6 x 7 In. 48.00
Water Lily, Bowl, Blue Satin, 9 In. 20.00
Water Lily, Bowl, Clear, Scalloped Edge, 3 ¼ x 9 In. 35.00
Water Lily, Rose Bowl, Blue Satin, 3 ¾ x 4 ¾ In. 30.00
Water Lily & Cattails, Bowl, French Opalescent, Scalloped Edge, 8 In. 45.00
Water Lily & Cattails, Tumbler, Chocolate Glass, 3 ⅞ x 2 ⅞ In. 345.00
Wheat, Vase, Cranberry, Ruby Overlay, Ruffled Edge, 7 ½ x 4 ⅝ In. 85.00

Fenton, Rose, Compote, Colonial Amber, 7 ½ x 6 In.
$26.00

Snow Domes
Snow domes were first made in the late nineteenth century in France. They almost always featured religious scenes with saints and churches. The first American patent for a dome was issued in 1927 for one that had a fish on a string floating in a seaweed patch.

Fenton, Silver Jamestown, Vase, Jack-In-The-Pulpit, 9 x 5 ¼ In.
$95.00

Fenton, Spiral Optic, Vase, Cranberry, Bottle Shape, 10 In.
$65.00

Fenton, Wild Rose & Bowknot, Vase, 7 ½ x 5 ¼ In.
$85.00

TIP
Repairs on standing figures or pitchers should be made from the bottom up.

Fiesta, Chartreuse, Cup, After Dinner
$100.00

Fiesta, Cobalt Blue, Pitcher, Disk
$70.00

Wild Rose & Bowknot, Vase, 7 ½ x 5 ¼ In. *illus* 85.00
Wild Strawberry, Candy Box, Cover, Green Satin, 9 x 5 In. 35.00

FIESTA, the colorful dinnerware, was introduced in 1936 by the Homer Laughlin China Co., redesigned in 1969, and withdrawn in 1973. It was reissued again in 1986 in different colors and is still being made. New colors, including some that are similar to old colors, are introduced regularly. The simple design was characterized by a band of concentric circles, beginning at the rim. Cups had full-circle handles until 1969, when partial-circle handles were made. Harlequin and Riviera were related wares. For more prices, go to Kovels.com.

Chartreuse, Bowl, Fruit, 5 ½ In. 21.00
Chartreuse, Casserole 92.00
Chartreuse, Chop Plate, 15 In. 61.00
Chartreuse, Coffeepot, Cover 300.00
Chartreuse, Cup, After Dinner *illus* 100.00
Chartreuse, Tidbit, 3 Tiers 65.00
Cobalt Blue, Bowl, Fruit, 5 ½ In. 23.00
Cobalt Blue, Candleholder, Bulb, Pair 30.00
Cobalt Blue, Candleholder, Tripod, Pair 150.00
Cobalt Blue, Chop Plate, 13 In. 22.00
Cobalt Blue, Coffeepot, After Dinner 275.00
Cobalt Blue, Coffeepot, Cover 90.00
Cobalt Blue, Mixing Bowl, Cover Only, No. 1 500.00
Cobalt Blue, Mixing Bowl, No. 6 140.00
Cobalt Blue, Mustard 35.00
Cobalt Blue, Nappy, 9 ½ In. 50.00
Cobalt Blue, Pitcher, Disk *illus* 70.00
Cobalt Blue, Pitcher, Ice Lip 40.00
Cobalt Blue, Plate, 6 In. 3.00
Cobalt Blue, Plate, 7 ½ In. 4.00
Cobalt Blue, Soup, Cream, Handles 65.00
Cobalt Blue, Sugar, 3 In. 10.00
Cobalt Blue, Sugar & Creamer 33.00
Cobalt Blue, Teapot, 8 Cup 132.00
Cobalt Blue, Tumbler, Juice, 3 ½ In. 6.00 to 10.00
Cobalt Blue, Vase, 8 In. 425.00
Cobalt Blue, Vase, 12 In. 500.00 to 650.00
Cobalt Blue, Vase, Bud 50.00
Gray, Ashtray 35.00
Gray, Bowl, Fruit, 5 ½ In. 21.00
Gray, Casserole 150.00
Gray, Chop Plate, 13 In. 25.00
Gray, Coffeepot, Cover 130.00 to 160.00
Gray, Pitcher, Disk 30.00
Gray, Plate, Salad, 7 In. 12.00
Gray, Sugar 25.00
Green, Vase, Bud 30.00
Ivory, Bowl, Fruit, 5 ½ In. 22.00
Ivory, Bowl, Fruit, 11 ¾ In. 160.00
Ivory, Candleholder, Bulb, Pair 55.00
Ivory, Candleholder, Tripod, Pair 500.00
Ivory, Carafe 100.00
Ivory, Coffeepot, After Dinner 175.00
Ivory, Coffeepot, Cover 95.00 to 120.00
Ivory, Compote, Sweets 50.00
Ivory, Marmalade 170.00
Ivory, Mixing Bowl, No. 2 55.00
Ivory, Nappy, 8 ½ In. *illus* 15.00
Ivory, Pitcher, Disk 30.00
Ivory, Plate, Compartment, 12 In. 60.00
Ivory, Soup, Onion, Cover 175.00 to 300.00
Ivory, Tumbler, Juice, 3 ½ In. 20.00
Ivory, Vase, 8 In. 275.00
Ivory, Vase, 10 In. 150.00 to 300.00
Ivory, Vase, 12 In. 700.00
Ivory, Vase, Bud 30.00

Light Green, Butter, ½ Lb. 85.00
Light Green, Candleholder, Bulb, Pair . . . . . 40.00 to 60.00
Light Green, Candleholder, Tripod 525.00
Light Green, Candleholder, Tripod, Pair 190.00
Light Green, Chop Plate, 15 In. 48.00
Light Green, Coffeepot, After Dinner 180.00
Light Green, Compote, Sweets 65.00
Light Green, Jug, Cover 100.00
Light Green, Mixing Bowl, No. 5. . . . . . 25.00
Light Green, Mixing Bowl, No. 6. . . . . . 60.00
Light Green, Sugar 20.00
Light Green, Teapot, 6 Cup 45.00
Light Green, Tumbler, Juice, 3 ½ In. 20.00
Light Green, Vase, 8 In. 225.00
Medium Green, Ashtray 170.00
Medium Green, Casserole, Cover 550.00
Medium Green, Chop Plate, 13 In.. . . . . . 160.00
Medium Green, Cup & Saucer 20.00
Medium Green, Jar, Cover, Kitchen Kraft, Large . . . . . *illus* 80.00
Medium Green, Plate, 9 In. 28.00
Medium Green, Plate, Dinner, 10 In. 175.00
Medium Green, Salt & Pepper 110.00
Medium Green, Sugar & Creamer . . . . . 110.00 to 120.00
Medium Green, Teapot, 6 Cup 50.00
Red, Ashtray 35.00
Red, Bowl, Fruit, 5 ½ In.. . . . . . 20.00
Red, Bowl, Salad, Footed, 11 ¼ In. . . . . . 100.00 to 120.00
Red, Bowl, Salad, Individual 74.00
Red, Butter 90.00
Red, Candleholder, Bulb, Pair. . . . . . 45.00 to 50.00
Red, Candleholder, Tripod, Pair. 160.00
Red, Canister, Individual, Kitchen Kraft 180.00
Red, Carafe. . . . . . 110.00 to 150.00
Red, Casserole. 50.00
Red, Compote, 12 In. . . . . . 45.00 to 100.00
Red, Creamer 25.00
Red, Cup & Saucer 10.00
Red, Jug, 2 Pt. 25.00
Red, Marmalade 160.00
Red, Mixing Bowl, No. 6 . . . . . 30.00
Red, Mustard. 120.00
Red, Nappy, 9 ½ In.. . . . . . 10.00
Red, Pitcher, 2 Pt. 40.00
Red, Pitcher, Water, Disk . . . . . 40.00 to 62.00
Red, Plate, Compartment, 12 In. 60.00
Red, Relish Tray, Multicolored Inserts. 50.00
Red, Sauceboat. 250.00
Red, Soup, Onion, Cover . . . . . 275.00 to 350.00
Red, Syrup, Lid . . . . . *illus* 140.00
Red, Tumbler, Juice, 3 ½ In.. . . . . . 20.00
Red, Tumbler, Water, 4 ¼ In. 40.00
Red, Vase, 8 In. 160.00
Red, Vase, Bud. 25.00
Rose, Bowl, Fruit, 4 ¾ In.. . . . . . 21.00
Rose, Bowl, Fruit, 5 ½ In.. . . . . . 21.00
Rose, Chop Plate, 13 In.. . . . . . 30.00
Rose, Coffeepot, Cover 130.00
Rose, Mug, Tom & Jerry . . . . . 25.00 to 30.00
Rose, Pitcher, Disk 40.00
Rose, Tumbler, Juice, 3 ½ In.. . . . . . 55.00
Turquoise, Ashtray. 15.00
Turquoise, Bowl, Fruit, 4 ¾ In. 18.50
Turquoise, Bowl, Salad, Footed. 130.00
Turquoise, Bowl, Salad, Individual. 62.00
Turquoise, Candleholder, Bulb, Pair 50.00
Turquoise, Candleholder, Tripod, Pair 350.00

Fiesta, Ivory, Nappy, 8 ½ In.
$15.00

Fiesta, Medium Green, Jar, Cover, Kitchen Kraft, Large
$80.00

TIP

Good tips for care of Fiesta and other heavy, color-glazed dishes of the 1930s. Most are oven safe for baking—up to 350 degrees. Do not use in a microwave or on a direct stove flame. Do not wash in an automatic dishwasher. The detergent may discolor the glaze. Do not scour. Store with felt between the stacked plates to avoid scratching. Early 1930 to 1942 dishes used a lead in the glazing, so do not use scratched dishes with acidic foods. Lead poisoning is possible with prolonged use.

Fiesta, Red, Syrup, Lid.
$140.00

Fiesta, Turquoise, Teapot, 6 Cup
$50.00

Fiesta, Turquoise, Vase, Bud
$50.00

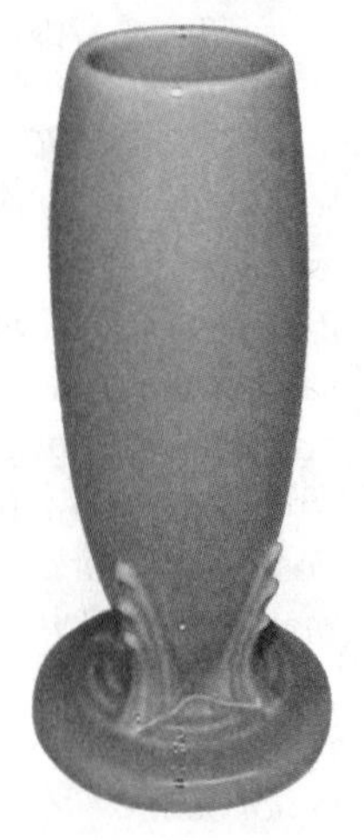

Fiesta, Yellow, Soup, Onion, Cover
$200.00

Turquoise, Coffeepot, After Dinner 55.00
Turquoise, Jug, 2 Pt. . . . . . 25.00 to 30.00
Turquoise, Marmalade 150.00
Turquoise, Nappy, 9 ½ In. 50.00
Turquoise, Plate, 6 In. 3.00
Turquoise, Salt & Pepper 100.00
Turquoise, Saucer 3.00
Turquoise, Sugar & Creamer 20.00
Turquoise, Teapot, 6 Cup . . . . . *illus* 50.00
Turquoise, Tumbler, Juice, 3 ½ In. 10.00
Turquoise, Tumbler, Water, 4 ¾ In. 40.00
Turquoise, Vase, 8 In. 250.00
Turquoise, Vase, 10 In. . . . . . 325.00 to 425.00
Turquoise, Vase, Bud . . . . . *illus* 50.00
Yellow, Bowl, Fruit, 4 ¾ In. 21.00
Yellow, Candleholder, Bulb 50.00
Yellow, Candleholder, Tripod, Pair. 225.00
Yellow, Casserole. 90.00
Yellow, Casserole, Cover 130.00
Yellow, Chop Plate, 13 In. 10.00
Yellow, Coffeepot, After Dinner 190.00
Yellow, Coffeepot, Cover . . . . . 50.00 to 65.00
Yellow, Creamer, Stick 20.00
Yellow, Cup & Saucer, Stick Handle. 22.00
Yellow, Eggcup 25.00
Yellow, Marmalade. 130.00
Yellow, Mixing Bowl, No. 5. . . . . . 188.00
Yellow, Pitcher, Disk. 100.00
Yellow, Plate, Compartment, 12 In. 45.00
Yellow, Red, Turquoise, Sugar & Creamer, Figure 8 Tray. 225.00
Yellow, Soup, Onion, Cover . . . . . *illus* 200.00
Yellow, Tumbler, Juice, 3 ½ In. 5.00
Yellow, Tumbler, Juice, 3 ¾ In. 7.00
Yellow, Tumbler, Water, 4 ¾ In. 40.00

FINCH, *see Kay Finch category.*

FINDLAY ONYX AND FLORADINE are two similar types of glass made by Dalzell, Gilmore and Leighton Co. of Findlay, Ohio, about 1889. Onyx is a patented yellowish white opaque glass with raised silver daisy decorations. A few rare pieces were made of rose, amber, orange, or purple glass. Floradine is made of cranberry-colored glass with an opalescent white raised floral pattern and a satin finish. The same molds were used for both types of glass.

Jar, Cover, Leaves, Flowers, Ball Finial, 5 ½ In. 4140.00
Spooner, Floradine, Oval, Opal, Flowers, 4 ½ In. 575.00
Sugar, Cover, Platinum, 5 ½ x 3 ½ In. 650.00
Syrup, Bulbous, Opal Handle, 7 In. 345.00
Toothpick, Cylinder Shape, Scalloped Rim, Silver Flowers, 3 In. 173.00
Tumbler, Barrel Shape, Opal, Silver Flowers, 6 In. 288.00

FIREFIGHTING equipment of all types is wanted, from fire marks to uniforms to toy fire trucks. It is said that every little boy wanted to be a fireman or a train engineer 75 years ago and the collectors today reflect this interest.

Alarm Box, Autocal Co., Cast Iron, Red Paint, Embossed, 13 x 9 x 5 ½ In. 150.00
Alarm Box, Gamewell, Cast Iron, Steel Plate, Red, Post, Box Stand, 73 In. 320.00
Bell, Fire Helmet Handle, Cast Iron, 4 ¼ In. 50.00
Belt, Leather, Excelsior, No. 1, Ax, Ladder, Red, Black, c.1865 . . . . . 325.00
Bucket, Gilt Eagle, Black, Red Paint, J.W. Sargent, Kennebunk, Maine, 1850, 14 In. 2133.00
Bucket, Leather, American Eagle Holding Banner, 13 In. 1175.00
Bucket, Leather, Black, H & L No. 2, Marked, No. 10, 20 In. 170.00
Bucket, Leather, Eagle, Henry Walton, Elmira, Paint, Multicolored, c.1851, 17 In. 38513.00
Bucket, Leather, Inscribed, F.A. Sumner, 1850s, 12 In. 660.00
Bucket, Leather, Painted, Red, No. 10, 19th Century, 12 In. 1404.00
Bucket, Painted, J.N. Marshall, 1797, 12 ½ In. 263.00
Bucket, Painted, Woman, Flower Crown, Bail Handle, 8 x 18 In. 6780.00

Bucket, Rubber, Canvas, Iron Strap, Black, Red, Mark, Haywood & Co., Conn., c.1868, 12 In.. 711.00
Bucket, Waggoner Sanatory, Pat. Feb. 5, 1905, Chicago, 12 x 18 In.. 440.00
Crock, Hand Painted Shield, No. 2 In Center, Tin Lid, 15 x 11 ½ In.. 500.00
Extinguisher, Pyrene, Brass, Hand Held, Newark, N.J., 14 In. 20.00
Fire Horn, Repousse Acorns, Silver, Presentation, R & W Wilson, 1868, 21 In. *illus* 9360.00
Fire Locator, Gamewell, Excelsior, Brass, Iron 660.00
Fire Marker, F.A., Old Paint, Cast Iron, Oval, 11 ½ In. 110.00
Fireplug Plate, F.A., Painted, Cast Iron, 18 x 12 In.. 50.00
Gong, Walnut, Moses Crane, 18 x 31 In. 5605.00
Grenade, American Electric Extinguisher, Yellow Amber, Ribs, 13 In. 5600.00
Grenade, C.&NW.RY, Clear Tube, Sheared, Ground, Cast Iron, 1885-1900, 18 In. 50.00
Grenade, Extincteur, Waffle, Systeme Labbe, L'Incombustibilte Paris, Yellow Amber, 6 ¾ In. 210.00
Grenade, Flagg's Fire Extinguisher, Orange Amber, Sheared Lip, 6 ⅜ In. 2800.00
Grenade, Harden, Hand, Star, Inside Star, Turquoise Blue, Sheared, Ground Lip, 6 ¼ In. 100.00
Grenade, Harden, Star, Embossed, Turquoise Blue, Ground Lip, c.1890, 6 ¾ In. *illus* 100.00
Grenade, Harden's, Star, Stopper, Turquoise, Qt. 224.00
Grenade, Harden's Hand, Star, Fire Extinguisher, Turquoise Blue, Qt. 134.00
Grenade, Hayward's Hand, Amber, Tooled Mouth, 6 ⅜ In. 308.00
Grenade, Hayward's Hand, Applied Band Top, 2, Medium Citron, c.1871, Pt. 392.00
Grenade, Hayward's Hand, Aqua, Tooled Mouth, 5 ¾ In. 364.00
Grenade, Hayward's Hand, Cobalt Blue, Tooled Lip, 1880-1900, 6 In. 410.00
Grenade, Hazelton's, High Pressure Chemical, Fire Keg, Amber, 11 In. 532.00
Grenade, Marden, Tubular, Star, 17 ½ In. 728.00
Grenade, UNIC, Extincteur, Medium Amber, Ribbed, France, 6 In.. 224.00
Helmet, Leather, Black, Newburyport, Mass., Eagle Bracket, Leather Shield, 15 x 9 In. 385.00
Helmet, Leather, Black, Poughkeepsee Exempt 1886, Shield, Lion Bracket, 14 x 10 In. 2065.00
Helmet, No. 1, Lake Hopatcong, N.J., Leather, Brass Eagle Head 225.00
Helmet, Shiffler Fire Co., No. 7, Red, Leather, Metal, Stamped, R. Necf, 1852, 9 x 15 x 11 In.. 935.00
Helmet, White Leather, Guardian 1 Hose, Fireman Bracket, Leather Shield, 14 x 10 In.. 2655.00
Hose Nozzle, Brass, Elkhart Chief, 8 ½ In. 215.00
Hose Nozzle, Imperial, Nickel Plated, Rubber Grips, Akron Brass Co., 1959, 20 ½ In. 20.00
Ladder, Hardwood, Collapsible, c.1870, 153 x 15 In. 165.00
Medallion, Fire Scene, Firemen Working, Celluloid, Brass Art Nouveau Frame, 1 ¾ In. 63.00
Parade Hat, Friendship Fire, Painted, James Remick, 1800s, 6 x 13 ½ In. *illus* 15210.00
Phone, Watchcase Receiver, In Case Of Fire, Red, Blue, Douglas Aircraft Co., 1935 350.00
Pumper, Hand, Model, Hand Painted Finial, Red, c.1890, 23 x 16 In. 5085.00
Siren, Hand Crank, Red, Nickel Plated Guard, No. 8094, Sterling Siren Horn, 12 In. 275.00
Speaking Horn, Nickel Plated, Tassel, 19th Century, 18 ¾ In. 200.00

FIREGLOW glass is attributed to the Boston and Sandwich Glass Company. The light-tan-colored glass appears reddish brown when held to the light. Most fireglow has an acid finish and enamel decoration, although it was also made with a satin finish.

Vase, Pedestal, Blue Blossoms, Fern, 18 ½ In. 150.00
Vase, Trumpet Form, Autumn Flowers, Satin, 18 In. 300.00
Vase, Victorian Courting Scene, Flowers, Enameled, 12 In. 77.00

FIREPLACES were used to cook food and to heat the American home in past centuries. Many types of tools and equipment were used. Andirons held the logs in place, firebacks reflected the heat into the room, and tongs were used to move either fuel or food. Many types of spits and roasting jacks were made and may be listed in the Kitchen category.

Andirons, Anchor Form, Cast Iron, Early 20th Century 165.00
Andirons, Bell Metal, Chippendale, Double Urn Top, Cabriole Legs, Claw Feet, 17 ¾ In. 250.00
Andirons, Bell Metal, Chippendale, Lemon Top, Spade Feet, 18th Century, 13 x 10 x 18 In. 350.00
Andirons, Bell Metal, Iron, Rope Shaft, Crosshatched, Spit Rests, 17th Century, 26 In. 1170.00
Andirons, Bell Metal, Iron, Scroll Base, Baluster, Ring Turned Shaft, 17th Century, 16 In. 3276.00
Andirons, Brass, Arts & Crafts, Floral Medallion, Open Work, Hammered, 26 In. 160.00
Andirons, Brass, Arts & Crafts, Hammered, Curled Design, 27 x 15 In. 1560.00
Andirons, Brass, Ball, Urn Finials, Baluster Shafts, 1800s, 20 x 16 In. 633.00
Andirons, Brass, Ball Finial, Baluster Shaft, Cabriole Legs, Claw Feet, c.1760, 17 In. 4446.00
Andirons, Brass, Ball Top, Arched Cabriole Legs, 14 ½ x 21 ½ In. 633.00
Andirons, Brass, Cannonball, Pagoda Feet, Iron Dogs, 16 ½ x 21 ½ In. 120.00
Andirons, Brass, Eagle, Sits On Base, 17 x 16 ½ x 9 ½ In.. 4600.00
Andirons, Brass, Federal, Ball Top, Baluster Turned Standard, Cabriole Legs, 15 x 21 In. 115.00
Andirons, Brass, Federal, Double Lemon Top, Early 19th Century, 19 x 9 x 17 ½ In. 200.00
Andirons, Brass, Federal, Impressed, R. Whittingham, N. York, 16 ½ In.. 1053.00

Firefighting, Fire Horn, Repousse Acorns, Silver, Presentation, R & W Wilson, 1868, 21 In.
$9360.00

Firefighting, Grenade, Harden, Star, Embossed, Turquoise Blue, Ground Lip, c.1890, 6 ¾ In.
$100.00

Firefighting, Parade Hat, Friendship Fire, Painted, James Remick, 1800s, 6 x 13 ½ In.
$15210.00

F

TIP

If you have an alarm system, program a strobe light attached to the outside of the house to go on if there is a break-in attempt. The light will frighten the burglar and will make it easy for the police to find the house.

Fireplace, Andirons, Bronze, Medieval Soldiers, 22 x 12 x 11 In.
$633.00

Fireplace, Andirons, Copper, Geometrics, Riveted, Patina, Prairie School, 20 x 30 ½ In.
$840.00

Fireplace, Andirons, Iron, Cast, Zoomorphic, Russel Wright, 1930, 15 ¾ x 6 x 22 In.
$5700.00

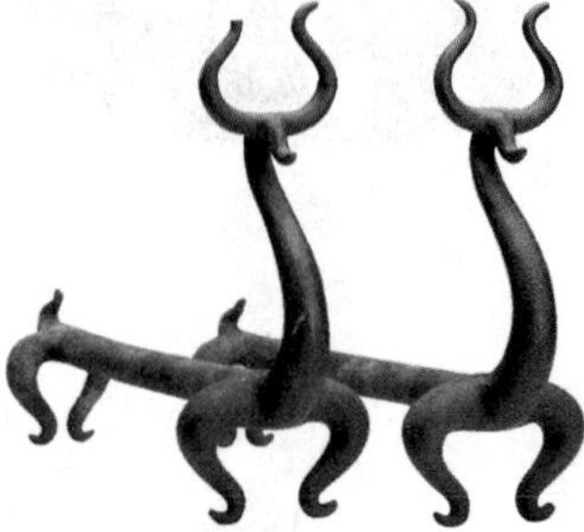

Andirons, Brass, Federal, Iron, Finial, Urn Shape, Ball Feet, c.1840, 18 x 11 In. 329.00
Andirons, Brass, Federal, Stamped, J. Davis, Boston, Early 19th Century, 15 ¼ In. 819.00
Andirons, Brass, Federal, Stamped, R. Wittingham, N.Y., 21 ½ In. 2340.00
Andirons, Brass, Federal, Steeple Top, Boston, c.1800, 21 In. 702.00
Andirons, Brass, Federal, Steeple Top, Urn, Turned, Scalloped Plinths, 17 x 10 ½ x 20 In.. . . . 896.00
Andirons, Brass, Fire Dogs, England, Arts & Crafts, 7 x 8 x 11 In. 210.00
Andirons, Brass, Gadrooned Urn Finial, Ionic Capitol, Fluted Column, Curved Feet, 27 In.. . . 259.00
Andirons, Brass, Hammered Steel, Pierced Medallions, Lotus Form, 27 In.. . . . . 2937.00
Andirons, Brass, Iron, Art Nouveau, 16 ½ In. 263.00
Andirons, Brass, Iron, Lobed Urn Finial, Penny Feet, c.1740, 16 ¾ In. 5616.00
Andirons, Brass, Iron, Queen Anne, Penn., c.1750, 17 x 10 In.. . . . . 4063.00
Andirons, Brass, Iron, Turned Finial, Shoe Base, c.1700, 17 ½ In.. . . . . 702.00
Andirons, Brass, Leaf & Acorn, 18 ¾ x 6 x 17 In.. . . . . 700.00
Andirons, Brass, Lemon Top Finials, Seamed Construction, Iron Billets, 17 ½ In. 294.00
Andirons, Brass, Molded, Stylized Scrolled Legs, Fan Pendant Center, Aesthetic Movement, 18 In. 1880.00
Andirons, Brass, Neoclassical, Cabriole Legs, Claw & Ball Feet, 23 x 12 x 20 In.. . . . . 384.00
Andirons, Brass, Scrolled Arches, Funnel Feet, 1800s, 19 In. 345.00
Andirons, Brass, Scrolled Legs, Button Feet, Iron Billet Bars, c.1850, 18 x 10 In. 1762.00
Andirons, Brass, Seamed, Over Iron, Urn Finials, Ball & Claw Feet, c.1800, 24 In.. . . . . 2585.00
Andirons, Brass, Seamed Construction, Iron Billets, c.1800, 17 ¾ In.. 205.00
Andirons, Brass, Swirled Finials, Beaded Standards, Arched Scalloped Feet, c.1875, 24 In.. . . . 3000.00
Andirons, Brass, Urn & Flame Tops, Ball & Claw Feet, 36 x 14 ½ In.. . . . . 250.00
Andirons, Brass, Urn Form, Acorn Finial, Arched Legs, Ball Feet, 21 x 22 In. 460.00
Andirons, Bronze, Ball Top, Queen Anne Style Legs, Iron Back, c.1900, 21 x 8 x 14 In. 187.00
Andirons, Bronze, Ball Top, Ribbed Column, Queen Anne Legs, 1900, 18 x 11 x 17 In. 220.00
Andirons, Bronze, Chippendale, Gilt, Fluted Pillar, Claw, Ball Feet, c.1885, 35 In. 177.00
Andirons, Bronze, Fluted Column, Urn Finial, 38 x 13 In.. . . . . 1880.00
Andirons, Bronze, Gilt, Flame Finials, Hairy Paw Feet, 30 In.. . . . . 800.00
Andirons, Bronze, Lions Supporting Base, Ball Stem, Finial, c.1880, 36 x 12 In. 1463.00
Andirons, Bronze, Medieval Soldiers, 22 x 12 x 11 In.. . . . . *illus* 633.00
Andirons, Bronze, Santa Claus, Cast Iron, c.1890, 18 In. 2185.00
Andirons, Bronze, Wrapped Wheat Stems, Fan Finial, Step Base, c.1937, 25 In. 23750.00
Andirons, Copper, Geometrics, Riveted, Patina, Prairie School, 20 x 30 ½ In. . . . . *illus* 840.00
Andirons, Duck, Shoulder Bust, Head Turns, Iron, Bronze, 11 ½ x 20 In.. . . . . 978.00
Andirons, Iron, Baroque, Brass Urn, Flame Finial, c.1905, 30 x 12 x 25 In. 920.00
Andirons, Iron, Billet Bars, Couple, Tropical Trees, Patent Feb. 1858, 18 ½ In.. . . . . 1410.00
Andirons, Iron, Brass, Chippendale, Twisted Shaft, New York, c.1770, 22 x 12 In. 5313.00
Andirons, Iron, Bronze Flowers, Incised Trifid Penny Feet, 1800s, 24 x 11 In. 960.00
Andirons, Iron, Cannonball Design, Bradley & Hubbard, 10 x 14 In. 420.00
Andirons, Iron, Cast, Acanthus Leaf, Scroll Base, c.1915, 26 x 24 In.. . . . . 420.00
Andirons, Iron, Cast, American Shields, Brass Finials, Black Paint, Late 1800s, 16 In.. . . . . . . 121.00
Andirons, Iron, Cast, Billets, Cat, Seated, Black Paint, c.1885, 17 In.. 705.00
Andirons, Iron, Cast, Dragon Head, Curved Neck, Feet, Bradley & Hubbard, c.1910, 27 x 30 In. 593.00
Andirons, Iron, Cast, Duck, Folk Art, 10 ½ x 17 ½ In.. . . . . 200.00
Andirons, Iron, Cast, Ducks, Memphis, 14 x 34 ¼ In.. . . . . 235.00
Andirons, Iron, Cast, Empire Forms, Urns, Flame Tops, Bronze Dore, Napoleon III, 10 In.. . . . 1470.00
Andirons, Iron, Cast, Face Of North Wind, Medallion, c.1880, 23 ½ x 22 ½ In.. . . . . 1250.00
Andirons, Iron, Cast, Hammered, Coiled Snakes Finial, Edgar Brandt, c.1925, 18 In. 20000.00
Andirons, Iron, Cast, Hessian, Dovetailed Billet Bars, 1800s, 19 ¾ x 22 ½ In. . . . . 316.00 to 410.00
Andirons, Iron, Cast, Indian Figures, Multicolored, Paint, 1890-1910, 13 x 7 ¼ In.. . . . . 2607.00
Andirons, Iron, Cast, Lighthouse, 14 ½ In. 250.00
Andirons, Iron, Cast, Owl, 15 x 9 x 13 In.. . . . . 80.00
Andirons, Iron, Cast, Owl, Black, 19th Century, 17 x 14 ⅜ In. 650.00
Andirons, Iron, Cast, Owl Shape, Branch Legs, P.S. & W. Co., Arts & Crafts, 16 x 16 In. 480.00
Andirons, Iron, Cast, Sailor On Crow's Nest, Holding Rigging, 26 x 22 ¼ In. 5750.00
Andirons, Iron, Cast, Zoomorphic, Russel Wright, 1930, 15 ¾ x 6 x 22 In.. . . . . *illus* 5700.00
Andirons, Iron, Curled Form, Patina, G. Stickley, 12 x 6 ½ x 34 In.. . . . . 18000.00
Andirons, Iron, Hammered, Applied Details, Orb Finial, Black, 24 x 13 In.. . . . . 390.00
Andirons, Iron, Hammered, Ball Finial, Oval Ring Pull, 21 ½ In. 960.00
Andirons, Iron, Indian Chief, Standing, Arms Folded, c.1900, 13 In.. . . . . 705.00
Andirons, Iron, Knife Blade, Brass Panels, Urn Finials, 17 ½ In.. . . . . 235.00
Andirons, Iron, Leaping Hare, Stylized Tree, c.1925, 14 In. 60000.00
Andirons, Iron, Owl, Glass Eyes, Marked, Howes, Boston, c.1900, 14 ½ x 9 ½ x 18 In.. . . . . . . 330.00
Andirons, Iron, Wrought, Arched Legs, Ball Feet, Log Holders, 18 ½ x 18 ½ In. 66.00
Andirons, Iron, Wrought, Ball Top, Mid 18th Century, 15 ¾ In.. . . . . 351.00
Andirons, Iron, Wrought, Brass Finial, Penny Feet, Early 18th Century, 23 In.. . . . . 4680.00

Andirons, Iron, Wrought, Brass Finials, Tapered Shaft, Flat Base, Early 1700s, 18 In. 702.00
Andirons, Iron, Wrought, Cast, Sunflowers, Arts & Crafts, T. Jeckyll, 1878-84, 34 x 11 In. 29900.00
Andirons, Iron, Wrought, Swan Neck Top, c., 1800, 18 ¾ In. 2340.00
Andirons, Knife Blade, Brass Finial, Trestle Base, Early 18th Century, 16 ¼ In. 1053.00
Andirons, Knife Blade, Brass Flame Finial, Penny Feet, c.1760, 20 ½ In. 1404.00
Andirons, Knife Blade, Faceted Ball & Flame Finials, Late 18th Century, 24 In. 11700.00
Andirons, Metal, Chippendale, Lemon Top Bell, Cabriole Legs, 20 x 18 In. 2300.00
Andirons, Metal, Hammered, Orb Finial, Black, 13x 24 In. 840.00
Andirons, Pierced Brass Rosette Finials, Shaped Flat Polished Steel Columns, 24 x 13 In. 201.00
Andirons, Steel, Polished, Flat Curved Columns, Brass Teardrops, 1900s, 22 x 11 In. 115.00
Bellows, Brass Nozzle, Fruit, Leaves, Multicolored Paint, 1800s, 18 In. 178.00
Bellows, Carved, Wood, Stenciled, Blue Leather, Brass Nozzle, 19th Century, 18 ½ x 7 In. 395.00
Bellows, Flowers, Yellow Ground, 19th Century, 17 ¾ In. 293.00
Bellows, Flowers, Yellow Ground, Stippled Border, 19th Century, 17 ½ In. 117.00
Bellows, Mahogany, Oak, Impressed, Pearsall & Pell, New York, 22 ½ In. 439.00
Bellows, Pine, Red Wash, Leather Bound, Oak Staves, Late 19th Century, 56 x 43 In. 230.00
Bellows, Stenciled Fruit, Red Ground, Leather, Overvarnish, 19th Century, 18 ⅜ In. 206.00
Bellows, Teardrop, Flowers, Leather, Tacks, 17 ½ x 7 ¾ In. *illus* 165.00
Bellows, Turtleback, Wood, Farmstead Scene, Brass Nozzle, 19th Century, 18 In. 470.00
Bellows, Walnut, Cupid, Flowers, Lion's Head Spout, Carved, Germany, 1900, 25 In. *illus* 770.00
Bellows, Warwick Castle, Painted, Signed, Beverly Stoppard, 1874, 17 In. 100.00
Bellows, Yellow, Fruit, Leaves, Wood, Leather, Metal, Eckstein & Richardson, 1800s, 19 In. 1755.00
Chenet, Andirons, Brass, Flower, Plinth Base, 18 x 15 In. 350.00
Chenet, Andirons, Brass, Leaf & Geometric Decoration, Russia, 22 ½ In. 720.00
Chenet, Andirons, Brass, Louis XVI, Flame Finial, Flower Swags, Continental, 1800s, 10 x 17 In. 230.00
Chenet, Andirons, Bronze, Fleur-De-Lis, Laurel Wreath, Regency, Gilt, Orb, Late 1800s, 20 ½ x 12 In. 5000.00
Chenet, Andirons, Bronze, Lion, Ormolu Sphere, Drapery Frieze Base, c.1780, 14 x 20 In. 17500.00
Chenet, Andirons, Bronze, Louis XV, Rearing Lion, Shield, Black, Gilt, c.1890, 16 x 14 In. 6875.00
Chenet, Andirons, Bronze, Louis XV, Seated Putti, Bird, Acorn Finial, Gilt, 1800s, 18 In. 1180.00
Chenet, Andirons, Ormolu, Military Frieze, 2 Ribbed Spheres, c.1807, 13 x 16 In. 50000.00
Coal Box, Rosewood, Mother-Of-Pearl Inlay, Handle, Syria, Early 20th Century, 18 In. 325.00
Coal Bucket, Hand Painted, Stenciled, Tin, Salesman Sample, 6 x 6 In. 110.00
Coal Bucket, Handle, Lid, Silver On Copper, 15 x 10 In. 94.00
Coal Grate, Brass, Iron, 29 x 28 x 14 In. 489.00
Coal Scuttle, Copper, Henry Loveridge & Co., 19 x 22 x 14 In. 450.00
Coal Scuttle, Helmet Shape, Delft Handle, 14 x 16 In. 35.00
Coal Scuttle, Hinged Lid, Cast Iron, Footed, 15 ½ In. 100.00
Coal Scuttle, Mahogany, Flower, Brass Handle, 19th Century, 13 ½ x 13 ½ In. 75.00
Coal Scuttle, Oak, Brass, Tin Insert, Late 19th Century, 14 x 13 ½ x 18 ½ In. 100.00
Coal Scuttle, Reverse Painted Panel, Tin, 19th Century, 19 x 19 x 13 In. 300.00
Coal Scuttle, Victorian, Walnut, Drop Front, Beveled Mirror, 1890s, 36 x 14 x 13 In. *illus* 143.00
Ember Carrier, Barrel Form, Mouse On Lid, Painted, Cast Iron, 4 x 7 ½ x 3 In. *illus* 55.00
Ember Carrier, Duck Foot Shape, Iron, 3-Footed, Hanger Hole, 2 x 7 ½ x 5 In. 11.00
Ember Carrier, Mouse Lid, Barrel Form, Air Holes, Iron, 3 ¾ x 7 ½ x 3 ½ In. 55.00
Fender, Brass, Gilded, Hunting Dog Ends, France, 8 ½ x 33 In. 1920.00
Fender, Brass, Onyx Balls, Panels, With 3 Utensils, 20th Century, 68 x 7 In. 264.00
Fender, Brass, Pierced, Claw Feet, Iron Floor, England, c.1820, 8 x 45 In. 374.00
Fender, Brass, Pierced, Metal Base, Paw Feet, c.1900, 9 x 49 x 13 ½ In. 275.00
Fender, Brass, Pierced Decoration, 50 ½ In. 168.00
Fender, Brass, Ribbed Ball Feet, Regency, 9 x 53 x 14 ½ In. 179.00
Fender, Brass, Steel, Patinated, Parcel Gilt, 8 x 34 x 3 ½ In. 1020.00
Fender, Bronze, Latticework, Ormolu, 2 Female Sphinx, Lions, 1820s, 10 x 41 In. 1600.00
Fender, Bronze, Putti Warming Hands, Flame Finials, Scrolls, 1800s, 14 x 65 In., 5 Piece 1265.00
Fender, Cast Brass, 4 Horizontal Bars, Leaf Tips, Flower, Leaf Spray, 10 ¾ x 69 In. 230.00
Fender, Corkscrew, Victorian, Iron, c.1890, 7 ½ x 36 ¾ x 12 ¼ In. 330.00
Fender, Empire Style, Mahogany, Marble Platforms, Urn, Sphinx, France, 63 x 20 In. 478.00
Fender, Federal, Brass, Wire, Serpentine Front, Ball Finials, c.1800, 15 x 54 In. 3276.00
Fender, Federal, Brass, Wire, Serpentine Front, Paw Feet, Turned Finial, c.1830, 16 x 53 In. 1053.00
Fender, George III, Brass, Serpentine, Late 18th Century, 5 ½ x 44 ½ In. 995.00
Fender, Iron Posts, Fencing, Brass Top, Ball Finials, 12 ½ x 41 ½ In. 360.00
Fender, Louis Philippe, Ormolu, France, c.1845, 18 x 38 In. 4375.00
Fender, Regency, Brass, Nickel, 57 In. 71.00
Fender, Wire, Brass Rail, Howard & Morse, Early 20th Century, 48 x 20 In. 294.00
Fender, Wire, Empire Finial Crown, Lion's Paw, England, 18 ¼ x 48 In., Pair 489.00
Fender, Wirework, Curls, Brass Finial, Iron, c.1790, 13 x 40 In. 518.00
Fire Rail, Brass, Shaped Gallery, England, c.1890, 10 x 43 x 15 In. 245.00

Fireplace, Bellows, Teardrop, Flowers, Leather, Tacks, 17 ½ x 7 ¾ In.
$165.00

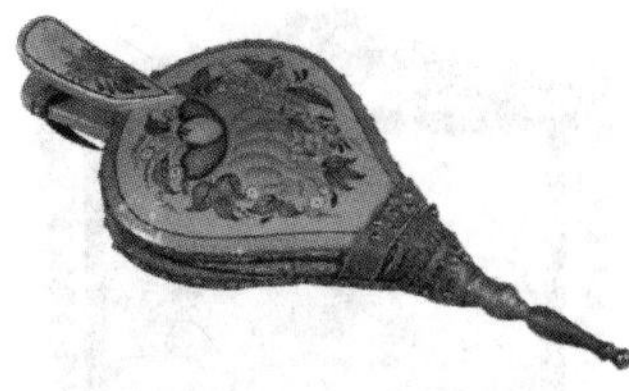

Fireplace, Bellows, Walnut, Cupid, Flowers, Lion's Head Spout, Carved, Germany, 1900, 25 In.
$770.00

Fireplace, Coal Scuttle, Victorian, Walnut, Drop Front, Beveled Mirror, 1890s, 36 x 14 x 13 In.
$143.00

Fireplace, Ember Carrier, Barrel Form, Mouse On Lid, Painted, Cast Iron, 4 x 7 ½ x 3 In.
$55.00

Fireplace, Screen, Mahogany, Rosewood, Highland Hunt Scene, Silk, 1800s, 49 x 33 x 16 In.
$770.00

Fireplace, Shovel, Wrought Iron, Round Shaft, Ball Terminal, 22 ¾ In.
$44.00

Fireplace, Surround, Federal, Yellow Pine, Walnut, White Paint, 1800s, 56 x 73 x 10 In.
$2010.00

Fireplace, Tongs, Wrought Iron, Button Terminal, Round Pinchers, 27 ½ In.
$11.00

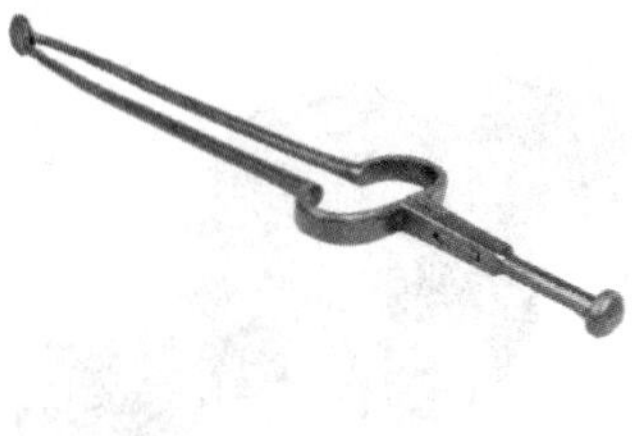

Item	Price
Fireback, Classical, Iron, Columns, Flame Topper, 13 ½ x 13 ¼ In.	550.00
Fireback, Hunters, Deer, Iron, 19th Century, 24 x 20 In.	605.00
Fireback, Neptune, Cast Iron, 25 ½ x 10 ½ In.	3900.00
Fireback, Tulip, Urn, Relief Column, 1765 Elisabeth Furnace, 1700s, 20 x 22 In.	1840.00
Fireboard, Pine, Angels, Tulips, Birds, Green Ground, Pa., c.1900, 46 x 61 In.	10530.00
Fireplace, Free-Standing, Log Holder, Screen, Tubes, Orange Enamel, c.1960, 30 x 75 In.	1200.00
Footman, Brass, Iron, Molded Edge, Shaped Apron, Curved Legs, Fat Knees, 12 x 16 In.	259.00
Fork, Iron, Brass Handle, 3 Tines, 50 In.	195.00
Fork, Renaissance Revival, Iron, Square Handle, Satyr Terminal, 39 In.	652.00
Log Basket, Hand Hammered, Rolled Corners, Iron, 6 ¾ x 11 ¾ In.	12.00
Poker, Victorian, Leg Handle, Cast Iron, 21 In.	220.00
Screen, 4 Panels, Landscape, Leaves, Flowers, 5 Ball Finials, Metal, 1900s, 32 x 46 In.	326.00
Screen, Aesthetic Movement, Ebonized, Leaded Glass, Flowers, 1800s, 49 x 25 In.	1200.00
Screen, Art Deco, Diagonal Grid, Spade Intersections, Iron, France, c.1925, 35 x 25 In.	652.00
Screen, Brass, Beveled Glass Center, 1900s, 31 x 21 x 8 In.	77.00
Screen, Brass, Fanning, Woman Holding Ball, Footed, 33 ¾ In.	90.00
Screen, Bronze, Winged Women, Leaded, Stained Glass Center, c.1880, 32 x 38 x 12 In.	3400.00
Screen, Cast Brass, Rococo Revival, Wire Mesh, Pierced Feet, 37 ½ x 26 ½ In.	403.00
Screen, Cherry, Pine, American Eagle, Wool Needlework, c.1850, 63 ½ In.	470.00
Screen, Fire, Canvas, Tree, Vines, Dogs, Birds, Mass., c.1790, 13 x 11 In.	5629.00
Screen, Flowering Branch, Stained & Leaded Glass, 3 Panels, 34 x 48 In.	160.00
Screen, French Provincial, Fruitwood, Frosted Etched Glass, Carved, c.1920, 44 x 24 In.	203.00
Screen, French Provincial, Walnut, Needlework Panel, Frame, Dome Crest, 38 x 28 In.	1920.00
Screen, G. Stickley, Leather, Tacks, Through Tenon Construction, 31 x 35 In.	1440.00
Screen, G. Stickley, Riveted Copper Hammered, 8 Panels, Patina, 28 x 37 x 5 In.	2000.00
Screen, George III, Mahogany, Sage Green Silk Panels, 19th Century, 44 x 42 In.	600.00
Screen, Gilt, Bronze, Bow, Wreath & Torch, 29 x 27 In.	700.00
Screen, Gilt, Bronze, Cherubs, 27 x 26 In.	600.00
Screen, Hand Held, Embroidered, Turned Ivory Handle, Victorian, 16 ¾ In.	60.00
Screen, Louis XV Style, Bronze, Lacquered, Black Mesh, Flower, c.1900, 30 x 29 x 9 In.	1200.00
Screen, Louis XVI, Giltwood, Fabric Panel, Stamped, Julieen, c.1780, 42 x 24 In.	1416.00
Screen, Louis XVI Style, Lacquered Brass, Fan Shape, Urn Finial, 27 x 40 In.	660.00
Screen, Mahogany, Oak, Turned Pole, Inlaid Flaring Legs, Shield Shape Silk Screen, 55 In.	235.00
Screen, Mahogany, Rosewood, Highland Hunt Scene, Silk, 1800s, 49 x 33 x 16 In. *illus*	770.00
Screen, Mahogany, Rosewood, Needlework, Hunt Scene, Victorian, 49 x 33 In.	805.00
Screen, Maple, Veneer, Inlaid Tripod Base, Asian Dragon Embroidery, 1800s, 53 In.	499.00
Screen, Needlepoint, Carved Mahogany, Crane In Marsh, Tripod Base, c.1885, 61 x 22 In.	411.00
Screen, Needlepoint, Flowers, Black Ground, Footed, c.1900, 40 ½ x 23 In.	146.00
Screen, Oak, Carved, Woman, Shield Crest, Griffins, Tapestry, 1880, 69 x 56 x 25 In.	4150.00
Screen, Papier-Mache, Mother-Of-Pearl, Persian Garden Scenes, Gilt Scrolls, Black Pole, 59 In.	236.00
Screen, Pinecone, Iron, Edgar Brandt, c.1925, 44 ½ In.	20000.00
Screen, Pole, Flowers, Victorian Style, Mahogany, Needlepoint, Tripod Feet, Kittinger Co.	170.00
Screen, Pole, George III, Mahogany, Needlework, Flower Bouquet, c.1760, 64 In.	6435.00
Screen, Pole, George III, Sliding Shield, Buildings, Trees, Urn, Tripod Base, 1800s, 62 x 13 In.	508.00
Screen, Pole, Mahogany, Flame Stitch Panel, Shield Form, England, Early 1800s, 21 In.	671.00
Screen, Pole, Queen Anne, Mahogany, Molded Frame, Silk Damask Panel, Tripod, 56 x 19 In.	240.00
Screen, Pole, Queen Anne, Mahogany, Needlework, 2 Figures, Flowers, c.1760, 61 ½ In.	3744.00
Screen, Pole, Queen Anne, Needlework, Mahogany, Acorn Finial, 11 x 13 x 56 In.	173.00
Screen, Pole, Rosewood, Pheasant, Flowers, England, 60 x 18 ½ In.	351.00
Screen, Regency, Mahogany, Adjustable, Needlepoint Panel, Octagonal, Pedestal, 35 x 18 In.	538.00
Screen, Regency, Mahogany, Trestle Form, Scroll Feet, Brocade Panel, 40 x 18 x 13 In.	1600.00
Screen, Rococo, Rosewood, Needlework Screen, Tripod Base, Alexander Roux, c.1865	2588.00
Screen, Stained, Leaded Glass, Stylized Flower, Late 19th Century, 32 In.	250.00
Screen, Victorian, Burl Walnut, Needlework, Figures, Landscape, Tripod, 54 x 23 ½ In.	415.00
Screen, Victorian, Mahogany, Floral Needlework On Linen, 45 x 27 In.	1645.00
Screen, Victorian, Needlepoint Insert, 44 x 29 In.	205.00
Screen, Walnut, Flame Torch, Devil's Mask, Shaped, Reeded, France, 1875, 42 x 29 In.	600.00
Screen, William IV, Rosewood, Needlework, Boy & Sheep, Tripod, 1875, 59 x 19 x 18 In.	850.00
Screen, Wood, Crest, Armorial Devices, Painted, Bracket Feet, 3-Fold, 35 x 44 In.	375.00
Shovel, Flat Handle, Rattail Terminal, Twisted Shaft, Flat Blade, Iron, 23 ⅛ In.	66.00
Shovel, Round Shaft, Ball Terminal, Bell Shape, Flat Blade, 25 ½ In.	11.00
Shovel, Wrought Iron, Round Shaft, Ball Terminal, 22 ¾ In. *illus*	44.00
Stand, Pot Hanger, Iron, Straight Bar, Arch Legs, Penny Feet, 17 ½ x 34 ½ In.	385.00
Stove Plate, Cast Iron, Woman Seated On Bench, Pine Grove, Pa., 18th Century, 22 x 29 In.	995.00
Surround, Federal, Yellow Pine, Walnut, White Paint, 1800s, 56 x 73 x 10 In. *illus*	2010.00
Surround, Oak, Garlands, Molded Mantel Top, Round Square Columns, 52 x 73 x 11 In.	400.00

Tongs, Coal, Round Pinchers, Spring Handle, Wrought Iron, 24 ½ In. 330.00
Tongs, Ember, Wrought Iron, Scrolled Handle, 19th Century, 21 ½ In. 1638.00
Tongs, Handle, Faceted Terminal, Wrought Iron, 25 In. 11.00
Tongs, Round Handle, Twisted, Button Finial, Shafts, Pinchers, Iron, 21 ¼ In.. .... 44.00
Tongs, Wrought Iron, Button Terminal, Round Pinchers, 27 ½ In. .... *illus* 11.00
Tool Set, Arts & Crafts, Hammered, Twisted, Tripod Base, Iron, 14 x 35 In. 480.00
Tool Set, Stand, 20th Century, 4 Piece, 32 In.. .... 175.00
Trammel, Sawtooth, Latch, Wood, Wire Hanger Hook, 23 In.. .... 413.00
Trammel, Sawtooth, Wrought Iron, Hooked Terminals, Adjustment, 11 ¼ In. 440.00
Trammel, Wrought Iron, Adjustable Ratchet, Upright Rod, Scroll, Heart Decoration, 37 x 12 In. 460.00

FISCHER porcelain was made in Herend, Hungary, by Moritz Fischer. The factory was founded in 1839 and continued working into the twentieth century. The wares are sometimes referred to as Herend porcelain.

Bear, Figurine, Seated, Purple, 3 ½ In. 165.00
Bowl, Cover, Rose Finial, 4 ⅛ x 7 ¼ x 3 ¾ In.. .... 90.00
Bowl, Green Flowers, Gilt, Scalloped Rim, 10 ¾ In. 75.00
Bowl, Queen Victoria, 8 ¾ x 7 ¾ In. 100.00
Bowl, Queen Victoria, Butterfly Form, 9 ½ x 10 In. 145.00
Bowl, Salad, Queen Victoria, Green Border, Square, Herend, 10 In. 418.00
Box, Flowers, Heart Form, Applied Flowers On Lid, Herend, 4 In. 40.00
Cachepot, Queen Victoria, Handles, Signed, 4 ¾ x 5 ½ In. 90.00
Candleholder, Queen Victoria, Round Base, Pair 165.00
Candlestick, Rothschild Bird, 2 Lights, White, Gilt, 9 x 5 In., Pair 293.00
Casserole, Cover, Queen Victoria, Handles, 4 ½ x 8 In. 450.00
Chess Pieces, Stylized Figure, Painted, Herend, 20th Century, 2 To 2 ⅜ In., 6 Piece 593.00
Chocolate Pot, Queen Victoria, Green Border, Herend, 9 ¼ In. 191.00
Coffeepot, Chinese Bouquet Rust, Herend, 10 ¼ In. 1062.00
Coffeepot, Rothschild Bird, Flower Finial, 8 ¾ In.. .... 180.00
Compote, Dancing Ladies, Cherubs, Gilt Handles, Herend, 3 ¼ x 3 ½ In. 50.00
Cooler, Cover, Flowers, Leaves, Butterflies, Scroll Handles, Gilt, Herend, 7 In. .... *illus* 265.00
Dinner Set, Rothschild Bird, Insects, Birds, Gold Trim, Herend, Hungary, 1900s, 88 Piece ... 6518.00
Dish, Indian Basket, Green, 3 Sections, Ruffled Rim, Handle, 5 x 13 ½ In. 185.00
Dish, Leaf Shape, Twig Handle, Basket Weave Border, Herend, 1900s, 9 ¼ In. 178.00
Figurine, Bird, Perched On Free-Form Base, Enamel, Mark, Herend, 1900s, 7 ½ In. 119.00
Figurine, Cat, Blue, White, Gold Feet, Red Ball, 5 x 5 In.. .... 205.00
Figurine, Cat, Orange, White, No. 5383, Marked, Herend, 4 ½ In. 100.00
Figurine, Cat, Purple, Gold, Blue Ball, 5 x 4 In. 150.00
Figurine, Cat, Seated, Orange Design, Gilt, Herend, 3 ½ In. 90.00
Figurine, Dancer, Enamel, Marked, Herend, 1900s, 8 ¼ In. .... *illus* 220.00
Figurine, Dancing Man, Polish Folk Costume, Herend, 11 ¼ x 6 In. 205.00
Figurine, Ducks, Entwined, Purple Fishnet, Multicolored Feathers, Herend, 6 In. 826.00
Figurine, Ducks, Entwined In Loving Embrace, Herend, 8 x 16 In. 469.00
Figurine, Elephant, Black, White, Gold, Mark, 10 x 14 In. 1265.00
Figurine, Elephant, Blue Printed Mark, Herend, 9 ¾ x 14 In. .... *illus* 1210.00
Figurine, Elephant, Orange Fishnet, Herend, 10 In. 944.00
Figurine, Foo Dog, Red On White, Gilt Feet, Red Tail, 10 In.. .... 760.00
Figurine, Kangaroo, Joey, Pink, White, Green, Gilt, 6 ½ In.. .... 250.00
Figurine, Leopard, Black Fishnet, Gold Paws, Nose, Herend, 17 In. 750.00
Figurine, Rabbit, Green Fishnet, Herend, 12 In. 944.00
Figurine, Rabbit, Green Fishscale, 5 In. 220.00
Figurine, Rhinoceros, Blue On White Ground, Gilt Feet & Horn, 6 ¾ x 13 ½ In.. .... 702.00
Figurine, Seahorse, Red, White, Blue, Yellow, Marked, Herend, Hungary, 4 In. 60.00
Figurine, Seminude Woman, Casually Draped, Hands In Hair, Marked, 22 x 8 ½ In. 1540.00
Figurine, Turtle, Orange Design, Aqua, Gilt, Herend, 1 ½ x 4 x 2 In. 90.00
Figurine, Young Cobbler, Hand Painted, Herend, 7 ½ x 3 x 4 ¼ In. 57.00
Group, Man On Donkey, Impressed, Markup B, Herend, 15 ½ x 11 x 5 In.. .... 355.00
Hors D'Oeuvre Dish, Shell Form, Fish, Blue Flowers, Gilt, Herend, 10 x 17 ½ In. 295.00
Lamp Base, Flowers, Butterflies, Queen Victoria, Herend, 20 In. 375.00
Platter, Orange Butterflies, Flowers, Orange & Gilt Borders, Removable Drain, Herend, 24 In. 460.00
Statue, Boxer, Fighting Pose, Blanc De Chine, Impressed Mark, Herend, 12 ½ In. 385.00
Teapot, Chinese Bouquet, Rust, Herend, 6 ¾ In. 1062.00
Tray, Chinese Bouquet, Green, Leaf Form, Handle, Signed, 9 x 8 ¾ In. 75.00
Tray, Chinese Bouquet, Green, Shell Form, Ruffled Rim, Signed, 9 x 8 ¾ In.. .... 75.00
Tray, Queen Victoria, 12-Sided, ¾ x 9 x 7 ½ In. 90.00
Vase, Bud, Butterflies, Flowers, 6 ¼ x 3 In. 33.00

TIP
Clean metal with a back-and-forth motion, not a circular motion. Use a soft, clean, lint-free cloth and turn it often to avoid reusing a soiled part.

F

Fischer, Cooler, Cover, Flowers, Leaves, Butterflies, Scroll Handles, Gilt, Herend, 7 In.
$265.00

Fischer, Figurine, Dancer, Enamel, Marked, Herend, 1900s, 8 ¼ In.
$220.00

Fischer, Figurine, Elephant, Blue Printed Mark, Herend, 9 ¾ x 14 In.
$1210.00

Fishy Gear
Think you found some valuable old fishing gear? If it has been stored, perhaps in an enclosed space, a tackle box or rod tube, it should smell musty and fishy. Examine everything. Almost anything old will be of value.

F

Fishing, Creel, George Lawrence, No. 15, Front Pocket Tillamook, Leather, Wicker, Stamp, Oregon, 14 In.
$2415.00

Fishing, Creel, Green, Indian, Moss Head Lake, Maine, c.1880, 9 ½ x 16 ½ x 8 ½ In.
$1600.00

Fishing, Fly Chest, Mahogany, 6 Drawers, Felt Lining, Brass Knobs, 20 x 14 x 11 In.
$230.00

FISHING reels of brass or nickel were made in the United States by 1810. Bamboo fly rods were sold by 1860, often marked with the maker's name. Lures made of metal, or metal and wood, were made in the nineteenth century. Plastic lures were made by the 1930s. All fishing material is collected today and even equipment of the past thirty years is of interest if in good condition with original box.

Boarding Pike, Bamboo Shaft, Hardy Bros., Alwick, England, 50 In. 173.00
Book, Compleat Angler, Izaak Walton, Illustrated, George G. Harrap, c.1931, 8 x 10 In.. ..... 546.00
Catalog, Creek Chub, Casting & Trolling Nature Lures, Catch More Fish, 1919, 8 Pages 173.00
Catalog, H.H. Kiffe, Fishing Tackle & Hunting Outfits, 1895, 166 Pages.................. 86.00
Catalog, Hardy Brothers, 50th Edition, 1928, 372 Pages.............................. 115.00
Catalog, Heddon, How To Catch More Fish, 1929, 32 Pages 259.00
Catalog, Heddon, How To Catch More Fish, 1930, 40 Pages 201.00
Catalog, Heddon, How To Catch More Fish, 1936, 36 Pages 173.00
Catalog, Iver Johnson, Fishing Tackle, Tents & Camping Goods, 1910, 192 Pages 40.00
Catalog, Iver Johnson, Fishing Tackle & Camp Outfits, 1905, 256 Pages................. 52.00
Catalog, Pfluger Tackle, No. 37, 1916, 394 Pages.................................... 201.00
Catalog, Shapleigh's, Sporting Goods, Spring & Summer, 1928, 228 Pages............... 52.00
Catalog, South Bend Bait Co., Fly Rod Lures, 1922, 32 Pages, 4 x 7 In.................. 259.00
Catalog, Wright & McGill, Fishing Tackle, 1953, 50 Pages, 6 ½ x 8 In.................. 60.00
Chest, Fly, Mahogany, Brass Trim, Canvas Cover, Interior Shelves, Hooks, 9 x 20 In. 613.00
Creel, A.E. Nelson, Split Willow, Leather, Interlocking Scallop Design, 15 x 5 x 10 In.. ...... 1265.00
Creel, Aluminum, Woven, 15 x 9 In... 109.00
Creel, Bulbous, Narrow Splint, Center Hole, Splint Hinged, 1800s, Maine, 8 ½ x 14 In. 385.00
Creel, Bulbous, Splint, Woven, Oval Wood Ends, Acorn Knob, Early 20th Century, 13 In...... 115.00
Creel, Clark, Woven, Split Willow, Leather Trim, 14 x 6 ½ x 11 In...................... 2645.00
Creel, Conway, Canvas Cover, Pouch, c.1950, England, 14 x 5 x 10 ½ In.................. 259.00
Creel, E. Robicheau, Wood, Slat Sides, 2 Painted Trout On Front, 1977, 8 x 15 In........... 855.00
Creel, George Lawrence, No. 15, Front Pocket Tillamook, Wicker, Stamp, Oregon, 14 In.... *illus* 2415.00
Creel, George Lawrence, Supreme, French Weave, Split Willow, Leather, 15 x 5 x 9 In........ 978.00
Creel, Green, Indian, Moss Head Lake, Maine, c.1880, 9 ½ x 16 ½ x 8 ½ In. .... *illus* 1600.00
Creel, Hardy Brothers, Double, Brass Hasp Closure, 14 x 6 x 12 In...................... 518.00
Creel, K.G. McKeeman, French Weave, Embossed Leather Trim, 15 x 5 ½ x 10 In. 690.00
Creel, Leather Shoulder Strap, Belt Attachment, 8 ¼ x 13 ½ x 6 In...................... 150.00
Creel, Pannier, Canoe, Wicker, Woven, 4 Wood Legs, 19 x 13 x 15 In..................... 40.00
Creel, Salmon, Ash Splint, Single Handle, Woven Splint Lid, c.1880, 19 x 20 In............. 209.00
Creel, Split Willow, Leather Straps, Green Paint, 16 x 10 In............................ 214.00
Creel, Tin, Faux Grain Paint, Rolled Edges, Blue Stencil, Trout, Leather Strap, 12 x 6 In. 431.00
Creel, Woven Strap, Green Paint, c.1920, 11 x 6 x 8 ¾ In............................ 176.00
Display, Diorama, Sailfish Leaping, Ocean Waves, Sky, Wood Frame, c.1935, 18 x 12 ½ In.... 345.00
Display, Heddon, Lures, 12 Assorted Torpedoes, Salesman's Board, 12 x 18 In.............. 230.00
Display, Pequea, 26 Lures, Metal & Mother-Of-Pearl, Oilcloth Covered Case............... 518.00
Display, Pequea, 58 Floats, Bobbers, Spinners, Salesman's Sample, Oilcloth Covered Case ... 2415.00
Display, Pequea, Hooks, Snelled, 6 Folding Panels, Carlisle, Sproat, Limerick, 10 x 30 In..... 259.00
Float, Kent Champion, Frog, Painted, Aluminum Props, Samuel Kent, c.1905 .... 604.00
Float, Minnow Torpedo Shape, Metal, Green Paint, Stenciled Decoration, 26 In. 460.00
Fly, Bass Devil, Indian Pattern, Orange & Yellow, 2 ¾ In................................ 259.00
Fly, Brown-Hackle Peacock Pattern, Walt Dette, ½ In., 4 Piece 35.00
Fly, Cree Spider Pattern, Walt Dette, 15 Piece 40.00
Fly, Dog Catcher Pattern, Walt Dette, 1 In., 3 Piece.................................. 58.00
Fly, Fan Wing Variation Of Royal Classic, Walt Dette, 12 Piece 201.00
Fly, Grizzly King Pattern, Winnie Dette, ¾ In., 11 Piece 46.00
Fly, Lady Beaverkill, ⅞ In., 2 Piece.. 58.00
Fly, Partridge Monarch, Brown Pattern, ⅞ In., 6 Piece 35.00
Fly, Quill Gordon Pattern, Winnie Dette, ¾ In., 10 Piece 58.00
Fly, Salmon, Golden Rogan, Yellow Tinseling, Alex Rogan, c.1925, 2 ½ In................. 144.00
Fly, Spent Wing, Adams Dry, Walt Dette, 1 In., 10 Piece 115.00
Fly, Three Peas In A Pod, Helen Shaw, Mounted In Shadowbox.......................... 316.00
Fly, Wet, Professor Pattern, Winnie Dette, ¾ In., Pair................................. 86.00
Fly Chest, Mahogany, 6 Drawers, Felt Lining, Brass Knobs, 20 x 14 x 11 In. .... *illus* 230.00
Fly Chest, Walnut, Oak, 18 Graduated Drawers, Paneled, 19th Century, 18 x 11 x 24 In...... 1840.00
Fly Wallet, Bray, Leather, Celluloid Holders, Felt Dividers, 1895........................ 259.00
Fly Wallet, George Lawrence, Leather, 9 ¾ x 4 ½ In.................................. 316.00
Gaff, George Hatch, Signed, 6 Ft. 5 In. 316.00
Hat, 25 Pennsylvania Fishing License Buttons, c.1960 .... 325.00
Lure, Anderson Animated Bait Co., Francois The Frog, Plastic, Glass Eyes, Box, 1948........ 920.00
Lure, Bagley, Miss Liberty, Red, White & Blue, Stars, Stripes, Box 173.00

Lure, Bagley, Super Grass Rat, SGR1, Orange, Yellow 144.00
Lure, C.R. Harris, Cork Floating Frog, Box, 4 In. 2415.00
Lure, Charmer, Minnow, White, Green Stripes, Glass Eyes, Patented Oct 11, 1910, 3 ¼ In. 920.00
Lure, Chippewa, Minnow, Bass Size, Sienna Crackle Back, Red Trim, 1910 .... 259.00
Lure, Clinton Wilt, Little Wonder, Red, Bronze Stripe, 2 In. 796.00
Lure, Coldwater Bait Co., Hell Diver, White Body, Red Chin, Glass Eyes, Box, Try One, 1920s .. 1150.00
Lure, Creek Chub, Baby Dingbat, No. 5238, Pearl Finish, Glass Eyes 86.00
Lure, Creek Chub, Baby Pikie Minnow, No. 906, Goldfish Scale 337.00
Lure, Creek Chub, Chautauqua Wiggler, Red Head White Body, Screw Eyes, 3 Hooks 1164.00
Lure, Creek Chub, Deluxe Wagtail, No. 806, Goldfish Scale Finish, Red Gills 582.00
Lure, Creek Chub, Gar Minnow, No. 2920, Glass Eye, 3 Hooks, Green Scales 354.00
Lure, Creek Chub, Green Gar Minnow, No. 2920, Green, Glass Eyes, 5 ¼ In. 201.00
Lure, Creek Chub, Husky Dinger, No. 5700, Pikie Finish, Gold Military Stencil 173.00
Lure, Creek Chub, Husky Injured Minnow, No. 3504, Gold Shiner Finish, Glass Eye ..... *illus* 521.00
Lure, Creek Chub, Husky Musky, No. 600, Red Head, White Body, Screw Eye 153.00
Lure, Creek Chub, Husky Musky, No. 600, Screw Eye, Green Scale Finish 368.00
Lure, Creek Chub, Injured Minnow, No. 1506, Special, Goldfish Finish, Hang Tag, 3 ¾ In. ... 345.00
Lure, Creek Chub, Midget Plunker, No. 5925, White Scale Finish, Red, Black, Yellow 153.00
Lure, Creek Chub, Pikie, No. 705, Black, Red, Silver Scales, Glass Eyes 259.00
Lure, Creek Chub, Pikie, Store Display, Red, Black, Gold, 2 Large Screws, 17 ½ In. 337.00
Lure, Creek Chub, Wiggler, No. 100, Glass Eye, Red Painted Gill Marks 86.00
Lure, Creek Chub, Wiggler, No. 206, Double Line Tie, Goldfish Scales 173.00
Lure, Creek Chub, Yellow Shiner Wiggler, No. 103, Painted Scales & Gills, Box 489.00
Lure, Creek Chub, Yellow Sucker, No. 3900Y, Glass Eyes, Box 316.00
Lure, E.C. Adams, Jersey Expert, Wood, Painted, Yellow Glass Eyes, 3 Hooks, Box, 1907 ...... 8855.00
Lure, Enterprise, Minnow, Muskellunge Trolling, Rubber, Feathered Treble Hook, 1890s, 7 In. 288.00
Lure, Fechter, Frog, Black Bead Eyes, Red Belly Weight, 1 11/16 In. 29.00
Lure, H.C. Brush, Trolling Spoon, Cork Float, Kidney Blade, Red Bucktail Hook, 1876 .... 175.00
Lure, Heddon, Black Sucker Minnow, No. 1300, Yellow, Green, Glass Eye 214.00
Lure, Heddon, Fuzzi-Bug, No. 75WR, White, Red, Bead Eyes, Feathers, Box 316.00
Lure, Heddon, Minnow, Underwater No. 100, Wood, Green Crackle Back, Box, c.1908 .... 1380.00
Lure, Heddon, Minnow, Underwater No. 150, Red, Gold, 5 Treble Hooks, Box .... *illus* 470.00
Lure, Heddon, Punkinseed, No. 740ROB, Floating Model, Finished In Rock Bass 337.00
Lure, Heddon, River Runtie, No. 750, Wood Body, Yellow Painted Eyes, Shiny Scales 276.00
Lure, J.D. Hosmer, Mechanical Froggie, Green, White Belly, Red Trim, Box, 1930s, 5 In. 17250.00
Lure, Joe Pepper, Roman Spider Bass & Pickerel, White, Red, Yellow Eyes, c.1915, 3 In. 633.00
Lure, Kalamazoo Tackle Co., Rhodes Mechanical Swimming Frog, Green, Box, c.1910 ...... 2415.00
Lure, Kimmich, Special Mouse, Wood Head, Black Bead Eyes, Bucktail Body, 1929, Box 230.00
Lure, Moonlight Bait Co. Dreadnought, 5 Hooks, c.1912 .... 1463.00
Lure, Neverfail Minnow, Metalized, Nickel Plated, Glass Eyes, Box 201.00
Lure, Neverfail Minnow, Wood, Red Head, White Body, Glass Eyes, Box 259.00
Lure, Pfleuger, Catalina Minnow, Metalized, Nickel Plated, Glass Eyes, 4 ½ In. 86.00
Lure, Pfleuger, Kent Champion Floater, Painted Spots, Nostrils & Mouth, Glass Eyes 173.00
Lure, Pfleuger, Maybug Spoon, Red & Black Body, Green & Gold Wings, On 5-In. Card 3450.00
Lure, Pfleuger, Monarch Minnow, Metalized, Nickel Plated, Glass Eyes, 3 In. 173.00
Lure, Pfleuger, Neverfail, Minnow, Green Crackle Back, Wooden Slide Box 345.00
Lure, Pfleuger, South Coast Minnow, Green Back, White Belly, Weights, Rear Hook, 3 In. 115.00
Lure, Shakespeare, Minnow, Musky Trolling, No. 972-8, Reed & Bucktail, Fluted Spinner 86.00
Lure, Shakespeare, Minnow, No. 23NP, Metalized, Nickel Plate, Glass Eyes 316.00
Lure, Shakespeare, Minnow, Slim Jim, No. 43GWJ, Wood, Green, Box, 3 ¾ In. 316.00
Lure, Shakespeare, Rhodes Mechanical Swimming Frog, Green, Spots, Box, Mich. ...... *illus* 1164.00
Lure, Shakespeare, Rhodes Wooden Minnow, Green Back, Box, Mich., 3 ¾ In. 919.00
Lure, Success Spinner Water Globe, Two Hook Model, Yellow, Gold Spots 368.00
Minnow Bucket, Blue Magic, No. 60, Falls City, Stenciled, Stylized Fish, 8 In. 288.00
Minnow Bucket, Climax, Cream City, Green, Stenciled Fish, Lily Pads, 8 x 9 ½ In. 201.00
Minnow Bucket, Copper, 2 Coiled Handles, c.1900, 16 In. 1250.00
Minnow Bucket, Copper, 2 Curled Bail Handles, Initials CG, 18 ½ x 9 ½ x 8 In. 288.00
Minnow Bucket, Swan Floating, Green, Stenciled, 10 x 8 ½ x 8 In. 978.00
Minnow Trap, Shakespeare, Glass, Wire Frame & Shaped Feet, Perforated Lid, 12 x 8 In. 86.00
Minnow Tube, Detroit, Glass, Celluloid Cap, Wire Leader Line, 4 Hooks, Box, c.1914 .... 978.00
Minnow Tube, Pfeiffer, Glass, Aluminum Cap, 4 Hooks, Box, Patented March 3, 1914 ...... 1725.00
Minnow Tube, Welch & Graves, Glass, Wire Leader, Cork Stopper, Wood Slide Box, 1893 .... 805.00
Net, Trout, Wrapped Handle, 9 x 17 In. 144.00
Pole, Bamboo, Barrel Reel, Tapered Shaft, Bakelite Inserts, c.1910, 81 ½ In. 170.00
Reel, A. Clerk & Co., 4 In. Marked Brass Ball Handle, Walnut Grasp, 2 ¼ In. 403.00
Reel, Abbey & Imbrie, Multiplying, Rim Mounted Drag, Marked Brass, 1 ⅞ In. 173.00
Reel, Abbey & Imbrie, Trout, German Silver Raised Pillar, Rubber Grasp, N.Y., 2 ¼ In. Diam. .. 575.00

Fishing, Lure, Creek Chub, Husky Injured Minnow, No. 3504, Gold Shiner Finish, Glass Eye
$521.00

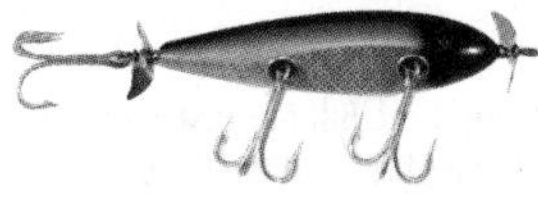

Fishing, Lure, Heddon, Minnow, Underwater No. 150, Red, Gold, 5 Treble Hooks, Box
$470.00

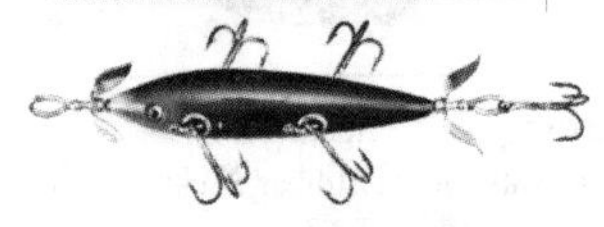

Fishing, Lure, Shakespeare, Rhodes Mechanical Swimming Frog, Green, Spots, Box, Mich.
$1164.00

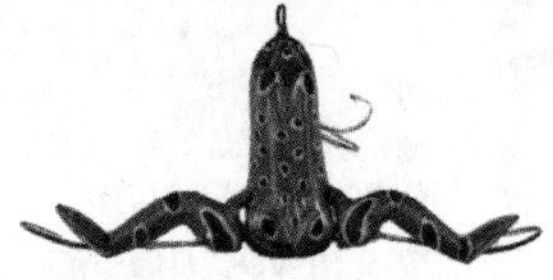

Fishing Lures
Lures are popular with collectors. Names to look for are Heddon, South Bend, Creek Chub, Paw Paw, Shakespeare, and Pflueger, according to a well-known auction house that specializes in fishing gear. There are sites online that will appraise antique fishing lures from a posted picture.

TIP
Worcestershire sauce is a good brass polish.

Fishing, Reel, Billinghurst Birdcage, Dual Patent Nickel Plated Mark, c.1873, 2 ⅞ In.
$826.00

Fishing, Reel, Pflueger, Kihoga, Salt Water, Hard Rubber, Nickel, Bulldog Logo, 450 Yd.
$115.00

TIP
Do not touch your coins. If you must, touch only the edge. The oil from your skin will damage the coin. There are cases where an actual fingerprint can be seen on the coin, etched by the oils put there years before. Wear white cotton gloves when examining the coins. Don't let people who are sneezing and coughing near the coins. Saliva will make carbon stains.

F

Reel, Abu Garcia Ambassadeur, Casting, Model No. 1750, Handle Mounted, Red. . . . 201.00
Reel, Ambassadeur, Trout, No. 178, Left Hand Wind, Signed, 3 ⅜ In. . . . 29.00
Reel, Arthur Walker, Trout, TR-2, Gold Finish, Rubber, Aluminum, 2 ¾ In.. . . . 2180.00
Reel, Billinghurst, Fly, Birdcage, Brass, Rosewood Grasp, Patent Aug. 9, 1859, 3 In. Diam. . . . 1495.00
Reel, Billinghurst, Fly, Brass Birdcage, c.1865, 2 ⅞ In. . . . 858.00
Reel, Billinghurst Birdcage, Dual Patent Nickel Plated Mark, c.1873, 2 ⅞ In. . . . *illus* 826.00
Reel, C.M. Clinton, Trout, Aluminum, German Silver, Pat. Oct. 29 '89, 2 ⅝ In. Diam.. . . . 6900.00
Reel, Coxon, Aerial, 4 Spokes, Rubber, 2 Horn Grasps, Marked Patent, 2 ⅞ In. Diam.. . . . 1150.00
Reel, Cozzone, Marbleized Hard Rubber Sides, German Silver, 6 Yd. Size, 2 ⅜ In.. . . . 2070.00
Reel, Cozzone, Trout, No. 980, German Silver, Marbleized Rubber Side Plates, Box . . . 920.00
Reel, Edward Vom Hofe, Trout, Peerless, Model 355, German Silver, Leather Case, 3 ½ In.. . . . 2588.00
Reel, Fly, Birdcage Style, Nickel Plated, 19 Ring, c.1902, 3 ⅜ In. . . . 575.00
Reel, G.S. Rinebolt, Night Casting, 8 Spokes, Indiana, 1927, 4 In. . . . 633.00
Reel, G.W. Gayle & Son, Trout, German Silver, Aluminum, Frankfort, Ky., c.1937, 2 ¼ Diam. . 8338.00
Reel, Go-Ite, Fly, Cast Foot, Egg-Shaped Cutouts, Twin Handles, Indiana, 3 ½ x 6 In.. . . . 403.00
Reel, H.L. Leonard, Fly, Bi-Metal, Bronze Foot, Pat. Jun. 12, 1877. . . . 8338.00
Reel, H.L. Leonard, Trout, Spool, Orange, Black Side Plates, Rubber, Silver, 3 In. . . . 8913.00
Reel, Hardy, Fly, Silex, No. 2, Alloy 3-Screw Spool Latch, Brass Foot, Box, 3 ¼ In. Diam.. . . . 374.00
Reel, Hardy, St. George Junior, Ribbed Aluminum Foot, Zipped Case, 2 ½ In. Diam.. . . . 805.00
Reel, Hardy, Trout, Perfect, Spool, Leather Case, 3 ⅜ In. . . . 575.00
Reel, Hardy, Trout, St. George MK2, Alloy Foot, Case, 3 ¾ In. . . . 316.00
Reel, Hardy, Trout, Super Silex, Alloy, Perforated Side, Ribbed Brass Foot, 3 ¼ In. Diam.. . . . 230.00
Reel, Henry Kenward, Brass, Nickel Plated Brass, 2 Wood Handles, Indiana, 1912 . . . 345.00
Reel, Henry Kiest, 6 Arms, Marbleized Plastic Handles, Off-Set Foot, Box, 1921, 7 In.. . . . 86.00
Reel, Horton Mfg., Trout, Meek No. 54, Smooth Brass Foot, c.1938, 2 ⅞ In.. . . . 214.00
Reel, J.C. Jeffries, Brass Line Guide, Cutouts, Signed, J.C.J., Indiana, Pat. May 6, 1924 . . . 201.00
Reel, James E. Oliver, Casting, Trolling, No. M300, Aluminum, 1951 . . . 173.00
Reel, Julius Vom Hofe, Trout, Hard Rubber Rim, German Silver, Size 3, c.1912, 2 ⅜ In.. . . . 14375.00
Reel, Julius Vom Hofe, Trout, Rubber, German Silver, Perforated, Pat. Oct. 8, '89 . . . 5405.00
Reel, K.C. Talbot, No. 100, German Silver, Aluminum, S-Handle, Ivory Grasp, Mo.. . . . 8625.00
Reel, Kelly, 4 Arms, Brass Cups, 2 Handle Grasps, Indiana, 1933 . . . 230.00
Reel, Kosmic, Fly, German Silver, Rubber, 1 x 2 ¼ In. . . . 2760.00
Reel, Leonard-Mills, Salmon, Raised Pillar, Adjustable Drag, S-Shaped Handle, 4 ¼ In. Diam. 748.00
Reel, Marryat, Gehrke's World Supreme, MR 8 A, Left Hand Wind, Gold, 3 ¼ In.. . . . 245.00
Reel, Nottingham, Star Back, Bone Handles, Brass Line Guide, Early 1900s, 3 In. . . . 550.00
Reel, Orvis, Trout, Nickel Plated, Patented May 12th, 1874, Fitted Walnut Case . . . 748.00
Reel, Pfleuger, Atlapac, German Silver, Rubber, Salt Water, Felt Bag, Case, Size 4/0 . . . 316.00
Reel, Pfleuger, Atlapac, No. 1960, Rubber, Nickel Plated, Diamolite Finish, Size 9/0. . . . 374.00
Reel, Pfleuger, Dixie, No. 1310, Salt Water, Rubber, Nickel Plated, Wood & Nickel Thumb Drag 403.00
Reel, Pflueger, Avalon, No. 2729, Salt Water, Rubber, Leather Thumb Drag, 1919. . . . 1495.00
Reel, Pflueger, Kihoga, Salt Water, Hard Rubber, Nickel, Bulldog Logo, 450 Yd.. . . . *illus* 115.00
Reel, Pflueger, Trout, Hawkeye, Rubber, Nickel Plated Silver, 100 Yd., 2 ¾ In. Diam. . . . 345.00
Reel, Rider, Casting, 4 Arms, Indiana, c.1908. . . . 115.00
Reel, Samuel L. Kuntz, 5 Arms, Cleats, Inward Folding Cups, Indiana, 1920. . . . 115.00
Reel, Seamaster, Fly, Mark III, Dual Mode, Salt Water, Black, Gold Finish, 12 Wt. Line. . . . 1265.00
Reel, Ustonson, Fly, Temple Bar, Brass, Raised Click Box, Brass Sheet Foot, London, c.1830. . . 4600.00
Reel, W.E. Carpentar Rod Co., Trout, Right Hand Wind, 3 In. . . . 805.00
Reel, Waltonian, Casting, New York Side Mount, Free Spool Lever, 100 Yd. Size. . . . 288.00
Reel, White-Ross Co., Trout, Follett Patent Automatic, Pat'd. Nov. 19 1889 . . . 1380.00
Reel, Willoughby, Molded Plastic, 6 Arms, Plastic Handles, Box, Indiana, 7 In.. . . . 316.00
Rod, Beaverkill, Parabolic 19, Gray Bag, Unmarked Tube, 8 Ft. . . . 735.00
Rod, C.F. Murphy, Calcutta Cane, Spiked Ferrules, 3/2, Case, 12 Ft.. . . . 1955.00
Rod, Carlson, Trout, 4-Lights, Flamed Cane, Red Silk Wraps, 2/2, Bag, Tube, 1979, 6 Ft. . . . 6431.00
Rod, Carpenter, Trout, Graphite, 4/1, Cork Reel Seat, Bag, Tube, 8 Ft. . . . 429.00
Rod, Caviello & Trucco, Trout, Dark Wood Spacer, 2/2, Bag, Tube, Label, 7 Ft. . . . 1610.00
Rod, Charles Wheeler, Trout, Calcutta Cane, Nickel Silver Slides, 3/2, Maine, 9 ½ In.. . . . 431.00
Rod, E.M. Holm, Deep Sea, Green Split Tonkin, Bamboo, Hand Finished, 6 Ft. 8 In.. . . . 6.00
Rod, F.E. Thomas, Bangor, 3/2, Red Wraps, Red Seat With Cap, Bag, Tube, 7 ½ Ft. . . . 1093.00
Rod, F.E. Thomas, Trout, 3/2, Cedar Reel Seat, Green Bag, Brass Capped Tube, 9 Ft.. . . . 490.00
Rod, Garrison, Salmon, No. 218, Cork Handle, 3/2, Bag, Tube, 10 Ft.. . . . 2144.00
Rod, Garrison, Salmon, No. 232, 3/2, Red Rubber Button, Bag, Tube, 9 Ft. . . . 1035.00
Rod, Gary Howells, Trout, 2/2, Bag, Tube, 7 Ft. 3 In. . . . 3450.00
Rod, Gary Howells, Trout, Flamed Cane, 2/2, Original Bag, Tube, 7 Ft. . . . 2185.00
Rod, Heddon, Deep Sea, No. 42, Checkered Walnut Handle, 6 Ft. 4 In. . . . 288.00
Rod, Leonard, Salmon, No. 92, 3/2, Canvas Bag, Tube, 11 Ft. . . . 490.00
Rod, Leonard, Trout, Model 50, Jasper Wraps, Pinched Snake Guides, 3/2, Bag, 8 Ft. . . . 1265.00

Rod, Leonard & Mills, Gold Wraps, Reverse Wells Grip, 9 Ft. 173.00
Rod, Montague, Salmon, 2/2, Exposed Cane Reel Seat, Bag, Crinkle Finish Tube, 8 ½ Ft. 2328.00
Rod, Orvis, Fly, Calcutta Cane, Red Wraps, 3 Sections, Original Cloth Bag, 1880s, 10 Ft. 115.00
Rod, Orvis, Fly, Wood, Turned, Sumac Handle & Seat, 3/2, Bag, Cedar Tube, 1882, 10 Ft...... 230.00
Rod, Orvis, Limestone Special, 2/2, Walnut Reel Seat, Bag, Tube, 8 ½ Ft.......... 575.00
Rod, Orvis, Trout, Battenkill, Walnut Spacer, 2/2, Bag, Tube, 8 Ft. 575.00
Rod, Orvis, Wes Jordan, Battenkill, No. 49974, Bamboo, 3/2, Bag, Tube, 8 Ft. 460.00
Rod, Orvis, Wes Jordan, Rocky Mountain Fly, No. 47007, Tube, 6 ½ Ft.. .... 949.00
Rod, Payne, Bait Casting, No. 304, 2/2, Stamped, Bag With Tag, Tube, 6 Ft.......... 201.00
Rod, Payne, Trout, 3/2, Cedar Reel Seat, Bag, Tube, 8 ½ In. 1041.00
Rod, Sam Carlson, Salmon, Quad, Walnut Spacer, 3/2, Bag, Tube, 9 Ft. 9 In. 1150.00
Rod, T & T, Salmon, Iliaska Special, 2/1, Bag, Labeled Tube, 9 Ft.......... 325.00
Rod, T & T, Trout, Firehole Graphite, 2/1, Bag, Label.......... 489.00
Rod, Wanigas, 2/2, Cork Reel Seat, Bag, Labeled Tube, 5 ½ Ft. 1840.00
Rod, Wheeldon, Trout, Tiger Stripe Flaming Cane, 2/1, Tube, England, 1992, 6 Ft. 9 In. 920.00
Tackle Box, Creek Chub Bait Co., Yellow, Pikie, Picture, c.1920, 5 x 2 In. 575.00
Tackle Box, F. Landsdown, Salt Water Hooks, Leaders, Leather, Brass, England, 14 x 18 In... 92.00
Tackle Box, Knickerbocker Case Co., Leather, 16 x 9 x 8 In.......... *illus* 288.00
Tackle Box, Mahogany, Brass Corners, Piano Hinge Latches, Canvas Cover, c.1945, 20 In. ... 633.00
Tackle Box, Trout Fisherman, Brass, 9 ½ In.......... 450.00
Tube, Rod Cover, Leather, Stamped, Punched Fish, Handle, Costa Rica, 60 x ¾ In.......... 518.00

FLAGS *are included in the Textile category.*

FLASH GORDON appeared in the Sunday comics in 1934. The daily strip started in 1940. The hero was also in comic books from 1930 to 1970, in books from 1936, in movies from 1938, on the radio in the 1930s and 1940s, and on television from 1953 to 1954. All sorts of memorabilia are collected, but the ray guns and rocket ships are the most popular.

Book, Pop-Up, Tournament Of Death, Alex Raymond, Pleasure Books, c.1935, 8 x 9 ½ In. ... 283.00
Book, Water World Of Mango, Big Little Book, Whitman, 1937.......... 25.00
Gun, Radio Repeater, Clicks, Red, Tin Lithograph, Marx, Box, 10 In.......... 935.00
Jigsaw Puzzle, Inlaid, Mac Raboy, Milton Bradley, 10 x 14 ½ In.. .... 73.00
Medals & Insignia, Blister Pack, 5 Piece.......... 50.00
Pistol, Arresting Ray, Clicks, Tin, King Features, c.1952, 10 In.. .... 226.00
Pistol, Signal, Sparks, Siren, Green, Red, Painted, Pressed Steel, Decal, Marx, 7 ¼ In.... *illus* 350.00
Rocket Fighter Ship, Sparks, No. 5, Red, Tin Lithograph, Marx, Box, 12 In.. .... 978.00 to 1650.00
Space Outfit, Belt, Wrist Compass, Goggles, Display Card, c.1951, 12 ½ x 8 ½ In. 260.00
Telephone, 2-Way, Tin, Display Card, King Features Syn., Marx, c.1940s, 4 ½ In.. .... 181.00
Toy, Action Figure, Dale Arden, Accessories, On Card, Mego, 1976, 8 ½ x 13 In.. .... 115.00
Toy, Figure, Ming The Merciless, Tin Lithograph, On Card 115.00
Toy, Ray Gun, Red, Gold, 1950s, 10 In. 70.00
Water Pistol, Plastic, Red, Original Stopper, Box, Marx, 7 In. 492.00

FLORENCE CERAMICS were made in Pasadena, California, from World War II to 1977. Florence Ward created many colorful figurines, boxes, candleholders, and other items for the gift shop trade. Each piece was marked with an ink stamp that included the name *Florence Ceramics Co.* The company was sold in 1964 and although the name remained the same, the products were very different. Mugs, cups, and trays were made.

Bust, Boy, White Matte Glaze, Marked, Ink Stamp, 9 ⅝ In. 45.00
Figurine, Clarissa, Muff, Green Dress, 8 In.......... 45.00
Figurine, Cleopatra, Stepped Base, Stamped, 11 ½ In. 275.00
Figurine, Lady Diana, Flowers, Purple & White Dress, Signed, 10 ½ In. 600.00
Figurine, Mardi Gras, Pink & White Dress, Signed, 10 ½ In.. .... 1000.00
Figurine, Sue Ellen, Muff, Pink Dress, 8 ½ In.......... 30.00
Figurine, Vivian, Pink Dress, Parasol, Signed, 10 ½ In.. .... 60.00

FLOW BLUE was made in England and other countries about 1830 to 1900. The dishes were printed with designs using a cobalt blue coloring. The color flowed from the design to the white body so that the finished piece has a smeared blue design. The dishes were usually made of ironstone china. More Flow Blue may be found under the name of the manufacturer.

Bone Dish, Grace, W.H. Grindley, c.1897, 2 Piece.......... 71.00
Bowl, Argyle, W.H. Grindley, Oval, Scalloped, Embossed, c.1842, 7 ¼ x 10 In. 89.00
Bowl, Beauty Roses, W.H. Grindley & Co., Open, c.1925, 12 In.......... 15.00
Bowl, Cambridge, New Wharf Pottery, c.1894, 9 ¼ In.......... 31.00

Fishing, Tackle Box, Knickerbocker Case Co., Leather, 16 x 9 x 8 In.
$288.00

Flash Gordon, Pistol, Signal, Sparks, Siren, Green, Red, Painted, Pressed Steel, Decal, Marx, 7 ¼ In.
$350.00

Dating Early Ironstone Plates

Ironstone patterns were copies of porcelain patterns until about 1830. Pieces were decorated with blue or Asian-inspired multicolored designs. Blue, pink, purple, green, black, and sepia transfers were used from about 1830 to 1845. Purple, black, and light blue were used until about 1850. Flow blue became very popular in the 1850s. Light-colored transfer prints of pink, green, light blue, or light purple were favored until about 1860. "Gaudy ironstone" was popular from about 1855 until 1865. It was decorated with orange and blue Imari-style designs. Luster-decorated ironstone, featuring Tea Leaf– or Chelsea Grape–type decorations, was made in the 1870–80 period. Plain white ironstone with raised decorations was most popular from about 1875 until 1900.

Flow Blue, Coffeepot, Snowflake Pattern, Bulbous, Dome Lid, Ironstone, 9 ¾ x 5 ½ In.
$143.00

Flow Blue, Cup & Saucer, Lahore, England, 2 ⅜ In. & 6 In.
$65.00

Flow Blue, Pitcher, Milk, Azalea, J. Kent, c.1913, 7 ¼ In.
$118.00

Flow Blue, Pitcher, Morning Glory, Copper Luster, Paneled, Ironstone, 5 ¼ In.
$120.00

F

Bowl, Columbia, Clementson & Young, 6 Pointed Sides, Embossed Handle, c.1846, 5 ½ In. . . 35.00
Bowl, Corinthian Flute, c.1905, 7 ¾ In. . . . 21.00
Bowl, Country Scenes, England, c.1891, 9 In. . . . 77.00
Bowl, Delph, Open, E. Bourne, J.E. Leigh, c.1908, 10 ½ In. . . . 11.80
Bowl, Elsa, W. & E. Corn, c.1891, 8 In. . . . 27.00
Bowl, Jenny Lind, Arthur Winklinson, c.1895, 7 ¾ In. . . . 35.00
Bowl, Keswick, Wood & Son, c.1898, 12 x 9 In. . . . 21.00
Bowl, Lahore Pattern, 9 ¼ In. . . . 71.00
Bowl, Navy, T. Till & Sons, Oval, c.1891, 7 x 9 ¾ In. . . . 32.00
Bowl, Open, Pierced Border, Grapes, Leaves, Blue Roses, C. Tielsch & Co., 11 ¼ In. . . . 71.00
Bowl, Scalloped Edge, Conway, New Wharf Pottery, c.1891, 9 In., 3 Piece . . . 35.00
Bowl, Trilby, Wood & Son, c.1907, 9 ½ In. . . . 18.00
Bowl, Victoria, Wood & Sons, c.1891, 10 ¼ In. . . . 11.80
Bowl, Windflower, Burgess & Leigh, Oval, c.1896, 7 ¼ x 9 ¾ In. . . . 24.00
Cake Plate, Gironde, W.H. Grindley, c.1891, 9 ½ x 10 ¾ In. . . . 59.00
Cake Plate, Pedestal, W. H. Grindley, Green Decor, c.1925, 4 ½ x 10 In. . . . 41.00
Cake Plate, Pierced Handles, 10 ¾ In. . . . 212.00
Chamber Pot, Cover, Doreen, W.H. Grindley, c.1891 . . . 150.00
Chamber Pot, Cover, Kelmscott, F. Winkle & Co., c.1910 . . . 15.00
Cheese Keeper, Acme, Sampson Hancock & Sons, c.1900. . . . 71.00
Coffeepot, Snowflake Pattern, Bulbous, Dome Lid, Ironstone, 9 ¾ x 5 ½ In. . . . *illus* 143.00
Compote, Byzantium, Brown Westhead Moore & Co., c.1900, 10 x 11 In. . . . 24.00
Creamer, Windmill, Blue, White, Gold Leafing, 4 ⅛ x 5 ¼ In. . . . 75.00
Cup & Saucer, Cecil, F. Till & Son, c.1891 . . . 53.00
Cup & Saucer, Haddon, Libertas Prussia, c.1900. . . . 11.80
Cup & Saucer, Hawthorne, Mercer Pottery Co., c.1890, 4 Piece . . . 11.80
Cup & Saucer, Lahore, England, 2 ⅜ x 6 In. . . . *illus* 65.00
Cup & Saucer, Take Ye A Cuppe O' Kindnesse For Auld Lang Syne, 5 ½ x 7 ¼ In. . . . 44.00
Dish, Sardine, Floral, Square, c.1895, 5 x 6 In. . . . 77.00
Gravy Boat, Derby, W.H. Grindley, c.1891 . . . 65.00
Gravy Boat, Marguerite, W.H. Grindley, c.1891 . . . 24.00
Gravy Boat, Underplate, Grace, W.H. Grindley, c.1897. . . . 47.00
Gravy Boat, Underplate, Hamilton, John Maddock & Sons, c.1896, 7 ¼ x 10 ¼ In. . . . 30.00
Jardiniere, Flowers, Leaves, Sebring Pottery, c.1887, 7 ¾ x 8 ½ In. . . . 100.00
Pitcher, Brush Stroke, Stem Design, Dot Flowers, Tulips, Twisted Handle, 9 In. . . . 10.00
Pitcher, Flowers, Keller & Guerin, Luneville, France, c.1900, 8 ¾ In. . . . 76.00
Pitcher, Milk, 3 Poppies, c.1900, 7 ¾ In. . . . 48.00
Pitcher, Milk, Alexandria, Purple, Multicolored, c.1875, 8 ½ In. . . . 26.00
Pitcher, Milk, Azalea, J. Kent, c.1913, 7 ¼ In. . . . *illus* 118.00
Pitcher, Milk, Columbia, Clementson & Young, c.1846, 7 ¾ In. . . . 106.00
Pitcher, Milk, Osborne, W.H. Grindley, c.1900, 6 ¾ In. . . . 195.00
Pitcher, Morning Glory, Copper Luster, Paneled, Ironstone, 5 ¼ In. . . . *illus* 120.00
Pitcher, Water, Oxford, William Adderly & Co., c.1905, 11 ½ In. . . . 89.00
Plate, Agra, F. Winkle & Co., c.1891, 10 In. . . . 35.00
Plate, Athens I, Charles Meigh, c.1840, 10 ¼ In. . . . 41.00
Plate, Athol, Burgess & Leigh, c.1910, 9 ¾ In. . . . 11.80
Plate, Avon War, Booths, c.1890, 9 In., 2 Piece . . . 41.00
Plate, Ayr, W. & E. Corn, c.1900, 9 In., Pair . . . 11.80
Plate, Belport, John Maddock & Sons, c.1986, 7 In., 3 Piece . . . 11.80
Plate, Bluebell & Grapes, Cherry Border, c.1865, 9 ½ In. . . . 136.00
Plate, Byzantium, BWM & Co., Westhead Moore & Co., 8 In. . . . 40.00
Plate, Canton, John Maddock, c.1855, 9 ½ In. . . . 18.00
Plate, Carlton, Royal Staffordshire, c.1907, 9 In. . . . 11.80
Plate, Chen-Si, John Meir, c.1835, 10 ½ In. . . . 30.00
Plate, Chusan, J. Clementson, c.1864, 9 ¼ In. . . . 11.80
Plate, Coronet, Sampson Hancock & Sons, c.1912, 9 In. . . . 77.00
Plate, Dessert, Shusan, F & R Pratt & Co., c.1865, 9 x 10 In. . . . 59.00
Plate, Elgar, Upper Henley Pottery Co., c.1910, 9 In. . . . 11.80
Plate, Flora, Cockson & Chetwynd, c.1867, 9 ½ In. . . . 100.00
Plate, Geisha, Upper Hanley Potteries, c.1901, 9 In., 2 Piece. . . . 18.00
Plate, Gladys, New Wharf Pottery, c.1891, 9 In. . . . 18.00
Plate, Grandmother's Flowers, Elsmore & Forster, c.1860, 10 In. . . . 11.80
Plate, Madras, Wood & Brownfield, Ironstone, 12-Sided, 10 ½ In. . . . 49.00
Plate, Man On Horse, Landscape Center, Flower Border, Marked, Washington, 7 ¾ In. . . . 225.00
Plate, Manilla, Podmore Walker & Co., c.1845, 10 In., Pair . . . 165.00
Plate, Multicolored, Keeling & Co., c.1936, 10 ½ In. . . . 11.80
Plate, Nankin, Ironstone, 6 Panels, c.1845, 9 ½ In. . . . 44.00

Plate, Pelew, E. Challinor, c.1840, 8 ¾ In., 2 Piece 65.00
Plate, Podmore, Washington Vase, 10 In. 125.00
Plate, Pomona, E.M. Co., c.1891, 8 In., 4 Piece 11.80
Plate, Rock, E. Challinor, c.1850, 9 ½ In., 3 Piece 59.00
Plate, Rouge Tone, c.1895, 9 In. 53.00
Plate, Salad, Arabesque, T.J. & J. Mayer, 14-Sided, c.1850, 10 ½ In. 21.00
Plate, Scinde, Oriental Stone, J. & G. Alcock, c.1840, 8 ½ In. 41.00
Plate, Shanghai, Grindley & Co., 9 In. *illus* 105.00
Plate, Snowflake, Mulberry, 9 ⅝ In. 121.00
Plate, Sobraon, Hill Pottery, c.1880, 10 ½ In., Pair 95.00
Plate, Soup, Circassia, J. & G. Alcock, c.1840, 10 ½ In. 18.00
Plate, Soup, Countess, T.R. & Co., c.1912 15.00
Plate, Soup, Cup, Handleless, Beauties Of China, Mellor Venable & Co., c.1851, 10 ¼ In. 53.00
Plate, Soup, Flowers, Leaves, Ironstone, Brush Stroke Design, Copper Luster, 5 ¼ In. 220.00
Plate, Soup, Indian Plant, Thomas Dimmock, 10 ½ In. 94.00
Plate, Soup, Spring, W.H. Grindley & Co., c.1842 15.00
Plate, Spanish Festivities, George Jones, c.1924, 9 ¼ In. 31.00
Plate, Touraine, Henry Alcock & Co., c.1898, 9 In., 9 Piece 65.00
Plate, Vinranka Percy, Gefle, Sweden, c.1967, 10 ¼ In. 18.00
Plate, Wire Basket, Flowers, Buds, Leaves, c.1890, 5 & 8 x 11 ½ In. 53.00
Plate Set, Lorne, Grindley & Co., c.1900, 10 In. 82.00
Platter, Asiatic Pheasants, Podmore, Blue Transferware, Scalloped Rim, 17 x 14 In. 150.00
Platter, Astral, W.H. Grindley, c.1891, 11 ½ x 16 ¼ In. 65.00
Platter, Buccleuce, c.1845, 14 ¾ x 18 ¼ In. 24.00
Platter, Burgess & Leigh, c.1870, 16 x 13 In. 15.00
Platter, Castle, Deep Well, c.1850, 12 ¾ x 16 ¼ In. 83.00
Platter, Chatsworth, Ford & Sons, c.1900, 13 ¾ x 18 ¾ In. 30.00
Platter, Chinese, Ashwork, Multicolored Chinoiserie, Luster, c.1880, 11 ½ x 14 ¼ In. 18.00
Platter, Clarendon, Henry Alcock & Co., 11 ¾ x 16 ¼ In. 35.00
Platter, Clover, W.H. Grindley, c.1925, 14 ½ x 10 ¾ In. 24.00
Platter, Dainty, John Maddock & Sons, c.1896, 11 ¼ x 14 ¾ In. 118.00
Platter, Derby, W.H. Grindley, c.1891, 9 x 12 In. 15.00
Platter, Dover, W.H. Grindley, 1920s, 10 ¼ x 14 In. 77.00
Platter, Eclipse, Johnson Bros., Oval, c.1891, 9 ¼ x 12 ½ In. 65.00
Platter, Erie, Bourne & Leigh, c.1900, 12 x 16 In. 30.00
Platter, Flora, Thomas Walker, c.1851, 12 x 15 ½ In. 47.00
Platter, Gironde, W.H. Grindley, c.1891, 10 ½ x 15 In. 77.00
Platter, Grace, W.H. Grindley, c.1842, 17 x 12 In. 189.00
Platter, Grosvenor, Moyatt Son & Co., c.1907, 14 ¾ x 18 ½ In. 47.00
Platter, Haddon, W.H. Grindley, c.1891, 12 x 8 ½ In. 27.00
Platter, Hong Kong, Charles Meigh, 8-Sided, c.1845, 13 ½ x 10 ¼ In. 242.00
Platter, Kelvin, Alfred Meakin, c.1891, 8 ¾ x 12 ¼ In. 118.00
Platter, Kin Shan, Edward Challinor, c.1855 207.00
Platter, Luray, Bishop & Stonier, c.1899 24.00
Platter, Lyndhurst, W.H. Grindley, c.1891, 11 ½ x 15 ¾ In. 83.00
Platter, Osborne, W.H. Grindley, c.1900, 10 ¼ x 14 ¼ In. 100.00
Platter, Peach, Johnson Brothers, c.1900, 9 ½ x 12 ¼ In. 71.00
Platter, Regent, 10 ½ x 8 ½ In. *illus* 65.00
Platter, Seville, New Wharf, Wood & Son, c.1894, 10 x 14 In. 94.00
Platter, Shapoo, Thomas Hughes, 1860-1870, 12 ½ x 9 ½ In. 165.00
Platter, Summer Flowers, Iron Stone Well, Tree, Sam Alcock & Co., 20 ¾ In. 264.00
Platter, Touraine, Henry Alcock & Co., c.1898, 7 x 10 ½ In. 38.00
Platter, Turkey, 21 x 24 In. 1400.00
Platter, Venice, Upper Hanley Pottery Co., Oval, c.1910, 11 ½ x 15 ½ In. 94.00
Platter, Vermont, Burgess & Leigh, Oval, c.1895, 8 ¼ x 11 ½ In. 35.00
Platter, Woodbine, Wood & Son, 14 x 10 ½ In. 53.00
Saucer, Oriental Scene, Scalloped Edge, Allertons England Willow, 5 ¾ In. 15.00
Sugar, Cover, Iris, A. Wilkinson, c.1907 18.00
Sugar, Cover, Neopolitan, Johnson Bros., c.1900 47.00
Sugar, Cover, Scinde, Thomas Walker, c.1847 118.00
Sugar, Cover, Wentworth, J. & G. Meakin, c.1907 35.00
Teapot, Lid, Lobelia, G. Phillips, c.1845, 9 In. 59.00
Teapot, Shapoo, Spout Lid, Thomas Hughes, 1860-70 354.00
Tureen, Cover, Aberdeen, E. Bourne & J.E. Leigh, c.1910 11.80
Tureen, Cover, Loraine, Leighton Pottery, c.1930, 8 x 11 In. 35.00
Tureen, Cover, Mongolia, Johnson Bros., c.1900, 9 ½ x 11 In. 366.00
Tureen, Sauce, Cover, Renown, Arthur Wilkinson Co., Oval, c.1907, 4 ½ x 9 In. 11.80

TIP
For emergency repairs to chipped pottery, try coloring the spot with a wax crayon or oil paint. It will look a little better.

Flow, Blue, Plate, Shanghai, Grindley & Co., 9 In.
$105.00

Flow Blue, Platter, Regent, 10 ½ x 8 ½ In.
$65.00

Country Name in Marks
If the name of a country is on the bottom, it was probably made after 1891. The United States government passed a law requiring that the name of the "country of origin" be in writing on each piece of pottery or porcelain imported into the United States. Some countries, like England, had used the country's name years earlier. If England is the mark the dish may have been made as early as 1850. The words "Made in..." were usually used after 1915.

Folk Art, Bird Tree, 7 Birds, Painted, Wood, 26 In.
$300.00

Folk Art, Bird Tree, Bird, Carved, Painted, c.1900, 6 ¾ In.
$1989.00

Folk Art, Sand Art, Layered, Eagle, Verse, Apothecary Jar, Andrew Clemens, 1889, 5 ¼ In.
$6600.00

Tureen, Soup, Cover, Regent, S.F. & Co., c.1939, 10 In. 27.00
Vase, Floral, Art Nouveau, Empire China, c.1915, 11 ¼ In. 112.00
Vase, Fruit, Gold Trim, 10 In. 30.00
Vase, Royal, William Adderly, c.1880, 8 ¾ In. 35.00
Waste Bowl, Calcutta, E. Challinor, 14-Sided, Paneled, c.1845. .... 59.00

FLYING PHOENIX, *see Phoenix Bird category.*

FOLK ART is also listed in many categories of this book under the actual name of the object. See categories such as Box, Cigar Store Figure, Paper, Weather Vane, Wooden, etc.

American Eagle, Perched, Shield, Base, Plaster Mold, Paul Bartlett, 1916, 13 In. 3555.00
Bear, Standing, Bottle Caps, On Wood, Clarence Woolsey, c.1960, 38 x 19 In. 2000.00
Bird, Cedar, Carved, Bead Eyes, Whittled Legs, Tree Branch Support, 1930, 6 x 11 In. 40.00
Bird, On Perch, Painted, Carved, Yellow, Red, Green, Spotted Base, Pa., Late 1800s, 6 In. 17550.00
Bird, On Stump, Painted, Carved, Yellow, Green, Red, 19th Century, 5 ½ In. 4212.00
Bird, Softwood, Wings, Glass Eyes, Wire Legs, Feet, Multicolored, 6 ¾ x 6 ¼ In. 154.00
Bird Tree, 7 Birds, Painted, Wood, 26 In. .... *illus* 300.00
Bird Tree, Bird, Carved, Painted, c.1900, 6 ¾ In. .... *illus* 1989.00
Bird Tree, Wood, Multicolored, Wings Form Hearts, Initials, WJG, c.1975, 18 ¾ In. 441.00
Birdcage, Mixed Woods, Stand, c.1900, 70 x 18 In. 99.00
Bottle, Sand, Patriotic, Eagle, American Flag, Dell & John Bergman, 1875, 10 ¾ In. 3400.00
Bowl, Carved, Horse Handles, Aqua, Red, Black, Scandinavia, 9 ¼ x 12 ½ x 9 In. 95.00
Box, Puzzle, Walnut, Incised Carving, Initials, Lock, 2 ½ x 6 In. 80.00
Box, Star, Geometric, Inlay, 6-Sided, Mirror, Lining, 1900s, 6 ¾ x 9 ¾ In. 575.00
Box, Wood, Hand Carved, Geometric Pattern, Hinged Lid, Metal Latch, Tray, 9 x 12 In. 390.00
Candlestand, Cherry, Round Top, Tripod Base, Black Paint, 27 x 18 In. 1840.00
Cat, Watercolor, Seated, Mouse In Mouth, Frame, Penn., 19th Century, 12 x 9 In. 19550.00
Diorama, Convict Ship, Oil Enamel, Carved Wood, Painted, Plaque, 1939, 17 x 22 In. 748.00
Dog, Chow, Painted Black, Gouge Carved, 3 ¾ x 4 ¾ x 1 ¾ In. 77.00
Dog, On Grass, Carved Softwood, Rust Red, Black, 5 x 7 ¼ x 1 ⅜ In. 55.00
Dove, Softwood, Beak, Wire Wound Legs, Feet, Multicolored, 4 ¾ x 10 x 3 ¼ In. 330.00
Eagle, Softwood, Glass Eyes, Wire Legs, Feet, Driftwood, Multicolored, 6 ¾ x 6 ¼ In. 198.00
Figurehead, Woman, Long Hair, Dress With Apron, Wood, 24 x 22 ½ In. 805.00
Fish, Wood Carving, Painted, Applied Metal Eyes, Metal Stand, 17 ½ x 23 In. 173.00
Fruit, Stone, Painted, Multicolored, Orange, Apple, Pa., 1 ¾ & 2 ¾ In., 2 Piece. 88.00
George Washington, Carved Horse, Blue, White, 1800s, 10 In. 3173.00
Landlord Collects Rent, Rural Scene, Farm Animals, Wood Carving, 32 ½ x 21 ¾ In. 960.00
Leopard, Painted, Leather Tail, Carved, Wood, 5 ⅛ In. 1645.00
Man's Head, Carved, Painted, Iron Base, 19th Century, 4 x 3 In. 40.00
Mirror, Carnival, Applied & Carved Designs, Glass Gems, Wood, c.1900, 39 x 34 In. 646.00
Moose, Brown Paint, Glass Eyes, Carved, Wood, Signed, Byron Smith, 11 In. 176.00
Oil On Canvas, Retablo, Madonna & Child, Spanish Colonial School, 29 x 21 In. 1058.00
Planter, Canoe Shape, Woven Twigs, Metal Insert, 7 x 30 x 7 In. 30.00
Policeman, 2 Handcuffed People, Dog, Lamp Post, Softwood, Base, 11 ½ x 12 x 4 In. 358.00
Rabbit, Standing, Bottle Caps, On Wood, Clarence Woolsey, c.1960, 46 ½ x 19 In. 3000.00
Rocket, Wood, Carved, Mounting Ladder, Base, Orange, Blue, 34 x 25 x 19 In. 316.00
Rooster, Crowing, Wood, Braces, Stand, c.1920, 30 In. 235.00
Rooster, Standing, Black, Green, Red, Yellow Body, Pine, Wilhelm Schimmel, 4 In. 22230.00
Rooster, Wood, Carved, Tack Eyes, Putty Comb, Signed, John Canfield, 1907, 17 ½ In. 235.00
Sand Art, Layered, Eagle, Verse, Apothecary Jar, Andrew Clemens, 1889, 5 ¼ In. .... *illus* 6600.00
Squirrel Cage, Tin, Wood, 27 In. 295.00
Tobacco Box, Wood, Inlay, Hand Carved, Smoking Items, 4 In. 140.00
Tray, Black Butler, Wood, Carved, Painted, 34 In. 70.00
Wall Pocket, Deer, Forest, Softwood, 14 ½ x 12 ½ x 4 In. 935.00
Whirligig, 2 Men Sawing, Red & Yellow Propeller, Green, 22 ½ x 18 ½ x 12 ½ In. 110.00
Whirligig, Bronco Buster, Painted, Iron Bracket, 11 x 15 ½ x 13 In. 55.00
Whirligig, Chatham Whale, Tail Spins, Black Paint, Wood, Carved, c.1920, 15 In. 330.00
Whirligig, Indian In Canoe, Wooden, Original Paint, c.1920, 10 ¼ In. 382.00
Whirligig, Man, Chopping Wood, Red, White, Brown, Hand Painted, Copper, 11 ½ In. 100.00
Whirligig, Man, On Bicycle, Pine, Metal, Carved, Painted Red, White, Blue, 1900s, 18 x 28 In. 9375.00
Whirligig, Man, Sawing, Red, White, Blue, 26 ½ In. 234.00
Whirligig, Man, Top Hat, Red Coat, Pine, Carved, Painted, c.1930, 20 In. .... *illus* 1872.00
Whirligig, Potter Turning Pottery Churn, Wood, Ceramic, Wire, Marked, 23 x 24 In. 144.00
Whirligig, Sailor, Painted, Pine, Splayed Leg Stand, New England, 20th Century, 43 ½ In. 1287.00

Whirligig, Soldier, Standing, Red Jacket, Painted, Wood, Carved, 20th Century, 69 In. 527.00
Whirligig, Soldier, Wood, Carved, Multicolored, Gray, Brass Tack Buttons, 1800s, 16 In. 999.00
Whirligig, Soldier, Wood, Carved, Red & White Paint, Paddle Arms, c.1890, 20 In. 2350.00
Whirligig, Soldier, Wood, Leather Hat, Wood Brim, c.1900, 19 ¼ In. 441.00
Whirligig, Uncle Sam, Carved, Painted, c.1945 .... 1500.00
Whirligig, Windmill, Man Sawing Wood, Painted, 39 In. 295.00
Whirligig, Windmill, Painted, 14 x 16 In. 150.00
Whirligig, Wood, Wheel Blade, 3 Sailors Holding Fans, 21 In. 5750.00

FOOT WARMERS solved the problem of cold feet in past generations. Some warmers held charcoal, others held hot water. Pottery, tin, and soapstone were the favored materials to conduct the heat. The warmer was kept under the feet, then the legs and feet were tucked into a blanket, providing welcome warmth in a cold carriage or church.

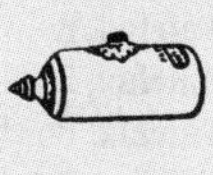

Tin, Pierced Sides & Top, Wire Handle, Tin Insert, 10 ½ In. 110.00
Tin, Punched, 19th Century, 5 ½ x 8 ¾ In. .... *illus* 101.00
Tin, Punched, Wood, Lap Joints, Wire Bail Handle, Hinged Door, Round, 6 x 9 ½ In. 143.00
Tin, Punched, Wood, Wire Bail Handle, Tag, H Foot, 5 ¾ x 9 x 7 ½ In. .... *illus* 88.00

FOOTBALL *collectibles may be found in the Card and the Sports categories.*

FOSTORIA glass was made in Fostoria, Ohio, from 1887 to 1891. The factory was moved to Moundsville, West Virginia, and most of the glass seen in shops today is a twentieth-century product. The company was sold in 1983; new items will be easily identifiable, according to the new owner, Lancaster Colony Corporation. Additional Fostoria items may be listed in the Milk Glass category.

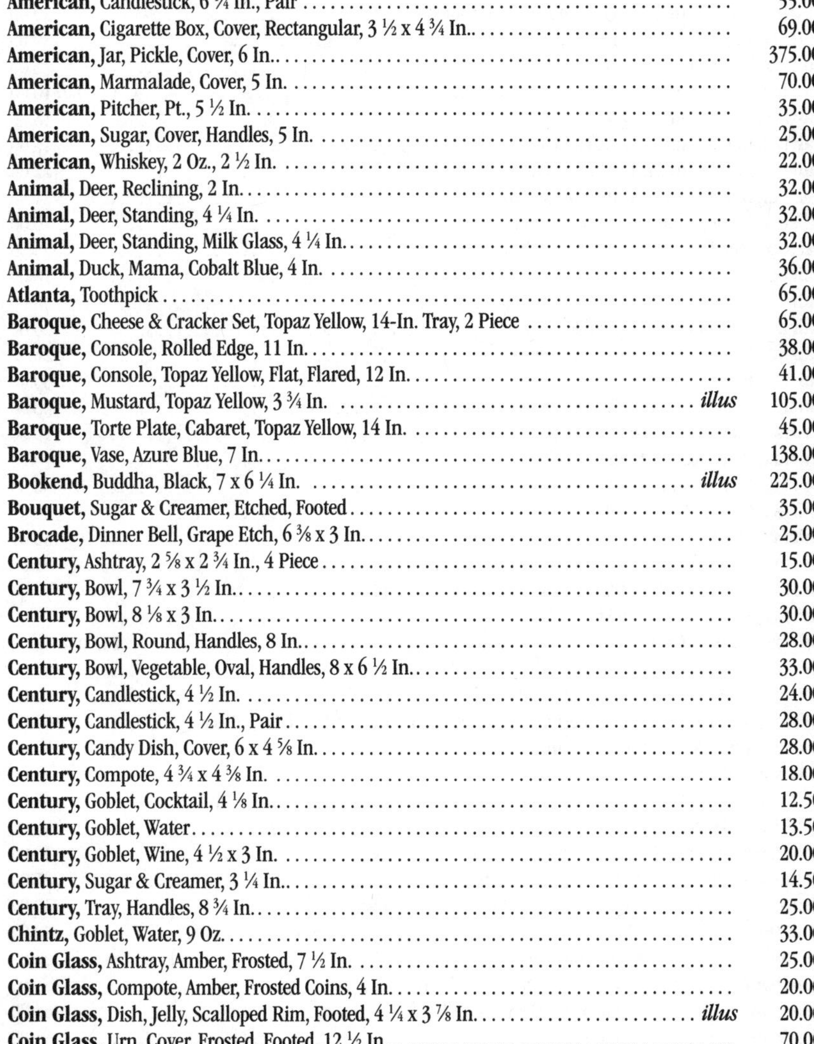

American, Candlestick, 6 ¼ In., Pair 55.00
American, Cigarette Box, Cover, Rectangular, 3 ½ x 4 ¾ In. 69.00
American, Jar, Pickle, Cover, 6 In. 375.00
American, Marmalade, Cover, 5 In. 70.00
American, Pitcher, Pt., 5 ½ In. 35.00
American, Sugar, Cover, Handles, 5 In. 25.00
American, Whiskey, 2 Oz., 2 ½ In. 22.00
Animal, Deer, Reclining, 2 In. 32.00
Animal, Deer, Standing, 4 ¼ In. 32.00
Animal, Deer, Standing, Milk Glass, 4 ¼ In. 32.00
Animal, Duck, Mama, Cobalt Blue, 4 In. 36.00
Atlanta, Toothpick 65.00
Baroque, Cheese & Cracker Set, Topaz Yellow, 14-In. Tray, 2 Piece 65.00
Baroque, Console, Rolled Edge, 11 In. 38.00
Baroque, Console, Topaz Yellow, Flat, Flared, 12 In. 41.00
Baroque, Mustard, Topaz Yellow, 3 ¾ In. .... *illus* 105.00
Baroque, Torte Plate, Cabaret, Topaz Yellow, 14 In. 45.00
Baroque, Vase, Azure Blue, 7 In. 138.00
Bookend, Buddha, Black, 7 x 6 ¼ In. .... *illus* 225.00
Bouquet, Sugar & Creamer, Etched, Footed 35.00
Brocade, Dinner Bell, Grape Etch, 6 ⅜ x 3 In. 25.00
Century, Ashtray, 2 ⅝ x 2 ¾ In., 4 Piece 15.00
Century, Bowl, 7 ¾ x 3 ½ In. 30.00
Century, Bowl, 8 ⅛ x 3 In. 30.00
Century, Bowl, Round, Handles, 8 In. 28.00
Century, Bowl, Vegetable, Oval, Handles, 8 x 6 ½ In. 33.00
Century, Candlestick, 4 ½ In. 24.00
Century, Candlestick, 4 ½ In., Pair 28.00
Century, Candy Dish, Cover, 6 x 4 ⅝ In. 28.00
Century, Compote, 4 ¾ x 4 ⅜ In. 18.00
Century, Goblet, Cocktail, 4 ⅛ In. 12.50
Century, Goblet, Water 13.50
Century, Goblet, Wine, 4 ½ x 3 In. 20.00
Century, Sugar & Creamer, 3 ¼ In. 14.50
Century, Tray, Handles, 8 ¾ In. 25.00
Chintz, Goblet, Water, 9 Oz. 33.00
Coin Glass, Ashtray, Amber, Frosted, 7 ½ In. 25.00
Coin Glass, Compote, Amber, Frosted Coins, 4 In. 20.00
Coin Glass, Dish, Jelly, Scalloped Rim, Footed, 4 ¼ x 3 ⅞ In. .... *illus* 20.00
Coin Glass, Urn, Cover, Frosted, Footed, 12 ½ In. 70.00

Folk Art, Whirligig, Man, Top Hat, Red Coat, Pine, Carved, Painted, c.1930, 20 In.
$1872.00

Foot Warmer, Tin, Punched, 19th Century, 5 ½ x 8 ¾ In.
$101.00

Foot Warmer, Tin, Punched, Wood, Wire Bail Handle, Tag, H Foot, 5 ¾ x 9 x 7 ½ In.
$88.00

As always, the edited listings in *Kovels' Antiques & Collectibles Price Guide 2010* aren't available on any website, but readers should visit Kovels.com for information on trends, tips, reproductions, marks, old prices, and more!

Fostoria, Baroque, Mustard, Topaz Yellow, 3 ¾ In.
$105.00

Fostoria, Bookend, Buddha, Black, 7 x 6 ¼ In.
$225.00

Fostoria, Coin Glass, Dish, Jelly, Scalloped Rim, Footed, 4 ¼ x 3 ⅞ In.
$20.00

TIP
Store glass right side up to protect the rims.

Colony, Bowl, Fruit, 10 In., Pair 310.00
Colony, Sugar & Creamer 19.00
Colony, Water Set, Green, 7 Piece 116.00
Crown Collection, Candleholder, Trindle, Luxemburg, 4 ¾ In. 130.00
Czarina, Toothpick 20.00
Eilene, Champagne, Saucer, Azure, Etched 30.00
Eilene, Goblet, Water, Azure, Etched 35.00
Fairfax, Bonbon, Rose, Turned Up Handles, 6 ¾ In. 22.00
Fairfax, Bouillon, Underplate, Azure, Handles, 5 Oz., 4 x 5 ¾ In. 20.00
Fairfax, Bowl, Azure, 3-Footed, 4 ½ x 2 ¼ In. 20.00
Fairfax, Bowl, Azure, 3-Toed, 6 ⅞ In. 25.00
Fairfax, Bowl, Dessert, Azure, Handles, 8 ½ In. 35.00
Fairfax, Bowl, Sweetmeat, Rose, Pointed Handles, 5 ½ In. 25.00
Fairfax, Bowl, Topaz Handles, 8 ½ In. 60.00
Fairfax, Bowl, Vegetable, Azure, Oval, 9 In. 55.00
Fairfax, Bowl, Vegetable, Rose, Oval, 9 In. 30.00
Fairfax, Bowl, Whipped Cream, Rose, Square Handles, 5 ½ In. 15.00
Fairfax, Cake Plate, Azure, Open Handles, 10 In. 40.00
Fairfax, Candleholder, Azure, 3-Footed, 2 In., Pair 35.00
Fairfax, Candleholder, Green, 3-Footed, 2 In., Pair 30.00
Fairfax, Candy Jar, Cover, Azure 75.00
Fairfax, Celery, Azure, Oval, 11 ½ In. 30.00
Fairfax, Celery, Rose, Oval, 11 ½ In. 28.00
Fairfax, Cocktail, Azure, 3 Oz., 5 In. 20.00
Fairfax, Compote, Topaz, 6 x 5 In. 24.00
Fairfax, Console, Azure, 3-Footed, 12 In. 35.00
Fairfax, Console, Rose, 3-Footed, 12 In. 55.00
Fairfax, Cup & Saucer, After Dinner, Green, Footed 20.00
Fairfax, Cup & Saucer, Amber, Footed 9.00
Fairfax, Cup & Saucer, Footed 18.00
Fairfax, Cup & Saucer, Green ..... 12.00 to 16.00
Fairfax, Cup & Saucer, Rose 18.00
Fairfax, Cup & Saucer, Rose, Footed 16.00
Fairfax, Cup & Saucer, Topaz, Footed 12.00
Fairfax, Dish, Pickle, Azure, Oval, 8 ½ In. 30.00
Fairfax, Goblet, Champagne, Topaz, 6 Oz., 6 In. 16.00
Fairfax, Icer, Liner, Azure, 2 ¾ x 4 ¾ In. 35.00
Fairfax, Ladle, 5 ½ In. 18.00
Fairfax, Plate, Bread & Butter, Azure, 6 In. 6.00
Fairfax, Plate, Bread & Butter, Rose, 6 In. 6.00
Fairfax, Plate, Lemon, Rose, Handles, 6 ¾ In. 26.00
Fairfax, Plate, Luncheon, 8 ½ In., 7 Piece 30.00
Fairfax, Plate, Luncheon, Azure, 9 ½ In. 26.00
Fairfax, Plate, Salad, Azure, 8 ¾ In. 10.00
Fairfax, Plate, Salad, Orchid Etch, 7 ½ In. 10.00
Fairfax, Plate, Salad, Topaz, 7 ½ In., 6 Piece 30.00
Fairfax, Relish, Rose, 2 Sections, 8 ½ In. 21.00
Fairfax, Salt & Pepper, Rose, Clear Top, Footed, 3 ½ In. 60.00
Fairfax, Saucer, Orchid 1.00
Fairfax, Sherbet, Waterfall Stem, Topaz, 6 In. 30.00
Fairfax, Sugar, Rose, Individual, Footed 15.00
Fairfax, Sugar & Creamer, Azure ..... 25.00 to 30.00
Fairfax, Sugar & Creamer, Topaz 35.00
Fairfax, Sugar & Creamer, Topaz, Individual 20.00
Fairfax, Sugar & Creamer, Underplate, Lemon Insert, Rose, 12-In. Plate, 4 Piece 160.00
Fairfax, Torte Plate, Azure, 13 ¾ In. 60.00
Fuchsia, Goblet, Water 42.00
Gold Lace, Bowl, Flame, Oval, 12 ½ x 7 ½ In. 35.00
Gold Lace, Sauce, 2 Sections, Handles, 12 ½ In. 25.00
Gold Lace, Sugar & Creamer, Baroque, Collar Foot, 3 ¾ & 3 ½ In. 30.00
Heather, Compote, Short Stem, 2 ½ x 5 ½ In. 25.00
Heather, Dish, Mayonnaise, 2 Sections, 2 Ladles, 6 ½ x 4 In. 30.00
Heather, Dish, Pickle, 8 ⅝ x 4 ⅛ In. 20.00
Heather, Tidbit, 3-Footed, Round, 8 In. 26.00
Heirloom, Bowl, Pink Opalescent, Oval, 11 x 6 ½ In. 55.00
Heirloom, Bowl, White Opalescent, Oval, 13 x 8 ⅝ In. 68.00
Heirloom, Candlestick, Pink, 9 In. 35.00

Heirloom, Vase, Bud, Amberina, 5 ¾ In. 45.00
Hermitage, Plate, Bread & Butter, 6 In. 8.00
Hermitage, Sherbet, Topaz 18.00
Horizon, Plate, Dinner, Cinnamon, 10 In. 32.00
Jamestown, Goblet, Water, Azure, 10 Oz., 5 ⅞ In. 12.00
Jamestown, Goblet, Wine, Blue, 4 Oz., 4 ⅜ In. 16.00
Jamestown, Salt & Pepper, Chrome Top, Pink, 3 ½ In. 45.00
Jamestown, Sherbet, Amber, 6 ½ Oz., 4 ¼ In. .... *illus* 12.00
Jamestown, Tumbler, Iced Tea, Blue, 11 Oz., 6 In. 20.00
Lafayette, Plate, Topaz, 8 ½ In. 16.00
Mayfair, Relish, Amber, Silver Plated Fork, 8 ½ x 5 ½ In. 20.00
Mayflower, Goblet, Water, 7 ¼ In. 22.00
Mayflower, Relish, Handles, 12 ½ In. 35.00
Mayflower, Sherbet, 4 ½ In. 10.00
Mayflower, Sugar & Creamer 24.00
Mayflower, Tumbler, Iced Tea, 6 ¼ In. 22.00
Mayflower, Tumbler, Juice, 5 In. 16.00
Mayflower, Tumbler, Water, 5 ½ In. 16.00
Meadow Rose, Nappy, Tricornered Handle, 4 ⅝ In. 35.00
Midnight Rose, Bowl, Scalloped Edges, 4-Footed, 10 ½ In. 65.00
Midnight Rose, Relish, 4 Sections, 10 x 8 ½ In. 25.00
Minuet, Plate, Luncheon, Topaz, Square, 8 ¼ In. 30.00
Monet, Goblet, Water, Lilac, 7 ½ In. 25.00
Navarre, Champagne, Saucer 28.00
Navarre, Dish, Pickle, 8 ½ In. 40.00
Navarre, Goblet, Water, 10 Oz., 7 ⅝ In. 36.00
Navarre, Sauce, Tricornered, 3-Toed, Handle, 4 ½ In. 28.00
No. 2470, Bonbon, Topaz, 7 In. 28.00
Oak Leaf, Bowl, Nasturtium, Brocade Etch, Pink, 10 In. 250.00
Persian, Toothpick, Gold Trim 80.00
Priscilla, Custard, Footed, Handles 20.00
Priscilla, Sugar & Creamer 45.00
Rib Optic, Compote, Rose, Waterfall Stem, 5 ½ x 6 ¼ In. 46.00
Rose, Console, Round, Flared, No. 2297, 3 Shaped Feet, 12 In. 26.00
Seville, Cup & Saucer, Etched, Footed 10.00
Seville, Plate, Bread & Butter, Amber, 6 In. 4.00
Seville, Plate, Salad, Amber, Etched, 7 ½ In. 4.00
Sonata, Dish, Mayonnaise, 2 Sections, 2 Ladles, 8 x 4 ½ In. 25.00
Straw Jar, Cover, 12 ½ In. 303.00
Versailles, Bowl, Green, 10 In. 238.00
Versailles, Bowl, Rose, Oval, 14 x 9 ½ In. .... *illus* 125.00
Versailles, Goblet, Gold Trim, 10 In. 205.00
Vesper, Cake Plate, Pedestal, Blue, Etched, 8 ½ x 2 ¾ In. 65.00
Vesper, Cup & Saucer, Amber .... *illus* 15.00
Vesper, Soup, Dish, Blue, Etched Rim, 8 In. 35.00
Victorian, Cordial, Empire Green, 3 ¼ In. 35.00
Vintage, Sauce, Cover, 5 ¼ x 4 ½ In. 25.00
Wheat Cuttings, Compote, 4 ½ x 5 ¼ In. 25.00
Willowmere, Tumbler, Iced Tea, Footed, 12 Oz., 5 ¾ In. 36.00
Wilma, Claret, Blue, 4 ½ Oz., 6 In. 120.00

FOVAL, *see Fry category.*

FRAMES *are included in the Furniture category under Frame.*

FRANCISCAN is a trademark that appears on pottery. Gladding, McBean and Company started in 1875. The company grew and acquired other potteries. It made sewer pipes, floor tiles, dinnerwares, and art pottery with a variety of trademarks. In 1934, dinnerware and art pottery were sold under the name Franciscan Ware. The company made china and cream-colored, decorated earthenware. Desert Rose, Apple, El Patio, and Coronado were best-sellers. The company became Interpace Corporation and in 1979 was purchased by Josiah Wedgwood & Sons. The plant was closed in 1984, but a few of the patterns are still being made. For more prices, go to Kovels.com.

Apple, Bowl, Fruit, 5 ¼ In. 10.00
Apple, Bowl, Salad, 10 ¼ In. 75.00
Apple, Coffeepot, Twig Handle, Cover 119.00
Apple, Compote, 3 ½ x 8 In. 65.00

TIP
Don't use ammonia on glasses with gold or silver decorations.

Fostoria, Jamestown, Sherbet, Amber, 6 ½ Oz., 4 ¼ In.
$12.00

Fostoria, Versailles, Bowl, Rose, Oval, 14 x 9 ½ In.
$125.00

Fostoria, Vesper, Cup & Saucer, Amber
$15.00

TIP
When the stopper of a glass decanter becomes too tight, a cloth wet with hot water and applied to the neck will cause the glass to expand so that the stopper may be easily removed.

Franciscan, Autumn, Cup & Saucer, c.1955
$8.00

Franciscan, Ivy, Plate, Bread & Butter, 6 In.
$10.00

Frankoma, Ashtray, Plainsman, Marked, F203, 12 ½ x 7 In.
$15.00

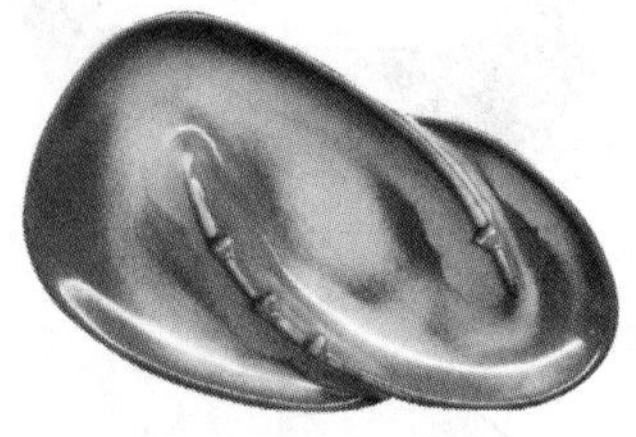

Frankoma, Teapot, Westwind, 6 ½ x 9 ½ In., 6 Cup
$65.00

Autumn, Bowl, Vegetable, Divided, 13 ½ x 6 ½ In.. . . . 20.00
Autumn, Cup & Saucer, c.1955 . . . *illus* 8.00
Coronado, Chop Plate, 12 In. . . . 21.00
Coronado, Relish, Satin, Coral, 9 ½ In. . . . 12.00
Desert Rose, Baker, 9 ½ x 8 ½ In.. . . . 145.00
Desert Rose, Bowl, Salad, 10 In.. . . . 40.00
Desert Rose, Plate, Dinner, 9 ½ In. . . . 10.00
Desert Rose, Soup, Dish, Rim, 8 ½ In. . . . 7.99
Desert Rose, Tumbler, Juice, 3 ¼ In. . . . 46.00
Duet, Creamer . . . 12.00
Duet, Platter, Oval, 13 x 9 ¼ In.. . . . 30.00
El Patio, Bowl, Fruit, Coral, 5 ¼ In. . . . 10.00
El Patio, Plate, Salad, Coral, 8 ¼ In.. . . . 10.00
El Patio, Sugar & Creamer, Coral . . . 25.00
Hacienda, Creamer, White, Yellow Band. . . . 9.00
Hacienda, Plate, Bread & Butter, Gold, 6 ⅝ In. . . . 4.00
Hacienda, Soup, Dish, Green, 6 ¼ In.. . . . 10.00
Ivy, Plate, Bread & Butter, 6 In. . . . *illus* 10.00
Madeira, Gravy Boat, Cover, Brown . . . 15.00
Madeira, Platter, Oval, Brown, 13 ½ In. . . . 25.00
Starburst, Bowl, Vegetable, Divided, 8 In. . . . 45.00
Starburst, Chop Plate, 13 In. . . . 55.00
Starburst, Cup & Saucer. . . . 18.00
Starburst, Plate, Bread & Butter, 6 In. . . . 9.00
Starburst, Plate, Dinner, 10 ½ In. . . . 20.00
Starburst, Platter, Oval, 13 In. . . . 40.00
Starburst, Salt & Pepper, 6 In. . . . 89.00
Starburst, Saucer . . . 7.00
Tiempo, Coffeepot, 7 ½ In.. . . . 75.00
Trio, Cup & Saucer. . . . 15.00
Trio, Plate, Bread & Butter. . . . 8.00
Trio, Plate, Dinner . . . 17.00
Trio, Plate, Salad . . . 12.00
Trio, Salt & Pepper. . . . 65.00
Trio, Sugar, Cover. . . . 40.00
Tulip Time, Gravy Boat, Attached Underplate, 7 In.. . . . 15.00
Tulip Time, Plate, Dinner, 10 ¾ In.. . . . 12.00

FRANKART, Inc., New York, New York, mass-produced nude *dancing lady* lamps, ashtrays, and other decorative Art Deco items in the 1920s and 1930s. They were made of white lead composition and spray-painted. *Frankart Inc.* and the patent number and year were stamped on the base.

Bookend, Nude, Seated, Leg Extended, Green, Spelter, 7 ¾ In. . . . 165.00
Bookends, Dog, Springer Spaniel, 5 ¾ In. . . . 80.00
Bust, Woman, Gold, Art Deco, 1940s, 7 In. . . . 500.00
Cardholder, Man, Holding Tray, Black Paint, Spelter, Art Deco, Signed, 10 In. . . . 75.00
Figurine, Nude, Upside Down, Black Paint, Spelter, Signed, 10 In.. . . . 400.00

FRANKOMA POTTERY was originally known as The Frank Potteries when John F. Frank opened shop in 1933. The factory is now working in Sapulpa, Oklahoma. Early wares were made from a light cream-colored clay from Ada, Oklahoma, but in 1956 the company switched to a red clay from Sapulpa. The firm made dinnerwares, utilitarian and decorative kitchenwares, figurines, flowerpots, and limited edition and commemorative pieces. John Frank died in 1973 and his daughter, Joniece, inherited the business. Frankoma went bankrupt in 1990. The pottery operated under various owners for a few years and was bought by Joe Ragosta in 2008.

ORIGINAL CREATION by FRANKOMA

Ashtray, Plainsman, Marked, F203, 12 ½ x 7 In. . . . *illus* 15.00
Charger, 2 Fish, White Glaze, Red Clay, 14 ⅜ In. . . . 55.00
Creamer, Mustard Yellow. . . . 15.00
Creamer, Plainsman, Prairie Green.. . . . 8.50
Cup, Mayan-Aztec, Desert Gold, Pacing Leopard Logo, 3 ¼ In. . . . 8.00
Figurine, Cat, Reclining, Brown & Green Glaze, 4 x 9 In. . . . 154.00
Plate, Christmas, 1972, Seeking The Christ Child, 8 ½ In. . . . 22.00
Plate, Christmas, 1977, Grace Madonna, 8 ¼ In.. . . . 20.00
Plate, Christmas, 1982, Wise Men Rejoice, 8 ¼ In.. . . . 20.00
Plate, Dinner, Lazybones, Prairie Green, Over Brown, 9 ¾ In. . . . 12.99
Plate, Dinner, Mayan-Aztec, Prairie Green, 10 ½ In. . . . 11.50

Plate, Salad, Mayan-Aztec, Desert Gold, 6 7/8 In. 7.00
Salt & Pepper, Westwind, Prairie Green, 3 1/4 In. 12.00
Saucer, Wagon Wheel, Prairie Green, 5 1/2 In. 4.00
Soup, Dish, Aztec, Desert Gold, 6 1/4 In. 7.00
Sugar, Cover, Plainsman, Desert Gold, 4 In. 10.99
Sugar, Open, Plainsman, Prairie Green, Individual. 8.00
Sugar & Creamer, Wagon Wheel, Prairie Green 24.00
Teapot, Plainsman, Desert Gold, 6 Cup, 7 1/2 In. 15.99
Teapot, Westwind, 6 Cup, 6 1/2 x 9 1/2 In. .... *illus* 65.00
Vase, Aztec Design, Molded, Green To Brown Glaze, 8 In. 55.00
Vase, Cactus, Desert, Prairie Green, Brown, Marked, 7 x 7 In. 45.00

FRATERNAL objects that are related to the many different fraternal organizations in the United States are listed in this category. The Elks, Masons, Odd Fellows, and others are included. Also included are service organizations, like the American Legion, Kiwanis, and Lions Club. Furniture is listed in the Furniture category. Shaving mugs decorated with fraternal crests are included in the Shaving Mug category.

Knights Templar, Creamer, Ascalon Commandery No. 59, Conclave, 3 x 4 In. .... 30.00 to 45.00
Knights Templar, Plate, Duquesne Commandery No. 72, Filigree, Gold Trim, 5 1/2 In. 55.00
Masonic, Apron, Gilt, Painted Kid Leather, Stamped, M. Wetherell, Early 1800s, 12 x 14 In. .. 403.00
Masonic, Apron, Initials, M.K.P., Embroidered Leaves, Eye, Fringe, 12 x 14 In. 115.00
Masonic, Birdhouse, Pine, Applied G, Painted, Early 20th Century, 11 3/4 In. .... *illus* 200.00
Masonic, Birdhouse, Pine, Compass & Square Form, Applied G, Painted, c.1920, 12 In. 235.00
Masonic, Box, Wood, Straw Inlay, 6 False Drawer Fronts, Symbols, 1700s, 3 x 12 x 9 In. 440.00
Masonic, Clock, Walnut, Yellow Pine, Inlay, Tulip, Symbols, Eagle, Heart, 87 x 20 In. 17250.00
Masonic, Ice Cream Mold, Pewter, Egyptian Woman's Head, Eppelsheimer & Co., 4 x 3 In. ... 100.00
Masonic, Jug, Symbols, Verse, Lusterware, Staffordshire, 9 In. 77.00
Masonic, Knights Templar Sword, Knight's Head Pommel, Grip, c.1923, 38 In. 413.00
Masonic, Medal, 14K Gold, Champleve Enamel, Engraved, Motto, Diamonds, 6 In. 1422.00
Masonic, Pitcher, Lodge, Flow Blue, Royal Doulton, Portland, Maine, 8 1/2 In. 173.00
Masonic, Walking Stick, Serpent Staff, Painted, c.1880 .... *illus* 1800.00
Modern Woodsmen Of America, Button, Stud, 10K Gold, Enamel Shield, 5/8 In. 15.00
Odd Fellows, Beehive, Pine, Painted Yellow, 10 x 10 x 8 1/2 In. 500.00
Odd Fellows, Medal, Silver, Glass Plumes, Prince Of Wales Lodge, 4 In. .... *illus* 240.00
Odd Fellows, Pin, New York World's Fair, Trylon & Perisphere, Metal, 1939, 3 1/2 In. 86.00
Odd Fellows, Staff, Painted, Late 19th Century, 64 In. 748.00
Odd Fellows, Trivet, Cast Iron, Horseshoe Shape, c.1875, 6 1/2 x 4 In. 33.00
Odd Fellows, Trivet, Horseshoe, Eagle 22.00
Patrons Of Husbandry, Pin, Celluloid, 2 Ribbons, Gold Metallic Fringe, c.1900. .... 35.00

FRY GLASS was made by the H.C. Fry Glass Company of Rochester, Pennsylvania. The company, founded in 1901, first made cut glass and other types of fine glasswares. In 1922 it patented a heat-resistant glass called Pearl Ovenglass. For two years, 1926–1927, the company made Fry Foval, an opal ware decorated with colored trim. Reproductions of this glass have been made. Depression glass patterns made by Fry may be listed in the Depression Glass category. Some pieces of cut glass may also be included in the Cut Glass category.

FRY GLASS

Butter, Cover, Star, Signed, 5 1/2 x 8 1/4 In. 500.00
Candlestick, Blue Opalescent, Signed, 4 x 4 In. 59.00
Casserole, Cover, Kidibake, Marked, Ovenglass, 4 1/2 In. 100.00
Casserole, Cover, Metal Server, Oval, Ovenglass, 6 1/4 x 11 3/4 x 6 1/4 In. 11.00
Grill Plate, Ovenglass, 10 1/2 In., 7 Piece. 55.00
Ice Tub, Intaglio Leaf & Berry Band, Fluted, Ribs, Signed, 5 3/4 x 6 3/4 In. .... *illus* 330.00
Loaf Pan, Kidibake, Bread Baker, Marked, Ovenglass, 5 In. 75.00
Nappy, Hobstar, Strawberry, Zipper, Crosscut Diamond, Fan, Signed, 6 In. 50.00
Pie Plate, Kidibake, Marked, Ovenglass, 5 In. 40.00
Plate, Japan Pattern, Square, 7 In. 248.00
Ramekin, Kidibake, Marked, Ovenglass, 2 1/2 In. 25.00
Sandwich Server, Diamond Optic, Center Handle, Marked, 6 x 10 1/2 In. 115.00
Sugar & Creamer, Hobstar, Strawberry Diamond & Fan, Notched Handles 138.00
Vase, Blue, Threaded, Flared, Controlled Bubble Ball, Footed, 8 In. 110.00
Vase, Pershing Pattern, Pinched Waist, 8 In. 121.00

FRY FOVAL

Bowl, Cobalt Blue, Ball Shape, Pinched Sides, Footed, 7 x 3 7/8 In. 358.00
Bowl, Fruit, Opal, Round, Jade Green Domed Foot, 5 1/2 x 9 1/2 In. 187.00
Candlestick, Opal, Delft Blue Threading, Signed, 10 1/2 In., Pair 275.00

Fraternal, Masonic, Birdhouse, Pine, Applied G, Painted, Early 20th Century, 11 3/4 In.
$200.00

Fraternal, Masonic, Walking Stick, Serpent Staff, Painted, c.1880
$1800.00

Fraternal, Odd Fellows, Medal, Silver, Glass Plumes, Prince Of Wales Lodge, 4 In.
$240.00

TIP
Check stored items once a year to be sure there is no deterioration or bugs.

F

Fry Glass, Ice Tub, Intaglio Leaf & Berry Band, Fluted, Ribs, Signed, 5 ¾ x 6 ¾ In. $330.00

Fry Glass,, Tea Set, Opal, Jade Green Handle, Spout, Finial, Signed, 6 Piece $230.00

Fulper, Vase, Blue Drip Over White Matte Glaze, Marked, 8 ¾ In. $345.00

Fulper, Vase, Frothy Cucumber Matte Over Mustard Crystalline Glaze, Marked, 9 x 11 In. $2160.00

Coffeepot, Cover, Cone Shape, Percolator, Opal, C Shape Handle, 10 In. 88.00
Coffeepot, Opal, Cobalt Blue, Handle Spout, Finial, 7 In. 144.00
Cup, Opal, Flared, Ribbed, Applied Cobalt Blue Handle, 4 ½ In., 6 Piece 426.00
Cup & Saucer, Opal, Bulbous, Delft Blue Handle, 2 ¼ & 5 ½ In., 4 Sets 99.00
Kettle, Hot Water, Cover, Opal, Jade Green, Ball Finial, 5 ¾ In. 220.00
Tea Set, Opal, Jade Green Handle, Spout, Finial, Signed, 6 Piece . . . . . *illus* 230.00
Teapot, Disc Cover, Opal, Delft Blue, Spout, Finial, Bulbous, 6 ¼ In. 66.00

FULPER Pottery Company was incorporated in 1899 in Flemington, New Jersey. It made art pottery from 1909 to 1929. The firm had been making bottles, jugs, and housewares from 1805. Doll heads were made about 1928. The firm became Stangl Pottery in 1929. Stangl Pottery is listed in its own category in this book.

Basket, Moss Green To Rose Flambe Glaze, 9 x 6 ½ In. 295.00
Bookends, Open Book On Top Of Closed Book, Holes For Pens, 1930, 5 ¼ x 4 ¾ In.. . . . . 125.00
Bowl, Center, Blue & Ivory Flambe Interior, Blue, Amber, Gray Matte, Marked, 5 x 13 In. 550.00
Bowl, Ibis, Blue & Green Flambe Glaze, Vertical Mark, 5 ½ x 10 ½ In.. . . . . 600.00
Bowl, Ribbed Diamond Shape, Undulating Rim, Blue, Green, c.1920, 4 In.. . . . . 89.00
Bowl, Scalloped Rim, Blue Crystalline Glaze, 7 x 12 In. 245.00
Cider Set, Tankard, 6 Mugs, Cafe-Au-Lait Glaze, 9 ½ In., 7 Piece. 840.00
Doorstop, Siamese Cat, Cream Over Mirror Black Glaze, c.1910, 5 x 9 In. 1840.00
Jug, Cobalt Blue, Bird, On Stump, 3 Gal., 15 ½ In.. . . . . 660.00
Lamp Base, Mouse Gray To Blue Flambe Glaze, 17 ¼ x 7 In. 1200.00
Lamp Base, Mushroom Shape, 2 Sockets, Leopard Skin Crystalline Glaze, 17 x 13 In. 1200.00
Pot, Green Crystalline Glaze, Handles, Round Racetrack Mark, 12 x 9 In.. . . . . 400.00
Vase, Apple Blossom & Black Flambe Glaze, Vertical Mark, 7 ½ x 7 In. 550.00
Vase, Avocado Green Drip Glaze, Shouldered, 7 In. 385.00
Vase, Blue Drip Over White Matte Glaze, Marked, 8 ¾ In. . . . . . *illus* 345.00
Vase, Blue Matte Glaze, Bulbous, 4 Loop Handles, Marked, 13 In.. . . . . 1400.00
Vase, Blue Over Blue Crystalline Drip, Scroll Handles, Marked, 11 In. 250.00
Vase, Blue Snowflake Crystalline Glaze, 2 Handles, 11 ⅛ In.. . . . . 374.00
Vase, Brown, Blue Flambe Glaze, Bulbous, Marked, 11 ¾ x 11 ½ In. 840.00
Vase, Brown, Tan & Green Flambe Glaze, 3 Handles, Marked, 6 ½ x 5 In. 325.00
Vase, Brown & Blue Vertical Design, Blue Mottled Ground, Bulbous, Narrow Neck, 12 In. 1800.00
Vase, Brown & Green Crystalline Glaze, Handles, Marked, 5 x 6 ½ In. 300.00
Vase, Brown Crystalline Glaze, Mustard Matte Drip, Vertical Mark, 8 x 10 In. 1100.00
Vase, Brown Crystalline Glaze, Yellow Matte, Squat, 8 x 10 In. 1320.00
Vase, Brownish Yellow Amber Glaze, 2 Handles, 6 ½ x 7 In. 225.00
Vase, Bud, Green Drip Over Blue, Quatrefoil Base, 8 ½ x 4 In. 185.00
Vase, Chinese Blue Crystalline Glaze, Flared Neck, Squat Base, 13 ½ In. 840.00
Vase, Cream & Tan Flambe Glaze, Pilgrim Bottle Form, Scroll Handles, Stamp Mark, 10 In. . . 275.00
Vase, Cucumber Crystalline Glaze, Oval, 16 x 6 In. 2520.00
Vase, Cucumber Crystalline Glaze, Silver Crystals, Squat, 5 ⅜ x 9 In.. . . . . 288.00
Vase, Flemington Green Glaze, 2 Handles, Marked, 6 In.. . . . . 316.00
Vase, Footed, Cream Over Blue Flambe Glaze, 2 Handles, Marked, c.1916, 9 In. 690.00
Vase, Frothy Cucumber Matte Over Mustard Crystalline Glaze, Marked, 9 x 11 In. . . . . . *illus* 2160.00
Vase, Green, Blue, Pink Flambe Glaze, 2 Handles, Footed, 9 x 9 In. 840.00
Vase, Green, Brown Crystalline Glaze, Bulbous, 2 Handles, Marked, 12 x 12 In. 390.00
Vase, Green & Blue Flambe Over Rose, Bullet Form, Marked, 6 ½ In. . . . . . *illus* 275.00
Vase, Mirror Black, Copperdust Crystalline Flambe Glaze, Marked, 12 In.. . . . . 275.00
Vase, Mirror Green Glaze, Buttressed, 13 ½ x 10 ½ In.. . . . . 3120.00
Vase, Mottled Gray Ground, Caramel Drip, Periwinkle Blue Crystals, 7 ¼ In. 288.00
Vase, Shouldered Shape, Brown, Green Glaze, 3 ½ x 4 ½ In.. . . . . 420.00
Vase, Tan, Green Flambe Glaze, Buttressed Shape, 9 x 6 ½ In. 420.00
Vase, Turquoise Crystalline Glaze, 33 x 11 In. 2280.00
Vase, Turquoise Crystalline Glaze, Footed, Vertical Stamp, 33 x 11 In. 1900.00
Vase, Wisteria Flambe Glaze, Gray, Maroon Crystals, Handles, 7 ⅞ In. 288.00
Vase, Yellow, Copper, Blue, Gunmetal Flambe Glaze, Ribs, Handles, Vertical Mark, 12 x 8 In. . 1100.00
Vase, Yellow Amber Glaze, 2 Handles, 7 x 7 In. 225.00

FURNITURE of all types is listed in this category. Examples dating from the seventeenth century to the 1970s are included. Prices for furniture vary in different parts of the country. Oak furniture is most expensive in the West; large pieces over eight feet high are sold for the most money in the South, where high ceilings are found in the old homes. Condition is very important when determining prices. These are NOT average prices but rather reports of unique sales. If the description includes the word *style*, the piece resembles the old furniture style but was made at a later time. It is not a period piece. Garden furniture is listed in the Garden Furnishings category. Related items may be found in the Architectural, Brass, and Store categories.

Armchairs are listed under Chair in this category.
Armoire, 2 Glass Doors, Chicken Wire Panels, Drawer, c.1880, 77 x 52 In. 598.00
Armoire, Art Deco, Burl, 3 Doors, Serpentine Front, France, c.1930, 85 x 80 In. 388.00
Armoire, Art Nouveau, Inlaid, Mirror, Drawer, 90 x 46 x 19 In. *illus* 1210.00
Armoire, Art Nouveau Inlaid Detail, Mirror Door, Drawer, 46 x 90 In. 1320.00
Armoire, Beveled Mirror Door, Shell Carving, Drawer, 4 Shelves, France, 43 x 92 In. 1200.00
Armoire, Burl, Veneer, Drawers, Converted To Bar, 84 x 63 In. 1955.00
Armoire, Empire Style, Mahogany, Fruitwood, 2 Doors, Pilasters, 84 x 46 x 20 In. 2880.00
Armoire, Federal, Mahogany, Paneled, Reeded, Ball Feet, c.1800, 84 x 48 In. 2350.00
Armoire, French Provincial, Oak, Leaf, Flower, Carved, 3-Panel Doors, 95 x 61 x 22 In. 3120.00
Armoire, Gothic Revival, Mahogany, Paneled Doors, Bracket Feet, 90 x 28 x 22 In. 1200.00
Armoire, Louis Philippe, Cherry, 2 Doors, 3 Panels, Shelves, 87 x 67 x 25 ½ In. 3780.00
Armoire, Louis XV, Fruitwood, Paneled Door, Cabochon, C-Scroll Border, 83 x 35 x 18 In. 1896.00
Armoire, Louis XV, Fruitwood, Walnut, Hatched Roundel, Scroll Feet, 1700s, 70 x 61 In. 2350.00
Armoire, Louis XV Style, Fruitwood, Doors, Shaped Panels, 89 x 57 x 25 In. 2640.00
Armoire, Louis XV Style, Walnut, 2 Mirror Doors, Crest, Parquetry, 101 x 64 x 21 In. 1725.00
Armoire, Louis XV/XVI, Cherry, Stepped Cornice, Pegged, 1800s, 78 x 58 In. 4200.00
Armoire, Louis XVI Style, Molded Cornice, Crested Leaves, Arching Panels, 86 x 54 In. 649.00
Armoire, Mahogany, 2 Flush Panel Doors, Reeded Shelves, 3 Drawers, 80 x 59 x 23 In. 3600.00
Armoire, Mahogany, Arched Doors, Flared Cornice, Drawers, c.1835, 96 x 83 In. 9187.00
Armoire, Mahogany, Brass Mounted, Paneled Doors, Drum Feet, c.1825, 84 x 55 In. 5287.00
Armoire, Mahogany, Carved Band, Paneled Door, Shaped Frame, 70 ½ x 39 x 19 In. 837.00
Armoire, Mahogany, Cornice, Doors, Columns, Drawers, Base, Ball Feet, 83 x 60 In. 2820.00
Armoire, Oak, 2 Doors, Removable Top, France, 19th Century, 95 x 58 ½ In. *illus* 1440.00
Armoire, Pine, Carved Panels, Shaped Apron, Scroll Carved Legs, France, 1700s, 50 x 18 In. 1680.00
Armoire, Rococo, Mahogany, Crest, Stepped Cornice, Mirrored Doors, c.1840, 99 x 73 In. 2937.00
Armoire, Rococo, Mahogany, Leaf Crest, Lobed Finials, Beaded Molding, c.1850, 110 x 59 In. 7800.00
Armoire, Shaped Case, Flat Top, Paneled Door, Cabriole Legs, France, c.1800, 35 x 18 In. 767.00
Armoire, Walnut, Carved, Beveled Mirror, Cherubs, France, c.1875, 119 x 105 x 23 In. 2478.00
Banquette, French Empire, Mahogany, Padded Scoop Seat, Floral Upholstery, 16 x 19 In. 167.00
Banquette, Louis XV, Walnut, Carved, Overupholstered, Leaf Carved Apron, Legs, 17 x 39 In. 504.00
Barstool, G. & Mira Nakashima, Walnut, 3 Legs, Footrest, Spindle Back, Widdicomb, 37 x 18 In. 2160.00
Bed, Arts & Crafts, 8-Slatted Headboard, Footboard, Tapered Legs, 45 x 80 x 45 In. 540.00
Bed, Arts & Crafts, Slats, 2-Arch Headboard, Paneled Footboard, Rail, 37 ½ x 44 ½ In. 120.00
Bed, Arts & Crafts, Wood, 4 Matching Slats, Panel Headboard, Footboard, 52 x 55 x 35 In. 450.00
Bed, Black, Red Grain, Yellow, Green Striping, Finials, Rope, c.1820, 50 x 71 In. 235.00
Bed, Blue Paint, Rope, Pa., c.1800, 32 x 74 x 49 ½ In. 819.00
Bed, Brass, Basket Medallion, Headboard, Footboard, France, Twin *illus* 200.00
Bed, Brass, Iron, c.1875, 64 x 54 x 76 In. 50.00
Bed, Brass, Iron, Painted, Leaftips, Scrolled, 7 Spindles, Head & Footboard, 54 x 53 In. 230.00
Bed, Brass, Steel Rails, Late 19th Century, 60 ½ x 54 In. 531.00
Bed, Brass Mounted, Canonball Finials, Posts, Rails, France, 20th Century, 48 x 92 x 55 In. 267.00
Bed, Campaign, Iron, Mid 19th Century, 70 x 41 In. 764.00
Bed, Canopy, Sheraton, Mahogany, Arched Headboard, Early 1800s, 60 x 69 In. 431.00
Bed, Canopy, Sheraton, Mahogany, Pencil Post, Arched Frame, Toile Fabric, 85 x 36 In., Pair. 1438.00
Bed, Cast Iron, Headboard, Footboard, Cream Paint, Open Scrolling, Double, 41 x 58 In. 209.00
Bed, Dog, Louis Philippe, Walnut, Upholstered Cushion, Paneled Sides, 15 x 33 x 18 In. 660.00
Bed, Eastlake, Walnut, Leaf Carved Crest, Full Size, 89 In. 132.00
Bed, English Regency, Mahogany, Urn Finials, c.1810, 55 x 71 ½ In. 230.00
Bed, Four-Poster, Canopy, Scrolled Headboard, Applied Cartouche, 115 x 78 In. 9200.00
Bed, Four-Poster, Federal, Curly Maple, Ring Turned, Paneled Headboard, c.1820, 92 x 80 In. 3760.00
Bed, Four-Poster, Federal, Mahogany, Reed Top, Flowers & Swag, 19th Century, 92 x 61 In. 1989.00
Bed, Four-Poster, Federal, Maple, Molded Square Tapered Rails, 77 ½ x 57 In. 1298.00
Bed, Four-Poster, Federal, Maple, Vase Turned Reeded Foot Posts, 1800s, 66 x 56 In. 822.00
Bed, Four-Poster, Gothic Revival, Oak, Carved, Pierced Canopy, England, 107 x 51 x 82 In. 9560.00
Bed, Four-Poster, Mahogany, Mixed Woods, Panel, Leaves, Rice Stalks, 93 x 52 In. 9300.00
Bed, Four-Poster, Mahogany, Oak, Carved, Tapered Posts, 1800s, 85 x 83 In. 920.00
Bed, Four-Poster, Mahogany, Vase-Form Finials, Rope Scroll Crest, c.1800, 92 x 78 x 58 In. 2115.00
Bed, Four-Poster, Maple, Canopy, Mortise & Tenon, Handmade, Signed, c.1960, King. 3995.00
Bed, Four-Poster, Maple, Carved, Hinged Side, Latches, c.1830, 45 x 27 In. 1292.00
Bed, Four-Poster, Neoclassical, Mahogany, Turned, Reeded Posts, 89 x 58 In. 8625.00
Bed, Four-Poster, Rococo Revival, Mahogany, Paneled Headboard, 113 x 59 x 77 In. 7200.00
Bed, Four-Poster, Sheraton, Canopy, Pineapple Top Posts, Twist Leaf Carving, 92 x 52 In. 2185.00
Bed, Four-Poster, Sheraton, Mahogany, Carved, Panel Headboard, 88 x 64 ½ x 80 In. 8030.00
Bed, Four-Poster, Sheraton, Maple, Ring Turned, Urn Form, 69 ½ x 39 ½ x 82 In. 1150.00
Bed, Four-Poster, Walnut, Ash, Lamb Decal, Ohio, 1875, 28 x 42 x 24 In., Child's *illus* 600.00
Bed, Four-Poster, Walnut, Cluster Posts, Paneled Headboard, 1800s, 111 x 72 In. 4700.00

Fulper, Vase, Green & Blue Flambe Over Rose, Bullet Form, Marked, 6 ½ In.
$275.00

Furniture, Armoire, Art Nouveau, Inlaid, Mirror, Drawer, 90 x 46 x 19 In.
$1210.00

Furniture, Armoire, Oak, 2 Doors, Removable Top, France, 19th Century, 95 x 58 ½ In.
$1440.00

Furniture, Bed, Brass, Basket Medallion, Headboard, Footboard, France, Twin
$200.00

F

Furniture, Bed, Four-Poster, Walnut, Ash, Lamb Decal, Ohio, 1875, 28 x 42 x 24 In., Child's
$600.00

Furniture, Bed, Half-Tester, Rococo, Rosewood, New Orleans, 1850, 126 x 85 x 67 In.
$60000.00

TIP
Experts say you should keep your furniture clean and dust-free, wax it once a year, and don't let it dry out.

Bed, Four-Poster, Walnut, Spool Turned, Victorian, 55 x 53 ½ In. . . . 189.00
Bed, Fruitwood, Post, Flower Marquetry, Dutch, 96 x 77 In. . . . 474.00
Bed, G. Stickley, No. 924, 12 Vertical Spindles, Signed, 37 x 79 x 58 In. . . . 3900.00
Bed, Gothic Revival, Iron, Rocker, Salesman's Sample, 9 x 14 x 15 In.. . . . 50.00
Bed, Half-Tester, Rococo, Rosewood, New Orleans, 1850, 126 x 85 x 67 In. . . . *illus* 60000.00
Bed, Louis XV Style, Cane Head & Footboard, Gilt, Late 1800s, 53 x 80 x 66 In. . . . *illus* 3100.00
Bed, Louis XV Style, Fruitwood, Carved, Paneled Headboard, 48 ½ x 41 x 76 In., Pair . . . 590.00
Bed, Louis XVI Style, Mahogany, Gilt Bronze, Cube Parquetry, c.1900, 47 x 87 In.. . . . 6250.00
Bed, Louis XVI Style, Walnut Veneer, Bronze Mounts, Early 1900s, 46 x 43 In., Pair . . . 230.00
Bed, Mahogany, Paneled Head & Footboard, Blocked Rail, Square Feet, Molding, 73 x 28 In. . 1920.00
Bed, Murphy, Oak, Quartersawn, Applied Carving, Mirrored Chifforobe, 77 x 53 In. . . . 468.00
Bed, Poplar, Red Paint, Diamond Headboard, Rope, c.1800, 27 x 37 x 73 In. . . . 1287.00
Bed, Red Paint, Ball Finials, Caster Wheels, Rope, 19 x 41 x 54 ½ In., Child's . . . *illus* 358.00
Bed, Rococo, Mahogany, Arched, Scalloped Headboard, Footboard, c.1960, 80 x 72 In. . . . 3525.00
Bed, Rococo Revival, Rosewood, Arched Top Rail, Leaf Carved Cartouche, 60 x 64 In. . . . 3120.00
Bed, Rococo Style, Fruitwood, Raised Panels, Shell Crested Footboard, 63 x 63 x 78 In. . . . 359.00
Bed, Shaped Wood, Headboard, Cutout Spindles, Blue Paint, c.1825, 27 x 42 x 20 In., Child's 235.00
Bed, Sleigh, Art Deco, Blond Wood, Baker Furniture, Queen, 43 x 87 In. . . . 777.00
Bed, Sleigh, Biedermeier, Bird's-Eye Maple, Plinth Base, Bracket Feet, 44 x 77 In. . . . 1180.00
Bed, Sleigh, Charles X, Mahogany, Round Crest Rail, Banding, Early 1800s, 41 x 64 In. . . . 1528.00
Bed, Sleigh, Empire, Mahogany, c.1840, 43 x 62 x 88 ½ In.. . . . 600.00
Bed, Tiger Maple, Cannonball, Twin, Mid 19th Century, Twin, 45 x 41 In. . . . 80.00
Bed, Trundle, Old Salmon Paint, Pa., c.1800, 13 x 34 x 50 ½ In. . . . 497.00
Bed, Walnut, Bottle Turned Legs, Arched Headboard, Rope, Pa., 1700s, 38 x 49 x 75 In. . . . 1404.00
Bed, Walnut, Pine, Turned Low Post, Folding, Rope, c.1800, 39 x 46 x 77 In.. . . . 1116.00
Bed Steps, George III, Mahogany, 3 Steps, c.1800, 24 x 32 ½ In. . . . 878.00
Bed Steps, William IV, Mahogany, 3 Steps, Chamber Pot, c.1835, 28 x 18 x 31 In. . . . *illus* 830.00
Bedroom Set, Art Deco, Enamel, Chrome, Simmons, c.1930, 7 Piece . . . 590.00
Bedroom Set, Scandinavian, Teak, 3 Chests Of Drawers, 2 Stands, Bed . . . 660.00
Bedroom Set, Victorian, Walnut, Marble-Top Dresser, Stand, 86 x 60-In. Bed . . . 7895.00
Bench, Arts & Crafts, Pyrographic Cattail Seat, 35 x 19 In. . . . 660.00
Bench, Black Forest, Mask Carved Crest, Lidded Seat, Animal Carved Arms, 47 x 48 In. . . . 478.00
Bench, Bucket, Pine, Collapsible, Slats, Sawbuck Legs, Gray Paint, 1900s, 16 x 46 x 20 In. . . . 176.00
Bench, Bucket, Pine, Cutout Legs, Late 19th Century, 30 x 42 In.. . . . 761.00
Bench, Bucket, Pine, Red Paint, 2 Tiers, Cross Brace, Trestle Feet, 1800s, 42 x 32 In. . . . 690.00
Bench, Bucket, Pine, Red Stain, 2 Doors, 19th Century, 36 x 38 In. . . . 2106.00
Bench, Bucket, Poplar, Scalloped, Cutout Feet, 2 Shelves, Red Paint, 1800, 48 x 35 x 14 In. . . 9945.00
Bench, Bucket, Softwood, Green Paint, 2 Shelves, V-Notched Leg, Pa., 36 x 39 x 12 In. . . . 4250.00
Bench, Bucket, Softwood, Salmon, Plank Back, Shelf, Curved Top, Cutout Legs, 37 x 30 In. . . 3190.00
Bench, Bucket, Softwood, Scrolled Back, 3 Drawers, Paneled Doors, Shelf, 54 x 41 In.. . . . 825.00
Bench, Chinese Chippendale, Blind Fretwork, Upholstered, X-Stretcher, 20 x 18 In. . . . 329.00
Bench, Chippendale, Mahogany, Loose Seats, Scrolled Arms, Claw & Ball Feet, 29 x 54 In. . . . 568.00
Bench, Cross Frame, Muslin Upholstery, Reeded Seat Rail, 22 x 48 In. . . . 259.00
Bench, Curule, Mahogany, Swan's Neck, Early 19th Century, 23 x 26 In.. . . . 1175.00
Bench, Curule, Neoclassical, Scroll Arms, Carved Flower, Upholstered, 1890s, 26 x 40 In. . . . 440.00
Bench, Elm, Lacquered, Rectangular, Chinese, 20 x 39 x 15 In. . . . 657.00
Bench, Fireside, Louis XV, Fruitwood, Serpentine Edge, Needlepoint Seat, 19 x 39 In.. . . . 633.00
Bench, G. McCabe, Chrome Frame, Black Vinyl Slat Back, Seat, 49 x 29 In. . . . 540.00
Bench, G. Nelson, Birch, Black Slatted Platform, Herman Miller, c.1950, 48 x 14 In. . . . 510.00
Bench, George III, Floral Lattice Upholstery, Padded Scroll Arms, Early 1900s, 28 x 47 In. . . . 239.00
Bench, Gothic Revival, Oak, Carved, Molded Crest Rail, Linenfold Panels, 36 ½ x 76 In. . . . 646.00
Bench, Gothic Revival, Walnut, Inverted Cathedral Arch, Storage, Upholstered, 9 Ft. . . . 4500.00
Bench, Hall, G. Stickley, No. 224, Chamfered, Lift Seat, Signed, 48 x 72 x 22 In. . . . *illus* 12000.00
Bench, Hall, Oak, Paneled, 4 Raised Arch Panels, Cabriole Legs, 18th Century, 35 x 58 x 26 In. 635.00
Bench, Judge's, Golden Oak, On Wheels, Late 19th Century, 90 x 46 In.. . . . 441.00
Bench, Limbert, No. 243, Square Cutouts, Signed, 24 x 24 ½ x 18 In. . . . 2500.00
Bench, Limbert, Window, Square Cutouts, Canted Legs, 24 x 24 ½ x 18 In.. . . . 3000.00
Bench, Louis IV, Fruitwood, Carved, Upholstered, 6 Cabriole Legs, c.1900, 18 x 36 In. . . . 777.00
Bench, Louis XV, Oak, Rolled Arms, Carved Legs, France, 1800s, 25 x 58 x 17 In. . . . 1495.00
Bench, Luggage, Regency, Mahogany, Rounded Mounts, Shaped Feet, 20 x 41 x 11 In. . . . 1320.00
Bench, M. Nakashima, Black Walnut, Hickory, Spindle Back, 32 x 66 x 30 ¾ In. . . . 6250.00
Bench, Mahogany, Satinwood, Serpentine, Upholstered, Square Legs, c.1900, 18 x 16 x 16 In. 470.00
Bench, Merklin, Mahogany, Brass Claw Feet, c.1885-95, 43 x 73 x 22 In. . . . 2300.00
Bench, Mortise, Tenon Joint, Beaded Edge Apron, c.1830, 17 x 72 In. . . . 149.00
Bench, Oak, Figural, Griffin Carved, Lift Top . . . 4313.00
Bench, Oak, Neoclassical, Lion's Head, Paw Feet, X Supports, 18 x 24 x 22 In. . . . 793.00

Bench, Oak, Trestle, Paneled Back, Oak Leaves, Birds, Shield, Scotland, 36 x 72 In. 3335.00
Bench, Peachwood, Chinese, 19th Century, 19 ½ x 25 ½ x 12 In. 448.00
Bench, Piano, Arts & Crafts, Walnut, Lift Top, Footed Base, Kunkle Furniture Co., 20 x 38 In. . 660.00
Bench, Piano, G. Stickley, No. 217, 22 x 36 x 12 ¾ In. 2040.00
Bench, Pine, Green Paint, Chamfered Legs, 17 x 70 In. 353.00
Bench, Pine, Lift Top, Shoe Feet, 18th Century, Go x 53 x 34 x 17 In. 2520.00
Bench, Prayer, Softwood, Flat Top, Skirt Sides, Arch-Cut Legs, Pa., 6 x 46 In. 220.00
Bench, Risom, Walnut Frame, Tufted White Vinyl Seat Cushion, 48 x 17 In. 780.00
Bench, Roycroft, Ali Baba, Carved Orb & Cross Mark, 19 x 42 In. 13200.00
Bench, Sam Maloof, Arms, Upholstered, c.1963, 18 x 16 In. 4500.00
Bench, School, Plank Seat & Back, Red Paint, Numbers, Pa., 34 x 71 x 16 In. 3850.00
Bench, Shaker, Pine, Plank Board Seat, Trestle Shape Base, 19th Century, 28 x 44 In. 295.00
Bench, Softwood, Beaded Crest, 2-Board Plank Seat, Tenon Joints, c.1800, 32 x 72 In. 5500.00
Bench, Softwood, Flat Top, Mortised Legs, 14 ½ x 139 x 14 ¾ In. 121.00
Bench, Softwood, Flat Top, Side Skirts, Shaped Legs, Arched Cutout Feet, 17 x 60 In. 1870.00
Bench, Softwood, Green Paint, Flat Top, Arched Cutout Feet, 18 x 52 In. 660.00
Bench, Softwood, Mortise & Tenon Joints, Blue Gray, 22 x 83 x 20 In. 8250.00
Bench, Softwood, Plank Seat & Back, Square Nail Construction, Pa., 19 x 46 x 12 In. 935.00
Bench, Vanity, Louis XVI, Fruitwood, Carved Scrolls, Crests, Upholstered, c.1910, 26 x 30 In. . 388.00
Bench, Vanity, Rococo Revival, Beech, Needlework Upholstery, c.1885, 20 x 18 In. 444.00
Bench, Walnut, End Supports, Iron Stretchers, Spain, 18 x 39 x 16 In. 780.00
Bench, Walnut, Upholstered, Flared Arms, Tapered Legs, Italy, 1700s, 32 x 74 x 21 In. 313.00
Bench, Window, Directoire Style, Chinoiserie, Scrolled Stiles, Turned Rungs, 30 x 36 In. 1035.00
Bench, Window, Louis XVI, Gilt, X Frame, Turned Arms, Upholstered, 24 x 30 In. 660.00
Bench, Window, Oak, Upholstered, Paine Furniture, 38 ½ x 46 x 17 In. 100.00
Bench, Window, Regency, Mahogany, Scrolled, Leaf Tips, Cushion, 51 ¾ x 22 ½ In. 3081.00
Bench, Windsor, Spindle Back, Bamboo Turned Arms, Legs, 19th Century, 34 x 77 x 21 In. . . . 1100.00
Bench, Windsor, Spindle Back, Scroll Arms, Dish Seat, 19th Century, 29 ½ x 73 In. 2350.00
Bench, Wood, Cat Silhouette Ends, Black & Blue Paint, 13 ½ x 22 ¾ In. 403.00
Bench, Wood, Deeply Carved Dragons, Clouds, Pierced Back, Arms, Chinese, c.1900, 43 x 50 In. 1062.00
Bench, Wood, Single Board, Beaded Edge, Tapered Ends, Shoe Feet, Late 1800s, 70 x 7 In. . . . 176.00
Bookcase, Art Deco, Breakfront, Stepped Pedestal, Glazed Sliding Door, 37 x 67 In. 1888.00
Bookcase, Arts & Crafts, 3 Doors, Applied Flowers, 12 Shelves, 58 x 57 In. 960.00
Bookcase, Arts & Crafts, 6 Glazed Panels, 2 Adjustable Shelves, 45 x 30 In. 1610.00
Bookcase, Arts & Crafts, Oak, Glass, 2 Doors, Gallery Top, 3 Shelves, 59 x 36 In. 504.00
Bookcase, Barrister, Mahogany, 2 Shelves, 6 Glazed Panels, Scroll Feet, c.1920, 55 x 51 In. . . 388.00
Bookcase, Barrister, Oak, 4 Sections, Leaded Glass Doors, 57 x 17 In. 1100.00
Bookcase, Barrister, Oak, 6 Shelves, Stack, Shaw-Walker, c.1930, 89 x 34 In. 1395.00
Bookcase, Biedermeier, Cherry, Gilt Bronze Mounted, Ebonized, 55 x 45 In. 4113.00
Bookcase, Chippendale, Cherry & Pine, Paneled Door, 1780s, 72 x 43 x 21 In. 3290.00
Bookcase, Chippendale Style, Mahogany, Dovetailed Drawers, Shelves, c.1950, 62 x 45 In. . . . 353.00
Bookcase, Edwardian, Satinwood, Broken Swan's Neck Pediment, c.1900, 106 x 88 In. 7680.00
Bookcase, Elm, Chinese, 75 x 33 x 15 In., Pair 1062.00
Bookcase, Empire, Mahogany, 3 Doors, Mullions Over Glass, c.1890, 57 x 75 x 17 In. 520.00
Bookcase, Empire Style, Mahogany, Blocked Cornice, Arched Frieze, 73 x 47 In. 3819.00
Bookcase, Empire Style, Mahogany, Gilt Bronze Mounted, 37 ½ x 31 ¾ x 8 ½ In. 948.00
Bookcase, Federal, Mahogany, Inlaid, 2 Glazed Doors, Hinged Drawer, c.1800, 90 In. 3750.00
Bookcase, G. Nelson, Walnut, Shelf, Steel Legs, Herman Miller, 24 x 34 In. 720.00
Bookcase, G. Stickley, 2 Doors, 12 Panes, Key & Tenon, Signed, 56 x 64 x 13 In. 12000.00
Bookcase, G. Stickley, No. 525, White Paint, 2 Doors, 3 Shelves, c.1901, 56 x 45 In. 6600.00
Bookcase, G. Stickley, No. 702, 2 Doors, Glass, 6 Shelves, 58 x 48 x 14 In. . . . . 8400.00 to 19200.00
Bookcase, G. Stickley, No. 715, 16-Pane Door, Copper Pull, Label, 56 x 36 x 13 In. 6000.00
Bookcase, G. Stickley, No. 716, 2 Doors, 8 Panes, Tenon, Signed, 56 x 45 x 13 In. 8400.00
Bookcase, G. Stickley, Oak, 2 Doors, Copper Pulls, 64 x 41 ½ In. 4140.00
Bookcase, George III, Frieze, Pendants, Geometric Mullions, Doors, c.1800, 94 x 53 In. 10575.00
Bookcase, George III, Fruitwood, 2 Parts, 4 Doors, 1800, 81 x 58 In. 6320.00
Bookcase, George III, Mahogany, Breakfront, 4 Astragal Glazed Doors, 100 x 98 In. 5760.00
Bookcase, George III, Mahogany, Mullioned Glass Doors, Shelves, 81 x 50 x 23 In. 8888.00
Bookcase, George III Style, Mahogany, 2 Astragal Doors, Drawers, 79 x 43 ½ x 15 In. 1220.00
Bookcase, George III Style, Multicolored, Arched, Reeded Frame, 89 x 40 In. 2640.00
Bookcase, George III Style, Pine, 2 Astragal Glazed Doors, Paneled, 1800s, 91 x 65 In. 5760.00
Bookcase, George IV, Breakfront, Cabinet, Rosewood, Burr Amboyna, 86 x 84 In. 5313.00
Bookcase, Gothic Revival, Mahogany, 2 Doors, Writing Desk, 85 x 47 x 24 In. 1320.00
Bookcase, Gothic Revival, Mahogany, Incised, Flowers, c.1870, 75 x 52 x 15 In. . . . . *illus* 1400.00
Bookcase, Gothic Revival, Oak, Carved, 2 Doors, 2 Shelves, c.1900, 63 x 70 x 16 In. 2300.00
Bookcase, L. & J.G. Stickley, Chestnut, Door, Chamfered Sides, Onondaga, 55 x 31 In. 2500.00

Furniture, Bed, Louis XV Style, Cane Head & Footboard, Gilt, Late 1800s, 53 x 80 x 66 In. $3100.00

Furniture, Bed, Red Paint, Ball Finials, Caster Wheels, Rope, 19 x 41 x 54 ½ In., Child's $358.00

Old Twins Are Rare

Although twin beds were made in the eighteenth century by Thomas Sheraton, the double bed was the most popular style through the nineteenth century. Few Victorian twins are found. The movie industry dictated the rule of twin beds after 1934, when the Hays Code discouraged showing a bedroom—and married people slept in separate beds. Magazines also promoted twin beds and never showed people sleeping together in a double bed. In 1959 a clever use of a split screen showed Doris Day and Rock Hudson in what looked like the same bed in the movie *Pillow Talk.*

Furniture, Bed Steps, William IV, Mahogany, 3 Steps, Chamber Pot, c.1835, 28 x 18 x 31 In.
$830.00

Furniture, Bench, Hall, G. Stickley, No. 224, Chamfered, Lift Seat, Signed, 48 x 72 x 22 In.
$12000.00

Furniture, Bookcase, Gothic Revival, Mahogany, Incised, Flowers, c.1870, 75 x 52 x 15 In.
$1400.00

Furniture
George Nakashima learned traditional joinery skills from a Japanese carpenter in a U.S. internment camp in Idaho during World War II.

Bookcase, L. & J.G. Stickley, No. 328, 2 Doors, 24 Panes, Original Hardware, 55 x 52 In. 9600.00
Bookcase, Library, Georgian Chippendale, Mahogany, Gothic Glazed Doors, 63 x 96 In. 2271.00
Bookcase, Library, Victorian, Walnut, Projecting Molded Edge Crown, 75 x 58 In. 896.00
Bookcase, Limbert, No. 323, 3 Doors, 9 Shelves, Arched Toe Board, 50 x 56 x 14 In. 4800.00
Bookcase, Limbert, No. 355, Cutout Panels, 3 Shelves, 47 ¾ x 33 x 12 In. 5400.00
Bookcase, Limbert, No. 359, 3 Doors, Signed, 57 x 67 x 15 In. . . . . *illus* 8400.00
Bookcase, Louis Philippe, Mahogany, Glazed Door, Drawer, 79 x 44 In. 3600.00
Bookcase, Louis Philippe, Mahogany, Pediment, Glazed Doors, Mid 1800s, 80 x 37 In. 980.00
Bookcase, Louis XVI Style, Mahogany, 2 Doors, Paneled, 71 x 50 In. 900.00
Bookcase, Louis XVI Style, Mahogany, Glazed Panel, Molded Crown, Early 1900s, 81 x 61 In. 956.00
Bookcase, Louis XVI Style, Star Carved Frieze, Shelves, Multicolored, 97 x 74 x 16 In. 3840.00
Bookcase, Mahogany, Breakfront, Crossbanded Cupboard, c.1800, 94 x 113 In. 8225.00
Bookcase, Mahogany, Inlaid, 2 Doors, 3 Shelves, Paine Furniture, 61 x 46 x 15 In. 950.00
Bookcase, Mahogany, Veneer, Hinged, Drawers, Ogee Bracket Feet, 80 x 42 ½ x 21 In. 504.00
Bookcase, Marble Top, 2 Doors, 2 Interior Shelves, Rosewood, Metal, 30 x 30 In., Pair 415.00
Bookcase, Oak, Figural Supports, Urns, Griffins, Flowers, Sections, c.1890, 76 x 116 x 24 In. . 2875.00
Bookcase, Oak, Walnut, Griffins, Shields, Caryatid Supports, Carved, 1880, 95 x 57 In. 7125.00
Bookcase, P. Hvidt, Teak, 5 Shelves, Soborg Mobler, Denmark, 36 x 34 In., Pair 1920.00
Bookcase, Regency, Mahogany, Bowfront, 2 Glass Doors, Drawers, 86 x 40 x 21 In. 1778.00
Bookcase, Regency Style, Mahogany, Breakfront, Molded Crown, 3 Doors, 79 x 75 In. 1062.00
Bookcase, Revolving, Cast Iron, Stamped, Norwich, Late 1800s, 52 x 16 In. . . . . *illus* 1320.00
Bookcase, Revolving, Library, Aesthetic Revival, Ebonized, Parcel Gilt, 73 In. 4148.00
Bookcase, Revolving, Oak, 4-Sided, Slanted Top, Casters, 47 x 18 In. 1035.00
Bookcase, Revolving, Oak, Rope-Molded Top, Bookstand, Slatted Tiers, 46 x 21 In. 1058.00
Bookcase, Revolving, Tabard Inn Library, Oak, Shields, 1902, 81 x 27 x 26 ½ In. . . . . . . *illus* 4640.00
Bookcase, Revolving, Walnut, Slatted Shelves, c.1900, 58 x 24 In. 1527.00
Bookcase, Rosewood, 2 Doors, 2 Drawers, 4 Shelves, c.1880, 85 x 52 x 16 In. 345.00
Bookcase, Roycroft, No. 84, Adjustable Shelves, Door, 60 x 31 In. 11400.00
Bookcase, Saarinen, Johnson Furniture, Michigan, c.1940, 24 x 30 In. 90.00
Bookcase, Stickley Bros., 3 Shelves, Open Side Slats, Signed, Quaint, 18 x 32 In. 720.00
Bookcase, Victorian, Oak, Curved Glass Door, Mirror, 71 x 38 x 16 In. 266.00
Bookcase, Victorian, Walnut, Arched Molded Cornice, Scrolled Crest, c.1875, 73 x 53 In. 1896.00
Bookcase, Walnut, 3 Doors, Blocked Plinth, Square Feet, Acorn Cornice, 99 x 86 In. 14100.00
Bookcase, Walnut, Glass, Scalloped Apron, Beaded Molding, 77 ½ x 56 In. . . . . *illus* 445.00
Bookcase, Wormley, Walnut, Dunbar Brass Tags, 25 x 27 In. 2280.00
Bookrack, G. Stickley, No. 74, Cutout Handles, V Trough, 30 ½ x 32 ½ x 10 In. 2160.00
Bookrack, G. Stickley, No. 74, Double V Trough, Cutout Sides, Black, 31 x 30 x 10 In. 4800.00
Bookstand, Dictionary, Victorian, Oak, Iron, Adjustable, Grate, Casters, 41 x 21 x 8 In. 200.00
Bookstand, Gothic Revival, Mahogany, Brass Mounts, Trefoils, 13 In. 174.00
Bookstand, Mahogany, Brass, Steel Mountings, Adjustable Height, Tilt Top, Shelf, 46 In. 1093.00
Bookstand, Neoclassical, Leather, Gilt Tooled, Serpentine Border, 11 x 17 In. 830.00
Bookstand, Reading, Georgian, Mahogany, Adjustable, Pad Feet, 1760, 43 x 23 In. . . . . . *illus* 2340.00
Boot Rack, Victorian, Mahogany, Arched Crest Rail, Turned Pegs, 12 Pegs, 39 x 30 In. 780.00
Bracket, Antler, Fallow Deer, Platform, White Paint, 21 x 23 In., Pair 633.00
Bracket, Neoclassical, Oak, Carved, Demilune, Leaf Pendant, 13 ½ x 23 ½ In. 900.00
Bracket, Renaissance Revival, Walnut, Carved Egg, Dart, Flowers, Putti, Italy, c.1890, 25 x 37 In. 3910.00
Brazier, Napoleon III, Bronze, Brass, Round Dish Top, Masks, Griffins, 30 x 16 In. 705.00
Breakfront, Adam Style, Mahogany, Acanthus, Garland, 1800s, 81 x 68 x 19 In. . . . . *illus* 4200.00
Breakfront, Chippendale, Mahogany, Glazed Doors, Glass Shelves, Baker Furniture, 91 x 73 In. 2115.00
Breakfront, Georgian, Mahogany, 3 Upper Doors, Drop Front, England, 1800s, 24 x 21 In. . . 575.00
Breakfront, Walnut, Broken Arch, Cartouche, Carved Fruit Baskets, 1800s, 121 x 108 In. . . . 8225.00
Buffet, Arts & Crafts, Oak, Carved, Shelves, Panels, Drawers, Doors, 62 x 67 ½ x 20 In. 1003.00
Buffet, Ash, Black Lacquer Steel, Plastic, 4 Drawers, Raised, Perriand, 1960, 32 x 123 In. 15625.00
Buffet, Empire Style, Fruitwood, Marble Top, 3 Drawers, Doors, 39 x 74 x 18 In. 6000.00
Buffet, French Provincial, Fruitwood, 2 Drawers, Felt Lined, 38 x 53 x 20 ½ In. 1475.00
Buffet, French Provincial, Fruitwood, Paneled Drawers, Doors, 42 x 72 x 24 In. 2400.00
Buffet, French Provincial, Louis XV, Oak, Fruitwood, Panels, Doors, Drawers, 90 x 55 x 24 In. 6900.00
Buffet, French Provincial, Pine, Panels, Cabriole Feet, 90 x 53 ½ x 21 ½ In. 3600.00
Buffet, Fruitwood, Paneled Doors, Diamond Accents, Italy, 40 x 53 x 24 In. 3840.00
Buffet, Louis XV Style, Fruitwood, Drawers, Shaped, Paneled Doors, 45 x 55 In. 3600.00
Buffet, Louis XVI Style, Multicolored Wood, 3 Drawers, 3 Doors, 43 x 76 ½ In. 9600.00
Buffet, Mahogany, Frieze Drawers, Shelf, Sauvrezy, c.1870, 73 x 46 In. 4375.00
Buffet, Oak, Marble Top, 2 Drawers, 2 Doors, Plinth Base, 38 x 53 x 25 In. 2400.00
Buffet, Pine, Multicolored, 4 Framed Paneled Doors, 36 x 63 x 25 In. 4080.00
Buffet, Queen Anne Style, Mahogany, 2 Drawers, 2 Doors, c.1930, 36 ½ x 48 x 19 In. 110.00
Bureau, Cherry, Inlaid, Bowfront, New England, C 1800s, 32 x 36 In. 1304.00

Furniture, Bookcase, Limbert, No. 359, 3 Doors, Signed, 57 x 67 x 15 In.
$8400.00

Names Are the Same

"Craftsman," "Arts & Crafts," "Roycroft," and finally "Crafts style" are all alternative names for Mission style furniture first popular from 1900 to 1920, then revived in the late 1980s.

Furniture, Bookcase, Walnut, Glass, Scalloped Apron, Beaded Molding, 77 ½ x 56 In.
$445.00

Furniture, Bookcase, Revolving, Cast Iron, Stamped, Norwich, Late 1800s, 52 x 16 In.
$1320.00

Furniture, Bookcase, Revolving, Tabard Inn Library, Oak, Shields, 1902, 81 x 27 x 26 ½ In.
$4640.00

Furniture, Bookstand, Reading, Georgian, Mahogany, Adjustable, Pad Feet, 1760, 43 x 23 In.
$2340.00

TIP

Rusty old lock in a drawer? Brush off the rust with a metal brush, then oil the lock. Test it before using it.

Furniture, Breakfront, Adam Style, Mahogany, Acanthus, Garland, 1800s, 81 x 68 x 19 In.
$4200.00

Furniture, Cabinet, Chinoiserie, Lacquer, Marble Top, Pagoda, Mid 1900s, 37 x 34 x 15 In.
$550.00

Furniture, Cabinet, Japonism, Burl, Black Trim, Marquetry, Victorian, 40 x 33 In.
$200.00

TIP
Brown shoe polish is good to cover scuffs and slight damage on furniture.

Bureau, Chippendale, Mahogany, Reverse Serpentine, Original Brass, Mass., c.1770, 31 x 36 In. 7703.00
Bureau, Dressing, Mahogany, 2 Mirrored Towers, Mirror, Marble Top, 95 x 44 x 22 In. 8125.00
Bureau, Dressing, Mahogany, Obelisk Supports, Mirror, Marble, Drawer, Doors, 80 x 41 In. . . 7500.00
Bureau, Faux Bois, Slant Front, Fitted Interior, 3 Long Drawers, Painted, 41 x 46 In. 5520.00
Bureau, G. Stickley, No. 902, V Backsplash, 50 ½ x 40 x 21 ¾ In. 8250.00
Bureau, George II, Walnut, Hinged Lid, Pigeonholes, Drawers, Handles, 37 x 24 x 18 In. 5750.00
Bureau, George III, Mahogany, Slant Front, 2 Over 3 Drawers, 42 x 44 x 22 In. 4800.00
Bureau, George III, Mahogany, Slant Front, Fitted Interior, Late 1700s, 42 x 41 In. 1528.00
Bureau, George III, Oak, Slant Front, Fitted Interior, Cupboard, 1800s, 43 x 44 In. 1680.00
Bureau, George III Style, Oak, Slant Front, Carved Border, Medallion, 40 x 36 x 19 In. 840.00
Bureau, Georgian, Oak, Hinged Door, Pigeonholes, Sliding Door, Drawers, 38 x 36 x 20 In. . . 1673.00
Bureau, Louis XV, Rosewood, Exotic Wood, Parquetry, Leather Inset, 37 x 33 In. 3480.00
Bureau, Louis XV Style, Rosewood, Slant Front, 2 Doors, Drawers, 55 x 29 x 19 In. 4800.00
Bureau, Louis XVI, Mahogany, Parquetry, Banded Top, Leather, Geometric, 29 x 46 In. 3290.00
Bureau, Louis XVI Style, Tulipwood Parquetry, Leaf Cast Mounts, 34 x 71 x 45 In. 3200.00
Bureau, Neoclassical, Walnut, Cherry, Compass Star, Slant Front, c.1800, 41 x 38 In. 2644.00
Bureau, Slant Front, Louis XV Style, Burgundy Lacquer, Parcel Gilt, Sabots, 35 x 27 x 15 In. . 2160.00
Bureau, Victorian, Walnut, 6 Drawers, Marble, Mirror, 80 x 42 x 20 In. 410.00
Bureau Bookcase, Queen Anne, Walnut, 3 Drawers, Double Bonnet, 1760, 86 x 44 In. 23000.00
Cabinet, Aesthetic Revival, Ebonized, Burl, Marquetry Panels, c.1880, 57 x 75 In. 4140.00
Cabinet, Anglo-Indian, Dark Hardwoods, 2 Doors, Shelves, Drawers, 1800s, 60 x 38 In. 470.00
Cabinet, Baroque Style, Fruitwood, Old Boards Over Hinged Doors, 45 x 41 In. 2510.00
Cabinet, Beech, Cream Paint, 2 Drawers Over Doors, Fluted Panels, 48 x 38 In. 4560.00
Cabinet, Biedermeier, Drawer, Door, 19th Century, 39 x 27 x 19 In. 325.00
Cabinet, Black Lacquer, Brass Mounts, Japan, 19th Century, 41 x 18 x 35 ½ In. 356.00
Cabinet, Black Lacquer, Painted Panels, Animals, Everyday Life, 1800s, 36 x 45 In. 600.00
Cabinet, Boulle, Brass, Tortoise Panel Door, 2 Flanking Glass Doors, 1800s, 47 x 66 In. 1093.00
Cabinet, Burled Elm, Continental, Mid 19th Century, 30 ¾ x 17 ¾ x 14 In. 502.00
Cabinet, C. Beatty, Wood, Parchment, Ebony, Metal Inlay, Paint, c.1900, 112 In. 74500.00
Cabinet, Cherry, Pyrography, Carved, Stiles, Drawer, c.1875, 31 x 20 In. 857.00
Cabinet, China, G. Stickley, No. 820, Door, 12 Panes, 62 ¾ x 36 x 15 In. 3000.00
Cabinet, China, Inlaid, 2 Upper Doors, Shelves, 2 Lower Doors, Drawer, 1900s, 52 x 46 In. . . . 518.00
Cabinet, China, Limbert, No. 1465, Door, Plate Rail, Marked, 58 ½ x 60 x 16 In. 2200.00
Cabinet, China, Mahogany, Carved, Bowfront, Glass Door, Shelves, 66 ½ x 50 x 19 In. 5463.00
Cabinet, China, Oak, 2 Glass Doors, Side Lights, Interior Shelves, c.1912, 57 x 37 In. 1185.00
Cabinet, China, Oak, Canted Front, Divided Glass Door, Bronze Pull, c.1900, 63 x 54 In. 2006.00
Cabinet, China, Oak, Carved Soldiers, Putti, Grotesques, Oriel Co., c.1909, 96 x 66 In. 24150.00
Cabinet, China, Oak, Curved Glass, Carved Leaves, Claw Feet, c.1880, 68 x 46 x 18 In. 2070.00
Cabinet, China, Oak, Drawer, Claw Feet, 66 x 36 x 17 In. 443.00
Cabinet, China, Oak, Triple Lobed, Molded Crown, Curved Glazed Panel Doors, 65 x 47 In. . . 508.00
Cabinet, China, Shop Of The Crafters, Door, Inlaid, Glass Panels, 64 x 43 x 16 In. 12000.00
Cabinet, China, Walnut, Carved, Bent Glass Sides, Burled, c.1870, 63 x 68 x 19 In. 4025.00
Cabinet, Chinoiserie, Lacquer, Marble Top, Pagoda, Mid 1900s, 37 x 34 x 15 In. . . . . . . *illus* 550.00
Cabinet, Chippendale, Mahogany, Dentil Molded Cornice, Fretwork, 73 x 36 In. 1440.00
Cabinet, Cocktail, Art Deco, Walnut, Pop-Up, Gilt Pull, Mirrored Interior, 44 x 25 In. 177.00
Cabinet, Corner, Biedermeier, Fruitwood, Ebonized, Glazed Door, c.1840, 63 x 35 x 21 In. . . . 590.00
Cabinet, Corner, Cherry, Door, 12 Glass Panels, c.1880, 84 x 38 In. 1265.00
Cabinet, Corner, Cherry, Door, Bracket Feet, 19th Century, 82 ½ x 43 x 18 In. 1800.00
Cabinet, Corner, Chippendale, Mahogany, Shell Carved, 2 Sections, Centennial. 2875.00
Cabinet, Corner, Display, Victorian, Graduated Shelves, Bowed Doors, 74 x 36 x 25 In. 1093.00
Cabinet, Corner, Federal, Oak, Parquetry, Door, 3 Shelves, c.1800, 40 x 34 ½ x 21 In. 400.00
Cabinet, Corner, George III, Pine, Wall, Early 19th Century, 44 x 29 x 17 In. 650.00
Cabinet, Corner, George III Style, Pine, Arched, 3 Shelves, 94 x 43 In., Pair 6250.00
Cabinet, Corner, Mahogany, Fitted Shelves, Inlaid, Stringing, Bracket Feet, 85 x 40 In. 1320.00
Cabinet, Corner, Mahogany, Stepped Dentil Frieze, Glazed Doors, Panel Doors, 74 x 36 In. . . . 660.00
Cabinet, Corner, Napoleon III, Mahogany, Marble Top, 2 Doors, 34 x 26 x 18 ½ In. 1440.00
Cabinet, Corner, Tiger Maple, 5 Drawers, 4 Doors, 77 x 55 In. 800.00
Cabinet, Cypress, Iron Mounts, Japan, 19th Century, 36 x 14 ½ x 33 ½ In. 711.00
Cabinet, Cypress, Lacquer, Iron Mounts, Japan, 19th Century, 39 x 38 x 18 ½ In. 356.00
Cabinet, Display, Arched Top, Glass Sides, Front, Applied Trim, 71 x 21 In. 350.00
Cabinet, Display, Courting Scene, Flowers, 2 Glass Shelves, Gilt, France, 65 x 26 In. 1250.00
Cabinet, Display, Louis XV Style, Gilt & Ivory Paint, 19th Century, 83 x 42 In. 3744.00
Cabinet, Display, Mahogany, Curved Panels, Queen Anne Legs, Mirror, 56 x 28 x 17 In. 472.00
Cabinet, Display, Metal Trim, Glass Sides, Door, 54 x 26 In. 375.00
Cabinet, Display, Oak, Crest, Medallion, Pilasters, Convex Panels, Animal Feet, 79 x 46 In. . . . 1180.00
Cabinet, Display, Rosewood, Paw Feet, Chinese, 19th Century, 84 x 45 ½ x 16 ½ In. 8295.00

Cabinet, Display, Walnut, Raised Doors, Drawers, Shelves, Marble Inserts, 107 x 64 In....... 4631.00
Cabinet, Distressed, Black Paint, 2 Doors, Shaped Apron, Chinese, 87 x 31 In.............. 2400.00
Cabinet, Eastlake, Mahogany, Double Rail, Glazed Panel Doors, c.1890, 70 x 49 In., Pair.... 2006.00
Cabinet, Ebonized, Boulle, Gilt Ormolu, France, c.1850-60, 46 x 31 x 14 In. 1495.00
Cabinet, Ebony, Marble, Ivory Scrolls, 3 Drawers, 2 Drop Front Drawers, 37 x 18 In......... 826.00
Cabinet, Elm, Iron Mount, Drawers, Paneled Doors, Chinese, 39 x 80 x 17 In............. 1680.00
Cabinet, Express Wood, Step Back, Japan, c.1800s, 100 x 77 In......................... 2115.00
Cabinet, Filing, Oak, 28 Drawers, 27 x 25 x 15 In., Pair 767.00
Cabinet, Filing, Oak, 4 Sections, Crowns, Base, Brass Pulls, 81 x 41 In................... 2750.00
Cabinet, Filing, Oak, Pullout Writing Surface, 27 Drawers, 2 Doors, c.1910, 82 x 34 In. 1320.00
Cabinet, Filing, Walnut, 2 Doors, 76 x 42 x 17 In.................................. 1035.00
Cabinet, Frank Lloyd Wright, Paneled Top, 2 Doors, Recessed Handles, Signed, 25 x 31 In.... 2160.00
Cabinet, Frank Lloyd Wright, Stacking, 2 Doors, Concentric Squares, 34 x 44 In., 2 Piece.... 1440.00
Cabinet, French Provincial, 2 Paneled Doors, Shaped Feet, 59 x 53 In.................. 1560.00
Cabinet, French Restauration, Mahogany, Marble Top, Drawer, 2 Doors, 1800s, 62 x 46 In. .. 920.00
Cabinet, G. Nelson, Rosewood, Thin Edge, Drop Front, Herman Miller, c.1952, 19 x 41 In.... 4200.00
Cabinet, G. Stickley, 2 Doors, 24 Panes, Gallery Back, Signed, 56 ½ x 36 x 14 In........... 6050.00
Cabinet, G. Stickley, No. 803, Door, Mirror, Glass, 3 Shelves, Arched Apron, 60 x 36 In. 6000.00
Cabinet, George III, Inlaid Mahogany, Starburst, Paneled Doors, 32 x 36 ½ x 22 In......... 1920.00
Cabinet, Gray Marble Top, Drawer, Paneled Door, Scroll Feet, Pa., c.1865, 34 x 36 In........ 2990.00
Cabinet, Green Paint, 2 Doors, 3 Shelves, Open Grid Work, Chinese, 87 x 31 In............. 1020.00
Cabinet, Hanging, Pine, Painted, Gray Blue, Fixed Shelf, Mid 1800s, 28 ½ x 19 In. 316.00
Cabinet, Hanging, Walnut, Cincinnati Art Carved Style, c.1880, 39 x 35 x 10 In. 460.00
Cabinet, Hanging, Walnut, Door, Early 19th Century, 18 ½ x 12 In...................... 410.00
Cabinet, Hanging, Walnut, Door, Pa., Early 19th Century, 18 ½ x 12 In.................. 410.00
Cabinet, Hepplewhite, Inlaid Mahogany, 2 Doors, Centennial, 69 x 36 In. 2300.00
Cabinet, Herb, 68 Drawers, Chinese Characters, Chinese, 65 x 55 x 23 In................. 3840.00
Cabinet, Herter Bros., Rosewood, Bamboo, c.1870, 30 ½ x 21 x 14 In.................... 5700.00
Cabinet, Japonism, Burl, Black Trim, Marquetry, Victorian, 40 x 33 In............... *illus* 200.00
Cabinet, Jean Royere, Ebony, Marble Top, 6 Doors, Interior Drawers, Bar, 39 x 118 In. 47500.00
Cabinet, Jewelry, Aesthetic Revival, Brass, Splayed Legs, Mirror, 1885, 32 x 11 In. ...... *illus* 3600.00
Cabinet, Jewelry, Mahogany, 8 Drawers, Door, Checkerboard Inlay, Pa., 12 x 17 x 12 In...... 1400.00
Cabinet, Lacquer Flowers, Bronze, 2 Doors, 6 Interior Drawers, Japan, 1900s, 18 In......... 413.00
Cabinet, Library, Ebonized Walnut, Tile Mounted, c.1880, 61 x 43 x 14 In................. 2844.00
Cabinet, Liquor, Hepplewhite, Mahogany, Bird's-Eye Maple, Inlaid, Decanters, 18 x 16 In. ... 3105.00
Cabinet, Liquor, Iron, Marble, Glass, 2 Doors, Etched Glass, 34 x 16 x 14 In. 889.00
Cabinet, Louis XV, Kingwood, Marble Top, 2 Doors, Cabriole Legs, 39 x 36 In. 2280.00
Cabinet, Louis XVI Style, Bonheur Du Jour, Marquetry, 2 Piece, 1900, 63 x 34 In. ...... *illus* 1980.00
Cabinet, Louis XVI Style, Kingwood, Mixed Woods, Marble Top, 2 Doors, 46 x 39 x 14 In. 3360.00
Cabinet, Louis XVI Style, Mahogany, Marble Top, Paneled Doors, 54 x 55 In............... 4080.00
Cabinet, Louis XVI Style, Marble Top, Bowfront, Floral Inlay, Drawers, 1900s, 9 x 17 In., Pair 460.00
Cabinet, Magazine, G. Stickley, No. 506, Tapered Sides, 39 x 15 ½ x 13 ½ In.............. 7500.00
Cabinet, Mahogany, 3 Drawers, Shelves, England, 54 x 15 ¾ x 18 In..................... 150.00
Cabinet, Mahogany, Graduated Drawers, England, 69 x 24 In.......................... 7900.00
Cabinet, Mahogany, Marquetry, Door, Interior Shelf, Octagonal, England, 23 x 14 ½ In...... 1000.00
Cabinet, Maple, Lift Top, Door, Drawer, Turned Legs, 34 x 17 ¾ In...................... 900.00
Cabinet, Metal, Galvanized, 2 Glazed Doors, Shelves, 78 x 47 x 17 ½ In.................. 1800.00
Cabinet, Milo Baughman, Olive Burl, 3 Flat Doors, T. Coggin, 66 x 23 In................. 1200.00
Cabinet, Music, Arts & Crafts, Wood, Incised Flowers, 3 Interior Shelves, 19 x 43 In. 60.00
Cabinet, Music, Door, Columns, Leaves, Peck & Hills Furniture, No. 1671, 36 x 24 In........ 66.00
Cabinet, Music, G. Stickley, No. 70, 2 Shelves, Amber Glass Door, 47 x 20 x 16 In. 3360.00
Cabinet, Music, G. Stickley, No. 70, 3 Shelves, Amber Glass Door, 47 ½ x 20 x 16 In. 3900.00
Cabinet, Music, G. Stickley, No. 70, 5 Shelves, Panel Door, 47 ½ x 20 x 16 In.............. 650.00
Cabinet, Music, Mahogany, Flowers, 6 Sheet Trays, Flat Legs, c.1910, 46 x 19 x 15 In........ 425.00
Cabinet, Napoleon III, Ebonized Mahogany, Brass Inlay, c.1870, 63 x 49 In. 7500.00
Cabinet, Napoleon III, Oak, Gilt, Cupboard, Putti, Flaming Urn, 1800s, 38 x 44 In.......... 3360.00
Cabinet, Neoclassical, Doors, Inset Oval Mirrors, Square Tapered Legs, 31 x 29 In., Pair..... 1200.00
Cabinet, Neoclassical, Harewood, Boxwood, Inlaid Walnut, Italy, 30 x 22 In. 770.00
Cabinet, Neoclassical, Mahogany, Ogee Drawer, Cupboard, Tapered Columns, 43 x 40 In..... 353.00
Cabinet, Oak, 2 Doors, Drawers, Shelf, 53 x 16 x 35 In................................ 4000.00
Cabinet, Oak, 6 Drawers, Cylinders, 37 x 23 In...................................... 1422.00
Cabinet, Oak, Carvings, Glazed Door, 2 Shelves, Drawer, Lion Pulls, c.1880, 57 x 41 In. 633.00
Cabinet, Oak, Recessed Panels, Arched Designs, Vertical Drop Doors, c.1900, 53 x 28 In...... 885.00
Cabinet, Peachwood, Doors, Shelves, Drawers, Chinese, 17th Century, 58 x 30 x 16 In....... 2360.00
Cabinet, Persimmon, Cypress, Iron Mounts, Rolling, Japan, 19th Century, 48 x 27 x 54 In. .. 2370.00
Cabinet, Pine, Doors, Drawers, Brass Pulls, Hardware, Chinese, 33 x 62 x 18 In. 1560.00

Furniture, Cabinet, Jewelry, Aesthetic Revival, Brass, Splayed Legs, Mirror, 1885, 32 x 11 In. $3600.00

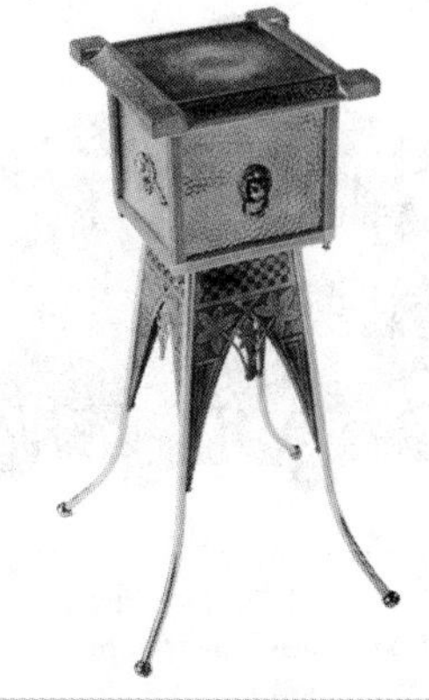

Furniture Definitions

A "Priscilla," is a small stand with a slanted peak top that can be lifted up on both sides. It has a handle at the top and is used as a sewing cabinet. It was named for the Priscilla sewing machine. "Borax" is the slang name for very cheap furniture. "Veneerite" is not wood veneer. It is a picture printed on thin paper that is glued to the wood. It is used only on very inexpensive furniture made since the 1980s and on plywood panels that are used on walls to imitate wood paneling.

Furniture, Cabinet, Louis XVI Style, Bonheur Du Jour, Marquetry, 2 Piece, 1900, 63 x 34 In. $1980.00

Furniture, Cabinet, Renaissance Revival, Rosewood, Inlaid, Moth, Leaves, Goddess, Gilt, c.1865
$41000.00

Furniture, Cabinet, Spice, Pine, Burl, 7 Dovetailed Drawers, Brown Paint, 13 x 8 ¾ x 4 In.
$425.00

Furniture, Cabinet-On-Stand, Empire Style, Mahogany, Eagles, Caryatids, Bronze, 60 x 34 In.
$2500.00

Cabinet, R.J. Horner, Corner, China, Oak, Carved, Signed 5750.00
Cabinet, Rectangular Outlines, 4 Doors, Korea, 54 x 36 In. 384.00
Cabinet, Regency, Mahogany, 2 Doors, Reeded Edge, Turned Legs, 35 ½ x 24 x 16 In. 1126.00
Cabinet, Regency, Mahogany, 2 Paneled Doors, Drawers, Bracket Feet, 36 x 40 x 15 In. 1778.00
Cabinet, Regency, Marble Top, Door, Plinth Base, Round, England, 28 x 15 In. 508.00
Cabinet, Renaissance Revival, Rosewood, Inlaid, Moth, Leaves, Goddess, Gilt, c.1865 ... *illus* 41000.00
Cabinet, Renaissance Revival, Walnut, Burled, Onyx Top, Secret Storage, 46 x 31 x 18 In. 2070.00
Cabinet, Robsjohn-Gibbings, Ebonized Wood, Drawer, 2 Doors, 1950, 26 x 24 x 17 In. 3250.00
Cabinet, Rococo Revival, Walnut, Carved, Pierced, Glass Door, 85 x 38 x 19 In. 478.00
Cabinet, Rosewood, Carved Dragons, Clouds, Chinese, 16 ¾ x 12 In. 474.00
Cabinet, Rosewood, Openwork Carved Dragons, Chinese, 64 x 24 x 16 ¾ In. 1770.00
Cabinet, S.B. Ali, Mahogany, 2 Doors, Recessed Panels, Sculptural Base, c.1940, 32 x 42 In. 780.00
Cabinet, Smoking, Black, White Leaded Glass Door, Applied Strap Pulls, Pipe Holder, 14 x 35 In. 960.00
Cabinet, Smoking, Oak, 2 Doors, Ebony Trim, Brass Mounts, 3 Interior Doors, England, 13 x 12 In. 403.00
Cabinet, Smoking, Regency, Burl, 3 Drawers, 2 Fitted Trays, 1800s, 15 In. 531.00
Cabinet, Softwood, 3 Floating Panels, Double Doors, Chinese, 39 x 91 In. 3360.00
Cabinet, Spice, 7 Drawers, Carved Back Panel, 12 ½ x 9 ½ x 5 ½ In. 120.00
Cabinet, Spice, 25 Drawers, Yellow Paint, Scalloped Base, Early 1900s, 14 x 14 ½ In. 350.00
Cabinet, Spice, English Oak, Dovetailed Case, Panel Door, 9 Drawers, 1700s, 20 x 18 In. 460.00
Cabinet, Spice, Federal, Cherry, Hinged Top, 4 Drawers, Bracket Feet, 1800s, 13 x 17 In. 316.00
Cabinet, Spice, Hanging, Cherry, 7 Drawers, Salt Box, Tennessee, 22 x 10 x 9 In. 450.00
Cabinet, Spice, Pine, Burl, 7 Dovetailed Drawers, Brown Paint, 13 x 8 ¾ x 4 In. .... *illus* 425.00
Cabinet, Step Back, 2 Sections, Mullioned Glazed Doors, Molded Drawers, 68 ½ x 22 In. 9600.00
Cabinet, Teak, 8 Drawers, Concave Front, Exposed Corners, Scandinavia, 76 x 35 In. 1680.00
Cabinet, Tuscan Style, Fruitwood, Glazed Doors, 4 Drawers Over Doors, 87 x 86 x 20 In. 6600.00
Cabinet, Walnut, Mahogany, Hinged, Folds, Drawers, Italy, 32 x 22 x 14 In. 2040.00
Cabinet, Walnut, Mixed Woods, Tambour Cupboard, Drawer, Italy, 31 x 19 x 12 In. 2640.00
Cabinet, Walnut, Pediment, Urn Carving, Paneled Door, Italy, 28 x 21 In. 2400.00
Cabinet, Wegner, Teak, Oak, 2 Drawers, Cane Shelf, 25 x 28 In. 510.00
Cabinet, William IV, Kingwood, Gilt, Bronze, Leather, 19th Century, 49 x 24 x 19 In. 3369.00
Cabinet-On-Stand, Anglo-Colonial, Mahogany, Brass Bound, Doors, Drawers, 57 x 35 In. 1200.00
Cabinet-On-Stand, Black Lacquer, Gilt Decorated, Chinese Export, 32 x 34 In. 5000.00
Cabinet-On-Stand, Empire Style, Mahogany, Eagles, Caryatids, Bronze, 60 x 34 In. ..... *illus* 2500.00
Cabinet-On-Stand, Renaissance Revival, Painted, Parcel Gilt, Carved Columns, 64 x 42 In. . 201.00
Cabinet-On-Stand, Scottish Baroque, Walnut, Arched Pediment, Doors, Shelves, 76 x 45 In.. 384.00
Candlestand, 2 Tin Candleholders, Maple, Adjustable, Round Top, Tripod Base, 1800s, 34 In. 1058.00
Candlestand, 2-Arm, Iron, 3-Footed, 51 ½ In. 702.00
Candlestand, 2-Arm, Iron, Tripod, 59 ¾ x 15 ¾ In. 1553.00
Candlestand, 2-Arm, Maple, Adjustable, Dish Top, Turned Standard, 32 In. 518.00
Candlestand, Cherry, Shaped Top, Turned Shaft, Cabriole Legs, 26 x 16 In. 411.00
Candlestand, Cherry, Square Top, Tripod Feet, 18th Century, 26 x 14 x 14 In. 1700.00
Candlestand, Chippendale, Cherry, Walnut, Scalloped Top, Slipper Feet, 26 x 14 In. 235.00
Candlestand, Chippendale, Mahogany, Dish Top, Tilt, Ball, Claw Feet, c.1780, 27 x 20 In. 5850.00
Candlestand, Chippendale, Mahogany, Dish Top, Urn Turned Support, 27 x 19 In. 863.00
Candlestand, Chippendale, Mahogany, Piecrust Top, Baluster Pedestal, 25 x 16 In., Pair 826.00
Candlestand, Chippendale, Mahogany, Scalloped Piecrust Top, Claw Feet, 32 x 14 In. 175.00
Candlestand, Chippendale, Mahogany, Tilt Top, Birdcage, Column Shaft, c.1770, 30 x 24 In. 764.00
Candlestand, Chippendale, Piecrust Tilt Top, New York, c.1770, 28 x 22 In. 46875.00
Candlestand, Chippendale, Walnut, Dish Top, Spiral Carved Urn Support, 1900s, 18 x 28 In. 382.00
Candlestand, Federal, Cherry, Birch, New England, c.1800, 29 x 16 In. 652.00
Candlestand, Federal, Cherry, Ring, Urn Turned Support, Arched Legs, 27 ½ x 19 ½ In. 563.00
Candlestand, Federal, Cherry, Tilt Top, Beveled, Turned Stem, Spider Legs, c.1800, 28 x 22 In. 940.00
Candlestand, Federal, Mahogany, Astragal, Tilt Top, Urn Turned Support, 29 x 26 In. 1380.00
Candlestand, Federal, Mahogany, Inlaid, Tilt Top, Dish Edge, Snake Feet, 25 x 16 ½ In. 558.00
Candlestand, Federal, Mahogany, Tilt Top, Baluster Turned Pedestal, 29 x 19 x 25 In. 299.00
Candlestand, Federal, Mahogany, Tilt Top, Oval, Tripod Base, Mass, c.1800, 29 x 25 x 15 In. . 1150.00
Candlestand, Federal, Maple, Square, Cutout Corners, 19th Century, 26 x 14 x 13 In. 150.00
Candlestand, Federal, Tiger Maple, Bulbous Ring Turned Standard, 28 x 18 In. 1150.00
Candlestand, George III, Mahogany, Round, Tilt Top, Urn Standard, 27 x 18 In. 153.00
Candlestand, Georgian, Mahogany, Tilt Top, 38 x 18 In. 266.00
Candlestand, Georgian, Mahogany, Tilt Top, Beech, Tripod Base, 1800s, 27 x 23 x 23 In. 375.00
Candlestand, Mahogany, Cherry, Cabriole Legs, Snake Feet, N.E., Early 1800s, 25 x 15 In. 700.00
Candlestand, Mahogany, Circle Of String Inlay, Tilt Top, c.1825, 29 x 24 x 16 In. 176.00
Candlestand, Mahogany, Dish Top, Tilt, Turned Base, Cabriole Legs, c.1800, 27 x 18 In. 529.00
Candlestand, Mahogany, Dish Top, Tilt, Turned Shaft, c.1780, 30 x 22 In. 5750.00
Candlestand, Mahogany, Tilt Top, Birdcage, Carved, Scalloped Dish Top, c.1900, 29 In. 499.00
Candlestand, Mahogany, Tilt Top, Piecrust, Claw & Ball Feet, England, 25 x 21 x 30 In. 920.00

Candlestand, Mahogany, Tilt Top, Serpentine, 3-Feet, Mass., c.1770, 29 x 20 In. 5333.00
Candlestand, Mahogany, Tilt Top, Turned Shafts, New York, c.1770, 27 x 24 In. 9375.00
Candlestand, Maple, Birch, 8-Sided, Basket, On Tripod Base, New England, c.1800, 27 x 18 x 18 In. 3910.00
Candlestand, Maple, Pine, 8-Sided Top, Crossed Shoe Base, N.E., c.1740, 24 x 12 ¾ In. 1170.00
Candlestand, Maple, Tilt Top, Turned Column, Curved Tripod Legs, Iron Spider Legs, 27 x 18 In. 345.00
Candlestand, Nutting, No. I-103, Ironwork, Brass Finial, Holder, Mark, 60 x 13 In.. . . . . 2530.00
Candlestand, Oak, Bentwood Side, X-Shape Base, 39 ½ x 14 x 12 In. . . . . *illus* 1760.00
Candlestand, Queen Anne, Cherry, Dish Top, Tilt, Baluster Shaft, 1700s, 26 x 20 In.. . . . . 2468.00
Candlestand, Queen Anne, Mahogany, Cherry Pedestal, Snake Feet, 27 x 16 x 16 In. 300.00
Candlestand, Queen Anne, Mahogany, Circular Top, Vase Pedestal, 27 x 17 In. 345.00
Candlestand, Queen Anne, Mahogany, Dish Top, Tilt, Cabriole Legs, c.1770, 27 x 21 In.. . . . . . 761.00
Candlestand, Queen Anne, Mahogany, Molded Lip, Ring & Baluster Pedestal, 27 x 16 In. . . . 598.00
Candlestand, Queen Anne, Mahogany, Tilt Top, Cabriole Legs, Snake Feet, 19 ⅜ In.. . . . . 3375.00
Candlestand, Queen Anne, Mahogany, Tilt Top, Slipper Feet, 29 x 19 ½ In. 800.00
Candlestand, Queen Anne, Maple, Black Paint, Notched Top, Conn., c.1795, 25 x 14 In.. . . . . 2340.00
Candlestand, Queen Anne, Maple, Tilt Top, Ring, Urn Shaft, 3 Legs, c.1770, 26 x 17 In.. . . . . 538.00
Candlestand, Queen Anne, Pine, Dish Top, Birdcage Support, Arched Legs, c.1750, 25 x 15 In. 381.00
Candlestand, Queen Anne, Walnut, Baluster Turned Standard, Tripod Base, 26 x 19 In.. . . . . 230.00
Candlestand, Queen Anne, Walnut, Dish Top, Tripod, Pad Feet, Mid 1700s, 27 x 18 In.. . . . . . 863.00
Candlestand, Regency, Beech, Mahogany, Tripod, Spade Feet, 28 ½ x 19 ¾ x 15 In. 978.00
Candlestand, Regency, Mahogany, Octagonal, Saber Legs, Ball Feet, 29 x 20 ½ In. 705.00
Candlestand, Regency, Mahogany, Ring Turned Standard, 3-Part Plinth, 26 x 21 In.. . . . . 920.00
Candlestand, Shaker, Cherry, Maple, Square Top, Baluster Shaft, Umbrella Base, 28 x 16 In.. 1645.00
Candlestand, Softwood, Center Post, T-Shape Base, Red Ocher, Adjustable, 27 x 12 x 9 In.. . . 1100.00
Candlestand, Tiger Maple, New England, 19th Century, 27 x 17 ¾ In. 1989.00
Candlestand, Tiger Maple, Tilt Top, Oval, Snake Feet, 30 x 22 x 15 ½ In. 4375.00
Candlestand, Tilt Top, Octagonal, Tripod Base, c.1890, 30 x 19 ½ In.. . . . . 173.00
Candlestand, Windsor, Mixed Wood, Turned Column, Legs, Red Paint, 26 x 15 In. 588.00
Candlestand, Windsor, Pine, Red Paint, Adjustable, Turned Post, Tripod Base, 33 In. 999.00
Canterbury, Mahogany, Drawer, Casters, England, Early 1800s, 17 ½ x 19 x 13 In.. . . . . 450.00
Canterbury, Mahogany, Drawer, Turned Legs, Casters, 19 ½ x 19 In. 204.00
Canterbury, Neoclassical, Mahogany, Lyre Ends, Compartments, Drawer, 22 x 18 x 15 In.. . . 1434.00
Canterbury, Regency, Mahogany, Scroll Inlay, 6 Lyre Fretwork Dividers, 22 x 21 In.. . . . . 207.00
Canterbury, Regency Style, Mahogany, 2 Drawers, Casters, England, 23 x 18 x 18 In.. . . . . . . 1300.00
Canterbury, Regency Style, Mahogany, 4 Compartments, Drawer, 25 x 19 In. 1320.00
Canterbury, Rosewood, Brass, Dividers, Cartouche, Drawer, Turned Legs, 1800s, 19 x 21 In. . 1880.00
Canterbury, Rosewood, Carved, Drawer, Casters, 22 x 20 x 15 In.. . . . . 700.00
Canterbury, Victorian, Walnut, Scrolling, Openwork Dividers, Drawer, 1800s, 19 x 21 In.. . . . 1554.00
Canterbury, Walnut, Line Inlay, 4 Carved Top Dividers, Drawer, 1800s, England, 19 x 20 In. . 1035.00
Canterbury, Walnut, Shell & Scroll Dividers, Inlaid, England, 1800s, 19 x 20 x 16 In. . . *illus* 990.00
Canterbury, William IV, Rosewood, X-Shape Slatted Divisions, c.1825, 20 x 19 In. 1298.00
Cellarette, Chippendale, Mahogany, Carved Top, Claw Feet, c.1890, 21 x 27 x 19 In.. . . . . 1400.00
Cellarette, Chippendale, Mahogany, Hinged Top, Fitted Interior, Handles, 26 x 24 In.. . . . . . . 920.00
Cellarette, Chippendale, Mahogany, Stand, Hinged Lid, Handles, England, c.1790, 30 x 16 In. 1035.00
Cellarette, Empire, Flame Mahogany, Divided Interior, Cast Brass Feet, 20 ½ x 26 In.. . . . . . . 6500.00
Cellarette, Federal, Inlaid Walnut, Hinged, Bottle Dividers, Stand, Early 1800s, 29 x 24 In. . . 6900.00
Cellarette, George III, Mahogany, Brass Handles, 27 x 19 In.. . . . . 2640.00
Cellarette, George III, Mahogany, Oval, Hinged, Brass Bands, c.1800, 26 x 23 x 16 In. 2820.00
Cellarette, George III, Satinwood, Painted, Octagonal, Banded, 28 x 25 x 20 In., Pair. 4112.00
Cellarette, Georgian, Mahogany, Stand, Hexagonal, 26 In. 660.00
Cellarette, Hepplewhite, Mahogany, Quarter Fan, Diamond & Line Inlay, Dividers, 27 x 16 In. 690.00
Cellarette, Jamestown Furn., Drop Front, Carved, Opens To Bar, 56 x 18 x 7 In.. . . . . *illus* 840.00
Cellarette, Mahogany, Carved, Banded, Fretted, Handles, Stand, 24 x 13 x 13 In.. . . . . 1020.00
Cellarette, Mahogany, William IV, Hinged Lid, Carved Scrolls, England, c.1875, 22 x 33 x 24 In. 2070.00
Cellarette, Queen Anne Style, Mahogany, Pine, Dovetailed, Divided Well, 34 x 19 In.. . . . . 705.00
Cellarette, Regency, Mahogany, Hexagonal, Brass Banded, Handles, 28 x 16 In. 1725.00
Cellarette, Regency, Mahogany, Hinged Lid, Interior Compartments, 23 x 19 In.. . . . . 1265.00
Cellarette, Victorian, Mahogany, Sarcophagus, Fitted Interior, Coffered Top, 25 x 30 In.. . . . . 2185.00
Cellarette, Walnut, Lift Top, Dovetailed, Scallopped Apron, Pa., 19th Century, 14 x 13 In.. . . . 671.00
Chair, 3 Vertical Slats, Spring Cushion, Arms, 37 x 27 x 23 In.. . . . . 330.00
Chair, 5 Slats, Writing Arm, Leather Seat, Signed, Roycroft, 25 x 39 In.. . . . . 780.00
Chair, A. Arbus, Mahogany, Gilt Bronze, Butternut Leather Upholstery, c.1947, 40 In. 15000.00
Chair, A. Dubreuil, Leopard-Spot Acetylene, Welded Sheet Steel, Paris, c.1991, 93 x 60 In.. . . . 7500.00
Chair, Adam Style, Mahogany, Walnut, Silk, Late 1800s, 36 x 23 In., Pair . . . . *illus* 920.00
Chair, Alvar Aalto, Birch, Bentwood, Brown, White Cowhide, ICF, 29 x 24 In., Pair 2280.00
Chair, American Rococo, Attributed To Belter, Rosewood, Carved, Upholstered, c.1850, 43 In.. 3877.00
Chair, Andrew Willner, Walnut, Curved, Hand Carved, 1972, 42 x 23 In. 1680.00

Furniture, Candlestand, Oak, Bentwood Side, X-Shape Base, 39 ½ x 14 x 12 In.
$1760.00

Furniture, Canterbury, Walnut, Shell & Scroll Dividers, Inlaid, England, 1800s, 19 x 20 x 16 In.
$990.00

Furniture, Cellarette, Jamestown Furn., Drop Front, Carved, Opens To Bar, 56 x 18 x 7 In.
$840.00

F

Furniture, Chair, Adam Style, Mahogany, Walnut, Silk, Late 1800s, 36 x 23 In., Pair
$920.00

Furniture, Chair, Barrel Form, 11 Slats, Saddle Seat, Signed, Michigan Chair Co., 31 x 23 In.
$1200.00

Furniture, Chair, Campaign, Eastlake, Canvas, Pierced Arms, Folding, 1890s, 36 x 22 x 17 In.
$300.00

Furniture, Chair, Campeachy, Walnut, Carved, Leaf, Upholstered, 1850s, 42 x 23 x 28 In.
$3300.00

Chair, Anglo-Colonial, Rosewood, Carved Crest, V-Shape Splat, Cane Seat, Saber Legs, Arms, 36 In. 4080.00
Chair, Arched Ladder Back, Rush Seat, Painted, Shaped Arms, Stretcher, 16 ½ x 50 In....... 770.00
Chair, Arched Slats, Mule Ear Back Stiles, Williamson Co., Tennessee, 1800s, 33 x 17 In. 281.00
Chair, Arrow Back, Painted, Yellow, Bamboo Turned Legs, Stretcher Base, 24 In............ 269.00
Chair, Arrow Back, Salmon Paint, Rush Seat, Arms, Pa., 1820, 17 ½ In., Child's............ 660.00
Chair, Art Deco, Maple, Leather, 29 ¾ x 18 In....................................... 600.00
Chair, Arts & Crafts, 3 Legs, Triangle, Diamond Cutout Back, Leather Seat, 36 x 16 In....... 390.00
Chair, Arts & Crafts, 5 Vertical Back Slats, Leather Seat Cushion, Arms, 27 x 39 In., Pair..... 1200.00
Chair, Arts & Crafts, Mahogany, Leather, 3 Back Slats, Cushion, Arms, 39 x 29 x 24 In....... 474.00
Chair, Arts & Crafts, Oak, Fabric, Cutout Back Slat, Triangle Cushion, c.1910, 42 x 16 In..... 257.00
Chair, Arts & Crafts, Oak, Trapezoid Seat, 3 Back Slats, 41 x 16 x 17 ½ In. 652.00
Chair, Arts & Crafts, Rope Design Spindles, Upholstered Back, Seat, 24 x 44 In., Pair........ 720.00
Chair, Ash, 3 Spindles, Baluster Turnings, 2 Box Stretchers, Arms, 1600s, 45 In.. .... 2233.00
Chair, B. Mathsson, Pernilla, Lounge, Bentwood, Webbing, K. Mathsson, Sweden, 36 x 25 In.. 1140.00
Chair, Bamboo, Cane, Ivory Mounted, Arms, Chinese Export, 1800s, Pair................ 2813.00
Chair, Bamboo, Cane Seat, Upholstered Cushions, Stretchers, 35 x 22 In., Pair 270.00
Chair, Bamboo, Corner, Stick & Ball, 31 ½ x 18 x 18 In.................................. 150.00
Chair, Banister Back, Shaped Crest, Turned Posts, Replaced Rush Seat, c.1815, 39 In........ 147.00
Chair, Barrel Form, 11 Slats, Saddle Seat, Signed, Michigan Chair Co., 31 x 23 In. ..... *illus* 1200.00
Chair, Belter, Laminated Rosewood, Office.. 4313.00
Chair, Belter, Rosalie, Rosewood, Upholstered, c.1840-60, 36 ½ x 16 In., Pair.............. 1955.00
Chair, Belter, Rosewood, Carved, Upholstered Seat, c.1847-58, 36 x 18 In.. .... 345.00
Chair, Belter, Rosewood, Carved, Upholstered Seat, c.1847-58, 47 ½ x 18 In. 978.00
Chair, Bergere, Empire, Walnut, Gilt Bronze, Carved, Silk Upholstery, Closed Arms, 1800s, 32 x 33 In. 1180.00
Chair, Bergere, French Empire Style, Mahogany, Gilt Metal, Scrolled Crest, 39 x 36 In....... 329.00
Chair, Bergere, Fruitwood, Pinecone Finials, Carved Scrolls, Tapered Legs, c.1775.......... 12500.00
Chair, Bergere, George IV, Mahogany, Cane, Drop-In Seat, Closed Arms, c.1820, Pair........ 16250.00
Chair, Bergere, Louis XV, Beech, Upholstered, Carved, Gris-De-Trianon, Closed Arms, 39 In... 840.00
Chair, Bergere, Louis XV, Carved Scrolled Crest, Upholstered, Closed Arms, c.1910, 41 x 29 In. 837.00
Chair, Bergere, Louis XV, Downswept Crests, Painted, Padded, Closed Arms, 34 x 26 In., Pair . 1673.00
Chair, Bergere, Louis XV Style, Fruitwood, Padded Seat, Domed, Closed Arms, 33 In......... 1680.00
Chair, Bergere, Louis XV Style, Walnut, Needlepoint, Closed Arms, 17 x 24 x 23 In., Pair..... 3851.00
Chair, Bergere, Louis XVI, Gilt, Bow Knot Crest, Upholstered, Closed Arms, c.1910, 37 x 25 In. 2270.00
Chair, Bergere, Louis XVI, Gilt, Multicolored, Padded Back, Domed, 36 In., Pair........... 4080.00
Chair, Bergere, Louis XVI, Walnut, Padded, Upholstered, Closed Arms, 39 x 27 x 23 In., Pair.. 4481.00
Chair, Bergere, Louis XVI Style, Domed, Padded Back, Closed Arms, 39 x 26 ½ In.......... 1560.00
Chair, Bergere, Louis XVI Style, Multicolored, Padded Oval Back, Shell Crest, Closed Arms, 39 In., Pair 8100.00
Chair, Bergere, Louis XVI Style, Painted, Medallion Back, Cushion, Closed Arms, 36 x 26 In., Pair 708.00
Chair, Bergere, Regency, Anglo-Colonial, Rosewood, Shaped Crest, Closed Arms, 35 In....... 940.00
Chair, Bergere, Regency, Ebony, Inlaid Mahogany, Cane, Arched Back, Closed Arms, c.1815, Pair 31250.00
Chair, Bergere, Restauration, Mahogany, Padded Rectangular Back, Closed Arms, 38 In. 2160.00
Chair, Bergere, Restauration, Walnut, Padded Back, Cushion, Scrolling Closed Arms, 36 In... 5040.00
Chair, Bergere, William IV Style, Mahogany, Cane, Cushion, 36 In., Pair................. 4800.00
Chair, Biedermeier, Bird's-Eye Maple, Lamb's Tongue, Saber Legs, Italy, 37 x 20 In., Pair 767.00
Chair, Biedermeier, Walnut, Inlaid Back, Carved Flowers, Hand Grip, c.1890, 37 x 18 In. 448.00
Chair, Biedermeier, Walnut, Scrolled Cornice, Padded, Cabriole Legs, 17 ½ In., Pair 119.00
Chair, Birch, Upholstered, Golden Yellow, Olive Green, c.1925, 34 ½ In. 6000.00
Chair, Black Lacquer, Yoke Back, Flowers, Landscape, Chinese, 39 ½ x 28 x 25 In.......... 960.00
Chair, Black Walnut, Flower Medallion, Carved Stiles, Spindles, 42 x 20 In., Pair........... 1840.00
Chair, Brunschwig & Fils, Upholstered Back, Enclosed Arms, 34 ½ x 35 ½ x 38 In. 384.00
Chair, Bugatti, Wood, Parchment, Metal Inlay, Silk Tassels, Italy, c.1900, 45 In............ 18750.00
Chair, Burl, Leather, Upholstered, France, c.1930, 33 ¾ In.. .... 5000.00
Chair, Butterfly, Leather, Iron Frame, Bonet-Kurchan-Ferrari, 31 x 29 In. 295.00
Chair, Campaign, Beehive Finials, Bamboo, Upholstered, Cherry, Folding, 40 In............ 150.00
Chair, Campaign, Eastlake, Canvas, Pierced Arms, Folding, 1890s, 36 x 22 x 17 In...... *illus* 300.00
Chair, Campeachy, Carved Walnut Crest, Scroll Arms, Leather Upholstery, c.1850, 42 In.. .... 3450.00
Chair, Campeachy, Federal, Mahogany, Leather, Inlaid, Hinge Wings, Arms, c.1815, 41 x 15 In. 8295.00
Chair, Campeachy, Walnut, Carved, Leaf, Upholstered, 1850s, 42 x 23 x 28 In.......... *illus* 3300.00
Chair, Caqueteuse, Renaissance Revival, Fruitwood, Carved Panel Back, Arms, 47 x 23 In.... 329.00
Chair, Carved, Dragons, Phoenix, Mythological Creatures, Ivory Eyes, Chinese 575.00
Chair, Carved Waves, Flowers, Snakes, Upholstered Back, Seat, c.1750, 40 x 27 In., Pair 25000.00
Chair, Chinoiserie, Black Lacquer, Oval Back, Upholstered Seat, Claw Feet, 41 In., Pair...... 1072.00
Chair, Chinoiserie, Ebonized, Spindled Back, Apron, Padded Seat, Saber Legs, 26 ¾ In.. ..... 1200.00
Chair, Chinoiserie, Pagoda Crest, Bell Carvings, Padded, Bulbous Feet, 28 In.. .... 2880.00
Chair, Chippendale, Mahogany, Acanthus, Arms, Silk Damask Upholstery, c.1910, 38 In. 1058.00
Chair, Chippendale, Mahogany, Carved, Figured, New York, c.1770, 39 In., Pair............ 7500.00
Chair, Chippendale, Mahogany, Carved, Open Arms, Veneered Splat, 1900s, 44 x 32 In.. ..... 546.00

Chair, Chippendale, Mahogany, Carved, Shell Mounts, Phila., 1770, 40 In., Pair 22500.00
Chair, Chippendale, Mahogany, Carved Splat, Shepherd Crook Arms, 1700s, 38 x 26 In. 1265.00
Chair, Chippendale, Mahogany, Claw & Ball Feet, c.1780, 38 ½ In. .... *illus* 1000.00
Chair, Chippendale, Mahogany, Green Seat, 1900s, 38 x 22 In., Pair 236.00
Chair, Chippendale, Mahogany, Oak, Interlaced Splat, Slip Seat, c.1785, 37 In. 764.00
Chair, Chippendale, Mahogany, Ribbonback, Upholstered, 37 x 20 x 18 In. 200.00
Chair, Chippendale, Mahogany, Ribbonback, Upholstered Seat, Arms, 1900s, 39 In., Pair 294.00
Chair, Chippendale, Mahogany, Serpentine Crest, Open Splat, c.1790, 39 x 18 In., Pair 12650.00
Chair, Chippendale, Mahogany, Serpentine Crest Rail, Leaf Carved Ears, c.1780, 38 In.. ..... 600.00
Chair, Chippendale, Mahogany, Shaped Crest Rail, Flared Pierced Splat, c.1780, 38 ½ In.. ... 288.00
Chair, Chippendale, Mahogany, Shell Carved Crest, Openwork Splat, Claw Feet, c.1780, 39 In. 1175.00
Chair, Chippendale, Mahogany, Upholstered, Arms, Early 1900s, 39 x 27 x 24 In.. .... 175.00
Chair, Chippendale, Shell Carved Crest, Open Splat, Pa., 1700s, 40 In., Pair 4140.00
Chair, Chippendale, Silk Damask Upholstery, c.1950, 38 x 20 x 27 In., Pair 690.00
Chair, Chippendale, Walnut, Figured, Shell Carving, Mass., c.1750, 39 In., Pair 38750.00
Chair, Chippendale, Walnut, Openwork Back, Arms, Virginia, c.1785, 46 x 26 In.. .... 6325.00
Chair, Chippendale, Walnut, Poplar Seat, Arms, Late 1700s, 46 x 26 x 22 In. .... *illus* 6050.00
Chair, Chippendale, Walnut, Shell Carved Crest, Pierced Splat, England, 1700s, 38 x 22 In. .. 431.00
Chair, Chippendale, Walnut, Shell Carving, Philadelphia, 1755-95, 40 In. 11850.00
Chair, Chippendale Style, Mahogany, Cabriole Legs, Arms, 40 ¾ x 25 ½ x 19 In., Pair 354.00
Chair, Chippendale Transitional, Mahogany, Serpentine Crest Rail, Pierced Splat, 39 In. 478.00
Chair, Cincinnati Art Carved, Walnut, Daisies, Heart On High Back, 16 x 41 In. 510.00
Chair, Club, Art Deco, Rosewood Frame, Cube Design, Upholstered, 29 x 33 In., Pair. 2160.00
Chair, Club, Brown Leather, Scallop Crest, Brass Studs, Velvet Cushion, Ball Feet, c.1900. .... 518.00
Chair, Club, Edwardian, Mahogany, Leather Upholstery, Tufted Back, Scrolled Arms, 38 In. .. 1920.00
Chair, Club, Frank Lloyd Wright, Mahogany, Taliesin Edge, Hexagonal, 42 x 48 x 17 In. 3480.00
Chair, Club, Maroon Leather, Brass Tack Trim, c.1935, 33 In.. .... 146.00
Chair, Colonial Revival, Mahogany, Pierced Splat, Shell Carved Rail, c.1936, 41 In., Pair 660.00
Chair, Colonial Revival, Walnut, Plank Seat, Late 1800s, 46 x 23 x 16 In. .... *illus* 1320.00
Chair, Commode, Georgian, Mahogany, Serpentine Crest Rail, Upholstered, 41 x 22 x 18 In. . 717.00
Chair, Concrete, Iron, Grand Confort, Sans Confort, Stefan Zwicky, Swiss, 1980, 26 x 27 In. .. 25000.00
Chair, Continental, Carved Scroll, Upholstered, H-Stretcher, Arms, 39 ½ x 25 x 28 In. 385.00
Chair, Corner, Baroque Style, Walnut, Carved Maiden's Head, Griffins, Italy, 32 In., Pair 2160.00
Chair, Corner, Chippendale, Mahogany, 19th Century .... *illus* 600.00
Chair, Corner, Chippendale, Mahogany, Bench Made, Rolled Pillow Crest, c.1900, 32 In.. .... 460.00
Chair, Corner, Chippendale, Mahogany, Pierced Splats, Cross Stretchers, Claw Feet, 33 In. ... 823.00
Chair, Corner, Chippendale, Mahogany, Slip Seat, Marlboro Legs, 18th Century. 550.00
Chair, Corner, Chippendale, Oak, Pierced Slats, Rolled Arms, Leather, England, 1700s, 33 x 30 In. 748.00
Chair, Corner, Georgian, Carved, 29 In. 270.00
Chair, Corner, Georgian, Walnut, Stepped Crest, Out-Turned Grips, Slip Seat, 33 x 18 In. 805.00
Chair, Corner, Mahogany, Oak, Corner Claw & Ball Leg, Upholstered Seat, 1700s, 32 In. 646.00
Chair, Corner, Maple, Hickory, Oak Split Seat, Mid 20th Century, 31 ½ In. .... *illus* 330.00
Chair, Corner, Maple, Hickory, Oak Split Seat, Western No. Carolina, c.1950s, 32 In. 316.00
Chair, Corner, Mixed Woods, Rush Seat, Black Over Red Paint, Arms, c.1800, 27 ½ In. 323.00
Chair, Corner, Pillow Crest Rail, Slip Seat, New England, c.1805, 19 x 33 In. 1080.00
Chair, Corner, Queen Anne, Cedar, Pierced, Fluted Slats, Slip Seat, Scalloped Frame, c.1750 .. 4446.00
Chair, Corner, Queen Anne, Mahogany, Upholstered, 18th Century, 35 x 30 ½ x 24 In. 300.00
Chair, Corner, Rosewood, Carved Cherry Blossom Branches, Chinese, 32 x 17 In., Pair 1298.00
Chair, Cromwellian, Walnut, Barley Twist Arms, Legs, Rails, 39 x 23 In. 209.00
Chair, Curule, Rosewood, Upholstered, X-Frame, Cuff Feet, c.1825, 18 x 24 In.. .... 2115.00
Chair, Desk, Barrel Back, Swivel, Velvet Upholstery, Button Tufted, 46 In., Pair. 956.00
Chair, Desk, Oak, Cane Seat & Back, Casters, 35 ½ In.. .... 193.00
Chair, Desk, Oak, Pressed & Slatted Back, Brass Rosettes, Cane Seat, Casters, 47 In.. .... 440.00
Chair, Directoire, Mahogany, Exposed Frame, Arms, Carved Rosettes, Fans, Brass, 1800s, 35 In. 264.00
Chair, Eames, Fiberglass, Gray, Swivel Base, Splayed, Dowel Legs, Arms, 17 In.. .... 1384.00
Chair, Eames, La Fonda, Fiberglass, Wool Upholstery, Herman Miller, 19 x 32 In., Pair 420.00
Chair, Eames, LCW, Molded Ash Plywood Seat, Back, Frame, Herman Miller, 22 x 27 In.. .... 1560.00
Chair, Eames, Lounge, High Back, Head Rest, Herman Miller, 21 x 21 x 18 In. 2200.00
Chair, Eames, Lounge, Leather Seat, Walnut Shell, Herman Miller, c.1950, 33 In. 1541.00
Chair, Eames, Lounge, Rosewood, Plywood, Molded, Leather Upholstery, 33 x 34 x 30 In. 2400.00
Chair, Eastlake, Oak, Padded Back, Upholstered, Carved Armrests, 38 ½ x 22 x 27 In. 179.00
Chair, Edwardian, Leather Upholstery, Block Feet, Brass Tack Accents, c.1900, Pair 2400.00
Chair, Edwardian, Sheraton Style, Mahogany, Panel, Battle Of Nile, Arms, 32 ½ In.. .... 1920.00
Chair, Edwardian, Sheraton Style, Parcel Gilt, Ebonized, Greek Key, Arms, 34 ½ In., Pair 2280.00
Chair, Eero Saarinen, Tulip, Florence Knoll, 31 ½ x 26 In., Pair 228.00
Chair, Egg, Arne Jacobsen, Model 3317, Black, Fritz Hansen, c.1960, 42 x 34 In.. .... 3960.00
Chair, Elizabethan Revival, Oak, Tall Back, Tapestry Panel, Box Stretcher, 50 In.. .... 840.00

Furniture, Chair, Chippendale, Mahogany, Claw & Ball Feet, c.1780, 38 ½ In.
$1000.00

Furniture, Chair, Chippendale, Walnut, Poplar Seat, Arms, Late 1700s, 46 x 26 x 22 In.
$6050.00

Furniture, Chair, Colonial Revival, Walnut, Plank Seat, Late 1800s, 46 x 23 x 16 In.
$1320.00

Furniture, Chair, Corner, Chippendale, Mahogany, 19th Century
$600.00

Furniture, Chair, Corner, Maple, Hickory, Oak Split Seat, Mid 20th Century, 31 ½ In.
$330.00

Furniture, Chair, Federal, Shieldback, Upholstered, Philadelphia, 1810, 39 x 21 In., Pair
$2420.00

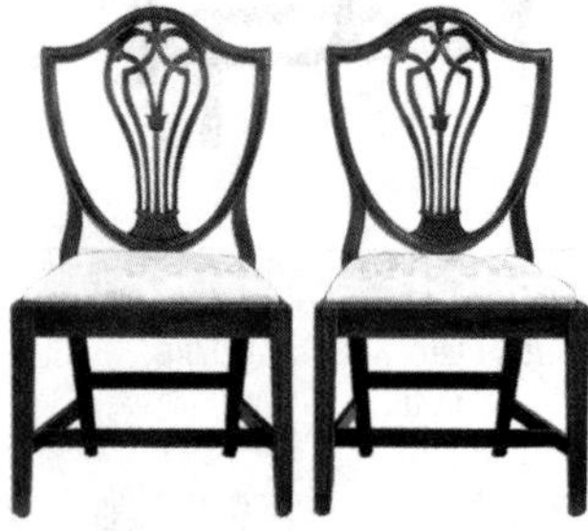

Shaker Chairs
Some Shaker chairs have a number impressed on the top of the front leg or back post. This indicated where the chair belonged. Each room had a number.

Chair, Elm, Lacquered, Horseshoe Back, Chinese, 18th Century, 35 x 36 In., Pair 885.00
Chair, Elm, Open Yoke Back, Arms, Chinese, 1800s, 36 In., Pair 299.00
Chair, Elm, Open Yoke Back, Black, Gold Symbols, Arms, Chinese, 1800s, 45 In., Pair 299.00
Chair, Empire, Mahogany, Carved, Scrolled Handholds, Upholstered, Arms, France, 37 In. 528.00
Chair, Empire Style, Sycamore, Brass Medallion, Downswept Arms, 31 In., Pair 9000.00
Chair, Exposed Frame, Oval Back, Carving, Fluted Legs, Upholstered, Arms, 38 In., Pair 646.00
Chair, Fauteuil, Charles X, Mahogany, Arched Scrolled Top Rail, Upholstered, 37 x 22 In.. . . . . 837.00
Chair, Fauteuil, Directoire, Cane, Molded Back, White Paint, Curved Arms, 34 ½ In. 1880.00
Chair, Fauteuil, Directoire, Mahogany, Fruitwood, Open Upholstered Arms, 35 x 21 x 19 In., Pair 2510.00
Chair, Fauteuil, Empire Style, Gilt Brass, Lion's Mask Open Upholstered Arms, 30 In., Pair . . . 2350.00
Chair, Fauteuil, Empire Style, Mahogany, Uprights, Open Upholstered Arms, 35 In., Pair 1800.00
Chair, Fauteuil, Louis XIV Style, Mahogany, Upholstered, Open Arms, 44 ½ In., Pair 4560.00
Chair, Fauteuil, Louis XV, Beech, Carved Crest, Rail, Open Upholstered Arms, 36 x 26 In., Pair 805.00
Chair, Fauteuil, Louis XV, Fruitwood, Cane Back, Flower Carved Crest, Open Arms, 35 x 23 In. 239.00
Chair, Fauteuil, Louis XV, Fruitwood, Cane Back, Seat, Open Upholstered Arms, 37 In. 2300.00
Chair, Fauteuil, Louis XV, Fruitwood, Cartouche Back, Open Upholstered Arms, 35 In., Pair . . 568.00
Chair, Fauteuil, Louis XV, Walnut, Cane, Carved Crest, Open Upholstered Arms, 34 ½ In., Pair 852.00
Chair, Fauteuil, Louis XV Style, Fruitwood, Open Upholstered Arms, 1800s, 32 ½ In. 345.00
Chair, Fauteuil, Louis XV Style, Fruitwood, Padded Back, Open Upholstered Arms, 34 x 25 In. 531.00
Chair, Fauteuil, Louis XV Style, Oak, Flower Crest, Open Upholstered Arms, 38 ½ In., Pair . . . 2640.00
Chair, Fauteuil, Louis XV Style, Walnut, Carved, Shaped, Open Upholstered Arms, 40 In., Pair 2400.00
Chair, Fauteuil, Louis XVI, Gilt, Carved Crest, Open Upholstered Arms, 42 In. 132.00
Chair, Fauteuil, Louis XVI Style, Carved, Open Upholstered Arms, 35 In. 240.00
Chair, Fauteuil, Louis XVI Style, Gilt, Carved Frame, Open Upholstered Arms, 39 x 24 In., Pair 600.00
Chair, Fauteuil, Louis XVI Style, Gilt, Open Upholstered Arms, Late 1800s, 36 In., Pair 2040.00
Chair, Fauteuil, Louis XVI Style, Multicolored, Open Upholstered Arms, 34 In., Pair. 1560.00
Chair, Fauteuil, Neoclassical, Mahogany, Shell & Scroll Crest, Open Upholstered Arms, 37 In. 1680.00
Chair, Fauteuil, Regency, Fruitwood, Cane Back, Seat, Open Upholstered Arms, 39 x 24 In., Pair 717.00
Chair, Federal, Inlaid Walnut, Carved, Geometric Design, c.1810, 34 x 19 In. 325.00
Chair, Federal, Mahogany, Carved Back, Upholstered Seat, Rhode Island, c.1790, 39 In., Pair. 8750.00
Chair, Federal, Mahogany, Shieldback, Arched Crest, Prince Of Wales Plum, 38 In., Pair. 5750.00
Chair, Federal, Mahogany, Square Back, Carved Fans, Upholstered Seat, c.1815, 34 In., Pair . 4113.00
Chair, Federal, Maple, Arched Crest, Pierced Vase Splat, H-Stretcher, 37 x 21 In.. . . . . 620.00
Chair, Federal, Pine, Stenciled Crest, Ears, Yellow Ground, Bamboo-Carved Legs, Arms, 34 In. 575.00
Chair, Federal, Shieldback, Upholstered, Philadelphia, 1810, 39 x 21 In., Pair . . . . *illus* 2420.00
Chair, Federal, Upholstered Seat, Carved Bowknot, New York, c.1807, 33 In., Pair 3318.00
Chair, Figured Veneered Tablet Back, Carved Stiles, Saber Legs, 31 x 18 In.. . . . . 1495.00
Chair, Finn Juhl, Teak, Bentwood Back, c.1945, 29 x 20 In., Pair 115.00
Chair, French Provincial, Tall Padded Back, Woven Lattice Upholstery, 45 ½ In. 881.00
Chair, Fritz Hansen, Laminated Walnut, Herman Miller, Denmark 365.00
Chair, Fritz Henningsen, Oak, Leather, Black, Arms, c.1935, 44 In. 43750.00
Chair, Fruitwood, Gilt, Domed Back, Padded, Cabriole Legs, Upholstered, 36 In., Pair 4080.00
Chair, Fruitwood, Writing Arm, Seat Swirls, Tripod Base, France, 19 ½ In. 474.00
Chair, G. Harcourt, Plastic, Leather Upholstery, Swivel Base, Artifort, 27 x 28 In., Pair. 2280.00
Chair, G. Mulhauser, Desk, Swirled Wood Arms, White Seat, Plycraft, c.1965, 27 x 23 In. 1320.00
Chair, G. Nakashima, Walnut, Slat Back, Solid Seat, Arms, c.1958, 31 x 30 In. 5700.00
Chair, G. Nelson, Steel, Enamel, Wood, Cushions, Orange, Herman Miller, 1960s, 27 x 29 In. . 450.00
Chair, G. Stickley, Cube, Spindles, Drop-In Spring Seat, 29 x 26 x 27 ½ In. 4500.00
Chair, G. Stickley, Fruitwood, Metal, Rush Seat, 39 x 16 ¾ x 16 In. 8400.00
Chair, G. Stickley, Morris, No. 332, Spring Seat, Black Leather, 41 x 31 x 38 In. 3360.00
Chair, G. Stickley, Morris, No. 336, Spring Seat, Bow Arms, 40 ½ x 36 x 30 In. 8400.00
Chair, G. Stickley, Morris, No. 369, Mahogany, 16 Spindles Under Arms, 40 x 33 x 38 In. 6000.00
Chair, G. Stickley, No. 318, 5 Vertical Slats, Drop-In Leather Seat, Arms, 37 x 27 In., Pair 1800.00
Chair, G. Stickley, No. 349, 3 Slats, Leather Seat, 38 x 26 x 22 In. . . . . *illus* 1130.00
Chair, G. Stickley, No. 349 ½A, Ladder Back, Rush Seat, Decal, c.1901, 38 x 26 In. . . . . . . *illus* 2640.00
Chair, G. Stickley, No. 352A, Ladder Back, Split Cane, Arms, 40 x 23 x 19 In., Pair 7200.00
Chair, G. Stickley, No. 354, 5 Vertical Slats, V-Back, Leather Seat, Signed, 35 x 19 In. 840.00
Chair, G. Stickley, No. 354 ½, 5 Vertical Slats, V-Back, Arms, Signed, 36 x 26 x 21 In. 610.00
Chair, G. Stickley, No. 361, Leather Seat & Back, Wheels, Label, Decal, 35 x 27 ½ In. 2100.00
Chair, G. Stickley, No. 394, H-Back, Drop-In Seat, 40 x 17 x 16 In. 265.00
Chair, G. Stickley, No. 394, H-Shape Back, Drop-In Seat, Flowers, 40 x 16 ½ In. 600.00
Chair, G. Stickley, No. 396 ½, Ladder Back, 3 Slats, Leather Seat, Signed, 17 x 36 In. 210.00
Chair, G. Stickley, No. 1291, Leather, Wood, Rabbit Ears, 2 Back Slats, 36 x 18 In. 1920.00
Chair, G. Stickley, No. 1299, Thornden, Ladder Back, Rush Seats, 35 x 17 x 16 In., Pair. 1800.00
Chair, G. Stickley, No. 2578, Broad Slat, Leather Seat, Marked, 29 In. 420.00
Chair, G. Stickley, Oak, Leather, H-Back, c.1912, 40 ¾ In. 267.00
Chair, G. Stickley, Willow, Loose Cushions, 42 x 31 ½ x 31 In. . . . . *illus* 2400.00

Chair, G. Ulrich, French Oak, Wool Cushions, Sculpted, 30 ½ x 25 ½ x 26 In., Pair 4200.00
Chair, Gainsborough, George III, Mahogany, Domed, Padded Back, Seat, Arms, 41 In. 960.00
Chair, Gainsborough, George III, Mahogany, Padded, Square Legs, 40 In.. . . . . 9600.00
Chair, George I, Walnut, Mahogany, Shepherd Crook Open Arms, 41 x 24 In., Pair 2530.00
Chair, George II, Mahogany, Carved, Upholstered, Cabriole Legs, c.1755 . . . . 31258.00
Chair, George II, Mahogany, Carved, Upholstered Back, Padded Arms, c.1755, Pair 74500.00
Chair, George II, Mahogany, Carved Bird Designs, Upholstered Seat, Arms, c.1890, 40 In. 1920.00
Chair, George II, Mahogany, Carved Splat, Legs, Upholstered Seat, c.1730. . . . . 3125.00
Chair, George II, Mahogany, Walnut, Needlework Drop-In Seat, Giles Grendy, c.1740 . . . . 18750.00
Chair, George II, Walnut, Escutcheon Backrest, Drop-In Oval Seat, Cabriole Legs, c.1735 . . . . 40625.00
Chair, George II, Walnut, Needlework Upholstery, Carved Seat Rail Mask, c.1745. . . . . 43750.00
Chair, George II, Walnut, Silk Upholstered Drop-In Seat, c.1740, Pair. 12500.00
Chair, George III, Chinese Influence, Mahogany, Pierced Backrest, Padded Seat 12500.00
Chair, George III, Chippendale, Gilt, Oval Back, Silk Upholstery, c.1775, Pair. 11250.00
Chair, George III, Mahogany, Backswept Reed Legs, Arms, Slip Seat, c.1770, 38 x 17 In. 633.00
Chair, George III, Mahogany, Carved, Leaf Crest Rail, Gothic Pierced Splat, 1700s, 37 In. 1528.00
Chair, George III, Mahogany, Carved Splat, Chain Link, Urn, Arms, c.1775, Pair 12500.00
Chair, George III, Mahogany, Family Crest, Pierced Backrest, Arms, c.1765. . . . . 5000.00
Chair, George III, Mahogany, Needlework Seat, Perching Owl, 38 ½ In., Pair 960.00
Chair, George III, Mahogany, Pierced Splat, Overupholstered Silk Seat, 1700s, 38 In. 294.00
Chair, George III, Mahogany, Serpentine, Chamfered Marlboro Front, Padded, 35 In. 236.00
Chair, George III, Mahogany, Serpentine Back, Upholstered, Downswept Arms, 17 ½ x 25 In.. 830.00
Chair, George III, Mahogany, Shieldback, Pierced, Carved Splat, Urn, Swags, 37 In.. . . . . 660.00
Chair, George III, Mahogany, Upholstered, Chamfered Square Legs, 38 ¾ In.. . . . . 3240.00
Chair, George III, Mahogany, Yoke-Form Crest, Overupholstered, 18 ½ In.. . . . . 593.00
Chair, George III, Open Shield Backrest, Painted Leaves, Scroll Arms, c.1820, 17 In. 1007.00
Chair, George III, Plume Open Back, Painted, Damask Upholstery, c.1950, 39 x 23 In., Pair. . 2868.00
Chair, George III Style, Domed Crest, Padded Seat, Shaped Apron, Arms, England 480.00
Chair, George III Style, Inlaid Mahogany, Painted Coat Of Arms Backrest, Arms, Pair 12500.00
Chair, George III Style, Mahogany, Leather, Flared Wings, 38 x 22 x 19 In.. . . . . 1793.00
Chair, George III Style, Upholstered, Leaf Carved Cabriole Legs, 23 x 19 In. 948.00
Chair, Georgian, Mahogany, Rolled Crest Rail, Pierced Splat, Cabriole Legs, 38 In., Pair 4025.00
Chair, Georgian, Mahogany, Swag & Tassel Crest, Eagle Heads, Floral Stiles, 1800s, 39 In. . . . 1645.00
Chair, Georgian, Walnut, Padded Back, Seat, Serpentine Arms, Cabriole Legs, 41 ½ In.. . . . . . 1348.00
Chair, Georgian Style, Mahogany, Leaf Carved Crest, Pierced Splat, Shaped Arms, 38 In.. . . . . 748.00
Chair, Georgian Style, Mahogany, Leather, Overstuffed Seat, Padded Arms, 38 x 26 x 24 In. . . 649.00
Chair, Georgian Style, Mahogany, Upholstered, Padded, Cabriole Legs, Arms, 39 x 29 In. 598.00
Chair, Georgian Style, Upholstered Back, Arms, Seat, Carved Cabriole Legs, 38 ½ In.. . . . . 180.00
Chair, Georgian Style, Walnut, Hand Holds, Cabriole Legs, Paw Feet, Arms, 18 In. 3081.00
Chair, Giancarlo Piretti, Plastic, Aluminum, Folding, One Piece, c.1970, 29 In. 60.00
Chair, Gilt, Curved Beaded Rails, Swags, Upholstered, Cream Paint, Italy, c.1790, 35 x 29 In., Pair 4063.00
Chair, Gothic Revival, Carved Quatrefoil Crest, Turned Stiles, Upholstered, c.1850, 55 In.. . . . . 390.00
Chair, Gothic Revival, Cast Iron, Square Back, Quatrefoils, Honeycomb Seat, Arms, 1800s, 35 In. 2937.00
Chair, Gothic Revival, Oak, Carved Owls, Glass Eyes, Trapezoid, c.1880, 38 x 19 In.. . . . . 2530.00
Chair, Gothic Revival, Rosewood, Pierced Trefoil Crest, Bobbin Stiles, 45 ½ In.. . . . . 2350.00
Chair, Gothic Revival, Trefoil Pierced Crest, Shaped Splat, Padded, 34 In., Pair 3360.00
Chair, Gothic Revival, Walnut, Carved, Padded Arms, Seat, c.1850, 58 x 23 x 22 In.. . . . . . *illus* 2000.00
Chair, Gothic Revival, Walnut, Upholstered, Pierced, Klismos Legs, Arms, 49 x 25 x 32 In. . . . 6250.00
Chair, Grotto, Gilt, Gesso, Carved, Seahorse, Shells, Venice, c.1895, 34 x 17 In., Pair 10350.00
Chair, Grotto, Gilt, Gesso, Carved Sea Creatures, Shells, Arms, Venice, c.1895, 31 x 22 In. 5500.00
Chair, Harden, 5 Back Slats, Leather Seat Cushion, Arms, 28 x 39 In. 300.00
Chair, Hardwood, Leather, Rosehead Nails, Curule Legs, 18th Century, 24 In.. . . . . 352.00
Chair, Hardwood, Slatted Back, Rolled Arms, Casters, 43 In.. . . . . 88.00
Chair, Heal & Son, Oak, Arms, c.1920, 39 ½ In., Pair 2000.00
Chair, Hepplewhite, Carved, Marquetry, Shieldback, Striped Upholstered Seat, 38 x 18 In.. . . . 230.00
Chair, Hepplewhite, Shield Shape Back, Vertical Splats, Padded, Cabriole Legs, 39 In. 295.00
Chair, Heywood, Wicker, Rolled Arms, Ball & Stick Detail, 37 x 28 In.. . . . . 595.00
Chair, Hickory, Arms, c.1930, 36 x 24 In. 450.00
Chair, Horn, Long Curved Horns Form Back & Arms, Upholstered Seat, c.1880, 36 In.. . . . . 323.00
Chair, Hunzinger, Walnut, Carved Spindles, 34 In. 374.00
Chair, Ice Cream, Wire, Wooden Arms, Heart Shape Back, 40 In.. . . . . 413.00
Chair, Invalid, Mahogany, Hinged Arms, Handles, Leg Extension, Folding, c.1875, 34 In. 857.00
Chair, Italian Neoclassical, Ivory Paint, Lyre Splat, Fluted Stiles, 34 In., Pair 900.00
Chair, Italian Renaissance, Walnut, Carved Flowers, Back, Stretcher, 54 x 32 x 17 In.. . . . . 3585.00
Chair, J. Adnet, Wood, Leather, Burnt Orange, Arms, 1950s, 27 In.. . . . . 17500.00
Chair, J. Hoffmann, Bentwood Back, Upholstered, Cafe Fledermaus, c.1907, 22 x 30 In., Pair. 1440.00
Chair, J. Hoffmann, Sitzmachine, No. 670, Beech, Adjustable, Bentwood, Arms, 40 ½ In.. . . . . 23750.00

Furniture, Chair, G. Stickley, No. 349, 3 Slats, Leather Seat, 38 x 26 x 22 In.
$1130.00

Furniture, Chair, G. Stickley, No. 349 ½A, Ladder Back, Rush Seat, Decal, c.1901, 38 x 26 In.
$2640.00

Furniture, Chair, G. Stickley, Willow, Loose Cushions, 42 x 31 ½ x 31 In.
$2400.00

F

Furniture, Chair, Gothic Revival, Walnut, Carved, Padded Arms, Seat, c.1850, 58 x 23 x 22 In.
$2000.00

Furniture, Chair, Lolling, Chippendale, Mahogany, Carved, Upholstered, Boston, c.1770, 43 In.
$59375.00

Furniture, Chair, Lounge, Walnut, Carved Roses, Incised, Footrest, 1890, 42 x 28 In.
$110.00

Chair, Jacobean, Oak, Carved Back, Stretcher Base, Late 17th Century, 40 In. 4446.00
Chair, Jean-Michael Frank, Oak, Upholstered Seat, c.1930, 33 In., Pair 32500.00
Chair, Kem Weber, Wood Frame, Leather Upholstery, Airline, c.1934, 31 x 25 In., Pair 22800.00
Chair, Kita, Lounge, Nickel-Plated Steel Frame, Upholstered, Swivel Base, 72 x 31 In. 875.00 to 1188.00
Chair, L. & J.G. Stickley, Leather Seat, Back, Tacks, Handcraft Decal, 39 x 18 In. 450.00
Chair, L. & J.G. Stickley, No. 420, Oilcloth Upholstery, Arms, 42 x 31 ½ x 29 In. 1080.00
Chair, L. & J.G. Stickley, No. 1313, Wood, Leather, 3 Slats, 16 x 37 In. 450.00
Chair, Ladder Back, 4 Slats, Baluster Arms, Rush Seat, Delaware Valley, 48 x 20 x 15 In. 325.00
Chair, Ladder Back, 4 Slats, Mushroom Cap Holds, Woven Seat, Black Paint, N.E., c.1740 .... 1872.00
Chair, Ladder Back, 5 Slats, Old Yellow Paint, Delaware Valley, c.1770 .... 305.00
Chair, Ladder Back, 5 Slats, Rush Seat, Arms, Oxblood Paint, Delaware Valley, c.1770 .... 9900.00
Chair, Ladder Back, Ash, Hickory, Painted, Ball Finials, 4 Curved Slats, Arms, 49 In. 588.00
Chair, Ladder Back, Maple, 3 Slats, Ball & Ring Stretcher, Late 1700s, 27 In., Child's 3978.00
Chair, Ladder Back, Maple, 5 Slats, Pa., Mid 18th Century 1170.00
Chair, Ladder Back, Maple, Turned Arms, Upholstered Seat, 1900s, 35 x 34 In. 230.00
Chair, Ladder Back, Oak, Horizontal Splats, Arms, Straight Stiles, Child's, 25 In. 177.00
Chair, Ladder Back, Oak, Split Seat, 4 Slats, Turned Finials, Shaped Arms, 42 In. 173.00
Chair, Limbert, 3 Back Slat, Brown Leather Cushion, Arms, Branded, 37 x 27 In. 420.00
Chair, Limbert, 5 Vertical Slats, Upholstered, Arms, Marked 220.00
Chair, Limbert, No. 837, 2 Vertical Slats, Leather Seat, Arms, Signed, 43 x 27 x 24 In. 510.00
Chair, Limbert, No. 901, Wide Slat, Signed, 37 x 17 x 17 In. 240.00
Chair, Lolling, Chippendale, Mahogany, Carved, Upholstered, Boston, c.1770, 43 In. ..... *illus* 59375.00
Chair, Lolling, Federal, Mahogany, Serpentine Crest, Outswept Arms, Stretcher, 40 x 27 In. ... 177.00
Chair, Lolling, Federal, Walnut, Serpentine Crest, H-Stretchers, Early 1900s, 42 x 28 In. 561.00
Chair, Lolling, Sheraton Style, Open Serpentine Arms, Brocade Upholstery, 48 In. 259.00
Chair, Louis Philippe, Mahogany, Domed, Downswept Crest, Padded, Tub Shape, 32 In. 1440.00
Chair, Louis XIII Style, Oak, Padded, Domed Back, H-Stretchers, 42 ½ In., Pair 840.00
Chair, Louis XIII Style, Walnut, Upholstered, Padded, Domed Flat Back, 44 ½ In. 2880.00
Chair, Louis XIV Style, Walnut, Carved, Nailed, Needlework, Overstuffed Seat, 46 x 25 x 22 In. 590.00
Chair, Louis XV, Fruitwood, Cane Back, Molded Frame, Cushions, Arms, 33 ¾ In. 1800.00
Chair, Louis XV, Fruitwood, Carved, Damask Upholstery, Cabriole Legs, Arms, c.1900, 35 x 25 In. 227.00
Chair, Louis XV, Fruitwood, Carved Crest, Upholstered, Scroll Feet, Arms, 1800s, 34 x 23 In. .. 269.00
Chair, Louis XV, Gilt, Velvet Upholstery, Curved Back, 35 In., Pair 2400.00
Chair, Louis XV, Gray Frame, Carved Flowers, Silk Upholstery, c.1750, 35 x 21 In., Pair 7500.00
Chair, Louis XV, Mahogany, Beige Paint, Striped Upholstery, c.1890, 49 x 27 In., Pair 4600.00
Chair, Louis XV, Walnut, Carved, Brown Padded Seat, Back, Folding, c.1750, 32 x 27 In. 10625.00
Chair, Louis XV, Walnut, Scalloped Floral Crest Rail, Arms, Mid 1700s, 37 ½ In., Pair 5640.00
Chair, Louis XV Style, Beech, Carved, Pierced Backrest, c.1895, 35 In., Pair 8125.00
Chair, Louis XV Style, Carved Crest, Seat Rail & Knees, Velvet Upholstery, 1800s, 36 In. 118.00
Chair, Louis XV Style, Fruitwood, Shaped Padded Back, Flower Crest, 37 In., Pair 2040.00
Chair, Louis XVI, Beech, Padded, Cushion, Fluted Frieze, Peg Feet, 32 ¾ In. 1800.00
Chair, Louis XVI, Carved Frame, Rosettes, Upholstered Back, Seat, Fluted Legs, 38 In. 216.00
Chair, Louis XVI, Fruitwood, Padded, Upholstered, Open Arms, 38 x 22 ½ In., Pair 649.00
Chair, Louis XVI, Gilt, Medallion Back, Open Arms, 37 x 22 ½ x 19 ½ In. 1180.00
Chair, Louis XVI, Gray, Carved Frame, Oval Back, Upholstered, c.1770, 39 x 24 In., Pair 10000.00
Chair, Louis XVI, Gray Paint, Carved Frame, Upholstered, M. Baudoin, c.1780, 35 x 22 In. 4375.00
Chair, Louis XVI Style, Fruitwood, Fluted Legs, Striped Silk Upholstery, 1900s, 28 x 18 In. 143.00
Chair, Louis XVI Style, Fruitwood, Molded Back, Fluted Legs, c.1925, 29 x 21 In., Child's 179.00
Chair, Louis XVI Style, Fruitwood, Padded, Square Legs, 34 In. 600.00
Chair, Louis XVI Style, Gilt, Padded, Cabriole Legs, 42 In. 2640.00
Chair, Louis XVI Style, Gilt, Padded, Rope Carved Frame, 40 In., Pair 1000.00
Chair, Louis XVI Style, Gilt, Padded, Rope Carved Frame, Fluted Legs, 40 In. 3120.00
Chair, Lounge, Upholstered, Flower Print, Late 1950s, 27 x 30 x 33 ¾ In. 598.00
Chair, Lounge, Walnut, Carved Roses, Incised, Footrest, 1890, 42 x 28 In. .... *illus* 110.00
Chair, Lounge, Walnut, Mechanical, 41 In. 1250.00
Chair, Lounge, Wood, Horn Shape Backrest, Striped Upholstery, Baker Furniture, 43 x 21 In. . 2160.00
Chair, M. Bailey, Lounge, Dark Stained Wood Frame, Upholstered, 27 x 30 In., Pair 2640.00
Chair, M. De Lucchi, Enameled, Wood, Metal, Memphis Milano Co., Italy, 1983, 35 In. 860.00
Chair, Mahogany, Arched Crest, Tapered Legs, England, 1800s, 37 x 20 In., Pair 460.00
Chair, Mahogany, Baluster Splats, Hickory Chair Co., 1900s, 35 x 18 In., Pair 179.00
Chair, Mahogany, Carved, Overupholstered, Cabriole Legs, Arms, 1700s 1185.00
Chair, Mahogany, Carved Dolphins, Arms 275.00
Chair, Mahogany, Carved Shield, Leaves, Endless Loop Design, Red Seat, Arms, 1800s, 37 In., Pair 265.00
Chair, Mahogany, Curved Splat, New York, c.1830, 34 x 19 In., Pair 345.00
Chair, Mahogany, Harp Back, Upholstered Seat, Paw Feet, N.Y., c.1815, 33 In., Pair 236500.00
Chair, Mahogany, Laminated, Carved, Pierced Back, Upholstered, Casters, Arms 1000.00
Chair, Mahogany, Marquetry, Twisted Columns, Arms, 50 x 24 x 19 In. 460.00

Chair, Mahogany, Pocahontas, Carved Figures, Animal-Head Arms, 41 x 27 x 22 In. 3680.00
Chair, Mahogany, Porcelain Plaque, Mother-Of-Pearl Inlay, Arms, Chinese, c.1900, 40 x 25 In. 1003.00
Chair, Maple, Ash, Banister Back, Scalloped Crest Rail, Rush Seat, 49 In. . . . . *illus* 850.00
Chair, Maple, Ash, Banister Back, Scalloped Crest Rail, Turned Stretchers, Arms, 49 In.. . . . . . 999.00
Chair, Maple, Birch, Banister Back, Rayed Fan Crest, Box Stretcher, 43 In. 3163.00
Chair, Maple, Leather Seat, Back, Spoon Splats, Rhode Island, c.1740, 40 In., Pair 14220.00
Chair, Marco Zanini, Fiberglass, Black, Arms, c.1986, 34 x 39 x 35 In.. . . . . 1800.00
Chair, Mario Bellini, Fiberglass Shell, Rubber Feet, Upholstered, c.1979, 33 In., Pair. 720.00
Chair, Mario Sabo, Lounge, Fiberglass Shell, Upholstered, Cutouts, c.1969, 24 x 36 In.. . . . . . 900.00
Chair, Mask & Scroll Carved Slats, Scrolled Ears, Split Spindles, Open Arms, 43 x 22 In.. . . . . 2415.00
Chair, McKinley, Leather, Spindle Sides, Phoenix Chair Co., 35 x 29 In., Pair 1800.00
Chair, McKinley, Leather Back, Seat, Slat Sides, Phoenix Chair Co., 29 x 35 In. 120.00
Chair, Meeks, Stanton Hall, Rosewood, Upholstered, Arms, Mid 1800s, 45 In., Pair 7475.00
Chair, Memento Mori, Fantasy, Seated Human Skeleton Shape, White Paint, 52 x 22 In.. . . . . 4406.00
Chair, Metal, Painted Geometric Shapes, c.1976, 43 ⅜ In. 34600.00
Chair, Milo Baughman, Black Vinyl Upholstery, Wood Legs, 30 x 27 In., Pair. 2640.00
Chair, Mixed Hardwood, Banister Back, Scalloped Crest Rail, Finials, Rush Seat, 43 In.. . . . . . 235.00
Chair, Mixed Wood, Arched Ladder Back, Rush Seat, Turned Urn Finials, Arms, 47 In.. . . . . . . 110.00
Chair, Mixed Wood, Banister Back, Shaped Crest, Red Paint, Rush Seat, 43 In., Pair 1116.00
Chair, Mixed Wood, Ladder Back, Red Paint, Rush Seat, Mid 1800s, 25 In., Child's 382.00
Chair, Moorish, Bone, Mother-Of-Pearl Inlay, Upholstered Seat, Arms, c.1900, 42 In., Pair . . . 633.00
Chair, Morris, Leather Cushion, Arch Seat, Bow Arms, 32 x 38 In. 1320.00
Chair, Morris, Oak, Corbel Supports, 5 Side Slats, Bent Arms, c.1907, 24 x 37 In.. . . . . 948.00
Chair, N. Ditzel, Molded Cutout Back, Turquoise, Fiberglass, Plastic, 22 x 31 In., Pair. 960.00
Chair, Napoleon III, Multicolored, Ebonized, Trefoil Pendants, Box Stretcher, Gilt, 32 In.. . . . . 420.00
Chair, Neoclassical, Fruitwood, U-Back, Carved, Strapwork Seat, Arms, Italy, c.1820 . . . . 889.00
Chair, Neoclassical, Mahogany, Arched Crest, Openwork Splat, Slip Seat, 37 x 20 In.. . . . . 418.00
Chair, Neoclassical, Mahogany, Curved Crest, Lyre Splat, Continental, 37 In., Pair. 2640.00
Chair, Neoclassical, Painted, Pumpkin Velvet Upholstery, Medallion Back, Italy, 34 In.. . . . . . . 657.00
Chair, Nutting, No. 492, Ladder Back, Arms, Rush Seat, Signed, 44 ½ In. 355.00
Chair, Nutting, Windsor, No. 301, Brace Back. 358.00
Chair, Nutting, Windsor, No. 303, Brace Back, Tapered Rhode Island Turnings, Label 358.00
Chair, Nutting, Windsor, No. 309, Comb Back, Mass. . . . . 248.00 to 385.00
Chair, Nutting, Windsor, No. 309, Fanback, Pa., Turnings, Label 220.00
Chair, Oak, 9 Spindles, Curved Back, Plank Seat, c.1900, 36 x 30 In.. 474.00
Chair, Oak, 11 Spindles, Scrolled, Pressed, 39 In.. . . . . 59.00
Chair, Oak, Cushion, Solid Back, Open Arms, Gordon Russel, c.1927, 38 In.. . . . . 5625.00
Chair, Oak, Rattan Sides, Back, Seat, Arms, Wilhelm Schmidt, c.1902, 29 In., Pair. 7250.00
Chair, Oak, Rush Seat, Square Legs, England, 1920s, 38 ¾ In.. . . . . 250.00
Chair, Oak, Upholstered, Square Legs, Arms, England, c.1910, 36 In.. 1625.00
Chair, Ottoman, Bergere, Louis XVI Style, Padded, Domed Back, Leaf Crest, 38 x 16 In.. . . . . . . 2160.00
Chair, Ottoman, Eames, Lounge, Leather, Plycraft Furniture, 1960s 275.00
Chair, Ottoman, G. Nakashima, Walnut, Cushion, Arms, 30 x 24 x 31 In.. . . . . *illus* 3360.00
Chair, Ottoman, G. Nakashima, Walnut Arms, 31 x 21 & 11 In.. . . . . 4200.00
Chair, Ottoman, G. Nelson, Coconut, Upholstered, Herman Miller, c.1955, 32 In.. . . . . 6250.00
Chair, Ottoman, Louis XV Style, Padded, Domed, Cushion, Cabriole Legs, 38 In. 1320.00
Chair, Ottoman, Plywood, Leather Upholstery, 32 x 33 x 34 In. 4688.00
Chair, Ottoman, Wegner, Teak, Adjustable, Orange Upholstery, 1954, 34 x 49 In.. . . . . 7500.00
Chair, P. Friedberg, Hand Shape, Gold, c.1964, 36 x 20 In. 14400.00
Chair, P. Tuttle, Super Z, Cherry, Stainless Steel, c.1996, 20 x 23 In.. . . . . 2400.00
Chair, Padded, Upholstered, Acanthine Carved Arms, Cabriole Legs, Peg Feet, 48 In., Pair. . . . 4560.00
Chair, Painted, Multicolored, Scroll Panel Back, Turned Legs, Arms, Sweden, 1790, 40 In. . . . 1541.00
Chair, Painted Stencil Back, Rush Seat, 1800s, 27 x 14 In., Pair. 896.00
Chair, Papavoine, Lomas, Steel Frame, Blue, Leather Upholstery, Montis, 28 x 29 In., Pair . . . 3000.00
Chair, Paul Laszlo, Lounge, Pale Wood Frame, c.1967, 33 x 28 In., Pair 9600.00
Chair, Paulin, Sling, Animal Skin Upholstery, Metal Frame, No. 444, c.1962, 38 x 33 In.. . . . . . 4500.00
Chair, Pierre Patout, Mahogany, Silk Cushions, Brass Sabots, c.1935, 35 x 20 x 18 In.. . . . . . . 9000.00
Chair, Pilgrim Style, Oak, Leather Seat & Back, Arms, c.1910, 22 In., Child's 118.00
Chair, Plank Seat, Shaped Crest, Supports, Red, Yellow, 9 x 5 ½ In., Child's 110.00
Chair, Porch, Mahogany, Cane Seat, Carved Crest, West Indies, 1800s, 42 x 29 In. . . . . . . *illus* 440.00
Chair, Posture, Grain Painted, Cane Seat, Turned Legs, 39 x 16 In., Child's. 633.00
Chair, Poul Kjaerholm, Wicker, Stainless Steel Frame, 1955, 29 In., Pair 5938.00
Chair, Queen Anne, Chamfered Yoke, Raked Ears, Solid Splat, Rush Seat, 39 ½ In. 294.00
Chair, Queen Anne, Hardwood, Yoke Crest Rail, Vase Shape Splat, Woven Seat, 40 In. 270.00
Chair, Queen Anne, Mahogany, Oxbow Crest, Pierced Slat, Stretchers, Salem, 38 x 23 In. 1495.00
Chair, Queen Anne, Mahogany, Stretchers, Silk Damask Upholstery, 47 x 32 In.. . . . . 826.00
Chair, Queen Anne, Mahogany, Yoke Crest, Shaped Splat, Pierced Heart, c.1750. . . . . 500.00

Furniture, Chair, Maple, Ash, Banister Back, Scalloped Crest Rail, Rush Seat, 49 In.
$850.00

Furniture, Chair, Ottoman, G. Nakashima, Walnut, Cushion, Arms, 30 x 24 x 31 In.
$3360.00

Furniture, Chair, Porch, Mahogany, Cane Seat, Carved Crest, West Indies, 1800s, 42 x 29 In.
$440.00

TIP

For a pollution-free furniture cleaner, use a mixture of 1 cup olive or vegetable oil and ½ cup lemon juice.

Furniture, Chair, Queen Anne, Open Splayed Arms, Upholstered, New York, c.1740, 36 In.
$146500.00

Furniture, Chair, Rene Gabriel, Lounge, Oak, Stained, Upholstered, 1940s, 28 In., Pair
$13750.00

Furniture, Chair, Rococo, Rosewood, Flowers, Grapes, Carved, Upholstered, 44 x 28 In.
$5500.00

TIP
Nuts and bolts on old furniture hardware should be removed carefully. Wrap pliers with masking tape to protect the brass. Old brass is often soft.

Chair, Queen Anne, Maple, Carved Crest, Cane Seat, Scroll Arms, Mass., c.1760, 42 In. 6044.00
Chair, Queen Anne, Maple, Cherry, Ash, Vase Shape Splat, Bristol, 40 In.. .... 206.00
Chair, Queen Anne, Maple, Compass Seat, Front Cabriole Legs, Pad Feet, Boston, c.1745..... 4680.00
Chair, Queen Anne, Maple, Mixed Wood, Shaped Splat, Black Over Red Paint, 40 In.. .... 353.00
Chair, Queen Anne, Maple, Painted, Vase Shape Slat, Rush Seat, 39 ½ In.. .... 518.00
Chair, Queen Anne, Maple, Pine, Sausage Turned Stretchers, Rope Seat, 41 In., Pair 764.00
Chair, Queen Anne, Maple, Poplar, Ash, Solid Splat, New England, 39 ¾ In. 264.00
Chair, Queen Anne, Maple, Shaped Crest, Carved Shell, Pierced, Rush Seat, c.1750, 38 In. ... 264.00
Chair, Queen Anne, Maple, Shaped Crest, Pierced Splat, Rush Seat, 39 In. 353.00
Chair, Queen Anne, Maple, Vase Shape Splat, Green Over Red Paint, 1700s, 40 In.. .... 323.00
Chair, Queen Anne, Maple, Vase Shape Splat, Turned Legs, Stretchers, 40 ½ In. 1351.00
Chair, Queen Anne, Maple, Yellow Splint Seat, Black Paint, Spanish Foot, 1700s, 41 x 18 In. . 770.00
Chair, Queen Anne, Open Splayed Arms, Upholstered, New York, c.1740, 36 In. .... *illus* 146500.00
Chair, Queen Anne, Walnut, Carved, Compass Seat, Pa., c.1760, 40 In., Pair. 15000.00
Chair, Queen Anne, Walnut, Carved, Upholstered Compass Seat, Boston, c.1750, 39 In.. ..... 15000.00
Chair, Queen Anne, Walnut, Carved Volutes, Figured, Phila., c.1760, 43 In. 71500.00
Chair, Queen Anne, Walnut, Compass Seat, Phila., c.1750, 40 In.. .... 23750.00
Chair, Queen Anne, Walnut, Flame Stitch Compass Seat, Mass., 1760, 39 In., Pair 56250.00
Chair, Queen Anne, Walnut, Serpentine Crest, Urn Shape Splat, Cabriole Legs, c.1750. ...... 2250.00
Chair, Queen Anne, Walnut, Serpentine Crest Rail, Vase Shape Splat, c.1770, 38 In.. .... 2300.00
Chair, Queen Anne, Walnut, Upholstered Compass Seat, Phila., c.1745, 40 In., Pair. 59375.00
Chair, Queen Anne, Walnut, Vase Shape Splat, Blocked Stretchers, Centennial, 41 In., Pair... 529.00
Chair, Queen Anne, Walnut, Vase Shape Splat, Slip Seat, 18 In., Pair. 1304.00
Chair, R. Venturi, Chippendale, Florence Knoll, c.1984, 38 x 23 In. 2400.00
Chair, Regency, Backswept Crest, Slatted Splat, Cane Seat, 33 In.. .... 1200.00
Chair, Regency, Concave Top Rail, Padded Seat, Bow Rail, Painted, Spade Feet, Arms, 34 In.. . 560.00
Chair, Regency, Ebonized, Parcel Gilt, Cane, Arms, c.1810, Pair 9375.00
Chair, Regency, Ebonized, Parcel Gilt, Scrolled Crest, Padded, Open Arms, 34 x 25 In., Pair .. 826.00
Chair, Regency, Ebonized, Parcel Gilt, Upholstered Seat, Back, Arms, Morel & Hughes, Pair .. 22500.00
Chair, Regency, Green Paint, Parcel Gilt, Cane, Padded Seat, c.1810 .... 21250.00
Chair, Regency, High Back, Tapestry Upholstery, Carved Open Arms, 19 x 20 In.. .... 948.00
Chair, Regency, Mahogany, Anthemia & Scrolled Crest, Rosettes, Fluted Legs, 1800s 1292.00
Chair, Regency, Mahogany, Curved Crest, Downswept Arms, Slip Seat, 36 In., Pair. 353.00
Chair, Regency, Mahogany, Gondola Form, Scrolled Crest, Cane, 19th Century, 33 In.. ...... 1560.00
Chair, Regency, Mahogany, Scrolled Arms, Reeded Front Legs, Raked Rear Legs, 44 In.. ..... 2938.00
Chair, Regency, Mahogany, Tablet Crest, Shaped Splat, Scroll Arms, Early 1800s, Pair. 551.00
Chair, Regency, Mahogany, Upholstered, Flat Back, Scroll Arms, Stretcher, 45 In., Pair 3360.00
Chair, Regency, Parcel Gilt, Cane Seat, Tapered Legs, England, Arms, 18 x 18 ½ x 16 In.. .... 1778.00
Chair, Regency, Simulated Bamboo, Rush Seat, Horizontal Splats, 34 ½ In.. .... 780.00
Chair, Regency, X-Shape Splats, Upholstered Seat, Tapered Legs, Arms, 34 In., Pair 1440.00
Chair, Regency Style, Mahogany, Upholstered, Flat Back, Scroll Legs, Arms, 42 ½ In., Pair ... 3480.00
Chair, Renaissance Revival, Brass, Bronze, Lion, Shield Finials, U-Shape Seat, Arms, 17 In... 1185.00
Chair, Renaissance Revival, Cupid Heads, Gilt, Upholstered, Folding, 1880, 39 x 25 In.. ..... 660.00
Chair, Renaissance Revival, Fruitwood, Padded, Lion Finials, Paw Feet, Italy, Arms, Pair. 2400.00
Chair, Renaissance Revival, Ivory Inlay, Pediment, Finials, Putti Splat, 50 x 19 In. 390.00
Chair, Renaissance Revival, Mahogany, Reticulated Back, Pendant Grapes, Padded Seat, 45 In. 210.00
Chair, Renaissance Revival, Walnut, Burl, Inlaid, Crested Back, Medallion, 42 In., Pair 3878.00
Chair, Renaissance Revival, Walnut, Burled Veneer, c.1875, 18 x 38 In.. .... 1200.00
Chair, Renaissance Revival, Walnut, Carved Dog's-Head Arm Grips, Upholstered, 37 In. 1610.00
Chair, Renaissance Revival, Walnut, Carved Shells, Leaves, c.1890, 40 x 13 In.. .... 431.00
Chair, Renaissance Revival, Walnut, Crests, Silk Damask, c.1860-75, 38 ½ x 17 In., Pair 1955.00
Chair, Renaissance Style, Walnut, Carved, Leather Panel, Seat, Folding, Italy, 42 In. 570.00
Chair, Rene Gabriel, Lounge, Oak, Stained, Upholstered, 1940s, 28 In., Pair. .... *illus* 13750.00
Chair, Restauration, Mahogany, Crest, Padded Back, Cushions, Paw Feet, 38 In., Pair. 2400.00
Chair, Restauration, Mahogany, Molded Rail, Reed & Acanthus Carving, 36 In., Pair 2880.00
Chair, Risom, Lounge, Walnut Frame, Upholstered, 2 Cushions, 30 x 30 In. 240.00
Chair, Rocker is listed under Rocker in this category.
Chair, Rococo, Rosewood, Flowers, Grapes, Carved, Upholstered, 44 x 28 In. .... *illus* 5500.00
Chair, Rococo Revival, Oak, Pierced, Carved Crest, Padded, Cabriole Legs, Iberia, Arms, 47 In. 2160.00
Chair, Rococo Revival, Rosewood, Laminated, Rosalie Pattern, 43 ½ In.. .... 3840.00
Chair, Rococo Revival, Upholstered, Carved, Overstuffed Seat, Arms, 42 x 30 x 22 In. 1046.00
Chair, Rococo Revival, Upholstered, Serpentine Rail, Arms, 42 x 30 x 22 In.. .... 1046.00
Chair, Rococo Revival, Walnut, Leaf & Shell Crest, Spindle Gallery, Mid 1800s, 35 In. 330.00
Chair, Rococo Revival, Walnut, Veneer, Carved, Scrolled Back, Upholstered Seat 375.00
Chair, Rococo Style, Painted, Scalloped Crest, Pierced Vase Shape Splat, 37 In., Pair 1410.00
Chair, Roman, Iron, Leather, Iron, Brass Finials, G. Poillerat, 32 x 25 In. 230.00
Chair, Rosewood, Laminated, Arched Crest, Scrolled, Silk Upholstery, Arms, c.1860, 27 In. ... 7200.00

Chair, Rosewood, Laminated, Shield Seat & Back, Swivel Base, Arms, c.1860, 37 In. 4313.00
Chair, Rosewood, Yoke Back, Bowed, Out-Curved Arms, Velvet Cushions, 47 In., Pair. 2640.00
Chair, Rosewood & Stone, Arms, Chinese, 38 x 24 ½ x 20 In. 299.00
Chair, Roycroft, Morris, No. 43, Macmurdo Feet, Carved Orb & Cross Mark, 45 x 32 In. 4800.00
Chair, Scholar's Hat, Curved Splat, Woven Splint Bamboo Cover, Chinese, 40 In., Pair 720.00
Chair, Shaker, Maple, Splint Seat, Conn., c.1840, 40 x 17 In. 296.00
Chair, Shaker, Maple, Tilters, Mid 1800s, 41 x 16 In. 2726.00
Chair, Shaker, Red Wash, Graduated Slats, Tape Seat, New Hampshire, c.1840, 40 In. 356.00
Chair, Shell Carved Crest, Openwork Splat, Slip Seat, Stretcher, Italy, 42 x 22 In., Pair 837.00
Chair, Sheraton, Beech, Cane Back, Cushion, Open Arms, 32 x 21 x 19 In., Pair. 1673.00
Chair, Sheraton, Mahogany, Carved, Padded, Overupholstered, Casters, 38 x 26 x 16 In. 761.00
Chair, Sheraton, Reeded, Ring-Turned Crest Rail, Rosette Stay Rail, Stuffed Seat, 32 In., Pair 538.00
Chair, Shield Shape, Ball Finials, Flat Top Rail, Reeded Legs, Arms, 19th Century, 34 In.. . . . . 236.00
Chair, Silvered, Slat Back, Scrolled Arms, Upholstered Seat, Italy, c.1780, 34 x 23 In., Pair . . . 7500.00
Chair, Skeleton Back, Wood, Open Rib Cage, Carved Skull, Bone Feet, 1900s, 53 x 24 In.. . . . . 3068.00
Chair, Sling Back, Painted, Continuous Metal Arm, 36 x 22 In. 203.00
Chair, Slipper, Charles X, Walnut, Floral Upholstery, 3-Lobed Openwork Back, 33 In., Pair . . . 567.00
Chair, Slipper, Lacquered, Mother-Of-Pearl Inlay, Spiral-Twist Stiles, Cane Seat, 40 In. 329.00
Chair, Slipper, Laminated Rosewood, Carved Crest, Silk Brocade, Casters, c.1855, 35 In. 920.00
Chair, Slipper, M. Taylor, Wood, Grid Frame, Silk Upholstery, Baker Furniture, 28 x 27 In., Pair 1200.00
Chair, Slipper, Renaissance Revival, Walnut, Masks Carved Crest Rail, 36 x 20 In., Pair 299.00
Chair, Slipper, Rococo, Laminated Rosewood, Fruit & Flower Crest, Cabriole Legs, c.1850, 44 In. 5875.00
Chair, Slipper, Rococo Revival, Rosewood, Laminated, Pierced Scroll Back, 39 In., Pair 1440.00
Chair, Slipper, Rosewood, Upholstered, Swan's Head, Medallion, c.1870, 32 x 21 x 22 In. 4800.00
Chair, Spindle Back, Rush Woven Seat, Arms, New York, c.1815, 33 x 17 In., Pair 470.00
Chair, Steel, Copper, Woven Rattan, Arms, Horseshoe Back, 30 x 24 In. 200.00
Chair, Stickley Bros., 3 Vertical Slats, Drop-In Seat, Signed, 42 x 17 x 17 In.. . . . . 480.00
Chair, Stickley Bros., Barley Twist Legs, Open Sides, Shoefoot Base, 17 x 40 In.. . . . . 150.00
Chair, Stickley Bros., Morris, Bowed Arms, Slatted Sides, Leather Upholstery, 37 x 32 In.. . . . . . 2400.00
Chair, Stickley Bros., No. 312 ½, Wood, 3 Back Slats, 14 x 38 In. 540.00
Chair, Swivel, Wegner, Teak, Metal, Leather, Wheels, Denmark, c.1955, 29 In.. . . . . 21250.00
Chair, Teak, Spindle Back, Upholstered Cushions, Arms, c.1950s, 27 x 29 In., Pair. 375.00
Chair, Thonet, High Back, Cane Seat, Back, Bent Arms, 24 x 45 In. 270.00
Chair, Throne, Carved, Arch Back, Hinged Storage Seat, Multicolored, 1800s, 78 x 26 In. 944.00
Chair, Throne, Gothic Revival, Mixed Wood, Openwork, Upholstered, Ball Grips, 55 x 26 In.. . 388.00
Chair, Throne, Renaissance Revival, Walnut, Carved, Classical Scenes, Lion Arms, Italy, 86 x 36 In. 4956.00
Chair, Tiger Maple, Tablet Crest, Scalloped Splat, Cane, 36 x 21 x 21 In. 826.00
Chair, Tub, Victorian, Mahogany, Continuous Arm, Leather Upholstery, Lyre Splat. 690.00
Chair, Twig, Split Branches For Seat, Nailed Construction, c.1910, 23 ½ In., Child's 59.00
Chair, Venetian, Carved Fantasy Bird, Upholstered Seat, 29 x 32 In.. . . . . 2040.00
Chair, Victorian, Gilt Frame, Needlework Back, Seat, Lion, Unicorn, Trees, c.1885, 40 In. 230.00
Chair, Victorian, Mahogany, Rounded Back, Padded Open Scrolled Arms, 39 In., Pair. 323.00
Chair, Victorian, Papier-Mache, Mother-Of-Pearl, Rush Seat, 33 x 18 ½ x 17 In. 239.00
Chair, Victorian, Walnut, 3 Conjoined Seats, Upholstered, 3 x 52 In. 2988.00
Chair, Victorian, Walnut, Balloon Back, Finger Mold Carving, Upholstered, Arms, 39 In.. . . . . 236.00
Chair, Victorian, Walnut, Carved, Tufted, Leather, Arms, c.1880, 44 ½ x 25 x 34 In. 440.00
Chair, W. Platner, High Back, Nickel Plated Wire Frame, Upholstered, Knoll, 41 x 40 In. 2160.00
Chair, Walnut, Carved Sides, Rolled Back, Arms, Tufted Leather, c.1875, 39 x 27 In.. . . . . 1610.00
Chair, Walnut, Crest Rail, Upholstered, Serpentine Seat, Arms, c.1840, 34 ½ In.. . . . . 1292.00
Chair, Walnut, Lacquered, Yoke, Arms, Chinese, 41 x 32 ½ x 17 In., Pair. 531.00
Chair, Walnut, Leaf Carved, Dome Crest, Vase Splat, Padded, Octagonal Feet, Dutch, 47 In. . . 1440.00
Chair, Walnut, Padded Back, Outscrolled Arms, Padded Seat, Late 1800s, 35 In., Pair 1920.00
Chair, Walter Lamb, Lounge, Adjustable, Black, White, Jordan Brown, c.1950, 45 x 24 In.. . . . . 2700.00
Chair, Wegner, Oak, Mixed Woods, Blue Upholstered Seats, 1952, 31 ½ In., Pair. 259.00
Chair, Wegner, Oak, Teak Armrests, Spindles, 42 x 27 ½ x 21 In., Pair. 3600.00
Chair, Wegner, Oak Frame, Curved Back, Rush Seat, Carl Hansen & Son, 27 x 29 In.. . . . . 900.00
Chair, Wegner, Papa Bear, Teak, Upholstered, 39 x 35 x 30 In.. . . . . 5700.00 to 6600.00
Chair, Wegner, Peacock, Ash Frame, Papercord Seat, P.P. Mobler, 1995, 30 x 42 In.. . . . . 3900.00
Chair, Wegner, Teak, Rattan Wrapped, Cane Seat, Arms, 30 x 25 x 19 In., Pair 2400.00
Chair, Wegner, Valet, Teak, Elm, Seat Opens To Storage, Copenhagen, 1953, 38 In. 10000.00
Chair, Wicker, Reed, Side Book Holder, Arms, 35 x 31 x 23 In. . . . . *illus* 240.00
Chair, William & Mary, 4 Slats, Buttressed Arms, Rush Seat, Sausage Stretchers, c.1740 . . . . . 702.00
Chair, William & Mary, Banister Slat Back, Rush Seat, Turned Stretchers, Arms, 47 In.. . . . . . . 230.00
Chair, William & Mary, Cane, Carved Crest, Turned Stiles, Stretchers, 48 x 18 In.. . . . . . . *illus* 230.00
Chair, William & Mary, Carved Scrolls, Flowers, Finials, Cane Back, 1800s, 44 x 20 In., Pair. . 269.00
Chair, William & Mary, Flemish Style, Carved Crest, Paneled Back, 53 x 19 In., Pair 489.00
Chair, William & Mary, Walnut, Arched Crest, Upholstered, Stretcher, 50 x 36 In.. . . . . 325.00

Wicker Labels

Date wicker furniture from the label. Wakefield Rattan Co. was used from 1855 to 1897; Heywood-Wakefield Co., 1868–97; Heywood Bros. & Wakefield Co., 1897–1921; Heywood-Wakefield Co., after 1921.

Furniture, Chair, Wicker, Reed, Side Book Holder, Arms, 35 x 31 x 23 In.
$240.00

Furniture, Chair, William & Mary, Cane, Carved Crest, Turned Stiles, Stretchers, 48 x 18 In.
$230.00

TIP

If you own a wicker chair that makes small popping noises when you sit in it, dampen it with water. It is too dry, and wicker may crack if not kept moist.

Furniture, Chair, William IV, Mahogany, Casters, England, 1800s, 39 x 26 x 27 In.
$5100.00

Furniture, Chair, Wycliff, Oak, Walnut, Rush Seat, c.1901, 39 ½ x 20 x 19 In.
$1560.00

TIP

If you reupholster an antique piece of furniture, save some of the original fabric. Put it in an envelope and tape it to the bottom of the seat so future owners can know more about the original appearance. When selling a piece, this sort of history will add to the value.

F

Chair, William & Mary, Walnut, Carved Dolphin Back, Stretcher, Arms, 1800s, 56 x 24 In., Pair 956.00
Chair, William IV, Mahogany, Cane, Carved, Upholstered, England, 1800s, 40 In. 5520.00
Chair, William IV, Mahogany, Casters, England, 1800s, 39 x 26 x 27 In. *illus* 5100.00
Chair, William IV, Mahogany, Reclining, Cane Seat & Back, Arms, c.1850, 42 x 54 In. 1320.00
Chair, William IV, Open Arms, Cartouche Back, Damask Upholstery, 42 x 24 In., Pair 236.00
Chair, Windsor, 5 Spindles, Bamboo Turnings, Stepped Crest, Stretcher, 27 ½ In. 374.00
Chair, Windsor, Arrow Back, Yellow Paint, Arms, 33 ½ In. 403.00
Chair, Windsor, Black Paint, New York, c.1775, 37 In. 2370.00
Chair, Windsor, Bow Back, 7 Spindles, Saddle Seat, Pa., Late 18th Century, 38 In. 403.00
Chair, Windsor, Bow Back, 9 Spindles, Beaded Edge, Continuous Arm, 36 ½ In., Pair 1645.00
Chair, Windsor, Bow Back, Bamboo Turnings, Saddle Seat, Stamped OC-W-A, c.1800, 35 In. 353.00
Chair, Windsor, Bow Back, Blue Paint, 1810, 36 In., Pair 1885.00
Chair, Windsor, Bow Back, Green, New England, Late 1700s, 36 In. 5925.00
Chair, Windsor, Bow Back, Maple, Hickory, Poplar, Turned, 35 In. 646.00
Chair, Windsor, Bow Back, Painted, Arms, New England, c.1790, 34 x 17 In. 470.00
Chair, Windsor, Bow Back, Pine Saddle Seat, Incised Crest Rail Reeding, 38 In. 132.00
Chair, Windsor, Bow Back, Saddle Seat, Turned Legs, Brown Paint, 38 x 18 In. 4740.00
Chair, Windsor, Brace Back, Continuous Arm, Green Paint, New York, 37 In. 4025.00
Chair, Windsor, Comb Back, 20th Century, 26 ½ In., Child's 144.00
Chair, Windsor, Comb Back, Bentwood Armrest, Saddle Seat, Spindle Supports, 39 In. 295.00
Chair, Windsor, Comb Back, Black Paint, Carved Ears, Arms, Signed, 1900s, 49 In. 411.00
Chair, Windsor, Comb Back, Mixed Wood, Graduated Spindles, Arms, 35 In. 269.00
Chair, Windsor, Continuous Arm, Yellow, New England, c.1810, 36 ½ In. 2726.00
Chair, Windsor, Fanback, Mixed Wood, 3 Tiers, New England, c.1830, 17 x 48 In. 360.00
Chair, Windsor, Fanback, Mixed Wood, Shaped Crest, Scrolled Ears, Grain Painted, 35 In. 470.00
Chair, Windsor, Fanback, Natural Wood, Shaped Crest, Plank Seat, Baluster Legs, Pair 275.00
Chair, Windsor, Fanback, Oak, Hickory, Tennessee, 20th Century, 35 ½ In., Pair 115.00
Chair, Windsor, Hoop Back, Painted, In-Curved Arms, Saddle Seat, Turned Legs, 1700s 1175.00
Chair, Windsor, Low Back, Rhode Island, c.1785, 28 In. 6250.00
Chair, Windsor, Mixed Wood, Bulbous, Tapered Spindles, Arms, 38 ½ In. 1540.00
Chair, Windsor, Outscrolled Arms, D-Shape Seat, Low Back, Arms, Late 1700s 3510.00
Chair, Windsor, Sack Back, 7 Spindles, Midrail, Baluster Turned Legs, 37 ½ In., Pair 1495.00
Chair, Windsor, Sack Back, Baluster Turnings, Black, Arms, 29 In. 118.00
Chair, Windsor, Sack Back, Brown, Green Paint, New England, Late 1800s, 37 ¾ In. 4148.00
Chair, Windsor, Sack Back, Elm, Spindle Back, Saddle Seat, Arm, 35 ½ In. 413.00
Chair, Windsor, Sack Back, Green Paint, Arms, Israel Schaaf, Ohio, 1900s, 34 ½ In. 705.00
Chair, Windsor, Sack Back, Maple, Ash, Pine, New England, c.1785, 37 In. 504.00
Chair, Windsor, Sack Back, Rounded Crest Rail, Wheel Carved Splat, Stretcher, 41 In. 177.00
Chair, Windsor, Scooped Seat & Swell, H-Stretcher, Child's, 25 ½ In. 176.00
Chair, Windsor, Spindles, Saddle Seat, Splayed Legs, 10 ½ x 24 ½ In., Child's 440.00
Chair, Windsor, Spindles, Saddle Seat, Turned Legs, Bentwood Armrests, 43 In. 354.00
Chair, Windsor, Wheel Back, Turned Spindles, Curved Arms, Shaped Saddle Seat 23.00
Chair, Windsor, Writing, Comb Back, Shaped Seat, Drawer, Bamboo Turnings, c.1800, 45 In. 352.00
Chair, Windsor, Writing, Drawer, Green Paint, Marked, D.W. Dimes, 44 x 36 x 33 In. 660.00
Chair, Windsor, Writing, Maple, Pine, Ash, Knuckle, Carved Ears, Arms, c.1780 2500.00
Chair, Wing, Chippendale, Mahogany, Claw & Ball Feet, Cabriole Legs, Arm, 46 In. 619.00
Chair, Wing, Chippendale, Mahogany, Scrolled Arms, Tapered Legs 813.00
Chair, Wing, Chippendale, Mahogany, Upholstered, Arms, 19th Century, 47 x 31 x 26 In. 200.00
Chair, Wing, Chippendale, Mahogany, Upholstered, Out-Swept Arms 8750.00
Chair, Wing, Chippendale, Maple, Birch Frame, Tapered Legs, Upholstered, 47 In. 1175.00
Chair, Wing, Chippendale, Nailed Leather, Button Tufted, Upholstered, 37 In., Pair 508.00
Chair, Wing, Chippendale, Upholstered, Serpentine Crest, Cut Velvet Upholstery, 46 In. 359.00
Chair, Wing, Chippendale Style, Carved Mahogany Legs, Drake Feet, c.1920, 45 ½ In. 705.00
Chair, Wing, Chippendale Style, Damask Upholstery, 48 x 36 x 31 In. 800.00
Chair, Wing, Chippendale Style, Hickory, Leather Upholstery, Brass Tacks, c.1980, 44 In. 646.00
Chair, Wing, Chippendale Style, Imitation Coverlet Upholstery, Arms, 45 In. 264.00
Chair, Wing, Chippendale Style, Leather Upholstery, Late 20th Century, 42 In. 294.00
Chair, Wing, Federal, Mahogany, Tapered & Reeded Legs, 46 x 23 x 19 In. 2350.00
Chair, Wing, George II, Mahogany, Needlepoint Cover, c.1740 8190.00
Chair, Wing, George III, Mahogany, Domed, Padded, Fluted Legs, 19th Century, 48 In. 3840.00
Chair, Wing, George III, Padded Back, Serpentine, Damask Upholstery, c.1900, 44 In. 805.00
Chair, Wing, George III Style, Mahogany, Tufted, Cushion, 19th Century, 43 In. 1320.00
Chair, Wing, Georgian, Walnut, Bargello Upholstery, Outscrolled Arms, 1900s, 44 x 31 In. 239.00
Chair, Wood Seat, Flat Crest, Paneled Splat, Shaped Arms, Wood Seat, England, 42 In. 600.00
Chair, Wormley, Leather, Enameled Wooden Frame, Dunbar, 22 x 24 ½ In., Pair 1800.00
Chair, Wormley, Low Arm, Floor Stretcher, Upholstered, Blue, Green, 28 x 23 In. 1020.00
Chair, Wormley, Slipper, Fabric, Wooden Frame, Dunbar, 31 x 22 x 29 In., Pair 4500.00

Chair, Wormley, Tall Man, Metal Legs, Upholstered, Dunbar, 29 x 38 In. 1200.00
Chair, Wormley, Upholstered, Dunbar, c.1952, 33 x 30 In. 1080.00
Chair, Wormley, Walnut, Upholstered, Dunbar, 27 x 33 x 34 In. 720.00
Chair, Wycliff, Oak, Walnut, Rush Seat, c.1901, 39 ½ x 20 x 19 In. *illus* 1560.00
Chair Set, Anglo-Indian, Cane, Inlaid Bone Panels, Ebonized, Arms, 20th Century, 4 4375.00
Chair Set, Art Deco, Lucite Tube Arm, Leg, Wide Back Slat, Upholstered Seat, 29 x 23 In., 4 563.00
Chair Set, Art Deco, Mahogany, Upholstered, Padded Back, Seat, 34 ½ In., 4 840.00
Chair Set, Arts & Crafts, Wood, Leather Back, Seat, 19 x 36 In., 6 1200.00
Chair Set, Baroque, Walnut, Fruitwood Inlay, Shaped Seat, Continental, 21 In., 6 2489.00
Chair Set, Baroque Revival, Upholstered Back, Seat, Barley Twist Legs, Stretcher, 37 In., 6 390.00
Chair Set, Biedermeier, Fruitwood, Inlaid Burl, Concave Crest, Padded Seat, 36 In., 12 3360.00
Chair Set, Carved, Pierced Crest, Upholstered Seat, Back, Norman Suite, 18 In., 6 2070.00
Chair Set, Cherry, Cane Seat, Saber Legs, 19th Century, 30 ¾ x 16 ½ In., 6 690.00
Chair Set, Cherry, Mahogany, Shaped Tablet Back, Lyre Splat, Cane Seat, Ky., 34 x 18 In., 6 489.00
Chair Set, Chippendale, Mahogany, Flower, Birds Needlepoint, c.1880, 40 x 21 In., 6 1840.00
Chair Set, Chippendale, Mahogany, Pierced Vase Splat, Upholstered, 36 In., 6 649.00
Chair Set, Chippendale Style, Mahogany, Carved, 2 Arm Chairs, 37 x 23 x 20 In., 8 *illus* 1700.00
Chair Set, Curly Maple, Cherry, Cane Seat, Scroll Crest Rails, Saber Legs, c.1830, 34 In., 8 1093.00
Chair Set, Eames DCM, Ash, Plywood, Metal, Molded Seat, Herman Miller, 30 x 20 In., 4 1080.00
Chair Set, Empire, Burled Walnut, Gondola Shape, Cane Seat, 36 In., 4 2160.00
Chair Set, Fauteuil, Charles X Style, Mahogany, Square, Stiles, Open Upholstered Arms, 36 In., 4 2350.00
Chair Set, Federal, Mahogany, Shieldback, Upholstered Seat, 37 ½ In., 8 2233.00
Chair Set, French Provincial, Fruitwood, Rush Seat, 5 In., 4 960.00
Chair Set, French Provincial, Shell & Leaf Carved, Cane Seat, 1900s, 14 *illus* 1980.00
Chair Set, G. Nakashima, Round Slatted Back, Solid Seat, c.1947, 30 x 22 In., 6 9600.00
Chair Set, G. Nelson, Birch, Green Leather, Herman Miller, 1950s, 31 x 19 In., 4 600.00
Chair Set, G. Nelson, Walnut, Upholstered, Herman Miller, 31 x 23 In., 8 *illus* 650.00
Chair Set, G. Stickley, 3 Vertical Back Slats, Rush Seat, Arch Apron, c.1905, 40 In., 6 2607.00
Chair Set, G. Stickley, No. 349 ½, Leather, Tacked Edge, 37 ¾ x 18 ½ x 17 In., 5 1920.00
Chair Set, G. Stickley, No. 3572, Slats, Leather Seat, Armchair, 36 In., 6 3000.00
Chair Set, George II, Walnut, William Hallett Style, Upholstered, Claw & Ball Feet, 4 10625.00
Chair Set, George III, Mahogany, Leaf Carved, Eared Crest, 39 In., 8 2160.00
Chair Set, George III, Mahogany, Shaped, Eared Crest, Padded Seat, 41 In., 8 6600.00
Chair Set, George III, Mahogany, Upholstered Seat, 2 Armchairs, c.1800, 8 3125.00
Chair Set, George III Style, Mahogany, Carved Backrest, Upholstered, Claw, Ball Feet, 10 3851.00
Chair Set, George III Style, Mahogany, Curved Crest, Padded Seat, 2 Armchairs, c.1900, 10 4560.00
Chair Set, Georgian, Mahogany, Carved Crest, Pierced Splats, Slip Seats, 38 In., 6 1880.00
Chair Set, Gothic Revival, Crest Pierced, Trefoils, Pointed Arch, 34 x 18 In., 9 8260.00
Chair Set, Gothic Revival, Mahogany, Arched, Molded Crest Rail, Slip Seat, Saber Legs, 6 938.00
Chair Set, Gothic Revival, Walnut, Carved, Pierced Back, Leaf, Scrollwork, 37 x 15 In., 6 5000.00
Chair Set, H. Brattrud, Scandia, Bentwood Slats, Rod Frame, Mobler, 38 x 19 In., 6 2040.00
Chair Set, Henry Clay, Rosewood, Belter, c.1840-60, 44 x 17 & 38 x 16 In., Armchair, 3 4025.00
Chair Set, Hepplewhite, Mahogany, Arched Crest, Damask Upholstery, Square Legs, 6 4140.00
Chair Set, Hepplewhite, Mahogany, Carved, Shieldback, Armchair, 38 In., 8 3600.00
Chair Set, Hepplewhite, Mahogany, Shieldback, Upholstered Seat, 17 ¾ In., 8 9775.00
Chair Set, Hepplewhite, Mahogany, Tobacco Leaf Spray, Pierced, 2 Armchairs, 10 6900.00
Chair Set, K. Kristiansen, Teak, Upholstered Seat, Backrest, c.1950, 30 In., 6 948.00
Chair Set, L. & J.G. Stickley, No. 342, Ladder Back, Armchair, 36 x 17 In., 6 3120.00
Chair Set, Lancashire, Shaped Yoke Crest Rail, Plank Seat, 1800-1900, 4 705.00
Chair Set, Leather, Padded Back, Seat, Legs, Stitched, Italy, 35 In., 4 478.00
Chair Set, Louis XVI, Cream Paint, Parcel Gilt, Upholstered, Fluted Legs, 35 ½ In., 6 948.00
Chair Set, Louis XVI, Gilt, Blue Damask Upholstery, c.1900, 40 In., 4 6250.00
Chair Set, Louis XVI Style, Multicolored, Lyre Splat, Padded, 34 ½ In., 8 5520.00
Chair Set, Louis XVI Style, Oval Back, Carved, Gilt, Upholstered, c.1900, 36 In., 4 646.00
Chair Set, Mahogany, Cane Back, Tapered Legs, 1900, 2 Armchairs, 37 ½ In., 8 7800.00
Chair Set, Mahogany, Carved, Scrolled Crest, Upholstered Seat, England, c.1850, 8 4993.00
Chair Set, Mahogany, Crest Rail, Floral Roundel, Pierced Splat, Rush Slip Seat, 34 In., 6 940.00
Chair Set, Mahogany, Pierced Back Splat, Upholstered Seat, 2 Armchairs, 37 In., 8 600.00
Chair Set, Mixed Wood, Dark Grained Ground, Mustard Stripes, Red Flowers, c.1850, 33 In., 4 529.00
Chair Set, Neoclassical, Mahogany, Scrolled Crest, Diamond Panel, Padded, 37 In., 6 5520.00
Chair Set, Neoclassical, Mahogany, Stepped Crest Rail, Urn Splat, c.1830, 33 In., 6 460.00
Chair Set, Nutting, No. 364, Carver, Side, Block Branded Signature, 45 In., 6 2640.00
Chair Set, Oak, Domed Crest, Ladder Back, Rush Seat, Ball Feet, England, 2 Armchairs, 10 1560.00
Chair Set, Oak, Ladder Back, Beveled Rails, Front Posts, Corn Husks Seat, 52 x 18 In., 6 1210.00
Chair Set, Old Hickory, Rocker, Wood Spindles, Leather Back, Seat, 34 x 25 In., 4 2400.00
Chair Set, Perriand, Rustic Wood Frame, Rush Seat, Sentu, c.1950, 30 x 15 In., 6 3600.00
Chair Set, Pine, Yellow Paint, Freehand Stripes, Stencil, Feather Graining, 33 ½ In., 6 1763.00

Furniture, Chair Set, Chippendale Style, Mahogany, Carved, 2 Arm Chairs, 37 x 23 x 20 In., 8
$1700.00

Furniture, Chair Set, French Provincial, Shell & Leaf Carved, Cane Seat, 1900s, 14
$1980.00

Furniture, Chair Set, G. Nelson, Walnut, Upholstered, Herman Miller, 31 x 23 In., 8
$650.00

Furniture, Chair Set, V. Panton, Plastic, Molded, Stamped, Herman Miller, 33 x 20 In., 8
$1010.00

As always, the edited listings in *Kovels' Antiques & Collectibles Price Guide 2010* aren't available on any website, but readers should visit Kovels.com for information on trends, tips, reproductions, marks, old prices, and more!

Furniture, Chair Set, Wegner, Beech, Rope Seat, Signed, Hansen, 28 x 22 In., 4
$2100.00

Furniture, Chair-Table, Pine, Birch, Drawer, Stained, Late 1700s, 28 ½ x 45 x 40 ½ In.
$3744.00

Furniture, Chaise Longue, Klaus Grabbe, Pine, Woven Straps, c.1949, 26 x 63 x 21 In.
$565.00

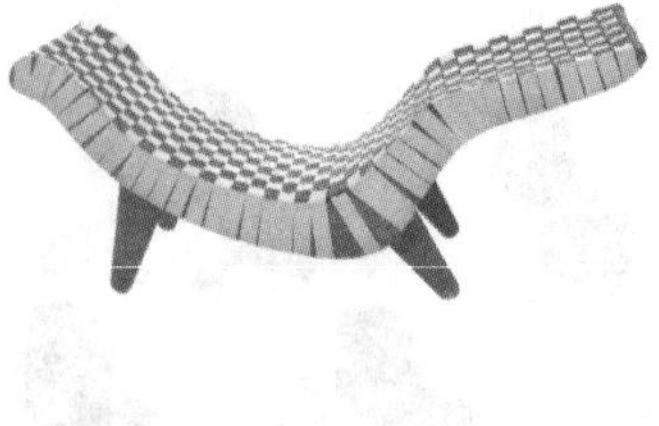

Furniture, Chaise Longue, Oak, Lion's Head, Claw Feet, Upholstered, c.1900, 26 x 74 In.
$189.00

Chair Set, Plywood, Tubular Chrome Legs, Shell Seat, 30 ¾ x 19 ¾ In., 6 .... 406.00
Chair Set, Queen Anne, Walnut, Upholstered Seat, c.1750, 41 x 18 In., 4 .... 17775.00
Chair Set, Queen Anne Style, Walnut, Open Arms, Yoke Crest, Vase Splat, 40 In., 6 .... 413.00
Chair Set, Regency, Mahogany, Carved, Leaf Slats, Damask Upholstery, 1800s, 33 In., 8 ..... 1410.00
Chair Set, Regency, Mahogany, Flame Veneered Cresting, Slip Seat, 18 In., 8 .... 948.00
Chair Set, Regency Style, Beech, Upholstered, Cabriole Legs, 2 Armchair, 45 In., 10 .... 9300.00
Chair Set, Rosewood, Leather Upholstery, Metal Tag, 32 x 19 ½ x 17 In., 8 .... 21600.00
Chair Set, Safari, Stained Elm, Leather, Collapsible, Kaare Klint, c.1930, 33 x 21 In., 4 ...... 920.00
Chair Set, Spindle Back, Rush Seat, Turned Stretcher, 4 Armchairs, 42 In., 8 .... 2300.00
Chair Set, Stacking, Metal Frame, Leather Upholstery, c.1960, 33 x 19 x 21 In., 6 .... 4800.00
Chair Set, Stickley Bros., No. 325 ½, 3-Slat Back, Saddle Seat, 17 x 37 In., 4 .... 2040.00
Chair Set, V. Panton, Plastic, Molded, Stamped, Herman Miller, 33 x 20 In., 8 .... *illus* 1010.00
Chair Set, Walnut, 4 Spindles, Egg & Dart Splat, 35 x 16 ½ x 13 ½ In., 6 .... 717.00
Chair Set, Wegner, Beech, Rope Seat, Signed, Hansen, 28 x 22 In., 4 .... *illus* 2100.00
Chair Set, Wegner, Teak, Cane Seat, Armchair, 30 x 24 ½ x 18 In., 6 .... 7800.00
Chair Set, Wegner, Teak, Padded Seat, 29 ½ x 25 x 20 In., 4 .... 3360.00
Chair Set, Windsor, Bamboo Turnings, Shaped Seat, c.1820, 35 In., 6 .... 2115.00
Chair Set, Windsor, Bow Back, 9 Spindles, Shaped Seat, 2 Armchairs, 6 .... 3173.00
Chair Set, Windsor, Bow Back, Black Paint, 35 In., 6 .... 1380.00
Chair Set, Windsor, Fanback, Black Paint, Serpentine Crest Rail, 35 In., 8 .... 4600.00
Chair Set, Windsor, Pine, Arrow Back, Green, Trumpet Flower Crest, c.1820, 33 ½ In., 6 ..... 969.00
Chair Set, Windsor, Spindle Back, Plank Seat, Turned Legs, Early 1800s, 37 x 21 In., 6 ...... 805.00
Chair Set, Windsor, Tablet Back, Painted Leaves, Faux Bamboo Spindles, 34 x 19 In., 6 ..... 3450.00
Chair-Table, Pine, Ash, Walnut, 2-Board Pine Top, Paint Trace, Early 1800s, 28 x 36 In. 2115.00
Chair-Table, Pine, Birch, Drawer, Stained, Late 1700s, 28 ½ x 45 x 40 ½ In. .... *illus* 3744.00
Chair-Table, Pine, Brown Wash, Bench Base, Hinged, Lift Seat, Recessed Panel, 28 x 54 In... 201.00
Chair-Table, Pine, Oak, Round Top, Applied Beaded Edge, Trestle Base, 1800s, 28 x 39 In.... 978.00
Chaise Longue, Art Deco, Upholstered Scroll Shape, 2 Wood Feet, c.1925, 24 x 74 In. 2844.00
Chaise Longue, Eames, ESI06, Metal, Leather, Herman Miller, 1968, 29 x 75 In.. .... 4800.00
Chaise Longue, Eames, Purple Aluminum Frame, Leather Cushions, Herman Miller, 18 x 29 In. 3600.00
Chaise Longue, Heywood-Wakefield, Woven Top, Turned Legs, Stretcher, 24 x 72 x 25 In. ... 195.00
Chaise Longue, Klaus Grabbe, Pine, Woven Straps, c.1949, 26 x 63 x 21 In.. .... *illus* 565.00
Chaise Longue, Leather, Padded Back, Seat, Cushion, Linda Sue Eastman, 39 x 59 x 24 In... 1534.00
Chaise Longue, Louis XV, Fruitwood, Flowers, Shell Carved, c.1900, 34 ½ x 72 In. 625.00
Chaise Longue, O. Mourgue, Bent Tubular Steel, Wool Upholstery, France, 67 x 25 In....... 1080.00
Chaise Longue, O. Mourgue, Bouloum, Zippered Upholstery, Arconas, Canada, c.1970...... 2640.00
Chaise Longue, Oak, Lion's Head, Claw Feet, Upholstered, c.1900, 26 x 74 In. .... *illus* 189.00
Chaise Longue, Pressed Oak, Upholstered, c.1900, 50 x 41 In.. .... 189.00
Chaise Longue, Regency Style, Painted, Upholstered Back, Arms, Seat, Splayed Feet, 63 In... 1320.00
Chaise Longue, Victorian, Padded, Shaped Back, Cushion, Cabriole Legs, Arms, 35 In....... 2280.00
Chaise Longue, Wegner, Teak, Adjustable Frame, Upholstered Pads, Footstool, Denmark, c.1960 3851.00
Chest, Art Deco, Burl Walnut, Bowfront, 3 Drawers, Bracket Feet, 33 x 48 x 20 In. 224.00
Chest, Arts & Crafts, Elm, Paneled Top, Carved Frieze, England, 28 x 40 x 18 ¾ In. 649.00
Chest, Bachelor's, Chippendale, Burl, 4 Drawers, Bracket Feet, 1750-80, 30 x 30 x 18 In. 8000.00
Chest, Bachelor's, Georgian, Crossbanded Walnut, Hinged Top, Drawers, 29 ¾ x 37 In....... 2370.00
Chest, Baroque Revival, 5 Arched Panels, Continental, 19th Century, 22 x 51 In. 354.00
Chest, Basswood, 4 Drawers, Red Over Red Grain Painted, Bun Feet, 10 ½ x 14 In. 440.00
Chest, Bench, Oak, Bootjack Ends, Cotter Pin Rattail Hinged Lid, 1650-1700, 23 x 35 In. 1080.00
Chest, Black Walnut, 10 Drawers, Curvilinear Panel Sliding Door, 48 x 48 In. 830.00
Chest, Blanket, Blue Paint, Cutout Feet, Thumb-Molded Lid, 1800s, 43 x 15 In. 823.00
Chest, Blanket, Bootjack Ends, Red Paint, Hinged, Early 1800s, 24 x 7 ¾ In. 940.00
Chest, Blanket, Bracket Base, Blue Paint, 48 x 19 x 24 In.. .... 690.00
Chest, Blanket, Chippendale, Dovetailed, 7 x 14 x 6 In.. .... 460.00
Chest, Blanket, Chippendale, Maple, 3 Drawers, 40 x 19 x 46 In. 518.00
Chest, Blanket, Federal, Pine, 2 Drawers, Hinged, Applied Molded Edges, 42 x 43 In. 201.00
Chest, Blanket, Federal, Walnut, Drawers, Dovetailed, Hinged, 31 x 49 In. 705.00
Chest, Blanket, Federal, Walnut, Hinged, Storage Well, Drawers, Late 1700s, 51 x 54 In. 448.00
Chest, Blanket, Grain Paint, Bootjack Feet, N.Y., 1800s, 9 x 12 ¾ x 6 ¼ In. 650.00
Chest, Blanket, Hepplewhite, 2 Drawers, 2 False Drawers, Dovetailed Feet................ 1595.00
Chest, Blanket, Jacobean, Oak, Carved Leaves, Footed, Late 17th Century, 22 x 37 In. 1000.00
Chest, Blanket, Mahogany, Oak, 2-Drawer Stand, Brass Ball Handles, 39 x 49 In.. .... 2115.00
Chest, Blanket, Mixed Woods, Columns, Turned Legs, 16 ½ x 21 x 12 ½ In. 2468.00
Chest, Blanket, Oak, Dome Top, 30 x 50 In. 720.00
Chest, Blanket, Oak, Paneled, 18th Century, 22 x 31 In. 518.00
Chest, Blanket, Pine, 3 Drawers, Molded Edges, Interior Well, 52 x 39 In. 575.00
Chest, Blanket, Pine, 6-Board, Bracket Feet, 19th Century, 22 x 44 x 17 In.. .... 189.00
Chest, Blanket, Pine, 6-Board, Bracket Feet, 21 x 35 x 21 In. 189.00

Chest, Blanket, Pine, 6-Board, Chip Carved Top, Blue Paint, Mass., c.1700, 28 x 48 In. 9480.00
Chest, Blanket, Pine, 6-Board, Poplar Till, Vinegar Sponged, Green Paint, 50 x 21 In. 1293.00
Chest, Blanket, Pine, 6-Board, Red Paint, Molded Lid, Applied Molding, 43 x 19 In. 1495.00
Chest, Blanket, Pine, 6-Board, Red Stain, Staple Hinges, T-Head Nails, 1800s, 47 x 16 In. 294.00
Chest, Blanket, Pine, 6-Board, Storage Well, Bracket Feet, Early 1800s, 23 x 43 In. 502.00
Chest, Blanket, Pine, Black, White, Smoke Imitation, Dovetailed, Bracket Feet, 38 x 15 In. 764.00
Chest, Blanket, Pine, Black Paint, Applied Lid Molding, Cutout Feet, 38 x 12 In. 676.00
Chest, Blanket, Pine, Blue, Red Paint, Dovetailed, Molded Edge, Till, 24 x 46 In. 1150.00
Chest, Blanket, Pine, Brass Escutcheon, Box Lock, Iron Hinges, 24 x 44 x 21 In. 154.00
Chest, Blanket, Pine, Flame Grain Painted, Cutout Feet, N.H., c.1840, 36 ½ x 16 ½ In. 2233.00
Chest, Blanket, Pine, Grain Painted, 6-Board, Dovetailed, Applied Lid, 48 ½ x 21 In. 518.00
Chest, Blanket, Pine, Green Paint, Lift Top, 2 Drawers, Bracket Feet, 1800s, 38 x 36 In. 5124.00
Chest, Blanket, Pine, Green Paint, Lift Top, Drawer, Bracket Feet, Late 1700s, 31 x 41 ½ In. .. 2574.00
Chest, Blanket, Pine, Ocher Grain Paint, Footed, Pa., 19th Century, 25 ½ x 42 In. 351.00
Chest, Blanket, Pine, Painted, Red & Black Stripes, 19th Century, 19 x 36 In. 1100.00
Chest, Blanket, Pine, Poplar, 3 Drawers, Compartment, Bracket Feet, 32 x 50 x 23 In. 7344.00
Chest, Blanket, Pine, Poplar, 6-Board, Till, Painted, Herringbone Design, c.1820, 37 x 22 In. . 470.00
Chest, Blanket, Pine, Red Grain Painted, Dovetailed, Bracket Feet, Molding, 40 x 19 In. 575.00
Chest, Blanket, Pine, Red Paint, Turned Legs, Pa., Mid 19th Century, 18 x 21 In. 1170.00
Chest, Blanket, Pine, Rosehead Nails, Red Paint, Black Pinwheels, 45 ½ x 17 In. 1293.00
Chest, Blanket, Pine, Yellow & Brown Swirl Design, Footed, Mid 1800s, 25 x 48 In. 475.00
Chest, Blanket, Poplar, 6-Board, Dovetailed, Turnip Feet, c.1825, 17 ½ x 32 x 14 In. 235.00
Chest, Blanket, Poplar, Applied Molding On Lid, Dovetailed, c.1850, 17 x 15 x 30 In. 411.00
Chest, Blanket, Poplar, Black & Red Paint, Dovetailed, Turned Feet, c.1840, 12 ⅜ x 17 In. 4313.00
Chest, Blanket, Poplar, Ocher Sponge Paint, Pa., c.1890, 21 x 48 In. 644.00
Chest, Blanket, Poplar, Red & Orange Design, Pa., 19th Century, 13 x 18 In. 2340.00
Chest, Blanket, Red Grain Painted, Bracket Feet, 44 x 20 In. 690.00
Chest, Blanket, Salmon Paint, 44 x 20 x 28 In. 633.00
Chest, Blanket, Softwood, Dovetailed, Brass Hinges, Lock, Ball Feet, 8 ¾ x 15 In. 1650.00
Chest, Blanket, Softwood, Drawers, Iron Strap Hinges, Jaw Lock, 32 x 51 x 25 In. 1100.00
Chest, Blanket, Softwood, Green Paint, Molded Lid, Dovetail Joints, 22 x 37 ½ In. 275.00
Chest, Blanket, Softwood, Molded Lid, Base, Bracket Feet, Strap Hinges, 26 x 51 In. 660.00
Chest, Blanket, Softwood, Molded Lid, Cast-Iron Hinges, 10 ¾ x 16 ¾ x 10 ⅜ In. 2090.00
Chest, Blanket, Softwood, Painted, Molded Lid, Base, Turned Feet, Pa., 26 x 50 In. 605.00
Chest, Blanket, Softwood, Red Ocher, Molded Lid, Interior Till, Drawers, 29 x 49 In. 605.00
Chest, Blanket, Sycamore, Walnut, Dovetailed Case, Interior Till, Turned Feet, 25 x 40 In. 1998.00
Chest, Blanket, Tombstone, 3 Drawers, Painted, Jonestown, Pa., 28 x 50 x 23 In. .... *illus* 37000.00
Chest, Blanket, Triple Tombstone, Diamond Banded Borders, Painted, 28 x 50 In. 40700.00
Chest, Blanket, Walnut, Dovetailed, Bracket Feet, Late 18th Century, 24 x 47 In. 527.00
Chest, Blanket, Walnut, Dovetailed, Strap Hinges, Bracket Feet, Early 1800s, 48 x 22 In. 441.00
Chest, Blanket, Walnut, Hinged Top, Interior Till, Ebonized, Piedmont, 25 x 44 In. 978.00
Chest, Blanket, William & Mary, Walnut, Iron Strap Hinges, 26 x 50 x 20 In. 2587.00
Chest, Blanket, Yellow Pine, Blue Paint, Lift Top, N.C., 19th Century, 24 x 44 x 18 In. 675.00
Chest, Bonnet, Cherry, c.1820-40, 42 x 52 In. 1200.00
Chest, Butler's, Biedermeier, Birch, Secretary Drawer, Fitted, 3 Drawers, 33 x 33 In. 508.00
Chest, Butler's, Campaign, Mahogany, String Inlay, Ebony, Satinwood, 36 x 33 In. 478.00
Chest, Butler's, Empire, Maple, Pillar & Scroll, Projecting Panel Drawer, 49 x 44 In. 299.00
Chest, Butler's, Federal, Walnut, False Double Front, 3 Drawers, Georgia, 44 x 41 In. 5290.00
Chest, Butler's, Regency, Mahogany, Drop Front, Scalloped Base, c.1840, 40 x 42 In. 1410.00
Chest, Campaign, Camphorwood, Brass Bound, Handles, 19th Century, 37 x 40 In. 770.00
Chest, Campaign, Camphorwood, Hinged, Brass Bound, c.1875, 13 x 29 In. 999.00
Chest, Campaign, Mahogany, 2 Drawers, Handles, 38 ½ x 41 ½ x 21 In. 2640.00
Chest, Campaign, Mahogany, Brass, 2 Over 3 Drawers, 39 x 18 ½ x 44 ½ In. 9750.00
Chest, Campaign, Teak, Brass Bound, 2 Short Over 3 Drawers, 40 x 34 x 17 ½ In. 1610.00
Chest, Captain's, Pine, Iron Mounts, Buddhist Angels, Lotus Plants, Japan, 15 x 13 x 17 In. .. 50.00
Chest, Carved, Chinese, c.1900, 18 x 57 x 24 In. 263.00
Chest, Charles II, Oak, Lift Top, Carved Paneled Front, England, 17th Century, 28 x 40 In. 2300.00
Chest, Cherry, 4 Graduated Drawers, Shaped Skirt, Bracket Feet, Tenn., 1800s, 39 x 42 In. 1495.00
Chest, Cherry, 6 Drawers, c.1760, 59 ½ x 38 In. 7605.00
Chest, Cherry, Poplar, 2 Over 3 Drawers, Shaped Skirt, Turned Feet, 46 x 43 x 20 In. 823.00
Chest, Cherry, Poplar, 2 Over 4 Drawers, Half Columns, Paint Decorated, 47 x 43 In. 1410.00
Chest, Cherry, Poplar, Walnut, Flowers, 6 Drawers, 1875, 47 x 43 x 20 In. .... *illus* 1200.00
Chest, Chippendale, 3 Over 2 Over 4 Drawers, Fluted Columns, Late 1700s, 62 x 43 In. 4230.00
Chest, Chippendale, 4 Drawers, 38 x 37 ½ x 21 In. 100.00
Chest, Chippendale, 6 Drawers, Bracket Base, 42 x 19 x 56 In. 2300.00
Chest, Chippendale, 6 Graduated Drawers, Incised Edges, Bracket Feet, 58 x 39 In. 1416.00
Chest, Chippendale, Birch, 4 Drawers, Bracket Base, 33 ½ x 40 x 21 In. 275.00

Furniture, Chest, Blanket, Tombstone, 3 Drawers, Painted, Jonestown, Pa., 28 x 50 x 23 In.
$37000.00

Furniture, Chest, Cherry, Poplar, Walnut, Flowers, 6 Drawers, 1875, 47 x 43 x 20 In.
$1200.00

Furniture, Chest, Chippendale, Walnut, Yellow Pine, 5 Drawers, 1820s, 39 x 40 x 19 In.
$935.00

TIP

When polishing the metal hardware on old chests of drawers, get a piece of stiff paper and slide it under the brass plate. This will protect the wood near the brass.

Furniture, Chest, Curly Maple, Cherry, Walnut, 4 Drawers, 1875, 38 x 30 x 19 In., Child's
$2100.00

Furniture, Chest, Dower, Chippendale Style, Painted, 3 Drawers, Panels, Pa., 26 x 51 x 22 In.
$1050.00

Golden Oak

Golden oak is Victorian, Mission and Art Deco. The Golden Oak period (1880–1920) is named for the wood that was most popular for furniture at the time. Walnut was used when Victorian-style furniture was first made, but it became harder to find. The most available wood was oak. Cabinetmakers began to use "quarter-cut" oak, which made a board with attractive grain patterns. The oak was given a light golden finish as well as darker finishes. The furniture was made not only of oak, but also had parts of ash, beech, maple, and hickory.

F

Chest, Chippendale, Birch, 4 Drawers, New England, 18th Century, 33 ½ x 36 In. 1053.00
Chest, Chippendale, Birch, Chestnut, 6 Graduated Drawers, Bracket Feet, 51 x 42 In. 8519.00
Chest, Chippendale, Cherry, 3 Short Drawers Over 5, Bracket Feet, 62 x 41 ¾ x 22 ½ In...... 2500.00
Chest, Chippendale, Cherry, 4 Drawers, Ogee Base, c.1790, 37 ¾ x 36 ½ x 18 In. 4000.00
Chest, Chippendale, Cherry, 4 Drawers, Ogee Bracket Feet, c.1780, 34 ½ x 38 In. 2106.00
Chest, Chippendale, Cherry, 4 Graduated Drawers, Bracket Feet, c.1780, 35 x 39 In. 1200.00
Chest, Chippendale, Cherry, 4 Graduated Drawers, Cutout Bracket Feet, c.1775-85 .... 425.00
Chest, Chippendale, Cherry, Bonnet Top, 2 Sections, 7 Drawers, Spiral Finials, 85 x 40 In. ... 3125.00
Chest, Chippendale, Cherry, Carved, 4 Drawers, Brass, Conn., c.1790, 33 x 36 In.. .... 28125.00
Chest, Chippendale, Cherry, Carved, 5 Drawers, Conn., c.1785, 38 x 39 In. 10000.00
Chest, Chippendale, Cherry, Chestnut, 6 Graduated Drawers, c.1800, 52 x 37 In. 1410.00
Chest, Chippendale, Cherry, Fluted Quarter Columns, Cock-Beaded Drawers, 35 x 41 In. 4700.00
Chest, Chippendale, Cherry, Oak, 5 Drawers, Rhode Island, c.1770, 42 ½ x 34 ½ In. 761.00
Chest, Chippendale, Cherry, Reverse Serpentine, 4 Drawers, Conn., c.1830, 32 x 37 In. 11258.00
Chest, Chippendale, Cherry, Serpentine Top, 4 Drawers, 32 x 35 ½ x 19 ¾ In.. .... 8125.00
Chest, Chippendale, Mahogany, 2 Over 3 Graduated Drawers, c.1780, 35 x 38 x 19 In. 1550.00
Chest, Chippendale, Mahogany, 3 Drawers, England, 1700s, 36 x 46 In. 1150.00
Chest, Chippendale, Mahogany, 4 Drawers, 1700s, 35 x 44 In. 2300.00
Chest, Chippendale, Mahogany, 4 Drawers, Dresser Top, Brass End Lifts, 12 x 24 In. 155.00
Chest, Chippendale, Mahogany, 4 Drawers, Ogee Bracket Feet, 32 ½ x 41 x 22 In. 375.00
Chest, Chippendale, Mahogany, Block Front, Figured, Mass., c.1770, 30 x 36 In. 28750.00
Chest, Chippendale, Mahogany, Bowfront, 4 Graduated Drawers, 42 x 39 In. 2300.00
Chest, Chippendale, Mahogany, Brass Figured, 4 Drawers, c.1780, 34 x 39 In. 194500.00
Chest, Chippendale, Mahogany, Molded Overhang, 4 Drawers, Pa., c.1780, 35 x 35 In. 1410.00
Chest, Chippendale, Mahogany, Pine, Bowfront, 4 Drawers, c.1780, 33 x 42 In. 3738.00
Chest, Chippendale, Mahogany, Reverse Serpentine, 30 x 40 x 21 In.. .... 1875.00
Chest, Chippendale, Maple, Late 1700s, 51 ½ x 18 ¾ In.. .... 5036.00
Chest, Chippendale, Maple, Pine, Molded Cornice, 2 Over 4 Drawers, 72 x 36 In. 3290.00
Chest, Chippendale, Maple, Pine, Molded Rectangle Top, 4 Drawers, c.1800, 39 x 38 In. 2585.00
Chest, Chippendale, Molded, 2 Faux Over 3 Graduated Drawers, Mid 1700s, 41 x 39 In. 708.00
Chest, Chippendale, Pine, Arches, Flowerpots, Iron Straps, Painted, 1775, 22 x 50 x 24 In. ... 1300.00
Chest, Chippendale, Poplar, Yellow Grain Paint, 8 Drawers, Pa., c.1790, 21 x 16 In.. .... 59375.00
Chest, Chippendale, Tiger Maple, 4 Drawers, Footed, Late 18th Century, 38 x 36 In.. .... 1464.00
Chest, Chippendale, Tiger Maple, 4 Drawers, Ogee Bracket Feet, c.1770, 33 x 32 In.. .... 7020.00
Chest, Chippendale, Tiger Maple, Cherry, 3 Over 4 Drawers, Ogee Feet, c.1780, 50 x 37 In. ... 585.00
Chest, Chippendale, Walnut, 2 Over 3 Cock-Beaded Drawers, c.1770, 35 x 37 x 20 In. 7700.00
Chest, Chippendale, Walnut, 2 Over 3 Drawers, Bracket Feet, Pa., c.1770, 40 x 38 In.. .... 1650.00
Chest, Chippendale, Walnut, 3 Over 5 Graduated Drawers, Fluted Pilaster, 61 x 43 In.. ...... 7170.00
Chest, Chippendale, Walnut, 5 Over 5 Drawers, Fluted Columns, Pa., c.1770, 68 x 39 In.. .... 9360.00
Chest, Chippendale, Walnut, 5 Over 5 Drawers, Ogee Bracket Feet, c.1775, 70 x 39 In.. ...... 6435.00
Chest, Chippendale, Walnut, 5 Short Drawers Over 3 Long, 50 x 40 ½ x 22 In. 1500.00
Chest, Chippendale, Walnut, Carved Shells, 11 Drawers, Pa., 1700s, 72 x 35 In. 4140.00
Chest, Chippendale, Walnut, Carved Shells, Pediment, 8 Drawers, Pa., 1700s, 86 x 40 In. 3220.00
Chest, Chippendale, Walnut, Dovetailed Drawers, Brass Pulls, Late 1700s, 61 x 43 In. 3910.00
Chest, Chippendale, Walnut, Molded Cornice, Pa., c.1780, 47 x 41 In. 480.00
Chest, Chippendale, Walnut, Pine, 3 Short & 3 Long Drawers, c.1775, 42 x 40 In. 2468.00
Chest, Chippendale, Walnut, Pine, 4 Dovetailed Drawers, Escutcheons, c.1800, 62 x 45 In. ... 352.00
Chest, Chippendale, Walnut, Reeded Columns, Ogee Bracket Feet, 62 ½ x 41 In. 2900.00
Chest, Chippendale, Walnut, Yellow Pine, 5 Drawers, 1820s, 39 x 40 x 19 In. .... *illus* 935.00
Chest, Chippendale Style, Mahogany, Bowfront, Inlaid, 34 ½ x 36 ¾ x 20 ½ In. 863.00
Chest, Colonial Revival, 3 Over 4 Graduated Drawers, Pilasters, 44 x 41 In. 295.00
Chest, Colonial Revival, Bird's-Eye Maple, Triple-Lobe Top, 3 Drawers, c.1910, 32 x 48 In. ... 299.00
Chest, Curly Maple, Cherry, Walnut, 4 Drawers, 1875, 38 x 30 x 19 In., Child's .... *illus* 2100.00
Chest, Directoire, Mahogany, 3 Drawers, Fluted Pilasters, Tapered Legs, 35 x 43 x 23 In...... 711.00
Chest, Dower, Chippendale, Painted, Hinged, Paneled Front, Drawers, 1700s, 26 x 52 In. 1093.00
Chest, Dower, Chippendale Style, Painted, 3 Drawers, Panels, Pa., 26 x 51 x 22 In...... *illus* 1050.00
Chest, Dower, Fir, Iron Hinges, Handles, Blue Field, Yellow, Red, Tulips, Va., c.1800 .... 1265.00
Chest, Dower, Fir, Yellow, Red Tulips, Black Ground, Va., 1790s, 18 x 41 x 23 In.. .... *illus* 1210.00
Chest, Dower, Hearts, Pine, Inscribed, LW D30 Novembre, 1798, 23 x 46 In. .... *illus* 11700.00
Chest, Dower, Pine, Clover Panels, Tulips, Pa., Late 18th Century, 22 x 51 In.. .... 468.00
Chest, Dower, Pine, Drawer, Grain Painted Yellow, Mennonite, c.1900, 29 x 46 In. 1725.00
Chest, Dower, Pine, Green Sponge Ovals, Orange Ground, Footed, 1820, 24 x 45 In. 1900.00
Chest, Dower, Pine, Paint Decorated, Applied Molding, Flowers, 22 ½ x 49 ½ In. 3450.00
Chest, Dower, Pine, Painted, Birds, Tulips, Hearts, Glass Panel, Drawer, c.1850, 12 x 16 In... 2937.00
Chest, Dower, Poplar, Molded Inset Panels, Green Paint, Ball Feet, c.1730, 24 x 48 In........ 8295.00
Chest, Dower, Softwood, Fraktur, Iron Hinges, Handles, 23 ½ x 51 x 23 ½ In.. .... 1100.00
Chest, Dower, Softwood, Tulip Panels, Red, Iron Strap Hinges, 21 ½ x 50 x 24 ½ In. 468.00

Chest, Dower, Sycamore, Dovetailed, Split Lip Drawers, Bracket Feet, 1700s, 38 x 51 In. 440.00
Chest, Dressing, Mahogany, Stiles, Capitals, Urn Finials, Mirror, Drawers, c.1825, 77 x 42 In. . . 1880.00
Chest, Dressing, Neoclassical, Mahogany, Mirror, Turned Stiles, c.1830, 83 x 42 In. 588.00
Chest, Dressing, Oak, Mirror, 3 Drawers, Knob Feet, Ambrose Heal, c.1925, 53 x 18 In. 94.00
Chest, Empire, 2 Drawers, Pilasters, Apron Heart Cutout, Paw Feet, c.1830, 15 x 12 In. 4112.00
Chest, Empire, Mahogany, 2 Drawer Top, 4 Drawers, Panel Stiles, 42 x 41 x 19 In.. . . . . 350.00
Chest, Empire, Mahogany, 4 Drawers, Backsplash, Mid 19th Century, 22 x 17 In., Child's 527.00
Chest, Empire, Mahogany, 4 Drawers, Embossed Glass Pulls, 41 x 42 x 22 In.. . . . . 384.00
Chest, Empire, Mahogany, 4 Drawers, Turned Pilasters, Block & Ball Feet, 42 x 43 In. 359.00
Chest, Empire, Mahogany, 4 Drawers, Writing Surface, c.1820-30, 29 x 33 x 15 ½ In. 600.00
Chest, Empire, Mahogany, 47 ½ x 44 x 20 In. 600.00
Chest, Empire, Mahogany, Carvings, 6 Drawers, Base Cornice Drawer, c.1820, 71 x 54 In.. . . . 560.00
Chest, Empire Style, Walnut, Yellow Pine, Poplar, Drawers, 47 x 36 x 21 In. 3955.00
Chest, English Oak, 4 Drawers, Geometric Panels, Bracket Feet, 38 x 39 x 22 ¾ In. 3840.00
Chest, Federal, Birch, Mahogany, Bowfront, Inlaid, 4 Drawers, c.1800, 37 x 42 In. 17500.00
Chest, Federal, Birch, Shaped Backsplash, 4 Dovetailed Drawers, 1800s, 45 x 42 In. 489.00
Chest, Federal, Carved, Inlaid, Brass Pulls, 3 Drawers, Mass., c.1815, 37 x 39 In. 1778.00
Chest, Federal, Cherry, 4 Dovetailed Drawers, Reeded Pilasters, 1800s, 38 x 40 In. 633.00
Chest, Federal, Cherry, 4 Drawers, Biscuit Corners, Reeded Columns, 1800s, 39 x 43 In. 1840.00
Chest, Federal, Cherry, 4 Graduated Dovetailed Drawers, French Feet, c.1800, 34 x 42 In.. . . . 3105.00
Chest, Federal, Cherry, 5 Drawers, Cock-Beaded, Turned Feet, Pa., 41 x 41 x 22 In. . . . . . *illus* 225.00
Chest, Federal, Cherry, Graduated Drawers, Pendant Stiles, c.1820, 47 x 41 In. 1175.00
Chest, Federal, Cherry, Mahogany, Maple Drawers, Brass, Scalloped, 43 x 43 x 20 In.. . . . . 2520.00
Chest, Federal, Cherry, Poplar Vine, Leaf Inlay, 4 Drawers, Kentucky, 1800s, 41 x 40 In.. . . . . . 5060.00
Chest, Federal, Cherry, Scroll Back, 4 Drawers, Turned Column Legs, 1800s, 45 x 42 In. 345.00
Chest, Federal, Lift Top, Inscribed, Glasgow, Ky., 19th Century, 28 x 43 In.. . . . . 518.00
Chest, Federal, Mahogany, 3 Drawers, Embossed Oval Brass Handles, c.1840, 42 x 37 In. 265.00
Chest, Federal, Mahogany, 4 Drawers, Line Inlay, New York, c.1800, 35 x 28 In. 2530.00
Chest, Federal, Mahogany, Bead Molding, 4 Drawers, 1800s, 41 x 42 x 20 ½ In. 490.00
Chest, Federal, Mahogany, Block & Scalloped Front, 4 Drawers, c.1810, 38 x 36 In. 5124.00
Chest, Federal, Mahogany, Bowfront, 4 Drawers, 1790-1810, 35 x 41 x 23 In. 1400.00
Chest, Federal, Mahogany, Bowfront, 4 Drawers, French Feet, c.1800, 37 ½ x 42 In.. . . . . 702.00
Chest, Federal, Mahogany, Bowfront, 4 Drawers, New Hampshire, c.1800, 38 x 40 In. 3910.00
Chest, Federal, Mahogany, Bowfront, 4 Inlaid Drawers, Bracket Feet, c.1805, 36 x 41 In.. . . . . 2808.00
Chest, Federal, Mahogany, Bowfront, Cock-Beaded, Reeded Stiles, Turned Feet, 41 x 40 In. . . . 1058.00
Chest, Federal, Mahogany, Bowfront, Graduated Drawers, Turned Legs, c.1800, 41 x 43 In.. . . 2468.00
Chest, Federal, Mahogany, Bowfront, Inlaid, 12 Drawers, 30 x 26 ½ x 13 ½ In. 350.00
Chest, Federal, Mahogany, Bowfront, Turreted Corners, Reeded Stiles, c.1820, 42 x 42 In.. . . . 2350.00
Chest, Federal, Mahogany, Cherry, 4 Drawers, New York, c.1810, 43 x 41 In.. . . . . 5313.00
Chest, Federal, Mahogany, Inlaid, 4 Drawers, Charleston, 1800, 38 x 44 x 20 In. 1500.00
Chest, Federal, Mahogany, Inlaid, Bowfront, c.1810, 37 x 38 In.. . . . . 4266.00
Chest, Federal, Mahogany, Inlaid, Bowfront, Reeded Edge, 2 Over 3 Drawers, 42 x 42 In. 478.00
Chest, Federal, Mahogany, Inlaid, Gilt, 2 Over 3 Drawers, 1800s, 41 x 40 x 18 In.. . . . . 440.00
Chest, Federal, Mahogany, Oval Corners, Rope-Twist Stiles, 4 Drawers, c.1800, 41 x 44 In. . . . 1880.00
Chest, Federal, Rosewood, Figured Mahogany, Drawers, Early 1800s, 16 x 13 In. 1380.00
Chest, Federal, Sheraton, Mahogany, Bowfront, 4 Drawers, c.1800, 41x 45 x 23 In. 550.00
Chest, Federal, Tiger & Bird's-Eye Maple, 4 Drawers, 19th Century, 43 x 41 x 18 In.. . . . . 375.00
Chest, Federal, Tiger Maple, 3 Over 5 Drawers, Pa., Early 19th Century, 65 x 43 In. 9200.00
Chest, Federal, Tiger Maple, Bird's-Eye Maple Case, 4 Drawers, New England, 38 x 42 In. 5520.00
Chest, Federal, Tiger Maple, Cherry, 4 Graduated Drawers, Tennessee, 1800s, 26 x 28 In. 805.00
Chest, Federal, Walnut, Fan & Barber Pole Inlaid Top, Graduated Drawers, 40 x 42 In.. . . . . . . 14900.00
Chest, Federal, Walnut, Figured, Bowfront, 4 Graduated Drawers, Early 1800s, 40 x 40 In. . . . 978.00
Chest, Federal, Walnut, Mahogany, Drawers, Fluted Columns, Early 1900s, 54 x 45 In. 2070.00
Chest, Federal, Yellow Pine, Figured Birch, 2 Over 3 Drawers, S.C., 41 x 40 In. 1093.00
Chest, Federal, Yellow Pine, Walnut, Inlaid, 4 Drawers, N.C., c.1800, 42 x 40 In.. . . . . 1840.00
Chest, Flame Grain Painted, 4 Drawers, 1 Overhanging, Ohio, c.1840, 47 x 43 In. 323.00
Chest, Flame Mahogany, 2 Over 4 Drawers, Mirror, 75 x 42 x 19 In.. . . . . 840.00
Chest, Flatware, Chippendale Revival, Mahogany, 3 Drawers, 38 x 23 In. . . . . *illus* 354.00
Chest, Frank Lloyd Wright, 4 Drawers, Recessed Handles, Signed, 25 x 33 In., Pair 1200.00
Chest, French Provincial, Shaped Front, 3 Drawers, Cabriole Feet, c.1825, 31 x 41 In.. . . . . 4800.00
Chest, G. Nelson, Oak Veneer, 3 Drawers, Door, Wire Pulls, Herman Miller, c.1965, 30 x 56 In. 504.00
Chest, G. Stickley, No. 626, 2 Over 3 Drawers, Inverted V Backsplash, 43 x 35 x 20 In. 3000.00
Chest, G. Stickley, No. 913, 6 Over 3 Drawers, Arched Toe Board, 50 ½ x 36 x 20 In.. . . . . 13000.00
Chest, George I, Oak, Carved, 2 Over 3 Drawers, Footed, Late 17th Century, 37 x 37 In. 995.00
Chest, George I, Walnut, Oyster Veneer, Molded Edge, 2 Drawers, 1900s, 30 x 36 In.. . . . . 2151.00
Chest, George II, Walnut, 2 Short Over 3 Long Drawers, Bracket Feet, 37 x 36 In.. . . . . 2040.00
Chest, George III, 6 Drawers, Banded, Bracket Feet, c.1775, 35 x 37 In. 2880.00

TIP

If the drawer in a cabinet sticks, buy some silicone spray at a craft store. Spray only the runners and the sides of the drawer. Do not let any spray get on the front finish of the cabinet.

F

Furniture, Chest, Dower, Fir, Yellow, Red Tulips, Black Ground, Va., 1790s, 18 x 41 x 23 In.
$1210.00

Furniture, Chest, Dower, Hearts, Pine, Inscribed, LW D30 Novembre, 1798, 23 x 46 In.
$11700.00

Furniture, Chest, Federal, Cherry, 5 Drawers, Cock-Beaded, Turned Feet, Pa., 41 x 41 x 22 In.
$225.00

Furniture Made Here
The center of furniture manufacturing in the United States in the late nineteenth century was Grand Rapids, Michigan.

Furniture, Chest, Flatware, Chippendale Revival, Mahogany, 3 Drawers, 38 x 23 In.
$354.00

Furniture, Chest, H. Probber, Walnut, Grasscloth Sliding Doors, Brass Feet, 30 ½ x 40 x 18 In.
$960.00

Furniture, Chest, Mixed Wood, Diamond Inlay, 3 Drawers, 13 x 13 x 8 In.
$375.00

Chest, George III, Fruitwood, Brushing Slide, 4 Drawers, 29 x 26 In., Pair . . . 1440.00
Chest, George III, Mahogany, 4 Cock-Beaded Drawers, French Feet, 35 x 35 x 18 In. . . . 850.00
Chest, George III, Mahogany, 4 Graduated Drawers, Ivory Escutcheons, 39 x 36 In. . . . 960.00
Chest, George III, Mahogany, 5 Drawers, Bracket Feet, c.1875, 39 x 46 In. . . . 1800.00
Chest, George III, Mahogany, Bowfront, 3 Drawers, Shaped Apron, c.1800, 36 x 43 In. . . . 1673.00
Chest, George III, Mahogany, Bowfront, 5 Drawers, Bracket Feet, 36 x 43 In. . . . 1920.00
Chest, George III, Mahogany, Bowfront Top, 3 Short Over 3 Long Drawers, 38 x 43 In. . . . 900.00
Chest, George III, Mahogany, Crossbanded Top, 2 Over 2 Beaded Drawers, 34 x 35 In. . . . 1440.00
Chest, George III, Mahogany, Inlaid, Serpentine Front, 3 Drawers, c.1775, 34 x 43 In. . . . 7500.00
Chest, George III, Mahogany, Inlaid, Serpentine Front, 4 Drawers, c.1780, 34 x 39 In. . . . 10000.00
Chest, George III, Mahogany, Short Drawers, Graduated Long Drawers, 33 x 45 x 22 In. . . . 1200.00
Chest, George III, Mahogany, Veneer, Serpentine, Dressing Slide, 4 Drawers, 34 x 23 x 37 In. . . 3525.00
Chest, George III, Oak, 2 Short Over 3 Long Graduated Drawers, Bracket Feet, 37 x 38 In. . . . 1560.00
Chest, George III, Red Lacquer, Oriental Landscape, 5 Drawers, c.1775, 38 x 41 In. . . . 4080.00
Chest, George III, Walnut, 2 Over 3 Drawers, Bracket Feet, c.1740-80, 39 x 37 x 21 In. . . . 2510.00
Chest, George III, Walnut, Mahogany, Pullout Brushing Slide, 3 Drawers, 35 x 38 x 21 In. . . . 2714.00
Chest, George III, Walnut, Oyster Veneers, 7 Drawers, Bracket Feet, 77 x 45 x 22 In. . . . 6000.00
Chest, George III Style, Hepplewhite, Mahogany, Line Inlay, Drawers, 41 ½ x 36 In. . . . 2040.00
Chest, George III Style, Mahogany, 2 Over 3 Drawers, Bracket Feet, 39 x 37 x 19 In. . . . 1560.00
Chest, George III Style, Mahogany, Drawers, 29 ½ x 24 x 15 In., Pair . . . 2150.00
Chest, George III Style, Mahogany, Inlaid, Bowed Front, 4 Drawers, 35 x 39 In. . . . 3125.00
Chest, George III Style, Mahogany, Serpentine, Cock-Beaded Drawers, 35 x 39 x 23 In. . . . 2903.00
Chest, Georgian, Burl Mahogany, Lift Top, 4 Drawers, c.1890, 36 x 31 x 17 In. . . . 300.00
Chest, Georgian, Walnut, Pine Inlay, Knobs, 4 Drawers, Shaped Feet, England, 1800s, 15 x 19 In. 403.00
Chest, Georgian Style, Mahogany, Inlaid, 4 Graduated Drawers, 33 x 27 In. . . . 1007.00
Chest, Georgian Style, Walnut, Herringbone Banded, 3 Drawers, 22 x 22 x 18 In., Pair . . . 1255.00
Chest, Grain, Mudejar, Carved Wood Flowers, Slant Front, Iron Band, India, 1800s, 16 In. . . . 708.00
Chest, H. Probber, Walnut, Grasscloth Sliding Doors, Brass Feet, 30 ½ x 40 x 18 In. . . . *illus* 960.00
Chest, Hardwood, Camphor, Carved, Lock, Chinese, 26 x 44 x 22 In. . . . 1652.00
Chest, Hepplewhite, Cherry, 4 Drawers, Flared Feet, c.1800, 39 x 41 In. . . . 764.00
Chest, Hepplewhite, Cherry, Bowfront, Drawers, French Feet, Early 1800s, 40 x 23 In. . . . 1528.00
Chest, Hepplewhite, Cherry, Curly Maple, 4 Drawers, c.1950, 22 x 20 In. . . . 323.00
Chest, Hepplewhite, Cherry, Poplar, Reed Band, 3 Over 2 Drawers, 64 x 43 In. . . . 1955.00
Chest, Hepplewhite, Cherry, Serpentine, Inlaid, 4 Graduated Drawers, 39 x 21 In. . . . 2115.00
Chest, Hepplewhite, Mahogany, 4 Drawers, Cross Bands, Bowed, c.1790, 31 x 33 In. . . . 265.00
Chest, Hepplewhite, Mahogany, 4 Drawers, England, 19th Century, 32 x 34 x 16 In. . . . 850.00
Chest, Hepplewhite, Mahogany, 5 Drawers, England, 19th Century, 42 x 43 x 20 In. . . . 650.00
Chest, Hepplewhite, Mahogany, 5 Drawers, Scalloped Skirt, 40 x 41 In. . . . 1175.00
Chest, Hepplewhite, Mahogany, Inlaid, Bowfront, 4 Drawers, 35 x 41 ½ x 23 In. . . . 1400.00
Chest, Hepplewhite, Mahogany, Pine, c.1820, 45 x 44 ¾ In. . . . 1610.00
Chest, Hepplewhite, Walnut, 5 Drawers, Beaded, c.1820, 12 x 13 In. . . . 323.00
Chest, Ice, Golden Oak, Paneled Doors, Porcelain Lined, 47 x 35 x 20 ½ In. . . . 531.00
Chest, Indo-European Colonial, Oak, Carved Figures, Columned Porticos, c.1900, 25 x 59 In. 649.00
Chest, Italian Renaissance Style, Walnut, Carved, Paw Feet, Continental, 26 x 60 x 27 In. . . . 1610.00
Chest, Jacobean, Panels, 3 Drawers, Extended Post Feet, Early 1900s, 37 x 40 In. . . . 2006.00
Chest, Johann Tapp, 3 Drawers, Acorn Drawer Pulls, Bracket Feet, 31 ½ x 38 In. . . . 5520.00
Chest, Kingwood, Mahogany, Inlaid Drawers, Bun Feet, Banded Top, 31 x 38 In. . . . 1020.00
Chest, Kittinger, 5 Shelves, Wood Pulls, Green, Stamped, 1940s, 16 x 27 In. . . . 720.00
Chest, Kittinger, Bachelor's, Mahogany, 4 Drawers, Pullout Slide, 31 x 31 x 18 In. . . . 1050.00
Chest, L. & J.G. Stickley, No. 97, 2 Over 3 Drawers, Brand Mark, 39 ½ x 38 x 18 In. . . . 2300.00
Chest, Lingerie, Alexander Roux, Rosewood, Inlaid, Drop Down, Signed, 1880, 53 x 25 In. . . . 14300.00
Chest, Lingerie, Louis XVI, Bookmatched Mahogany, Marble Top, Early 1900s, 46 x 19 In. . . . 978.00
Chest, Louis XV, Chinoiserie, 2 Drawers, Marble Top, Brass Mounts, Black, 1900s, 33 x 46 In. . . 690.00
Chest, Louis XV, French Provincial, 4 Carved Drawers, Shaped Feet, 33 x 49 x 22 In. . . . 3081.00
Chest, Louis XV, Marquetry, Marble Top, Drawers, Rosewood Band, 59 x 38 In. . . . 748.00
Chest, Louis XV, Marquetry, White & Gray Marble Top, 2 Drawers, 1900s, 34 x 41 In., Pair . . . 1292.00
Chest, Louis XVI, Mahogany, Marble Top, 7 Drawers, Bronze Pulls, France, c.1900, 56 x 24 In. 1265.00
Chest, Louis XVI, Walnut Veneer, Marble Top, 2 Over 4 Drawers, Early 1900s, 50 x 34 In. . . . 460.00
Chest, Mahogany, 2 Over 3 Dovetailed Drawers, Brass Pulls, c.1885, 13 x 7 x 14 In. . . . 646.00
Chest, Mahogany, 2 Short Over 4 Long Drawers, Turned Half Columns, Feet, 43 x 42 x 20 In. . . 688.00
Chest, Mahogany, 4 Drawers, Fluted Corner Columns, Ogee Bracket Feet, 36 x 37 In. . . . 9560.00
Chest, Mahogany, 4 Drawers, Serpentine Feet, Brass Handles, Mass., c.1790, 33 x 41 In. . . . 5750.00
Chest, Mahogany, 5 Drawers, Base Molding, Bracket Feet, Mid 1800s, 39 x 18 In. . . . 3450.00
Chest, Mahogany, 5 Drawers, Columns, Paw Feet, 54 x 49 x 28 In. . . . 660.00
Chest, Mahogany, 7 Drawers, Corner Columns, c.1820, 20 x 17 x 7 ¼ In. . . . 960.00
Chest, Mahogany, Bowfront, 4 Dovetailed Drawers, Scalloped Apron, 1800s, 43 x 22 In. . . . 822.00
Chest, Mahogany, Bowfront, 4 Drawers, Flared Feet, String Inlay, c.1800, 38 x 43 In. . . . 1528.00

Chest, Mahogany, Bowfront, Frieze Drawers, Floral Stiles, Drawers, Scotland, 49 x 50 In. 1080.00
Chest, Mahogany, Bowfront, Inlaid, 5 Drawers, French Feet, England, c.1800, 41 x 40 In. 1265.00
Chest, Mahogany, Cherry, Crossbanded Drawers, Bulbous Feet, c.1830, 47 x 43 In. 587.00
Chest, Mahogany, Gadrooned, 2 Over 2 Drawers, Pineapple Carved Columns, 31 x 46 x 25 In. 944.00
Chest, Mahogany, Graduated Drawers, Bead Molding, 30 ½ x 35 ½ x 20 ¾ In. 25095.00
Chest, Mahogany, Marble Top, Ormolu, 2 Doors, Brass Fluted Legs, France, 45 x 53 In. 22500.00
Chest, Mahogany, Oak, Pine, 2 Over 3 Drawers, Bracket Base, 1700s, 42 x 40 In. 863.00
Chest, Mahogany, White Marble Top, 4 Drawers, Frieze, Gold, N.Y., c.1820, 40 x 51 In. 43700.00
Chest, Mahogany Veneer, Oak, White Marble Top, Drawers, 37 x 50 In. 1175.00
Chest, Maple, 3 Drawers, Fan Carving, Shaped Apron, c.1790, 70 x 39 ½ In. 6038.00
Chest, Maple, Cherry, Walnut Drawer Dividers, Ogee Molding, Ohio, c.1840, 38 x 30 x 19 In. 2468.00
Chest, Mirror, Black Walnut, 9 Drawers, Curvilinear Panel, Raised Frame, c.1950, 32 x 78 In. 415.00
Chest, Mirror, Mahogany Veneer, Scalloped Crown, Handkerchief Drawers, 20 x 44 In. 381.00
Chest, Mixed Wood, Diamond Inlay, 3 Drawers, 13 x 13 x 8 In. .... *illus* 375.00
Chest, Mixed Wood, Edge-Molded Top, 3 Drawers, Rosehead Decoration, 32 x 35 In. 1175.00
Chest, Mule, Pine, 2 Lower Drawers, Cutout Feet, Black Over Yellow Paint, 37 x 19 In. 4935.00
Chest, Mule, Pine, Lift Top, Drawer, Shaped Apron, Bracket Feet, Green, Brown, c.1810, 38 x 37 In. 1920.00
Chest, Mule, Pine, Red Stain, 2 Faux Over 2 Dovetailed Drawers, Lift Top, 36 x 19 In. 863.00
Chest, Mule, Pine, Single Board Lid, Strap Hinges, Bracket Feet, 18 x 31 ½ x 32 In. 2938.00
Chest, Mule, Poplar, Chestnut, Lift Top, 2 False Over 2 Working Drawers, 45 x 40 In. 441.00
Chest, Napoleon III, Kingwood, Marble Top, 5 Drawers, 33 x 16 x 10 In., Pair 1680.00
Chest, Napoleon III, Kingwood, Matchbook Veneers, 6 Drawers, 48 x 17 x 11 In. 720.00
Chest, Neoclassical, Adam Style, Parquetry, Drawers, Doors, 47 x 35 ½ x 21 In. 260.00
Chest, Neoclassical, Mahogany, 4 Drawers, Paneled Doors, Acanthus Carved, 49 x 49 In. 600.00
Chest, Neoclassical, Mahogany, 5 Drawers, Ionic Pilasters, Bun Feet, c.1825, 42 x 47 In. 1762.00
Chest, Neoclassical, Mahogany, Carved, 4 Drawers, 2 Paw Feet, New York, c.1825, 12 x 13 In. 1750.00
Chest, Neoclassical, Mahogany, Graduated Drawers, Blocked Stiles, Drawer, 34 x 37 In. 1410.00
Chest, Neoclassical, Tiger Maple, Mahogany, Pine, 19th Century, American, 49 x 47 In. 805.00
Chest, Nutting, Oak, Sunflower, Banded Drawers, 40 ½ x 45 In. 7020.00
Chest, Oak, Maple, Pine, Joined, Molding, 4 Drawers, Mass., c.1690, 38 x 52 In. .... *illus* 28125.00
Chest, Oak, Pine, Reeded Edge, Line Inlay, Dovetailed Drawers, Early 1800s, 51 x 45 In. 294.00
Chest, Oak, Shaped Front, Undulating Uprights, Square Feet, Dutch, 33 x 33 x 21 In. 4320.00
Chest, Oyster-Cut Veneer, 2 Short Over 2 Long Drawers, Bracket Feet, 31 x 38 In. 1440.00
Chest, Painted, Lift Top, Scalloped Base, T-Head & Rosehead Nails, c.1700 .... 4900.00
Chest, Pine, 4 Drawers, Glove Drawers, Scrolled Pilasters, Legs, 15 ½ x 13 x 6 ½ In. 558.00
Chest, Pine, 5 Drawers, Bun Feet, c.1800, 38 x 42 x 18 In. 266.00
Chest, Pine, 5 Over 3 Drawers, Red Stain, Bracket Feet, c.1800, 47 ½ x 42 In. 1287.00
Chest, Pine, Blanket, Hinged Lid, Brass Corners, c.1925, 13 x 31 x 15 In. 127.00
Chest, Pine, Blanket, Lift Top, Dovetailed, Interior Till, Bracket Base, Pa., 24 x 44 In. 604.00
Chest, Pine, Blanket, Lift Top, Iron Mountings, Bun Feet, Folk Art Designs & Flowers, 20 x 45 In. 403.00
Chest, Pine, Blanket, Painted, Harbor Scene, Flower Urns, Nailed, Interior Till, 1800s, 19 x 40 In. 1150.00
Chest, Pine, Bowed Top, Cityscape, Country Life, Drawers, 31 x 44 ½ x 23 In. 4080.00
Chest, Pine, Brown & Ocher Paint, Lift Top, Pa., 1820s, 28 x 50 x 22 ½ In. 1200.00
Chest, Pine, Drawer, Blue Paint, New England, 31 x 41 In. 1304.00
Chest, Pine, Poplar, Drawer, Painted, Early 1800s, 30 x 41 In. 1126.00
Chest, Pinwheels, Hearts, Painted, Red Ground, Yellow, Green, Scalloped Base, 27 x 38 In. 40700.00
Chest, Poplar, 4 Drawers, Paneled Sides, Shaped Front, 1800s, 24 x 19 In. 978.00
Chest, Poplar, Drawers, High Valance Base, Red Paint, Conn., c.1765, 43 x 38 In. 2963.00
Chest, Queen Anne, 7 Drawers, Carved Fan, 1700s, 74 x 41 In. 16415.00
Chest, Queen Anne, 8 Over 4 Drawers, Dovetailed, Cabriole Legs, Pad Feet, 77 x 40 In. 1150.00
Chest, Queen Anne, Cherry, Chestnut, Pine, Fan Carving, 1700s, 76 x 44 In. 920.00
Chest, Queen Anne, Maple, Pine, 7 Drawers, Cabriole Legs, c.1760, 72 ½ x 38 In. 1380.00
Chest, Queen Anne, Maple, Pine, 9 Drawers, Cabriole Legs, Mass., c.1730, 68 x 39 In. 3172.00
Chest, Queen Anne, Maple, Pine, Shaped Skirt, New England, c.1750, 73 x 41 In. 4700.00
Chest, Queen Anne, Tiger Maple, 7 Drawers, 1700s, 73 ½ x 40 x 20 In. .... *illus* 15400.00
Chest, Queen Anne, Tiger Maple, 9 Drawers, Cabriole Legs, Drake Feet, 63 x 41 In. 3000.00
Chest, Queen Anne, Walnut, Crossbanded Top, Inlaid, 5 Drawers, c.1780, 33 x 41 x 33 In. 3500.00
Chest, Queen Anne, Walnut, Pine, Inlaid, Flat Top, 2 Over 4 Over 4 Drawers, 74 x 35 In. 7638.00
Chest, Red Paint, Latticework Design, Iron Handles, c.1850, 20 x 38 In. 518.00
Chest, Regency, Bowfront, 4 Drawers, Serpentine Apron, Flared Feet, 39 x 42 In. 443.00
Chest, Regency, Mahogany, Banded, 5 Drawers, Splayed Feet, 42 x 42 x 20 In. 1500.00
Chest, Regency, Mahogany, Bowfront, 2 Over 3 Graduated Drawers, 42 x 43 In. 2880.00
Chest, Regency, Mahogany, Bowfront, 2 Short Over 3 Long Drawers, 41 x 41 In. 1680.00
Chest, Regency, Mahogany, Bowfront, 5 Drawers, Bracket Feet, 40 x 41 x 20 In. 1200.00
Chest, Regency, Mahogany, Bowfront, Inlaid, 3 Short Drawers Over 3, 44 x 48 x 22 In. 2400.00
Chest, Regency, Mahogany, Line Strung, Top Banded, Ebonized, 41 x 42 In. 2640.00
Chest, Regency Style, Mahogany, Bowfront, 2 Short Drawers Over 3, c.1880, 40 x 42 In. 2640.00

TIP

When removing a lock on an old piece of furniture, make a diagram of the lock. Tape each screw on the proper place on the diagram so you can return each one to its original hole. Old screws may be different lengths, and putting a long screw in a short hole could cause damage.

Furniture, Chest, Oak, Maple, Pine, Joined, Molding, 4 Drawers, Mass., c.1690, 38 x 52 In. $28125.00

Furniture, Chest, Queen Anne, Tiger Maple, 7 Drawers, 1700s, 73 ½ x 40 x 20 In. $15400.00

TIP
Felt tops on card tables and desks attract moths. Vacuum tops carefully at least once a year.

F

Furniture, Chest, Sugar, Federal, Cherry, Hinged Top, Drawer, Early 1800s, 30 x 38 x 18 In.
$4840.00

Furniture, Clothes Tree, Softwood, Green Paint, 32 Dowel Hangers, Virginia, 72 ½ x 17 In.
$605.00

TIP
Polish leather tabletops with saddle soap. Apply the soap, wait 30 minutes, then buff with a cloth for a high shine.

Chest, Renaissance Revival, Burl Walnut, Drawer, 2 Doors, Columns, 1800s, 52 x 41 In. 299.00
Chest, Renaissance Revival, Oak, Spiral Twist Columnar Supports, Late 1800s, 28 x 54 In. ... 627.00
Chest, Renaissance Revival, Walnut, Frieze, Drawers, Doors, Masks, 38 x 55 x 20 In. 1076.00
Chest, Rococo, 4 Drawers, Burl Fronts, Applied Pulls, Victorian, 50 x 41 In. 177.00
Chest, Rococo, Bombe, Multicolored, Serpentine Top, Drawers, Blue Ground, 33 x 44 In. 1896.00
Chest, Rococo, Rosewood, Crossband Mahogany, Bombe, Dutch, 36 x 40 ½ x 25 In. 5036.00
Chest, Rococo, Rosewood, Marble Top, Carved Crest, Drawers, 77 x 47 ½ x 24 In. 3450.00
Chest, Rosewood, 3 Drawers, Denmark, c.1952, 24 x 30 In. 1020.00
Chest, Rosewood, 6 Drawers, Octagonal Pulls, Scroll & Vine Appliques, c.1840, 50 x 47 In. ... 2350.00
Chest, Roycroft, No. 097, Copper Strap Hinges, Patina, Signed, 26 x 38 ½ x 21 In. 26000.00
Chest, Sheraton, Cherry, 4 Drawers, Footed, 19th Century, 46 x 44 ¾ In. 234.00
Chest, Sheraton, Cherry, 5 Drawers, Applied Pilasters, Turned Feet, c.1825, 42 x 40 In. 353.00
Chest, Sheraton, Cherry, Poplar, 4 Drawers, Turned Feet, 43 x 38 x 19 In. 1293.00
Chest, Sheraton, Cherry, Poplar, Inlaid, 4 Drawers, c.1815, 43 x 41 x 19 In. 764.00
Chest, Sheraton, Curly Maple, Pine, Poplar, 4 Drawers, Shaped Skirt, 49 x 38 x 24 In. 4348.00
Chest, Sheraton, Mahogany, Bowfront, 4 Drawers, c.1815, 40 x 42 In. 761.00
Chest, Sheraton, Mahogany, Bowfront, Reeded Pilasters, c.1815, 40 x 41 In. 995.00
Chest, Sheraton, Mahogany, Inlaid, Bowfront, 5 Drawers, 1860s, 42 x 42 x 21 In. 1430.00
Chest, Sheraton, Mahogany, Inlaid, Crossbanded Top, 5 Drawers, Splay Feet, 1840s, 39 In. ... 1210.00
Chest, Sheraton, Mahogany, Molded Edge Top, 2 Drawers, Scalloped Apron, 31 x 36 In. 657.00
Chest, Sheraton, Pine, Black On Red Graining, Splashboard, 4 Drawers, 47 x 42 x 21 In. 1410.00
Chest, Sheraton, Scalloped Apron, Casters, 43 x 20 x 37 In. 2300.00
Chest, Spice, Federal, Mahogany, 2 Flame Maple Doors, 5 Drawers, c.1805, 17 x 13 In. 4680.00
Chest, Spice, Hardwood, Carved, Painted Front Panels, Flowers, 12 x 24 ½ x 13 In. 210.00
Chest, Spice, Paint, Green, 1 Long Over 12 Square Drawers, 24 x 12 x 24 In. 863.00
Chest, Spice, William & Mary, Walnut, 5 Drawers, Door, Bun Feet, c.1730, 17 x 13 In. 3978.00
Chest, Sugar, Cherry, Drawer, 33 x 30 x 18 ½ In. 9350.00
Chest, Sugar, Cherry, Hinged, Open Interior, Center Divider, Diamond Design, 37 x 29 In. 4830.00
Chest, Sugar, Cherry, Poplar, Dovetailed Drawer, Turned Feet, c.1840-50, 28 x 27 x 14 In. 2200.00
Chest, Sugar, Cherry, Poplar, Hinged Top, Drawer, Turned Legs, 1800s, 30 x 34 x 21 In. 4400.00
Chest, Sugar, Cherry, Poplar, Walnut, Fold-Back Lid, Dovetailed Drawers, 38 x 20 x 37 In. ... 2938.00
Chest, Sugar, Federal, Cherry, Dovetailed Drawer, Shaped Skirt, Tenn., c.1850, 32 x 37 In. ... 7480.00
Chest, Sugar, Federal, Cherry, Hinged Top, Drawer, Early 1800s, 30 x 38 x 18 In. .... *illus* 4840.00
Chest, Sugar, Federal, Pine, Dovetailed, Turned Legs, 1800s, 38 x 34 x 19 In. 5405.00
Chest, Sugar, Hepplewhite, Cherry, Drop Front, Fitted Bins, Kentucky, c.1800, 31 x 30 In. 2702.00
Chest, Sugar, Hepplewhite, Cherry, Poplar, Slant Front, Dovetailed, 30 x 30 x 17 In. 5288.00
Chest, Sugar, Softwood, Green Paint, Giles Co., Leather Hinges, 20 x 20 ½ In. 1045.00
Chest, Teak, Shaped Pulls, 6 Drawers, Screw-Out Legs, Denmark, c.1950, 30 x 72 In. 593.00
Chest, Tiger Graining, 3 Drawers, 11 x 7 x 12 In. 403.00
Chest, Tiger Maple, Cherry, Mahogany, Swell Front, Shaped Back, Brass Pulls, c.1820, 42 x 41 In. 2489.00
Chest, Victorian, Cherry, 6 Drawers, Side Lock, New York, 63 x 37 In. 1035.00
Chest, Walnut, 3 Over 4 Drawers, Fluted Columns, Base Molding, 37 x 41 In. 3585.00
Chest, Walnut, Canted Corners, Eagle, Leaf Medallion, 3 Drawers, Square Legs, 37 x 50 In. .. 3360.00
Chest, Walnut, Dentil Edge, Paneled, Shield, Paw Feet, Late 1600s, 22 x 61 In. 2040.00
Chest, Walnut, Inlaid Pine, Poplar Designs, 4 Drawers, 1800s, 45 x 41 In. 2760.00
Chest, Walnut, Marquetry, Figures On Horseback, Paw Feet, 1800s, 27 x 76 In. 3600.00
Chest, Walnut, Molded Lid, Dovetailed, Lock, Tin Escutcheon, 12 x 16 x 11 ½ In. 468.00
Chest, Walnut, Poplar, 3 Over 2 Over 4 Drawers, Bracket Feet, 65 ½ x 43 x 23 In. 7200.00
Chest, Walnut, Poplar, Lift Top, Scrolled Bracket Feet, Tenn., 1800s, 20 x 40 In. 863.00
Chest, Walnut, Scrolled Backsplash, 3 Drawers, 1800s, 17 x 13 In. 546.00
Chest, Walnut, Stenciled Gilt Birds, Flowers, Yellow Scallops, Pa., 1840, 22 x 40 In. 176.00
Chest, Walnut, Yellow Pine, Lift Top, Dovetailed, Bracket Feet, 24 x 24 x 14 In. 11500.00
Chest, Wellington, Pine, Painted, 4 Drawers, Carved Corner-Block Pilasters, 44 x 14 In. 299.00
Chest, White Pine, Figured Maple, 3 Graduated Drawers, New England, 1700s, 38 x 39 In. 1265.00
Chest, William & Mary, Mahogany, 5 Over 3 Drawers, Bracket Feet, c.1740, 41 x 39 In. 1872.00
Chest, William & Mary, Oak & Pine, 4 Graduated Drawers, Late 1600s, 49 x 43 In. 1410.00
Chest, William & Mary, Olive Wood, Inlaid, 2 Over 3 Drawers, Ball Feet, 36 x 39 In. 17500.00
Chest, William & Mary, Pine, Poplar, 5 Drawers, c.1715, 40 x 38 In. 390.00
Chest, William & Mary, Walnut, Veneers, 8 Drawers, 6 Trumpet Legs, c.1725, 60 x 37 In. 3995.00
Chest, William & Mary Style, Oak, 5 Drawers, Recessed Starburst Inlay, 35 x 37 In. 2040.00
Chest, William IV, Mahogany, 5 Drawers, Reeded & Leaf Carving, Turned Feet, 46 x 42 In. 1093.00
Chest, William IV, Mahogany, Cock-Beaded Drawers, Scalloped Base, 41 x 36 In. 1410.00
Chest, William IV, Walnut, 4 Drawers, Plinth Base, 30 ½ x 15 ¾ x 20 ½ In., Pair 2400.00
Chest, Wine, Eagle Lid Inlay, Front Fan Inlay, 12 Dividers, Turned Legs, c.1890, 24 x 21 In. .. 2300.00
Chest, Wormley, Walnut, Brass Pulls, Dunbar, 34 ½ x 38 x 18 In. 1200.00
Chest, Yellow Pine, Hinged Lift Top, Interior Till, Bracket Feet, 22 x 42 In. 518.00
Chest, Yellow Pine, Lift Top, Blue Green Paint, Hinged, Turned Feet, 25 x 36 In. 518.00

Chest-On-Chest, Chippendale, Mahogany, 11 Drawers, S.C., 1750-70, 72 x 44 x 24 In. 41000.00
Chest-On-Chest, Chippendale, Mahogany, Cornice, 2 Over 3 Drawers, Greek Key, 76 x 48 In. .. 3105.00
Chest-On-Chest, Chippendale, Mahogany, Figured, Flame Finial, c.1770, 89 x 42 In. 230500.00
Chest-On-Chest, Federal, Mahogany, Bonnet Top, 8 Drawers, Bracket Feet, 1800s, 82 x 37 In. 1195.00
Chest-On-Chest, Federal, Walnut, 3 Over 4 Drawers, Bracket Feet, 76 x 41 x 21 In. 5677.00
Chest-On-Chest, George II, Mahogany, 8 Drawers, c.1760, 71 x 44 In. 7500.00
Chest-On-Chest, George III, Mahogany, 2 Short, 3 Long Drawers, Bracket Feet, 70 x 43 x 21 In. 2607.00
Chest-On-Chest, George III, Mahogany, 5 Drawers, Bracket Feet, 77 ½ x 49 x 21 In. 4800.00
Chest-On-Chest, George III, Mahogany, Brass Inlay, 10 Drawers, c.1760, 83 x 47 In. 5625.00
Chest-On-Chest, George III, Mahogany, Carved Frieze, 5 Drawers, 68 x 42 In. 3186.00
Chest-On-Chest, George III, Mahogany, Molded Cornice, 5 Over 3 Drawers, 72 x 41 In. 1998.00
Chest-On-Chest, Georgian, Mahogany, Pine, 2 Over 3 Drawers, Early 1800s, 81 x 43 In. 1265.00
Chest-On-Chest, Georgian, Shaped Cornice, 3 Short Over 3 Long Drawers, 68 x 39 In. 1080.00
Chest-On-Chest, Victorian, Mahogany, Pine, 4 Over 3 Drawers, 83 x 49 x 22 In. 2415.00
Chest-On-Frame, George I, Walnut, 2 Over 3 Drawers, Bun Feet, 49 ½ x 35 x 20 ¾ In. 2360.00
Chest-On-Frame, Queen Anne, Maple, 5 Drawers, Cabriole Legs, 51 x 37 ½ In. 4025.00
Chest-On-Frame, Queen Anne, Maple, 5 Graduated Drawers, 18th Century, 60 x 38 In. 5175.00
Chest-On-Frame, Queen Anne, Maple, Pine, 5 Graduated Drawers, c.1780, 65 x 40 In. 4600.00
Chest-On-Frame, Walnut, Yellow Pine, 4 Graduated Drawers, Late 1700s, 46 x 28 In. 7130.00
Chiffonier, Ormolu, Marble Top, Inlaid Flowers, Pierced Rim, Door, c.1775, 28 x 13 In. 5938.00
Chiffonier, Parquetry, Tambour Door, Ormolu Rim, Mounts, France, c.1770, 31 x 20 In. 74500.00
Chiffonier, Regency, Rosewood, Crossband Mahogany, Gallery, Drawers, 42 x 36 x 14 In. 2015.00
Clothes Tree, Softwood, 6 Hanger Posts, Ogee Legs, Claw Feet, 69 x 24 In. 143.00
Clothes Tree, Softwood, Green Paint, 32 Dowel Hangers, Virginia, 72 ½ x 17 In. .... *illus* 605.00
Coat Rack, Arts & Crafts, 3 Men In Powdered Wigs Scene, 12 Pegs, Rings, 12 ½ x 22 In. 240.00
Coat Rack, Costumer, G. Stickley, No. 53, Double, 6 Iron Hooks, 72 x 13 x 22 In. 3240.00
Coat Rack, Merklin-Hunzinger, Mahogany, Twisted, Flame Top, 1880, 83 x 16 In. 770.00
Coat Rack, Victorian, 3 Lion Mask Carvings, Leaf Decoration, 61 x 71 In. 431.00
Coat Rack, Wall Mount, Metal Frame, Color Balls, Mirror, Umbrella Base, c.1950, 68 x 19 In. 178.00
Coffer, Gothic, Oak, Plank Top, Paneled, Heraldic, Continental, 25 ½ x 59 ½ x 20 In. 2280.00
Coffer, Henri II, Fruitwood, Carved Figures, 8 Panels, Iron Hinges, 28 x 51 x 23 In. 1888.00
Coffer, Jacobean, Oak, 17th Century, 22 ½ x 47 In. 427.00
Coffer, Oak, Carved Leaves & Panels, Geometric Design, Hinged, 18th Century, 27 x 47 In. ... 737.00
Coffer, Oak, Iron Hardware, Arched, Leaf Carved Frieze, 4 Carved Panels, 57 x 24 In. 1680.00
Coffer, Walnut, Carved, Text Frieze, Paneled Sides, Runner Feet, 28 x 54 x 24 In. 4320.00
Coffer, Walnut, Oak, Geometric, Carved, Hinged, Plant Legs, 27 x 41 x 21 ½ In. 2880.00
Commode, American Aesthetic Revival, Maple, Faux Bamboo, 1890s, 39 x 36 x 21 In. .. *illus* 1100.00
Commode, Arched Sides, Scrolled Arm, Sliding Seat, Access Door, Red, 1800s, 42 x 21 In. 382.00
Commode, Baroque, Burl, Marble Top, 3 Drawers, Italy, c.1790, 33 x 43 In. 1725.00
Commode, Biedermeier, Fruitwood, Pine, Dovetailed Drawers, Germany, c.1800s, 29 x 38 In. 1610.00
Commode, Biedermeier, Mahogany, Marble Top, Door, 28 ½ x 15 In. 720.00
Commode, Burl Walnut, Double Banded, Inlaid Star, 4 Drawers, 37 x 47 x 23 In. 5760.00
Commode, Continental Rococo, Marble Top, Drawer, Figural Door, Gilt, c.1885, 27 x 16 In. .. 657.00
Commode, Empire, Mahogany, Marble Top, 3 Drawers, Bronze Mounts, c.1860, 34 x 28 In. .. 1610.00
Commode, Empire Style, Cherry, Marble Top, 3 Drawers, 33 x 36 x 19 In. 2640.00
Commode, Flame Mahogany, 3 Steps, England, Mid 1800s, 27 x 31 x 17 In. .... *illus* 450.00
Commode, French Empire Revival, Mahogany, Brass Mounted, Drawers, 38 x 48 In. 2489.00
Commode, French Provincial, Walnut, Marble Top, Frieze Drawer, 4 Drawers, 39 x 47 In. ... 299.00
Commode, Fruitwood, 3 Drawers, Ebonized Feet, Escutcheons, Continental, 1800s, 15 x 19 In. 575.00
Commode, George II, Mahogany, Rosewood, Bombe, Casters, c.1755, 36 x 42 In. 31250.00
Commode, George III, Mahogany, ¾ Handle Gallery, Doors, Drawers, 32 In. 1080.00
Commode, George III, Mahogany, 3-Piece Gallery, Paneled Doors, Drawer, 31 x 21 x 17 In. .. 2400.00
Commode, George III, Mahogany, Gallery, Tambour Cupboard, Drawer, 31 x 18 x 20 In. 2160.00
Commode, Kingwood, Bronze, Marble, Rope Drawers, Chamfered Stiles, 1900, 38 x 50 In. ... 2644.00
Commode, Lannuier, Mahogany, Marble, Psyche & Eros, Long Island, c.1820, 39 x 51 In. .... *illus* 41000.00
Commode, Louis Philippe, Mahogany, Marble Top, Drawers, Block Feet, 37 x 52 x 24 In. 2880.00
Commode, Louis Philippe, Walnut, Molded Edge, 4 Drawers, Mid 1800s, 30 x 32 In. 2400.00
Commode, Louis XIV, Walnut, 2 Over 2 Long Drawers, Carved, 32 x 50 x 23 In. 8365.00
Commode, Louis XV, Burl Veneer Panels, Green Marble Top, Drawers, 37 x 64 In. 646.00
Commode, Louis XV, Demilune, Marble Top, 2 Drawers, String Inlay, c.1880, 29 x 27 In. 239.00
Commode, Louis XV, Exotic Woods, Marble Top, Ormolu, 5 Drawers, c.1730, 33 x 57 In. 13750.00
Commode, Louis XV, French Provincial, Walnut, 4 Drawers, Fluted Legs, 32 x 42 x 21 In. 1422.00
Commode, Louis XV, Kidney Shape, Rose Marble Top, 2 Drawers, c.1900, 30 x 24 In., Pair ... 1265.00
Commode, Louis XV, Kingwood, Parquetry, Gallery Top, 20 x 15 In., Pair 598.00
Commode, Louis XV, Marble Top, 2 Inlaid Drawers, Bronze Mounts, 1900s, 33 x 46 In. 748.00
Commode, Louis XV, Marble Top, 3 Drawers, Marquetry, Gilt Mounts, c.1800s, 36 x 48 In. ... 1135.00
Commode, Louis XV, Marble Top, Inlaid, Jasperware Medallion, 30 x 27 In., Pair ...... *illus* 2070.00

Furniture, Commode, American Aesthetic Revival, Maple, Faux Bamboo, 1890s, 39 x 36 x 21 In.
$1100.00

Furniture, Commode, Flame Mahogany, 3 Steps, England, Mid 1800s, 27 x 31 x 17 In.
$450.00

TIP

If you see any numbers or letters on the frame of a wooden piece of furniture, do not remove or erase them. They may refer to a catalog, and eventually you may be able to attribute the piece to the proper manufacturer.

TIP
Glue weather stripping to the bottom of a chair rocker to protect the floor.

Furniture, Commode, Lannuier, Mahogany, Marble, Psyche & Eros, Inscribed, Long Island, c.1820, 39 x 51 In.
$41000.00

Furniture, Commode, Louis XV, Marble Top, Inlaid, Jasperware Medallion, 30 x 27 In., Pair
$2070.00

TIP
Be sure the big furniture you buy is small enough to go through the door into your room.

Commode, Louis XV, Marquetry, Marble Top, 5 Drawers, France, 37 x 52 In. 3450.00
Commode, Louis XV, Marquetry, Marble Top, Relief Panel, Putti, Birds, 34 x 40 In. 2415.00
Commode, Louis XV, Oak, Concave & Convex Drawers, Hoof Feet, 34 x 51 In. 11163.00
Commode, Louis XV, Oak, Marble Top, 2 Drawers, Bronze Mounts, France, 1900s, 33 x 33 In. 690.00
Commode, Louis XV, Serpentine Front, Marquetry, c.1890, 36 x 46 x 21 In. 4900.00
Commode, Louis XV, Walnut, Bronze Mounted, Marble Top, Cabriole Legs, 36 x 41 x 21 In. . . 2489.00
Commode, Louis XV Style, Kingwood, Bombe, Serpentine Edge, 2 Drawers, 35 x 49 In. 295.00
Commode, Louis XV Style, Kingwood, Marble, Drawers, Matchbook Veneers, 35 x 33 x 18 In.. 2400.00
Commode, Louis XV Style, Mahogany, Bombe, Serpentine, Hinged Door, 41 x 30 x 18 In. 388.00
Commode, Louis XV Style, Mahogany, Kingwood, Drawers, Tapered Legs, 29 x 14 x 11 In. ... 540.00
Commode, Louis XV Style, Mahogany, Ormolu, Parquetry, Marble, 32 x 39 In., Pair 4080.00
Commode, Louis XV Style, Mixed Wood, String Inlay, Marble Top, Drawers, 32 x 23 In.. ..... 1175.00
Commode, Louis XV Style, Parquetry, Bombe, 2 Drawers, 35 x 48 x 20 In. 777.00
Commode, Louis XV Style, Parquetry, Patinated, Bronze Mounted, Marble Top, 38 x 58 In. .. 1998.00
Commode, Louis XVI, Mahogany, Bronze, Marble, Cabinet, Paw Feet, 36 x 84 In. 38775.00
Commode, Louis XVI, Mahogany, Marble Top, 3 Drawers, Ormolu Mounts, 34 x 23 In. 28750.00
Commode, Louis XVI, Painted, Marble Top, Drawer, Scenic Panels, Door, 46 x 35 In. 960.00
Commode, Louis XVI Style, Oak, 3 Drawers, Paneled, Carved, 41 x 49 x 21 In. 4320.00
Commode, Louis XVI Style, Parquetry, Gilt Metal Mounted, Marble Top, 34 x 48 In. 1440.00
Commode, Mahogany, 3 Steps, Turned Legs, Slide Hinge, c.1850, 31 x 17 In. 531.00
Commode, Mahogany, Empire, 3 Drawers, Brass Sphinx Pilasters, France, c.1890, 32 x 40 In. 575.00
Commode, Mahogany, Hinged, Sham Drawers, Turned Legs, c.1820, 18 x 19 In. 940.00
Commode, Mahogany, Marble, Round Corners, Disc Feet, c.1835, 30 x 16 x 16 In. 1175.00
Commode, Mahogany, Marquetry, 2 Drawers, Marble Top, France, 1890, 35 x 56 x 24 In. 18400.00
Commode, Mahogany, Marquetry, Bowed, Drawers, Scalloped Apron, 26 x 28 x 15 In. 3840.00
Commode, Mahogany, Marquetry, Hinged Top, Drawer, Pedestal, Mid 1800s, 35 x 17 In. 1225.00
Commode, Marble Top, Painted Flowers, Birds, Ormolu, France, c.1745, 34 x 32 In. 43750.00
Commode, Marquetry, Wood Flower Inlay, 2 Drawers, Leather, Brass Mounts, 28 x 26 In. 3750.00
Commode, Napoleon III, Mahogany, Kingwood, Parquetry, Marble Top, 50 x 36 In. 600.00
Commode, Neoclassical, Mahogany, 3 Drawers, Ebonized Maiden's Head, 35 x 49 In. 2880.00
Commode, Neoclassical, Painted, Marble Top, Breakfront Slab, Carved Frieze, 35 x 49 In. ... 1135.00
Commode, Oak, Drawers, Diamond Panels, Reeded, Bellflowers, 45 x 54 x 24 In. 8700.00
Commode, Pine, Scrolling Highlights, Flower Sprays, Hinged, c.1800, 30 x 29 x 16 In. 236.00
Commode, Regency, Kingwood, Ormolu Mounted, Marble Top, Bowfront, 33 x 45 In. 6518.00
Commode, Regency, Oak, Rectangular, Molded Edge, 3 Long Drawers, 36 x 56 In. 3120.00
Commode, Regency Style, Fruitwood, Oak, Bombe, Marble Top, 9 Drawers, 33 x 53 x 28 In.. . 5280.00
Commode, Renaissance Revival, Burl Walnut, Carved Marble Top, Lion Heads 1955.00
Commode, Renaissance Revival, Walnut, Carved, Drawer, Door, Bracket Feet, 37 x 30 In. 2232.00
Commode, Rococo, Tiger Maple, Rosewood, Marble Top, Mid 1800s, 30 x 26 In. 7344.00
Commode, Rococo, Walnut, Serpentine Molded Edge, Paneled Doors, Continental, 36 x 29 In. 388.00
Commode, Rococo Style, Walnut, Bombe, Drawers, Cabriole Legs, Dutch, 36 x 57 x 28 In. ... 2640.00
Commode, Rosewood, Carved, Marble, Drawer, Casters, c.1835, 31 x 18 In. 940.00
Commode, Rosewood, Mahogany, Marble Top, Portugal, 35 ½ x 44 ½ x 21 ½ In. 2880.00
Commode, Sheraton, Mahogany, Bowfront, Drawer, Door, England, 1800, 34 x 18 x 23 In. .. 200.00
Commode, Sycamore, Amaranth, Marble, Ormolu Mounts, Saunier, c.1775, 34 x 42 In.. .... 15000.00
Commode, Tulipwood, Purplewood Parquet, Marble Top, 3 Drawers, Ormolu Mounts, 33 x 52 In. 6875.00
Commode, Victorian, Walnut, 3 Drawers, Carved Pulls, 37 x 28 x 16 In. 212.00
Commode, Victorian, Walnut, Marble Top, Recessed Panel, Backsplash, 42 x 35 x 17 In. 354.00
Commodes, Walnut, Serpentine Front, 3 Drawers, Bracket Feet, Italy, 25 x 21 x 13 In., Pair . . 2640.00
Console, Painted, Marble Top, 2 Grill Inset Doors, Flattened Ball Feet, 42 x 57 In. 720.00
Cradle, Canoe Form, Gold Flowers, Wood Slats, Wheels, Ford Johnson & Co., 1876, 26 In.. ... 440.00
Cradle, Chippendale, Mahogany, Cutout Handles, c.1770 .... 165.00
Cradle, Federal, Cherry, Pegged, John Gillespie, Tenn., 1800s, 27 x 44 In. 115.00
Cradle, Federal, Cherry, Poplar, Pine, Turned Slats, Charleston, 1800s, 38 x 42 In.. .... 1035.00
Cradle, Federal, Cherry, Poplar Slats, Scrolled Rockers, 1800s, 38 x 36 x 42 In. .... *illus* 990.00
Cradle, Poplar, Heart Cutout, Scalloped Sides, 1820s, 20 x 43 x 14 ½ In.. .... *illus* 220.00
Cradle, Poplar, Hinged Arm, Heart Cutout, Dovetailed, Pennsylvania, c.1800, 22 x 41 In. 206.00
Cradle, Softwood, Green Paint, Shaped Top Hoop, Bentwood Sides, 19 ½ x 35 ½ In. 605.00
Cradle, Swinging, 2 Wheels, Ribbed, Patent October 17, 1876, Ford Johnson Co. 1400.00
Cradle, Walnut, Slatted, Pierced Handle, France, 10 ½ x 37 x 16 In. 300.00
Credenza, Art Moderne, Parchment, Gilt Doors, Brass Mount, Mid 1900s, 35 x 55 In. 9900.00
Credenza, Biedermeier, 4 Doors, Molded, 29 x 75 x 18 ½ In. 657.00
Credenza, Florence Knoll, Teak, 3 Doors, 6 Drawers, Black Base, 24 x 108 In. .... *illus* 1920.00
Credenza, George III, Mahogany, Bowed Top, 2 Drawers, Paneled Doors, 36 x 68 x 21 In.. ... 3360.00
Credenza, Mahogany, Mirrored Door, Interior Shelves, Lattice Band, 45 x 38 In. 325.00
Credenza, Pedersen, Teak, Sliding Tambour Doors, Denmark, 31 x 82 x 20 In. 1200.00
Credenza, Renaissance Revival, Maple, Satinwood, Rosewood, c.1890, 48 x 72 x 23 In. 10950.00

Credenza, Rosewood, Marquetry, Pottier & Stymus 8050.00
Credenza, Teak, Sliding Doors, Shelves, 4 Drawers, Lip Pulls, 1960, 33 x 93 x 20 In. 2675.00
Credenza, V. Kagen, Roll Top, Chrome Platform, Wood Case, 6 Drawers, 96 x 30 In. 1020.00
Credenza, Victorian, Mahogany, Marble Top, Doors, Inlaid, 34 ¾ x 63 x 15 In. 1080.00
Credenza, Wegner, Rosewood, Tambour Doors, Shelves, 32 x 78 ¾ x 19 In. 4200.00
Crib, Rococo, Walnut, Carved, Acorn Finials, Arched Crest, Rocker Base, c.1850, 39 x 42 x 26 In. 2820.00
Cupboard, Cherry, 2 Drawers, 4 Doors, 19th Century, 87 x 45 x 18 In. .... *illus* 4600.00
Cupboard, Cherry, 2 Sections, 4 Panels, Drawers, Doors, c.1820, 87 x 42 x 19 In. 3600.00
Cupboard, Cherry, Poplar, Chamfered Corners, Reeded, Bead Molding, 86 x 52 x 21 In. 4406.00
Cupboard, Cherry, Walnut, 4 Paneled Doors, 64 x 41 ½ x 19 ½ In. 2310.00
Cupboard, Chestnut, Pine, Step Back, Painted, Decorated Hearts, Early 1900s, 76 x 33 In. ... 920.00
Cupboard, Chimney, Chestnut, Door, Blue Paint, Early 1900s, 66 x 14 In. 748.00
Cupboard, Chimney, Pine, Raised Panel Door, Drawer, Brown Stain, c.1840, 81 x 35 In.. .... 1150.00
Cupboard, Chimney, Yellow Pine, Grain Painted, Double Panel Door, 1800s, 82 x 29 In. 2990.00
Cupboard, Chippendale, Curly Maple, Dentil Molding, 2 Paneled Doors, c.1770, 41 x 37 In. . 1140.00
Cupboard, Chippendale, Stepped Cornice, Raised Panel Doors, c.1840, 85 x 48 In. 1725.00
Cupboard, Corner, 4 Doors, Drawer, Grain Paint, Yellow Interior, Pa., 80 x 48 x 28 In. 3750.00
Cupboard, Corner, Baroque, Arch Door, Lion, Cherub Carvings, England, c.1890, 30 x 27 In.. 575.00
Cupboard, Corner, Cherry, 2 6-Pane Doors, 2 Paneled Doors, c.1830, 82 x 49 In.. .... 2350.00
Cupboard, Corner, Cherry, Molded Cornice, Arch Shape Base, c.1830, 83 x 34 In. 1725.00
Cupboard, Corner, Cherry, Pine, Broken Arch Pediment, Carved, 8-Pane Doors, 95 x 50 In... 1528.00
Cupboard, Corner, Cherry, Poplar, Double Panel Doors, Shelf, 82 ½ x 44 x 28 ½ In. 1880.00
Cupboard, Corner, Chippendale, Poplar, Early 1800s, 90 x 52 x 26 ½ In. .... *illus* 1540.00
Cupboard, Corner, Chippendale, Poplar, Reed Paneled Doors, 1800s, 90 x 52 In.. .... 1610.00
Cupboard, Corner, Empire, Cherry, Glazed Door, 12-Pane Doors, Drawers, 83 x 56 In. 1175.00
Cupboard, Corner, Empire, Cherry, Poplar, 10-Pane Doors, Bowfront, 100 x 57 In. 2703.00
Cupboard, Corner, Federal, Cherry, 3 Doors, 12 Panes, c.1800, 85 x 46 x 22 In. 850.00
Cupboard, Corner, Federal, Cherry, Paneled Doors, Shelves, Thomas Lincoln, 90 x 48 In.. ... 3220.00
Cupboard, Corner, Federal, Cherry, Scrolling Broken Arch Crest, 1800s, 96 x 48 In.. .... 1680.00
Cupboard, Corner, Federal, Walnut, Drawer, 4 Shelves, Over 2 Doors, c.1800, 85 x 50 In. 3318.00
Cupboard, Corner, Hanging, Birch, Peaked Crest, Glass Pane Doors, Sweden, 36 ½ x 22 In... 403.00
Cupboard, Corner, Hanging, Chippendale, Walnut, 3 Shelves, 38 x 30 x 18 In.. .... *illus* 1100.00
Cupboard, Corner, Hanging, Georgian, Oak, 3-Panel Door, England, 39 x 28 x 16 In.. ...... 375.00
Cupboard, Corner, Hanging, Georgian, Oak, Door, 3 Shelves, England, 36 x 24 x 12 In. 400.00
Cupboard, Corner, Hanging, Georgian, Oak, England, 19th Century, 28 x 26 x 15 In. 325.00
Cupboard, Corner, Hanging, Old Green Paint, c.1820, 41 ½ x 29 ½ In.. .... 585.00
Cupboard, Corner, Hanging, Pine, Door, Shelves, Blue Paint, Red Trim, c.1785, 46 x 31 In... 2820.00
Cupboard, Corner, Hanging, Walnut, Door, Canted Sides, c.1770, 34 x 30 In.. .... 3510.00
Cupboard, Corner, Mahogany, Dentil Molding, Astragal Glazed Door, c.1800, 40 x 32 In. 767.00
Cupboard, Corner, Mahogany, Pine, Bowfront, Glazed Door, c.1900, 78 x 46 In. 2070.00
Cupboard, Corner, Nutting, No. 945, Pine, Signed, 80 x 38 x 19 In.. .... 3300.00
Cupboard, Corner, Paint Decoration, Blind Door, Molded Cornice, Panel Doors, 80 x 48 In... 4125.00
Cupboard, Corner, Pine, Dentil Molded Cornice, 2 Doors, Varnished, c.1780, 95 x 37 In.. .... 1872.00
Cupboard, Corner, Pine, Molded Cornice, Arched Doors, Blue Paint, c.1790, 93 x 62 In. 3290.00
Cupboard, Corner, Pine, Raised Panel, 42 x 22 x 85 In. 690.00
Cupboard, Corner, Pine, Scalloped Shelves, Door, Blue Gray Paint, Pa., c.1800, 82 x 49 In. .. 3744.00
Cupboard, Corner, Poplar, 2 12-Pane Doors, Over 2 Doors, Painted, c.1850, 85 x 49 In. 5288.00
Cupboard, Corner, Poplar, 2 Sections, Carved, c.1790, 87 ½ In. 2133.00
Cupboard, Corner, Red Paint, Door Over Drawer, Early 19th Century, 65 x 34 In. 527.00
Cupboard, Corner, Softwood, Molded Cornice, Arched Glazed Door, 95 x 53 In. 1870.00
Cupboard, Corner, Softwood, Molded Cornice, Raised Panel Blind Door, 81 x 42 In. 5500.00
Cupboard, Corner, Tiger Maple, 12 Panes, 2 Doors, Turned Feet, 91 x 44 x 23 In. 3300.00
Cupboard, Corner, Walnut, 12 Panes, Lower Blind Doors, 80 x 52 In. 1058.00
Cupboard, Corner, Walnut, 2 Molded Paneled Doors, 3 Ball Feet, c.1770, 72 x 45 In.. .... 1175.00
Cupboard, Corner, Walnut, Blind Door, Raised Panels, Red, Blue Interior, 83 x 45 In.. ...... 1410.00
Cupboard, Corner, Walnut, Cove Molded Cornice, Fluted Frieze, Paned Doors, 90 x 52 In. ... 4140.00
Cupboard, Corner, Walnut, Glazed Doors, Cornice, c.1800, 77 ½ x 44 In. 1180.00
Cupboard, Corner, Walnut, Yellow Pine, Stepped, Cornice, Glazed Panel Doors, 88 x 49 In. .. 2990.00
Cupboard, Corner, Yellow Pine, c.1780, 82 x 38 In. .... *illus* 5616.00
Cupboard, Corner, Yellow Pine, Cut Nails, Lower Doors, Plate Rails, 1800s, 75 x 36 In.. ..... 920.00
Cupboard, Corner, Yellow Pine, Cut Nails, Panel Doors, 1800s, 83 x 49 In.. .... 2415.00
Cupboard, Corner, Yellow Pine, Painted, Red, Cornice Molding, Panel Doors, 86 x 49 In. 3450.00
Cupboard, Corner, Yellow Pine, Walnut, Pine Safe Top, Punched Tin Panels, 85 x 46 In. 920.00
Cupboard, Country, Pine, Glazed Doors, Interior Shelves, Lower Paneled Doors, 87 x 56 In.. . 1652.00
Cupboard, Distressed Wood, Cream Paint, Hinged Storage, Scandinavia, 35 x 73 x 9 In.. .... 2160.00
Cupboard, Ellinger, 2 Sections, Molded Cornice, 2 Glazed Doors, 79 x 42 x 12 In. 2125.00
Cupboard, Federal, Cherry, Broken Arch Pediment, Doors, Early 1800s, 84 x 49 In.. .... 1593.00

Furniture, Cradle, Federal, Cherry, Poplar Slats, Scrolled Rockers, 1800s, 38 x 36 x 42 In.
$990.00

Furniture, Cradle, Poplar, Heart Cutout, Scalloped Sides, 1820s, 20 x 43 x 14 ½ In.
$220.00

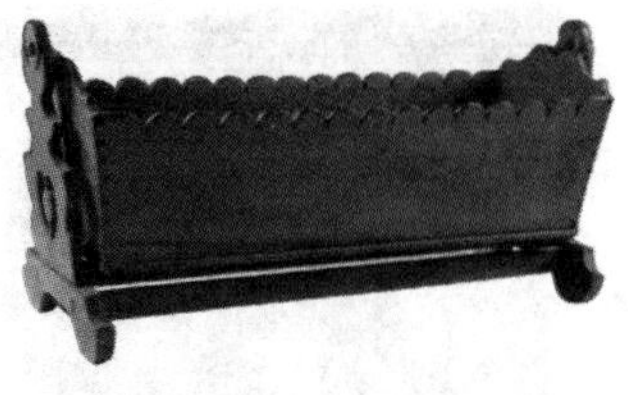

Furniture, Credenza, Florence Knoll, Teak, 3 Doors, 6 Drawers, Black Base, 24 x 108 In.
$1920.00

Furniture, Cupboard, Cherry, 2 Drawers, 4 Doors, 19th Century, 87 x 45 x 18 In.
$4600.00

A Dovetail Substitute

Dovetails that held drawers and other parts of wooden furniture together were hand cut in the eighteenth century. With the abundance of new tools and the availability of electricity and other power sources in the nineteenth century, inventors improved many products. In 1867, Charles Knapp invented a substitute for the dovetail joint: a scallop and peg joint. The "pegs" went into a hole in the center of each scallop cut into the side of the drawer front. Knapp invented a machine to cut all the pieces.

Furniture, Cupboard, Corner, Chippendale, Poplar, Early 1800s, 90 x 52 x 26 ½ In.
$1540.00

Furniture, Cupboard, Corner, Hanging, Chippendale, Walnut, 3 Shelves, 38 x 30 x 18 In.
$1100.00

Furniture, Cupboard, Corner, Yellow Pine, c.1780, 82 x 38 In.
$5616.00

Furniture, Cupboard, Jelly, Pine, 19th Century, 60 ½ x 40 In.
$1168.00

Furniture, Cupboard, Pine, Door, Dovetailed, Blue Paint, 19th Century, 30 x 20 x 15 In.
$700.00

Furniture, Cupboard, Pine, Step Back, Old Green Paint, Early 1800s, 78 x 38 In.
$2340.00

Furniture, Cupboard, Softwood, Brown, Yellow Ground, Lancaster Co., 45 x 37 x 18 In.
$3750.00

Cupboard, Fruitwood, Drawers, Paneled Door, Bracket Feet, Italy, 34 x 26 x 12 In. 3840.00
Cupboard, Gothic Revival, Carved, Parcel Gilt, Linenfold, Tracery, 1800s, 59 x 39 In. 1093.00
Cupboard, Hanging, Jacobean, Oak, Molded Door, Late 17th Century, 22 x 37 In. 1900.00
Cupboard, Hanging, Jacobean, Oak, Molded Door, Sides, Late 17th Century, 36 x 29 In. 2223.00
Cupboard, Hanging, Poplar, Door, Ram's-Horn Hinges, Red Paint, c.1740, 36 x 25 x 14 In. . . 18720.00
Cupboard, Hanging, Poplar, Red Paint, Reeded Pilasters, 33 ½ x 38 In. 2106.00
Cupboard, Hanging, Softwood, Red Paint, Molded Cornice, Panel Door, 36 x 27 In. 1540.00
Cupboard, Hanging, Stick & Ball, Glass Sides, Doors, Shelves, 37 12 x 21 In. 375.00
Cupboard, Hanging, Walnut, Raised Panel Door, Rattail Hinges, Pa., Late 1700s, 31 x 29 In. . 3510.00
Cupboard, Jelly, 2 Drawers, 2 Doors, Red, Black Paint, 19th Century, 49 x 50 x 21 In. 550.00
Cupboard, Jelly, Molded Top, Recessed Panels, Shelves, Scrolled Skirt, 64 x 39 x 14 In. 935.00
Cupboard, Jelly, Pine, 19th Century, 60 ½ x 40 In. . . . . *illus* 1168.00
Cupboard, Jelly, Pine, 2 Doors, Gallery Top, Bracket Feet, 48 x 30 x 14 In. 195.00
Cupboard, Jelly, Pine, 2 Doors, Late 19th Century, 48 x 44 In. 336.00
Cupboard, Jelly, Pine, Drawer Over 2 Doors, Bracket Feet, 58 ½ x 41 x 18 In. 305.00
Cupboard, Jelly, Poplar, Grain Painted, 2 Drawers, 2 Doors, 1800s, 50 x 45 x 18 In. 550.00
Cupboard, Jelly, Red Paint, Flat Backsplash, Ogee Sides, Drawer, 18 x 14 In. 6050.00
Cupboard, Jelly, Softwood, Backsplash, Drawer, Paneled Doors, 59 ⅝ x 42 x 19 ½ In. 1210.00
Cupboard, Mahogany, Pylon Form, Pedestal, Plinth Base, 31 x 15 In. 1175.00
Cupboard, Milk, Softwood, Grain Painted, Paneled Door, Shelves, 1900s, 47 x 37 In. 110.00
Cupboard, Milk, Yellow Ground, Brown-Rag Grain Painted, Paneled Door, 45 x 38 In. 4125.00
Cupboard, Mixed Woods, 2 Sections, Cream Paint, 88 x 19 x 45 ¾ In. 1028.00
Cupboard, Painted, Molded Cornice, Raised Panel Door, c.1860, 68 x 42 In. 1045.00
Cupboard, Pine, Applied Cornice, Wire Hinges, Crazed Paint, c.1885, 30 x 17 In. 646.00
Cupboard, Pine, Door, Dovetailed, Blue Paint, 19th Century, 30 x 20 x 15 In. . . . . *illus* 700.00
Cupboard, Pine, Door, Valanced Top, Molded Slats, 4 Shelves, 77 x 42 In. 575.00
Cupboard, Pine, Mixed Wood, Reeded Sides, Molded Edge, 82 x 55 In. 2233.00
Cupboard, Pine, Open Front, Shaped Cornice, 3 Shelves, 2 Drawers, 2 Doors, 71 x 46 In. 330.00
Cupboard, Pine, Overhung Cornice, 2 Doors, Drawers Over 2 Doors, Canada, c.1880, 78 x 57 In. 1645.00
Cupboard, Pine, Paneled Doors, Drawers, Bracket Feet, 19th Century, 57 x 46 x 18 In. 354.00
Cupboard, Pine, Paneled Doors, High Legs, Shelves, Plate Grooves, 71 x 50 x 13 In. 382.00
Cupboard, Pine, Step Back, 4 Doors, 2 Drawers, 19th Century, 73 x 41 In. 976.00
Cupboard, Pine, Step Back, Old Green Paint, Early 1800s, 78 x 38 In. . . . . *illus* 2340.00
Cupboard, Pine, Step Back, Open Shelf, 19th Century, 73 ½ x 48 x 18 In. 660.00
Cupboard, Pine, Step Back, Pierced, Scalloped Frieze, Open Shelves, 78 x 45 In. 531.00
Cupboard, Pine, Step Back, Red & Blue Paint, Blind Paneled Doors, 1700s, 42 x 20 In. 2233.00
Cupboard, Poplar, Federal, Red Paint, Pa., c.1840, 86 x 51 In. 18750.00
Cupboard, Raised Panel, Double Doors, Red Paint, 36 x 14 x 71 In. 1898.00
Cupboard, Renaissance Revival, Oak, 2 Over 2 Paneled Doors, 88 x 69 x 30 In. 4560.00
Cupboard, Shaker, Pine, Buttermilk Blue Paint, Wide Board Door, 1800s, 42 x 18 In. 5750.00
Cupboard, Softwood, Brown, Yellow Ground, Lancaster Co., 45 x 37 x 18 In. . . . . *illus* 3750.00
Cupboard, Softwood, Flame Grain Painted, Recessed Panel Doors, Pa., 42 x 43 In. 1650.00
Cupboard, Softwood, Red Paint, Molded Top, Dovetailed Drawer, 59 ½ x 36 In. 4950.00
Cupboard, Softwood, Red Paint, Step Back, 3 Shelves, Cabinet Top, 79 x 44 In. 9900.00
Cupboard, Tulips, Flowers, Blind Door, Drawer, 1828, 29 x 23 x 12 In. . . . . *illus* 1000.00
Cupboard, Walnut, 2 Paneled Doors, Shelves, Plate Grooves, 58 x 37 x 13 In. 1058.00
Cupboard, Walnut, Molded Cornice, 2 6-Pane Doors, Drawer, Panel Doors, 81 x 44 In. 881.00
Cupboard, Walnut, Open Top, Beaded Molding, Tongue & Groove Backboard, c.1830, 76 In. . 1410.00
Cupboard, Walnut, Parquetry Diamond, Drawer, Italy, 38 x 31 x 14 In. 1800.00
Cupboard, Walnut, Raised Panel Doors, 76 ½ x 17 ½ x 36 In. 1058.00
Cupboard, Yellow Pine, Open Top, Shelves, Lower Door, 1800s, 81 x 39 In. 805.00
Cupboard, Yellow Pine, Paneled, Blue Green Paint, Interior Shelves, 1800s, 49 x 55 In. 748.00
Cupboard, Yellow Pine, Poplar, Step Back, Panel Doors, Shelves, 1800s, 75 x 54 In. 4600.00
Cupboard, Yellow Pine, Red Stain, Stepped Cornice, Panel Doors, c.1900, 85 x 53 In. 1840.00
Cupboard, Yellow Pine, Step Back, 2 Doors, Shelves, Blue Paint, Late 1800s, 81 x 37 In. 805.00
Cupboard, Yellow Pine, Step Back, Door, Open Interior, Late 1800s, 59 x 33 In. 633.00
Daybed, Cane Platform, Round Headrest, Drawers, Pierced Panels, Chinese, 28 x 66 In. 450.00
Daybed, Directoire, Mahogany, Scrolled Head & Footboard, c.1900, 30 x 74 In. 1180.00
Daybed, Directoire, Mahogany, Scrolled Head & Footboard, Spindles, Splats, 63 x 21 In. 2233.00
Daybed, Directoire Style, French Provincial, Walnut, Acorn Finials, 29 x 25 In. 1800.00
Daybed, Directoire Style, Outscrolled Side, Fluted Uprights, 47 x 79 x 30 ½ In. 2400.00
Daybed, Empire, Mahogany, Flower & Lotus Carved, Bolsters, Pillows, 42 x 81 In. 2160.00
Daybed, Empire, Mahogany, Gilt Classical Figures, France, c.1850, 45 x 80 x 49 In. 12650.00
Daybed, Empire, Mahogany, Ormolu Mounts, Bust, Urn Finials, France, 51 x 80 x 49 In. 4600.00
Daybed, Empire, Mahogany, Padded, Upholstered, Cushion, 36 x 82 x 32 In. 1016.00
Daybed, Empire Style, Fruitwood, Ebonized, Paneled, 1890s, 46 x 74 x 40 In. . . . . *illus* 400.00

Furniture, Cupboard, Tulips, Flowers, Blind Door, Drawer, 1828, 29 x 23 x 12 In.
$1000.00

Furniture, Daybed, Empire Style, Fruitwood, Ebonized, Paneled, 1890s, 46 x 74 x 40 In.
$400.00

Furniture, Daybed, Empire Style, Sleigh, White, Green Paint, 1910, 37 x 74 x 26 In.
$1300.00

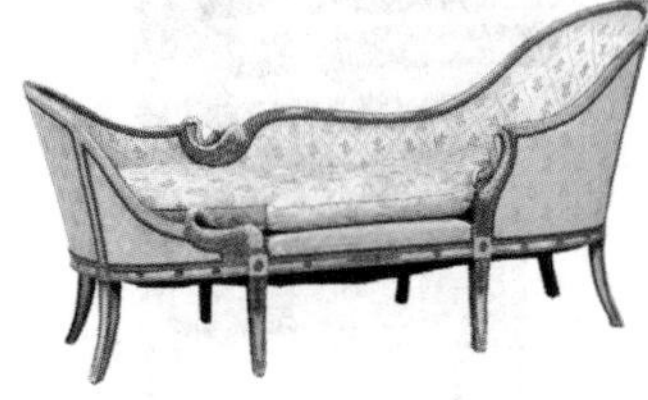

Furniture, Daybed, French Provincial, Fruitwood, Silk, 19th Century, 37 x 81 x 28 In.
$1955.00

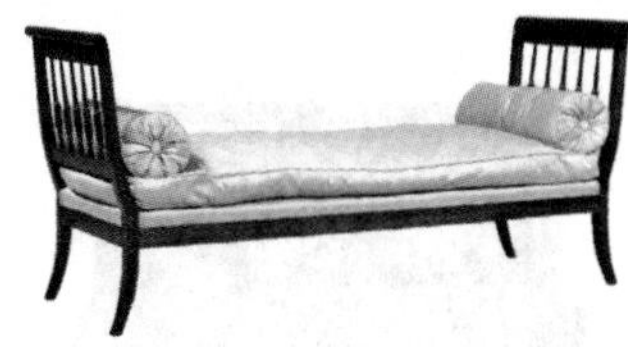

F

Furniture, Daybed, William & Mary, Banister Back, Black Over Green, c.1730
$4212.00

Furniture, Desk, Chippendale, Slant Front, Walnut, C, 1775, 42 x 38 In.
$2440.00

Furniture, Desk, Davenport, Faux Bamboo, Slant Front, England, 1890s, 44 x 23 x 19 In.
$425.00

Furniture, Desk, Federal, Mahogany, 2 Tambour Doors, 2 Sections, 1810, 47 x 39 x 20 In.
$2530.00

Daybed, Empire Style, Sleigh, White, Green Paint, 1910, 37 x 74 x 26 In. *illus* 1300.00
Daybed, French Provincial, Fruitwood, Silk, 19th Century, 37 x 81 x 28 In. *illus* 1955.00
Daybed, G. Stickley, Slatted, Rope Foundation, 34 x 83 x 36 In. 3000.00
Daybed, Iron, Sleigh, Front Rail, Gilt, Green Patina 300.00
Daybed, L. & J.G. Stickley, No. 292, 4 Vertical Slats, Flared Legs, Signed, 28 x 80 x 30 In. 3950.00
Daybed, Oak, Carved Crest, Spiral Turned, Block Stiles, Legs, Stretchers, England 748.00
Daybed, Painted, Carved Parcel Gilt, Spiral Fluted Legs, Silk Pillows, 36 x 75 In. 9375.00
Daybed, Peter Hvidt, Teak, Red, Orange Cushion, France & Sons, 16 x 75 In. 600.00
Daybed, Saporiti, Adjustable Suede Back, Color Swirl Missoni Upholstery, Italy, 36 x 28 In. 4200.00
Daybed, Victorian, Wood, Mirror, Striped Upholstery, Carved Serpents, Ball Detail, 75 x 76 In. 1680.00
Daybed, William & Mary, Banister Back, Black Over Green, c.1730 *illus* 4212.00
Desk, Architect's, Double Ratcheting Support, Pullout Writing Surface, c.1760, 32 x 36 In. 5280.00
Desk, Architect's, Mahogany, Ratcheted Top, Inlaid, 2 Drawers, England, c.1800, 32 x 30 In. 3220.00
Desk, Arts & Crafts, Oak, 2 Drawers, Copper Pulls, Side Slats, c.1905, 29 x 50 In. 237.00
Desk, Arts & Crafts, Oak, Drawer, Copper Pulls, Lower Shelf, Tenons, c.1910, 30 x 48 In. 652.00
Desk, Arts & Crafts, Slant Front, Oak, 41 x 32 x 16 In. 135.00
Desk, Burl, Bombe, Italy, Late 19th Century, 86 x 45 ½ x 19 In. 1700.00
Desk, Burl Walnut, Double Pedestal, Leather Inset, Drawers, c.1880, 31 x 53 In. 2640.00
Desk, Butler's, Cherry, Inlaid, 3 Drawers, Dovetailed, N.Y., 44 x 47 x 21 In. 1150.00
Desk, Butler's, Mahogany, Felt, 4 Drawers, Ring & Ball Feet, c.1840, 48 x 43 x 22 In. 750.00
Desk, Butler's, Regency, Mahogany, Rope Inlaid Drawers, Drop Front, Early 1900s, 42 x 46 In. 1528.00
Desk, Campaign, Brass Banded Drawers, Mahogany, 40 x 37 In. 3995.00
Desk, Campaign, Mahogany, Inset Leather, 29 ¾ x 52 x 24 ¾ In. 1920.00
Desk, Chippendale, Drop Front, Cherry, 41 x 20 In. 3163.00
Desk, Chippendale, Mahogany, Brass Hardware, Slant Front, Mass., 1780, 44 x 41 In. 7500.00
Desk, Chippendale, Mahogany, Brass Mounted, Slant Front, Tooled Leather, 33 x 43 In. 1840.00
Desk, Chippendale, Mahogany, Pedestal, Leather, Carved, 7 Drawers, 1700s, 30 x 48 In. 1150.00
Desk, Chippendale, Mahogany, Pierced Gallery, Slant Front, 4 Drawers, 1700s, 37 x 37 In. 633.00
Desk, Chippendale, Slant Front, Birch, Bird's-Eye Maple, Drawers, 35 ½ In. 2650.00
Desk, Chippendale, Slant Front, Cherry, 4 Drawers, Fitted Interior, c.1760, 41 x 37 In. 823.00
Desk, Chippendale, Slant Front, Cherry, Drawers, Pilaster Fronts, c.1790, 45 x 40 In. 2133.00
Desk, Chippendale, Slant Front, Curly Maple, Fitted Interior, Pigeonholes, c.1760, 41 x 36 In. 2820.00
Desk, Chippendale, Slant Front, Fitted Interior, 3 Drawers, Painted, c.1775, 32 x 21 In., Child's 4406.00
Desk, Chippendale, Slant Front, Mahogany, 2 Over 3 Drawers, c.1780, 43 x 47 x 21 In. 4000.00
Desk, Chippendale, Slant Front, Mahogany, 4 Drawers, 18th Century, 40 x 37 x 19 In. 1000.00
Desk, Chippendale, Slant Front, Mahogany, 42 ¾ x 40 ¾ x 21 ½ In. 6250.00
Desk, Chippendale, Slant Front, Mahogany, 5 Drawers, Bracket Feet, c.1800, 44 x 22 In. 495.00
Desk, Chippendale, Slant Front, Mahogany, String Inlay, 45 x 41 x 25 In. 2400.00
Desk, Chippendale, Slant Front, Maple, Pine, Dovetailed, Fitted Interior, c.1785, 43 x 40 In. 1058.00
Desk, Chippendale, Slant Front, Tiger Maple, 3 Drawers, Bracket Feet, c.1780, 16 x 13 In. 4914.00
Desk, Chippendale, Slant Front, Tiger Maple, 44 ¾ x 38 x 19 In. 5175.00
Desk, Chippendale, Slant Front, Tiger Maple, 7 Drawers, New England, 1780s, 45 x 39 In. 5451.00
Desk, Chippendale, Slant Front, Walnut, 4 Drawers, Bracket Feet, c.1780, 41 x 38 In. 3600.00
Desk, Chippendale, Slant Front, Walnut, C, 1775, 42 x 38 In. *illus* 2440.00
Desk, Chippendale, Slant Front, Walnut, Cubbyholes, Drawers, 42 x 39 ¾ x 21 In. 2990.00
Desk, Chippendale Style, Mahogany, Lion Mask, Compartments, 32 x 9 x 50 ½ In. 3840.00
Desk, Danish Modern, Rosewood, c.1970, 29 x 79 In. 1920.00
Desk, Davenport, Burl Walnut, Lift Top, Leather Inset, 4 Side Drawers, 33 x 21 In. 720.00
Desk, Davenport, Faux Bamboo, Slant Front, England, 1890s, 44 x 23 x 19 In. *illus* 425.00
Desk, Davenport, Victorian, Walnut, Leather, Drawers, Partitions, England, 46 x 24 x 22 In. 2596.00
Desk, Double Pedestal, Burled Oak Veneers, Ebonized, 96 x 48 x 25 In. 1840.00
Desk, Drop Front, Pine, Drawers, Breadboard Top, Pigeonholes, 44 x 22 x 22 In. 384.00
Desk, Ebonized, Carved Panels, England, Japonisme, 48 x 30 x 20 ½ In. 805.00
Desk, Edwardian, Satinwood, Painted, Flower Garland, Cupids, 37 x 54 In. 8519.00
Desk, Empire, Bird's-Eye Maple, 7 Drawers, 49 x 42 x 20 In. 525.00
Desk, Empire, Drop Front, Mahogany, Raised Panel Top, 19th Century, 54 ½ x 32 In. 1121.00
Desk, Escritoire, Louis XV, Walnut, Shell Carved Knees, Cabriole Legs, Hoof Feet, 29 x 34 x 23 In. 2467.00
Desk, Escritoire, Louis XVI, Kidney Shape, Gilt Bronze, Leather, c.1920, 30 x 47 In. 1645.00
Desk, Federal, Cherry, Lift Top, Drawer, Signed, Baltimore, 1860, 46 x 28 x 25 In. 1500.00
Desk, Federal, Drop Front, Mahogany, Cherry, Slotted, Baize, Turned Legs, 53 x 33 x 22 In. 1880.00
Desk, Federal, Mahogany, 2 Tambour Doors, 2 Sections, 1810, 47 x 39 x 20 In. *illus* 2530.00
Desk, Federal, Mahogany, Inlaid, Fold Flap, 2 Doors, 3 Drawers, c.1800, 47 x 39 In. 2530.00
Desk, Federal, Mahogany, Slant Front, Inlaid, Figured, Pa., c.1800, 15 x 13 In. 3750.00
Desk, Federal, Mahogany, Tambour, 2 Sections, 4 Drawers, Scrolled Skirt, 51 x 39 In. 2350.00
Desk, Federal, Slant Front, Mahogany, 4 Graduated Drawers, Early 1800s, 46 x 46 In. 590.00
Desk, Federal, Slant Front, Pine, 3 Drawers, Fitted Interior, Oval Brass Pulls, 41 x 35 In. 501.00
Desk, Florence Knoll, Birch, 3 Drawers, Signed, 1950s, 29 x 50 x 28 In. *illus* 890.00

Desk, French Rococo, Roll Top, Rosewood, Carved, Pull Down Surface, c.1870, 40 x 21 In.... 2530.00
Desk, Fruitwood, Long Drawer, 2 Short Drawers, 30 x 40 ½ x 21 In. 325.00
Desk, G. Nelson, Single Pedestal, Herman Miller, c.1964, 30 x 66 In. 4500.00
Desk, G. Redfield, Mahogany, Applied Mahogany Dolphins, Ebony Stretchers, 27 x 43 In. 385.00
Desk, G. Stickley, No. 713, Roll Top, 6 Drawers, Decal, c.1903, 46 x 60 x 32 In. .... *illus* 7200.00
Desk, G. Stickley, No. 732, Drop Front, 4 Drawers, Slab Sides, Brass Hardware, 44 x 32 In. 2160.00
Desk, George II, Slant Front, Mahogany, Marquetry, Landscapes, Hunters, 40 x 39 In. 2340.00
Desk, George III, Slant Front, Mahogany, 4 Drawers, 19th Century, 40 x 36 In. 644.00
Desk, George III, Slant Front, Mahogany, Fitted Interior, 4 Drawers, England, c.1795, 42 x 38 In. 1150.00
Desk, George III Style, Mahogany, Kneehole, 7 Drawers, 29 x 40 ½ x 19 In. 1380.00
Desk, Georgian, Mahogany Pedestal, Inset Leather Top, Frieze Drawer, 30 x 48 In. 474.00
Desk, Georgian Style, Slant Front, Walnut, Breadboard Ends, Drawers, 43 x 41 In. 299.00
Desk, Greta Grossman, Top Storage Unit, Glenn, c.1955, 41 x 48 In. 21600.00
Desk, Hepplewhite, Mahogany, 3 Drawers, Fan, Line Inlay, England, 1800s, 31 x 37 In. 1610.00
Desk, Hepplewhite, Mahogany, Inlaid, 5 Drawers, England, c.1880, 32 x 49 x 24 In. 633.00
Desk, Hepplewhite, Slant Front, Curly Maple, Cherry, Poplar, Dividers, 46 x 42 x 34 In. 3173.00
Desk, Hepplewhite, Slant Front, Walnut, 4 Graduated Drawers, French Feet, 46 x 39 In. 1410.00
Desk, Hepplewhite, Slant Front, Walnut, 52 x 38 x 22 ½ In. 1760.00
Desk, Limbert, No. 736, Gallery Top, Mark, 38 x 30 x 20 In. .... *illus* 1920.00
Desk, Limbert, Oak, Arts & Crafts, 2 Drawers, Wooden Knobs, 29 x 48 x 29 In. 418.00
Desk, Louis XV, Slant Front, Amaranth, Parquetry, Fitted Interior, 35 x 51 In. 16250.00
Desk, Louis XV Style, Fruitwood, Planked Top, End Drawers, 29 x 65 ⅜ x 28 In. 2160.00
Desk, Louis XV Style, Kingwood, Bureau Du Roi, Gilt, Bronze, Marquetry, 1950s .... *illus* 6050.00
Desk, Louis XVI, Gilt Metal Mounted, Gallery Top, Drawers, Fluted Legs, 38 x 36 In. 660.00
Desk, Louis XVI Style, Drop Front, Kingwood, Mahogany, Drawers, 31 x 52 x 26 In. 3120.00
Desk, Louis XVI Style, Roll Top, C Roll, Pierced Brass Gallery, Marble Top, 1800s, 44 x 35 In. . 1150.00
Desk, Mahogany, Burl, Pedestals, Drawers, Victorian, 30 x 48 x 28 ½ In. 3360.00
Desk, Mahogany, Carved Flowers, Doors, Drawers, Crest, Chinese, c.1900, 53 x 48 In. 826.00
Desk, Mahogany, Inlaid, Drawers, Tambour Doors, c.1890, 46 x 63 x 31 In. 4600.00
Desk, Mahogany, Slant Front, Oak, 4 Drawers, Pigeonholes, 42 x 36 x 21 In. 2530.00
Desk, Neoclassical, Roll Top, Drawers, Marble, Turned Legs, c.1835, 39 x 63 In. 2937.00
Desk, Neoclassical, Slant Front, Walnut, Inlaid, 3 Short 3 Long Drawers, 38 x 30 x 18 In. 2370.00
Desk, Oak, Gilt Metal, Inset Leather Top, 3 Drawers, France, c.1950, 29 x 46 In. 22500.00
Desk, Officer's, Mahogany, 8 Drawers, 2 Doors, Green Writing Surface, c.1860, 60 x 51 In. 440.00
Desk, Partners, Edwardian, Oak, Leather, Drawers, c.1890, 31 x 61 In. 1997.00
Desk, Partners, R.J. Horner, Mahogany, Carved, Cabriole Legs, 31 ½ x 54 x 30 In. 4025.00
Desk, Partners, Renaissance Revival, Oak, Lion Mask Stiles, Rosettes, 30 x 59 In. 1880.00
Desk, Pedestal, Balloon Flight Scenes, 8 Drawers, Plinth Bases, 30 x 50 x 31 In. 1725.00
Desk, Plantation, Cherry, Double Slant Front, Fitted Interiors, Drawers, 51 x 60 In. 2990.00
Desk, Plantation, Pine, Slant Front, Shaped Backsplash, Fitted Interior, 44 x 36 In. 650.00
Desk, Plantation, Yellow Pine, Painted, Panel Doors, Shelves, 1800s, 62 x 41 In. 863.00
Desk, Queen Anne, Slant Front, Cherry, 2 Drawers, Bun Feet, c.1730, 21 x 18 x 11 In. 5616.00
Desk, Queen Anne, Slant Front, Curly Maple, Maple, Pine, Compartments, 43 x 39 x 19 In. .. 4406.00
Desk, Queen Anne, Slant Front, Tiger Maple, 3 Drawers, Early 1900s, 36 x 25 x 16 In. 550.00
Desk, Queen Anne, Slant Front, Walnut, Fitted Interior, Tapered Legs, c.1750, 34 x 34 In. 822.00
Desk, Queen Anne, Slant Front, Walnut, Shell Carved Apron, c.1900, 39 x 28 x 20 In. 820.00
Desk, R.J. Horner, Mahogany, Molded Edge, 5 Drawers, 30 x 54 x 34 In. 4600.00
Desk, Regency, Mahogany, 3 Drawers, Reeded Edge, Casters, 37 x 42 x 24 In. 826.00
Desk, Regency, Mahogany, Tooled Leather, Drawers, Trestle Base, Baker Furniture, 35 x 42 In. 546.00
Desk, Regency, Roll Top, Mahogany, 2 Drawers, Casters, c.1810, 40 x 36 In. 3042.00
Desk, Renaissance Revival, Walnut, Carved, Italy, 1890s, 59 x 34 x 23 In. .... *illus* 3500.00
Desk, Renaissance Revival, Walnut, Carved, Leather, Drawers, Scroll Feet, 31 x 81 x 36 In. 5500.00
Desk, Renaissance Revival, Walnut, Pedestal, Ornate Oak Carvings, Leather, c.1800, 31 x 59 In. 944.00
Desk, Rococo, Rosewood, Acanthus, Pierced Gallery, Barley Twist, 51 x 34 In. 1058.00
Desk, Rococo, Walnut, Pedestal, 3 Drawers, 2 Cabinets, Relief Carving, 64 x 35 In. 3819.00
Desk, Rococo Revival, Mahogany, Drawer, Germany, 1850, 54 x 40 x 26 In. 502.00
Desk, Rohde, Paldao, Double Pedestal, 6 Drawers, Vinyl, Herman Miller, 1940s, 29 x 56 In. .. 5400.00
Desk, Roll Top, C Roll, 3 Drawers, Gilt Pilasters, Baker Furniture, c.1950s, 44 x 42 In. 690.00
Desk, Roll Top, C Roll, Mahogany, Shaped Back, Top Shape Feet, c.1820, 53 ½ x 50 In. 5287.00
Desk, Rosewood, Chrome Border, Pullout Writing Surface, 3 Drawers, c.1950, 29 x 72 In. 1067.00
Desk, Rosewood, Kingwood, Leather Top, Bronze Mounted, c.1900, 29 x 60 x 29 In. 1610.00
Desk, Roycroft, 5 Drawers, Copper Pulls, Carved Orb & Cross Mark, 29 x 53 In. 14400.00
Desk, Roycroft, No. 91, Drop Front, Carved Orb & Cross Mark, 44 x 37 In. 4800.00
Desk, Satinwood, Burl Veneers, Kidney Shape, Painted, c.1930s, 29 x 48 In. 489.00
Desk, School, Amish, Slant Front, Pine, Green Paint, Backboard, 31 x 51 In. 550.00
Desk, School, Poplar, 19th Century, 31 x 42 In. 200.00
Desk, School, Slant Front, Pine, Green Paint Over Red Ocher, 31 x 51 x 17 In. .... *illus* 550.00

Furniture, Desk, Florence Knoll, Birch, 3 Drawers, Signed, 1950s, 29 x 50 x 28 In.
$890.00

Furniture, Desk, G. Stickley, No. 713, Roll Top, 6 Drawers, Decal, c.1903, 46 x 60 x 32 In.
$7200.00

Furniture, Desk, Limbert, No. 736, Gallery Top, Mark, 38 x 30 x 20 In.
$1920.00

Furniture, Desk, Louis XV Style, Kingwood, Bureau Du Roi, Gilt, Bronze, Marquetry, 1950s
$6050.00

F

Furniture, Desk, Renaissance Revival, Walnut, Carved, Italy, 1890s, 59 x 34 x 23 In.
$3500.00

Furniture, Desk, School, Slant Front, Pine, Green Paint Over Red Ocher, 31 x 51 x 17 In.
$550.00

Furniture, Desk, Wooton, Bird's-Eye Maple, Signed, Rue Jackson, 1884, 72 x 42 x 29 In.
$7763.00

Roll-Top Patent

The first American patent for a horizontal tambour roll-top desk was issued in 1850 to Abner Cutler. The Cutler desk became the best-known commercial desk in the United States in the late nineteenth century.

Desk, Schoolmaster's, Slant Front, Cherry, Gallery, Scrolled, Pigeonholes, 44 x 33 In. 2970.00
Desk, Sheraton, Slant Front, Cherry, 4 Drawers, 39 ½ x 40 x 19 ½ In. 600.00
Desk, Shop Of The Crafters, No. 281, Pencil Post, Drawer, 30 x 42 In. 1080.00
Desk, Slant Front, Birch, Stenciled, Drawer, Signed, F.A. Pals, 37 ½ x 29 ½ x 19 In. 1100.00
Desk, Slant Front, Cherry, 4 Drawers, Fitted Interior, Pinstripe Inlay, Pa., c.1790, 39 x 45 In. . . 1062.00
Desk, Slant Front, Figured Maple, Dovetailed, Fitted Interior, 1700s, 40 x 36 In. 575.00
Desk, Slant Front, Maple, Inlaid, Fitted Interior, 6 Drawers, Cubbyholes, 61 x 40 In. 403.00
Desk, Slant Front, Poplar, 3 Drawers, Crotch Grain Design, French Feet, c.1800, 41 x 40 In. . . 18700.00
Desk, Spinet, Walnut, Ivory Inlay, Drawers, Doors, Burl Panels, 37 ½ x 46 x 24 In. 550.00
Desk, Stand Up, Pine, Lift Top, Dovetailed Gallery, Drawer, c.1800, 53 x 22 x 22 In. 2468.00
Desk, Tiger Maple, Cotton Factor, 4 Interior Drawers, Cherry Arcade, Southern, 51 x 36 In. . . 2760.00
Desk, Victorian, Roll Top, C Roll, Walnut, Derby Desk Co., 19th Century, 51 x 54 x 33 In. 750.00
Desk, Walnut, Carved, Kneehole, Cubbyholes, Slots, c.1880, 60 x 55 x 35 In. 7480.00
Desk, Walnut, Trestle, 3 Drawers, Stretcher, Carved Legs, 1900s, 32 x 94 x 37 In. 440.00
Desk, William & Mary, Slant Front, Walnut, 4 Drawers, Bun Feet, c.1730, 42 x 36 In. 7605.00
Desk, William & Mary, Slant Front, Walnut, 4 Graduated Drawers, 41 x 35 In. 6463.00
Desk, Wooton, Bird's-Eye Maple, Signed, Rue Jackson, 1884, 72 x 42 x 29 In. . . . . *illus* 7763.00
Desk, Wooton, Walnut, Burled Walnut Panels, Brass Hardware, Standard Model, c.1874, 72 x 43 In. 10350.00
Desk, Wormley, Mahogany, Gallery, 3 Drawers, Pedestal, Tapered Legs, 29 x 48 In. 1020.00
Desk, Wormley, Rosewood, Walnut, Tambour Compartments, Dunbar, 35 x 75 x 29 In. 6000.00
Desk-Bookcase, Butler's, Georgian, Mahogany, Glazed Doors, Drawers, 1800s, 74 x 41 In. . . 1380.00
Desk-Bookcase, Federal, Mahogany, Glazed Doors, 4 Drawers, Finials, c.1805, 82 x 43 In. . . . 2252.00
Desk-Bookcase, Federal, Mahogany, Tambour, Inlaid, 2 Doors, 3 Drawers, c.1815, 68 x 42 In. 4740.00
Desk-Bookcase, Gothic Revival, Mahogany, 19th Century, 89 x 49 ½ In. 6169.00
Desk-Bookcase, Mahogany, Carved, Top Cupboard, 4 Drawers, c.1825, 85 x 45 In. 13035.00
Desk-Bookcase, Mahogany, Ogee Cornice, Mirrored Doors, c.1850, 85 x 41 In. 1645.00
Desk-Bookcase, William IV, Mahogany, Beaded Cornice, Shelves, Early 1800s, 74 x 53 In. . . . 823.00
Desk-Bookcase, Yellow Pine, Broken Scroll Pediment, Fan Carving, 1800, 92 x 49 In. 3450.00
Dinette Set, Eero Saarinen, Aluminum, 5 Tulip Chairs, 6 Piece. 1353.00
Dining Set, Edgar Brandt, Mahogany, Drop Leaf Table, 29 x 60 In., 5 Piece 550.00
Dining Set, Heywood-Wakefield, Drop Leaf Table, 29 x 63 x 42 In., 7 Piece . . . . *illus* 502.00
Dresser, Chippendale, Mahogany, 4 Drawers, Dovetailed, 35 ½ x 40 x 21 In. 690.00
Dresser, Eastlake, Walnut, Marble Top, 3 Drawers, Mirror, Shelves, c.1875, 75 x 41 In. 325.00
Dresser, Empire, Mahogany, Marble Insert, Glass Pulls, c.1840-50, 60 x 36 ½ x 20 In. 570.00
Dresser, Empire Style, Cherry, Drawers, Pilasters, Torpedo Feet, 32 x 64 x 21 In. 3840.00
Dresser, Louis XVI, Figured Walnut Veneers, Marble Top, Bronze Mounts, 34 x 49 In. 920.00
Dresser, Mahogany, Mirror, 6 Drawers, Stencils, Carved Paw Feet, c.1825, 70 x 39 In. 2530.00
Dresser, Marble Top, 12 Drawers, Bernhardt Furniture, 36 ½ x 67 ½ x 20 In. 800.00
Dresser, McCobb, Mahogany, 11 Drawers, Brass Cross Stretcher, Calvin, 53 x 36 In. 1020.00
Dresser, Neoclassical, Mahogany, Mirror, 4 Drawers, 1870s, 70 x 26 x 21 In. . . . . *illus* 1210.00
Dresser, Neoclassical, Mahogany, Swan & Leaf Carved Mirror Supports, 71 x 36 In. 1265.00
Dresser, Nutting, No. 922, Oak Welsh, Iron Hardware, Handmade Nails 16500.00
Dresser, Oak, Elm, Open Shelves, 2 Drawers, Ring Stiles, England, c.1800, 80 x 49 In. 3738.00
Dresser, Oak, Scalloped, Pierced Frieze, Shelves, 2 Drawers, Spade Feet, 80 x 54 x 17 In. 4080.00
Dresser, Oak, Shelves, Hooks, Drawers, Arched, Cupboards, England, 68 x 62 x 17 In. 1800.00
Dresser, Oak, Welsh, Flared Cornice, Reeded Stiles, Drawers, Doors, c.1775, 59 x 57 In. 2467.00
Dresser, Oak, Welsh, Shaped Apron, Mid 1800s, 82 x 66 ½ x 18 ½ In. . . . . *illus* 2415.00
Dresser, Princess, Renaissance Revival, Walnut, Carved, Marble Top. 2875.00
Dresser, Renaissance Revival, Walnut, Mirror, Carved Crests, Marble, c.1870, 106 x 59 In. . . . 767.00
Dresser, Saarinen, Birch, 5 Drawers, Johnson Furniture, 46 x 32 x 20 In. . . . . *illus* 650.00
Dresser, Victorian, Mahogany, Carved Cherub Crest, 5 Drawers, 79 x 55 x 27 In. 590.00
Dresser, Victorian, Walnut, 3 Drawers, Glove Boxes, 38 x 40 x 18 In. 236.00
Dresser, Victorian, Walnut, 3 Drawers, Marble Top, Handkerchief Boxes, 70 x 39 x 18 In. 266.00
Dresser, Victorian, Walnut, 3 Drawers, Mirror, Glove Boxes, Marble Top, 85 x 41 x 19 In. 472.00
Dresser, Victorian, Walnut, 4 Drawers, Handkerchief Boxes, Swivel Mirror, 70 x 40 x 18 In. . . 413.00
Dresser, Victorian, Walnut, Mirror, 4 Drawers, Shelf, c.1900, 63 x 36 x 19 In. . . . . *illus* 154.00
Dresser, Walnut, 5 Drawers, Wood Knobs, Mirror, Kunkle Furniture Co., 76 x 54 In. 510.00
Dresser Base, George I, Oak, 3 Drawers, Backsplash, Arched Apron, 35 ½ x 68 ½ In. 4183.00
Dresser Base, Oak, 3 Drawers, Scalloped Apron, Squared Legs, England, 32 x 72 x 19 In. . . . 4183.00
Dresser Base, Queen Anne, 3 Drawers, Cabriole Legs, Pad Feet, 30 x 64 In. 1410.00
Dry Sink, Green Paint, Door, 33 x 41 x 20 In. 500.00
Dry Sink, Oak, Painted, Metal Latches, Bracket Feet, 29 ½ x 23 ½ x 11 In. 770.00
Dry Sink, Pine, Cupboard, Painted, 2 Parts, Ocher Grain, Pa., Mid 1800s, 81 x 43 In. 7020.00
Dry Sink, Pine, Door, Wainscot Base, 19th Century, 33 x 35 x 19 In. . . . . *illus* 201.00
Dry Sink, Pine, Gray Over Green Paint, Early 19th Century, 36 x 39 In. 1170.00
Dry Sink, Pine, Plank Board Top, 2 Doors, Shelves, England, 38 ¾ x 45 ½ x 22 In. 590.00
Dry Sink, Pine, Raised Drawer, 2 Paneled Doors, 33 x 48 ¾ x 19 ¾ In. 189.00

Dry Sink, Pine, Sponged Door, Cutout Bracket Feet, Red Paint, Pa., 30 x 27 ½ In. 11000.00
Dry Sink, Pine, Weathered Red Paint, New England, c.1880, 30 x 58 In. 999.00
Dry Sink, Pine, Yellow Paint, Drawer, 2 Doors, Bracket Feet, Pa., Mid 1800s, 38 x 40 In. 4212.00
Dry Sink, Poplar, Gallery Top, 2 Drawers, Mid 1800s, 44 x 40 In. 1035.00
Dry Sink, Red & Yellow Paint, Door, Cutout Base, 32 x 32 x 17 In. 300.00
Dry Sink, Softwood, Backsplash, Shaped Sides, Red, Bracket Feet, 33 ¾ x 42 ¾ In. 1980.00
Dry Sink, Softwood, Red, Zinc Lined, Backsplash, Recessed Panel Doors, 36 x 46 In. 2420.00
Dry Sink, Softwood, Red Paint, Bead Molded, Recessed Panel Door, Shelf, 35 x 34 In. 1320.00
Dry Sink, Tiger Maple, Drawer, Door, Wayne Timpson, N.J., 22 x 24 x 14 In. 385.00
Dry Sink, Trench Form, Splayed Legs, Red Paint, 19th Century, 33 ½ x 51 In. . . . . *illus* 878.00
Dry Sink, Walnut, Grain Painted, Cream, Blue Panels, Scalloped Base, 35 x 38 In. 805.00
Dry Sink, Walnut, Yellow Paint, Berks County, Pa., 40 ½ x 43 ¾ x 21 ½ In. 1540.00
Dry Sink, Zinc Lined, Dovetailed, Drawers, Paneled Doors, Turned Feet, 35 x 38 In. 5225.00
Drying Post, Maple, Turned Urn Finial, Inset Paneled Rods For Dyeing Bottler, 1920 . . . . 350.00
Dumbwaiter, Chippendale, Mahogany, 3 Dish Tops, 3-Footed, 1890s, 42 x 21 ½ In. 600.00
Dumbwaiter, George III, Mahogany, 2 Tiers, Tripod Base, 39 ½ x 26 In. 413.00
Dumbwaiter, Georgian Style, Mahogany, 2 Tiers, Revolving, 3-Footed, B. Ferber 150.00
Dumbwaiter, Georgian Style, Mahogany, 3 Tiers, 3-Footed, 19th Century, 44 x 26 In. 450.00
Dumbwaiter, Mahogany, Beaded, Molded, 3 Tiers, Carved, 1800s, 28 x 27 x 17 In. 2585.00
Dumbwaiter, Regency, Mahogany, 2 Tiers, Brass Columns, Casters, c.1810, 45 x 22 In. 1638.00
Dumbwaiter, Regency, Mahogany, 2 Tiers, Dish Top, Brass, 3-Footed, c.1810, 45 x 22 In. 1400.00
Easel, Faux Bamboo, Gilt, Arched Spindled Crest, c.1875, 77 In. 980.00
Easel, Hong Mu, Cobras, Figures, Carved, Spindle Guard, British Colonial, 73 In. 4740.00
Easel, Louis XV Style, Asymmetrical Crest, 3 Supports, Holding Pegs, 82 In. 1920.00
Easel, Mahogany, Aesthetic Revival, Hinged, Upper & Lower Spindle Gallery, 68 x 21 In. 2160.00
Easel, Mahogany, Brass Mounted, Adjusting Crank, Stretchers, Shoe Feet, 62 x 26 In. 4025.00
Easel, Renaissance Revival, Walnut, Ebonized, Gilt, Spindle Crest, Medallion, c.1870, 77 x 36 In. 3600.00
Easel, Rosewood, A-Frame, Carved Vines, Flowers, Buds, Grape Clusters, 90 x 35 In. 4080.00
Easel, Victorian, Walnut, Storage, Gilt, 77 x 36 In. 880.00
Easel, Walnut, Gilt Incised, Bronze, Ebonized, Medallion, c.1870, 77 x 36 In. . . . . *illus* 3000.00
Etagere, Corner, Walnut, Victorian, Figural Craved Doors, Shelves, 24 x 77 In., Pair 2415.00
Etagere, Edwardian, Mahogany, Gilt, Label, London, 1895, 68 ½ x 41 In. . . . . *illus* 660.00
Etagere, Empire Style, Mahogany, Bronze Mounted, Tiers, Brass Gallery, 22 x 14 In. 940.00
Etagere, Federal, Mahogany, 4 Shelves, Turned Finials, Columns, Feet, 1800s, 63 x 18 In. . . . 2070.00
Etagere, Fruitwood, 3 Shelves, Continental, 19th Century, 47 In. 938.00
Etagere, Louis XVI Style, Burl Walnut, Parquetry, Ormolu Mounts, 33 x 21 x 14 In. 3081.00
Etagere, Mahogany, Carved Scrolls, Crest, Demilune Base, Scalloped Mirror, 1800s, 48 x 18 In. 560.00
Etagere, Regency, Black Lacquer, Gilt, Brass, 19th Century, 43 x 17 x 10 In. . . . . *illus* 1500.00
Etagere, Regency, Mahogany, Turned, Bulbous Supports, 3 Shelves, Drawer, 59 x 21 In. 4560.00
Etagere, Regency, Rosewood, Balustrade Gallery, 12 Spindles, Frieze Drawer, 54 x 36 In. 3680.00
Etagere, Rococo, Rosewood, Console Base, Marble Top, c.1850 . . . . 11500.00
Etagere, Rosewood, 6 Shelves, 2 Doors, Drawer, Chinese, 35 x 31 ½ x 10 In. 538.00
Etagere, Rosewood, Crest, Mirror, Trefoil Arch, Marble, 76 x 57 In. 8812.00
Etagere, Rosewood, Mirrored, Carved, Alexander Roux, c.1855 . . . . 9775.00
Etagere, Victorian, Bamboo, Shaped Crest, 4 Tiers, 53 x 22 In. 204.00
Etagere, Victorian, Corner, 4 Tiers, Twist Supports, Casters, 52 ½ In. 180.00
Etagere, Victorian, Rosewood, Shaped Top, Corner Finials, Shelves, 34 x 24 In. 1080.00
Etagere, Victorian, Walnut, 5 Tiers, Scalloped Edges, 1880s 150.00
Etagere, William IV, Mahogany, 4 Slatted Shelves, Bulbous Finials, 57 ½ x 60 x 17 In. 2400.00
Fainting Couch, Victorian, Walnut, Spindles, Leaves, Upholstered, 32 x 34 x 20 In. 235.00
Fernery, Neoclassical, Mahogany, Ebonized, Parcel Gilt, Center Urn, Scrolling, 40 x 24 In. . . . 384.00
Footstool, Arts & Crafts, 7 Vertical Spindles, Leather Top, 21 x 15 In. 210.00
Footstool, Arts & Crafts, Oak, Leather, Upholstery Tacks, Woodcraft Guild, 18 x 21 x 14 In. . . 415.00
Footstool, Arts & Crafts, Slatted Sides, Tacked Leather Upholstery, 14 x 21 In. 210.00
Footstool, Beaded, Floral Needlework, Multicolored, Round, 4 ½ x 11 In., Pair 431.00
Footstool, Bronze, Reeded Frame, Needlepoint Cushion, 19th Century, 4 x 15 In., Pair 176.00
Footstool, Empire, Mahogany, Serpentine Case, Upholstered, 18 ½ x 20 x 17 ½ In. 366.00
Footstool, Empire, Mahogany Veneer, Pine, Needlework, Signed, Perin, 15 x 17 x 36 In. 470.00
Footstool, Federal, Mahogany, Leather, Baluster Turned Legs, c.1825, 8 x 15 In. 411.00
Footstool, Frank Lloyd Wright, 6-Sided, Upholstered, 6 Casters, Henredon, 18 x 29 In. 325.00
Footstool, G. Stickley, No. 300, Leather Cover, c.1905, 15 x 20 x 16 In. 1440.00
Footstool, Gilt Brass Mounted, Upholstered, Cloven Hooves, 8 x 14 x 14 In. 510.00
Footstool, Green Paint, Cutout Ends, Mortised, 7 x 17 x 7 In. 85.00
Footstool, Louis XV Style, Beech, Silk Damask Upholstery, France, 8 x 14 x 13 In. 450.00
Footstool, Louis XV Style, Gilt, Blue Floral Needlepoint, Guilloche, 6 x 18 In., Pair 1470.00
Footstool, Louis XVI Style, Gilt, Upholstered Seat, Top Shape Feet, 7 ½ x 15 In., Pair 247.00
Footstool, Mahogany, Carved, Reeded Scroll Ends, Faux Leather, Turned Legs, c.1830, 10 x 18 In. 398.00

TIP
To remove fresh food stains from rugs and upholstery, sprinkle cornstarch on the spot. It will act as a blotter. Vacuum.

F

Furniture, Dining Set, Heywood-Wakefield, Drop Leaf Table, 29 x 63 x 42 In., 7 Piece
$502.00

Furniture, Dresser, Neoclassical, Mahogany, Mirror, 4 Drawers, 1870s, 70 x 26 x 21 In.
$1210.00

Furniture, Dresser, Oak, Welsh, Shaped Apron, Mid 1800s, 82 x 66 ½ x 18 ½ In.
$2415.00

Furniture, Dresser, Saarinen, Birch, 5 Drawers, Johnson Furniture, 46 x 32 x 20 In.
$650.00

Furniture, Dresser, Victorian, Walnut, Mirror, 4 Drawers, Shelf, c.1900, 63 x 36 x 19 In.
$154.00

Furniture, Dry Sink, Pine, Door, Wainscot Base, 19th Century, 33 x 35 x 19 In.
$201.00

Dressing Tables

Dressing tables are back in style. In the seventeenth and eighteenth centuries, dressing tables with adjustable mirrors, candleholders, drawers, and shelves were made, most to be used by men. The idea of a special table to hold cosmetics and toilet articles went out of fashion in the nineteenth century when separate bathrooms became available. In the 1920s, dressing tables came back, usually as a long shelf between two stacks of drawers. Modern dressing tables in many styles are being made today.

Furniture, Dry Sink, Trench Form, Splayed Legs, Red Paint, 19th Century, 33 ½ x 51 In.
$878.00

Furniture, Easel, Walnut, Gilt Incised, Bronze, Ebonized, Medallion, c.1870, 77 x 36 In.
$3000.00

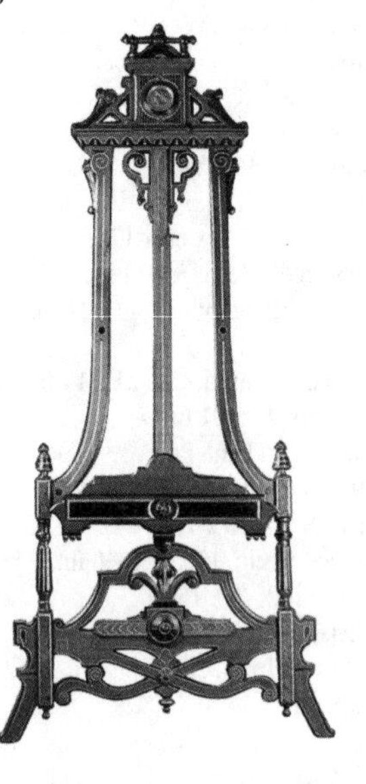

Furniture, Etagere, Edwardian, Mahogany, Gilt, Label, London, 1895, 68 ½ x 41 In.
$660.00

Furniture, Etagere, Regency, Black Lacquer, Gilt, Brass, 19th Century, 43 x 17 x 10 In.
$1500.00

Furniture, Footstool, Mahogany, Removable Slip Seat, Upholstered, c.1830, 15 x 19 x 16 In.
$495.00

Footstool, Mahogany, Curule Frame, Silk Upholstery, Green, c.1845, 15 x 19 x 16 In. 518.00
Footstool, Mahogany, Flared Square Seat, Upholstered, Bracket Feet, c.1840, 12 x 15 In., Pair 470.00
Footstool, Mahogany, Removable Slip Seat, Upholstered, c.1830, 15 x 19 x 16 In. . . . . . . *illus* 495.00
Footstool, Mahogany, Upholstered, Scroll Fretwork, Gadrooned Border, 15 x 22 x 22 In.. . . . . 1020.00
Footstool, Metal Base, Velvet Upholstery, Fringe, 14 x 11 In.. . . . . 40.00
Footstool, Neoclassical, Mahogany, Molded Frame, Bracket Feet, c.1830, 15 x 17 In., Pair . . . 1293.00
Footstool, Neoclassical, Mahogany, Padded Seat, Molded Frieze, Paw Feet, c.1825, 9 x 15 In. . 294.00
Footstool, Pig Shape, Turned Legs, Leather Ears, Gold Paint, Early 1900s, 7 x 12 In.. . . . . 575.00
Footstool, Pine, Painted, Scroll, Green, Red, Yellow, Stars, Stripes, W.L.H., 8 x 16 In. . . . . *illus* 2585.00
Footstool, Pine, Red Paint, Yellow, Black Trim, Cutout Feet, 1800s, 7 ½ x 16 In. 489.00
Footstool, Renaissance Revival, Walnut, Burl, Upholstered Seat, Stretchers, Casters, 15 x 17 In. 588.00
Footstool, Softwood, Altar Coffer, Shaped Apron, Drawer, Iron Pull, Chinese, 12 x 25 In. 180.00
Footstool, Stickley Bros., No. 394 ½, Black Leather Cushion, Notched Feet, 17 x 20 In.. . . . . . 300.00
Footstool, Stickley Bros., No. 5674, Wide Slat Sides, Brown Cushion, Signed, 8 x 18 In.. . . . . . 660.00
Footstool, Victorian, Walnut, Serpentine, Overupholstered, Cabriole Legs, 14 x 19 In., Pair . . 360.00
Footstool, Walnut, Mortised Construction, Cutouts, 7 x 15 x 7 In.. . . . . 2233.00
Footstool, Windsor, Pine, Bamboo Turnings, Red & Black Paint, Gold Trim, c.1820, 6 x 12 In. 499.00
Frame, Art & Crafts, Hammered Copper, Wood, Oval Opening, 8 ¼ x 6 ¾ In. 360.00
Frame, Figured, Maple, Gilt Gesso Borders, 41 x 36 In.. . . . . 190.00
Frame, Giltwood, Carved, Beaded & Bellflower Inner Border, 50 x 40 In., Pair 881.00
Frame, Giltwood, Raised Flower Bands, 33 ¾ x 39 In.. . . . . 1440.00
Frame, Harp, Cherub, Flowers, Reticulated, Painted, Iron, No. 8003, CJO, 6 x 4 In. . . . . . *illus* 145.00
Frame, Leaves, Wood, Black Forest, c.1900, 39 x 46 In.. . . . . 750.00
Frame, Louis XVI, Gilt Metal, Stand, 10 ½ x 8 ¾ In. 120.00
Frame, Softwood, Gold Stars, Red Ground, Stenciled Back, W.H. Logan, c.1860, 17 x 12 In. . . 1998.00
Frame, Walnut, Carved, Tapestry, Village Scene, 48 x 40 In.. . . . . 142.00
Frame, Wood, Painted Yellow, Red Leaves, Lancaster County, Penn., c.1910, 22 x 22 In. 353.00
Gun Case, Stand, Mahogany, Brass Hardware, Paper Lining, England, c.1850, 36 x 18 In. . . . 881.00
Hall Seat, Oak, Umbrella Stand, Drawer, Early 1900s, 30 x 28 x 12 In.. . . . . *illus* 198.00
Hall Seat, Spindles, Michigan Chair Co., 35 ¾ x 41 ¾ x 21 In.. . . . . *illus* 1080.00
Hall Stand, Art Nouveau, Irises, Marquetry, Mirror, Signed, Galle, 85 x 34 In. . . . . *illus* 1195.00
Hall Stand, G. Stickley, No. 66, Peaked Top, Mirror, 4 Iron Hooks, Signed, 28 x 36 In.. . . . . . . 2000.00
Hall Stand, L & J.G. Stickley, No. 65, Arched Top, Mirror, Iron Hooks, Signed, 26 ½ x 40 In. . . 840.00
Hall Stand, Molded Cornice, Beveled Mirror, Carved Dragons, Shelf, England, 76 x 41 In. . . . 360.00
Hall Stand, R.J. Horner, Mahogany, Carved, Mirror, Cupids, Griffin Arms, c.1885. . . . . 15525.00
Hall Stand, Rococo Revival, Carved Leaves, Drawer, Mirror, Marble, 1890s, 89 x 43 In.. . . . . . 305.00
Hall Stand, Victorian, Walnut, Marble, Glove Box, Umbrella Holder, 81 x 34 x 9 In. 236.00
Hall Tree, Arts & Crafts, Oak, 3-Slat Base, Michigan Chair Co., 66 x 28 In.. . . . . 275.00
Hall Tree, Arts & Crafts, Oak, Quartersawn, Horn Hooks, Metal Tips, c.1900, 80 In.. . . . . 1560.00
Hall Tree, Black Forest, Carved, Mountain Goat, Eagle, 101 In.. . . . . 12650.00
Hall Tree, Black Forest, Standing Bear At Base, Cub Up Tree, 101 In.. 6900.00
Hall Tree, Renaissance Revival, Walnut, 101 x 48 x 16 In.. . . . . 1840.00
Hall Tree, Victorian, Umbrella Holder, Cast Iron, Scrolls, 75 In.. . . . . 425.00
Hall Tree, Victorian, Walnut, Carved, Marble Top, Mirror, 84 x 32 In. . . . . *illus* 200.00
Hat Rack, Arts & Crafts, Mirrored Spindled Back, Bench Seat, Brass Hooks, 24 x 30 In.. . . . . . 330.00
Headboard, Louis XV Style, Brass, Upholstered, 3 Arches, Floral Swag, c.1935, 81 In. 470.00
Headboard, Painted, Cherubs, Incised, Gilt, Acanthus Leaves, Venetian, 75 x 67 ½ In. 4800.00
Highboy, Chippendale, Maple, Bonnet Top, Carved Fan, 3 Finials, c.1785, 85 x 41 In. 31250.00
Highboy, Chippendale Style, Mahogany, Dovetailed, Old Dominion Label, 85 x 38 In.. . . . . 5287.00
Highboy, Queen Anne, Cherry, Bonnet Top, Finials, Carved Fan, Conn., c.1780, 83 x 41 In.. . . . 6250.00
Highboy, Queen Anne, Cherry, Carved, Bonnet Top, c.1780, 52 x 41 In.. . . . . 31250.00
Highboy, Queen Anne, Cherry, Drawers, Cabriole Legs, 70 In.. . . . . 6490.00
Highboy, Queen Anne, Mahogany, Carved, Bonnet Top, Figured, c.1780, 80 x 42 In. 8125.00
Highboy, Queen Anne, Maple, Birch, 6 Drawers, c.1760, 70 x 38 ½ In. 3510.00
Highboy, Queen Anne, Maple, Pine, 5 Graduated Drawers, Cabriole Legs, 77 x 37 x 20 In. . . . 7050.00
Highboy, Queen Anne, Tiger Maple, 9 Drawers, 98 x 34 x 19 ½ In.. . . . . 3000.00
Highboy, Queen Anne, Walnut, 9 Drawers, Legs, Pad Feet, c.1760, 72 x 37 In.. . . . . 18720.00
Highboy, Queen Anne, Walnut, Cherry, Bonnet Top, Flame Finials, Pad Feet, 77 x 39 In.. . . . . 2400.00
Highchair, Barrel Back, Rose, White, Yellow Lines, Green Paint, 32 In. . . . . *illus* 650.00
Highchair, Chippendale, Mahogany, Pierced Vase Shape Splat, Tray, Early 1900s, 39 x 18 In.. 359.00
Highchair, George III Style, Oak, Scrolled Arms, Square Legs, England, 35 ½ In.. . . . . 1080.00
Highchair, Ladder Back, Green Paint, Tapered Feet, Woven Seat, c.1830, 35 In.. . . . . 735.00
Highchair, Limbert, No. 871, Windsor, Bow Back, Leather Seat, 39 x 19 x 18 In. 600.00
Highchair, Maple, Hickory, Ladder Back, Red Paint, Splayed Leg, Early 1800s, 36 In. 646.00
Highchair, Original Green Paint, Round Finials, Woven Seat, New England, c.1830, 35 In. . . 734.00
Highchair, Pine, Ladder Back, Black Paint, Rush Seat, Shaped Footrest, 20 x 33 In. 470.00
Highchair, Risom, Spruce Frame, Plastic Woven Straps, Florence Knoll, c.1940, 14 x 32 In.. . 270.00

Furniture, Footstool, Pine, Painted, Scroll, Green, Red, Yellow, Stars, Stripes, W.L.H., 8 x 16 In.
$2585.00

Furniture, Frame, Harp, Cherub, Flowers, Reticulated, Painted, Iron, No. 8003, CJO, 6 x 4 In.
$145.00

Furniture, Hall Seat, Oak, Umbrella Stand, Drawer, Early 1900s, 30 x 28 x 12 In.
$198.00

Furniture, Hall Seat, Spindles, Michigan Chair Co., 35 ¾ x 41 ¾ x 21 In.
$1080.00

Furniture, Hall Stand, Art Nouveau, Irises, Marquetry, Mirror, Signed, Galle, 85 x 34 In.
$1195.00

Furniture, Hall Tree, Victorian, Walnut, Carved, Marble Top, Mirror, 84 x 32 In.
$200.00

TIP
Antique mirrors can be cleaned with a piece of newspaper dipped in a solution of equal parts white vinegar and water.

F

Highchair, Rush Seat, Ladder Back, Green, Paintball Finials, Turned Legs, 39 x 16 In. 1430.00
Highchair, Slat Back Rail, Shaped Plank Seat, Turned Supports, Pa., 1800s, 35 x 16 In. 468.00
Highchair, Windsor, Pine, Plank Seat, Black Paint, Early 1800s, 28 In. *illus* 530.00
Highchair, Wood, Adjustable, Upholstered, Iron Gears, Victorian, c.1890, 37 x 25 In. 173.00
Humidor, Mahogany, Marble Top, Applied Gilt Swags, 33 x 14 In. 205.00
Huntboard, Federal, Poplar, Yellow Pine, 3 Drawers, 3 Doors, Ga., 1800s, 48 x 60 In. 6900.00
Huntboard, Kittinger, Federal, 3 Drawers, Mid 1900s, 41 x 57 In. 1980.00
Huntboard, Pine, Scrolled Backsplash, 2 Drawers, Square Legs, Early 1800s, 48 x 48 In. 6435.00
Huntboard, Yellow Pine, 2 Drawers, Turned Legs, North Georgia, 1800s, 4 x 58 In. 5520.00
Kas, Gumwood, Mahogany Veneer, 2 Doors, Drawer, Bun Feet, 2 Parts, 1700s, 76 x 59 In. 8000.00
Kneeler, Art Nouveau, Flowers, Vines, Early 20th Century, 32 x 23 In. 117.00
Kneeler, Prie-Dieu, Blackwood, Carved Apron, Scrolling Vines, Berries, 46 x 22 x 30 In. 2160.00
Kneeler, Prie-Dieu, Oak, Carved, Italy, 17th Century, 36 x 26 In. 1404.00
Kneeler, Prie-Dieu, Walnut, Baroque, Hinged Top, Bracket Feet, 1600s, 38 x 27 In. 1527.00
Lap Desk, Burl Walnut, Inlaid Escutcheon, Brass, Shield, 6 ½ x 15 ¾ In. 195.00
Lap Desk, Campaign, William IV, Rosewood, Ink Bottle Wells, 36 ½ x 21 x 21 In. 2160.00
Lap Desk, Chinoiserie, Lacquered, Exotic Bird, Embossed Flowers, 4 ¾ x 14 In. 100.00
Lap Desk, Chippendale Style, Rosewood, Stand, Brass, c.1860, 24 x 19 x 12 In. 1760.00
Lap Desk, Ebony, Scrimshaw, England, c.1850, 6 ½ x 10 x 17 In. 526.00
Lap Desk, Mahogany, Brass, Marked JAL, Label, England, Early 1800s, 8 x 24 In. 1067.00
Lap Desk, Mahogany, Leather Writing Surface, Hinged, Drawers, 19 x 11 ½ x 7 In. 1250.00
Lap Desk, Mahogany, Milk Glass Inkwell, Velvet Pen Case, 12 ½ x 9 In. 175.00
Lap Desk, Mahogany, Side Drawer, Leather Writing Surface, Inkwell, Stand, 25 x 18 x 11 In. 920.00
Lap Desk, Mahogany, Writing Surface, Lift-Out Tray, Brass, England, 6 x 19 x 12 In. 660.00
Lap Desk, Maple, Inlaid Piano Image, New England, 19th Century, 5 x 16 ½ In. 439.00
Lap Desk, Maple, Shell Inlaid Lid, Geometric Borders, Drawer, Handle, 1821, 6 x 20 In. 805.00
Lap Desk, Papier-Mache, Mother-Of-Pearl, Gilt Decoration, Inkwell, Pen, 10 ½ In. 225.00
Lap Desk, Papier-Mache, Mother-Of-Pearl Inlay, Scalloped Canted Lid, 3 ¾ x 12 In. 170.00
Lap Desk, Parquetry, Geometric, Repeating Patterns, 5 ½ x 12 In. 225.00
Lap Desk, Regency, Figured Walnut, Brass Inlay, 3 Hidden Drawers, 6 ¾ x 19 ½ In. 575.00
Lap Desk, Rosewood, Brass, Mother-Of-Pearl Inlay, 2 Inkwells, L&S, 1907, 14 x 9 In. 201.00
Lap Desk, Rosewood, Stand, Rosewood, Inlaid Brass Flowers, Compartments, c.1880, 20 x 20 ½ In. 558.00
Lap Desk, Victorian, Inlaid Wood Mosaic, Bands, Medallion, Escutcheon, Hinged, 5 x 14 In. 239.00
Lazy Susan, Mixed Woods, Octagonal, 6 Revolving Shelves, 3 Legs, 106 x 31 In. 7344.00
Lectern, Mahogany, 3 Tiers, Lift Top, Drawer, Footed, Brass Sconces, 1800s, 42 x 20 In. 2115.00
Lectern, Oak, Tooled Leather, c.1880, 63 x 31 ½ x 19 ½ In. 3000.00
Lectern, Poplar, Red Over Mustard Graining, Black Marbleized Top, c.1900, 34 x 16 In. 489.00
Library Ladder, Charles X, Gothic Revival, Oak, Brass Mounted Steel, c.1830, 84 x 31 In. 17500.00
Library Ladder, Iron, Wood, Spiral, 71 In. 100.00
Library Ladder, Mahogany, Folding, 7 Rungs, England, 79 x 10 ½ In. 1320.00
Library Ladder, Mahogany, Folding, Ladder Form, Brass Mounts, 5 Rungs, 90 x 16 In. 708.00
Library Ladder, Pine, Iron Top Hooks, Lower Brackets, 8 Rungs, 1800s, 94 x 32 In. 418.00
Library Ladder, Regency, Mahogany, Hinged, 5 Graduated Rungs, 57 x 20 In. 840.00
Library Ladder, Regency Style, Mahogany, Brass, Inlaid, Folding, Spiral, Pole, 24 x 54 In. 2703.00
Library Ladder, Wood, Hinged, Spiral, England, c.1900, 145 x 13 In. 1645.00
Library Steps, George III, Mahogany, Door, Leather, 3 Steps, Legs, c.1810, 26 x 20 x 30 In. 1000.00
Library Steps, Mahogany, Dovetailed Case, Turned Legs, Leather Inserts, 17 x 28 In. 1093.00
Library Steps, Oak, 5 Steps, Carved Supports, 46 x 21 ¾ x 37 ½ In. 2280.00
Library Steps, Regency Style, Mahogany, Brass, Inlaid, Folding, 88 x 24 In. *illus* 2300.00
Linen Press, 2 Parts, Floor Unit, Press Top, 4 Shelves, Drawer, Belgium, c.1900. 542.00
Linen Press, Ambrose Heal, Oak, 2 Drawers, Doors, c.1900, 80 x 60 x 24 In. 6000.00
Linen Press, Bird's-Eye Maple, Paneled Doors, 2 Short Over 2 Long Drawers, 83 x 49 In. 2040.00
Linen Press, Chippendale, Cherry, 2 Doors, Dentil Molding, Drawers, c.1785, 77 x 48 In. 1410.00
Linen Press, Chippendale, Mahogany, Dentil, Fret Work, 2 Doors, Slides, 3 Drawers, 65 x 49 In. 1840.00
Linen Press, Federal, Cherry, Paneled Doors, 3 Fixed Interior Shelves, 1800s, 68 x 41 In. 633.00
Linen Press, Federal, Mahogany, Frieze, Paneled Doors, 4 Drawers, Scallop, 92 x 53 x 23 In. 4112.00
Linen Press, George III, Dentil Cornice, 3 Doors, 3 Over 2 Drawers, c.1780, 83 x 65 In. 1645.00
Linen Press, George III, Mahogany, Molded Cornice, Panel Doors, Drawers, 74 x 50 In. 472.00
Linen Press, George III, Mahogany, Pine, 2 Doors, Sliding Trays, c.1760, 78 x 48 In. 2530.00
Linen Press, Georgian, Mahogany, Inlaid, Pediment Cornice, Bellflower Swag, 80 x 50 In. 2644.00
Linen Press, Georgian, Yew, 2 Case, Dovetailed, Panel Doors, 2 Over 2 Drawers, 81 x 55 In. 920.00
Linen Press, Mahogany, 2 Doors, 4 Interior Slides, 4 Drawers, N.Y., c.1800, 86 x 52 In. 5520.00
Linen Press, Maple, Arched Doors, 4 Drawers, Fluted Columns, Ogee Feet, 78 x 47 x 18 In. 2880.00
Linen Press, Sheraton, Mahogany, Bowfront, 4 Drawers, England, 1830s, 82 x 49 x 24 In. 2600.00
Linen Press, Victorian, Pine, Paneled Doors, Drawers, 89 x 52 In. 1680.00
Linen Press, Walnut, Poplar, 2 Paneled Doors, 2 Drawers, c.1840, 50 x 50 x 23 In. 705.00
Linen Press, William IV, Cove Molded Cornice, Arched Paneled Doors, c.1830, 83 x 57 In. 2573.00

Liquor Cabinet, Victorian, Rosewood, Campaign Style, 4 Bottles, Mid 1900s, 7 3/8 x 8 In. 1140.00
Liquor Cabinet, William IV, Mahogany, Ivory Knobs, 6 Decanters, 10 x 11 In. 900.00
Love Seat, Hvidt & Molgaard-Nielsen, Leather, Wood, 3 Cushions, Denmark, 31 x 53 In. 900.00
Love Seat, L. & J.G. Stickley, No. 785, Double Crest Rails, Oilcloth, 37 x 48 x 22 In. 2640.00
Love Seat, Rococo, Rosewood, Laminated Floral, Pierced, Meeks. 10350.00
Love Seat, Takahama, Wool Upholstery, Chrome Plated Feet, Knoll, 61 x 26 In. 480.00
Love Seat, Wood, Woven Seat, 2 Slats, Arms, New England, Early 19th Century, Child's. 410.00
Lowboy, Georgian Style, Mahogany, Drawers, Cabriole Legs, 31 x 32 x 22 ½ In. 239.00
Lowboy, Nutting, No. 691, Maple, Shell Carving, 2 Drawers, 29 ½ x 39 x 20 In. 2650.00
Lowboy, Oak, Drawer, Dovetailed, Shaped Skirt, England, 1800s, 28 ½ x 37 x 20 In. 850.00
Lowboy, Queen Anne, Mahogany, Burl Veneer Top, Crossbanded, Sutton, 1900s, 31 x 33 In. .. 1293.00
Lowboy, Queen Anne, Oak, 3 Drawers, Scrolled Apron, Spoon Feet, 1800s, 30 x 33 In. 708.00
Lowboy, Queen Anne, Walnut, 2 Short & 1 Long Drawer, Shaped Skirt, 27 x 30 In. 960.00
Lowboy, Queen Anne, Walnut, 5 Drawers, Cabriole Legs, Pad Feet, 1890, 30 x 42 x 23 In. 1400.00
Lowboy, Queen Anne Style, Mahogany, Projecting Corner, Molded Edge Top, 29 x 32 In. 299.00
Lowboy, Rococo Style, Burl Walnut, Serpentine, Drawers, Dutch, 30 x 30 x 19 In. 1126.00
Luggage Rack, Roycroft, Chestnut, Branded Orb & Cross Mark, 26 x 30 In. 840.00
Mirror, Aesthetic Revival, Wood Gesso, Naturalistic Design, Flowers, Berries, 32 In. 518.00
Mirror, Art Nouveau, Gilt, Reverse Painted, Oval, Arabesque, Early 1900s, 46 x 33 In. 885.00
Mirror, Arts & Crafts, Hammered Copper, Flowers, Central Jewel, England, 22 x 30 In. 2640.00
Mirror, Baluster, Reverse Painted, Fruit Basket, New England, c.1825, 26 x 13 In. 176.00
Mirror, Baroque Style, Giltwood, Plumes, Swagged Crest, Scrolling, 1800s, 33 ½ x 26 In. 360.00
Mirror, Beech, Parcel Gilt, Painted, Landscape, 33 ½ x 19 ½ In. 1680.00
Mirror, Beveled Glass, Spider Web Form, 1950-60, 28 x 32 In. 650.00
Mirror, Biedermeier, Early 19th Century, 55 x 25 In. 800.00
Mirror, Bone, Rayed Round Flowers, Arch, 60 x 48 In. 2160.00
Mirror, Brass, Hammered, Octagonal Shape, England, c.1900, 22 In. 1188.00
Mirror, Brass, Hammered, Rectangular, Scotland, c.1900, 19 ¾ x 12 In. 375.00
Mirror, Brass, Hammered, Scotland, c.1900, 26 ¾ x 22 In. 2125.00
Mirror, Bronze, Leaf Shape, Phoenixes, Lotus Plants, Chinese, 11 In. 5036.00
Mirror, Bronzed Wood, Carved, Sunburst, 16 Giltwood Rays, Italy, 49 x 46 In. 6300.00
Mirror, Burl, Lacquered, Metal, Second Half 20th Century, 34 x 20 In. 500.00
Mirror, Cheval, Arts & Crafts, Beveled, Shoefoot Base, 60 ½ x 30 In. 390.00
Mirror, Cheval, Brass, Claw Feet, 62 x 26 ½ x 21 In. 1150.00
Mirror, Cheval, Come-Packt, A-Frame Supports, 67 x 25 x 18 In. .... *illus* 2100.00
Mirror, Cheval, Empire Style, Flame Mahogany, Turned Stretcher Base, 64 x 37 x 23 In. 605.00
Mirror, Cheval, Glasgow Style, Inlaid Roses, Shoe Feet, 69 x 32 In. .... *illus* 2880.00
Mirror, Cheval, Louis XVI Style, Painted, Parcel Gilt, Carved, Early 1900s, 69 x 41 In. 236.00
Mirror, Cheval, Mahogany, Beveled Glass, c.1900, 70 x 26 In. 442.00
Mirror, Cheval, Mahogany, Rounded Molding, Beveled Glass, 70 x 28 In. 633.00
Mirror, Chippendale, Gilt, Carved Eagle, Scrolls, Shells, England, c.1750, 51 x 29 In. 12650.00
Mirror, Chippendale, Gilt Molded Slip, Scrolled Crest, Mid 1700s, 31 x 17 In. 1380.00
Mirror, Chippendale, Giltwood, Phoenix Crest, Scrolling Openwork, 1800s, 56 x 28 In. 2032.00
Mirror, Chippendale, Mahogany, Cutout Scrolls, Beveled, 19th Century, 41 x 22 In. 300.00
Mirror, Chippendale, Mahogany, Figured, James Stokes, Pa., c.1795, 29 x 16 In. 10625.00
Mirror, Chippendale, Mahogany, Figured, Leaftip Gilt, Scrolled Crest, 34 x 18 In. 518.00
Mirror, Chippendale, Mahogany, Gilt, Apex Mythical Creature, England, c.1780, 51 x 23 In. .. 7500.00
Mirror, Chippendale, Mahogany, Giltwood, Scrolled Crest, Medallion, 36 ½ x 19 In. 594.00
Mirror, Chippendale, Mahogany, Molded Frame, Gold Paint, Late 1700s, 26 x 15 In. 259.00
Mirror, Chippendale, Mahogany, Parcel Gilt, Phoenix, c.1770-90, 23 x 50 In. 7080.00
Mirror, Chippendale, Mahogany, Parcel Gilt, Scrolled Crest, 41 x 22 In. 1783.00
Mirror, Chippendale, Mahogany, Scalloped, Scrolling Ears, Phoenix, 21 ½ x 12 In. 575.00
Mirror, Chippendale, Mahogany, Scalloped Crest, c.1770, 38 In. 761.00
Mirror, Chippendale, Mahogany, Scrolled Crest, Base, Phoenix, Late 18th Century, 30 In. 936.00
Mirror, Chippendale, Mahogany, Scrolled Crest, Flower Baskets, Late 1700s, 41 In. 497.00
Mirror, Chippendale, Mahogany, Scrolls, Gilt, c.1790, 36 In. 195.00
Mirror, Chippendale, Mahogany, Scrolls, Leaves, Late 18th Century, 40 In. 585.00
Mirror, Chippendale, Mahogany Veneer, Phoenix Crest, Gilt Liner, 1700s, 30 x 14 In. 411.00
Mirror, Chippendale, Phoenix At Center, England, Late 1700s, 33 x 19 ½ In. 489.00
Mirror, Chippendale, Walnut, Carved, Gilt, Broken Arch, Plume, 1860, 43 x 24 In. 1450.00
Mirror, Chippendale, Walnut, Parcel Gilt, Scrolls, Leaves, Urn Crest, c.1750, 51 x 29 In. 2489.00
Mirror, Chippendale, Walnut, Scrolling Fretwork, Rectangular, 19th Century, 27 x 14 In. 147.00
Mirror, Chippendale, Walnut Veneer, Gilt Gesso, Scrolled, 1700s, 45 x 24 In. 1304.00
Mirror, Chippendale Style, Burl, Broken Arch, Gilt Finial, Molding, 1900s, 53 x 27 In. 323.00
Mirror, Chippendale Style, Mahogany, Gilt Phoenix, Liner, Early 20th Century, 43 In. 115.00
Mirror, Chippendale Style, Mahogany, Phoenix, Beveled, England, 35 ½ x 20 In. 260.00
Mirror, Copper, Hammered, Oval, Hanging Chain, England, c.1900, 31 x 21 In. 2125.00

Furniture, Highchair, Barrel Back, Rose, White, Yellow Lines, Green Paint, 32 In.
$650.00

Furniture, Highchair, Windsor, Pine, Plank Seat, Black Paint, Early 1800s, 28 In.
$530.00

Furniture, Library Steps, Regency Style, Mahogany, Brass, Inlaid, Folding, 88 x 24 In.
$2300.00

TIP

Ordinary beer is great for cleaning a gilded mirror frame. Just pour it on a soft rag, rub gently, and dry.

Furniture, Mirror, Cheval, Come-Packt, A-Frame Supports, 67 x 25 x 18 In.
$2100.00

Furniture, Mirror, Cheval, Glasgow Style, Inlaid Roses, Shoe Feet, 69 x 32 In.
$2880.00

Mirror, Copper, Hammered, Shields, Arrows, 27 ¾ x 40 In. . . . 313.00
Mirror, Courting, Pine, Glass Panels, Reverse Painted, c.1800, 17 x 11 ½ In. . . . 588.00
Mirror, Courting, Pine, Shaped Crest, Reverse, Painted Glass, Flower Basket, 17 x 11 In. . . . 3643.00
Mirror, Curly Maple, Scrolled Crest, Molded Frame, 30 In. . . . 793.00
Mirror, Damascene, Bird & Flower Carved Crest, Beaded, c.1850, 63 x 32 ½ In. . . . 3525.00
Mirror, Desk, Antelope, Bronze, Nickeled, Emile-Jacques Ruhlman, c.1925, 17 ¼ In. . . . 3750.00
Mirror, Directoire, Paneled Crest, Applied Pierced Patera Mount, 83 x 41 In. . . . 2160.00
Mirror, Dresden, Rope Twist, Flowers, Gilt Trim, Applied Birds, Flowers, c.1850, 44 x 31 In. . . 2082.00
Mirror, Dressing, Biedermeier Style, Arched Panel, Columns, Drawers, Baker, 36 x 25 In. . . . 489.00
Mirror, Dressing, Federal Style, Mahogany, Inlaid, Drawer, Benchmade, 20 x 16 x 7 In. . . . 240.00
Mirror, Dressing, G. Stickley, Tapered Stand, Shoefoot Base, 21 x 24 x 7 In. . . . 1400.00
Mirror, Dressing, George I, Walnut, Inlaid, Drawer, Bracket Feet, c.1700s, 28 x 16 In. . . . 443.00
Mirror, Dressing, Gothic Revival, Walnut, Arched Mirror, Scroll Supports, Finial, 27 ½ x 12 In. 529.00
Mirror, Dressing, Hepplewhite Style, Satinwood, Shield Shape, 24 ⅝ x 18 ⅜ In. . . . 356.00
Mirror, Dressing, Regency, Mahogany, Inlaid, Swivel Frame, Early 1800s, 25 x 24 In. . . . 266.00
Mirror, Dutch Baroque Style, Giltwood, Pierced Gilt, Scrolling Crest, 64 x 40 In. . . . 2160.00
Mirror, Empire, Carved, Columns, Rosette Corners, Black, Gold, c.1820, 31 x 48 In. . . . 1912.00
Mirror, Empire, Giltwood, Part Ebonized, Mask, Dolphin Heads, Italy, 40 x 20 In. . . . 1007.00
Mirror, Empire, Paint Decoration, 4 Stamped Brass Medallions, c.1835, 13 x 11 In. . . . 529.00
Mirror, Federal, Carved, Circular, Spread Wing Eagle, Leaves, c.1810, 48 x 25 In. . . . 15275.00
Mirror, Federal, Gilt, Acorn, Shell, Rosette Carvings, White House Print, c.1900s, 43 x 25 In. . 431.00
Mirror, Federal, Gilt, Cornice, Reverse Painted, Fluted Columns, c.1810, 46 x 24 In. . . . 1016.00
Mirror, Federal, Gilt, Reverse Painted, Fruit Basket, J. Todd Looking Glass Co., c.1825, 19 x 13 In. 593.00
Mirror, Federal, Giltwood, Landscape, Reverse Painted, c.1820, 30 x 19 In. . . . 235.00
Mirror, Federal, Giltwood, Molded, Rope Twist, c.1825, 20 x 11 In. . . . 1541.00
Mirror, Federal, Giltwood, Oval, Cornucopia, Eagle Crest, c.1840, 23 x 26 In. . . . 2300.00
Mirror, Federal, Giltwood, Reverse Painted, Ship, Dingy, 35 x 20 In. . . . 600.00
Mirror, Federal, Mahogany, Parcel Gilt, Carved, Leaves, Fruit Finial, c.1805, 69 x 28 In. . . . 53125.00
Mirror, Federal, Mahogany, Parcel Gilt, Urn, Rosettes, Carved Fretwork, 61 x 24 In. . . . 4720.00
Mirror, Federal, Mahogany, Reverse Painted, Memorial To Washington, c.1800, 33 In. . . *illus* 1035.00
Mirror, Federal, Mahogany Inlay, Parcel Gilt, 55 ½ x 22 ¾ In. . . . 6875.00
Mirror, Federal, Molded, Kite Table, Reverse Painted, Boy, Black, Gold, c.1850, 35 x 16 In. . . . 588.00
Mirror, Federal, Pilasters, Rope Twist, Cornice Detail, Applied Grapevine, 33 x 21 In. . . . 431.00
Mirror, Federal, Pine, Glass, Gilt, Gesso, Acorn Drops, Cornucopia, Boston, c.1840, 43 x 26 In. 411.00
Mirror, G. Stickley, No. 66, 4 Hooks, 28 x 36 In. . . . 1950.00 to 3360.00
Mirror, George II, Giltwood, Carved, c.1755, 50 x 25 In. . . . 11875.00
Mirror, George II, Mahogany, Ogee, Scrolling Fretwork, 26 ½ x 16 In. . . . 472.00
Mirror, George III, Giltwood, Carved, Oval, c.1760, 42 x 24 In., Pair . . . 40625.00
Mirror, George III, Giltwood, Leaves, C-Scroll Surround, 1770, 37 ½ x 25 In. . . . 976.00
Mirror, George III, Mahogany, Pine, Gilt Liner, Openwork, Gilt Shell Crest, 36 x 19 In. . . . 470.00
Mirror, George III Style, Giltwood, Carved, Urn Finials, 66 x 36 In. . . . 8125.00
Mirror, George III Style, Giltwood, Leaf Crest, Oval Plate, 48 x 20 ½ In. . . . 660.00
Mirror, George V Style, Sterling Silver, Inlaid, Leaves, Walker & Hall, 1929, 9 ½ In. . . . 225.00
Mirror, Georgian, Gilt, Gesso, Flower Basket Crest, Beveled Glass, 40 x 22 In. . . . 1840.00
Mirror, Georgian, Giltwood, Broken Swan-Neck Pediment, Extending Ears, 51 x 25 In. . . . 1076.00
Mirror, Georgian, Rococo, Giltwood, Crest, Pendant, Scrolling Leaf Tips, 44 x 24 In. . . . 1778.00
Mirror, Gilt, Reverse Painted, House & Pond, Half Turnings, Black Paint, 1800s, 25 x 13 In. . 176.00
Mirror, Gilt Bronze, Plateau, 2 Parts, Leaf Border, Urn Handles, 1800s, 40 x 21 In. . . . 6462.00
Mirror, Gilt Gesso, Carved, Multicolored, Continental, Late 1700s, 21 x 10 In. . . . 711.00
Mirror, Giltwood, Argente, 2 Carved Sunburst Panels, c.1900, 27 ½ In. . . . 4080.00
Mirror, Giltwood, Baluster, Leaves, Rosettes, Beveled, c.1840, 38 x 25 In. . . . 646.00
Mirror, Giltwood, Carved, Octagonal, 34 ¾ In. . . . 240.00
Mirror, Giltwood, Carved, Pierced Carved Grapevine Overlay, 23 x 21 In. . . . 1140.00
Mirror, Giltwood, Carved, Scrolling Vine Borders, Oval, 19th Century, 14 In., Pair . . . 510.00
Mirror, Giltwood, Carved, Scrolls, Leaves, Late 18th Century, 40 ½ x 34 ½ In. . . . 1989.00
Mirror, Giltwood, Carved, Turned Half Column Stiles, Rosette Corners, 68 x 32 In. . . . 1292.00
Mirror, Giltwood, Gesso, Flower Basket, c.1930, 20 x 7 In. . . . 400.00
Mirror, Giltwood, Leaf Crest, Pierced Leaf & Flower Frame, 45 x 32 ½ In. . . . 1680.00
Mirror, Giltwood, Leaf Crest, Rounded Top, 45 x 27 In. . . . 228.00
Mirror, Giltwood, Marquetry, A.J. Rowley Landscape, c.1930, 31 x 10 In. . . . 625.00
Mirror, Giltwood, Marquetry, Landscape, c.1920, 20 x 16 In. . . . 813.00
Mirror, Giltwood, Oval Cartouche, Rose Garland, c.1900, 38 x 51 ½ In. . . . 176.00
Mirror, Giltwood, Plaster, Carved, Leaf Scrolls, 90 x 50 ½ In. . . . 1920.00
Mirror, Giltwood, Plaster, Infant, Seated, Flower Basket, Pedestal, Italy, 68 x 36 x 7 In. . . . 3840.00
Mirror, Giltwood, Reverse Painted, Rosettes, Woman, Stenciled Leaves, c.1850, 34 x 18 In. . . . 646.00
Mirror, Giltwood, Shaped, Pierced Leaf Crest, Scrolled Frame, 40 x 24 In. . . . 660.00
Mirror, Giltwood, Shaped Crests, Scrolls, Dragons, Mirror Borders, c.1715, 53 x 30 In. . . . 25000.00

Mirror, Giltwood, Shaped Plate, Leaf Carved, 35 x 24 In. 240.00
Mirror, Giltwood, Shell Crest, 19 x 16 In., Pair 900.00
Mirror, Giltwood, Shield Plate, Carved Flowers, Scrolls, Italy, c.1750, 39 x 30 In., Pair 22500.00
Mirror, Giltwood, Sienna, Yellow Sponge Paint, Cottage Landscape, c.1830, 29 x 13 In. 356.00
Mirror, Giltwood, Split Baluster, Rosette Blocked Corners, c.1830, 38 x 26 In. 940.00
Mirror, Giltwood, Stag Crest, Rope Twist, Leaves, Convex, Thomas Fentham, England, c.1800, 41 In. 4446.00
Mirror, Giltwood, Sun Shape, Radiating Metal Segments, Convex, 19 In. 120.00
Mirror, Giltwood, Sun Shape, Radiating Metal Segments, Convex, 28 In. 180.00
Mirror, Girandole, Eagle, Scrolling Arms, Gilt Metal Candle Cups, 19th Century, 35 x 21 In.. . 4112.00
Mirror, Girandole, Giltwood, Ribbon Bowknot, Crest, Candle Arms, Oval, c.1800, 45 x 33 In. . 2702.00
Mirror, Girandole, Neoclassical, Gilt, Carved, Eagle Mount, Ebonized, c.1815, 58 x 34 In.. . . . 8750.00
Mirror, Gothic Revival, Cast Iron, Crocket Finials, c.1850, 23 In.. . . . . 235.00
Mirror, Hepplewhite, Mahogany, Gilt, Urn, Flowers, Broken Arch Crest, 54 x 32 In. 529.00
Mirror, Inlaid, Eagle, Scrolling, Early 19th Century, 32 x 16 In.. . . . . 3220.00
Mirror, Iron, Protruding Rock Figures, Beveled Glass, c.1975, 30 x 37 In.. . . . . 219.00
Mirror, Italianate, Wood, Plaster, Carved, Flowers, Woman's Heads, Painted, 29 x 39 In., Pair 1645.00
Mirror, Japonisme, Wood, Lacquer, Flower Design, Early 20th Century, 38 x 25 In. 59.00
Mirror, L. & J.G. Stickley, Dark Finish, 17 x 56 In. 790.00
Mirror, Louis Philippe, Giltwood, Cream Paint, Flower & Beaded Border, 54 x 32 In., Pair . . . 3600.00
Mirror, Louis XV, Giltwood, Carved Garland, Flower Spray, 30 x 21 In. 3120.00
Mirror, Louis XV Style, Giltwood, Leaf Crest, Scrolling Frame, Asymmetrical, 63 x 32 In. 5760.00
Mirror, Louis XV Style, Gold Paint, Gesso, C-Scrolls, Rocaille, 27 In., Pair. 415.00
Mirror, Louis XVI, Gilt, Blue, Ivory, Ornate Carvings, 1900s, 56 x 41 In. 1840.00
Mirror, Louis XVI, Giltwood, Carved, Flowers, Garlands, Animals, c.1900, 56 x 38 In. 2300.00
Mirror, Louis XVI, Giltwood, Composition, Leaves & Bird Crest, Flowers, 42 x 27 In. 1304.00
Mirror, Louis XVI Style, Giltwood, Leaf, Carved Scroll Crest, c.1900, 68 x 38 x 5 In. 2280.00
Mirror, Mahogany, Blond, Brass Mounted, Matchbook Veneer, 39 x 29 ½ In. 960.00
Mirror, Mahogany, Brass Rosettes, Carved Columns, c.1830, 30 x 13 In.. . . . . 130.00
Mirror, Mahogany, Reverse Painted, Scenic, Brass Rosettes, c.1930, 37 x 18 In. 130.00
Mirror, Mahogany, Scalloped, Early 19th Century, 12 ¾ x 8 ¾ In.. . . . . 527.00
Mirror, Max Ingrand, Glass, Brass, Blue, 1956, 29 In.. . . . . 6250.00
Mirror, Molded Edges, Multicolored Birds, Flowers, 12 ¾ x 10 ¾ In. 165.00
Mirror, Multiple Glass Flower Border, Round, Italy, 20th Century, 26 ½ In., Pair 4320.00
Mirror, Napoleon III, Argente, Molded, Leaf Accents, Oval, 44 x 33 In. 600.00
Mirror, Napoleon III, Empire Style, Giltwood, Wreath, Carved Crest, 93 x 51 In.. . . . . 2880.00
Mirror, Napoleon III, Giltwood, Annulated Frame, Mid 1800s, 31 x 26 In., Pair 1560.00
Mirror, Napoleon III, Giltwood, Carved, Plaster, Inset Glass Panels, 70 x 42 In. 2280.00
Mirror, Napoleon III, Giltwood, Medallion, Swags, Corinthian Columns, 71 x 61 In.. . . . . 2040.00
Mirror, Napoleon III, Giltwood, Plaster, Oval, Flower Spray, 40 x 29 In. 900.00
Mirror, Napoleon III, Giltwood, Reeded, Mid 1800s, 34 x 27 In.. . . . . 480.00
Mirror, Napoleon III, Giltwood, Spiral Flutes, Mid 1800s, 44 x 29 ½ In. 1440.00
Mirror, Napoleon III, Louis XVI Style, Giltwood, Carved, Oval, 53 x 37 In.. . . . . 2280.00
Mirror, Napoleon III, Louis XVI Style, Giltwood, Domed, 81 x 48 In. 3840.00
Mirror, Neoclassical, Giltwood, Burnished, Molded, Late 1800s, 41 x 25 In. 529.00
Mirror, Neoclassical, Giltwood, Eagle, Laurel Branches, Cornucopia, Oval, 22 x 26 In. 356.00
Mirror, Neoclassical, Giltwood, Ebonized, Winged Griffin Crest, Anthemions, 42 x 24 In. *illus* 470.00
Mirror, Neoclassical, Giltwood, Swags, Plums, Roses, Shield Shape, c.1950, 27 x 13 In., Pair 508.00
Mirror, Neoclassical, Giltwood, Tabernacle, Guilloche Frieze, 48 x 35 In. 236.00
Mirror, Neoclassical, Giltwood, Urn Crest, Gilt Metal Finials, Swags, 54 x 21 In.. . . . . 1062.00
Mirror, Neoclassical, Giltwood, Vase, Flowers, Laurel Leaf Cluster, 70 x 29 In. 1680.00
Mirror, Neoclassical, Parcel Gilt, Green Paint, Ribbon, Medusa, Mid 1800s, 60 x 31 In.. . . . . . 6875.00
Mirror, Neogrecque, Walnut, Giltwood, Ebonized, Bust, Laurel Crown, c.1875, 54 x 60 In. . . . 1880.00
Mirror, Oak, Eagle, Cornucopia, Lion, Scroll, 1870s, 41 ½ x 48 In. . . . . *illus* 1760.00
Mirror, P. Venini, Iridescent, Milan, c.1948, 39 x 26 In.. . . . . 16250.00
Mirror, Pewter, Hammered, Enamel, c.1900, 29 x 21 In.. . . . . 5250.00
Mirror, Pewter, Hammered, Enamel Inset, Leaves, England, 1900, 18 ½ x 14 In. 625.00
Mirror, Pier, Directoire Style, Multicolored, Molded, 84 x 32 In.. . . . . 960.00
Mirror, Pier, Empire, Gilt, Rope Carved, Cream Paint, Divided Mirror, 45 x 22 In. 1470.00
Mirror, Pier, George II, Gilt Gesso, Carved, Broken Pediment, c.1740, 53 x 33 In.. . . . . 18750.00
Mirror, Pier, George II, Giltwood, Carved, Oval, Palladian Style, c.1745 . . . . 28750.00
Mirror, Pier, George II, Giltwood, Shell Pendent, c.1740, 66 x 40 In.. . . . . 11875.00
Mirror, Pier, George II, Rococo, Giltwood, Carved, Beveled Edge, 76 x 39 In. 46875.00
Mirror, Pier, George II Style, Giltwood, Broken Pediment, Flower Urn, 64 x 30 In., Pair 11875.00
Mirror, Pier, George III, Gilt Gesso, Broken Pediment, Center Cartouche, 50 x 28 In.. . . . . 6875.00
Mirror, Pier, Gilt, Lotus-Leaf Carved Columns, Scrolled Corners, Mid 1800s, 61 x 32 In. 748.00
Mirror, Pier, Gilt Gesso, Reverse Painted, Patriotic Scene, Ring Columns, c.1816, 6 x 40 In. . . 3318.00
Mirror, Pier, Giltwood, c.1843, 62 ½ x 31 ½ In.. . . . . 1880.00

Furniture, Mirror, Federal, Mahogany, Reverse Painted, Memorial To Washington, c.1800, 33 x 21 In.
$1035.00

Furniture, Mirror, Neoclassical, Giltwood, Ebonized, Winged Griffin Crest, Anthemions, 42 x 24 In.
$470.00

TIP

Early mirrors, those made before 1850, had thin glass. To judge the thickness of a mirror, hold a pencil point against the glass. The difference between the point and the reflection is the thickness.

As always, the edited listings in *Kovels' Antiques & Collectibles Price Guide 2010* aren't available on any website, but readers should visit Kovels.com for information on trends, tips, reproductions, marks, old prices, and more!

Furniture, Mirror, Oak, Eagle, Cornucopia, Lion, Scroll, 1870s, 41 ½ x 48 In.
$1760.00

F

Furniture, Mirror, Roycroft, Wood, Hanging, Chains, 23 ¾ x 33 ¾ In.
$1560.00

Furniture, Mirror, Shaving, Walnut, Incised, Candle Shelves, Late 1800s, 32 ½ In.
$110.00

Furniture, Mirror, Wood, Sunburst, Carved, Gilt, Carvers Guild, Mass., 1900s, 47 In.
$2070.00

Mirror, Pier, Giltwood, Colonnettes, Blocked Corners, Roundels, c.1800, 62 x 36 In. 1997.00
Mirror, Pier, Giltwood, Female Mask Crest, Urn Finials, Marble Base, 144 In. 2880.00
Mirror, Pier, Louis XVI Style, Giltwood, Multicolored, Molded Cornice, c.1900, 77 x 48 In. ... 3360.00
Mirror, Pier, Louis XVI Style, Ribbon, Draped Leaf, Painted, France, c.1900, 78 x 49 In. 4080.00
Mirror, Pier, Neoclassical, Mahogany, Maple, Acorns, Brass Rosettes, c.1840, 39 x 22 In. 411.00
Mirror, Pier, Neogrecque, Giltwood, Egyptian Bust, Marble Plinth, c.1870, 115 x 37 In. 3760.00
Mirror, Pier, Rococo Revival, Giltwood, Leaf Crest, Bellflower Mounted, Victorian, 59 x 43 In. 826.00
Mirror, Pier, Walnut, Carved, Bust, Footed Marble Step, c.1870, 109 x 31 In. 1180.00
Mirror, Pier, Wood, Carved, Gilt, Arch, 1800s, 63 x 31 In. 633.00
Mirror, Pine, Gilt, Applied Turnings, Corner Blocks, Yellow, Black Paint, 11 x 9 In. 353.00
Mirror, Pine, Reverse Painted, Crown Molding, Fluted Columns, c.1815, 20 x 12 In. 146.00
Mirror, Queen Anne, Burl Walnut Veneer, Applied Gilt Gesso Trim, 1750s, 13 x 28 In. 690.00
Mirror, Queen Anne, Mahogany, Pierced, Gilt Shell Crest, Liner, 43 ½ x 17 In. 18800.00
Mirror, Queen Anne, Mahogany, Pine, Gilt Shell, Scroll Cut Crest, 42 x 17 In. 823.00
Mirror, Queen Anne, Mahogany, Scalloped, Scrolled Crown, c.1730, 34 x 17 In. 763.00
Mirror, Queen Anne, Pine, Mahogany Veneer, Mid 18th Century, 21 x 10 In. 382.00
Mirror, Queen Anne, Walnut, Gilt Gesso, Scrolled Crest, Prince Of Wales, 1725, 35 In. 1570.00
Mirror, Queen Anne, Walnut, Parcel Gilt, Figured, 2 Glass Parts, England, c.1759, 49 x 18 In. 8125.00
Mirror, Queen Anne, Walnut, Scrolled Crest, Molded Surround, 1700s, 36 x 18 In. 345.00
Mirror, Queen Anne Style, Shaped Crest, Beveled Glass, 2 Parts, 51 x 26 In. 204.00
Mirror, Regency, Giltwood, Arched, Flowers, Bird Scrolls, c.1715, 71 x 41 In. 28750.00
Mirror, Regency, Giltwood, Bull's-Eye, Carved, Ebonized Rabbit, Eagle, 34 x 24 In. 2350.00
Mirror, Regency, Giltwood, Reeded, Ebonized Slip, Carved, Convex, Round, 26 In. 1560.00
Mirror, Regency, Giltwood, Reeded, Scrolling Candle Arms, Eagle, 1800s, 32 In. 3290.00
Mirror, Regency Style, Pine, Waxed, Reeding, Applied Bead, Convex, 31 ½ In. 1320.00
Mirror, Renaissance Revival, Giltwood, Composition, Mask Fretwork, Burnished, 27 x 52 In.. 413.00
Mirror, Reverse Painted, Applied Half Turnings, Acorn Drops, 1800s, 40 x 24 In. 176.00
Mirror, Rococo, Chinoiserie, Parcel Gilt, Scrolled, Painted, Robed Woman, 33 In. 1080.00
Mirror, Rococo, Giltwood, Carved, Cartouche Plate, Openwork, 1700s, 31 x 19 In. 474.00
Mirror, Rococo, Giltwood, Carved, Pierced Crest, Continental, Early 19th Century, 51 x 23 In. 460.00
Mirror, Rococo, Giltwood, Leaf, Scroll Pediment, 1900s, 47 x 49 In. 920.00
Mirror, Rococo, Giltwood, Leaf Crested Scrolled Pediment, Continental, 47 x 29 In. 215.00
Mirror, Rococo, Giltwood, Rocaille, Scrolled, Carved, Continental, 48 x 31 In. 1126.00
Mirror, Rococo, Giltwood, Scrolls, Flowers, Cartouche, Italy, c.1730, 63 x 31 In. 6250.00
Mirror, Rococo, Painted, Cartouche Crest, Fruited Urn, Scrolling, Continental, 49 x 25 In.... 239.00
Mirror, Rococo, Walnut, Carved, Flowers, Pierced, 47 In. 1725.00
Mirror, Rococo Revival, Giltwood, Bells, Whistles, Egg & Dart Border, Swag, 56 x 36 In. 2645.00
Mirror, Rococo Style, Giltwood, Ebonized, Openwork Crest, Cartouche, 40 x 28 In. 179.00
Mirror, Roycroft, Wood, Hanging, Chains, 23 ¾ x 33 ¾ In. .... *illus* 1560.00
Mirror, Rustic, Wood, Carved Ruined Greek Temple, Swiss, 1800s, 22 x 14 In. 1150.00
Mirror, Shaving, Federal, Mahogany, 3 Drawers, Early 19th Century, 20 x 21 ½ In. 117.00
Mirror, Shaving, Federal, Mahogany, 4 Drawers, Early 1800s, 24 x 21 x 8 ½ In. 100.00
Mirror, Shaving, Federal, Mahogany, Pine, Dovetailed Drawers, Early 1900s, 16 x 14 In. 176.00
Mirror, Shaving, Queen Anne, Mahogany, 18th Century, 16 ½ x 9 ¾ In. 1404.00
Mirror, Shaving, Walnut, Incised, Candle Shelves, Late 1800s, 32 ½ In. .... *illus* 110.00
Mirror, Shell Crest, Acanthine Stiles, Putti, Strapwork Cartouche, 68 x 52 In. 9694.00
Mirror, Sheraton, Giltwood, Applied Rosettes, Basket Of Fruit, 38 x 18 In. 600.00
Mirror, Sheraton, Reverse Painted, Peacock, On Branch, Reeded Column, 22 x 13 In. 165.00
Mirror, Sheraton, Tablet, House, Ship, Wood, Label, John Daggett, Roxbury, 46 In. 440.00
Mirror, Stick & Ball, 1869, 35 x 36 In. 500.00
Mirror, Tortoiseshell Veneer, Copper Leaf Corner Mounts, 19 ¾ x 17 In. 1560.00
Mirror, Vanity, Bronze, Patinated, Demilune, Dancing Girl, Butterflies, Erte, 9 x 15 In. 478.00
Mirror, Venetian, Etched, Segmented Frame, Octagonal, c.1880, 38 x 22 In. 294.00
Mirror, Venetian Rococo Style, Giltwood, Carved, Italy, 22 ½ x 15 In. 960.00
Mirror, Walnut, Parcel Gilt, Beveled, Continental, 31 x 21 In. 780.00
Mirror, Wood, Gilt Gesso, Convex Glass, c.1800s, 43 In. 2370.00
Mirror, Wood, Gilt Gesso, Faux Patina, Broken Pediment, 32 x 25 In. 224.00
Mirror, Wood, Parcel Gilt, Pinecone Finials, Portrait Bust Oval Medallion, 39 In. 2032.00
Mirror, Wood, Sunburst, Carved, Gilt, Carvers Guild, Mass., 1900s, 47 In. .... *illus* 2070.00
Mirror, Wood, White Paint, Carved Bowknot, Scandinavia, 82 x 38 In. 2040.00
Modular Unit, McCobb, Walnut, Metal Frame, 5 Shelves, Doors, Directional, 99 x 87 In. 3360.00
Ottoman, Eames, No. 671, Rosewood, Brown Leather Cushion, Herman Miller, 26 x 17 In. .. 720.00
Ottoman, Ebonized Wood, Cloverleaf Shape, Red Upholstery, Velvet Tassels, 14 ½ In. 444.00
Ottoman, Faux Leopard, Pouf, Upholstered, Footed, 36 In. Diam. 75.00
Ottoman, Finn Juhl, Teak, Black Leather Seat, c.1950, 14 x 24 In. 237.00
Ottoman, G. Nakashima, Greenrock, Walnut, Chenille Cover, 1982, 15 x 21 x 21 In. 6875.00
Ottoman, G. Nakashima, Walnut, Chenille Cover, Hand Stitched, Walnut, 1982. .... 6875.00

Ottoman, G. Nakashima, Walnut, Webbing, Chenille Upholstery, 15 x 21 x 21 In. 6875.00
Ottoman, Neoclassical Style, Argente, Rectangular Seats, Dolphin Feet, 20 x 37 In., Pair 3173.00
Ottoman, Turkish Style, Wool Plush Upholstery, 2 Tiers, Casters, 17 x 62 In., Pair.......... 2350.00
Ottoman, Victorian, Mahogany, Padded, Upholstered, Needlework, 19 x 22 x 23 In. 1920.00
Ottoman, Walnut, Ebonized, Incised Gilt, Upholstered, Allen & Bros., 19 x 19 In. .... *illus* 690.00
Ottoman, Wegner, Teak, Blue Wool Upholstery, 16 x 27 ½ x 15 In. 2400.00
Overmantel Mirror see Architectural category.
Panel, Louis XVI Style, Gesso Crest, Floral Basket, Scrolling, 31 x 60 In. 1680.00
Panel, Walnut, Relief Carved, Classical Couple, Putto, 17 ¾ x 32 ½ In.................... 2040.00
Parlor Set, Bamboo, Lacquered, Settee, 2 Side Chairs, Bowed Back, 3 Piece.............. 3120.00
Parlor Set, Empire, Ebonized, Serpentine, France, 1870, 47-In. Settee, 4 Chairs .... *illus* 1100.00
Parlor Set, French Empire, Mahogany, Upholstered, Applied Gilt, 7 Piece 7475.00
Parlor Set, Louis Philippe, Needlepoint Upholstery, c.1860, 11 Piece 18700.00
Parlor Set, Louis XV Style, Walnut, Parcel Gilt, Aubusson Tapestry, 9 Piece 16450.00
Parlor Set, Louis XVI Style, Gilt, 4 Chairs, 2 Chairs, Settee, Padded, 7 Piece............... 8100.00
Parlor Set, Rococo Revival, Rosewood, Love Seat, Armchair, 4 Side Chairs, 6 Piece......... 20700.00
Parlor Set, Victorian, Rosewood, Carved Crests, Exposed Frame, Padded, Upholstered, 3 Piece 499.00
Pedestal, Anglo-Indian, Carved, Square Molded Top, Fluted, Carved Frieze, 40 x 12 In.. ...... 179.00
Pedestal, Biedermeier, Burl, Round Top, Cylindrical, Socle Base, 43 x 24 In. 2880.00
Pedestal, Brass, 5 Onyx Columns, Bronze Accents, c.1900, 44 x 14 In.. .... 1380.00
Pedestal, Ebonized, Multicolored, Hexagon Top, Gesso Birds, Flowers, 42 x 14 In., Pair 840.00
Pedestal, G. Stickley, No. 27, Square, Flared Base, Extended Feet, Signed, 36 x 19 In.. .... 3600.00
Pedestal, George III, Mahogany, Carved, 30 x 18 In., Pair 5000.00
Pedestal, Gilt, Blackamoor Standard, Multicolored, Scalloped Frieze, 42 x 16 In. 3120.00
Pedestal, Gothic Revival, Oak, Revolving Rectangular, Paneled Column, 48 x 22 In.. .... 960.00
Pedestal, Imitation Marble, Wood Top, Round & Socle Base, 1800s, 41 ½ x 13 In.. .... 1200.00
Pedestal, Kingwood, Octagon Top, Ormolu Flower, Ram Mounts, c.1820, 46 x 14 In., Pair... 31250.00
Pedestal, L. & J.G. Stickley, No. 27, Corbels, Signed, 36 x 19 In. .... *illus* 3600.00
Pedestal, Limbert, No. 267, Circular Top, Corbel Base, 32 x 14 In.. .... 1560.00
Pedestal, Louis XIV Style, Gilt, Circular, Gadrooned, Carved Bands, 59 x 19 In. 1440.00
Pedestal, Louis XVI, Ebonized, Gilt Metal Mount, Tapered Support, 53 x 16 In. 538.00
Pedestal, Neoclassical, Faux Tortoiseshell Ground, Arrow Supports, 37 x 12 In., Pair 2468.00
Pedestal, Oak, Molded Edge, Stepped Square Top, Raised Panels, 1800s, 39 x 18 ½ In. 575.00
Pedestal, Pine, Painted, Chamfered Top, Molded Paneled Base, 33 ½ x 10 ½ In. 86.00
Pedestal, Regency Style, Tulipwood, Marquetry, Gilt Bronze Mounted, 54 In., Pair 7050.00
Pedestal, Renaissance Revival, Walnut, Burl, Gilt, Chamfered Stem, Stepped Base, 38 x 14 In. 940.00
Pedestal, Renaissance Revival, Walnut, Buttressed Support, Plinth, Block Legs, c.1875, 38 In. 1410.00
Pedestal, Rococo, Painted, Parcel Gilt, Cabochon, Scrolling Leaf, Continental, 30 x 19 In.... 568.00
Pedestal, Roycroft, No. 61, Carved Orb & Cross Mark, 39 In. 3600.00
Pedestal, Victorian, Mahogany, Carved, Swan, Inset Marble Top, 38 x 20 x 15 In. 2000.00
Pedestal, Victorian, Marble, Square Top, Spiral & Acanthus Carved Column, 43 x 12 In. 978.00
Pedestal, Walnut, Carved, Capitals, Center Shields, c.1880, 47 x 12 In., Pair 2300.00
Pew, Oak, 2 Seats, Hinged Flap Well, Hinged Flap Book Support, 39 x 46 x 21 In.. .... 1500.00
Pie Safe, Cherry, Pierced Flowers, c.1850, 64 x 46 In. 1116.00
Pie Safe, Cherry, Poplar, Punched Tin Panels, 2 Drawers, 2 Doors, c.1850, 51 x 39 In. 1998.00
Pie Safe, Doors, 6 Punched Tin Panels, Chrome Yellow Paint, Ohio, 60 ½ x 41 In. 3850.00
Pie Safe, French Provincial, Pine, Doors, Drawers, Wire Grill, 88 x 44 x 24 In.. .... 2880.00
Pie Safe, Pine, 2 Drawers, Shelves, 60 x 40 x 12 In.. .... 325.00
Pie Safe, Poplar, Blue Green Paint, 2 Tin Doors, Shelves, Late 1800s, 55 x 33 In. 1035.00
Pie Safe, Poplar, Dovetailed Drawer, Punched Tin Panel Doors, Shelves, 54 x 43 In. 1763.00
Pie Safe, Poplar, Painted, 6 Punched Tin Panels, Shaped Skirt, High Legs, c.1850, 67 x 45 In. 3878.00
Pie Safe, Poplar, Red Paint, Drawer, Punched Tin Panels, Shelves, 54 x 43 x 17 In.. .... 1763.00
Pie Safe, Poplar, Red Wash, Flower, Punched Tin Panels, 2 Drawers, Doors, 1850, 46 x 53 In. 2100.00
Pie Safe, Poplar, Yellow Pine, 6 Punched Tin Philflot Panels, 19th Century, 49 x 38 In. 1404.00
Pie Safe, Red Stain, Drawer, 4 Punched Panels, 2 Doors, Va., 19th Century, 53 x 35 In.. ..... 2106.00
Pie Safe, Red Stain, Punched Tin Panels, Drawer, Virginia, 53 x 35 In.. .... 1700.00
Pie Safe, Softwood, 4-Star Pierced Panels, Painted, 2 Doors, Drawers, Pa., 58 x 56 x 19 In. .. 650.00
Pie Safe, Softwood, Punched Tin Face, Stars, Yellow, 60 ½ x 41 x 16 ¾ In. .... *illus* 3650.00
Pie Safe, Yellow Pine, Blue Gray Paint, Doors, Interior Shelf, 1800s, 68 x 49 In. 1093.00
Planter, Arts & Crafts, 4 California Art Scenic Tiles, Oak, 10 ½ In.. .... 345.00
Planter, Arts & Crafts, Slats, Metal Liner, 30 ½ x 33 x 14 ½ In.. .... 115.00
Planter, Fruitwood, Inlaid, Scroll Legs, Tin Liner, 3-Sided Base, Continental, 13 ¾ In. 400.00
Planter, Louis XV, Kingwood, Bronze Mount, Metal Liner, c.1890, 29 x 25 x 14 In........... 1950.00
Planter, Regency, Hardwood Tripod Base, Chains, Lion's Head Mounts, 34 In. 403.00
Planter, Regency Style, Hardwood, Lion's Heads, Chains, 3-Footed, Marked, 34 In. ...... *illus* 385.00
Planter, Softwood, Green Paint, Metal Casters, Wood Wheels, 24 x 36 x 18 In. .... *illus* 348.00
Planter, Softwood, Green Paint, Rabbit-Joint Well, Turned Legs, Stretchers, 24 x 36 In.. ..... 348.00

Furniture, Ottoman, Walnut, Ebonized, Incised Gilt, Upholstered, Allen & Bros., 19 x 19 In.
$690.00

Furniture, Parlor Set, Empire, Ebonized, Serpentine, France, 1870, 47-In. Settee, 4 Chairs
$1100.00

Furniture, Pedestal, L. & J.G. Stickley, No. 27, Corbels, Signed, 36 x 19 In.
$3600.00

Furniture, Pie Safe, Softwood, Punched Tin Face, Stars, Yellow, 60 ½ x 41 x 16 ¾ In.
$3650.00

Furniture, Planter, Regency Style, Hardwood, Lion's Heads, Chains, 3-Footed, Marked, 34 In.
$385.00

Furniture, Planter, Softwood, Green Paint, Metal Casters, Wood Wheels, 24 x 36 x 18 In.
$348.00

Furniture, Press, Jackson, Walnut, Punched Tin, Virginia, 19th Century, 87 x 46 x 20 In.
$4830.00

Furniture, Recamier, Mahogany, Silk Upholstery, Philadelphia, 1890s, 34 x 72 x 23 In.
$1500.00

Planter, Wirework, Wall Mounted, Demilune, Scalloped Top, 1800s, 10 x 17 In. ... 153.00
Press, Jackson, Walnut, Punched Tin, Virginia, 19th Century, 87 x 46 x 20 In. ... *illus* 4830.00
Pulpit, Arts & Crafts, Oak, Carved, 67 x 40 x 30 In. ... 200.00
Rack, Baking, 4 Iron Shelves, Berry Design, Ball Feet, 1900s, 78 x 42 In. ... 239.00
Rack, Baking, Brass, Iron, 3 Shelves, Scrolls, c.1880, 97 x 35 ½ x 18 ½ In. ... 830.00
Rack, Baking, Brass, Iron, Scroll Crown & Supports, 4 D-Shape Shelves, 91 x 61 x 18 In. ... 275.00
Rack, Baking, Iron, Brass, 3 Shelves, 72 x 60 x 18 In. ... 150.00
Rack, Baking, Iron, Wood, Brass, Cutting Board Shelf, Parquetry, Wine Rack, 90 x 48 In. ... 805.00
Rack, Drying, Pine, Mortised Bars, Screws, Shoe Feet, Late 1800s, 31 x 17 ¾ In. ... 323.00
Rack, Magazine, G. Stickley, No. 79, Cutout Pulls, 40 x 14 x 10 In. ... 1920.00
Rack, Magazine, Renaissance Revival, Wood, Inlaid, Instruments, c.1870, 21 x 16 x 12 In. ... 330.00
Rack, Plate, Hanging, Oak, Scroll Sides, 3 Shelves, 2 Rails, 36 x 29 In. ... 206.00
Rack, Quilt, Hardwood, Blue Gray Paint, Chamfered, Tapered Uprights, 64 x 39 In. ... 633.00
Rack, Quilt, Pine, 3 Mortised & Pegged Panels, Hinged, 19th Century, 66 x 36 In. ... 176.00
Recamier, Carved Back, Arms, Upholstered, Boston, 1825-35, 34 x 86 x 25 In. ... 3200.00
Recamier, Federal Style, Mahogany, Ebonized, Brass, Upholstered, Baker, 34 x 80 x 27 In. ... 225.00
Recamier, Mahogany, Carved Shell Detail, Rolled Arms, 72 x 32 In. ... 2420.00
Recamier, Mahogany, French Empire, Gilt Mounts, Asymmetric, c.1830, 34 x 75 In. ... 2032.00
Recamier, Mahogany, Silk Upholstery, Philadelphia, 1890s, 34 x 72 x 23 In. ... *illus* 1500.00
Recamier, Neoclassical, Mahogany, Carved, Blue & Gold Silk Upholstery, 34 x 72 In. ... 1725.00
Rocker, Art Deco, Chrome Plated, Tubular, Flat Steel, Upholstered, 36 x 29 x 34 In., Pair ... 3450.00
Rocker, Arts & Crafts, Oak, 4 Vertical Back Slats, Flat Arms, 3 Side Slats, Leather Seat, 28 x 18 In. 119.00
Rocker, Cherry, Curved Crest Rail, Woven Seat & Back, c.1875, 32 In. ... 558.00
Rocker, Eames, Fiberglass Seat, Eiffel Tower Rod, Birch Rockers, Herman Miller, c.1950, 27 In. 474.00
Rocker, Eames, RAR, Fiberglass, Molded, Wire, Birch, Herman Miller, 27 x 25 In. ... *illus* 890.00
Rocker, G. Stickley, Craftsman, Oak, 4 Vertical Back Slats ... 675.00
Rocker, G. Stickley, No. 311, 5 Vertical Slats, V-Back, Leather Seat, Arms, 33 x 27 x 26 In. ... 650.00
Rocker, G. Stickley, No. 323, Ebonized, Slatted Sides, Cushions, 38 x 29 x 29 In. ... 3360.00
Rocker, G. Stickley, Oak, 3 Slats, Woven Seat, No Arms, 34 x 25 In. ... 100.00
Rocker, Herman Miller, Enamel, Striped Upholstery, Multicolored, 29 x 23 In., Pair ... 840.00
Rocker, L. & J.G. Stickley, No. 815, Vertical Slats, Drop-In Seat, Decal, 40 x 27 In. ... *illus* 2640.00
Rocker, L. & J.G. Stickley, No. 1321, 13 Spindles, Leather Seat, 42 x 31 x 32 In. ... *illus* 1080.00
Rocker, Ladder Back, Red, Ball Finials, 4 Arched Splats, Cheese Cutter Rockers ... 11.00
Rocker, Laurel Twig, c.1930, 30 x 24 In. ... 900.00
Rocker, Lifetime, Wood, Curved, Slat Back, 29 x 42 In. ... 660.00
Rocker, Limbert, No. 1646, 5 Slats, Spring Cushion, Signed, 36 x 30 x 28 In. ... 1950.00
Rocker, Lincoln, Rococo, Walnut, Carved, Leafy Crest, Shaped Back, Upholstered, 46 In. ... 764.00
Rocker, Lincoln, Swan's Head Armrests, Cane Seat, 29 In., Child's ... 94.00
Rocker, Mahogany, Carved, Upholstered, Mid 19th Century, 45 In. ... 2880.00
Rocker, Maple, 3 Arched Slats, Split Oak Seat, Arms, Tennessee, c.1860, 38 x 22 In. ... 365.00
Rocker, McKinley, Slat Sides, Leather Back, Seat, Phoenix Chair Co., 29 x 31 In. ... 450.00
Rocker, Multicolored, Cane Seat, Flowers, 28 In., Child's ... 142.00
Rocker, Orange & Ocher Graining, Stenciled Locomotive & Town, Crest Rail, N.E., c.1850 ... 1638.00
Rocker, Plank Seat, Turned Spindles, 24 In., Child's ... 71.00
Rocker, Red Paint, 2 Spindles, 17 ¾ x 10 ½ x 15 ½ In., Child's ... 40.00
Rocker, Roycroft, No. 020, 5 Vertical Slats, Leather Seat, Tacks, 28 x 17 x 17 In., Child's ... 720.00
Rocker, Roycroft, No. 107, Red Oilcloth Seat, 35 x 22 In. ... 1800.00
Rocker, Rustic Old Hickory, Branch Construction, Cane Seat, 1930s, 40 x 26 In. ... 975.00
Rocker, Selig, Round, Swivel Base, Yellow Upholstery, 40 x 37 In., Pair ... 2160.00
Rocker, Shaker, 3 Back Slats, Taped Red Seat, Shawl Rail, Mt. Lebanon, c.1890, 34 x 15 In. ... 323.00
Rocker, Shaker, 3 Backslats, Ball Finials, Cheese Cutter Rockers, 33 In. ... 11.00
Rocker, Shaker, Birch, Turned Finials, Blue, Cream Woven Seat, Back, c.1900, 34 x 20 In. ... 144.00
Rocker, Shaker, Mixed Wood, Wool Twill Tape, Blue Paint, Mt. Lebanon, Late 1800s, 43 In. ... 88.00
Rocker, Shaker, No. 4, Shawl Rail & Arms, Tape Seat, Mt. Lebanon, 34 ¼ x 22 In. ... 316.00
Rocker, Shaker, No. 6, Tape Seat, Indian Red Finish, Mt. Lebanon, c.1880, 16 x 41 In. ... 499.00
Rocker, Shaker, No. 7, 4 Arched Slats, Tape Seat, Arms, Mt. Lebanon, 1900, 41 In. ... 640.00
Rocker, Stickley Bros., No. 715, 5 Vertical Slats, Arms, Cushion, 35 x 39 x 28 In. ... 1100.00
Rocker, Teak, Cushions, Franz Reenskaug, 1958, 32 x 25 ½ x 33 In. ... 1500.00
Rocker, Twig, Orange & White Paint Traces, Southern, Early 1900s, 42 x 24 In. ... 230.00
Rocker, Victorian, Stenciled Griffin, 41 x 23 x 28 In. ... 50.00
Rocker, Victorian, Walnut, Carved Back Crest, Upholstered, 40 In. ... 130.00
Rocker, Victorian, Walnut, Medallion Back, Folding, 24 In., Child's ... 59.00
Rocker, Wegner, Wool Cushion, c.1960, 32 x 23 x 18 In., Pair ... 1200.00
Rocker, Windsor, Black On Red Graining, Arms, Stencil By P.P. Billings N.Y., c.1835, 44 In. ... 1292.00
Schrank, Cherry, Poplar, 2 Dovetailed Doors, Hooks, Shelf, W.H. Carr, c.1840, 82 x 70 In. ... 840.00
Schrank, Chippendale, Walnut, Paneled Doors, Iron Hinges, 77 x 70 x 23 In. ... 8800.00
Schrank, Walnut, 2 Doors, Astragal Panels, Molded, Pilasters, Bun Feet, 1762, 81 x 72 In. ... 19890.00

Schrank, Walnut, Poplar, Raised Panels, Recessed Feet, Shelf, Hooks, 83 x 63 x 26 In. 1645.00
Screen, 2-Panel, Carved Phoenixes, Flowers, Red Insert, Bone Flowers, c.1895, 75 x 64 In.... 374.00
Screen, 2-Panel, Hardwood Inlay, Mother-Of-Pearl, Woman, Child, Dog, Japan, 34 x 72 In... 119.00
Screen, 2-Panel, Wood, Gilt, Openwork Bird Decoration, Chinese 266.00
Screen, 3-Panel, Arts & Crafts, Mahogany, Leaded Amber Glass, 72 x 189 In.............. 390.00
Screen, 3-Panel, Arts & Crafts, Wood, Fabric, 57 x 198 In. 390.00
Screen, 3-Panel, Black Lacquer, Ivory Inlay, Japan, 30 x 30 In. 117.00
Screen, 3-Panel, Chinoiserie, Painted, Water Lilies, Birds, Ebonized, 66 x 60 In. 173.00
Screen, 3-Panel, Dressing, Regency, Painted, Flowers, Satinwood, c.1880, 67 x 51 In........ 270.00
Screen, 3-Panel, Faux Bamboo, 3 Curved Tube Arches, Tube Links, Gilt Metal, 1900s, 73 In... 237.00
Screen, 3-Panel, Flowers, 68 x 19 ¾ In. 540.00
Screen, 3-Panel, Gothic Revival, Walnut, Tapestry, Carved Leaf, Birds, 75 x 75 In........... 4444.00
Screen, 3-Panel, Leather, Painted, Flowers, Scrolling, Roman Art Screen Co., 68 x 54 In..... 259.00
Screen, 3-Panel, Louis XV, Leather, Landscape, Couple, Gold Border, France, 1800s, 69 x 60 In. 978.00
Screen, 3-Panel, Regency Style, Leather, Oak, Parrot On Swing, 74 ½ x 81 In............. 3120.00
Screen, 3-Panel, Risen Christ, Scrolled Wood, Gilt, Metal, 2 Angels, Stand, France, 1800s, 19 In. 590.00
Screen, 3-Panel, Satinwood, Inlaid, c.1910, 72 x 66 In. .... *illus* 1300.00
Screen, 3-Panel, Teak, Carved, Early 20th Century, 62 ½ In. 175.00
Screen, 3-Panel, Varnished Paper, Oriental Scenes, Women In Garden, 68 x 51 In.......... 431.00
Screen, 3-Panel, Victorian, Painted Canvas, Playing Putti, Rocaille Borders, 59 x 60 In...... 770.00
Screen, 4-Panel, Adam Style, Canvas, Pastoral Scene, Flower Swags, 53 x 98 In. 1440.00
Screen, 4-Panel, Black Lacquer, Bone Inlay, Courtyard Scenes, Chinese, 1800s, 72 x 72 In. .. 3450.00
Screen, 4-Panel, Brocade, Gilt Frame, Chinese, 93 x 80 In. 1920.00
Screen, 4-Panel, Burl Walnut, Sport Scenes, Signed, 1894, 72 In. .... *illus* 9000.00
Screen, 4-Panel, Chinoiserie, Silk, Wool, Multicolored, Allegorical, 64 x 104 In. 22500.00
Screen, 4-Panel, Faux Marble, Monkey, Landscape, Verse, 20th Century, 76 x 72 In. 1920.00
Screen, 4-Panel, Lacquer, Landscape, Figures, Flowers, Black Ground, Chinese, 70 x 64 In... 305.00
Screen, 4-Panel, Louis XVI Style, Gilt, Aubusson Tapestry, Late 1800s, 78 x 66 In. 5000.00
Screen, 4-Panel, Louis XVI Style, Gilt, Painted, Figural Group, 56 x 68 In................. 2596.00
Screen, 4-Panel, Mahogany, Carved, Ebonized, Pierced Flowers, c.1915, 69 In. 826.00
Screen, 4-Panel, Scenes From Ramayana, 65 x 60 ½ In. 415.00
Screen, 4-Panel, Wood, Carved, Brass Inlay, India, 20th Century, 72 x 78 In............... 225.00
Screen, 4-Panel, Wood, Greek Letters, Key Design, Gold, 1940s, 68 x 76 In................ 2520.00
Screen, 5-Panel, Silk, Painted Oriental Design, Birds, Flowers, 77 ½ x 84 ½ In............ 235.00
Screen, 6-Panel, Lacquer, Black, Flowers, 15 Recessed Panels, Stone, Chinese, 72 x 96 In. ... 850.00
Screen, 6-Panel, Scenic, Women In Garden, Cinnabar Red, Wood Frame, Chinese, 102 x 77 In. 6756.00
Screen, 6-Panel, Table, Crane, Wood, Brass Mounted, Japan, c.1920, 23 ¾ In. 590.00
Screen, 6-Panel, Temple, Figures, Black Lacquer, Hardstone, Ivory Inlay, 74 In. 2750.00
Screen, 8-Panel, Coromandel, Black Lacquer, Deity, Chinese, 20th Century, 96 x 136 In. 885.00
Screen, 8-Panel, Coromandel, Carved Court Scene, Chinese, 96 x 140 In.................. 472.00
Screen, 8-Panel, Coromandel, Painted Scene, Lacquer, Chinese, 147 In.................. 1170.00
Screen, 10-Panel, Eames, FSW, Molded Birch Plywood, 86 x 68 In...................... 4800.00
Screen, Matchstick, Bamboo, Portable, Vertical Slats, Twine Joined, c.1950, 62 x 84 In. 593.00
Screen, Queen Anne, Mahogany, Needlework Panel, Carved Cabriole Legs, 48 In. 1063.00
Screen, Regency, Silk, Needlework, Mahogany, Pole Mounted, 55 ½ In. 360.00
Screen, Table, Framed Mirror, Fretwork, Mortise & Tenon, Trestle Base, 36 x 25 In......... 316.00
Screen, Table, Jade, Wood, Carved, Reticulated, Chinese, 15 x 11 In..................... 995.00
Screen, Table, Marble, Carved, Rosewood Frame, Chinese, 19th Century, 34 In............ 296.00
Screen, Teak, Carved, 8 Sections, Panel Insert, Figures, Scenes, 70 x 106 In. 2640.00
Secretary, Birch, Lacquered, Drop Front, Shelves, Drawers, Sweden, 54 x 14 In. 8750.00
Secretary, Burl Walnut, Ebonized, Drop Front, Domed Pediment, 91 x 43 x 20 ¾ In. 6300.00
Secretary, Butler's, Mahogany, Poplar, Pine, Writing Surface, Hinges, 52 x 45 x 22 In. 1175.00
Secretary, Chippendale, Cherry, Drop Front, Pigeonholes, Drawers, 89 x 42 x 22 In......... 3738.00
Secretary, Chippendale, Mahogany, Bonnet Top, Goddard Townsend, 97 x 43 x 24 In. 23000.00
Secretary, Chippendale, Walnut, Slant Front, Paneled Doors, Shelves, 75 x 36 x 18 In....... 3600.00
Secretary, Federal, Mahogany, 2 Doors, 6 Drawers, Bun Feet, 84 x 45 x 21 In............. 475.00
Secretary, Federal, Mahogany, Bookcase Doors, Fitted Interior, Mass., c.1800, 53 x 36 In..... 588.00
Secretary, Federal, Mahogany, Glazed Panel Doors, Early 1800s, 79 x 43 In. 1673.00
Secretary, Federal, Mahogany, Maple, Cherry, Drop Front, Drawers, 59 x 41 x 18 In......... 2880.00
Secretary, Federal, Mahogany, Veneers, 2 Gothic Doors, Writing Flap, 5 Drawers, 67 x 43 In.. 1150.00
Secretary, French Provincial, Fruitwood, Drop Front, 6 Stacking Drawers, 44 x 33 x 15 In... 915.00
Secretary, Fruitwood, Marble Top, Inlaid Drop Front, France, c.1795, 59 x 37 In. 2530.00
Secretary, George III, Chinoiserie, Black Lacquer, 87 x 35 x 20 In. 4560.00
Secretary, George III, Mahogany, Astragal Glazed Doors, 83 x 38 In. 5280.00
Secretary, George III, Mahogany, Cubbyholes, Drawers, Glazed Doors, 84 x 38 x 21 In. 5280.00
Secretary, George III, Mahogany, Dentil Cornice, Fluted Frieze, 91 x 41 In................ 4320.00
Secretary, George III, Mahogany, Drop Front, Doors, Drawers, 89 x 49 x 23 In............. 2880.00

Furniture, Rocker, Eames, RAR, Fiberglass, Molded, Wire, Birch, Herman Miller, 27 x 25 In.
$890.00

Furniture, Rocker, L. & J.G. Stickley, No. 815, Vertical Slats, Drop-In Seat, Decal, 40 x 27 In.
$2640.00

Furniture, Rocker, L. & J.G. Stickley, No. 1321, 13 Spindles, Leather Seat, 42 x 31 x 32 In.
$1080.00

Furniture, Screen, 3-Panel, Satinwood, Inlaid, c.1910, 72 x 66 In.
$1300.00

F

Furniture, Screen, 4-Panel, Burl Walnut, Sport Scenes, Signed, 1894, 72 In.
$9000.00

Furniture, Secretary, Victorian, Oak, Drop Front, Mirror, c.1900, 68 x 32 x 18 In.
$300.00

Furniture, Semainier, Louis XVI Style, Mahogany Veneer, Parquetry, Marble Top, 55 x 24 x 15 In.
$1210.00

Furniture, Serving Cart, Cees Braakman, Rolo, Birch, Red Top, UMS Pastoe, 27 x 31 x 18 In.
$1200.00

Secretary, George III, Mahogany, Slant Front, Glazed Doors, Cubbyholes, Drawers, 88 x 42 In. 4080.00
Secretary, George III, Secretary, Mahogany, Inlaid, 2 Glazed Doors, Shelves, 84 x 42 In...... 1150.00
Secretary, George III Style, Mahogany, Glazed Doors, Drawers, 80 x 42 In.. .... 1800.00
Secretary, Georgian, Broken Arch Pediment, Glazed Doors, Drop Front, Drawers, 96 x 41 In. 1020.00
Secretary, Hardwood Veneers, 2 Doors, 3 Shelves, Letter Slots, Drawer, 46 x 34 x 12 In. 1067.00
Secretary, Lincoln Style, Walnut, 2 Glass Doors, 2 Panel Doors, 42 x 90 In. 1650.00
Secretary, Louis Philippe, Mahogany, Marble, Doors, Drawers, 57 x 38 x 17 In.. .... 2450.00
Secretary, Mahogany, Drop Front, Wedgwood Plaques, Ormolu, c.1810, 55 x 34 In. 20000.00
Secretary, Mahogany, Glass Doors, Pillar & Scroll Base, c.1850, 74 x 47 In. 1003.00
Secretary, Mahogany, Glazed Doors, Fold-Down Drawer, 94 x 50 x 24 In.. .... 4800.00
Secretary, Mahogany, Roll Top, Panel Cupboard Doors, Pigeonholes, 92 ½ x 46 In. 1725.00
Secretary, Mahogany, Satinwood Inlay, Drop Front, Dutch, 63 x 41 x 21 In.. .... 2300.00
Secretary, Marble Top, 4 Drawers, Inlaid Drop Front, Bronze Pulls, France, 1900s, 52 x 24 In. 805.00
Secretary, Napoleon III, Galleried Marble Top, Drop Front, 47 x 25 In.. .... 1416.00
Secretary, Neoclassical, Mahogany, Carved Cornice, Glazed Doors, 1820s, 93 x 49 In.. ...... 4600.00
Secretary, Neoclassical, Mahogany, Drawers, Cubbyholes, Block Feet, 48 x 41 x 18 In. 1920.00
Secretary, Neoclassical, Mahogany, Panel Doors, Drop Front Drawer, 79 x 43 In. 568.00
Secretary, Queen Anne Style, Maple, Drop Front, Pigeonholes, 65 x 24 x 15 In.. .... 230.00
Secretary, Regency, Mahogany, Inlaid, Glazed Doors, Drawers, Scotland, 89 x 48 In. 2938.00
Secretary, Regency, Mahogany, Satinwood, Cubbyholes, 45 x 43 x 22 In. 2160.00
Secretary, Renaissance Revival, Walnut, Bird's-Eye Maple, Drop Front, 57 x 37 x 23 In...... 6325.00
Secretary, Rococo Revival, Walnut, Circular Glazed Panels, Writing Surface, 107 x 50 In. ... 3000.00
Secretary, Sheraton, Mahogany, Eagle Finial, Line Inlay, Paneled Doors, 71 x 41 In. 1870.00
Secretary, Swedish Biedermeier, Drop Front, Drawers, 1900s, 48 x 46 In.. .... 212.00
Secretary, Tiger Maple, Cherry, Lift Top, 4 Graduated Drawers, 39 x 22 In.. .... 3738.00
Secretary, Victorian, Oak, Drop Front, Mirror, c.1900, 68 x 32 x 18 In. .... *illus* 300.00
Secretary, Wooton, Standard Grade, Ladies, 36 In. 17250.00
Semainier, Biedermeier, Mahogany, 7 Drawers, Step Top, 54 x 27 ⅝ x 16 In. 1830.00
Semainier, Burl Walnut, Ebony Inlaid, Bun Feet, 7 Drawers, c.1850, 66 x 41 In. 2280.00
Semainier, Louis Philippe, Mahogany, Canted Corners, 7 Drawers, 54 x 28 x 15 In. 2040.00
Semainier, Louis XVI, Walnut, Amboyna Inlay, Sarcophagus Plinth, 7 Drawers, 65 x 42 In... 3642.00
Semainier, Louis XVI Style, Mahogany Veneer, Parquetry, Marble Top, 55 x 24 x 15 In... *illus* 1210.00
Semainier, Napoleon III, Kingwood, Marble Top, 7 Drawers, 51 ½ x 23 x 14 In. 840.00
Server, Art Deco, Chamfered, Long Doors, 3 Drawers, France, 40 x 47 x 20 In. 239.00
Server, Arts & Crafts, Drawer, Lower Shelf, Signed, Kunkle Furniture, 34 x 36 In. 540.00
Server, Chippendale, Mahogany, Brass Gallery, Drawer, England, 1890, 49 x 82 x 29 In...... 2000.00
Server, Federal, Mahogany, Central Oval, String Inlay, Quarter Fans, c.1795, 36 x 46 In. 7110.00
Server, Federal, Mahogany, Gadroon, Bowfront, Backsplash, Carved Spiral, 40 x 46 In.. ..... 717.00
Server, Federal, Mahogany, Inlaid, Arched Apron, 5 Drawers, c.1800, 34 x 40 In. 3760.00
Server, Fruitwood, 3 Tiers, Canted Edge, 28 x 31 ¾ x 14 ½ In. 1200.00
Server, G. Stickley, No. 818, 3 Drawers, Oval Pulls, 39 ½ x 48 x 20 In. 3900.00
Server, G. Stickley, Oak, 3 Drawers, Copper Pulls, Shelf, Drawer, c.1912, 39 x 48 In.. .... 2607.00
Server, G. Stickley, Oak, Back Rail, 2 Drawers, V Pulls, Arch Apron, Low Shelf, c.1908, 40 x 41 In. 3318.00
Server, George III, Mahogany, Inlaid, 3 Frieze Drawers, 32 x 108 In.. .... 13750.00
Server, George III, Mahogany, Inlaid, Serpentine, 3 Drawers, 32 x 48 x 29 In. 1896.00
Server, Henri II, Rosewood, Carved, Drawer, Marble Lined, 40 x 44 x 24 In. 2300.00
Server, Hepplewhite, Mahogany, Inlaid, Crossbands, Bowfront, 3 Drawers, c.1900, 33 x 41 In. 1058.00
Server, Mahogany, Scrolled Backsplash, Carved Columns, 4 Drawers, 2 Doors, c.1835, 48 x 47 In. 353.00
Server, Marquetry, Gilt Metal Mounted, 4 Drawers, Leaf & Geometric Designs, 38 x 58 In. ... 2280.00
Server, Oak, 2 Drawers, Copper Pulls, Low Shelf, Whitehead Furniture Co., c.1906, 37 x 40 In. 5925.00
Server, Oak, Rectangular Top, 2 Drawers, Cabriole Legs, England, 31 x 49 x 20 In. 1778.00
Server, Oak, Serpentine Front, 3 Drawers, Late 19th Century, 36 x 40 x 22 ½ In. 146.00
Server, Regency, Mahogany, Galleried Top, Frieze Drawers, Baluster Legs, 39 x 39 In. 1195.00
Server, Regency Style, Mahogany, Inlaid, Bowfront, Drawers, c.1930, 31 x 36 In.. .... 1150.00
Server, Rosewood, Marble Top, c.1865, 70 x 49 x 16 In. 1840.00
Server, Sheraton, Mahogany, 3 Drawers, Spiral Legs, 19th Century, 36 x 36 ½ x 21 In. 600.00
Server, Walnut, Burl Walnut, Bird's-Eye Maple, Inset Mirror, c.1920, 44 x 66 x 24 In. 805.00
Server, William IV, Mahogany, Tiers, ¾ Gallery, Corner Finials, Casters, 47 x 47 In.. .... 1500.00
Serving Cart, Cees Braakman, Rolo, Birch, Red Top, UMS Pastoe, 27 x 31 x 18 In...... *illus* 1200.00
Serving Cart, William IV, Mahogany, 3 Tiers, 44 x 41 x 17 ½ In. 2040.00
Settee, Arrow Back, Plank Seat, Baluster Supports, Bamboo Turned Legs, 34 x 82 x 23 In. ... 413.00
Settee, Banister Back, 9 Vertical Stayrails, Arched Crest, Slip Seat, 1900s, 45 x 52 In.. ...... 384.00
Settee, Beech, Trisected Back, Bulbous Turned Crests, Cushions, 35 x 63 x 22 In.. .... 4320.00
Settee, Biedermeier, Fruitwood, Oval Splats, Chairbacks, Upholstered, Arms, 1800s, 72 In. ... 1495.00
Settee, Biedermeier, Fruitwood, Oval Splats, Rolled Arms, c.1855, 33 x 72 In.. .... 1300.00
Settee, Borge Mogensen, Beech, Slat Back, Adjustable Sides, Cushions, Denmark, 1964, 34 x 34 In. 2160.00
Settee, Brass Veneer Frame, Upholstered, 1975, 27 ½ x 54 x 33 In., Pair 5000.00

Settee, Charles II Style, Walnut, Needlework Upholstery, 40 ½ In. 3125.00
Settee, Cherry, Carved, Turned Supports, Stylized Flowers, Late 1800s, 35 x 43 In. . . . . . . *illus* 830.00
Settee, Chippendale, High Back, Wings, Loose Cushion, Velvet Upholstery, 50 x 43 In. 588.00
Settee, Chippendale, Mahogany, Double Chairback, Carved, Flame Stitch Seat, 42 x 41 In. . . . 235.00
Settee, Chippendale, Mahogany, Double Chairback, Carved, Pierced, c.1880, 38 x 45 In. 568.00
Settee, Chippendale, Mahogany, Double Chairback, Needlework Seat, England, 1700s, 38 x 45 In. 3335.00
Settee, Chippendale, Mahogany, Padded Cabriole Legs, Animal Feet, c.1700, 39 x 46 In. 2596.00
Settee, Chippendale, Mahogany, Strapwork Splat, Damask Upholstery, 38 x 55 In. 2645.00
Settee, Chippendale Style, Mahogany, Double Chairback, Openwork Splats, 1900s, 25 x 30 In. . 209.00
Settee, Chippendale Style, Mahogany, Double Chairback, Philadelphia, Early 1900s, 38 x 52 In. 978.00
Settee, Chippendale Style, Mahogany, Upholstered, Ireland, 1800s, 42 x 67 x 22 In. . . . . . *illus* 2010.00
Settee, Edwardian, Mahogany, Inlaid, Mother-Of-Pearl, Inlaid Splats, Cushion, 33 x 39 In. . . 568.00
Settee, Empire Style, Mahogany, Upholstered, Falcon Claw Feet, 34 x 89 x 26 In. 1350.00
Settee, Empire Style, Mahogany, Upholstered, Hairy Paw Carved Feet, 36 x 54 x 20 In. 825.00
Settee, Empire Style, Rosewood, Gilt, Padded, Cushions, 32 x 90 x 33 ½ In. 3100.00
Settee, French Provincial, Blue Paint, Shaped Crest, Stretchers, Rush Seat, 37 x 74 In. 230.00
Settee, George II Style, Mahogany, Double Chairback, Padded, 41 ½ x 51 x 24 In. 2880.00
Settee, George III, Mahogany, Rococo, Domed, Padded Back, 34 x 70 x 23 In. 1800.00
Settee, Grotto, Gilt, Gesso, Carved Sea Creatures, Shells, Venice, c.1895, 43 x 41 In. 11500.00
Settee, Irish Chippendale, Mahogany, Rolled Arms, Leaf Carved, Paw Feet, 42 x 67 In. 2185.00
Settee, Limbert, 8 Vertical Slats, Spring Cushion, Arms, Signed, 37 x 47 x 25 In. 890.00
Settee, Louis XIV Style, Fruitwood, Padded Back, Scroll Carved, Arms, 49 x 64 In. 2400.00
Settee, Louis XIV Style, Gilt, Domed, Padded, Carved Crest, 50 ½ x 69 x 27 In. 2400.00
Settee, Louis XV, Ivory Paint, Chairback, Rush Seat, 41 x 42 In. 840.00
Settee, Louis XV, Wood, Cane Panels, Cream Paint, Carved Flower Backrest, Legs, 54 x 30 In. . 1416.00
Settee, Louis XVI, Mahogany, Carved, Arched Crest Rail, Roses, Scrolled Arms, 40 x 51 In. . . . 823.00
Settee, Louis XVI Style, Beech, Carved, Painted, Padded, Cushions, 35 x 61 In. 3360.00
Settee, Louis XVI Style, Fruitwood, Padded, Molded, Fluted Apron, 37 x 58 x 25 In. 4320.00
Settee, Louis XVI Style, Gilt, Padded, Domed Back, Closed Arms, 38 x 72 x 24 In. 2880.00
Settee, Louis XVI Style, High Back, Distressed Paint, Maison Jansen, 48 x 46 x 23 In. 700.00
Settee, Louis XVI Style, Verdigris Finish, Carved, Early 1900s, 32 x 32 x 31 In. . . . . *illus* 365.00
Settee, Mahogany, Carved Mermaid Top, Claw & Ball Foot, Yellow Upholstery, 58 x 44 In. 960.00
Settee, Mahogany, Pierced Triple Chairback, Claw & Ball Feet, Ireland, c.1755, 77 In. 8750.00
Settee, Mahogany, Scalloped Crest, Upholstered, Bracket Feet, c.1830, 32 x 46 In. 881.00
Settee, Meridienne, Rococo, Rosewood, Carved, Serpentine Arms, c.1850, 41 x 56 In. 6462.00
Settee, Meridienne, Upholstered, Knuckle Feet, 1820s, 49 ½ x 60 x 26 In. . . . . *illus* 978.00
Settee, Mixed Woods, Cream Ground, c.1815, 17 x 33 x 48 ½ In. 1998.00
Settee, Molded Back, Seat, Carved Flowers, Scrolls, Padded, 1800s, 32 x 39 In., Pair 5938.00
Settee, Nanna & Jorgen Ditzel, Black Back, White Seat, c.1962, 29 x 56 In. 1320.00
Settee, Neoclassical, Fruitwood, Double Chairback, Slip Seat, Tapered Legs, Italy, 34 In. 948.00
Settee, Neoclassical, Fruitwood, Ebonized, Swan, Stylized Lyre Splats, 18 x 30 In. 652.00
Settee, Neoclassical, Mahogany, Nailed Upholstered, Bowed Crest Rail, 1900s, 41 x 79 In. 657.00
Settee, Regency Style, Maple, Curved Rail, Scroll Arms, Upholstered, 6 Legs, 33 x 42 In. 825.00
Settee, Rococo, Walnut, Crest, Grape Clusters, Vines, Serpentine Seat Rail, c.1850, 42 x 64 In. 2350.00
Settee, Rococo Revival, Espresso Velvet, Fringe, Down-Swept Padded Back, 32 x 60 In. 478.00
Settee, Rosewood, 2 Chairbacks, Scrolling, Cabriole Legs, Upholstered, c.1850, 39 x 64 In. . . . 403.00
Settee, Rosewood, Arched Pierced Crest, Flowers, Serpentine Arms, Cabriole Legs, 47 x 65 In. . 5581.00
Settee, Rosewood, Carved Crest, Curved Back, Rose Fabric, Arms, N.Y., c.1860, 40 x 68 In. . . . 3335.00
Settee, Rosewood, Spindle Back, Plank Seat, Scrolled Arms, Rocker, 30 x 73 x 31 In. 550.00
Settee, Sheraton, Pine, Painted, Spindled Chairback Rail, Pa., c.1830, 35 x 59 In. 920.00
Settee, Slats, Spindles, Leather Cushion, Brooks, 33 x 58 x 29 In. *illus* 2620.00
Settee, Softwood, Painted, Shaped Crest Rail, Urn Splats, Scrolled Arms, 15 x 24 In. 1760.00
Settee, Wendel Castle, Molar, Fiberglass, Red High Gloss, Beylerian, 26 x 50 x 33 In. . . . . *illus* 1800.00
Settee, Windsor, Arrow Back, Cane Seat, Painted, 35 x 77 In. 875.00
Settee, Windsor, Bamboo, Medallion, 3 Sections, Spindles, Plank Seat, 10 Legs, 75 In. 3375.00
Settee, Windsor, Birdcage, Bamboo Turnings, Green Paint, c.1820 . . . . 3510.00
Settee, Windsor, Fruit, Bird, Ribbon Crest, Scroll Ears, Painted, 1880s, 37 x 45 x 16 In. 650.00
Settee, Windsor, Mixed Wood, 20 Spindles, Arrow Back, Yellow Paint, c.1810, 33 x 17 In. 1880.00
Settee, Windsor, Pine, Bamboo Turnings, Black Paint, Yellow Trim, c.1800, 81 x 36 In. 1998.00
Settee, Windsor, Spindle Back, Plank Seat, Continuous Arm, Early 1900s, 36 x 63 In. 1093.00
Settee, Wood, Arrow Back, Dutch Flower & Bird Crest, Bamboo Turned Legs, 26 x 36 In. 248.00
Settle, G. Stickley, No. 22, Rope Frame, Even Arm, 39 x 76 x 29 In. 6600.00
Settle, G. Stickley, No. 171, 6 Legs, Through Tenon Construction, 27 x 78 x 33 In. . . . . . . *illus* 4800.00
Settle, G. Stickley, No. 291, Spindled Cube, Drop-In Seat, Marked, 31 x 78 x 30 In. . . . . . . *illus* 9600.00
Settle, L. & J.G. Stickley, 7 Vertical Slats, Leather Cushion, Arms, Marked, 36 x 72 x 26 In. . . . 2500.00
Settle, L. & J.G. Stickley, No. 232, 5 Back Slats, Black Leather Cushion, 72 x 28 In. 2160.00
Settle, L. & J.G. Stickley, No. 775, Paneled, Cushion, Marked, 40 x 84 x 32 In. 7400.00

Furniture, Settee, Cherry, Carved, Turned Supports, Stylized Flowers, Late 1800s, 35 x 43 In.
$830.00

Furniture, Settee, Chippendale Style, Mahogany, Upholstered, Ireland, 1800s, 42 x 67 x 22 In.
$2010.00

Furniture, Settee, Louis XVI Style, Verdigris Finish, Carved, Early 1900s, 32 x 32 x 31 In.
$365.00

Antimacassar
An antimacassar is a doily or cover put on the top of the upholstered back of a chair. It was used to keep hair oil used by men from staining the upholstery. Hair oil used in the nineteenth century was said to have been imported from Macassar in the East Indies.

Furniture, Settee, Meridienne, Upholstered, Knuckle Feet, 1820s, 49 ½ x 60 x 26 In.
$978.00

Furniture, Settee, Slats, Spindles, Leather Cushion, Brooks, 33 x 58 x 29 In.
$2620.00

Furniture, Settee, Wendel Castle, Molar, Fiberglass, Red High Gloss, Beylerian, 26 x 50 x 33 In.
$1800.00

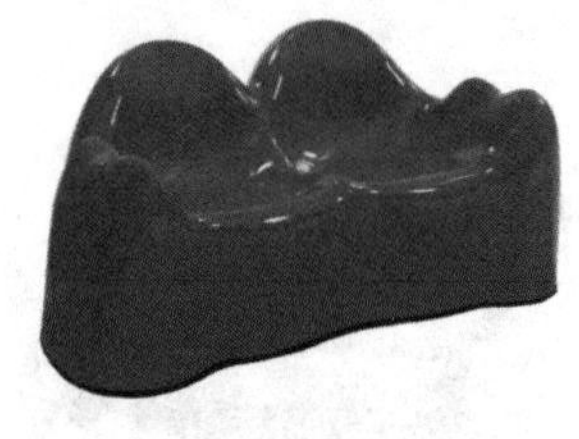

Furniture, Settle, G. Stickley, No. 171, 6 Legs, Through Tenon Construction, 27 x 78 x 33 In.
$4800.00

Furniture, Settle, G. Stickley, No. 291, Spindled Cube, Drop-In Seat, Marked, 31 x 78 x 30 In.
$9600.00

Settle, Oak, Molded Crest, Inset Panels, Cushioned Seat, Scrolled Arms, 1700s, 46 x 73 In. 1800.00
Settle, Pine, 10 Raised Panels, Lollipop Arms, Blue Paint, Late 1700s, 61 x 75 In. 32760.00
Settle, Pine, Scrolled Crest, Spindle Back, Paneled Seat, Late 18th Century, 39 x 69 In. 2808.00
Settle, Pine, Tongue & Groove Canted Backboards, Shaped Arms, 1800s, 53 x 60 In. 1410.00
Settle, Pine, Wing, Rosette Carved Crest, Lift Seat, Holds Oil Lamp, 49 x 50 In. 805.00
Settle, Stickley, No. 172, Leather Seat, Back, Signed, 54 x 21 In. 7800.00
Settle, Stickley Bros., Knock-Down Form, 3 Vertical Slat Arms, Pull Peg, 35 x 80 In. 1750.00
Settle, Wood, Green Paint, 19th Century, 58 x 49 In. 550.00
Shelf, Corner, Hanging, Mahogany, 7 Tiers, Scalloped Sides, Late 1700s, 42 ½ In. 5850.00
Shelf, Corner, Hanging, Pine, Rosehead Nails, Dovetailed, Shelves, Beaded Edges, 40 x 19 In.. 999.00
Shelf, Crock, 6 Shelves, Green Paint, Reed Trim, Diagonal Back Stretcher, 80 x 49 x 52 In.... 675.00
Shelf, Directoire, Metal, Bronzed, 3 Tiers, Tubular Legs, 32 x 25 x 12 ¾ In. 2400.00
Shelf, French Provincial, Fruitwood, Turned, Carved, Baluster Rail, 31 x 25 In. 1560.00
Shelf, George III, Mahogany, 4 Shelves, 2 Marquetry Drawers, 1790, 39 x 40 In. 1638.00
Shelf, Hanging, Black Forest, Wood, Deer, Antlers, 16 x 13 In. 460.00
Shelf, Hanging, Federal, Chinoiserie, Black Ground, Pastoral Scene, 20 x 21 In. 403.00
Shelf, Hanging, Figural, Head, Plaster, 20 x 16 x 15 In. 95.00
Shelf, Hanging, Gilt, Leaf Scroll Bracket, Carved Flowers, c.1730, 10 x 7 In., Pair 2000.00
Shelf, Hanging, Mahogany, Whale Tail, 4 Shelves, 19th Century 550.00
Shelf, Hanging, Pine, Scalloped Sides, Pierced Tulips, 1890s, 16 x 9 x 6 In. .... *illus* 2223.00
Shelf, Hanging, Triangular, 3 Shelves, Blue Paint, 19th Century, 26 x 29 ¾ In. 518.00
Shelf, Mahogany, Whale Tail, 19th Century, 33 x 28 In. 995.00
Shelf, Pine, 3-Sided, 3 Shelves, Scalloped Rim, Old Red & Green Paint, Early1800s, 34 In. 1638.00
Shelf, Pine, Painted, 3 Tiers, 1800s 1540.00
Shelf, Pine, Scalloped Sides, Plate Racks, 6 Pegs, Early 19th Century, 23 x 42 In. 4446.00
Shelf, Plate, Hanging, Softwood, Arch Cut Sides, Molded Strips, 36 ¾ x 31 x 9 In. 330.00
Sideboard, Arts & Crafts, Mirror, Phoenix Furniture Co., 65 x 60 x 24 In. .... *illus* 4100.00
Sideboard, Cherry, Charak Furniture Co., c.1942, 72 x 40 In. 1380.00
Sideboard, Cherry, Walnut, Stepped, Mirrored Backsplash, Drawers, Doors, 61 x 73 In. 4370.00
Sideboard, Chippendale, Mahogany, Carved, Cove Molding, Mass., c.1770, 30 x 48 In. 13750.00
Sideboard, Ebonized, Burl Inlay, Central Door, 43 x 65 x 19 In. 5175.00
Sideboard, Edwardian, Burr Walnut, Carved Roses, 1900s, 104 x 85 x 28 In. .... *illus* 1050.00
Sideboard, Edwardian, Fruitwood, Harewood, Inlaid, Crossbanded Mahogany, 37 x 72 In.... 4148.00
Sideboard, Edwardian, Hepplewhite Style, Mahogany, Inlaid, Brass Gallery, 55 x 59 In. 978.00
Sideboard, Edwardian, Mahogany, Banding, Fans, Center Drawer, 2 Cabinets, 48 x 60 In. 1035.00
Sideboard, Edwardian, Mahogany, Demilune, Drawer, 2 Doors, c.1900, 36 x 54 x 24 In. 2040.00
Sideboard, Empire, Bird's-Eye Maple, Walnut, Drawer, Doors, Backsplash, 52 x 42 x 22 In. .. 690.00
Sideboard, Empire, Mahogany, 3 Drawers, Claw Feet, c.1860, 48 x 56 x 22 ½ In. 450.00
Sideboard, Empire, Mahogany, Carved, Mirrored, Step Back, Drawers, Panel Doors, 63 x 71 In. 837.00
Sideboard, Federal, Cherry, 4 Drawers, Frieze, Tapered Legs, c.1790, 38 x 77 In. 7931.00
Sideboard, Federal, Cherry, Ivory Inlay, Drawers, Cellarettes, Boston, 43 x 61 In. 9560.00
Sideboard, Federal, Mahogany, Bird's-Eye Maple Inlay, Boston, c.1806, 42 x 68 In. 41475.00
Sideboard, Federal, Mahogany, Brass Gallery, Band Inlay, Bowed Drawers, 72 x 24 In. 1763.00
Sideboard, Federal, Mahogany, Crossbanded, Figured Veneers, c.1800, 54 x 71 x 25 In. 4406.00
Sideboard, Federal, Mahogany, Inlaid, 3 Drawers, Bowfront, 39 x 74 x 27 In. 3738.00
Sideboard, Federal, Mahogany, Inlaid, 4 Drawers, 2 Doors, Southern, c.1800, 40 x 69 In. 3680.00
Sideboard, Federal, Mahogany, Inlaid, 5 Drawers, 2 Doors, Reeded Legs, 42 x 56 x 24 In. 9375.00
Sideboard, Federal, Mahogany, Inlaid, Serpentine Front, c.1820, 40 x 66 x 22 In. 2750.00
Sideboard, Federal, Mahogany, Inlaid, Serpentine Top, Drawers, Bottle Drawers, 39 x 73 In. . 1315.00
Sideboard, Federal, Mahogany, Line Inlay, 5 Drawers, 4 Doors, Carved, Mass., c.1810, 39 x 66 In. 2370.00
Sideboard, Federal, Mahogany, Satinwood Flower Inlay, Figured, c.1800, 40 x 75 In. 15000.00
Sideboard, Federal, Mahogany, Serpentine Top, Bowfront Drawers, 1900s, 39 x 72 In. 1955.00
Sideboard, Federal, Mahogany, String Inlay, 2 Doors, 5 Drawers, c.1800, 40 x 64 In. 1175.00
Sideboard, Federal, Tiger Maple, Drawers, Doors, 1830s, 55 x 57 x 22 In. .... *illus* 4640.00
Sideboard, Federal, Walnut, Poplar, Inlaid, Drawer, 4 Doors, N.C., 40 x 70 x 23 In. 3600.00
Sideboard, Federal Style, Curly Maple, Pegged, Dovetailed, Panel Doors, 38 x 62 In. 1175.00
Sideboard, Federal Style, Mahogany, 2 Swelled Drawers, Bowfront, 37 x 61 x 24 In. 1076.00
Sideboard, Frank Lloyd Wright, Taliesin Design Edge, 66 x 36 In. 3360.00
Sideboard, French Provincial, Walnut, Shaped Front, 2 Drawers, Cabinet Doors, 41 x 53 In. . 2640.00
Sideboard, G. Nakashima, Walnut, Sliding Doors, Interior Shelves, 1970s, 32 x 60 In. 11875.00
Sideboard, G. Stickley, No. 816, Plate Rack, 45 x 48 x 18 In. 2280.00
Sideboard, G. Stickley, Oak, Plate Rail, 3 Drawers, Cabinet Doors, 1908, 46 x 49 In. 2844.00
Sideboard, George III, Hepplewhite Style, Walnut, Bowfront, Faux Front, 37 x 67 In. 2832.00
Sideboard, George III, Mahogany, 4 Doors, Stringing, Square Tapered Legs, 36 ½ x 65 In.... 660.00
Sideboard, George III, Mahogany, Bowfront, Line Inlay, 4 Drawers, 1780s, 36 x 72 In. 7605.00
Sideboard, George III, Mahogany, Inlaid, 2 Drawers, Cupboards, c.1790, 39 x 98 In. 10625.00
Sideboard, George III, Mahogany, Inlaid, Bowfront, Frieze Drawer, Doors, 35 x 57 x 28 In. .. 4444.00

Sideboard, George III, Mahogany, Inlaid, Drawers, Door, c.1800, 38 x 67 In. 1265.00
Sideboard, George III, Mahogany, Inlaid, Drawers, Doors, Inlaid Shells, 42 x 28 x 77 In. 2963.00
Sideboard, George III Style, Flatware Drawer, Tambour Drawer, 36 x 78 x 25 In. 1534.00
Sideboard, George III Style, Mahogany, 2 Drawers, 2 Doors, Henredon, c.1950, 38 x 72 In. 1075.00
Sideboard, George III Style, Mahogany, Bowfront, Flatware Drawer, 37 x 60 x 24 In. 3600.00
Sideboard, George III Style, Mahogany, Brass Back Piece, Drawers, 34 x 60 x 25 In. 5760.00
Sideboard, Georgian, Mahogany, Inlaid Yew Crossbanding, Drawers, Bellflowers, 36 x 72 In. 1020.00
Sideboard, Georgian Style, Mahogany, 2 Frieze Drawers, 36 x 60 In. 5625.00
Sideboard, H. Probber, Walnut Veneers, Cane, Drawers, Sliding Doors, Shelves, 32 x 78 In. 652.00
Sideboard, Hepplewhite, Burl, Rosewood, Serpentine Top, Drawers, 1900s, 36 x 72 In. 1955.00
Sideboard, Hepplewhite, Mahogany, Inlaid, 3 Drawers, 4 Doors, 42 x 71 x 22 In. 1400.00
Sideboard, Hepplewhite, Mahogany, Serpentine, Drawers, Doors, 39 x 58 In. 18213.00
Sideboard, Hepplewhite, Mahogany, Veneer Banding, 2 Cabinets, Early 1900s, 36 x 80 In. 2070.00
Sideboard, Hepplewhite, Pine, Poplar, 3 Drawers, Paneled Doors, 49 x 75 x 19 In. 3738.00
Sideboard, Hepplewhite, Walnut, Stringing, Bottle Drawer, Ga., c.1800, 38 x 71 In. 2875.00
Sideboard, L. & J.G. Stickley, 2 Doors, 2 Drawers, Strap Hinges, 46 x 60 x 22 In. 2640.00
Sideboard, L. & J.G. Stickley, No. 709, Plate Rail, 6 Drawers, 2 Doors, 48 x 54 x 22 In. 2400.00
Sideboard, L. & J.G. Stickley, No. 734, Plate Rack, Copper Pulls, 44 x 48 x 20 In. 1800.00
Sideboard, Louis XVI Style, Mahogany, Marble Top, Drawers, Paneled Doors, 43 x 59 In. 1800.00
Sideboard, Mahogany, 3 Drawers, Cabriole Legs, Pad Feet, England, 29 x 68 In. 2880.00
Sideboard, Mahogany, 5 Drawers, Lion & Ring Handles, Tapered Legs, Spade Feet, 33 x 46 In. 1680.00
Sideboard, Mahogany, Carved Columns, Drawers, Doors, Claw Feet, c.1830, 61 x 43 In. 708.00
Sideboard, Mahogany, Flower Inlay, Metal, White Furniture Co., 38 x 64 x 18 In. *illus* 720.00
Sideboard, Mahogany, Inlaid, Green Marble, Open Shelf, Reeded Feet, 1900s, 40 x 50 In. 2100.00
Sideboard, Mahogany, Marble, Drawers, Gothic Arch, Plinth Base, Ball Feet, c.1830, 40 x 60 In. 2644.00
Sideboard, Majorelle, Carved, Marble Top, Mirror, 2 Drawers, 2 Doors, Shelf, 48 x 63 In. 1800.00
Sideboard, Neoclassical, Cherry, Poplar, Center Drawer Opens To Desk, c.1835, 77 x 46 In. 764.00
Sideboard, Neoclassical, Mahogany, Figured, Pilaster Doors, Pedestal, c.1820, 59 x 71 In. 2300.00
Sideboard, Neoclassical, Mahogany, Galleried Top, Drawer, Panel Doors, c.1830, 59 x 63 In. 384.00
Sideboard, Neoclassical, Mahogany, Tiered Mirrored Backsplash, Arched Doors, 55 x 71 In. 1920.00
Sideboard, Oak, Carved Figures, Center Door, Curved Side Panels, Nut, Berry, 124 x 74 x 26 In. 3450.00
Sideboard, Oak, Carved Women, Cupid Riding Dolphin, Fruit, Nuts, c.1890, 104 x 66 In. 2070.00
Sideboard, Oak, Mirror, Shelf, 2 Doors, Drawer, Northern Furniture Co., c.1912, 56 x 48 In. 356.00
Sideboard, Oak, Red Paint, Ocher, Backsplash, Drawer, Doors, Bedford Co., 39 x 43 In. 2200.00
Sideboard, Parzinger, Lacquer, Milk Glass Inserts, 4 Drawers, 28 x 68 x 16 In. 9000.00
Sideboard, Parzinger, Rectangular, 4 Doors, Ring Pulls, Charak Modern, 32 x 65 In. 6600.00
Sideboard, Regency, Mahogany, Inlaid, 3 Drawers Over Doors, 36 x 42 ½ x 27 In. 2875.00
Sideboard, Regency, Mahogany, Serpentine Case, Brass Top, Drawer, 1900s, 51 x 77 In. 2151.00
Sideboard, Regency, Mahogany, String Inlay, 3 Drawers, Cutout Lower Shelf, 34 x 48 In. 705.00
Sideboard, Robsjohn-Gibbings, Walnut, 3 Flat Doors, Widdicomb, 70 x 31 In. 660.00
Sideboard, Roycroft, Leaded Glass, Carved Orb & Cross Mark, 45 ½ x 42 In. *illus* 13200.00
Sideboard, Roycroft, Plate Rack, Leaded Glass, Carved Orb, 45 x 42 In. 13200.00
Sideboard, Sheraton, Mahogany, Bowfront, Ribbon Inlay, Bellflower, c.1840, 36 x 79 In. 5200.00
Sideboard, Sheraton, Mahogany, Inlaid, Drawer, 2 Doors, Spade Feet, c.1860, 37 x 59 In. 4200.00
Sideboard, Sheraton, Mahogany, String Inlay, Brass Mounted, Banded, 60 x 59 In. 1200.00
Sideboard, Sheraton, Walnut, 7 Drawers, Dovetailed, c.1870, 44 x 44 x 21 In. 1725.00
Sideboard, Victorian, Mahogany, Walnut, Pedestal, Drawers, Mirror, 90 ½ x 84 x 28 In. 575.00
Sideboard, Walnut, Burl, Feather Inlay, 4 Drawers, England, 34 ½ x 59 x 20 In. 350.00
Sideboard, Walnut, Carved, Atlas, Cherubs, Griffins, c.1880, 94 x 88 x 23 ½ In. 9775.00
Sideboard, Walnut, Carved, Lion's Head Door, Fruit, Mirror, c.1880, 113 x 79 x 25 In. 5175.00
Sideboard, Walnut, Frosted Glass Doors, Mirrored, N.C., 1880s, 70 ½ x 22 ½ In. 1995.00
Sideboard, Walnut, Sunflower & Leaf Frieze, Leaf Carved Columns, Marble, c.1880, 94 x 60 In. 2115.00
Sideboard, Warren Hile Studios, Arts & Crafts, Oak, Through Tenon, 46 ½ x 60 x 21 In. 1400.00
Sofa, Art Deco, Banquet Shape, Trapezoid Arm, Back, Ebonized Feet, 32 x 86 In. 189.00
Sofa, Art Deco, Painted Wood, Upholstered, Black, Silver Lines, Oval Base, 82 In. 889.00
Sofa, Borge Mogensen, No. 2252, Beech, Upholstered, Leather Straps, 39 x 55 In. *illus* 1050.00
Sofa, Celadon Crushed Velvet, Brass Feet, Dunbar, 28 x 108 x 31 In. 2760.00
Sofa, Chesterfield, Edwardian, Mahogany, Tufted Leather, c.1900, 29 x 86 x 38 In. 6300.00
Sofa, Chesterfield, Nailed Leather, Button Tufted, Seat, Rollover Back, 28 x 84 In. 1195.00
Sofa, Chippendale, Crest, Rolled Arms, Mahogany Legs, 1790s, 40 x 97 x 24 In. *illus* 14200.00
Sofa, Chippendale, Large Crest, Rolled Arms, Mahogany Legs, New York, 40 x 97 In. 1380.00
Sofa, Chippendale, Mahogany, Camelback, Carved Arms, Legs, Upholstered, c.1890, 36 x 83 In. 3680.00
Sofa, Chippendale, Mahogany, Serpentine Back, Rolled Arms, Scrolled Feet, 1800s, 37 x 78 In. 1093.00
Sofa, Chippendale, Serpentine Back, Outscrolled Arms, Brocade, Kittinger, 82 In. 3055.00
Sofa, Chippendale Style, Camelback, Block Legs, Plaid Upholstery, Late 1900s, 72 x 36 In. 118.00
Sofa, Chippendale Style, Camelback, Padded Crest, Stretcher Base, 35 x 75 In., Pair 1180.00
Sofa, Chippendale Style, Camelback, Silk Upholstery, 90 x 34 In. 235.00

Furniture, Shelf, Hanging, Pine, Scalloped Sides, Pierced Tulips, 1890s, 16 x 9 x 6 In.
$2223.00

Furniture, Sideboard, Arts & Crafts, Mirror, Phoenix Furniture Co., 65 x 60 x 24 In.
$4100.00

Furniture, Sideboard, Edwardian, Burr Walnut, Carved Roses, 1900s, 104 x 85 x 28 In.
$1050.00

Furniture, Sideboard, Federal, Tiger Maple, Drawers, Doors, 1830s, 55 x 57 x 22 In.
$4640.00

F

Furniture, Sideboard, Mahogany, Flower Inlay, Metal, White Furniture Co., 38 x 64 x 18 In.
$720.00

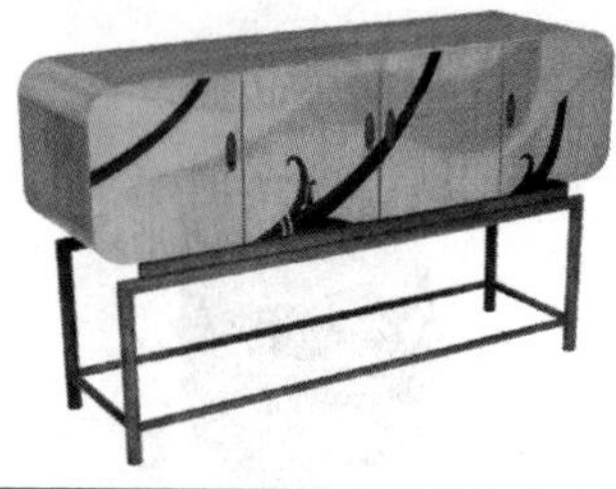

Furniture, Sideboard, Roycroft, Leaded Glass, Carved Orb & Cross Mark, 45 ½ x 42 In.
$13200.00

Furniture, Sofa, Borge Mogensen, No. 2252, Beech, Upholstered, Leather Straps, 39 x 55 In.
$1050.00

Furniture, Sofa, Chippendale, Crest, Rolled Arms, Mahogany Legs, 1790s, 40 x 97 x 24 In.
$14200.00

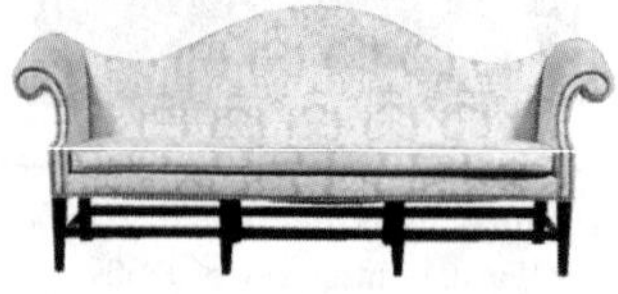

Furniture, Sofa, Frank Lloyd Wright, Taliesin Design, 2 Sections, 30 x 63 x 32 In.
$2520.00

Sofa, Contemporary, Box Shape, Upholstered Rail, Late 20th Century, 30 x 67 In., Pair...... 767.00
Sofa, Duncan Phyfe, Mahogany, Carved, N.Y., 1792-1815, 77 ½ In....................... 30810.00
Sofa, Duncan Phyfe, Mahogany, Scrolled Crest Rail, Bowknot Panels, 35 x 84 In........... 1180.00
Sofa, Dutch Neoclassical, Rosewood, Marquetry, Scrolling Crest, Arms, c.1840, 37 x 99 In.... 1315.00
Sofa, Eames, Slab Seat, Folding Back, Orange Vinyl Upholstery, Herman Miller, c.1962, 72 x 34 In. 960.00
Sofa, Edwardian, Chesterfield, Mahogany, Leather Upholstery, Tufted, 28 x 82 x 36 In....... 2880.00
Sofa, Empire, Mahogany, Carved, Cornucopia, Upholstered, Claw Feet, 1825, 37 x 88 In. 940.00
Sofa, Empire Style, Flame Mahogany, Acanthus Carved, 19 x 93 x 23 In. 1200.00
Sofa, Federal, Mahogany, Scrolled Arms, Upholstered, Reeded Feet, c.1815, 36 x 78 In....... 2574.00
Sofa, Federal, Reeded, Arched Crest, Curved Arms, Tapered Legs, Early 1800s, 38 x 79 In..... 9200.00
Sofa, Federal, Reeded Arms & Leg Supports, Damask Upholstery, 19th Century, 79 In........ 6440.00
Sofa, Federal Style, Camelback, Padded, Upholstered, Outscrolled Arms, 36 x 81 x 31 In. 531.00
Sofa, Federal Style, Mahogany, Upholstery Tack Frame, Fluted Tapered Legs, 34 x 78 In...... 900.00
Sofa, Frank Lloyd Wright, 4 Sections, Upholstered Cushions, Henredon, 31 x 153 In......... 2400.00
Sofa, Frank Lloyd Wright, Taliesin Design, 2 Sections, 30 x 63 x 32 In................ *illus* 2520.00
Sofa, Frank Lloyd Wright, Taliesin Edge, Upholstered, Paper Label, 96 x 27 In.............. 4200.00
Sofa, George III, Gilt, Arched Back, Silk Upholstery, c.1785, 72 In....................... 17500.00
Sofa, George III, Mahogany, Fluted & Leaf Carved Arms, Silk Upholstered Back, 38 x 75 In... 748.00
Sofa, George III, Mahogany, Padded, Domed Back, Leaf Carved, Ireland, 36 x 88 In......... 1920.00
Sofa, George III Style, Mahogany, Green Striped Silk Upholstery, Fluted Legs, 77 In. 3750.00
Sofa, Georgian, Camelback, Tufted Leather Upholstery, Marlboro Legs, 86 In. 1126.00
Sofa, Hand Shape, 8-Finger Backrest, Red Velour Upholstery, Plastic Feet, 75 x 39 In........ 1200.00
Sofa, Hardwoods, Slope Back, Carvings, Gold Upholstery, c.1830, 50 x 60 In. 978.00
Sofa, Hepplewhite, Upholstered Back, Arms, Seat, Tapered Fluted Legs, 63 In............... 720.00
Sofa, Jelliff, Burl Walnut, Velour, Bronze Medallion, Victorian, 44 x 78 In. 550.00
Sofa, Knoll, Armless, Steel Frame, 3 Cushions, Orange, Blue Upholstery, 31 x 84 In. 960.00
Sofa, Knoll, No. 53, Parallel Bar, Upholstered, c.1960, 86 In. 1300.00
Sofa, Le Corbusier, LC 3, Tan, Leather Cushions, Steel Frame, 1980s, 67 x 23 In. 1560.00
Sofa, Louis XV, Parcel Gilt, Fortuny Fabric, Serpentine Back, 20 ½ x 53 In................ 770.00
Sofa, Louis XV Style, Beech, Cream Paint, Domed, Padded Back, 36 x 83 x 32 In............ 9600.00
Sofa, Louis XV Style, Fruitwood, Red & White Striped Upholstery, 33 x 51 In. 826.00
Sofa, Louis XVI Style, Gilt, Carved, Cushions, Padded, 32 x 66 ½ x 31 In. 1920.00
Sofa, Louis XVI Style, Gilt, Ribbon & Vine, Flower Crest, Padded Arms, 42 x 37 In........... 6169.00
Sofa, Louis XVI Style, Gilt, Upholstered, Fluted Legs, Bulb Feet, 38 x 66 x 11 In............ 500.00
Sofa, Mahogany, Carved, Scroll Arms, Back, Feet, Red Silk Upholstery, c.1830, 32 x 93 In..... 649.00
Sofa, Mahogany, Carved Scrolls, Crests, Legs, Rolled Arms, Boston, c.1825, 33 x 76 In. 1495.00
Sofa, Mahogany, Crest Rail, Outswept Arms, Melon Feet, Bolster Base, c.1825, 38 x 94 In..... 8519.00
Sofa, Mahogany, Scrolled Ends, Leaf Arved Arms, Rosettes, Cornucopia Legs, 81 In.......... 1875.00
Sofa, Mahogany, Slope Back, 1 Arm, Pink Striped Upholstery, c.1870, 35 x 73 x 26 In., Pair .. 1840.00
Sofa, Mahogany, Upholstered Seat, 3 Back Cushions, Square, 39 x 85 x 26 In............. 6875.00
Sofa, Neoclassical, Mahogany, Barrel Crest Rail, Scroll Arms, Silk Upholstery, 35 x 89 In..... 2588.00
Sofa, Neoclassical, Mahogany, Eagle Heads, Cornucopia Arms, Seat Rail, c.1800, 36 x 81 In. . 3819.00
Sofa, Neoclassical, Mahogany, Horsehair Upholstery, Curved Scrolled Back, 89 x 39 In. 1725.00
Sofa, Neoclassical, Mahogany, Rolled Crest, Outscrolled Arms, Paw Feet, Upholstered, 80 In. . 851.00
Sofa, Neoclassical, Mahogany, Scroll Arms, 1 Cushion, Damask Upholstery, c.1810, 74 In.... 528.00
Sofa, Neoclassical, Mahogany, Scroll Crest Rail, Boston, 1825, 33 x 76 x 24 In. .... *illus* 1430.00
Sofa, Neoclassical, Mahogany, Upholstered, Box Shape, c.1825, 36 x 75 In. 767.00
Sofa, Neogrecque, Mahogany, Scrolled Crest Rail, Bolster, c.1832, 32 x 83 In.............. 18213.00
Sofa, Oak, Carved, Bookcase Sides, Acanthus, Upholstered, 1880, 63 x 98 x 37 In........... 8800.00
Sofa, Oak, Walnut, Silk Upholstery, Paris, c.1930, 31 x 62 In........................... 6250.00
Sofa, Overstuffed, Scrolled Arm, Yellow Chinoiserie Damask Upholstery, 42 x 88 In. 1793.00
Sofa, P. Piva, Alanda, Leather Upholstery, Adjustable Arms, Back, B & B Italia, 83 x 31 In.... 3000.00
Sofa, Pottier & Stymus, Walnut, Tufted, Inlaid Crest Rail, c.1880, 43 x 74 x 32 In.......... 480.00
Sofa, Reeded Edge, Spade Feet, Wood Frame, Floral Brocade Upholstery, 1800s 805.00
Sofa, Regency, Mahogany, Bronze Mounted, Scrolled Back & Arms, c.1820, 66 In........... 1880.00
Sofa, Regency, Mahogany, Gadrooned Tablet Crest, Scrolled Arms, Early 1800s, 36 x 94 In. .. 1175.00
Sofa, Renaissance Revival, Molded, Horsehair Upholstery, Chairback, c.1870, 44 x 71 In..... 738.00
Sofa, Renaissance Revival, Walnut, Crowned Women, Triple Back, Turned Legs, c.1860, 42 x 76 In. 2585.00
Sofa, Restauration, Fruitwood, Domed, Cushioned, Upholstered, 35 x 78 x 26 In. 3360.00
Sofa, Risom, Walnut, Tan Upholstery, 3 Cushions, 30 x 62 In. 900.00
Sofa, Risom, Walnut Frame, Tan Upholstery, 33 x 80 In................................ 1680.00
Sofa, Rococo, Rosewood, Laminated, Charles Boudoin, c.1860............................ 7475.00
Sofa, Sheraton, Mahogany, Barrel Turned Crest, Carved, Early 1900s, 33 x 84 In. 575.00
Sofa, Sheraton, Mahogany, Black Silk Upholstery, Turned Legs, 34 ½ x 71 ½ x 26 In. 780.00
Sofa, Sheraton, Mahogany, Inlaid, Padded Back, Curved Arms, Upholstered Seat, 72 In...... 2875.00
Sofa, V. Kagen, Free-Form, Green Upholstery, 2 Platform Bases, Lucite Legs, 94 x 29 In. 4800.00
Sofa, Victorian, Mahogany, Carved Crest, Scalloped, c.1850, 74 x 36 In. 649.00

Sofa, Victorian, Mahogany, Molded Crest, Velvet Upholstery, 1800s, 30 x 81 In. 173.00
Sofa, Victorian, Walnut, Serpentine Scrolled Crest Rail, Downswept Arms, c.1860, 52 In. 230.00
Sofa, William & Mary, Gilt, Velvet Upholstery, Scrolled Arms, Early 1700s, 78 In. 2370.00
Sofa, Wormley, Beige Upholstery, 6 Loose Cushions, 6 Metal Legs, 108 x 27 In. 5400.00
Sofa, Wormley, Mahogany, 7 Tufted Cushions, Signed, Dunbar, 28 ½ x 90 In. 2760.00
Stand, Bent Twig, Heart Shape, Wooden Top, Painted, c.1915, 22 x 15 x 24 In. 176.00
Stand, Birch, Red Wash, Pillar Stem, Octagonal, 3 Legs, New Hampshire, c.1815, 30 In. 1422.00
Stand, Bradley & Hubbard, Brass, Enamel Top, Cylinder, Splayed Legs, c.1870, 34 x 14 In. ... 3600.00
Stand, Carved, Pierced, 5-Sided Top, Rose Marble Insert, Chinese, c.1900, 35 ½ In. 323.00
Stand, Cherry, Curly Maple, 2 Drawers, Turned Legs, c.1820, 29 x 22 In. 441.00
Stand, Cherry, Curly Maple, Poplar, Turned Legs, 2 Over 3 Drawers, 28 x 26 x 18 In. 1998.00
Stand, Cherry, Curly Maple, Scratch-Beaded Drawer, c.1820, 28 x 22 In. 840.00
Stand, Cherry, Dovetailed Drawer, Spiral Twist Legs, Drawer, Compass Star, c.1840, 30 x 24 In. 900.00
Stand, Cherry, Dovetailed Skirt Drawer, Tapered Legs, 24 x 17 In. 248.00
Stand, Cherry, Inlaid Lightwood Stringing, 3 Drawers, Woodford County, 29 x 21 ½ In. 6000.00
Stand, Cherry, Line, Dot Inlaid Top, Drawer, Chestnut Vines Flowers, 1800s, 25 x 15 In. 1035.00
Stand, Cherry, Poplar, Dovetailed, Beveled Front, Drawer, Turned Legs, 1800s, 29 x 20 In. 489.00
Stand, Cherry, Poplar, Single Drawer, Scalloped Top, Blue Glass Knob, c.1835, 27 x 22 In. ... 470.00
Stand, Chippendale, Tiger Maple, Pine, Pullout Candle Slide, Drawer, 27 x 30 x 19 In. 920.00
Stand, Corner, Gothic Revival, Oak, Pierced & Carved Apron, 1750, 27 x 15 In. 570.00
Stand, Corner, Pine, Maple, Drawer, Tapered Legs, Bulb Feet, 41 ¾ x 17 x 15 In. 130.00
Stand, Curly Bird's-Eye Maple, Poplar, Sandwich Glass Knobs, Drawers, c.1830, 31 x 21 In. .. 999.00
Stand, Curly Maple, Cock-Beaded Top, Canted Apron, Dovetailed Drawer, 26 x 18 x 17 In. ... 1645.00
Stand, Curly Maple, Mahogany Banding, 2 Drawers, Turned Legs, c.1824, 29 x 22 In. 2820.00
Stand, Curly Maple, Poplar, Board Top, Drawer, Half Round Feet, 20 x 18 x 30 In. 940.00
Stand, Drop Leaf, Federal, Tiger Maple, Drawer, 19th Century, 29 x 18 In. 300.00
Stand, Drop Leaf, Walnut, Bird's-Eye Maple, Poplar, Drawer, c.1845, 29 x 17 In. 374.00
Stand, Drop Leaf, Walnut, Butterfly Supports, Drawer, Turned Legs, 25 x 34 In. .... *illus* 450.00
Stand, Empire, Flame Mahogany, 2 Drawers, Wheels, 19th Century, 31 x 22 x 17 In. 425.00
Stand, Federal, Birch, Pine, Single-Board Top, Dovetailed Drawer, New England, c.1825, 28 In. 205.00
Stand, Federal, Cherry, Drawers, Turned Legs, Tenn., 19th Century, 29 x 25 In. 489.00
Stand, Federal, Mahogany, Drawer, Dovetailed, Tapered Square Legs, 1800s, 30 x 17 In. 805.00
Stand, Federal, Mahogany, Drawer, Early 19th Century, 29 x 18 ½ x 16 In. 497.00
Stand, Federal, Rosewood, 2 Drawers, Reeded Legs, Early 19th Century, 30 x 20 x 17 In. 300.00
Stand, Fern, Aesthetic Revival, Brass, Onyx Top, Glazed Shelf, Paw Feet, 34 ½ x 23 In. 1410.00
Stand, Fern, Brass, 3 Shelves, Marble Inserts, 44 In. 500.00
Stand, Fern, Eastlake, Walnut, Marble Top, Tree Shape, Tripod, Victorian, 30 x 17 ½ In. 495.00
Stand, Fern, Limbert, Oak, Ebonized, Square Top, Signed, 30 x 11 ¾ In. 3600.00
Stand, Fern, Louis XVI, Gilt, Onyx, Leaf Border, Paw Feet, 1800s, 41 ½ x 14 In. 2937.00
Stand, Fern, Mahogany, Reeded Column, 34 x 12 ½ In. 45.00
Stand, Fern, Napoleon III, Egyptian Revival, Ebonized, Bronze, Sphinxes, 35 x 11 In., Pair .. 470.00
Stand, Fern, Rococo Style, Mahogany, Marble Top, 19 x 14 x 14 In., Pair 106.00
Stand, Fern, Victorian, Walnut, Carved, Square Top, Tripod Base, 29 x 12 x 16 In. 130.00
Stand, Fern, Victorian, Walnut, Elk Heads, 32 ½ x 13 In. 224.00
Stand, Fern, Victorian, Walnut, Figural Mountain Goat, 31 x 12 In. .... *illus* 413.00
Stand, Fern, Victorian, Walnut, Marble Top, Scalloped Legs, 30 x 15 x 15 In. 142.00
Stand, Fern, Victorian, Walnut, Scrolled Legs, Octagonal Marble Top, 29 x 15 x 15 In. 130.00
Stand, Fern, Wood, Carved, Lion's Head Serpent On Pedestal, Chinese, c.1910, 15 x 37 In. 382.00
Stand, Folio, Aesthetic Revival, Burl Walnut Panels, 46 x 24 In. 2749.00
Stand, Folio, Hardwood, Carved Flowers, Carved Shoe Feet, 29 x 24 ½ x 27 In. 1997.00
Stand, Folio, Renaissance Revival, Walnut, Gilt Incised, Hinged, Trestle Base, c.1850, 38 x 26 In. 1645.00
Stand, Folio, Victorian, Mahogany, Burl, Adjustable, Carved Figure, c.1870, 44 x 32 In. 2695.00
Stand, Frank Lloyd Wright, Iron, Warren MacArthur, Biltmore Hotel, Arizona, c.1928, 26 x 7 ½ In. 4800.00
Stand, Galle, Marquetry, Frog Sitting On Leaves, Playing Stringed Instrument, 13 x 42 In. 3450.00
Stand, Galle, Oak, Inlaid Chestnut Leaves, Signed, 45 x 17 ½ In. .... *illus* 4800.00
Stand, Georgian, Mahogany, Inlaid, Dish Top, Cabriole Legs, 62 x 19 In. 460.00
Stand, Gilt, Carved, Incised, Victorian, Marble, 32 In. 2090.00
Stand, Gospel, Bronze, Enamel Medallions, St. Joseph, Mary, Agnus Dei, Gilt, France, 1899s, 11 In. 767.00
Stand, Hepplewhite, Bead-Molded Drawer, Square Tapered Legs, Green Paint, 29 x 20 In. 323.00
Stand, Hepplewhite, Birch, Pine, Drawers, X-Stretcher, Early 19th Century, 28 x 15 In. 431.00
Stand, Hepplewhite, Curly Maple, Overhanging Top, Drawer, 1800s, 28 x 18 In. 1175.00
Stand, Hepplewhite, Curly Maple, Poplar, Drawer, c.1800, 25 x 21 x 17 In. 940.00
Stand, Hepplewhite, Mahogany, 2 Drawers, Tapered Legs, 29 x 17 x 15 ½ In. 250.00
Stand, Hepplewhite, Mixed Wood, Drawer, Tapered Legs, c.1800, 28 x 27 x 21 In. 441.00
Stand, Hepplewhite, Pine, Carved Yoke, Molded Stiles, Spanish Feet, 41 In. 235.00
Stand, Hepplewhite, Pine, Drawer, Square Top, Applied Molded Edge, 29 x 15 In. 115.00
Stand, Hepplewhite, Pine, Drawer, Tapered Legs, Bead Molded Apron, Red Paint, 28 x 21 In. .. 999.00

Furniture, Sofa, Neoclassical, Mahogany, Scroll Crest Rail, Boston, 1825, 33 x 76 x 24 In.
$1430.00

Furniture, Stand, Drop Leaf, Walnut, Butterfly Supports, Drawer, Turned Legs, 25 x 34 In.
$450.00

Furniture, Stand, Fern, Victorian, Walnut, Figural Mountain Goat, 31 x 12 In.
$413.00

Furniture, Stand, Galle, Oak, Inlaid Chestnut Leaves, Signed, 45 x 17 ½ In.
$4800.00

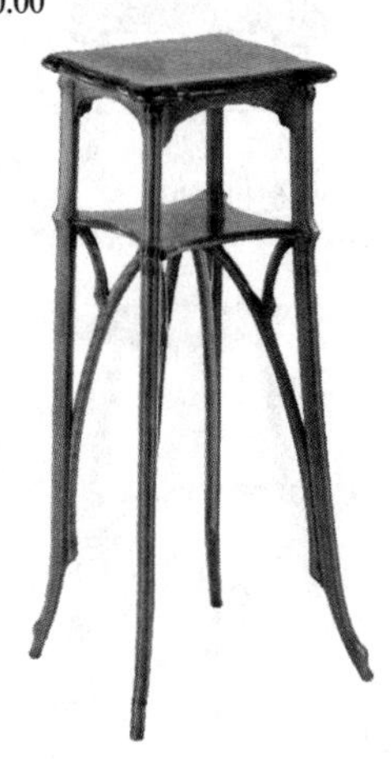

Furniture, Stand, Music, Mahogany, Lyre, 3 Shelves, Early 1900s, 36 x 22 x 13 ½ In.
$350.00

Furniture, Stand, Telephone, Gray Laminate, Steel, Enamel, E. Noyes, 1957, 22 ½ x 13 In.
$385.00

Furniture, Stand, Victorian, Walnut, Mahogany, Marble Top, Drawer, Door, 32 x 20 In.
$325.00

Furniture, Stool, Esherick, Walnut Seat, Ash Legs, 1966, 19 ½ In.
$5500.00

F

Stand, Hepplewhite, Pine, Maple, Square Tapered Legs, Red Paint, 28 ½ x 17 In. 294.00
Stand, Hepplewhite, Pine, Single-Board Top, Gallery Edge, Dovetailed Drawer, Painted, 28 In. 470.00
Stand, Kettle, Chinese Chippendale, Mahogany, Pierced Gallery, Apron, Stretchers, 13 x 13 In. 558.00
Stand, Kettle, Queen Anne, Fruitwood, Walnut, Dish Top, Late 1700s, 22 ½ x 15 In. 460.00
Stand, Lacquer, Red, Rectangular, Flowers, 19 ¾ In. 1554.00
Stand, Louis XV, Kidney Shape Marble Top, Bronze Mounts, Drawer, 29 x 20 x 12 In. 425.00
Stand, Louis XV, Mahogany, Gilt Metal, Porcelain Mounted, Drawer, Late 1800s, 38 x 16 In... 337.00
Stand, Louis XV Style, Walnut, Marble Top, Drawers, c.1900, 29 x 12 In. Square, Pair 840.00
Stand, Louis XVI, Faux Drawers, Carved Wreath, 1700s, 34 x 17 In., Pair 2596.00
Stand, Magazine, Arts & Crafts, Cherry, 5 Shelves, Ornate Iron Sides, 31 x 17 In. 1020.00
Stand, Magazine, G. Stickley, No. 54, Panels, 3 Shelves, Beveled Top, 35 x 15 In. 3360.00
Stand, Magazine, G. Stickley, No. 79, 4 Shelves, D-Cutouts, Arched Base, 40 x 14 x 10 In. 2530.00
Stand, Magazine, Goatskin Shelf Over Wood, Metal Frame, 2 Handles, Singer, 19 x 29 In. 420.00
Stand, Magazine, L. & J.G. Stickley, No. 45, Curved Apron, 4 Shelves, 45 ½ x 21 x 12 In. 2000.00
Stand, Magazine, L. & J.G. Stickley, No. 346, Ash, 4 Shelves, 4 Vertical Slats, 42 x 20 In. 1090.00
Stand, Magazine, L. & J.G. Stickley, No. 464, Wood, Shelves, Slats, 21 x 42 In. 1320.00
Stand, Magazine, Stickley Bros., No. 4604, Heart Cutout, 5 Shelves, 44 ½ x 14 x 13 In. 1920.00
Stand, Magazine, Stickley Bros., No. 4702, 3 Shelves, Vertical Spindles, 32 x 27 x 12 In. 8400.00
Stand, Mahogany, Brass Mounts, 3 Drawers, Oval, c.1900, 28 x 16 ¾ x 12 ½ In. 431.00
Stand, Mahogany, Carved, Iron, Inset Marble, 3-Part Pedestal, c.1900s, 36 In. 269.00
Stand, Mahogany, Feathered, Shell & Leaf Carving, 2 Tiers, 34 x 25 In. 180.00
Stand, Mahogany, Ormolu Design, Marble Top, Early 20th Century, 22 ½ x 16 In. 644.00
Stand, Maple, Pine, Drawer, Square Legs, Black Graining, Square Nails, 28 x 14 In. 2115.00
Stand, Mixed Woods, Bird's-Eye Maple Drawer, Brass Knob, 28 ½ x 19 x 15 ½ In. 441.00
Stand, Mixed Woods, Chalky Blue Paint, Peg, Nailed, Bead Drawer, 32 x 18 x 29 In. 558.00
Stand, Music, Brass, Eagle Lectern, Stamped, R. Geissler, Late 19th Century, 57 In. 1287.00
Stand, Music, Iron, Brass, c.1900, 24 x 16 In. 176.00
Stand, Music, Mahogany, Lyre, 3 Shelves, Early 1900s, 36 x 22 x 13 ½ In. .... *illus* 350.00
Stand, Music, Maple, Doors, Drawer, Brass Floral Pulls, Cabriole Legs, 34 In. 330.00
Stand, Music, Queen Anne, Mahogany, Turned Standard, Pad Feet, Late 1700s, 42 ½ In. 1170.00
Stand, Music, Rosewood, Bas Relief, Carved, Turned Stiles, 1800s, 54 x 27 x 14 In. 4700.00
Stand, Music, Rosewood, Gilt, Pierced, Stencil Painted, c.1890, 35 x 22 In. 231.00
Stand, Neoclassical, Mahogany, Veneer, 3 Drawers, Adjustable Writing Surface, 31 x 24 In... 206.00
Stand, Nutting, No. 653, Oak, Splayed Legs 550.00
Stand, Oak, Parquet, Marble Top, Drawer, Door, Shelf, 1900, 44 ½ x 16 x 16 In. 110.00
Stand, Pine, Black On Red Grain, Green, Yellow Stripes, Board Top, 29 x 19 x 15 In. 588.00
Stand, Pine, Butternut, Mahogany, Bird's-Eye Maple, Drawers, Glass Pulls, 29 x 22 x 17 In... 4113.00
Stand, Pine, Decorated, Square Top, Black Over Yellow Smoke, Tapered Legs, 30 x 16 In. 382.00
Stand, Pine, Drawer, Cut Nail, Dovetailed, Tapered Legs, North Carolina, 27 x 27 In. 715.00
Stand, Pine, Drawer, Grain Paint, Pa., c.1830, 29 x 21 ¾ In. 819.00
Stand, Pine, Mixed Wood, Drawer, Black On Red Graining, Stripes, 1800s, 28 x 20 In. 353.00
Stand, Pine, Single Board Top, Gray Paint, Turned Legs, Vase Feet, Late 1800s, 18 x 18 In. ... 460.00
Stand, Plant, Arts & Crafts, Knights On Horseback, California Art Tiles, 28 ¾ In. 403.00
Stand, Plant, Brass, 3 Satyrs Supporting Round Top, Faux Marble Wood Base, 20 x 12 In. ... 780.00
Stand, Plant, Cast Iron, Brass Openwork Basket, Tapered Shaft, Rings, Gilt, Mark, 60 In. 518.00
Stand, Plant, G. Stickley, No. 11, Tile Top, c.1901, 23 ½ x 15 In. 2760.00
Stand, Plant, G. Stickley, No. 44, Cloud-Lift Aprons, c.1901, 30 x 12 ¾ In. 1440.00
Stand, Plant, G. Stickley, No. 48, Chestnut Top, Cloud-Lift Aprons, c.1902, 26 x 13 In. 2400.00
Stand, Plant, Half Round, 3 Tiers, Green Paint, Stepped, 37 In. 170.00
Stand, Plant, Iron, Forged, 3 Branches, 43 x 23 ½ In. 375.00
Stand, Plant, Louis XV, Walnut, Carved Apron, Cabriole Legs, c.1890, 39 x 14 In. 300.00
Stand, Plant, Rosewood, Marble Top, Pierced Neck, Frieze, Prunus Branches, 27 In. 360.00
Stand, Plant, Stickley Bros., No. 135, Square Top, Notched Apron, Stretcher, 34 x 14 In. 720.00
Stand, Plant, Victorian, Bone Inlay, 4 Swing-Out Pot Ledges, Middle Shelf, 27 x 20 In. 179.00
Stand, Plant, Victorian, Wirework, 3 Tiers, 36 x 39 x 25 In. 50.00
Stand, Plant, Walnut, Carved, Winged Griffin, Tripod Base, c.1880, 44 ½ x 20 In. 880.00
Stand, Plant, Wirework, 2 Semicircular Tiers, 2 Smaller Tiers, Painted, c.1900, 40 x 62 In. .. 206.00
Stand, Plant, Wirework, 3 Tiers, Oval Troughs, Geometric Designs, 44 In. 590.00
Stand, Plant, Wood, Brass Hoops, Slatted Bucket, 3 Leg Base, Woodcraft, 27 x 12 ½ In. 120.00
Stand, Plant, Wood, Carved, Marble, Chinese, 15 x 14 In. 234.00
Stand, Poplar, Dovetailed Drawer, Turned Legs, Ball & Spike Feet, Tenn., c.1820, 30 x 27 In. . 618.00
Stand, Poplar, Green Over Red Paint, Drawer, Turned Legs, c.1840 .... 881.00
Stand, Renaissance Revival, Bronze, 3 Winged Griffin, Leaves, A. Hoehn, 9 ⅛ In. 178.00
Stand, Renaissance Revival, Ebonized, Gilt, Marquetry, 1870, 42 x 38 x 12 In. 1840.00
Stand, Rococo Revival, Walnut, Marble Top, Scrolled Legs, 29 ½ x 15 In. 266.00
Stand, Rosewood, Carved, Marble Top, Cabriole Legs, Scrolling Vines, Chinese, 19 In. 201.00
Stand, Rosewood, Red Marble, Round Top, Openwork Apron, Chinese, 36 x 12 In. 1534.00

Stand, Shaker, Maple, Arched Tripod, Mt. Lebanon, c.1830, 24 x 14 In. 9480.00
Stand, Shaving, Arts & Crafts, Mirror Back, Single Drawer, 63 ½ x 19 In. 900.00
Stand, Shaving, Federal, Mahogany, Oval, Cyma Curved Arms, c.1810, 17 x 8 In. 403.00
Stand, Shaving, Georgian, Mahogany, 30 x 15 ¾ x 26 ½ In. 207.00
Stand, Shaving, Hepplewhite, Cherry, Mahogany Inlay, Drawer, Mirror, 21 x 19 In. 154.00
Stand, Shaving, Oak, Mirror, Drawer, 64 In. 354.00
Stand, Shaving, Rosewood, Mirror, Oval, Pierced Crest, Marble, Drawer, c.1850 1920.00
Stand, Shaving, Sheraton, Mahogany, String Inlaid Posts, Urn Finials, Drawers, 21 x 19 In. 418.00
Stand, Sheraton, Bird's-Eye & Tiger Maple, 2 Drawers, Tray Top, c.1830, 22 x 22 In. 4313.00
Stand, Sheraton, Bird's-Eye Maple, Cherry Top, Drawer, c.1820, 26 x 18 In. 546.00
Stand, Sheraton, Bird's-Eye Maple, Drawer, Spiral Twist Legs, 27 ½ x 18 ½ x 18 In. 960.00
Stand, Sheraton, Cherry, Curly Maple, 2 Drawers, 28 ½ x 19 x 18 ¾ In. 863.00
Stand, Sheraton, Cherry, Curly Maple, Ohio, Early 1800s, 30 x 20 In. 323.00
Stand, Sheraton, Cherry, Drawer, 19th Century, 27 x 20 In. 175.00
Stand, Sheraton, Curly Maple, Cherry, Poplar, 2 Drawers, Turned Legs, 29 x 21 In. 969.00
Stand, Sheraton, Mahogany, Fluted, Reeded Column, Tripod Base, Early 1900s, 64 x 19 In. 230.00
Stand, Sheraton, Mahogany, String Inlay, Pagoda Form, 3 Tiers, c.1900, 39 In. 405.00
Stand, Sheraton, Pine, Drawer, Black Marble Top, Turned Legs, c.1820, 28 x 20 x 20 In. 5148.00
Stand, Sheraton, Pine, Overhang Top, Drawer, Old Stain, Tapered Legs, c.1810, 28 x 18 In. 823.00
Stand, Sheraton, Walnut, Reeded Corners, 2 Drawers, Turned Legs, c.1830, 27 x 19 x 19 In. 470.00
Stand, Sheraton Style, Mahogany, Biscuit Corners, 2 Drawers, Reeded Legs, 30 x 21 In. 863.00
Stand, Smoking, Art Deco, Onyx, Chrome, 29 In. 71.00
Stand, Smoking, Art Nouveau, Iron, 1920s. 35.00
Stand, Smoking, Iron, Figural, Black Man In Red Tails, Holding Brass Tray, 1930s, 35 ½ In. 460.00
Stand, Smoking, Iron, Flamingo Standing By Vine, Footed Base, 24 x 8 In. 978.00
Stand, Telephone, Gray Laminate, Steel, Enamel, E. Noyes, 1957, 22 ½ x 13 In. *illus* 385.00
Stand, Tiger Maple, 2 Dovetailed Drawers, Turned Legs, 1800s, 29 x 22 x 18 ½ In. 950.00
Stand, Tiger Maple, Drawer, New England, Early 1800s, 26 ¾ x 17 ½ In. 1778.00
Stand, Tiger Maple, Urn & Vase Shape, Pedestal, Arched Legs, c.1820, 28 x 23 In. 480.00
Stand, Twigs, Yellow, Black Paint, Half-Round Skirt, H.E. Burger, 1894, 37 x 22 x 23 In. 264.00
Stand, Victorian, Brass, Marble, Glass, Masks, Fretwork, Columns, 72 x 52 In. 837.00
Stand, Victorian, Mahogany, Stained Poplar, Pedestal, 4-Footed, 35 x 13 In. 70.00
Stand, Victorian, Walnut, Mahogany, Marble Top, Drawer, Door, 32 x 20 In. *illus* 325.00
Stand, Victorian, Wire, White Paint, 3 Tiers, 71 ¾ x 38 ½ x 27 In. 200.00
Stand, Walnut, Drawer, Turned Splayed Legs, Red Stain, Pa., 1825, 29 x 20 ½ In. 6600.00
Stand, Walnut, Poplar, Canted Apron, Drawer, Splayed Legs, 28 ½ x 22 x 21 ½ In. 470.00
Stand, White Pine, 2 Tiers, Applied Molded Top, Trumpet Turned Feet, 1800s, 28 x 23 In. 288.00
Stand, Wig, Regency, Lignum Vitae, Turned Bowl, Base, Early 1800s, 27 x 5 In. 120.00
Stand, Yellow Paint Over Red, Dovetailed Drawer, Mid 1800s, 29 x 27 In. 1840.00
Stand, Yellow Pine, Blue Paint, Turned Legs, 48 x 24 In. 259.00
Stool, Aalto, Birch, 1933, 17 ½ x 13 ½ In., Pair 531.00
Stool, Arts & Crafts, Slat Seat, Curved, Rope Design Legs, 20 x 22 In. 240.00
Stool, Bar, Windsor, Black Over Red Finish, Late 1900s, 49 ½ In., 3 Piece 705.00
Stool, Chippendale, Mahogany, Upholstered, Cabriole Legs, Claw & Ball Feet, 16 x 10 In. 775.00
Stool, Chippendale Style, Beech, Upholstered, Shell & Flower Knees, 16 x 19 x 15 In. 1500.00
Stool, Chippendale Style, Mahogany, Acanthus, Upholstered, 1890s, 19 x 24 x 19 In. 650.00
Stool, Cricket, Red & Black Grained, 8 In. 345.00
Stool, Eames, Rosewood, Tufted Black Leather Cushion, Herman Miller 450.00
Stool, Elm, Lacquered, Square, Apron, Shaped Stretchers, Chinese, 21 x 17 In., Pair 531.00
Stool, English Oak, Hinged, Open Interior, Carved Vine, Shaped Ends, 1800s, 19 x 18 In. 540.00
Stool, Esherick, Walnut Seat, Ash Legs, 1966, 19 ½ In. *illus* 5500.00
Stool, Frank Lloyd Wright, Copper Clad, Cushions, 17 x 19 x 17 In. *illus* 1080.00
Stool, George II, Gilt, Upholstered, Cabriole Legs, Scrolled Toes, 17 x 22 In. *illus* 5206.00
Stool, George II, Walnut, Drop-In Seat, Carved Legs, Pad Feet, c.1750 8750.00
Stool, George II, Walnut, Needlepoint, Claw & Ball Feet, c.1745 7500.00
Stool, Gilt, Seated Blackamoor, Padded Seat, Paint, Venice, c.1875, 25 x 26 In., Pair 34375.00
Stool, Goncalo Alves, Turned Stretcher, Upholstered, 17 ¾ In. 450.00
Stool, Gout, Mahogany, Upholstered, Scroll Base, c.1830, 17 x 14 In. 705.00
Stool, Jacobian, Oak, Chestnut, Square Top, Frieze, Baluster Legs, c.1830, 19 x 14 In. 1150.00
Stool, Louis XV, Multicolored, Flower Needlework Upholstery, Scroll Toes, 10 x 32 In. 1560.00
Stool, Louis XV Style, Padded, Needlework, 18 ½ x 20 x 16 In., Pair 2040.00
Stool, Louis XV Style, Padded, Needlework, Shaped Shell Carved Frieze, 19 x 20 x 16 In. 2040.00
Stool, Mahogany, Serpentine, Upholstered, Bracket Feet, 17 x 18 x 18 In., Pair 780.00
Stool, Mahogany, Upholstered, Saddle Seat, Fan Carved Legs, 16 ½ x 18 x 15 ½ In. 1375.00
Stool, Milking, Cutout Center, 4-Footed, Patina 40.00
Stool, Molded Top, Side Skirts, Orange, Blue, Cutouts, Splayed Legs, 7 ½ x 18 ½ In. 248.00
Stool, Organ, Wood, Cast Iron, 20 In. 35.00

Furniture, Stool, Frank Lloyd Wright, Copper Clad, Cushions, 17 x 19 x 17 In.
$1080.00

Furniture, Stool, George II, Gilt, Upholstered, Cabriole Legs, Scrolled Toes, 17 x 22 In.
$5206.00

Furniture, Stool, Windsor, Wood, Brown Paint, White & Hubbard, 1825, 32 x 15 In.
$475.00

Revival Furniture

In the years following World War I (1914–18), Americans turned to different revival styles of furniture that sparked memories of the past. Almost every old style—from Windsor chairs, Chippendale chests, and wing chairs to bulky, William and Mary dining room sets and Empire pieces—was slightly changed and marketed to the general public at reasonable prices.

House of Cards
Charles and Ray Eames, famous for furniture and other designs in the 1950s and after, invented the game House of Cards. It was a deck of large cards that could be used to build "houses."

F

Furniture, Table, Baker's, Iron & Brass, Scrolled Base, Marble Top, Casters, 31 x 39 x 25 In.
$4113.00

Furniture, Table, Card, Federal, Mahogany, Inlaid, Veneer, Demilune Top, 28 x 17 ½ In.
$499.00

TIP
If you spill nail polish on furniture, try this cure: Rub the spot with 0000-grade steel wool dipped in liquid wax polish. Wipe, then rewax with your usual furniture polish.

Stool, Perriand, Wood, 3 Legs, c.1951, 18 x 12 In. 2160.00
Stool, Piano, Mahogany, Upholstered, Scalloped Apron, Paw Feet, c.1850, 21 x 14 x 14 In. 411.00
Stool, Piano, Neoclassical, Marquetry, Floral Medallion, Swivel Base, 32 x 14 In. 708.00
Stool, Piano, Oak, Claw & Ball Feet .... 65.00 to 90.00
Stool, Piano, Windsor, Glass Ball & Claw Feet, 34 In. 59.00
Stool, Pine, Fruit, Ivory Ground, Black Pinstriped, Signed, J.A. Haskell, 3 x 5 ¾ x 3 In. 410.00
Stool, Queen Anne, Cuban Mahogany, Slip Seat, Spanish Feet, c.1740, 17 x 17 In. 4680.00
Stool, Queen Anne, Walnut, Upholstered, Cabriole Legs, Pad Feet, 23 x 20 ½ x 17 In. 920.00
Stool, Regency, Parcel Gilt, Painted, Upholstered Seats, 17 x 23 In., Pair 1080.00
Stool, Regency, Rosewood, Padded, Needlework Seat, Leaf Carved Stretcher, 17 x 25 x 19 In. 1680.00
Stool, Regency Style, Walnut, Concave Padded Seat, Lion's Mask Toes, 18 x 23 In. 900.00
Stool, Regency Style, Walnut, Padded, Needlework, Putti, Flower Garlands, 16 x 18 In. 1560.00
Stool, Rohde, Vanity, Leather Seat, Wavy Wood Frame, Herman Miller, c.1936, 17 x 20 In. 600.00
Stool, Rosewood, Mother-Of-Pearl Inlay, Barrel Form, Open, Chinese, 1900s, 21 x 14 In. 375.00
Stool, Softwood, Gray Paint, Double Skirt, V-Shape Cutout Feet, 7 ½ x 12 x 5 In. 50.00
Stool, Stickley, Oak, Through Tenon Construction, Tagged, 15 x 15 x 15 In. 635.00
Stool, Thebes, Mahogany, Concave Seat, Tapered Legs, Late 19th Century, 14 ½ x 16 In. 711.00
Stool, Tooth Form, Plastic, White, 1980s. 44.00
Stool, Vanity, Georgian Style, Mahogany, Upholstered Seat, Cabriole Legs, 19 x 24 In. 830.00
Stool, Vanity, Louis XV, Beech, Needlepoint, Leaf Carved Frame, 18 ½ x 20 In. 356.00
Stool, Vanity, Lucite, One Piece, Upholstered, c.1950, 17 x 22 In. 120.00
Stool, Vanity, Queen Anne, Walnut, Overupholstered Velvet Seat, Early 1700s, 17 x 23 In. 2015.00
Stool, Victorian, Cast Iron, Needlepoint Seat, c.1880 .... 88.00
Stool, Victorian, Mahogany, Bronze, 3 Humans Shape Legs, Shoe Feet, 20 In. 1793.00
Stool, William & Mary, Walnut, Cross Stretcher, Upholstered, 17 x 16 x 13 In. 600.00
Stool, William & Mary, White Oak, Turned Splayed Legs, c.1710, 22 x 18 In. 5382.00
Stool, William III, Walnut, Upholstered, Carved Legs, Stretcher, c.1700 .... 5000.00
Stool, William IV, Mahogany, Upholstered Seat, Turned Legs, c.1820, 18 x 16 In., Pair 1528.00
Stool, Windsor, Mixed Woods, Bamboo Turnings, Brown Paint, Early 1800s, 32 x 16 In. 558.00
Stool, Windsor, Wood, Brown Paint, White & Hubbard, 1825, 32 x 15 In. .... *illus* 475.00
Stool, Windsor, Yellow Paint, Upholstered, 19th Century, 16 In. 58.00
Stool, Wood, Grain Painted, Mortise & Tenon Joints, Splayed Legs, 5 ½ x 14 In. 132.00
Stool, Wood, Mottled, Rivered Blond Ground, Random Black Marks, 19 ½ x 13 In. 390.00
Table, 3 Tiles, Painted, Southwestern Scene, Indian On Horse, 24 x 12 In. 3120.00
Table, 4 Green Tiles, Lower Shelf, 21 x 21 x 26 In. 840.00
Table, Aesthetic Revival, Malachite Top, Ebonized Wood, Galleried Shelf, 26 x 32 In. 518.00
Table, Altar, Pine, Panel, 3 Drawers, Leaf Pulls, Horse Hoof Feet, Chinese, 37 x 48 x 12 In. 1560.00
Table, Altar, Walnut, 3 Drawers, Beaded Apron, Red, Black, Mongolia, c.1790, 34 x 62 In. 657.00
Table, Altar, Walnut, Carved Birds, Rabbit, Dragon, Flowers, Chinese, 39 x 78 x 22 In. 3835.00
Table, Antico Marble Top, Multicolored, Carved Frieze, Sweden, Late 1800s, 31 x 36 In. 1920.00
Table, Art Deco, Figured Round Top, Plain Frieze, Tapered Legs, Early 1900s, 29 x 30 In. 960.00
Table, Art Deco, Peach Mirrored Glass Top, Bent, Scrolled Lucite Base, 17 x 18 In. 119.00
Table, Art Deco, Wood, Multicolored, Drawers, Shelves, Spade Feet, 36 x 32 x 14 In. 1560.00
Table, Art Deco, Wood Burl, Ebonized, Birch Inserts, Metal Band, 29 x 45 In., Pair 8888.00
Table, Art Moderne, Gilt Metal, Glass, Elongated Oval, Tubular Supports, 29 x 59 x 18 In. 4800.00
Table, Art Nouveau, Galle Style, Fruitwood, Marquetry, Landscapes, 2 Tiers, 30 x 30 In. 1778.00
Table, Arts & Crafts, Color Geometric Tile Top, Curled Black Iron Base, 18 x 24 In. 360.00
Table, Arts & Crafts, Oak, Chamfered Edge, Frieze, Stretcher Base, Early 1900s, 30 x 47 In. 266.00
Table, Arts & Crafts, Round Leather Top, Tacks, Shelf, Floor Stretcher Base, 30 x 30 In. 330.00
Table, Arts & Crafts, Wood, Circular, 4 Legs, 30 x 30 In. 840.00
Table, Arts & Crafts, Wood, Leather, Drop Front Door, Strap Hinges, Slats, 25 x 30 In. 600.00
Table, Baker's, Iron & Brass, Scrolled Base, Marble Top, Casters, 31 x 39 x 25 In. .... *illus* 4113.00
Table, Baker's, Metal, Cream, Gray Marble Top, Steel Base, Casters, France, 31 x 61 x 28 In. 2596.00
Table, Baker's, Wood, 2 Drawers, 5 Cutting Boards, c.1900, 32 x 60 x 24 In. 720.00
Table, Bamboo, Brass, Tray, Applied Handles, Collapsible Stand, 25 x 27 x 20 In. 1320.00
Table, Bamboo, Decoupage, Square Top, c.1900, 28 x 22 ½ x 22 ½ In. 480.00
Table, Bench, Pine, Green Paint, c.1800, 28 x 64 x 42 ½ In. 6435.00
Table, Bench, Pine Top, Red Paint, Mortise & Tenon Joints, Plank Seat, 30 x 60 In. 1540.00
Table, Biedermeier, Dovetailed, Diamond Shape Inlay, Supports, German, 1800s, 27 x 69 In. 1495.00
Table, Biedermeier, Fruitwood, Circular, Triangular Shelf, Splayed Legs, c.1835, 26 x 19 In. 356.00
Table, Biedermeier, Fruitwood, Tin Lined, Faceted Sides, Cabriole Legs, 33 ½ In. 1025.00
Table, Biedermeier, Round Parquetry Top, Drawer, 3 Tapered Saber Legs, 17 x 14 ½ In. 598.00
Table, Bistro, Molded Edge, Wood Top, Painted Cast-Iron Base, 30 ½ x 42 ½ In. 144.00
Table, Black Forest, Walnut, Tilt Top, Carved Deer, Leaves, Tripod Base, c.1890, 29 x 30 In. 889.00
Table, Black Lacquer, Floating Panel, Squared Legs, 30 ½ x 109 x 42 In. 7200.00
Table, Black Walnut, c.1910, 23 x 17 In. 475.00
Table, Brass, Glass Tops, Fretwork Brackets, Square Legs, 20th Century, 28 x 26 In., Pair 443.00

Table, Brass, White Marble Top, Cast Base, Portrait Medallions, 23 ½ x 26 ½ In. 264.00
Table, Brass Frame, Glass Top, Kasco Products, Finland, 19 x 19 In., Pair.......... 360.00
Table, Burl, Tilt Top, Oval, Scrolled Legs, Leaf Decoration, 20 x 46 ½ In.......... 1020.00
Table, Butcher, Cast Iron, Marble Top, Scrolling Supports, Stretchers, 31 x 50 x 29 In. 1920.00
Table, Card, Art Deco, Rosewood, Chrome Mounted, Swivel Top, 30 x 35 x 22 In.......... 1800.00
Table, Card, Birch, Salmon Paint, Breadboard Ends, Drawer, 30 x 35 ½ In. 2185.00
Table, Card, Burl, Rotating Oval Top, 4 Scroll Legs, Leaf Carving, 1800s, 42 x 28 In. 708.00
Table, Card, Directoire, Fruitwood, Gilt Metal, Felt Lined, Swivel, 27 x 32 x 16 In. 448.00
Table, Card, Empire, Walnut, Serpentine Top, Lyre Base, Casters, 30 In. 135.00
Table, Card, Federal, Birch, Bird's-Eye Maple, Shaped Top, Early 1800s, 31 x 34 In.......... 1265.00
Table, Card, Federal, Cherry, Banding, Tapered Legs, 29 ½ x 35 x 17 In. 3738.00
Table, Card, Federal, Cherry, Serpentine Top, Turned Legs, 29 ½ x 36 x 18 ½ In. 303.00
Table, Card, Federal, Inlaid, Demilune, Flip Top, Felt Surface, Early 1800s, 29 x 36 In. 1150.00
Table, Card, Federal, Mahogany, 5 Legs, New York, c.1810, 30 x 36 In.......... 1185.00
Table, Card, Federal, Mahogany, Carved, Brass Animal Paw Casters, c.1820, 30 x 36 In. 322.00
Table, Card, Federal, Mahogany, Carved, Satinwood Inlay, Boston, c.1812, 30 x 37 In........ 2844.00
Table, Card, Federal, Mahogany, Carved Serpentine, Tapered Legs, c.1795, 28 x 36 In........ 2015.00
Table, Card, Federal, Mahogany, Figured, Inlaid, Charleston, c.1810, 30 x 36 In.......... 6440.00
Table, Card, Federal, Mahogany, Inlaid, Bellflowers, Tapered Legs, 34 x 17 In.......... 1035.00
Table, Card, Federal, Mahogany, Inlaid, Hinged Lid, Bowed, Late 1700s, 29 x 36 In.......... 1035.00
Table, Card, Federal, Mahogany, Inlaid, Hinged Top, Crossbanded, 29 x 34 ½ x 17 In........ 748.00
Table, Card, Federal, Mahogany, Inlaid, Serpentine Top, Tapered Legs, 30 x 36 x 18 In....... 1000.00
Table, Card, Federal, Mahogany, Inlaid, Veneer, Demilune Top, 28 x 17 ½ In.......... *illus* 499.00
Table, Card, Federal, Mahogany, Inlaid, Walnut Fly Leg, Midatlantic, c.1800, 30 x 36 In...... 2300.00
Table, Card, Federal, Mahogany, Pine, Diamond Inlaid Bands, Hinged Top, 29 x 36 x 17 In... 2232.00
Table, Card, Federal, Mahogany, Shaped Top, Baltimore, c.1820, 33 x 38 In.......... 2133.00
Table, Card, Federal, Mahogany, Tiger Maple, Inlaid, Mass., c.1795, 30 x 35 In.......... 3081.00
Table, Card, Federal, Mahogany, Veneered, Shaped Top, Tapered Legs, 29 x 36 x 17 In. 593.00
Table, Card, Federal, Mahogany Inlay, Demilune, 28 ½ x 35 ¾ x 17 In.......... 5000.00
Table, Card, Federal, Satinwood, Inlaid Acorn, Oakleaf, Hinged Top, 29 ½ x 35 ½ In. 4312.00
Table, Card, Federal Style, Mahogany, Inlaid, Veneered, Oval Corners, 29 x 35 x 17 In. 4888.00
Table, Card, Hepplewhite, Birch, Walnut, Crossbanded Inlaid Skirt, 30 x 36 In.......... 441.00
Table, Card, Hepplewhite, Cherry, Flame Mahogany, Swing Leg, c.1790, 28 x 36 x 19 In...... 1430.00
Table, Card, Hepplewhite, Mahogany, Demilune, Inlaid, Flip Top, 30 x 38 x 19 In.......... 500.00
Table, Card, Hepplewhite, Mahogany, Inlaid Shell, Leather Top, England, c.1790s, 29 x 38 In. 2415.00
Table, Card, Hepplewhite, Mahogany, Pine, Inlaid, Demilune, Folding Top, 29 x 30 In. 1116.00
Table, Card, Mahogany, Flip Top, Reeded Edge, 29 x 36 x 18 In.......... 406.00
Table, Card, Neoclassical, Stenciled, Flip Top, Scroll Legs, Boston, 1825, 29 x 36 x 18 In....... 2000.00
Table, Card, Oak, Iron, Milwaukee, Pat. Dec. 8, 1896, 30 x 36 In.......... *illus* 660.00
Table, Card, Queen Anne, Mahogany, Demilune, Flip Top, Swing Leg, 1700s, 28 x 18 In...... 1150.00
Table, Card, Sheraton, Birch, Casters, Kentucky, Early 1800s 200.00
Table, Card, Sheraton, Mahogany, Acanthus Carved, Reeded Legs, 29 x 40 x 18 ½ In. 805.00
Table, Card, Walnut, Square Leather Top, Upholstered Chairs, 1930s, 5 Piece.......... 425.00
Table, Cast Brass, Demilune, Inset Glass Top, 33 x 29 x 16 In. 165.00
Table, Cast Iron, Glass Top, Phoenix Bird Base, 20 x 48 In.......... 225.00
Table, Center, Biedermeier, Scrolled Legs, 19th Century, 31 x 46 x 31 ½ In.......... 205.00
Table, Center, Carved Winged Dragons, Serpents, Cabriole Legs, 19th Century, 33 x 53 In. ... 2415.00
Table, Center, Ebonized, Inlaid Top, c.1880, 29 x 36 x 24 In.......... 780.00
Table, Center, Empire, Mahogany, Marble Top, Molded Frieze, 3 Scrolling Supports.......... 598.00
Table, Center, Fruitwood, Concave Top, Flower, Bird Inlay, Medallion, 32 x 44 x 34 In. 2160.00
Table, Center, George III Style, Mahogany, Circular, 4 Splayed Cabriole Legs, 72 In.......... 3840.00
Table, Center, George III Style, Satinwood, Ebony, Painted, Landscape, 30 x 38 x 26 In....... 711.00
Table, Center, Louis XV Style, Mahogany, Kingwood, Sunburst Inlay, 40 x 30 In.......... 2880.00
Table, Center, Louis XVI Style, Oak, Tapered Square Legs, Feet, 29 ½ x 36 x 31 In. 1560.00
Table, Center, Louis XV-XVI Style, Fruitwood, Parquetry, Cabriole Legs, 30 x 35 In.......... 508.00
Table, Center, Mahogany, Carved Woman Lifting Tabletop, Drapes, Tassels, 1800s, 25 x 35 In. 8850.00
Table, Center, Mahogany, Egyptian Marble Top, Carved Shells, Stretcher, 31 x 45 In......... 1880.00
Table, Center, Mahogany, Roses Wreath, Black Ground, Gadrooned, 30 x 28 In......... *illus* 5036.00
Table, Center, Neoclassical, Burl Walnut, Circular, Continental, 26 ¾ x 29 In. 3840.00
Table, Center, Neoclassical, Mahogany, Cartouche Top, Scrolled Supports, 30 x 35 In........ 460.00
Table, Center, Oak, Bulbous Legs, Ball Feet, Spain, 28 x 34 x 25 In.......... 1200.00
Table, Center, Regency, Rosewood, Tilt Top, Carved Paw Feet, 19th Century, 31 x 50 In....... 3600.00
Table, Center, Regency Style, Burl, Greek Key Inlay, 30 x 72 In. 4320.00
Table, Center, Renaissance Revival, Burl Walnut, Geometric Inlay, Gameboard, 31 x 33 In. .. 5287.00
Table, Center, Renaissance Revival, Ebonized, Inlaid, c.1860, 30 x 41 In. 3105.00
Table, Center, Renaissance Revival, Specimen Marble, Semiprecious Stone, 32 x 64 In...... 10575.00
Table, Center, Renaissance Revival, Walnut, Burl, Inset Marble Top, 31 x 43 x 25 In......... 863.00

TIP
The marble top of a table can be shined with putty powder (zinconium oxide) from a cemetery monument works. Put the powder on a piece of damp felt and rub the marble until it shines.

Furniture, Table, Card, Oak, Iron, Milwaukee, Pat. Dec. 8, 1896, 30 x 36 In. $660.00

Furniture, Table, Center, Mahogany, Roses Wreath, Black Ground, Gadrooned, 30 x 28 In. $5036.00

Furniture, Table, Center, Rococo Revival, Rosewood, Dog, Marble Top, 1870s, 30 x 32 x 20 In. $990.00

TIP

Never clean marble with either vinegar or lemon juice. They will damage the marble. If someone spills lemonade on your marble topped table, wipe it up immediately and wash the area with ammonia and water to neutralize the acid.

Furniture, Table, Coffee, Arthur Court, Glass Top, Aluminum Antler Base, 52 x 15 In.
$3240.00

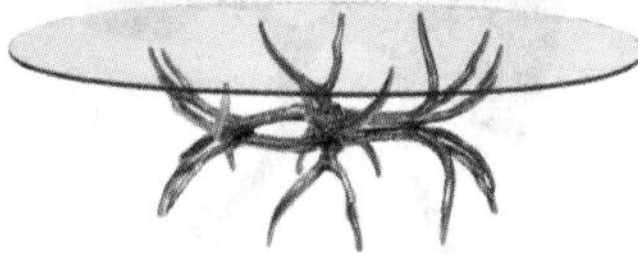

Furniture, Table, Coffee, W. Platner, Nickel Plate, Wire Base, Round Glass Top, Knoll, 42 x 15 In.
$1200.00

Cocktail or Coffee
When Prohibition ended in 1933, furniture makers started to sell low "cocktail tables" to be used in front of sofas to serve the newly legal mixed drinks. The public objected to the name, so it was renamed a "coffee table."

Table, Center, Restauration, Mahogany, Marble Top, Columnar Standard, 31 x 39 In. 3120.00
Table, Center, Rococo, Rosewood, Marble Top, Cartouche Form, 1850s, 31 x 44 x 29 In. 8600.00
Table, Center, Rococo, Walnut, Marble Top, 29 x 47 ½ x 26 In.. .... 1437.00
Table, Center, Rococo, White Marble Top, Carved Dolphin Legs, c.1850, 30 x 27 In. 575.00
Table, Center, Rococo Revival, Gilt, Composition, Porcelain Mounted, 31 x 29 In. 1304.00
Table, Center, Rococo Revival, Rosewood, Dog, Marble Top, 1870s, 30 x 32 x 20 In. ...... *illus* 990.00
Table, Center, Rococo Revival, Rosewood, Marble Top, Tortoise Shape, 30 x 38 x 27 In. 1560.00
Table, Center, Rosewood, Oak, Inlaid Patterns, Tortoise, Panels, 25 x 27 x 17 In. 2640.00
Table, Center, Victorian, Pine, Carved, Late 19th Century, 31 ¾ x 17 ½ In. 29.00
Table, Center, Victorian, Rosewood, Bulbous Standard, Splayed Supports, 30 x 59 x 42 In. 2640.00
Table, Center, Victorian, Walnut, Marble Top, Scrolled Legs, Turned Finials, 30 x 22 In. 472.00
Table, Center, Walnut, Barley Twist Legs, Finial, Spain, 31 x 76 x 38 In. 7500.00
Table, Center, William IV, Rosewood, Tilt Top, Circular, Carved Paw Feet, 41 ½ In. 7500.00
Table, Cercasian Walnut, Serpentine Top, Frieze, Scroll Carved, Continental, 19 x 39 In.. .... 227.00
Table, Cherry, Birch, Pine, Red, Drawer, New England, Late 1700s, 26 ½ x 32 ½ In. 8295.00
Table, Cherry, Drawer, Turned Legs, c.1850s, 29 x 28 In. 345.00
Table, Cherry, Inlaid, Stringing On Tapered Leg, Elliptical, c.1820, 28 x 47 In., Pair 1920.00
Table, Cherry, Snake Feet, England, 29 ½ x 58 In. 660.00
Table, Chinese Chippendale, George III Style, Mahogany, 24 x 22 x 14 In., Pair 1440.00
Table, Chippendale, Mahogany, 3 Tiers, Claw & Ball Feet, 35 ½ In. 80.00
Table, Chippendale, Mahogany, Dish Tilt Top, Tripod Base, Pa., 1700s, 29 x 33 In. 7130.00
Table, Chippendale, Mahogany, Figured, Hinged Top, Molded Edges, c.1770, 29 x 34 In. 480.00
Table, Chippendale, Mahogany, Leather, Cross Stretcher, England, 1890, 27 x 34 x 22 In. 950.00
Table, Chippendale, Mahogany, Tilt Top, Piecrust Edge, Early 20th Century, 45 x 31 In. 250.00
Table, Chippendale, Pine, Peg, Oval Corner Top, Square Legs, Inside Chamfer, 28 x 26 In. 294.00
Table, Chippendale, Tilt Top, Tripod, Birdcage, Pad Feet, 27 ½ x 28 In. 296.00
Table, Chippendale, Walnut, Oval Top, Drop Sides, Ball & Claw Feet, Pa., 1700s, 29 x 50 In. .. 1093.00
Table, Chippendale Revival, Mahogany, Scalloped Top, Tripod Base, 30 x 18 x 22 In. 142.00
Table, Chrome, Glass, Double Support, Label, Office Archives Inc., 1990, 27 x 60 x 36 In. 865.00
Table, Cincinnati Art Carved, Walnut, Serpent, Flowers, Lower Shelf, 3 Legs, 18 x 21 In. 450.00
Table, Coffee, Alvin Lustig, Glass Top, Cross Frame, Wood Shelf, c.1947, 15 x 44 In. 7800.00
Table, Coffee, Arthur Court, Glass Top, Aluminum Antler Base, 52 x 15 In. .... *illus* 3240.00
Table, Coffee, B. Schaefer, Walnut, 6 Curved Supports, Travertine Top, Singer & Sons, 60 x 15 In. 960.00
Table, Coffee, Christopher Maier, Gilt, Box Form, Ribbed Bun Feet, 17 x 37 x 25 In. 7500.00
Table, Coffee, Concave, Glass Cutout Top, Black Base, 1960s, 43 x 15 In.. .... 600.00
Table, Coffee, Danish Modern, Rosewood, c.1968, 20 x 62 In.. .... 1440.00
Table, Coffee, Florence Knoll, Divided Walnut Top, White Enamel Steel Legs, 40 x 16 In.. .... 180.00
Table, Coffee, Frank Lloyd Wright, Mitered Drop Ends, Slab Base, Henredon, 14 x 60 In. 3000.00
Table, Coffee, Frank Lloyd Wright, Overhanging Taliesin Edge, 60 x 14 In. 2040.00
Table, Coffee, Frank Lloyd Wright, Square, Cruciform Base, Signed, Henredon, 15 ½ x 33 In.. 4200.00
Table, Coffee, Frankl, Free-Form Cork Top, 4 Flared Mahogany Legs, 72 x 15 In. 4200.00
Table, Coffee, G. Nakashima, Rosewood, Arrow Shape, Slab Top, c.1958, 16 x 64 In. 12000.00
Table, Coffee, G. Nelson, Glass, Chrome, Steel, Herman Miller, c.1963, 15 x 36 In. 2760.00
Table, Coffee, Galvanized Metal, Marble Top, Shelf, Tubular Supports, 34 x 24 x 7 In. 1440.00
Table, Coffee, Iron, Variegated Travertine Top, Scroll Legs, 19 ½ x 51 In. 1293.00
Table, Coffee, Knut Hesterberg, Propeller, Aluminum, Glass, 1964, 15 x 43 In. 1700.00
Table, Coffee, L. & J.G. Stickley, Spindle Base, 44 x 17 In. 1320.00
Table, Coffee, Louis XVI Style, Gilt Metal, Faux Marble, Fluted Legs, 18 x 47 In. 1560.00
Table, Coffee, Louis XVI Style, Gilt Metal, Glass, 17 ½ x 39 x 19 ¾ In. 2760.00
Table, Coffee, Lucite Top, Greek Key Base, 1967, 8 x 28 x 48 In. 12600.00
Table, Coffee, Marble, Enameled, c.1960, 16 ¾ x 36 In.. .... 60.00
Table, Coffee, Milo Baughman, Wood Top, Black Frame, T. Coggin, c.1965, 17 x 35 In. 480.00
Table, Coffee, Red, Yellow, Enamel Metal, Sculpted Wood Base, 38 x 19 In. 210.00
Table, Coffee, Robsjohn-Gibbings, White Marble Top, Widdicomb, 40 x 12 In. 840.00
Table, Coffee, Round, Rubber Top, Metal Base, B & B Italia, 48 x 17 In.. .... 300.00
Table, Coffee, Saarinen, Round White Marble Top, Plastic, Metal Base, Knoll, 54 x 15 In. 2280.00
Table, Coffee, Satinwood, Hardwood Marquetry, Ribbon Mahogany Base, 18 x 48 In. 1200.00
Table, Coffee, V. Kagan, Sculptural Walnut Base, Glass Top, 3 Legs, 3 Supports, 55 x 16 In. ... 1800.00
Table, Coffee, W. Platner, Nickel Plate, Wire Base, Round Glass Top, Knoll, 42 x 15 In.. .. *illus* 1200.00
Table, Coffee, Warren McArthur, Biltmore, Irregular Top, c.1928, 24 x 24 In. 2160.00
Table, Coffee, William & Mary Style, Oak, 20th Century, 21 x 40 ½ x 35 In. 146.00
Table, Coffee, Wormley, Walnut, Hexagon Top, Paper Label, Dunbar, 77 x 17 In. 2640.00
Table, Conservatory, Iron, Marble Top, Shaped End Supports, Late 1800s, 29 x 38 In. 720.00
Table, Console, Art Deco, Marble Top, Ebonized Wood, Chrome Frame, 34 x 64 In., Pair 3840.00
Table, Console, Art Nouveau, Mahogany, Scalloped Fan Carved Apron, 33 x 43 In.. .... 940.00
Table, Console, Carved, Green Marble Top, France, 36 x 56 x 19 In.. .... 500.00
Table, Console, Charles X Style, Mahogany, Marble Top, Frieze Drawer, 34 x 39 In., Pair 3819.00

Table, Console, Christopher Maier, Gilt, Tapered Legs, 34 ½ x 72 x 14 In. 2640.00
Table, Console, Elm, Green Lacquer, Drawers, Cabriole Legs, Chinese, 33 x 48 x 17 In. 531.00
Table, Console, Empire, Mahogany, Flip Top, D-Shape, Hinged, Molded Frieze, 29 x 36 In. 269.00
Table, Console, Empire, Mahogany, Pillar & Scroll, Gadrooning, S-Scrolls, 36 x 41 In. 413.00
Table, Console, Empire Style, Mahogany, Ebonized, Leaf, Flower Medallion, 32 x 37 x 18 In. . . 2032.00
Table, Console, French Provincial, Short & Long Drawers, Concave Shelf, 33 x 59 In. 1020.00
Table, Console, Fruitwood, Marble Top, Frieze Drawer, 35 ½ x 42 x 20 ¾ In.. .... 150.00
Table, Console, George III, Gilt, Marble Top, Flower Head, Swag Draped, 32 x 25 x 12 In. 1076.00
Table, Console, George III, Mahogany, Carved, Shaped Top, 3 Drawers, 34 x 46 In. 2640.00
Table, Console, Georgian Style, Mahogany, Molded Top, Blind Fretwork, 32 ½ x 60 In. 2350.00
Table, Console, Gillows, Regency, Rosewood, Parcel Gilt, Marble Top, c.1810, 33 x 43 In. 10000.00
Table, Console, Gilt, Carved, Marble Top, Painted, Flower Medallion, 40 x 66 x 22 In. 2100.00
Table, Console, Gilt, Marble, Flower Carved Skirt, Mask, c.1875, 36 x 58 In. 2644.00
Table, Console, Gothic Revival, Oak, Column Supports, Round Plinth, 32 x 74 x 33 In.. ...... 826.00
Table, Console, Gray Marble Top, Gilt Swags, Urns, Demilune, Swiss, c.1780, 36 x 64 In.. .... 31250.00
Table, Console, Jansen, Marble Top, Beveled Edge, Double Pedestal, 35 ½ x 102 x 18 ½ In.... 1700.00
Table, Console, Jean Royere, Oak, Naugahyde Insets, 3 Drawers, c.1946, 35 In. 35000.00
Table, Console, Lifetime, Puritan, 6 Legs, Corbel Supports, Drawer, 31 x 67 In.. .... 6600.00
Table, Console, Louis XV, Gilt, Marble Top, Carved Bouquet, Painted, c.1750, 31 x 45 In.. .... 12500.00
Table, Console, Louis XV, Oak, Carved, White Paint, Faux Marble Top, Frieze, 36 x 37 In. 1067.00
Table, Console, Louis XV, Oak, Marble Top, Carved Scrolls, Flowers, c.1750, 33 x 56 In. 37500.00
Table, Console, Louis XV Style, Gilt, Serpentine Carrara Slab, Lattice Frieze, 34 x 29 In. 472.00
Table, Console, Marble Top, Curved, Scrolled Support, Gilt, France, c.1750, 31 x 52 In. 13750.00
Table, Console, Marble Top, Frieze Drawer, Carved Scroll, Shell Supports, Painted, 36 x 50 In. 4375.00
Table, Console, Mirror, Louis XVI, Gilt Metal, Porcelain Mounted, 29 x 35 In.. .... 840.00
Table, Console, Neoclassical, Gilt, Demilune, Garland Swags, Wreath, 34 x 42 x 19 In. 2124.00
Table, Console, Pine, Long Leaf, White Glazed Terra-Cotta Baluster Base, 34 x 90 In. 345.00
Table, Console, Red Marble, Acanthus Border, Winged Sphinx Standards, 32 x 60 In. 3231.00
Table, Console, Regency, Painted Marble Top, Scrolled, Carved Base, Gray, c.1730, 39 x 65 In. 3585.00
Table, Console, Restauration, Mahogany, Marble Top, Mirrored Back, 32 x 43 x 14 In. 1673.00
Table, Console, Sheraton, Mahogany, String Inlay, Molded Backsplash, Drawers, 37 x 40 In... 538.00
Table, Console, Walnut, Marble Top, Triform Pedestal, Animal Form Feet, c.1900, 32 x 36 In... 944.00
Table, Console, Walnut, Pine, Scalloped Edge, Breadboard Ends, 2 Drawers, France, 28 x 51 In. 1150.00
Table, Console, William IV, Walnut, Marble, Doors, Mirrors, c.1850, 32 ½ x 45 In. 587.00
Table, Console, Wormley, Birch, Demilune, Drawer, Dunbar, 48 In. 1800.00
Table, Console, Wormley, Walnut, Drawer, Cross-Legged Base, Dunbar, 29 x 72 x 19 In.. ..... 1560.00
Table, Contemporary, Oak, Revolving, Double Helix Shape, 40 x 16 ½ In.. .... 900.00
Table, Contemporary, Rosewood, Square Top, Open Trellis Pedestal, 27 x 24 In.. .... 179.00
Table, Corner, Pine, Black Paint, Shaped Top, Scrolled Serpentine Frieze, 32 x 29 In. 652.00
Table, Cream Paint, Single Plank, Squared Legs, 38 x 77 x 14 In. 2160.00
Table, Cricket, Pine, Circular Top, Aprons, 3 Legs, 19th Century, 27 In. 531.00
Table, Crouched Atlas, Walnut, Carved, Venice, c.1900, 32 In.. .... 11500.00
Table, Dining, Art Deco, Laminated, Chrome, 2 Pedestals, Ebonized, c.1930, 30 x 60 In. 443.00
Table, Dining, Baroque Revival, Glass Top, Painted, Metal Scroll Base, 28 x 30 In.. .... 203.00
Table, Dining, Baroque Revival, Oak, 5 Leaves, Twist Legs, 1800s, 29 x 111 ½ In. 179.00
Table, Dining, Chippendale, Mahogany, Carved Edge, Round, Baker, 1950s, 30 x 84 In. 3910.00
Table, Dining, Chippendale, Mahogany, Hinge Top, Rhode Island, c.1770, 28 x 44 In.... *illus* 11850.00
Table, Dining, Chippendale Style, Extending, Double Baluster Pedestals, 30 x 73 In. 1534.00
Table, Dining, Drop Leaf, Cherry, Spider Legs, 29 ½ x 42 x 16 ½ In.. .... 132.00
Table, Dining, Drop Leaf, Cherry, Turned Legs, Mid 1800s, 45 x 67 In.. .... 115.00
Table, Dining, Drop Leaf, Chippendale, Mahogany, Claw Feet, Mass., c.1770, 28 x 28 In. 5333.00
Table, Dining, Drop Leaf, Chippendale, Mahogany, Rosehead Nails, 28 x 60 In. 1170.00
Table, Dining, Drop Leaf, Chippendale, Maple, Red Stain, c.1780, 27 x 45 ½ x 16 In.. .... 468.00
Table, Dining, Drop Leaf, D-Ends, Reeded Tapered Legs, 19th Century, 88 x 47 In. 2160.00
Table, Dining, Drop Leaf, Federal, Mahogany, Saber Legs, Mass., c.1800, 28 x 51 In. 1265.00
Table, Dining, Drop Leaf, Federal, Walnut, 3 Parts, Tapered Legs, 1810, 42 x 20 In. 785.00
Table, Dining, Drop Leaf, Georgian, Mahogany, Oval, Pad Feet, 53 x 20 In.. .... 2585.00
Table, Dining, Drop Leaf, Maple, Pine, Swing Legs, 27 ½ x 36 x 12 In.. .... *illus* 500.00
Table, Dining, Drop Leaf, Scalloped Leaves, Tapered Legs, Red, Late 1700s, 28 x 19 x 37 In. .. 1500.00
Table, Dining, Drop Leaf, Walnut, New England, c.1750, 29 x 48 In. 2015.00
Table, Dining, Drop Leaf, William & Mary, Oak, Drawer, Fly Leg, 20 x 58 x 24 In.. .... 800.00
Table, Dining, E. Saarinen, Marble Top, Aluminum Base, Black, Knoll, 49 x 54 In. ..... *illus* 3240.00
Table, Dining, Empire Style, Mahogany, Round, 4-Footed, Late 1800s, 29 x 52 In. 1638.00
Table, Dining, Federal, Mahogany, 2 Pedestals, Rosewood Bands, 28 x 54 x 53 In. 460.00
Table, Dining, Fruitwood, Demilune Ends, Cabriole Legs, 49 x 94 In. 3000.00
Table, Dining, G. Nakashima, Oval, Dark, Wood, 3 Leaves, Widdicomb, c.1958, 29 x 54 In.... 3000.00
Table, Dining, G. Stickley, No. 632, Round Top, 4 Leaves, 5 Legs, 28 x 48 In. 1100.00

Furniture, Table, Dining, Chippendale, Mahogany, Hinge Top, Rhode Island, c.1770, 28 x 44 In.
$11850.00

Furniture, Table, Dining, Drop Leaf, Maple, Pine, Swing Legs, 27 ½ x 36 x 12 In.
$500.00

Furniture, Table, Dining, E. Saarinen, Round, Marble Top, Aluminum Base, Black, Knoll, 49 x 54 In.
$3240.00

Furniture, Table, Dining, Stickley Bros., Pedestal, 4 Drop-Down Legs, Leaves, Casters, 30 x 60 In.
$5100.00

F

Furniture, Table, Drafting, F. Kramer, Adjustable Steel Frame, Wood Top, Dutch, 41 x 30 In.
$1560.00

Furniture, Table, Dressing, Pine, Ivory, Yellow Stripes, Stenciled, 1830s, 35 x 33 x 16 In.
$425.00

Furniture, Table, Drop Leaf, Chippendale, Mahogany, Drawer, 1790s, 28 x 18 x 30 In.
$1210.00

Marquetry
Furniture with marquetry designs is always expensive. Best are pieces made of walnut, then mahogany, then oak. Flower marquetry designs are more common than bird or insect designs.

Table, Dining, G. Stickley, No. 632, Wood, 3 Leaves, 5 Legs, 30 x 48 In. 2400.00
Table, Dining, G. Stickley, No. 634, Round, Leaves, 5 Legs, 54 x 34 In. 8400.00
Table, Dining, G. Stickley, No. 634, Round Top, Cross Stretcher, 6 Leaves, Signed 16800.00
Table, Dining, G. Stickley, Oak, Round, 2 Leaves, 5 Legs, Paper Label, c.1904, 30 x 48 In. 2015.00
Table, Dining, George III, Accordion Extension, 3 Supports, Down Swept Legs, 49 x 105 In. .. 3600.00
Table, Dining, George III, Burl Walnut, Double Pedestal, Paw Feet, Oval, 1800s, 28 x 72 In. .. 1315.00
Table, Dining, George III, Mahogany, 2 Pedestals, Brass Casters, 23 x 29 x 51 In. 4148.00
Table, Dining, George III, Mahogany, Rectangular Top, Reeded Edge, 52 x 125 In. 5040.00
Table, Dining, George III Style, Mahogany, 2 Pedestals, 3 Splayed Legs, 29 x 49 x 51 In. 2160.00
Table, Dining, George III Style, Mahogany, 3 Pedestals, Leaves, 32 x 156 x 54 In. 6900.00
Table, Dining, I. Noguchi, Round, Laminate, Wood, Wire Struts, Iron Base, Knoll, 29 x 36 In. 900.00
Table, Dining, John McGuire, Clustered Rattan, Octagonal, Bevel Edge Glass Top, 29 x 80 In.. 708.00
Table, Dining, L. & J.G. Stickley, No. 716, Prairie Style, Pedestal, 4 Leaves, 29 x 48 In. 4250.00
Table, Dining, Laverne, Enamel, Bronze, Pewter, Courtyard Scene, c.1979, 92 In. 35000.00
Table, Dining, Limbert, No. 1499-A, Pedestal Base, Round Top, 6 Leaves, Signed, 30 x 48 In. . 2300.00
Table, Dining, Louis XV Style, Oak, Drawers, Shell Centered Frieze, 31 x 41 x 63 In. 3840.00
Table, Dining, Mahogany, 2 Curved Base Supports, 3 Leaves, 96 x 31 In. 330.00
Table, Dining, Mahogany, Round, Fluted Pedestal, 6 Leaves, c.1875, 30 x 60 In. 4994.00
Table, Dining, Neoclassical, Double Reeded Urn Pedestals, 3 Leaves, Baker, 29 x 68 In. 2938.00
Table, Dining, Neoclassical, Mahogany, Reeded Edge Frieze, Stretcher, 21 x 98 In. 227.00
Table, Dining, Philip Johnson, Walnut, Baker Furniture, c.1952, 29 x 72 In. 10000.00
Table, Dining, Philippe Starck, Green Glass Top, Aluminum Tapered Legs, Driade, 83 x 28 In. 1800.00
Table, Dining, Poul Kjaerholm, PK 54, Round Marble Top, Steel Frame, 1963, 26 In. 8125.00
Table, Dining, Queen Anne Style, Mahogany, Oval, 2 Pedestals, 31 x 114 x 48 In. 1000.00
Table, Dining, Regency, Mahogany, 2 Pedestals, 3 Leaves, c.1810, 28 x 115 In. 13750.00
Table, Dining, Regency, Mahogany, Cumberland Action, c.1815, 29 x 30 x 14 In. 17500.00
Table, Dining, Regency, Mahogany, Double Pedestal, Down Swept Legs, 29 x 69 In. 4425.00
Table, Dining, Regency, Mahogany, Inlaid, Extending, 2 Leaves, c.1810, 29 x 108 In. 15000.00
Table, Dining, Regency, Walnut, Pedestal, Casters, England, 19th Century, 28 x 55 In. 885.00
Table, Dining, Regency Style, Mahogany, Inlaid, 4 Saber Legs, 30 x 54 x 54 In. 125.00
Table, Dining, Regency Style, Mahogany, Metamorphic, Round, Pedestal, 30 x 72 In. 11258.00
Table, Dining, Smith & Watson, Mahogany, Radial Banded, 4-Footed, 29 x 60 In. 2500.00
Table, Dining, Stickley Bros., Pedestal, 4 Drop-Down Legs, Leaves, Casters, 30 x 60 In. .. *illus* 5100.00
Table, Dining, Stinkwood, Shaped Top, Cross Stretcher, S. Africa, c.1900, 30 x 70 x 41 In. 750.00
Table, Dining, Victorian, Mahogany, Extension, Gadroon Edge, Paw Feet, 1800s, 29 x 53 In.. . 837.00
Table, Dining, Victorian, Mahogany, Figured, 5 Pedestals, Late 1800s, 28 x 169 In. 7080.00
Table, Dining, William IV Style, Mahogany, 3 Pedestals, Splayed Legs, 30 x 48 x 124 In. 5280.00
Table, Dining, Wormley, Walnut, Mahogany, Brass, 3 Leaves, Dunbar, 1950s, 29 x 72 In. 7200.00
Table, Drafting, Edwardian, Fruitwood, Oak, Adjustable, c.1900, 44 x 47 x 32 In. 2040.00
Table, Drafting, F. Kramer, Adjustable Steel Frame, Wood Top, Dutch, 41 x 30 In. ...... *illus* 1560.00
Table, Drafting, George III, Mahogany, Lift Top, 2 Swing Legs, Inlaid Doors, 37 x 48 In. 8190.00
Table, Drafting, Georgian, Mahogany, Square, Adjusting Top, Shelf, 33 x 24 In. 1135.00
Table, Dressing, Cherry, Drawer, Cabriole Legs, c.1770, 31 x 33 ½ x 20 In. 13145.00
Table, Dressing, Chippendale, Cherry, Pierced Brasses, 1700s, 29 x 35 In. 5750.00
Table, Dressing, Chippendale, Mahogany, Batwing Brasses, Salem, 18th Century, 31 x 33 In. . 9200.00
Table, Dressing, Chippendale, Walnut, 4 Drawers, Cabriole Legs, c.1770, 30 x 32 In. 11700.00
Table, Dressing, Empire, Mahogany, Brass Mounted, Mirror, Drawers, 70 x 38 ½ In. 3437.00
Table, Dressing, Empire, Mahogany, Pedestal, Mirror, Sconces, c.1830, 81 x 43 x 23 In. 780.00
Table, Dressing, Federal, Cherry, Veneer, Step Back, Drawers, Early 1800s, 35 x 32 In. 176.00
Table, Dressing, G. Stickley, No. 632, 5 Drawers, Copper Sconces, Label, 57 x 54 x 22 In. 3900.00
Table, Dressing, George I, Elm, 3 Drawers, c.1720, 28 ½ x 17 ¾ In. 5625.00
Table, Dressing, Georgian Style, Mahogany, Shield Shape Mirror, 3 Drawers, 25 x 19 In. 192.00
Table, Dressing, Hepplewhite, Mahogany, Oval Inlay, Split Top, 2 Drawers, 29 x 24 In. 2200.00
Table, Dressing, Louis XV Style, Marquetry, 3-Panel Top, Mirror, Drawers, 1900s, 30 x 31 In. . 472.00
Table, Dressing, Louis XVI Style, Kingwood, Mahogany, 3 Hinged Lids, Mirror, 29 x 31 x 18 In. 805.00
Table, Dressing, Mahogany, 4 Drawers, Brass Knob Pull, 37 x 42 x 22 In. 1434.00
Table, Dressing, Maple, Bird's-Eye Maple, Lift Top, Drawer, Early 20th Century, 29 x 22 In.... 70.00
Table, Dressing, Maple, Triangular Carved Feet, Finials, 4 Drawers, c.1745, 29 x 34 In. 9375.00
Table, Dressing, Napoleon III, Rosewood, Ebonized, Serpentine Lid, 1800s, 43 x 24 In. 1298.00
Table, Dressing, Pine, Drawers, Molded Edge, Teardrop Pulls, Slipper Feet, 29 In. 840.00
Table, Dressing, Pine, Ivory, Yellow Stripes, Stenciled, 1830s, 35 x 33 x 16 In. .... *illus* 425.00
Table, Dressing, Pine, Overhanging Top, Drawer, Painted, c.1760, 29 x 30 In. 499.00
Table, Dressing, Pine, Stenciled Oak Leaves, Fruit, Striping, Backsplash, c.1830, 35 x 33 In... 499.00
Table, Dressing, Queen Anne, Birch, Cherry, Carved Fan, 4 Drawers, c.1770, 31 x 34 In. 15000.00
Table, Dressing, Queen Anne, Maple, Fan Carving, 4 Drawers, c.1795, 13 x 37 In. 15000.00
Table, Dressing, Queen Anne, Maple, Scalloped Apron, Drawer, Cabriole Legs, 28 x 31 In..... 5175.00
Table, Dressing, Queen Anne, Mixed Wood, 3 Drawers, Shaped Skirt, 30 x 35 In. 660.00

Table, Dressing, Queen Anne, Walnut, 1 Over 2 Drawers, Spoon Feet, 1700s, 29 x 30 In. 295.00
Table, Dressing, Queen Anne, Walnut, 3 Drawers, Scroll Cut, Cock-Beaded, 32 x 31 In. 6169.00
Table, Dressing, Queen Anne, Walnut, 3 Drawers, Shaped Skirt, c.1900, 30 x 34 In. 748.00
Table, Dressing, Queen Anne, Walnut, 3 Drawers, Spanish Feet, c.1750, 28 x 30 In. 22230.00
Table, Dressing, Queen Anne, Walnut, 4 Drawers, Carved, Boston, c.1770, 31 x 33 In. 15000.00
Table, Dressing, Queen Anne, Walnut, Bookmatched Veneer, Drawer, 29 x 30 In. 1239.00
Table, Dressing, Queen Anne, Walnut, Maple, 5 Drawers, Boston, c.1745, 30 x 32 In. 12500.00
Table, Dressing, Regency, Mahogany, Pine, Inlaid, Drawers, 1800s, 30 ½ x 46 In.. . . . . 264.00
Table, Dressing, Rosewood, Caryatid Supports, Mirror, Marble, Twist Supports, 63 x 42 In. . . . 4112.00
Table, Dressing, Sheraton, Mahogany, Mirrorplate, Drawers, c.1825, 55 x 35 x 18 ½ In. 1150.00
Table, Dressing, Sheraton, Pine, Yellow, Scroll Backsplash, 3 Drawers, 1820, 39 x 36 In. 644.00
Table, Dressing, Sheraton, Splashguard, Drawer, Swelled Turned Legs, 37 ¾ x 36 ½ In. 234.00
Table, Dressing, Yellow Paint, Decorated, 36 x 15 x 29 In.. . . . . 575.00
Table, Drop Leaf, Baroque Style, Oak, Gateleg, Ball Turned Legs, 26 x 52 x 44 In.. . . . . 299.00
Table, Drop Leaf, Cherry, Kidney Shape, Swing Leg, Ball & Spike Feet, 30 x 46 x 45 In. 1012.00
Table, Drop Leaf, Cherry, Swelled Turned Legs, 19th Century, 28 ½ x 40 x 46 In. 234.00
Table, Drop Leaf, Chippendale, Cherry, Drawer, 1800, 27 x 42 x 32 In.. . . . . 1800.00
Table, Drop Leaf, Chippendale, Mahogany, Drawer, 1790s, 28 x 18 x 30 In.. . . . . *illus* 1210.00
Table, Drop Leaf, Chippendale, Walnut, Drawer, c.1780, 29 x 18 x 35 In.. . . . . 2808.00
Table, Drop Leaf, Chippendale Style, Walnut, Cabriole Legs, Claw, Ball Feet, 30 x 49 x 22 In. . 299.00
Table, Drop Leaf, Curly Maple, Spiral Turned Legs, Ball Feet, 29 x 58 In.. . . . . 705.00
Table, Drop Leaf, Drawer, Spiral Turned Legs, Peg Feet, Casters, 28 x 36 x 44 In. 1250.00
Table, Drop Leaf, Empire, Grained, Pedestal Base, 42 x 19 x 28 In. 288.00
Table, Drop Leaf, Empire, Mahogany, Drawer, Gilt Winged-Lion Paw Feet, 29 x 54 x 28 In. . . . 956.00
Table, Drop Leaf, Empire, Mahogany, Drawers, Claw Feet, 1840s, 29 x 18 In. . . . . *illus* 440.00
Table, Drop Leaf, Empire, Walnut, Rule-Joined Leaves, 2 Frieze Drawers, 30 x 51 In. 177.00
Table, Drop Leaf, Federal, Mahogany, Dovetailed Drawer, Virginia, 1800s, 28 x 22 In. 863.00
Table, Drop Leaf, Federal, Mahogany, Inlaid, 2 Parts, Demilune, 28 x 50 x 97 In.. . . . . 6490.00
Table, Drop Leaf, Federal, Mahogany, Maple, Drawer, 25 x 20 x 36 In.. . . . . 500.00
Table, Drop Leaf, Federal, Mahogany, Rounded Corner Leaves, String Inlay, 30 x 38 In. 472.00
Table, Drop Leaf, Federal, Walnut, Jointed, Stacking Drawers, 27 ½ x 18 x 18 In.. . . . . 388.00
Table, Drop Leaf, Federal, Walnut, Shaped Apron, Cabriole Legs, c.1950, 29 x 48 In. 956.00
Table, Drop Leaf, George II, Mahogany, Shell Carved Legs, Mid 1700s, 28 x 14 In. 1100.00
Table, Drop Leaf, George III, Mahogany, Molded Top, Skirt, Drawer, Claw Feet, 30 x 16 In. . . . 1058.00
Table, Drop Leaf, George III Style, Mahogany, 27 x 25 x 42 In.. . . . . 125.00
Table, Drop Leaf, George IV, Mahogany, 2 Drawers, 28 ½ x 57 ½ x 31 ½ In. 650.00
Table, Drop Leaf, Georgian, Mahogany, D-Shape Leaves, 18th Century, 27 x 14 x 38 In. 410.00
Table, Drop Leaf, Handkerchief, Chippendale, Mahogany, Swivel, Tripod, England, 28 x 18 In. 1100.00
Table, Drop Leaf, Handkerchief, Kittinger, Mahogany, Scrolled Apron, 28 x 34 In. 823.00
Table, Drop Leaf, Hepplewhite, Walnut, Scalloped Apron, Early 1800s, 30 x 47 x 44 In. 176.00
Table, Drop Leaf, Jacobean, Oak, Gateleg, 25 ½ x 36 x 30 ½ In.. . . . . 2252.00
Table, Drop Leaf, Mahogany, Acanthus Carved Base, Pedestal Base, Paw Feet, 30 x 41 In. 805.00
Table, Drop Leaf, Mahogany, Carved, Curved Plinth, Paw Feet, Casters, 37 x 23 In. 1762.00
Table, Drop Leaf, Mahogany, Carved, Drawers, Spiral & Reeded Legs, c.1830, 29 x 37 In.. . . . . 1410.00
Table, Drop Leaf, Mahogany, Carved, New York, c.1815-20, 34 ¾ x 22 In.. . . . . 2489.00
Table, Drop Leaf, Mahogany, Drawer, Paw Feet, c.1810, 28 ½ x 37 In.. . . . . 1762.00
Table, Drop Leaf, Mahogany, Drawer, Pedestal Base, Md., c.1810, 28 x 25 In. 1035.00
Table, Drop Leaf, Mahogany, Pegged, Deep Curved Drops, Cabriole Gatelegs, 28 x 36 In.. . . . . 518.00
Table, Drop Leaf, Mahogany, Round Tapered Legs, Pad Feet, 28 x 17 In.. . . . . 510.00
Table, Drop Leaf, Mahogany, Tray, 2 Tiers, 3-Footed, Casters, 19th Century, 31 x 20 In. 263.00
Table, Drop Leaf, Maple, Swing Arm Supports, Turned Legs, Leaves, c.1835, 29 x 38 In.. . . . . . 411.00
Table, Drop Leaf, Neoclassical Style, Bird's-Eye Maple, Pedestal, Plinth, 28 x 33 x 27 ½ In. . . . 561.00
Table, Drop Leaf, Oak, Gateleg, England, 19 ¾ x 27 ½ In.. . . . . 2000.00
Table, Drop Leaf, Old Blue Paint, Scrubbed, 52 x 22 x 39 In. 95.00
Table, Drop Leaf, Pine, Grain Paint, Red Wash, Turned Legs, 29 ½ x 36 x 15 In.. . . . . 70.00
Table, Drop Leaf, Queen Anne, Double Ogee Apron, New England, 1700s, 27 x 39 In.. . . . . 1121.00
Table, Drop Leaf, Queen Anne, Mahogany, Mid 1700s, 27 x 41 In. 2726.00
Table, Drop Leaf, Queen Anne, Mahogany, Pad Feet, Ireland, 1790s, 29 x 35 x 15 In. 525.00
Table, Drop Leaf, Queen Anne, Mahogany, Pad Feet, Signed, 25 x 42 x 21 In. 800.00
Table, Drop Leaf, Queen Anne, Mahogany, Rectangular Top, Hinged, 27 x 15 ½ x 48 In. 1150.00
Table, Drop Leaf, Queen Anne, Mahogany, Rounded Ends, Demilune, 30 x 58 In. 3120.00
Table, Drop Leaf, Queen Anne, Mahogany, Shaped Skirt, Cabriole Legs, 27 x 48 In. 805.00
Table, Drop Leaf, Queen Anne, Maple, Demilune Leaves, Cabriole Legs, 27 x 15 x 40 In. 2415.00
Table, Drop Leaf, Queen Anne, Maple, Oak, Rounded Corners, Swing Legs, 28 x 42 In. 1763.00
Table, Drop Leaf, Queen Anne, Maple, Pine, Cabriole Legs, Mid 1700s, 27 ½ x 12 In. 588.00
Table, Drop Leaf, Queen Anne, Maple, Red & Black, Grain Painted, c.1760, 27 x 42 In. 633.00
Table, Drop Leaf, Queen Anne, Maple, Rounded Leaves, Turned Legs, 27 x 45 In.. . . . . 470.00

TIP

To clean oil-based paint off old brass fixtures or hardware, use vegetable oil. Paint the oil on it, let the oil rest for 15 minutes or more, then wipe off the oil with a rough cloth. If necessary, repeat.

Furniture, Table, Drop Leaf, Empire, Mahogany, Drawers, Claw Feet, 1840s, 29 x 18 In.
$440.00

Furniture, Table, Drop Leaf, William & Mary, Oak, Oval Top, England, 27 x 9 x 22 In.
$515.00

Furniture, Table, Eastlake, Walnut, Burled, Oval Marble Inset, Shaped Apron, 31 x 34 In.
$300.00

Furniture, Table, G. Stickley, No. 436, Curved Cross Stretchers, c.1902, 28 x 24 In. $2760.00

Furniture, Table, Game, Queen Anne, Mahogany, Triple Top, Gateleg, 1700s, 31 x 31 In. $2500.00

TIP

If you accidentally dust off a bit of veneer, a loose screw, or a piece of metal mounting, immediately put it in an envelope in a drawer or tape or pin it to the back of the furniture. When you have time, decide if you or an expert should do the needed restoration. These small pieces should be carefully saved because they can never be exactly duplicated.

Table, Drop Leaf, Queen Anne, Walnut, Circular Legs, Pad Feet, 29 x 44 x 44 In. 413.00
Table, Drop Leaf, Queen Anne, Walnut, Rectangular Leaves, 1800s, 19 x 27 In., Miniature ... 411.00
Table, Drop Leaf, Queen Anne, Walnut, Scalloped Apron, Pad Feet, c.1760, 28 x 16 x 42 In. .. 468.00
Table, Drop Leaf, Queen Anne, Walnut, Turned Legs, Pad Feet, 27 ¾ x 50 In. 460.00
Table, Drop Leaf, Regency, Mahogany, Carved Saber Legs, Casters, 29 x 21 In. 805.00
Table, Drop Leaf, Regency, Mahogany, Pine, Straight Apron, Faux Drawer, 29 x 39 In........ 264.00
Table, Drop Leaf, Regency, Mahogany, Top Shape Feet, 31 ½ x 48 x 22 In. 2400.00
Table, Drop Leaf, Rococo Revival, Walnut, Gatelegs, Victorian, 28 x 36 x 48 In. 300.00
Table, Drop Leaf, Rosewood, Gateleg, Leaves, Norway, 29 x 69 In. 1020.00
Table, Drop Leaf, Sheraton, Mahogany, D-Shape Leaves, Rope-Twist Legs, 30 x 20 x 52 In.... 403.00
Table, Drop Leaf, Sheraton, Mahogany, Early 19th Century, 29 x 46 x 59 In............... 351.00
Table, Drop Leaf, Sheraton, Mahogany, Reeded Legs, c.1820, 30 x 42 In.................. 500.00
Table, Drop Leaf, Sheraton, Rope Turned Legs, 36 x 20 In............................. 230.00
Table, Drop Leaf, Softwood, Pie Board Ends, Drawer, 27 ½ x 53 x 41 ½ In................. 660.00
Table, Drop Leaf, Stickley Bros., No. 2636, Wood, 13 x 28 ½ In. 840.00
Table, Drop Leaf, Tiger Maple, Red Wash, Drawer, 36 x 18 x 29 In........................ 1035.00
Table, Drop Leaf, Victorian, Burl Walnut, Pierced, Swing Legs, Casters, 29 x 30 x 14 In...... 195.00
Table, Drop Leaf, Victorian, Mahogany, Ebonized Stringing, Splayed Legs, 42 x 39 In........ 2640.00
Table, Drop Leaf, Victorian, Rosewood, Demilune, 29 x 24 x 9 In. 660.00
Table, Drop Leaf, Victorian, Rosewood, Openwork Trestle, 28 x 35 x 39 In................ 711.00
Table, Drop Leaf, Walnut, Drawer, Leather Top, 1890s, 30 x 36 In........................ 495.00
Table, Drop Leaf, Walnut, Painted, Swing Arms, Early 1800s, 28 ½ x 14 In. 823.00
Table, Drop Leaf, William & Mary, Oak, Oval Top, England, 27 x 9 x 22 In. .... *illus* 515.00
Table, Drop Leaf, William & Mary, Oak, Oval Top, Turned Legs, England, 1800s, 27 x 9 In.... 546.00
Table, Drop Leaf, William & Mary, Walnut, 2 Drawers, Gateleg, c.1740, 28 x 20 x 48 In. 3000.00
Table, Drop Leaf, William & Mary, Walnut, Drawer, Gateleg, Stretchers, 29 x 22 In.......... 935.00
Table, Drum, Empire, Flame Mahogany, Drawer, Claw Feet, 28 x 27 In. 1600.00
Table, Drum, Federal, Tambour Door, Tripod Base, Casters, c.1950, 30 x 28 In. 299.00
Table, Drum, George III Style, Mahogany, Drawers, Splayed Legs, 30 x 36 In................ 6000.00
Table, Drum, Louis XV, Marquetry, Galleried, Trompe L'Oeil, Drawers, 1800s, 30 x 14 In. 944.00
Table, Drum, Mahogany, Carved, Leather Top, 5 Drawers, 3-Footed, B. Ferber, 28 x 34 In..... 2600.00
Table, Drum, Regency, Mahogany, Green Leather, 4 Drawers, Legs, England, 29 x 48 In...... 2900.00
Table, Drum, Regency, Mahogany, Leather Top, 8 Drawers, Early 1800s, 31 x 48 In. 3978.00
Table, Eames, IR-1, Birch Top, Chrome Folding Legs, Herman Miller, 22 x 18 In., Child's.... 780.00
Table, Eastlake, Walnut, Burled, Oval Marble Inset, Shaped Apron, 31 x 34 In.......... *illus* 300.00
Table, Eastlake, Walnut, White Marble Top, Shaped Corners, Victorian, 30 x 25 In. 90.00
Table, Edwardian, Neoclassical, Painted, D-Shape Top, Figural Plaque, 32 x 46 x 19 In...... 944.00
Table, Edwardian, Rosewood, Inlaid, Round Top, 4 Drawers, Lower Shelf, 29 x 30 In........ 690.00
Table, Edwardian, Satinwood, Mahogany, Multicolored, Classical Figures, 18 In. Sq......... 2160.00
Table, Elm, Brown Lacquer, Square Top, Circular Legs, 21 x 29 ½ In. Sq. 598.00
Table, Elm, Lacquered, Shanxi Province, Chinese, c.1800, 33 ½ x 38 In.................. 568.00
Table, Elm, Marble Top, Mother-Of-Pearl Inlay, Oval, 32 x 58 x 38 In.................... 1200.00
Table, Empire Style, Bookmatched Mahogany Veneer, Ormolu-Mounted Skirt, 29 x 36 In. ... 201.00
Table, Empire Style, Ebonized, Gilt Metal, Octagonal, Turned Legs, 18 x 20 x 20 In.......... 840.00
Table, Empire Style, Gilt Bronze, Round Marble Top, Metal Frame, Hoof Feet, 27 x 28 In..... 8400.00
Table, Farm, Black Painted Base, Scrubbed Top, 85 x 35 x 29 In........................ 805.00
Table, Farm, Cherry, Breadboard Ends, T-Stretcher, Square Legs, France, 30 x 71 In......... 3163.00
Table, Farm, Curly Maple Top, Breadboard Ends, Green Stretcher Base, 31 x 38 In.......... 1763.00
Table, Farm, Fruitwood, Plank Top, Apron Drawer, H-Stretcher, France, 28 x 71 In.......... 1495.00
Table, Farm, Mixed Wood, Overhanging Top, Round Edge, Drawer, France, 1800s, 31 x 67 In. 1935.00
Table, Farm, Oak, Breadboard Ends, H-Stretcher, Drawer, 1800s, 29 x 74 x 33 In. 900.00
Table, Farm, Pine, Plank Apron, Turned Legs, 30 ½ x 75 In............................ 1200.00
Table, Farm, Pine, Scrubbed, Painted, Plain Frieze, Tapered Legs, 1800s, 28 x 68 In......... 413.00
Table, Farm, Pine, Scrubbed Top, Tapered Legs, c.1880, 73 x 31 In...................... 822.00
Table, Farm, Softwood, 3-Board Top, Turned Legs, 30 x 59 ½ x 34 ½ In.................. 195.00
Table, Farm, Spruce, Rectangular, 3-Board Top, X-Shape Base, c.1920, 29 x 35 x 83 In. 627.00
Table, Farm, Walnut, 2-Board Top, Deep Overhang, Tapered Legs, 1800s, 27 x 38 x 72 In..... 382.00
Table, Federal, Bird's-Eye Maple, Cherry Top, Drawer, Dovetailed, c.1830, 29 x 22 In. 575.00
Table, Federal, Cherry, Mahogany, Tilt Top, Brass Latch, Ogee Legs, 30 x 26 x 18 In. 110.00
Table, Federal, Cherry, Tiger Maple, Drawers, Turned Legs, Mid-Atlantic, 1800s, 29 x 24 In. .. 748.00
Table, Federal, Cherry, Yellow Pine, 2 Drawers, Turned Legs, 1800s, 31 x 26 In. 546.00
Table, Federal, Inlaid Walnut, Skirt Drawer, Square Tapered Legs, c.1790, 29 x 36 In........ 823.00
Table, Federal, Mahogany, 2 Pedestals, Fluted, Turned, Saber Legs, 1900s, 30 x 72 In........ 575.00
Table, Federal, Mahogany, 3 Pedestals, 3 Pineapple Supports, 1800s, 36 x 107 x 30 In. 1265.00
Table, Federal, Mahogany, Band Inlay, 2 Leaves, 45 x 70 In............................ 3250.00
Table, Federal, Mahogany, Tilt Top, Acanthus Leaf Stem, Tripod Feet, c.1820, 29 x 26 In. 384.00
Table, Federal, Walnut, Dovetailed Drawer, Sugar Bin, Till, Ky., Early 1800s, 27 x 18 In. 1150.00

Table, Federal, Walnut, Drawer, Dividers, Poplar Inlay, Turned Legs, Southern, 30 x 25 In. . . . 431.00
Table, Federal, Walnut, Tilt Top, Round, Birdcage, Baluster Pedestal, 1700s, 30 x 38 In. 359.00
Table, Federal Style, Mahogany, Galleried Tray, Conforming Trays, 29 x 21 In., Pair 649.00
Table, Finn Juhl, Wood, Inlaid Circle, Rounded Corners, 29 ½ x 76 x 46 In. 310.00
Table, Frank Lloyd Wright, Hexagonal Top, Taliesin Edge, Marked, 22 x 20 x 17 In. 1680.00
Table, Frank Lloyd Wright, Round Slate Top, Cruciform Base, Marked, Henredon, 22 x 17 In. 4200.00
Table, French Provincial, Louis XV Style, Oak, Multicolored Frieze, 30 x 37 x 29 In. 2400.00
Table, French Provincial, Oak, Fruitwood, Planked, Frieze Drawer, 28 x 35 In. 1440.00
Table, French Provincial, Oak, Parquetry, Draw Leaf, Splayed Rings, 28 x 68 x 29 In. 189.00
Table, French Provincial, Walnut, Drawers, Stretchers, 31 x 112 x 29 ½ In. 3346.00
Table, Fruitwood, 2 Pedestals, Inverted Acorn, 30 ½ x 120 x 54 In. 4080.00
Table, Fruitwood, Carved, Inlaid, Tilt Top, Apollo In Chariot, c.1920, 31 x 31 ¾ In. 6250.00
Table, Fruitwood, Leather Inset, Frieze Drawer, Lower Shelf, 26 x 16 In. 840.00
Table, Fruitwood, Multicolored, Tapered Legs, Bulbous Feet, 25 x 38 x 22 In. 1320.00
Table, Fruitwood, Serpentine Gallery, Drawers, Shaped Apron, 29 x 16 x 12 In. 777.00
Table, Fruitwood, Tapered Legs, Gilt Leaf Carving, Italy, 25 x 38 In. 1320.00
Table, Fruitwood, Tilt Top, Black Distressed Paint, 3 Splayed Legs, 30 x 44 In. 1320.00
Table, G. Nakashima, Burl Oak, Butterfly Keys, 1987, 22 ½ x 29 ¾ x 27 ½ In. 85000.00
Table, G. Nelson, Walnut, Steel Legs, Herman Miller, 30 x 59 In. 1560.00
Table, G. Poillerat, Iron, Wood, Round, Black Base, Double Rope Motif, 29 x 63 In. 1955.00
Table, G. Stickley, No. 436, Curved Cross Stretchers, c.1902, 28 x 24 In. . . . . *illus* 2760.00
Table, G. Stickley, No. 449, Eastwood, Stacked Stretcher, Signed, 22 x 24 In. 3850.00
Table, G. Stickley, No. 656, Round, Pedestal Base, Leaves, Signed, 29 ½ x 54 In. 3200.00
Table, G. Stickley, Round Leather Top, Stacked Stretcher, Signed, 40 x 30 In. 3240.00
Table, Galle, Inlaid Flowers, Lower Shelf, Turned Legs, 29 x 15 ½ In. 1080.00
Table, Game, Ash, Top Parcheesi Board, Drawer, c.1890, 20 x 25 In. 3447.00
Table, Game, Burl, Inlaid Checkers, Chessboard, Knopped Stem, 8 ¼ x 10 In. 652.00
Table, Game, Checkerboard, Carved, Marquetry, 30 x 19 In. 201.00
Table, Game, Chinese Rosewood, Hung-Mu, Floating Panel, Horse Hoof Feet, 31 x 36 In. 2880.00
Table, Game, Chippendale, Mahogany, Carved, Drawer, Boston, c.1760, 29 x 32 In. 10000.00
Table, Game, Chippendale, Mahogany, Carved, Figured, Claw & Ball Feet, 29 x 30 In. 28125.00
Table, Game, Chippendale, Mahogany, Flip Top, Double Fly-Leg Support, 29 x 36 In. 1840.00
Table, Game, Chippendale, Walnut, Flip Top, Swing Leg, Late 1700s, 29 x 31 x 16 In. 2875.00
Table, Game, Chippendale Style, Inlaid Mahogany, Banded Flip Top, 28 x 33 In. 1058.00
Table, Game, Chippendale Style, Mahogany, Drawer, X-Stretcher, 1890s, 28 x 18 x 23 In. 475.00
Table, Game, Drop Leaf, Regency Style, Mahogany, Backgammon Board, 30 x 18 x 29 In. . . . 474.00
Table, Game, Empire, Mahogany, Flip Top, 29 x 36 ¾ x 19 In. 425.00
Table, Game, Empire, Mahogany, Flip Top, Scroll Feet, c.1840, 30 x 36 In., Pair. 504.00
Table, Game, Federal, Mahogany Top, Swag, Flower Inlay, N.Y., c.1800, 29 x 36 In. 6210.00
Table, Game, Federal, Rosewood, Mahogany, Birch, Mass., c.1805, 30 x 21 In. 8750.00
Table, Game, Floral Marquetry, Chessboard, Fluted, Tapered Legs, 29 ½ x 28 In. 800.00
Table, Game, Fruitwood, Parquetry, Chessboard Top, Tripod, Geometric Motif, 30 x 20 In. . . . 267.00
Table, Game, George III, Inlaid, Shaped Flip Top, Inlaid Apron, 29 x 35 In. 510.00
Table, Game, George III, Mahogany, Carved, Green Felt, c.1715, 29 x 34 x 17 In. 178.00
Table, Game, George III, Mahogany, Serpentine Top, Leaf Carved, 1800s, 29 x 34 In. 2115.00
Table, Game, George III, Walnut, Turreted Corners, Hinged, Cabriole Legs, 30 x 44 x 22 In. . . 2640.00
Table, Game, George III Style, Mahogany, Inlaid, Banded, Square Legs, 29 x 35 x 19 In. 1020.00
Table, Game, George III Style, Mahogany, Rosewood, 31 ¾ x 35 ½ x 17 ¾ In. 1320.00
Table, Game, Georgian, Mahogany, Flip Top, 9 Cups Interior, 1800s, 18 x 23 x 44 In. 546.00
Table, Game, Georgian, Mahogany, Flip Top, Crossbanding, 29 x 38 In. 360.00
Table, Game, Kittinger, Chippendale, Mahogany, Half Round, Flip Top, 32 x 32 In. 4230.00
Table, Game, Louis Philippe, Mahogany, Flip Top, Inset Felt Surface, 30 x 33 In. 1140.00
Table, Game, Louis Philippe, Mahogany, Flip Top, Molded Skirt, 1800s, 30 x 32 In. 919.00
Table, Game, Louis Philippe, Mahogany, Inlaid, Gilt Metal, Swivel Top, 30 x 26 In. 1200.00
Table, Game, Louis XVI, Parquetry, Gilt Bronze Mounted, Accordion Action, 30 x 33 In. 1185.00
Table, Game, Mahogany, Birch, Inlaid, Figured, Mass., c.1805, 21 x 36 In. 20000.00
Table, Game, Mahogany, Carved Pedestal, 4 Claw Feet, c.1830, 30 x 36 In. 944.00
Table, Game, Mahogany, Flip Top, Carved Festoon, 30 x 32 In. 325.00
Table, Game, Mahogany, Flip Top, Chessboard, Lined Interior, Boston, c.1840, 30 x 36 In. . . . 5925.00
Table, Game, Mahogany, Leaf Carved Stretcher, Knees, Claw Feet, c.1820, 30 x 37 In. 1062.00
Table, Game, Mahogany, Ormolu Mounts, Lyre, Brass Casters, c.1825, 29 x 36 In. 2015.00
Table, Game, Mahogany, Triple Top, Scrolled Skirts, 1700s, 31 x 31 x 16 In. 2760.00
Table, Game, Napoleon III, Ebonized, Parquetry Panels, Leaf Design, 30 x 34 ½ x 17 In. 840.00
Table, Game, Queen Anne, Mahogany, Triple Top, Gateleg, 1700s, 31 x 31 In. . . . . *illus* 2500.00
Table, Game, Queen Anne Style, Mahogany, Drawer, Pad Feet, 29 x 36 ½ x 18 In. 2400.00
Table, Game, Regency, Black, White Penwork, Flowers, Checkerboard, Lyres, c.1820, 30 x 18 In. 2645.00
Table, Game, Regency, Mahogany, Demilune, Veneered, Banded, 29 x 35 x 18 In. 2400.00

TIP

If the screw holding a hinge is loose, try this old-fashioned remedy. Break the heads off several large wooden kitchen matches. Put the wooden strips in the hole with some glue, then screw the old screw back into place.

Furniture, Table, George III, Mahogany, Tilt Top, Plate Wells, Wheat Stalks, 1780s, 42 x 34 In.
$1320.00

Furniture, Table, J. Hoffmann, Beech, 8 Spindle Legs, Brass Base Ring, c.1908, 26 x 29 In.
$2160.00

TIP
Examine a piece of furniture and look for unexplained holes, stains, and fade marks. They may indicate a fake.

F

Furniture, Table, L. & J.G. Stickley, No. 508, Round, Shelf, Signed, 24 ½ x 24 ½ In.
$2100.00

All Stickley Is Not the Same
Gustav Stickley is the most famous of the Arts & Crafts furniture makers in the Stickley family. But his brothers Charles, Albert, John George, and Leopold had their own firms. Gustav's furniture was marked with the "Craftsman" trademark. His brothers used the marks "Stickley Brothers Company," "L. & J.G. Stickley," and "Stickley & Brandt Chair Company." Gustav also used "Gustav Stickley Company," "Stickley & Simonds Company," "United Crafts," and "Craftsman Workshops." L. & J.G. Stickley, Inc., is still making furniture.

Table, Game, Regency, Mahogany, Lacquered, Decoupage Banding, 21 In. Sq. 3120.00
Table, Game, Rococo Revival, Rosewood, Maple Lined, Cabriole Legs, 29 x 33 x 18 In. 1140.00
Table, Game, Rosewood, Flip Top, Green Leather Interior, Scrolls, England, c.1830s, 39 x 35 In. 575.00
Table, Game, Sheraton, Birch, Mahogany, Bowfront, Cookie-Corner Top, 1810, 40 x 17 In.. . . 900.00
Table, Game, Square, 4 Swing-Out Chip Compartments, Chairs, Dunbar, 28 x 36 In., 5 Piece. 1800.00
Table, Game, Walnut, Fruitwood, Parquetry, Cabriole Legs, Italy, 29 x 35 In. 4080.00
Table, Gateleg, Mahogany, Round Edge, Oval Top, Tapered Legs, Pad Feet, 28 x 54 In.. . . . . . . 1380.00
Table, Gateleg, Oak, Single-Board Oval Top, Vase Turned Legs, England, 1700s, 40 x 45 In. . . 881.00
Table, George II, Mahogany, Brass Inlay, Tilt Top, Tripod, 27 x 22 In. 15000.00
Table, George II, Mahogany, Hinged Rectangular Top, Frieze Drawer, 27 x 23 x 20 In.. . . . . . . 1298.00
Table, George II, Mahogany, Shaped Top, Shell Carved Apron, Leaf Carved Legs, 28 x 29 In.. . 533.00
Table, George II, Mahogany, Tilt Top, Baluster Pedestal, Claw & Ball Feet, 46 x 30 In. 384.00
Table, George II, Mahogany, Tilt Top, Carved, Fluted Urn Pedestal, Snake Feet, 41 x 24 In. . . . 325.00
Table, George II, Mahogany, Tilt Top, Tripod, Claw Feet, c.1760, 28 x 27 In. 13750.00
Table, George III, Mahogany, Demilune, Stringing, Tapered Legs, 33 x 52 In.. . . . . 3200.00
Table, George III, Mahogany, Round Tilt Top, Tripod, Piecrust Edge, 1800s, 29 x 21 In.. . . . . . 2040.00
Table, George III, Mahogany, Tilt Top, Plate Wells, Wheat Stalks, 1780s, 42 x 34 In.. . . . . *illus* 1320.00
Table, George III, Mahogany, Tilt Top, Scalloped, Molded Tray, Cabriole Legs, 25 x 22 In. 1673.00
Table, George III, Mahogany, Tilt Top, Scalloped Shell Form, 3 Splayed Legs, 38 x 28 In.. . . . . 2640.00
Table, George III, Mahogany, Tilt Top, Splayed Legs, Leaf Carved, Pad Feet, 39 x 29 In. 1920.00
Table, George III, Mahogany, Tripod, Round, Dish Tilt Top, 28 ½ x 20 In.. . . . . 720.00
Table, George III, Oak, Drawer, Brass Pulls, Chamfered Edge, Late 1700s, 28 x 35 In. 561.00
Table, George III, Shell Inlay, Tray, Oval Galleried Top, Painted Flowers, 25 x 28 In. 1200.00
Table, George III Style, Demilune, Marble Top, Carved Frieze, Fluted Legs, 31 x 50 x 25 In.. . . 4320.00
Table, George III Style, Ebonized, Gilt, Landscape, Flower Border, 30 x 48 x 24 In., Pair 7500.00
Table, George III Style, Mahogany, Satinwood, D-Shape Top, 28 x 48 x 24 In., Pair 1673.00
Table, George III Style, Mahogany, Tilt Top, Splayed Legs, Reeded Feet, 29 x 52 x 39 In. 2040.00
Table, George III Style, Painted Wood, Marble Top, Square, Legs, 34 x 41 ½ x 16 ¾ In. 3120.00
Table, George IV, Parcel Gilt, Mahogany, Stretcher, c.1820, 33 x 24 In., Pair 11875.00
Table, George Mathias, Laminate, Brass, c.1970, 12 x 49 x 29 ½ In.. 7500.00
Table, George V, Rosewood, Carved Pedestal, Tripod, c.1825, 29 x 15 In., Pair. 20000.00
Table, Georgian, Mahogany, Carved, Round Top, Columnar Cage, Tripod, 31 x 32 In. 209.00
Table, Georgian, Mahogany, Cock-Beaded Drawer, Molded Chamfered Legs, c.1770, 29 x 35 In. 881.00
Table, Georgian, Mahogany, Tray, Gallery Top, Pierced Grips, 23 x 28 In. 748.00
Table, Georgian Style, Mahogany, Round Tilt Top, Turned Post, Splayed Feet, 30 In. 192.00
Table, Gilt, Carved, Top Painted Black, Gold Putti Pedestal, c.1900s, 27 x 24 In.. . . . . 1265.00
Table, Gilt, Multicolored, Mother-Of-Pearl, Papier-Mache, Scalloped Top, Scalloped Top, 29 x 28 In. 1320.00
Table, Green Marble Top, 2 Leaping Deer Base, Cast Metal, P. Sega, France, c.1925, 27 In.. . . . 1121.00
Table, Grotto, Gilt, Gesso, Carved Dolphins, Shells, Venice, c.1895, 28 x 34 In. 5750.00
Table, Gueridon, Louis XVI Style, Kingwood, Marble Top, Starburst Shelf, 32 x 26 In. 3360.00
Table, Gueridon, Mahogany, Fruitwood, Tilt Top, Marble, Brass Border, c.1780, 28 x 28 In.. . . 9375.00
Table, H. Probber, Hexagon Composite Top, Brass Inserts, Tapered Mahogany Legs, 22 x 18 In. 840.00
Table, Hardwood, Octagonal, Banded, Geometric & Leaf Inlay, North Africa, 21 x 20 In. 1440.00
Table, Harvest, Pine, Painted, Turned Legs, Pullout Supports, Red Paint, 29 x 20 In.. . . . . 2233.00
Table, Harvest, Scrubbed Top, Turned Legs, 73 x 24 x 28 In.. . . . . 690.00
Table, Harvest, Walnut, Yellow Pine, Maple, Drawer, Southern, c.1825, 29 x 47 x 33 In.. . . . . . 1380.00
Table, Hepplewhite, Cherry, Pine, Overhang Top, Drawer, String Inlay, c.1820, 29 x 31 In. . . . 294.00
Table, Hepplewhite, Cherry, Softwood, Serpentine Top, 2 Drawers, 29 x 35 ½ x 21 In. 999.00
Table, Hepplewhite, Mahogany, Kingwood Crossbanded, Gateleg, 1700s, 28 ½ x 34 In. 1750.00
Table, Hepplewhite, Mahogany, Projecting Plinth Top, String Inlay, 29 x 21 In., Pair. 359.00
Table, Hunt, Blue Paint, Yellow Pine, Virginia, 36 x 44 In. 1438.00
Table, Hunt, George III, Mahogany, Hinged, c.1770, 29 x 79 In.. . . . . 9375.00
Table, Hunt, Poplar, Drawer, Pegged, Cut Nail, Tapered Square Legs, 1800s, 37 x 28 In.. . . . . . 8050.00
Table, Iron, Multicolored Tiles, X-Shape Stretcher, Continental, 19 x 21 x 15 In. 1416.00
Table, Iron, White Paint, Oval Glass Top, Vine & Leaf Detail, 18 x 30 In., Pair 201.00
Table, Italian Style, Marble Top, Brass, Turned Legs, Mid 20th Century, 15 ½ x 60 In. 115.00
Table, J. Hoffmann, Beech, 8 Spindle Legs, Brass Base Ring, c.1908, 26 x 29 In.. . . . . *illus* 2160.00
Table, Jacobean Style, Square Paneled Top, Draw Leaf, Bulbous Supports, 29 ½ In.. . . . . 236.00
Table, Jansen, Brass, Marble Top, c.1960, 15 x 35 In.. . . . . 5615.00
Table, Japanese Style, Ebonized, Onyx Top, Victorian, 30 x 39 ½ x 26 ½ In. 2400.00
Table, Jean Prouve, Compass, Wood Top, Black Frame, c.1950, 31 x 59 In.. . . . . 6600.00
Table, Jean Royere, Oak, Iron, Yo-Yo Feet, 1950s, 29 x 33 In. 13750.00
Table, Joe D'Urso, Mahogany Planks, Steel Base, Casters, 28 ½ x 12 x 30 In.. . . . . 4375.00
Table, Killian Bros., Medallion Inlay, 1876 Philadelphia Exhibition, 1870s, 31 x 25 In.. . . . . . 13800.00
Table, L. & J.G. Stickley, No. 508, Round, Shelf, Signed, 24 ½ x 24 ½ In. . . . . *illus* 2100.00
Table, L. & J.G. Stickley, Oak, Round Top, Low Shelf, 4 Square Legs, 1916, 29 x 18 In. 652.00
Table, Laverne, Ming, Round, Shelf, 3 Legs, Figures, Label, 1960s, 22 x 24 In. 4800.00

Table, Laverne, Shang Ti Pair, Enamel, Bronze, Blue Flowers, 1960s, 20 In., Pair. 6875.00
Table, Lazy Susan, Southern Pine, Round Revolving Plateau, Late 1800s, 32 x 53 In. 294.00
Table, Library, Adam, Mahogany, Oval Leather Top, Drawers, 19th Century, 31 x 96 In.. . . . . . 2990.00
Table, Library, Art Deco, Black Lacquered Plinth Top, Pedestal Shelving, 27 x 36 In. 177.00
Table, Library, Arts & Crafts, Oak, Frieze Drawer, Bookshelf Ends, 1915-20, 30 x 43 x 27 In. . . 400.00
Table, Library, Baroque Style, Mahogany, Bead Carved Frieze, Trestle Base, 30 x 87 In. 472.00
Table, Library, Colonial Revival, Fumed Oak, Carved Apron, c.1875, 28 x 29 In.. . . . . 173.00
Table, Library, Federal, Pine, Turned Legs, H-Stretcher, 1800s, 21 x 47 In.. . . . . 748.00
Table, Library, G. Stickley, No. 613, 2 Drawers, Hammered Copper Pulls, 30 x 36 x 24 In. 1200.00
Table, Library, G. Stickley, No. 636, Round Top, Curved Stretchers, 29 ½ x 44 In. 2700.00
Table, Library, G. Stickley, No. 653, Drawer, Stretcher, Label, 29 x 48 x 30 In. 1080.00
Table, Library, George III, Chippendale, Mahogany, Center Drawer, Pedestals, 31 x 54 In. 53125.00
Table, Library, Georgian, Mahogany, Inset Leather Top, Drawers, Spade Feet, 30 x 94 In. 2056.00
Table, Library, Herter Bros., Aesthetic Revival, Ebonized, Gold Incised, c.1880 . . . . 8050.00
Table, Library, L. & J.G. Stickley, No. 563, Hexagonal Top, Wagon Wheel, 28 ½ x 48 In. 5100.00
Table, Library, L. & J.G. Stickley, Oak, Drawer, Shelf, Red Signature, 1910, 29 x 42 In. 1840.00
Table, Library, Limbert, Cutout Sides, Corbels, 29 x 50 x 28 In. 2040.00
Table, Library, Limbert, No. 153, Turtle Top, Blind Drawer, Cutout Sides, 29 x 48 x 30 In. 2300.00
Table, Library, Limbert, No. 647, 2 Drawers, Panel Shelf Stretcher, 29 x 48 In. 900.00
Table, Library, Limbert, No. 1132, Blind Drawer, Signed, 29 x 48 x 28 In. 1100.00
Table, Library, Limbert, Oak, Turtle Top, Drawer, Cane Slab Sides, Ebony Detail, 48 x 29 In.. . 3900.00
Table, Library, Louis XV Style, Walnut, Skirt Drawer, Mid 1800s, 30 x 43 In. 1103.00
Table, Library, Mixed Wood, Plank Top, 4 Divided Wells, Turned Legs, 38 x 75 In. 354.00
Table, Library, Nutting, No. 637, Maple, Drawer, Signed, 30 x 50 x 30 In. 550.00
Table, Library, Oak, Gargoyle Supports, 72 In. 4025.00
Table, Library, P. Jeanneret, Teak, Illuminated, Metal, Frosted Glass, c.1966, 47 x 96 x 48 In. . 301000.00
Table, Library, Regency, Bird's-Eye Maple, Mahogany, Stringing Line, Drawers, 30 x 37 In.. . . 1800.00
Table, Library, Rosewood, Round Corners, Molded Edges, 34 ½ x 82 x 41 ½ In. 4025.00
Table, Library, S. Karpen Bros., Rectangular, Cutout Sides, 29 ¾ x 41 ½ x 35 In. . . . . *illus* 3000.00
Table, Library, Stickley, Brown Leather Top, Brass Tacks, Drawer, Label, 30 x 48 x 29 In.. . . . . 2185.00
Table, Library, Victorian, Oak, Frieze, End Drawers, Turned Legs, 30 ½ x 83 In. 830.00
Table, Library, Walnut, Scallop-Carved Edge, Lion Supports, Paw Feet, c.1800, 29 x 71 In. . . . 2702.00
Table, Library, William IV, Rosewood, Inset Leather, Drawer, Splayed Legs, 30 x 39 x 21 In.. . . 4080.00
Table, Limbert, Ash, Square Top, Cane Shelf, Signed, 29 x 29 In. 510.00
Table, Limbert, No. 146, Ash, Oval Top, Lower Shelf, Cutout Side Slats, 45 x 30 In.. . . . . 2400.00
Table, Limbert, No. 148, Round Top, Cutout Stretcher, Signed, 29 x 30 In. . . . . *illus* 2880.00
Table, Limbert, No. 251, Cutouts, 8-Sided Top, Signed, 24 x 17 In. 3250.00
Table, Limbert, No. 429, Square Top, Round Corners, Cutout Sides, Shelf, 20 x 31 In. 2160.00
Table, Limestone, Iron, Square Top, Scroll Shape Supports, 20 x 38 In.. . . . . 866.00
Table, Louis Philippe, Mahogany, Ormolu, Marble Top, Column Legs, 28 x 26 In. 1560.00
Table, Louis XIV Style, Gilt, Black Lacquered Top, Fluted Legs, 32 x 40 x 22 In.. . . . . 1800.00
Table, Louis XV, Carvings, Putti Plaque, 2 Lift Tops, France, c.1890, 32 x 36 In. 1035.00
Table, Louis XV, French Provinical, Pine, Overhang Top, Scalloped Apron, 1700s, 26 x 29 In. . 1998.00
Table, Louis XV, Fruitwood, Drawer, Cabriole Legs, 28 x 33 ½ In. 1175.00
Table, Louis XV, Mahogany, Gilt Bronze Mounted, Parquetry, c.1880, 30 x 55 In. 6250.00
Table, Louis XV, Mahogany, Kingwood, Oval Top, Brass Gallery, 29 x 28 ¾ x 17 In.. . . . . 4080.00
Table, Louis XV, Oak, Marble Top, Leaf Carved, Scalloped Frieze, Pad Feet, 30 x 33 In. 2280.00
Table, Louis XV, Walnut, Gilt Tooled Leather, Frieze Drawer, 27 x 33 ½ In. 1126.00
Table, Louis XV, Walnut, Molded Top, Scalloped Apron, Drawer, Cabriole Legs, 28 x 33 In.. . . . 2115.00
Table, Louis XV, Walnut, Paneled Top, Scalloped Apron, Drawer, Cabriole Legs, 29 x 32 In. . . . 2233.00
Table, Louis XV, Walnut, Scalloped Dish Top, Skirt, Hoof Feet, 29 x 24 In. 4994.00
Table, Louis XV, Walnut, Scalloped Skirt, Drawer, Cabriole Legs, Hoof Feet, 26 x 37 In. 4113.00
Table, Louis XV, Walnut, Scalloped Skirt, Drawer, Late 1700s, 27 x 25 ½ In. 3525.00
Table, Louis XV Style, Fruitwood, Tiers, Cabriole Legs, 32 x 21 x 13 In. 2040.00
Table, Louis XV Style, Kingwood, Mahogany, Marble Top, Drawer, 28 x 11 x 8 ½ In.. . . . . 420.00
Table, Louis XV Style, Mahogany, Ormolu Mounted, Bouquet Inlay, Drawer, 20 x 22 x 15 In. . 1560.00
Table, Louis XV Style, Oak, Shaped Frieze, Corners, Drawer, Cabriole Legs, 30 x 52 In.. . . . . . 1680.00
Table, Louis XV Style, Rosewood, Kingwood, Round Top, Drawer, Sabots, 28 x 15 In. 2400.00
Table, Louis XVI, Gilt Metal Mount, Parquetry, Galleried Top, 30 x 26 In. 1135.00
Table, Louis XVI, Mahogany, Bronze Putto Panel, Marble Top, c.1920, 20 x 25 In. 266.00
Table, Louis XVI, Mahogany, Marble, Kidney Shape Top, Brass Gallery, 29 x 24 In.. . . . . 1440.00
Table, Louis XVI, Mahogany, Marble Top, Pierced Gallery, Leather Inset Slides, 29 In. 1920.00
Table, Louis XVI, Mahogany, Marble Top, Round, Pierced Brass Gallery, 29 x 26 In.. . . . . 1800.00
Table, Louis XVI Style, Burl, Flower Marquetry, Lift Top, Bag Drawer, 30 x 17 In. . . . . *illus* 633.00
Table, Louis XVI Style, Fruitwood, Bookmatched Top, Leather Interior, 30 x 34 In.. . . . . 1880.00
Table, Louis XVI Style, Gallery Top, Round Marble Inset, Drawer, Shelf, 31 x 24 In. 450.00
Table, Louis XVI Style, Gilt, Marble Top, Round, Carved Frieze, 31 x 48 In. 2160.00

Furniture, Table, Library, S. Karpen Bros., Rectangular, Cutout Sides, 29 ¾ x 41 ½ x 35 In.
$3000.00

Furniture, Table, Limbert, No. 148, Round Top, Cutout Stretcher, Signed, 29 x 30 In.
$2880.00

Furniture, Table, Louis XVI Style, Burl, Flower Marquetry, Lift Top, Bag Drawer, 30 x 17 In.
$633.00

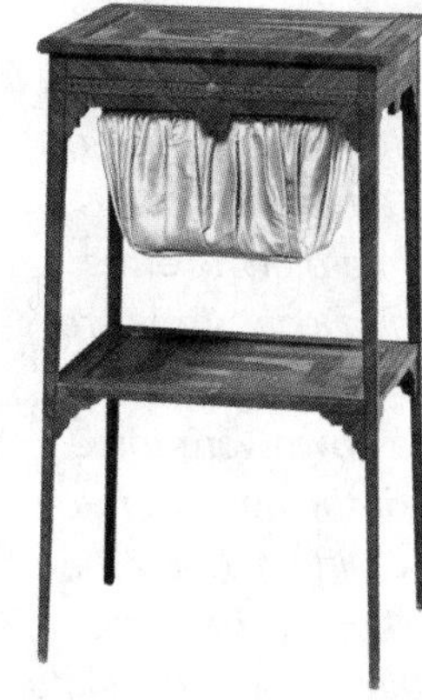

TIP
Never carry a marble tabletop flat. It can break under its own weight. Carry it in a vertical position.

Furniture, Table, Mahogany, Flame Veneer, Tilt Top, Carved Claw Feet, Round, Pa., c.1825, 29 x 46 In.
$4740.00

Furniture, Table, Mahogany, Marble Top, 3-Footed, Paw Feet, Phila., 31 ½ x 36 In.
$13200.00

TIP

Most furniture should be moved by two people. Ask for help. Dragging a table or chair is hard on its arms and legs. Arms are made to withstand a downward force, not the upward force of lifting. Carry the chair by the bottom frame. Large cabinets should not be pushed across a floor. Remove drawers and loose shelves, lock any doors or tie them shut. If possible, lift the piece off the floor to move it.

Table, Louis XVI Style, Gilt Brass, Mirrored, Reeded Supports, 18 x 13 x 11 ½ In. 960.00
Table, Louis XVI Style, Gilt Metal, Oriental Scenes, 2 Shelves, 24 x 17 x 18 In., Pair 3120.00
Table, Louis XVI Style, Kingwood, White, Gray Marble Top, 26 x 22 In., Pair 1440.00
Table, Louis XVI Style, Mahogany, Inlaid, Flower, Ribbon, 27 x 29 ½ x 21 In. 3840.00
Table, Louis XVI Style, Marble Top, ¾ Brass Gallery, Drawer, 25 x 18 In., Pair 1020.00
Table, Louis XVI Style, Marquetry, Parquetry, Hinged, Divided Top, Drawer, 29 x 23 In. 1470.00
Table, Louis XVI Style, Rosewood Border, Parquetry, Flower Design, 29 x 28 ½ In. 230.00
Table, Louis XVI Style, Walnut, Crossbanded, Drawers, Cabriole Legs, 30 x 20 x 15 In. 329.00
Table, Mahogany, 6-Lobed Top, Shamrocks, Alligators, Tripod, Block Legs, 21 x 17 In. 177.00
Table, Mahogany, Carved, Mass., c.1815, 35 ½ x 30 In. 3318.00
Table, Mahogany, Carved, N.Y., 1830-40, 35 ½ In. Diam.. .... 3318.00
Table, Mahogany, Carvings, 3 Frieze Drawers, England, 1800s, 31 x 60 ½ x 21 In. 3680.00
Table, Mahogany, Circular, Tilt Top, 3-Footed, Cabriole Legs, Beaded, 10 x 14 ½ In.. .... 1200.00
Table, Mahogany, Drawer, Column Base, Saber Legs, 1800s, 28 x 48 In. 1725.00
Table, Mahogany, Figured, Shaped Leaves, Turned Reeded Legs, Casters, 1800s, 29 x 39 In. .. 690.00
Table, Mahogany, Flame Veneer, Tilt Top, Carved Claw Feet, Pa., c.1825, 29 x 46 In. .... *illus* 4740.00
Table, Mahogany, Galleried Top, Drawer, Pad Feet, Ireland, c.1755, 29 x 14 ½ In. 6250.00
Table, Mahogany, Gallery, Tray, Open Handles, Crossbuck Stand, Web Straps, 36 x 22 In. 575.00
Table, Mahogany, Gilt Bronze Mounted, Marble Top, Drawer, c.1890, 28 x 17 In. 9375.00
Table, Mahogany, Gray, White Marble Top, Frieze Drawer, Door, 37 ½ x 32 x 17 In. 2160.00
Table, Mahogany, Hinged Opening To Basin, 2 Drawers, Cabinet, c.1830, 33 x 24 In.. .... 1955.00
Table, Mahogany, Inlaid, Baltimore, c.1795, 35 ½ x 18 In. 3081.00
Table, Mahogany, Inlaid, Medallion, Card Players, Birds, Bulbous Standard, 30 x 39 In. 3600.00
Table, Mahogany, Marble Top, 36 ½ x 39 ½ In. 2585.00
Table, Mahogany, Marble Top, 3-Footed, Paw Feet, Phila., 31 ½ x 36 In. .... *illus* 13200.00
Table, Mahogany, Ormolu Mounted, Drawers, Tapered Square Legs, 30 x 48 x 30 In.. .... 2880.00
Table, Mahogany, Swivel Top, Acanthus Corners, Paw Feet, c.1825, 47 x 23 In.. .... 4920.00
Table, Mahogany, Tilt Top, Carved Wheat, Plate Wells, Tripod Base, c.1775, 42 x 34 In. 1416.00
Table, Mahogany, Tilt Top, Circular, Carved Animal Shape Legs, Claw Feet, 30 x 45 In. 1840.00
Table, Mahogany, Tilt Top, Column Support, Carved Paw Feet, c.1825, 30 x 36 In. 2070.00
Table, Mahogany, Tilt Top, Dish Shape, Tripod Legs, c.1770, 26 x 22 In. 1645.00
Table, Mahogany, Tilt Top, Enclosed Birdcage, Arched Legs, Snake Feet, 28 x 31 In.. .... 1188.00
Table, Mahogany, Tilt Top, Piecrust Edge, Pedestal Base, Carved Knees, 29 x 26 In. 374.00
Table, Mahogany, Tray, Hinged, X-Shape Stand, Turned Legs, Late 1800s, 33 x 19 In. 230.00
Table, Mahogany, Tray, Stand, Cutout Handholds, Turned Stand, 21 ½ x 20 In. 441.00
Table, Mahogany, Turned Base, Figural Mounted, Drawer, X-Stretcher, Marklin 2013.00
Table, Mahogany Veneer, Black Marble Top, Pedestal, c.1830-40, 29 ½ x 36 In. 1020.00
Table, Mahogany Veneer, Cheval, Marble Top, Pedestal, 30 ½ x 35 x 35 In. 920.00
Table, Marble Top, Cream, Painted Flower, Cabriole Legs, 16 x 17 In., Pair 478.00
Table, Marble Top, Round, Iron Spiral, Arched Tassel, Leaves, 6 Legs, 17 ½ x 40 In.. .... 345.00
Table, Marquetry, Demilune, Drawer Fronts, Marble Top, 29 x 26 x 13 In., Pair 1434.00
Table, Marquetry, Mahogany Veneer, 6 Drawers, Pullout End, 67 x 39 In. 881.00
Table, Mashrabiya, Mixed Metal, Brass, Silver Inlay, Glass Top, Egypt, 20 x 31 In. Diam...... 225.00
Table, Ming Style, Distressed Yellow Paint, Open Frieze, Chinese, Late 1800s, 21 x 42 In...... 237.00
Table, Mixed Wood, Square Tapered Legs, 1 Leaf, c.1830, 29 x 43 In. 299.00
Table, Mixing, Mahogany, Marble, Cock-Beaded Drawer, Reeded, 32 x 25 x 23 In. 7343.00
Table, Napoleon III, Inlaid, Ormolu Mounted, Boulle, Ebony, 31 x 46 In. 690.00
Table, Napoleon III, Louis XV Style, Japonesque, Kidney Shape, 23 x 19 In., Pair 2160.00
Table, Neoclassical, Cocoa Slab Marble Top, Turned Legs, Teal Paint, c.1790, 28 x 25 In. 1075.00
Table, Neoclassical, Inlaid, Inset Leather, 2 Drawers, Late 1800s, 28 x 15 ¾ In. 443.00
Table, Neoclassical, Mahogany, Gilt, Fluted Band, Edge, Bail Feet, 27 x 44 In.. .... 7800.00
Table, Neoclassical, Mahogany, Marble Top, Cyma-Molded Frieze, Pedestal, 31 x 35 In.. ..... 3840.00
Table, Neoclassical, Pedestal Base, Inset Tooled Leather Panel, Saber Legs, 25 x 22 In. 239.00
Table, Neoclassical Style, Wave-Carved Frieze, Turned Legs, c.1815, 27 x 32 In. 2880.00
Table, Nesting, Art Deco, Marquetry, Sunburst, 3 Quarter Stretchers, 26 x 24 x 17 In., 3 Piece 502.00
Table, Nesting, Black Lacquer, Multicolored, Gesso Leaf, Bird Scene, 30 x 23 x 15 In., 3 Piece. 2160.00
Table, Nesting, Burl Walnut, Carved, Cabriole Legs, c.1920, 22 ½ x 24 x 17 In., 3 Piece 710.00
Table, Nesting, Floral Marquetry, Tapered Legs, England, 25 x 28 In., 4 Piece 359.00
Table, Nesting, Old Hickory, 2 Side Handles, Cross Stretcher, 30 x 24 In., 2 Piece 1320.00
Table, Nesting, Wormley, Walnut, Brass Stretchers, Dunbar, 22 x 28 In., 3 Piece 1320.00
Table, Oak, Bulbous Legs, X-Stretcher, Ball Feet, Spain, 28 x 34 x 25 In. 1200.00
Table, Oak, Cream Paint, Side Drawer, Fluted Square Legs, Peg Feet, 29 x 30 x 20 In. 3360.00
Table, Oak, Cut Corner Rectangular Top, Lower Shelf, c.1905, 29 x 18 In.. .... 711.00
Table, Oak, Frieze, Drawer, X-Stretcher, Square Legs, 19 ½ x 40 ½ x 36 In. 1200.00
Table, Oak, Pegged, Dovetailed, Overhang Top, Molded Edge Drawers, Stretcher, 32 x 45 In.. . 805.00
Table, Oak, Plank Top, Legs, Side Drawer, H-Stretcher, 61 x 32 In. 1200.00
Table, Oak, Scalloped Front, Frieze Drawer, Pad Feet, Early 1900s, 28 x 29 In. 2040.00

Table, Oak, Spiral Columns, Draw Leaf, Finland, 18th Century, 30 x 50 x 23 ½ In. 960.00
Table, Onyx, Bronze, Demilune, Pierced Front, Female Figure Legs, c.1950, 32 x 23 In. 767.00
Table, Oscar Bach, Iron, Bronze, Marble, Women Holding Geese, 34 x 73 x 31 In. 2185.00
Table, P. Evans, Cityscape, Glass Top, Chrome Base, c.1970, 29 x 93 In. 6000.00
Table, P. Evans, Glass, Square, Metal Clad, Raised Base, Signed, 15 In. 3120.00
Table, P. Evans, Stalagmite, Round, Glass Top, Composition, Metal Base, c.1970, 40 In. 1534.00
Table, P. Friedberg, Gilt, Glass, 3 Footed Base, 3 Hands Under Top, 1960s, 20 x 24 In. 12500.00
Table, Papier-Mache, Mother-Of-Pearl, Flowers, Black, Gilt, Pedestal, Italy, 23 x 28 In. 220.00
Table, Papier-Mache, Mother-Of-Pearl Inlay, Tilt Top, Pedestal Base, 1800s, 42 x 23 In. 478.00
Table, Parcel Gilt, Ebonized Bamboo, Tray, Tole, Bird, Flowers, 19 x 30 In. 354.00
Table, Parcel Gilt, Tray Top, 3 Swan Legs, Painted, Italy, c.1820, 29 x 18 In., Pair....... *illus* 17500.00
Table, Partner, Arts & Crafts, Leather Top, 2 Drawers, Paneled Sides, Shoefoot Base, 52 x 30 In. 2040.00
Table, Parzinger, Triangle, Leather, Mahogany, Shelf, Green, 55 x 18 In., Pair 6600.00
Table, Pedestal, Empire Style, Mahogany, Octagonal Base, 29 ½ x 36 In. Square 460.00
Table, Pedestal, G. Stickley, No. 656, Oak, Label, Early 1900s, 29 ½ x 54 In. 1500.00
Table, Pembroke, Chippendale, Cherry, Pine, Shaped Top, Serpentine Leaves, 28 x 18 In. 1116.00
Table, Pembroke, Chippendale, Mahogany, 2 Leaves, Drawer, 18th Century, 35 In. 1270.00
Table, Pembroke, Chippendale, Mahogany, c.1780, 30 x 29 x 21 In. 936.00
Table, Pembroke, Chippendale, Mahogany, Drawer, Molded Legs, Late 1700s, 27 x 20 In. 3200.00
Table, Pembroke, Chippendale, Mahogany Top, Drawer, 1700s, 39 x 23 In. 4140.00
Table, Pembroke, Chippendale, Walnut, Molded Frieze, Drawer, c.1770, 38 x 34 In. 978.00
Table, Pembroke, Drawer, Line Inlay, c.1810, 29 x 32 In. 748.00
Table, Pembroke, Federal, Cherry, Hinged Leaves, Drawer, 28 x 19 x 31 In. 403.00
Table, Pembroke, Federal, Mahogany, Inlaid, Drawer, New York, c.1800, 28 x 32 In. ..... *illus* 10625.00
Table, Pembroke, Federal, Mahogany, Inlaid, Early 1900s, 29 x 33 In. 690.00
Table, Pembroke, Federal, Mahogany, Inlaid Eagles, Figured, c.1950, 28 x 22 In. 1875.00
Table, Pembroke, Federal, Mahogany Inlay, 28 ½ x 37 ¾ x 30 In. 4750.00
Table, Pembroke, George III, Mahogany, Carved Stretcher, c.1765, 37 x 19 In. 2813.00
Table, Pembroke, George III, Mahogany, Faux Drawers, 1800s, 30 x 39 In. 1440.00
Table, Pembroke, George III, Mahogany, Fitted Drawer, X-Stretcher, 28 x 39 In. 10625.00
Table, Pembroke, George III, Mahogany, Inlaid, X-Stretcher, c.1790, 29 x 45 In. 6250.00
Table, Pembroke, George III, Mahogany, Oak Inlay, c.1790, 28 x 21 In. 575.00
Table, Pembroke, George III, Mahogany, Overhang Top, Drawer, Shelf, Casters, 28 x 35 In. .. 7500.00
Table, Pembroke, George III, Mahogany, Rosewood, c.1775, 29 x 37 x 30 In. 1554.00
Table, Pembroke, George III, Satinwood, Scalloped Medallion, Ebonized Stringing, 29 x 30 In. 299.00
Table, Pembroke, Hepplewhite, Country, Birch, Red Paint, 39 x 16 In. 690.00
Table, Pembroke, Hepplewhite, Mahogany, Inlaid, Serpentine Top, c.1800, 28 x 16 x 35 In. .. 529.00
Table, Pembroke, Hepplewhite, Old Finish, Cross Stretchers, 31 x 18 In. 1725.00
Table, Pembroke, Hepplewhite, Walnut, Pine, Tapered Legs, Drawer, Leaves, 1800s, 43 x 36 In. 264.00
Table, Pembroke, Mahogany, Beaded Drawers, Urn Pedestal, Paw Feet, 42 x 38 In. 235.00
Table, Pembroke, Mahogany, Drawer, c.1780, 28 ½ x 20 ½ x 29 In. 1755.00
Table, Pembroke, Mahogany, Fruitwood Inlaid, Frieze Drawer, Dutch, 28 x 33 x 44 In. 2844.00
Table, Pembroke, Mahogany, Inlaid, Ogee Corners, 28 x 22 x 32 In. 920.00
Table, Pembroke, Mahogany, Pine, Rosehead Nails, Shaped Leaves, Reeded Legs, 29 In. 764.00
Table, Pembroke, Regency, Mahogany, Satinwood Banding, Inlaid, c.1920, 32 x 20 In. 206.00
Table, Pembroke, Sheraton, Bird's-Eye Maple, Delaware Valley, c.1840, 28 x 21 In. 1955.00
Table, Pembroke, Sheraton, Cherry, Poplar, Turned Legs, Ball Feet, 29 x 37 x 19 In. 558.00
Table, Pembroke, Sheraton, Mahogany, Shell Inlay, Drawer, 1790s, 28 x 33 x 35 In. 2750.00
Table, Philip Webb, Oak, Round, 3 Legs, c.1870, 24 x 24 In. 938.00
Table, Phillip Powell, Walnut, Cherry, c.1955, 19 ½ x 30 x 19 ¾ In., Pair 6875.00
Table, Pier, Egyptian Revival, Carving, Drawer, Mirror, 35 x 37 x 22 In. 1422.00
Table, Pier, Empire, Gilt Bronze Mounted, Onyx Top, Classical Designs, 37 x 47 In. 2726.00
Table, Pier, Federal, Mahogany, Marble Top, Column, Claw Feet, 36 x 19 x 39 In. 6325.00
Table, Pier, George III Style, Mahogany, Inlaid, Demilune Top, Shelf, 34 x 52 In. 1875.00
Table, Pier, Mahogany, Gilt, Dolphin Supports, Mirror Back, Melon Feet, 38 x 45 x 20 In. 3231.00
Table, Pier, Mahogany, Gilt Stenciled, Marble, Gadrooned Molding, c.1815, 38 x 42 In. 11162.00
Table, Pier, Mahogany, Marble, Cove Frieze, Acanthus Supports, c.1800, 36 x 42 In. 3172.00
Table, Pier, Mahogany, Marble Top, 37 ½ x 36 x 20 In. 3000.00
Table, Pier, Mahogany, Marble Top, Molded Skirt, Paw Feet, 6 Drawers, 35 x 44 In. 16450.00
Table, Pier, Mahogany, Marble Top, Ormolu Mounts, New York, c.1820, 41 x 19 In. ..... *illus* 8750.00
Table, Pier, Mahogany, Marble Top, Scrolled Ends, Shaped Platform, 36 x 42 x 20 In. 1875.00
Table, Pier, Mahogany, Scrolled Supports, Mirror Back, Scroll Feet, c.1860, 37 x 42 In., Pair .. 1956.00
Table, Pier, Mahogany, Variegated Marble, S-Scroll, Mirror, Gilt, c.1830, 37 x 42 In. 1175.00
Table, Pier, Neoclassical, Rosewood, Paint, 3 Drawers, N.Y., c.1825, 33 x 35 In. 2370.00
Table, Pier, Regency, Ebonized, Marble Top, Griffin Supports, Mirror Back, 39 x 46 In. 3643.00
Table, Pier, Serpentine Boulle Front, White Marble Top, Ormolu Lion, 1800s, 31 x 53 In. 633.00
Table, Pine, 3 Square Slate Slabs, Scrolling Iron Stretchers, 31 x 41 In. 1800.00

TIP

If you have an old wooden table of little value, you might want to try adding color with Rit dye. The color can never be removed, so don't use this on any good antiques.

Furniture, Table, Parcel Gilt, Trapezoid Tray Top, 3 Swan Legs, Painted, Italy, c.1820, 29 x 18 In., Pair
$17500.00

Furniture, Table, Pembroke, Federal, Mahogany, Inlaid, Drawer, New York, c.1800, 28 x 32 In.
$10625.00

Furniture, Table, Pier, Mahogany, Marble Top, Ormolu Mounts, New York, c.1820, 41 x 19 In.
$8750.00

TIP
Animal-hide glue was usually used on furniture made before the 1900s. The glue was made by boiling animal heads—which explains the saying about taking the horse to the glue factory. The glue is strong but not water resistant. You can dissolve and remove the old glue with hot water, then re-glue the joints. New glues will not work unless the wood is cleaned.

Furniture, Table, Poplar, Old Blue Paint, 2-Board Top, Drawer, 1860s, 29 x 51 x 30 In.
$625.00

TIP
A drawer that is stuck can be helped by heat. Remove any nearby drawers, then aim a blow dryer set on medium at the wood. Once the drawer is opened, rub the runners with paraffin or a candle.

Table, Pine, Demilune, Turned Legs, 1800s, 31 x 46 In. . . . 1955.00
Table, Pine, Stained, Demilune, 28 x 42 x 21 ½ In. . . . 1659.00
Table, Poplar, Dovetailed Drawer, Marble Top, c.1893, Tenn., 31 x 24 In. . . . 805.00
Table, Poplar, Old Blue Paint, 2-Board Top, Drawer, 1860s, 29 x 51 x 30 In. . . . *illus* 625.00
Table, Poplar, Painted, Ocher Grain Paint, Late 1800s, 29 x 37 In. . . . *illus* 1755.00
Table, Pub, Walnut, Tile Top, Oval, Swinging & Hinged Base, 29 x 55 In. . . . 240.00
Table, Pub, Wood Top, Beveled Edge, Cast-Iron Trestle Base, 1800s, 28 x 49 In. . . . 460.00
Table, Pub, Wood Top, Round, Cast Iron, Britannia Pattern, Scrolled Legs, 24 In. . . . 940.00
Table, Queen Anne, Cherry, Round Dish Tilt Top, Birdcage Support, 30 x 34 In. . . . 403.00
Table, Queen Anne, Drawer, Turned Legs, Pad Feet, 1740, 28 x 44 In. . . . 600.00
Table, Queen Anne, Mahogany, Tray Top, Drawer, Brass Pull, c.1750, Ireland, 29 x 30 In. . . . 2300.00
Table, Queen Anne, Walnut, 2 Drawers, Ball Feet, Pa., 30 x 51 x 31 In. . . . *illus* 1600.00
Table, Queen Anne, Walnut, Dish Top, Birdcage Support, Urn Standard, c.1770, 29 x 35 In. . . . 1560.00
Table, Queen Anne, Walnut, Tilt Top, Columnar Pedestal, Tripod Base, 48 ½ x 35 x 29 In. . . . 329.00
Table, Red Lacquer, Chinese, 19th Century, 18 x 47 x 25 ½ In. . . . 2032.00
Table, Red Lacquer, Inlaid Stone, Round Legs, Shaped Stretchers, Chinese, 21 x 28 In. . . . 540.00
Table, Refectory, Jacobean Style, Walnut, Plank Top, Drawers, Baluster Legs, 29 x 79 In. . . . 2057.00
Table, Refectory, Oak, Oval Corners, Scalloped Stretchers, c.1720, 29 x 85 x 29 In. . . . 7020.00
Table, Refectory, Pine, Oak, Red Stain, 18th Century, 27 x 87 ½ x 29 ½ In. . . . 995.00
Table, Refectory, Walnut, Carved Apron & Legs, Paw Feet, Dentil Top, 33 x 89 x 36 In. . . . 5581.00
Table, Refectory, Walnut, Marble Top, Carved, Pierced Stretcher, Italy, c.1890, 29 x 55 In. . . . 1495.00
Table, Regency, Bamboo, Tray, Tole, Raised Edge, 2 Handles, Cityscape, 20 x 30 x 22 In. . . . 2400.00
Table, Regency, Bamboo, Tray, Tole, Raised Edge, Gilt, Figural Seascape, 20 x 33 x 26 In. . . . 2480.00
Table, Regency, Mahogany, Elm, Brass Mounted, Oval Top, Pierced Gallery, 30 x 24 x 11 In. . . . 4080.00
Table, Regency, Mahogany, Figured, Revolving, 4 Drawers, 4 Faux Drawers, 30 x 48 In. . . . 2115.00
Table, Regency, Mahogany, Gilt Tooled Leather, Writing Surface, 31 x 35 x 26 In. . . . 1200.00
Table, Regency, Mahogany, Tooled Leather, Cock-Beaded Drawers, c.1800, 28 x 43 In. . . . 3525.00
Table, Regency, Painted, Parcel Gilt, 2 Drawers, Leafy X-Shape Supports, 29 x 28 In. . . . 1080.00
Table, Regency, Papier-Mache, Tilt Top, Oval, Scalloped, Abalone, 29 x 29 x 24 ½ In. . . . 230.00
Table, Regency, Rosewood, Parcel Gilt, Marsh & Tatham, Early 1800s, 26 x 18 In., Pair . . . 23750.00
Table, Regency, Rosewood, Round Top, Column Pedestal, Bun Feet, 27 ¾ x 21 In. . . . 1920.00
Table, Regency, Walnut, Round, Concentric Banding, England, Late 1900s, 30 x 84 In. . . . 2596.00
Table, Regency Style, Carved, Animal Shapes, Masks, Marble Top, Hoof Feet, 27 x 39 In. . . . 2160.00
Table, Regency Style, Mahogany, 3 Tiers, Frieze Drawer, 2 Gallery Tray Shelves, 31 x 18 In. . . . 568.00
Table, Regency Style, Mahogany, Cross Banding, Inlaid, Downswept Legs, 19 x 48 In., Pair . . . 679.00
Table, Regency Style, Mahogany, Splayed Legs, Brass Caps, Casters, 28 x 54 x 35 In. . . . 2540.00
Table, Regency Style, Mahogany, String Inlay, Tilt Top, Reeded Edge, Paw Feet, 31 x 42 In. . . . 529.00
Table, Renaissance Revival, Mahogany, Scrolling Leaf Carved Edge, Drawer, 31 x 48 In. . . . 598.00
Table, Renaissance Revival, Oak, Inset Leather, Italy, 30 ½ x 54 ½ In. . . . 4800.00
Table, Renaissance Revival, Oak, Leaf Carved, Caryatid Legs, 32 x 105 In. . . . 1495.00
Table, Renaissance Revival, Rosewood, Ebonized, Inlaid, Circular, Scroll Legs, c.1875, 30 x 32 In. 4200.00
Table, Renaissance Revival, Walnut, Carved Frieze, Gadrooned, Dolphin, 29 x 30 x 18 In. . . . 1422.00
Table, Renaissance Revival, Walnut, Figural, Standing Dog, Paw Feet, Marble Top . . . 1150.00
Table, Renaissance Revival, Walnut, Inlaid, Ebonized, Musical Trophee, 29 x 28 In. . . . 1998.00
Table, Richard Neutra, Camel, Wood, Adjustable Metal Legs, c.1954, 12 x 80 x 42 In. . . . 24000.00
Table, Robsjohn-Gibbings, Free-Form Glass, Mahogany Base, Widdicomb, c.1950, 54 x 18 In. 3900.00
Table, Robsjohn-Gibbings, Round, Tapered, Curved Legs, 3 Leaves, Widdicomb, 1955, 44 x 29 In. 1800.00
Table, Robsjohn-Gibbings, Round Top, Lower Shelf, 3 Curved Legs, Widdicomb, 30 x 20 In. . . . 960.00
Table, Rococo, Gilt, Floral Pietra Dura, Marble Top, c.1880 . . . 6038.00
Table, Rococo, Walnut, Drawer, Cabriole Legs, Continental, 28 x 28 x 17 ¾ In. . . . 444.00
Table, Rococo, Walnut, White Marble, Leaf, Scroll Post, Carved Legs, c.1860, 29 x 42 In. . . . 1955.00
Table, Rococo Revival, Rosewood, Drawer, Cabriole Legs, 33 x 21 x 16 In. . . . 1140.00
Table, Rococo Revival, Rosewood, Lid, Mirror, Drawer, Cabriole Legs, 29 ¾ x 24 x 18 In. . . . 780.00
Table, Rococo Revival, Walnut, Gadrooned Serpentine Top, Floral Inlay, 31 x 51 In. . . . 7963.00
Table, Roger Capron, Metal, Ceramic, Black, Orange, White, c.1960, 16 x 48 In. . . . 7500.00
Table, Rosewood, Carved, Openwork Apron, Chinese, 31 ½ x 15 x 12 In. . . . 1416.00
Table, Rosewood, Carved, Plant Tendrils, Inset Marble Top, Chinese, 19th Century, 30 In. . . . 2607.00
Table, Rosewood, Marble Top, Pedestal, Round, Pierced Grape & Leaf, 33 x 50 In. . . . 17600.00
Table, Rosewood, Rectangular, Beaded Apron, Chinese, 12 x 41 x 24 ¾ In. . . . 418.00
Table, Rosewood, Tilt Top, Scrolling Leaf, Flowers, Bulbous Standard, 28 ¾ x 53 In. . . . 5280.00
Table, Rosewood, Veneers, Flowers, Bronze Mounts, Stretcher Urn, France, c.1855, 30 x 53 In. 4600.00
Table, Round, Brass, Black Marble Round Top, Scrolled Tripod Base, 1900s, 29 x 31 In. . . . 518.00
Table, Round, Burr Elm, Marble Top, Shelf, Lion Heads, Ormolu Mounts, 29 x 15 In. . . . 25000.00
Table, Round, Empire Style, Mahogany, Brass Mounted, Eagle's Heads, c.1900, 30 x 2 ½ In. . . . 1680.00
Table, Sansone, Metal, PVC Tubing, Projecting Grid, Red, Black, c.1987, 17 x 66 In. . . . 10560.00
Table, Sawbuck, Pine, Board Top, Breadboard Ends, Red Paint, 1700s, 26 x 34 In. . . . 1495.00
Table, Sawbuck, Pine, Red Paint, Early 19th Century, 27 ¾ x 62 x 24 ¾ In. . . . 3276.00

Table, Sawbuck, Pine, Weathered Brown, New England, c.1790, 26 x 69 In. 1778.00
Table, Sawbuck, Pine, X Supports, Stretcher, 1800s, 29 x 31 In. 354.00
Table, Sawbuck, Red Paint, Ocher, Scrubbed Top, Mortised Stretcher, 28 x 72 In.. . . . . 1430.00
Table, Sawbuck, White Pine, Green Paint Over Red Wash, Maine, 1800s, 30 x 34 In. 1380.00
Table, Sawbuck, Yellow Pine, Oak, Cut Nails, Blue Paint Trace, 1800s, 29 x 47 In. 489.00
Table, Sewing, Belter, Mahogany, Carved, Hinged Top, 32 x 21 x 16 ½ In. 345.00
Table, Sewing, Biedermeier, Fruitwood, Ebonized Bands, Dovetail, 1800s, 31 x 22 In. 1093.00
Table, Sewing, Black Japanned, Gilt, Shaped Top, Fitted Interior, Asia, 28 x 26 In. 1920.00
Table, Sewing, Cherry, 2 Dovetailed Drawers, Turned Legs, 19th Century, 30 x 33 In. 323.00
Table, Sewing, Chestnut, Turned Feet, Drawer, 2 Tiers Spool Holders, 12 ¾ x 10 ¾ In. 345.00
Table, Sewing, Chinoiserie, Mother-Of-Pearl Inlay, 19th Century, 30 x 21 ½ x 16 In. 1800.00
Table, Sewing, Drawer, Teal Paint, Tapered Legs, 27 x 20 x 20 ½ In. . . . . *illus* 2090.00
Table, Sewing, Drop Leaf, 2 Drawers, Raised Spiral Legs, c.1800, 29 x 33 In. 413.00
Table, Sewing, Drop Leaf, Empire, Mahogany, 2 Drawers, Cloth Basket, c.1850, 30 x 19 In. . . . 489.00
Table, Sewing, Drop Leaf, G. Stickley, No. 630, 2 Drawers, Label, 28 x 18 x 18 In. 1680.00
Table, Sewing, Drop Leaf, Mahogany, 2 Serpentine Drawer Fronts, c.1840, 29 x 15 In.. . . . . . . 266.00
Table, Sewing, Drop Leaf, Mahogany, Drawers, Incurved Plinth, c.1835, 29 x 18 x 18 In. 1410.00
Table, Sewing, Drop Leaf, Mahogany, Gadrooned, 2 Drawers, c.1840, 29 x 18 In. 472.00
Table, Sewing, Drop Leaf, Neoclassical, Mahogany, Molded Edge Top, Drawers, 29 x 17 In. . . . 179.00
Table, Sewing, Empire, Mahogany, Faux Drawer, Interior Compartments, 30 x 18 In. 472.00
Table, Sewing, Empire, Walnut, Drop Leaf, 2 Drawers, Basket, 29 ½ x 19 x 18 In. . . . . . . *illus* 518.00
Table, Sewing, Federal, Mahogany, Dovetailed Drawers, Spiral Legs, Early 1800s, 29 x 19 In. . 805.00
Table, Sewing, Federal, Mahogany, Figured, Satinwood Inlay, Mass., c.1800, 30 x 17 In. 11250.00
Table, Sewing, Federal, Mahogany, Hinged Lid, Fitted Interior, 2 Drawers, c.1830, 30 x 18 In.. 345.00
Table, Sewing, Federal, Mahogany, Outset Corners, Turned Legs, c.1825, 29 x 20 In. 1292.00
Table, Sewing, Federal, Mahogany, Pine, Drawer, Writing Board, Compartments, 29 x 18 In. . 5060.00
Table, Sewing, Federal, Maple, Frieze Drawer, Splayed Legs, Late 1700s, 24 x 17 In. 227.00
Table, Sewing, Federal, Tiger Maple, Turned Legs, 2 Drawers, c.1825, 29 x 22 In. 1778.00
Table, Sewing, George III, Kingwood, Inlaid, Drawer, Casters, 29 x 24 In. 5625.00
Table, Sewing, Hardwood, Inlaid, Mother-Of-Pearl, Octagonal, Hinged, North Africa, 25 x 19 In. 1500.00
Table, Sewing, Japanned, Drawers, Block Stem, Pedestal, Painted, 1800s, 28 x 20 In.. . . . . 1175.00
Table, Sewing, Mahogany, 2 Drawers, Turned, Carved Legs, c.1820, 21 x 18 In. 590.00
Table, Sewing, Mahogany, Carved, 2 Columns, Drawers, Brass Handles, c.1825, 31 x 22 In. . . 1121.00
Table, Sewing, Mahogany, Drawers, Acanthus Carved Baluster Support, c.1825, 30 x 22 In. . . 7050.00
Table, Sewing, Mahogany, Drawers, Carved Corners, Paw Feet, c.1830, 30 x 19 In. 1997.00
Table, Sewing, Mahogany, Gilt Bronze, Jasperware Medallion, Early 1900s, 28 x 16 In. 9375.00
Table, Sewing, Mahogany, Lift Top, Drawers, Scroll Supports, 29 x 21 ¾ In. 1292.00
Table, Sewing, Mahogany, String Inlay, Folding Top, Swivel, 28 x 13 ¾ In. 235.00
Table, Sewing, Maple, Single-Board Top, Breadboard Ends, Painted, Pa., c.1850, 26 x 43 In. . . 881.00
Table, Sewing, Neoclassical, Burl, Lift Top, Interior Work Surface, Maryland, c.1825, 32 x 22 In. 2489.00
Table, Sewing, Neoclassical, Mahogany, Lift Top, Fitted Interior, Drawers, Scroll Feet, 29 x 20 In. 470.00
Table, Sewing, Pine, 4-Board Top, Oak Base, Legs, England, c.1900, 30 x 96 In. 1763.00
Table, Sewing, Pine, Breadboard Ends, Painted Base, 2 Drawers, Scalloped Edge, 30 x 48 In. . 230.00
Table, Sewing, Pine Top, Salmon Paint, 3 Drawers, 50 x 36 In. 2300.00
Table, Sewing, Regency, Mahogany, Ebony, Drawer, Bag Drawer, 29 x 25 x 19 In. 2749.00
Table, Sewing, Restauration, Mahogany, Lift Top, Inside Mirror, Leather Surface, 30 x 21 In.. 1800.00
Table, Sewing, Rosewood, Drawer, Slide-Out Basket, G. Tanier, Denmark, 23 x 21 In. 360.00
Table, Sewing, Rosewood, Hinged Top, Compartments, 29 x 21 ½ x 17 In. 600.00
Table, Sewing, Shaker, Pine, Birch, 12 Drawers, Pullout Work Surface, c.1860, 39 x 31 In. . . . 18960.00
Table, Sewing, Shaker, Poplar, Dovetailed Drawers, Tapered Legs, 30 x 22 In.. . . . . 4700.00
Table, Sewing, Sheraton, Cherry, Skirt, Banded, Turned Legs, c.1820, 29 x 23 In. 4112.00
Table, Sewing, Sheraton, Mahogany, Inlaid, Glove Box, Drawers, 37 x 20 x 19 In. 978.00
Table, Sewing, Sheraton, Maple, Birch, Drawer, Bag Drawer, 26 x 17 ¾ x 20 In. 575.00
Table, Sewing, Softwood, Grain Painted, Drawer, Turned Legs, Yellow Ocher, 31 x 28 In. 110.00
Table, Sewing, Teal Green Paint, Drawer, Dovetailed, Tapered Legs, 27 x 20 In. 2090.00
Table, Sewing, Walnut, Burl Veneer, Lift Top, 28 x 24 x 15 ½ In.. . . . . 489.00
Table, Sewing, Walnut, Iron, Drawers, Column Supports, Quatrefoil Base, c.1840, 31 x 25 In. 2937.00
Table, Sewing, Walnut, Lift Top, Burl Trim, Carved, 28 x 22 In. 660.00
Table, Sewing, Walnut, Octagonal Lift Top, Fitted Interior, Tapered Base, Victorian, 28 ½ In. . . 330.00
Table, Sewing, Walnut, Single Board Top, Tapered Legs, Ohio, Late 1800s, 38 x 26 In. 206.00
Table, Sewing, William IV, Rosewood, Swivel Top, Inset Leather, Trestle Base, c.1825, 29 x 21 In. 1527.00
Table, Shaker, Walnut, Tiger Maple, Drawer, Wood Pull, New York, c.1865, 30 x 30 In. 4444.00
Table, Sheraton, Mahogany, Carved Legs, 38 x 21 x 29 In. 374.00
Table, Sheraton, Pine, Tray Top, 2 Chamfered Drawers, Turned Legs, c.1840, 31 x 19 In. 230.00
Table, Side, American Maple, Rectangular Top, 2 Drawers, Cabriole Legs, 30 x 22 In. 120.00
Table, Side, Cast Iron, Starburst, Cabriole Legs, Cartouche Knees, c.1850, 27 x 23 In. 1292.00
Table, Side, Chippendale, Mahogany, Door, Drawer, England, 1890, 33 x 14 x 14 In. 375.00

Furniture, Table, Poplar, Painted, Ocher Grain Paint, Late 1800s, 29 x 37 In. $1755.00

Furniture, Table, Queen Anne, Walnut, 2 Drawers, Ball Feet, Pa., 30 x 51 x 31 In. $1600.00

Furniture, Table, Sewing, Drawer, Teal Paint, Tapered Legs, 27 x 20 x 20 ½ In. $2090.00

Furniture, Table, Sewing, Empire, Walnut, Drop Leaf, 2 Drawers, Basket, 29 ½ x 19 x 18 In. $518.00

As always, the edited listings in *Kovels' Antiques & Collectibles Price Guide 2010* aren't available on any website, but readers should visit Kovels.com for information on trends, tips, reproductions, marks, old prices, and more!

F

Furniture, Table, Tavern, Maple, Pine, Oval Top, Black Paint, 1820s, 24 x 22 ½ x 28 In.
$2500.00

Furniture, Table, Tavern, Queen Anne, Maple, Pine, Breadboard Ends, Drawers, 1700s, 26 x 37 In.
$633.00

Furniture, Table, Tavern, Queen Anne Style, Maple, Poplar, Green Paint, 27 x 29 x 20 In.
$325.00

TIP
A white ring on a tabletop is in the finish, a black ring is in the wood. It is easier to remove a damaged finish than a wood stain.

F

Table, Side, Edwardian, Mahogany, Boxwood, Hardwood Inlay, Kidney Shape, 30 x 21 x 15 In. 6518.00
Table, Side, George III Style, Mahogany, Carved Frieze, Cabriole Legs, 32 x 36 x 19 In. 3840.00
Table, Side, Gothic Revival, Mahogany, Later Top, Trestle Base, c.1830, 29 x 30 In. 1057.00
Table, Side, Grossman, Walnut, Plastic, Enamel, Steel, Black, 2 Triangle Tiers, Glenn, 20 x 18 In. 1140.00
Table, Side, Jacobean, Oak, Paneled Frieze Drawer, Ring Turned Legs, 28 ½ x 32 ¾ In. 4740.00
Table, Side, Louis XVI Style, Parquetry, Gilt Metal Mounts, 28 x 23 x 17 In., Pair 1554.00
Table, Side, Regency Style, Mahogany, Step Form, Brass, Leather, 1920s, 27 x 15 x 25 In. 425.00
Table, Side, Rococo, Serpentine Front, Frieze Drawer, Arched Apron, 27 x 24 x 17 In. 830.00
Table, Side, Teak, Carved, Marble Top, 20th Century, 23 x 18 In. 403.00
Table, Side, Walnut, Demilune Top, Scrolling Supports, Spain, 31 x 40 x 20 In. 1020.00
Table, Side, Walnut, Frieze, 3 Drawers, Tapered Legs, 34 x 66 x 27 In. 4320.00
Table, Side, Walnut, Leather, Glass, c.1930, 27 x 26 In. 5625.00
Table, Silas Seandel, Cube, Metal Patchwork Over Wood, 14 x 14 In. 600.00
Table, Silvered Edge, Projecting Corners, Drawer, X-Stretcher, 31 x 44 In. 2160.00
Table, Slab Slate Top, Cast Iron Base, 32 ½ x 61 In. 345.00
Table, Sofa, Drop Leaf, Mahogany, 2 Drawers, Trestle Base, 1800s, 29 x 32 x 30 In. 2645.00
Table, Sofa, Drop Leaf, Regency, Mahogany, Drawers, Early 20th Century, 29 x 58 In. 940.00
Table, Sofa, Mahogany, Carved, 2 Drawers, Inlaid Crossbanding, England, c.1820, 30 x 48 In. 2252.00
Table, Softwood, 3 Splayed Legs, Triangle Shelf, 25 x 29 In. 276.00
Table, Softwood, Blue Paint, T-Shape Bracket Legs, Feet, 29 x 96 In. 1430.00
Table, Softwood, Pieboard Top, Drawer, Wood Pull, Stretcher Base, 29 x 33 x 25 ½ In. 330.00
Table, Stacked Books Shape, Tooled Morocco Leather, Black Base, 17 x 42 In., Pair 2350.00
Table, Stickley, Oak, Round, Through Tenon Construction, 30 x 30 In. 805.00
Table, Stickley, Wood, Circular, Spindle Slab Sides, Shoefoot, 29 x 29 In. 600.00
Table, Stickley Bros., No. 2504, Circular Top, Square Apron, Shelf, 29 ¾ x 26 In. 1560.00
Table, Stickley Bros., No. 2608, Shelf Supported By Cross Stretcher, Round, 32 x 30 In. 720.00
Table, Sunderland, Rosewood, Gadrooned Edge, Melon Supports, c.1840, 32 x 38 In. 2644.00
Table, Sunderland, Rosewood, Trestle Base, Concentric Ends, c.1840, 29 x 38 In. 1175.00
Table, Sutherland, Mahogany, Molded Edge, Turned Gatelegs, Victorian, 28 x 33 In. 518.00
Table, Tavern, Beech, Single Board Pine Top, Breadboard Ends, Drawer, 29 x 45 x 27 In. 734.00
Table, Tavern, Birch, Pine Top, Red Paint, Tapered Legs, Early 1800s, 28 x 22 In. 2350.00
Table, Tavern, Birch, Single Board Pine Top, Frame, Chamfered Legs, 25 x 32 x 21 In. 1410.00
Table, Tavern, Black Paint, Box Stretcher, Baluster Legs, N.E., Late 1770s, 26 x 34 In. 16380.00
Table, Tavern, Brown Stain, Splayed Legs, New England, 26 x 35 In. 1645.00
Table, Tavern, Federal, Pine, Birch, Overhang Top, Red Paint, New England, c.1790, 29 x 26 In. 652.00
Table, Tavern, Hepplewhite, Walnut, Pine, Overhang Top, 2 Drawers, c.1760, 28 x 58 In. 558.00
Table, Tavern, Maple, Breadboard Ends, Turned Legs, New England, 1700s, 26 x 23 In. 823.00
Table, Tavern, Maple, Pine, Oval Top, Black Paint, 1820s, 24 x 22 ½ x 28 In. *illus* 2500.00
Table, Tavern, Maple, Pine, Oval Top, Box Stretcher Base, Black Paint, 24 x 23 In. 2938.00
Table, Tavern, Maple, Pine, Round, Triangular Lower Shelf, Old Paint, Round, 1800s, 28 x 27 In. 1293.00
Table, Tavern, Oak, Overhang Top, Long Drawer, Scalloped Apron, Turned Legs, 1710, 29 In. 587.00
Table, Tavern, Pine, Maple, Poplar, Breadboard Top, Dovetailed Drawer, 1800s, 35 x 25 In. 822.00
Table, Tavern, Pine, Maple, Red Stain, Oval Top, Splayed Legs, 18th Century, 26 x 30 In. 2106.00
Table, Tavern, Pine, Maple, Scrubbed Top, Breadboard Ends, Drawer, 1700s, 26 x 37 ½ In. 2115.00
Table, Tavern, Pine, Maple, Scrubbed Top, Breadboard Ends, Drawer, Red Paint, 28 x 40 In. 2232.00
Table, Tavern, Pine, Maple, Walnut, Breadboard Ends, Drawer, 44 x 29 In. 1380.00
Table, Tavern, Pine, Oval, Red Paint, Turned Legs, Button Feet, 1770, 25 x 36 x 26 In. 3042.00
Table, Tavern, Pine, Oval Top, Splayed Legs, Painted, 27 x 30 In. 705.00
Table, Tavern, Pine, Red, Blue Paint, Drawer, Stretcher Base, 1890s, 30 x 46 x 28 In. 475.00
Table, Tavern, Pine, Scrub Top, 3-Legged Base, 28 ½ x 27 x 26 In. 499.00
Table, Tavern, Queen Anne, Breadboard Top, Button Foot, 25 x 39 x 26 In. 1898.00
Table, Tavern, Queen Anne, Maple, Oval, Splayed Legs, Paint, N.E., c.1745, 25 x 32 x 23 In. 7020.00
Table, Tavern, Queen Anne, Maple, Pine, Breadboard Ends, Drawers, 1700s, 26 x 37 In. *illus* 633.00
Table, Tavern, Queen Anne, Maple, Pine, Oval, Box Stretcher, c.1770, 24 x 29 ½ In. 2574.00
Table, Tavern, Queen Anne, Pine, Blue, Lift-Off Top, Drawer, Pad Feet, c.1760, 28 x 27 In. 1430.00
Table, Tavern, Queen Anne, Walnut, Breadboard Ends, Drawers, 25 x 32 ¾ x 20 ¾ In. 4375.00
Table, Tavern, Queen Anne, Walnut, Drawer, Tapered Legs, Pad Feet, Late 1700s, 28 x 26 In. 633.00
Table, Tavern, Queen Anne Style, Maple, Poplar, Green Paint, 27 x 29 x 20 In. *illus* 325.00
Table, Tavern, Queen Anne Style, Maple, Poplar, Turned Legs, 27 x 20 ½ In. 382.00
Table, Tavern, Queen Anne Style, Pine, Drawer, Shaped Skirt, Turned Legs, 29 x 35 In. 403.00
Table, Tavern, Walnut, Rectangular Top, Drawer, Baluster Turned Legs, 29 x 37 ½ In. 14040.00
Table, Tavern, Walnut, Tilt Top, Oval, Cross Stretcher, Cabriole Legs, 1730s, 28 x 49 In. 1053.00
Table, Tavern, William & Mary, Pine, Drawer, Baluster Legs, c.1740, 29 x 43 x 29 In. 3276.00
Table, Tavern, William & Mary, Walnut, Drawer, Baluster Legs, c.1740, 27 x 45 x 25 In. 5382.00
Table, Tea, Black Paint, Birdcage, Tilt Top, Conn., c.1750, 28 x 31 In. 3555.00
Table, Tea, Cherry, Tray Top, Scroll Skirt, Cabriole Legs, Pad Feet, c.1900, 26 x 27 x 18 In. 4817.00
Table, Tea, Chippendale, Birdcage, Cherry, Dish Top, Pedestal, Snake Feet, 29 x 23 In. 2645.00

Table, Tea, Chippendale, Dish Tilt Top, Birdcage, 28 ½ x 34 In. 2350.00
Table, Tea, Chippendale, Mahogany, Birdcage, 3-Footed, 1790s, 28 x 35 x 35 In. 550.00
Table, Tea, Chippendale, Mahogany, Carved, Cabriole Legs, Stamped Sutton, 27 x 32 In. 1998.00
Table, Tea, Chippendale, Mahogany, Carved, Piecrust, Tilt Top, Birdcage, 28 x 25 In. 2760.00
Table, Tea, Chippendale, Mahogany, Tilt Top, Fan & Bellflower Inlay, 1800s, 27 x 36 In. 748.00
Table, Tea, Chippendale, Mahogany, Tray Top, Cabriole Legs, 1700s, 27 x 32 x 21 In. *illus* 55000.00
Table, Tea, Chippendale, Mahogany, Tray Top, Cabriole Legs, Mass., 1700s, 17 x 32 In. 57500.00
Table, Tea, Chippendale, Piecrust, Tilt Top, Carved Knees, Ball, Claw Feet, 1800s, 29 x 34 x 33 In. 5750.00
Table, Tea, Chippendale, Walnut, Tilt Top, Birdcage, Claw Feet, 1770, 28 x 33 In. 17600.00
Table, Tea, Chippendale, Walnut, Tilt Top, Delaware, c.1770, 29 x 34 In. 5000.00
Table, Tea, Chippendale Style, Piecrust Top, Tripod, 1800s, 29 x 34 x 33 In. *illus* 5500.00
Table, Tea, Drop Leaf, Dutch Neoclassical, Walnut, Marquetry, Oval Top, 29 x 47 In. 448.00
Table, Tea, G. Stickley, No. 654, Round, Notched Stretcher, 28 x 24 In. 1860.00
Table, Tea, George II, Mahogany, Carved Edge, Frieze, Legs, Claw & Ball Feet, 28 x 30 In. 26250.00
Table, Tea, George II, Mahogany, Raised Edge, Pad Feet, c.1745, 26 x 31 In. 6875.00
Table, Tea, George II, Mahogany, Shell Carved Cabriole Legs, Trifid Feet, 29 x 32 In. 1888.00
Table, Tea, George II, Mahogany, Tilt Top, Mid 18th Century, 26 ½ x 31 In. 380.00
Table, Tea, George III, Neoclassical, Mahogany, Inlaid, Adams, c.1760, 29 x 32 In. 34375.00
Table, Tea, Kittinger, Queen Anne Style, Mahogany, Tray Top, Shaped Skirt, Pad Feet, 27 x 31 In. 460.00
Table, Tea, Kittinger, Queen Anne Style, Tray Top, Williamsburg Reproduction, 26 x 18 In. 705.00
Table, Tea, Louis XV, Marble Top, Greek Key Banding, Mask Mounts, c.1890, 29 x 23 In. 6333.00
Table, Tea, Mahogany, Piecrust, Flip Top, Collapsing, British Patent, 30 x 36 In. 345.00
Table, Tea, Mahogany, Piecrust Edge, Tilt Top, Tripod Base, Claw & Ball Feet, 1800s, 30 In. 822.00
Table, Tea, Mahogany, Tilt Top, Cabriole Legs, Snake Feet, 27 x 31 ½ x 30 ¾ In. 375.00
Table, Tea, Mahogany, Tilt Top, Round, Spiral Turned Support, Cabriole Legs, c.1775, 31 x 27 In. 881.00
Table, Tea, Mahogany, Tilt Top, Round, Triangular Plinth, Scroll Feet, c.1830, 28 ½ x 31 In. 3407.00
Table, Tea, Mahogany, Tilt Top, Tripod Base, Slipper Feet, 1700s, 29 x 29 x 28 In. 690.00
Table, Tea, Maple, Octagonal Top, Turned Standard, 3 Shaped Feet, 27 ½ In. 192.00
Table, Tea, Marquetry, Circular, Medallion, Tripod Base, Scroll Feet, c.1800, 27 x 19 ¾ In. 708.00
Table, Tea, Queen Anne, Birch, Maple, Porringer Top, Cabriole Legs, 1700s, 27 x 35 In. 6325.00
Table, Tea, Queen Anne, Mahogany, Dish Top, Baluster Pedestal, 30 x 35 In. 1035.00
Table, Tea, Queen Anne, Mahogany, Tilt Top, Birdcage, Snake Feet, c.1770, 29 ½ x 31 In. 11700.00
Table, Tea, Queen Anne, Mahogany, Tray Top, Cabriole Legs, Pad Feet, 26 ½ x 19 ½ In. 705.00
Table, Tea, Queen Anne, Tilt Top, Urn Shape, Turned Standard, Slipper Feet, 27 x 30 In. 633.00
Table, Tea, Queen Anne, Walnut, Tilt Top, Birdcage, Pad Feet, c.1760, 30 x 33 In. 3276.00
Table, Tea, Queen Anne Style, Mahogany, 2 Candleslides, Cabriole Legs, 27 x 19 x 30 In. 239.00
Table, Tea, Queen Anne Style, Mahogany, Oak, Tilt Top, Snake Feet, 28 x 29 In. 455.00
Table, Tea, Queen Anne Style, Walnut, Tray Top, Scalloped Apron, 27 x 30 In. 230.00
Table, Tea, Rosewood, Hinged Top, 4 Lidded Canisters, Scroll Feet, England, 1800s, 33 x 18 In. 575.00
Table, Tea, Tilt Top, Turned Standard, Cabriole Legs, Pad Feet, c.1760, 28 x 32 ½ In. 671.00
Table, Tea, Victorian, Rosewood Veneer, Hinged Top, England, 1800s, 32 x 18 x 15 In. *illus* 605.00
Table, Teak, Hand Carved, Marble Top, 1800s, 17 x 22 In. 351.00
Table, Tiger Maple, Drawer, Turned Legs, New England, c.1825, 30 x 33 ¾ In. 3510.00
Table, Tilt Top, Papier-Mache, Painted Flowers, Birds, Brown Ground, Multicolored, c.1850, 21 x 24 In. 177.00
Table, Tilt Top, Papier-Mache, Painted Flowers, Gold, White, Mother-Of-Pearl, c.1850, 25 x 30 In. 708.00
Table, Tilt Top, Papier-Mache, Painted Flowers, Mother-Of-Pearl, c.1850, 24 x 28 In. 826.00
Table, Tilt Top, Papier-Mache, Scalloped, Mother-Of-Pearl, Flowers, Scroll Feet, c.1950, 17 x 30 In. 206.00
Table, Tray, Chippendale, Piecrust Edge, Mahogany, c.1775, 20 In. 518.00
Table, Tray, Tole, Reticulated Rim, Flowers, Bird, c.1900, 18 ¾ x 26 In. 235.00
Table, Trestle, 4-Board Pine Top, Oak Trestles & Stretchers, 1740, 105 x 30 In. 1560.00
Table, Trestle, Baroque Style, Walnut, Frieze Drawer, 31 x 29 x 18 In. 850.00
Table, Trestle, Baroque Style, Walnut, Molded, Faux-Painted Top, 31 x 86 In. 3220.00
Table, Trestle, David T. Smith, Round Corners, Arched Feet, Painted, Ohio, c.1970, 78 x 36 In. 352.00
Table, Trestle, Leaves, Square Legs, Late 1700s, 29 x 71 In. 1180.00
Table, Trestle, Lifetime, No. 935, Shelf, Through Tenon Construction, Signed, 29 x 54 x 32 In. 1820.00
Table, Trestle, Maple, Chestnut, Breadboard Ends, Painted, c.1800, 23 x 21 x 37 In., Child's 382.00
Table, Trestle, Oak, Breadboard Ends, 19th Century, 29 ½ x 66 x 29 ¾ In. 250.00
Table, Trestle, Oak, Breadboard Ends, Plank Top, Bulbous Column Base, 31 x 76 In. 1265.00
Table, Trestle, Pine, Beech, Through Tenon Construction, 33 x 78 x 31 In. 800.00
Table, Trestle, Stickley & Brandt, Low Shelf, Shoefoot Base, Signed, 48 x 29 In. 1920.00
Table, Trestle, Walnut, Iron Brace, 63 x 29 In. 1175.00
Table, V. Kagan, Rosewood, Aluminum, Glass, 1967, 29 x 98 ½ x 40 In. 8750.00
Table, V. Kagan, Tri-Symmetric, Ausubo, Glass, c.1960, 18 ¾ x 28 x 22 ¾ In. 2500.00
Table, Victorian, Elm, Oval Top, Tripod Base, Turned Pedestal, 31 x 44 In. 780.00
Table, Victorian, Mahogany, Tilt Top, Tripod, Turned Standard, Scrolled Toes, 29 x 25 In. 2160.00
Table, Victorian, Oak, Glass, Claw Feet, 30 x 36 In. 177.00
Table, Victorian, Papier-Mache, Tray, Serpentine Edges, Leaves, 16 x 20 x 16 In. 948.00

Furniture, Table, Tea, Chippendale, Mahogany, Tray Top, Cabriole Legs, 1700s, 27 x 32 x 21 In.
$55000.00

Furniture, Table, Tea, Chippendale Style, Piecrust Top, Tripod, 1800s, 29 x 34 x 33 In.
$5500.00

Furniture, Table, Tea, Victorian, Rosewood Veneer, Hinged Top, England, 1800s, 32 x 18 x 15 In.
$605.00

TIP

Permanent marker stains can be removed from most wood or textiles by wiping with a cloth soaked in rubbing alcohol.

TIP
If your wicker furniture is very dusty, take it to the gas station and blow the dust away with the air hose.

Furniture, Table, Victorian, Walnut, Incised, Inset Marble Top, c.1875, 30 x 22 x 16 In.
$330.00

Furniture, Tabouret, Limbert, No. 234, Slab Sides, Signed, 18 x 16 x 16 In.
$2320.00

TIP
When removing a stain from fabrics or marble or any other surface, apply the stain cleaner from the edge to the center to avoid spreading the stain.

Table, Victorian, Rosewood, Marquetry, Circular, Ebonized, c.1870, 29 x 27 ½ In. 2400.00
Table, Victorian, Walnut, Burl Veneers, Tilt Top, 3 Splayed, Molded Legs, 28 ½ In. 2400.00
Table, Victorian, Walnut, Incised, Inset Marble Top, c.1875, 30 x 22 x 16 In.. .... *illus* 330.00
Table, Victorian, Walnut, Marble Top, 29 x 29 ½ In. 403.00
Table, Victorian, Walnut, Marble Top, Burl Panels, Turned Rosettes, 30 x 23 x 16 In.. .... 354.00
Table, Victorian, Walnut, Oval Marble Top, Scalloped Legs, 30 x 17 x 22 In. 177.00
Table, Walnut, Banded Square Top, Recessed Frieze, Italy, 29 x 31 In. 1440.00
Table, Walnut, Burl Veneer, Red Marble Top, 30 x 28 x 20 In. 330.00
Table, Walnut, Carved, Cock-Beaded, 2 Dovetailed Drawers, Spiral Legs, c.1830, 29 x 21 In... 1462.00
Table, Walnut, Carved, Tripod Base, Scroll Feet, Marble Top, 36 x 19 In. 7250.00
Table, Walnut, Drawer, Poplar Turned Legs, Tenn., 1800s, 28 x 22 In. 575.00
Table, Walnut, Exotic Wood Inlay, Hexagonal Top, Scalloped Frieze, 27 ½ x 19 ½ In.. .... 900.00
Table, Walnut, Lacquered, Black, Red, Shaped Apron, Chinese, 32 x 42 x 17 In. 708.00
Table, Walnut, Leaf, Egg, Dart-Carved Edge, Spain, 30 ½ x 28 x 49 In. 3840.00
Table, Walnut, Oval Top, Inlaid Medallion, Pad Feet, 20 x 47 In. 300.00
Table, Walnut, Parquetry, Scrolled Ends, Stretcher, Brass, Iron Base, 31 x 75 In. 1333.00
Table, Walnut, Poplar, Overhang Top, Drawer, Tapered Legs, Early 1800s, 27 x 20 In. 805.00
Table, Walnut, Satinwood Inlay, Tilt Top, Hunting Scenes, Swiss, 31 x 46 x 32 In. 1150.00
Table, Walnut, Square Top, Rectangular Legs, Stretchers, Chinese, 17th Century, 29 x 22 In. . 472.00
Table, William & Mary, Maple, Red Paint, Gateleg, 2 Drawers, Mass., c.1740, 27 x 48 In. 9480.00
Table, William & Mary, Oak, X-Stretcher, Drawer, c.1800, 28 x 41 In.. .... 2937.00
Table, William & Mary, Oak Top, Gateleg, Baluster, Turned Legs, c.1720, 27 x 43 In. 1175.00
Table, William & Mary, Walnut, Feather Inlay, Drawer, 29 x 31 x 19 In.. .... 502.00
Table, William & Mary Style, Oak, Gateleg, Bowed, Baluster Turned Legs, 30 x 89 x 59 In. ... 956.00
Table, William IV, Mahogany, Marble Top, Carved Front Legs, Paw Feet, c.1860, 33 x 44 In. .. 2963.00
Table, William IV, Mahogany, Tilt Top, Splayed Legs, Brass Caps, Casters, 29 x 64 x 42 In. 4120.00
Table, William IV, Rosewood, Corner Finials, Lower Shelf, Reeded Feet, 26 x 16 In. 840.00
Table, Wine, Baroque Style, Walnut, Tilt Top, Italy, 64 x 47 In. 2510.00
Table, Wood, Acid Etched, Bronze, Patinated Scenic Top, Tubular Legs, 24 x 47 In. 6518.00
Table, Wood, Lacquered, Floating Panel, Horse Hoof Feet, 30 x 84 x 41 In. 6000.00
Table, Wormley, Constellation, Marquetry, Ebonized Top, Walnut Base, 19 x 13 In. 7200.00
Table, Writing, Adjustable Lift Top, Pen Stop, Pullout Candle Shelf, Tripod, 31 x 22 In. 1140.00
Table, Writing, Anglo-Indian, Arched Apron, Drawers, Late 20th Century, 32 x 79 In. 708.00
Table, Writing, Chippendale, Mahogany, Tapered Legs, Molded Feet, 30 x 53 x 27 In.. .... 250.00
Table, Writing, Federal, Mahogany, Bowed Front, Frieze Drawer, 30 x 34 In. 1093.00
Table, Writing, Federal, Mahogany, Slant Front, Raised Back Corner Drawers, 36 x 53 In.. .... 478.00
Table, Writing, Fruitwood, Drawers, Bulbous Legs, 28 x 37 In. 1440.00
Table, Writing, George II, Padouk, Inlaid, c.1745, 28 ½ x 36 In.. .... 6250.00
Table, Writing, Georgian, Mahogany, 2 Drawers, Casters, England, 39 x 40 x 19 In. 850.00
Table, Writing, Georgian, Mahogany, Drawer, England, 1890s, 27 x 31 x 21 In. 650.00
Table, Writing, Georgian, Rosewood, Mahogany Banded, Drawers, 29 x 49 ½ x 28 In. 2963.00
Table, Writing, Jacobean Style, Oak, Frieze Drawers, Leaf Paneling, 30 ½ x 72 x 28 In. 2015.00
Table, Writing, Louis XV, Ormolu Rim, Mounts, Drawer, Cabriole Legs, 1754, 28 x 24 In.. .... 5000.00
Table, Writing, Louis XVI Style, Marble Top, Frieze Drawers, Early 1900s, 30 x 43 In.. .... 575.00
Table, Writing, Mediterranean Style, Trestle Base, Stretcher, Chair, Spain, 34 x 48 & 40 In. ... 598.00
Table, Writing, Neoclassical, Mixed Woods, Inlaid, Continental, c.1910, 30 x 34 In. 717.00
Table, Writing, Regency, Mahogany, Inset, Leather, 2 Drawers, Circular Legs, 30 x 51 x 42 In.. 3120.00
Table, Writing, Regency, Mahogany, Red Leather, Drawer, England, 1800s, 31 x 24 x 16 In. .. 900.00
Table, Writing, Regency Style, Mahogany, Leather, Splayed Legs, Brass Caps, 29 x 72 x 34 In.. 2400.00
Table, Writing, Walnut, Molded Edge, Frieze, 2 Drawers, Iron Stretchers, 32 x 63 x 28 In. 4080.00
Table, Writing, William IV, Mahogany, Inset Leather, Drawers, 28 ¾ x 47 x 35 In. 3600.00
Table, Zinc Top, Cast Iron Column Base, 19th Century, 31 x 68 In. 805.00
Tabouret, Arts & Crafts, Carved, Geometric Design, 6-Sided, Multicolored, 21 x 17 In. 420.00
Tabouret, Carved, Mother-Of-Pearl Inlay, Painted, 8 Sides, 1894-1923, 16 ½ x 20 In. 300.00
Tabouret, G. Stickley, No. 53-T, Inset Grueby Tiles, Cut Corners, Label, 22 x 17 In.. .... 10000.00
Tabouret, G. Stickley, No. 449, Eastwood, Round Top, Decal, 22 x 24 In.. .... 4250.00
Tabouret, L. & J.G. Stickley, No. 560, Cut Corners, Curved Stretchers, 18 ½ x 16 In. 1800.00
Tabouret, L. & J.G. Stickley, No. 561, Cut Corners, Arched Stretcher, 20 x 18 x 18 In. 600.00
Tabouret, Limbert, No. 234, Slab Sides, Signed, 18 x 16 x 16 In. .... *illus* 2320.00
Tabouret, Louis XVI, Carved Frieze, White Paint, Fluted Legs, Pad Top, c.1780, 17 x 16 In., Pair 7500.00
Tabouret, Rosewood, Bamboo Inset Top, Red Marble, Chinese, 19th Century, 37 In. 444.00
Tabouret, Rosewood, Carved Berries, Vines, Flowers, Red Marble Top, Chinese, 19 In.. .... 474.00
Tabouret, Rosewood, Carved Butterflies, Dragons, Inset Marble Top, Chinese, 35 ½ In.. .... 533.00
Tabouret, Rosewood, Carved Dragons, Fish, Flowers, Red Marble Inset Top, Chinese, 32 In... 1541.00
Tabouret, Rosewood, Carved Foo Dog Heads, Flowering Plants, Marble Top, Chinese, 18 In. . 385.00
Tabouret, Rosewood, Marble Inset, Fruiting Vines, Chinese, 19th Century, 37 In.. .... 770.00
Tabouret, Stickley Bros., Stretcher Base, 18 x 12 x 12 In. 360.00

Tabouret, Teak, Marble Insert, Carved Base, Chinese, Early 20th Century, 37 In. . . . . *illus* 390.00
Tabouret, White, Parcel Gilt, Upholstered Seat, Sides, Saber Legs, c.1800, 27 x 28 In., Pair . . . 6250.00
Tea Cart, Louis XVI, Mahogany, Satinwood, Gilt Metal, Serpentine Edge, Handles, 28 x 34 In. 480.00
Tea Cart, Louis XVI Style, Brushed Brass, Glass, Leaves, France, 31 x 18 x 30 In. 3360.00
Umbrella Stand, Art Deco, Copper, Bronze, Demilune Top, Columnar Base, 25 x 19 In. 299.00
Umbrella Stand, Black Forest, Bear, Standing, Linden Wood, Swiss, c.1920, 20 In. 3220.00
Umbrella Stand, Black Forest, Standing Bear Cub, Holding Rustic Hoop, 37 x 17 In. 1320.00
Umbrella Stand, Brass, Turtle Relief Work, 24 In. 385.00
Umbrella Stand, Cast Iron, Antlers, Paw Feet, Germany, 31 ½ x 19 ½ In. 1020.00
Umbrella Stand, Cast Iron, Dog, Holding Double-Looped Whip, Pedestal, 23 x 20 x 13 In. . . 1438.00
Umbrella Stand, G. Stickley, No. 80, Tapered, Copper Base, Patina, 27 x 13 In. 10800.00
Umbrella Stand, G. Stickley, No. 100, Slats, Riveted Rings, 24 x 11 In. . . . . *illus* 960.00
Umbrella Stand, Horn, Antlers, Hexagonal Base, Paw Feet, Cast Iron, Germany, c.1900, 32 x 20 In. 1020.00
Umbrella Stand, Lucite, Tube Spiral, 22 In. 119.00
Umbrella Stand, Porcelain, Blue & White, Pierced Sides, Birds, Flowers, Japan, 1800s, 24 In. 207.00
Umbrella Stand, Shell Decorated, Turtle Feet, Cast Iron, 1867 . . . . 3500.00
Umbrella Stand, Victorian, Cast Iron, Allegorical, Youth With Serpent, 33 x 20 In. 1020.00
Umbrella Stand, Victorian, Oak, Carved, Cast-Iron Drip Pan, 37 x 14 In. 75.00
Umbrella Stand, Victorian, Walnut, Cast-Iron Drip Pan, 36 In. 212.00
Vanity, Neoclassical, Rosewood, Exotic Veneer, Mirror Stand, Pullout Slide, 32 x 32 In. 489.00
Vanity, Queen Anne Style, Walnut, Mirror, England, 28 In. 777.00
Vitrine, Biedermeier, Mahogany, Ebonized, Pediment Cornice, Columns, 76 x 45 In., Pair . . . 4406.00
Vitrine, Edwardian, Checkerbanded Satinwood, Silk Lining, 28 x 16 In. 652.00
Vitrine, Edwardian, Mahogany, Inlaid Satinwood, Multicolored Scrolls, 42 x 32 In. 236.00
Vitrine, Empire Style, Mahogany, Brass Mounts, 67 x 2 x 16 ½ In. 690.00
Vitrine, George II, Chinese Chippendale, Lacquered, Gilt, Gothic Arch, 63 x 23 In. 1016.00
Vitrine, Georgian, Mahogany, Banding, Inlaid, Glazed Doors, Bowfront Base, 53 In. 960.00
Vitrine, Hammered Brass, Tray Top, X-Stretcher, Contemporary, 31 x 19 In. 418.00
Vitrine, Italian Rococo, Gilt, Shell Carved, Scrolling Leaves, Putti, 53 x 36 x 4 In. 1770.00
Vitrine, Louis Philippe, Ebony, Bronze, Gilt Mounts, Putti, Door, France, 1800s, 46 x 35 In. . . 1380.00
Vitrine, Louis XV, Gilt Metal Mounted, Rectangular, Cabriole Legs, 30 ½ In. 1080.00
Vitrine, Louis XV, Kingwood, Marquetry, Gilt Metal Mount, Bombe, 68 x 27 In. 1434.00
Vitrine, Louis XV, Pine, Domed Crest, Doors, Grilled Panel, 65 x 41 x 16 In. 1320.00
Vitrine, Louis XV Style, Gilt, Door, Cabriole Legs, 77 x 35 x 17 In. 1800.00
Vitrine, Louis XV Style, Mahogany, Serpentine Top, Fitted Sides, Glass Panels, 38 x 18 x 18 In. 415.00
Vitrine, Louis XV Style, Oak, Egg & Dart Molded Cornice, 89 x 59 x 24 In. 3360.00
Vitrine, Louis XV Style, Pine, Domed Crest, Doors, Cabriole Legs, 64 ½ x 41 x 15 ½ In. 1320.00
Vitrine, Louis XVI, Breccia Marble Top, 55 x 26 In. 960.00
Vitrine, Louis XVI, Gilt, Triangular, Glass Insert, Fluted Legs, 39 x 23 In. 2300.00
Vitrine, Louis XVI, Mahogany, Ormolu, Lined, Paneled Frieze, 32 x 38 x 23 In. 2160.00
Vitrine, Louis XVI, Sloped Cornice, Green Velvet Lining, 65 x 28 In. 1560.00
Vitrine, Louis XVI, Veneer, Glazed Doors, Painted Scene Panels, 65 x 27 In. 1440.00
Vitrine, Louis XVI Style, Ebonized, Ormolu, Hinged Top, 31 x 37 x 24 In. 3120.00
Vitrine, Louis XVI Style, Gilt Brass, Oval, Mirrored, Bowfront, 66 ½ x 30 x 17 In. 460.00
Vitrine, Mahogany, 3 Compartments, Bowed X-Shape Legs, Stretchers, 19 x 41 In. 1320.00
Vitrine, Mahogany, Marquetry, Parquetry, Gilt Bronze Mounted, c.1900, 55 x 47 In. 6875.00
Vitrine, Mahogany, Molded Cornice, 2 Glazed Doors, Mullions, 50 x 40 x 13 In. 1315.00
Vitrine, Napoleon III, Kingwood, Parquetry, Glass Panel, 96 x 43 x 20 In. 1920.00
Vitrine, Napoleon III, Louis XVI Style, Mahogany, Marble Top, Glazed, 59 x 28 In. 780.00
Vitrine, Neoclassical, Glass Case, Lined Interior, Tapered Legs, 1900s, 27 x 55 In. 295.00
Vitrine, Oak, Bowfront, Curved Glass, Mirrored Back, Glass Shelves, 80 x 54 In. 1725.00
Vitrine, Parzinger, Enameled, Glass Doors, Shelves, Brass Hardware, 85 x 36 x 15 In. 3900.00
Vitrine, Rococo Revival, Mahogany, Reserves, Mirrored Back, Cabriole Legs, 65 x 50 x 18 In. . 384.00
Wardrobe, Arts & Crafts, Mirror Door, 2 Copper Repousse Panel Doors, England, 67 x 82 In. . 3120.00
Wardrobe, Edwardian, Mahogany, Leaf Inlay Frieze, Paneled, 4 Drawers, 90 x 101 In. 4800.00
Wardrobe, French, Provincial, Fruitwood, Serpentine Panels, Mid 1700s, 80 x 44 In. 1062.00
Wardrobe, George III, Mahogany, Dentil Molded, Swan's Neck, c.1840, 93 x 59 In. 1438.00
Wardrobe, Paint Decorated, Cornice Molding, 2 Doors, Inset Panels, 82 ½ x 61 In. 960.00
Wardrobe, Pine, 2 Paneled Doors, Molded Plinth Base, England, 88 x 52 ½ x 20 In. 354.00
Wardrobe, Poplar, Dovetailed, Paneled Doors, Red & Black Paint, Mid 1800s, 63 x 43 In. 3819.00
Wardrobe, Poplar, Ocher Grain Paint, Door, 2 Drawers, 19th Century, 74 ½ x 36 In. 936.00
Wardrobe, Renaissance Revival, Walnut, Step-Molded Crown, Glazed Door, 80 x 40 In. 212.00
Washstand, Bird's-Eye & Tiger Maple, Demilune Crest, Top Shape Feet, 40 x 27 x 19 In. 3172.00
Washstand, Chippendale, George II, Mahogany, Chinese, 30 x 13 x 13 In. 738.00
Washstand, Chippendale, Mahogany, Ring Turned Top, 2 Drawers, 1790, 31 x 22 x 21 In. . . . 550.00
Washstand, Corner, Regency, Mahogany, Rounded Backsplash, Shelf, c.1800, 41 x 22 In. 582.00
Washstand, Corner, Sheraton, Cherry, Bowfront, Dovetailed, Curved Doors, c.1820, 49 x 28 In. 499.00

TIP
Don't ship furniture from a hot to a cold climate or a wet to a dry climate, if it can be avoided. The wood will expand or contract, causing cracks and other damage.

F

Furniture, Tabouret, Teak, Marble Insert, Carved Base, Chinese, Early 20th Century, 37 In.
$390.00

Furniture, Umbrella Stand, G. Stickley, No. 100, Slats, Riveted Rings, 24 x 11 In.
$960.00

Furniture, Washstand, Federal, Walnut, Backsplash, Drawer, c.1800, 34 x 28 x 18 In.
$360.00

Furniture, Washstand, Gothic Revival, Oak, Tile Backsplash, c.1900, 35 x 46 x 21 In.
$495.00

Furniture, Washstand, Yellow, Black, New England, c.1830-40, 37 x 17 x 17 In.
$510.00

Furntiture, Workbench, Yellow Pine, Lift Top, 6 Compartments, 1800s, 22 x 29 x 15 In.
$195.00

Washstand, Corner, Sheraton, Mahogany, Bowfront, Drawer, 2 Faux Drawers, c.1820, 33 In. . 264.00
Washstand, Federal, Cherry, Scalloped Backsplash, Shelf, c.1820, 35 x 20 x 19 In. 764.00
Washstand, Federal, Walnut, Backsplash, Drawer, c.1800, 34 x 28 x 18 In.. . . . . *illus* 360.00
Washstand, Georgian, Mahogany, Tambour Door, Drawer, England, 1890, 37 x 21 x 18 In. . . 250.00
Washstand, Gothic Revival, Oak, Tile Backsplash, c.1900, 35 x 46 x 21 In.. . . . . *illus* 495.00
Washstand, Hepplewhite, Pine, Painted, Ocher, Striping, Backsplash, Shelf, 36 x 17 In. 575.00
Washstand, Mahogany, Backsplash, Ionic Columns, Paw Feet, 1800s, 38 x 29 In. 2115.00
Washstand, Mahogany, Lift Top, Corner, 32 ½ x 28 x 20 In.. . . . . 585.00
Washstand, Mahogany, Marble, Drawer, Doors, Scroll Feet, 39 x 33 In.. . . . . 940.00
Washstand, Mahogany, Scroll Backsplash, Shelf, Drawer, c.1810, 37 x 26 In.. . . . . 325.00
Washstand, Maple, 2 Drawers, Bail Capitals, Casters, Bulb Feet, England, 37 x 42 x 22 In. . . . 620.00
Washstand, Pine, 3 Shelves, Shaped Ends, Braces, Early 1900s, 57 x 12 ½ In. 374.00
Washstand, Pine, Green Paint, Cutout Sides, 3 Stepped Shelves, 1900s, 40 x 14 In. 489.00
Washstand, Pine, Poplar, Striping, Dovetailed Gallery, Stenciled Fruit, Drawer, 36 x 18 In.. . 294.00
Washstand, Poplar, Yellow Paint, Flowers, Drawer, Scroll Backsplash, 1800s, 34 x 27 In. 3744.00
Washstand, Regency, Mahogany, Dovetailed Gallery, Basins, Shelf, 35 x 38 In. 235.00
Washstand, Regency, Mahogany, Recessed Top, Drawers, Backsplash, 38 x 19 x 16 In. 325.00
Washstand, Regency, Mahogany, Tiers, Cutouts, Drawers, Turned Legs, 15 x 15 In.. . . . . 230.00
Washstand, Renaissance Revival, Walnut, Marble Top, 3 Drawers, 35 x 29 x 17 In.. . . . . 480.00
Washstand, Rococo Revival, Rosewood, Carved, Cupboard, Marble, c.1850, 41 x 36 In. 1292.00
Washstand, Sheraton, Mahogany, Hole For Washbasin, Backsplash, 37 x 26 In. 489.00
Washstand, Sheraton, Maple, Scalloped, Drawer, Shelf, 35 ½ x 25 ½ x 17 In. 805.00
Washstand, Victorian, Mahogany, High Backsplash, Shelf, Drawer 350.00
Washstand, Victorian, Walnut, Towel Bars, Backsplash, 34 x 32 x 17 In. 83.00
Washstand, Walnut, Backsplash, Marble, Leaf Design, 36 x 30 In.. . . . . 250.00
Washstand, Walnut, Dovetailed Gallery, Lower Shelf, Turned Legs, 1800s, 30 x 22 x 17 In.. . . 176.00
Washstand, Yellow, Black, New England, c.1830-40, 37 x 17 x 17 In. . . . . *illus* 510.00
Wastebasket, G. Stickley, No. 94, Slats, Riveted Iron Hoops, Signed, Label, 14 x 12 In. 1090.00 to 3100.00
Whatnot Shelf, Anglo-Indian, Tropical Hardwood, Gallery, 3 Shelves, Cupboard, 51 x 50 In.. 1880.00
Whatnot Shelf, Corner, Victorian, Walnut, 5 Graduated Shelves, 61 In. 106.00
Whatnot Shelf, Walnut, Turned, Scroll Cut, 4 Graduated Shelves, 55 In. 106.00
Window Seat, Directoire Style, Padded, Outscrolled Lyre, Crest, 30 x 38 x 13 In. 1200.00
Window Seat, G. Stickley, No. 177, V Seat, Tacked-On Leather, 26 x 25 x 18 ½ In. 3500.00
Window Seat, George III, Gilt, Outscrolled Arms, Upholstered, 27 x 48 In.. . . . . 4375.00
Window Seat, George III, Mahogany, Scrolled Ends, Square Legs, c.1780, 26 ½ x 39 In.. . . . . 1872.00
Window Seat, Louis XVI Style, Mahogany, Cane Seat, 28 x 26 x 16 In. 1200.00
Window Seat, Neoclassical, Mahogany, Carved, Leather Cushions, 36 x 64 x 28 In. 3360.00
Window Seat, Regency, Gilt Metal, Rosewood Grain, Parcel Gilt, Cane, Pair 11250.00
Wine Cooler, Regency, Figured Mahogany, Reeded Feet, Metal Liner, 20 x 32 ½ In.. . . . . 2400.00
Workbench, Yellow Pine, Lift Top, 6 Compartments, 1800s, 22 x 29 x 15 In. . . . . *illus* 195.00

G. ARGY-ROUSSEAU is the impressed mark used on a variety of objects in the Art Deco style. Gabriel Argy-Rousseau, born in 1885, was a French glass artist. In 1921, he formed a partnership that made pate-de-verre and other glass. He worked until 1952 and died in 1953.

G-ARGY-ROUSSEAU

Fairy Lamp, Flowers, Wrought Iron Base, Marked, 5 ½ x 8 ¼ In. . . . . *illus* 7200.00
Lamp, 2 Tigers, Hidden By Foliage, Purple, Pate-De-Verre, Signed, 1921, 8 In. 4400.00
Lamp, Dune Flowers, Purple, Amber, Roses, Leaves, Pate-De-Verre, 13 In.. . . . . 690.00
Luminaire, Eels Heads, Pink, Purple, Pate-De-Verre, Hammered Metal Stand, 9 x 7 In. 9660.00
Night-Light, Aquatic, Red To Purple, Tentacles, 3 Ball Feet, 7 ½ In.. . . . . 4600.00
Night-Light, Stylized Leaves, Deep Purple, Pate-De-Verre, Stand, Signed, 6 In.. . . . . 3800.00
Paperweight, 2 Butterflies, Green, Purple Highlights, Signed, 1921, 2 ½ x 2 In. 2200.00
Paperweight, 2 Moths, Mottled Green, Pate-De-Cristal, 2 ¾ In.. . . . . 1100.00
Pendant, Purple Crane, Blue Scroll Work, Pink Tassel Cord, 3 In.. . . . . 1840.00
Pendant, Purple Moth, Pink Ground, Pate-De-Verre, Pink Silk Cord, 2 ½ x 18 In.. . . . . 2013.00
Vase, Amber & Red, Mottled, Pate-De-Verre, Signed, 7 In. 5175.00
Vase, Magenta, Brown, Vertical Lines, Footed, Signed, c.1921, 5 ¼ In. 2000.00
Vase, Stylized Flowers, Purple Ground, Signed, Signed, 6 ¾ In. 6000.00
Vase, Vertical Lines, Magenta, Brown, White, Signed, c.1921, 5 ½ In.. 3520.00

GALLE was a designer who made glass, pottery, furniture, and other Art Nouveau items. Emile Galle founded his factory in France in 1874. After Galle's death in 1904, the firm continued to make glass and furniture until 1931. The name *Galle* was used as a mark, but it was often hidden in the design of the object. Galle glass is listed here. Pottery is in the next section. His furniture is listed in the Furniture category.

Atomizer, Cherry Blossoms, Leafy Branches, Signed, 7 In. 690.00
Bowl, Amber, Crimson Flowers, Footed, Trifold Shape, Cameo, Signed, 6 ½ In.. . . . . 1150.00

Bowl, Red Roses, Yellow Ground, Oblong, Gentle Wave Edge, Cameo, 9 In. 2040.00
Box, Cover, Blue, Brown Dragonflies, Lilies, Signed, 7 In. 7475.00
Compote, Red Flowers, Leafy Stems, Yellow Flared Frosted Rim, Tapered, Signed, 8 In. 3390.00
Decanter, Blue Forget-Me-Nots, Dragonflies, Ribbons, Enameled, Blown Stopper, 10 ¼ In. . . 2588.00
Decanter, White Cut To Purple, Purple Foot, Cameo, Stopper, 11 ¾ In. 2106.00
Ewer, Red & Yellow Flowers, Amber Ground, Enameled, Sinuous Handle, Stopper, 12 ½ In. . . 6038.00
Lamp, Ceiling, 6 Iris, Red Leaf Rim, Citron, Oval, Cameo, Signed, 14 In. 3450.00
Lamp, Mushroom Shade, Green Flowers, Pink Ground, Bronze, Ivory, Woman Base, 18 ½ In. 8625.00
Lamp, Pinecone & Needles Shade, Yellow, Green, Lighted Wood Base, Signed, 4 ½ In. 660.00
Lamp Base, Leaves, Brown, Orange, Yellow, Bulbous, Cameo, Signed, 11 x 5 In. 720.00
Lamp Base, Mauve-Brown Fuchsia, Cameo, Pedestal Base, 9 In. 420.00
Night-Light, 3 Turquoise Butterflies, Citron Domed Shade, Metal Base, Cameo, 5 In. 633.00
Powder Jar, Flowers, Pink, Gray, Blue, Green, Cameo, Signed, 6 In. 1300.00
Vase, Acorns, Green, Oak Leaves, Cinnamon Frosted Ground, Flared Rim, Cameo, 4 ½ In. . . . 776.00
Vase, Amber, Leaves, Berries, Stems, Frosted Ground, Fire Polished, 2 ¾ x 4 In. 960.00
Vase, Amber, Nasturtium, Cameo, Signed, 18 x 6 ½ In. 2040.00
Vase, Amber, Yellow Flowers, Frosted Pink Ground, Cameo, 12 ½ In. 1265.00
Vase, Amber Tiger Lilies, Yellow Ground, Cameo, Signed, 13 In. 2070.00
Vase, Amethyst, Hydrangea Blossom, Lavender, Olive Green, Frosted Ground, 9 ⅝ In. 1380.00
Vase, Amethyst Leaves, Blue & Purple Fuchsia, Yellow Ground, Cameo, 8 ½ In. 4370.00
Vase, Banjo, Branches, Olive Green, Orange Ground, Signed, 8 In. 978.00
Vase, Banjo, Chartreuse To Pink, Green, Stemmed Branch, Seed Pods, Cameo, Signed, 7 In. . . 949.00
Vase, Banjo, Dangling Pea Pods, Lime Green, Orange, 6 ⅝ In. . . . . *illus* 805.00
Vase, Banjo, Flowers, Blue, Multicolored Mottled Ground, Bulbous, Cameo, 7 ⅞ In. 1870.00
Vase, Banjo, Green, Pink, Stylized Leaf, 6 ½ In. 605.00
Vase, Banjo, Green Fern, Frosted, Cameo, Signed, 6 ¾ In. 403.00
Vase, Banjo, Lavender, White Flowers, Leaves, Stems, Frosted Ground, 6 ¾ In. 2645.00
Vase, Banjo, Lavender Flowers, Olive Leaves, Frosted Peach Ground, Signed, 6 In. 720.00
Vase, Barrel, Pressed, Wheat Stalks, Red, Yellow, Green, Gold Trim, Enameled, 8 In. 7475.00
Vase, Bleeding Hearts, Leaves, Maroon, Frosted Amber Ground, Cameo, Signed, 9 In. . . . *illus* 2950.00
Vase, Bleeding Hearts, Leaves, Translucent Maroon Foot, Yellow Ground, Cameo, 16 ½ In. . . . 4428.00
Vase, Bleeding Hearts, Squat, Cameo, c.1900, 6 ¾ x 6 ½ In. 3276.00
Vase, Bleeding Hearts, Vines, Brown, Salmon, Yellow Ground, Cameo, 17 ¾ In. 8625.00
Vase, Blossoming Branches, Violet, Lemon Ground, Cameo, Signed, 4 ½ In. 900.00
Vase, Blue, Cascading Royal Blue Wisteria, Footed, Shouldered, Cameo, Signed, 10 In. 518.00
Vase, Blue Gooseberries, Purple Leaves, Yellow To Purple Ground, Bulbous, Cameo, 10 In. . . . 9775.00
Vase, Branches, Berries, Olive Green, Purple, Blue, Tan To Yellow Ground, Cameo, 8 ¼ In. . . . 3600.00
Vase, Branches, Leaves, Berries, Amber, Cameo, Signed, 13 ½ In. 2040.00
Vase, Brown, Black Leaves, Red Berries, Red Ground, Cameo, 16 ½ In. 8050.00
Vase, Brown, Tan, Berries, Leaves, Frosted Amber Ground, Cameo, 5 ¾ In. 660.00
Vase, Brown, White Ground, Berries, Leaves, Vines, 2 ¾ In. 600.00
Vase, Brown Columbine, Gold To Tan Ground, Cameo, Signed, 6 In. 646.00
Vase, Brown Flowers, Stems, Leaves, Chartreuse Ground, Amethyst Foot, 6 ¼ In. 540.00
Vase, Brown Flowers, Stems, Leaves, Orange Ground, 5 ¾ In. 575.00
Vase, Bud, Branches, Leaves, Purple, Pink Ground, Cameo, 2 x 6 In. 390.00
Vase, Bud, Pink, Flower Buds, Leaves, Cameo, Signed, 6 ½ In. 715.00
Vase, Bud, Purple Blossoms, Amber Ground, Cameo, Signed, 8 ¾ x 3 ¾ In. 1680.00
Vase, Bulbous, Brown Leaves, Citron Ground, Cameo, Signed, 4 ½ In. 460.00
Vase, Butterfly, Leaves, Green Frosted Ground, Cameo, 6 ½ In. 8625.00
Vase, Clematis, Gray, Citrine, Plum Overlay, Cameo, c.1915, 10 In. 2124.00
Vase, Clematis, Purple, Yellow Ground, Blown Out, Signed, c.1900, 6 ½ In. 3750.00
Vase, Cyclamen, Dark Red To Cream To Green, Cameo, c.1900, 3 ¾ x 3 ½ In. 1638.00
Vase, Daffodils, Yellow, Green Leaves, Windowpane, Frosted Ground, Cameo, 21 ¾ In. 6325.00
Vase, Dragonflies, Pond, Flowers, Orange, Caramel, Pale Blue, c.1885, 22 In. 8225.00
Vase, Ferns, Purple, Lemon Ground, Tapered, Cameo, 7 In. 840.00
Vase, Fishing Ships, Birds, Yellow Ground, Cameo, Signed, 20 ½ In. 4313.00
Vase, Flower, Lavender, Olive Green, Buds, Frosted, Blue Ground, 2 ⅛ In. 489.00
Vase, Flower Overlay, Gold Enameled, Cream, Long Neck, Chinese Signature, c.1880, 13 ½ In. 4250.00
Vase, Flowers, Brown, Amber, Apricot & Cream Shaded Ground, Cameo, 13 ½ In. 3450.00
Vase, Flowers, Green, Amethyst Pink, Purple Crown Rim, Footed, Cameo, 19 In. 4313.00
Vase, Flowers, Leaves, Vines Overlay, Etched, c.1900, 16 In. 5625.00
Vase, Flowers, Purple, Bronze Foot, 7 x 4 ½ In. 3480.00
Vase, Flowers, Red, Stems, Leaves, Frosted Yellow Ground, Windowpane, Cameo, 6 ¼ In. 3450.00
Vase, Flowers, Russet Blossoms, Leaves, Stems, White Ground, 2 ¾ x 2 ¼ In. 480.00
Vase, Flowers, Yellow, Gray, Amethyst, Ruffled Edge, Cameo, Signed, 13 ½ In. 1600.00
Vase, Frosted, Amethyst, Pink Flowers, Blown Out, 4-Footed Base, Glass, Metal, 10 ½ In. 633.00
Vase, Frosted & Pink, Leafy Green Flowers, Cameo, Signed, 12 In. 1610.00
Vase, Frosted Amber, Crimson Stemmed Flowers, Oval, Signed, Cameo, 3 ¾ In. 776.00

G. Argy-Rouseau, Fairy Lamp, Flowers, Wrought Iron Base, Marked, 5 ½ x 8 ¼ In.
$7200.00

Galle, Vase, Banjo, Dangling Pea Pods, Lime Green, Orange, 6 ⅝ In.
$805.00

Galle, Vase, Bleeding Hearts, Leaves, Maroon, Frosted Amber Ground, Cameo, Signed, 9 In.
$2950.00

TIP

Do not wash or rinse gold-decorated glass with very hot water or strong soap. It will remove some of the gold.

Galle, Vase, Landscape, Amber, Orange, Yellow Frosted Ground, Cameo, Signed, 1900, 14 In.
$4800.00

Galle, Vase, Plums, Purple Leaves, Amber, Orange Ground, Cameo, Signed, 1905, 13 x 8 In.
$9600.00

Galle, Vase, Pond Scene, Blue, Green, Yellow To Frosted Ground, Cameo, Signed, 7 x 5 In.
$1010.00

Vase, Gold, Brown Flower, Green Transparent Ground, Cameo, Signed, 7 In. 6600.00
Vase, Green & Gold Leaf Overlay, Frosted Ground, Signed, c.1910, 3 ⅞ In.. .... 325.00
Vase, Irises, Plum, Stems, Leaves, Bud, Yellow Frosted Ground, 3 ¾ In. 540.00
Vase, Irises, Purple Leaves, Frosted Ground, Cameo, Signed, 10 In. 8912.00
Vase, Jack-In-The-Pulpit, Clear, 13 ¼ x 5 In. 2040.00
Vase, Japanese Peach Blossoms, Blue, Yellow Ground, Cameo, Signed, 5 In. 4800.00
Vase, Landscape, Amber, Orange, Yellow Frosted Ground, Cameo, Signed, 1900, 14 In. . . *illus* 4800.00
Vase, Landscape, Black Pine Trees, Rocky Shore, White Shaded To Yellow Ground, Cameo, 8 In. 4600.00
Vase, Landscape, Lake Como, Mountains, Black, Green, Blue, Aqua To Peach Ground, Cameo, 8 In. 5750.00
Vase, Landscape, Misty, Cameo, Signed, 10 In. 2760.00
Vase, Landscape, Purple Pine Trees, Blue Mountains, White Ground, Cameo, 5 ¼ In. 2818.00
Vase, Landscape, Tree, Blue Lake, Shore, Frosted Yellow Sky, Footed Cylinder, Signed, 14 In... 5600.00
Vase, Landscape, Tree Lined Lake, Amber Overlay, Frosted Ground, Cameo, c.1910, 3 ½ In.... 708.00
Vase, Leafy Plants, Transparent Green, Amber Ground, Metal Footed, 17 x 6 ¼ In.. .... 4200.00
Vase, Leaves, Flowering Pods, Olive Green, Pink, Yellow, Frosted Ground, 2 ⅝ x 6 In. 978.00
Vase, Leaves, Flowers, Red, Yellow Shaded To White Ground, Cameo, 6 In. 2530.00
Vase, Lilies, Gray, Amber, Green, Cameo, c.1915, 18 In. 2596.00
Vase, Lily Pads, Iris, Dragonflies, Brown Stems, Seashells, Yellow Ground, Cameo, 16 In. 9200.00
Vase, Mums, Leafy Stems, Frosted, Urn, Footed, Cameo, Signed, 8 In. 1380.00
Vase, Orange Flowers, Leaves, Apricot Frosted Ground, Fire Polished, Engraved, Cameo, 7 In.. 2880.00
Vase, Orange Leafy Flowers, Frosted, Shouldered, Chinese Signature, Cameo, 7 In. 1495.00
Vase, Orange Poppies, Cameo, 2 ½ In. 354.00
Vase, Orchids, Leaves, Frosted, Footed, Purple, Cameo, 5 In. 575.00
Vase, Pillow, Purple Flowers, Caramel Ground, Funnel Neck, 7 In.. .... 4135.00
Vase, Plums, Leaves, Yellow Ground, Blown Out, Signed, c.1920, 16 x 3 ⅝ In.. .... 14000.00
Vase, Plums, Purple Leaves, Amber, Orange Ground, Cameo, Signed, 1905, 13 x 8 In. ... *illus* 9600.00
Vase, Pond Lily Scene, Blue, Frosted To Citron, Cameo, 10 ½ In. 1725.00
Vase, Pond Lily Scene, Blue, Green Frosted, Oval, Cameo, 2 ½ In. 575.00
Vase, Pond Scene, Blue, Green, Yellow To Frosted Ground, Cameo, Signed, 7 x 5 In. .... *illus* 1010.00
Vase, Pond Scene, Iris, Blue, Green, Yellow Ground, Bulbous, Cameo, 5 x 7 In.. .... 1020.00
Vase, Poppies, Serpentine Stems, Coral, Orange, Frosted Ground, Cameo, 17 ¼ In. 1265.00
Vase, Prickly Thistle Plants Circling Body, Green, Frosted & Pink Ground, Flared, 5 In....... 635.00
Vase, Purple Clematis, Frosted Lavender Ground, Cameo, Fire Polished, 5 In.. .... 1955.00
Vase, Purple Flowers, Stems, Leaves, Frosted Ground, 2 ½ In.. .... 480.00
Vase, Purple Leaf, Berries, Frosted Green Ground, Flared Rim, Cameo, Signed, 6 In. 690.00
Vase, Red To Yellow, Flowers, Tapered, Round Base, Cameo, Signed, c.1900, 5 In.. .... 1007.00
Vase, Red Windowpane Flowers, Yellow Ground, Bulbous, Cameo, Signed, 8 In. 6000.00
Vase, Red Windowpane Flowers, Yellow Ground, Teardrop Shape, Cameo, Signed, 10 In...... 3600.00
Vase, Rio De Janeiro, Russet Tropical Scene, Mountains, Cameo, Signed, 14 In. 9600.00
Vase, Roses, Red, Frosted Cream Shaded To Yellow, Windowpane, Cameo, Signed, 10 ½ In.... 5175.00
Vase, Seagulls, Conical, Pulled Stem & Foot, Rolled Lip, Signed, c.1920, 6 ½ In.. .... 3500.00
Vase, Stick, Amethyst Flower Overlay, Frosted Ground, c.1910, 20 In.. .... 2242.00
Vase, Stick, Citron, Red Stemmed Leafy Flowers, Footed, Cameo, Signed, 7 In. 920.00
Vase, Stick, Green Leaves, Seed Pods, Frosted Cinnamon, Cameo, Signed, 12 In.. .... 1495.00
Vase, Thistles, Crimson, Gold Stemmed, Textured, Etched, Cameo, 10 In. 1770.00
Vase, Thistles, Flared Rim, Footed, Frosted & Pink Ground, 4 ⅜ In. 633.00
Vase, Thistles, Leaves, Apricot, Frosted Ground, 2 x 3 In. 374.00
Vase, Trumpet, Trees Silhouetted, Mountains, Lake, Frosted Blue To Amber, Cameo, 12 ½ In.. 2990.00
Vase, Violet Blossoms, Buds, Leaves, Chocolate Brown, Sulfur Yellow, Cameo, 3 ¼ In. 546.00
Vase, Water Lilies, Purple Buds, Stems, Yellow Mottled Ground, Cameo, Signed, 7 In.. .... 1689.00
Vase, White Polar Bear, Iceberg, Coupe Shape, Signed, 11 In. 2400.00
Vase, Windowpane Blue Clematis, Lavender Leaves, Yellow Ground, Cameo, 13 In. 6600.00
Vase, Wisteria, Blossoms, Vines, Frosted, Saffron, Amethyst Ground, 17 ¼ In. 1955.00
Vase, Wisteria Vine, Cascading, Flowers, Lavender, Olive Green, Coral, 22 ⅞ In. 2645.00

GALLE POTTERY was made by Emile Galle, the famous French designer, after 1874. The pieces were marked with the initials *E. G.* impressed, *Em. Galle Faiencerie de Nancy*, or a version of his signature. Galle is best known for his glass, listed above.

Inkwell, Red European Village, Enameled, Flowers, Signed, 3 In. 230.00
Vase, Dianthus, Butterflies, Twigs, Gold Enameled, Signed, Label, 8 ¼ x 6 In. .... *illus* 1800.00
Vase, Flying Phoenix, Relief, Gold Enameled, Signed, 6 x 5 x 2 ¾ In. .... *illus* 485.00

GAME collectors like all types of games. Of special interest are any board games or card games. Transogram and other company names are included in the description when known. Other games may be found listed under Card, Toy, or the name of the character or celebrity featured in the game.

Admiral Byrd's South Pole, Spinners, Game Pieces, Parker Bros., Board, Box, 13 x 17 ¼ In. 330.00
All Star Basketball, Player Shoots Baskets, Marx-O-Matic, Marx, Box 90.00
Auto Game, Spinner, Game Pieces, Milton Bradley, Board, Box, 1906, 11 In. 55.00
Babe Ruth's Baseball, Toy Town Corp., Box, 1940s, 25 x 19 In. 675.00
Ball Toss, Man's Bust, Fur Hat, Painted, Wood Backboard, Composition, 12 ½ x 27 In. 230.00
Baseball, 52 Player Picture Cards, Pat. March 25, 1913 .... *illus* 1955.00
Baseball, Field, Bat, Players, Cardboard, Realistic Game & Toy Co., Box, c.1925, 18 x 18 In. 115.00
Baseball, Major League, Spinner, Playing Field, Hinged Wooden Box, c.1920 .... 360.00
Baseball, Zimmer's Base Ball Game, McLoughlin Bros., Board, 1894, 21 x 21 In. 19975.00
Batman & Robin Marble Maze, Plastic Tray, Instructions, Box, c.1966, 12 x 12 In. 822.00
Bear, Target Game, Seated, Plays Drums, Tin, Battery Operated, Modern Toys, 9 In. 375.00
Bingo, Super Heroes, Hasbro, 1976, 11 ¾ x 7 In. 22.00
Board, Blondie Goes To Leisureland, Westinghouse, Premium, c.1935 .... 75.00
Board, Checkered Game Of Life, Paper Lithograph, Milton Bradley, 15 x 16 In. 173.00
Board, Checkers, 2-Sided, Applied Gallery Edge, Black, Red, Mustard, 13 ½ x 13 ½ In. 646.00
Board, Checkers, Brown, Black, Brown & Gray Ground, Molding, 18 ½ x 19 In. 978.00
Board, Checkers, Gold, Black, Landscape, Gilt Gesso Frame, 19th Century, Square, 25 In. 1440.00
Board, Checkers, Painted, Black, Yellow, 12 x 12 In. 374.00
Board, Checkers, Painted, Red, Black, Sliding Lids, Compartments, 22 ½ x 15 In. 345.00
Board, Checkers, Pine, Black, Yellow, 1908, 15 x 15 In. 1410.00
Board, Checkers, Red, Black, 2-Sided, Applied Molding, Cutout, 28 ½ x 16 ½ In. .... *illus* 504.00
Board, Checkers, Red, Black, Slate, c.1900, 20 x 20 In. 220.00
Board, Checkers, Reverse Painted Glass, Abalone, Multicolored, 1890s, 20 ¼ x 20 ¼ In. 1126.00
Board, Checkers, Wood, Applied Molding, c.1800, 11 x 11 In. 444.00
Board, Checkers, Wood, Painted Yellow, Black, c.1800, 16 x 27 In. 563.00
Board, Checkers, Yellow & Black Squares, Walnut, c.1900, 15 ¾ x 15 ½ In. .... *illus* 410.00
Board, Checkers & Backgammon, Wood, Red, Cream, Black, 1800s, 22 x 21 In. 1067.00
Board, Checkers & Parcheesi, Dividers, Yellow Ground, 30 ¾ x 19 In. 495.00
Board, Checkers & Parcheesi, Walnut, M.C. White, 19 x 19 ½ In. 1528.00
Board, Chess, Ebony, Tulip Wood, Drawer, France, c.1900, 3 x 18 x 18 In. 234.00
Board, Parcheesi, Multicolored, Mid 20th Century, 20 x 20 In. 88.00
Board, Parcheesi, Painted, Folding, c.1900, 16 x 16 In. 336.00
Board, Parcheesi, Slate, Marble Inlay, c.1900, 22 x 22 In. .... *illus* 527.00
Board, Parcheesi, Wood, Ivory, Inlaid, Molding, 1890-1910, 20 ¼ x 20 ¼ In. 504.00
Board, Parcheesi & Backgammon, Painted, Wood, Applied Molding, 20 ½ x 20 In. .... *illus* 889.00
Board, Parcheesi & Backgammon, Slate, 20 x 20 In. 225.00
Board, Slate, Painted & Stone Squares, Applied Decal Corners, c.1885, 20 x 20 In. 235.00
Board, Spider's Web, McLoughlin Bros., Box, 1898, 11 x 19 ¼ In. 115.00
Bowling Set, Wood, Incised Band, Painted, Bittersweet, Black, 10-In. Pin, 10 Piece .... *illus* 275.00
Captain Kidd, Junior Walking The Plank, Parker Bros., Board, 1920s, 12 x 11 In. 90.00
Chess Set, Carved Wood, Board, Modern, c.1965 .... 1800.00
Chess Set, Ebonized Pearwood, Carved Pieces, Oak Box, Josef Hartwig, Bauhaus, c.1924 .... 3750.00
Chess Set, Enameled, Bejeweled Silver, Military Theme, Austro-Hungarian, c.1900 .... 15925.00
Chess Set, Ivory, Box, Chinese, 9 x 18 In. & 5 ¾ x 2 ¾ In., 32 Piece 354.00
Chess Set, Ivory, Carved Figures, Temples, Case Converts To Game Board, 18 x 18 x 1 ¾ In. 920.00
Chess Set, Wood, Sliding Box, Jones, African-American Mass., 54th Infantry, 6 x 3 In. 590.00
Chiromagica, Answer Game, Pointer, Board, Inserts, McLoughlin, Box, 1870, 11 ½ x 11 ½ In. 115.00
Chiromagica, Hand Of Fate, McLoughlin, Board, 1901, 12 In. 355.00
Chuck-A-Luck Game, Dice, J. Chein, No. 176, 1930s 300.00
Circus Game, Spinner, Wood Pieces, Parker Bros., Board, 1897, 15 x 8 ¾ In. 82.00
Cycling Tour, Fold-Out Base, Spinner, Playing Pieces, J.W. Spear & Co., 8 x 10 ½ In. 144.00
Dart, Rocky Colavito's, Baseball, Bowling, Darts, 1960, 22 x 25 In. 95.00
Dice Chimney, Distressed Wood, Felt Lined, 5-Sided, Dice, 10 x 9 x 7 In. 249.00
Dice Spinner, Nickel, Chrome, 12 In. 20.00
Elmer Layden's Scientific Football Game, Cadaco, Board, 1936, 10 x 20 In. 50.00
Fun At The Circus, Wood Pieces, McLoughlin, Board, Box, 16 ¾ In. 275.00
Gambler's Box, Roulette, Chuck-O-Luck Dice, Checkers Horse Race, Cards, Chips, 14 x 5 In. 83.00
Game Of Jaws, Ideal Toy Corp., Board, Sealed, 1975, 7 x 15 In. 80.00
Game Of Shopping, Strawbridge & Clothier, Board, 1879, 17 x 17 In. 375.00
Hare & Hound, Spinner, Wood Pieces, Parker Bros., Board, 1895, 12 ¾ In. 110.00
Hold The Fort, Parker Brothers, Board, 1895 .... 95.00
Home Fish Pond, 2 Poles, 30 Fish, McLoughlin, Board, Box, 15 ½ In. 77.00
India, An Oriental Game, Spinner, Wood Pieces, McLoughlin, Board, Box, 14 x 15 In. 88.00
International Automobile Race, European Map, Tokens, Cards, Parker Bros., 11 x 20 ½ In. 410.00
Jeu De Course, Racehorses, Mechanical, M.J. & Cie, Late 19th Century 275.00
Jigsaw Puzzle, Battleship Oregon, McLoughlin Bros., Box, c.1900, 12 ¾ x 10 ½ In. 88.00

Galle Pottery, Vase, Dianthus, Butterflies, Twigs, Gold Enameled, Signed, Label, 8 ¼ x 6 In.
$1800.00

Galle Pottery, Vase, Flying Phoenix, Relief, Gold Enameled, Signed, 6 x 5 x 2 ¾ In.
$485.00

Game, Baseball, 52 Player Picture Cards, Pat. March 25, 1913
$1955.00

G

Game, Board, Checkers, Red, Black, 2-Sided, Applied Molding, Cutout, 28 ½ x 16 ½ In.
$504.00

Game, Board, Checkers, Yellow & Black Squares, Walnut, c.1900, 15 ¾ x 15 ½ In.
$410.00

Game, Board, Parcheesi, Slate, Marble Inlay, c.1900, 22 x 22 In.
$527.00

Game, Board, Parcheesi & Backgammon, Painted, Wood, Applied Molding, 20 ½ x 20 In.
$889.00

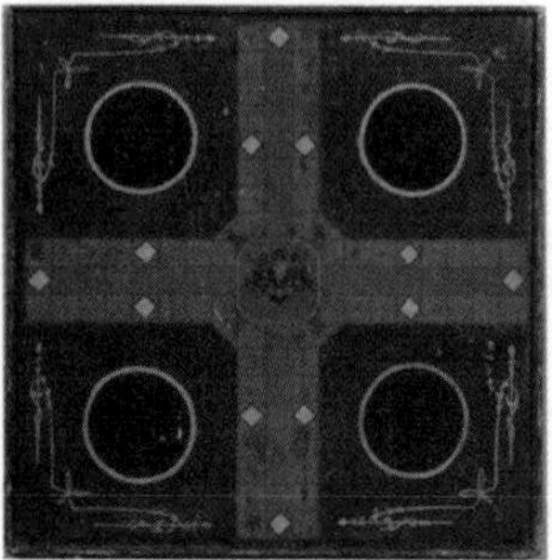

Jigsaw Puzzle, Bewitched, Entitled Along For The Ride, 1964, 14 x 24 In. 100.00
Jigsaw Puzzle, Christmas, Santa Claus Picture, Milton Bradley. 500.00
Jigsaw Puzzle, Dissected Map Of United States, McLoughlin Bros., Box, 25 x 18 In.. .... 55.00
Jigsaw Puzzle, Fire Engine, 2 Horses, Firemen, Paper On Board, McLoughlin, Box, 1887, 21 x 27 In. 365.00
Jigsaw Puzzle, Going Home, Cowboys On Horses, Jaymar, 1949, 11 x 14 In.. .... 45.00
Jigsaw Puzzle, Jig Of Jiggs, Queen's Page, Maxfield Parrish, Box, 1920, 9 ½ x 12 In., 250 Piece 144.00
Jigsaw Puzzle, Little Golden Picture Puzzle, No. 2991, 2 Trains, c.1951 .... 95.00
Jigsaw Puzzle, Locomotive, Paper On Board, McLoughlin, Box, 1887, 22 x 29 In. 330.00
Jigsaw Puzzle, Old Homestead, Country Farm Scene, 14 ½ x 17 In. 144.00
Jigsaw Puzzle, Santa Claus, Milton Bradley Co., c.1890-1900, 13 x 9 ¼ In. 325.00
Jigsaw Puzzle, SS Werra, Sailing Ship, McLoughlin Bros., Box, c.1882, 22 ½ x 17 In. 88.00
Jigsaw Puzzle, Victory, River Outing, Wood, Signed, J. Wilson, Box, 10 ⅜ x 14 In. 11.00
Junior Auto Race, Spinner, All-Fair, Board, Box 6.00
Kentucky Derby Race, Hinged Box, Chein, 1920s, 8 x 8 In. 143.00
Lawn, 4-4 Arm Boomerangs, 2 Round Nets, Marked, Brist, Box, 1902, 14 x 16 In. 82.00
Little Shoppers Game, Gibson Game Co., Board, 1915, 20 x 14 In. 55.00
Mah-Jongg, Case, Chinese, 6 ½ x 9 ¼ x 6 ½ In.. .... 357.00
Mah-Jongg, Chinese Carved Wood, Ivory Pieces, 10 x 7 x 9 In. 175.00
Mah-Jongg, Lid, Lizard Mount, Bone, Bamboo Tiles, Black, Lacquered Case, c.1900, 7 x 10 In. 115.00
Major League Indoor Baseball, Player Photos, Philadelphia Game Co., Board, 1910, 19 x 13 In. 1645.00
Man From U.N.C.L.E., Illya Kuryakin, Milton Bradley, Cards, 1966 .... 8.00
Marble, Frying Pan Form, Gold Paint, Clown Handle, Marked, Pat Apl 1884, 10 In.. .... 518.00
Merry-Go-Round, Chaffee & Selchow, Board, Box, 1898, 13 In. 880.00
Monkees, Guitar Version, Box, Transogram, Board, 1967, 9 x 17 ½ In. 221.00
Moon Mullins, Kayo Startling Turkey, 5 Characters, Milton Bradley, Cards, Board, 1927 .... 175.00
Munsters Masquerade Party, Spinner, Die Cut Player Pieces, Board, 1964, 9 ½ x 19 In.. .... 383.00
Over There, Spinner, Game Pieces, Milton Bradley, Board, Box, 9 x 14 ¾ In. 165.00
Parlor Football Game, Illustrated, McLoughlin Bros., Board, 1890s, 20 x 10 In. 900.00
Pinky Lee & The Runaway Frankfurters, Lisbeth Whiting Co., Board, Box, 1954, 16 x 13 ½ In. 66.00
Poker, Chips, Mother-Of Pearl, 5 Dollar, 86 piece. 165.00
Poker, Chips, Mother-Of-Pearl, Playing Cards, Leather Box, 13 x 3 In.. .... 354.00
Poker Chips, Bakelite, Red, Green, Yellow, Case 220.00
Pro Baseball, Roulette Type Spinner, Board, 1940, 9 x 5 x 9 ½ In. 50.00
Punch Board, What's Cookin'?, 1940-50, 15 x 9 ½ In. .... *illus* 87.00
Put The Teeth In Pickaninny, 2 Black Boys In Bathtub, Tin, Glass, 2 ⅝ In. 250.00
Race To The Moon, Wood Stands, Rockets, Balls, All-Fair, Board, Box, c.1932. .... 1582.00
Ring The Pin, Parker Brothers, Box. 30.00
Ring Toss, Camel, Cardboard, Die Cut, Lithograph, Japan, 1950s, 6 x 3 In.. .... 18.00
Rival Policemen, McLoughlin, Board, 1896 .... 125.00
Shooting Gallery, Rubber Balls, Gun, Paper Lithograph, Schoenhut, 22 In. 280.00
Shooting Range, Arcade, Marx, Box, 8 x 21 In.. .... 80.00
Table Croquet Set, 8 Wooden Mallets, 8 Brass Wickets, 8 Ivory Balls, Stand, 14 ¾ In.. .... 345.00
Target, Arcade, Masked Clown, Painted, Cast Iron, Dickman, 1911, 20 x 16 In. .... *illus* 21850.00
Target, Black Man's Head, Open Mouth, Carved, Painted, c.1900, 31 In. 1638.00
Target, Carnival, Spinning Disc, Cast Iron, Electric, W.F. Mangles Co., N.Y., 20 x 16 In. 863.00
Target, Growling Tiger, Tail Wags, Tin Lithograph, Eldon, Box. 55.00
Target, Hostellerie, Cardboard On Wood, Marked, No. 421, 14 x 20 In. 495.00
Target, Merry-Go-Round Hunting, Cork Firing Gun, Windup, Parker Bros., 12 x 12 In.. .... 220.00
Target, Pigeon Sporting, Dart Board Style, Wood, Metal, Box 70.00
Target, Red Indian Shooting, Paper Over Cardboard, Chad Valley, Harborne, England, Box .. 66.00
Tiddlywinks, McLoughlin, 850A, 5 ½ x 4 ½ In. 40.00
Toonerville Trolley, Milton Bradley, Board, 1927, 8 ½ x 16 ½ x 1 In. 11.00
Uncle Sam's Postman, Spinner, Milton Bradley, Box, 10 ¼ x 20 In.. .... 110.00
Walter Johnson Base Ball Game, Autographed, May Co., Cleve., Board, c.1940, 10 x 14 In.. 1293.00
Welcome Back Kotter, Ideal, Board, 1976 .... 11.00
Wheel, Gambling, 12-Point Star, Red, Dice, Painted, Cast, H.C. Evans & Co., c.1900, 86 x 60 In. 1800.00
Wheel, Gambling, Horse Race, Wood & Cast Iron, Odds Indicator, H.C. Evans, 1940s, 84 x 60 In. 9000.00
Wheel, Gambling, Roulette, Flapper Arm, 1940s, 35 ½ In. 588.00
Wheel, Gambling, Roulette, Flapper Arm, Yellow, World War II Era, 31 ½ In. 676.00
Wheel, Gambling, Roulette, Myers Lake Amusement Park, 20 In. 125.00
Wheel, Gambling, Roulette, Painted, Cast Iron Base, Signed, Evans, Chicago, 47 x 23 x 22 In. 475.00
Wheel, Gambling, Roulette, Wood, Hand Painted, Domino Design, Red Flapper Arm, 1940s, 30 In. 445.00
Wheel, Gambling, Turned Wood, Cast Iron Base, c.1910, 60 x 32 In. 605.00
Wilder's Baseball, Spring Loaded Wooden Bat, Lead Runner, Wilder Mfg., Board, 1936 .... 195.00
Wolf Man Mystery, Hasbro, Board, 1963, 15 x 18 In. 210.00
Wonderful Wizard Of Oz, Parker Bros., Board, 1921, 19 ½ x 10 In.. .... 132.00

GAME PLATES are plates of any make decorated with pictures of birds, animals, or fish. The game plates usually came in sets consisting of twelve dishes and a serving platter. These sets were most popular during the 1880s.

Birds, Cream Shoulder, Multicolor Reserve, Gilt Rim, Coalsport, 9 ⅛ In., 12 In. 779.00
Birds, Dark Green & Gold Border, Royal Vienna, 9 In., 3 Piece 316.00
Birds, Gilt Floral Enamel Border, Royal Doulton, Tiffany & Co., 9 In., 6 Piece 1440.00
Birds, Hand Painted, Signed, Coronet Limoges, 10 ¾ In. 115.00
Birds, Other Animals, Gilt Border, Mansard, France, 9 In., 6 Piece 207.00
Birds, Signed, Dubois, Limoges, 10 In., 6 Piece 259.00
Fish, Various Fish Types, Pastel Scalloped Border, Gilt Rim, Limoges, 8 ¼ In., 12 Piece 227.00
Game Birds, Various, Gilt Rim, Lazeyas Rosenfeld Lehman, Limoges, c.1900, 9 ½ In., 13 Piece. 1135.00
Partridge, Painted, Bavaria, 10 In. 30.00
Quail, Woodcock, Grouse, Goose, Pheasant, Turkey, Duck, Boehm, 10 ¾ In. 115.00
Retriever, Game Bird, Signed Valenum, Limoges, 12 ½ In. 184.00

GARDEN FURNISHINGS have been popular for centuries. The stone or metal statues, wire, iron, or rustic furniture, urns and fountains, sundials, and small figurines are included in this category. Many of the metal pieces have been made continuously for years.

Armillary Sphere, Man Holding Sphere, Arrow, iron, Green Paint, Mid 20th Century, 29 In. . 234.00
Basin, Grotto, Demilune, Leaf Carved Exterior, White Marble, Copper Drain, 6 x 30 In. 4113.00
Bench, Arlington, Curtain Style, 3 Panels, Scroll Arms, Cast Arms, c.1880, 42 In., Pair 3308.00
Bench, Fern, Scroll Reticulated Seat, Cast Iron, c.1880, 33 x 49 ½ In., Pair 9988.00
Bench, Grapes, Leaves, Hand Painted, Green, Black, Cast Iron, 42 x 30 In. 480.00
Bench, Grapes, White Enamel, Cast Iron, 28 x 31 In. 75.00
Bench, Grapevine, Barrel Shape Back, White Paint, Cast Iron, John McLean, N.Y., 48 In. 1763.00
Bench, Lattice & Ivy, Cast Iron, John F. Riley, Charleston, Late 1800s, 27 x 41 In., Pair 5500.00
Bench, Openwork, Cast Iron, N. American Ironworks, 1891, 36 x 45 x 18 In. 495.00
Bench, Passion Flower, Fretwork, Branch Legs, Cast Iron, c.1880, 33 x 37 In. 4920.00
Bench, Pine, Slat Seat, Trestle Shape Base, Cast Iron, 20 x 71 ½ x 10 ¼ In. 1062.00
Bench, Rococo, Pierced Seat, Flowers, Leaves, Painted, Cast Iron, 36 x 43 x 17 In. 1920.00
Bench, Rococo, Scalloped Crest, Arched Back, Scrollwork Seat, Cast Iron, c.1880, 36 x 46 In. . 1593.00
Bench, Rustic, Reticulated, Painted, Cast Iron, c.1870, 33 x 49 In., Pair 7050.00
Bench, Scroll Arabesques, Bird & Berry Brackets, Hoof Feet, Cast Iron, c.1850, 39 x 66 In. ... 2520.00
Bench, Serpent Shape, Wood, Plank, Cast Iron Supports, Continental, 33 x 40 x 24 In. 1440.00
Bench, Twig & Oak Leaf, Green Paint, Cast Iron, Wise Foundry, Ohio, 1900s, 38 x 32 In. 323.00
Birdbath, 2 Seahorses, Cement, 35 x 34 In. 110.00
Birdbath, Putti Holding Bath, White, Cast Iron, 19th Century, 32 ½ In. 475.00
Birdbath, Square Top, Marble, Carved, c.1900, 38 In. 585.00
Birdhouse, 8-Sided, Bird Finial, Cast Iron, Impressed, Miller Iron Co., R.I., 1888, 15 In. 1170.00
Birdhouse, Architectural, Wood, Painted, ½ Round Design, Shingle Roof, 1900s, 50 x 40 In. . 1265.00
Birdhouse, Bucket Form, Added Perches, Ladders, Wood, Tin Cone Roof, c.1885 .... 1292.00
Birdhouse, Schoolhouse Shape, Wood, Painted, 21 x 27 In. 375.00
Boot Scraper, Dog, Boxer, Cast Iron, 15 x 18 ½ In. 80.00
Boot Scraper, Dog, Dachshund, Curly Tail, Cast Iron, 7 x 21 In. 110.00
Boot Scraper, Dog, Pointer, Cast Iron, Painted, 15 x 18 x 11 In. 165.00
Boot Scraper, Dog, Spaniel, Shoe Brushes, Cast Iron, 17 x 18 In. 303.00
Boot Scraper, Double Ram's Horn Terminals, Stone Block, Cast Iron, 1800s, 16 x 14 In. 264.00
Boot Scraper, Double Ram's Horns, Stone Base, Cast Iron, 7 x 7 x 4 In. 250.00
Boot Scraper, Duck, Cast Iron, 15 In. 135.00
Boot Scraper, Duck, Cast Iron, c.1890, 4 x 6 In. 770.00
Boot Scraper, Flat, Scrolled Sides, Arched Blade, Cast Iron, 8 ½ x 11 ¾ In. 99.00
Boot Scraper, Lyre Form, Scalloped Edge Base, Cast Iron, 7 ¾ In. 44.00
Boot Scraper, Rococo Shell, Acanthus Leaf Edges, Cast Iron, 11 x 8 ½ In. 365.00
Boot Scraper, Round, Pointed Terminals, Arched Blade, Cast Iron, 8 ¾ x 6 ½ In. 143.00
Boot Scraper, Scrolled Sides, Faux Marble Painted Wood Base, Cast Iron, 6 x 11 In. 187.00
Boot Scraper, Shell, 2 Dolphins, Black Paint, 19th Century, Cast Iron, 10 ½ In. .... *illus* 275.00
Chair, Fern, Arm Supports, Leg Brackets, Pierced Seat, Cast Iron, 35 In. 960.00
Chair, Morning Glory, Round Seat, 3 Legs, Cast Iron, c.1880, 33 In., Pair 881.00
Chair, White Paint, Cast Iron, Arms, Victorian, 29 x 15 ½ In., Pair. 823.00
Chair, White Paint, Cast Iron, Victorian, 31 x 14 ½ In., Pair 266.00
Chair, Wirework, Balloon Back, White Paint, Victorian, 40 In., Pair 294.00
Chair Set, Domed Crest, Slat Back, Scrolled Arms, Lattice Woven Seat, Cast Iron, 38 In., 4 piece 1020.00
Chair Set, Metal, Domed Crest, Sloping Arms, Lattice Seat, Wrought Iron, 40 In., 6 piece 1800.00
Clippers, Grass, Aluminum, Red, c.1960 .... 12.00
Faucet Knob, Squirrel, Bronze, 3 ½ In. 50.00

Game, Bowling Set, Wood, Incised Band, Painted, Bittersweet, Black, 10-In. Pin, 10 Piece, $275.00

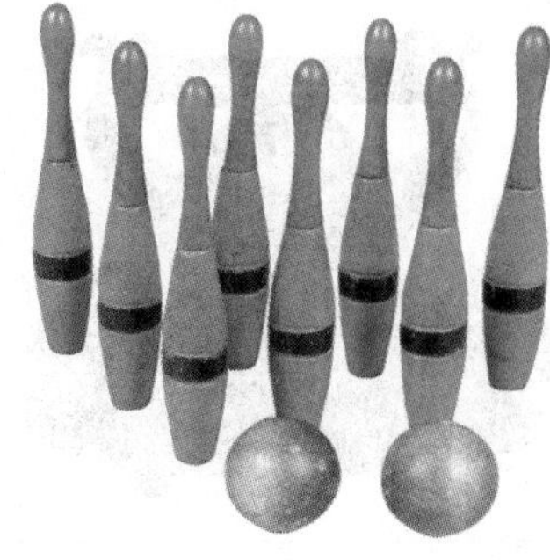

Game, Punch Board, What's Cookin'?, 1940-50, 15 x 9 ½ In. $87.00

Game, Target, Arcade, Masked Clown, Painted, Cast Iron, Dickman, 1911, 20 x 16 In. $21850.00

TIP

Set your sundial at noon on June 15. Place it so the shadow falls on the 12.

Garden, Boot Scraper, Cast Iron, Shell, 2 Dolphins, Black Paint, 19th Century, 10 ½ In.
$275.00

G

Garden, Figure, Girl, Curly Hair, Holding Bowl, White Paint, Terra-Cotta, 1890s, 34 x 14 In.
$605.00

Garden, Figure, Horses, Bronze, Green Patina, Stone Base, Late 1900s, 32 x 38 In.
$1298.00

Figure, Asian Woman, With Fan, Concrete, 40 In. 25.00
Figure, Boy, Hand On Hip, Painted, Iron, France, 1900s, 38 In. 275.00
Figure, Bulldog, Black Paint, Cast Iron, 15 ½ x 27 In. 288.00
Figure, Bust, Boy, Stone, Mounted On Rod, 8 ¾ In. 40.00
Figure, Cherub, Flower Garland, Plinth, Concrete, 35 In. 45.00
Figure, Cherub, Holding Drape, Concrete, Pedestal Base, 46 In. 275.00
Figure, Classical Warrior, Concrete, 36 In. 150.00
Figure, Cranes, Iron, 40 x 11 ½ x 13 ¾ In. 322.00
Figure, Deer, Cast Iron, Fisk, 62 In. 5003.00
Figure, Dog, Whippet, Lying On Plinth, Cast Stone, 15 ½ x 10 ½ x 26 In., Pair 1800.00
Figure, Foo Dog, Scrolled Lotus, Marble, Carved, Plinth Base, 23 x 10 In., Pair 1380.00
Figure, Frog, Bronze, 6 ½ In. 175.00
Figure, Fruit Basket, Woven Base, Fruit Cover, Painted, Glazed, Pottery, Italy, 23 ¾ In. 1100.00
Figure, Girl, Curly Hair, Holding Bowl, White Paint, Terra-Cotta, 1890s, 34 x 14 In. .... *illus* 605.00
Figure, Girl, Holding Urn, Concrete, 30 In. 70.00
Figure, Greek Woman, Draped, Concrete, 40 In. 70.00
Figure, Horse, Reclining, Cement, 23 x 34 In., Pair 1100.00
Figure, Horses, Bronze, Green Patina, Stone Base, Late 1900s, 32 x 38 In. .... *illus* 1298.00
Figure, Lion, Reclining, Cement, 22 x 27 ½ In., Pair 125.00
Figure, Lion, Reclining, Plinth Base, Cast Iron, Signed, W.W. Jennings, 1800s, 34 x 55 In. 5060.00
Figure, Lion, Seated, Shield, Cast Iron, 38 x 27 x 18 In., Pair 550.00
Figure, Medici Venus, Cast Stone, 19th Century, 31 In. 1020.00
Figure, Pegasus, Lead, Wheeler Williams, c.1946, 38 x 25 In. 6325.00
Figure, Putti, Holding Flower Over Head, Lead, Marble Base, c.1900, 30 In. 439.00
Figure, Rabbit, Painted White, Cast Iron, Early 1900s, 11 ½ In., Pair 633.00
Figure, Roman Centurion, Armor, Plumed Helmet, Concrete, Columnar Pedestal, 52 ½ In. .. 65.00
Figure, Rooster, Painted, White, Red, Green, Concrete, 25 In. 40.00
Figure, Running Putto, Holding Serpent, Lead, England, 25 In. 1320.00
Figure, Stag, Rectangular Base, Cast Iron, J.W. Fiske, c.1875, 61 x 52 In. 9988.00
Finial, Acanthus, Cast, Concrete, White Paint, 9 ¼ x 4 ½ In., Pair .... *illus* 143.00
Fountain, 2 Tiers, Figures Holding Bowl, Bronze, 14 Ft. 10 In. x 4 Ft. 4700.00
Fountain, 3 Cranes Holding Bowl, 2 Cranes In Bowl, Bronze, 63 x 33 In. 990.00
Fountain, Acanthus, Cattails, Water Lilies, Cranes, Cast Iron, 39 x 35 In. 2644.00
Fountain, Baroque Style, Scalloped Rims, Putti Figures, Bronze, 3 Tiers, 118 x 63 In. 6000.00
Fountain, Basket Shape, Galvanized Metal, Wirework, Iron Legs, 1800s, 37 x 26 In. 764.00
Fountain, Bird, Aquamarine, Ball Finial, Rigaree, Round Foot, 6 ½ In. 147.00
Fountain, Boy, Goose, Flowers, Lobed, Plinth Base, Cast Iron, 87 x 51 In. 1540.00
Fountain, Boy, Holding Bowl On Head, 3-Footed Dolphin Base, Cast Iron, 1900, 68 x 36 In. .. 550.00
Fountain, Boy, Holding Bowl On Head, 8-Sided, Cast Iron, 1900s, 75 x 37 In. 950.00
Fountain, Boy, Playing Flute, Lead, Marked, Florentine Craftsmen, Mid 20th Century, 32 In. . 175.00
Fountain, Boy, With Jug, Cast, Concrete, 20 x 9 x 11 In. 50.00
Fountain, Cherubs, Bronze, 2 Tiers, 54 x 25 In. 11000.00
Fountain, Figural, Holding Jug, Grapes, Bronze, 20th Century, 37 x 26 x 21 In. 1100.00
Fountain, Fish, Cresting Wave, Open Mouth Spout, Cast Stone, 1900s, 31 x 13 In. 58.00
Fountain, Garland Draped Bowl, Scrolls, Tripod, Plinth Base, Bronze, 45 x 26 In. 2200.00
Fountain, Hexagonal Bowls, 4 Birds, 2 Tiers, Cast Iron, Continental, 50 ½ x 31 In. 1560.00
Fountain, Lion's Head, Cement, Painted White, 10 x 8 ½ In. 350.00
Fountain, Lion's Head Spout, Cast Iron, 57 x 32 x 21 In. 340.00
Fountain, Lobed Basin, Dolphins, Lion's Mask, Paw Feet, Square Plinth, Bronze, 57 x 48 In. . 5581.00
Fountain, Lobed Bowl, Mermaid, Fish Spout, Putti, Egret Base, Bronze, 2 Tiers, 88 x 45 In. .. 7931.00
Fountain, Round Scalloped Bowl, Scrolled Griffin Leaf Supports, Tripod Base, Indiana, 49 x 46 In. 5290.00
Fountain, Tree Shape, Squirrels, Leaves, Acorns, Owls Around Basin, Cast Iron, 56 x 46 In. .. 22325.00
Fountain, Wall, 2 Sections, Black Paint, Lion's Head Spout, Basin, Cast Iron, 30 In. 88.00
Fountain, Wall, Classical, Scrolled Back, Lion's Mask Spout, Bronze, 51 x 24 In. 2703.00
Fountain, Wall, Lion's Mask Spout, 3 Scallop Shells, Scrolled Frame, Cast Metal, 67 x 63 In. . 575.00
Fountain, Women Playing Instruments, Holding Vases, Bronze, 90 x 46 In. 6600.00
Fountain Head, Bearded Man, Cast Iron, 16 ½ x 12 ½ In. 150.00
Fountain Head, Cherub Wrestling, Serpent, Cast Metal, Victorian, 23 ½ In. 201.00
Gate, Acorn & Leaves, Arched, Cast Iron, White Enamel, 54 x 43 In., 2 Piece 180.00
Gate Lock, Violin Shape, Cast Iron, 15 ⅛ In. 657.00
Gate Weight, Star, Raised Letters, Red Paint, Cast Iron, 9 x 7 ¼ In. .... *illus* 275.00
Gate Weight, Star Shape, 4-Point, Iron, Ring At Top, Incised, 843, Penn., 5 Lb., 9 x 7 ¼ In. .. 275.00
Gnome, Standing, Iron, Painted, Late 19th Century, 13 ½ In. 176.00
Hitching Post, Eagle, Cast Iron, 53 In. 770.00
Hitching Post, Eagle, Cast Iron, J.W. Fiske, New York, c.1870, 48 In. 4000.00
Hitching Post, Eagle, On Ball, Iron, 53 In. 700.00
Hitching Post, Gnome, Painted, Cast Iron, 46 x 11 In. 940.00

Hitching Post, Gnome, Painted, Iron, 46 x 11 In. 978.00
Hitching Post, Horse Head, 2-Part, Iron, Rod, Acanthus, 13 ¼ x 7 In. 220.00
Hitching Post, Horse Head, Black, Nose Ring, Wall Mount, Iron, 16 x 3 ½ In. 99.00
Hitching Post, Horse Head, Cast Iron, 50 In. .... 165.00 to 175.00
Hitching Post, Horse Head, Green Paint, Ring, Urn Base, Cast Iron, 15 ½ x 5 ½ In. .... *illus* 495.00
Hitching Post, Horse Head, Nose Ring, Iron, 15 ½ x 5 ½ In. 495.00
Hitching Post, Horse Head, Ring, Green Paint, Cast Iron, New England, 15 ½ x 5 ½ In. 450.00
Hitching Post, Jockey, Arm Extended, Blue Vest, Cast Iron, 30 In. 330.00
Hitching Post, Jockey, Arm Extended, Plinth Base, Painted, Cast Iron, Late 1800s, 37 ½ In. 395.00
Hitching Post, Jockey, Black, Red Vest, Blue Pants, Cast Iron, Late 1800s, 23 In. 410.00
Hitching Post, Jockey, Painted, Cast Iron, Signed, McKittrick Foundry Co., 46 In. 750.00
Hitching Post, Ram's Head, Cast Bronze, 6 x 7 ½ In. 495.00
Hitching Post, Tree Stump Shape, 19th Century, 56 In. 322.00
Hitching Post, Tree Trunk Form, Vines, Iron, 1800s, 65 In. 1410.00
Insect Sprayer, Fly Tox, Metal, Painted, c.1955, 13 In. 18.00
Jardiniere, Oak, Copper, c.1900, 29 ¾ x 12 ¾ In. 250.00
Lamp, Pagoda, Domed, Hexagonal Roof, Mushroom, Recessed Panels, Granite, 36 x 37 In. 2875.00
Lamp, Pagoda, Granite, Square Stepped Base, 42 In. 375.00
Lavabo, Flowers, Scrolls, 3-Footed, Iron, Copper, France, 80 In. 880.00
Lawn Sprinkler, Frog, Tongue Directs Water Spray, Cast Iron, 4 x 4 In. 275.00
Lawn Sprinkler, Mallard Duck, Painted, Cast Iron, 13 ¼ In. .... *illus* 345.00
Lawn Sprinkler, Rocket, Red, Cast Iron, Marked, F, 10 x 12 In. 195.00
Lawn Sprinkler, Wood Duck, Painted, Multicolored, Cast Iron 1100.00
Mower, Sickle Bar, Brass Wheels, Gears, Walter A. Woods, N.Y., Salesman's Sample, 20 x 22 In. 9775.00
Nozzle, Hose, Brass, c.1955, 3 ¼ In. 7.00
Patio Set, Empire, Iron, Square, Swan Supports, Paw Feet, 2 Chairs, 32 x 16 In. 920.00
Patio Set, Marble, Round Table, Carved, Dragons, 4 Elephant Shape Chairs, Chinese, 29 x 39 In. 4900.00
Pedestal, Hand Painted Flowers, Multicolored, Iron, 20 x 54 In. 780.00
Plant Stand, see Furniture, Stand, Plant.
Planter, Birdhouse Style Front, Copper Helmet, Open Back Box, 26 x 15 In. 518.00
Planter, Cast Metal, Painted, Black, 47 In., Pair 863.00
Planter, Footed, Scalloped Shell Shape, Shallow Bowl, Coral, 11 x 21 x 15 In. 118.00
Planter, Lantern Shape, Scrolled Support Arm, Verdigris, Metal, Italy, 1800s, 16 x 7 In. 214.00
Planter, Scroll Design, Cast Iron, White Paint, Zinc Liner, 9 x 22 ½ In., Pair 150.00
Seat, Blue, White, Chinese Export, 20th Century, 17 ½ In. .... 146.00 to 263.00
Seat, Blue, White, Chinese Export, 20th Century, Pair 263.00
Seat, Blue & White, Porcelain, Flowers, Hexagonal, Chinese, 11 In., Pair 590.00
Seat, Famille Rose, Multicolored Flowers, Chinese, 11 ¼ In. 330.00
Seat, Hexagonal, Flower Filigreed Panels, Chinese, 19 x 15 In. 150.00
Seat, Imari, Birds, Flowers, Brocade, Japanese Style, Chinese, 20 In., Pair 1076.00
Stake, Mutt & Jeff, Plywood, Painted, 2-Sided, c.1940, 29 In., Pair 69.00
Stool, Brass, Enamel, Barrel Form, Reserves, Flowers, Yellow Ground, Chinese, 17 ¼ In. 650.00
Sundial, Brass, Footed, Square, Marked, France, 5 x 6 In. 400.00
Sundial, Inscribed, Time Is Fleeting, Latin, Copper, Brass, 12 In. 385.00
Sundial, Pierced Concentric Sections, Zodiac, Arabic, Bronze, 53 x 32 In. 4750.00
Sundial, Stone Plinth, Cast Metal Dial, Stone, 10 x 20 x 19 In. 352.00
Table, Cast Iron, Marble, Wood, Lion's Head, Paw Feet, Late 1800s, 30 x 40 x 18 In. .... *illus* 880.00
Table, Wirework, Round, Gallery Edge, Green Paint, Porcelain Casters, Victorian, 29 x 24 In. .. 264.00
Terrarium, Bird Finials, Urn, 4 Swing Arms, Green Aluminum, c.1900, 51 x 26 In. 3600.00
Trough, Corner, Cast Iron, Embossed, Fiske, New York, 11 ½ x 16 ½ In. 60.00
Urn, 4 Sections, Cast Iron, White Paint, Inscribed, Walbridge & Co., 28 x 22 In. 200.00
Urn, Applied Handles, Cast Iron, White Paint, c.1900, 17 In., Pair 353.00
Urn, Bacchanalian Design, Footed, Bronze, Patinated, c.1950, 30 x 30 In., Pair 2832.00
Urn, Campagna, Lion's Mask, Ruffled Rim, Cast Iron, 21 x 22 In., Pair 350.00
Urn, Classical Style, Lobed Body, Pineapple Finial, Handles, Terra-Cotta, 62 In., Pair 2350.00
Urn, Classical Style, Square Base, Cast Iron, White, 25 x 19 In., Pair 150.00
Urn, Flower Garlands, Footed, Cement, 25 In., Pair 225.00
Urn, Fluted, Acanthus Band, Handles, Pedestal, Cast Iron, White Paint, c.1850, 38 x 30 In. 2350.00
Urn, Fruit, Flower, Garlands, Cement, 30 x 12 In. 66.00
Urn, Fruit, Lion's Head, Square Base, Concrete, 27 ½ x 19 ½ In. 200.00
Urn, Grapevine & Putti, Ram's Head Handles, Cast Iron, Late 19th Century, 27 ½ In., Pair 995.00
Urn, Lion, Seated, Urn On Head, Concrete, c.1970, 35 ½ In., 2 Piece 150.00
Urn, Lobed Body, Square Plinth, Cast Iron, White, c.1890, 29 x 24 In., Pair 1093.00
Urn, Melon Ribs, Applied Handles, Relief Molded, Green, Bronze, Black Patina, 29 In., Pair 354.00
Urn, Ribbed Neck, Terra-Cotta, 36 x 16 In., Pair 1080.00
Urn, Ruffled Edge, Putti Support, Square Pedestal, Multicolored, 24 x 12 In., Pair 960.00
Urn, Scroll Design, Relief, Lion Handles, Bronze, 38 x 25 ½ In., Pair 2800.00

Garden, Finial, Acanthus, Cast, Concrete, White Paint, 9 ¼ x 4 ½ In., Pair
$143.00

Garden, Gate Weight, Star, Raised Letters, Red Paint, Cast Iron, 9 x 7 ¼ In.
$275.00

Garden, Hitching Post, Horse Head, Green Paint, Ring, Urn Base, Cast Iron, 15 ½ x 5 ½ In.
$495.00

TIP
Set heavy garden urns or statues on a foundation, usually a cement block set in the ground.

Garden, Lawn Sprinkler, Mallard Duck, Painted, Cast Iron, 13 ¼ In.
$345.00

Garden, Table, Cast Iron, Marble, Wood, Lion's Head, Paw Feet, Late 1800s, 30 x 40 x 18 In.
$880.00

Gardner, Bowl, Flowers, Lavender Ground, Red Eagle Mark, Cipher, Mid 19th Century, 7 In.
$250.00

TIP

Ivory, bone, horn, wood, and mother-of-pearl handled tableware should never be washed in a dishwasher. The heat and soaking will crack these materials.

Urn, Square Handles & Base, Cast Iron, Kramer, 37 x 21 ½ In. 150.00
Urn, Stand, Cast Iron, Mott, 19th Century, 31 ½ x 32 ½ In. 488.00
Watering Can, Cover, Painted, Herons, Swamp Plants, Japanesque Style, 15 x 7 ¾ In. 1020.00
Watering Can, Galvanized Steel, Round, 1940s, England, 11 x 22 In. 140.00
Watering Can, Multicolor Flowers, Black Ground, Tin, 12 In. 201.00

GARDNER Porcelain Works was founded in Verbiki, outside Moscow, by the English-born Francis Gardner in 1766. The Gardner family retained ownership of the factory until 1891 and produced porcelain tablewares, figurines, and faience.

ΓΑΡΔΗΕΡΖ

Bowl, Flowers, Lavender Ground, Red Eagle Mark, Cipher, Mid 19th Century, 7 In. ..... *illus* 250.00

GAUDY DUTCH pottery was made in England for the American market from about 1810 to 1820. It is a white earthenware with Imari-style decorations of red, blue, green, yellow, and black. Only sixteen patterns of Gaudy Dutch were made: Butterfly, Carnation, Dahlia, Double Rose, Dove, Grape, Leaf, Oyster, Primrose, Single Rose, Strawflower, Sunflower, Urn, War Bonnet, Zinnia, and No Name. Other similar wares are called Gaudy Ironstone and Gaudy Welsh.

Bowl, Sunflower, 3 ¼ x 6 ½ In. 330.00
Coffeepot, Single Rose, 12 ½ In. 3744.00
Creamer, Grape, 4 ¼ In. 585.00
Creamer, Oyster, 4 ¼ In. 1521.00
Creamer, Urn, 4 ¾ In. 556.00
Cup, Grape, Cobalt Blue Band, Hearts, 2 ½ x 3 ½ In. 300.00
Cup & Saucer, Butterfly, Handleless, 2 ½ x 3 ¾ In. .... 323.00 to 770.00
Cup & Saucer, Carnation, Vine Border, Handleless 303.00
Cup & Saucer, Double Rose 263.00
Cup & Saucer, Dove, Handleless 234.00
Cup & Saucer, Oyster, Handleless 322.00
Cup & Saucer, Single Rose, Handleless 206.00
Cup & Saucer, Sunflower, Handleless .... 382.00 to 556.00
Cup & Saucer, Urn, Paneled Border, Handleless, 2 ½ x 3 ⅝ In. 385.00
Cup & Saucer, War Bonnet, Handleless, 9 ¾ In. 468.00
Oyster Plate, 6 ½ In. 380.00
Plate, Carnation, 5 ¾ In. 154.00
Plate, Carnation, 8 ¾ In. 303.00
Plate, Carnation, Vine Border, 6 ⅜ In. 220.00
Plate, Double Rose, 7 ⅝ In. 165.00
Plate, Double Rose, 10 In. 1521.00
Plate, Dove, 19th Century, 9 ¾ In. 183.00
Plate, Dove, 8 ¼ In. 410.00
Plate, Grape, Vine Border, 7 ¼ In. .... 154.00 to 198.00
Plate, Leaf, Flowers, Red, Blue, Gold, Green, 19th Century, 7 ¾ In. 14040.00
Plate, Primrose, 19th Century, 8 ¼ In. .... *illus* 2106.00
Plate, Single Rose, 19th Century, 8 ¼ In. 176.00
Plate, Strawflower, 19th Century, 8 ½ In. 1112.00
Plate, Sunflower, 7 ½ In. 248.00
Plate, Sunflower, Zigzag & Vine Border, 8 ⅜ In. 303.00
Plate, Urn, 7 ⅜ In. 351.00
Plate, Urn, 8 ¼ In. 351.00
Plate, Urn, Riley Mark, 7 ⅜ In. 350.00
Plate, War Bonnet, 6 In. 303.00
Plate, War Bonnet, 8 In. 380.00
Plate, War Bonnet, 9 ¾ In. 305.00
Plate, War Bonnet, Flowers, Paneled Border, 7 ¼ In. 248.00
Plate, Zinnia, Impressed, Riley, 8 ¼ In. 4680.00
Soup, Dish, Butterfly, 7 ¼ In. 995.00
Soup, Dish, Butterfly, 8 ⅜ In. 878.00
Soup, Dish, Double Rose, 9 ¾ In. 468.00
Soup, Dish, War Bonnet, 9 ¾ In. 761.00
Teapot, Carnation, 6 In. 1755.00
Teapot, Single Rose, 6 ¾ In. 3744.00
Teapot, Single Rose, 6 In. 995.00
Teapot, Urn, 9 ¾ In. 3416.00
Toddy Plate, Primrose, 4 ⅝ In. 4446.00
Waste Bowl, Double Rose, 2 ¾ x 5 ¼ In. 351.00
Waste Bowl, Oyster, 3 x 6 ¼ In. 146.00
Waste Bowl, Single Rose, 3 x 5 ½ In. 263.00
Waste Bowl, Urn, 3 ¼ x 6 ⅜ In. 527.00

GAUDY IRONSTONE is the collector's name for the ironstone wares with the bright patterns similar to Gaudy Dutch. It was made in England for the American market after 1850. There may be other examples found in the listing for Ironstone or under the name of the ceramic factory.

Bowl, Ribbed, Red, Blue, Green, Flowers, Gold Luster, 6 In. 35.00
Compote, Red Flowers, Scalloped Rim, Footed, 5 ¼ x 9 In. 85.00
Plate, Aurora, Red, Brown Transfer Scrolls, Medallions, Flowers, 9 In. 85.00
Plate, Aurora, Red, Leaves, Flowers, Blue, Yellow, Green, 9 ½ In. 39.00
Plate, Aurora, Red, Maroon, Blue, Yellow, Green, 8 ½ In. 32.00
Plate, Leaves, Flowers, Red, Maroon, Blue, Yellow, Green, 8 In. 32.00
Plate, Old Japan Vase, On Table, Flowers, Transfer, Black, Burnt Orange, 10 In. 255.00
Plate, Sponge Decorated, Red Flower Heads, Blue Bands, c.1890, 9 In. 105.00
Plate, Willow, Mulberry Transfer, Red, Pink, Green, Salmon, Brown, 8 ¾ In. 85.00

GAUDY WELSH is an Imari-decorated earthenware with red, blue, green, and gold decorations. Most Gaudy Welsh was made in England for the American market. It was made from 1820 to about 1860.

Basin, Blue & White Flowers, Impressed, Stevenson, c.1820, 4 ¼ x 13 In. 374.00
Cake Plate, Sunflower, Orange, Green, Pink, Copper Luster, c.1860, 7 ¾ In. 195.00
Cup & Saucer, Oyster, Cobalt Blue, Rust, Green, Luster, c.1912, 5 ¾ In. 80.00
Cup & Saucer, Venus, Green, Orange, Pink, Blue Underglaze, c.1860 195.00
Dish, Grape, c.1840, 4 ½ In., Pair 65.00
Jug, Barmouth, Flower, Gadrooned, Cobalt Blue, Rust, Gold, Handle, 9 ½ x 8 In. 285.00
Jug, Flowers, Poppies, Orange, Blue, Green Leaves, Pink, Copper Luster, 4 In. 350.00
Jug, Marigold, c.1850, 4 ½ In. 350.00
Jug, Poppy, Blue, Orange, Green, Copper, Pink Luster, 7 ¼ In. 350.00
Mug, Forget-Me-Not, Swansea, Pearlware Glaze, Pink, Copper Luster, 3 x 3 In. 65.00
Plate, Lotus, 9 In. 195.00
Platter, Strawberry, 8 ¼ x 10 ⅝ In. 759.00
Platter, Willow, Blue & White, 10 ¼ x 13 ¼ In. 110.00
Teapot, Boston, Cobalt Blue, Gold Swirls, White Panels, Orange Flowers, 6 ½ x 9 In. 150.00
Teapot, Flow Blue, Scalloped Edge, Fancy Handle, Lid, 7 In. 65.00
Vase, Bud, Urn, Holes On Top, Handles, 19th Century, 7 In. *illus* 556.00

GEISHA GIRL porcelain was made for export in the late nineteenth century in Japan. It was an inexpensive porcelain often sold in dime stores or used as free premiums. Pieces are sometimes marked with the name of a store. Japanese ladies in kimonos are pictured on the dishes. There are over 125 recorded patterns. Borders of red, blue, green, gold, brown, or several of these colors were used. Modern reproductions are being made.

Berry Bowl, Oriental Scene, 5 x 1 ¼ In. 13.00
Biscuit Jar, Cover, Cobalt Blue Edge, 7 x 5 In. 50.00
Bowl, Tab Handle, Oriental Scene, 5 ¾ x 1 ¼ In. 9.00
Chocolate Pot, 7 ½ x 3 ½ In. 75.00
Chocolate Pot, 9 x 5 x 6 ½ In. 110.00
Creamer, Oriental Scene, Figures, 3 ½ x 2 ⅜ In. 13.00
Creamer, Oriental Scene, Silk Screen, Painted Red Rim, 4 In. 12.00
Cup & Saucer, Women In Garden, 2 x 2 & 4 ⅜ In. 10.00
Mask, White Face, Black Hair, Cherry Blossoms, 8 ½ x 8 In. 45.00
Mug Cup, Blue, 2 ⅞ x 2 In. 8.00
Purse, Paper Fabric, Foldover, Inside Pocket, 5 ¼ In. 8.00
Saucer, Silk Screen, Painted, Oriental Scene, Painted Red Rim, 5 ½ In. 3.00
Spice Shaker, Red Paint, Oriental Scene 5.00
Sugar, Cover, Women In Kimonos, 5 ½ In. 55.00
Toothpick, 2 ⅜ x 1 ⅞ In. 9.00
Toothpick, Pointed Edge, 3 ¾ In. 20.00
Vase, Wisteria, 3 ¾ In. 20.00
Wall Pocket, 3 ⅛ x 2 ½ In. 35.00

GENE AUTRY was born in 1907. He began his career as the "Singing Cowboy" in 1928. His first movie appearance was in 1934, his last in 1958. His likeness and that of the Wonder Horse, Champion, were used on toys, books, lunch boxes, and advertisements.

Boots, Cowboy, Rain, Rubber, 4 Clasps, Box 165.00
Cap Gun, Short Barrel, Cast Iron, Engraved, Orange Grips, Kenton, 1952, 6 ½ In. 519.00
Cap Gun, Western Pistol, Gene Autry 44, Leslie-Henry Products, Box, 11 In. 220.00
Cap Gun, White Handle, c.1930. 66.00

Gaudy Dutch, Plate, Primrose, 19th Century, 8 ¼ In.
$2106.00

Metric Dinnerware Sizes

The metric system was adopted in the United States by an Act of Congress in 1988, but sizes were not quickly changed. Dishes imported into the United States after that were often in metric sizes. A new metric dinner plate may be about ¼ inch too large to fit the shelf in a standard 1950s kitchen cabinet. Old patterns made from old molds are still made with sizes measured in inches.

Gaudy Welsh. Vase, Bud, Urn, Holes On Top, Handles, 19th Century, 7 In.
$556.00

TIP

You can remove stickers from most things by spraying them with a lubricant.

Gene Autry, Comic Book, Mile High Pedigree, No. 5
$1430.00

Gillinder, Bust, Abraham Lincoln, Milk Glass, Frosted, Centennial Exhibition, 1890s, 6 In.
$265.00

Old Milk Glass

It is difficult to determine the age of a piece of milk glass. Many old milk glass pieces have a c-shaped rough spot on the foot of the glass. Known as a straw mark or lap line, it was formed when the glass cooled after it was snipped into the mold. The plain surfaces of old milk glass items are often marked with concentric circles, a result of uneven cooling in the mold. Old milk glass has less blue in it, the texture is less oily, and the glass is heavier.

Comic Book, Mark Of Cloven Hoof, No. 1, Fawcett, 1942 . . . . . 3000.00
Comic Book, Mile High Pedigree, No. 5 . . . . . *illus* 1430.00
Comic Book, Mystery Of Paint Rock Canyon, No. 5, Fawcett, 1943 . . . . . 2800.00
Comic Book, Secret Of The Aztec Treasure, No. 3, Fawcett, 1942 . . . . . 515.00
Display, Cap Gun, 2 Guns, Holsters, Cuffs, Spurs, Bandanna, De-Luxe Premium Corp., 1957 . 440.00
Double Gun & Holster Set, Red Leather, Marked, Gene Autry 44, 11 In. 165.00
Guitar, Raised Images, Plastic, Emenee, 1950s, 32 In.. . . . . 44.00
Lunch Box, Melody Ranch, Cowhide Back, Thermos, Universal, Box, 1954 . . . . . 771.00
Movie Poster, Cow Town, Autry Riding Champion, 1956, 1 Sheet, 27 x 41 In. 127.00
Wristwatch, Gene, Holding Gun, Paper Dial, Leather Band, Swiss, 1948, 1 ¼ In. 88.00
Wristwatch, Gene, On Rearing Horse, Off-White, Green Numbers, Leather Band, 1 ¼ In. 154.00
Wristwatch, Gene Autry Image, Wilane Watch Co., Box, 1948, 5 x 5 In. 506.00

GIBSON GIRL black-and-blue decorated plates were made in the early 1900s. Twenty-four different 10 ½-inch plates were made by the Royal Doulton pottery at Lambeth, England. These pictured scenes from the book *A Widow and Her Friends* by Charles Dana Gibson. Another set of twelve 9-inch plates featuring pictures of the heads of Gibson Girls had all-blue decoration. Many other items also pictured the famous Gibson Girl.

Postcard, On The Dock, May 9, 1913 . . . . . 6.00
Postcard, Studies In Expression, c.1907. . . . . . 24.00
Postcard, Turning Of The Tide, Couple Kissing, 1905 . . . . . 30.00
Print, Au Montmartre, 1901, 17 ¼ x 11 ¼ In. 25.00
Print, His Christmas Gift, c.1901. . . . . . 55.00
Print, In Germany, 1898, 17 ¼ x 11 ¼ In. 25.00
Print, Prince & Duke, 1898, 17 ¼ x 11 ¼ In. 28.00
Print, Unexpected Encounter, 1899, 17 ¼ x 11 ¼ In.. . . . . 28.00
Shaving Mug, Silhouette. 75.00
Stickpin, Woman, Wide Brim Hat, High Neck Blouse, 2 ⅜ In. 140.00
Vase, Head, Ivory, Gold, Black, 3 ½ x 2 ¾ In. 65.00

GILLINDER

GILLINDER pressed glass was first made by William T. Gillinder of Philadelphia in 1863. The company had a working factory on the grounds at the Centennial and made small, marked pieces of glass for sale as souvenirs. They made a variety of decorative glass pieces and tablewares.

Bread Tray, Luck & Puck. 195.00
Bust, Abraham Lincoln, Milk Glass, Frosted, Centennial Exhibition, 1890s, 6 In. . . . . . *illus* 265.00
Bust, William Shakespeare, Frosted, Round Plinth, Embossed, Centennial, 1890s, 5 x 2 In. . . 132.00
Cup, Lion, 2 In. 110.00
Dish, Daisy & Button, Canoe Shape, 10 ½ In.. . . . . 230.00

GIRL SCOUT collectors search for anything pertaining to the Girl Scouts, including uniforms, publications, and old cookie boxes. The Girl Scout movement started in 1912, two years after the Boy Scouts. It began under Juliette Gordon Low of Savannah, Georgia. The first Girl Scout cookies were sold in 1928.

Camera, Jem Jr. 120, Art Deco Design, Aluminum, 1940, 5 x 5 In. 40.00
Doll, Ginny, Walker, Brown Sleep Eyes, Jointed, Vogue, No. 7104, Box 110.00
Handbook, Scouting For Girls, Cloth Covers, First Edition, 1920, 7 x 5 In. 30.00
Lunch Pail, Scout Leader, Girls Playing Sports, Tin, Green, Bail Handle, 1930. . . . . . 75.00

GLASS-ART. Art glass means any of the many forms of glassware made during the late nineteenth or early twentieth century. These wares were expensive when they were first made and production was limited. Art glass is not the typical commercial glass that was made in large quantities, and most of the art glass was produced by hand methods. Later twentieth-century glass is listed under Glass-Contemporary, Glass-Midcentury, or Glass-Venetian. Even more art glass may be found in categories such as Burmese, Cameo Glass, Tiffany, and other factory names.

Atomizer, Cranberry, Flower, Frosted Ground, Gilt Metal Top, Nancy, Signed, 6 ½ In.. . . . . 250.00
Biscuit Jar, Pink Satin, Globular, c.1900, 7 x 5 In., Pair 205.00
Biscuit Jar, Quilted Satin, Pink, c.1890, 7 x 6 In.. . . . . 117.00
Biscuit Jar, Twisted Handle, Pink Ground, Flowers, England, c.1880, 8 ½ In.. . . . . 175.00
Bottle, Scent, Ruby, Engraved, Flowers, Leaves, Blown Stopper, 4 ½ In. 460.00
Bowl, Amber, Pink, Striated, Crimped Top, Stemmed Flowers, Egret, 7 In. 3700.00
Bowl, Black Amethyst, White Rim, Rose, Signed, 5 ¾ x 11 In.. . . . . 200.00
Bowl, Centerpiece, Cobalt Blue, Gilt Metal Mounts, Enameled, Handles, 6 ⅛ x 6 ¾ x 10 In.. . . 205.00
Bowl, Cranberry Opalescent, Vaseline, Square, 3 x 4 ½ In. 125.00

Bowl, Iridescent Gold, Scalloped Rim, 3 ¾ x 10 In. .... 994.00 to 1170.00
Bowl, Iridescent White, Green Base, 5 x 11 In. 235.00
Bowl, Mottled White, Purple, Quatrefoil Rim, Enameled, Violets, France, 5 ⅜ In. 3346.00
Bowl, Opalescent, White Stripe, Red Wide Rim, Etched Flowers, c.1905, 3 x 10 In. 474.00
Box, Hinged Cover, Blue, Highlights, Egg Shape, 5 In. 200.00
Compote, Lobed Top, Border Enameled Flowers, Gold, Scrolls, 6 x 10 x 6 In. 316.00
Compote, Peach Opalescent, Optic Ribbed, Scalloped Rim, 4 In. 115.00
Cordial Set, Art Deco, Geometric Black Enameling, Etched, Frosted, 11 ½ In., 7 Piece 1062.00
Decanter, Enameled Flower Cartouche, Gold Leaves Bands, Black Vines, Stopper, 27 In. 518.00
Epergne, 3-Lily, Lavender Opalescent, Ruffled Rim, Amber Leaves, Victorian, 17 In. 173.00
Epergne, 3-Lily, Opalescent, Ruffled Rims & Base, c.1880, 18 x 9 ½ In. .... *illus* 117.00
Epergne, Lily, Green Yellow Opalescent, Baskets, Clear Twist Arms, England, 17 In. 478.00
Ewer, Iridescent Green Body, Shoulder, Silver Lid, Raised Flowers, 7 In. 240.00
Figurine, Tulip Arrangement, 12 Flowers, Black, Gold, Silver, Black Bowl, Art Deco, 12 In. 441.00
Goblet, Amber Iridescent, Gold Blue, Threaded, Tapered Stem, 8 In., Pair 173.00
Martini Set, Emerald Green, Gold Base, Abercrombie & Fitch, 1940s, 5 Piece 400.00
Pitcher, Amber, Leaf Mold, Blue Rope Twist Handle, 7 ¾ In. 140.00
Pitcher, White, Melon Rib, Yellow Ribbed Handle, 8 In. 70.00
Plate, Dancing Nude Figures, Frosted, Clear Glass, 8 In., Pair 58.00
Punch Pot, Green, Gilt Wrought & Cast Iron Mount, 22 x 25 In. 3120.00
Sugar, Opaque Green, Applied Handles, 3 ½ In. 489.00
Vanity Set, Tweety Bird, Green Frosted, Bakelite Lid, Tray, 2 Bottles, 4 In. 185.00
Vase, Amber, Red Berry Form Cabochons, France, 6 ¾ In. 150.00
Vase, Blue Opalescent, Ruffled Edge, Applied Feet, Stem, Leaves, 6 ¾ x 7 ½ In. .... *illus* 230.00
Vase, Bud, Gold, Black Mottled Base, 6 ¼ In. 105.00
Vase, Bud, Iridescent, Gold, Pink, Green, Metal Base, 1880-1910, 12 ½ In. 920.00
Vase, Bulbous, Iridescent Blue & Purple Finish, 4-Fold Rim, Ground Pontil, 4 x 4 ½ In. 180.00
Vase, Cover, Mercury, Oval, Etched, Dome Foot, England, Early 1900s, 25 In., Pair 561.00
Vase, Diagonal Bands, Iridescent Blue Feather, Gold Green Interior, 3 ½ In. 316.00
Vase, Emerald Green Body, Iridescence, Pulled Loop, Austria, 9 In. 633.00
Vase, Etched Oval, Paper Label, O.S. Palquist, 5 ¼ In. 250.00
Vase, Frosted Mottled Ground, Olive Green, Globular, Flared Rim, France, 7 ¾ In. 598.00
Vase, Gold Highlights, Medallion Portraits, Girls, Pedestal, 10 ¾ In., Pair 750.00
Vase, Green Opalescent Stripe, Vaseline Base, Tulip Shape, 6 In. 100.00
Vase, Iridescent, Millefiori, Amber, Applied Drippings, Mottled Green Base, 11 In. 920.00
Vase, Iridescent Blue, Gold, Scalloped Rim, Ground Bottom, 6 x 8 In. 660.00
Vase, Iridescent Blue, Green, Pulled Line Leaf, Pontil, 4 In. 575.00
Vase, Iridescent Blue, Hooked Feather, Purple Iridescent Ground, 7 In. 86.00
Vase, Iridescent Gold, Footed Ribbed Body, Magenta Highlights, Signed, Nash, 4 In. 345.00
Vase, Iridescent Gold Organic Threading, Art Nouveau Metal Frame, 12 In. 690.00
Vase, Iridescent Green, Amethyst, White, Swirls, 10 In. 86.00
Vase, Iridescent Green, Art Nouveau Woman, Enameled, 4-Sided, 10 ½ In. 633.00
Vase, Iridescent Purple Lily Pad, Green & Gold Iridescent Ground, Handle, 8 ¼ In. 406.00
Vase, Milk Glass, Painted, Iridescent Golden Salmon, Gold Enameled, Baluster Shape, 10 ½ In. 155.00
Vase, Mythological Figure, Engraved, Sweden, 9 ¼ x 5 ½ In. 1440.00
Vase, Opalescent, Uranium, Cylindrical, Thorns, Leaf Foot, Stourbridge, c.1880, 40 In. 212.00
Vase, Peach Satin, Stretch Neck, Ruffled Edge, c.1880, 11 ¼ In. 70.00
Vase, Pulled Flowers, Yellow Ruffled Frosted Rim, Short Stem, Footed, 6 In. 356.00
Vase, Raised Leaves, Berries, Blue, Red Matte, Handles, 10 x 17 In. 510.00
Vase, Stick, Bulbous, Iridescent Purple, Threading, Pallme-Koenig, 11 In. 86.00
Vase, Trevais, Pulled Feather, Green & Gold Iridescent, Yellow Ground, 5 In. .... 604.00 to 920.00
Vase, Trumpet, Blue Opaque, White Garland, 12 In. 90.00
Vase, Trumpet, Pastel Turquoise, White, Ribbed, Yellow, Green Knop, Footed, 14 ¼ In. 1434.00
Vase, Trumpet, Pulled Feather, Iridescent Gold, Green, Pink, Gilt Bronze, 11 ½ In. 1610.00
Vase, Zipper Pattern, Cream Ground, Conical Base, Handles, 12 ½ In. 1793.00

GLASS-BLOWN. Blown glass was formed by forcing air through a rod into molten glass. Early glass and some forms of art glass were hand blown. Other types of glass were molded or pressed.

Bell Jar, 15 ½ In. 657.00
Bowl, Aqua, Tapered, Folded Rim, Domed Base, Pontil, c.1800, 7 ¼ x 11 In. 339.00
Bowl, Bottle Green, Straight Sides, Domed Base, Pontil, c.1825, 5 ½ x 7 In. 248.00
Bowl, Centerpiece, Blue, Threaded Rim, 4 ½ x 11 ½ In. 117.00
Bowl, Conical Cover, Ball Finial, Clear, Baluster Stem, c.1800, 14 In. 117.00
Bowl, Folded Rim, 1800s, 11 ¾ x 10 In. 173.00
Bowl, Linear Flower, Clear, Yellow, A. Jablonski, Poland, 17 In. 70.00

Glass-Art, Epergne, 3-Lily, Opalescent, Ruffled Rims & Base, c.1880, 18 x 9 ½ In.
$117.00

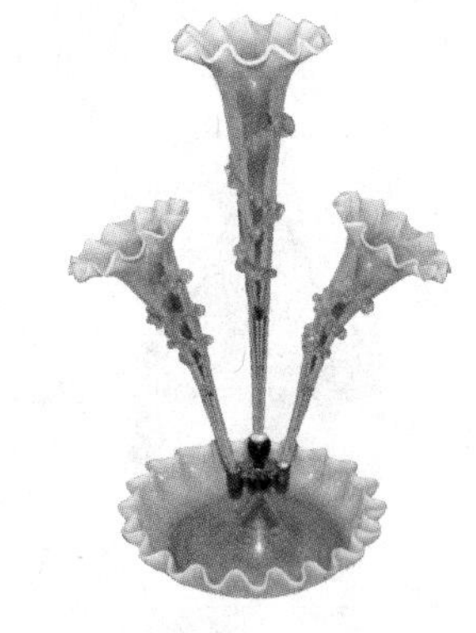

Glass-Art, Vase, Blue Opalescent, Ruffled Edge, Applied Feet, Stem, Leaves, 6 ¾ x 7 ½ In.
$230.00

Glass-Blown, Carafe, Cobalt Blue, Ribbed, Flared Lip, Applied Neck Ring, Pontil, c.1850, 6 ⅝ In.
$228.00

Glass-Blown, Cuspidor, Amber, Flared Rim, Pontil, 1830-80, 1 ⅝ x 2 ¾ In.
$440.00

G

Glass-Blown, Decanter, Clear, Applied Chain Bands, 3 Rings, Wheel Stopper, Pontil, 1813-30, 9 In. $295.00

Glass-Blown, Jug, Cobalt Blue, Threaded, Bulbous, Applied Handle, S. Jersey, 1835-60, 7 In. $11000.00

Glass-Blown, Salt, Expanded Diamonds, Footed, Pontil, 3 x 2 ⅜ In. $44.00

TIP

Switch dishwasher detergent brands periodically. This helps to keep the inside of the dishwasher and the dishes free of any chemical buildup.

Canister, Aqua, Tin Cover, 1800s, 3 x 6 ½ In. 230.00
Canister, Clear, Tin Cover, 1800s, 3 x 7 In. 230.00
Carafe, Cobalt Blue, Ribbed, Flared Lip, Applied Neck Ring, Pontil, c.1850, 6 ⅝ In. *illus* 228.00
Celery Vase, Clear, 3-Piece Mold, Applied Foot, Tooled Rim, Pontil, 7 In. 2530.00
Celery Vase, Clear Cable, Hexagonal, Beaded, Six Scalloped Rim, c.1875, 8 ⅜ In. 96.00
Cheese Dome, Pale Green Tint, c.1800, 13 ½ x 15 In. 147.00
Compote, Beehive, Clear, Tooled Rim, Ground Pontil, 7 ¼ x 8 In. 748.00
Compote, Light Green, Blue, Star Base, Stand, 9 x 17 In. 82.00
Compote, Ribbed, Tooled Rim, Baluster Stem, Pontil, c.1850, 6 ⅞ In. 339.00
Cordial, Clear, Cotton Twist Stem, 1900s, 4 In., 6 Piece 118.00
Creamer, Aquamarine, Pear Shape, Applied 3-Rib Handle, 5 ⅝ x 4 In. 735.00
Creamer, Clear, Applied Handle, Tooled Rim, Pontil, c.1815, 4 ¼ In. 748.00
Creamer, Green, Spiral Threading, Bulbous, Flared Rim, C-Shape Handle, 4 ½ In. 440.00
Creamer, Medium Violet, Squat, Pulled Spout, Applied Handle, Pontil, 1800s, 3 In. 791.00
Cuspidor, Amber, Flared Rim, Pontil, 1830-80, 1 ⅝ x 2 ¾ In. *illus* 440.00
Decanter, Clear, Applied Chain Bands, 3 Rings, Wheel Stopper, Pontil, 1813-30, 9 In. *illus* 295.00
Decanter, Clear, Rings, Diamonds, Ribs, Pontil, Stopper, c.1825, 6 In. 108.00
Decanter, Olive, 3-Piece Mold, c.1800, 7 In. 587.00
Dish, Clear, Ribbed, Ruffled Edge, Applied Cobalt Trim, Knop Stem, 5 ¾ x 5 ¼ In. 529.00
Float, Glass, Pink, Applied Plug, 3 In. 56.00
Float, Purple, 11 In. 1456.00
Funnel, Moonstone, Ribbed, Swirled, Folded Rim, c.1800, 7 In. 36.00
Goblet, Fedora, Loop, Amethyst, Pontil, c.1840, 5 ⅞ In. 791.00
Jar, Cover, Chicken Finial, Aqua, Applied Lily Pad On Base, Gallery Rim, c.1900, 9 In. 147.00
Jug, Cobalt Blue, Threaded, Bulbous, Applied Handle, S. Jersey, 1835-60, 7 In. *illus* 11000.00
Jug, Cobalt Blue, Threaded, Footed, Tooled Rim, Handle, Whitney Glass, c.1835, 6 In. 11300.00
Pan, Amber, Folded Rim, Domed Base, Pontil, c.1800, 4 ¼ x 10 In. 1469.00
Parade Cane, Gold, Red, White, Blue Spirals, c.1850, 66 ½ In. 375.00
Pitcher, Clear, Applied Handle, Pontil, c.1875, 8 ½ In. 113.00
Pitcher, Clear, Cable, Applied Handle, Pontil, c.1875, 8 ½ In. 904.00
Pitcher, Clear, Tooled Rim, Ribbed Handle, Pontil, 3 Piece Mold, c.1815, 4 ¾ In. 575.00
Pitcher, Green, Swirled Ribs, Applied Ribbed Handle, c.1800, 5 ⅞ In. 5405.00
Pitcher, Lily Pad, Threading, Green, Applied Handle, 5 ¾ In. 264.00
Salt, Blue, Flared Rim, Pedestal, Pontil, c.1850, 2 x 2 ¾ In. 102.00
Salt, Double Ogee, Medium Amethyst, Sheared Rim, Pontil, 2 ⅜ In. 1590.00
Salt, Expanded Diamonds, Footed, Pontil, 3 x 2 ⅜ In. *illus* 44.00
Salver, Clear, Footed, Folded Rim, Pontil, Flint, c.1800, 4 ½ x 6 ¼ In. 621.00
Salver, Gallery Rim, Silesian Stem, Domed Foot, Tooled Edge, Pontil, 6 x 10 In. 360.00
Smoke Bell, Kerosene, Gauffered, Opaque White, Cobalt Rim, 7 In. 60.00
Stringholder, Clear, Cobalt Rim & End, c.1850, 4 ½ x 4 ½ In. 352.00
Sugar, Ball Cover, Aqua, Gallery Rim, c.1850, 8 In. 735.00
Sugar, Ball Cover, Aquamarine, Pontil, c.1845, 7 ¾ x 8 ½ In. 15820.00
Sugar, Cover, Aqua, Bulbous, Threaded, Applied Handles, 1845-65, 8 In. *illus* 15400.00
Sugar, Cover, Sapphire Blue, Milk Glass Looping, Bulbous, Gallery Rim, 6 ¾ In. 1093.00
Tumbler, Amber, 6 Flutes, Pontil, c.1850, 3 ⅜ In. 192.00
Tumbler, Clear, Footed, Hexagonal Stem, Pontil, c.1875, 4 ¼ In. 906.00
Tumbler, Flip, Clear, Engraved Flowers, Vines, Swags, 2 Fluted Sides, 4 x 6 In., 3 Piece 3356.00
Tumbler, Flip, Clear, Engraved Rim, 6 In. 264.00
Tumbler, Flip, Clear, Tooled Rim, 3-Piece Mold, Pontil, c.1815, 5 ¾ In. 138.00
Tumbler, Flip, Green, 12 In. 293.00
Tumbler, Opalescent, 8 Flute, Pontil, c.1850, 3 ¼ In. 254.00
Twine Holder, Clear, Applied Cobalt Top Ring & Lower Rim, c.1850, 4 ¼ In. 169.00
Vase, Amethyst, 12 Arched Flutes, Pontil, 1830-60, 8 ¼ In. *illus* 4050.00
Vase, Trumpet, Amethyst, Inverted Baluster Stem, Footed, Pontil, c.1875, 11 ⅞ In. 847.00
Vase, Trumpet, Molded, 5 Petal Rosette, Jade Green, c.1850, 6 ¼ In. 508.00
Vase, Witch's Ball Cover, Clear, White Loops, Pontil, 1850-70, 15 ½ x 7 In. *illus* 1870.00
Vase, Witch's Ball Cover, Lockport Blue, Flared, Bulbous, Pontil, 1850-70, 10 ¾ In. *illus* 9350.00
Wedding Beaker, Shield, Female Figure, Small Cup, F. Heckert, Nurnberg, 7 ½ In. 776.00
Whimsy, Hat, Cobalt Blue, Early 19th Century, 2 ¼ In. 323.00
Whiskey Taster, Aqua, Pressed Foot, Tooled Rim, Pontil, c.1820, 1 ¾ In. 374.00
Wine, Aqua, Bell-Shape Bowl, Tapered Low Knop Stem, 1800s, 4 ½ In. 960.00
Wine, Clear, Double Cotton Twist Stem, 5 ½ In. 382.00
Witch's Ball, Amber, 5 ½ In. 112.00
Witch's Ball, Medium Blue, Top Pontil, c.1840-70, 5 In. 123.00
Witch's Ball, Milk Glass, Pink, Blue, Splotches, Egg Shape, c.1840-70, 5 ¼ In. 364.00
Witch's Ball, Red, 3 ¼ In. 235.00

Witch's Ball, Red Amber, Tooled Rim, On Knopped Stand, Pontil, 1840-60, 10 ¼ In. 1480.00
Witch's Ball, White Looping, Tooled Rim, On Stand, Pontil, 1840-60, 14 ¼ In. 800.00

GLASS-BOHEMIAN. Bohemian glass is an ornate overlay or flashed glass made during the Victorian era. It has been reproduced in Bohemia, which is now a part of the Czech Republic. Glass made from 1875 to 1900 is preferred by collectors.

Basket, Swirled Ribs, Amberina, Amber Rigaree Handle, Blue Flower Feet, Ginkgo, 11 In.. . . . 633.00
Bowl, Frosted Iridescence, Purple Threading, Spots, Ruffled Rim, 11 In.. . . . . 115.00
Box, Cover, Green Malachite, Embossed Nude, 2 ½ x 5 In.. . . . . 200.00
Box, Opal Cover, White Scrolls, Amber Ground, Children, Metal Base, Feet, Oval, 7 In.. . . . . . . 173.00
Candy Dish, Cover, Amber, White, Gold Enameled Flowers, Leaves, 6 ¼ In. 50.00
Candy Dish, Cover, Pinwheel, Winding Bands, Scalloped Edge, Footed, 4 ½ x 9 In. 75.00
Casket, Flowers, Blue, Pink, White, Enameled, c.1885, 3 ¾ In. . . . . 600.00 to 690.00
Cigarette Holder, Amber, Etched, 3 In. 20.00
Compote, Cover, Steeple Finial, Hexagonal Base, Rolled Rim, 15 ½ In., Pair 403.00
Compote, Silver Lake, Shepherd Family, Metal Overlay, 11 In.. . . . . 115.00
Cooler, White Cased, Cranberry, Enameled & Transfer, Women's Busts, 11 x 8 ⅛ In. 2370.00
Cruet, Amber, Blue Applied Rope Handle, Faceted Stopper, 7 ⅝ x 4 In., Pair 1095.00
Decanter, Cut & Engraved, Deer, Forest Scene, Bulbous, Stopper, 10 x 5 ½ In. 215.00
Decanter, Ruby Cut To Clear, Farmers, Grape & Vine, Frosted Ground, Verse, 1800s, 12 In.. . . 2252.00
Dresser Box, Cranberry, White, 4 Brass Ball Feet, Round, c.1885, 3 ½ In.. . . . . 400.00
Dresser Box, Flowers, Sapphire Blue Enamel, c.1900, 6 ½ In. . . . . *illus* 176.00
Dresser Box, Iridescent Purple, Gold Stemmed Enameled Flowers, Round, 5 ½ In.. . . . . 201.00
Epergne, Rose Shaded To Opal, c.1890, 13 In. . . . . *illus* 415.00
Flask, Amber, Engraved Deer & Monogram, L.L.S., Ribbed Edges, Oval, 1837, 7 ⅜ In. 267.00
Girandole, Flowers, Enameled, Opalescent Cased, 13 ¾ In., Pair. 150.00
Goblet, Bell Shape, Cranberry Cut To Clear Bird, Flowers, 1900, 8 In., 10 Piece 948.00
Goblet, Green Cut To Clear, Facets, Disc Foot, Early 1900s, 8 ¼ In. . . . . *illus* 2032.00
Jar, Cover, Ball Finial, Amethyst, Wavy Blue Bands, Kralik, 6 In.. . . . . 575.00
Jar, Cover, Frosted Yellow To Clear, Guba Ducks, Gold Filigree, Harrach, 4 In.. . . . . 1725.00
Jar, Metal Cover, Cobalt, Iridescent, Blue Undulating Bands, Handle, Kralik, 7 In. 230.00
Night-Light, Leaves, Red, Black, Urn Shape, Metal Base, Kralik, 11 In.. . . . . 115.00
Pitcher, Amberina, Flower Sprays, Melon Ribbed, Rope Handle, 1900, 8 In.. . . . . *illus* 550.00
Pitcher, Peachblow, Oval, Square Mouth, Applied Amber Handle, 7 In.. . . . . 58.00
Pitcher, Prussian Blue, Optic Ribbed, Amber Handles, Harrach, 8 In.. 58.00
Pokal, Cavalier, Staff, Amber, Enamel, Prunts, Theresienthal, c.1880, 17 In. 253.00
Pokal, Cover, Engraved, Woodland Scene, Pedestal, 13 x 4 ⅛ In.. . . . . 425.00
Pokal, Cover, Trumpet Shape, Faceted Knop Stem, 15 ¾ In.. . . . . 598.00
Pokal, Enameled Coat Of Arms, Gold Bands, Early 20th Century, 11 In. 2280.00
Pokal, Trumpet Shape, Cartouche, Cherub, Holding Basket, 7 ⅛ In.. . . . . 478.00
Powder Box, Blue Scrolls, White, Enameled, Footed, c.1885, 5 In.. . . . . 275.00
Urn, Ruby Cut To Clear, Bronze Gold Dore Base, 3-Footed, 35 In., Pair 819.00
Vase, 6 Nude Women, Molded Green, Malachite, 5 In. . . . . *illus* 275.00
Vase, Amber Rim, Applied Lizard, Ribbed, Gold Enameled, 1900, 10 In., Pair 504.00
Vase, Cobalt Blue, Gold Enameled, Scenes, 13 x 6 In. 695.00
Vase, Cobalt Blue Cut To Clear, Oval, Signed, Reidl, 14 In. 60.00
Vase, Flowers, Pinched, Clear To Green, 10 In.. . . . . 1195.00
Vase, Frog, Flower, Yellow, Blue Handles, Enameled, Austria, 1890s, 12 In. . . . . *illus* 1200.00
Vase, Frosted, Green, Yellow Leaves, Wilhelm Kralik, Signed, Carpe, 9 In. 575.00
Vase, Green, White Flowers, Branches, Enameled, 12 In.. . . . . 80.00
Vase, Iridescent, Gold Oil Spot, Bulbous, Flared, Austria, 5 ½ In. 115.00
Vase, Iridescent Green, Variegated Pulled Feathers, Rindskopf, 8 In. 115.00
Vase, Opal, Variegated Crimson Pulled Leaves, Swags, Footed, 10 In.. 115.00
Vase, Red Aventurine, Green Threading, Josephinenhuette, 12 In. 230.00
Vase, Ruby Cut To Clear, Farmer, Vines, Grape, 1800s, 12 In. 2252.00
Vase, Ruby Cut To Clear, Intaglio, Figural Cameo, Knights & Crest, 1870s, 6 ½ In.. . . . . 500.00
Vase, Ruby Flashed, Enameled Deer, Bird, Etched, Bulbous, Flared Rim, c.1890, 10 In. 250.00
Vase, Salamander, Blue Berries, Drip, Amber, Gold, Enameled, Wide Mouth, c.1900, 7 In.. . . . 296.00
Vase, Trumpet, White Over Cranberry, Rolled Rim, 12 ½ In.. . . . . 250.00

GLASS-CONTEMPORARY includes pieces by glass artists working after 1970. Many of these pieces are free-form, one-of-a-kind sculptures. Paperweights by contemporary artists are listed in the Paperweight category. Earlier studio glass may be found listed under Glass-Midcentury or Glass-Venetian.

Basket, Byrdes, Medallions, Engraved Birds, Hofbauer, 10 ¾ x 8 ½ In. 100.00

Glass-Blown, Sugar, Cover, Aqua, Bulbous, Threaded, Applied Handles, 1845-65, 8 In.
$15400.00

Glass-Blown, Vase, Amethyst, 12 Arched Flutes, Pontil, 1830-60, 8 ¼ In.
$4050.00

Glass-Blown, Vase, Witch's Ball Cover, Clear, White Loops, Pontil, 1850-70, 15 ½ x 7 In.
$1870.00

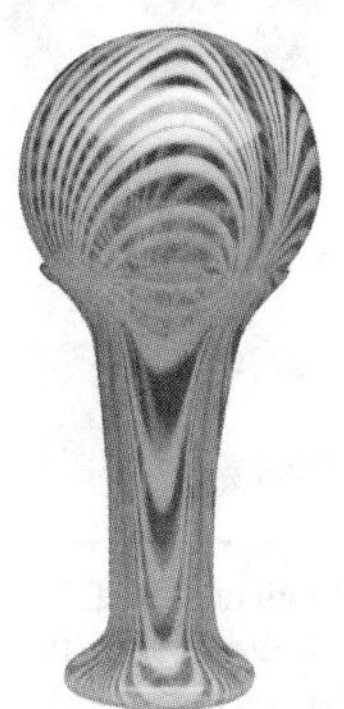

Dale Chihuly
Dale Chihuly (1941–) is the best-known of the late twentieth-century studio glassmakers. Chihuly blew early pieces himself, but after several injuries, he had others do the glassblowing. He still designs the pieces.

G

Glass-Blown, Vase, Witch's Ball Cover, Lockport Blue, Flared, Bulbous, Pontil, 1850-70, 10 ¾ In.
$9350.00

Glass-Bohemian, Dresser Box, Flowers, Sapphire Blue Enamel, c.1900, 6 ½ In.
$176.00

Glass-Bohemian, Epergne, Rose Shaded To Opal, c.1890, 13 In.
$415.00

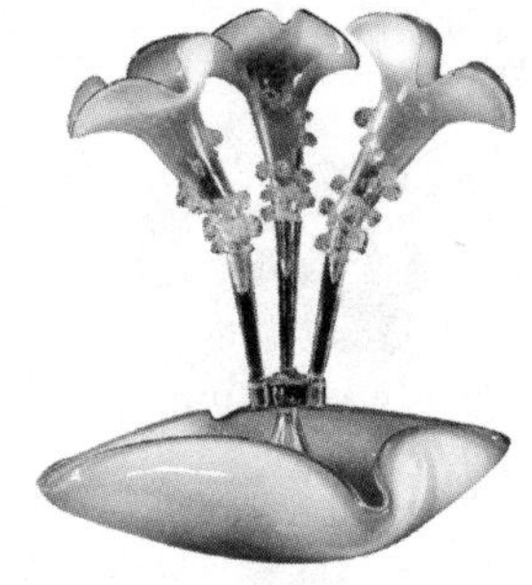

Glass-Bohemian, Goblet, Green Cut To Clear, Facets, Disk Foot, Early 1900s, 8 ¼ In.
$2032.00

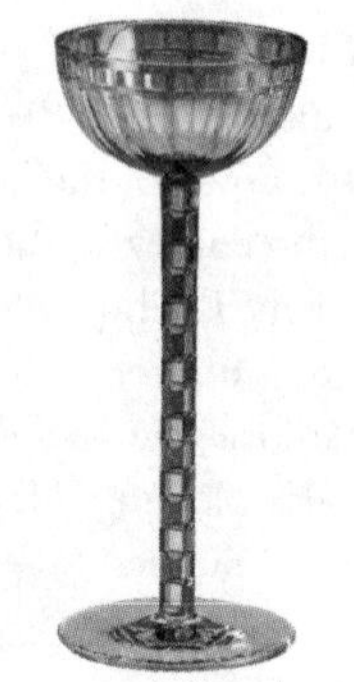

Bowl, Blue, Green, Iridescent Feather, Opal Ground, Cobalt Interior, Daniel Lotton, 1995, 7 In.. 920.00
Bowl, Blue Ground, Brown Mottling, Yellow Interior, Signed, White, 1997, 16 In.. 144.00
Bowl, Centerpiece, Swirl, Blue, Red, 6 x 23 In. 702.00
Bowl, Opal, Pulled Cobalt, Collar, 1995, 5 In.. 288.00
Candy Jar, Lid, Pink Satin, Epic, Viking, 5 x 5 In. 45.00
Decanter, Clear, Cut, 2-Sided Spout, Stopper, Sweden, 1960-80, 11 x 3 In. 150.00
Decanter Set, Gourd Shape, Cranberry, Black, Goblets, Stopper, 17 ¾ In., 5 piece 1016.00
Figure, Owl, Red, Dominick Labino, c.1974, 4 ⅛ x 2 ¾ In. 527.00
Figurine, Donkey, Pilgrim, Green, 5 x 4 ¼ In. 23.00
Figurine, Duck, Bluenique, Epic, Viking, 5 In.. 30.00
Figurine, Duck, Ruby Red, Epic, Viking, 5 In. 36.00
Figurine, Fish, Persimmon, Epic, Viking, 10 In.. 50.00
Jug, Green, Ruby Blush, Finger Grip, Dominick Labino, 1974, 4 ⅜ In. 374.00
Obelisk, Skyscraper Style, Metal Mount, Internal Blue Ribbon, Lynn Tissot, 11 ½ In. 500.00
Pedestal, Cobalt Blue, Pilgrim, 30 x 12 In.. 234.00
Perfume Bottle, Flowers, Citron, Oval, Red Flowers, Stems, Charles Lotton, 7 In. 978.00
Pitcher, Kanawha, Thumbprint, Amberina, 3 ½ x 3 In. 30.00
Platter, Brown, Mahogany, Blue Swirl, Signed, Ipsen, 1979, 20 In. *illus* 1250.00
Sculpture, Neodymium, Hot Pink, White, John Lotton, c.1988, 10 In. 1610.00
Urn, Iridescent Blue, Wavy Coil, Footed, Orient & Flume, 11 In. 288.00
Vase, Amber, Burgundy, White Combed, Orient & Flume, 8 In. 230.00
Vase, Blue, Green, Bottle Shape, Signed, Labino, 1980, 7 x 3 ½ In. 510.00
Vase, Blue, White Ground, Red, Orange Abstract, Bulbous, D. Edler, 1974, 5 x 9 In. 90.00
Vase, Blue Iridescent, Gold, Platinum Swags, Oval, Rolled Rim, Charles Lotton, 5 In. 863.00
Vase, Blue Iridescent, Split Leaves, Pink Flowers, Bulbous, Charles Lotton, 8 ½ In.. 748.00
Vase, Blue Iridescent, Textured, Orient & Flume, 4 ¼ In.. 207.00
Vase, Blue Pulled Leaf Design, Silver Sheen, Bulbous, M. Peiser, 4 x 5 In. 360.00
Vase, Bronze Color, Pulled Plumes, Yellow, Opal Tipped, Orient & Flume, 4 ⅛ In.. 207.00
Vase, Bulbous, Pastel Boats, M. Peiser, 1975, 6 x 8 In. 3900.00
Vase, Bulbous, Yellow, Applied Red Threads, D. Edler, 1993, 5 x 6 In. 90.00
Vase, Burgundy Feathering, Gold, Orient & Flume, 4 ⅛ In.. 138.00
Vase, Byrdes, Footed Cornucopia, Engraved Birds, Hofbauer, 6 In. 60.00
Vase, Calla Lilies, Plants, Blue Ground, c.1997, 12 In. 863.00
Vase, Checkerboard, Ladder, Relief, Amber, Frosted, Flowers, 6 ¼ x 7 ¾ In. 1035.00
Vase, Cherry Red, Blue Iridescent, Split Leaves, Opal, Charles Lotton, 6 ½ In. 1035.00
Vase, Cinnamon, Translucent, Pink Flowers, Leaves, Oval, 5 In. 863.00
Vase, Cobalt Blue, Split Leaves, Black Stems, Flowers, Cylindrical, Charles Lotton, 9 In.. 1438.00
Vase, Embossed Wavy Ridge, Blue, Gold Highlights, Lundberg, c.1980, 10 In. 501.00
Vase, Etched, Oval, Signed, Samuel J. Herman, 1969, 11 In. 250.00
Vase, Flowers, Amethyst, Pink Clematis, David Lotton, 8 In. 518.00
Vase, Flowers, Crimson Leaves, Vines, Bulbous Shoulder, Charles Lotton, 7 ½ In. 1495.00
Vase, Flowers, Leaves, Gold, White, Green, Charles Lotton, 1986, 5 ½ x 5 ½ In. 780.00
Vase, Free-Form, Horizontal Stripes, Peach, Pink, Chihuly, c.1980, 8 x 9 In. 4680.00
Vase, Fuchsia Red, Black Vines, Globular, Charles Lotton, c.1989, 4 ¼ In. 978.00
Vase, Geometrics, Blue, Gold, Transparent, Charles Lotton, 1982, 4 ½ x 4 In. 660.00
Vase, Gold, Brown, Blue Iridescent Pulled Heart, Vine, Cypriot, 5 ½ In. 690.00
Vase, Gold, Dangling Leaves, Tangled Vines, Lundberg, 5 ⅛ In. 138.00
Vase, Gold Iridescent, Blue Pulled Feathers, Smoke Stack, Lundberg, 12 ½ In. 201.00
Vase, Gold Iridescent, Cobalt Blue Vines, Charles Lotton, c.1988, 5 ¾ In. 633.00
Vase, Gold Iridescent, Draped Swags, Bulbous, Charles Lotton, 8 ¼ In. 518.00
Vase, Gold Iridescent, Pink Pulled & Swirled Feather, Escobedo, 11 In. 115.00
Vase, Gold Iridescent, Pulled Feathers, Bulbous, Alabaster, 6 ½ In.. 633.00
Vase, Green, Frosted, White Flowers, Blue Iridescent Vines, Charles Lotton, 6 ½ In. 690.00
Vase, Green, Purple Iridescent, Brown, Oval, M. Peiser, 1970, 4 x 5 In.. 510.00
Vase, Green Iridescent, Ric Rac, Bulbous, c.1974, 3 ½ In. 230.00
Vase, Hunters Chasing Deer, Oval, Flared Lip, Signed, Savata, 15 ¼ In. 1210.00
Vase, Inari, Mold Blown, Cut, Signed, Tapio Wirkkala, 1967, 7 x 14 ½ In. *illus* 1400.00
Vase, Iridized Cranberry, Pink Flowers, Cascading Leaves, Charles Lotton, 7 ½ In. 805.00
Vase, Lavender Pink, Silvery Blue Leaves, Charles Lotton, c.1987, 7 In. 546.00
Vase, Leaves, Flowers, Vines, Pink, Black, Charles Lotton, 10 In.. 1495.00
Vase, Mandarin Yellow, Blue Swags, Charles Lotton, 1975, 3 In. 575.00
Vase, Melon Shape, Lavender, Custard Ground, c.1984, 5 In. 115.00
Vase, Mottled Cream, Green, White, Iridescent Gold, Charles Lotton, 6 In.. 1035.00
Vase, Mottled Red, Blue Vines, Ruby Leaves, Lip Wrap, John Lotton, 7 ⅙ In.. 1380.00
Vase, Multiple Layers, Multicolored, Lisa & Peter Ridabock, 8 ¾ x 11 ¼ In. 345.00
Vase, Opal White Ground, Flowers, Rolled Rim, Charles Lotton, c.1997, 10 ⅝ In. 2875.00
Vase, Organic Shape, Clear, All Over Iridescence, F. Warren, 1981, 8 x 4 In. 350.00

Vase, Oval, Variegated Swirling, Amber & Purple, Opalescent, Signed, Mark Peiser, 5 In. 460.00
Vase, Paperweight, Green Shaded To Blue, Random Bubbles, 6 In. 575.00
Vase, Pulled Leaf, Red, Blue, Green, Iridescent, Charles Lotton, 1993, 5 x 6 In. 660.00
Vase, Red, Black, Opaque, Charles Lotton, 1975, 5 ¾ x 3 ½ In. 720.00
Vase, Red, Iridescent, Bottle Shape, Signed, Labino, 1983, 6 ¼ x 3 ½ In. 510.00
Vase, Ribbed, Pulled Feather, Gold, Blue, Magenta, Lundberg, 9 ½ In. 150.00
Vase, Spiral, Red, Blue, Green, White, Charles Lotton, 1985, 8 x 7 In. 900.00
Vase, Swirl Design, Red, Pulled Gooseneck, Charles Lotton, 1979, 12 x 4 In. 1560.00
Vase, Teardrop, Pink, Spring Green, c.1970, 6 In. 288.00
Vase, Timberline, Snow Storm, Red, c.1994, 13 In. 1150.00
Vase, Trumpet, Emerald Green Feathers, c.1973, 11 ¼ In. 805.00
Vase, Trumpet, Fluted, Opalescent Peach, Pulled Feathers, Lundberg, 13 In. 288.00
Vase, Trumpet, Mottled, Gold To Blue, Lundberg, 11 ¼ In. 115.00
Vase, White Opaque, Pulled Iridescent Color, Orient & Flume, 5 x 7 In. 240.00

GLASS-CUT, *see Cut Glass category.*

GLASS-DEPRESSION, *see Depression Glass category.*

GLASS-MIDCENTURY refers to art glass made from the 1940s to the early 1970s. Some glass factories, such as Baccarat or Orrefors, are listed under their own categories. Earlier glass may be listed in the Glass-Art and Glass-Contemporary categories. Italian glass may be found in Glass-Venetian.

Bowl, Gray Tint, Signed, Holmegaard Glassworks, Denmark, 1960, 3 ½ x 7 In. 68.00
Bowl, Opaline, Gray Splashes, Benny Motzfeld, Scandinavian, 7 In. 86.00
Decanter, Modern Cutting, Stopper, Johansfors, Sweden, 11 x 3 In. 150.00
Mobile, Fused Glass, 22 Pieces, Copper, Signed, Higgins, 22 x 18 In. ..... *illus* 1750.00
Pitcher, Amber, Squat Base, Narrow Neck, Spout, Clear Handle, 4 In. 26.00
Plate, Higgins, Concentric Circles, Random Dots, Dashes, 8 ½ In., Pair 375.00
Vase, Blown, Marbleized, Brown, Amber, Rectangular, Per Lutken, Denmark, 7 x 4 ¾ In. 130.00
Vase, Blue, Pinched Body, Long Slender Neck, Zeller, 30 x 11 In. 127.00
Vase, Frosted Green Leaves, Oval, Cameo, Kelsey Pilgrim, 9 In. 316.00
Vase, Handkerchief, Clear, Green Rim, Poland, 13 x 9 In. 176.00

GLASS-PRESSED, *see Pressed Glass category.*

GLASS-VENETIAN. Venetian glass has been made near Venice, Italy, since the thirteenth century. Thin, colored glass with applied decoration is favored, although many other types have been made. Collectors have recently become interested in the Art Deco and fifties designs. Glass was made on the Venetian island of Murano from 1291. The output dwindled in the late seventeenth century but began to flourish again in the 1850s. Some of the old techniques of glassmaking were revived, and firms today make traditional designs and original modern glass. Since 1981, the name *Murano* may be used only on glass made on Murano Island. Other pieces of Italian glass may be found in the Glass-Contemporary and Glass-Midcentury categories of this book.

Beverage Set, Continental Scenes, Amethyst, Murano, 7 Piece 288.00
Bird, Multicolored, Clear Base, Murano, 16 ¾ In., Pair 510.00
Bookends, Teardrop, Blue, Swirl, Label, Murano, 7 ½ x 4 x 5 In. 180.00
Bowl, Canne Transversale, Yellow, Blue, White, Archimede Seguso, Murano, 4 In. 600.00
Bowl, Gold, Spiral Threading, Round, Footed, Dino Martens, Murano, 6 In. 400.00
Bowl, Green, Folded Rim, Applied Lavender & Yellow Iris Handles, 10 ¾ x 3 ½ In. 59.00
Bowl, Green Rugiadoso Glass, Sea Plant Base, Gold, Barovier, 9 ½ x 17 In. 1680.00
Bowl, Leaf Shape, Black, Red, Copper Fleck, Fratelli Toso, Murano, 11 ½ x 9 In. 100.00
Bowl, Leaf Shape, Milky Green, Gold Aventurine, Archimede Seguso, Murano, 9 x 4 In. 850.00
Bowl, Red, Blue, White Swirl, Oval, Murano, 4 ½ x 11 ½ In. 130.00
Bowl, Tortoiseshell, Yellow, Black, Wide Rim, Murano, 3 ¼ x 10 ½ In. 55.00
Bowl, White, Gold Flecks, Barbini, Murano, 11 ½ x 10 ¼ In. 150.00
Candlestick, Yellow, Rigaree Band, Swans, Purple Powdered Finish, 15 In., Pair 1150.00
Candy Jar, Cover, Opalescent Blue, Pear, Fratelli Toso, 4 ¾ x 3 ⅝ In. 500.00
Casket, Cranberry, Enameled, Moser Style, 8-Sided, 1800s, 4 ¼ x 3 ¼ In. 165.00
Chalice, Cover, Snake Stem & Finial, 15 ½ In. 4329.00
Compote, Latticed Cover, Green Swirling Aventurine, Multicolored Fruit, V. Barovier, 8 In. 7000.00 to 7500.00
Compote, Orange, Gold Flecks, Ribbed Pedestal, Barbini, 7 x 7 In. 350.00
Compote, Red, Applied Gold Grape Clusters, Flared, Footed, Murano, 9 ⅛ x 6 In. 200.00
Console Set, Bird, Iridescent, Clear, Diamond Acid Stamp, Iridato, 4 ½ In., 3 Piece 575.00
Cordial, Clear Bowl, Twisted Gem-Colored Stem, 5 ¾ In., 8 Piece 145.00
Decanter, Amber, Tiered, Opaque Red, Black Foot, Stopper, 11 ½ In. 550.00

Glass-Bohemian, Pitcher, Amberina, Flower Sprays, Melon Ribbed, Rope Handle, 1900, 8 In.
$550.00

Glass-Bohemian, Vase, 6 Nude Women, Molded Green, Malachite, 5 In.
$275.00

Glass-Bohemian, Vase, Frog, Flower, Yellow, Blue Handles, Enameled, Austria, 1890s, 12 In.
$1200.00

G

Glass-Contemporary, Platter, Brown, Mahogany, Blue Swirl, Signed, Ipsen, 1979, 20 In.
$1250.00

Glass-Contemporary, Vase, Inari, Mold Blown, Cut, Signed, Tapio Wirkkala, 1967, 7 x 14 ½ In.
$1400.00

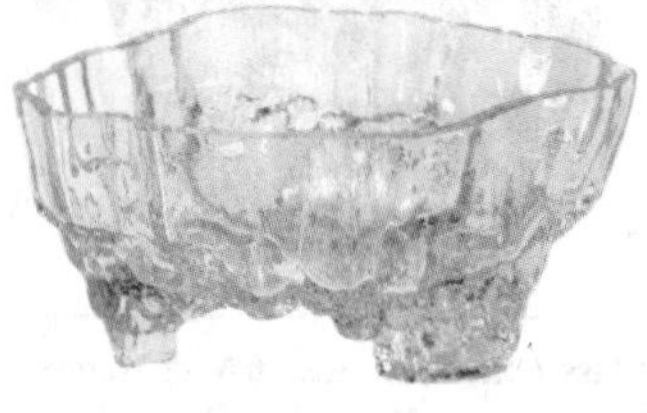

Glass-Midcentury, Mobile, Fused Glass, 22 Pieces, Copper, Signed, Higgins, 22 x 18 In.
$1750.00

Glass-Venetian, Sculpture, Aquarium, 3 Tropical Fish, Seaweed, Cenedese, 5 x 9 In.
$360.00

Decanter, Clear, Hollow Blown Stopper, Applied Prunts, Rings, Rigaree, 10 ¼ In. 300.00
Decanter, Gold Overlay, Flowers, Stopper, Handles, c.1930, 14 In., Pair.......... 760.00
Decanter, Pink, Gold Flecks, Rocket Shape, Barbini, Murano, 1950s, 20 x 5 ½ In.......... 3200.00
Dish, Leaf Shape, Free-Form, Applied Brown Swirls, Fulvio Bianconi, 2 ¼ x 5 ½ In.......... 876.00
Figurine, Bird, Blue, Clear Base, Engraved, Salviati L. Gaspari, 18 ⅞ In.......... 650.00
Figurine, Clown, Green Coat, Red Tie, Buttons, Striped Outfit, Murano, 20 In.......... 355.00
Figurine, Clown, Juggling, Murano, 12 In.......... 50.00
Figurine, Clown, Ribbon Canes, Gold Leaf, Murano, 9 ¾ In.......... 575.00
Figurine, Duck, Pink, Spotted, Gold Flecks, Fratelli Toso, Murano, 4 ¾ x 4 ¾ In.......... 120.00
Figurine, Duck, Red, Orange, White & Green, Archimede Seguso, Murano, 13 x 7 In.......... 950.00
Figurine, Duck, Whimsical, Green, Red, Murano, 15 x 5 In.......... 385.00
Figurine, Elephant, Trunk Raised, Balancing On Ball, Signed, Zanetti L., 17 In.......... 400.00
Figurine, Frog, Amethyst, Etched, Signed, Lino Zanetti, 5 In.......... 485.00
Figurine, Geese, Signed, 12 ¾ x 19 In., Pair.......... 351.00
Figurine, Man, Carrying Fruit, Blue, Red, Gold Leaf Sections, 13 ¼ In.......... 500.00
Figurine, Man On Base, Blue, Milk Glass, Fulvio Bianconi, 15 ½ In.......... 1000.00
Figurine, Parrot, Red To Gold Dust, Clear Perch, Murano, 12 ½ In. 250.00
Figurine, Pheasant, Cased White, Blue, Gold Flecks, Barbini, Salviati, 13 ½ x 9 In.......... 750.00
Figurine, Pheasant, Graffito, Green, Gold Flecks, Barovier, Murano, 9 x 6 ½ In. 1200.00
Figurine, Polar Bear Family, White, Gold Specks, Murano, 12 In. 550.00
Figurine, Tiger, Ruby, Black Stripes, Applied Details, Barovier, 7 x 16 ¼ In. 1200.00
Figurine, Toucan, Fish, Pink & Gold, Italy, 13 ½ In.......... 420.00
Figurine, Woman In Skirt, Bubbles, Gold Leaf, 11 ¾ In.......... 1550.00
Flute, Champagne, Clear, Pulled Blue Feather, Murano, 10 x 4 In.......... 117.00
Goblet, Clear Bowl, Pink Ribbons, White Lattice, Gold Aventurine, 6 In., 6 Piece 345.00
Goblet, Cranberry Bowl, Molded, Enameled, Gold Leaf, 1800s, 8 x 3 ½ In., 8 Piece 1600.00
Goblet, Ruby Bowl, Base, Clear Knobbed Stem, c.1920, 6 In., 5 Piece.......... 410.00
Jar, Cover, Cased Blue, Gold Flecks, Barbini, Murano, 10 ½ x 6 ½ In.......... 720.00
Lamp, Gold & Purple, Barovier Zebratti, Murano, 28 In.......... 1000.00
Lamp, White, Red, Meza Filigrana, Brass Base, Dino Martens, 12 x 5 In.......... 1000.00
Paperweight, Rainbow Satin, Murano, 3 ⅜ In.......... 75.00
Pitcher, Bowl, Dino Martens, Red, Clear, 14 x 10 & 15 x 3 ½ In., 2 Piece.......... 3000.00
Plate, Girl In Low Cut Dress, Frame, Shadowbox, 16 x 16 In.......... 248.00
Powder Box, Cover, Flame Finial, Cased Pink, Gold Flecks, Bubbles, Barbini, Murano, 9 x 7 In. 600.00
Sconce, Pink Finial, Barovier & Toso, 11 In. 1500.00
Sculpture, Aquarium, 3 Tropical Fish, Seaweed, Cenedese, 5 x 9 In.......... *illus* 360.00
Sculpture, Nude, Abstract, Signed, Murano, 26 x 6 x 5 In.......... 990.00
Sculpture, Orb, Green, Spherical, Internal Bubbles, 7 ½ In.......... 4250.00
Timer, Venini Yellow, Triangle, Clessidre, Murano, 7 ¼ x 3 In. 1200.00
Vase, Applied Matte Red Murines To Amber Top, Signed, Venini, Murano, 22 In.......... 960.00
Vase, Black Amethyst, Iridescent, Enameled Hawaiian Luau Scene, 11 ¾ In. 1250.00
Vase, Cased Amber, Red Layers, Label, Flavio Poli, 11 ⅜ In. 2000.00
Vase, Clear, Blue Interior, Murano, c.1950, 15 x 7 In. 82.00
Vase, Clear, Gold Aventurine, Pedestal Foot, Vittorio Zecchen, Venini, Murano, 8 In.......... 1250.00
Vase, Clear, Purple, Yellow Vertical Stripes, Scavo, Cenedese, Murano, 13 x 10 In.......... 950.00
Vase, Cranberry Overlay, 4-Fold Rim, Footed, Fired Gold, Murano, 14 x 7 In. 410.00
Vase, Diamond Pattern, Violet, Cobalt Blue Foot, Murano, 12 x 7 In.......... 100.00
Vase, Fan, Pale Amber, Gold Fleck, Applied Fish Handles, Ribbed Knop Stem, 8 In.......... 82.00
Vase, Fenicio Amethyst Decoration, Ercole Barovier, c.1950, 16 In. 500.00
Vase, Flower Form, Blue, Gold, Red, Flared, Murano, 1940s, 14 ½ x 15 In. 650.00
Vase, Flower Shape, Pink, Murrhina, Trails, Fratelli Floreale, 5 In. 1800.00
Vase, Fused, Pierced, Cinesi Shape, Murano, 13 ¼ x 9 ½ In.......... 6000.00
Vase, Fused Layers, Opaque, Translucent, Gold Leaf, 10 ¾ In.......... 6500.00
Vase, Geometric Patchwork, Pezzato, Signed, F. Bianconi, 8 x 7 ¾ In.......... *illus* 11140.00
Vase, Gold, A Canne, Signed, Barovier Toso, Murano, 9 ½ x 5 In.......... 2600.00
Vase, Gourd, Aubergine, White, Gold Glitter, Crosshatching, Murano, 12 x 7 In.......... 1810.00
Vase, Green, Internal Yellow Design, Label, Cenedese, 6 ¼ x 7 ½ In. .... *illus* 120.00
Vase, Green To Clear, Signed, Fulvio Bianconi, 1963, 10 x 6 ½ In.......... 875.00
Vase, Hourglass Shape, Amber, Mauve, Murano, Cenedese, c.1965, 11 x 8 In.......... 720.00
Vase, Jack-In-The-Pulpit, Green, Ribs, Gold Leaf, Murano, 12 ¾ In.......... 200.00
Vase, Lavender, Red Stripe, Murano, 6 x 3 ¼ In.......... 439.00
Vase, Loose Bag Shape, Green Trails Over Bubbles, Flavio Poli, c.1940, 5 ½ In.......... 2500.00
Vase, Multicolored, Gilt, Abstract Design, Round Base To Square Top, Italy, 20 In. 115.00
Vase, Multicolored Stripes, Fulvio Bianconi, c.1950, 6 ½ In.......... 815.00
Vase, Opal Yellow, Flared Top, Barovier Toso, Murano, 9 ⅝ x 6 In.......... 1200.00
Vase, Red, Silver Leaf Inclusion, Gold Draping, Fratelli Toso, 1920, 16 x 5 ½ In.......... 850.00
Vase, Sculptured, Loop Shaped, Lavender, Clear Base, Signed, Seguso Livia, 12 ¾ x 13 In.......... 1200.00
Vase, Serpent, Coiled Tail, Green, Gold Flecks, Napoleon Martini, 3 In.......... 130.00

Vase, Silver Swirled, Scalloped Handles, Gold Foil Inclusions, Barovier, 14 x 8 In. 2520.00
Vase, Spirolato, Spirals, Red, Black, T. Stearns, Venini, c.1960, 11 x 9 In.. .... 1020.00
Vase, Teardrop Shape, Cased Blue, Green Layers, Flavio Poli, 10 ¼ In.. .... 1500.00
Vase, Veronese, Gold Threaded, Bubbles, Zecchin Venini, Murano, 11 ⅜ x 8 ½ In. 6000.00
Vase, Yellow Marks On Clear Glass, Over Green Center, Cenedese, Murano, 7 x 6 In.. .... 180.00

GLASSES for the eyes, or spectacles, were mentioned in a manuscript in 1289 and have been used ever since. The first eyeglasses with rigid side pieces were made in London in 1727. Bifocals were invented by Benjamin Franklin in 1785. Lorgnettes were popular in late Victorian times. Opera Glasses are listed in their own category.

Cat's-Eye, Bakelite, Butterscotch, Wavy Lines, Vogue, 1950s 55.00
Cat's-Eye, Rhinestones, Black, Square, Green Vinyl Case, c.1940, 5 x 6 In. 100.00
Gold, Side Spangle Drops, Leather Case, Gastone Novelli, GEM, Milan, 1968. .... 12500.00
Lorgnette, Platinum, 68 Diamonds, 23 Sapphires, Rock Crystal, Victorian. 4602.00
Lorgnette, Platinum, Diamonds, Filigree, Link Chain, Hinged Frame. 1560.00
Lorgnette, Silver, Rose Cut Diamond, Scrolled, Chain, Art Nouveau, 7 In. 840.00
Lorgnette, Sterling Silver, Green Enamel, Classical Design, 6 In.. .... 316.00
Spectacles, Coin Silver, Rounded Rectangular Lenses, Collapsible Arms, D. Moody, 5 x 5 In. . . 345.00
Sunglasses, Plastic, Rhinestones, Off-White, Light Brown Overlay, Mid 1900s .... *illus* 49.00
Tortoiseshell, Carved, Gothic Style, Case, 5 x 2 ¼ x ½ In. 780.00

GLIDDEN Pottery worked in Alfred, New York, from 1940 to 1957. The pottery made stoneware, dinnerware, and art objects.

Platter, 3 Sections, Palm Trees, Lion, Marked, 12 x 9 In.. .... 150.00
Server, Turquoise, Handle, Marked, 10 In. 55.00
Teapot, Moderne, Blue Green, Abstract Scene, Wood Handle, Copper, Marked, 9 In. 82.00
Teapot, Moderne, Seafoam Blue Green, Marked, 9 In.. .... 75.00
Tray, Rooster, Square, Marked, 35, 5 ½ In. 10.00
Vase, Sandstone, Speckled, Gray, Rust & Mauve Bands, 9 ½ In. 225.00
Vase, Speckled Green, Square Top, Round Sides, 7 ¼ In.. .... 85.00

GOEBEL is the mark used by W. Goebel Porzellanfabrik of Oeslau, Germany, now Rodental, Germany. The company was founded by Franz Detleff and William Goebel in 1871. It was known as F&W Goebel. Slates, slate pencils, and marbles were made. Soon the company began making porcelain tableware and figurines. Hummel figurines were first made in 1935 and are now being made by another company. Goebel is still in business. Old pieces marked Goebel Hummel are listed under Hummel in this book.

Figurine, Babysitter, No. 66, Girl Holding Baby, Byj, 5 In. 130.00
Figurine, Bachman, Woman, In Flowing Dress, Hat, 1972, 8 In. 115.00
Figurine, Barn Owl, c.1975, 6 ¼ In. 135.00
Figurine, Blumenkinder, Accompanist, Girl Strumming Banjo, 7 ½ In. 95.00
Figurine, Blumenkinder, First Date, Imprinted, 1970, 9 x 4 In. 175.00
Figurine, Boy, Trouble Shooter, Doctor Outfit, Needle, Red Hair, 5 ¼ In. 95.00
Figurine, Cardinal, Red Bird, White, Black, 3 ½ x 2½ x 2 ¼ In. 30.00
Figurine, Cat, Siamese, Walking, 9 ¾ In. 140.00
Figurine, Co-Boy, Fritz, Wine Merchant, Bee On Base, 1972-79, 8 In. 79.00
Figurine, Co-Boy, Holding Bee Sign, 1971, 7 ½ In. 85.00
Figurine, Dog, Boxer, Preparing To Scratch, 4 ½ In. 75.00
Figurine, Horse, Brown, White On Front Legs, 6 ¾ x 7 In. 48.00
Figurine, Horse, Running, Black, White Blaze, 8 x 11 In. 400.00
Figurine, Peacock, Spread Tail, Marked, 1979, 9 In. 56.00
Figurine, Penguin, Standing, 3 ¼ In. 30.00
Figurine, Ram, 5 In. 5.85
Figurine, Sleeping Pigs, 1 ¼ x 4 ½ In. 36.00
Pitcher, Harlequin Clown, 8 In.. .... 75.00
Plate, Bird, Robin, Sitting On Branch, 1973. .... 25.00
Salt & Pepper, Chimney Sweep. 18.00
Salt & Pepper, Friar, West Germany, 3 x 2 In. 15.00

GOLDSCHEIDER was founded by Friedrich Goldscheider in Vienna in 1885. The family left Vienna in 1938 and the factory was taken over by the Germans. Goldscheider started factories in England and in Trenton, New Jersey. The New Jersey factory started in 1940 as Goldscheider-U.S.A. In 1941 it became Goldscheider-Everlast Corporation. From 1947 to 1953 it was Goldcrest Ceramics Corporation. In 1950 the Vienna plant was returned to Mr. Goldscheider and the company continues in business. The Trenton, New Jersey, business, called Goldscheider of Vienna, imports all of the pieces.

Glass-Venetian, Vase, Geometric Patchwork, Pezzato, Signed, F. Bianconi, 8 x 7 ¾ In.
$11140.00

Glass-Venetian, Vase, Green, Internal Yellow Design, Label, Cenedese, 6 ¼ x 7 ½ In.
$120.00

Top Ten Glass Categories

Hundreds of thousands of users visit our website, Kovels.com, each month. There are over 170 glass categories listed. The glass categories that are the most popular among our visitors are:

1. Depression Glass
2. Fenton
3. Heisey
4. Cobalt Blue Glass
5. Lalique
6. Fostoria
7. D'Aurys (cameo)
8. Ruby Glass
9. Czechoslovakia Glass
10. Goofus Glass

As always, the edited listings in *Kovels' Antiques & Collectibles Price Guide 2010* aren't available on any website, but readers should visit Kovels.com for information on trends, tips, reproductions, marks, old prices, and more!

Glasses, Sunglasses, Plastic, Rhinestones, Off-White, Light Brown Overlay, Mid 1900s
$49.00

Goldscheider, Figurine, Woman, Seated, Marked, Early 1900s, 10 ¼ In.
$660.00

Graniteware, Coffeepot, Burgundy, White, Green, Yellow, Blue, Pink, 9 In.
$400.00

Graniteware, Pitcher, Ice Water, Speckled Blue Mottle, Quadruple Plate, Late 1800s, 10 In.
$88.00

G

Bust, Woman, In Bonnet, Terra-Cotta, Marked, Early 1900s, 28 x 18 In. 990.00
Bust, Woman, Wearing Hood, Marked, Early 1900s, 25 In. 1430.00
Clock, Art Nouveau, Figural, Man & Woman Holding Hands, Hammered Copper Face. 6613.00
Figurine, Boy, Sitting In Chair, Painted, Terra-Cotta, c.1895, 25 In.. .... 1000.00
Figurine, Boy, With Fish Tank, Painted, Terra-Cotta, c.1895, 25 In.. .... 1500.00
Figurine, Bust, Black Woman, Aqua Hat, Base, Art Deco, 5 In. 150.00
Figurine, Bust, Woman, Aqua Curls, Red Lips, Art Deco, 5 In. 250.00
Figurine, Bust, Woman, Aqua Draped Hood, Red Lips, Art Deco, 10 In. 100.00
Figurine, Dancer, Arms Stretched, Blue Skirt, Art Deco, Marked, Wien, 15 ½ In. 800.00
Figurine, Fisherman, Painted, Terra-Cotta, c.1895 .... 2500.00
Figurine, Flamingo, Pink, Green Base, c.1950, 14 In., Pair 300.00
Figurine, Man, With Pipe, Painted, Terra-Cotta, c.1895, 25 In. 3500.00
Figurine, Queen, Blue Dress, Art Deco, 8 In. 125.00
Figurine, Woman, Pink Skirt, Black Blouse, Long White Gloves, Oval Base, 15 In.. .... 250.00
Figurine, Woman, Rose Skirt, Black Top, Summer Hat, Paper Label, 14 ¾ In. 500.00
Figurine, Woman, Seated, Marked, Early 1900s, 10 ¼ In. .... *illus* 660.00

GOLF, *see Sports category.*

GONDER Ceramic Arts, Inc., was opened by Lawton Gonder in 1941 in Zanesville, Ohio. Gonder made high-grade pottery decorated with flambe, drip, gold crackle, and Chinese crackle glazes. The factory closed in 1957. From 1946 to 1954, Gonder also operated the Elgee Pottery, which made ceramic lamp bases.

Candleholder, Fish, Yellow, Brown, Marked, 2 ⅜ x 5 In., Pair 11.00
Figurine, Leopard, Yellow, Brown, No. 210, Marked, 19 In. 44.00
Planter, Oriental Girl With Buckets, Green, Red Glaze, Paper Label, 14 In.. .... 66.00
Vase, Flowers, Leaves, Pink Matte Glaze, Pinched Waist, 12 ½ In.. .... 55.00
Vase, Pink Interior, White, Looping Handles, Lobed Rim, Marked, 9 In.. .... 22.00
Vase, Ribbon Candy Form, Yellow, 11 In. 66.00
Vase, Shell Form, Lavender, No. J60, Marked, 8 x 11 In.. .... 55.00

GOOFUS GLASS was made from about 1900 to 1920 by many American factories. It was originally painted gold, red, green, bronze, pink, purple, or other bright colors. Many pieces are found today with flaking paint, and this lowers the value.

Grapes, Vase, Brown, Green, Gold, 9 In., Pair. 45.00
Seascape, Vase, Red, Green, Gold Ground, 9 ½ In., Pair 25.00
Ship, Vase, Red, Brown, Green, Gold Ground, 9 ½ In., Pair. 30.00

GOUDA, Holland, has been a pottery center since the seventeenth century. Two firms, the Zenith pottery, established in the eighteenth century, and the Zuid-Hollandsche pottery, made the brightly colored art pottery marked *Gouda* from 1898 to about 1964. Other factories followed. Many pieces featured Art Nouveau or Art Deco designs. Pattern names in Dutch, listed here, seem strange to English-speaking collectors.

Bowl, Flowers, Leaf Vines, Green Ground, Marked, Arnhem, Holland, 1927, 5 x 11 In. 232.00
Charger, Red Poppies, Green Leaves, Marked, Zuid, PZH, c.1927, 13 ½ In. 255.00
Charger, Rembrandt, Green Border, Marked, Ivora, c.1925, 14 ½ In.. .... 280.00
Ewer, Mary Pattern, Signed, 1923, 9 ¼ x 6 ¼ In. 225.00
Jar, Cover, Art Nouveau Flowers, Black Ground, Marked, 4297, Cassa, 996 Lazuid, 7 In.. ..... 135.00
Jardiniere, Flowers, Scrolls, Signed, 7 ½ x 11 In. 200.00
Pitcher, Art Nouveau Flowers, Black Ground, Marked, Regina, Lydia, 795, 6 In.. .... 115.00
Tile, Ships, Blue, White, Brant Jes-Purmerend, Frame, 6 In. 400.00
Vase, Lindus Pattern, Flowers, Multicolored, Handles, c.1923, 14 In. 440.00
Vase, Maas, High Glaze, 1921, 7 ¾ x 4 In.. .... 265.00
Vase, Mary Pattern, Signed, c.1923, 7 x 4 In. 145.00
Vase, Shouldered, Anchors, Footed, Marked, 6 ¾ In. 230.00
Vase, Shouldered, Tulip, Multicolored, Mark, Jaap Branger, c.1905, 12 ½ x 6 In. 480.00
Vase, Zomer, Flowers, Leaves, Signed, 1923, 7 x 4 ½ In. 100.00

GRANITEWARE is an enameled tinware that has been used in the kitchen from the late nineteenth century to the present. Earlier graniteware was green or turquoise blue, with white spatters. The later ware was gray with white spatters. Reproductions are being made in all colors.

Berry Bucket, Lid, Bail Handle, Blue 60.00
Bucket, Blue Swirl, Wood Handle 110.00

Can, Cream, Blue & White Swirl, Wood Handle, 7 ½ x 5 In. 69.00
Coffee Boiler, Tin Lid, 12 ½ x 9 ¾ In.. .... 80.00
Coffeepot, Agate, 9 In. 44.00
Coffeepot, Black & White, 10 In.. .... 25.00
Coffeepot, Burgundy, White, Green, Yellow, Blue, Pink, 9 In. .... *illus* 400.00
Coffeepot, Hinged Lid, Multicolored, 9 In.. .... 230.00 to 431.00
Cooker, Gary, Pierced Insert, Twisted Handle, Agate-Nickel Steel Ware, 8 x 21 x 9 In.. .... 80.00
Cream Can, Blue & White Swirl, Wire Bail Handle, Replaced Lid, 4 ¾ x 7 ¾ In.. .... 100.00
Flour Bin, Lid, White, Black Letters, Handles, 10 ¼ In. 65.00
Mixing Bowl, Turquoise, Mottled, 1960s, 5 x 12 In.. .... 11.00
Muffin Pan, Gray, 12 Cup, 10 ½ x 14 In. 11.00
Pitcher, Ice Water, Speckled Blue Mottle, Quadruple Plate, Late 1800s, 10 In. .... *illus* 88.00
Pitcher, Milk, 4 ½ x 5 In. 21.00
Plate, Red Bunny Rabbit, Running In Field Of Flowers, 8 In., Child's 30.00
Pot, Hot Water, Burgundy Spatter, Green, Blue, White, Gooseneck Spout, Qt.. .... 220.00
Roaster, Mottled Gray, Swirl, Oblong, 15 ¾ x 9 In. 70.00
Slop Bucket, Blue Swirl, White Interior, 9 ¾ x 11 In. 38.50
Sugar Shaker, Lid, Chrysanthemum Swirl, Blue, Satin Finish, 4 ½ In.. .... 490.00
Teapot, Statue Of Liberty, Blue, White, Wood Handle, 8 In. 173.00

GREENTOWN glass was made by the Indiana Tumbler and Goblet Company of Greentown, Indiana, from 1894 to 1903. In 1899, the factory became part of National Glass Company. A variety of pressed glass was made. Additional pieces may be found in other categories, such as Chocolate Glass, Holly Amber, Milk Glass, and Pressed Glass.

Austrian, Goblet, 6 ⅛ In., 6 Piece 45.00
Dolphin, Dish, Chocolate Glass, Smooth Rim 100.00
Squirrel, Pitcher, Water, 9 In. 102.00
Troubadour, Mug, Nile Green, 4 ¾ In. .... *illus* 80.00
Wheelbarrow, Salt, Amber, Diamond On Front, 1920s, 17 x 15 In. 155.00

GRUEBY Faience Company of Boston, Massachusetts, was incorporated in 1897 by William H. Grueby. Garden statuary, art pottery, and architectural tiles were made until 1920. The company developed a green matte glaze that was so popular it was copied by many other factories making a less expensive type of pottery. This eventually led to the financial problems of the pottery. Cuerda seca and cuenca are techniques explained in the Tile category.

GRUEBY FAIENCE Co. BOSTON, U.S.A.

Bowl, Blue Matte, Glossy Green Interior, Marked, 5 ¾ In. 395.00
Bowl, Brown, Green Matte To High Glaze, Label, 6 x 2 In.. .... 395.00
Bowl, Center, Drip Brown Matte Glaze, Glossy Green Interior, 2 ¼ x 8 ¼ In. 895.00
Bowl, Cream Matte, Circular Impressed Mark, 4 ½ x 1 ¾ In. 350.00
Bowl, Drip Brown Glaze To Glossy Green, Marked, 2 x 8 In. 450.00
Bowl, Drip Brown Matte Over Bisque, Glossy Green Interior, 8 ¼ In. 395.00
Bowl, Green Matte, Glossy Interior, Applied Rows Of Leaves, 4-Sided, 3 x 9 In. 2750.00
Bowl, Green Matte Glaze, Exposed Clay, Round, Marked, 3 ⅞ In. 259.00
Bowl, Green Matte Glaze, Ribbed, Squat, Marked, 3 ¼ x 5 ¼ In.. .... 474.00
Flower Bowl, Leaves, Green Matte Glaze, Copper Ikebana Insert, Stamped, 9 In. .... *illus* 3360.00
Tile, Candle Sconce, Candle, 6 x 4 ½ In. 2280.00
Tile, Landscape, Painted, Blue, Green, Carved, Oak Frame, Signed, PS, 12 x 12 In.. .... 4200.00
Tile, Rabbit, In Lettuce Field, Green, Ivory, Metal Mount, Cuenca, Signed, 6 x 6 In. .... *illus* 4800.00
Tile, Ship, Cuenca, 8 x 8 In. 1800.00
Tile, Tulip, Cuenca, Marked, 6 x 6 In. 1440.00
Tile, Yellow Tulip, Green Ground, Dust-Pressed, Cuerda Seca, 8 x 8 In. 1080.00
Vase, Arches, Green Matte Glaze, Paper Label, 4 x 3 In. 895.00
Vase, Blue Green Glaze, Bottle Shape, Carved & Applied Leaves, c.1908, 6 ½ In. 1680.00
Vase, Butterscotch Glaze, Bud & Leaf, Squat, Signed, 6 ½ x 9 ¼ In. 5500.00
Vase, Curdled Green Matte Glaze, Bulbous, 11 In. 2495.00
Vase, Daffodils, Green Leaves, Gourd, Stamped, 4 ½ x 5 In. .... *illus* 4200.00
Vase, Green Glaze, Modeled Tulips, 5 ½ In.. .... 1035.00
Vase, Green Matte Glaze, Arch Designs, Paper Label, 4 ¼ In.. .... 895.00
Vase, Green Matte Glaze, Carved Broad Leaf Leaves, Folded Rim, 4 ½ x 5 ¾ In. 2195.00
Vase, Green Matte Glaze, Carved Leaves & Buds On Bottom, Marked, 6 x 4 In. 1300.00
Vase, Green Matte Glaze, Carved Vertical Leaves, Marked, 10 x 7 In. 3600.00
Vase, Green Matte Glaze, Hand Carved Broad Leaf Design, Folded Rim, 4 ½ In. 2195.00
Vase, Green Matte Glaze, Impressed Leaves, Round, Faience, 7 ¾ In.. .... 4500.00
Vase, Green Matte Glaze, Leaves, Buds, 8 ½ x 4 In.. .... 1920.00
Vase, Green Matte Glaze, Leaves, Buds, Carved, Tapered, Marked, 11 ½ x 5 ½ In. 1860.00

Greentown, Troubadour, Mug, Nile Green, 4 ¾ In.
$80.00

Grueby, Flower Bowl, Leaves, Green Matte Glaze, Copper Ikebana Insert, Stamped, 9 In.
$3360.00

Grueby, Tile, Rabbit, In Lettuce Field, Green, Ivory, Metal Mount, Cuenca, Signed, 6 x 6 In.
$4800.00

Grueby, Vase, Daffodils, Green Leaves, Gourd, Stamped, 4 ½ x 5 In.
$4200.00

Gundersen, Fairy Lamp, Burmese, Ruffled, 1960-70, 5 ½ In.
$225.00

Gustavsberg, Jar, Seminude Woman, Green Ground, Gilt, Signed, Kage, 1930, 9 ½ In.
$1320.00

Haeger, Figurine, Bull, Charging, Sandpaper Glaze, Black Base, 7 ¾ x 14 In.
$143.00

Haeger, Vase, Art Nouveau, Brown, Black, Marked, 5066, 7 ¼ x 6 ¼ In.
$33.00

Vase, Green Matte Glaze, Leaves, Buds, Marked, 4 x 7 ¾ In. 1440.00
Vase, Green Matte Glaze, Leaves, Squat, 5 x 7 In. 6600.00
Vase, Green Matte Glaze, Rounded Leaves, Squat, 2 ¼ x 5 ¾ In. 1440.00
Vase, Green Matte Glaze, Carved & Applied Leaves, 7 ¾ In. 2040.00
Vase, Green Matte Glaze, Uncurling Leaves On Neck, Marked, 10 In. 259.00
Vase, Green Matte Glaze, Yellow Buds, Leaves, Bulbous, 7 ½ x 4 ¼ In. 7800.00
Vase, Green Matte Glaze, Yellow Buds, Molded Leaves, 6 ¼ In. 3300.00
Vase, Green Matte Glaze, Yellow Ground, Leaves, Experimental, Signed, c.1900, 16 x 11 In. . . 9300.00
Vase, Mustard Matte Glaze, Frothy, Leaves, Squat, 3 ¼ x 6 In. 2280.00

GUNDERSEN glass was made at the Gundersen Glass Works of New Bedford, Massachusetts, from 1939 to 1952 and by its successor, Gundersen/Pairpoint, from 1952 to 1957. Gundersen Peachblow is especially famous.

Bowl, Peachblow, Red To Pink, White Interior, Rolled Crimped Edge, Pontil, 7 In. 40.00
Fairy Lamp, Burmese, Ruffled, 1960-70, 5 ½ In. . . . . *illus* 225.00
Rose Bowl, Peachblow, Red To Pink Matte, Rolled Crimped Edge, Broken Pontil, 3 In. 25.00

GUSTAVSBERG ceramics factory was founded in 1827 near Stockholm, Sweden. It is best known to collectors for its twentieth-century artwares, especially Argenta, a green stoneware with silver inlay.

Gustafsberg

Bowl, Draping, White On Tan Ground, Signed, Stig L, Early 1900s, 5 ⅛ x 8 In. 195.00
Bowl, Fish, Green-Blue Ground, Argenta, 1 ½ x 6 In. 165.00
Bowl, Green Glaze, Shell Shape Handles, Sterling Silver Band, Argenta, 3 x 6 In. 598.00
Bowl, Mermaid, On Fish, Turquoise, Silver Inlay, Marked, Argenta, 1 ½ x 9 ¼ In. 220.00
Console Set, Candlesticks, Bowl, 4-Sided, Blue-Green Iridescent, Gilt, Signed, 1931 . . . . 90.00
Jar, Lid, Green Glaze, Gold Woman, Torch, Scrolls, 2 Handles, W. Kage, 1930, 10 In. 416.00
Jar, Seminude Woman, Green Ground, Gilt, Signed, Kage, 1930, 9 ½ In. . . . . *illus* 1320.00
Plaque, 2 Dolphins, Bubbles, Glossy Blue Glaze, Silver Inlay, Signed, Erret, 9 x 19 In. 220.00
Plaque, Blue Glossy Glaze, Silvery Inlay, Swimming Fish, Bubbles, Signed, 19 x 9 In. 230.00
Trivet, Abstract Tree, Gray, Red, Oval, 11 In. 155.00
Vase, Bouquet, Green, Silver Inlay, Round, Footed, Argenta, 9 x 8 ½ In. 275.00
Vase, Fish, Bubbles, Silver, Mottled Green Ground, Scalloped Rim, 5 In. 316.00
Vase, Geometric Leaves, Turquoise, Silver Overlay, Argenta, Marked, Sweden, 4 ¼ In. 190.00
Vase, 2 Nudes Running, Green, Silver Inlay, Cutout Base, Wilhelm Kage, 9 x 7 In. 550.00
Vase, Lion, Crowns, Turquoise, Silver Inlay, Argenta, Marked, Wilhelm Kage, 7 ¼ In. 330.00
Vase, Man & Woman On Balcony, Gilt Scroll Handles, Oval, c.1860, 22 ½ In. 800.00
Vase, Nude, Green, Silver Inlay, Footed, Handles, Argenta, 10 x 7 In. 220.00
Vase, Sterling Silver Inlaid Dragon, Green Glaze, Wilhelm Kage, c.1930, 5 ¾ In. 956.00

GUTTA-PERCHA was one of the first plastic materials. It was made from a mixture of resins from Malaysian trees. It was molded and used for daguerreotype cases, toilet articles, and picture frames in the nineteenth century.

Collar Box, Masonic, 4 ½ x 4 ¾ In. 30.00
Golf Ball, Case, c.1890 . . . . 100.00

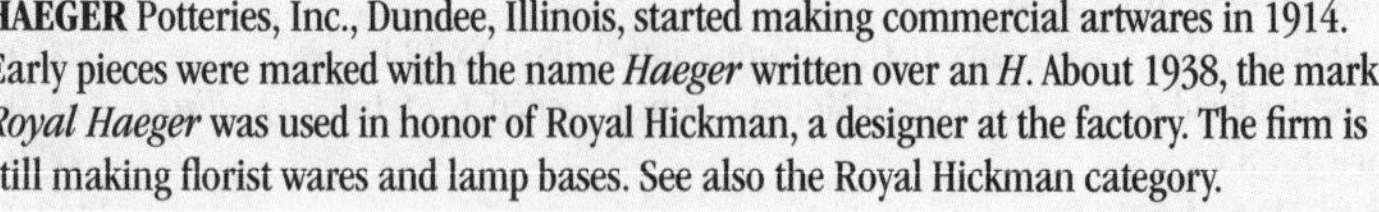

HAEGER Potteries, Inc., Dundee, Illinois, started making commercial artwares in 1914. Early pieces were marked with the name *Haeger* written over an *H*. About 1938, the mark *Royal Haeger* was used in honor of Royal Hickman, a designer at the factory. The firm is still making florist wares and lamp bases. See also the Royal Hickman category.

Candy Dish, Cover, Dotted & Spotted, 7 ¼ x 3 In. 9.00
Figurine, Bull, Charging, Sandpaper Glaze, Black Base, 7 ¾ x 14 In. . . . . *illus* 143.00
Figurine, Cat, Seated, Dark Orange, Red Luster Glaze, Marked, 1940s, 15 ½ In., Pair 385.00
Lamp, Electric, Television, Gazelle, Ebony Agate, Planter, Phi-Mar, 9 ¾ x 15 ½ In. 50.00 to 80.00
Lamp, Panther, Black, White, Royal Haeger, 18 In. 100.00
Lamp, Panther, Red, Royal Haeger, 18 In. 100.00
Vase, Aquatic, Relief, Mottled Green, 11 x 12 ½ In. 121.00
Vase, Art Deco, Earth Wrap, Marked, 1970s, 12 In. 95.00
Vase, Art Nouveau, Brown, Black, Marked, 5066, 7 ¼ x 6 ¼ In. . . . . *illus* 33.00
Vase, Bud, Orange Peel, Mottled Volcanic Glaze, 1970s, 7 x 3 In. 65.00
Vase, Classic Shape, Earth Wrap, Brown, Orange, Yellow Glaze, Mark, 1970s, 13 x 6 In. 95.00
Vase, Classic Shape, Mandarin Orange, 9 x 4 In. 85.00
Vase, Dancing Girl, Turquoise, 7 ¾ In. 27.00
Vase, Earth Wrap, Brown, Orange High Glaze, 1970s, 12 x 9 In. 95.00
Vase, Earth Wrap, Caramel High Gloss Glaze, 1970s, 11 x 5 In. 125.00

Vase, Epergne, Centerpiece, Triple Trumpet, Turquoise, Glazed, 16 x 10 In.. . . . . . 82.00
Vase, Fern Agate, Earth Wrap, Olive Green, Marked, 1970s, 8 x 8 In. 85.00
Vase, Marigold Agate, High Gloss Earth Wrap, 11 In. 100.00
Vase, Pillow, Green, Agate, 1970s, 7 ¾ In. 150.00
Vase, Sailfish, Green, Marked, 9 x 12 ½ In. 30.00
Vase, Swan, Marked, 8 ¾ In., Pair . . . . *illus* 25.00

HALF-DOLL, *see Pincushion Doll category.*

HALL CHINA Company started in East Liverpool, Ohio, in 1903. The firm made many types of wares. Collectors search for the Hall teapots made from the 1920s to the 1950s. The dinnerwares of the same period, especially Autumn Leaf pattern, are also popular. The Hall China Company is still working. For more prices, go to Kovels.com. Autumn Leaf pattern dishes are listed in their own category in this book.

HALL'S SUPERIOR QUALITY KITCHENWARE

Acacia, Creamer, 2 ½ In. . . . . . . *illus* 10.00
Bricks & Ivy, Coffeepot, Drip-O-Lator, 6 Cup 25.00
Cadet Blue, Mixing Bowl, 9 In. 19.00
Cameo Rose, Plate, Dinner, 10 In. 20.00
Gaillardia, Casserole, Cover Only, Radiance 10.00
Medallion, Mixing Bowl, Ivory, 8 ½, 7 ½, 6 In., 3 Piece. 70.00
Poppy, Custard 6.00
Poppy, Leftover, Loop Handle, No Cover, 8 x 5 ½ In. 55.00
Red Kitchenware, Salt & Pepper 14.00
Red Poppy, Egg Plate, 12 Wells, Center Handle, 10 In. 85.00
Red Poppy, Jug, No. 5. . . . . . . 30.00
Red Poppy, Pie Bird, 5 In. 75.00
Red Poppy, Salt & Pepper, Handle, Cover, Blue, 7 In. 15.00
Refrigerator Ware, General Electric, Casserole, Lid, Tab Handle 35.00
Refrigerator Ware, General Electric, Refrigerator Set, Yellow & Gray, 7 Piece. 350.00
Refrigerator Ware, Westinghouse, Baker, Open, Cadet Blue, White Interior 28.00
Refrigerator Ware, Westinghouse, Water Server, Green, Art Deco, 8 ½ In. 44.00
Rose Parade, Jug, Water, Cadet Blue, 7 ½ In. 50.00
Rose Parade, Salt & Pepper, Cork Stoppers, 4 In. . . . . . . 15.00 to 17.50
Rose White, Casserole, Cover, Round, 10 In. 38.00
Rose White, Casserole, Cover, Tab Handle, 5 ¼ x 10 In. 20.00
Rose White, Mixing Bowl, Straight Sides, 9 In. 20.00
Rose White, Salt & Pepper, Sani-Grid. 28.00
Serenade, French Baker, Fluted 14.00
Serenade, Sugar & Creamer, 8 Oz. 52.00
Springtime, Cake Plate, 9 ½ In. . . . . . . 16.00 to 24.00
Springtime, Creamer, 3 In. 7.00
Springtime, Plate, Bread & Butter, 6 In. . . . . . . 4.90 to 6.00
Springtime, Plate, Dinner, 9 In. . . . . . . 3.00 to 8.00
Springtime, Soup, Dish, 8 ½ In. . . . . . . 7.00 to 8.00
Springtime, Sugar, Cover, 4 ½ In. 8.40
Teapot, Aladdin, Black, 3 Piece Tea Strainer, Gold Mark, 6 Cup . . . . *illus* 33.00
Teapot, Aladdin, Cobalt 65.00
Teapot, Automobile, Canary 55.00
Teapot, Boston, Warm Yellow 12.00
Teapot, Donut, Chinese Red. 110.00
Teapot, French, Cadet Blue, 6 Cup 48.00
Teapot, Hook, Cadet Blue, Gold Stars, 6 Cup 10.00
Teapot, Lipton, Maroon, 4 Cup 25.00
Teapot, Melody, Chinese Red, 6 Cup . . . . *illus* 77.00
Teapot, Parade, Canary, 6 Cup 88.00
Teapot, Rhythm, Canary 86.00
Teapot, Windshield, Ivory, Gold Polka Dots, 6 Cup . . . . *illus* 44.00
Tulip, Saucer, D-Style. 6.00
Tulip, Saucer, St. Denis Shape, 6 In. 6.00
White Bakeware, Nesting Bowls, Ivory, 9, 7, 6 In., 3 Piece. 65.00
Wildfire, Cup & Saucer 15.00
Wildfire, Gravy Boat. 38.00
Wildfire, Plate, Soup, 7 In. 10.00
Wildfire, Saucer, 6 In. 4.00
Yellow Rose, Custard. 7.00
Yellow Rose, Shaker, Pepper, Handle 20.00

Haeger, Vase, Swan, Marked, 8 ¾ In., Pair
$25.00

Hall China, Acacia, Creamer, 2 ½ In.
$10.00

Hall China, Teapot, Aladdin, Black, 3 Piece Tea Strainer, Gold Mark, 6 Cup
$33.00

Hall China, Teapot, Melody, Chinese Red, 6 Cup
$77.00

Hall China, Teapot, Windshield, Ivory, Gold Polka Dots, 6 Cup
$44.00

Halloween, Boot Scraper, Witch, On Broom, Cast Iron, Albany Foundry Co., 7 x 10 ½ In.
$1610.00

Halloween, Jack-O'-Lantern, Painted, Papier-Mache, Wire Handle, 7 In.
$120.00

Halloween, Mask, Pig's Head, Painted, Pressed Paper, 9 x 9 In.
$29.00

Halloween, Toy, Squeaker, Cat, Black, Composition, Glass Eyes, Germany, 6 ½ In.
$160.00

Zeisel, Fantasy, Platter, 9 ¾ In. 23.00

HALLOWEEN is an ancient holiday that has changed in the last 200 years. The jack-o'-lantern, witches on broomsticks, and orange decorations seem to be twentieth-century creations. Collectors started to become serious about collecting Halloween-related items in the late 1970s. The papier-mache decorations, now replaced by plastic, and old costumes are in demand.

Black Cat, On Jack-O'-Lantern, Celluloid, Viscoloid, 3 ½ x 2 In. 198.00
Boot Scraper, Witch, On Broom, Cast Iron, Albany Foundry Co., 7 x 10 ½ In. .... *illus* 1610.00
Costume, Lily Munster, Mask, Hair, Yvonne DeCarlo's Silver Streak, Ben Cooper, 1964 .... 210.00
Costume, Thor, Vacuform Plastic Mask, Box, Ben Cooper, c.1966, Large 12-14 .... 348.00
Costume, Wonder Woman, Vacuform Plastic Mask, Box, Ben Cooper, c.1966, Medium 8-10 .... 173.00
Goblin, Stingy Jack, Witch, Bat, 2-Sided, Cream, Celluloid, 4 x 2 In. 275.00
Jack-O'-Lantern, Black Cat, Growling, Green Eye Paper, Molded, Painted, Pulp, 5 In. 140.00
Jack-O'-Lantern, Devil Head, Molded Papier-Mache, Painted, Germany, 1900s, 4 ½ In. 900.00
Jack-O'-Lantern, Devil Head, Papier-Mache, 4 ½ x 4 ½ In. 1035.00
Jack-O'-Lantern, Happy-Sad, 2-Sided, Celluloid, 4 x 1 ¾ In. 330.00
Jack-O'-Lantern, Moon Face, Molded Cardboard, Painted, Parade, Germany, 1890s, 4 In. 2500.00
Jack-O'-Lantern, Painted, Papier-Mache, Wire Handle, 7 In. .... *illus* 120.00
Jack-O'-Lantern, Paper Facial Insert, Papier-Mache, Painted, Wire Handle, 7 In. 132.00
Jack-O'-Lantern, Pig Nose, Molded, Painted, Papier-Mache, Muslin Inserts, 11 In. 440.00
Jack-O'-Lantern, Playing Saxophone, Display, Die Cut, Embossed, 1920s, 12 x 25 In. 690.00
Jack-O'-Lantern, Potato Head, Papier-Mache, Painted, Parade, Germany, 1890s, 5 In. 3250.00
Jack-O'-Lantern, Watermelon, Painted, Composition, Paper Inserts, 6 ½ x 3 ½ In. 475.00
Mask, Pig's Head, Painted, Pressed Paper, 9 x 9 In. .... *illus* 29.00
Mold, Chocolate, Witch, On Broom, 10 x 5 x 1 ½ In. 200.00
Pumpkin Head Man, Dressed As Chef, Red, White, Celluloid, 2 ¼ x 1 ¾ In. 625.00
Pumpkin Moon Face, Cardboard, 4 x 4 ½ In. 2875.00
Scarecrow, Yellow, Celluloid, Viscoloid, 3 x 2 In. 50.00
Toy, Black Cat, Arched Back, Red Bow, Celluloid, 4 x 3 ¼ In. 400.00
Toy, Cat, Noisemaker, Painted, Wood, Composition, 8 x 4 x 1 ½ In. 188.00
Toy, Folk Cat, Witch, Accordion, Squeaks, 10 x 6 In. 230.00
Toy, Pumpkin Head, Cloth Outfit, Holds Bells, Does Splits, Windup, 11 In. 1150.00
Toy, Roly Poly, Witch, Orange, Black, Blue, Celluloid, Viscoloid, 3 x 1 ½ In. 250.00
Toy, Squeaker, Cat, Black, Composition, Glass Eyes, Germany, 6 ½ In. .... *illus* 160.00
Toy, Squeeze, 2 Faces, Papier-Mache, Leather, 2 In. 58.00
Witch, Flying Over Crescent Moon, Die Cut, Metal, Swivels, Bell, Bracket, 20 In. 633.00
Witch, In Pumpkin, Movement, Composition, Orange, Green, Black, 26 x 36 In. 770.00

HAMPSHIRE pottery was made in Keene, New Hampshire, between 1871 and 1923. Hampshire developed a line of colored glazed wares as early as 1883, including a Royal Worcester–type pink, olive green, blue, and mahogany. Pieces are marked with the printed mark or the impressed name *Hampshire Pottery* or *J.S.T. & Co., Keene, N.H.* Many pieces were marked with city names and sold as souvenirs.

Bowl, Artichoke, Green Matte Glaze, Marked, c.1905, 3 x 4 ¾ In. 382.00
Bowl, Leaves, Green Matte Glaze, Flared, 3 x 6 In. .... *illus* 395.00
Bowl, Raised Poppy, Leaves, Green Matte Glaze, Marked, 3 x 10 In. 595.00
Ewer, Green Glaze, 9 ½ In. 395.00
Lamp, Green Glaze, Beige Paneled Shade, Electrified, 19 In. 1400.00
Lamp, Water Lilies, Green Matte Glaze, Squat, Wicker & Ivory Fabric Shade, 18 ½ x 16 In. 1320.00
Pitcher, Green Matte Glaze, Yellow Interior, Arts & Crafts, 5 x 6 In. 70.00
Vase, Blue Matte Glaze, Incised Arches, Marked, 4 ½ x 3 ¼ In. .... *illus* 175.00
Vase, Green Matte Glaze, Ruffled Rim, 11 x 6 In. 850.00
Vase, Green Matte Glaze, Squat, 3 x 6 In. 625.00
Vase, Leaves, Shouldered, Green Glaze, 9 ½ x 7 ½ In. 700.00
Vase, Mottled Green Over Blue Matte Glaze, Marked, 4 ⅜ In. 288.00
Vase, Raised Corn, Green Matte Glaze, Marked, 6 x 6 In. 625.00
Vase, Tulips, Green Glaze, Bulbous, 8 ½ x 6 ½ In. 550.00

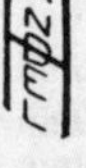

HANDEL glass was made by Philip Handel working in Meriden, Connecticut, from 1885 and in New York City from 1893 to 1933. The firm made art glass and other types of lamps. Handel shades were made not only of leaded glass in a style reminiscent of Tiffany but also of reverse painted glass. Handel also made vases and other glass objects.

Candlestick, Teroma, Windmill, Shore, F. Gubisch, 8 In., Pair 1093.00
Chandelier, Teroma, Parrot, Blue, Gold Iridescent, Tassel, Bronze, 29 In. 5750.00

Humidor, Camel, Bedouin, Osiris Symbol, Shriner Hat, Cigar On Cover, Cylindrical, 6 In. . . . 518.00
Humidor, Cover, Owl, Handelware Marked, 5 x 3 ½ In. . . . 400.00
Jar, Cover, Frog, Lily Pad, Dragonflies, Amber, Cylindrical, Signed, 8 In. . . . 748.00
Lamp, 3 Panels, Slag Glass Shade, Geometric Border, Weighted Base, 51 In. . . . 1980.00
Lamp, 3-Light, 3 Pond Lily Shades, 2 Buds, Green, White Lily Pad Base, 3 Acorn Pulls, 18 In. . 4200.00
Lamp, 6 Panels, Alternating Nudes, Columns, Fish Scale, 3-Arm Base, Art Deco, 20 In. . . . 1920.00
Lamp, 6 Panels, Bronze Overlay, Fish Scale, Slag Glass, 5 ¾ In., Pair . . . 443.00
Lamp, 6 Panels, Filigree Overlay, Oak Leaf, Pink, Butterscotch, 16 In. . . . 2875.00
Lamp, 6 Panels, Landscape, Multicolored Glass, Bronze, Signed, 15 ½ x 9 In. . . . 2000.00
Lamp, 6 Panels, Metal Overlay, Sunset Palm, Amber Slag Glass, Tree Trunk, Base, c.1910, 16 In. 2645.00
Lamp, 8 Panels, Aquarium, Bronze Candelabra Base, 21 In. . . . 7590.00
Lamp, 8 Panels, Metal Overlay, Cattail, Leaves, Yellow Slag, Bulbous Foot, 60 In. . . . 9775.00
Lamp, 8 Panels, Metal Overlay, Cattails, Caramel Slag Glass, Signed, 22 In. . . . 8775.00
Lamp, 8 Panels, Metal Overlay, Pine Needle, Caramel & Green Slag Glass, c.1915, 24 In. . . . 3231.00
Lamp, 8 Panels, Pine Trees, Poppy Base, Marked, 25 x 22 In. . . . *illus* 25200.00
Lamp, 9 Panels, Metal Overlay, Hawaiian Sunset, S-Band Border, 20 x 25 In. . . . 4025.00
Lamp, Bell Shade, 6 Panels, Brass Overlay, Slag Glass, Metal Base, Signed, 14 In. . . . 1333.00
Lamp, Bell Shade, Green, Bronze Base, 56 In. . . . 440.00
Lamp, Bridge, Opal Glass, Bronze, Cast Iron Base, 57 In. . . . 2300.00
Lamp, Chipped Ice Shade, 4 Panels, Pink Flowers, Forest Base, 14 ¼ x 7 In. . . . 1680.00
Lamp, Chipped Ice Shade, Bamboo, Cranes, Bronze Base, Signed, 24 In. . . . 10200.00
Lamp, Chipped Ice Shade, Flower Border, 6 Shaped Feet, Acorn Pulls, c.1919, 24 In. . . . 3600.00
Lamp, Chipped Ice Shade, Wooded Landscape, Bronze Base, 22 ½ x 16 In. . . . 4600.00
Lamp, Desk, Chipped Ice Shade, Persian Border, Turquoise, Green, Swivel Base, 8 In. . . . 900.00
Lamp, Desk, Green Mosserine Shade, Adjustable Base, Acorn Pull, 14 In. . . . 900.00
Lamp, Desk, Green Mosserine Shade, Leaf Border, 11 x 10 In. . . . 3480.00
Lamp, Domed Shade, Birds In Flight, Landscape, 23 ½ x 17 ¾ In. . . . 8400.00
Lamp, Domed Shade, Black Birds, Multicolored, Black Ground, 3-Scroll Base, 24 In. . . . 12650.00
Lamp, Domed Shade, Bronze Metal Base, Signed, 7 x 15 ½ In. . . . 900.00
Lamp, Domed Shade, Caramel Slag, Bell Shaped Harp, c.1910, 57 In. . . . 1422.00
Lamp, Domed Shade, Chipped Glass, Pink Roses, Copper Enameled Base, 20 x 14 In. . . . 1800.00
Lamp, Domed Shade, Chipped Ice, Grecian Ruins, Signed, 24 x 18 In. . . . 6000.00
Lamp, Domed Shade, Chipped Ice, Landscape, Signed, 15 In. . . . 2500.00
Lamp, Domed Shade, Chipped Ice, Parrots, Butterfly, Black Ground, Bronze Base, 18 In. . . . 11000.00
Lamp, Domed Shade, Chipped Ice, Stylized Roses, Pink, Green, Signed, 1923, 25 x 18 In. . . . 9800.00
Lamp, Domed Shade, Desert Scene, Nomad, Camel, Bronze Base, 3 Phoenix, 25 In. . . . 22600.00
Lamp, Domed Shade, Flowers & Butterflies, Pink, Yellow, Blue Ground, Scroll Legs, 23 In. . . . 11500.00
Lamp, Domed Shade, Harbor Scene At Sunset, Acorn Pulls, c.1915, 18 In. . . . 7475.00
Lamp, Domed Shade, Ivory, Blue Flower & Scroll Border, Ochre, Black Base, 18 x 24 In. . . . 4500.00
Lamp, Domed Shade, Jungle Bird, Bronze Baluster Base, 24 In. . . . 15813.00
Lamp, Domed Shade, Landscape In Moonlight, 18 In. . . . 7700.00
Lamp, Domed Shade, Leaded Glass, Grapes, Green Ground, Copper Base, 65 x 24 In. . . . 3600.00
Lamp, Domed Shade, Metal Overlay, Landscape, Trees, Copper Patina, Signed, 20 x 14 In. . . . 1700.00
Lamp, Domed Shade, Moonlit Harbor, Metal, c.1923, 24 x 18 In. . . . 2370.00
Lamp, Domed Shade, Moonlit Landscape, Trees, Lake, House, 24 In. . . . 5463.00
Lamp, Domed Shade, Moonlit Water Landscape, Tan & Gray, Bronze Base, 14 x 23 ½ In. . . . 3450.00
Lamp, Domed Shade, Opal Glass, Blue, Green Ground, 23 ¾ x 18 ½ In. . . . 5700.00
Lamp, Domed Shade, Parrots, Tassels, 3-Column Base, 24 In. . . . 15813.00
Lamp, Domed Shade, Ship, Ocean, Palms, Moon, Blue, Bronze Trumpet Base, 18 In. . . . 14400.00
Lamp, Domed Shade, Woodland In Moonlight, Bronze Base, c.1910, 14 x 20 In. . . . 2006.00
Lamp, Double Green Hearts, Rookwood Pottery Base, 20 In. . . . 4600.00
Lamp, Flared Shade, Caramel & White Slag Glass, Cutout Stem, Bronze Base, Chains, 21 x 28 In. 12000.00
Lamp, Geometric Shade, Greek Key Border, 26 ½ x 22 In. . . . 4500.00
Lamp, Globe Shade, Vertical Drip Design, Orange, Green, Tripod Base, 18 x 25 In. . . . 7475.00
Lamp, Hanging, 8 Panels, Metal Overlay, Tropical Scene, Bronze, Pink Ground, 19 x 12 ½ In. 7800.00
Lamp, Hanging, Curved Panels, Metal Overlay, Diamond Design, Caramel Slag Glass, 24 In. . 1500.00
Lamp, Hanging, Geometric Design, Orange & Frosted Glass Shade, Bronze Shaft, 20 In. . . . 2400.00
Lamp, Hanging, Globe, Bird, Caramel, 31 In. . . . 1300.00
Lamp, Hanging, Globe, Birds, Trees, Bronzed, Metal Fittings, c.1920, 10 In. . . . 3450.00
Lamp, Hanging, Globe, Birds In Flight, Iridescent Ground, 30 x 9 In. . . . 9200.00
Lamp, Hanging, Globe, Birds In Flight, Signed, Bedigie . . . 3738.00
Lamp, Hanging, Globe, Chipped Ice, Parrots, Leafy Branches, Tassel, 27 x 9 In. . . . 4800.00
Lamp, Hanging, Leaded Glass, Grapes, Fruit, Round, Brass Mount, Marked, 12 ½ In. . . . 1430.00
Lamp, Hanging, Schoolhouse Globe, Birds, Flowers, Iridescent Ground, 31 x 12 In. . . . 8625.00
Lamp, Hanging, Slag Glass Panels, Palm Tree, Tropical Sunset, 47 x 24 In. . . . 7200.00
Lamp, Landscape, Egyptian, Elephantine Island, Nile River, Palm Trees, Bedigie, 24 In. 5175.00 to 8625.00
Lamp, Landscape, Seagull, Billowy Clouds, Lobed Shade, Basket Weave Exterior, 15 x 23 In. . . 4200.00

Hampshire, Bowl, Leaves, Green Matte Glaze, Flared, 3 x 6 In. $395.00

Hampshire, Vase, Blue Matte Glaze, Incised Arches, Marked, 4 ½ x 3 ¼ In. $175.00

Handel, Lamp, 8 Panels, Pine Trees, Poppy Base, Marked, 25 x 22 In. $25200.00

The Drilled Hole

In the 1930s, lamps were often assembled using antique porcelain or glass pieces. Some lamps were mounted on a stand with a rod at the back that went up to hold the bulb and the shade. Others were drilled. A hole lowers the value of the antique part of a lamp. Many of these lamps have been dismantled, and the separated vases and figurines have hit the auction market with holes that lower their value.

Handel, Lamp, Leaded Glass Shade, 6 Panels, Cattails, Bronze Base, Patina, 24 ½ x 8 In.
$8400.00

Handel, Lamp, Shade, Sun Setting Over Lake, Marked, 22 ½ x 18 In.
$4100.00

Handel, Tobacco Jar, Opaline Glass, Horse & Rider, Brown, Green, Enamel, Stamped, 1890, 7 In.
$475.00

Lamp, Landscape, Trees, Mountain, Reeded Stem, Metal Spread Base, c.1917, 13 In. 960.00
Lamp, Landscape In Sunset, Cylindrical Bronze Base, 15 x 19 In. 2185.00
Lamp, Landscape In Sunset, Marsh, Trees, Lobed Metal Base, c.1924, 18 x 25 In. 4888.00
Lamp, Landscape In Sunset, River, Tall Trees, Bronze Base, c.1924, 24 x 18 In. 4025.00
Lamp, Leaded Glass Shade, 6 Panels, Cattails, Bronze Base, Patina, 24 ½ x 8 In. .... *illus* 8400.00
Lamp, Leaded Glass Shade, Flowers, Metal Base, Patina, Acorn Pulls, Signed, 23 ½ x 18 In. ... 1760.00
Lamp, Leaded Glass Shade, Metal Overlay, Lattice, Caramel Slag, Scalloped Rim, 16 x 24 In. . 1140.00
Lamp, Leaded Glass Shade, Panels, Green, Pink, 56 x 10 In. 1920.00
Lamp, Mushroom Shade, Poppy, Flared Brass Base, Art Nouveau, 21 In. 1440.00
Lamp, Piano, Pond Lily Globe, Glass & Metal Bud, Green, White, 10 x 17 In. 2400.00
Lamp, Piano, Purple Flowers, 14 In. 2250.00
Lamp, Piano, Yellow, Scroll Design, 13 ½ x 10 In. 1000.00
Lamp, Shade, Chinese Pheasant, Multicolored, Blue Ground, Column Base, Rings, 23 In. ... 27600.00
Lamp, Shade, Cone Shape, Reverse Painted, Daffodil, Green Stems, Bronze Base, 22 In. 4715.00
Lamp, Shade, Daffodils, Green Ground, Fleur De Lis Heat Cap, Bronze Urn Base, 24 In. 7705.00
Lamp, Shade, Egyptian Figures, Multicolored, Column Base, 28 ½ x 20 ½ In. 9600.00
Lamp, Shade, Green & Red Slag Glass, Bronze Frame, 6 ½ In., 4 Piece 345.00
Lamp, Shade, Green Mosserine, Adjustable Goose Neck, c.1910, 51 In. 1659.00
Lamp, Shade, Landscape, Multicolored, Bronze Base, Signed, 24 x 18 In. 7200.00
Lamp, Shade, Metal Overlay, 8-Sided, 24 Slag Glass Panels, Acorn Pull, Leaf Base, 17 x 21 In. 2588.00
Lamp, Shade, Metal Overlay, Palm Trees, Slag Glass Panels, Sunset, Forest Base, 15 x 10 In.. . 1800.00
Lamp, Shade, Metal Overlay, Slag Glass Panels, Caramel, Green, Red, 3-Footed, 60 x 14 In. .. 3120.00
Lamp, Shade, Mosserine, Chain Design, Brown, Ribbed Stem, Square Base, Signed, 14 In. ... 1150.00
Lamp, Shade, Mountains, Pine Trees, Art Nouveau Base, Signed, 7 x 12 In. 1955.00
Lamp, Shade, Pansies, Butterflies, Multicolored, Bronze Base, Signed, 14 ½ x 8 ½ In. 720.00
Lamp, Shade, Pine Tree, Yellow, Pink, Green, Scalloped Border, Bulbous Base, 25 In. 8625.00
Lamp, Shade, Sun Setting Over Lake, Marked, 22 ½ x 18 In. .... *illus* 4100.00
Lamp, Shade, Sunflowers, Multicolored, 3 Supports, Bronze Base, Signed, 65 x 27 In. 22800.00
Lamp, Student, Copper Finish, Scrolled Arms, 20 x 21 ½ In. 1920.00
Lamp, Student, Cylindrical Shade, Palm Tree, Ship, Moon, Adjustable Gooseneck Base, 14 In. 3600.00
Lamp, Student, Domed Shade, Double, Yellow, Arts & Crafts, 18 ½ x 21 In. 3250.00
Lamp, Student, Double, Glass Shades, Paneled, Bronze Base, 21 ½ x 15 In. 3600.00
Lamp, Tapered Shade, Cast Metal Candlestick Base, Patinated, 8 x 23 In. 4255.00
Lamp, Textured Shade, Autumn Leaves Border, c.1916, 18 x 26 In. 6325.00
Lamp, Textured Shade, Leaf & Vine Border, Bronze Base, Acorn Pulls, 25 x 18 In. 3738.00
Lamp, Venetian Scene, Watercolor Palette, Arts & Crafts Base, 18 x 23 In. 2243.00
Lamp, Water Landscape, Blue, Green, Bronze Base, Acorn Pulls, 15 x 23 In. 1093.00
Sconce, Geometric Shade, Green, Bronze Base, Cylindrical, Marked, 4 x 10 ½ In., Pair 2160.00
Sconce, Hanging, Cylindrical Chipped Ice Lantern, Green, Frosted, Bronze, 14 x 10 In. 1020.00
Shade, Bent Panel, Slag Glass, Rose To Dark Purple, Green, Signed, 8 x 3 ¼ In., Pair 690.00
Shade, Boudoir, Egg Shape, Pink Crackle Glass, Painted Garland, 7 In., Pair 518.00
Shade, Chipped Ice, Orange & Tan, Enameled Trees, Flared, Rolled Edge, 4 x 7 In. 390.00
Tobacco Jar, Opaline Glass, Horse & Rider, Brown, Green, Enamel, Stamped, 1890, 7 In. .. *illus* 475.00

HARDWARE, *see Architectural category.*

HARKER Pottery Company of East Liverpool, Ohio, was incorporated in 1890 in East Liverpool, Ohio. The Harker family had been making pottery in the area since 1840. The company made many types of pottery but by the Civil War was making quantities of yellowware from native clays. It also made Rockingham-type brown-glazed pottery and whiteware. The plant was moved to Chester, West Virginia, in 1931. Dinnerwares were made and sold nationally. In 1971 the company was sold to Jeannette Glass Company, and all operations ceased in 1972. For more prices, go to Kovels.com.

Alpine, Platter, 13 ½ In. 10.00
Amy, Bean Pot, Bakerite, 2 ¼ In. 7.00
Amy, Pie Server 18.00
Amy, Rolling Pin, Stopper, 13 In. 99.00
Amy, Utility Bowl 32.00
Basket Of Flowers, Plate, Dessert, Decal, 6 ⅛ In. 6.00
Basket Of Flowers, Spoon, Decal, 9 In. 18.00
Blue Basket, Creamer, 3 In. 5.00
Cameoware, Bowl, Scalloped, Blue, 9 In. 9.99
Cameoware, Saucer, Blue, 4 ½ In. 4.95
Chesterton, Cup & Saucer, Gray 8.00
Chesterton, Plate, Dinner, Celadon, 10 ¼ In. 7.50
Colonial Lady, Pie Baker, 9 In. 18.00

Compass Rose, Creamer, 4 ⅝ In. 7.00
Corinthian, Plate, Bread & Butter, Teal Green, 6 ¼ In. 3.37
Currier & Ives, Pie Lifter, 9 In. 18.00
Deco Dahlia, Cake Lifter, 9 ¼ In. 18.00
Deco Dahlia, Plate, 7 In. 6.00
Emmy, Rolling Pin, 14 ½ In. 99.00
English Ivy, Batter Jug, Lid, 7 In. 25.00
Godey, Bowl, Dessert, 6 ⅛ In. 3.00
Heritance, Dish, Vegetable, Cover, Divided, c.1940 .... 50.00
Intaglio, Sugar, Cover, Parchment Beige 13.50
Jewel Weed, Custard, 2 x 3 ⅜ In. 6.00
Laurelton, Creamer, 3 ⅛ In. 5.00
Laurelton, Cup & Saucer 5.00
Laurelton, Plate, Dinner, 10 In. 5.00
Laurelton, Salt & Pepper, 3 ¾ In. 4.00
Mallow, Rolling Pin, Stopper, 15 In. 99.00
Modern Tulip, Cake Plate, Metal Holder 13.00
Pastel Tulip, Bean Pot, Individual, 3 In. 12.00
Pate-Sur-Pate, Creamer, Teal, Applied White, Gadroon Edge 15.00
Pate-Sur-Pate, Gravy Boat, Underplate, Teal, 9 x 5 ¼ In. 22.00
Pate-Sur-Pate, Sugar, Cover, Teal .... *illus* 16.00
Persian Key, Plate, Dinner, 10 In. 8.00
Petit Point, Pie Dish, Floral, 9 In. 30.00
Petit Point, Plate, Dinner, 9 ¼ In. 9.50
Petit Point, Rolling Pin, 15 In. 45.00
Petit Point, Spoon 20.00
Pink Poppy, Pie Lifter, 9 In. 18.00
Provincial Tulip, Plate, Salad, 7 ¼ In. 4.00
Provincial Tulip, Platter, 11 ¼ x 9 ¼ In. 8.00
Quaker Maid, Creamer, Rawhide 15.00
Quaker Maid, Plate, Dinner, Rawhide, 10 In. 7.50
Red Apple, Cheese Plate, 11 In. 50.00
Sea Fare, Plate, Bread & Butter, 1950s, 6 In. 5.50
Shadow Rose, Plate, 6 ¼ In. 3.00
Shell Pink, Creamer 8.00
Spring Time, Cup & Saucer 7.00
Spring Time, Plate, Salad, 7 ¼ In. 4.00
Stone China, Plate, Dinner, Blue Mist, 10 In. 7.50
White Rose, Pie Plate, Cameo, Blue, 9 In. 22.00

HARLEQUIN dinnerware was produced by the Homer Laughlin Company from 1938 to 1964, and sold without trademark by the F. W. Woolworth Co. It has a concentric ring design like Fiesta, but the rings are separated from the rim by a plain margin. Cup handles are triangular in shape. Seven different novelty animal figurines were introduced in 1939. For more prices, go to Kovels.com.

Blue, Plate, Bread & Butter, 6 ¼ In. 4.95
Chartreuse, Bowl, Oatmeal, 36s, 6 ½ In. 20.00
Chartreuse, Cup & Saucer 20.00
Gray, Eggcup 43.00
Light Green, Bowl, Fruit, 5 ⅛ In. 40.00
Light Green, Jug, 22 Oz. 125.00
Medium Green, Cup 15.00
Medium Green, Cup, 3 In. 25.00
Red, Creamer, 1 ¼ x 2 ¼ In. 25.00
Red, Plate, Bread & Butter, 6 ¼ In. 12.00
Rose, Cup 7.00
Rose, Cup, After Dinner 65.00
Rose, Cup & Saucer 15.00
Rose, Plate, Salad, 7 In. 10.00
Rose, Sugar 25.00
Turquoise, Cup .... *illus* 7.00
Turquoise, Cup & Saucer 12.50
Turquoise, Plate, Luncheon, 9 In. 12.00
Turquoise, Plate, Salad, 7 In. 6.95
Turquoise, Sugar 5.00
Yellow, Creamer, Individual 18.00

Harker, Pate-Sur-Pate, Sugar, Cover, Teal
$16.00

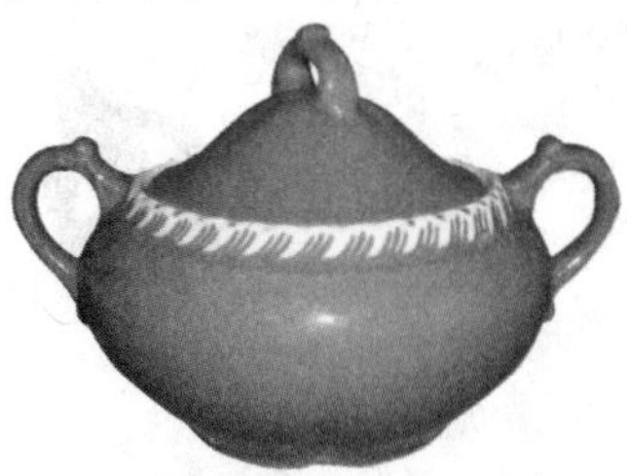

April Fool's Day

April Fool's Day probably started in 1564 in France. The New Year's celebration back then had been an eight-day celebration ending on April 1. When the Gregorian calendar was introduced, New Year's Day became January 1.
But in those days of slow communications, many country folk continued to celebrate New Year's on April 1. Those who knew about the new calendar called the others "April Fools," and the custom of playing jokes began.
The idea spread around the world and was known in the American colonies in the eighteenth century. Holiday collectibles are popular today, and Christmas, Easter, Halloween, or other holiday items of all ages sell well.
But for April Fool's Day, the only mementos seem to be postcards.

Harlequin, Turquoise, Cup
$7.00

Hatpin, Silver Bear, Hallmarked, Birmingham, England, 1909, 5 ¾ In.
$250.00

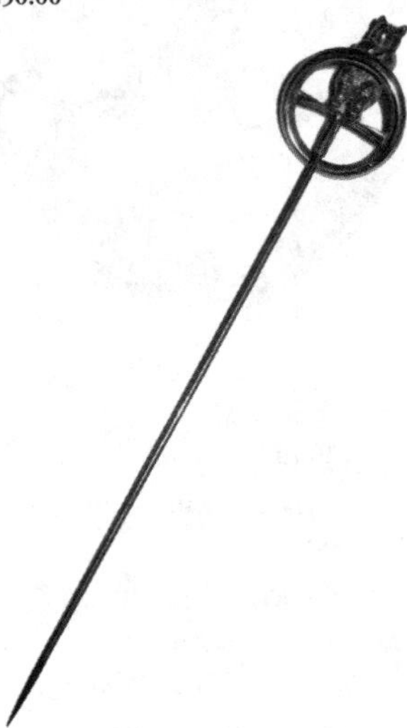

Hatpin Holder, Red Clay, Greek Key Design, Rounded Corners, Dome Top, 2 ¼ x 5 In.
$55.00

TIP

Don't use gold- or silver-decorated glasses if the trim has turned chalky gray. This is a source of lead poisoning.

Yellow, Cup 7.50
Yellow, Pitcher, Ball 50.00

HATPIN collectors search for pins popular from 1860 to 1920. The long pin, often over four inches, was used to hold the hat in place on the hair. The tops of the pins were made of all materials, from solid gold and real gemstones to ceramics and glass. Be careful to buy original hatpins and not recent pieces made by altering old buttons.

Art Deco, Bakelite, Cube Shape, Yellow, 1920s, 9 ½ In. 50.00
Art Deco, Wood, Carved, Geometric, Painted Black, Angled Shaft, 1930s. 35.00
Art Nouveau, Sterling Silver, Heart Shape, Woman's Face, Flowing Hair, Poppies, 8 In. 150.00
Bakelite, Red, Angular, 3 ½ In. 28.00
Bakelite, Red, Cube Shape, Art Deco, Brass Shank, 1930s, 9 ½ In. 50.00
Black Glass, Cabochon, c.1900, 7 In. 22.00
Bone, Carved, Brass, 3 Spheres, 7 In.. . . . . . 10.00
Copper, Melon Ribbed, Sphere Top, c.1910, 9 In. 48.00
Enamel, Hunting Dog & Fowl, Blue Ground, Brass Relief, Brass Shank, 1890s, 7 In. 138.00
Enamel, Puttin' On The Ritz, Top Hat, Cane, White Gloves, 1940s, 2 ½ In. 54.00
Gold Plate, Scroll Sides, Flat Oval Plain Shield, Brass Shank, c.1890, 8 ¾ In. 138.00
Green Glass, Shaped Cabochon, 3 ¼ In. 27.00
Green Rhinestone, Bulb Shape, Filigree, Openwork, Facet Cut, 5 ¼ In. 50.00
Rhinestone, Clear, Faceted, Brass Base, Shank, 10 ½ In. 50.00
Rhinestone, Clear, Prong Set, Openwork Diamond Shape, 11 In. 135.00
Rhinestone Cluster, Dome Shape, 1890s, 9 In.. . . . . . 50.00
Serpent, Lotus, Turquoise, Enamel, Gold Mount, Egyptian Revival, c.1905. . . . . . 593.00
Silver, Mother-Of-Pearl, Blue Enamel, Oval, c.1915, 9⁄16 In.. . . . . . 48.00
Silver Bear, Hallmarked, Birmingham, England, 1909, 5 ¾ In. . . . . . *illus* 250.00

HATPIN HOLDERS were needed when hatpins were fashionable from 1860 to 1920. The large, heavy hat required special long-shanked pins to hold it in place. The hatpin holder resembles a large saltshaker, but it often has no opening at the bottom as a shaker does. Hatpin holders were made of all types of ceramics and metal. Look for other pieces under the names of specific manufacturers.

Art Nouveau, Porcelain, Light Blue, 6 Ribs, Scalloped Base, Gold Leaf Dots, 5 In. 75.00
Carnival Glass, Grape & Cable, Amethyst, 3-Footed, Northwood, 6 ¾ In. 150.00
Celluloid, Tulip Shape, 4-Pointed Bottom, Ivaleur & Royalton, 7 ⅛ x 3 ⅛ In. 68.00
Porcelain, Blue Rising Sun, Scalloped Edge, Raised Swirl, Nippon, c.1910, 4 ¼ In.. . . . . . 125.00
Porcelain, Coat Of Arms, c.1910, 4 ½ In. 100.00
Porcelain, Forget-Me-Not, Square, Ruffled Edge, Gold Top, Bavaria, 3 ⅞ x 2 ¾ In. 100.00
Porcelain, Japanese Garden Scene, Multicolored, Nippon, 4 x 2 ¼ In. 138.00
Porcelain, Jester, Staffordshire, 6 x 3 In. 52.00
Porcelain, Painted Flowers, Raised Gold Beading, Scalloped Edge, c.1900, 4 In. 100.00
Porcelain, Painted Stylized Flowers, Relief Gold Leaves, Nippon, c.1906, 4 ¾ In. 100.00
Porcelain, Ring Tree Bottom, Apple Blossoms, Lavender, Gold Accents, Nippon, 5 x 4 In. 138.00
Porcelain, Spanish Moss, Open. 129.00
Porcelain, White, Pink Flowers, 6-Sided Base, Scalloped Rim, R.S. Prussia, 4 ⅜ In. 180.00
Porcelain, White Ground, Gold Leaf Flowers, Cobalt Blue Border, 4 ¾ In. 49.00
Porcelain, White Ground, Painted Pink & Blue Flowers, Gold Top, Bavaria 35.00
Porcelain, White Ground, Painted Rose, Signed, Royal Rudolstadt, 5 In. 105.00
Porcelain, White Ground, Pink Flower, Gold Leaf, Pedestal Base, Bavaria, 4 ¼ In.. . . . . . 129.00
Porcelain, White Ground, Stylized Multicolored Flowers, Gold Accent, 5 In. 125.00
Red Clay, Greek Key Design, Rounded Corners, Dome Top, 2 ¼ x 5 In. . . . . . *illus* 55.00

HAVILAND china has been made in Limoges, France, since 1842. The factory was started by the Haviland Brothers of New York City. Pieces are marked *H & Co.*, *Haviland & Co.*, or *Theodore Haviland*. It is possible to match existing sets of dishes through dealers who specialize in Haviland china. Other factories worked in the town of Limoges making a similar chinaware. These porcelains are listed in this book under Limoges.

HAVILAND & CO.

Berry Bowl, Pink & White Wild Roses, Gold Scalloped Rim, 5 In. 30.00
Bone Dish, Pink Roses, Gold Scalloped Rim, 6 In. 34.00
Bowl, Caroline Shape, Gold Trim, 9 ¾ In.. . . . . . 45.00
Bowl, Green Border, Gold Trim, 6 ½ x 5 ¼ In. 75.00
Bowl, Green Leaves, Gold Trim, Oval, 9 In. 110.00
Bowl, Pale Blue Flowers, Double Gold Trim, Embossed, 5 In. 36.00
Bowl, Pink Morning Glories, Ranson Shape, 5 In. 32.00
Bowl, Romeo, Double Gold Trim, Scalloped, 9 ⅜ In. 38.00

Bowl, Star Shape, 8-Sided, Gold Trim, 9 ¼ In. 56.00
Butter Chip, Gold Trim, Caroline Shape, 3 In.. .... 32.00
Butter Chip, Pink & Blue Roses, Embossed Gold Trim, 3 In., 8 Piece 140.00
Butter Chip, Violets, Scalloped Rim, 3 In. 25.00
Butter Chip, Wild Roses, Gold Trim, Scalloped Rim, 3 In. 32.00
Cake Plate, Pink Morning Glories, Ranson Shape, 11 In.. .... 118.00
Chocolate Set, Pot, 2 Demitasse Cups & Saucers, 9 ⅜ & 5 x 2 ¾ In. 225.00
Chocolate Set, White, Gold Trim, Pot, Lid, 8 Cups & Saucers, c.1900, 8 ¾ & 3 In. 599.00
Compote, White, Pedestal, Reticulated, 9 x 7 ¼ In. 240.00
Compote, White, Pink Band, Gold Trim, c.1880, 5 x 9 ¾ In.. .... 75.00
Creamer, Apple Blossoms, Gold Trim, 4 ½ In. 75.00
Creamer, Peach & Blue Flowers, Gold Trim, 5 ½ In. 78.00
Creamer, Pitcher Shape, Pink Floral, Green Leaves, Melon, Ribbed Embossed, 5 ⅛ In. 68.00
Cup & Saucer, Baltimore Rose, Scalloped Base, 2 Handles, 3 ½ x 5 ¼ In.. .... 65.00
Cup & Saucer, Cabbage Roses, Gold Trim, 4 x 5 ½ In. .... *illus* 45.00
Cup & Saucer, Demitasse, Dark Pink Flowers, Double Gold Trim, 2 ¼ x 5 In. .... *illus* 32.00
Cup & Saucer, Demitasse, Pink Roses, Princess Shape, 5 In. 55.00
Cup & Saucer, Demitasse, Romeo, Double Gold Trim, Scalloped Base, 2 ½ x 5 In.. .... 36.00
Cup & Saucer, Flowers, Pink, Yellow, White, 3 ¼ x 4 ¾ In.. .... 36.00
Cup & Saucer, Pale Green Flowers, Gold Trim, Embossed, 4 ⅜ x 6 In. 48.00
Cup & Saucer, Pink, Lavender, Yellow Flowers, 3 ½ x 5 ½ In. 36.00
Cup & Saucer, Pink & Blue Roses, Scalloped Star Shape, 3 ⅝ x 5 ⅜ In. 45.00
Cup & Saucer, Pink & Green Floral Leaf Band, 2 Handles, 5 ½ x 3 ½ In. 25.00
Cup & Saucer, Pink Apple Blossoms, Ranson Shape, 3 ½ x 5 ⅜ In.. .... 50.00
Cup & Saucer, Pink Carnations, 3 ⅜ x 5 ⅜ In. 32.00
Cup & Saucer, Pink Morning Glories, Ranson Shape, 3 ⅜ x 5 ⅜ In. 45.00
Cup & Saucer, Pink Rose Garlands, 5 ¾ In. 52.00
Cup & Saucer, Pink Roses, Gold Trim, 3 ⅜ x 5 ¼ In. 46.00
Cup & Saucer, Pink Roses, Gold Trim, 5 ¾ In. 48.00
Cup & Saucer, Romeo, Double Gold Trim, Scalloped Base, 4 x 6 In. 42.00
Cup & Saucer, Romeo Shape, Double Gold Trim, 4 ⅛ In.. .... 52.00
Cup & Saucer, Rose Clusters, Pink, Green Scrolls, 3 ½ x 5 ½ In. 48.00
Cup & Saucer, Roses, Pink, Gold Trim, Scalloped Base, 3 ¾ x 5 ⅜ In.. .... 38.00
Cup & Saucer, Scalloped, Double Gold Trim, 3 ⅝ x 5 ½ In. 50.00
Cup & Saucer, White Blossoms, 3 ⅜ x 5 ⅜ In.. .... 55.00
Cup & Saucer, Wild Roses, Green Shaded To White, 3 ¾ x 5 ¼ In.. .... 46.00
Dinner Service, Palais Oriental, Mozart Shape, Charles Field, 10 ¾ In., 36 Piece 269.00
Eggcup, Green Leaves, Gold Trim, Scalloped Base, 3 ⅝ In. 35.00
Gravy Boat, Attached Underplate, Trailing Oak Leaf, Rose Vine, 7 ½ x 3 In. 75.00
Gravy Boat, Underplate, White, Green Band, Gold Scroll Work & Trim 23.00
Ice Cream Set, Violets, Oval, Platter, 10 Plates, 15 x 8 ⅝ & 7 ¼ In., 11 Piece 340.00
Pitcher, Chocolate, Flower, Blue, Yellow, Gilt, Scalloped Rim, Base, 1880, 9 ½ x 6 In. 76.00
Pitcher, Draped Leaf, White, Embossed, 9 ¼ In.. .... 175.00
Pitcher, Pink Rose Garlands, Footed, Double Gold Trim, 4 ¼ In. 95.00
Pitcher, St. Lazare, Peach & Blue Flowers, Gold Trim, 9 In. 190.00
Place Setting, Gloria, Cup & Saucer, Dinner, Salad, Bread & Butter Plates, Bowl. 90.00
Plate, American Beauty Roses, Ranson Shape, Gold Trim, 7 ½ In. 40.00
Plate, Baltimore Rose, Scalloped Rim, 7 ½ In. .... 30.00 to 45.00
Plate, Blue Floral Spray, Scalloped Rim, 8 ½ In. .... *illus* 28.00
Plate, Blue Roses, Pink Flowers, Gold Trim, Scalloped Rim, 8 ¾ In. 40.00
Plate, Bread & Butter, Albany, Greek Key Band, 6 ⅛ In.. .... 18.00
Plate, Bread & Butter, Blue Flowers, Torse Shape, Margaux, 6 ⅜ In. 5.00
Plate, Dark Pink Flowers, Double Gold Trimmed Star, 8 ½ In. 45.00
Plate, Dinner, Pink & Yellow Roses, Gold Trim, 10 In. 45.00
Plate, Dinner, Pink Roses, Gold Trim, Scalloped Rim, 10 In. 48.00
Plate, Dinner, Pink Roses, Princess Shape, 9 ¾ In. 40.00
Plate, Dinner, Trailing Oak Leaf, Rose Vine, 9 ½ In. 35.00
Plate, Double Gold Trim, Scalloped Rim, 7 ½ In.. .... 45.00
Plate, Flowers, Pink, Yellow, White, 6 ⅛ In. 34.00
Plate, Gold Trim, Caroline Shape, 9 ¾ In. 48.00
Plate, Green Clover, Scalloped, Gold Trim, 7 ⅝ In.. .... 40.00
Plate, Green Scrolls, Pink Roses, Gold Trim, 8 ½ In. 45.00
Plate, Lavender & Pink Sprays, Double Gold Trim, 8 ⅝ In.. .... 50.00
Plate, Pale Blue Flowers, Double Gold Trim, Embossed, 8 ¾ In.. .... 46.00
Plate, Pink & White Wild Roses, Gold trim, Scalloped Rim, 9 ⅝ In. 48.00
Plate, Pink & Yellow Roses, Gold Trim, 9 In. 44.00

The Haviland Family
Pieces marked "Johann Haviland" were made in Germany from 1907 to 1924. They are not the famous French Haviland china made by Theodore Haviland Company or Haviland & Company. These are marked with variations of the name "Theodore Haviland" or "Haviland."

Haviland, Cup & Saucer, Cabbage Roses, Gold Trim, 4 x 5 ½ In.
$45.00

Haviland, Cup & Saucer, Demitasse, Dark Pink Flowers, Double Gold Trim, 2 ¼ x 5 In.
$32.00

Haviland, Plate, Blue Floral Spray, Scalloped Rim, 8 ½ In.
$28.00

Haviland, Ramekin Set, Ivy, Green, Scalloped Rim, 3 ½ x 5 ⅛ In., 2 Piece
$62.00

Hawkes, Bowl, Hobstar, Cane & Fan, 3 ½ x 8 ¾ In.
$165.00

Hawkes, Charger, Panels, Signed, 15 In.
$20190.00

Hawkes, Ginger Jar, Diamond, Amber To Clear, 3 Panels, Garland, Urns, 9 In.
$3850.00

Plate, Pink Apple Blossoms, Ranson Shape, 8 ½ In. 48.00
Plate, Pink Flowers, Gray Shadow Flowers, Gold Trim, Scalloped Rim, 8 ⅝ In. 48.00
Plate, Pink Flowers, Scalloped Rim, 8 In. 35.00
Plate, Pink Flowers, Scroll & Lattice Border, 3 ⅝ x 5 ⅜ In. 52.00
Plate, Pink Morning Glories, Ranson Shape, 6 ⅛ In. 36.00
Plate, Pink Rose Garlands, Double Gold Trim, 8 ½ In. 48.00 to 50.00
Plate, Pink Roses, 11 ½ In. 95.00
Plate, Pink Roses, Double Gold Trim, Scalloped Rim, 8 ½ In. 48.00
Plate, Pink Roses, Gold Trim, 5 In. 30.00
Plate, Pink Roses, Gold Trim, Scalloped Rim, 7 ½ In. 42.00
Plate, Pink Roses, Romeo Shape, Double Gold Trim, 9 ¾ In. 52.00
Plate, Pink To White Roses, Romeo Shape, Double Gold Trim, 9 ¾ In. 52.00
Plate, Pink To White Roses, Romeo Shape, Gold Trim, 7 ⅝ In. 45.00
Plate, Roses, Gold Trim, Scalloped Rim, 8 ⅝ In. 52.00
Plate, Roses, Pink, Green Leaves, Gold Trim, 8 ½ In. 55.00
Plate, Soup, Roses, Pink, 9 ⅛ In. 42.00
Plate, St. Germain Shape, Double Gold Trim, 6 ¼ In. 40.00
Plate, St. Germain Shape, Double Gold Trim, 8 In. 48.00
Plate, White, Gold Border, Silver Highlights, 8 ¾ In. 50.00
Plate, Wild Roses, Embossed, Scalloped Rim, 8 ½ In. 38.00
Plate, Wild Roses, Gold Trim, Star Shape, 3 ⅝ x 5 ⅜ In. 48.00
Plate, Wild Roses, Gold Trim, Star Shape, 8 ½ In. 46.00
Plate, Wild Roses, Green Shaded To White, 8 ½ In. 45.00
Plate Set, Le Tanneur Le Grand Depot, Green, Red Flowers, Gold, G. Remy, 11 In., 12 Piece 351.00
Platter, Albany, Greek Key Band, Yellow Outline In Black, 11 ¼ x 8 ½ In. 40.00
Platter, Blue Flowers, Torse Shape, Oval, 14 In. 75.00
Platter, Cake, Pink Roses, Round, Scalloped Rim, Embossed, 11 ¾ In. 110.00
Platter, Green Leaf Border, Gold Trim, Scalloped Rim, 11 ¾ In. 120.00
Platter, Lambelle, Flowers, Deep Pink To White, 16 ⅜ In. 136.00
Platter, Pink & Blue Roses, Star Shape, Scalloped Rim, 11 ½ In. 95.00
Platter, Pink Flowers, Green Leaves, Lacy Embossed Gold Trim, Scalloped Rim, 14 In. 88.00
Platter, Pink Roses, Double Gold Trim, Scalloped Rim, 12 In. 120.00
Platter, Pink Roses, Gold Trim, 12 ¾ In. 110.00
Platter, Pink Roses, Gold Trim, Scalloped Rim, 13 ¾ In. 120.00
Platter, Pink Roses, Oval, 16 In. 130.00
Platter, Pink Roses, Princess Shape, 12 ¼ In. 120.00
Platter, Pink Roses, Princess Shape, 16 ¼ In. 140.00
Platter, Rose Clusters, Pink, Embossed, Gold Trim, Scalloped Rim, 14 ⅝ In. 112.00
Platter, Roses Border, 12 In. 124.00
Platter, Tarascon, Violets, 11 ½ & 13 ½ & 17 ½ In., 3 Piece 340.00
Ramekin, Blue Flowers, Pink & White, 3 ½ x 5 ¼ In., 2 Piece 48.00
Ramekin, Gold Trim, Embossed Shape, 3 ⅝ x 5 ¼ In., 2 Piece 78.00
Ramekin, Pink & Yellow Roses, Gold Trim, 3 ½ In. 32.00
Ramekin Set, Ivy, Green, Scalloped Rim, 3 ½ x 5 ⅛ In., 2 Piece *illus* 62.00
Ramekin Set, Pale Blue Flowers, Double Gold Trim, Embossed, 3 ⅝ In., 2 Piece 58.00
Ramekin Set, Pink Roses, Princess Shape, 3 ⅝ x 5 ¼ In., 2 Piece 76.00
Relish, Pink & Yellow Roses, Gold Trim, 8 ¾ In. 80.00
Soup, Cream, Saucer, Blue & White Flowers, Gold Trim, 2 Handles, 3 ½ x 5 ½ In. 38.00
Soup, Cream, Saucer, Gold Trim, Embossed, Scalloped Rim, 2 Handles, 3 ¾ x 5 ⅜ In. 50.00
Soup, Cream, Saucer, Yellow Flowers, Ranson Shape, 2 Handles, 3 ¾ x 5 ⅜ In. 32.00
Soup, Dish, Baltimore Rose, Scalloped Rim, 7 ½ In. 55.00
Soup, Dish, Pale Blue Flowers, Double Gold Trim, Embossed, 7 ½ In. 36.00
Sugar, Pink Rose Garlands, Footed, Double Gold Trim, 5 In. 110.00
Sugar & Creamer, Pink & Blue Flowers, Gold Trim, Scalloped Rim, 2 ¼ x 4 ½ In. 110.00
Tea Set, Flowers, Blue & Brown, Gold Trim, Teapot, Cup & Saucers, Plates, Child's, 14 Piece 200.00
Teapot, Cover, Lambelle, White, Embossed, Bows, Scalloped Rim, 9 ⅝ In. 275.00
Tureen, Cover, Double Gold Trimmed Star, 10 ¼ In. 150.00
Tureen, Cover, Pink Roses, 9 ⅝ In. 124.00

HAWKES cut glass was made by T. G. Hawkes & Company of Corning, New York, founded in 1880. The firm cut glass blanks made at other glassworks until 1962. Many pieces are marked with the trademark, a trefoil ring enclosing a fleur-de-lis and two hawks. Cut glass by other manufacturers is listed under either the factory name or in the general Cut Glass category.

Bottle, Thistle, Engraved, Sterling Silver Cap, 11 ½ In. 110.00
Bowl, Centerpiece, Gladys Pattern, Pinched Neck, Flared Rim, 7 x 12 In. 1320.00
Bowl, Dragon, Engraved, Scalloped Rim, Signed, E. Palme, 3 ¾ x 9 In. 4212.00

Bowl, Garland & Medallion, Engraved, Greek Key Border, 3 ¼ x 8 In. 44.00
Bowl, Grecian Pattern Variant, Rounded Square, Scalloped Edge, 8 ¾ In. 440.00
Bowl, Hobstar, Cane & Fan, 3 ½ x 8 ¾ In. .... *illus* 165.00
Bowl, Irises, Gravic Glass, 3-Footed, 6 x 8 In. 150.00
Bowl, Kensington Pattern, 3 x 6 ¾ In. 358.00
Bowl, Lorraine Pattern, Signed, 3 ¾ x 9 In. 850.00
Bowl, Star-Petaled Flowers, Scalloped & Notched Rim, 4 ½ x 10 ¼ In. 644.00
Bowl, Whipped Cream, Hobstar & Crosscut Diamond, Signed, 2 ½ x 6 In. 60.00
Charger, Panels, Signed, 15 In. .... *illus* 20190.00
Cocktail Shaker, Sterling Silver Rim, Cap, 10 In. 234.00
Cookie Jar, Sterling Silver Cover, 5 ½ x 9 In. 300.00
Cruet, Gladys Pattern, Pattern Cut Stopper, Hobstar Base, 6 ½ In. 200.00
Cup & Saucer, Engraved Flower Garland, Signed 110.00
Decanter, Bourbon, Scotch, Stand, c.1900, 11 x 10 In., Pair 234.00
Decanter, Flute, Long Neck Handle, Signed, 14 ½ In. 100.00
Decanter, Signed, 12 ½ In. 70.00
Dish, Pedestal, Blown Mold, Hobstar Motif, Ray Base, Signed 4 x 6 ½ In. 175.00
Ginger Jar, Diamond, Amber To Clear, 3 Panels, Garland, Urns, 9 In. .... *illus* 3850.00
Goblet, Delft Diamond, Square Foot, 8 In., 8 Piece 410.00
Luster, Gladys Pattern, Bobeche, Prisms, Domed Scalloped Foot, 9 In., Pair 3575.00
Nappy, Chrysanthemum Pattern, Handle, 6 In. 138.00
Nappy, Diamond Point, Engraved Thorn & Berry Border, 5 In. 165.00
Pitcher, Juno Pattern, 7 ½ In. .... *illus* 138.00
Pitcher, Marriage, Man & Woman, Flower Wreath, Engraved, Dec. 4, 1901, 11 ½ In. 7020.00
Pitcher, Martini, Fighting Cocks, Stir Stick, Signed, 16 In. 200.00
Plate, Plum, Engraved, Gravic, 8 ½ In. 330.00
Plate, Vintage, Engraved, Gravic, 8 ½ In. 303.00
Powder Box, Cover, Florence Pattern, 3 ½ In. 200.00
Rose Bowl, Venetian Pattern, 4 ⅞ In. 196.00
Sherry, Crosscut Diamond & Fan, 4 ¼ In., 6 Piece 400.00
Sugar & Creamer, Millicent Pattern, Engraved Basket, Cornucopia Medallions 275.00
Tazza, Panels, Solid Stem, Scalloped Hobstar Base, 9 x 13 In. 4950.00
Tidbit, Flowers, Engraved, Band Border, 2 Tiers, Sterling Stem & Handle, 6 ½ x 9 In. 55.00
Tumbler, Whiskey, Brunswick Pattern, Signed, 2 ¾ In. 210.00
Vase, Bell Shape, Engraved Leaf Swag, Air Bubble Stem, Silver Foot, c.1910, 15 In. 474.00
Vase, Blue To Clear, Flowers, Engraved, Gold Rim, Signed, 10 x 9 In. 200.00
Vase, Bull's-Eye, Step Cut, Hobstar Base, Signed, 8 In. 250.00
Vase, Butterfly, Flowers & Leaves, Engraved, 7 ½ In. 615.00
Vase, Engraved Flowers & Leaves, Scalloped Rim, 9 ½ In. 695.00
Vase, Flower & Fruit, Signed, 14 ¾ In. 350.00
Vase, Flowers, Intaglio Leaves, 7 ¼ In. 690.00
Vase, Hobstar, Long Thumbprint, Ray Base, Pedestal, Signed, 9 ¾ In. 40.00
Vase, Trumpet, Brunswick Pattern, Hobstar Base, 16 In. 550.00
Wine, Russian Pattern, Clear Buttons, Faceted Stem, Rayed Base, 4 ⅝ In. 33.00

HEAD VASES, generally showing a woman from the shoulders up, were used by florists primarily in the 1950s and 1960s. Made in a variety of sizes and often decorated with imitation jewelry and other lifelike accessories, the vases were manufactured in Japan and the U.S.A. Less elaborate examples were made as early as the 1930s. Religious themes, babies, and animals are also common subjects. Other head vases are listed under manufacturers' names and can be located through the index in the back of this book.

Barbie, Blond Hair, Blue Eyes, Ceramic Arts Studio, 7 ¼ In. 22.00
Carmen Miranda, Fruit Bowl On Head, Furrowed Brow, Marti Of Hollywood, 7 ⅛ In. 45.00
Ermyn Trude, Black Hair, Yellow Hat, Dress, Betty Lou Nichols, 8 ½ In. 250.00
Indian Boy, Closed Eyes, Feathered Headdress, Inarco, 5 ½ In. 44.00
King, Curly Beard, Gold Crown, Inarco, 5 ¾ In. 77.00
Mary Lou, Black Hat, Yellow Ruffled Dress, Betty Lou Nichols, 7 ¾ In. .... *illus* 247.00
Teen, Ash Blond, Blue Hair Ribbon, Pearl Necklace & Earrings, Enesco, 5 ½ In. 55.00
Teen, Ash Blond, Pearl Earring, Yellow Bow, Napcoware, 5 ¾ In. 22.00
Teen, Ash Blond, Pigtails, Closed Eyes, Long Eyelashes, Pink Lips, Japan, 5 ½ In. 55.00
Teen, Blond Page-Boy, Pink Flower In Hair, Pearls, Nancy Pew, 5 ¾ In. 33.00
Teen, Blond Pigtails, Black Bands, Pearl Earrings, Rubens, 5 ½ In. .... *illus* 88.00
Valerie, Black Hair, Blue & White Hat, Blue Dress, Ruffle, Betty Lou Nichols, 8 In. 275.00
Woman, Ash Blond, Blue Eyes, Red Lips, Brown Fur Collar, Enesco, 6 In. 66.00
Woman, Beehive Hat, Applied Roses, Raised Arms, Pearl Necklace, Relpo, 4 ¾ In. 44.00
Woman, Black Hat, Openwork On Brim, White Bow, Black Glove Hand, Napco, 6 ½ In. 66.00

Hawkes, Pitcher, Juno Pattern, 7 ½ In.
$138.00

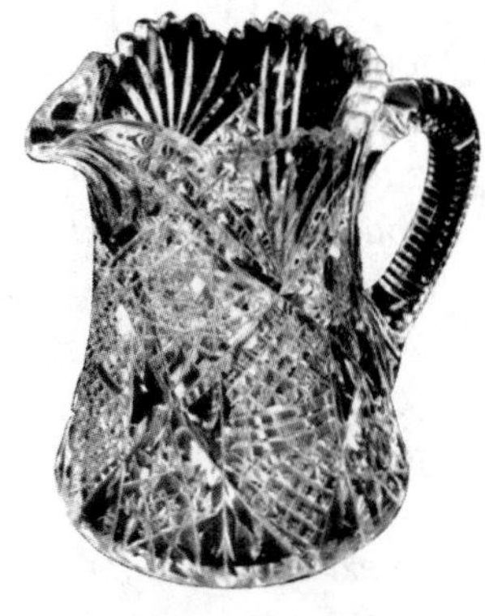

Head Vase, Mary Lou, Black Hat, Yellow Ruffled Dress, Betty Lou Nichols, 7 ¾ In.
$247.00

Head Vase, Teen, Blond Pigtails, Black Bands, Pearl Earrings, Rubens, 5 ½ In.
$88.00

TIP

Bone china is a special type of porcelain that has bone ash added to the clay. This makes a stronger, whiter porcelain.

Woman, Blond, Black Dress, Pearl Necklace, Earring, Napcoware, 6 In. 25.00
Woman, Blond, Black Hat, Blue Bow, Pearl Necklace & Earrings, Relpo, 9 ¼ In. 77.00
Woman, Blond, Brown Eyes, Hanging Pearl Earring, Ruffled Collar, Inarco, 5 In. 88.00
Woman, Blond, Eyelashes, White Scarf Around Head & Neck, Inarco, 5 ½ In. 132.00
Woman, Blond, Turquoise, Hand On Face, Eyelashes, Earrings, Necklace, Rubens, 6 In. 210.00
Woman, Blond Curls, White Open-Collar Striped Shirt, Relpo, 4 ½ In. 88.00
Woman, Blond Curly Bangs, Flower Wreath In Hair, Pearl Necklace, Napco, 5 ½ In. 33.00
Woman, Blond Streaked Hair, Green Bow, Pearl Necklace & Earring, Napco, 5 ½ In. 39.00
Woman, Bonnet Baby, Blond, Pink Cheeks, White Cap, Relpo, 6 In. 11.00
Woman, Brown Hair, Lashes, Earrings, Daisy Collar, Blue Glove Hand, Napcoware, 7 In. 127.00
Woman, Brown Updo, Lashes, Pearls, Upturned Hand, Black Ruffles, Dress, Inarco, 7 In. 204.00

HEDI SCHOOP Art Creations, North Hollywood, California, started about 1945 and was working until 1954. Schoop made ceramic figurines, lamps, planters, and tablewares.

Hedi Schoop

Bowl, Leaf Form, Yellow, Scratched Black Interior, 12 In. 66.00
Chip & Dip, Figurine, Woman, Holding Bowls, Blue, Green, White, 1962, 9 ¾ x 13 ½ In. 400.00
Figurine, Boy Playing Horn, Signed, 10 ½ In. 22.00
Figurine, Exotic Lady, Light Green & Black Dress, Gilt, Marked, 1940s, 12 ½ In. 150.00
Planter, Rooster, Green, 14 x 11 In. 44.00
Plaque, Fish, Pink, Scratched Black Design, No. 472, 8 ¼ In. 30.00

HEINTZ ART Metal Shop used the letters *HAMS* in a diamond as a mark. Otto Heintz took over the Arts & Crafts Company in Buffalo, New York, in 1903. By 1906 it had become the Heintz Art Metal Shop. It remained in business until 1930. The company made ashtrays, bookends, boxes, bowls, desk sets, vases, trophies, and smoking sets. The best-known pieces are made of copper, brass, and bronze with silver overlay. Similar pieces were made by Smith Metal Arts and were marked *Silver Crest*. Some pieces by both companies are unmarked.

HAMS

Bell, Dinner, Flowers, Applied, Sterling On Bronze, Patina, 5 ½ x 3 In. 360.00
Bookends, Applied Palm Trees, Sterling On Bronze, Patina, 5 x 3 In. .... *illus* 300.00
Bookends, Applied Sterling Leaves, Bronze, Green, Arch Shape, Impressed Mark, 5 x 5 In. 210.00
Bookmark, Nature Design, Sterling On Bronze, 5 In., 5 Piece 450.00
Bowl, Applied Leaf, Berry Design, Sterling On Bronze, Impressed Mark, 14 x 7 In. 180.00
Bowl, Applied Leaf, Berry Design, Sterling On Bronze, Silver Patina, 2 x 6 In. 150.00
Bowl, Applied Leaf Design, Sterling On Bronze, 9 x 3 In. 390.00
Bowl, Applied Organic, Sterling Silver On Bronze, Green Patina, 2 ½ x 7 In. 490.00
Bowl, Applied Organic Design, Sterling On Bronze, 3 x 9 In. 210.00
Bowl, Flowers, Leaves, Sterling On Bronze, 3 ½ x 9 In. 180.00
Bowl, Leaves, Sterling On Bronze, Flared, Impressed Mark, 9 x 3 In. 210.00
Box, Applied Design, Sterling Silver On Bronze, Green Patina, 2 x 4 In. 220.00
Box, Applied Design, Sterling Silver On Bronze, Patina, Marked, 1 x 4 In. 185.00
Box, Applied Flowers, Sterling On Bronze, Patina, Marked, 3 x 6 In. .... *illus* 480.00
Box, Bamboo, Sterling On Bronze, Impressed Mark, 11x 4 In. 360.00
Candlestick, Applied Design, Sterling Silver On Bronze, Patina, 11 x 5 In., Pair 360.00
Candlestick, Applied Grape Design, Sterling On Bronze, 4 ½ x 3 ½ In., Pair 330.00
Candlestick, Silver On Bronze, Art Nouveau, Patina, 15 In., Pair 890.00
Frame, Applied Flowers, Sterling On Bronze, Patina, Marked, 4 ¾ x 4 ¾ In. 175.00
Frame, Applied Leaves & Berries, Sterling Silver On Bronze, 5 ½ x 7 ½ In. 230.00
Humidor, Geometric Design, Sterling On Bronze, Green, Impressed Mark, 6 x 5 ½ In. 330.00
Humidor, Geometric Design, Sterling On Bronze, Impressed Mark, 6 x 5 ½ In. 390.00
Humidor, Hunting Scene, Sterling On Bronze, Patina, Marked, 6 In. .... *illus* 660.00
Humidor, Landscape, Sterling Silver On Bronze, Green Patina, 6 ½ x 5 In. 720.00
Humidor, Silver On Bronze, 6 ¼ x 4 In. 400.00
Lamp, Applied Lilies, Sterling Silver On Bronze, Cutout Shade, Mica, Patina, 12 In. 1920.00
Lamp, Flowers, Helmet Shade, Sterling On Bronze, 15 x 13 In. 1080.00
Lamp, Helmet Shade, Sterling Silver On Bronze, 9 x 13 In. 1080.00
Lamp, Poppy Design, Sterling On Bronze, Mica Shade, Green, 10 x 8 ½ In. 1800.00
Spoon, Twisted Stem, Buffalo On Tip, Sterling Silver, 1896, 2 ½ In. 60.00
Tray, Bird Dog, Silver On Bronze, Handle, 7 In. 70.00
Vase, 2 Handles, Green, Sterling Silver Grapes, Leaves Overlay, 8 In. 83.00
Vase, Applied Cattail Design, Sterling On Bronze, Green Patina, 3 x 6 In. 240.00
Vase, Applied Daffodils, Sterling On Bronze, Patina, 14 ½ In. .... *illus* 1420.00
Vase, Applied Design, Sterling Silver On Bronze, Patina, Marked, 8 x 3 In. 320.00
Vase, Applied Flower, Sterling On Bronze, Marked, Aug 27, '12, 8 In. 575.00
Vase, Applied Flowers, Sterling On Bronze, Cylindrical, Patina, Marked, 6 x 2 In. 310.00
Vase, Applied Flowers, Sterling On Bronze, Green Patina, 5 ½ x 5 In. 240.00

TIP
You can check to see if the light intensity is too strong for your antique pictures and fabrics. Take a light meter used with a camera and check the exposure values (EV) and lux. The maximum level for watercolors, paper, and other easily damaged items is 50 lux. Glass, stone, and metal is safe up to 300 lux.

Heintz, Bookends, Applied Palm Trees, Sterling On Bronze, Patina, 5 x 3 In.
$300.00

Heintz, Box, Applied Flowers, Sterling On Bronze, Patina, Marked, 3 x 6 In.
$480.00

TIP
The words "bone china" were first used as a mark on dishes about 1915.

Vase, Applied Flowers, Sterling On Bronze, Patina, Impressed Mark, 7 x 3 In. 300.00
Vase, Applied Flowers, Sterling Silver On Bronze, 11 x 3 ½ In. 86.00
Vase, Applied Flowers, Sterling Silver On Bronze, Patina, 5 x 3 In. 270.00
Vase, Applied Flowers, Sterling Silver On Bronze, Patina, Marked, 12 x 5 In. 240.00
Vase, Applied Leaf & Berry, Sterling Silver On Bronze, Patina, Flared, 4 x 3 In. 150.00
Vase, Applied Poppy Design, Sterling On Bronze, Orange Patina, 3 x 6 In. 270.00
Vase, Applied Thistle, Sterling Silver On Bronze, Marked, 8 x 3 In. 260.00
Vase, Applied Tree, Sterling Silver On Bronze, Green Patina, 12 ½ x 5 In. 960.00
Vase, Bud, Applied Design, Birds On Branches, Sterling Silver On Bronze, 4 x 11 ½ In. 345.00
Vase, Flower, Leaves, Sterling Silver On Bronze, 5 x 3 In. 235.00
Vase, Flowers, Sterling On Bronze, Impressed Mark, 3 x 4 ½ In. 150.00
Vase, Grapevine, Sterling On Bronze, Patina, Stamped, 7 ¾ In. 225.00
Vase, Trees, Sterling Silver On Bronze, Patina, Marked, 3 ½ x 2 ½ In. 465.00

HEISEY glass was made from 1896 to 1957 in Newark, Ohio, by A. H. Heisey and Co., Inc. The Imperial Glass Company of Bellaire, Ohio, bought some of the molds and the rights to the trademark. Some Heisey patterns have been made by Imperial since 1960. After 1968, they stopped using the *H* trademark. Heisey used romantic names for colors, such as Sahara. Do not confuse color and pattern names. The Custard Glass and Ruby Glass categories may also include some Heisey pieces.

African, Goblet, Clear Bowl, Moongleam Stem & Foot 50.00
African, Goblet, Flamingo, 8 ¼ In. 40.00
Albermarle, Wine, 2 Oz. 55.00
Animal, Bull 750.00
Animal, Clydesdale horse 160.00
Animal, Donkey 70.00
Animal, Elephant, Amber 2300.00
Animal, Flying Mare 2300.00
Animal, Giraffe, Head Looking Back 160.00
Animal, Hen 320.00
Animal, Piglet, Seated 110.00
Animal, Rooster .... 250.00 to 270.00
Animal, Sow 425.00
Animal, Sparrow 35.00
Animal, Swan 260.00
Aristocrat, Candlestick, 7 In., Pair 35.00
Aristocrat, Lamp, Metal Spider Web, Satin Shade, 9 In. 700.00
Athena, Candlestick, 2-Light 15.00
Athena, Relish, Sections 5.00
Banded Picket, Basket, Hawthorne, 7 ½ In. 300.00
Beaded Panel & Sunburst, Creamer 15.00
Beaded Panel & Sunburst, Spooner 5.00
Beaded Swag, Spooner, Gold Trim, Green Bands 15.00
Beaded Swag, Sugar, Cover, Enameled, Opal .... *illus* 85.00
Beaded Swag, Tumbler, Opal, Enameled Cornflower 13.00
Beaded Swag, Wine, Ruby Stain, Engraved Mother 1902 .... 10.00
Beehive, Plate, Moongleam, 5 In. 8.00
Bethal, Cigarette Holder 15.00
Bonnet, Basket, 9 In. .... 150.00 to 170.00
Bookends, Doe Head 325.00
Bookends, Horse Head 80.00
Bookends, Rearing Horse, 8 ¾ In. 44.00
Cascade, Candlestick, 3-Light 10.00
Cathedral, Vase, Alexandrite, 8 In. 1050.00
Cathedral, Vase, Antarctic Etch, 8 In. 250.00
Cathedral, Vase, Flamingo, 8 In. 525.00
Cathedral, Vase, Moongleam, 8 In. 750.00
Cherub, Candlestick 450.00
Coarse Rib, Plate, 11 In. 10.00
Cobel, Cocktail Shaker, Tally Ho Etch, Qt. 85.00
Colonial, Basket, Round, 7 In. .... 65.00 to 100.00
Colonial, Bottle, Water, Scalloped Rim 15.00
Colonial, Butter, Cupped, Scalloped 20.00
Colonial, Cruet, Clear 30.00
Colonial, Toothpick Tray 65.00
Continental, Bottle, Water, Flamingo 175.00

Heintz, Humidor, Hunting Scene, Sterling On Bronze, Patina, Marked, 6 In. **$660.00**

Heintz, Vase, Applied Daffodils, Sterling On Bronze, Patina, 14 ½ In. **$1420.00**

TIP

You can use an empty vase as a bookend if you weight it. Put a resealable plastic bag in the vase. Fill the bag with sand, then seal it. The vase should be about half full. This is also a good way to keep a vase with an irregular base from tipping.

Heisey, Beaded Swag, Sugar, Cover, Enameled, Opal
$85.00

Heisey, Crystolite, Cigarette Holder
$18.00

Heisey, Double Rib & Panel, Basket, Flamingo, 6 In.
$235.00

Country Club, Tumbler, Soda, 10 Oz. 10.00
Coventry, Goblet, Zircon, 7 In. 100.00
Creole, Champagne, 7 Oz. 75.00
Creole, Tumbler, Soda, Alexandrite, Footed, 12 Oz. 70.00
Crystolite, Bowl, Floral, 12 ½ In. 20.00
Crystolite, Bowl, Floral, Oval, 13 In. 45.00
Crystolite, Bowl, Gardenia, Square, 10 In. 30.00
Crystolite, Candleblock, Pair. 10.00
Crystolite, Candlestick, 3-Light, Pair 25.00
Crystolite, Candy Dish 10.00
Crystolite, Cigarette Holder *illus* 18.00
Crystolite, Lamp, Hurricane 55.00
Crystolite, Relish, 3 Sections, 9 ¾ In. 35.00
Crystolite, Relish, 5 Sections, Round, 10 In. 40.00
Crystolite, Torte Plate, 11 In. 35.00
Crystolite, Tray, Oval 25.00
Diamond Point, Bowl, 2 ⅝ In. 16.00
Dolphin, Candlestick, Amber. 675.00
Double Rib & Panel, Basket, Flamingo, 6 In. *illus* 235.00
Double Rib & Panel, Basket, Hawthorne, 6 In. 300.00
Double Rib & Panel, Basket, Moongleam, 6 In. 110.00
Emogene, Vase, Bud, Moongleam, 9 In. 130.00
Empress, Bonbon, Sahara, 6 ½ In. 15.00
Empress, Bowl, 3 Dolphin Feet, Camellia Etch, 11 In. 110.00
Empress, Bowl, 3 Dolphin Feet, Minuet Etch, 11 In. 110.00
Empress, Candlestick, 3 Dolphin Feet, Sahara, Pair 125.00
Empress, Celery Dish, Sahara, 10 In. 25.00
Empress, Mustard, Moongleam, 3 ¾ x 2 ¼ In. 75.00
Empress, Nappy, Flamingo, 8 In. 15.00
Empress, Nappy, Moongleam, 8 In. 35.00
Empress, Plate, Alexandrite, Square, 7 In. 100.00
Empress, Plate, Arctic Etch, Footed, 9 In. 35.00
Empress, Plate, Moongleam, 10 ½ In. 35.00 to 40.00
Empress, Plate, Moongleam, 12 In. 55.00
Empress, Plate, Sportsman Etch, 8 ¼ In., 8 Piece 150.00
Empress, Plate, Tangerine, Square, 6 In. 45.00
Empress, Platter, Flamingo, Oval, 14 In. 35.00
Empress, Relish, Triplex, Silver Overlay, 10 In. 23.00
Empress, Sandwich Server, Center Handle, Fuchsia Cutting. 35.00
Empress, Sugar & Creamer, Sahara 90.00
Fancy Loop, Cruet 25.00
Fancy Loop, Nappy, Crimped Edge, 9 ½ In. 20.00
Fancy Loop, Rose Bowl, 7 In. 80.00
Fancy Loop, Toothpick 25.00
Fancy Loop, Toothpick, Emerald Green 30.00
Fandango, Bowl, Footed, 9 In. 70.00
Fandango, Cake Basket, Gold Trim, Footed 80.00
Fandango, Celery Dish, 11 In. 30.00
Fandango, Dish, Jelly, Footed, 4 In. 55.00
Fandango, Dish, Jelly, Handle 15.00
Fandango, Nappy, 3-Sided, 9 In. 40.00
Fandango, Nappy, Crimped Edge, 9 In. 20.00
Fandango, Nappy, Ruffled Edge, 7 In. 10.00
Fandango, Sugar & Creamer, Pair 35.00
Fandango, Toothpick. 13.00
Fern, Candlestick, 2-Light, Poppy Etch, Pair. 195.00
Fern, Plate, 8 In. 25.00
Fern, Plate, Etched, 8 In. 50.00
Fern, Sugar & Creamer, Etched, Clear. 75.00
Flamingo, Spoon 45.00
Flat Panel, Bowl, Floral, Moongleam, Octagonal, 12 In. 35.00
Four Leaf, Candlestick, Pair 30.00
Frog, Cheese Plate, Flamingo 65.00
Gallagher, Pitcher, Diamond Optic, Moongleam 135.00
Gascony, Tumbler, Tangerine Bowl, Clear Foot 100.00
Greek Key, Cruet, 4 Oz. 55.00
Greek Key, Ice Tub, Underplate. 65.00

Greek Key, Sherbet, Straight Sides 5.00
Groove & Slash, Cruet, Stopper, 6 In. 55.00
Groove & Slash, Rose Bowl, 4 In. 130.00
Hartman, Claret, 5 Oz. 25.00
Helmet, Basket, Flamingo, 10 ½ In. 275.00
Herringbone, Bowl, Cereal, Clear, 7 ½ In., 4 Piece 10.00
Hexagon, Basket, Etched, 8 In. 85.00
Hi Lo, Vase, Cobalt Blue, 8 In. 300.00
Hi Lo, Vase, Flamingo, 8 In. 350.00
Ipswich, Candy Dish, Cover, 9 ½ In. 80.00
Ipswich, Tumbler, Juice, 3 ⅜ In. 15.00
Ipswich, Tumbler, Juice, Footed, 4 ⅝ In. 20.00
Jamestown, Cordial, 1 Oz. 5.00
Jamestown, Parfait, Narcissus Cutting, 5 Oz. 110.00
Janice, Vase, Flamingo 45.00
Joyce, Vase, Footed, Hawthorne, 9 ¼ In. 65.00
Kalonyal, Compote 25.00
Kalonyal, Dish, Jelly, Footed, 5 In. 30.00
Kimberly, Cordial, Zircon, 3 ⅞ In. 250.00
Lariat, Candlestick, Pair 10.00
Lariat, Dish, Mayonaisse, Underplate, Ladle . . . . . *illus* 44.00
Lariat, Punch Set, 14-In. Bowl, Cups, 19-In. Underplate, Ladle, 15 Piece . . . . . 165.00 to 225.00
Lariat, Relish, 3 Sections, 10 In. 20.00
Lariat, Sugar & Creamer 35.00
Lariat, Torte Plate, 14 In. 45.00
Locket On Chain, Compote 35.00
Locket On Chain, Wine 10.00
Lokay, Basket, Etched, 8 In. 165.00
Marlboro, Candlestick, 9 In. 25.00
Marshall, Decanter, Moonglo Cutting, Pt. 50.00
McGrady, Syrup, Flamingo, 7 Oz. 45.00
McGrady, Syrup, Sahara, 7 Oz. . . . . . 35.00 to 65.00
Narrow Flute, Cruet 5.00
Narrow Flute, Mustard, Cover 30.00
Narrow Flute, Nappy, 7 ½ In. 10.00
Narrow Flute, Nappy, 8 In. 10.00
Narrow Flute, Nappy, Flared, 9 ½ In. 25.00
Narrow Flute, Nappy, Shallow, 10 In. 25.00
New Era, Cordial 5.00
New Era, Plate, 9 In. 20.00
Newton, Tumbler, Soda, Sahara, 12 Oz. 15.00
Oak Leaf, Coaster, Flamingo 13.00
Octagon, Basket, Moongleam, 3 In. 185.00
Octagon, Bonbon, Flamingo 15.00
Octagon, Candlestick, 7 In., Pair 50.00
Octagon, Dish, Mayonnaise, Hawthorne 10.00
Octagon, Nut Dish, Hawthorne 15.00
Octagon, Nut Dish, Moongleam 20.00
Octagon, Rum Pot, Ribbed 350.00
Octagon, Tray, Arctic Etch, Handle 35.00
Old Colony, Dish, Pickle & Olive, Sahara, Sections, 13 In. 62.00
Old Sandwich, Cruet, Oil, Sahara 35.00
Old Sandwich, Sherbet 1.00
Old Williamsburg, Relish, 5 Sections, 13 In. 25.00
Orchid Etch, Bowl, Floral, 12 In. 65.00
Orchid Etch, Bowl, Gardenia, Waverly, 13 x 3 In. 50.00
Orchid Etch, Bowl, Lily, Queen Anne, 7 In. 50.00
Orchid Etch, Candlestick, 2-Light, Trident 45.00
Orchid Etch, Cheese & Cracker Set, Queen Anne, 12-In. Plate, 2 Piece 120.00
Orchid Etch, Cocktail Shaker, Sterling Silver Base, 1 Qt. . . . . . *illus* 270.00
Orchid Etch, Cruet, Stopper . . . . . 55.00 to 60.00
Orchid Etch, Dish, Jelly, Flared, Footed, 7 In. 32.00
Orchid Etch, Dish, Jelly, Queen Anne, Loop Handles, 4-Footed, 6 In. 35.00
Orchid Etch, Dish, Mayonnaise, Sections, Tab Handles, Oval, 6 ½ In. 60.00
Orchid Etch, Pitcher, 73 Oz. 275.00
Orchid Etch, Plate, Cabaret, Waverly, Turned Up Edge, 14 In. 40.00
Orchid Etch, Platter, Etched, 13 In. 30.00

Heisey, Lariat, Dish, Mayonnaise, Underplate, Ladle
$44.00

Heisey, Orchid Etch, Cocktail Shaker, Sterling Silver Base, 1 Qt.
$270.00

TIP

When moving, wrap dishes in bubble wrap and pack on edge. If you have no bubble wrap, put each dish in a plastic bag to keep it clean, then wrap in newspaper and pack on edge. Put about three inches of crumpled paper on the bottom of the carton.

Heisey, Pineapple & Fan, Tumbler, Emerald Green, Gold Trim
$115.00

Heisey, Pleat & Panel, Compote, Cover, Pink, 8 In.
$95.00

Heisey, Punty Band, Salt & Pepper, Souvenir
$120.00

TIP
If your stainless steel knife blades stain in a dishwasher, rinse them, then dry or clean them with silver polish.

Orchid Etch, Sauce, Queen Anne, 3-Footed, 7 ½ In. 45.00
Orchid Etch, Torte Plate, Waverly, 10 In. 15.00
Orchid Etch, Tumbler, Juice, Tyrolean, Footed, 5 Oz. 25.00
Patio, Tumbler, Sultana, Footed 130.00
Patrician, Candelabrum, 2-Light, 16 In. 45.00
Patrician, Candlestick, 5 In. 30.00
Patrician, Candlestick, Toy, 5 In. 10.00
Peerless, Vase, Orchid, 6 In.. 15.00
Peerless, Vase, Swing, 14 In. 30.00
Peerless, Vase, Swing, 17 In. 30.00
Petal, Sugar & Creamer, Flamingo 30.00
Petal, Sugar & Creamer, Moongleam 30.00
Picket, Basket, Etched, 8 In.. 85.00
Pillows, Mustard 5.00
Pillows, Rose Bowl, Footed 35.00
Pineapple & Fan, Cake Plate, Footed 20.00
Pineapple & Fan, Sugar & Creamer 5.00
Pineapple & Fan, Tankard, Opal 15.00
Pineapple & Fan, Tankard, Petoskey, ½ Pt. 5.00
Pineapple & Fan, Toothpick, Emerald. 20.00
Pineapple & Fan, Tumbler, Emerald, Gold Trim *illus* 115.00
Pineapple & Fan, Vase, 12 In.. 35.00
Pinwheel & Fan, Bowl, 8 ¾ In.. 10.00
Pinwheel & Fan, Bowl, Vaseline, 8 ¾ In. 1650.00
Pinwheel & Fan, Powder Box 5.00
Plantation, Bowl, 8 In. 30.00
Plantation, Bowl, Fruit, Crimped Edge, 9 ½ In.. 20.00
Plantation, Candleblock, Pair 95.00
Plantation, Cocktail, 3 Oz. 13.00
Plantation, Compote, 7 In.. 40.00
Plantation, Dish, Mayonnaise, Underplate 30.00
Plantation, Marmalade, Cover 65.00
Plantation, Platter, Ivy Etched, 14 In. 20.00
Plantation, Relish, 5 Sections, Oval 45.00
Plantation, Salt & Pepper 25.00
Plantation, Sandwich Server, 14 In.. 20.00
Plantation, Tumbler, Iced Tea, 12 Oz. 10.00
Plantation, Vase, Footed, 9 In. 175.00
Pleat & Panel, Compote, Cover, Pink, 8 In. *illus* 95.00
Pleat & Panel, Cruet, Oil, Amber 675.00
Pleat & Panel, Cruet, Oil, Moongleam 35.00
Prince Of Wales, Toothpick 45.00
Prince Of Wales Plumes, Punch Bowl Base, 5 ¼ x 6 In. 200.00
Prison Stripe, Toothpick. 18.00
Provincial, Candlestick, 2-Light 20.00
Provincial, Candlestick, 3-Light 10.00
Punty & Diamond Point, Biscuit Jar, Cover 190.00
Punty & Diamond Point, Bottle, Mucilage, Sterling Silver Top 110.00
Punty & Diamond Point, Cologne, Sterling Silver Top 50.00
Punty & Diamond Point, Cruet 25.00
Punty Band, Salt & Pepper, Souvenir *illus* 120.00
Puritan, Candlestick, Pair 10.00
Puritan, Cocktail, 3 Oz. 20.00
Puritan, Compote, 7 In.. 35.00
Puritan, Compote, 9 ½ In.. 35.00
Puritan, Cruet, Stopper, 4 Oz. 15.00
Puritan, Dish, Jelly, Footed, 5 In.. 15.00
Puritan, Tankard, Qt.. 60.00
Queen Anne, Bowl, Floral, Barcelona Cutting, 12 In. 30.00
Queen Anne, Dish, Lemon, Farber Metal Holder 10.00
Queen Anne, Pitcher, Ice Lip, 80 Oz. 30.00
Queen Anne, Torte Plate, Orchid Etch, 10 In. 30.00
Recessed Panel, Basket, 7 In. 30.00
Recessed Panel, Candy Jar, Cover, 9 In. 10.00
Recessed Panel, Candy Jar, Cover, 13 In. 80.00
Recessed Panel, Candy Jar, Cover, Emerald Green, 9 In. 950.00
Revere, Cracker Tray, 10 In. 15.00

Revere, Dish, Spice, 2 Handles, 7 In. 10.00
Revere, Sauceboat, Underplate, French Dressing, Moongleam *illus* 125.00
Ridgeleigh, Bowl, Centerpiece, 8 In. 25.00
Ridgeleigh, Bowl, Floral, Swan Handles 140.00
Ridgeleigh, Bowl, Fruit, 12 In. 5.00
Ridgeleigh, Candleholder, 3 In., Pair 15.00
Ridgeleigh, Candlestick, 2 In., Pair 60.00
Ridgeleigh, Celery Dish, 12 In. 20.00 to 35.00
Ridgeleigh, Coaster 12.00
Ridgeleigh, Coaster, Sahara 8.00
Ridgeleigh, Plate, 6 In. 7.00
Ridgeleigh, Sandwich Server, 13 ½ In. 15.00
Rococo, Relish, 5 Sections, Footed 8.00
Rooster, Strainer, Stopper 25.00
Rose Etch, Bowl, Waverly, Seahorse, Footed, 11 In. 30.00
Rose Etch, Sandwich Server, Center Handle, Waverly 50.00
Rose Etch, Torte Plate, Waverly, 13 ½ In. 15.00
Saturn, Mustard, Paddle 30.00
Saturn, Vase, 7 ½ In. 35.00
Sheffield, Candlestick, 9 In., Pair 210.00
Spanish, Champagne, Cobalt Blue Bowl, Clear Stein & Foot, 6 Oz. 90.00
Stanhope, Tumbler, Footed, Etched, 5 In. 10.00
Suez, Cocktail, Midwest Cutting, 3 Oz. 25.00
Suez, Cordial, Peachtree Cutting, 1 Oz. 55.00
Suez, Goblet, Clear Bowl, Sultana Stem 250.00
Sunburst, Bowl, Clear, 7 ½ In. 5.00
Sunburst, Butter, Cover 20.00
Sunburst, Dish, Jelly, Footed, 5 In. 30.00
Sunburst, Nappy, 5 In. 8.00
Sunburst, Toothpick 50.00
Sunflower, Bowl, Flared, 12 ½ In. 25.00
Sunflower, Candlestick, 3 ½ In., Pair 15.00
Sunflower, Candy Dish, Cover 35.00
Sunflower, Torte Plate, 14 In. 15.00
Sunflower, Tumbler 15.00
Sussex, Goblet, Moongleam Bowl, Clear Stem & Foot 35.00 to 49.00
Sussex, Wine, Moongleam 20.00
Swan, Bowl, Floral, Flower Frog, Sahara 110.00
Swan, Candlestick, Moongleam, 6 ½ In. 250.00
Swan, Candlestick, Sahara, 6 ½ In. 90.00
Symphone, Goblet, Minuet Etch 30.00
Tricorn, Candlestick, 3-Light 20.00
Trident, Candlestick, 2-Light, Pair 23.00
Triplex, Candlestick, 3-Light, Pair 80.00
Trojan, Goblet, 8 ½ In. 10.00
Tudor, Creamer, Moongleam 45.00
Tudor, Oyster Cocktail, 4 Oz. 5.00
Tudor, Sugar Dispenser 55.00
Tulip, Vase, Sahara, 9 In. 155.00
Twist, Bowl, Floral, Alexandrite, 12 In. 500.00
Twist, Bowl, Floral, Moongleam, 9 In. 55.00
Twist, Bowl, Nasturtium, Marigold 110.00
Twist, Celery Dish, Flamingo, 12 In. 5.00
Twist, Compote, Flamingo, 7 In. 135.00
Twist, Cruet, Oil & Vinegar 10.00
Twist, Cruet, Oil & Vinegar, Flamingo 45.00
Twist, Cruet, Oil & Vinegar, Moongleam 55.00
Twist, Cruet, Oil & Vinegar, Sahara 35.00
Twist, Goblet, Marigold, 7 In. 23.00
Twist, Mustard, Cover 45.00
Twist, Nappy, Moongleam, 4 ½ In. 35.00
Twist, Relish, Flamingo, 10 In. 20.00
Twist, Underplate, 4 In. 23.00
Verlys, Bowl, Seagulls & Fish, 13 ½ In. 60.00
Victorian, Cigarette Box, Cover, 6 In. 25.00
Victorian, Goblet, 1 Ball Stem, 9 Oz. 20.00
Victorian, Plate, Luncheon, 7 ½ In., 8 Piece 20.00

TIP
Remove stains from dishes with hydrogen peroxide or bicarbonate of soda, not with bleach, which was the suggested way years ago. The bleach may damage the finish.

Heisey, Revere, Sauceboat, Underplate, French Dressing, Moongleam
$125.00

Heisey, Warwick, Vase, Cobalt Blue, 7 ¼ In., Pair
$330.00

TIP
A ground-glass perfume bottle stopper should be turned gently to the right for a snug fit. To remove the stopper, first turn it to the left to "unlock it" before pulling it out.

Heisey, Yeoman, Puff Box, Flamingo, 3 ¾ x 4 In.
$95.00

TIP

Microcrystalline waxes, like Quake Wax or Quake Hold or the wax used by dentists to keep braces from hurting, are good to stick ceramics and glass on shelves, but don't use them on soft unglazed ceramics like Indian pots. They may leave an oil stain.

Heubach, Vase, Portrait, Art Nouveau, Blue, Gilt, 7 In.
$250.00

Victorian, Tumbler, Juice, 4 In. 6.00
Wabash, Goblet, Hawthorne, 5 ½ In. 15.00
Wabash, Wine, Hawthorne, 4 ¾ In.. . . . . 5.00
Warwick, Vase, 5 In.. . . . . 18.00
Warwick, Vase, 5 In., Pair 20.00
Warwick, Vase, 8 ½ In.. . . . . 43.00
Warwick, Vase, Cobalt Blue, 7 ¼ In., Pair. . . . . *illus* 330.00
Warwick, Vase, Sahara, 7 In.. . . . . 60.00
Waverly, Bowl, Crimped Edge, 12 In. 45.00
Waverly, Bowl, Floral, 12 ½ In. 25.00
Waverly, Candlestick, Epergnette, 5 In.. . . . . 5.00
Waverly, Cigarette Jar, Cover, Engraved, Monogram 25.00
Waverly, Compote, 6 In.. . . . . 20.00
Waverly, Cruet, Clear 45.00
Waverly, Dish, Mayonnaise, Oval, Sections, Handle, 6 ½ In.. . . . . 20.00
Waverly, Relish, 3 Sections, Oval. 10.00
Waverly, Torte Plate, 13 In. 10.00
Waverly, Torte Plate, Rolled Edge, 14 In. 35.00
Whaley, Beer Mug, Fox Chase Etch 55.00
Whaley, Pretzel Jar, Drinking Scene Etch 28.00
Whirlpool, Candleblock, Pair 25.00
Wide Flat Panel, Lavender Jar, 2 ½ Oz. 70.00
Winchester, Tumbler, 6 ¾ In. 30.00
Winged Scroll, Ashtray, Ivorina Verde 95.00
Winged Scroll, Cigarette Holder, Emerald Green 135.00
Winged Scroll, Match Holder, Ivorina Verde 75.00
Winged Scroll, Pitcher, Tankard, Emerald Green, Gold Trim. 200.00
Yeoman, Bonbon, Flamingo, Bowtie, Handle, 5 In. 20.00
Yeoman, Bowl, Oval, Hawthorne, 9 In. 25.00
Yeoman, Casserole, Flamingo 25.00
Yeoman, Compote, Flamingo 6.00
Yeoman, Compote, Hawthorne 15.00
Yeoman, Cup & Saucer, Hawthorne 13.00
Yeoman, Plate, Hawthorne, Acorn & Leaves, 2 Piece 13.00
Yeoman, Puff Box, Flamingo, 3 ¾ x 4 In. . . . . . *illus* 95.00
Yeoman, Relish, Moongleam, 3 Sections, 13 In. 78.00
Yeoman, Soup, Dish, Flat Rim, 9 In.. . . . . 40.00
Yeoman, Sugar & Creamer 20.00

HEREND, *see Fischer category.*

HEUBACH is the collector's name for Gebruder Heubach, a firm working in Lichten, Germany, from 1840 to 1925. It is best known for bisque dolls and doll heads, the principal products. The company also manufactured bisque figurines, including piano babies, beginning in the 1880s, and glazed figurines in the 1900s. Piano Babies are listed in their own category. Dolls are included in the Doll category under Gebruder Heubach and Heubach. Another factory, Ernst Heubach, working in Koppelsdorf, Germany, also made porcelain and dolls. These will also be found in the Doll category under Heubach Koppelsdorf.

Figurine, 2 Black Boys, Standing Against Fence, Telling A Secret, 6 In. 250.00
Figurine, Dancing Girl, Blond, Flower Dress, Bisque, Gilt, Marked, 12 In.. . . . . 165.00
Figurine, Dog, Seated Upright, Shaggy, White, Incised Mark, c.1900, 6 In. 110.00
Figurine, Man, Playing Lute, Bisque, Gilt, Marked, 13 In.. . . . . 195.00
Figurine, Putti, Playing Flute, Bird, 7 x 4 ½ In.. . . . . 121.00
Plaque, Konigin Louise, Queen Louise, Signed, Stamped, Gilt Frame, 6 x 4 ⅜ In.. . . . . 748.00
Vase, Portrait, Art Nouveau, Blue, Gilt, 7 In. . . . . . *illus* 250.00

HIGBEE glass was made by the J. B. Higbee Company of Bridgeville, Pennsylvania, about 1900. Tablewares were made and it is possible to assemble a full set of dishes and goblets in some Higbee patterns. Most of the glass was clear, not colored. Additional pieces may be found in the Pressed Glass category by pattern name.

Bowl, Alfa, Scalloped Edge, 2 x 6 ½ In. 30.00
Bowl, Feathered Medallion, 3 ¾ x 8 ¾ In. 30.00
Bowl, Rosette & Palms, 10 In. 25.00
Cake Plate, Arrowhead-In-Oval, Madora, 10 ¼ x 10 ¼ In. 30.00
Compote, Fortuna, 6 ¾ x 8 In. 30.00
Cruet, Twin Teardrop, Stopper, 6 x 3 In. 35.00

Pitcher, Owl, 7 ¼ In. 192.00
Pitcher, Owl, Opaque White, Faceted Eyes, 1890s, 7 ¼ In. *illus* 135.00
Spooner, Toy, Menagerie Fish, Blue, 1890s, 3 ½ In. *illus* 283.00
Toothpick, Hawaiian Lei, Clear 13.00
Tray, Condiment, Alfa, 3-Footed, 1 ¾ x 6 ½ In. 30.00

HISTORIC BLUE, *see factory names, such as Adams, Ridgway, and Staffordshire.*

HOBNAIL glass is a style of glass with bumps all over. Dozens of hobnail patterns and variants have been made. Clear, colored, and opalescent hobnail have been made and are being reproduced. Other pieces of hobnail may also be listed in the Duncan & Miller and Fenton categories.

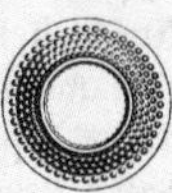

Basket, Blue Opal, White Ruffled Edge, Clear Handle, 8 In. 12.00
Bottle, Barber, Amber, Ringed Neck, 7 In. 12.00
Bowl, Amethyst, White Ruffled Edge, 10 In. 138.00
Bowl, Green, 3-Footed, 3 ½ x 4 ½ In. 18.00
Bowl, White Opalescent, Ruffled Edge, 8 In. 23.00
Cake Plate, Blue, Victorian 115.00
Creamer, Opalescent, 5 In. 17.00
Dish, Fan Shape, Blue 17.00
Dish, Underplate, Blue, Ruffled Edge 46.00
Lamp, Hurricane, Milk Glass, 8 In. 138.00
Pitcher, Amber, Gold, Polished Pontil, 11 ⅛ In. 20.00
Pitcher, Amber, Tapered, 6 In. 25.00
Pitcher, Amethyst, Pulled Hobs, 7 ¼ In. 18.00
Pitcher, Green, Tapered, 5 ¾ In. 25.00
Plate, Luncheon, Pink, 8 ½ In. 9.00
Shade, Aqua, Ruffled, 4 In. 58.00
Shade, Ruby, Ruffled, 4 In. 69.00
Sherbet, Pink 6.00
Syrup, Blue, Metal Lid, Pear Shape, 7 In. 144.00
Tumbler, Juice, Footed, 5 Oz., 3 ½ In. 4.00
Vase, Amber, Pulled Hobs, Ruffled Rim, 7 In. 13.00
Vase, Amber, Pulled Hobs, Snipped Edge, 5 ½ In. 25.00
Vase, Clear, Barrel Shape, 3 ½ In. 14.00
Vase, Olive Green, Snipped Edge, 5 ¾ In. 13.00
Vase, Top Hat, Cranberry Flashed, Kanawha, 2 ½ x 4 ¼ In. 30.00

HOLLY AMBER, or golden agate, glass was made by the Indiana Tumbler and Goblet Company of Greentown, Indiana, from January 1, 1903, to June 13, 1903. It is a pressed glass pattern featuring holly leaves in the amber-shaded glass. The glass was made with shadings that range from creamy opalescent to brown-amber.

Bowl, 8 ½ x 3 In. 662.00
Compote, 7 ¾ x 8 ¼ In. 900.00
Nappy, Handle, 4 ½ In. 475.00
Toothpick, 2 ¼ x 2 ½ In. 40.00
Tray, Square, 7 ¼ In. 600.00
Tumbler, 4 In. *illus* 196.00

HOLT-HOWARD was an importer that started working in 1949 in Stamford, Connecticut. The company sold many types of table accessories, such as condiment jars, decanters, spoon holders, and saltshakers. The figures shown on some of its pieces had a cartoon-like quality. The company was bought out by General Housewares Corporation in 1969. Holt-Howard pieces are often marked with the name and the year or *HH* and the year stamped in black. The *HH* mark was used until 1974. There was also a black and silver label. Production of Holt-Howard ceased in 1990. Similar pieces by the same Holt-Howard designer are being made today and are marked *GHA*.

Butter, Cover, Coq Rouge, Rooster, 1960 85.00
Butter Chip, White, 2 Holly Leaves, 2 Berries, Ruffled Rim, 1959, 4 Piece 35.00
Candleholder, Cherubs, Sitting On Flower Frog Base, Ivory, 1958, 4 x 3 ½ In., Pair 25.00
Candleholder, Figural, Girl, Yellow Dress, Bow In Hair, 1950s, 4 ½ In. 25.00
Candleholder, Green, Fluted, Applied Holly & Berries, Double Rim, 1964, 2 In., Pair 20.00
Candleholder, Santa Claus, Sitting On Red Tile Roof, 1958, 6 x 3 ¼ In., Pair 85.00
Candleholder, Spaghetti Art, Domed Shape, Scalloped Edge, Gold Trim, 1 ¼ x 4 In. 5.00
Cookie Jar, Coq Rouge, Rooster, White Ground, Yellow & Red Rooster, 8 In. 105.00
Decanter, Jeeves, Bowtie, Holds Shape Sign, 10 ¼ In. 145.00

Higbee, Pitcher, Owl, Opaque White, Faceted Eyes, 1890s, 7 ¼ In.
$135.00

Higbee, Spooner, Toy, Menagerie Fish, Blue, 1890s, 3 ½ In.
$283.00

Holly Amber, Tumbler, 4 In.
$196.00

Hopalong Cassidy, Game, Shooting Gallery, Tin, Windup, Automatic Toy Co.
$173.00

Hopalong Cassidy, Sign, Hopalong, Embossed, Tin, Diecut, C&P Signs, 1950s, 36 x 34 In.
$1955.00

Hopalong Cassidy, Toy, Range Rider, Lasso, Gun, Tin, Windup, Marx, 11 In.
$403.00

Horn, Cup, Birds, Flowers, Hearts, Engraved, 20th Century, 3 ½ In.
$96.00

Eggcup, Coq Rouge, Rooster, Flips To Juice Cup, 4 ¾ In. 25.00
Eggcup, Man's Head, Removable Hat Salt, Marked, 6 In., 2 Piece. 75.00
Figurine, Christmas Girl, Green Stylized Tree, Snow, 1959, 6 ½ In. 85.00
Head Vase, Woman, Holly & Berry Hair, Ball Earrings, Long Neck, Pearls, 4 In. 44.00
Jar, Cocktail Olives, 1958, 5 In. 55.00
Mug, Abstract Design, Red, Orange, Lime Green, Black, 1969, 4 In., 4 Piece 25.00
Mug, Tall, Pink & Orange Geometric Design, Footed, 1967, 6 In. 6.00
Napkin Holder, Coq Rouge, Rooster, Red, Yellow, Tan, 1960, 5 ½ In. 40.00
Nut Dish, Blueberries, c.1963, 4 In., 4 Piece. 29.00
Ornament, Bell, Holly Berries, Applied Holly & Berries, Red Handle, 1960s, 3 ½ In. 9.00
Salt & Pepper, Beatnik, Boy With Guitar, Girl With Peace Sign, 3 ½ In. 22.00
Salt & Pepper, Coq Rouge, Rooster, 1964, 4 ½ In. 40.00
Salt & Pepper, Figural, Tomatoes, Red, Green Stem, 2 x 2 ¾ In. 20.00
Salt & Pepper, Girl, Ponytail With Flower, Holding Flower Fan, 1955, 3 ½ In. 32.00
Salt & Pepper, Kids, With Umbrellas, In Rain, 4-Sided, 1964, 4 In. 18.00
Stringholder, Cozy Kitten, Pink Plaid Bow, 1958, 4 ¾ In. 78.00
Tea Set, Tan, Orange & Rust Stripes, Teapot, 4 Mugs, 1972, 5 Piece. 83.00
Trivet, Flower Power Cat, Tea Tile, Scrolled Cast Iron Frame, 1970s, 9 ¼ x 6 ¼ In. 20.00
Trivet, Tea Tile, Seahorse, Cast Iron Openwork Frame, 9 ½ x 5 ½ In. 15.00

HOPALONG CASSIDY was a character in a series of twenty-eight books written by Clarence E. Milford, first published in 1907. Movies and television shows were made based on the character. The best-known actor playing Hopalong Cassidy was William Lawrence Boyd. His first movie appearance was in 1919, but the first Hopalong Cassidy film was not until 1934. Sixty-six films were made. In 1948, William Boyd purchased the television rights to the movies, then later made fifty-two new programs. In the 1950s, Hopalong Cassidy and his horse, named Topper, were seen in comics, records, toys, and other products. Boyd died in 1972.

Barrette, Metal, c.1950 .... 75.00
Book, Pop-Up, c.1950. .... 125.00
Bottle, O'Fallon Milk, Black Decals, Qt., 9 ½ In. 60.00
Breakfast Set, Bowl, Cup, Box 270.00
Button, Hopalong, Topper, 1 ¾ In. 18.00
Button, Saving Rodeo, Red, Black, White, c.1950, 1 ½ In. 20.00
Can, Potato Chip, White, Hopalong & Topper Image, Kuehmann Foods, 1950 .... 35.00
Cap Gun, Double Holster, Medallions, Conchas, c.1950, 27 In. 358.00
Ceiling Fan Hanger, Hopalong Ice Cream, Cardboard, 1950. .... 22.00
Comic Book, DC, Night Raiders Of Twin Rivers, No. 95, Nov. 1954. .... 25.00
Crayon, Black, 3 ⅜ x ⅝ In. 20.00
Doll, Cloth, Stuffed, Rubber Head, Hands, Oil Cloth Boots, c.1950, 20 ½ In. 345.00
Figurine, Hopalong On Topper, Plastic, Jointed, Box, 1950, 2 ¼ x 4 ¾ x 5 In. 115.00
Game, Lasso, Transogram, 1950, 15 ½ x 12 In. 150.00
Game, Shooting Gallery, Tin, Windup, Automatic Toy Co. .... *illus* 173.00
Gun & Holster Set, Gold Plated Gun, Black Holster, 9 In. 220.00
Jacket, Jean, Steer Head On Pockets, Blue Bell, Child's 65.00
Lamp, Aladdin, Hopalong Cassidy, Ranch House, Alacite, Marked, 7 ½ In. 325.00
Lamp, Aladdin, Hoppy Decal, Gun In Holster, Alacite Opaque Glass, c.1950, 10 x 4 In. 525.00
Lamp, Gun In Holster Shape, Wall, 1950s .... 100.00 to 110.00
Lunch Box, Thermos, Aladdin, Nashville, Tenn., U.S.A., 1950 .... 295.00
Mug, Milk Glass, Red Graphics, Hazel Atlas, c.1950, 3 x 2 ¾ In. 35.00
Pen, Ballpoint, Signature On Barrel, Box, 1950, 6 In. 45.00
Pin, Hopalong & Topper, Red, White & Purple Ribbons, 1 ¾ In. 20.00
Poster, Riders Of The Deadline, Sleeve, United Artists, 27 x 41 In. 295.00
Puzzle, Television, Milton Bradley, 1950, 12 x 12 In., 4 Piece 150.00
Radio, Hoppy On Topper, Red Steel Case, Silver Foil, c.1950, 8 ¼ x 5 ¼ In. 848.00
Record, Hopalong Cassidy & The Singing Bandit, Capitol Records, 1950 .... 35.00
Sign, Hopalong, Embossed, Tin, Diecut, C&P Signs, 1950s, 36 x 34 In. .... *illus* 1955.00
Straw Dispenser, Hoppy's Favorite Sunshine Straws, Glass, Chromed Metal, 1950s, 6 In. 30.00
Thermos, Yellow, Red Cap, Aladdin, 6 ¼ In. 40.00
Toothpick, Glass, Wm. Boyd 18.00
Toy, Chow Set, Image Of Hoppy, Stainless Steel, Box, 1950 .... 175.00
Toy, Hopalong & Topper, Hat In Hand, 5 In. 195.00
Toy, Range Rider, Lasso, Gun, Tin, Windup, Marx, 11 In. .... *illus* 403.00

HORN was used to make many types of boxes, furniture inlays, jewelry, and whimsies.

Cigar Cutter, Black, Spiral, Metal, 13 ¾ In. 150.00

Cup, Birds, Flowers, Hearts, Engraved, 20th Century, 3 ½ In. . . . . *illus* 96.00
Cup, Libation, 3 Sinuous Chilong Climbing Over Masks, Triangular, Incised, Chinese, 3 ¼ In. 275.00
Cup, Libation, Chilong & Taotie Mask Band, Brown, Chinese, 7 In. 110.00
Cup, Libation, Rhinoceros, Taotie Masks, Qilin, Key Fret Rim, Dragon Head Handle, 3 ½ In. . . 4130.00
Cup, Sitting Bull, Engraved, Makms, April, 71, 4 ½ In. 225.00
Cup, Tapered, Applied Bottom, Round, 3 ⅞ x 3 ½ In. 33.00
Figurine, Fish, Glass Eyes, Inserted Fins, Carved, Metal Base, 15 In. 250.00
Vinaigrette, Coiled Mull Shape, Amethyst Tip, Chased Silver Lid, Thistle, Chain & Loop, 2 In. 630.00
Vinaigrette, Hunting Horn Shape, Chased Silver Mount, Thistles, Amethyst Tip, 2 In. 315.00
Vinaigrette, Mull Shape, Cairngorm Stone, Engraved Hinged Cover, 1 ¾ In. 604.00

HOWARD PIERCE began working in Southern California in 1936. In 1945, he opened a pottery in Claremont. He moved to Joshua Tree in 1968 and continued making pottery until 1991. His contemporary-looking figurines are popular with collectors. Though most pieces are marked with his name, smaller items from his sets often were not marked.

Figurine, 2 Quails In Tree, Gray, 9 x 5, 1950s. 115.00
Figurine, Deer, Resting, 5 ½ In. 70.00
Figurine, Dog, Droopy Ears, Large & Small Dog, Stamped, 8 & 6 In., 2 Piece 150.00
Figurine, Dove, Black To Blue Drip Glaze, Marked, 7 In. 115.00
Figurine, Dove, Blue, 4 x 9 In. 60.00
Figurine, Duck, Ivory, Shaded Brown, 8 ½ In. 26.00
Figurine, Girl With Basket, Signed, 9 ½ In. 43.00
Figurine, Goose, Brown, Off-White, Stamped, 14 In. 44.00
Figurine, Madonna & Child, 8 In. 100.00
Figurine, Madonna & Child, 13 ½ In. 85.00
Figurine, Owl, Brown, Marked, 5 In. 55.00
Figurine, Owl, Gray, 3 In. 40.00
Figurine, Quail Family, Mother, 2 Chicks, Marked, 6, 4, & 2 ½ In., 3 Piece 65.00
Figurine, Roadrunner, Male, Brown Matte Finish, Stamped, 12 In. 100.00
Vase, Brown, Off-White, Flared Mouth, 6 ¼ In. 25.00
Water Vase, Tree Trunk Shape, Birds On Branches, c.1960, 9 In. 75.00

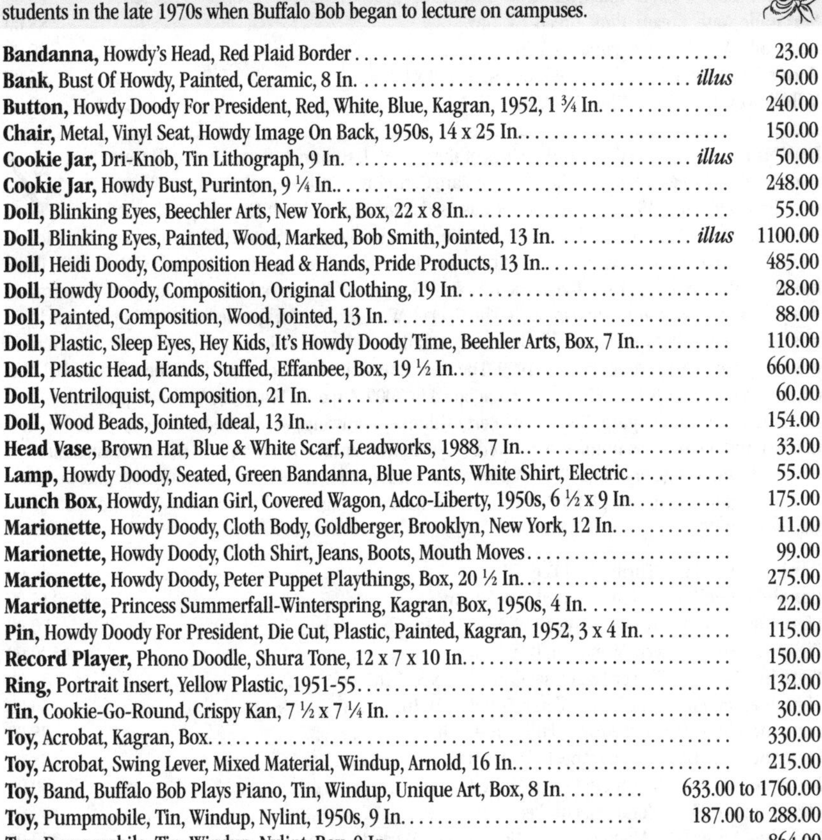

HOWDY DOODY and Buffalo Bob were the main characters in a children's series televised from 1947 to 1960. Howdy was a redheaded puppet. The series became popular with college students in the late 1970s when Buffalo Bob began to lecture on campuses.

Bandanna, Howdy's Head, Red Plaid Border 23.00
Bank, Bust Of Howdy, Painted, Ceramic, 8 In. . . . . *illus* 50.00
Button, Howdy Doody For President, Red, White, Blue, Kagran, 1952, 1 ¾ In. 240.00
Chair, Metal, Vinyl Seat, Howdy Image On Back, 1950s, 14 x 25 In. 150.00
Cookie Jar, Dri-Knob, Tin Lithograph, 9 In. . . . . *illus* 50.00
Cookie Jar, Howdy Bust, Purinton, 9 ¼ In. 248.00
Doll, Blinking Eyes, Beechler Arts, New York, Box, 22 x 8 In. 55.00
Doll, Blinking Eyes, Painted, Wood, Marked, Bob Smith, Jointed, 13 In. . . . . *illus* 1100.00
Doll, Heidi Doody, Composition Head & Hands, Pride Products, 13 In. 485.00
Doll, Howdy Doody, Composition, Original Clothing, 19 In. 28.00
Doll, Painted, Composition, Wood, Jointed, 13 In. 88.00
Doll, Plastic, Sleep Eyes, Hey Kids, It's Howdy Doody Time, Beehler Arts, Box, 7 In. 110.00
Doll, Plastic Head, Hands, Stuffed, Effanbee, Box, 19 ½ In. 660.00
Doll, Ventriloquist, Composition, 21 In. 60.00
Doll, Wood Beads, Jointed, Ideal, 13 In. 154.00
Head Vase, Brown Hat, Blue & White Scarf, Leadworks, 1988, 7 In. 33.00
Lamp, Howdy Doody, Seated, Green Bandanna, Blue Pants, White Shirt, Electric 55.00
Lunch Box, Howdy, Indian Girl, Covered Wagon, Adco-Liberty, 1950s, 6 ½ x 9 In. 175.00
Marionette, Howdy Doody, Cloth Body, Goldberger, Brooklyn, New York, 12 In. 11.00
Marionette, Howdy Doody, Cloth Shirt, Jeans, Boots, Mouth Moves 99.00
Marionette, Howdy Doody, Peter Puppet Playthings, Box, 20 ½ In. 275.00
Marionette, Princess Summerfall-Winterspring, Kagran, Box, 1950s, 4 In. 22.00
Pin, Howdy Doody For President, Die Cut, Plastic, Painted, Kagran, 1952, 3 x 4 In. 115.00
Record Player, Phono Doodle, Shura Tone, 12 x 7 x 10 In. 150.00
Ring, Portrait Insert, Yellow Plastic, 1951-55 . . . . 132.00
Tin, Cookie-Go-Round, Crispy Kan, 7 ½ x 7 ¼ In. 30.00
Toy, Acrobat, Kagran, Box. 330.00
Toy, Acrobat, Swing Lever, Mixed Material, Windup, Arnold, 16 In. 215.00
Toy, Band, Buffalo Bob Plays Piano, Tin, Windup, Unique Art, Box, 8 In. . . . . 633.00 to 1760.00
Toy, Pumpmobile, Tin, Windup, Nylint, 1950s, 9 In. . . . . 187.00 to 288.00
Toy, Pumpmobile, Tin, Windup, Nylint, Box, 9 In. 864.00

Howdy Doody, Bank, Bust Of Howdy, Painted, Ceramic, 8 In.
$50.00

Howdy Doody, Cookie Jar, Dri-Knob, Tin Lithograph, 9 In.
$50.00

Howdy Doody, Doll, Blinking Eyes, Painted, Wood, Marked, Bob Smith, Jointed, 13 In.
$1100.00

Hull, Ebb Tide, Pitcher, Fish, Pink, Turquoise, 13 ⅞ In.
$143.00

Hull, Parchment & Pine, Pitcher, Marked, 14 ⅜ In.
$44.00

Hummel, Figurine, No. 71, Stormy Weather, Full Bee, 6 ¼ In.
$198.00

Toy, Time Teacher, Unopened, Schwab, 18 x 10 In. 6.00
Toy, Tool Box, Ranch House, Tin Lithograph, 14 In., 5 Piece.......... 132.00
Toy, Tricycle, Hard Plastic Head, Wood, Pull Toy, 8 ¼ In.......... 170.00
Wristwatch, Ever Ticking, Glows In Dark, Red Band, On Original Card, Kagran 49.00
Wristwatch, Moving Eyes, Numbers Inside Letters For Howdy Doody, Green Band.......... 88.00

HULL pottery was made in Crooksville, Ohio, from 1905. Addis E. Hull bought the Acme Pottery Company and started making ceramic wares. In 1917, A. E. Hull Pottery began making art pottery as well as the commercial wares. For a short time, 1921 to 1929, the firm also sold pottery imported from Europe. The dinnerwares of the 1940s (including the Little Red Riding Hood line), the high gloss artwares of the 1950s, and the matte wares of the 1940s are all popular with collectors. The firm officially closed in March 1986.

Acorn & Oak Leaves, Vase, Experimental, Handles, 1930s, 8 ¼ x 5 ¾ In.......... 2200.00
Blossom Flite, Pitcher, Metallic, Pink Interior, Twisted Rope Handle, 1955, 9 x 4 ½ In.......... 575.00
Bow Knot, Basket, Blue, 12 x 11 In. 875.00
Bow Knot, Jardiniere, Pink, Green, 9 ⅜ In. 275.00
Bow Knot, Plaque, Blue Border, 10 In. .... 375.00 to 405.00
Bow Knot, Vase, Blue, Pink, Yellow, Label, 7 x 5 In.......... 195.00
Bow Knot, Wall Pocket, Iron, Blue Glaze, 6 x 4 In. 225.00
Butterfly, Pitcher, Cream, 1957, 9 x 8 In.......... 75.00
Corky Pig, Bank, Gold Ears, No Cork, Marked, 1957, 4 In.......... 88.00
Dogwood, Ewer, Cream, Blue, 519, 13 ½ In.......... 175.00 to 195.00
Ebb Tide, Pitcher, Fish, Pink, Turquoise, 13 ⅞ In. .... *illus* 143.00
Gingerbread Man, Tray, Brown Glaze, 10 In. 5.00
Little Red Riding Hood, Cookie Jar, Flower Border, Open Basket, 13 In. 350.00
Little Red Riding Hood, Saltshaker, 5 ½ In.......... 125.00
Magnolia, Ewer, Pink, Blue, 1946, 13 ½ In.......... 40.00
Magnolia, Vase, Scalloped Rim, 6 In. 30.00
Open Rose, Vase, Handles, Green, Pink, 5 x 4 In.......... 65.00
Open Rose, Vase, Scalloped Rim, 6 ¼ In.......... 30.00
Parchment & Pine, Ewer, Green, 14 In. 20.00
Parchment & Pine, Pitcher, Marked, 14 ⅜ In.......... *illus* 44.00
Parchment & Pine, Vase, Cornucopia, Green, 12 In.......... 20.00
Planter, Siamese Cat & Kitten, Marked, 12 In.......... 25.00
Serenade, Vase, Cream, Pink, Green 7 x 4 In. 85.00
Serenade, Vase, Orange, Pink, 7 x 7 In. 85.00
Water Lily, Vase, Yellow, Cream, White, Handles, 9 x 6 In.......... 95.00
Wildflower, Ewer, Pink, Blue, 1946, 13 ½ In.......... 100.00

HUMMEL figurines, based on the drawings of the nun M. I. Hummel (Berta Hummel) were made by the W. Goebel Porzellanfabrik of Oeslau, Germany, now Rodental, Germany. They were first made in 1935. The Crown mark was used from 1935 to 1949. The company added the bee marks in 1950. The full bee with variations was used from 1950 to 1959; stylized bee, 1957 to 1972; three-line mark, 1964 to 1972; last bee, sometimes called vee over gee, 1972 to 1979. In 1979 the V bee symbol was removed from the mark. U.S. Zone was part of the mark from 1946 to 1948; W. Germany was part of the mark from 1960 to 1990. The Goebel, W. Germany mark, called the missing bee mark, was used from 1979 to 1990; Goebel, Germany, with the crown and WG, originally called the new mark, was used from 1991 through part of 1999. The newest version of the bee mark with the word Goebel, the current mark or Goebel with full bee, was adopted in 2000. A special Year 2000 backstamp was also introduced. Porcelain figures inspired by Berta Hummel's drawings were introduced in 1997. These are marked BH followed by a number. They were made in the Far East, not Germany. Goebel discontinued making Hummel figurines in 2008, but they will continue to be made by Manufaktur Rodental GmbH. Other decorative items and plates that feature Hummel drawings have been made by Schmid Brothers, Inc., since 1971.

Bank, No. 118, Little Thrifty, Full Bee, 5 In. 46.00
Candleholder, Silent Night, Stylized Bee, 3 ½ In.......... 115.00
Figurine, No. 6/0, Sensitive Hunter, Full Bee, 7 ½ In.......... 70.00
Figurine, No. 7/x, Merry Wonderer, Bee, 32 In. 6500.00
Figurine, No. 10/1, Flower Madonna, Child, 8 ¼ x 5 ¾ In.......... 82.00
Figurine, No. 11/2/0, Merry Wanderer, Full Bee, 10 In.......... 50.00
Figurine, No. 16/2/0, Little Hiker, Full Bee, 4 ¼ In.......... 75.00
Figurine, No. 21/0, Heavenly Angel, Crown Mark, 4 In.......... 125.00
Figurine, No. 23/1, Adoration, Crown Mark, 6 ¼ In.......... 250.00
Figurine, No. 23/1, Adoration, Full Bee, 7 In.......... 109.00
Figurine, No. 46/111, Madonna, With Halo, Crown Mark, 15 ¼ In.......... 200.00

Figurine, No. 47/0, Goose Girl, Stylized Bee, 4 ¾ In. . . . 94.00
Figurine, No. 51/0, Village Boy, Crown Mark, 6 In. . . . 110.00
Figurine, No. 52, Going To Grandma's, Crown Mark, 6 ½ In. . . . 374.00
Figurine, No. 71, Stormy Weather, Full Bee, 6 ¼ In. . . . *illus* 198.00
Figurine, No. 79, Globe Trotter, Crown Mark, 5 ¼ In. . . . 325.00
Figurine, No. 84/0, Worship, Crown Mark, 5 ½ In. . . . 200.00
Figurine, No. 141/1, Apple Tree Girl, Full Bee, 6 ¼ In. . . . *illus* 77.00
Figurine, No. 143/0, Boots, Full Bee, 6 In. . . . 250.00
Figurine, No. 145, Little Guardian, Stylized Bee, 3 ¾ In. . . . 70.00
Figurine, No. 163, Whitsuntide, Crown Mark, 7 In. . . . 575.00
Figurine, No. 176, Happy Birthday, Crown Mark, 5 ½ In. . . . 170.00
Figurine, No. 184, Latest News, Crown Mark, 5 ½ In. . . . 475.00
Figurine, No. 186, Sweet Music, Crown Mark, 5 ½ In. . . . 375.00
Figurine, No. 201/1, Retreat To Safety, 3-Line Mark, 5 ½ In. . . . 70.00
Figurine, No. 473, Ruprecht, New Mark, 6 In. . . . 450.00
Figurine, No. 620, Story From Grandma, New Mark, 8 In. . . . 1000.00
Figurine, No. 635, Welcome Spring, New Mark, 6 ½ In. . . . 800.00
Holy Water Font, Child Praying, 5 In. . . . 50.00

HUTSCHENREUTHER Porcelain Company of Selb, Germany, was established in 1814 and is still working. The company makes fine quality porcelain dinnerwares and figurines. The mark has changed through the years, but the name and the lion insignia appear in most versions.

Bowl, Art Nouveau, White, 3 ¼ x 12 In. . . . 115.00
Bowl, Art Nouveau, White, Embossed Leaves, Marked, 12 In. . . . 115.00
Box, Woman, Long Brown Hair, Oval, Gilt Metal, 5 x 6 ½ In. . . . 633.00
Cake Plate, Noblesse, Handles, White, Light Blue Border, c.1966, 11 In. . . . 59.99
Candelabrum, 4-Light, Figural, 2 Children, Flutes, Signed, Tutter, 6 ½ x 16 In. . . . 165.00
Figurine, Cardinal, Signed, 6 ½ x 5 In. . . . 60.00
Figurine, Moose, Running, K. Tutter, 9 ½ x 11 In. . . . 125.00
Figurine, Mythological Horse & Rider, 8 ½ In. . . . 55.00
Figurine, Nude Sun Child, On Gold Ball, Karl Tutter, 1938, 12 ¼ In. . . . 475.00
Figurine, Parrot On Stump, Art Deco, c.1940, 15 In. . . . 117.00
Group, Bird Feeding 2 Baby Birds, On Branch, 5 ½ In. . . . 100.00
Group, Boy Riding Horse Bareback, 20th Century, 12 ½ In. . . . 60.00
Group, Nude Woman Feeding Fawn, 10 x 12 ½ In. . . . 300.00
Plaque, Elegant Lady, Carved Gilt Leaf Frame, Oval, 7 ¾ In. . . . 690.00
Plaque, Maiden In Green Robe, Arms Behind Head, 6 x 4 In. . . . 920.00
Plaque, Portrait, Nude Woman, Frame, 12 ½ x 11 In. . . . 588.00
Plaque, Portrait, Woman, On Porcelain, Gilt Frame, E. Valk, c.1910, 5 ½ x 3 ¾ In. . . . 550.00
Plaque, Woman, Reflexion, Signed, Wagner, Marked, Gilt Frame, c.1875, 5 x 4 In. . . . 1495.00
Plate, Biblical Ruth, Holding Sheath Of Wheat, Cobalt Blue Border, 10 In. . . . 978.00
Plate, Figures, Trystians Tod, Late 19th Century, 9 ¾ In. . . . 351.00
Plate, Gilded Frame, Germany, 19th Century, 10 In., Pair. . . . 960.00
Plate, Roman Scene, Transfer, Gold Border, Green Mark, 12 ⅞ In. . . . *illus* 99.00
Plate, Serving, White, Gold Feathery Scrolls At Rim, Handles, 1920, 11 In. . . . 29.00
Plate, Woman, Gold Urns, Flowering Scrolls, Shells, Cobalt Blue Border, 9 ⅜ In. . . . 1150.00

ICONS, special, revered pictures of Jesus, Mary, or a saint, are usually Russian or Byzantine. The small icons collected today are made of wood and tin or precious metals. Many modern copies have been made in the old style and are being sold to tourists in Russia and Europe and at shops in the United States. Rare, old icons have sold for over $50,000.

3-Handed Mother Of God, Embroidered Riza, Gilt Wood Frame, Russia, c.1800, 12 x 10 In. 1121.00
Annunciation, Repousse Silvered Metal Oklad, Painted, Tempera On Wood, Greece, 11 x 8 ¼ In. 472.00
Birth Of The Mother Of God, Vivid Colors, Arched Border, 1800s, 12 x 10 In. . . . 2006.00
Christ As Ruler, Oil On Panel, Gilt Halo, Enameled Rays, Silver Oklad, Russia, 1800s, 7 x 6 In. 489.00
Crowned Mary, Christ, St. John, 2 Angels, Gold Borders, Multicolored, c.1890, 31 x 26 In. . . . 10030.00
Elijah, Saint, Kneeling Before Cave, 3 Small Figures, Riding Chariot, Russia, 7 x 5 ¼ In. . . . 148.00
Feodorovskaya Mother Of God, Repousse Metal Riza, 1900s, 25 x 19 In. . . . 2596.00
Holy Trinity, Angels, Greek Inscriptions, Gilt, Wood Panel, 6 ¾ x 4 ¾ In. . . . 173.00
Kasperov Mother Of God, Silver Gilt, Marked, N.G., Russia, c.1908-17, 8 ¾ x 7 In. . . . *illus* 1760.00
Kazan Mother Of God, 4 Evangelists In Corners, Gilt Copper, Moscow, 1900s, 49 x 38 In. . . . 5900.00
Korsun Mother Of God, Chased Silver, Gilt, Enamel, Cyrillic Mark, c.1900, 16 x 14 In. . . . 64900.00
Lord Almighty, Jesus Blessing, Book, Silver Repousse Overlay, 1884, 12 x 11 In. . . . 25960.00
Madonna, Standing, Wood, Carved, Marked, G. Denunsky, 23 x 5 In. . . . 99.00

Hummel, Figurine, No. 141/1, Apple Tree Girl, Full Bee, 6 ¼ In.
$77.00

Hutschenreuther, Plate, Roman Scene, Transfer, Gold Border, Green Mark, 12 ⅞ In.
$99.00

Icon, Kasperov Mother Of God, Silver Gilt, Marked, N.G., Russia, c.1908-17, 8 ¾ x 7 In.
$1760.00

As always, the edited listings in *Kovels' Antiques & Collectibles Price Guide 2010* aren't available on any website, but readers should visit Kovels.com for information on trends, tips, reproductions, marks, old prices, and more!

I

Icon, Madonna & Child,
Silver Plate Over Copper, Gilt, Enamel,
Russia, 10 x 8 ½ In
$935.00

Icon, Resurrection,
Christ Descends To Hades, 19th Century,
12 ½ x 10 ½ In.
$1430.00

Imari, Bowl, Dutch Figures, Central Tree,
Gilt, 19th Century, 3 ¾ x 8 ⅜ In.
$495.00

Imari, Bowl, Phoenixes, Birds,
Flowers, Fish, Scalloped Rim, Late 1800s,
5 ¼ x 12 In.
$450.00

Madonna & Child, Silver Plate Over Copper, Gilt, Enamel, Russia, 10 x 8 ½ In. .... *illus* 935.00
Madonna & Christ, Loving Sorrowful Mother & Christ From Cross, Chalkware, 19 x 14 In.. 770.00
Mary, Sts. Dimitri, George, Nicholas, 4 Parts, Crucifix In Center, c.1825, 16 x 13 In. 236.00
Mother Of God, Mary, Jesus, Border, Bible Figures, Cyrillic Text, c.1800, 16 x 13 In. 3068.00
Mother Of God To All Who Suffer, Tempera, Gold Leaf, Linen, On Wood, Russia, 8 ¾ x 8 In. 177.00
Old Testament Trinity, Round Gilt Panel, Russia, 1900s, 39 In. 6844.00
Processional, 2-Sided, Archangel Michael, Christ With Angels, Russia, 1700s, 17 x 15 In. ... 837.00
Resurrection, Christ Descends To Hades, 19th Century, 12 ½ x 10 ½ In. .... *illus* 1430.00
Resurrection & Descent With Feast Days, Small Religious Scenes, c.1780, 21 x 18 In..... 3540.00
Resurrection With Feasts, Gilt Metal Oklad, Tempera, Gesso, On Wood, Russia, 12 x 10 ¾ In. 413.00
Saint, Staff, Engine Turned Riza, Giltwood Frame, Box, 1882, 7 x 6 In. 563.00
Saints, Full View, Scrolling Border, Signed, A.G. Smeyekalin, Russia, 1915, 12 x 10 In. 21240.00
St. Eusebius, Full View, Biography Text Surround, Christ Cameo, Palekh School, 1800s, 14 x 12 In. 7080.00
St. John The Baptist, Holding Scroll, Life Scenes Surround, Russia, 1800s, 12 x 11 In. 2242.00
St. Nicholas, Silver Gilt, Books, Blessing Pose, Stole, Cloisonne, c.1906, 12 x 11 In.......... 70800.00
St. Peter, St. Paul, Book, Keys, Sword, Silver Gilt Repousse, Enamel, c.1910, 12 x 11 In. 35400.00
St. Seraphim, Life Scenes, Decorated Borders, Russia, c.1902, 21 x 17 In. 2006.00
Theotokos Mother Of God, Engraved Silver, Marked, Moscow, Russia, 1896, 9 x 7 In...... 2880.00
Tikhvin Mother Of God, Mary Jesus, Cyrillic Text, Gold, Black, Red, 1700s, 19 x 16 In. 4484.00
Traveling, 15 Panels, Religious Figures, Red, Gold Borders, 1800s, 21 x 51 In.. .... 15340.00
Traveling, Deisis, Mary, Jesus, St. John Busts, Red, Gold, Cyrillic Text, 1700s, 9 x 22 In...... 11800.00
Triptych, Trinity Middle Panel, 2 Fathers Of Church Panels, Gilt Riza, Russia, 11 x 4 In. 4720.00
Unexpected Supreme Joy, Ivan Khlebnikov, Cyrillic Writing, 12 ½ x 10 ½ In. 3220.00
Virgin Mary, Crown, Robe, Turquoise, Gilt, Signed, Luis Barra, 27 In.. .... 275.00
Vladimir Mother Of God, Gold, Red, Black, 1800s, 14 x 10 In. 1888.00
Vlakhernskaya Mother Of God, Gilt Silver, Enamel, Pearls, Moscow, 1899, 12 x 10 In..... 35400.00

IMARI porcelain was made in Japan and China beginning in the seventeenth century. In the eighteenth century and later, it was copied by porcelain factories in Germany, France, England, and the United States. It was especially popular in the nineteenth century and is still being made. Imari is characteristically decorated with stylized bamboo, floral, and geometric designs in orange, red, green, and blue. The name comes from the Japanese port of Imari, which exported the ware made nearby in a factory at Arita. Imari is now a general term for any pattern of this type.

Bowl, Birds, Butterflies, Flowers, Fluted Body, Cobalt Blue, Gilt, 3 ¼ x 10 In.. .... 104.00
Bowl, Birds, Fish, Interior Molded Panels, Scalloped Edge, Flared Rim, 1910s, 5 ¼ x 12 In. .. 518.00
Bowl, Cartouches Of Landscapes, Flowers, Birds, Hand Painted, 9 ¾ In. 150.00
Bowl, Crisscross Rim, Late 19th Century, Japan, 3 ¾ x 7 ¼ In. 94.00
Bowl, Dutch Figures, Central Tree, Gilt, 19th Century, 3 ¾ x 8 ⅜ In. .... *illus* 495.00
Bowl, Fans, Chrysanthemums, Crane, Conifers, Double Gourd, 5 ¾ x 15 In.. .... 1380.00
Bowl, Phoenixes, Birds, Flowers, Fish, Scalloped Rim, Late 1800s, 5 ¼ x 12 In. .... *illus* 450.00
Cachepot, Landscape, Phoenix, Japan, Early 20th Century, 4 In. 546.00
Charger, Birds, Flowers, Multicolored, 18 In. 150.00
Charger, Blossoming Peonies, Bamboo, Iron Red, Blue & Gilt Enamel, 12 ½ In. 460.00
Charger, Center Flower Urn, Flower Cartouche Rim, 19th Century, 18 ½ In. 403.00
Charger, Flowers, Beasts, Center Medallion, 4 Reserves, 24 ¾ In.. .... 480.00
Charger, Flowers, Peony Border, Scrolling Lotus, Scalloped, Fluted, Early 1900s, 2 ½ x 18 In. 633.00
Charger, Flowers, Waves, Blue, White, 19th Century, 14 ½ In. 305.00
Charger, Peonies, Verso, Scrolling Lotus, Scalloped Rim, 1890s, 2 ½ x 18 ¼ In. .... *illus* 550.00
Charger, Scenic, Women In Boat, Cranes, Eight Precious Objects, Impressed Mark, 21 In. ... 646.00
Charger, Scrolling Vine, Peonies, Cartouches, Prunus Tree, Lotus, Early 1900s, 2 ¾ x 22 In. . 575.00
Dish, Condiment, Figural, Wood Box, Japan, Late 1800s, 5 ½ In., 14 Piece 239.00
Dish, Fan Shape, Japan, 10 ¼ x 13 In., Pair 236.00
Jar, Cover, Blue Geometrics, Multicolored, Japan, c.1840, 10 x 8 In. 585.00
Jar, Cover, Buddhist Lions, Kiku, Scrolling Lotus Ground, Flowering Trees, 17 ½ In., Pair 1380.00
Lamp Base, Ginger Jar, Horses, Phoenix Birds, Flowers, Red & Blue, 10 ¾ In. 948.00
Lamp Base, Vase, Flowers & Leaves Panels, Iron Red, Blue Enamels, 1800s, 11 ⅝ In. 326.00
Plate, Flight Into Egypt, Honeycomb Border, 8 ⅝ In. .... *illus* 2200.00
Plate, Flower & Brocade, Scalloped Rim, Ribbed, Multicolored, 8 ½ in., Pair 720.00
Plate, Flowers, Blue, Red, Japan, 19th Century, 7 ¼ In. 117.00
Plate, Lotus Shape Cavetto, Flowers, Fence & Floral Center, 10 ½ In.. .... 1554.00
Platter, Eagle On Rocks, Red Cranes, Clouds, Octagonal, 19th Century, 15 x 11 ¾ In. 690.00
Platter, Fish Form, Blue Fins, Tail, 1800s, 16 ½ In. 275.00
Platter, Flowers, Multicolored, 13 ¼ x 10 ½ In., Pair 179.00
Platter, Oval, Blue, Rust, Wide Border, Pierced, Japan, 1800s, 16 x 12 ½ In. 230.00
Platter, Well & Tree, Stamped, 15 ¾ x 19 ¾ In. 225.00

Potpourri, Flowers, Pierced Border, Ormolu Mounts, Japan, c.1740, 10 x 9 In. 25000.00
Serving Dish, Flower Basket Design, Phoenix, Landscape, Iron Red, Gilt, Square, 13 x 13 In. 900.00
Umbrella Stand, Blue, White, 19th Century, 24 x 15 ½ In. 375.00
Umbrella Stand, Flowers, Cobalt Blue, Bittersweet, c.1860, 25 In.. .... 1700.00
Vase, Geishas, Flowers, Blue Ground, Cinnabar, c.1900, 42 In. 990.00
Vase, Lakeside Pavilions, Mandarin Ducks, Oval, Solid Base, c.1900, 15 ¾ In., Pair 1265.00

IMPERIAL GLASS Corporation was founded in Bellaire, Ohio, in 1901. It became a subsidiary of Lenox, Inc., in 1973 and was sold to Arthur R. Lorch in 1981. It was sold again in 1982, and went bankrupt in 1984. In 1985, the molds and some assets were sold. The Imperial glass preferred by the collector is freehand art glass, carnival glass, slag glass, stretch glass, and other top-quality tablewares. Tablewares and animals are listed here. The others may be found in the appropriate sections.

Animal Dish, Duck Cover, Caramel Slag, 5 In. .... *illus* 75.00
Animal Dish, Rabbit Cover, Lacy Base, Purple Slag, 7 ½ In.. .... 495.00
Art Glass, Vase, Cobalt Blue, Zippered Panels, 5 x 2 ¾ In.. .... 20.00
Art Glass, Vase, Iridescent Green, Variegated Blue Heart, Vines, Rim, 7 In. 805.00
Art Glass, Vase, Jewel, Bronze Color, Flared & Stretched Rim, 3 ⅝ x 10 ¼ In. 184.00
Art Glass, Vase, King Tut, Cobalt Blue, Pulled Cream Design, Green & Orange Detail, 9 In.... 920.00
Art Glass, Vase, Opaque Orange, Green Leaves, Flared, 7 ½ x 4 In.. .... *illus* 600.00
Art Glass, Vase, Pulled Swags, Oval, Red Handles, 7 In.. .... 518.00
Beaded Block, Compote, Crimped, Tricornered Edge, Peach Opalescent. 60.00
Beaded Block, Creamer. 12.00
Beaded Block, Dish, Jelly, Pink, Handles, 4 ¾ In. 30.00
Bel-Aire, Tray, Rose Pink, Handles, 11 In.. .... 45.00
Broken Arches, Punch Bowl Base, Imperial, 6 x 5 In. 45.00
Candlewick, Bowl, Dessert, 5 In.. .... 16.00
Candlewick, Bowl, Fruit, Heart Shape, 5 In. 20.00
Candlewick, Candleholder, Beaded Foot, 3 In. .... *illus* 14.00
Candlewick, Candlestick, 2-Light, 5 x 6 ¾ In., Pair. 40.00
Candlewick, Candlestick, Mushroom, 3 ½ In. 33.00
Candlewick, Candlestick, Rolled Edge, 3 ½ In., Pair. 46.00
Candlewick, Cocktail, 4 Oz., 3 ½ In.. .... 16.00
Candlewick, Creamer, Beaded Handle, 6 Oz. 8.00
Candlewick, Dish, Mayonnaise, Underplate, Sections, 2 Ladles 85.00
Candlewick, Dish, Mayonnaise, Underplate, Star Etched, 3 Sections, 5 & 7 ½ In.. .... 55.00
Candlewick, Fork & Spoon Set 35.00
Candlewick, Ladle, Mayonnaise, 3 Ball, 5 ¾ In. 15.00
Candlewick, Plate, Dinner, 10 ½ In.. .... 45.00
Candlewick, Plate, Gold Beaded, Handles, 7 In.. .... 12.00
Candlewick, Punch Bowl, Underplate, Cups, 14 In. 310.00
Candlewick, Relish, Sections, 6 ½ In.. .... 25.00
Candlewick, Sherbet, 6 Oz.. .... 14.00 to 18.00
Candlewick, Soup, Cream, Handles, 5 ¼ In. 55.00
Candlewick, Sugar, 3 ½ In.. .... 12.00
Candlewick, Tray, Ruby, 12 In. Diam. .... *illus* 725.00
Candlewick, Tray, Wafer, 6 In.. .... 31.00
Candlewick, Tumbler, Iced Tea, 12 Oz., 5 ½ In.. .... 22.00
Cape Cod, Berry Bowl, Ruby, Avon, 5 x 1 ¾ In.. .... 4.00
Cape Cod, Bowl, Flared, Smooth Edge, 12 ½ x 6 ¾ In. 70.00
Cape Cod, Bowl, Fruit, Flared, 10 ¾ x 4 In. 35.00
Cape Cod, Butter, Cover, Ruby, Avon, 3 ¼ x 7 In. 12.00
Cape Cod, Candy Dish, Ruby, Footed, Avon, 3 ¼ x 6 In.. .... 8.00
Cape Cod, Cruet, Round Handle, Stopper, 4 Oz., 5 ¼ In. 30.00
Cape Cod, Cup & Saucer, Ruby, Avon, 4 ⅝ x 5 ½ In. 9.00
Cape Cod, Dish, Baked Apple, Rolled, Edge, 6 In.. .... 11.00
Cape Cod, Dish, Sundae, 6 Oz., 4 In.. .... 6.00
Cape Cod, Finger Bowl, Flared, 5 In.. .... 8.00
Cape Cod, Goblet, Water, Fancy Ball Stem, 9 Oz., 5 ½ In. 10.00
Cape Cod, Goblet, Water, Ruby, Avon, 6 x 3 ½ In.. .... 6.00
Cape Cod, Mustard, Cover, Ladle, 3 ½ In. 35.00
Cape Cod, Parfait, 6 Oz., 5 ¾ In. 10.00
Cape Cod, Pitcher, Ruby, Footed, Avon, 8 ¼ x 7 ¾ In. 22.00
Cape Cod, Plate, Bread & Butter, 6 ¾ In. 6.00
Cape Cod, Plate, Cabaret, Cupped Edge, 13 ½ In. 50.00
Cape Cod, Plate, Dinner, Ruby, Avon, 10 ¼ In. 15.00

Imari, Charger, Peonies, Verso, Scrolling Lotus, Scalloped Rim, 1890s, 2 ½ x 18 ¼ In.
$550.00

Imari, Plate, Flight Into Egypt, Honeycomb Border, 8 ⅝ In.
$2200.00

Imperial Glass, Animal Dish, Duck Cover, Caramel Slag, 5 In.
$75.00

Imperial Glass, Art Glass, Vase, Opaque Orange, Green Leaves, Flared, 7 ½ x 4 In.
$600.00

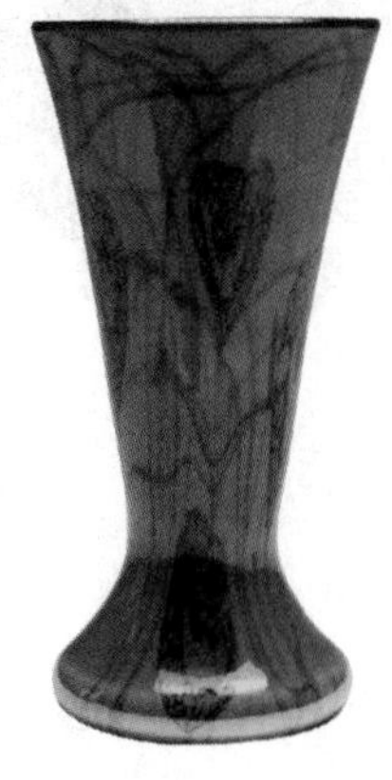

TIP
Never allow water to evaporate in a glass vase. It will leave a white residue that may be impossible to remove.

Imperial Glass, Candlewick, Candleholder, Beaded Foot, 3 In.
$14.00

Imperial Glass, Candlewick, Tray, Ruby, 12 In. Diam.
$725.00

Imperial Glass, Feathers, Dish, Red Slag, 4 In.
$45.00

Cape Cod, Relish, Oval, 3 Sections, 9 ½ In. 23.00
Cape Cod, Relish, Sections, Ruby, Avon, 5 ½ x 9 ⅜ In. 15.00
Cape Cod, Salt & Pepper, Footed, Tapered, 4 In. 16.00
Cape Cod, Salt & Pepper, Ruby, 4 ¾ In. 6.00
Cape Cod, Soup, Dish, Ruby 12.50
Cape Cod, Sugar & Creamer, Ruby, 3 ¼ x 3 ½ & 3 ½ x 5 ¼ In. 7.00
Cape Cod, Sugar & Creamer, Tray, 3 ½ & 7 In. 45.00
Cape Cod, Tumbler, Iced Tea, Ruby, Avon, 5 ½ x 3 In. 8.00
Cape Cod, Tumbler, Juice, Footed, 6 Oz., 5 ¼ In. 7.00
Cape Cod, Tumbler, Old Fashioned, 8 Oz., 3 ½ In. 10.00
Cape Cod, Wine Set, Decanter, Stopper, Ruby, Avon, 9 ½ x 3 ½ In., 8 Piece 35.00
Colonial Crystal, Mug, Footed, Canary Yellow, 9 Oz., 5 ¼ In. 55.00
Diamond Block, Bowl, Green, Oval, Handles, 6 ½ In. 20.00
Diamond Block, Bowl, Lily, Pink, 5 In. 18.00
Diamond Block, Bowl, Pink, Oval, Handles, 6 ½ In. 20.00
Diamond Block, Creamer, Green 15.00
Diamond Block, Jug, 16 Oz. 25.00
Diamond Block, Nappy, Green, Handle, 4 ½ In. 16.00
Diamond Quilted, Bowl, Black, Crimped Edge, 7 In. 20.00
Diamond Quilted, Bowl, Pink, 7 In. 20.00
Diamond Quilted, Bowl, Soup, Cream, Black, 4 ¾ In. 22.00
Diamond Quilted, Candlestick, Black 18.00
Diamond Quilted, Candlestick, Black, Gold Trim, Pair 35.00
Diamond Quilted, Candlestick, Blue 25.00
Diamond Quilted, Candlestick, Green 15.00
Diamond Quilted, Candlestick, Green, Domed Foot 25.00
Diamond Quilted, Candlestick, Pink, 4 ¼ In., Pair 30.00
Diamond Quilted, Compote, Cover, Green, 11 ½ In. 140.00
Diamond Quilted, Creamer, Black 17.00
Diamond Quilted, Creamer, Pink 12.00
Diamond Quilted, Cup, Black 17.00
Diamond Quilted, Nappy, Black, Handle, 5 ½ In. 18.00
Diamond Quilted, Nappy, Pink, Handle, 5 ½ In. 15.00
Diamond Quilted, Plate, Luncheon, Green, 8 In. 12.00
Diamond Quilted, Plate, Luncheon, Pink, 8 In. 12.00
Diamond Quilted, Plate, Sherbet, Blue, 6 In. 8.00
Diamond Quilted, Punch Bowl Base, Green 250.00
Diamond Quilted, Soup, Cream, Black, 4 ¾ In. 25.00
Diamond Quilted, Sugar, Black 17.00
Diamond Quilted, Sugar, Green 10.00
Diamond Quilted, Sugar & Creamer, Green 22.00
Doeskin, Pitcher, Dutch Scenes, Milk Glass, Branch Handle, 5 ½ x 3 ¾ In. 25.00
Feathers, Dish, Red Slag, 4 In. . . . . *illus* 45.00
Floral Optic, Cake Plate, Pink Iridescent Glaze, 3-Footed, 10 ½ In. 10.00
Four Seventy Four, Vase, Octagonal Foot, 12 x 5 In. 100.00
Grape, Plate, Amethyst, Scalloped Rim, 8 ½ In. 33.00
Hobnail, Cologne, Stopper, Pink 95.00
Hobstar & Arches, Bowl, 3 ½ x 7 ⅜ In. 35.00
Indian Sunset, Creamer, 4 x 2 ½ In. 25.00
Lace Edge, Plate, Stiegel Green, 7 ⅜ In. 20.00
Logan Berry, Vase, Green, Scalloped Edge, 10 In. 77.00
Mt. Vernon, Creamer 8.00
Newbound, Bowl, Fruit, Stiegel Green, Footed, 10 In. 55.00
Newbound, Candlestick, 2-Light, Cobalt Blue, Pair 30.00
Newbound, Candlestick, 2-Light, Pink 15.00
Newbound, Candlestick, 2-Light, Stiegel Green, Pair 30.00
Niagara, Sandwich Server, Milk White, Grapevine Handle, Leaf & Grape Design On Bottom . . 22.00
No. 212, Bowl, Olive, Scalloped Edge, Handle, 6 ½ x 2 In. 23.00
No. 499, Bowl, Scalloped Edge, Handles, 10 x 2 ½ In. 30.00
Nu-Cut, Creamer, 4 x 5 In. 25.00
Nu-Cut, Sugar, 6 x 3 In. . . . . 18.00 to 25.00
Nu-Cut, Vase, 10 x 4 ¾ In. 45.00
Octagon, Muffin Basket, Azure Blue, 15 x 5 In. 25.00
Packard, Console Set, Rose Pink, 3 Piece 95.00
Pillar Flute, Celery Dish, Blue Glow, 8 ½ In. 15.00
Pillar Flute, Sugar & Creamer, Blue Glow, 3-Toed 35.00

Provincial, Goblet, Turquoise, 12 Oz., 6 ½ In. 18.00
Reeded, Pitcher, Stiegel Green, Clear, Applied Handle, Ice Lip, 8 In. .... 65.00 to 95.00
Reeded, Tumbler, Iced Tea, Cobalt Blue, 15 Oz. 24.00
Reeded, Vase, Bud, Stiegel Green, 6 In. 35.00
Scroll Fluted, Sugar & Creamer, Blue Opalescent 55.00
Shaeffer, Vase, Rose Bowl, Stiegel Green, 6 In. 75.00
Spoon, Salad, Crystal, 9 ½ In. 10.00
Spoon & Fork, Salad, Crystal, 9 ½ In. 30.00
Square, Server, Black Amethyst, Center Handle, 10 ½ In. 45.00
Square, Sugar & Creamer, Red 45.00
Star & File, Compote, 6 ½ x 6 In. 40.00
Stretch Glass, Sandwich Server, Rose Ice, Center Handle, 4 ½ x 10 ⅝ In. 85.00
Stretch Glass, Sherbet, Blue, 3 ⅜ x 3 ⅝ In. 10.00
Three In One, Toothpick 20.00
Tiara, Candy Dish, Cover, Ruby 85.00
Twisted Optic, Bowl, Pink, 10-Sided, Handles 35.00
Twisted Optic, Candy Dish, Cover, Green, 9 In. 35.00
Twisted Optic, Cheese Compote, Green 12.00
Twisted Optic, Plate, Luncheon, Blue, 8 In. 12.00
Twisted Optic, Plate, Luncheon, Canary Yellow, 8 In. 12.00
Twisted Optic, Sherbet, Canary Yellow 15.00
Vase, Maize, Bulbous, 9 x 7 In. 70.00
Windmill, Bowl, Green, Ruffled Edge, 8 ¾ In. 28.00

INDIAN art from North America has attracted the collector for many years. Each tribe has its own distinctive designs and techniques. Baskets, jewelry, pottery, and leatherwork are of greatest collector interest. Eskimo art is listed under Eskimo in this book.

Adze, Mangaia, Carved, Pierced Base, c.1950, 21 ½ In. 420.00
Armband, Pueblo, Hide, Orange, Zigzag Pattern, 5 ½ x 11 In., Pair 294.00
Armband, Sioux, Beaded, Quilled, Rawhide, Yellow, Red, Purple, c.1900, 11 In., Pair 764.00
Awl Case, Apache, Beaded Hide, Black, White, Yellow, Cobalt, Rose, Tin Cones, Drops, 13 In. 1265.00
Ax, Great Lakes, Hand Wrought, Cutout Blade, Brass Tacked Haft, 6 ½ x 16 In. 316.00
Bag, Central Plains, Beaded, Quilled Hide, Multicolored Geometric, Danglers, 18 ½ x 14 In. 7703.00
Bag, Cree, Cloth, Beaded, Thread Sewn Applique, Flowers, Delia In Beads, 4 ¾ x 4 ⅝ In. 230.00
Bag, Document, Arapaho Style, Beaded, Fringe, Tin Cone Suspensions, 8 ⅝ x 8 ⅝ In. 403.00
Bag, Great Lakes, Charm, Thunderbird, Underwater Panthers, 3 ⅝ In. 2252.00
Bag, Great Lakes, Horse, Running, Rider, Leather, Flap, Fringes, Light Blue Ground, 19 x 6 In. 248.00
Bag, Nez Perce, Husk, Dyed, Polished Cotton Lining, Internal Pockets, 20 ¼ x 17 In. 805.00
Bag, Nez Perce, Storage, Hemp Root, Woven, 7 x 12 ½ x 14 In. 138.00
Bag, Northern Plains, Beaded, White Ground, Red Felt, Brass Beads, 9 ¼ x 7 In. 2530.00
Bag, Octopus, Northwest Coast, Beaded, Cloth, Bifurcated Tabs, Multicolored Flowers, 21 In. 4148.00
Bag, Plains, Beaded Pinwheel, 9 ½ In. 235.00
Bag, Plateau, Beaded, Rose, Blue Ground, 8 ⅜ x 7 ¼ In. 316.00
Bag, Plateau, Beaded, Roses, Deer, 10 x 8 ½ In. 633.00
Bag, Sioux, Beaded, Flags, Figures, Multicolored, Leather Handles, 8 x 14 x 6 In. 4800.00
Bag, Sioux, Tobacco, Beaded, Quill Fringe Slats, c.1900, 18 x 8 In. 2310.00
Bag, Sioux, Tobacco, Hide, Beaded, Diamonds, Triangles, Quillwork, Fringe, 1800s, 32 x 7 In. 1952.00
Bag, Sioux, Tobacco, Hide, Beaded, Sinew Sewn, Triangular Tabs, Fringe, 28 In. .... *illus* 1610.00
Bag, Sioux, Tobacco, Quilled Rawhide Slats, Glass Beads, c.1915, 30 In. 1527.00
Bag, Southern Cheyenne, Tobacco, Hide, Beaded, Sinew Sewn, Fringe, 20 In. 4888.00
Bag, Winnebago, Otter Skin, Beaded, Cloth, Abstract Flowers, 41 ½ In. 4444.00
Bag, Yakima, Buckskin, Beaded, Portrait, 8 In. 460.00
Bandolier, Central Plains, Carved Deer Hoof, Brass Spacer, Quilled Leather Loop, 38 In. 4444.00
Bandolier, Central Plains, Carved Deer Hoof Pendant, Wrist Band, 34 ½ In. 3851.00
Bandolier, Chippewa, Bag, Beaded, Thread Sewn, Flowers, c.1900, 41 x 14 ½ In. 3172.00
Bandolier, Chippewa, Beaded, Gray Ground, Asymmetrical Flowers, 41 x 15 In. 1725.00
Bandolier, Great Lakes, Beaded, 43 x 12 In. 1430.00
Bandolier, Ojibwa, Trade Cloth, Beaded, Multicolored Geometric, Tassels, 38 In. 4444.00
Bandolier, Seminole, Beaded Cloth, c.1835, 8 x 7 In. 17775.00
Bandolier, Winnebago, Loom Beaded, Braided Strands, Wool, Silk Ribbon, 40 ½ In. 3738.00
Basket, Apache, Bowl, Coiled, 4 Rows Human, Animal Figures, 15 ½ In. 8888.00
Basket, Apache, Burden, Woven Sumac, Double Rim, Geometric Bands, Leather, Fringe, 13 x 13 In. 448.00
Basket, Apache, Cover, Stepped Diagonal, Imbricated, Coiled, 11 x 12 ½ In. 889.00
Basket, Apache, Figural, Riveted Copper Collar, 12 x 16 In. 4200.00
Basket, Apache, Yucca Root Design Border, c.1920, 5 ¾ x 16 ¼ In. 2702.00
Basket, Burden, Apache, Woven, Reverse Design, Cone Shape, 9 x 12 ¾ In. 259.00

TIP
To remove the brown deposits found in old vinegar cruets, fill the cruets with diluted ammonia for a few hours, then rinse.

Indian, Bag, Sioux, Tobacco, Hide, Beaded, Sinew Sewn, Triangular Tabs, Fringe, 28 In.
$1610.00

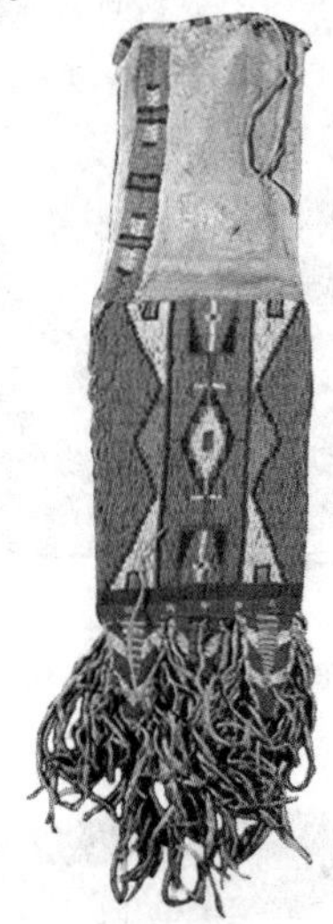

TIP
Clean silver with any acceptable commercial polish. Don't use household scouring powder on silver, no matter how stubborn the spot may be. Use a tarnish-retarding silver polish to keep your silver clean. It will not harm old solid or plated wares. Do not use "instant" silver polishes.

Indian, Basket, Chippewa, Cover, Sweet Grass, Liner, Strap, 5 ¾ x 8 In. $121.00

Indian, Basket, Chitimacha, Geometrics, Square To Round, Early 1900s, 3 ¾ In. $685.00

Indian, Basket, Hupa, Shades Of Brown, 8 ½ x 8 ¾ In. $495.00

Indian, Basket, Taconic, Friendship, Splint, 19th Century, 3 x 4 In. $550.00

Basket, Cherokee, Buttocks, Plaited Weave, Bent Ash Handle, 12 x 17 x 14 ½ In. 92.00
Basket, Cherokee, River Cane, Brown, Orange Weavers, Bentwood Oak Handle, Rim, 16 x 19 In. 633.00
Basket, Cherokee, River Cane, Red, Brown Weavers, Diamond Pattern, Oak Lock Handle, 12 x 14 In. 546.00
Basket, Cherokee, River Cane, Red, Brown Weavers, Diamond Pattern, Oak Lock Handle, 12 x 15 In. 460.00
Basket, Cherokee, Splint, Oval, Oak Handle, 14 ¼ x 27 ½ In. 345.00
Basket, Cherokee, Storage, Cover, Handles, 18 ¼ x 18 In. 230.00
Basket, Chippewa, Cover, Sweet Grass, Liner, Strap, 5 ¾ x 8 In. .... *illus* 121.00
Basket, Chitimacha, Double Woven, Geometrics, Square To Round Rim, c.1910, 4 In. 719.00
Basket, Chitimacha, Double Woven, Lid, Snake Design, 6 ¾ x 6 In. 3680.00
Basket, Chitimacha, Geometrics, Square To Round, Early 1900s, 3 ¾ In. .... *illus* 685.00
Basket, Chitimacha, Natural, Red, Yellow & Black Cane, Turtle Necklace Pattern, 6 ½ In. ... 1880.00
Basket, Chitimacha, Natural, Red & Black Cane, Bull's-Eye Pattern, Cover, 7 x 5 ½ In. 1762.00
Basket, Hopi, Bowl, Woven, Coiled, Corn Design, c.1975, 3 x 14 ¾ In. 431.00
Basket, Hopi, Coiled, Multicolored Dogs, Geometric Designs, 3 In. 230.00
Basket, Hopi, Wicker Weave, Mesa Plaque, Swirling Pattern, Multicolored, 14 In. 230.00
Basket, Hupa, Beige, Tan, Black, c.1930, 5 x 7 In. 250.00
Basket, Hupa, Shades Of Brown, 8 ½ x 8 ¾ In. .... *illus* 495.00
Basket, Klickitat, Hard Sided, Inverted Cone Shape, c.1900, 12 x 10 x 13 In. 150.00
Basket, Klickitat, Hard Sided, Inverted Cone Shape, c.1900, 16 x 13 In. 575.00
Basket, Navajo, Wedding, 3 Colors, c.1910, 10 ½ In. 86.00
Basket, Nootka, 2 Colors, Whale Forms, Cover, c.1900, 2 ¾ x 4 In. 863.00
Basket, Northwest, Baleen, Cover, Ivory Knob, Bear Attacking Seal, Ivory Plaque, 4 x 4 In. ... 1896.00
Basket, Northwest, Thompson River, Square, Inbricated Weaved, Zigzags, 5 ½ In. 288.00
Basket, Paiute, Beaded, Lid, Finial, Concentric Stars, Geometric Designs, 5 x 8 In. 1725.00
Basket, Paiute, Bowl, Beaded, Warrior In Headdress, Butterfly, Blue, Amber Ground, 3 x 6 In. 7703.00
Basket, Paiute, Bowl, Woven, Bulbous, Red Fern Geometric X Design, c.1900, 4 ½ x 8 In. 1035.00
Basket, Paiute, Seed, Cone Shape Bottom, 11 x 6 In. 259.00
Basket, Penobscot, Woven Sweet Grass, Soft Bark Bottom, Early 1900s, 3 ¾ x 9 ¾ In. 177.00
Basket, Pima, Canted Sides, Human Figures, 5 x 9 ¼ In. 235.00
Basket, Pima, Lightning Step Pattern, Black, Brown, 6 ¼ x 15 In. 1955.00
Basket, Pima, Multicolored, Oval, Angled, Crosses, 6 In. 374.00
Basket, Pima, Twist Weave, Double Banded, Fringe, Beads, 10 x 12 In. 259.00
Basket, Pomo, Bowl, Woven, Coiled, Parallel Step Design, c.1900, 3 x 6 ¼ In. 316.00
Basket, Pomo, Figural, Flattened Shape, Men, Ravens, Whirling Logs, 2 x 7 ½ In. 1150.00
Basket, Salish, Cover, Handles, 3 Colors, Diamond Design, Early 1900s, 9 x 14 x 9 In. 230.00
Basket, Salish, Cover, Valero Star, Chevron, Drum Shape, 10 ½ x 13 In. 345.00
Basket, Salish, Hard Sided, 2 Colors, Rectangular, 11 ½ x 17 ¾ x 12 ½ In. 633.00
Basket, Salish, Rim Loops, Handle, Figural Designs, 7 x 17 ¼ x 7 ¼ In. 219.00
Basket, Salish, Top Knot Cover, 2 Colors, Imbricated, 5 x 7 ⅝ In. 150.00
Basket, Santa Clara, Pottery, Twist Handle, Blackware, Carved Avanyu Figure, 6 x 5 In. 138.00
Basket, Taconic, Friendship, Splint, 19th Century, 3 x 4 In. .... *illus* 550.00
Basket, Taconic, Splint, Oak, Arched Swing Handle, c.1890, 8 ½ x 14 In. 423.00
Basket, Taconic, Splint, Oak, Double Wrapped Rim, Swing Handle, c.1890, 9 x 12 In. 413.00
Basket, Tlingit, Painted Geometrics, Pacific Northwest, 8 x 10 ½ In. 440.00
Basket, Tlingit, Twined Rattle Top, Multicolored Geometric Bands, 8 x 6 ¼ In. 2963.00
Basket, Tray, Pima, Geometric Blossom Design, Ticked Rim, c.1925, 2 ¼ x 10 ¼ In. 259.00
Basket, Twined Hat, Northern California, Brown, Yellow, Quilled Geometric, 3 ¼ x 6 ¾ In. ... 1422.00
Basket, Twined Hat, Northern California, Multicolored, Brown Geometric, 3 x 7 In. 948.00
Basket, Washo, Bowl, Woven, Globular, Red, Geometric Forms, Zigzag Band, c.1900, 5 ½ x 10 In. 1840.00
Basket, Woodlands, Splint, Blue, Salmon, Yellow, Bands, Wood Handles, 12 x 14 x 2 ½ In. 382.00
Basket, Woodlands, Splint, Blue, Salmon, Yellow, Wood Handles, 11 ½ x 13 ½ x 5 In. 235.00
Basket, Wounaan, Butterfly, Bird, Globular, 4 ½ x 6 In. 115.00
Basket, Wounaan, Rain Forest, 38 Butterflies, Globular, 6 x 7 ½ In. 230.00
Basket, Yokuts, Bowl, Coiled, Flared Sides, Stacked Triangles, 10 x 19 ¾ In. 1541.00
Basket, Yokuts, Chalice, Gap Stitched, Rattlesnake Design, Multicolored, 5 ¼ x 6 ¼ In. 480.00
Basket, Yokuts, Jar, Coiled, Bottleneck, Geometric Bands, Human Holding Hands, 4 x 7 In. .. 5925.00
Basket, Yokuts, Rattlesnake Design, Multicolored, 4 ½ x 7 ½ In. 2588.00
Belt, Navajo, 10 Oval Conchas, Silver Inlay, Inlaid Diamond Design, 20th Century, 45 In. 266.00
Belt, Navajo, Concha, Butterflies, Round Turquoise, 4 Turquoise Belt, 2 ⅕ x 3 ¾ In. 1920.00
Belt, Navajo, Concha, Silver First Phase, 1870s, 36 x 4 In. 28440.00
Belt, Northern Plain, Beaded, Buffalo Hide, Sinew Sewn, Glass Beads, Eagle, c.1890, 34 In. .. 1116.00
Belt, Southwest, Leather, Silver, Turquoise, Oval Medallions, Buckle, 46 In. 797.00
Blanket, Lakota, Saddle, Beaded, Crosses, Geometrics, Hide, Fringe, 1800s, 66 x 23 In. 4392.00
Blanket, Lakota, Saddle, Hide Panels, Multicolored Geometrics, Canvas, 69 x 31 In. 2133.00
Blanket, Navajo, Diamonds, Yellow, Gray, Brown, Cream, 65 x 45 In. 585.00
Blanket, Navajo, Double Saddle, Orange, Black, Red, Striped, Hooked Diamonds, 33 x 54 In. .. 633.00

I

Blanket, Navajo, Eye Dazzler, Red, Orange, Black, Purple, Figures, Crosses, 61 x 83 In. 6038.00
Blanket, Navajo, Eye Dazzler, Red, Orange, Brown, Cream, Green, Wool, Geometric, 101 x 56 In. 2415.00
Blanket, Navajo, Saddle, Central Box Zigzag Border, Red Ground, c.1925, 26 x 35 In. 1035.00
Blanket, Navajo, Saddle, Wool, Banded Design, Feathers, Blocked Corners, c.1900, 25 x 30 In. 881.00
Blanket, Navajo, Serape, Red, Blue, Green, Orange, Serrated Diamonds, 51 x 73 In. 31050.00
Blanket, Navajo, Single Ply, Hand Spun, Salmon, Blue, Cream, c.1880, 69 x 48 In. 15275.00
Blanket, Navajo, Transitional, Hand Spun Wool, Alternating Bands, 68 x 53 ½ In. 1840.00
Blanket, Navajo, Wool, Red, Blue, Cream, Crosses, Zigzags, Poles, 50 x 30 In.. . . . . 14100.00
Blanket, Navajo, Woven, Multicolored, Crosses, Diamonds, Germantown, 53 x 36 In. 4700.00
Blanket, Rio Grande River Valley, Wool, Red, Pink, Yellow, Blue, Gray Bands, 76 x 54 In. 863.00
Blanket, Sioux, Saddle, Beaded Geometric Design, Buckskin, Bead Fringe, 30 x 51 In. 3190.00
Blouse, Navajo, Velvet, Silver, Rickrack Trim, Pocket, c.1920, 13 ½ In. 881.00
Bolo, Navajo, Peyote Bird, Turquoise, c.1950, 32 In. 316.00
Bolo, Navajo, Silver, Turquoise, Matching Tips, c.1970, 4 ¾ In. 840.00
Bolo, Zuni, Inlaid, Knifewing Figure, Fleur-De-Lis Mark, Frank Vacit, 1950s, 1 ¾ In. 420.00
Bolo, Zuni, Mudhead, Infant On Back, Coral, Marked, Matching Tips, c.1970, 3 x 2 In. . . *illus* 646.00
Bottle, Makah, Basketry, Multicolored, Plaited Weaving, Eagle, Sea Monster, 11 x 3 ½ In. 288.00
Bow, Plains, Blue & Red Panels, 19th Century, 37 ½ In. 819.00
Bowl, Anasazi, Salada Gila, Pottery, Multicolored, 7 x 12 ½ In. 489.00
Bowl, Apache, Coiled, Dark Circle, Stepped Design, Black Rim, 1800s, 5 ½ x 18 In. 2574.00
Bowl, Apache, Coiled, Round Medallion, Stepped Striped Boxes, 1800s, 4 ½ x 15 In. 2808.00
Bowl, Blackware, Maria Martinez, c.1950, 2 ½ x 5 In.. . . . . 1610.00
Bowl, Dough, Zuni, Wood, Stylized Rainbirds, Scalloped Line Wraps Rim, c.1870, 5 ½ x 16 In. 1292.00
Bowl, Haida, Horn, Mountain Sheep, Golden Amber, Incised Face, 6 ½ x 4 ½ In. 6900.00
Bowl, Haida, Oil, Seal Shape, Carved Wood, Abalone Inlay, 8 In. 3300.00
Bowl, Hopi, Brown & Orange Abstract Designs, White Ground, 3 ¼ In. 58.00
Bowl, Hopi, Flowers In Square Frame, c.1900, 3 ½ x 11 In. 9400.00
Bowl, Hopi, Low, Squat, Geometric Design, 3 ½ x 8 ¼ In.. . . . . 118.00
Bowl, Hopi, Squat Shape, Orange, Black Abstract Design, Signed, Corn Tassel, Pollen, 4 In. . . 115.00
Bowl, Hupa, Geometric Design, Banded Stacked Triangle Pattern, 4 ¾ x 7 ½ In. 748.00
Bowl, Maidu, Coiled, Basket, c.1900, 4 ½ x 7 ¼ In. 1287.00
Bowl, Northwest Coast, Wood, Beaver Shape, Abalone Eyes, Nostrils, Beads, 16 In.. . . . . 5333.00
Bowl, Northwest Coast, Wood, Flat Bottom, Canoe Shape, Upswept Ends, 22 ¼ In.. . . . . 5925.00
Bowl, Pima, Woven, Geometric Design, Fine Patina, 12 ¼ In.. . . . . 205.00
Bowl, San Ildefonso, Pottery, Bird, Blackware, 2 ¾ x 3 ½ In. 460.00
Bowl, San Ildefonso, Pottery, Blackware, Radiating Feathers, 3 x 5 In. 431.00
Bowl, San Ildefonso, Pottery, Leaf, Blackware, 4 ½ x 5 ¼ In. 805.00
Box, Navajo, Silver, Turquoise, Coral, Lapis, Lid, Legs, W. Muskett Jr., c.1975, 3 x 2 x 1 ½ In. . . 1495.00
Box, Northwest Coast, Bentwood, Abstract Animals, Paint, Tag, 9 ½ x 9 x 12 In. 1896.00
Bracelet, Hopi, Cuff, Sterling Silver, Spider & Web, Turquoise, c.1970 . . . . 5629.00
Bracelet, Hopi, North American Wild Animals, Nelson Piaso, Man's, 6 ¾ x 1 ¼ In. . . . . . *illus* 330.00
Bracelet, Navajo, Bangle, Turquoise, Tiger Eye, Leaves, Stamped, Late 1900s, 2 ¾ In. . . *illus* 121.00
Bracelet, Navajo, Cuff, Pitted, Red Coral, c.1990 . . . . 294.00
Bracelet, Navajo, Sterling Silver, Hammered, Repousse Band, c.1920s 948.00
Bracelet, Navajo, Sterling Silver, Turquoise, Beaded, Oval Stones Set On Square Wires, c.1930 1126.00
Bracelet, Navajo, Sterling Silver, Turquoise, Hammered, Applied Repousse Decorations, c.1950 1422.00
Bracelet, Southwest, Cuff, Silver, Burnished, Bezel Set Turquoise, J. Begat, 2 ½ In. 472.00
Bracelet, Zuni, Silver, Turquoise Needlepoint, Coral, Mother-Of-Pearl, Open End, 1 ⅝ In.. . . . 384.00
Breast Plate, Lakota, Otter Skin, Canvas, Trade Cloth Trim, Bead Edge Mirrors, Sequins, 41 In. 5925.00
Buckle, Hopi, Sterling Overlay, Man In The Maze, c.1970, 3 x 2 In.. . . . . 173.00
Buckle, Navajo, Turquoise, Jet, Mother-Of-Pearl, Spondolus, Inlay, 1950s, 2 x 2 ½ In. 60.00
Buckle, Navajo, Turquoise, Repousse, Trapezoid Setting, Silver, 3 ¾ In. 1304.00
Canteen, Hopi, Knob Handles, Feather Design, Bulging Belly, c.1900, 2 ½ x 4 ¾ In.. . . . . 705.00
Canteen, Navajo, Tobacco, Copper, Chain, Wood Stopper, 3 ⅛ In. 415.01
Canteen, Navajo, Tobacco, Silver, Applied Arrow, Pinpricked Eagle, 1920s, 3 ¼ x 2 ⅜ In. 705.00
Canteen, Navajo, Tobacco, Silver, Engraved Stylized Flower On Each Side, 1930s, 3 x 2 In.. . . 646.00
Cap, Mohawk, Cloth, Flowers, Multicolored Beads, c.1870, 4 ½ x 7 ½ In.. . . . . 711.00
Charm Bag, Mesquakie, Loom Beaded, Nested Diamonds, Rayed, Panther, 3 ¾ x 5 In. 5750.00
Chest Plate, Lakota, Beads, Bones, Bison Horns, 15 x 27 In. 234.00
Cigarette Holder, Haida, Carved, Bone, Eagle & Bear Totemic Figures, c.1925, 3 ½ In.. . . . . . . 173.00
Club, Plains, Stone Head, Wood Handle, Blue Pigmented Hide, c.1875, 27 ½ In.. . . . . 1410.00
Club, Plains, War, Oval Shape Stone, Wood Handle, Painted Orange Hide, 30 In. 403.00
Club, Sioux, War, Beaded, 19th Century, 28 In.. . . . . 439.00
Coat, Plains, Painted, Calumet Style Pipes, 54 In. 7110.00
Cradle, Nupa, Woven, Open Weave, Bear Grass, Maidenhair Fern Wrappings, 27 x 11 In. 2300.00
Cradle, Ute, Hide, Woven Visor, Beadwork, Multicolored, 16 ½ In. 960.00

TIP

If you are having antique jewelry repaired, be sure the jeweler uses old stones. New ones are cut differently and will seem brighter. Pearls and turquoise change color with age.

Indian, Bolo, Zuni, Mudhead, Infant On Back, Coral, Marked, Matching Tips, c.1970, 3 x 2 In.
$646.00

Indian, Bracelet, Hopi, North American Wild Animals, Nelson Piaso, Man's, 6 ¾ x 1 ¼ In.
$330.00

TIP

Broken silver jewelry may have melt-down value. Check to see if the metal is really silver.

Indian, Bracelet, Navajo, Bangle, Turquoise, Tiger Eye, Leaves, Stamped, Late 1900s, 2 ¾ In.
$121.00

Indian, Frame, Great Lakes, Flowers, Velvet, Beaded, c.1820, 11 ¼ x 11 In.
$198.00

Indian, Moccasins, Great Lakes, Beaded, Child's, c.1890-1910, 6 In.
$220.00

Indian, Moccasins, Plains, Beaded, Leather, Fringe, c.1930
$500.00

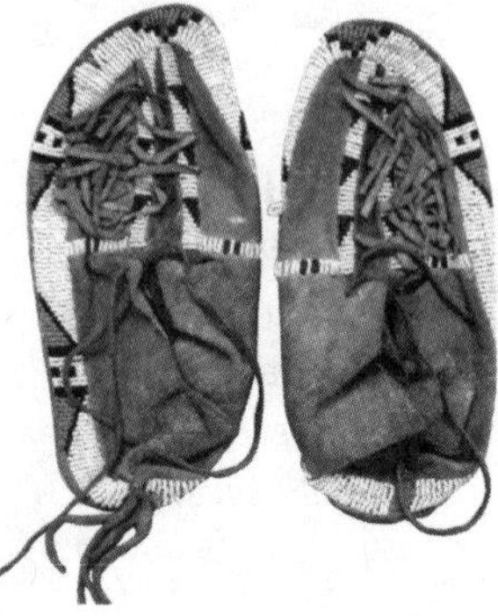

Cradle Cover, Plains, Tanned Hide, Beaded, Geometric, Fringe, Late 1800s, Size 6. . . . . 345.00
Cradle Cover, Sioux, Beaded, Buffalo Hide, Canvas Lined, c.1880, 27 ½ In. 8812.00
Cradle Cover, Sioux, Multicolored Beads, 11 In. 176.00
Cup, Sioux, Buffalo Horn, Dyed Quill Work, Openwork, Cut Parfleche, 19th Century 1100.00
Dagger, Northwest Coast, Totem, Fish Fin Blade, Cedar Handle, Abalone Inlaid, 37 ½ In. 200.00
Dance Rattle, Pueblo, Gourd, Hand Hewn Handles, c.1900, 9 ½ x 10 In., Pair. 489.00
Doll, Cradle, Cheyenne, Buckskin, Beaded, Board, Stick Backboard, 1900s, 11 x 4 In. 345.00
Doll, Northern Cree, Hide, Quilled Flower Jacket, Beads, Composition, c.1900, 18 In.. . . . . 764.00
Doll, Northern Plains, Thread Sewn, Human Hair, c.1870, 14 In.. . . . . 4406.00
Doll, Plains, Beaded War Shirt, Leggings, Moccasins, 14 x 5 In. 178.00
Doll, Plateau, White Buckskin, Beaded Shirt, Leggings, Moccasins, Pipe Bag, 10 x 6 In.. . . . . . 230.00
Doll, Sioux, Cloth Body, Beaded, Horse Hair, c.1875, 13 ½ In. 1292.00
Doll, Zuni, Beaded, Multicolored, c.1950, 11 In.. . . . . 235.00
Dress, Blackfoot, Trade Cloth, Lazy Stitch, Green, White, Pink Beads, Woman's Small 127.00
Dress, Plains, Deerskin, Deer Tail Pendant, Fringed, 51 In.. . . . . 6518.00
Dress, Plateau, Beaded, Flowers, Moose Hide, Buckskin, Fringe, Woman's Small, 54 In. 184.00
Dress, Sioux, Buckskin, Beaded, Girl's, 36 x 40 In.. . . . . 1380.00
Dress, Spokane, Muslin, Fringe, Woman's, 42 In. 127.00
Drum, Plains, 2-Sided, Painted, Beater, 17 In.. . . . . 316.00
Drum, Plateau, Cottonwood, Hide, 1900s, 20 x 19 In. 230.00
Earrings, Zuni, Petit Point Turquoise, Silver, c.1950, 1 ½ In.. . . . . 127.00
Figure, Northwest Coast, Effigy, Inscribed, Klaskimo B. Col., Early 20th Century, 19 ½ In.. . . . 5148.00
Figurine, Northwest Coast, Haida, Argillite, Children, Bears, 6 ½ In. 6518.00
Figurine, Northwest Coast, Haida, Argillite, Human, Nursing Bear Cubs, 7 ½ In.. . . . . 5629.00
Fire Bag, Columbia River, Seed Beads, Wool, Prairie Chickens, 14 ¾ x 9 ¾ In.. . . . . 5100.00
Flute, Sioux, Courtship, Cedar, Carved, 13 ½ x 1 ⅝ In. 345.00
Frame, Great Lakes, Flowers, Velvet, Beaded, c.1820, 11 ¼ x 11 In. . . . . *illus* 198.00
Frame, Great Lakes, Glass Beads, Paperboard, Leaves, Union Jack Flag, 10 x 7 ½ In.. . . . . 248.00
Gauntlets, Northern Plains, Beaded, Hide, Swallow On Cuffs, Multicolored, c.1915, 17 In.. . . . 2585.00
Gauntlets, Shoshone, Beaded, Abstract Flowers, Multicolored, 13 In. 830.00
Gloves, Cree, Beaded, Moose Hide, Rose, Mid 1900s, 10 x 4 ½ In.. . . . . 115.00
Gloves, Crow, Beaded, Tanned Buckskin, 1930, Pair 167.00
Hair Extender, Plains, Human, 6 Hangs, Ornamental Buttons, c.1860, 5 x 29 In.. . . . . 4112.00
Hair Roach, Plains, Red Dyed Whitetail Deer Hair, Black Turkey Beard, Mid 1800s, 11 In.. . . . 2300.00
Hat, Klamath, Woven, 3 ¾ x 6 ½ In. 311.00
Hat, Tohono O'Odham, Geometric Design, Woven, Wide Brim, 10 ½ In. 201.00
Horse Collar, Crow, Beaded, Cloth Insets, Hide, Geometric, 31 In.. . . . . 3555.00
Jacket, Chimayo, Wool, Zipper, Black Buckles, Size 10 ½ 144.00
Jar, Acoma, Black, Orange, Enclosed Rim, Round Shoulders, 5 ½ x 8 ½ In. 1265.00
Jar, Acoma, Fineline Hatching, Checkered Boxes, c.1900, 12 x 15 In.. . . . . 1150.00
Jar, Acoma, Globular, Constricting Neck, Fluted Rim, Birds, Geometrics, Strap Handles, c.1910, 13 In. 1762.00
Jar, Acoma, High Shoulder, Animal Figures, 14 In.. . . . . 264.00
Jar, Acoma, High Shoulder, Signed, Mrs. Ruby Shronlate, N.M., 10 In.. . . . . 206.00
Jar, Acoma, Orange, Black, Buff, Bear, Antelope, Deer, Pottery, 6 ½ x 8 In.. . . . . 1955.00
Jar, Acoma, Orange, Black Geometric Designs, White Ground, Flared, Lug Handle, 6 ¾ In.. . . . 690.00
Jar, Acoma, Parrot, Geometric, Leaves, Flared Neck, Multicolored, 10 x 9 ½ In. 1422.00
Jar, Acoma, Twisted Flowers, Multicolored, Banded Strap Handles, 11 ½ x 8 ¼ In. 1265.00
Jar, Hopi, Low, Narrow Neck, Flared Rim, Signed, Osuana Nampeyo, 8 x 13 ½ In. 1175.00
Jar, Hopi, Orange, Black, Beige, Geometric, Wide Shoulder, 3 x 5 ¾ In.. . . . . 460.00
Jar, Mata Ortiz, Sgraffitto, Butterflies, Curvilinear, Multicolored, 11 x 9 In.. . . . . 127.00
Jar, San Ildefonso, Geometric Step Design, Blackware, 3 In.. . . . . 472.00
Jar, Santa Clara, Wedding, Multicolored, c.1860, 8 ½ x 4 ½ In.. . . . . 167.00
Jar, Santa Domingo, Bird & Feather Design, Wide Mouth, Multicolored, c.1925, 9 ½ x 7 In. . . 633.00
Jar, Seed, Hopi, Mid 1900s, 4 ½ x 5 ½ In. 288.00
Jar, Seed, Hopi, Squat, Black, Red, White Ground, Abstract Design, 5 ¼ In. 10925.00
Jar, Water, Anasazi, Pottery, Double Neck, Handle, 4 ¾ x 6 x 5 ¼ In. 316.00
Jar, Zia, Bird, Flowers, Turtle, Multicolored, 10 x 7 ½ In.. . . . . 518.00
Kachina, Hopi, Ahote, Cottonwood, Multicolored, Leather, Shells, Feather, 12 ½ In.. . . . . 431.00
Kachina, Hopi, Balsa Wood, Painted, Feathers, Signed, H. Shelton, Oraibi, Arizona, 20 In. . . . 150.00
Kachina, Hopi, Butterfly Maiden, c.1950, 15 ½ In. 316.00
Kachina, Hopi, Cottonwood Root, Carved, Painted, 7 x 3 In. 316.00
Kachina, Hopi, Cottonwood Root, Piggyback Clown, Carved, 17 In.. . . . . 207.00
Kachina, Hopi, Drummer, Cottonwood Root, c.1960s, 15 In. 201.00
Kachina, Hopi, Kokopi Doll, Carved, Painted, 18 x 9 In.. . . . . 184.00
Kachina, Hopi, Tube Mouth, Cotton Near Ears, Qoia Navajo, c.1930, 7 ¾ In.. . . . . 1116.00
Kachina, Hopi, White Mask, Colored Mouth Lines, Polik Mana, c.1925, 13 In.. . . . . 840.00

Kachina, Hopi, Woman, Holding Plate, 12 x 3 In. 127.00
Kachina, Zuni, Horned Head, Tube Shaped Mouth, c.1950, 14 In. 374.00
Kepi, Sioux, Beaded, Multicolored, c.1900, 2 ¾ x 8 In. 822.00
Knife, Cheyenne, Sheath, Sinew Beadwork, Buffalo Hide, c.1880, 9 ½ In. 1035.00
Knife, Great Lakes, Crooked, Carved Handle, Dog Face, Walnut, Steel Blade, 8 ½ In. 1150.00
Knife, Northeast, Wood, Metal, Brass Wire Wrap, Woman's Lower Torso, 5-Point Star, 8 ½ In.. 1185.00
Knife Sheath, Crow, Beaded, Hide, Parfleche, Silver Concha, 12 ½ x 4 ½ In. 5750.00
Knife Sheath, Sioux, Beaded, Hide, Sinew Sewn, Holds 1800s Kitchen Knife, 9 ½ In. 2875.00
Leggings, Cheyenne, Glass Beads, Sinew Sewn, Fringe, c.1890, 20 ½ In. 5875.00
Leggings, Northern Plains, Hide, Appliqued Strip, Couched Beadwork, Fringe, 29 In. 720.00
Leggings, Sioux, Beaded, Fringe Seam, Multicolored, c.1890, 13 ¼ In. 1292.00
Leggings, Southern Plains, Yellow Skin, Yellow, Green, Red, Blue Beading, 36 x 14 In. 2530.00
Loom Sampler, Navajo, Geometric Pattern, Germantown, c.1800, 17 ½ x 18 In.. .... 294.00
Martingale, Plateau, Beaded, Flowers, Wool, Patterned Cotton, Brass Hawk Bells, 44 x 24 In. 1680.00
Mask, Lakota, Horse, Porcupine Quill, Seed Beads, Buffalo Hide, 12 ¼ x 22 In. 3163.00
Mask, Northwest Coast, Carved, Painted, 19 ½ x 12 ½ In. 352.00
Moccasins, Cheyenne, Pictorial, American Flag, Teepees, Tin Cones On Fringe, 11 In. 1430.00
Moccasins, Crow, Beaded, Hide, Abstract Flowers, Multicolored, Cuffed, c.1875, 9 ½ In. 1175.00
Moccasins, Crow, Sinew Sewn, Beaded, Buffalo Hide, Flowers, Cotton Edge Cuffs, 10 In. 1955.00
Moccasins, Great Lakes, Beaded, Child's, c.1890-1910, 6 In. .... *illus* 220.00
Moccasins, Plains, Beaded, Leather, Fringe, c.1930 .... *illus* 500.00
Moccasins, Plains, Buckskin, Beaded, c.1910, 12 In.. .... 303.00
Moccasins, Plains, Crosses, Beaded, Hide, Painted Soles, 19th Century, 10 ¾ In. 1098.00
Moccasins, Sioux, Beaded, Buffalo Soles, Bifurcated Tongues, 10 ½ In. 1840.00
Moccasins, Sioux, Ceremonial, Symbols, Beaded, Silver, 2-Tone Green, 10 In. 2090.00
Moccasins, Sioux, Sinew Sewn, Glass Beads, Hide, Multicolored, c.1890, 10 ¼ In. 2115.00
Moccasins, Southern Plains, Kiowa, Hard Sole, Geometric, Fringes, Multicolored, 9 ½ In. 5333.00
Moccasins, Southern Plains, Sinew Sewn, Hard Sole, Tanned, Painted Yellow, 10 ½ In. 690.00
Model, Cradle, Plateau, Red & White Beads, 16 ½ In. 323.00
Necklace, Navajo, Cast Naja, Star Terminals, Beads, Sterling Silver, 19 In. 4148.00
Necklace, Navajo, Graduated 2 Piece Bench Made Beads, Silver, c.1900, 24 In. 374.00
Necklace, Navajo, Silver, Buffalo Nickel Cross, 22 In. 176.00
Necklace, Navajo, Squash Blossom, Crescent Shape, Silver, Turquoise Beads, 15 In. 472.00
Necklace, Navajo, Squash Blossom, Naja, Silver, Coral, 10 Beads, 13 In.. .... 767.00
Necklace, Navajo, Squash Blossom, Naja, Silver, Turquoise, Fleur-De-Lis, 12 Beads, 15 In. 708.00
Necklace, Navajo, Squash Blossom, Silver, Turquoise, 10 Nugget Naja, 14 Beads, 13 In. 590.00
Necklace, Navajo, Squash Blossom, Silver, Turquoise, c.1950, 29 In.. .... 499.00
Necklace, Navajo, Squash Blossom, Silver, Turquoise, Cast Naja, 14 Beads, c.1930, 14 In.. .... 826.00
Necklace, Navajo, Squash Blossom, Silver, Turquoise, Horseshoe Naja, 120 Beads, 14 In. 649.00
Necklace, Navajo, Squash Blossom, Silver, Turquoise, Mid 1900s, 29 ½ In. .... *illus* 1210.00
Necklace, navajo, Squash Blossom, Silver, Turquoise, Naja, Mid 1900s, 15 ½ In. .... *illus* 720.00
Necklace, Navajo, Squash Blossom, Sterling Silver, Turquoise, Hand Wrought, 1940s, 13 ½ In. 388.00
Necklace, Navajo, Squash Blossom, Sterling Silver, Turquoise, Hollow Beads, c.1920, 15 ¾ In. 2844.00
Necklace, Navajo, Squash Blossom, Turquoise Stone, Horseshoe Naja, 24 x 3 ½ x 3 ¼ In. 403.00
Necklace, Navajo, Squash Blossom, Wrought Silver Beads, Turquoise Stones, 28 In. 546.00
Necklace, Northern Plains, Whiteheart Beads, Tack, 9 Strands, 25 x 4 In.. .... 104.00
Necklace, Plateau, Dentalium Shell, Blue & Red Pony Beads, Incised, 22 Strands, 22 In. 2185.00
Necklace, Santo Domingo, Turquoise Fetish, Heshi, 10 Strands, 28 In. 150.00
Necklace, Zuni, Double Pendant, Blood Coral Cluster, Sterling Silver Bead Chain, 32 In. 316.00
Necklace, Zuni, Naja, Kachina Inlaid, Turquoise, Coral, 8 Figural Beads, 14 In. 885.00
Necklace, Zuni, Rosette Pendant, Silver, Turquoise, Coral, Stylized Wings, c.1970, 14 In. 649.00
Necklace, Zuni, Silver Inlaid, Turquoise, Coral, Naja, Red Cardinal, 12 Beads, Birds, 13 ½ In. 708.00
Necklace, Zuni, Squash Blossom, Crescent Shape, Silver, Coral, Turquoise Beads, 15 ½ In.. .... 561.00
Olla, Acoma, Black, Cream, 11 ½ x 13 ½ In.. .... 259.00
Olla, Acoma, Black & Red Bird, Leaf Forms, White Slip, 8 ½ x 10 In. 316.00
Olla, Acoma, Multicolored, Fingernail Trim, Black Bird Wing, 12 x 9 In.. .... 167.00
Olla, Acoma, Stylized Flowers, Orange, Tan, Brown, Bulbous, 9 ½ x 10 ½ In. 2520.00
Olla, Acoma, Teardrop, Geometrics, Marked, Ruby Shroulote, c.1950, 16 x 15 In. 940.00
Olla, Acoma, Terra-Cotta, Bold Geometric Design, Orange, Black, Brown, Signed, 10 x 12 In.. 900.00
Olla, Apache, Coiled Over Rods, Devils Claw, Triangle, c.1900, 7 ¼ x 6 ¼ In. 450.00
Olla, Hopi, Feathers, Geometrics, c.1940, 6 ½ x 9 In. 330.00
Olla, Laguna, Black, Orange, Cream, 10 x 10 In. 489.00
Olla, San Ildefonso, Scrolls, Abstract Designs, Bulbous, Flared Rim, c.1900, 10 x 12 ½ In.. .... 2963.00
Olla, Santo Domingo, Bird, Geometric, 13 x 12 ½ In. 2875.00
Olla, Zia, Birds, Leaves, Red Lines, Multicolored, 10 x 11 In.. .... 5036.00
Olla, Zuni, Abstract Geometric, Kachina Face, Multicolored, c.1900, 4 x 11 ¼ In. 2370.00

Indian, Necklace, Navajo, Squash Blossom, Silver, Turquoise, Mid 1900s, 29 ½ In.
$1210.00

Indian, Necklace, Navajo, Squash Blossom, Silver, Turquoise, Naja, Mid 1900s, 15 ½ In.
$720.00

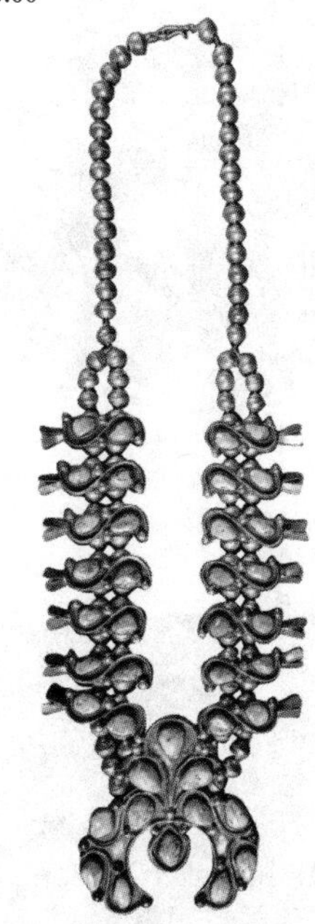

TIP

Turquoise is porous. Remove rings and bracelets before doing dishes, cleaning, or using hand lotion.

Skookum Apple Heads
Skookum Indian dolls were made with apple heads from about 1915 to 1920 and had no feet. The body was a block of wood. In the 1920s, a few had shoes. In the 1930s, leather-over-wood moccasins were used. Composition masks were used as part of the heads from the late teens to the 1940s.

Indian, Pouch, Chippewa, Beaded, Hide, Thread Sewn, Flowers, Cotton Lining, 9 ¼ x 9 In.
$345.00

Indian, Rug, Navajo, Diamonds, Orange, Cream, Brown, c.1920, 88 x 55 In.
$1920.00

Olla, Zuni, Pottery, High Shoulder, Flared Rim, Birds, 10 ½ In. 2820.00
Olla, Zuni, Sloping Rim, Red & Brown Geometric Design, White Ground, 9 In. 2185.00
Olla, Zuni, Stylized Volute, Medallion, 9 ¾ x 13 ½ In. 4444.00
Paddle, Northwest Coast, Carved, Painted, 35 ½ In. 822.00
Pants, Sioux, Sinew Sewn, Glass Beads, Gingham Waist, Multicolored, c.1900, 12 x 13 In. 3055.00
Parfleche, Blackfoot, Painted, Multicolored, Geometric, 24 x 13 ½ In. 2252.00
Parfleche, Case, Crow, Multicolored, Geometric, Elk Hide Fringe, Tapered, Cylindrical, 34 In. 1150.00
Parfleche, Northern Plains, Envelope, Stacked Diamonds, Multicolored, 24 ½ x 13 In. 1304.00
Pendant, Hopi, Badger Claw, Turquoise, Silver, c.1960, 25 x 2 ¼ In. 3055.00
Pendant, Navajo, Turquoise, Spider Web, Silver, Oval, c.1980, 1 ¾ x 2 ¼ In. 161.00
Pill Box, Navajo, Silver, Turquoise, Rocker Engraved, c.1950, 3 ½ x 2 ¾ In. 127.00
Pillow, Great Lakes, Heart Shape, Corduroy, Glass Beads, British, French Flags, 9 x 8 In. 22.00
Pillow, Great Lakes, Multicolored Glass Beads, Antelope, Bird, Rabbit, Tassels, 12 x 11 In. 154.00
Pillow, Great Lakes, Velvet, Cloth Back, Glass Beads, Tulip, Tassels, Hanger Loop, Square, 6 ½ In. 22.00
Pin, Navajo, Concha, Silver, Turquoise, Repousse Center, Scalloped & Perforated Edges, 3 In.. 444.00
Pin, Zuni, Oxblood Red Coral, Silver, c.1950, 2 ½ In. 196.00
Pin, Zuni, Stone To Stone Inlay, Spiny Oyster, Rainbow God, c.1974, 2 ½ In. 345.00
Pipe, Cheyenne, Catlinite Bowl, Ash Wood Stem, Horsehair, c.1800, 26 ½ In. 3163.00
Pipe, Plains, Ash Wood, Catlinite Bowl, Beaded Hide Case, Fringe, c.1880, 25 ¼ In. 7475.00
Pipe, Plateau, Catlinite Head, Brass Tacked Stem, Woman's, 2 ⅝ x 4 ½ x 10 ¾ In. 690.00
Pipe, Sioux, Scalloped Ash Wood Stem, Catlinite Bowl, Inlaid Lead, Steatite, 1920s, 28 In. 489.00
Pipe Bag, Lakota, Beaded Panels, Multicolored Geometric, Rawhide Slats, Fringes, 34 In. 1304.00
Pipe Stem, Plains, Branded Parallel Lines & Dots, Yellow, Wood, c.1890, 12 In. 720.00
Pitcher, Anasazi, Black On White, Squared Corners, Animal Handle, 4 ¾ x 4 ½ In. 575.00
Pitcher, Anasazi, Pinedale, Black On White, Bands, 6 x 6 In. 431.00
Plate, Hopi, Corn Maiden Kachina, Pottery, c.1915, 10 In. 1380.00
Plate, Northwest Coast, Haida, Argillite, Stylized Animal Heads, Halibut, Oval, 10 ⅛ In. 4740.00
Pot, Acoma, High Shoulders, Ruffled Rim, Impressed Collar, Deer, Bears, Flowers, 8 ½ In. 115.00
Pot, Acoma, Shouldered, Flared Rim, Geometric Design, 6 ½ In. 529.00
Pouch, Athabascan, Sealskin, Beaded, Flower Cutout Patterns, Hide Thong, 5 ½ x 2 In. 978.00
Pouch, Chippewa, Beaded, Hide, Thread Sewn, Flowers, Cotton Lining, 9 ¼ x 9 In. ..... *illus* 345.00
Pouch, Plains, Hide, Beaded, White, Red, Blue, Late 19th Century, 10 ½ x 16 In. 3276.00
Pouch, Plains, Paint, Multicolored Geometric, Brick Stitch, 4 ½ In. 948.00
Puppet, Sioux, Buckskin, Painted Face, 9 x 6 In. 288.00
Rattle, Great Lakes, Snapping Turtle, 20th Century, 17 In. 69.00
Rattle, Hopi, Dance, Gourd, Painted Face, Applied Design, 1970, 16 x 10 In. 100.00
Rattle, Northwest Coast, Eagle, Cedar, Painted, Carved, c.1970, 4 x 12 ½ x 3 In. 259.00
Ring, Navajo, 2 Frogs, Sterling Silver, Turquoise, Late 20th Century, 11 ¾ In. 40.00
Ring, Navajo, Silver, Landers Turquoise, Elongated Oval, c.1980, 2 ½ In., Size 8 .... 748.00
Ring, Navajo, Silver, Turquoise Stone, Oval, Size 10 ¼ 230.00
Ring, Zuni, Snake Figure, Silver, 2 Turquoise Stones, Size 10 .... 115.00
Robe, Plains, Sun Symbol, Abstract Feathers, Geometric Border, Multicolored, 85 x 65 In. 9480.00
Rug, Navajo, 2 Gray Hills, woven, 19 x 13 In. 167.00
Rug, Navajo, 3 Yei Figure Cornstalks, Hand Loomed, 1970s, 16 x 24 In. 92.00
Rug, Navajo, 3 Yei Figures, Gold, Black Border, Wool, 31 x 39 ½ In. 259.00
Rug, Navajo, 4 Yei Figures, Cornstalks, Heather Ground, c.1960, 57 x 31 In. 374.00
Rug, Navajo, Diamonds, Gray, Red, Black & White Bands, c.1940, 67 x 60 In. 2006.00
Rug, Navajo, Diamonds, Orange, Cream, Brown, c.1920, 88 x 55 In. .... *illus* 1920.00
Rug, Navajo, Ganado, Diamonds, Zigzags, c.1940, 58 x 40 In. 374.00
Rug, Navajo, Geometric, 36 x 60 In. 200.00
Rug, Navajo, Geometric, Red, Black, Gray, Ivory, 79 ½ x 50 ½ In. 880.00
Rug, Navajo, Natural Dye, Rabbit Brush, Soft Tones, Churro Wool, 1930s, 83 x 51 In. 748.00
Rug, Navajo, Serrated, Homespun, Natural Colors, c.1950, 176 x 62 In. 2588.00
Rug, Navajo, Serrated Diamonds, Red, Brown, Ivory, 69 ¼ x 42 ¾ In. 1112.00
Rug, Navajo, Stepped Interior, Red, Black, Gray, Cream, 48 x 83 In. 702.00
Rug, Navajo, Tapestry Weave, Yei Figure, c.1970s, 14 ½ x 16 ½ In. 150.00
Sash, Great Lakes, Beaded, 19th Century, 29 x 4 ¼ In. 878.00
Sash, Great Lakes, Chevron, White Pony Beads, Braided Fringe, 108 In. 9480.00
Sash, Great Lakes, Red Wool, Beaded, Central Band, Horse Track, Braided Ends, 44 In. 4444.00
Sash, Iroquois, Finger Woven, Beaded, Geometric, Braided Fringe, 71 & 73 x 3 In., Pair 1495.00
Sash, Plains, Loom Beaded, Tassels, White, Blue, Red, Yellow, 21 In. 86.00
Scabbard, Crow, Rifle, Beaded, Tanned Hide, Sinew Sewn, Red Wool, Long Fringe, 46 In. 9775.00
Scabbard, Northern Plains, Beaded Hide, Fringe, Trade Cloth Inset, Multicolored, 46 In. 5333.00
Scale, Plains, Hanging, Buffalo Hide, Pendulum, 2 Weights, 1800s 460.00
Scraper, Plains, Elk Antler Hide, Etched Pictographs, 11 ¾ In. 474.00
Shirt, Blackfoot, War, Buckskin, Beaded Strips, Ermine Tail, Fringe, 33 ½ x 63 In. 4025.00

Shirt, Ute, Pony Beaded Cloth, Hide, Fringe, Hide Beaded Strips, Man's, 30 In. 6518.00
Shot Pouch, Sioux, Beaded, Teardrop Shape, 7 x 5 ¼ In. 201.00
Snowshoes, Micmac, Rawhide Weaving, Dyed Wool Pompons, 41 In. 316.00
Spoon, Abenaki, Birch, Dog's Head Finial, 1 ¾ In. 1896.00
Spoon, Great Lakes, Effigy, Wood, Wide Scoop, Tapered Handle, Horse Head Finial, 10 In. 948.00
Spoon, Hopi, Pottery, Geometric Design, c.1940, 4 ½ x 7 In. 69.00
Spoon, Northwest Coast, Haida, Carved Horn, Beaver, Bird Handle, 7 ½ In. 1541.00
Spoon, Northwest Coast, Haida, Carved Horn, Stylized Animal, Abalone Eyes, 10 In. 2607.00
Spoon, Northwest Coast, Horn, Incised, Hatched, Round Designs, Tapered Handle, 11 In. 345.00
Spoon, Northwest Coast, Stylized Animals, Tapered Handle, 8 ¾ In. 444.00
Tableta, Hopi, Butterfly Shape, Head Strap, Multicolored, c.1950, 15 x 13 In. 431.00
Tomahawk, Plains, Forged Iron, Barrel Shape Pipe Bowl, Ash Handle, Brass Tack, 22 ¼ In. 11850.00
Tomahawk, Plains, Steel, Hardwood Handle, c.1875, 18 In. 3172.00
Totem, Haida, Northwest Coast, Argillite, Human, Animal, Bird Figures, 19 ½ In. 4740.00
Totem, Northwest Coast, Carved, 2 Figures, Bird, Original Black Paint, 14 In. .... *illus* 529.00
Totem, Northwest Coast, Carved, 3 Faces, Painted, 16 ½ x 7 ¾ In. 2115.00
Totem, Northwest Coast, Carved, Beaver, Frog, Raven, Flat Back, 13 In. 1725.00
Totem, Northwest Coast, Carved, Painted, c.1900, 33 In. 7605.00
Totem, Northwest Coast, Carved Walrus Ivory, Animals, Bird Finial, Tapered Shaft, 15 In. 830.00
Tray, Navajo, Wedding, Concentric Sawtooth Design, 15 In. 403.00
Tray, Pima, Coiled, American Eagle, 1924, 16 ½ x 14 ½ In. 1287.00
Tray, Pima, Coiled, Willow, Devil's Claw Design & Rim, Hooked Frets, 3 ¾ x 16 ¾ In. 863.00
Tray, Pima, Man In Maze Pattern, Woven, 10 In. 1035.00
Vase, Acoma, Baluster Form, Flared & Ruffled Rim, 6 ½ In. 176.00
Vase, Acoma, Pottery, New Mexico, 7 ¼ x 7 ½ In. 117.00
Vase, Cochiti, Black Curvilinear, Red Ground, Tapered Neck, Handles, 10 ¾ In. 830.00
Vase, Hopi, Wedding, Frog Woman, Double Neck, Birds, 12 ½ x 6 ½ In. 575.00
Vase, Maricopa, Round, Slender Neck, Flared, Black, Orange Ground, c.1969, 22 ½ In. 863.00
Vase, Mata Ortiz, Wedding, Double Spout, Handle, Black, Red, Blue, White Clay, 10 x 7 In. 92.00
Vase, Navajo, Wedding, Embossed, 6 x 6 In. 127.00
Vase, Pima Maricopa, Rustic, Tree, Dark Slip, Red Body, Handle, c.1912, 7 x 4 In. 230.00
Vase, San Ildefonso, Blackware, Signed, Diaz, 7 ¼ x 5 In. 380.00
Vase, Santa Clara, Wedding, Double Neck, Carved Avanyu, Late 1900s, 7 ⅝ x 6 ½ In. 460.00
Vase, Santo Domingo, Flowers, Birds, Blackware, Marked, 10 ½ In. 206.00
Vase, Toltec, Effigy Pot, 3-Footed, Quattamundi Head, Late 1900s, 5 x 5 x 6 ½ In. 29.00
Vest, Eastern Sioux, Hide, Flower Quillwork, Velveteen, Cotton Lining, 21 ½ x 40 In. 920.00
Vest, Great Lakes, Beaded, American Flags, Leather, Blue Bead Ground, Doll, 5 ¼ x 2 ¼ In. 330.00
Vest, Plains, Beaded, Quilled, Flowers, Purple, Red, White, Green, Fringe, 1800s 5500.00
Vest, Sioux, Beaded, Hide, Sinew Sewn, Tipi Designs, Forked Devices Fringe, 21 x 38 In. 2415.00
Vest, Sioux, Beaded, Sinew Sewn, Sheepskin, Flags, Teepees, Fringe, Child's, 15 ½ In. .... *illus* 1610.00
Vest, Sioux, Fully Beaded, 2 Hands, Indian, Yellow, White, Blue, Red, Green, 1800s 26000.00
Vest, Sioux, Glass Beads, Cotton, Multicolored, c.1900, 13 In., 24-In. Chest 1410.00
Vest, Sioux, Thread & Sinew Sewn, Glass Beads, Ribbon Fringe, Multicolored, c.1900, 12 x 26 In. 2820.00
Victory Staff, Sioux, Carved Buffalo Effigy, Horn Tip, c.1880, 36 ½ In. 805.00
Wall Pocket, Great Lakes, Slipper Shape, Velvet, Clear Beads, Star, Bird, 8 ¼ x 3 ¾ In. 44.00
Wand, Kwakiutl, Wood, Sea Serpent, Red, Black, White, c.1890, 25 In. 1680.00
Water Drum, Chippewa, Cedar Log, Carved, 16 x 9 ½ In. 575.00
Weaving, Navajo, 3rd Phase, Red, Black, Cream, Saltillo Design, 58 x 70 In. 5520.00
Weaving, Navajo, 5 Stylized Yei Dancers, Variegated Ground, Wool, 63 ½ x 43 ½ In. 948.00
Weaving, Navajo, 7 Yei Figures, Brown Ground, c.1920, 55 x 36 In. 2015.00
Weaving, Navajo, American Flag, Cream, Aniline Blue, Red, 50 Stars, 58 x 37 In. 1527.00
Weaving, Navajo, Beige, Red, Brown, Cross, Whirling Logs, 50 ½ x 99 ½ In. 1293.00
Weaving, Navajo, Black, Red, Tan, Center Diamonds, X Border, 56 x 84 In. 5175.00
Weaving, Navajo, Corn Stalks, Yei Heads, Variegated Ground, Wool, c.1920, 71 x 42 In. 4740.00
Weaving, Navajo, Crystal, Brown, Cream, Diamond, Sawtooth Border, 64 x 82 In. 1380.00
Weaving, Navajo, Crystal, Interlock Border, Gray, Serrated Diamond, Spirit Line, 55 x 32 In. 259.00
Weaving, Navajo, Diamond Pattern, Red & Black On Gray & Cream, 38 x 55 In. 440.00
Weaving, Navajo, Ganado, Red, Brown, Double Diamonds, Sawtooth Border, 46 x 60 In. 575.00
Weaving, Navajo, Ganado, Stacked Diamonds, Crosses, Wool, Aniline Dye, 82 x 48 In. 1265.00
Weaving, Navajo, Geometric Design, Red & Black On Gray, 53 ½ x 85 In. 1763.00
Weaving, Navajo, Germantown, Diamond, Angular Border, Zigzags, 109 ½ x 51 In. 2760.00
Weaving, Navajo, Horn Toad People, Hand Spun Wool, Red Antway Chant, 44 x 52 In. 1725.00
Weaving, Navajo, Natural, Aniline Red, Stacked Diamonds, Hooked Border, c.1920, 78 x 42 In. 780.00
Weaving, Navajo, Red Mesa, Serrated Outlined Zigzags, Hand Spun Wool, 71 ½ x 45 In. 978.00
Weaving, Navajo, Stylized Horned Figure, Lightning, Variegated Ground, 64 x 46 ½ In. 1896.00
Weaving, Navajo, Yeis With Concha Belts, Stepped Border, Wool, 43 x 62 ½ In. 1265.00
Weaving, Navajo, Zigzag Bands, Rows Of Crosses, Late 1800s, 51 x 72 In. 4700.00

TIP

Wool rugs that are hung on the wall should be treated with moth repellent, perhaps even put in the sun for a few hours in the spring and fall.

Indian, Totem, Northwest Coast, Carved, 2 Figures, Bird, Original Black Paint, 14 In.
$529.00

Indian, Vest, Sioux, Beaded, Sinew Sewn, Sheepskin, Flags, Teepees, Fringe, Child's, 15 ½ x 15 In.
$1610.00

TIP

Keep art, paintings, prints, and textiles away from sunny windows.

Inkstand, Bronze, Bust, Diana, Red Marble Base, Gilt Feet, Signed, Falguiere, 1890s, 8 In.
$857.00

TIP

Clean a glass inkwell carefully. The old ink may cover a crack. Wash in warm water with mild dishwashing liquid or soap, never dishwasher detergent. Don't use ammonia if the glass is decorated or iridescent.

Inkwell, Glass, Cover, Aqua, Globular, Knop Stem, Pontil, 1840-70, 5 ⅝ In.
$1760.00

Inkwell, Milk Glass, Boat, Opalescent Flowers, Pat'd Aug. 9, 1870, c.1890-1910, 2 ½ In.
$186.00

INDIAN TREE is a china pattern that was popular during the last half of the nineteenth century. It was copied from earlier Indian textile patterns that were very similar. The pattern includes the crooked branch of a tree and a partial landscape with exotic flowers and leaves. Green, blue, pink, and orange were the favored colors used in the design.

Bowl, Coalport, 6 ½ In., 12 Piece 69.00
Bowl, Coalport, 10 x 3 In. 58.00
Bowl, Dessert, Tan Border, Band, Greek Key, Soho Pottery 15.00
Cup & Saucer, Demitasse, Coalport, c.1760 .... 50.00
Pitcher, Lamberton, Albert Pick & Co., Stamped, 4 x 4 In. 45.00
Plate, Dinner, English Ironstone, Minton, 10 ¼ In., 12 Piece 403.00
Plate, Dinner, Shenango Pottery, Staffordshire, 10 ½ In. 10.00
Plate, Pink & Blue Flowers, Floral Border, Ironstone, Early 1900s, 10 ¼ In., 12 Piece 411.00
Plate, Spode, c.1820, 9 In. .... 195.00 to 265.00
Platter, Coalport, 18 ½ x 14 ½ In. 86.00
Platter, Ironstone, 17 ½ x 14 In. 63.00
Platter, Ironstone, Oval, 14 x 17 ½ In. 55.00
Sugar & Creamer, Green Greek Key Border, Johnson Brothers, 1979-82 .... 35.00
Tea Set, Teapot, Cover, Sugar, Creamer, WR Midwinter Ltd., 3 Piece 35.00
Teapot, Transferware, 5 ¾ In. 17.00
Tureen, Cover, Underplate, Spode, 11 x 13 In. 403.00

INKSTANDS were made to be placed on a desk. They held some type of container for ink, and possibly a sander, a pen tray, a pen, a holder for pounce, and even a candle to melt the sealing wax. Inkstands date to the eighteenth century and have been made of silver, copper, ceramics, and glass. Additional inkstands may be found in these and other related categories.

Brass, Paw Feet, Lion Head Details, c.1900, 12 ½ x 5 In. 264.00
Bronze, 2 Inkwells, Liners, Pierced Platform, Scroll, Shell Pediment, 1875, 12 x 18 x 13 In. 805.00
Bronze, Bust, Diana, Red Marble Base, Gilt Feet, Signed, Falguiere, 1890s, 8 In. .... *illus* 857.00
Bronze, Dore, Green Veined Marble, 3 Pots, round, Laurel Wreath, Acorn Finials, 8 x 13 In. 1527.00
Bronze, Fox, Duck In Mouth, 2 Stump Wells, Red Marble Base, After Leonard, 7 x 18 In. 1725.00
Cast Iron, Double Font Revolving, Milk Glass & Cobalt Snail Fonts, c.1870, 3 ½ In. 219.00
Cast Iron, Inkwell, Glass Snail Fonts, Ground Lips, Penholders, c.1875, 4 x 5 x 8 In. 196.00
Cast Iron, Pierced, Openwork Tray, Handles, Late 19th Century, 19 ½ In. 49.00
Louis XVI Style, Gilt Bronze, Oval Stand, Shell Form Bowls, c.1900, 4 ¾ x 8 ¾ In. 75.00
Porcelain, Hand Painted, Multicolored, Fischer & Mieg, c.1875, 6 x 6 ¾ x 8 ¼ In. 176.00
Silver, Chased, 2 Glass Pots, Lids, Rolling Calendar, Pen Tray, Octagon, Gorham, c.1910, 15 In. 4063.00
Silver, Sheffield, Marked, Henry Wilkinson & Co., c.1878, 6 ½ x 14 x 9 In. 1495.00
Silver Plate, Ellkington, 2 Inkwells, Masks, 2 Children, Lidded Box, Candle Post, 1897, 6 x 15 In. 431.00
Standish, Silver Bronze, Horn, Oak, Dolphin Shape, Cut Glass Inkwell, 13 ½ x 7 In. 1020.00

INKWELLS, of course, held ink. Ready-made ink was first made about 1836 and was sold in bottles. The desk inkwell had a narrow hole so the pen would not slip inside. Inkwells were made of many materials, such as pottery, glass, pewter, and silver. Look in these categories for more listings of inkwells.

Bear, Coleslaw Mane, Redware, Shenandoah Valley, 19th Century, 7 ¼ In. 11700.00
Bird, Green, Globular, Applied Head Wings & Tail, Drawn Stem, Pontil, 4 ¾ In. 158.00
Blue Satin Glass, Victorian, 2 In. 50.00
Brass, 3 Dogs, Seated, Ball Top, Chains, 4 ½ In. 180.00
Brass, Double, Curvilinear Shape, Flowers, Art Nouveau, 3 ½ x 10 In. 180.00
Brass, Double Well, Claw Foot, Glass Inserts, Victorian, 3 ¾ x 10 ½ x 6 ¼ In. 75.00
Brass, Malachite, Amboyna Wood, Cut Glass, Baronial Style, Round Base, c.1880, 8 ¼ In. 470.00
Bronze, 3 Squatting Satyrs Holding Putti Finial, Lid, Wood Base, 10 In. 805.00
Bronze, Arts & Crafts Style, Enameled, Multicolored, Marked, 4 x 3 In. 600.00
Bronze, Blotter, Masks, Marked Stingle, Vienna, Late 19th Century, 5 In. 147.00
Bronze, Dore, Lid, Urn Shape, 20th Century, 6 ¾ x 6 In. 783.00
Bronze, Gargoyle, Penholder In Mouth, Spread Wings, N. Muller, 6 x 6 In. 230.00
Bronze, Oak, Bulldog, Glass Eyes, Arthur Court, 1979, 6 x 4 ½ In. 200.00
Bronze, Turkey, Oak, Signed, Arthur Court, 7 x 5 x 6 In. 175.00
Cast Brass, Double Urns, Hinged, Women's Heads, Art Nouveau, c.1900, 5 ½ x 12 In. 66.00
Cast Iron, Buffalo, Hump Opens To Well, 9 x 6 In. 240.00
Cast Iron, Dog, Dead Game, c.1900, 4 x 11 In. 358.00
Cast Iron, Greyhound Head, Figural, 7 In. 190.00
Cast Iron, Horse Head & Horseshoe, Double, Victorian, 5 ⅜ x 6 ¼ In. 60.00
Cast Iron, Katz Drug Co., c.1910, 7 x 4 ½ In. 715.00
Clear Glass, Etched Flowers, Leaves, Silver Collar, Friction Lid, Tiffany & Co., 5 x 5 In. 1920.00

Copper, Lid, Double Wells, Enamel Green, Blue Flowers, Arts Crafts Shop, 7 x 4 In. 450.00
Cut Glass, Brass Hinged Lid, Turquoise Blue, Faceted Corners, 3 ⅛ In. 134.00
Genie With Aladdin Lamp, Hinged Lid, Capo-Di-Monte 121.00
Glass, Acorn Embossed Lid, 4-Sided Pyramid, Blue Iridescent, Amethyst Shards, Bohemia, 3 In. 374.00
Glass, Aquamarine, Pontil, Pedestal, c.1840, 5 ⅝ x 3 ½ In. 1808.00
Glass, Clear, Brass Hinged Lid, Neck Ring, Ribs, Horizontal Red, White Bands, 1 ⅝ In. 258.00
Glass, Clear, Brass Hinged Mushroom Lid, Neck Ring, Applied Green Threading, 2 ⅛ In. 255.00
Glass, Cover, Aqua, Globular, Knop Stem, Pontil, 1840-70, 5 ⅝ In. .... *illus* 1760.00
Glass, Embossed Lid, 4-Sided, Pyramid, Gold Iridescent, Amber Shards, Kralik, Bohemia, 3 In. 288.00
Glass, Embossed Lid, Amethyst Shards, Gold Iridescent, Kralik, Bohemia, 3 ½ In. 431.00
Glass, Embossed Lid, Melon Ribbed, Gold Iridescent, Amber Shards, Kralik, Bohemia, 3 ½ In. 345.00
Glass, Embossed Lid, Wide Threading, Oval, Squat, Green Iridescent, Kralik, Bohemia, 3 In. . 86.00
Glass, Flip Lid, Melon Ribbed, Gold Iridescent, Amber Shards, Kralik, Bohemia, 5 ¼ In. 345.00
Glass, Hinged Lid, Square, Concave Panels, Iridescent Amethyst, Brass Neck Ring, 3 ¼ In. 364.00
Glass, Metal Lid, Embossed Mask, Green Iridescent, Metal Frame, Bohemia, 3 In. 173.00
Glass, Metal Swivel Lid, Swirl Shape, Scrolled Ormolu Base, France, 10 In. 115.00
Glass, Mushroom Shape, Stopper, Millefiori, Paperweight Type, Tooled Mouth, 5 ⅛ In. 420.00
Horse Head, Bronze, Gilt Interior, Glass Liner, Wooden Plinth, 7 x 7 ½ In. 1763.00
Metal, 3 Monkeys, Cat On Barrel, Opalescent Glass Insert 150.00
Metal, Boar's Head, Porcelain Insert, Wood Base, 6 ½ x 8 ¼ In. 370.00
Metal, Cat, Glass Eyes, Glass Insert, 3 ¾ x 5 In. 165.00
Metal, Owl, Porcelain Insert, 4 x 9 ½ In. 160.00
Metal, Porcelain, Cat, Wearing Bonnet, 6 In. 201.00
Milk Glass, Boat, Opalescent Flowers, Pat'd Aug. 9, 1870, c.1890-1910, 2 ½ In. .... *illus* 186.00
Milk Glass, Horseshoe, Pen Rest At Bottom, 2 ¼ x 3 ⅜ In. 79.00
Paperweight, Millefiori, Glass, Stopper, England, 5 In. 1050.00
Porcelain, 2 Wells, Bird, Footed, Herend, 4 ½ x 5 ½ In. 292.00
Porcelain, Snail, Leaf, Twig Pen Rest, Late 19th Century, 4 ½ x 6 ½ In. .... *illus* 275.00
Porcelain, Snail, Twig Pen Rest, White, Yellow, Pink, c.1890, 5 x 7 x 7 In. 288.00
Porcelain, Snail, White, Brass Swivel Stand, Drip Tray, Pen Rack, c.1900, 3 x 5 In. 125.00
Pottery, Dog, Reclining, Staffordshire, 5 x 3 ¾ In. 144.00
Pottery, Prunus Blossoms, Orbs, Rookwood, c.1888, 3 In. 207.00
Pottery, Sleeping Shepherdess, Dark Brown Glaze, Larkin Bros., E. Liverpool, Ohio, 3 ½ x 5 In. 120.00
Ram's Horn, Buck, Germany, c.1920, 14 In. 250.00
Shell, Brass, Copper Wash, Glass, 4 x 10 ½ In. .... *illus* 138.00
Silver, Cut Glass, Shield Reserve, Square Body, Victorian, 3 ½ x 3 In. 173.00
Silver, Porcelain Well, Pocket Watch Within Lid, Flared Base, Wm. Comyns, England, 1909, 3 x 5 In. 717.00
Silver Plate, 2 Glass Inserts, Sheffield, 3 ¼ x 4 ¼ In. 104.00
Silver Plate, Greyhound, Sitting In Doghouse, Hinged Roof, Brick Style Base, 5 x 4 ½ In. 120.00
Spelter, Glass, Gothic Bird, Cast Iron Lid, Mueller, 1800s, 6 x 6 ½ In. 330.00
Spelter, Hunting Dog, Porcelain Liner, Marked, Kaiser, 5 x 10 x 4 In. 195.00
Stoneware, 8 Quill Holes, Great Western Devonshire, 3 ½ In. 58.00
Stoneware, Book Form, Cobalt Blue, Incised Heart, Pinwheel, Early 1800s, 1 ½ x 3 In. 9945.00
Wood, Bird & Stump, Carved, Late 19th Century, 5 ½ x 8 ¼ In. 275.00
Wood, Devil's Head, Red Face, Black Beard, Yellow Glass Eyes, Black Forest, c.1890, 3 ¾ In. .. 850.00
Yellowware, Incised Banding, Round, 5 Holes, Orange Glaze, 1 ½ x 3 ½ In. 77.00

INSULATORS of glass or pottery have been made for use on telegraph or telephone poles since 1844. Thousands of different styles of insulators have been made. Most common are those of clear or aqua glass; most desirable are the threadless types made from 1850 to 1870.

E.C. & M. Co., S.F., Teal Blue, White Dot, 4 ¼ In. 476.00
Harloe's Pat., Mar 21, '99, Mar 12, '01, Dec., '02, White, Glazed, Pottery, 3 ½ In. .... *illus* 240.00
Star, Side Wire Groove, Single Petticoat, Smooth Base, Aqua 12.00

IRISH BELLEEK, *see Belleek category.*

IRON is a metal that has been used by man since prehistoric times. It is a popular metal for tools and decorative items like doorstops that need as much weight as possible. Items are listed here or under other appropriate headings, such as Bookends, Doorstop, Kitchen, Match Holder, or Tool. The tool that is used for ironing clothes, an iron, is listed in the Kitchen category under Iron and Sadiron.

Anvil, Painted, Bittersweet, 3 ¾ x 8 In. 55.00
Aquarium, Glazed Panels, Finials, Octagonal, Painted, Victorian, 25 x 27 In. 1076.00
Ashtray, Boy With Basket, Hubley, 5 ¼ x 6 ¼ x 7 In. 57.00
Bird Spit, Wrought, Adjustable Rack, 3-Footed Base, c.1770, 27 ¼ In. 1521.00

TIP

Do not display glass inkwells in a window or sunny location. The glass may turn slightly purple.

Inkwell, Porcelain, Snail, Leaf, Twig Pen Rest, Late 19th Century, 4 ½ x 6 ½ In.
$275.00

Inkwell, Shell, Brass, Copper Wash, Glass, 4 x 10 ½ In.
$138.00

Insulator, Harloe's Pat., Mar 21, '99, Mar 12, '01, Dec., '02, White, Glazed, Pottery, 3 ½ In.
$240.00

I

IRON

Iron, Bootjack, Lyre Form, Black Paint, 2 ¼ x 12 In. $90.00

Iron, Card Holder, Wire, Star, Boot Form Feet, 3 x 3 ½ x 2 ¾ In. $198.00

Iron, Paperweight, French Bulldog, Bulging Eyes, 3 ½ x 4 In. $144.00

TIP

Small nicks and scratches in decorative iron pieces can be covered with black crayon. Wipe off the excess with paper. Don't do this on pots and pans you may use for cooking.

I

Book Press, Black Paint, Gold Trim, 3 ⅝ x 3 ⅜ x 2 ⅜ In. 325.00
Bootjack, Cricket, 9 ½ In. 55.00
Bootjack, Cutout Heart, 10 ¼ x 4 ¾ In. 60.00
Bootjack, Lyre Form, Black Paint, 2 ¼ x 12 In. .... *illus* 90.00
Bootjack, Naughty Nellie, Painted, Late 19th Century, 10 In. 99.00
Bootjack, Openwork Heart, U-Shape Top, Penn., 2 ½ x 9 ½ In. .... 250.00 to 275.00
Bootjack, Pistol Form, 8 In. 125.00
Candleholder, Lamp, Stand, 3 Splayed Feet, Round Base, 17 x 8 In. 303.00
Candlestand, Wrought, Tripod Base, Penny Feet, Spring Held Crossbar, Early 1800s, 37 ¾ In. 940.00
Cannon, Signal, Wood Base, 17 In. 300.00
Card Holder, Wire, Star, Boot Form Feet, 3 x 3 ½ x 2 ¾ In. .... *illus* 198.00
Card Holder, Wire Spring, Star & Boot Shape Feet, 3 x 3 ½ In. 198.00
Cigar Cutter, Enterprise, Medium Plug, Champion Improved, 1871, 17 ½ In. 120.00
Cigar Cutter, Griswold, Gold Accents, 1870, 18 ½ In. 225.00
Cigar Cutter, Pig, Figural, Painted, Base, Marked, Pat Appld For, 3 ¾ x 8 x 5 ¾ In. 350.00
Cigarette Holder, Elephant, 6 x 8 In. 70.00
Coin Counter, Lamson, Victorian, Pat. July 7, 1891, 7 x 11 ¼ x 11 ½ In. 400.00
Cuspidor, Turtle, Electroplated, Tin Shell, Golden & Jacobson, 14 x 10 x 5 ¼ In. 345.00
Cuspidor, Turtle Shape, Copper Flashed, Removable Pan, Golden Jacobs, Chicago, 4 x 11 x 13 In. 300.00
Figure, Birds, Lizards, Leaves, Stylized, 37 x 34 In. 190.00
Figure, Boy, Holding Goose, Paint, Rocaille Base, Cast, 39 In. 300.00
Figure, Devil's Head, Forehead Hole, Cigarette Holder, Pool Hall Aid, Porcelain, Red Paint, 3 x 4 In. 354.00
Figure, Dog, Spaniel, Seated, 34 x 33 x 17 ¼ In., Pair 633.00
Figure, Dog, Terrier, Multicolored Cold Painted, 19th Century, 22 ¼ In. 5040.00
Figure, Eagle, Spread Wings, Painted, Yellow Beak, White Head, 13 x 31 In. 336.00
Figure, Frog, Horse Tether, Original Green Paint, 30 Lbs. 1930.00
Figure, Indian, Shooting Arrow, Die Cut, Painted, c.1900, 10 x 7 In. 295.00
Figure, Nude Man, Standing, 32 x 18 x 11 In. 176.00
Figure, Puppy, 10 x 14 In. 380.00
Figure, Yale Bulldog, Painted Black, Life Size, 15 x 26 In. 418.00
Lantern Bracket, Edwardian, Wrought, Regency Gothic Style, Quatrefoil, 33 x 31 In., Pair .. 570.00
Leg Irons, Bean, Key, Owned By Houdini, Engraved With Name. 8400.00
Light Holder, Rope, Turned Wood Base, Flat Clamp, Curved Handle, 10 ¾ In. 248.00
Ornament, Wrought, Multicolored Flowers, Petal Base, 19th Century, 19 ¼ In. 235.00
Paperweight, 2 Bobwhites, On Grassy Knoll, Multicolored Paint, Hubley, 2 ⅝ x 3 In. 250.00
Paperweight, Atta Boy, Hubley Manufacturing Co., 4 ⅝ In. 403.00
Paperweight, Dolly Dimple, Hubley, 2 ½ In. 201.00
Paperweight, Duck Decoys, Mallard, Canvasback, Green Winged Teal, Hubley Co., 3 ½ In., 3 Piece 144.00
Paperweight, Flapper, Duck, Rain Hat, Galoshes, Domed Base, Hubley, c.1922, 3 ¾ x 2 ¾ In. 495.00
Paperweight, French Bulldog, Bulging Eyes, 3 ½ x 4 In. .... *illus* 144.00
Paperweight, Frog, Male & Female, Painted Green, White, Red, 3 x 2 ⅞ In., Pair 198.00
Paperweight, Girl Skater, Hubley Manufacturing Co., 3 ¼ In. 173.00
Paperweight, Mouse With Biscuit, Bradley & Hubbard, 4 x 2 ⅜ In. 403.00
Paperweight, Ski Jumper, No. 130, Hubley Manufacturing Co., 2 ½ In. 345.00
Paperweight, Swing Band, 6 Musicians, Hubley, 2 ⅝ In. 403.00
Pipe Tongs, Blacksmith Made, Pennsylvania, c.1750 .... 350.00
Plaque, Eagle, Spread Wings, Flag Banner, Painted, Red, White, Blue, 4 ¾ x 7 ½ In. 121.00
Safe, Star, 3 ½ x 2 ½ x 2 ½ In. 66.00
Safe, Victor Safe & Lock Co., Hand Painted, Victorian, Footed, H.C. Hoffman, 21 x 14 x 15 In. .. 440.00
Safe, Wood Grain Paint, Ship, Standard Safe & Lock, Des Moines, Wheels, 27 x 16 In. .. *illus* 220.00
Sconce, 3 Platforms, Scrolled & Twisted, 47 In., Pair 431.00
Shooting Gallery Target, Turkey Hen Form, Painted, Cast, 5 ½ x 4 ½ In. 143.00
Sign, Wall St., New St., Corner Frame, Cast, Model T-128, 13 x 30 In. 1760.00
Smokehouse Hanger, Crown Of Thorns, 3 Hanger Hook, Wrought, 11 ¾ x 13 ½ In. 165.00
Stamp, Notary, Hand, Cast, 12 x 7 In. .... *illus* 1500.00
Stringholder, Cast, Revolves On Base, c.1900, 6 In. 88.00
Stringholder, Woman's Face, Red, Yellow, 8 ⅛ x 6 ½ In. 317.00
Target Shooting Gallery, Turkey Hen, Painted, 5 ½ x 4 ½ In. 130.00
Tobacco Shredder, Cast, Wood, Roller Bar, Footed, Marked, Gesetzlich-Gesmutzt, 8 x 12 ½ In. 180.00
Tree Guard, 68 x 20 In., Pair 75.00
Vase, Scenic Landscape, Horizontal Ribs, Baluster, Cast, Japan, Early 1900s, 12 ½ In. 240.00
Windmill Weight, Crescent Moon, Marked, Eclipse A13, Morse & Co., Chicago, c.1875, 10 In. 118.00
Windmill Weight, Crescent Moon, Raised Numerals 417, Stand, c.1920, 12 x 7 In. 563.00
Windmill Weight, Horse, 19th Century, Iron, 8 ½ In. 936.00
Windmill Weight, Rooster, Red Paint, Hummer, E 184, 8 In. 650.00
Windmill Weight, W, Althouse-Wheeler Co., Wisconsin, c.1915, 13 x 22 In. 326.00
Windmill Weight, Warship, Monitor, Cement, Baker Mfg., c.1918, 7 ½ x 28 ¼ In. 4100.00

IRONSTONE china was first made in 1813. It gained its greatest popularity during the mid-nineteenth century. The heavy, durable, off-white pottery was made in white or was decorated with any of hundreds of patterns. Much flow blue pottery was made of ironstone. Some of the decorations were raised. Many pieces of ironstone are unmarked, but some English and American factories included the word *Ironstone* in their marks. Additional pieces may be listed in other categories, such as Chelsea Grape, Chelsea Sprig, Flow Blue, Gaudy Ironstone, Mason's Ironstone, Moss Rose, Staffordshire, and Tea Leaf Ironstone.

Basin, Meakin, Staffordshire, 15 x 4 ½ In. 95.00
Basin, Prairie, J. Clementson, Staffordshire, 13 x 4 ¾ In. 150.00
Bowl, Toddy, Fleur-De-Lis Handles, Staffordshire, 10 x 8 In. 100.00
Butter Drainer, 4 ½ In. 25.00
Coffeepot, George Washington Vignette, Elsmore & Forster, 10 ¾ In. 488.00
Compote, Flow Blue, Open Handles, Footed, 11 ¼ In. 60.00
Compote, Flowers, Scalloped Edge, Embossed, Staffordshire, 10 ½ x 6 In. 250.00
Compote, Fluted, Scalloped Edge, 9 x 6 In. 275.00
Compote, Fluted Hops, Pedestal, Scalloped, Ruffled Rim, 11 x 4 In. 325.00
Compote, Gothic, J. Meir, Staffordshire, 9 x 4 ¾ In. 225.00
Compote, Melon Ribbing, Pedestal, 8 ⅝ x 5 In. 245.00
Compote, Pedestal, 8 ¾ In. 210.00
Compote, Pedestal, Edward Clark, 8 ¾ x 4 In. 230.00
Compote, Square, Pedestal, Embossed, Ruffled Rim, John Maddock, 7 ⅝ In. 285.00
Drainer, Oval, 10 In. 120.00
Drainer, Oval, 14 ⅝ In. 260.00
Food Mold, Grape Cluster, 6 ½ x 2 ¾ In. 75.00
Gravy Boat, Bow & Tassel, Burgess & Goddard, 9 ¼ x 5 ¼ In. 118.00
Gravy Boat, Ribbed Raspberry, J. & G. Meakin, 8 x 5 ¾ In. 142.00
Gravy Boat, Sydenham, Anthony Shaw, 8 x 5 ½ In. 112.00
Gravy Boat, Wheat & Clover, Embossed, 8 x 5 ½ In. 136.00
Ladle, Rope & Ring, Staffordshire, 3 ½ x 8 In. 99.00
Ladle, Sauce, Blue Band, Gold Highlights, 3 x 5 In. 25.00
Ladle, Sauce, Staffordshire, 2 ⅓ x 6 In. 95.00
Ladle, Sauce, Staffordshire, 3 x 5 ¾ In. 75.00
Ladle, Soup, Staffordshire, 4 ¼ x 11 In. 125.00
Mold, Flower, Oval, Melon Ribbing, 6 ¾ x 3 ¾ In. 115.00
Mold, Flower, Ribbed Sides, Scalloped, 7 In. 145.00
Mold, Flower, Scalloped, 6 x 4 In. 115.00
Mold, Grapes, Scalloped Border, 6 ½ In. 92.00
Mold, Roses, Oval, Scalloped, 6 x 3 ¼ In. 125.00
Mold, Strawberry, 8 ½ x 3 ½ In. 110.00
Pitcher, Arcaded Panels, Staffordshire, 12 In. 350.00
Pitcher, Basin, Blue & White, Landscape, Victoria Ware, 13 ½ & 14 ½ In. 263.00
Pitcher, Bowl, White, 11 x 13 In. 250.00
Pitcher, Cable & Ring, Embossed, Cockson & Seddon, 12 ¾ In. 260.00
Pitcher, Ceres, Melon Ribbed, Turner & Goddard, 6 In. 162.00
Pitcher, Chain Of Tulips, J. & G. Meakin, 12 ¾ In. 300.00
Pitcher, Clover, Beaded, Flower Thumb Rest, Cockson & Seddon, 12 ¾ In. 300.00
Pitcher, Couple, Leaves, Flowers, Blue, Sydenham Clementson, Eagle Mark, 12 In. 110.00
Pitcher, Draped Leaf, Bridgwood & Clarke, 13 In. 225.00
Pitcher, Dresser, Full Ribbed, Pankhurst, Staffordshire, 8 In. 275.00
Pitcher, Embossed Scrolling, East Liverpool, 12 In. 240.00
Pitcher, Fig, J. Wedgwood, Staffordshire, 11 In. 300.00
Pitcher, Flared, Scalloped Base & Rim, 8 ¼ In. 175.00
Pitcher, Flowers, Leaves, Scalloped Rim, 19th Century, 9 In. .... *illus* 60.00
Pitcher, Fuchsia, Embossed, Flowers, Meakin, Staffordshire, 12 In. 300.00
Pitcher, Gothic, Octagonal, 13 In. 95.00
Pitcher, Hyacinth, J. Wedgwood, 8 ½ In. 160.00
Pitcher, Leaves, Fruit Thumb Rest, Edward Clark, 12 In. 175.00
Pitcher, Lion's Head, J. Edwards, Staffordshire, 12 ½ In. 100.00
Pitcher, Melon Ribbed, Scalloped Rim, Johnson Bros., 6 In. 156.00
Pitcher, Ribbed Body, Embossed Leaf, Miniature, Red Cliff, 3 ¼ In. 74.00
Pitcher, Ribbed Raspberry, Bloom, Concave Ribs, J. & G. Meakin, 6 In. 98.00
Pitcher, Scalloped Rim, Bailey Walker, 5 ½ In. 85.00
Pitcher, Serpent Handle, Staffordshire, 11 In. 125.00
Pitcher, Tracery Shape, Embossed Leaf & Scroll, Johnson Bros., 5 ¾ In. 148.00
Pitcher, Victorian, Footed, Embossed, Scalloped Rim, 7 ¾ In. 192.00
Pitcher, Victorian, Melon Ribbed, Scalloped Rim, Johnson Bros., 9 In. 180.00

Iron, Safe, Wood Grain Paint, Ship, Standard Safe & Lock, Des Moines, Wheels, 27 x 16 In.
$220.00

Iron, Stamp, Notary, Hand, Cast, 12 x 7 In.
$1500.00

Ironstone, Pitcher, Flowers, Leaves, Scalloped Rim, 19th Century, 9 In.
$60.00

TIP

Clean dirt and rust from an old iron piece by spraying it with oven cleaner. Put it in a sealed bag for an hour or two, then rub the spray off with a nylon scouring pad.

Ironstone, Punch Bowl, Ribbed, Raised Foot, Stamped, J. Pankhurst, c.1860, 12 x 8 In.
$240.00

Ironstone, Puzzle Pitcher, Transfer, Harlequin, Green Marble Ground, Elsmore & Forster, 8 ¼ In.
$352.00

Ironstone, Toothbrush Holder, Aesthetic Transfer, Abeona, 3 ½ x 11 In.
$45.00

TIP

Beware of using some rust and stain removers on ironstone. The chemical could remove both the rust and the glaze, ruining the piece. It can also seep into the glaze and make the piece unfit for use with food.

Pitcher, Water & Bowl, J. & G. Meakin, 11 ½-In. Pitcher 50.00
Plate, 1851 Octagon Shape, Boote, Staffordshire, 10 ½ In. 50.00
Plate, Alternate Sprig, Washington, Powell & Bishop, 11 In. 25.00
Plate, Angels, Green Transfer, 9 ½ In. 25.00
Plate, Berry Cluster, Berlin Gothic, Classic Border, Paneled, 8 ½ In. 25.00
Plate, Cambridge, Scalloped Decagon, J. Wedgwood, 10 ½ In. 75.00
Plate, Copper Luster, Raised Flower Border, 8 ¾ In., 8 Piece 170.00
Plate, Dinner, Full Ribbed, Pankhurst, Staffordshire, 9 ½ In. 50.00
Plate, Fig, J. Wedgwood, 8 ½ In. .... 25.00 to 75.00
Plate, Fig, J. Wedgwood, Staffordshire, 9 ¾ In. 125.00
Plate, Gothic, Luster Band, 12-Sided, 10 In. 65.00
Plate, Gothic, Paneled Rim, 7 In. 40.00
Plate, Imari Colors, 19th Century, 10 In., 4 Piece 29.00
Plate, Ladies' Cabin, Handles, Boston Mails, 10 In. 120.00
Plate, Luster, Livesley & Powell, 10-Sided, 8 ½ In. 50.00
Plate, Luster Band, 10-Sided, Livesley & Powell, 8 ½ In. 45.00
Plate, Luster Band, Gothic, 10 ¾ In. 50.00
Plate, Luster Band, Livesley Powell & Co., 8 ½ In., 4 Piece 125.00
Plate, Neva, Paneled, Black Transfer, 10 ½ In., 12 Piece 220.00
Plate, New York, J. Clementson, Staffordshire, 8 ½ In. 50.00
Plate, Oak Leaf, Flowers, Red, Green, Blue, Black, 9 ¾ In. 95.00
Plate, Scalloped Rim, Furnival, Staffordshire, 10 ¼ In. 50.00
Plate, Soup, Baltic, Rimmed, 10-Sided, Wooliscroft, 10 In. 65.00
Plate, Soup, Berlin Gothic, Flared Ribs, 12-Sided, J. Wedgwood, 10 ¾ In. 45.00
Plate, Soup, Berlin Gothic, Rimmed, Flared Ribs, 12-Sided, 10 ¾ In. 65.00
Plate, Soup, Wheat & Hops, Meakin, Staffordshire, 10 In. 25.00
Plate, Yellow, Blue Flower Border, England, 9 ½ In., 12 Piece 590.00
Platter, 8-Sided, Marked, R. Boote, 20 in. 55.00
Platter, Augusta, Raised Ridge, J. Clementson, Staffordshire, 16 x 12 In. 225.00
Platter, Bird In Tree, 17 In. 750.00
Platter, Castles, Gazelles, Coach, Horses, Brown Transfer, Marked, c.1840, 14 x 17 ½ In. 180.00
Platter, Chinese Pavilions, Multicolored Overglaze, 21 x 17 ½ In. 240.00
Platter, Cranes, Flowers, Butterflies, 8-Sided, c.1822, 19 ¼ x 14 ¾ In. 413.00
Platter, Embossed Border, Scalloped Blank, William Brunt Pottery, 16 ¼ In. 82.00
Platter, Embossed Flower, Scalloped Blank, 14 ¼ In. 124.00
Platter, Fig, J. Wedgwood, Staffordshire, 15 ¾ x 12 ¼ In. .... 250.00 to 300.00
Platter, Flowers, Green Border, Gilt, Scalloped Rim, Ashworth Bros., 16 ½ x 21 In. 90.00
Platter, Gothic, 8-Sided, Wooliscroft, Staffordshire, 17 ¼ x 14 In. 175.00
Platter, Gothic 8-Sided, Green Dotted, 13 x 10 In. 150.00
Platter, Gypsy, Purple Transfer, Coral, Scroll Border, 10 x 12 ⅞ In. 132.00
Platter, Imari, Oval, Ashworth Label, England, Early 1800s, 12 ½ x 15 ½ In. 176.00
Platter, Octagonal, Raised Border, Furnival, 15 ½ x 12 In. 100.00
Platter, Oriental Flowers, Blue & White, Ashworth Bros., 20 x 16 ½ In. 360.00
Platter, Plain, Oval, James Edwards, Staffordshire, 14 ½ x 10 In. 40.00
Platter, Ruins, Mountain Peaks, Mansion, Bridge, Blue, 8-Sided, 1800s, 10 x 13 In. 85.00
Platter, Square Ridged, Ridge Border, Alcock, 16 In. 118.00
Platter, Star Flower, 17 In. 168.00
Platter, Sydenham, T. & R. Boote, Staffordshire, 14 x 11 In. 175.00
Platter, Sydenham, T. & R. Boote, Staffordshire, 16 x 12 In. 95.00
Platter, Tree Of Life, Pheasant, Multicolored, Marked, c.1870, 21 x 17 In. 470.00
Platter, Well & Tree, Flow Blue, Oval, Marked, 19th Century, 16 ¾ x 22 In. 90.00
Platter, Well & Tree, Flowers, Parrot, Booths Of England, 16 x 20 In. 150.00
Punch Bowl, Furnivals, Footed, 9 ½ In. 351.00
Punch Bowl, Ribbed, Raised Foot, Stamped, J. Pankhurst, c.1860, 12 x 8 In. .... *illus* 240.00
Punch Cup, Pearl Sydenham, Pedestal, 3 ⅝ In. 60.00
Punch Cup, Sydenham Variation, Pedestal, 4 In. 60.00
Puzzle Pitcher, Transfer, Harlequin, Green Marble Ground, Elsmore & Forster, 8 In. ... *illus* 352.00
Relish, Embossed, Burgess & Goddard, 8 ½ In. 72.00
Relish, President, Embossed Flower Bud, J. Edwards, 9 ¼ In. 98.00
Relish, President, Lobed, J. Edwards, 9 ½ In. 75.00
Relish, Scalloped, Open Handles, Pankhurst, 8 ⅝ In. 55.00
Relish, Wheat & Hops, Thumbprint Center, J. & G. Meakin, Staffordshire, 8 ½ In. 45.00
Sauceboat, Fig, J. Wedgwood, Staffordshire, 9 x 4 ½ In. 99.00
Sauceboat, Grape Octagon, Crabstock Handle, Staffordshire, 8 x 4 ¾ In. 125.00
Sauceboat, Hidden Motif, Twined Crabstock Handle, Furnival, 9 x 4 In. 85.00
Sauceboat, Vintage, Medallions, Vines, Challinor, 9 x 5 In. 75.00

Sauceboat, Wheat & Hops, Staffordshire, 8 x 4 ¾ In. 80.00
Soap Dish, Slab, Vodrey Bros. & Co., 4 ½ x 3 ½ In. 40.00
Soap Dish Drainer, 4 ¾ x 3 ½ In. 25.00
Sugar, Cover, Full Ribbed, Scroll Handles, Daisy Finial, Pankhurst, 8 In. 145.00
Sugar, Cover, Botanical Finial, Hexagonal, Ridgway Staffordshire, 3 ¾ x 3 ⅛ In. 100.00
Sugar, Cover, Gelson, Eagle, Diamond Thumbprint Shape, 3 ½ In. 35.00
Teapot, Cover, Cable & Ring, Rope Handle & Finial, J. & G. Meakin, 9 ¾ In. 230.00
Teapot, Cover, Memnon, J. Meir & Son, 10 ¼ In. 215.00
Teapot, Cover, Leaf Fan Shape, Pearson, Staffordshire, 3 ½ In. 35.00
Teapot, Cover, Plain Looped, 3 ½ In. 25.00
Toddy Bowl, E. Clarke, Staffordshire, 10 x 8 In. 225.00
Toddy Plate, Ceres, Pearson's, 4 ½ In. 25.00
Toothbrush Holder, Acanthus Leaves, Mercer Pottery, 5 ¼ In. 76.00
Toothbrush Holder, Aesthetic Transfer, Abeona .... *illus* 45.00
Tray, Flowers, Cobalt Blue, Bittersweet, Yellow, 4-Sided, Handles, c.1860, 7 x 9 In., Pair 300.00
Tureen, Cover, Box Shape, Serpentine Handles, Finial, John Maddock, 9 ⅜ In. 178.00
Tureen, Cover, Chain Of Tulips, J. & G. Meakin, 11 In. 145.00
Tureen, Cover, Chinese Shape, Leaf Design, T. & R. Boote, 8 x 7 In. 170.00
Tureen, Cover, Underplate, Flowers, c.1880, 10 x 15 x 12 In. 925.00
Tureen, Cover, Wheat & Hops, Pedestal Base, J. & G. Meakin, 11 In. .... *illus* 198.00
Tureen, Indian Scroll, Handles, 11 x 11 In. 300.00
Tureen, Sauce, Cover, 1851 Octagon, T. & R. Boote, 7 ½ x 7 ½ In. 195.00
Tureen, Sauce, Cover, Fig Cousin, J. Wedgwood, Staffordshire, 7 ½ In. 75.00
Tureen, Sauce, Cover, Ring O' Hearts, Livesley & Powell, 9 x 7 In. 125.00
Tureen, Sauce, Cover, Underplate, Adams Scallop, Staffordshire, 9 ½ x 6 ½ In. 225.00
Tureen, Sauce, Cover, Underplate, Baltic, J. Meir, Staffordshire, 8 x 8 ¼ In. 85.00
Tureen, Sauce, Sydenham, T.R. Boote, 8 x 5 In. 95.00
Tureen, Sauce, Underplate, Ceres, Elsmore & Forster, 8 ½ x 7 ½ & 9 x 7 In. 225.00
Tureen, Sauce, Underplate, Grape Octagon, E. Challinor, 8 ½ In. 75.00
Tureen, Sauce, Underplate, Oval Rim, E. Burgess, Staffordshire, 9 ⅓ x 6 ½ In. 35.00
Tureen, Soup, Cover, Ball & Stick, James Edwards, 10 x 12 In. 525.00
Tureen, Soup, Cover, Underplate, Arched Forget-Me-Not, Staffordshire, 14 In. 500.00
Tureen, Soup, Monogram, Melon Finial, Scroll Handles, 16 x 13 In. 275.00
Tureen, Soup, Underplate, 1851 Octagon, Boote, Staffordshire, 15 ¼ In. 125.00
Tureen, Soup, Underplate, Corn, Pankhurst, Staffordshire, 14 In. 125.00
Tureen, Stew, Cover, Paris, Flared Ribs, Melon Finial, 13 x 8 In. 175.00
Tureen, Vegetable, Columbia, Clementson, Staffordshire, 8 x 7 ½ In. 275.00
Tureen, Vegetable, Cover, Bellflower, Floral Sprays, Edwards, 10 ½ x 5 ½ In. 195.00
Tureen, Vegetable, Cover, Fig, Crabstock Band, J. Wedgwood, 12 x 7 In. 275.00
Tureen, Vegetable, Cover, Fig, No. 4, J. Wedgwood, 12 x 7 In. 200.00
Tureen, Vegetable, Cover, Florence, Furnival, 11 ½ x 7 In. .... *illus* 100.00
Tureen, Vegetable, Cover, Fluted Pearl, J. Wedgwood, 12 x 7 In. 245.00
Tureen, Vegetable, Cover, Gooseberry Border, Staffordshire, 12 x 6 ½ In. 195.00
Tureen, Vegetable, Cover, Gourd, James Edwards, Staffordshire, 10 x 6 In. 125.00
Tureen, Vegetable, Cover, Grape Octagon, Furnival, Staffordshire, 7 ¼ In. 195.00
Tureen, Vegetable, Cover, Hyacinth, Embossed Sprigs, J. Wedgwood, 11 ½ x 6 In. 125.00
Tureen, Vegetable, Cover, Jumbo, Staffordshire, 13 x 13 In. 75.00
Tureen, Vegetable, Cover, Leaf Border, Staffordshire, 11 x 7 In. 195.00
Tureen, Vegetable, Cover, Lily-Of-The-Valley, Edwards, 11 x 6 ½ In. 175.00
Tureen, Vegetable, Cover, Niagara Fan, Anthony Shaw, Staffordshire, 12 x 8 In. 225.00
Tureen, Vegetable, Cover, Prairie, J. Clementson, 13 x 7 ¼ In. 195.00
Tureen, Vegetable, Cover, Prize Bloom, 6-Sided, Mayer, 12 x 9 In. 350.00
Tureen, Vegetable, Cover, Rose, Twined Crabstock Finial, 14 x 7 In. 125.00
Tureen, Vegetable, Cover, Rosebuds, Crabstock Handle, Staffordshire, 13 x 7 In. 125.00
Tureen, Vegetable, Cover, Scalloped Decagon, Staffordshire, 11 ½ x 7 ½ In. 250.00
Tureen, Vegetable, Cover, St. Louis, Looping Ovals, James Edwards, 12 x 6 In. 149.00
Tureen, Vegetable, Cover, Sydenham, Boote, Staffordshire, 9 x 9 In. 250.00
Tureen, Vegetable, Cover, Virginia, Staffordshire, 10 x 8 ½ In. 175.00
Tureen, Vegetable, Gothic, 8-Sided, Staffordshire, 11 In. 95.00
Tureen, Vegetable, Star Flower, Pankhurst, Staffordshire, 11 x 6 ½ In. 145.00
Tureen, Vegetable, Wheat & Hops, Furnival, Staffordshire, 12 In. 35.00
Tureen Cover, Cable & Bar, 7 In. 20.00
Tureen Cover, Staffordshire, Child's, 3 ¼ In. 25.00
Tureen Cover, Washington Shape, Staffordshire, 6 ⅓ In. 35.00
Tureen Cover, Wheat & Hops Shape, Staffordshire, 6 ¼ x 4 ¾ In. 40.00
Tureen Underplate, Atlantic, T.R. Boote, 9 x 6 ½ In. 65.00

TIP

If you have an alarm system, set it each time you leave the house, not just at night. Most home burglaries take place during the day or early evening.

Ironston, Tureen, Cover, Wheat & Hops, Pedestal Base, J. & G. Meakin, 11 In.
$198.00

Ironstone, Tureen, Vegetable, Cover, Florence, Furnival, 11 ½ x 7 In.
$100.00

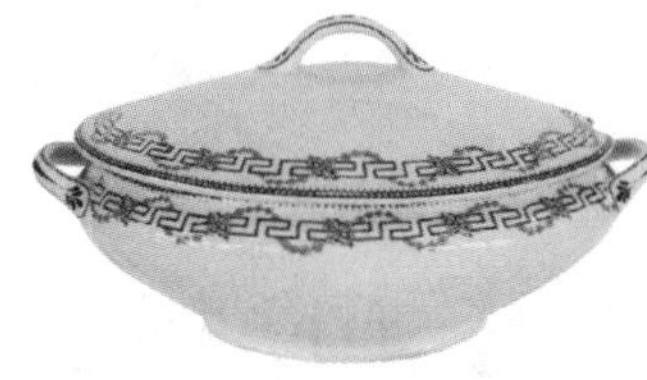

Ironstone, Vase, Flowers, Multicolored, England, 19th Century, 17 ¾ In.
$300.00

Ispanky, Figurine, Donkey Heads, Bisque, Signed, 7 x 5 In.
$117.00

Ivory, Card Case, Victorian, Book Shape, Carved Spine, Fore-Edge, Late 1800s, 4 ¼ In.
$178.00

TIP

Decorate with the neighborhood burglar in mind. Large windows can be made less attractive to intruders if you put shelves holding plants or collectibles across the window. Decorative shelves and grilles are made for this. Of course, be sure you can open the windows in case of fire.

Tureen Underplate, Ceres, Elsmore & Forster, Staffordshire, 9 x 7 In. 30.00
Tureen Underplate, Wheat & Hops, Meakin, Staffordshire, 9 ¼ x 6 In. 25.00
Tureen Underplate Pedestal, Gothic, Raised Handles, J. Alcock, 8 ½ In. 65.00
Underplate, Tulip, Elsmore & Forster, Staffordshire, 9 x 7 In. 35.00
Vase, Flowers, Lion's Head Handles, Bottle Shape, England, c.1890, 5 ⅞ In. 88.00
Vase, Flowers, Multicolored, England, 19th Century, 17 ¾ In. .... *illus* 300.00
Vase, Red, Blue, Black, Flowers, Gilt, England, 1800s, 7 In. 489.00

ISPANKY figurines were designed by Laszlo Ispanky, who began his American career as a designer for Cybis Porcelains. In 1966, he established his own studio in Pennington, New Jersey; since 1976, he has worked for Goebel of North America. He works in stone, wood, or metal, as well as porcelain. The first limited edition figurines were issued in 1966.

Bust, Joshua, Holding Horn Above Head, Limited Edition, 18 ¾ x 10 In. 385.00
Bust, Madonna, Gold Halo, Limited Edition, Marked, 12 x 9 x 6 In. 55.00
Figurine, Aaron, Red Mark, Limited Edition, 13 ¼ In. 400.00
Figurine, Annabell Lee, Limited Edition, Signed, 15 In. 140.00
Figurine, Dianne, Holding Flower, Red Mark, Limited Edition, 12 In. 150.00
Figurine, Donkey Heads, Bisque, Signed, 7 x 5 In. .... *illus* 117.00
Figurine, Elizabeth, Signed, 8 ¼ x 5 ½ In. 66.00
Figurine, Hands Holding Arm, Holding Pipe, Bronze, Marble, Signed, 1973, 13 In. 850.00
Figurine, Hawaiian Princess, Red Flowers, Limited Edition, Signed, 11 ½ In. 145.00
Figurine, Jessemy, Limited Edition, 12 ½ In. 150.00
Figurine, Man With Sword, Woman, Child, Bronze, Marble Base, 1975, 18 In. 600.00
Figurine, Mr. & Mrs. Otter, Holding Hands, Limited Edition, 13 In. 120.00
Figurine, Orchid Flower Girl, 8 ½ In. 65.00
Figurine, Queen Of Spring, Limited Edition, 11 ½ In. 170.00

IVORY from the tusk of an elephant is thought by many to be the only true ivory. To most collectors, the term *ivory* also includes such natural materials as walrus, hippopotamus, or whale teeth or tusks, and some of the vegetable materials that are of similar texture and density. Other ivory items may be found in the Scrimshaw and Netsuke categories. Collectors should be aware of the recent laws limiting the buying and selling of elephant ivory and scrimshaw.

Box, Cover, Grisaille Figures, Oval, Chinese, 6 In. 354.00
Box, Cricket, Chinese, 5 ½ In. 643.00
Box, Dragon, Wave, Japan, 19th Century, 4 ½ In. 356.00
Box, English Regency, 8-Sided, 9 Compartments, 2 ½ x 11 x 9 ¼ In. 1080.00
Box, Putti, Silver Mounted, Mythological Beasts, Pearls, Gems, Austria, c.1880, 12 In. 17500.00
Brushpot, Carved, Bear, Eagle, In Tree, 7 ¼ In. 352.00
Brushpot, Carved, Low Relief, Ribbed, Leafy Branches, Shoots, Wood Stand, Mid 1800s, 6 In. 360.00
Brushpot, Mountain Landscape, Incised, 3 Squat Legs, Ivory Plug, Chinese, 3 ¼ x 2 ¼ In. ... 330.00
Bust, African Woman, Exotic Hairstyle, Wood Base, 4 ¼ In. 146.00
Candlestick, Turned On Lathe, 19th Century, 4 x 2 In., Pair 425.00
Card Case, Carved, Figures, Leaves, Removable lid, 4 ¼ x 2 ¾ x ⅜ In. 259.00
Card Case, Landscape, Lozenge, Key Fret Border, Chinese, 4 ½ x 3 In. 240.00
Card Case, Victorian, Book Shape, Carved Spine, Fore-Edge, Late 1800s, 4 ¼ In. ...... *illus* 178.00
Censer, Animal Mask Handles, Feet, Foo Dog Finial, Pavilions, Chinese, 20th Century, 10 In. . 1778.00
Censer, Carved, 3-footed, Foo Dog Lid, Handles, Fitted Wood Base, 1900s, 12 In. 1170.00
Dresser Set, Carved, Serge Obolensky, Early 20th Century, 6 Piece 234.00
Elephant Bridge, Carved, 5 ½ x 22 In. 702.00
Figurine, 2 Buddhist Saints, Lion, Chinese, 19th Century, 5 ½ x 4 In. 8295.00
Figurine, 2 Monkeys, Dancer's Fan & Rattle, Japan, 19th Century, 3 In. 119.00
Figurine, Angel, On Fisherman's Shoulder, Holding Harpoon, 9 ¼ In. 1265.00
Figurine, Ariadne, Panther, Ebonized Wood Plinth, Germany, c.1850, 5 x 6 In. 1121.00
Figurine, Asian Man, Poppy Between Teeth, Wood Stand, 6 In. 325.00
Figurine, Barrel Maker, Japan, 13 x 4 In. 702.00
Figurine, Bearded Scholar, Holding Staff, Tugging At Beard, Early 1900s, 1 ¾ In. 120.00
Figurine, Bird, Hatching From Egg, 1 ½ x 2 In. 130.00
Figurine, Bird, Perched On Branch, 8 ½ In. 292.00
Figurine, Boat, Dragon Bowhead, Mast, Sails, Fishing Figures, Playing Instruments, Japan, 6 In. 508.00
Figurine, Boat, Dragon Figurehead, Mast, Sails, Figures Fishing, Drinking Sake, Japan, 15 In. 1195.00
Figurine, Boat, Dragon Shape, Pagoda, Pierced Panels, Figures, Wood Stand, 1900s, 18 In. ... 7080.00
Figurine, Boy, With Sake Decanter, Japan, 19th Century, 1 ½ In. 178.00
Figurine, Buddha, 5 Attendants, Chinese, 1900s, 6 In. 3225.00
Figurine, Buddha, Seated, Chinese, 19th Century, 5 ¾ In. 178.00

Figurine, Buddha, Seated, Upstretched Arms, Ink Details, 7 ½ In. 235.00
Figurine, Buddha, Standing, On Lotus Blossom Platform, Ink Details, Wood Base, 9 In. *illus* 1528.00
Figurine, Buddhist Monk, Chinese, c.1940, 10 In. 585.00
Figurine, Buddhist Monk, Holding Child, Chinese, c.1940, 10 In. 702.00
Figurine, Carpenter, Sawing Wood, Japan, 19th Century, 3 ½ In. 178.00
Figurine, Chick, In Shell, Chinese, 1 ¾ In. 88.00
Figurine, Clipper Ship, Fully Rigged, Laminated, 19th Century, 6 x 8 ½ x 2 In. 385.00
Figurine, Confucius, Smiling Scholar, Draped Robe, Elephant Ivory, Signed, 13 ½ In. 750.00
Figurine, Dragon, Tapered Masked Feet, Wine Vase Shape, Chinese, 7 In. 204.00
Figurine, Dragon Boat, Figures, Pavilion, Chinese, 19th Century, 22 In. 13035.00
Figurine, Empress, Fan, Wood Plinth, Chinese, c.1935, 14 In. 1003.00
Figurine, Farmer, With Basket, Japan, Early 20th Century, 7 ¼ In. 527.00
Figurine, Female Nude, Art Deco, Green Marble Base, c.1915, 9 In. 826.00
Figurine, Fisherman, Basket, Wood, Japan, 13 x 12 In. 5265.00
Figurine, Fisherman, Chinese, 6 In. 88.00
Figurine, Fisherman, Chinese, 10 x 2 In. 351.00
Figurine, Fisherman, Fish, Crabs, 19th Century, 9 In. *illus* 1476.00
Figurine, Fisherman, Net, Japan, Mid 20th Century, 5 ½ In. 322.00
Figurine, Fisherman, Oriental, Creel, Spear, Fish, Ink Details, Mid 1800s, 7 ¾ In. 575.00
Figurine, Fisherman, Seated, Basket, 3 Fish On Pole, Oriental, 7 In. 441.00
Figurine, Fisherman, Splashing Waves, Basket Of Fish, Japan, 17 ½ In. 2300.00
Figurine, Fisherman, With Basket, Crab, Japan, 7 In. 1185.00
Figurine, Foo Dog, Wood Plinth, Chinese, c.1940, 5 In., Pair 472.00
Figurine, Geisha, Wood Stand, Japan, 11 In. 1404.00
Figurine, General Kwan Yu, Seated, Holding Folded Book, Holding Hair, 6 ¼ In. 6900.00
Figurine, God Of Wealth, Chinese, 18th Century, 9 In. 356.00
Figurine, Goddess, Seated On Platform, Flowers, Chop Marks, 9 In. 900.00
Figurine, Head Of Buddha, Chinese, 19th Century, 9 x 4 In. 1287.00
Figurine, Horse, Hand Carved Wood Stand, 3 x 3 ¾ In. 88.00
Figurine, Horse, Prancing, Chinese, c.1950, 5 In., Pair 472.00
Figurine, Hotei, 5 In. 263.00
Figurine, Immortal, Holding Bamboo Staff, Chinese, 9 In. 295.00
Figurine, Immortal, Male & Female, Chinese, 19th Century, 11 In. 652.00
Figurine, Imperial, Dragon Robes, Holding Sword, Hat Finial, Base, Chinese, 12 In. 294.00
Figurine, Japanese House, Contents, Mahogany Platform, c.1900, 6 ½ In. 885.00
Figurine, Lion, Stalking, Carved, Chinese, 1 ¾ x 6 ¾ x 1 ½ In. 400.00
Figurine, Lion, Stalking, Stylized Mane, Faux Gemstone Eyes, Chinese, 9 ½ In. 176.00
Figurine, Madonna, Wood Base, India, 4 In. 47.00
Figurine, Male, Dancer, With Tambourine, Renaissance Clothing, Continental, c.1880, 8 In. 558.00
Figurine, Man, 2 Sticks Attached To Rope, 2-Character Mark, Japan, 1890s, 4 ½ In. *illus* 275.00
Figurine, Man, Carrying Wood Bundle, Child, 11 In. 1955.00
Figurine, Man, Dandy, Standing, 1700s Clothes, With Flower, Walking Stick, 6 ⅜ In. 770.00
Figurine, Man, Holding Branch With Nuts, 3 Squirrels, 7 In. 633.00
Figurine, Man, Holding Fish, 6 x 1 ¼ x 1 ½ In. 146.00
Figurine, Man, Holding Pipe & Staff, Early 1900s, 2 In. 120.00
Figurine, Man, Seated, Wood, Japan, 9 x 9 In. 4680.00
Figurine, Man, Woman, Erotic Position, 1 ½ x 2 In. 293.00
Figurine, Man, Wood, Japan, c.1920, 10 In. 1053.00
Figurine, Mandarin Horse, Saddle, Stand, Chinese, 7 x 7 In., Pair 1117.00
Figurine, Mary, Wearing Robe, Rosary, Standing On Flowered Base, Signed, Chinese, 8 In. 529.00
Figurine, Medicine Lady, Chinese, 20th Century, 5 ½ In. 354.00
Figurine, Meiren, Holding Lotus Flower & Vase, Signed, 11 ¾ In. 445.00
Figurine, Military Horseman, Horse, Jewels, Wood Plinth, 1900s, Chinese, 13 In. 767.00
Figurine, Mother, Suckling Child, Resting On Leaf, 2 ⅝ x 1 ⅝ In. 425.00
Figurine, Musical Instruments, Chinese, 9 In., Pair 761.00
Figurine, Napoleon, Military Dress, Crossed Arms, Cannon Balls, Late 1800s, 12 ⅝ In. 2252.00
Figurine, Nefertiti, Bust, 7 In. 499.00
Figurine, Old Man, Chinese, 22 In. 2106.00
Figurine, Old Man, Walking With Staff, Holding Basket Of Flowers, 2 Pigeons, 5 ⅜ In. 575.00
Figurine, Paysan, Holding Staff, Bottle, Turned Ivory & Wood Base, Continental, 5 ¾ In. 359.00
Figurine, Peddler, Smiling, Carrying Baskets, Japan, 14 In. 648.00
Figurine, People, In Boat, Chinese, c.1900, 3 In. 88.00
Figurine, Priest, Staff, Chinese, c.1940, 11 x 3 In. 644.00
Figurine, Puppeteer, Wood, Japan, c.1920, 14 In. 2340.00
Figurine, Quan Yin, Flower Basket, Chinese, 27 In. 4387.00
Figurine, Quan Yin, Holding Scepter, Reclining, Long Robes, Beaded Jewelry, Chinese, 12 In. 1416.00

Ivory, Figurine, Buddha, Standing, On Lotus Blossom Platform, Ink Details, Wood Base, 9 In.
$1528.00

Ivory, Figurine, Fisherman, Fish, Crabs, 19th Century, 9 In.
$1476.00

Ivory, Figurine, Man, 2 Sticks Attached To Rope, 2-Character Mark, Japan, 1890s, 4 ½ In.
$275.00

Ivory, Jar, Cover, Dragons, Dragon Finials, Lion Mask Jump Rings, Chinese, 19th Century, 8 In., Pair
$1896.00

Ivory, Okimono, Shinto Priest With Rake, Japan, 19th Century, 5 In.
$119.00

TIP
Don't soak ivory in water. It will soften any glue and damage the patina.

Jackfield, Creamer, Cow, Lid, Black Glaze, Gilt Accents, England, Early 1800s, 6 ½ In.
$88.00

Figurine, Quan Yin, Standing, Long Robes, Veil, High Chignon, Chinese, 12 In. 944.00
Figurine, Rat Catcher, Japan, 19th Century, 3 In. 770.00
Figurine, Sage, With Staff, Japan, 11 ⅜ In. 1195.00
Figurine, Shou Lao, Chinese God Of Longevity, Holding Peach, Staff, Ink Details, Stand, 5 ¾ In. 118.00
Figurine, Sword Smith, Working, Japan, 19th Century, 2 In. 296.00
Figurine, Tiger, Stalking, Carved Stripes, Inked Eyes, Wood Base, Signed, Chinese, 8 ½ In. 264.00
Figurine, Warlord, Seated, 7 x 4 In. 1521.00
Figurine, Warrior, Bearded, Holding Spear, Sword, Wood Stand, Chinese, 20th Century, 8 ½ In. 175.00
Figurine, Warrior, With Sword, Halberd, Chinese, 19th Century, 9 ½ In. 385.00
Figurine, Wiseman, Holding Stick, Marked, Chinese, 11 ⅞ In. 990.00
Figurine, Woman, Dancer, Leaning Back, Right Foot Off Ground, Carved, Stand, Chinese, 7 In. 625.00
Figurine, Woman, Dancer, Leaning Forward, Foot Off Ground, Stand, Chinese, 7 In. 625.00
Figurine, Woman, Dancer, Leaning Forward, Left Foot Back, Stand, Chinese, 7 In. 575.00
Figurine, Woman, Fan, Carved, Signed, Japan, c.1900, 7 ½ In. 410.00
Figurine, Woman, Holding Fan, Chinese, 19th Century, 10 ½ In. 3851.00
Figurine, Woman, Holding Paddle, Flower, Headband, Embellished Garment, 6 ⅜ In. 489.00
Figurine, Woman, Lotus Blossoms, 1900s, 17 In. 1180.00
Figurine, Woman, Lotus Branch, 1900s, 9 In. 413.00
Figurine, Woman, Lotus Branch, Black Hair, Wood Plinth, 1900s, 19 In. 413.00
Figurine, Woman, Nude, Classical Style, Venus, Draped Urn, Wood Base, 7 In. 675.00
Figurine, Woman, Parasol, Lantern, Signed, Meizan, Japan, 19th Century, 7 ¼ In. 1126.00
Figurine, Woman, Phoenix Headdress, Fan, Flowering Branch, Ink Details, Base, Chinese, 13 In. 764.00
Figurine, Woman, Raised Sword, 14 In. 610.00
Figurine, Woman By Table, Japan, 3 x 2 In. 117.00
Frame, Dragons, Scalloped Easel Shape, Chinese, 1800s, 4 x 4 In. 390.00
Group, 2 Boys, 1 With Flute, Seated On Water Buffalo, Signed, Chinese, 10 ½ x 7 ½ In. 1410.00
Group, Boy, Man, Using Pole To Scare Birds, Japan, 7 In. 330.00
Group, Boy & Girl In Flowers, Teakwood Stand, Chinese, 8 ¼ x 6 ½ In. 1638.00
Group, Man, Child, Seated, Japan, 20th Century, 5 In. 585.00
Group, Man, Child, With Bale Of Rice, Japan, 19th Century, 2 ½ In. 296.00
Group, Woman, Parasol, Carved, Teakwood Stand, c.1880, 3 x 12 In. 1287.00
Group, Woman & Child, Water Jug, Lifting Edge Of Sarong, 2-Tier Base, 16 ½ In. 460.00
Jar, Cover, Dragon, Ring Handles, Chain Hanger, Oval, Bulbous, Wood Base, 14 ½ x 6 ½ In. 413.00
Jar, Cover, Dragons, Lion Mask Jump Rings, Chinese, 19th Century, 8 In., Pair *illus* 1896.00
Jar, Scenic, People On Porch, Threaded Lid, Removable Spoon In Finial, Chinese, 4 ½ In. 118.00
Jewelry Box, Carved, 2 ¼ x 3 ½ In. 263.00
Magnifying Glass, Brass, Rectangular, Ivory Handle, 10 ½ In. 30.00
Okimono, Beggar, Standing, Carrying Man, Woman In Basket, Japan, 9 ½ In. 448.00
Okimono, Boy Holding Large Fish, 14K Gold Mount, Early To Mid 1900s, 3 In. 325.00
Okimono, Carpenters, Signed, Japan, 1800s, 2 ¼ x 4 ½ In. 439.00
Okimono, Farmer, Child, Signed, Japan, 6 In. 777.00
Okimono, Farmer, Holding Rooster, Signed, Japan, 8 ½ In. 777.00
Okimono, Fisherman, Basket On Shoulder, Signed, Japan, 8 ½ In. 717.00
Okimono, Fisherman, Standing On Rocks, Fishing Net, Hat, Japan, 8 In. 531.00
Okimono, Geisha, Holding Umbrella, Signed, Japan, 6 ¼ In. 598.00
Okimono, Man, Holding Flower, Staff, Child Reaching For Flower, Signed, Japan, 4 ¾ In. 538.00
Okimono, Man, Seated With Child, Drums, Signed, Japan, 5 ½ In. 568.00
Okimono, Peasant, Holding Flower Branch, Basket, Japan, 7 In. 330.00
Okimono, Peddler, Carrying Bamboo Pole With Baskets, Signed, Japan, 7 ½ In. 657.00
Okimono, Scribe, Holding Book, Tool, With Bucket, Leaf Filled Vase, Signed, Japan, 8 In. 717.00
Okimono, Sennin Holding Oni, Feeding Pomegranates To Monkeys, Japan, 8 ¼ In. 8295.00
Okimono, Shinto Priest With Rake, Japan, 19th Century, 5 In. *illus* 119.00
Okimono, Woman, Kimono, Holding Basket, Flowering Branch, Japan, 6 ½ In. 384.00
Page Cutter, Chinese, 19th Century, 1 ¾ x 17 ⅞ In. 351.00
Page Turner, Perched Bird, Silver Mounting Joint, 19 ½ x 2 In. 480.00
Page Turner, Thomas Jefferson, Masonic Symbols, Silver Handle, 17 In. 8962.00
Picture, Gentleman, ½ Length Portrait, Continental, Brass Frame, c.1699, 4 ½ x 3 ½ In. 390.00
Plaque, Figures, Blossoming Branch, Chinese, 2 x 7 ¾ In. 1170.00
Plaque, Immortals Inset, Clouds, Rosewood Frame, Chinese, 19th Century, 6 In., Pair 504.00
Plaque, Phoenix, Nesting On Mountain Ledge, Inscription, Wood Stand, 10 In. 1292.00

JACKFIELD ware was originally a black glazed pottery made in Jackfield, England, from 1750 to 1775. A yellow glazed ware has also been called Jackfield ware. Most of the pieces referred to as Jackfield today are black-glazed, red-clay wares made at the Jackfield Pottery in Shropshire, England, in Victorian times.

Creamer, Cow, Lid, Black Glaze, Gilt Accents, England, Early 1800s, 6 ½ In. *illus* 88.00

Mug, Blaze Glaze, Baluster, late 1800s, 5 In. 140.00
Pitcher, Black Glaze, Applied Loop Handle, c.1770, 4 In. 245.00
Vase, Art Deco Zigzag, Black, Orange, Victorian Shape, 1930, 6 In. 58.00

JACK-IN-THE-PULPIT vases, shaped like trumpets, resemble the wild flower named jack-in-the-pulpit. The design originated in the late Victorian years. Vases in the jack-in-the-pulpit shape were made of ceramic or glass, and the complete list of page references can be found in the index.

Vase, Blue & White Pulled Feather, Blue Iridescent Ground, 16 In. 690.00
Vase, Cobalt Blue, Glass, Charles Lotton, c.1991, 15 ¾ In. 1495.00
Vase, Green Translucent, Glass, Striated, Pulled Feathers, 16 In. 460.00
Vase, Iridescent Blue, Glass, Ribbed Neck, Ruffled Rim, 19 In. 1380.00
Vase, Iridescent Gold, Glass, Pulled Heart & Vine, Lundberg, 7 In. 690.00
Vase, Iridescent Gold, Pulled Feather, Applied Button Pontil, 12 In. 173.00

JADE is the name for two different minerals, nephrite and jadeite. Nephrite is the mineral used for most early Oriental carvings. Jade is a very tough stone that is found in many colors from dark green to pale lavender. Jade carvings are still being made in the old styles, so collectors must be careful not to be fooled by recent pieces. Jade jewelry is found in this book under Jewelry.

Belt Hook, Dragon Head, Raised Chilong On Top, Mounted As Magnifying Glass, Chinese, 5 In. 2160.00
Bowl, Cafe-Au-Lait, Wood Base, Chinese, 4 ¼ In. 230.00
Bowl, Chrysanthemum, Carved, Spinach Green, Chinese, 19th Century, 8 ¾ In. . . . . *illus* 3081.00
Bowl, Translucent White, Russet, Chinese, 5 ⅛ In. 1434.00
Bowl, White, Carved, Chinese, 1 ¾ x 4 ¼ In. 143.00
Box, Celadon Stone, Carved Dragons, Silver Mounts, Chinese, 19th Century, 3 x 2 In. . . . *illus* 948.00
Box, Kylin, Square Vase On Back, Dragon, Chinese, 20th Century, 4 ½ In. 7110.00
Box, Spinach Green, 1 ⅞ x 3 ½ x 5 ⅞ In. 643.00
Box, White, Round, Chinese, 18th-19th Century, 2 ¼ In. 4740.00
Brushpot, Boy Under Tree, Bamboo Shape, Celadon, Chinese, 20th Century, 6 ¼ In. 767.00
Brushpot, Celadon, Peach Shape, Bat Decoration, Stand, Chinese, 8 In. 5900.00
Brushpot, Cylindrical, Carved Figures Under Tree, Chinese, 6 ½ x 5 In. 1652.00
Brushpot, Gray, Tree Trunk, Bird On Flowering Branch, Chinese, 20th Century, 4 x 6 In. 1180.00
Brushpot, Lotus, Apple Green, Chinese, 19th Century, 6 ¼ In. 1422.00
Brushpot, Wood Base, Chinese, 1 ½ x 3 x 4 In. 439.00
Burial Relic, Foo Dog, Chinese, 3 x 2 In. 234.00
Candleholder, Calligraphy Bamboo, Flower, Spinach Green, Chinese, 15 ½ In., Pair 6490.00
Censer, Boat Shape, Spinach Green, Foo Dog Finial, Chinese, 5 In. 478.00
Censer, Cover, 3-Footed, Glin Shape Handles, Chinese, 4 ¾ In. 717.00
Censer, Dragons, Clouds, Yellow, White Stone, Carved, Hardwood Stand, 6 x 5 ½ In. 2489.00
Censer, Figure, Seated, Dragons, Scrolls, Ring Handles, 6 Parts, 30 ½ In. 875.00
Censer, Gray Stone, Animal Form Handles, Chinese, 18th Century, 6 In. 1185.00
Censer, Immortals Under Pine Tree, 3-Footed, Celadon, Carved, Chinese, 4 ½ In. 1554.00
Cup, Mutton Fat, Carved, Footed, 1 ¾ In., Pair 1725.00
Cup, Rhyton, Winged Animal, Mask, Celadon Green, Russet, 2 ¼ In. 711.00
Cup, Squirrel, Leaf Handle, Melon Shape, Silver Cover, Chinese, 17th Century, 4 ½ In. 889.00
Cup, Trees, Scholars In Garden, Translucent Celadon, Chinese, 18th Century, 5 ½ In. 2252.00
Dish, Mutton Fat, Footed, Chinese, 6 In., 5 Piece 6325.00
Figurine, Bird, Dark Olive Green, Tan, Chinese, 20th Century, 7 ½ In., Pair . . . . *illus* 178.00
Figurine, Bird, Green, Stand, Burma, c.1900, 5 x 5 In., Pair. 1053.00
Figurine, Bird, Spinach Green, Chinese, 20th Century, 10 In., Pair 224.00
Figurine, Birds, Exotic, Carved, Wood Base, 7 In., Pair 175.00
Figurine, Birds, Sitting On Branch, Extended Tails, Spinach Green, Wood Stand, 10 In., Pair. 660.00
Figurine, Boy, Short Coat, Holding Oval Tray, Celadon, Chinese, 2 ¾ In. 1416.00
Figurine, Butterfly, Cream, Carved, Dark Wood Stand, 6 x 7 In. 760.00
Figurine, Carp, Leaping, Carved, Wood Base, 15 x 10 ½ In. 5124.00
Figurine, Chimera, Gray, White, Chinese, 19th Century, 2 ¼ x 4 ½ In. 2006.00
Figurine, Dog, Pup, Jade, Gray White, Carved, Chinese, 19th Century, 1 ¼ x 2 ½ In. 232.00
Figurine, Dog, Winged, Raised Front Paw, Flowing Mane, Teak Stand, Oriental, 9 ½ x 14 ¾ In. 115.00
Figurine, Dragon, Black, Carved, Chinese, 8 In. 3422.00
Figurine, Dragon, Sword, Stand, Carved, Chinese, 13 x 24 In. 936.00
Figurine, Dragon, White, Gilt, Chinese, 2 ¾ x 5 In. 351.00
Figurine, Dragon Carp, Yellow Celadon, Chinese, 20th Century, 7 ½ In. 711.00
Figurine, Fisherman, Gray, White, 19th Century, 1 ¾ In. 1541.00
Figurine, Frog, Children, White, Chinese, 2 x 4 In. 561.00
Figurine, Goddess Of Mercy, Standing, Lotus Stand, Yellow, Green, Gray Swirls, Chinese, 22 In. 1067.00

Jade, Bowl, Chrysanthemum, Carved, Spinach Green, Chinese, 19th Century, 8 ¾ In.
$3081.00

Jade, Box, Celadon Stone, Carved Dragons, Silver Mounts, Chinese, 19th Century, 3 x 2 x 1 In.
$948.00

Jade, Figurine, Bird, Dark Olive Green, Tan, Chinese, 20th Century, 7 ½ In., Pair
$178.00

TIP

Install locks on all garage doors and windows. Keep front hedges and fences under three feet in height so prowlers or break-ins can be seen from the street. See-through fences are best.

Jade, Figurine, Horse, Pale Celadon, Chinese, 19th Century, 4 In. **$711.00**

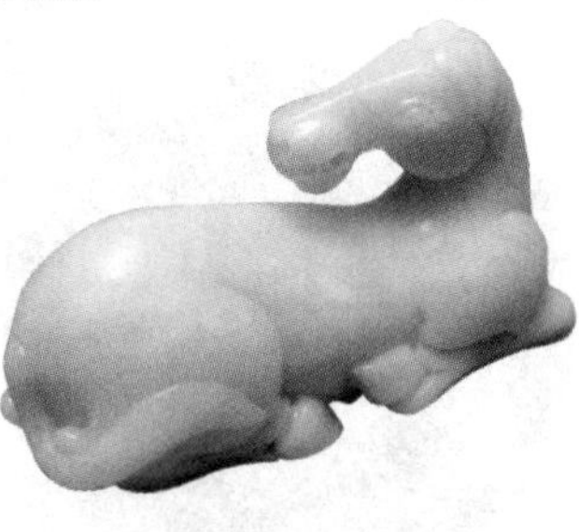

Jade, Vase, Cover, Kylin, Vapor From Mouth, Double Jump Rings, Green, White, Chinese, 5 ½ In. **$5925.00**

Jasperware, Cheese Dish, Cover, Dark Blue, Paneled, Applied Cherubs, Acorns, 10 ½ In. **$300.00**

TIP
Rub Bakelite hard for 30 seconds, then sniff it. You will soon learn to recognize its distinctive smell.

Figurine, Horse, Ceremonial Trappings, Dark Green, Chinese, 35 x 28 In. 5850.00
Figurine, Horse, Pale Celadon, Chinese, 19th Century, 4 In. *illus* 711.00
Figurine, Hotei, Seated, Laughing, Lavender, Stand, 3 In. 936.00
Figurine, Immortal, Boulder, Deer, Trees, Nephrite, Carved, Chinese, 4 ¾ In. 840.00
Figurine, Intertwined Arches, White, Carved, Chinese, 2 ½ x 2 In. 644.00
Figurine, Koro, Mutton Fat, Chinese, 8 x 8 In. 1521.00
Figurine, Mongolian Pony, Reclining, Carved Mane, Tail, Hair, Chinese, 7 In. 2160.00
Figurine, Qilin, Chinese, 5 x 4 ¼ In. 2950.00
Figurine, Quan Yin, Serpentine, 7 ¾ x 3 ¼ In. 117.00
Figurine, Rat, Bag On Back, Chinese, 5 ½ In. 1180.00
Figurine, Rhinoceros, Celadon, Chinese, Early 19th Century, 3 ¾ x 6 In. 1298.00
Figurine, Tangerine Tree, Hardstone, Chinese, 30 ½ x 18 In. 205.00
Figurine, Tree, Leaves, Pink Flowers, Cloisonne Pot, 22 x 18 In. 351.00
Figurine, Water Buffalo, Reclining, Wood Platform, Chinese, 11 x 4 In. 146.00
Figurine, Winged Beast, Horns, Chinese, 18th Century, 2 ½ In. 2015.00
Figurine, Woman, Asian, Holding Flowers, Stork, Carved, 8 ¾ x 5 ½ In. 198.00
Figurine, Woman, Elderly, Holding Large Fruit, Peony Sprig Over Shoulder, 2 ¾ In. 633.00
Group, 2 Women Divinities, Man, Attendant, Lavender, Pale Green, Chinese, 9 ½ x 7 ½ In. 948.00
Group, 3 Fencers, Swords, White Stone, Forest Green, Chinese, 20th Century, 9 ¾ x 7 In. 830.00
Group, Figures Under Pine Tree, Mountainous Landscape, Celadon, Chinese, 7 ½ In. 1725.00
Group, Pu Tai, Dragons, Foo Dogs, Cloud, Yellow, Green Stone, Chinese, 6 In. 504.00
Group, Water Buffalo, Reclining, Child, Celadon Stone, Brown Inclusions, 5 ¼ In. 1920.00
Hairpin, Celadon, Carved Finial, 18th-19th Century, 5 In. 119.00
Incense Burner, Spinach Green, Handle, Footed, Carved Foo Dog Finial, Chinese, 7 x 8 ½ In. 5925.00
Jar, Cover, Birds In Flowering Tree, Pale Green Stone, Brown Skin, Chinese, 1800s, 7 In. 1185.00
Jar, Cover, Stylized Lotus, Gray Stone, 19th Century, 3 In. 356.00
Jar, Cover, White, Black Streaks, Flower Shaped Handle, Finial, Chinese, 18th Century, 10 In. 9480.00
Joss Stick Holder, Celadon, Fluted Base, Drip Ring, Chinese, 7 In., Pair 2124.00
Paperweight, Elephant, Carrying Scepter, Carved, Round, Chinese, 1 ½ In. 1800.00
Pi Disk, Carved, Round, Brown, High Relief, Chih Dragons, Rice Grain Design, 1722, 8 ⅛ In. 6000.00
Scepter, White Jade Plaques, Rosewood Inset, Chinese, 19th Century, 21 ½ In. 267.00
Screen, Rosewood, 4 Panels, Carved, Pierced Frames, 11 x 18 In. 1140.00
Seal, Mythical Animal, Gray, Brown Veining, 1 ½ In. 652.00
Tray, Green, Tan, Lotus Leaf, Hardwood Stand, Chinese, 19th Century, 10 ½ In. 1304.00
Tray, Lotus Pad, Frog, Snail, Translucent, 19th Century, 2 ½ In. 3200.00
Urn, cover, Carved, Blue Bird On Top, 2 Handles, Smoky Gray, Chinese, 3 x 4 In. 164.00
Urn, Cover, Pale Green, Elephant Finial, Chains On Handles, 7 x 4 In. 527.00
Vase, Carved, Oval, Translucent, Splayed Base, Bird Handles, Button Top, Chinese, 7 ½ In. 7800.00
Vase, Cover, Carved Wood Stand, Chinese, 7 x 14 ½ In. 1298.00
Vase, Cover, Flowering Branch, Celadon, Flattened Baluster Shape, Ring Handles, 7 In. 176.00
Vase, Cover, Immortals, Animals, Pavilions, Trees, Relief Carved, Pale Celadon, 8 ½ In. 5925.00
Vase, Cover, Kylin, Vapor From Mouth, Jump Rings, Green, White, Chinese, 5 ½ In. *illus* 5925.00
Vase, Cover, Raised & Pierced Carving, Animals, Bats, Foo Dog Finial, Chinese, 4 ¼ In. 180.00
Vase, Cover, White, Flattened Oval, Carved, Confronting Phoenix, Chinese, 8 ½ In. 885.00
Vase, Cover, White, Flattened Oval, Pierced Body, Elephant, Chinese, 10 In. 2360.00
Vase, Cover, White, Ring & Mask Shape Handles, Incised Dragon, Chinese, 5 In. 1003.00
Vase, Dragons, Ring Handles, Gray, Russet Marbled, Chinese, 5 ½ In., Pair 478.00
Vase, Fang Ku Form, Scrolling, Carved, Celadon, Chinese, 12 ½ In. 2133.00
Vase, Green, Applied White Handles, 10 ½ In., Pair 1265.00
Vase, Moghul White, Flattened Oval, Flower Head, Scrolling Leaf Handles, Chinese, 6 ¾ In. 1793.00
Water Coupe, Goose, 2 Goslings, Hardwood Stand, Chinese, 3 In. 2726.00
Water Coupe, Lotus, Dragonfly, Celadon, Chinese, 5 ½ In. 6300.00
Water Coupe, Oval, Gray, Green, Brown, Scrolls, Chinese, 19th Century, 4 In. 178.00
Wrist Rest, Translucent White, Green, Brown, Bamboo, Scholars, Landscape, Chinese, 9 In. 7768.00

JAPANESE CORALENE is a ceramic decorated with small raised beads and dots. It was first made in the nineteenth century. Later wares made to imitate coralene had dots of enamel. There is also another type of coralene that is made with small glass beads on glass containers.

Bowl, Ivory, Gold Trim, Beaded Rim, 3 Gold Trimmed Feet, 3 ½ x 7 In. 135.00
Cup & Saucer, Ivory, Cream Rim, Gold & Coralene Flowers, Scrolls, 2 x 5 ½ In. 40.00
Dresser Jar, Cover, Heart Shape, White & Green, Green & Pink Flowers, 2 x 4 In. 39.00
Vase, Art Nouveau Style, Floral, Kinran, c.1909, 16 x 8 In. 1750.00
Vase, Dandelion, Buds, Leaves, Green & Yellow Ground, Handles, 8 In. 297.00
Vase, Portrait, Pastoral Scene, Scrolling Flowers, Signed, LeRoy, Buttel, 19 ½ In. 2995.00

JAPANESE *Woodblock Prints are listed in this book in the Print category under Japanese.*

JASPERWARE can be made in different ways. Some pieces are made from a solid-colored clay with applied raised designs of a contrasting colored clay. Other pieces are made entirely of one color clay with raised decorations that are glazed with a contrasting color. Additional pieces of jasperware may also be listed in the Wedgwood category or under various art potteries.

Cheese Dish, Cover, Dark Blue, Paneled, Applied Cherubs, Acorns, 10 ½ In. .... *illus* 300.00
Cheese Dome, Dark Blue, White, Classical Figures, 11 x 11 In. 250.00
Jardiniere, Adams Tunstall, Equestrian Scene, Blue, White, England, c.1890, 8 x 9 In. 88.00
Pancake Server, Fern & Cattail, Blue, White, c.1900, 12 ½ In. .... *illus* 143.00
Plaque, Woman In Swing, Cherubs, Green, White, Oval, 7 ½ In. 40.00

JEWELRY, whether made from gold and precious gems or plastic and colored glass, is popular with collectors. Values are determined by the intrinsic value of the stones and metal and by the skill of the craftsmen and designers. Victorian and older jewelry have been collected since the 1950s. More recent interests are Art Deco and Edwardian styles, Mexican and Danish silver jewelry, and beads of all kinds. Copies of almost all styles are being made. American Indian jewelry is listed in the Indian category. Tiffany jewelry is listed here.

Bangle, Love, Signed, Cartier, 8 ¾ In. 1896.00
Bar Pin, Platinum On Yellow Gold, Diamond, Seed Pearl, Edwardian, 2 In. 329.00
Belt, Silver, Oval, Rope, Silver Domes, Malachite, 36 ½ In. 207.00
Belt, Silver, Winged Cherubs, Plaques, Openwork Spacers, Oval, c.1901, 26 ¾ In. 805.00
Belt Buckle, Arrow Shape, Silver, Hammered, Pierced, Turquoise Enamel, Liberty, c.1908, 4 In. 415.00
Belt Buckle, Jade, Dragon Final, Kylin, Yellow White, Chinese, 19th Century, 3 ½ In. 1778.00
Bracelet, 10 Rectangular & Oval Panels, Platinum, 275 Cut Diamonds, Art Deco, c.1930, 7 In. 5581.00
Bracelet, 16 Graduated Ball Links, 14K Gold, Diamonds, Van Cleef & Arpels, c.1940, 7 In. ... 3240.00
Bracelet, 2 Ovals, Oblong Links, Screw Closure, Sterling Silver, Hans Hansen, 7 In. 356.00
Bracelet, Alternating Beads & Black Onyx, Sterling Silver, Tiffany & Co. 71.00
Bracelet, Amber Glass & Lucite Stones, Faceted, Flattened Gold Metal Mount, c.1945, 1 x 7 In. 168.00
Bracelet, Arched Panels, Trace Links, Geometric, Sterling Silver, Georg Jensen, 7 In. 770.00
Bracelet, Art Deco, Camphor Glass, Rhodium, Filigree, Marcasite, 6 ⅝ In. 140.00
Bracelet, Art Deco, Clamper, Camphor Glass, Rhodium, Rhinestones, Topaz, ¾ x 2 ¼ In. 175.00
Bracelet, Bakelite, Bangle, Artichoke Carving, Hinged, 1 ½ In. 235.00
Bracelet, Bakelite, Bangle, Black, Carved Leaves, 1940s, ⅞ In. 225.00
Bracelet, Bakelite, Bangle, Bowtie, Black, Cream, ¾ x 3 ¼ In. .... *illus* 1600.00
Bracelet, Bakelite, Bangle, Butterscotch, 12 Red Polka Dots, 1940s, 1 ⅝ In. 595.00
Bracelet, Bakelite, Bangle, Butterscotch, Shell Carving, 1 ½ In. 176.00
Bracelet, Bakelite, Bangle, Marbleized Blue Moon, 1 ¾ x 3 In. .... *illus* 100.00
Bracelet, Bakelite, Bangle, Marbleized Red, Carved, 1 ½ In. 323.00
Bracelet, Bakelite, Bangle, Orange, Carved, Flowers, Leaves, 1 ⅛ In. 235.00
Bracelet, Bakelite, Bangle, Red, Faceted, 1 In. 245.00
Bracelet, Bakelite, Bangle, Zigzag Design, Marbleized Yellow & Green, 1940s, 1 In. 195.00
Bracelet, Bakelite, Brown, Carved, Flowers & Leaves, ⅞ In. 294.00
Bracelet, Bakelite, Brown, Flower Carving, 1 ¼ In. 176.00
Bracelet, Bakelite, Butterscotch, 8 Cream Polka Dots, Belle Kogan, ⅝ In. 353.00
Bracelet, Bakelite, Chevron Carving, Cream, 1 ½ x 3 In. .... *illus* 100.00
Bracelet, Bakelite, Cuff, Cherry, Brass, 2 Seahorses, France, c.1937 .... 688.00
Bracelet, Bakelite, Green, Rust, Laminated, 1 ¼ In. 118.00
Bracelet, Bakelite, Ladybugs, Green, 7 ½ In. .... *illus* 350.00
Bracelet, Bakelite, Orange, Rope Twist, Carved, Crosshatch, 1 ¼ In. 206.00
Bracelet, Bakelite, Polka Dot, Marbleized Red, Yellow Polka Dots, ½ In. 382.00
Bracelet, Bakelite, Red, Carved, ¾ In. 118.00
Bracelet, Bangle, Black Jade, Confronting Dragons, 14K Yellow Gold Hinge & Clasp 1265.00
Bracelet, Bangle, Coiled, 3 Loops, 18K Gold, Michael Good, 7 ⅝ In. 2963.00
Bracelet, Bangle, Hinged, 18K Gold, Fire Opal, Diamond Cabochons, Roberto Coin, 7 In. 4183.00
Bracelet, Bangle, Hinged, Leaf Openwork, 14K Gold, Diamonds, Victorian .... *illus* 3850.00
Bracelet, Bangle, Hinged, Platinum, Pave, 55 Diamonds, 18K Gold, Oscar Heyman, 6 ¼ In. .. 3555.00
Bracelet, Bangle, Hinged, Sterling Silver, Rock Crystal, Sweden, 6 ½ In. 267.00
Bracelet, Bangle, Hinged Leaf, Openwork, Platinum Over Gold, Edwardian 2040.00
Bracelet, Bangle, Links, Amethyst & Pink Tourmaline Cabochons, Vacheron Constantin 3381.00
Bracelet, Bangle, Love, 18K Gold, Aldo Cipullo, Cartier, 6 ⅞ In. 2015.00
Bracelet, Bangle, Mabe Pearl, 18K Gold, Belcher Links, Asprey, 6 ⅜ In. 3200.00
Bracelet, Bangle, Molded Waves, Gold Plated Silver, 925, TR & Co., Mexico, 1960s 750.00
Bracelet, Bangle, Openwork Scrolls, Hinged, 3 Sapphires, 2 Diamonds, Fritschze & Co., 7 In. 1422.00
Bracelet, Bangle, Peridot, Amethyst, Sterling Silver, 14K Gold, David Yurman, 6 ¾ In. 563.00
Bracelet, Bangle, Platinum, 22K Gold, Diamond, Cathy Waterman, 6 ⅝ In. 3437.00
Bracelet, Bangle, Split Pearls, Turquoise, Silver, Gold, Margaret Rogers, c.1935, 7 ¼ In. 5629.00

Jasperware, Pancake Server, Fern & Cattail, Blue, White, c.1900, 12 ½ In.
$143.00

Jewelry, Bracelet, Bakelite, Bangle, Bowtie, Black, Cream, ¾ x 3 ¼ In.
$1600.00

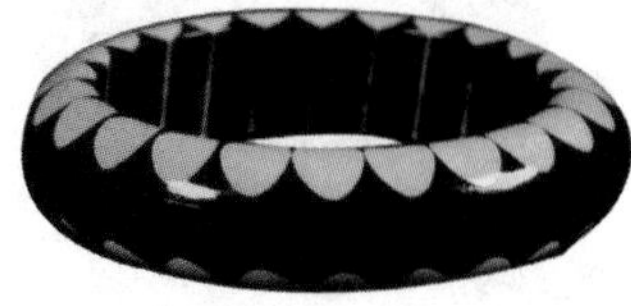

Jewelry, Bracelet, Bakelite, Bangle, Marbleized Blue Moon, 1 ¾ x 3 In.
$100.00

Jewelry, Bracelet, Bakelite, Chevron Carving, Cream, 1 ½ x 3 In.
$100.00

Jewelry, Bracelet, Bakelite, Ladybugs, Green, 7 ½ In.
$350.00

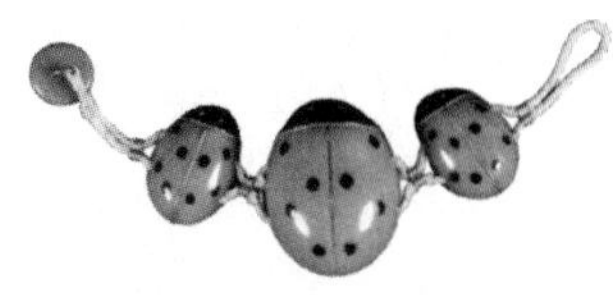

Jewelry, Bracelet, Bangle, Hinged, Leaf Openwork, 14K Gold, Diamonds, Victorian
$3850.00

Jewelry, Bracelet, Charm, Sterling Silver, 25 Charms, 7 ½ In.
$165.00

Jewelry, Bracelet, Sterling Silver, Sculpted, Links, Marked, Federico Serranol, Mexico, 2 ½ In.
$425.00

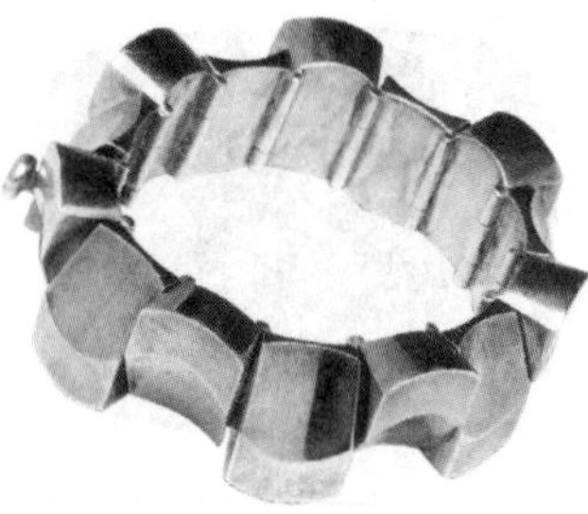

Clamper Bracelets
"Clamper" bracelets, hinged plastic bracelets that open to be put around a wrist, were originally made from umbrella handles. Albert Weiss & Company made the first bracelets sold under the name "Bon-Bonn."

Bracelet, Bangle, Tiger, Alternating Enamel & Rhinestone Stripes, Green Eyes, K.J. Lane 625.00
Bracelet, Bangle, Wood, 18K Gold Plaques, Van Cleef & Arpels, 2 ¾ In. 4508.00
Bracelet, Beads, 5 Strands, Emerald Cabochon, Diamond Melee Clasp, 18K Gold, Emis, 7 In. 3851.00
Bracelet, Celluloid, Pink & Cream Flowers, Green Leaves, c.1940, ½ In. 55.00
Bracelet, Charm, 4 Fruits Of Summer, 18K Gold, Bicolor, Cartier 6518.00
Bracelet, Charm, Platinum, Aquamarine, Citrine, Diamond, Boucheron, Cartier, 7 ½ In. 659.00
Bracelet, Charm, Platinum, Elephant, Ghost, Dachshund, Terrier, Diamonds, Art Deco, 7 ⅜ In. 6814.00
Bracelet, Charm, Sterling Silver, 25 Charms, 7 ½ In. .... *illus* 165.00
Bracelet, Cuff, Amber, Sterling Silver, Denmark, 2 ½ x 1 ¼ In. 80.00
Bracelet, Cuff, Amber & Purple, Faceted Stones, Gold Metal Openwork Frame, c.1965 .... 188.00
Bracelet, Cuff, Coil, Baroque Pearls, Filigree Caps, Tassels, Silvertone Metal, c.1945 .... 128.00
Bracelet, Cuff, Flexible, 18K Gold, Patinated Steel, Bulgari 4148.00
Bracelet, Cuff, Hinged, 22K Gold, Hammered, Zolotas 2963.00
Bracelet, Cuff, Manca, Bud, Leaf, Sterling Silver, 4 In. 593.00
Bracelet, Cuff, Ribbed, 18K Gold, Diamond Terminals, Dorfman, 6 ½ In. 1659.00
Bracelet, Cuff, Sterling Silver, Hammered, 18K Gold Butterfly, Tiffany & Co., 6 In. 385.00
Bracelet, Diamond, Cabochon Rubies, Platinum Mount, 1930s, 7 ¼ In. 7130.00
Bracelet, Diamond, Leafy Engraved Edges, Platinum, Art Deco, 7 ⅛ In. 5925.00
Bracelet, Faux Sapphires, Square & Channel Set, Pave Rhinestones, Art Deco, 7 ¼ In. 813.00
Bracelet, Flexible, Turquoise Cabochons, 14K Gold, Early 1905, 7 ¼ In. 3910.00
Bracelet, Garnet Cabochon, Diamond Crests, 18K Gold, c.1870, 7 ½ x ⅞ In. 2400.00
Bracelet, Glass Beads, 2 Strands, Blue Tint, Rose Montee Floral Clasp, Miriam Haskell, 7 In. .. 225.00
Bracelet, Glass Panels, Frosted & Clear, Arched, Infant Bacchantes, Lalique, 8 In. 837.00
Bracelet, Grapes, Leaves, Sterling Silver, Georg Jensen, No. 30 .... 3200.00
Bracelet, Intaglio, Black Basalt Medallions, Oval, Wedgwood & Bentley, 6 ¼ In. 1896.00
Bracelet, Jade, Immortal Faces, Carved, Green, White, 8 Oval Beads, Chinese, 1 In. 825.00
Bracelet, Jade, White, Spiral Carved, 3 In. 4444.00
Bracelet, Jadeite, Pi Disc & Round Links, Chinese Characters, 20K Gold, 7 ¼ In. 296.00
Bracelet, Jadeite Tablets, Flowers, Leaves, 18K Gold, Tiffany & Co., c.1935, 7 In. 3674.00
Bracelet, Leather, Red, 2 Straps, Silvertone H Buckle, Sliding Closure, Hermes 207.00
Bracelet, Link, Arched & Reverse Arch, Retro, 14K Gold, 8 In. 2133.00
Bracelet, Link, Black Enamel, Green Enamel Spacers, Diamonds, Art Deco, 7 ½ In. 1996.00
Bracelet, Link, Bombe, Green Enamel Panels, Gold Ribs & X's, Schlumberger, Paris 9016.00
Bracelet, Link, Chevron, Flexible, Line Of Sapphires, 18K Gold, Cartier, c.1940, 6 ½ In. 5635.00
Bracelet, Link, Curved, Goldtone Metal, Germany, 1940s, 7 ½ x 1 In. 406.00
Bracelet, Link, Filigree, 14K Gold, Carved Carnelian, Art Deco, 7 ¾ In. 598.00
Bracelet, Link, Gold, Dangling Urn Finials, Watch, Harman, c.1940, 11 x ½ In. 469.00
Bracelet, Link, Goldtone Metal, Square Faux Aquamarines, Rhinestones, c.1940, 7 ½ In. 219.00
Bracelet, Link, Medallions, Women, Soldiers, Sterling Silver, G.W. Shiebler, 1880, 8 In. 1304.00
Bracelet, Link, Pyramid, Square, 14K Gold, Tiffany & Co., c.1940, ⅝ x 7 ½ In. 1562.00
Bracelet, Link, Ribbed, Rectangular, Sterling Silver, Hermes, Box, 7 ¾ In. 600.00
Bracelet, Link, Shaped, Applied Beads, Art Nouveau, Marcus & Co., 18K Gold, 6 ⅜ In. 3555.00
Bracelet, Link, Tapered, 18K Gold, Jadeite, Diamonds, Enamel, Art Deco, 7 ¼ In. 3555.00
Bracelet, Medallion, Woman's Head, 21K Gold, 1899, 8 In. 353.00
Bracelet, Panther, Gold Plated, Brushed Platinum, 7 In. 40.00
Bracelet, Pearls, Dove, Flowers, Sterling Silver, Georg Jensen, 7 ¼ In. 1541.00
Bracelet, Pearls, Scrolling Leaves, 18K Gold, Hooper Bolton, England, c.1970, 6 ½ In. 1541.00
Bracelet, Peridot, Citrine, Gold, Scrolling, Art Nouveau, Sidney Smith & Co., 7 In. 474.00
Bracelet, Plaques, Bloodstone & Nephrite Tablets, Bicolor Gold, Bippart, Griscom & Osborne, 7 In. 1541.00
Bracelet, Plaques, Bulrushes, Oak Leaf, Acorns, Grapevines, Mixed Metal, Everett Oaks, 7 In.. 5629.00
Bracelet, Platinum, Geometric, Enamel, Diamonds, Art Deco, 6 ⅞ In. 6844.00
Bracelet, Ribs, Curved Ribs, Diamond Melee, 14K Gold, Jose Hess, 7 In. 3081.00
Bracelet, Scottish Agate, Amber, Goldtone Metal, Victorian 173.00
Bracelet, Sterling Silver, Enamel, Box Clasp, Safety Chain, Marked, Mexico, 7 ½ x ¾ In. 115.00
Bracelet, Sterling Silver, Leaf Shaped Links, Carnelian, Georg Jensen, 7 ¼ In. 1304.00
Bracelet, Sterling Silver, Marcasite, Onyx, Coral, Art Deco, Theodor Fahrner, 7 ½ In. 948.00
Bracelet, Sterling Silver, Sculpted, Links, Marked, Federico Serranol, Mexico, 2 ½ In. .. *illus* 425.00
Bracelet, Sterling Silver Twisted Rope, 14K Gold Bands, 2 Orange Citrine, D. Yurman, 3 x 2 ½ In. 633.00
Bracelet, Train Track, Sterling Silver, Mexico 125.00
Bracelet & Earrings, Bakelite, Drop, Yellow, Carved, Flowers, Leaves, ⅞ In. 353.00
Bracelet & Earrings, Cuff, Leopard Spots, Rhinestones, Gold, Kenneth Jay Lane, 5 ¼-In. Cuff 594.00
Charm, Dachshund, Platinum, Rose Cut Diamonds, Art Deco, ¾ In. 533.00
Charm, Stanhope Church, Sterling Silver, c.1949 .... 35.00
Charm, Turtle, Platinum, 36 Round Diamonds, Art Deco, 34 In. 705.00
Chatelaine, Neoclassical Garden Design, Festoons, Tricolor Gold, c.1900, 3 ⅜ In. 1320.00
Chatelaine, Pencil, Note Holder, Container, Bottle, Coin Purse, Sterling Silver, Tiffany .. *illus* 805.00
Chatelaine, Pencil Holder, Pin Back, Ketcham & McDougall, c.1910, 18 ½ In. 39.00

Chatelaine, Perfume Bottle, Teardrop Shape, Sterling, Gold Washed, Engraved Clip, Victorian, 9 In. 289.00
Chatelaine, Sterling Silver, Philadelphia, 1800s . . . . *illus* 519.00
Chatelaine, Vinaigrette, Courting Couple, Swan, Man On Horse, Enamel, Marked, LP, 5 In. . . 1320.00
Chatelaine, Vinaigrette, Teapot Shape, Repousse, A. Jacobi, Baltimore, c.1880, 4 x 2 In. 761.00
Cigarette Case, Diamond, Sapphire, France, 18K Gold, Art Deco, 3 ⅞ x 2 ⅞ x ⅝ In. 5100.00
Cigarette Case, Enamel, Geometric Borders, Cylindrical, Silver, Russia, 1882, 3 ½ In. 2726.00
Cigarette Case, Enamel, Silver, Blue & Green Cloisonne, Rectangular, Russia, 3 ½ In. 805.00
Cigarette Case, Geometrics, Sapphires, 18K Gold, Art Deco, 2 ½ x 1 ¾ x ⅜ In.. . . . . 2880.00
Clip, Bumble Bee, Onyx Eyes, 18K Yellow & White Gold, Hermes, c.1960, 1 ½ In. 2479.00
Clip, Butterfly, Ruffled Wings, Pave Rhinestones, 12K Gold, Retro, c.1940, Pair 313.00
Clip, Dog, Fox Terrier, Ruby Eye, Diamond & Onyx Eye, Cartier, c.1950, 1 ¼ In. 4508.00
Clip, Dress, Diamonds, Sapphires, Platinum Scrolled Mount, Chaumet, c.1935, 2 In., Pair . . . 3156.00
Clip, Dress, Flower, Green Stone Center, Eisenberg Original, 2 ½ In., Pair 59.00
Clip, Dress, Hand, Silver, Red Enamel Nails, Rhinestone, Adolph Katz, Coro, c.1944. . . . . 215.00
Clip, Flower, Diamonds, Onyx Bombe Petals, 18K White Gold, Van Cleef & Arpels, 1 In. 4283.00
Clip, Flower, Ruby, Diamond Melee, 18K Gold, Tiffany & Co., 1 ⅝ In. 948.00
Clip, Flower Bouquet, Rubies, Diamond Centers, 18K Gold, Van Cleef & Arpels, ¾ In.. . . . . . . 6762.00
Clip, Hummingbird, Diamond Eye & Accents, 18K Gold, Cartier, c.1950, 1 ¾ In.. . . . . 8453.00
Clip, Lapel, Shield, 14K Yellow & Rose Gold, Guilloche Enamel, Cartier, 1945, Pair 2818.00
Clip, Lingerie, Vinaigrette, Filigree, White Metal, Box, 6 x ¼ In., 4 Piece 74.00
Clip, Shield Shape, Red & Clear Rhinestones, Gold Washed Silver, Mazer, c.1940, Pair. 188.00
Cuff Links, 3 Vices, Enamel, Gold Mount, Marked, GH, ⅝ In.. . . . . 1185.00
Cuff Links, Celtic Design, Oval, 14K Gold, Geo. Street & Sons, New York, c.1900. . . . . 1385.00
Cuff Links, Crystal, Pheasant, Water Birds, 14K Gold, c.1875. . . . . 480.00
Cuff Links, Eagle, Enamel, Sapphire Eyes, 18K Gold, Tiffany & Co. 1800.00
Cuff Links, Fish, Blue Enamel, 14 Diamonds, 18K Gold, Tiffany & Co. 1900.00
Cuff Links, Golf Bag, Clubs, 14K Gold, 1950s, 1 In. 360.00
Cuff Links, Hematite, Sterling Silver, Georg Jensen, No. 10. . . . . 750.00
Cuff Links, Links, Double Pyramid, Enamel, 18K Gold, Schlumberger 1778.00
Cuff Links, Lion's Head, 5 White Gold Strips, Emerald Eyes, 18K Gold, Tiffany & Co.. . . . . 1800.00
Cuff Links, Music Staffs, Clefs, Linked Oval Tablets, Engraved, 14K Gold, Cartier. 711.00
Cuff Links, Owl, Enamel, Diamonds, 18K Gold, Tiffany & Co. 1800.00
Cuff Links, Regiment Badge, Cheshire, Brass 46.00
Cuff Links, Studs, Lapis Lazuli, 2-Sided, Button Shape, 14K Yellow Gold, c.1900 . . . . 179.00
Cuff Links, Sunburst, Sapphire, Oval, 14K Gold, Tiffany & Co., Box. 400.00
Cuff Links, Tiger, Enamel, Emerald Eyes, 18K Gold, Tiffany & Co.. . . . . 2100.00
Cuff Links, Tsavorite Garnets, 2 Diamonds, Bombe Shape, Bar Links, 18K Gold, M. Burgener 2266.00
Cuff Links, Wave, Gold, Georg Jensen, No. 153. . . . . 750.00
Cuff Links, Weave Design, Oval, 18K Yellow Gold, Cartier. 500.00
Cuff Links, Woman, Holding Poppy, Flowing Hair, 14K Gold, c.1900. . . . . 925.00
Earrings, 3 Diamonds, Platinum, Art Deco 2040.00
Earrings, Abalone, Enamel, Multicolored, Tricolor 14K Gold, Earl Pardon, 1 In. 1185.00
Earrings, Agate, Shell Shape, Pearl Accents, 18K White Gold, Verdura 6231.00
Earrings, Alligator, 18K Gold, Pouch, Barry Kieselstein-Cord. 1422.00
Earrings, Amethyst, Pear Shape, Diamond Surround, Purple Jadeite Drop, M. Burgener 8497.00
Earrings, Amethyst Rhinestone, Cluster, Faux Baroque Pearls, Gold Filigree Mount, DeMario 344.00
Earrings, Amethyst Teardrop, Sterling Silver, Mexico, 1 ¾ x ¾ In.. . . . . 161.00
Earrings, Aventurine Quartz, 18K Gold, Angela Cummings 1541.00
Earrings, Biwa Pearl, Calligraphic, X Shape, 18K Gold, Christopher Walling, 1 ¾ In. 2489.00
Earrings, Bow, Brown Rhinestones, Green & Gold Speckled Drop, Dior. 281.00
Earrings, Christmas Tree, Enamel, Rhinestones, Goldtone Metal, Clip-On, 1 In. 25.00
Earrings, Citrine, Oval, Clip-On, 1970, 1 x ¾ In. 1912.00
Earrings, Citrine, Round, Suspended Pink Tourmaline, 18K Gold, Marina B 3606.00
Earrings, Coral, Onyx, Diamond, Platinum & Gold Mount, Art Deco 415.00
Earrings, Cushion Shape, Sterling Silver, 18K Gold Accents, Tiffany & Co., 1 In. 326.00
Earrings, Daffodil, 18K Gold, c.1990, Tiffany & Co., 1 In. 720.00
Earrings, Dangling, Coral Glass, Miriam Haskell 125.00
Earrings, Dangling, Pear Shape Amethyst, Clip-On, 18K Gold, P. Picasso 3585.00
Earrings, Diamond, Full Cut, White Gold, Studs, Hammerman Bros. 1541.00
Earrings, Diamond, Reversible, Pomellato, 18K Bicolor Gold, ¾ In. 1067.00
Earrings, Diamond Melee, 18K White Gold, Bulgari, ⅞ In.. . . . . 3200.00
Earrings, Diamonds, 18K Gold, Paloma Picasso, Tiffany & Co., Italy, 2 ⅛ In. 1659.00
Earrings, Diamonds, Onyx, 18K Gold, Clip-On, Van Cleef & Arpels, 1 In.. . . . . 2750.00
Earrings, Diamonds, Rubies, Pave Set, Ruffled Form, 18K Gold, Mauboussin, 1 In.. . . . . 2963.00
Earrings, Double Loop, Draped, Screwback, Goldtone Metal, Napier, 1 ⅜ In. 18.00
Earrings, Drop, Graduated Onyx Plaques, Pave Diamond Spacers, Art Deco, 3 In.. . . . . 3172.00
Earrings, Drop, Ruby, Diamonds, Chandelier, 18K White Gold, Art Deco, 1 ¾ In. 3824.00

The Duchess of Windsor's Charms

The Duchess of Windsor's charm bracelet designed about 1935 by Cartier sold in 1987 for a record price of £235,000 (about $376,000) The diamond bracelet had nine charms shaped like crosses set with diamonds, amethysts, emeralds, and sapphires and inscribed with references to special occasions, like the Duchess's 1944 appendectomy.

Jewelry, Chatelaine, Pencil, Note Holder, Container, Bottle, Coin Purse, Sterling Silver, Tiffany
$805.00

Jewelry, Chatelaine, Sterling Silver, Philadelphia, 1800s
$519.00

As always, the edited listings in *Kovels' Antiques & Collectibles Price Guide 2010* aren't available on any website, but readers should visit Kovels.com for information on trends, tips, reproductions, marks, old prices, and more!

J

Jewelry, Earrings, Marcasite, Silver, Art Deco, 3 ¼ In.
$330.00

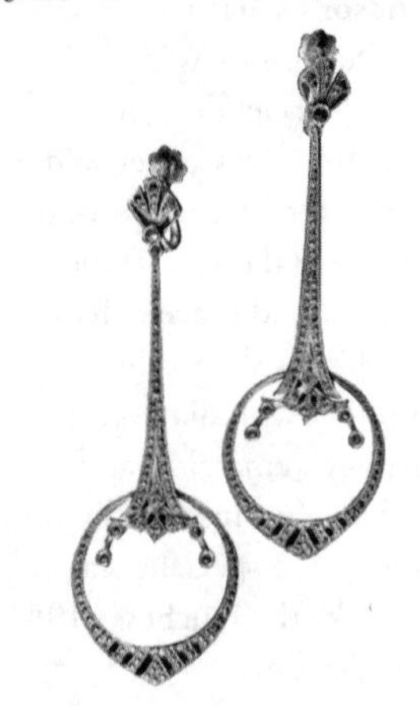

Jewelry, Necklace, Amethysts, Victorian, 15K Gold, 14 In.
$540.00

Jewelry, Necklace, Bakelite, Cigarettes, Matches, Martha Sleeper, 2 ⅜ In.
$1700.00

TIP
If a thin chain becomes tangled, dust it with talcum powder and the untangling should be easier.

Earrings, Drop, Wire, Brass, Copper, Art Smith, 1960s, 2 ⅝ In. 1126.00
Earrings, Emerald Cabochon, Rope Twist Border, 22K Gold, Tracy Dara Kamenstein, 1 In. 1304.00
Earrings, Fire Opal, 18K Gold, Paloma Picasso, Tiffany & Co. 1896.00
Earrings, Flower, Coral, Scrolls, Applied Beads, Etruscan Revival, 2 ⅛ In. 1185.00
Earrings, Flower, Mother-Of-Pearl, 18K Gold, Angela Cummings, 1 ⅛ In. 1185.00
Earrings, Flower, Purple Pansy, Clip-On, 18K Gold, JAR 2963.00
Earrings, Garnet, Square Cut, 18K Yellow Gold Mount, David Yurman, 9 ⅛ In. 1035.00
Earrings, Glass, Intaglio, Seed Pearls, 18K Gold, Elizabeth Locke, 1 ⅜ In. 1185.00
Earrings, Grape Clusters, Pearls, Diamonds, c.1950, 1 ¼ x ¾ In. 840.00
Earrings, Half Hoop, 18K Gold, Diamonds, Cartier 4148.00
Earrings, Hammered, Domed Shape, Raised Concentric Circles, 18K Gold, Ilias Lalaounis 2607.00
Earrings, Heart, Diamonds, Studs, 18K White Gold, Chopard 830.00
Earrings, Hoop, Double G Design, 18K Yellow Gold, Gucci 350.00
Earrings, Hoop, Open, Diamonds, 18K Gold, Cartier 6762.00
Earrings, Hoop, Sterling Silver Twist, 18K Gold, David Yurman, 1 In. 175.00
Earrings, Knot Shape, 18K Gold Accents, Signed, Van Cleef & Arpels, 1 In. 1659.00
Earrings, Lapis Plaque, 18K Gold, Angela Cummings, 1984, ¾ In. 1422.00
Earrings, Leaf, Pave Set Diamonds, 18K Gold Border, M. Ostier, 1 ¼ In. 4740.00
Earrings, Malachite, Triangular, Sterling Silver, Los Castillo, Mexico, 1 ½ x ¾ In. 69.00
Earrings, Marcasite, Silver, Art Deco, 3 ¼ In. *illus* 330.00
Earrings, Mother-Of-Pearl, Agate, Black Jade Intarsia, 18K Gold, Angela Cummings, ¾ In. 1541.00
Earrings, Onyx, Seed Pearls, 14K Yellow Gold, Victorian, 1 ½ In. 295.00
Earrings, Open Panels, Japoneseque, Leaves, Tricolor Gold, Tiffany & Co., c.1878 2640.00
Earrings, Parcel-Gilt Silver, Gold, Kinetic Brush, J.R. Soto, GEM, Milan, 1967, 4 In. 18750.00
Earrings, Paste, Enamel, Portrait, Star, Rope Bezel, Seed Pearls, Scallop Shells, 14K Gold 353.00
Earrings, Pearl, White & Black Diamond Cones, 18K White Gold, M. Burgener 5410.00
Earrings, Pendant, Suspended Pearl, 18K Gold, Janiye 533.00
Earrings, Ruby, Briolette Cut, Pear Shaped Diamond Drop, 18K White Gold, Art Deco, 1 ¾ In. 2390.00
Earrings, Ruby Cabochon Center, 4 Green Cabochons, Goldtone Metal, Chanel, 1980 469.00
Earrings, Sapphire, Old Cut Diamond Surround, c.1950 3965.00
Earrings, Sapphire, Turquoise Cabochon Flowerhead, Goldtone Metal, Clip, 1960s 620.00
Earrings, Scribble, 18K Yellow Gold, Paloma Picasso, Tiffany & Co., 1 ½ In. 295.00
Earrings, Tortoise Cabochon, Steel Posts, Avon, 1980, ¾ In. 18.00
Earrings, White Enamel, Door Knocker Style, 18K Gold, David Webb 2950.00
Hair Ornament, Rhinestone, Lacquer, Banded Silver Tone Metal Swirl, Pink, Blue, 1950s, 6 ¾ In. 38.00
Hatpins are listed in this book in the Hatpin category.
Key Chain, Stylized Wave, Malachite, Link Chain, Oval, 18K Gold, c.1970 785.00
Kilt Pin, Cairngorm, Agate, Sterling Silver, Circle, Crowned, Victorian, Scotland 230.00
Kilt Pin, Cairngorm, Amethyst, Pendant Loop, Sterling Silver, Victorian 115.00
Kilt Pin, Shield Shape, Stones, Sterling Silver, Victorian, Scotland 201.00
Lavaliere, 3 Diamonds, Round, Pear Shape Links, Art Deco, 1 ⅞ In. 1080.00
Lavaliere, Diamonds, Filigree, 2 Strands, 14K Gold Chain, Art Deco 720.00
Lipstick Case, Ladybug, Enamel, Convex Top, Silver, Gold Trim, 2 ¼ In. 2040.00
Locket, Leafy Scroll, Fleur-De-Lis, Garnet, 14K Gold, Monogram, Art Nouveau, 1 ⅛ In. 323.00
Locket, Victorian Woman, Diamond, 14K Yellow Gold, Round, Photo 590.00
Necklace, 3 Alexandrite Stone Nuggets, Purple, Thick Gold, Givenchy 265.00
Necklace, 5 Amethyst Drops, Amethyst Stones, Faux Pearls, Dior, 1960 750.00
Necklace, Abstract Links, Sterling Silver, Georg Jensen, 16 ¾ x 1 ⅝ In. 4148.00
Necklace, Amethysts, Victorian, 15K Gold, 14 In. *illus* 540.00
Necklace, Anchor, Twisted Trace Links, Sterling Silver, Hermes, 16 ¾ In. 1126.00
Necklace, Angelskin Coral Beads, Graduated, 14K Gold, 24 ½ In. 474.00
Necklace, Aquamarine, Heart Shape, Scrolling Leaves, Vines, 18K Gold, Art Nouveau, 2 x 18 In. 3081.00
Necklace, Aquamarine Beads, Wirework, Box Clasp, 18K Gold, Rebecca Koven, 16 In. 3911.00
Necklace, Bakelite, 13 Green Leaves, Blue Celluloid Chain, 16 In. 264.00
Necklace, Bakelite, Charm, Superstition, 5 Charms, Metal Chain 1175.00
Necklace, Bakelite, Cigarettes, Matches, Martha Sleeper, 2 ⅜ In. *illus* 1700.00
Necklace, Bakelite, Green Carved Tubes, Apple Juice Beads, Clasp, 20 In. 264.00
Necklace, Bakelite, Heart & Arrow, Red, ¾-In. Hearts *illus* 440.00
Necklace, Bakelite, Red, Beads, 20 In. 250.00
Necklace, Bakelite, Tooth, Red, Green, Black, Butterscotch, Red Celluloid Chain, 17 In. 382.00
Necklace, Ball Spacers, Flower Links, Sterling Silver, Pearls, Georg Jensen, 16 ¾ In. 948.00
Necklace, Bar Links, Sterling Silver, Georg Jensen, 20 In. 385.00
Necklace, Beads, 3 Strands, Glass, Clear & Frosted, Laguna, 1950s, 11 In. 45.00
Necklace, Beads, 4 Strands, Clear Glass, Seed Pearl, Miriam Haskell 425.00
Necklace, Beads, Black Jasper, Applied White Flowers, Silver Chain, Wedgwood, 36 In. 1007.00
Necklace, Beads, Milk Glass, Arrow Shape, Faceted, Rhinestone Rondels, Art Deco, 17 In. 148.00
Necklace, Beads, Milk Glass, Gold Metal Filigree Beads, Judy Lee, c.1955, 23 In. 148.00

Necklace, Beads, Red, Goldtone Clasp, Trifari, 1940s, 22 In. 22.00
Necklace, Beads, Sterling Silver, Barrel Shape, Mother-Of-Pearl, Sylvia Gottwald, 20 In. 538.00
Necklace, Beads, Venetian Glass, Gold, Blue, Pink, Cranberry, Flowers, Early 1900s, 15 In. 190.00
Necklace, Beads, Venetian Glass, Pearl, Gold Dust, Copper, Aventurine, Pink, Blue, Red, 19 In. 225.00
Necklace, Bib, Coral Beads, Barrel Shape, Gold Center Plaque, Spacers, 16 ½ In. 711.00
Necklace, Bracelet & Earrings, Link, Flexible, Tapered, 18K Yellow & White Gold, Cartier 6199.00
Necklace, Celluloid, Figural Fruit & Leaves, Celluloid Chain, Metal Clasp, 1930s, 15 In. 145.00
Necklace, Chain, Snake, 4 Strands, Knots, Gold, Marked, Yves St. Laurent, 1970s. 2125.00
Necklace, Chain, Stone, 7 Sterling Silver Disc Surrounds, Silver, Denmark, c.1950, 2 x 27 In. 107.00
Necklace, Choker, Beads, Flowers, 6 Strands, Wiener Werkstatte, 13 In. 2844.00
Necklace, Choker, Faux Pearls, Rhinestone Rings, Fish Hook Clasp, 1950s, 12 In. 65.00
Necklace, Choker, Interlaced Links, 14K Yellow Gold, Tiffany & Co., 16 In. 10800.00
Necklace, Choker, Rock Crystals, Beaded Rosettes, Gilt Filigree, Edwardian, c.1910, 8 In. *illus* 266.00
Necklace, Choker, Roses, Goldtone Metal, Monet, 18 In. 11.00
Necklace, Collar, Flexible, 18K Gold, Beaded, Boucheron, 12 x ½ In. 3226.00
Necklace, Collar, Ram's Horn Links, 18K Gold, Lalaounis, 16 x ⅞ In. 6573.00
Necklace, Collar, Sterling Silver, Rolled Edges, Art Smith, 13 ⅜ In. 2726.00
Necklace, Cultured Pearls, Graduated Sizes, Mabe Pearl Clasp, 14K Gold, 21 ½ In. 474.00
Necklace, Curved Shape, Flexible Fringe, 18K Gold, Bulgari, 14 In. 3555.00
Necklace, Enamel, Charles River View In Autumn, Silk Cord, 18K Gold, Janiye, 1974 2370.00
Necklace, Enamel, Double Scroll, Sterling Silver, Marked, Mexico. 104.00
Necklace, Faux Aquamarines, Baguette & Round Rhinestones, Trifari, 1950 281.00
Necklace, Flowers, Blue Stones, Pave Rhinestone 5 Pendant Drops, Trifari, 1950s 438.00
Necklace, Freshwater Pearls, Enamel, Bippart, Griscom & Osborn, Art Nouveau, 16 ½ In. 533.00
Necklace, Freshwater Pearls, Enamel Festoon, Seed Pearls, 14K Gold, Art Nouveau, 17 In. 1659.00
Necklace, Fringe, 11 Strands, Fuchsia Paste Stones, Bezel Set, Brass Mount, c.1900, 16 In. 238.00
Necklace, Fringe, Amethyst, Pear Cut, Coiled Links, Gold Mount, 13 ½ In. 593.00
Necklace, Fringe, Cascading Flower Heads, Brass, Spring Ring Clasp, c.1800, 15 ¼ In. 95.00
Necklace, Fringe, Herringbone Chain, 18K Gold, M. Buccellati, 16 ¾ In. 4148.00
Necklace, Garnet, Foil Back, Collet Set, Pear Shape Fringe, Gold Mount, Georgian, 15 In. 2370.00
Necklace, Lariat, Woven Chain, Lion's Head Terminals, 18K Gold, Zolotas, 40 ½ In. 2726.00
Necklace, Link, Flexible, Clear & Peridot Rhinestones, Goldtone Metal, Hobe, 16 ½ In. 168.00
Necklace, Link, Leaves, Articulated, Crystal Center, Glass Spacers, Duane, c.1945, 16 In. 128.00
Necklace, Locket, Sterling Silver, Birmingham, England, 19th Century, 2 x 1 ¼ In. 100.00
Necklace, Maguey, Sterling Silver, Hector Aguilar, Taxco, 1940s, 6 ½ In. *illus* 7100.00
Necklace, Mother-Of-Pearl Nugget Shape Clusters, Black Spacers, c.1955, 16 In. 168.00
Necklace, Opals, Graduated, Crystal Rondels, Diamond Barrel Clasp, Art Deco, 17 ¼ In. 720.00
Necklace, Pearl, Baroque, Goldtone Chains, Push Clasp, Miriam Haskell, 31 In. 285.00
Necklace, Pearls, Cultured, 2 Strands, Mikimoto, 17 In. 2868.00
Necklace, Pearls, Cultured, 3 Strands, Rose Tint, Mikimoto, 16 ¼ In. 7703.00
Necklace, Pendant, Butterfly, Cloisonne Enamel, Silver, Box Form Clasp, Sallyann Wekstein, 17 In. 178.00
Necklace, Pendant, Diamonds, Pear Cut, 2 Fetter Link Chains, Edwardian, 2 ½ x 1 ⅝ In. 4800.00
Necklace, Pendant, Free-Form Disc, Pierced, Silvered Rhodium, Gold, G. Pomodoro, 1967, 18 In. 4750.00
Necklace, Pendant, Graduated Rings, Silvered Rhodium, Aluminum, E. Sottsass, Milan, 1967, 9 In. 6250.00
Necklace, Pendant, Hematite, Fringe, Seed Pearls, Silver, Theodor Fahrner, 19 ½ & 3 In. 1422.00
Necklace, Pendant, Hematite Beads, Sterling Silver, 14K Gold, Earl Pardon, 18 In. 2489.00
Necklace, Pendant, Incised Crown, Intertwined C's, Gold, Oval, Chanel 688.00
Necklace, Pendant, Jasper, Hardstone, Trace Link Chain, 18K Gold, Elsa Peretti, 27 x 1 In. 1778.00
Necklace, Pendant, Micromosaic, Fringe Design, Flowers, Birds, Beetles, S-Clasp, Gold, c.1870 16273.00
Necklace, Pendant, Pierced Ball, Silvered Rhodium, Hinged Rods, G. Pomodoro, GEM, 1967, 20 In. 6250.00
Necklace, Pendant, Rainbow Zigzag, Silvered Rhodium, Gold, Aluminum, Del Pezzo, 1968, 10 In. 6875.00
Necklace, Puffed Heart, Baton Link Chain, Sterling Silver, Georg Jensen 593.00
Necklace, Sautoir, Cobalt Blue & Green Glass Loops, Faux Pearls, Archimede Seguso, 1970 344.00
Necklace, Sautoir, Panel, Diamond Center, Diamond Chain, Platinum, Art Deco, 25 In. 3900.00
Necklace, Sautoir, Shaped Links, Gray Glass Loops, Archimede Seguso, 1970. 375.00
Necklace, Snake, Flexible Link, Looped, Rhinestone Accents, Goldtone Metal, 1920s 750.00
Necklace, Triangles, Gold Stripes, Woven Chain, Goldtone, Art Deco Style, 1980s, 16 In. 32.00
Necklace, Turquoise, Leafy Frame, Paperclip Chain, 14K Gold, Arts & Crafts, 1 ¾, 16 In. 3674.00
Necklace, Turquoise & Blue Teardrop Stones, Green Accents, Silver Chain, 1960 313.00
Necklace, Turquoise Stones, Lattice Rope Chain, Fringe, 18K Gold, Persian, c.1930. 1680.00
Necklace & Bracelet, Celluloid Chain, Navy Blue, Sliced Loops, Black, 1930s, 16 ½ In. 235.00
Necklace & Bracelet, Green Hardstone, Sterling Silver, Felipe Martinez, 14 ⅝ & 7 In. 2015.00
Necklace & Bracelet, Pearls, Multicolored, Diamonds, Etienne Perret, 19 & 7 ½ In. 9560.00
Necklace & Bracelet, Strap, Diamonds, Chain, 18K Gold, Bulgari, 8 ⅜ & 15 ½ In. 4385.00
Necklace & Earrings, Beads, Turquoise & Rhinestones, 2 Strands, Gripoix, France, 1960 1063.00
Necklace & Earrings, Faux Aquamarine, Garnet, Marked, Schreiner, N.Y. *illus* 150.00
Necklace & Earrings, Pansies, Amethyst Rhinestones, Gold Leaves & Filigree, DeMario. 500.00

TIP
Don't wear jewelry when swimming. Both salt and chlorine damage some types of stones, like opals or emeralds. Sand will scratch coral, pearl, opal, lapis, turquoise, and other stones. Base metals will corrode.

Jewelry, Necklace, Bakelite, Heart & Arrow, Red, ¾-In. Hearts
$440.00

Jewelry, Necklace, Choker, Rock Crystals, Beaded Rosettes, Gilt Filigree, Edwardian, c.1910, 8 In.
$266.00

Jewelry, Necklace, Maguey, Sterling Silver, Hector Aguilar, Taxco, 1940s, 6 ½ In.
$7100.00

J

Jewelry, Necklace & Earrings, Faux Aquamarine, Garnet, Marked, Schreiner, N.Y.
$150.00

Jewelry, Pendant, Weeping Willow, Sheaf Of Wheat, Hair, Gold Frame, Chain, 1800
$1000.00

Jewelry, Pin, 78 Diamonds, Platinum Mount, Double Clip, Edwardian, 2 ¼ x 1 ⅜ In.
$6050.00

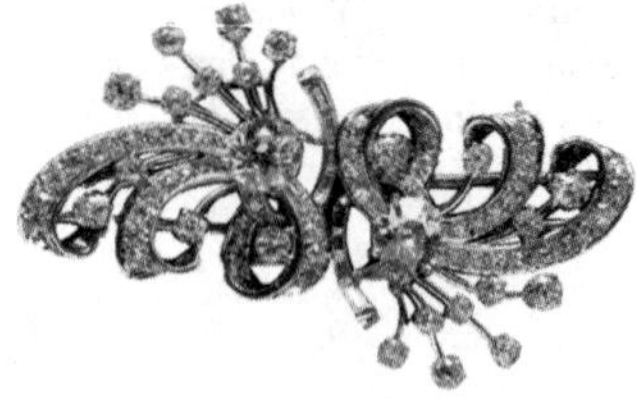

Necklace Set, Coral, Button & Drop Pendants, 18K Yellow Gold, Victorian, 4 Piece 920.00
Pendant, 2 Foo Dogs, Rhinoceros Horn, Chinese. 1062.00
Pendant, 4-Leaf Clover, Sapphires, Diamond, 14K Gold, Cartier 250.00
Pendant, 9 Diamonds, Pave Surround, Pearl Drop, 18K White Gold, Chopard 7889.00
Pendant, Amethyst, Diamonds, Platinum, 14K White Gold Chain, Edwardian, 2 In. 1422.00
Pendant, Arts & Crafts, Cutout, Hand Wrought Nickel, Cross Section, Newcomb, 1910, 2 In.. . 646.00
Pendant, Cameo, 3 Images, Swivels, Agate Reverse, Scrolling, 14K Gold, Victorian, 1 ½ In. . . 118.00
Pendant, Demantoid Garnet, Diamond, Platinum, Edwardian, 1 In. 8888.00
Pendant, Dendridic Agate, Bezel Set, Abstract Shape, Sterling Silver, Denmark, 1965, 2 ⅞ In. 237.00
Pendant, Egg, 14K Yellow Gold, Granulation, ⅝ In. 531.00
Pendant, Enamel, Courtesan, Masked Eyes, Diamonds, 14K Gold, c.1880, 3 ½ x 2 In.. .... 4800.00
Pendant, Enamel, Egyptian Design, Ra, Scarab, 18K Gold, 1 ½ x 1 ¼ In. 353.00
Pendant, Gibson Girl, Sterling Silver, High Relief Repousse, 1 ⅞ x 1 ½ In. 135.00
Pendant, Glass, Tiger Lilies, Green, Molded, Green Cord, Lalique, 2 ⅛ In.. .... 1067.00
Pendant, Heart, Diamond Melee, 18K White Gold, Judith Ripka, ¾ In. 711.00
Pendant, Heart, Pave Diamonds, Sterling Silver, David Yurman, 2 x 1 ¾ In. 425.00
Pendant, Jade, 8-Sided, 2 Circles, Yin Yang Symbol, 14K Yellow Gold Bail, 2 ¼ x 2 In.. .... 2185.00
Pendant, Jade, Child, Dragon, Phoenix, Pierced, Carved, 2 ¾ In.. .... 2252.00
Pendant, Jade, Chinese Yellow, Double Dragon, Chinese, 3 ¾ In.. .... 1180.00
Pendant, Jade, Double Dragon Finial, 13 Characters, Inlaid Gold, Green, White, Chinese, 2 ¾ In. 652.00
Pendant, Jade, Double Gourd Plant, White, Tan, 1 ¾ In. 770.00
Pendant, Jade, Dragon, White, Green, Chinese, 20th Century, 3 In. 237.00
Pendant, Jade, Dragons, Characters, Pale Celadon, Chinese, 19th Century, 3 ¾ x 3 In. 889.00
Pendant, Jade, Gray, Tan, Dragon Finial, Scholar In Landscape, 1 ¾ In.. .... 296.00
Pendant, Jade, Green, White, 2 Dragons, Character, Flowers, 3 ½ x 2 ¾ In. 1659.00
Pendant, Jade, Mandarin Duck, Lotus Plant In Beak, White, 2 ½ In.. .... 1422.00
Pendant, Jade, Monkey With Money Bag, White, 2 ¼ In.. .... 2133.00
Pendant, Jade, Pebble Shaped, Fish, Lotus Plants, White, 2 In.. .... 2133.00
Pendant, Jade, Russet, Quan Yin, Emerald, Apple Green, Celadon, Chinese, 3 In.. .... 598.00
Pendant, Jade, Taotie Mask, 2 Stylized Dragons, Calcified, Chinese, 3 ½ x 4 In. 1003.00
Pendant, Jade, Translucent Nephrite, Carved, Archaic Dragon, Phoenix Swirling Around, 1 ½ In. 5629.00
Pendant, Jade, White, Catfish, Ling Chih Plant, 18th Century, 1 ½ In.. .... 4148.00
Pendant, Jade, White, Woman, Looking At Window, Poem, 19th Century, 1 ½ In.. .... 5629.00
Pendant, Locket, Chinoiserie Scene, Enamel, Seed Pearls, Etruscan Revival, 26 In.. .... 652.00
Pendant, Micro Mosaic, Agnus Dei, 18K Yellow Gold, Etruscan Revival, 1800s, 2 x 2 In. 4600.00
Pendant, Micro Mosaic, Scarab, White Ground, Blue Star Border, 18K Yellow Gold, 1 ½ In. . . 1150.00
Pendant, Old Mine Diamond, 23 Single Cut Diamond Surrounds, Gold Filigree, 1800s, 1 ½ In. 5175.00
Pendant, Open Heart, 18K Gold, Diamond, Elsa Peretti, Tiffany & Co., 1 ½ In.. .... 2370.00
Pendant, Pearls, 11 Freshwater, Shield, Wreath, Ribbon, Black Enamel, 14K Gold, c.1860 . . . 316.00
Pendant, Rhinoceros Horn, Stylized Dragons, Chinese, 2 ½ In. 460.00
Pendant, Shell Shape, Black Enamel Decoration, Chain, 18K Gold, Switzerland, 1828, 1 x ¾ In. 1418.00
Pendant, St. Christopher, Sapphires, 14K Gold, Cartier. 200.00
Pendant, Star Of David, 30 Diamonds, Platinum, 14K White Gold Chain, 18 In. 264.00
Pendant, Syria Temple, Carved, Moonstone, Diamond Encrusted, Rubies, Star Drop, 2 ¼ In.. 294.00
Pendant, Turquoise, Leaves, Branches, 18K Gold, Art Nouveau, Georges Fouquet, 2 ¼ x 17 in. 3081.00
Pendant, Vinaigrette, Egg Shape, Engraved, Sterling Silver, Gold Scissors Accents On Grille, 1 In. 394.00
Pendant, Vinaigrette, Enamel, Courting Couples, Pear Shape, Lift Out Grille, Victorian, 1 In. 236.00
Pendant, Vinaigrette, Enamel, Courting Scene, Teardrop Shape, Hinged Cap, Victorian, 1 ½ In. 289.00
Pendant, Vinaigrette, Portrait On Ivory, Gold Mount, Engine Turned, France, 1 ¼ x 1 In.. . . . 315.00
Pendant, Weeping Willow, Sheaf Of Wheat, Hair, Gold Frame, Chain, 1800 .... *illus* 1000.00
Pendant & Earrings, Aquamarine, Garnet, Imitation, Silvertone Mounts, Schreiner, 13 ¼ In. 173.00
Pendant Pin, Snowflake, Diamonds, Platinum Over 18K Gold Mount, Edwardian, 1 In.. . . . . 1422.00
Pin, 2 Eagles On Branch, 16 Diamond, Pearls, 22K Gold, 1 ½ x 2 ½ In.. .... 1540.00
Pin, 2 Flowers, Pave Rhinestone Petals, Green Enamel Leaves, Tremblant, Coro, 1930s. 281.00
Pin, 2 Tulips, Moonstone, Sterling Silver, Georg Jensen, No. 1008. .... 850.00
Pin, 3 Birds On Branch, Pave Diamonds, Ruby Eyes, 18K Gold, Van Cleef & Arpels. 10143.00
Pin, 3 Coins, Classical Overlapping, Sterling Silver, Art Nouveau, Shiebler 296.00
Pin, 3 Flowers, Pave Rhinestones, Enameled Leaves, Silver Metal, Coro, 1930s 344.00
Pin, 4 Birds On Branch, Aquamarines, Diamonds, Rubies, 18K Gold, Van Cleef & Arpels, 2 In. 7325.00
Pin, 10 Cabochon Semi-Precious Stones, Sterling Silver, Wiener Werkstatte, 2 x 3 In. 4250.00
Pin, 78 Diamonds, Platinum Mount, Double Clip, Edwardian, 2 ¼ x 1 ⅜ In. .... *illus* 6050.00
Pin, 1876, Philadelphia, Memorial Hall, Black, Glass, Embossed, Oval, 1 ⅛ x 1 ⅜ In. . . . *illus* 55.00
Pin, Abstract, Wrapped Ribbon, 18K Gold, Barry Kieselstein-Cord, 1 ½ In.. .... 1422.00
Pin, Alice In Wonderland, Caterpillar, Mushroom, Diamonds, 14K Gold, 2 x 1 ⅝ In. 316.00
Pin, Amber, Leaf & Berry Frame, Sterling Silver, Georg Jensen 830.00
Pin, Amber Stone, Triangular Dangling Stones, Goldtone Metal, c.1900s, 2 x 3 In.. .... 165.00
Pin, Amethyst, 3 Drops, Pierced 14K Yellow Gold Mount, 1 ¾ In. 411.00

J

Jewelry, Pin, 1876, Philadelphia, Memorial Hall, Black, Glass, Embossed, Oval, 1 ⅛ x 1 ⅜ In.
$55.00

Jewelry, Pin, Bakelite, Dog, Begging, Leather Ears, Glass Eye, 3 ¼ In.
$220.00

Jewelry, Pin, Bakelite, Dog, Ears Move, Lucite Accents, 3 In.
$275.00

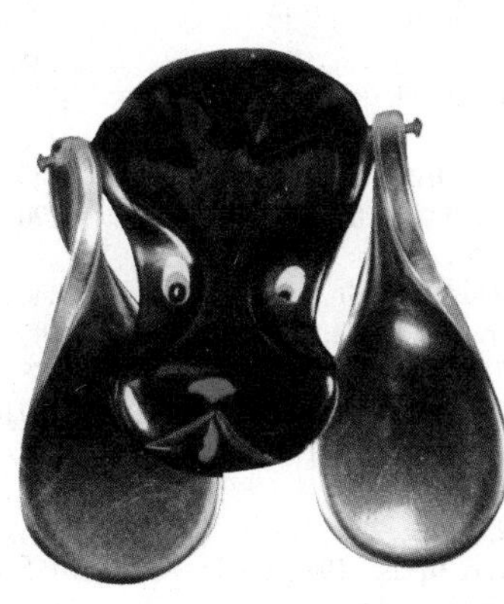

Jewelry, Pin, Bakelite, Doghouse, Dog's Head, House, 3 In.
$550.00

Jewelry, Pin, Bakelite, United States, Red, White, Blue, Lucite Rhinestones, 3 In.
$2250.00

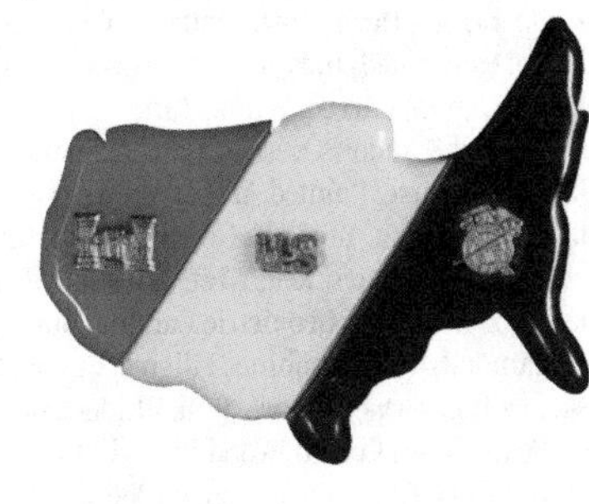

Jewelry, Pin, Bow, Gold, Amethyst, Retro, 3 ½ In.
$250.00

Jewelry, Pin, Cameo, Woman, Heart Shape, Shell, Carved, 10K Gold, c.1900, 1 ½ In.
$220.00

Jewelry, Pin, Cameo, Woman, Shell, Diamonds, Filigree, 14K White Gold, 2 x 1 ½ In.
$440.00

Jewelry, Pin, Christmas Tree, Rhinestone Ornaments, Goldtone Metal, Hedy, 2 ¼ In.
$30.00

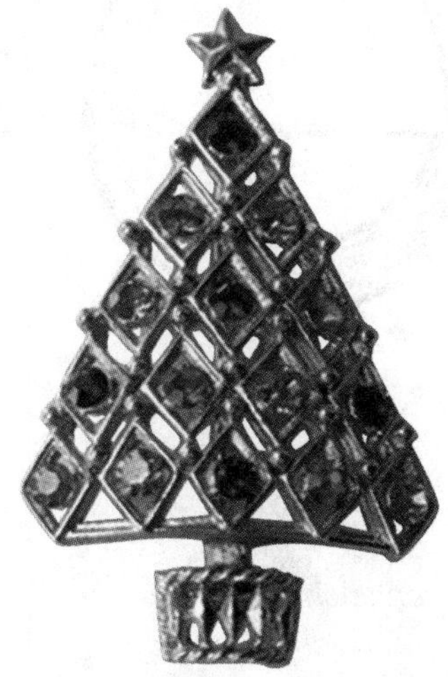

Jewelry, Pin, Dragonfly, Plique-A-Jour, 14K Yellow Gold, Art Nouveau, Masriera, 2 x 3 ½ In.
$3910.00

Jewelry, Pin, Enamel Over Brass, Marked, Molli Juin, 2 ½ In.
$360.00

Jewelry, Pin, Horseshoe, Diamond, Platinum, Art Deco, c.1920, 1 x 1 In.
$1760.00

J

TIP

Bakelite buyers must be sure to check condition. Avoid any obvious chips, cracks, crazes, pits, scrapes, scuffs, or fading. Run your fingernail over the edges to check for tiny chips, and look out for internal cracks. Any type of crack is the worst kind of damage, because eventually it will break. Scrapes and scuffs cannot be buffed off without damaging the patina.

Pin, Angel Skin Coral, Sapphire, Phoenix, 14K Gold, 2 In. 147.00
Pin, Apple, Rhinestones, Enamel Leaves, Silver Metal, Francoise, Coro, 2 ½ x 2 In. 165.00
Pin, Aquamarine, Bezel Set Crystals, Rhodium Plated Metal, Reja, 2 ¼ x 1 In. 150.00
Pin, Arabesque, Lotus, Enamel, Rope & Bead Border, Yellow Gold, Box, Tiffany, 1 ½ In. 978.00
Pin, Artist's Palette, Seed Pearls, 14K Yellow Gold, Retro, 1 ¾ In. 83.00
Pin, Axe Shape, Agates, Sterling Silver, Scotland, Victorian 69.00
Pin, Aztec God, Turquoise, Sterling Silver, Mexico, 3 ¾ x 2 ½ In. 115.00
Pin, Bakelite, Anchor, Painted Globe, Red White & Blue Tassel, Wood Top, 2 In. 176.00
Pin, Bakelite, Bambi, Butterscotch, 1940s, 3 x 2 x ¼ In. 325.00
Pin, Bakelite, Bird Flying, Red, Carved Feathers, Pearlized Eye, 3 In. 59.00
Pin, Bakelite, Dangling Cherries, 8 Red Cherries, 4 Green Leaves, 1940s 110.00
Pin, Bakelite, Dog, Begging, Leather Ears, Glass Eye, 3 ¼ In. .... *illus* 220.00
Pin, Bakelite, Dog, Ears Move, Lucite Accents, 3 In. .... *illus* 275.00
Pin, Bakelite, Doghouse, Dog's Head, House, 3 In. .... *illus* 550.00
Pin, Bakelite, Donkey, Carved, Wood, Button Eyes, Plastic & String Harness, Tail, 3 In. 235.00
Pin, Bakelite, Dragon, Green, Marbleized, Scrolled Brass Mount, 3 x 1 ½ In. 94.00
Pin, Bakelite, Flamingo, Flying, Yellow, Carved, Glass Eye, 5 In. 206.00
Pin, Bakelite, Fruit, Orange, Apple, Peach, Banana, Strawberry, Celluloid Leaves, 3 In. 1293.00
Pin, Bakelite, Giraffe, Swing Neck, 3 In. 1116.00
Pin, Bakelite, Hand, Butterscotch, Painted Nails, Cuff, Gold Chain, 4 ½ In. 588.00
Pin, Bakelite, Hat, Flared Brim, Applied Flowers, Carved, 3 In. 353.00
Pin, Bakelite, Hat, Red, Green Bird On Top, c.1935, 1 ¼ x 2 ⅞ In. 435.00
Pin, Bakelite, Horse's Head, Rust, Leather Collar, Brass Chain, 3 ½ x 3 In. 185.00
Pin, Bakelite, Laminate Bands, Mustard, Green, Rust, 1 ½ In. 206.00
Pin, Bakelite, Lemon, Carved, Yellow, 2 In. 59.00
Pin, Bakelite, Red & Yellow Overdye, Carved Flowers, Leaves, 3 ½ x 2 ¼ In. 323.00
Pin, Bakelite, Seahorse, Painted, Yellow, Brown, Carved, 3 ½ In. 529.00
Pin, Bakelite, Swordfish, Yellow & Green Overdye, Glass Eye, 4 In. 1116.00
Pin, Bakelite, United States, Red, White, Blue, Lucite Rhinestones, 3 In. .... *illus* 2250.00
Pin, Bakelite, Zigzag, Red, Geometric Carving, Bubbles, 3 ½ x 1 In. 176.00
Pin, Bar, Diamond, Bow, Sapphires, Filigree, Curved Ends, 14K Gold, 2 ½ In. 118.00
Pin, Basket Of Roses, Open Weave, Pink Rhinestones, Goldtone, 1 ¾ x 1 ½ In. 16.50
Pin, Bear, Pears, Resin Coated, Wood Bar, 3 ¼ In. 264.00
Pin, Bird, 18K Gold, Giacomo Manzu, c.1966, 1 x 2 ¼ In. 5400.00
Pin, Bird, Ferns, Sterling Silver, Georg Jensen, 2 ⅜ In. 385.00
Pin, Bird Of Paradise, Diamond Beak, Ruby Eye, Enamel, 18K Gold, Nardi, 3 ½ x 2 In. 3000.00
Pin, Bow, Diamond In Flower, Navette Shape, 14K Gold, c.1940, 3 ¼ x 2 ½ In. 3240.00
Pin, Bow, Gold, Amethyst, Retro, 3 ½ In. .... *illus* 250.00
Pin, Bow, Triple, Monet, 1 ¾ In. 8.00
Pin, Butterfly, Plique-A-Jour, 102 Round Diamonds, Ruby, 1 ¾ x 3 ½ In. 316.00
Pin, Butterfly, Red & Blue Rhinestones, Goldtone Metal, 1960s, 2 x 1 ½ In. 20.00
Pin, Butterfly, Textured, Brushed, Turquoise, Ruby Eyes, 14K Yellow Gold, 3 ¾ In. 679.00
Pin, Butterfly Shape, Watermelon Toumaline, 14K Gold 948.00
Pin, Calla Lilly, Rock Crystal, Enamel, Yellow Sapphire, Diamond, 18K Gold, Emis, 4 In. 4740.00
Pin, Cameo, Col. Randal McGavock, 18K Gold Mount, Saulini, c.1851, 2 ⅜ x 2 In. 7400.00
Pin, Cameo, Woman, Carved Grapevine Garland, c.1890, 2 x 1 ⅝ In. 845.00
Pin, Cameo, Woman, Heart Shape, Shell, Carved, 10K Gold, c.1900, 1 ½ In. .... *illus* 220.00
Pin, Cameo, Woman, Shell, Carved, Copper Vermeil, 1 ⅛ x ⅞ In. 75.00
Pin, Cameo, Woman, Shell, Diamonds, Filigree, 14K White Gold, 2 x 1 ½ In. .... *illus* 440.00
Pin, Cameo, Woman Holding Lamb, With Sheep, Dog, Gold Frame, Victorian, 2 ¼ x 2 In. 695.00
Pin, Cameo, Women, 3 Flowing Gowns, Holding Hands, Shell, Oval, Gilt Frame, 4 ½ x 4 In. 978.00
Pin, Camphor Glass, Art Deco, Rhodium, Red Stone, C Clasp, 1 ½ x 1 ¼ In. 49.00
Pin, Cat, Black Enamel Stripes, Emerald Eyes, 18K Gold, Van Cleef & Arpels, 1 ¾ In. 4508.00
Pin, Cat, Seated, Orange Agate Belly, Pewter, 1960s, 1 ¾ x ¾ In. 48.00
Pin, Cat, Wire Frame Outline, Goldtone Metal, Marked, AJC, 2 ¾ In. 13.00
Pin, Chick, Textured, Sapphire Eye, Pearl, 18K Gold, Van Cleef & Arpels, c.1964, 1 ½ In. 156.00
Pin, Chinese Man Shape, Carnelian, Malachite, 18K Bicolor Gold, 2 ⅜ In. 1062.00
Pin, Christmas Tree, 2 Layers, Rhinestones, Hollycraft, 2 ¼ In. 95.00
Pin, Christmas Tree, Abstract Piercings, Multicolored Rhinestones, Gold Metal, Marked, ART, 2 In. 65.00
Pin, Christmas Tree, Clear Rhinestone Base, Rhinestone Ornaments, Goldtone Metal, 2 In. 25.00
Pin, Christmas Tree, Rhinestone Ornaments, Goldtone Metal, Hedy, 2 ¼ In. .... *illus* 30.00
Pin, Christmas Tree, Glass Molded, Rhinestones, Trifari, c.1966, 2 ¼ In. 275.00
Pin, Christmas Tree, Rhinestone Ornaments, Baguette Candles, Victorian Style, Weiss, 2 In. 150.00
Pin, Christmas Tree, Rhinestone Streamers, Enamel Gifts, Goldtone Metal, Warner, 2 In. 165.00
Pin, Christmas Tree, Rhinestones Candles, Goldtone Metal, Weiss 2 ¾ In. 250.00
Pin, Christmas Tree, Rope Twist Garland, Rhinestones, Goldtone Metal, Pakula, 2 ¼ In. 80.00
Pin, Christmas Tree, Stained Glass, Goldtone Metal, Austria, 2 In. 165.00
Pin, Christmas Tree, Star & Rhinestone Border, Gold Plate, Tancer, 3 In. 60.00

Pin, Circle, Pearl, Granulated Leaves, Enamel Vines, 18K Gold, Giacinto Melillo, 2 In. 5333.00
Pin, Circle, Rubies, Diamond Blossoms, Platinum, Oscar Heyman. 1778.00
Pin, Croquet Mallet, 18K Yellow Gold, 2 In. 177.00
Pin, Cushion Cut Emeralds, Diamonds, Openwork Mount, Platinum, Art Deco, 2 ¼ In. 4740.00
Pin, Daisy, Enamel, Orange, White Center, 1960s, 1 ¾ In. 9.00
Pin, Diamond, 3 Drop Pendants, Platinum & 18K Yellow Gold, Bow Shape, 1 ¼ x 1 ¼ In. 1725.00
Pin, Diamond, 74 Bead Set, Rectangular Panel, Pierced, Art Deco, 1 ¾ x ⅝ In. 1560.00
Pin, Diamond, Pave Bombe Flowerhead, Stem, Leaf, 18K Gold, c.1960, 2 ⅝ In. 5100.00
Pin, Diamond, Platinum, 14K Gold, Art Deco, ¾ x 3 In. 1680.00
Pin, Diamond, Platinum, Square, Openwork, 14K Gold Pin Stem, 1 ½ x 1 ½ In. 5290.00
Pin, Dog, Long Hair, Rubies, Diamonds, 18K Gold, Van Cleef & Arpels, c.1963, 1 ¾ In. 4508.00
Pin, Dragonfly, Plique-A-Jour, 14K Yellow Gold, Art Nouveau, Masriera, 2 x 3 ½ In. ...... *illus* 3910.00
Pin, Dragonfly, Tortoiseshell Wings, Sterling Silver, William Spratling, c.1964, 2 In. 504.00
Pin, Duck, Sapphire Torso, 18K Gold Head & Feet, Van Cleef & Arpels, c.1960, 1 In. 2254.00
Pin, Elephant, Diamond, Round Ruby Eyes, 18K Yellow Gold, 1 ⅜ In. 797.00
Pin, Enamel, Orange Tulip, White Ground, Oval, Silver Mount, L. Nesbit, 1975. .... 178.00
Pin, Enamel Over Brass, Marked, Molli Juin, 2 ½ In. .... *illus* 360.00
Pin, Feather Shape, 17 Round Diamonds, 18K Bicolor Gold, 2 ½ In. 767.00
Pin, Flag, Rhinestones, Red, White, Blue, Goldtone Metal, 1970s, 2 In. 38.00
Pin, Flamingo, Standing, Painted, Yellow, Glass Eye, Carved, 4 ½ In. 323.00
Pin, Flower, 18K Gold, Tiffany & Co., 1 ½ In. 1304.00
Pin, Flower, Amethyst, Clear Rhinestones, Goldtone Metal, c.1930, 3 ½ x 2 In. 100.00
Pin, Flower, Blue Stone Center, Green Stone Petals, Rhinestones, Silver Metal, Jomaz, 4 In. .. 469.00
Pin, Flower, Diamonds, Enameled Edges, Georgian, 1 ⅜ x 1 ½ In. 900.00
Pin, Flower, Green & White Enamel, Blue Rhinestones, Leaves, Goldtone, c.1930, 4 In. 185.00
Pin, Flower, Marcasite, Frosted Glass Buds, Rhinestones, Silver Metal, Art Deco, Marked, BPCD 813.00
Pin, Flower, Pave Rhinestones, Chrome Plated Metal, Crown Trifari, 1930s. 500.00
Pin, Flower, Rhinestones, Rhodium, Goldtone, c.1930, 3 In. 125.00
Pin, Flower Shape, Twisted Wire, 7 Round Rubies, Art Deco, 2 ½ In. 413.00
Pin, Flower Spray, Faux Pearl, Bow, Trumpet Style Fastener, 1940s, 3 ½ x 2 ¼ In. 35.00
Pin, Flowers, Carnelian Cabochons, Sterling Silver, Georg Jensen, 1 ½ In. 533.00
Pin, Flowers, Citrine, Diamond, Silver Top, Victorian, 1 $^5/_{16}$ x 1 In. 956.00
Pin, Flowers, Feathered Scroll, Grape Cluster, Sterling Silver, Georg Jensen, No. 217A 475.00
Pin, Flowers, Green Beryl Leaves, Cushion Cut, Citrine, Iradj Moini, 3 x 3 ½ In. 948.00
Pin, Flowers, White Enamel, Summer Magic, Silver Metal, Sarah Coventry, 1960s, 2 ¾ x 2 ¾ In. 33.00
Pin, Fly, Pave Diamonds, Ruby Eyes, 14K Gold, ¾ In., Pair 1007.00
Pin, Forget-Me-Not, Ruby Melee Blossoms, Diamonds, Van Cleef & Arpels. 4740.00
Pin, Frog, Aventurine, Carved, Pearls, Seaman Schepps, Gold Studs, Pyramid, 18K Gold, 3 ⅜ In. 1778.00
Pin, Frog, Playing Banjo, Singing, Enamel & Rhinestone Accents, Goldtone Metal, 2 ½ In. ... 115.00
Pin, Fronds, Tendrils, Diamond, Oval Cut Sapphires, Gold Mount, Arts & Crafts, 2 ¼ In. 2489.00
Pin, Fruit Salad, Flowers & Leaves, Pave Rhinestone Apple Juice Plastic Frame, c.1930 .... 188.00
Pin, Garnet, Quatrefoil, Vinaigrette Covered Compartment, 16K Yellow Gold, Scotland 288.00
Pin, Gazelle, Rhinestones, Goldtone Metal, Art Deco, 1930s, 3 ½ x 2 In. 95.00
Pin, Ginko Leaf, Diamond Pave Stem, 18K Matte Gold, Tiffany & Co., 2 x 1 ⅝ In. 660.00
Pin, Girl, Rock Crystal Head, Rubies, Sapphires, 18K Gold Wire Hair, Van Cleef & Arpels 4508.00
Pin, Glass, Reverse Painted, Miniature Pinscher, Gold Mount, Tiffany, c.1880, 1 ⅛ in. 2370.00
Pin, Glass, Sleeping Child, Silver Mount, Frosted, Polished Accent, Lalique 415.00
Pin, Guitar Player, Sterling Silver, Mexico, 2 ⅜ In. 207.00
Pin, Hand, Holding Flower, Diamonds, Black Lacquer, 18K Gold, Cartier, c.1930 .... 9016.00
Pin, Heart, Opal, Diamonds, Garnets, Edwardian, 1 ½ x 1 ¼ In. 4200.00
Pin, Heart, Red Cabochons, Rhinestone Ribbon, Iradj Moini 1188.00
Pin, Heart, Ruby Cabochons, Rhinestones, Braid, Pearl Border, Gold Metal, Scaasi, 1960 .... 281.00
Pin, Heart, Yellow & Clear Rhinestones, Gold Rope Twist Lattice, Corocraft, 1950s 156.00
Pin, Horseshoe, Diamond, Platinum, Art Deco, c.1920, 1 x 1 In. .... *illus* 1760.00
Pin, Kitten, Silver Bow, Rhinestone Tail, Paw, Eye & Ball, Gold Metal, 2 ¼ In. 10.00
Pin, Knot, Textured, Tassels, 14K Gold, 2 ½ In. 900.00
Pin, Leaf, Double, Multicolored, Rhinestones, Joseff Of Hollywood, 1950s, 2 ½ x 1 ¼ In. 35.00
Pin, Leaf, Enamel Ladybug, Diamond Dew Drop, Frosted Rock Crystal, Tiffany, 2 ¼ In... *illus* 2015.00
Pin, Leaf, Heart Shape, Aurora Borealis, Multicolored Rhinestones, 1950s, 2 ½ x 1 ⅜ In. 38.00
Pin, Leaf, Mother-Of-Pearl, Moss Agate, Japanese Stick Pearl, Sylvia Gottwald 359.00
Pin, Leaf, Ruby & Diamond, Platinum & 18K Gold Mount, Tiffany & Co., 1 ¾ In. 6518.00
Pin, Leaf, Sterling Silver, Green Onyx, Georg Jensen, 2 ¼ In. 2726.00
Pin, Leaf & Fruit, Oval, Amber, Chrysophase, Silver, Georg Jensen, No. 18 .... 2600.00
Pin, Leopard, Black Enamel Spots, Emerald Eyes, 18K Gold, Van Cleef & Arpels, 2 In. 5635.00
Pin, Lion, Articulated, Sapphire Cabochon Eyes, Ruby Nose, 18K Gold, 3 In. 323.00
Pin, Lizard, Garnet, Diamond, Ruby Eyes, Edwardian, 2 In. 2844.00
Pin, Lobster, Lucite Claws, Wood Body, Glass Eyes, 3 In. 147.00

Jewelry, Pin, Leaf, Enamel Ladybug, Diamond Dew Drop, Frosted Rock Crystal, Tiffany, 2 ¼ In.
$2015.00

Jewelry, Pin, Micro Mosaic, Etruscan Revival Style, 18K Gold, 1800s, 2 x 1 ⅞ In.
$4400.00

Jewelry, Pin, Mourning, Hair, Woven, Under Glass, 14K Gold, 2 x 1 ½ In.
$115.00

Jewelry, Pin, Pear Cut Citrine, Diamonds, Gold Mount, Retro, Tiffany & Co., 2 ¾ In.
$2726.00

Jewelry, Pin, Pearls, Wreath & Ribbon, Black Enamel, 14K Gold, c.1860, 2 x 1 ¼ In.
$330.00

Jewelry, Pin, Sunburst, Diamonds, 14K Gold, Edwardian, 1 ½ In.
$316.00

Jewelry, Pin, Swallow, Diamond Dangling From Beak, 33 Diamonds On Wings, 18K Gold
$1093.00

Jewelry, Pin, Woman, Amethyst, Pearls, Sapphires, 14K Gold, M. Zimmerman, Box, 1 ⅝ In.
$3120.00

J

Pin, Love Sickness, Red Bakelite Heart, Wood First Aid Kit, Wood Bar, 2 ½ x 3 ¼ In. 118.00
Pin, Malachite, Diamond Melee, 18K Gold, R. Stone, 2 ⅜ In. 4444.00
Pin, Man In The Moon, Red, Clear & Blue Rhinestones, Gold Metal, c.1940, 3 In. 625.00
Pin, Micro Mosaic, Architectural Ruins, Twisted Border, 20K Yellow Gold, 4 x 2 In. 2530.00
Pin, Micro Mosaic, Etruscan Revival Style, 18K Gold, 1800s, 2 x 1 ⅞ In. .... *illus* 4400.00
Pin, Modern Head, Enamel Dots, Pin Back, Loop, R. Lichtenstein, c.1963, 3 x 2 ¼ In. 3900.00
Pin, Moonstone, Garnet Retro Flowers, 14K Gold, 1 ½ In. 147.00
Pin, Mosaic, Flowers, Geometric, Copper Mount, Fluted Edges, Italy, 1 x 1 In. 40.00
Pin, Moth, Arts & Crafts, Cutout, Silver, Newcomb, Early 1900s, 1 ½ In. 470.00
Pin, Mourning, Gold, Enamel, Pearls, c.1848, 1 ½ x 1 ¼ In. 150.00
Pin, Mourning, Hair, Woven, Under Glass, 14K Gold, 2 x 1 ½ In. .... *illus* 115.00
Pin, Native American Style, Turquoise, Ruby, Diamonds, Van Cleef & Arpels, 1 ⅝ In. 3200.00
Pin, Opal, Bezel Set, European Cut Diamonds, Flower Swags, Platinum, Art Deco 411.00
Pin, Opal, Pear Shape Cabochon, 21 Diamonds, 18K Yellow Gold Mount, 1 ½ x 1 ½ In. 805.00
Pin, Orb, Cross Top, Green, Red & Blue Stones, Faux Pearls, Gold Metal, Trifari, 1953 .... 406.00
Pin, Order Of The Garter, Coldstream Guard Badges, Motto, Enamel, 14K White Gold 1610.00
Pin, Oval, Pierced, Chain Link, 3 Diamonds, Platinum, Belle Epoque, 1 ⅛ x ⅞ In. 2760.00
Pin, Owl, Geometric Design, Big Eyes, Goldtone Metal, 1 In. 6.50
Pin, Owls, Perched On Branch, Diamond Melee, Emerald Eyes, 18K Gold, Kurt Wayne 948.00
Pin, Painter's Palette, Etched, Toledo Ware, Spain, Goldtone Metal, 1950s, 2 ¼ In. 85.00
Pin, Pansy, Black Enamel, Whiteside & Blank, 14K Gold, Art Nouveau, 2 In. 474.00
Pin, Peacock Feather, Enamel, Green Onyx, Silver, Arts & Crafts, Mildred Watkins, 2 In. 1422.00
Pin, Pear Cut Citrine, Diamonds, Gold Mount, Retro, Tiffany & Co., 2 ¾ In. .... *illus* 2726.00
Pin, Pearl, Clear Rhinestones, Open Center, Goldtone Metal, Hand Wired, Originals By Robert, 2 In. 135.00
Pin, Pearl, Peridot, Round, Openwork Mount, 14K Gold, Art Nouveau, 1 ½ In. 1035.00
Pin, Pearl Buds, Leaves, Vines, Blue Enamel Ground, Sterling Silver, Wiener Werkstatte, 1 ¾ In. 7406.00
Pin, Pearls, 3 Heart Cluster, 18K White Gold, Mikimoto, 1 In. 267.00
Pin, Pearls, Wreath & Ribbon, Black Enamel, 14K Gold, c.1860, 2 x 1 ¼ In. .... *illus* 330.00
Pin, Pendant, Courtship Scene, Transfer, Painted, Gold Twisted Rope Frame, Limoges, 1 ⅛ x 1 In. 85.00
Pin, Pendant, Diamonds, Pearls, Platinum Over 18K Gold Mount, Edwardian, 2 ⅝ In. 3081.00
Pin, Pendant, Figurine, Profile Scrolls, Abstract Shape, 23K Gold, Jean Cocteau, 2 ¼ In. 7406.00
Pin, Pendant, Free-Form Linear Shape, Gold, Ibram Lassaw, c.1957, 2 x 2 In. 420.00
Pin, Pendant, Horseshoe, Rhinestones, Pink, White, Gold Center Ball, 1930s, 1 ¾ x 1 ⅝ In. .. 30.00
Pin, Pendant, Pineapple, Autumn Haze, Sarah Coventry, 1960s, 1 ¾ In. 68.00
Pin, Phoenix, Sterling Silver, Frederick Davis, Mexico, 5 In. 1126.00
Pin, Pinecone, Needles, Lapis Cabochons, 18K Gold, Arts & Crafts, Heintz, 2 ¾ x 3 In. 1541.00
Pin, Plastic, Ice Skates, Silver, White, 1 ¾ x 1 ⅜ In. 10.00
Pin, Plastic, Old-Fashioned Ice Skates, Silver Blades, White, 1 ¾ x 1 ⅜ In. 10.00
Pin, Porcelain, Flowers, Basket, Painted, Scrolled Frame, Oval, Goldtone, 2 x 2 ½ In. 11.00
Pin, Quiver, Bow & Arrows, Rubies, Diamonds, 18K Gold, Cartier, c.1949 .... 2489.00
Pin, Rabbit, Holding Carrot, Ruby Eyes, Cartier, c.1950, 18K Gold, 1 ¼ In. 5410.00
Pin, Rabbit, Twisted Rope, Emeralds, Rubies, Diamonds, 18K Gold, Van Cleef & Arpels, 1 In. . 2479.00
Pin, Raccoon, Diamond Melee, Enamel, Platinum, 18K Gold, McTeigue, 1 In. 563.00
Pin, Ribbon, 23 Round & Full Diamonds, Cut, Sapphires, Platinum, 2 x ⅜ In. 920.00
Pin, Rooster, Buff Top Rubies, Sapphires, Emeralds, Enamel, Platinum, Art Deco, 2 In. 7406.00
Pin, Rose, Carved, Amethyst, Sterling Silver, William Spratling, 1945, 2 ⅜ x 1 ⅜ In. 295.00
Pin, Rose, Circles, Blue Zircon Center, Green Enamel Leaves, Acorn Catch, 14K Gold, Retro, 1 ½ In. 88.00
Pin, Roses, Carved, Thorny Branch, Pink Quartz, Silver, Mexico, 2 ⅝ x 2 ¾ In. 115.00
Pin, Salamander, Pave Rhinestones, Faux Ruby Eyes, Green Enamel Feet, Coro, 1930s 344.00
Pin, Sapphire, Cushion Cut, 12 Diamonds, Art Deco, 2 ¼ In. 840.00
Pin, Sapphires, Diamonds, Emeralds, Openwork, Platinum, Art Deco, 2 ⅝ In. 3318.00
Pin, Saturn, Blue Moonstone, Rhinestone Ring, M.B. Boucher, 1 x 1 ¾ In. 185.00
Pin, Scarecrow, Green Agate Head, Rubies, Sapphires, 18K Gold, Van Cleef & Arpels, 2 ¼ In... 5072.00
Pin, Scepter Shape, Agates, Cairngorm Thistle, Sterling Silver, Scotland, Victorian, c.1845 ... 81.00
Pin, Sea Creature, Emerald Eye, 18K Gold, David Webb, 3 ⅜ x 2 In. 1778.00
Pin, Shovel, Gold Rush, Riveted, Quartz Crystals, Inlaid Green Stone, 14K Gold, 3 ¼ In. 830.00
Pin, Squares, Interlaced, Polished & Textured, Emmons, 1950s, 2 x 2 In. 20.00
Pin, St. Simon Anchor, Wrapped In Rope, Sterling Silver, Scotland, Victorian 58.00
Pin, Star, Rhinestones, Blue, Pink, Purple, Goldtone Mount, Coro, 1 ¼ In. 65.00
Pin, Starburst, Diamonds, 14K Gold, Edwardian, 1 ⅞ In. 3555.00
Pin, Starburst, Garnet Center, Clear Rhinestones, Kenneth Jay Lane, 3 x 2 ¼ In. 275.00
Pin, Sterling Silver, Abstract Shape, Pin Loop, Sigi Pineda, Mexico, 1994, 2 ¼ In. 207.00
Pin, Strawberry, Fuchsia Rhinestones, Gold Stems & Leaves, Eisenberg, 1 ¼ x 1 ½ In. 50.00
Pin, Stylized Star, Red Cabochons, Gold Metal Openwork, Sarah Coventry, 1970s, 2 ¼ In. 55.00
Pin, Sunburst, Diamonds, 14K Gold, Edwardian, 1 ½ In. .... *illus* 316.00
Pin, Swallow, Diamond Dangling From Beak, 33 Diamonds On Wings, 18K Gold .... *illus* 1093.00
Pin, Swan, Flying, Elongated Wingspan, Mottled Silvertone, 1970s, 2 ½ x 3 In. 30.00

Pin, Swirl, Faux Pearl Center, Silvertone Rhodium, Sarah Coventry, 1960s, 2 ½ In. 65.00
Pin, Toucan, Enamel, 18K Bicolor Gold, Italy, 2 ¼ In. 2478.00
Pin, Toucan, Faux Yellow Topaz, Rhinestones, Blue & Yellow Enamel, Corocraft, 1930s 563.00
Pin, Turtle, Marcasite, 1 ¾ In. 15.00
Pin, Turtle, Rhinestones, Enamel, Amber, Orange, 1 ¼ x 2 In. 28.00
Pin, Twin Figures, Faceted Sapphires, 18K Gold, Franco Cannilla, 1 ½ x 1 ¾ In. 3120.00
Pin, Woman, Amethyst, Pearls, Sapphires, 14K Gold, M. Zimmerman, Box, 1 ⅝ In. *illus* 3120.00
Pin, Woman, Leaves, Berries, Sterling Silver, Kerr & Co., 2 ¾ x 2 ½ In. *illus* 120.00
Pin, Wreath Shape, Scrolls, Moonstones, Sterling Silver, Georg Jensen, 2 In., No. 159. 605.00
Pin & Earrings, 5 Mine Cut Diamond, Diamond & Turquoise, Etruscan Revival, 1800s 1495.00
Pin & Earrings, Flowers, Ruby Baguettes, Rhinestones, Gold Metal, Duette, Coro 250.00
Pin & Earrings, Geometrics, Multicolored Enamel, Round, Sterling Silver, Kalo 2400.00
Pin & Earrings, Geometrics, Sterling Silver, Marked, Kalo, 1 ¾-In. Pin. *illus* 2400.00
Pin & Earrings, Glass Stone, Filigree, Dangling Chains, Goldtone Metal, Clip-On, c.1850, 6-In. Pin 400.00
Pin & Earrings, Leaf Form, Doves, Sterling Silver, Georg Jensen, 1 ¾-In. Pin 711.00
Pin & Earrings, Leopard Head, Black Enamel, Rhinestones, Green Cabochon Eyes, J. Mazer. 438.00
Pin & Earrings, Maple Leaf, Bicolor Gold, Cartier, 2-In. Pin, 1-In. Earrings. 3674.00
Pin & Earrings, Moonstone, Cabochons, Lily Pad Design, Sterling Silver Balls, 1940s, 2 & 1 In. 236.00
Pin & Earrings, Pendant, Flowers, Coral, Carved, 14K Gold Wire, 1 ½-In. Pin 1380.00
Pin & Earrings, Sphinx, Rhinestones, Enamel Berries, 2 ½-In. Pin, ¾-In. Earrings 165.00
Pin & Earrings, Turquoise, Diamonds, 20K Gold, Etruscan Revival, 1 x 2 ⅛-In. Pin *illus* 1430.00
Ring, 3 European Cut Diamonds, Diamonds Surround, Filigree, Art Deco, Size 5 ¾. 823.00
Ring, 4 Projecting Cylinders, Rhodium Plated Silver, E. Sottsass, GEM, Milan, 1967, Size 7 ¼-8. 4375.00
Ring, 7 Bands, Diamonds, 18K Bicolor Gold, Neiman Marcus, Size 6 ¼. 770.00
Ring, 9 Diamonds, Filigree, 14K White Gold, Art Deco, c.1925, Size 7 ¼ 323.00
Ring, Amethyst, Oval, 23 Diamond Surround, Yellow Gold, Mid 19th Century 418.00
Ring, Amethyst, Seed Pearls, 14K Rose Gold, 1920s, Size 6 ¼ 425.00
Ring, Amethyst, Turquoise, Pear Shape, Pave Diamonds, Platinum Mount, Cartier, 1950 6762.00
Ring, Amethyst Cabochon, Enamel, 18K Gold, David Webb, Size 5 ½. 2973.00
Ring, Anodized Aluminum, Gold, Box, Gastone Novelli, GEM, Italy, 1968, Size 7. 8750.00
Ring, Aquamarine, Diamonds, Platinum, Shreve Crump & Low, Size 6 ½. 2607.00
Ring, Aquamarine Cabochon, 18K White Gold, Bulgari, Size 6 ½. 1126.00
Ring, Bakelite, Butterscotch, Domed, Diamond Cut Facets, Size 5 89.00
Ring, Bamboo, Pave Diamonds, Black Enamel Inlay, 18K Rose Gold, Enigma, Size 6 ½ 5098.00
Ring, Band, Manhattan Skyline, Sapphire Baguettes, Diamonds, Platinum, Size 6 ½ 8850.00
Ring, Bands, White Enamel, Diamonds, 18K Gold Mount, David Webb, Size 6 7889.00
Ring, Black Diamond, Pearls, Diamonds, Leaf Mount, Pierced, Chased, Art Deco, Size 7 4500.00
Ring, Blue Diamond, Round, Brilliant Cut, 14K White Gold, Size 6 ½ 1200.00
Ring, Bombe Shape, 3 Diamonds, 18K Gold Rope Twist Mount, Boucheron, c.1930 3945.00
Ring, Bombe Shape, Diamonds, 28 Brilliant Cut, 18K Gold, Tiffany & Co., 1965, Size 5 3000.00
Ring, Bombe Shape, Diamonds, Ribbed, 18K Gold, David Webb, Size 7 ¼ 4029.00
Ring, Cameo, Center Diamond, Flips To Black Onyx, 14K White Gold, Habille, Size 6. 395.00
Ring, Carnelian Cabochon, Oval, Engraved, Shoulders, 14K Gold, Cartier, c.1940, Size 3 207.00
Ring, Cat's Eye, Chrysoberyl, Enamel, Diamond, 18K Gold, Elizabeth Gage, Size 6 ¾. 948.00
Ring, Cat's Eye, Green, Pewter, No. 230, Georg Jensen, Adjustable, Size 7. 65.00
Ring, Checkerboard, Diamond, Sapphire Bombe, Platinum, c.1960, Size 6 ½. 3480.00
Ring, Citrine, Brown & Yellow, Teardrop Shape, 18K Gold, Tapered, Bulgari, Size 6 1916.00
Ring, Citrine Cabochon, Red Basse Taille Enamel, 18K Gold, DeVroomen, Size 7 ¼. 1126.00
Ring, Citrine Stylized Scarab, 18K Gold, Burle Marx, Size 6 ¼ 1422.00
Ring, Cocktail, Diamond, European Cut, 8 Full Cut, 14K White Gold, Art Deco, Size 4 ¾. 176.00
Ring, Diamond, Cushion Cut, Art Nouveau, c.1885, Size 7 ½ 1560.00
Ring, Diamond, European Cut, 14K White Gold, Edwardian, Size 8 *illus* 375.00
Ring, Diamond, European Cut, Sapphires, French Cut, Art Deco, Size 7 ¼ 2468.00
Ring, Diamond, Filigree, White Gold, 1920s *illus* 265.00
Ring, Diamond, Navette Shape, Beaded Edge, Platinum, Art Deco, Size 4 ¼ 1185.00
Ring, Diamond, Rose Cut Diamonds, Silver Over 14K Gold, Victorian, Size 6 ¾ 1912.00
Ring, Diamond, White & Black, 2 Cross-Over Hearts, 18K White Gold, M. Burgener, Size 7 4079.00
Ring, Diamond Cluster, Melee, Baguettes, 18K Gold, Kurt Wayne 1422.00
Ring, Flower, Ruby, 14K Bicolor Gold, Retro, Size 6 ¾. 237.00
Ring, Jade, Sterling Silver, David Anderson, Norway, Box, ¾ In. *illus* 510.00
Ring, Jadeite, Diamond, Bow Shape Shoulders, Platinum, Size 6 ¾. 5036.00
Ring, Kunzite, Pear Cut, Bezel Set, 18K Gold, Miye For Janiye, Size 4 1422.00
Ring, Lapis Lazuli, Sterling Silver, Georg Jensen, Size 7. 444.00
Ring, Lavender Jade, Cabochon, 14K Yellow Gold, Art Deco, Size 7. 633.00
Ring, Lion's Head, Ruby Eyes, Textured Mane, 18K Gold, David Webb, Size 6 4508.00
Ring, Mabe Pearl, 7 Diamonds, Openwork, Carved Leaves, 18K Yellow Gold, Size 10 1121.00
Ring, Memorial, Engraved Accents, Black Enamel, 18K Gold, 1835, 1837, Size 7 ½, Pair 652.00

Jewelry, Pin, Woman, Leaves, Berries, Sterling Silver, Kerr & Co., 2 ¾ x 2 ½ In.
$120.00

Jewelry, Pin & Earrings, Geometrics, Sterling Silver, Marked, Kalo, 1 ¾-In. Pin.
$2400.00

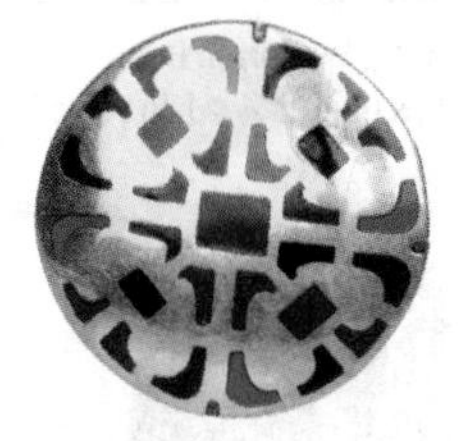

Jewelry, Pin & Earrings, Turquoise, Diamonds, 20K Gold, Etruscan Revival, 1 x 2 ⅛-In. Pin
$1430.00

Jewelry, Ring, Diamond, European Cut, 14K White Gold, Edwardian, Size 8
$375.00

Jewelry, Ring, Diamond, Filigree, White Gold, 1920s
$265.00

Jewelry, Ring, Jade, Sterling Silver, David Anderson, Norway, Box, ¾ In.
$510.00

Jewelry, Ring, Memorial, Hair, Braided, 14K Gold, 1 ⅛ x 1 In., Size 7
$115.00

John Rogers, Group, Matter Of Opinion, Woman Patient, Doctor, Husband, 1884, 19 In.
$325.00

Ring, Memorial, Hair, Braided, 14K Gold, 1 ⅛ x 1 In., Size 7 .... *illus* 115.00
Ring, Multicolored Stones, Gold Metal, Leaf, Sarah Coventry, c.1970, Size 5 .... 32.00
Ring, Oak Leaves, Turquoise, Gold, Beads, Silver, Everett Oakes, c.1935, Size 3 ¾ 1304.00
Ring, Ram's Head, Ruby, 18K Gold, Zolotas, Size 7 ½ 593.00
Ring, Ruby, Eternity Band, Platinum, Tiffany & Co., Size 6 .... 978.00
Ring, Ruby, Oval Cut, Diamond, Platinum, 18K Gold, c.1920, Size 3 ½ 960.00
Ring, Saddle, Amethyst Cabochon, 18K White Gold, Size 6 ½ 830.00
Ring, Sapphire, 8 Diamonds, 14K Gold, Victorian, Size 4 ¾ 294.00
Ring, Sapphire, Diamond, Rounded Knot Design, Cartier, Size 6 ½ 195.00
Ring, Sapphire, Rectangular Diamond Surround, Platinum Mount, Art Deco, Size 5 ¼ 4395.00
Ring, Sapphire, Round, 13 Round Diamonds, 14K Bicolor Gold, Edwardian, Size 6 .... 748.00
Ring, Sapphires, 17 Square, 13 Diamonds, X Design, Tiffany & Co., Size 6 ¾ 1121.00
Ring, Scarab, Faience, Applied Wirework, Swivels, 18K Gold, Size 7 ½ 444.00
Ring, Scarab, Poison, Diamond Eyes, Rope Twist, 14K Gold, Art Nouveau, Size 4 ½ 2133.00
Ring, Star Sapphire, Diamond Melee, Platinum, Art Deco, Size 5 ¼ 3437.00
Ring, Star Sapphire Cabochon, Diamond, Platinum, 1935, Size 7 .... 840.00
Ring, Stylized Wave, Polished, Textured, 14K Gold, Ed Wiener, Size 9 ½ 593.00
Ring, Tahitian Pearl, Diamond, Black, 18K White Gold, Size 6 ¼ 2645.00
Ring, Tourmaline, Diamond Baguette, Platinum, Art Deco, Size 6 ¾ 2400.00
Ring, Tourmaline, Pink, 18K Gold, Cellino, Size 6 ¼ 569.00
Ring, Wedding Band, Diamond, Wheat Chasing, Platinum, Edwardian 418.00
Ring, Zircon, Green, Diamond, Octagonal, 14K Gold, Art Deco, c.1930, Size 6 ¾ 660.00
Shoehorn, 14K Gold, Gorham 600.00
Stickpin, Bedouin Figure, Enamel, Diamonds, 14K Gold, Art Nouveau 356.00
Tiara, Coral Beads, Faceted, Gilt Wirework Mount, 1 ⅜ In. 3318.00
Watches are listed in their own category.
Wristwatches are listed in their own category.

JOHN ROGERS statues were made from 1859 to 1892. The originals were bronze, but the thousands of copies made by the Rogers factory were of painted plaster. Eighty different figures were created. Similar painted plaster figures were produced by some other factories. Rights to the figures were sold in 1893, and the figures were manufactured for several more years by the Rogers Statuette Co. Never repaint a Rogers figure because this lowers the value to collectors.

Group, Charity Patient, Doctor, Woman, Child, 22 x 12 ¼ x 8 In. 575.00
Group, Checkers Up At The Farm, 20 x 17 In. .... 250.00 to 325.00
Group, Chess, 2 Men, Woman Pouring Tea, Clay, Signed, 21 ½ In. 480.00
Group, Coming To The Parson, Sitting At Desk, Couple Standing, Signed, 1870, 22 In. 250.00
Group, Council Of War, Lincoln, Grant & Stanton, 23 x 14 In. 1025.00
Group, Foundling, Man Holding Baby, Woman, Clay, Signed, 21 In. 750.00
Group, Going For The Cows, Horse, Boy, Dog, Clay, Signed, 11 ½ In. 190.00
Group, Innocence Protected, Soldier, Woman, Child, Painted, 21 In. 300.00
Group, Is It So Nominated In The Bond, 23 In. 200.00
Group, Matter Of Opinion, Woman Patient, Doctor, Husband, 1884, 19 In. .... *illus* 325.00
Group, Neighboring Pews, Plaster, 19 x 15 In. 50.00
Group, Parting Promise, 21 ½ x 10 In. 25.00
Group, Phrenology At The Fancy Ball, 20 x 9 ½ In. 425.00
Group, Rip Van Winkle At Home, 18 x 10 In. 200.00
Group, School Days, Man, Monkey, 2 Children, Signed, 1877, 21 ½ x 15 In. 275.00
Group, Weighing The Baby, Doctor, Mother, Baby, Boy, Signed, 1876, 21 x 15 ⅜ In. 550.00
Group, Why Don't You Speak For Yourself, 22 ½ x 17 In. 165.00
Group, Wounded Scout, Friend In The Swamp, Signed, 23 x 11 x 9 In. .... 600.00 to 1000.00
Group, Wounded To The Rear, One More Shot, Soldier Standing, Man Seated, 24 In. 450.00

JOSEF ORIGINALS ceramics were designed by Muriel Joseph George. The first pieces were made in California from 1945 to 1962. They were then manufactured in Japan. The company was sold to George Good in 1982 and he continued to make Josef Originals until 1985. The company was then sold to Southland Corporation. The name is now owned by Applause, and the Birthday Girl series is still being made.

Figurine, Birthstone, Girl, April, Turquoise Raincoat, Hood, Umbrella, 1953, 4 ¼ In. 43.00
Figurine, Birthstone, Girl, August, Holds Flower, Peridot Center, 4 In. 22.00
Figurine, Birthstone, Girl, July, Yellow Dress, 1960s, 3 In. 16.50
Figurine, Birthstone, Girl, March, Flower Basket, Aquamarines, 1960s, 4 In. 28.00
Figurine, Bride, Flowers, Veil, Marked, 6 ¼ In. 150.00
Figurine, Bride & Groom, Flowers, Veil, Marked, 4 In. 150.00
Figurine, Dinner Belle, Girl With Cake, 4 In. 35.00
Figurine, Girl, Charmaine, Blue Ruffled Dress, Dove On Wrist, 5 ½ In. 85.00

Figurine, Girl, Happy Anniversary, Bonnet, Bouquet, Gold Bow, 4 ½ In. 35.00
Figurine, Girl, Tina The Gypsy, Bright Blue, Yellow, Pink, 1940s, 5 ¾ In.. .... 195.00
Figurine, Girl With Pekingese Dog, Brown & Turquoise Gown, 5 In. 195.00
Figurine, International, Girl, China, White & Turquoise Kimono, Fan, Flowers, 6 ½ In. 155.00
Figurine, International, Girl, Greece, Blue Iridescent Dress, 10 ½ In. 690.00
Figurine, International, Girl, Japan, Pink Kimono & Umbrella, 4 In. 95.00
Figurine, International, Girl, Poland, Floral Headdress, Gold Trim, 4 ¼ In. 295.00
Figurine, International, Girl, Portugal, 4 In. 90.00
Figurine, Midnight Snack, New Mother, Pink Robe, Curlers, Holding Bottle, 4 In. 21.00
Figurine, Nursery Rhyme, Cinderella, Ball Gown, 4 In. 295.00
Figurine, Nursery Rhyme, Miss Muffet, 4 In. 185.00
Figurine, Ostrich, Mama & Baby, Seated, 5 ½ In. 45.00
Figurine, Wee Japanese Kabuki, Playing Tategoto Harp, Pink Dress, 3 ½ In.. .... 135.00
Pie Bird, Grandma, Pie Baker, Holding Mixing Bowl & Spoon, 1980s, 3 ¼ In. 120.00
Pin Tray, Sprite, Flowers, Scalloped, Gold Trim, Footed, 2 ¾ x 4 ½ In.. .... 115.00
Salt & Pepper, Owls, Wide-Eyed, 3 ½ In. 20.00
Soap Dish, Girl's Face In Relief, 5 Flowers, Yellow Stone Centers, Blue, Yellow, 6 In. ..... *illus* 75.00

JUDAICA is any memorabilia that refers to the Jews or the Jewish religion. Interests range from newspaper clippings that mention eighteenth- and nineteenth-century Jewish Americans to religious objects, such as menorahs or spice boxes. Age, condition, and the intrinsic value of the material, as well as the historic and artistic importance, determine the value.

Bowl, Cameo, Cobalt Blue Glass, Silver Plated Trim, Base, Mohr, 4 ¾ x 6 In. 325.00
Box, Art Nouveau, Silver, Flower Design, Footed, Marked, c.1890, 9 In. 1440.00
Box, Bessamin, Havdalah, Silver, 8 In. 2925.00
Box, Etrog, Silver, Hallmarked, 1856, Continental, 4 x 6 In. 450.00
Candlestick, Caricature Face, Bone, Silver, Marked, Jones, Paris & London, c.1850, 4 x 3 In. . 1760.00
Candlestick, Havdalah, Silver, Hebrew Words, Flat Top, Base, 3 ½ x 3 ½ In. 25.00
Candlestick, Shabbat, Silver, Baluster, Skirted Stem, Square Base, c.1859, 13 In., Pair 2520.00
Candlestick, Shabbat, Silver, England, 1920, 14 In., Pair 1185.00
Candlestick, Shabbat, Silver, Marked, Fraget W. Warsawie, Poland, 11 ¾ In., Pair 125.00
Charger, Brass, Stylized Flowers, Star Of David, No. 2031, Bezalel Mark, Jerusalem, 1910, 15 ½ In. 2607.00
Charity Box, Silver, Brass, Inlay, Hexagonal, Domed Lid, 8 ¾ In. 877.00
Charity Box, Silver, Leaves, English Text, Hennegan, Bates & Co., Baltimore, 1917, 5 In. 948.00
Clock, Bronze, Star Of David, 2 Lions, Hebrew Numbers, Georg Luz, c.1910, 6 ½ In. 474.00
Crown, Torah, Silver, Chased Fruit, Flowers, Scrolls, 1900s, 11 In.. .... 1541.00
Cup, Kiddush, Glass, Beaker Shape, Engraved Hebrew, Red, Bohemia, c.1900, 5 In. 711.00
Cup, Kiddush, Silver, Beaker Shape, Chased Jerusalem Scenes, Flared Rim, Moscow, c.1860, 3 In. 1126.00
Cup, Kiddush, Silver, Chased Town Scenes, Beaker Shape, Hebrew, Russia, c.1860, 3 In. 356.00
Cup, Kiddush, Silver, Copper Inlay, Beaker Shape, Damascene, 4 In. .... *illus* 830.00
Cup, Kiddush, Silver, Engraved Flowers, Flared Rim, Skirted Stem, Marked, Vilna, 1873, 7 In. 1185.00
Cup, Kiddush, Silver, Hebrew Dedication, Beaker Shape, Sweden, c.1842, 3 In. 1007.00
Cup, Kiddush, Silver, Hebrew Wine Blessing, Tapered, L. Wolpert, New York, 1900s, 9 In. 1659.00
Cup, Kiddush, Silver, Repousse Flowers, Hebrew Text, Panels, Domed Base, Marked, 4 In. 770.00
Cup, Kiddush, Silver, Turquoise, Marked, I.M., Israel, 7 ½ In. 450.00
Dish, Havdalah, Silver, Lazarus Posen, Engraved, c.1890, 12 In. 7200.00
Egg Holder, Seder, Porcelain, Multicolored Transfers, Scrolled Feet, c.1900, 6 In. 385.00
Etrog Box, Hinged Lid, Brass, Gold, Silver, Rabbi & Torah, 1890s, 5 x 8 x 5 ½ In.. .... 700.00
Etrog Box, Hinged Lid, Silver, Footed, Bird Finial, 5 ¾ x 5 ¼ x 5 ½ In. 1300.00
Etrog Box, Hinged Lid, Silver, Footed, Flower Finial, 5 x 6 x 5 In. 850.00
Etrog Box, Silver, Deer Finial, Oval, Key, Austria, c.1890, 6 In. 830.00
Etrog Box, Silver, Hinged Lid, Animal Shape, Red Eyes, Poland, 1800s, 6 ½ In. 3851.00
Goblet, Presentation, Silver Plate, Germany, c.1890, 9 ½ In. 2400.00
Goblet, Star Of David, Grapevines, Sterling Silver, Marked, 6 In. 60.00
Goblet, Wedding, Amber, Blown Glass, Ribs, Gilt Overlay, 10 ½ In.. .... 1783.00
Goblet, Wine, Silver, Flowers, Scrolls, Hebrew Text, Dome Lid, Bell Shape, c.1950, 8 ½ In.. ... 474.00
Inkwell, Silver, Vines & Flowers, Mishniac Saying, Round, c.1915, 3 ½ In. 7200.00
Kovsch, Presentation, Silver, Gilt, Engraved, No. 84, St. Petersburg, Russia, 9 x 16 In. 8625.00
Megillah, Silver, Gilt Tube, Twisted Filigree, Pointer, Box, c.1850, 9 In. 14400.00
Menorah, Brass, Lyre, Candleholder, Oil Font, Drip Pan, Poland, c.1800, 8 In. 1304.00
Menorah, Brass, Pierced Backplate, Flowers, Birds, Candle Cups, Poland, c.1800, 9 In.. ...... 2133.00
Menorah, Bronze, Arch Shape, Priest, Trees, Lions Oil Tray, Italy, c.1700, 11 In. 3555.00
Menorah, Pierced Scrolls, Grapes, Pitcher, Pot, Portugal, c.1900, 13 x 10 In. 1126.00
Menorah, Silver, 4 Lion Paws, Seated Lion Wick Holders, Marked, c.1900, 10 In. 6000.00
Menorah, Silver, Animals, Hinged Cover, Marked, Frankfurt, 7 In. .... *illus* 3851.00
Menorah, Silver, Crown, Lions, Shield, Oil, Candle Cups, Scroll Feet, Vienna, 13 In. 9480.00

Josef Originals, Soap Dish, Girl's Face In Relief, 5 Flowers, Yellow Stone Centers, Blue, Yellow, 6 In.
$75.00

Judaica, Cup, Kiddush, Silver, Copper Inlay, Beaker Shape, Damascene, 4 In.
$830.00

Judaica, Menorah, Silver, Animals, Hinged Cover, Marked, Frankfurt, 7 In.
$3851.00

Jukebox, Wurlitzer, Bubbler, Lights, Revolves, 78 RPM
$4600.00

Jukebox, Wurlitzer, Model 81, Key, 57 x 23 x 19 In.
$13000.00

Jukebox, Wurlitzer, Model 102, 50 Cent, 25 Cent, 10 Cent, 45 RPM, 1957
$1955.00

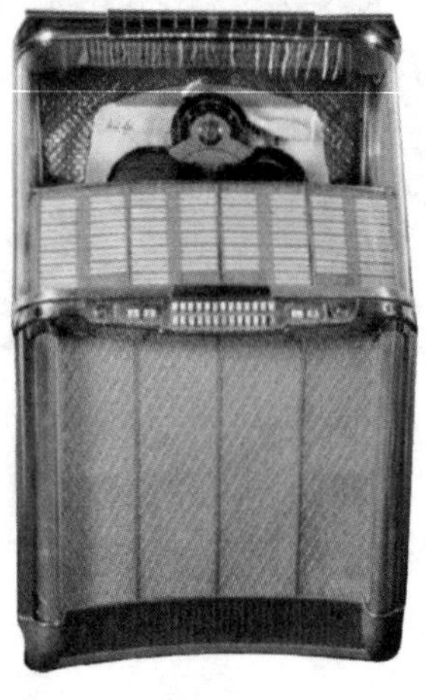

Menorah, Sterling Silver, Parcel Gilt, Scrolled Feet, 8 Lion Shape Lamps, 12 ¾ In. 1912.00
Menorah, Stone, Stylized Tree, Carved, Candle Holes On Top, 8 In. 533.00
Menorah, Traveling, Sterling Silver, Flower Form, 1 ½ In. 110.00
Menorah, Tree Form, Stamped, Walberg, 1950s, 13 ¼ x 9 ⅛ In. 200.00
Mezuzah, Bronze, Hinged Flap, Poland, c.1910, 8 In. 948.00
Pendant, Moses, With Tablets, Enamel, Multicolored, Marked, Sh'ma, 1800s, 1 In. 296.00
Plate, Havdalah, Star Of David, Blue, Porcelain, Limoges, France, 1900s, 10 In. 444.00
Plate, Seder, P. Kuchler, Star Of David, Opalescent, Gilt, Bohemia, Karlsbad, 1900s, 11 In. 415.00
Plate, Seder, Sterling Silver, Embossed, 7 x 14 In. 2925.00
Poster, Jewish Welfare Board, United War Work, New York, 1918, 14 x 22 In. 1659.00
Salt, Passover, Silver, Scrolled Rim, Russia, 1844, 3 In. 652.00
Scroll, Esther, Illuminated, Hand Lettered, Fruitwood Rollers, Italy, c.1790, 8 In. 13035.00
Scroll, Esther, Silver Case, 6 In. 1521.00
Spice Tower, Silver, Austria-Hungary, c.1900, 8 In. 409.00
Spice Tower, Silver, Filigree, Bell Skirt Base, Knob, Pennant, Frenk, Warsaw, c.1889, 10 In. .. 1185.00
Spice Tower, Silver, Filigree, Ribbed Knob, Pennant, Stamped, Berlin, c.1850, 10 In. 593.00
Spice Tower, Silver, Flowers, Latticework, Engraved, c.1925, 11 ¾ In. 960.00
Spice Tower, Silver, Flowers, Pierced, 3 Tiers, Door, Top Pennant, Oval, Poland, 1800s, 9 In. . 2489.00
Spice Tower, Silver, Gilt, Fruit Branch, Flowers, Bells, Birds, Round Base, 1900s, 13 In. 1896.00
Tile, Israeli Statehood, Blue, Green, English, Hebrew Text, Ceramic, c.1948, 6 x 6 In. 95.00
Torah Breastplate, Silver, Cartouche Shape, Lions, Crowns, Tablet, 8 In. 563.00
Torah Breastplate, Silver, Tablet Shape, Lion, Globe, E. Viner, Sheffield, c.1950, 12 In. 2133.00
Torah Curtain, Silk, Velvet Embroidery, Crown, Hebrew Text, 1800s, 64 x 44 In. 178.00
Torah Finial, Engraved, Morocco, c.1900, Pair 4200.00
Torah Pointer, Silver, Meerschaum Stem, Loop, Chain, Beaded Endcap, 5 In. 296.00
Torah Pointer, Silver, Spread Wing Eagle Top, Eastern Europe, 10 ¾ In. 400.00
Torah Pointer, Sterling Silver, 18K Gold, Parcel Gilt, Index Finger, Repousse, 8 ¼ In. 568.00
Torah Pointer, Sterling Silver, Index Finger, Filigree Barrel Top, 1900s, 12 In. 191.00
Torah Pointer, Yad, Sterling Silver, Star Of David, Garnet, Ivory Shaft, Marked, Russia, 12 In. 125.00
Torah Shield, Silver, Bells, Lazarus Posen, Marked, c.1890, 9 ½ In. 5400.00
Torah Shield, Silver, Cartouche Shape, 2 Birds, Spread Wing, Lions, c.1810, 10 In. 24200.00
Torah Shield, Silver, Lions, The Decalogue, Gilt, c.1890, 14 In. 4200.00
Wall Hanging, Theodor Herzl, Sun Setting, Cotton, Jerusalem, c.1930, 56 x 24 In. 1126.00

JUGTOWN Pottery refers to pottery made in North Carolina as far back as the 1750s. In 1915, Juliana and Jacques Busbee set up a training and sales organization for what they named Jugtown Pottery. In 1921, they built a shop at Jugtown, North Carolina, and hired Ben Owen as a potter in 1923. The Busbees moved the village store where the pottery was sold to New York City. Juliana Busbee sold the New York store in 1926 and moved into a log cabin near the Jugtown Pottery. The pottery closed in 1959. It reopened in 1960 and is still working near Seagrove, North Carolina.

JUGTOWN WARE

Candlestick, Chamber, Caramel, Black & Yellow Design, Handle, 7 In. Diam. 38.00
Jar, 4 Handles, Green Frogskin Glaze, 8 ½ x 7 ½ In. 475.00
Pitcher, Frogskin Glaze, Intertwining Line Decoration, Impressed Mark, 6 ¼ In. 40.00
Pitcher, Squat, Strap Handle, Cobalt Blue Design, Incised, Salt Glaze, Stamped, 5 ¼ In. 121.00
Vase, 4 Applied Handles, Pumpkin Orange Glaze, Round Stamp Mark, 8 ½ In. 220.00
Vase, Blue Green Glaze, Red Clay, 4 ⅛ In. 475.00
Vase, Bulbous, Waisted, Mottled Green, Red, White Glaze, Marked, 7 x 5 In. 600.00
Vase, Tapered, 4 Pinched Handles, Dogwood, Salt Glaze, Stamp Mark, 1930, 6 ½ In. 220.00
Vase, Wide Mouth, White Glaze Over Red Earthenware, Impressed Mark, c.1920s, 5 x 7 In. ... 130.00

JUKEBOXES play records. The first coin-operated phonograph was demonstrated in 1889. In 1906 the Automatic Entertainer appeared, the first coin-operated phonograph to offer several different selections of music. The first electrically powered jukebox was introduced in 1927. Collectors search for jukeboxes of all ages, especially those with flashing lights and unusual design and graphics.

Rock-Ola, Model 1422, Art Deco, Illuminated Pilasters, Swirling Colors, c.1946, 28 x 59 In. .. 9200.00
Rock-Ola, Model 1426, 20 Selections, 78 RPM Records, 1946 .... 5750.00
Rock-Ola, Model 1497, Empress, Front Door, Cash Box, Key, 120 Selections, 1962 .... 2944.00
Rock-Ola, Series C, DE39 S50807, 20 Selections, 78 RPM Records, 55 x 36 x 26 In. 900.00
Seeburg, Model 146M, Symphonola, Trash Can, Red, 20 Selections, 78 RPM, 1948 .... 2400.00
Seeburg, Model 220S, Stereophonic Select-O-Matic, 100 Selections, 1958-59 .... 2070.00
Seeburg, Model M-1008, 55 x 34 x 27 In. 990.00
Seeburg, Wall-O-Matic, 200 Selections, 14 ½ In. 180.00
Wurlitzer, Bubbler, Lights, Revolves, 78 RPM .... *illus* 4600.00
Wurlitzer, Model 81, Key, 57 x 23 x 19 In. .... *illus* 13000.00

Wurlitzer, Model 81, Mae West Stand ... 15600.00
Wurlitzer, Model 102, 50 Cent, 25 Cent, 10 Cent, 45 RPM, 1957 ... *illus* 1955.00
Wurlitzer, Model 412, c.1934 ... 2500.00
Wurlitzer, Model 500, 1938, 59 x 35 x 29 In. ... 9424.00
Wurlitzer, Model 800, Keys, 59 x 38 x 28 In. ... 5700.00
Wurlitzer, Model 1100, Multi-Selector, Red Trim, 78 RPM, 1948 ... 988.00
Wurlitzer, Model 2200, 200 Selections, 45 RPM, 1958, 53 ½ x 36 x 28 In. ... 446.00
Wurlitzer, Model 2250, High Fidelity Music, Yellow Sides, 200 Selections ... 1140.00
Wurlitzer, Model 2500, Stereophonic Music, Multi-Selector ... 472.00
Wurlitzer, Model 2900, Art Deco, 200 Selections, 11 x 9 x 14 ½ In. ... 86.00
Wurlitzer, Victory, 1942-45, 38 x 66 x 27 ½ In. ... 16950.00

KATE GREENAWAY, who was a famous illustrator of children's books, drew pictures of children in high-waisted Empire dresses. She lived from 1846 to 1901. Her designs appear on china, glass, and other pieces.

Diorama, Kate Wizard's Workbench, Little Tommy, Bisque Head Doll, c.1889, 11 x 5 In. ... 86.00
Jewelry Box, Silver Plate, Figure, Swing, Velvet, Middletown Plate Co., 12 x 7 In. ... 2160.00
Match Holder, Girl On Bench, Basket, Bronze, 3 ¼ x 3 ½ In. ... 75.00
Napkin Ring, Silver Plate, Figural, 2 Girls, Ladder, Simpson, Hall, Miller & Co. ... 1900.00
Napkin Ring, Silver Plate, Figural, Boy, Lying On Clip, Roses, James W. Tufts ... *illus* 75.00
Napkin Ring, Silver Plate, Figural, Boy, Riding Toboggan, James W. Tufts ... 1900.00
Napkin Ring, Silver Plate, Figural, Boy With Ball, Arched Draped Ribbon, J.W. Tufts ... 748.00
Napkin Ring, Silver Plate, Figural, Girl, Boy, Parasol, Hoop, James W. Tufts ... 1000.00
Napkin Ring, Silver Plate, Figural, Girl, Boy, Seesaw, Leaves, Toronto Silver Plate ... 1900.00
Napkin Ring, Silver Plate, Figural, Girl, Large Hat, Long Coat, Muff ... 58.00
Salt & Pepper, Silver Plate, Boy & Girl, Long Coats, Meriden B. Co. ... *illus* 144.00

KAY FINCH Ceramics were made in Corona Del Mar, California, from 1935 to 1963. The hand-decorated pieces often depicted whimsical animals and people. Pastel colors were used.

Kay Finch
CALIFORNIA

Bank, Pig, Sassy, Strawberries, 4 ½ x 3 ½ In. ... 75.00 to 100.00
Bank, Pig, Winkie, Winking One Eye, Shamrocks & Flowers, 4 x 3 ¾ In. ... 225.00
Candleholder, Angel, Blond Hair, Purple Trim, Holding Candle, 8 ½ In., Pair ... 350.00
Figurine, Angels, Blond Hair, 3 ¾ In., Pair ... 65.00
Figurine, Baby Giraffe, Seated, Tan, Brown, 7 ½ In. ... 45.00
Figurine, Burro, Gray, 10 In. ... 46.00
Figurine, Cat, Ambrosia, Seated, Ivory Pink, Marked, 10 ½ In. ... 150.00 to 330.00
Figurine, Cat, Baby Ambrosia, Marked, 5 ½ In. ... 78.00
Figurine, Cat, Hear No Evil, 1950s, 3 ¼ In. ... 65.00
Figurine, Cat, Hear No Evil, See No Evil, Do No Evil, 1948, 3 In., 3 Piece ... 375.00
Figurine, Cat, Mr. Tom, 18 In. ... 1840.00
Figurine, Cat, Muff, 3 ¼ In. ... 75.00
Figurine, Cat, Seated, Ivory, Pale Pink, 10 ½ In. ... 150.00
Figurine, Chinese Princess, 1950s, 23 In. ... 130.00
Figurine, Choir Boy, Brunette, Kneeling, 5 ½ In. ... 25.00 to 65.00
Figurine, Dog, Pekingese, Pink, White, Marked, 13 In. ... 165.00
Figurine, Dog, Yorkshire Terrier, 11 In. ... 165.00
Figurine, Duck, Mama, 4 ½ In. ... 199.00
Figurine, Duck, Peep, 1950s, 4 In. ... 46.00 to 65.00
Figurine, Elephant, Pink Ears, Purple & Green Flowers, Purple Toes, Seated, 6 In. ... 52.00
Figurine, Girl, Scandie, 5 In. ... 52.00
Figurine, Godey, Man & Woman, Victorian Couple, 7 ½ In., Pair ... *illus* 28.00
Figurine, Lamb, Kneeling, Green Trim, 2 ¾ In. ... 15.00 to 75.00
Figurine, Mr. & Mrs. Bird, Pink, c.1950, 4 ½ In. & 3 In., Pair ... 175.00
Figurine, Owl, Hoot, Brown, Brown Eyes, Beige Tail, 3 ¼ In. ... 38.00
Figurine, Owl, Hoot, Gold Leaf, 8 ½ In. ... 82.00
Figurine, Owl, Hoot, Purple, Blue & Turquoise Tail, 8 ⅜ In. ... 27.00
Figurine, Owl, Tootsie, Pearl Gray, Brown Eyes, 3 ¾ In. ... 55.00
Figurine, Owl, Tootsie, Pink, Mauve, Violet Eyes, 3 ¼ In. ... 10.00
Figurine, Peasants, Black Hair, 6 ½ In., Pair ... 126.00
Figurine, Peasants, Blond Hair, 6 ½ In., Pair ... 124.00
Figurine, Penguin, Pee-Wee, 1949, 3 ¼ In. ... 65.00
Figurine, Rooster, Chanticleer, 10 ¾ In. ... 76.00
Figurine, Rooster & Hen, Butch & Biddy, 8 & 5 ¼ In. ... 185.00
Flower Bowl, Swan, 6 ½ x 9 In. ... 125.00

Kate Greenaway, Napkin Ring, Silver Plate, Figural, Boy, Lying On Clip, Roses, James W. Tufts
$75.00

Kate Greenaway, Salt & Pepper, Silver Plate, Boy & Girl, Long Coats, Meriden B. Co.
$144.00

Kay Finch, Figurine, Godey, Man & Woman, Victorian Couple, 7 ½ In., Pair.
$28.00

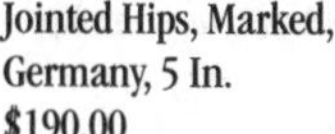

Kewpie, Bisque, 5-Piece Body, Jointed Hips, Marked, Paper Shield, Germany, 5 In.
$190.00

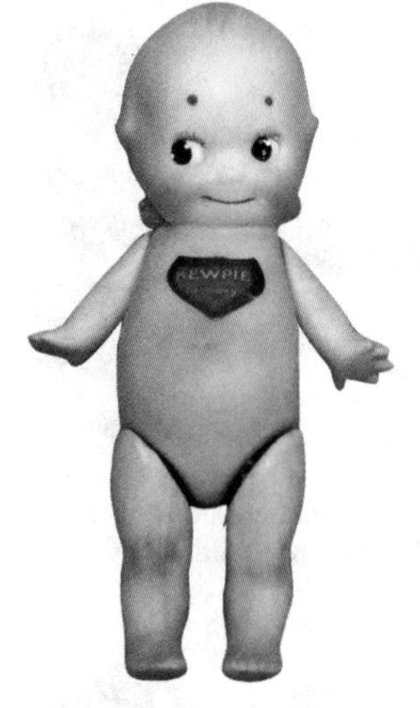

Kewpie, Bisque, Seated On Green Chair, Ball, Marked, 5 In.
$2750.00

Kewpie, Clock, Romping Kewpies, Green Ground, Jasperware, Brass, Germany, 4 In.
$225.00

Planter, Bassinet, Baby's First, From California, Pink, Baby, 6 ½ In. 45.00
Planter, Rabbit Book Nursery, Blue Rabbit, 6 ½ In. 95.00
Plaque, Seahorse, 16 In. 56.00
Plate, Santa Claus, c.1950, 6 ½ In. .... 26.00 to 95.00
Powder Box, Raised Pink & Blue Flowers, Round, 2 x 3 ½ In. 11.00
Punch Bowl, Holiday Wreath, Gold Trim, 5 ½ x 11 In. 33.00
Vase, Green Glaze, Bulbous, Footed, Marked, 5 ½ x 7 In. 49.00

KAYSERZINN, *see Pewter category.*

KELVA glassware was made by the C. F. Monroe Company of Meriden, Connecticut, about 1904. It is a pale, pastel-painted glass decorated with flowers, designs, or scenes. Kelva resembles Nakara and Wave Crest, two other glasswares made by the same company.

Box, Bishop's Hat, Flowers, Peach, 4 In. 300.00
Box, Bishop's Hat Mold, Flowers, Peach, 4-Sided, 1920s, 4 In. 165.00
Dresser Box, Pink Roses, Enamel Dots, Scrolls, Olive Green, Stamped, Kelva, 2 ⅜ In. 165.00
Jewelry Box, Hinged Cover, Blue Flowers, Pink Mottled Ground, Round, Signed, 6 In. 400.00
Vase, Flowers, Dark Green Ground, Metal Base, Signed, 8 ½ x 3 In. 295.00
Vase, Pink Flowers, Dark Green Ground, Filigree Metal Base, Signed, 3 x 9 In. 303.00
Vase, Pink Flowers, Pale Green Ground, Divided Base, 4 x 13 In. 177.00
Vase, Red, White, Stemmed Flowers, Mottled Green, Metal Dolphin Feet, 13 ½ In. 978.00

KEMPLE glass was made by John Kemple of East Palestine, Ohio, and Kenova, West Virginia, from 1945 to 1970. The glass was made from old molds. Many designs and colors were made. Kemple pieces are usually marked with a *K* on the bottom. Many milk glass pieces were made with or without the mark.

Bowl, Moon & Star Variant, Milk Glass, Scalloped Edge, Footed, 5 ⅝ x 8 ⅜ In. 35.00
Candlestick, Green Ivy, Milk Glass, No. 125, 4 ½ x 4 In. 25.00
Compote, Aztec, Amber, 4 ¾ x 7 In. 23.00
Nut Dish, Toltec, Blue, Footed, 3 ⅜ x 4 ¾ In. 20.00
Plate, Inverted Heart, Milk Glass, Painted, 7 ¼ In. 25.00
Sugar, Coal Bucket, Green, 4 x 2 ¾ In. 30.00
Vase, Sunburst, Milk Glass, 5 ½ x 4 In. 24.00

KENTON HILLS Pottery in Erlanger, Kentucky, made artwares, including vases and figurines that resembled Rookwood, probably because so many of the original artists and workmen had worked at the Rookwood plant. Kenton Hills opened in 1939 and closed during World War II.

Box, Bear, 2 Stars, Marked, Unica, David Seyler, 3 ⅜ In. 250.00
Box, Cover, Portrait Of Brown Bear, 2 Stars, White Ground, Marked, 3 ½ In. 260.00
Figurine, Mammy, Infant, Metallic Brown Glaze, Rose Dickman, 6 ½ In. 660.00
Tray, Horse Head, White, Pink, 4 ½ x 5 ¼ In. 66.00
Vase, 4 Birds, Trees, Grass, Pedestal Base, Signed, Unica, David Seyler, 5 ¾ In. 275.00
Vase, Stylized Flowers, Cream, Bulbous, Flared Rim, Signed, Stratton, 12 ½ In. 165.00
Vase, Stylized Flowers, Leaves, Blue, Black, White Ground, Signed, Stratton, 8 In. 375.00

KEW BLAS is the name used by the Union Glass Company of Somerville, Massachusetts. The name refers to an iridescent golden glass made from the 1890s to 1924. The iridescent glass was reminiscent of the Tiffany glass of the period.

Vase, Cream Iridescent, 4 Gold Pulled Feathers, Signed, 6 In. 550.00
Vase, Gold Iridescent, Purple & Green Highlights, Ground Pontil, 8 ¼ In. 633.00
Vase, Iridescent, Green Pulled Feather, Gold Tip Opal, Flared, Signed, 5 In. 374.00
Vase, Pulled & Spotted, Green, Gold, White Ground, Signed, 6 ¼ x 3 ¾ In. 440.00
Vase, Stick, Gold Iridescent, Bulbous Base, Signed, 8 In. 201.00

KEWPIES, designed by Rose O'Neill, were first pictured in the *Ladies' Home Journal.* The figures, which are similar to pixies, were a success, and Kewpie dolls and figurines started appearing in 1911. Kewpie pictures and other items soon followed. Collectors search for all items that picture the little winged people.

Bisque, 5-Piece Body, Jointed Hips, Marked, Paper Shield, Germany, 5 In. .... *illus* 190.00
Bisque, Bellhop, Blue Jacket, Pink Wings, Right-Glancing Eyes, c.1912, 4 In. 795.00
Bisque, Brown Forelock, Jointed Arms, Side-Glancing Eyes, Germany, c.1912, 9 In. 470.00
Bisque, Chef, Crepe Paper Apron, Hat, Jointed Arms, Signed, O'Neill, 1915, 5 In. 317.00
Bisque, Doodle Dog, Black Spots, Blue Wings, Left-Glancing Eyes, 3 In. 1575.00

Bisque, English Bobby, Jointed Arms, Right-Glancing Eyes, c.1912, 4 In. 1290.00
Bisque, Hero, Jointed Arms, Gold Medallion, Helmet, Side-Glancing Eyes, c.1914, 4 In. 890.00
Bisque, Hero, Painted Belt, Rifle, Helmet, Sack, Right-Glancing Eyes, c.1914, 4 In. 950.00
Bisque, Huggers, Paper Label, Signed, O'Neill, 1915, 3 ½ In. 173.00
Bisque, Jointed Arms, Costume, Straw Hat, Marked, O'Neill, 1915, 4 ½ In. 460.00
Bisque, Jointed At Shoulders, Decal On Back, c.1900, 7 ½ In. 285.00
Bisque, Jointed At Shoulders, Incised, Rose O'Neill, J.D. Kestner Co., c.1913, 7 ½ In. 288.00
Bisque, Lying On Stomach, Side-Glancing Eyes, Doodle Dog On Back, c.1912, 3 In. 1120.00
Bisque, Messenger, Jointed Arms, Right-Glancing Eyes, c.1912, 4 In. 450.00
Bisque, Seated On Green Chair, Ball, Marked, 5 In. .... *illus* 2750.00
Bisque, Soldier, Bursting From Eggshell, Helmet, Rifle, Germany, 1915, 4 In. 3540.00
Bisque, Soldier, Jointed Arms, Right-Glancing Eyes, c.1912, 4 ½ In. 840.00
Bisque, Teddy Bear, Side-Glancing Eyes, Germany, c.1912, 4 In. 675.00
Bisque, Traveler, Doodle Dog, Umbrella, Leash, Side-Glancing Eyes, 3 ½ In. 2010.00
Candy Container, Bisque, Guitar, Side-Glancing Eyes, Eggshell Container, c.1912, 4 In. 1250.00
Clock, Romping Kewpies, Green Ground, Jasperware, Brass, Germany, 4 In. .... *illus* 225.00
Doll Head, Bisque, Blue Wings, Blue Side-Glancing Eyes, Germany, c.1912, 5 In. 2392.00
Doorstop, White, Black Base, Cast Iron, 13 ⅞ x 6 ¾ In. 345.00
Frame, Kewpie, Standing, Foot Out, Lilies, 2 Frames, Ivory, Marked. 1700.00
Inkwell, Bisque Figure, Holding Pen, Sticker, Rose O'Neill, 1915, 3 In. 288.00
Letter Opener, Pewter, 6 ¼ In. 36.00
Mold, Chocolate, Hinged, 5 ¾ x 3 ½ In., 2 Piece 55.00
Nut Dish, Seated Kewpie, Side-Glancing Eyes, Mandolin, Pottery, c.1912, 2 ½ x 3 In. 575.00
Postcard, 6 Kewpies Doing Wash, Rose O'Neill, Klever Kard, 1914. .... 66.00
Tea Set, Child's, Signed, Rosie O'Neill, Marked, Bavaria, 21 Piece 550.00
Tray, Albany Ice Cream, Kewpie On Peach, 13 ½ x 13 ½ In. 320.00
Tray, Moglia's Ice Cream, Kewpies On Strawberry, 13 ½ x 13 ½ In. 310.00
Vase, Bud, Kewpie With Guitar, Right-Glancing Eyes, Bisque, Germany, c.1915, 5 In. 495.00

KING'S ROSE, *see Soft Paste category.*

KITCHEN utensils of all types, from eggbeaters to bowls, are collected today. Handmade wooden and metal items, like ladles and apple peelers, were made in the early nineteenth century. Mass-produced pieces, like iron apple peelers and graniteware, were made in the nineteenth century. Also included in this category are utensils used for other household chores, such as laundry and cleaning. Other kitchen wares are listed under manufacturers' names or under Advertising, Iron, Tool, or Wooden.

Apple Slicer, Wood, 5 x 32 In. 1984.00
Baker, Yellow, Oval, Pyrex, 10 Oz. 8.00
Basket, Egg, Wire, Round, Heart Form Handles, Footed, 15 x 10 ½ In. .... *illus* 132.00
Batter Bowl, Green Glass, Hocking, 7 In. 28.00
Batter Bowl, Green Glass, Spiraled, Hocking, 7 In. 60.00
Batter Bowl, Milk Glass, Fruit & Floral, Federal, 7 ½ x 7 ½ In. 35.00
Bean Pot, Plastic Cover, Blue, Glasbake, McKee. 10.00
Beater Jar, Mayonnaise, Wesson Oil, c.1950, 8 ¼ x 3 ¼ In. 50.00
Beater Jar, Pyrex, Red Top, JAJ, Box, c.1950, 8 ½ In., Pt. 38.00
Board, Cheese, Cheese & Mouse, Porcelain, Wood, 1950s, 7 x 6 ½ In. 20.00
Board, Cheese, Yellow Pine, Rough Hewn, Footed, 19th Century, 7 ½ x 28 ½ In. 173.00
Board, Cutting, Maple, Lollipop Shape, Turned Handle, Pa., 15 ¾ x 9 ¾ In. 700.00
Board, Cutting, Painted, Marked, Paula Kloppel, 27 In. Diam. 12.00
Board, Dough, Parrot, Seated, Carved, 4 x 6 ¾ In. 66.00
Board, Dough, Tiger Maple, Applied Ends, Penn., 25 ½ x 20 In. .... 375.00 to 413.00
Board, Scrub, Pine, 1830s, 12 x 8 x 2 ¾ In. 110.00
Board, Slaw, Oak, Metal Plate, Acme Novelty Co., N.J., 24 In. 30.00
Board, Slaw, Tiger Maple, Heart Cutout, Pa., 19th Century, 19 x 6 ½ In. .... *illus* 1404.00
Board, Slaw, Walnut, Heart Shape Cutout, 22 ½ x 7 ½ In. 121.00
Bowl, Dough, Maple, Curly Maple, Utensils, 1800s, 16 In. 177.00
Bowl, Dough, Wood, 7 x 42 x 22 In. 85.00
Bowl, Dough, Wood, Hand Hewn, 19th Century, 5 x 13 x 33 In. 88.00
Bowl, Dough, Wood, Red Stain, 19th Century, 7 ¾ x 22 In. 550.00
Bowl, Egg, Ceramic, Stack Of Eggs Lid, Basket Weave Base, 9 x 9 In. 46.00
Bowl, Flowers, Enamel, Blue, Orange, Czechoslovakia, c.1940, 9 ¾ In. 25.00
Bowl, Fruit, Wood, Aqua Exterior, Painted Fruit Interior, 3 Ball Feet, 12 In. 14.00
Bowl, Heart Shape, Safe Bake, Saben, 6 ½ In. 15.00
Bowl, Heart Shape, Safe Bake, Saben, 10 In. 25.00
Bowl, Pyrex, Milk Glass, Pour Spout, Ovenware, Marked, 1 ½ Pt. 16.00

Kitchen, Basket, Egg, Wire, Round, Heart Form Handles, Footed, 15 x 10 ½ In.
$132.00

Kitchen, Board, Slaw, Tiger Maple, Heart Cutout, Pa., 19th Century, 19 x 6 ½ In.
$1404.00

K

TIP

Graniteware and other enameled kitchenwares should be cleaned with water and baking soda. If necessary, use chlorine bleach.

Kitchen, Butter Paddle, Maple, Concave Scoop, Hooked End, 9 x 5 ¼ In.
$90.00

Kitchen, Butter Stamp, Acorns, Leaf, Hardwood, Carved, Case, 4 ¾ x 4 ¾ In., 2 Piece
$180.00

Kitchen, Butter Stamp, Stylized Pineapple, Serrated Border, Carved, Wood, 6 x 4 ⅞ In.
$700.00

Kitchen, Cake Board, Horse & Rider, Softwood, Relief Carved, 2-Sided, 1707, 35 x 20 In.
$99.00

Bowl, Sunburst, Anodized Aluminum, Gold, c.1960, 5 ¼ In. 6.00
Bowl, Sunburst, Anodized Aluminum, Red, c.1960, 5 ¼ In. 8.00
Bowl, Vegetable, Yellow, Square, Pyrex, 2 ½ Qt., 9 x 9 In. 16.50
Bundt Pan, Frank Hay, Cast Iron, March 10, 1891 .... 350.00
Bundt Pan, Spring Form, Aluminum, c.1955, 6 ¼ x 2 ⅛ In. 18.00
Butcher's Block, Inlaid Hardwoods, Bracketed Corners, Drawers, France, 31 x 40 x 36 In. 418.00
Butcher's Block, Maple, Turned Legs, c.1910, 25 x 25 x 20 In. 144.00
Butcher's Block, Wood, Iron Band, Turned Legs, 3-Footed, 26 In. 125.00
Butter, Cover, Blue, Clear, Plastic, Blisscraft Plastics, c.1960, 7 ½ x 2 ¾ In. 15.00
Butter Mold, look under Mold, Butter in this category.
Butter Paddle, Burl, Hook Handle, 19th Century, 9 In. 176.00
Butter Paddle, Curly Maple, Bird's-Eye Maple, Scrubbed, Hook Handle, 1800s, 9 ½ In. 206.00
Butter Paddle, Curly Maple, Hook, Patina, 19th Century, 10 ½ In. 147.00
Butter Paddle, Maple, Carved, Round Scoop, Handle, Natural Finish, 7 x 4 ¼ In. 33.00
Butter Paddle, Maple, Concave Scoop, Hooked End, 9 x 5 ¼ In. .... *illus* 90.00
Butter Paddle, Maple, Hook Handle, Carved Faces, Initials, 19th Century, 10 In. 71.00
Butter Scoop, Curly Maple, Tapered, Hooked Handle, Mid 19th Century 90.00
Butter Stamp, Acorn, Leaf, Poplar, Banded Border, 2 ¼ x 3 ¾ In. 66.00
Butter Stamp, Acorns, Leaf, Hardwood, Carved, Case, 4 ¾ x 4 ¾ In., 2 Piece .... *illus* 180.00
Butter Stamp, Amish, Pyrex, 7 x 3 ½ In. 17.00
Butter Stamp, Butterfly Gold, Pyrex, 7 x 2 ¼ In. 12.00
Butter Stamp, Dove, Wood, Sawtooth Border, 2 ¼ x 4 In. 165.00
Butter Stamp, Fish, Poplar, Serrated Edges, 1 ½ x 4 ⅜ In. 358.00
Butter Stamp, Flower, Leaves, 6-Sided, 2 ¾ In. 66.00
Butter Stamp, Pineapple, Half Moon, 7 In. 288.00
Butter Stamp, Pinwheel, Wood, Serrated Border, 1 x 4 ½ In. 935.00
Butter Stamp, Scallops, Incised, Concave Side Grooves, 3 ¾ In. 44.00
Butter Stamp, Stylized Pineapple, Serrated Border, Carved, Wood, 6 x 4 ⅞ In. .... *illus* 700.00
Butter Stamp, Swan, Hatched Border, Incised, Lollipop, 2 ⅞ In. 154.00
Butter Stamp, Swan, Wood, 3 ½ In. 115.00
Butter Stamp, Thistle, Double Banded Border, Round Handle, 2 ¾ x 3 ½ In. 33.00
Butter Stamp, Thistle, Pine, Serrated Border, Round, 1 ½ x 3 ¾ In. 165.00
Butter Stamp, Thistle, Wood, Serrated Border, 1 ¼ x 3 ⅞ In. 523.00
Butter Stamp, Tulip, Stars, Rooster, Serrated Borders, 2-Sided, 5 ⅜ x 2 ½ In. 605.00
Butter Stamp, Wheat Sheaves, Turned Oak Handle, Incised Band, Serrated Border, 5 x 4 In. 44.00
Cake Board, Cat, Dog, Maple, 19th Century, 17 In. 863.00
Cake Board, Horse & Rider, Softwood, Relief Carved, 2-Sided, 1707, 35 x 20 In. .... *illus* 99.00
Cake Board, Knight On Horseback, Wood, Carved, 10 x 7 In. 115.00
Cake Board, Man & Woman, Mortised, 2-Sided, 1800s, 30 x 8 In. 360.00
Cake Board, Punch & Judy, Woman, Carrying Bottle, Man In Top Hat, Oak, 27 ½ x 9 ¾ In. 66.00
Cake Board, Saint Nicholas, Sinterklass, Continental, 12 ¾ x 5 In. 489.00
Cake Pan, Angel Food, Katzinger Swans Down, Tin, Tab Handles, c.1945, 8 ½ In. 40.00
Cake Pan, Calumet, Aluminum, c.1959, 10 ¼ In. 15.00
Cake Pan, Ovenex, Aluminum, Square, c.1940, 9 In. 15.00
Cake Pan, Swans Down, Aluminum, Square, c.1945, 8 In. 15.00
Can Opener, Can-O-Matic, Plastic, 1950s 20.00
Canister, 4 Ribbed Column, Yellow Cover, Square, 6 ¾ x 3 ⅜ In. 20.00
Canister, Burl, Turned, Late 18th Century, 19 In. 234.00
Canister, Cereal, Forest Green, Ribs, Glass, Metal Lid, Owens-Illinois, 7 In. .... 40.00 to 75.00
Canister, Coffee, Forest Green, Ribs, Glass, Metal Lid, Owens-Illinois, 7 In. .... 52.00 to 90.00
Canister, Coffee, Jadite, Square, Screw Lid, 28 Oz. 210.00
Canister, Cookie, Ribbed Glass, Screw Lid, Hocking, 64 Oz., 8 x 6 In. 95.00
Canister, Cover, Green Vaseline, Ribbed, Hocking, 40 Oz. 110.00
Canister, Flour, Forest Green, Owens-Illinois, 7 In. .... 52.00 to 75.00
Canister, Glass Lid, Hocking Glass, 47 Oz., 8 ½ x 4 In. 75.00
Canister, Green, Flat Panel, Metal Screw Lid, 10 Oz., 4 ¾ In. 40.00
Canister, Green, Flat Panel, Metal Screw Lid, 20 Oz., 6 In. 50.00
Canister, Green, Flat Panel, Metal Screw Lid, 40 Oz., 8 In. 65.00
Canister, Lid, Wood, Barrel Form, Ribbed Lines, Turned Knob, Red Paint, Treen, 12 ½ x 9 ½ In. 300.00
Canister, Lid, Wood, Pine, Yellow Flower, Green Ground, Stripes, Footed, Pa., Late 1800s, 8 ½ In. 410.00
Canister, Rice, Forest Green Glass, Diagonal Ridge, Owens-Illinois 38.00
Canister, Rice, Green, Square, Diagonal Ridge, Owens-Illinois, 5 ¼ x 2 ¾ In. .... 39.00 to 55.00
Canister, Sugar, Green, Square, Diagonal Ridge, Owens-Illinois, 7 x 3 ½ In. .... 40.00 to 75.00
Canister, Tea, Forest Green, Oval, Owens-Illinois, 6 ½ In. 48.00
Canister, Tea, Forest Green, Owens-Illinois, 5 ¼ In. 55.00
Canister, Tea, Green, Square, Diagonal Ridge, Owens-Illinois, 5 ¼ x 2 ¾ In. 39.00
Canister, Tea, Hoosier, Napanee Style, Vertical Ridges, Arches, 5 ½ x 3 ¼ In. 55.00

K

Canister Set, Kromex, Aluminum, Black Top, c.1960, 5, 6, 7 & 8 In., 4 Piece 45.00
Carafe, Coffee, Gold Spears, Black Plastic Handle, Lid, Pyrex, 8 Cup 25.00
Carafe, Coffee, Star Design, Black Plastic Handle, Lid, Warming Stand, 8 ½ In. 12.50
Carafe, Jeannette, Glasbake, 6 In., Pair 25.00
Casserole, Aqua Blue Snowflake, Oval, Divided, Pyrex 12.50
Casserole, Cover, Corning Ware, Cornflower, 4 Qt. 30.00
Casserole, Cover, Corning Ware, Cornflower, 5 Qt. 40.00
Casserole, Cover, Glasbake, Colonial, Yellow, 3 ¼ x 3 ¼ In. 12.00
Casserole, Cover, Glasbake, Crystal, Silver Handles, Chrome Holder 45.00
Casserole, Cover, Pyrex, Black Snowflake, 1 ½ Qt. 25.00
Casserole, Saben, Cupid & Arrow, Sweetheart 143.00
Casserole Set, Pyrex, Old Orchard, Flat Lids, Box, Qt., 1 ½ Qt., 2 ½ Qt., 6 Piece 48.00
Cauldron, Cast Iron, Footed, Handle, Stamped, Savery & Co., Phila., 19th Century, 14 ¾ x 20 In. 322.00
Cauldron, Iron, Ring Handles, Scrolling Lotuses, Chinese, 1900s, 14 x 17 x 16 In. 489.00
Cheese Cutter, Counter Balance, Glass Cover, Edward Smith, Wisconsin, 26 x 41 In. 990.00
Cheese Safe, Oak, Computing Cheese Cutting Company, 22 x 13 In. 495.00
Cheese Server, Brown Bakelite Handle, 6 ⅝ x 1 ½ In. 4.00
Cheese Slicer, Brown Mottled Bakelite Handle, 8 ¾ x 3 ⅛ In. 9.00
Cheese Slicer, Curved, Brown Mottled Bakelite Handle, 7 ½ x 3 ⅛ In. 5.00
Cheese Trolley, Mahogany, Dovetailed, Brass, Leather Casters, Quatrefoil Cutouts, 8 x 21 In.. 546.00
Cherry Pitter, Aluminum, Chrome Plated, Fairgrove, Original Package, c.1975 . . . . 12.00
Cherry Pitter, Enterprise, No. 1, 1883 . . . . 20.00
Chopping Block, Carved, 1789, 27 ½ x 13 ¾ In. 146.00
Chopping Block, Master Built, Detroit, Michigan, 60 x 28 x 30 In. 220.00
Churn, Barrel Form, Crank Handle, c.1900, 14 ½ In. . . . . *illus* 77.00
Churn, Blanchard, Wood, Crank Handle, Stand, 33 x 18 ½ In. 95.00
Churn, Dasher, Blue Paint, 24 In. 173.00
Churn, Dasher, Wood, 19th Century, 38 In. 130.00
Churn, Dazey, Embossed, Glass, Metal, Crank, Dazey Churn & Mfg. Co., 6 ½ In., ½ Pt. 99.00
Churn, Dazey, Embossed, Glass, Metal, Crank, Dazey Churn & Mfg. Co., 8 ½ In., Pt. 77.00
Churn, Dazey, Glass, Square, St. Louis, USA, 14 x 5 ¾ In. 50.00
Churn, Dazey, No. 4, Red Handle, 12 ½ In., Gal. 60.00
Churn, Dazey, No. 60, Glass, St. Louis, 14 ¾ In. 60.00
Churn, Glass, Metal, Embossed, Crank Handle, 12 ¼ In., 2 Qt. 26.00
Churn, Square Base, Round Rim, 10 In., Qt. 88.00
Churn, Wood, Dasher, 19th Century, 38 In. . . . . *illus* 130.00
Churn, Wood, Rockers, 37 x 46 ½ x 17 ¼ In. 286.00
Coffee Grinders are listed in the Coffee Mill category.
Coffeepot, Agate, Gray, Handle, Bail Handle, 13 ½ In. 20.00
Coffeepot, Lady Vanity, Electric, c.1950, 11 In. 19.00
Coffeepot, Tin, Wrigglework, Hannah Reinert, Stamped, W. Shade, Late 1700s, 10 ½ In. 11700.00
Coffeepot, Wrigglework, Flowerpots, Swags, Stamped, Ketterer, 1800s, 11 In., Pair . . . . . *illus* 4914.00
Colander, Enamel, Blue, White, Handles, Footed, c.1950, 10 In. 25.00
Condiment Set, Green Plastic Holder, Spoons, Tops, Federal Glass, 4 x 6 In. 23.00
Cookie Cutter, Abraham Lincoln, Tin, 6 x 3 In. 55.00
Cookie Cutter, Baron Steigel, Tin, 19th Century, 8 In. 99.00
Cookie Cutter, Bird, Seated, Tin, Flat Back, 3 ½ x 6 ¼ In. 99.00
Cookie Cutter, Bird, Tin, Flat Back, Center Hole, Pa., 3 ½ x 6 ¼ In. 90.00
Cookie Cutter, Chick, Tin, Pine, Square Nails, 3 ½ x 3 ¾ In. 330.00
Cookie Cutter, Chick, Tin Strip, Wood, Square Nails, Pa., 3 ½ x 3 ¾ In. 300.00
Cookie Cutter, Eagle, Tin, Flat Back, Center Hole, 1 x 4 ½ x 4 ¾ In. 20.00
Cookie Cutter, Elephant, Trunk Raised, Tin, 3 ¾ x 6 In. 44.00
Cookie Cutter, Fire Parade Trumpet, Tin, 4 ¼ x 3 In. 33.00
Cookie Cutter, Ghost, Tin, 3 ¼ x 2 ¾ In. 4.00
Cookie Cutter, Guitar, Tin, 5 x 2 ¼ In. 44.00
Cookie Cutter, Hand, Tin, 3 ½ x 2 ½ In. 44.00
Cookie Cutter, Heart, Tin, 3 ¾ x 3 In. 11.00
Cookie Cutter, Horse, Standing, Tin, Flat Back, 5 x 6 ½ In. 154.00
Cookie Cutter, Horse, Tin, 7 ¼ x 5 In. 77.00
Cookie Cutter, Horse, Tin, Flat Back, Pa., 1 ¼ x 5 x 6 ½ In. 140.00
Cookie Cutter, Horse, Walking, Tinned Sheet Iron, 19th Century, 9 ½ x 11 ½ In. 1760.00
Cookie Cutter, Horse & Rider, Tinned Sheet Iron, 19th Century, 9 x 10 ¼ In. 1870.00
Cookie Cutter, Indian, Drinking, Tin, Flat Back, Holes, 8 ¼ x 4 In. 220.00
Cookie Cutter, Indian Head, Tin, 4 ½ x 5 In. 195.00
Cookie Cutter, Man, In Hat, Waistcoat, Tin, 9 ½ x 3 ⅝ In. 44.00
Cookie Cutter, Man, In Top Hat, Tinned Sheet Iron, 19th Century, 13 ¾ In. 1540.00
Cookie Cutter, Man, Riding Horse, Tin, 5 x 5 ⅜ In. 185.00

Kitchen, Churn, Barrel Form, Crank Handle, c.1900, 14 ½ In.
$77.00

Kitchen, Churn, Wood, Dasher, 19th Century, 38 In.
$130.00

Kitchen, Coffeepot, Wrigglework, Flowerpots, Swags, Stamped, Ketterer, 1800s, 11 In., Pair
$4914.00

K

Kitchen, Cookie Cutter, Rabbit, Tin, Pine, 4 ¼ x 4 ⅞ x ¾ In.
$523.00

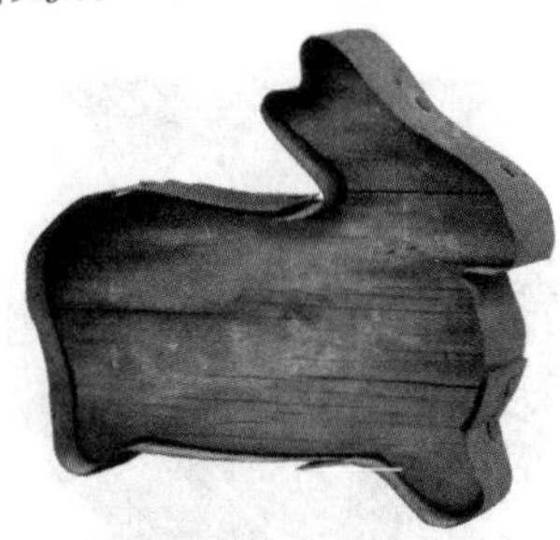

Kitchen, Cookie Cutter, Reindeer, Tin, Late 1800s, 8 In.
$2106.00

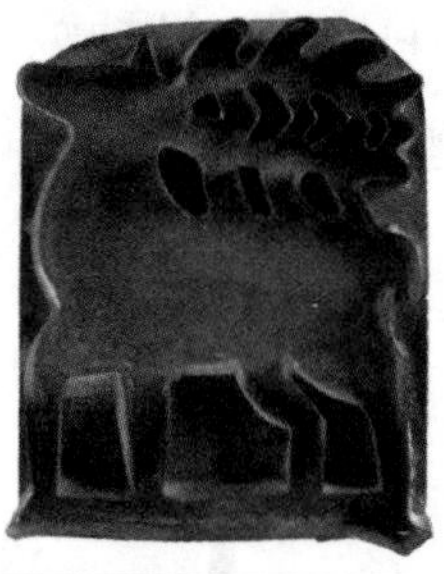

K

Kitchen, Dough Scraper, Wrought Iron, Bell Form Blade, Round Handle, 2 ⅞ x 4 x 3 In.
$110.00

TIP

To clean stained aluminum, boil it in a pot with water and grapefruit or lemon rind for about 30 minutes. Another method of cleaning stained aluminum is to put 2 heaping tablespoons of cream of tartar in a pot of water and boil the aluminum in the mixture for 30 minutes.

Cookie Cutter, Pregnant Woman, Tin, 7 x 3 ¼ In. 110.00
Cookie Cutter, Rabbit, Tin, Pine, 4 ¼ x 4 ⅞ x ¾ In. .... *illus* 523.00
Cookie Cutter, Reindeer, Iron, Late 19th Century, 8 In. 2106.00
Cookie Cutter, Reindeer, Tin, 5 ½ x 4 ½ In. 195.00
Cookie Cutter, Reindeer, Tin, Late 1800s, 8 In. .... *illus* 2106.00
Cookie Cutter, Rooster, Tin, Pine, Penn., 5 x 4 ¾ In. 660.00
Cookie Cutter, Rooster, Tin, Wood, Square Nails, Pa., 5 x 4 ¾ In. 450.00
Cookie Cutter, Seal, Tin, 6 x 6 In. 77.00
Cookie Cutter, Tulip, Tin, 3 ¾ x 3 ⅓ In. 44.00
Cookie Cutter, Whale, Tin, 4 x 1 ¾ In. 33.00
Corn Holder, Bakelite, Butterscotch, Elongated Pentagon, 2 Prongs, 3 ¼ In., 8 Piece 130.00
Crumb Sweeper, Fuller Brush, Tidy Sweeper, 1950s, 3 x 6 In. 25.00
Cup, Sifter, Applied Handle, Perforated Lid, Tin, Japanned, Round, 3 ½ x 2 ¾ In. 11.00
Cutlery Tray, Canted Sides, Wood, Black, Red, Yellow Paint, New England, 1800s, 2 ½ x 8 ¾ In. 411.00
Cutlery Tray, Walnut, Center Divider, Heart Cutout, Dovetailed, c.1825, 6 x 10 x 14 In. 470.00
Dipper, Aluminum, Wood Handle, Green Paint, Mirro, c.1958, 13 In. 18.00
Dipper, Ash, Burl, Figured Bowl, Patina, 19th Century, 16 ½ In. 470.00
Dipper, Coconut, Ivory Inlaid Handle, 16 In. 375.00
Dipper, Coconut, Ivory Inlay, Patina, 14 ½ In. 500.00
Dipper, Enamel, Black, White, c.1950, 13 In. 18.00
Dipper, Enamel, Green, Cream, c.1940, 14 In. 14.00
Dipper, Enamel, Red, White, c.1955, 13 x 5 In. 20.00
Dipper, Maple, Early 19th Century, 4 x 7 ½ x 17 In. 75.00
Double Boiler, Enamel, Blue, White, c.1958, 4 ¼ In. 50.00
Dough Box, Cover, Wood, Blue Milk Paint, 2 Sections, 30 x 42 x 19 In. 700.00
Dough Box, French Provincial, Chestnut, Hinged Top, Scalloped Skirt, 29 x 53 In. 1293.00
Dough Box, Pine, Footed, 19th Century, 28 ¾ x 39 ¾ x 17 In. 322.00
Dough Box, Poplar, Handles, 19th Century, 9 x 26 In. 117.00
Dough Box, Sheraton, Dovetailed Case, Scalloped Apron, c.1840, 28 x 40 In. 575.00
Dough Box, Softwood, Painted Red Ocher, Dovetailed Joints, Molded Base, 29 ½ x 38 In. 1650.00
Dough Scraper, Brass, Iron, Initials, Peter Derr, 1850, 4 ¼ In. 1287.00
Dough Scraper, Brass, Iron, Stamped, P.D., Mid 19th Century, 2 ½ x 3 ¾ In. 468.00
Dough Scraper, Iron, Arched Blade, Bent Handle, Penn., 3 ¼ x 3 ¼ In. 176.00
Dough Scraper, Iron, Arched Handle, 3-Sided Blade, 4 x 2 In. 88.00
Dough Scraper, Iron, Heart Cutout, 19th Century, 4 In. 1170.00
Dough Scraper, Iron, Heart Cutout, Pa., 19th Century, 3 In. 761.00
Dough Scraper, Iron, Triangle Blade, Rounded Handle, 1885, 2 ⅝ x 3 ¾ In. 66.00
Dough Scraper, Wrought Iron, Bell Form Blade, Round Handle, 2 ⅞ x 4 x 3 In. .... *illus* 110.00
Dough Tray, Softwood, Red Ocher Paint, Tapered Sides, Handle, 7 ½ x 23 ½ In. 358.00
Dutch Oven, Corning Ware, Cornflower, 4 Qt. 47.00
Dutch Oven, Iron, Tin, Roasting Spit, 1800s, 19 x 8 ½ x 16 ½ In. 323.00
Flatiron, Trivet, Nickel Plated, Brass Posts, Wood Handle, France, 1928, 8 In. 263.00
Flue Cover, Victorian Girl, Blond Hair, 6 In. 50.00
Food Chopper, Heart Cutout, Iron, Turned Wood Handle, 11 x 5 ½ In. 200.00
Food Chopper, Maple Handle, Heart Cutout, 19th Century 495.00
Food Chopper, Nut, Metal Hopper, Handle, Hazel Atlas, 1940s, 6 ¼ x 3 In. 15.00
Food Chopper, Nut, Plastic Top, 7 ½ x 3 ½ In. 15.00
Food Chopper, Pamco, Glass Measuring Cup, Red Plastic Handle, Wood Block, 11 In. 15.00
Food Grinder, Nut, Hazel Atlas, Red, Flower Decal, Glass Jar, Red Handle, 1950, 6 ½ In. 20.00
Food Grinder, Spice, Little Tot, Wood, Cast Iron Top, Drawer, 1880, 2 ½ x 2 ½ In. 55.00
Food Grinder, Spice, Little Tot, Wood Box, Cast Iron Top & Embossed Drawer, c.1880, 3 x 4 In. 55.00
Food Grinder, Spice, Treen, Storage Compartment, Tin Grater, Plate, 19th Century, 9 ½ In. 1112.00
Food Chopper, Nutmeg, Decal, Metal Hopper, Handle, Hazel Atlas, 1930s, 6 ¼ x 3 ¼ In. 17.50
Fork, Flesh, Iron, Engraved, Tulip Vine, Pierced Heart, c.1800, 18 ½ In. 761.00
Fork, Flesh, Iron, Inlaid Brass & Copper Bands, Punched Star, 1821, 16 ½ In. 4446.00
Fork, Toasting, 2-Tine, Forged Iron, 14 ½ x 2 ¼ In. 20.00
Fork, Toasting, 3-Tine, Iron, Mahogany Handle, Brass Ferrule, Patina, 27 x 4 In. 45.00
French Casserole Set, Blue, Yellow, Red, Handle, Glasbake, McKee, 3 ¼ x 5 In., 3 Piece. 45.00
Fruit Press, Griswold, No. 2, Cast Iron 70.00
Frying Pan, Grand Union Tea Co., 10 ¼ In. 19.00
Grater, Aluminum, Oval, Handle, c.1958, 4 x 2 ½ In. 5.00
Grease Can, Aluminum, Strainer, Italy, c.1960, 5 ¼ x 3 ½ In. 25.00
Grease Jar, Black Shield, Milk Glass, Black Letters, Hazel Atlas, 4 x 3 In. 95.00
Griddle, Scroll & Heart Design, Iron, Early 19th Century, 24 ½ In. 644.00
Gridiron, Movable Grid, Iron, 3 Legs, Penny Terminal, Oval, Flat Handle, Wrought, 3 ¼ x 11 In. 88.00
Gridiron, Wrought Iron, Wavy Grid, Rotates, Geometrics, Rattail Loop End, 3 x 13 In. .. *illus* 120.00
Grill, Basting, Cast Iron, Enamel, c.1800, 22 x 9 ¾ In. 55.00

Hanger, Metal, Landers, c.1960, 3 ¾ In. 8.00
Ice Cream Freezer, Up To Date, Wood, Metal, O.A. Lappe Co., Pat. 1896, 11 x 20 In. 330.00
Ice Cream Packer, Excelsior, Patent Ap, 9 ½ In. 99.00
Icebox, Fake Ice Block, Alaska Ice Box Salesman's, Sample, Iron, White Paint, 9 x 11 In. 531.00
Icebox, Oak, 4 Door, Porcelain, Lined, Bohn Syphon Refrigerator, c.1900, 56 x 36 In. 1320.00
Icebox, Oak, 4 Door, Porcelain Lined, Alaska-Muskegon, Mich., c.1910, 54 x 44 In. 1100.00
Iron, Brass, Turned Wood Handle, Slide Back, Initials, E.I.D.B., 1794, 4 ½ x 5 x 3 In. *illus* 190.00
Iron, Cross Rib, Thinkbase, 3 ½ In. 22.00
Iron, Electric, Baby Betsy Ross, Box, 4 In. 22.00
Iron, Fluter, American, Heater, c.1879. 22.00
Iron, Fluter, Geneva, c.1866. 22.00
Iron, Fluter, Hand, Star, American Machine Co., Cast Iron, Yellow, Red, Black, 1895, 302.00
Iron, Fluter, Nickel, Heater, North Bros., Phila., 3 Piece. 22.00
Iron, Fluter, Roller Type, Shepard Hardware, Buffalo, N.Y., 4 Piece 22.00
Iron, Gas, Diamond Akron Ohio Lamp Co. 22.00
Iron, Gas, Revolving, Late 1800s, 6 In. *illus* 1750.00
Iron, Goffering, Brass, 6 In. 22.00
Iron, Goffering, Kenrick, England, 5-In. Barrel 22.00
Iron, H Improved Progress, Cast Iron, Pat. Feb. 4, 1913, 6 In. 177.00
Iron, J.C. Stevens, No. 8, Star, Wood Handle, c.1888, 3 In. 22.00
Iron, Pressing, Brass, Original Slug Insert, Miniature, 19th Century, 3 ⅝ In. 225.00
Iron, Sensible, No. 4, Nickel Plated 22.00
Iron, Smoothing Board, Hardwood, Carved Horse Handle, Multicolored, 1807, 27 x 7 In. 413.00
Iron, Smoothing Board, Horse Handle, Green Paint, Continental, Signed, c.1854, 28 In. 748.00
Iron, Smoothing Board, Softwood, Oblong, Molded, Carved Cherry Handle, 29 x 6 ½ In. 22.00
Iron, Steam, Stewardess, Universal, Landers Frary & Clark, No. 1675, Instruction, Box, 1960s 35.00
Iron Warmer, Lid, Pierced Compass Star, Bail Handle, Feet, 8-Sided, Iron, 3 x 4 In. 411.00
Jar, Storage, Clear Lid, Yellow, 501-B, Pyrex, 1 ½ Cup 10.00
Jar, Storage, Metal Lid, Wave, Hazel Atlas, 6 ½ x 4 ¾ In. 25.00
Jar, Utility, Lefferts, Cast Iron, Baked Enamel Interior, Thumb Screw, c.1860, Qt. *illus* 840.00
Jar Opener, Embossed, Best S. Co., Lancaster, Pa., 7 ½ In. 176.00
Juicer, Quem Nichols Co., Aluminum, Kwicky, c.1955, 6 In. 12.00
Kettle, Apple Butter, Copper, 19th Century, 18 x 26 In. 263.00
Kettle, Sugar, Cast Iron, Flared Rim, c.1850, 15 x 36 In. 1997.00
Knife, Fruit, Depression Glass, Stonex, Box, 8 ½ In. 29.00
Knife Sharpener, Hardwood, Footed Cast Iron Frame, Mountable, 19 x 18 In. 431.00
Ladle, Mayonnaise, Amber, Gold Trim, Flat Bottom, 5 In. 20.00
Ladle, Mayonnaise, Glass, Blue, 5 In. 35.00
Laundry Stove, 6 Flat irons, Demas & F. Co., 22 In. 2750.00
Mangle, Triumph, Cast Iron Frame, 2 Hardwood Roller, 40 In. 387.00
Match Holders can be found in their own category.
Match Safes can be found in their own category.
Meal Bin, Cover, Pine, Grain Paint, Split Lift Top, Scroll Sides, 2 Sections, 34 x 50 x 20 In. 400.00
Measuring Cup, 3-Spout, Hazel Atlas, 1 Cup 12.00
Measuring Cup, Custard, McKee, 4 Cup, 6 In. 145.00
Measuring Cup, Green, Embossed, Sellers, U.S. Glass, 1 Cup 95.00
Measuring Cup, Green Glass, Hazel Atlas, Embossed, 3 Spout 25.00
Measuring Cup, Hazel Atlas, 4 x 4 ¼ In. 18.00
Measuring Cup, Jadite Clambroth, Hocking, 2 Cup, 3 ¾ In. 235.00
Measuring Cup, Milk Glass, 3 Spouts, Hazel Atlas 25.00
Measuring Cup, Milk Glass, McKee, 2 Cup 45.00
Measuring Cup, Red Letters, Fire-King, 16 Oz., 2 Cup 10.00
Measuring Cup, Skokie Green, McKee, 2 Cup 76.00
Measuring Cup Set, Jennyware, Ultramarine, Cup, ½ Cup, ⅓ Cup, ¼ Cup, 4 Piece 245.00
Measuring Spoon Set, Chilton, Aluminum, Original Package, c.1965, 4 Piece 10.00
Meat Hook, Cast Iron, Cow Finial, Eclipse Mfg., Pittsburg, Penn., 30 x 16 In. 1650.00
Meat Rack, Gloeklers, Curled Ends, Metals, C. Bliber & Co., Omaha, Neb., Pat. 1889, 8 Ft. 880.00
Meat Rack, Iron, Scrolled Design, 6 Hooks, 23 x 26 In. 115.00
Meat Slicer, U.S. Slicing Machine Company, Chain Mall Glove, Cheese, Red, 1912, 34 x 35 In. 6050.00
Meat Slicer, Vegetables, Starrett Tool, 16 x 14 x 12 In. 165.00
Meatball Maker, Aluminum, c.1955, 7 x 2 In. 8.00
Mixer, Chrome, Red Bakelite Handle, Red Cord, Owens-Illinois, 3 Cup 45.00
Mixer, Electric, Electromix, Model E-50, 3-Footed Beater Bowl, Meljax, Box, 7 ½ In. 85.00
Mixer, Electric, Electromix, Model E-50, Meljax, Box, Instruction 55.00
Mixer, Electric, Wood Panhandle Grip, Footed Pitcher, Weinig Made-Rite, Cleveland 65.00
Mixer, Glass, Hand Crank, S & S Hutchinson & Ny, 9 In. 330.00
Mixer, Handy Whip, Model 34-109-A, Embossed, Jadite, Chicago Electric 75.00

Kitchen, Gridiron, Wrought Iron, Wavy Grid, Rotates, Geometrics, Rattail Loop End, 3 x 13 In.
$120.00

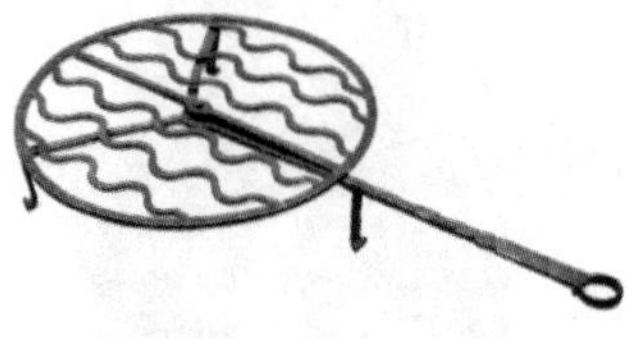

Kitchen, Iron, Brass, Turned Wood Handle, Slide Back, Initials, E.I.D.B., 1794, 4 ½ x 5 x 3 In.
$190.00

Kitchen, Iron, Gas, Revolving, Late 1800s, 6 In.
$1750.00

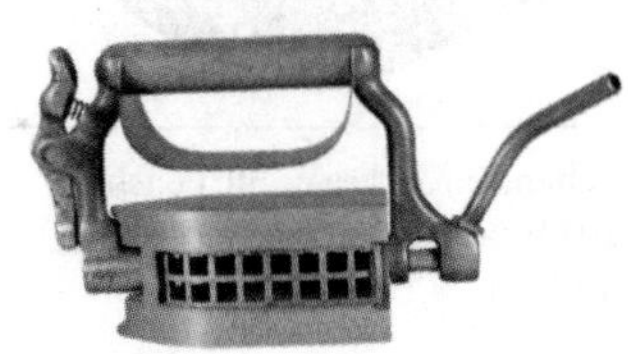

Kitchen, Jar, Utility, Lefferts, Cast Iron, Baked Enamel Interior, Thumb Screw, c.1860, Qt.
$840.00

K

Kitchen, Mold, Cake, Santa Claus, Cast Aluminum, 12 In., 2 Piece
$144.00

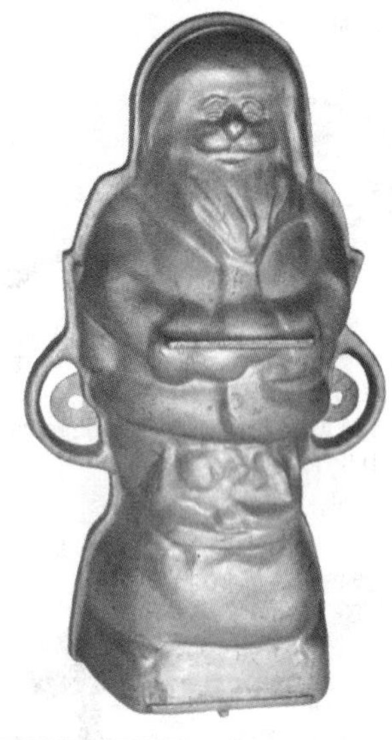

Kitchen, Mold, Cake, Scalloped Rim, Orange Glaze, Yellow Band, Redware, 2 ¾ x 8 ¾ In.
$170.00

Kitchen, Mold, Cheese, Tin, Punched, Heart Form, Applied Handle, 3-Footed, 4 x 4 ¼ In.
$132.00

Mixer, Kenmore, Electric, White, Blue Wood Grip Knob, 3-Cup Glassbake Measure 45.00
Mixer, KM, Electric, White, Red Bakelite Handle, Switch, 3-Cup Measure, Knapp Monarch ... 50.00
Mixer, Mayonnaise, Universal, Clip Fastens To Table, Glass, Metal, Frary & Clark, 13 In...... 115.00
Mixer, Milk Shake, Hand Crank, Porcelain Base, Brass, 13 x 24 In. 3390.00
Mixer, Milk Shake, Porcelain Base, Hamilton Beach, 3 Cup, 18 In. 210.00
Mixer, Milk Shake, Rising Sun, Mounts On Fountain Counter, Cast Iron, Belt, 25 x 26 In..... 7150.00
Mixer, Moderne, Electric, Ivory & Green, 4 Cup Measure, Knapp Monarch 75.00
Mixer, Naxon, Electric, 100-125 Volt, 60 Cycle, 2 Cup Measure, Green 55.00
Mixer, Transparent Green Wood Grip Knob, Better Homes, 2 Cup Nazon Measure 55.00
Mixer, Vidreo, Wood Panhandle Grip, 2 Cup Measure, Transparent Green................. 55.00
Mixer, Whipper, Freezer, Jewel, Glass, Metal, Wire Handle, Gravity Twin Box Co., 10 ½ In..... 316.00
Mixer, Whirlpool, Hocking 2 Cup Measuring Pitcher, Box, Instructions.................. 75.00
Mixing Bowl, Amber, Federal, 9 ¾ x 4 ½ In. 30.00
Mixing Bowl, Blue Dot, Pyrex, 9 In.. 14.25
Mixing Bowl, Blue Flower, Pyrex, 8 ½ In. 7.50
Mixing Bowl, Cattail, Milk Glass, Hazel Atlas, 2 Qt., 7 ½ In............................ 18.00
Mixing Bowl, Cellar, White, Embossed Grape & Vine Rim, 10 x 5 ½ In.. .... 15.50
Mixing Bowl, Cinderella, 1 ½ Pt. 6.00
Mixing Bowl, Crisscross, Hazel Atlas, 4 ½ x 9 ½ In.. .... 28.00
Mixing Bowl, Glass, Cobalt Blue, Ribbed, Hazel Atlas, 7 ⅝ x 3 ⅛ In. 40.00
Mixing Bowl, Glass, Pink, Ribbed, Federal, 10 ½ x 4 ½ In.. .... 45.00
Mixing Bowl, Green, Hocking, 7 ½ In.. 30.00
Mixing Bowl, Green, Slick Handle, Cover, U.S. Glass, 10 In. 145.00
Mixing Bowl, Green Ivy, Hazel Atlas, 8, 7, 4 ¾ In., 3 Piece 55.00
Mixing Bowl, Milk Glass, Aqua Stars, Federal, 7 & 8 & 9 In., 3 Piece.................... 45.00
Mixing Bowl, Milk Glass, Dutch Decal, Hazel Atlas, 7 In. 20.00
Mixing Bowl, Milk Glass, Gold Wheat, Hazel Atlas, 5 In.. .... 7.50
Mixing Bowl, Milk Glass, Paneled, Hazel Atlas, 8 ¾ In.. .... 14.00
Mixing Bowl, Milk Glass, Turquoise Fruit, Federal, 3 x 6 In. 12.50
Mixing Bowl, Modern Tulips, Fire-King, Black & Red, 8 ½ In. 50.00
Mixing Bowl, Set, Rest Well, Green, Hazel Atlas, 8, 7, 6, 5 In., 4 Piece 105.00
Mixing Bowl, Skating Dutch, White, Red Figures, Hazel Atlas, 4 ½ x 9 In. 35.00
Mixing Bowl, Space Age, White, Turquoise Design, Federal, 5 ¾ In. 18.00
Mixing Bowl, Town & Country, Cinderella, Pyrex, 2 ½ Qt. 12.00
Mixing Bowl, White, Black Flower, Red Yellow & Orange Bands, Hazel Atlas, 9 In.. .... 50.00
Mold, Butter, Geometrics, Drain Holes, Pegged, Handle, 15 In.......................... 110.00
Mold, Cake, Bundt, Scalloped, Redware, 3 ¼ x 9 ½ In. 50.00
Mold, Cake, Fish Form, Scales, Center Post, Orange Glaze, Green, Yellow, Redware, 2 ½ x 12 In. 413.00
Mold, Cake, Little Princess, Glasbake, McKee, 4 ⅝ x 1 ½ In. 10.00
Mold, Cake, Raised, Spiral Grooves, Center Post, Brown Ground Glaze, Redware, 3 ½ x 7 In. . 55.00
Mold, Cake, Round, Center Post, Umber Glaze, Brown Splatter, Redware, c.1899, 2 x 4 ¾ In. . 275.00
Mold, Cake, Santa Claus, Cast Aluminum, 12 In., 2 Piece .... *illus* 144.00
Mold, Cake, Scalloped Edges, Grooves, Center Post, Orange Glaze, Redware, 2 x 8 In. 11.00
Mold, Cake, Scalloped Rim, Orange Glaze, Yellow Band, Redware, 2 ¾ x 8 ¾ In. .... *illus* 170.00
Mold, Cake, Scalloped Rim, Spiral Grooves, Pumpkin Orange Ground Glaze, Redware, 3 ¼ x 10 In. 44.00
Mold, Cake, Swirl, Rim, Redware, 4 x 9 ¾ In.. .... 35.00
Mold, Candle, see Tinware category.
Mold, Cheese, Tin, Heart, Hand Punched, Loop Handle, 1810, 4 ½ x 8 ½ x 6 ½ In.. .... 175.00
Mold, Cheese, Tin, Punched, Heart Form, Applied Handle, 3-Footed, 4 x 4 ¼ In. .... *illus* 132.00
Mold, Chocolate, 8 Flower Cups, Aluminum, c.1958, 12 ½ x 6 ¼ In. 20.00
Mold, Chocolate, Boy, Full Figure, Clay, 3-Footed, 13 ¼ x 4 ¼ x 3 ½ In.. .... 25.00
Mold, Chocolate, Copper, Gothic Spire Shape, Fabt. Mouliste Breuelle Trottier, 16 x 5 ⅜ In. .. 420.00
Mold, Chocolate, Egg, Cracked, Metal, Hinged, 7 In. 20.00
Mold, Chocolate, Grape Bowl, Clay, 3-Footed, 12 ¾ x 8 x 3 ¾ In. 25.00
Mold, Chocolate, Lobster, Clay, 3-Footed, 12 ¾ x 8 x 3 ¾ In. 25.00
Mold, Chocolate, Pear Designs, Clay, 3-Footed, 11 ½ x 8 ½ x 3 ½ In. 20.00
Mold, Cookie, Cornucopia, Cast Iron, Oval, 19th Century, 5 ½ In. 58.00
Mold, Fluted, Aluminum, c.1955, 8 x 2 ¼ In. 12.00
Mold, Ice Cream, see also Pewter category.
Mold, Jelly, Lamb, Kidney Bean Form, Orange, Black Spatter, Redware, 2 x 4 ½ x 3 In. .. *illus* 150.00
Mold, Jelly, Molded Grooves Rim To Center, Orange Glaze, Black Spatter, Redware, 1 ¾ x 4 ⅛ In. 88.00
Mold, Sugar, Maple Sugar, House, 6 ¾ x 6 ½ x 5 ¾ In. 95.00
Molds may also be found in the Pewter and Tinware categories.
Mortar & Pestle, Brass, 3 x 2 ½ In. 129.00
Mortar & Pestle, Brass, Chain, 3 x 4 ¼ In. 50.00
Mortar & Pestle, Brass, Handles, 8 ¼ x 4 ⅜ In.. .... 10.00
Mortar & Pestle, Maple, Carved, October 23, 1754 .... 450.00

Mortar & Pestle, Maple, Red Paint, Incised Medial Rings, Late 1800s, 13 ½ In.. . . . . 201.00
Mortar & Pestle, Softwood, Cone Shape, Black Stain, 4 x 3 ½ In.. . . . . 303.00
Mortar & Pestle, Walnut, Carved, 7 ¼ In. 82.00
Mortar & Pestle, Wood, Turned, Old Blue Paint, Late 18th Century, 8 In.. . . . . 644.00
Napkin Holder, Bakelite, Yellow Scottie Dog 35.00
Orange Squeezer, Juice-O-Mat, White, Rival, 1939, 8 ½ x 7 In.. . . . . 45.00
Pan, Bread, Chilton, Aluminum, Plastic Cover, Label, 4 ¼ x 7 ½ In. 10.00
Pan, Bread, Loaf, Blue Flower, Milk Glass, Glasbake, Jeannette. 12.00
Pan, Bread, Loaf, Nature's Bounty, Anchor Hocking, 5 x 9 In.. . . . . 10.00
Pan, Corn Stick, Beauty Bake, Glass, 12 x 6 ¼ In. 45.00
Pan, Corn Stick, Griswold, No. 273, Cast Iron, 7 Sticks 15.00
Pan, Graniteware, Red & White, c.1958, 7 ½ x 2 ½ In. 12.00
Pan, Graniteware, Red & White, c.1958, 7 x 1 ½ In.. . . . . 10.00
Pan, Graniteware, Red & White, c.1958, 8 ¾ x 3 In.. . . . . 15.00
Pan, Graniteware, Red & White, c.1958, 9 x 2 ¾ In.. . . . . 18.00
Pan, Loaf, Provincial, Cover, Ocher Glaze, Tobacco Drip Accents, Handles, 3 ¾ x 5 In.. . . . . 120.00
Pan, Muffin, Aluminum, 8 Cup, c.1955, 13 ¾ x 7 In.. . . . . 18.00
Pan, Muffin, Griswold, No. 10, Cast Iron, 11 Cup 20.00
Pan, Muffin, Griswold, No. 18, Cast Iron, 6 Cup 50.00
Pan, Muffin, Wagner, No. 1330, 8 Cup. 14.00
Pan, Popover, Kreamer, Aluminum, 6 Cup, c.1965, 11 ½ x 5 ½ In.. . . . . 15.00
Pan, Rehruecken, Aluminum, Germany, c.1955, 12 x 4 ¾ In.. . . . . 9.00
Pan, Sauce, Copper, Iron Handle, France, Early 20th Century, 2 ¾ x 7 ¼ In.. . . . . 150.00
Pan, Saute, Copper, Brass Handle, France, Early 20th Century, 26 ½ x 11 In. 510.00
Pan, Tart, Aluminum, 6 Shells, c.1955, 10 ¾ x 7 In. 12.00
Peach Stoner, Cast Iron, Sinclair Scott Co., Baltimore. 50.00
Peel, Pine, Round Paddle, Handle, 89 ½ In.. . . . . 1560.00
Peeler, Apple, Wood, Blue Green Paint, Black Pinstripe, Maine, 28 x 6 In.. . . . . 173.00
Peeler, Potato, Cast Iron, Nu-Way Automatic, St. Louis, 6 x 12 ½ In.. . . . . 20.00
Percolator, Cornflower, Corning Ware, Electric, Plastic Footed Stand, 10 Cup 49.00
Percolator, Glasbake, Manhattan, Black Plastic Handle, 4 Cup. 33.00
Pestle, Wood, Carved, Acorn Finial, Diamond Banding, 11 ⅜ x 2 ¼ In.. 44.00
Pie Crimper, Forged Iron, Bone Knob, 7 In.. . . . . 201.00
Pie Crimper, Forged Iron, Brass Wheel, 7 In.. . . . . 144.00
Pie Crimper, Serpent Handle, Copper Wheel, Wrought Iron, 1820s, 6 In. . . . . *illus* 1404.00
Pie Pan, Acme, Tin, c.1950, 9 In.. . . . . 12.00
Pie Pan, Ekcoloy, Silver Beauty, c.1950, 9 ½ In.. . . . . 10.00
Pie Pan, Hagelstein Bakery, Aluminum, c.1960, 9 In.. . . . . 12.00
Pie Pan, Mrs. Wagner's, Aluminum, c.1950, 9 In. 12.00
Pie Pan, Shenandoah, Aluminum, c.1955, 9 In. 12.00
Pie Plate, Deep, Scalloped Inside Edge, Anchor Hocking, Qt., 9 In. 10.00
Pie Plate, Lemon Yellow, Glasbake, McKee, 9 ½ In.. . . . . 12.00
Pie Plate, Milk Glass, Flamingo Pink, Pyrex, 9 In. 12.00
Pie Server, Anodized Aluminum, Gold, c.1950, 9 ½ In.. . . . . 10.00
Pie Server, Stainless Steel, Brown & Black Bakelite Handle, Sta-Brite, 9 ⅛ x 1 ½ In.. . . . . 5.00
Pitcher, Cocktail, Metal Base, Band, Frosted Bands, 1950s, 8 ½ x 2 ¾ In. 20.00
Plate Warmer, Painted, Footed, 19th Century, 26 ¼ In.. . . . . 293.00
Popsicle Maker, Popsicle Service Center, Metal, Makes 12, c.1931, 8 x 18 In.. . . . . *illus* 358.00
Popsicle Mold, Brass, Iron Frame, 18 In.. . . . . 995.00
Pot, Copper, Round, Side Handles, Early 20th Century, 6 ¾ x 11 ½ In.. . . . . 210.00
Pot, Fish Poacher, Brass, Oval, Suspension Handle, 15 x 24 In.. . . . . 900.00
Pot, Fish Poacher, Copper, Iron, Oval, Swing Handle, 5 ½ x 25 In. 720.00
Pot, Iron, Indigo, Canted Handles & Feet, 14 ½ x 24 In. 352.00
Pot, Iron, Indigo, Rim With Knobs, American, 21 x 33 ½ In. 1080.00
Pot Hanger, Wrought Iron, Straight Bar, Arched Legs, Penny Feet, 17 ½ x 34 ½ x 15 In.. . . . . . 350.00
Pot Stand, Tripod, Round, 3 Supports, Leaf Accents, Wrought Iron, Scotland, 75 x 16 In.. . . . . 3360.00
Potato Masher, Mortar & Pestle, Softwood, Bell Shape, Footed, Blue, 8 In.. . . . . *illus* 121.00
Potato Masher, Mortar & Pestle, Softwood, Round, Footed, Pedestal, 5 ¼ In. 209.00
Pressure Cooker, Wear-Ever Aluminum, Instructions, 2 Weights, 1940s, 7 Qt. 30.00
Reamers, are listed in their own category.
Refrigerator, Stoll Manufacturing, Portable, 21 x 20 In.. . . . . 86.00
Refrigerator Box, Cover, Aluminum, Frigidaire, c.1955, 5 ¼ x 4 ¼ In.. 8.00
Refrigerator Dish, Amber, Federal, 8 ½ x 4 In.. . . . . 25.00
Refrigerator Dish, Butter Print, Pyrex, 4 ½ x 3 ¼ In. 12.00
Refrigerator Dish, Butterfly Gold, Pyrex, 6 ¾ x 4 ¼ In.. . . . . 12.00
Refrigerator Dish, Butterscotch, Pyrex, Small 8.75
Refrigerator Dish, Cover, Enamel, Red, Becoware, c.1950, 8 x 5 In.. . . . . 25.00

Kitchen, Mold, Jelly, Lamb, Kidney Bean Form, Orange, Black Spatter, Redware, 2 x 4 ½ x 3 In.
$150.00

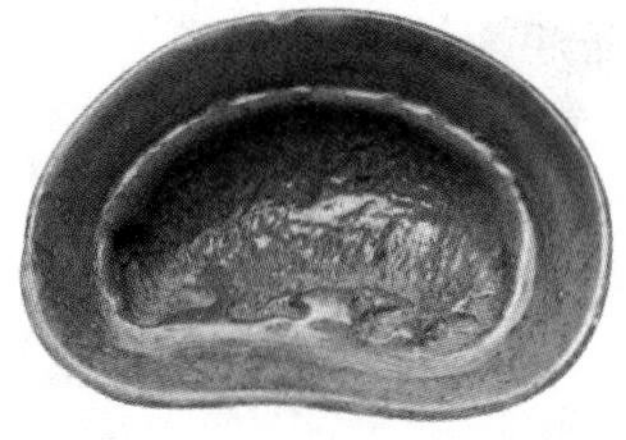

Kitchen, Pie Crimper, Serpent Handle, Copper Wheel, Wrought Iron, 1820s, 6 In.
$1404.00

Kitchen, Popsicle Maker, Popsicle Service Center, Metal, Makes 12, c.1931, 8 x 18 In.
$358.00

Kitchen, Potato Masher, Mortar & Pestle, Softwood, Bell Shape, Footed, Blue, 8 In.
$121.00

K

Kitchen, Rolling Pin, Poplar, Turned Round Handles, PA., 3 ½ x 25 ½ In.
$88.00

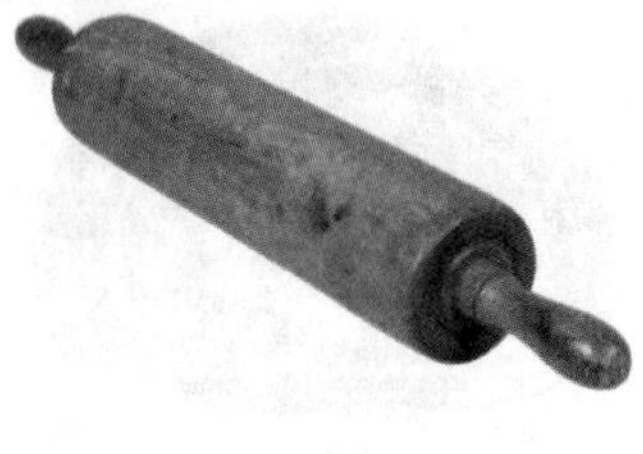

Kitchen, Scoop, Ice Cream, Fletcher Mfg. Co., Copper, Toronto, 10 In.
$300.00

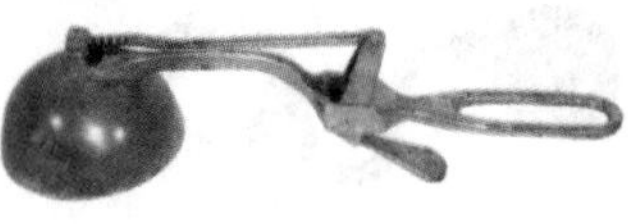

Kitchen, Scoop, Serrated Tulips, Central Star, Carved, Wood, 9 ½ x 2 ¾ In.
$225.00

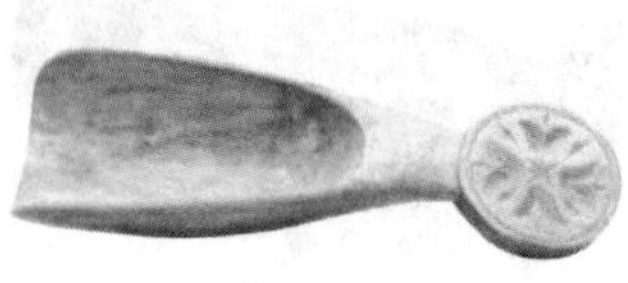

Kitchen, Serving Set, Cake, Checkerboard, Bakelite, Box, 2 Piece
$50.00

Refrigerator Dish, Cover, Enamel, White, Black Edge, c.1950, 5 x 4 In. 15.00
Refrigerator Dish, Cover, Stainless Steel, Revere, c.1958, 7 ¾ x 4 In. 15.00
Refrigerator Dish, Early American, Pyrex, 4 ½ x 3 ¼ In. 10.00
Refrigerator Dish, Old Orchard, Pyrex, 1 ½ Qt. 15.00
Rolling Pin, Double Rollers, Wood, Turned Handle, 19th Century, 12 ½ In. 527.00
Rolling Pin, Glass, Cobalt Blue, 15 ¾ In. 80.00
Rolling Pin, Glass, Pink, 14 In. 30.00
Rolling Pin, Nantucket, Bone Ends, 10 In. 75.00
Rolling Pin, Poplar, Turned Round Handles, Pa., 3 ½ x 25 ½ In. .... *illus* 88.00
Rolling Pin, Tiger Maple, 3 ½ x 17 ½ x 3 ½ In. 15.00
Rolling Pin, Tiger Maple, Bold Stripes, Early 1800s 250.00
Rolling Pin, Wood, Ivory Tips, 19th Century, 10 In. 330.00
Salt & Pepper Shakers are listed in their own category.
Salt Bowl, Maple, 18th Century, 2 ¾ x 5 ¾ In. 173.00
Saucepan Set, Cornflower, Corning Ware, Cover, 1 ½ In., 4 Piece 8.00
Sauerkraut Slicer, Wood, Iron Blade, Square Nails, 19 ½ x 6 ¾ In. 25.00
Sausage Stuffer, Wagner Stuffer, 45 x 16 In. 120.00
Sausage Stuffer, Wood, Tin, 21 x 42 ¾ In. 20.00
Scoop, Ice Cream, Aluminum, Copper Color, c.1958, 8 In. 9.00
Scoop, Ice Cream, Dover Mfg. Co., Size 10, Round Bowl, Patent, Feb. 1924, 11 ½ In. 495.00
Scoop, Ice Cream, Erie Specialty Co., Size 12, Cone Shape Bowl, 10 ½ In. 330.00
Scoop, Ice Cream, Fletcher Mfg. Co., Copper, Toronto, 10 In. .... *illus* 300.00
Scoop, Ice Cream, Geer Mfg. Co., Nickel Plated, Round, 9 ½ In. 33.00
Scoop, Ice Cream, Gilchrist, No. 34, Oval Bowl, 11 ½ In. 440.00
Scoop, Ice Cream, H.S. Greer, Nickel Plated, Wooden Handle, Cone Shape, 9 In. 1100.00
Scoop, Ice Cream, Icypi Automatic, Square, Wood Handle, Springless, German, 11 In. 187.00
Scoop, Ice Cream, Rolette Plunger Style, Brass, Wood Handle, 7 ½ In. 385.00
Scoop, Ice Cream, Victor, Nickel Plated, Round Bowl, Wooden Handle, 1908, 10 ½ In. 77.00
Scoop, Measuring, Aluminum, Copper Color, Color Craft, c.1958, ¼ Cup, 5 In. 7.00
Scoop, Metal, Wood Handle, c.1920, 9 x 3 ½ In. 200.00
Scoop, Serrated Tulips, Central Star, Carved, Wood, 9 ½ x 2 ¾ In. .... *illus* 225.00
Scoop, Softwood, Carved Handle, Dark Patina, 19th Century, 10 ½ In. 147.00
Scoop, Wood, Carved, Squared, Curved Handle, Shaft, 13 ½ x 3 ¼ In. 22.00
Scoop, Wood, Nabisco Grain Company, 12 x 29 In. 330.00
Serving Set, Cake, Checkerboard, Bakelite, Box, 2 Piece .... *illus* 50.00
Shaker, Flour, Milk Glass, Diagonal Red Stripes, McKee, 5 In. 65.00
Shaker, Glass, Clambroth, Paneled, Cone Shape, 4 ¾ x 3 In. 85.00
Shaker, Glass, Green, Paneled, Jeannette, 4 ½ x 3 In. 145.00
Shaker, Green, Square, Metal Lid, Hocking, 8 Oz. 29.00
Shaker, Nut Meats, Block Design, Owens-Illinois, 8 Oz. 29.00
Shaker Set, Cherry, White Trellis Stand, 8 Piece 214.00
Shaver, Chocolate, Cast Iron, Wood, 3 Blades, 8 x 13 In. 550.00
Sieve, Iron, Brass, Flat Handle, Hook End, 18 x 5 In. 66.00
Sieve, Pestle, Stand, Funnel Shape, Aluminum, c.1940, 9 ½ In. 25.00
Sifter, Triple Screen, Eames, White, Red Plastic Handle, Androck, c.1965, 5 x 5 ¼ In. 15.00
Sifter, Triple Screen, White, Flowers, Red Wood Handle, Androck, c.1950, 5 x 5 ¼ In. 20.00
Skewer Set, Iron, 6 Skewers, Hook 671.00
Skillet, Copper Bowl, Iron Handle, c.1790 .... 185.00
Skillet, Griswold, No. 0, Cast Iron 80.00
Skillet, Griswold, No. 2, Slant 475.00
Skillet, Griswold, No. 3 .... 7.00
Skillet, Griswold, No. 8 .... 20.00
Skillet, Griswold, No. 13, Block 1475.00
Skillet, Griswold, No. 14, Block 200.00
Skillet, Savery & Co., Cast Iron, 3-Footed, 21 ½ In. 300.00
Skimmer, Brass, Iron, Punched Star Pan, Copper Rivets, 17 In. 633.00
Slicer, Cake, Black Bakelite Handle, 11 x 3 ¾ In. 12.00
Slicer, Cake, Brown Mottled Bakelite Handle, 10 ½ x 3 ¾ In. 7.50
Spatula, Burl, Bone Edge, 4 ½ x 4 ¾ x ½ In. 95.00
Spatula, Iron, Brass, Flat Handle, Rattail End, Riveted Bell Blade, 16 In. 44.00
Spatula, Round Shaft, Sunburst, Iron, Flat Handle, Blade, Hanging Hole, 16 ½ In. 55.00
Spatula, Tin, Pierced Heart, Pa., 19th Century, 14 x 5 In. 400.00
Spatula, Wrought Iron, Bell Form, Round Shaft, Rattail End, 19 x 3 ½ In. .... *illus* 160.00
Spice Box, Walnut, 6 Compartments, Slide Lid, Late 19th Century, 3 x 9 x 5 ½ In. 105.00
Spice Box, Walnut, George I, c.1720, 40 x 20 In., 2 Piece .... *illus* 5148.00
Spice Box, Walnut, Pennsylvania, 1700s 950.00
Spice Box, Wood, 7 Drawers, Porcelain Labels, Knobs, Germany, 9 ½ x 8 ¼ x 2 In. 75.00

Spice Box, Wood, Strawberries, Flowers, Salmon Ground, Cylindrical, Turned, Painted, Lehn, 5 In. 1170.00
Spice Set, Cosmos, Yellow Flower, Tipp City, 2 ¼ In., 7 Piece 95.00
Spice Set, Kromex, Rack, Aluminum, Aqua Plastic Top, c.1960, 4 ¼ In., 9 Piece 150.00
Spice Set, Kromex, Rack, Aluminum, Black Plastic Top, c.1960, 3 ½ x 2 In., 9 Piece 40.00 to 65.00
Spoon, Tasting, Brass, Iron, Pa., Mid 19th Century, 7 ¾ In. 468.00
Spoon, Tasting, Iron, Brass, Flat Handle, Copper Rivets, 12 ¾ x 2 ¼ In. 190.00
Spoon, Tasting, Iron, Brass, Round Shaft, Flat Handle, 8 ½ x 2 ⅜ In. 22.00
Spoon, Tasting, Iron, Brass, Round Shaft, Flat Handle, Rattail End, 10 ¼ In.............. 99.00
Spoon, Tasting, Iron, Square Shaft, Flat Handle, Rattail Loop End, 9 ⅛ x 2 ⅛ In. 11.00
Spoon Rack, Oak, Nailed Construction, Shaped Crests, Mid 1800s, 12 ½ x 5 ½ In. 345.00
Spoon Rack, Wood, Incised Tulips, Hearts, Pinwheels, 3 Holders, 29 ½ x 11 ½ In.......... 110.00
Spoon Rack, Wood, Painted, Freehand Flowers, Holds 12 Spoons, 1800s, 15 x 8 In. 780.00
Spoon Rack, Wood, Red Paint, 19th Century, 23 ½ x 12 ¼ In.......................... 819.00
Spoon Rest, Aluminum, Copper Color, Tidy, c.1960, 5 In............................. 10.00
Spoon Rest, Double, Hen Sitting In Center, Ceramic, Avocado Green, California Ware, 9 ⅜ In. 12.00
Stocking Dryer, Softwood, Patina, Child's, 20 x 3 ¾ In. .... *illus* 99.00
Strainer, Cottage Cheese, Wood, Banded, 8-Sided, Lid, 10 In. Diam. 66.00
Strainer, Enamel, Blue, White, Handle, c.1950, 6 ¼ x 4 ½ In. 20.00
Stringholder, Eugene The Jeep, Figural, Plaster, Incised, 1949, 8 ½ x 7 x 2 In. 690.00
Sugar Nippers, Hand Forged, c.1800, 9 ½ x 3 ¼ In.................................. 110.00
Syrup, Green Vaseline, Paneled, Hinged Metal Lid, Hocking, 4 ¼ In..................... 65.00
Teapot, Griswold, No. 576, Cast Iron, Marked, 5 ¼ x 4 ½ In............................ 726.00
Teapot, Iron, Copper, Globular, Swing Bail Handle, Signed, Japan, 8 ½ In................. 143.00
Timer, Lux, White, Red Numbers, Box, c.1955, 3 ½ x 4 ¾ In. 28.00
Toaster, 2 Slice, Chrome, Bakelite Handles, Dial & Base, Electric, 1940s, 7 ½ x 10 ½ In...... 44.00
Toaster, 2 Slice, Chrome, Brown Bakelite, Toastmaster 1B14, Electric, 1947............... 85.00
Toaster, Art Nouveau, Hotpoint, Pat. Date February 22, 1910, Edison Electric, 14 In......... 79.00
Toaster, Drop Sides, Fostoria, No. 72, Chrome, Bersted Mfg. Co., 1930s 38.00
Toaster, Flip Flop, Series 680, Black Wood Handles, Son-Chief Electrics, Inc............... 24.00
Toaster, Iron, Brass Cup, Copper Rivets, Round Shaft, Flat Handle, 12 ¾ In. 209.00
Toaster, Iron, Pierced Uprights, Riveted Feet, Turned Wood Handle, 8 x 15 In.............. 144.00
Toaster, Kick, Wrought Iron, Twisted Arch Holders, 3-Footed, 6 x 14 x 13 In. .... *illus* 143.00
Toaster, Knapp-Monarch Reverso, No. 510, Chrome, Black Base, 1930s, 7 x 4 x 6 In......... 18.00
Toaster, Movable Top, Arch Holders, Snake Like Heads, 3-Footed, Wrought Iron, 6 x 14 x 13 In. 143.00
Toaster, Revolving, Westinghouse, Electric, East Pittsburgh............................ 55.00
Toaster, T-Shape, Spiraled Arches, 3-Footed, 1800s, 23 ¼ In............................ 375.00
Toaster, Wood Handle, Lititz Bakery, A.R. Keller, 14 In................................ 88.00
Tongs, Fish, 5 Prongs, Aluminum, Androck, Original Package, c.1955, 8 ½ In.............. 18.00
Towel Bar, White Glass, Double, Swivel, 14 In. 68.00
Trivet, see Trivet category.
Waffle Iron, Griswold, No. 8, Cast Iron.. 18.00
Waffle Iron, Griswold, No. 18, Hearts & Stars, Cast Iron.............................. 25.00
Waffle Iron, Hibbard, No. 8, Cast Iron 9.00
Waffle Iron, Norra Hammar, Hearts, Cast Iron 18.00
Waffle Iron, Rey-O-Noc, No. 8, Cast Iron, High Base.................................. 14.00
Waffle Iron, Skillet, Swivel Base, No. 67, Cast Iron, Marked, P & B Mfg. Co., 12 In.......... 60.00
Waffle Iron, Victor, No. 8, Cast Iron 35.00
Waffle Iron, Wagner Ware, No. 0, Nickel 90.00
Waffle Iron, Wrought Iron, Mold, Round Shaft, Flattened Handles, 19 x 8 In............... 66.00
Wash Board, Asco Junior, Wood, Metal, American Stores Co., 1920s, 15 In. 39.00
Wash Board, Badger Zip Junior, Wood, Metal, 1905, 15 In. 33.00
Wash Board, Glass, Wood, 1900s, 18 x 10 In. 10.00
Wash Board, Oak, Cutout Heart Handle, Chamfered Sides, c.1800, 34 ¾ x 8 In. 1080.00
Waste Can, Red Poppy, Pedal, Metal, 13 x 11 In...................................... 225.00

KNIFE collectors usually specialize in a single type. In the 1960s, the United States government passed a law that required knife manufacturers to mark their knives with the country of origin. This seemed to encourage the collectors, and knife collecting became an interest of a large group of people. All types of knives are collected, from top quality twentieth-century examples to old bone- or pearl-handled knives in excellent condition.

Bayonet, Steel, Horn Handle, Scabbard, Leather, Finial, 15 In.......................... 1150.00
Bolo, U.S. Model 1910, Scabbard, 10 In.. 259.00
Bowie, Bone Handle, Engraved, 19th Century 702.00
Bowie, Celluloid Handle, German Silver Sheath, Wolstenholm, 5-In. Spear Point Blade 550.00
Bowie, Henry Huber, Stag Handle, c.1832, 8 ¼ In.................................. 17250.00
Bowie, Horn Handle, Silver Name Plate, Pommel, Leather Scabbard, Edward Barnes & Sons 350.00
Bowie, Horn Scales, Mother-Of-Pearl Insert, Sheath, Manson Sheffield, 4 ¾-In. Blade 250.00

Kitchen, Spatula, Wrought Iron, Bell Form, Round Shaft, Rattail End, 19 x 3 ½ In.
$160.00

Kitchen, Spice Box, Walnut, George I, c.1720, 40 x 20 In., 2 Piece
$5148.00

Kitchen, Stocking Dryer, Softwood, Patina, Child's, 20 x 3 ¾ In.
$99.00

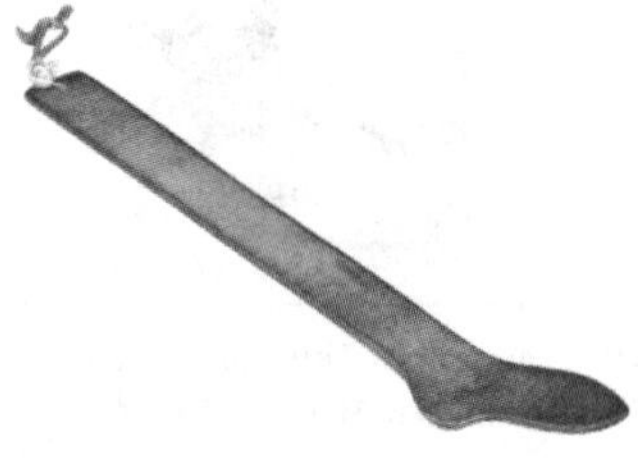

Kitchen, Toaster, Kick, Wrought Iron, Twisted Arch Holders, 3-Footed, 6 x 14 x 13 In.
$143.00

Kosta, Vase, Seaweed, Clear, Green, Signed, Lindstrand, c.1950, 11 In. $195.00

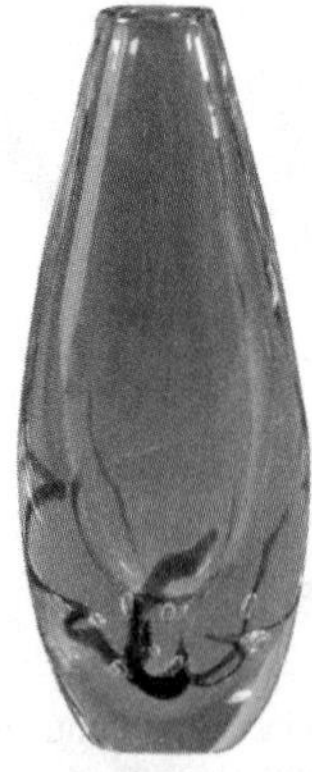

KPM, Cup & Saucer, Cornflowers, Wheat, Blue, Gilt, Mid 1800s $230.00

KPM, Figurine, Woman, Seated, Flower Basket, Blue Scepter Mark, 5 ⅞ In. $245.00

KPM, Lamp, Brass, Lithophane, 6 Panels, Women, Children, Stamped, 10 ⅛ In. $633.00

Bowie, Iron D-Guard, Clip Point Blade, Hickory Handle, 13-In. Blade 350.00
Bowie, Mother-Of-Pearl Handle, Scabbard, Leather, W. & S. Butcher, c.1840, 9 In. 40250.00
Bowie, Sterling Silver Handle, George Wolstenholm, 18 ½ In. 468.00
Dagger, Bone Grip, Acanthus Pommel, Turk's Head Ferrule, Italy, c.1570, 17 In. 1126.00
Dagger, Iron, Silver Plate, Inlaid, Chiseled Brass Hilt, c.1690 .... 1422.00
Dagger, Ivory Handle, Scrolls, Diced Panels, Steel, Scabbard, 9 ½ In. 1495.00
Dagger, Sheath, Chrome Hardware, German SA, Marked, 14 ½ In. 550.00
Dagger, Sheath, Enamel Scabbard, German SS, Stamped, HACO, 14 ¾ In. 650.00
Dagger, Walrus Ivory Handle, Scabbard, Silver, Will & Finck, c.1849, 4 ¼ In. 34500.00
Dirk, Battelle, Horn Oval Handle, Scabbard, Silver, c.1849, 10 ¾ In. 12650.00
Folding, Multi-Blade, Stainless, Mother-Of-Pearl Handle, c.1935, 4 ¾ In. 4025.00
Ivory, Elephant Handle, Mounted, E. Gross, 5-In. Kershaw Blade, c.1988, 11 In. 1150.00
No. 2, Brass Knuckle, Metal Scabbard, U.S., 1918, 6 ½ In. Blade 475.00
Pocket, Silver, Embossed Handle, c.1900, 3 In. 96.00
Rifleman's, Ames Mfg. Co., Walnut Handle, Scabbard, Leather, c.1849, 9 ½ In. 14950.00
Safari Set, Mitchell Monarch, Elephant, Rhinoceros, Lion, Tiger, Water Buffalo, Case 2013.00
Staghorn Handle, Scabbard, Leather, World War I, 14 ⅛ In. 1093.00
Trench, Model 1917, Knuckle Bow, Leather Scabbard, 9-In. Triangular Blade 425.00

KNOWLES, TAYLOR & KNOWLES *items may be found in the KTK category.*

KOREAN WARE, *see Sumida.*

KOSTA, the oldest Swedish glass factory, was founded in 1742. During the 1920s through the 1950s, many pieces of original design were made at the factory. Kosta and Boda merged with Afors in 1964 and created the Afors Group in 1971. In 1976, the name Kosta Boda was adopted. The company merged with Orrefors in 1990 and is still working.

KOSTA

Goblet, Woman's, Light Blue, Dashes On Base, Signed, Kosta Boda, 7 ¾ In. 25.00
Paperweight, Bubble Spray, Round, Vicke Lindstrand, 4 In. 84.00
Paperweight, Deer In Woods, Signed, 6 In. 200.00
Paperweight, Mouse, Signed, Lindstrand, 2 ½ x 4 ½ x 2 In. 50.00
Tumbler, Yellow Flowers, Green Leaves, Signed, Kosta Boda, 4 ⅛ In. 50.00
Vase, Blue, Red, Clear, Signed, Goran Warff, 10 ¾ In. 154.00
Vase, Blue Iridescent, Swirled, Blue & White Waves, Signed, 10 In. 275.00
Vase, Sailing Ship, Tapered, Octagonal, Intaglio Design, Signed, Kjellander, 5 In. 465.00
Vase, Seaweed, Clear, Green, Signed, Lindstrand, c.1950, 11 In. .... *illus* 195.00

KPM refers to Berlin porcelain, but the same initials were used alone and in combination with other symbols by several German porcelain makers. They include the Konigliche Porzellan Manufaktur of Berlin, initials used in mark, 1823–1847; Meissen, 1723–1724 only; Krister Porzellan Manufaktur in Waldenburg, after 1831; Kranichfelder Porzellan Manufaktur in Kranichfeld, after 1903; and the Krister Porzellan Manufaktur in Scheibe, after 1838.

K.P.M

Bowl, Vegetable, Flowers, Cream Ground, 2 ¼ x 9 ½ In. 230.00
Box, Cover, Apple Green Reserve, Raised Gilt Garlands, Painted Flower Roundel, 2 ⅝ In. 72.00
Chest, Garden, Corner Cherub, Gilt Bronze, Porcelain Cover, Base, Footed, 10 x 6 In. 2990.00
Cup & Saucer, Cornflowers, Wheat, Blue, Gilt, Mid 1800s .... *illus* 230.00
Dish, Leaf Form, Flowers, Latticed Edge, Handle, 6 x 4 In. 100.00
Figurine, Bird, Art Nouveau Style, Crested, Imperial Necklace, Stylized Feet, 8 ¼ In. 5925.00
Figurine, Child, Berry Seller, Blue Underglaze, 19th Century, 3 ½ In. 180.00
Figurine, Woman, Child At Side, 11 In. 450.00
Figurine, Woman, Seated, Flower Basket, Blue Scepter Mark, 5 ⅞ In. .... *illus* 245.00
Figurine, Woman, Seated, Flower Basket, Marked, 5 ⅞ In. 259.00
Group, Fawn Holding Fruit Basket, Signed, W.W. Demann, 12 ¾ In. 1200.00
Jar, Flower Bouquet, Painted, Gilt Border, Cobalt Blue Ground, Oval, Flat Lid, 11 ½ In., Pair 3081.00
Jardiniere, Flowers, Palace, Painted, Blue Ground, 14 x 6 In. 444.00
Lamp, Brass, Lithophane, 6 Panels, Women, Children, Stamped, 10 ⅛ In. .... *illus* 633.00
Lithophane, see also Lithophane category.
Plaque, Bearded Man, Smoking Pipe, Monks, Marked, Late 1800s, 11 x 13 In. 6250.00
Plaque, Jesus & Rabbis, Porcelain, Gilt Frame, Stamped, 19th Century, 7 ½ x 10 In. 4500.00
Plaque, Judith, Holding Sword, Holofernes' Head, After August Reidel, 1890s, 15 x 12 In. 11258.00
Plaque, Lithophane, Mary, Jesus, Joseph Traveling By Donkey, Intaglio, White, 5 ¾ x 4 ¼ In. 80.00
Plaque, Lithophane, Religious Scene, Cobalt Blue, Red, Leaded Glass, 1930s, 9 ½ x 14 In. 295.00
Plaque, Melon Eaters, Impressed Mark, Scepter, Frame, 9 ¾ x 12 In. 4900.00
Plaque, Mother & Child, Giltwood Frame, Late 19th Century, 9 x 6 In. 4375.00
Plaque, Odalisque, After Wagner, Giltwood Frame, Shadowbox, Oval, 5 x 4 In. 1200.00

Plaque, St. Jerome, Bearded Saint At Prayer, Giltwood Frame, c.1885, 12 x 10 In. 2844.00
Plaque, Virgin Mary, Blue Cape, Oval, Stamped, 19th Century, 7 x 5 In. 1000.00
Plaque, Virgin Mary, Child, Black Forest, Carved Frame, 1800s, 10 x 8 In. 3422.00
Plaque, Woman, Long Hair, Blue Ribbon, Frame, Signed, Wagner, Marked, 6 ¾ x 5 In. . *illus* 2320.00
Plaque, Woman, Ruth, Sword Verso, Gilt Frame, Signed, Wagner, 7 x 5 In.. .... 2185.00
Plaque, Woman, With Paper, Asceive De Vircine, Oval, Marked, 6 ⅞ x 5 ⅛ In. 1100.00
Plate, Dog, Terrier, White, Gilt, Scalloped Rim, 1866, 8 In. 175.00
Platter, Flowers, Pastel, Gold Trim, 10 ⅞ x 7 ¾ In. 24.00
Stein, Face On Neck, Star Pattern, Blue, White, Pewter Lid, Berlin, 2 ½ Liter. 138.00
Tureen, Cover, Oval, Figural Finial, Blue Underglaze Scepter, Red KPM & Globe, 16 In.. ..... 840.00
Urn, Allegory Of Putto, Goat, Lion, Masks, Blue Scepter Mark, Red Orb, 22 ½ In. .... *illus* 360.00
Vase, Courting Couple, Triple Trumpet, Blue KPM Mark, 5 ¼ x 4 x 3 In. 70.00

KTK are the initials of the Knowles, Taylor & Knowles Company of East Liverpool, Ohio, founded by Isaac W. Knowles in 1853. The company made many types of utilitarian wares, hotel china, and dinnerwares. It made the fine bone china known as Lotus Ware from 1891 to 1896. The company merged with American Ceramic Corporation in 1928. It closed in 1934. Lotus Ware is listed in its own category in this book.

K.T.& K. CHINA

Bowl, Fruit, Ivory, Flowers, Orange Trim, Gloria Shape, Late 1920s, 5 ½ In. 3.00
Casserole, Cover, Gold Swags, Victory Shape, Footed, 1922, 10 In. 25.00
Cuspidor, Ivy, Blossoms, Swirl, Blue Transfer, White, Semi-Vitreous, Early 1900s, 5 ¾ x 8 In. . 22.00
Gravy Boat, Orange & Black Bird, Flowers, Orange Trim, 1930s 18.00
Pitcher, Ice Water, Flowers, Ironstone, Gray Stamp, c.1900, 6 ½ In.. .... 55.00
Plate, Alpha, Flow Blue, c.1900, 11 ¾ x 15 ¼ In. 35.00
Plate, Dinner, Gloria Shape, Yellow, Red & Blue Flower Bouquets, Orange Trim. 7.50
Plate, Luncheon, Ramona, Green Flowers, Gold Trim, Marked 7.50
Platter, Ivory, Orange Oriental Flowers, Gloria Shape, 1930s, 15 ½ In. 25.00
Platter, Plymouth Shape, Scalloped Rim, Gold Highlights, c.1905, 13 In.. .... 20.00
Sauceboat, Underplate, Pink Roses, Black Band, Double Handle & Spout, 1909, 6 ½ In. 25.00
Vase, Flowers, White, Applied, Dark Green Ground, Grecian, Handle, Lotus Ware Mark, 6 In. . 605.00

KU KLUX KLAN items are now collected because of their historic importance. Literature, robes, and memorabilia are seen at shows and auctions. Laws passed in 1870 and 1871 caused the decline of the Klan. A second group calling itself the Ku Klux Klan emerged in 1915. There are still local groups using the name.

Button, KKK, White Ground, Red Letters, 1 In.. .... 41.00
Flag, Realm Of Alabama, Frame, 1916, 20 x 36 In. 165.00
Matchbox, Wraparound, 1 Flag, 1 Language, 1 School, 1 Country, 1 ½ x 2 ¼ In.. .... 168.00
Pin, Hooded Man, On Hooded Horses, Wielding Sword, Black Ground, ⅜ x ½ In. 127.00
Pin, Klan Day, Robed Klansman Holds Burning Cross On Robed Horse, ⅞ In.. .... 172.00
Pin, Klan Day, Robed Klansman With Burning Cross, Robed KKK Horse, Pa., 1920, 2 In.. .... 442.00
Pin, Opposing Former Klansman Daid Duke, Klansman In Center, Red Border, 1992, 2 In.... 25.00
Postcard, Klansmen On Horseback At Night, Real Photo, Postmarked Oklahoma 172.00
Postcard, Parade, Washington, D.C., Photograph, August 18, 1925. .... 431.00
Printing Block, Wood, 2 Men Hanging, Carpetbag Labeled Ohio, Mule, 1869, 1 ¾ x 5 In. ... 550.00
Sticker, Secret Member, Never Accept Busing, Denham Springs La., 12 In., 5 Piece 55.00
Sword, Ceremonial, With Scabbard, Hilt With Klansman On Horse, Black Enamel Grip 55.00

KUTANI porcelain was made in Japan after the mid-seventeenth century. Most of the pieces found today are nineteenth-century. Collectors often use the term *Kutani* to refer to just the later, colorful pieces decorated with red, gold, and black pictures of warriors, animals, and birds.

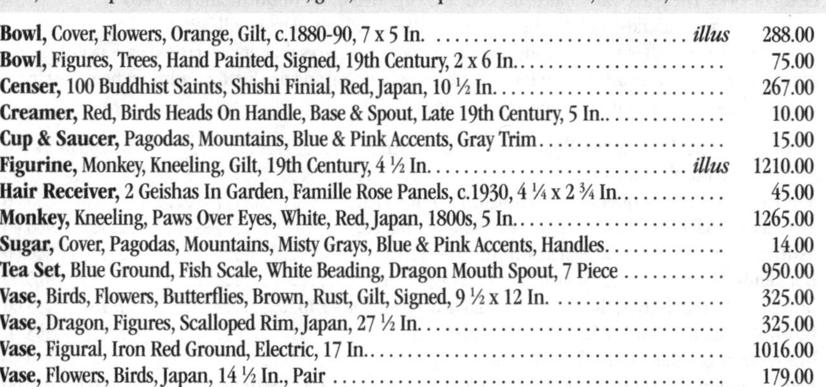

Bowl, Cover, Flowers, Orange, Gilt, c.1880-90, 7 x 5 In. .... *illus* 288.00
Bowl, Figures, Trees, Hand Painted, Signed, 19th Century, 2 x 6 In. 75.00
Censer, 100 Buddhist Saints, Shishi Finial, Red, Japan, 10 ½ In. 267.00
Creamer, Red, Birds Heads On Handle, Base & Spout, Late 19th Century, 5 In.. .... 10.00
Cup & Saucer, Pagodas, Mountains, Blue & Pink Accents, Gray Trim 15.00
Figurine, Monkey, Kneeling, Gilt, 19th Century, 4 ½ In. .... *illus* 1210.00
Hair Receiver, 2 Geishas In Garden, Famille Rose Panels, c.1930, 4 ¼ x 2 ¾ In. 45.00
Monkey, Kneeling, Paws Over Eyes, White, Red, Japan, 1800s, 5 In. 1265.00
Sugar, Cover, Pagodas, Mountains, Misty Grays, Blue & Pink Accents, Handles. 14.00
Tea Set, Blue Ground, Fish Scale, White Beading, Dragon Mouth Spout, 7 Piece 950.00
Vase, Birds, Flowers, Butterflies, Brown, Rust, Gilt, Signed, 9 ½ x 12 In. 325.00
Vase, Dragon, Figures, Scalloped Rim, Japan, 27 ½ In. 325.00
Vase, Figural, Iron Red Ground, Electric, 17 In. 1016.00
Vase, Flowers, Birds, Japan, 14 ½ In., Pair 179.00

KPM, Plaque, Woman, Long Hair, Blue Ribbon, Frame, Signed, Wagner, Marked, 6 ¾ x 5 In.
$2320.00

KPM, Urn, Allegory Of Putto, Goat, Lion, Masks, Blue Scepter Mark, Red Orb, 22 ½ In.
$360.00

Kutani, Bowl, Cover, Flowers, Orange, Gilt, c.1880-90, 7 x 5 In.
$288.00

As always, the edited listings in *Kovels' Antiques & Collectibles Price Guide 2010* aren't available on any website, but readers should visit Kovels.com for information on trends, tips, reproductions, marks, old prices, and more!

Kutani, Figurine, Monkey, Kneeling, Gilt, 19th Century, 4 ½ In.
$1210.00

Lacquer, Box, Game, Black Gilt, 12 Trays, Chinese, 19th Century, 5 x 15 x 12 In.
$880.00

Lalique, Bowl, Chene, Oak Leaves, Gondola Shape, Etched, Frosted, 4 x 7 In.
$293.00

TIP

Never wash lacquered wood. Just wipe it clean with a damp cloth. Water could seep into the base wood and cause damage.

Vase, Flowers, Orange, White, Green, 2 Mounted Handles, Japan, c.1890, 14 In. 239.00
Vase, Immortals, Kylins, Molded, Red Ground, Painted, 20th Century, 11 ¾ In. 125.00
Vase, Squares, Calligraphy, White Ground, Gilt, Handles, 9 ½ In. 550.00

L.G. WRIGHT Glass Company of New Martinsville, West Virginia, started selling glassware in 1937. Founder "Si" Wright contracted with Ohio and West Virginia glass factories to reproduce popular pressed glass patterns, like Rose & Snow, Baltimore Pear, and Three Face, and opalescent patterns, like Daisy & Fern and Swirl. Collectors can tell the difference between the original glasswares and L.G. Wright reproductions because of colors and differences in production techniques. Some L.G. Wright items are marked with an underlined W in a circle. Items that were made from old Northwood molds have an altered Northwood mark—an angled line was added to the N to make it look like a W. Collectors refer to this mark as "the wobbly W." The L.G. Wright factory was closed and the existing molds sold in 1999.

W

Daisy & Button, Bowl, Amber, Footed, 2 ½ x 5 ½ In. 12.50
Daisy & Button, Nappy, Amber, Handle, 2 x 6 ⅝ In. 17.50
Daisy & Button, Sugar & Creamer, Amber 25.00
Moon & Star, Banana Bowl, Green, 4 ¾ x 9 In. 30.00
Moon & Star, Candlestick, Amberina, 6 ¼ x 4 In. 35.00
Moon & Star, Compote, Amber, Scalloped Edge, 4 x 7 ½ In. 25.00
Moon & Star, Compote, Amberina, 6 ¾ x 8 In. 34.00
Moon & Star, Compote, Cover, Amberina, 10 In. 52.00
Moon & Star, Compote, Ruby, Amberina, 6 ½ x 6 ¼ In. 25.00
Moon & Star, Decanter, Red, Clear, Stopper, 1960s 288.00
Moon & Star, Lamp, Courting, Ruby 55.00
Moon & Star, Toothpick, Green, 2 ⅜ x 2 In. 10.00
Paneled Grape, Wine, Blue, 4 x 2 In. 10.00
Stars & Stripes, Tumbler, Cranberry Opalescent, 3 ⅝ x 2 ⅞ In. 77.00

LACQUER is a type of varnish. Collectors are most interested in the Chinese and Japanese lacquer wares made from the Japanese varnish tree. Lacquer wares are made from wood with many coats of lacquer. Sometimes the piece is carved or decorated with ivory or metal inlay.

Bowl, Courtyard, Harbor People, Black, Gilt, Chinese, 1800s, 14 x 7 In., Pair 633.00
Box, Food, Gilt Brown, Hollyhocks In Circle, Paktong Water Vase, 21 x 12 In. 856.00
Box, Food, Gilt Brown, Paktong Container, Hollyhocks In Circle, 20 x 11 ½ In. 649.00
Box, Game, Black Gilt, 12 Trays, Chinese, 19th Century, 5 x 15 x 12 In. .... *illus* 880.00
Box, Mother-Of-Pearl Inlay, Black, Riverscape, Gold Plated Interior, Japan, 5 ¾ x 16 ½ In. 266.00
Seal Case, Boat, Willow Tree, 5 Sections, 19th Century, Japan, 3 ½ In. 1896.00
Seal Case, Carriage, Insect, Gold Sprinkled Lacquer, 4 Sections, Pearl Inlay, Japan, 3 ½ In. ... 2252.00
Seal Case, Peacocks, Autumn Flowers, 5 Sections, Gold Sprinkled Lacquer, Japan, 3 ½ In. 2133.00
Sewing Box, Black, Lake Scene On Lid, Flowers, Original Contents, 5 ½ x 4 x 2 ¼ In. 135.00
Shrine, Black, Gilt, Calligraphy, 2 Sections, Doors, Stepped, Japan, 45 x 20 In. 1062.00
Stand, Cosmetic, Black, Gilt, Mon & Leaves, 4 Drawers, Chinese, 13 x 11 ½ In. 443.00
Tray, Bordeaux, Maroon Reserve, Gilt, Plants, Birds, 22 x 28 In. 420.00
Tray, Oval, Black, Allover Flowers, Fluted, 10 x 13 ½ In. 185.00
Tray, Regency, Black, Gilt, Figural Scene, Brown Reserve, 22 ¼ In. 360.00
Tray, Silver Mounted, Elongated Octagonal Shape, Handles, Chinoiserie, 23 x 32 In. 3600.00

LADY HEAD VASE, *see Head Vase.*

LALIQUE glass was made by Rene Lalique in Paris, France, between the 1890s and his death in 1945. The glass was molded, pressed, and engraved in Art Nouveau and Art Deco styles. Pieces were marked with the signature *R. Lalique*. Lalique glass is still being made. Pieces made after 1945 bear the mark *Lalique*. Some pieces that are advertised as ring dishes or pin dishes were listed as ashtrays in the Lalique factory catalog and are listed as ashtrays here. Jewelry made by Rene Lalique is listed in the Jewelry category.

R.LALIQUE

Ashtray, Archers, Deep Amber, Engraved, c.1922, 4 ½ In. .... 823.00 to 840.00
Ashtray, Ark Royal, Ship, 3 ½ In. 41.00
Ashtray, Bluets, Cornflowers, Clear, Frosted, 4 x 5 In. 58.00
Ashtray, Grenade, Art Deco, Deep Amber, 1928, 5 ½ In. 960.00
Ashtray, Moineau, Sparrow, Seated, Green, 1925, 4 In. 840.00
Bookends, Reverie, Frosted, Signed, 9 ¼ x 5 ¼ x 3 ½ In. 925.00
Bowl, Chene, Oak Leaves, Gondola Shape, Etched, Frosted, 4 x 7 In. .... *illus* 293.00
Bowl, Marguerites, Daisies, Signed, Paper Label, 3 x 14 In. 355.00
Bowl, Mesanges, Band Of Birds, 3 ¾ x 9 In. 380.00
Bowl, Nemours, Flower Heads, Enameled, Clear, Frosted, c.1929, 3 ⅞ x 10 In. .... 575.00 to 1020.00

Bowl, Nogent, Frosted Birds Base, Clear Bowl, c.1966, 3 ½ x 5 ½ In. 234.00
Bowl, Paons, Peacock, Feathers, Tapered Sides, 4 ¾ x 9 ½ In. 275.00
Bowl, Paons, Peacock Feathers, Etched, Blown, Clear, 2 ½ x 12 In. 600.00
Bowl, Perruches, Parakeets, Clear, Frosted, Blue, Green, R. Lalique, 4 ¼ x 9 ½ In. 5400.00
Bowl, Pinsons, Finches, Swirled Knot Design, Clear, Frosted, 4 x 9 In. .... 173.00 to 380.00
Bowl, Pissenlit, Dandelion Leaves, Clear, Mark, 9 x 3 In. 300.00
Bowl, Primaveres, Primroses, Cover, Molded, R. Lalique, 5 ¾ In. 1250.00
Bowl, Sirenes, Mermaids, Opalescent, c.1920, 14 In. 7800.00
Bowl, Volubilis, Morning Glory, Footed Shape, Yellow, Etched, Signed, 2 ¼ x 8 ½ In. 510.00
Box, Cover, Dancing Figures, Frosted, Signed D'Orsay, 3 ¾ In. 390.00
Box, Quatre Papillions, Lid, 4 Butterflies, Sepia, c.1900, 2 x 3 In. 2070.00
Candy Dish, Cyprins, Fish, Flowers, Leaves, Amber, Silk Lined Base, 1920s, 10 In. 1020.00
Carafe, Stopper, Sirenes & Grenouilles, Mermaids & Frogs, Clear, Frosted, Green Patina, 15 In. 2880.00
Centerpiece, Marguerites, Daisies, Sunburst Design, Clear, 3 x 13 In. 936.00
Charger, Cote D'Or, Nudes, Signed, 15 ¾ In. 750.00
Clock, Dahlia, Art Deco, Black Enamel Painted, Frosted, 1926, 7 In. 3840.00
Clock, Inseparables, Birds On Branches, Blue Patina, c.1926, 4 In. .... *illus* 3120.00
Clock, Moineaux, Sparrows, Frosted, Brown Patina, Ato Electrique Movement, 8 ½ x 6 ½ In. .. 2760.00
Compote, Nogent, 4 Sparrows, Clear, Frosted Stem, 3 ¼ x 5 ½ In. 150.00
Decanter, Coquilles, Shell Shape Stopper, Double Ring Neck, 1920, 13 ½ In. 3000.00
Decanter, Deux Danseuses, 2 Dancers, c.1912, 13 ½ In. 4750.00
Decanter, Masques, Silver Stopper, Grapes, Sepia Bacchus Face, 12 In. 2760.00
Decanter, Satyr, Satyr Bust, Handle, Brown, Patina, Stopper, 10 In. 1725.00
Figurine, 2 Fish, 11 ¼ In. 1080.00
Figurine, Angel, Clear, Gold Wings, 3 In. 176.00
Figurine, Angelfish, Teal Blue, Frosted, Signed, 2 In. 60.00
Figurine, Antelope, Frosted, Charcoal Gray Patina, Art Deco, 1929, 3 ½ In. 390.00
Figurine, Bird, 9 ½ x 11 ½ In. 292.00
Figurine, Bird, Head Down, 1 ¾ x 4 In., Tail Up, 1 ½ x 4 ¾ In., Pair 70.00
Figurine, Blue Jay, 4 ½ x 4 ½ In. 117.00
Figurine, Bull, Head Down, Leg Raised, Rectangular Base, Acid Etched, 3 ½ In. 192.00
Figurine, Chat Assis, Cat Seated, Frosted Body, Signed, 8 In. .... 438.00 to 644.00
Figurine, Chat Couche, Cat Crouching, Frosted, Molded, Inscribed, c.1960, 9 In. 708.00
Figurine, Danseuse, Nude Female Dancer, Frosted, 5 x 9 In. 585.00
Figurine, Deux Poissons, 2 Fish, 11 ½ In. 2232.00
Figurine, Dolphin, 4 ¼ x 4 ¼ In. 235.00
Figurine, Duck, Clear Frosted, Signed, 4 ½ In. 50.00
Figurine, Eagle, Clear, Frosted, Signed, 9 ½ In. 475.00
Figurine, Eagle Head, Clear, Frosted, Etched, Signed, 4 ½ In. 225.00
Figurine, Elephant, Raised Head & Trunk, 6 x 6 In. 263.00
Figurine, Female Nude, Frosted, Raised Arms, Clear Glass Base, Signed, 1900s, 9 In. 711.00
Figurine, Floral, Nude Figure, Female, Seated, 3 ½ In. .... 140.00 to 180.00
Figurine, Lion, Seated, 8 x 7 In. 646.00
Figurine, Lion Cubs, Reclining, Frosted, 3 x 5 In. 263.00
Figurine, Owl, Clear, 3 ½ In. 117.00
Figurine, Owl, Frosted, Clear, 4 x 2 In., Pair 176.00
Figurine, Rabbit, Frosted, 2 ¾ x 3 ½ In. 117.00
Figurine, Rabbit, Frosted, Textured, Crouching, 5 ½ In. 176.00
Figurine, Salamander, Emerald Green, Signed, Lalique, 3 x 6 ¾ x 2 ¼ In. 220.00
Figurine, Salamander, Green, Frosted, Signed, 6 ½ In. 80.00
Figurine, Siglavy Horse, Frosted, Clear, Stand, 6 x 7 In. 263.00
Figurine, Sirene, Opalescent Glass, c.1920, 4 In. 3360.00
Figurine, Stallion, 4 ½ In. 150.00
Figurine, Thais, Nude, Woman, Holding Drapery, Wood Base, 8 ½ In. 2400.00
Figurine, Toad, Clear, 3 x 4 In. 263.00
Figurine, Toba, Rhinoceros, Clear, 1990, 11 In. 300.00
Figurine, Turtle, Amber, 2 x 4 ½ In. 234.00
Figurine, Woman, Holding Lamb, 4 ½ x 2 ¼ In. 146.00
Flower Frog, Dove, Signed, 8 In. 425.00
Hood Ornament, Chrysis, Woman, Kneeling, Hair Flowing, 1931, 5 ½ In. .... 1680.00 to 2596.00
Hood Ornament, Coq Nain, Rooster, Smoky Topaz, c.1928, Incised, R. Lalique, 8 x 5 In. ... *illus* 1800.00
Hood Ornament, Perche, Fish, Clear & Frosted, c.1928, 3 ⅞ x 6 ⅛ In. 345.00
Hood Ornament, Sirene, Iridescent, Presentation Base 1955.00
Inkwell, Biches, Does In Forest, Amber, R. Lalique, c.1912, 4 ¼ x 5 ¾ In. 1800.00
Inkwell, Biches, Does In Forest, Gray Patina, 1912, 6 In. Square 2700.00
Inkwell, Colbert, Warblers, Clear, Frosted, Sepia Patina, c.1924, 10 ¼ In. 6600.00

TIP
Shallow nicks and rough edges on glass can sometimes be smoothed off with fine emery paper.

Lalique, Clock, Inseparables, Birds On Branches, Blue Patina, c.1926, 4 In.
$3120.00

Lalique, Hood Ornament, Coq Nain, Rooster, Smoky Topaz, c.1928, Incised, R. Lalique, 8 x 5 In.
$1800.00

Lalique, Inkwell, Myrtilles, Clear, Frosted, Black Enamel, c.1924, 8 ¼ In.
$3360.00

L

Lalique, Perfume Bottle, Gabilla, La Violette, Clear, Frosted, Enamel, R. Lalique, c.1925, 3 In.
$3600.00

Lalique, Plate, Algues, Seaweed, Black Amethyst, Marked, Lalique France, 7 ⅝ In., 5 Piece
$385.00

Lalique, Vase, Acanthes, Acanthus Leaves, Blue, Signed, R. Lalique, 11 In.
$16100.00

Inkwell, Myrtilles, Clear, Frosted, Black Enamel, c.1924, 8 ¼ In. . . . *illus* 3360.00
Inkwell, Nenuphar, Water Lily, Lemon Yellow, 1910, 2 ¾ In. . . . 2400.00
Inkwell, Quatre Sirenes, 4 Mermaids On Cover, Patina, 1920, 6 ¼ In. . . . 3600.00
Inkwell, Serpents, Snakes, Opalescent, Sepia Patina, c.1920, 6 ¼ In. . . . 2880.00
Inkwell, Trois Sirenes, 3 Mermaids, Swirls, Opalescent, Blue, 1921, 9 In. . . . 9600.00
Lamp, Mesanges, 2 Birds At Base, 7 x 14 In. . . . 322.00
Letter Seal, Poisson, Fish, Multicolored, 1912, 2 In., 6 Piece . . . 270.00
Mirror, Naiade, Water Nymph, Clear, Gold Foil Backing, Metal Frame, 3 ½ x 2 ¼ In. . . . 3600.00
Paperweight, Barbillon, Fish, Art Deco, 1930, 3 ¾ In. . . . 330.00
Paperweight, Moineau Sournois, Sparrow, Sepia Patina, 1930, 5 In. . . . 210.00
Paperweight, Pommes, Apple, 5 ½ In. . . . 179.00
Paperweight, Taureau, Bull, 3 ½ x 4 ½ In. . . . 146.00
Pendant, Muguet, Lily Of The Valley, Molded, Opalescent, Silk Cord . . . 533.00
Perfume Bottle, Amphitrite, Shell, Blue Patina, Figurine Stopper, c.1920, 3 ¾ In. . . . 2280.00
Perfume Bottle, Amphitrite, Shell, Green, Figurine Stopper, c.1920, 3 ½ In. . . . 5100.00
Perfume Bottle, Amphitrite, Shell, White, Figurine Stopper, c.1920, 3 ½ In. . . . 2400.00
Perfume Bottle, Bouchon Cassis, Clear, Red Enamel & Stopper, R. Lalique, 4 ½ In. . . . 14500.00
Perfume Bottle, Clairefontaine, Lily-Of-Valley Stopper, Clear, Frosted, Signed, 4 ¼ In. . . . 100.00
Perfume Bottle, Corday, Tzigane, Frosted, Clear, Vertical Zipper, Brown Enamel Letters, 4 In. 240.00
Perfume Bottle, Danseuses Egyptiennes No. 1, Clear, Frosted, Orange Enamel, c.1926, 5 In. . 1140.00
Perfume Bottle, Deux Fleurs, Overlapping Discs, Pierced Stopper, 4 x 4 In., Pair . . . 263.00
Perfume Bottle, D'Orsay, Roses, No. 3, Clear, Frosted, Sepia Patina, c.1912, 4 In. . . . 3360.00
Perfume Bottle, Forvil, Les Cinq Fleurs, Flowers, Stems, Cylinder, Stopper, 4 In. . . . 1380.00
Perfume Bottle, Gabilla, La Violette, Clear, Frosted, Enamel, R. Lalique, c.1925, 3 In. . . *illus* 3600.00
Perfume Bottle, Marquila, Impressed Artichoke Design, Green Patina, Signed, Stopper, 3 In. 1140.00
Perfume Bottle, Molinard, Bacchantes, Engraved, 1929, 4 ¾ In. . . . 1440.00
Perfume Bottle, Molinard, Figural, Bacchantes, Sepia Patina, Atomizer, 1927, 5 ½ In. . . . 720.00
Perfume Bottle, Molinard, Le Baiser Du Faune, Clear, Frosted, c.1928, 5 ¾ In. . . . 4800.00
Perfume Bottle, Pan, Classical Masks, Clear, Frosted, Sepia Patina, c.1920, 5 In. . . . 2520.00
Perfume Bottle, Pan, Classical Masks, Flowers, Brown Patina, Signed, Stopper, 5 In. . . . 1955.00
Perfume Bottle, Perles, Clear, Frosted, Brown Patina, c.1926, 5 ¾ In., Pair . . . 660.00
Perfume Bottle, Roger & Gallet, Flausa, No. 3, Clear, Frosted, Sepia Patina, 4 ¾ In. . . . 4200.00
Perfume Bottle, Roger & Gallet, Le Jade, No. 15, Green, Gray Patina, 3 ¼ In. . . . 2400.00
Perfume Bottle, Volnay, Ambre De Siam, Woman & Thorns Stopper, Frosted, 4 ¾ x 3 In. . . . 25200.00
Perfume Burner, Papillons, Butterflies, Opalescent, Blue, Green Patina, R. Lalique, c.1920, 7 ½ In. 4500.00
Perfume Burner, Sirenes, Mermaids, Clear, Frosted, R. Lalique, c.1920, 6 ¾ In. . . . 2040.00
Plaque, Tree, Black, Signed, 11 ½ In. . . . 125.00
Plate, Algues, Seaweed, Black Amethyst, Marked, Lalique France, 7 ⅝ In., 5 Piece . . . *illus* 385.00
Plate, Annual, 1965, Deux Oiseaux, 2 Birds, Clear, 8 In. . . . 380.00 to 585.00
Plate, Annual, 1967, Fish Ballet, 5 Swimming Fish, Clear, 1967, 8 In. . . . 146.00
Plate, Annual, 1971, Hibou, Owl, 8 ¼ In. . . . 94.00
Plate, Annual, 1972, Coquillage, Shell, 8 ¼ In. . . . 117.00
Plate, Annual, 1973, Petit Geai, Jayling, Bird Head, 8 In. . . . 70.00
Plate, Annual, 1975, Duo De Poisson, Fish Duet, 8 ¼ In. . . . 117.00
Plate, Antelope, Clear, Etched, 1965-76, Box, 8 ½ In., 12 Piece . . . 480.00
Plate, Asters, Stenciled, R. Lalique, c.1930, 10 ¾ In. . . . 500.00
Plate, Coquilles, 4 Shells, Clear, Opalescent, Signed, 6 ¾ In. . . . 300.00
Plate, Fleurons, Stenciled, R. Lalique, c.1930, 10 ½ In. . . . 400.00
Plate, Ondes, Waves, Opalescent, Acid Etched, R. Lalique, c.1935, 10 ¾ In. . . . 600.00
Plate, Ondines, Water Nymphs, Opalescent, 1921, 10 ¾ In. . . . 1200.00
Plate, Oursins, Sea Urchin, Stenciled, R. Lalique, c.1930, 11 In. . . . 500.00
Plate, Pinsons, Finches, Stenciled, R. Lalique, c.1930, 10 ¾ In. . . . 450.00
Powder Box, Duncan, Figural, Female Nude, Green Patina, 1931, 3 ¾ In. Square . . . 720.00
Powder Box, Nina Ricci, Figural, 3 Nude Neoclassical Women, 1950s, 4 ½ In. . . . 390.00
Sconce, Dahlias, Frosted, c.1921, 8 In., Pair . . . 2640.00
Swizzle Stick, Barr, Masks, Clear, Frosted, Leather Box, c.1931, 5 In., 12 Piece . . . 2880.00
Vase, Acacia, Gray, Signed, R. Lalique, c.1930, 8 In. . . . 1000.00
Vase, Acanthes, Acanthus Leaves, Blue, Signed, R. Lalique, 11 In. . . . *illus* 16100.00
Vase, Ajaccio, Sleeping Impalas, Raised Stars, Green Patina, Signed, 7 ⅞ In. . . . *illus* 2300.00
Vase, Albert, Clear, 2 Falcon Handles, 7 In, Pair. . . . 3450.00
Vase, Archers, Dark Amber, Intaglio Molded, Impressed, Signed, R. Lalique, 10 ½ In. . . . 6000.00
Vase, Avallon, Impressed Birds, Branches, Fruit, Blue Patina, 1927, 6 In. . . . 1955.00 to 2400.00
Vase, Avallon, Impressed Birds, Branches, Fruit, Opalescent, Blue Patina, 6 In., Pair . . . 4500.00
Vase, Bacchantes, Encircling Female Nudes, Black, 9 ⅝ In. . . . 4800.00
Vase, Bacchantes, Encircling Female Nudes, Frosted, c.1946, 10 In. . . . 1770.00 to 3738.00
Vase, Bacchantes, Encircling Female Nudes, Opalesent, Blue, Green, c.1927, 9 In. . . . 25000.00

Vase, Biskra, Palm Leaves, Blue, Frosted, 1932, 11 ½ In. 1800.00
Vase, Bouchardon, Bulbous Body, Figural Female & Flower, Handles, 5 In. 4025.00
Vase, Camargue, 4 Cartouches, Horses Rearing, Frosted, Scalloped Border, 11 ¼ In. 6900.00
Vase, Campanule, Bellflower, Frosted, Petals, Clear Ground, 6 x 4 In. 546.00
Vase, Ceylan, Paired Birds, Opalescent, Marked, R. Lalique, 9 ½ In., Pair 5500.00
Vase, Chamarande, Wild Roses, Handles, Topaz, White Patina, 7 ¾ In. 2880.00
Vase, Claude, Long Stem, Bulbous Base, Frosted, 14 x 6 In. 263.00
Vase, Coqs Et Plumes, 12 Strutting Cock Roosters, Blue Patina, Engraved, 6 In. 1610.00 to 1783.00
Vase, Coquilles, Overlapping Scallop, Shells, Opalescent, 7 ¼ In. 2400.00
Vase, Coquilles, Overlapping Scallop Shells, Blue Patina, Signed, 7 In. 1610.00
Vase, Damiers, Radiating Black Squares, Etched Ground, Signed, 9 ¼ In. 5750.00
Vase, Dampierre, Protruding Birds, 2 Handles, Clear, Frosted, Pedestal, 5 x 5 In. 146.00 to 351.00
Vase, Davos, Bubble Clusters, Cylinder Shape, Tapered Base, Marked, 1900s, 11 In. 711.00
Vase, Davos, Bubble Clusters, Opalescent, 10 x 7 In. 4973.00
Vase, Dentele, Notched Ribs, Clear & Frosted, c.1912, 7 ½ In. 720.00
Vase, Deux Moineaux Bavardant, 2 Sparrows On Branches, Sepia Patina, 1920, 8 ¼ In. 1800.00
Vase, Domremy, Raised Thistle, Emerald Green, Leaves, White Patina, 8 ¼ In. 5750.00
Vase, Druide, Overlapping Mistletoe Branches, Emerald, White Patina, R. Lalique, 6 ¾ In. 3900.00
Vase, Druide, Overlapping Mistletoe Branches, Opalescent, White, Engraved, R. Lalique, c.1930, 7 In. 1400.00
Vase, Elisabeth, Protruding Birds, Branches, Frosted Clear, Pedestal, 5 x 5 In. 293.00 to 410.00
Vase, Epis, Leaves & Flared Ribs, Mid 20th Century, Signed, 7 In. 189.00
Vase, Espalion, Allover Ferns, Green, Opalescent, 7 In. 1955.00
Vase, Espalion, Stylized Ferns, Frosted Blue, Signed, R. Lalique, 7 ½ In. *illus* 2400.00
Vase, Eucalyptus, Vertical Overlapping Leaves, Green Patina, Molded, R. Lalique, c.1920, 6 ½ In. 1500.00
Vase, Fontainebleau, Molded Grapevines, Cobalt Blue, Flared Rim, c.1930, 6 ⅝ In. 431.00
Vase, Formose, Swirling Carp, Red, 6 ½ In. 8190.00
Vase, Gobelet, 6 Figurines, Women Holding Bouquets, Olive Green, 8 In. 3795.00
Vase, Graines, Molded Seed Pods At Base, Acid Etched, R. Lalique, c.1940, 7 ¾ In. 2000.00
Vase, Grenade, Amber, Engraved, Bulbous, R. Lalique, 4 ½ x 4 ½ In. 2880.00
Vase, Gros Scarabees, Molded Beetles, Gray Ground, Narrow Mouth, Round, Signed, 12 In. 7200.00
Vase, Guirlandes, Overlapping Crimped Bands, Flaring Clear Rim, Opalescent Foot, 8 ½ In. 3220.00
Vase, Hiboux, Owls, Art Deco, Marie-Claude, 5 ¼ In. 385.00
Vase, Luxembourg, Cherubs, Garlands, 10 ½ In. 600.00
Vase, Malines, Pointed Leaves, Frosted, Clear, 4 ¾ In. 400.00
Vase, Meandres, Wavy Bands, Frosted, 6 ½ In. 1755.00
Vase, Moissae, Overlapping Raised Leaves, Deep Amber, Stenciled, R. Lalique, c.1927, 5 ⅛ In. 275.00
Vase, Monnaie Du Pape, Money Plant, Cased Opalescent, Blue, c.1914, R. Lalique, 9 x 6 In. *illus* 4500.00
Vase, Mossi, Large Hobnails, Signed R. Lalique, 8 In. 604.00
Vase, Narcisse, Abstract Swirl, 10 ½ In. 877.00
Vase, Ondines, Water Nymphs, Etched, Clear, 9 ½ x 7 ½ In. 1170.00
Vase, Orleans, Molded Flower Heads Around Flared Rim, Opalescent, 8 x 9 In. 1113.00
Vase, Ormeaux, Overlapping Elm Leaves, Globular, Blue Opalescent, 1926, 6 ¼ In. 1440.00
Vase, Ormeaux, Overlapping Elm Leaves, Globular, Charcoal Gray, 1926, 6 ½ In. 1800.00
Vase, Ornis, Opalescent Birds, Handles, Foot, Signed, 7 ¼ In. 4313.00
Vase, Palmes, Overlapping Palm Leaves, Cased Yellow, c.1923, 4 ⅜ In. 2040.00
Vase, Perruches, Parakeets, Clear, Frosted, 1919, 10 In. 2160.00
Vase, Piriac, Fish & Waves At Base, Smoky Green, Signed, 7 ¼ In. 3795.00
Vase, Piriac, Fish & Waves At Base, Topaz, 8 In. 2760.00
Vase, Plumes, Ostrich Feathers, Brown Patina, Molded, R. Lalique, c.1928, 8 In. 1250.00
Vase, Poissons, Overlapping Spiky Fish, Creamy White, Gray Patina, Signed, 9 In. 5175.00
Vase, Poivre, Pepper Berries, Dark Topaz, Molded, R. Lalique, c.1937, 9 ¾ x 3 ½ In. 4600.00
Vase, Poivre, Pepper Berries, Topaz, White Patina, c.1921, 9 ½ x 9 ¼ In. 3600.00
Vase, Rampillion, Cabochons & Flowers, Green Patina, Marked, R. Lalique, c.1930, 5 x 4 ¼ In. 1000.00
Vase, Ronces, Thorny Branches, Blue, Japanese Sake Flask Shape, 1921, 9 ½ In. 7800.00
Vase, Royat, Vertical Molded Ridges, Tapered Shapes, Turned Rim, 6 x 8 In. 234.00
Vase, Saint-Francois, Finches On Branches, Frosted Ground, 7 In. 3450.00
Vase, Saint-Francois, Finches On Branches, Frosted Ground, Green Patina, 7 In. 1725.00
Vase, Saint-Francois, Finches On Branches, Opalescent, c.1940, 7 x 6 ¾ In. 2106.00
Vase, Saint-Marc, Birds On Horizontal Bands, Clear, Frosted, Patina, R. Lalique, c.1939, 6 ¾ In. 1125.00
Vase, Sauge, Sage Leaves, Clear & Frosted, Green Patina, c.1923, 10 In. 1680.00
Vase, Sauterelles, Grasshoppers, Swordlike Leaves, Sky Blue, Marked, 10 ¾ In. 10062.00
Vase, Scarabees, Beetles, Clear, 2 Ear Handles Holding 2 Gray Scarab Rings, 13 In. 3163.00
Vase, Silenes, Pan Heads Among Leaves, 8 x 7 In. 2106.00
Vase, Six Figurines Et Masques, Sepia Tint, Opalescent, R. Lalique, 9 ½ In. 6850.00
Vase, Stopper, Douze Figurines Avec Bouchon, Sepia Patina, 1920, 11 ¼ In. 6000.00
Vase, Sylvie, 2 Birds, Clear, Flower Frog, 1970s, 8 x 5 In., 2 Piece 644.00

Lalique, Vase, Ajaccio, Sleeping Impalas, Raised Stars, Green Patina, Signed, 7 ⅞ In.
$2300.00

Lalique, Vase, Espalion, Stylized Ferns, Frosted Blue, Signed, R. Lalique, 7 ½ In.
$2400.00

Lalique, Vase, Monnaie Du Pape, Money Plant, Cased Opalescent, Blue, c.1914, R. Lalique, 9 x 6 In.
$4500.00

Lalique, Water Set, Jaffa, Amber, Frosted, 9-In. Pitcher, 4 ¾-In. Tumbler, Tray, 8 Piece
$4313.00

Lamp, Argand, 2-Light, Hooper, Bronze, Cut Pattern Pendants, Etched, 1820s, 18 ½ In.
$1045.00

Lamp, Argand, Satyr Masks, Cut Glass, Frosted, Bronze, J. & I. Cox, 1880s, 17 ½ In.
$1320.00

Lamp, Betty, Double, Forged Reservoirs, Suspended Lamp Hook, 13 x 5 ½ In.
$29.00

Vase, Tournai, Leaf Panels, Gray, Green Patina, 1924, 5 In. 390.00
Vase, Tournesols, Sunflowers, Electric Blue, R. Lalique, c.1927, 4 ½ In. 3600.00
Vase, Tournesols, Sunflowers, Raised Centers, Wide Neck, Blue Patina, Opalescent, 1927, 4 ½ In. 1800.00
Vase, Tournesols, Sunflowers, Raised Centers, Wide Rim, Yellow Patina, 1927, 4 ¾ In. 1440.00
Water Set, Jaffa, Amber, Frosted, 9-In. Pitcher, 4 ¾-In. Tumbler, Tray, 8 Piece *illus* 4313.00

LAMPS of every type, from the early oil-burning Betty and Phoebe lamps to the recent electric lamps with glass or beaded shades, interest collectors. Fuels used in lamps changed through the years; whale oil (1800–1840), camphene (1828), Argand (1830), lard (1833–1863), turpentine and alcohol (1840s), gas (1850–1879), kerosene (1860), and electricity (1879) are the most common. Other lamps are listed by manufacturer or type of material.

Aladdin, B-52, Washington Drape, Crow's Foot, Amber, Chimney, 1940, 9 In. 70.00
Aladdin, B-75, Lincoln Drape, Crow's Foot, Alcacite, Chimney, 1940-49, 10 ¼ In. 275.00
Aladdin, B-76A, Simplicity, Alcacite, Chimney, 1948-1953, 10 In. 100.00
Aladdin, B-77, Tall Lincoln Drape, Crow's Foot, Ruby Amber, 1940-49, 10 ¼ In. 400.00 to 450.00
Aladdin, B-83, Beehive, Ruby Amber, Chimney, 10-In. Ruby Half-Shade, 8 ½ In. 300.00
Aladdin, B-88, Vertique, Yellow Moonstone, Model B Burner, Kerosene, c.1938 495.00
Aladdin, B-116, Corinthian, Pink Opaque, Chimney, 8 ½ In. 200.00 to 318.00
Aladdin, G-43, Alacite, Silk Shade, Fired On Coral Base, Silk Shade, 17 In. 75.00
Aladdin, Model B, Quilt Pink, White Moonstone, 1935-36 404.00
Aladdin, Model B, Vertique, Yellow Moonstone, 8 ¾ In. 465.00
Aladdin, Model B-115, Corinthian, Green Moonstone, 1935-36 247.00
Aladdin, Treasure, Chromium 35.00
Aladdin, Washington Drape, Crystal, Plain Stem 65.00
Argand, 2-Light, Bronze, Baluster, Crystal Shades, Tripod Feet, c.1850, 21 In. 3231.00
Argand, 2-Light, Classical, Bronze, Baluster Shades, Urn Shape Reserves, 17 x 18 In., Pair 2056.00
Argand, 2-Light, Hooper, Bronze, Cut Pattern Pendants, Etched, 1820s, 18 ½ In. *illus* 1045.00
Argand, Gilt Lacquered Brass, Spring-Loaded Burner, c.1850, 22 In. 575.00
Argand, Satyr Masks, Cut Glass, Frosted, Bronze, J. & I. Cox, 1880s, 17 ½ In. *illus* 1320.00
Art Nouveau, Hyacinth Shade, Tree Trunk Metal Base, Green, Pink, Brown, 1910s, 26 In. 1200.00
Arts & Crafts, Frog, Holding Tulip Shade, 12 x 10 x 6 In. 1088.00
Astral, Cornelius, Brass, Patina, Red Glass Shade, c.1845, 35 In. 940.00
Betty, Copper, Iron, Impressed P.D., Peter Derr, 1835, 6 In. 4680.00
Betty, Copper, Iron, Impressed P.D., Peter Derr, 1842, 5 ¾ In. 3744.00
Betty, Double, Forged Reservoirs, Suspended Lamp Hook, 13 x 5 ½ In. *illus* 29.00
Betty, Maple, Turned, Black Paint, 18th Century, 6 In. 3510.00
Betty, Tin, Teardrop Shape, Hanging Hook, Chain, Wick Holder, 5 x 4 x 3 In. 88.00
Bouillote, 3-Light, Red Tole Shade, Dish Base, 30 ¼ In. 518.00
Bouillote, 4-Light, Brass, Tole Shade, 25 ¾ In. 120.00
Bouillote, 4-Light, Tole Shade, Neoclassical Brass Base, Early 20th Century, 28 In. 385.00
Bradley & Hubbard lamps are included in the Bradley & Hubbard category.
Chandelier, 3-Light, Art Nouveau, Leaded Glass Shades, Pink, Blue, France, c.1900, 23 x 35 In. 2530.00
Chandelier, 3-Light, Copper Patinated Brass, Frosted Globe, Ribbon Swags, 61 x 28 In. 2070.00
Chandelier, 3-Light, Louis XV Style, Bronze Dore, Swags, Ribbons, 34 In. *illus* 1650.00
Chandelier, 3-Light, Louis XVI, Iron, Rose Opaline Glass, Cut Drops, 21 x 12 In. 720.00
Chandelier, 4-Light, 4 Antlers, Chains, Brass Canopy, Shades, Germany, 30 In. 330.00
Chandelier, 4-Light, Art Nouveau, Opal Shades, Green Pulled Feathers, 3-Chain Brass Base, 56 In. 1495.00
Chandelier, 4-Light, Arts & Crafts, Iron, Slag Glass, 20 x 26 In. 750.00
Chandelier, 4-Light, Central Urn, Shades, Blue, Gilt, Tin, 17 In. 425.00
Chandelier, 4-Light, Louis XV Style, Gilt Bronze, Crystal Drops, 45 ½ x 26 In. 658.00
Chandelier, 4-Light, Louis XVI, Brass, Cut Glass, Faux Candles, Early 1900s, 29 x 19 In. 2400.00
Chandelier, 4-Light, Louis XVI Style, Silver Plate, Amethyst Pendalogues, France, 39 x 16 In. 1920.00
Chandelier, 4-Light, Tin, Black, 20th Century, 21 In. 29.00
Chandelier, 5-Light, Brass, Milk Glass, Embossed, Acorn Finial, Early 1900s, 21 In. *illus* 440.00
Chandelier, 5-Light, Glass Spheres, Black Enameled Sleeves, Brass Ceiling Cap, 34 x 15 In. 1200.00
Chandelier, 6-Light, Carved Wood, Baluster Shape, Scrolled Supports, Italy, 29 x 27 In. 940.00
Chandelier, 6-Light, Cone Shape, Black & White, c.1960, 28 In. 1020.00
Chandelier, 6-Light, Crystal, Tiered Support, Scrolled Arms, Prisms, 20th Century, 25 x 22 In. 403.00
Chandelier, 6-Light, Empire Style, Bronze, Patinated, Gilt Lacquered Brass, 18 ¾ x 19 In. 2160.00
Chandelier, 6-Light, George III, Brass, 22 x 24 In. 819.00
Chandelier, 6-Light, Green Glass, Ormolu Band, Rosette Knop, Russia, c.1813, 28 In. 37500.00
Chandelier, 6-Light, Iron, Shells, Candleholders, Electrified, 40 x 26 In. 1080.00
Chandelier, 6-Light, Louis XVI Style, Cut Glass Jewel Chains, Gilt Brass, 21 x 23 In. 780.00
Chandelier, 6-Light, Regency, Gilt, Patinated Metal, Cut Glass, 38 x 24 In. 13750.00
Chandelier, 6-Light, Renaissance Revival, Gilt, Hexagonal Arms, Beaded, Leaves, 37 x 32 In. 3600.00
Chandelier, 6-Light, Renaissance Revival, Iron, Leaf & Spiral Accent, 33 In. 593.00
Chandelier, 6-Light, Rock Crystal Prisms & Drops, Metal Frame, Painted Silver, c.1910, 32 x 31 In. 7050.00

Chandelier, 8-Light, Andre Arbus, Glass, Gilt, 1940s, 33 In. 18750.00
Chandelier, 8-Light, Blanc-De-Chine, Green Pottery, Eglomise, Cut Glass, Brass, 18 x 15 In. 1680.00
Chandelier, 8-Light, Bronze, Crystal, Prism Drop Finials, Round Frame, c.1890, 40 In. 748.00
Chandelier, 8-Light, Cast Metal, Cased Glass Standard, Cage Shape, Prisms, Finials, 43 In. 3600.00
Chandelier, 8-Light, Cast Metal, Gilt, Candle Style Mounts, c.1900, 20 In. 587.00
Chandelier, 8-Light, Empire Style, Gilt Metal, Cut Glass, Leaf Corona, Faceted Beads, 39 In. 840.00
Chandelier, 8-Light, Gates Moore, Wooden Ball, Waxed Candle Covers, Electrified, 1900s, 25 x 12 In. 147.00
Chandelier, 8-Light, Gothic, Iron, 25 x 30 In. 550.00
Chandelier, 8-Light, Silver Plated Branches, Williamsburg, 19th Century, 22 x 22 In. 715.00
Chandelier, 8-Light, Venetian, Scrolled Arms, Glass Drops, Amethyst Rosettes, 31 x 31 In. 1610.00
Chandelier, 8-Light, White Enameled, Glass Bobeches, Italy, 39 ½ x 22 In. 1800.00
Chandelier, 9-Light, Louis XV Style, Brass, Cage Shape, Clear Glass, Scrolled Arms, Prisms, 38 In. 1304.00
Chandelier, 9-Light, Louis XVI, Gilt Brass, Gold Spangles, Frosted Glass, France, 42 x 24 In. 1920.00
Chandelier, 10-Light, Bronze, Patina, Parcel Gilt Brass, France, 36 ½ x 22 In. 1680.00
Chandelier, 10-Light, Iron Arms, Wooden Center, D. Smith, Ohio, 1900s, 36 x 20 In. 440.00
Chandelier, 12-Light, 2 Tiers, Brass, Scrolled Arms, Dutch, 18th Century, 26 In. 1700.00
Chandelier, 12-Light, Caramel Slag Glass Panel Shade, Bronze Scrolls, Chains, Cap, 30 x 56 In. 8050.00
Chandelier, 12-Light, Wood, Brass, Patina, Multicolor, Carved, Gilt, 39 x 30 In. 1800.00
Chandelier, 14-Light, Antlers, Elk, Caribou, Candleholders, Electrified, Austro-German, 36 x 58 In. 6000.00
Chandelier, 14-Light, Bronze Dore, Basket Shape, Prism Swags, Central Drop Finial, 72 In. 2875.00
Chandelier, 15-Light, Cut Glass, Prisms, Spikes, Tiered Candlearms, 35 x 29 ½ In. 6900.00
Chandelier, 15-Light, Louis XV, Bronze, Clear & Amethyst Glass, Serpentine, 30 In. 770.00
Chandelier, 18-Light, Neoclassical, Gilt Brass, Cut Glass, 3 Tiers, Spears & Drops, 36 x 33 In. 4800.00
Chandelier, 24-Light, Wirework, Tiered, S Shape Arm, 43 x 46 In. 450.00
Chandelier, Arts & Crafts, Cast Images, Pink Slag, Square Brass Frame Shades, 22 x 12 In. 420.00
Chandelier, Brass, Cut Glass Prisms, Acanthus Scroll Arms, Brass Fonts, 1800s, 36 x 47 In. 1410.00
Chandelier, Brass Dome, Cutout Detail, 4-Sided, Slag Glass, X Overlay Design, 36 x 22 In. 1800.00
Chandelier, Kalmar, Clear Glass Beaded Strings, Silver Frame, 56 x 23 In. 3900.00
Chandelier, Lobmeyer, Enameled Metal, Crystal Rays, Brass Shaft, c.1960, 52 x 13 In. 5400.00
Chandelier, Louis XVI Style, Gilt Metal, Baluster Shape, Sevres Style, Porcelain, 42 x 35 In. 5760.00
Chandelier, Louis XVI Style, Gilt Metal, Crystal, Leaf Corona, Beaded Prisms, 33 x 10 ½ In. 472.00
Chandelier, Lucite, Pressed Glass Drops, Brass Frame, 23 x 22 In. 2640.00
Chandelier, Radiating Glass Rays, Brass Frame, 38 x 27 In. 6000.00
Chandelier, Silver, Steel Acorn Drop Finials, Brass Chains, Continental, 8 x 12 ½ In., Pair 978.00
Chandelier, Stained Glass, Amber & Green Panels, Grapes, Apples, Pears, Green Stems, 27 In. 115.00
Chandelier, Victorian, Brass, Shades, 19th Century, 37 x 29 In. 780.00
Chandelier, Vistosi, Snowball, Clear Glass Plates, Opaque Inclusions, Italy, 1960, 22 x 20 In. 1680.00
Electric, 2-Light, Arts & Crafts, 2 Lanterns, Triangle Shade, Iron Overlay, Base, Stem, 20 x 19 In. 960.00
Electric, 2-Light, Bronze Cherub, Garland, Marble Base, Eagle Feet, c.1900, 24 In. 805.00
Electric, 2-Light, Copper, Bronze Leaf Arms, Mosaic Glass Dome, Austria, c.1910, 20 x 10 In. 1304.00
Electric, 2-Light, Copper, Mica Shade, Bronze, 20 ¾ x 16 In. 6000.00
Electric, 2-Light, Domed Glass Shade, 16 Bent Petal Panels, Green, Red, Metal Base, 20 x 16 In. 1304.00
Electric, 2-Light, Octagon Yellow Slag Glass, Metal Overlay, Bulbous Base, c.1905, 18 x 20 In. 711.00
Electric, 3-Light, Bullet Shape Center, Sailboat Decoration, Silver Plated Frame, 18 In. 175.00
Electric, 3-Light, Domed Shade, Pierced Rim, Cutouts, Bronze Base, Stone Nuggets, 24 x 15 In. 2252.00
Electric, 3-Light, Mosaic Glass, Lilies, White, Green Ground, Drum Shade, Metal, 1900s, 18 x 23 In. 1304.00
Electric, 4-Light, Jeweled Crystal Prisms, Amethyst Chimes, Silver Base, Leaves, Deco, 31 In. 6900.00
Electric, A & W, Hanging, Tiffany Style, 1960s, 21 x 47 In. 305.00
Electric, A. & P. Giacomo Castiglioni, Gatto Piccolo, Plastic, Metal, Italy, c.1960, 12 x 7 In., Pair 720.00
Electric, A. Court, Tortoiseshell Shape, Backlit, Aluminum, Paper Label, 22 x 33 In. 1800.00
Electric, A. Lelii, Metal, Brass, Marble, Black, Brown, White, c.1950, 78 In. 8750.00
Electric, A. Masson, Glazed Ceramic, Geometric Openings, White, Orange, c.1950, 31 In. 6000.00
Electric, Abet Print, Laminated Covered Wood, Chrome Plated Metal, Italy, c.1979, 98 In. 15000.00
Electric, Abstract, Curved Arm, Orange & White Shade, Brass, Stone Base, Austria, c.1920, 17 In. 444.00
Electric, Acrylic, Spiral Staircase, Footed Beveled Base, Chocolate Shade, 36 In. 900.00
Electric, Action Corp., Motion, Niagara Falls, Cast-Iron Top, Base, Chicago, 9 ¼ In. 100.00
Electric, Arredoluce, Easel, Enamel, Metal, Brass, c.1965, 82 In. 10000.00
Electric, Art Deco, Alabaster Shade, Dancing Figure, Gilt Bronze Base, Germany, 15 ½ In. 510.00
Electric, Art Deco, Amethyst Crystal, Chromed Steel, Pad Feet, Linen Shade, 21 In. 1680.00
Electric, Art Deco, Dancing Woman, Amethyst Frosted Glass Shade, 12 ½ In. *illus* 403.00
Electric, Art Deco, Empire State Building, Metal, Glass Shade, Geometric, Frosted, 69 In., Pair 1659.00
Electric, Art Deco, Figural, Dutch Boy, Pushing Ball, 12 x 9 In. 510.00
Electric, Art Deco, Gold Iridescent Glass Shades, Figural Woman, Flowing Dress, Rocky Ledge, 29 In. 374.00
Electric, Art Deco, Iron, Bronze, Square Base, 6-Panel Shade, 67 ½ In. 960.00
Electric, Art Deco, Woman Holding Torch, Skyscraper, Semimatte Ivory Glaze, 64 In. 4600.00
Electric, Art Glass, Metal, Bonnet Shape Shade, Puffy, Roses, Multicolored, 13 ½ In. 2510.00
Electric, Art Glass Shade, Flowers, Bronze Base, 1910, 57 ½ In. 705.00

Lamp, Chandelier, 3-Light, Louis XV Style, Bronze Dore, Swags, Ribbons, 34 In.
$1650.00

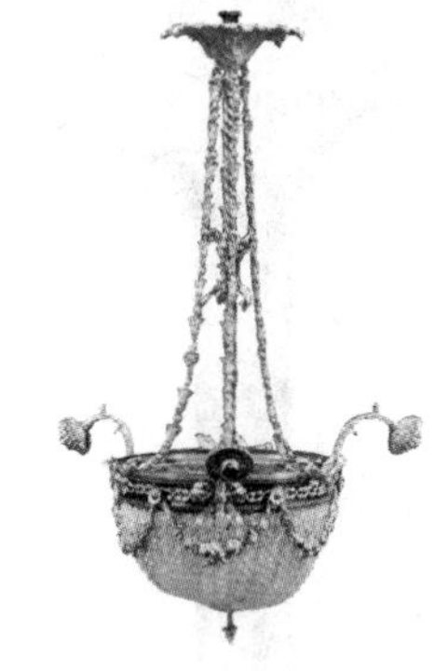

Lamp, Chandelier, 5-Light, Brass, Milk Glass, Embossed, Acorn Finial, Early 1900s, 21 In.
$440.00

Lamp, Electric, Art Deco, Dancing Woman, Amethyst Frosted Glass Shade, 12 ½ In.
$403.00

L

Lamp, Electric, Arts & Crafts, Leaded Glass, 12 Panels, Oak, c.1910, 77 x 26 ½ In.
$8250.00

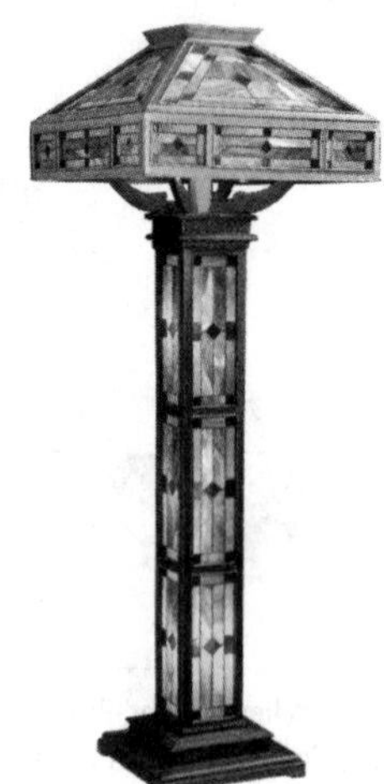

Lamp, Electric, Bigelow & Kennard, Leaded Glass, Flowers, Bronze Base, 23 x 18 In.
$14400.00

Lamp, Electric, Duffner & Kimberly, Leaded Glass, Water Lilies, Patina, 3 Sockets, 26 x 19 In.
$6000.00

Electric, Art Nouveau, Bent Metal, Glass, Amber Cone Shape Panels, Embossed Metal Base, 22 In. 259.00
Electric, Art Nouveau, Glass Flame Shade, Brass Lily Pad Base, Stems, Flowers, 31 x 5 ¾ In. . 1560.00
Electric, Art Nouveau, Glass Shade, Leaves, Flowers, Trunk Stem, Bronze, 1900s, 22 In. 1185.00
Electric, Art Nouveau, Slag Glass, 4 Panels, Spelter Base, Overlay, 22 x 12 In.. . . . . 325.00
Electric, Art Nouveau, Slag Glass, 8-Panel Shade, Bronze, Flower Shaft, 21 ½ x 14 In. 856.00
Electric, Arteluce, Chrome, Steel, Black Frame, Spherical Light Elements, H-Shape Base, 59 ¾ In. . 360.00
Electric, Arts & Clay Co., Classic No. 2, Hammered Copper Base, Mica Lined Shade, 23 x 25 In. 1020.00
Electric, Arts & Crafts, 4-Panel Slag Glass Shade, Oak Base, 17 x 23 In. 600.00
Electric, Arts & Crafts, 6-Panel Mica Shade, Hammered Copper Base, 16 x 20 In. 900.00
Electric, Arts & Crafts, 8-Panel Slag Glass Shade, Metal Leaf Overlay, Bronze Base, 19 x 24 In. 480.00
Electric, Arts & Crafts, Caramel Slag Glass Shade, Copper Overlay, Column Base, 17 x 11 ½ In. 1560.00
Electric, Arts & Crafts, Hammered Iron, Steel, Leaves, 56 x 14 In. 790.00
Electric, Arts & Crafts, Hanging Lantern, Vellum Shade, Tripod, Leaf Base, Iron, 68 In.. . . . . . 540.00
Electric, Arts & Crafts, Iron, Tree Shape, 10 ½ In. 2160.00
Electric, Arts & Crafts, Leaded, Yellow & White Slag, Vertical Panels, Geometric, 15 x 22 In. . . 748.00
Electric, Arts & Crafts, Leaded Glass, 12 Panels, Oak, c.1910, 77 x 26 ½ In. . . . . *illus* 8250.00
Electric, Arts & Crafts, Slag Glass Shade, 6 Panels, Metal & Column Shaft, Square Base, 21 x 14 In. 207.00
Electric, Arts & Crafts, Slag Glass Shade, Metal Overlay, Copper Organic Base, 19 x 20 In. . . . 960.00
Electric, Arts & Crafts, Up-Lighter, 3-Light, Hammered Copper, 18 x 15 In.. . . . . 600.00
Electric, Baluster, Heart, Vine, Iridescent Orange, Midnight Blue, 1920s, 22 In. 575.00
Electric, Baluster, Taupe Linen Shade, Wood, Ivory Paint, Distressed, Italy, 16 ½ In., Pair. . . . 240.00
Electric, Baluster, Yellow Glass Shade, Pink Flowers, Victorian, 27 In., Pair 1062.00
Electric, Baroque Style, Giltwood, Ribbed Standard, Elongated Leaf Tips, Round Foot, 51 In.. 267.00
Electric, Baroque Style, Tripod Base, Oval Cartouches, Cupid Heads, Floral Swags, Early 1900s, 88 In. 863.00
Electric, Bent Metal, Slag Glass, Amber & Blue Panels, Scrolling Metal Frame, 26 In. 345.00
Electric, Bigelow & Kennard, Leaded Glass, Flowers, Bronze Base, 23 x 18 In. . . . . *illus* 14400.00
Electric, Black Lacquer, Gilt, Mon & Leaf Decoration, Japan, 40 In., Pair 443.00
Electric, Brass, Adjustable Shade, Fabric Facing, Round Base, Shaft, 1900s, 20 In., Pair 259.00
Electric, Brass, Fluted Column, Marble Base, Cut Glass Shade, Prisms, 31 In. 882.00
Electric, Brazzoli & Lampa, Alba, Metal, Plastic, H. Guzzini, Italy, 1970s, 64 x 18 In.. . . . . 2040.00
Electric, Bronze, Arab, Seated, Drinking Tea In Tent, Geschutzt, Vienna, 14 In. 11500.00
Electric, Bronze, Arab Man, Washing Feet At Fountain, Geschutzt, Vienna, 12 In. 9200.00
Electric, Bronze, Patinated Brass, Iron, Pleated Silk Shade, 16 ½ x 23 ½ In. 1200.00
Electric, Bronze, Reclining Woman, Harem Room, Boy Servant, Namgreb, Vienna, 17 ¼ In. . 14900.00
Electric, Bronze, Silk Cream Shade, Wood Base, Asia, 9 x 32 In. 900.00
Electric, Brown Basket Weave Shade, Rose Highlights, Metal Base, 19 x 16 In.. . . . . 150.00
Electric, Bulbous Iridescent Yellow Glass Shade, Patinated Metal, Figural Shaft, 24 In.. . . . . . 1062.00
Electric, Caramel Slag Bent Panels, Hammered Metal Design, 22 In. 350.00
Electric, Caramel Slag Inserts, Drop Panel Shade, Baluster Base, Flowers, 25 ¼ In.. . . . . 690.00
Electric, Cast Metal, Columnar, Acanthus Leaf, 15 In.. . . . . 510.00
Electric, Ceiling, Art Deco, Blue Twist Ribs, Bead Chain, 11 In. 165.00
Electric, Ceiling, Art Deco, Copper, Glass, Bead Chain, 11 ½ In.. . . . . 225.00
Electric, Ceiling, Art Deco, Pink Twist Ribs, Bead Chain, 11 In. 165.00
Electric, Ceiling, Art Deco, Ribbed Dome, Bead Chain, 6 In.. . . . . 155.00
Electric, Ceiling, Art Deco, Star & Bead Edge, Bead Chain, 11 In.. . . . . 165.00
Electric, Ceiling, Parchment Scroll, Raised Fleur-De-Lis Scroll, Bead Chain, 11 ¼ In.. . . . . 165.00
Electric, Ceiling, Purcell & Elmslie, Bronze, White Glass, 1917, 14 x 25 In. 8750.00
Electric, Celeste Blue Glass, Columnar, Geometric Panel Overlay, Brass, Early 1900s, 38 In. . . 480.00
Electric, Chotka, Bronze, Cold Painted, Arabic Man, Donkey, Monkey, Mosque Dome, 16 In. . 4025.00
Electric, Classical, Bronze, Intaglio Cut Glass Globe, Frosted, 68 In. 431.00
Electric, Classique, Patinated Metal, Silver Overlay, Heart Design, 11 In. 460.00
Electric, Classique, Reverse Painted, Domed Shade, Rose Ground, Forest, Urn Base, 23 In.. . . 1208.00
Electric, Cranberry Hobnail Glass, Diamond Quilted, Amber Prisims, 22 In. Illus. 767.00
Electric, Cut Glass, Hobstar, Engraved Flowers, Butterflies, Vesica & Fan Base, 13 In. 1320.00
Electric, Desk, Architect's, Brass, Emeralite Glass, Extending, 32 In.. . . . . 390.00
Electric, Desk, Arts & Crafts, Emeralite Glass, Adjustable Shade, Matte Finish, 1920, 19 In. . . 1020.00
Electric, Desk, Serge Mouille, Metal, Brass, Attachable Clamp, Black, c.1958 23 In.. . . . . 6250.00
Electric, Dome Flower, Leaf Glass Shade, Multicolored, Pastel Ground, 6 Sockets, Metal Base, 79 In. 1265.00
Electric, Donald Deskey, Chromium Plated, c.1930, 64 ½ In.. . . . . 7500.00
Electric, Dorflinger, Hanging, Globe, Shade, Geometric Glass, Chromed Plate, Applied Wings, 26 In. 593.00
Electric, Duffner & Kimberly, Leaded Glass, Water Lilies, Patina, 3 Sockets, 26 x 19 In. . . *illus* 6000.00
Electric, Duffner & Kimberly, Louis XV, Leaded Glass, Filigree Shade, 29 x 22 In. . . . . . *illus* 38000.00
Electric, Duffner & Kimberly, Metal, Patina, Pull Chain, c.1920, 23 ½ In.. . . . . 3500.00
Electric, Duffner & Kimberly, Multicolored Geometric Shade, Thistle Base, 3 Sockets, 24 In. . 10350.00
Electric, Duffner & Kimberly, Owl, Leaded Glass, Acorn Pulls, 15 x 22 In.. . . . . 5750.00
Electric, Duffner & Kimberly, Peony Shade, Tan, Red, Blue, Yellow, Bronze Base, 32 In. 57500.00
Electric, Duffner & Kimberly, Pink & Yellow Dogwood Shade, Bronze Base, 22 In.. . . . . 10350.00

Electric, Duffner & Kimberly, Pussy Willow, Tuck-Under-Shade, Yellow, Striated Glass, 19 x 24 In. 7475.00
Electric, Edward F. Caldwell & Co., Gilt, Patinated Bronze, Baluster, Early 1900s, 30 In. 3750.00
Electric, Edwardian, Mahogany, Fluted Standard, Leaf & Greek Key Carving, c.1900, 73 ½ In. 570.00
Electric, Edwardian, Multicolored, Paneled, Bulbous, Hexagon Base, c.1900, 62 In. 720.00
Electric, Elizabeth Burton, Water Lily, Copper, Abalone, Patina, 17 x 10 In. *illus* 1320.00
Electric, Emeralite Glass, Metal, Adjustable, 60 In. 900.00
Electric, Figural, 2 Bronze Girls, Glass Globe, Stepped Marble Base, 10 ¼ x 10 In. 720.00
Electric, Figural, Arabian Musician, Spelter, Cold Painted, Red & Green Glass Panels, c.1925, 13 In. 646.00
Electric, Figural, Seminude Woman, Holding Globe, Jewel Shade, 29 ¾ In. 1434.00
Electric, Figural, Shell, Open To Nude Woman Holding Pearl, Alabaster, 24 x 20 x 14 In. 1750.00
Electric, Figural, Woman, Cast Bronze, Flowing Gown, Flower Stem, Pulled Flower Shade, 28 In. 230.00
Electric, Figure, Seated With Basket, Gilt, France, Late 19th Century, 30 In. 1404.00
Electric, Frosted Glass, Nude Figures, Green Reeded Cylinder Shade, 11 x 5 ½ x 3 In. 138.00
Electric, G. Nakashima, Burl, Signed, 7 ½ In. 450.00
Electric, G. Stickley, Hammered Copper, Wicker, Fabric Shade, 23 x 18 ½ In., Pair 8400.00
Electric, Gerald Thurston, Black Metal Frame, Bamboo Shade, 17 x 18 In., Pair 3600.00
Electric, Gilt Brass, 4 Ram Masque Monopods, Hoof Feet, Gilt Edged Shades, 66 In. 2880.00
Electric, Gilt Brass, Campana Shape, Palm Sprays, Fabric Shade, 22 ½ In., Pair 1200.00
Electric, Gilt Bronze, Steel, Ebony, 22 ¼ x 9 x 5 In. 2160.00
Electric, Ginger Jar, Scenic, Oriental Warriors, Horses, Wood Base, 13 In. 144.00
Electric, Globe, Apothecary, Leaded, Victorian Design, Red, Pink, Green, Geometric Panels, 19 In. 2875.00
Electric, Gone With The Wind Style, Satin Red, Drapery, 20th Century, 24 In. 531.00
Electric, Gorham Co., Leaded Shade, Poppies, Leaves, Butterflies, Bronze Base, 6 Sockets, 37 In. 47150.00
Electric, Gothic, Gilt, Brass, Fluted Pedestal, Marble Plinth, Etched Shade, c.1850, 24 In. 1080.00
Electric, Gunnar Nyland, Glazed Porcelain, 1940s, 24 ¼ In. 2500.00
Electric, H. Weese, Aluminum Support, Black Enamel Base, Black Rectangular Shade, c.1950, 23 In. 600.00
Electric, Hanging, Arts & Crafts, Curled Iron, Opalescent Glass Shade, 26 x 15 In. 840.00
Electric, Hanging, Arts & Crafts, Glass Shade, Flowers, Multicolored, 19 x 7 In. 540.00
Electric, Hanging, Arts & Crafts, Hammered Brass, 4 Sockets, Chain, Ceiling Cap, 32 ½ x 12 In. 960.00
Electric, Hanging, Bat Shape, Cast Bronze, Verdigris, Early 1900s, 21 x 25 In., Pair 7475.00
Electric, Hanging, Bradley & Hubbard, Bronze Overlay, Glass Panels, Marked, 14 x 18 In. 3120.00
Electric, Hanging, Brass, Mica, Scrolls, Cylindrical Shade, c.1950, 31 In., Pair 431.00
Electric, Hanging, Camphor Glass, Art Deco, Drop, Dome Shade, 9 x 20 In. 695.00
Electric, Hanging, G. Sciolari, Chrome, Brass, Lucite, Curved Plates, Rods, Label, 27 In. 1920.00
Electric, Hanging, Hammered Square, Hipped Roof, Over Caramel Slag Glass, 23 x 10 In. 593.00
Electric, Hanging, Inverted Bell Shape, Clear Glass, Prisms, Brass, 3 Sockets, 1950s, 29 In. 1035.00
Electric, Hanging, Iron Frame, 6-Sided, Hinged Door, Amber Stretched Glass Inserts, 18 x 9 ½ In. 1320.00
Electric, Hanging, John Morgan & Sons, Mosaic, Geometric Panels, Yellow, Green, 26 In. 1185.00
Electric, Hanging, Man, Shimmying Down Rope, Wood, Carved, c.1900, 47 x 14 In. 305.00
Electric, Hanging, Red Shade, Brass Frame, Faceted Jewels, Prisms, Amberina, 14 x 6 In. 29900.00
Electric, Hanging, Stickley Bros., Peacocks, Green, Caramel Slag Glass, Copper, 10 x 19 In. 2300.00
Electric, Hanging, Tin & Glass, Moravian Star, 18 Points, 1900s, 15 In. 118.00
Electric, Hanging, Vistosi, Orange Cased Glass Globe, Gold Chain, Italy, 13 x 11 In. 330.00
Electric, Harlequin, Blue & White, Vase Shape, Chinese Porcelain, Wood Base, 1900s, 18 ¾ In. 296.00
Electric, Heissner, Gnome Holding Lantern, Painted Chalkware, Label, W. Germany, 16 x 11 In. 55.00
Electric, Jefferson, 2-Light, Tree Lined Landscape, Yellow Sky, Bulbous, Green Glass, 22 x 18 In. 3600.00
Electric, Jefferson, Reverse Painted, Landscape, Sunset, Boat, Water, c.1915, 22 ¼ In. 1265.00
Electric, Jefferson, Reverse Painted, Scenic, Lake, Shoreline, 2 Sockets, Pull Chains, 16 x 21 In. 2185.00
Electric, Jefferson, Reverse Painted Shade, Lake Scene, 2 Sockets, No. 1377, 24 x 18 In. *illus* 2500.00
Electric, Joe Colombo, Coupe, Orange Enamel Metal Shade, Base, Adjustable, Floor, 58 In. 1140.00
Electric, Koch & Lowry, Chrome Shade, Tripod Base, Black Leather Handle, 34 x 58 In. 570.00
Electric, Kurt Versen, Copper Plated Brass, Aluminum, c.1930, 54 ½ In. 5000.00
Electric, L. & J.G. Stickley, No. 510, Wicker Shade, Pull Chains, 4 Sockets, 60 x 30 In. 7200.00
Electric, Lamb Brothers, Leaded Glass, Flower Border, 18 In. 1595.00
Electric, Laurel, Lucite Box, Chrome Stacked Shapes, Replaced Shade, 34 In., Pair 1200.00
Electric, Laurel Lamp Co., Aluminum, Chrome, Domed Shade, 1960s, 34 x 17 In., Pair 840.00
Electric, Leaded Glass, Flowers, Tree Trunk Base, Chicago Mosaic, 24 In. 4255.00
Electric, Leaded Glass, Mosaic, Roses, 3 Sockets, Shell Feet, c.1900, 29 x 22 In. *illus* 1050.00
Electric, Leaded Glass, Pink Apple Blossoms, 4 Sockets, Brass Base, 31 x 22 ½ In. 5400.00
Electric, Lightolier, Black Metal Rods, 9 Black, Tan & White Shades, 1950s, 60 In. *illus* 1080.00
Electric, Luis Barragan, Bulbous, Pale Green Glass, Parchment Shade, c.1950, 35 x 29 In. 35000.00
Electric, Magel Anthouard, Bronze, Marble, Stamped, France, 18 In., Pair 3240.00
Electric, Maison Desny, Chrome, Glass, Cone, Ring, Stem, Ecru Shade, Paris, c.1930, 10 In. 25000.00
Electric, Metal, Wood, Relief Panels, Bird & Flower, Mask Ring Handles, 1920s, 25 ½ In. 270.00
Electric, Michael Ashford, Rippled Glass Shade, 4-Arm Base, Wood, 15 x 21 In. 390.00
Electric, Millefiori Glass Shade, Mushroom Shape, 13 In. 120.00
Electric, Miller, Slag Glass, Metal Base, Leaf Petal Design, 3 Fixtures, 8 Panels, 18 ½ x 22 ½ In. 660.00

Lamp, Electric, Duffner & Kimberly, Louis XV, Leaded Glass, Filigree Shade, 29 x 22 In.
$38000.00

Lamp, Electric, Elizabeth Burton, Water Lily, Copper, Abalone, Patina, 17 x 10 In.
$1320.00

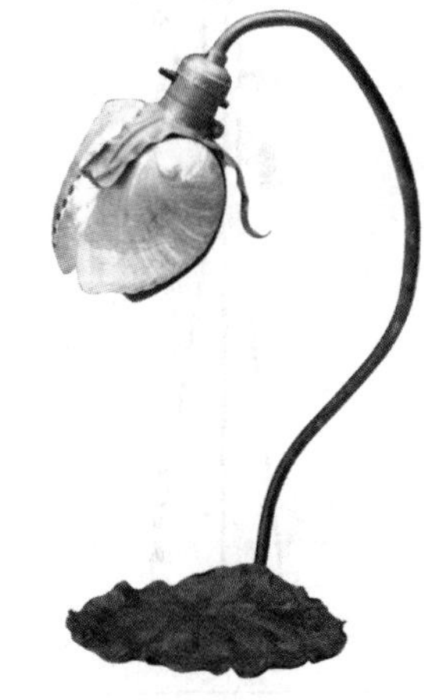

Lamp, Electric, Jefferson, Reverse Painted Shade, Lake Scene, 2 Sockets, No. 1377, 24 x 18 In.
$2500.00

L

Lamp, Electric, Leaded Glass, Mosaic, Roses, 3 Sockets, Shell Feet, c.1900, 29 x 22 In.
$1050.00

Lamp, Electric, Lightolier, Black Metal Rods, 9 Black, Tan & White Shades, 1950s, 60 In.
$1080.00

Lamp, Electric, Monk, Seated Below Street Lamp, Cast, Early 1900s, 19 In.
$135.00

Electric, Moe Bridges, Leaded Glass, 8 Panels, Domed Shade, Beaded Fringe, Bronze, 31 In... 780.00
Electric, Moe Bridges, Reverse Painted, River Landscape, Trees, Shoreline, 20 In. 1680.00
Electric, Monk, Seated Below Street Lamp, Cast, Early 1900s, 19 In. *illus* 135.00
Electric, Moravian Star Shape, Glass, Colored Panes, Electric, 19 In. 58.00
Electric, Murano Glass, Vertical Pillow Shape, Caramel Glass Center, c.1950, Italy, 15 In. 563.00
Electric, Neoclassical, Bronze Mounted, Cut Crystal, c.1910, 32 In. 1347.00
Electric, Neoclassical, Rock Crystal, Columnar, Gilt Metal Mounts, Malachite Veneer, 44 In., Pair 4080.00
Electric, Neoclassical, Turned Standard, Ivory Paint, Square Base, Linen Shade, 28 In., Pair. 840.00
Electric, Newel Post, 3-Light, Fruits Of Automne, Woman, Lily Branch, 800s, 28 In. 1121.00
Electric, Newel Post, 4-Light, LeRevel, Woman, Lily, Bronze, Black Marble Plinth, c.1900, 30 In. 767.00
Electric, Octagonal Shade, Ocher Slag Glass, Bronze Base, 25 x 17 ¾ In. 590.00
Electric, Octagonal Shade, Slag Glass Panels, 4-Arm Support, Cylindrical, 20 x 14 ½ In. 575.00
Electric, Old Mission, Hammered Copper, Mica Shade, 4 Panels, Stamped, 19 x 22 In. *illus* 5100.00
Electric, Old Mission Kopperkraft, Hammered Copper Shade, Base, Original Patina, 13 x 18 In. 1140.00
Electric, Opal Glass, Sea Scene, Flying Seagulls, Wave Tossed Sea, Victorian, 26 In. 443.00
Electric, Opalescent Glass, Metal, Wood, Flower Shape, Ribbed, Silver Gilt Base, 36 In. 1007.00
Electric, Opaque Glass Shade, Filigree Brass Frame, Blue Prisms, Victorian, 30 In. 295.00
Electric, Oscar Bach, Brass Shade, Grape, Leaf Overlay, Mica, Scroll Arms, 2 Bacchus Heads, 20 In. 805.00
Electric, Oscar Bach, Metal, Patinated, Openwork Globe, Figural Finial, c.1925, 70 ½ In., Pair 5000.00
Electric, Owl, Bronze, Glass Beads, c.1920 1035.00
Electric, Parrot, Beaded, Venetian, c.1920 *illus* 1200.00
Electric, Pastoral Scene, Red, Painted Base, Cylinder Shape, 14 In., Pair 259.00
Electric, Paul Evans, Brass, Chrome, Wood, Shade, 16 x 30 In. 720.00
Electric, Peacock, Blue, Green, Gold, Metal, 15 x 15 In. 2100.00
Electric, Phoenix, Reverse Painted Shade, Landscape, Cottage, Water, Brass, 23 x 17 In. 990.00
Electric, Piano, 3-Leg Base, Etched Globular Shade, Victorian, 67 In. 384.00
Electric, Piano, Brass, Tripod Base, Telescoping, 66 In. 1180.00
Electric, Piano, Quezal Shade, Opal Pulled Feathers, 11 In. 403.00
Electric, Pittsburgh, 2-Sided Landscape-Painted Glass Shade, Green Ground, 23 x 14 In. 900.00
Electric, Pittsburgh Lamp Co., Reverse Painted, Maple Leaf, Bronze Owl Base, c.1910, 18 x 23 In. 2875.00
Electric, Porcelain, Ginger Jar, Flowers, Famille Rose Enamel, Calligraphy, 25 ½ In. 1800.00
Electric, Porcelain, Sevres Style, Gilt, Oval, Blue Ground, Cartouche, 2 Cherubs, 30 ¼ In. 1673.00
Electric, Radio, Czech Art Glass, Spelter, Dancing Figures, Early 1900s, 12 In. *illus* 224.00
Electric, Red Slag Glass Shade, Bronze Figural, Arabian Trader, Seated, Cold Paint, c.1920, 11 In. 440.00
Electric, Reverse Painted, Americans Indians Along Streams, Indian Panels, 27 In., Pair 8050.00
Electric, Reverse Painted, Domed Shade, Lakeside Landscape, Multicolored, 23 & 15 ¾ In. 585.00
Electric, Reverse Painted, Pastel Flowers, Metal, 23 x 16 In. 384.00
Electric, Reverse Painted Landscape, Domed Shade, Copper Patinated Metal Base, 1915, 21 In. 900.00
Electric, Rispal, U-Shape, Wood Pierced Stem, 2 Tan Modern Shades, c.1950, 65 In. 3600.00
Electric, Rococo, Brass, Marble, Leaves, Scroll, Snowflake Prisms, Etched Glass, c.1860, 19 In. 999.00
Electric, Roland Smith, Victor, Metal Base, Adjustable Boom Arm, c.1948, 48 x 44 In. 900.00
Electric, Rubina Hobnail Shade, Jeweled Brass Frame, Crystal Prisms, 30 In. 885.00
Electric, Samuel Yellin, Wrought Iron, Paw Feet, Mica Shade, Stamped, 30 In., Pair *illus* 13200.00
Electric, Schoolboy, With Books, Cast Metal, Bronze Finish, Early 1900s, 19 ½ In. *illus* 250.00
Electric, Sconce, 2-Light, Art Deco, Cloth Shade, Brass, Ebonized, 14 x 11 In., Pair 1440.00
Electric, Sconce, 2-Light, Neoclassical, Gilt Brass, Cut Glass, Jewels, Spears, Sweden, 16 x 7 In., Pair 600.00
Electric, Sconce, 4-Light, Consular Style, Bronze, Patinated Brass, Electrified, 25 x 16 In., Pair 3120.00
Electric, Sconce, Louis XVI Style, Beechwood, Carved, Verdigris Pickled, 41 x 20 In. 2400.00
Electric, Serge Mouille, Tres Grand Signal, Upright, Brushed Aluminum Steel, 1963, 80 x 12 In. 55250.00
Electric, Silver Plate, Columnar, 26 ½ In., Pair 600.00
Electric, Silver Plate, Columnar, Wreath Decoration, Stepped Base, 30 In. 510.00
Electric, Skating Woman, 2-Tone Alabaster, Onyx Base, 32 x 8 x 10 In. 1725.00
Electric, Slag Glass, 8 Panels, 24 In. 1450.00
Electric, Slag Glass, Gold Finish, Classical Overlay, 26 In. 190.00
Electric, Slag Glass, Metal, Filigree, Leaf Tip, Domed Shade, 24 x 16 ½ In. 403.00
Electric, Slag Glass, Metal Spider Web Overlay, 20 ½ In. 633.00
Electric, Slag Glass, Stylized Flower, 8-Panel Shade, Bronze, Multicolored, 22 In. 299.00
Electric, Stained Glass, Domed Shade, Red Dogwood Blossoms, Green Stems, Bronze Base, 32 In. 4830.00
Electric, Stained Glass, Leaded, Domed Shade, Raised White Panels, Yellow Ground, 1920s, 16 x 24 In. 259.00
Electric, Stickley, 3-Sided Shade, Slag Glass, Hammered Copper, Oak Base, 16 x 10 x 8 In. 3750.00
Electric, Stickley, Cast & Hammered Copper, Leaded Slag Glass Shade, 27 ¾ x 13 ½ In. 6000.00
Electric, Stickley, Triangular Shade, Slag Glass, Hammered Copper, Oak Base, 16 x 10 In. *illus* 3750.00
Electric, Stickley Bros., 6 Panels, Peacocks, Hammered Copper, 2 Sockets, 21 x 17 In. *illus* 2400.00
Electric, Stickley Bros., Hammered Copper, Peacocks, Slag Glass, 2 Handles, 2 Sockets, 21 In. 2000.00
Electric, Student, Bronze, Pink Shades, 1920, 25 ¼ x 19 x 11 In. 275.00
Electric, Student, Gold Iridescent Shades, Flared Stem, 4-Leg Base, Cast Brass, 21 In. 420.00
Electric, Sunflower Head, Pomegranate, Steel, Brushed, Parcel Bronze, 28 ¼ x 9 ¼ In. 1440.00

Electric, T. Bonan, Lucite, Chrome, Aluminum Drum Shade, 15 x 25 In. 480.00
Electric, Television, Fountain Of Youth, Celluloid, Boy Fishing, Brass Mount, 8 In. 125.00 to 147.00
Electric, Television, Gazelle, Leaping, Head Thrust Back, Ebony Cascade 55.00
Electric, Television, Monkey, Playing Banjo, Art Deco, 7 In. 200.00
Electric, Television, Shell, Biomorphic, Green Drip 16.00
Electric, Television, Waterfalls, Glass Insert, Bronze Base, Cylindrical, 1930s 75.00
Electric, Tulip Glass Shade, Pink, Green Slag, Baluster Base, Bronze Patina, 22 ½ In.. . . . . . . 575.00
Electric, Unique Art Glass Co., Leaded Shape, Tulips, Brass Base, 23 In. 4600.00
Electric, Unique Glass Co., Leaded Glass, Tulips, Bronze Base, 18 In.. 2645.00
Electric, Urn, Bronze, Putti, Goat Head Handles, Red Griotte Marble, France, c.1900, 38 x 9 In., Pair. 5750.00
Electric, Urn, Green Quartz, Red, Gold, Carved, Glass Shade, Chinese, c.1900, 26 In.. . . . . 702.00
Electric, Urn, Tapered Base, Paw Feet, Lion's Head Rings, Painted, Black Shade, 31 In., Pair . 1093.00
Electric, Vase Shape, Wood, Painted, 2 Handles, Linen Shade, 30 ¼ In., Pair 2400.00
Electric, Viking, Owl, Amber, Glimmer Candlelight 27.00
Electric, W. Von Nessen, Stainless Steel, Enamel, 2 Adjustable Shades, 25 x 29 In. 420.00
Electric, Whaley, Tulip Shade, Leaded Glass, Bronzed Base. 2243.00
Electric, Wicker, Half Domed Shade, Openwork Stem, Table Half Way Down, Painted, c.1910, 67 In. 176.00
Electric, Wiener Werkstatte, Cone Shade, White Glass, Green, Yellow Panels, 25 ¾ In.. . . . . . . 885.00
Electric, Wiley Post, Will Rogers Portraits, Planes, Green Globes, Spelterware Base, 17 In., Pair 489.00
Electric, Wilkinson, Leaded Glass, Flowers, Bronzed Base, 20 In. 2990.00
Electric, Wilkinson, Leaded Glass, Geometric, Yellow, Red, White. 2300.00
Electric, Wilkinson, Stained Glass, Water Lily, Blue Ground, Yellow, Rose, Orange, Pink, 20 x 28 In. 6058.00
Electric, Wilkinson, Yellow Daffodil, Green Leaves, Asymmetrical Purple Tiles, 26 In. 11500.00
Electric, Williamson, Hanging, Leaded Glass, Stained, Roses, Early 1900s, 26 In. . . . . . *illus* 940.00
Electric, Winged Metal Nymph, Filigree Bronze Pierced Scrolled Shade, c.1900, 30 In. 2596.00
Fairy, 2-Arm, Frosted Green, Frosted Blue, Crimped Lamp Cup, Signed, Clarke, 14 ½ x 16 In.. 403.00
Fairy, 3-Arm, Cut Glass Standard, Blue To White, Cased, English Robin, Clarke, 18 x 14 In. . . 690.00
Fairy, Aladdin, Ruby Shade, Creamware Base, Aladdin, Diamond Candle Co., 6 ¼ In. 86.00
Fairy, Aladdin Style, Creamware Base, Ruby, Germany, 6 ¼ In.. . . . . 86.00
Fairy, Amber Domed Shade, Reverse Thumbprint Pattern, Crimped Base, Rigaree Waist, 6 In. 230.00
Fairy, Blue, White & Frosted Crystal Stripes, Cleveland Pattern, Pedestal, Clarke's, 11 In. . . . 3163.00
Fairy, Blue, White & Frosted Stripes, Pedestal, Frosted Cup, 11 In. 3163.00
Fairy, Blue, White Satin Diamond Domed Shade, Ruffled Top, Matching Cup Vase, 7 In.. . . . . 144.00
Fairy, Blue Nailsea, Blue Ground, White Looping, Clear Cup, Clarke, 5 ½ In. 180.00
Fairy, Blue Satin, Cased, Reverse Drape, Crystal Cup, 5 In. 115.00
Fairy, Blue Satin, Diamond Quilted, Mother-Of-Pearl Satin Stripe, Puckered Top Rim, 5 ⅜ In. 144.00
Fairy, Blue Satin, Embossed Rib, White Lining, Clarke, 5 ¼ In. 144.00
Fairy, Blue Satin, Flared Piecrust Top Rim, Ribbon Swirl, Blue Shaded To White, 5 In. 460.00
Fairy, Blue Satin Pyramid, Cased, Ormolu Mirrored Stand, Clarke, 6 ¾ In.. . . . . 575.00
Fairy, Blue Satin Pyramid, Thorn Pattern, Scalloped Edges, 3-Leg Brass Holder, 7 ¾ In. 316.00
Fairy, Blue Satin Shaded To White, Butterscotch & White Bowl, Pedestal, Clarke, 11 ¼ In. . . . 690.00
Fairy, Blue To White Satin, Multicolored Flowers, Frosted Ruffled Edges, 7 x 8 In., 3 Piece . . . 690.00
Fairy, Blue To White Satin, Multicolored Flowers, Ribbon Candy Edges, 7 x 8 ¼ In., 3 Piece . . 690.00
Fairy, Bowl, Rose Color, Cased, Clear Candleholder, 4 ¾ In. 1035.00
Fairy, Bristol, White, Birds, Flowers, Cup, Underbowl, Crimped Edge, 5 ¼ In., Pair, ... 58.00
Fairy, Cased Rose Satin Ribbed, Diamond Quilted, Mother-Of-Pearl, Metal Holder, 10 In. 288.00
Fairy, Cat, Bisque, Gray, Green Glass Eyes, Basket Weave, Triangular, 4 x 4 In. 288.00
Fairy, Cat, Bisque, Painted, Blue Bow, Green Transparent Eyes, Black Fur, 4 x 3 ½ In. 173.00
Fairy, Cat, Bisque, Painted, Gray, Green Eyes, 3 ½ x 3 ½ In., Pair. 460.00
Fairy, Cat, Bisque, Painted, Green Eyes, Pink Rope, Tassels, 3 ½ In. 100.00
Fairy, Cat, Owl, Dog, 3 Faces, Bisque, Painted, Signed, KPM, 4 x 4 ½ In. 518.00
Fairy, Cat, Owl, Dog, Faces, Blue Rope, Tassels, Stamped, KPM, 4 In. 130.00
Fairy, Chartreuse, Cased, Satinized, Reverse Drape, Signed Crystal Cup, Clarke, 5 In.. . . . . 230.00
Fairy, Chartreuse, Diamond Quilted, Mother-Of-Pearl, Downward Ruffle, Clarke, 6 ¾ In. 450.00
Fairy, Child's Head, Smiling, Crying, 2-Sided, Frosted, Clarke Fairy Pyramid, 4 ¾ In. 200.00
Fairy, Chimney, Bulbous, Embossed, Opaque Dome, Fluted, Ruffled Rim, 6 ½ In. 690.00
Fairy, Cleveland Pattern, Frosted Crystal, Ribbed, Satinized, Pink & White Stripes, 5 In. 690.00
Fairy, Coralene Shade, Pink Ground, Metal Holder, Handle, 4 ¾ In.. . . . . 288.00
Fairy, Cottage, Porcelain, Thatched Roof, 4 x 5 In. 288.00
Fairy, Cranberry, Overshot Crown Shade, Pewter Pedestal, Figural Handle, 7 ½ In. . . . . . *illus* 173.00
Fairy, Cranberry, Satinized, White Enameled Flowers, Fluted Rim, 7 In. 230.00
Fairy, Cranberry Flower Shape, Clear Dome, Tooled Petals, Pressed Base, Clarke, 4 ¾ x 7 In. . 201.00
Fairy, Cranberry Overshot Crown, Signed, 4 ½ In. 173.00
Fairy, Cranberry Waffle, Embossed Ribs, Applied Finger Hold, Clarke's Cricklite, 5 In. 518.00
Fairy, Diamond Quilted, Mother-Of-Pearl, Yellow, 5 In. 200.00
Fairy, Diamond Quilted, Mother-Of-Pearl, Yellow Shaded To White, 5 ½ In. 230.00
Fairy, Double Arm, Standard, Crystal, Base, Clarke's Cricklite, 19 x 15 In., Pair 805.00

Lamp, Electric, Old Mission, Hammered Copper, Mica Shade, 4 Panels, Stamped, 19 x 22 In.
$5100.00

Lamp, Electric, Parrot, Beaded, Venetian, c.1920
$1200.00

Lamp, Electric, Radio, Czech Art Glass, Spelter, Dancing Figures, Early 1900s, 12 In.
$224.00

Lamp, Electric, Samuel Yellin, Wrought Iron, Paw Feet, Mica Shade, Stamped, 30 In., Pair
$13200.00

Lamp, Electric, Schoolboy, With Books, Cast Metal, Bronze Finish, Early 1900s, 19 ½ In.
$250.00

Lamp, Electric, Williamson, Hanging, Leaded Glass, Stained, Roses, Early 1900s, 26 In.
$940.00

Lamp, Electric, Stickley, Triangular Shade, Slag Glass, Hammered Copper, Oak Base, 16 x 10 In.
$3750.00

Lamp, Electric, Stickley Bros., 6 Panels, Peacocks, Hammered Copper, 2 Sockets, 21 x 17 In.
$2400.00

Lamp, Fairy, Cranberry, Overshot Crown Shade, Pewter Pedestal, Figural Handle, 7 ½ In.
$173.00

Lamp, Fairy, Finger, Vaseline Opalescent, 3 Rows Applied Petals, 3 ¾ x 4 ¾ In.
$460.00

Lamp, Fairy, Opaline, Children, Flowers, Cylindrical Dome, Ruffled Top, Fluted Rim, 6 ¾ In.
$180.00

Lamp, Fat, Hanging, Wrought Iron, Twisted, Chained Wick Pick, Swivel, 6 ½ x 4 ½ In.
$100.00

Lamp, Fluid, Kosmos Brenner, Pressed Tin, Glass, Reflector, Teal Paint, 8 ½ x 3 ¾ In.
$99.00

Fairy, Finger, Vaseline Opalescent, 3 Rows Applied Petals, 3 ¾ x 4 ¾ In. . . . . *illus* 460.00
Fairy, Flower Shape, Cranberry To Clear Dome, Tooled Crystal Petals, Base, 4 ¾ x 7 In. 201.00
Fairy, Frog, Brown, Amber Eyes, Sloping Rear, 4 ½ x 5 ½ In. 575.00
Fairy, Green, Jeweled, Satin Globular Dome, Brass Fittings, Ruffled Rim, 5 ½ & 6 In., Pair . . . 120.00
Fairy, Hobbs Brockunier, Frosted Yellow Dome, Swirled, Crystal Base, Ribbed Edging, 5 ¼ In.. 374.00
Fairy, Jeweled, Multicolored Ball Shade, Ruffled Top, Brass Retainers, 6 In. 300.00
Fairy, Light Pink Cased Glass, Clear Lamp Cup, Dark Pink Folded Base, Mark, 6 In.. . . . . 345.00
Fairy, Lighthouse, Frosted Pedestal Base, Integral Shade Cup, Paneled, Threaded, 12 ½ In. . . 1035.00
Fairy, Multicolored Flowers, Pink, Gold Trim, Roof Vents, Top Knob, Handle, Footed, 7 ¼ x 4 In. 115.00
Fairy, Nailsea, Blue Satin Shade, Cup, 4 ⅜ In. 115.00
Fairy, Nailsea Dome, Swirled Diamond Pattern, 3 ¼ In. 2530.00
Fairy, Nailsea Type, Dome, 2 Tiers, Red, White Looping, 11 In. 750.00
Fairy, Nailsea Type, Dome, Rose Glass, Frosted, White Stripes, Flared Rim, 6 ¼ In.. . . . . 375.00
Fairy, Nailsea Type, Satin Glass, Cranberry, Clear Base, Clarke's, 5 In. 120.00
Fairy, Opalescent, Domed Shade, Ruffled Rim, Cranberry Swirl Design, Clarke Criklite, 7 In. . 575.00
Fairy, Opalescent, Paneled, Threaded Amber Shaded To White, Clear Cup, Clarke's, 4 ¾ In. . . 420.00
Fairy, Opaline, Children, Flowers, Cylindrical Dome, Ruffled Top, Fluted Rim, 6 ¾ In. . . *illus* 180.00
Fairy, Owl, Bisque, Glass Eyes, Painted, Bavaria, 7 ½ In. 50.00
Fairy, Owl, Bisque, Painted, Gray, Blue Tassel, Amber Eyes, 3 ½ x 3 ½ In. 489.00
Fairy, Pastel Rainbow, Diamond Quilted, Mother-Of-Pearl, Clear Cup, Clarke's, 5 In.. . . . . 3335.00
Fairy, Pink & White, Satinized Pink Shaded To Rose Dome, White Loopings, 4 ½ In. 210.00
Fairy, Pink Cased, Tapestry, Blue, Yellow, Purple, Clarke, 5 ¼ In. 805.00
Fairy, Pink Embossed Swirl, Candy Stripes, Lined White, Crystal Cup, 5 In.. . . . . 345.00
Fairy, Pink Opalescent, Impressed Diamonds, Paneled Shoulder, 5 ½ In. 201.00
Fairy, Pink Satin, Rose Shaded To Pink, Puckered Top Rim, Crystal Cup, Clarke's, 5 In. 230.00
Fairy, Pink Satin Pucker Dome, 3-Jewel Inserts, Ruffled Dish Base, Clear Glass Cup Holder, 5 In. 201.00
Fairy, Pink Satin Reverse Swirl Ribs, Frosted, Swirled Cup, Pink Pedestal Base, 13 In. 450.00
Fairy, Plateau, Cased Satin, Shaded Butterscotch, Raindrop Pattern Cup, Clarke's, 6 ¾ In. . . . 575.00
Fairy, Pressed Glass, Crystal Ribbed Pyramid Shade, Embossed Standards, 12 In., Pair 58.00
Fairy, Rainbow Satin Glass, Cased, Diamond Quilted Mother-Of-Pearl, Ribbon Candy Edge, 7 In. 4025.00
Fairy, Raspberry Satin Pucker Shade, Brass Holder, Stem, Floral Porcelain Wafer Base, 8 In. . 288.00
Fairy, Red Nailsea, White Loopings, Crystal Cups, 5 In., 3 Piece 258.00
Fairy, Rose, Diamond Quilted, Mother-Of-Pearl, Satin Lined White Dome, Crystal Cup, 4 ¾ In. 345.00
Fairy, Rose Bowl, Threaded Exterior, Clear Cup, Signed, Clarke's, 4 ¾ In. 1035.00
Fairy, Rose Nailsea, Double Arm, Cut Glass, Bud Vases, Clarke's Cricklite, 19 ¼ x 15 In.. . . . . 575.00
Fairy, Rose Nailsea, Rose Ground, White Loopings, Clear Cup, Clarke's, 5 ¼ In. 360.00
Fairy, Rose Nailsea, White Loopings, Clear Cup, Marked, Clarke's, 5 ½ In.. . . . . 300.00
Fairy, Rose Nailsea, White Loopings, Ruffled Rim, Clarke's, 5 ¾ In. 173.00
Fairy, Rose Satin, Embossed Rib Dome, White Lining, Crystal Cup, 4 ¾ In.. . . . . 115.00
Fairy, Satin, Yellow To White, Cone Dome, Cased, Fluted, Ribbed Top, 6 In.. . . . . 230.00
Fairy, Silo, Bisque, Brown, Gold, Green Ground Cover, Trees, Signed, 6 ½ In. 518.00
Fairy, Stevens & Williams, Cased Dome, Red & Peach Swirl, Puckered Top Rim, 5 In. 920.00
Fairy, Wee, Red Nailsea, Swirled Diamond, Marked, 3 ¼ In. 2530.00
Fairy, White, Blue Swirled Satin Dome, Scalloped Base, Applied Frosted Branch Feet, 7 In. . . . 403.00
Fairy, White Nailsea, Satinized Dome, 3 ⅛ & 3 ¼ In., Pair 201.00
Fairy, White Swirl Ruffled Satin Shade, Pinched White Swirl Satin Base, 4 x 6 In. 633.00
Fairy, Woman's Head, Blue Eyes, Yellow Hair, Blue Bonnet, 3 Pink Feet, 3 ½ x 4 In. 460.00
Fairy, Yellow, Diamond Quilted, Mother-Of-Pearl, White Lining, Rim Waisted, Fluted, 5 In.. . . 201.00
Fairy, Yellow, Frosted, White & Opaque Swirl, Cleveland Pattern, Piecrust Edge, 6 In. 625.00
Fairy, Yellow Satin, Cased, Scalloped Top Dome, Enamel Flowers, Butterflies, Brass Base, 7 In. 86.00
Fairy, Yellow Satin, Cone Dome, Cased, Fluted, Ruffled Top Rim Edge, 6 In. 230.00
Fat, Brass, Gimbal, Footed, 19th Century, 10 ½ In.. . . . . 1053.00
Fat, Copper, Iron, Gimbal, 4-Footed, 19th Century, 7 ¼ In. 819.00
Fat, Copper, Iron, Gimbal, Footed, 19th Century, 10 ¾ In. 819.00
Fat, Hanging, Wrought Iron, Twisted, Chained Wick Pick, Swivel, 6 ½ x 4 ½ In. . . . . . . *illus* 100.00
Fat, Peter Derr, Brass, Iron, Impressed, 1848, 6 In.. . . . . 3978.00
Fluid, Bronze, Raised Dragons, Chinese, 1800s, 22 In.. . . . . 140.00
Fluid, Kosmos Brenner, Pressed Tin, Glass, Reflector, Teal Paint, 8 ½ x 3 ¾ In. . . . . *illus* 99.00
Fluid, Peg, Cut Overlay Glass, Opaque Blue Cut To Clear, Brass Collars, 6 ¾ In., Pair. 823.00
Fluid, Sinumbra, Blown Glass Shade, Flowers, Tapered Footed Brass Column, 36 In.. . . . . 1265.00
Fluid, Sinumbra, Brass, Cut, Frosted Shade, c.1840, 26 x 11 In. 2702.00
Fluid, Sinumbra, Brass, Rosettes, Prisms, Etched Glass Shade, Triangular Base, 37 x 14 In. . . 1410.00
Fluid, Sinumbra, Frosted Cut To Clear Shade, Large Prisms, Square Base, 4 Brass Turned Feet, 29 In. 1725.00
Fluid, Sinumbra, Gilt Bronze, Cut & Etched Blown Glass Shade, Marble Base, 18 In. 2160.00
Fluid, Sinumbra, Glass Column, Frosted, Cut Leaf, Berry Shade, Prisms, Brass Base, 29 In. . . 690.00
Fluid, Triple Scallop, Rib Swag Font, Brass & Marble Base, 11 ¾ In. 44.00
Gas, Gasolier, Etched Shade, Prisms, Gilt Metal, 24 In. 50.00

Lamp, Kerosene, Admiral Dewey's Bullet, Copper, Opaque Ball Shade, 5 ¾ x 8 ¾ In.
$180.00

Lamp, Kerosene, Arts & Crafts, Stylized Berries, Green, Red Glass, Crystals, 24 x 16 In.
$1560.00

Lamp, Kerosene, Atterbury Loop, Yellow-Green Translucent, Double Burner, 8 ¼ x 4 In.
$255.00

Lamp, Kerosene, Finger, Cobalt Blue, Coolidge Drape, Taplin-Brown Collar, 5 ⅞ x 5 In.
$270.00

Lamp, Kerosene, Gone With The Wind, Red & Pink Flowers, Green, Early 1900s, 26 In.
$295.00

Lamp, Kerosene, Nara, Opaque White, Pink, Cream Ground, Gilt, Flowers, Scrolls, 8 x 3 In.
$102.00

Grease, Tin, Cylindrical, Tube Stem, Round Base, Flat Loop Handle, Pa., 6 ½ x 6 In. 110.00
Grease, Tin, Cylindrical Reservoir, Tube Stem, Round Dish Base, Loop Handle, 6 ½ x 6 ½ In. 121.00
Handel, lamps are included in the Handel category.
Kerosene, Adams, No. 405, Opaque White Font Base, Drip Catcher, Brown Collar, c.1875, 5 ½ In. 330.00
Kerosene, Admiral Dewey's Bullet, Copper, Opaque Ball Shade, 5 ¾ x 8 ¾ In. *illus* 180.00
Kerosene, Amethyst Base, Fine Line Collar, Clear, Brass Connector, c.1850, 10 ½ x 4 In. 203.00
Kerosene, Arts & Crafts, Stylized Berries, Green, Red Glass, Crystals, 24 x 16 In. *illus* 1560.00
Kerosene, Atterbury, Finger, Embossed Base, Patent Information, 1862, 3 ⅝ In. 96.00
Kerosene, Atterbury, Hexagonal Base, Opaque White, Screw Socket, c.1850, 8 ¼ x 4 In. 48.00
Kerosene, Atterbury, Shelley, Starch Blue, Baroque Base, c.1875, 9 ¾ In. 132.00
Kerosene, Atterbury Filley, Ribbed Band, Collar, c.1850, 3 ⅛ In. 23.00
Kerosene, Atterbury Loop, Yellow-Green Translucent, Double Burner, 8 ¼ x 4 In. *illus* 255.00
Kerosene, Baroque Base, Gilt, Star & Quatrefoil, Ruby Cased Font, c.1850, 13 In. 480.00
Kerosene, Berkshire, Applied Handle, Collar, c.1875, 2 ¾ x 3 ½ In. 132.00
Kerosene, Berkshire, Finger, Applied Handle, c.1880, 2 ¾ x 3 ½ In. 132.00
Kerosene, Blue, Peacock Feather, c.1875, 3 ½ x 4 In. 158.00
Kerosene, Blue Opalescent, Swirl, Taplin-Brown Collar, c.1900, 3 In. 282.00
Kerosene, Bull's-Eye, Brass Collar, Square Base, c.1875, 9 ⅞ In. 56.00
Kerosene, Bull's-Eye, Green, Taplin-Brown Collar, Safety Handle, Footed, c.1875, 5 ½ In. 144.00
Kerosene, Clear, Pear Shape Font, Gilt Leaves, White Stepped Base, c.1875, 14 ¼ x 5 In. 180.00
Kerosene, Clear, Poppy Band, Taplin-Brown Collar, Footed, c.1900, 6 ⅝ x 4 ½ In. 102.00
Kerosene, Clear, Prisms, Applied Handle, c.1875, 3 ½ x 4 In. 11.00
Kerosene, Clear, Ruby Bird & Leaf, Clambroth Baroque Base, Gilt Band, Brass, c.1875, 9 In. 120.00
Kerosene, Clear, Single Rib Collar, Applied Handle, c.1875, 3 x 3 ¾ In. 34.00
Kerosene, Clear, Torpedo, Taplin-Brown Collar, c.1875, 3 ½ x 3 ¾ In. 45.00
Kerosene, Clear Applied Handle, Swirled Segments & Vines, c.1875, 3 ⅛ x 3 ¾ In. 34.00
Kerosene, Clear Font & Stem, Red Base, Brass Connector, c.1875, 10 ½ x 4 In. 60.00
Kerosene, Cleveland & Thurman On Shade, c.1888, 13 In. 478.00
Kerosene, Cobalt Blue Baroque Base, Honeycomb, Fine Line Collar, c.1850, 10 ⅜ In. 147.00
Kerosene, Cobalt Blue Cut To Clear, Cast Brass Base, Swan's Head, Scrolled Tripod, 42 In., Pair 2300.00
Kerosene, Coolidge Drape, Cobalt Blue, Footed, c.1900, 3 ¼ x 3 ⅛ In. 254.00
Kerosene, Cranberry Opalescent Font, Sheldon Swirl, Dotted Band Collar, c.1900, 7 ¼ In. 204.00
Kerosene, Cranberry Swirl, Applied Ruffled Rim, Petal Footed, 7 In. 225.00
Kerosene, Cut Diamonds, Oval Mitered Panels, Marble Base, Silver Plated Stem, c.1850, 11 In. 270.00
Kerosene, Cut Glass, Mushroom Shape Top, 3 Brass Arms, Candlestick Base, 17 ½ In. 345.00
Kerosene, Deep To Light Pink Glass, Embossed, Foreign Burner, 10 In. 460.00
Kerosene, Deep To Light Yellow Glass, Embossed, Foreign Burner, 10 In. 920.00
Kerosene, Diamond, Sunburst, Clear, Applied Handle, Taplin-Brown Collar, c.1875, 3 ¼ In. 30.00
Kerosene, Dietz, Monarch, 13 ½ In. 12.00
Kerosene, Eason, Opalescent Font, Opaque Black Base, Fine Line Collar, c.1900, 8 x 4 In. 192.00
Kerosene, Finger, Cobalt Blue, Coolidge Drape, Taplin-Brown Collar, 5 ⅞ x 5 In. *illus* 270.00
Kerosene, Finger, Cup & Saucer, Taplin-Brown Collar, c.1885, 3 x 5 ⅛ In. 102.00
Kerosene, Finger, Diamond Band & Shield, Cobalt Blue, Applied Handle, Pinwheel, c.1880, 3 ¼ In. 480.00
Kerosene, Finger, Footed, Applied Handle, Taplin-Brown Collar, Chicago, c.1900, 4 ¾ In. 34.00
Kerosene, Finger, Iron Base, Embossed, Taplin-Brown Collar, Barries Patent, Aug. 24, 1875, 6 ¼ In. 158.00
Kerosene, Finger, Poppy Band, Footed, Taplin-Brown Collar, c.1900, 6 ⅝ In. 102.00
Kerosene, Finger, Recessed Drip Catcher Shoulder, Ribs, c.1871-87, 3 ⅛ In. 45.00
Kerosene, Frosted Font, Riverside Clinch Collar, No. 537, c.1900, 5 ½ x 4 ⅝ In. 108.00
Kerosene, Gilt Bronze, Faux Marble, Mask, Draped Mantle, Handles, Late 1800s, 35 x 10 In., Pair 5000.00
Kerosene, Globe, Blue, White, Moorish Window Stand, Marble Base, c.1870, 15 In. 1293.00
Kerosene, Goddess Of Liberty, Milk Glass, Black, Brass Collar, 1868 Screw Connector, 6 In. 215.00
Kerosene, Goddess Of Liberty, Milk Glass, Opaque Black, Frosted Font, Brass Collar, 10 In. 242.00
Kerosene, Gone With The Wind, Beaded Iris, Frosted, Embossed, 27 In. 385.00
Kerosene, Gone With The Wind, George Washington, Abraham Lincoln's Bust, Pink, White, 30 In. 225.00
Kerosene, Gone With The Wind, Red, Cream, 22 In. 172.00
Kerosene, Gone With The Wind, Red & Pink Flowers, Green, Early 1900s, 26 In. *illus* 295.00
Kerosene, Gone With The Wind, Satin Glass, Red, Electrified, 18 In. 230.00
Kerosene, Gone With The Wind, Scroll & Crosshatch, Green Opaque, 20 In. 512.00
Kerosene, Gone With The Wind, Urn, Globular Shade, Red, Pink, Victorian, 26 In. 295.00
Kerosene, Green To Clear Font, Marble Base, Reeded Brass, No. 2 Collar, c.1875, 11 ¼ In. 508.00
Kerosene, Hanging, Opalescent Art Glass, Floral Bronze Fixture 1495.00
Kerosene, Hanging, Ribbed Cranberry Shade, Victorian, 9 In. 201.00
Kerosene, Hanging, Stained Glass, Mushroom Shape, Paneled, Brass, Bronze Dore, 31 x 27 In. 546.00
Kerosene, Hanging, Toleware, Wire Loop, Wide Wick, Push-Up Riser, Filler Spout, 13 In. 29.00
Kerosene, Hobbs, Blackberry Base, Diamond Cluster, Melon, c.1850, 9 x 3 ¼ In. 60.00
Kerosene, Hobbs, Snowflake, No. 341, Footed, Cranberry, Applied Handle, c.1900, 4 ⅞ x 4 ¼ In. 734.00
Kerosene, Hobbs, Snowflake, No. 341, Opalescent, Taplin-Brown Collar, c.1900, 3 In. 270.00

Kerosene, Jensen, Opalescent Font, Blue Base, c.1900, 6 ¾ x 4 In. 367.00
Kerosene, Lampada, Brass, Russia, Late 19th Century, 9 ¾ In. 295.00
Kerosene, Leaf & Jewel, Opalescent Coin Dot Font, Taplin-Brown Collar, c.1900, 9 ⅜ In. 180.00
Kerosene, Log Cabin, Finger, Milk Glass, Hornet Burner, Embossed 1868 Patent Date, 3 ¼ In. 1115.00
Kerosene, Lomax Globe, Clear, Pontil, Fine Line Collar, c.1870, 4 x 3 ¾ In. 34.00
Kerosene, Louis XVI Style, Gilt Bronze, Marble, Urn Shape, Satyr Mask Handles, c.1895, 17 In., Pair 5000.00
Kerosene, Miniature, Pink Satin, Raindrop, Mother-Of-Pearl, Ribbed, Frosted Shell Skirt, 9 ½ In. 2358.00
Kerosene, Nara, Opaque White, Pink, Cream Ground, Gilt, Flowers, Scrolls, 8 x 3 In. *illus* 102.00
Kerosene, New Martinsville Glass Co., Clear, Nosegay, Ebling Collar, Applied Handle, c.1875, 3 In. 36.00
Kerosene, Opaque Blue, Embossed, Swan, Cattails, 7 ¾ x 2 ¾ In. *illus* 1243.00
Kerosene, Parlor, Pull-Down, Milk Glass Shade, Opal Glass Font, Victorian, 18 In. 83.00
Kerosene, Pattern Molded, English Peg, Teal Blue, Band Of Flutes, c.1875, 3 ¾ x 4 ½ In. 11.00
Kerosene, Pattern Molded, Footed, Applied Handle, c.1875, 3 x 2 ¾ In. 90.00
Kerosene, Peachblow, Cased, Flowers, 6 In. 300.00
Kerosene, Peg, Wall Mounted, Green Optic Paneled Fonts, Fleur-De-Lis Embossed, 9 ½ In., Pair 345.00
Kerosene, Polka Dot, Swirled Base & Stem, Taplin-Brown Collar, c.1875, 10 ¾ In. 181.00
Kerosene, Princess Feather, Cobalt Blue, No. 2 Taplin-Brown Collar, c.1900, 9 ½ In. 226.00
Kerosene, Quartered Block, Ebling Collar, c.1875, 3 ⅝ x 3 ¾ In. 68.00
Kerosene, Queen Heart, Clear, Ebling Collar, c.1875, 3 ⅝ x 4 ⅝ In. 102.00
Kerosene, Red Satin, Embossed, Electrified, 11 ¾ In. *illus* 270.00
Kerosene, Ripley, Double Handle, Footed, 2 Font Support, Circles, 1868 Patent, c.1875. 72.00
Kerosene, Rows Of Beads, Fine Line Collar, Clear, c.1850, 6 ¼ x 4 ⅛ In. 90.00
Kerosene, Shield & Star, Translucent Starch Green Base, c.1850, 8 ½ x 3 ¾ In. 216.00
Kerosene, Silver Plate, Mercury Fluted Column Stem, Slate Base, Ring Punty, c.1875, 8 ¾ In. 68.00
Kerosene, Sitzendorf, Putto, Dolphin Pedestal, Applied Flowers, Etched, c.1900, 26 In. *illus* 550.00
Kerosene, Skater's, Red Stained Globe, Brass Font & Mount, Bail Handle, c.1900, 7 In. 540.00
Kerosene, Square, Stippled Stem, Clear, Fine Line Collar, 1868, 5 x 3 ⅝ In. 72.00
Kerosene, Square Stem, Stippled Brackets, Clear, Pontil, 1868, 5 ¼ x 3 ¾ In. 102.00
Kerosene, Starch Blue, Pattern Molded Font, Black Base, Faux Marble, c.1860-80, 9 ¼ In. 360.00
Kerosene, Student, Double, Brass, 2 Fonts, White Milk Glass Shades, 13 ½ In. 420.00
Kerosene, Student, Double, Liberty Bell, Brass Bell Shape Holder Tanks, 1880s, 20 x 27 In. 4700.00
Kerosene, Student, Lion's Heads, Cast Brass, 17 x 8 x 6 ½ In. 330.00
Kerosene, Student, Miller Lamp Co., Yellow Shades, Brass, Electified, 21 In. 350.00
Kerosene, Student, Rochester, Butterscotch, Opaque White Cased, Gilt, Brass, 20 ½ In. *illus* 1200.00
Kerosene, Student, Urn Shape Fonts, Gilt, Black Ground, Electrified, 19th Century, 18 In. 587.00
Kerosene, Sunken Window Stand, Clear, Taplin-Brown Collar, c.1900, 8 ¾ x 5 In. 102.00
Kerosene, U.S. Glass Co., Blue Font, Opaque White Base, Taplin-Brown Collar, c.1900, 8 In. 113.00
Kerosene, Vaseline Opalescent Stripes, Applied Flowers, Red & Pink, 7 ¾ In. *illus* 1955.00
Kerosene, Washington Stand, Cut Overlay, White, Clear Etched Glass Shade, Brass, c.1870, 13 In. 235.00
Kerosene, Westmoreland Specialty, Finger, Daisy, Taplin-Brown Collar, c.1885, 3 ¾ In. 300.00
Kerosene, White, Blue Flowers Glass Shade, Double Overlay Quatrefoil Stand, Brass, 1870, 13 In. 1175.00
Kerosene, White Cut, Green Alabaster Globe, Double Overlay Quatrefoil Stand, Brass, c.1870, 10 In. 940.00
Kerosene, White Loop Threaded Glass Shade, Brass Stem, Marbrie Loop Stand, c.1870, 9 In. 300.00
Kerosene, White Satin Rain Drop, 5 In. 150.00
Kerosene, White Spiraled Threads, Marble Base, Fine Line Collar, c.1875, 8 ¼ x 4 In. 570.00
Kerosene, White To Clear, Black Base, Gilt, Roughed Leaves, No. 1 Collar, c.1875, 9 ¼ In. 124.00
Kerosene, Zipper Loop, Marigold, Taplin-Brown Collar, c.1900, 7 ¼ In. 367.00
Oil, 3-Light, Gilt Bronze, Leaf Branches, Flower Drip Pan, c.1850, 9 ½ In., Pair 881.00
Oil, Altar Light, Neoclassical, Hanging, Nickel Silver, Continental, Early 1900s, 43 x 18 In. 2880.00
Oil, Amber Pressed Glass, Victorian, 20 In. 71.00
Oil, Amber Shaded To Clear, Applied Cranberry Threading, Applied Feet, 10 ¼ In. 3738.00
Oil, Amberina Glass, Applied Leaf, Nutmeg Burner, Amber Feet, 9 In. 575.00
Oil, Applied Flower, Vaseline Opalescent Striped, Red & Pink Flowers, 7 ¾ In. 1955.00
Oil, Artichoke, Blue Aquamarine Satin Glass, Nutmeg Burner, 8 In. 690.00
Oil, Blue, Spanish Lace, Nutmeg Burner, 7 ¾ In. 1840.00
Oil, Blue Cased, Embossed Floret, Quilted Phlox, 7 In. 460.00
Oil, Blue Enamel, Translucent, White Enamel Flowers, 9 ¾ In. 115.00
Oil, Blue Satin, Diamond Quilted, Mother-Of-Pearl, Ball Shade, 5 ½ In. 115.00
Oil, Blue Satin, Pansy Ball Shade, Melon Ribbed, Nutmeg Burner, 7 In. 575.00
Oil, Brady's Night Lamp, Green Satin Glass Shade, Base, Embossed Swirls, Nutmeg Burner, 8 In. 288.00
Oil, Brass, Canister Shape, Hanger Hook, Drip Spout, Copper Handle, 8 x 4 ½ In. *illus* 210.00
Oil, Brass, Cover, Bird Finial, Wick Spout, Wire Wick Pick, Gaff Hanger, 4 ¼ x 3 x 5 In. 99.00
Oil, Brass, Dome Top, Incised Grape Leaves, Anthemion Handle, Tole Plinth, c.1800s, 9 x 19 In. 1880.00
Oil, Brass, Iron, Hanger Hook, Disc Reservoir, Wick Hole, 21 x 4 ½ In. 275.00
Oil, Brass, Iron, Hanger Hook, Disc Shape Reservoir, 10 ½ x 10 ½ In. 66.00
Oil, Bronze, Cloisonne, Brass Font, Square Brass Base, Silk Shade, Electrified, Asia, 40 In. 575.00
Oil, Cabbage Rose, Green Bowl, Clear Chimney, 19 ½ In. 44.00

Lamp, Kerosene, Opaque Blue, Embossed, Swan, Cattails, 7 ¾ x 2 ¾ In.
$1243.00

Lamp, Kerosene, Red Satin, Embossed, Electrified, 11 ¾ In.
$270.00

Lamp, Kerosene, Sitzendorf, Putto, Dolphin Pedestal, Applied Flowers, Etched, c.1900, 26 In.
$550.00

Lamp, Kerosene, Student, Rochester, Butterscotch, Opaque White Cased, Gilt, Brass, 20 ½ In.
$1200.00

Lamp, Kerosene, Vaseline Opalescent Stripes, Applied Flowers, Red & Pink, 7 ¾ In.
$1955.00

Lamp, Oil, Brass, Canister Shape, Hanger Hook, Drip Spout, Copper Handle, 8 x 4 ½ In.
$210.00

Oil, Candy Stripes, Pink, White Cased, Satin, 10 In. 2760.00
Oil, Cased Satin Glass, Raspberry To Pink, Ruffled Saucer, 3-Footed, 12 ½ In., 3 Piece. 748.00
Oil, Chartreuse, White, Gold, Orange Enamel Flowers Shade, Base, Nutmeg Burner, 8 In. 863.00
Oil, Clear Glass, Rainbow Swirl Pattern, Hornet Burner, Crystal Applied Leaf Feet, 9 In. 2185.00
Oil, Cone Shape, Cranberry Reverse, Spangled Foot, Victorian, 19 In. 212.00
Oil, Consolidated Glass Co., Basket, Yellow Cased, Embossed, 7 In. 805.00
Oil, Consolidated Lamp, Melon Ribbed, Cased Interior Shade, Yellow Base, 7 ¼ In. 460.00
Oil, Cox Argand, Artichoke Finial, Urn With Swags, 2 Frosted Globes, Prisms, c.1865, 20 In., Pair 2875.00
Oil, Cranberry, Opalescent, Clear Pedestal Base, Nutmeg Burner, 7 ½ In. 690.00
Oil, Cranberry, White Enamel Flowers, Gold Banding, 9 ¾ In. 115.00
Oil, Cranberry Chimney, Ribbed, Ruffled Shade, Ribbed Base, Applied Feet, 9 ½ In. 3105.00
Oil, Cut Glass, Silver Plate, Columnar, Fluted Shaft, Corinthian Capital, Clear Font, 32 In. . . . 382.00
Oil, Cut Glass Mushroom Shade, Base, Prisms, Silver Plated Collar, 10 x 12 In. 1265.00
Oil, Dithridge & Co., Versailles, Milk Glass, Roses, Pink, Green, Yellow, Ribbon, 1900, 15 In. . . 30.00
Oil, Double Crusie, Brass, Engraved, Filigree, Dutch, 14 ½ In. 695.00
Oil, End Of Day, Beige, Brown, Beaded, Embossed, Swirling Design, 8 ¾ In. 115.00
Oil, Etched Glass, Greek Key Design, Brass Base, Blue Glass Chips, Electrified, 33 In. 59.00
Oil, Finger, Log Cabin, Milk Glass, Embossed 1868, 1875, 3 ¼ x 2 ¾ In. 1015.00
Oil, Finger, Satin Glass, Rose Shaded To Pink, Embossed, Applied Reeded Handle, 3 ¼ x 3 ¼ In. 288.00
Oil, Finger, White Milk Glass, Cigar Light Shade, Lock On Burner, 7 ¼ In., 3 Piece 115.00
Oil, Frosted, Celeste Blue Stand, Victorian, 22 In. 153.00
Oil, Glass, Greek Key On Frosted Glass Globe, Opal Font, Blue Base, 8 ½ In. 115.00
Oil, Glossy Melon Ribbed Rainbow Glass Shade, Applied Clear Base Shells, Silver Plate, 10 In. 4600.00
Oil, Goofus Glass, Red Flowers, Green Leaves, Gold Paint, 17 ¾ In. 220.00
Oil, Green Satin Drape, Acorn Burner, 8 ¼ In. 173.00
Oil, Iron, 2 Parts, Teardrop Drip Tray, Swivel, 8 x 6 ½ x 4 In. 44.00
Oil, Iron, 2-Light, Adjustable Arm, Center Post, Tripod, Penny Feet, 1800s, 22 ½ In. 978.00
Oil, Iron, Adjustable Plate, Slotted Wick Holder, Stand, 3 Scroll Feet, 1800s, 21 In. 1035.00
Oil, Iron, Lollipop Shape Reservoir, Hinged, Wick Pick, Gaff Hanger, 4 ¾ x 4 ¼ In. 121.00
Oil, Jadeite, Globe, Octagonal Base, 1900s, 10 In. 150.00
Oil, Kosmos-Brenner, Cranberry Satin Glass, Square Base, Ruffled Rim 978.00
Oil, Kosmos-Brenner, Dark To Light Pink Satin Glass, Brass Holder, 12 In. 1610.00
Oil, Magnet Co., Nickel Finish, Globe 20.00
Oil, Milk Glass, Embossed Fishnet, Flowers, Painted, Nutmeg Burner, 7 ¾ In., Pair 58.00
Oil, Mother-Of-Pearl, Cased Glass, Satin Raindrop Pattern, Shade, Nutmeg Burner, 8 In. 345.00
Oil, Mother-Of-Pearl, Diamond Quilted, Blue Satin Shade, Silver Plated Base, Foreign Burner, 11 In. 259.00
Oil, Mother-Of-Pearl, Diamond Quilted, Melon Ribbing, Dark To Light Pink, Frosted Feet, 10 In. 1725.00
Oil, Mother-Of-Pearl, Embossed White Satin Raindrop Pattern, Nutmeg Burner, 8 In. 460.00
Oil, Pink & White Spatter Glass, Swirled Ribbing, Nutmeg Burner, 6 In. 633.00
Oil, Pink Satin, Cased, Ruffled Top, White Herringbone Shade, 6 ¾ In. 345.00
Oil, Porcelain, Teal Ground, Glass Globe, Ormolu Mount, Continental, 25 In., Pair 388.00
Oil, Pressed Glass, Cornflower Blue, Tooled Mouth, Tin Burners, 5 ⅜ In., Pair 2645.00
Oil, Pressed Glass, Wedding, Opal, Match Holder, Mid 1800s, 20 In. . . . . *illus* 490.00
Oil, Queen Mfg. Pressed Glass, Fan Pattern, 16 ½ In. 100.00
Oil, Raspberry Satin, Mother-Of-Pearl, Diamond Pattern, 6 In. 748.00
Oil, Red Enamel, White Enamel Flowers, 6 ⅛ In. 518.00
Oil, Red Satin, Embossed, 11 ¾ In. 270.00
Oil, Ribbed Ruby Chimney, 9 ¼ In. 374.00
Oil, Ruby Glass Font, Floral Etched Shade, Brass, 19th Century, 24 In. . . . . *illus* 165.00
Oil, Satin Blue Milk Glass, Embossed Ribs, Nutmeg Burner, 8 ½ In. 920.00
Oil, Satin White Milk Glass, Embossed Ribs, Shell, Flowers, Hornet Burner, 7 ¾ In. 288.00
Oil, Sinumbra, Cut Glass, Bronze, Marble Base, Early 1800s, 23 In. . . . . *illus* 495.00
Oil, Sinumbra, Cut Glass, Frosted, Faceted Prisms, Gilt Lacquered Brass, 30 ¼ x 14 In. 960.00
Oil, Sinumbra, Cut Leaf & Berry, Opalescent Column, Gilt, Brass Font, Base, 29 In. . . . . *illus* 660.00
Oil, Softwood Stand, Oval, 3 Square Legs, 6 ¾ x 9 ½ x 4 ¾ In. 248.00
Oil, Street Light, Wood Stand, Iron Base, Metal Head, c.1900 . . . . . 200.00
Oil, Thumbprint & Fern, Brass & Marble Base, 11 In. 125.00
Oil, Tin, Cone Shape, Cast Metal, 2 Wick Holders, 5 ½ x 3 In. 44.00
Oil, Tin, Dome, Screw Top Wick Holder, Side Fill Spout, Cap, C-Shape Handle, 3 ¾ x 2 ½ In. . . 33.00
Oil, Tin, Kettle, Cylinder Reservoir, Wick Holder, Swivel Base, Stand, 8 x 4 ¼ In. 275.00
Oil, Tin, Sheath, Well, Wick Spout, Handle, Latch Cover, 5 ½ x 3 ¼ x 1 ½ In. 220.00
Oil, Tin, Stand, Cylinder Reservoir, Raised Banding, 7 ¼ x 7 In. 121.00
Oil, Torchere, Wrought Iron, 3-Light, Twisted Shaft, Tripod Base, 56 In., Pair 863.00
Oil, Transparent Red, Gold, Blue, White Enamel, 10 In. 2530.00
Oil, Urn Shape Reservoir, Ribbed, Pedestal, Claw Feet, Victorian, 69 x 15 In. 443.00
Oil, White Milk Glass, Embossed, Owl Shape, Nutmeg Burner, 8 In. 805.00
Oil, Workman's, Tin, Screw Top, Cone Shape Body, Chain & Hanger Hook, Handle, 8 x 9 In. . . 88.00

Oil, Yellow Cased, Orange & Gold Flowers, Nutmeg Burner, 8 In. 805.00
Oil, Yellow Pansy Ball Shade, Yellow Melon Ribbed Base, Nutmeg Burner, 7 In. 288.00
Oil, Yellow Swirled, Ribbed, Recessed Medallions, Applied Feet, Acorn Burner, 8 ¼ In. 978.00
Pairpoint lamps are In the Pairpoint category.
Rush, Iron, Brass Finial, Candle Cup, Late 18th Century, 34 In. 1521.00
Rush, Iron, Combination, Forged, Counterbalance, Twisted, Turned Wood Base, 8 In. 120.00
Sconce, 2-Light, Blue Celeste Porcelain Oval, 2 Romantic Figures, Bronze, c.1900, 19 In. 885.00
Sconce, 2-Light, Edwardian, Gilt Brass, Furled Bowknot, 5 Bellflowers, 22 In. 1080.00
Sconce, 2-Light, Empire, Gilt Bronze, Cut Glass, Glass Chains, Ram's Head, 28 ½ In., Pair 2963.00
Sconce, 2-Light, Empire Style, Bronze Dore, Brazier Escutcheon, 20th Century, 14 In., Pair 177.00
Sconce, 2-Light, George III Style, Giltwood, Eagle, Ribboned, Tassels, 36 x 15 In., Pair 6875.00
Sconce, 2-Light, Green Glass Arms, Lucite, Brass Sockets, Stars, Shells, Italy, 14 x 12 In., Pair 540.00
Sconce, 2-Light, Louis XV, Gold Ribbon Tied Backplate, Porcelain Flowers, 15 x 14 In., Pair 9375.00
Sconce, 2-Light, Louis XVI, Gilt Metal, Ribbon Shape, Oval Plaque, Scenic, 14 In., Pair 1800.00
Sconce, 2-Light, Louis XVI Style, Iron, Rusted Matte White, 16 x 11 ½ In., Pair 2040.00
Sconce, 2-Light, Silver Plate, Scrolled Arms, Fruit Basket Backplate, 14 ½ In., Pair 1840.00
Sconce, 3-Light, Cast Brass, Lyre Pediment, Removable Arms, 1800s, 11 In., Pair 546.00
Sconce, 3-Light, Cast Iron, Twisted Standard, Leaf Decoration, 37 ¼ In., Pair 360.00
Sconce, 3-Light, Tin, Oval Back, 19th Century, 9 x 13 In., Pair 4680.00
Sconce, 5-Light, J. Royere, 5 Shades, Gilt, Iron, c.1950, 26 In., Pair 20000.00
Sconce, Brass, Candle, Scrolled Arm, Round Bracket, Drip Pan, Early 1800s, 9 In., Pair 2415.00
Sconce, Candle, Arched, Crimped Reflectors, 19th Century, 11 ¼ In., Pair 206.00
Sconce, Cast Brass, Mirrored, Sunburst Shape Pine Backs, Etched Faces, Cut Rays, 15 In., Pair 6463.00
Sconce, Coral Shape, Enameled Brass, 2 Arms, 20th Century, 15 In., Pair 353.00
Sconce, Iron, Branch, Flowers, Scrolls, 10 Candle Spikes, Black, 55 In. 374.00
Sconce, Pierre Fargette, Nickel Plated Metal, Colored Glass, c.1940, 15 x 11 In., Pair 823.00
Sconce, Sabino, Art Deco, Triangular Shape, 14 In., 3 Piece 3120.00
Sconce, Silver Plate, Swan Arms, Floral Garlands, France, c.1900, 16 In., Pair 2115.00
Sconce, Tin, Candle Cup, Scalloped Top, Cutout Round Mirror, 19th Century, 14 ½ In. 3510.00
Sconce, Tin, Ridged Back, Crimped Crest, 19th Century, 9 ¾ In., Pair 470.00
Sconce, Tin, Round, Rayed Back, Crimped Candle Cups, 19th Century, 9 ½ In., Pair 441.00
Sconce, Tin, Round Reflectors, Candleholder, Mid 18th Century, 9 ¼ In. 3978.00
Sconce, 2-Light, Brass, Crystal, Ram's Head Cast Drop Finial, 4 Arms, Prisms, c.1900, 24 In., Pair 2990.00
Sconce, Bronze Dore, 3-Light, Leaves, Flowers, France, 1800s, 22 x 25 x 17 In. 875.00
Solar, Brass, Bronze Hexagonal Column, Pear Shape Font, Oregon Shade, 15 ½ x 26 In. 805.00
Solar, Brass, Gilt, Globular Cut Glass Shade, Marble Base, 29 In. 2644.00
Solar, Dietz & Co., Frosted, Cut Shade, Blue Alabaster Reeded Stem, Marble Base, c.1860, 15 In. 420.00
Solar, H. Hudson, Frosted, Cut Shade, Metal Stem Mounts, Pull Chain, Marble Base, c.1850, 16 In. 360.00
Solar, Patinated Brass, Gothic Arches, Crockets, Tracery, Globular Etched Shade, 29 In. 2467.00
Solar, Rococo, Gilt, Lacquered Brass, Flower Decorations, Prisms, c.1850, 21 In. 1527.00
Tiffany lamps are listed in the Tiffany category.
Torchere, 7-Light, Carved, Ebony, Gilt Blackamoor, Stamped, Italy, 1900s, 80 x 24 x 21 In. 1380.00
Torchere, Art Deco, Ebonized, Round Silver Metal Bowl Shade, Cone Shape Base, 68 x 24 In. 944.00
Torchere, Brass, Iron, Marble Base, Acid Cut Shades, c.1920, 68 In., Pair 1380.00
Torchere, Bronze Dore, Leaves, Faces, Marble Base, 40 x 10 In., Pair 748.00
Torchere, Edgar Brandt, Bronze, Snake Shape, Round Base, 61 In., Pair 1320.00
Whale Oil, Alabaster, Clambroth, Hexagonal, 2-Tube Burner, c.1850, 10 In. 621.00
Whale Oil, Applied Handle, No. 1 Collar, J. Sangster Patent, 1862, c.1875, 3 ⅜ In. 228.00
Whale Oil, Applied Handle, Pewter Collar, Burner, 3-Printie Block, c.1850, 3 ⅛ In. 147.00
Whale Oil, Brass, 3 Horizontal Bands, Turned Stem, Egg Shape Font, Round Foot, 8 ¼ In. 180.00
Whale Oil, Brass, Iron, Nautical, 5 x 3 ¼ In. 465.00
Whale Oil, Brass, No. 60, 7 x 3 ½ In. 275.00
Whale Oil, Canary, Hexagonal, Pewter Collar, Waisted Loop, c.1840, 8 ¾ In. 452.00
Whale Oil, Clambroth, Hexagonal, Star & Punty, No. 1 Collar, c.1850, 10 ⅛ In. 570.00
Whale Oil, Clear Glass, Hand Formed, Drip Tray, Cork & Pewter Burner, 8 In. .... *illus* 365.00
Whale Oil, Double Burners, Pewter Bobeches, Circular Plinths, Roswell Gleason, 10 In., Pair 805.00
Whale Oil, Etched Wheat Sheath, 13 ½ In., Pair 470.00
Whale Oil, Globe, Medial Pattern Band, Peg, c.1825, 4 ½ In. 147.00
Whale Oil, Molded Handle, Moon & Star, No. 1 Collar, c.1875, 3 ¾ In. 120.00
Whale Oil, Star & Punty, 6-Sided, Bell Shape, Handle, No. 1 Collar, 4 ¾ x 4 ½ In. .... *illus* 120.00
Whale Oil, Tin, Red Paint, 8 x 8 In. 135.00
Whale Oil, Tin, Ring Handle, Cylindrical Shaft, Tray, Reservoir, 7 ¼ x 8 ¾ x 6 ⅛ In. 110.00
Whale Oil, Used At Mammoth Cave, Ky., c.1930, 13 ½ In. 748.00

LAMPSHADE

Acorn, Leaded Glass, Yellow Mottled, Cream Ground, Geometric, 16 In. 5750.00
Art Glass, Bell Shape, Gold Iridescent, Pink Highlights, Ribbing, Gold Interior, 6 ¼ x 8 In. 345.00

Lamp, Oil, Pressed Glass, Wedding, Opal, Match Holder, Mid 1800s, 20 In.
$490.00

Lamp, Oil, Ruby Glass Font, Floral Etched Shade, Brass, 19th Century, 24 In.
$165.00

Lamp, Oil, Sinumbra, Cut Glass, Bronze, Marble Base, Early 1800s, 23 In.
$495.00

L

Lamp, Oil, Sinumbra, Cut Leaf & Berry, Opalescent Column, Gilt, Brass Font, Base, 29 In.
$660.00

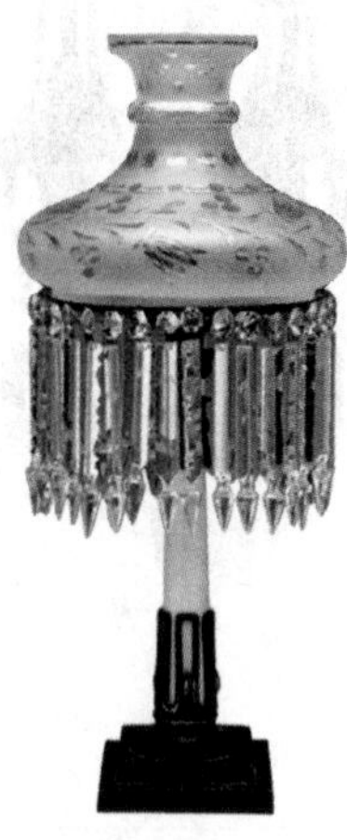

Lamp, Whale Oil, Clear Glass, Hand Formed, Drip Tray, Cork & Pewter Burner, 8 In.
$365.00

Lamp, Whale Oil, Star & Punty, 6-Sided, Bell Shape, Handle, No. 1 Collar, 4 ¾ x 4 ½ In
$120.00

Art Glass, Blue Pulled Feather, Gold Border, Ivory Ground, 5 x 3 ¼ In. 288.00
Art Glass, Calcite, Tulip Shape, 5 In., 4 Piece 90.00
Art Glass, Dome, Gold Fishnet, White Ground, 3 x 8 In. 1265.00
Art Glass, Dome, Gold Iridescent, Applied Glass Pods, Signed, 5 x 7 ½ In. 345.00
Art Glass, Gold Iridescent, Brown Feathering, Ribbed Body, 5 ½ In. 58.00
Art Glass, Gold Pulled Feather, Iridescent Green, Gold Interior, Ruffled Edge, 7 x 2 ¼ In. 115.00
Art Glass, Hooked Feather, Bullet Shape, Cream Ground, Gold Iridescent Threading, 9 In. 690.00
Art Glass, Mushroom Shape, Blue, Platinum Iridescent Ovals, Green, Tan Ground, 10 x 8 In. 173.00
Art Glass, Pulled Feather, Green Iridescent, Ruffled Edges, Gold Interior, 6 x 2 ¼ In., Pair 230.00
Art Glass, Threaded Leaf & Vine, Gold, On Cream, Iridescent, 10 In. 1323.00
Art Glass, Uneven Border, Tiles, Flowers, Green, Yellow, Pink, Duffner & Kimberly, 20 In. 2645.00
Art Glass, White, Gold, Green Iridescent Pulled Feather, Scalloped Edge, 4 In. 177.00
Bronzed Metal Frame, Inlaid Panels, 6-Sided, Stylized & Geometric, 15 x 23 In. 900.00
Coralene Glass, Iridescent Orange, Mountain Scene, Dome, c.1910, 8 ½ x 7 ½ In. 595.00
Cut Glass, Hobstar, Vesica & Circles, Ball Shape, 6 In. 440.00
Fiberglass, Metal, Gold Paint Spatters, Gold String, 4 ½ x 4 ⅛ In. 10.00
Glass, Frosted, Tulip Shape, Flared Ruffled Top, 4 ½ x 6 In. 15.00
Glass, Painted Birds, Flowers, Blue Inside, Textured & Embossed Swirls, 5 ½ In. 65.00
Gold Iridescent Glass, Opal Snakeskin, Green & Gold Pulled Design, 5 ¼ x 2 ¼ In. 288.00
Gold Iridescent Glass, White & Green Feathered Design, Signed, 4 ¼ In., Pair 275.00
Hurricane, Engraved, Flowers, Flared Lip, George IV, 23 x 8 ½ In. 660.00
Iridescent Glass, Gold, Etched Pansies, Bell Shape, Early 1900s, 5 ¼ x 5 In., 4 Piece 174.00
Leaded Glass, 6-Sided, Caramel Slag, Grapevine Overlay, Beading, Open Edge Chainwork, 14 In. 540.00
Mercury Glass, Blue, Diamond Pattern Inside, c.1890-1910, 6 In. 145.00
Milk Glass, Globe, Scalloped Edge, 5 x 5 In. 22.00
Owl, Glass, Brown, Art Deco, Screw-In Base, 7 In. 150.00
Pittsburgh, Domed Shade, Reverse Painted, Red & Orange Winter Farm Scene, 16 In. 288.00
Silver, Pierced, Gorham, 4 ¼ x 7 In., Pair 24.00
Stained Glass, Bird, Fruit, Leaves, 16 x 27 ¼ In. 354.00
Tin, Pierced, Art Nouveau, Irises In Relief, Pomegranate Glass Bead Fringe, 6 In. 40.00
Yellow Pulled Feather, Cream Ground, Iridescent, Green Outline, 7 ½ In. 690.00

LANTERNS are a special type of lighting device. They have a light source, usually a candle, totally hidden inside the walls of the lantern. Light is seen through holes or glass sections.

Allen, Brass, Fire Truck, 7, 20 In., Pair 819.00
Arts & Crafts, Leaded Glass, 4-Sided, Prairie Design, 7 x 9 In. 360.00
Brass, Dietz, Convex, Kerosene, Folding Handles, 5 ⅞ x 3 ⅜ x 2 ¼ In. .... *illus* 55.00
Brass, Glass, Cobalt, Ruby, Cupola Vents, Vase Shape, England, 26 ½ x 13 x 8 ½ In. 1800.00
Brass, Glass, Inverted Bowl Shape, England, 11 ¾ In. 420.00
Bronze, Dragons, Shishi, Japan, 24 In. 326.00
Candle, Copper, Wire Hanger, Vent Holes, 6 Glass Panes, 13 x 8 ½ In. 66.00
Candle, Tin, Octagonal, Glass Sides, Wavy Mounts, Wire Hanger, 5 x 3 ⅜ In. 88.00
Candle, Tin, Ring Handle, Crimped Roof, Glass Pane, Hinged Door, Hasp, 13 x 3 ¾ In. 6.00
Candle, Tin, Wire Handle, 3 Glass Windows, Slide Door, 13 x 6 x 6 In. 99.00
Cast Metal, Brass, Twist Rod Support, Lighting Element, 4-Sided Frame, 57 In. 300.00
Chunk Jewel, Multicolored, Diamond Shape, 14 In. 230.00
Contemporary, Wirework, Linen Lined, Globular, Japonesque Style, 34 x 20 In. .... 96.00 to 150.00
Copper, Frosted Glass, Mounted, Arts & Crafts, Pair, 9 ½ x 11 ½ In. 1320.00
Copper, Zinc, Lemon Finial, Stepped Copper Top, Glazed Panels, Late 1800s, 44 x 20 In. 1380.00
Dietz, Brass, Red Globe, 18 ¼ In. 210.00
Dietz, Fire King, Nickel Plated, 14 ¾ In., Pair 150.00
Eclipse, Red Globe, Nickel Plated Brass, Bale, 20 In. 1475.00
Entrance, Georgian Style, Copper, Glass, Iron, Hexagonal, Black Matte, 41 x 28 In. 2160.00
Firehouse, Dietz King, Brass, August 27, 1907 .... 355.00
G. Stickley, Hammered Copper, Amber Glass Inserts, Geometric Overlay, Handle, 10 x 6 In. 1800.00
G. Stickley, Hammered Copper, Amber Liner, Hanging, Chain, 36 x 8 ½ In. 2500.00
G. Stickley, Hammered Copper, Umber Slag Glass, Hanging, Chain, 12 ½ x 7 In. 2000.00
G. Stickley, Iron, Pierced Design, Glass Panels, Chain, Ceiling Cap, Yates Hotel, N.Y., 30 x 9 In. 2160.00
Gas, Red Glass, 36 In., Pair 550.00
Hanging, Copper, Patina, Tapered Square, 3 Candlelights, 4 Side Panels, 1800s, 18 x 10 In. 329.00
Hanging, Cylindrical, Cone Top, Tin, Horn Panels, Dormer Vents, England, 1700s, 17 In. 633.00
Iron, Painted, Pierced, Leaf Shape Crown, Scrolled Arms, Early 1900s, 46 x 23 In. 978.00
Japanese, Ni-O Figurative, Man Holding Finial On Head, Black, Red, Edo Period, 70 In., Pair 598.00
Justrite, Engraved, Jack Fuller From Bertie, Tin Container, 5 Keys, Box. 260.00
Kerosene, Bail Handle, Pierced Dome Top, Bulbous Globe, Tin, 13 ¾ x 5 ¾ In. 33.00
Moroccan, Tin, Colored Glass, 19th Century, 17 ½ x 8 In., Pair 115.00

Parade, Wood Stick, 56 In. 100.00
Reflector, Painted Green, Gilford, Maine, 13 x 13 x 23 In. 2013.00
Reflector, Tinned Sheet Iron, Dome Top, Red & Yellow Paint, 19th Century, 13 In. 1053.00
Ring Handle, Cone, Smokestack Vent, Hinged Door, Tin, 15 ¼ x 5 ½ In. 88.00
Temple, Cast Iron, 19th Century, 51 x 15 ½ In. 475.00
Tin, 4-Sided, Corner, Mirrored, Early 19th Century, 14 ¾ x 9 In. 108.00
Tin, 6 Wicks, Handle, 2 Gal., 9 x 8 ½ In. 70.00
Tin, Candle, Cylindrical, Ring Handle, Crimped Vent Cover, 4 Panels, 11 x 4 In. 198.00
Tin, Punched, Cylindrical, Hinged Door, Paul Revere Style, 19th Century, 17 In. 475.00
Tin, Punched Bottom, Glass Thumb Lamp, Mirror Reflector, Dec. 10, 1867, 16 x 6 ½ In. 200.00
Wood, Hexagonal Frame, Fretwork Rails, Reverse Painted Flowers, Chinese, 19 ½ In. 8050.00

LE VERRE FRANCAIS is one of the many types of cameo glass made by the Schneider Glassworks in France. The glass was made by the C. Schneider factory in Epinay-sur-Seine from 1918 to 1933. It is a mottled glass, usually decorated with floral designs, and bears the incised signature *Le Verre Francais*.

Le Verre Français

Pitcher, Kalanchoe, Brown, Orange Ground, Purple Handle, Signed, 8 In. 1760.00
Vase, Berries, Leaves, Orange, Cobalt Blue, Knob Stem, Footed, 7 In. 805.00
Vase, Butterfly, Blue & Brown Mottled, Aqua, Cream Ground, Footed, 3 ¼ In. 1800.00
Vase, Crimson Border, Branching Stems, Flared Rim, Footed, 9 ¾ In. 1035.00
Vase, Dahlia, Amethyst, Mottled Purple Stems, Leaves, Mottled Pink, 17 ¼ In. 1200.00
Vase, Fougeres, Orange Tendrils, Signed, 4 ⅜ x 6 In. 1210.00
Vase, Mottled Powder Blue, Royal Blue, 18 ½ In. 2128.00
Vase, Orange, Flowers, Branches, Signed, 16 In. .... *illus* 2588.00
Vase, Orange Cherries, Leaves, Mauve Ground, Shouldered, 17 In. 4200.00
Vase, Orange Flowers, Frosted Ground, Purple Mottled Foot, 9 ¼ In. 1323.00
Vase, Pebble Base, Flowers, Multicolored, Egg Shape, Flat Rim, 7 In. 920.00
Vase, Pods Of Grapes, Footed, Mottled Purple, Orange Ground, Footed, Oval, 5 ½ In. 633.00
Vase, Poppies, Orange, Mottled Yellow, Brown Pebbled Base, 9 ½ In. 1100.00
Vase, Red Art Deco Flowers, Mottled Yellow Ground, Footed Urn, Signed, 6 In. 518.00
Vase, Seed Pods, Leaves, Tortoiseshell, Amber Ground, Pebbled Base, 10 ¾ In. 1093.00

LEATHER is tanned animal hide and it has been used to make decorative and useful objects for centuries. Leather objects must be carefully preserved with proper humidity and oiling or the leather will deteriorate and crack. This damage cannot be repaired.

Holster, Artillery, For 5.5-In. Colt Single Action, Embossed U.S., Initials 900.00
Racket Case, Brass Mounted, Holds 2 Rackets, England, 19th Century, 28 ½ x 10 ½ In. 86.00
Saddle, Hereford Brand Tex Tan, Hand Tooled, Suede Seat, Yoakum, 24 x 21 In. 2900.00
Saddlebag, Tooled, Floral & Leaf Design, Foldover Flap, Double Closure, 11 x 12 In. 230.00
Wallet, Gift Of Hen Drinker To Caspar Wistar, June 30, 1760, 4 ¾ x 7 ¼ In. 2574.00

LEEDS pottery was made at Leeds, Yorkshire, England, from 1774 to 1878. Most Leeds ware was not marked. Early Leeds pieces had distinctive twisted handles with a greenish glaze on part of the creamy ware. Later ware often had blue borders on the creamy pottery. A Chicago company named Leeds made many Disney-inspired figurines. They are listed in the Disneyana category.

LEEDS POTTERY.

Candlestick, Reticulated, Square, c.1900, 7 In., Pair 644.00
Coffeepot, Flowers, Blue, Tan, Soft Paste, Loop Handle, Miniature .... *illus* 375.00
Creamer, Flower & Leaf, Helmet Shape, Multicolored, 5 ⅜ In. 198.00
Creamer, Sunflower, Helmet Shape, Soft Paste, Scalloped Rim, 5 ⅛ In. .... *illus* 475.00
Pepper Pot, Green, Ribbed Band, 4 ½ In. 140.00
Pitcher, Milk, Flower, Acorn, Green Edge, Leaf & Fish Scale Border, Bulbous, 7 ¾ In. 605.00
Plate, 4-Bud Cluster, Scalloped Feather Edge, Soft Paste, 5 ¾ In. 950.00
Plate, Eagle, Green Feather Edge, c.1820, 6 ½ In. 995.00
Plate, Eagle, Shield, Green Rim, Soft Paste, 8 In. 950.00
Plate, Flower Basket, Green Feather Edge, Scalloped Rim, 8 ⅛ In. 1650.00
Plate, Flower Bouquet, Green Feather Edge, c.1820, 9 ½ In. 380.00
Plate, Flowers, Leaves, Flower Border, Canary Yellow, 8 ¾ In. 468.00
Plate, House, Trees, Blue Feather Edge, 4 ¼ In. 450.00
Plate, Peafowl, On Branch, Blue Feather, Scalloped Rim, Soft Paste, 8 In. 450.00
Plate, Peafowl, On Branch, Feather Edge, 8-Sided, Soft Paste, 4 In. 600.00
Plate, Peafowl, Tree, Green Feather Edge, Scalloped Rim, 19th Century 800.00
Platter, 3 Flowers, Leaves, Feather Edge, Blue, White, c.1820, 12 ½ x 17 In. 2340.00
Platter, Flower, Fish Scale Border, Multicolored, Soft Paste, 1 ¼ x 12 ¼ x 9 ½ In. 1100.00
Platter, Flower Basket, Oval, Blue Scalloped Edge, Soft Paste, 1 ¼ x 14 x 10 ½ In. 1000.00
Toddy Plate, Eagle, Blue Feathered Rim, 19th Century, 5 In. 380.00

Lantern, Brass, Dietz, Convex, Kerosene, Folding Handles, 5 ⅞ x 3 ⅜ x 2 ¼ In.
$55.00

Le Verre Francais, Vase, Orange, Flowers, Branches, Signed, 16 In.
$2588.00

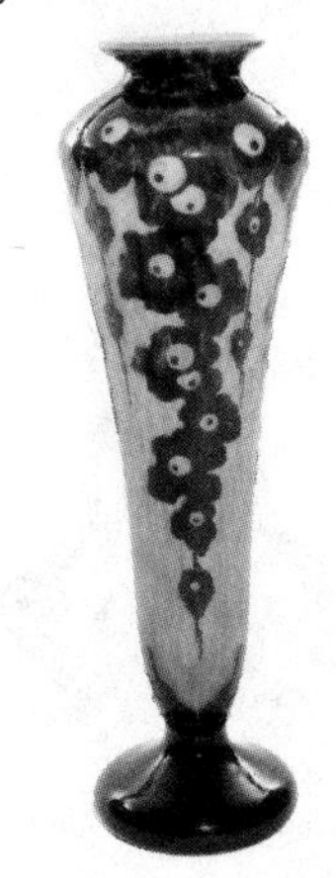

Leeds, Coffeepot, Flowers, Blue, Tan, Soft Paste, Loop Handle, Miniature
$375.00

Leeds, Creamer, Sunflower, Helmet Shape, Soft Paste, Scalloped Rim, 5 ⅛ In.
$475.00

L

Lefton, Salt & Pepper, Miss Priss
$25.00

Legras, Vase, Grapes On The Vine, Textured Ground, Spattered With White, 6 ¾ In.
$403.00

Legras, Vase, Lake, Trees, Cameo, Signed, 8 ¼ In.
$175.00

LEFTON is a mark found on pottery, porcelain, glass, and other wares imported by the Geo. Zoltan Lefton Company. The company began in 1941 and is still in business. It was restructured in 2002 and is now called The Lefton Company. The company mark has changed through the years, but because marks have been used for long periods of time, they are of little help in dating an object.

Birthday Girl, 3 Years, Holding Doll, Sticker, Medallion 20.00
Birthday Girl, 4 Years, Holding Flower Basket, Sticker, Medallion 22.00
Birthday Girl, 9 Years, Holding Bluebird, Sticker, Medallion 23.00
Bowl, Roses, Pink, Oval, Footed, Bisque, Pearl Interior, c.1953, 8 x 4 ½ In. 225.00
Candy Cane Holder, Snow Woman, 6 In. 22.00
Coffeepot, Green Heritage, Marked, 9 In. 140.00
Cookie Jar, Miss Priss 50.00
Cup, Golden Wheat, Square Handle, 6 Oz. 5.00
Figurine, Christmas Angel, Playing Drum, Pink, Gold Trim, 4 In. 12.00
Figurine, Clown, Bird In The Hat Trick, No. 02355, Bisque, 7 In. 35.00
Figurine, Girl, With Basket, Skipping, Stamped, 5 ½ In. 10.00
Figurine, Parakeet, Blue, Green, 5 In. 27.00
Figurine, Snow Bird, 3 ½ In. 16.00
Figurine, Spring Flowers, Bouquet Bold, Orange, Pink, Yellow, 3 ½ In. 20.00
Head Vase, Woman, Green Hat, Long Gloves, Hand On Chin, No. 4228, 5 ⅝ In. 44.00
Napkin Holder, Mr. Toodles, 5 In. 24.00
Nut Dish, Leaf Shape, Roses, Gold Trim, 6 x 5 ½ In. 6.00
Pitcher, Saucer, Holly, White, Gold Trim, Mark, 4 x 4 In. 10.00
Salt & Pepper, Miss Priss .... *illus* 25.00
Salt & Pepper, Mr. Toodles 25.00
Salt & Pepper, Owls, Rhinestone Eyes, Stamped, Foil Label, 3 ½ In. 17.00
Soap Dish, Flower Bouquet, Mint Green, Scalloped Edges, Gold Trim, 6 ½ x 5 In. 12.00
Sugar, Cover, Pink Roses, Green Leaves, Gilt 16.00
Toothpick, Salt & Pepper, Christmas Tree, 1950s, 7 ¼-In. Toothpick, 3 Piece 75.00
Trinket Box, Sunflower, Yellow, Orange, Green, Marked, c.1984, 3 x 4 In. 9.00

LEGRAS was founded in 1864 by Auguste Legras at St. Denis, France. It is best known for cameo glass and enamel-decorated glass with Art Nouveau designs. Legras merged with Pantin in 1920 and became the Verreries et Cristalleries de St. Denis et de Pantin Reunies.

Vase, Acorn, Green Chipped Ice, Gold Enameled, Bulbous, Flared, c.1900, 15 ¾ x 7 ¾ In. 1540.00
Vase, Brown Leaves, Amber To Orange, Fluted Rim, 9 In. 205.00
Vase, Camel, Pyramids, Palm Trees, Orange, 10 ⅛ In. 230.00
Vase, Emerald Green, Bulbous, Gold Trim, Signed, 8 In. 2000.00
Vase, Flowers, Blue Enamel Green, Cameo, Signed, 4 In., Pair 431.00
Vase, Flowers, Vines, Red Crackle, Milky White Ground, Cameo, Signed, 1920, 15 In. 495.00
Vase, Grapes On The Vine, Textured Ground, Spattered With White, 6 ¾ In. .... *illus* 403.00
Vase, Grapevine, Purple, Apricot Shaded To Clear To Apricot, Cameo, 13 ¾ In. 518.00
Vase, Green, White Flowers, Flattened Oval, Cameo, Signed, 4 ½ x 5 ¼ In. 800.00
Vase, Lake, Trees, Cameo, Signed, 8 ¼ In. .... *illus* 175.00
Vase, Leaves, Red Shaded To Yellow, Orange, 6 In. 300.00
Vase, Light Green Ground, Dark Green Sycamore, Cameo, Signed, 13 ½ In. 700.00
Vase, Mistletoe, Green Blue, Amber Opalescent, Cone Shape, Cameo, Signed, 7 In. 633.00
Vase, Pond Lily, Red Flower, Leaf, Fire Polished, Cameo, Signed, 3 In. 275.00
Vase, Purple Leaves, Berries, Enameled, Signed, 14 In., Pair 633.00
Vase, Scenic, Lake, Leaves, Enameled, Cameo, Square, 7 In. 480.00
Vase, Swan, Lake, Trees, Enameled, Cameo, Signed, 11 ½ In. 325.00
Vase, Trees, Leaves, River, Mountains, Coral, Olive Green, Yellow, Cameo, 13 ¾ In. 863.00
Vase, Trumpet, Orange Mottled, Green Trees, Amethyst Shoreline, Footed, Cameo, 21 In. 1840.00
Vase, White Flowers, Green Ground, Flattened Oval, Cameo, Signed, 4 ½ x 5 ¼ In. 825.00
Vase, Winter Scene, Enameled, Slender, 4-Sided Base & Rim, Signed, c.1920, 12 In. 200.00
Vase, Winter Scene, Frosted White Ground, Enameled, Pinched Neck, 13 In. 300.00

LENOX porcelain is well-known in the United States. Walter Scott Lenox and Jonathan Coxon Sr. founded the Ceramic Art Company in Trenton, New Jersey, in 1889. In 1906, Lenox left and started his own company called Lenox. The company makes porcelain that is similar to Irish Belleek. In 2009, after a series of mergers, Lenox became part of Clarion Capital Partners. The marks used by the firm have changed through the years, so collectors can date the ceramics. Related pieces may also be listed in the Ceramic Art Co. category.

Bowl, Centerpiece, Underplate, Cardinal, Winter Greenery 59.00
Casserole, Cover, Blue Breeze, Temperware, 1 ¼ Qt. 80.00

Casserole, Cover, Sprite, Temperware, c.1978, 10 x 6 ½ x 4 In. 90.00
Chop Plate, Orleans, Round, c.1969, 12 ⅞ In.......... 120.00
Coffeepot, Fall Bounty, Temperware, 7 Cup, 7 ⅜ In. 35.00
Creamer, Sketchbook, Temperware 15.00
Cup, Quakertown, Temperware 4.00
Cup & Saucer, Blue Breeze, Temperware 8.00
Cup & Saucer, Country Blue, Chinastone 13.00
Cup & Saucer, Dewdrops, Temperware 8.00
Cup & Saucer, Fall Bounty, c.1978 .... 7.50
Cup & Saucer, Merriment, Temperware 5.00
Cup & Saucer, Rhodora 20.00
Cup & Saucer, Wheat 15.00
Dinner Set, Olympia, Gold Band, 61 Piece 468.00
Fondue Pot, Stand, Fall Bounty, Temperware, 2 Qt. 72.00
Plate, Bread & Butter, Cinderella, 6 ½ In.......... 11.00
Plate, Bread & Butter, Rhodora, 6 ¼ In. 14.00
Plate, Bread & Butter, Temperware, c.1983, 6 ⅜ In.......... 5.00
Plate, Bread & Butter, Wheat, 6 ⅜ In. 12.00
Plate, Dinner, Dewdrops, Temperware, 10 In.......... 12.00
Plate, Dinner, Fall Bounty, Temperware, 10 ¾ In. 12.00
Plate, Dinner, Green Scalloped, 10 ½ In., 12 Piece 826.00
Plate, Dinner, Maldon, Gold Border, Oxford, 10 ⅝ In., 12 Piece 526.00
Plate, Dinner, Merriment, 10 ⅜ In. 12.50
Plate, Dinner, Orleans, c.1969, 10 ½ In. 37.00
Plate, Dinner, Quakertown, Temperware, 10 ¼ In. 12.00
Plate, Dinner, Summer Spice, Temperware, 10 ¼ In. 12.00
Plate, Luncheon, Mayfair, 1930s 32.00
Plate, Salad, Decor, 7 In. 8.00
Plate, Salad, Sprite, Temperware, 8 In.......... 8.00
Plate, Salad, Summer Spice, Temperware, 7 ⅞ In. 9.00
Plate Set, Boehm Bird, Bird Center, Gold Rim, c.1975, 10 ½ In., 12 Piece 263.00
Plate Set, Jeweled Flowers, Blue Ground, 10 ½ In., 12 Piece 805.00
Stein, Monks, Transfer, Sterling Lid, Marked C.A.C., ½ Liter 311.00
Sugar, Cover, Orleans, c.1969 .... 68.00
Sugar & Creamer, Dewdrops, Temperware, 1970s 32.00
Tureen, Soup, Autumn, 8 ¼ x 11 ½ In.......... 205.00
Vase, Bud, Pink Rose, Gold Leaves, Bulbous, Thin Flared Neck, 1930s, 7 ⅞ In. 49.00
Wine, Smoke Blue, Hexagon, 5 ⅛ x 4 In. 9.00

LETTER OPENERS have been used since the eighteenth century. Ivory and silver were favored by the well-to-do. In the late nineteenth century, the letter opener was popular as an advertising giveaway and many were made of metal or celluloid. Brass openers with figural handles were also popular.

Acanthus, Sterling Silver, Georg Jensen, 10 In. 112.00
Art Nouveau, Jack-In-The-Pulpit Center, Ivory, Silver, Opal, 1900s, 11 In. .... *illus* 275.00
Baltimore, Md., Monuments, Germany, 1910 .... 18.00
Bone, Malachite Handle, 11 In. 82.00
Bulldog Head Top, Bronze, 9 ½ In. 220.00
Bust Of Dante, Ivory, Bronze, 19th Century, 12 In.......... 358.00
Cicada, Silver Plated, Bakelite, Green, Flat, Art Deco, 8 In. 82.00
Coiled Snake Finial, Ivory, Rosewood Handle, 19th Century, 13 ½ In. 660.00
Elephant Tip, Jade, Nephrite, Enamel, Diamonds, Sapphires, Faberge, Case, 9 ¾ In.. .... 6050.00
Faberge, Diamonds, Sapphire, Enamel, Nephrite Jade, 9 ¾ In. .... *illus* 6435.00
Flowers, Monogram, Sterling Silver, Openwork, Flowers, Flowers, Black, Starr & Frost, 8 In. 29.00
Frog & Snake, Tree Branch, Mixed Metal, Gilt Highlights, Japan, 1920s, 9 ¾ In. 275.00
Gui Carved Handle, Jade, 10 In. 695.00
Horse Head, Sterling & Jade, Box, 10 In. 1500.00
Horse Head, Sterling Silver, Agate Blaze, Russia, c.1910, 9 ½ In. 715.00
Indian Chief, Sterling Silver, 10 ½ In. 413.00
Ivory, Enamel Inlay, Early 1900s, 10 In. 295.00
Lily, Sterling Silver, Stainless Blade, Art Nouveau, Whiting, 1902, 7 ¾ In. 55.00
Man & Woman On Sleigh, Pulled By Horses, Relief, Silver, c.1850, 10 x 2 In. 850.00
Mice, Bone, Carved, Germany, 7 ½ In.......... 55.00
Mouse, Bronze, Vienna, 10 ⅝ In.......... 275.00
Mouse On Feather, Bronze, 9 In. 80.00
Nude Woman Lying Down, Legs Crossed, Gilt Metal, House Of Silz, 7 In. 158.00

Retired Plates
The collector of limited editions knows that "retired" means no longer made by the company and never again to be made. The only way to get a limited edition after it is retired is to buy it on the "secondary market"—kind of like buying a used car.

Letter Opener, Art Nouveau, Jack-In-The-Pulpit Center, Ivory, Silver, Opal, 1900s, 11 In.
$275.00

Letter Opener, Faberge, Diamonds, Sapphire, Enamel, Nephrite Jade, 9 ¾ In.
$6435.00

TIP
Whiten bone-handled knives with a piece of soft cloth dipped in hydrogen peroxide and water.

L

Libbey, Carafe, Cranberry Cut To Clear, Harvard, American Brilliant, 8 In.
$1650.00

Libbey, Tray, Aztec, Cut Glass, American Brilliant, Signed, 10 In.
$6150.00

Lighter, Cigar, Elephant, Cigar Cutter, Painted, Cast Iron, Glass Globe, 10 ½ In.
$1430.00

Lighter, Cigar, Lamp, Nickel Plated Brass, Emerald Shade, Zigara 5 Cent Cigar, 10 x 8 ½ In.
$575.00

Owl, Bronzed Silver, 8 In. 42.00
Pierced Gold Peony Leaf Handle, Silver Blade, G. Shiebler Co., c.1890, 12 In. 1315.00
Revolutionary War Soldier, Sterling Silver, Dudley & Co., England, 10 ¼ In. 220.00
Round Head Top, Glass Eyes, Black Beak, Bakelite, Marbled Brown, 6 In. 55.00
Silver, Stylized Leaf, Berry, Georg Jensen, 5 ½ In. 353.00
Sterling & Ivory, Signed Byron On Handle, 1918, 12 In. 32.00
Tortoiseshell, Silver Beaded Edge, 12 ½ In. 24.00
Woman's Face, Ivory, Bronze Scarf Mount, Holly, Berries, Art Nouveau, 8 In. 550.00
Woman's Head, Hair Pulled Back, Bronze, Art Deco, 12 In. 193.00

LIBBEY Glass Company has made many types of glass since 1888, including the cut glass and tablewares that are collected today. The stemwares of the 1930s and 1940s are once again in style. The Toledo, Ohio, firm was purchased by Owens-Illinois in 1935 and is still working under the name Libbey Inc. Maize is listed in its own category.

Atomizer, Cranberry Cut To Clear, Harvard Pattern, Hobstar Base, 9 In. 175.00
Bowl, Amberina, Oval, Scalloped Rim, 3-Footed, Signed, 4 In. 173.00
Bowl, Bread, Stratford, 11 ½ In. 193.00
Bowl, Hobstar, 6-Point Hobstar Cluster Center, Signed, 4 x 8 In. 60.00
Bowl, Hobstar, Prism & Fan, Notched 6-Scalloped Edge, 4 x 8 In. 88.00
Bowl, Marcella, Square, 3 ½ x 9 ½ In. 200.00
Bowl, Melrose, 2 x 9 In. 110.00
Bowl, Whipped Cream, Zenda, 7 In. 138.00
Bowl, Wisteria, 6 In. 500.00
Butter, Cover, Daisy & Button, Amberina, 7 In. 173.00
Candlestick, Airtwist Stems, 8 ½ In. 495.00
Carafe, Cranberry Cut To Clear, Harvard, American Brilliant, 8 In. .... *illus* 1650.00
Carafe, Ellsmere, 8 ¼ In. 275.00
Cider Set, Venetia, 7-In. Jug, 5 Piece 330.00
Compote, Amberina, Pedestal, 4 x 6 ¼ In. 985.00
Compote, Engraved Flower, Teardrop Stem, Signed, 7 ¾ x 7 In. 150.00
Compote, Poinsettia, Twist Stem, Signed, 5 ½ x 7 ½ In. 125.00
Compote, Wisteria, Signed, 4 ½ x 7 In. 600.00
Cordial, Fernwood, Icicle Stem, Rock Sharp, 5 ¼ x 2 ¾ In., 6 Piece 130.00
Cordial, Harvard, Apple Core Stem, Rayed Base, 4 ¼ In., 4 Piece 303.00
Cuspidor, Amberina, Ladies, Pinched Waist, Optic Scalloped Rim, 5 ½ In. 144.00
Decanter, Intaglio Flowers, Faceted Cut Stopper, 12 ¼ In. 130.00
Decanter, Whiskey, Engraved Wheat, 13 In. 578.00
Dish, Daisy & Button, Boat Shape, Amberina, 8 In. 144.00
Dish, Ice Cream, Harvard, 6 In., 4 Piece 25.00
Finger Bowl, Wedgmere, Signed, 2 ½ x 4 ½ In. 275.00
Goblet, Fernwood, Flowers, Icicle Stem, Faceted Discs, Rock Sharp, 5 ¼ x 2 ¾ In., 6 Piece 130.00
Ice Tub, Scalloped Hobstar, Crosscut Diamond, Strawberry Diamond, Handles, 5 x 10 In. 300.00
Mug Set, Sports, Baseball, Football, Golf, Tennis, Box, c.1985, 4 Piece 20.00
Nappy, File, Engraved Flowers, Handle, 6 In. 138.00
Perfume Bottle, Black Cut To Clear, Engraved Peacock, Signed, 8 ¼ In. 900.00
Pitcher, Hobstar, Strawberry Diamond, 24-Point Hobstar Base, Wide, 8 ¾ In. 400.00
Sugar, Harvard, Oval, 4 ½ In. 44.00
Toupee Stand, Hobstar, Cane Vesica & Fan, 3 ½ x 6 ¼ In. 990.00
Tray, Aztec, Cut Glass, American Brilliant, Signed, 10 In. .... *illus* 6150.00
Tray, Princess, Round, 10 In. 175.00
Vase, Amberina, Flared Rim, 6 x 6 In. 950.00
Vase, Amberina, Optic Ribbed, Footed, Flared Ruffled Rim, 10 In. 288.00
Vase, Flower Shape, Black Cut To Clear, Crossed Lines, Ovals & Dots, Marked c.1930, 9 In. 189.00
Vase, Heron In Marsh, Engraved, Flared, 18 In. 3850.00
Vase, Hobstar, Strawberry Diamond, Vesica & Fan, Triple Notch Handle, 10 In. 400.00
Vase, Thistles, Engraved, Ruffled Rim, Flared, Footed, Signed, 10 In. 132.00
Vase, Trumpet, Harvard, 8 In. 60.00
Vase, Trumpet, Hobstar, Prism & Fan, Ray Base, Signed, 11 ¾ In. 150.00
Vase, Trumpet, Princess, Hobstar Base, 9 In. 110.00
Water Set, Harvard, 8-In. Carafe, 2 Piece 175.00

LIGHTERS for cigarettes and cigars are collectible. Cigarettes became popular in the late nineteenth century, and with the cigarette came matches and cigarette lighters. All types of lighters are collected, from solid gold to the first of the recent disposable lighters. Most examples found were made after 1940. Some lighters may be found in the Jewelry category in this book.

Airplane, Figural, Chrome, Hamilton, 1950s, 3 x 6 In. 50.00

Airplane, Spelter, 10-In. Wingspan ... 1098.00
Artichoke Head, Sterling Silver, Italy, 3 ½ In. ... 185.00
Boy Lighting Cigarette, Figural, A. De Rianery, France, 22 In. ... 862.00
Butterfly Airplane, Figural, Negbaur, No. 95, Box, 1940s, 3 x 6 ¼ In. ... 100.00
Card Shark, Card Suits, c.1940, 3 In. ... 20.00
Cigar, Crane, Marsh, Milk Glass, Brass, Cast Iron Base, Apt. June 23, 1863, 8 In. ... 160.00
Cigar, Eagle, Claw Feet, Brass, 7 ½ In. ... 77.00
Cigar, Elephant, Cigar Cutter, Painted, Cast Iron, Glass Globe, 10 ½ In. ... *illus* 1430.00
Cigar, Lamp, Nickel Plated Brass, Emerald Shade, Zigara 5 Cent Cigar, 10 x 8 ½ In. ... *illus* 575.00
Cigar, Lamppost, Brass Marble Ashtray Base, Alcohol, 10 x 7 In. ... 44.00
Cigar, Monkey, Silver, Russia, c.1980, 5 In. ... 1888.00
Dunhill, Car, MG, M-Type, Hood Lifts Up, Stainless Steel, 6 In. ... 1150.00 to 1400.00
Dunhill, Engraved, c.1930, 4 x 3 ¼ In. ... 330.00
Dupont, Yellow Gold, 20 Microne, 1 ⅞ x 1 ½ In. ... 110.00
Emken Malt Products, Embossed, Established 1884 ... 29.00
Knight, Figural, Metal, 1940s, 8 ½ In. ... 50.00
Knight, Music Box, Figural, Chrome, Plastic, 1940s, 7 ¾ In. ... 50.00
Knight In Armor, Figural, Spelter, 8 ¼ In. ... 110.00
Midland Jump Spark, Davenport Mfg. Co., Patent 1920, 15 In. ... 468.00
Monte Carlo Roulette Wheel, Spins, Box, 1950s ... 20.00
Mythological Figure, Claw Base, Cast Metal, Burns Alcohol, c.1890, 8 ½ x 5 In. ... 385.00
Pepper, Shape, Sterling Silver, Buccellati, 5 ½ x 3 In. ... 455.00
Pistol, Candle Arm, George III, Brass, Iron, 18th Century, 4 ¾ x 7 In. ... 1980.00
Pistol, Piezo Modern, Electric Gas, Box ... 30.00
Rocket, Space, Tin, Key, Nibo, Box, 2 ⅞ In. ... 20.00
Ronson, Futura, Silver Finish ... 25.00
Ronson, Touch Tip, Dispenser, Chrome, Enamel, Marked, c.1940, 4 ½ x 8 ¾ In. ... *illus* 82.00
Royal Haeger, Aqua, Flared Top & Bottom, Art Nouveau, 10 ½ x 4 In. ... 65.00
Scripto, Trojan Horse, U.S. Pat. No. 2, c.1960 ... 19.00
Ship's Wheel Mounted On Front, Chrome Plated Spelter, U.S.A., c.1940, 5 In. ... 30.00
Street Light, Brass, 9 ¼ In. ... 100.00
Urn Shape Font, Flower Sprays, Cast Iron, Brass Wash, Cobalt Blue Glass Shade, 11 ½ In. ... 495.00
Violin, Brass, 2 ½ In. ... 11.00
Woman On Medallion, Cast Metal, Marble Base, Cobalt Blue Glass Globe, 10 In. ... 523.00
Zippo, Nipper Forever, Box ... 10.00 to 15.00

LIGHTNING RODS AND LIGHTNING ROD BALLS are collected. The glass balls were at the center of the rod that was attached to the roof of a house or barn to avoid lightning damage.

LIGHTNING ROD

Copper Rod, Milk Glass Ball, Cast Iron Stand, Impressed, Hawkeye, 68 In. ... 135.00
Twisted Rod, Copper, Iron, Slag Glass, Directional, Star Finial, 72 In. ... 485.00
Twisted Rod, Quilted Ball, Blue Rigaree, Panel, Spear, Kretzner, 1900s, 59 In. ... 165.00
Cobalt Blue, Embossed, Chrome, J.F.G., 19 ½ In. ... *illus* 175.00
Moon & Stars, Ruby Red, 5 In. ... *illus* 275.00

LIGHTNING ROD BALL

Blue Milk Glass, Molded Stars, 4 ¼ In. ... 22.00
Cobalt Blue, Marked, Shinn-System, 4 ¼ In. ... 88.00
Diddie Blitzen, Ruby Red, 4 In. ... *illus* 250.00
Green Glass, 5 x 4 ¼ In. ... 77.00
Red Chestnut, 4 ½ In. ... *illus* 350.00

LIMOGES porcelain has been made in Limoges, France, since the mid-nineteenth century. Fine porcelains were made by many factories, including Haviland, Ahrenfeldt, Guerin, Pouyat, Elite, and others. Modern porcelains are being made at Limoges and the word *Limoges* as part of the mark is not an indication of age. Haviland, one of the Limoges factories, is listed as a separate category in this book.

Berry Bowl, Flowers, Gilt Ground, Footed, Signed, M. Blanche Lenzi, Pa., 3 ⅛ x 4 ⅞ In. ... 66.00
Bowl, Art Nouveau, Tulip, Gilt Highlights, Signed, Shoner, 4 ¼ x 10 ¼ In. ... 345.00
Bowl, Vegetable, Cover, Round, Handles, Gerard Dufraisseix & Abbot, 9 ½ x 8 ½ In. ... 75.00
Box, Casket, 7 Round Panels, Putti With Garland, Bows, Liner, 6 Leaf Feet, 9 ½ x 6 ¾ In. ... 2750.00
Box, Hand Painted, Flowers, Gilt, 3 x 5 In. ... 41.00
Cake Plate, Purple Irises, Scalloped Rim, Gilt, Handles, Signed, E.W. Finer, 1900, 10 ¼ In. ... 55.00
Centerpiece, Tray, Flowers, Pink, White, Gilt, 3 x 14 In. ... 70.00
Charger, Ahrenfeldt, Scalloped Edge, Gold Rim, Higgins & Seiter, 13 ½ In. ... 159.00

Lighter, Ronson, Touch Tip, Dispenser, Chrome, Enamel, Marked, c.1940, 4 ½ x 8 ¾ In.
$82.00

Lightning Rod, Cobalt Blue, Embossed, Chrome, J.F.G., 19 ½ In.
$175.00

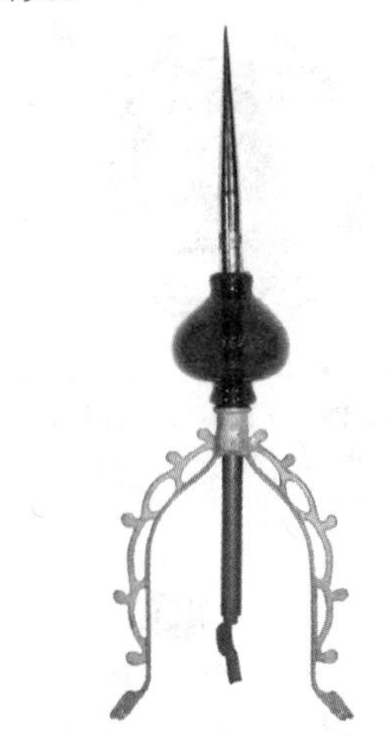

Lightning Rod, Moon & Stars, Ruby Red, 5 In.
$275.00

Lightning Rod Ball, Diddie Blitzen, Ruby Red, 4 In.
$250.00

L

Lightning Rod Ball, Red Chestnut, 4 ½ In.
$350.00

Limoges, Dresser Box, Horseman, Flowers, Black Ground, Blowout Panels, Enamel, 4 ½ In.
$500.00

Limoges, Pitcher, Penguin, Marked, Signed, Edouard Marcel Sandoz, Early 1900s, 6 ⅝ In.
$135.00

Limoges, Vase, Seminude Woman, Pool, Flowers, Gilt, Early 1900s, 14 ½ In.
$2000.00

Limoges, Washbowl, Flowers, Rose Ground, Marked, c.1900, 22 ½ In.
$440.00

Charger, White, Gold Highlights, Courting Scene, 12 In. 200.00
Chocolate Set, Rose, Pink, Red, Gold, White, c.1930, 13 Piece.... 380.00
Chop Plate, Coronet, Roses, 12 ½ In.... 20.00
Compote, Enamel, Art Nouveau, Mottled, Red, Brown, Yellow, Hammered Frame, 10 ½ In. .. 6900.00
Cup & Saucer, Demitasse, Courtship Scenes, Gilt, 2 x 4 ¼ In. 16.00
Dish, George & Martha Washington, Mount Vernon, Square, c.1907, 4 ¾ x 4 ¾ In. 55.00
Dish, Lobster, Marked, M.I.R. 84, c.1875.... 100.00
Dish, Spring Flowers, Vines, Gold Trim, Scalloped Foot, Jean Pouyat, 3 ½ x 1 ½ In. 55.00
Dresser Box, Hinged Lid, Flowers, Gilt, Marked, Pate De Limoges, 3 x 7 ¼ x 5 ¾ In. 85.00
Dresser Box, Horseman, Flowers, Black Ground, Blowout Panels, Enamel, 4 ½ In. .... *illus* 500.00
Ewer, Multicolored Flowers, Gilt Scrolled Handles, France, c.1900, 15 In., Pair.... 237.00
Ewer, Pairpoint, Poppies, Pastels, Marked, 16 In.... 403.00
Fernery, Purple Irises, Green Ground, Gilt, Footed, 4 ¼ x 7 ¾ In. 154.00
Fish Platter, Scalloped, Multicolored Fish, Water Lilies, Gilded Rim, c.1890, 24 x 10 ½ In.... 200.00
Ginger Jar, Stand, Aquatic Scene, Marked 500.00
Ice Cream Set, Flower Transfer, Children's Faces, Gilt, Plates, Platter, 13 Piece 356.00
Jug, Lid, Pour Spout, Cork Bottom, Old English Lettered H, Bulbous, 6 ½ x 5 In. 95.00
Pipe, White, Courtship Scene, Reddish Rim, Gold Trim, 3 ½ x 2 ⅔ In.... 35.00
Pitcher, Grape & Vines, Purple, Green, Yellow, 7 In.... 72.00
Pitcher, Leaves, Ruffled Spout, Lizard Handle, Jean Pouyat, c.1900, 14 ½ In. 117.00
Pitcher, Oranges, Stems, O. Shouet, Signed, 14 In. 885.00
Pitcher, Penguin, Marked, Signed, Edouard Marcel Sandoz, Early 1900s, 6 ⅝ In. .... *illus* 135.00
Plaque, 2 Birds, Yellow Ground, Trees, Ferns, Gold Scalloped Rim, Signed, 11 ½ In. 225.00
Plaque, 2 Green Birds On Branch, Flowers, Gold Scalloped Rim, Marked, 12 ½ In. 225.00
Plaque, Figures At Table, Enameled, Later Frame, 1800s, 9 ½ x 12 In. 4740.00
Plaque, Quail, Flying, Pond, Ferns, Gold Rim, Signed, Bizumy, 12 ½ In.... 225.00
Plaque, Woman, Red Dress, Enamel On Copper, Frame, 6 ¾ x 5 ½ In. 660.00
Plate, Cobalt Blue Border, Gold Filigree Trim, Flower Center, 6 ¼ In.... 32.00
Plate, Courtship Scene, Blue Rim, Gold Trim, 4 ½ In.... 25.00
Plate, Dessert, Gilt, Cowell & Hubbard, Cleveland, 1894, 8½ In. 191.00
Plate, Floral & Green Borders, Gold Trim, Scalloped, 8 ⅝ In. 55.00
Plate, Gold Trim, Green Rim, Gold Overlay, Delinieres & Cie, 8 ½ In. 60.00
Plate, Green, Yellow To Light Orange Flowers, Gold Trim, Tressemann & Vogt Mark, 8 ¼ In. . 23.00
Plate, Lavender & Pink Flowers, Backstamp, 10 ⅜ In.... 18.00
Plate, Multicolored Orchid Center, Raised Flower, Leaf Border, c.1890, 9 In., 12 Piece 3081.00
Plate, Purple Flowers, White Ground, Marked, 8 In. 15.00
Plate, Une Journee Au Bord De L'Eau, Country Scene, Michel Julien, 11 x 8 ½ In. 60.00
Plate, White, Multicolored Floral Bouquet, Embossed Rim, 1940, 8 In.... 15.00
Platter, Flowers, Scalloped Edge, Gold Trim, Blake & Henderson, c.1914, 16 x 9 ½ In.... 300.00
Platter, Pheasants, Handles, Green Border, c.1900, 12 x 18 In.... 146.00
Punch Bowl, Grape Design, Gilt Trim, Footed, Marked, J.P.L., France, 8 ½ In., 2 Piece 336.00
Stein, Figural Gold Handle, Victorian Woman, Sherratt's, Early 1900s, 5 x 6 In.... 95.00
Sugar, Cover, Creamy Yellow & Green, Flowers, Swags, Roses, Gold Trim, 2 x 5 ¼ In.... 15.00
Sugar, Cover, Flowers, Blue, Green, Ahrenfeldt, 1894-1930s, 6 x 6 In. 33.00
Sugar, Creamer, Seal Of United States, Hand Painted, Gilt, c.1890, 3 x 5 In. 230.00
Tankard, Figural Portrait, Monk, Smelling Flower, Jean Pouyat, 5 In. 295.00
Tankard, Figural Portrait, Portly Man, Wineglass, Tressemann & Vogt, c., 1907, 5 ½ In.... 350.00
Tidbit, Flowers, Gilt, Hand Painted, 2 Tiers, 22 ¾ In.... 130.00
Trinket Box, Hinged Lid, Cat In Chair, Yellow, Brown, White, 2 ¼ In. 30.00
Trinket Box, Purse Shape, Painted, Pink, Purple, Blue, Green, Gold, 2 ¼ x 1 ½ In.... 145.00
Vase, Bassin De Bain, Floral Medallions, Rose, Blue, c.1900, 23 In. 472.00
Vase, Bud, Bulbous, Slender Neck, Flared Opening, Courtship Scene, 2 ½ In. 30.00
Vase, Roses, Pink, White, Green Ground, Hand Painted, Marked, T & V, 22 In. 2500.00
Vase, Seminude Woman, Pool, Flowers, Gilt, Early 1900s, 14 ½ In. .... *illus* 2000.00
Vase, Shouldered Shape, Metal Rim, Foot, Poppies, Multicolored, Mark, 8 x 3 In.... 360.00
Washbowl, Flowers, Rose Ground, Marked, c.1900, 22 ½ In. .... *illus* 440.00

LINDBERGH was a national hero. In 1927, Charles Lindbergh, the aviator, became the first man to make a nonstop solo flight across the Atlantic Ocean. In 1932, his son was kidnapped and murdered, and Lindbergh was again the center of public interest. He died in 1974. All types of Lindbergh memorabilia are collected.

Bank, Cast Metal, Gilt, Marked Lindy Bank By G & T, McKeesport, Pa., 6 ½ x 4 In. 125.00
Bookends, Aviator, Arched, Cast Iron, 5 ½ In. 75.00
Bookends, Charles Lindbergh, Aviator Hat, Bust, Painted, Metal, 5 In. 175.00
Bookends, Lindbergh In Flight Cap, Metal, Painted, 5 In. 150.00
Bottle, Great American Series, Wheaton, Blue Carnival Glass, 1970s, 8 ½ In. 9.00

Candy Container, Spirit Of St. Louis, Glass, Tin, 6 ½ In. . . . . *illus* 345.00
Cloth, Charles Lindbergh, First Trans-Atlantic Flight, Red, White, 1927, 16 ½ x 16 ½ In. 250.00
Frame, Paris Flight, Embossed Headlines, Composition, 8 x 6 ½ In. 285.00
Game, Hop-Off Airplane Game, Metal Pieces, Wood Cups, Parker Bros, Box 195.00
Medallion, Bust, Inscription, Flight Path, N.Y. To Paris, Bronze, G. Prudhomme, 2 ¾ In. 50.00
Medallion, Charles Lindbergh, Bust, Bronze, N.Y., Paris Aetatis Svae XXV, 1927, 3 In. 55.00
Mug, Lindbergh Air Fair, 1983, Little Falls, Minn., 3 ½ x 3 In. 19.95
Paperweight, Bust, Cast Iron, 3 ⅞ x 1 ⅝ In. 112.00
Plate, Lindbergh, Eiffel Tower, Plane, Pewter, International Silver Co., 1970s, 8 In. 16.00
Postcard, Lindbergh In Flight Jacket, Divided Back, C. Underwood, Unused. 15.00
Postcard, Lindbergh Riding In Car In Parade, Real Photo, May 1927. . . . . 45.00
Sheet Music, Like An Angel You Flew Into Everyone's Heart, Copyright 1927 . . . . . 18.00
Silhouette, Black & Gold Border, Wood Frame, Brass Hanger, 1920s, 4 ⅛ x 5 ⅛ In. 85.00
Stereo Card, Lindbergh & Spirit Of St. Louis, Keystone Card 25.00
Tapestry, Charles Lindbergh, Paris Flight, 1927, 20 x 54 In. 165.00
Tapestry, Portraits, Early Aviators, Map Flight, 19 x 53 In. 330.00
Toy, Airplane, Lindy, NR-211, Pilots, Red, Black Paint, Cast Iron, Hubley, 10 ½ In. . . . . *illus* 2200.00
Toy, Spirit Of St. Louis Round About, 2 Planes, Painted, Tin, Steel, Electric, 19 In. 1210.00

LITHOPHANES are porcelain pictures made by casting clay in layers of various thicknesses. When a piece is held to the light, a picture of light and shadow is seen through it. Most lithophanes date from the 1825–75 period. A few are still being made. Many lithophanes sold today were originally panels for lampshades.

Cup, Demitasse, Saucer, Geisha, Shoza Style, Gilt Scrolls & Flowers, Footed Cup, Kutani 48.00
Cup & Saucer, Black, Geisha Lithophane, Raised Rim Saucer, Andrea By Sadek, Pair. 35.00
Cup & Saucer, Tea, Geisha, Red, Gold & Black Trim, Mori China, Japan. 45.00
Fairy Lamp, 4-Panel Dome, Flared White, Feather, Angel Top, Clear Base, Mark, 4 In. 288.00
Fairy Lamp, Fleur-De-Lis, 4 Fan Shape Feet, Air Holes, 7 ¼ x 5 In. . . . . *illus* 600.00
Fairy Lamp, Little Miss Muffet, Porcelain, 2 Panels, Candleholder, 4 ½ In., Pair 546.00
Fairy Lamp, Newel Post Dome, Air Holes, Pressed Glass Pedestal Base, 8 ¼ In., Pair 575.00
Lampshade, Genessee Falls, Rochester, Painted Metal Hexagonal Frame, PPM, 6 x 9 In. 300.00
Lampshade, Hexagonal Frame, Panels, Figures, Animals, c.1875, 6 x 9 In. 339.00
Picture, 3 Children In Barn, Cat & Kittens, Pressed Wood Frame, 1950s, 4 ¾ x 4 In. 195.00
Tankard, 2 Women Reading Letter, Hand Painted, Flowers, Germany, 19th Century, 5 ½ In. . 149.00
Tea Warmer, Scenic Panels, Nickel Plated Frame, Kerosene Burner, 4 x 4 ⅝ In. 120.00

LIVERPOOL, England, has been the site of many pottery and porcelain factories since the eighteenth century. Color-decorated porcelains, transfer-printed earthenware, stoneware, basalt, figurines, and other wares were made. Sadler and Green made print-decorated wares from 1756. Many of the pieces were made for the American market and feature patriotic emblems, such as eagles, flags, and other special-interest motifs. Liverpool pitchers are always called Liverpool jugs by collectors.

Bowl, Delft, Fazackerly, Flower Vine, Blue, Green, Red, Yellow, Mid 1700s, 3 ½ x 9 In. 1404.00
Bowl, George Washington, B. Franklin, Captions, Symbols, Black Transfer, c.1785, 10 In. 4200.00
Creamer, Ship, Creamware, Early 19th Century 6720.00
Figurine, Cow & Maiden, Pearlware, c.1800, 5 ¾ In. 1638.00
Figurine, Nun, Reading Bible, Flower Over Yellow Habit, Puce Veil, c.1760, 4 ½ In. 1440.00
Jug, Apotheosis, Peace, Plenty & Independence, Early 1800s, 10 In. 5382.00
Jug, Creamware, Liberty, Indians, Patriotic Portraits, c.1790, 9 ¾ x 6 In. 2950.00
Jug, Creamware, Washington In Glory, America In Tears, c.1800, 9 ½ x 5 In. 2205.00
Jug, Eagle, 16 State Rings, Verse, Clasped Hands, Ship Medallion, Black Transfer, 11 In. 764.00
Jug, Eagle, Shield, Multicolored Enamel, Creamware, Black Transfer, J. Berry, c.1820, 9 In. . . 1541.00
Jug, George Washington, America In Tears, Black Transfer, c.1800, 8 ½ In. . . . . 2000.00 to 3500.00
Jug, George Washington, General, Crowned With Laurels By History, Symbols, c.1794, 8 In. . . 1800.00
Jug, George Washington, Patriotic Symbols, Black Transfer, 7 In. 5100.00
Jug, John Adams, Liberty, Justice, Prosperity Figures, Black Transfer, 10 In. 5676.00
Jug, John Adams, Success To America, Ship, Patriotic Symbols, Figures, c.1820, 12 In. 8400.00
Jug, Mariner's Compass, Sailing Ship, Red Transfer, c.1800, 8 x 6 x 5 ¼ In. 400.00
Jug, Masonic Arms, Black Transfer, Creamware, Signed, Kennedy, Early 1800s, 11 ½ In. 550.00
Jug, Sailor's Farewell, Ship, Woman, Black Transfer, 19th Century, 9 ½ x 10 In. 225.00
Jug, Thomas Jefferson, States, Sailing Vessel, Transfers, Black, Blue, Red, 9 ¾ In. 8962.00
Jug, Thomas Jefferson Portrait, Reverse Side Poetic Ode, Black Transfer, 7 In. 3585.00
Jug, Transfer, Hope, Woman With Anchor, Sailing Ship, 9 In. 5750.00
Jug, Transfers, God-Like George Washington, Apotheosis, Cherubs, Ship, Eagle, c.1810, 11 In. 2520.00
Jug, Washington, Adams, Jefferson, Black Transfer, 1790s, 9 ½ In. 2868.00

Lindbergh, Candy Container, Spirit Of St. Louis, Glass, Tin, 6 ½ In.
$345.00

Lindbergh, Toy, Airplane, Lindy, NR-211, Pilots, Red, Black Paint, Cast Iron, Hubley, 10 ½ In.
$2200.00

Lithophane, Fairy Lamp, Fleur-De-Lis, 4 Fan Shape Feet, Air Holes, 7 ¼ x 5 In.
$600.00

L

Wooden Molds Are Hot

Early glass was made from wooden molds. The mold was soaked in water, then hot glass was blown into it. Each was used 100 to 1,000 times; after that, it would be burned and useless. The hot glass and water created steam that polished the glass.

Liverpool, Jug, Washington In Glory, Map, Black Transfer, Early 1800s, 9 ¼ In.
$1896.00

Lladro, Figurine, Angel With Clarinet, No. 1232, 1972, 9 ¾ In.
$216.00

Lladro, Figurine, Kiyoko, No. 1450, 1893, 7 In.
$209.00

Lladro, Figurine, Opening Night, No. 5498, 6 ¼ In.
$88.00

Lladro, Figurine, Young Harlequin, No. 1229, 1972, 9 ¾ In.
$143.00

Jug, Washington Bust, Figures, 15 States, Ship, Creamware, Transfer, c.1800, 9 ⅞ In. 8000.00
Jug, Washington In Glory, Map, Black Transfer, Early 1800s, 9 ¼ In. . . . . *illus* 1896.00
Jug, Washington In Glory, America In Tears, U.S. Symbols, Patriots, c.1800, 8 In.. . . . . 4130.00
Mug, Washington, Adams, Jefferson, Banner, Slogans, Transfer, 1790s, 6 In. 2868.00
Punch Bowl, John Adams, 5 Patriotic Transfers, Red, Black, Blue, Creamware, 13 x 6 In.. . . . 15535.00
Punch Bowl, Washington, Franklin, Patriotic Symbols, Color Transfer, 5 x 11 In. 5079.00
Punch Bowl, Washington & Franklin, Warship, U.S. Flag, Black Transfer, 4 ¾ x 11 In.. . . . . . 4250.00
Tankard, George Washington, Sacred To Memory Of, Straight Side, 6 x 3 ¾ In.. . . . . 1434.00

LLADRO is a Spanish porcelain. Juan, Jose, and Vicente Lladro opened a ceramics workshop in Almacera in 1951. They soon began making figurines in a distinctive, elongated style. In 1958 the factory moved to Tabernes Blanques, Spain. The company makes stoneware and porcelain figurines and vases in limited and unlimited editions.

LLADRÓ

Bust, Lola, No. 2078, 13 In. 293.00
Bust, Maja, No. 4668, 12 In.. . . . . 205.00
Bust, Pensive Clown, No. 5130, 9 In. 234.00
Figurine, Angel With Clarinet, No. 1232, 1972, 9 ¾ In. . . . . *illus* 216.00
Figurine, Balloon Seller, No. 5141, 10 ½ In.. . . . . 82.00
Figurine, Boy & Girl Dancing, Now & Forever, 10 ½ In. 175.00
Figurine, Boy From Madrid, No. 4898, 8 ½ In.. . . . . 125.00
Figurine, Boy With Dog, No. 4522, 7 ½ In. 100.00
Figurine, Boy With Lambs, No. 4509, 10 ½ In.. . . . . 105.00
Figurine, Bride, No. 5439, Black Legacy Collection, 12 In. 176.00
Figurine, Carnival Couple, No. 4882, 10 ¼ In.. . . . . 105.00
Figurine, Chrysanthemum, No. 4990, 11 ½ In. 105.00
Figurine, Curious, No. 5009, 9 In.. . . . . 60.00
Figurine, Death Of The Swan, No. 4855.3G, 5 In. 82.00
Figurine, Dentist, No. 6450, Signed, 12 In. 125.00
Figurine, Don Quixote Standing, No. 4854, 11 ½ In.. . . . . 263.00
Figurine, Elephant, No. 2110, 16 ¾ In.. . . . . 885.00
Figurine, Eloise, No. 5005, 16 ½ In. 165.00
Figurine, Flower Peddler, No. 5029, 16 ¼ In. 263.00
Figurine, Geisha, No. 4807, 12 In.. . . . . 146.00
Figurine, Girl On Carousel Horse, No. 1469, 15 In. 300.00
Figurine, Girl Tennis Player, No. 4798, 12 ½ In. 60.00
Figurine, Girl With Bonnet, No. 1147, 8 ½ In. 121.00
Figurine, Girl With Dove, No. 4909, 7 ¾ In. 50.00
Figurine, Girl With Flower, No. 4596, 6 In.. . . . . 94.00
Figurine, Girl With Sparrow, No. 4758, 11 ½ In. 146.00
Figurine, Girl With Wheelbarrow, No. 4816, 9 ¾ In. 175.00
Figurine, Hamlet, No. 4729, 15 ¾ In. 400.00
Figurine, Harmony, No. 5159, Black Legacy Collection, 12 ¼ In. 293.00
Figurine, Hebrew Scholar, No. 6029, 9 ¼ In. 205.00
Figurine, High Society, No. 1430, 14 ½ In. 125.00
Figurine, Idyl, No. 1017, 14 ¼ In. 118.00
Figurine, King Balthasar's Page, No. 1516, Black Legacy Collection, 13 ½ In. 936.00
Figurine, Kiyoko, No. 1450, 1893, 7 In. . . . . *illus* 209.00
Figurine, Lamplighter, No. 5205, 18 ¼ In. 110.00
Figurine, Little Sailor Boy, No. 6314, 9 In. 82.00
Figurine, Little Senorita, No. 5054, 10 ½ In. 205.00
Figurine, Little Sleepwalker, No. 6482, 10 In.. . . . . 80.00
Figurine, Lupida, No. 1058, 7 ¾ In. 118.00
Figurine, Miss Valencia, No. 1422, 7 ½ In. 82.00
Figurine, Moses, No. 5170, 16 ½ In.. . . . . 205.00 to 225.00
Figurine, Mother & Child, No. 4701, 13 ½ In. 153.00
Figurine, Mother & Children, No. 4575, 9 ½ In. 100.00
Figurine, My Little Pet, No. 4994, 11 ¾ In. 80.00
Figurine, My Precious Bundle, No. 5123, 10 ½ In.. . . . . 70.00
Figurine, New Friend, No. 6211, 5 In. 130.00
Figurine, Nuns, No. 4611, 13 In. 150.00
Figurine, Opening Night, No. 5498, 6 ¼ In. . . . . *illus* 88.00
Figurine, Oriental Girl, No. 4840, 7 ½ In.. . . . . 125.00
Figurine, Pan With Cymbals, No. 1006, 10 ½ In.. . . . . 220.00
Figurine, Predicting The Future, No. 5191, 11 ¾ In.. . . . . 110.00
Figurine, Prissy, No. 5010, 9 ¾ In. 88.00
Figurine, Puppy Love, No. 1127, 9 ¾ In.. . . . . 99.00

L

Figurine, Re-Encounter, No. 5012, 17 In. 300.00
Figurine, Regatta, No. 6248, 14 In. 146.00
Figurine, Sad Clown, No. 5611, 8 ¼ In. 250.00
Figurine, Seesaw, 7 ¾ In. 125.00
Figurine, Shepherd, No. 4659, 7 ½ In. 47.00
Figurine, Sweet Symphony, No. 6243, 9 ½ In. 175.00
Figurine, Turtle Dove, No. 276.12, 11 x 8 In. 59.00
Figurine, Waltz Time, No. 4856, 9 ½ In. 146.00
Figurine, Woman, No. 4761, 14 In. 118.00
Figurine, Yachtsman, No. 5206, 13 ¼ In. 82.00
Figurine, Young Harlequin, No. 1229, 1972, 9 ¾ In. .... *illus* 143.00

LOCKE ART is a trademark found on glass of the early twentieth century. Joseph Locke worked at many English and American firms. He designed and etched his own glass in Pittsburgh, Pennsylvania, starting in the 1880s. Some pieces were marked *Joe Locke*, but most were marked with the words *Locke Art*. The mark is hidden in the pattern on the glass.

Pitcher, Poppies, Fern Fronds, Grass, Ribs, Marked, 8 In. 950.00
Vase, Roses, Ruffled Rim, Ribs, Footed, Marked, 7 In. 850.00
Vase, Stork, Reeds, Rushes, Rectangular, Amberina, 4 ½ In. .... *illus* 1480.00

LOETZ glass was made in many varieties. Johann Loetz bought a glassworks in Austria in 1840. He died in 1848 and his widow ran the company; then in 1879, his grandson took over. Most collectors recognize the iridescent gold glass similar to Tiffany, but many other types were made. The firm closed during World War II.

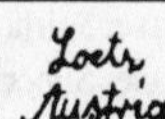

Atomizer, Green Iridescent, Striated, Gold Iridescent Wreaths, 5 In. 288.00
Basket, Empire, Fan, Green, Iridescent Gold Handle, Raspberry Prunts, Swags, 12 In. 518.00
Basket, Oil Spot, Blue Iridescent, Ruffled Edge, 6 x 5 ½ In. 425.00
Bowl, Blue Iridescent, Silver Overlay, Scalloped Rim, 2 ¾ x 4 In. 1072.00
Bowl, Green, Gold Scrolls, Cupped Ruffled Rim, Footed, 7 In. 195.00
Bowl, Papillon, Iridescent Blue, Reticulated Metal Rim, Oval, Gold, 6 ½ In. 144.00
Bowl, Yellow, Navy Blue, Green, Cameo, 7 ¾ x 4 ½ In. 2200.00
Candlestick, Gold, Purple, Green Iridescent, 13 In. 250.00
Chandelier, 4-Light, Gilt Metal, Iridescent Glass, 1901, 35 In. 938.00
Epergne, 1-Lily, Red & Green Iridescent Bowl, Silver Plated Base, Pedestal, 16 ½ In. 425.00
Jar, Cover, Papillon, Oil Spot, Iridescent Blue, 6-Sided, Oval, 5 ½ In. 575.00
Lamp, Oil, Hammered Metal, Embossed, Alfred Daguet Style, 22 In. 900.00
Lamp, Oil Spot, Amber Domed Shade, Swirling, Art Nouveau Base, 7 x 16 ½ In. 1320.00
Rose Bowl, Pink, Opaline, Scalloped Rim, Applied Iridescent Blue Snake, Leaf Foot, 3 In. 690.00
Shade, Gold Iridescent, Pulled Design, Ruffled Rim, 5 ¾ x 5 ½ In. 120.00
Shade, Oil Spot, Gold Iridescent, Ruffled Rim, 6 x 6 In. 120.00
Vase, Agate, Gold Gingko Flowers, Border, Footed, Cupped Pinched Sides, 6 ¼ In. 201.00
Vase, Amethyst, Mask, Jeweled Eyes, Mouth, Copper Overlay, Pinched Sides, 8 ½ In. 1610.00
Vase, Blue & White Stripes, Flared Rim, c.1930, 9 In. 275.00
Vase, Blue Green Iridescent, Copper Handles, Base & Rim, 5 ¾ x 9 ½ In. 2520.00
Vase, Blue Iridescent, Flared Rim, Bulbous, Polished, 6 ⅞ In. 385.00
Vase, Blue Leaf, Dots, Cranberry Ground, Signed, 7 In. 2185.00
Vase, Cobalt Blue, Green & Blue Swirl, Iridescent, Sterling Silver Overlay, Scroll, 7 In. 1725.00
Vase, Conch Shell, Neptune, Iridescent, Green Foot, 5 x 8 In. .... *illus* 1560.00
Vase, Crater, Gold Iridescence, Blue, Pink Highlights, 3 In. 180.00
Vase, Cytisus Iridescent Peach, Cobalt Blue Bands, Gold Spatter, Pinched Collar, 8 In. 3450.00
Vase, Diaspora, Blue Gold, Dimpled, 9 ½ In. 1150.00
Vase, Diaspora, Gold Iridescent, Tricornered Rim, 5 ¼ x 4 ½ In. 270.00
Vase, Emerald Green, Silver Overlay, Art Nouveau, Shouldered, 5 In. 431.00
Vase, Gold Aventurine, Spattered Pink & White, Speckled Dolphin Feet, 6 ⅝ In. 127.00
Vase, Gold Iridescent, Flared, Short Neck, Shouldered, Signed, c.1908, 8 In. 2015.00
Vase, Gold Iridescent, Folded Tricornered Rim, c.1902, 5 ¼ x 4 ⅕ In. 270.00
Vase, Gold Iridescent, Ribbed, 3 Handles, Green Stem, Round Base, c.1910, 8 In. 1304.00
Vase, Gold Iridescent, Squat, Bulbous, Pedestal, Flared Rolled Rim, 7 ½ x 8 In. 270.00
Vase, Green, Blue Iridescent, Applied Decoration, Bulbous, Pinched Neck, Shaped Lip, 6 ¾ In. 326.00
Vase, Green Iridescent, Blue & Silver Flowers, Vines, Pinched Sides, Rolled Edge, 5 ¾ In. 2520.00
Vase, Green Iridescent, Blue Waves, Applied Metal Ribbon Scrolls, Flower Flame, 10 In. 690.00
Vase, Green Iridescent, Clear Handles, Footed, Signed, 7 In. 225.00
Vase, Green Iridescent, Cupped Scalloped Rim, 7 ½ In. 75.00
Vase, Green Iridescent, Pinched Waist, Dimpled, 6 In. 110.00
Vase, Jack-In-The-Pulpit, Gold Iridescent, 18 x 9 ¾ In. 3120.00
Vase, Jack-In-The-Pulpit, Gold Iridescent, Stretched Pink, Green Rim, 12 x 7 In. 1140.00

Locke Art, Vase, Stork, Reeds, Rushes, Rectangular, Amberina, 4 ½ In.
$1480.00

Loetz, Vase, Conch Shell, Neptune, Iridescent, Green Foot, 5 x 8 In.
$1560.00

Loetz, Vase, Oil Spot, Green & Amber, Dimpled, Squat, Flower Shaped Rim, 8 x 12 ½ In.
$2040.00

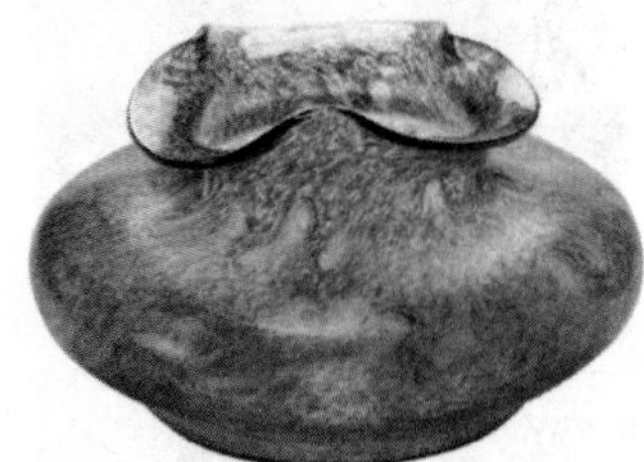

Loetz, Vase, Pampas, Cobalt Blue, Twisted, 9 ½ x 5 ½ In.
$1300.00

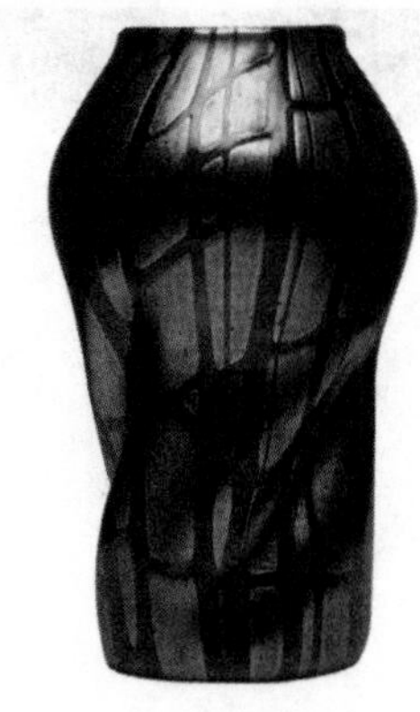

Loetz, Vase, Yellow Iridescent Amber, Ruffled Rim, Bronze Base, c.1900, 9 ¼ In.
$5080.00

Lone Ranger, Toy, Lone Ranger, Silver, Hat, Guns, Hartland, Box, 9 In.
$310.00

Longwy, Bowl, Primavera, Stylized Flowers, Incised, Painted, Footed, 4 ¼ x 9 ½ In.
$240.00

Vase, Moon Crater, Square Shape, Green Iridescent, 8 In. . . . 275.00
Vase, Oil Spot, Amber, Blue Iridescent, Pinched Sides, Tricornered Rim, 8 ½ In. . . . 2300.00
Vase, Oil Spot, Blue, Silver Mounts, 9 ⅛ In., Pair . . . 1320.00
Vase, Oil Spot, Gold, Iridescent, Amber, Oval, Signed, 6 In. . . . 431.00
Vase, Oil Spot, Gold Iridescent, Dimpled, Pinched Rim, 6 ¼ In. . . . 250.00
Vase, Oil Spot, Green, Blue Iridescent, Flowers, Ball Shape, 4 In. . . . 425.00
Vase, Oil Spot, Green & Amber, Dimpled, Squat, Flower Shaped Rim, 8 x 12 ½ In. . . . *illus* 2040.00
Vase, Opalescent, Cased, Fluted, Footed, 6 In. . . . 59.00
Vase, Pale Green, Silver Overlay Scrolls, Shouldered, 3 In. . . . 374.00
Vase, Pampas, Cobalt Blue, Twisted, 9 ½ x 5 ½ In. . . . *illus* 1300.00
Vase, Papillon, Blue Iridescent, Cobalt Blue, Footed, Urn Shape, 7 ¾ In. . . . 489.00
Vase, Papillon, Cobalt Blue, Oil Spot, Reeded Handles, 8 In. . . . 144.00
Vase, Papillon, Green, Squat, c.1900, 6 ½ In. . . . 94.00
Vase, Papillon, Ribbed, Citron, Squared Rim, 11 ¾ In. . . . 546.00
Vase, Phanomen, Pink, Blue, Orange, Gold Iridescent Ground, Pinched Waist, 6 x 4 In. . . . 1200.00
Vase, Phanomen, Transparent Pink, Pulled Feather Spirals, 9 ½ In. . . . 650.00
Vase, Platinum Iridescent Pulls, Amber Ground, Flared Lip, 6 In. . . . 518.00
Vase, Purple Iridescent, Baluster, Handles, Disc Foot, 9 ½ In. . . . 180.00
Vase, Red Iridescent, White & Green, Bulbous, Flared, 1900, 10 In. . . . 300.00
Vase, Rusticana, Green, Iridescent Gold Interior, Squared Rim, Squat, 5 In. . . . 225.00
Vase, Salmon, Orange Iridescent Wave, Platinum, Blue Oval Spots, 5 In. . . . 966.00
Vase, Silberiris, Iridescent Gold, Dimples Around Shoulder, Ground Pontil, 5 ½ In. . . . 200.00
Vase, Silberiris, Iridescent Gold, Straight Rim, Polished Pontil, 6 ½ In. . . . 225.00
Vase, Silberiris, Red Orange, Iridescent Gold Art Nouveau Flowers, Cameo, Oval, 4 In. . . . 1150.00
Vase, Tadpole, Pulled Wave Over Honey Amber, Gold Streaks, Sterling Silver Rim, 9 ¼ In. . . . 4750.00
Vase, Yellow, Round, Ruffled Rim, 5 ¼ In. . . . 330.00
Vase, Yellow Iridescent Amber, Ruffled Rim, Bronze Base, c.1900, 9 ¼ In. . . . *illus* 5080.00

LONE RANGER, a fictional character, was introduced on the radio in 1932. Over three thousand shows were produced before the series ended in 1954. In 1938, the first Lone Ranger movie was made. Television shows were started in 1949 and are still seen on some stations. The Lone Ranger appears on many products and was even the name of a restaurant chain for several years.

Belt & Holster, Rubber, CBS Toys, 1978, 29 In. . . . 11.00
Book, Lone Ranger & The Silver Bullets, 1946 . . . 66.00
Comic Book, No. 1 . . . 605.00
Comic Book, No. 2, March-April . . . 88.00
Comic Book, No. 6 . . . 296.00
Costume & Mask, Box, Child's, Size 4-6 . . . 25.00
Doll, Hat, Holster, Guns, Badge, Stuffed Body, Dollcraft, 1938, 15 In. . . . 865.00
Gun & Holster, Die Cast Pony Boy, Nickel, Ivory Grips, Leather, Box, Esquire, c.1947 . . . 305.00
Harmonica, 1947, 4 In. . . . 35.00
Holster, Double, Lone Ranger, Silver Conchas, Studs . . . 165.00
Jigsaw Puzzle, Lone Ranger & Tonto, 1974, 5 ½ In. . . . 22.00
Jigsaw Puzzle, The Legend Of Lone Ranger, 250 Pieces, 1980, 19 x 13 In. . . . 10.00
Pin, Lone Ranger Riding Silver, Colorful, U.S. Treasury Bonds, c.1959, 1 ¼ In. . . . 75.00
Pocket Knife, Lone Ranger, Hi-Yo Silver, 2 Blades, Red, Camco, Rail City Museum, 1940s, 3 In. 101.00
Poster, Lone Ranger & The Lost City Of Gold, Clayton Moore, Movie, 1958, Half Sheet . . . 285.00
Puppet, Hand, Cloth Body, Felt Hands, Rubber Head, National Mask & Puppet Co., 9 ¾ In. . . . 115.00
Puppet, Lone Ranger, Tonto, Vinyl, Wrather Corp., 1966, 10 ½ In., Pair . . . 95.00
Record Player, Lone Ranger & Tonto Image, Official Seal, Wood Case, 1950s, 10 x 12 In. . . . 253.00
Ring Toss, Target, 4 Rings, Instruction Sheet, Box, Rosebud, 9 ½ In. . . . 153.00
Sign, Merita Bread, It's Enriched, Lone Ranger On Silver, Tin, 14 ¼ x 9 ¾ In. . . . 143.00
Toy, Lone Ranger, Silver, Hat, Guns, Hartland, Box, 9 In. . . . *illus* 310.00
Toy, Lone Ranger, Vibrates, Lasso Spins, With Gun, Tin, Marx, c.1938, 9 In. . . . 396.00 to 540.00
Wristwatch, Lone Ranger On Silver, Hi-Yo Silver, Gold Dial, Black Band, 1 In. . . . 330.00

LONGWY Workshop of Longwy, France, first made ceramic wares in 1798. The workshop is still in business. Most of the ceramic pieces found today are glazed with many colors to resemble cloisonne or other enameled metal. Many pieces were made with stylized figures and Art Deco designs. The factory used a variety of marks.

Bowl, Primavera, Stylized Flowers, Incised, Painted, Footed, 4 ¼ x 9 ½ In. . . . *illus* 240.00
Lamp, Elephant, Crackle Glaze, Cloisonne Style, Wood Base, 13 In. . . . 690.00
Sconce, Gas, Brass, Etched Ruffle Shade, 14 x 11 ½ In. . . . 330.00
Sugar Shaker, Flowers, Blue, Red, Yellow, Black, Green, White, c.1920, 5 In. . . . 100.00

Vase, Primavera, Black Waves, Circles, Deck Blue Ground, Art Deco, 11 ½ In. 1035.00
Vase, Primavera, Green, Yellow Wave Panels, Black Lines, Crackle Glass, 10 ½ In. .... *illus* 1150.00
Vase, Tiger, Surrounded By Flames, 15 In. .... *illus* 1725.00

LONHUDA Pottery Company of Steubenville, Ohio, was organized in 1892 by William Long, W. H. Hunter, and Alfred Day. Brown underglaze slip decorated pottery was made. The firm closed in 1896. The company used many marks; the earliest included the letters *LPCO*.

LONHUDA

Jug, Corn, Green Ground, Marked, LF Shield, 5 ⅝ In. 275.00
Sugar & Creamer, Clovers, Brown Glaze, Marked. .... *illus* 275.00
Vase, Birds In Tree, Brown Glaze, Bulbous, Handles, Marked, JC, 9 ⅜ In. 1650.00
Vase, Daisies, Faience, Marked, 6 ¾ In. 88.00
Vase, Leaf & Berry, Green Glaze, Pillow Shape, 4-Footed, Marked, LF, 7 ½ In. 420.00
Vase, Man Herding Oxen, Brown Glaze, Pillow Shape, 4-Footed, Marked, 11 ½ x 11 In. 1275.00
Vase, Pink Roses, Green Ground, Marked, AH, Shield Logo, 3 ¾ x 6 ¾ In. 299.00
Vase, Trailing Nasturtium, Marked, Jessie R. Spaulding, 1892, 5 ½ In. 360.00

LOSANTI was made by Mary Louise McLaughlin in Cincinnati, Ohio, about 1899. It was a hard paste decorative porcelain. She stopped making it in 1906.

Losanti

Vase, Blossoms, White Glaze, Oxblood Flashes, Bulbous, Marked, Incised, 55, 5 x 3 ½ In. 29000.00
Vase, Lilies, Blue & White Ground, Bulbous, Shouldered, Signed, McLaughlin, 8 In. 16500.00
Vase, Roses, Carved, Stippled, Painted, Peach Ground, Marked, McLaughlin, 5 In. 8800.00

LOTUS WARE was made by the Knowles, Taylor & Knowles Company of East Liverpool, Ohio, from 1890 to 1900. Lotus Ware, a thin porcelain that resembles Belleek, was sometimes decorated outside the factory..

Bowl, Jewel Work, Turquoise Enamel, Gilt Ground, Reticulated Medallion, KTK, 3 In. 650.00
Bowl, Shell Shape, Vines, Pink Flowers, Ruffled Edge, Gilt, 3 Twig Feet, 8 x 2 ¼ In. 490.00
Ewer, Tiberian, White Glaze, Twig Handles, Mark, 7 In.. .... 700.00
Pitcher, Bulbous, Opal Porcelain, Multicolored Flowers, Branch Handle, Late 1800s, 7 In. ... 115.00
Pitcher, Painted, Flowers, Turquoise, Gold Detail, 4 ½ x 6 In. 550.00
Pitcher, White, Applied Net Pattern, Twisted Rope Handle, c.1890, KTK, 5 x 7 ¼ In. 550.00
Tray, Shell Shape, Painted, Yellow Flowers, Ruffled Edge, KTK, 5 In. 650.00
Vase, Grecian, Green Glaze, Applied White Flowers, Knowles Taylor Knowles, 6 x 4 In. 633.00

LOW art tiles were made by the J. and J. G. Low Art Tile Works of Chelsea, Massachusetts, from 1877 to 1902. A variety of art and other tiles were made. Some of the tiles were made by a process called "natural," some were hand-modeled, and some were made mechanically.

J.&J.G.LOW

Paperweight, Hotel Bell Shape, Ceramic, Brass, Label, 3 x 3 ½ In. 375.00
Tile, Bearded Man, Wearing Cap, Golden Brown Glaze, 6 In.. .... 90.00
Tile, Bird In Corner, Flowers, Checkers, Brown High Glaze, Marked, Frame, 6 In.. .... 140.00
Tile, Flower, 4 Petals, Embossed, Amber Crackle Glaze, Brass Frame, Marked, 8 In. 1000.00
Tile, Old Man In Relief, Long Hair, Beard, When Age Steals On, Green Glaze, Frame, 11 x 7 In. 690.00

LOWESTOFT was a factory in Suffolk, England, which from 1757 to 1802 made many commemorative gift pieces and small, dated, inscribed pieces of soft paste porcelain. Related items may be found in the Chinese Export category.

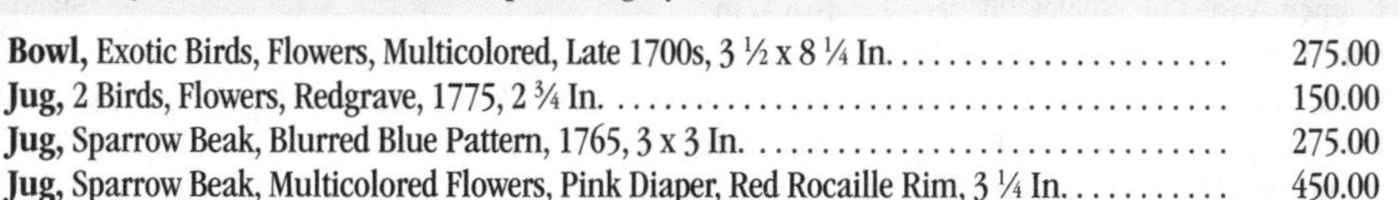

Bowl, Exotic Birds, Flowers, Multicolored, Late 1700s, 3 ½ x 8 ¼ In. 275.00
Jug, 2 Birds, Flowers, Redgrave, 1775, 2 ¾ In. 150.00
Jug, Sparrow Beak, Blurred Blue Pattern, 1765, 3 x 3 In. 275.00
Jug, Sparrow Beak, Multicolored Flowers, Pink Diaper, Red Rocaille Rim, 3 ¼ In. 450.00

LOY-NEL-ART, *see McCoy category.*

LUNCH BOXES and lunch pails have been used to carry lunches to school or work since the nineteenth century. Today, most collectors want either early tobacco advertising boxes or children's lunch boxes made since the 1930s. These boxes are made of metal or plastic. Boxes listed here include the original Thermos bottle inside the box unless otherwise indicated. Movie, television, and cartoon characters may be found in their own categories. Tobacco tin pails and lunch boxes are listed in the Advertising category.

LUNCH BOX

Astronaut, Space Ships, Lunar Surface Scene, Steel, King Seeley, c.1960, 9 In.. .... 181.00
Banana Splits, Playing Instruments, Vinyl, Thermos, King Seeley Thermos Co., 1969 ...... 253.00
Barbie, Metal Thermos, Red Plastic Cap, Mattel, King Seeley Thermos Co., 1962 .... 175.00

Longwy, Vase, Primavera, Green, Yellow Wave Panels, Black Lines, Crackle Glass, 10 ½ In.
$1150.00

Longwy, Vase, Tiger, Surrounded By Flames, 15 In.
$1725.00

Lonhuda, Sugar & Creamer, Clovers, Brown Glaze, Marked
$275.00

TIP

Beware if you're sending precious gemstones and pearls through the mail. The Department of Homeland Security has encouraged a mail sterilization process that can discolor glass, pearls, and gemstones.

L

Luster, Copper, Bowl, Yellow, Blue, Green, Mid 1800s, 3 ½ x 6 ½ In.
$225.00

Luster, Copper, Pitcher, Andrew Jackson, Hero Of New Orleans, Blue Ground, 7 In.
$8963.00

Lustres, Canary Yellow, Diamond Point & Honeycomb, Petal Foot, 1890, 11 In., Pair
$1650.00

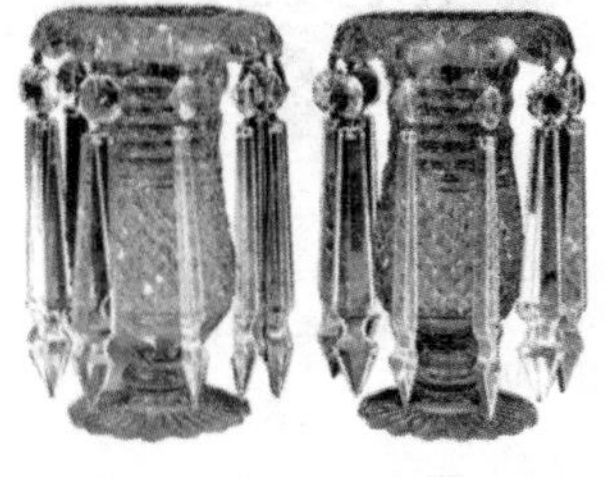

Lustres, Green Flash, White Cased, Trumpet Form, Bohemian Glass, Late 1800s, 11 ½ In.
$660.00

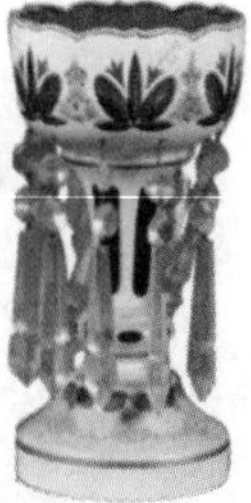

TIP
Sculptures should be dusted with a clean, dry paintbrush. Never use water.

Batman, Robin, TV Show, Tin, Aladdin Industries, 1966, 7 x 8 x 4 ¾ In. 40.00
Battlestar Gallactica, Cylons, Spaceships, Yellow, Metal, Thermos, Aladdin, 1978 .... 185.00
Bobby Sherman, Playing Guitar, Hearts, Metal, Thermos, King Seeley, 1972 .... 173.00
Bugaloos, Pink, Thermos, Krofft Productions Inc., 1971 .... 35.00
Circus Wagon, Dome Top, Tin Lithograph, Plastic Handle, Thermos Brand 90.00
Globe Trotter, Dome Top, Metal, Thermos, Aladdin, 1959 .... 175.00
Grizzly Adams, Life & Times, Cabin, Bear, Dome Top, Tin, Aladdin, 1977, 6 ½ x 9 In. 40.00
Gunsmoke, Matt Dillon, Gunfight, Metal, Thermos, Aladdin, 1973 .... 144.00
Incredible Hulk, Steel, Thermos, 1978 .... 54.00
James Bond 007, Metal, Thermos, Gildrose Productions, 1966 .... 60.00
Laugh-In, Cast, Tin, Thermos, Aladdin Industries, 1968, 7 x 8 x 3 ¾ In. 40.00
Man From U.N.C.L.E., Jack Davis, Metal, Thermos, King Seeley Thermos Co., 1966 .... 383.00
Marvel Comics Super Heroes, Metal, Thermos, Aladdin, 1976 .... 115.00
Munsters, Riding In Car, Tin, Kayro-Vue Productions, 1965, 7 x 8 ¾ x 4 In. 625.00
My Little Pony, Ponies, Rainbow, Pink, Plastic, Thermos, Aladdin, 1986 .... 15.00
Tarzan, Fighting Lion, Tin, Thermos, Aladdin Industries, 1966, 7 x 8 x 4 In. 30.00
Tom Corbet, Space Cadet, Blue, Tin, Aladdin Industries, 7 x 8 x 3 ¾ In. 50.00
Wayne Gretzky, Blue, Plastic, Thermos, Aladdin, 1980s 50.00
Wee Pals, Kid Power, Plastic Thermos, King Features, American Thermos, 1974 .... 30.00
World Of Dr. Seuss, Cat In Hat Juggling, Blue, Vinyl, Thermos, Aladdin, 1970 .... 201.00
Wrinkles, Red, Plastic, Thermos, Ganz Brothers, 1984 .... 12.00

LUNCH BOX THERMOS

Get Smart, Glass Interior, Thermos Brand, No. 2891, 1966 .... 10.00
Tom Corbet, Space Cadet, Red Plastic Screw Top, Aladdin, 1952 .... 55.00

LUNEVILLE, a French faience factory, was established about 1730 by Jacques Chambrette. It is best known for its fine biscuit figures and groups and for large faience dogs and lions. The early pieces were unmarked. The firm was acquired by Keller and Guerin and is still working.

Plate, Asparagus, Majolica, 9 In., Pair 138.00
Vase, Leaves, Pink, Red Ground, Green Interior, Gilt, Flared Rim, Marked, 14 x 6 In., Pair, ... 176.00

LUSTER glaze was meant to resemble copper, silver, or gold. The term luster includes any piece with some luster trim. It has been used since the sixteenth century. Some of the luster found today was made during the nineteenth century. The metallic glazes are applied on pottery. The finished color depends on the combination of the clay color and the glaze. Blue, orange, gold, and pearlized luster decorations were used by Japanese and German firms in the early 1900s. Tea Leaf pieces have their own category.

Copper, Bowl, Yellow, Blue, Green, Mid 1800s, 3 ½ x 6 ½ In. .... *illus* 225.00
Copper, Creamer, Marbleized, Gilt Handle, Foot, Rim, 5 ½ In. 59.00
Copper, Mug, American Eagle, Blue, White Porcelain, 1850s, 3 ¾ In. 418.00
Copper, Pitcher, Andrew Jackson, Hero Of New Orleans, Blue Ground, 7 In. .... *illus* 8963.00
Copper, Pitcher, Bulbous, Young Andrew Jackson, Hero Of America, White, Red, 5 In. 3585.00
Copper, Pitcher, Cornwallis Resigning Sword, Lafayette, Early 1800s, 5 ¼ In. 575.00
Copper, Pitcher, General Jackson, Hero Of New Orleans, Enoch Wood & Sons, 6 ¾ In. 7475.00
Copper, Teapot, Eagle On Handle, Blue Lid, Base, 6 In. 777.00
Copper, Waste Cup, Goblet, Pitchers, 2 ¼ To 5 ¾ In. 59.00
Fairyland Luster is included in the Wedgwood category.
Pink, Bulb Pot, Buildings, Gilt, 3 Holders, Footed, 19th Century, 7 ¼ x 9 In., Pair 936.00
Pink, Mug, Canary Ground, Pink Landscape, Building Scene, 2 x 2 ¼ In. 178.00
Sunderland Luster pieces are in the Sunderland category.
Tea Leaf Luster pieces are listed in the Tea Leaf Ironstone category.

LUSTRES are mantel decorations or pedestal vases with many hanging glass prisms. The name really refers to the prisms, and it is proper to refer to a single glass prism as a lustre. Either spelling, luster or lustre, is correct.

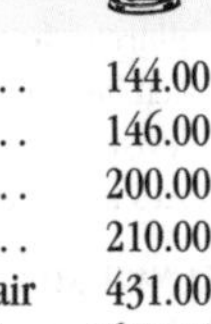

Amber Cut To Clear Base, Crystal Prisms, Pair 144.00
Blue, Bristol, Victorian, Clear Prisms, c.1870, 9 ½ x 4 ½ In. 146.00
Bohemian, Cobalt Blue Cut To Clear, Cut Flowers, 11 x 6 In., Pair 200.00
Bohemian, Cranberry, Gilt, Long Prisms, 11 In., Pair 210.00
Brass, Cut Glass Shade, Column Standard, Acanthus Leaf Base, Crystal Prisms, 24 ½ In., Pair 431.00
Canary Yellow, Diamond Point & Honeycomb, Petal Foot, 1890, 11 In., Pair .... *illus* 1650.00
Cased Glass, Pink Over White, Gilt Highlights, 19th Century, 14 x 6 ½ In., Pair 978.00
Cobalt Blue Cut To Clear, Gold Decoration, Crystal Prisms, 18 ¾ In., Pair 200.00

Cranberry, Gilt, 18 In., Pair 150.00
Cranberry Flashed, Shade, Tapered Stem, Faceted Drops, 26 In., Pair 1304.00
Cut Glass Prisms, c.1830, 13 x 13 In., Pair 6500.00
Cut Glass Prisms, Shaped Pedestal, Bulbous Bowl, Scalloped Edge, 15 In., Pair 690.00
Engraved, Leaves, Deer, Castles, Sunbursts, Prisms, 12 ¼ x 5 ¾ In., Pair 1550.00
French Blue Opaline, Bulbous Bowls, Ruffled Rim, Crystal Prisms, Pair 184.00
Green Flash, White Cased, Trumpet Form, Bohemian Glass, Late 1800s, 11 ½ In. ..... *illus* 660.00
Green Glass, Enameled, Prisms, Gilt Accents, Late 1800s, 12 ½ In., Pair 354.00
Green Glass, Tapered Tulip Shape, Cut Glass Prisms, Gilt Highlights, 12 In., Pair 518.00
Green Satin Glass, Gold Flowers, Crystal & Metal Base, Crystal Prisms, c.1930, 30 In., Pair . 81.00
Hand Cut English Crystal, Shaped Base, Facet Cut Prisms, Late 1800s, 6 ¾ x 4 In., Pair.... 447.00
Pink, Bristol, Gold Enameled, Scalloped Rim, Brass Plinth, Mid 1800s, 24 x 13 ½ In., Pair... 288.00
Pink, Gold & White Enamel Decoration, Crystal Prisms, 14 ½ x 7 In. 230.00
Pink Opaque Glass, Crystal Prisms, Pedestal, Bulbous Bowl, 13 ½ In., Pair 259.00
Porcelain, Ivory Ground, Pink & Flower Detail, Crystal Prisms, Pair 173.00
Ruby Red, Scalloped Edge, Crystal Prisms, 15 In., Pair 345.00
Ruby Red, Victorian, Gilt Decoration, Crystal Prisms, c.1890, 14 In., Pair 489.00
Satin Lilac, Cased, Cut To Clear Panels, Gilt, Enameled Flowers, 10 ½ In., Pair 1500.00
Shade, Iridescent White Glass, Green Pulled Feather, Iridescent Gold Ground, 5 x 2 ¼ In., Pair 240.00
Vase, White, Green, Gilt, Cut Glass Prisms, 15 ½ In., Pair 460.00
White Cased, Green Flashed, Trumpet Shape, Flowers, 11 ½ In., Pair 711.00
White Glass Ground, Green & Pink Painted Flowers, Black Interior, Prisms, Metal Base, Pair 86.00
White Porcelain, Gold Flowers, Crystal Prisms, Bronze Base, 14 ½ In., Pair 115.00

LUTZ glass was made by Nicolas Lutz working at the Boston and Sandwich Glass Company from 1870 to 1888. He made delicate and intricate threaded glass of several colors. Similar wares made by other makers are now known by the generic name Lutz.

Bowl, Cranberry, Amber Threading, Clear Rigaree, Tricornered, Ruffled Rim, 8 In. 58.00
Bowl, Cranberry, Enameled Flower, Thorn Feet, 4 In. 58.00
Cruet, Stopper, Blue, Yellow, Green, Red Plain & Gold Accented Twisted Stripes, 7 ½ In. 86.00

MAASTRICHT, Holland, was the city where Petrus Regout established the De Sphinx pottery in 1836. The firm was noted for its transfer-printed earthenware. Many factories in Maastricht are still making ceramics.

Bowl, Footed, Oriental Scenes, Greens, Reds, Stamped Petrus Regout & Co., 8 ¼ In. 48.00
Plate, Cherries, Red Brown Ground, Backstamp, Petrus Regout & Co., 9 ½ In. 37.00
Plate, Duck, Embossed Green Border, Backstamp, Petrus Ragout & Co., 8 ½ In. 45.00
Plate, President Franklin D. Roosevelt, Gold Gilt, Petrus Regout, 10 ½ In. 25.00
Plate, Timor Oriental Design, Holland, 8 ¼ In. 28.00

MACINTYRE, *see Moorcroft category.*

MAIZE glass was made by W.L. Libbey & Son Company of Toledo, Ohio, after 1889. The glass resembled an ear of corn. The leaves were usually green, but some pieces were made with blue or red leaves. The kernels of corn were light yellow, white, or light green.

Celery Vase, White, Green Leaves, 6 ⅜ In. 80.00
Muffineer, Custard Glass, Yellow Leaves, 5 ½ In. 250.00
Saltshaker, Custard Glass, Yellow & Gilt Leaves, 4 In. 250.00
Sugar Shaker, Custard Glass, Brown & Green Leaves, 5 ½ In. .... *illus* 110.00
Toothpick, Oval, 2 ¼ In. 365.00
Vase, White, Green Leaves, 6 ½ In. 100.00

MAJOLICA is a general term for any pottery glazed with an opaque tin enamel that conceals the color of the clay body. It has been made since the fourteenth century. Today's collector is most likely to find Victorian majolica. The heavy, colorful ware is rarely marked. Some famous makers include Minton; Griffen, Smith and Hill (marked *Etruscan*); and Chesapeake Pottery (marked *Avalon* or *Clifton*). Majolica made by Wedgwood is listed in the Wedgwood category.

Ashtray, Wild Rose, Rope, Cobalt Blue Center, Oval, Branch Handles, 15 ½ In. 150.00
Asparagus Set, Drainer, Tray, Plates, St. Clement, 15-In. Tray, 10 ¼-In. Plate, 7 Piece 173.00
Bank, Baby, Crying Painted, Glazed, 3 ⅜ In. 201.00
Bank, Border Guard, Handle, 3 ⅜ In. 69.00
Bank, Bulldog, Smoking, Red Coat, 4 ½ In. 57.00
Bank, Girl, Wearing Hat, Hand Painted, Glazed, 3 ⅝ In. 58.00
Bank, Hen On Nest Shape, 4 In. 29.00

Bottoms-up Cup

The bottoms-up cup was patented in 1929. It is a drinking cup that has a nude woman holding the large cup against her stomach, her hands and feet clinging to the sides of the cup. The bottom of the cup is the round bottom of the woman. Once it is filled, usually with whiskey, it cannot be put down before it is emptied. A later version was made with a flat bottom. The pottery cups were made by White Cloud Farms Pottery Company of Rock Tavern, New York. McKee Glass made two similar green glass cups. The earliest, made about 1934, is called the "split leg flapper." The other, made later, is known as the "closed leg flapper."

Maize, Sugar Shaker, Custard Glass, Brown & Green Leaves, 5 ½ In.
$110.00

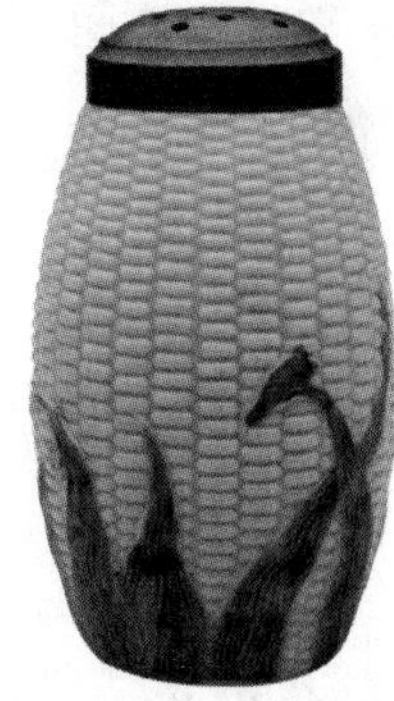

TIP

The value of lustres with hanging prisms is not changed if a few of the prisms have been replaced.

Majolica, Basket, Shell, Seaweed, Basket Weave, Rope Handle, 8 ¾ In.
$460.00

Majolica, Butter Chip, Begonia Leaf On Wicker
$69.00

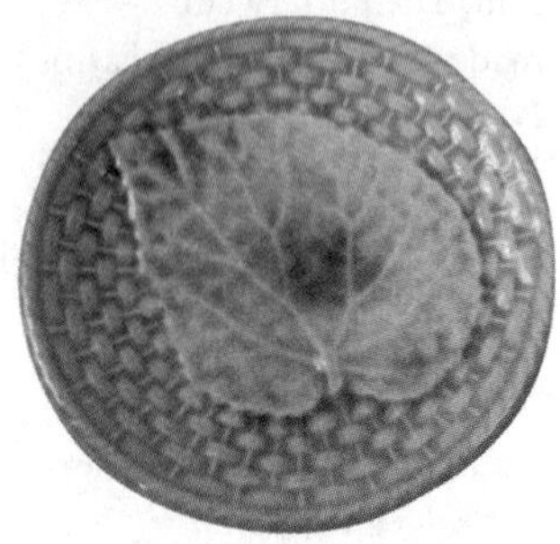

Majolica, Celery Vase, Basket Weave, Flowers, Clifton, 6 ½ In.
$92.00

TIP

To remove gum, put an ice cube in a zip-up plastic bag, then set it on the gum. When the gum hardens, hit it with a hammer and it will break off.

Bank, Woman In Bonnet, Glazed, Painted, Austria, c.1900, 3 ⅝ In. 144.00
Basket, Basket Weave, Bamboo, Banks & Thorley, 9 ½ In. 81.00
Basket, Blackberries, Yellow Ground, Pink Inside, Flat Sides, 7 ½ In. 196.00
Basket, Shell, Seaweed, Basket Weave, Rope Handle, 8 ¾ In. *illus* 460.00
Basket, Sunflower, Begonia, Leaves, Vine Handle, 7 x 12 In. 150.00
Biscuit Barrel, Brown Barrel Form, Grapevines, Branch Loop, Handle, G. Jones, 8 In. 345.00
Biscuit Barrel, Turquoise, Yellow Flowers, Bird Finial, Attached Underplate, G. Jones, 8 In. 1725.00
Bottle, Scenic, Dogs In Relief, Green, Tan, Square, 10 In. 12.00
Bowl, Apple Blossom, Cobalt Blue Ground, Handles, George Jones, 3 ¾ In. 345.00
Bowl, Leaves, Turquoise Ground, George Jones, 5 x 10 In. 230.00
Bowl, Oak Leaves, Overlapping, Acorns, Etruscan, 12 ¼ In. 161.00
Bowl, Salad, Silver Rim, Artichoke Feet, 8 ¾ In. 104.00
Bowl, Shell Shape, Mottled, Pink Interior, 10 In. 58.00
Bread Plate, Harvest, Brownfield, 11 In. 201.00
Bread Plate, Wheat, Eat Thy Bread With Thankfulness, 12 ½ In. 196.00
Butter, Cover, Artichoke, Bird Finial, 7 In. 115.00
Butter, Cover, Fan, Insect, Scrolls, Turquoise, Flower Finial, 7 ½ In. 115.00
Butter, Cover, Pineapple, Cow Finial, 5 x 6 In. 316.00
Butter Chip, Begonia Leaf On Wicker *illus* 69.00
Butter Chip, Blackberries, Clifton 69.00
Butter Chip, Cobalt Blue, Basket Weave, Flowers 81.00
Butter Chip, Fish Head 69.00
Butter Chip, Geranium Leaf, Dark Green, George Jones 46.00
Butter Chip, Green Leaf On Basket Weave 69.00
Butter Chip, Maple Leaf, Etruscan 46.00
Butter Chip, Morning Glory, Wheat, Ribbon, Bow, Fielding 23.00
Butter Chip, Morning Glory On Napkin, Handle 80.00
Butter Chip, Pansy, Etruscan, 4 Piece 230.00
Butter Chip, Pansy, Turquoise, Red 46.00
Butter Chip, Pond Lily, Dark Green, George Jones 46.00
Butter Chip, Pond Lily, Etruscan 69.00
Butter Chip, Pond Lily, George Jones 58.00
Butter Chip, Shell, Seaweed, Etruscan 58.00
Cachepot, Bamboo, Turquoise Ferns, Elephant Handles, Wardle, 5 ½ In. 173.00
Cachepot, Brown, Mottled, Yellow Flowers & Rim, 8 x 8 In. 219.00
Cachepot, Morning Glories, Swags, Tassels, 6 ¾ In. 173.00
Cachepot, Morning Glory, Picket Fence, France, 5 ½ In., Pair 161.00
Cachepot, Palissy Ware, France, 3 ¼ In. 92.00
Cachepot, Portrait Medallion, England, 7 In. 92.00
Cake Plate, Begonia, Overlapping Leaves, Footed, 5 ¼ x 9 In. 92.00
Cake Plate, Maple Leaves, Pink, Footed, Etruscan, 9 In. 81.00
Cake Plate, Pond Lily, Mottled Foot, 4 ¼ x 8 ¾ In. 127.00
Cake Plate, Pond Lily, Stork Base, 6 x 9 ¾ In. 288.00
Cake Plate, Stork, Compote Form, Green, Stippled, Holdcroft, 19th Century, 10 ½ In. 118.00
Candleholder, Flowers, France, 6 In. 104.00
Candleholder, Fruit & Leaf, Italy, Cantelier, 3 In., 4 Piece 12.00
Candlestick, Busts Of Men & Women, Swags, Cobalt Blue, 12 In., Pair 207.00
Candlestick, Parrot, Figural, Metal Mount, Mid 19th Century, 14 ½ In., Pair 325.00
Carafe, Water, Pineapple, 8 ½ In. 173.00
Caviar Server, Fish Shape, Scrolled Fins, Center Well, Wilhelm Schiller & Sons, 20 In. 460.00
Celery Vase, Basket Weave, Flowers, Clifton, 6 ½ In. *illus* 92.00
Celery Vase, Lily, Etruscan, 8 ½ In. 805.00
Centerbowl, Oval, Continental, Pink Flamingoes, Laurel Garland, c.1880, 22 ½ In. 5000.00
Charger, Neptune Center, Scrolling Border, Masques, Dolphins, Late 1800s, 14 ¾ In. 767.00
Charger, Palissy Ware, Fish, Snakes, Lizard, Shells, Ferns, 1880, 16 In. 2300.00
Cheese Dish, Dome Top, Fish, Dragonflies, Lilies, Cattails, Kingfisher Finial, 14 x 12 ½ In. 5500.00
Cheese Keeper, Apple Blossom, Turquoise, Basket Weave Bottom, George Jones, 13 In. 1208.00
Cheese Keeper, Leaves, Ferns, Shell Rim, Goat On Wheat Finial, George Jones, 14 In. 8855.00
Cheese Keeper, Lily Of The Valley, Fern, Rope, Samuel Lear, 12 x 12 In. 1150.00
Cheese Keeper, Rope & Fern, Lavender, 9 x 11 In. 460.00
Cheese Keeper, Wild Rose, Cobalt Blue, Branch Handle, 11 x 12 In. 690.00
Cigarette Holder, Striker, Cat, Flower, 6 In. 325.00
Compote, Bacchanal, Cobalt Blue, Putti Holding Bowl, Leaves, George Jones, 5 x 8 In. 1333.00
Compote, Basket Weave, Compote, Leaves On Base, 8 ½ In. 81.00
Compote, Chestnut, Turquoise Ground, George Jones, 9 In. 374.00
Compote, Daisies, Yellow, Red, Pedestal Form, Etruscan, Late 1800s, 5 ½ In. *illus* 177.00
Compote, Daisy, White Ground, Etruscan, 9 In. 138.00
Compote, Eichwald, Cobalt Blue, Shell Shape, Leaves & Flowers, 13 x 8 In. 104.00

Compote, Green Glaze, Basket Border, France, c.1920, 2 x 9 In. 35.00
Compote, Green Glaze, Scenic, Man Climbing Ladder, 5 x 10 ¼ In. 81.00
Compote, Green Leaf, Yellow, Basket Weave, Etruscan, c.1880, 9 In. 236.00
Compote, Pond Lilies, Red, Green Mottled, Holdcroft, 10 ½ In. 236.00
Compote, Shell Shape, Flowers, 11 ½ x 17 ½ In. 81.00
Creamer, Barrel Shape, Flowers, 4 ¼ In. 58.00
Creamer, Flowers, Wheat, 4 ¾ In. 58.00
Creamer, Lion, Frie Onnaing, 4 ½ In. 58.00 to 104.00
Creamer, Water Lily, Turquoise, Holdcroft, 4 In. 58.00
Cup & Saucer, Bamboo & Fern, Yellow Ground, Wardle 104.00
Cup & Saucer, Blackberry, Basket Weave, Yellow Ground 81.00
Cup & Saucer, Cauliflower, Etruscan *illus* 138.00
Cup & Saucer, Flower, Basket Weave 69.00
Cup & Saucer, Pineapple 104.00
Cup & Saucer, Wild Rose, Rope 69.00
Cuspidor, Flowers, Basket Weave, 5 ½ In. 92.00
Cuspidor, Mottled, Shell Border, 9 In. 58.00
Cuspidor, Shell & Seaweed, Etruscan, 6 ½ In. 115.00
Decanter, Rooster, St. Clement, 13 In. 104.00
Dessert Set, Green Flower Shape, Platter, 6 Plates, 11 ½ & 7 ¼ In., 7 Piece 60.00
Dessert Set, Tray, Plates, Reticulated Border, Germany, 12 & 7 ½ In., 6 Piece 81.00
Dish, Begonia, 9 In. 104.00
Dish, Cover, Hare, Mallard, Oak Leaves, Basket Weave, Minton, c.1890, 12 In. 561.00
Dish, Game, Basket Bottom, Oak Leaves, Dead Rabbit, Duck, Quail On Cover, Minton, 14 In. 805.00
Dish, Holly, Bird Handle, George Jones, 7 ¾ In. 748.00
Dish, Leaf, Figural Black Rabbit, Worm, George Jones, 6 ¼ In. 920.00
Dish, Pickle, Daisy, Oval, Pink Interior, Etruscan, 7 ¼ In. 161.00
Dish Base, Game, Trellis, George Jones, 12 In. 69.00
Egg Basket, Log Shape, Cobalt Blue Top, Branch Handle, 7 In. 92.00
Eggcup Holder, Double, 2 Eggcups, Green Center Handle, 4 Leafy Feet, 4 ½ In. *illus* 184.00
Ewer, Palissy, Lizards, Shells, Leaves, Cobalt Ground, George Jones, c.1873, 16 ¾ In. 6250.00
Figurine, Cat, Googly Eyes, Arched Back, Blue, Green Dotted, 1970s, 3 x 2 ⅜ In. 89.00
Figurine, Cockatoo, Choise-Le-Roi, Hautin Boulander & Co., c.1870, 18 ½ In. 5000.00
Flask, Pilgrim, Renaissance Revival, Painted, Baluster Shape, Mask Handles, 15 ½ In. 889.00
Fox, Lying Down, 10 x 19 x 8 In. 64.00
Garden Seat, Elephant, Signed, Edie, 1976, 21 x 10 x 13 In. 205.00
Garniture Set, Egyptian, Sphinx, G. Jones, 8-In. Bowl, 6-In. Candleholder, 3 Piece 5750.00
Humidor, Blackamoor Wearing Head Scarf, 5 ¾ In. 58.00
Humidor, Devil's Head, 7 In. 69.00
Humidor, Dog's Head, Bulldog, Alice, 4 ¼ In. 69.00
Humidor, Elephant Wearing Red Smoking Jacket & Pipe, 7 In. 184.00
Humidor, Engineer Wearing Hat, Smoking Cigar, 6 In. 69.00
Humidor, Fox Dressed As Clown, Figural, 5 In. *illus* 173.00
Humidor, Frog, Red Smoking Jacket, Continental, 6 ½ In. 81.00
Humidor, Head, Tier, Green Hat, Dick 5 In. 104.00
Humidor, Hippo, 5 x 7 In. 316.00
Humidor, Indian, Seated, Painted Indian Profile On Attached Tray, 5 x 5 x 9 In. 138.00
Humidor, Indian Chief, Continental, 5 ½ In. 81.00
Humidor, Knight, Helmet, 6 ½ In. 81.00
Humidor, Man, Beanie Hat, Bowtie, 5 In. 69.00
Humidor, Man, Green Cape, Purple Hat, Cigar, 8 In. 92.00
Humidor, Man, Green Hat, Turned Up Rim, 6 In. 69.00
Humidor, Man, Mustache, Hunting Hat, 5 ¾ In. 81.00
Humidor, Man, Purple Smoking Jacket, Green Hat, 8 In. 104.00
Humidor, Man's Head, Mustache, Hat With Feather, Rope Band, Impressed, 9 x 7 In. 300.00
Humidor, Man's Head, Purple Cap, Tassel, Brown Eyes, Impressed, Austria, 8 ½ x 5 In. 300.00
Humidor, Monkey Wearing Suit & Cap, 6 In. 46.00
Humidor, Owl On Branch, 7 In. 58.00
Humidor, Scottish Man, Beard, Blue Hat, 6 In. 81.00
Humidor, Skeleton's Head, Wearing Red, White & Blue Hat, 6 ½ In. 259.00
Humidor, Tiger's Head, 4 ½ In. 127.00
Humidor, Woman's Head, 4 ½ In. 104.00
Inkwell, Turquoise, Flowers, Square Through Tenon Frame, Geschutzt, 3 ½ In. 115.00
Jam Jar, Basket Weave, Rope Rim, Cow On Leaves Finial, George Jones, 5 In. 1438.00
Jar, Tree Trunk, Ivy Covered, Brownfield, 3 ½ In. 46.00
Jardiniere, Bird, Leaves, Green Interior, France, 6 ½ x 13 ½ In. 316.00
Jardiniere, Boat Shape, Applied Flowers, Longchamp, 13 In. 58.00
Jardiniere, Butterflies, Bugs, Flowers, Ferns, Lion's Mask Handles, Oval, England, 12 In. 84.00

Majolica, Compote, Daisies, Yellow, Red, Pedestal Form, Etruscan, Late 1800s, 5 ½ In.
$177.00

Majolica, Cup & Saucer, Cauliflower, Etruscan
$138.00

Majolica, Eggcup Holder, Double, 2 Eggcups, Green Center Handle, 4 Leafy Feet, 4 ½ In.
$184.00

Majolica, Humidor, Fox Dressed As Clown, Figural, 5 In.
$173.00

Majolica, Jardiniere, Pedestal, Bird, Berry, Bamboo, Dolphins, Embossed, 47 x 16 In.
$1500.00

Majolica, Pedestal, Leaf Carved Base, Eagle, Garland, Cobalt Blue, Green, 45 x 15 In., Pair
$4000.00

Majolica, Pitcher, Asparagus, Figural, Frie Onnaing, 8 In.
$173.00

Jardiniere, Chrysanthemums, Cobalt Blue Ground, France, 13 In. 805.00
Jardiniere, Dragon, Green, Turquoise Ground, 3 Claw Feet, C. Dresser, 14 x 13 In. 4255.00
Jardiniere, Embossed Bird, Berry & Bamboo, Dolphin Corners, 47 x 16 In., 2 Piece 1500.00
Jardiniere, Figural, Tree Stump, Oak Leaves, Acorns, France, 8 In. 403.00
Jardiniere, Lion's Head Handles, Multicolored, c.1910, 12 x 20 ½ In. 234.00
Jardiniere, Neoclassical, Eichwald, Oval, Relief Figure, Lavender Rim, Base, 12 In.. . . . . . . 91.00
Jardiniere, Pedestal, Bird, Berry, Bamboo, Dolphins, Embossed, 47 x 16 In. . . . . . . *illus* 1500.00
Jardiniere, Pedestal, Molded Lip, Applied Satyr Masque Handles, Italy, 39 x 21 In., Pair 1140.00
Jardiniere, Shaped Body, Molded Leaf Decoration, Blue Interior, Teal, Ocher, Gilt, 23 In. 239.00
Jardiniere Pedestal, Cobalt Blue, 17 In. 104.00
Jardiniere Stand, Storks, Relief Base, Mottled, 20 ½ In. 35.00
Jug, Multicolored Scroll, Flowers, Tin Glaze, c.1750, 10 In. 1007.00
Jug, Wine, Cobalt Blue, Water Lilies, Mermaid Handle, Holdcroft, 9 In. 1553.00
Lavabo, Sea Creature, Shell Shape Basin, 24 x 14 ½ In. 764.00
Match Striker, Austrian Lady, Seated, Baskets In Field, 7 ½ In. 69.00
Match Striker, Water Fountain, Doves, 5 ½ In. 104.00
Matchbox, Turquoise, Rope Trim, George Jones, 3 In.. . . . . . . 431.00
Matchbox, Wild Rose, Rope, Striker On Base, 4 In. 219.00
Muffin Keeper, Turquoise, Apple Blossom, Dome Cover, Vine Handle, G. Jones, 6 x 10 In. 1265.00
Mug, Lily, Etruscan, 4 In. 115.00
Mug, Shaving, Wheat, Daisy, Ribbon, Bow, Fielding, 3 ½ In. 69.00
Mug, Water Lily, Etruscan, 3 ½ In.. . . . . . . 92.00
Pedestal, Copeland, Classical Figures, Blue Ground, Flower Swags, c.1870, 24 In. 5000.00
Pedestal, Leaf Carved Base, Eagle, Garland, Cobalt Blue, Green, 45 x 15 In., Pair . . . . . . *illus* 4000.00
Pedestal, Sunflowers In Cartouche, Turquoise Ground, England, 26 In.. . . . . . . 288.00
Pitcher, Artichoke, Figural, Brown Handle, Green Foot, 7 ½ In. 316.00
Pitcher, Asparagus, Figural, Frie Onnaing, 8 In. . . . . . . *illus* 173.00
Pitcher, Bamboo & Fern, Wardle, 7 In. 58.00
Pitcher, Bamboo & Wheat, Rope Handle, 8 ¾ In. 58.00
Pitcher, Bird & Fan, Wardle, 7 ½ In. 104.00
Pitcher, Blue Ground, Pink Interior, Flowers, c.1870, 7 In.. . . . . . . 70.00
Pitcher, Brown, Grape & Basket Weave, Fruit, 8 In.. . . . . . . 46.00
Pitcher, Calla Lily, George Jones, 7 In. 1438.00
Pitcher, Cat Holding Mandolin, France, 9 ¼ In. 316.00
Pitcher, Cobalt Blue, Flower, Branch Handle, 6 ½ In. 104.00
Pitcher, Corn, 7 ¼ In. 69.00
Pitcher, Corn, 8 ½ In. 138.00
Pitcher, Dog's Head, Spaniel, 4 In. 104.00
Pitcher, Duck, Wing Handle, 11 In.. . . . . . . 575.00
Pitcher, Elephant, Palm Trees, Drum Shape, Vine Bail Handle, 9 ½ In.. . . . . . . 1955.00
Pitcher, Elephant & Palm Tree, Bamboo Handle, 7 ½ In. 316.00
Pitcher, Fish, 11 ½ In. 104.00
Pitcher, Fish, Morley & Co., 8 ½ In. 230.00
Pitcher, Fish, Multicolored, Boch Freres Keramis, 9 ¾ In.. . . . . . . 81.00
Pitcher, Flower, Frie Onnaing, 7 ½ In. . . . . . . *illus* 69.00
Pitcher, Flowers, Leaves, Brown, Green, Pink, Etruscan, 1800s, 6 x 8 ½ In.. . . . . . . 234.00
Pitcher, Flowers, Yellow Top, Bottom, England, 6 ½ In. 69.00
Pitcher, Lily Of The Valley, Ferns, Rope Handle, 11 In. 259.00
Pitcher, Lobster, 7 ½ In.. . . . . . . 1035.00
Pitcher, Man, Basket, Holding Rabbit, 8 In. 69.00
Pitcher, Monkey, Baby Monkey, Flower On Handle, 10 In.. . . . . . . 58.00
Pitcher, Monkey, Bamboo Handle, 9 ½ In. . . . . . . *illus* 633.00
Pitcher, Mottled Eagle, On Branch, Fox Hunt Scene, 9 ½ In. 58.00
Pitcher, Owl, Figural, Morley & Co., 8 ½ In.. . . . . . . 259.00
Pitcher, Owl, Green, Hand Painted, 8 ¾ In. 100.00
Pitcher, Parrot, Multicolored, 19th Century, 10 In. 295.00
Pitcher, Parrot, St. Clement, 13 In. 104.00
Pitcher, Pineapple, 7 ½ In. 374.00
Pitcher, Pond Lily, 7 In. 81.00
Pitcher, Pond Lily, Pink Top, 7 ½ In.. . . . . . . 69.00
Pitcher, Rooster, Chante Clair Pour La France, Frie Onnaing, 9 In. 230.00
Pitcher, Rooster, St. Clement, 11 In. 92.00
Pitcher, Shell & Seaweed, Etruscan, 6 In. . . . . . . 104.00 to 150.00
Pitcher, Stork, In Water, France, 8 ½ In.. . . . . . . 81.00
Pitcher, Trunk & Floral, Aqua, Pink Flowers, Trunk Handle, 1930, 8 In. 275.00
Pitcher, Water Lily, Iris, Turquoise Ground, George Jones, 7 In. 2300.00
Pitcher, Water Lily, Yellow Scalloped Top, Bulbous Bottom, Bamboo Handle, Lear, 7 In. 161.00
Pitcher, Wheat, Pink Ground, George Jones, 8 ¼ In. 1150.00

Pitcher, Wild Rose, On Tree Bark, 7 In. . . . 58.00
Pitcher, Wild Rose, Tree Bark, Branch Handle, 9 In. . . . 58.00
Pitcher, Wild Rose, Turquoise Ground, Branch Trim & Handle, George Jones, 8 In. . . . 575.00
Planter, Morning Glory, Basket Weave, Oval, Cobalt Blue, Yellow, Green, 6 ¼ x 3 In. . . . 91.00
Planter, Pointed Leaves, Bamboo Corners, Rectangular, George Jones, 5 ½ x 13 In. . . . 690.00
Plaque, Crab, Seaweed, Starfish, Round, Palissy, 17 In. . . . 863.00
Plaque, Figural, Duck, Cobalt Blue Accents, 11 ½ In., Pair . . . 35.00
Plaque, Fish, White Ground, Oval, Morley & Co., 13 In. . . . 1035.00
Plaque, Lizard, Toad, Butterflies, Crab, Grass Ground, Jose Cunha, Palissy, 10 In. . . . 920.00
Plaque, Madonna, Child, Blue, Green, White, Italy, 1800s, 20 x 17 In. . . . 819.00
Plaque, Man, Woman Busts, Embossed Green Stem, Flowers, 14 In., Pair . . . 649.00
Plaque, Overlapping Fish, Snake, Snails, Leaves, Barbizet, Palissy, Round, 13 In. . . . 3105.00
Plate, Asparagus, Artichoke, Luneville, 9 In. . . . 104.00
Plate, Asparagus, Cradle Shape, Bed Of Leaves Underplate, France, 14 In. . . . 219.00
Plate, Asparagus, Oval, Asparagus Handles, 16 In. . . . 161.00
Plate, Asparagus, Ribbons, Ruffled Shape, 14 ½ In. . . . 184.00
Plate, Bamboo, Fern, Cobalt Center, James Wardle & Co., 7 ¾ In. . . . 58.00
Plate, Banana Leaf, Bow Handle, 8 ¾ In. . . . 196.00
Plate, Cobalt Blue Blackberry, 8 In. . . . 104.00
Plate, Daisy, Wheat, Ribbon & Bow, S. Fielding & Co., 7 ½ In. . . . 115.00
Plate, Dog, Scalloped Rim, 10 ¾ In. . . . 60.00
Plate, Geranium, Brown Ground, 9 ¼ In. . . . 104.00
Plate, Hunt Scene, Reticulated Border, France, 19th Century, 9 ¼ In., Pair . . . 58.00
Plate, Leaf Center, Green, Pink Edge, Cobalt Blue Ground, 9 ¼ In. . . . 184.00
Plate, Leaves, Fern, Flowers, Basket Weave Border, 8 ¾ In. . . . 69.00
Plate, Maple Leaf, Cobalt Blue Ground, Holdcroft, 8 ½ In. . . . 184.00
Plate, Maple Leaf, On Basket, Etruscan, 9 In. . . . 81.00 to 92.00
Plate, Napkin, Chestnut Leaf, Pink Ground, George Jones, 9 In. . . . 431.00
Plate, Napkin, Morning Glory, 9 In. . . . 69.00
Plate, Pansy, Choise-Le-Roi, 8 In. . . . 58.00
Plate, Rabbit With Wheelbarrow In Garden, France, 9 In. . . . 259.00
Plate, Reticulated Border, Green Center, Portrait, Rubles, 9 In. . . . 104.00
Plate, Shell Shape, George Jones, c.1873, 8 ½ In. . . . 230.00
Plate, Strawberry, Minton, 8 In. . . . 207.00
Plate, Turkey, Oyster, 5 Wells, Stangl Pottery, 9 In. . . . 460.00
Plate, Water Lily, 8 ½ In. . . . 104.00
Plate, White Asparagus, Flowers, Cradle Shape, Underplate, 14 In. . . . 316.00
Plate, Yellow Fish, Daisy, Joseph Holdcroft, 8 ½ In. . . . 230.00
Platter, Bamboo, Wicker Center, Oval, 11 In. . . . 213.00
Platter, Barrel & Staves, Flowers, Leaves, Branch Handles, 10 ½ In. . . . 92.00
Platter, Bird & Fan, Bamboo Rim, Oval, 11 ½ In. . . . 81.00
Platter, Blooming Pond Lily, Handles, c.1890, 13 In. . . . *illus* 354.00
Platter, Deer & Dog, Yellow Ground, 11 In. . . . 104.00
Platter, Dog, Doghouse, Scalloped Edge, Handles, 11 In. . . . 138.00
Platter, Lizard On Rock, Leaves, Flowers, Shells, T. Sergent, Palissy, Oval, 8 In. . . . 690.00
Platter, Mackerel, Eel, Leaves, Mussels, Snails, Turtle, Worms, Palissy, Oval, 17 In. . . . 2300.00
Platter, Neptune, Victorian, Leda & The Swan, Figure Of Mercury, c.1865, 15 x 12 ¾ In. . . . 345.00
Platter, Pineapple, Brown Center, Round, 13 In. . . . 288.00
Platter, Pond Lily, Lavender Ground, Oval, 13 In. . . . 460.00
Platter, Shell & Seaweed, Etruscan, 13 ¾ In. . . . 324.00
Platter, Water Lily, Pink Shell Ends, 13 ¼ In. . . . 299.00
Platter, Wheat, Vine, Leaves, Basket Weave, 13 In. . . . 489.00
Punch Bowl, Punch Lying Down, Holding Bowl, Cobalt Blue, George Jones, 9 x 11 In. . . . 8625.00
Punch Pot, 16th Century Style, Cylindrical, Birds, Deer, Dogs, Italy, 16 x 16 In. . . . 840.00
Salt, Dolphin, Shell, 4 ½ In. . . . 58.00
Salt, Figural, Brown Dog Holding Salt Basket, 6 In., Pair . . . 460.00
Sandwich Tray, Oak Leaves, Acorns, Turquoise, Squirrel Handle, George Jones, 12 In. . . . 1553.00
Sardine Box, Flowers, Bulrush, Overlapping Fish On Cover, Pink Ground, 5 In. . . . 230.00
Sardine Box, Pineapple, 3 Fish On Cover, Attached Underplate, 8 ½ In. . . . *illus* 431.00
Sardine Box, Water Lily, Pink, Swan Finial On Cover, Underplate, Etruscan, 9 In. . . . 690.00
Sconce, Bust, Bearded Man, Holding Torch, Oval Cartouche, c.1865, 18 ½ In. . . . 5000.00
Server, 3 Sections, Handle, Minton, c.1860, 3 x 10 In. . . . 92.00
Spoon Warmer, Turquoise, Tub Form, George Jones, 3 ¼ x 6 ¼ In. . . . 374.00
Statue, Gargoyle, Blood Glaze, c.1900, 23 x 18 x 16 In. . . . 600.00
Strawberry Server, 2 Water Lily Wells, Vine Handle, George Jones, 10 In. . . . 1093.00
Strawberry Server, Bird's Nest Sugar & Cream Wells, Bird Handle, 11 In. . . . 633.00
Strawberry Server, Turquoise Napkin, Pink Sugar & Creamer, George Jones, 14 In. . . . 345.00
Sugar, Corn, 4 In. . . . 81.00

Majolica, Pitcher, Flower, Frie Onnaing, 7 ½ In.
$69.00

Majolica, Pitcher, Monkey, Bamboo Handle, 9 ½ In.
$633.00

Majolica, Platter, Blooming Pond Lily, Handles, c.1890, 13 In.
$354.00

Majolica, Sardine Box, Pineapple, 3 Fish On Cover, Attached Underplate, 8 ½ In.
$431.00

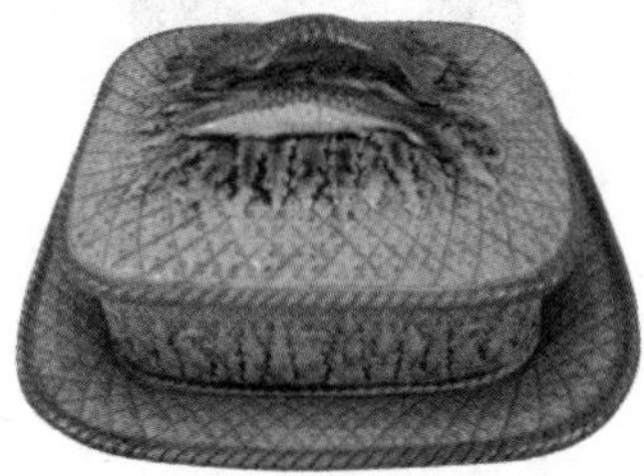

M

Majolica, Syrup, Red Flowers, Pink Bow, Conical Form, Late 1800s, 9 In.
$413.00

Wall Pocket, Figural, Bull's Head, Cobalt Blue Trim, T. Sergent, 5 ¾ In., Pair
$748.00

Malachite, Perfume Bottle, Flowers, Cupids, Garland, Czechoslovakia, 6 In.
$121.00

Sugar, Daisy, Wheat, Morning Glory, Fielding, 6 In. 92.00
Sugar, Melon Shape, Cover, Holdcroft, 5 In. 104.00
Sugar & Creamer, Cauliflower, Etruscan 173.00
Sugar & Creamer, Wild Rose 138.00
Sweetmeat, Conch Shell, 2-Dolphin Stem, Intertwined Tails, Minton, 9 ¼ In. 805.00
Syrup, Blackberry Albino, Pewter Top, Bennet's, 8 In. 104.00
Syrup, Corn, Pewter Lid, 9 In. 230.00
Syrup, Mottled Brown, Cobalt Blue, Yellow, Pewter Top, 4 ¼ In. 35.00
Syrup, Red Flowers, Pink Bow, Conical Form, Late 1800s, 9 In. .... *illus* 413.00
Syrup, Sunflower, Yellow, Blue Ground, Etruscan, c.1900, 8 In. 354.00
Table, Bulbous, Cartouche, Leaf Decor, Scrolling Feet, Teal, Ocher Glaze, Gilt, 21 x 16 In. 227.00
Tankard Set, Corn, 12-In. Tankard, 5 ¾-In. Mug, 7 Piece 288.00
Tea Set, Yellow Basket Weave & Bamboo, Morley & Co., 3 Piece 316.00
Teapot, Bow, Leaf, Flowers, Basket Weave, Brown Spout & Handle, Fielding, 5 ½ In. 374.00
Teapot, Cauliflower, Etruscan, 5 ¼ In. 55.00
Teapot, Cobalt Blackberry, Basket Weave, 7 x 11 In. 92.00
Teapot, Fish Swallowing Fish, Figural, Brown, Green, Yellow, 11 In. 184.00
Teapot, Pineapple, 8 In. 374.00
Tobacco Jar, Figural, Monkey With Spoon, Cat In Cauldron, T. Sergent, 7 ½ In. 575.00
Tobacco Jar, Leaves, Shells, Snail Finial, T. Sergent, Palissy, c.1870, 6 In. 345.00
Toothpick, Beetle, Butterfly, 4-Sided, 2 ¾ In. 29.00
Toothpick, Flowers, Cobalt Blue Ground, 2 In. 17.00
Tray, Begonia Leaf, Basket Weave, Round, 12 In. 207.00
Tray, Bird, On Leaf, 10 In. 69.00
Tray, Chestnut Leaf, Cobalt Blue, Mottled, Squirrel Handle, 9 ½ In. 230.00
Tray, Corn, Basket Weave, Leaf Border, 13 In. 345.00
Tray, Fish, George Morley, 13 In. 127.00
Tray, Leaves, Pink Ground, Fox Handle, 11 In. 1035.00
Tray, Oak Leaf, Purple Rim, Etruscan, 12 In. 173.00
Tray, Oak Leaves, Acorns, Cobalt Blue Ground, Oval, Stretched Handles, 9 ½ In. 150.00
Tray, Singing Frog, Gnome With Guitar, Under Mushroom, Wilhelm Schiller & Son, 7 In. 29.00
Tureen, Basket Form, 3 Dove & Oak Branch Feet, White Dove Finial, Minton, 11 In. 8625.00
Tureen, Fish, Cover, Boat Shape, Winged Beast, Oval, c.1870, 21 In. 8750.00
Tureen, Game, Wheat & Leaves, Dead Quail On Cover, Round, George Jones, 11 ¾ In. 690.00
Tureen, Tray, Corn, Portugal, 13 In., 2 Piece 17.00
Umbrella Stand, Blackberry Border, 20 In. 100.00
Umbrella Stand, Cobalt Blue, Green, Cream, Black, 22 In. 81.00
Umbrella Stand, Figural, Heron, Flowers, Frog, 36 x 19 x 16 In. 400.00
Umbrella Stand, Multicolored, Early 20th Century, 18 ¾ x 10 In. 176.00
Umbrella Stand, Stork In Fan, Bamboo Ground, Fielding, 23 In. 518.00
Umbrella Stand, Water Lily, Leaves, Shaded, 19 ½ In. 46.00
Umbrella Stand, Wheat Wreath, Ribbon & Bow, High Relief Butterflies, 24 In. 104.00
Urn, Grape Clusters, Vine Leaves, Gilt, Handles, George Jones, 1860-1970, 10 ½ In. 420.00
Urn, Mask, Flower, Swag Mounts, Color, Wilhelm Schiller & Sons, c.1880, 12 In., Pair 1135.00
Vase, Bud, Triple, Bamboo, Holdcroft, 4 ½ In. 81.00
Vase, Bud, Triple, Owl, Brown, 4 ½ In. 173.00
Vase, Bud, Triple, Stems, Flower Border, Leafy Foot, 5 In. 374.00
Vase, Cadinen, Knights, Battle, Painted Enamel, Molded Medusa Head Handles, c.1900, 8 In. 652.00
Vase, Cobalt Blue, Grape Clusters, Leaves, Branch Handles, T. Sergent, Palissy, 14 ½ In. 575.00
Vase, Figural, Minton, Classical Maiden, Reading Book, c.1872, 19 ½ In. 7500.00
Vase, Garniture, Double Serpent Handle, Mythological Figure Reserves, 30 x 13 In., Pair 2640.00
Vase, Hand Holding Ear Of Corn, 8 In. 403.00
Vase, Hand Holding Pineapple, England, 7 ¾ In. 518.00
Vase, Spill, Dolphin Holding Shell, 8 In. 288.00
Vase, Tree Trunk, Flowers, Butterfly, 5 In. 104.00
Wall Pocket, Applied Flowers, Leaves, 12 In. 104.00
Wall Pocket, Bird & Nest Shape, Branch, Leaves, England, 11 ¼ In. 184.00
Wall Pocket, Butterfly Shape, Yellow, Gold Detail, 8 In. 69.00
Wall Pocket, Figural, Bull's Head, Cobalt Blue Trim, T. Sergent, 5 ¾ In., Pair .... *illus* 748.00
Wall Pocket, Sunflower, Begonia Leaf, 13 ½ In. 1035.00
Waste Bowl, Shell & Seaweed, Etruscan, 5 In. 259.00

MALACHITE is a green stone with unusual layers or rings of darker green shades. It is often polished and used for decorative objects. Most malachite comes from Siberia or Australia.

Ashtray, 8 x 6 In. 117.00
Basket, Glass, 5 ½ x 5 ¾ In. 94.00
Box, Cover, Strips Of Gilt Bronze Inlay, Round, 20th Century, 3 ¾ In. 100.00

Box, Vinaigrette, 18K Gold Rectangular Mount, Punched & Engraved Grill, c.1820, 1 In. 341.00
Brush Holder, Chinese, Early 10th Century, 4 In. 443.00
Easter Egg, Bronze, Dore, Fleur-De-Lis, Footed, Nicholas II, Russia, c.1900, 9 ¼ In. 2000.00
Figurine, Bird, Carved, Bezel Set Diamond Eyes, Jasper Beak, Bronze Feet, 3 x 2 In. 411.00
Figurine, Horse, Chinese, c.1900, 7 In. 325.00
Figurine, Hotai, God Of Wealth, Carrying Treasure Sack, Mallet, Carved, 2 ½ In. 50.00
Group, 2 Meiren, With Fan, Chinese, 6 In. 201.00
Perfume Bottle, Flowers, Cupids, Garland, Czechoslovakia, 6 In. .... *illus* 121.00
Perfume Bottle, Green Glass, Raised Flowers On Base & Stopper, 3-Sided, 4 In. 80.00

MAPS of all types have been collected for centuries. The earliest known printed maps were made in 1478. The first printed street map showed London in 1559. The first road maps for use by drivers of automobiles were made in 1901. Collectors buy maps that were pages of old books, as well as the multifolded road maps popular in this century.

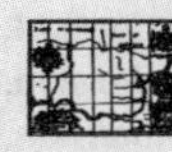

Americas, Johann Baptiste, Nuremberg, Hand Colored, Engraved, Frame, 1730, 19 x 23 In. 538.00
Atlas, Massachusetts, O.W. Walker, Folio, 1891 .... 1422.00
Canada, English Colonies, Zatta, Hand Colored, Frame, c.1778, 15 ¾ x 19 ¾ In. 431.00
Charleston Harbor, Hand Tinted Lithograph, 1841, 9 ½ x 11 In. 374.00
England & Wales, M. Jackson, Embroidered, Multicolored, 1781, 25 x 21 In. 695.00
Globe, Celestial, Engraved, 12 Multicolored Gores, 2 Polar Calottes, Plaster, Wilson, 13 x 18 In. 7703.00
Globe, Celestial, Terrestrial, Compass, Mahogany, Tripod Base, Brass Feet, 31 ½ x 13 In. 10158.00
Globe, Terrestrial, 12 Gores, Plaster Sphere, Mahogany Stand, Wilson, 13 x 29 In. 6518.00
Globe, Terrestrial, 12 Paper Gores, 2 Polar Calottes, Art Deco Base, Hammond, 21 In. 207.00
Globe, Terrestrial, 12 Paper Gores, Plaster, Tripod, Rand McNally, 18 In. 385.00
Globe, Terrestrial, Georgian Style, Walnut, Tripod Base, Rand McNally, 38 x 22 In. 110.00
Globe, Terrestrial, Gregorian, Zodiacal Calendars, 12 Gores, Mahogany Legs, 9 x 14 ½ In. 6518.00
Globe, Terrestrial, H.B. Nims & Co., Tripod Base, Cast Iron, 15 In. 500.00
Globe, Terrestrial, Kittinger, Wood Stand, 15 ½ In. 375.00
Globe, Terrestrial, Red Trim, Iron Top Pointer, C.F. Delamarche, 1835, 19 x 13 In. 1760.00
Globe, Terrestrial, Stand, Rand McNally, 46 x 24 In., 18-In. Globe 3744.00
Illinois, Hand Colored, W. Graham Arander III, c.1856 .... 8500.00
Long Island, Courtland Smith, 1961, 19 ¾ x 26 ¾ In. 2040.00
Massachusetts, Official Topographical Atlas Walling & Gray, Hand Colored, c.1871 .... 533.00
New York, Original Surveys, Paper, On Canvas, 1860, 69 x 73 In. 220.00
North & South Carolina, Johnson & Ward, Hand Colored Inset Views, 17 ⅜ x 24 In. 460.00
North America, 18th Century, American Atlas, Engraved, John Reid, c.1796, 16 ½ x 19 In. 230.00
North America, Eastern Seaboard, Hand Colored, Amsterdam, c.1720, 15 x 20 In. 2124.00
North America, Pownall, Thomas Jeffery's American Atlas, c.1763, 22 x 48 In. 2185.00
Paris, Jardin Des Tuileries, Lithograph, Charles Fichot, Frame, Late 1800s, 20 x 32 ½ In. 478.00
Scandinavia, Overton, Multicolored, England, Frame, c.1717, 33 x 23 In. .... *illus* 920.00
Scotland, Hand Colored, Frame, John Senex, 1721, 23 x 19 In. 359.00
South Carolina, Indian Villages, Hand Colored, I. Low, New York, 1799, 8 x 10 In. .... *illus* 820.00
Tennessee, Early Settlement, Carey, Frame, c.1814, 18 ½ x 29 In. 920.00
United States, Post Revolutionary War, Laurie & Whittle, c.1794, 19 ¼ x 26 In. 575.00
University Of Michigan, Ann Arbor, Hardboard, Color, Gertrude Strickler, 1901, 39 x 31 In. 248.00
World, Double Hemisphere, Copper Engraving, 2 Celestial Models, 1746, 18 x 21 In. 1057.00
World, Ink, Watercolor, September 14, 1825, 18 ½ x 23 In. 3042.00

MARBLE collectors pay highest prices for glass and sulphide marbles. The game of marbles has been popular since the days of the ancient Romans. American children were able to buy marbles by the mid-eighteenth century. Dutch glazed clay marbles were least expensive. Glazed pottery marbles, attributed to the Bennington potteries in Vermont, were of a better quality. Marbles made of pink marble were also available by the 1830s. Glass marbles seem to have been made later. By 1880, Samuel C. Dyke of South Akron, Ohio, was making clay marbles and The National Onyx Marble Company was making marbles of onyx. The Navarre Glass Marble Company of Navarre, Ohio, and M. B. Mishler of Ravenna, Ohio, made the glass marbles. Ohio remained the center of the marble industry, and the Akron-made Akro Agate brand became nationally known. Other pieces made by Akro Agate are listed in this book in the Akro Agate category. Sulphides are glass marbles with frosted white figures in the center.

Clambroth, White Line, Deep Amethyst, 1 $^{15}/_{16}$ In. 7475.00
Gutta-Percha, 1 $^{11}/_{16}$ In. 1210.00
Joseph's Coat, 1 $^{15}/_{32}$ In. 1150.00
Joseph's Coat, England, $^{13}/_{16}$ In. 316.00
Joseph's Coat, Swirl, Red, Orange, Yellow, Green Swirls, Aventurine, England, $^{25}/_{32}$ In. 330.00
Latticinio, Aqua, Oxblood, White Swirl, $^{27}/_{32}$ In. .... *illus* 189.00

TIP
A heavy odor from smoke or mildew lowers the value of a collection of paper.

Map, Scandinavia, Overton, Multicolored, England, Frame, c.1717, 33 x 23 In.
$920.00

Map, South Carolina, Indian Villages, Hand Colored, I. Low, New York, 1799, 8 x 10 In.
$820.00

TIP
Small cracks in marble can be concealed with a mixture of colored wax and chalk dust. The same mixture can be used to make a new nose or finger for a damaged marble figure.

Marble, Latticinio, Aqua, Oxblood, White Swirl, 27/32 In.
$189.00

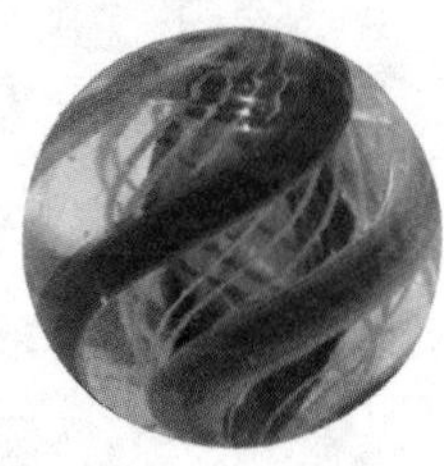

Marble, Latticinio, Red Jelly Core, Yellow Swirl, Red, White, Green Yellow Bands, 11/16 In.
$495.00

Marble, Latticinio, White Core, Aqua Case, Red, White, 29/32 In.
$550.00

Marble, Onionskin, Mica, Blue, Red, Yellow, White, 2 1/4 In.
$385.00

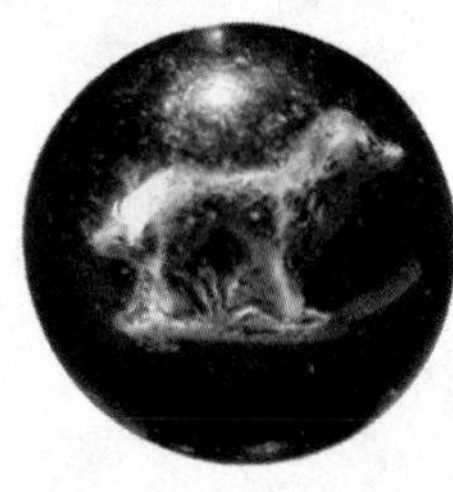

Marble, Sulphide, Dog, Lavender Tint, Early 20th Century, 2 In.
$201.00

Latticinio, Orange, White, Ribbon Swirl, 27/32 In. 30.00
Latticinio, Red, Orange, Olive, Blue, Gray & White Swirls, 1 1/16 In. 550.00
Latticinio, Red Jelly Core, Yellow Swirl, Red, White, Green Yellow Bands, 11/16 In. *illus* 495.00
Latticinio, Swirl, 4 Stages, White, Blue, Yellow, Red Bands, 27/32 In. 403.00
Latticinio, Swirl, Multicolored, 2 1/16 In. 173.00
Latticinio, Swirl, Stages, Blue Tint, 2 1/32 In. 173.00
Latticinio, White Core, Aqua Case, Red, White, 29/32 In. *illus* 550.00
Latticinio, White Core, Yellow, Red, Green, Black Swirls, 7/8 In. 29.00
Latticinio, Yellow Core, 1 13/32 In. 230.00
Onionskin, 4 Panel, 1 5/8 In. 173.00
Onionskin, Cubist Clown, Multicolored, Pontil, 1 3/8 In. 5000.00 to 5750.00
Onionskin, Mica, Blue, Red, Yellow, White, 2 1/4 In. *illus* 385.00
Onionskin, Mica, Multicolored, 4 Lobes, 2 1/8 In. 575.00
Onionskin, Mica, Pink, Speckled, 7/8 In. 110.00 to 115.00
Onionskin, Mica, Yellow, Green, Red, 1 1/16 In. 115.00
Red & Yellow Swirl, 3 Stages, Pontil, 1 1/16 In. 440.00
Sulphide, Boy, With Sailboat, 1 3/4 In. 84.00
Sulphide, Dog, Lavender Tint, Early 20th Century, 2 In. *illus* 201.00
Sulphide, Dog, Standing, Pontil, 1 3/4 In. 161.00
Sulphide, Donkey, Pontil, 1 1/2 In. 92.00
Sulphide, Fox, Crouching, Pontil, 1 3/8 In. 92.00
Sulphide, Lamb, Lying Down, Clear, 1 1/2 In. 94.00
Sulphide, Lamb, Standing, 2 1/8 In. 242.00
Sulphide, Rabbit, 1 5/8 In. 130.00
Sulphide, Rabbit, Running, Pontil, 1 1/2 In. 58.00
Sulphide, Shetland Pony, 2 In. 330.00
Sulphide, Squirrel, Holding Nuts, 2 In. 224.00
Sulphide, Squirrel, Standing Eating, Pontil, 1 5/8 In. 207.00
Swirl, Aventurine, 5/8 In. 58.00
Swirl, Broken Core, 3 Latticinio Ribbons, Red, Yellow, Blue Turquoise, 2 1/16 In. 403.00
Swirl, Ribbon Core, Multicolored, 13/16 In. 403.00
Swirl, Yellow Inner, Red, Blue, Green With White Swirls, 1 1/2 In. 70.00
White Core, Multicolored Swirl Bands, Pontil, 2 In. 180.00

MARBLE CARVINGS, such as large or small figurines, groups of people or animals, and architectural decorations, have been a special art form since the time of the ancient Greeks. Reproductions, especially of large Victorian groups, are being made of a mixture using marble dust. These are very difficult to detect and collectors should be careful. Other carvings are listed under Alabaster.

Basin, Cupped Hands, Cut Drain Hole, 11 x 18 In. 999.00
Box, Table, Black, Ocher Variegated, Silvered Metal Mounts, Ball Feet, 3 x 6 1/4 In. 420.00
Bust, Apollo, Base, 19th Century, 13 In. 500.00
Bust, Apollo, Looking Over Shoulder, Tunic, Gray Veined Pedestal, 27 x 33 1/2 In. 4740.00
Bust, Belvedere Apollo, Socle, Column, 32 x 39 1/2 In. 4025.00
Bust, Blackamoor, Bearded, Onyx Turban, Socle Base, 1900s, 29 In. 649.00
Bust, George Washington, 1800s, 14 In. 296.00
Bust, Girl, Peasant Attire, Kerchief, Gray Veined, White, 10 In. 1495.00
Bust, Man, Roman, Curled Hair, Cropped Beard, Folded Tunic, Pedestal, 24 x 40 In. 1007.00
Bust, Pan, Satyr, Pipe, Grapes, White, Gray Marble Pedestal, 1800s, 64 In. 9375.00
Bust, Renaissance Woman, Pedestal, 19th Century, 24 In. 2360.00
Bust, Savonarola, Italy, 19th Century, 8 1/4 In. *illus* 165.00
Bust, Woman, Art Nouveau Mandolin Pedestal, 1900s, 26 In. 413.00
Bust, Woman, Lacy Collar, Rose, Signed, E. Fortin, 16 x 22 1/2 In. 4500.00
Bust, Woman Wearing Bonnet, Italy, 14 1/2 In. 413.00
Bust, Woman With Braided Hair, Socle, Pedestal, c.1850, 68 1/2 In. 1762.00
Bust, Young Woman, With Cap, E. Villanis, 26 In. 2185.00
Bust, Youth, Maiden, Drapery, Circular Base, 25 & 23 In., Pair 1320.00
Obelisk, Bronze Mounts, Red, White, France, 24 x 6 In. 468.00
Obelisk, Metal Detail, Gray, Red, Yellow, 26 x 6 In. 293.00
Pedestal, Columnar, Veined, Hexagonal Top, 46 In. 2360.00
Pedestal, Dark Gray & White, 2 Sections, 29 1/2 In. 2199.00
Pedestal, Green, Fluted, 3 Sections, 19th Century, 42 In. 150.00
Pedestal, Square, Linear Design, 40 In. 300.00
Pedestal, Square Top, Banded Column Shaft, Square Base, 6 Sections, 36 x 14 In. 275.00
Pedestal, Square Top, Round Banded Top, Bottom, Square Base, 43 x 8 3/4 In. 220.00
Pedestal, Twist Stem, Octagonal Base, 35 In. 900.00

Pedestal, White, Striated, 3 Columns, Acanthus Capital, Trefoil Top, Bottom, 35 In. 431.00
Plaque, Angel, White, Carrara, Italy, 18 x 16 x 5 In. .... *illus* 550.00
Statue, 2 Putti, Cup, Reed Instrument, Carrara, Italy, c.1885, 34 In. 7500.00
Statue, Bacchante, Reclining, Nude, Tambourine, Snake, 1800s, 16 x 29 In. 7500.00
Statue, Boy, Reading, On Ledge, c.1880, 31 In. 3450.00
Statue, Buddha, Multicolored, Burma, 28 ½ In. 850.00
Statue, Buddha, Seated, Eyes Down, Long Earlobes, Holding Jar, 18 x 11 In. 350.00
Statue, Cleo, Muse Of History, Seated, Pointing At Scroll, 38 In. 9200.00
Statue, Faun, Reclining, Lion Skin, Pillow, Italy, c.1825, 11 x 34 In. 18750.00
Statue, Female Nude, Kneeling, P. Barranti, Florence, c.1885, 34 x 12 In. 5463.00
Statue, Foo Dog, Male & Female, Seated, On Carved Plinth, 29 x 11 x 18 In., Pair 575.00
Statue, Foo Dog, Seated, Base, Chinese, 24 x 13 x 9 In., Pair 425.00
Statue, Foo Dog, Seated, On Base, White, 24 x 10 x 13 In., Pair 375.00
Statue, Gautama Buddha Head, 8 x 5 ½ In. 50.00
Statue, Horse, Tang Style, Standing, Jade Green, China, 19 In. 275.00
Statue, Inverno, Cesare Lapini, c.1893, 26 In. 6250.00
Statue, Leda & The Swan, G. Gerujinsky, 1937, 12 In. 3081.00
Statue, Lion, Sitting, Paw On Globe, White, Base, 27 x 23 In., Pair 5581.00
Statue, Lion, Stalking, Green Glass Eyes, Base, c.1920, 11 x 16 ½ x 5 In. 175.00
Statue, Mother Holding Infant, Son Alongside, Plinth, 19th Century, 16 ½ In. 764.00
Statue, Olympic Wrestlers, White, Carrara, Italy, Late 20th Century, 18 x 7 x 8 In. 425.00
Statue, Pig, Reclining, Signed, R. Angelletti, Perugia, 1896, 10 x 22 x 12 In. 650.00
Statue, Rebecca At The Well, C. Fontana, Italy, c.1825, 41 In. 7670.00
Statue, Shepherdess, Sheep, Cane, Hand Over Eyes, Signed, P. Bazzanti, 16 x 5 ½ In. 500.00
Statue, Torso, Male, Truncated Limbs, Robert Graham Style, 24 In. 2115.00
Statue, Woman, Holding Rose Bouquet, Carrara, Italy, 21 In. 1020.00
Statue, Woman, Nude, Art Nouveau, c.1900, 24 In. 1725.00
Statue, Woman, Reclining, 19th Century, 23 x 31 ½ In. 2106.00
Statue, Woman, Seated, 19th Century, 20 ½ x 10 In. 4112.00
Statue, Woman Dancer, Pink Clothing, Cape, Art Deco Style, 60 x 14 x 46 In. 2350.00
Statue, Young Boy, With Staff, P. Borranti, Marked, Italy, 19th Century, 25 In. 2090.00
Statue, Young Girl, Carrying Basket, Italy, 19th Century, 42 In. 9350.00
Urn, Carved, Lamp Mounted, Italy, c.1900, 15 In. 263.00
Urn, Cover, Classical Style, Bronze Mounts, Scrolled Handles, 28 x 12 In. 410.00
Urn, Lid, Louis XVI, Fleur De Pecher, Gilt Bronze Mounts, Paris, c.1895, 21 In., Pair 8625.00
Urn, Louis XVI, White Baluster Form, Bronze Mounts, Eagle Finials, 18 In. 472.00
Urn, Rouge, Gilt Metal, Lion's Mask Ring Pulls, Mounted As Lamps, 35 In., Pair 1560.00
Urn, White, Rose & Black, Satyr Mask Ormolu Fittings, 14 In., Pair 999.00
Vase, Asian Figure, Black, Bronze Dragon Handles, France, 1800s, 12 In., Pair 1422.00

MARBLEHEAD Pottery was founded in 1905 by Dr. J. Hall as a rehabilitative program for the patients of a Marblehead, Massachusetts, sanitarium. Two years later it was separated from the sanitarium and it continued operations until 1936. Many of the pieces were decorated with marine motifs.

Bowl, Band Of Blueberries & Leaves, Dark Blue Matte Ground, Marked, 2 x 6 In. 1035.00
Bowl, Blue Matte Glaze, Signed, 9 x 3 In. 330.00
Bowl, Green Matte Glaze, Green Glossy Glaze Interior, Mark, c.1930, 2 x 5 In. 207.00
Bowl, Undulating Rim, Glossy Teal Glaze, Teal Matte Interior Glaze, c.1930, 12 In. 148.00
Candleholder, Yellow Matte Glaze, Original Paper, 4 x 5 In. 295.00
Flowerpot, Cobalt Blue, Mark, 5 x 6 In. 245.00
Flowerpot, Golden Brown, Glaze Skip Inside Rim, Mark, 5 x 6 In. 245.00
Flowerpot, Ribbed Design, Blue Glaze, A.E. Baggs Mark, 5 x 6 In. 265.00
Humidor, Green Matte Ground, Black Flower Lid, 4 ¼ In. 3240.00
Mug, Grape Leaves, Vines, Blue, Green, Gray, Blue, 6 x 4 ¾ In. 2520.00
Tile, Fish, Incised, Waves On Gray Matte Ground, Frame, 6 In. Square 12000.00
Tile, Landscape, Incised, Trees, Pond, Frame, 6 In. Square 114000.00
Tile, Rooster, Incised, Speckled Gray Ground, Round, 5 In. 3240.00
Tile, Ship, Sea, Mustard Orange Glaze, Square, Paper Label, c.1930, 4 In. 119.00
Tile, Trees, Sunset, Silhouette, Green, Yellow, Original Drawing, 8 In. .... *illus* 14400.00
Vase, Bird Medallions, Brown, Speckled Green Ground, Tapered, 5 ¾ x 3 ¾ In. 2040.00
Vase, Blue, Sea Gulls In Flight, Semigloss Ground, 1911, 4 ¼ x ¾ In. 2880.00
Vase, Blue Matte Glaze, 9 ¼ x 6 ¾ In. 1560.00
Vase, Blue Matte Glaze, Cylindrical, Impressed Mark, 10 x 3 ½ In. 150.00
Vase, Blue Matte Glaze, Oval, Mark, 7 ½ In. 403.00
Vase, Bulbous, Lavender Matte, Mark, 4 x 6 In. 375.00
Vase, Bulbous, Raised Lip, Blue Matte Glaze, Mark, c.1930, 5 In. 296.00

Marble Carving, Bust, Savonarola, Italy, 19th Century, 8 ¼ In.
$165.00

Marble Carving, Plaque, Angel, White, Carrara, Italy, 18 x 16 x 5 In.
$550.00

Marblehead, Tile, Trees, Sunset, Silhouette, Green, Yellow, Original Drawing, 8 In.
$14400.00

M

Marblehead, Vase, Stylized Trees, Blue Green Ground, Speckled, Beaker Form, 3 ½ In.
$4500.00

Martin Brothers, Jar, Grotesque Bird, Leather Liner, Signed, 1899, 11 ¼ x 5 ¾ In.
$36000.00

Martin Brothers, Vase, Grotesque Fish, Sea Life, 4-Sided, Incised, Marked, 1913, 6 x 3 In.
$3000.00

Vase, Classical Shape, Mauve Matte Glaze, 4 In. 350.00
Vase, Cover, Cylindrical, Blue Seaweed, Ivory To Blue Ground, 13 ¼ x 5 ¼ In. 8400.00
Vase, Cylindrical, Blue Matte Glaze, Mark, c.1930, 4 In. 415.00
Vase, Cylindrical, Slanted Rim, Olive Green Matte Glaze, c.1920, 4 In. 356.00
Vase, Cylindrical, Yellow, Brown Matte Glaze, 3 x 2 In. 325.00
Vase, Egg Shape, Stylized Lemon Trees, Blue Ground, 4 ½ x 3 ½ In. 2040.00
Vase, Green Glaze, Squat, Signed, 3 x 5 In. 200.00
Vase, Incised, Top Border Painted Leaves, Pink Flowers, Green Matte, 7 ½ In. 1800.00
Vase, Light Blue & Purple, Impressed Ship Mark, 5 ⅛ x 7 ⅝ In. 330.00
Vase, Orange, Amber, Yellow Mottled Glaze, Faceted, 8 ¼ x 8 In. 5400.00
Vase, Organic, Green Matte Glaze, Flower Vine, Incised, Mark, 7 ½ In. 900.00
Vase, Oval, Blue & Gray, Stylized Flowers, Gray Ground, 5 ¼ In. 1920.00
Vase, Persian Blue Glaze, Ribbed, Oval, 11 x 7 In. 3240.00
Vase, Roses, Green, Red, Blue Matte Ground, Tapered, 3 ½ x 3 ¾ In. 1920.00
Vase, Scottish Roses, Green, Yellow, Blue, Gray Ground, 3 ⅛ In. 748.00
Vase, Stylized Blossoms, Purple Ground, Squat, 3 x 5 ¼ In. 1800.00
Vase, Stylized Blossoms, Speckled Brown Ground, Wide Mouth, 3 ¾ In. 1920.00
Vase, Stylized Trees, Blue Green Ground, Speckled, Beaker Form, 3 ½ In. *illus* 4500.00
Vase, Tapered, Green Matte Glaze, Impressed Mark, 4 x 7 In. 420.00

MARTIN BROTHERS of Middlesex, England, made Martinware, a salt-glazed stoneware, between 1873 and 1915. Many figural jugs and vases were made by the three brothers. Of special interest are the fanciful birds, usually made with removable heads. Most pieces have the incised name of the artists plus other information on the bottom.

Jar, Grotesque, Gremlin, Lid, Signed, 1888, 8 x 5 In. 13000.00
Jar, Grotesque Bird, Leather Liner, Signed, 1899, 11 ¼ x 5 ¾ In. *illus* 36000.00
Jug, Smiling Face, Incised, Signed, c.1898, 7 ¾ In. 9000.00
Pencil Holder, Scotsman, Wearing Tam, Figural, 3 ½ x 3 In. 750.00
Vase, Bird, Interior Signed, TWM S, c.1898, 15 In. 43200.00
Vase, Bird, Signed, Martin Bros London & Southall, 12 In. 50400.00
Vase, Dragons, 1901, 11 ½ x 3 ¾ In. 3000.00
Vase, Grotesque Fish, Sea Life, 4-Sided, Incised, Marked, 1913, 6 x 3 In. *illus* 3000.00
Vase, Incised Thistles, Amber Ground, Painted, Signed, 1905, 10 ¼ x 5 In. 2400.00
Vase, Incised Vultures, Marked, c.1884, 9 ¼ In. 10800.00
Vase, Orchids, Incised Hummingbirds, Dragonflies, Brown, London & Southall, 1898, 9 ½ In. 3920.00

MARY GREGORY is the name used for a type of glass that is easily identified. White figures were painted on clear or colored glass as the decoration. The figures chosen were usually children at play. The first glass known as Mary Gregory was made about 1870. Similar glass is made even today. The traditional story has been that the glass was made at the Sandwich Glass works in Boston by a woman named Mary Gregory. Recent research suggests that it is possible that none was made at Sandwich. In general, all-white figures were used in the United States, tinted faces were probably used in Bohemia, France, Italy, Germany, Switzerland, and England. Children standing, not playing, were pictured after the 1950s.

Barber Bottle, Palm Tree, Green, Tooled Mouth, c.1885-1925, 8 In. 2420.00
Box, Cover, Boy Waving To Bird, Cranberry Glass, Gold Rim, 5 In. 75.00
Pitcher, Woman Picking Grapes, Iridescent Amber, Amethyst Twist Handle, 13 In. 115.00
Powder Jar, Boy Walking, Cranberry Glass, 4 ½ In. 100.00
Powder Jar, Woman Holding Lyre, White, Cranberry Glass, Gold Flowers, 3 ¼ In. 295.00
Vase, Boy With Flower, Girl With Fan, Green, Gold, Scalloped & Flared Rim, 13 In. 100.00
Vase, Girl At Water Pump, Green Satin, 12 ¼ In., Pair 250.00
Vase, Jack-In-The-Pulpit, Clear Shaded To Amber, Scrolls, 5 ½ In. 55.00
Vase, Jack-In-The-Pulpit, Vaseline Opalescent, Purple Trim, Scrolls, 5 ½ In. 65.00
Vase, Roman Children, Purple, Optic Ribbed, Urn Shape, Scroll Handles, 12 In., Pair 403.00
Vase, Victorian Women, Cranberry Glass, Footed Urn, 9 ½ In., Pair 173.00
Vase, Women, Blue, Scalloped Edge, 17 ½ In., Pair 1150.00
Water Set, Cranberry Glass, 8 In., 8 Piece 146.00

MASONIC, *see Fraternal category.*

MASON'S IRONSTONE was made by the English pottery of Charles J. Mason after 1813. Mason, of Lane Delph, was given a patent for this improved earthenware. He usually called it Mason's Patent Ironstone China. It resisted chipping and breaking so it became popular for dinnerwares and other table service dishes. Vases and other decorative pieces were also made. The ironstone was decorated with orange, blue, gold, and other colors, often in Japanese inspired designs. The firm had financial difficulties, but the molds and the name Mason were used by many owners through the years, including Francis Morley, Taylor Ashworth, George L. Ashworth, and John Shaw. Mason's joined the Wedgwood group in 1973 and the name is still found on dinnerwares.

Cake Plate, Square, 2 Handles, Watteau Scene, 10 ¼ In. 199.00
Cheese Dish, Stand, Cover, Round, Blue Mandalay, 11 ¾ In. 96.00
Pitcher, Ming Tree Form, Cobalt Blue, Gilt, 8-Sided Base, Marked, 11 ½ In. 175.00
Plate, Flowers, Cobalt Blue, Red, Gilt, Imari Style, Marked, 1820s, 10 In. 80.00
Plate, Oriental Design, Flowers, Cobalt Blue Ground, Gilt, Marked, 10 ½ In. 40.00
Platter, Oriental Flowers, Scenery, 19th Century, 13 x 10 ½ In. 81.00
Platter, Red Transfer, Flowers, Birds, Multicolored, England, c.1850, 17 In. 863.00
Tureen, Lid, Stand, c.1900, 10 x 14 In. 293.00
Tureen, Platter, No Lid, Mandarin Pattern, Handles, c.1870, 8 ½ x 10 In. 1000.00
Vase, Blue Mandalay, 13 In., Pair 168.00

MASSIER a French art pottery, was made by brothers Jerome, Delphin, and Clement Massier in Vallauris and Golfe-Juan, France, in the late nineteenth and early twentieth centuries. It has an iridescent metallic luster glaze that resembles the Weller Sicardo pottery glaze. Most pieces are marked *J. Massier*. Massier may also be listed in the Majolica category.

J.Massier fils

Centerbowl, Mottled, Oval, Majolica, 10 In. 58.00
Charger, Peacock Feathers, Iridescent Metallic Glaze, Marked, Vallauris, 14 ½ In. 1080.00
Figurine, Parrot, Perched On Branch, Majolica, France, c.1900, 13 In. 480.00
Planter, Pansy, Purple, Yellow, Blue, Marked, 17 ½ x 15 ½ x 9 ⅜ In. 800.00
Wall Pocket, Lavender Daisy, Majolica 58.00

MATCH HOLDERS were made to hold the large wooden matches that were used in the nineteenth and twentieth centuries for a variety of purposes. The kitchen stove and the fireplace or furnace had to be lit regularly. One type of match holder was made to hang on the wall, another was designed to be kept on a tabletop. Of special interest today are match holders that have advertisements as part of the design.

Adriance Farm Machinery, Corn Binder, Tin Lithograph, 4 ¾ In. 250.00
Alligator, Hinged Lid, Bronze, c.1910, 10 ½ In. .... *illus* 575.00
American Eagle, Shield, 7 ¼ In. 275.00
Ashtray, Claridge Hotel, Atlantic City, Hall China, 4 In. 29.00
Baby, In Top Hat, Opaque White, Black, Late 19th Century, 4 ¼ x 4 In. .... *illus* 226.00
Baby, In Top Hat, Underside Match Striker, Milk Glass, 1920s, 4 x 3 In. 135.00
Baking Soda, Cast Iron, Copper Flashed, 5 x 4 x 4 In. 412.00
Bear, Carved Wood, Standing, Box In Hand, Figural, Incised, c.1890, 9 In. 385.00
Bear, Seated, Holding Tree, Glass Eyes, Brass, Figural, 3 In. 100.00
Bear, Walking, Bronze, Cigar Holder, 4 ¼ x 8 ½ In. 200.00
Bird, Branch, Figural, 4 ½ x 5 ½ x 3 ½ In. 30.00
Bird, Spread Wings, Nose Down, Figural, 5 x 4 ¾ x 2 ¾ In. 40.00
Boot, Cast Iron, 5 In. 20.00
Boot, Woonsocket Rubber Co., A Match For You, None For Woonsocket, 3 ¼ In. 45.00
Boy, Between Baskets, Watering Can, Porcelain, Austria, 3 ½ x 3 ⅛ In. 65.00
Boy, On Bucket, Concours Dlizy Oureq, Onyx Base, 5 ¾ In. 400.00
Boy, With Rabbits & Birds, Conta & Boehme, Porcelain, 5 ¾ In. 130.00
Brass, Elephant Shape, Head Opens, Scratch Back, Vesta, 2 ¼ x 1 ½ In. 119.00
Brass, Mice In Boot, Marked, Peerage England, 1 ⅝ x 3 In. 45.00
Bull Dog Cut Plug Tobacco, Tin Lithograph, 7 x 3 ¼ In. .... *illus* 805.00
Butterfly, Yellow, Cast Iron, 4 ¾ In. 431.00
Camel, Reclining, Figural, 4 ¼ x 6 ½ x 5 ¼ In. 150.00
Cat, On Kettle, Metal, Slate Base, 3 ½ In. 100.00
Cat, On Tray, c.1911, 3 x 5 x 4 In. 140.00
Ceresota Flour, Ceresota Kid Slicing Bread, Tin Lithograph, 5 ½ In. 360.00
Cherub, Strike Under Lid, Metal, Footed, 4 x 5 ⅝ In. 45.00
Chick, Rabbit Heads, Basket Form, Milk Glass, Hanging, 2 ¼ x 4 ¼ In. 25.00
Chickens, Stump, Brass, Nickel Plated, 2 ⅜ x 4 ⅜ In. 110.00
Child, In Boot, With Spur, Brass, 4 ¼ x 4 ¾ In. 125.00
Child's Head, Painted, Bisque, Victorian, 3 In. 10.00
Coal Scuttle, Holyoke Coal & Wood Co., Tel. 137-2, Cast Iron, 5 x 3 ⅞ In. 45.00
Columbia Mills, Woman In Patriotic Outfit, Tin Lithograph, 5 ½ In. 360.00
Crescent Stoves, Cup, Attached Underplate, Japanned Metal, Cutout, 1901, 2 x 3 In. 70.00
DeLaval Cream Separator, 1 Million In Use, Embossed, Tin, 6 ½ x 4 In. .... *illus* 240.00
Dog, Cast Brass, 3 ¾ x 3 ¼ In. 175.00
Dog, In Barrel, Bronze, 3 ½ In. .... *illus* 350.00

Match Holder, Alligator, Hinged Lid, Bronze, c.1910, 10 ½ In.
$575.00

Match Holder, Baby, In Top Hat, Opaque White, Black, Late 19th Century, 4 ¼ x 4 In.
$226.00

Match Holder, Bull Dog Cut Plug Tobacco, Tin Lithograph, 7 x 3 ¼ In.
$805.00

Match Holder, DeLaval Cream Separator, 1 Million In Use, Embossed, Tin, 6 ½ x 4 In.
$240.00

M

Match Holder, Dog, In Barrel, Bronze, 3 ½ In.
$350.00

Match Holder, Gatling Gun, Bronze, Gilt, Hinged Lid, Late 19th Century, 6 ½ In.
$767.00

Match Holder, Shoe, Victorian, Bird, Leaves, Hinged Lid, Black Paint, Gilt, 1 ½ x 3 x 1 In.
$33.00

TIP
When you cancel your paper before you leave on a trip, don't tell why you want the paper stopped. Call to restart it when you return.

Dog, Top Hat In Mouth, Metal, Slate Base, 5 In. 120.00
Donkey, Figural, Cast Iron, Bryant & May, c.1860 .... 99.00
Dr Pepper, Green, Tin, P.N. Co., Fulton, Ill., 6 x 3 ¼ x 3 ¼ In. 200.00
Dutch Boy Painter, Tin, Embossed, 6 ½ In. 345.00
Elephant, In Suit, Hands In Pockets, Bronze, 4 ½ In. 500.00
Enterprise Glass Co., Jenny Lind, Figural, c.1880, 4 ⅜ x 2 ⅝ In. 55.00
Flowers, Hanging, Cast Iron, 9 ¼ x 3 In. 45.00
Fly, Figural, Brass, 2 ½ x 4 In. 77.00
Game Animals, Horn, Pouch, 2 Red Men, Painted, Cast Iron, 5 x 11 In. 330.00
Gatling Gun, Bronze, Gilt, Hinged Lid, Late 19th Century, 6 ½ In. .... *illus* 767.00
Girl, Japan, Pottery, c.1950, 5 ¼ In. 10.00
Girl, Vase On Back, Porcelain, Germany, 5 ¾ In. 15.00
Grover Cleveland, Bust, Embossed, Cast Iron, 5 ½ In. 239.00
Hammered Sterling Silver, F.W.P. Monogram, Kalo, 1 x 2 In., 4 Piece 180.00
Hat, Brass, Art Nouveau, Wall Mount, 13 x 5 In. 88.00
High Button Shoe, Cast Iron, 5 ¼ In. 20.00
Hogarth Boy, Majolica, Minton, 8 In. 80.00
Jennie Wade House, High Water Mark Monument, Hanging 55.00
Julie Marlowe, Porcelain, c.1890, 3 ¾ In. 55.00
Luzianne Mammy, Wall Mount, Ceramic, Painted, 11 ½ In. 25.00
Man, In Slipper, Painted, Porcelain, 3 ¼ x 5 ¼ In. 77.00
Man, Laughing, Metal, 4 ¼ In. 100.00
Man, Wearing Cap, Hands In Pockets, Potbelly, Bronze, 4 ¼ In. 130.00
Monkey, Basket, Fence, Cast Iron, Marked, Corneau Fes Charleville, France, 8 x 5 In. 140.00
Nude, Art Deco, White Metal, Copper Patina, 4 ¾ x 11 In. 187.00
Old Hickory Wagons, Farm Wagon, Tin Lithograph, 4 ¾ In. 275.00
Old Woman, Basket On Back, Cast Iron, Slate Base, 6 ⅛ In. 90.00
Oriental Man, Hat, Figural, Porcelain Insert, 4 x 4 ½ x 3 In. 60.00
Outcault Comic Character, Serving Bread, Tin Lithograph, 6 ¾ In. 325.00
Owl, Glass Eyes, Brass, Figural, 2 ¾ In. 85.00
Pabst's Okay Specific, Bald Man's Face, Celluloid, 2 x 1 ½ In. 27.00
Rabbit, Basket On Back, Standing, Brass Bowl, 5 ¼ x 3 x 1 ¾ In. 40.00
Rabbit, Seated, Brass Bowl, 3 ¼ x 3 ¼ x 2 In. 30.00
Republican Elephant, Lifting Head, Signed Stevens, 4 ½ In. 172.00
Sharples Separator, Child Helping Mom, Tin Lithograph, 6 ¾ In. 165.00
Sharples Separator, Farm Wife At Work, Tin Lithograph, 6 ¾ In. 135.00
Shepherdess, Porcelain, 4 ½ In. 35.00
Shoe, Victorian, Bird, Leaves, Hinged Lid, Black Paint, Gilt, 1 ½ x 3 x 1 In. .... *illus* 33.00
Shoe Shine, 8 ½ In. 75.00
Soldier, Bronze, Continental, Strike, Early 1900s, 3 In. 80.00
Statler Hotel, Teal Glaze, Pottery 35.00
Topsy Hosiery, Bathing Beauty At Beach, Tin Lithograph, 4 ¾ In. 300.00
Turtle, Grand Rapids Brass Co., Souvenir, Grand Rapids, Mich., 5 In. 50.00
Turtle, Old Red Paint, Cast Iron, Marked, Golden's, 4 ½ In. 25.00
Vulcan, Bearded Man, Apron, Painted, Tin Lithograph, c.1900-10, 8 x 2 ½ In. 748.00
Vulcan Plows, Blacksmith By Anvil, Tin Lithograph, 7 ¾ In. 185.00
What Cheer, Devil's Mask, Funny Face, 2-Sided, Stoneware, Marked, 2 ¼ x 3 ½ In. 210.00
William Tell Flour, Ansted & Burk Co., Sack, Tin, Ohio, 4 x 5 In. 275.00
Woman's Boot, Cast Iron, Base, c.1870, 4 ¾ In. 65.00

MATCH SAFES were designed to be carried in the pocket. Early matches were made with phosphorus and could ignite unexpectedly. The matches were safely stored in the tightly closed container. Match safes were made in sterling silver, plated silver, or other metals. The English call these "vesta boxes."

Anheuser-Busch, Letter A, Eagle, Nickel, 2 ¾ x 1 ½ In. 176.00
Art Nouveau, Monogram, Sterling Silver, 2 ½ In. 200.00
Ballerina, F.A. Brecht, Brass 140.00
Book Shape, Bryant & May Ltd., Tin 65.00
Dog, Clown Outfit, Hinged Bottom, Silver, England, 2 ¼ In. .... 99.00 to 200.00
Flowers, Enamel, Copper, c.1940, 2 ½ x 1 ½ In. 40.00
Geisha, With Umbrella, Rooster Being Attacked, Brass, Japan 165.00
Maple Leaf, Enamel, Gun Metal, Turquoise Button 195.00
Monkey, Smoking Pipe, Bottom Release, Nickeled Silver, 2 ¾ In. 110.00
Muriel Cigars, Mild Habana Blend, Woman, Red Scarf, Celluloid, 2 ½ In. 92.00
Plaid, 14K Gold, Slide Lid, Engraved c.1920 .... 495.00

Pont A Mousson, Niello, Enamel 395.00
Pool Table, Striker On Base, Wood, 2 ½ In. 115.00
Press Club Cigar, Flask Form, Hand With Cards, Brass, Des Moines, Iowa, 3 In. 165.00
Quails, Sterling Silver, American Match Safe, 2 ½ In. 200.00
R. Blackinton & Co., Sterling Silver, Leaf Border, Hinged, c.1900 .... 195.00
Round Oak Stoves, Ranges, Furnaces, Celluloid, Nickel Plated Brass, 3 x 1 In. .... *illus* 560.00
San Felice Cigars, Metal, Oval, Celluloid, 2 ⅜ In. 425.00
Scroll Design, Sterling Silver, Hinged, Birmingham, c.1911 .... 105.00
Scrolls, Primroses, Square, Sterling Silver, Late Victorian 195.00
Scrolls, Script Monogram, Sterling Silver, 2 ¾ x 1 ½ In. 175.00
Shield, Sterling Silver, Early 1900s, 1 ¾ x 1 ¾ In. 145.00
Shoe Shape, Wood, Cardboard, Hinged, Match Strike Sole, Black, 1 x 3 ¼ In. 33.00
Silver, Scrolls, Flowers, Leaves, Art Nouveau, 2 ⅞ x ¾ In. 89.00
Silver, Trotting Pig, Lift Up Head, Hinged, c.1975, 4 In. 472.00
Silver Plate, Leaves, Chased, Ring For Chain, c.1919, 1 ⅝ x 1 ⅞ In. 145.00
Stainless Steel, Round, 3 In. 23.00
Standard Oil Company, Celluloid, 2 ¾ In. 495.00
Sterling Silver, Leopard's Head, Lion Passant, London, c.1475, 2 In. 950.00
Sterling Silver, Repousse, Hinged Top, 2 ½ In. 35.00
Sterling Silver, Script Initials, Art Nouveau, 2 ¾ x 1 ¾ In. 195.00
United Cigars, c.1935 .... 35.00
Wildlife Birds, Sterling Silver 123.00
Woman, Smoking, Silveroid, Art Nouveau, c.1910 .... 85.00

MATT MORGAN, an English artist, was making pottery in Cincinnati, Ohio, by 1883. His pieces were decorated to resemble Moorish wares. Incised designs and colors were applied to raised panels on the pottery. Shiny or matte glazes were used. The company lasted less than two years.

Charger, Art Nouveau, Draped Woman, Clouds, Green Dimpled Ground, 14 In. 173.00
Charger, Art Nouveau, Draped Woman, Waves, Cobalt Blue Dimpled Ground, 14 ¼ In. 500.00
Charger, Butterflies, Raised Fleur-De-Lis, Gold Highlights, 16 ½ In. 500.00
Charger, Swallows, In Flight, Incised, Gilt Flowers, 11 ½ In. 259.00
Cup, Orange Ground, Slip Decorated Flowers, Mark, 3 ⅝ In. 61.00
Ewer, Swallows, Mauve & Green Ground, Gilt Accents, Red Clay, Mark, 6 ¾ In. 173.00
Jug, Corn, Embossed, Blue High Glaze, Gold Trim, Mark, 6 ¼ x 5 ¾ In. 143.00
Pitcher, Incised Leaves, Glazed Interior, Signed, Matt Daly, 7 ½ x 6 ½ In. 127.00
Umbrella Stand, Art Nouveau, Painted, Landscape, Clouds, Leaves, 20 x 13 In. 600.00
Vase, Gold, Incised, Gilt Trim, Signed, 5 ½ x 5 ½ In. 92.00
Vase, Painted, Birds, White, Orange Dogwood Blossoms, Gold Bands, 15 x 12 In. 600.00
Vase, Painted, Cherry Blossom, 2 Handles, Signed, Matt Daly, 9 x 8 ¾ In. .... *illus* 440.00

McCOY pottery was made in Roseville, Ohio. Nelson McCoy and J.W. McCoy established the Nelson McCoy Sanitary and Stoneware Company in Roseville, Ohio, in 1910. The firm made art pottery after 1926. In 1933 it became the Nelson McCoy Pottery Company. Pieces marked *McCoy* were made by the Nelson McCoy Pottery Company. Cookie jars were made from about 1940 until December 1990, when the McCoy factory closed. Since 1991 pottery with the McCoy mark has been made by firms unrelated to the original company. Because there was a company named Brush-McCoy, there is great confusion between Brush and Nelson McCoy pieces. See Brush category for more information.

Bank, Keebler Elf 85.00
Bank, Seaman 55.00
Bank, Smiley Face 25.00
Basket, Leaves & Berries, Green Gloss, Brown Highlights, 9 x 7 In. 135.00
Bean Pot, Cover, Brown Drip, Tab Handles, Marked, Overproof, 6 x 6 In. 28.00
Birdhouse, Hanging, Squat 82.00
Bowl, Butterfly, White, Marked, NM, 8 In. 25.00
Bowl, Vegetable, Coupe Form, Beige Flowers, Brown Antique Rose, 1959, 8 ¾ In. 18.00
Casserole, Brown Glaze, Embossed, Individual, Stick Handle, 1930s, 5 In. 10.00
Casserole, Cover, Brown Drip, Flat Panels, Ovenproof, 10 x 5 In. 10.00
Casserole, Divided, Brown Drip, Oval, 12 x 6 ⅝ In. 18.00
Cookie Jar, 2 Owls, 10 ¾ In. 44.00
Cookie Jar, Aunt Jemima, White, Red, Black, 10 In. 60.00
Cookie Jar, Bananas 165.00
Cookie Jar, Chilly Willy, Penguin, Yellow Hat, Scarf & Feet 44.00
Cookie Jar, Cook Stove, Kettle On Burner, 10 In. 17.00
Cookie Jar, Dalmation, Rocking Chair, No. 189, Marked, 10 In. .... *illus* 44.00

Match Safe, Round Oak Stoves, Ranges, Furnaces, Celluloid, Nickel Plated Brass, 3 x 1 In.
$560.00

Matt Morgan, Vase, Painted, Cherry Blossom, 2 Handles, Signed, Matt Daly, 9 x 8 ¾ In.
$440.00

McCoy, Cookie Jar, Dalmation, Rocking Chair, No. 189, Marked, 10 In.
$44.00

M

TIP
China can be washed in warm water with mild soapsuds. The addition of ammonia to the water will add that extra sparkle.

McCoy, Pitcher, Donkey, White Semimatte Glaze, Marked, NM, 6 ½ x 7 ¼ In.
$295.00

McCoy, Planter, Wild West Rodeo, Cowboy, On Bronco, Marked, 5 x 7 ¾ In.
$121.00

McCoy, Vase, Lily, White, Green, Brown High Glaze, Marked, 8 ½ x 7 ¼ In.
$210.00

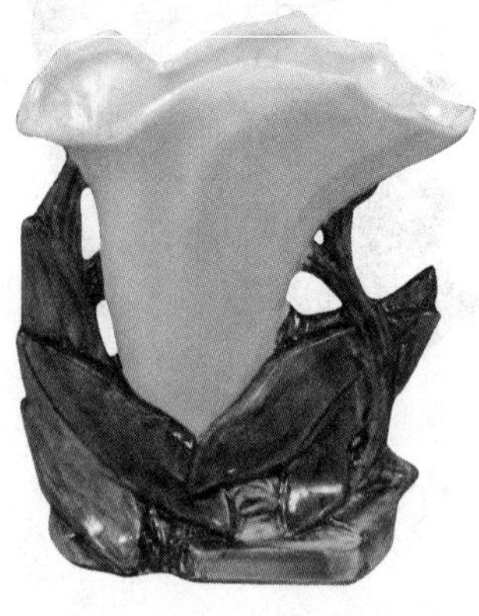

M

Cookie Jar, Honey Bear, 1950s, 8 ½ In. . . . 245.00
Cookie Jar, Indian, No. 50, Marked. . . . 70.00
Cookie Jar, Mammy, Ivory Apron, Red Scarf 165.00
Cookie Jar, Mammy, No. 17, 10 ⅞ In. . . . 33.00
Cookie Jar, Mammy, White Outfit, Green Trim, Red Hat, Signed, 10 ¾ In. . . . 72.00
Cookie Jar, Sad Clown, Multicolored, Signed, 9 ½ In. . . . 170.00 to 187.00
Cookie Jar, Smiley Face, Have A Happy Day, Round, Yellow, Ball Finial 165.00
Cookie Jar, Train Engine, 1962-64, 11 ½ In. . . . 65.00
Creamer, Brown Drip, 4 ¾ In. . . . 14.50
Figurine, Pelican, Gloss White, 3 ½ In. . . . 45.00
Flower Holder, Aqua Matte Glaze, 3 In. . . . 80.00
Flower Holder, Hat, Cobalt Blue, 1940s, 4 In. . . . 40.00
Flowerpot, Basketweave, Green, Attached Saucer, 1950s, 3 ¼ x 3 ⅜ In. . . . 20.00
Flowerpot, Quilted, Blue, Attached Saucer, 1950s, 3 ⅜ x 4 In. . . . 25.00
Frog Planter, Reclining, Green, Brown & Ivory Matte, 9 ½ x 4 In. . . . 75.00
Jar, Oil, Blue, Handle, 17 ¾ x 13 ½ In. . . . 215.00
Jar, Oil, White Matte Glaze, Stoneware, 13 In. . . . 130.00
Jardiniere, Birds, Brown, Green, Footed, 7 In. . . . 60.00
Lamp Base, Gloss Green, Stoneware, 1930s, 9 In. . . . 350.00
Mug, Happy Face, Yellow, 1971, 4 In. . . . 15.00
Mug, Wood Grain, Brown Glaze, 1970s 6.00
Pitcher, Batter, Ribs, c.1945, 5 ¼ In. . . . 25.00
Pitcher, Chicken, Aqua, c.1943 . . . . 39.00
Pitcher, Donkey, White Semimatte Glaze, Marked, NM, 6 ½ x 7 ¼ In. . . . *illus* 295.00
Planter, Anvil, Green, White, 1953, 9 In. . . . 28.00
Planter, Cornucopia, 1940s, 5 In. . . . 23.00
Planter, Driftwood, 1957, 8 ½ x 3 ½ In. . . . 24.00
Planter, Frog, Green, 6 In. . . . 25.00
Planter, Goose, With Cart, 1940, 8 x 4 ¾ In. . . . 40.00
Planter, Swan, White, Marked, 815 USA, 4 x 3 In., Pair. . . . 12.00
Planter, Trivet, Maroon, Metallic Base, 1953 . . . . 35.00
Planter, Turquoise, 1953, 8 In. . . . 17.00
Planter, White Matte, 9 ½ In. . . . 50.00
Planter, Wild West Rodeo, Cowboy, On Bronco, Marked, 5 x 7 ¾ In. . . . *illus* 121.00
Soup, Coupe, Beige Flowers, Brown Antique Rose, 1959, 7 ½ In. . . . 6.00
Stein, League Boot, 1970s, 7 In. . . . 70.00
Teapot, Leaves, Green, Cream Ground, Branch Handle, 7 ¾ x 9 ⅞ x 6 ½ In. . . . 38.00
Umbrella Stand, Green Matte Glaze, Arts & Crafts, 17 In. . . . 100.00
Umbrella Stand, Independence Hall, Red, White, Blue, 1776, 22 In. . . . 350.00
Umbrella Stand, White Matte, 1940s, 10 x 14 In. . . . 350.00
Vase, Amaryllis, Cobalt Blue, Yellow, 4 ¾ In. . . . 85.00
Vase, Aqua Glaze, Handles, 9 x 7 In. . . . 95.00
Vase, Art Deco, Aqua Glaze, Ribs, 9 x 7 In. . . . 90.00
Vase, Art Deco, High Gloss Yellow Glaze, Decorative Handles, 9 x 8 In. . . . 85.00
Vase, Bird, Yellow, Flower, High Gloss Yellow, 8 x 7 In. . . . 85.00
Vase, Birds & Berries, Pink, Tab Handles, Footed, 1940s, 8 ¼ In. . . . 42.00
Vase, Bittersweet, Cream White, 8 In. . . . 95.00
Vase, Blossom Time, White Matte, 6 ½ In. . . . 65.00
Vase, Bud, Lily, White, Marked, 8 x 5 In. . . . 115.00
Vase, Butterfly, Aqua, 1940s, 6 x 3 In. . . . 95.00
Vase, Butterfly, Pink, Handles, 10 ½ In. . . . 50.00
Vase, Cornucopia, Yellow 12.00
Vase, Double Tulip Shape, Yellow, 8 x 7 In. . . . 115.00
Vase, Fan, Lime & Green Gloss, 10 In. . . . 85.00
Vase, Fan, Yellow, Art Deco 10 x 7 In. . . . 100.00
Vase, Feather, 1954, 8 ½ In. . . . 59.00
Vase, Garden Club, Black Matte, Ruffled Lip, 5 In. . . . 60.00
Vase, Garden Club, White Matte, 7 In. . . . 55.00
Vase, Grapes, Leaves, Marked, 15 x 7 In. . . . 170.00
Vase, Green & Rose Matte, Glo-Art, 1930s, 7 ½ In. . . . 105.00
Vase, Green Matte, 8 In. . . . 140.00
Vase, Jadite, Green Matte, 7 In. . . . 45.00
Vase, Leaf & Berry, Brown, No. 523, Marked 25.00
Vase, Lily, White, Green, Brown High Glaze, Marked, 8 ½ x 7 ¼ In. . . . *illus* 210.00
Vase, Magnolia, Flower Shape, Ivory, Green, Brown & Rose Gloss, 8 ¼ In. . . . 215.00
Vase, Pale Green Glaze, Peach, Handles, 9 x 7 In. . . . 100.00
Vase, Palm, White Matte, 14 In. . . . 175.00

Vase, Pink, Handles, 1940s, 2 ½ In. 60.00
Vase, Ribbon Handles, Light Blue, Marked, 9 x 7 In. 95.00
Vase, Ringware, White Matte, 6 In. 65.00
Vase, Swan, White Matte, 10 x 7 In. 100.00
Vase, Tulip, Aqua Matte, 8 In. 85.00
Vase, Urn, Aqua Gloss, 12 In., Pair. 235.00
Vase, Vestal, Duo-Tone, 8 x 5 ½ In. . . . . . *illus* 70.00
Vase, Vestal Virgin, Yellow, Brown, Footed, 10 In. 200.00
Vase, Wheat Design, Green Caramel High Gloss, No. 298, 8 x 6 In. 125.00
Vase, White Gloss, 8 In. 120.00
Vase, White Gloss, 9 In. 80.00
Vase, White Matte, 6 In. 65.00
Vase, Wild Rose, Yellow, 6 x 4 ½ In. 60.00
Vase, Yellow Gloss, 7 In. 45.00
Wall Pocket, Dog, Boxer, Green & Light Brown Gloss, 10 x 7 ½ In. 75.00
Wall Pocket, Lily, White, 8 x 5 In. 115.00
Wall Pocket, Lily, Yellow, 8 x 5 In. 95.00

McKEE is a name associated with various glass enterprises in the United States since 1836, including J. & F. McKee (1850), Bryce, McKee & Co. (1850 to 1854), McKee and Brothers (1865), and National Glass Co. (1899). In 1903, the McKee Glass Company was formed in Jeannette, Pennsylvania. It became McKee Division of the Thatcher Glass Co. in 1951 and was bought out by the Jeannette Corporation in 1961. Pressed glass, kitchenwares, and tablewares were produced. Jeannette Corporation closed in the early 1980s. Additional pieces may be included in the Custard Glass and Depression Glass categories.

McKee

Batter Jug, Measuring, Jade Green, 2 Cup 65.00
Bowl, Autumn, Seville Yellow, Oval, Footed, 5 ½ x 3 ¾ In. 30.00
Bowl, Bulb, Colonial, Jade Green, 7 In. 65.00
Bowl, Cereal, Blue, Green, Red, Yellow, White Interior, Glasbake, 5 In., 4 Piece 14.50
Bowl, Egg Beater, Sailboats, Red, Child's, 3 x 4 In. 65.00
Bowl, Floral, Black, Oval, Handles, 10 ½ In. 55.00
Bowl, Floral, Colonial, Caramel, Footed, 11 ½ In. 40.00
Bowl, Floral, Colonial, Seville Yellow, Oval, Handles, 12 In. 35.00
Bowl, Hickman, Green, Spade Shape, Tree Handle, 6 ¼ x 4 ¾ In. 20.00
Bowl, Jade Green, Impressed Leaves, Flowers, Scrolls, 8 In. . . . . . *illus* 48.00
Bowl, Puritan, Seville Yellow, 2 Qt., 10 ½ In. 90.00
Bowl, Salad, Puritan, Seville Yellow, Flared, 3-Footed, 10 In. 65.00
Bowl, Valtec, Precut, 8 ¼ In. 20.00
Bowl, Wiltec, Square, Sawtooth Edge, Precut, 7 ¾ In. 15.00
Canister, Cereal, Cover, Jade, 40 Oz., 5 In. . . . . . 100.00 to 125.00
Canister, Cereal, Round, Jade, Clear Cover, 48 Oz., 5 ½ In. 95.00
Canister, Coffee, Jade, Round, 40 Oz., 5 In. 100.00
Canister, Sugar, Cover, Jade, Round, 48 Oz. 75.00
Canister, Sugar, Jade, Clear Cover, 40 Oz. 95.00
Console, Autumn, Black, Handles, Oval, Footed, 9 In. 45.00
Console, Autumn, Jade Green, Handles, Oval, Footed, 9 In. 125.00
Cup, Glasbake, Square, Carol. 7.50
Custard Cup, Cover, Honey Pot Shape, Seville, Yellow, Glasbake, 4 ½ In. 5.50
Eggcup, Jade, Footed 39.00
Mixing Bowl, Delphite, Ribbed, 8 In. 150.00
Planter, Lion, Jade 135.00
Plate, Old Rose, Octagon, 8 ¼ In. 12.00
Refrigerator Dish, Cover, Jade, 4 x 5 In. 30.00
Refrigerator Jar, Delphite, Cover, 4 x 4 In. 45.00
Salt & Pepper, Chintz 119.00
Salt & Pepper, Roman Arches, Black, Metal Screw Lid 55.00
Salt & Pepper, Roman Arches, Red, Green, 3 ¾ In. 65.00
Saltshaker, Range, Jade Green, 1930s, 4 ¾ In. . . . . . *illus* 48.00
Saltshaker, Roman Arch, Jade 75.00
Shaker, Range, Delphite, Basket Weave, Pair 18.00
Toothpick, Sunbeam, Blue 10.00
Tumbler, Bottoms Up, Custard, Legs Together 162.00
Vase, I-H-C Pattern, BPCO Credit Kings, 6 ¼ x 3 In. 25.00

MECHANICAL BANKS *are listed in the Bank category.*

McCoy, Vase, Vestal, Duo-Tone, 8 x 5 ½ In.
$70.00

McKee, Bowl, Jade Green, Impressed Leaves, Flowers, Scrolls, 8 In.
$48.00

McKee, Saltshaker, Range, Jade Green, 1930s, 4 ¾ In.
$48.00

TIP

Glass plates that are cloudy can sometimes be cleaned with silver polish and a plastic scouring pad. If a plate is scratched, it might look better for display if it is coated with a non-yellowing floor wax and then lightly buffed. Of course, then you can't use it for food.

Medical, Model, Eye, Ophthalmologist, Blown Glass, Papier-Mache, Painted, Wood, 7 In.
$800.00

Medical, Phrenology Head, Earthenware, White, Marked In Black, Freda, c.1850, 12 In.
$1150.00

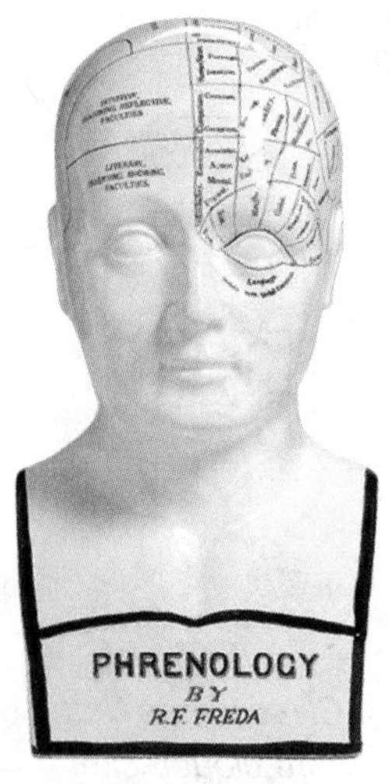

Medical, Sign, Doctor's Office, 2-Sided, 3-D Horse, Buggy & Doctor, Metal, 13 x 16 In.
$403.00

MEDICAL office furniture, operating tools, microscopes, thermometers, and other paraphernalia used by doctors are included in this category. Veterinary collectibles are also included here. Medicine bottles are listed in the Bottle category. There are related collectibles listed under Dental.

Accident Case, Seabury's, Laboratory, Factories, Image, Tin, Hinged Lid, 8 ½ x 5 x 4 In. 405.00
Amputation Set, Saw, 3 Knives, Tourniquet, Case, W. & H. Hutchison, England, 16 ½ In..... 1185.00
Bag, Doctor's, Crocodile, Brass Hinges, Locks, Leather Handle, 18 x 14 In. ... 207.00
Breast Exhauster, Elastic Tube, Metal Nipple Shields, Box, 3 ½ x 6 In.. ... 357.00
Breast Pump, Dr. O.H. Needham, Patent Improved, B.B. & J. Haggerty, N.Y., Box, 1874 ... 178.00
Brush, Flesh, Dr. Scott's, Electric, Plastic, Embossed Coat Of Arms, Box, 2 ½ x 5 In. ... 176.00
Cabinet, Apothecary, Georgian, Mahogany, Molded Top, Drawers, Panel Doors, 19 x 16 In.. ... 316.00
Cabinet, Apothecary, Mahogany, 15 Drawers, Patina, 24 x 45 x 8 In. ... 660.00
Cabinet, Apothecary, Mahogany, 16 Bottles, Contents, 2 Drawers, 9 ½ x 10 ½ In. ... 1067.00
Cabinet, Apothecary, Mahogany, Gold Leaf Labels, 25 Drawers, 2 Doors, 1800s, 57 x 59 In.. ... 1459.00
Cabinet, Apothecary, Pine, 10 Drawers, Glass Pull, Latin Inscriptions, 28 x 25 In. ... 748.00
Cabinet, Apothecary, Pine, 24 Drawers, 19th Century, 47 x 44 ½ In. ... 1700.00
Cabinet, Apothecary, Pine, 24 Drawers, Blue Paint, Graduated Drawers, 33 x 28 In. ... 2415.00
Cabinet, Apothecary, Pine, 36 Drawers, Blue Paint, Yellow Numbers, 34 ½ x 24 In. ... 1840.00
Cabinet, Apothecary, Pine, Grain Paint, Crown Molding, 90 Drawers, 1800s, 62 x 83 In. ... 3630.00
Cabinet, Apothecary, Poplar, 143 Drawers, Wooden Knobs, 1800s, 57 x 83 x 12 In. ... 2585.00
Cabinet, Apothecary, Traveling, Brass Mounted, Lift-Out Tray, 9 x 12 ¾ x 6 In. ... 420.00
Cabinet, Door, 6 Shelves, Egg & Dart Frieze, O.G. Poor, 27 x 45 x 10 In. ... 86.00
Cabinet, Walnut, Poplar, 20 Drawers, Tennessee, c.1860, 28 x 25 x 12 In. ... 1200.00
Chest, Apothecary, Mahogany, Fitted Interior, Bottles, Dr. Samuel Fisk Green, 16 In. ... 652.00
Chest, Traveling, Leather Covered, 49 Glass, 4 China Bottles, Drawer, Eagle Lock, 15 x 9 In... 267.00
Emergency Case, For Tourists, 7 Bottles, Tin, Hinged Lid, Utica, N.Y., 6 x 3 ¾ In. ... 33.00
Jar, Camphora, Stopper, Footed, W.R. Warner & Co., Phila'd Patd Sept. 18, 1875, 10 ¾ In. ... 60.00
Lancette, Spring, Brass, Cased, Cherry Wood Box, Engraved, D. Scheirman, c.1860, 4 In. ... 1995.00
Leech Jar, Cover, Porcelain, White, Black Lettering, 2 Handles, c.1895, 7 ½ x 4 In. ... 7800.00
Medicator, Cures Catarrh, Headache, Bottle, Label, Box, Pat'd Feb 16, 1897, 3 ½ x 2 In. ... 50.00
Medicine Case, Wood, Glass Vials, Leather Cover, 7 x 9 ¼ In.. ... 144.00
Model, Eye, Ophthalmologist, Blown Glass, Papier-Mache, Painted, Wood, 7 In. ... *illus* 800.00
Model, Teaching, Human Head, Plaster, Cutaway, Numbered, Clay Adams, 11 x 14 In. ... 119.00
Model, Teaching, Human Mandible, Papier-Mache, Cut-Away, 8 Teeth, Clay Adams, 13 In. ... 326.00
Mortar & Pestle, Brass, Handles, 4 ¼ x 4 ¾ In.. ... 65.00
Mortar & Pestle, Wood, Red Stain, 6 ½ x 5 In. ... 110.00
Phrenology Head, Earthenware, White, Marked In Black, Freda, c.1850, 12 In. ... *illus* 1150.00
Pill Counter, Wood, 24 Holes, Heart Oil, 10 In. ... 275.00
Pill Tile, 0-24 Graduation Lines, Eagle, Wedgwood, 6 x 8 In. ... 1760.00
Saddlebag, Doctor's, Leather, Straps, Pockets, Panel, Flaps, 24 Glass Containers, 1860s ... 432.00
Sign, Doctor's Office, 2-Sided, 3-D Horse, Buggy & Doctor, Metal, 13 x 16 In. ... *illus* 403.00
Specie Jar, Houblon, Green Cardboard Lid, Pontil, 11 ½ x 4 ¾ In.. ... 132.00
Stitching Instrument, Surgical, 3 Needles, Spools, Case, Label, Singer, 1942 ... 59.00
Surgeon's Kit, 15 Instruments, Dr. Lewis Whiting, Civil War ... 9200.00
Syringe, Self-Injection, Male Urethral, Gonorrhea Treatment, McElroy's, c.1872, 5 ¼ In. ... 195.00
Tablets, Sharp & Dohme's, Chocolate Coated Sedative, Baer's, Glass, c.1900, 3 ¼ In. ... 65.00
Test Kit, Ophthalmic, Various Lenses, Silk Lined, Fitted, Walnut Case, c.1915, 20 In. ... 178.00
Tin, Bronchial Lozenges, Parke, Davis & Co., Hinged Lid, 8 ½ x 5 x 5 In.. ... 300.00
Tin, Gibson's Linseed Liquorice & Chlorodyne Cough Lozenges, Mortar, Pestle, 9 x 5 In. ... 88.00
Trapanning Set, Bone Handles, Mahogany Case, Stamped Saglee & Co., 8 In.. ... 2726.00
X-Ray Machine, Mili-Ampmeter Dial, Decal, Mahogany Case, Campbell, c.1920. ... 2015.00

MEISSEN is a town in Germany where porcelain has been made since 1710. Any china made in the town can be called Meissen, although the famous Meissen factory made the finest porcelains of the area. The crossed swords mark of the great Meissen factory has been copied by many other firms in Germany and other parts of the world. Pieces of Meissen dinnerware in the Onion pattern are listed in their own category in this book.

Bird, Yellow & Black, Orange Beak, Leaf Stumps, 18th Century Style, 10 ¼ In., Pair ... 1080.00
Bowl, Center Flower Medallion, Cobalt Ground, Border Mounts, Marked, c.1900, 3 x 12 In... 403.00
Bowl, Flowers, Navy, Gold, Pink, Yellow, 1900s, 13 In. ... 322.00
Bowl, Peach, Fruit & Flower Ground, 1 ½ x 9 ½ In.. ... 75.00
Bowl, Turquoise Ground, Flower Sprays, Landscape Reserves, Gilt, 1800s, 3 ¼ x 6 ½ In. ... 885.00
Bread Tray, Oval, Gilt, Marked c.1900, 12 In. ... 94.00
Candelabra, 3-Light, Cherubs Holding Fish, 12 ½ In., Pair ... 1057.00
Chandelier, 6-Light, 6 Floral Bouquets, Garlands, Green, Rose, c.1950, 33 x 27 In. ... 3585.00

Clock, Mantel, Children, Flowers, 19th Century, 22 x 20 In. 2925.00
Coffeepot, Flowers, Burgundy, Gilt, Figural Spout, 10 ½ x 9 ½ In. 225.00
Coffeepot, Lid, Turquoise Ground, Turkish Merchant, Man, Donkey Panels, c.1740, 9 In. 10000.00
Compote, Flowers In Relief, Children Surrounding Stem, c.1900, 11 x 9 In. 1872.00
Cup & Saucer, Blue Ground, Monkeys Making Tools, Birds, Flowers, c.1760, 5 In. 8125.00
Cup & Saucer, Cartouches, Indian Birds & Flowers, Crossed Swords, c.1785, 4 ¾ In. 1645.00
Cup & Saucer, Classical Courting Couples, Reserves, Gold 75.00
Cup & Saucer, White, Gold Accents 75.00
Figurine, 2 Dancing Clowns, Stamped Underside, 8 ½ In. 7475.00
Figurine, Bacchic Satyr, Riding Goat, Drinking From Wine Jug, Grapevine, 7 ½ In. 1304.00
Figurine, Boy, Barefoot, With Grapes In Cone Shape Basket, Blue Sword Mark, 4 ¾ In. 400.00
Figurine, Boy, Carrying Goat, 6 ½ In. 956.00
Figurine, Carriage, Horses, Driver, Passengers, 11 ½ x 24 In. 1170.00
Figurine, Centaur, Holding Child, Tambourine, Rocky Base, 19th Century, 7 ½ In. 1300.00
Figurine, Cherub, Blind Faith, Blue Crossed Swords Mark, 7 ½ In. .... 800.00 to 1100.00
Figurine, Cherub, Kneeling, Cooking Pot On Chimney, Blue Crossed Swords, 5 In. 1000.00
Figurine, Cherub, Putting Bird In Cage, Holding Bird, Blue Crossed Swords, 5 In. 1100.00
Figurine, Cherub, Sewing Broken Heart, Blue Crossed Swords Mark, 6 ½ In. .... 850.00 to 1100.00
Figurine, Cherub, Winged, Lighting Torch, Flaming Hearts, Garlands, Motto, 5 ⅜ In. 889.00
Figurine, Cherub Gardener, Digging With Spade, Topiaries, 4 ⅝ In. 770.00
Figurine, Child, Selling Fruit, Barefoot, Gilt Rocaille Base, Blue Underglaze, c.1850, 5 ½ In. 720.00
Figurine, Cupid, Arrows, Blue Crossed Swords Mark, 8 In. .... 800.00 to 1200.00
Figurine, Cupid, Blacksmith Forging Heart, Late 19th Century, 7 ¼ In. 2242.00
Figurine, Cupid, Hiding His Heart, Blue Crossed Swords Mark, 6 ½ In. .... 800.00 to 1000.00
Figurine, Cupid, Seated, Table, Bowl, Flower Base, 1800s, 7 In. 896.00
Figurine, Cupid, Sleeping, White & Gilt Bed, Pink Flower Pillow, 4 ½ In. 750.00
Figurine, Demeter, Standing, Holding Sickle, Sheaf Of Wheat, Diadem Of Wheat, 8 In. 652.00
Figurine, Dog, Empress Catherine II Of Russia, Crouched On Cushion, c.1850, 16 In. 8125.00
Figurine, Eagle, Banc De Chine, On Rock, Black Base, 15 In. 440.00
Figurine, Eagle, Perched, On Craggy Pinnacle, Incised Initials, 16 In. 1422.00
Figurine, Elegant Woman, Holding Back Of Chair, Foot On Pillow, 19th Century, 14 In. 500.00
Figurine, Flower Vendor, 18th Century Rococo Style, Blue Persian Glaze, c.1825-50, 5 In. 180.00
Figurine, Man, Gathering Grapes, 6 In. 240.00
Figurine, Man, Selling Seafood, c.1850, 5 ½ In. 1140.00
Figurine, Nude, Flora, Marked, Blue Crossed Swords, Walter Schott, 1902-05, 15 In. 6200.00
Figurine, Shepherd, Shepherdess, Boy Playing Recorder, Girl Holding Grapevine, 6 ¼ In. 1185.00
Figurine, Venus, In Chariot, Wheeled Shell, Flower Garland, Early 1900s, 6 ¾ In. .... *illus* 2370.00
Figurine, Venus & 2 Cupids, Quiver & Arrows, Pink Ribbon, 9 In. 2700.00
Figurine, Woman, Barefoot, Holding Flower Basket, 5 In. 425.00
Figurine, Woman, Holding Basket, Cobalt Blue Crossed Sword Mark, 5 In. 242.00
Figurine, Woman, Ice Skating, Marked, c.1900-25, 8 In. 3840.00
Figurine, Woman, Keeping The Books, Period Attire, Basket, Food, 6 ¼ In. 2070.00
Figurine, Woman, On Alligator, Feathered Outfit, Blue Crossed Swords Mark, 11 ½ In. 3525.00
Figurine, Woman, Selling Fish, Blue Underglaze, Marked, c.1850, 5 ¼ In. 1140.00
Figurine, Woman, With Cherub, Raised Flowers, Floral Dress, 13 x 8 In. .... *illus* 995.00
Figurine, Woman At Dressing Table, Looking In Mirror, Gilt Accents, 5 ¾ In. 1304.00
Group, Barefoot Lovers, On Rock, Marked, Blue Crossed Swords, 19th Century, 13 ¼ In. 690.00
Group, Birth Of Venus, Venus, Swirled Wrap, Shell, Mermaids, Dolphins, 1800s, 9 In. 2596.00
Group, Card Players, Blue Crossed Swords Mark, 5 ¼ In. .... *illus* 1760.00
Group, Children, Around Barrel Of Grapes, Blue Underglaze, 1850-75, 7 x 7 x 6 In. 1200.00
Group, Children, Playing With Lambs, Blue Underglaze, c.1850, 7 ½ x 6 In. 840.00
Group, Clown & Piano, Dog, Blue Underglaze, c.1925, 3 ⅛ In., 2 Piece 420.00
Group, Country Dancers, Blue Underglaze, 1850-75, 9 x 7 x 5 In. 3840.00
Group, Couples Around Tree, Oval Base, Gilt Guillouche, 19th Century, 18 In. 2370.00
Group, Europia, Handmaidens, Bull, c.1890, 8 x 8 ½ x 5 ½ In. 2937.00
Group, Fawn & Cupid With Robe, 19th Century, 7 In. 1200.00
Group, Figures Draping Bull In Flowers, Crossed Swords Mark, 9 x 8 x 4 In. 1210.00
Group, Man, Old Woman, Looking In Trunk, Pan, Blue Crossed Swords Mark, 5 ¾ In. 1300.00
Group, Man & Woman With New Baby, Elliptical Base, Blue Underglaze, c.1875, 7 In. 2880.00
Group, Musicians, Family, Scroll Feet, Crossed Swords Mark, 8 x 9 In. 2300.00
Group, Mythological, Neptune, Chariot, Hippocampi, Ormolu Mounts, c.1750, 17 In. 31250.00
Group, Neptune & Nude Girl, Net, 19th Century, 7 ¾ x 15 ½ x 11 In. 3750.00
Group, Oceanic, Women, Net, Children, Sea Animals, Mark, No. 24, 13 x 10 x 6 In. 5750.00
Group, Putti, Seated Female, Egg Shape Base, Blue Underglaze, 1825-50, 5 ¾ x 4 ½ In. 840.00
Group, Silenus, On Donkey, Nude Boys, Donkey, Girl, Flowers, 9 x 9 In. 1463.00
Group, Tailor, Riding Goat, Holding Scissors, Flower Jacket, Blue Crossed Swords, 9 In. 1800.00

Meissen, Figurine, Venus, In Chariot, Wheeled Shell, Flower Garland, Early 1900s, 6 ¾ In.
$2370.00

Meissen, Figurine, Woman, With Cherub, Raised Flowers, Floral Dress, 13 x 8 In.
$995.00

Meissen, Group, Card Players, Blue Crossed Swords Mark, 5 ¼ In.
$1760.00

Common Myth
The crossed sword mark was used only on German porcelain made by Meissen. NOT TRUE. The mark is the most copied mark found on porcelain and was used on English, French, and other wares as well as dishes made by other German companies.

Meissen, Tazza, Exotic Birds, Dragons, Gilt, Blue Crossed Swords Mark, 8 ¾ In. $400.00

Meissen/Dresden China What's in a Name?
The word "Meissen" should mean any type of ceramic made at the original Meissen factory from 1710 to the present time. The English refer to Meissen as "Dresden," the French use the word "Saxe." People sometimes refer to Meissen porcelain as Dresden china. Dresden sold today is not made by the famous original Meissen factory. Until the mid-nineteenth century the term "Dresden china" was used to refer to porcelain made in the Meissen factory; then it was used for other porcelains that resembled the work of the famous factory. Most of it is from factories in or near the city of Dresden, which is 15 miles from Meissen. French, Italian, English, and other factories copied Meissen china. These pieces are Meissen-type or Dresden-type.

Group, Winemakers, Blue & White, 3 Bucolic Figures, Bird In Cage, 8 ½ In., Pair 2844.00
Inkwell, Cover, Tray, Blue & White 58.00
Inkwell, Underplate, Green & Black Ivy Design At Rim, Marked, 5 ¾ x 2 ½ In. 175.00
Mirror, 2 Cherubs, Figural, Beaded Rim, Multicolored, 19th Century, 12 In., Pair 950.00
Paperweight, Sphinx, Gilt Trim, Enameled Flowers, Crossed Swords, c.1885, 8 In. 1422.00
Pitcher, Hot Water, Lid, Martial Scene, Gilt Scroll, Insects, c.1740, 7 In. 11250.00
Plate, Blue Floral, Porcelain, Reticulated Border, 10 In. 35.00
Plate, Cabinet, Birds, Branches, Turquoise Ground, Pierced Border, 1800s, 10 In., 2 Piece ... 299.00
Plate, Dessert, Scattered Flowers, Reticulated Border, Gilt, 8 In., 2 Piece 359.00
Plate, Soldier On Horse, Basket Weave Border, Leafy Branches, Gold Trim, 1800s, 9 In. 732.00
Plate, Soup, Couples, Flowers, Black Ground, Gilt Border, Hand Painted, c.1890, 9 In., 2 Piece 179.00
Platter, Spring Flowers, Gilt, Scalloped Rim, Blue Crossed Swords Mark, 1900s, 15 In. 150.00
Salt, Shell Shape, Painted Flowers, Scenes, 3 Scroll Feet, Gilt Rim, c.1735, 4 In., Pair 31250.00
Sculpture, Stallion, Rearing, White, Blue Swords Mark, Erich Oehme, 1949, 20 x 16 ½ In. .. 1650.00
Soldier, Hand On Hip, White & Gilt Base, 6 In. 300.00
Sugar & Creamer, Blue & White, 4 & 6 In. 587.00
Sweetmeat, Putti, Flower Swags, Multicolored Flowers, Gilt Border, 8 x 6 x 5 In. 1560.00
Sweetmeat, Woman Reclining, 6 ½ x 12 x 6 ½ In. 500.00
Tazza, Exotic Birds, Dragons, Gilt, Blue Crossed Swords Mark, 8 ¾ In. .... *illus* 400.00
Tea Bowl & Saucer, Churches, Landscapes, Puce Ground, Gilt Border, c.1740, 5 In. 6250.00
Tea Canister, Lid, Figures, Landscape, Flower Knop, Yellow Ground, Gilt Edge, c.1740, 5 In. ... 9375.00
Teapot, White Ground, Pink Flowers, Early 20th Century, 6 In. 293.00
Tray, 2 Handles, Square, White, Flowers, Shells, Marked, 16 In. 500.00
Tray, Flowers, Painted, Cutout Handles, Gilt, 19th Century, 14 ½ x 14 ½ In. 500.00
Tureen, Sauce, Cover, Oval, Pink Bouquets, Molded Ozier Rim, Underplate, 9 ¼ In., Pair 652.00
Urn, Multicolored, Gilt Border, Serpent Handle, Flowers, 19th Century, 19 x 13 In. 1762.00
Vase, Bud, Classical, Applied Bisque Flowers, Marked, Crossed Swords, 1700s, 5 In., Pair 764.00
Vase, Mantel, Blue Ground, Medallions, Courting Scenes, Flowers, Gold, 13 In., Pair 413.00
Vase, Schneeballen, Oval, Flower Branches, Marcolini, Early 1800s, 16 In., Pair 5605.00
Wall Pocket, Figural, Boy & Girl On Ledge Looking Into Basket, 6 ½ x 6 ½ In. 350.00

MERCURY GLASS, or silvered glass, was first made in the 1850s. It lost favor for a while but became popular again about 1910. It looks like a piece of silver.

Candlestick, Ribbed, Scalloped Base, 4 In. 40.00
Globe, Stand, Late 19th Century, 10 ½ x 6 ½ In. 300.00
Goblet, Pair 125.00
Tieback, Embossed, Victorian, 2 ½ In., Pair 27.00
Tieback, Embossed, Victorian, 3 In., Pair 12.00
Tieback, Etched Floral, Victorian, 3 ¼ In., Pair 12.00
Tieback, Etched Grapevine, Victorian, 3 ¾ In., Pair 12.00
Tieback, Victorian, 3 ¾ In., Pair 12.00
Vase, Bulbous, Flared Rim, Footed, 10 x 4 In. 60.00

MERRIMAC POTTERY Company was founded by Thomas Nickerson in Newburyport, Massachusetts, in 1902. The company made art pottery, garden pottery, and reproductions of Roman pottery. The pottery burned to the ground in 1908.

Bowl, Scalloped Rim, Green & Gunmetal Mottled Glaze, Stamped Fish Mark, 3 x 7 In. 465.00
Humidor, Frothy Mottled Green Matte Glaze, 3 Handles, Marked, 6 ½ x 5 ½ In. 880.00
Jardiniere, Lotus Leaves, Feathered Crystalline Green Glaze, Incised, EB, 5 x 8 ½ In. 2750.00
Vase, Bulbous, Feathered Green & Gunmetal Glaze, Stamped Fish Mark, 6 x 4 ¾ In. 1870.00
Vase, Bulbous, Green, Black Crystalline Glaze, Marked, 17 x 18 In. .... *illus* 5700.00
Vase, Frothy Semimatte Green Glaze, Squat, Long Neck, Handle, Stamped, 4 x 4 In. 770.00
Vase, Gunmetal & Green Mottled Glaze, 3 Handles, Marked, 15 x 6 In. 16500.00
Vase, Leaf Rows, Green Matte Glaze, Impressed Fish & Merrimac, 4 ½ x 6 In. 1540.00
Vase, Oval, Bright Yellow & Orange Peel Matte Glaze, Marked, 6 ½ x 3 ½ In. 2060.00
Vase, Oval, Frothy Yellow Matte Glaze, Stamped Fish Mark, 9 ½ x 4 ¾ In. 3100.00
Vase, Speckled Indigo Matte Glaze, Shouldered, Stamped Fish Mark, 5 ¼ x 3 ¼ In. 1099.00
Vase, Squat, Feathered Green Matte Glaze, Paper Label, 4 ¼ x 5 In. 1980.00

METLOX POTTERIES was founded in 1927 in Manhattan Beach, California. Dinnerware was made beginning in 1931. Evan K. Shaw purchased the company in 1946 and expanded the number of patterns. Poppytrail (1946-1989) and Vernonware (1958-1980) were divisions of Metlox under E.K. Shaw's direction. The factory closed in 1989.

American Heritage, Sugar, No Lid 11.00
Antiqua, Bowl, Fruit, c.1970, 6 ½ In. 6.00

Antique Grape, Bowl, 9 ¾ In. 40.00
Antique Grape, Cup & Saucer 12.00
Bandero, Plate, Bread & Butter, 6 ½ In. 7.00
Bandero, Salt & Pepper 12.00
California Ivy, Bowl, Divided, Stem Handle, 9 x 5 In. 45.00
California Ivy, Bowl, Vegetable, Stem Handle 40.00
California Ivy, Plate, Dinner, 10 ¼ In. 10.00 to 18.00
California Ivy, Platter, 10 ¼ x 13 ¼ In. 38.00
California Ivy, Teapot, Poppy Trail 100.00
California Peach Blossom, Cup & Saucer 6.00
California Strawberry, Bowl, Vegetable, Divided, 8 In. 15.00
California Strawberry, Plate, Dinner, 10 ¼ In. 10.00
Camelia, Plate, Dinner, 10 In. 8.50
Colorstax, Butter, Cover, Apricot 46.00
Colorstax, Creamer, Apricot, 4 In. 20.00
Colorstax, Plate, Apricot, 10 ¾ In. 15.00
Colorstax, Plate, Salad, Sand, 7 ¾ In. 10.00
Colorstax, Sugar, Cover, Turquoise 20.00
Cookie Jar, Cat, White, Yellow Bow, Hat, Blue Eyes, Meow Box, Marked 120.00
Cookie Jar, Chilly Willy Penguin 40.00
Cookie Jar, Clown, Yellow, Big Smile, Poppy Trail 39.00
Cookie Jar, Cow, Purple, Poppy Trail 66.00
Cookie Jar, Cow, Yellow, Marked 50.00
Cookie Jar, Gingham Dog, Blue, Poppy Trail 72.00
Cookie Jar, Mammy, Washtub, Marked R 600.00
Cookie Jar, Mona, Pink, Stegasaurus, Marked, USA By Vincent 85.00
Cookie Jar, Mona, Yellow, Stegasaurus, Marked, USA By Vincent 180.00 to 198.00
Cookie Jar, Pretty Ann, Marked, Poppy Trail 50.00
Cookie Jar, Puddle Duck, Wearing Yellow Raincoat, Hat 35.00 to 39.00
Cookie Jar, Rabbit, On Cabbage, Marked, 11 ½ In. 50.00
Cookie Jar, Raccoon, Cookie Bandit, Poppy Trail 22.00
Cookie Jar, Walrus, White, Blue Hat, Scarf, Marked 40.00 to 44.00
Della Robbia, Bowl, Vegetable, 9 ½ In. 14.00
Della Robbia, Platter, Oval, 14 ½ In. 16.00
Fruit Basket, Plate, Salad, 7 ½ In. 6.00
Gold Dahlia, Bowl, Vegetable, 9 ¼ In. 25.00
Golden Blossom, Platter, 12 ¾ x 12 ¾ In. 26.00
Homestead Provincial, Creamer 14.00
Homestead Provincial, Hen On Nest, Blue & White, Poppy Trail, 6 ½ x 5 x 6 In. 59.00
Homestead Provincial, Sugar, Cover, Green Handles 27.00
La Mancha, Platter, Gold, Scalloped Edge, Black Trim, 14 ¼ In. 18.50
Lotus, Mug, Yellow, Poppy Trail, 4 ¼ In. 9.00
Lotus, Plate, Salad, Scalloped Rim, Peach, 8 In. 12.00
Marina, Plate, Dinner, Speckled Gray, Green & Brown Border, Poppy Trail, 10 ⅝ In. 8.00
Mission Verde, Platter, Oval, 13 x 10 In. 18.00
Navajo, Plate, Salad, 7 ¾ In. 8.00
Navajo, Sugar, Cover 10.00
Peach Blossom, Gravy Boat, Underplate, 11 In. 28.00
Peach Blossom, Plate, Dinner, 10 ⅜ In. 14.00
Provincial Fruit, Bowl, Cereal, 7 ⅛ In. 8.00
Provincial Fruit, Place Setting, 5 Piece 15.75
Provincial Fruit, Platter, Oval, 13 ¼ In. 21.00
Red Rooster, Butter, Cover 16.50
Red Rooster, Condiment Tray, Divided, Handle, Poppy Trail, 12 x 5 ½ In. 45.00
Red Rooster, Creamer 10.00
Red Rooster, Plate, Dinner, 10 In. 12.00 to 15.00
Red Rooster, Saltshaker, 4 In. 22.00
Red Rooster, Sugar & Creamer, Cover, Green Handles 50.00
Rose-A-Day, Creamer, c.1960, 4 In. 9.00
Rose-A-Day, Gravy Boat, c.1960, 3 ½ In. 174.00
Sculptured Daisy, Creamer 9.00
Sculptured Daisy, Plate, Bread & Butter, 6 ¼ In. 3.00
Sculptured Daisy, Platter, Oval, 11 In. 20.00
Sculptured Grape, Bowl, Vegetable, Cover, 2 Qt. 89.00
Sculptured Grape, Dish, Condiment, Divided, Handle, 8 ½ In. 18.00
Sculptured Grape, Vase, 7 ¼ In. 34.00
Sculptured Zinnia, Bowl, Vegetable, Divided, 9 ⅜ In. 24.00

Merrimac, Vase, Bulbous, Green, Black Crystalline Glaze, Marked, 17 x 18 In.
$5700.00

Mettlach, Stein, No. 1562, 5 ½ Liter, Trumpeter Of Sackigen, 21 ¾ In.
$920.00

Mettlach, Stein, No. 1577, 4 ½ Liter, 12 People At Dinner, 20 ½ In.
$1100.00

As always, the edited listings in *Kovels' Antiques & Collectibles Price Guide 2010* aren't available on any website, but readers should visit Kovels.com for information on trends, tips, reproductions, marks, old prices, and more!

Mettlach, Stein, No. 1786, ½ Liter, St. Florian, Village, Pewter Lid, Dragon Handle, 10 In.
$485.00

Mettlach, Stein, No. 2382, ½ Liter, Thirsty Rider, Etched, Inlaid Lid, H. Schlitt
$520.00

Mettlach, Tankard, No. 1159, 6 Liter, Music, Dancing, Tavern Scenes, Marked, 16 ¼ In.
$500.00

Sculptured Zinnia, Cup & Saucer 6.00
Sculptured Zinnia, Plate, Dinner, 10 ½ In.. . . . . 7.50
Tickled Pink, Plate, Bread & Butter, 6 ½ In. 7.00
Tropicana Pineapple, Platter, Footed, Label, 3 x 16 In. 185.00
Vineyard, Creamer 9.00
Wild Poppy, Bowl, Cereal, 6 ½ In.. . . . . 10.00
Wild Poppy, Plate, Dinner, 11 In. 12.00
Woodland Gold, Casserole, Cover, 2 Qt. 40.00
Woodland Gold, Plate, Dinner, 10 In. 9.00
Woodland Gold, Platter, Oval, 13 ¼ x 10 In. 15.00

METTLACH, Germany, is a city where the Villeroy and Boch factories worked. Steins from the firm are marked with the word *Mettlach* or the castle mark. They date from about 1842. *PUG* means painted under glaze. The steins can be dated from the marks on the bottom, which include a date-number code. Other pieces may be listed in the Villeroy & Boch category.

Cigar Holder, No. 354, Woman, Holding Basket, 6 ½ In. 299.00
Drinking Horn, Steer, Brass Metal Fittings, Set-On Lid, 15 ¾ In.. . . . . 460.00
Loving Cup, No. 2169, Men In Forest, Etched, Handles, 6 In. 253.00
Mirror, No. 6007, Faience, 25 x 16 In.. . . . . 978.00
Pitcher, No. 1638, Mosaic, Repeating Design, Etched, Flowers, Blue Ground, 5 In.. . . . . 114.00
Pitcher, No. 1800, Mosaic, Footed, White Ground, 11 ½ In. 184.00
Plaque, No. 1044-131, Freiburg, PUG, B. Munster, 12 In. 115.00
Plaque, No. 1044-147, Liechtenstein, Hand Painted, 14 In. 150.00
Plaque, No. 1044-219, Burghof Und Burgfried, Wartburg, PUG, 12 In. 150.00
Plaque, No. 1044-221, Munchen, Hand Painted, 14 In.. . . . . 265.00
Plaque, No. 1097, Men Fighting, 16 In. 196.00
Plaque, No. 1290-3225, Elks, Purple, Brown, PUG. 345.00
Plaque, No. 2361A, Wartburg Castle, Etched, 17 ½ In.. . . . . 477.00
Plaque, No. 2362, Heidelburg Castle, Etched, 17 ½ In. 403.00
Plaque, No. 2443, Trojan Woman, Servants, Cameo, Signed, Stahl, 19 In. 296.00
Plaque, No. 5148B, Ship With Sails, Delft, 12 ½ In.. . . . . 115.00
Plaque, No. 5179, Landscape, Windmill By River, Delft, 18 In. 138.00
Plaque, No. 5185, William Burggraf, After Rembrandt, Delft, 19 In. 350.00
Plaque, No. 7048, Chess Game, 3 Children, Phanolith, 14 ½ In. 504.00
Plaque, No. 9041, Landscape, River, Mountains, 12 In.. . . . . 357.00
Stein, No. 1033-2333, ½ Liter, Dancing Elves, Toasting Mugs, PUG Pewter Lid 161.00
Stein, No. 1101-1526, ½ Liter, Barmaid, Relief, PUG, Pewter Lid 115.00
Stein, No. 1273-1909, ½ Liter, Drunken Man, Monkey, Cat, Pewter Lid, PUG. 265.00
Stein, No. 1395, ½ Liter, French Card, Etched, Inlaid Lid 460.00
Stein, No. 1476, ½ Liter, Art Nouveau, Hooded Men, Tying Vines, Etched, Inlaid Lid. 489.00
Stein, No. 1519, ½ Liter, Scull Racing, Etched, Inlaid Lid 546.00
Stein, No. 1526, ½ Liter, Man, Holding Stein, Transfer, Enamel, Pewter Lid. 98.00
Stein, No. 1527, ½ Liter, 4 Men Drinking, Etched, Inlaid Lid, Signed, Warth 235.00
Stein, No. 1562, 5 ½ Liter, Trumpeter Of Sackigen, 21 ¾ In. . . . . . *illus* 920.00
Stein, No. 1577, 4 ½ Liter, 12 People At Dinner, 20 ½ In. . . . . . *illus* 1100.00
Stein, No. 1655, ½ Liter, Man, Woman Dancing, Etched, Inlaid Lid 345.00
Stein, No. 1725, ½ Liter, Lovers, Cupid 326.00
Stein, No. 1742, ½ Liter, Scene Of Gottingen, Etched, Inlaid Lid. 115.00
Stein, No. 1786, ½ Liter, St. Florian, Village, Pewter Lid, Dragon Handle, 10 In. . . . . . *illus* 485.00
Stein, No. 1861, ½ Liter, Wilhelm II, Etched, PUG, Inlaid Lid 345.00
Stein, No. 1909, ¼ Liter, Pschorr-Brau Munchen, Relief, Pewter Lid 311.00
Stein, No. 1914, ½ Liter, Man Holding Flag, Dumbbell, 4F, Etched, Inlaid Lid 444.00
Stein, No. 1998, ½ Liter, Trumpeter, Pewter Lid 237.00
Stein, No. 2001A, ½ Liter, Book Stein For Law, Glazed, Hand Painted, Inlaid Lid. 506.00
Stein, No. 2001B, ½ Liter, Book Stein For Medicine, Glazed, Hand Painted, Inlaid Lid 475.00
Stein, No. 2008, ½ Liter, Trumpeter, Etched, Inlaid Lid 196.00
Stein, No. 2009, ½ Liter, Werner & Margarete, Dancing, Etched, Inlaid Lid. 489.00
Stein, No. 2024, ½ Liter, Berlin Shield, Etched, Pewter Lid 144.00
Stein, No. 2036, ½ Liter, Owl, Inlaid Lid 253.00
Stein, No. 2052, ¼ Liter, Munich Child, Etched, Inlaid Lid 207.00
Stein, No. 2082, William Tell, Inlaid Lid, Etched, c.1897 . . . . . 385.00
Stein, No. 2083, ½ Liter, Boar Hunt, Etched, Inlaid Lid 834.00
Stein, No. 2091, Pouring Water On Man's Head, Etched, St. Florian. 652.00
Stein, No. 2092, ½ Liter, Keeper Of Clock Tower, Etched, Inlaid Lid 345.00
Stein, No. 2126, 5 ½ Liter, Symphonia, Pewter Lid, 22 In. 4140.00
Stein, No. 2140-792, ½ Liter, Mounted Officer, Horse, Text, Pewter Lid. 489.00

Stein, No. 2140-941, ½ Liter, Man Outside Pointing, PUG, Pewter Lid 138.00
Stein, No. 2230, ½ Liter, Man, Barmaid, Etched, Inlaid Lid, Schlitt 237.00
Stein, No. 2277, ⅓ Liter, Heidelberg, Etched, Inlaid Lid.................... 196.00
Stein, No. 2382, ½ Liter, Thirsty Rider, Etched, Inlaid Lid, H. Schlitt .... *illus* 520.00
Stein, No. 2402, ½ Liter, Courting Of Siegfried, Etched, Inlaid Lid 518.00
Stein, No. 2520, ½ Liter, Student & Barmaid, Etched, Inlaid Lid .... 460.00 to 480.00
Stein, No. 2530, ½ Liter, Boar Hunt, Cameo, Pewter Lid, Stahl 374.00
Stein, No. 2716, ½ Liter, Tavern Scene, Etched, Inlaid Lid, F. Quidenus 489.00
Stein, No. 2752, ½ Liter, 2 Men Drinking, Inlaid Lid, Schlitt.................... 518.00
Stein, No. 2778, ¼ Liter, Carnival, Etched, Inlaid Lid, Schlitt 329.00
Stein, No. 2833, ⅓ Liter, Man In Red Cape, Etched, Inlaid Lid 180.00
Stein, No. 2886, ½ Liter, Notables, Inlaid Lid 489.00
Tankard, No. 1159, 6 Liter, Music, Dancing, Tavern Scenes, Marked, 16 ¼ In. .... *illus* 500.00
Tureen, Cameo, Cover, Stoneware, Silver Ladle 1380.00
Vase, No. 1573, Mosaic, Terra-Cotta Ground, 6 ½ In.................... 161.00
Vase, No. 1841, Flowers On Vine, White Ground, 12 ¾ In.................... 334.00
Vase, No. 1981, Mosaic, 3 In. 115.00
Vase, No. 2301, Children, Scalloped Rim, Multicolored, 12 ½ In.................... 184.00
Vase, No. 2328, Square, Panels, Woman With Child, 4 Feet, Etched, 14 In.. .... 230.00
Vase, No. 3017-376, Japanese Women, Transfer, Enamel, 7 ½ In.................... 207.00
Vase, No. 7021, Mythological Scene, Flared Sides, Cameo Relief, 14 ¼ In.................... 356.00

MILK GLASS was named for its milky white color. It was first made in England during the 1700s. The height of its popularity in the United States was from 1870 to 1880. It is now correct to refer to some colored glass as blue milk glass, black milk glass, etc. Reproductions of milk glass are being made and sold in many stores. Related pieces may be listed in the Cosmos, Vallerysthal, and Westmoreland categories.

Ashtray, Stylized Cat, Green, Houzex 35.00
Banana Boat, Teardrop, Indiana, 8 x 11 In.................... 30.00
Bonbon, Figural, Czar Nicholas II, Sheared & Ground Base, French, c.1890, 12 ⅝ In.. .... 476.00
Bonbon, Figural, Egg On Basket, Lid, Group Lip, c.1895, 12 ¼ In.. .... 2240.00
Bottle, Figural, Metal Cap, U.S. Grant Bust, Capital Building Base, 10 In.................... 239.00
Bowl, Daisy & Button, L.E. Smith, 3 ½ x 6 In. 23.00
Box, Figural, Book Shape, Cover, Opalescent, 1920s, 4 ½ x 2 x 3 ¾ In.. .... 80.00
Box, Figural, Gingerbread House, Opaque Jade Green, Gilt Enameled, 1890s, 4 x 4 In. .. *illus* 360.00
Breakfast Set, Fan & Leaf, Gold Trim, Tray, Fitted Salt, Eggcups, 10 ½ In., 8 Piece 288.00
Butter, Cow & Milkmaid Cover, Oval, Cow Standing At Feeding Rough, 5 ½ In. 82.00
Butter, Cow & Wheat Cover, 4 Panels, Wheat Surrounding A Recumbent Cow, 7 In.. .... 80.00
Butter, Cow Cover, Oval, Beaded Ring, 24 Panels, 3 ¾ In.. .... 145.00
Cake Stand, Grapes, Pedestal, Scalloped Edge, 11 In.................... 122.00
Condiment Set, Jar, Salt & Pepper Shakers, Original Lids 220.00
Dish, Baker Boy, Cover, Clambroth, 7 ½ In. 75.00
Dish, Battleship Cover, Remember The Maine, 3 ½ In. 125.00
Dish, Boy Washing Dog, Cover, Double Wash Tub Base, 4 ¼ x 3 ½ In. 255.00
Dish, Butterfly Cover, 3 Double Legs, 3 Floral Panels, 6 x 4 ½ In.................... 310.00
Dish, Ceres Swan Cover, 4 ⅞ x 3 ¼ In. 80.00
Dish, Clamshell Cover, 4 Shell Feet, Shall Finial, 4 ¼ In.. .... 120.00
Dish, Dewey On Cover, Scroll Base, Golf Trim, 1890s, 5 x 3 ½ x 5 ½ In. .... *illus* 91.00
Dish, Dewey On Ribbed Base Cover, Gold Trim, 4 ¾ In.. .... 220.00
Dish, Dog On Cushion On Wicker Basket Cover, Caramel, 4 x 3 4 In.. .... 242.00
Dish, Dog On Steamer Trunk Cover, Yellow, Gold Trim, 1890s, 4 ⅞ x 4 ¾ In. .... *illus* 204.00
Dish, Elephant With Rider Cover, Frosted, 5 ½ x 3 ½ In.................... 83.00
Dish, Figural, Walking Bear, 20th Century, 4 ½ In. 288.00
Dish, Fox On Log Cover, 5 ½ In.. .... 163.00
Dish, Girl Emerging From Shell Cover, 6 ½ In. 175.00
Dish, Lady's Slipper, 5 In.................... 163.00
Dish, Moses In The Bulrushes Cover, 3 ¾ In. 45.00
Dish, Mother Eagle Cover, Raised Wing, 3 Eaglets At Side, Basket Weave Base, 6 x 5 In....... 39.00
Dish, Pope Leo Cover, 5 ¼ In.. .... 90.00
Dish, Rabbit Emerging From Egg Cover, Embossed Easter, 5 In.. .... *illus* 67.00
Dish, Robin On Nest Cover, 3 Legs, 6 ¼ In.................... 152.00
Dish, Rocking Horse Cover, Satin Finish, 5 In.................... 410.00
Dish, Spaniel Cover, Lattice & Striped Base, 3 ¾ In.................... 141.00
Dish, Startled Doe Cover, Fighting Stag On Base, 5 ½ In. 203.00
Dish, Swan Cover, Block Flange, Star Base, Glass Eyes, 6 ½ In.. .... 45.00
Dish, Wolf Dog Cover, Vegetation On Front, 5 ½ In.................... 555.00

Milk Glass, Box, Figural, Gingerbread House, Opaque Jade Green, Gilt Enameled, 1890s, 4 x 4 In.
$360.00

Milk Glass, Dish, Dewey On Cover, Scroll Base, Golf Trim, 1890s, 5 x 3 ½ x 5 ½ In.
$91.00

Milk Glass, Dish, Dog On Steamer Trunk Cover, Yellow, Gold Trim, 1890s, 4 ⅞ x 4 ¾ In.
$204.00

Milk Glass, Dish, Rabbit Emerging From Egg Cover, Embossed Easter, 5 In.
$67.00

TIP

Rub salt inside old tea and coffee cups to remove stains.

M

Milk Glass, Figurine, Lion, Black, Oval, Ribbed Edge, 1890s, 4 ¾ In.
$475.00

Milk Glass, Mustard, Figural, Bull's Head, Opaque Blue, Glass Eyes, Ladle, Atterbury & Co., 4 ¼ In.
$270.00

Milk Glass, Plate, Easter Sermon, Child, Reading To 3 Rabbits, 6 ⅜ In.
$113.00

Minton, Garden Seat, Orientalist, Dragons, Sancai, Marked, 18 ½ x 16 x 13 In.
$8000.00

Eggcup, Apple Tree, 2 ¼ In., Pair ... 11.00
Ewer, Red Flowers, Blue Ground, Spelter Foot, Top, Gold Paint, 12 In., Pair ... *illus* 60.00
Figurine, Lion, Black, Oval, Ribbed Edge, 1890s, 4 ¾ In. ... *illus* 475.00
Jar, Figural, Baker Man, Cover, 1840s, 8 ½ In. ... 192.00 to 218.00
Jar, Figural, French Chef Cover, Embossed Portieux, 8 ¼ In. ... 242.00
Jar, Figural, Little Golfer Cover, Hats, 5 ¾ In. ... 62.00
Jar, Figural, Queen Victoria, Bust, Embossed Coat Of Arms, 8 ½ In. ... 408.00
Lamp, Green, Houzex, 8 In. ... 60.00
Lamp, Radio, Banana Split, Electric, 1930s, 4 x 4 ⅛ In. ... 113.00
Mug, Liberty Bell, Embossed 1776 Between Bells, c.1976, 2 In. ... 120.00
Mustard, Figural, Bull's Head, Opaque Blue, Glass Eyes, Ladle, Atterbury & Co., 4 ¼ In. *illus* 270.00
Paperweight, Hand & Turtle, Frosted, Floral Band, Rays & Diamonds, 4 ¼ x 2 ¾ In. ... 150.00
Paperweight, Mastiff, Stepped Oval Base, 2 x 2 ⅞ In. ... 367.00
Pin Tray, Figural, Woman With Open Apron, Seated On Bale Of Straw, 6 ¼ In. ... 50.00
Plate, Chick In Shell, 7 ¼ In. ... 30.00
Plate, Easter Sermon, Child, Reading To 3 Rabbits, 6 ⅜ In. ... *illus* 113.00
Plate, Jefferson Davis, C-Scroll Border, Embossed Name, 9 In. ... 68.00
Rocker Blotter, Scotty, Green, Houzex ... 35.00
Rose Bowl, Ribbon Swags, Scalloped Edge, Pedestal Foot, 4 x 5 In. ... 12.50
Salt, Cow On Round Tub Cover, Wooden Tub Base, 2 x 2 In. ... 125.00
Salt, Figural, Flying Fish, Kirk Repousse Sterling Silver Spoon, 2 ½ In. ... 135.00
Saltshaker, Figural, Young Columbus, Embossed Columbus, 3 ½ In. ... 85.00
Shaving Mug, Scuttle, President Garfield, Lucretia Garfield, 3 x 5 In. ... 227.00
Vase, Flower Garlands, Blue Ribbons, Hand Painted, 21 In. ... 325.00

MILLEFIORI means, literally, a thousand flowers. Many small pieces of glass resembling flowers are grouped together to form a design. It is a type of glasswork popular in paperweights and some are listed in that category.

Basket, 2 Layers, Different Design Inside & Out, Clear Applied Handle, 4 ¾ In. ... 60.00
Basket, Double Sided, Clear Applied Handle, Different Design Inside & Out, 4 ¾ In. ... 60.00
Bowl, Yellow, White, Red, 4 Concentric Rings, Canes, Whitefriars, Footed, 4 $\frac{9}{16}$ In. ... 750.00
Figurine, Mouse, Green, Blue, Red, Yellow, White, Clear Ears, 4 ¼ In. ... 28.00
Pill Box, Iridescent Foil Inclusion, Canes, Round, 2 x 1 ¼ x ¾ In. ... 35.00
Sugar & Creamer, Swirled Colors, 3 In. ... 350.00
Vase, Cog Canes, Tapered, Flared Rim, Concentric Rings Base, Whitefriars, 8 ½ In. ... 700.00
Vase, Handkerchief, Rough Pontil, 3 In. ... 50.00

MINTON china has been made in the Staffordshire region of England from 1793 to the present. The firm became part of the Royal Doulton Tableware Group in 1968, but the wares continued to be marked Minton. In 2009 the brand was bought by KPS Capital Partners of New York and became part of WWRD Holdings. Many marks have been used. The word *England* was added in 1891. Minton majolica is listed in this book in the Majolica category.

Bouillon, Princess, Double Handle, 2 x 4 In. ... 10.00
Bowl, Flower, Mauve, Green, Square, Ironstone, Late 1800s, 2 ½ x 8 ⅝ In. ... 100.00
Bowl, Grasmere, Flower Urns & Scrolls Border, 9 In. ... 38.00
Bust, Richard Green, Draped, Parian, Waisted Circular Pedestal, England, c.1864, 11 In. ... 296.00
Butter, Cover, Flowers, Leaves, Blue Transfer, Gilt, Marked, 4 ½ x 8 ⅜ In. ... 132.00
Charger, Birds, Yellow Ground, Enameled, c.1872, 13 ½ In. ... 823.00
Charger, Nymphs, Waterscape, Hand Painted, Blue Underglaze, c.1882, 15 In., Pair ... 1007.00
Charger, Palissy, Lobster, Multicolored, 11 ¾ In. ... 351.00
Creamer, 22K Gold Design, 1875, 4 ¾ In. ... 125.00
Creamer, Marlow, Oval, Globe Mark, c.1930, 3 x 5 ¼ In. ... 90.00
Cup & Saucer, Green Leaf Vine, Gold Trim, Demitasse ... 25.00
Dish, Haddon Hall, 4 ½ In. ... 12.50
Figurine, Hera & Peacock, White, Gilt, c.1990, 9 In. ... 99.00
Figurine, Venus & Cupid, Reclining, Parian, Flower Oval Base, c.1865, 8 ¾ In. ... 533.00
Flower Trough, Picket Fence, Curved, c.1870, 10 In. ... 104.00
Garden Seat, Orientalist, Dragons, Sancai, Marked, 18 ½ x 16 x 13 In. ... *illus* 8000.00
Jardiniere, Stand, Ferns, Hollyhocks, Morning Glories, Multicolored, Handles, 18 ¾ In. ... 3850.00
Jug, Moon, Blue & White, Bulbous Neck, Scrolling Applied Handles, 14 ½ x 10 In. ... 230.00
Pedestal, Flow Blue, 19th Century, 30 In. ... 500.00
Plate, Bird, W. Mussill, Gilman Collamore & Co., c.1900, 9 ½ In., 4 Piece ... 575.00
Plate, Bread & Butter, Beaumaris, 6 ½ In. ... 16.00
Plate, Bread & Butter, Malta, 6 ¼ In. ... 10.00
Plate, Chinese Marine, Blue Transfer, Gadrooned Edge, Staffordshire, 10 ¼ In. ... 150.00
Plate, Dinner, Marlow, Floral Sprays, Gold Trim, c.1952, 10 ¾ In. ... 35.00

Plate, Flowers, Garlands, Pink, Blue, c.1910, 10 In., Pair 263.00
Plate, Navy Gold, Urns & Scrolls Border, 10 ½ In. 40.00
Platter, Willow, Blue Transferware, 18 x 14 ½ In. 250.00
Salt & Pepper, Marlow, Pink & Yellow Flowers, Scalloped Gold Trim, 2 ⅞ In. 42.00
Serving Dish, Cover, White, Molded Scale Design, Gold Trim, Marked, 5 ¾ In. 160.00
Tile, Earthenware, Bird, Leaves, Flower, Multicolored Enamel, Black Print, C. Dresser, 8 In. . . 948.00
Tile, Moon & Child, Pinecones, Stamped, c.1910, 6 ⅝ x 6 ⅝ In. 450.00
Tile, Musketeer, Brown Glaze, England, China Works, 12 x 6 In. 148.00
Tile, Stylized Leaf, Blue, Tan, White, Marked, Minton & Co., 6 x 6 In. 88.00
Urn, Cover, Figure, Cameo, Blue, Gilt, Handles, Square Base, 13 In. 3000.00
Vase, 3 Cherubs, Gilt, Pillow, Late 19th Century, 7 ½ In. 540.00
Vase, Blue Celeste, Multi-Spout, Marked, Christopher Dresser, 10 ¼ In. . . . . . *illus* 4850.00
Vase, Flowers, Green Glaze, Bottle Shape, Ribbed, 8 In. 431.00
Vase, Pate-Sur-Pate, Louis Solon, Blue, White Slip, Putti, Woman, Anchor, c.1889, 21 In. 52140.00
Vase, Pink Glaze, Enameled Flowers, Vines, Gold & Black Bands, 7 ½ x 3 ¼ In. 510.00
Vase, Stylized Flora, Turquoise Ground, Secessionist Ware, c.1905, 5 In. 450.00

MOCHA pottery is an English-made product that was sold in America during the early 1800s. It is a heavy pottery with pale coffee-and-cream coloring. Designs of blue, brown, green, orange, black, or white were added to the pottery and given fanciful names, such as Tree, Snail Trail, or Moss. Mocha designs are sometimes found on pearlware. A few pieces of mocha ware were made in France, the United States, and other countries.

Bowl, Brown Pinstripe Rim, Blue Band, Leaves, Crow's-Foot Base, 4 x 7 In. 440.00
Bowl, Cat's-Eye, Brown, White, Butterscotch Band, Pearlware, 3 x 5 ½ In. 200.00
Bowl, Cat's-Eye, Earthworm, Tapered, Lattice Banding, Multicolored, 5 x 9 ¾ In. 700.00
Bowl, Cat's-Eye, Green, Rust, 7 In. 690.00
Bowl, Earthworm, 19th Century, 3 x 6 ½ In. . . . . . *illus* 671.00
Bowl, Earthworm, Blue Border, Black Lines, Gray Band, Pearlware, c.1830, 4 x 7 ½ In. 180.00
Bowl, Earthworm, Wide Blue Band, Blue, Brown, White, Cat's-Eye Design, Pearlware, 6 In. . . 165.00
Bowl, Salmon, Green, Blue & Double Brown Bands, Creamware, 6 ½ In. 240.00
Bowl, Seaweed, Brown Band, Pearlware, 3 ¼ x 6 ½ In. 150.00
Bowl, White Band, 2 Stripes, Yellowware, 5 ¼ x 10 In. 60.00
Creamer, Marbleized, Brown, Blue, White, Bulbous, Applied Handle, 3 ⅞ x 3 In. . . . . . *illus* 1980.00
Creamer, Orange, Blue, Brown Bands, 19th Century, 3 ¾ In. 380.00
Jar, Condiment, Cover, Cat's-Eye, Handle, 19th Century . . . . . *illus* 576.00
Jug, Earthworm, Applied Loop Handle, Cracked, Repair, Signed, 4 Clews, 7 In. . . . . . *illus* 1320.00
Muffineer, Seaweed, Yellow, 4 ½ In., Pair 1495.00
Mug, Brown, Green, Orange, England, 1800s, Qt., 5 ½ In. 1067.00
Mug, Cat's-Eye, 5 In. 1150.00
Mug, Cat's-Eye, Pale Gold Bands, Acanthus Leaf Handle, c.1875, 5 In. 587.00
Mug, Earthworm, Blue, 4 In. 1725.00
Mug, Earthworm, Blue, Gray, Black, 4 In. 460.00
Mug, Earthworm, Blue Band, Triple Black Bands, 19th Century, 6 In. 458.00
Mug, Earthworm, White Ground, Brown Bands, 3 ⅞ In. 415.00
Mug, Leaf Design, 3 ½ In. 345.00
Mug, Seaweed, Blue, 5 In. 173.00
Mug, Seaweed, Blue, 6 In. 863.00
Mug, Seaweed, Brown Bands, Blue Band Rim, Creamware, 2 ⅝ In. 200.00
Mug, Seaweed, Green, 5 In. 978.00
Pepper Pot, Earthworm, Blue, Brown Bands, Footed, 4 ¼ In. 3744.00
Pepper Pot, Earthworm, Cat's-Eye, Blue, Tan, Black, 4 ¾ x 2 ¼ In. . . . . . *illus* 2019.00
Pitcher, Bands, Brown, Yellowware . . . . . *illus* 118.00
Pitcher, Bands, Sunburst, Bulbous, C-Shape Handle, Multicolored, 8 ¼ x 6 ¾ In. 6250.00
Pitcher, Cat's-Eye, Bulbous, Footed, C-Shape Handle, Multicolored, 7 ¼ x 5 ¾ In. 1000.00
Pitcher, Checkerboard Band, Blue, 19th Century, 9 In. 146.00
Pitcher, Earthworm, Bulbous, C-Shape Handle, Multicolored, 4 ¾ x 4 In. 650.00
Pitcher, Earthworm, Cat's-Eye, Blue, 6 ¾ In. 805.00
Pitcher, Earthworm, Coggled Bands, Black, Orange, Blue, Brown, 6 x 3 In. 4840.00
Pitcher, Earthworm, Double, Blue, 8 In. 3450.00
Pitcher, Seaweed, Alternating Pumpkins, Acanthus Leaf Handle, c.1870, 7 In. 1058.00
Pitcher, Seaweed, Blue, Bulbous, Applied Loop Handle, Yellowware, 6 ½ In. . . . . . *illus* 275.00
Pitcher, Seaweed, Orange Ground, 5 ½ In. 978.00
Pitcher, Wavy Slip Lines, Acanthus Leaf Handle, c.1875, 6 In. 1292.00
Salt, Seaweed, Pedestal, 2 In. 633.00
Sugar, Cover, Marbleized, Pink, Black, Ivory, Footed, 19th Century, 4 ¾ In. 275.00
Syrup, Agate, Blue, 5 ½ In. 345.00

Minton, Vase, Blue Celeste, Multi-Spout, Marked, Christopher Dresser, 10 ¼ In.
$4850.00

Mocha, Bowl, Earthworm, 19th Century, 3 x 6 ½ In.
$671.00

Mocha, Creamer, Marbleized, Brown, Blue, White, Bulbous, Applied Handle, 3 ⅞ x 3 In.
$1980.00

Mocha, Jar, Condiment, Cover, Cat's-Eye, Handle, 19th Century
$576.00

Mocha, Jug, Earthworm, Applied Loop Handle, Cracked, Repair, Signed, 4 Clews, 7 In.
$1320.00

Mocha, Pepper Pot, Earthworm, Cat's-Eye, Blue, Tan, Black, 4 ¾ x 2 ¼ In.
$2019.00

Mocha, Pitcher, Bands, Brown, Yellowware
$118.00

Mocha, Pitcher, Seaweed, Blue, Bulbous, Applied Loop Handle, Yellowware, 6 ½ In.
$275.00

MONMOUTH Pottery Company started working in Monmouth, Illinois, in 1892. The pottery made a variety of utilitarian wares. It became part of Western Stoneware Company in 1906. The maple leaf mark was used until 1930. If *Co.* appears as part of the mark, the piece was made before 1906.

Vase, Black Gloss Glaze, Stamp, 10 x 6 In. 50.00
Vase, Green Matte Glaze, Handles, Western Ware, 26 In. 175.00

MONT JOYE, *see Mt. Joye category.*

MOORCROFT pottery was first made in Burslem, England, in 1913. William Moorcroft had managed the art pottery department for James Macintyre & Company of England from 1898 to 1913. The Moorcroft pottery continues today, although William Moorcroft died in 1945. The earlier wares are similar to the modern ones, but color and marking will help indicate the age.

Bowl, Cover, Columbine, Purple, Red, Mottled Green Ground, Marked, W.M., 6 ¾ In. 275.00
Bowl, Cover, Dark, Light Blue Glaze, Large Multicolored Flowers, 6 In. 115.00
Bowl, Iris, Red, White, Green, Blue Ground, Signed, 10 ½ In. 225.00
Bowl, Pink Flower, Green, 5 In. 125.00
Bowl, Red Flowers, Green Leaves, Blue Ground, Signed, 9 In. 170.00
Bowl, Yellow Glaze, c.1913, 8 In. 60.00
Box, Cover, Anemone, Yellow, Orange, Brown, Flambe Glaze, Impressed Mark, 5 ¼ In. 330.00
Box, Cover, Clematis, Red, Blue, Green, Round, Impressed Mark, 9 ¼ In. 365.00
Canister, Tea, Dome Lid, Cylindrical Shape, Fruit, Signed, c.1950, 5 In. 2844.00
Charger, Carousel Design, 14 In. 513.00
Clock, Anemone, Cobalt Blue Ground, Battery Powered, 1993, 6 ¼ In. 184.00
Clock, Anemone, Cobalt Blue Ground, c.1993, Marked, 6 ¼ In. 259.00
Compote, Claremont, Silver Overlay, Trefoils, Handles, Marked, c.1905, 6 ¾ In. 20400.00
Ginger Jar, Cover, Winds Of Change, Rachel Bishop, 6 ¼ In. 355.00
Jug, Poppy, Blue, Macintyre, 3 In. 211.00
Lamp, Cluny, Trees, Green, Pink Ground, 10 ½ In. 220.00
Lamp, Hazelden, Blue, White, Signed, W. Moorcroft, c.1905, 12 In. 2500.00
Lamp, Oberon, Flowers, Pink, Yellow Green Blue Ground, 11 In. 220.00
Pitcher, Anemone, Blue, Green Leaves, White Ground, Florian, Marked, Macintyre, 5 ¼ In. 582.00
Pitcher, Leaf & Berry, Blue, Green, Aqua, Impressed Mark, 4 ½ In. 310.00
Planter, Mottled Green, 2 Handles, Art Nouveau, 5 ½ In. 98.00
Plate, Violet, Sally Tuffin, 10 ¼ In. 158.00
Powder Box, Cover, Red, White Flowers, Green Leaves, Blue Ground, Stamped, 6 In. 170.00
Tazza, Pomegranate, 8 ¾ In. 197.00
Vase, Amazon, Frogs, Lizard, Black Ground, Red, Green Blue, 5 In. 341.00
Vase, Anemone, Green Ground, 5 ¼ In. 177.00
Vase, Apples, Brown Ground, 5 ½ In. 197.00
Vase, Avalon, Butterflies, Vivid, White, Black, Orange, 8 In. 362.00
Vase, Bulbous, Cobalt Blue, Florets, Leafy Vine, 9 ½ In. 69.00
Vase, Bulbous, Flower, Cobalt Blue, Green Glaze, Paper Label, 5 In. 173.00
Vase, Cobalt Blue, Red Poppies, Green Leaves, Signed, Impressed, 7 In. 172.00
Vase, Cornflower, Yellow, Green, Black, Signed, 21 In. 7200.00
Vase, Daydreams, 7 ½ In. 335.00
Vase, Eventide, Tree, Blue Ground, Marked, 14 ½ In. 3600.00
Vase, Fiji, Emma Bossons, 8 ¼ In. 295.00
Vase, Flambe, Apple Blossoms, Egg Shape, Marked, 5 ¾ x 3 In. 960.00
Vase, Flambe, Honesty Pattern, 8 ⅝ In. 748.00
Vase, Flambe, Spring Flowers, 8 In. 414.00
Vase, Flambe, Studio Compressed, 12 In. 296.00
Vase, Florian, 2 Handles, Relief Flowers, Leaves, Blue Glaze, 10 In. 3680.00
Vase, Florian, Peacock Feather, 10 ¾ In. 1380.00
Vase, Florian, Poppies, Forget-Me-Knots, Marked, 12 In. 1840.00
Vase, Florian, Yellow Tulips, Jas. Macintyre & Co., 11 In. 7800.00
Vase, Flowers, Cobalt Blue Ground, 4 ½ In. 205.00
Vase, Flying Geese, Black Ground, Marked, 5 In. 591.00
Vase, Glazed Spring Flowers, Oval, Round Foot, c.1940, 6 In. 826.00
Vase, Hairy Health, E. Bossons, 8 ¼ In. 296.00
Vase, Hibiscus, Bulbous, Blue Ground, 9 ½ In. 690.00
Vase, Knightwood, Rachel Bishop, 7 ¼ In. 276.00
Vase, Leaf & Berry, Blue, Green, Aqua, Matte Glaze, Impressed, 10 In. 563.00
Vase, Minuet, 7 ½ In. 355.00
Vase, Orchid, Flambe Glaze, Impressed Mark, 9 ½ In. 760.00
Vase, Orchid, Red Flower, Dark Blue Ground, 6 In. 426.00

Vase, Pomegranate, c.1922, 8 ½ In. . . . *illus* 460.00
Vase, Pomegranate, Red, Brown, Impressed, Cobridge, 6 ¼ In. . . . 549.00
Vase, Quiet Waters Fish, 7 ¾ In. . . . 572.00
Vase, Rainforest, Sally Tuffin, c.1992, 8 ¼ In. . . . 414.00
Vase, Shouldered, Clematis, Purple Ground, Multicolored, Mark, 4 x 2 ½ In. . . . 360.00
Vase, Simeon, 8 ¼ In. . . . 256.00
Vase, Solomon's Seal, Flowers On Blue & Cream Ground, 10 In. . . . 394.00
Vase, Spirazia, Emma Bossons, c.1999, 7 ¾ In. . . . 513.00
Vase, Spring Flowers, Purple, Pink, Yellow, Green Ground, Signed, 6 In. . . . 488.00
Vase, Tapered, Flared Lip, Glossy Blue, Turquoise, Yellow Glaze, 7 ¾ In. . . . 533.00
Vase, Winds Of Change, White, Blue Brown Swirls, 7 ½ In. . . . 238.00
Vase, Wisteria, Multicolored, Cobalt Blue Ground, 12 ⅜ In. . . . 345.00
Vase, Woodlands Farm, Barren Tree, Rural Scene, Blue, White Brown, 5 ½ In. . . . 638.00

MORGANTOWN GLASS WORKS operated in Morgantown, West Virginia, from 1900 to 1974. Some of the wares are marked with an adhesive label that says *Old Morgantown Glass.*

Adams, Vase, Green, Slant, 12 In. . . . 75.00
Art Moderne, Goblet, Shamrock Green, 10 Oz. . . . 8.00
Chanticleer, Cocktail, 3 Oz. . . . 48.00
Chanticleer, Cocktail, Amber, 3 Oz. . . . 45.00
Crinkle, Berry Bowl, Amethyst & Green, 4 In. . . . 28.00
Crinkle, Pitcher, Peacock Blue, 80 Oz., 8 In. . . . 195.00
Crinkle, Pitcher, Tijuana, Green, 7 ½ In. . . . 135.00
Crinkle, Pitcher, Tijuana, Topaz, 7 ½ In. . . . 125.00
Crinkle, Plate, Dinner, Ice, 9 In. . . . 48.00
Crinkle, Plate, Gloria Blue, 7 ½ In. . . . 24.00
Crinkle, Plate, Topaz, 6 ½ In. . . . 19.00
Crinkle, Sherbet, Peacock Blue . . . 26.00
Crinkle, Sherbet, Topaz, 7 ½ In. . . . 23.00
Crinkle, Tumbler, Amethyst, 4 In. . . . 22.00
Crinkle, Tumbler, Footed, Amethyst, 5 In. . . . 35.00
Crinkle, Tumbler, Harlequin . . . 35.00
Crinkle, Tumbler, Juice, Amethyst & Green, 4 In. . . . 18.00
Crinkle, Tumbler, Juice, Moss Green, 4 In. . . . 14.00
Crinkle, Tumbler, Old-Fashioned, Amethyst, 5 ½ Oz. . . . 28.00
Crinkle, Tumbler, Ruby, 5 In. . . . 29.00 to 35.00
Crinkle, Vase, Snowball, Green, 7 In. . . . 200.00
Crinkle, Wine, Pink, 3 In. . . . 62.00
El Mexicano, Cup & Saucer, Spanish Red . . . 24.00
El Mexicano, Dinner Plate, Seaweed, 9 In. . . . 48.00
El Mexicano, Salad Plate, Seaweed, 7 ½ In. . . . 32.00
El Mexicano, Tumbler, Iced Tea, 5 ½ In. . . . 45.00
Golf Ball, Champagne, Ritz Blue Bowl, Clear Stem, 5 ½ Oz., 5 In. . . . 35.00
Golf Ball, Cocktail, Spanish Red, Clear Stem, 3 Oz., 4 ½ In. . . . 45.00
Golf Ball, Cordial, Anna Rose, 1 ½ Oz., 3 ½ In. . . . 8.00
Golf Ball, Cordial, Spanish Red, 1 ½ Oz., 3 ½ In. . . . 35.00
Golf Ball, Goblet, Ruby, 4 In. . . . 40.00
Golf Ball, Sherry, Amethyst, 2 ½ Oz., 4 ⅝ In. . . . 10.00
Gypsy Fire, Console Set, 3 Piece . . . 100.00
Jewel, Champagne, Spanish Red, 6 Oz. . . . 10.00
Jockey, Champagne, Amber Stem, Clear Bowl, Foot, 5 ½ In. . . . 35.00
Laura, Vase, Burgundy, 10 x 2 ½ In. . . . 30.00
Laura, Vase, Smoky Gray, 10 In. . . . 30.00
Queen Anne, Goblet, Aqua Marine, 9 Oz. . . . 10.00
Serenade, Vase, Bud, Jade Green, 10 In. . . . 65.00
Summer Cornucopia, Cordial, Clear, Oz. . . . 5.00
Top Hat, Cocktail, 3 Oz. . . . 150.00
Trudy, Tumble-Up, Turquoise, 6 ½ In., 2 Piece . . . 135.00

MORIAGE is a special type of raised decoration used on some Japanese pottery. Sometimes pieces of clay were shaped by hand and applied to the item; sometimes the clay was squeezed from a tube in the way we apply cake frosting. One type of moriage is called Dragonware by collectors.

Humidor, Cover, Swans In Lake, Leaves, Nippon, 5 ½ In. . . . 201.00
Humidor, Horse Head, Oval Cartouche, Shamrocks, Nippon, 6 ½ In. . . . 325.00
Plaque, Chief Sitting Bull, Moriage Bands, Crossed Arrows, Nippon, 10 In. . . . 3776.00

TIP

Modern bleach can damage eighteenth century and some nineteenth century dishes. To clean old dishes, try hydrogen peroxide or bicarbonate of soda. Each removes a different type of stain.

Moorcroft, Vase, Pomegranate, c.1922, 8 ½ In.
$460.00

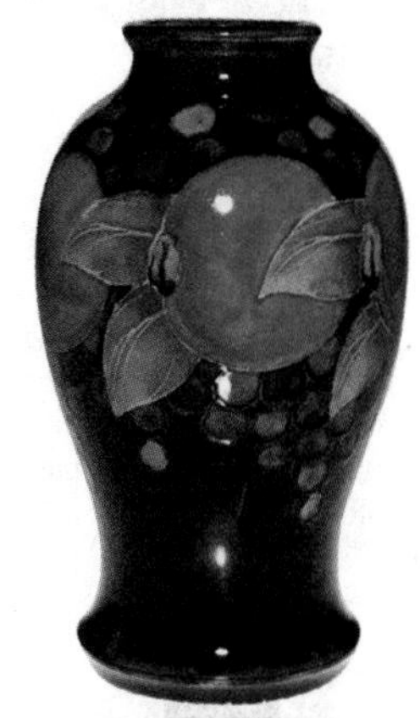

Moriage, Urn, Cover, Flowers, Flower Ground, Handles, Nippon, 11 ½ In.
$605.00

M

Moser, Box, Cranberry Glass, Gold Enameled, Scrolls, Daisies, Rigaree Footed, c.1890, 6 ½ In.
$825.00

Moser, Vase, Amethyst To Clear, Flowers, Engraved, Signed, 10 In.
$400.00

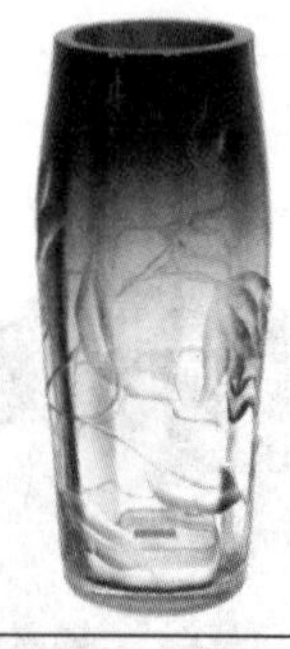

Moser, Vase, Cobalt Blue, Gilt Intaglio Band, Classical Women, Playing Music, Signed, 11 In.
$489.00

Moser, Vase, Green Crackle, Fish, Seaweed, Dimples, Enameled, Late 1800s, 6 ⅝ In.
$200.00

Plaque, Squirrel, Moriage Peanuts, Nippon, 10 ¾ In. 266.00
Plaque, Woodland, Mountains, Trees, Nippon, 8 ⅝ In. 266.00
Plate, Woodland, Lakeshore, Cobalt Rim, Nippon, 9 ⅜ In. 354.00
Urn, Cover, 2 Handles, Oval Footed, Scrolled Leaves, Jewels, Nippon, 9 In. 1062.00
Urn, Cover, Flowers, Flower Ground, Handles, Nippon, 11 ½ In. *illus* 605.00
Urn, Flowers, Purple, Green Stems, Yellow To Amethyst Ground, Handles, Nippon, 9 In. 978.00
Vase, Birds In Flight, Melon Ribbed, Oval, Scrolls, Nippon, 8 ½ In. 767.00
Vase, Egret, Poppy Blossoms, Ruffled Rim, Nippon, 11 ¼ In. 3540.00
Vase, Flowers, Leaves, Purple, Yellow Ground, Oval, Applied Gold Handles, Nippon, 5 In. 403.00
Vase, Pink & Purple Flowers, Green, Crimped Rim, Handles, 4-Footed, 8 In. 100.00
Vase, Portrait, Queen Louise, Enameled Lacy Overlay, Scrolled Leaves, Nippon, 10 In. 3540.00
Vase, Swans In Lake, Tapestry, Grape Leaf, Clusters, Handles, Nippon, 6 ½ In. 2242.00

MOSAIC TILE COMPANY of Zanesville, Ohio, was started by Karl Langerbeck and Herman Mueller in 1894. Many types of plain and ornamental tiles were made until 1959. The company closed in 1967. The company also made some ashtrays, bookends, and related giftwares. Most pieces are marked with the entwined *MTC* monogram.

Figurine, Bear, Black Matte Glaze, Green, Impressed, 5 ½ x 9 ½ In. 165.00
Figurine, Bear, Walking, Marked, 9 ½ In. 173.00
Figurine, German Shepard, Seated, Plinth, Tan Matte Glaze, 9 In. 115.00
Paperweight, Abraham Lincoln, Blue, White, 6-Sided, Marked, 3 In. 40.00
Pin Tray, Hunting Dog, Emerald Green, Gunmetal Glaze, Marked, 5 x 8 In. 150.00
Pin Tray, Hunting Dog, Green Black Glaze, Marked, 5 x 8 ½ In. 95.00
Pin Tray, Turtle, Light Blue Matte Glaze, Marked, 4 ½ In. 25.00
Tile, Ship, Single Mast, Waves, Arts & Crafts, Signed, 6 In. 650.00

MOSER glass is made by a Bohemian (Czech) glasshouse founded by Ludwig Moser in 1857. Art Nouveau-type glassware and iridescent glassware were made. The most famous Moser glass is decorated with heavy enameling in gold and bright colors. The firm, Moser Glassworks, is still working in Karlovy Vary, Czech Republic. Few pieces of Moser glass are marked.

Moser Karlsbad

Bottle, Ribbed, Gold Scrolling, Blue, Red, Pink Flowers Band, Faceted Stopper, 9 ¼ In. 345.00
Bowl, Amber, Gilt Intaglio Roman Warrior Band, Signed, Moser Karlsbad, 4 In. 138.00
Box, Cranberry Glass, Gold Enameled, Scrolls, Daisies, Rigaree Footed, c.1890, 6 ½ In. *illus* 825.00
Box, Raised Purple Rectangles, Gold, Cut Panels, Hinged Cover, Metal Rims & Clasp, 5 In. 655.00
Chalice, Amethyst Shaded To Clear Bowl, Etched Wreath, Gold, Long Stem, 12 ½ In. 365.00
Cordial, Green, Gilt Intaglio, Panels, Blue & Red Peacock Eyes, 12-In. Decanter, 5 Piece 460.00
Cruet, Gemel, Green, 2 Spouts, Enameled Bird Stoppers, 11 In. 250.00
Cup, Green Crackle, Enameled, Bird, Water Lily, Leaves, c.1885, 4 In. 200.00
Cup & Saucer, Gold Enameled Scrolling, Translucent Green, Cranberry Glass, 5 ½ In. 345.00
Cup & Saucer, Green, Enameled Gold Flowers, Footed, 3 In. 58.00
Decanter, Clear, Amethyst Panels, Gilt Intaglio Band, Stopper, 12 In. 500.00
Decanter, Creme De Menthe, Enameled Insects, Bird, Leaves, Cranberry Glass, Stopper, 14 In. 546.00
Dish, Opalescent Purple, Shell Shape, Gold Scrolls, Trim, 10 In. 201.00
Dresser Jar, White Medallions, Gold Scrolls, Amber Ground, 3-Footed, Metal Base, Oval, 5 In. 144.00
Finger Bowl, Underplate, Cloverleaf Shape, Green, Gold Scrolling, 6 ¼ In. 58.00
Goblet, Amber To Cranberry, Applied Grapes, Leaves, Multicolored Vineyard, 6 In. 1035.00
Goblet, Blue Yellow Leaves, Green, Coralene, Jeweled Baluster Stem, 7 In. 144.00
Goblet, Cobalt Blue To Clear, Faceted, Gilt Intaglio Roman Warrior Frieze, 6 ½ In., 6 Piece 1035.00
Goblet, Green, Applied Grapes, Multicolored Grape Leaves, Gold Vines, 8 In. 374.00
Goblet, Green, Coralene, Blue & Yellow Leaves, Jeweled Stem, Baluster Stem, 7 In. 395.00
Jar, Cover, Amber, Gilt Intaglio Roman Warrior Frieze, Oval, Signed, Moser Karlsbad, 6 In. 403.00
Liquor Set, Clear To Green, Pyramid Shape, Prism Cut, Gold Stencil, 11-In. Decanter, 5 Piece 475.00
Liquor Set, Gilt Intaglio Bands, Gold Swags, Ribbed Stopper, Handles, 8-In. Decanter, 6 Piece 863.00
Mug, Ruby Footed, Pedestal, Gold Leafy Scrolling, 5 In. 201.00
Pitcher, Clear, Padded, Grapes, Leaves, Silver Plated Stem, Spout, Lid, 8 In. 1610.00
Pitcher, Clear Crackle, Enameled, Bird, Water, Cattails, c.1885, 5 ¾ In. 550.00
Pitcher, Green, Multicolored Scrolls, Leaves, Peacock Eyes, Gold Tracery, 13 In. 690.00
Pitcher, Green, Scrolling, Flowers, Baluster, 12 In. 690.00
Pitcher, Green Crackle, Bird, Water, Flowers, Enameled, Vaseline Twisted Handle, c.1885, 8 In. 800.00
Pitcher, Prussian Blue, Multicolored, Gold, Borders, Bulbous, Notched Rim, 10 ½ In. 2013.00
Pitcher, Raised Enamel Flowers, Leaves, Faceted Neck, c.1885, 8 In. 444.00
Sherbet, Scenic, Cut To Clear, Amethyst, Blue, Amber, Cranberry, 5 In., 8 Piece 345.00
Tumbler, Clear, Ribbed, Gold Wash Leaf Band, c.1950, 6 In., 6 Piece 86.00
Tumbler, Cranberry Glass, Floral, Footed, c.1870, 5 ¼ In., Pair 288.00
Tumbler, Gold Scrolling, Gold Handle, Oak Leaves, Applied Acorns, 4 In. 460.00

Tumbler, Green, Enameled, Gilt Intaglio Band, Triangular Design, 4 In. 125.00
Tumbler, Juice, Cranberry Glass, Gold Enameled, Reserves, Flowers, 3 ⅝ x 2 ¼ In. 350.00
Tumbler, Ocean Blue, Gold Leaves, White Flowers, 4 ⅛ x 3 In. 125.00
Tumbler, Whiskey, Clear, Gold & Colored Oak Leaves, 3 ¼ In., Pair 300.00
Vase, Amber, Black Intaglio Fruit, Band, 11 ½ In. 50.00
Vase, Amber, Enameled, 4 Reeded Feet, c.1885, 7 ½ In. 863.00
Vase, Amber, Gilt Intaglio Sovereign Band, Women Warriors, Footed, Signed, Moser Karlsbad, 7 ⅝ In. 300.00
Vase, Amber, Gilt Intaglio Sovereign Band, Women Warriors, Signed, Moser Karlsbad, 13 ⅜ In. 475.00
Vase, Amber, Gold Intaglio Roman Warrior Frieze, Urn, Signed, Moser Karlsbad, 8 In. 489.00
Vase, Amethyst, Gilt Intaglio Roman Warrior Frieze, Faceted Urn, Signed, Moser Karlsbad, 8 In. 345.00
Vase, Amethyst, Moorish Panel, Flowers, Cranberry Jewels, Gold Tracery, Hexagonal, 12 In. 1438.00
Vase, Amethyst To Clear, Flowers, Engraved, Signed, 10 In. *illus* 400.00
Vase, Applied Acorns, Flowers, Butterfly, Enameled, 4-Footed, 1910, 4 ⅝ In. 200.00
Vase, Blue, Coraline, Enameled Flowers, Gilt, 1890, 10 ½ x 5 In. 880.00
Vase, Blue, Gold Elephants, Palm Trees, Ring Base, Cameo, Signed, Moser Karlsbad, 12 In. 1955.00
Vase, Cobalt, Gilt Intaglio Roman Warrior Frieze, Footed Urn, Signed, Moser Karlsbad, 10 In. 662.00
Vase, Cobalt Blue, Gilt Intaglio Band, Classical Women, Playing Music, Signed, 11 In. *illus* 489.00
Vase, Cranberry, Engraved Flowers, 12-Sided, 6 ¼ In. 175.00
Vase, Dragons, Enameled, Footed, Light Blue Ruffled Rim, Handles, Signed, 1890, 7 x 8 In. 220.00
Vase, Fish, Enamel, Handles, Round, Long Neck, 7 ½ In. 85.00
Vase, Gold Angel Fish, Enameled, Footed, Cut Diamonds, Signed, 8 ¼ x 4 In. 225.00
Vase, Gold Enameled Fish, Underwater Scene, 8 In. 920.00
Vase, Green, Twisted Rectangle, Jeweled Flowers, Butterflies, Gold, 11 In. 1150.00
Vase, Green Crackle, Fish, Seaweed, Dimples, Enameled, Late 1800s, 6 ⅝ In. *illus* 200.00
Vase, Green To Clear, Flowers, Engraved, Square, 6 ¼ In. 40.00
Vase, Rosaline, Pink, Shaded, Applied Jewels, Gold Enameled, c.1920, 11 In. 1300.00
Water Set, Green, Yellow Flowers, 16 In., 7 Piece *illus* 550.00
Wine, Green Prunt Cabochons, Multicolored Grapes, Vines, Ball Stem, 7 In., Pair 288.00

MOSS ROSE china was made by many firms from 1808 to 1900. It has a typical moss rose pictured as the design. The plant is not as popular now as it was in Victorian gardens, so the fuzz-covered bud is unfamiliar to most collectors. The dishes were usually decorated with pink and green flowers.

Butter, Dome Cover, 4 x 6 ½ In. 15.00
Cuspidor, Ironstone, 19th Century, 5 x 7 In. 85.00
Tureen, Cover, Handles, Ironstone, 9 x 16 In. 95.00

MOTHER-OF-PEARL GLASS, or pearl satin glass, was first made in the 1850s in England and in Massachusetts. It was a special type of mold-blown satin glass with air bubbles in the glass, giving it a pearlized color. It has been reproduced. Mother-of-pearl shell objects are listed under Pearl.

Basket, Herringbone, Blue, Ruffled Rim, Handle, 5 x 4 ¾ In. 195.00
Jar, Cover, Diamond Quilted, Cranberry, Oval, 5 ¼ In. 374.00
Lamp, Diamond Quilted, Pink, Metal, Melon Ribbed Base, 8 ½ x 17 In., Pair 1150.00
Lamp, Herringbone, Rainbow, Pinched Base, Domed Shade, 16 In. 316.00
Lamp, Rainbow, Applied Clear Rigaree, 9 ¾ In. 2818.00
Perfume Bottle, Peacock Eyes, Blue, Oval, Sterling Silver Twist Lid, 4 In. 805.00
Pitcher, Bubble Zigzag, Rainbow, Reeded Handle, 9 ½ In. *illus* 167.00
Pitcher, Diamond Quilted, Pink, Ruffled Rim, Reed Handle, 9 In. 230.00
Pitcher, Diamond Quilted, Rainbow, Bulbous, 4-Fold Rim, Reeded Handle, 11 In. 1725.00
Pitcher, Rainbow, Bulbous, Ruffled Rim, Caramel Reeded Handle, 9 In. 115.00
Rose Bowl, Diamond Quilted, Rainbow, Clear Panels, Patent, Signed, 3 In. 403.00
Spooner, Diamond Quilted, Pink, 5 In. *illus* 150.00
Vase, Diamond Quilted, Blue, Hexagonal Shouldered, 6 In. 86.00
Vase, Diamond Quilted, Blue, Ruffled Rim, 6 x 4 ½ In. 275.00
Vase, Diamond Quilted, Blue, Ruffled Rim, Camphor, Lip, 9 ½ x 6 ½ In. 450.00
Vase, Diamond Quilted, Blue To White, Flowers, 9 ½ In. *illus* 518.00
Vase, Diamond Quilted, Peach, Bulbous, Bulging Collar, 11 In. 173.00
Vase, Diamond Quilted, Peach, Bulbous, Triple Ring Collar, 11 In. 69.00
Vase, Herringbone, Apricot Shaded To White, 7 ¼ In. 86.00
Vase, Herringbone, Pink, Gold Branches, Urn Shape, Handles, 11 In. 201.00
Vase, Herringbone, Rainbow, Tricornered Rim, 8 In. 604.00
Vase, Stick, Diamond Quilted, Peach, Bulbous Base, Scalloped Rim, 6 In. 52.00
Vase, Stick, Hobnail, Pink, Bulbous Base, 9 In. 316.00

Moser, Water Set, Green, Yellow Flowers, 16 In., 7 Piece
$550.00

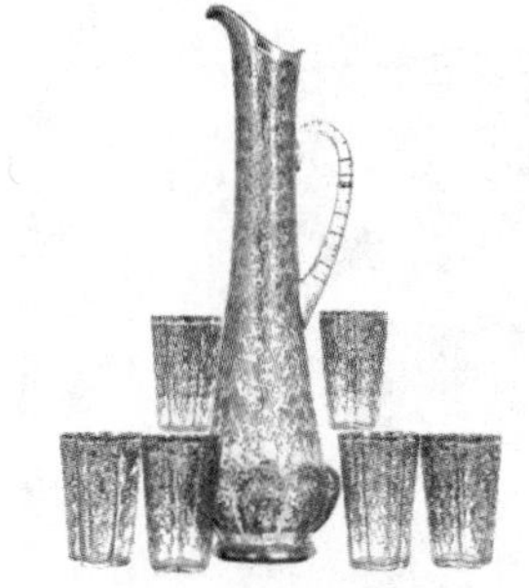

Mother-Of-Pearl, Pitcher, Bubble Zigzag, Rainbow, Reeded Handle, 9 ½ In.
$167.00

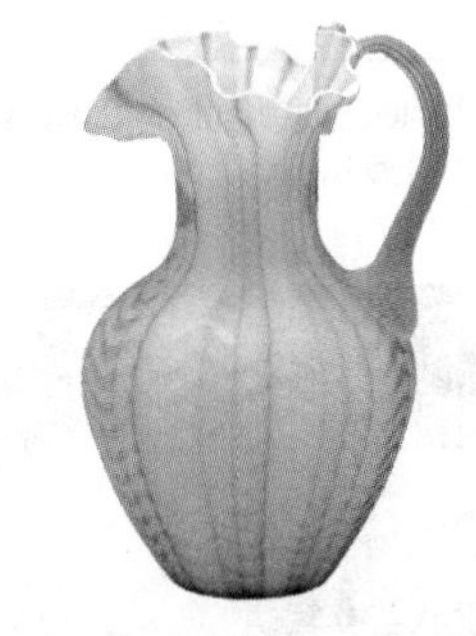

Mother-Of-Pearl, Spooner, Diamond Quilted, Pink, 5 In.
$150.00

Mother-Of-Pearl, Vase, Diamond Quilted, Blue To White, Flowers, 9 ½ In.
$518.00

Movie, Poster, Big Sleep, Humphrey Bogart, Lauren Bacall, 1946, 27 x 41 In. $2124.00

Movie, Poster, Pillow Talk, Rock Hudson, Doris Day, 1959, 27 x 41 In. $240.00

Movie, Poster, Vertigo, James Stewart, Kim Novak, Hitchcock, 1958, 27 x 41 In. $4425.00

MOTORCYCLES and motorcycle accessories of all types are being collected today. Examples can be found that date back to the early twentieth century. Toy motorcycles are listed in the Toy category.

Brochure, Neracar Motorcycle, 1922 . . . . . 50.00
Coil Cover, Chrome, Live To Ride, Ride To Live, Eagle Spirit, 5 ½ x 6 x 4 ½ In. 63.00
Harley-Davidson, Screamin' Eagle, Thunder Mountain Sterling RM, 103 Cu. In. 9200.00
Wrench, Indian 20.00

MOUNT WASHINGTON, *see Mt. Washington category.*

MOVIE memorabilia of all types are collected. Animation Art, Games, Sheet Music, Toys, and some celebrity items are listed in their own section. A lobby card is 11 by 14 inches. A set of lobby cards includes seven scene cards and one title card. A one sheet, the standard movie poster, is 27 by 41 inches. A three sheet is 81 by 40 inches. A half sheet is 22 by 28 inches. A window card, made of cardboard, is 14 by 22 inches. An insert is 14 by 36 inches. A herald is a promotional item handed out to patrons. Press books, sent to exhibitors to promote a movie, contain ads and lists of what is available for advertising, i.e., posters, lobby cards. Press kits, sent to the media, contain photos and details about the movie, i.e., stars' biographies and interviews.

Badge, Ribbon, Gone With The Wind, Clark Gable, Vivien Leigh, 1939, 1 ¾ & 3 ½ In. 2277.00
Costume, Danny Kaye's, The Court Jester, Green Suede, Leather Collar, 1955 . . . . . 1075.00
Figurine, Creature From The Black Lagoon, 1954, 76 In. 2925.00
Game, Scarlett O'Hara, Gone With The Wind, Promotion, Box, 1939 . . . . . 125.00
Herald, Black Magic, Orson Welles, 1948 . . . . . 8.00
Herald, Westworld, Yul Brynner, 1973 . . . . . 8.00
Insert, It's A Wonderful Life, James Stewart, 1946, 14 x 36 In. 8496.00
Insert, Mr. Deeds Goes To Town, Gary Cooper, Jean Arthur, Columbia, 1936, 36 x 14 In. 2360.00
Insert, The Trail Of The Lonesome Pine, Sylvia Sidney, Fred MacMurray, 1936, 14 x 36 In. 415.00
Lobby Card, Bride Of Frankenstein, Boris Karloff, Elsa Lancaster, 1935, 11 x 14 In. 944.00
Lobby Card, Guys & Dolls, Marlon Brando, 1955, 11 x 14 In. 115.00
Lobby Card, Mary Of Scotland, Katharine Hepburn, 1936, 11 x 14 In. 944.00
Lobby Card, Private Life Of Henry VIII, Charles Laughton, 1933, 11 x 14 In. 561.00
Lobby Card, Thin Man, William Powell, Myrna Loy, 1934, 11 x 14 In. 3835.00
Mug, Figural, Bing Crosby, Pipe Forming Handle, Barclay, c.1940, 6 In. 115.00
Photo, Gone With The Wind, Clark Gable, 1939, 8 x 10 In. 863.00
Photo, Jerry Lewis, 1960, 8 x 10 In. 13.00
Photo, The Prince & The Show Girl, Marilyn Monroe, 1937, 8 x 10 In. 64.00
Poster, Bachelor & The Bobby Soxer, Cary Grant, Shirley Temple, 1947, 41 x 81 In. 354.00
Poster, Big Sleep, Humphrey Bogart, Lauren Bacall, 1946, 27 x 41 In. . . . . . *illus* 2124.00
Poster, Breakfast At Tiffany's, Audrey Hepburn, 1961, 1 Sheet 5310.00
Poster, Bus Stop, Marilyn Monroe, 1956, 81 x 40 In. 1534.00
Poster, Century Christmas Number, Louis John Rhead, Color Lithograph, Frame, c.1894, 18 x 12 In. 299.00
Poster, Chinatown, Jack Nicholson, Faye Dunaway, 1974, 27 x 41 In. 295.00
Poster, Demetrius & The Gladiators, Victor Mature, 1954, 27 x 41 In. 118.00
Poster, Dirty Dozen, Lee Marvin, Ernest Borgnine, 1967, 27 x 41 In. 35.00
Poster, Frankie & Johnny, Elvis Presley, Signed, 1966, 81 x 40 In. 826.00
Poster, Help, Beatles, 1965, 1 Sheet, 27 x 41 In. 480.00
Poster, Metropolis, Fritz Lang, Reissue, 1968, 27 x 41 In. 150.00
Poster, Mr. District Attorney, Dennis O'Keefe, Adolphe Menjou, 1947, 27 x 41 In. 143.00
Poster, Night At The Opera, Marx Brothers, 1935, 22 x 28 In. 1298.00
Poster, North By Northwest, Cary Grant, A. Hitchcock, 1959, 27 x 41 In. 1180.00
Poster, One Million Years B.C., Raquel Welch, 1966, 27 x 41 In. 177.00
Poster, Pillow Talk, Rock Hudson, Doris Day, 1959, 27 x 41 In. . . . . . *illus* 240.00
Poster, Psycho, Anthony Perkins, Janet Leigh, Hitchcock, 1965, 1 Sheet 354.00
Poster, Sea Hawk, Errol Flynn, 1940, 27 x 41 In. 9440.00
Poster, Slave Girl, Yvonne DeCarlo, George Brent, 1947, 27 x 41 In. 126.00
Poster, The Bamboo Blond, Frances Langford, RKO, 1946, 27 x 41 In. 143.00
Poster, The Mummy's Curse, Lon Chaney Jr., Linen Backed, 1944, ½ Sheet. 4500.00
Poster, The Ten Commandments, Charlton Heston, 1956, 27 x 41 In. 177.00
Poster, The Wyoming Bandit, Allan Rocky Lane, 1949, 27 x 41 In. 295.00
Poster, Theater, Under The Red Robe, Paper Lithograph, Mat, Glass, Frame, c.1900, 38 x 27 In. 230.00
Poster, Theater, When Knighthood Was In Flower, Plexiglas, Frame, c.1900, 30 x 40 In. 29.00
Poster, This Gun For Hire, Veronica Lake, Alan Ladd, 1942, 27 x 41 In. 30680.00
Poster, Trapeze, United Artists, Burt Lancaster, Tony Curtis, 1956, 27 x 41 In. 472.00
Poster, Vertigo, James Stewart, Kim Novak, Hitchcock, 1958, 27 x 41 In. . . . . . *illus* 4425.00
Poster, Yellow Submarine, Beatles, 1968, 27 x 41 In. 510.00

Poster, Young Frankenstein, Peter Boyle, Gene Wilder, 1974, 27 x 41 In. 71.00
Press Book, A Walk With Love & Death, Angelica Huston, 1968 .... 9.00
Press Book, The Brotherhood, Kirk Douglas, 1969 .... 10.00
Press Kit, The Star Chamber, Michael Douglas, 1983 .... 12.00
Program, Absence Of Malice, Paul Newman, 1981 .... 48.00
Window Card, Mississippi Gambler, Tyrone Power, 1953 .... 46.00
Window Card, Night Of The Hunter, Robert Mitchum, 1955 .... 107.00

MT. JOYE is an enameled cameo glass made in the late nineteenth and twentieth centuries by Saint-Hilaire Touvier de Varraux and Co. of Pantin, France. This same company made De Vez glass. Pieces were usually decorated with enameling. Most pieces are not marked.

Vase, Flowers, Green, Gold Enameled, 12 ¼ In. 225.00
Vase, Frosted Purple, Green, Blue Thistles, Enameled, Bottle Shape, Signed, c.1900, 10 In. 800.00
Vase, Green, Gold Acorns & Leaves Overlay, Goblet Shape, c.1900, 13 ⅞ In. 750.00
Vase, Irises, Enameled, Gold, Signed, L.C., 20 In. 1000.00
Vase, Pansies, Red, Yellow, Violet Stems, Gold Rim, Curved, Tapered, Signed, 1900, 7 In. 650.00
Vase, Purple Flowers, Stems, Leaves, Gold Highlights, 7 ½ In. .... *illus* 420.00
Vase, Purple Iris, Icicle Trim Rim, Bulbous Stove Pipe Shape, Textured, Signed, 8 In. 546.00
Vase, Stemmed Gold Flowers, Flower Border, Textured, Signed, 12 In. 1093.00
Vase, Textured Amethyst, Stemmed Gold Flowers, Cameo, Footed, 6 In. 230.00

MT. WASHINGTON Glass Works started in 1837 in South Boston, Massachusetts. In 1870 the company moved to New Bedford, Massachusetts. Many types of art glass were made there until 1894, when the company merged with Pairpoint Manufacturing Co. Amberina, Burmese, Crown Milano, Cut Glass, and Peachblow are each listed in their own category.

Bowl, Pink Over White, Romanesque Women Medallion, Scrolling, Cameo, 9 In. 403.00
Bride's Basket, Blue Over White, Cameo, Square Ruffled Rim, Footed, 15 In. 891.00
Candlestick, Dolphin, Starch Blue, Clambroth, Sanded, 1845-70, 10 ½ In., Pair .... *illus* 495.00
Carafe, Bedford Cutting, Hobstar Base, Prism Neck, c.1885 .... 295.00
Carafe, Bristol Rose, 8 In. 175.00
Cruet, Pink, White Cased, Stopper, Applied Handle 100.00
Dish, Sweetmeat, Melon Ribbed, Jewels, Silver Plate, Cover, 4 x 5 In. 1300.00
Ewer, Herringbone, Apricot, Satin, White Lining, Applied Camphor Handle, 9 x 6 In. 100.00
Jar, Ivory, Flowers, Flower Lid, Butterfly Finial, 6 In. 425.00
Mustard, Christmas Cactus Blossoms, Pink, Thumb Lift Cover, 4 In. 259.00
Pitcher, Oval, Verse, Rose Frame, 4 ½ In. 1150.00
Salt, Flat Side, Milk Glass, Embossed, Columbian 1893 Exhibition, 1 ¾ In. 136.00
Salt & Pepper, Colonial Ware, Scenic, Snowy Landscape, Country House 86.00
Salt & Pepper, Flowers, Light Blue, Egg Shape .... *illus* 75.00
Saltshaker, Chick, Pink & Yellow Pansies, Metal Head, 2 ¼ In. 374.00
Saltshaker, Ribbed, Blue, Pink Flower 25.00
Shaker, Egg Shape, Green Shaded To Beige, Pansies, Vining, 4 ½ x 3 ½ In. 650.00
Sugar Shaker, Colonial Ware, Shell Mold, Gold Enameled Flowers, 5 In. 230.00
Sugar Shaker, Crosscut Diamond & Fan, Egg Shape, 4 ¼ In. 175.00
Sugar Shaker, Egg Shape, Colonial Ware, Blue & Yellow, Pink Flowers, 4 ¼ In. 100.00
Sugar Shaker, Fig, Blue, White Daisies, Yellow To Peach Shading, 4 In. 863.00
Sugar Shaker, Fig, Custard, Blue & Pink Asters, 4 In. 115.00
Syrup, Bulging Loop, Cream & Blue, Flowers, Silver Plate Top, 4 In. 200.00
Toothpick, Diamond Quilted, Crimped Rim, Applied Yellow Rigaree Trim, 2 In. 805.00
Toothpick, Spider Mum, Yellow, Colonial Ware, Square Rim, 2 ⅜ x 1 ¾ In. 785.00
Vase, Colonial Ware, Guba Ducks, Mauve, Bulbous, Gold Scroll, Handles, 11 In. 2415.00
Vase, Colonial Ware, Pictures Of Venice, Applied Twist Dolphin Handles, 15 ¼ In. 5175.00
Vase, Colonial Ware, Pink Thistles, Leaves, Webs, Squared Gold Rim, 14 In. 920.00
Vase, Lava, Black Ground, Red, Green Shards, Pinched Waist, 6 ½ In. 1093.00
Vase, Lava, Multicolored Shards, Flat Rim, 3 ½ In. 4830.00
Vase, Rose Amber, Scalloped Rim, Bulbous Base, 6 ½ x 4 ½ In. 550.00

MUD FIGURES are small Chinese pottery figures made in the twentieth century. The figures usually represent workers, scholars, farmers, or merchants. Other pieces are trees, houses, and similar parts of the landscape. The figures have unglazed faces and hands but glazed clothing. They were originally made for fish tanks or planters. Mud figures were of little interest and brought low prices until the 1980s. When the prices rose, reproductions appeared.

2 Men Sitting At Table, Books, Pipe, 2 ½ x 2 ¾ In. 16.00
Chinese Man, Signed On Base, 12 x 11 In. 150.00
Chinese Man, Sitting, Book, Basket Of Flowers, 9 ½ In. 66.00

Mt. Joye, Vase, Purple Flowers, Stems, Leaves, Gold Highlights, 7 ½ In.
$420.00

Mt. Washington, Candlestick, Dolphin, Starch Blue, Clambroth, Sanded, 1845-70, 10 ½ In., Pair
$495.00

Mt. Washington, Salt & Pepper, Flowers, Light Blue, Egg Shape
$75.00

TIP

To remove stains from a glass vase, fill it with a mixture of ammonia and water and let it stand for a few hours.

M

Muller Freres, Vase, Blooming Vines, Purple, Green, Ivory, Handles, Signed, 5 ¾ In.
$1080.00

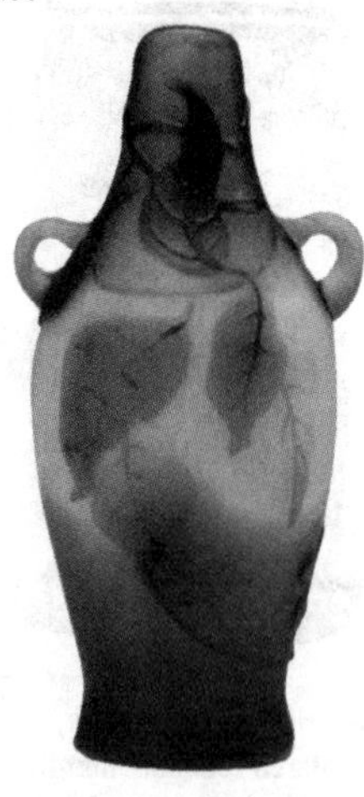

Muller Freres, Vase, Butterflies, Vines, Mottled Yellow, Orange, Black, Cameo, 1900s, 13 In.
$1100.00

Muller Freres, Vase, Trees, Mountain Lane, Chateau, Broken Pine, Egg Shape, 15 ¾ In.
$3740.00

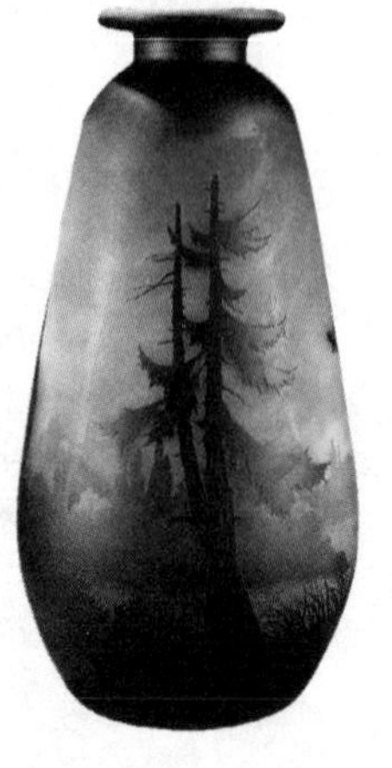

Chinese Man, With Token, Glazed, 20th Century, 23 In. 60.00
Fisherman, Carrying Fish, China, 8 ½ In. 45.00
Fisherman, Kneeling, 5 ¼ x 3 ½ In. 48.00
Fisherman, Kneeling, Reaching In Barrel, Holding Fish, 7 In. 22.00
Oriental Man, Red Robe, Holding Sword, 17 x 7 x 9 In. 25.00
Shalao, Boy, Impressed, 10 ¾ In. 90.00
Woman, Pierced Nose, Eyes & Ears, Blue & Green Glaze, c.1900, 4 ¾ In. 55.00
Woodsman, Chinese, 9 ¼ In. 55.00

MULBERRY ware was made in the Staffordshire district of England from about 1850 to 1860. The dishes were decorated with a reddish brown transfer design, now called mulberry. Many of the patterns are similar to those used for flow blue and other Staffordshire transfer wares.

Cup & Saucer, Flora, Thomas Walker, c.1845 .... 24.00
Cup & Saucer, Jardiniere, Paul Utschneider, 16-Sided, Paneled, c.1891 .... 30.00
Cup & Saucer, Kyber, John Meir, Handleless, c.1870 .... 47.00
Plate, Pelew, Transfer, Ironstone, Staffordshire, 10 In. 75.00
Plate, Vincennes, John Alcock, c.1857, 10 ½ In. 165.00
Platter, Correlia, 8-Sided, Staffordshire, 9 ⅜ x 12 ¼ In. 40.00
Platter, Middle Eastern Scene, Palm Trees, Camels, Marked, Oriental Over WR, 17 In. 300.00
Platter, Rhone Scenery, T. J. & J. Mayer, c.1850, 18 x 14 In. 118.00
Platter, Romantic Scene, Landscape, Scalloped Rim, Staffordshire, 14 ½ x 17 ½ In. 165.00
Platter, Spanish Villa, Oval, Staffordshire, Early 19th Century, 20 ½ In. 250.00
Platter, Transfer, Palm Trees, Camels, People, Oriental WR Mark, 1800s, 17 In. 316.00
Sauce Set, Corean, Podmore Walker & Co., 1840-50, 3 Piece 100.00
Saucer, Chinoiserie, 4 In. 39.00
Soap Dish, Peruvian, John Wedgwood, c.1849, 3 Piece 59.00
Sugar & Creamer, Marked M, c.1855, Miniature 53.00

MULLER FRERES, French for Muller Brothers, made cameo and other glass from about 1895 to 1933. Their factory was first located in Luneville, then in nearby Croismare, France. Pieces were usually marked with the company name.

Bowl, Red Roses, Mottled Amethyst, Yellow, Green Ground, Square Rim, Cameo, 5 In. 920.00
Bowl, Square, Tapered, Art Deco, Signed, 3 ½ x 6 ½ In. 175.00
Chandelier, 4-Light, Dome Center Shade, Sunset, Signed, 28 x 28 ½ In. 1500.00
Chandelier, Art Deco, Hexagonal Bowl, Bird Pattern, Pendants, 36 x 24 In. 649.00
Chandelier, Orange & Blue Shades, Gilt Bronze, France, c.1920, 31 x 20 In. 1770.00
Lamp, Hanging, Rose Petal Shade, Bronze, Cupid, Holding 2 Lights, Signed, 24 x 9 In. 275.00
Vase, Blooming Vines, Purple, Green, Ivory, Handles, Signed, 5 ¾ In. .... *illus* 1080.00
Vase, Brown Forest, Ponds, Orange Ground, 9 ¾ In., Pair 1725.00
Vase, Brown Trees, Green Mountains, Orange Lake, 2 ¾ In. 431.00
Vase, Butterflies, Vines, Mottled Yellow, Orange, Black, Cameo, 1900s, 13 In. .... *illus* 1100.00
Vase, Butterfly, Snake, Enameled, Purple Shaded To Yellow, 6 ¼ In. 1725.00
Vase, Dragonfly, Violet, Cameo, 6 ½ In. 2500.00
Vase, Flowers, Leaves, White Ground, Cameo, Signed, 12 x 4 In. 1760.00
Vase, Landscape, Brown, Frosted, Orange, Cameo, Signed, 3 In. 550.00
Vase, Leaf Branches, Flowers, Ruffled Rim, White, Brown, Signed, 4 x 6 In. 800.00
Vase, Purple Shaded To Peach, Stems, Leaves, Flowers, 15 ¼ In. 1800.00
Vase, Red Flowers, Mottled Blue, Yellow, Oval, Signed, 8 In. 2875.00
Vase, Red Greek Mythology Scene, Shouldered, Cameo, Signed, 8 In. 805.00
Vase, Red Roses, Leaves, Twigs, Cameo, Signed, 1910, 11 ⅝ x 11 In. 2860.00
Vase, Scenic, Enameled, Brown, Gray, Green To Amber Ground, 7 ¾ In. 460.00
Vase, Shouldered, Yellow & Blue Mottled, Red Flowers, Leafy Stems, 7 In. 2185.00
Vase, Silhouetted Forest, Orange Sky, Signed, 7 ⅝ In. 1725.00
Vase, Sparrows, Twigs, Cameo, Signed, 1910, 13 x 11 In. 3000.00
Vase, Stick, Blue, Lake Scene, Trees, Purple Shoreline, Footed, 9 ½ In. 633.00
Vase, Trees, Mountain Lane, Chateau, Broken Pine, Egg Shape, 15 ¾ In. .... *illus* 3740.00
Vase, Vines, Purple, Green, Orange, Ivory, 5 ¾ x 2 ¾ In. 1080.00

MUNCIE Clay Products Company was established by Charles Benham in Muncie, Indiana, in 1922. The company made pottery for the florist and giftshop trade. The company closed by 1939. Pieces are marked with the name *Muncie* or just with a system of numbers and letters, like *1A*.

MUNCIE

Candleholder, Spanish Line, Pumpkin Orange, 3 x 4 In. 125.00
Lamp, Art Deco, Yellow, Green, Square Base, 6 In. 250.00
Lamp Base, Dancing Nudes, Green Matte Over Pumpkin, 10 x 9 In. .... *illus* 295.00
Pitcher, Blue Over Pink, Ruffled Rim, 5 In. 30.00

Vase, Blue, Lavender, Rose Drip Matte Glaze, 6 x 4 In. 100.00
Vase, Classical Shape, Orange, 10 x 5 In. 175.00
Vase, Double Bud, Arch Gate Joining, White Drip To Blue, Gray Base, Mark, 5 x 9 In. 100.00
Vase, Fan Shape, Pink To Green Matte Glaze, 8 x 8 In. 125.00
Vase, Flared Rim, Green, Lavender, Matte, 5 x 6 In. 95.00
Vase, Flowing Blue Glaze, 7 x 5 In. 145.00
Vase, Green Drip Glaze Over Lavender, Square, Rounded Corners, 4 Handles, c.1930, 6 In. 165.00
Vase, Pillow, Tan Drip To Orange Glaze, 2 Handles, 9 x 9 In. 185.00
Vase, Rombic Geometric, Brown, Green, 4 x 6 In. 395.00
Vase, Ruba Rombic, Black High Glaze, 6 x 4 In. 115.00
Vase, Ruba Rombic, Blue Matte Glaze, 4 In. 460.00
Vase, Ruba Rombic, Purple, Green, 6 In. 400.00
Vase, Yellow Glaze, 9 x 4 In. 95.00

MURANO, *see Glass-Venetian category.*

MUSIC boxes and musical instruments are listed here. Phonograph records, jukeboxes, phonographs, and sheet music are listed in other categories in this book.

Accordion, Horner Concerto, No. 3, Red, White, Case 70.00
Banjo, Cheese Box, Homemade, 5-String, Fretless, c.1920, 35 In. .... 660.00 to 705.00
Banjo, Deering, Golden Era, 5-String, Mother-Of-Pearl Inlay Neck, Curly Maple, Case 950.00
Banjo, Dobson, Flapper Girl, Blond Hair, 6-String, Drum Painted, c.1920. .... 400.00
Banjo, Harmony, Roy Smeck, 33 ½ In. 55.00
Banjo, Slingerland Maybell, Tenor, Mother-Of-Pearl Inlay, Open Back, c.1925, 22 In. 191.00
Banjo, Woman's, Black Face Vaudeville, 5-String, Celluloid Pegs, Ivory Inlay, c.1900, 28 In. 411.00
Box, Basket, Birds, Fruit, 2 Butterflies, Revolves, Dome, Stand, France, c.1880, 22 In. 920.00
Box, Brass Cylinder, 8 Tunes, 31 Teeth, Steel Comb, Wood Case, Paris, LM, France 542.00
Box, Cast Silver, Scenes, Instruments, Cherubs, Birds, Germany, 1 ½ x 4 x 2 ½ In. 2875.00
Box, Criterion, Mahogany Case, Double Comb, Plaque, 13 Discs, c.1895, 11 ½ x 27 x 24 In. 4025.00
Box, Crown Shape, Pewter, Jewels, Velvet Lining, Plays Fleidermaus, Thorens, 11 ¼ In. 354.00
Box, Cylinder, Brass, 6 Bells, Lady Of Geneva Watercolor, Wood, 123 Teeth, 30 x 13 In. 2316.00
Box, Cylinder, Grained Case, Mermod Freres, 6 Tunes, Swiss, c.1890, 4 ¾ x 13 In. 708.00
Box, Cylinder, Inlaid Wood Case, Hinged Top, Front, Handles, 12 Tunes, Swiss, 9 x 31 x 11 In. 2478.00
Box, Cylinder, Nicole Freres, Key Wind, 7 ½ In. 2530.00
Box, Cylinder, Rosewood Case, Inlay, 8 Tunes, 3 Bells, Swiss, c.1900, 18 ½ In. .... *illus* 715.00
Box, Cylinder, Zither, Inlaid Case, 10 Tunes, 11 In. 50.00
Box, Dancing Dolls, 15 Key Organ, 10 Tunes, Double Spring Motor, 24 ½ x 9 In. 2844.00
Box, Forte Piccolo, Brass Cylinder, Wood Case, Inlays, 77 Teeth, Swiss, 8 Tunes, 25 x 12 In. 1937.00
Box, Grand Piano Form, Enameled, Austria, 3 x 3 ½ x 5 In. 3217.00
Box, Imperial Symphonion, Double Combs, Mahogany Case, 14 ½-In. Disc 3318.00
Box, Imperial Symphonion, Mahogany, Disc, 27 x 22 x 12 In. 6000.00
Box, Ivory, Carved, Elizabethan Courting Scenes, Key, Bellows, 5 x 2 ¾ In. 1175.00
Box, Ivory, Painted Interior Scene, Plays Viennese Blood Waltz, 2 ⅝ x 6 ½ In. 275.00
Box, Lochmann, 12 Tubular Bells, Base Cabinet, 24 ½-In. Disc 18000.00
Box, Mermod Freres, Mahogany, Carved Feet, Table, 18 In. 5500.00
Box, Mira, Double Comb, Disc Player, Mahogany Case, 22 12-In. Discs, 11 x 22 x 18 In. 3190.00
Box, New Century, Shifter Duplex Comb, 18 ½ In. 15000.00
Box, Nicole Freres, 4 Overture Melody Brass Cylinders, 188 Teeth, Walnut Case, c.1835 .... 10846.00
Box, Nicole Freres, Brass Cylinder, 6 Tunes, 106 Teeth, Swiss, c.1870, 18 x 7 In. 1317.00
Box, Olympia, Double Comb, Oak Case, Disc, 15 ½ In. 1700.00
Box, Olympia, Mahogany, Disc, Inlaid Eagle, 28 In. 28000.00
Box, Olympia, Mahogany, Single Comb, Dome Lid, 15 ½ In. 2800.00
Box, Pianoforte, 2 Piece Comb, Key Wind, Walnut Case, Rosewood Inlay, 17 In. 1541.00
Box, Polyphon, Disc, Inlaid Lid, 11 In. 1650.00
Box, Polyphon, Disc, Rosewood, Coin-Operated, c.1900, 43 In. .... *illus* 3530.00
Box, Polyphon, Glass Door, 20 Discs, Coin-Operated, Germany, 30 ¾ x 43 ½ x 18 In. 2358.00
Box, Regina, Bird's-Eye Maple, Double Comb, Zinc Discs, 15 ½ In. 4200.00
Box, Regina, Bowfront, Glass Door, Gilt, Drawer, Cabriole Legs, c.1900, 60 ½ In. 16380.00
Box, Regina, Double Comb, Mahogany Case, 15 ½ In. 1300.00
Box, Regina, Double Comb, Oak, European Court Scene, 11-In. Disc, 17 x 11 x 15 In. 748.00
Box, Regina, Double Comb, Oak Case, Brass Paw Feet, 45 Discs, 21 x 9 x 19 In. 1380.00
Box, Regina, Double Comb Cylinder, Mahogany Case, Rope Twist Border, Discs, 11 x 21 In. 2300.00
Box, Regina, Double Combs, Oak Case, Double Doors, 20 27-In. Discs, 41 x 75 In. 6221.00
Box, Regina, Dragonfront, Oak, Carved Dragons, Door, 27 In. 23500.00
Box, Regina, Mahogany, Drum, Floor Model, Rookwood Decorated, 14 30-In. Discs 27255.00
Box, Regina, Mahogany, Fan Scroll, Lyre, 26 Discs, 67 ½ x 27 x 22 In. .... *illus* 13200.00
Box, Regina, Orchestral, Upright, Single Play, Style 4, Mahogany Base, 25 27-In. Discs. 22500.00

Muncie, Lamp Base, Dancing Nudes, Green Matte Over Pumpkin, 10 x 9 In.
$295.00

Music, Box, Cylinder, Rosewood Case, Inlay, 8 Tunes, 3 Bells, Swiss, c.1900, 18 ½ In.
$715.00

Music, Box, Polyphon, Disc, Rosewood, Coin-Operated, c.1900, 43 In.
$3530.00

Music, Box, Regina, Mahogany, Fan Scroll, Lyre, 26 Discs, 67 ½ x 27 x 22 In.
$13200.00

Music, Harp, Rosewood, Gilt, Composition, Erard Facateur Du Painos, 1835, 67 x 34 In.
$3800.00

Music, Piano, Player, Baby Grand, Steinway, Style O, Mahogany, 200 Rolls, 58 In.
$6600.00

Music, Piano, Player, Nickelodeon, Organ, Reproduco Coinola, Mahogany, 1900s, 58 x 60 In.
$3930.00

Box, Regina, Serpentine Case, Stained, Double Comb, 68 Discs, 13 ½ x 22 In. 3220.00
Box, Regina, Style 6, Mahogany, Folding Top, Base Cabinet, 27 In.. .... 16000.00
Box, Regina, Tabletop, Mahogany, Double Comb, 7 21-In. Discs, 28 x 13 x 24 In.. .... 2760.00
Box, Regina Corona, Carved Oak, Dragon Front Case, 27-In. Disc Changer. 21850.00
Box, Regina Disc, Double Comb, c.1910, 9 x 18 x 21 In. 1755.00
Box, Rosewood, Faux Grain Paint, Symphonion, 14 Discs, 3 ½ x 6 ½ In.. .... 1150.00
Box, Rosewood, Marquetry Inlay, 12 Tunes, 14 x 31 x 15 In. 3875.00
Box, Singing Bird, 2 Birds, In Cage, Ebonized Wood Cage, 14 In. 475.00
Box, Singing Bird, Cage, Brass, Germany, c.1930, 11 ½ x 6 ½ In. 468.00
Box, Singing Bird, Going-Barrel Movement, Domed Brass Cage, 10 ½ In. 207.00
Box, Singing Bird, Going-Barrel Movement, Enameled Case, Pastoral Scenes, Griesbaum, 4 In. 4444.00
Box, Singing Bird, Grand Piano, Sterling Silver, Marked, 925, 3 ¼ x 6 ½ x 4 In. 4400.00
Box, Singing Bird, In Cage, Germany, 11 In.. .... 633.00
Box, Singing Bird, Red, Black, Brass Perch, Domed Brass Cage, 12 x 6 ½ In.. .... 776.00
Box, Singing Bird, Shell, Etched Brass Lid, 4 x 2 ½ In.. .... 2900.00
Box, Singing Bird, Wings Flap, Triple Bellow Windup, Repousse Metal, KM, Germany, 4 In.. .. 863.00
Box, Singing Birds, Double, Moving Heads, Beaks, Tails, Cage, Bontemps, 19 ½ In. 1541.00
Box, Stella, Double Comb, Mahogany, 10 16-In. Discs, 27 x 12 In. 1898.00
Box, Stella, Mahogany, Acorn, Leaf, Scroll Panel, Disc, 13 ½ x 29 x 22 In.. .... 2970.00
Box, Stella, Upright, Mahogany, Coin Or Manual Operation, 30 26-In. Discs, 78 x 36 In. 16100.00
Box, Sublime Harmony, Nickel Plated Movement, Grained Case, Handles, 34 x 19 In. 3318.00
Box, Upright Piano, Walnut, Henry W. Hill, 20th Century, 12 x 15 ½ x 8 In. 1020.00
Drum, Marching, Metal, Painted Red White & Blue, Wood, Early 1900s, 14 x 14 ½ In. 189.00
Drum, Painted Wood, Black, White, Chinese, 18 x 18 In. 70.00
Drum, Snare, Brass, Wood Rim, Rope Ties, Painted Hoops, 19th Century, 10 ½ x 16 In. 263.00
Fife, Wood, 4 Interlocking Sections, Marked, Firth, Pond & Co., N.Y., 19th Century, 24 In.. ... 100.00
Graphophone, Columbia, Oak, Silver Horn, Type A Cylinder, Crank, Reproducer 1870.00
Harmonica, Hohner Trumpet, No. 222, Paperwork, Box 350.00
Harmonica Holder, Bent Wire, Softwood Supports, Springs, 9 x 7 ½ In. 6.00
Harmony Piccolo, Mermod Freres, Cylinder Box, 4 Cylinders 7700.00
Harp, Carved, Painted Indian Head Column, Leaves, Raven Top, c.1910, 49 In. 2937.00
Harp, Empire, Rosewood, Giltwood, Fluted Column, Anthemion, Lyres, Winged Angels, 67 In. 3600.00
Harp, Gothic Style, Rosewood Veneer, Gilt, Composition, Erard, Louis Philippe, 67 x 34 In.. .. 4370.00
Harp, Rosewood, Gilt, Composition, Erard Facateur Du Painos, 1835, 67 x 34 In. .... *illus* 3800.00
Harp, Rosewood, Sebastian Erard, Patent No. 4596, c.1825 .... 7920.00
Harp, Tiger Maple, Spruce, Gilt, Unstrung, Schweiso & Co., 67 ½ x 33 In.. .... 2100.00
Horn, Tin, Cone Shape, Metal Reed Mouthpiece, Penn., 28 x 4 In.. .... 77.00
Kalliope, Bells, Case, 13 ½-In. Disc 3750.00
Mandolin, Alvarez, Mother-Of-Pearl Inlaid Head, Maple, Spruce Body, Case, 28 x 11 In. 633.00
Mandolin, Cylinder, Lever Wind, 6 Tunes, 17 ¼ In. 2860.00
Mandolin, Gibson Style A, Junior, Sheraton Brown Finish, Oval Hole, c.1925, 26 ¼ In. 1195.00
Melodeon, Rosewood, Beaded, Shaped Stretcher, Lyre Shaped Trestles, c.1860, 29 x 37 In. ... 180.00
Music Rolls, Hupfeld Animatics, 88 Note Scale, Used In Instruments, 22 Piece 1085.00
Nickelodeon, Seeburg, Leaded Glass, Piano, Mandolin, c.1920, 54 x 37 x 23 In. 4023.00
Nickelodeon Pianola, Coinola Cupid, No Keyboard, 10 Tunes, A Rolls, Wood, Chicago, c.1920 2555.00
Orchestration Rolls, Weber UnikaWaldkirch, Black Forest, 15 Piece 1859.00
Organ, Band, 48 Keys, Wilhelm Bruder Sohne, Model 79, Metal Bells, Music Book, c.1921 ... 62500.00
Organ, Band, Wurlitzer, Electric Blower, Mozart Figure, Moving Arms, Head, 125 Rolls 4028.00
Organ, Barrel, 25 Keys, North Tonawanda, Lake Scene 3850.00
Organ, Gem Roller, 4 Cobs, Original Stenciling, 15 x 8 In. 138.00
Organ, Roller, Improved Celestine, Walnut Case, Paper Roll 575.00
Organ, Roller, Wood Cob, See-Through Glass Cover 300.00
Organette, Roller, Mechanical, Paper Roll 325.00
Piano, Baby Grand, Baldwin, Upholstered Stool, Paris, Grand Prix, 1904, 38 x 62 In. 2585.00
Piano, Baby Grand, Steinway, Bench, c.1900, 37 x 70 x 56 In. 8260.00
Piano, Baby Grand, Steinway, Mahogany, c.1912. .... 8625.00
Piano, Baby Grand, Steinway & Sons, Black Lacquered Case, Bench 8400.00
Piano, Coin-Operated Barrel, Dale Forty, Spring Powered, Mahogany Case, England. 958.00
Piano, Coin-Operated Barrel, Magnan Freres, Painted Gondola Panel, France, 51 Key 2324.00
Piano, Grand, Parlor, Steinway, c.1911, 72 x 58 x 39 In. 6900.00
Piano, Grand, Rosewood, Carved Shell, Scroll Legs, Late 19th Century, 94 x 61 In. 4800.00
Piano, Grand, Steinway, Mahogany, Model M, 1918, 67 In.. .... 9400.00
Piano, Grand, Steinway, Model A, Carved, Tiger Oak, Bench, 41 x 82 x 61 In. 37600.00
Piano, Parlor, Burlwood, Gilt Scroll Candle Arms, Klingmann, Germany, 1800s, 59 x 50 In.. . 590.00
Piano, Player, Baby Grand, Ivers & Pond, Ebonized Case, Bench, 24 Rolls, c.1914 .... 1200.00
Piano, Player, Baby Grand, Steinway, Style O, Mahogany, 200 Rolls, 58 In. .... *illus* 6600.00

Piano, Player, Mahogany Foot Pump, Electric Suction Box, 190 Rolls ... 399.00
Piano, Player, Nickelodeon, Organ, Reproduco Coinola, Mahogany, 1900s, 58 x 60 In. ... *illus* 3930.00
Piano, Player, Upright, York Piano Weaver Co., Glass Panels, Door, Electric, 48 x 65 In. ... 660.00
Piano, Steinway, Parlor, Bench, Ebonized, No. 67281 ... 3437.00
Piano Rolls, Great Collection, 88 Note, Classical To Dance Music, c.1920 ... 697.00
Piano Stand, Hepplewhite, Inlaid Mahogany, Tapered Legs, John Broadwood, 35 x 61 In. ... 2645.00
Pianoforte, Alphonse Malignon, Cylinder Box, Key Wind, 17 ½ In. ... 2400.00
Seal, Barrel Operated, Central Wound Top Ring, Lateral Slide Music Control, Gold, Swiss, c.1890 2944.00
Stand, Classical, Mahogany, Brass Mounts, Double Lyre Shape, Adjustable, 52 x 18 In. ... 345.00
Stand, Lyre Form, Brass, Round Foot, 40 In. ... 77.00
Symphonion, Diametric Combs, Walnut Case, Ormolu Handles, 11 ¾-In. Disc, 18 In. ... 1541.00
Symphonion, Harmonie Disc, Case, 13 ⅝ In. ... 5000.00
Symphonion, Longue Marche, Veneer, 8 Tunes, 141 Teeth, 45 x 18 ½ x 11 In. ... 25300.00
Symphonion, Mahogany, Discs, Double Comb, Brass Plaque, 13 ½ x 18 ½ x 17 In. ... 1955.00
Symphonion, Oak, Eroica, Discs, Germany, c.1895, 104 In. ... *illus* 86000.00
Trumpet, Fireman's, Silver Plate, Engraved Ferns, Coral Bells, Hook & Ladder, c.1900, 22 In. 2115.00
Trumpet, J.W. Pepper Perfected, Brass, Leaves, Philadelphia, 1740 ... 234.00
Ukulele, Gibson, Style 1, Case, 24 ½ In. ... 390.00
Ukulele, Kamaka Hawaiian, Pineapple Decal, Canvas Case, 1930s, 21 x 6 x 2 ½ In. ... 495.00
Violin, Bow, Curly Maple Sides, Hand Carved Scroll, Label, c.1800, 23 x 8 In. ... 546.00
Violin, Jofredys Cappa Fecit Salvtvs Anno 1630, 2 Bows, Double Case, 23 x 29 In. ... 8338.00
Violin, John Murdoch, Wood From Ship Orion, Applied Scrimshaw, Bow, Case, 1865, 24 x 8 In. 3819.00
Violin, Maple, Spruce, Label, Berlin, String Inlay, Ebony Tuners, Hardshell Case, 31 In. ... 374.00

MUSTACHE CUPS were popular from 1850 to 1900 when the large, flowing mustache was in style. A ledge of china or silver held the hair out of the liquid in the cup. This kept the mustache tidy and also kept the mustache wax from melting. Left-handed mustache cups are rare but are being reproduced.

Bamboo Style, Yellow Violets, Metallic Gold, Footed, 3 ⅜ x 3 ¼ In. ... 75.00
Barber Pole, Hand Painted, Saucer, Lefton, 3 ½ x 3 ½ & 4 In. ... 45.00
Firefighter, Brothers Of The Brush, Oregon Bicentennial Shield, 1959 ... 19.00
Flowers, Pink, Gold, 3 ½ In. ... 22.00
Gay Nineties, Gold Trim, Enesco, 4 x 3 ¾ In. ... 68.00
Gold Rose Spray, Gold Interior, Saucer, 3 ¼ In. ... 65.00
Hand Painted, Flowers, Blue, Tan Ground, Victorian, 3 ¼ x 3 ½ In. ... 35.00
Husband, Gilt Band, Fancy Handle, Saucer, 3 ½ x 3 ½ & 6 In. ... 145.00
Pink Dogwood, Green Leaves, Scrolled Handle, Nippon, 3 ½ x 4 In. ... 30.00
Pink Luster, Children Picking Cherries, 3 ¼ x 3 ½ In. ... *illus* 35.00
Present, Cobalt Blue, Saucer, 1900s ... 45.00
Roses, Gold Trim, Embossed, 3 x 3 ½ In. ... 39.00
Roses, Swirls, Dots, Bows, Scalloped, Handle, Victorian ... 85.00
Viking, Milk Glass, Laurel Wreath ... 295.00

MZ AUSTRIA is the wording on a mark used by Moritz Zdekauer on porcelains made at his works in Altrolau, Austria, from 1884 to 1909. The mark was changed to *MZ Altrolau* in 1909, when the firm was purchased by C.M. Hutschenreuther. The firm operated under the name Altrolau Porcelain Factories from 1909 to 1945. It was nationalized after World War II. The pieces were decorated with lavish floral patterns and overglaze gold decoration. Full sets of dishes were made as well as vases, toilet sets, and other wares.

Bowl, 3 Cherubs, Fruit, Cranberry Border, Scalloped Rim, 7 ½ In. ... 10.00
Chocolate Pot, Pink Flowers, Gilt, Blown-Out Body, Marked, 10 x 6 ½ In. ... 35.00
Pin Tray, Blue Flowers, Gilt, Oval, Marked, 6 In. ... 10.00
Plaque, Geese In Flight, Gilt Rim, Hand Painted, Signed, A.B. Owen, 1910, 12 ½ In. ... 35.00
Plate, Portrait, Constance, Woman, Flowers, Burgundy, Scalloped Rim, Marked, 9 ½ In. ... 25.00
Plate, Portrait, Woman, Maroon, Green, Gilt, Scalloped Rim, 9 ½ In. ... 35.00
Platter, Pheasant, Flower Border, Scalloped Rim, 17 In. ... 25.00
Tray, Dresser, Flower Garland, Gold Handles, Hand Painted, 6 x 18 In. ... 25.00

NAILSEA glass was made in the Bristol district in England from 1788 to 1873. It was made by many different factories, not just the Nailsea Glass House. Many pieces were made with loopings of either white or colored glass as decoration.

Bowl, Cranberry, Ruffled Rim, Oval, 5 In. ... 173.00
Bowl, Prussian Blue, White Swags, Footed, Tricornered Ruffled Rim, 7 In. ... 431.00
Decanter, Olive Green, White Twisted Splotch, Tooled Mouth, Spout, Handle, 5 In. ... 672.00
Fairy Lamp, Blue, Draped Loopings, Clarke, 4 ¾ In. ... 225.00

Music, Symphonion, Oak, Eroica, Discs, Germany, c.1895, 104 In.
$86000.00

TIP
Never try to play a disc on your music box that was not made for that box. The machine will be damaged and the disc ruined.

Mustache Cup, Pink Luster, Children Picking Cherries, 3 ¼ x 3 ½ In.
$35.00

Nailsea, Fairy Lamp, Red, White Loopings, Ribbed, 11 In. $750.00

Nailsea, Lamp, Kerosene, Rose Verre Moire Shade, Font, 7 ½ In. $1323.00

Nakara, Dresser Box, Pink Roses, Marked, 5 ¼ x 8 ¼ In. $495.00

TIP
Never put a modern collector plate in a dishwasher or microwave oven. The glaze may be damaged.

Fairy Lamp, Blue, Signed, Clarke, 4 ¼ In. 150.00
Fairy Lamp, Blue, White Draped Loopings, Clarke, 4 ¾ In. 225.00
Fairy Lamp, Citron, White Loopings, Clear Cup, Upright Fluted Rim, 5 ¾ In. 300.00
Fairy Lamp, Citron, White Swags, Scalloped Base, 5 In. 719.00
Fairy Lamp, Cranberry, White Swags, Scalloped Base, Mark, Clarke, 5 In. 633.00
Fairy Lamp, Pink, White Loopings, Clarke, Cricklite Mark, 4 ¾ In., 3 Piece 200.00
Fairy Lamp, Red, Draped Loopings, Ruffled Base, Frosted Foot, Clarke, Cricklite, 7 x 8 In. 575.00
Fairy Lamp, Red, White Loopings, Ribbed, 11 In. *illus* 750.00
Fairy Lamp, Rose, Draped Loopings, Clarke, Pyramid Mark, Candle, 3 ½ In. 110.00
Fairy Lamp, Rose, Draped Loopings, Frosted, Fluted Base, 4 ½ In. 150.00
Fairy Lamp, Rose Ground, White Loopings, Clear Base, Fluted Rim, Clarke's, 5 ½ In. 201.00
Fairy Lamp, Yellow, Draped Loopings, Clear Base, Piecrust Rim, Clarke, 5 ½ In. 375.00
Fairy Lamp, Yellow, Draped Loopings, Clear Base, Scalloped Rim, Clarke, 5 In. 375.00
Fairy Lamp Base, Red & White, Ruffled, Tricornered Base, Applied Foot, 8 In. 518.00
Flask, Clear, Cranberry Flashed White Looping, Tooled Mouth, Pontil, c.1870, 8 In. 265.00
Flask, Clear, Ribbed, Red & Blue Splotches, Sheared Mouth, Pontil, c.1870, 8 In. 138.00
Flask, Deep Olive Amber, White Splotch, Tooled Mouth, Pocket, 5 ⅛ In. 392.00
Flask, Free-Blown, White & Green Loopings, Sheared Lip, Pontil, 7 ¼ In. 280.00
Flask, Milk Glass, Cranberry Splotches, Teardrop, Tooled Mouth, c.1870, 7 In. 207.00
Flask, Milk Glass, Red & Blue Loopings, Tooled Mouth, c.1870, 5 In. 242.00
Gemel, Opalescent Looping, Applied Rigaree, Blue Rim, 1800s, 8 ½ In. 144.00
Jug, Deep Olive Green, White Splotch, Applied Double Collar, Handle, Pontil, 5 ½ In. 840.00
Jug, Olive Green, White Twisted Splotch, Tooled Mouth, Spout, Applied Handle, 6 ⅞ In. 476.00
Lamp, Kerosene, Rose Verre Moire Shade, Font, 7 ½ In. *illus* 1323.00
Lamp, Kerosene, Rose Verre Moire Shade, White, Frosted Applied Flowers, 10 ¾ In. 690.00
Pitcher, Green, White Splotch, Pontil, Tooled Rim, Spout, c.1820, 6 In. 748.00
Rolling Pin, Blue & White Pulled Loopings, 15 In. 100.00
Vase, Cranberry, White Loopings, Scalloped & Ruffled Rim, 5 In. 100.00
Whimsy, Bellow Shape, Cranberry, White Loopings, Rigaree, Applied Clear Handles, 1 In. 86.00
Wine, Olive Amber, White Splotch, 3 Coggle Wheels, Sheared, Tooled Mouth, 6 ¾ In. 1344.00

NAKARA

NAKARA is a trade name for a white glassware made about 1900 by the C. F. Monroe Company of Meriden, Connecticut. It was decorated in pastel colors. The glass was very similar to another glass, called Wave Crest, made by the company. The company closed in 1916. Boxes for use on a dressing table are the most commonly found Nakara pieces. The mark is not found on every piece.

Ashtray, Gilt Brass Mounted, Blue, Pink & White Flowers, Marked, C.F. Monroe, 3 x 7 In. 431.00
Biscuit Jar, Cover, Blue, Pink Roses, Bail Handle, 7 ½ In. 2832.00
Biscuit Jar, Wave Crest, Pink, White Daisy Wreath, Bail Handle, 7 ½ In. 2875.00
Box, Painted, Queen Louise, Blue, Ivory, Round, Marked, 8 x 3 ½ In. 2013.00
Box, Painted, Scenic, 2 Women, Pink, Ivory, Round, C.F. Monroe, 7 x 3 ½ In. 1208.00
Dresser Box, Bishop's Hat, Apricot, Painted Flowers, 4 ½ x 4 In. 385.00
Dresser Box, Painted, Green, Square Top, Hinged, C.F. Monroe, 2 In. 270.00
Dresser Box, Pink Roses, Marked, 5 ¼ x 8 ¼ In. *illus* 495.00
Dresser Box, Woman, Garden On Lid, Satin Lining, Marked, 8 x 4 In. 550.00
Fernery, Gilt Brass Mounted, Blue, White & Pink Flowers, C.F. Monroe, 2 ½ x 8 In. 144.00
Hair Receiver, Cream, Floral, Gold Rim, Marked, C.F. Monroe, 2 ¾ x 4 ⅜ In. 435.00
Handkerchief Box, Pink, White Lily, Blown Out Rococo Swirls, 4 ½ x 7 ½ In. 1495.00
Jewelry Box, Gilt Brass, Green, Applied Flowers, Octagonal, C.F. Monroe, 3 ¼ x 4 In. 293.00
Jewelry Box, Gilt Brass, Pink, Blown Out, Round, C.F. Monroe, 4 x 8 In. 878.00
Pin Tray, Gilt Brass, Handles, Footed, Green, 5 x 2 In. 385.00
Tray, Tilt Mirror, Beveled Plate, C.F. Monroe, Late 1800s, 5 x 4 ½ In. 270.00
Vase, Blue Satin Finish, Blue Sailing Boats, Ormolu Feet, Handles, 13 In. 1333.00

NANKING is a type of blue-and-white porcelain made in Canton, China, since the late eighteenth century. It is very similar to Canton, which is listed under its own name in this book. Both Nanking and Canton are part of a larger group now called Chinese export porcelain. Nanking has a spear-and-post border and may have gold decoration.

Compote, Pagodas, River, Blue, Flared Pedestal, Leaves, Lattice Border, 1800s, 4 x 9 ¼ In. 250.00
Compote, River, Pagodas, Flared Pedestal, Leaves, Latticework Border, 4 x 9 ¼ In. 225.00
Gravy Boat, River Scene, Pagodas, 3 ½ x 5 ½ In. 70.00
Plate, Orange Peel Glaze, River Scene, Pagodas, Octagonal, 9 ¼ In. 75.00
Platter, Pagodas, River, Trees, Blue, White, Oval, Diaper Border, 17 ½ x 20 ½ In. 275.00
Platter, Well & Tree, Pagodas, c.1770, 17 ½ x 13 In. 325.00
Tureen, Lid, Pagodas, Houses, Landscape, Blue, White, 8 ½ x 14 In. 365.00

Underplate, House, Boats On Lake, Bridge, Mountains, Reticulated Underplate, c.1760, 9 In. 175.00

NAPKIN RINGS were in fashion from 1869 to about 1900. They were made of silver, porcelain, wood, and other materials. They are still being made today. The most popular rings with collectors are the silver plated figural examples. Small, realistic figures were made to hold the ring. Good and poor reproductions of the more expensive rings are now being made and collectors must be very careful.

Bakelite, Bird, Red 75.00
Bakelite, Elephant, Butterscotch 90.00
Crystal, Blue, Yellow, Green, Amethyst, Hans Turnwald, 2 ½ x 2 ¼ In., 4 Piece 800.00
Pewter, Flowers, Vines, Engraved, c.1850, Pair 185.00
Silver Plate, Figural, 4 Ball Feet, Cast Rose On Top, F. Whiting Co., c.1880, 2 In. 131.00
Silver Plate, Figural, Angel, Blowing Horn, Branches, Leaves, Flowers 86.00
Silver Plate, Figural, Baby Chick, Rustic Base, Triangular, Wilcox Silver Plate Co. 201.00
Silver Plate, Figural, Bakelite, Bird, Green, Yellow, Red, 2 ½ In., 6 Piece 154.00
Silver Plate, Figural, Barrel, Leaves, Crossed Branches, 2 Piece 29.00
Silver Plate, Figural, Bird, Perched On Knife Rest 201.00
Silver Plate, Figural, Boy, Riding Turtle, Middletown Plate Co. 100.00
Silver Plate, Figural, Boy, Sits Pulling Off Sock, Shoes By Feet, Derby Silver Co. 210.00
Silver Plate, Figural, Boy, Stealing Eggs From Nest, Meriden 150.00
Silver Plate, Figural, Brownie, Crawling Over Ring, Oak Leaves, Acorns, Palmer Cox 225.00
Silver Plate, Figural, Brownie, Pushing Ring, Oval Base, Palmer Cox, Marked, Anchor 100.00
Silver Plate, Figural, Cat, Sheet Music, Oval Base, Ball Feet, James W. Tufts 978.00
Silver Plate, Figural, Cherub, Artist, Draped, On Leaves, Branches 288.00
Silver Plate, Figural, Cherub, Butterfly, Leaves, Chains, Ball Feet 175.00
Silver Plate, Figural, Cherub, Glass Vase, Footed Base, Meriden 201.00
Silver Plate, Figural, Cherubs, Holding Painter's Palette, Footed, Hall Elton & Co. 173.00
Silver Plate, Figural, Chick, Pulling Ring On Wheels 288.00
Silver Plate, Figural, Conquistador, Holding Rifle, Toronto Silver Plate 225.00
Silver Plate, Figural, Coral & Shell, Meriden B. Co. 86.00
Silver Plate, Figural, C-Scroll, Flowers, Beaded Band, Wood & Hughes, N.Y., c.1867, 2 In. 120.00
Silver Plate, Figural, Dachshund, Ring On Back, Figural, 4 In. 220.00
Silver Plate, Figural, Deer, Pulling Napkin Ring 690.00
Silver Plate, Figural, Dog, Butterfly 316.00
Silver Plate, Figural, Dog, Pulling Ring On Wheels, Simpson Hall Miller & Co. 518.00
Silver Plate, Figural, Dog, Pulling Sled, Meriden Silver Plate Co. 144.00
Silver Plate, Figural, Dog, With Bucket, James W. Tufts 125.00
Silver Plate, Figural, Dog, With Bucket, Seated By Barrel 144.00
Silver Plate, Figural, Draped Woman On Scroll, Meriden *illus* 100.00
Silver Plate, Figural, Fireman's Helmet, Square Earthen Base, Pairpoint Mfg. Co. 1610.00
Silver Plate, Figural, Foxes, Chasing Bird 115.00
Silver Plate, Figural, Game Bird, Walking, Marked, Meriden Silver Plate 115.00
Silver Plate, Figural, Gargoyle, Hoop, Round Domed Base, Meriden 86.00
Silver Plate, Figural, Goat, Walking, Ball Footed Base, Meriden 259.00
Silver Plate, Figural, Grapes, Over Barrel, Leaf Base, Standard Silver Co. 86.00
Silver Plate, Figural, Greyhound, Seated Next To Ring, Oval Base, Reed & Barton 575.00
Silver Plate, Figural, Halloween Cat, William Rogers Mfg. Co. 259.00
Silver Plate, Figural, Humming Bird, Cutout Base, Van Berg Silver Plate Co. 87.00
Silver Plate, Figural, Hunting Dog, Crouched, Ring On Back, Simpson Hall Miller & Co. 259.00
Silver Plate, Figural, Lamb, Lying, Flat Base, Aurora Silver Plate Co. 144.00
Silver Plate, Figural, Little Red Riding Hood, Reed & Barton 450.00
Silver Plate, Figural, Monkey, Tricornered Hat, Coat, Middletown Plate Co. 50.00
Silver Plate, Figural, Morning Glory Bud Vase, Oriental Fan, Butterfly, Bamboo Leaves *illus* 86.00
Silver Plate, Figural, Mouse, Flowers, James W. Tufts 115.00
Silver Plate, Figural, Mouse With Flower & Vine, James W. Tufts, 1800s 610.00
Silver Plate, Figural, Naked Child & Bird, Flat Base, Meriden B. Co. 403.00
Silver Plate, Figural, Owl, Glass Eyes, Ring Body, Moon, Stars 175.00
Silver Plate, Figural, Owl, On Branch, Aurora Mfg. Co. 86.00
Silver Plate, Figural, Peacock, Long Tail Is Support, Meriden 86.00
Silver Plate, Figural, Rabbit, Crouching, Log, Leaves, Berries, Simpson Hall Miller & Co. 633.00
Silver Plate, Figural, Rabbit, Standing, Leaning On Ring, 4 ½ In. 259.00
Silver Plate, Figural, Rabbit, Standing, Openwork 460.00
Silver Plate, Figural, Rooster, Stands On 3-Tier Base 230.00
Silver Plate, Figural, Rosebud, Hanging, Leaves, Arched Branches 58.00
Silver Plate, Figural, Sitting Hen, Meriden *illus* 288.00
Silver Plate, Figural, Sphinx, Ring On Back, Meriden B. Co. 75.00

Napkin Ring, Silver Plate, Figural, Draped Woman On Scroll, Meriden
$100.00

Napkin Ring, Silver Plate, Figural, Morning Glory Bud Vase, Oriental Fan, Butterfly, Bamboo Leaves
$86.00

Napkin Ring, Silver Plate, Figural, Sitting Hen, Meriden
$288.00

TIP
The English use this old system for cleaning silver: Put the silver in a bowl, cover it with sour milk, and let it stand overnight. Rinse it in cold water the next morning; dry with a soft cloth.

N

Napkin Ring, Sterling Silver, Ships, 3 Amethyst Flags, Stamped, Watkins, 1 ¼ x 1 ¾ In.
$1920.00

TIP

Go to antiques shows early; there may be plenty of antiques left at the end of the show, but the dealers are tired and not as eager to talk to customers.

Nautical, Canteen, Robin's-Egg Blue Paint, Bulbous, Applied Ends, Carved, M, 12 x 6 ½ In.
$550.00

Nautical, Chronometer, Marked, Charles Frodsham, No. 2513, Box, 1860, 5 ½ In. Diam.
$3600.00

Silver Plate, Figural, Squirrel, On Pouch, Maple Leaf, Acorns, James W. Tufts . . . 144.00
Silver Plate, Figural, Stag, Looking Back, Round Base, Fluted Edge, Rockford . . . 745.00
Silver Plate, Figural, Stork, Walking, Ring On Back, Simpson Hall Miller & Co., 4 ½ In. . . . 920.00
Silver Plate, Figural, Triton, Blowing Conch Shell, Rogers & Bros. . . . 600.00
Silver Plate, Figural, Viking, Club, Dog, Diamond Shape Base, Footed, Manhattan Silver. . . . 144.00
Silver Plate, Figural, Winged Cherub, Riding Dolphin . . . 201.00
Silver Plate, Vase, Bud, Black, Scroll Work, White Flowers, Oval Footed Base, Rogers . . . 460.00
Sterling Silver, Banded Oval, Scrolled, Beaded, Georg Jensen, 1 ⅛ In., 12 Piece . . . 1837.00
Sterling Silver, Chased Flowers, Marked, Unger Bros., N.J., c.1900, 2 x 2 In. . . . 538.00
Sterling Silver, Classical Medallion, Floral Repousse, Reeded Band, c.1865, 2 In. . . . 418.00
Sterling Silver, Classical Portrait, Flowers, Leaves, Engraved, Gorham, c.1855, 2 In., Pair . . . 508.00
Sterling Silver, Monogram, Beaded Edges, Embossed Flowers, Early 1900s, 1 ⅜ In. . . . 34.00
Sterling Silver, Monogram, Leaf Pattern, 1 ¾ In. . . . 36.00
Sterling Silver, Ships, 3 Amethyst Flags, Stamped, Watkins, 1 ¼ x 1 ¾ In. . . . *illus* 1920.00
Sterling Silver, Trumpet Bud Shape Top, Birds, Vines, Footed, 1873, 4 ¼ In. . . . 895.00

NASH glass was made in Corona, New York, from about 1928 to 1931. A. Douglas Nash bought the Corona glassworks from Louis C. Tiffany in 1928 and founded the A. Douglas Nash Corporation with support from his father, Arthur J. Nash. Arthur had worked at the Webb factory in England and for the Tiffany Glassworks in Corona.

Bowl, Gold Iridescent, Ribbed, Scalloped Rim, Footed, 6 In. . . . 1900.00
Compote, Chintz, Clear, Green Tint, Red Rim, Purple, 4 x 7 ½ In. . . . 850.00
Vase, Chintz, Cypriot Signed, 7 In. . . . 805.00

NAUTICAL antiques are listed in this category. Any of the many objects that were made or used by the seafaring trade, including ship parts, models, and tools, are included. Other pieces may be found listed under Scrimshaw.

Anchor, Cast Iron, Ring At Top, Black Paint, Early 1900s, 45 In. . . . 353.00
Bell, Ship's, Civil War Ship, Fulton, Pittsburgh, c.1860, 15 In. . . . 2340.00
Bell, Ship's Dolphin Stand, Cast Iron, Dun Rovin, c.1940 . . . 3650.00
Blubber Skimmer, Whale Boat, 98 x 15 In. . . . 2250.00
Bowl, Mess, Sailor's, Pewter, Engraved, Ship & Initials R.C.R., Stamped Boston, 1700s . . . 585.00
Box, Whalebone, Carved, Basket Weave, 1900s, 3 ½ x 3 ¼ In. . . . 550.00
Bridge Telegraph, Brass, 2 Faces, Handles, J.W. Ray & Co., Liverpool, London, 45 In. . . . 1050.00
Bucket, U.S. Lighthouse Service, Boston No. 61, Red, Rope Detail, 17 x 17 x 14 In. . . . 225.00
Cane, Captain's, Cocobolo Shaft, Ivory Knob, Early 1800s, 33 In. . . . 330.00
Canoe, Birch Bark, Octa Style, Ribbed Interior, 3 Thwarts, Pine Paddles, 1930s, 6 Ft. . . . 1150.00
Canoe, Paddle, Lapstrake Construction, Fiberglass Coat, Mahogany, 1930s, 13 Ft. . . . 1840.00
Canteen, Robin's-Egg Blue Paint, Bulbous, Applied Ends, Carved, M, 12 x 6 ½ In. . . . *illus* 550.00
Chest, Pine, Hinged, Applied Molding, Painted, Full Rigged Ship, Dolphins, 16 x 46 In. . . . 1150.00
Chest, Seaman's, Camphor, Brassbound, 13 ½ x 40 ½ x 20 ¼ In. . . . 805.00
Chest, Writing, Captain's, Brass Inlaid, 20 x 10 In. . . . 144.00
Chest, Writing, Captain's, Fitted Interior, 8 x 11 x 20 In. . . . 805.00
Chronometer, Brass, 8-Day Movement, Gimbaled Mahogany Case, Waltham, c.1910, 5 x 5 In. 822.00
Chronometer, Brass, Silver Dial, Chadwick, No. 386, 2 Day, Mahogany Case, 8 x 8 In. . . . 1438.00
Chronometer, Double Cased, Gimbaled Case Marked Kupoba, 1984, 9 ½ x 9 ¾ In. . . . 382.00
Chronometer, Marked, Charles Frodsham, No. 2513, Box, 1860, 5 ½ In. Diam. . . . *illus* 3600.00
Cigar Cutter, Ship's Wheel, Brass, 5 In. . . . 150.00 to 280.00
Clock, Barometer, Compass, Crossed Oars, Sailor's, Wood Base, 10 ½ x 13 ¼ In. . . . 439.00
Clock, Chelsea Clock Co., Chrome, Hinged Bezel . . . 275.00
Clock, Chelsea Clock Co., Constitution Model, Ship's Bell, Silvered Brass Case, c.1987, 9 In. . . . 474.00
Clock, Chelsea Clock Co., U.S. Maritime, Boston Ships, Black, Plastic, 5 In. . . . 225.00
Clock, Desk, Captain's, Trapezoidal Base, Winding Keys, 10 ½ x 8 ½ x 11 ½ In. . . . 6000.00
Clock, Merrill Co., Bronze, Boston, 10 ½ In. . . . 475.00
Clock, Parkinson & Frodsham, Chronometer, Change Alley, London, c.1822. . . . 5610.00
Clock, Seth Thomas, Ship's Bell, Brass, Gilt Spelter, Conn., c.1880, 9 In. . . . 711.00
Clock, Seth Thomas, Ship's Bell, Hinged Bezel, Kelvin White Co., Boston & New York, 7 In. . . . 245.00
Clock, Shelf, Chelsea Clock Co., Ship's Bell, Weighted Brass Case, Silvered Dial, Early 1900s, 7 ¼ In. 444.00
Clock, Shipley, Bronze, Brooklyn, N.Y., 10 In. . . . 600.00
Clock, Ship's Bell, Yacht Wheel On Base, 8-Day, Hinged Bezel, Mahogany . . . 1320.00
Clock, Smith Astral, Ship's Bell, Engine Room, Brass, England, c.1920, 10 In. . . . 205.00
Clock, Waterbury, Ship's Wheel, 5 In. . . . 44.00
Compass, E. & G.W. Blunt, Wood Bowl, Slide-Lid Box, 19th Century, 6 ½ In. Diam. . . . 125.00
Compass, Hardwood Base, Cast Iron, Ballast Balls, 58 x 32 In. . . . 1210.00
Compass, Kelvin & Wilfid, 10 ½ x 15 In. . . . 110.00

Compass, Mariner's, Tell Tale, Printed Card Compass, Brass Case, R. King, N.Y., 6 ¼ In. 2963.00
Compass, Navigation, Brass Case, Engraved Dial, Cover, England, Late 1700s, 16 ¾ In. 598.00
Desk, Captain's, Camphor, Inlaid, Ebony Stringing, Drawers, Chinese Export, 33 x 49 ½ In... 5750.00
Desk, Captain's, Regency, Inlaid Rosewood, Sliding Slant Front, Drawers, 32 x 24 In. 940.00
Dipper, Abalone Shell, Carved Bone Handle, New England, 19th Century, 15 ¼ In. 173.00
Diving Helmet, Copper, Brass Trim, 1900s, 19 x 18 In. 495.00
Diving Helmet, Cylindrical, 3 Glass Panels, Late 19th Century, 15 x 14 In. 770.00
Eagle, From Pilot House, Pine, Carved Boards, Paint Traces, New York, c.1850, 56 x 39 In.... 2468.00
Fid, Bone, Old Patina, 19th Century, 12 ½ In. 770.00
Frame, Sailor's Macrame, Wood Base, Braided Corners, Oval Opening, 26 x 23 In. 3450.00
Half-Model, Alternating Laminations, Pine Backboard, Early 1900s, 9 x 51 In. 920.00
Half-Model, Wood, Blue Paint, 26 ¼ In. 105.00
Harpoon, Darting, Acute Barb, 31 In. 250.00
Harpoon, Darting, Iron, Acute Barb, J Macy Jr., 19th Century, 33 In. 600.00
Harpoon, Darting, Iron, Acute Barb, Marked, Peters, New Bedford, 19th Century, 37 In. 700.00
Harpoon, Double Fluke, Arctic, 19th Century, 35 In. 700.00
Harpoon, Iron, Whaling, Wrought, Signed, Macy, 19th Century, 34 ½ In. 3000.00
Harpoon, Temple Form, Marked, 19th Century, 37 ½ In. 600.00
Harpoon, Toggle, Iron, Acute Barb, 29 In. 400.00
Harpoon, Whaling, Iron, Toggle, Rope Loop, 24 ½ In. 294.00
Harpoon Projector, CC Brand, 19th Century, 38 x 1 ¼ In. 4000.00
Hat, Parade, Sailor's, Tin, Brass Overlay, Jack Tar, Early 1800s, 13 x 15 In. 385.00
Headlight, Mast, Black Metal, Early 1900s, 14 In. 50.00
Lantern, Ship's, Brass, Wood, Glass, 18 x 12 In. 117.00
Lantern, Ship's, Copper, Bail Handle, Brass Mounts, William Harvey & Co., Glasgow, 28 In... 239.00
Lantern, Ship's, Lake Erie, Brass, Cobalt Blue Glass Shade, 13 ½ x 10 ½ x 9 ½ In. 90.00
Lantern, Ship's, Oil, Brass, Alderson & Glyde, Birmingham, England, 1800s, 16 In., Pair 322.00
Lantern, Signal, U.S. Navy, Black Paint, 14 x 10 ½ In. 44.00
Life Preserver, USS W. Va., 1st Div., Fire & Rescue, Red, White, Rope, 1941 .... 1870.00
Life Preserver, USS West Virginia Battleship, BB-48, IWB, Rope, 1941 .... 675.00
Light, Ship's Masthead, Birmingham Engineering Co., England, 12 In. 115.00
Log Book, Nantucket Ship, Manchester, 1871 .... 600.00
Log Book, Whaling, Bark Hiram, E. Phinney Master, New Bedford, 1838-41 .... 2000.00
Model, Ship, 1902 Mackeral Schooner, Variety Of Woods, c.1982, 29 x 6 In. 2370.00
Model, Ship, Bone, Napoleonic Prisoner-Of-War, 19th Century, 16 ¾ x 22 In. 9360.00
Model, Speedboat, Mahogany, Maple Trim, Gas Engine, Carl B. Seaman, 16 x 43 x 12 In. 7475.00
Model, Tether Boat, Ice Racing, Stand, c.1940s, 54 x 48 In. 990.00
Model, USS Constitution, Wood, Cloth, String, Etched Deck, Cannon, 26 x 40 In. 180.00
Octant, C.G. King Instrument Maker, Spencer Browning, Step-Up Box, 19th Century 425.00
Octant, L. Van DerVoodt, Brass, Wood, Signed, 19th Century, 10 In. 550.00
Pond Boat, Carved Wood, Partial Rigging, Linen Sails, Named Henry, c.1900, 48 x 31 In. 646.00
Pond Boat, X Class, William Wadsword, Camden, Maine, 74 x 94 In. 1093.00
Pond Boat, Yacht, Kathleen, Stand, c.1940, 76 x 55 In. 990.00
Pond Boat, Yacht, Shamrock V, Base, c.1950, 47 x 36 In. 440.00
Pond Boat, Yacht, Skylight In Cabin, Stand, England, 1905, 23 x 24 In. 825.00
Sailor's Valentine, Hand Set Shells, 8-Sided, Wood Box, 9 ½ x 2 ½ In. 4025.00
Sailor's Valentine, Woman's 18th Century Shoe Form, Shells, Pearls, c.1880, 3 x 7 In. 120.00
Sextant, Negretti & Zambra, Brass, 7 Filters, Mahogany Box, 1850, 11 In. .... *illus* 430.00
Sextant, Wood Case, Paper Label, A. Hurliman, France, 1920s 275.00
Ship In Bottle, 3-Masted, British Naval Union Jack Flag, Wyeth & Bro., 7½ In. 30.00
Ship In Bottle, 3-Masted, Clipper, Andromeda, 13 In. 130.00
Ship In Bottle, Faux Painted Stand, Small Town Scene, c.1900, 14 x 7 ½ In. 1750.00
Ship Model, see Nautical, model.
Ship's Wheel, Bronze, No. Ed 90282, Handle, 36 In. 300.00
Ship's Wheel, Metal, Wood, 6 Spokes, Turned Handles, 9 ½ In. 29.00
Ship's Wheel, Oak, 8 Spokes, Iron Bound, 44 In. 230.00
Ship's Wheel, Oak, 9 Spokes, Mounted, Early 20th Century, 64 In. 508.00
Ship's Wheel, Teak, 8 Spokes, Brass Hub, 42 In. 145.00
Ship's Wheel, Teakwood, Brass Hub, 24 In. 105.00
Ship's Wheel, Tugboat, Bronze, Brass, 19th Century, 54 In. 550.00
Ship's Wheel, Wood, 8 Spokes, Brass Trim, Ring, Hub, 36 In. 350.00
Ship's Wheel, Wood, Painted, 19th Century, 30 In. 75.00
Ship's Wheel, Wood, Steel, Red Paint, 19th Century, 42 In. 75.00
Sign, American Frigate Constitution, Wood, Painted, c.1885, 23 x 32 In., 2 Piece 2820.00
Spotlight, Brass, Gas Burner, Tripod Feet, Hoffmans, 1910, 9 x 11 ½ In. 200.00
Spyglass, Captain's, Tiger Maple, Brass Fittings, c.1790-1820. .... 550.00
Table, Ship's Wheel, Lantern Base, 36 In. Diam. 200.00

Nautical, Sextant, Negretti & Zambra, Brass, 7 Filters, Mahogany Box, 1850, 11 In.
$430.00

Shell Work
Shell work has a long history. Elaborate floral bouquets, figures, and pictures were made in the eighteenth century, when shell work was an elegant parlor pastime for "genteel" ladies.
"Sailor's valentines," made of framed shell groupings, were souvenirs for travelers to the West Indies and other islands. Shell-covered trinket boxes, pincushions, and souvenir items came into vogue around 1850. Most were made of cardboard covered with plaster of Paris, then decorated with shells, marbleized paper, lithographed scenes, fabric, or mirrors. They took the form of cottages, shoes, miniature furniture, and other imaginative shapes. Shell-decorated souvenirs are still made but differ in style and construction from old ones. Most new shell pieces are made from Pacific Ocean shells rather than West Indies shells.

Netsuke, Boxwood, Tortoise, Signed, 18th Century, 1 ¾ In.
$1007.00

Netsuke, Hardwood, Demon's Head, Movable Jar, Inlaid Eyes, 19th Century, 1 ½ In.
$1304.00

Netsuke, Ivory, Chick, In Cracked Shell, Movable, Signed, Mitsuhiro, 1900s, 1 ¾ In.
$120.00

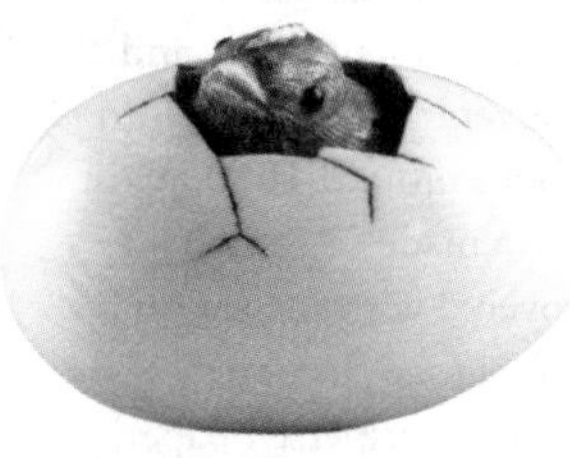

Netsuke, Ivory, Karako, Boy, On Tortoise, Signed, 19th Century, 2 In.
$267.00

Taffrail, Brass, John Bliss Co. 150.00
Tally Slate, Sailor's, Painted, Raised Wood Panels, Star & Compass, 13 x 9 In. 2640.00
Telegraph, Ship's, Brass, Side Lantern, J.R. Ray & Co., 46 x 24 In. 2750.00
Telescope, Harbor Master, T. Evans, London, c.1900 . . . . . . 644.00

NETSUKES are small ivory, wood, metal, or porcelain pieces used as toggles on the end of the cord that held a Japanese money pouch or inro. The earliest date from the sixteenth century. Many are miniature, carved works of art. This category also includes the ojime, the slide or string fastener that was used on the inro cord.

Basket Of Fish, Artist Signed 240.00
Basketry, Brass Chrysanthemum Jump Ring, 19th Century, 2 In. 474.00
Bone, South Sea Islander, Holding Cymbal, 19th Century, 3 ½ In. 326.00
Boxwood, Boy With Mirror, Signed, 18th Century, 1 ¾ In. 176.00
Boxwood, Dragon, Ivory Horns, Whirling, 2 ¼ In. 1185.00
Boxwood, Groom With Horse, 19th Century, 1 ½ In. 237.00
Boxwood, Man On Horseback, Blowing Horn, 19th Century, 1 ¼ In. 178.00
Boxwood, Tortoise, Signed, 18th Century, 1 ¾ In. . . . . . *illus* 1007.00
Elephant, Red, Blue, Aqua Stones, Signed 240.00
Hardwood, Cat, Inlaid Mother-Of- Pearl Eyes, 19th Century, 1 ½ In. 148.00
Hardwood, Demon's Head, Movable Jar, Inlaid Eyes, 19th Century, 1 ½ In. . . . . . *illus* 1304.00
Hornbill, Hen & Chicks, Winnowing Basket, Signed, 19th Century, 2 In. 415.00
Ivory, 2 Monkeys, Giant Peach, 19th Century, 1 In. 711.00
Ivory, 3 Men, Signed, 2 x 2 x 1 In. 200.00
Ivory, 5 Masks, Signed, 19th Century, 1 ½ In. 474.00
Ivory, 10 Figures Fording Stream, Signed, Shunzan, 3 ½ In. 1422.00
Ivory, Arm Wrestling Frogs, Signed, 1 ¾ In. 585.00
Ivory, Bearded Man, Riding Frog, Carved, Signed, 2 ¼ In. 995.00
Ivory, Bird, Nest Of Eggs, Signed, 2 In. 205.00
Ivory, Boar, Sleeping, Leaves, Signed, Masatsugu, 1 ¾ In. 4444.00
Ivory, Boy, Sleeping, 2 x 2 In. 153.00
Ivory, Buddha, Reclining, Rosewood Stand, Signed, 3 In. 175.00
Ivory, Chick, Hatching From Egg, Signed, Early 20th Century, 2 ½ In. 220.00
Ivory, Chick, In Cracked Shell, Movable, Signed, Mitsuhiro, 1900s, 1 ¾ In. . . . . . *illus* 120.00
Ivory, Chick, Peeping Out Of Egg, Signed, 1 ¼ x 1 ½ In. 150.00
Ivory, Cicada, On Leaf Wrapped Log, 19th Century, 2 ⅜ In. 761.00
Ivory, Demon, Under Table With Book, 19th Century, 1 ½ In. 148.00
Ivory, Demon Musician, Dancing Skeletons, 2 ¼ In. 118.00
Ivory, Doll Maker, 1 ½ In. 293.00
Ivory, Dragon, 2 In. 176.00
Ivory, Dragon Turtle, Signed, 1 x 1 ¾ In. 100.00
Ivory, Duck, Preening, 19th Century, 1 ½ In. 119.00
Ivory, Elephant, 1 ½ In. 176.00
Ivory, European, Flageolet, Signed, 19th Century, 4 ⅛ In. 497.00
Ivory, Figure With Tambourine, Child, Signed, 18th Century, 2 ½ In. 474.00
Ivory, Foo Dog, Figure In Mouth, 1 ½ In. 293.00
Ivory, Foo Dog, On Ball, Multicolored, 1 ½ In. 82.00
Ivory, Fox, Dressed As Priest, Carved, Signed, 19th Century, 3 ½ In. 702.00
Ivory, God Of Contentment, Carrying Child On Shoulder, Walking Through Stream, 2 ¼ In. . . 563.00
Ivory, God Of Contentment & Children, Bag Of Wealth, Signed, 19th Century 296.00
Ivory, Hermit Sage, Gnarled Staff, Signed, 19th Century, 3 ¾ In. 1404.00
Ivory, Horse, Grazing, Carved, Japan, 1 ⅞ In. 585.00
Ivory, Karako, Boy, On Tortoise, Signed, 19th Century, 2 In. . . . . . *illus* 267.00
Ivory, Man, Demon Face Shield, Signed, 2 x ¼ In. 100.00
Ivory, Man, Mask Maker, 2 In. 323.00
Ivory, Man, Reclining On Mat, Signed, Minkoku, 2 ½ In. 207.00
Ivory, Man, With Monkey, 18th Century, 2 ½ In. 148.00
Ivory, Man & Child Behind Screen, 1 ½ In. 146.00
Ivory, Man Holding Fan, With Child, 1 ½ In. 117.00
Ivory, Man Pruning Tree, 1 ½ In. 235.00
Ivory, Mandarin Duck, 19th Century 356.00
Ivory, Manju, 19th Century, 1 ¾ In. 585.00
Ivory, Mermaid, Ningyo, 19th Century, 4 ⅛ In. 936.00
Ivory, Mice, Hiding, Signed, 1 ¾ In. 1287.00
Ivory, Monkey, Octopus, 19th Century, 1 ¾ In. 119.00
Ivory, Mouse, In Basket, 19th Century, 1 ½ In. 652.00
Ivory, Okimono, 3 Crying Demons, Signed, Gyokumin, 3 In. 652.00

Ivory, Okimono, 7 Gods Of Luck In Boat, Signed, Masamitsu, 4 ½ In. 830.00
Ivory, Old Man, Carrying Sake Flask, 19th Century, 2 ½ In. .... *illus* 120.00
Ivory, Old Man, Standing, Mother-Of-Pearl Inlay, 19th Century, 1 ½ In. 770.00
Ivory, Pouch Shape, Applied Bronze Bamboo, Signed, 19th Century, 2 In. 234.00
Ivory, Samurai Warrior, 2 In. 293.00
Ivory, Skeleton, Wrestling A Snake, On Human Skull, Signed, 1 ¾ In. .... *illus* 264.00
Ivory, Skull, Snake, Japan, 1 ¼ In. 88.00
Ivory, Tower Of 3 Turtles, 1 ½ In. 118.00
Ivory, Turtle, 5 Babies, Signed, ¾ In. 235.00
Ivory, Warrior, 2 Attendants, Tying Up Demons, Signed, 19th Century, 2 In. 356.00
Ivory, Warrior Fending Off Demons, Signed, 2 ¼ x 1 ⅜ In. 150.00
Ivory, Woman, In Shell, Lying Down, Signed, 2 In. 1404.00
Ivory, Zodiac, Chinese, 1 ¾ x 2 In. 205.00
Magic Pearl, 2 Foo Dogs, Signed 250.00
Porcelain, Man, Standing, 2 ½ In. 119.00
Wood, Dancer Holding Rattle, Lacquered, 19th Century, 1 ¾ In. 504.00
Wood, Dried Salmon, 18th-19th Century, 3 In. 474.00
Wood, Elder With Monkey, 19th Century, 3 ¾ In. 439.00
Wood, Man, Bearded, Rope, 19th Century, 5 ¼ In. 1638.00
Wood, Rat, Glass Eyes, Signed, 19th Century, 1 ½ In. 4095.00
Wood, Wasp Eating Rotted Pear, Signed, Kogetsu, 1 ¾ In. .... *illus* 2015.00

NEW HALL Porcelain Manufactory was started at Newhall, Shelton, Staffordshire, England, in 1782. Simple decorated wares were made. Between 1810 and 1825, the factory made a glassy bone porcelain sometimes marked with the factory name. Do not confuse New Hall porcelain with the pieces made by the New Hall Pottery Company, Ltd., a twentieth-century firm.

New Hall

Bowl, Flower Swags & Sprays, 5 ¾ Diam. 280.00
Cup & Saucer, Flowers, Swags, Pink, Green, Blue, Rust, Black Rim, Marked, Handleless 40.00
Punch Bowl, Chinoiserie, Figures, Flowers, Center Scene In Medallion, 4 ¾ x 11 ½ In. 1200.00
Teapot, Flowers, Pink, Puce, Oval, Ribs, Marked, 19th Century, 6 ½ x 4 x 8 In. 150.00

NEW MARTINSVILLE Glass Manufacturing Company was established in 1901 in New Martinsville, West Virginia. It was bought and renamed the Viking Glass Company in 1944. In 1987 Kenneth Dalzell, former president of Fostoria Glass Company, purchased the factory and renamed it Dalzell-Viking. Production ceased in 1998.

Addie, Cup, Green, Lorelei Lace Etch 25.00
Addie, Cup & Saucer, Amethyst .... 14.00 to 20.00
Addie, Plate, Luncheon, Amethyst, 8 In. .... 12.00 to 13.00
Addie, Sandwich Server, Amber, 14 In. 35.00
Addie, Sugar, Amber 10.00
Addie, Sugar & Creamer, Ruby, Footed 30.00
Addie, Tumbler, 9 Oz. 24.00
Addie, Tumbler, Jade 24.00
Addie, Vase, Fan, Amber, 12-Point Rim, 6 In. 25.00
Addie, Vase, Fan, Green, 12-Point Rim, 11 In. 75.00
Cozy, Decanter, Amber, Clear Stopper, 16 Oz., 6 ½ In. 40.00
Crystal Eagle, Candlestick, 2-Light, Amber, 6 x 7 ¼ In. 45.00
Diamond, Puff Box, Cover, 6 x 4 In. 95.00
Florentine, Console, Flared, 3-Toed, 12 In. 50.00
Georgian, Bowl, Avocado Green, Footed, 5 ¾ x 8 ¾ In. 35.00
Hostmaster, Cup & Saucer, Cobalt Blue 20.00
Hostmaster, Cup & Saucer, Ruby 18.00
Hostmaster, Goblet, Cordial, Amber, 1 ⅞ In. 20.00
Hostmaster, Plate, Luncheon, Cobalt Blue, 8 In. 18.00
Hostmaster, Plate, Luncheon, Ruby, 8 In. 18.00
Hostmaster, Sugar & Creamer, Amber 24.00
Hostmaster, Tumbler, Iced Tea, Cobalt Blue, 14 Oz., 5 ¾ In. 25.00
Hostmaster, Tumbler, Whiskey, Harlequin, 2 Oz., 4 Piece 48.00
Janice, Basket, Blue, Clear Handle, 6 ½ x 9 In. 145.00
Janice, Bowl, Swan, Cobalt Blue Neck & Head, 10 In. 50.00
Janice, Cake Plate, 25th Anniversary, Tab Handles, 11 In. 19.00
Modernistic, Sugar & Creamer, Undertray, Pink, 3 Piece 225.00
Modernistic, Vase, Pink, Peony Etch, 3-Sided, Footed, 8 ½ In. 195.00
Moondrops, Bowl, Roberto Etch, 3-Legged, 9 ¾ In. 195.00
Moondrops, Candlestick, Blue, Lions Etch, Footed, 4 ½ In. 45.00

Netsuke, Ivory, Old Man, Carrying Sake Flask, 19th Century, 2 ½ In.
$120.00

Netsuke, Ivory, Skeleton, Wrestling A Snake, On Human Skull, Signed, 1 ¾ In.
$264.00

Netsuke, Wood, Wasp Eating Rotted Pear, Signed, Kogetsu, 1 ¾ In.
$2015.00

N

New Martinsville, Moondrops, Decanter, Evergreen, 12 x 4 ¾ In.
$795.00

New Martinsville, Oscar, Pitcher, Blue, 9 ⅜ In.
$95.00

New Martinsville, Radiance, Sugar & Creamer, Ruby,
$70.00

Moondrops, Cordial, Amber, 1 Oz. 15.00
Moondrops, Decanter, Evergreen, 12 x 4 ¾ In. *illus* 795.00
Moondrops, Plate, Dinner, Ruby, 9 ½ In. 35.00
Moondrops, Plate, Ruby, 6 ½ In. 12.00
Moondrops, Sugar & Creamer, Amber 28.00
Moondrops, Sugar & Creamer, Amber, Roberto Etch 60.00
Moondrops, Tumbler, Whiskey, Handle, Cobalt Blue, 2 Oz., 2 ¼ In. 19.50
Muranese, Bride's Bowl, Caramel, Yellow To Pink Peachblow, Ruffled Rim, 8 In. 11.00
Muranese, Nappy, Salmon, Ruffled Rim, 6 In. 30.00
No. 18, Dresser Set, Pink, 3 Piece 175.00
No. 18-2, Perfume Bottle, Light Blue, 5 ½ In., Pair 95.00
No. 18-2, Powder Jar, Black & Jade, 5 ½ In. 95.00
Oscar, Pitcher, Blue, 9 ⅜ In. *illus* 95.00
Prelude, Butter, Cover, Oval, 6 ½ In. 40.00
Prelude, Plate, Lemon, 3-Toed, 7 In. 24.00
Prelude, Sandwich Server, Center Handle, 11 ½ In. 40.00
Queen Anne, Dresser Set, Amber, Cologne, Powder Box, 18 ½-In. Tray, 3 Piece 150.00
Queen Anne, Powder Jar, Cover, Pink, 6 In. 45.00
Radiance, Candy Jar, Amber 45.00
Radiance, Condiment Set, Ruby, 5 Piece 225.00
Radiance, Plate, Luncheon, Ruby, 8 In. 20.00
Radiance, Plate, Ruby, 11 In. 55.00
Radiance, Salt & Pepper, Ruby 110.00
Radiance, Sugar & Creamer, Ruby, *illus* 70.00
Rocket, Vase, Cupped Rim, Amethyst, 3-Legged 60.00
Rocket, Vase, Cupped Rim, Clear, Pink, 3-Legged 50.00
Rocket, Wine Set, Cobalt Blue, Clear, Fan Shape Stopper, 9 Piece 350.00
Rocket, Wine Set, Ruby, Clear Fan Shape Stopper, 9 Piece 250.00

NEWCOMB Pottery was founded at Sophie Newcomb College, New Orleans, Louisiana, in 1895. The work continued through the 1940s. Pieces of this art pottery are marked with the printed letters *NC* and often have the incised initials of the artist and potter as well. A date letter code was printed on pieces made from 1901 to 1941. Most pieces have a matte glaze and incised decoration.

Bowl, Band Of Blossoms, Purple Ground, Pink Overglaze, c.1916, 8 In. 840.00
Bowl, Blue, Darker Blue Trim, 4 Raised Points, Sadie Irvine, 1912, 9 ¼ In. 1895.00
Bowl, Daffodils, Alma Mason, c.1914, 2 ½ x 5 In. 1175.00
Bowl, Flower Band, Marked, 2 ⅛ x 5 In. 575.00
Bowl, Pink Flowers, Green Leaves, H. Bailey, 1917, 3 x 6 In. 1095.00
Clock, Mantel, Iris, Sadie Irvine, 11-Jewel Clock Movement, c.1916, 8 ½ x 7 ⅝ In. 30550.00
Coffeepot, Pine Trees, A.F. Simpson, 1909, 10 ¾ x 5 In. *illus* 5100.00
Creamer, Flower Band, Blue, Green, Yellow, High Glaze, Marie Hoa LeBlanc, 3 ½ x 3 In. 1780.00
Creamer, Marie LeBlanc, 1905, 4 x 4 In. 3250.00
Inkwell, Trees, Blue, Green, Yellow Ground, Liner, L. Nicholson, 1908, 2 ½ x 3 ¼ In. 2520.00
Jar, Ali Baba, Bulbous, Turquoise Drip, Orange, High Gloss, Marked, c.1905, 4 In. 593.00
Jar, Bulbous, Blue Upper, Green Lower, Red Clay Body, Matte Glaze, Marked, c.1902, 4 In. 415.00
Jar, Cover, Blooming Dogwood Branches, Blue Ground, Pear Shape, c.1898, 6 ½ In. 3900.00
Jar, Cover, Dogwood Branches, Blue Ground, White, Pear Shape, H. Joor, 1898, 6 ½ In. 3250.00
Jardiniere, Crepe Myrtle Trees, Blue, Blue Green, Yellow, c.1907, 7 ¼ x 9 ¼ In. 21150.00
Lamp, Irises, Bulbous Trumpet Base, Mushroom Shade, Sadie Irvine, c.1916, 19 ½ In. 11750.00
Mug, Box Turtles, C-Handle, Henrietta Bailey, c.1910, 3 ⅞ In. 1410.00
Mug, Dutch Girls, Holding Hands, Olive Dodd, c.1902, 4 ¼ In. 3675.00
Mug, Incised Blue Green Bands, Blue Handle, Glossy Glaze, Marked, 1906, 5 In. 1067.00
Mug, Incised Narcissus, Lily, Blue, Green, Marked, 1907, 5 In. 2015.00
Pitcher, Yellow Flowers, Green Arrowheads, Black Outline, Marked, 1902, 7 In. 1422.00
Plaque, Cottage, Pine Trees, Henrietta Bailey, Frame, 12 ¼ x 8 ¼ In. 10800.00
Plaque, Pine Tree, Blue, Green, Carved, Signed, Henrietta Bailey, 10 x 6 In. 5500.00
Plaque, Pine Trees, Henrietta Bailey, 10 x 6 In. 6600.00
Plate, Blue Incised Freesia Border, Glossy Glaze, Marked, 1909, 8 In. 1007.00
Plate, Flower Border, Blue Green High Glaze, Henrietta Bailey, 9 In. 840.00
Trivet, Vellum Glaze, Spanish Moss Design, Signed, Anna Frances Simpson, 1928, 6 In. 5520.00
Vase, 2 Handles, Calendula, Leona Nicholson, c.1907, 8 In. 9400.00
Vase, Abstract Design, Blue & Green Underglaze, Pinched Neck, Marked, c.1904, 6 In. 9106.00
Vase, Allamanda Vine, Globular, Anna Simpson, c.1927, 9 ¼ In. 5875.00
Vase, Band Of Girl In Dutch Dress Holding Hands, c.1902, 4 ½ In. 3675.00
Vase, Bayou Scene, Oak Trees, Full Moon, Blue, Sadie Irvine, c.1932, 3 ¾ x 4 In. 2400.00

N

Vase, Blossoms, White, Waxy Green Ground, Bulbous, Harriet Joor, 1912, 9 x 3 ¼ In. 3250.00
Vase, Blue, Green Iris Relief, Wide Mouth, Bulbous Base, Marked, 1911, 8 In. 2133.00
Vase, Blue & Green, Matte Glaze, Moon & Moss, Marked, c.1920, 6 ¼ In. 2467.00
Vase, Brown Mottled Drip To Green Glaze, 6 x 4 In. 975.00
Vase, Carved, Moon, Trees, Moss, Blue & White, S. Irvine, 4 x 5 In. 3360.00
Vase, Cherokee Rose, Blue, Green Underglaze, Sadie Irvine, c.1929, 5 ½ x 4 ¼ In. 1175.00
Vase, Coreopsis, Blue, Green, Yellow, Matte Glaze, c.1917, 4 ¼ x 6 ¼ In. 1175.00
Vase, Cream Flowers, Hand Tooled, Blue & Green, Anna Simpson, 1928, 3 ½ x 3 ¼ In. 1750.00
Vase, Crocus, Painted, Flared Foot, Esther Huger Elliot, 1903, 6 ¼ In. *illus* 1010.00
Vase, Daffodil, Blue, Green, Yellow Underglaze, Relief, Squat, c.1913, 6 ¼ In. 2467.00
Vase, Daffodils, Squat, C. Littlejohn, 5 x 5 ½ In. 2040.00
Vase, Daisies, White, Yellow, Green, Blue Ground, Alma Mason, 6 x 4 In. 1300.00
Vase, Espanol, Blue, Sadie Irvine, 1927, 4 ¾ x 5 In. 2300.00
Vase, Flowering Rice Plants, Marked, 6 ½ In. 1495.00
Vase, Flowers, Purple, Yellow, Blue, Sadie Irvine, 1917, 2 ½ x 5 ½ In. 1200.00
Vase, Flowers On Shoulder, Painted, Sadie Irvine, 1924, 5 In. 1725.00
Vase, Forest At Night, Full Moon, Moss Branches, 6 ⅛ In. 5175.00
Vase, Iris, Green, Blue, White, Yellow, Cylindrical, Signed, Henrietta Bailey, 9 In. 3600.00
Vase, Irises, Blue, Green & Pink Underglaze, Squat, c.1926, 4 ¾ In. 4700.00
Vase, Jonquil, Satin Glaze, Blue, Yellow, Green, Sadie Irvine, c.1912, 9 ¾ x 4 ½ In. 3290.00
Vase, Mallow Branches, Blue, Pink, Yellow, Green Satin Glaze, Cynthia, c.1914, 6 ¾ In. 1175.00
Vase, Moon & Moss, Anna Simpson, c.1923, 8 In. 3231.00
Vase, Moon & Moss, Bulbous, Sadie Irvine, c.1927, 7 ½ In. 4112.00
Vase, Morning Glories, Pale Blue, Sadie Irvine, 1910, 7 ¼ x 6 ½ In. 2100.00
Vase, Multicolored Blooms, Sadie Irvine, Squat, c.1917, 2 ½ x 5 ½ In. 1440.00
Vase, Oak Trees, Spanish Moss, Blue, Green, Squat, A.F. Simpson, 1920, 3 ¾ x 5 In. 1200.00
Vase, Oak Trees, Spanish Moss, Carved, A.F. Simpson, 1930, 5 x 5 ½ In. *illus* 3480.00
Vase, Oak Trees, Spanish Moss, Moon, Blue, Tapered, Anna Frances Simpson, 9 x 5 In. 6200.00
Vase, Oak Trees, Spanish Moss, Squat, c.1920, 3 ¾ In. 1440.00
Vase, Paperwhites, Leafy Ground, Alma Mason, c.1913, 5 ½ In. 3600.00
Vase, Pine Trees, Blue, Green, Yellow, Marie De Hoa LeBlanc, 1906, 12 x 5 In. 15000.00 to 18000.00
Vase, Pines Under Full Moon, Blue, Sadie Irvine, 1917, 9 x 3 ¾ In. 6000.00
Vase, Pink Trumpet Flower & Leaf Bands, Blue Ground, Carved, Simpson, 7 In. 1400.00
Vase, Raised Flowers, Pink & Purple Glaze, Marked, Jonathan Hunt, 4 ½ In. 2000.00
Vase, Spanish Moss, Blue, White Moon, Tapered, Wide Mouth, Marked, c.1910, 9 In. 5925.00
Vase, Stylized Oak Trees, Bulbous, Multicolored, c.1905, 5 In. 18212.00
Vase, Stylized Trees, Blue, Green, Yellow, Bottle Form, Rebecca Kennon, 1905, 9 In. 8000.00
Vase, Stylized Trees, Bottle Shape, c.1905, 9 In. 9600.00
Vase, Trumpet Flowers, Pink, Blue, No. 97, A. Simpson, 7 ¼ x 4 In. *illus* 1920.00
Vase, Variegated Arrowhead, Green, White, Pinched Neck, Handles, c.1895, 9 x 7 In. 29375.00
Vase, Water Lilies, Ivory, Yellow, Blue, Green Ground, 2 Handles, 3 ½ x 4 ½ In. 4500.00
Vase, White Blossoms, Waxy Green Ground, Bulbous, c.1912, 9 In. 3900.00
Vase, White Flowers, Hand Tooled, Green Ground, A. Simpson, 1928, 4 x 3 In. 1995.00
Vase, Willow Trees, Blue, Green, White Underglaze, Cylindrical, c.1925, 4 In. 4112.00

NILOAK Pottery (Kaolin spelled backward) was made at the Hyten Brothers Pottery in Benton, Arkansas, between 1910 and 1947. Although the factory did make cast and molded wares, collectors are most interested in the marbleized art pottery line made of colored swirls of clay. It was called Mission Ware. By 1931 the company made castware, and many of these pieces were marked with the name *Hywood.*

NILOAK

Bowl, Mission Ware, Brown, Blue, Rust, Beige, Interior Glaze, 4 x 1 ½ In. 125.00
Vase, Blue, Brown, Cream, Incised, Mid 1900s, 10 ½ In. *illus* 154.00
Vase, Bud, Marbleized, Multicolored, Marked, 8 ¼ In. 92.00
Vase, Marbleized, Blue, Orange, White, Bulbous, 10 x 6 In. 275.00
Vase, Marbleized, Brown, Blue, Cream, Pinched Waist, 10 In. 85.00
Vase, Marbleized, Dark Blue, Orange, White, Early Mark, 9 x 5 In. 250.00
Vase, Marbleized, Multicolored, Tapered, Flared Rim, Marked, 10 x 5 ½ In. *illus* 265.00

NIPPON porcelain was made in Japan from 1891 to 1921. Nippon is the Japanese word for "Japan." A few firms continued to use the word *Nippon* on ceramics after 1921 as a part of the company name more than as an identification of the country of origin. More pieces marked *Nippon* will be found in the Dragonware, Moriage, and Noritake categories.

Bowl, Cartouches, Chrysanthemums, Cobalt Blue Ground, Gilt Trim, 3 x 10 ¼ In. 46.00
Bowl, Footed, Painted Flowers Inside Bowl, 2 x 5 In. 12.00
Bowl, Gold Tapestry Ground, Flowers, Butterflies, 7 In. 80.00

Newcomb, Coffeepot, Pine Trees, A.F. Simpson, 1909, 10 ¾ x 5 In.
$5100.00

Newcomb, Vase, Crocus, Painted, Flared Foot, Esther Huger Elliot, 1903, 6 ¼ In.
$1010.00

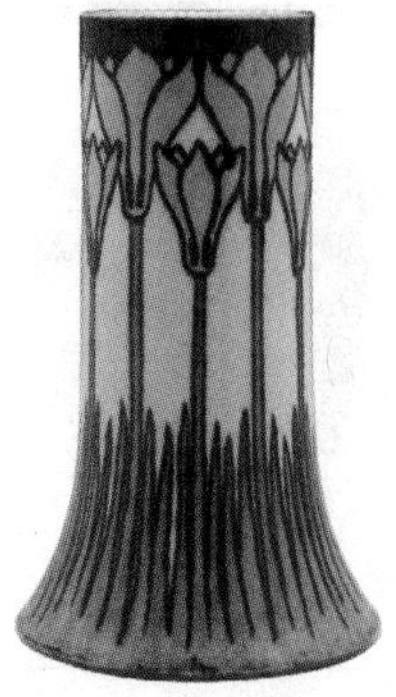

Newcomb, Vase, Oak Trees, Spanish Moss, Carved, A.F. Simpson, 1930, 5 x 5 ½ In.
$3480.00

Newcomb, Vase, Trumpet Flowers, Pink, Blue, No. 97, A. Simpson, 7 ¼ x 4 In.
$1920.00

N

Niloak, Vase, Blue, Brown, Cream, Incised, Mid 1900s, 10 ½ In.
$154.00

Niloak, Vase, Marbleized, Multicolored, Tapered, Flared Rim, Marked, 10 x 5 ½ In.
$265.00

Nippon, Plaque, Cardinal, Portrait, Gilt Border, Green Maple Leaf Mark, 1900s, 9 ½ In.
$9472.00

Nippon, Smoking Set, Trees, Swallows, Green M Mark, 1900s, 10-In. Tray, 5 Piece
$590.00

Chocolate Pot, Flower Bands, Gold Trim, Blue Leaf Mark, 12 ½ In. 90.00
Chocolate Pot, Pink & White Flowers, Gilt, 12 In. 120.00
Chocolate Pot, Violets, Gilt Leaves, Cups, Saucers, 9 Piece 443.00
Fernery, Houses, Island, Figures, Bridge, Lake, 3-Sided, Handles, Rising Sun Mark, 4 x 6 In. 75.00
Hair Receiver, Ivory, Black, Gilt, 3-Footed, 3 ¼ x 4 In. 25.00
Hatpin Holder, Flowers, Gilt, Signed, 4 In. 25.00
Jug, 4 Dancers, Olive Satin Ground, Handle, Stopper, 9 ½ In. 354.00
Match Holder, Dog Scene, Raised Enamel Trim, Attached Underplate, 3 x 5 In. 70.00
Plaque, 2 Buffalo, 10 ¾ In. 384.00
Plaque, 5 Horseheads, Enameled Border, 11 ⅝ In. 472.00
Plaque, Basket, Acorns, Handle, 8 In. 236.00
Plaque, Cardinal, Portrait, Gilt Border, Green Maple Leaf Mark, 1900s, 9 ½ In. *illus* 9472.00
Plaque, Cherry Tree, Mountain Lake, 10 In. 885.00
Plaque, Cows In Stream, Raised Rim, Jeweled Border, 10 ½ x 8 ¼ In. 885.00
Plaque, Dog, St. Bernard, Enameled, Jeweled Border, 10 ¼ In. 708.00
Plaque, Dogs, Collie, Terrier, In Field, 10 ½ In. 384.00
Plaque, Egyptian Sailboat, Enameled Border, 10 In. 354.00
Plaque, Egyptian Scene, Figures Along Nile, 10 ¼ In. 472.00
Plaque, Egyptian Scene, Ostriches, Gilt Border, 10 In. 236.00
Plaque, Elk, Bellowing, Wooded Lake, 10 ¾ In. 325.00
Plaque, Farmhouse, Horse, Cart, Jeweled Enameled Rim, 11 ¼ In. 443.00
Plaque, Indian, On Horseback, Firing Rifle, 10 ¾ In. 384.00
Plaque, Indian Chiefs, 10 ¾ In. 885.00
Plaque, Indian Hunter, Goose, Water Marsh, 10 ¾ In. 1062.00
Plaque, Lion, Lioness, Prowling, 11 ⅝ In. 295.00
Plaque, Moose, Bellowing, Pastoral Scene, 10 ⅝ In. 354.00
Plaque, Mug, Desert Scene, Camel Riders, 10 ¼ & 5 ½ In. 413.00
Plaque, Woman, Horse, Geometric Border, 10 In. 1121.00
Plate, Flowers, Trees, Water, Gold Trim, 10 In. 25.00
Plate, Queen Louisa, Red & Pink Border, Gold & Enamel Jewels, 10 In. 400.00
Plate, Queen Louisa Portrait, Red & Pink Border, Gold, Enamel, Jewels, 10 In. 400.00
Punch Bowl, House, Landscape, Gilt, 12 ¼ x 10 ¼ In., 2 Piece 125.00
Smoking Set, Trees, Swallows, Green M Mark, 1900s, 10-In. Tray, 5 Piece *illus* 590.00
Toothpick, Gold, Flowers 12.00
Toothpick, Scenic 12.00
Urn, Cover, Scenic, Early 20th Century, 30 x 11 In. 4680.00
Vase, 6-Sided, 2 Handles, Green, White Flowers, 11 In. 150.00
Vase, Chrysanthemums, Coralene Beaded, Melon Rib, Satin Ground, 10 In. 2360.00
Vase, Chrysanthemums, Red, Pink, Cobalt Blue Rim, 18 In. 826.00
Vase, Cottage, Flowers, Tapestry, Handle, 7 ½ In. 1180.00
Vase, Flower, Raised Enamel, Handle, 8 ½ In. 153.00
Vase, Flowers, Coralene, Beaded Glass, Magenta Mark, 1909, 8 ½ In. *illus* 880.00
Vase, Flowers, Gold Trim, Beading, 14 ⅞ In. 173.00
Vase, Geese, Gilt, Signed, 12 ½ x 7 ¼ In. 350.00
Vase, Lake, Gilt Scrolled, Jeweled, Black Ground, 14 ½ In. 590.00
Vase, Lake Scene, 4 Reserves, Gilt Arched Handles, 8 ½ In. 590.00
Vase, Mountains, Lake, Gilt, Enameled, 8 ½ In. 266.00
Vase, Roses, Flower Medallions, Raised Gold, White Dots, Handles, Blue Leaf Mark, 6 In. 100.00
Vase, Roses, Red, Yellow, Cobalt Rim, Base, 10 In. 248.00
Vase, Scenic Panels, Trees, Plants, Water, Raised Dot Lines, Gold Trim, 2 Handles, 5 ½ In. 50.00
Vase, Stylized Flowers, Blue Satin Ground, Coralene, Magenta Mark, 1909, 9 In. *illus* 2019.00
Vase, Vase, Seaside Cottage, Gilt Ribbon Handles, 11 ½ In. 266.00
Vase, Water Lilies, Blossoming, Shaded Satin Ground, Coralene, Handles, 12 In. 944.00
Vase, Waterfall, Rocks, Trees, Jewel Gold Trim, Handles, Signed, 12 x 6 In. 110.00
Vase, Woman, Flowing Gown, Doves, Jeweled, Gilt Canopy, 12 In. 885.00

NODDERS, also called nodding figures or pagods, are figures with heads and hands that are attached to wires. Any slight movement causes the parts to move up and down. They were made in many countries during the eighteenth, nineteenth, and twentieth centuries. A few Art Deco designs are also known. Copies are being made. A more recent type of nodder is made of papier-mache or plastic. These often represent sports figures or comic characters. Sports nodders are listed in the Sports category.

Big Boy, Brown Hair, Curl, Red & White Checkered Overalls, 7 ½ In. 275.00
Cat, Chalkware, Yellow, Red, 19th Century, 4 x 8 In. *illus* 3510.00
Chef, Holding Frying Pan & Bird, Bisque, Unger Schneider, Germany, c.1970, 6 In. 88.00

Chinese Man, Sitting, Hands & Head Nod, Dresden Porcelain, 10 x 10 In. 330.00
Dalmation Fire Dog, Red Scarf & Hat, Bell, 5 In. 24.00
Denny Dimwit, Painted, Composition, Box, 10 In. 121.00
Duck, Yellow, Orange Beak, Papier-Mache, Cardboard, Germany, 9 In. 33.00
Elephant, Green Overalls, Pottery, Japan, 1960s, 5 ½ In. 22.00
Elf, Green Hat, Yellow Jacket, Composition, 11 In. 55.00
Girl, Holding 2 Cats Under Arms, White Dress, Cobalt Flowers, Porcelain, c.1920, 5 ½ In. 55.00
Happy Hooligan, Red Coattail Jacket, Blue Pants, Painted, Composition, 8 In. 139.00
Hula Girl, Double, Dancing, Playing Ukulele, Grass Skirts, Composition, Aloha, 5 x 4 In. 182.00
Man Playing Accordion, Exaggerated Eyes, Bowler Hat, Celluloid, Tin Base, Japan, 7 In. 440.00
Monkey, Moving Tongue, Bisque, Painted, Germany, Early 1900s, 4 In. 173.00
Monkey, Wearing Fez, Playing Squeezebox, Porcelain, 1930s, 3 In. 35.00
Mr. Twee Deedle, Oversized Flower Petal Head, Papier-Mache, Early 20th Century, 6 In. 239.00
Nanny Nursing Baby, Bisque, Blue Dress, White Apron & Bonnet, Nods & Sways, 8 In. 10.00
Oliver Hardy, Green Suit, Papier-Mache, Germany, 1930s, 5 ½ In. 66.00
Pinup Girl, Reclining In Chaise, Legs Up, Holding Fan, Fan & Legs Nod, Porcelain, 5 x 3 In. 22.00
Salt & Pepper shakers are listed in the Salt & Pepper category.
Samurai, Sitting, Banko, Japan, 1920s, 3 ¾ In. 110.00
Tiger, Reclining, Glass Eyes, Painted, Composition, 9 ½ In. .... 10.00 to 11.00
Woman, Holding Tea Cup, Green Dress, Ruffled Apron, Porcelain, England, 6 In. 289.00

NORITAKE porcelain was made in Japan after 1904 by Nippon Toki Kaisha. The best-known Noritake pieces are marked with the M in a wreath for the Morimura Brothers, a New York City distributing company. This mark was used until the early 1950s. There may be some helpful price information in the Nippon category, since prices are comparable. Noritake Azalea is listed in the Azalea category in this book.

Ashtray, Clown, Seated, Black, Red, Orange, Green M In Wreath, 6 x 4 In. 225.00
Bonbon, Handle, Flower Design, Gold Trim, 6 ½ In. 22.00
Coffee Set, Chintz, Demitasse, 6 Cups & Saucers, Coffeepot, Sugar & Creamer 92.00
Creamer, Winthrop, Pink Flowers, 2 ⅝ In. 15.00
Cup & Saucer, Starburst, Iridescent White, Royal Blue Band, Gold Trim 33.00
Dresser Box, Cover, Figure Holding Umbrella Finial, 6 In. 150.00
Goblet, Spotlight Ruby, Red, Square Base, Impressed Interverted 8s, 5 x 2 ½ In., 6 Piece 42.00
Gravy Boat, Kilkee 35.00
Gravy Boat, Underplate, Marywood, 10 ¼ In. 50.00
Humidor, Tobacco, Silhouettes Of Woman 500.00
Inkwell, Woman, Gold Dress, Flowers, Luster, Art Deco, 5 In. 200.00
Napkin Ring, Flapper Girl, Red Coat, White Fur Trim, Blue Luster, 2 x 1 ⅝ In. 99.00
Nappy, Yellow Cartouches, Multicolored Flowers, c.1920, 7 ¼ x 1 ½ In. 55.00
Nut Bowl, Chestnuts, 8 In. 118.00
Plate, Dinner, Happy Time, Flowers, Blue, Yellow, Green, Rust, 10 ⅝ In. 14.00
Plate, Salad, Shasta, 7 ½ In. 10.00
Platter, Chelsea, Oval, 13 ¾ In. 30.00
Platter, Croyden, Oval, 13 ¾ x 10 ¼ In. 42.00
Platter, Parkridge, Oval, 14 x 10 ½ In. 40.00
Saucer, Flowers, Peach & Yellow Bands, Blue, Green, Pink, Orange, Gold, 5 ½ In. 5.50
Saucer, Starburst, Iridescent White, Royal Blue Band, Gold Trim 11.00
Shaker, Tree In Meadow, 6 ½ In. 45.00
Soup, Dish, Corsage, 7 ¾ In. 9.79
Sugar & Creamer, Cover, Country House Scene, Lake, 4 & 3 ¼ In. 38.00
Sugar Shaker, Woman, Green Dress, Flowers, Art Deco, 6 In. 400.00
Teapot, Romance 159.00
Toothpick, Tree By The Lake, 2 ½ In. 30.00
Vase, Farmhouse By Lake, Handles, Green M In Wreath, 8 In. 70.00
Wall Pocket, Lady In Garden, Blue Border 350.00
Wall Pocket, Tree In Meadow, Blue Luster 115.00
Wine, Ruby, Square Base, Pressed Interverted 8s, 5 x 2 ½ In., 6 Piece 42.00

NORSE Pottery Company started in Edgerton, Wisconsin, in 1903. In 1904 the company moved to Rockford, Illinois. The company made a black pottery, which resembled early bronze relics of the Scandinavian countries. The firm went out of business in 1913.

Jardiniere, 3 Handles, Black Gloss Glaze, White Markings, 6 x 9 In. 395.00
Jardiniere, Scandinavian Design, Black Gloss Glaze, 8 ½ x 9 In. 325.00
Jug, Sea Serpent Design, Black Glaze, 7 x 5 In. 425.00
Vase, Primitive Scandinavian Design, Black Glaze, 10 x 9 In. 850.00

Nippon, Vase, Flowers, Coralene, Beaded Glass, Magenta Mark, 1909, 8 ½ In.
$880.00

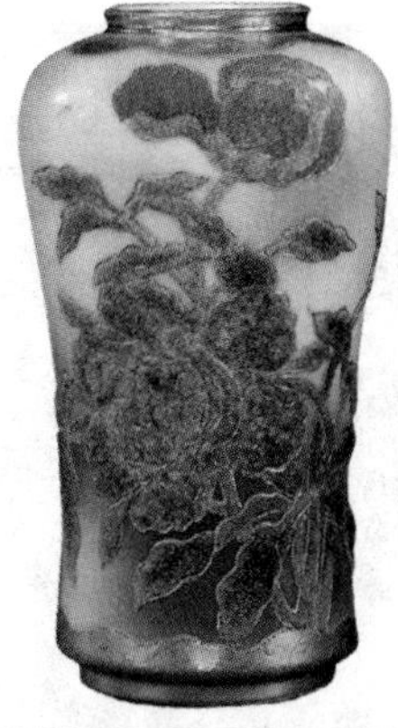

Nippon, Vase, Stylized Flowers, Blue Satin Ground, Coralene, Magenta Mark, 1909, 9 In.
$2019.00

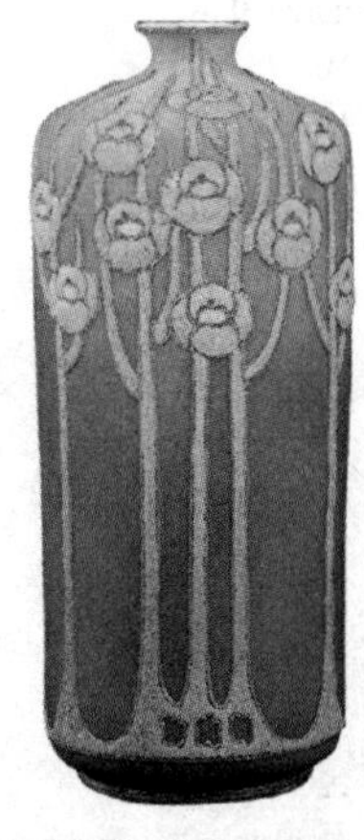

Nodder, Cat, Chalkware, Yellow, Red, 19th Century, 4 x 8 In.
$3510.00

TIP
Don't clean a brass mortar and pestle. It lowers the value.

North Dakota School of Mines, Vase, Painted Flowers, Shouldered Shape, Signed, Huckfield, 11 x 6 In.
$510.00

Northwood, Pull-Up, Vase, Ruby, Coral, Custard Interior, 9 In.
$570.00

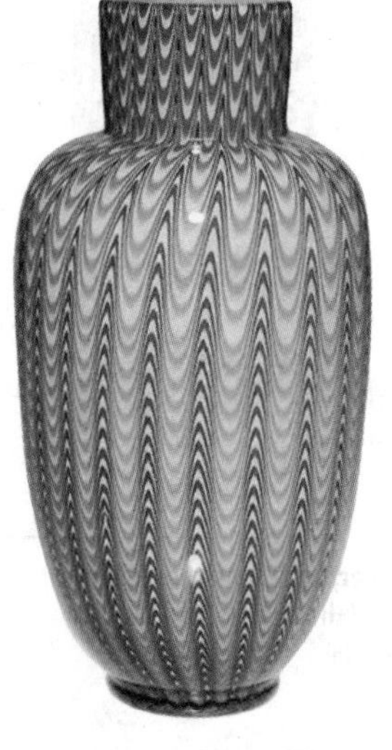

Nutcracker, Squirrel, Cast Iron, Spring Loaded, Tail, Paws, 8 In.
$200.00

NORTH DAKOTA SCHOOL OF MINES was established in 1892 at the University of North Dakota. A ceramic course was included and pieces were made from the clays found in the region. Students at the university made pieces from 1909 to 1949. Although very early pieces were marked *U.N.D.*, most pieces were stamped with the full name of the university.

Ewer, Rose Spout, Gray, White Base, Signed Hagness 58, 15 x 8 In. 200.00
Lamp Base, Lavender Glaze, Signed, 9 x 5 In. 165.00
Vase, Arabian Night Scene, Black, Caramel Ground, c.1930, 7 ¾ x 6 In. 7800.00
Vase, Black Lions, Mustard Ground, 1936, 6 x 5 ¾ In. 5700.00
Vase, Bulbous, Green Mottled, Julia Mattson, 5 x 5 In. 550.00
Vase, Cover, Gazelles, Trees, Indigo, Buff Ground, 1956, 10 ½ x 6 In. 2280.00
Vase, Cover, Red To Blue Glaze, Signed, 8 x 6 In. 545.00
Vase, Cylinder Shape, Green Matte Glaze, Signed, 5 x 9 In. 330.00
Vase, Fish, Swirling Ground, Teal, Green, Gray Glaze, 7 ½ x 8 ½ In. 6000.00
Vase, Fish, Tree Trunk, Blue, Black Flambe Glaze, Bottle Shape, 7 In. 950.00
Vase, Globular, Margaret Cable, 4 ½ In. 805.00
Vase, Iris Panels, Green Glaze, Stamped, L.M. Barlow, 9 x 5 In. 750.00
Vase, Lid, Leaping Gazelles, Blue, Buff Ground, Rimestad, 10 x 6 In. 1300.00
Vase, Light Blue, Yucca, Incised, Margaret Cable, 5 ¾ In. 420.00
Vase, Mauve Flowing To Blue Glaze, Middleton, 1963, 4 x 4 In. 225.00
Vase, Multicolored Stripes, Black Glaze, Incised, 8 x 5 In. 695.00
Vase, Native American Design, 3 x 4 In. 695.00
Vase, Orange Flower, Brown Glaze, 3 x 3 In. 795.00
Vase, Oxen, Wagons, Green Brown Glaze, Huck, 3 x 5 In. 570.00
Vase, Painted Flowers, Shouldered Shape, Signed, Huckfield, 11 x 6 In. .... *illus* 510.00
Vase, Prairie Rose, Light Green, Cream, Margaret Cable, 7 x 6 In. 595.00
Vase, Ribbed Cabinet, Brown Glaze, 2 In. 225.00

NORTHWOOD glass was made by the H. Northwood Co., founded in Wheeling, West Virginia, in 1901 by Harry Northwood. He worked for the Hobbs-Brockunier and LaBelle firms in the 1880s before operating his own glass plants in Martins Ferry, Ohio, and Ellwood City and Indiana, Pennsylvania. At the Wheeling factory, Harry Northwood and his brother Carl manufactured pressed and blown tableware and novelties in many colors that are collected today as custard, opalescent, goofus, carnival, and stretch glass. Pieces made between 1905 and about 1915 may have an underlined *N* trademark. Harry Northwood died in 1919, and the plant closed in 1925.

Aurora, Sugar, Rubina, Ball Shape, 3 ¼ In., 1890s 250.00
Block, Bowl, Whimsey, Cobalt Blue, Opalescent, Ruffled Edge, 9 In. 65.00
Leaf Mold, Toothpick, Yellow, Red & White Spatter 32.00
Pull-Up, Bowl, Yellow, Red Loopings, Oval, Pinched, Ruffled Rim, 9 ½ In. 920.00
Pull-Up, Plate, Shell Shape, Blue Satin, Brown Loopings, 6 In. 690.00
Pull-Up, Vase, Ruby, Coral, Custard Interior, 9 In. .... *illus* 570.00
Pull-Up, Vase, Tan, Purple Stripes, Blue Interior, Marked, Patent, 7 In. 1725.00
Royal Ivy, Lamp, Kerosene, Rubina, Frosted, Nutmeg Burner, 6 ½ In. 518.00
Royal Ivy, Toothpick, Rubina, Satin 125.00
Strawberry, Bowl, Ruffled Edge, Amethyst, Early 20th Century, 9 In. 125.00
Stretch Glass, Bowl, Green, Cupped Rim, No. 714, 4 ½ x 9 ¼ In. 45.00

NUTCRACKERS of many types have been used through the centuries. At first the nutcracker was probably strong teeth or a hammer. But by the nineteenth century, many elaborate and ingenious types were made. Levers, screws, and hammer adaptations were the most popular. Because nutcrackers are still useful, they are still being made, some in the old styles.

Bear, Wood, Carved, Black Forest 90.00
Cat, Wood, Carved, Black Forest 100.00
Coachman, Wood, Carved, Continental, 12 In. 770.00
Dog, Cast Iron, Headlight Stoves & Ranges, L.A. Althoff Mfg. Co., 6 x 11 x 4 In. 110.00
Dog, Collie, Cast Iron, Walnut Base, Ratchet, Nickel Finish, c.1920, 5 In. 288.00
Dog, Standing, Cast Iron, Lift Tail To Open Jaws, c.1900, 5 In. 170.00
Eagle Head, Cast Iron, Feather Handle, Spring Loaded, c.1900, 6 In. 288.00
Elephant, Cast Iron, Art Deco, 1930s, 4 ¾ In. 115.00
Lion, Bronze, Plinth Base, 6 x 7 In. 55.00
Man Riding Horse, Cast Iron, Beetee, 7 In. 14.00
Man's Face, Wood, Carved, 8 ⅛ x 2 ⅞ In., Pair 250.00
Parrot, Cast Iron, Green, Red Crest, 12 In. 44.00
Parrot, Cast Iron, Standing On Platform, Ratchet Action, c.1900, 6 In. 173.00
Skull & Crossbones, Cast Iron, England, Impressed, RD 740410, 6 In. 44.00
Squirrel, Cast Iron, Serrated Teeth, c.1900, 6 In. 173.00

Squirrel, Cast Iron, Spring Loaded, Tail, Paws, 8 In. . . . . . *illus* 200.00
Squirrel, Walnut, Long Eared, Gouge Highlights, Articulated Jaw, Glass Eye, Swiss, 7 In. 44.00
Woman's Legs, Bolted At Hip, Metal, Gold Finish, 5 In. 25.00

NYMPHENBURG, *see Royal Nymphenburg.*

OCCUPIED JAPAN was printed on pottery, porcelain, toys, and other goods made during the American occupation of Japan after World War II, from 1945 to 1952. Collectors now search for these pieces. The items were made for export. Ceramic items are listed here. Toys are listed in the Toy category in this book.

Cachepot, Girl, Resting, Multicolored, 2 ¾ x 4 ¾ In. 13.00
Cachepot, Yellow Duck, 3 ¼ x 4 ¾ In. 13.00
Camera Lighter, Compass, c.1940 . . . . . . 38.00
Candy Dish, Angel Pedestal, Bisque, 4 ¾ x 4 ½ In. 28.00
Creamer, Flowers, Gold Trim, 3 ¾ In. 28.00
Cup & Saucer, Imari, Cobalt Blue, Red, Gilt, 3 ¼ x 2 ⅝ & 1 ¼ In. 48.00
Dish, Trinket, Shell Shape, Scalloped Edge, Painted, Waving Cherubs 50.00
Figurine, Boy, Carrying Birdcage, 5 x 1 ¾ In. 28.00
Figurine, Boy, Carrying Stool, 4 ¾ In. 23.00
Figurine, Boy, Playing Mandolin, 7 ½ In. 25.00
Figurine, Boy, With Umbrella, 3 x 2 In. 13.00
Figurine, Colonial Couple, 2 ⅜ In. 8.00
Figurine, Colonial Couple, 3 ¼ In. 13.00
Figurine, Colonial Man, 5 x 1 ¾ In. 28.00
Figurine, Colonial Man, Sitting In Chair, 3 x 1 ¾ In. 10.00
Figurine, Colonial Man, Sitting On Bench, Flowers, 2 ¾ In. 8.00
Figurine, Dolly Dingle, 4 x 2 In. 40.00
Figurine, Man & Dog, 3 x 2 In. 48.00
Figurine, Man Playing Accordion, 5 In. 30.00
Figurine, Woman, Blue, Yellow Dress, 3 x 3 In. 23.00
Jug, Cowboy Handle, Hanging On Barrel, 5 ¾ x 2 ½ In. 27.00
Planter, Dutch Girl, Seated, 4 ¼ x 3 ¾ In. 15.00
Plate, Center Flower, Leaves, Fluted, Scalloped, 4 ½ In. 8.00
Plate, Forest Scene, 2 Swans In Pond, 7 ¼ In. 35.00
Salt & Pepper, Children, 2 In. 25.00
Salt & Pepper, Nodders, Koi Fish, On Aquarium Sugar Bowl, Porcelain 57.00
Salt & Pepper, Windmills, Blue, White, 2 In. 25.00
Sardine Box, Seashells, Brown, Red, Blue, Gray, 5 x 3 ¾ x 2 ¾ In. 65.00
Serving Bowl, Cover, Yellow, Laurel Leaves, Flowers, 10 ⅜ x 6 In. 32.00
Tea Set, Painted, Flowers, White Ground, Hata China Mark, 11 Piece 75.00
Teapot, Lid, Flowers, 7 ½ x 7 ¼ In. 45.00
Toothpick, Dog, On Front Paws, Glancing Back, 2 ½ x 1 ¾ In. 20.00
Vase, Figurine, Ballerina, White, Burgundy, 8 x 7 x 5 In. 125.00
Vase, Painted, Branches & Berries, Square, Straight Sides, Mark, 12 ¼ In. 15.00
Vase, Painted, Flowers, Pink, Yellow, Purple, Fluted Neck, Gilt Handles, Mark, 10 In. 13.00
Wall Pocket, Parrot On Tree, 5 ¼ x 4 In. 75.00
Watering Can, Flower, Ceramic, 3 ¼ x 6 In. 9.00

OFFICE TECHNOLOGY includes office equipment and related products, such as adding machines, calculators, and check-writing machines. Typewriters are in their own category in this book.

Adding Machine, Locke Adder, 1901 . . . . . . *illus* 369.00
Addressing Machine, Elliot Addressing Machine, Boston, 1925 . . . . . . *illus* 123.00
Calculating Machine, Twin-Odhner Calculator, Double Spokewheel, c.1937 . . . . . . 1860.00
Calculating Machine, 4 Operations, Levers, Mercedes-Euklid, No. 1, Germany, 1905 . . . . . . 1162.00
Calculating Machine, Addo Mod. 2, Feed Rack Adder, Wood Base, Sweden, 1920 . . . . . . 1162.00
Calculating Machine, Arithmometer, No. 1489, Case, Charles Thomas, France, c.1875 . . . . . . 4632.00
Calculating Machine, Arithmometer, Stepped Drum, No. 1788, Case, Germany, 1907 . . . . . . 3098.00
Calculating Machine, Burkhardt-Arithmometer, Wood Case, Brass Emblem, 1878 . . . . . . 3673.00
Calculating Machine, Burrough's, No. 9, 3 Glass Sides, Prints, c.1900 . . . . . . *illus* 308.00
Calculating Machine, Comptator, 9 Digit, Case, 1908 . . . . . . 116.00
Calculating Machine, Eclair, Suresnes Disc, France, 8 In. 465.00
Calculating Machine, Electric, Oak, Ivory Keys, Patent Model, C. Winter, 1859 . . . . . . 46481.00
Calculating Machine, Fowler's Magnum, Manual, c.1915, 4 ¾ In. . . . . . *illus* 154.00
Calculating Machine, Hannovera, Spokewheel, 20 Digit, Germany, 1921 . . . . . . 1210.00

OJ Colors
Experts say the color of the mark on a piece of Occupied Japan china does not indicate age or value.

Office Technology, Adding Machine, Locke Adder, 1901
$369.00

Office Technology, Addressing Machine, Elliot Addressing Machine, Boston, 1925
$123.00

Office Technology, Calculating Machine, Burrough's, No. 9, 3 Glass Sides, Prints, c.1900
$308.00

Office Technology, Calculating Machine, Fowler's Magnum, Manual, c.1915, 4 ¾ In.
$154.00

Ohr, Bowl, Indigo Sponge Glaze, Speckled, Raspberry, Green Interior, Stamped, 2 x 5 In.
$9000.00

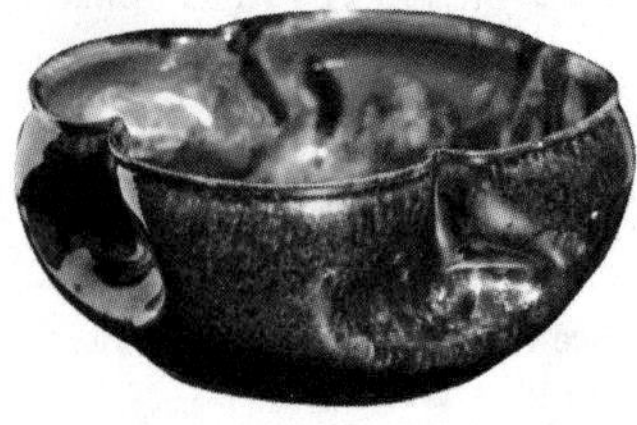

Ohr, Teapot, Gunmetal Brown Glaze, Bulbous, Uneven Rim, Dimple, Stamped, 6 x 8 In.
$4200.00

Ohr, Vase, Ribbon Handles, Mottled, Gunmetal, Amber Glaze, Red, Green Flashes, 8 ¼ In.
$36000.00

TIP
Always put plastic dishes on the top rack of the dishwasher. Test any old dishes to be sure they will not warp or melt in the dishwasher.

Calculating Machine, Original Patent Model, Oak, C. Winter, Ohio, 1859, 11 x 9 In. 4648.00
Calculating Machine, Quixsum Fractional Adding Machine, 4-Disc, 1924, 16 x 6 In. 620.00
Calculating Machine, Stepped Drum, Badenia, St. Georgen Schwarzwald, c.1905 .... 278.00
Calculating Machine, Stepped Drum, No. 229, Case, Label, Germany, 1907 .... 2247.00
Calculating Machine, Thatcher's, No. 1740, Serial No. 773, Keuffel & Esser, 1881, 21 In. 1304.00
Check Writer, Williams Automatic Bank Punch, Wood Box, c.1885 .... 496.00
Cipher Machine, Enigma Type A, Eclectic, 1941.................................... 38734.00
Dictating Machine, Electric, Parlograph, 2 Phonograph Cylinders, Berlin, c.1910......... 1472.00
Stapler, Hotchkiss, No. 2, Staples, Patd. 1896, 2 ¾ x 11 ½ In........................ 195.00
Stock Ticker, Edison, No. 9775, Western Union, Glass Dome, Cast Iron Base, c.1880, 13 In... 9200.00
Stock Ticker Tape Machine, Western Union, Cast Iron Base, Glass Dome, c.1920, 14 x 8 In. 4750.00
United States Check Punch, No. 2171, Box, 1888................................. 697.00

OHR pottery was made in Biloxi, Mississippi, from 1883 to 1906 by George E. Ohr, a true eccentric. The pottery was made of very thin clay that was twisted, folded, and dented into odd, graceful shapes. Some pieces were lifelike models of hats, animal heads, or even a potato. Others were decorated with folded clay "snakes." Reproductions and reworked pieces are appearing on the market. These have been reglazed, or snakes and other embellishments have been added.

Ashtray, Flower Form, Mottled Gunmetal, Green Glaze, Stamped, 1 ½ x 4 ¾ In. 1985.00
Bowl, 4-Lobed, Piecrust Edge, Green Speckled Glaze, Marked, 1 ¾ x 3 ¼ In................ 2880.00
Bowl, Black Glaze, Signed, 3 ½ x 4 In. 977.00
Bowl, Indigo Sponge Glaze, Speckled, Raspberry, Green Interior, Stamped, 2 x 5 In. .... *illus* 9000.00
Cup, Black Olive Green, Mottled Glaze, Redware, 1 ¾ In. 504.00
Hat, Gun Metal & Green Glaze, Marked, 2 ¼ x 4 ¾ In. 1440.00
Mug, Puzzle, Brown Glaze, Holes In Rim, 3 ½ In. 1610.00
Pitcher, Bisque, Folds, Ear Shape Handle, 3 ½ x 5 In.............................. 3240.00
Pitcher, Blue Purple Glaze, Bulbous, Flared Rim, Scroll Handle, Signed, 6 ¾ In............ 6900.00
Pitcher, Yellow & Green Glaze, Signed, 3 ¾ In. 2400.00
Teapot, Gunmetal Brown Glaze, Bulbous, Uneven Rim, Dimple, Stamped, 6 x 8 In. .... *illus* 4200.00
Teapot, Lid, Ear Shape Handle, Serpentine Spout, Green, Brown Flambe Glaze, 7 x 7 ¾ In. .. 7200.00
Vase, 2 Handles, Brown Gunmetal Glaze, 4 x 3 ½ In.................................. 2880.00
Vase, Amber, Sponge Green, Brown Glaze, Oval, Twisted Body, 7 ½ x 3 ¼ In................ 5400.00
Vase, Bulbous, Olive Green, Amber & Rasberry Flambe Glaze, 4 ¾ x 6 In.................. 3240.00
Vase, Cover, Gunmetal Sponged Glaze, Bottle Green, Squat, 3 ¾ x 4 ¼ In.................. 12000.00
Vase, Dark Green Glaze, 6 x 4 ¼ In... 2300.00
Vase, Deep Body Twist, Blue Purple Matte Glaze, Periwinkle, Stamped, 4 ½ x 4 In.......... 6600.00
Vase, Gunmetal Glaze, Textured, Pinched Rim, 3 ½ x 4 In.............................. 3600.00
Vase, Mottled Brown, Crimped Edge, Signed, 2 ½ x 4 ½ In.............................. 2875.00
Vase, Pebbled Matte, Metallic Mahogany, Tapering, Squat, Bulbous, Crimped Rim, 6 x 3 ¾ In. 3120.00
Vase, Pinched Waist, Brown Glaze, Signed, 6 ½ In. 1995.00
Vase, Ribbon Handles, Mottled, Gunmetal, Amber Glaze, Red, Green Flashes, 8 ¼ In. .... *illus* 36000.00
Vase, Twisted, Folded Rim, Black Matte Glaze, 4 ½ In................................ 4500.00
Vase, Waisted Shape, Pinched Rim, Brown, Green Glaze, 6 x 5 In........................ 3900.00

OLD IVORY china was made by the Ohme Porcelain Works in Silesia, Germany, a factory working from 1882 to 1928. The china had an ivory matte background and was usually decorated with flowers or fruit. Dinner sets, fish sets, mustache cups, and souvenir pieces were made. Pieces were marked with a crown, the cipher OH, and the word *Silesia*. Some pieces are also marked with the words *Old Ivory*. The pattern numbers appear on the base of many pieces.

Cake Plate, Silesia Holly Berry, Open Handle, 10 In.................................. 175.00
Cup & Saucer, Green Leaves, Pink Berry Band, 2 ¼ x 4 ¼ In. 19.00
Plate, Roses, 9 In.. 57.00
Plate, Salad, SY77, 7 ⅛ In.. 15.00
Saucer, No. 55, 4 ½ In.. 6.00

OLD PARIS, *see Paris category.*

OLD SLEEPY EYE, *see Sleepy Eye category.*

ONION PATTERN, originally named bulb pattern, is a white ware decorated with cobalt blue or pink. Although it is commonly associated with Meissen, other companies made the pattern in the late nineteenth and the twentieth centuries. A rare type is called red bud because there are added red accents on the blue-and-white dishes.

Bowl, Blue, Shell Shape, Meissen, 8 ¼ In.. 175.00
Bowl, Blue & White, Bavaria, 1920s, 9 ½ In.. 65.00

Candlestick, Blue, Chamber, Meissen, 2 ¾ In. 70.00
Coffeepot, Cover, Blue, Flower Bud Finial, Meissen, 9 ½ x 7 ¼ In. 240.00
Compote, Blue & White, Shaped Foot, Scalloped Edge, Germany, 16 x 9 ½ In. 161.00
Creamer, Blue Danube, Blue & White, 8 In. 19.00
Cup & Saucer, Blue, Scalloped, Meissen, 5 ½ x 2 ½ In. 90.00
Gravy Boat, Blue, Attached Plate, Meissen, 8 ½ In. 117.00
Jar, Cover, Blue, Meissen, 1 ½ x 3 In. 146.00
Jardiniere, Pedestal, Blue & White, 28 In. 120.00
Plate, Blue, Scalloped, Meissen, 8 In. 60.00
Plate, Dessert, Blue & White, c.1890, 7 ½ In., 6 Piece 150.00
Plate, Dinner, Blue, Scalloped, Meissen, 10 In. .... 60.00 to 90.00
Plate, Salad, Blue & White, Blue Danube, c.1951, 8 ¾ In. 7.00
Platter, Blue, Triangular, Meissen, 1 ½ x 9 ½ x 10 ¼ In. 82.00
Platter, Blue & White, Triangular, 9 ½ x 10 ¼ In. 81.00
Platter, Flowers, Blue, White, Scalloped Rim, Oval, Meissen, 9 ½ x 13 ¼ In. 50.00
Platter, Flowers, Blue, White, Scalloped Rim, Tab Handles, Oval, Meissen, 11 ½ x 15 ½ In. 50.00
Platter, Oval, Blue & White, Marked, Meissen, 12 x 16 In. 890.00
Relish, Blue, Handle, Meissen, c.1930, 13 ½ In. 239.00
Teapot, Blue, Flower Bud Finial, Meissen, 5 ¾ x 9 ¾ In. 240.00
Teapot, Blue, Rosebud Finial, Meissen, c.1900, 5 ½ In. 300.00
Teapot, Cover, Blue & White, Rosebud Finial, Meissen, c.1900, 5 ½ x 10 In. 345.00
Tray, Blue, Molded Scrolls, Shells, 2 Handles, Meissen, c.1855, 17 x 17 In. 288.00
Tray, Blue & White, Square, Meissen, c.1890, 7 x 7 In. 115.00
Tray, Scrolls, Cartouches, Shells, Crossed Swords, Meissen, 1860s, 16 ½ In. .... *illus* 288.00
Trivet, Blue & White, Meissen, c.1920, 5 ¾ x 1 ¼ In. 225.00
Tureen, Cover, Blue & White, Signed, Juger, 12 x 9 In. 52.00
Tureen, Soup, Underplate, Blue & White, Meissen, c.1920, 15 x 10 & 16 x 10 ½ In. 1800.00
Vase, Porcelain, Blue & White, Gilt Trim, Signed, 10 ¾ x 5 In., Pair 431.00

OPALESCENT GLASS is translucent glass that has the tones of the opal gemstone. It originated in England in the 1870s and is often found in pressed glassware made in Victorian times. Opalescent glass was first made in America in 1897 at the Northwood glassworks in Indiana, Pennsylvania. Some dealers use the terms opaline and opalescent for any of these translucent wares. More opalescent pieces may be listed in Hobnail, Northwood, Pressed Glass, and other glass categories.

Buttons & Braids, Water Set, Blue, Pitcher, 6 Tumblers 110.00
Coin Dot, Water Set, Blue, Bulbous, 8 ½-In. Pitcher, 3 Piece 143.00
Coinspot, Pitcher, Blue, Flowers, Applied Clear Handle, 5 In. 30.00
Daisy & Fern, Cruet, Blue, Applied Handle, 7 x 3 In. .... *illus* 110.00
Daisy & Fern, Cruet, Blue, Applied Handle, Clear Faceted Stopper, 1890s, 7 x 3 In. 99.00
Daisy & Fern, Sugar Shaker, Cranberry, 4 ½ In. 375.00
Mephistopheles, Mug, Blue, Dragon Handle, c.1890, 3 ⅜ In. 79.00
Opaque Brocade, Sugar Shaker, Canary, 4 ½ In. 200.00
Seaweed, Pitcher, Cranberry Opalescent, 8 ¾ In. .... *illus* 375.00
Tokyo, Compote, Jelly, Blue, 5 x 5 In. 30.00
Tokyo, Dish, Blue, 7 ½ In. 28.00
Tokyo, Pitcher, Blue, 9 x 8 In. 150.00

OPALINE, or opal glass, was made in white, green, and other colors. The glass had a matte surface and a lack of transparency. It was often gilded or painted. It was a popular mid-nineteenth-century European glassware.

Box, Enameled, Hinged, Birds, Flowers, Acorn Finial, Blue, Pink, Yellow, 4 ¾ x 3 ¼ In. 295.00
Box, Green, Crystal Lid, 5 Cupids, 2 Goats, France, c.1890, 4 ½ x 9 x 5 ¾ In. 2100.00
Box, Hinged Lid, Lion, Scrolls, Gilt, Enamel, 19th Century, 5 In. 800.00
Candlestick, Blue, Round Base, 6 ½ In., Pair 250.00

OPERA GLASSES are needed because the stage is a long way from some of the seats at a play or an opera. Mother-of-pearl was a popular decoration on many French glasses.

Aluminum, Case, Marked, Tiffany & Co. 351.00
Blue Guilloche Enamel, Flowers, Silver Fleur-De-Lis, Brass, France, 1800s, 4 In. 300.00
Brass, Tortoiseshell, Blue Silk Lined Leather Case, G. Fisher, Munich, 1800s, 3 ½ In. 235.00
Enamel On Silver, Courting Couple, Leather Case, 4 In. 374.00
Folding, Black Leather, Chrome Trim, Marked Skyline, Red Box, 4 ¼ x 2 ½ In. 39.00
Hammered Silver Plate, Flowers, Bugs, Case, Field, Asheville, No. Car., 1900s, 2 x 4 In. 173.00
Lizard Skin Barrels, Prism Lens, C.P. Goerz, Berlin, Germany, 1902, 4 x 2 ½ In. 150.00
Mother-Of-Pearl, Brass, Le Pert, Leather Case, c.1900, 2 ¼ x 4 In. 117.00

Onion Pattern, Tray, Scrolls, Cartouches, Shells, Crossed Swords, Meissen, 1860s, 16 ½ In.
$288.00

Opalescent Glass, Daisy & Fern, Cruet, Blue, Applied Handle, 7 x 3 In.
$110.00

Opalescent Glass, Seaweed, Pitcher, Cranberry Opalescent, 8 ¾ In.
$375.00

As always, the edited listings in *Kovels' Antiques & Collectibles Price Guide 2010* aren't available on any website, but readers should visit Kovels.com for information on trends, tips, reproductions, marks, old prices, and more!

Orrefors, Vase, Ariel, Cobalt Blue, Amber, Signed, Ohrstrom, 1962, 7 ⅜ In.
$1870.00

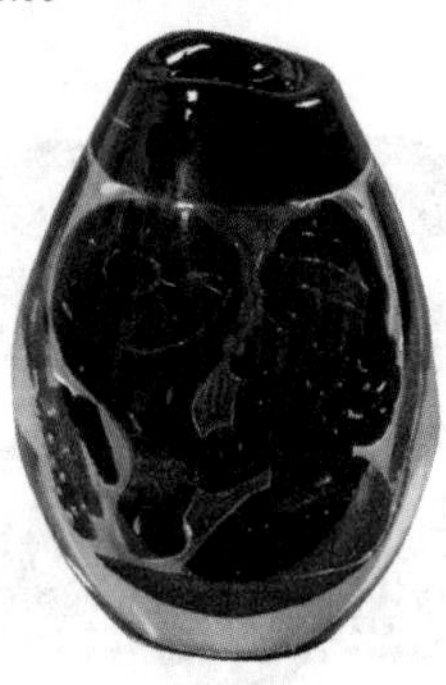

Orrefors, Vase, Smoky Fish Graal, Bulbous, Short Neck, Signed, Ohrstrom, 7 In.
$330.00

Overbeck, Figurine, Dog, Blue, Yellow, Red, Incised, OBK, 3 ¾ x 2 ⅞ In.
$385.00

Overbeck, Vase, Organic Design, Blue & Brown Matte Glaze, Incised, Signed, EF, 7 ½ In.
$8400.00

Mother-Of-Pearl, Brass, Marked, Paris, France, c.1800, 4 In. 60.00
Mother-Of-Pearl, Handle, 6 In. 132.00
Mother-Of-Pearl, Lemoire, c.1900, 3 x 4 In. 409.00
Nacre, Gilt Brass, 19th Century, 4 ¼ x 2 ⅜ In. 25.00

ORPHAN ANNIE first appeared in the comics in 1924. The redheaded girl, her dog Sandy, and her friends have been on the radio and are still on the comic pages. A Broadway musical show and a movie in the 1980s made Annie popular again, and many toys, dishes, and other memorabilia are being made.

Badge, Decoder, Brass, Ovaltine Premium, c.1935, 1 ¼ In. 41.00
Book, Annie & Jumbo The Circus Elephant, Pop-Up, 1935 .... 135.00
Game, Little Orphan Annie, No. 4082, Milton Bradley, 1930s, 12 x 17 ¾ In. 115.00
Nodder, Annie & Sandy, Painted, Bisque, Germany, 3 ½-In. Annie, 1-In. Sandy 235.00
Pin, Portrait, Annie In Winter Outfit, Some Swell Sweater, 1928, 1 ¼ In. 98.00
Toy, Orphan Annie, Jumps Rope, Tin Lithograph, Windup, Marx, Box, 8 In. 550.00
Toy, Sandy, Tin, Key Wind, 4 x 5 In. 90.00
Toy, Sandy, Walker, Tin Lithograph, Windup, Marx, Box 88.00
Toy, Sandy, Walks With Valise, Paperboard Doghouse, Windup, Marx. 650.00
Toy, Sandy's Doghouse, Tin Lithograph, Steel, Lever, Box, 8 In. 250.00
Toy, Stove, Green, Yellow, Pressed Steel, Electric, 1930s, 8 ½ x 9 In. 110.00
Wristwatch, New Haven, 1935, 4 x 7 x 1 In. 222.00

ORREFORS Glassworks, located in the Swedish province of Smaaland, was established in 1898. The company is still making glass for use on the table or as decorations. There is renewed interest in the glass made in the modern styles of the 1940s and 1950s. In 1990, the company merged with Kosta Boda. Most vases and decorative pieces are signed with the etched name *Orrefors*.

Orrefors

Bowl, Blue, Allover Frit, 2 ⅞ x 5 ¼ In. 22.00
Bowl, Clear, 4-Footed, 4 x 11 In. 41.00
Bowl, Cut Art Glass, 9 Panels, Signed, c.1930, 9 x 6 In. 250.00
Chalice, Alternating Bands, Yellow & Blue, Signed, Cyren, 7 ¼ In. 805.00
Decanter, Clear, Cut Stopper, Double Spout, 11 x 3 In. 125.00
Decanter, Clear, Flattened Stopper, 1 In. 41.00
Decanter, Folded Hands Holding Nude Women, Etched, 16 In. 819.00
Decanter, Marine & Sailor Scenes, Engraved, Clear, Flattened, Signed, Landberg, 1938, 10 ½ In. 250.00
Figurine, Elephant, Clear, 3 ½ & 6 ½ In., Pair 117.00
Figurine, Rabbit, Clear, Signed, 3 x 5 In. 20.00
Vase, Ariel, Cobalt Blue, Amber, Signed, Ohrstrom, 1962, 7 ⅜ In. .... *illus* 1870.00
Vase, Blossom Shape, Clear, 4 x 5 In. 175.00
Vase, Blue To Green, 13 In. 351.00
Vase, Bud, Fish Graal, Green Interior Scene, Signed, c.1950, 6 ½ x 5 In. 351.00
Vase, Fish Graal, Swimming, Oval, Signed, Edvard Hald, 6 In. 600.00
Vase, Fish Graal, Underwater Landscape, Black Fish, Starfish, Oval, Signed, E. Hald, 6 ¼ In. .. 500.00
Vase, Fish Graal, Underwater Landscape, Brown Fish, Plants, Bowl Form, Signed, E. Hald, 4 x 8 In. 425.00
Vase, Flying Geese, Engraved, Clear, Signed, 7 ¾ In. 25.00
Vase, Green, White Stripe, Clear Base, Signed, F.M.V. Johannsson, 9 ¾ In. 120.00
Vase, Smoky Fish Graal, Bulbous, Short Neck, Signed, Ohrstrom, 7 In. .... *illus* 330.00
Vase, Underwater Scene, Diving Figure, Engraved, Clear, 6 x 7 In. 450.00

OTT & BREWER Company operated the Etruria Pottery at Trenton, New Jersey, from 1871 to 1892. It started making belleek in 1882. The firm used a variety of marks that incorporated the initials *O & B*.

Bust, Parian, Elaine, Signed, Isaac Broome, c.1876, 15 x 9 ½ In. 4200.00
Cup & Saucer, Light Green, Pink Interior, New Orleans Exposition, c.1885, 2 x 6 In. 546.00
Sugar & Creamer, Pink Flowers, Green Leaves, Belleek, Signed, 2 x 4 ⅜ & 3 In. 144.00
Vase, Gilt, Gilded Branch Handles, Applied Pierce Vase, Belleek, 9 ¼ In. 633.00

OVERBECK pottery was made by four sisters named Overbeck at a pottery in Cambridge City, Indiana. They started in 1911. They made all types of vases, each one-of-a-kind. Small, hand-modeled figurines are the most popular pieces with today's collectors. The factory continued until 1955, when the last of the four sisters died.

Figurine, Dog, Blue, Yellow, Red, Incised, OBK, 3 ¾ x 2 ⅞ In. .... *illus* 385.00
Pitcher, Blue, Gray Stylized Trees, Brown Matte Ground, 4 ¾ x 9 ½ In. 3120.00
Vase, Fierce Blue Jays, Carved, Blue & Green Matte Glaze, 8 ½ In. 8287.00
Vase, Flowers, Bees, Green, Blue, 2 x 6 ½ In. 460.00

Vase, Organic Design, Blue & Brown Matte Glaze, Incised, Signed, EF, 7 ½ In. .... *illus* 8400.00
Vase, Stylized Birds, Branches, Raspberry Ground, Incised, OBK E F, 7 x 4 In. .... *illus* 4800.00

OWENS Pottery was made in Zanesville, Ohio, from 1891 to 1928. The first art pottery was made after 1896. Utopian Ware, Cyrano, Navarre, Feroza, and Henri Deux were made. Pieces were usually marked with a form of the name Owens. About 1907, the firm began to make tile and discontinued the art pottery wares.

Ewer, Dandelions, Brown Glaze, Yellow, White Flowers, H. Larzelere, 7 x 4 In.. .... 245.00
Ewer, Utopian, Flowers, Silver Overlay, Marked 773, Signed, 6 ½ In. 720.00
Jardiniere, Pedestal, 3 Eagles, Flowers, Leaves, Radford, 32 x 17 In. 115.00
Jardiniere, Pedestal, Women, Henri Deux, Art Nouveau, 26 ¼ In. .... *illus* 1980.00
Jardiniere, Utopian, Tulips, Blue Matte, White, 7 ⅝ x 9 ¾ In. .... *illus* 495.00
Jug, Utopian, Corn, Dark Brown Glaze, Yellow, Green, Ear Of Corn, No. 1266, 9 x 5 In. 225.00
Jug, Utopian, Currents, Ivory Ground, Marked, 6 ⅛ In. 127.00
Lamp Base, Utopian, Nasturtiums, Marked, 10 In. 115.00
Poster Mug, Incised Serpent, Marked, J.B. Owens, 7 ⅛ In. 695.00
Vase, Embossed Lotus, Grapes, Leaves, Black Matte Ground, 8 ¾ In. 374.00
Vase, Green Matte Glaze, Buttress Shape, 4 x 7 In. 425.00
Vase, Henri Deux, Woman's Face, Back Of Head, Flowing Hair, 2 Handles, 9 In. 489.00
Vase, Indian Chief Profile, Oval, Marked, 10 ½ In.. .... 1440.00
Vase, Kittens, Bottle Shape, 10 ½ In. 3450.00
Vase, Lotus, Abstract Leaf Relief, Blue, Pink, Orange, Green, Bulbous, c.1907, 7 In. 326.00
Vase, Lotus, Cranes In Flight, Clouds, Moon, Handles, 14 ¾ In. 4025.00
Vase, Lotus, Flying Cranes, Marked, 14 ¼ In. 1955.00
Vase, Lotus, Lavender, 5 In. 75.00
Vase, Lotus, Poppies, Flared Base & Rim, Ivory Ground, 14 ⅛ In.. .... 2185.00
Vase, Opalescent Inlaid, Symmetrical Flowers, Coralene Ground, 10 ⅛ In. 633.00
Vase, Poppies, Painted, Bulbous, White, Green, No. 1146, 4 x 13 In. 600.00
Vase, Poppies, White, Pink, Green, Bulbous Shape, E. Jenkins, No. 1039, 16 x 8 In.. .... 420.00
Vase, Soudaneze, Stork, Tan Beak, Legs, Against Black Ground, 7 ¾ In.. .... 259.00
Vase, Sylvan, Molded Flowers, Trees, Leaves, Dark Green Matte Glaze, 9 In.. .... 173.00
Vase, Utopian, Boy Wearing Feathered Hat, Pillow, 8 ⅜ In. 345.00
Vase, Utopian, Brown Glaze, Wild Rose, 3 ½ x 7 In. 86.00
Vase, Utopian, Brown Glaze, Yellow, Orange Flowers, 2 Handles, No. 953, 5 x 5 In. 215.00
Vase, Utopian, Brown Matte Glaze, Painted Rose, No. 127, 7 x 3 In. 145.00
Vase, Utopian, Brown Matte Glaze, Pale Yellow Tulips, 8 ½ x 9 ½ In. 875.00
Vase, Utopian, Brown Matte Glaze, Pink Rose, No. 123, 13 x 6 In. 195.00
Vase, Utopian, Brown Matte Glaze, Yellow Flower, Green Leaves, W. Long, 15 x 5 In.. .... 425.00
Vase, Utopian, Cherries, Leaves, Twisted, Matte, 13 ½ x 4 ½ In. 330.00
Vase, Utopian, Cheyenne, Chief Wolf Robe, Pinched Waist, 13 ¾ x 7 ¼ In. 1200.00
Vase, Utopian, Cheyenne Chief Soaring Eagle, Portrait, 11 In. 1900.00
Vase, Utopian, Daffodils, Bottle Shape, Slip, Marked, No. 1076, Signed, 12 ¼ In.. .... 121.00
Vase, Utopian, Double Handles, Brown Glaze, Pansy, 4 ¾ x 4 ½ In. 173.00
Vase, Utopian, Ear Of Corn, Husk, 8 ½ In. 184.00
Vase, Utopian, Flowers, Signed, Backwards E, Marked, No. 1118, 10 ¾ In.. .... 250.00
Vase, Utopian, Globular, Native American, Headdress, Marked, 12 In. 4600.00
Vase, Utopian, Horse, 9 In. 690.00
Vase, Utopian, Hunting Dog In Collar, Marked, Owensart Utopian, 15 ½ x 8 In. 1540.00
Vase, Utopian, Indian Chief, Painted, Bottle Shape, 15 ½ x 4 ½ In. 1680.00
Vase, Utopian, Milkweed, 11 ⅜ In.. .... 104.00
Vase, Utopian, Pansies, Square, Marked, 5 ⅞ In. 127.00
Vase, Utopian, Pink & White Flowers, Blue To Pink Ground, 4 ½ In. 60.00
Vase, Utopian, Pitcher, Wading Stork, Green, White, Gray, No. 4, 6 x 8 In. 325.00

OYSTER PLATES were popular from the 1880s. Each course at dinner was served in a special dish. The oyster plate had indentations shaped like oysters. Usually six oysters were held on a plate. There is no greater value to a plate with more oysters, although that myth continues to haunt antiques dealers. There are other plates for shellfish, including cockle plates and whelk plates. The appropriately shaped indentations are part of the design of these dishes.

4 Wells, Majolica, Basket Weave, Pink Wells, Rectangular, Rounded, Minton, 9 In. 2300.00
4 Wells, Majolica, Shells, Green, Handle, J.W. Boteler, 8 ½ In.. .... 3795.00
5 Wells, Fish, Shellfish, Crustaceans, Outlined Gilt, Limoges, 9 In., Pair 460.00
5 Wells, Flowers, Cream, Green, Signed, Limoges, 9 In. .... *illus* 50.00
5 Wells, Flowers, Gerard Dufraisseix & Abbot, Limoges, 8 ¾ In. 46.00
5 Wells, Flowers, Haviland, 8 ¾ In. 29.00

Overbeck, Vase, Stylized Birds, Branches, Raspberry Ground, Incised, OBK E F, 7 x 4 In.
$4800.00

Owens, Jardiniere, Pedestal, Women, Henri Deux, Art Nouveau, 26 ¼ In.
$1980.00

Owens, Jardiniere, Utopian, Tulips, Blue Matte, White, 7 ⅝ x 9 ¾ In.
$495.00

TIP

If you live in an old house and the locks are old, check the new types. There have been many improvements, and new locks provide much better security.

O

Oyster Plate, 5 Wells, Flowers, Cream, Green, Signed, Limoges, 9 In.
$50.00

Oyster Plate, 6 Wells, Majolica, Pink, White Center, George Jones, 9 In.
$978.00

Canadian Pressed Glass
Pattern glass was made in Canada. Patterns were similar to the glass pieces made in the United States. Companies that made pressed glass in Canada include the Burlington Glass Works of Hamilton, Ontario (1875–1909); the Excelsior Glass Company, St. Johns (1878–80) and Montreal (1881–85), Quebec; Humphreys Glass Works, Trenton, Nova Scotia (1890–1914); Napanee Glass House, Napanee, Ontario (1881–83); Nova Scotia Glass Company, Trenton, Nova Scotia (1881–92); and the Sydenham Glass Company, Ltd., Wallaceburg, Ontario (1895–1913).

5 Wells, Gold Blackberry Decoration, Haviland Limoges, 8 ¾ In. . . . 29.00
5 Wells, Gold Flowers, Haviland, 9 In. . . . 69.00
5 Wells, Majolica, Gold Flowers, 8 ½ In. . . . 69.00
5 Wells, Majolica, Seaweed, Magenta, Pink Wells, Crescent Shape, 10 In. . . . 489.00
5 Wells, Majolica, Seaweed, Turquoise, Crescent Shape, Copeland, 9 ½ In. . . . 748.00
5 Wells, Majolica, Square, Gold Border, 9 In. . . . 23.00
5 Wells, Pistachio Green Ground, Gold, T & V, Limoges, 9 In. . . . 175.00
5 Wells, Seaweed, Fish, Square, Limoges, 8 In. . . . 196.00
5 Wells, Turkey, Large Wells, Pink Ground, 8 ¾ In. . . . 173.00
5 Wells, Turkey, Pink Ground, Gold Trim, C. Tielsch, 9 In., 4 Piece . . . 546.00
5 Wells, Wave, White, Gold Trim, Haviland, 1880s, 9 In. . . . 99.00
6 Wells, Alternating Flowers, Mountain Landscapes, Green, Gold Trim, 9 In. . . . 135.00
6 Wells, Center Sauce Well, Pink Flowers, William Guerin, Limoges, c.1900, 9 ½ In. . . . 299.00
6 Wells, Fish, Turtle, Seaweed, Shells, Haviland Limoges, 9 In. . . . 184.00
6 Wells, Flower Mold, Victoria Karlsbad, Austria, c.1885, 9 ⅛ In. . . . 145.00
6 Wells, Gray To White Flowers, Green & Gold Border, Haviland, 9 In. . . . 85.00
6 Wells, Majolica, Alternating Pink & Green Wells, Cobalt Center, 10 In. . . . 173.00
6 Wells, Majolica, Basket Weave, Longchamp, Stoneware, 9 ½ In. . . . 35.00
6 Wells, Majolica, Blue & White, Bombay, 9 ½ In. . . . 325.00
6 Wells, Majolica, Brown, France, 9 ½ In. . . . 6.00
6 Wells, Majolica, Cobalt Blue, White Center, George Jones, 8 ¾ In. . . . 2013.00
6 Wells, Majolica, Earth Tones, Serpentine Border, St. Clement, France, 9 ½ In. . . . 85.00
6 Wells, Majolica, Fish & Seaweed, Minton, 11 In. . . . 2300.00
6 Wells, Majolica, Fishnet Ground, 8 ½ In. . . . 46.00
6 Wells, Majolica, Green, Gien, 9 ¾ In., Pair . . . 59.00
6 Wells, Majolica, Ivory Wells, Pink & Green Border, Cracker Well, Minton, 9 In. . . . 104.00
6 Wells, Majolica, Leaves & Berries, Cobalt Ground, France, 10 In. . . . 219.00
6 Wells, Majolica, Mottled Green, White Shell Dividers, Minton, 9 In. . . . 8863.00
6 Wells, Majolica, Oriental Flowers, Birds, 9 In. . . . 35.00
6 Wells, Majolica, Oyster Decorated Shell, 9 ½ In. . . . 58.00
6 Wells, Majolica, Pink, White Center, George Jones, 9 In. . . . *illus* 978.00
6 Wells, Majolica, Sarreguemines, 10 In. . . . 23.00
6 Wells, Majolica, Scenic, Man & Woman In Center, Flowers, 9 ½ In. . . . 91.00
6 Wells, Majolica, Seamist Green, White Shell Dividers, Minton, 9 In. . . . 316.00
6 Wells, Majolica, Shaded Green Shells, Green Branch Handle, Choisy-Le-Roi, 10 In. . . . 1035.00
6 Wells, Majolica, Turquoise, Cracker Well, Minton, 9 ½ In. . . . 575.00
6 Wells, Majolica, Turquoise, George Jones, 8 ½ In. . . . 1265.00
6 Wells, Majolica, Turquoise Glaze, Shell, Seaweed, 1873, 9 In. . . . 472.00
6 Wells, Majolica, Union Porcelain Works, 9 ½ In. . . . 288.00
6 Wells, Majolica, White, Pink, Blue, Tan, Victoria Pottery, 9 ½ In. . . . 184.00
6 Wells, Majolica, White, Seaweed, Turquoise Wells, 9 ¼ In. . . . 259.00
6 Wells, Majolica, Yellow Wells, White Shell Dividers, Minton, 9 In. . . . 2875.00
6 Wells, Mottled Pink, Green & Cream Shells, Gold Center Bands, 9 In. . . . 35.00
6 Wells, Pink & White Shaded Shells, 9 In., Pair . . . 46.00
6 Wells, Pink & Yellow Roses, Gold Trim, Haviland, 8 ⅜ In. . . . 210.00
6 Wells, Pink Iridescent, Gold Spiral & Ruffled Ivory Shells, C.H. Pillivuyt & Cie, 9 ½ In. . . . 485.00
6 Wells, Shell Shape, Haviland, 9 In. . . . 29.00
6 Wells, Snail, Shrimp, Clam Sea Creatures, Embossed, Giraud Limoges France, 10 In. . . . 89.00
6 Wells, Turquoise, Swags, Flowers, Handle, 10 ½ In. . . . 288.00
6 Wells, Wave, Cobalt Blue, Gold Leaves, Haviland, 1880s . . . 825.00
6 Wells, Yellow, Pink Edge, Blue Center Well, Haviland Limoges, c.1890, 9 In. . . . 175.00
9 Wells, Turquoise, Conch & Clam Shell Spacers, Minton, 9 ¾ In. . . . 440.00
Haviland, Wild Roses, 8 ¼ In. . . . 210.00
Majolica, Flowers, Victoria Karlsbad, 8 ½ In. . . . 58.00
Majolica, Pink, Minton, c.1879, 9 In. . . . 805.00
Pink Rose Garlands, Gold Trim, Scalloped, Haviland, 9 In. . . . 225.00
Urn & Flowers, Haviland, Limoges, 9 In. . . . 81.00

PADEN CITY Glass Manufacturing Company was established in 1916 at Paden City, West Virginia. The company made over twenty different colors of glass. The firm closed in 1951. Paden City Pottery is not listed here. Some Paden City Pottery may be listed in Dinnerware.

Crow's Foot, Candlestick, 3-Light . . . 17.00
Crow's Foot, Candlestick, 3-Light, Ruby, Irwin Etch . . . 95.00
Crow's Foot, Candy Dish, Cover, Cobalt Blue, Silver Overlay, 3 Sections . . . 295.00
Crow's Foot, Candy Dish, Cover, Gold Trim, 3 Sections . . . 75.00

Crow's Foot, Cheese & Cracker, Lattice Flower Overlay 65.00
Crow's Foot, Compote, Ruby, 3 ½ x 6 ¼ In. 30.00
Crow's Foot, Console, Cobalt Blue, Silver Overlay, 11 ½ In. 175.00
Crow's Foot, Creamer, Ruby, Footed 18.00
Crow's Foot, Cup & Saucer, Pink, Footed 12.00
Crow's Foot, Cup & Saucer, Ruby, Footed 24.00
Crow's Foot, Plate, Pink, Square, 8 ½ In. 8.00
Crow's Foot, Plate, Red, Handles, 10 ½ In. 45.00
Crow's Foot, Soup, Cream, Ruby, 4 ½ In. 30.00
Crow's Foot, Sugar, Ruby 18.00
Cupid, Dish, Mayonnaise, Green 145.00
Daisy Cross, Bowl, Square, Handles, 10 In. 75.00
Eden Rose, Creamer, Green 45.00
Figurine, Chinese Pheasant, 13 x 16 In. 110.00
Figurine, Horse, 12 In. 40.00
Figurine, Rabbit, Cotton Ball Dispenser, Satin, 5 ¼ In. .... *illus* 60.00
Fruit, Pie Baker, Decal, 9 ¾ In. 18.00
Gazebo, Candy Dish, Cover, Gold Trim, 3 Sections 75.00
Gazebo, Sugar & Creamer 45.00
Glades, Compote, Ruby, 7 ½ x 5 ½ In. 75.00
Glades, Soup, Cream, Underplate, Ruby 45.00
Glades, Sugar, Ruby 30.00
Glades, Tumbler, Ruby, 9 Oz. 65.00
Gothic Garden, Dish, Sweetmeat, Yellow, Square, 7 ½ In. 45.00
Largo, Candlestick, Copen Blue, 5 In. 45.00
Largo, Compote, Copen Blue, 10 x 6 ½ In. 45.00
Largo, Cup, Cobalt Blue 35.00
Largo, Sugar & Creamer, Ruby 120.00
Lucy, Dish, Mayonnaise, 3-Footed, 3 ¾ In. 20.00
Maya, Console, Blue, 12 In. 75.00
Maya, Plate, Dinner, Ruby, 9 In., 4 Piece 270.00
Maya, Sandwich Server, Ruby, Handles, 11 ½ In. 125.00
Mr. B., Candlestick, 2-Light, Pam's Floral, Etch, Pair 120.00
Mr. B., Candy Dish, Cover, Heart Shape, Floral Cutting, 3 Sections, 7 ½ In. 35.00
Mr. B., Candy Dish, Cover, Ruby, Footed 75.00
Mrs. B., Cheese & Cracker Set, Yellow, Ardith Etch, 5 x 2 ½ In. 95.00
Mrs. B., Sugar, Yellow, Ardith Etch 60.00
Mrs. B., Vase, Ebony, Silver Overlay, 9 In. 200.00
Party Line, Candlestick, Aqua, 4 ½ In., Pair .... *illus* 65.00
Party Line, Creamer, Green 12.00
Party Line, Cup, Green 9.00
Party Line, Cup, Pink 10.00
Party Line, Dresser Set, Amber, Tray, Powder Dish, Perfume, Stopper .... *illus* 30.00
Party Line, Parfait, Green, Footed, 5 Oz., 5 ½ In. 16.00
Party Line, Salt Shaker, Amber 25.00
Party Line, Sherbet, Amber 8.00
Party Line, Sherbet, Green 10.00
Party Line, Sugar, Cover, Hotel, Amber 20.00
Party Line, Sugar, Pink 12.00
Party Line, Tumbler, Soda, Pink, 8 Oz. .... 15.00 to 18.00
Peacock & Wild Rose, Bowl, Console, 14 In. 55.00
Peacock & Wild Rose, Cheese & Cracker, Plate, Pink, 10 ½ In. 65.00
Peacock & Wild Rose, Plate, Dinner, Cheriglo, 10 ½ In. 35.00
Peacock & Wild Rose, Sugar & Creamer, Green 105.00
Peacock & Wild Rose, Vase, Green, Elliptical, 8 ¼ In. 295.00
Penny, Bowl, Finger, Ruby, 4 ⅜ x 2 ¼ In. 20.00
Penny, Cordial, Ruby, 1 Oz. 30.00
Penny, Cup, Primrose 12.00
Penny, Cup, Ruby 10.00
Penny, Plate, Luncheon, Royal Blue, 8 In. 14.00
Penny, Plate, Luncheon, Ruby, 8 In. 10.00
Penny, Sandwich Server, Ruby, Center Handle, 10 ½ In. 60.00
Penny, Saucer, Royal Blue 4.00
Penny, Saucer, Ruby 4.00
Penny, Sherbet, Red, 6 Oz. 12.00
Penny, Tumbler, Iced Tea, Amber, 12 Oz., 5 ¼ In. 8.00
Penny, Tumbler, Iced Tea, Ruby, 12 Oz., 5 ¼ In. 15.00

TIP
Never leave the key under the door mat.

Paden City, Figurine, Rabbit, Cotton Ball Dispenser, Satin, 5 ¼ In.
$60.00

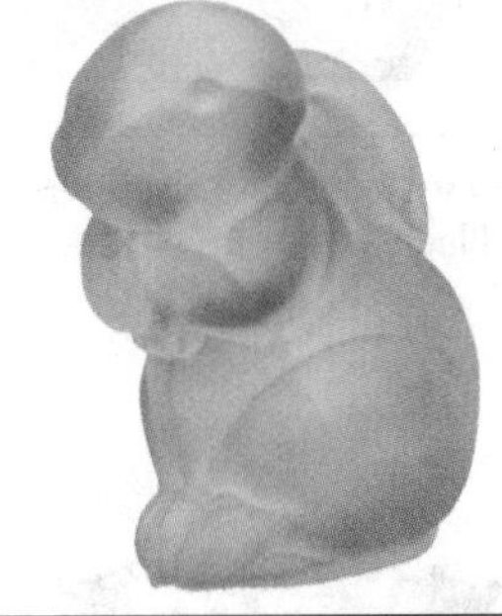

Paden City, Party Line, Candlestick, Aqua, 4 ½ In., Pair
$65.00

Paden City, Party Line, Dresser Set, Amber, Tray, Powder Dish, Perfume, Stopper
$30.00

TIP
Pet doors should be less than 6 inches across to keep out small children who might then open a regular door for a burglar.

Paden City, Rambler Rose, Dish, Mayonnaise, Underplate, Cheriglo, 3 ¼ x 7 In.
$60.00

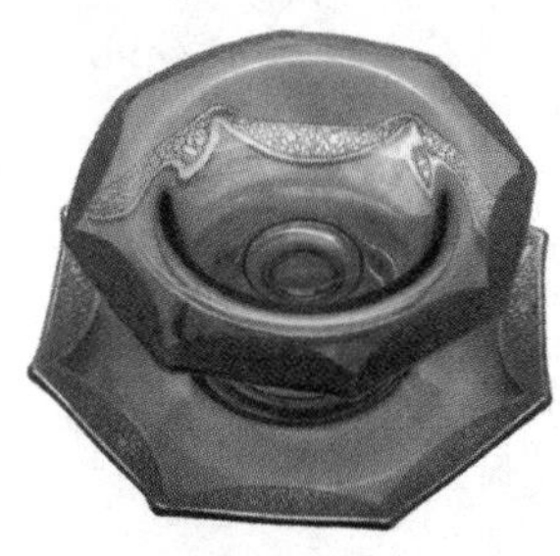

Paden City, Vermillion, Candy Dish, Copen Blue, 9 ¾ x 6 ¼ In.
$30.00

Painting, On Copper, Landscape, Pond, Signed, Eros, Frame, 5 ⅝ x 7 In.
$140.00

Painting, Reverse On Glass, Eagle, Flags, Banner, Boy In Oval, Frame, 9 ½ x 11 ½ In.
$99.00

Penny, Tumbler, Juice, Royal Blue, 5 Oz., 3 ⅞ In. 15.00
Penny, Tumbler, Water, Ruby, 10 Oz., 4 ⅛ In. 12.00
Penny, Tumbler, Whiskey, Ruby, 3 Oz., 2 ¾ In. 10.00
Popeye & Olive, Saucer, Ruby 15.00
Popeye & Olive, Sherbet, Ruby 18.00
Rambler Rose, Dish, Mayonnaise, Underplate, Cheriglo, 3 ¼ x 7 In. .... *illus* 60.00
Regina, Candlestick, Amber, 4 x 4 In. 32.00
Regina, Console, Green, 10 ⅞ In. 30.00
Spire, Sandwich, Server, Bridal Basket Etch, Center Handle, 11 In. 45.00
Spring Orchard, Decanter Set, Scotch, Rye, Whiskey, 3 Piece 195.00
Vermillion, Candy Dish, Copen Blue, 9 ¾ x 6 ¼ In. .... *illus* 30.00

PAINTINGS listed in this book are not works by major artists but rather decorative paintings on ivory, board, or glass that would be of interest to the average collector. Watercolors on paper are listed under Picture. To learn the value of an oil painting by a listed artist you must contact an expert in that area.

Acrylic, Charleston Rooftops, Paolo, Frame, 1900s, 36 x 36 In. 3910.00
Gouache On Paper, Train Run By Devils, Night Scene, Painted Frame, 1900s, 22 x 32 In. 118.00
Miniature, On Ivory, Priest, Seated, Holding Red Book, Black Wood Frame, 6 x 5 In. 5.50
Miniature, On Ivory, Taj Mahal, Multicolored, Oval Metal Frame, 4 ¾ x 6 ½ In. 165.00
Miniature, On Ivory, Young Woman, With Crown, Velvet Mat, Frame, 6 ½ x 4 ¾ In. 99.00
Oil On Board, Man Hunting, On Farmstead, Multicolored, Penn., 23 ½ x 35 In. 660.00
Oil On Board, Mountain & River Scene, Signed Meurer, Frame, 16 x 12 In. 500.00
Oil On Board, Still Life, Grapes, Peaches, Cake, Wineglass, Frame, 10 ½ x 15 In. 633.00
Oil On Canvas, 2 Raptor Hawks, On Tree Branches, Frame, Early 1900s, 27 ¾ x 19 In. 690.00
Oil On Canvas, Blindman's Bluff, War Caricature, Color, Gilt Frame, 1942, 18 x 24 In. 489.00
Oil On Canvas, Cattle Grazing, Stormy Sky, Johannes De Haas, Signed, c.1884, 20 x 28 In. 4994.00
Oil On Canvas, Chinese Man Seated, Yellow Dragon Robe, Carved, Frame, 1800s, 15 x 10 In. 8125.00
Oil On Canvas, Family Portrait, 3 People, Blue, Black, Red Stains, Chinese, c.1960, 25 x 30 In. 598.00
Oil On Canvas, Figures In Stream During Deer Hunt, Gilt Frame, 31 x 22 ½ In. 2467.00
Oil On Canvas, Geo. Washington, Uniform, Portrait, Profile, Frame, c.1900, 31 x 26 In. 1058.00
Oil On Canvas, House By Stream, William Fisher, Frame, c.1930, 8 x 10 In. 720.00
Oil On Canvas, Landscape, Building On Hill, New York, c.1855, 35 x 47 In. 21250.00
Oil On Canvas, Man, Seated, Seascape In Nearby Window, c.1830, 36 x 29 In. 470.00
Oil On Canvas, Memorial Portrait, Little Girl, With Roses, 31 ¼ x 25 ¼ In. 900.00
Oil On Canvas, Portrait Of Young South African, Face Of Black Woman, A. Lewis, 16 x 12 In. 6573.00
Oil On Canvas, River Landscape, 19th Century, 29 ½ x 19 ½ In. 431.00
Oil On Canvas, River Valley, Fishermen, Cottages, Castle, Wood Frame, 14 x 18 In. 7110.00
Oil On Canvas, Rowboats, Sea Captain Image, Frame, J. Gabin, 1900s, 30 x 43 In. 118.00
Oil On Canvas, Sheep, Old Norfolk Breed, Late 19th Century, Frame, 32 x 25 In. 748.00
Oil On Canvas, Summertime, Houses, Field, Emil Thulin, c.1950, 22 x 28 In. 330.00
Oil On Canvas, Winter Morning, Victor Korecki, Frame, c.1930, 23 x 36 In. 1800.00
Oil On Masonite, The Trumpeteer, Green, Blue, White, H. Falkner, 14 x 10 In. 2530.00
Oil On Oak Panel, Seascape, Storm, Rocky Coastline, Wrecked Galleon, 10 x 12 ½ In. 403.00
On Copper, Landscape, Pond, Signed, Eros, Frame, 5 ⅝ x 7 In. .... *illus* 140.00
On Ivory, 1800s Woman, Plumed Hat, Miller, Frame, 4 ½ x 3 In. 187.00
On Ivory, Josephine Bonaparte, Filigree Frame, 1800s, 3 ¼ In. 413.00
On Ivory, Napoleon Bonaparte, In Uniform, Renior, Frame, 4 ¾ x 3 In. 154.00
On Ivory, Portrait, Thomas Shinn Ridgeway, Burlington, N.J., 1779-1857, 2 ¾ x 2 In. 936.00
On Silk, Radha, Krishna, Tree Grove, Surrounding Attendants, Frame, Indian, 14 x 17 In. 58.00
Reverse On Glass, Eagle, Flags, Banner, Boy In Oval, Frame, 9 ½ x 11 ½ In. .... *illus* 99.00
Reverse On Glass, Portrait, Duc De Cordeaux, Young Man, Military Outfit, 12 x 9 ½ In. 288.00

PAIRPOINT Manufacturing Company started in 1880 in New Bedford, Massachusetts. It soon joined with the glassworks nearby and made glass, silver-plated pieces, and lamps. Reverse-painted glass shades and molded shades known as "puffies" were part of the production until the 1930s. The company reorganized and changed its name several times but is still working today. Items listed here are glass or glass and metal. Silver-plated pieces are listed under Silver Plate.

Biscuit Jar, Opal, Faceted, Mold, Blown, Enameled, Sailing Ships, Metal Lid, 6 ½ In. 546.00
Biscuit Jar, Pink, White, Enameled Flowers, Silver Plate Lid & Bail, 6 In. 300.00
Biscuit Jar, Pink, White, Gold Enameled Flowers, Silver Plate Cover, Square, 7 ½ In. 575.00
Biscuit Jar, Yellow Ground, Courting Scene, Gold Trim, Silver Plate Lid, Bail, 5 In. 400.00
Bowl, Nevada Pattern, Violet, Pedestal, 7 In. 275.00
Bride's Basket, White, Flowers, Pink Interior, Crimped, Ruffled Rim, Metal Frame, 11 In. 350.00
Candlestick, Amber, Clear Strawberry Ball, 10 ¾ In., Pair 220.00

P

Candlestick, Colias Cutting, Vaseline, 16 In., Pair 990.00
Card Holder, Engraved Flowers, 5 In. 99.00
Chalice, Clear Cutting, Controlled Bubble Stem, 12 In. 180.00
Chalice, Colias Cutting, Apple Green, Clear Controlled Bubble Stem, 11 ¾ In. 550.00
Compote, Amethyst, Clear Bubble Ball Connector, Flat Wafer Base, 4 ⅝ x 8 In. 250.00
Compote, Colias Cutting, Amber, 7 ¼ x 8 ¼ In. .... *illus* 165.00
Compote, Colias Cutting, Apple Green, 7 ¼ In., Pair .... *illus* 175.00
Compote, Colias Cutting, Vaseline, 8 x 7 In. 330.00
Compote, Marina Blue, Clear Bubble Ball Connector, Footed, 6 x 10 In. 375.00
Compote, Rosaria, Diamond Quilted, Hollow Stem, Domed Foot, 8 x 9 In. 750.00
Compote, Ruby Twist, Clear Stem, Applied Wafer Base, 8 x 4 ⅝ In. 525.00
Goblet, Colias Cutting, Apple Green, 6 ¼ In., 6 Piece 248.00
Lamp, Beehive Shade, Brown, Multicolored, Tropical Birds, Scrolling, 22 In. 3910.00
Lamp, Beehive Shade, Flying Cranes, Lake, Moon, Embossed Metal Base, Stem, 16 In. 1265.00
Lamp, Bombay Shade, Farm Scene, Fleur-De-Lis Top, Baluster Bronze Base, 22 In. 2875.00
Lamp, Bombay Shade, Lake Scene, 21 In. 2760.00
Lamp, Drapery Shade, Flower Swags, Textured, Cast Iron Base, 13 x 21 In. 489.00
Lamp, Exeter Shade, Four Seasons, Brass Base, 22 In. 2473.00
Lamp, Kerosene, Paneled Milk Glass, Delft Scene, Acorn Burner, 8 ¼ In. 288.00
Lamp, Lucca, Shade, Oriental Poppies, Brass Base, 14 x 23 In. 5175.00
Lamp, Mushroom Shade, Green, Chrysanthemum, Silver Plate Base, Marked, 21 ½ x 12 In. 450.00
Lamp, Piano, Mozart Shade, Mauve Flowers, Gold, Brass Base, Wreath, Garlands, 14 In. 1553.00
Lamp, Plymouth Shade, Basket, Flowers, Acorn Pulls, Marked Base, 16 x 13 In. 2588.00
Lamp, Pompey Shade, Floral Serpentine, Metal Base, c.1920, 20 In. 2300.00
Lamp, Portsmouth Shade, Apricot Ground, Flowers, 8 x 14 In. 3163.00
Lamp, Puffy, Apple Tree Blossoms, Bumblebees, Butterflies, Tree Trunk Base, 21 x 16 In. 32200.00
Lamp, Puffy, Azalea, Silver Plate Base, 4-Footed, 21 x 10 In. 17250.00
Lamp, Puffy, Birds, Roses, Plaid Ground, 2-Light, Gold Metal Base, 23 x 14 In. 4200.00
Lamp, Puffy, Cabbage Rose, Victorian Scrollwork, White, Cream, 19 ¾ In. 4200.00
Lamp, Puffy, Flowers, Butterflies, Pinstripes, Brass Footed Base, 15 ½ In. 7475.00
Lamp, Puffy, Hollyhocks, Metal, Reeded Column, Base, 21 ⅜ In. .... *illus* 4120.00
Lamp, Puffy, Hummingbird, Red Flowers, Strawberry Top, 16 In. 9100.00
Lamp, Puffy, Lilac, Butterfly, Marked, 8 In. 3410.00
Lamp, Puffy, Papillion, Flowers, Butterflies, Brass Footed Base, Signed, 16 In. 7475.00
Lamp, Puffy, Papillon, Butterflies, Geometrics, Silver Plate Base, 14 ½ x 7 ½ In. .... *illus* 1600.00
Lamp, Puffy, Papillon, Flowers, Butterflies, Yellow, Pink, Blue, Paw Feet, 8 x 14 ½ In. 4312.00
Lamp, Puffy, Papillon, Red Flowers, Monarch Butterflies, 14 x 20 In. 3795.00
Lamp, Puffy, Red Roses, Green Leaves, Brass Base, Marked, 17 In. 575.00
Lamp, Puffy, Rose, Red, Yellow, Wood Baluster, Base, Signed, 10 In. 115.00
Lamp, Puffy, Rose Bonnet, Pink, Yellow, Cream, Green Ground, Artichoke Base, 14 ½ In. 1150.00
Lamp, Puffy, Rose Bonnet, Red & Yellow Roses, Blue & White Lattice, 10 x 15 In. 316.00
Lamp, Puffy, Square, Pansies, Roses, Poppies, Daisies, Seafoam Ground, 14 In. 2300.00
Lamp, Puffy, Stratford Shade, Flowers, Hummingbird, Blue Lattice, Marked, 23 x 15 In. .... *illus* 3950.00
Lamp, Puffy, Stratford Shade, Pink, Black, Flowers, Frosted Glass, Brass Base, 14 In. 5175.00
Lamp, Puffy, Stratford Shade, Roses, Dogwoods, 14 x 8 In. 5175.00
Lamp, Puffy, Yellow Roses, Green Ground, Handles, Marked, 11 In. 230.00
Lamp, Reverse Painted, Allover Rose, Green, Bronze, Gold Dore, Oak Leaf, Acorn, 10 x 22 In. 4888.00
Lamp, Reverse Painted, Birds, Flowers, Bronze Open Base, 18 x 22 In. 1920.00
Lamp, Reverse Painted, Chestnut Tree, Pink, Yellow, Green, Urn Shape Base, 20 x 24 In. 2760.00
Lamp, Reverse Painted, Farm Landscape, Cottages, Bulbous, 23 ½ x 18 In. 3360.00
Lamp, Reverse Painted, Geese, Blue Sky, 3-Dolphin Base, 15 x 20 In. 4200.00
Lamp, Reverse Painted, Landscape, Lake, Urn Shape Base, 23 ¼ x 18 In. 1920.00
Lamp, Reverse Painted, Landscape, Stone Wall Shade, Silvered Base, 22 x 15 In. .... 2300.00 to 4500.00
Lamp, Reverse Painted, Leaf Design, Patinated Bronze Base, Paneled Urn, Marked, 21 ¼ In. 978.00
Lamp, Reverse Painted, Meadow, Butterflies, Daisies, Yellow Sky, Cast, Metal Base, 15 x 8 In. 165.00
Lamp, Reverse Painted, Mill Scene, Forest Ground, Colonna Closed Top, Signed, 15 In. 1400.00
Lamp, Reverse Painted, Parrots On Branch, 22 ¼ x 7 ¼ In. 3360.00
Lamp, Reverse Painted, Seascape, Ships, Dolphin Base, Shade Signed, C. Durand, 16 x 24 In. 4025.00
Lamp, Reverse Painted, Ships On Stormy Sea, Orange, Yellow Sky, Dolphin Base, 15 x 8 In. 2760.00
Lamp, Windsor Shade, Sailing Boat, Cabins, Trees, Person, 5 x 10 In. 2530.00
Paperweight, Pear, Controlled Bubbles, Applied Red Stem, 3 x 2 ½ In. 40.00
Paperweight, Rose, 18 Petals, Burmese, Green Leaves, 6 Facets, Signed, 3 ¼ In. .... *illus* 180.00
Pickle Castor, Cranberry, Coin Spot, Enameled Flower, 11 In. 400.00
Pickle Castor, Pink Satin, Diamond Quilted, Signed, 12 ½ In. 525.00
Pitcher, Amethyst, Applied Handle, Marked, 5 ¼ In. 90.00
Plate, Colias Cutting, Apple Green, 8 ½ In., Pair 28.00
Salt, Vintage Cutting, Cobalt Blue, Pedestal, 3 x 4 ¼ In. 175.00

Pairpoint, Compote, Colias Cutting, Amber, 7 ¼ x 8 ¼ In.
$165.00

Pairpoint, Compote, Colias Cutting, Apple Green, 7 ¼ In., Pair
$175.00

Pairpoint, Lamp, Puffy, Hollyhocks, Metal, Reeded Column, Base, 21 ⅜ In.
$4120.00

Pairpoint, Lamp, Puffy, Papillon, Butterflies, Geometrics, Silver Plate Base, 14 ½ x 7 ½ In.
$1600.00

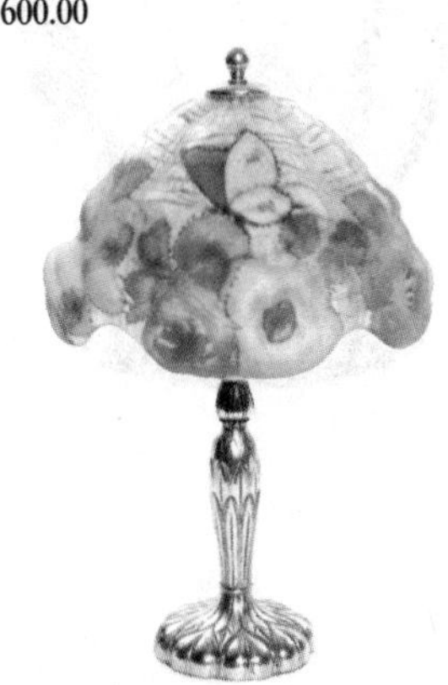

P

Pairpoint, Lamp, Puffy, Stratford Shade, Flowers, Hummingbird, Blue Lattice, Marked, 23 x 15 In.
$3950.00

Pairpoint, Paperweight, Rose, 18 Petals, Burmese, Green Leaves, 6 Facets, Signed, 3 ¼ In.
$180.00

Pairpoint, Vase, Vintage Cutting, Amethyst, Footed, 7 In.
$82.00

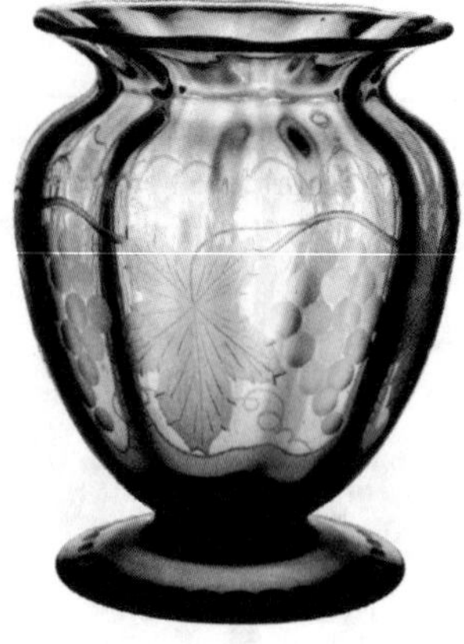

Shade, Bonnet, Pansies, Multicolored, 1907, 7 In. 7130.00
Shade, Carlisle, Mottled Cream, Multicolored Indian Design, 14 In. 690.00
Shade, Puffy, Palermo, Green, Lilac Clusters, Leaves, 15 In. 3105.00
Sugar & Creamer, Pink, Flowers, Opal, Opalescent Handles, 3 ½ In. 115.00
Sugar Shaker, Opal, Crimson Flowers, Barrel Shape, Marked, 6 ¾ In., Pair. 288.00
Tray, Oval, Reticulated, Green, Rust, Pink Flowers, Marked, 12 ¼ In. 60.00
Tray, Vintage Cutting, Apple Green, Round, 15 ½ In. 55.00
Vase, Ambero, Flower Form, Red Flowers, Textured Yellow Ground, Footed, Signed, 6 In. 518.00
Vase, Apple Green, Butterfly, Web & Flower Cutting, Footed, 11 In. 400.00
Vase, Burmese, Lily Shape, Multicolored Flowers, 4 In., Pair. 81.00
Vase, Clear, Figural, Winged Cherub, Footed, Stem, Gilt, Silver Plate, 7 ¼ In. 345.00
Vase, Leaf Mold Top, White, Daisies, 2 Handles, Marked, 7 In. 225.00
Vase, Vaseline, Butterfly & Web Cutting, Footed, 8 ¼ In. 550.00
Vase, Vintage Cutting, Amethyst, Footed, 7 In. *illus* 82.00

PALMER COX, BROWNIES, *see Brownies category.*

PAPER collectibles, including almanacs, catalogs, children's books, some greeting cards, stock certificates, and other paper ephemera, are listed here. Paper calendars are listed separately in the Calendar category. Paper items may be found in many other sections, such as Christmas and Movie.

Birth Record, Watercolor, Flower Vase, Rebecca Prickitt, Feb. 9 1856, Frame, 13 x 11 In. 999.00
Book, Denslow's Zoo, Pictorial Wraps, Color Illustrated, W.W. Denslow, 1903 325.00
Book, Mop Top, Cloth, Color Illustrated, Don Freeman, 7 ½ x 10 In. 175.00
Book, My Little ABC, Cloth, Photo Illustrated, Gilbert Cousland, 1934, 7 ½ x 9 ½ In. 400.00
Book, Pop-Up, Goldilocks, Blue Ribbon Press, 1934 65.00
Bookplate, 3 Birds In Tree, Ink, Watercolor, Henrey Bucher, Samuel May, 1809, 6 ½ x 4 In. 2200.00
Bookplate, Bird, Yellow, On Branch, Watercolor, On Paper, 1800s, 2 ¾ x 4 ⅜ In. 353.00
Bookplate, Carnation, Monochromatic, Ink, Watercolor, Lebanon County, c.1820, 8 ½ x 6 ½ In. 129.00
Bookplate, Charl M. Jug, Multicolored, Geometric Borders, Leather Bound, c.1842, 7 In. 11.00
Bookplate, Fraktur, Bird, 2 Tulip Vines, Religious Texts, Lancaster, Pa., 1792, 3 ¾ x 6 In. 995.00
Bookplate, Fraktur, Watercolor, Music Pages, Frame, Abraham Meyer, 15 x 10 ½ In. 2760.00
Bookplate, Fraktur, Watercolor, Yellow Dog Chasing 4 Birds, Frame, 1800s, 3 x 4 ½ In. 24500.00
Bookplate, Heinrich Diener, Peil Taunschip, Illuminated, Geometrics, Frame, 1852, 9 x 11 In. 110.00
Bookplate, Joseph Smith, Lebanon County, Multicolored Flower Border, c.1864, 6 ¾ In. 248.00
Bookplate, Magdalena Schmerrle, Multicolored, Birds, Flowers, c.1824, 6 ¾ In. 330.00
Bookplate, May, Leaves, Samuel Witmer, Illuminated, Frame, 1848, 11 ½ x 9 ½ In. 99.00
Bookplate, Trapezoidal, Flower & Leaf Border, Watercolor, c.1810, 3 ¼ x 3 ¾ In. 288.00
Bookplate, Watercolor, Geometric Design, Maddi Mellinger, c.1843, 3 ¼ x 4 ½ In. 633.00
Broadside, Rally! A War Meeting, Black Freemen Recruitment, Civil War Era, 14 x 10 In. 1003.00
Catalog, L.L. Bean, 1949, Fall, Camping, Travel, Hunting & Fishing Outfits, 90 Pages 45.00
Catalog, Mallory, Wheeler & Co. Lock Making, 1871, 227 Plates 6850.00
Catalog, Rambler Bicycles, Embossed Cover, 1896, 7 x 8 In., 40 Pages 230.00
Certificate, Confirmation, German Text, Trumpeting Angel, Frame, c.1829, 9 ¾ x 7 ¾ In. 11.00
Certificate, Merit, Spencerian, Praying Child, Henery, J. Cook, Frame, 1860, 25 x 20 In. 235.00
Cutwork, Birds, Sunburst, Watercolor, Mary Reyder, 5 ½ x 3 ½ In. 264.00
Cutwork, Family Record, Cyrus Wells, Vase, Flowers, J.B. Walker, 1881, 31 x 25 In. 353.00
Cutwork, Hand, Blue Band, Red, Blue Hearts, Braided Hair, Forget-Me-Not, Frame, 4 ¾ x 3 ¾ In. 1495.00
Cutwork, Scherenschnitte, 2 Distlefinks, Flower Medallion, Frame, 16 x 16 In. 529.00
Cutwork, Scherenschnitte, 4 Blocks Of Nesting Birds, Frame, 9 x 11 In. 250.00
Cutwork, Scherenschnitte, Birds, Nests, Lined Paper, 4 Blocks, Wood Frame, 9 x 11 In. 275.00
Cutwork, Scherenschnitte, Cupid At Temple Of Love, Walnut Frame, Mid 19th Century, 14 x 12 In. 1755.00
Cutwork, Scherenschnitte, Rooster, Birds, Flowers, Initials, J.R., Pa., Frame, 12 ½ x 12 ½ In. 190.00
Cutwork, Scherenschnitte, Tulips, Heart, Serrated Border, Text, Frame, 1845, 11 x 13 In. *illus* 275.00
Dance Card, Boar's Head, Carnival Mistick Krewe Of Comus, 1881 *illus* 500.00
Document, Benjamin Manny, Birds, Tulip, Heart, Ulster, N.Y., 7 ¾ x 8 In. 235.00
Fraktur, 2 Mermaids Above Pond, Fish, Tulip Vines, Pa., Early 1800s, 7 ¼ x 8 ¼ In. 19890.00
Fraktur, Adam & Eve, Verse, Hand Colored, Frame, Baumann, 15 ¼ x 12 ½ In. 322.00
Fraktur, Bird Perched On Flower, Red, Green, Yellow, Signed, D. Ellinger, Frame, 5 x 4 In. 720.00
Fraktur, Birth, Catherine Moyer, Watercolor, Pencil, On Paper, 11 ½ x 9 In. 558.00
Fraktur, Birth, Elam Tout, Lancaster County, Watercolor, c.1844, 9 x 7 In. 130.00
Fraktur, Birth, Johan Peter Trion, Laid Paper, Georg F. Speyer, c.1790, 13 x 16 In. 1528.00
Fraktur, Birth, Tobias Kreider, Vases, Flowers, Birds, Fans, 11 ⅛ x 9 In. 4950.00
Fraktur, Birth, Watercolor, Blue, Tulips, Pelicans, Heart, Text, Frame, 11 x 13 12 In. 353.00
Fraktur, Birth, Watercolor, Columns, Flowers, Printed Heart, Text, Ohio, c.1807, 13 x 16 In. 499.00
Fraktur, Birth, Watercolor, Elizabeth Groff, Flowers, c.1850, 4 ¾ x 8 In. 264.00

Fraktur, Birth, Watercolor, Ink, Grain Painted Frame, Penn., c.1836, 21 x 17 In. 705.00
Fraktur, Birth, Watercolor, Northumberland County, Penn., c.1818, 15 x 12 In. 823.00
Fraktur, Birth, Watercolor, Tulips, Birds, Pinwheels, Frame, c.1806, 15 x 17 In. 470.00
Fraktur, Birth & Baptism, Ester Frey, Multicolored, Rockland Twp., Berks County, c.1839, 16 x 13 In. 77.00
Fraktur, Birth & Baptism, Hanna Dormeyer, Sawtooth Border, Northampton County, c.1806, 18 x 20 In. 935.00
Fraktur, Birth & Baptism, Johanna Jacob, Northampton County, Penn., Friedrich Krebs, 15 x 17 ¾ In. 2200.00
Fraktur, Birth & Baptism, John Sala, Trumpeting Angels, Flowers, German, Ohio, 17 x 21 In. 88.00
Fraktur, Birth & Baptism, Maria Rebner, Angel, Birds, Bucks County, c.1844, 18 ½ x 15 ½ In. 121.00
Fraktur, Brodbeck Family, 2 Women, Flower Vines, Verse, Signed, Frame, 12 x 15 In. 5850.00
Fraktur, Classe De 1885 Canton De Truchtersheim, Man, Oxen, Watercolor, 1800s, 20 x 16 In. 558.00
Fraktur, Flower Vase, Watercolor, Script, Frame, 1837, 10 x 7 ¾ In. .... *illus* 1112.00
Fraktur, Friederich Schafner, Angels, Illuminated, Frame, 1825, 17 ½ x 14½ In. 44.00
Fraktur, Hearts, Flower Vines, Johann Jacob Friedrich Krebs, 1784-1812, Frame, 12 x 16 In. . 380.00
Fraktur, Jerimias Bayer, Angels, Birds, Illuminated, Frame, Berks Co., 1840, 18 x 15 In. 44.00
Fraktur, Marriage Certificate, Watercolor, Frame, Schuykill Township, 1810, 10 x 15 In. 1116.00
Fraktur, Pelican, Feeding 2 Babies In Nest, Flowers, Watercolor, Ink, 1800s, 7 ¼ x 6 In. 1100.00
Fraktur, Roosters With Swords, Watercolor, Frame, 8 x 9 ½ In., Pair 550.00
Fraktur, Susanna Yergin, Angels, Birds, Illuminated, Frame, 1840, 16 x 15 In. 44.00
Fraktur, Watercolor & Ink, Heart, German Script, Signed, Johan Lohr, Frame, 1821, 12 x 12 In. 225.00
House Blessing, Cherubs, Birds, German Text, Illuminated, Johann Ritter, 18 x 15 In. 44.00
Invitation, New Orleans Carnival Ball, Owl, Phunny Phorty Phellows, 1896 .... *illus* 1000.00
Land Grant, Camden County, Georgia, Wax Seal, George Matthews, Frame, 1700s, 15 x 12 In. 478.00
Magazine, Field & Stream, 27576 .... 6.00
Magazine, Sports Illustrated, No. 1 First Issue, 1952 .... 766.00
Marriage Certificate, William Moor & Margaret Locke, Watercolor, Frame, 1800, 8 x 9 In. .. 936.00
Menu, Holsten's, Sopranos Final Episode, Red, White, Blue, Signed, 2007, 9 x 11 In. 1175.00
Mortgage Bond, Antonio Lopez De Santa Anna, A. Mortgage Co., c.1866, 13 x 18 In. 118.00
Passenger List, Titanic, 2nd Class, White Star Line, First Sailing April 12, 1912 .... 33900.00
Print Sheet, Gregorian Chant, Antiphonary, Colored Pigments, Ink, Frame, 19 x 13 In., Pair 551.00
Reward Of Merit, Perched Birds, Pencil, Yellow, Orange, Laid Paper, Frame, 8 x 6 In. 209.00
Reward Of Merit, Peter Yoder, Sun, Bird, On Heart, Tulip Vine, Watercolor, 1811, 4 x 3 ¼ In. 1210.00
Silhouette, Lady, Head Cover, Black, Gray Highlight, Mrs. Rease L'Noir, c.1847, 7 x 6 In. 165.00
Silhouette, Seated Woman, Knitting, Mrs. Chas Adams, 65 Years, Wood Frame, 15 x 13 In. . . 44.00
Wallpaper, Dagobert Peche, Wiener Werkstatte, Iridescent, Chevron, c.1920, 14 x 15 In. 295.00

PAPER DOLLS were probably inspired by the pantins, or jumping jacks, made in eighteenth-century Europe. By the 1880s, sheets of printed paper dolls and clothes were being made. The first paper doll books were made in the 1920s. Collectors prefer uncut sheets or books or boxed sets of paper dolls. Prices are about half as much if the pages have been cut.

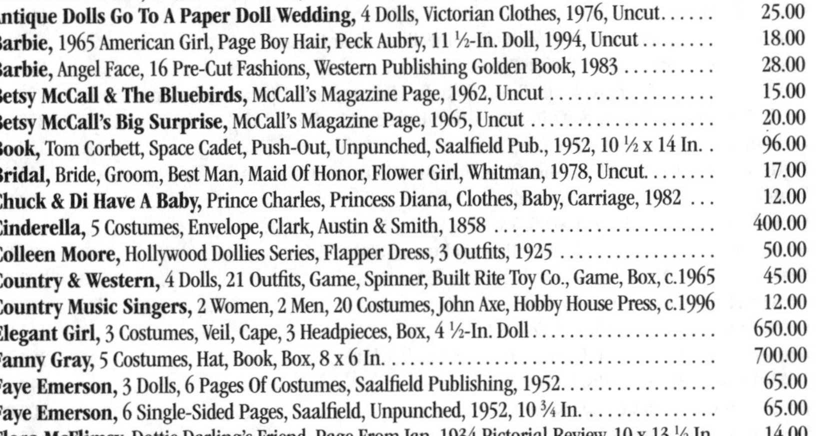

Annette Funicello, Punch-Out Clothes, Cardboard, Kit O. 4621, Whitman, 1962, 10 In. 100.00
Antique Dolls Go To A Paper Doll Wedding, 4 Dolls, Victorian Clothes, 1976, Uncut 25.00
Barbie, 1965 American Girl, Page Boy Hair, Peck Aubry, 11 ½-In. Doll, 1994, Uncut 18.00
Barbie, Angel Face, 16 Pre-Cut Fashions, Western Publishing Golden Book, 1983 .... 28.00
Betsy McCall & The Bluebirds, McCall's Magazine Page, 1962, Uncut 15.00
Betsy McCall's Big Surprise, McCall's Magazine Page, 1965, Uncut 20.00
Book, Tom Corbett, Space Cadet, Push-Out, Unpunched, Saalfield Pub., 1952, 10 ½ x 14 In. . 96.00
Bridal, Bride, Groom, Best Man, Maid Of Honor, Flower Girl, Whitman, 1978, Uncut 17.00
Chuck & Di Have A Baby, Prince Charles, Princess Diana, Clothes, Baby, Carriage, 1982 ... 12.00
Cinderella, 5 Costumes, Envelope, Clark, Austin & Smith, 1858 .... 400.00
Colleen Moore, Hollywood Dollies Series, Flapper Dress, 3 Outfits, 1925 .... 50.00
Country & Western, 4 Dolls, 21 Outfits, Game, Spinner, Built Rite Toy Co., Game, Box, c.1965 45.00
Country Music Singers, 2 Women, 2 Men, 20 Costumes, John Axe, Hobby House Press, c.1996 12.00
Elegant Girl, 3 Costumes, Veil, Cape, 3 Headpieces, Box, 4 ½-In. Doll 650.00
Fanny Gray, 5 Costumes, Hat, Book, Box, 8 x 6 In. 700.00
Faye Emerson, 3 Dolls, 6 Pages Of Costumes, Saalfield Publishing, 1952 .... 65.00
Faye Emerson, 6 Single-Sided Pages, Saalfield, Unpunched, 1952, 10 ¾ In. 65.00
Flora McFlimsy, Dottie Darling's Friend, Page From Jan. 1934 Pictorial Review, 10 x 13 ½ In. 14.00
Gone With The Wind, 5 Dolls, From Movie, Merrill Publishing, 1940, Unpunched 328.00
Hood's Pills, Family, Mother, Father, 3 Girls, Clothing, Original Envelope, 1894 .... 225.00
Jenny Lind, 10 Costumes, 8 Headpieces, Box, 4-In. Doll 1800.00
Lucille Ball, Saalfield Publishing Co., 1944, Unpunched 328.00
Miss Sunbeam, Doll, 4 Dresses, Sunbeam Bread, Quality Bakers, Grocery Store Giveaway, 1950s 15.00
Pebbles, Flintstones, Playpen, Buggy, Toys, Whitman, Punched Out 39.00
Raggedy Ann & Andy, Cardboard Dolls, Plastic Stands, 30 Outfits, Whitman, Box, 1975 .... 17.00
Sandra Dee, Saalfield Publishing Co., Unpunched 107.00
Sister Singing Star Duet Dolls, Patience & Prudence, Bonnie Books Pub., Unpunched 56.00

Paper, Cutwork, Scherenschnitte, Tulips, Heart, Serrated Border, Text, Frame, 1845, 11 x 13 In.
$275.00

Paper, Dance Card, Boar's Head, Carnival Mistick Krewe Of Comus, 1881
$500.00

Paper, Fraktur, Flower Vase, Watercolor, Script, Frame, 1837, 10 x 7 ¾ In.
$1112.00

Paper, Invitation, New Orleans Carnival Ball, Owl, Phunny Phorty Phellows, 1896
$1000.00

P

Skipper, Super Teen, 1980, 12 ¾ x 10 In., Uncut.......... 26.00
Snow White & Prince, Magic Dolls, Dolls, Stands, 23 Outfits, Plastic Scissors, Whitman, Box, 1972 36.00
Sunny, Dolly Dingle's Friend, Grace Drayton, 1926, 10 x 14 In.......... 25.00
Tom Tierney's Cupies, 2 Dolls, Boy, Girl, 14 Outfits, Mushroom, Bee, Clown, Indian, 1984 .. 20.00
Trish, Doll 6, Stand, Clothes, 1920s.......... 22.00
Twiggy, Western Publishing Company, 1967, Unpunched.......... 191.00

PAPERWEIGHTS must have first appeared along with paper in ancient Egypt. Today's collectors search for every type, from the very expensive French weights of the nineteenth century to the modern artist weights or advertising pieces. The glass tops of the paperweights sometimes have been nicked or scratched, and this type of damage can be removed by polishing. Some serious collectors think this type of repair is an alteration and will not buy a repolished weight; others think it is an acceptable technique of restoration that does not change the value. Baccarat paperweights are listed separately under Baccarat.

Advertising, Atlantis, Scale Weights, Clear, Silver Knob Finial, 2 ¾ x 2 ½ In.......... 110.00
Advertising, Buckeye Harvesting Machinery & Binder Twine, c.1900s, 3 In.......... 193.00
Advertising, Color Picture Of Rocky Glen Sanatorium, Glass, 4 In.......... 59.00
Advertising, Dr Pepper 100 Years, 1885-1985, Silver Dollar, Plexiglas, 3 x 3 In.......... 40.00
Advertising, Dump Truck, Recessed Base, The Hug Co. Highland, Ill., c.1925, 3 x 3 x 3 In.... 144.00
Advertising, Furst Bros. & Co., Moldings, Pictures, Domed, Metal Covering, 1 ½ x 3 In. 75.00
Advertising, J.B. Cogan Cork Importer, Glass, Woman's Image, Round, 3 x 1 ½ In.......... 213.00
Advertising, J.H. Lesher & Co., Tailors Trimmings, Chicago, Milk Glass Base, 3 In. 58.00
Advertising, Knickerbocker Fuel Co., Coal, Smokeless, Painted, Cast Metal, 1910, 2 x 3 ½ x 3 In. 144.00
Advertising, Nipper, Cast Iron, Box.......... 30.00
Advertising, Rectangular Victor, His Master's Voice.......... 20.00
Advertising, Russell Cream Co., Polk & Bush Sts., San Francisco, Glass, 4 x 2 ½ In.......... 56.00
Advertising, S.T. Alcus Beverages, Built To Last Bottle Boxes, Copper.......... 50.00
Advertising, Vetrerie & Mosaici Salviati, 2 x 3 ½ In.......... 480.00
Ayotte, Double Pansy Bouquet, Mauve, Ladybug, Signed, 1988, 3 $^{11}/_{16}$ In. 1650.00
Black, Jockey, Red Vest Hat, White Pants, Shirt, Cast Iron, Hubley, 3 ⅜ x 1 ⅞ In. 245.00
Bohemian, Millefiori, Pink, Blue, Green, Yellow, White, Green Ground, Mica, 2 ¾ In.......... 575.00
Bohemian, Millefiori, Pink, Green, Blue, White, Clear Ground, 2 ¼ In.......... 518.00
Bohemian, Millefiori, Red, White, Blue, Yellow, Green, Clear Ground, 2 ½ In. 173.00
Bohemian, Millefiori, White Latticinio, 2 ¼ In.......... 400.00
Bronze, Bird, Lying On Back, 5 In. 219.00
Bronze, Dragon, Figural, On Layered Coin Mound, 4 In. 175.00
Bronze, Figural, Woman's Hand, France, 7 ¼ x 4 ¼ In. 154.00
Clichy, Millefiori, Concentric, Florets, Canes, Green, Pink, Blue, White, 1 ⅝ In. 460.00
Clichy, Millefiori, Nosegay, Pink, Blue, Russet, Green Leaves, 2 ⅜ x 1 ¾ In.......... 345.00
Clichy, Millefiori, Open Concentric, Amethyst, Green, Pink, Blue, White, 2 x 1 In.......... 270.00
Clichy, Millefiori, Rose Garland, 2 ½ In.......... 900.00
Clichy, Millefiori, Star Shape, Green, White, Blue, Pink, Clear Ground, 3 In.......... 345.00
Clichy, Pansy, Purple, Yellow & Blue Petals, 2 In.......... 805.00
Daniel Salazar, Christmas, White, Green Holly, Red Berries, Gold Threading, 2 ½ In.......... 90.00
David Lotton, Floral, Pink & White, Blue Green Iridescent Dichroic Bed, 3 x 2 In. 250.00
Dominick Labino, Green, 1971, 2 x 3 In. 117.00
Figural, Lion, Black Amethyst, Milk Glass, Recumbent Figure, 2 ¾ x 2 In. 141.00
Fratelli Toso, Millefiori, Satino Handle, 5 x 3 In. 400.00
Fratelli Toso, Twisted Cane, Footed, 5 x 3 In.......... 225.00
George Washington, Clear, Frosted, Houdon Bust, c.1880, 2 ⅞ In. 124.00
Glass, Presidents McKinley, Roosevelt, Sepia, 2 ½ x 4 ¼ In. 179.00
Grover Cleveland, Clear, 2 ½ x 4 In.......... *illus* 90.00
Grover Cleveland, Milk Glass, 1890s, 3 In.......... 143.00
Grover Cleveland, Pottery, Portrait, Transfer, Black, White, 3 In.......... 203.00
J. Winfisky, Seascape, 1980s, 4 x 2 ½ In. 140.00
Jay Strongwater, Flower, Enameled, Jewels, Leaves 100.00
Kanawha, Owl, Amberina, 4 ⅝ In.......... 25.00
Kansas Jayhawk, Painted, Cast, Lead, 2 ½ x 2 ¼ x 1 In. 33.00
Millville, Umbrella, White, Red, Green, Blue Spatters, Applied Clear Pedestal, 3 ¾ In.......... 300.00
Murano, Multicolored Millefiori Canes, Pink Over White, 5 Facets, 3 In.......... 115.00
New England Glass Co., Blown Apple, Rust To Yellow, Cookie Base, 3 ¼ x 2 ¾ In. 460.00
New England Glass Co., Blue Poinsettia, White Swirl Latticinio Ground, 2 ⅞ In.......... 300.00
New England Glass Co., Fruit Bouquet, Pink, Yellow, Pears, Cherries, Leaves, 2 ⅝ In. 300.00
New England Glass Co., Millefiori, 2 Garlands, White, Red, Blue, Green, Yellow, 2 ⅝ In. 780.00
New England Glass Co., Millefiori, Concentric, Blue, Pink, Yellow, White, 2 ⅜ In. 288.00
New England Glass Co., Millefiori, Concentric, Swirl Latticinio, 12 Facets, 2 ⅝ In.......... 115.00

TIP
Paperweights that are displayed on a wooden table in front of a sunny window may magnify the sun's rays enough to scorch the tabletop.

Paperweight, Grover Cleveland, Clear, 2 ½ x 4 In.
$90.00

Paperweight, New England Glass Co., Poinsettia, 10 Red Petals, Green Leaves, Stem, 2 ½ In.
$288.00

TIP
Rub tartar-control toothpaste on your scratched snow dome paperweights. It will remove the smaller scratches.

P

New England Glass Co., Millefiori, Scramble, Multicolored, Running Rabbits, 2 ¼ In. 201.00
New England Glass Co., Millefiori, Scrambled, 1852 Cane, 2 ¼ In. 259.00
New England Glass Co., Millefiori, Spiral Latticinio Ground, 2 ⅝ In. 288.00
New England Glass Co., Poinsettia, 10 Red Petals, Green Leaves, Stem, 2 ½ In. . . . . . *illus* 288.00
Orient & Flume, Dragonfly, Pulled Leaves, Magenta, Purple, Gold, 2 ¾ In. 374.00
Orient & Flume, Frog, Iridescent Gold, 3 ½ In. 115.00
Orient & Flume, Frog, Red Spotted, On Stone, 2 ¾ x 3 ⅜ In. 431.00
Orient & Flume, Green Spider, Millefiori Body, Blue Flower, Maroon Web, 2 ⅛ In. 207.00
Orient & Flume, Millefiori, Green, Ground, Signed, 2 ½ In. 360.00
Orient & Flume, Peacock Feathers, Combed, 1978, 2 ½ In. 207.00
Orient & Flume, Penguin, Black, White, Box, Signed, 4 In. 173.00
Paprabelle, Millefiori, White, Amethyst, Green, Red, Red Ground, 2 ¾ In. 201.00
Perthshire, Golfer, Millefiori, Twists, 3 In. 380.00
Portraits, Cleveland, Stevenson, Milk Glass, Clear Glass, N.Y., 1892, 4 x 3 In. 239.00
Portraits, Parker, Davis, Red, White, Blue, 1904, 3 In. 538.00
Portraits, Roosevelt, Fairbanks, Parker, Davis, Glass, Color, 1904, 3 In., Pair 1315.00
Portraits, Roosevelt, Fairbanks, Sepia, 1904 . . . . . . 155.00
Portraits, Roosevelt, Fairbanks, Symbols, Penn., Milk Glass, 1904, 4 x 3 In. 508.00
Portraits, Roosevelt, Franklin, Symbols, Sepia, Crystallography, 3 In. 448.00
Ray Banford, Pink Rope Roses, Green Leaves, Stems, 5 Side Facets, 2 ¼ In. 403.00
Ribbon, Looped, Powder Blue, Red, White Bubble, England, 5 ½ In. 210.00
Rosessler, Morning Glory, Blossoms, Orange, Purple, Green, Stems, 1980s, 2 ⅜ In. 180.00
St. Louis, Bouquet, 4 Blossoms, 6 Side Facets, 2 ⅝ In. 2280.00
St. Louis, Fruit Bouquet, Pears, Cherries, Leaves, Spiral Latticinio Basket, 2 ½ In. 575.00
St. Louis, Heart Shape, Coeur Filet, St. Louis, 3 ½ x 3 ¾ In. 176.00
St. Louis, Millefiori, Crown, Red, Blue Twist Ribbons, White Twist Filigrees, 2 ⅛ In. 960.00
St. Louis, Millefiori, Open Concentric, Red, White, Blue, Yellow, Pink, Green, 2 ¾ In. 460.00
St. Louis, Millefiori, Scrambled, Multicolored Twist, Clear Ground, 3 x 1 ¾ In. 288.00
St. Louis, Miniature, Pink, Green, White, Blue, 1 ¾ In. 345.00
St. Louis, Nosegay, Green Leaves, 3 Millefiori Florets, Red, White, Blue, 2 In. 230.00
Sulphide, White Eagle, Blue Mottled Ground, Signed, c.1969, 2 ⅞ In. 17.00
Viking Arat Glass, Rabbit, Bluenique, 4 ⅛ x 2 ½ In. 25.00
Whitefriars, Millefiori, Blue, White, Teal, Red, 3 ⅛ In. 230.00
Whitefriars, Millefiori, Close Pack, Cobalt Blue Flash Overlay, 5 Facets, 3 ⅛ In. 360.00
Whitefriars, Millefiori, Concentric, Applied Pedestal, Star Cut Base, 2 ¾ x 3 In. 575.00
Whitefriars, Millefiori, Concentric, White, Green, Blue, Pink, Triplex, 1951, 2 ⅜ In. 403.00
Whittemore, Hummingbird, Green, White, Brown, Bluebell, Signed, 2 ¼ In. . . . . . *illus* 259.00
Zachary Taylor, White Military Portrait, Wine Colored Sulfide Glass, 3 x 2 In. 1435.00

PAPIER-MACHE is made from paper mixed with glue, chalk, and other ingredients, then molded and baked. It becomes very hard and can be painted. Boxes, trays, and furniture were made of papier-mache. Some of the nineteenth-century pieces were decorated with mother-of-pearl. Papier-mache is still being used to make small toys, figures, candy containers, boxes, and other giftwares. Furniture made of papier-mache is listed in the Furniture category.

Bowl, Vines, English Victorian, c.1850, 11 ½ x 14 ½ In. 88.00
Cabinet, Writing, Mother-Of-Pearl Inlays, Gilt, Drop Front, Dividers, Pen Rests, c.1850, 14 In. 649.00
Case, Jewelry, Mother-Of-Pearl, Warwick Castle, 11 ½ In. . . . . . *illus* 600.00
Figure, Bulldog, Wheels On Feet, Barks When Chain Is Pulled, 15 x 27 In. 725.00
Figure, Peacock, Yellow, Green, Blue Eyes, Brass Stand, Sergio Bustamante, 65 ½ In. 3068.00
Figure, Rabbit, Blue Dress, Pink Apron, Carrying Egg, Yellow Basket On Back, 8 In. 121.00
Figure, Stylized Rooster, Modern, 20th Century, Italy, 39 In. 235.00
Folio Cover, Victorian, Ebonized, Inlaid, Mother-Of-Pearl, Shadowbox Frame, 12 x 9 In. 81.00
Horn, Pig, Pillbox Hat, 16 In. 201.00
Milliner's Head, Woman, Painted Multicolored, France, 19th Century, 15 In. 1763.00
Roly Poly, Clown, Red, 5 ¾ In. 69.00
Roly Poly, Clown, Skull Cap, Germany, 14 In. 316.00
Tray, Black, Inlayed Mother-Of-Pearl, Gilt, Scalloped Edge, 10 ½ In. 190.00
Tray, Black Ground, Multicolored Flowers, Oblong, England, 19th Century, 10 In. 205.00
Tray, Black Lacquer, Scalloped, Raised Edge, Vining, Victorian, 22 x 32 In. 720.00
Tray, Dog Portrait, Mother-Of-Pearl, Gold Highlights, Raised Rim, Oval, 24 x 30 In. 920.00
Tray, Flowers, Brown Ground, Metal Base, 24 x 31 In. 264.00
Tray, Gilt, Green, Flowers, Birds, Peacock, England, Early 1800s, 25 x 32 In. 3081.00
Tray, Hand Painted Flowers, Occupied Japan, 14 x 12 In. 95.00
Tray, Stylized Branches, Black, Gilt, Jennens & Bettridge, 1865, 25 x 31 In. . . . . . *illus* 978.00
Tray, Wood Stand, Abbey Scene, Mother-Of-Pearl Inlay, Scalloped Rim, c.1850, 20 x 28 In. 885.00

PARASOL, *see Umbrella category.*

Paperweight, Whittemore, Hummingbird, Green, White, Brown, Bluebell, Signed, 2 ¼ In.
$259.00

Papier-Mache, Case, Jewelry, Mother-Of-Pearl, Warwick Castle, 11 ½ In.
$600.00

Papier-Mache, Tray, Stylized Branches, Black, Gilt, Jennens & Bettridge, 1865, 25 x 31 In.
$978.00

TIP

If your papier-mache doll heads or furniture are cracking, you might try arresting the cracks with a thin coat of white household glue.

Parian, Bust, Woman, Summer, Copeland Tint, Enamel, Gilt, Owen Hale, 1885, 17 ½ In.
$1430.00

Paris, Planter, Landscape Panels, Sheep, Windmills, Green Base, Gilt Highlights, 1800s, 5 In., Pair
$805.00

Paris, Tureen, Cover, Platter, Columbine Sprays, Bouquets, Gilt, Handles, 12-In. Tureen
$600.00

TIP

If you use plate hangers to display your plates, be sure they are not too tight. The clips should be covered with a soft material. Otherwise the end clips may scratch or chip the plate.

PARIAN is a fine-grained, hard-paste porcelain named for the marble it resembles. It was first made in England in 1846 and gained in favor in the United States about 1860. Figures, tea sets, vases, and other items were made of Parian at many English and American factories.

Bust, Bearded Lincoln, White, c.1864, 9 In. 1434.00
Bust, Byron, Black Glaze, Circular Base, E.W. Wyon, England, c.1890, 16 In. 415.00
Bust, John Bunyan, Signed, E.W. Wyon, 13 ¾ In. 550.00
Bust, Theodore Roosevelt, Suit, Tie, c.1900, 9 In. 354.00
Bust, Ulysses S. Grant, Military Uniform, White, 8 In. 1195.00
Bust, Woman, Elaborate Hair, Stand-Up Collar, Mid 19th Century, 23 In. 470.00
Bust, Woman, Summer, Copeland Tint, Enamel, Gilt, Owen Hale, 1885, 17 ½ In. ...... *illus* 1430.00
Ewer, Dolphin Handle, Applied Flowers, Grapes, Leaves, Ruffled Spout, c.1850, 20 In. 510.00
Figurine, Angel Praying, 13 x 11 In., Pair 175.00
Figurine, Atlas, Supporting Globe, Astrological Symbols, Impressed Mark, 1800s, 10 ½ In. 646.00
Figurine, Ladies, Beatrice, Maidenhood Symbol, Multicolored, Pastels, Gilt, c.1875, 22 In., Pair 948.00
Figurine, Little Red Riding Hood, Painted, 19th Century, 6 ½ In. 40.00
Figurine, Nude Female, Standing, Greek Slave Bound By Chains, c.1850, 16 x 4 In. 1610.00
Figurine, Nude Woman, Washing Foot, 32 In. 1320.00
Figurine, Seminude Maiden, Holding Cup, Marble Plinth, 19 In. 336.00
Figurine, Wolfhound & Farm Boy, White, 7 ½ In. 110.00
Figurine, Woman, Child & Dogs, 13 ½ x 9 ½ In. 11.80
Figurine, Woman, Seated On Rock Pile, Marked, 211, Late 1800s, 13 x 6 x 5 In. 187.00
Group, Three Graces, 3 Nude Women, Oval Plinth, c.1850, 12 x 7 In. 570.00
Jug, Cobalt Blue Design, Relief, Marked, 9 In. 44.00
Plaque, 2 Men, Woman, Classical, Relief, Frame, 11 ½ In. Diam. 20.00
Vase, Bearded Lincoln Portrait, Blue, White, 7 ¾ In. 717.00
Vase, Figural, Woman, Cherub, Leaves, Flowers, Scrolls, 8 ¾ x 7 ¼ x 6 ½ In. 77.00

PARIS, Vieux Paris, or Old Paris, is porcelain ware that is known to have been made in Paris in the eighteenth or early nineteenth century. These porcelains have no identifying mark but can be recognized by the whiteness of the porcelain and the lines and decorations. Gold decoration is often used.

Basket, Center, Gold & White, Navette Shape, Gilded Border, Wheat Sheaf, 10 x 12 In. 900.00
Cachepot, Cherubs, Platinum Glaze, 19th Century, 7 ½ In., Pair 1210.00
Cachepot, Flowers, Yellow Ground, Gilt, Handles, 8 x 8 In. 50.00
Cup, Henry Clay, Portrait, Gold Leaf Trim, White, Black, Hand Painted, 4 In. 13145.00
Cup & Saucer, Daniel Webster, Portrait, Gold Leaf Trim, White, Black, c.1840, 3 ¼ In. 4481.00
Dessert Service, Floral Sprays, Pink & Gilt Borders, Compote, Tazza, 12 Plates, Dish, 9 ¼ In. 360.00
Dessert Stand, 2 Tiers, Double Cobalt Blue Bands, Gilt Lines, Early 1800s, 14 ½ x 11 In. 294.00
Planter, Landscape Panels, Sheep, Windmills, Green Base, Gilt, 1800s, 5 In., Pair ...... *illus* 805.00
Plate, Chateau De Combreux, Chateau De Grimaldi, Blue Border, Footed, c.1840, 8 ¾ In., Pair 1920.00
Tea Set, Italianate Scene, Gilt Highlights, 40 Piece 575.00
Teapot, Cover, Napoleon Portrait, Green Ground, Gilt Spout, Handle & Border, 1800s, 8 ¼ In. 385.00
Tureen, Cover, Platter, Columbine Sprays, Bouquets, Gilt, Handles, 12-In. Tureen ..... *illus* 600.00
Urn, Courting Couple, Landscape, Flowers, Painted, Gilt, Campana Form, 1800s, 10 ¾ In. 400.00
Urn, Cover, Federal Eagle, Banner, White, Magenta, Gold Accents, c.1820, 9 ¼ In. 4780.00
Urn, Deer, Landscape, Hut, Gold, Arch Handles, Mid 19th Century, 14 ½ In. 700.00
Urn, Figures, Landscape, Painted, Gilt, Brass Mounts, Footed, Early 20th Century, 23 In. 250.00
Urn, Floral Bouquets, Green Ground, Gilt Highlights, c.1890, 17 In., Pair 4600.00
Urn, Flowers, Flared, Square Foot, c.1830, 9 In., Pair 445.00
Urn, Gilt, Campana Shape, Scenic Reserves, 13 In., Pair 720.00
Urn, Gilt, Oval, Painted, Landscape, Scroll Handles, Square Base, c.1820, 12 ¾ In., Pair 531.00
Urn, Gold Handles, Neck, Base, Peasants On Road, Painted Panels, France, c.1890, 13 In., Pair 1955.00
Urn, Hand Painted Flowers, Purple Ground, 2 Gilt Satyr Head Handles, 1800s, 13 In., Pair... 633.00
Urn, Reserves, Birds, Landscape, Yellow Ground, Black Bands, Gilt Highlights, 1800s, 5 In., Pair 4230.00
Vase, Asian Figures, Flowers, 2 Gilt Winged Dragon Handles, c.1890, 16 In., Pair 3689.00
Vase, Blue & White, Gilt, Cities & Castles On The Rhine, Openwork Handles, 17 In., Pair. 4200.00
Vase, Bottle Shape, Lovers, Woodland Panels, Applied Flowers, Fruits, Insects, c.1900, 12 In., Pair 920.00
Vase, Classical Style, Ormolu Stand, Blue Ground, Painted, Roman Man Profile, 12 ½ In. ... 95.00
Vase, Etruscan Revival, Balustroid, Cup Shape Neck, Vine Bands, Medallions, 18 ½ In. 119.00
Vase, Garniture, Gilt, Green Accents, Royal Blue Ground, Painted Reserves, 1800s, 18 In., Pair 1680.00
Vase, Romantic Scenes, Flowers, Scrolling Plinths, Gilt, c.1890, 11 ½ x 8 ½ In., Pair 520.00
Vase, Turquoise Ground, Barrel Shape, Loop Handles, Mother & Child, Gilt, 8 ⅜ In., Pair 326.00

PATE-DE-VERRE is an ancient technique in which glass is made by blending and refining powdered glass of different colors into molds. The process was revived by French glassmakers, especially Galle, around the end of the nineteenth century.

Figurine, Fish, Blue, Orange, Green, Amber, Marked, Decorchemont, 7 ¼ In. .... *illus* 2040.00
Figurine, Fish, Waves, Gold, Blue, Green, Impressed Seal, Decorchemont, 8 In. 2280.00
Pendant, Beetle, Rose To Milk Ground, Taupe Silk Double Cord, Wood Bead, c.1900 .... 1007.00
Tray, Lily Pad, Large Beetle, Green, Amber, Mark, c.1900, 9 In. 1035.00
Vase, Urn Shape, 2 Swag Handles, Fruit, Mottled, Green, Amber, Decorchemont, 7 In. 633.00

PATENT MODELS were required as part of a patent application for a United States patent until 1880. In 1926 the stored patent models were sold as a group by the U.S. Patent Office and individual models are now appearing in the marketplace.

Artificial Leg, No. 71197, Abner McOmber, Schenectady, N.Y., 1867, 9 In. 880.00
Biscuit Maker, No. 39972, J.R. Treadwell, Sept. 15, 1863 .... 275.00
Chair, Folding, No. 167098, Francis Hickman, Aug. 1875 .... 130.00
Gas Apparatus, Brass, Tin, No. 228848, Tag, 1880, 10 x 12 In. 600.00
Harness Equipment, Leather, Cast Steel Ham Type Harness Mount, J.H. Garret Inventor, 7 x 11 In. 117.50
Improved Refrigerator, Grain Painted, Tags, Patent Papers, Peter Vogt, 1866, 11 ½ x 10 In. 1100.00
Inkstand, S. Darling, Patent Office Tags, January 9th 1866, Reissued 1870, 1876 .... 425.00
Ironing Board, Wood, No. 183807, J.M. Kendall, Oct. 31, 1876 .... 300.00
Sled, Walnut, Front Steering, No. 381665, Samuel Leeds Allen, 1888, 13 ½ In. 400.00

PATE-SUR-PATE means paste on paste. The design was made by painting layers of slip on the ceramic piece until a relief decoration was formed. The method was developed at the Sevres factory in France about 1850. It became even more famous at the English Minton factory about 1870. It has since been used by many potters to make both pottery and porcelain wares.

Flask, Moon, Girl On Swing, Woodland Scene, Brown, Gilt, 8 ⅛ In. 431.00
Plaque, Allegorical, Wind, Olive Ground, Late 1800s, 9 ½ x 7 In. 748.00
Plaque, Classical, Disguised Woman, Cupids, Blue Ground, Birks, 5 ⅜ x 2 ⅜ In. 1150.00
Plaque, Green, Cameo Of Young Woman, Oval, 9 ¼ In. 400.00
Plaque, Le Collier, Classical Figure, Putting Spiked Collar On Cupid, 7 In. 1955.00
Plaque, Woman, Cherub, Purple, Green, 5 ⅛ In. Diam. 265.00
Plaque, Woman & Angel With Flowers, Gilt, 5 ⅛ In. 250.00
Plate, Reticulated Greek Key Borders, Birds, Flowers, Pink Ground, 9 ¾ In., Pair 978.00
Urn, Bust, Art Nouveau, Woman, Flowers, Scarf, Olive Ground, Gilt, 10 In. 575.00
Vase, 2 Cherubs, Green, White Enamel, 6-Sided, Branch Handles, Pierced Neck, 8 In. 150.00
Vase, Girl Carrying Basket, Blue, White, Gilt, Egg Form, Signed, 5 ½ In. 250.00
Vase, Green Medallion, Flowers, Ivory, Reticulated Rim, Snake Handles, 4 ¼ In. 210.00
Vase, Lid, Pink, White, Gilt, Oval, Crown Top, Handles, 15 ½ In., Pair 125.00
Vase, Neoclassical Maiden, White, Mint Ground, Sterling Overlay, Handles, 5 ½ In. 275.00
Vase, Salmon Pink, Raised White Birds In Flight, Cattails, Reticulated Rim, Flat, 7 In. 800.00
Vase, Woman, White Gown, Green Cartouche, Mother-Of-Pearl Ground, Gold, 7 In. 250.00

PAUL REVERE POTTERY was made at several locations in and around Boston, Massachusetts, between 1906 and 1942. The pottery was operated as a settlement house program for teenage girls. Many pieces were signed S.E.G. for Saturday Evening Girls. The artists concentrated on children's dishes and tiles. Decorations were outlined in black and filled with color.

Bookends, Snowy Landscape, Dead Matte Glaze, Gray Ground, c.1926, 4 x 5 In. 1560.00
Bowl, 2-Tone Light Blue Gloss Glaze, Mark, Signed HE, 2 x 4 In. 195.00
Bowl, Blue Over Orange, Yellow Gloss Glaze, Mark, 2 x 5 In. 345.00
Bowl, Clusters Of Geese, Blue Ground, 2 x 6 In. 570.00
Bowl, Double Rabbit, Yellow, S.E.G., Signed LS, 1909, 5 In. .... *illus* 465.00
Bowl, Incised Flower Border, Yellow Glaze, S.E.G., 9 x 3 In. 450.00
Bowl, Roosters, Green, Cuerda Seca, S.E.G., Signed, 1909, 2 x 5 ½ In. 4500.00
Cup Plate, Blue Mottled Glaze, Signed WB, 39929, 4 In. 75.00
Cup Plate, Green Mottled Glaze, Mark, 4 In. 75.00
Cup Plate, Olive Green Matte, 4 In. 75.00
Cup Plate, Orange Matte Glaze, P.R.P. Mark, 4 In. 75.00
Cup Plate, Yellow Mottled Matte Glaze, 4 In. 65.00
Mug, Brown Over Blue, White Glaze, Paper Label, 4 x 5 In. 395.00
Mug, Roosters, Green Ground, Early Bird, Mark, S.E.G, 4 x 4 In. .... *illus* 14400.00
Pitcher, Squirrel, White Matte Glaze, Black Outline, Signed, 3 In. 415.00
Pitcher, Yellow, White, Black Band, Signed L.M., 39892, 8 x 11 In. 495.00
Plate, Cup, Brown Houses, Tree Rim, Mustard Glaze, Round, c.1905, 8 In. 474.00
Plate, Flower Border, Blue, Green, Black Outline, c.1901, 8 In. 356.00
Plate, Painted Center Landscape, Blue, Green, Mark, 1936, 8 In. 600.00
Salt, Satiny Matte Glaze, No. 345, Signed R. Bacchini, ½ x 2 ½ In. 95.00

Pate-De-Verre, Figurine, Fish, Blue, Orange, Green, Amber, Marked, Decorchemont, 7 ¼ In.
$2040.00

Paul Revere Pottery, Bowl, Double Rabbit, Yellow, S.E.G., Signed LS, 1909, 5 In.
$465.00

Paul Revere Pottery, Mug, Roosters, Green Ground, Early Bird, Mark, S.E.G., 4 x 4 In.
$14400.00

TIP

If you own a wicker chair that makes small popping noises when you sit in it, dampen it with water. It is too dry, and wicker may crack if not kept moist.

Peachblow, Bride's Bowl, Diamond Quilted, Metal Holder, Rope Ormolu, c.1890, 7 In.
$250.00

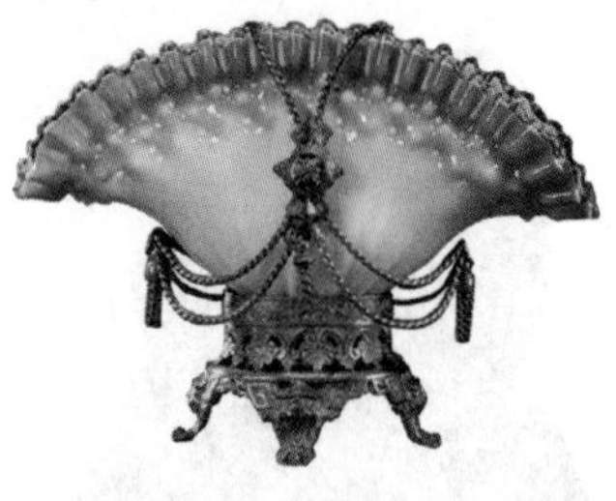

Peachblow, Toothpick, Glossy, Kate Greenaway Holder, Marked, Tufts, 3 ½ In.
$740.00

Peachblow, Vase, Morgan, Griffin Base, Hobbs, Brockunier, New England, 10 In.
$2390.00

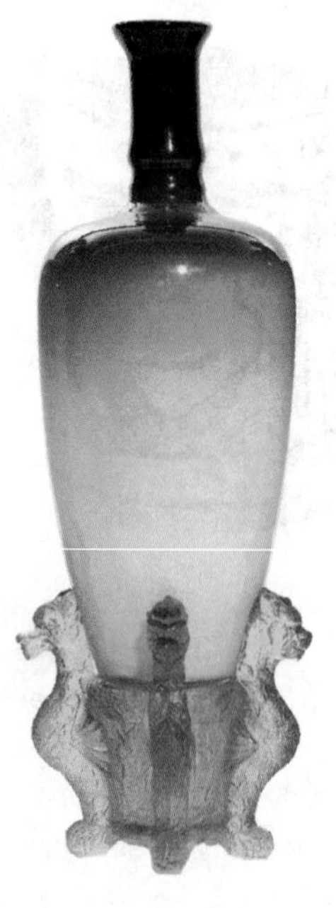

Salt & Pepper, Green, 2 x 3 In. 195.00
Tile, Hull Street Galloupe House, 3 ¾ In. Square 10200.00
Tile, Paul Revere's House North Square, 3 ¾ In. Square 3000.00
Tumbler, Blue Glaze, Mark, 40010, A.G., 4 In. 33.00
Vase, High Blue Glaze, 12-23 Mark, 7 x 4 In. 295.00
Vase, High Blue Glaze, Paper Label, 5 x 4 In. 165.00
Vase, Light Blue Matte Glaze, 1929, 14 In. 540.00

PEACHBLOW glass was made by several factories beginning in the 1880s. New England peachblow is a one-layer glass shading from red to white. Mt. Washington peachblow shades from pink to bluish-white. Hobbs, Brockunier and Company of Wheeling, West Virginia, made Coral glass that they marketed as Peach Blow. It shades from yellow to peach and is lined with white glass. Reproductions of all types of peachblow have been made. Related pieces may be listed under Gunderson and Webb Peachblow.

Bride's Bowl, Diamond Quilted, Metal Holder, Rope Ormolu, c.1890, 7 In. .... *illus* 250.00
Creamer, Oval, Satin, Hobbs, Brockunier, 4 In. 575.00
Cruet, Bulbous, Stickneck, Amber Handle, Faceted Stopper, Hobbs, Brockunier, 7 In. 360.00 to 546.00
Cruet, Melon Ribbed, Teardrop Stopper, Mt. Washington, 7 In.. .... 1380.00
Cup & Saucer, Mt. Washington, 4 ½ In. 230.00
Decanter, Bulbous, Reeded Handle, Faceted Stopper, Hobbs, Brockunier, 10 In. 2300.00
Dish, Condiment, Silver Plated Cover, Silver Undertray, New England, 5 In. 345.00
Ewer, Ruffled Rim, Mt. Washington, 5 ½ x 4 In.. .... 50.00
Finger Bowl, Hobbs, Brockunier, 4 In. 259.00
Jug, Claret, Reeded Handle, Rigaree Collar, Hobbs, Brockunier, 10 In. 1380.00
Pitcher, Enameled, Butterfly, Flowers, James Montgomery Verse, Mt. Washington, 7 In. 40250.00
Pitcher, Milk, Oval, Glossy, Hobbs, Brockunier, 5 In.. .... 288.00 to 345.00
Plate, Rolled Edge, 9 In.. .... 40.00
Toothpick, Glossy, Kate Greenaway Holder, Marked, Tufts, 3 ½ In. .... *illus* 740.00
Tumbler, Glossy, New England, 3 ½ In.. .... 201.00
Vase, Bud, Hobbs, Brockunier, 8 ¾ In.. .... 225.00
Vase, Bulbous, Glossy, Hobbs, Brockunier, 6 ½ In. 834.00
Vase, Double Gourd, Glossy, Hobbs, Brockunier, 8 In. 1150.00
Vase, Double Gourd, Glossy, Mt. Washington, 10 In.. .... 2415.00
Vase, Double Gourd, Hobbs, Brockunier, 7 ½ In. 1380.00
Vase, Flowers, Enameled, Ruffled Tricornered Rim, Mt. Washington, 7 ½ In. 90.00
Vase, Glossy, Hobbs, Brockunier, 4 In. 201.00
Vase, Glossy, Morgan, Griffin Base, Hobbs, Brockunier, 10 In. 978.00
Vase, Gourd, Enameled Daisies, Leaves, Gourd, New England, 6 In. 316.00
Vase, Jack-In-The-Pulpit, Ruffled Edge, Footed, Mt. Washington, 7 ¼ In. 825.00
Vase, Lily, Base, New England, 10 x 4 In.. .... 1050.00
Vase, Lily, Gold Enameled Flowers, Vines, Tricornered Rim, Mt. Washington, 10 ¼ In. 2100.00
Vase, Lily, Tricornered Rim, 9 x 3 ½ In.. .... 985.00
Vase, Morgan, Griffin Base, Hobbs, Brockunier, New England, 10 In. .... *illus* 2390.00
Vase, Snipped Edge, Enameled, Bluebird, Branch, New England, 6 In.. .... 316.00
Vase, Square Mouth, Glossy, Hobbs, Brockunier, 4 In. 431.00
Vase, Squat, Flowers, 4 ¼ In. 100.00
Vase, Stick, Cupped Rim, New England, 9 x 4 ½ In. 1275.00
Vase, Stick, Glossy, Bulbous, Base, Hobbs, Brockunier, 11 In. 460.00
Vase, Stick, Glossy, Bulbous, Hobbs, Brockunier, 8 ¼ In. 345.00
Vase, Teardrop Shape, Glossy, Hobbs, Brockunier, 9 In. 2013.00
Water Bottle, Cone Shape, Ring Collar, Glossy, Hobbs, Brockunier, 8 In. 920.00

PEANUTS is the tile of a comic strip created by cartoonist Charles M. Schulz (1922–2000). The strip, drawn by Schulz from 1950 to 2000, features a group of children, including Charlie Brown and his sister Sally, Lucy Van Pelt and her brother Linus, Peppermint Patty, and Pig Pen, and an imaginative and independent beagle named Snoopy. The Peanuts gang has also been featured in books, television shows, and a Broadway musical.

Book, Peanuts Holiday Super Coloring & Activity Book, Landoll Inc., 10 x 8 In. 9.00
Clock, Snoopy On Dog House, Glass, Metal Bezel, Battery, 10 x 1 ½ x 10 In. 20.00
Clock, Wall, Swiss Chalet, Citizen, Charlie Brown, Lucy, Swinging Woodstock, 15 x 13 x 7 In.. 350.00
Comic Strip, Peanuts Daily, Charlie, Linus, For Al With Friendship, 27268, 7 x 28 In. 16500.00
Comic Strip, Peanuts Daily, Snoopy Acts As Revolving Door For Linus, 19591, 6 x 28 In. 21000.00
Cookie Jar, Charlie Brown Finial, Peanut Gang Around Base, UFS 15.00
Doll, Linus, Vinyl, Clothes, Accessories, In Bag, Determined Products, 1960s, 7 In. 80.00
Jar, Insulated, Charlie Brown On Lid, Orange, Plastic, Thermos, 1969, 3 ½ x 4 In. 18.00

Mug, I'm Not Worth A Thing Before Coffee Break, 3 ⅛ x 3 9/16 In. 14.00
Mug, Snoopy, Woodstock, At Times Life Is Pure Joy, Fire-King .... *illus* 24.00
Music Box, Figural, The Doctor Is In, Wood, Charlie Brown, Lucy, Anri, Italy, 1968, 9 In. 221.00
Music Box, Snoopy, Astronaut, Painted, Wood, Figural, Schmid, 8 x 5 In. 145.00
Music Box, World War I Flying Ace, Painted, Wood, Figural, Schmid, 8 x 4 ¾ In. 506.00
Nodder, Charlie Brown, Painted, c.1960s, 6 x 5 In. .... *illus* 145.00
Nodder, Charlie Brown, Red Shirt, Black Shorts, 1960s, 6 In. 145.00
Nodder, Lucy, Red Dress, Papier-Mache, 1952, 3 ½ In. 25.00
Original Comic Art, 3 Panels, Daily Strip, Charlie Brown, Sally, 40175, 1992, 10 x 24 In. 12245.00
Ornament, Linus On Sled, Hallmark, Box, 1995 .... 13.00
Ornament, Snoopy Holding Woodstock In Nest, Ceramic, Flat, 2 ¾ In. 24.00
Pendant, Snoopy, Woodstock, Joint Parade, Enamel, 1 x 1 ½ In. 22.00
Pin, Charlie Brown, Holding Mitt, 1 ¼ In. 10.00
Shoe Bag, Snoopy, Woodstock, Sleeping On Mailbox, c.1972, 29 ½ x 17 In. 12.00
Telephone, Snoopy, Woodstock, Rotary, Yellow Receiver, 1976-79, 13 ½ x 9 ½ x 8 ½ In. 250.00
Thermos, Charlie Brown On Lid, United Feature Syndicate Inc., 1969, 3 ½ x 4 In. 18.00
Thermos, Snoopy With Bat, Charlie Brown, Lucy, Schroeder, Metal, 1966. .... 10.00
Wristwatch, Woodstock On Dial, Peanuts Gang On Box Top, Armitron, c.1980 .... 69.00

PEARL items listed here are made of the natural mother-of-pearl from shells. Such natural pearl has been used to decorate furniture and small utilitarian objects for centuries. The glassware known as mother-of-pearl is listed by that name. Opera glasses made with natural pearl shell are listed under Opera Glasses.

Card Case, 4 x 3 In. 35.00
Card Case, Abalone, Tortoiseshell, Inlaid Diamond, Brass Rope Twist Edge, 3 ⅝ In. 178.00
Card Case, Mother-Of-Pearl, Abalone, Shell, Diamond Inlay, Brass, 1890s, 3 ⅝ In. .... *illus* 175.00
Card Case, Shell Cameo Bone, Ebony Inlaid Checkerband, Mounted, 3 ½ In. 237.00
Magnifying Glass, Parasol Handle, Victorian, 16 ½ In. 117.00
Mirror, Handle, George Washington Portrait, c.1790 .... 450.00

PEARLWARE is an earthenware made by Josiah Wedgwood in 1779. It was copied by other potters in England. Pearlware is only slightly different in color from creamware and for many years collectors have confused the terms. Wedgwood pieces are listed in the Wedgwood category in this book. Most pearlware with mocha designs is listed under Mocha.

Pearl

Cistern, Bear Holding Dog, c.1800, 12 ½ In. 6435.00
Coffeepot, Cover, Mosque & Camel, Blue Transferware, 11 x 9 In. 425.00
Creamer, 7 Men At Table, 2 Figures At Well, Hound Handle, 19th Century, 5 In. 527.00
Cup, American Flag, Red, White, Blue, Handleless, 19th Century, 2 ½ x 4 In. 380.00
Figurine, Couple, Rural Pastime, Bagpiper, Tambourine, c.1810, 8 In., Pair 1500.00
Figurine, Sailor's Farewell, Return, Period Couple, c.1822, 10 In., Pair. 3438.00
Figurine, Squirrel, Eating Nut, Yellow, Brown Streaked Glaze, Green Stand, c.1795, 7 In. 7500.00
Figurine, Tee Total, Family, Table, Tea, Turrets, Table Base, c.1830, 8 In. 5000.00
Jug, Mask, Multicolored, 7 In. 230.00
Loving Cup, Peafowl, 2-Sided, Handles, Footed, 19th Century, 5 ½ In. 410.00
Mug, Asian Scene, Brown Transfer, Cobalt Blue Trim, c.1815, 4 ½ In. 88.00
Mug, Blue Willow, Transfer, England, Mid 19th Century, 4 ¾ In. 59.00
Pitcher, Hunt Scene, Copper Highlights, Impressed, Wood & Caldwell, 1820s, 7 ½ In. 150.00
Pitcher, Landscape, Blue, Rust & Green Stripes, 6 ¾ In. 819.00
Pitcher, Red Flowers, Leaves, 6 x 5 In. 110.00
Plate, Boston State House, Blue Transfer, Rogers, 10 In. 250.00
Plate, Chinese Fisher, Blue Transfer, 10 In. 200.00
Plate, Flower Basket, 6 Panels, Relief Eagles & Flower Spray Rim, Early 1800s, 7 ¼ In. 1000.00
Plate, Raised Trophy Border, Star, Multicolored Enamel, Dawson Pratt Type, 1800, 6 ⅜ In. 593.00
Platter, Tendril, Flowers & Vine, Scalloped, Blue Transfer, 17 x 11 ½ In. 150.00
Teapot, Chinoiserie, Blue, White, c.1800, 11 ¾ In. 176.00
Teapot, Cover, Lozenge Shape, Flower Swags, Sprays, Swan Finial, 6 ½ In. 179.00
Teapot, Cover, Shepherd & Sheep, Blue Transferware, 10 x 6 In. 300.00
Teapot, Flowers, 4-Sided, Swan Finial, Late 18th Century, 6 In. .... *illus* 225.00
Teapot, Round Diamond Shape, Tapered, Paneled Spout, Swan Finial, 6 In. 259.00
Teapot, Tin Lid, White, Vine Detail, 5 In. 98.00
Tureen, Grouse, Nest Form Base, Red, White, Green, c.1865, 9 In. 767.00

PEKING GLASS is a Chinese cameo glass first made popular in the eighteenth century. The Chinese have continued to make this layered glass in the old manner, and many new pieces are now available that could confuse the average buyer.

Peanuts, Mug, Snoopy, Woodstock, At Times Life Is Pure Joy, Fire-King
$24.00

Peanuts, Nodder, Charlie Brown, Painted, c.1960s, 6 x 5 In.
$145.00

Pearl, Card Case, Mother-Of-Pearl, Abalone, Shell, Diamond Inlay, Brass, 1890s, 3 ⅝ In.
$175.00

Pearlware, Teapot, Flowers, 4-Sided, Swan Finial, Late 18th Century, 6 In.
$225.00

P

Peking Glass, Vase, Lion Masks, Leaves, Stylized Dragons, Yellow, Carved, 1800s, 9 ⅞ In.
$2420.00

Peking Glass, Vase, Pheasant, Lotus Branch, Ice Blue, White Opal, Cameo, Early 1900s, 6 In.
$300.00

Pen, Fountain, Conklin, Endura, Sapphire Blue, c.1925, 5 ¼ In.
$470.00

Bottle, Blue, C-Scroll Carving, 2 In. 144.00
Bowl, Leaves, White Ground, Green Rim, Wood Stand, 3 x 7 In., Pair 293.00
Bowl, White & Yellow, 2 ½ x 6 ⅛ In. 293.00
Snuff Bottle, Amorous Couple, White & Orange, 3 ½ x 2 In. 146.00
Snuff Bottle, Carved, Red, Free Form Design, Jade Stopper, c.1925, 3 x 2 In. 82.00
Snuff Bottle, Ivory & Black, 2 ½ x 2 In. 88.00
Vase, Amethyst, Double Gourd, Stand, 13 In. 1300.00
Vase, Applied Leaves, Green, Double Gourd, 9 x 4 In. 644.00
Vase, Butterfly, Flowers, Green, White Ground, Double Gourd, Rosewood Stand, 10 In. 300.00
Vase, Green Over White, Bulbous, Flared Rim, 9 ½ In. 75.00
Vase, Lion Masks, Leaves, Stylized Dragons, Yellow, Carved, 1800s, 9 ⅞ In. .... *illus* 2420.00
Vase, Mustard, Carved, c.1920, 10 In. 527.00
Vase, Pheasant, Lotus Branch, Ice Blue, White Opal, Cameo, Early 1900s, 6 In. .... *illus* 300.00
Vase, White & Yellow, 6 x 2 ¾ In. 117.00
Vase, White Ground, Black Vining, Red Berries, 9 x 4 In. 47.00

PELOTON glass is a European glass with small threads of colored glass rolled onto the surface of clear or colored glass. It is sometimes called spaghetti, or shredded coconut, glass. Most pieces found today were made in the nineteenth century.

Bowl, Clear, White, Red, Blue, Yellow Threads, Scalloped Rim, Footed, Kralik, 6 In. 175.00
Vase, Blue, Milk Glass Threads, Ruffled Rim, Sample, c.1982-83, 5 In. 325.00
Vase, Cranberry, Yellow Threads, Ribs, Ruffled Rim, Sample, c.1982-83, 4 ½ In. 110.00
Vase, White, Rainbow Threads, Crimped & Ruffled Rim, 6 ⅜ In. 173.00

PENS replaced hand-cut quills as writing instruments in 1780, when the first steel pen point was made in England. But it was 100 years before the commercial pen was a common item. The fountain pen was invented in the 1830s but was not made in quantity until the 1880s. All types of old pens are collected. Float pens that feature small objects floating in a liquid as part of the handle are popular with collectors. Advertising pens are listed in the Advertising section of this book.

PENS
Fountain, Conklin, Endura, Sapphire Blue, c.1925, 5 ¼ In. .... *illus* 470.00
Fountain, Gold Filled Repousse, c.1900, 5 ¼ In. .... *illus* 121.00
Mont Blanc, Fountain, Stainless Steel, Papers, Box 300.00
Mont Blanc, Fountain, Sterling Silver, Gold, Box 250.00
Parker, Fountain, Duofold Senior, Lucky Curve, Red, c.1926, 5 ⅜ In. 150.00

PEN & PENCIL
Bradley, Gold Tipped 47.00
Cross, Ballpoint, Mechanical, Box, 1960 .... 30.00
Cross, Stainless Finish, Box 95.00
Sheaffer, Ballpoint, Mechanical, Goldtone, Box 95.00
Sheaffer, Black, Marbleized Pearl Gray, Silver Nickel Trim, Case, 1930-40s 125.00
Sheaffer, Snorkel, Marked, Box 80.00
Waterman's, Fountain, Mechanical, Marbleized Gray & Green, Box, 1930s 90.00
Waterman's, Pearlized, Case, Thermometer, Pouch, 1948 .... 125.00

PENCILS were invented, so it is said, in 1565. The eraser was not added to the pencil until 1858. The automatic pencil was invented in 1863. Collectors today want advertising pencils or automatic pencils of unusual design. Boxes and sharpeners for pencils are also collected. Advertising pencils are listed in the Advertising category. Pencil boxes are listed in the Box category.

PENCIL
Mechanical, 10-Sided Barrel, Brown-Tex Mfg. Co., c.1930, 5 In. 18.00
Mechanical, Eversharp, Masonic, Morning Star Lodge, Black Plastic, 5 In. 15.00
Mechanical, Eversharp, Plastic, Black, Metal Cap, Goldtone, Mason, 5 In. 15.00
Mechanical, Floater RCA 35.00
Mechanical, Gold Filled, Black Enamel Insert, c.1870, 4 ½ In. 95.00
Mechanical, Hamilton, Amber Celluloid, Brown Stripes, Brass Fittings 15.00
Mechanical, Jewel Barrel, Blackamoor Head, Goldtone Turban, Florenza, 4 In. 58.00
Mechanical, Marbled, Red Vein, Swan Holder, Black Base 35.00
Mechanical, Mascot USA, 10K Gold Plate, Turquoise Stone, White Enamel Daisies, 3 ⅝ In. 25.00
Mechanical, Sheaffer, Orange, Gray Case, USA 35.00
Mechanical, Sterling, Chatelaine, Beveled, Jeweled Glass Seal, Engraved 195.00
Mechanical, Telescoping, Rubicon Stretch, Gold Tone, Chain Loop, 1950s, 4 In. 40.00
Mechanical, Twist, Enameled, Swirl Pattern, c.1900 .... 18.00
Mechanical, Twist, Plastic, Black & Cream, 3 ⅝ In. 30.00

Mechanical, Victor Cornelius Theatrical Advertising, Pearlized, c.1930, 5 ¼ In. 18.00
Mechanical, Wahl, Eversharp, Gold Filled, Model No. 177c 45.00
Mechanical, Wahl Eversharp, Gold Filled, 3 ⅞ In. 45.00
Pin On, Blue, Silver Metal, K & McD Inc., 5 In. 35.00
Propelling, Cone Shape, 1 ¼ In.. .... 135.00
Propelling, Lee Enfield Rifle Shape, Germany, c.1905, 4 ¾ In.. .... 65.00
Propelling, Silver, Amber Inset Stones, c.1875, 4 In.. .... 125.00
Ticonderoga, Dixon, 1388-2, Yellow, Green, 68 x 3 In. 200.00
Trick, Reddy Kilowatt Magic Holetite, Kansas Power & Light, c.1950 .... 13.00

PENCIL SHARPENER

Antique Phone, Cast Iron, Brown, 2 x 2 ½ In.. .... 45.00
Automatic Pencil Sharpener Co., Chicago, Pat '06 & '08, 5 ⅜ x 4 ½ In. 138.00
Car, 1917 License Plate, Metal, Hong Kong 9.00
Cast Iron, Wood Handle, Gould & Cook, Leominster, Ma., 1886, 8 x 7 In. .... *illus* 225.00
Chicken, In Hat, 2 ⅝ In. 30.00
Elmer Elephant, Celluloid, Painted, Japan, 1930s, 2 ½ In. 139.00
Felix The Cat, Relief, Spelter, Black & White Enamel, 1 ¼ x 1 ½ In. 115.00
Gun, Bakelite, Orange, Brown, Marbled, 2 In. 5.00
Jupiter Model, Mechanical, Favor Ruhl & Co., Wood Base, 13 x 6 x 6 In.. .... 55.00
Paddleboat, Mark Twain, Metal 9.00
Plane, Bakelite, Green, U.S. Army, 1940s, 2 ¼ x 2 ¾ In.. .... 65.00
Rocket, Lionel 6407 Flatcar, Silver & Blue Nose Cones, Sterling Logos 452.00
Vacuum Base, APSCO 15.00
Wendy's, Frosty, c.1992 .... 5.00

PENNSBURY Pottery worked in Morrisville, Pennsylvania, from 1950 to 1971. Full sets of dinnerware as well as many decorative items were made. Pieces are marked with the name of the factory.

Pennsbury Pottery

Creamer, Amish Lady & Heart, 2 ½ In.. .... 18.00
Creamer, Yellow Rooster, 4 ½ In. 45.00
Plate, B & O Railroad Veterans, Phil., 1955, 5 ¾ x 7 ¾ In. 65.00
Plate, Baltimore & Ohio R.R., Brown, Black, Yellow, Maroon, Green Trim, 1837, 8 x 5 ¾ In.. . 25.00
Plate, Rotary Club, Washington Crossing, Penn., Earth Tones, 4 ^15^⁄~16~ In. 14.00
Tip Tray, Yellow Rooster, 6 x 8 In. 49.00

PEPSI-COLA, the drink and the name, was invented in 1898 but was not trademarked until 1903. The logo was changed from an elaborate script to the modern block letters in 1963. Several different logos have been used. Until 1951, the words *Pepsi* and *Cola* were separated by 2 dashes. These bottles are called "double dash." In 1951 the modern logo with a single hyphen was introduced. All types of advertising memorabilia are collected, and reproductions are being made.

PEPSI-COLA

Bottle, Hutchinson, Escambia, Embossed, 6 ½ In.. .... 920.00
Bottle, Hutchinson, Escambia, Embossed, 7 ¾ In.. .... 288.00
Bottle, Registered, 8-Sided, Crown Top, 8 In. 616.00
Bottle, Straight-Sided, c.1915-20, 7 ½ In.. .... 201.00
Clock, Double Dash, Time For Pepsi-Cola, Blue, Red, White, Square, 14 ¼ In. 170.00
Clock, Light-Up, Dualite, Plastic, c.1950, 17 In. 316.00
Clock, Neon, Square, Center Bottle Cap Image, Red Edge, 1940s, 15 ½ x 15 ½ In. 403.00
Clock, Oak, Double Dash, Sparkling, Nickel Drink Worth A Dime, 34 ½ x 14 x 5 In.. .... 550.00
Coin Changer, Side Lever, 59 ½ In. 575.00
Cooler, Insulated, Countertop, Dispenser, c.1940, 15 x 27 x 13 In. 863.00
Cooler, Pepsi-Cola, Bottle Cap, White, 1940s, 13 x 12 x 8 In. .... *illus* 144.00
Cooler, Radio, Transistor, c.1960s-70s, 12 x 5 ½ In.. .... 345.00
Crate, Wood, 18 x 12 In.. .... 48.00
Dispenser, Pepsi-Cola Fountain, Musical, Pepsi Jingle, Double Dash Pepsi Bottle Cap, 19 In.. 805.00
Door Push, Bottle Caps, Prenez Un Pepsi, Merci Au Revoir, 2-Sided, Metal, 31 ½ In. 60.00
Door Push, Enjoy Iced Pepsi-Cola, Thank You Call Again, Yellow, Red, Porcelain, 31 In. 60.00
Door Push, Pepsi-Cola, Buvez Glace, Red, White, Yellow, Porcelain, 32 In.. .... 50.00
Door Push, Pepsi-Cola, Enjoy Iced, Thank You Call Again, 2-Sided, Porcelain, 31 ½ In.. .... 60.00
Door Push, Pick A Pepsi, Tin, c.1940s, 2 ¾ x 10 In. 403.00
Door Push, Prenez Un Pepsi, 2 Bottle Caps, Merci An Revoir, Porcelain, 31 ½ In. 60.00
Door Push, Tin, Canada, c.1940s, 3 ½ x 13 ½ In. 805.00
Key Chain, Bottle Cap Center, Drink Pepsi-Cola, Single Dot, Metal 65.00
Menu Board, Pepsi-Cola Hits The Spot, Tin Lithograph, 30 x 19 ½ In. 55.00
Napkin Holder, Ceramic, 7 x 5 x 4 ½ In. 805.00
Radio, Bottle Shape, Plastic, 33 In. 468.00

Pen, Fountain, Gold Filled Repousse, c.1900, 5 ¼ In.
$121.00

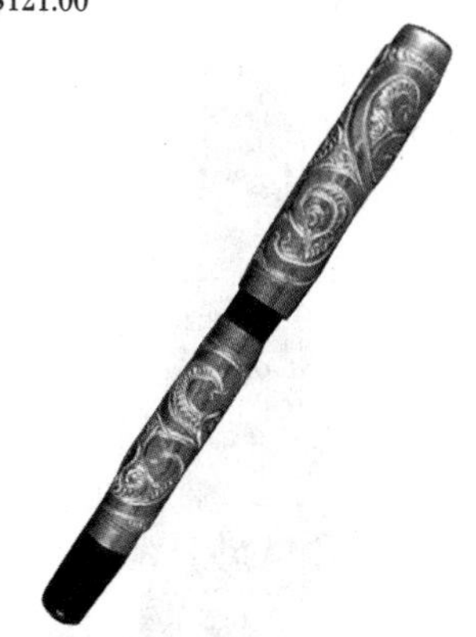

Pencil Sharpener, Cast Iron, Wood Handle, Gould & Cook, Leominster, Ma., 1886, 8 x 7 In.
$225.00

Pepsi-Cola, Cooler, Pepsi-Cola, Bottle Cap, White, 1940s, 13 x 12 x 8 In.
$144.00

TIP

You can remove rust from a tin by using an ink eraser. If you can't find an old one, use the type that comes on a ballpoint pen.

Pepsi-Cola, Sign, Bottle, 5 Cent, Diecut, Tin, c.1940, 29 ½ x 8 In.
$345.00

Pepsi-Cola, Tip Tray, Victorian Woman, Pink Dress, I Love Its Flavor, Oval, 6 x 4 ⅜ In.
$1475.00

TIP

To hang an old Coca-Cola tray, use a wire plate holder. The bent parts of the holder that touch the tray should be covered with plastic tubing. Thin plastic tubing is sold for use in fish aquariums.

Sign, Ask For Pepsi-Cola, The Perfect Mixer, Cardboard, Red, White, Blue, Celluloid, 9 In. 75.00

Sign, Bottle, 5 Cent, Die Cut, Tin, c.1940, 29 ½ x 8 In. .... *illus* 345.00

Sign, Bottle, Die Cut, Metal, c.1930, 29 ½ x 8 ⅛ In. 322.00

Sign, Bottle, Nickel Drink Worth A Dime, Celluloid Over Tin, 1930s, 12 ½ x 5 In. 1093.00

Sign, Bottle Cap, Pepsi-Cola, Red, White, Blue, Scalloped Rim, Tin, 19 ½ In. .... 85.00 to 130.00

Sign, Bottle Cap, Plastic, Metal, c.1950s, 16 In. 288.00

Sign, Bottle Cap, Prenez Un Pepsi, Tin, Yellow, Red, White, Blue, France, 29 ¼ In. 45.00

Sign, Bottle Cap, Red, White, Blue, Tin, Stoudt Co., St. Louis, 19 ½ In. 130.00

Sign, Celluloid, Tin, Cardboard, c.1930s, 5 ½ x 12 ½ In. 1955.00

Sign, Drink Pepsi-Cola, Cup, Bottle Cap, Revolving, Metal, Plastic, 1950s, 10 x 20 x 7 In. 460.00

Sign, Drink Pepsi-Cola, Light Refreshment, Light-Up, Glass, Aluminum, 1950s, 15 In. 748.00

Sign, Ice Cold Pepsi-Cola Sold Here, Double Dash, Tin, 2-Sided, Flange, 10 In. 130.00

Sign, Santa Claus Dancing, Red Outfit, Cardboard, Cutout, 1960s, 31 x 24 In. 110.00

Sign, Sidewalk, Curb Service, Embossed, Tin, c.1940s, 20 x 28 In. 403.00

Sign, Tops, Multiple Bottle Caps, Aluminum, Red, Blue, Yellow, 1940s, 14 x 36 In. 403.00

Straw Box, Drinking Straws, c.1930s, 11 In. 288.00

Strawholder, Dispenser, Ceramic, 1940s, 9 ½ In. 748.00

Thermometer, Bottle Cap, Any Weather's Pepsi Weather, White, Tin, 1950s, 27 x 8 In. 125.00

Thermometer, Bottle Cap, Light Refreshment, Red, White, Blue, Tin, 27 In. 140.00

Thermometer, Bottle Cap, Say Pepsi Please, Yellow, Tin, 1950s, 27 x 7 In. 45.00

Thermometer, Buy Pepsi-Cola, Big, Big Bottle, Blue, White, Red, Tin, 1940s, 27 x 7 In. 500.00 to 518.00

Thermometer, Have A Pepsi, Bottle Cap, Yellow, Tin, 27 x 7 ¼ In. .... 80.00 to 110.00

Thermometer, Have A Pepsi, Yellow, Red, White, Blue, Tin, 27 In. 132.00

Thermometer, Say Pepsi Please, Yellow Ground, Tin, 1969, 28 In. 30.00

Tip Tray, Victorian Woman, Blue Dress, Holding Cup, Oval, 6 x 4 ½ In. 440.00

Tip Tray, Victorian Woman, Pink Dress, I Love Its Flavor, Oval, 6 x 4 ⅜ In. .... *illus* 1475.00

Tip Tray, Woman In Green Dress, Green Trim, Oval, 6 x 4 In. 1100.00

Toy, Truck, Pepsi-Cola, Sparkling, Satisfying, Wood, Tin, Buddy L, 7 x 16 x 5 In. 2950.00

Toy, Truck, Tin, Friction, Japan, 5 ½ In. 145.00

Tray, Bigger & Better, Bottle, Yellow, Green, Red, 10 ½ x 13 In. 121.00

Tray, Victorian Woman, Green Dress, Hat, Holding Cup, Oval, 13 ½ x 11 ¼ In. 550.00

Tray, Victorian Woman, Holding Glass, c.1909, 13 ½ x 11 In. 5175.00

Tumbler, Christmas, Ponderosa Steakhouse, Libbey, 6 x 3 ½ In. 8.00

Tumbler, Flared, Embossed Diamonds, Pepsi-Cola In Script, 1950s, 4 ¾ In., 6 Piece 29.00

Vending Machine, 10 Cent, Blue, Dolly On Back, No. PC27B, 52 In. 1500.00

PERFUME BOTTLES are made of cut glass, pressed glass, art glass, silver, metal, enamel, and even plastic or porcelain. Although the small bottle to hold perfume was first made before the time of ancient Egypt, it is the nineteenth- and twentieth-century examples that interest today's collector. DeVilbiss Company has made atomizers of all types since 1888 but no longer makes the perfume bottle tops so popular with collectors. These were made from 1920 to 1968. The glass bottle may be by any of many manufacturers even if the atomizer is marked *DeVilbiss*. The word *factice,* which often appears in ads, refers to store display bottles. Glass or porcelain examples may be found under the appropriate name such as Lalique, Czechoslovakia, Glass-Bohemian, etc.

Amber, Tapered Cylinder, Vertical Embossed, 8 In. 48.00

Amber Glass, Cylinder, Vertical Embossed Stars, 8 In. 39.00

Atomizer, Emerald Green, Drop Leaves Over Gold, D. Lotton, 6 ⅞ In. 288.00

Balmain, Ivoire, Clear, Stopper, 4 ½ In. 2070.00

Black Glass, Chrome Atomizer, 6 ½ In. 196.00

Brown Over Cream, Bleeding Heart, Ball, Tassel, Atomizer, 6 ½ In. 299.00

Bullicante, Gold Aventurine, Bulbous, Barovier, 5 In. 500.00

Cameo Glass, Brown Over Clear Over Blue, Daisies, Leaves, Atomizer, 7 ¼ In. 253.00

Clear Cut Glass, Frosted Stopper, Man & Woman, 8 In. 230.00

Clear Glass, Jeweled Metalwork Frieze, Screw-On Dabber, 2 ½ In. 92.00

Clear Glass, Stopper, Metal Framework, Blue Medallions, Portrait, 6 In. 403.00

Cologne, 16 Vertical Ribs, 20 Fluted Panels, Sapphire Blue, Flared Mouth, Pontil, 5 ¼ In. 633.00

Cologne, Amethyst, Thumbprint Sides, Herringbone, Tooled Lip, 9 In. 392.00

Cologne, Aqua, Barrel Shape, Ribs, 3 In. 59.00

Cologne, Barrel Form, Monogram In Cartouche, Oval Panel, Folded Lip, c.1850, 4 ⅜ In. 45.00

Cologne, Bunker Hill Monument, Amethyst, Tooled Mouth, Label, c.1865, 9 ⅞ In. 1265.00

Cologne, Bust, Knight, Mirror, Clear, Round, 5 In. 39.00

Cologne, Clear, Silver Overlay, Stopper, Initials, c.1900, 2 ½ In. 112.00

Cologne, Clear Glass, Swirled Silver Overlay, Stopper, M Monogram, N.Y., c.1900, 3 In., Pair . 120.00

Cologne, Cobalt Blue, 8-Sided, Rolled Lip, c.1860, 4 ⅛ In. 265.00

Cologne, Pinched Waist, Amethyst, 8-Sided, Tooled Lip, c.1860, 4 ⅝ In. 345.00

Cologne, Fleur-De-Lis, Clear, 3-Mold, Pinched Waist, 4 In. 195.00

Cologne, Flowers, Greek Key, Clear, 3-Piece Mold, Flared Lip, Footed Base, 4 In. 295.00
Cologne, Flowers, Logo, Woman Paper Label, Clear, Barrel Shape, Pontil, 4 In. 329.00
Cologne, Indians, Aqua, Embossed, 4-Sided, Inrolled Lip, Open Pontil, 4 In. 269.00
Cologne, Knight, Standing, Roman Column, Blue Aqua, 3 ⅞ In. 79.00
Cologne, Lavender Blue, Ribs, Necking, 3-Piece Mold, Sandwich Type, 5 In. 179.00
Cologne, Milk Glass, 12-Sided, Rolled Lip, c.1860, 11 In. 196.00
Cologne, Monument, Fountains, Embossed, Lion's Head Finials, Blue Milk Glass, 4 ⅝ In. 1265.00
Cologne, Plumes, Floral Sprays, Aqua, Flared Lip, Pontil, 4 ½ In. 212.00
Cologne, Shell Shape, Aqua, Scalloped Edges, Rolled Lip, Pontil, 3 ¾ In. 308.00
Cologne, Teal Blue, Vertical Ribs, Tooled Mouth, Pontil, Pinched Neck, c.1815, 2 In. 345.00
Cologne, Teal Green, Tapered Cylinder, Neck Ring, 7 In. 69.00
Cologne, Victorian Gothic Column, Clear, Embossed, 9 In. 239.00
Coty, Ambre Antique, Frosted, Clear, Stopper, Women Posing, 6 In. 2875.00
Coty, Muguet, Clear, Stopper, Box, 2 ¾ In. 161.00
Cranberry Glass, Flower Silver Overlay, Round Stopper, Bulbous, Signed, 1900s, 9 In. 1067.00
Cranberry Glass, Flowers, Enamel, 3 ¾ In. *illus* 175.00
Cranberry Glass, Stopper, Art Nouveau, Sterling Overlay, 3 ½ In. 94.00
Cut Glass, Brass Hinged Top, Late 1800s, 2 ¾ x 1 ¼ In. 48.00
Cut Glass, Cobalt Blue To Clear, Silver Repousse Top, 4 x 2 In. 495.00
Cut Glass, Diamond, Cranberry To Clear, Silver Repousse, 4 x 4 ½ In. 745.00
Cut Glass, Russian Pattern, Silver Plated Screw Top, Laydown, 8 ½ In. 358.00
Daniel R. Bradley & Son, Jockey Club, Rose Geranium, Binoculars, 4 In. 360.00
De Marcy, L'Orange, 8 Glass Orange Segments, Ceramic Orange Holder, c.1925, 2 ½ In. 1840.00
DeVilbiss, Atomizer, Blue Glass, 7 ¼ In. 299.00
DeVilbiss, Atomizer, Engraved, Black Round Body, Stylized Flowers, Gilt, Black Bulb, 6 ¾ In. 115.00
DeVilbiss, Atomizer, Gilt Etched Panels, Black Cabochon, Bulb, 9 ¾ In. 259.00 to 316.00
DeVilbiss, Atomizer, Satin Glass, Amber, Ginger Jar, Cover, 6 ¼ In. 173.00
DeVilbiss, Atomizer, Yellow Shading To Blue, Gold Metal Casing, 7 In. 4600.00
DeVilbiss, Atomizer, Yellow To Blue, Imperial Glass, Signed, 7 In. *illus* 4600.00
Elizabeth Arden, My Love, Snowman, Metal, Glass, Plastic, 1 ½ In. *illus* 299.00
Elizabeth Arden, On Dit, Frosted, Inner Stopper, 2 Women Whispering, 4 ¼ In. 518.00
Enamel, Flower, Cranberry, 3 ¾ In. 175.00
Givenchy, L'Interdit, Flower Brocade Casket, Silver Mounts, 7 ¾ x 4 In. *illus* 150.00
Glass, Basket Weave, Pewter Screw Top, Stopper, c.1800, 3 ¼ In. 288.00
Glass, Engraved, Enamel, Bulbous Body, Cut Ovals, Sterling Silver Collar & Cap, 4 In. 288.00
Glass, Jewels, Metalwork Frieze, Screw-On Dabber, 2 ½ In. *illus* 92.00
Glass, Peppermint Swirl, Pink, White, Frosted Bands, Stevens & Williams, 5 In. 489.00
Glass, Red, Silver Scroll Overlay, 3 ½ x 2 ¾ In. *illus* 495.00
Gold Iridescent, Sterling Overlay, Quezal, Signed, 4 ½ In. 150.00
Helena Rubenstein, Water Lily, Black Glass, Label, Signed, Box, 3 ½ In. *illus* 460.00
Houbigant, Clear, Stopper, Vertical Panels, Scenic, Shepherdess, Sleep, 4 In. 230.00
Houbigant, La Bell Saison, Clear, Frosted, Stopper, Woman, Flowers, Box, 3 ¾ In. 5750.00
House Of Tre-Jur, Suivez Moi, Woman, Wide Skirt, Bonnet, Frosted, 1925, 4 ¼ In. 480.00
Jay Thorpe, Jaytho, Clear, Frosted, Bud Stopper, Molded Tulip Bouquet, 4 In. 920.00
Jovan, Sculptura, Frosted Glass, Atomizer, Black Plastic Stand, 7 ½ In. 92.00
La May, Je Suis L'Ame, Clear, Enameled Stopper 374.00
Malachite, Birds Kissing, Dabber, 7 ½ In. *illus* 2530.00
Mary Chess, Souvenir D'Un Soir, Frosted, Stopper, Fountain Shape, 3 ½ In. 633.00
Paperweight, White & Pink Flowers, Paperweight Stopper, 8 ½ In. 23.00
Parfumerie Moderne, Gilt Metal Stopper, Classic Figures, 4 ¾ In. 1560.00
Paul P. Rosine, Aladdin, Metal, Patina, Chain Handle, Ivory Stopper, 1922, 2 ½ In. 390.00
Pink Satin, Diamond Quilted, Gilt Ormolu Fitting, 4 In. 500.00
Porcelain, Chinese Woman, Blue, Yellow, Metal Stopper, 3 ½ In. *illus* 288.00
Premet, Brise Imperiale, Napoleon Statue As Roman Emperor, 1924, 6 ⅛ In. 1440.00
Prince Matchabelli, Duchess Of York, Red Glass, Gold Enamel, Label, 3 ¼ In. *illus* 7863.00
Red Seal Company, Peacock Blue, Cylinder, Metal Shaker Top, 6 In. 89.00
Rosine, Metal, Cork Stopper, Flower Bouquet, 3 In. 115.00
Rosine, Spirit Of Saint-Louis, Label, Contents, Box, 4 ⅛ In. *illus* 24150.00
Sandwich Glass, 12 Side Panels, Blue Opalescent, c.1850, 8 ¾ In. 323.00
Schiaparelli, Shocking, Dress-Dummy Form, Glass, Stopper, Dome, 4 ½ In. *illus* 242.00
Silver, Basket Trompe L'Oeil, Green Cabochon Twist Cap, Moscow, 1892, 4 In., Pair. 1180.00
Solon Palmer, Violet Bloom, Clear, Stopper, Gold Label, Box, 4 ¼ In. 219.00
St. Louis, Cranberry To Clear, Victorian, 6 In. 720.00
Sterling Silver Overlay, Art Nouveau, Monogram, Stopper, 3 ¼ In. 86.00
Sterling Silver Overlay, Bulbous Stopper 20.00
Sterling Silver Overlay, Green Glass, Monogram, 3 ½ x 2 ¼ In. 374.00
Vanity, Cut Crystal, Art Deco, Stopper, 8 In. 165.00

Perfume Bottle, Cranberry Glass, Flowers, Enamel, 3 ¾ In.
$175.00

Perfume Bottle, DeVilbiss, Atomizer, Yellow To Blue, Imperial Glass, Signed, 7 In.
$4600.00

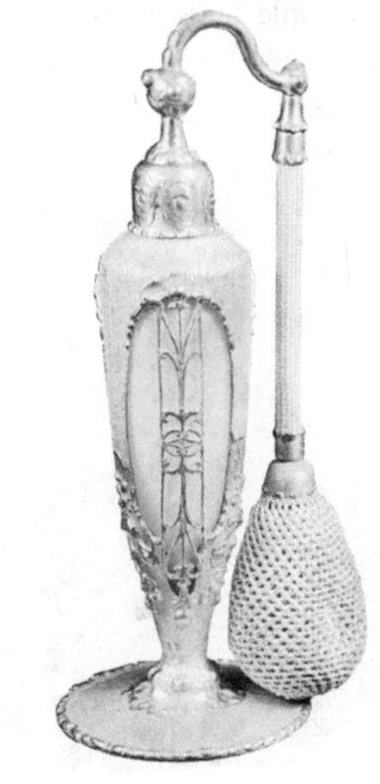

Perfume Bottle, Elizabeth Arden, My Love, Snowman, Metal, Glass, Plastic, 1 ½ In.
$299.00

Perfume Bottle, Givenchy, L'Interdit, Flower Brocade Casket, Silver Mounts, 7 ¾ x 4 In.
$150.00

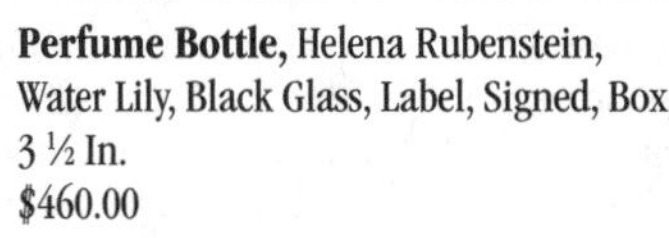

Perfume Bottle, Helena Rubenstein, Water Lily, Black Glass, Label, Signed, Box, 3 ½ In.
$460.00

Perfume Bottle, Prince Matchabelli, Duchess Of York, Red Glass, Gold Enamel, Label, 3 ¼ In.
$7863.00

Perfume Bottle, Glass, Jewels, Metalwork Frieze, Screw-On Dabber, 2 ½ In.
$92.00

Perfume Bottle, Malachite, Birds Kissing, Dabber, 7 ½ In.
$2530.00

Perfume Bottle, Rosine, Spirit Of Saint-Louis, Label, Contents, Box, 4 ⅛ In.
$24150.00

Perfume Bottle, Glass, Red, Silver Scroll Overlay, 3 ½ x 2 ¾ In.
$495.00

Perfume Bottle, Porcelain, Chinese Woman, Blue, Yellow, Metal Stopper, 3 ½ In.
$288.00

Perfume Bottle, Schiaparelli, Shocking, Dress-Dummy Form, Glass, Stopper, Dome, 4 ½ In.
$242.00

Vantine's, Chypre, Clear, Spherical, Block Top, Oriental Woman, Fan, France, 2 ½ In........ 546.00
Victorian, Painted, Flowers, Violet Lining, Stopper, 4 ½ In............................ 92.00
Woodworth, Woman, Violet, Clear, Labels, Embossed Flower Box, 1910, 3 ¾ In........... 600.00

PETERS & REED Pottery Company of Zanesville, Ohio, was founded by John D. Peters and Adam Reed in 1897. Chromal, Landsun, Montene, Pereco, and Persian are some of the art lines that were made. The company, which became Zane Pottery in 1920 and Gonder Pottery in 1941, closed in 1957. Peters & Reed pottery was unmarked.

Bowl, Dragonfly, Blue Glaze, 5 In............ 50.00
Bowl, Landsun, Brown Mottled Glaze, 8 ½ x 2 ½ In............ 75.00
Bowl, Moss Aztec, Wiped-On Green, Brown Clay, Incised, Ferrell, 1912-18, 8 ½ In............ 60.00
Case, Blue, Yellow Swirls, 6-Sided, 9 In............ 60.00
Flower Frog, Green Crystalline Glaze, 2 x 5 In............ 45.00
Tobacco Jar, Cover, Marbleized, 7 ¾ x 6 ¼ In............ 220.00
Vase, Green Turquoise Glaze, 3 Twisted Handles, c.1899-1912, 16 In............ 175.00
Vase, Landsun, Blue, Creme Glaze, 5 x 4 In............ 75.00
Vase, Landsun, Blue, Green, Yellow, Fire Nozzle Form, 10 In............ *illus* 121.00
Vase, Landsun, Dark Green, Blue Swirls, 6 x 7 In............ 235.00
Vase, Landsun, Green, Blue Zigzag Glaze, 8 x 4 In............ 215.00
Vase, Landsun, Nozzle, 9 ½ In............ 184.00
Vase, Landsun, Yellow, Black Mottled Glaze, 8 x 6 In............ 215.00
Vase, Lion Heads, Flower Garland, Pinched Neck, Brown Drip Glaze, 14 In............ 127.00
Vase, Marbleized, Earth, 8 ⅛ x 5 ½ In............ *illus* 220.00
Vase, Marbleized, Fluted, Squared Handles, 13 ½ In............ 230.00
Vase, Marbleized, Multicolored, Flared Rim, 12 In............ 75.00
Vase, Montene, Soft Green, Blue Glaze, 5 ½ x 3 In............ 80.00
Vase, Moss Aztec, Brown, Flared Rim, 8 In............ 75.00
Vase, Raised Wisteria Rim, Blue Matte Glaze, c.1912-18, 12 In............ 100.00
Vase, Road Climbing Up Mountain, 8 ⅜ In............ 345.00
Vase, Shadow Ware, Black Drip Glaze Over White, Mark, 10 x 5 In............ 115.00
Vase, Shadow Ware, Light Green Over Dark Green, No. 785, 12 x 7 ½ In............ *illus* 800.00
Vase, Standard Ware, Garland, 4 x 5 ½ In............ *illus* 38.00
Vase, Wilse Blue, Flared Rim, 12 In............ 125.00
Vase, Yellow & Green Swirls, Cream Ground, 9 In............ 60.00

PETRUS REGOUT, *see Maastricht category.*

PEWABIC POTTERY was founded by Mary Chase Perry Stratton in 1903 in Detroit, Michigan. The company made many types of art pottery, including pieces with matte green glaze and an iridescent crystalline glaze. The company continued working until the death of Mary Stratton in 1961. It was reactivated by Michigan State University in 1968.

PEWABIC

Bowl, Red, Brown, Luster Glaze, Green Interior, c.1950, 3 x 4 In............ 176.00
Bowl, Sink, Flower, Blue, Green, 6 x 16 ½ In............ 560.00
Box, Cover, Green Luster, 2 x 3 ½ In............ 322.00
Plate, Ducks On Water, Blue & White Ground, Crackleware, 9 In............ 840.00
Plate, Green, Orange Border, c.1910, 7 ½ In............ 234.00
Tile, Occupations, 4 & 7 In., 6 Piece............ 88.00
Tile, Scenic, Oak Frame, 17 In............ 198.00
Vase, Blue, Green, Purple Metallic Glaze, Hand Thrown Form, Marked, 4 x 4 In............ 690.00
Vase, Blue, Purple, c.1920, 8 In............ 1053.00
Vase, Brown, Green, Blue, c.1920, 11 In............ 1404.00
Vase, Coil, Orange, Signed, Seal, c.1920, 7 In............ 468.00
Vase, Gray, Blue, c.1920, 12 In............ 526.00
Vase, Green, Gray, Iridescent, c.1920, 8 In............ 1404.00
Vase, Mottled Luster Glaze, 4 ⅞ In............ 374.00
Vase, Multitoned Brown Metallic Glaze, Shouldered, Marked, 10 x 6 In............ 600.00
Vase, Orange, Yellow Interior, c.1940, 5 ¼ x 6 In............ 730.00

PEWTER is a metal alloy of tin and lead. Some of the pewter made after 1840 has a slightly different composition and is called Britannia metal. This later type of pewter was worked by machine; the earlier pieces were made by hand. In the 1920s pewter came back into fashion and pieces were often marked *Genuine Pewter*. Eighteenth-, nineteenth-, and twentieth-century examples are listed here.

Basin, Blakslee Barnes, Partial Touchmark, Philad., c.1815, 9 ¼ In............ 206.00
Basin, Flat Molded Rim, 3 ½ x 14 ½ In............ 30.00

Peters & Reed, Vase, Landsun, Blue, Green, Yellow, Fire Nozzle Form, 10 In.
$121.00

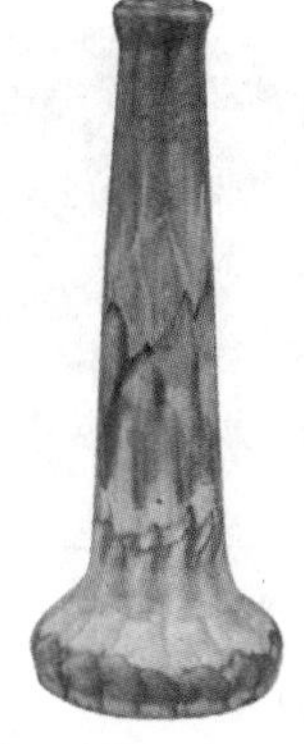

Peters & Reed, Vase, Marbleized, Earth, 8 ⅛ x 5 ½ In.
$220.00

Peters & Reed, Vase, Shadow Ware, Light Green Over Dark Green, No. 785, 12 x 7 ½ In.
$800.00

Peters & Reed, Vase, Standard Ware, Garland, 4 x 5 ½ In.
$38.00

P

Pewter, Charger, Oval, Flat Rim,
1 x 17 x 12 ¾ In.
$110.00

Pewter, Measure,
Shell Shape Thumbpiece, England,
19th Century, 12 ¾ In.
$235.00

Pewter, Pot, Bell Form, Raised Rose,
Locking Lid, Spout, Ring Handle,
A.G.I., 1721, 9 x 5 In.
$190.00

TIP
Don't display pewter on a wooden shelf. Paint and wood give off gases that damage pewter.

Basin, Love, Philadelphia, Late 18th Century, 11 In. 468.00
Basin, Ship, Crowned Rose, Marked ND, Stamped Initials On Rim, 14 ½ x 2 ½ In. 173.00
Basin, Thomas Compton, Hammered Bouge, Partial Touchmark, London, c.1885, 11 In. 235.00
Basin, Wm. Danforth, Touchmark, Conn., c.1800, 8 In. 646.00
Bedpan, Curved Sides, Screw Handle, Round, 2 ¾ x 12 In. 55.00
Bottle, Nursing, Bulbous Shape, Nipple Top, England, 1899s, 6 In. 352.00
Bowl, F. Widmer Handarbeit, Hammered, 4 Scroll Feet, Stamped, 1935, 3 ½ x 11 In. 500.00
Box, Hinged Lid, Sunken Wire Ring Pulls, ⅞ x 3 x 2 ¼ In. 44.00
Canister, Ball Screw Top, Rubber Stopper, Cylindrical, 13 ½ x 4 In. 33.00
Centerpiece, Winged Women, Leaf Handles, Blue Glass, Germany, WMF, c.1905, 8 x 13 In. 2400.00
Chalice, Bell Shape, Footed, 6 ⅞ x 3 ¾ In., Pair 88.00
Chalice, Flared Rim, Castle Over Lion, Footed, ½ Pt. 33.00
Chamber Pot, Bulbous, Rounded Rim, Applied Handle, 5 ½ x 9 In. 121.00
Charger, Flared, Molded Rim, Wriggle Work Border, Flowers, Lions, 1 ½ x 12 ⅛ In. 1100.00
Charger, Hammered Bouge, Early 19th Century, 16 ½ In., Pair 460.00
Charger, Kayserzinn, Relief Border, Butterflies, 1 ¾ x 15 ¾ In. 201.00
Charger, Oval, Flat Rim, 1 x 17 x 12 ¾ In. *illus* 110.00
Charger, Thomas Badger, Touchmark, Boston, 15 In. 323.00
Charger, William Billings, Touchmark, Providence, 13 ¼ In. 353.00
Coffeepot, Pyriform, 3 Legs, Wooden Handle, Domed Lid, Fluted Shell Hinge, c.1800, 9 In. 59.00
Coffeepot, R. Dunham, Gooseneck, Signed, 8 ¾ In. 40.00
Coffeepot, Roswell Gleason, Lighthouse Shape, Black Handle, Dorchester, Mass., 10 ¾ In. 499.00
Creamer, Plate, Cover, Bulbous, Scrolled Handle, 6 ⅜ & 8 In. 154.00
Cup, Cover, Sculpted Lion, Shield Finial, Austria, 15 In. 189.00
Desk Set, Standish, Sanders, Galleried Base, Candle Sockets, Hinged Ink, 3 x 7 ½ In. 323.00
Dipper, Ivory Handle, Early 1800s, 14 In. 250.00
Dispenser, Water, Wall Mount, Half Split Baluster, Removable Lid, 14 x 10 x 4 ¾ In. 22.00
Ewer, Ram's Head Finials, Applied Flower, Touchmark, Swiss, 8 In. 86.00
Flagon, Cover, Ball Finial, Heart Form Spout, 12 ¼ x 5 ½ In. 220.00
Flagon, Diamond Shape Lid, Thumbpiece Hinged, Handle, Bulbous, 10 ½ x 5 ¾ In. 55.00
Flagon, Dome Lid, Thumbpiece Hinged, Arched Handle, Bulbous, 8 ½ x 4 ½ In. 121.00
Flagon, Heart Form Spout, Ball Finial, Incised, G.M. 18 Bruder, 11 In. 200.00
Flagon, Hinged Dome Lid, Ball Thumbpiece, S-Form Handle, Flared Base, 13 ¾ x 5 ⅞ In. 165.00
Flagon, Hinged Lid, Wriggle Work Spout, Applied Handle, Splayed Base, 11 ¾ x 6 ¼ In. 44.00
Flagon, Religious Design, Relief, c.1870, 1 ½ Liter, 14 ½ In. 311.00
Foot Warmer, Oval, Cylindrical Cup Well, Screw Top, Handle, 4 ½ x 12 ½ x 7 ½ In. 55.00
Garment Rack, Finial Top, Sliding Hooks, Cast Iron Base, 1900s, 74 x 19 In. 215.00
Lamp, Finger, Fuel, Rosewell, Dunham, Acorn Fonts, Mark, Dish Base, Mass., c.1850s, 6 ½ In. 444.00
Lamp, Oil, Hinged Lid, Wire Chain, Wick Pick, Stand, Oval Handle, 8 ¾ x 4 ¾ In. 66.00
Lamp, Whale Oil, Brook Farm, Signed, 9 ½ x 3 ¾ In. 275.00
Lamp, Whale Oil, Pontil, 2-Tube Burner, c.1850, 6 ¼ In. 79.00
Lamp, Whale Oil, Round Foot, Cylinder Reservoir, Double Tube Burner, 7 ¾ In. 92.00
Lamp, Whale Oil, Taunton Brothers, Signed, 10 x 6 In. 440.00
Lamp, Whale Oil, Turned Column Stem, Cylindrical Font, Bulging Body, Saucer Foot, 10 In. 109.00
Lamp Filler, Gooseneck Spout, Push Valve Fill, Stamp, 6 In. 58.00
Light Switch Cover, Girl, Bonnet, Watering Can, Sea Gull, Canada, 2 ½ x 4 ½ In. 20.00
Measure, Cylindrical, Squared Handle, Molded Top, Bottom Rims, Liter, 7 ¼ x 4 ⅛ In. 44.00
Measure, Shell Shape Thumbpiece, England, 19th Century, 12 ¾ In. *illus* 235.00
Measure Set, Tavern Spirit, England, Quart To Quarter Gill, 1800s, 6 Piece 465.00
Mold Candle, 24 Tube, W. Webb, Mixed Wood Frame, 19th Century, 18 x 21 1/4 In. 1150.00
Pitcher, Boardman & Hall Philad, Impressed, c.1845, 10 In. 468.00
Pitcher, Side Spout, Center Banding, C-Shape Handle, Footed, Molded, Pt., 5 x 3 ⅜ In. 66.00
Pitcher, T.D. Boardman, Lid, Straining Holes, Lion Touchmark, Conn., c.1840, 10 In. 411.00
Plate, Benjamin & Joseph Harbeson, 1765-1800, 7 ¾ In. 995.00
Plate, Jacob Whitmore, Touchmark, Conn., 8 In., Pair 235.00
Plate, Love, Philadelphia, Late 18th Century, 8 ½ In. 293.00
Plate, Nicholson, Single Reed, Hammered, Family Crest, Marked, c.1725, 10 In., 4 Piece 690.00
Plate, William Will, Touchmark, 1764-1798, 8 ⅜ In. 2223.00
Plate Warmer, Hollow, Round, Concave Top, Handles, Marked, Made In London, 2 x 8 In. 40.00
Plate Warmer, Hollow Round, Concave Top, Hinged D-Shape Handles, 1 ¾ x 8 In. 44.00
Platter, Fish, Kayserzinn, Oval, 21 In. 475.00
Porringer, John Ingram Jr., Crown Shape Handle, Touchmark, c.1820, 5 In. 323.00
Porringer, Old English Handle, Stamped Initials, Early 19th Century, 3 ½ In. 59.00
Porringer, Round Bowl, Handles, Scallop Shells, 1 ¼ x 9 ¾ x 6 In. 66.00
Pot, A. Porter, Bulbous, Dome Lid, Wood Wafer Finial, Black Handle, c.1840, 12 In. 546.00
Pot, Applied Handles, Straight Sides, Lion Stamps, C.M.H. 1824, 2 ¾ x 8 ½ In. 33.00

Pot, Bell Form, Raised Rose, Locking Lid, Spout, Ring Handle, A.G.I., 1721, 9 x 5 In. ... *illus* 190.00
Pot, Locking Hinged Lid, Bell Form Spout, Ring Handle, Wriggle Work, 9 ¼ x 4 ⅞ In. 209.00
Pot, O. Trask, Raised Rings, Engraved Bands, Touchmark, Mass., c.1827, 11 In. 411.00
Salt Cellar, 8-Sided, Molded, 1 ⅜ x 4 x 2 ⅞ In. 50.00
Sugar & Creamer, Sugar Lid, Scroll Handles, c.1800, 7 In. 353.00
Tankard, Cover, Tulip Shape, Heart Cutout Thumbpiece, Early 19th Century, 8 In. 646.00
Tankard, Dome Lid, Bulbous, Hinged Shell Thumbpiece, Handle, Footed, 9 ⅛ x 5 In. 66.00
Tankard, Fillet Bandings, Scroll Handle, Footed Base, Qt., 6 ¼ x 4 ⅜ In. 44.00
Tankard, General Elliot Allbridge, Banding, Molded Base, Applied Handle, 6 x 4 ¾ In. 88.00
Tankard, H.T. Eichler, Hinged Lid, Urn Thumbpiece, Footed Base, 8 ½ x 5 In. 413.00
Tankard, Hinged Dome Lid, Curled Thumbpiece, Scrolled Handle, 8 x 4 ¾ In. 99.00
Tankard, Hinged Dome Lid, Urn Finial, Handle, 8 ¾ x 4 ¾ In. 99.00
Tankard, Presentation, Hinged Lid, Lion Stamp, Curled Thumbpiece, Glass Bottom, 8 In. 90.00
Tankard, Scrolled Handle, Banded Rim, c.1815, Qt. 206.00
Tankard, Townsend & Compton, WR, Crown, Impressed, London, Late 1700s, 6 ¼ In. 1053.00
Tea Canister, Engraved Designs, Wood Base, Chinese, 7 ¼ In., Pair 23.00
Teapot, Alberti, Queen Anne, Chased Vines, Flowers, Birds, Wood Handle, 6 ¼ In. 35100.00
Teapot, J. Munson, Gooseneck Spout, Scroll Handle, Signed, 9 In. ... *illus* 176.00
Teapot, Kayserzinn, Fish, Snail, Hammered, 11 x 9 In. 633.00
Teapot, Pear Shape, Black Handle, Finial, Early 1800s, 7 In. 294.00
Teapot, Reed & Barton, Ebonized Wood Handle, Late 19th Century 60.00
Teapot, Rufus Dunham, Black Handle & Finial Wafer, Westbrook, Maine, c.1861, 7 In. 323.00
Teapot, Samuel Pierce, Pear Shape, Paneled Spout, c.1830, 7 In. 823.00
Teapot, Savage, Footed, Marked, 8 ¾ x 10 ½ In. 160.00
Teapot, Williams, Gooseneck Spout, Scrolled Handle, 10 ½ In. 209.00
Tray, Hugo Leven, Water Lily Center, Dragonfly Handles, 1898, 11 x 18 In. 3140.00
Urn, Tudric, Faceted, Buttressed Feet, Stamped, 8 ¼ x 3 ¾ In. ... *illus* 1440.00
Vase, Cover, Regency, Painted, Handles, Flower Garland, Leaf Spray, 13 x 9 ½ In. 3600.00
Vase, Kayserzinn, Angel, Child, Octopus, Country Club Presentation, 1902, 11 x 11 In. 805.00
Vase, Kayserzinn, Angel, Child, Octopus, Flowers, Marked, No. 4093, 11 ½ x 11 In. ... *illus* 770.00
Vase, Screw Top, Bulbous, Ring Finial, Footed, Side String Cleats, 5 ¾ x 2 ¼ x 2 In. 110.00
Vase, Trophy, Kayserzinn, Hammered, Organic Designs, 3 Handles, c.1903, 6 ½ x 10 In. 144.00
Warmer, Hot Water, Rudolph Wehrli, Liberty For All, 4-Footed, Touchmark, 2 ¾ x 10 In. 450.00

PHOENIX BIRD, or Flying Phoenix, is the name given to a blue-and-white dinnerware popular between 1900 and World War II. A variant is known as Flying Turkey. Most of this dinnerware was made in Japan for sale in the dime stores in America. It is still being made.

Cup & Saucer, Blue & White, Birds, Occupied Japan 18.00
Cup & Saucer, Blue & White, Birds, Occupied Japan, 4 Sets 45.00
Mug, Blue & White, Birds, Myott Staffordshire, 2 ¼ In. 15.00
Salt & Pepper, Birds, Blue & White, Japan, 2 ¾ In. 18.00
Soup, Dish, Blue & White, Birds, Myott Son & Co., 7 ⅝ In. 20.00

PHOENIX GLASS Company was founded in 1880 in Pennsylvania. The firm made commercial products, such as lampshades, bottles, and glassware. Collectors today are interested in the "Sculptured Artware" made by the company from the 1930s until the mid-1950s. Some pieces of Phoenix glass are very similar to those made by the Consolidated Lamp and Glass Company. Phoenix made Reuben Blue, lavender, and yellow pieces. These colors were not used by Consolidated. In 1970 Phoenix became a division of Anchor Hocking, then was sold to the Newell Group in 1987. The company is still working.

Lightning Globe, Hobstar, Lozenges, Fans, 7 ½ In. 690.00
Vase, Bachelor Buttons, Red Ground, Iridescent White, 7 ½ x 6 ½ x 4 In. 55.00
Vase, Daisies, Blue, White, Frosted, 9 ⅛ In. 165.00
Vase, Dancing Nymph, Lavender Ground, 11 ½ In. 110.00
Vase, Dancing Nymphs, Peach Ground, 11 ½ In. 185.00
Vase, Dogwood, Blue Ground, 10 ½ In. 125.00
Vase, Dogwood, Yellow, Green, Brown, White Ground, 11 In. 70.00
Vase, Fern, Red Ground, Iridescent White, Bulbous, 7 x 6 In. 44.00
Vase, Freesia, Blue, White, Trumpet, 7 ½ In. 175.00
Vase, Star Flower, Cream Ground, 6 ¾ In. 80.00
Vase, Thistle, Blue Ground, White Trim, Bulbous, 17 ½ x 9 ½ In. 55.00
Vase, Thistle, White Ground, Bulbous, 17 ½ x 9 ½ In., Pair 555.00
Vase, Virgin Mary, Silhouette, White, Pink Ground, 12 In. 100.00
Vase, Wild Geese, Brown Ground, Pillow Shape, 9 ½ In. 160.00
Vase, Wild Geese, Lime Green Ground, Pillow Shape, Oval, 9 ½ In. 99.00

Pewter, Teapot, J. Munson, Gooseneck Spout, Scroll Handle, Signed, 9 In.
$176.00

Pewter, Urn, Tudric, Faceted, Buttressed Feet, Stamped, 8 ¼ x 3 ¾ In.
$1440.00

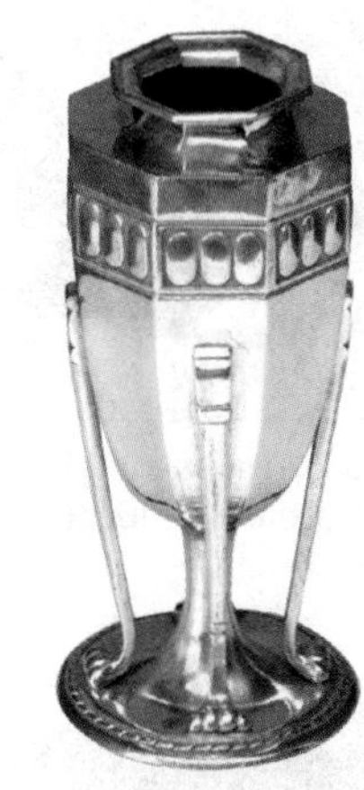

Pewter, Vase, Kayserzinn, Angel, Child, Octopus, Flowers, Marked, No. 4093, 11 ½ x 11 In.
$770.00

TIP
Don't put pewter in a newly painted room until the paint smell is gone. Paint fumes will attach to the pewter.

Phonograph, Columbia, Regent, Desk, Carved Claw Feet, 32 x 46 x 29 In.
$550.00

Phonograph, Gramophone, Morning Glories, Red, Japanned, Oak, c.1900
$495.00

Phonograph, Lamp, 8-Sided, Fabric, Tassels, Copper, Burns Pollack Co., 1915, 26 x 16 In.
$1870.00

Phonograph, Universal, Talking Machine, Windup, Oak, c.1900
$950.00

PHONOGRAPHS, invented by Thomas Edison in 1877, have been made by many firms. This category also includes other items associated with the phonograph. Jukeboxes and Records are listed in their own categories.

B Z N, Hornless Talking Machine, Tabletop Model, Openwork Grille, c.1910, 13 x 10 In. 1265.00
Berliner, Zon-O-Phone, No. 1330, Turntable, Brass Horn, Oak Case, 14 ½ x 16 x 9 In. 2133.00
Climax, Oak Case, Drawer, Black Horn, Records 590.00
Columbia, BC, Cylinder, Wood Case, Brass Horn, Label, 58 In., 1905 . . . . 3099.00
Columbia, BO, Cylinder, 10 Panels, Morning Glory Horn 775.00
Columbia, Cylinder, Lyre Reproducer, Crank 300.00
Columbia, Graphophone, Type AZ, Cylinder, Reproducer, Witch's Hat Horn, Cover 700.00
Columbia, Majestic, BD Disc, Morning Glory Horn, Nickel, 24 In. 550.00
Columbia, Oak, Floor Model, Vertical Inside Louvers, Inside Horn 50.00
Columbia, Oak Case, Table Model, Inside Horn, Louvered Speakers 150.00
Columbia, Q Cylinder, Key, Reproducer 150.00
Columbia, Regent, Desk, Carved Claw Feet, 32 x 46 x 29 In. . . . . *illus* 550.00
Columbia, Type B, Cylinder, Key, Reproducer, Cover 275.00
Columbia, Type N, Coin-Operated Graphophone, American Graphophone Co., D.C. 5333.00
Edison, Amberola, 30 Cylinder, Babson Floor Model, Cabinet, 4 Shelves 450.00
Edison, Cylinder, Lunch Box Style, Dome Lid, 384739, 13 x 12 In. 420.00
Edison, Diamond Disc C-19, Mahogany, Key 10.00
Edison, Fireside, Model A, Cylinder, K Reproducer, Cygnet Horn 1150.00
Edison, Model A, Opera, Double Spring Motor, Oak Case, Dome Lid, Horn, 18 In.. . . . . 4148.00
Edison, Model C, Cylinder, Oak Case, Red Flowers On Horn, 13 x 13 x 23 In. 550.00
Edison, Model C-200, Diamond Disc, Floor Model, Mahogany Cabinet 50.00
Edison, Speaking Parlor Model, Tinfoil Phonograph, Glass Cabinet, 1878 . . . . 22515.00
Edison, Standard, 2 & 4 Minute Ear, 10-Petal Black Cygnet Horn, Crane, 1 Cylinder 2336.00
Edison, Standard, H Reproducer, Crane, Blue Morning Glory Horn, Pink Roses 850.00
Edison, Standard, Model A, 2-Minute Cylinders, Oak Case, Lid, Brass Horn. 620.00
Edison, Triumph, Cylinder, C Reproducer, Crank, Cover, Witch's Hat Horn 575.00
Edison, Triumph, Model B, Cylinder, Shaver, C Reproducer, Crane, Horn, 30 In.. . . . . 700.00
Edison, Triumph, Model E, Triple Spring Motor, Oak Case, Dome Lid, Cygnet Horn, 18 In. . . . 1067.00
Gramophone, Morning Glories, Red, Japanned, Oak, c.1900 . . . . *illus* 495.00
Graphophone, Columbia Type, AJ Disc, Turntable, Oak Case, Handle, 11 In. Square. 1304.00
Kompact, Portable, Crank Handle, Self Containing Box. 100.00
Lamp, 8-Sided, Fabric, Tassels, Copper, Burns Pollack Co., 1915, 26 x 16 In. . . . . *illus.* 1870.00
Lifesavers, Model Sp-15, Red, Yellow, Green, Orange Stripes, Handle 45.00
Reginaphone, Music Box, Double Combs, Morning Glory Horn, 28 x 47 In. 5629.00
Universal, Talking Machine, Windup, Oak, c.1900 . . . . *illus* 950.00
Victor, Disc, Table Model, Case, Back Bracket, Turntable, Motor. 160.00
Victor, Electrola Type, Electric Motor, Mahogany Case, 2 Doors, Records, 49 In. 1778.00
Victor, No. 4, Mahogany, Spear Point Horn. 1500.00
Victor, Talking Machine, Type B, No. 8979, Black Horn, Gold Pinstriping, Oak Case, c.1901 . . 5629.00
Victor, Type P, Disc, Brass Bell Horn, Crank, 20 x 11 In.. . . . . 850.00
Victor, VV-50, Oak Case, Portable, Victrola No. 2 Reproducer 210.00
Victor, VV-410, Mahogany, Disc, No. 4 Reproducer. 400.00
Victor, VV-IX, Mahogany, Disc, Crank, Exhibition Reproducer 100.00
Victor Talking Machine Co., No. 43555, 4 Figures Musical Figures, Camden, N.J. 1770.00
Victor Victrola, Upright, Mahogany, c.1900, 42 In. . . . . *illus* 110.00
Victrola, Model VV XVI, No. 121895H, Mahogany Cabinet, 2 Over 2 Doors, 51 In.. . . . . 1304.00
Victrola, No. 788, 3-Spring Motor, Mahogany Horn, Cabinet, Flat Lid, 47 In. 4740.00
Zon-O-Phone, Concert Grand, Disc, Brass Horn, Rear Mount 1150.00
Zon-O-Phone, Type A, Universal Talking Machine Co., New York, 3 Records 9480.00
Zon-O-Phone, Type C, Brass Bell Horn, Front Mount 1100.00

PHONOGRAPH NEEDLE CASES of tin are collected today by music and phonograph enthusiasts and advertising addicts. The tins are very small, about 2 inches across, and often have attractive graphic designs lithographed on the top and sides.

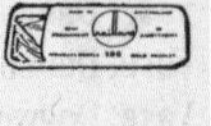

Leading Always, Running Dog, Frisbee, Tin, 1 ⅝ x 1 ¼ In. 36.00
Marschall Forte, Red, Yellow, White, Tin, 1 ⅝ x 1 ⅝ In. 36.00
Songster, Bird On Branch, Sun, Tin, Gold Color, 2 x 1 ¼ In.. . . . . 37.00

PHOTOGRAPHY items are listed here. The first photograph was a view from a window in France taken in 1826. The commercially successful photograph started with the daguerreotype introduced in 1839. Today all sorts of photographs and photographic equipment are collected. Albums were popular in Victorian times. Cartes de visite, popular

P

after 1854, were mounted on 2 ½-by-4-inch cardboard. Cabinet cards were introduced in 1866. These were mounted on 4 ¼ by 6 ½-inch cards. Stereo views are listed under Stereo Card. The cases for daguerreotypes are listed in the Gutta-Percha category. Stereoscopes are listed in their own section.

Albumen Print, Clean Shaven Lincoln, Oval, R. Cole, c.1858, 7 x 5 In.. 2640.00
Albumen Print, Seated A. Lincoln, Inscribed, A. Gardner, 1865, 15 x 19 In. 34663.00
Albumen Print, Veta Pass With Trains, Mat, Frame, 26 x 31 In. *illus* 6463.00
Ambrotype, Girl Standing Next To Chair, 4 5/16 x 5 1/16 In. 210.00
Ambrotype, Gold Mining, 6 Miners, Pressed Leather Case, ½ Plate, 4 ¼ x 5 ½ In. 4025.00
Ambrotype, Hombre & Dude Sharing A Glass Of Beer, Seated, Leather Case, 1/6 Plate. 180.00
Ambrotype, Man, Tinted Cheeks, 1/6 Plate *illus* 11.00
Ambrotype, Man With Dog On Lap, Paper Case, 1/6 Plate 190.00
Ambrotype, Mother, Infant Seated On Lap, Bakelite Case, 1800s, 3 ¾ x 3 ¼ In. 44.00
Ambrotype, Painter, Paint Brush, Ladder, Case, 1/16 Plate *illus* 242.00
Ambrotype, Soldier, Gun, Baxter Jordan, Dixie Boys, Alabama Infantry, Civil War, ½ Plate. 4994.00
Ambrotype, Young Man In Lab Coat, Paper Case, 1/9 Plate 35.00
Cabinet Card, Bicycle, Man, High Wheeler, Tool Bag, c.1881, 6 x 4 In. 121.00
Cabinet Card, Kiowa Child, Cradleboard, Irwin & Mankins, Silver Gelatin, 15 x 12 In. 288.00
Cabinet Card, Man & Horse In Front Of Barn 45.00
Cabinet Card, Toddler Sitting In Rocking Chair 40.00
Cabinet Card, Young Girl Holding Doll 40.00
Cabinet Card, Young Girl Wearing Bonnet On Bench With Doll 15.00
Camera, Graflex, Crown Pacemaker, 3 x 4 In. 44.00
Camera, Nikon, S, No. 6103728, Nippon Kogaku, 1951 *illus* 443.00
Camera, Rolleiflex, 35 mm, No. 1129497, Black, 5 ¾ x 3 ½ x 3 ¾ In. 121.00
Carte De Visite, Abraham Lincoln, April 17, 1863. 836.00
Carte De Visite, Elizabeth B. Custer, Geo. Custer Wife, c.1875 1175.00
Carte De Visite, George A. Custer, Major General, 2 Cent Stamp, May 23, 1865 2640.00
Carte De Visite, Greeley & Brown, Grant & Wilson, 1872, 2 x 4 In., Pair. 956.00
Carte De Visite, Horse-Drawn Wagon, Store, John Kalla, Toledo, Oh. *illus* 77.00
Carte De Visite, Lincoln & Son, Bouve 273.00
Carte De Visite, Men Standing On Main Road, Gibsonville, Calif., 1870s 518.00
Carte De Visite, Tom Thumb & Wife, Trimmed To Oval, 3 3/8 x 2 3/8 In. 55.00
Carte De Visite, Zaluma Agra, P.T. Barnum Exhibition Act, 1860s, 4 x 2 ½ In. 125.00
Cinematograph, Film Camera, Projector, Printer In 1, Louis Lumiere, c.1895 30000.00
Daguerreotype, 2 Cigar Smoking Men, Color Tint, 6 Plate, Frame, Mat 660.00
Daguerreotype, 2 Girls, Posed In Dresses, Gutta Percha Case, 1/16 Plate *illus* 176.00
Daguerreotype, Gentleman, Crossed Arms, Top Hat, 1/6 Plate 200.00
Daguerreotype, Girl, Leaning On Table, Case, 1/6 Plate *illus* 44.00
Daguerreotype, Man, Glasses, 6 Plate, Brass Mat, Leather Case, R. Cornelius, c.1842 5875.00
Daguerreotype, Mother & Daughter, Seated, 1/6 Plate. 65.00
Daguerreotype, Older Man Holding Cane, 1/6 Plate. 75.00
Daguerreotype, Portrait, Gentleman, Brass Mat, Pressed Paper Case, c.1825, 1/6 Plate 470.00
Daguerreotype, Young Man, Bushy Hair, 1/6 Plate. 90.00
Daguerreotype, Young Woman, Lace Bonnet, Heavy Coat, 1/6 Plate. 50.00
Ferrotype, Black Girl, Seated, Embossed Leather Case, 4 5/8 x 3 ¾ In. 110.00
Photograph, Beaumont Newhall, Chase Bank, Black & White, c.1928, 16 x 22 In. 780.00
Photograph, Bird Pageant, Fiber Based Paper, Signed, Eudora Welty, Frame, 37 x 28 In. 2530.00
Photograph, Edward Curtis, Apache Women Fording, 1903, 6 x 8 In. 2280.00
Photograph, Frank Zappa, Black & White, Michael Matlese, 24777, 20 x 16 In.. 311.00
Photograph, George Custer, Sleigh, Buffalo Robes, 4-Horse Team, Oval, Frame, 10 x 13 In. 3819.00
Photograph, Indian Council At Driving Of Last Spike Of NPRR, F.J. Hayes, 1883, 7 x 9 In. 1410.00
Photograph, Orotone, Prayer To The Stars, Edward S. Curtis, Frame, 18 ¾ x 15 ¾ In. 1880.00
Photograph, Panoramic, Zeppelin, U.S. Navy, Shenandoah, c.1925, Frame, 41 x 11 In. 575.00
Photogravure, Vanishing Race, Navaho, Edward Curtis, 17 ½ x 22 In.. 2875.00
Silver Print, Oyster, Theodore Fonville Winans, Mounted, c.1939, 16 x 20 In. 1880.00
Silver Print, Paris, Les Halles, A. Kertesz, 2 Men, Dog, 1928, 8 x 9 In. 2700.00
Silver Print, Waiting, Woman, Child By Shore, Nancy Cones, Frame, c.1908, 16 x 12 In. 480.00
Tintype, Armed Union Soldier, Bearded, Knapsack, Full Case, 1/6 Plate *illus* 245.00
Tintype, Atkins, Baseball, Player By Backdrop, 1889 360.00
Tintype, Doll Posed On Chair, 2 x 3 1/8 In.. 125.00
Tintype, Drugstore, Men, Log Crosswalk, ½ Plate 294.00
Tintype, Home, Family, Dog, Building, 1800s, 8 ½ x 6 ½ In. *illus* 121.00
Tintype, Indian Bust, Union Soldier, Gutta Percha Case, 2 x 2 In. 140.00
Tintype, Man On Bicycle In Front Of Shack, ¼ Plate, 3 ¾ x 4 7/8 In.. 150.00
Tintype, Man Showing Horse, 2 ½ x 3 7/8 In.. 75.00
Tintype, Men On Buckboard In Front Of Store, 2 ½ x 3 ½ In.. 100.00

Phonograph, Victor Victrola, Upright, Mahogany, c.1900, 42 In.
$110.00

Photography, Albumen Print, Veta Pass With Trains, Mat, Frame, 26 x 31 In.
$6463.00

Photography, Ambrotype, Man, Tinted Cheeks, 1/6 Plate
$11.00

As always, the edited listings in *Kovels' Antiques & Collectibles Price Guide 2010* aren't available on any website, but readers should visit Kovels.com for information on trends, tips, reproductions, marks, old prices, and more!

Photography, Ambrotype, Painter, Paint Brush, Ladder, Case, 1⁄16 Plate
$242.00

Photography, Camera, Nikon, S, No. 6103728, Nippon Kogaku, 1951
$443.00

Photography, Carte De Visite, Horse-Drawn Wagon, Store, John Kalla, Toledo, Oh.
$77.00

Found Photographs

In the 1990s a few dealers and galleries "discovered" photographs by amateurs. They searched boxes of snapshots, pored over work by news and sports photographers, and looked for other sources of photographs of daily life. The best were matted, framed, and hung in galleries to be sold to collectors as art. These are known as "found photographs," and many show remarkable artistic talent and photographic skill.

Photography, Daguerreotype, 2 Girls, Posed In Dresses, Gutta Percha Case, 1⁄16 Plate
$176.00

Photography, Daguerreotype, Girl, Leaning On Table, Case, 1⁄6 Plate
$44.00

Photography, Tintype, Armed Union Soldier, Bearded, Knapsack, Full Case, 1⁄6 Plate
$245.00

Tintype, Postmortem, Girl, Tinted Flowers, 2 Views, Brass Mats, ½ Plate, c.1870 . . . . 353.00
Tintype, Woman Seated Holding Book, Paper Case, ½ Plate 90.00

PIANO BABY is a collector's term. About 1880, the well-decorated home had a shawl on the piano. Bisque figures of babies were designed to help hold the shawl in place. They range in size from 6 to 18 inches. Most of the figures were made in Germany. Reproductions are being made. Other piano babies may be listed under manufacturers' names.

Baby, Crawling, Intaglio Eyes, All White, Marked, 5 x 3 ½ In. 150.00
Baby, Crawling, On Knees, Blond Hair, 1 Hand Out, 4 In. 41.00
Baby, Emerging From Egg, Bisque, Skin Tones, Blond Hair, Brown Eyes, 2 ½ In. 172.00
Baby, Googly Eyes, Bonnet, 5 In. 95.00
Baby, Holding Mirror, Germany, 13 In. 690.00
Baby, Holding Pear, Germany15 In. 345.00
Baby, Intaglio Eyes, Large Ears, Open-Close Mouth, 8 In. 825.00
Baby, Lying Down, Blue Eyes, On Pillow With Puppy, 5 In. 149.00
Baby, Lying On Back, Bisque, Blond, White Bonnet, Marked, 5 ½ In. 195.00
Baby, Reclining, Brown Hair, Blue Eyes, Thumb By Mouth, 14 ½ In. 225.00
Baby, Sitting, Bisque, Blond, White Underwear, Sunburst Mark, c.1915, 5 In. 80.00
Baby, Sitting, Bisque, Brown Hair, White Underwear, Sunburst Mark, c.1915, 8 In. 300.00
Baby, Sitting, Blue Eyes, Pinafore & Bonnet, Finger To Lips, 6 In. 21.00
Baby, Sitting, Girl, Blond Curls, Ruffled Romper, Bisque, Painted, Victorian, 7 In. 120.00
Baby, Sitting, In Shoe, Bisque, Blue Eyes, Marked, 5 In. 300.00
Baby, Sitting, White Bisque, Reading Large Book, 1900, 4 ¾ In. 49.00
Baby, Sitting, With Shovel, 3 In. 39.00
Baby, With Cat, White, Marked, 1900s, 6 x 4 In. 59.00
Boy, Finding His Fingers & Toes, 6 In. 100.00
Boy, Sitting, Reading Book, c.1900, 4 ½ In. 40.00
Dutch Boy, Sitting, Arm Wrapped Around Rope, c.1890, 5 ¾ In. 120.00
Girl, Bonnet With Bow On Top, 6 ½ In.. . . . . 50.00
Girl, Crawling, 10 x 6 ½ In. 175.00
Girl, Holding Flower, Bisque, 13 In.. . . . . 175.00
Girl, Lying Down, Holding A Bunch Of Grapes, 1900s, 5 x 3 In. 33.00
Girl, Sitting, Off The Shoulder Nightgown, Pink Bows, Pointy Curls, Bisque, 7 In. 120.00
Girl, Sleeping, Holding Teddy Bear, 7 ½ x 5 ¼ In. 75.00
Girl, Wearing Burnt Red Bonnet & Dress, 8 ½ In. 75.00
Girl Twins, Long Hair, Rosy Cheeks, Blue Eyes, Red Lips, White Gowns, 1900s, 5 In. 399.00

PICKARD China Company was started in 1893 by Wilder Pickard. Hand-painted designs were used on china purchased from other sources. In the 1930s, the company began to make its own china wares in Chicago, Illinois. The company now makes many types of porcelains, including a successful line of limited edition collector plates.

Bell, Christmas, The First Noel, Gold Decorated, 1977 . . . . 27.00
Bowl, Pergola By Lake, Mountains, Oval, Signed, Yeschel, 9 In. 100.00
Bowl, Poppy, Hand Painted, Signed, Wagner, 9 ½ x 3 ½ In.. . . . . 495.00
Bowl, Vegetable, Oval, Brown Rose, 9 x 6 ¾ In. 45.00
Cup & Saucer, Cattails 18.50
Cup & Saucer, Damask 32.00
Cup & Saucer, Enchantment 22.00
Cup & Saucer, Fleurette 27.00
Pitcher, Poppy, 5 ¾ In.. . . . . 288.00
Plate, Bread & Butter, Fleurette, 6 ¼ In. 15.00
Plate, Dessert, Wishbones, 4-Leaf Clover, Hand Painted, White, Gold, Black, Green, 7 ¾ In.. . . 15.00
Plate, Dinner, Fleurette, 11 In.. . . . . 35.00
Plate, Pastoral Scene, Signed, E. Challinor, 8 ½ In. 30.00
Plate, Pergola By Lake, Moonlight Scene, Signed, C. Marker, 8 ½ In. 40.00
Plate, Salad, Brown Rose, 8 In. 20.00
Plate, Salad, Damask, Platinum Trim, 8 In.. . . . . 24.00
Plate, Salad, Sunflower, 8 ¼ In.. . . . . 12.00
Sugar Basket & Creamer, Gold Baroque, 4 ½-In. Sugar, 2 ⅝-In. Creamer, 1920-30s. 115.00
Vase, Bud, 24K Gold Rim At Neck & Base, Greek Letter Gold Symbol, 6 ¾ In. 35.00

PICTURES, silhouettes, and other small decorative objects framed to hang on the wall are listed here. Sandpaper pictures are black and white charcoal drawings done on a special sanded paper. Some other types of pictures are listed in the Print and Painting categories.

TIP

Daguerreotype cases can be polished with liquid shoe wax (not polish).

Photography, Tintype, Home, Family, Dog, Building, 1800s, 8 ½ x 6 ½ In.
$121.00

Picture, Centaur, Boy, Archery, Shell Cameo, Brass Frame, Millefiori, Late 1800s, 5 x 4 In.
$2320.00

Picture, Needlework, 3 Kittens, Bowl, Wool, Frame, 19th Century, 12 ½ x 16 ½ In.
$310.00

Picture, Needlework, Eagle Over Ship's Life Ring, 2 Flags, Silk, Frame, Late 1800s, 17 x 19 In.
$520.00

Picture, Silhouette, Man In Suit, Red, Black Sash, German Text, 16th March 54, Frame, 5 x 4 In.
$180.00

Picture, Silhouette, Mother & Child, Frame, 1830s, 10 x 7 In.
$825.00

TIP

The center of a hanging picture should be about 66 to 68 inches from the floor or 12 to 16 inches above the top of a piece of furniture.

Bird, On Flowering Branch, Potted Flower, Miller, Frame, 9 ¾ x 8 ¾ In. 110.00
Centaur, Boy, Archery, Shell Cameo, Brass Frame, Millefiori, Late 1800s, 5 x 4 In. *illus* 2320.00
Cut Paper, Ships, Storms, Ship Paul Jones At Sandy Hook, 15 ½ x 18 ½ In. 46800.00
Drawing, Pencil, Tomb Of Harrison, Frame, 19th Century, 16 ¼ x 12 ½ In. 345.00
Glass Beads On Net, Romantic Scene, River, Sailboat, Buildings, Gilt Frame, c.1810, 7 x 11 In. 176.00
Gouache, Alpine Scene, Milo Winter, Jr. American, Frame, c.1940, 20 x 14 In. 540.00
Ink, Paper, Trees, Rocks, Signed, Carl Schmidt, Frame, c.1920, 20 ½ x 14 ½ In. 1080.00
Marquetry, Art Nouveau, Woman, Feeding Dove, Wood, Mother-Of-Pearl, 23 x 18 In. 489.00
Nautical Chart, Martha's Vineyard, Engraved, Mat, Gilt Wood Frame, 33 x 23 ½ In. 288.00
Needlework, 3 Kittens, Bowl, Wool, Frame, 19th Century, 12 ½ x 16 ½ In. *illus* 310.00
Needlework, Alphabet, Flowers, Magdalena Shirk, Wool, Frame, 1867, 16 ¾ x 18 In. 527.00
Needlework, Alphabet, Verse, Amanda Searing, Aged 12, N.J., April 28 1848, 18 x 19 In. 1035.00
Needlework, Charles II, Knights In Battle, Gilt Frame, Late 17th Century, 17 ¼ x 21 In. 10530.00
Needlework, Crocheted Animals, Tree, Wool, Cotton, Tweed Ground, 30 x 30 In. 353.00
Needlework, Eagle Over Ship's Life Ring, 2 Flags, Silk, Frame, Late 1800s, 17 x 19 In. *illus* 520.00
Needlework, Embroidered, Painted, Boy In Tunic, Branch, Stormy Landscape, Frame, 12 x 9 ½ In. 403.00
Needlework, Embroidered, St. Catherine Of Alexandria, Classical Attire, Silk, Frame, 21 x 15 In. 259.00
Needlework, French Nun, Holding Book, Garden, Silk, Watercolor, c.1820, 11 x 9 ½ In. 176.00
Needlework, Lady Of The Lake, Embroidery, Silk, Chenille, Painted, Eglomise Mat, 18 x 25 In. 3910.00
Needlework, Man Leaning On Cannon, Frame, 14 x 10 ½ In. 81.00
Needlework, Parrot, Silk, On Paper, Perched On Basket, Frame, 11 x 8 In. 264.00
Needlework, Patriotic, Silk Thread On Silk, Flags, Eagle, Military Items, 1800s, 35 x 28 In. 2355.00
Needlework, Petit Point, Meeting In The Garden, Silk, Linen Canvas, 1800s, 21 x 32 In. 353.00
Needlework, Silk, Eagle, Embroidered E Pluribus Unum, Red Ground, 20 x 33 In. 315.00
Needlework, Silk, Painted Details, Young Woman, Empire Gown, Lute, 1800s, 7 ½ x 9 In. 431.00
Needlework, Silk & Ink On Silk, Woman, 1700s Dress, Windmill, Gilt Frame, c.1795, 9 x 8 In. 822.00
Needlework, Silk Embroidery, House, Trees, Work'd By Lydia G. Day, Frame, 22 x 24 In. 705.00
Needlework, Silk On Linen, Mother & Daughter, Frame, 19th Century, 9 x 12 In. 402.00
Needlework, Silk Thread, Farm Scene, Eglomise Mat, Oval Aperture, Frame, 11 x 13 In. 472.00
Oil On Canvas, Saint Barbara, Spanish School, 19th Century, 30 x 24 In. 1410.00
Pastel, On Paper, Sky Studies, House, Clouds, Pierce Rice, c.1965, 24 x 18 In. 191.00
Pastel, On Paper, Still Life, Fruit, Gilt Wood Frame, 1800s, 16 ¾ x 12 ¾ In., Pair 748.00
Pastel, Paper On Board, Pine Forest, G.A. Sartorio, Italy, 1927, 12 x 23 In. 12650.00
Pencil & Ink, Woman, In Bonnet, Laid Paper, Gilt Frame, Early 1800s, 5 x 4 ¼ In. 206.00
Scroll, Ink, On Paper, Tree, Poem, Chinese, 68 x 38 In. 1920.00
Silhouette, Man In Cap, Greyhound, Bird's-Eye Maple Frame, c.1840, 10 ½ x 12 ½ In. 1265.00
Silhouette, Man In Suit, Red, Black Sash, German Text, 16th March 54, Frame, 5 x 4 In. *illus* 180.00
Silhouette, Mother & Child, Frame, 1830s, 10 x 7 In. *illus* 825.00
Silhouette, Portrait, Girl, M. Honeywell, Cut By Mouth, Bird's-Eye Maple Frame, 7 x 6 In. 575.00
Sketch, Pencil, Duke Of Wellington's Flagship, Frame, Mid 1800s, 20 ½ x 17 In. 173.00
Theorem, Basket Of Roses, Morning Glory, Butterfly, Gilt Frame, c.1825, 14 x 17 In. 411.00
Theorem, Compote Of Fruit, Watercolor On Velvet, Boghese Label, Gilt Frame, 19 x 21 In. 176.00
Theorem, Flowers, Presented To Isabel Perrine, From Rebecca J., 10 x 11 ½ In. 1265.00
Theorem, Glass Bowl, Fruit, Blue, Red, Green, Stenciled Frame, New England, c.1820, 10 x 13 In. 575.00
Theorem, Parrot, On Tree Branch, Label, Chagrin Falls, Ohio, 1800s, 18 ½ x 14 ½ In. 940.00
Theorem, Parrot, Stencil, On Paper, Charles Cotton, August 1846, Frame, 9 ⅝ x 7 ¼ In. 323.00
Theorem, Still Life, Fruit, Glass Compote, Freehand, Stenciled, Gilt Frame, c.1825, 22 x 27 In. 1175.00
Theorem, Watercolor, On Paper, Basket Of Fruit, Cutout, Gilt Frame, 9 ¾ x 11 ⅜ In. 633.00
Theorem, Watercolor, On Paper, Flowers, Purple, Red, Yellow, Green, 1800s, 15 x 19 In. 259.00
Theorem, Watercolor, On Velvet, Basket Of Fruit, Crested Bird, Multicolored, 16 ½ x 21 In. 1058.00
Theorem, Watercolor, On Velvet, Basket Of Fruit, Strawberries, Grapes, Frame, 11 ½ x 14 ¾ In. 118.00
Theorem, Watercolor, On Velvet, Bowl Of Fruit, Vegetables, Seaweed Type, 19 ¼ x 23 ¾ In. 9988.00
Theorem, Watercolor, On Velvet, Fruit Bowl, 2 Birds, Multicolored, Frame, 15 x 18 ½ In. 209.00
Theorem, Watercolor, On Velvet, Owl On Oak Branch, Multicolored, Frame, 15 x 13 ¼ In. 55.00
Theorem, Watercolor, Shepherd, Sheep, House, Cherry Frame, 11 ½ x 15 ½ In. 192.00
Tinsel, Birds, In Flowering Wreath, Reverse Painted, Frame, Late 1800s, 25 x 19 In. *illus* 323.00
Tinsel, Cat, Crinkled Tin Foil, Stuffed, On Velvet Background, Frame, 1800s, 24 x 22 In. 1380.00
Wall Hanging, Silk, Painted, Birds-Of-Paradise, Rain Forest, c.1940, 48 x 52 In. 239.00
Watercolor, Angel, Multicolored, Red, Black, Frame, T.J. Graham, 13 ¼ x 13 ¼ In. 77.00
Watercolor, Backyards, James Sessions, Frame, 1936, 16 x 18 In. 1800.00
Watercolor, Bird, Perched On Heart, Folk Art, Multicolored, Frame, Late 1800s, 6 x 3 ¾ In. 382.00
Watercolor, Bird On Flower, Grain Painted Frame, c.1830, 10 x 8 ½ In. 205.00
Watercolor, Cat With Ball, Ink, Red, Black Corner Block Frame, French, 14 x 17 In. 330.00
Watercolor, Docked Tanker, Reginald Marsh, Frame, 1936, 14 x 20 In. 5625.00
Watercolor, Dove On Mound, Flowers, Sawtooth Border, Multicolored, 8 ¼ x 8 ½ In. 605.00
Watercolor, Equestrian Lady, Papier-Mache Frame, Continental, 1800s, 6 x 6 In. 147.00
Watercolor, Forest Scene, Robert Root, Frame, c.1900, 9 ½ x 6 ½ In. 1020.00

Watercolor, Ghost, Tombstone, Vine Border, C. Hopf, Vinegar Painted Frame, 7 x 7 In.	143.00
Watercolor, Grapevine, Franz Aulich, c.1890, 20 x 14 In.	780.00
Watercolor, Landscape, Edgar Forkner, Frame, c.1920, 12 x 22 In.	1200.00
Watercolor, Landscape, Mountains, Signed, J.B. Sword, Phil., Frame, c.1890, 7 x 10 In.	144.00
Watercolor, Man In Sombrero, Donald Ruf, Frame, c.1940, 14 x 10 In.	240.00
Watercolor, Maria Howard Weeden, Portrait, Black Woman, Signed, Oval, Frame, 10 x 8 In.	4600.00
Watercolor, Memorial, Col. Henry Gerrish, Frame, May 18 1806, 12 ¾ x 11 ¼ In.	270.00
Watercolor, On Ivory, Man, Black Tie, Oval, Locket Gilt Frame, 1800s, 3 x 2 In.	518.00
Watercolor, On Ivory, Man, Oval, Wood Frame, Late 1700s, 2 x 1 ½ In.	385.00
Watercolor, On Ivory, Man, Red Hair, Oval, Gilt Frame, 1800s, 2 ½ x 2 In.	489.00
Watercolor, Peacock, Flowers, Elligen, Love, Frame, Heart Blocks, 16 x 20 In.	1380.00
Watercolor, Pont Neuf, Reginald Marsh, Paris Scene, Frame, 1938, 12 x 18 In.	8750.00
Watercolor, Portrait, Child, Blond, Blue Dress, White Rose, Molded Frame, 9 x 8 In.	2760.00
Watercolor, Portrait, Gentleman, Black Painted Brass Oval Frame, Continental, 5 ½ x 4 In.	173.00
Watercolor, Portrait, Gentleman, Black Suit, Full Length, Mat, Frame, England, c.1850, 14 x 12 In.	205.00
Watercolor, Portrait, Woman In Black, White Bonnet, Eglomise Mat, Frame, 6 x 5 In.	235.00
Watercolor, Pot Of Flowers, Birds, Mahogany Veneer Frame, 9 x 10 ⅞ In.	288.00
Watercolor, Profile Portrait, Richard Colbath, J.H. Davis, Frame, 1835, 10 x 8 In.	5938.00
Watercolor, River Landscape, Town, Covered Bridge, Frame, c.1880, 11 x 15 In.	176.00
Watercolor, Rooster On Mound, Red, Black, Yellow Sponge, Frame, 8 ½ x 10 ½ In.	550.00
Watercolor, Shining Sea, Ship Deck, James Sessions, Frame, c.1937, 16 x 21 In.	5050.00
Watercolor, Study For Porcelain Vase, Franz Aulich, c.1890, 20 x 14 In.	390.00
Watercolor & Ink, Court Lady, Woman, Characters, Chinese, c.1950, 50 x 25 In.	837.00
Watercolor & Ink, Lion, Black, Yellow, Red Corner Block Frame, France, 14 x 17 In.	165.00
Watercolor & Ink, Parrot, Flowers, Elliger, Green Corner Block Frame, 8 x 6 ¾ In.	2750.00
Watercolor & Ink, Portrait, Black Girl, With Basket, Sister Devola, c.1840, 7 ½ x 5 ½ In.	2415.00
Watercolor & Ink, Turkey, Pumpkin, Corner Block Frame, French, 15 x 15 In.	248.00
Wax, Portrait, Indigo Jones, Signed, John Flaxman, Shadowbox Frame, 7 x 8 In.	633.00
Woolie, Yarn Work, Tower Bridge Of London, Flags, Britain, 21 ½ x 34 In.	6143.00

PICTURE FRAMES *are listed in this book in the Furniture category under Frame.*

PIERCE, *see Howard Pierce category.*

PIGEON FORGE Pottery was started in Pigeon Forge, Tennessee, in 1946. Red clay found near the pottery was used to make the pieces. Molded or thrown pottery with matte glaze and slip decoration was made. The pottery closed in 2000.

Candleholder, Olive Green Matte Glaze, E. Ownby, 1950s-60s, 4 ¼ In.	15.00
Coaster Set, Gray Blue, 2 Wheat Designs, 2 Snowflake Designs, Set Of 4	22.00
Figurine, Black Bear, Satin Matte Glaze, Incised, Signed, D. Ferguson, 4 In.	34.00
Figurine, Raven, Black, Douglas Ferguson, Incised, 1984, 10 x 13 In.	200.00
Jar, Cover, Dogwood Blossom, 4 ¼ In.	12.00
Jar, White, Blue Lid, Wheat Design On Lid, D. Ferguson, 3 ¾ x 5 ⅜ In.	43.00
Pin Dish, Hand Thrown, E. Ownby, 1 ⅜ x 4 ¼ In.	15.00
Pitcher, Dogwood Blossom, 3 ¾ In.	12.00
Vase, Bud, Double, Beige & White, Dogwood Blossom, 7 ¾ In.	30.00
Vase, Dogwood Blossom, Narrow Neck, Bulbous, 3 ½ In.	9.00
Vase, Souvenir, Dogwood Blossoms, Beige & White, 3 ¾ In.	7.00
Wall Pocket Vase, Dogwood Blossom, 4 ¼ x 4 In.	10.00

PILKINGTON Tile and Pottery Company was established in 1892 in England. The company made small pottery wares, like buttons and hatpins, but soon started decorating vases purchased from other potteries. By 1903, the company had discovered an opalescent glaze that became popular on the Lancastrian pottery line. The manufacture of pottery ended in 1937. Pilkington's Tiles Ltd. has worked from 1938 to the present.

Tea Bowl, Crocuses, Gold, Green, Blue, Royal Lancastrian, 1909, 2 ½ x 4 In.	650.00
Vase, Crystalline Glaze, Double Gourd, Blue, c.1910, 7 In.	800.00
Vase, Flowers, Metallic Luster Glaze, 3 ⅞ In.	690.00
Vase, Repeating Shamrocks, Tab Handles, Footed, Geometric, 4 ½ x 2 In.	495.00

PILLIN pottery was made by Polia (1909–1992) and William (1910–1985) Pillin, who set up a pottery in Los Angeles in 1948. William shaped, glazed, and fired the clay, and Polia painted the pieces, often with elongated figures of women, children, flowers, birds, fish, and other animals. Pieces are marked with a stylized *Pillin* signature.

W+P
Pillin

Picture, Tinsel, Birds, In Flowering Wreath, Reverse Painted, Frame, Late 1800s, 25 x 19 In.
$323.00

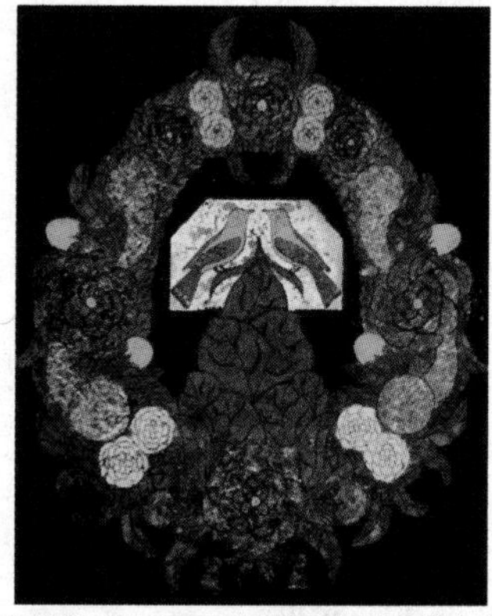

Pillin, Tray, Fish, Signed, 6 ¼ In.
$395.00

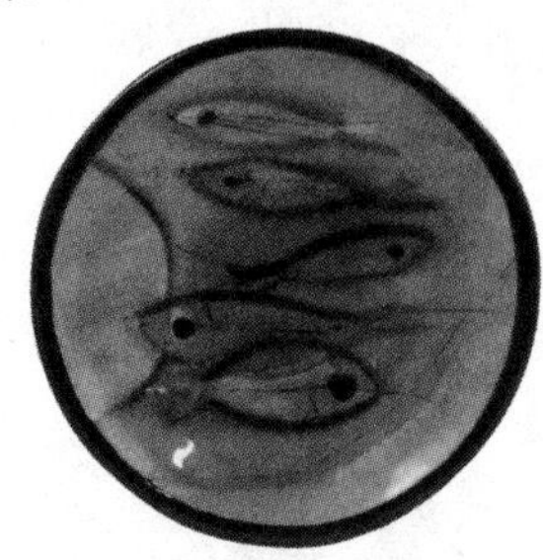

Pillin, Vase, Birds, Pastel Underglaze Design, Oval, Signed, 4 ¼ In.
$385.00

Pillin, Vase, Woman With Balloons, Pastel Underglaze Design, Cylindrical, Signed, 10 In.
$990.00

P

Pincushion Doll, Spanish Woman, No. 10016, 6 ½ In. |
$275.00

Pincushion Doll, Woman, Yellow Dress, Brown Hair, Blue Mark, G.H. Macheleid, 5 In.
$295.00

Pipe, Meerschaum, American Indian, On Horse, Mountain Lion, 4 x 9 ¼ In.
$1820.00

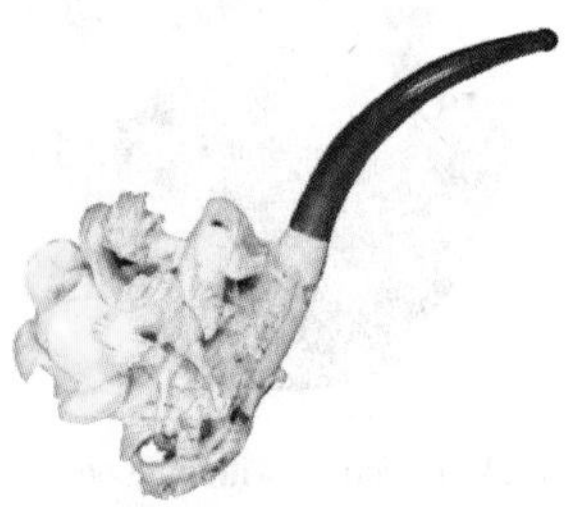

Pisgah Forest, Jug, Green, Lid, Marked, Pisgah Forest 38, 2 ⅞ In.
$27.00

Bowl, Birds, Multicolored Patchwork Ground, Curved, 3 ¾ x 10 ½ In. 1800.00
Chalice, Colorfully Painted Horses, Blue Ground, 4 x 5 In. 420.00
Tray, 2 Women, Blue, White, Yellow, 10 In. 650.00
Tray, Fish, Signed, 6 ¼ In. *illus* 395.00
Tray, Fish, Woman, Abstract, 4-Sided, 5 In. 450.00
Tray, Horse, Abstract, 5 In. 350.00
Vase, 3 Women, Holding Scarves, Vivid Colors, 4 x 8 In. 780.00
Vase, 3 Women, Shouldered, Narrow Opening, Blue, Gray Ground, 6 x 11 In. 1140.00
Vase, 4 Birds, 3 ½ In. 175.00
Vase, 4 Dancers, Yellow Glaze, Blue, Black, White, Cylindrical, Mark, 7 x 4 In. 695.00
Vase, Birds, Pastel Underglaze Design, Oval, Signed, 4 ¼ In. *illus* 385.00
Vase, Colorful Painted Women's Heads, Roosters, Red, Purple, Bulbous, 4 x 3 In. 510.00
Vase, Dancers, Woman, Mandolin, Pale Underglaze, Orange Collar, Cylindrical, Base, 14 In. 1416.00
Vase, Spotted Horses, Pink, Yellow, White, Brown, White Ground, Squat Shouldered, 7 x 6 In. 660.00
Vase, Swimming Fish, In Size Order, Brown Glaze, Yellow, White, Mark, 5 x 4 In. 495.00
Vase, Woman, Balloons, Pale Blues, Pinks, Cylindrical, Signed Polia Pillin, c.1950, 10 In. 1062.00
Vase, Woman With Balloons, Pastel Underglaze Design, Cylindrical, Signed, 10 In. *illus* 990.00
Vase, Woman With Flower, Woman With Bird, Blue, Yellow, Red, White, Triangular, 8 x 4 In. 900.00
Vase, Women Holding Fish In Net, Painted, Signed, 14 ½ x 6 ¼ In. 2400.00

PINCUSHION DOLLS are not really dolls and often were not even pincushions. Some collectors use the term "half-doll." The top half of each doll was made of porcelain. The edge of the half-doll was made with several small holes for thread, and the doll was stitched to a fabric body with a voluminous skirt. The finished figure was used to cover a hot pot of tea, powder box, pincushion, whiskbroom, or lamp. They were made in sizes from less than an inch to over 9 inches high. Most date from the early 1900s to the 1950s. Collectors often find just the porcelain doll without the fabric skirt.

Spanish Woman, No. 10016, 6 ½ In. *illus* 275.00
Woman, Yellow Dress, Brown Hair, Blue Mark, G.H. Macheleid, 5 In. *illus* 295.00

PINK SLAG *pieces are listed in this book in the Slag Glass category.*

PIPES have been popular since tobacco was introduced to Europe by Sir Walter Raleigh. Carved wooden, porcelain, ivory, and glass pipes may be listed here.

Figural, Faux Ivory, Lion, Baring Teeth, Stand, Early 20th Century, 6 In. 176.00
Ivory, Elephant, Incised Abstract Design, Carved, 4 ½ In. 20.00
Meerschaum, American Indian, On Horse, Mountain Lion, 4 x 9 ¼ In. *illus* 1820.00
Meerschaum, Bearded Man, Long Hair, Hat, Box, 6 ½ In. 30.00
Meerschaum, Bearded Man, Tassled Hat, Inland Products Inc., Box, 7 In. 60.00
Meerschaum, Bearded Man, Wearing Cap, Birch Stem, Carved Bowl, 3 ½ x 1 ¼ In. 75.00
Meerschaum, Cavalier Plume In Hat, Carved, Leather Case, 14 In. 117.00
Meerschaum, Dog, Pheasant In Mouth, Pearlized Brown & Tan Stem, Ring, Case, 5 ½ In. 30.00
Meerschaum, English Nobleman, Reclining, Amber Stem, Silver Band, 3 Star Case, 6 ½ In. 60.00
Meerschaum, Flowers, Carved, Cigar Holder, 4 ½ In. 30.00
Meerschaum, Lion, Prowling, Amber Stem, 1900s, 8 In. 205.00
Meerschaum, Stag, Running, Carved, Amber Stem, C.P.F., Case, 4 ¾ In. 50.00
Meerschaum, Stag, Running, Carved, Amber Stem, F. Benz, Case, 4 ¼ In. 60.00
Meerschaum, Woman, Wearing Hat, Carved, Stand, Early 20th Century, 3 ½ In. 234.00
Porcelain, Skull, White, Black, Wood Stem, 3 x 4 In. 253.00
Wood, Hand, Thumb Lifts, Carved, 5 x 3 In. 110.00

PISGAH FOREST pottery was made in North Carolina beginning in 1926. The pottery was started by Walter B. Stephen, who had been making pottery in that location since 1914. The pottery continued in operation after his death in 1961. The most famous kinds of Pisgah Forest ware are the cameo type with designs made of raised glaze and the turquoise crackle glaze wares.

Cookie Jar, Blue, Ear Handles, 8 In. 440.00
Cup, Indian, Buffalo, Blue Matte, Pink Interior, Signed, Stephen, 1951, 3 ⅜ In. 330.00
Jug, Green, Lid, Marked, Pisgah Forest 38, 2 ⅞ In. *illus* 27.00
Mug, Fiddler, Dog, Olive Green Matte, Pink Interior, Signed, Stephen, 3 ½ In. *illus* 242.00
Teapot, Purple Matte Glaze, Rolled Edge, Flattened Finial, 1945, 5 x 9 In. 300.00
Vase, Ivory To Ocher Ground, Blue Crystalline Glaze, W.B. Stephen, 12 x 8 In. 650.00
Vase, Tan, Blue Crystalline Glaze, Squat, c.1938, 4 In. 345.00
Vase, White, Blue, Crystalline Glaze, Runny Olive Green Glaze, Marked, c.1941, 6 ½ In. 345.00

PLANTERS PEANUTS memorabilia are collected. Planters Nut and Chocolate Company was started in Wilkes-Barre, Pennsylvania, in 1906. The Mr. Peanut figure was adopted as a trademark in 1916. National advertising for Planters Peanuts started in 1918. The company was acquired by Standard Brands, Inc., in 1961. Standard Brands merged with Nabisco in 1981. Some of the Mr. Peanut jars and other memorabilia have been reproduced and, of course, new items are being made.

Bank, Mr. Peanut, Cast Iron, 3 x 3 x 11 In. 30.00
Bank, Mr. Peanut With Top Hat, Red, White, Blue, Plastic, 1950s, 8 ½ In. 950.00
Book, Famous Men, Story & Paint, 1935, 7 ⅜ x 10 ⅜ In. 60.00
Bookmark, Mr. Peanut, Greetings From Mr. Peanut, Cardboard, 1940s, 7 In. .... 15.00 to 18.00
Bracelet, Charm, Mr. Peanut, Red, White, Blue, Plastic, 8 In. 25.00
Coaster, Mr. Peanut, Greetings, Tin, 3 ½ In. Diam. 7.00
Container, Mr. Peanut, Yellow, Black, Papier-Mache, 12 ½ In. 375.00
Cookie Jar, Planters Peanuts, 5 Cent, Salted, Cobalt Blue, Molded, 6-Sided, 12 In. 35.00
Cruet, Oil & Vinegar, Mr. Peanut, 7 In., Pair 40.00
Display, Rack, Peanut Specialties, Tin Lithograph, Red, Yellow, Black, White, 1940s, 14 x 8 In. 805.00
Display Stand, Planters Peanut Specialties, Z-Shape, Tin Lithograph, 4 ½ x 14 In. 250.00
Doll, Mr. Peanut, Wood, Jointed, Painted, c.1930, 8 ½ In. .... *illus* 213.00
Figure, Mr. Peanut, Painted, Papier-Mache, 12 ½ In. .... *illus* 202.00
Jar, 4-Sided, Embossed, c.1930, 9 ½ x 7 x 7 In. 173.00
Jar, Embossed, Planters Peanuts, Square, 7 ½ In. 50.00
Jar, Lid, 75th Anniversary, Clear, 1981, 7 ¾ In. 15.00
Jar, Lid, Streamline, Embossed, Planters Peanuts, 10 In. 170.00
Letter Opener, 2 Peanuts, Figural, Embossed, Metal, Wilkes-Barre, c.1920, 8 ½ In. 202.00
Mask, Mr. Peanut, Santa Hat, Celluloid, 11 In. 50.00
Measuring Cup, Mr. Peanut, Plastic, Clear, 3 ¾ In. 40.00
Measuring Cup, Tin Lithograph, Blue Ground, Red, Black, White, 1930s, 2 ¾ In., 3 Piece 403.00
Nut Set, Tin, 1939, 5 Piece 25.00
Nutcracker, Mr. Peanut, Wood, Carved, 20th Century, 8 In. 195.00
Pail, Planters Peanut Butter, Tin, 25 Lb., 9 ½ In. .... *illus* 173.00
Paperweight, Mr. Peanut, Painted, Iron, 1940-50, 7 ½ In. .... *illus* 460.00
Pen, Mr. Peanut On Barrel, Blue, Bic, c.1970, 6 In. 10.00
Salt & Pepper, Mr. Peanut, Plastic, Pink, 3 In. 18.00
Sign, Mr. Peanut, Salted Peanuts, Embossed, Tin, 1930-40, 10 x 23 In. .... *illus* 202.00
Tin, Mr. Peanut's, Barking Dog, Instruments, Yellow, Bail Handle, 4 x 3 ½ In. 485.00
Toothpick, Mr. Peanut, 4 In. 95.00
Toothpick, Mr. Peanut, On Peanut Shell, Bisque, 4 In. 90.00
Toothpick, Mr. Peanut, Standing Next To Half Peanut Shell, Noritake, 4 In. 80.00
Wristwatch, Mr. Peanut, Calendar, Blue, Yellow, c.1970, 1 ½ x 9 In. 173.00

PLASTIC objects of all types are being collected. Some pieces are listed in other categories; gutta-percha cases are listed in photography, celluloid in its own category.

Bowl, Confetti, Aqua & Black, Melmac, Dallas Plastics Mfg., c.1960, 8 In. 25.00
Bowl, Confetti, Melmac, Texasware, 10 In. 35.00
Box, Green Bakelite, Flowers, 5 x 8 In. 30.00
Cigarette Holder, Butterscotch, Bakelite, 1 ⅝ x ½ In. 8.00
Coaster Set, Yellow, Scalloped Edge, Blisscraft, c.1950, 3 In., 17 Piece 12.00
Dish, Butter, Clear & Yellow, Blisscraft Plastics Of Hollywood, 7 ½ In. 8.00
Napkin Holder, Teapot Shape, Yellow, Rogers Plastic Co., 4 ½ x 6 In. 18.00
Poker Chips, Red, Green, Butterscotch, Bakelite, Case, 4 ½ x 7 ¼ In. .... *illus* 200.00
Sculpture, Lucite, Jan De Swart, Cylindrical, Swirls, Crystal Highlights, c.1948, 12 In. 1320.00
Tie Rack, Hollywood Tie Keeper, Folding, Holds 32 Ties, 15 ¼ x 2 In. 15.00

PLATED AMBERINA was patented June 15, 1886, by Joseph Locke and made by the New England Glass Company. It is similar in color to amberina, but is characterized by a cream colored or chartreuse lining (never white) and small ridges or ribs on the outside.

Bowl, 3 ¼ x 8 In. 14850.00
Creamer, 5 ½ In. 15000.00
Finger Bowl, 2 ½ x 5 In. 5850.00
Pitcher, Lemonade, Amber Applied Handle, 5 In. 4600.00
Punch Cup, Inverted Thumbprint, Applied Reeded Handle, 2 ½ In. 60.00
Saltshaker, Ribbed Body, Spelter Lid, 4 In. 4025.00
Sugar, Oval, Applied Amber Handles, 6 In. 10000.00
Tankard, Applied Amber Handle, 5 ⅜ In. 4600.00
Vase, Lily, Ruffled Rim, Amber Disc, 7 In. 7763.00

Pisgah Forest, Mug, Fiddler, Dog, Olive Green Matte, Pink Interior, Signed, Stephen, 3 ½ In.
$242.00

Planters Peanuts, Doll, Mr. Peanut, Wood, Jointed, Painted, c.1930, 8 ½ In.
$213.00

Planters Peanuts, Figure, Mr. Peanut, Painted, Papier-Mache, 12 ½ In.
$202.00

Planters Peanuts, Pail, Planters Peanut Butter, Tin, 25 Lb., 9 ½ In.
$173.00

Planters Peanuts, Paperweight, Mr. Peanut, Painted, Iron, 1940-50, 7 ½ In.
$460.00

Planters Peanuts, Sign, Mr. Peanut, Salted Peanuts, Embossed, Tin, 1930-40, 10 x 23 In.
$202.00

Plastic, Poker Chips, Red, Green, Butterscotch, Bakelite, Case, 4 ½ x 7 ¼ In.
$200.00

Water Set, 7-In. Pitcher, 7 Piece .... *illus* 36750.00

PLIQUE-A-JOUR is an enameling process. The enamel is laid between thin raised metal lines and heated. The finished piece has transparent enamel held between the thin metal wires. It is different from cloisonne because it is translucent.

Bowl, Brass Rim, Enamel Flowers, Chinese, c.1870, 2 ½ x 5 In. 234.00
Bowl, Red & Yellow Flowers, Green Leaves, Flared Lip, 5 In. 100.00
Bowl, Scalloped Top, Birds, Flowers, Red, Blue, Green, Yellow, 6 x 3 In. 120.00
Box, Lid, Blue, Brown, Flowers, Leaves, Carved, Round, 2 In. 469.00
Brushpot, Red & Yellow Flowers, Green Leaves, Cylindrical, 5 In. 100.00
Spoon, Silver, Multicolored 210.00
Spoon, Silver Wire Frame, Gold Wash, Georg Adam Scheid, 4 ½ In. 100.00

POLITICAL memorabilia of all types, from buttons to banners, are collected. Items related to presidential candidates are the most popular, but collectors also search for material related to state and local offices. Memorabilia related to social causes, minor political parties, and protest movements are also included here. Many reproductions have been made. A jugate is a button with photographs of both the presidential and vice presidential candidates. In this list a button is round, usually with a straight pin or metal tab to secure it to a shirt. A pin is brass, often figural, sometimes attached to a ribbon.

Ashtray, Calvin Coolidge For President, Black, White, H. Davis Co., Chicago, 1920s, 5 In. 67.00
Ashtray, Theodore Roosevelt, African Safari, Art Nouveau, Brass, c.1910, 5 x 7 In. 173.00
Badge, Bryan, 16 To 1, Antitrust, Brass, Enamel Stars, 1900, 1 ⅛ In. 28.00
Badge, Bryan, Democracy Stands For, 1900, 1 ¼ In. 172.00
Badge, Bryan, Sound Money, Silver, Gold Nuggets, 1 ⅝ In. 155.00
Badge, Campaign, Henry Clay, Portrait, Pewter Rim, 1844, 2 ½ In. 3346.00
Badge, Cleveland, Stevenson, Ribbon, Eagle, Brass Shell Frame, 1892, 3 In. 658.00
Badge, Eisenhower, Nixon, Inauguration, Brass Framed Hanger, Jugate, 1953, 3 x 7 In. 411.00
Badge, Geo. McClellan, Cardboard, Brass, Red, White, Blue, 1864, 1 x 3 In. 1314.00
Badge, Grant, Cardboard, Photo Under Glass, Brass Rim, 1868, 1 ⅛ In. 487.00
Badge, Hancock & English Jugate, My Choice, Tin Shield, 1880, 1 x 1 In. 1076.00
Badge, Harrison, Morton, Ribbon, 1888, 2 ½ x 1 ¼ In. .... *illus* 239.00
Badge, Lincoln, Ferrotype, Ribbon, Flag, Brass, 1864, 2 In. 2629.00
Badge, Lincoln, Mourning, Photo, Tintype, Black Silk, 1 ½ In. .... *illus* 900.00
Badge, Lincoln, Mourning, Silk Ribbon, Red, White, Blue, Black, 4 In. 1912.00
Badge, Lincoln, Portrait, Flag, Brass Shell Frame, 1864, 1 x 1 ¼ In. 4481.00
Badge, McKinley, Commercial Tribune, Hurrah!, Brass, Cardboard, 1896, 5 In. .... *illus* 158.00
Badge, McKinley, Roosevelt, Rough Rider, Inaugural, Jugate, 1901, 1 ¾ x 9 In. 660.00
Badge, Vote Truman For President, Portrait, Philadelphia, 1948, 3 ½ In. 2868.00
Badge, William McKinley, Bell Shape, 1900 National Convention, 1 ½ x 2 ½ In. 72.00
Badge, Wm. Henry Harrison, Blue Glazed Medallion, Brass Fringe, 7 ½ In. 311.00
Badge, Wm. J. Bryan, 1896 Silver Dollar, Openwork Silver Text, Ribbon, 2 x 5 In. 2629.00
Badge, Wm. J. Bryan, 1908 Democratic Convention, Portrait, Ear Of Corn, Celluloid, 6 In. 1912.00
Badges, Bryan, McKinley, Portrait, Ribbon, Red, White, Blue, 3 ¾ In., Pair 538.00
Bandanna, Bryan, Presidential Campaign, Black, White, 1908 .... 180.00
Bandanna, Frame, Jugate, Bryan, Sewell, Slogans, Silk, 1896, 16 x 16 In. 96.00
Bandanna, George Washington, Centennial, Contemporary Frame, c.1876, 27 x 20 In. 382.00
Bandanna, George Washington, Red, White, Blue, Frame, c.1876, 25 x 17 In. .... *illus* 325.00
Bandanna, Harrison, Morton, Protection & Prosperity, Stars, Red, White 700.00
Bandanna, Henry Clay, Portrait, Stars, 1844 .... 2500.00
Bandanna, Mounted, Jugate, McKinley, Hobart, Campaign, Silk, 1896, 16 x 16 In. 120.00
Bandanna, Roosevelt, Fairbanks, Slogans, Red, White, Frame, 1904, 25 x 23 In. 717.00
Bandanna, Theodore Roosevelt, Red, Teddy Bears, Big Stick, 1912 .... 655.00
Bandanna, TR, Hat In Ring, Bull Moose, Big Sticks, Bears, Red, White, 1912, 17 x 27 In. 360.00
Bandanna, W.H. Harrison, On Horseback, Log Cabin Campaign, Red, White, c.1840, 27 x 25 In. 575.00
Bandanna, Washington, Lincoln Portraits, Black, White, 1876 .... 11000.00
Bandanna, Wm. H. Harrison, Harrison & Reform, Log Cabin, Black, White, Frame, 15 x 17 In. 3300.00
Bank, Eggman, Taft Caricature, Cast Iron, Painted Gold, Arcade, 4 ⅛ In. 2185.00
Bank, McKinley, Teddy, Elephant, Embossed Portraits, Painted Gold, c.1900, 2 ½ In. 748.00
Bank, President Roosevelt, New Deal, Cast Iron, Nickel Finish, Kenton, 5 In. 345.00
Bank, Teddy Roosevelt, Rough Rider Uniform, Bust, Pedestal, 1919, 5 In. 282.00
Bank, Teddy Roosevelt, Bust, Cast Iron, Gold Paint, A.C. Williams Co., Ohio, c.1919, 5 In. 215.00
Banner, Harrison, Morton, Eagle, Stars, Shield, Red, White, Blue, Frame, 20 x 38 In. 986.00
Banner, Thomas Jefferson, Inaugural Speech, Silk, Early 19th Century, 21 x 15 In. 3851.00
Bell, Harding Face, Metal, c.1920, 1 In. 36.00

Book, Cartoon History Of Roosevelt's Career, By Albert Shaw, Pub. 1910, 254 Pages . . . 120.00
Book, Profiles In Courage, John F. Kennedy, Signed, Inscribed, Cloth, c.1956 . . . 3200.00
Book, White House Gallery Of Official Portraits Of The Presidents, Gravure, c.1906 . . . 681.00
Bookmark, Bryan Photo, Heart Shape, Silver, Gold Tassel, c.1896, 2 ½ In. . . . 33.00
Bottle, Beer, Harry S. Truman, Souvenir, Autograph, Blatz, Milwaukee, c.1950, 10 In., Pair . . 478.00
Bottle, Pig, Earthenware, Grover Cleveland Campaign, Slip Stoneware, 1880, 8 x 4 In. . . . 1725.00
Bottle, Whiskey, Old Mr. Boston, Eisenhower Inauguration, c.1953, 11 ½ In. . . . 35.00
Bowl, Fr. Matthew, Temperance Preacher, c.1850, 2 In. . . . 231.00
Box, Benjamin Harrison Portrait, Amber Glass, Hinged Lid, Brass Rim, 4 In. . . . 1793.00
Box, Great Washington To Thee We Owe Our Liberty, Blue, Enamel, Battersea, 2 In. . . . 2032.00
Box, Sewing, Andrew Jackson Portrait Inside, Rainbow Paper, Slogan Outside, 5 x 3 In. . . . 2868.00
Box, Sewing, J. Adams Portrait Inside, Rainbow Paper, Slogan Outside, 1828, 5 x 3 In. . . . 2390.00
Bread Plate, Cleveland, Hendricks, 1884 Campaign, Frosted Glass, 11 ½ In. . . . 263.00
Broadside, Lincoln Funeral, Mourning Borders, c.1865, 6 x 18 ½ In. . . . 1041.00
Bunting, Cleveland, Thurman, Let The Eagle Scream, Red & White, c.1888, 22 x 14 In. . . . 1139.00
Bunting, Teddy Roosevelt's Train, Red, White, Blue, Shield, Stars, 1904, 15 x 22 In. . . . *illus* 220.00
Bust, Wm. McKinley, Parian, Wood Pedestal, Late 1800s, 10 In. . . . 1315.00
Button, Adlai, Estes Vote Straight Democratic, Celluloid, Jugate, 1956, 3 ½ In. . . . 396.00
Button, Adlai & Estes, Right Will Prevail, Clover, Jugate, 1956, 2 ¼ In. . . . 460.00
Button, Adlai Stevenson, Vote Democratic, Red, White, Blue, Picture, 1 In. . . . 335.00
Button, African-Americans For Gore Liebermann 2000, Red, White, Blue, Celluloid, 2 In. . . . 4.00
Button, Al Smith, Derby Shape, Brown, 1928, 1 In. . . . 41.00
Button, Al Smith, Liberty We Want Beer, 1928 . . . 45.00
Button, Al Smith, No Oil On Al, Celluloid, 1924, 1 In. . . . 465.00
Button, Al Smith, Republican Club, Celluloid, 1928, 1 In. . . . 110.00
Button, Alf Landon, Photo, Sunflower, Yellow, White, 1936, 3 ½ In. . . . 1075.00
Button, Alf Landon, Sunflower, Iridescent Petals, Portrait, Celluloid, 1936, 1 ¼ In. . . . 600.00
Button, Alf Landon, Sunflower, Landon Across Front, 2 ¼ In. . . . 597.00
Button, Alfred E. Smith, For President, 1 ¼ In. . . . 29.00
Button, All The Way With Adlai, Red, White, Blue, Celluloid, 1950s, 6 In. . . . 39.00
Button, Alton Parker, Henry Davis, Celluloid, Red, White, Blue, Rooster, Jugate, 1904, 1 In. . . 450.00
Button, America's Hope, Wendell Willkie, Black, White, Transfer, Celluloid, 1940, 1 In. . . . 20.00
Button, Au H2O 1964, Pink Ground, Orange Flowers, Black Letters, 2 ½ In. . . . 24.00
Button, Berger, Gaylord, Socialists For Congress, Jugate, Capitol Dome, Wisconsin, 1 In. . . . 120.00
Button, Bryan, Biblical Verse, Matthew 7:19, Hand Holding Shovel, 1908, ⅞ In. . . . 506.00
Button, Bryan, Commoner Guarantee Of Bank Deposits, Safe, Photo, 1900, 1 ¼ In. . . . 375.00
Button, Bryan, Danforth, Celluloid, Jugate, National Equipment Back Paper, 1900, 2 In. . . . 905.00
Button, Bryan, Free Silver, Daisy, Celluloid, 1896, 13/16 In. . . . *illus* 173.00
Button, Bryan, Kern, Broom, Clean Sweep For Democracy, 1908, 1 In. . . . 1650.00
Button, Bryan, Presidential Campaign, Anti Expansionism, Color, 1900, 1 ½ In. . . . 1500.00
Button, Bryan, Sewell, Pitchfork, Gold Bugs, Slogan, Jugate, Celluloid, 1 In. . . . 269.00
Button, Bryan, Stevenson, Red, White, Blue, Celluloid, Newell Bros., Jugate, 1896 . . . 200.00
Button, Bryan, Stevenson, Red, White, Blue, Liebmann Back Paper, Jugate, 1900, 1 In. . . . 73.00
Button, Bryan From Denver To Washington, Car, Woman Driver, Celluloid, 1908, 1 In. . . . 1162.00
Button, Bury Goldwater, Anti Goldwater, Blue, Gold, Celluloid, 1964, 1 In. . . . 31.00
Button, Bush, George Bush President, Photo, 1980, 3 In. . . . 44.00
Button, Bush, Quayle '92, Celluloid, 2 In. . . . 2.00
Button, Carry On With Roosevelt, Lithograph, 1940, 1 In. . . . 13.00
Button, Carter, I Work For, Picture Of Peanuts, Celluloid, Cream, Brown, 1976, 1 ¾ In. . . . 66.00
Button, Carter, Mondale, Green, White, Celluloid, c.1976, 2 In. . . . 3.00
Button, Carter '76, Celluloid, 2 In. . . . 3.00
Button, Charles E. Hughes Our Choice For President, Black, White, 1908, 1 ¾ In. . . . 1188.00
Button, Chas. Hughes, Our Member For President, Photo, 1 ¼ In. . . . 956.00
Button, Chas. Hughes, Photo, Whitehead & Hoag Backpaper, 1 ¾ In. . . . 1434.00
Button, Churchill, Stalin, FDR, World War II, Maple Leaves, Trigate, 1 ¼ In. . . . 3444.00
Button, Cleveland & Hendricks, Photo Of Mouth On Shield, Jugate, 1884, 2 ½ x 5 ¾ In. . . . 145.00
Button, Clinton, Alamo Rally, Bill, Hillary, Mountain, Celluloid, 1996, 3 In. . . . 16.00
Button, Clinton, Gore, Blue Shirts, Color Photo, White Rim, 1996, 2 ¼ In. . . . 89.00
Button, Clinton, Gore 92, Celluloid, 2 In. . . . 2.00
Button, Coolidge, Dawes, Lithograph, 1924, 1 In. . . . 10.00
Button, Coolidge, Firm As The Rock Of Ages, Photo, Whitehead & Hoag, 1922, 1 In. . . . 360.00
Button, Cox, Roosevelt, Names, White Ground Red Edge, 1920, ⅞ In. . . . 1195.00
Button, Davis, Bryan, Celluloid, Bastian Bros., Jugate, 1924, ⅞ In. . . . 4481.00
Button, Davis, Teapot Dome, Oil Dispenser Cans, 1924, 1 ½ In. . . . 510.00
Button, Debs, Convict No. 9653 For President, Socialist Party, Photo, 1920, 1 In. . . . 1210.00
Button, Debs, Hanford, Rural Setting, Multicolored, Jugate, 1904, 1 ¼ In. . . . 544.00
Button, Debs, Seidel, Socialist Party, Celluloid, Jugate, 1912, 1 ¼ In. . . . 840.00

Plated Amberina, Water Set, 7-In. Pitcher, 7 Piece
$36750.00

Political, Badge, Harrison, Morton, Ribbon, 1888, 2 ½ x 1 ¼ In.
$239.00

Political, Badge, Lincoln, Mourning, Photo, Tintype, Black Silk, 1 ½ In.
$900.00

Political, Badge, McKinley, Commercial Tribune, Hurrah!, Brass, Cardboard, 1896, 5 In.
$158.00

P

Political, Bandanna, George Washington, Red, White, Blue, Frame, c.1876, 25 x 17 In.
$325.00

Political, Bunting, Teddy Roosevelt's Train, Red, White, Blue, Shield, Stars, 1904, 15 x 22 In.
$220.00

Political, Button, Bryan, Free Silver, Daisy, Celluloid, 1896, 13/16 In.
$173.00

Button, Debs, Stedman Statue Of Liberty, Blue Ground, Jugate, 1920, 1 In. . . . 1755.00
Button, Dewey, Bricker, 1944, 1 In. . . . 823.00
Button, Dewey, Bricker, For Prosperity, Celluloid, Jugate, 1944, 6 In. . . . 335.00
Button, Dewey, Bricker, Red, White, Jugate, 1944, 1 ½ In. . . . 264.00
Button, Dewey, Warren, District Of Columbia, 1948, ⅞ In. . . . 41.00
Button, Dewey, Warren, Jugate, 1948, 1 ¼ In. . . . 63.00
Button, Dewey For President, Celluloid, 1948, 1 In. . . . 10.00
Button, Draft Stevenson, Sticker Over Celluloid, 1960, 3 In. . . . 66.00
Button, Dukakis, Bentsen, Flag, Celluloid, 1988, 2 In. . . . 3.00
Button, Dwight Eisenhower, I Like Ike, Time For A Change, Blue, White, Celluloid, 1 ¼ In. . . . 140.00
Button, Eisenhower, Herter, Red, White, Blue, Celluloid, 1956, 2 In. . . . 15.00
Button, Eisenhower, Nixon, Red, White, Blue, Jugate, 1950s, 1 ¼ In. . . . 480.00
Button, Elect Bobby Kennedy President, Photo, White Ground, Red Text, 1968, 3 ½ In. . . . 656.00
Button, Equality, TR, B.T. Washington, 1st Black Presidential Diner, Celluloid, 2 In. . . . 1888.00
Button, FDR, Gardner Return Our Country To The People, Jugate, 1940, 1 In. . . . 1064.00
Button, FDR Photo, Red, White, Blue Stars, Stripes On Rim, c.1940, 3 ½ In. . . . 799.00
Button, For The Love Of Ike Vote Republican, Photo, Red, White, Blue, 1950s, 2 ¼ In. . . . 21.00
Button, Ford, Betty, Gerald Photo, 1976, 2 ¼ In. . . . 66.00
Button, Ford, Dole, Photo, Celluloid, 1976, 2 ¼ In. . . . 121.00
Button, Ford, Dole, Photo, Red, White, Blue, Celluloid, 1976, 1 ¾ In. . . . 66.00
Button, Ford, Dole, Yellow Rim, Red, White, Blue, Committee Pin, 1976, 1 ¾ In. . . . 26.00
Button, Ford, Model T For President, Red, White, Blue, Celluloid, c.1976, 3 In. . . . 238.00
Button, Forward With President Truman No Retreat, Red, White, Blue, 1948, 2 In. . . . 1315.00
Button, Franklin D. Roosevelt, A Gallant Leader, Black, White, Union Bug Stamp, ⅞ In. . . . 20.00
Button, Franklin Delano Roosevelt, Garner, Lithograph, Jugate, 1932, ⅞ In. . . . 230.00
Button, G.B. M'Clellan, For President, Ferrotype Portrait, Brass, 1864, 11/16 In. . . . *illus* 489.00
Button, Geo. Washington, Inaugural, Eagle With Sunburst, Brass, 1 In. . . . 1680.00
Button, Geo. Washington, Inaugural, Long Live The President, Wreath, Brass, 1789, ¾ In. . . . 2520.00
Button, Georgetown Class Of 1968, FOB, Red, White, Blue, 1996, 1 ¾ In. . . . 55.00
Button, Get The Cabot Habit Vote Lodge, Black, White, 1960, 4 In. . . . 107.00
Button, Goldwater, I Am Big On Barry, Red, White, Celluloid, 1 ¾ In. . . . 560.00
Button, Goldwater, In Your Heart You Know He's Right, Photo, Red, White, 3 ½ In. . . . 1135.00
Button, Goldwater, It's Barry Pickin' Time, White, Black, Celluloid, 1964, 2 ½ In. . . . 436.00
Button, Goldwater, Man Of Courage, Celluloid, 1964, 3 In. . . . 1463.00
Button, Goldwater In 1964, Photo, Stars, Gold, White, 3 ½ In. . . . 1075.00
Button, Goldwater Press, Celluloid, 1964, 1 ¾ In. . . . 436.00
Button, H.S. Truman, Signature, Photo, 1922 District Judge Campaign, 4 In. . . . 8365.00
Button, Hanoi Needs McGovern & Fonda, 1968, 2 ¼ In. . . . 33.00
Button, Harding, Celluloid, Metal Frame, 1920, 1 ¼ In. . . . 165.00
Button, Harding For Governor, Profile Photo, Ohio, Celluloid, 1910, 1 ¼ In. . . . 2900.00
Button, Harriman Is The Man, Democrat, Lithograph, 1952, 2 In. . . . 5.00
Button, Harrison & Protection, Portrait, Painted Tin, 1892, 1 ¼ In. . . . 182.00
Button, Harry S. Truman, Inauguration, Jan. 20, 1949, Portrait, Black, White, 4 In. . . . 2032.00
Button, Harry S. Truman For President, Black & White, 1948, 1 ¾ In. . . . 55.00
Button, Harry Truman, Photo, Draped Flags, Celluloid, 1940s, 9 In. . . . 254.00
Button, Help Kennedy Stamp Out Private Enterprise, 1960, 1 ¾ In. . . . 143.00
Button, Henry Ford For President, Donkeyphant, Uniting Both Parties, 1916, 2 In. . . . 2244.00
Button, Herbert C. Hoover, For President, Photo, Red, White Blue, 1 ¼ In. . . . 86.00
Button, Hoover, Allen, Young, Trigate, 13/16 In. . . . 40.00
Button, Hoover, Curtis, U.S. Shield, Presidential Seal, Jugate, 1932, 1 ¼ In. . . . 900.00
Button, Hoover, For President, Photo, Black, Cream, Celluloid, 1928, 1 In. . . . 166.00
Button, Hoover, Who But Hoover, Photo, 1928, 1 In. . . . 43.00
Button, Hubert Humphrey Is A Fink, Anti HHH, 1968, 2 ¼ In. . . . 145.00
Button, Huey Long, Every Man A King, Share Wealth Society, Long Back Paper, 1 In. . . . 209.00
Button, Hughes, Fairbanks, Famous Beards, Black, White, Jugate, 1916, 1 ¾ In. . . . 799.00
Button, I Am A Democrat For Willkie, Red, White, Blue, Lithograph, 1940, 1 In. . . . 3.00
Button, I Am A Playboy Bunny For Carter, Name In Shape Of Bunny, 1976, 2 ½ In. . . . 19.00
Button, I Am For Bob LaFollette, Photo, 1924, 1 In. . . . 556.00
Button, I Am For Levin & LBJ, Portrait, Coattail, Black, Red, White, 1964, 1 ½ In. . . . 432.00
Button, Ike, Draft Eisenhower For President League, Celluloid, 1952, 1 ½ In. . . . 99.00
Button, Ike, I Like Mamie, Lithograph, c.1953, 1 In. . . . 18.00
Button, Ike, Mamie, Photo, No Text, c.1953, 3 ½ In. . . . 33.00
Button, Ike, Man Of The Hour, Photo, Red, White, Blue, Celluloid, c.1953, 13 ½ In. . . . 16.00
Button, Ike, New York For Ike, State Outline, Celluloid, 1952, 1 ½ In. . . . 213.00
Button, Ike, Time For A Change, I Like Ike, Baby, Diaper, Blue, White, 1952, 1 ½ In. . . . 145.00
Button, Ike Dick, They're For Us, Red, White, Blue, 1950s, 3 ½ In. . . . 892.00
Button, In Your Guts You Know He's Nuts, Goldwater Photo, 1964, 3 ½ In. . . . 704.00

Button, J.A. Garfield, Ferrotype, Eagle Brass Shell Frame, 1880, 1 x 2 In. 1673.00
Button, JFK, Next President, Photo, Flag, Celluloid, 1960, 1 ¾ In. 905.00
Button, Jimmy Carter, Jimbo For President, Smiling Hobo, 1976, 2 ½ In. 484.00
Button, John W. Davis For President Club, Celluloid, White, Red Trim, 1924, 1 In. 646.00
Button, Johnson, Draft Johnson, Blue, Gray, Celluloid, 1968, 1 ¼ In. 16.00
Button, Kennedy, Election Night Press, Black, White, 1960, 3 ½ In. 4183.00
Button, Kennedy, Johnson, Vote Straight Democratic Ticket, Lithograph, Jugate, 1960, 3 In. 1315.00
Button, Kennedy & Johnson, Red, White, Blue, Lithograph, 1960, 1 In. 4.00
Button, Kennedy For President, Blue, White, Celluloid, 1960, 1 In. 19.00
Button, Kennedy For President, Ted Kennedy, Red, White, Blue, Celluloid, 1972, 3 In. 5.00
Button, Labor For Stevenson, White, Blue, Celluloid, 1950s, 2 In. 29.00
Button, Landon, It's Landon, Blue, White, 1936, ⅞ In. 837.00
Button, Landon, Knox, St. Louis Button Co., Black Ground, Jugate, 1936, 1 ¼ In. 2390.00
Button, Landon For President, Celluloid, 1 In. 25.00
Button, LBJ, HHH National Maritime Union, 2 Photos, Celluloid, 1964, 3 ½ In. 330.00
Button, LBJ, Ladies For Lyndon, Western Hat, Gold, Red, 1964, 3 ½ In. 55.00
Button, Let's Clean House With Ike & Dick, Lithograph, Red, White, Blue, 1950s, 1 In. 6.00
Button, Lincoln & GOP, 50th Anniversary, Celluloid Oak Tree, 1904, 1 ¼ x 2 ⅛ In. 144.00
Button, Lincoln For President, Ferrotype, Reverse Johnson, 1864, 1 ¼ In. 1496.00
Button, McGovern, Come Back America, Plane, Bombs, Dove, Olive Branch, 1972, 3 In. 839.00
Button, McGovern, Eagleton, Blue, White, Lithograph, 2 In. 4.00
Button, McGovern '72, Green, Dove, Lithograph, 1 In. 3.00
Button, McGovern For Senate, South Dakota, c.1960, 1 ¾ In. 116.00
Button, McKinley, Photo, Flag On Corner, Celluloid, 1904, 3 In. 196.00
Button, McKinley, Roosevelt, Broom Shape, 1904, 2 ½ In. 107.00
Button, McKinley, Roosevelt, Coattail, Trigate, 1 ¼ In. 191.00
Button, McKinley, Roosevelt, Jugate, Frame, 1 ¼ In. 167.00
Button, McKinley, White, Black, Back Paper, Celluloid, 1900, 1 In. 20.00
Button, McKinley, Yes, Commercial Traveler, Suitcase, Celluloid, c.1900, 1 ¼ In. 240.00
Button, Me Gusta Lindsay, John Lindsay, Democrat, Black, White, Celluloid, 1972, 1 In. 4.00
Button, Mill Liberty, Full Figure, Jugate, 1904, 1 ¼ In. 420.00
Button, Mondale, Ferraro, Transfer, Celluloid, 1984, 3 In. 9.00
Button, Neglected Husbands For Nixon, Red, White, Blue, 1968, 1 ½ In. 297.00
Button, Nixon For President, Blue, White, Celluloid, 1960s, 1 In. 13.00
Button, No Man Is Good 3 Times, Anti FDR, 1940, 3 In. 613.00
Button, No Third Term, Lithograph, Anti FDR, 1940, 1 In. 3.00
Button, Not For Sale, Elect Nixon, Anti JFK, 1960, 4 In. 300.00
Button, Nurses For Clinton Gore, Republican, Blue, White, Celluloid, 1992, 2 In. 6.95
Button, Ohio For Taft, Republican, Lithograph, 1952, 1 In. 7.00
Button, OK America Play Safe With Hoover, Red, White, Blue, Photo, 1928, 1 ¼ In. 1862.00
Button, Parker, Celluloid, Laurel Branches, 1904, 1 ¼ In. 243.00
Button, Parker, Colorized Photo, Celluloid, 1904, 1 ¾ In. 116.00
Button, Parker, Davis, Democratic Candidates, Celluloid, Jugate, 1904, 1 In. 399.00
Button, Parker, Davis, Eagle, Flag, Jugate, 1904, 1 ¼ In. 165.00
Button, Parker, Davis, International Badge Back Paper, Jugate, 1904, 1 In. 436.00
Button, Parker, Davis, Liberty Cap Design, Celluloid, Paper, Jugate, 1904, 1 In. 1207.00
Button, Parker, Davis, Shield, Jugate, 1904, 2 In. 341.00
Button, Parker, Davis, Uncle Sam's White Elephant, 1904, 1 ¼ In. 634.00
Button, Philander Knox For President, Photo, Sepia, Cream, 1908, 1 ¾ In. 935.00
Button, Prohibition, Vote Dry, Vote Yes, Black Umbrella, White Ground, c.1920, 1 In. 24.00
Button, Quayle For VP, Signed, Color, Picture, Celluloid, 1992, 3 In. 4.00
Button, Reagan, Bush, Unite The Party, Yellow Ground, Blue Letters, 1980, 2 ½ In. 56.00
Button, Reagan, Bush '84, Red, White, Blue, Celluloid, 2 In. 3.00
Button, Reagan, End Voo Doo Economics Oust Reagan, c.1984, 1 ¾ In. 52.00
Button, Reagan, For Acting Governor, Yellow, Blue, c.1967, 1 ¼ In. 22.00
Button, Reagan, Kemp, Black, White, 1980, 2 In. 3.00
Button, Reagan, Starry Night Ground, Red Letter, Celluloid, 1980s, 2 ½ In. 118.00
Button, Reagan, Thatcher, The Right Stuff, Cartoon Portraits, 1980s, 1 ½ In. 238.00
Button, Ribbon, Cox Home Country Club, Celluloid, Butler Co., Ohio, 1920, 1 ¾ In. 6810.00
Button, Richard Nixon, Man Of Steel, Photo, 1960, 3 ½ In. 353.00
Button, Richard Nixon, Photo, Vice President Staff, Celluloid, 1950s, 3 ½ In. 1016.00
Button, Robert F. Kennedy For President, Democrat, Transfer Photo, Celluloid, 1968, 2 In. 6.00
Button, Ron Paul Libertarian For President, Libertarian Party, Celluloid, 1988, 2 In. 5.00
Button, Roosevelt, Fairbanks, Lady Liberty, Color, Jugate, 1904 .... 140.00
Button, Roosevelt, Garner, Celluloid, Jugate, 1932, 1 ¼ In. 40.00
Button, Roosevelt, Garner, Jugate, c.1932, 1 In. 179.00
Button, Roosevelt, Lewis Bring Back Beer, Business, Red, White, Blue, 1932, 1 ⅜ In. 3430.00

Political, Button, G.B. M'Clellan, For President, Ferrotype Portrait, Brass, 1864, ¹¹⁄₁₆ In.
$489.00

Top Ten Political Buttons

Hundreds of thousands of users visit our website, Kovels.com, each month. The slogans on the political buttons that are the most popular among our visitors are:

1. Truman Was Screwy To Build A Porch For Dewey, 1948, 1 In.
2. Parker, Davis, Uncle Sam's White Elephant, 1904, 1 ¼ In.
3. If I Were 21 I'd Vote For Kennedy, 1968, 4 In.
4. Wilson, Preparedness, Peace, Prosperity, Red, White, Blue, 1916, ⅞ In.
5. Eugene Debs, For President, Convict No. 9653, 1920
6. Ike, Dick, Peace, Prosperity, Progress, Green On White, 1956, 1 ¼ In.
7. Remember The Maine, 1898, 2 In.
8. Boycott Non-union Lettuce, Red, Black, White, UFW Eagle, early 1970s, ¼ In.
9. Shirley Chisholm, President, Catalyst For Change, 1972
10. Nixon Eats Lettuce, Black, Green, Eagle On Bottom, early 1970s, 1 ¼ In.

Political, Button, Theodore Roosevelt, Bull Moose, Sepia, Ribbon, Cardboard, 1 ¼ In.
$488.00

Political, Button, Truman, Barkley, Inaugural, Jugate, 1949, 1 ¾ In.
$777.00

Political, Cap Bomb, William McKinley Bust Shape, Name, Metal, 2 In.
$717.00

Button, Roosevelt, National Progressive Party, Bull Moose, Celluloid, 1912, 1 ¼ In. 792.00
Button, Roosevelt, National Unity, Advancement, Celluloid, 1904, 1 ¼ In. 446.00
Button, Roosevelt, Truman, Black, White, Jugate, Celluloid, 1944, 1 ¼ In. 2363.00
Button, Roosevelt, Wallace, Lithograph, 1940, 1 In. 25.00
Button, Roosevelt & Hitt, Our Choice, Photo, 2 ⅛ In. 2068.00
Button, Samuel Whitaker, Pennypacker, Seal On Back, ⅞ In. 10.00
Button, SDS, Anti Vietnam, c.1968, 1 In. 56.00
Button, Shank, George Washington, Memorable Era, Inaugural, Brass, 1789, 1 ⅜ In. 1195.00
Button, Spanish American War, Yankee Pig Dancing On Cuba, Celluloid, 1 In. 161.00
Button, Stevenson, Portrait, 2 In. 172.00
Button, Stevenson, Vote Democratic Don't Let Them Take It, c.1950, 2 ¼ In. 726.00
Button, Stop Johnson Now, Anti Vietnam, LBJ, Celluloid, c.1968, 1 In. 4.00
Button, T.R., Fear God & Take Your Own Part, Navy, Gold, Progressive, 1916, 1 In. 2572.00
Button, T.R., My Hat Is In The Ring, Black, White, Celluloid, 1912, 1 In. 1461.00
Button, T.R., Progressive, Thou Shalt Not Steal, Dead Elephant, Donkey, 1912, 1 In. 1392.00
Button, T.R., Won't You Be My Teddy Bear, Cream, Red, Back Paper, c.1900, 1 ¼ In. 53.00
Button, Taft, Sherman, Celluloid, Oval, Jugate, 1908, 1 In. 300.00
Button, Taft, Sherman, Lady Liberty, Celluloid, Jugate, 1908, ⅞ In. 155.00
Button, Taft, Sherman, Red, White Stripes, Blue, White Stars, Jugate, Celluloid, 1908, 1 In. 1155.00
Button, Taft, Sherman, The Exporters, White Ribbon, Color Celluloid, 1908, 2 In. 657.00
Button, Teddy Bear, Wearing Glasses, Die Cut, Tin Lithograph, Embossed, c.1912, 2 In. 288.00
Button, Teddy Roosevelt, Photo, Blue, Gold, 1912, 2 In. 837.00
Button, Teddy Roosevelt, Photo, Bull Moose Party, Red, White Rim, 1912, 2 In. 2868.00
Button, Teddy Roosevelt, Portrait, Eagle, 1 ¼ In. 167.00
Button, Teddy Roosevelt, Portrait, Multicolored, Celluloid, 1904, 1 ¼ In. 85.00
Button, Teddy Roosevelt, Red, White Stripes, Photo, c.1905, 1 ¼ In. 3978.00
Button, Teddy Roosevelt Photo, Moose, National Progressive Party, Sepia, 1912, 1 In. 1315.00
Button, Temperance, I Am On The Water Wagon Now, Wagon, Horses, Driver, 1 In. 22.00
Button, Theodore Roosevelt, Bull Moose, Sepia, Ribbon, Cardboard, 1 ¼ In. *illus* 488.00
Button, Theodore Roosevelt, Celluloid, Gold, c.1900, 1 ¼ In. 55.00
Button, Theodore Roosevelt, Eagle On Rocks, c.1904, 1 ¼ In. 657.00
Button, Theodore Roosevelt, Hat In The Ring, Black, White, Celluloid, 1912, ⅞ In. 475.00
Button, Theodore Roosevelt, National Equipment Co., c.1912, 1 ¾ In. 227.00
Button, Theodore Roosevelt, Preparedness, Portrait, Paperback, 1916, ⅞ In. 120.00
Button, Theodore Roosevelt, Sepia Portrait, Attached Flag, 1 ¾ In. 263.00
Button, Tom Watson, Photo, Eagle, Gilt Frame, c.1800, 1 ½ In. 311.00
Button, Trade In Your Ford In 76, Gerald Ford In Edsel Car, 2 ½ In. 135.00
Button, True To Truman, Truman Democratic Club Of Wash., White, Blue, 1948, 1 ¼ In. 1554.00
Button, Truman, All 48 In 48 Young Democrats, Lithograph, Tab, 1948, 1 In. 116.00
Button, Truman, Barkley, Black, White, Celluloid, Jugate, 1948, 1 In. 514.00
Button, Truman, Barkley, Donkey, Orange, 1948, 1 ¼ In. 1434.00
Button, Truman, Barkley, Inaugural, Jugate, 1949, 1 ¾ In. *illus* 777.00
Button, Truman, Barkley, Lithograph, 1948, 1 In. 35.00
Button, Truman, Forrest Smith, Coattail, White, Blue Letters, 1948, 2 In. 2270.00
Button, Truman, No Retreat, ⅞ In. 110.00
Button, Truman, Photo, 60 Million People Working Why Change, Sepia, c.1948, 2 In. 19718.00
Button, Truman, Wild About Harry, Donkey, Brown, Plastic, 1948, 2 ½ In. 273.00
Button, Truman & Civil Rights, White Ground, Blue Letters, 1 ¼ In. 896.00
Button, Truman For President, Barkley For Vice President, Jugate, 1948, 1 ¼ In. 514.00
Button, Truman In '48, White Ground, Blue Letters, 1 ¼ In. 2032.00
Button, Truman Photograph, Red, White & Blue Ribbon, Plastic Donkey, 1 ¼ In. 48.00
Button, United Christian Party, Sword, Cross, Star, Celluloid, c.1900, ⅞ In. 413.00
Button, Viet Nam, Voting Age, You Fight & Die But Can't Drink At 18, c.1970, 1 In. 18.00
Button, Vietnam, Draft Beer Not Students, Celluloid, 1 ¾ In. 25.00
Button, Vote Socialist, Socialist Party, Red, White, Celluloid, c.1940, 1 In. 9.00
Button, Washington Citizens For Colin Powell, Republican, Celluloid, 1996, 3 In. 9.00
Button, Washington For Bush, Apple, Red, White, Celluloid, 1988, 3 In. 13.00
Button, Wendell Willkie, Photo, Metal Easel Stand, 1940, 4 In. 660.00
Button, Wendell Willkie For President, Photo, Celluloid, 1940, 1 In. 253.00
Button, Willkie, I'm For Willkie, Joe Lewis, Lewis Photo, 1940, 1 In. 1075.00
Button, Willkie, No New Deal We Want A Square Deal, Green, White, Celluloid, 1940, 1 ¼ In. 16.00
Button, Willkie, Republican Victory Year Life Begins In 40, Celluloid, 1 In. 9.00
Button, Willkie For President, 2 ½ In. 28.00
Button, Wilson, Photo, Flag, Celluloid, Back Paper, c.1908, 1 In. 85.00
Button, Win With Nelson Rockefeller, Republican, Red, White, Blue, Celluloid, 1964, 4 In. 9.00
Button, Win With Wilson, Celluloid, 1912, 1 In. 40.00
Button, Wm. J. Bryan, Biblical Verse Matthew 7:19, 1908, ⅞ In. 506.00

Button, Wm. J. Bryan, Clockface Portrait, Celluloid, Back Paper D.A. Mills, c.1900, 1 In. 1064.00
Button, Women's Rights, 2 Women's Feet, Dress Hem, 1 In. 19.00
Button, Woodrow Wilson, Man Of The Hour, Blue, Gold, Celluloid, 1916, 1 ¼ In. 900.00
Calendar, FDR, Wall Display, Funeral Director Imprint, Cardboard, c.1934, 4 x 9 In. 52.00
Campaign Ribbon, Lincoln, Free Homes For The People, 1860, 2 x 5 In. 3360.00
Campaign Ticket, Lincoln & Hannibal Hamlin, Virginia, Elector's List, 8 ½ x 11 In. 142.00
Cap Bomb, William McKinley Bust Shape, Name, Metal, 2 In. ..... *illus* 717.00
Card, Cigarette, Teddy Roosevelt Poses, Frame, 8 x 24 In., 6 Piece 1912.00
Card, Communist Party, Nikita Khrushchev, Signed, Leather Case, 1956, 3 x 2 In. 510.00
Card, Playing, Andrew Jackson As Jack Of Spades, Horse, Sword Drawn. 287.00
Card, Playing, Theodore Roosevelt, On Horse, Directions, Box, 1900s, 6 x 45 In. 478.00
Card, Window, Roosevelt, Truman, Cardboard, Vote Democratic For Lasting Peace, 11 x 14 In. 974.00
Chair, D. Eisenhower, Cherry Hill Club President, Denver, Metal, Wood, Leather, 1950s, 32 In. 411.00
Cigar Band, National Candidates, Color, Frame, Jugate, 1896-1900 ..... 215.00
Cigar Box, Chester A. Arthur, La Flor De General Arthur, Holiday Greetings 50.00
Cigar Box, Cleveland, Stevenson, Wood, 1892, 1 ¾ x 4 ¾ x 3 In. 70.00
Cigar Box, Label, Parker, Davis, Symbols, Multicolored, Frame, 1904, 13 x 12 In. 311.00
Cigar Cutter, Betsy Ross, Painted Portrait, Pat.1906, A.S. Valentine, Philadelphia, 6 x 9 In. 472.00
Cigar Cutter, Teddy Roosevelt, Progressive Party, Bullmoose, Hole, Round, 2 Parts 215.00
Clicker, Teddy Roosevelt, Zig Zag Candy, Two Winners, Liberty, Color, Celluloid, 1 In. 1434.00
Clock, Bronze, McKinley Bust, Sound Money Slogan, Wood Base, 1896, 15 In. 570.00
Clock, F.D.R., Man Of The Hour, Electric, Brass Cover, United, 1930s, 4 x 9 x 14 In. 417.00
Clock, Shelf, Boy In Costume, Happy Days, Electric, c.1933, 3 ¼ x 11 x 12 ½ In. 500.00
Clock, Shelf, Oak, William McKinley, Gingerbread Portrait, Symbols, 22 ¾ In. 418.00
Clock, Shelf, Teddy Roosevelt On Rearing Horse, Figural 538.00
Clock, Theodore Roosevelt, Rough Rider, Base Metal, Bronze, 10 ¼ In. 508.00
Coffin Shape Novelty, Silver, Mechanical, Billy Bryan, c.1896, 1 1/16 In. ..... *illus* 215.00
Collar Box, Hayes & Wheeler Tin Lithograph, Portraits, Wire Handle, c.1877, 4 x 3 x 2 In. 418.00
Collar Box, Tin, Hayes, Wheeler Inauguration, Mar. 4, 1877, 4 ¾ x 3 ½ In. 896.00
Collar Box, Wood, Gutta Percha, Portrait Lid, Garfield, Arthur, 1880, 4 x 4 In. 627.00
Collar Box, Wood, Gutta Percha, Portrait Lid, Hancock, 1880, 4 x 4 In. 836.00
Container, Glass, Full Dinner Pail, McKinley, Bail Handle, Tin Cup Lid, Albert Pick Co. 448.00
Costume, Uncle Sam, Parade, Long Legged, Blue Vest, Striped Pants, 1895. ..... 495.00
Creamer, William Henry Harrison, Log Cabin Pattern, Brown & White, 1840, 6 ½ x 5 In 287.00
Cup, Milk Glass, Bryan, McKinley, Portrait, Campaign, Flowers, 1896, 3 ¾ In., Pair 657.00
Cup, Silver Plate, Relief Portraits, McKinley, Hobart, 1896, 3 ½ In. 179.00
Derby, Al Smith, Photo Campaign Pin Attached, Brown, 1928, 6 x 3 In. 220.00
Dish, Lincoln, Bas Relief, Crisscross Border, Milk Glass, Oval, 6 ½ x 8 ¼ In. 191.00
Doll, F. Roosevelt, E. Roosevelt, Composition, Painted, Formal Attire, 9 ½ In., Pair 478.00
Door, Pine, Inlay Base, Frosted Glass Top, Etched McKinley Portrait, Brass, 30 x 78 In. 1912.00
Fan, Lincoln Mourning, Hand Painted Lincoln Life Scenes, Medallion, 22 In. 15535.00
Fan, Manheim National Bank, Presidents Of The United States, Paddle, 14 ½ In. 20.00
Fan, Question Mark, Bryan, Taft, Uncle Sam, Color, Starr Piano Co., 1908, 8 x 14 In. 263.00
Fan, Women's Suffrage, Keep Cool Massachusetts, Nov. 6 ..... *illus* 311.00
Ferrotype, Grant, Colfax, Brass, 1868, 1 In. 1160.00
Ferrotype, Grant, Colfax, Frame 636.00
Ferrotype, Lincoln, Hamlin, Campaign, 1860, 1 In. 717.00
Ferrotype, Lincoln, Hamlin, Portraits, Brass Frames, 1 In. 2629.00
Ferrotype, Lincoln, Oval Portrait, Eagle Pin, Brass Frame, 1864, 1 ½ In. 4481.00
Figurine, Donkey, Sitting, Truman & Stevenson Names, Plaster, c.1952, 5 ½ In. 131.00
Figurine, Elephant, Carrying Hoover & Curtis Portraits, Cast Metal, 5 ¼ x 5 ½ In. 657.00
Figurine, Elephant, Taft For President, Profile Insert, Celluloid, Cast Iron, 4 ½ x 7 In. 420.00
Figurine, Log Cabin, Benjamin Harrison, Chalk, Painted, 3 x 3 ½ x 2 ½ In. ..... *illus* 33.00
Figurine, Policeman, Baby Suffragist Crying, I Want A Vote, Bisque, c.1910, 6 In. 1140.00
Flag, American, 47 Stars, Hand Sewn, Wool, Cotton, Admission Of New Mexico, 1912, 48 x 86 In. 1645.00
Flag, Garfield, Arthur, Cotton, 1880, 24 x 17 In. 5378.00
Flag, Grant, Wilson, 1872 Campaign, Original 10-In. Stick, 7 x 5 In. 5079.00
Flag, Hayes Wheeler, Campaign, 1 Star, Stripes, Handmade, 1876 ..... 425.00
Flag, R.B. Hayes, W.A. Wheeler, 36 Border Stars, Stick, Oilcloth, 1876, 18 x 26 In. 2040.00
Flag, The Hero Of Tippecanoe, Gen. Harrison Portrait, 12 Stars, Frame, 1840, 30 x 33 In. 16800.00
Flag, Theodore Roosevelt, Portrait, God Save Our President Music, Flag Border, 9 x 12 In. 150.00
Flask, Bryan, Stevenson, Symbols, Label Inside, Metal Cap, Jugate, 1900, 4 In. 3107.00
Flask, McKinley, Hobart, Metal Cap, Gold Standard Whiskey, 1896, 5 ½ In. 1673.00
Flask, McKinley, Roosevelt, Symbols, Label, Metal Cap, Jugate, 1900, 4 In. 2090.00
Flask, Whiskey, Bryan & Sewall Sure Winner, Blue, Silver, White Label, Cap, 1896, 6 In. 717.00
Flue Cover, President & Mrs. McKinley, Portrait, Flowers, Multicolored, 1896, 14 x 10 In. 125.00
Greeting Card, Christmas, Gov. FDR, Eleanor, Dog, Seated Fireside, 1930s, 5 x 7 In. 128.00

Political, Coffin Shape Novelty, Silver, Mechanical, Billy Bryan, c.1896, 1 1/16 In.
$215.00

Political, Fan, Women's Suffrage, Keep Cool Massachusetts, Nov. 6
$311.00

Political, Figurine, Log Cabin, Benjamin Harrison, Chalk, Painted, 3 x 3 ½ x 2 ½ In.
$33.00

Political, Hat, Bryan & Sewell, McKinley & Hobart, Paper, Boston Sunday Globe, 1896
$72.00

P

Political Ribbons
Mass-produced printed ribbons for political campaigns were first manufactured in the United States in 1813.

Political, Parasol, McKinley & Hobart, Red Panels, 33 In.
$600.00

Political, Pitcher, McKinley, Hobart, 1896 Campaign, White, Black Transfer, 7 In.
$311.00

Political, Poster, Lyndon Johnson, U.S. Senator, Harris County, Cardboard, 22 x 13 In.
$230.00

Handbill, Daily Star Extra, Peace Headline, Feb. 4, 1865, Faded Ribbon Backing, 3 x 7 In. 837.00
Hard Hat, Spiro T. Agnew, White, Blue & Red Stickers, c.1970 .... 86.00
Hat, Bryan & Sewell, McKinley & Hobart, Paper, Boston Sunday Globe, 1896 .... *illus* 72.00
Invitation, National Inaugural Ball, Lincoln, Johnson Portraits, Eagles, 1865, 8 x 10 In. 3346.00
Knife Set, Bone Handle Lafayette, Washington, Franklin, Wood Stand, 1700s, 10 x 13 In. 3300.00
Label, Cigar Box, Smoke McKinley & Hobart Cigars, Color, Frame, 1896, 14 x 12 In. 120.00
Lamp, Electric, Teddy Roosevelt, Doves, White House, Red, Green, White, Glass, Metal Base, 25 In. 3346.00
Lamp, F.D.R., New Deal, Candlestick, We Do Our Part, Overstuffed Chair, 1930s, 5 x 6 In. 452.00
Lamp, Kerosene, Glass, Bryan Portrait, Berries, Leaves, Bronze Base, 1896, 21 In. 1912.00
Lamp, Kerosene, Glass, McKinley Portrait, Berries, Leaves, Clear, 16 ½ In. 1076.00
Lamp, Kerosene, Glass, McKinley Portrait, Relief Leaves, Gold Leaf Dollar Signs, Yellow, 15 ¾ In. 3346.00
Lantern, McKinley & Roosevelt, Full Dinner Pail, Punched Tin, 1900, 9 In. 2868.00
Lantern, Parade, McKinley, Hobart, Etched Glass, Flags, Shield, Tin, Handle, 18 In. 2629.00
Lantern, Tin, Fillmore & Donelson, Pierced Star Motif, Flat Back, Handle, 11 ½ x 4 In. 10755.00
Lapel Pin, Teddy Roosevelt Riding G.O.P. Elephant, Pressed Metal, c.1900, 1 ¼ In. 657.00
License Plate, Willkie The Hope Of Our Country, Metal, 11 x 6 ½ In. 85.00
License Plate Attachment, FDR For President, Blue, White, 1936 .... 110.00
License Plate Attachment, Hoover For President, Red, Black, White, Metal, 12 In. 82.00
License Plate Attachment, I'm For Dewey, Sketch, Red, White, Blue, Metal, 3-D, 1948, 11 In. 399.00
License Plate Attachment, I'm For Truman, Sketch, Red, White, Blue, Metal, 3-D, 1948, 11 In. 1089.00
License Plate Attachment, JFK 464, California, Black, Gold, c.1962, 4 In. 33.00
License Plate Attachment, Uphold Prohibition, Black, Gold, Metal, 11 ½ In. 120.00
License Plate Attachment, Wendell Willkie, Life Begins In 40, Metal, 1940, 10 In. 165.00
License Plate Attachment, Win With Truman, Sketch Portrait, 9 ½ In. 1315.00
Lighter, Cigarette, Truman Photo, Signature, Glass, Chrome, St. Louis, 1940s, 4 In. 418.00
Lunch Pail, Lid, McKinley, Roosevelt, Full Dinner Pail, Tin, Wire Handle, 1900, 6 x 8 In. 633.00
Match Safe, Teddy Roosevelt, Rough Rider, Color Paper Lithographed, Glass, Vesta 956.00
Match Safe, Wm. H. Taft Breakfast Event, El Paso, Silver, Engraved, 1909, 3 In. 837.00
Matchbox, Geo. McClellan, Ceramic, Portrait, 1864, 1 ¾ x 1 In. 1434.00
Mirror, First 25 Presidents Of The United States, Sepia, Oval, Pocket, 2 ¾ x 1 ¾ In. 130.00
Mug, FDR, Happy Days Are Here Again, Green, Ceramic, 4 ½ In. 34.00
Mug, Geo. Washington Portrait, Blue, White, W.T. Copeland & Son, 1876, 3 x 3 In. 179.00
Mug, Jas. Monroe Name, Eagle, Flowers, Black, White, Pink Luster Accents, 2 ½ x 3 In. 9560.00
Mug, McKinley, Bryan, Portrait Transfer, 2 Handles, Penn., Late 1800s, 4 ¾ In. 388.00
Mug, William Henry Harrison Campaign, Log Cabin, Luster, Copper, Orange, 3 In. 3585.00
Mug, Zachary Taylor, Black Military Portrait, Gold Highlights, c.1847, 3 In. 1560.00
Napkin Ring, Roosevelt, Fairbanks, Riker Mount, Pink Celluloid, 2 x 1 ½ In. 239.00
Nodder Set, Jack & Jackie Kennedy, Kissing, Painted, 5 In., Pair 702.00
Parasol, McKinley & Hobart, Red Panels, 33 In. .... *illus* 600.00
Pardon, Signed, Ulysses S. Grant, Frame, 1871 .... 1140.00
Pass, Lincoln Conspirators' Trial, Washington, Manuscript Form, 39949, 1865, 4 x 3 In. 3107.00
Pass, Lincoln Funeral, Springfield, Mat, Frame, 3 x 2 In. 2629.00
Pass, Lincoln Funeral, White House Green Room, Black Border, 3 x 5 In. 8365.00
Pennant, Bryan, Kern, Regular Democratic Nominations, Eagle, Flag, Blue, Felt, 1908 .... 1020.00
Pennant, C. Coolidge, White Letters, Blue Felt, Multicolored Portrait, 1924, 25 In. 450.00
Pennant, Debs, Seidel, Red Ground, Candidate Cameos, Torches, 1912, 25 In. 3722.00
Pennant, John W. Davis, Portrait, Green Felt, 1924, 25 In. 660.00
Pennant, Ohio Is Going Dry, Prohibition Reform, Yellow, White Letters, c.1920 .... 100.00
Pennant, Teddy Roosevelt, Symbols, John Brown Celebration, Kansas, Felt, 1910, 20 In. 143.00
Pennant, Welcome To Fulton, Truman, Churchill, Westminister Address, 1946, 28 In. 1195.00
Photo Album, Teddy Roosevelt, Velvet Back, Brass Clasp, Celluloid, 8 x 11 In. 1673.00
Picture, Abraham Lincoln, Bearded, Openwork Walnut Frame, Easel, 7 x 5 In. 167.00
Pill Box, Jas. Polk, Portrait, Name, Original Pills, Glass, Foil, Papier-Mache 4481.00
Pin, Gold Bug, McKinley & Hobart, Jugate, 1896, 1 In. 567.00
Pin, Ike, Brass, Clutch Back, 1 In. 3.00
Pin, Lapel, C.E. Hughes For President, Black, White Picture, 1916, 1 x 2 In. 300.00
Pin, McKinley, On Gold Throne Pinning Opponent Bryan, Color, 1896, ⅞ In. 2400.00
Pin, Mechanical, Theodore Roosevelt, Brass, 1 ¾ In. 287.00
Pin, Patriotic, Union Shield, Torah Scroll, Faith Hope & Charity, c.1860 .... 919.00
Pin, Ribbon, Hoover 1932 Election Day, Celluloid, Red, White, Blue, 2 In. 396.00
Pin, Tab, McKinley For Protection, Red, White, Blue, 1896, 5 x 3 ¾ In. 896.00
Pipe, Abraham Lincoln, Portrait, Wreath, Stars, Clay, 3 In. 478.00
Pipe, Buck, Cannon, Symbols For Buchanan, Clay, Late 1850s, 1 ½ In. 299.00
Pipe, Clay, Harrision, Cleveland Portraits, Slogans, White, 6 x 5 In., Pair 215.00
Pipe, Franklin Pierce Portrait On Head, Clay, 2 In. 131.00
Pipe, Millard Fillmore, Laurel Wreath, Clay, 1 ¾ In. 72.00
Pipe, Pressed Mold Clay, Henry Clay Bust On Front, White, Stem, 3 In. 155.00

Pipe Bowl, McClellan Bust, Leafy Branches, c.1864, 2 ¼ In. 388.00
Pitcher, A. Jackson, Hero Of New Orleans Transfer, Blue Ground, Copper Luster, 5 In. 3107.00
Pitcher, Civilian Ulysses S. Grant, Blue, Green, Brown, Rose, Majolica, 1870s, 10 In. 508.00
Pitcher, Cleveland, Stevenson, Red, Transfer, 1892, 6 ¼ In. 667.00
Pitcher, J.A. Garfield, Profile, Relief Garlands, Bennington Style, Brown Glaze, 9 In. 359.00
Pitcher, McKinley, Hobart, 1896 Campaign, White, Black Transfer, 7 In. *illus* 311.00
Pitcher, Taft, Ceramic, Painted, Figural, Holding Cigar, Molded Handle, c.1908, 4 ½ x 3 In. 58.00
Pitcher, Taft & Sherman, Portraits, Ceramic, 7 ½ In. 239.00
Pitcher, William Henry Harrison, Log Cabin Scene, Columbian Star, 1840, 6 ¾ In. 466.00
Pitcher, Wm. H. Harrison Campaign, Log Cabin, Ceramic, White, c.1840, 5 ½ In. 780.00
Pitcher, Wm. Henry Harrison, Log Cabin, Cider Barrel, Flag, White, Salt Glaze, 6 In. 1554.00
Plaque, Teddy Roosevelt, Lady Liberty, Washington, Patriotic Symbols, Bronze, 1905, 7 In. 538.00
Plate, Bryan, Sewell Campaign, Portraits, Sepia, 1896, 9 In. 131.00
Plate, Campaign, Grover Cleveland, Portrait, Bubble Border 179.00
Plate, Cleveland, Hendricks Campaign, Transfer Portraits, Gold Trim, 1884, 8 In., Pair 167.00
Plate, Cleveland, Stevenson Campaign, Portraits, Blue, White, 1892, 8 In. 179.00
Plate, Garfield & Arthur, Portraits, Names, Symbols, Black, White Transfer, 1880, 9 In. 836.00
Plate, General Winfield Scott, Portrait, Hand Colored, Embossed ABC Border, 5 In. 311.00
Plate, Harrison 1840 Campaign, Portrait, Slogans, White, Pink, 10 In. 1553.00
Plate, Lincoln White House, White, Purple Gold, Eagle, Text, Haviland, 9 ½ In. 14100.00
Plate, McKinley, Bryan, Portrait, Color, Wave Border, Green, White, 1896, 9 In., Pair 179.00
Plate, McKinley, Hobart, Black, White Transfer, 1896, 9 ¾ In., Pair 120.00
Plate, McKinley, Hobart, Portrait, Campaign, Sepia, 1896, 7 ½ In., Pair 167.00
Plate, McKinley, Hobart, Portraits, Dresden, Purple Transfer, 1896, 8 In. 131.00
Plate, McKinley, Roosevelt, Portraits, Milk Glass, Brown Transfer, Blue Lattice Edge, 5 In. 131.00
Plate, McKinley & Roosevelt, Portraits, Milk Glass, c.1900, 5 ½ In. 124.00
Plate, Taft, Sherman, Portraits, Wash., D.C. Scenes, Blue, Staffordshire, 1908, 10 In. 90.00
Plate, Teddy Roosevelt, Portrait, Fort Scott Kansas Bank, Color, Tin, 1905, 10 In. 508.00
Plate, Theodore Roosevelt As President, Flow Blue, Portrait, 9 In. 73.00
Plate, William McKinley, Hand Painted, Portrait, Black, Red, Signed Francis, 10 In. 1195.00
Plate, William McKinley, Portrait, Symbols, Pink Openwork Border, 8 In. 215.00
Plate, Zachary Taylor, Portrait, Red & Green Flower Border, Pasteware, c.1848, 6 In. 2629.00
Platter, Cleveland, Thurman, Portraits, Black, White Transfer, 1888, 14 ½ In. 657.00
Platter, Columbian Star, Wm. H. Harrison Campaign, Log Cabin, Blue, White, 1840, 13 x 17 In. 900.00
Platter, U.S. Presidents To McKinley, Portraits, White House, Seals, Multicolored, 13 In. 598.00
Platter, Wm. Henry Harrison, Blue On White, Log Cabin, Farm, Star Border 310.00
Playbill, John Wilkes Booth, Broadside, The Robbers, Boston, 1862, 6 x 15 In. 776.00
Pocket Knife, Teddy Roosevelt, Our Rough Rider President, Embossed, J.A. Henckels, 3 In. 956.00
Postcard, FDR, Our Quarterback, FDR Standing As Football Player, U.S. Capitol, 1932 53.00
Postcard, Goldwater, Miller, Vote, In Your Heart You Know He Is Right, 1964 41.00
Postcard, Teddy Roosevelt, Cameo Rough Rider, Candidate, Capitol Building, 1908 30.00
Postcard, Teddy Roosevelt, On Seesaw, White Fur Bear, Mechanical, 3 ½ x 5 ½ In. 247.00
Poster, Bill Clinton, Inaugural, Peter Max, Mixed Media, Jan. 19, 1993, 24 x 36 In. 196.00
Poster, Bobby Kennedy, 18 ¾ x 12 ¼ In. 144.00
Poster, Byran, Stevenson, Portraits, J.A. Graham & Co., Frame, 1900, 34 x 26 In. 2629.00
Poster, Clinton, Gore, Win In 96, Peter Max, Mixed Media, c.1996, 24 x 34 In. 127.00
Poster, Cox, Roosevelt, Peace-Progress-Prosperity, Frame, 1920, 19 x 15 In. 956.00
Poster, Edmund G. Brown, Attorney General, California Election, 1946, 11 x 14 In. 125.00
Poster, Lyndon Johnson, U.S. Senator, Harris County, Cardboard, 22 x 13 In. *illus* 230.00
Poster, Gays For Carter, Benefit Party, Handbill, Galaxy 21, c.1976, 17 x 22 & 9 x 11 In. 115.00
Poster, Gene McCarthy, Democrat, A Breath Of Fresh Air, 1968, 11 x 17 In. 33.00
Poster, Harrison, Morton, Blaine, Free Trade Policy, Color, Frame, 1888, 25 x 19 In. 3107.00
Poster, Harry S. Truman, Civil Rights Rally, Cardboard, Oct.11, 1952, 11 x 14 In. 717.00
Poster, I Am Counting On You, Don't Discuss Troop Movements, Mounted, 1943, 20 x 28 In. 440.00
Poster, John Lindsay, GOP Loser, Peter Max, c.1968, 10 x 15 In. 506.00
Poster, LBJ, HHH, Dynamic Duo Exposed, Batman Inspired, Day Glo, 1966, 23 x 35 In. 173.00
Poster, Lincoln, Johnson, Portraits, 1864 Campaign 550.00
Poster, Logan, Blaine, Black, White, Campaign, 1884 550.00
Poster, McKinley, Bryan, Buffalo Bill, A Bunch Of Big Bills, Frame, 1900, 36 x 48 In. 2629.00
Poster, McKinley & Roosevelt Prosperity, Portraits, Lady Liberty, Color, 28 x 40 In. 6000.00
Poster, McKinley Cyclists Vs. Cleveland Cyclists, Yellow, Black, Frame, 1896, 31 x 40 In. 2520.00
Poster, Mondale, Ferraro, Vote Democratic, Cardboard, 1984, 14 x 22 In. 19.00
Poster, Octopus, Symbols, Bryan Portrait, Multicolored, Frame, 1900, 26 x 36 In. 8365.00
Poster, Roosevelt, Fairbanks, Portraits, Flag, Vivid Color, Frame, 15 x 35 In. 3346.00
Poster, Ted Kennedy, To Sail Against The Wind, c.1980, 23 x 31 In. 420.00
Poster, Tilden, Hendricks, Portraits, 1876 Centennial Celebration, Colored, 25 x 21 In. 7170.00
Poster, Truman, Barkley, Beat High Prices, Photos, 1948, 21 x 28 In. 327.00

Political, Razor, Straight, Zachary Taylor, Rough & Ready, Cannon, Tally Ho, Case, 5 ⅞ In.
$389.00

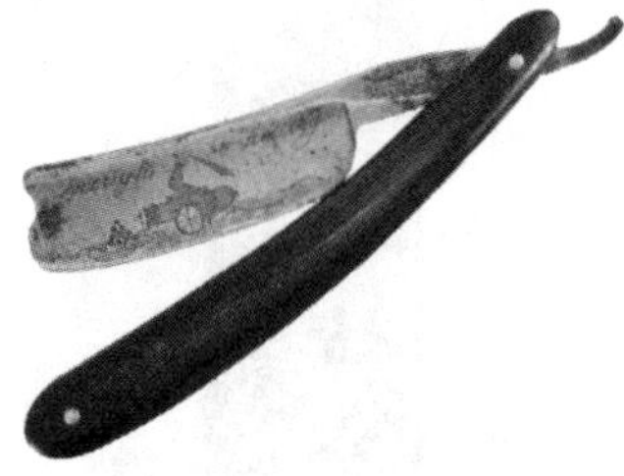

Political, Ribbon, Abraham Lincoln, Eagle, Shield, Mat, Frame, 8 ¼ x 2 In.
$419.00

Political, Ribbon, Button, Eisenhower, Nixon, New York State Citizens, 8 In.
$173.00

Political, Ribbon, Harrison, Morton, Young Men's Republican Club, Brass Tassels, 11 x 3 In.
$288.00

Political, Stickpin, Teddy Roosevelt, Cartoon Like, Clay, Glossy, Bowtie, Figural, 2 ¾ In.
$149.00

Political, Sugar, Lid, William Henry Harrison, 4 Medallions, 1840, 6 ¾ x 5 ¾ In.
$600.00

Political, Textile, William Henry Harrison, Hero of Tippecanoe, Frame, 4 ¾ x 6 ¾ In.
$335.00

Poster Stamp, Roosevelt & Garner, Happy Days Are Here Again, 1932, 1 ⅛ x 1 ³⁄₁₆ In. 38.00
Print, Kellogg, Stephen Douglas, Multicolored, Frame, 1860, 11 x 15 In. 335.00
Print, Lincoln Family Around Table, Black, White, Currier, 13 ½ x 10 ¼ In. 143.00
Program, Truman, Barkley Photos, Inaugural Dinner, Diner Lists, 9 x 11 In. 55.00
Radio, Cardboard, W. Willkie, We Want Willkie, Talk-A-Box, 1940, 3 In. 717.00
Razor, Straight, Benjamin Harrison Portrait On Handle, Campaign 1888 .... 167.00
Razor, Straight, Harrison, Horn Handle, Engraved Slogans, Symbols, 1840, 6 ¼ In. 568.00
Razor, Straight, McKinley, Roosevelt On Handle, Flags, 1900 .... 191.00
Razor, Straight, T. Roosevelt, C.W. Fairbanks, Flags, Shield, Portraits, Plastic Handle, No. 735R 125.00
Razor, Straight, Teddy Roosevelt Portrait, Etched, Germany, c.1901 .... 119.00
Razor, Straight, Theodore Roosevelt, Portrait, Etched, Germany, 1901 .... 100.00
Razor, Straight, Wilson, Marshall, Photos On Blade, Flowers, M. Thomas, Boston 388.00
Razor, Straight, Zachary Taylor, Rough & Ready, Cannon, Tally Ho, Case, 5 ⅞ In. ..... *illus* 389.00
Ribbon, Abraham Lincoln, Eagle, Shield, Mat, Frame, 8 ¼ x 2 In. .... *illus* 419.00
Ribbon, B. Harrison, Portrait, Red Ground, White, Blue, Philadelphia, 3 x 10 In. 568.00
Ribbon, Bryan, Sewell, Portraits, Free Silver 16-1, Arrow Bar Pin, Slogans, 25 x 7 In. 598.00
Ribbon, Bryan, Young Democracy, Flag Ribbon, Cameo Photo, c.1896, 2 ½ In. 216.00
Ribbon, Buchanan, Light Green, 1856, 5 In. 519.00
Ribbon, Button, Eisenhower, Nixon, New York State Citizens, 8 In. .... *illus* 173.00
Ribbon, Button, Hanger, Teddy Roosevelt, Reception, Montana, Red, White, Blue, 1903, 8 In.. 508.00
Ribbon, Campaign, Abraham Lincoln, Brady Portrait, Scalloped Border, 1860, 2 x 7 In. 3107.00
Ribbon, Campaign, Henry Clay, Silk, Clay As Farmer Of Ashland, 1844, 8 ¾ In. 335.00
Ribbon, Campaign, Henry Clay, Silk, Youthful Clay, Moss Convention, 1844, 7 ¼ In. 657.00
Ribbon, Campaign, Lincoln, Hamlin, Black, Salmon Silk, Merrill & Sons, 5 ½ x 2 In. 1416.00
Ribbon, Campaign, Lincoln, Johnson, Red, White, Blue, Woven Cotton, 1864, 2 ½ x 5 ½ In.. . 7767.00
Ribbon, Cleveland, Hendricks, 1884, 2 ½ x 5 ¾ In. 145.00
Ribbon, Cleveland, Stevenson Photo, Purple, Gold, Fringe, 1893, 10 In. 450.00
Ribbon, Convention Delegate, Ike, Nixon Metal Profiles, Blue Cloth, 1956, 2 ½ In. 53.00
Ribbon, Dewey, For President, Republican, White Ribbon, Celluloid, 1940s, 3 ½ In. 89.00
Ribbon, Douglas, Johnson, Democratic Candidates, Silk, 1858, 6 ¾ In. 2151.00
Ribbon, Flag, Abraham Lincoln's Photo, Silk, Brass Shell Frame, 1864, 5 In. 690.00
Ribbon, Geo. McClellan, 1864 Campaign, Paper, Multicolored, Frame, 8 ½ x 13 In. 2270.00
Ribbon, George Washington, Centennial Of His Birth, 1832, 2 x 7 In. 185.00
Ribbon, Greeley, Metal Hat, Brown, 1872 Election 318.00
Ribbon, Harrison, Morton, Raccoon With Hatchet By Neck Of English Rooster, 1889 .... 212.00
Ribbon, Harrison, Morton, Young Men's Republican Club, Brass Tassels, 11 x 3 In. .... *illus* 288.00
Ribbon, Harrison & Reid National Club, Organized June 11, 1892, Brass Top, 2 x 8 In. 86.00
Ribbon, Illinois 1960 GOP Convention, Lincoln Medal, Gold, White, Blue, 2 ½ In. 69.00
Ribbon, John Fremont, Black, White Transfer, 1856, 7 In. 568.00
Ribbon, Lincoln, Beardless, 1864 Campaign, Paper, Multicolored, Frame, 8 ½ x 13 In. 2390.00
Ribbon, Lincoln, Hamlin, Free Homes For The People, Silk, Frame, 1860, 2 ¼ x 5 In. 956.00
Ribbon, Lincoln, July 4th 1865, Washington, July 4th 1776, Ferrotype, Purple, Brass. 378.00
Ribbon, Lincoln, Railsplitter Of 1830 President Of U.S., Tan, Silk, 1861, 6 In. 1434.00
Ribbon, Lincoln, The People's Choice, Transfer, Yellow, Silk, 1864, 6 In. 3107.00
Ribbon, Lincoln Portrait, Beardless, Slogans, Red, Silk, Frame, 1860, 2 x 4 In. 2032.00
Ribbon, Martin Van Buren, Free Soil Candidate, Frame, 1848, 9 ½ In. 837.00
Ribbon, McKinley, Hobart, Portraits, Liberty Atop Flying Eagle, 2 ¼ x 6 In. 155.00
Ribbon, McKinley, Patriotism Protection Prosperity Win, 1896, 2 ¼ x 5 ¾ In. 82.00
Ribbon, McKinley, White Cloth, Michigan, 1896, 10 ½ In. 82.00
Ribbon, Mourning, Abraham Lincoln, 2 ⅛ x 9 In. 288.00
Ribbon, Paper, Lincoln, Hamlin, Portraits, Slogans, Split Rail Fence, Frame, 12 x 15 In. 3346.00
Ribbon, Perry's Victory, 1813, Single Day, Erie, Pa., 3 x 6 In. 202.00
Ribbon, Polk, Dallas, Portraits, 1844, 3 x 9 In. 2032.00
Ribbon, Teddy Roosevelt, Forest Park, St. Louis, Color Photo, Red, 1907 .... 218.00
Ribbon, Tip O'Neill For Vice President, White, 10 In. 238.00
Ribbon, Willkie Train, Red, White, Blue Stripe, Campaign Pass, 1940, 2 ½ In. 288.00
Ring, Teddy Roosevelt, Cameo Portrait, White, Ornate, Onyx, Gold 1195.00
Scale, Cleveland, Harrison, Wrapped In Flags, Hung From Wood Bar, c.1875, 6 In. 836.00
Scale, Harrison, Cleveland, Weighs The Candidates, Multicolored, Bisque, 1888, 6 In. 1075.00
Scissors, Teddy Roosevelt, Taft, On Handle, Germany 49.00
Scissors, Theodore Roosevelt, Edith, Portrait, Embossed, Metal, Solingen Co. 160.00
Scissors, Theodore Roosevelt, Howard Taft, Busts, Metal, Germany 40.00
Shadow Box, Teddy Roosevelt, Wife Edith, Velvet, Wax, c.1902, 30 x 29 In. 900.00
Sheet Music, Abe Lincoln's Union Wagon, Lincoln Portrait, Liberty, Multicolored, 13 x 9 In. . 311.00
Sheet Music, League Of Nations Song, Lady Liberty, Cox, Roosevelt, 1920, 10 x 12 In. 2760.00
Sheet Music, Susan B. Anthony For President, Women Voters At Poll, 1869, 10 x 13 In. 1673.00
Shell, Carved, George Washington Profile, c.1810 .... 100.00

Sign, Wilson, World War II Leaders, Maps, Flags, Slogans, Color, Tin Lithograph, 27 In. 1075.00
Snuffbox, Martin Van Buren Portrait, Capitol Building, Papier-Mache, 3 ½ In. Diam. 1600.00
Snuffbox, Van Buren, Portrait On Lid, Papier-Mache, 3 ½ In. 1912.00
Song Book, Lincoln Portrait Cover, 47 Pages, 1860, 4 x 6 In. 1793.00
Spoon, Bryan Portrait In Bowl, Clover On Handle, Silver Plate, NF Co., 1896, 5 ¾ In. 84.00
Spoon, Demitasse, Wm. McKinley Handle Portrait, U.S. Symbols, Sterling, 4 ½ In. 49.00
Spoon, Grover & Mrs. Cleveland On Handle, Baby Ruth In Spoon Bowl, Sterling, 7 In. 90.00
Spoon, Teddy Roosevelt, Rifles, Arrows, Broncos On Handle, Eliza In Bowl, Sterling, 6 In. 131.00
Spoon, U.S. Grant Bust On Handle, Defender Of His Country, Sterling, 6 In. 72.00
Spoon, Wm. J. Bryan, Sterling Silver, Enamel Portrait Handle, Demitasse, 4 In. 287.00
Stamp Holder, Wm. McKinley Portrait, 1901 Inaugural, Silver Plate, 2 x 3 In. 388.00
Stein, Teddy Roosevelt, On Safari, High Relief Imagery, Multicolored, Germany, 12 ½ In. 3107.00
Stein, Teddy Roosevelt, Rifle, Elephant, Jungle Imagery, Black, White, Green, Metal Lid, 6 ½ In. 478.00
Sticker, Roosevelt, Garner, Anchors Away Sailing To Victory, Ship, 1932, 5 ½ x 8 In. 196.00
Sticker, Window, Cox, Roosevelt, Harding, Coolidge, Portraits, Slogans, Color, 7 x 6 In., 2 Piece 508.00
Sticker, Window, Nixon, Lodge, Red, White, Blue, 1960, 4 x 6 In. 3.00
Stickpin, Andrew Johnson Profile, Ivory, 3 ½ In. 1315.00
Stickpin, Bryan, McKinley, Skeleton, Slogan, Opens To Portraits, Brass, 1896, 2 In., Pair 2270.00
Stickpin, Bryan, Nation's Commoner, Ears Of Corn, Celluloid, c.1900, 1 In. 600.00
Stickpin, Cox, Roosevelt, Man, Horse, Pennant On Stick, Beige Paint, 1920, 1 ¾ In. 2151.00
Stickpin, Hayes, Paper Photo, Brass Shell Frame 478.00
Stickpin, Hayes, Wheeler, 1872 Campaign, Photos, Brass Shell Frame, 1 In. 1195.00
Stickpin, McKinley, Bryan, Oval Celluloid Portraits, Bunting, 1896, 2 In., Pair 179.00
Stickpin, McKinley, Flag, Photo, 1896, 2 ⅝ In. 165.00
Stickpin, Roosevelt, Pop-Up Hills Of San Juan Sign, Striped Bow, Gilt Brass, 1898, 3 In. 2270.00
Stickpin, Teddy Roosevelt, Cartoon Like, Clay, Glossy, Bowtie, Figural, 2 ¾ In. .... *illus* 149.00
Sugar, Cover, Harrison, Frontier Scenes, Red, White, Porcelain, 1840, 6 ¾ In. 1075.00
Sugar, Lid, William Henry Harrison, 4 Medallions, 1840, 6 ¾ x 5 ¾ In. .... *illus* 600.00
Tag, Harding, Photo, Elephant, Don't Throw Your Vote Away, 1920, 1 x 1 In. 538.00
Teapot, Harrison, Log Cabin, Cider Barrels, Red, White, Porcelain, 1840, 6 ½ In. 3107.00
Telescope, Teddy Roosevelt, Rough Riders, Hallett Alsop Borrowe, Spanish American War ... 748.00
Textile, Apotheosis Of Franklin, Lady Liberty, Franklin, Cotton, Red, c.1790, 20 x 30 In. 2950.00
Textile, National American Fillmore Donelson Ticket, Silk, Frame, c.1853, 23 x 16 In. 620.00
Textile, Washington Coronation By Victory, Patriotic Symbols, Chintz, Fragment, c.1783, 66 x 60 In. 4130.00
Textile, William Henry Harrison, Hero of Tippecanoe, Frame, 4 ¾ x 6 ¾ In. .... *illus* 335.00
Ticket, 39876, 1865, Inauguration, Washington, D.C., 4 x 3 In. 14340.00
Ticket, Electoral, Belva Lockwood, Marietta Stow, New York, 1884, 3 x 12 In. 896.00
Ticket, Electoral, Fillmore, Donelson, 1856 .... 115.00
Ticket, FDR, Wallace Inauguration, 1941 .... 55.00
Ticket, Gene Debs, Socialist Event, Photo, St. Louis, c.1920, 5 In. 82.00
Tie, Alton Parker, Campaign Photo, Large Red, White, Blue Stripes, 1904 .... 128.00
Tile, Wm. Henry Harrison, Hero Of The Thames 1813, Blue Transfer, Ceramic, 6 ½ In. 896.00
Tintype, John Fremont, 1856, 1864 Candidate, Thermoplastic Case, 2 x 2 In. 657.00
Tip Tray, Taft, Sherman, Portraits, 1800s Republican Presidents Border, Color, Tin, 10 In. 263.00
Tip Tray, Taft, Sherman, Portraits, Symbols, Lithographed, Color, Tin, 4 In. 120.00
Tire Cover, Franklin D. Roosevelt, A Big Man For A Big Job, 1932, 28 ½ In. 1800.00
Toby Jug, Wm. McKinley As Potbellied Napoleon, Hat Spout, 1890s, 4 In. To 11 In., 4 Piece .. 780.00
Toothpick, Parker, Davis, Portraits, Custard Glass, White, Green, 1904, 2 In. .... *illus* 567.00
Tray, Bryan, Stevenson, Symbols, Eberle Brewing Co., Tin, 1900, 16 In. 1554.00
Tray, McKinley, Roosevelt, Portraits, Bunting, Eagle, White House, Color, Oval, 1900, 13 x 16 In. 450.00
Tray, McKinley, Roosevelt, Tin, 1900, 16 In. 1315.00
Tray, Teddy Roosevelt, Rough Rider Attire, Aluminum, 3 x 5 In. 120.00
Tray, Wm. Jennings Bryan, Tin, Lithograph, Red Edge, 12 ¼ x 17 In. 49.00
Trunk, John Q. Adams, Campaign Broadside Lining, Wood, Painted, 1820, 14 x 6 In. 1554.00
Tumbler, Cigar Band Glass, 1864-1901 Presidential Portraits, 4 In. 120.00
Tumbler, Roosevelt, Fairbanks, Portraits, Patriotic Symbols Etched, 3 ¾ In. 179.00
Vase, Gen. W. Scott, Whig Campaign, Color Portrait, White, Gold, Ceramic, 1852, 6 In. 4481.00
Watch, Ingersoll, Roosevelt, Fairbanks, Metal Stand, Pocket, 1904, 2 In. 2390.00
Watch, John F. Kennedy Profile, Gruen, Leather, 1976 .... 155.00
Watch, McKinley, Roosevelt, Washington, Lincoln, Nude Women, Silver Case, 2-Sided, 2 In. .. 1912.00
Watch, Washington, Lincoln, Wreath, Fob, Amethyst, Gold, American Watch Co., 1 ¼ In. 7768.00
Watch Fob, Bryan, Kern, Enamel On Brass, Spread Winged Eagle, Flags, 1908, 1 ¼ In. 40.00
Watch Fob, Teddy Roosevelt, Admiral Evans, Silver, Leather, U.S. Fleet, 1907, 2 In. 96.00
Watch Fob, Theodore Roosevelt, 1912-1916, Figural R, Bull Moose Party, 1 ⅜ In. .... *illus* 135.00
Whistle, Cleveland, Thurman, Wood, Paper Label With Photos, 4 ½ In. .... *illus* 896.00
Whistle, G. Cleveland, Rooster, Democrat Symbol, Gold, Blue, Red, Metal, 1884, 3 x 2 In. 657.00
Whistle, Horace Greeley, Metal, 1872, 2 In. 1195.00

Political, Toothpick, Parker, Davis, Portraits, Custard Glass, White, Green, 1904, 2 In.
$567.00

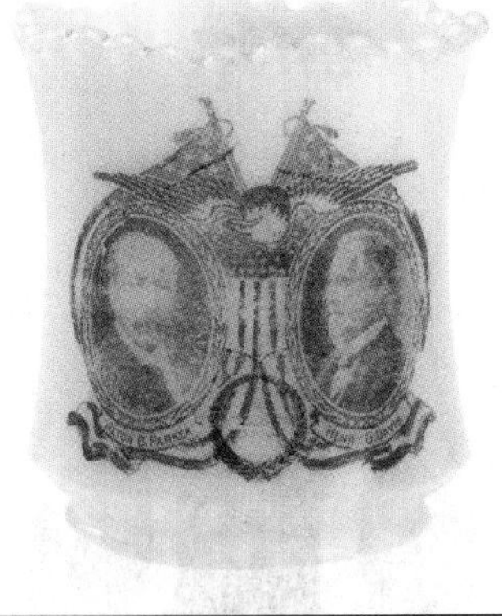

Political, Watch Fob, Theodore Roosevelt, 1912-1916, Figural R, Bull Moose Party, 1 ⅜ In.
$135.00

Political, Whistle, Cleveland, Thurman, Wood, Paper Label With Photos, 4 ½ In.
$896.00

P

Popeye, Doorstop, Painted, Cast Iron, Hubley, Signed, 9 x 4 ⅜ In.
$5750.00

Popeye, Toy, Brutus, Hops, Head Bobs, Tin, Windup, Linemar, Mean Man Box, 5 In.
$1150.00

Popeye, Toy, Olive Oyl, Hops, Head Bobs, Tin, Windup, Linemar, Box, 5 In.
$1725.00

POMONA glass is a clear glass with a soft amber border decorated with pale blue or rose-colored flowers and leaves. The colors are very, very pale. The background of the glass is covered with a network of fine lines. It was made from 1885 to 1888 by the New England Glass Company. First grind was made from April 1885 to June 1886. It was made by cutting a wax surface on the glass, then dipping it in acid. Second grind was a less expensive method of acid etching that was developed later.

Toothpick, Tricornered Rim, 2 ⅝ In. .... 173.00 to 259.00

PONTYPOOL, *see Tole category.*

POOLE POTTERY was founded by Jesse Carter in 1873 in Poole, England, and has operated under various names since then. The pottery operated as Carter & Co. for several years and established Carter, Stabler & Adams as a subsidiary in 1921. The company specialized in tiles, architectural ceramics, and garden ornaments. Tableware, bookends, candelabra, figures, vases, and other items have also been made. The name Poole Pottery Ltd. was taken in 1963. The company went bankrupt in 2003, but is in business today with new owners.

Bowl, Free-Form Bowl, Green, Gray, Red Bands, Marked, 12 ½ In. 94.00
Butter, Cover, Flowers, White, Blue & Aqua Trim, Round, Knop On Lid, Marked, 6 ¾ In. 25.00
Charger, Delphis, Stylized Sunflower, Yellow, Orange, Green, A. Godfrey, c.1967, 17 In. 362.00
Charger, Leaves, Gray, Blue Dots, Yellow Orange, Black, Red Ground, Art Deco, 16 In. 143.00
Cup & Saucer, Flowers, Gilt, 1940-52 .... 25.00
Dish, Dolphin, Swimming In Water, 7 In. 15.00
Dish, Galaxy, Red, Orange, Black Ground, 10 ½ In. 75.00
Egg Cup, Ivory Exterior, Brown Interior, Marked, 1 ¾ In. 20.00
Jam Dish, Lilac, Pink, Yellow, Teal & Light Green 24.00
Jug, Stylized Flowers, Multicolored, White, Scroll Handle, 8 In. 75.00
Pin Dish, Flowers, Blue, 4 In. 15.00
Toast Rack, 6-Slice, Peach, 1930s, 8 x 2 ¾ In. 50.00
Vase, Cylindrical, Flowers, Orange & Red Living Glaze Ground, Marked, 8 In. 94.00
Vase, Stylized Flowers, Hand Painted, Impressed Factory Mark, Initials, 20 In. 239.00

POPEYE was introduced to the Thimble Theatre comic strip in 1929. The character became a favorite of readers. In 1932, an animated cartoon featuring Popeye was made by Paramount Studios. The cartoon series continued and became even more popular when it was shown on television starting in the 1950s. The full-length movie with Robin Williams as Popeye was made in 1980. KFS stands for King Features Syndicate, the distributor of the comic strip.

Ashtray Stand, Popeye, Smoking Pipe, Blue, Black, White, Painted, Wood, 29 In. 100.00
Badge, Navy Admiral, Brass, 1930s, 1 ½ In. 230.00
Bank, Popeye's Head, Corn Cob Pipe, Pottery, Marked, Thermos, 8 In. 100.00
Bank, Wimpy, Painted, Cast Iron, U.S., 8 In. 60.00
Cookie Jar, Popeye's Head, Corn Cob Pipe, American Bisque, 10 ¼ In. 440.00
Cracker Box, Popeye The Sailor, Sunshine Biscuits, 1935, 3 x 5 In. 280.00
Doll, Popeye, Composition, Jointed, Painted, 14 In. 132.00
Doll, Popeye, Composition, Wood, Jointed, Posable, Chein, 1932, 8 In. 305.00
Doll, Popeye, Composition, Wood, Jointed, Posable, Ideal, 12 In. 170.00
Doll, Popeye, Seated In Chair, Foam Stuffed, 52 In. 260.00
Doll, Popeye, Wood, Jointed, c.1935, 11 x 6 In. 236.00
Doorstop, Painted, Cast Iron, Hubley, Signed, 9 x 4 ⅜ In. .... *illus* 5750.00
Flashlight, Popeye, Whistling, Battery Operated, Bantam Lite, 1960s, 4 ¾ x 8 In. 94.00
Lamp, Popeye, Figural, Olive Oyl & Popeye On Shade, Painted, Metal, 15 In. 165.00
Lamp Shade, Popeye, Olive Oyl, Wimpy, Cardboard, King Features, 1935, 6 x 8 In. 1437.00
PEZ, Popeye, Blue, Black, Marked, Austria, 1950s, 4 ⅛ In. 115.00
Poster, Popeye, The Sailor Man, Mess Production, Red, White, Blue, Frame, 42 x 28 In. 225.00
Stringholder, Bluto, Figural, Painted, Incised, 206, 1950s, 8 x 6 In. 689.00
Stringholder, Eugene The Jeep, Full Body, Plaster, Painted, Incised Whitman, 1938, 6 x 10 In. 1075.00
Thimble Theatre, Original Characters, Porcelain, King Features, Davidson, Box, 9 Piece ... 480.00
Toy, Barnacle Bill, Walker, Tin Lithograph, Windup, Chein, 6 In. 195.00
Toy, Boat, SS Popeye, Die Cut, Wood, Paper Lithograph, Pull Toy, 15 ½ In. 250.00
Toy, Boat Fleet, Wood, Celluloid Sails, Box, Transogram, King Features Syn., c.1929, 3 ½ In. . 271.00
Toy, Brutus, Dippy Dumper, Tin Lithograph, Celluloid, Windup, Marx, Box, 9 ¼ In. 1210.00
Toy, Brutus, Hops, Head Bobs, Tin, Windup, Linemar, Mean Man Box, 5 In. .... *illus* 1150.00
Toy, Bubble Blowing, Spinach Pipe, Tin, Battery Operated, Linemar, Box, 1950, 12 In. 1921.00
Toy, Colorforms, Cartoon Kit, No. 116, King Features, c.1957, 11 x 16 In. 115.00
Toy, Olive Oyl, Ballet Dancer, Tin Lithograph, Pull Lever, King Features, Linemar, 6 In. 1640.00
Toy, Olive Oyl, Hops, Head Bobs, Tin, Windup, Linemar, Box, 5 In. .... *illus* 1725.00

P

Toy, Olive Oyl, Sports Roadster, Kaiser Darrin Car, Vinyl Head, Tin, Linemar, 8 In. 339.00
Toy, Olive Oyl, Squeaks, Pop Up, Composition, Tin, Wire, Linemar, 7 In. 863.00
Toy, Pirate Gun, Clicker, Tin Lithograph, Characters On Barrel, Marx, Box, 10 In. 605.00
Toy, Popeye, Acrobat, Swings Back & Forth, Base Rocks, Tin, Windup, 13 In.. .... 1978.00
Toy, Popeye, Aeroplane, Pilot, Tin, Windup, Linemar, 6 In. 2825.00
Toy, Popeye, Aeroplane, Pilot, Tin, Windup, Linemar, Box, 6 In. 4130.00
Toy, Popeye, Bag Puncher, Floor Bag, Tin Lithograph, Windup, Chein, Box, 7 ½ In. 1540.00
Toy, Popeye, Barrel Walker, Tin, Windup, Chein, 1930s, 7 In. .... 418.00 to 440.00
Toy, Popeye, Barrel Walker, Tin, Windup, Chein, Box, 1930s, 7 In. 576.00
Toy, Popeye, Basketball Player, Tin, Cloth, Windup, Linemar, Box, 9 In. .... 977.00 to 1320.00
Toy, Popeye, Bicycle, Tin Lithograph, Windup, Linemar, Box, 7 In. 4313.00
Toy, Popeye, Bubbles, Blowing, Spinach, Pipe, Tin, Battery Operated, Linemar, 1950s, 12 In.. . 750.00
Toy, Popeye, Carrying, Tin Lithograph, Windup, Marx, 8 ¼ In.. .... 295.00
Toy, Popeye, Champ, Boxing Ring, Tin, Celluloid, Windup, Marx, Box, 7 x 7 In.... 1130.00 to 2588.00
Toy, Popeye, Dippy Dumper, Tin, Lithograph, Celluloid, Windup, Marx, 9 In. 825.00
Toy, Popeye, Drummer, Wood, Metal, Fisher-Price, No. 488, 1939, 10 In.. .... 225.00 to 260.00
Toy, Popeye, Express, Parrot, Pops In & Out Of Trunk, Tin, Windup, Marx, 8 In. .. 475.00 to 520.00
Toy, Popeye, Express, Popeye Pushing Trunk, Bird Pops In & Put, Tin, Marx, 8 In. 475.00
Toy, Popeye, Head Goes Up & Down, Celluloid, Windup, 1930s, 8 In. 390.00
Toy, Popeye, Head Goes Up & Down, Celluloid, Windup, Japan, Box, 8 ½ In. 512.00
Toy, Popeye, Heavy Hitter, Tin, Windup, Chien, 1930s, 7 x 12 In 2006.00
Toy, Popeye, Hops, Head Bobs, Tin, Windup, Linemar, Box, 5 In. .... *illus* 1150.00
Toy, Popeye, Horse Drawn Cart, Tin, Celluloid, Windup, Marx, Box, 7 ½ In.. .... 825.00
Toy, Popeye, In Rowboat, Pressed Steel, Hoge Mfg., 14 In. 1092.00
Toy, Popeye, In Spinach Can, Jack-In-The-Box, Tin Lithograph, Plastic, Mattel, 1957, 7 In ... 275.00
Toy, Popeye, Lantern, Tin, Glass, Rubber, Battery Operated, Linemar, Box, 7 In. 275.00
Toy, Popeye, On Wagon, Rings Bell, Painted, Wood, Fisher-Price. 633.00
Toy, Popeye, On Wagon, Rings Bell, Painted, Wood, Fisher-Price, No. 700, 1935, 10 In. 550.00
Toy, Popeye, Pilot, No. 47, Tin, Windup, Marx, 7 ¾ In. .... 550.00 to 700.00
Toy, Popeye, Pilot, Red, Blue, Yellow, Tin Lithograph, Windup, 6 ½ In.. .... 440.00
Toy, Popeye, Pop Up, Push Down, Squeaks, Cloth, Composition Shoes, Linemar, 7 In. 1265.00
Toy, Popeye, Rowboat, Metal Oars, Tin Rudder, Battery Operated, Japan, 10 In. 3430.00
Toy, Popeye, Rowboat, Tin Lithograph, Windup, Hoge, 1930s, 15 In. 4200.00
Toy, Popeye, Skating Waiter, Tin, Windup, Linemar, 6 In. .... *illus* 440.00
Toy, Popeye, Smoking On Spinach Can, Tin, Battery Operated, Linemar, Box, 9 In. 1870.00 to 4025.00
Toy, Popeye, Sparkler, Tin Lithograph, Windup, Chein, Box, 5 ½ In.. .... 275.00
Toy, Popeye, Spins Olive Oyl In Chair, Tin, Windup, Linemar, Japan, 9 In. 1380.00
Toy, Popeye, Tricycle, Tin, Cloth, Linemar, 6 ¾ In. 660.00
Toy, Popeye, Tricycle, Tin Lithograph, Celluloid Arms, Legs, Windup, Linemar, 4 x 4 In.. ..... 575.00
Toy, Popeye, Unicyclist, Cloth, Tin Lithograph, Windup, Linemar, 6 In. 2070.00
Toy, Popeye, Vibrates, Head Bobs, Celluloid, Windup, Japan, 9 In.. .... 403.00
Toy, Popeye & Olive Oyl, Dancing On Roof, Tin, Windup, Marx, 1936s, 10 In. .... 373.00 to 763.00
Toy, Popeye & Olive Oyl, Dancing On Roof, Tin, Windup, Marx, Box, 1930s, 10 In. 1250.00
Toy, Popeye & Olive Oyl, Fliers, 2 Airplanes, Tower, Tin, Windup, Marx, 1930, 8 x 17 In.. ..... 1250.00
Toy, Popeye & Olive Oyl, Handcar, Tin Lithograph, Windup, Marx, Box, 11 x 9 In. 600.00
Toy, Popeye & Olive Oyl, Juggling, Tin, Windup, Linemar, 9 In.. .... 4025.00
Toy, Popeye & Olive Oyl, Juggling, Tin, Windup, Linemar, Box, 3 x 10 In. 3245.00
Toy, Popeye & Olive Oyl, Playing Ball, Windup, 19 x 4 ½ In. 2185.00
Toy, Popeye Bag Puncher, Chein, Box 2195.00
Toy, Puppets, Popeye & Olive Oyl, Kohner, 1960s, 4 In. 22.00
Toy, Spinach Cycle, Cast Iron, Hubley, 1930s, 5 ½ In.. .... 675.00
Toy, Spinach Motorcycle, Cast Iron, Hubley, 1935, 5 ½ In.. .... 418.00
Toy, Truck, Popeye Transit Co., Tin Lithograph, Linemar, 12 ½ In. .... *illus* 385.00
Toy, Wimpy, Hops, Head Bobs, Tin, Windup, Linemar, Box, 5 In. .... *illus* 1150.00
Toy, Wimpy, Tricycle, Tin Lithograph, Celluloid Limbs, Windup, Linemar, Box, 4 In. 715.00 to 863.00
Toy, Wimpy, Twists, Celluloid, Windup, Japan, Box, 7 In. 440.00
Toy, Wimpy, Walker, Celluloid, Windup, Japan, 7 In. 403.00
Toy, Wimpy, Walker, Plastic, KFS, Marx, Box, c.1964, 4 ¾ In.. .... 102.00
Watering Can, Popeye's Spinach Farm, Olive Oyl, Sweet' Pea, Tin, Cohn, 6 ¾ In. 141.00

PORCELAIN factories that are well known are listed in this book under the factory name. This category and the two following list pieces made by the less well-known factories. Porcelain-Contemporary lists pieces made by artists working after 1975. Porcelain-Midcentury includes pieces made from the 1940s to the 1980s.

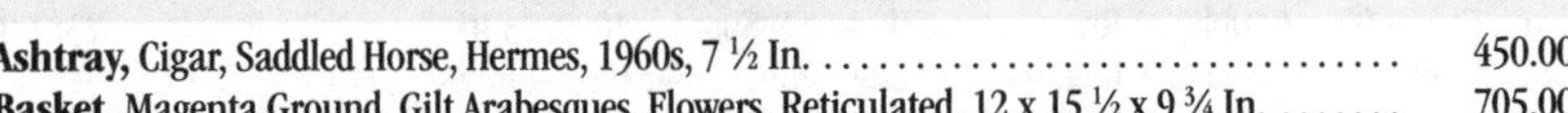

Ashtray, Cigar, Saddled Horse, Hermes, 1960s, 7 ½ In. 450.00
Basket, Magenta Ground, Gilt Arabesques, Flowers, Reticulated, 12 x 15 ½ x 9 ¾ In. 705.00

Popeye, Toy, Popeye, Hops, Head Bobs, Tin, Windup, Linemar, Box, 5 In.
$1150.00

Popeye, Toy, Popeye, Skating Waiter, Tin, Windup, Linemar, 6 In.
$440.00

Popeye, Toy, Truck, Popeye Transit Co., Tin Lithograph, Linemar, 12 ½ In.
$385.00

Popeye, Toy, Wimpy, Hops, Head Bobs, Tin, Windup, Linemar, Box, 5 In.
$1150.00

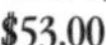

Porcelain, Cheese Keeper, Demi, Lying Wedge Shape, Flowers, Vine Handle, c.1875, 8 x 10 In.
$53.00

Porcelain, Figurine, Girl With Flower Basket, Pink, Blue, Rex Valencia, Spain, 10 In.
$59.00

Porcelain, Figurine, Grecian Lady, Seated, Leaning On Column, Jacob Petit, c.1850, 8 ¾ In.
$367.00

Biscuit Jar, Wild Flowers, Silver Plated Lid & Bail, England, 7 In. 50.00
Bottle, Peach Bloom, Chinese, 7 ½ In. 767.00
Bough Pot, Multicolored, Reticulated Rim & Base, c.1850, 6 ¼ x 7 ½ In. 587.00
Bowl, Blue & White, Dragon Decoration, Chinese, Qing Dynasty, 6 ½ In. 478.00
Bowl, Blue & White, Fish, Flowers, Leaves, Chinese, 8 ½ In. 354.00
Bowl, Blue & White, Floral & Leaf Decoration, Exterior Cafe Au Lait, 6 ¼ In. 538.00
Bowl, Centerpiece, Multicolored, Chinese, 20th Century, 3 x 16 ¾ In. 117.00
Bowl, Cover, 6 Characters, Robin's Egg Blue Glaze, Chinese, 7 ¼ In., Pair 296.00
Bowl, Cover, Blue Band Rim, Leaf Medallion, Red Ground, Japan, 4 ¾ In., 15 Piece 295.00
Bowl, Cover, Multicolored, Chinese, c.1900, 5 x 10 In. 762.00
Bowl, Eggplant Glaze, Incised Decoration, 6 Character Reign Mark, Chinese, 3 In. 390.00
Bowl, Eggshell, Engraved Dragons, Pearls, 4 Character, Moon White, Chinese, 5 ¼ In. 119.00
Bowl, Fans, Adrift On Water, Blue & White, Japan, 19th Century, 12 In. 178.00
Bowl, Footed, Large Colorful Fruit Design, N. Brunt, Aynsley, 10 In. 74.00
Bowl, Fruit, Calla Lilies, Germany, 1930s, 5 x 2 ½ In. 13.00
Bowl, Fruit, Water Lilies, Blue Ground, c.1900, 10 ½ In. 94.00
Bowl, Gu Style, White Crackled Glaze, Scalloped Edge, Chinese, 6 In. 354.00
Bowl, Lotus Scrolls, Red, Green Enamels, Chinese, 19th Century, 8 ¾ In. 119.00
Bowl, Mythical Animals, Red, Blue Underglaze, Chinese, 19th Century, 6 ¼ x 9 ½ In. 830.00
Bowl, Prunus Blossoms, Brass Rim, Yellow Glaze, Japan, 19th Century, 6 In. 385.00
Bowl, Vegetable, Cover, Blue & White, Rectangular, Monogram Shield, c.1790, 9 ½ x 8 In. 649.00
Bracket, Shelf, White, Bouquet, Tassel Bottom, c.1950, 9 x 6 ½ In. 94.00
Brushpot, Cylindrical Body, Red, Geometric Borders, Fruit, Chinese, 5 ½ x 5 In. 840.00
Brushpot, Family Under Tree, Chinese, 7 ¼ x 7 ¾ In. 409.00
Bust, Woman, Art Nouveau, Pastel Hued Glaze, Large Hat, Austria, 21 In. 561.00
Cachepot, Painted, Flowers, Gilt Banding, Lion's Mask Handles, 8 ½ x 7 ½ In., Pair 353.00
Cachepot, Vista Alegre, Orange Field, White Cameo, Gilt, Mottahedeh, 1980s, 6 x 7 In., 3 Piece 205.00
Cake Compote, Blue Border, Central Bouquet, Schumann, Germany, 11 In. 29.00
Cake Plate, Georgian, Square, Stylized Feather Design, Cobalt Blue, Orange, 10 ½ In. 206.00
Censer, Blue & White, Calligraphy Decoration, Chinese, 8 In. 269.00
Centerpiece, Sevres Style, Gilt Brass Mounted, Elliptical, Flowers, 11 ½ x 16 ¼ In. 540.00
Charger, Blue & White, Flowers, Japan, 15 ½ In. 224.00
Charger, Blue & White, Peacocks, Prunus Tree, Floral, Diamond, Japan, 3 ¼ x 22 ½ In. 115.00
Charger, Cobalt Flow Blue Underglaze, Flowers, Chinese, 13 ½ In. 173.00
Charger, Gold Rondelet, Fitz & Floyd, 12 In., 10 Piece 439.00
Charger, Japanese Warrior, Blue, White, 13 ½ In. 22.00
Charger, Overlapping Fans, Cranes, Conifers, Lions, Peonies, Japan, 18 In. 633.00
Charger, Painted Scene, Blue & White, Japan, Late 19th Century, 14 ¾ In. 94.00
Cheese Keeper, Demi, Gilt, Pink Flowers, c.1890, 7 x 10 In. 82.00
Cheese Keeper, Demi, Lying Wedge Shape, Flowers, Vine Handle, c.1875, 8 x 10 In. *illus* 53.00
Cheese Keeper, Demi, Red, Green, Stylized Flowers, c.1880, 8 ½ In. 88.00
Cheese Keeper, Demi, Wedge Shape, Cherries, White Ground, c.1890, 8 x 9 In. 88.00
Coffeepot, Embossed, Applied Floral Lift, Germany, 10 ¼ In. 15.00
Compote, Blue & White, Scenic, Chinese, 4 ½ x 6 ¼ In. 702.00
Compote, Crockets, Quatrefoils, Gilt, c.1850, 5 ¾ x 9 ¼ In. 210.00
Compote, Figural, Children Picking Apples, Reticulated, Von Schierholz, c.1930, 13 x 9 In. 176.00
Compote, Sepia, Gilt, Grapevine Friezes, Marked, 1825, 5 ½ x 8 ¾ In. 1645.00
Cup & Saucer, Blanc De Chine, Chinese, 4 x 6 In. 105.00
Cup & Saucer, Montroyal, Adderley, 2 ¾ x 5 ½ In. 20.00
Cup & Saucer, White, Gold Trim, Winged Figure Handle, Toga Clad Man, 4 ¾ In. 115.00
Dish, 3-Part, Fruits, Flowers, White Ground, Morning Glory Handle, 16 ½ In. 264.00
Dish, 4-Footed Figures, Holding Bowl, Von Schierholz, 5 x 9 In. 88.00
Dish, Dragons, Pearls, Clouds, Blue Underglaze, 19th Century, 6 ¾ In. 148.00
Dish, Green Flowers, 8 Precious Emblems Border, Yellow Ground, Chinese, 6 ¼ In. 770.00
Dish, Imperial Yellow, Aoguang, Chinese, 6 ¾ In. 295.00
Dish, Reticulated, Oval, Enameled, Gilt, Flowers, Pierced Rim, Japan, 8 ½ x 10 In., Pair 1200.00
Dish, Robin Egg, Flower Shape, Chinese, 19th Century, 10 ¾ In. 472.00
Dish, Shallow, Blue & Copper Red, Reticulated Border, Peach Tree, 8 ½ In. 131.00
Dish, Sitting Hen, Marked, c.1875, 8 ¾ x 6 ½ In. 674.00
Dish, Sweetmeat, 4 Wells, Flowers, Scalloped Edge, Grapevine Arabesques, c.1850, 13 In. 264.00
Dish, Sweetmeat, Meissen Style, Putti Base, Pierced Basket, Early 1900s, 10 In., Pair 224.00
Dish, Yellow Glazed, Incised Dragons, Chinese, 4 ¼ In. 330.00
Dresser Jar, Chelsea House, Green, Late 20th Century, 6 x 6 x 4 In., Pair 35.00
Easter Egg, Painted, 3 Bouquets Of Wildflowers, Blue Ground, Ribbon, Russia, 4 In. 826.00
Ewer, Cobalt Blue, Couple On River, Bronze Handle & Spout, c.1800, 23 In. 236.00
Ewer, Double Gourd Shape, White, Incised Lotus Petal, Flower Head, Chinese, 8 ¼ In. 384.00
Ewer, Grisaille & Green, Flowers, Dragon Shape Handle, 9 In., Pair 649.00

Ewer, Maiden Supporting Spout, Flowers, Green, Blue, Ernst Wahliss, 8 In. 2300.00
Ewer, Roses, Black Border, Hand Painted, Gilt, Japan, c.1900, 11 In. 146.00
Figurine, Blanc De Chine, Quan Yin, Chinese, 20 In. 70.00
Figurine, Dog, Seated, Holding Baskets Of Puppies & Kittens, Blue & Gilt, 7 ½ x 6 ½ In. 546.00
Figurine, Duck, Chinese, 4 ½ x 5 ½ In., Pair 99.00
Figurine, Fisherman, Basket Of Fish, Italy, 10 x 10 In. 409.00
Figurine, Girl With Flower Basket, Pink, Blue, Rex Valencia, Spain, 10 In. .... *illus* 59.00
Figurine, Girl With Flower Baskets, Rex Valencia, Spain, 10 In. 94.00
Figurine, Goddess Of Mercy, Seated, Robes, Throne, Blue Underglaze, Chinese, 10 ¾ In. 711.00
Figurine, Grecian Lady, Seated, Leaning On Column, Jacob Petit, c.1850, 8 ¾ In. .... *illus* 367.00
Figurine, Hofburg Wein 1926, Military Officer, White Horse, Stand, Vienna, c.1940, 10 x 8 In. 585.00
Figurine, Horse, Brown Green Glaze, Japan, 5 ¾ In., Pair 266.00
Figurine, Leda & The Swan, Germany, c.1930, 12 In. 176.00
Figurine, Man, Woman, French Style Stand, Pitcher, Mugs, 7 ½ x 7 ½ In. 90.00
Figurine, Man & Woman, Hand Decorated, Green Transfer Anchor Mark, 1900s, 18 In., Pair. 382.00
Figurine, Mother With Child In Cradle, Germany, c.1890, 17 ½ In. 117.00
Figurine, Napoleon, On Rearing Horse, Austria, 15 ½ x 11 In. 263.00
Figurine, Napoleonic General, On Horseback, Dorsenne, Germany, 12 x 8 In. 322.00
Figurine, On Horseback, Scholars, In Study, Oriental, 19th Century, 17 ¾ In. 441.00
Figurine, Plateau, Horse Drawn Carriage, Driver, Fabris, c.1930, 5 x 14 In. 526.00
Figurine, Pug, Brown, Tan, White Collar, Applied Bells, Seated, Facing, 7 ¼ x 8 In., Pair..... 518.00
Figurine, Skunk, Baby, Hand Painted, 1950s, ¾ x 1 ½ In. 9.00
Figurine, Skunk, Papa, Hand Painted, 1950s, 1 ¾ x 1 In. 11.00
Figurine, Sleeping Satyr, Pate-Sur-Pate Band, Bacchus Heads, Vines, 7 x 8 In. 403.00
Fish Service, Imperial Crown, 8 Plates, Sauceboat, Underplate, Tray, Austria, 23 In. 510.00
Flask, Moon, Blue & White, Flattened Oval, Tree, Flowers, Rat Shape Handles, Korea, 9 In.... 3585.00
Flask, Moon, Sancai, Flattened Round Body, Ruyi Scepter Handles, Chinese, 1 In. 472.00
Ginger Jar, Blue & White, Globular, Scrolling Vines, Flowers, Chinese, 1800s, 11 In. 120.00
Ginger Jar, Cover, Blue & White, Early 20th Century, 6 ¼ x 5 ½ In. 35.00
Group, Fall, Winter, Spring Figures, Period Dress, Obelisk, H. Damm, c.1850, 15 In. 3125.00
Group, Man & Woman Harvesters, Continental, Early 20th Century, 8 ½ In. 177.00
Incense Burner, Figural, Courtier & Lady, Scrolled Base, c.1850, 12 ½ In., Pair 881.00
Incense Burner, Scenic, Chinese, 20th Century, 14 x 8 In. 47.00
Jar, Cover, Bats, Shou Characters, Lotus Meanders, Turquoise Ground, Chinese, 7 ½ In. 652.00
Jar, Cover, Blue & White, Oval, Flowering Prunus, Crackled Ice Ground, Chinese, 12 In. 679.00
Jar, Cover, Blue & White, Silver Mounted, Chinese, 6 ¼ In. 649.00
Jar, Fruits, Pomegranates, Peaches, Buddha's Hand, Blue Underglaze, Chinese, 5 ½ In. 326.00
Jar, Powder Blue, 2 Concentric Circles, Wood Lid, 20th Century, Chinese, 9 ¾ In. 633.00
Jar, Storage, Brown Glaze, Globular, Strap Handles, Bulbous, Chinese, 5 ½ In. 270.00
Jardiniere, Band Of Arabesques, Pearled & Gilt Borders, Black Ground, Continental, 7 In., Pair 858.00
Jardiniere, Blue, White, Landscape, Geometric, Inverted Rim, Chinese, 13 ¾ x 21 In. 351.00
Jardiniere, Flowers, Birds, Multicolored, Japan, 13 x 17 ½ In. 323.00
Jardiniere, Gold Stencil Highlights, Tapestry Scenic Home, Bonn, 7 x 10 In. 250.00
Jardiniere, Multicolored, Teakwood Stand, Japan, 12 x 11 In. 88.00
Jardiniere, Rocaille Top, Scroll Handles, Gilt, Undertray, 19th Century, 9 ¼ In. 764.00
Jardiniere, Rosewood Stand, Chinese, c.1950, 31 x 20 In. 439.00
Jardiniere, Sevres Style, Flower Sprays, Scrolling, Intertwining Lines, Round, 11 ¾ In. 510.00
Jewelry Box, Blue, Gilt, Multicolored Flowers, Egg Shape, 8 x 7 ½ x 11 ½ In. 325.00
Joss Stick Holder, Figural, Famille Verte, Foo Dog Shape, Chinese, 7 In., Pair 896.00
Joss Stick Holder, Green Glazed, Recumbent Lion Shape, Dragon Disc, Chinese, 19 In., Pair 470.00
Lamp, Bottle Shape, Flower Encrusted, Spelter Mount, 17 ¾ In., Pair 288.00
Lantern, Marriage, Famille Rose, Chinese, 19th Century, 11 ¾ In., Pair 896.00
Nodder, Seated Man, Chinese, Early 20th Century, 4 In. 59.00
Pastry Stand, Louis XVI Style, Girl Finial, Reticulated, Tiered, 14 ½ x 10 ½ In., Pair 510.00
Planter, Dragon Design, White Ground, Flower, Chinese, 6 x 6 In. 527.00
Planter, Oval, Gilt Ormolu, Cherub Handles, Tapestry Terrace & Flower Scene, 14 x 20 In.... 800.00
Plaque, Nymph, Seminude, Scrolling Brass Frame, Easel Back, Frame, 11 In. 652.00
Plaque, Pavilions By Lake Shore, 20th Century, Chinese, 15 ¼ x 10 ¼ In. 948.00
Plaque, Woman In Green Dress & Yellow Ribbons, Painted, 6 ½ x 3 ¾ In. 80.00
Plate, Birds In Marsh, Green Border, Flowers, Scroll Gold, 9 In., Pair 33.00
Plate, Cabinet, Blue, Swirled Flower Border, Flower Center, Multicolored, Gilt, 17 ¾ In. 448.00
Plate, California Quail, Pink Border, Gold Band, Sterling, Singer & Otto, 7 ¾ In. 14.00
Plate, Cobalt Blue, Fired Gold, Crescent & Sons, 10 ¼ In., 4 Piece 70.00
Plate, Dessert, Flowers, Rose, Square, Schumann Bavarian, 8 In., 6 Piece 105.00
Plate, Empire Paris, Melon Ground, Red Neoclassical, France, c.1810, 8 ½ In. 720.00
Plate, Marie Antoinette, Blue Borders, Flowers, 9 ½ In. 176.00
Plate, Napoleon Crowning Josephine, Austria, 9 ½ In. 288.00

Bisque Doll Heads
Bisque, unglazed porcelain that may be tinted or painted, was often used to make doll heads and sometimes their bodies.

Porcelain, Plate, Royal Vienna Style, Exotic Beauty, Bien Etre, Cobalt Blue, Gilt, 1900, 9 In.
$750.00

Porcelain, Urn, Campagna, Multicolored Flowers, Gilt, Mask Loop Handles, c.1825, 11 x 8 In., Pair
$822.00

P

TIP
Tell your neighbors when you will be away for a long time. Ask them to remove any newspapers or mail left in front of the house and to check on any trucks, especially unmarked trucks, that are in the driveway.

TIP

Either Coca-Cola or Tang can be used to remove stains from porcelain.

Porcelain, Vase, Raised Leaves, Yellow, Green, Blue, Brown, Signed, U. Ekeby, Sweden, 8 In.
$130.00

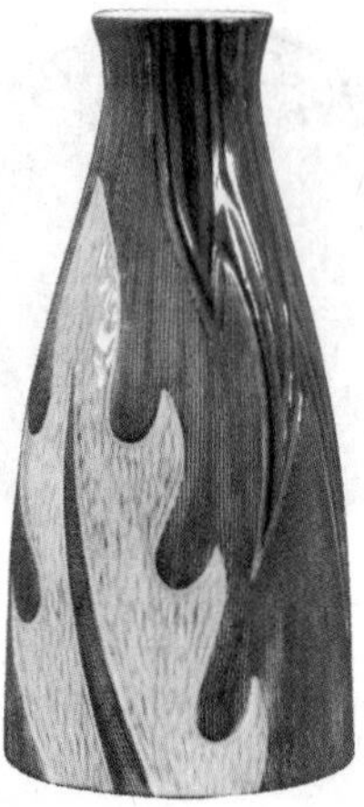

Top Ten Pottery & Porcelain Categories
Hundreds of thousands of users visit our website, Kovels.com, each month. There are over 300 pottery and porcelain categories on the site. The most popular among our visitors are:

1. Limoges
2. Royal Doulton
3. Czechoslovakia Pottery
4. Occupied Japan
5. Nippon
6. Haviland
7. Haeger
8. RS Germany
9. Lefton (an importer)
10. Majolica

Plate, Royal Vienna Style, Exotic Beauty, Bien Etre, Cobalt Blue, Gilt, 1900, 9 In. . . . . . . *illus* 750.00
Plate, Seated Woman, Birds, Pink Border, Wagner, Marked, c.1900, 9 ½ In. 295.00
Plate, Spode, Transfer, University Of Chicago Scenes, 10 ½ In., 12 Piece 480.00
Plate, Woman, Plumed Hat, Frame, 8 In. Diam. 50.00
Platter, Fish, White, Gold, Elliptical, Neoclassical Style, 11 ½ x 24 ¾ In., Pair 840.00
Platter, Sevres Style, Blue Celeste Border, Oval, Figural Reserve, France, 22 x 15 ¼ In. 660.00
Platter, Turkeys, Windsorware, 15 ½ x 20 In.. . . . . 205.00
Powder Box, Figures, Landscapes, Flowers, Metal Mounts, c.1775, 2 ½ In.. . . . . 382.00
Punch Bowl, Apple Green, Gilt Band, Footed, c.1850, 5 ¾ x 14 ¼ In. 857.00
Saucer, Monogram, Russian Imperial, 19th Century, 6 In.. . . . . 263.00
Saucer Dish, Flower Scrolls, Phoenixes, Blue, White, Chinese, 6 ¼ In. 504.00
Soup, Dish, Gold Rim, Heinrich & Co., Bavaria, 7 ½ In., 10 Piece 351.00
Soup, Dish, Handles, Saucer, Birds, Flowers, Divington Brothers, 9 In., 12 Piece. 86.00
Sugar, Cover, Multicolored, Gilt Decorated, Lid, Summer Bouquets, 7 ¼ x 6 In. 235.00
Sugar, Gilded, Circular Cushion Form, 2 Handles, 4 ½ x 5 ½ In. 180.00
Tazza, Dresden Style Flower, Latticed Bowl, Base, Applied Stem, Gilt Trim, 8 ½ In. 160.00
Tea Bowl & Saucer, Ogee Shape, Scalloped Rim, Peacocks, Gilt, England, 1700s, 2 ¾ In. . . . 240.00
Teapot, Blue & White, Oval, Flower Heads, Scrolling Leaves, Chinese, 6 ¼ In.. . . . . 767.00
Temple Jar, Cover, Blue & White, Foo Dog, Chinese, 19th Century, 16 In., Pair. 388.00
Tureen, Soup, Pig Shape, Flowers, Apple In Mouth, Italy, 24 In.. . . . . 439.00
Urn, Cabinet, Bronze Dore, Painted Putti, Champleve Feet, Neck Band, 10 ¾ In. 747.00
Urn, Campagna, Multicolored Flowers, Gilt, Mask Loop Handles, c.1825, 11 x 8 In., Pair *illus* 822.00
Urn, Cover, Figures, Capo-Di-Monte Style, France, c.1950, 20 ½ In.. . . . . 1287.00
Urn, Cover, Footed, 2 Handles, Pedestal Base, Transfer Portraits, Gilt, c.1891, 17 In. 94.00
Urn, Cover, Mythological Scene, Diana, Von Schierholz, Germany, 28 x 16 In. 1989.00
Urn, Cover, Rococo Style, Hand Painted, Gilt, France, 15 x 8 In., Pair 146.00
Urn, Cover, Sevres Style, Flower Basket, Tambourine, Tools, Flower Swags, 9 ¼ In., Pair 687.00
Urn, Cover, Sevres Style, Hand Painted, Man, Courting Woman, France, Signed, 16 ¾ In. 819.00
Urn, Cover, Sevres Style, White Ground, Scenic, Gold Handles, c.1920, 7 ½ x 3 ½ In. 234.00
Urn, Multicolored Pastoral Cameo Scene, Dark Blue Ground, Gold Highlights, 41 In. 74.00
Urn, Sevres Style, Oval, Napoleonic Figures, Blue, Transfer Painted, Gilt, 6 ½ x 12 In. 144.00
Urns, Figures, Landscape, Sevres Style, Cobalt Blue, Gilt Metal Base, Swan Mounts, 24 In., Pair 236.00
Vase, 4 Women Holding Basket Of Flowers, Frankenthal, 18th Century, 14 In. 644.00
Vase, Beaker, Acanthus Leaves, Blue Underglaze, Chinese, 19th Century, 10 In. 356.00
Vase, Bird Shape, Yellow, Chinese, 7 ½ In.. . . . . 354.00
Vase, Blanc De Chine, Baluster Shape, Ram's Head Handles, Royal Berlin, 6 ¾ In.. . . . . 72.00
Vase, Blanc De Chine, Oval, Foo Dog Handles, Chinese, 5 In. 177.00
Vase, Blue & White, Baluster Shape, Applied Foo Dog Handles, 20th Century, 23 In., Pair 540.00
Vase, Blue & White, Cylindrical, Landscape, Chinese, 17 ¼ x 6 In. 936.00
Vase, Blue & White, Figural Decoration, Chinese, 19th Century, 13 ½ In. 228.00
Vase, Blue & White, Round, Footed, Gilt, Japan, c.1930, 11 ½ x 9 ½ In. 176.00
Vase, Blue & White, Trumpet Baluster, Phoenixes, Flowers, Chinese, 1800s, 16 In. 230.00
Vase, Bottle Shape, Gilt, Pomegranate Branch, Calligraphy, Chinese, 1700s, 6 ⅛ In. 212.00
Vase, Bottle Shape, Green Glazed, Chinese, 18th Century, 5 ½ In.. . . . . 472.00
Vase, Cong Form, Blue, Gilt, Rondels, Flower Heads, Brocade, 11 ½ In., Pair 717.00
Vase, Copper Red, Baluster Shape, High Shoulders, 19th Century, 5 ½ In.. . . . . 295.00
Vase, Copper Red, Bulbous, Narrow Neck, 19th Century, 7 In.. . . . . 472.00
Vase, Copper Red, Squat Base, Narrow Neck, Flared Lip, Chinese, Qing Dynasty, 7 In. 299.00
Vase, Cover, Black, Gilt, Shaped Cartouche, Flowering Lotus Branches, Chinese, 8 In. 388.00
Vase, Cover, Blue & White, Oval, Dragons, Chasing Flaming Pearl, Chinese, 1800s, 18 In. 885.00
Vase, Cover, Sevres Style, Bronze Dore Mounted, 18 In., Pair 807.00
Vase, Double Gourd, Beige, Brown, Relief Cloud Decoration, Chinese, 7 ¾ In. 236.00
Vase, Double Gourd, Black Glaze, Brown Speckling, Chinese, 19th Century, 5 In.. . . . . 72.00
Vase, Double Gourd, Yellow Glaze, Chinese, 19th Century, 9 ½ In.. . . . . 531.00
Vase, Flambe, Lotus Petal, Garlic Mouth, High Relief, Molded Dragon, 10 ½ In.. . . . . 388.00
Vase, Flask Shape, Orange & White, Gilt Handles, Chinese, 6 ¾ x 5 In. 410.00
Vase, Flowers, Leaves, High Relief, Multicolored, Longchamp, 12 ½ In., Pair 17.00
Vase, Flowers, Scrolling Leaves, Blue & White, Oval, Japan, 10 ½ In.. 236.00
Vase, Foo Dogs, Peonies, Oval, 19th Century, Chinese, 14 ½ In. 948.00
Vase, Funerary, Yingqing, Tan Color, Row Of Attendants, Dragon, 15 In.. . . . . 270.00
Vase, Garniture, Franco Bohemian, Rococo Style, Flowers, Handles, 9 x 6 ½ In., Pair 180.00
Vase, Garniture, Gilt Brass, Champleve Enamel Mounted, Handles, 13 ½ x 4 In. 270.00
Vase, Garniture, Louis XVI Sevres Style, Gilt Brass Mounted, River Landscape, 27 ½ In.. . . . . . 660.00
Vase, Gourd, Blue & White, Riverscape, Vietnam, 9 In., Pair 239.00
Vase, Green & Black, Floral & Scrolling Leafy Decoration, Chinese, 11 ¼ In. 329.00
Vase, Hawthorne, Dark Blue Ground, White Figures, 19th Century, 9 In.. . . . . 88.00
Vase, Lady In Shawl, Vine Handles, Multicolored, Gilt, c.1850, 12 ¼ In.. . . . . 235.00

Vase, Moon Flask, Sang De Boeuf, Chinese, 10 ½ In. 777.00
Vase, Multicolored, Gilt Decorated, Painted, Bouquets, Leaf Handles, 16 x 12 In., Pair 94.00
Vase, Palace, Flowers, Leaves, Multicolored, Wood Stand, Asian, 37 In., Pair 936.00
Vase, Peach Bloom Chrysanthemum, Oval Body, Strawberry Glaze, Speckled, Chinese, 6 ½ In. 690.00
Vase, Potpourri, Blanc De Chine, Goat Masque Handles, Garlands, 11 x 5 In., Pair 780.00
Vase, Prunus, Blue Ground Underglaze, Chinese, 19th Century, 17 ¼ In. 711.00
Vase, Raised Leaves, Yellow, Green, Blue, Brown, Signed, U. Ekeby, Sweden, 8 In. .... *illus* 130.00
Vase, Raised Red Dragons, Blue Waves, Kangxi Underglaze Blue Marks, Early 1900s, 16 In. .. 294.00
Vase, Rouleau, Turquoise, Incised Leaf Decoration, 19th Century, 9 In. 502.00
Vase, Sang De Boeuf, Bottle Shape, Strawberry Glaze, White Rim, Chinese, 12 ½ In. 920.00
Vase, Turquoise Glaze, Chinese, 19th Century, 14 In. 590.00
Vase, White, Monochrome, Oval, Molded, Deer Under Pine Tree, Moon, 7 ¾ In. 657.00
Vase, White, Oval Shape, Flared Mouth, Chinese, 16 ½ In. 325.00
Vase, Woman, Roses, Keine Rosen Ohne Dornen, Enamel, Gilt, Shield Mark, 16 In. .... *illus* 1000.00
Vase, Wucai, Painted, Children Playing, Mountain Landscape, Qing, Dynasty, 9 ½ In. 299.00
Vase, Yellow, Bulbous Base, Tapered Neck, Chinese, 12 ½ x 10 In. 585.00
Vase, Yen Yen, Blue & White, Pine Tree, Bamboo, Flowering Prunus Tree, 1900s, 14 ½ In. 215.00
Wine Cup, Doucai, For The Pleasure Of The Lover Of Lotus, Chinese, 2 ¾ In. 897.00
Wine Pot, Landscapes, Flowers, Hexagonal, 4 ½ In. 119.00

PORCELAIN-CONTEMPORARY lists pieces made by artists working after 1975.

Glove Forms, White High Glaze, Stamped, Richard Ginori, 14 In., 3 Piece .... *illus* 510.00
Moonpot, Ivory Over Mustard Matte Glaze, Toshiko Takaezu, 5 In. 3600.00
Moonpot, Matte Glazes, Inner Rattle, Signed, Toshiko Takaezu, 7 x 5 ¾ In. 1920.00
Vase, Stands, Boxes, Flowers, Back With Inscription, Red Stamp, c.1980, 9 ½ In. 235.00

PORCELAIN-MIDCENTURY includes pieces made from the 1940s to about 1975.

Bowl, Bronze Glaze, Blue Band, Plum Foot, Lucie Rie, Signed, Mid 1970s, 2 ¼ x 6 In. 4500.00
Candy Dish, Grimwades, Pink, Gray Ground, Royal Winton, 6 ¾ x 4 ¼ In. 36.00
Figurine, Peacocks, A.K. Kaiser, 8 x 7 In. 29.00
Figurine, Serenade, Borsato, Glazed, 9 x 7 In. 176.00
Tureen, Cover, Painted Flowers Allover, Gilt Accents, Cmielow, Poland, 7 In., Pair 418.00
Vase, Cottage Garden, Double Handles, Aynsley, 3 ¼ x 3 ¼ In. 10.00

POSTCARDS were first legally permitted in Austria on October 1, 1869. The United States passed postal regulations allowing the card in 1872. Most of the picture postcards collected today date after 1910. The amount of postage can help to date a card. The rates are: 1872 (1 cent), 1917 (2 cents), 1919 (1 cent), 1925 (2 cents), 1928 (1 cent), 1952 (2 cents), 1958 (3 cents), 1963 (4 cents), 1968 (5 cents), 1971 (6 cents), 1973 (8 cents), 1975 (7 cents), 1976 (9 cents), 1978 (10 cents), March 1981 (12 cents), November 1981 (13 cents), 1985 (14 cents), 1988 (15 cents), 1991 (19 cents), 1995 (20 cents), 2001 (21 cents), 2002 (23 cents), 2006 (24 cents), 2007 (26 cents), 2008 (27 cents), 2009 (28 cents). While most postcards sell for low prices, a small number bring high prices. Some of these are listed here.

Albany Railroad Station, Americhrome, Albany News Co., N.Y., Postmarked Mar. 3, 1913 .. 4.00
Anheuser-Busch Brewery, Tropical House, Flora, Fauna, Tampa 1.00
Atlantic City, Beach, Regent, Schiltz, Almanac, 4 Panels, c.1910, 4 ¾ x 8 ¼ In. 115.00
Baseball Player, C. Mathewson, PC796, Sepia, 1910, 4 x 6 In. 4406.00
Baseball Player, Ty Cobb, A.C. Dietsche, Rookie, Detroit Tigers, 1907, 4 x 6 In. 823.00
Baseball Player, Walter Johnson, Sepia, PC796, 1910, 4 x 6 In. 1645.00
Boy Scouts, 2 Scouts & Woman, Always Be Polite, 1916 .... 35.00
Christmas, Collie Dog In Crisscross Frame, May You Have A Merry Christmas 18.00
Field Artillery, Photo By U.S. Army Signal Corps., Linen, Postmarked 1942 .... 10.00
Fourth Of July, Lithographed, Red, White & Blue, Boy Shooting Pistol, Girl With Toy 22.00
Gibson Girl, Studies In Expression, 1907 .... 24.00
Hotel San Carlos, Yuma, Ariz., Old Cars Parked In Front, 1940 .... 10.00
Little Lady Demure, 1907 .... 35.00
Merry Christmas, Faces Of 4 Angels Above Church Scene, Divided Back, Tuck 5.00
New Orleans Mardi Gras, 1940s 45.00
Satchel Paige, Autographed, 1948 .... 960.00
Schlitz Brewing Plant, Tampa, 1959 .... 10.00
Split Rock Lighthouse, 200 Feet Above Lake Superior 8.00
St. Anthony's Hospital, Oklahoma City, 1940 .... 10.00
St. Patrick's Day, Girl, Green Umbrella, Boy, Drum, 2 Piece .... *illus* 12.00
Victorian Hunting Dog, Silk Fringe 6.00
Warner Bros. Studio, Joan Crawford On Front, Marked October 8, 1947 .... 13.00

Porcelain, Vase, Woman, Roses, Keine Rosen Ohne Dornen, Enamel, Gilt, Shield Mark, 16 In.
$1000.00

Porcelain-Contemporary, Glove Forms, White High Glaze, Stamped, Richard Ginori, 14 In., 3 Piece
$510.00

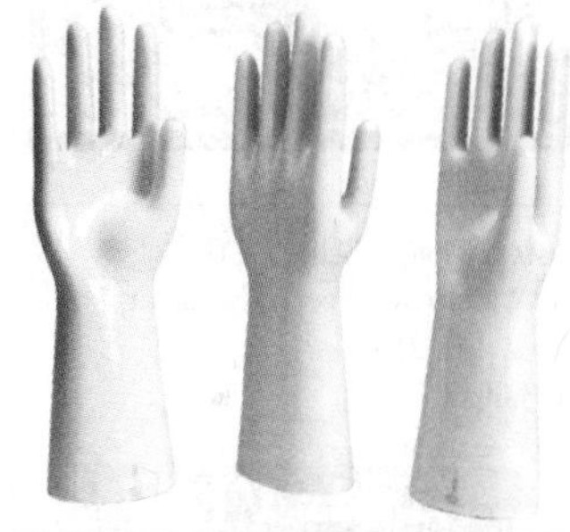

Postcard, St. Patrick's Day, Girl, Green Umbrella, Boy, Drum, 2 Piece
$12.00

TIP
American postcards from long-gone towns have extra value to collectors.

P

Poster, Carter Magician, Cardboard, Frame, 1920-30, 22 x 14 In.
$173.00

Poster, Ringling Bros. & Barnum & Bailey Circus, Frame, 1940-50, 28 x 42 In.
$144.00

Poster, Ripley's Believe It Or Not, Bob Wallace As Popeye The Sailor, Paper, 28 x 21 In.
$173.00

TIP

Paper must "breathe." Don't glue it to a backing. It expands and contracts and eventually it will tear.

Women, Large Feather Hat, 1900s. 15.00

POSTERS have informed the public about news and entertainment events since ancient times. Nineteenth-century advertising or theatrical posters and twentieth-century movie and war posters are of special interest today. The price is determined by the artist, the condition, and the rarity. Other posters may be listed under Movie, Political, and World War I and II.

Alexander Magic, Paper Lithograph, Glass, Frame, c.1910-20, 28 x 42 In.. . . . . 316.00
Allevard Les Bains, Jean Julien, Lithograph, Scenic Landscape, 42 ½ x 30 ¾ In. 374.00
Amazing Kirma, Magic, He Can Tell You, Theater, 14 x 22 In.. . . . . 115.00
Association, Fillmore Auditorium, Green, Pink, c.1966, 14 x 20 In. 508.00
Balloon Girl, Theater, 27 x 41 In.. . . . . 67.00
Barnum & Bailey Circus, Dancing Bears, Glass, Frame, 1916, 30 x 40 In. 403.00
Big Brother & The Holding Company, Fillmore West, c.1968, 14 x 22 In.. . . . . 478.00
Carter Magician, Cardboard, Frame, 1920-30, 22 x 14 In. . . . . *illus* 173.00
Chambre De Commerce, Gustave Umbdenstock, France, 38 x 24 In. 1440.00
Circus, American Presidents, Storybook Characters, Horses, Parade, Frame, 46 x 38 In. 11950.00
Circus, Clowns, Horses, Cowboy Movie Star, Jack Hoxie, c.1937, 27 ½ x 40 ½ In. 192.00
Circus, King Of The Carnival, Big Top Scene, Linen Mounted, 3 Sheet, c.1955, 41 x 80 In. . . . 144.00
Circus, Only Genuine Living Hippopotamus, c.1910, 40 x 50 In.. . . . . 510.00
Cole Bros. Circus, 24 Performing Elephants, c.1938, 27 x 40 In. 633.00
Cole Bros. Circus, Boxing Horses, Clown Ring, c.1944, 27 x 41 In.. . . . . 348.00
Cole Bros. Circus, Horses, Elephants, Seals, Scenes, Linen Backed, c.1940, 28 x 41 In.. . . . . . 460.00
Concert, McGovern, Carole King, Barbra Streisand, James Taylor, 1972, 25 x 38 In. 506.00
Concert, Rare Earth, Cardboard, Field House, Villa Nova Univ., c.1970, 14 x 28 In.. . . . . 288.00
Cote D'Azur, Birds, Sea, Trees, Lithograph, H. Deschamps, Frame, Signed, c.1950, 39 x 26 In. 359.00
Country & Western Show, George Jones, Tammy Wynette, Cardboard, c.1970, 22 x 28 In. . . 115.00
Cream, Paul Butterfield Blues Band, Fillmore, Bonnie MacLean, c.1967, 14 x 21 In.. . . . . 359.00
Cuckoo, Theater, Paper Lithograph, Mat, Glass, Frame, c.1900, 18 x 28 In. 58.00
Dailey Bros. Circus, Big 5 Ring Railroad, Clown, 21 x 28 In.. . . . . 99.00
Dailey Bros. Circus, Big 5 Ring Railroad, Wild Animal, 28 x 42 In.. . . . . 55.00
Dr. Korda Ra Mayne, Mystic, He Sees Unseen, Cardboard, Lakewood Theatre, 1930s, 14 x 22 In. 259.00
Elephant Race, Circus, c.1910, 40 x 50 In. 720.00
Ephrata Park, 4th Of July, Spring Garden Band, 1939, 22 In.. . . . . 30.00
Fine Feathers, Theater, Paper Lithograph, Glass, Frame, c.1900, 20 x 28 In.. . . . . 58.00
Fogg's Ferry, Plexiglas, Graphics, Frame, Paper Lithograph, c.1900, 27 x 41 In. 115.00
Glasgow Institute Of Fine Arts, Stylized Woman, Color Lithograph, Frame, c.1896, 11 x 4 In. 840.00
Great Arabian Caravan Of 20 Dromedaries & Camels Circus, c.1910, 40 x 50 In.. . . . . . 660.00
Hagenbeck-Wallace Circus, Seals, Playing Drums, Tuba, Banjo, Lamp, 27 ½ x 40 ½ In. . . . 411.00
How's Your Control, Self Control Is Job Control, Charles Mather, 47 ½ x 36 ½ In.. . . . . 4320.00
Human Be-In, Gathering Of The Tribes, Summer Of Love, San Francisco, c.1967, 14 x 20 In. 717.00
I Want You For The U.S. Army, Metal, 2-Sided, J.M. Flagg, 1950s, 25 x 38 In.. . . . . 756.00
Imperial Burlesquers, Theater, Paper Lithograph, Mat, Glass, Frame, c.1900, 20 x 27 In.. . . 86.00
Jimi Hendrix Experience, Fillmore, Winterland, Rick Griffin, c.1968, 14 x 22 In. 1195.00
Job, Cigarettes, Leonetto Cappiello, Man In White & Turban, c.1933, 24 ½ x 23 In. 720.00
Kiss V, Signed, Roy Lichtenstein, Frame, 30 ½ x 30 ½ In.. . . . . 1400.00
La Revue Des Folies-Bergere, Frame, France, 1905, 35 ½ x 50 In. 1440.00
Leland McNamee's Minstrels, Chromolithograph, Stretcher, c.1930, 84 x 48 In.. . . . . 173.00
Leopard Men Of Africa, Paper, African Cannibals At Home & Play, c.1940, 28 x 42 In. 201.00
Lincoln Center, 4th New York Film Festival, Roy Lichtenstein, 24351, 45 x 29 In.. . . . . 1560.00
Livemont, Michiels Freres, Art Nouveau Woman, Pear, Tree Nursery Ad, c.1902, 34 x 20 In.. . . 1495.00
Magic, Alexander The Man Who Knows, Black, White, Red, 1 Sheet, 1920s, 28 x 42 In.. . . . . . 330.00
Magic, Alexander The Man Who Knows, Question Mark Turban, 3 Sheet, 1920s, 42 x 81 In.. . 420.00
Manheim Lion's Club Carnival, With Ranger Joe, May 30-31, 28 ½ In.. . . . . 350.00
Millersville State College, Senior Dance, Band, 40091, 1935, 11 In.. . . . . 20.00
Minstrels, Al. G. Field, Rody Jordan In Blackface, Dean Of Drollery, 19 ½ x 26 In.. . . . . 1179.00
Montana Frank Shows, On Horse, c.1910, 21 x 27 In. 460.00
Monterey Pop Festival, Silver Tone, c.1967, 12 ½ x 21 ¼ In. 1793.00
Mt. Gretna Grand Ole Opry, Grandpa Jones, 28 ½ In. 200.00
Myles Aroon Play, Under Glass, Frame, c.1900, 28 x 28 In.. . . . . 86.00
New Baby, Theater, Paper Lithograph, Glass, Frame, c.1900, 21 x 26 In.. . . . . 29.00
Orpheum Show Play, Under Glass, Frame, c.1900, 26 x 38 In.. . . . . 58.00
Ostende, Bains De Mer, 3 Panels, Floris Van Acker, June, 1901, 10 x 48 ¼ In.. . . . . 3000.00
Paper Sir, Newspapers Offered To Man In Top Hat, 48 ¼ x 30 ¼ In. 1440.00
Paris Londres, Glass, Graphics, Frame, c.1900, 29 x 42 In.. . . . . 230.00
Perfect Finish, Sailboat, Frank Beatty, 44 x 36 In. 4080.00
Ringling Bros. & Barnum & Bailey Circus, Frame, 1940-50, 28 x 42 In. . . . . *illus* 144.00

Ringling Bros. & Barnum & Bailey Circus, Animal Graphics, Erie Litho Co., c.1928, 26 x 40 In. 1657.00
Ringling Bros. & Barnum & Bailey Circus, Magyars Acrobats, 27 x 39 ½ In. 403.00
Ringling Bros. & Barnum & Bailey Circus, Pallenberg's Wonder Bears, c.1925, 27 x 40 In. 607.00
Ringling Bros. & Barnum & Bailey Circus, Tiger, Greatest Show, c.1942, 27 x 39 ½ In. 115.00
Ripley's Believe It Or Not, Armless Knife Thrower, Red, Black, White, c.1940, 21 x 28 In. 345.00
Ripley's Believe It Or Not, Bob Wallace As Popeye The Sailor, Paper, 28 x 21 In. *illus* 173.00
Ripley's Believe It Or Not, Girl With A Radio Mind, Blue, Black, White, c.1940, 21 x 28 In. 144.00
Ripley's Believe It Or Not, Hindu Quarter Man, Paper, 1940, 42 x 28 In. *illus* 633.00
Ripley's Believe It Or Not, Medusa Child Of The Sea, Orange, Black, c.1940, 28 x 42 In. 748.00
San Francisco, Haight-Ashbury, Hippie Summer Camp, Sparta Graphics, c.1968, 32 x 41 In. 345.00
Seils Sterling 4 Ring Circus, Man Killing Gorilla, 20 x 28 In. 55.00
Shadows Of A Great City, Theater, Paper Lithograph, Mat, Glass, Frame, c.1900, 24 x 36 In. 86.00
Shakespeare Theater, Figures, Poodle, Signed Rene Peau, France, Frame, 1899, 32 x 24 In. 518.00
Shepherd Of Shanty Run, Theater, 27 x 41 In. 55.00
Shore Acres, Theater, Paper Lithograph, Glass, Frame, c.1900, 28 x 42 In. 173.00
Touchdown, You're Out To Win, Hal Depuy, 1929, 43 ½ x 36 In. 6500.00
U.S. Army, I Want You, c.1917, 30 x 40 In. 6572.00
Uncle Tom's Cabin, Glass, Theater, Frame, c.1900, 21 x 28 In. 58.00
White Star Line, Types Of World Famous Liners, Liverpool Printing, 1920s, 40 x 25 In. 3050.00
Woman & Wine, Theater, Paper Lithograph, Glass, Frame, c.1900, 30 x 40 In. 288.00
Wooing Of Mrs. VanCott, Theater, Paper Lithograph, Glass, Frame, c.1900, 36 x 26 ½ In. 86.00

POTLIDS are just that, lids for pots. Transfer-printed potlids had their heyday from the 1840s to the early 1900s. The English Staffordshire potteries made ceramic containers with decorative lids for bear's grease, shrimp or meat paste, cold cream, and toothpaste. Printed advertising and pictures of historical events, portraits of famous people, or scenic views were designed in black and white or color. Reproductions have been made.

A.M. Cole, Cold Cream, Nevada, 1878, 2 ¾ In. 840.00
Garden Scene, Man On Bended Knee Offering Bouquet To Woman, Frame, 6 ¼ In. 60.00
Vantine's Cherry Blossom Tooth Paste, Oriental Woman, Holding Fan, Milk Glass, 3 x 3 In. 358.00

POTTERY and porcelain are different. Pottery is opaque; you can't see through it. Porcelain is translucent. If you hold a porcelain dish in front of a strong light, you will see the light through the dish. Porcelain is colder to the touch. Pottery is softer and easier to break and will stain more easily because it is porous. Porcelain is thinner, lighter, and more durable. Majolica, faience, and stoneware are all pottery. Additional pieces of pottery are listed in this book in the categories Pottery-Art, Pottery-Contemporary, Pottery-Midcentury, and under the factory name. For information about pottery makers and marks, see *Kovels' Dictionary of Marks—Pottery & Porcelain: 1650–1850* and *Kovels' New Dictionary of Marks—Pottery & Porcelain: 1850 to the Present.*

Bowl, Chinese Blue Matte Glaze, Wave Borderings, Earthenware, 3 ½ x 9 In. 303.00
Bowl, Crane Design, Yellow Ground, Turquoise, White, Chinese, 4 ¼ x 10 ¼ In. 468.00
Bowl, Pedestal, Silla Period, Korea, 3 ½ x 4 In. 94.00
Dish, Art Nouveau, Leaf Shape, Vein Relief, Black Glaze, Mark, France, 14 In. 119.00
Eggcup, EGG In Red Letters, Red Pin Stripe, White, Hornsea, 1 ¾ x 1 ½ In., Pair 10.00
Ewer, Turquoise Glaze, Pierced, Carved, Strap Handle, 11 In. 593.00
Figurine, Bird Whistle, Cinnamon Lead Glaze, Blow & Sound Holes, Earthenware, 3 ½ In. 55.00
Figurine, Camel, Demon Mask Saddlebags, Multicolored, 26 x 20 In. 770.00
Figurine, Chicken, Blue Feldspathic Glaze, Sawtooth Feathers, Body Details, Earthenware, 8 x 7 In. 248.00
Figurine, Dog, Cocker Spaniel, England, 11 x 10 In., Pair 440.00
Figurine, Dog, Spaniel, Begging, Rust Nutmeg Glaze, Curled Tail, Earthenware, 8 ½ In. 330.00
Figurine, Dog, Spaniel, Reclining, Tooled Fur, Tan Clay, Late 19th Century, 7 x 9 ½ In. 431.00
Figurine, Dog, Spaniel, White, Open Front Legs, Resting, Creamy Glaze, 9 ½ In. 1528.00
Figurine, Dragon, Crouching, Brown, Chinese, 6 x 21 x 3 In. 10.00
Figurine, Lion, Lying Down, Stepped Base, White Glaze, Cobalt Details, c.1875, 5 x 9 In. 1116.00
Figurine, Woman, Holding Bowl, Multicolored Feldspathic Glaze, Earthenware, 11 In. 303.00
Flower Frog, Female Nude, Emerging From Blossom, White, Germany, 1920s, 6 ½ In. 80.00
Jar, Edgefield, 2 Lug Handles, Green, Purple Glaze, South Carolina, 1850s, 15 In. 633.00
Jar, Rust, Black, Red Lead Glaze, Earthenware, 12 ½ x 32 In. 5280.00
Jar, Square Rim, Lid Ledge, Olive Streaking, c.1875, 10 In. 358.00
Jar, Storage, 4 Loop Handles, Unglazed Foot, Brown Glaze, Chinese, 19th Century, 11 ¾ In. 90.00
Jar, Storage, Gray, Horizontal Rows, Dome Shape, 3 Bear Feet, Chinese, 13 ½ In. 300.00
Jar, Storage, Green, Brown, Drip Glazed, Vertical Chain Bands, Leaf Sprays, 30 x 25 ½ In. 660.00
Jug, Bell Shape, Olive Lime, Shoulder Handle, Inner Lid Ledge, Gloss Glaze, c.1900, 13 ½ In. 220.00
Jug, Bulbous, C-Handle, Dark Rust Chocolate Glaze, c.1935, 3 ⅛ In. 44.00
Jug, Cylindrical Neck, No Rim, Slope Shoulder, Slant Handle, c.1950s, 3 ½ In. 77.00
Jug, Red Lead Glaze, Manganese Splotches, Grooved Handle, Earthenware, 4 ¼ In. 33.00

Date Your Postcard

Postcard collectors have a dating system of their own. First was the Pioneer Era (1893–1898), then the Private Mailing Card Era (1898–1901) and Postcard Era (1901–1907). All of these postcards had a photo and message on one side, the address on the other (the Undivided Back Era, 1893–1907). Next came the Divided Back Era (1907–1914), when the message and address were on the same side of the postcard. The White Border Era (1915–1930) was next, then the Linen Era (1930–1944) and the Photochrome Era (1945 to the present).

Poster, Ripley's Believe It Or Not, Hindu Quarter Man, Paper, 1940, 42 x 28 In.
$633.00

Pottery, Plate, St. Charles, Coggled Rim, Slip Design, 10 ¼ In.
$375.00

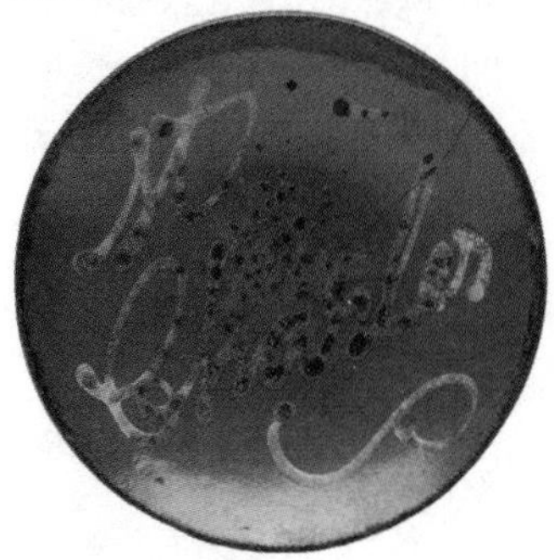

P

Pottery-Art, Bowl, Anthemion Border, Purple, Green Blue Crystalline Glaze, Marjorelle, 3 x 12 x 8 In.
$660.00

Pottery-Art, Charger, Fish, Slip Decorated, Blue, Green, C.H. Brannum, Barnstaple, 9 ⅞ In.
$345.00

Pottery-Art, Figurine, Alice & Ugly Duchess, Signed, Edris Eckhardt, 1930s, 5 ⅞ In.
$595.00

TIP
Don't use rubber gloves when washing figurines with protruding arms and legs. The gloves may snag and cause damage.

Mug, Children Spinning Tops, Black Transfer, Canary Yellow, England, 1800s, 2 ¼ In. 263.00
Pitcher, Cobalt Blue, Green Over Orange, No Spout, Lines, Drooling, Earthenware, 11 ⅛ In. . 880.00
Pitcher, Light Green Glaze, Hound Handle, 7 ¼ In.. .... 100.00
Pitcher, Oval Top, Albany Slip Glaze, c.1900, 11 In.. .... 66.00
Planter, Cinnamon, White Lead Glaze, Grooves, Flat Rim, Drain Hole, Earthenware, 11 x 15 ½ In. 44.00
Plaque, Madonna, Child, Fruits, Flowers, Della Robbia, Italy, 22 In. 292.00
Plate, St. Charles, Coggled Rim, Slip Design, 10 ¼ In. .... *illus* 375.00
Platter, Lake, Boat, Building, Minarets, Blue & White, England, c.1845, 11 x 15 In.. .... 439.00
Statue, Monk Carrying Bowl, 23 In. 33.00
Teapot, Caramel Red Lead Glaze, Rebekah Biblical Scene, Handle, Spout, Earthenware, 7 ¼ x 7 In. 523.00
Tureen, Marble Glaze, Tortoiseshell Palette, Gloss Ocher, France, 10 ½ x 9 In. 240.00
Umbrella Stand, Applied Ovals, Embossed Eagles, 25 In., 2 Piece 646.00
Vase, Bottle, Tea Dust, Oval, Elongated Neck, Japan, 17 In. 236.00
Vase, Brown Glaze, Signed, Japan, 9 x 9 ½ In. 266.00
Vase, Chrome Red Glaze, Handles, Multicolored, Tapered, Earthenware, 23 ¾ In. 880.00
Vase, Glossy Green, Orange Red Lead Glaze, Green Drooling, Earthenware, 3 ½ In. 385.00
Vase, Hand Painted, Landscape, Multicolored, Harmersbach, Germany, 20th Century, 4 In. . . 117.00
Vase, Maroon, Turquoise Lead Glaze, 3 Handles, Grooved Lug Handles, Earthenware, 3 ½ In. 77.00
Vase, Multicolored Red Lead Glaze, Double Ribbon Handle, Earthenware, 10 ⅞ In. 935.00
Vase, Olive, Incised Flowers & Oak Leaves, Alkaline Glaze, 8 In. 248.00
Vase, Red, Aqua Chinese Blue Glaze, Bulbous, Albany Slip Glaze, Earthenware, 4 ¾ In. 1210.00
Vase, Satin Gloss, Chinese Blue Glaze, Spout, Flat Style Handle, Earthenware, 4 ¼ In. 88.00
Vase, Storm Cloud, Rain, Lightning, Blackware, 5 In. 283.00
Vase, Teardrop, Pear Shape Body, Flared Base, Hare's Foot Glaze, Chinese, 3 ¾ In. 210.00

POTTERY-ART Art pottery was first made in America in Cincinnati, Ohio, during the 1870s. The pieces were hand thrown and hand decorated. The art pottery tradition continued until the 1930s when studio potters began making the more artistic wares. American, English, and Continental art pottery by less well-known makers is listed here. Most makers listed in *Kovels' American Art Pottery*, such as Arequipa, Ohr, Rookwood, Roseville, and Weller, are listed in their own categories in this book. More recent pottery is listed under the name of the maker or in another pottery category.

Ashtray, Organic Form, Red, Marked, Piccaso, Madoura, France, 5 ½ x 6 ½ x 4 In. 330.00
Beverage Set, Yale Football Players, Avon Pottery, 7 Piece 517.00
Bowl, Anthemion Border, Purple, Green Blue Crystalline Glaze, Marjorelle, 3 x 12 x 8 In. . . *illus* 660.00
Bowl, Arts & Crafts, Brown Glaze, Flowers, Unglazed Inside, 10 In. 18.00
Bowl, Calla Lily, Low, Common Ground, Signed, Eric Olson, 12 In. 201.00
Bowl, Chamberstick, Blue, Green Glaze, Brown Accents, North Carolina, 5 x 8 In. 95.00
Bowl, Flat Matte Glaze, Vontury, 1957, 2 ¾ x 7 ½ In.. .... 69.00
Bowl, Hampshire, Flared, Leaf, Green Matte Glaze, 6 x 3 In.. .... 316.00
Bowl, Low Dragonfly Relief, Matte Green Glaze, T.J. Wheatley, 1880, 2 x 6 In. 326.00
Bowl, Round, Abstract Faces, Blue, Green, Purple, E. Scheier, 1995, 8 x 10 In. 2015.00
Candelabrum, 3-Holder Shape, Green Matte Glaze, Mark, 15 x 7 ½ In. 270.00
Candlestick, Norse, Trumpet Shape, Incised Snake, 11 ½ In., Pair 403.00
Charger, Embossed Hands, Cupping Fish, Glazed Faience, Piccaso, Madoura, France, 12 ¾ In. 3900.00
Charger, Fish, Slip Decorated, Blue, Green, C.H. Brannum, Barnstaple, 9 ⅞ In. .... *illus* 345.00
Charger, Flower Border, Radiating Lines, Charlotte Rhead, Bursley Ware, 14 In. 341.00
Decanter, Lid, Blue, Brown, Black, John Glick, Plum Tree Pottery, 17 In. 146.00
Figurine, Alice & Ugly Duchess, Signed, Edris Eckhardt, 1930s, 5 ⅞ In. .... *illus* 595.00
Figurine, Woman, Water Jug, Large Dux, 19 In. 288.00
Green Matte Glaze, Tan To Blue Rim, Incised Zark, 7 x 4 In. 650.00
Group, Fantasy, Seated Maiden, Cat, Magpie, Charles Vyse, c.1938, 8 ⅜ In. 5250.00
Jardiniere, Bracket, Barbotine, Floral Garlands, France, Early 1900s, 28 x 40 In., Pair...... 6250.00
Jardiniere, Carved, Thistle, Green Matte Glaze, 12 x 1 In. 1020.00
Mug, Green Hues, Matte Glaze, Zark, Bringhurst Label, 4 x 5 In. 240.00
Pitcher, Ducks, Brown Ground, Enamel Design, 2-Sided, Jervis, 5 ¼ In. 88.00
Planter, Art Nouveau, Irises, Purple, Pink, Petal Handles, Maussier, 8 ¾ In. 210.00
Plate, Cabinet, Swirling Reticulated Floral Border, Persian Floral, Multicolored, Gilt, 18 In.. . 191.00
Tea Service, Modernist, Tray, Teapot, Creamer, Sugar, 6 Cups, Fraunfelter, 12 x 19 In. 2013.00
Teapot, Blue, Yellow, Green Design, Cambridge, Marked, Ink Stamp, 5 ⅛ In. .... *illus* 44.00
Umbrella Stand, Art Deco, Yellow Ground, Maroon, Brown Oval Designs, 12 x 23 In.. .... 330.00
Vase, 4-Sided, Green, Red, Blue Matte Glaze, Dalpayrat, Signed, 9 x 4 In. 960.00
Vase, Art Nouveau, Earthenware, Molded, Wildflowers, Multicolored, Gilt, 6 ½ In. 119.00
Vase, Art Nouveau, Earthenware, Organic Rim, Vining, Maiden & Bird, 27 ½ In. 237.00
Vase, Arts & Crafts, 2 Handles, Green Matte Glaze, 9 x 8 In. 165.00
Vase, Blue & Plum Flambe Crystalline Glaze, Signed, T Doat Sevres, 1907, 3 In. .... *illus* 3000.00
Vase, Blue Green Matte Glaze, Lines, Bulbous, Flared Lip, Clivia Calder, 1909, 4 In. 80.00

P

Vase, Blue Lily, Green Ground, Yellow Band, Santa Barbara Ceramic, 5 x 4 In. 175.00
Vase, Brown, Tan Matte Glaze, Green Crystals, Handle, Pierrefonds, 10 x 11 In. 420.00
Vase, Brown Glaze, Linear Gold Design, Incised Zack B, Ozark, 10 x 4 In. 1495.00
Vase, Bulbous, 6 Cats, Common Ground, Eric Olson, 8 ½ x 7 ¾ In. 1035.00
Vase, Bulbous, Brown Glaze, Painted Flowers, Rozane, 4 x 7 ½ In. 86.00
Vase, Bulbous, Calla Lilly, Peach Ground, Eric Olson, Common Ground, 7 x 8 In. 270.00
Vase, Bulbous, Red, Turquoise Glaze, Marked, Dalpayrat, 5 x 3 In. 300.00
Vase, Bulbous, Thick Blue, Brown, Ivory Drip Glaze, Adelaide Robineau, 1919, 5 x 3 In. 3620.00
Vase, Burley Winter, Glendale Mold, Blue Glaze, Mark 2, 8 x 5 In. 115.00
Vase, Burley Winter, Red, Blue Mottled Glaze, 8 x 5 In. 125.00
Vase, California Faience, Shouldered, Red Matte Glaze, 6 x 10 In. 120.00
Vase, Carved Vertical Leaves, Mottled Green Matte Glaze, Label, Arts & Clay Co., 8 x 21 In. 780.00
Vase, Cobalt Blue, Pink Tulips, Double Swirl Art Nouveau Handles, Austria, 19 In. 173.00
Vase, Flared, Mottled Blue, Green, Black Matte Glaze, Dalpayrat, 4 x 6 In. 240.00
Vase, Flowers, Butterflies, Transfer, Gilt, Stand, Faience Mfg. Co., 659, 16 x 9 In. .... *illus* 2880.00
Vase, Flowers, Water, Grass, Verse, 3-Sided, Squeezebag, Signed, Avon, 9 x 4 In. .... *illus* 1920.00
Vase, Green Crystalline Glaze, Bulbous, Long Neck, Signed, Pierrefonds, 7 In. 250.00
Vase, Hammered Copper, Dragonflies, Turquoise Glaze, Signed, Baudin, 3 In. .... *illus* 1320.00
Vase, Iris, Shouldered, Common Ground, Eric Olson, 5 x 10 ½ In. 460.00
Vase, Leave & Buds, Green Crystalline, Tapered, Arts & Clay Co., 4 ½ x 11 ½ In. 489.00
Vase, Milky White Over Yellow Glossy Glaze, Footed, Frank Reuss Kelley, 2 ⅝ In. 259.00
Vase, North State, 4 Handles, Charcoal, Green Glaze, Mark, 9 x 10 In. 390.00
Vase, Norwetta, Shouldered, Ivory Glaze, Blue Crystal Highlights, 3 x 4 In. 360.00
Vase, Rust Exterior Glaze, Green, Orange Interior, Footed, Frank Reuss Kelley, 3 In. 173.00
Vase, Shouldered, Green Matte Glaze, Hampshire, 5 x 12 In. 805.00
Vase, Shouldered, Orange, Cream Swirl Design, Evans, Dexter, Missouri, 9 x 17 In. 420.00
Vase, Slate Blue, Crane Amidst Marsh Grass, Leafy Vine, Berries, Baluster, 7 In. 660.00
Vase, Squat, 2 Handles, Green Glaze, Marked Zark, 3 x 7 In. 475.00
Vase, Vertical Leaves, Yellow Buds, Green Matte Glaze, Arts & Clay Co., 5 x 12 In. 345.00
Vase, Vertical Leaves, Yellow Buds, Green Matte Glaze, Arts & Clay Co., 6 ½ x 15 In. 546.00
Waffle Service, Modernist, Iron, Bowl, Spoon, Syrup Jar, Tray, Fraunfelter, 14 x 21 In. 1495.00
Water Jug, Abstract Bird Shape, Picasso, Madoura, France, 9 ¼ x 8 ¾ In. 3000.00

POTTERY-CONTEMPORARY lists pieces made by artists working after 1975.

Bowl, Chartreuse, Brown Volcanic Glaze, Earthenware, J. Lovera, Signed, 2 ¼ x 8 In. 840.00
Bowl, Cylindrical Stand, Metallic Teal Luster Glaze, Beatrice Wood, 4 ½ x 4 ¾ In. 1500.00
Bowl, Yellow Glaze, Lucie Rie, Impressed, c.1960, 3 In. 9375.00
Figurine, Jacked Up Pants, Signed, Theo Portnoy, 27 x 6 ½ x 6 In. 9600.00
Figurine, Zebra, Arabia, Marked, 5 ¾ In. 50.00
Figurine, Zebra, Hand Painted, Marked, Taisto Kaisinen, Finland, 5 ¾ In. 90.00
Jardiniere, Verdigris Glaze, Signed, William Daley, 10 ¼ x 16 In. 1560.00
Teapot, Orange, Large Painted Brown Eye, Michael Lucero, New York, 12 x 16 x 7 ½ In. 9775.00
Vase, Beatrice Wood, Gourd Shape, Metallic Glaze, Multicolored, Signed, Beato, 4 x 9 In. 1400.00
Vase, Glazed Ceramic, Fern Leaves, Brown, Tan, Peter Voulkos, 1953, 9 In. 4800.00
Vase, Incised Wheat, Green Matte Glaze, Signed, T. Eberhardt, 13 ¼ x 5 In. 510.00
Water Set, Geometrics, Stamped, Deruta, 12-In. Pitcher, 9 Piece .... *illus* 360.00

POTTERY-MIDCENTURY includes pieces made from the 1940s to about 1975.

Bowl, 10 Sides, 5 Bird Medallions, Green, Brown, L. Anderson, 1972, 7 x 3 In. 780.00
Bowl, City Scene, Yellow, Brown, White, 4-Sided, Harris Strong, 12 In. 150.00
Bowl, Cone Shape, White Pitted Glaze, Lucie, Stoneware, Rie, c.1974, 15 ⅝ In. 43000.00
Bowl, Flared Shape, Brown Glaze, L. Anderson, 1978, 3 x 10 In. 720.00
Bowl, Geometrics, Stars, White Ground, Oval, Marked, Ede, Calf, 2 x 22 ¾ In. 33.00
Bowl, Irregular Form, Yellow, Blue Circle, G. Gambone, Italy, 2 ½ x 4 In. 290.00
Bowl, Orange & Brown Glaze, Marked, Natzler, 2 x 5 ½ In. .... *illus* 1420.00
Charger, Kingfishers, Tube Lined, Maling Ware, 7 In. 190.00
Container, Lid, Orange, Yellow, Tyrone Larson, Cranbrook Academy, 17 x 6 In. 88.00
Ewer, Ruddy Brown Glaze, Maigon Daga, No. 64, 9 x 3 In. 145.00
Ewer, Stick Handle, Mottled Green Glaze, M. Daga, 8 x 5 In. 115.00
Figurine, Pigeon, Perched On Base, Black, White, Carl Waters, Stonelain, 9 In. 800.00
Figurine, Rooster, Carl Waters, Stonelain, 10 ¾ x 8 In. .... *illus* 121.00
Pitcher, Face, Brown, Black, Tan, Mark, Pablo Picasso, 13 x 6 In. 4200.00
Pitcher, Glazed Ceramic, White, Red Interior, Pol Champbost, France, c.1950, 11 In. 7500.00
Pitcher, Green, Black Handle Lid, Arts & Crafts, Marked, Catalina Pottery, Ca., 8 In. 200.00
Pitcher, Green, Embossed Flower Band, Scalloped Foot, 5 In. 15.00
Pitcher, Picador, Man, Horse, Spear, Picasso, 5 In. 2530.00

TIP
Remove stains from plastic dishes with paste silver polish.

Pottery-Art, Teapot, Blue, Yellow, Green Design, Cambridge, Marked, Ink Stamp, 5 ⅛ In.
$44.00

Pottery-Art, Vase, Blue & Plum Flambe Crystalline Glaze, Signed, T Doat Sevres, 1907, 3 In.
$3000.00

Pottery-Art, Vase, Flowers, Butterflies, Transfer, Gilt, Stand, Faience Mfg. Co., 659, 16 x 9 In.
$2880.00

P

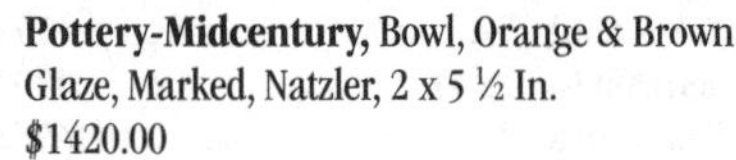
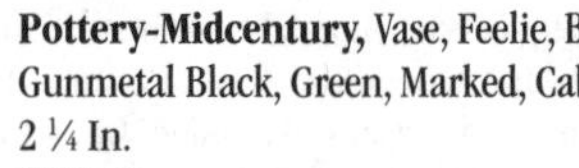

Pottery-Art, Vase, Flowers, Water, Grass, Verse, 3-Sided, Squeezebag, Signed, Avon, 9 x 4 In.
$1920.00

Pottery-Art, Vase, Hammered Copper, Dragonflies, Turquoise Glaze, Signed, Baudin, 3 In.
$1320.00

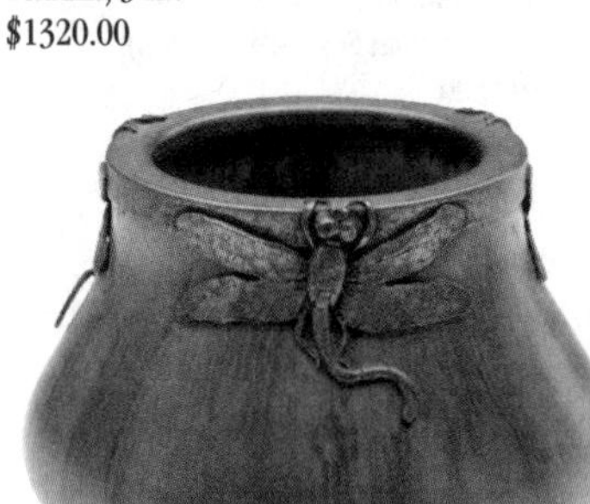

Pottery-Midcentury, Bowl, Orange & Brown Glaze, Marked, Natzler, 2 x 5 ½ In.
$1420.00

Pottery-Midcentury, Figurine, Rooster, Carl Waters, Stonelain, 10 ¾ x 8 In.
$121.00

Pottery-Midcentury, Vase, Feelie, Blue, Gunmetal Black, Green, Marked, Cabat 39, 2 ¼ In.
$440.00

Pottery-Midcentury, Vase, Tan & Turquoise Volcanic Glaze, Signed, Beato, 6 ½ x 3 In.
$1640.00

Pottery-Contemporary, Water Set, Geometrics, Stamped, Deruta, 12-In. Pitcher, 9 Piece
$360.00

TIP

"Cold-painted" items like some glass and porcelain, especially cookie jars, should never be put in a dishwasher. Just wipe them with a damp cloth.

P

Planter, Bathtub, Footed, Earth Tones, California Original, 10 1/12 x 4 3/4 In. 15.00
Plate, Toros, 2 Bulls, Green & Blue Ground, Picasso, Valluris, France, 1952, 7 3/4 In. 1030.00
Teapot, Black Cat, Shafford, 8 Oz., 5 1/2 In. 25.00
Teapot, Black Cat, Shafford, 20 Oz., 6 In. 45.00
Tray, City Scene, Brown, Heart Shape, Harris Strong, 10 In. 25.00
Vase, Acropolis, Lekythos Style, Green, Clay, c.1962, 7 1/2 In. 15.00
Vase, Blue, Scalloped Rim, Footed, Embossed Flower, USA, 8 1/2 In. 18.00
Vase, Feelie, Black Clay, Blue, Green Drip Glaze, Small Foot, Cabat, 2 x 2 In. 600.00
Vase, Feelie, Blue, Gunmetal Black, Green, Marked, Cabat 39, 2 1/4 In. .... *illus* 440.00
Vase, Feelie, Brown, Blue, Green Drip Glaze, Cabat, 2 x 3 In. 780.00
Vase, Feelie, Bulbouse, Blue, Lavender Speckled Glaze, Rose Cabat, 2 x 3 In. 660.00
Vase, Feelie, Raised Figures, Green, Blue Glaze, Rose Cabat, 2 x 4 In. 660.00
Vase, Flared Lip, Teal Glaze, Brown Speckle, Women, Gold Discs, E. Cazaux, 11 In. 1007.00
Vase, Gray, Gunmetal Mottled Matte Glaze, Earthenware, Signed, F. Carlton Ball, 20 x 12 In. . 1800.00
Vase, Green Crystalline Glaze, Squat, Handles, Carolina Cole Pottery, 5 In. 60.00
Vase, Melon Shape, Incised Brown, White, Lines, C. Conover, 13 x 13 In. 5290.00
Vase, Oxblood Glaze, Catalina, 8 5/8 In. 196.00
Vase, Slope Shouldered Shape, Red Metallic Glaze, Kahler, 13 x 10 In. 510.00
Vase, Tan & Turquoise Volcanic Glaze, Signed, Beato, 6 1/2 x 3 In. .... *illus* 1640.00
Vase, Tapered, Earthenware, Multicolored, Gambone, c.1950, 16 x 12 x 3 In. 1800.00

POWDER FLASKS AND POWDER HORNS were made to hold the gunpowder used in antique firearms. The early examples were made of horn or wood; later ones were of copper or brass.

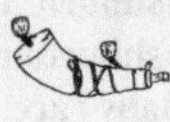

POWDER FLASK

Brass, Copper Spout, c.1775, 10 x 3 1/2 In. 201.00
Copper, Bag Shape, c.1862, 6 1/2 x 2 In. 85.00
Copper, Batty, c.1850 .... 625.00
Copper, Brass, Italy, 9 1/4 In. 215.00
Copper, Brass, Raised Linear Design, 7 3/4 x 3 1/4 In. 25.00
Copper, N.P. Ames 1838 .... 665.00
Copper, Ornate Design, 7 1/2 x 3 1/2 In. 60.00
Glass, Sterling Cap, Repousse Flowers, 19th Century, 7 1/2 In. 165.00
Leather, Brass, Flask Cap Co., c.1800s 50.00
Leather, Brass Pourer, c.1850 .... 180.00
Leather, Geometric Design, Rolled Brass Top, Chain, 19th Century, 6 1/2 x 2 3/4 In. 225.00
Leather, Hunting Scene, 19th Century, 9 x 4 In. 45.00
Metal, Brass Top, Hunting Scene, 6 1/4 In. 67.00
Metal Spout, Carved Coconut, Church, Castle, Flowers, Grapes, 5 In., Pair. 575.00

POWDER HORN

2 Sailing Ships, Engraved, 18th Century, 15 In. 761.00
American, c.1780, 13 1/4 In. 293.00
Engraved, Crown, Mermaid, Anchor, England, 1800s, 12 1/2 In. 940.00
Engraved, Harbor Scene, Sailing Vessel, Structures, Landscape, 1800s, 16 1/2 In. 805.00
Engraved, Scenes, Ship, Buildings, John Newell His Horn May 8, 1859 .... 800.00
Engraved, Towns, Coat Of Arms, Cannons, Flags, Drums, N.Y., 11 In. .... *illus* 4500.00
Glass, White, Applied Mouth & Neck Ring, Pontil, c.1850, 13 In. 68.00
Health To Huntsman, Eagle, Hunter, Dog, Game, Engraved, 1776, 14 In. 1872.00
Lone Star State, Texas, 2 Dogs, Horse, Sheep, Relief Carved, c.1900, 9 In. 237.00
Mounted Soldier, Carved, 1807, 8 1/2 In. 234.00
Pinwheels, Inscribed, John Price, Belford, Engraved, 1771, 17 In. 439.00
Scrimshaw, Bird, Inscribed, Joseph Wills, Late 18th Century, 13 In. 439.00
There Bidh Ballard, 1776, Frigate & Geometrics, Engraved, Mass., Late 1700s, 18 In. 936.00
Whaling Scene, Engraved, Mid 19th Century, 12 1/2 In. 644.00

PRATT ware means two different things. It was an early Staffordshire pottery, cream-colored with colored decorations, made by Felix Pratt during the late eighteenth century. There was also Pratt ware made with transfer designs during the mid-nineteenth century in Fenton, England. Reproductions of the transfer-printed Pratt are being made.

PRATT
FENTON

Figurine, Farmer & Cow, Early 19th Century, 6 In. 1989.00
Pitcher, Berries, 6 1/2 In. 374.00
Pitcher, Mischievous Sport, Sport Vs. Innocent, Heart Medallion, Blue, Yellow, Gilt, 6 In. 150.00
Sugar, Cover, Classical Figures, Leaves, Swan Finial, England, c.1890, 6 x 5 In. 154.00
Sugar, Cover, Figures, Flowers, Leaves, Swan Finial, Late 1700s, 5 1/2 x 4 1/2 In. .... *illus* 1541.00

Powder Horn, Engraved, Towns, Coat Of Arms, Cannons, Flags, Drums, N.Y., 11 In.
$4500.00

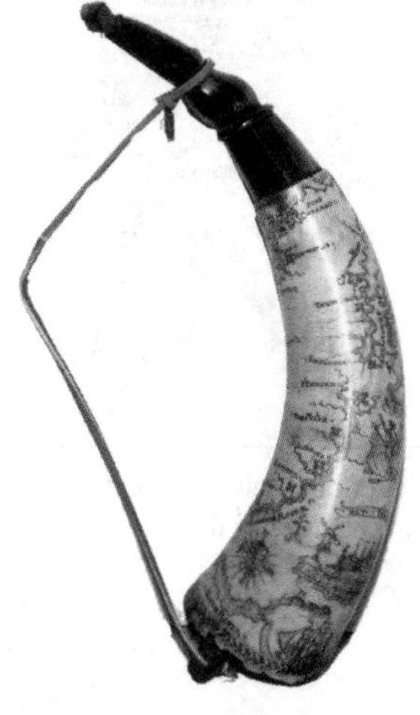

Pratt, Sugar, Cover, Figures, Flowers, Leaves, Swan Finial, Late 1700s, 5 1/2 x 4 1/2 In.
$1541.00

TIP

Don't post the name of your alarm company on your house. Use a generic sign that says the house has an alarm system. The name of the alarm company aids a burglar trying to break in.

As always, the edited listings in *Kovels' Antiques & Collectibles Price Guide 2010* aren't available on any website, but readers should visit Kovels.com for information on trends, tips, reproductions, marks, old prices, and more!

Pressed Glass, Alabama, Tumbler, Souvenir, Ruby Stain, Omaha Exposition, 1899, 4 x 3 In.
$120.00

Pressed Glass, Baby Face, Butter, Cover, Frosted, 8 ½ x 6 ⅜ In.
$204.00

Pressed Glass, Bellflower & Vine, Tumbler, Handle, Flint, 3 x 2 ½ In.
$550.00

Pressed Glass, Bohemian, Cologne, Rose Stain, 4 Footed, 9 ¾ In.
$102.00

Teapot, Blue, Yellow, Relief Swag, Girl Finial, c.1800, 4 ¾ In. 702.00
Teapot, Seated Man, Multicolored, Arm Handle, Arm Spout, c.1800, 7 ¾ In. 237.00
Watch Hutch, Man & Woman Next To Tall Case Clock, Early 19th Century, 8 ½ In. 1521.00

PRESSED GLASS was first made in the United States in the 1820s after the invention of glass pressing machines. Hundreds of patterns of pressed glass were made in complete table settings. Although the Boston and Sandwich Works was the most famous of the pressed glass factories, there were about sixteen other factories making pressed glass from 1830 to 1850, and still more from 1850 to 1900, when pressed glass reached its greatest popularity. It is now being widely reproduced. The pattern names used in this listing are based on the information in the book *Pressed Glass in America* by John and Elizabeth Welker. There may be pieces of pressed glass listed in this book in other categories, such as Lamp, Ruby, Sandwich, and Souvenir.

Acanthus pattern is listed here as Ribbed Palm.
Actress, Cheese Dish, Cover, Frosted, 6 ½ x 8 ½ In. 68.00
Actress, Goblet, Lota & Kate Claxton, Frosted, 6 ½ In. 135.00
Alabama, Tumbler, Souvenir, Ruby Stain, Omaha Exposition, 1899, 4 x 3 In. . . . . . *illus* 120.00
Alaric, Tray, Rectangular, Octagon, Bryce Higbee, 11 x 7 ½ In. 65.00
Amazon, Butter, No Cover, 7 x 5 In. 25.00
Arched Ovals, Pitcher, 4 ¼ In. 35.00
Arched Ovals, Pitcher, 6 ⅜ In. 30.00
Ashburton, Tumbler, Applied Handle, Polished Pontil, 3 In., Pair . . . . . . 90.00 to 102.00
Ashburton, Tumbler, Jelly, Flared Rim, Polished Pontil, 5 In., 4 Piece. 136.00
Baby Face, Butter, Cover, Frosted, 8 ½ x 6 ⅜ In. . . . . . *illus* 204.00
Baby Thumbprint pattern is listed here as Dakota.
Barrel Honeycomb, see the related pattern Honeycomb.
Beaded Bull's-Eye & Drape pattern is listed here as Alabama.
Bellflower & Vine, Tumbler, Handle, Flint, 3 x 2 ½ In. . . . . . *illus* 550.00
Bird & Strawberry, Goblet, 6 ½ In. 423.00
Birds, Pitcher, 7 ½ x 3 ¾ In. 245.00
Bleeding Heart, Wine, 4 In., 4 Piece 110.00
Block, Finger Bowl, Amber Stain, 3 x 4 ⅝ In. 50.00
Block & Fine Cut pattern is listed here as Fine Cut & Block.
Block & Pruntie, Vase, Amethyst, Ruffled Edge, c.1870, 9 In. 546.00
Bluebird pattern is listed here as Bird & Strawberry.
Bohemian, Cologne, Rose Stain, 4 Footed, 9 ¾ In. . . . . . *illus* 102.00
Brazen Shield, Goblet, 6 In. 33.00
Bringing Home The Cows, Pitcher, 10 ½ In. 678.00
Bucket pattern is listed here as Oaken Bucket.
Buckle, Eggcup, 3 ⅝ In. 40.00
Bull's-Eye, Tumbler, Flint, Pontil, 3 ¾ x 3 ¾ In. . . . . . *illus* 121.00
Bull's-Eye & Button, Cruet, Stopper, Emerald Green, 4 Eyes, 7 ½ x 3 ½ In. 245.00
Bull's-Eye & Wishbone, Goblet, Flint, 6 ⅛ In. . . . . . *illus* 165.00
Bull's-Eye With Diamond Point, Goblet, 6 ¾ In. . . . . . 56.00 to 96.00
Bull's-Eye With Diamond Point, Spooner, Gold Trim, 5 ½ In. 80.00
Bull's-Eye With Diamond Point, Tumbler, Whiskey, Pontil, c.1875, 3 ¼ In. 144.00
Button Arches, Creamer, 2 ¾ x 3 In. 40.00
Cabbage Leaf, Sugar, Cover, Amber, 6 ½ x 5 ½ In. . . . . . *illus* 295.00
Cabbage Rose, Wine, 6 Piece 67.00
Cable, Celery Vase, Hexagonal, Ribbed, Flint, 8 ⅜ x 5 In. . . . . . *illus* 66.00
Cable, Goblet, 6 ½ In., Pair 90.00
Canadian, Wine, 4 ⅛ In., 4 Piece 90.00

Candlewick, as a pressed glass pattern is properly named Banded Raindrop. There is also a pattern called Candlewick, which has been made by Imperial Glass Corporation since 1936. It is listed in this book in the Imperial Glass category.

Caryatid, Candlestick, Canary Yellow, 8-Sided Socket, 9 ¾ In., Pair . . . . . . *illus* 3190.00
Chain With Diamonds pattern is listed here as Washington Centennial.
Chilson, Goblet, 6 ½ In. 203.00
Chippendale Krystol, Pitcher, 4 ¾ x 5 ¼ In. 24.00
Classic, Bowl, Cover, Frosted, Log Feet, 1890s, 9 x 8 ½ In. 110.00
Classic, Goblet, Frosted, 6 In. . . . . . *illus* 165.00
Columbian Coin, Ale, 6 ¾ In. 79.00
Columbian Coin, Finger Lamp, Footed, 5 x 3 ½ In. 367.00
Columbian Coin, Syrup, Frosted, Tin Lid, 6 ⅜ x 3 In. 226.00
Comet, Goblet, 6 In. . . . . . 102.00 to 124.00
Compact pattern is listed here as Snail.

Co-Op No. 2, Cheese Dish, Cover, Ruby Stain, 5 ½ x 8 In. . . . . *illus* 91.00
Cord & Tassel, Finger Lamp, Applied Handle, 5 x 3 ¾ In. 136.00
Cord & Tassel, Mug, Applied Handle, 4 ½ x 3 ½ In. 68.00
Cord & Tassel, Syrup, Applied Handle, 6 ¾ In. 113.00
Cord & Tassel, Wine, 3 ⅞ In., 8 Piece 34.00
Cosmos pattern is listed in this book as its own category.
Crane pattern is listed here as Stork.
Cube With Fan pattern is listed here as Pineapple & Fan.
Cupid & Venus, Cruet, Footed, Applied Handle, Stopper, 7 ¾ In. 68.00
Cupid & Venus, Wine, 3 ¾ In., 4 Piece 79.00
Currant, Compote, Cover, 13 ½ In. 57.00
Daisy & Almond Band, Butter, Cover, Amber, 6 ½ x 7 In. 125.00
Dakota, Goblet, 6 ½ In., 8 Piece 60.00
Deer & Dog, Bowl, Cover, Oval, Frosted, Etched, 7 ¼ In. 339.00
Deer & Dog, Pitcher, Water, 10 In. 136.00
Deer & Dog, Sugar, Cover, Frosted, 9 ½ In. 396.00
Deer & Oak Tree, Pitcher, 8 ⅝ In. 170.00
Delaware, Banana Boat, Emerald Green, Gold Trim, Oval, 11 ¾ x 7 ¼ In. 79.00
Diamond & Pineapple, Vase, 10 ½ x 5 ½ In. 55.00
Diamond Point, Pitcher, 8-Panel Base, Applied Handle, Pontil, Flint, 9 x 4 In. . . . . *illus* 99.00
Diamond Point, Sugar & Creamer, Cover, Finial, 8 In. & 6 ¾ In. 124.00
Diamond Thumbprint, Goblet, 6 ¾ In. 1017.00
Diamond Thumbprint, Tumbler, 3 ¾ In. 102.00
Diamond Thumbprint, Tumbler, Lemonade, Applied Handle, 3 In. 855.00
Dogwood Flower & Leaves, Sugar & Creamer, 7 ¼ x 3 & 6 x 3 ¼ In. 50.00
Dolphin, Compote, Blue, 9 ¾ In. 231.00
Dolphin, Creamer, Frosted, 6 ¾ In. 102.00
Eagle, Butter, Cover, Frosted, Tab Handles, Footed, 7 ⅜ In. . . . . *illus* 66.00
Egg & Groove, Vase, Flared, 6-Scallop Rim, Pontil, 6 x 3 ¾ In. . . . . *illus* 44.00
Eight Panel, Celery Vase, Tulip, Fiery Opalescent, Clear Foot, 8 ½ In. . . . . *illus* 1430.00
Eight Panel, Sugar, Cover, Cobalt Blue, Acorn Finial, Pontil, 8 ¾ In. . . . . *illus* 920.00
Elegant, Compote, Pedestal Foot, 6 ½ x 7 ⅛ In. 20.00
Elk Medallion, Goblet, 6 ¼ In. 67.00
Empress, Cruet, Green, Gold Trim, 7 x 3 ¼ In. . . . . *illus* 60.00
Esther, Sauce, Amber, 2 x 4 ¼ In., 4 Piece 68.00
Etched Alligator, Goblet, 6 ¼ In. 135.00
Etched Dakota pattern is listed here as Dakota.
Etched Stork Feeding, Goblet, 6 ¼ In. 45.00
Etched Three Presidents, Goblet, 6 ¼ In. 101.00
Excelsior, Goblet, Hexagonal Stem, 6 ⅛ In., 6 Piece 67.00
Falling Leaves, Butter Cover, Federal, 5 ¾ x 7 ¼ In. 65.00
Feeding Swan, Cake Stand, Scalloped Rim, 8-Point Star, Swirled Stem, 5 ½ In. 79.00
Fine Cut & Block, Finger Bowl, Amber Stain, 3 x 4 ⅝ In. . . . . *illus* 40.00
Fine Cut & Block, Shaker, Amber, Tall, 4 ½ In. 113.00
Flamingo, Goblet, 6 ¼ In. 121.00
Fleur-De-Lis, Celery Vase, 2 Handles, Ruffled Edge, 6 ¼ x 6 ¼ In. 60.00
Flying Birds, Goblet, 5 ¾ In. 158.00
Flying Robin pattern is listed here as Hummingbird.
Four Block Printie, Vase, Green, Hexagon Base, 8 ¾ In. 588.00
Frosted patterns may also be listed under the name of the main pattern.
Frosted Eagle, Marmalade, Cover, 8 ½ x 3 ½ In. 45.00
Frosted Lion, Compote, Cover, Rampant Lion With Stump Finial, Frosted, 1890s, 13 x 8 In. . 121.00
Frosted Roman Key pattern is listed here as Roman Key, Frosted.
Galloway, Creamer, 4 ¼ x 4 In. 15.00
Giant Sawtooth, Goblet, 6 ½ In. 124.00
Girl With Fan, Goblet, 5 ¾ In. 67.00
Good Luck pattern is listed here as Horseshoe.
Grand Army Of The Republic pattern is listed here as Historical.
Heart Plume, Pitcher, 8 ½ x 8 In. 80.00
Heart With Thumbprint, Goblet, Ruby Stained, 5 ⅞ In. 508.00
Hearts Of Loch Laven pattern is listed here as Shuttle.
Hero, Tumbler, Ruby Stained, 3 ⅜ In., 4 Piece 45.00
Hexagonal Block, Tumbler, Ruby Stained, 4 In., 4 Piece 68.00
Historical, Berry Bowl, Honoring John Davis, Atlas Glass Co., c.1924, 3 ¾ In. 179.00
Historical, Mug, Civil War, Union Forever, 4 In. 523.00
Historical, Tray, Campaign, Blaine, Logan, Handles, Pressed Glass, 8 ½ x 11 ½ In. . . . . *illus* 170.00
Historical, Tray, Campaign, Cleveland, Hendricks, Handle, 9 ½ x 11 ½ In. . . . . *illus* 250.00

Pressed Glass, Bull's-Eye, Tumbler, Flint, Pontil, 3 ¾ x 3 ¾ In.
$121.00

Pressed Glass, Bull's-Eye & Wishbone, Goblet, Flint, 6 ⅛ In.
$165.00

Pressed Glass, Cabbage Leaf, Sugar, Cover, Amber, 6 ½ x 5 ½ In.
$295.00

Pressed Glass, Cable, Celery, Vase, Hexagonal, Ribbed, Flint, 8 ⅜ x 5 In.
$66.00

Pressed Glass, Caryatid, Candlestick, Canary Yellow, 8-Sided Socket, 9 ¾ In., Pair
$3190.00

Pressed Glass, Classic, Goblet, Frosted, 6 In.
$165.00

Pressed Glass, Co-Op No. 2, Cheese Dish, Cover, Ruby Stain, 5 ½ x 8 In.
$91.00

Pressed Glass, Diamond Point, Pitcher, 8-Panel Base, Applied Handle, Pontil, Flint, 9 x 4 In.
$99.00

Historical, Tumbler, Civil War, c.1875, 4 ¾ In. 311.00
Hobnail pattern is in this book as its own category.
Hobstar, Creamer, 4 x 5 ¾ In. 30.00
Holly, Compote, Hexagonal, Faceted Stem, Stepped Foot, 8 ½ In. 355.00
Holly, Sugar & Creamer 220.00
Honeycomb, Pitcher, Towering Applied Handle, 11 ½ In. 215.00
Horn Of Plenty, Champagne, c.1875, 5 ¼ In. 124.00
Horn Of Plenty, Decanter, Diamond Point Stopper, 11 In. 285.00
Horn Of Plenty, Goblet, 6 ¼ In., 4 Piece 158.00
Horse, Cat & Rabbit, Goblet, 6 ⅜ In. 621.00
Horseshoe, Bread Tray 46.00
Horseshoe, Cheese Dish, Woman Churning, 5 ⅝ x 7 ½ In. 23.00
Horseshoe, Goblet, 6 In., 6 Piece 79.00
Hummingbird, Tumbler, 3 ¾ In. 90.00
Inverted Fern, Tumbler, Flint, 3 ½ In. . . . . *illus* 143.00
Jacob's Ladder, Goblet, 6 ½ In., 6 Piece 90.00
Jewel, Toothpick, Emerald Green, 2 ¼ x 2 ¼ In. 25.00
Jewel & Crescent, Goblet, 5 ¾ In. 254.00
Jewel & Crescent, Wine, 4 ¼ In. 124.00
Jumbo, Bowl, Cover, Elephant, 10 ⅜ x 10 ½ x 5 In. . . . . *illus* 180.00
King Arthur Variant, Water Set, 9 ⅞-In. Pitcher, 7 Piece 68.00
King's Crown, Cake Stand, 7 x 9 In. 45.00
King's Crown, Caster Set, 4 Bottles, 9 ¼ In. 57.00
Klondike, Spooner, Amber Stain, Frosted, 3 ½ In. . . . . *illus* 40.00
Leaf & Vines, Tankard, Engraved, Applied Handle, 13 x 7 In. 100.00
Lily Of The Valley, Pitcher, Milk, Applied Handle, 8 In. 45.00
Lincoln Drape With Tassel, Goblet, 6 In. 146.00
Lion, Compote, Cover, Frosted, Rampant Lion Finial, 13 In. 124.00
Log Cabin, Pitcher, 8 ½ In. 495.00
Loop & Arch, Tumbler, Translucent Blue, c.1850, 3 ½ In. 181.00
Loops & Drops, Bowl, 3 ½ x 10 In. 45.00
Lotus, Compote, Cover, Wafer Stem, High, 11 ⅞ In. 147.00
Massachusetts, Card Tray, 2 ⅜ x 8 ⅝ In. 40.00
Monkey, Butter, Cover, Rayed Base, 6 x 7 ⅜ In. 136.00
Monkey, Mug, Deep Amethyst, Plain Handle, Diamond Band At Foot, 3 ¾ In. 113.00
Monkey, Table Set, Fiery Opalescent, Butter, Creamer, Spooner, 3 Piece 1356.00
Monkey, Toothpick, Frosted, Brass Cover, Gilt Brass Frame, 4 In. 1017.00
New England Pineapple, Tumbler, Pontil, c.1875, 3 ¾ In. 84.00
New York Honeycomb, Candlestick, Fiery Opalescent, Hexagonal, 7 ¾ In. 508.00
Oaken Bucket, Pitcher, Amethyst, 8 ⅛ In. 90.00
Ohio Star, Sugar & Creamer, 6 x 3 ½ & 6 x 3 In. 225.00
Ohio Star, Tankard, 10 In. 195.00
Ohio Star, Vase, 9 ¾ x 4 ½ In. 200.00
Ohio Star, Vase, Scalloped Edge, 10 In. 225.00
Old Abe pattern is listed here as Frosted Eagle.
Owl pattern is listed here as Bull's-Eye With Diamond Point.
Palmette, Syrup 154.00
Panama, Compote, 6 ¼ x 8 In. 55.00
Paneled Acorn Band, Creamer, Footed, 6 x 5 ⅜ In. 55.00
Paneled Dogwood, Green, Gold Trim, 12 In. 45.00
Peacock Eye, Vase, Olive Green, 6-Flute Rim, 9 ¼ x 4 In. . . . . *illus* 990.00
Pennsylvania Thumbprint, Celery Vase, 5 Flared Scallops, 9 x 5 In. 119.00
Pennsylvania Thumbprint, Tumbler, 3 ⅞ In. 135.00
Pillar & Bull's-Eye pattern is listed here as Thistle.
Pinafore pattern is listed here as Actress.
Pineapple & Fan, Toothpick, Flared Rim 12.00
Plain Smocking pattern is listed here as Smocking.
Plume, Pitcher, Water, 9 ¼ In. 90.00
Polar Bear, Tray, Water, Frosted, Egg & Dart Border, 11 x 15 ¼ In. 113.00
Polar Bear, Waste Bowl, Frosted, Flared Rim, 3 x 5 In. . . . . *illus* 130.00
Powder & Shot, Goblet, 6 In., 6 Piece 169.00
Prayer Rug pattern is listed here as Horseshoe.
Prism & Thumbprint, Goblet, Flint, 6 ¼ In. . . . . *illus* 165.00
Puritan, Pitcher, Water, Ruby Stained, Gold Trim, 8 ½ In. 113.00
Reverse Torpedo, Pitcher, Engraved Leaf Band, 10 ¼ In. 56.00
Ribbed Ellipse, Bowl, Scalloped Edge, 3 ¼ x 8 ¼ In. 35.00
Ribbed Grape, Compote, 36 Even Scalloped Rim, 5 ¼ In. 33.00

P

Pressed Glass, Eagle, Butter, Cover, Frosted, Tab Handles, Footed, 7 ⅜ In.
$66.00

Pressed Glass, Egg & Groove, Vase, Flared, 6-Scallop Rim, Pontil, 6 x 3 ¾ In.
$44.00

Pressed Glass, Eight Panel, Celery Vase, Tulip, Fiery Opalescent, Clear Foot, 8 ½ In.
$1430.00

Pressed Glass, Eight Panel, Sugar, Cover, Cobalt Blue, Acorn Finial, Pontil, 8 ¾ In.
$920.00

Pressed Glass, Empress, Cruet, Green, Gold Trim, 7 x 3 ¼ In.
$60.00

Pressed Glass, Fine Cut & Block, Finger Bowl, Amber Stain, 3 x 4 ⅝ In.
$40.00

Historical, Tray, Campaign, Blaine, Logan, Handles, Pressed Glass, 8 ½ x 11 ½ In.
$170.00

Historical, Tray, Campaign, Cleveland, Hendricks, Handle, 9 ½ x 11 ½ In.
$250.00

Pressed Glass, Inverted Fern, Tumbler, Flint, 3 ½ In.
$143.00

Pressed Glass, Jumbo, Bowl, Cover, Elephant, 10 ⅜ x 10 ½ x 5 In.
$180.00

Pressed Glass, Klondike, Spooner, Amber Stain, Frosted, 3 ½ In.
$40.00

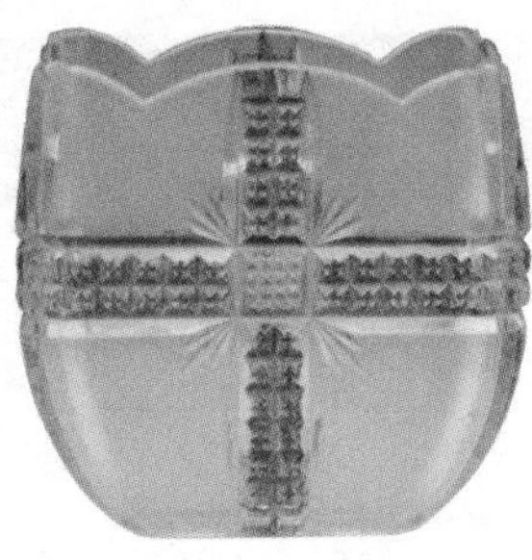

Pressed Glass, Peacock Eye, Vase, Olive Green, 6-Flute Rim, 9 ¼ x 4 In.
$990.00

Pressed Glass, Polar Bear, Waste Bowl, Frosted, Flared Rim, 3 x 5 In.
$130.00

Pressed Glass, Prism & Thumbprint, Goblet, Flint, 6 ¼ In.
$165.00

Pressed Glass, Shield & Anchor, Goblet, 6 ⅛ In.
$99.00

Pressed Glass, Swan, Jar, Pickle, 6 ½ x 3 In.
$82.00

Pressed Glass, Thistle, Candlestick, Turquoise Translucent, Sanded, Pewter Insert, 9 ¾ In.
$209.00

Pressed Glass, Three Face, Goblet, Frosted, Engraved, Leaves, 6 ¼ In.
$113.00

Pressed Glass, Toy, Berry Set, Inverted Strawberry, 1890s, 4 Piece
$102.00

Pressed Glass, Toy, Cup & Saucer, Cat & Dog, Blue
$75.00

Pressed Glass Machines

Pressed glass machines were invented in the 1820s. Molds were made of brass, iron, or other metal. A plunger forced the glass into the mold.

By the 1840s, American glasshouses were firepolishing their glass. It was reheated after shaping, "melting" the seams a little and smoothing the surface.

Ribbed Ivy, Tumbler, Whiskey, 2 ¾ In. 79.00
Ribbed Palm, Pitcher, Applied Handle, 9 In. 169.00
Ribbed Palm, Pitcher, Applied Handle, Clear, c.1875, 9 In.. . . . . 158.00
Ribbon Glass, Creamer, 6 In. 95.00
Ribbon Glass, Pitcher, Water, 8 ½ In.. . . . . 125.00
Ring & Block, Goblet, Engraved, 6 ½ x 3 In. 59.00
Roman Key, Frosted, Champagne, c.1875, 5 In. 96.00
Roman Key, Goblet, Frosted, 6 In.. . . . . 67.00
Rose In Snow, Compote, Cover, 10 x 8 In. 33.00
Rose In Snow, Water Set, 8 ¾-In. Pitcher, 7 Piece. 56.00
Ruby Rosette pattern is listed here as Hero.
Sawtooth, Creamer, Applied Handle, 6 ¾ In. 180.00
Sawtooth Band pattern is listed here as Amazon.
Scarab, Goblet, Plain Foot, 6 ¼ In. . . . . 57.00 to 90.00
Scarab, Goblet, Rayed Foot, 6 ¼ In. 102.00
Seahorse, Butter, Cover, 5 ¼ In. 135.00
Shield & Anchor, Goblet, 6 ⅛ In. . . . . *illus* 99.00
Shuttle, Goblet, 4 In., Pair. 30.00
Singing Birds, Goblet, 6 In. 146.00
Singing Birds, Pitcher, 8 ⅝ In. 203.00
Six Panel, Cake Stand, Amber Stained, 7 x 10 ½ In. 56.00
Six Panel, Pitcher, Milk, Amber Stained, 7 ¾ In. 90.00
Smocking, Creamer, Applied Handle, 5 ¼ In.. . . . . 90.00
Snail, Spooner, 6 x 3 ¾ In.. . . . . 45.00
Spanish Coin pattern is listed here as Columbian Coin.
Stork, Sugar, Cover, Stork Finial, Oval & Bar Border, 9 In. 203.00
Swan, Bowl, Scalloped Rim, Oval Footed, Cover, 6 ½ x 5 In.. . . . . 135.00
Swan, Jar, Pickle, 6 ½ x 3 In. . . . . *illus* 82.00
Swan, Pitcher, 9 ¾ In. 56.00
Swimming Swan, Goblet, 6 In. 423.00
Tennessee, Tumbler, Water, 4 In. 169.00
Texas, Compote, Cover, 10 x 6 In. 214.00
Thistle, Candlestick, Turquoise Translucent, Sanded, Pewter Insert, 9 ¾ In. . . . . *illus* 209.00
Three Face, Butter, 7 ¾ In. 79.00
Three Face, Celery Vase, Engraved Leaf Band, 1880, 9 In. 169.00
Three Face, Champagne, Hollow Stem, 4 In.. . . . . 904.00
Three Face, Claret, Engraved Flowers, Monogram, 4 ¾ In. 101.00
Three Face, Goblet, 6 ¼ In., 4 Piece. 282.00
Three Face, Goblet, Frosted, Engraved, Leaves, 6 ¼ In. . . . . *illus* 113.00
Three Face, Lamp, Kerosene, Frosted Font, Brass No. 1 Atwood Collar, 16 In. 1582.00
Three Face, Table Set, Engraved Ivy, Butter, Sugar, Creamer & Spooner, 4 Piece 955.00
Three Graces, see the related pattern Three Face.
Three Sisters pattern is listed here as Three Face.
Thumbprint, Compote, Cover, Footed, Flint, 9 In. 29.00
Thumbprint, Compote, Scallops, Stepped Hollow Stem, 12 Flutes, 9 ¾ In. 300.00
Torpedo, Lamp, Stand, 8 ¾ In. 33.00
Torpedo, Table Set, 4 Piece 67.00
Toy, Berry Set, Inverted Strawberry, 1890s, 4 Piece . . . . . *illus* 102.00
Toy, Cup & Saucer, Cat & Dog, Blue . . . . . *illus* 75.00
Toy, Cup & Saucer, Lion . . . . . *illus* 57.00
Toy, Mug, Mephistopheles, Translucent Opalescent Blue, Dragon Handle . . . . . *illus* 79.00
Toy, Nappy, Rooster . . . . . *illus* 68.00
Toy, Punch Set, Colonial, 7 Piece . . . . . *illus* 102.00
Toy, Punch Set, Nursery Rhyme, Opaque White, 1890s, 7 Piece . . . . . *illus* 102.00
Toy, Punch Set, Tulip & Honeycomb, 7 Piece . . . . . *illus* 68.00
Toy, Table Set, Acorn, 4 Piece . . . . . *illus* 395.00
Toy, Table Set, Beaded Swirl, 4 Piece . . . . . *illus* 181.00
Toy, Table Set, Doyle's No. 500, 1890s, 5 Piece . . . . . *illus* 75.00
Toy, Table Set, Drum, Frosted, 4 Piece . . . . . *illus* 226.00
Toy, Table Set, Grapevine & Ovals, 4 Piece . . . . . *illus* 147.00
Toy, Table Set, Lion, Frosted, 4 Piece . . . . . *illus* 226.00
Toy, Table Set, Rooster, Frosted, 4 Piece . . . . . *illus* 339.00
Toy, Table Set, Tulip & Honeycomb, 4 Piece . . . . . *illus* 68.00
Transverse Ribs, Compote, Round Bowl, Square Foot, 7 x 8 In. 55.00
Tree Of Life, Compote, Apple Green, Wafer, 9 x 9 In. . . . . *illus* 205.00
Tree Of Life, Pitcher, Water, Applied Handle, 9 ½ In.. . . . . 282.00
Twinkle Star pattern is listed here as Utah.

Pressed Glass, Toy, Cup & Saucer, Lion
$57.00

Pressed Glass, Toy, Mug, Mephistopheles, Translucent Opalescent Blue, Dragon Handle
$79.00

Pressed Glass, Toy, Nappy, Rooster
$68.00

Pressed Glass, Toy, Punch Set, Colonial, 7 Piece
$102.00

Pressed Glass, Toy, Punch Set, Nursery Rhyme, Opaque White, 1890s, 7 Piece
$102.00

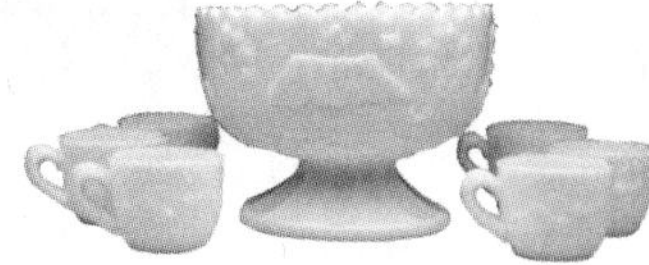

Pressed Glass, Toy, Punch Set, Tulip & Honeycomb, 7 Piece
$68.00

Pressed Glass, Toy, Table Set, Drum, Frosted, 4 Piece
$226.00

Pressed Glass, Toy, Table Set, Rooster, Frosted, 4 Piece
$339.00

Pressed Glass, Toy, Table Set, Acorn, 4 Piece
$395.00

Pressed Glass, Toy, Table Set, Grapevine & Ovals, 4 Piece
$147.00

Pressed Glass, Toy, Table Set, Tulip & Honeycomb, 4 Piece
$68.00

Pressed Glass, Toy, Table Set, Beaded Swirl, 4 Piece
$181.00

Pressed Glass, Toy, Table Set, Lion, Frosted, 4 Piece
$226.00

Pressed Glass, Tree Of Life, Compote, Apple Green, Wafer, 9 x 9 In.
$205.00

Pressed Glass, Toy, Table Set, Doyle's No. 500, 1890s, 5 Piece
$75.00

TIP

If you wash vintage dishes in a dishwasher, use a no- or low-phosphate (under 1.7 percent) dishwashing product. Read the label. Also remember that lemon-oil products are not good for silverware.

Two Owls, Compote, Cover, 13 ¼ In. 90.00
Two Owls, Sugar, Cover, 9 In. 282.00
U.S. Coin, Sauce, 3 ⅞ In. 79.00
U.S. Coin, Sugar, 6 ¾ In. 79.00
Utah, Pitcher, Footed, 9 ⅜ x 4 ½ In. 40.00
Valentine, Goblet, 5 ¾ In. 45.00
Waffle, Dish, Sweetmeat, Cover, Octagonal Finial, 8 ⅛ x 6 ½ In. 68.00
Waffle & Thumbprint, Celery Vase, Faceted Knop Stem, Flared Rim, Footed, 9 ¼ In. 110.00
Waffle & Thumbprint, Goblet, Faceted Knop Stem, 6 ¼ In. 68.00
Waffle & Thumbprint, Goblet, Flint, Pontil, 1870s, 6 ¾ x 3 ½ In. .... *illus* 60.00
Waffle & Thumbprint, Jug, Applied Handle, Qt., 9 In. 1074.00
Washington, Bowl, Cover, Low Foot, Wafer Stem, 6 ½ x 6 ½ In. 155.00
Washington Centennial, Pitcher, Applied Handle, 8 ½ In. 67.00
Westward Ho, Creamer, 7 In. 146.00
Westward Ho, Creamer, Frosted, 1890s, 7 In. 143.00
Westward Ho, Mug, Opaque White, 3 ½ In. 1017.00
Westward Ho, Mug, Opaque White, 3 ½ x 2 ⅞ In. 990.00
Westward Ho, Pitcher, Frosted, 1890s, 9 ⅜ x 5 In. 154.00
Wooden Pail pattern is listed here as Oaken Bucket.
Zippered Block, Compote, Cover, 12 ½ x 8 In. .... *illus* 100.00
Zippered Swirl & Diamond, Table Set, 4 Piece 67.00

PRINT, in this listing, means any of many printed images produced on paper by one of the more common methods, such as lithography. The prints listed here are of interest primarily to the antiques collector, not the fine arts collector. Many of these prints were originally part of books. Other prints will be found in the Advertising, Currier & Ives, Movie, and Poster categories.

Audubon bird prints were originally issued as part of books printed from 1826 to 1854. They were issued in two sheet sizes, 26 ½ inches by 39 ½ inches and 11 inches by 7 inches. The quadrupeds were issued in 28-by-22-inch prints. Later editions of the Audubon books were done in many sizes, and reprints of the books in the original size were also made. The words *After John James Audubon* appear on all of the prints, including the originals, because the pictures were made as copies of Audubon's original oil paintings. The bird pictures have been so popular they have been copied in myriad sizes by both old and new printing methods. This list includes originals and later copies because Audubon prints of all ages are sold in antiques shops.

J.W.Audubon

Audubon, Barn Owl, J. Whatman, Frame, 1836, 38 x 25 ¼ In. .... *illus* 18400.00
Audubon, Black & White Creeper, R. Havell, Engraved, c.1831, 38 ⅛ x 25 ⅝ In. 830.00
Audubon, Broad-Winged Hawk, R. Havell, Etching, Aquatint, c.1827, 38 ⅝ x 25 ⅝ In. 3851.00
Audubon, Canada Porcupine, J.T. Bowen, Lithograph, c.1844, 27 x 21 ¼ In. 2133.00
Audubon, Cat Squirrel, J.T. Bowen, Lithograph, c.1843, 26 ⅜ x 21 In. 711.00
Audubon, Common American Shrew Mole, J.T. Bowen, Lithograph, c.1843, Full Sheet 652.00
Audubon, Common Osprey Fish Hawk, Royal Octavo, Plate 15, c.1844, 8 ½ x 6 In. 920.00
Audubon, Cougar, Male, J.T. Bowen, Lithograph, c.1846, 21 ¾ x 27 ⅛ In. 4444.00
Audubon, Great Horned Owl, R. Havell, Engraved, c.1829, 38 ½ x 25 ⅜ In. 17775.00
Audubon, Key West Dove, R. Havell, Engraved, c.1833, 24 x 29 ¾ In. 889.00
Audubon, Large Tailed Skunk, J.T. Bowen, Lithograph, Frame, c.1846, Full Sheet 2133.00
Audubon, Little Chief Hare, J.T. Bowen, Lithograph, c.1846, 20 x 25 ¼ In. 326.00
Audubon, Little Owl, R. Havell, Engraved, c.1834, 38 x 24 ¾ In. 1185.00
Audubon, Long-Tailed Deer, Male, J.T. Bowen, Lithograph, c.1847, 21 ⅝ x 27 ¼ In. 1778.00
Audubon, Long-Tailed Duck, R. Havell, Engraved, c.1836, 25 ⅜ x 35 ⅝ In. 1304.00
Audubon, Mallard Duck, J. Bien, Chromolithograph, c.1860, 27 ¾ x 39 In. 1304.00
Audubon, Migratory Squirrels, Frame, 25 x 18 In. 550.00
Audubon, Mockingbird, R. Havell, Frame, c.1827, 36 ¾ 25 ¼ In. 5925.00
Audubon, Musk Ox, Imperial Quadrupeds, Plate CXI, Stone Lithograph, c.1847, 23 x 27 In. 1380.00
Audubon, Rathbone Warbler, R. Havell, Engraved, c.1831, 38 ¼ x 25 ¾ In. 1422.00
Audubon, Razor Billed Auk, R. Havell, Engraved, c.1836, 24 ¼ x 36 In. 1186.00
Audubon, Red-Bellied Squirrel, J.T. Bowen, Lithograph, 27 x 21 ¼ In. 593.00
Audubon, Ruddy Duck, R. Havell, Engraved, c.1836, 20 ¾ x 30 ¾ In. 1778.00
Audubon, Tawny Thrush, Aquatint, Hand Colored, Frame, c.1838, 31 x 22 In. 460.00
Audubon, Towhe Bunting, R. Havell, c.1831, 38 ⅛ x 25 ¾ In. 2489.00
Audubon, Uria Brunnichii, Havell Edition, CCXLV, c.1835, 28 x 38 In. 2300.00
Audubon, Vigor's Warbler, R. Havell, Lithograph, c.1831, 38 ⅛ x 25 ⅜ In. 1185.00
Audubon, White Heron, Engraved, Aquatint, Havell, Frame, c.1837, 25 x 37 In. 6900.00
Audubon, Yellow Bellied Woodpecker, Havell Edition, CXC, 29 ½ x 20 In. 2300.00
Baille, Zachary Taylor, Hero Of Buena Vista, Hand Colored, Frame, 1848, 9 x 13 In. 287.00
Barton, Mt. Rainier, Paradise Valley, c.1910, 13 x 10 In. 120.00
Benecke, Sleighing In New York, Lithograph, 30 ½ x 38 In. 58.00

Pressed Glass, Waffle & Thumbprint, Goblet, Flint, Pontil, 1870s, 6 ¾ x 3 ½ In. $60.00

Pressed Glass, Zippered Block, Compote, Cover, 12 ½ x 8 In. $100.00

P

TIP

Flies are not toilet-trained and they leave bits of their meals on pictures and paintings. These flyspecks can be removed with a knife blade.

TIP
Don't write on the back of a print with either pencil or ink. Eventually the writing will bleed through to the front.

Print, Audubon, Barn Owl, J. Whatman, Frame, 1836, 38 x 25 ¼ In.
$18400.00

Print, Icart, Woman, Cat, No. 247, Limited Edition, Frame, Stamped, 1920, 14 x 15 In.
$2400.00

TIP
Spray glass cleaner on a cloth, then wipe the glass on a framed print. Do not spray the glass because the liquid may drip and stain the mat or print.

Benjamin Franklin, Portrait, Beaver Hat, French Text, c.1777, 8 x 6 In. 767.00
Bouchoz, Botanical, Histoire Universelle Du Regne Vegetal, Frame, 22 x 17 In., 12 Piece 6250.00
Bradley, Trees, Green, Yellow, Ault & Wiborg Co., Oak Frame, 1900, 14 ¼ x 17 ¼ In. 480.00
Catesby, Mark, Arbor Foliis, Vipera Nigra, Engraved, Hand Colored, Laid Paper, Frame, 9 ½ x 13 In. 805.00
Catesby, Mark, Bastard Baltimore Bird, Catalpa Tree, Hand Colored, Engraved, Frame, 14 x 10 In. 1265.00
Catesby, Mark, Crested Jay, Hand Colored, Frame, 1754, 9 ¾ x 14 In.. .... 2185.00
Catesby, Mark, Red Mottled Rock Crab, Hand Colored, Frame, 1809, 14 x 10 In. 1035.00
Catesby, Mark, Sea Hermit Crab, Hand Colored, Frame, Late 1700s, 13 x 10 In. 978.00
Chandler, Landscape Pastel, Evening Golden Sunset Scene, c.1854-1928, 26 x 14 In. 210.00
Davidson, Babbling Brook, c.1915, 20 x 16 In. 35.00
Davidson, Diadem Aisle, Hillside Garden, c.1915, 48 x 24 In. 100.00
Davidson, Juliet Escaping, Woman On Porch, c.1915, 5 x 7 In. 88.00
Davidson, Lambs May Feast, Sheep Graze In Lakeside, c.1915, 13 x 16 In. 88.00
Dow, Arthur Wesley, Village Roofs, Ipwich Prints, Series K, Frame, c.1901, 4 x 5 ¾ In. 173.00
Erte, Costume Design, Signed, 28 x 19 In. 472.00
Erte, Slave, Signed, Silkscreen, 33 ½ x 25 ½ In. 354.00
Erte, Three Graces, Signed, Silkscreen, Embossed, 30 x 20 In. 443.00
Fox, R. Atkinson, Enchanted Steps, Garden, c.1920, 16 x 20 In. 55.00
Frodin, Eiders A Duvet, Lithography, Triple Mat, Aluminum Frame, 1900s, 21 x 26 ½ In. 35.00
Garrison, Santa Monica, c.1910, 16 x 10 In. 66.00
Gould, Great Crested Coquette Hummingbird, Gold Leaf Over Paint, c.1861, 21 x 14 In. 460.00
Gutmann, Bessie Pease, Awakening, Child Print, c.1916, 17 x 14 In.. .... 88.00
Gutmann, Bessie Pease, My Honey, African-American Child, c.1916, 17 x 14 In. 330.00
Gutmann, Bessie Pease, When I Was Sick & Lay A Bed, c.1910. .... 77.00
Higgins, Confidences, c.1900, 14 x 11 In. 50.00
Higgins, Indian Maiden, c.1900, 7 x 11 In.. .... 175.00
Higgins, Woodland Path In Winter, c.1900, 9 x 11 In.. .... 35.00
Higgins, Woodland Path In Winter, c.1900, 16 x 20 In. 45.00
Hurley, E.T., Apple Orchard, c.1899, 9 ½ x 13 ¾ In.. .... 431.00
Hurley, E.T., Autumn Woods, Brown Ink, Signed, c.1913, 12 x 6 ½ In.. .... 115.00
Hurley, E.T., Kentucky Scene, Brown Ink, Signed, c.1895, 9 x 12 In. 58.00

Icart prints were made by Louis Icart, who worked in Paris from 1907 as an employee of a postcard company. He then started printing magazines and fashion brochures. About 1910 he created a series of etchings of fashionably dressed women and he continued to make similar etchings until he died in 1950. He is well known as a printmaker, painter, and illustrator. Original etchings are much more expensive than the later photographic copies.

Icart, Don Juan, Masked Man Holding Woman, Frame, 1920s, 29 ½ x 21 In. 900.00
Icart, Etching, Nude Woman, Stockings, Heels, White Cat, Signed, Frame, 19 ½ x 11 ½ In.... 920.00
Icart, Loulou, Oval, Signed, Frame, 17 x 12 In. 550.00
Icart, Lying In The Moonlight, Signed, Frame, 8 ¼ x 6 In. 490.00
Icart, Masked Woman & Man, Aqua Tint, Signed, Frame, 1920, 15 x 18 In. 750.00
Icart, Masque Chinois, No. 66, Signed, Gilt Wood Frame, 18 x 14 In.. .... 690.00
Icart, Thais, Woman, Leopards, Aquatint, Signed, Frame, 17 x 21 ½ In. 1900.00
Icart, Woman, Cat, No. 247, Limited Edition, Frame, Stamped, 1920, 14 x 15 In. ...... *illus* 2400.00
Icart, Woman With Horned Devil, Aqua Tint, Signed, Frame, 1921, 15 x 19 In.. .... 750.00

Jacoulet prints were designed by Paul Jacoulet (1902–1960), a Frenchman who spent most of his life in Japan. He was a master of Japanese woodblock print technique. Subjects included life in Japan, the South Seas, Korea, and China. His prints were sold by subscription and issued in series. Each series had a distinctive seal, such as a sparrow or butterfly. Most Jacoulet prints are approximately 15 x 10 inches.

Jacoulet, Geisha With Teapot, Signed, Stamped, Frame, 11 ½ x 15 ½ In. 575.00
Jacoulet, Le Mandarin Aux Lunettes, Man Holding Spectacles, Frame, 25 ½ x 21 ½ In.. ..... 345.00
Jacoulet, Les Joueurs Chinois, 2 Men Playing Game, Pencil Signed, Frame, 11 ¾ x 15 ¼ In. . 711.00
Jacoulet, Les Vieux Manuscrits, Pencil Signed, Faux Bamboo Frame, 20 ½ x 17 In.. .... 402.00
James Hall, Thomas McKenney, Wa-Na-Ta, Grand Chief Of Sioux, Lithograph, Frame, 17 x 11 In. 1315.00

Japanese woodblock prints are listed as follows: Print, Japanese, name of artist, title or description, type, and size. Dealers use the following terms: Tate-e is a vertical composition. Yoko-e is a horizontal composition. The words Aiban (13 by 9 inches), Chuban (10 by 7 ½ inches), Hosoban (13 by 6 inches), Koban (7 by 4 inches), Nagaban (20 x 9 inches), Oban (15 by 10 inches), Shikishiban (8 x 9 inches), and Tanzaku (15 x 5 inches) denote approximate size. Modern versions of some of these prints have been made. Other woodblock prints that are not Japanese are listed under Print, Woodblock.

Japanese, Azechi, Umetaro, Autumn, Mat, Frame, 20th Century, 13 ½ x 10 ½ In. 173.00

Japanese, Hasui, Kawase, Spring Rain, Woman With Parasol, Bamboo Frame, 14 x 9 In. 360.00
Japanese, Hiroshige, Hot Springs, Near Shuzen Temple, Woodblock, Mat, Frame, 21 x 17 In.. 161.00
Japanese, Hoshi, Spring, Woodblock, Snow Covered Tree, Gold Wood Frame, 10 ½ x 8 In. ... 575.00
Japanese, Saito Kiyoshi, Flowering Shrub, Kamakura, c.1950, 15 x 21 In. ... 448.00
Japanese, Yoshitora, Utagawa, Triptych, Harbor Scene, Frame, Late 19th Century, 20 x 34 In. 323.00
Keep, Portland Head Light, Seascape Lighthouse, c.1905, 10 x 8 In. ... 88.00
Kurz & Allison, Battle Between The Monitor & Merrimac, Mat, c.1889, 22 x 28 In. ... 690.00
Kurz & Allison, Battle Of Atlanta, Mat, c.1888, 22 x 28 ¼ In. ... 690.00
Kurz & Allison, Battle Of Bull Run, Mat, c.1889, 22 x 27 In. ... 460.00
Kurz & Allison, Battle Of Chattanooga, Mat, c.1888, 22 ⅝ x 28 ¼ In. ... 489.00
Kurz & Allison, Battle Of Corinth, Mat, Frame, c.1891, 20 ¾ x 27 ¾ In. ... 322.00
Kurz & Allison, Battle Of Five Forks, Mat, c.1886, 21 ½ x 28 ¼ In. ... 460.00
Kurz & Allison, Battle Of Franklin, Mat, c.1891, 21 ¾ x 28 In. ... 348.00
Kurz & Allison, Battle Of Gettysburg, Mat, Frame, c.1884, 21 x 28 In. ... 431.00
Kurz & Allison, Battle Of Lookout Mountain, Mat, c.1889, 21 ¼ x 27 ¾ In. ... 431.00
Kurz & Allison, Battle Of Olustree, Florida, Mat, c.1894, 22 x 28 In. ... 316.00
Kurz & Allison, Battle Of Resaca, Mat, c.1889, 22 x 28 In. ... 1840.00
Mourlot, Flower, Chromolithograph, Josef Nigg, Mat, Frame, 39 ½ x 34 ¼ In. ... 59.00

Nutting prints are now popular with collectors. Wallace Nutting is known for his pictures, furniture, and books. Nutting prints are actually hand-colored photographs issued from 1900 to 1941. There are over 10,000 different titles. Wallace Nutting furniture is listed in the Furniture category.

Nutting, Affectionately Yours, c.1915, 12 x 10 In. ... 35.00
Nutting, Apple Pool, Signed, Frame, 1930-35, 20 x 30 In. ... 550.00
Nutting, April In The Sheep Pasture, c.1900, 20 x 8 ½ In. ... 210.00
Nutting, At The Ford, Original Mat, Signed, Frame, 1905-10, 11 x 14 In. ... 770.00
Nutting, Autumn Days, c.1915, 16 x 13 In. ... 270.00
Nutting, Bonny Dale, Stream Runs Through Green Meadow, c.1915, 18 x 22 In. ... 135.00
Nutting, Capture Of A Red Coat, c.1915, 10 x 12 In. ... 120.00
Nutting, Cloud Capped Towers, Signed, Mat, Frame, 1900-10, 17 x 14 In. ... 475.00
Nutting, Cluster Of Zinnias, Floral Still Life, c.1930, 16 x 20 In. ... 176.00
Nutting, Coming Out Of Rosa, Little Rosa & Mother Under Trellis, c.1915, 16 x 13 In. ... 66.00
Nutting, Connecticut Homestead, c.1915, 12 x 10 In. ... 90.00
Nutting, Enticing Waters, Signed, Original Mat, Frame, 1930-35, 20 x 30 In. ... 550.00
Nutting, Errand, Signed, Original Mat, Frame, 1915-25, 17 x 13 In. ... 550.00
Nutting, Errand, Young Girl At Open Gate, c.1915, 13 x 17 In. ... 550.00
Nutting, Four O'Clock, Cows On Hillside, c.1900, 14 x 17 In. ... 310.00
Nutting, Garden Steps, c.1930, 9 x 11 In. ... 130.00
Nutting, Garden Temple, Montibello, Va., Mat, Frame, c.1915-25, 13 x 16 In. ... *illus* 650.00
Nutting, Girl Leans On Fence, Pen & Ink Silhouette, Frame, c.1927, 4 x 4 In. ... 66.00
Nutting, Going Forth Of Betty, c.1900, 14 x 17 In. ... 55.00
Nutting, Guardian Mother, 1905-10, Frame, 14 x 7 In. ... 940.00
Nutting, Hide & Seek Cottage, Signed, Original Mat, Frame, 1920, 12 x 14 In. ... 210.00
Nutting, Home Among The Roses, Frame, 1915-25, 15 x 12 In. ... 550.00
Nutting, Larkspur, Thatch-Roofed Cottage Scene, 1915, 14 x 17 In. ... 110.00
Nutting, Little Washer Women, Amalfi, Signed, Mat, Frame, 1915-25, 16 x 13 In. ... 770.00
Nutting, Mexican Zinnias, Signed, Original Mat, Frame, 1930-35, 16 x 13 In. ... 440.00
Nutting, Midsummer Vale, Original Mat, Signed, Frame, Ireland, c.1920, 22 x 18 In. ... 77.00
Nutting, On The Teith, Frame, 1915-25, 14 x 17 In. ... 154.00
Nutting, Orchard Brook, Blossom Trees Beside Rippling Stream, c.1930, 20 x 16 In. ... 88.00
Nutting, Palms By The Pool, c.1915, 12 x 15 In. ... 275.00
Nutting, Patti's Favorite Walk, c.1915, 17 x 14 In. ... 165.00
Nutting, Purity & Grace, c.1930, 17 x 22 In. ... 145.00
Nutting, Reading From Arabian Nights, Frame, c.1900-10, 13 x 16 In. ... 165.00
Nutting, Rhode Island Coast, Rhode Island Seascape With Calm Water, c.1915, 26 x 14 In. ... 330.00
Nutting, Roses & Larkspur, Signed, Original Mat, Frame, 1930-35, 13 x 16 In. ... 330.00
Nutting, Sailing Among Windmills, c.1915, 16 x 12 In. ... 175.00
Nutting, Shaded Bridge, Signed, Original Mat, Frame, 1915-25, 14 x 17 In. ... 275.00
Nutting, Smoke Of Evening Fires, c.1915, 16 x 10 In. ... 88.00
Nutting, Spinning At Eight-Four, Signed, Mat, Frame, 1900-10, 14 x 16 In. ... 330.00
Nutting, Stitch In Time, c.1930, 11 x 9 In. ... 110.00
Nutting, Swarthmore, Signed, Original Mat, Frame, 1915-25, 16 x 13 In. ... 358.00
Nutting, Three Chums, Scene With Cats, c.1915, 20 x 16 In. ... 330.00
Nutting, Tiger Lilies & Elder, Garden, c.1915, 13 x 16 In. ... 165.00
Nutting, Tower At Swords, Original Mat, Signed, Frame, 1915-25, 22 x 17 In. ... 830.00
Nutting, Tree At The Bridge, Mat, Frame, c.1915-25, 13 x 16 In. ... *illus* 130.00

Print, Nutting, Garden Temple, Montibello, Va., Mat, Frame, c.1915-25, 13 x 16 In.
$650.00

Print, Nutting, Tree At The Bridge, Mat, Frame, c.1915-25, 13 x 16 In.
$130.00

Kurz and Allison

Most Kurz and Allison prints were pictures of Civil War battlefields. Louis Kurz immigrated to the United States from Austria in 1852. He founded the Chicago Lithographing Co. in 1863. He was a Union solder whom President Lincoln asked to record war scenes. He made 36 color lithographs. He and Alexander Allison were partners from 1880 to 1903. They made hundreds of colored and black and white lithographs of battles and of animals, people, religious subjects, and scenery.

Test the Picture
You can often take a painting, print, or photograph home from a shop or show to see how it will look on your wall. Sometimes pictures or furniture can be too big for your house, too large for the space, too high to get in the room, or just plain wrong to your eyes. Talk to the dealer and see if it is okay to give the picture a trial. Pay for the piece and get a signed paid bill that says you can return it. If you love a heavy collectible and can't lift it, you might even make a deal to have it delivered to your home if you live nearby.

Print, Woodblock, Norton, Elizabeth, Gated Field Of Trees, Signed, Frame, 1922, 6 x 4 ½ In.
$650.00

TIP
Mold is living and will spread. Keep "foxed" prints away from any others.

Nutting, Under Table Rock, Signed, Original Mat, Frame, 1900-10, 10 x 8 In. 330.00
Nutting, Warm Spring Day, Grazing Sheep, c.1915, 22 x 15 In. 154.00
Nutting, Watching For Papa, Signed, Original Mat, Frame, 1915-25, 17 x 14 In. 550.00
Nutting, Water Paths Of Venice, Signed, Mat, Frame, 1915-25, 14 x 10 In. 610.00
Nutting, Wayside's Colonial Dignity, c.1915, 12 x 9 In. 330.00
Nutting, Winslow Water, c.1905, 17 x 14 In. 88.00

Parrish prints are wanted by collectors. Maxfield Frederick Parrish was an illustrator who lived from 1870 to 1966. He is best known as a designer of magazine covers, posters, calendars, and advertisements. His prints have been copied in recent years.

Parrish, Air Castles, Frame, 19 x 15 In. 100.00
Parrish, Daybreak, Frame, Early 1900s, 17 ½ x 29 ½ In. 145.00 to 250.00
Parrish, Daydream, Frame, 23 x 35 In. 225.00
Parrish, Evening, Frame, 16 ¼ x 13 ½ In. 100.00
Parrish, Garden Of Allah, Frame, Early 1900s, 14 ½ x 29 ½ In. 120.00 to 250.00
Parrish, Garden Scene, Woman At Pool, Frame, 15 x 30 In. 225.00
Parrish, Lute Players, Frame, 10 x 18 In. 195.00
Parrish, Morning, Original Mat, Frame, c.1922, 9 ½ x 6 In. 110.00
Parrish, Talking Oak, c.1908, 9 x 11 In. 99.00
Parrish, Triptych, Canyon, Daybreak, Wild Geese, Frame, c.1920, 20 x 54 In. 405.00
Parrish, Triptych, Old King Cole, Frame, 6 ½ x 8 ½ In. 330.00
Ritchie, Alexander Hay, 3 Members Of Temperance Society, Black & White, Frame, 22 x 29 In. 144.00
Sawyer, Acadia National Park, c.1910, 11 x 9 In. 66.00
Sawyer, Adirondacks, Lake Champlain, c.1910, 11 x 9 In. 99.00
Sawyer, Echo Lake, c.1910, 12 x 10 In. 50.00
Sawyer, February Morning, Winter Snow Scene, c.1910, 7 x 8 In. 99.00
Sawyer, Mount Katahdin, Birch Trees, Lake, c.1910, 9 x 7 In. 198.00
Sawyer, Mt. Chocorua, c.1910, 16 x 13 In. 55.00
Sawyer, Mt. Washington, c.1910, 13 x 10 In. 175.00
Sawyer, Thunder Hole, c.1910, 8 x 10 In. 330.00
Standley, Aspens, Colorado, c.1920, 13 x 15 In. 120.00
Standley, Pikes Peak From Woodland Park, c.1910, 18 x 22 In. 385.00
Thompson, Milady Fair, c.1900, 11 x 17 In. 66.00
Thompson, Minuet, Colonial Interior Scene With Man & Piano, c.1900, 17 x 14 In. 187.00
Thompson, Priscilla Spinning, c.1900, 17 x 14 In. 55.00
Thompson, Rock Bound Coast, Surf Crashes Over Rocks, c.1900, 16 x 13 In. 35.00
Thulstrop, Sheridan's Ride, Winchester, Signed, Frame, c.1880, 17 x 20 ¾ In. 385.00
Thulstrop, Sherman's March To The Sea, Frame, c.1883, 27 x 38 In. 330.00
Ward, T., Livery Stable, Colored, Brown Horse, Shown To Man & Woman, Gilt Frame, 21 x 29 In. 150.00
Wight, Gulls Along The Shore, c.1900, 12 x 10 In. 121.00

Woodblock prints that are not in the Japanese tradition are listed here. Most were made in England and the United States during the Arts & Crafts period. Japanese woodblock prints are listed under Print, Japanese.

Woodblock, Astronomy, Hand Colored, Mat, Frame, Mid 1800s, 16 x 15 In., 18 Piece 8750.00
Woodblock, Hyde, Helen, Woman, Child, Landscape, Signed, Frame, 5 ½ x 4 ½ In. 420.00
Woodblock, Hyde, Helen, Woman, Child In Window, Signed, Frame, 1913, 8 x 8 In. 600.00
Woodblock, Hyde, Helen, Woman & Infant, Mat, Signed, Frame, 1909, 9 x 6 In. 375.00
Woodblock, Lum, Bertha, 4 Girls, Trees, Signed, Frame, 1913, 17 x 12 In. 830.00
Woodblock, Mystic River, Art & Crafts, Green, White, Frame, 8 x 6 In. 325.00
Woodblock, Norton, Elizabeth, Gated Field Of Trees, Signed, Frame, 1922, 6 x 4 ½ In. . . *illus* 650.00
Woodblock, Woman, Wiping Hands On Cloth, Laid Rice Paper, Silk Mat, Japan, Frame, 14 x 10 In. 46.00
Woodcut, Glen Ellyn Woods, Henry Foot, Multicolored, Frame, c.1930, 16 x 17 ½ In. 1200.00

PURINTON POTTERY COMPANY was incorporated in Wellsville, Ohio, in 1936. The company moved to Shippenville, Pennsylvania, in 1941 and made a variety of hand-painted ceramic wares. By the 1950s Purinton was making dinnerware, souvenirs, cookie jars, and florist wares. The pottery closed in 1959.

Apple, Bowl, Dessert, 4 In. 9.00
Apple, Cookie Jar, Cover, 9 ½ In. 70.00
Apple, Creamer, Cover, Handle, 6 ½ In. 20.00
Apple, Grease Jar, Cover, 5 ½ In. 28.00
Apple, Plate, Breakfast, 8 ½ In. 10.00
Apple, Salt & Pepper, Jugs, 2 ¾ In. 12.00
Apple, Sugar, Cover. 9.50
Apple, Tea Set, Teapot, Lid, Covered Sugar, Creamer 160.00

Apple, Teapot, 4 In., 2 Cup 50.00
Cornucopia, Vase, Floral Pattern, Stamped, 6 In. 25.00
Fruit, Canister, Coffee, Cover, 9 In. 35.00
Fruit, Sugar & Creamer, Cover 16.00
Fruit, Teapot, Individual, 2 Cup 50.00
Fruit, Tumbler, Water, 12 Oz., Pair 40.00
Heather Plaid, Plate, Dinner, 9 ½ In.. .... 6.50
Intaglio, Bowl, Dessert, Brown, 4 In.. .... 6.00
Intaglio, Mug, Brown, 8 Oz.. .... 25.00
Intaglio, Mug, Brown, 16 Oz.. .... 13.50
Intaglio, Plate, Dinner, Brown, 9 ¾ In.. .... 12.50
Intaglio, Platter, Brown, 12 ½ In. 32.00
Intaglio, Snack Set, Brown, 8 ½ In. 12.50
Intaglio, Sugar, Cover, Brown 33.00
Ivy, Honey Jug, 6 ½ In. 35.00
Mountain Rose, Planter, Basket Form, 6 ½ In. 50.00
Mountain Rose, Teapot, 2 Cups, 4 In. 45.00
Normandy Plaid, Beer Mug, 16 Oz. 35.00
Normandy Plaid, Cup 10.00
Normandy Plaid, Plate, Dinner, 9 ½ In.. .... 8.50 to 12.50
Normandy Plaid, Salt & Pepper, Jug Shape, Cork Stopper 12.50
Normandy Plaid, Sugar, No Lid, Handles 10.00
Petals, Honey Jug, Loop Handle, 7 In. 45.00
Shooting Star, Vase, 6 In. 25.00

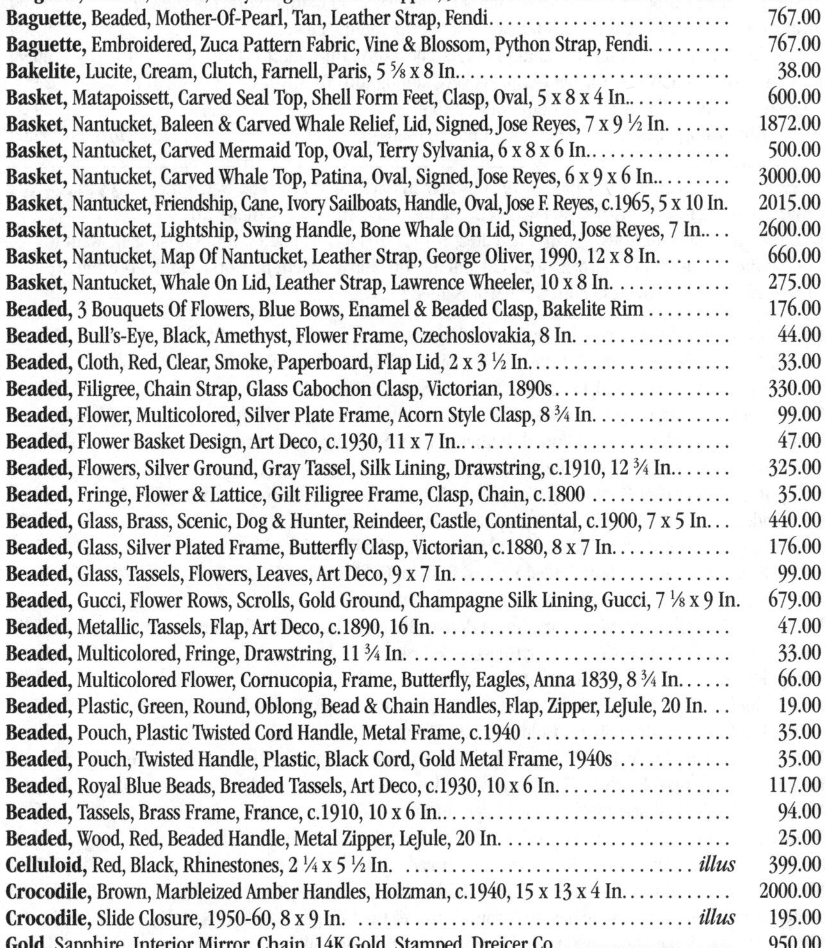

PURSES have been recognizable since the eighteenth century, when leather and needlework purses were preferred. Beaded purses became popular in the nineteenth century, went out of style, but are again in use. Mesh purses date from the 1880s and are still being made. How to carry a handkerchief and lipstick is a problem today for every woman, including the Queen of England.

Alligator, Leather, Brown, Baby Alligator Hide Wrapped, 9 ¾ In. .... *illus* 150.00
Baguette, Beaded, Mother-Of-Pearl, Tan, Leather Strap, Fendi 767.00
Baguette, Embroidered, Zuca Pattern Fabric, Vine & Blossom, Python Strap, Fendi 767.00
Bakelite, Lucite, Cream, Clutch, Farnell, Paris, 5 ⅝ x 8 In.. .... 38.00
Basket, Matapoissett, Carved Seal Top, Shell Form Feet, Clasp, Oval, 5 x 8 x 4 In.. .... 600.00
Basket, Nantucket, Baleen & Carved Whale Relief, Lid, Signed, Jose Reyes, 7 x 9 ½ In. 1872.00
Basket, Nantucket, Carved Mermaid Top, Oval, Terry Sylvania, 6 x 8 x 6 In.. .... 500.00
Basket, Nantucket, Carved Whale Top, Patina, Oval, Signed, Jose Reyes, 6 x 9 x 6 In.. .... 3000.00
Basket, Nantucket, Friendship, Cane, Ivory Sailboats, Handle, Oval, Jose F. Reyes, c.1965, 5 x 10 In. 2015.00
Basket, Nantucket, Lightship, Swing Handle, Bone Whale On Lid, Signed, Jose Reyes, 7 In... 2600.00
Basket, Nantucket, Map Of Nantucket, Leather Strap, George Oliver, 1990, 12 x 8 In. 660.00
Basket, Nantucket, Whale On Lid, Leather Strap, Lawrence Wheeler, 10 x 8 In. 275.00
Beaded, 3 Bouquets Of Flowers, Blue Bows, Enamel & Beaded Clasp, Bakelite Rim 176.00
Beaded, Bull's-Eye, Black, Amethyst, Flower Frame, Czechoslovakia, 8 In. 44.00
Beaded, Cloth, Red, Clear, Smoke, Paperboard, Flap Lid, 2 x 3 ½ In. 33.00
Beaded, Filigree, Chain Strap, Glass Cabochon Clasp, Victorian, 1890s 330.00
Beaded, Flower, Multicolored, Silver Plate Frame, Acorn Style Clasp, 8 ¾ In. 99.00
Beaded, Flower Basket Design, Art Deco, c.1930, 11 x 7 In.. .... 47.00
Beaded, Flowers, Silver Ground, Gray Tassel, Silk Lining, Drawstring, c.1910, 12 ¾ In.. .... 325.00
Beaded, Fringe, Flower & Lattice, Gilt Filigree Frame, Clasp, Chain, c.1800 .... 35.00
Beaded, Glass, Brass, Scenic, Dog & Hunter, Reindeer, Castle, Continental, c.1900, 7 x 5 In... 440.00
Beaded, Glass, Silver Plated Frame, Butterfly Clasp, Victorian, c.1880, 8 x 7 In. 176.00
Beaded, Glass, Tassels, Flowers, Leaves, Art Deco, 9 x 7 In. 99.00
Beaded, Gucci, Flower Rows, Scrolls, Gold Ground, Champagne Silk Lining, Gucci, 7 ⅛ x 9 In. 679.00
Beaded, Metallic, Tassels, Flap, Art Deco, c.1890, 16 In. 47.00
Beaded, Multicolored, Fringe, Drawstring, 11 ¾ In. 33.00
Beaded, Multicolored Flower, Cornucopia, Frame, Butterfly, Eagles, Anna 1839, 8 ¾ In. 66.00
Beaded, Plastic, Green, Round, Oblong, Bead & Chain Handles, Flap, Zipper, LeJule, 20 In. .. 19.00
Beaded, Pouch, Plastic Twisted Cord Handle, Metal Frame, c.1940 .... 35.00
Beaded, Pouch, Twisted Handle, Plastic, Black Cord, Gold Metal Frame, 1940s 35.00
Beaded, Royal Blue Beads, Breaded Tassels, Art Deco, c.1930, 10 x 6 In. 117.00
Beaded, Tassels, Brass Frame, France, c.1910, 10 x 6 In.. .... 94.00
Beaded, Wood, Red, Beaded Handle, Metal Zipper, LeJule, 20 In. 25.00
Celluloid, Red, Black, Rhinestones, 2 ¼ x 5 ½ In. .... *illus* 399.00
Crocodile, Brown, Marbleized Amber Handles, Holzman, c.1940, 15 x 13 x 4 In. 2000.00
Crocodile, Slide Closure, 1950-60, 8 x 9 In. .... *illus* 195.00
Gold, Sapphire, Interior Mirror, Chain, 14K Gold, Stamped, Dreicer Co. 950.00

Purse, Alligator, Leather, Brown, Baby Alligator Hide Wrapped, 9 ¾ In.
$150.00

Purse, Celluloid, Red, Black, Rhinestones, 2 ¼ x 5 ½ In.
$399.00

Purse, Crocodile, Slide Closure, 1950-60, 8 x 9 In.
$195.00

Purse, Mesh, Enamel On Silver Plate, Whiting & Davis, 6 x 5 In.
$52.00

Purse, Wood, Glitter Bugs, Leather Handles, Enid Collins, 1960s, 5 ½ x 11 In.
$95.00

Types of Compacts

Flapjacks

Flapjacks are oversized compacts about 4 to 6 inches in diameter. They were popular in the 1930s and made of plastic as well as metal, often with modern designs.

Minaudiere

A minaudiere is a jeweled box-purse often of gold that became popular in the 1930s. It is expensive, valuable for its gold and jewels and workmanship, and cleverly designed.

Necessaire

A necessaire is an expensive vanity case used for formal events. The case, usually silver and enamel, had compartments for powder, rouge, lipstick, and cigarettes. They were popular from 1915 into the 1930s.

Tango

A tango is a small purse or lipstick case attached to a chair with a finger loop. It was popular in the 1920s and '30s to be carried when dancing.

Vanity Cases

A vanity case is a compact plus more. It is a case, perhaps a small purse or box, for a dressing table. It holds rouge, mascara, powder, puff, mirror, lipstick, etc.

Gold, Woven, Diamond Melee Clasp, Clutch, Mirrored Interior, 18K Gold, Italy. 9006.00
Gold Link, Cathedral Style, Art Deco, Engraved Flower On Mounting, 1920s 165.00
Kidskin, Turquoise Ornament, Gilt, Onyx Border, Clutch, Cartier, c.1925, 5 ½ x 9 In. 6000.00
Leather, Beige Quilted, Red Patent Trim, Gold Tone Strap, Chanel, Box 1475.00
Leather, Black, Alligator Head Clasp, Strap, Feet, Barry Kieselstein-Cord . . . . 593.00 to 1304.00
Leather, Black, Kelly, Lock, Hermes, 8 ½ x 12 x 5 In.. . . . . 1900.00
Leather, Black, Quilted Exterior, Gold Tone Hardware, Chanel, Box 2360.00
Leather, Black, Sailboat Clasp, Clutch, Hermes, 6 ½ In. 120.00
Leather, Blue, Clutch, Blue, Leather, 18K Gold Fittings, Hermes, 5 x 9 In.. . . . . 495.00
Leather, Box Shape, Burgundy, Flap Closure, Sleeves, Pockets, Mirror, 26 x 18 x 4 In.. . . . . 474.00
Leather, Ivory, Flap, Sleeves, Pockets, Mirror, Hermes, 26 x 18 x 4 In.. . . . . 474.00
Leather, Kelly, Black, Goldtone Hardware, Shoulder Strap, Hermes, Box, 1975. . . . . 830.00
Leather, Kelly, Orange, Goldtone Hardware, Shoulder Strap, Hermes, Box, 1994 . . . . 4148.00
Leather, Leonor, Strap, Suede Interior, Louis Vuitton 1067.00
Leather, Quilted, Sleeper Bag, Chanel, Box, 13 ½ In.. . . . . 1185.00
Leather, Rhinestone, Gilt Metal Shoulder Strap, Compact, Judith Leiber, 5 ¼ In. Purse, 2 Piece 1440.00
Lucite, Amber, 2 Handles, Stamped, France, 11 ¼ x 8 ½ x 4 ⅜ In.. . . . . 55.00
Mesh, 14K Gold, Flower Openwork Frame, Acorn Clasp, Blue Stones, Link Handle, 5 x 6 In. . . 3335.00
Mesh, Aluminum, Off White Satin Lining, Double Chain, Whiting & Davis, Box, 8 x 7 In.. . . . . 81.00
Mesh, Chatelaine, Diamonds, Rubies, Drawstring, 18K Gold, c.1900, 11 In. 1800.00
Mesh, Enamel On Silver Plate, Whiting & Davis, 6 x 5 In.. . . . . *illus* 52.00
Mesh, Gold, Wrist Strap, Whiting & Davis, 5 x 5 In.. . . . . 11.00
Mesh, Peafowl, Multicolored Enamel, Flowers, Scroll, Fringe, Hinged, Mandalian, 8 ¾ In. . . . 275.00
Mesh, Row Of Rubies, Diamond, Rose Cut, 14K Gold, No. 42834, Edwardian 7110.00
Mesh, Sterling Silver, Blue Enamel, c.1920, 4 ½ In.. . . . . 60.00
Mesh, Sterling Silver, Repousse Top, Expands, Chain Handle, 3 In. 190.00
Mesh, Sterling Silver, Scroll Top, Beaded Sides, Gorham. 400.00
Needlepoint, Flower Vase, Multicolored, Black Ground, Chain, 7 In.. . . . . 22.00
Satin, Black, Damask, Rhinestone Clasp, Evening Bag, 1930s 65.00
Silver, Egg Shape, Engraved Fish Scales, Interior Folds, Coin Purse, Russia, c.1880, 3 In.. . . . . 590.00
Silver, Jugendstil, Amethyst Cabochons, Mother-Of-Pearl, Mesh Body, Chain Link Handle. . . . 356.00
Snakeskin, Crown, Gold Tone Closure, Shoulder Strap, Judith Leiber. 797.00
Snakeskin, Rhinestone, Chrome, Chain Link Handle, Coin Purse, Judith Leiber, 4 ½ x 6 In. . 2160.00
Sterling Silver, Cabochon Garnet Clasp, Pockets, Monogram, Tiffany & Co., 3 ½ x 2 ¾ In. . . 323.00
Tapestry, Flowers, Plastic Frame, Coin Purse, c.1950 . . . . 24.00
Wood, Glitter Bugs, Leather Handles, Enid Collins, 1960s, 5 ½ x 11 In. . . . . *illus* 95.00

Quezal

QUEZAL glass was made from 1901 to 1924 by Martin Bach, Sr., in Queens, New York. Other glassware by other firms, such as Loetz, Steuben, and Tiffany, resembles this gold-colored iridescent glass. Martin Bach died in 1921. His son-in-law, Conrad Vahlsing, Jr., went to work at the Lustre Art Company about 1920 and his son, Martin Bach, Jr., worked at the Durand Art Glass division of the Vineland Flint Glass Works after 1924.

Bowl, Green Pulled Feather, Iridescent, Gold, White Ground, Footed, 4 x 6 ½ In. . . . . *illus* 5750.00
Candlestick, Iridescent Blue, Baluster, Footed, Signed, 7 In. . . . . *illus* 425.00
Candlestick, Iridescent Gold, Coil, Opal, Baluster, Signed, 7 In.. . . . . 518.00
Chandelier, 4-Light, King Tut Shades, Cast Bronze, Dolphin Arms, 8 x 30 In. . . . . 920.00 to 1725.00
Compote, Flower Shape, Green Pulled Feathers, Zipper Stem, Signed, 6 In. 2300.00
Compote, Gold Over Opaque White, Rolled Rim, 5 In. 650.00
Compote, White Pulled Feather, Applied Saucer Foot, Iridescent Gold Zipper, 6 x 6 ½ In. 1438.00
Cup, Iridescent Gold, Blue Highlights, Applied Gold Handle, 2 In. 180.00
Cup & Saucer, Iridescent Gold, Rainbow, Magenta, Scrolled Handle, 2 & 4 In.. . . . . 575.00
Cup & Saucer, Iridescent Gold Pulled Hooked Feather, Gold Handle, 5 x 2 ½ In. . . . . . . *illus* 270.00
Epergne, 3-Lily, Trumpet, Center, White Iridescent, 7 x 12 In. 1035.00
Lamp, 2-Light, Helmet Shades, Ivory, Green Hooked Feather, Hammered Cross Base, 20 In. . . 5175.00
Lamp, Desk, Tulip Shade, Gold Zipper, Gooseneck, Brass, 11 ¾ In.. . . . . 1610.00
Lamp, Flower Shape Shade, Iridescent Gold, Curved Leaf, Vine Arm, 11 In.. . . . . 444.00
Lamp, Gold & Cobalt Blue Pulled Feather & Hook, Iridescent Opal Ground, 12 x 25 In. 1495.00
Lamp, Hanging, Teardrop Shade, Gold & Cream Fishnet, 9 ¼ x 6 ¼ In.. . . . . 2588.00
Lamp, Mushroom Shade, King Tut, Gold Iridescent, Green Ground, Highlights, 13 x 10 In. . . 5750.00
Lamp, Yellow Hooked Feather, White Ground, Iridescent Gold, Green Outline, 27 In.. . . . . 1725.00
Perfume Bottle, Iridescent Gold, Cone Shape, 4 Ribs, 6-Sided Stopper, Signed, 8 In. 776.00
Rondel, Iridescent Gold, Center Hole, Stretched Rim, Pink & Blue Detail, 12 In. 1610.00
Shade, Bell Shape, Opal, Gold Hearts, Overall Threading, Ribbed, Signed, 4 ½ In.. . . . . 201.00
Shade, Cream, Gold Interior, Applied Green, Gold Leaves, Threading, 5 ½ x 2 ¼ In. 200.00
Shade, Dome Shape, White Opalescent Ground, Allover Gold Zipper, Cased, 11 x 10 In.. . . . . . 3335.00
Shade, Flower Shape, Blue, Gold Pulled Feather Design, Opalescent, 5 x 6 In., Pair. 900.00

Shade, Gold Hooked Feather, Ivory Ground, Signed, 5 ½ x 4 In. 230.00
Shade, Gold Pulled Feather, Green Trim, Opalescent Ground, Ribbed, 5 ¼ x 5 ½ In., Pair. 259.00
Shade, Green & Platinum Pulled Feather, Emerald Green Ground, Ribbed, 5 ⅛ In., Pair 3738.00
Shade, Green Flower, Gold Iridescent Vertical Heart & Vine, White Ground, 5 In. 2300.00
Shade, Green Pulled Feather, Gold Trim, Iridescent Ivory, Signed, 5 In., 3 Piece 403.00
Shade, Green Pulled Feathers, Iridescent, Orange, Gold Interior, Signed, 2 ½ In. 95.00
Shade, Iridescent Gold, Green Pulled Feather, Opal, Ribbed, Signed, 3 ¾ x 2 ¼ In., Pair 480.00
Shade, Iridescent Gold, Platinum, Pink Highlights, Red Detail, Ribbed, 5 ¼ In. 173.00
Shade, Iridescent Gold, Pulled Feather, Glass, Ribbed, 5 ¼ x 5 In., Pair 360.00
Shade, Iridescent Gold, Pulled Feather, Green Trim, Ribbed Opal Ground, 5 ½ x 2 ¼ In. 115.00
Shade, Iridescent Gold, Pulled Feather, White Ground, Opalescent, Ribbed, 6 x 2 ¼ In., Pair 920.00
Shade, Iridescent Gold, Ribbed, 4 ½ In., Pair 250.00
Shade, Iridescent Gold, Threading, White Pulled Feathers, Metal Rings, 8 In., 4 Piece 403.00
Shade, Iridescent Gold Finish, Scalloped Edge, White Opalescent, Ribbed, 4 ¼ In., Pair 403.00
Shade, Iridescent Gold Zipper, Opalescent, Pinched Waist, 4 x 2 ¼ In., 6 Piece 1150.00
Shade, Iridescent White, Custard Interior, Ruffled Edge, Signed, 6 ¾ x 5 In., Pair 201.00
Shade, Lily, Pulled Feather, Green & White Opalescent, Gold, Signed, 4 ½ In. 500.00
Shade, Opal, Iridescent Gold Zipper, Signed, 4 ½ x 2 ¼ In. 86.00
Shade, Opal, Ribbed, Gold Luster Interior, Signed, 5 ¼ x 2 ¼ In., Pair 230.00
Shade, Opalescent, Pulled Iridescent Gold, Bulbous, Signed 4 x 4 In., Pair 720.00
Shade, Platinum Pulled Feather, Green Striped Ground, Iridescent Interior, Signed, 5 x 2 In. 1610.00
Shade, Pulled Feather, White Pulled Feather, Iridescent Gold Ground, Ribbed, 6 ¼ In. 210.00
Shade, Pulled Heart, White, Gold Threading, Scalloped Rim, Signed, 5 ¼ In. 125.00
Shade, Snake Skin, Green, Iridescent Platinum, Fitted Rim, Signed, 7 In. 3600.00
Shade, Trumpet, Gold Hooked Feather, Ivory Ground, Rib, Optic, Scalloped Rim, 2 x 7 In. 518.00
Shade, Tulip Shape, Green, Gold Pulled Feather Design, Opalescent, Ribbed, 5 x 5 In., Pair 720.00
Shade, Tulip Shape, Opalescent, Ribbed, Signed, 5 x 5 In., Pair 300.00
Shade, White, Gold Interior, Iridescent Gold Threading, Pulled Heart, 5 In. 125.00
Shade, White, Threading, Signed, 5 ⅜ In. 166.00
Shade, White Opalescent, Iridescent Gold Zipper, Bulbous Shoulder, 4 ½ x 2 ¼ In., Pair 230.00
Shade, Yellow & Iridescent Gold, Hooked Feather, Signed, 3 ⅛ In. 460.00
Shades, White, Gold, Iridescent Threading, Pulled Heart, 6 ¼ In., Pair 275.00
Vase, Flower Shape, Green Leaf, Iridescent Gold, White Pulled Feather, 4 In. 1265.00
Vase, Flower Shape, Green Pulled Feathers, Opal Ground, Pinched Waist, Scalloped Rim, 6 In. 1495.00
Vase, Flower Shape, Iridescent Gold Ribs, Red Detail, Foot, 10 ¼ In. 2760.00
Vase, Flower Shape, Iridescent Green, Gold, Pulled & Hooked Feather, 10 In. 3162.00
Vase, Flower Shape, Pulled Feathers, Gold Tipt, Onion Skin Gold Interior, Footed, 6 ¼ In. 431.00
Vase, Gold, Iridescent Magenta, Bulbous, 3 Pulled Handles, 8 In. 660.00
Vase, Gold & Blue Leaves, Gold Threads, Flared Rim, Marked, 6 ½ In. 863.00
Vase, Gold Hooked Feather, Cream Ground, Hooked Border, Signed, 6 ¾ In. 2818.00
Vase, Green, Pink, Pulled Feather, Elongated Neck, c.1910, 6 x 5 In. 293.00
Vase, Green, Urn Shape, Gold Iridescent Rolled Rim, Handle, Signed, 5 ¾ In. 3910.00
Vase, Green & White Pulled Feather, Iridescent Gold Pulled Feather, Signed, 3 ¾ In. 6325.00
Vase, Green Hooked Feather, Iridescent Gold, Rolled Rim, 7 In. *illus* 6613.00
Vase, Iridescent, Pulled Green Feathers, Gold Lattice, Ribbed, Scalloped Rim, Footed, 7 In. 3450.00
Vase, Iridescent Amber, Silver, Green Flowers, Gold Stems, Opalescent, Signed, 4 In. 1150.00
Vase, Iridescent Gold, Green, Opal Pulled Feather, Shouldered, Signed, 6 In. 3048.00
Vase, Iridescent Gold, Hooked Feather, Squat, Flared Neck, Signed, 5 ¼ In. 7475.00
Vase, Iridescent Gold, Hooked Feather, White Ground, 4 ½ In. 2300.00
Vase, Iridescent Gold, Lattice, Pulled Green Feather, Flared Gold Rim, Signed, 9 In. 3163.00
Vase, Iridescent Gold, Opal, Coil, Cone Shape, Flared Rim, Signed, 7 In. 748.00
Vase, Iridescent Gold, Pink Detail, Pinched Waist, Flared, 14 ¾ In. 660.00
Vase, Iridescent Gold, Pulled Feathers, Green Tips, Opal, Bulbous, Squat, Signed 4 In. 1495.00
Vase, Iridescent Gold, White Pulled Feather, Flared Ruffled & Stretched Rim, 6 In. 1020.00
Vase, Iridescent Gold, Wide, Pinched Waist, Flared Rim, Signed, 8 In. 460.00
Vase, Iridescent Gold & Purple Bands, Silver Overlay, Double Gourd Shape, 5 ¾ In. 1800.00
Vase, Iridescent Green, Gold Double Hooked Feathers, Opal, Shouldered, 5 In. 3450.00
Vase, Iridescent Green, Pulled Feather, Gold Fishnet, Applied Gold Foot, 6 ⅜ In. 1440.00
Vase, Iridescent Green, Pulled Feathers, Bulbous, Elongated Neck, 5 ½ x 5 In. 352.00
Vase, Iridescent Green To Pink Luster, Bulbous, c.1910, 5 x 4 In. 468.00
Vase, Iridescent Platinum, Heart & Vine, Iridescent Green Ground, 5 ½ In. 4200.00
Vase, Jack-In-The-Pulpit, Gold Luster Blossom, Purple To Emerald Stem, 14 In. 3120.00 to 5170.00
Vase, Jack-In-The-Pulpit, Green Pulled Feathers, Pinched Waist, Flared, Scalloped Rim, 8 In. 4025.00
Vase, Jack-In-The-Pulpit, Iridescent Gold, Green, Gold Pulled Feather, 6 ½ x 4 ¼ In. 3360.00
Vase, Jack-In-The-Pulpit, Iridescent Gold, Pulled Feather, Onion Skin Rim, 12 ½ In. 2128.00
Vase, Jack-In-The-Pulpit, Iridescent Yellow & Purple, 13 x 9 ⅛ In. 3000.00
Vase, King Tut, Gold, Pink, Blue, Iridescent, Flower Silver Overlay, 10 In. 3680.00

Quezal, Bowl, Green Pulled Feather, Iridescent, Gold, White Ground, Footed, 4 x 6 ½ In.
$5750.00

Quezal, Candlestick, Iridescent Blue, Baluster, Footed, Signed, 7 In.
$425.00

Quezal, Cup & Saucer, Iridescent Gold Pulled Hooked Feather, Gold Handle, 5 x 2 ½ In.
$270.00

Quezal, Vase, Green Hooked Feather, Iridescent Gold, Rolled Rim, 7 In.
$6613.00

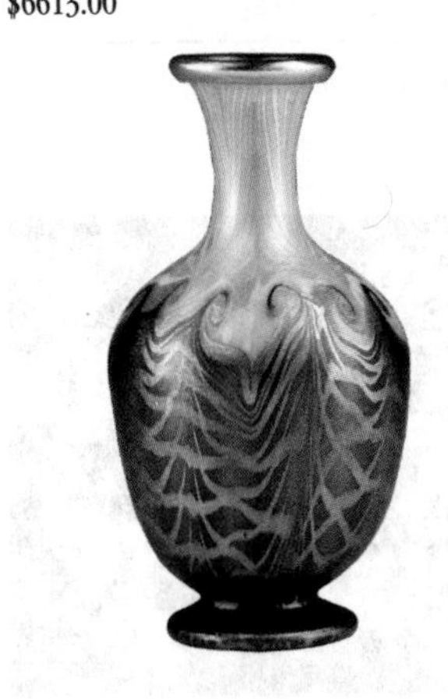

Quilt, Appliqued, Diamond, Multicolored, Flower Backing, 90 x 80 In.
$88.00

Quilt, Appliqued, Geometric Sampler, Multicolored, Houndstooth Back, 82 x 80 In.
$1760.00

Quilt, Appliqued, Triple Irish Chain, Yellow, Green, Red, Arch Border, Penn., 80 x 76 In.
$935.00

Quilt, Crazy, Multicolored, Victorian, 58 x 58 In.
$582.00

Vase, King Tut, Oil Spot, Gold Iridescent, Green & White, 6 ¼ In. 2760.00
Vase, Opal, Iridescent Gold Pulled Feathers, Green Tips, 6 ½ In. 604.00
Vase, Smoky, Iridescent Gold Body, White Pulled Feather, Ruffled Rim, 6 ¼ In. 633.00
Vase, Trumpet, Iridescent Gold, Footed, Ribbed, 6 In. 633.00
Vase, Trumpet, Iridescent Gold, Platinum Foot Band, Signed, 9 In. 230.00
Whimsy, Darning Egg, Iridescent Gold, Engraved, 4 ½ In. 460.00

QUILTS have been made since the seventeenth century. Early textiles were very precious and every scrap was saved to be reused. A quilt is a combination of fabrics joined to a filler and a backing by small stitched designs known as quilting. An appliqued quilt has pieces stitched to the top of a large piece of background fabric. A patchwork, or pieced, quilt is made of many small pieces stitched together. Embroidery can be added to either type.

Amish, Bar, Blue, Green, Brown, Early 20th Century, 73 x 80 In. 4680.00
Amish, Bar, Blue, Purple, Square Corners, Mid 20th Century, 84 x 85 In. 468.00
Amish, Bars, Old Order, Purple, Brown, Blue, Maroon, c.1940, 70 x 70 ½ In. 1265.00
Amish, Diamond, Red, Green, Sawtooth Border, 1900s, 80 x 79 In. . . . . 6000.00 to 6435.00
Amish, Diamond Center, Purple, Blue, Maroon, Square Corners, 78 x 79 In. 2574.00
Amish, Diamond In Square, Blue, Green, Purple, Printed Back, Pa., c.1930, 78 x 78 In. 3525.00
Amish, Double Nine, Pink, Red, Blue, Green, Square Corners, Rayon, Wool, 80 x 79 In. 3744.00
Amish, Irish Chain, Green, Brown, c.1920, 65 x 78 In. 585.00
Amish, Jacob's Ladder, Multicolored, Light Green Ground, Early 20th Century, 83 x 74 In. . . . 585.00
Amish, Log Cabin, Brown, Black, Early 20th Century, 77 x 77 In. 1760.00
Amish, Log Cabin, Mulitcolored, Brown Border, c.1920, 93 x 77 In. 1170.00
Amish, Patchwork, 9-Patch, Red, Blue, Black, Early 20th Century, 80 x 67 In. 3276.00
Amish, Patchwork, Sunshine & Shadows, Wool, Cotton Sateen, Rayon Crepe, 76 x 80 In. 345.00
Amish, Pineapples, Red, Blue, Brown, Green, Early 1900s, 80 x 80 In. 5500.00
Amish, Tumbling Blocks, Double Border, Black, Mustard, Olive, Wool, c.1925, 62 x 74 In. . . . 705.00
Appliqued, 4 Blocks, Eagles & Roses Border, Flowers, Pomegranates, c.1856, 94 x 94 In. 2585.00
Appliqued, 4 Flower Sprays, Red, Green, Vine Border, Cream Ground, 19th Century, 78 x 79 In. 761.00
Appliqued, American Eagle, Bellflowers & Egg Cartouche, Red, Green, Yellow, 94 x 79 In. . . . 460.00
Appliqued, Baskets, Red, Green, White Ground, 1950s, 86 ½ x 86 ½ In. 350.00
Appliqued, Central Star, Brown Flower, Diamond Stitch, Maroon, Yellow, Green, 76 x 76 In. . 198.00
Appliqued, Christmas Tree, Green, White, 85 x 67 In. 100.00
Appliqued, Diamond, Multicolored, Flower Backing, 90 x 80 In. . . . . *illus* 88.00
Appliqued, Diamond, Red, Yellow, Green, Diamond Stitch, 78 x 76 In. 110.00
Appliqued, Diamond & Wreath, Swag Border, 86 x 104 In. 999.00
Appliqued, Double Rose, Eagles, Stars, Jacquard, Blue, White, Wool, Cotton, 1845, 90 x 82 In. 385.00
Appliqued, Eagle, Oak, Grapevine Border, 80 x 80 In. 358.00
Appliqued, Feather, Black, Red, Yellow, Sawtooth Border, Early 20th Century, 86 x 84 In. 3744.00
Appliqued, Flowers, Buds, Red, Green Leaves, Vine Border, Cotton, c.1860, 84 x 101 In. 558.00
Appliqued, Geometric, Black, Red, Pink, Green, Diamond Stitch, 78 x 78 In. 99.00
Appliqued, Geometric Sampler, Multicolored, Houndstooth Back, 82 x 80 In. . . . . *illus* 1760.00
Appliqued, Grandmother's Tulip, Red, Green, White, Late 19th Century, 75 x 79 In. 410.00
Appliqued, Hawaiian, Aloha, Red Leaves, Branches, White, Cotton, c.1891, 83 x 92 In. 18750.00
Appliqued, Indian, With Bow, Arrow, 4 Panels, Red, Yellow, 95 x 89. . . . . 7020.00
Appliqued, Indian Plumes, 6-Point Stars, Pink, Blue, Sawtooth & Plume Border, 101 x 91 In. 2200.00
Appliqued, Leafy Hearts, Red Berries, Vined Arcaded Border, White Ground, 76 x 91 In. 764.00
Appliqued, Patchwork, Centennial, Red, White, Blue, Cotton, Illinois, 1876, 77 x 88 In. 8125.00
Appliqued, Patchwork, Flowers, Red, Green, Orange, c.1860, 92 x 94 In. 1080.00
Appliqued, Poppies, Red, Green Leaves, 88 x 76 In. 150.00
Appliqued, President's Wreath, Red, Green, Orange, White Ground, 19th Century, 94 x 92 In. 2574.00
Appliqued, Princess Feather, Red, Yellow, Green, 19th Century, 82 x 80 In. 3276.00
Appliqued, Rolling Stone, Blue, Green, Brown, Zigzag Border, c.1900, 98 x 82 In. 527.00
Appliqued, Schoolhouse, Red, White, Blue, Early 20th Century, 90 x 70 In. 1872.00
Appliqued, Star In A Star, Quadruple Rows, Multicolored, Cotton, c.1850, 102 x 102 In. 940.00
Appliqued, Star Of Bethlehem, Black, Red, Yellow, Double Sawtooth Border, 1900s, 88 x 88 In. 3300.00
Appliqued, Star Of Bethlehem, Blue, Sawtooth Border, E. Landers, 1933, 80 x 78 In. 975.00
Appliqued, Star Of Bethlehem, Yellow, Pink, Blue, Brown, Yellow, Purple Ground, c.1900, 77 x 75 In. 234.00
Appliqued, Sunbonnet Girl, Red, Blue, Pink Print Lattice, 64 x 81 In. 145.00
Appliqued, Tree Of Life, Yellow, Blue, Green, White Ground, Scalloped Edge, 75 x 91 In. 427.00
Appliqued, Triple Irish Chain, Yellow, Green, Red, Arch Border, Penn., 80 x 76 In. . . . . *illus* 935.00
Appliqued, Tulip, Green, Pink, Peach, Red, 1920s, 82 x 94 ½ In. 425.00
Appliqued, Whig Rose, 9 Squares, Green, Red, 1900s, 88 x 86 In. 575.00
Appliqued, Whig Rose, Red, Green, White Ground, Swag Border, 19th Century, 88 x 85 In. . . . 2340.00
Appliqued, Whig Rose, Red, Yellow, Green, Pink, Double Diamond Border, 1800s, 74 x 75 In. . 1872.00
Appliqued, Whig Rose, White Ground, Diamond Pattern, Mid 1800s, 70 x 75 In. 690.00

Appliqued, Wreath, Star Center, Red, Green, Orange, 19th Century, 78 x 86 In. 600.00
Crazy, Flowers, Animals, Multicolored, Cotton, Wool, Early 1900s, 65 x 65 In. 345.00
Crazy, Flowers, Black, Rust, Yellow, Gray, White, Wool, 1918, 69 x 85 In. 450.00
Crazy, Multicolored, Victorian, 58 x 58 In. .... *illus* 582.00
Crazy, Wagon Wheel, 9 Squares, Green & Black Ground, Wool, 1875, 84 x 82 In. 1425.00
Hawaiian, Comb Of Kaiulana, 8-Rayed Combs, Maroon, 1850, 72 x 72 In.. .... 2300.00
Lone Star, Pieced, Vines, Flowers, 2 Eagles, Cotton, Muslin Back, Pa., c.1850, 90 x 96 In. 294.00
Patchwork, 16 Squares, Double Star, Calico, Late 19th Century, 79 x 80 In.. .... 770.00
Patchwork, 4 Eagles, Yellow, Green, Red Calico Ground, c.1900, 79 x 79 In. 2200.00
Patchwork, Album, Quilted Hearts, Charlotte Jane Prindle, c.1858, 89 x 79 In. 431.00
Patchwork, Baptist Fan, Red & White, c.1900, 74 x 80 In. 550.00
Patchwork, Bar, Blue, Green, Yellow, Orange, Red, Mid 20th Century, 85 x 76 In. 1540.00
Patchwork, Diamonds, Pink Border, 76 x 80 In. .... *illus* 150.00
Patchwork, Dresden Plate, White Ground, Red, 66 x 75 In. 145.00
Patchwork, Flower Basket, Dresden Plate Yellow, White, 19th Century, 72 x 84 In. 413.00
Patchwork, Geometric, Medallion, Outer Fan, Francois Barnes, 62 x 60 In. 403.00
Patchwork, Grandmother's Flower Garden, 6-Sided Printed Blocks, 1880, 78 x 83 In. 410.00
Patchwork, Log Cabin, Barn Raising, Wool, Cotton Dress Print, c.1890, 32 x 31 ½ In. 115.00
Patchwork, Log Cabin, Multicolored, 19th Century, 115 x 98 In.. .... 250.00
Patchwork, Log Cabin, Multicolored, Red Border, Early 20th Century, 50 ½ x 41 In.. .... 410.00
Patchwork, Log Cabin, Red, Green, Blue, White, Double Border, Cotton, c.1900, 80 x 80 In.. . 403.00
Patchwork, Lone Star, Multicolored, Dark Blue Ground, Cotton, Hanging Grid, 82 x 84 In. . . 3162.00
Patchwork, Mariner's Compass, Red, Orange, Teal Ground, 19th Century, 81 x 81 In. 1890.00
Patchwork, Mariner's Star, Yellow, Red Ground, Early 20th Century, 71 x 83 In. 1430.00
Patchwork, Mosaic, Star, Diamonds, Red, White, Blue, Yellow, Felt, Late 1800s, 84 x 96 In. . . 3042.00
Patchwork, Orange Slices, Red, Blue, Triangle & Arch Border, Floral Back, Penn., 72 x 72 In. 330.00
Patchwork, Pavement, c.1900, 67 x 68 In. .... *illus* 819.00
Patchwork, Pinwheel, Green, Yellow, Orange, Plaid Back, 2 Piece, c.1820, 85 x 74 In. 474.00
Patchwork, Schoolhouse, 1930, 76 x 76 In. .... *illus* 322.00
Patchwork, Star, Green, Yellow, Print, Flannel, 72 x 83 In. 150.00
Patchwork, Star Of Bethlehem, Diamonds, Red, Blue Green, Pink, Cotton, c.1890, 91 x 91 In. 385.00
Patchwork, Star Of Bethlehem, White Ground, Borders, Cotton, Charleston, 1700s, 78 x 79 In. 316.00
Patchwork, Tree Of Life, Brown, Green, Cream, c.1860, 70 x 80 In.. .... 546.00
Patchwork, Trip Around The World, Yellow, Black, Blue, Brown, Border, 1900s, 81 x 85 In. . . 468.00
Patchwork, Triple Irish Chain, Red, Green, Yellow, Cream, c.1900, 81 x 84 In. 575.00
Patchwork, Triple Irish Chain, Yellow, Green, Red Squares, Floral Back, Penn., 80 x 76 In. . . 935.00
Patchwork, Wagon Wheel, Dark Green, Orange, Blue, Cotton, Wool, Penn., c.1875, 85 x 83 In. 1422.00
Patchwork & Appliqued, South Carolina Lily, Stems, Leaves, Double Border, c.1937, 42 x 43 In. 225.00
Pyrotechnics, Pieced, Blue, Orange, Black Square, 1898, 67 x 88 In. 1725.00
Squares, Plumed Wreaths, Pieced, Blue, Yellow, Pink, White Ground, Cotton, c.1875, 78 x 97 In. 440.00
Star, Diamonds, Rows, Pierced, Red, Blue, Pink, Yellow, Brown, 102 x 102 In. 940.00
Template, Tin, Interlocking Line Shape, Painted Olive Green, Penn., 7 ¾ x 15 ¾ In.. .... 175.00

QUIMPER pottery has a long history. Tin-glazed, hand-painted pottery has been made in Quimper, France, since the late seventeenth century. The earliest firm, founded in 1685 by Jean Baptiste Bousquet, was known as HB Quimper. Another firm, founded in 1772 by Francois Eloury, was known as Porquier. The third firm, founded by Guillaume Dumaine in 1778, was known as HR or Henriot Quimper. All three firms made similar pottery decorated with designs of Breton peasants and sea and flower motifs. The Eloury (Porquier) and Dumaine (Henriot) firms merged in 1913. Bousquet (HB) merged with the others in 1968. The group was sold to a United States family in 1984. The American holding company is Quimper Faience Inc., located in Stonington, Connecticut. The French firm has been called *Societe Nouvelle des Faienceries de Quimper HB Henriot* since March 1984.

HR Quimper

Basket, Breton Man, Swan Neck, Signed, 8 In. 110.00
Basket, Footed, Handle, 1922, 11 ½ x 9 ½ In.. .... 600.00
Bean Pot, Lid, Mustard Yellow Glaze, 2 Handles, 1930s-40s 36.00
Bowl, Fluted, Breton Man, Pine Tree Center, Stylized Flower Border, Bands, Dots, 9 x 3 In. . . . 86.00
Bowl, Porringer, Petit Breton Pattern, Yellow Glaze, 7 In. 38.00
Butter, Breton Man, Red, Green & Blue Border 375.00
Butter, Underplate, Lid, Breton Peasant Bride, Cobalt Blue Acanthus, Signed, 5 In. 140.00
Butter Bell, Liner, Breton Couple On Lid, Flowers On Sides, 3 x 7 In. 48.00
Butter Chip, Octagonal Shape, 2 In. 95.00
Clock, Breton Couple, Flowers Line Border, 9 ¼ In. 200.00
Cup & Saucer, Breton Man, 1900s 85.00
Cup & Saucer, Breton Man With Pipe, 2 ¾ x 5 ½ In. 99.00
Figurine, Dancers, Breton Man & Woman, 4 In. 66.00

Quilt, Patchwork, Diamonds, Pink Border, 76 x 80 In.
$150.00

Quilt, Patchwork, Pavement, c.1900, 67 x 68 In.
$819.00

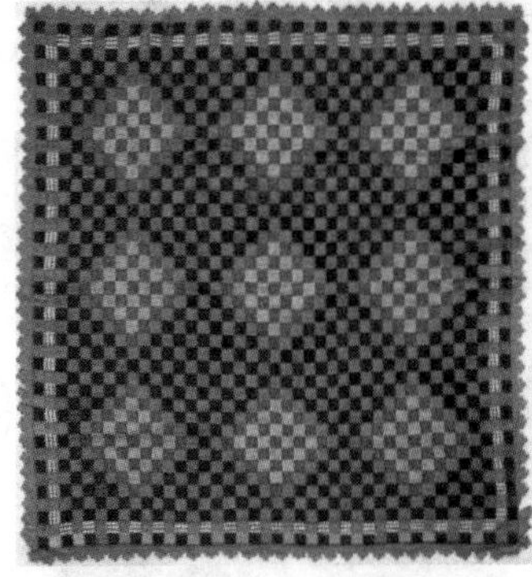

Quilt, Patchwork, Schoolhouse, 1930, 76 x 76 In.
$322.00

TIP
Do not dry clean an old quilt. The chemicals will damage the fabric.

Radio, Addison, Model 2C, Marbleized Butterscotch, Red, No. R5A1, 6 x 10 ¼ In.
$3480.00

Radio, Addison, Model 5F, Bakelite, c.1940, Table, 12 ½ In.
$700.00

Radio, Fada, Model 1000, Bullet, Catalin, 10 ½ x 6 In.
$950.00

Radio, Gridiron, Football, Green, Aluminum, c.1930
$978.00

TIP
A household window cleaner with ammonia can be used to clean Bakelite.

Figurine, Swan, 7 x 3 ½ In. ... 285.00
Figurine, Virgin Mary & Child, Sainte Vierge, Signed, 11 ½ In. ... 50.00
Jardiniere, Breton Man, Coat Of Arms, Cornucopia Feet, Signed, 3 ½ x 10 ½ In. ... 175.00
Oyster Plate, 6 Wells, Flowers, Breton Woman, In Center, 9 ½ In. ... 46.00
Oyster Plate, 6 Wells, Orange, Black Outline, Chain Decoration, 9 ¼ In. ... 35.00
Oyster Plate, 24 Wells, Black, Hand Painted Seashells & Grass, 16 ½ In. ... 172.00
Oyster Plate, Fish Shape, 1934, 10 In. ... 225.00
Plate, Beige Ground, Female Breton, Floral Rims, Brown Band, Pre 1942, 5 ½ In. ... 125.00
Plate, Bird Design, Marked, 1920s, 10 In. ... 96.00
Plate, Breton Couple, 8 ½ In. ... 20.00
Plate, Flowers, Signed HB Quimper RD, 11 In. ... 25.00
Plate, Flowers & Insects, White Ground, Border, Signed HB Quimper, 9 ½ In. ... 28.75
Plate, Seated Peasant Woman, Scalloped Edge, 1900s, 8 ¼ In. ... 85.00
Plate, Stylized Flowers, Flower & Band Border, Signed HB Quimper RD, 11 In. ... 28.75
Platter, Fish, Blue, Green, Rust & Yellow, Signed, 19 ½ x 9 In. ... 225.00
Platter, Musicians Entertaining Women At Well, Elaborate Border, 8-Sided, 13 ½ x 18 In. ... 339.00
Porridge, Mayflower, Flying French Flags, 1930s, 5 In. ... 350.00
Salt & Pepper, Breton Woman & Tree Salt, Man & Tree Pepper, Yellow, 3 ½ In. ... 25.00
Sugar, Henriot Soliel, Yellow, Floral Garlands, 6-Sided, 1930s, 6 x 6 ½ In. ... 175.00
Teapot, Large Bird, Flowers, White Body, Blue Handle & Finial, Late 1900s, 6 ⅞ x 5 In. ... 45.00
Tray, 2 Figures, Flower & Leaf Border, Yellow, Green, Blue, Signed, 8 ¾ x 24 In. ... 77.00
Tray, Breton Man & Woman, Gathering Fish, 8-Sided, Signed, 9 x 12 In. ... 425.00
Tray, Breton Man & Woman, Stylized Flowers, Signed, 24 x 8 ¾ In. ... 81.00
Trivet, Breton Woman, Ivoire Basket Pattern, Beige Ground, 8-Sided, Mid 1900s, 8 ½ In. ... 45.00
Vase, Armorial, Couple In Garden, Bretagne Coat Of Arms, Flowers On Reverse, c.1994, 12 In. 90.00
Vase, Breton Man & Woman, Flowers, Fan Form, Dolphin Base, Signed, 8 In. ... 325.00
Vase, Breton Man & Woman, Moon, Flowers, Flask Form, Signed, 155, 8 In. ... 140.00
Vase, Breton Woman, 1930s, 3 ½ In. ... 225.00
Vase, Breton Woman, Flowers, Hand Painted, 2 Applied Handles, 9 x 6 In. ... 146.00
Vase, Fleur-De-Lis, Breton Man, Flowers, Coat Of Arms, Signed, 10 ½ In. ... 100.00
Vase, Stylized Birds & Flowers, Yellow & Blue, White Ground, 2 Handles, 10 ¼ In. ... 200.00
Vase, Wall, Shoe, Flowers, Blue Sponge Border, Late 19th Century, 9 ½ In. ... 325.00
Wall Pocket, Cornet, Breton Man Smoking Pipe, Geometric Design, Florals, 1900. ... 475.00

RADFORD pottery was made by Alfred Radford in Broadway, Virginia; Tiffin and Zanesville, Ohio; and Clarksburg, West Virginia, from 1891 until 1912. Jasperware, Ruko, Thera, Radura, and Velvety Art Ware were made. The jasperware resembles the famous Wedgwood ware of the same name. Another pottery named Radford worked in England and is not included here.

RADURA.

Pitcher, Cornucopia, Embossed Flowers, Fruit, Rim & Handle, Mottled Tan Matte, 7 x 8 In. ... 95.00
Pitcher, Pastel Blue, Anemones, Purple, Red, Green Leaves, 9 In. ... 95.00
Thera, Green Matte Body, Slip Decorated Berries, Leaves, Signed, 14 ⅛ In. ... 690.00
Vase, Radura, Green Matte Glaze, 4 Handles, 10 ¼ In. ... 546.00
Vase, Thera, Shaded Green, Painted Red & Green Flowers, Impressed, 1900s, 9 In. ... 138.00
Vase, Velvety, Green, Painted Rose, 9 ⅞ In. ... 330.00

RADIO broadcast receiving sets were first sold in New York City in 1910. They were used to pick up the experimental broadcasts of the day. The first commercial radios were made by Westinghouse Company for listeners of the experimental shows on KDKA Pittsburgh in 1920. Collectors today are interested in all early radios, especially those made of Bakelite plastic or decorated with blue mirrors. Figural advertising radios and transistor radios are also collected.

Addison, Model 2, Waterfall Grille, Catalin, Maroon, Yellow, 1940, 10 x 6 In. ... 1140.00
Addison, Model 2C, Marbleized Butterscotch, Red, No. R5A1, 6 x 10 ¼ In. ... *illus* 3480.00
Addison, Model 5, Courthouse, Catalin, Pale Green, Yellow, 1940, 12 x 8 ¾ In. ... 1560.00
Addison, Model 5, Courthouse, Catalin, Red, Yellow, 1940, 12 x 8 ¾ In. ... 240.00
Addison, Model 5F, Bakelite, c.1940, Table, 12 ½ In. ... *illus* 700.00
Advertising, Dr Pepper, Transistor, Vending Machine Form, Chevron Logo, 1960s, 7 x 3 In. ... 150.00
Advertising, Dr Pepper, Wood, Mesh Over Speaker, White, Red, 1930s, 7 ¾ x 12 x 7 ¼ In. ... 1700.00
Air King, Model 52, Skyscraper, Ivory, Clock Insert, c.1933, 11 ¾ x 8 ¾ x 6 ¾ In. ... 5700.00
Airline, Model 311, Movie Dial, 1938, 37 ½ x 21 ½ x 10 ½ In. ... 1700.00
Airline, Model 409, Multicolored Dial, 1938, 40 x 24 x 11 ½ In. ... 1750.00
Astor Mickey, Plaskon, Cream, 1939-40, 7 x 10 x 7 In. ... 900.00
Atwater Kent, Model 84, Cathedral, Super Heterodyne, Walnut, 1930s, 19 In. ... 275.00
Atwater Kent, Model 165, Cathedral, Table Top, 1933, 19 ¼ x 16 x 9 ¾ In. ... 275.00
Atwater Kent, Model 217, Table, Barn Top, 1933, 17 x 14 x 10 ½ In. ... 978.00
Atwater Kent, Model 447, Tombstone, 1933, 21 ½ x 16 x 11 In. ... 1000.00
AWA, Radiolette Fisk Skyscraper, Bakelite Case ... 900.00

AWA, Skyscraper, c.1936, 11 x 11 In. 960.00
Barbarossa Beer, Bottle Form, Bakelite, Electric, 1934, 23 In. 165.00
Belmont, Model 6D14Bakelite, Art Deco, Ivory, 12 In. 250.00
Bendix, Catalin, Model 115, Polystyrene, Cream, Red, 1948, Table 1020.00
Bendix, Model 526MC, Catalin, Green, Black Swirls, 1946, Table 660.00
Bendix, Model 55P3U, Bakelite, 2 Tone Brown, 1949, 11 ½ In. 100.00
Catalin, Tom Thumb, Butterscotch, 1937 .... 2400.00
Crosley, Model 10-136E, Bakelite, Art Deco, Brown, 12 ½ In. 110.00
Crosley, Model 58, Buddy Boy, Cathedral, 1931 .... 575.00
Crosley, Model 127, Adventurer, 1931, 13 In. 1200.00
Crosley, Model D25 MN, Clock, Bakelite, Art Deco, 1953, 13 In. 60.00
Cyarts, Model B, Bullet Style, Lucite, Art Deco, 1946, Table 1100.00
Detrola, Model 281, Catalin, Marbleized Oxblood, Handle, Grilles, Knobs, 1940s 1020.00
Dewald, Model A-502, Catalin, 1946, 6 ½ x 10 x 6 ½ In. 3000.00
Emerson, Catalin, Model 400, Patriot, Red, White, Blue, 1940, Table .... 2040.00 to 4800.00
Emerson, Model 400, Aristocrat, Catalin, Brown, Marbleized, 1940 .... 720.00
Emerson, Model 564, Slot Grille, Oxblood, Catalin, Art Deco Dial, 1940, Table 1080.00
Emerson, Model 744B, Art Deco, Red, Gray, 1954, 11 ½ In. 200.00
Emerson, Model AU-190, Cathedral, Alabaster, Catalin, Herringbone Grille Cloth, 1938 .... 840.00
Emerson, Model AU-190, Tombstone, Catalin, Ivory, Yellow, 1937 .... 2160.00
Emerson, Model AX-235, Little Miracle, Catalin, Onyx Green, Ivory, 5 ¼ x 8 ⅞ In. 1080.00
Emerson, Model BT-245, Tombstone, Burgundy, White, Torpedo Knobs, 1938, 10 In. 1680.00
Fada, Model 5F60, Catalin, Butterscotch, Louvered Grille, 1939, 8 x 5 ½ In. 1800.00
Fada, Model 115, Streamliner Bullet, Marbleized Blue, Butterscotch, 1940, 6 x 10 In. 5700.00
Fada, Model 189, Blue & White Marbleized, Red Knob, Yellow Dial, 1942 .... 5400.00
Fada, Model 711, Catalin, Onyx Green, Dip Top Midget, Polystyrene, Handle, 1947, 8 x 11 In. 480.00
Fada, Model 1000, Bullet, Catalin, 10 ½ x 6 In. .... *illus* 950.00
Fada, Model L-56, Catalin, Burgundy, Butterscotch Grille, Handle, Fluted Knobs, 1939, 6 x 9 In. 1200.00
Freed Eisemann, Model NR7, Headphones, 1925, Table 30.00
Gilfillan, Model 63, Tombstone, 1935, 12 x 7 In. 920.00
Globe, Navigator, Black, Bakelite, 1940, 5 x 9 ¾ In. 220.00
Gridiron, Football, Green, Aluminum, c.1930 .... *illus* 978.00
Grunow, Model 1291, Wood, 1936, 42 ½ x 28 x 14 ½ In. 1900.00
Imperial, Model 57A, Chrome, Ultra Deco, 1935, Table 600.00
Jackson Bell, Model 88, Tulip, Tombstone, Art Deco, Black Lacquer, 1933, 15 ½ In. 225.00
Microphone, RCA, 4030-E 1200.00
Microphone, RCA, BK-5B 1900.00
Microphone, RCA, PB-90 .... 900.00
Microphone, RCA, PB-90A2 .... 900.00
Microphone, Western Electric, 387 W 2800.00
Microphone, Western Electric, 600, Double Button, Carbon 800.00
Microphone, Western Electric, 618, Moving Coil 2600.00
Microphone, Western Electric, 618A 900.00
Microphone Form, WVKO 94-7 FM, White, Red, Bakelite, Plastic, 14 x 8 In. 90.00
Mitchell's El Paso Beer, Bottle Shape, Bakelite, Electric, 23 In. 330.00
Motorola, Model 50-XC, Circle Grille, Catalin, Red, Butterscotch, 1940, Table 7200.00
Motorola, Model 51X15, S Grille, Catalin, Black, Red, Handle, Art Deco, 1940, Table 4200.00
Motorola, Model 53H2, Bakelite, Ivory, 1954, 11 In. 50.00
Philco, Model 16B, Cathedral, Mahogany, 1933, 19 ½ In. 250.00
Philco, Model 37-60, c.1937, Table 1035.00
Philco, Model 39-70, Battery, Console, 37 ½ x 23 x 10 In. 1200.00
Philco, Model 50, Cathedral, 1931, 15 ¾ x 14 ½ x 7 ¾ In. 70.00
Philco, Model 70B, Cathedral, 1931, Table 225.00
Philco, Model 90, Cathedral, 1931, Table 625.00
Philco, Model 90, Super Heterodyne 9, Cathedral, Tag .... *illus* 413.00
Philco, Model 118B, Slide Rule Dial, 1935, 40 x 26 x 13 In. 2200.00
Philco 45, Table Model, Butterfly, c.1934, 16 x 9 x 8 ¼ In. 1035.00
Philco 65, Floor Model, c.1929, 28 x 40 x 14 ½ In. 863.00
Pilotuner, Model T-601, Broadcast, 1933, 19 x 16 x 11 In. 1400.00
Radiola, Model 60, Separate Speaker, Table, 1930, 11 ½ x 30 x 10 ½ In. 700.00
RCA Victor, Model 66X1, Bakelite, Ivory, 1946, 15 In. 45.00
RCA Victor, Model 66X11, Super Heterodyne, Bakelite, Art Deco, 1947, 14 In. 60.00
Sentinel, Model 194UTI, Bakelite, Ivory, 1940s, 10 ½ In. 110.00
Silvertone, No. 6641, Chairside, Floor Model, c.1946, 28 x 22 In. 920.00
Smokerette, Model SR-600W, Humidor, Pipe Stand, 1947, 21 ½ In. 60.00
Sparton, Bluebird, Model 506, Mirror, Cobalt Blue, Art Deco Disc, Chrome Bands, 1936, 15 x 14 In. 2450.00
Sparton, Model 506, Blue Bird, Chrome, c.1936, 14 ¼ In. 3360.00

Radio, Philco, Model 90, Super Heterodyne 9, Cathedral, Tag
$413.00

Radio, Zenith, Model 5H40, Trans-Oceanic, c.1940
$72.00

Radio, Zenith, Model 9-S-262, 9 Tube, Shutter Dial, 1937
$375.00

As always, the edited listings in *Kovels' Antiques & Collectibles Price Guide 2010* aren't available on any website, but readers should visit Kovels.com for information on trends, tips, reproductions, marks, old prices, and more!

R

Railroad, Lantern, Dietz, Vesta, B & M Railroad, Etched Red Shade, 10 ½ In.
$295.00

Railroad, Sign, Crossing, Light On Iron Post, Gaylord, Mich., 89 x 18 In.
$105.00

Butter Chip
A 1900 railroad butter chip marked "Santa Fe Route" on top sold for $6,247. Wow!

Sparton, Model 557, Sled, Cobalt Blue, Chrome Fins, Art Deco, 1936, 18 x 9 x 8 ¼ In. 1560.00
Sparton, Model 558-B, Sled Rail, Chrome, 1937, 8 ½ x 17 ½ In. 3000.00
Sparton, Model 1186, Nocturne, Cobalt Blue, Chrome, Tubes, Shortwave, c.1936, 46 x 42 In. 51000.00
Westinghouse, Model H-126, Refrigerator Shape, 1948, Portable, 9 In. 60.00
Westinghouse, Model H-127, Refrigerator Shape, 1946, Portable, 9 In. 403.00
Zenith, Model 5H40, Trans-Oceanic, c.1940 *illus* 72.00
Zenith, Model 6-D-615, Walnut, 1942, 14 In. 120.00
Zenith, Model 9-S-262, 9 Tube, Shutter Dial, 1937 *illus* 375.00
Zenith, Model J402R, Plug For Battery, 1952, 8 ¼ x 11 ½ x 5 ½ In. 30.00

RAILROAD enthusiasts collect any train memorabilia. Everything is wanted, from oilcans to whole train cars. The Chessie system has a store that sells many reproductions of their old dinnerware and uniforms.

Badge, Police, Southern Pacific, Star, c.1910, 2 ¼ In. 150.00
Bell, Locomotive, Boston & Maine 1000.00
Bell, Locomotive, Diesel, Bronze 300.00
Bowl, Cereal, Adam, Blue, Denver & Rio Grande Railroad, Syracuse China Co., 5 In. 35.00
Butter Chip, B & O Railroad, Centenary Pattern, Marked, Shenango China, 3 ⅛ In. 55.00
Calendar, Missouri Pacific Lines, Removable Numbers, Green, Tin, c.1900, 19 x 13 In. 205.00
Cuspidor, Union Pacific Railroad, Brass, Raised Logo On Front, 10 In. 46.00
Fire Bucket, Pennsylvania Railroad, Red 75.00
Fire Bucket, PRR Insignia, Bail Handle, 1900s 60.00
Hat, Conductor's, NYC & HRRR, Black, Yellow Trim 99.00
Key, Switch Lock, B & O Adlake Railroad, Hollow Barrel, 2 In. 28.00
Lamp, Inspector, PRR Logo, Handle, Raised Letters, Dietz Fitall, NY, USA On Globe, 14 ½ In. 119.00
Lantern, Adelake, Non-Sweating, Red, Blue 66.00
Lantern, B & ORR Plate, Embossed, Red & Green Lenses, Handlan, St. Louis, 15 In. 296.00
Lantern, CHRVRY., No. 39, Handle, 15 In. 250.00
Lantern, CM STP & PRR, Tin, Red Globe, Adams & Westlake Co., 9 ½ In. 119.00
Lantern, Caboose, Raised Letters On Shade & Base, Handlan, St. Louis, 18 In. 119.00
Lantern, D & RGWR., Adams & Westlake, Tin, Amber Globe, Etched, 9 In. 148.00
Lantern, Dietz, Vesta, B & M Railroad, Etched Red Shade, 10 ½ In. *illus* 295.00
Lantern, Dressel, 4-Way, 2 White, Yellow, Gold, Enamel Saucers, Blue & Amber Lenses 70.00
Lantern, Long Island, LIRR., Tin, Glass Globe, Rubber Covered Wire Handle, 10 ¼ In. 59.00
Lantern, Signal, B. & ORR., Safety First, Glass Globe, N.Y., 10 ¼ In. 267.00
Lantern, Switch, Pressed Steel, Red & Green Lenses, Non-Sweating, Adlake, Chicago, 16 In. 119.00
Lock, Switch, Steel, F.S. Hardware Co., 4 ½ In. 85.00
Number Plate, Locomotive, No. 3597, Black, Yellow, Cast Iron 650.00
Paperweight, Locomotive, Streamlined Hudson Type, Used In 20th Century Service 88.00
Plate, Dinner, Canadian Pacific, Blue Heron, Blue, White, Stamped, 8 ½ In. 219.00
Plate, Engine Portraits, Potomac Valley, Lamberton China Co., 8 ½ In. 59.00
Sign, Brotherhood Of Railroad Train Men, Paper, Frame, 1883, 27 x 22 In. 200.00
Sign, Crossing, Light On Iron Post, Gaylord, Mich., 89 x 18 In. *illus* 105.00
Sign, Crossing, Look & Listen, Cast Iron, 48 In. 296.00
Sign, Missouri Pacific Lines Railroad, Aluminum, Red, White Letters, 24 In. Diam. 148.00
Sign, New Jersey Central Line, Speed, Iron, 1800s 975.00
Sign, Rail-Road, White, Black, Cast Iron, 9 x 48 In. 33.00
Sign, Railway Express Agency, Red & Gold Letters, Steel, Enamel, 60 In. 296.00
Sign, Railway Express Agency Inc., Black, Yellow, Enamel, c.1900, 12 x 72 In. 165.00
Sign, Southern Railroad, Southern Serves The South, Painted Aluminum, 32 x 32 In. 95.00
Spike, Cast Iron, 3 ⅞ x ⅜ In. 11.00
Spoon Rest, Pacific Railroad, Historical Pattern, Syracuse China, 4 ¾ x 4 ¼ In. 225.00
Teapot & Creamer, Canadian Pacific, Empress Pattern, 6-In. Teapot 187.00
Tumbler, Pennsylvania Railroad 4902, Train, 2 ½ x 2 ½ In. 25.00
Tumbler, Pennsylvania Railroad 4902, Train, 4 ¼ x 3 ½ In. 25.00
Whistle, PRR, Brass, Stenciled, 1800s, 17 In. 550.00

RAZORS were used in ancient Egypt and subsequently wherever shaving was in fashion. The metal razor used in America until about 1870 was made in Sheffield, England. After 1870, machine-made hollow-ground razors were made in Germany or America. Plastic or bone handles were popular. The razor was often sold in a set of seven, one for each day of the week. The set was often kept by the barber who shaved the well-to-do man each day in the shop.

Blue Steel, Wood Grain Plastic Handle, Metal, Iowa, 6 In. 20.00
Gem, Snap Front, Stainless Steel Blades, Plastic Case, Instructions, 1950s, 4 In. 23.00
Keen Kutter, No. K419, Royal, Engraved Blade, Black Plastic Handle, Box, 6 ¼ In. 30.00
Straight, Faultless, No. 110, Cuticut Co., Germany, Box, 9 ⅜ x 5 ⅜ In. 355.00

Twin Works, No. 415, J. Henckels, Mother-Of-Pearl Handle, Inlay, Germany, Box, 6 In. 20.00
Winchester, No. WII, Engraved Blade, Celluloid Handle, Metal Ends, Box, 6 ¾ In. 30.00
Yankee Cutlery Co., No. 090, Art Nouveau, Nude Woman, White, Green, 6 ⅛ In. 60.00

REAMERS, or juice squeezers, have been known since 1767, although most of those collected today date from the twentieth century. Figural reamers are among the most prized.

Aluminum, Handle With Nose, Foley, c.1950, 8 x 4 In. 16.00
Figural, Clown, Japan, 2 Piece, c.1940 . . . . 155.00 to 197.00
Glass, Amber, Federal Glass Co., 5 x 3 ½ In. 20.00
Glass, Clear, Draining Holes, Scalloped, Tab Handle, 5 x 3 In. 12.00
Glass, Clear, Easley's Improved Reamer, Tab Handle, 4 ½ x 2 ¼ In. 47.00
Glass, Clear, Loop Handle, Ribbed, Hocking Glass, c.1950, 6 ¼ x 4 In. 15.00
Glass, Clear, Pitcher, 2 Piece, c.1930, 6 x 3 In. 20.00
Glass, Clear, Tab Handle, Thumb Ridge, 1 ¼ x 8 In. 9.00
Glass, Clear, Vertical Ribs, Tab Handle, 2 ½ x 8 In. 14.00
Glass, Crisscross, Draining Holes, Hazel Atlas, 2 ¼ 6 In. 20.00
Glass, Crisscross, Hazel Atlas, 4 x 7 ¾ In. . . . . 9.00 to 12.00
Glass, Crisscross, Hazel Atlas, c.1950, 6 x 2 ¼ In. 20.00
Glass, Custard, Sunkist, McKee 75.00
Glass, Custard Glass, McKee Glass Co., c.1940, 7 x 3 ¼ In. 85.00
Glass, Delphite, Blue, 6 In. . . . . 20.00 to 36.00
Glass, Delphite Blue, Spout, Handle, Barnes, 2 Piece, 3 ½ x 3 ½ In. 38.00
Glass, Green, Draining Holes, 4 ¼ In. 18.00
Glass, Green, Hazel Atlas, Crisscross, Pitcher, 2 Piece, 2 ¾ x 8 ¼ In. 32.00
Glass, Green, Indiana Glass, 7 ¼ In. 25.00
Glass, Green, Lemon, Hazel Atlas, Tab Handle 15.00
Glass, Jadite, Jeannette Glass Co., c.1930, 8 x 4 In. 30.00
Glass, Jeannette, Green, 8 In. . . . . *illus* 28.00
Glass, Juice, Ribbed Panel, Loop Handle, Hocking Glass, 8 In. 23.00
Glass, Juice, Ribbed Panel, Tab Handle, Hocking Glass, 8 In. 23.00
Glass, Lime Green, Hocking Co., 5 x 8 ¼ In. 20.00
Glass, Milk Glass, Embossed Sunkist, McKee 25.00
Glass, Orange, Amber, Federal 45.00
Glass, Orange, Crisscross, Pink, Hazel Atlas 325.00
Glass, Orange, Delphite, Blue, Jeannette 75.00
Glass, Orange, Green, Jeannette 60.00
Glass, Pink, 8 x 3 ½ In. 50.00
Glass, Pink, Tab Handle, Hazel Atlas 35.00
Glass, Sunkist, Seville Yellow . . . . 60.00 to 68.00
Measuring Cup, Slick Handled, Green Frosted, U.S. Glass, 16 Oz. . . . . 55.00 to 65.00
Plastic, Pink, Lustroware, c.1955, 6 In. 15.00
Plastic, Red, 6 In. 12.00
Porcelain, Figural, Clown, Japan, Crown Mark, 2 Piece, c.1925, 6 x 5 ½ In. . . . . *illus* 75.00
Porcelain, Multicolored, Crisscross, Green Leaf Design, Japan, 4 x 3 In. 24.00
Porcelain, Yellow Ducks Jumping Rope, Hand Painted, Orange Juice, Japan, 3 ¾ x 3 ¼ In. . . 28.00
Potlay, Jack & Jill, 2 Handles, Japan, 4 ½ In. . . . . *illus* 142.00
Pottery, Figural, Child's Face, 2 Piece, 3 In. 165.00
Pottery, Figural, Citrus Face, Yellow, Japan, 2 Piece, c.1940, 5 ¼ In. . . . . 197.00 to 210.00
Pottery, Figural, Duck, Japan, 2 ½ In. 165.00
Pottery, Figural, Duck, Lusterware, Japan, c.1940, 3 ½ In. 155.00
Red, Plastic, Westland, 6 In. 10.00
Sunkist, Black, Embossed, Pat. No. 68764, 8 ½ In. . . . . *illus* 500.00
Sunkist, White, Embossed MCK, 6 In. . . . . 10.00 to 18.00
Sunkist, White, Footed, Embossed MCK, 6 In. 36.00

RECORDS have changed size and shape through the years. The cylinder-shaped phonograph record for use with the early Edison models was made about 1889. Disc records were first made by 1894, the double-sided disc by 1904. High-fidelity records were first issued in 1944, the first vinyl disc in 1946, the first stereo record in 1958. The 78 RPM became the standard in 1926 but was discontinued in 1957. In 1932, the first 33 ⅓ RPM was made but was not sold commercially until 1948. In 1949, the 45 RPM was introduced. Compact discs became available in the U.S. in 1982 and many companies began phasing out the production of phonograph records.

Abbott & Costello, Who's On First, Baseball Hall Of Fame, Cooperstown, Signed, 1956 . . . . . . 3819.00
Chuck Berry, Great Twenty-Eight, Sugar Hill Records, Signed, 33 RPM, 1982 . . . . 173.00
Dean Martin, Everybody Loves Somebody, Hit Version, Reprise, Signed, 45 RPM, 1964 . . . . . . 115.00
Gary Lewis & The Playboys, Everybody Loves A Clown, 45 RPM, 2 Records 3.00

Reamer, Glass, Jeannette, Green, 8 In.
$28.00

Reamer, Porcelain, Figural, Clown, Japan, Crown Mark, 2 Piece, c.1925, 6 x 5 1/2 In.
$75.00

Reamer, Potlay, Jack & Jill, 2 Handles, Japan, 4 1/2 In.
$142.00

Reamer, Sunkist, Black, Embossed, Pat. No. 68764, 8 ½ In.
$500.00

R

TIP

Rub the base of a candlestick with a little olive oil before lighting a candle. Any wax that drips can easily be peeled off the oiled base.

Red Wing, Bob White, Teapot, 8 In.
$53.00

Red Wing, Magnolia, Plate, Dinner, 10 ½ In.
$10.00

Red Wing, Random Harvest, Cup & Saucer
$7.50

TIP
Check the metal strips holding any heavy wall-hung shelves. After a few years, the shelf holder may develop "creep" and gradually bend away from the wall.

Glenn Miller, Army Air Force Band, Limited Edition, Volume II, Gold, 45 RPM . . . 35.00
John Denver & The Muppets, Christmas Together, RCA Records, 1979 . . . 29.00
Lennon Sisters, Shake Me I Rattle, One Day A Little Girl, 45 RPM . . . 3.00
Perry Como, Christmas Music For Children, 45 RPM . . . 5.00
Ricky Nelson, Stood Up, Waitin' In School, Imperial, 45 RPM, 1958 . . . 139.00
Rudolph The Red Nosed Reindeer, RCA Victor, 45 RPM . . . 10.00
Song Hits Of 1933, 78 RPM, 4 Records . . . 12.00
Stevie Wonder, My Cherie Amour, Yester-Me Yesterday, 45 RPM . . . 4.50
The Lovin Spoonful, Do You Believe In Magic, 2 Record Set . . . 3.00
Trini Lopez, Free With A Carton Of Fresca, 45 RPM . . . 9.00
Voices From The Moon, Philco Records, Apollo 11, 1969 . . . 27.00

RED WING Pottery of Red Wing, Minnesota, was a firm started in 1878. The company first made utilitarian pottery, including stoneware jugs and canning jars. In the 1920s art pottery was introduced. Many dinner sets and vases were made before the company closed in 1967. Rumrill pottery made by the Red Wing Pottery for George Rumrill is listed in its own category. For more prices, go to Kovels.com.

Advertising, Bowl, It Pays To Mix With Hoeck's Grocery, Iowa, Sponge Panel, 7 In. . . . 165.00
Advertising, Rolling Pin, Complements Of C.J. Buckley, Blue, White, 15 ½ x 2 ½ In. . . . 275.00
Advertising, Stoneware, Bean Pot, Tan & Brown Glaze, Bulbous, Handles, 5 ¾ x 7 In. . . . 55.00
Advertising, Stoneware, Jug, Hanlen Brothers, White Ground, Handle, 6 ½ x 3 ½ In. . . . 110.00
Advertising, Stoneware, Jug, Shoulder, Old Rose Distilling Co., Chicago, ½ Gal. . . . 125.00
Advertising, Stoneware, Jug, Wm. Steinmeyer Co. Wine Merchants, Milwaukee, Wis., Pt. . . . 105.00
Blossom Time, Plate, Bread & Butter, Lexington Shape, 6 ¼ In. . . . 8.00
Blossom Time, Saucer, Speckled Ivory, Casual Shape, 12 In. . . . 15.00
Bob White, Bowl, Vegetable, Divided, 14 ¼ x 6 ¼ In. . . . 25.00
Bob White, Bowl, Vegetable, Lug, Handle End, 9 ¼ x 9 In. . . . 22.00
Bob White, Casserole, Cover, Handle, Individual, 6 ½ x 4 ¼ In. . . . 55.00
Bob White, Casserole, Cover, Handles, 2 Qt. . . . 12.00
Bob White, Cup, 3 In. . . . 12.00
Bob White, Pitcher, 60 Oz., 12 ½ In. . . . 115.00
Bob White, Pitcher, Ice Lip, 11 ¾ In. . . . 75.00
Bob White, Plate, Bread & Butter, 6 ½ In. . . . 10.00
Bob White, Plate, Dinner, 11 In. . . . 17.50
Bob White, Plate, Salad, 7 ¼ In. . . . 60.00
Bob White, Platter, 13 ½ In. . . . 60.00
Bob White, Salt & Pepper, Cork Stoppers, 6 In. . . . 40.00
Bob White, Teapot, 8 In. . . . *illus* 53.00
Brushware, Jardiniere, 8 In. . . . 120.00
Casual, Relish, 5 Sections, 12 In. . . . 40.00
Churn, Large Wing, Lid, 2 Gal. . . . 300.00
Cookie Jar, Chef Pierre, Tan Glaze . . . 25.00
Cookie Jar, Chef Pierre, Yellow Glaze . . . 158.00
Cooler, Stag, Cobalt Blue, Cover, 10 Gal. . . . 775.00
Cooler, Water, Double Birch Leaf . . . 325.00
Creamer, Chartreuse, Colonial Shape, 3 ½ x 7 In. . . . 15.00
Crock, Bread Baker, Cover, Trees . . . 300.00
Crock, Cobalt Blue Design, Salt Glaze, Ear Handles, 1 ½ Gal. . . . 125.00
Crock, Cover, Bail Handle, 20 Gal. . . . 100.00
Crock, Large Wing, Mark, 15 Gal. . . . 70.00
Cuspidor, Spongeware, Red, Blue, Brown, Yellow Glaze, 4 ½ x 7 ½ In. . . . 11.00
Damask, Tidbit, 7 ⅜ In. . . . 26.00
Frontenac, Cup & Saucer . . . 17.00
Frontenac, Gravy Boat, Underplate, 7 x 4 ¾ In. . . . 34.00
Frontenac, Plate, Dinner, 10 ⅞ In. . . . 17.00
Jug, Oval, Brown, 5 Gal. . . . 150.00
Lexington Rose, Plate, Dinner, 10 ¼ In. . . . 25.00
Lotus, Cup & Saucer . . . 22.50
Lotus, Plate, Dinner, 10 In. . . . 22.00
Lotus, Saucer, 6 ¼ In. . . . 11.00
Lute Song, Butter Cover Only, 5 ½ In. . . . 10.00
Lute Song, Cup & Saucer . . . 15.00
Lute Song, Plate, Bread & Butter . . . 10.00
Lute Song, Plate, Salad, 7 ½ In. . . . 10.00
Magnolia, Cup & Saucer . . . 12.00
Magnolia, Plate, Dinner, 10 ½ In. . . . *illus* 10.00

Magnolia, Platter, 13 ½ x 11 ½ In. 15.00
Magnolia, Saucer 3.00
Pitcher, Blue Sponge, Band, Molded 200.00
Pompeii, Bowl, Salad, Duo-Tone, 6 In. 6.00
Random Harvest, Bowl, Fruit, 5 ¼ In. 3.50
Random Harvest, Cup & Saucer .... *illus* 7.50
Random Harvest, Plate, Bread & Butter, 6 ⅞ In. 2.50
Random Harvest, Relish, Divided, 13 x 5 ¼ In. 18.00
Reed, Cup & Saucer, Orange 30.00
Rose, Plate, Dinner, 10 ¾ In. 5.00
Smart Set, Platter, Warming, 19 ¾ In. 150.00
Sponge Band, Casserole, 8 In. 150.00
Stoneware, Ashtray, Stylized, Horse's Head, Green, 8 ½ x 8 ¾ In. 35.00
Stoneware, Ashtray, Wing Shape, Red Glaze, 9 ½ x 4 In. 198.00
Stoneware, Bowl, Shoulder, Albany Slip, 17 In. 165.00
Stoneware, Bowl, Shoulder, Blue, 7 In. 115.00
Stoneware, Bowl, Shoulder, Blue, 9 In. 85.00
Stoneware, Bowl, Sponge Panel, 8 In. .... 60.00 to 75.00
Stoneware, Bowl, Sponge Panel, 9 In. 70.00
Stoneware, Bowl, Sponge Panel, 11 In. 135.00
Stoneware, Bowl, Sponge Panel, Dark Blue, 8 In. 195.00
Stoneware, Bowl, White Sponge, 5 In. 75.00
Stoneware, Bowl, White Sponge, 10 In. 80.00
Stoneware, Churn, Butter, Cover, Albany Slip Glaze, Ear Handles, 1 Gal. 650.00
Stoneware, Churn, Butter, Cover, Birch Leaf, Union Oval, 2 Gal. 335.00
Stoneware, Churn, Butter, Cover, Wing & Ski Oval Over Wing, 4 Gal. 300.00
Stoneware, Churn, Cover, Wing & Oval, 2 Gal. 270.00
Stoneware, Churn, Cover, Wing & Oval, 3 Gal. 155.00
Stoneware, Churn, Cover, Wing & Oval, 4 Gal. 185.00
Stoneware, Crock, 3-Rib Cage, 20 Gal. 200.00
Stoneware, Crock, Butter, 20 Lb. 700.00
Stoneware, Crock, Cover, 2 Gal. 20.00
Stoneware, Crock, Cover, Pickle, Blue Bands, Bail Handle 100.00
Stoneware, Crock, Double Leaf, 20 Gal. 400.00
Stoneware, Crock, Rib Cage, 5 Gal. 185.00
Stoneware, Crock, Single Leaf, 6 Gal. .... 100.00 to 190.00
Stoneware, Crock, Single Leaf, 10 Gal. 235.00
Stoneware, Crock, Union Oval, Elephant Ear Handles, 4 Gal. 95.00
Stoneware, Crock, Upturned Leaf, 20 Gal. 400.00
Stoneware, Crock, Wing, Oval, No. 6, 10 Gal. 95.00
Stoneware, Crock, Wing, Oval, No. 6, 30 Gal. 235.00
Stoneware, Cuspidor, Daisy & Rope Design 65.00
Stoneware, Jar, Canning, Lid, 2 Gal. 55.00
Stoneware, Jar, Pantry, Lid, 5 Lb. 255.00
Stoneware, Jar, Pantry, Lid, Gal. 220.00
Stoneware, Jar, Stone Mason Fruit Jar, 2 Qt. 175.00
Stoneware, Jar, Stone Mason Fruit Jar, Qt. 220.00
Stoneware, Jug, Beehive, Rib Cage, Target, 5 Gal. 500.00
Stoneware, Jug, Beehive, Target, 5 Gal. 500.00
Stoneware, Jug, Beehive, Wing & Union, Oval, 5 Gal. 225.00
Stoneware, Jug, Dome Top, 2 Gal. 75.00
Stoneware, Mason Fruit Jar, Stone, Union, Cream, Pat. Jan. 24, 1899, Qt. .... *illus* 186.00
Stoneware, Mason Fruit Jar, Stone, Union, Screw Lid, Minn., Jan., 1899, 6 ⅝ In., Qt. 90.00
Stoneware, Pitcher, Blue & White Sponged Bands 170.00
Stoneware, Sponge, Casserole, Band, 7 In. 35.00
Stoneware, Vase, Impressed Flower, Gold, Black, 2 Handles, Brushware, 7 x 8 In. 95.00
Stoneware, Vase, Nokomis, Mountain Lions, Golden Glaze, Stamp, 8 x 7 In. 175.00
Stoneware, Vase, Orange & Bay Glaze, Molded Handles, 6 In. 105.00
Stoneware, Water Cooler, Lid, 4 Gal. 95.00
Stoneware, Water Cooler, Wing & Union Oval, 4 Gal. 185.00
Stoneware, Water Cooler, Wing & Union Oval, 5 Gal. .... 155.00 to 265.00
Stoneware, Water Cooler, Wing & Union Oval, 10 Gal. 115.00
Tampico, Bowl, Underplate 25.00
Tampico, Saucer 4.00
Town & Country, Cup & Saucer, Dusk Blue, Eva Zeisel 25.00
Town & Country, Relish, Lazy Susan Insert, Dusk Blue, Eva Zeisel, 7 ½ In. 35.00
Vase, Brushware, 2 Handles, 7 In. 100.00

TIP
A dental mirror is useful when checking for damage or repairs inside a teapot or clock.

Red Wing, Stoneware, Mason Fruit Jar, Stone, Union, Cream, Pat. Jan. 24, 1899, Qt.
$186.00

Red Wing, Wall Pocket, Bird, Brushware, 10 ½ In.
$55.00

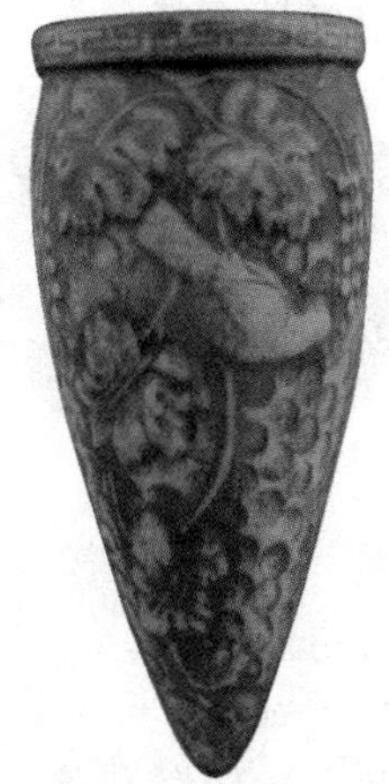

TIP
Bakelite needs special care. Avoid extreme heat sources like an electric stove or hot hair dryer. Wash by hand, never in a dishwasher.

R

Redware, Batter Bowl, Coggled Rim, Orange Glaze, Black Drip Glaze, Spout, Applied Handle, 4 x 6 In.
$330.00

Redware, Creamer, Bulbous, Orange, Brown Mottled Glaze, Handle, 3 ½ x 3 In.
$110.00

Redware, Cuspidor, Concave Top, Center Hole, Orange Ground, Black Spatter, 1 ½ x 4 In.
$220.00

TIP

You might be able to remove the warp from a 78 rpm record. Put it between two pieces of glass in a sunny window for a day. Let it cool. This should straighten the record.

Vase, Green & Brown Crystalline Glaze, 2 Handles, 4 ½ x 10 In. 345.00
Vase, Oval, Blue Gray, 10 In. 82.00
Vase, Raised Designs, Matte Brown & Blue Crystalline Glaze, 10 In. 46.00
Wall Pocket, Bird, Brushware, 10 ½ In. .... *illus* 55.00

REDWARE is a hard, red stoneware that originated in the late 1600s and continues to be made. The term is also used to describe any common clay pottery that is reddish in color. Redware molds are listed in Kitchen.

Baking Dish, Wild Slip, England, c.1800, 14 In. 16865.00
Bank, Bird, Seated, Jug Shape, Blue Wings, Black Sponging, James Seagreaves, 7 ½ In. 110.00
Bank, Black Man's Face, Painted, 19th Century, 3 ¼ x 3 ½ In. 527.00
Bank, Coggled Bands, Rounded Finial, Slot, Bulbous, Green Splotch Glaze, c.1890, 5 x 4 In. 1265.00
Bank, Lion, Coleslaw Mane, Green, Brown, Yellow Mottled Slip, c.1860, 6 ¼ In. 5616.00
Bank, Round, Sawtooth Border, 4-Knop Base, Initialed, NS, c.1830, 7 ¾ In. 4914.00
Bank, Spaniel, 19th Century, 3 ½ In. 497.00
Bank, Spaniel, Seated, Owl Eyed, Molded Fur, Orange Glaze, Manganese, 5 ¼ In. 345.00
Barrel, Brandy, Marbleized Glaze, Inscribed, E. Sheets, Philadelphia, 1853, 5 ½ In. 468.00
Basin, Round, Cone Shape, Orange Glaze Interior, 7 ½ x 15 ½ In. 55.00
Batter Bowl, Coggled Rim, Orange Glaze, Black Drip Glaze, Spout, Handle, 4 x 6 In. .... *illus* 330.00
Bean Pot, Bulbous, Flared Rim, Orange Glaze, Reeded C-Shape Handle, 5 x 5 In. 33.00
Bean Pot, Cover, Bulbous, Spiral Splotched Brown Manganese, Lug Handles, c.1824, 9 In. 3555.00
Bean Pot, Cover, Bulbous, Spiraled Splotches Of Brown Manganese, 1855, 9 In. 3555.00
Bean Pot, Cover, Orange Glaze, Round Finial, Spout, Applied Handle, 6 ½ x 6 In. 220.00
Bean Pot, Flared, Bulbous, Orange Glaze, Black Base, 2 Applied C-Shape Handles, 5 x 4 ¾ In. 176.00
Bell, Dome Shape, Incised Bands, Orange Glaze, Applied Handle, Foltz, 7 ½ x 4 ¾ In. 143.00
Bottle, Cylindrical, Tapered, Brown Glaze, 8 x 3 ⅝ In. 55.00
Bowl, Avanyu Among Rain Clouds, Signed, San Ildefonso, c.1900, 4 x 8 ½ In. 600.00
Bowl, Barber, Yellow Slip, Tulips, Comb, Scissors, Late 18th Century, 2 ½ x 8 In. 878.00
Bowl, Blocked Geometrics, San Ildefonso, c.1925, 5 ¾ x 10 In. 5287.00
Bowl, Flared, Ringed Base, Manganese, c.1850, 3 x 6 In. 381.00
Bowl, Flared Molded Rim, Yellow Wavy Line, 2 ½ x 9 In. 220.00
Bowl, Flared Rim, Dash, Dot, Black, White Slip Bands, Penn., 1800s, 4 x 14 In. 575.00
Bowl, Glazed Interior Yellow, Green, Brown, 1800s, 7 x 2 In. 235.00
Bowl, Green Exterior, Brown Interior Glaze, c.1825, 2 x 5 In. 2015.00
Bowl, Incised Band, Green, Brown Glaze, John Bell, Penn., c.1850, 3 x 8 In. 770.00
Bowl, Olive Green & Orange Glaze, Brown Daubs, 1800s, 10 x 3 ½ In. 352.00
Bowl, Olive Green Glaze, Orange Spots, 1800s, 11 ½ In. 323.00
Bowl, Oval, Flared, Orange Ground, Black Manganese Drip, 2 x 10 x 8 In. 44.00
Bowl, Round, Orange Glaze, Manganese Black Mottled Glaze, 2 x 3 ¾ In. 275.00
Bowl, Round, Orange Ground, Brown Mottled Glaze, 1 ¼ x 7 In. 88.00
Bowl, Slip Decorated, Yellow Bands, Wavy Lines, c.1824, 3 x 11 In. 1185.00
Bowl, Tapered Sides, Cogged Rim, Orange Ground Glaze, 1 x 3 ½ In. 413.00
Bowl, Yellow & Green Squiggles, Manganese Stripes, Moravian, 2 ½ x 8 ½ In. 1872.00
Butter Print, Cut Star, Orange Glaze, Early 19th Century, 3 ½ In. 2340.00
Butter Print, Heart Form, Roses, Heart, Compass, Unglazed, Inscribed, Jacob Berger, 5 In. 3042.00
Butter Print, Sophia Butter Mold, Amber Glaze, Pa., Incised 1851 X, 6 In. 2585.00
Canister, Fox, Coleslaw Mane, Holding Cup, Late 1800s, 10 ½ In. 2340.00
Charger, Bird, Yellow Slip, Pennsylvania, 11 ¼ In. 550.00
Charger, Coggled Rim, 3 Wavy Yellow Lines, Orange Ground, Oval, 3 x 17 ¼ x 13 In. 1210.00
Charger, Coggled Rim, Orange Glaze, 3-Line Slip, Curled Yellow Slip, 2 x 12 ½ In. 880.00
Charger, Coggled Rim, Whirligig Design, Yellow Slip, 19th Century, 13 ¼ In. 1035.00
Charger, Coggled Wheel Rim, Orange Slip Glaze, Yellow Lined Wave, 2 ½ x 14 ½ In. 935.00
Chicken, Oval Base, Pinwheel, Black Sponged, James Seagreaves, 6 ¾ x 8 ½ In. 132.00
Churn, Bulbous, Flared Lid Rim, C-Shape Handles, 5 Gal., 17 ½ x 10 In. 143.00
Colander, Basket Form, Cylindrical, Handle, 19th Century, 15 In. 400.00
Colander, Round Rim, Diamond, Center Circle, Orange Glaze, Footed, 4 ¾ x 8 ½ In. 220.00
Creamer, Brown Glaze, c.1850, 4 ½ In. 176.00
Creamer, Bulbous, Orange, Brown Mottled Glaze, Handle, 3 ½ x 3 In. .... *illus* 110.00
Creamer, Yellow Squiggle Lines, 19th Century, 3 ½ In. 2808.00
Crock, Apple Butter, Bulbous, Black Manganese Glaze, Applied Handle, 6 ½ x 5 In. 77.00
Crock, Apple Butter, Bulbous, Orange, Mottled Manganese, Handle, 6 x 4 ½ In. 209.00
Crock, Apple Butter, Bulbous, Orange Glaze, Black Mottled Highlight, 6 ¼ x 5 In. 110.00
Crock, Apple Butter, Orange Glaze, Manganese Mottled, Drip Glaze, 6 x 4 ¼ In. 154.00
Crock, Black Splotch Slip Decoration, Closed Handles, c.1870, 9 ½ In. 115.00
Crock, Bulbous, Rolled Rim, Incised Bands, Black Mottled Glaze, 5 ½ x 5 ¼ In. 523.00
Crock, Butter, Bulbous, Banding, Rolled Rim, Black Manganese Glaze, 5 ½ x 4 ¼ In. 22.00

Crock, Flared Rim, Incised Ring, Brown Lead Glaze, Manganese Daubs, 13 In. 144.00
Crock, Green Running Glaze, Double Strap Handles, 19th Century, 17 ½ In. 88.00
Crock, Oval, Black Mottled Glaze, Closed Handles, c.1850, 8 In. 127.00
Crock, Storage, Round, Rim, Banding, Unglazed, Stamped John Bell, 7 ¾ x 6 ½ In. 220.00
Crock, Yellow Glaze, Sgraffito Crosses, Rope Twist Handles, 19th Century, 7 ¾ In. 1521.00
Crock, Yellow Wavy Slip, Handles, 19th Century, 11 In. 2574.00
Cup, Bulbous, Flared Rim, Orange Glaze, Black Spatter, Applied Handle, 3 ½ x 4 ¼ In. 99.00
Cup, Flared Rim, Brown Glaze, Black Mottled Drip, Applied Handle, 2 ½ x 3 ¾ In.. . . . . 66.00
Cup, Golden Brown Glaze, Manganese Streaks, c.1824, 2 x 4 In. 830.00
Cuspidor, Concave Top, Center Hole, Orange Ground, Black Spatter, 1 ½ x 4 In. . . . . *illus* 220.00
Cuspidor, Molded, Raised, Cord Banding, Concave Top, Oval Waste Hole, 3 ¾ x 8 ½ In. 55.00
Custard Cup, Tapered, Brown, Black Glaze Interior, Unglazed Exterior, 2 ¼ x 3 ⅜ In.. . . . . 55.00
Custard Cup, Tapered, Orange Glaze, Black Spatter, 2 ½ x 3 ⅝ In. 44.00
Dirt Dish, Bouge Style, c.1850, 2 x 10 In.. . . . . 523.00
Dirt Dish, Oval, Square Rim, c.1875, 1 ½ x 10 In.. . . . . 193.00
Dish, Crisscrossed Lines, 11 ⅝ In. 15210.00
Dish, Loaf, Coggled Rim, Wavy Line, Dot Yellow Slip, c.1825, 3 x 10 In.. . . . . 593.00
Dish, Loaf, Oblong, Wavy Lines, Dots, Yellow Slip, c.1825, 2 x 9 In. 504.00
Dish, Loaf, Orange Glaze, Yellow Slip Polka Dots, Mid 19th Century, 4 ¼ In.. . . . . 3744.00
Figurine, Bird, On Base, Multicolored, Signed, James Seagreaves, 7 ¼ x 12 ¼ In. 176.00
Figurine, Cat, Reclining, 19th Century, 5 ½ x 10 ½ In.. . . . . 1638.00
Figurine, Dog, Holding Basket With Bottle, 19th Century, 5 ½ In. 2400.00
Figurine, Dog, Standing, Curly Tail, 19th Century, 3 ¾ In.. . . . . 2640.00
Figurine, Lion, Full-Bodied, Brown Glaze On Mane, Tail, Face, Breininger, c.1981, 7 In.. . . . . . 460.00
Figurine, Rabbit, Long Ears, Hollow, Brown & Black Mottled Glaze, Ned Foltz, 11 ½ x 10 In. . 176.00
Figurine, Sow, 3 Piglets, Louis Brown, North Carolina, 1930s, 2 To 3 In.. . . . . 316.00
Figurine, Turkey, Spread Tail, Brown Ground, Yellow, Green Mottled Glaze, Hollow, 9 ¾ x 9 In. 143.00
Flask, Fish, Full-Bodied, Brown Glaze, Bottom Fins Are Stand, 19th Century, 11 ½ In.. . . . . . . 115.00
Flask, Oval, Black Manganese Glaze, 8 x 4 ½ x 2 ¾ In.. . . . . 99.00
Flask, Ring Form, Hollow, Bottle-Like Rim Spout, Brown Manganese Glaze, 3 x 10 In. 44.00
Flower Frog, Bird, On Mound, Green Wings, Black Sponged, James Seagreaves, 6 x 6 In.. . . . 165.00
Flower Frog, Bird On Mound, Green Wings, Signed, James Seagreaves, 5 ½ x 5 ¼ In.. . . . . . . 66.00
Flowerpot, Applied Flower Pinwheel, Yellow, Green, Tab Handles, 1800s, 12 x 13 In.. . . . . 380.00
Flowerpot, Bulbous, Crimped Rim, Orange Ground, Brown Glaze, Greg Shooner, 9 x 8 In.. . . 275.00
Flowerpot, Coggled Rim, Green, Brown & Orange Glaze, 5 ¾ In. 990.00
Flowerpot, Cone Shape, Crimped, Banding, Drip Tray, Drain Hole, 5 ½ x 6 In.. . . . . *illus* 220.00
Flowerpot, Cone Shape, Tapered, Brown Ground, Splotched, Drip Tray, 3 ⅞ x 4 ½ In.. . . . . 77.00
Flowerpot, Crimped Rim, Cylindrical, Banding, Orange Glaze, Black Manganese, 6 ¼ In. . . . 33.00
Flowerpot, Flared Saucer Base, Orange Glaze, Brown Mottled Highlights, 4 ½ x 5 In.. . . . . 77.00
Flowerpot, Manganese Splotch Design, Stamped, W. Smith Womelsdorf, 5 ¾ In.. . . . . 1320.00
Flowerpot, Pie Crimped Rim, Cone Shape, Orange Glaze, Drain Holes, 6 ⅞ x 7 ½ In. 99.00
Flowerpot, Undertray, Sgraffito, Bird, Tulip, Pinched Edge, Breininger, c.1986, 6 In.. . . . . 110.00
Hotplate, Manganese Splash, 19th Century, 7 ½ In. 110.00
Jar, Bulbous, Banding, Unglazed, Orange Glaze Interior, C-Shape Handles, 4 ⅛ In. 55.00
Jar, Bulbous, Concave Collar, Rounded Rim, Incised Band, H. Fulton, 9 x 7 In.. . . . . 385.00
Jar, Bulbous, Green & Brown Glaze, Incised Shoulder, Signed, Stahl, c.1939, 5 ¾ In.. . . . . 198.00
Jar, Butter, Round, Flat Rim, Brown, Orange Ground, Mottled Black, Handle, 6 ⅛ x 5 In. 143.00
Jar, Canning, Straight-Sided, Mustard Glaze, Round Shoulder, Stamped John Bell, c.1850, 7 In. 205.00
Jar, Coggled Neck, 2-Pinched Lugs, Manganese Design, 11 In.. . . . . 520.00
Jar, Cover, 3-Color Slip Linear Design, Handles, Signed, Greg Schooner, 11 In.. . . . . 764.00
Jar, Cover, Cylindrical, Incised Band, Black Glaze, 9 ¼ x 5 ½ In. . . . . *illus* 225.00
Jar, Cover, Oval, Brown Manganese, New England, c.1825, 11 In.. . . . . 1067.00
Jar, Cover, Oval, Green Glaze, c.1855, 7 In.. . . . . 13035.00
Jar, Cover, Oval, Incised Neck Lines, Brown Manganese Streaked Glaze, c.1820, 6 In.. . . . . 1541.00
Jar, Cover, Oval, Molded Neck Bands, Streaked, Brown Manganese Glaze, Handle, c.1830, 8 In. 3555.00
Jar, Cover, Oval, Streaked Brown Manganese Glaze, c.1824, 7 In.. . . . . 1896.00
Jar, Cover, Straight-Sided, Incised Bands, Green, Brown Glaze, Orange Accents, c.1825, 8 In. . 830.00
Jar, Manganese Daubed Glaze, c.1875, 6 In.. . . . . 205.00
Jar, Oval, Incised Shoulder Lines, Streaked Brown Manganese Glaze, c.1825, 8 In.. . . . . 2726.00
Jar, Red Speckles, Golden Brown Manganese Glaze, Handle, c.1835, 8 In.. . . . . 1541.00
Jar, Spotted Glaze, Green, Orange, New Hampshire, 19th Century, 9 In.. . . . . 575.00
Jar, Storage, Bulbous, Glazed Brown Interior, Unglazed Exterior, 5 ¼ x 5 ¼ In. 66.00
Jar, Storage, Bulbous, Rounded Rim, Brown Ground, Black Spatter, 6 ½ x 5 ¾ In.. . . . . 33.00
Jar, Storage, Cloth Lid, Cylindrical, Rim, Orange Glaze, Black Spatter, 6 ⅜ x 4 ⅛ In. 66.00
Jar, Storage, Dome Lid, Flared Rim, Button Finial, Orange Ground Glaze, 7 ¾ x 6 ¼ In. 110.00
Jar, Straight-Sided, Incised Bands, Transparent Green Glaze, Orange Halos, c.1824, 7 In.. . . . . 830.00
Jar, Tapered Cylinder, Mottled Green Copper Glaze, Lug Handles, c.1800, 11 In.. . . . . 2133.00

Redware, Flowerpot, Cone Shape, Crimped, Banding, Drip Tray, Drain Hole, 5 ½ x 6 In.
$220.00

Redware, Jar, Cover, Cylindrical, Incised Band, Black Glaze, 9 ¼ x 5 ½ In.
$225.00

Redware, Jelly Mold, Pinwheel, Scalloped Sides, Brown Ground Glaze, 2 ¾ x 5 ⅛ In.
$44.00

TIP
Don't overclean hardware, andirons, or other old brass objects. Clean off the worst, but don't try to make them look brand new.

Redware, Mug, Swan Handle Base, Inscribed, J.A. Mench, 1827, 4 ¼ In.
$1638.00

Redware, Pitcher, Bulbous, Black Manganese Glaze, Handles, 4 x 5 ½ In.
$120.00

TIP
Doormats at every door catch the dirt and keep it from creating dust and pollution in the house. Shake out, wash, or vacuum the mats frequently.

Jelly Mold, Pinwheel, Scalloped Sides, Brown Ground Glaze, 2 ¾ x 5 ⅛ In. .... *illus* 44.00
Jelly Mold, Rosette Center, Fluted, Scalloped, Orange Ground Glaze, 2 ⅛ x 5 ½ In. 66.00
Jelly Mold, Scalloped Rim, Grooves To Center, Orange Glaze, 1 ¼ x 5 ½ In. 55.00
Jelly Mold, Scalloped Rim, Spiral Grooves, Center Post, Manganese Glaze, 2 x 5 ¼ In. 22.00
Jug, Albany, Slip Glaze, Bulbous, Ear Handle, 4 ¼ In. 303.00
Jug, Albany Slip Glaze, Bulbous, Molded Shaped Handle, 6 ¼ In. 110.00
Jug, Albany Slip Glaze, Ear Handle, 6 ½ In. 110.00
Jug, Bulbous, Rounded Rim, Brown, Black Manganese Glaze, C-Shape Handle, 5 ¾ In. 88.00
Jug, Bulbous, Rounded Rim, Brown Glaze, C-Shape Handle, 4 ¼ x 4 In. 88.00
Jug, Face, 3 Horns, Question Mark Ears, Rosette On Handle, James Seagreaves, 4 In. 990.00
Jug, Incised Rim Bands, Brown Manganese Accents, Handle, c.1825, 8 In. 1185.00
Jug, Long Oval, Green, Brown To Red Brown Glaze, Strap Handle, c.1825, 7 ½ In. 4740.00
Jug, Make Do, Bulbous, Tapered Rim, Yellow Ocher, Mottled, Tin Handle, 3 x 3 In. 1540.00
Jug, Olive, 2 Mid Ridges, Brown Red Glaze, Handle, 10 ⅞ In. 880.00
Jug, Orange Glaze, Black Manganese, Yellow & Green Slip, Late 1800s, 2 ½ In. 1872.00
Jug, Oval, Golden, Green Glaze, Orange Halo, c.1824, 9 In. 1007.00
Jug, Oval, Green, Orange, Manganese, Mottled Glaze, Applied Strap Handle, 5 ½ In. 690.00
Jug, Oval, Running Red & Green Glaze, Manganese Spots, Applied Strap Handle, 12 ¾ In. 235.00
Jug, Red Brown Manganese Glaze, c.1824, 5 In. 385.00
Lamp, Fat, 3 Wicks, Handle, Pa., 19th Century, 2 ¼ x 5 ¾ In. 644.00
Lamp, Fat, Black Manganese Overall, Pa., 7 ¼ In. 556.00
Lamp, Fat, Dark Brown, 19th Century, 8 ¼ In. 1521.00
Loaf Pan, Coggled Rim, Yellow Slip, Mid 19th Century, 3 ½ x 11 ½ In. 1410.00
Milk Pan, Round, Rolled Rim, Coggled Banding, Black Drip Highlights, 3 ¾ x 9 ¼ In. 248.00
Mixing Bowl, Rounded Rim, Banding, Orange Glaze, Black Sponged Drip, 5 x 10 ¾ In. 248.00
Mug, Brown & Green Splotches, 19th Century, 3 In. 1170.00
Mug, Green, Orange Mottled Ground, Trailing Yellow Slip, Strap Handle, c.1800, 3 ½ In. 5148.00
Mug, Manganese Splash, Beaded Bands, 19th Century, 4 ¾ In. 410.00
Mug, Orange & Green Glaze, 19th Century, 3 In. 351.00
Mug, Orange Glaze, Yellow Slip Diagonal Lines, 19th Century, Child's, 2 ¾ In. 2808.00
Mug, Swan Handle Base, Inscribed, J.A. Mench, 1827, 4 ¼ In. .... *illus* 1638.00
Mug, Tapered, Orange Glaze, Black Manganese Drip Spatter, C-Shape Handle, 4 x 4 ¾ In. ... 88.00
Mug, Yellow & Green Slip Curlicue, 19th Century, 6 In. 761.00
Oil Lamp, Green & Orange Glaze, c.1900, 2 ¾ In. 527.00
Pail, Milk, Tapered Sides, Incised Banding, Applied Arched Handles, 5 ¼ x 11 ¾ In. 154.00
Pie Plate, Coggled Rim, Yellow Slip, 1800s, 7 In. 529.00
Pie Plate, Coggled Rim, Yellow Slip, 1800s, 12 In. 646.00
Pie Plate, Coggled Rim, Yellow Slip, Wavy Lines, 11 ¼ In. 406.00
Pie Plate, Coggled Rim, Yellow Slip Design, 19th Century, 10 In. 460.00
Pie Plate, Coggled Rim, Yellow Slip Lines, c.1875, 10 ¼ In. 382.00
Pie Plate, Yellow & Brown Slip, Stamped, W. Smith Womelsdorf, 7 ½ In. 2200.00
Pitcher, Bulbous, Black Manganese Glaze, Handles, 4 x 5 ½ In. .... *illus* 120.00
Pitcher, Bulbous, Collar Top, Black Mottled Glaze, Applied C-Shape Handle, 10 x 7 In. 275.00
Pitcher, Bulbous, Collar Top, Pour Spout, Fluted C-Shape Handle, 8 ¼ x 6 ½ In. 165.00
Pitcher, Cover, Coggled Band, Bulbous, Orange Glaze, Sponged, C-Shape Handle, 7 ½ x 6 In. 77.00
Pitcher, Eagle, Spread Wings, Jacob Medinger, Late 19th Century, 7 ¼ In. 1755.00
Pitcher, Flared, Bulbous, Orange Glaze, Black Base, C-Shape Handle, 5 ¼ x 4 ¾ In. 110.00
Pitcher, Flared Rim, Brown Glaze, Applied C-Shape Handle, 6 ½ In. 77.00
Pitcher, Large Circles, Dark Band At Rim, England, 1700s, 5 In. 12870.00
Pitcher, Oval, Sponged Manganese Glaze, Flowers, Strap Handle, 11 ½ In. 235.00
Pitcher, Paneled, Bulbous, Garland, Variegated Brown, Yellow Glaze, Handle, 7 ½ In. 33.00
Pitcher, Relief Birds & Stars, Black Manganese Glaze, Initials, JF, c.1805, 10 ½ In. 6435.00
Plate, 6-Point Star, 7 Astrisks Border, Initials, HBL, Scalloped Border, Early 1800s, 7 In. 1755.00
Plate, Bird, On Flower Vine, Sawborder, Sgraffito, HR, Montgomery, Pa., 1776, 12 In. 28080.00
Plate, Coggled Rim, 3 Yellow Wavy Lines, Sprig, Orange Glaze, 1 ½ x 9 In. 770.00
Plate, Coggled Rim, Brown Ground, Stylized Sprig, Round, 1 ⅛ x 5 In. 154.00
Plate, Coggled Rim, Orange, 4 Yellow Slip Lines, Black Wavy Central Line, 1 ½ x 10 In. 495.00
Plate, Coggled Rim, Orange Glaze, 3 Yellow Lines, ⅞ x 4 ⅜ In. 121.00
Plate, Coggled Rim, Orange Ground Glaze, Wavy Line, 2 x 10 In. 198.00
Plate, Coggled Rim, Tulip, Brown & Green Slip, Dryville, 7 ¾ In. 3080.00
Plate, Coggled Rim, Woman, Riding Horse, Flowers, Yellow Ground, Green, 12 ½ In. 33.00
Plate, Coggled Rim, Yellow Slip, Inscribed, Apple Pie, c.1825, 10 In. 5629.00
Plate, Coggled Wheel Rim, 3-Line Yellow Slip, 1 ½ x 9 ¾ In. 358.00
Plate, Eagle, Spread Wings, Sgraffito, Green, Initialed, NM, 1811, 12 In. 12870.00
Plate, Moravian, Slip Decorated, Brown Glaze, Red, Green, c.1800, 10 ⅛ In. 14375.00
Plate, Round, Orange Slip Glaze, Yellow Slip Dot, 6 ½ In. 132.00

R

Plate, Sgraffito, Multicolored Glaze, Ivory Ground, Pa., c.1800, 11 ½ In. 470.00
Plate, Tulip Vine, Birds, Pinwheels, Sgraffito, Squiggle Rim, Inscribed, 39958, 1828, 12 In. .. 11115.00
Plate, Yellow Slip, Apple Pie, 19th Century, 10 In. 263.00
Porringer, Flat Rim, Bulbous, Orange Glaze, Black Spatter, 4 ¼ x 5 ½ In. .... *illus* 66.00
Porringer, Tapered Sides, Brown Mottled Glaze, Pour Spout, 3 ½ x 5 ½ In. 77.00
Puzzle Jug, Bird Spout, Brown Manganese Glaze, White Dots, 19th Century, 6 In. 8775.00
Stein, Hunt Scene, Dogs, Deer, Multicolored, Pewter Foot, Lid, Germany, 7 In. 415.00
Sugar, Cover, Brown Glaze, White Dot Slip, Bead & Scrolls, Twisted Handles, c.1830, 7 In. ... 12870.00
Sugar, Cover, Finial, Bulbous, Flared Rim, Orange Ground Glaze, Handle, 4 ¾ x 4 In. 132.00
Sugar, Roll Rim, Rust Brown Glaze, Loop Handles, 5 ⅝ x 6 ⅛ In. 1265.00
Toddy Plate, Free-Form, Mottled Yellow Slip, Green Splotches, Early 19th Century, 5 In. 3276.00
Toddy Plate, Yellow & Green Splotch Design, Connecticut, 19th Century, 5 In. 439.00
Toddy Plate, Yellow Slip Flag, Mid 19th Century, 5 In. 1170.00
Wall Pocket, Bird, Flowers, Mottled Green & Brown Glaze, Strasburg, Va., 1800s, 5 ½ In. 3510.00
Wall Pocket, Cone Shape, Incised Band, Mushroom Finial, Orange Glaze, 7 In. .... *illus* 121.00
Waste Bowl, Tapered Sides, Manganese Black & Brown Glaze, 3 ⅜ x 6 ⅜ In. 66.00
Whistle, Bird, Bell Form Base, Black Sponge, James Seagreaves, 5 x 6 In. 275.00
Whistle, Bird, Multicolored, Sponged Highlights, James Seagraves, 2 ¾ x 6 In. 88.00
Whistle, Chicken Form, 3 ¾ In. 950.00
Wigstand, Mottled Orange Glaze, Early 19th Century, 7 ¼ In. 936.00

REGOUT, *see Maastricht category.*

RICHARD was the mark used on acid-etched cameo glass vases, bowls, night-lights, and lamps made by the Austrian company Loetz after 1918. The pieces were very similar to the French cameo glasswares made by Daum, Galle, and others.

Vase, Ferns, Cupped Rim, Exotic Flowers, 8 ½ In. .... *illus* 489.00
Vase, Flowers, Amethyst, Pink, Footed, Oval, Cameo, Signed, 5 In. 403.00
Vase, Flowers, Pink, Magenta Overlay, Elongated Cylindrical Neck, 7 ½ In. 130.00
Vase, Frosted, Green Chateau, Tall Trees, Lake, Mountains, Barrel Shape, 14 ½ In. 1955.00

RIDGWAY pottery has been made in the Staffordshire district in England since 1808 by a series of companies with the name Ridgway. The transfer-design dinner sets are the most widely known product. They are still being made. Other pieces of Ridgway may be listed under Flow Blue.

Bowl, Etruscan Festoon, Pink, Black, 1835, 2 ¼ x 5 ½ In. 175.00
Bowl, India Temple, Blue, Pedestal, 9 ½ x 4 In. 300.00
Butter, Cover, Flowers, Leaves, Blue, Green, Scroll Border, Marked, 8 ¼ x 4 In. 58.00
Dish, Oriental Pattern, Oval, 14 x 3 In. 9.95
Gravy Boat, Underplate, Olga, Flow Blue, c.1912 .... 11.80
Gravy Boat, Verona, Flow Blue, c.1910. .... 30.00
Jug, Blue Flowers, Chester Pattern, Cream Ground, 11 In. 44.00
Jug, Lion, Boar Hunt Scene, Green, Stoneware, c.1835, 6 In. 575.00
Pitcher, Coaching Days, Craqueleur, Silver Overlay, Handle, 7 ½ In. 100.00
Pitcher, Parian, Relief, Hunting, Tavern Scenes, W. Ridgeway & Co., 1835, 10 In. 115.00
Plate, Amoy, Blue, 9 ¼ In. 125.00
Plate, Brown, Grecian, Transfer, Marked, 1802, 9 In. 250.00
Plate, Delaware, Flow Blue, 14-Sided, 10 ¾ In. 75.00
Plate, Etruscan Festoon, Pink, Brown, 9 ¼ In. 200.00
Plate, Flosculous, Brown, Scalloped Rim, 9 In. 125.00
Plate, Gainsborough, Raised Design, Embossed Rim, Flow Blue, c.1900, 9 In. 45.00
Plate, Napier, Blue, 9 In. 125.00
Plate, Napier, Purple, 7 ½ In. 95.00
Plate, Philadelphia Library, Blue, 8 In. 140.00
Plate, Ruggles House, Hudson River, Blue, 10 In. 175.00
Plate, Soup, Harpers Ferry, Potomac Side, Black, 9 In. 125.00
Plate, Soup, Indus, Brown, 9 ½ In. 95.00
Platter, Berlin Vase, Flow Blue, c.1850, 10 ½ x 12 ¾ In. 11.80
Platter, Italian Flower Garden, Blue, 11 x 9 ½ In. 250.00
Platter, University, Blue, 12 ¼ x 9 ½ In. 225.00
Platter, Verona, Flow Blue, c.1910, 10 ¼ x 13 ¾ In. 83.00
Platter, Windsor Festoon, Gadrooned Rim, c.1879, 19 x 16 In. 501.00
Platter, Wreath, Flowers, Pink, Blue, Yellow, 14 x 11 In. 125.00
Tureen, Cover, Attached Underplate, Flowers, Handles, Ironstone, England, c.1870, 12 In. 200.00
Tureen, Devonshire, Brown, 11 x 5 ½ In. 175.00

Redware, Porringer, Flat Rim, Bulbous, Orange Glaze, Black Spatter, 4 ¼ x 5 ½ In.
$66.00

Redware, Wall Pocket, Cone Shape, Incised Band, Mushroom Finial, Orange Glaze, 7 In.
$121.00

Richard, Vase, Ferns, Cupped Rim, Exotic Flowers, 8 ½ In.
$489.00

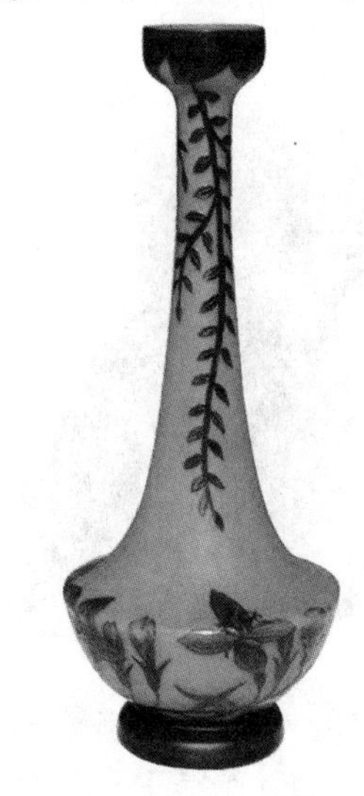

R

RIVIERA dinnerware was made by the Homer Laughlin Co. of Newell, West Virginia, from 1938 to 1950. The pattern was similar in coloring and in mood to Fiesta and Harlequin. The Riviera plates and cup handles were square. For more prices, go to Kovels.com.

Green, Casserole, Cover, 10 ½ In. 66.00
Green, Sugar & Creamer 7.50
Ivory, Tumbler, Handle 70.00
Mauve Blue, Tumbler, Handle 60.00
Red, Casserole, Cover, Handles, 10 ½ In. 91.00

ROBLIN Art Pottery was founded in 1898 by Alexander W. Robertson and Linna Irelan in San Francisco, California. The pottery closed in 1906. The firm made faience with green, tan, dull blue, or gray glazes. Decorations were usually animal shapes. Some red clay pieces were made.

Vase, Bisque, Tooled Carved Foot, Impressed, Marked, 2 x 3 In. 270.00
Vase, Crayfish, Applied, Pinched Neck, Bisque, 5 x 4 ½ In. 1320.00
Vase, Green, Brown Glaze Drip, Marked, Rolled Lip, 5 x 5 ½ In. .... *illus* 2520.00

Roblin, Vase, Green, Brown Glaze Drip, Marked, Rolled Lip, 5 x 5 ½ In.
$2520.00

ROCKINGHAM, in the United States, is a pottery with a brown glaze that resembles tortoiseshell. It was made from 1840 to 1900 by many American potteries. Mottled brown Rockingham wares were first made in England at the Rockingham factory. Other types of ceramics were also made by the English firm. Related pieces may be listed in the Bennington category.

Bank, Boot, Yellowware, Glazed, 3 ½ x 5 ½ In. 77.00
Bank, Dog, Boxer, Seated, Brown Glaze, Square Base, 7 ⅜ In. 86.00
Batter Jug, Man, Seated, Smoking Pipe, Yellowware, Wire Handle, 10 In. .... *illus* 990.00
Creamer, Cow, Yellowware, Lid, 1847-56, 5 ¼ x 6 ¼ In. 431.00
Cuspidor, Shield & Eagles, Hexagonal, Embossed, 1850, 4 x 6 In. 295.00
Doorstop, Dog, Spaniel, Seated, Curly Tail, Embossed Figures, c.1865, 12 x 10 In. 1265.00
Doorstop, Dog, Spaniel, Yellowware, Flower Base, c.1875, 11 ½ In. 1610.00
Figurine, Cat, Seated, Oval Base, Late 1800s, 11 In. 1469.00
Figurine, Dog, Hound, Seated, Yellowware, 19th Century, 6 x 6 In. 115.00
Figurine, Dog, Spaniel, Seated, 5 ¾ In. .... *illus* 275.00
Figurine, Dog, Spaniel, Seated, Base, Late 19th Century, 10 ¾ In. 125.00
Figurine, Lion, Reclining, Brown Glaze, 19th Century, 6 x 12 In., Pair 878.00
Figurine, Man, 2 On Keg, Yellowware, 9 In. 143.00
Foot Warmer, Oval, Center Hole, Raised Block Letters, J.L. Rue Pottery, 7 x 9 ½ In. 820.00
Inkstand, Yellowware, Sponged Glaze, Cartouche, Marked Sharpe, 12 x 6 In. 230.00
Jug, Falstaff, Seated, Stamped, A. Cadmus, Congress Pottery, 1850s, 7 In. 1650.00
Nappy, Yellowware, 4 Piece 88.00
Pitcher, Ale, Cover, Molded Cartouche, Pierced Spout, Hound Handle, c.1850s, 10 In. 633.00
Pitcher, Ale, Cover, Riders & Hounds, Molded Branch Handle, 1850s, 9 In. 720.00
Pitcher, Ale, Presentation, John De Molitor, Dog Handle, c.1850, 10 ¼ In. 173.00
Pitcher, Boar, Stag Hunt, Hound Handle, Harker, Taylor, Ohio, c.1850, 10 In. 633.00
Pitcher, Boar, Stag Hunt, Teal, Brown, Hound Handle, Harrison, Ohio, c.1853, 11 In. 2875.00
Pitcher, Grapes, Branch Handle, 1849-54, 11 ½ In. 1210.00
Pitcher, Grapes, Branch Handle, D. Greatbatch, N.J., c.1850, 12 In. 1265.00
Pitcher, Heron, Goat's Head Under Spout, Twig Handle, 1850-58, 8 ½ In. 510.00
Pitcher, Hound Handle, 1847-58, 4 Qt. 978.00
Pitcher, Hunt Scenes, Hound Handle, Salamander Works, 8 In. 374.00
Pitcher, Ice, Cover, Stag, Leaping, Rabbits, Eagles, Hound Handle, c.1860, 12 In. 270.00
Pitcher, Ice, Heron Attacking Snake, Leaves, Acorn Finial, Twig Handle, c.1847, 9 In. 1495.00
Pitcher, Ice, Presentation, Grapes, Vines, Branch Handle, JPB, 1850s, 9 ½ x 14 In. 5650.00
Pitcher, Marsh, Herons, Goat Head, Snake Handle, Bennett, Baltimore, c.1855, 9 In. 546.00
Pitcher, Pheasant, Gamekeeper, Landscape, Branch Handle, Bennett, c.1850, 8 In. 546.00
Pitcher, Stag, Boar Hunt, Hound Handle, Bennett, Baltimore, c.1850, 10 In. 489.00
Pitcher, Strainer, Grapes & Vines, Branch Finial, 1850s, 9 ⅝ In. 6038.00
Pitcher, Toby, Ben Franklin, 5 ⅞ In. 225.00
Urn, Lid, Flowers, Pink, White, Gilt, Ram Head Mounts, Mark, England, 1800s, 15 In. 1725.00
Window Sash Rest, Wigged Man, Unglazed, 1800s, 5 In., Pair 230.00

Rockingham, Batter Jug, Man, Seated, Smoking Pipe, Yellowware, Wire Handle, 10 In.
$990.00

Rockingham, Figurine, Dog, Spaniel, Seated, 5 ¾ In.
$275.00

ROGERS, *see John Rogers category.*

ROOKWOOD pottery was made in Cincinnati, Ohio, from 1880 to 1960. All of this art pottery is marked, most with the famous flame mark. The R is reversed and placed back to back with the letter P. Flames surround the letters. After 1900, a Roman numeral was added to the

TIP

If something looks strange or not quite right when you come home, don't be shy. Risk embarrassment and go to the neighbors for assistance.

mark to indicate the year. The company went bankrupt in 1941. For several years various owners tried to revive the pottery, but by 1967 it was out of business. The name and some of the molds were bought by a collector in 1984. The molds were kept in his basement until 2006 when a group of investors bought them and revived the pottery. The Rookwood Pottery Co. currently makes fireplaces, tiles, and bookends in old designs and special items for limited edition vases and steins for Christmas.

Ash Receiver, Frog, Open Mouth, Green Glaze, c.1950, 2 ⅞ In. 345.00
Ashtray, Crocodile, Dark Blue Matte Glaze, c.1922, 2 x 6 ¼ In. 633.00
Basket, Flowers, Standard Glaze, Red Label, 1891, 4 In. 69.00
Biscuit Jar, Mice, c.1893, 6 x 6 In. 1560.00
Bookends, Beagles, Heads Down, Red Commandel Glaze, 4 ½ In. 460.00
Bookends, Bear, Seated, Brown High Glaze, Louise Abel, 1948, 4 ¼ In. 2070.00
Bookends, Colonial Women, Standing, Gray Matte Glaze, Impressed, 1915, ... 316.00
Bookends, Dog, Seated, Celadon Glaze, 1945, 5 x 6 In. 173.00
Bookends, Dutch Boy & Girl, Sallie Toohey, 1953, 6 x 4 ¼ In. 144.00
Bookends, Elephant, Trunks Down, Brown Matte Glaze, 1922, 5 ½ x 7 In. 403.00
Bookends, Elephants, Ivory Matte Glaze, c.1931 .... 374.00
Bookends, Elephants, Raised Trunks, Green Gray Matte, 1929, 7 ¼ In. 1035.00
Bookends, Elephants, Raised Trunks, Nubian Black Glaze, 1951, 7 ½ In. 1035.00
Bookends, Flower Basket, Multicolored, Glossy Glaze, 1927 .... 288.00
Bookends, Flower Basket, Multicolored, Pottery, c.1927, 6 In. .... *illus* 546.00
Bookends, Flower Basket, Multicolored Matte Glaze, 1927, 6 ⅛ In. 230.00
Bookends, Giraffe, Reclining, Olive Over Brown Matte Glaze, 1940, 5 x 6 ½ In. 1380.00
Bookends, Giraffe, Reclining, Turquoise Glaze, 1940, 5 x 7 In. 748.00
Bookends, Horse Head, Nubian Black Glaze, W. McDonald, c.1954, 6 In. 259.00
Bookends, Jay Bird, Blue Matte Glaze, Pottery, Impressed, 1937, 5 In. 230.00
Bookends, Kingfisher, Green Matte Glaze, 1925, 5 ¾ In. 431.00
Bookends, Lion, Reclining, Brown Glaze, Signed, 6 x 5 ½ x 4 In. 600.00
Bookends, Lion, Seated, Ivory Matte Glaze, c.1928, 6 ½ In. 575.00
Bookends, Monkey On Book, Black & Tan Mottled Glaze, 3 ¾ In. 518.00
Bookends, Nude Woman, Kneeling, Cream High Glaze, 1959, 7 In. 2530.00
Bookends, Owl, Tan & Blue Matte Glaze, c.1929, 5 ¾ In. 288.00
Bookends, Owl Seated On Book, Matte Green Glaze, 1942, 5 ½ In. 288.00
Bookends, Panther, Reclining, Tan Glaze, Wm. McDonald, 1946, 5 ½ x 6 In. 230.00
Bookends, Peacock, White, Blue, 1921 .... 375.00
Bookends, Rook, Blue Gray Glaze, c.1921, 5 ¼ In. 248.00
Bookends, Rook, Dark Blue, 1920, 6 In. 110.00
Bookends, Rook, Leaves, Berries, Blue Matte Glaze, Wm. McDonald, 1946, 5 ¼ In. 230.00
Bookends, Rook, Standing, Leaves & Berries, Green Mottled Glaze, 5 ½ In. 259.00
Bookends, Ships, Blue Matte Crystalline Glaze, Impressed, 4 ¾ In. 316.00
Bookends, Ships, Full Sail, Cream Glaze, Marked, c.1936, 5 ½ In. 360.00
Bookends, St. Francis Of Assisi, c.1945, 8 In. 705.00
Bookends, Water Lilies, White Matte Glaze, 3 ¾ x 5 ½ In. 110.00
Bookends, Water Lily, Ivory Matte Glaze, c.1941, 3 ½ x 5 ½ In. 173.00
Bowl, 2 Female Nudes, Arched, Cream Matte Glaze, Oval, Footed, 1928, 8 In. 95.00
Bowl, Band Of Ducks, Molded, Rose Matte Glaze, Production, c.1920, 2 x 4 ¾ In. 196.00
Bowl, Butterflies, Black Opal, Sara Sax, c.1926, 7 ⅜ In. .... *illus* 1725.00
Bowl, Dragonflies, Light Blue Ground, c.1917, 3 x 9 In. 431.00
Bowl, Flower Band, Yellow, Green, Brown Shaded To Maroon, c.1915, 4 ½ In. 270.00
Bowl, Flowers, Yellow To Rose, Black Slip Outline, Flared, D. Workum, 6 ½ x 2 ½ In. 345.00
Bowl, Fowl, White, Black, Brown, Footed, Gilt, 9 ¼ In. 770.00
Bowl, Geometric, Blue & Tan Matte Glaze, c.1923, 2 ⅜ In. 150.00
Bowl, Green Glaze, c.1915, 2 ½ In. 81.00
Bowl, Pinecones, Reticulated, Embossed, Deep Green Matte Glaze, c.1909, 2 ¾ In. 633.00
Bowl, Stylized Design, Blues & Browns, Blue Ground, Squeezebag, c.1928, 5 x 6 In. 960.00
Bowl, Stylized Flowers, Maroon Ground, Sara Sax, c.1920, 2 ½ x 6 In. 1495.00
Bowl, Yellow To Rose, Slip, Flared, Workum, 1927, 2 ½ x 6 ½ In. .... *illus* 360.00
Box, Bisque, Hollow Body, Oval, Gray Glossy Glaze, 1884, 5 x 4 x 4 In. 575.00
Box, Cover, Maroon High Glaze, Jet Black, 6-Sided, 1 ⅞ x 5 ½ In. 184.00
Cachepot, Green, Incised, Footed Pedestal, c.1922, 4 ¾ x 6 In. 94.00
Candelabrum, Aventurine Glaze, 1920, 23 ⅝ In. 863.00
Candleholder, Art Deco, Green Matte Glaze, c.1929, 2 ¾ In., Pair 138.00
Candleholder, Lavender Glaze, Handle, c.1924, ¾ x 5 In. 104.00
Candlestick, Production, Impressed, c.1928, 1 ½ x 3 ½ In., Pair 84.00
Centerpiece, Flowers, Geometrics, Multicolored, Milky Overglaze, 1930 .... 1380.00
Charger, Giraffe, Palm Tree, River, Mountain, Landscape, Wax Matte Glaze, 2 ¼ x 14 In. 2070.00
Charger, Stylized Lily, Green, Blue, Brown, 12 ¼ In. .... *illus* 1800.00

Rookwood, Bookends, Flower Basket, Multicolored, Pottery, c.1927, 6 In.
$546.00

Rookwood, Bowl, Butterflies, Black Opal, Sara Sax, c.1926, 7 ⅜ In.
$1725.00

Rookwood, Bowl, Yellow To Rose, Slip, Flared, Workum, 1927, 2 ½ x 6 ½ In.
$360.00

Rookwood, Charger, Stylized Lily, Green, Blue, Brown, 12 ¼ In.
$1800.00

Rookwood, Figurine, Chow Chow, Tan Glaze, c.1936, 7 ¾ In. $1380.00

Rookwood, Figurine, Kitten, Turquoise High Glaze, 1943, 2 x 3 ½ In. $720.00

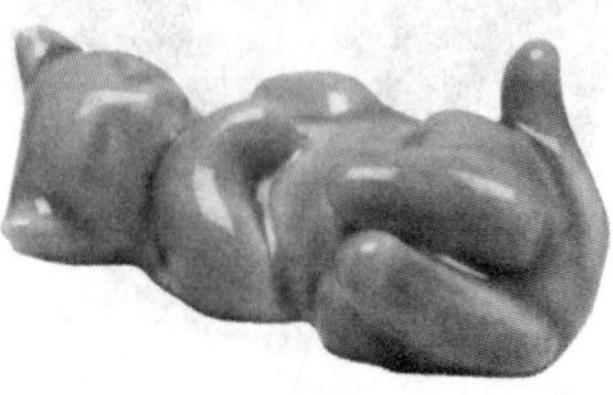

Rookwood, Flower Holder, Bird, Seated On Stump, Dark Blue High Glaze, 1924 $431.00

TIP

Do not put an alabaster figure or vase outside. It is softer than marble and will eventually fall apart if exposed to rain.

Clock, Supine Panther, Green Glaze, c.1950, 7 ⅝ In. 460.00
Creamer, Daffodils, Leaves, Yellow, Shaded Brown, Green, c.1890, 7 In. 81.00
Cruet, Daisies, Carrie Steinle, c.1902, 5 ⅜ In.. . . . . 374.00
Dish, Lyre, Faun, Playing Flute, Figural, Marked, c.1927, 4 x 5 ¼ In.. . . . . 86.00
Dish, Rose Spray, Pink, Blue Ground, Jones, 1923, 11 In. 711.00
Ewer, Clover Leaves, White Flowers, Brown Shaded To Green To Orange, 6 ½ In. 316.00
Ewer, Cornflowers, Standard Glaze, Carl Schmidt, 1899, 5 In. 150.00
Ewer, Daffodils, Scrolled Sterling Overlay, 1898, 11 In. 2875.00
Ewer, Flower, Leaves, Handles, Standard Glaze, Impressed, B. Horsfall, 1900, 4 ½ In.. . . . . 316.00
Ewer, Flying Geese, Standard Glaze, Shirayamadani, 12 ⅛ In. 1725.00
Ewer, Holly, Standard Glaze, Lenore Asbury, 1899, 9 ½ In. 316.00
Ewer, Irises, Yellow, Matthew Daly, c.1889, 12 In.. . . . . 1495.00
Ewer, Laurel Leaves, Berries, Ruffled Rim, c.1892, 10 In. 575.00
Ewer, Mother & Baby Birds, Brown To Gold, K. Shirayamadani, c.1893, 8 x 15 In. 4025.00
Ewer, Prunus Blossoms, Mahogany Glaze, c.1887, 13 ¼ In. 374.00
Ewer, Purple Iris, Standard Glaze, Impressed, Edith Felten, 1903, 6 ½ In.. . . . . 374.00
Ewer, Red Cherries, Caroline Steinle, c.1901, 6 In.. . . . . 403.00
Ewer, Roses, Yellow, Silver Overlay, Ruffled Spout, c.1893, 10 ¾ In. 2070.00
Ewer, Sea Eagle On Pine Bough, Crashing Waves, Matte Finish, 26 ½ In. 16100.00
Ewer, Sweet Peas, c.1894, 6 In. 316.00
Ewer, Wild Rose, E. Lincoln, c.1894, 6 ¼ In. 403.00
Ewer, Yellow Flowers, Green Leaves, Brown Ground, Bulbous, Stamped, 10 In.. . . . . 403.00
Ewer, Yellow Roses, c.1891, 8 ⅞ In. 150.00
Figurine, Angel, Holding Song Book, Louise Abel, 3 ⅝ In. 345.00
Figurine, Beagle Puppy, Seated, c.1943, 5 x 6 In.. . . . . 380.00
Figurine, Bird, Brown, Red, Green High Glaze, K. Shirayamadani, c.1945, 7 ½ x 6 ½ In. 230.00
Figurine, Chow Chow, Tan Glaze, c.1936, 7 ¾ In. . . . . *illus* 1380.00
Figurine, Cockatoo, Yellow, White Green, Shirayamadani, c.1944, 9 In. 288.00
Figurine, Dog, Seated, Runny Blue Glaze, c.1930, 4 ½ In. 345.00
Figurine, Egret, Nubian Black, Claire De Lune Glaze, 1940s, 9 In.. . . . . 374.00
Figurine, Honey Bear, Seated, Nubian Black, c.1948, 4 In. 920.00
Figurine, Kitten, Turquoise High Glaze, 1943, 2 x 3 ½ In. . . . . *illus* 720.00
Figurine, Polar Bear, Ivory Matte Glaze, 1934, 4 In.. . . . . 690.00 to 978.00
Figurine, Sacred Heart Of Jesus, Pink, Brown, Cream Ground, c.1946, 14 ½ In.. . . . . 518.00
Figurine, Sea Nymph, On Rock, Holding Shell To Ear, Blue Glaze, c.1921. . . . . 805.00
Figurine, Woman, In Long Skirt, Tan High Glaze, 1946, 7 ½ In. 127.00
Flower Frog, Turtle On Top, Blue Matte Glaze, c.1928, 2 ¾ In. 518.00
Flower Holder, Bird, Seated On Stump, Dark Blue High Glaze, 1924 . . . . *illus* 431.00
Flower Holder, Frog, Mottled Blue & Gray, Shirayamadani, c.1927, 2 ⅛ In.. . . . . 460.00
Flower Holder, Pansies, Uplift Handles, Mary Nourse, c.1895, 1 ¾ x 5 ½ In. 460.00
Flower Holder, Woman, Nude, Resting Arm On Mushroom, Blue High Glaze, 6 ¼ In.. . . . . 259.00
Flower Holder, Woman, Seminude, Yellow Matte Glaze, 1921, 5 ¾ In. 196.00
Ginger Jar, Gray Glaze, Cover, c.1916, 11 In. 219.00
Inkwell, Oak Leaves, Acorns, Pink, Green Matte Glaze, 1905, 11 x 6 In.. . . . . 600.00
Inkwell, Sphinx, Brown Matte Glaze, c.1922, 10 x 9 In. 960.00
Jar, Cover, Dogwood, Footed, Handles, c.1889, 7 In. 489.00
Jar, Tea, Birds, Branches, c.1884, 4 ½ In. 219.00
Jardiniere, Owl In Branch, Crescent Moon, Blue, Yellow, Gold, Gilt Border, 8 x 11 In. 1416.00
Jardiniere, Roses, Pink, White, Green Leaves, Blue, Green Ground, 13 x 17 In. 1438.00
Jug, Birds In Flight, Limoges Glaze, Martin Rettig, c.1883, 3 ½ x 4 ¾ In.. . . . . 230.00
Jug, Black Birds, Rose Ground, Signed NJH, c.1893, 5 In. 403.00
Jug, Corn, Wheat, Standard Glaze, Impressed, Lenore Asbury, 1900, 9 ⅜ In. 546.00
Jug, Ear Of Corn, Matte Glaze, Carved, Handle, Rose Fechheimer, c.1905, 6 x 7 In.. . . . . 546.00
Jug, Flower, Art Deco Style, Yellow Matte Glaze, W. Rehm, c.1929, 8 ½ x 8 In. 805.00
Jug, Grapes, Blue, Stopper, c.1898, 8 ¾ In. 920.00
Jug, Hops, Silver Overlay & Stopper, E. Lincoln, c.1896, 6 ¾ In. 2530.00
Jug, Whiskey, Corn, Standard Glaze, Jeanette Swing, Marked, 1899, 7 In. 633.00
Lamp, Fern Fronds, Paneled Green Leaded Glass, 18 x 14 In. 3000.00
Loving Cup, Cuddling Monkeys, 3 Handles, Bruce Horsfall, c.1895, 7 ⅞ In. 2300.00
Loving Cup, Sioux Indian, 3 Handles, c.1900, 5 In.. . . . . 1320.00
Match Holder, Owl Striker, Dark Green, Light Green Matte Glaze, 1909, 1 ½ x 2 ½ In. 288.00
Medallion, Madonna & Child, White Glaze, c.1959, 5 In. Diam. 115.00
Mug, Cincinnati Cooperage Co., c.1882, 7 ¼ In.. . . . . 288.00
Mug, Eagle Crest, Band Of Seahorses, c.1907, 7 In. 546.00
Mug, Flowers, Maroon Ground, Vellum, c.1905, 6 ⅞ In. 575.00
Mug, Indian, Conquering Deer Portrait, Edith Felten, c.1900, 5 ⅛ In. 2185.00
Mug, Indian, Feather Headdress, Standard Glaze, A. Van Briggle, 1897, 5 In. 546.00

Mug, Indian, Standard Glaze, Frederick Laurence, 1896, 5 ¼ x 5 ¾ In. 2160.00
Mug, Indian, Standard Glaze, Sadie Markland, 1897, 5 ¼ x 5 ¾ In. 1560.00
Mug, Poppies, Wheat, Sara Sax, c.1899, 5 ⅝ In. 690.00
Mug, Puppy, E.T. Hurley, c.1933, 4 ¾ In. 1020.00
Mug, Star & Crescent Moon, Green Matte Glaze, Alpha Delta Phi Sorority, 5 ½ x 5 In. 201.00
Paperweight, Bird, Dark Blue, Black Matte Glaze, 1909, 3 x 4 ½ In. 374.00
Paperweight, Bulldog, Reclining, White Opal Glaze, 1934, 2 ½ x 5 In. 431.00
Paperweight, Bunny, Ivory Matte Glaze, Louise Abel, 1954 .... 345.00
Paperweight, Burro Carrying Baskets, Tan Glaze, c.1935, 4 In. 288.00
Paperweight, Cat, Dripped Brown Matte Glaze, William Hentschel, c.1927, 5 ¼ In. 575.00
Paperweight, Cat, Glossy Black Glaze, 1949, 6 ¾ In. 690.00
Paperweight, Cat, Seated, Brown, White, Blue Glossy Glaze, c.1935, 4 ½ In. 748.00
Paperweight, Cat, Seated, Dark Blue Matte Glaze, William Hentschel, 1927, 5 ¼ In. 1150.00
Paperweight, Dog, Ivory Matte Finish, c.1928, 4 ⅞ In. 173.00
Paperweight, Dog, Red, Brown, Green Matte Glaze, 1928, 4 ⅞ In. 460.00
Paperweight, Dog, Seated, Tan Matte Glaze, 1928 .... 316.00
Paperweight, Elephant, Blue High Glaze, Arthur Conant, 1945, 3 ½ In. .... 259.00 to 518.00
Paperweight, Fox, Reclining, Aventurine Glaze, 1937, 2 ¼ x 5 ¾ In. 633.00
Paperweight, Gazelle, Blue High Glaze, 1936, 4 ⅞ In. 518.00
Paperweight, Gazelle, Ivory Matte Glaze, Louise Abel, 1935, 4 ⅛ In. 374.00
Paperweight, Goat, Wine Madder Glaze, Louise Abel, 1945, 6 ¼ x 4 ⅝ In. .... *illus* 115.00
Paperweight, Hawk, Blue Crystalline Glaze, c.1936, 4 ½ In. 633.00
Paperweight, Leopard, Tan High Glaze, William McDonald, 1946, 3 x 6 ½ In. 489.00
Paperweight, Man, Playing Violin, Terra-Cotta, Signed, Louise Abel, c.1940, 6 ¼ x 7 In. 460.00
Paperweight, Monkey, Seated On Book, Brown Mottled Glaze, 1924, 3 ⅝ In. .... 288.00 to 316.00
Paperweight, Mythical Creature, Brown Matte Glaze, Blue Crystals, c.1924, 4 x 2 ¾ In. 633.00
Paperweight, Nude Girl, Seated On Plinth, Art Deco, c.1930 .... 219.00
Paperweight, Nude Woman, Seated, Cream Glaze, Louise Abel, 1932, 5 x 4 In. .... 175.00 to 220.00
Paperweight, Pelican, Orange Glossy Glaze, Shirayamadani, 1965, 2 ¾ x 6 In. 374.00
Paperweight, Pigeon, Kay Le, c.1946, 2 x 7 In. 748.00
Paperweight, Potter At The Wheel, Green Matte Glaze, 1940, 3 ⅝ In. 173.00
Paperweight, Rabbit, Brown Glaze, 3 ½ x 3 ½ In. 259.00
Paperweight, Rabbit, Mustard Seed Glaze, c.1961, 3 In. 403.00
Paperweight, Radio Singers, David Seyler, 1948, 4 ¾ In. 288.00
Paperweight, Rook, Blue & Tan Matte Glaze, c.1931, 2 ¾ In. 288.00
Paperweight, Rooster, Ivory Matte Glaze, Plinth, c.1928, 5 In. 288.00
Paperweight, Rooster, Multicolored Matte Glaze, 1929, 4 ⅝ In. .... 259.00 to 489.00
Paperweight, Rooster, Red, Yellow, Orange, Black Gloss Glazes, 1943, 5 In. 345.00
Paperweight, Seal, Aventurine Glaze, Shirayamadani, c.1928, 3 In. .... *illus* 978.00
Paperweight, Ship, 1929, 3 ½ In. 460.00
Paperweight, Turtle, Pink Matte Haze, Green Glaze, c.1920, 2 ⅛ In. 345.00
Pin Tray, Languid Nude Female, Green Matte Glaze, c.1927, 1 ¾ x 4 ½ In. 575.00
Pitcher, Clover, Iris Glaze, Silver Plate Handle & Rim, Sara Sax, c.1905, 5 x 5 In. 1380.00
Pitcher, Ducks, Swimming In Lotus Pond, Cobalt Blue, Gray Clay, Laura Fry, 8 ¾ In. 1438.00
Pitcher, Leaf & Berries, Glazed, Leona Van Briggle, c.1901, 6 x 6 ½ In. 374.00
Pitcher, Lid, Green Matte Glaze, Finial, c.1904, 9 ½ In. .... *illus* 259.00
Pitcher, Orient Trees, Clouds, Albert Valentien, c.1883, 8 ½ In. .... *illus* 374.00
Pitcher, Roses, Yellow, Branches, c.1888, 8 ⅜ In. 805.00
Plaque, Along The East Fork, Vellum Glaze, E.T. Hurley, c.1921, 13 ½ x 9 ½ In. 2530.00
Plaque, Along The River, Vellum Glaze, Fred Rothenbusch, Frame, c.1920, 16 ½ x 14 In. 4025.00
Plaque, Along The Swanee River, Landscape, Ed Diers, 1912, 16 x 21 In. 20400.00
Plaque, Glimpse Of The Sea, Vellum Glaze, Charles McLaughlin, Frame, c.1915, 11 x 9 In. 4600.00
Plaque, Landscape, Late Autumn, Vellum Glaze, F. Rothenbusch, Frame, 9 x 5 ½ In. 4025.00
Plaque, Landscape, Moonlight, Fred Rothenbusch, Frame, 10 x 12 In. 4025.00
Plaque, Landscape, Pastel, Vellum Glaze, E.T. Hurley, Frame, 1912, 9 ½ x 13 In. 2040.00
Plaque, Landscape, Vellum Glaze, Fred Rothenbusch, Frame, 1904, 20 x 15 In. 12000.00
Plaque, Misty Morning, Harbor, Vellum Glaze, Carl Schmidt, Frame, c.1921, 16 ½ x 13 In. 8050.00
Plaque, Moonlight Sailboat Scene, Green Vellum Glaze, Frame, c.1912, 11 x 9 ½ In. 10350.00
Plaque, Morning Glow, Vellum, Frame, 1913, 10 ½ x 8 ½ In. 4800.00
Plaque, Tree Lined Landscape, River, Vellum Glaze, Asbury, Frame, 1922, 13 x 11 In. 19000.00
Plaque, Winter, Pond, In The Woods, Vellum Glaze, S.E. Coyne, Frame, 9 x 13 In. 1725.00
Plaque, Winter, Mountain, Landscape, Vellum Glaze, Rothenbush, Frame, 1927, 10 x 12 In. 12500.00
Plate, Mice, Brown, Irregular Edge, Sallie Toohey, c.1891, 7 In. 805.00
Stein, Sprig, Cherry, Glazed, Commercial Club Of Cincinnati, Presentation, 1894, 6 ¾ In. 2300.00
Tankard, Black Boy, Incised, 5 In. 400.00
Tile, 2 Tulips, Green Glaze, Carved, Faience, Frame, Marked, 1347Y, 6 In. 840.00
Tile, 2 Tulips, Tan, Brown, Blue Ground, Carved, Faience, Frame, Marked, 6 In. 720.00

Rookwood, Paperweight, Goat, Wine Madder Glaze, Louise Abel, 1945, 6 ¼ x 4 ⅝ In.
$115.00

Rookwood, Paperweight, Seal, Aventurine Glaze, Shirayamadani, c.1928, 3 In.
$978.00

Rookwood, Pitcher, Lid, Green Matte Glaze, Finial, c.1904, 9 ½ In.
$259.00

Rookwood, Pitcher, Orient Trees, Clouds, Albert Valentien, c.1883, 8 ½ In.
$374.00

Rookwood, Tray, Owl, Forest Green Glaze, Marked, 1946, 4 ⅛ x 6 ½ In.
$121.00

Rookwood, Trivet, Grapevine, Turquoise, Blue, Stylized Star Shape, c.1924, 6 ¼ In.
$173.00

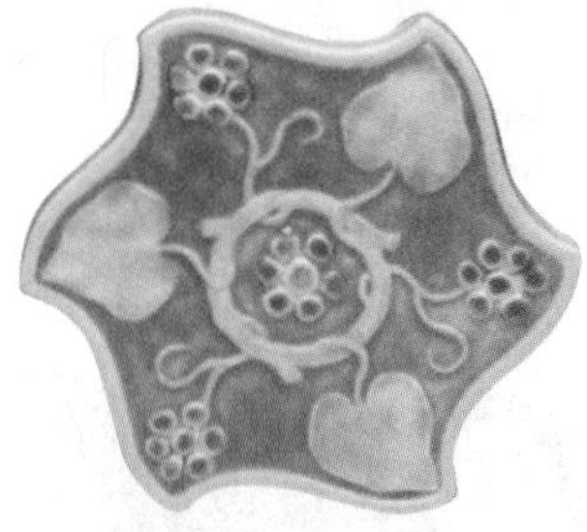

Rookwood, Vase, Aventurine, Tiger's Eye Green Glaze, Marked, 1920, 6 ¼ In.
$855.00

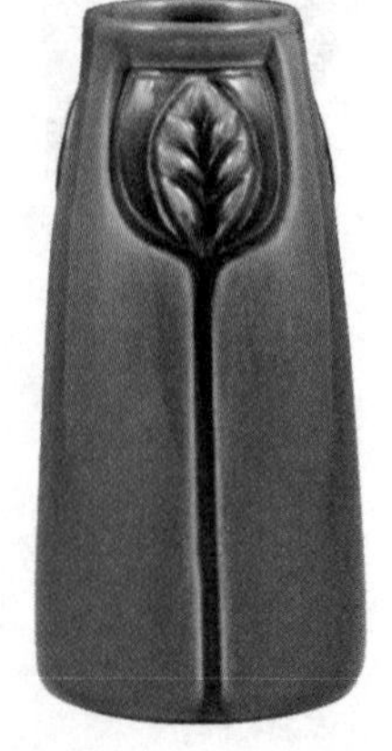

R

Tile, Blue Bird, Yellow Branches, Cream Ground, 1918, 5 ¾ In. Diam. ... 150.00
Tile, Geese, White, Tree, Lake, Green, Yellow, c.1926, 5 x 5 In. ... 316.00
Tile, Knight On Horse, Matte Glaze, 1920, 5 ⅞ In. ... 288.00
Tile, Mule, Leaves, Blue & Ivory Ground, Frame, 6 In. ... 960.00
Tile, Multicolor, Stylized Design, Frame, 8 x 8 In. ... 259.00
Tile, Owl & Crest Shape, Faience, Frame, 7 x 7 ½ In. ... 403.00
Tile, Parrot, Flowering Tree, Multicolored, Frame, c.1929, 5 x 5 In. ... 431.00
Tile, Poppy, Blue Ground, Matte Glaze, Faience, Frame, c.1904, 8 ½ x 8 ½ In. ... 3450.00
Tile, Rook, Blue, 3 ¾ x 7 ½ In. ... 110.00
Tile, Sailing Ship, Blue & Green Matte, Frame, 6 x 6 In. ... 460.00
Tile, Ship With Sails, Matte Glaze, 1920, 5 ⅞ In. ... 288.00
Tile, Tea, Parrot, Impressed, 1920, 5 ½ In. ... 207.00
Tile, The Mission, Frame, c.1925, 6 x 6 In. ... 690.00
Tile, Woman, Carrying Bucket, Blue, White Matte Glaze, Impressed, 1919, 5 ¼ In. ... 316.00
Tobacco Jar, Seashells, Cigarettes, Cigar, Matches, Silver Overlay Lid, c.1899, 5 ⅛ In. ... 546.00
Tray, Fruit, Leaves, Black Matte Glaze, White Cirrus Glaze, 1953, 2 x 14 In. ... 518.00
Tray, King Of Diamonds, Sallie Toohey, 9 ⅝ In. ... 115.00
Tray, Owl, Forest Green Glaze, Marked, 1946, 4 ⅛ x 6 ½ In. ... *illus* 121.00
Tray, Roses, Yellow, Ed Abel, c.1891, 1 ¾ In x 9 In. ... 288.00
Tray, Seal, Seated, Tan High Glaze, 1942, 4 x 6 ½ In. ... 489.00
Tray, Violet Gray Shaded Glaze, 4 ¾ In. ... 1035.00
Trivet, Dutch Woman, Children, c.1927, 5 ¾ x 5 ¾ In. ... 144.00 to 210.00
Trivet, Dutch Woman, Pail, Birds, Blue, Brown, Glaze, Oak Frame, 1920, 11 x 11 In. ... 120.00
Trivet, Grapevine, Turquoise, Blue, Stylized Star Shape, c.1924, 6 ¼ In. ... *illus* 173.00
Trivet, Stylized Geometrics, Pink, Blue, Purple, Frame, 1922, 6 In. ... 300.00
Urn, Blue, Tan Matte Glaze, Handles, Impressed, Production, 1921, 5 ¾ In. ... 178.00
Urn, Stand, Terra-Cotta, Italian Renaissance, Blue Engobe, 43 x 26 In. ... 5700.00
Vase, 3 Aztec Figures, Red, Brown Matte Glaze, Bulbous, 1910, 5 x 8 In. ... 540.00
Vase, 3 Fish, Vellum Glaze, Flared, E.T. Hurley, c.1907 ... 1035.00
Vase, 3 Gothic Figures, Gray & Blue Matte Glaze, c.1916, 12 ½ x 5 ½ In. ... 633.00
Vase, 4 Palm Tree Panels, Mottled Mauve, Green, Marked, 7 In. ... 172.00
Vase, American Indian, Brown Glaze, Handles, 1901, 8 x 8 ½ In. ... 1200.00
Vase, American Indian, Glazed, Handles, E.T. Hurley, c.1898, 5 x 4 ¾ In. ... 2415.00
Vase, Apple Blossom Bough, Vellum Glaze, 8 ¼ In. ... 345.00
Vase, Apple Blossoms, Pink, Vellum Glaze, 6 ⅜ In. ... 489.00
Vase, Art Deco, Green, Brown, Incised, 11 ½ In. ... 345.00
Vase, Autumn Leaves, Standard Glaze, Squat, Handles, L. Van Briggle, 1899, 3 x 5 ½ In. ... 316.00
Vase, Aventurine, Tiger's Eye Green Glaze, Marked, 1920, 6 ¼ In. ... *illus* 855.00
Vase, Aztec Design, Pink To Lavender, Angular Handles, 4 ½ In. ... 201.00
Vase, Baluster, Oxblood Glaze, c.1928, 7 ¼ In. ... 345.00
Vase, Bearded Man, Pillow, c.1896, 6 ½ In. ... 1035.00
Vase, Bellflowers, Incised, Charles Todd, c.1920, 9 ¼ In. ... 1610.00
Vase, Bellflowers, Light Brown Matte Glaze, Molded Handle, c.1920, 8 ½ In. ... 345.00
Vase, Berries, Blue, White Blossoms, Vellum Glaze, R. Fechheimer, c.1905, 4 ½ x 8 ½ In. ... 863.00
Vase, Berries, Leaves, Vines, Loretta Holtkamp, 1945, 6 ⅜ In. ... 431.00
Vase, Berries, Red, Leaves, Trellis, Gray Ground, Sara Sax, 1918, 10 In. ... 3565.00
Vase, Berries, Vines, Aquamarine, Matte Glaze, Katherine Jones, 5 In. ... 540.00
Vase, Birch Trees, Riverbank, Pink Sky, Purple Trees, Vellum Glaze, E.T. Hurley, 3 x 6 In. ... 1725.00
Vase, Birds, Hunting Gear, Silver Overlay, K. Shirayamadani, c.1892, 12 x 6 ½ In. ... 10925.00
Vase, Birds, In Flight, Purple To Orange High Glaze, 6 x 8 ½ In. ... 259.00
Vase, Birds, On Branches, Purple, Vellum Glaze, 1915, 8 x 3 ¾ In. ... *illus* 1020.00
Vase, Birds, On Magnolia Branches, Porcelain Glaze, Jens Jensen, c.1948, 7 x 11 ¾ In. ... 2875.00
Vase, Birds, Perched In Leafy Trees, Brown Slip, White Ground, c.1943, 4 ⅝ In. ... 288.00
Vase, Birds On Branches, Forest Scene, Pillow, c.1881, 10 ¼ In. ... 460.00
Vase, Black-Eyed Susans, Standard Glaze, Leona Van Briggle, 1903, 7 ¼ In. ... 345.00
Vase, Blossoming Branches, Glazed, Leona Van Briggle, c.1903, 3 x 7 ½ In. ... 374.00
Vase, Blossoms, Blue & Pink Matte Glaze, Bulbous, Flared Lip, 8 ⅛ In. ... 1422.00
Vase, Blossoms, Mottled Blue Over Pink Matte Ground, Handles, c.1928, 6 ¼ In. ... 546.00
Vase, Blue Jay, On Apple Blossom Branch, c.1900, 7 x 5 In. ... 1680.00
Vase, Bottle Shape, Handles, Production, c.1912, 8 ¼ In. ... 360.00
Vase, Bud, Purple Mottled Glaze, c.1920, 7 In. ... 150.00
Vase, Bulbous, Black Gloss Finish, c.1918, 15 ¼ In. ... 316.00
Vase, Bulbous, Carved, Painted Green Flower, Blue Matte, Signed, 1905, 6 x 10 In. ... 4200.00
Vase, Butterfly, Beige Matte Glaze, Bulbous, 3 ½ x 4 ½ In. ... 70.00
Vase, Calla Lilies, c.1894, 12 ⅛ In. ... 1035.00
Vase, Carnations, Green Crackle Glaze, Elongated, Bulbous, 12 ⅜ In. ... 1896.00
Vase, Cherries, Leaves, Tan Ground, Handles, W. Hentschel, c.1930, 13 In. ... 2530.00

Vase, Cherries, Red, Around Rim, Vellum Glaze, Blue, E. McDermott, c.1917, 5 ⅝ In. 575.00
Vase, Cherry Blossoms, Iris Glaze, Black To Green To Pink, Tapered, c.1911, 4 x 7 In. 1265.00
Vase, Cherry Blossoms, Vellum Glaze, E.T. Hurley, c.1910, 4 x 8 ½ In. 748.00
Vase, Cherry Design, Matte Glaze, c.1904, 4 ⅝ In. 805.00
Vase, Chick, Yellow, Standard Glaze, Caroline Steinle, 1896, 5 ½ In. 546.00
Vase, Chrysanthemums, Yellow, Green Ground, Matt Daly, c.1899, 12 ⅞ In. 4485.00
Vase, Clover, Swirling Ribbed Body, Pinched Fluted Top, c.1893, 3 ½ In. 184.00
Vase, Cranes, Flying, Orange, Swirling Clouds, Marked, Shirayamadani, c.1891, 4 x 7 In..... 2640.00
Vase, Crocus, Iris Glaze, Ed Diers, c.1902, 6 ⅞ In. 1265.00
Vase, Crocus, Yellow, Green Matte Glaze, A. Valentien, 1901, 4 x 9 In.. .... 4800.00
Vase, Crocus Blossoms, Blue, Pink, Vellum Glaze, E. Wildman, c.1912, 7 In. 470.00
Vase, Crocus Blossoms, Iris Glaze, Carl Schmidt, c.1907, 3 x 7 ¼ In. 2013.00
Vase, Currants, Red, Standard Glaze, Marianne Mitchell, 1902, 5 ⅝ In.. .... 316.00
Vase, Cyclamen, Blue To Green Ground, Iris Glaze, c.1911, 8 ¾ In. 1955.00
Vase, Cyclamen Flowers, Leaves, Blue Ground, 3-Footed, c.1901, 4 ⅜ In.. .... 518.00
Vase, Daffodils, Standard Glaze, Marked, Strafer, 5 ¾ x 4 In. .... *illus* 485.00
Vase, Daisies, Handles, Harriet Wilcox, c.1893, 8 ½ In. 288.00
Vase, Dandelions, Iris Glaze, c.1903, 4 ¾ In. 863.00
Vase, Dark Blue Matte Glaze, Production, 1925, 5 In. 161.00
Vase, Deer, Grazing, Anniversary Glaze, Jens Jensen, 1944, 6 ¼ In. .... 1265.00 to 1380.00
Vase, Dentil Design, Green Mottled Shaded To Pink, Marked, c.1918, 5 In. 115.00
Vase, Dog, Portrait, Standard Glaze, E.T. Hurley, 1899, 4 ⅝ In. 920.00
Vase, Dogwood Flowers, Blue To Pink, Brown Stems, Green Leaves, 8 In.. .... 1200.00
Vase, Dogwood Flowers, Double Vellum Glaze, c.1933, 6 ¾ In. 345.00
Vase, Dogwood Flowers, Purple Matte Glaze, Production, c.1914, 6 ⅞ In. 690.00
Vase, Dragonflies, Flowering Plants, Vellum Glaze, c.1917, 7 ¼ In. 2760.00
Vase, Drip Design, Green, Blue, Pink, Yellow, Pink Matte Ground, Free-Form, 6 ½ In. 460.00
Vase, Dutch Windmill Scene, Blue, Cream, Vellum Glaze, Ed Diers, 1912, 6 x 5 In.. .... 2106.00
Vase, Elderly Woman, Gold, Brown, Deep Brown Ground, 1890, 12 ½ x 3 ½ In. 600.00
Vase, Fan Shape, Yellow Matte Glaze, Flared, Lorinda Epply, 1930, 5 ½ In. 345.00
Vase, Fauns, Blue On Ivory Ground, 1948, 6 ½ x 6 In.. .... 1200.00
Vase, Flower, Vine, Yellow, Shaded Yellow Ground, Marked, c.1886, 6 In. 374.00
Vase, Flower Band, Red, Blue, Red Brown Matte Glaze, c.1930, 10 ¾ In. 1265.00
Vase, Flower Band, Vellum Glaze, L. Epply, c.1915, 17 In. 4112.00
Vase, Flower Blossoms, Leaves, Multicolored, c.1882, 4 ⅜ In. 173.00
Vase, Flower Garden, Matte Glaze, Delia Workum, 1927, 7 ½ In. 690.00
Vase, Flowers, Amber, Orange Ground, Standard Glaze, S. Toohey, 1899, 15 ½ x 5 ¾ In. 4200.00
Vase, Flowers, Around Shoulder, Arthur Conant, c.1922, 8 ⅜ In. 2415.00
Vase, Flowers, Art Deco, Vellum Glaze, Leonore Asbury, c.1924, 8 ½ In. 2760.00
Vase, Flowers, Black Opal Glaze, Sara Sax, c.1926, 5 ⅜ In. 1725.00
Vase, Flowers, Blue, Gray To Peach Ground, 1945, 9 ½ x 4 ¼ In. 1560.00
Vase, Flowers, Blue, Silver Overlay, Bulbous, 1891, 7 x 4 ½ In. 2400.00
Vase, Flowers, Gold Ground, Ana Marie Bookprinter, c.1886, 3 ½ x 8 In. 863.00
Vase, Flowers, Green Matte Glaze, Louise Abel, 1920, 7 x 4 In. 540.00
Vase, Flowers, Green Matte Glaze, Sallie Coyne, c.1930, 4 x 4 ¾ In. 374.00
Vase, Flowers, High Glaze, Margaret McDonald, c.1946, 4 ½ x 6 ¼ In. 316.00
Vase, Flowers, Incised, Blue To Tan, Tapered, Rolled Edge, 9 ½ In.. .... 518.00
Vase, Flowers, Leaves, Column Shape, Narrow Lip, Shirayamadani, 1902, 17 In. 1541.00
Vase, Flowers, Leaves, Red, Brown, Milky White Glaze, c.1945, 14 ⅜ In.. .... 1955.00
Vase, Flowers, Leaves, Standard Glaze, Albert Valentien, 1892, 17 ¼ In.. .... 863.00
Vase, Flowers, Leaves, Stems, Black Outline, Vellum Glaze, Ed Diers, 1929, 4 In.. .... 805.00
Vase, Flowers, Lotus Blossoms, Butterfly, Gray, Blue, Red Glaze, Kay Ley, 1946, 13 In.. .... *illus* 633.00
Vase, Flowers, Multicolored, Blue Ground, Squat, Vellum Glaze, c.1927, 4 ⅞ In.. .... 1610.00
Vase, Flowers, On Shoulder, Black Trim, French Red, Sara Sax, 1922, 6 In. 3680.00
Vase, Flowers, Orange, Yellow, Brown Shaded To Green, Ribbed Swirl, 11 ¼ In. 920.00
Vase, Flowers, Pink, Green, Production, 1938, 4 In. 138.00
Vase, Flowers, Pink, Green Matte Glaze, 1928, 6 x 9 In. 210.00
Vase, Flowers, Purple, Pink, Multicolored Mottled Ground, Flared Rim, 1914, 22 x 8 ½ In. 1320.00
Vase, Flowers, Raised, Blue, Incised, 7 ½ In. 288.00
Vase, Flowers, Relief, Blue Matte Glaze, Tapered, 1916, 9 In. 296.00
Vase, Flowers, Tan Matte Glaze, Tapered, 1919, 5 x 11 In. 240.00
Vase, Flowers, Yellow, Green, Black Glaze, White Ground, S. Sax, 1926, 6 ⅛ In.. .... 3220.00
Vase, Flying Swallows, Pillow, Albert Valentien, c.1882, 7 ⅞ In. 288.00
Vase, Forest, Snowy, Birds In Flight, Vellum Glaze, E.T. Hurley, 9 ¼ In. 5100.00
Vase, Forget-Me-Nots, White, Blue, Gold, Shirayamadani, 1887, 6 In. 1150.00
Vase, Forsythia, M. Daly, c.1902, 12 ½ In. 2300.00
Vase, Fruit Blossoms, Flowers, Turquoise, Dark Blue Ground, Green, S. Sax, 14 ½ In. 4255.00

Rookwood, Vase, Birds, On Branches, Purple, Vellum Glaze, 1915, 8 x 3 ¾ In.
$1020.00

Rookwood, Vase, Daffodils, Standard Glaze, Marked, Strafer, 5 ¾ x 4 In.
$485.00

Rookwood, Vase, Flowers, Lotus Blossoms, Butterfly, Gray, Blue, Red Glaze, Kay Ley, 1946, 13 In.
$633.00

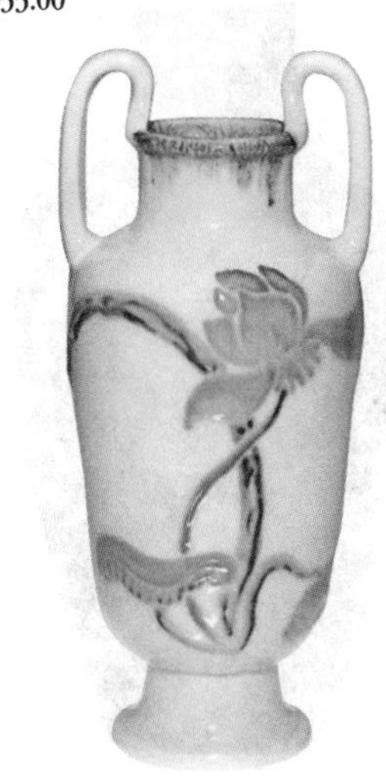

R

Rookwood, Vase, Geese, Striated Yellow Ground, Production, c.1937, 4 ¾ In.
$207.00

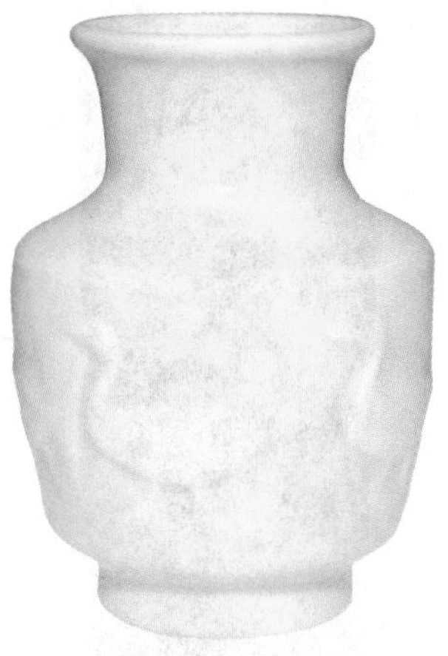

Rookwood, Vase, Horses, Peacocks, William Hentschel, 9 ½ x 6 In.
$1800.00

Rookwood, Vase, Lotus Blossoms, Leaves, Orange, Black Ground, Bulbous, Matt Daly, c.1902, 15 In.
$2400.00

Vase, Fuchsia, Yellow Matte Glaze, Shouldered, Tapered, 1928, 12 x 5 In. 330.00
Vase, Geese, Striated Yellow Ground, Production, c.1937, 4 ¾ In. *illus* 207.00
Vase, Geometric, Chocolate Brown Slip, Brown Ground, c.1928, 14 In. 230.00
Vase, Geometric, Green, Blue, Brown, Flared, 1931, 7 x 5 ½ In. 3240.00
Vase, Geometric, Raised, Green Matte Glaze, c.1929, 2 ½ x 5 ¾ In. 259.00
Vase, Geometric Band, Incised, Blue Mottled Glaze, Marked, c.1921, 6 ¾ In. 259.00
Vase, Geranium, Tan Glaze, Tapered, Edith Noonan, c.1906, 3 ½ x 6 ¾ In. 403.00
Vase, Green Over Brown Matte Glaze, Squat, c.1912, 4 ½ In. 489.00
Vase, Hawthorne Branches, Laura Fry, c.1887, 10 ¼ In. 748.00
Vase, Hawthorne Branches, Red, c.1923, 10 ¾ In. 1265.00
Vase, Holly Leaves, Berries, Handles, Sara Sax, c.1898, 5 ¾ In. 207.00
Vase, Hollyhocks, Iris Glaze, c.1907, 7 ¾ In. 1265.00
Vase, Horses, Peacocks, William Hentschel, 9 ½ x 6 In. *illus* 1800.00
Vase, Hyacinth, Iris Glaze, Olga Reed, c.1902, 8 ½ x 4 In. 1495.00
Vase, Hydrangea Cluster, Bulbous, Handles, 10 x 10 ½ In. 3360.00
Vase, Incised Stylized Flower, Blue, c.1930, 9 ¼ x 5 In. 322.00
Vase, Iris, Blue, Bulbous, Anna Valentien, c.1898, 12 ⅝ In. 1093.00
Vase, Iris, Grapes On Vine, Carved, 10 ½ In. 6043.00
Vase, Jonquil, Pink, Double Vellum Glaze, Blue, Black Glaze, 1935, 6 ⅜ In. 920.00
Vase, Jonquils, Sallie Coyne, c.1900, 8 ⅞ In. 288.00
Vase, Landscape, Birch Trees, Lake, Vellum Glaze, E.T. Hurley, c.1916, 11 In. 2185.00
Vase, Landscape, Blue, Green, Porcelain Glaze, McDonald, c.1939, 11 ½ In. 1840.00
Vase, Landscape, Blue Ground, Clear Glaze, c.1922, 8 ¼ In. 4600.00
Vase, Landscape, Iris Glaze, F. Rothenbusch, c.1921, 7 ½ In. 1610.00
Vase, Landscape, Silhouetted Trees, Vellum Glaze, Frederick Rothenbusch, c.1913, 14 ½ In. 2300.00
Vase, Landscape, Snow Covered, Canoe On Riverbank, Sallie Coyne, c.1920, 9 In. 2875.00
Vase, Landscape, Snow Covered, Vellum Glaze, Sallie Coyne, c.1920, 13 In. 4313.00
Vase, Landscape, Trees, River, Mountain, Vellum Glaze, Van Horne, c.1914, 11 In. 1208.00
Vase, Landscape, Vellum Glaze, Carl Schmidt, c.1917, 8 ½ In. 3220.00
Vase, Landscape, Water Scene, Blue Ground, E. Hurley, 1938, 11 In. 1896.00
Vase, Leaves, Berries, Aubergine Rose, Matte Glaze, M. McDonald, c.1926, 8 In. 805.00
Vase, Leaves, Berries, Intaglio Carved, Ivory Glaze, Stippled Ground, 18 ½ In. 575.00
Vase, Leaves, Berries, Yellow, Pink, Purple Ground, E. McDermott, 1917, 4 x 6 In. 600.00
Vase, Leaves, Feathered Green To Yellow Glaze, Bulbous, 1912, 12 ½ In. 1560.00
Vase, Leaves, Flowers, Incised, Mottled Blue Glaze, 6 In. 230.00
Vase, Leaves, Glazed, Applied Silver Overlay, Handles, H. Wilcox, c.1893, 4 x 5 ½ In. 3163.00
Vase, Leaves, Raised, Green, Flared Lip, 13 In. 1380.00
Vase, Leaves, Turquoise Matte Glaze, Cylindrical, c.1923, 3 ½ x 5 ¼ In. 144.00
Vase, Leaves, Yellow Ground, Handles, Sara Sax, c.1915, 7 ⅞ In. 1265.00
Vase, Lilies, Orange, Standard Glaze, Leona Van Briggle, 6 In. 460.00
Vase, Lilies Of The Valley, Iris Glaze, 7 ½ In. 518.00
Vase, Lotus Blossoms, Leaves, Orange, Black Ground, Bulbous, Matt Daly, c.1902, 15 In. *illus* 2400.00
Vase, Magnolia, White, Gray Ground, c.1904, 8 ¼ In. 1725.00
Vase, Magnolias, Lavender, Purple Matte Glaze, W. Hentschel, c.1930, 5 x 10 ½ In. 1208.00
Vase, Man Wearing Hat, Portrait, Pillow, c.1896, 7 ¾ In. 920.00
Vase, Misty Forest Landscape, Vellum Glaze, Flame Marks, E.T. Hurley, c.1908, 8 ½ In. 2520.00
Vase, Modern People, Brown On Cream, Square, Footed, J. Jensen, c.1946, 6 In. 920.00
Vase, Mountains, Lake, Vellum Glaze, E.T. Hurley, c.1914, 11 ¾ In. 2400.00
Vase, Multicolored Matte Glaze, Carved, Tapered, Cylindrical, 1912, 9 In. 920.00
Vase, Mums, Pink, Bulbous, c.1924, 9 In. 1320.00
Vase, Mushrooms, Iris Glaze, Carl Schmidt, c.1902, 5 x 10 ½ In. 7188.00
Vase, Nude Figure, Flowers, Porcelain Glaze, Jens Jensen, c.1948, 3 ½ x 6 ½ In. 4025.00
Vase, Oak Leaves, Globular, c.1922, 10 ¼ In. 1610.00
Vase, Oranges, Blue Ground, Footed, Handles, H. Wilcox, c.1927, 9 ¾ In. 3910.00
Vase, Organic Design, Pink & Blue Matte Glaze, E. Lincoln, c.1921, 3 ¾ x 8 ¼ In. 633.00
Vase, Panels, Blue & Tan Matte Glaze, Production, c.1923, 9 In. 489.00
Vase, Pansies, Dark Amber Glaze, Flared, 1890, 5 x 6 In. 240.00
Vase, Pansies, Purple, White, Blue Rim, Edward Hurley, 4 ½ x 3 ¾ In. 650.00
Vase, Pansies, Sara Sax, c.1899, 7 ½ In. 460.00
Vase, Pansy, Blue Ground, Vellum Glaze, Bulbous, Ed Diers, c.1924, 7 x 4 ½ In. 978.00
Vase, Parrots, In Palm Trees, Blue Ocean, Vellum Glaze, Sara Sax, 1916, 15 ½ In. 6043.00
Vase, Peacock Feathers, 4 Panels, Sara Sax, c.1928, 11 ⅞ In. *illus* 9200.00
Vase, Peacock Feathers, Brown, Green Crystalline Matte Glaze, c.1922, 6 ¼ In. 403.00
Vase, Peacock Feathers, Green, Pink, Green Ground, Tapered, 1914, 8 x 4 ¼ In. 6600.00
Vase, Peacock Feathers, Tinted Porcelain Glaze, Ed Diers, c.1923, 6 ½ In. 1150.00
Vase, Peacocks, Feathers Around Base, Blue Tinted Glaze, Sara Sax, c.1920, 12 ¼ In. 8050.00

Vase, Peonies, Blooming, Standard Glaze, Amelia Brown Sprague, 1896, 9 In. 1495.00
Vase, Peonies, Vellum Glaze, Lenore Asbury, c.1904, 10 ½ In. 978.00
Vase, Pinecone, Branches, Green & Brown Matte Glaze, Pierced, 1960s, 8 In. 355.00
Vase, Pinecones, Carved, Vellum Glaze, Carved, Lorinda Epply, c.1909, 3 x 6 In. 1265.00
Vase, Pinecones, Needles, Drippy Blue Matte Glaze, Production, 1919, 6 ⅜ In. 316.00
Vase, Poinsettias, 3 Panels, Carvrd, Matte Glaze, c.1913, 7 ⅞ In. 978.00
Vase, Poppies, Geometric Design On Neck, c.1940, 13 ¼ In. 1035.00
Vase, Poppies, Green Over Pink Matte Glaze, Production, Shirayamadani, 11 ¾ In. 345.00
Vase, Poppies, Spiraling Ribbing, Globular, K. Shirayamadani, c.1891, 8 In. 805.00
Vase, Poppies, Standard Glaze, Edith Noonan, 1905, 7 ¼ In. 431.00
Vase, Poppy, Matte Glaze, Bulbous, Kataro Shirayamadani, c.1930, 5 ½ x 6 ½ In. 920.00
Vase, Poppy, Pink Rim, Vellum Glaze, Mary Grace Denzler, c.1914, 6 ¾ In. 230.00
Vase, Poppy, Sea Green Glaze, Carved, Matt Daly, c.1899, 4 x 6 ¾ In. 7480.00
Vase, Poppy Blossoms, Orange On Brown Ground, c.1899, 7 In. 431.00
Vase, Rasberry Glaze, Footed, Handles, c.1928, 13 In. 288.00
Vase, Red Aventurine Glaze, Tapered, c.1928, 4 x 7 ¼ In. 345.00
Vase, Ring Handles, Green, Pink Matte Glaze, Shouldered, c.1914, 4 x 8 In. 240.00
Vase, Ring Of Fruit Around Rim, Yellow Glaze, Molded, c.1948, 4 ¼ In. 92.00
Vase, River Scene, Vellum Glaze, Footed, c.1917, 9 In. 805.00
Vase, River Scene, Vellum Glaze, Fred Rothenbush, c.1928, 11 In. 1920.00
Vase, Rook, 5-Sided, Green, White & Green Highlights, Signed, c.1923, 4 ½ In. 360.00
Vase, Rook, Branch, 5-Sided, Blue Crystalline Matte Glaze, Production, 3 ½ In. 431.00
Vase, Rook, Yellow Matte, 5-Sided, Marked, 1928, 4 ¾ In. .... *illus* 330.00
Vase, Rooks, In Flight, Iris Glaze, E.T. Hurley, c.1906, 6 ½ In. 2280.00
Vase, Rose Hips, Standard Glaze, Sallie Coyne, 1903, 7 In. 575.00
Vase, Roses, Blue, Red, Green, Pink, Green Mottled Ground, 1911, 9 ¼ x 3 ¾ In. 1140.00
Vase, Roses, Blue Matte Glaze, Katherine Jones, c.1926, 4 ¼ x 8 ½ In. 805.00
Vase, Roses, Buds, Yellow, Standard Glaze, Carrie Steinle, 1907, 4 In. 259.00
Vase, Roses, Pink, Green Ground, Iris Glaze, Ed Diers, c.1902, 6 ¼ In. 518.00
Vase, Roses, Red, Blue Ground, Square, c.1931, 6 In. 460.00
Vase, Roses, Red, Standard Glaze, Impressed, 1901, 6 In. 403.00
Vase, Runny Brown Matte Glaze, Molded, c.1926, 9 ½ In. 345.00
Vase, Sailboats, Clouds, Wave Caps, Blue, Gray Sky, Iris Glaze, S. Laurence, 11 ⅝ In. 5290.00
Vase, Sailboats On Lake, Vellum Glaze, Oval, Fred Rothenbusch, c.1908, 10 ¾ In. 1560.00
Vase, Scenic, Birch Trees, Landscape, Vellum Glaze, E.T. Hurley, 1915, 9 ½ In. 1380.00
Vase, Seahorse, Navy Matte Glaze Band, Column Shape, 1924, 7 In. 267.00
Vase, Sea Gulls In Flight, Shore, Waves, Vellum Glaze, c.1905, 12 ½ In. 3565.00
Vase, Ship Medallions, Carved, Wide Mouth, c.1911, 8 ½ x 8 ½ In. 1680.00
Vase, Spanish Ship, Pinta, Standard Glaze, Sturgis Laurence, 1899, 9 In. 8050.00
Vase, Spider, Insects, Flared Lip, 17 ¼ In. 1778.00
Vase, Spider Mums, Standard Glaze, Squat, Fred Rothenbusch, 1898, 3 In. 403.00
Vase, Stylized Flower, Turquoise, A. Conant, 1917, 9 x 4 In. 1020.00
Vase, Stylized Flowers, Blue, Green Matte, 4 Carved Panels, 5 x 5 In. 240.00
Vase, Stylized Flowers, Blue Matte Ground, Marked, c.1924, 10 ¼ In. 1380.00
Vase, Stylized Flowers, Blue Vellum Glaze, Mauve Interior, Sara Sax, 6 In. 1100.00
Vase, Stylized Flowers, Green Matte Glaze, Carved, Albert Pons, 1907, 7 x 7 In. 900.00
Vase, Sunflowers, Green Leaves, Green Shaded To Brown Ground, c.1905, 6 ½ In. 575.00
Vase, Trees, Rolling Landscape, Blue Gray & Cream Ground, Marked, 1913, 14 In. 2300.00
Vase, Trumpet Flowers, Red, Flame Mark, K. Shirayamadani, 1931, 7 x 5 In. .... *illus* 1560.00
Vase, Tulip, Incised, Pink Ground, Green Mottled, c.1919, 5 ¼ In. 144.00
Vase, Tulips, Green, Yellow, Orange, Shirayamadani, 1894, 19 In. 2070.00
Vase, Tulips, Iris Glaze, Bulbous, Tapered, Lenore Asbury, c.1910, 6 x 9 ½ In. 4370.00
Vase, Tulips, Red, Brown, Gold, Stamped, L. Van Briggle, c.1902, 7 In. 411.00
Vase, Tulips, Red Matte Glaze, Green, Shouldered, Molded, 1917, 10 x 5 In. 270.00
Vase, Tulips, Tapered, Margaret McDonald, c.1936, 5 ¼ x 13 In. 374.00
Vase, Turquoise & Pink Glaze, Bulbous, c.1932, 2 ¾ x 5 In. 115.00
Vase, Urn Shape, Blue, Rolled Rim, c.1927, 5 ¼ In. 117.00
Vase, Vertical Leaves, Rose, Green Matte Glaze, Raised, Bulbous, 1910, 4 x 7 In. 300.00
Vase, Vertical Ribs, Pink & Green Matte Glaze, c.1912, 4 x 9 ¼ In. 288.00
Vase, Vines, Pillow, Harriet Strafer, c.1895, 7 ¼ In. 460.00
Vase, Water Lilies, Standard Glaze, 14 ¾ x 5 ½ In. 1440.00
Vase, White Grapes, Pale Green Ground, Vellum Glaze, c.1927, 9 ½ In. 1495.00
Vase, Windmills, Landscape, Vellum Glaze, Oval, 6 ¼ x 2 ½ In. 2160.00
Vase, Winter Landscape, Vellum Glaze, 1915, 12 x 6 In. 4800.00
Vase, Wisteria, Gathered Neck, Vellum Glaze, Ed Diers, c.1923, 9 ¼ In. 2300.00
Vase, Wisteria Blossoms, Leaves, Pink Matte Glaze, Applied Handles, 8 ¾ In. 2070.00

Rookwood, Vase, Peacock Feathers, 4 Panels, Sara Sax, c.1928, 11 ⅞ In.
$9200.00

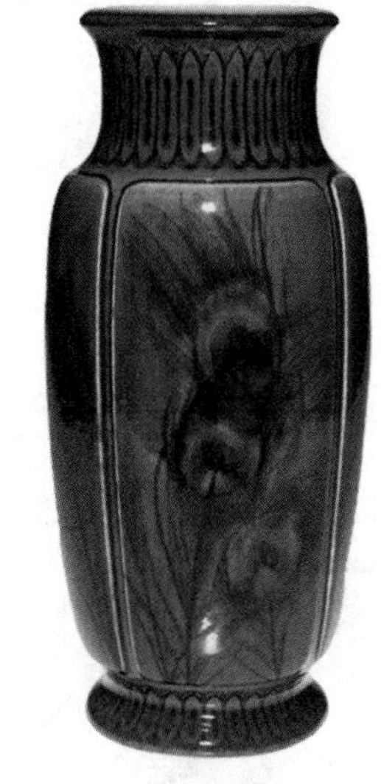

Rookwood, Vase, Rook, Yellow Matte, 5-Sided, Marked, 1928, 4 ¾ In.
$330.00

Rookwood, Vase, Trumpet Flowers, Red, Flame Mark, K. Shirayamadani, 1931, 7 x 5 In.
$1560.00

Rookwood, Wall Pocket, Poppies, Blue-Green Matte Glaze, c.1923, 12 ½ In.
$690.00

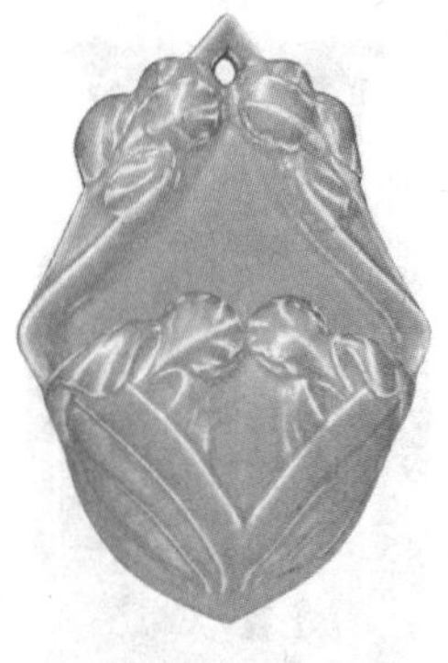

Rorstrand, Vase, Blossoms Ivory, Cobalt Blue Ground, Brown Stems, 14 ¾ x 6 ¼ In.
$3240.00

Rose Mandarin, Tureen, Cover, Buddhist Symbols, Figures, Courtyard, 1800s, 5 x 9 x 8 In.
$403.00

Rose Medallion, Candlestick, Gilt, 1800s, 9 ½ In., Pair
$550.00

Vase, Woman, Standing, Moon, Aerial Blue Glaze, Bruce Horsfall, c.1894, 8 ¾ In. 4600.00
Vase, Wooded Landscape, Snow Covered, Sallie Coyne, c.1922, 9 ¼ In. 1725.00
Vase, Zinnia, Blue Matte Glaze, Elizabeth Barrett, 1924, 6 ½ In. 690.00
Wall Pocket, Poppies, Blue-Green Matte Glaze, c.1923, 12 ½ In. .... *illus* 690.00

RORSTRAND was established near Stockholm, Sweden, in 1726. By the nineteenth century Rorstrand was making English-style earthenware, bone china, porcelain, ironstone china, and majolica. The company is still working. The three crown mark has been used since 1884.

Pitcher & Bowl, Swedish Line, 3 Crowns, 2 ¼-In. Pitcher 45.00
Vase, Blossoms Ivory, Cobalt Blue Ground, Brown Stems, 14 ¾ x 6 ¼ In. .... *illus* 3240.00
Vase, Woman, Holding Bird, Hand Painted, 5 In. 40.00

ROSE CANTON china is similar to Rose Mandarin and Rose Medallion, except no people or birds are pictured in the decoration. It was made in China during the nineteenth and twentieth centuries in greens, pinks, and other colors.

Dish, Lozenge Shape, Footed, Chinese, 14 ½ x 10 ¾ In. 177.00
Vase, Rectangular, Dragon Handles, Flared Rim, 12 ¼ In., Pair 1020.00

ROSE MANDARIN china is similar to Rose Canton and Rose Medallion. If the panels in the design picture only people and not birds, it is Rose Mandarin.

Bough Pot, Handles, Canted, Square, Cover, c.1785, 7 ¾ In., Pair 5313.00
Charger, Courtyard Scene, People, Flowers, Multicolored, Wood Stand, 15 In. 1150.00
Dish, Scalloped, Figures, Chinese, 19th Century, 9 ¼ In. 179.00
Pitcher, Figures, Flowers, c.1840 .... 351.00
Plate, 4 Women, On Terrace, Blue Geometric Inner Border, Dragons, 9 ¾ In. 173.00
Punch Bowl, Courtyard Scene, Butterflies, Flowers, Gilt Rim, 1800s, 18 ½ x 9 In. 8519.00
Punch Bowl, Flowers, Rust Ground, c.1780, 10 In. 1180.00
Tureen, Cover, Buddhist Symbols, Figures, Courtyard, 1800s, 5 x 9 x 8 In. .... *illus* 403.00
Vase, Molded & Gilt Mask Handles, c.1850, 12 In., Pair 763.00

ROSE MEDALLION china was made in China during the nineteenth and twentieth centuries. It is a distinctive design with four or more panels of decoration around a central medallion that includes a bird or a peony. The panels show birds and people. The background is a design of tree peonies and leaves. Pieces are colored in greens, pinks, and other colors. It is similar to Rose Canton and Rose Mandarin.

Bowl, Vegetable, Knop Finial, Exotic Birds, Chinese, 5 ¼ x 9 ¼ In. 288.00
Candlestick, Bird, 1940s, 7 In., Pair 1380.00
Candlestick, Gilt, 1800s, 9 ½ In., Pair .... *illus* 550.00
Candlestick, Lighthouse Form, Flared Bobeche, Flared Foot, 7 ½ In., Pair 720.00
Candlestick, Lizard, 6 ½ In. 100.00
Compote, Figures, Scenes, Bronze Ormolu Mounts, c.1840, 8 x 14 In., Pair 3850.00
Dish, Lobed, Ribbed Sides, c.1850, 11 x 9 In., Pair 518.00
Garden Bench, Flowers, Figures, Cutouts, 6-Sided, Early 19th Century, 19 x 11 In. 1900.00
Jar, Applied Dragon, Pearl, Lion Lid Finial, Gilt, 15 ¼ In., Pair 3680.00
Jardiniere, Hexagonal, Stand, c.1840, 5 ¾ In. 2006.00
Lamp, Baluster, Vase, Electrified, 18 In., Pair 2160.00
Lamp, Electrified, Base, c.1910, 14 In. 178.00
Planter, Hexagonal Shape, Flat Flared Edges, Scenic, 5 x 7 In. 690.00
Platter, Late 1800s, 11 ¾ x 14 ¾ In. 144.00
Punch Bowl, 6 Scenes, 19th Century, 5 ½ x 13 ¼ In. 671.00
Punch Bowl, Domestic Life, Birds, Flowers, Panels, 6 x 14 ¾ In. 805.00
Punch Bowl, Flowers, Mandarin Scenes Inside & Out, c.1850, 14 ½ In. 1527.00
Sauceboat, Footed, Intertwined Strap Handle, 19th Century, 3 ¼ x 7 ½ In. 58.00
Sweetmeat Set, Round, 6 Sectional Dishes, Center Dish, Early 1900s, 12 ¾ In. 60.00
Teapot, c.1900, 7 In. 150.00
Tray, Triangular Shape, Chinese, c.1840, 10 ½ In. 176.00
Tureen, Bulbous, Lid, Lotus Finial, Strap Handles, 6 x 8 In., Pair 460.00
Tureen, Cover, c.1920, 4 x 8 x 10 In. 59.00
Urn, Cover, 15 ½ x 8 In. 117.00

ROSE O'NEILL, see Kewpie category.

ROSE TAPESTRY porcelain was made by the Royal Bayreuth factory of Tettau, Germany, during the late nineteenth century. The surface of the porcelain was pressed against a coarse fabric while it was still damp, and the impressions remained on the finished porcelain. It looks and feels like a textured cloth. Very skillful reproductions are being made that even include a variation of the Royal Bayreuth mark, so be careful when buying.

Basket, Pink Rose, Royal Bayreuth, 5 ¼ In. 150.00
Dish, Leaf, Roses, 4 ¼ x 5 In. 175.00
Hair Receiver, Pink Roses, Misty Green Ground 195.00
Hair Receiver, Roses, Peach, Pink, Muted Daisies 379.00

ROSEMEADE Pottery of Wahpeton, North Dakota, worked from 1940 to 1961. The pottery was operated by Laura A. Taylor and her husband, R.I. Hughes. The company was also known as the Wahpeton Pottery Company. Art pottery and commercial wares were made.

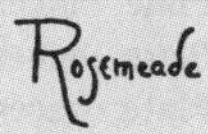

Candleholder, Blue, 1 ¾ x 3 In. Square, Pair 82.00
Figurine, Pheasant, Tail Up, 3 x 3 ½ In. 50.00
Flower Holder, Heron, 1950, 6 ¾ In. 87.00
Salt & Pepper, Black Cat, 3 In. 89.00
Salt & Pepper, Brown Bear, 3 ¼ & 4 In. 77.00
Salt & Pepper, Flamingos, 4 ¼ x 3 ¼ In. 185.00
Salt & Pepper, Greyhound, 2 ½ In.. .... 82.00
Salt & Pepper, Pheasant, 3 In. 10.00
Salt & Pepper, Pheasant, Squatting, 1 ¾ x 5 ½ In. 99.00
Salt & Pepper, Pheasants, 3 In. 45.00
Salt & Pepper, Prairie Rose, 3 Holes, 1950, 2 ½ In.. .... 65.00
Salt & Pepper, Rooster, Chicken, Mauve, 3 ½ x 2 ¼ In. 45.00
Shaker, Duck, Salmon, 3 Holes, 2 ½ In. 19.00
Sugar & Creamer, Corn, 2 ½ & 2 In. 49.00
Vase, Green, Flared, Ruffled Edge, 3 x 2 ¾ x 4 ¼ In. 68.00
Vase, Wheat, Feathered Glaze, Cylindrical, 7 In.. .... 60.00

ROSENTHAL porcelain was made at the factory established in Selb, Bavaria, in 1880. The factory is still making fine-quality tablewares and figurines. A series of Christmas plates was made from 1910. Other limited edition plates have been made since 1971. In 1998 Rosenthal was acquired by the Waterford Wedgwood Group.

Ashtray, Elegance, White To Gray, Platinum Trim, c.1956, 5 ⅜ In. 13.00
Bowl, Dignity, Cobalt Blue, Gold Wheat Center, Square, 9 In. 255.00
Bowl, Fruit, Ceres, Gray Trim, 5 ⅛ In.. .... 16.00
Bowl, Fruit, Japanese Quince, 5 In. 17.00
Bowl, Moliere, Flowers, Pink & Green, Gray & Maroon Trim, Footed, Stamped 85.00
Bowl, Vegetable, Orchid Blossom, Pink, Purple, Yellow, Oval, 10 ½ x 7 ½ In.. .... 18.00
Butter Chip, Orchid Blossom, Pink, Purple, Yellow Flowers, 3 ¼ In. 8.50
Celery Dish, Donatello, Gold Encrusted, Cobalt Blue Band, 10 ⅜ x 4 ⅜ In. 15.00
Charger, Phoenix Bird, Red Ground, Silver Overlay, 20th Century, 13 ⅛ In. 200.00
Coffeepot, Bettina, Rose & Platinum Trim, 7 ⅜ In., 6 Cup 65.00
Coffeepot, Geisha, Gray, Black & Pink Sprigs, Gold Trim, 7 ⅛ In. 45.00
Creamer, Ceres, Gray Trim, 5 ⅛ In.. .... 24.00
Cup & Saucer, Dignity, Cobalt Blue, Gold Wheat, 4 ⅛ In.. .... 17.50
Cup & Saucer, Japanese Quince 17.00
Cup & Saucer, Romance, Pedestal Cup, Blue Medallions, 4 ¾ In. 28.00
Cup & Saucer, Rosenthal Rose 18.00
Cup & Saucer, White, Gilt, Marked, 1930 .... 25.00
Decanter, Cut Glass, Sterling Silver Liquor Tags, England, 10 ¼ In., 6 Piece 270.00
Figurine, Baby Elephant, 5 In. 150.00
Figurine, Bird, Long Tail, Signed, T. Karner, 6 ½ x 4 ¾ In. 66.00
Figurine, Dog, Dachshund Puppy, 6 x 6 In. .... *illus* 220.00
Figurine, Duck, Signed, 5 ½ x 6 ½ In. 120.00
Figurine, Horse, On Hind Legs, White, 15 x 16 In. 700.00
Figurine, Nude, On Horseback, Horse Rearing, 9 ¼ x 9 ½ In.. .... 325.00
Figurine, Nude Woman, Arm Raised, Resting On Head, No. 7655, 14 ¼ In.. .... 275.00
Figurine, Nude Woman, Crouching, White Bisque, Germany, 13 x 7 In. 234.00
Figurine, Rooster, Signed, 6 ½ x 8 In.. .... 150.00
Figurine, Sea Lion, Signed, 3 x 4 x 3 ½ In.. .... 77.00
Figurine, Siamese Dancer, Dramatic Pose, Signed, Holzer-Defanti, 16 ½ In.. .... 1838.00
Figurine, Siamese Dancer, Signed, c.1925, 16 ½ In. .... *illus* 1500.00

Rosenthal, Figurine, Dog, Dachshund Puppy, 6 x 6 In.
$220.00

Rosenthal, Figurine, Siamese Dancer, Signed, c.1925, 16 ½ In.
$1500.00

Rosenthal, Soup, Cream, Vienna, Gold Trim, 6 ⅛ In.
$55.00

TIP

Mother was right: Have a place for everything and everything in its place. Don't stack old dishes or crowd vases on a shelf. Proper spacing prevents nicks and breaks in pottery or porcelain.

Roseville, Baneda, Vase, Blue, Green, 6 In.
$355.00

Roseville, Blackberry, Basket, Hanging, 4 ½ x 5 In.
$390.00

Roseville, Creamware, Tea Set, Landscape, Ships, Windmills, 3 Piece
$176.00

Roseville, Dahlrose, Basket, Hanging, 5 x 8 ¼ In.
$110.00

Gravy Boat, Underplate, Moss Rose Pompadour, 10 x 5 ½ In. 65.00
Group, Eros, Nude Man & Woman, Passionate Kiss, Aigner, 13 ½ In. 652.00
Group, Lioness, Dragging Gazelle, Signed, T. Karner, 1918, 12 ½ x 4 x 25 In. 2320.00
Group, Wolfhounds Playing, 5 ½ x 7 ½ In. 125.00
Group, Woman & Elf, Friedrich Gronau, 11 ¼ In. 275.00
Jar, Cover, Flowers, White, Hexagonal, 6 x 6 In. 35.00
Planter, Flowers, Blue & White Stripes, Yellow Band, Gilt, 8 In. 100.00
Plate, Bread & Butter, Parisian Spring, 6 ¼ In. 4.00
Plate, Bread & Butter, Rosenthal Rose, 6 ¼ In. 10.00
Plate, Cobalt Blue Rim, Gilt Latticework, Etched Rim, 10 ⅜ In., 12 Piece 770.00
Plate, Dinner, Bettina, Rose & Platinum Trim, Continental Line, c.1970, 9 ¾ In. 17.50
Plate, Dinner, Park Lane, Pink Rose Buds, Gold Trim, Scalloped Edge, 10 ¼ In. 32.00
Plate, Grapes & Flowers, Scalloped Edge, Hand Painted, Signed, c.1900, 8 ¾ In. 165.00
Plate, Salad, Dignity, Cobalt Blue, Gold Wheat Center, 7 ¾ In. 35.00
Plate, Salad, Elegance, White To Gray, Platinum Trim, Marked, 7 ⅝ In. 7.99
Plate, Salad, New Wave, Multicolored Geometrics, Pastels, 7 ⅞ In. 30.00
Plate, Salad, Platinum Crossing Lines, Charcoal Ground, Platinum Trim, Marked, 7 ⅝ In. 22.00
Plate, Salad, Vignettes Of Couples, Turquoise Inner Band, Gold Overlay, 7 ¾ In. 30.00
Plate, Wild Violets, Pink, Yellow, Green, Orange, Kimmel, c.1930, 6 ⅞ In. 25.00
Platter, Malmaison, Pink Rose Spray, Garlands, Scalloped Rim, c.1900, 13 In. 85.00
Platter, Moss Rose Pompadour, 14 ½ x 11 In. 75.00
Saucer, Park Lane, Pink Rose Buds, Scalloped Rim, 5 In. 15.00
Server, Flower Center, Cobalt Blue Rim, Gold Trim, Footed, Marked, 9 ½ In. 150.00
Soup, Cream, Saucer, Elegance, White To Gray, Platinum Trim, 5 ⅛ In. 15.00
Soup, Cream, Vienna, Gold Trim, 6 ⅛ In. .... *illus* 55.00
Sugar, Cover, Ceres, Gray Trim, 2 ⅞ x 3 ½ In. 26.00
Sugar, Cover, Romance, Blue Medallions, Demitasse, 3 ½ In. 40.00
Teapot, Carmen, Chrysanthemum, Green Ink Mark, 8 ¼ In. 48.00
Tureen, Soup, Cover, Moss Rose Pompadour, 11 x 14 In. 350.00
Vase, Blue-Green Craqueleure, Bulbous, Gilt Rim, Marked, 8 In. 150.00
Vase, White Leaves, Blue Ground, Stem, Bisque, 12 x 8 In. 117.00

ROSEVILLE Pottery Company was organized in Roseville, Ohio, in 1890. Another plant was opened in Zanesville, Ohio, in 1898. Many types of pottery were made until 1954. Early wares include Sgraffito, Olympic, and Rozane. Later lines were often made with molded decorations, especially flowers and fruit. Most pieces are marked *Roseville*. Many reproductions made in China have been offered for sale the past few years.

Roseville U.S.A.

Abstract, Bowl, Green, Tan, Brown Circles, Blue Ground, 3-Sided, Raymor, 12 ¾ In. 40.00
Apple Blossom, Console, Green, 8 In. 100.00
Apple Blossom, Jardiniere, Pedestal, Rose, 24 ½ x 8 In. 330.00
Apple Blossom, Vase, Handles, 19 In. 325.00
Apple Blossom, Window Box, Green, 8 In. 75.00
Aztec, Vase, Applied Flowers, Blue & Green, Bulbous, Flared, 4 ¼ x 7 ¼ In. 374.00
Aztec, Vase, Applied Flowers, Broad Blue Rim, Footed, 5 ¼ x 10 ½ In. 518.00
Azurean, Vase, Sailboat, Steamship On River, Hills, 7 ⅝ In. 632.00
Baneda, Rose Bowl, Green 250.00
Baneda, Vase, Blue, Green, 6 In. .... *illus* 355.00
Baneda, Vase, Flower & Leaf Band, Green, Footed, Handles, 15 ¾ In. 2280.00
Baneda, Vase, Pink, Footed, Handles, 6 ⅛ In. 236.00
Baneda, Vase, Pink, Handles, 7 ½ x 9 ¼ In. 460.00
Blackberry, Basket, Footed, Handle, 6 ½ In. 649.00
Blackberry, Basket, Hanging, 4 ½ x 5 In. .... *illus* 390.00
Burmese, Candleholder, Woman's Head, White, Pair 90.00
Bushberry, Vase, Footed, Handles, 8 In. 90.00
Bushberry, Wall Pocket, Blue, Fan, 8 In. 324.00
Carnelian II, Vase, Blue, Green Glaze, 5 In. 161.00
Carnelian II, Vase, Bud, Raspberry, 6 In. 125.00
Cherry Blossom, Vase, Brown, Tan, Foil Label, Bulbous, Double Handles, 7 x 5 In. .... 150.00 to 201.00
Cherry Blossom, Vase, Gourd, Cherry Red To Green, Handles, 10 ¼ In. 708.00
Chloron, Wall Pocket, Green Matte Glaze, Stylized Flowers, 10 ¼ x 6 ½ In. 480.00
Clemana, Bowl, Oval, 13 x 9 In. 555.00
Clemana, Vase, Brown, Bulbous, 6 ½ In. 225.00
Clematis, Basket, Brown, 7 ½ x 7 In. 100.00
Clematis, Basket, Brown, 10 ½ x 10 In. 80.00
Clematis, Bowl, Brown, Handles, 4 x 6 In. 70.00
Clematis, Candlestick, Brown, 2 x 5 In., Pair 50.00

Clematis, Cookie Jar, Lid, Handles, 10 ¾ In. 165.00
Clematis, Cornucopia, Orange, Brown, 8 ¼ In. 11.00
Clematis, Planter, Hanging, 5 x 8 In. 53.00
Clematis, Rose, Bowl, 2-Tone Blue, 4 In. 55.00
Clematis, Vase, Bud, Double, 5 In. 50.00
Columbine, Basket, Brown, Blue Flowers, Handle, 8 In. 177.00
Creamware, Brush Holder, 5 In. 50.00
Creamware, Chamber Pot, Cover, 13 ¼ x 12 ½ In. 245.00
Creamware, Tea Set, Landscape, Ships, Windmills, 3 Piece *illus* 176.00
Creamware, Teapot, Dutch Line, C-Shape Handle, 5 ¼ In. 153.00
Daffodil, Purple Ground, Handles, 8 ¾ In. 4200.00
Dahlrose, Basket, Hanging, 5 x 8 ¼ In. *illus* 110.00
Dahlrose, Jardiniere, Pedestal, Daisies, Oval, Handles, 20 x 13 In., 2 Piece 625.00
Dahlrose, Vase, Brown, Double Handles, 7 x 10 In. 240.00
Dahlrose, Vase, Cylindrical, Handles, 12 In. 384.00
Dahlrose, Wall Pocket, 8 ½ In. 160.00
Dawn, Bookends, Green, 5 ¼ x 4 ¼ In. 118.00 to 350.00
Della Robbia, Vase, Cavaliers, Forest, Greens, Brown, Pink, 14 x 10 ¼ In. 7800.00
Donatello, Candlestick, 8 ⅛ In., Pair *illus* 121.00
Falline, Vase, Blue To Green, Ribbed Bottom, Handles, 9 ⅛ In. 1180.00
Falline, Vase, Pea Pod, Yellow, Blue, Handles, 15 ¼ In. 2160.00
Ferella, Vase, Cutout Design, Mottled Red & Green, Double Handles, 4 ¼ x 9 ¼ In. 1725.00
Ferella, Vase, Red, Globular, Handles, 8 ⅛ In. 885.00
Ferella, Wall Pocket, Red, 3 Sections, 6 ½ In. 708.00
Florentine, Bowl, Grape Bunches, Crackle Glaze, Square Handles, 2 ½ x 8 In. 100.00
Florentine, Jardiniere, Pedestal, 28 ½ In. 248.00
Florentine, Umbrella Stand, Handles, 20 In. 300.00
Foxglove, Basket, Mauve, Pink, Marked, 8 ½ x 7 In. *illus* 132.00
Foxglove, Planter, Blue, 12 In. 110.00
Freesia, Cookie Jar, Blue, Handles 400.00
Freesia, Flowerpot, Blue, Hanging, 5 ½ x 7 ½ In. 125.00
Freesia, Pitcher, Green, Blue, Pink, Cutaway Spout, c.1945, 11 In. 70.00
Freesia, Vase, Blue, 6 ¼ In. 66.00
Freesia, Vase, Footed, Low Handles, 10 In. 90.00
Freesia, Vase, Handles, 6 ½ x 5 ½ In. 215.00
Fuchsia, Flower Frog, Brown, 3 ⅛ x 4 ½ In. 145.00
Fuchsia, Jardiniere, Pedestal, Green, 25 ⅝ In. 1265.00
Futura, Basket, Gray, Pink, Hanging, 5 In. 750.00
Futura, Bowl, Pedestal, Tan, Blue Matte Glaze, 4 Buttressed Handles, 4 In. 575.00
Futura, Bowl, Yellow, Green, 4 In. 2000.00
Futura, Console, Flower Frog, Angled, Green & Brown Mottled Glaze, 12 ½ x 3 ½ In. 748.00
Futura, Jardiniere, Brown, Multicolored Leaves, Double Handle, 8 ½ x 6 ¼ In. 288.00
Futura, Jardiniere, Pink, Multicolored Leaves, Double Handle, 12 x 8 In. 575.00
Futura, Vase, 6-Point Star Shape, Ribs, Green & Pink Highlights, 8 ½ x 3 ¾ In. 633.00
Futura, Vase, Beehive, Brown, Green, Leaves, 8 ¼ In. 1035.00
Futura, Vase, Blue, Green, Tan, Flared, 4-Sided, 3 ½ x 8 ¼ In. 1035.00
Futura, Vase, Blue, Tan, Oval, 4-Footed, Square Base, 7 ⅜ In. 354.00
Futura, Vase, Crocus, Purple, 9 In. 750.00
Futura, Vase, Geometrics, Green, Blue Fan, 9 x 6 ¼ In. 403.00
Futura, Vase, Green, Ribbed Neck, Square Handles, 9 In. 354.00
Futura, Vase, Inverted Triangle, Geometric, Blue, 4 ½ x 9 In. 863.00
Futura, Vase, Mottled Brown & Tan, Flowers, Footed, Square, 4 ¼ x 5 ¼ In. 259.00
Futura, Vase, Tan, Blue, Stepped Rim, Square Handles, 6 ¼ In. 165.00
Futura, Vase, Tan, Brown, Green, Ribbed Neck, Square Handles, 9 In. 767.00
Futura, Vase, Vee, Red, Pink, Footed, 7 In. 250.00
Imperial, Basket, Grapes, Leaf, Green Matte Glaze, 5 ¾ x 5 ½ In. 66.00
Imperial, Vase, Handles, 9 ¾ In. 66.00
Imperial, Vase, Turquoise Glaze, Raised Yellow Design, 8 ½ x 7 In. 173.00
Iris, Wall Pocket, Pink, Impressed Mark, 8 ¼ In. 590.00
Ixia, Lamp, Pumpkin Textured Ground, 8 In. 400.00
Jonquil, Wall Pocket, Marked, 8 ⅜ x 6 ⅜ In. *illus* 595.00
Juvenile, Cup & Saucer, Puppy, Glossy, 2 ⅜ In. 85.00
Juvenile, Plate, Chicks, Marked, RV, 7 ⅛ In. *illus* 121.00
Juvenile, Plate, Nursery Rhyme, Baby Bunting, Rolled Edge, 7 ⅝ In. 60.00
Laurel, Vase, Orange, Tab Handles, 7 In. 175.00
Luffa, Jardiniere, Brown, Green, Double Handles, 7 x 5 In. 240.00
Luffa, Vase, Green, Caramel, Square Handles, 6 ⅛ In. 130.00

Roseville, Donatello, Candlestick, 8 ⅛ In., Pair
$121.00

Roseville, Foxglove, Basket, Mauve, Pink, Marked, 8 ½ x 7 In.
$132.00

Roseville, Jonquil, Wall Pocket, Marked, 8 ⅜ x 6 ⅜ In.
$595.00

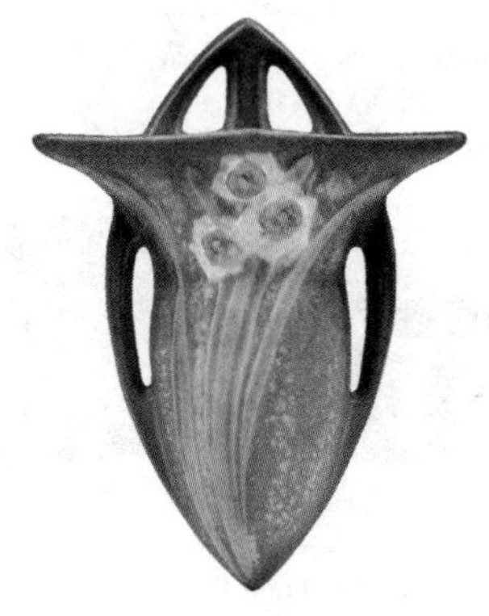

Roseville, Juvenile, Plate, Chicks, Marked, RV, 7 ⅛ In.
$121.00

Roseville, Mostique, Wall Pocket, 10 In.
$99.00

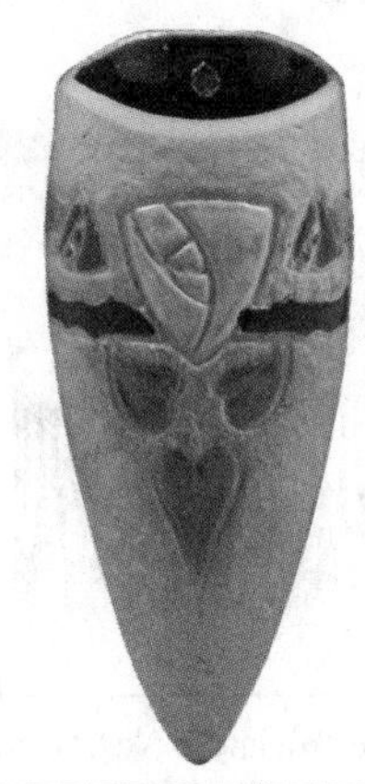

Roseville, Peony, Jardiniere, Pedestal, Pink, Green, 24 ⅜ x 11 ½ In.
$440.00

Roseville, Pine Cone, Bookends, Planter, Brown, 5 ¼ x 5 ¼ In.
$440.00

Roseville, Pine Cone, Vase, Marked, Red Crayon, 10 ⅜ In.
$143.00

Luffa, Vase, Green & Brown, Shouldered, Double Handles, 8 x 8 In. 345.00
Magnolia, Cookie Jar, Brown, Green, White, Handles 200.00
Magnolia, Vase, Blue, 6 ¼ In. 66.00
Montacello, Vase, Blue, Green & Brown Mottled Glaze, Double Handles, 5 x 4 In. 201.00
Morning Glory, Vase, Flowers, Pink, Green, Handles, 8 In. 400.00
Morning Glory, Vase, White, Double Handles, 7 ½ x 9 ½ In. 748.00
Morning Glory, White, Flared Bottom, 10 ¼ In. 413.00
Moss, Vase, Blue, Bulbous, 8 x 6 In. 120.00
Moss, Vase, Blue, Bulbous, Double Handles, 9 ½ x 6 ¼ In. 230.00
Moss, Vase, Blue, Bulbous, Foil Label, 8 x 6 ¼ In. 230.00
Moss, Vase, Blue, Tapered, Double Handles, 7 x 8 ½ In. 316.00
Moss, Vase, Pink, Green, Double Handles, 9 x 14 ½ In. 863.00
Mostique, Bowl, Standard Matte Glaze, Green Interior, 8 In. 80.00
Mostique, Umbrella Stand, Beige, Brown, 22 In. 225.00
Mostique, Wall Pocket, 10 In. .... *illus* 99.00
Orion, Vase, Turquoise, Double Handles, 5 x 8 In. 240.00
Panel, Lamp Vase, Nudes, Green, 10 ⅛ In. 1150.00
Pauleo, Umbrella Stand, Squared Form, Trees, Leaves, Hillside, 22 ½ In. 1770.00
Peony, Jardiniere, Pedestal, Pink, Green, 24 ⅜ x 11 ½ In. .... *illus* 440.00
Peony, Pitcher, Yellow, 7 ½ In. 120.00
Peony, Tea Set, Yellow, Green, Teapot, Sugar & Creamer 230.00
Persian, Bowl, Yellow, Green, 3 Handles, 2 ½ x 7 In. 65.00
Persian, Candlestick, White Ground, 9 ⅞ In. 189.00
Pine Cone, Ashtray, Brown, 4 ¾ In. 94.00
Pine Cone, Basket, Brown, Handle, 9 ½ x 12 ½ In. 403.00
Pine Cone, Basket, Flower Frog, Brown 390.00
Pine Cone, Bookends, Planter, Brown, 5 ¼ x 5 ¼ In. .... *illus* 440.00
Pine Cone, Bowl, Yellow, Brown, Oval, 9 In. 150.00
Pine Cone, Ewer, Blue, Handles, 7 x 15 ½ In. 1725.00
Pine Cone, Toothpick, Pair 175.00
Pine Cone, Vase, Blue, 7 In. 125.00
Pine Cone, Vase, Blue, 18 In. 2200.00
Pine Cone, Vase, Blue, Bulbous, 7 ½ x 6 ½ In. 375.00
Pine Cone, Vase, Brown, 10 In. 550.00
Pine Cone, Vase, Cylindrical, Handles, c.1930, 10 ½ In. 236.00
Pine Cone, Vase, Green, Red, Orange, Stand, 6 x 6 In. 146.00
Pine Cone, Vase, Marked, Red Crayon, 10 ⅜ In. .... *illus* 143.00
Pine Cone, Vase, Pillow, Brown, Handles, Marked, 10 x 9 In. 360.00
Pine Cone, Wall Pocket, Brown, 9 In. 625.00
Poppy, Vase, Green, 8 x 10 In. 180.00
Rosecroft, Wall Pocket, Nude, Brown Matte Glaze, 7 In. 324.00
Rozane, Candlestick, Daffodil, Applied Ceramic Seal, 9 ⅛ In. 132.00
Rozane, Pitcher, Trumpet Flowers, 9 ⅜ In. 69.00
Rozane, Umbrella Stand, Multicolored Flowers, Creme Ground, 1917, 19 x 9 In. 595.00
Rozane, Vase, Flowers, Blue, 4-Sided, Bisque Ground, 8 ¾x 2 ½ In. 3120.00
Rozane, Vase, Honeysuckle, Gussie Gerwick, 12 ¾ In. 286.00
Rozane, Vase, Jonquil, 8 In. 207.00
Rozane, Vase, Nasturtiums, Virginia Adams, 7 ⅜ In. 69.00
Rozane, Vase, Pillow, Dog, Holding Pheasant, Handles, 9 ⅜ x 11 In. 374.00
Rozane Aztec, Vase, Squeezebag, 10 In. 300.00
Rozane Royal, Vase, Pharaoh's Horses, c.1902, 21 In. 4720.00
Sign, Blue, Cream Script Logo, 7 ⅞ x 4 ½ In. 1550.00
Silhouette, Vase, Nude, Fan, 7 In. 275.00
Snowberry, Jardiniere, Pedestal, Blue, 16 x 9 In. 525.00
Snowberry, Teapot, Green, Marked, 7 x 10 In. 150.00
Snowberry, Vase, 12 In. 320.00
Snowberry, Wall Pocket, Blue, 8 In. 125.00
Sunflower, Lamp, Blue, Green Matte Ground, Leather Shade, 6 In. 690.00
Sunflower, Vase, 8 ½ In. 863.00
Sunflower, Vase, Globular, Handles, 9 ⅛ In. 1180.00
Sunflower, Vase, Green, Blue, Double Handles, 4 x 5 In. 316.00
Sunflower, Vase, Handles, 5 In. 275.00
Sunflower, Vase, Waisted, Brown, Green, 7 x 8 ½ In. 690.00
Sunflower, Vase, Yellow, Green, 5 In. 300.00
Sunflower, Wall Pocket, Rolled Lip, 7 ¼ In. 649.00
Teasel, Console, Blue, 12 In. 70.00
Teasel, Ewer, Thistle, Blue, 8 x 18 ½ In. 230.00

Thorn Apple, Vase, 10 In. 155.00
Tuscany, Vase, Pink, Double Handles, 7 x 9 In. 90.00
Tuscany, Vase, Urn, Handles, c.1920, 9 ½ In. 212.00
Velmoss, Vase, Leaves, Green Matte Glaze, Globular, Flared Lip, 5 ⅞ In. 649.00
Velmoss, Vase, Raised Vertical Leaves, Green & Yellow Matte Glaze, Swollen, 10 x 7 In. 220.00
Velmoss Scroll, Wall Pocket, 11 In. 125.00
Vista, Basket, 6 x 8 In. 489.00
Vista, Vase, Palm Trees, Green, Pink, 12 x 6 In. 450.00
Vista, Vase, Swollen Shape, 12 x 5 ½ In. 518.00
Water Lily, Bowl, Rose, 6 x 10 In. 77.00
White Rose, Vase, Loop Handles, 8 x 4 In. 185.00
Wincraft, Ewer, Marked, 8 In. 60.00
Wincraft, Tea Set, Blue, 8 ½-In. Teapot, 3 Piece 374.00
Wincraft, Vase, Handles, 11 In. 130.00
Windsor, Candlestick, Brown, White, 4 In., Pair 225.00
Windsor, Vase, Blue, Sweeping Handles, 7 ¼ In. 1298.00
Wisteria, Vase, Blue, 6 ⅛ x 4 ¾ In. *illus* 355.00
Wisteria, Vase, Blue, Bulbous, Handles, 9 ⅛ In. 649.00
Wisteria, Vase, Blue, Squat, Handles, 4 In. 275.00
Wisteria, Vase, Brown, Double Handles, Foil Label, 6 x 7 ¼ In. 374.00
Wisteria, Vase, Brown, Double Handles, Foil Label, 7 x 15 ¼ In. 1495.00
Wisteria, Vase, Brown, Purple, Green, Handles, Paper Mark, 9 x 7 ½ In. 420.00
Zephyr Lily, Bowl, Brown, 10 In. 150.00
Zephyr Lily, Ewer, Blue, 10 In. 345.00

ROWLAND & MARSELLUS Company is part of a mark that appears on historical Staffordshire dating from the late nineteenth and early twentieth centuries. Rowland & Marsellus is the mark used by an American importing company in New York City. The company worked from 1893 to about 1937. Some of the pieces may have been made by the British Anchor Pottery Co. of Longton, England, for export to a New York firm. Many American views were made. Of special interest to collectors are the plates with rolled edges, usually blue and white.

Cup & Saucer, Blue & White 110.00
Plate, 1000 Islands New York, 7 Views, Rolled Edge, Blue & White, 10 In. 110.00
Plate, Alaska-Yukon-Pacific Exposition, Blue & White, 10 In. 135.00
Plate, American Poets, Roses, Banner, Cobalt Blue, 10 In. 85.00
Plate, Bridgeport, Connecticut, 7 Scenes, Blue & White, 10 In. 110.00
Plate, Brooklyn, New York, Blue Transfer, Marked, 10 ⅛ In. 55.00
Plate, Great American Poets, 7 Portraits, Blue & White, 10 In. 184.00
Plate, Harrisburg, Pa., 4 Views, Blue & White, 10 In. 71.00
Plate, Longfellow, 6 Views, 10 In. 110.00
Plate, Minneapolis, 7 Scenes, Blue & White, 10 In. 89.00
Plate, Myles Standish Monument, Blue & White, 9 ¾ In. 52.00
Plate, Plymouth Rock, 6 Oval Views, Blue & White, 10 In. 89.00 to 110.00
Plate, St. Louis, 7 Scenes, Rolled Edge, Blue & White, 10 In. 74.00
Plate, St. Louis Centennial, Rolled Edge, Blue & White, 1909, 10 In. 157.00
Plate, View Of Denver, Blue & White, 10 In. 110.00
Salt Lake City, 7 Scenes, Blue & White, 10 In. 110.00
Soup, Blue Willow, Blue & White, 8 ¼ In. 25.00

ROY ROGERS was born in 1911 in Cincinnati, Ohio. In the 1930s, he made a living as a singer; in 1935, his group started work at a Los Angeles radio station. He appeared in his first movie in 1937. From 1952 to 1957, he made 101 television shows. The other stars in the show were his wife, Dale Evans, his horse, Trigger, and his dog, Bullet. Roy Rogers memorabilia, including items from the Roy Rogers restaurants, are collected.

Camera, Flash, Herbert George Co., Box, 1950s, 4 x 5 x 9 In. 320.00
Cap Gun, Double Holster, Horse Heads, Conchas, c.1950, 29-In. Waist 330.00
Christmas Card, Roy Rogers & Dale Evans, Fan Club, Members Only, 1950s 65.00
Cowboy Suit, Cream, Blue Trim, Nudie's Rodeo Tailors, Late 1940s, Size 38-40 3450.00
Guitar, 6 Strings, Plastic Handle, Liner, Case, 33 In. 230.00
Guitar, Child, 1950s, 28 ½ In. 83.00
Guitar, Jefferson, Box, 28 In. *illus* 144.00
Guitar, Roy, Trigger, Jefferson, Box, 28 In. 135.00
Guitar, Roy, Trigger, Red, Black, Range Rhythm, Box, 30 In. 135.00
Gun, Double Holster, 31 Bullets, c.1980, 45 x 19 ½ x 4 ¾ In. 1440.00
Gun, Double Holster, Rivets, c.1950, 29 In. *illus* 300.00
Harmonica, King Of The Cowboys, 4 ⅛ In. 65.00

Roseville, Wisteria, Vase, Blue, 6 ⅛ x 4 ¾ In.
$355.00

Roy Rogers, Guitar, Jefferson, Box, 28 In.
$144.00

Roy Rogers, Gun, Double Holster, Rivets, c.1950, 29 In.
$300.00

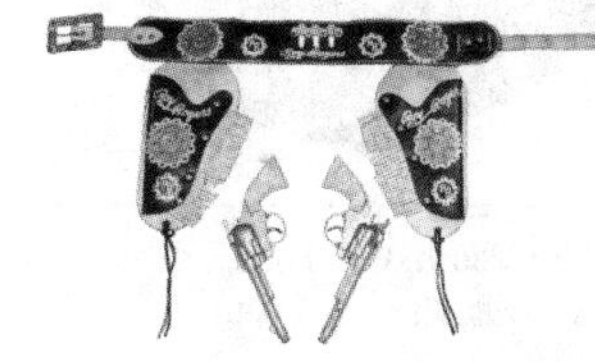

TIP

If your home is water-damaged, ask friends to help. Time is critical. Hire a company that specializes in water-damage restoration. Experts have the necessary equipment to circulate air to keep out mold, mildew, and fungi.

Royal Bayreuth, Hatpin Holder, Poppy, 4 ¼ In.
$400.00

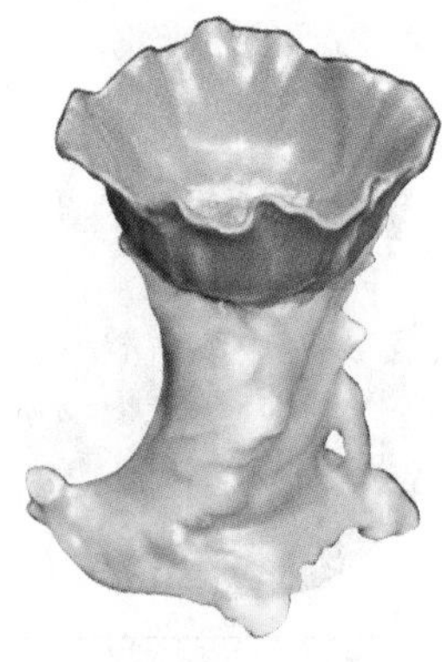

Royal Bayreuth, Stringholder, Rooster, Blue Mark, 6 ¼ In.
$170.00

Royal Bayreuth, Wall Pocket, Devil & Cards, Blue Mark, 3 In.
$275.00

Horseshoe, Rubber, Pair 34.00
Lobby Card, Roy Rogers, Trigger, Under Western Stars, Green, 1938, 11 x 14 In. 213.00
Lunch Box, Double R Bar Ranch, Metal, Thermos, Thermos Brand 230.00
Lunch Box, Roy Rogers & Dale Evans, Double R Ranch, Metal, Thermos, 1953 .... 230.00
Paper Doll, Roy Rogers & Dale Evans, 12 x 10 In. 15.00
Record Player, Trigger, Images, Metal, RCA Victor, 1950s, 9 ½ x 9 ½ x 4 ½ In. 518.00
Ring, Cannon, Gabby Hayes, Brass, Quaker Premium, c.1951 .... 85.00
Saddle, Leather, Roy Rogers Logo, Child's 425.00
Spurs, Child's, Kilgore 95.00
Tie, Roy Rogers & Trigger, Child's 85.00
Toy, Bow, Arrows, Quill, Ben Pearson 110.00
Toy, Chuck Wagon, Steel, Wood Bed, Canvas Cover, Pull, Steger Co., 1950s, 17 x 40 In. 345.00
Toy, Nellybelle Jeep, Trailer, Pressed Steel, Tin, Marx, Box, 15 In. 440.00
Toy, Quick Shooter, Hat, Ideal, Box, 12 In. 110.00
Toy, Roy Rogers, On Trigger, 2 Pistols, Hard Plastic, Hartland 60.00
Tricycle, Roy Rogers, Trigger Head, Horsehair Tail, Metal, Cardboard, 1950s, 18 x 35 In. 863.00
T-Shirt, Roy Rogers & Trigger, Old Store Stock, Child's, c.1950 .... 95.00
Wristwatch, Dale Evans, Girls, Bradley Time, Box, 1954 .... 325.00

ROYAL BAYREUTH is the name of a factory that was founded in Tettau, Bavaria, in 1794. It has continued to modern times. The marks have changed through the years. A stylized crest, the name *Royal Bayreuth,* and the word *Bavaria* appear in slightly different forms from 1870 to about 1919. Later dishes may include the words *U.S. Zone,* the year of the issue, or the word *Germany* instead of *Bavaria.* Related pieces may be found listed in the Rose Tapestry, Sand Babies, Snow Babies, and Sunbonnet Babies categories.

Basket, Pink Roses, Green Ground, Gold Trim, Blue Mark, 4 x 4 ½ In. 100.00
Bowl, Cover, Tomato, 3 ½ x 4 In. 199.00
Bowl Set, Lobster, Graduated, Cover, c.1900, 7 ¾ In., 3 Piece 822.00
Creamer, Cows In Pasture, 4 ½ In. 55.00
Creamer, Elk, 4 ½ In. 60.00
Creamer, Moose, Marked, Austria, 1900s, 4 ½ In. 250.00
Creamer, Tomato, Marked Switch Back, Souvenir Of Railroad, Pa., 1866-77 .... 300.00
Creamer, Turkeys, Gold Handle, Rim, Blue Mark, 4 In. 20.00
Creamer, Victorian Lady, 4 In. 70.00
Dresser Box, Courting Couple, 2 ½ x 3 ½ In. 295.00
Hatpin Holder, Poppy, 4 ¼ In. .... *illus* 400.00
Hatpin Holder, Porcelain, Rose Tapestry 295.00
Jar, Lid, Lobster, Painted, 8 In. 275.00
Pitcher, Devil & Cards, Green Mark, 2 ¾ In. 195.00
Pitcher, Goats Grazing, 6 ½ In. 185.00
Pitcher, Grapes, Yellow, White Satin, Gold Highlights, Blue Mark, 6 x 9 In. 125.00
Pitcher, Toby, Red, Black, White, 1900s, 5 In. 40.00
Planter, Woman Holding Tray, Basket, House, Handles, 2 ¾ x 3 ½ In. 65.00
Plate, Girl With Ducks, 6 In. 10.00
Plate, Rose Tapestry, Pink, Red, Yellow, Orange, Scalloped Rim, Blue Mark, 9 ½ In. 175.00
Shoe, Rose Tapestry, Pink Roses, Green Ground, Gold Accents, Blue Mark 150.00
Stringholder, Rooster, Blue Mark, 6 ¼ In. .... *illus* 170.00
Tobacco Jar, Figures, Greek Key Design, Red, Green, 6 ½ x 6 In. 187.00
Toothpick, Flowers, 3 Handles 20.00
Toothpick, Greek Key Band, Man, Black, Orange Interior, Footed, Marked, 2 ¾ In. 25.00
Toothpick, Turquoise, Gilt Rim, U.S. Zone Germany 14.00
Vase, Bathing Nymphs, 19th Century, 10 In. 250.00
Vase, Bud, Lady With Horse, Queen Anne's Lace Ground, 6 In. 60.00
Vase, Desert Oasis, Green Mark, 7 In. 475.00
Vase, Fishermen At Sea, Footed, Marked, 4 ½ In. 70.00
Vase, Pastoral Scene, Ruffled Rim, 6-Sided, Signed, 3 ¾ In. 50.00
Vase, Stag, Cream, Pink, Green, Handles, Marked, 3 In. 35.00
Vase, Woman Leaning On Horse, Tapestry, Gilt, Handles, 4 ¾ In. 198.00
Wall Pocket, Devil & Cards, Blue Mark, 3 In. .... *illus* 275.00

ROYAL BONN is the nineteenth- and twentieth-century trade name used by Franz Anton Mehlem, who had a pottery in Bonn, Germany, from 1836 to 1931. Porcelain and earthenware were made. The factory was purchased by Villeroy & Boch in 1921 and closed in 1931. Many marks were used, most including the name *Bonn,* the initials *FM,* and a crown.

Charger, Roses, Pink, Yellow, Green, Signed, 13 In. 40.00

Clock, Ansonia, Flowers, Turquoise, Signed, c.1900, 15 ½ In. . . . *illus* 531.00
Clock, Ansonia, Ormolu, Cast Iron, Pinched Waist, Scrolled Legs, 13 ½ In. . . . 148.00
Clock, Ansonia, Shelf, Blue, Flowers, c.1900, 12 In. . . . 531.00
Clock, Ansonia, Shelf, Flower Spray, Green To Rose, Open Handle, c.1900, 15 In. . . . 130.00
Clock, Ansonia, Shelf, Flowers, Green To Rose, 11 In. . . . 885.00
Clock, Ansonia, Shelf, Flowers, Pink, Marked, 12 In. . . . 600.00
Clock, Ansonia, Shelf, Flowers, Turquoise, Open Handle, c.1900, 15 ½ In. . . . 1534.00
Clock, Ansonia, Shelf, Iris, Yellow, Blue, White, Crimson, c.1900, 12 In. . . . 590.00
Clock, Ansonia, Shelf, Morning Glories, Crimson, c.1900, 11 In. . . . 708.00
Clock, Ansonia, Shelf, Multicolored, Open Handle, 14 In. . . . 1003.00
Clock, Ansonia, Shelf, Mums, Crimson, Yellow, Pink, 11 In. . . . 325.00
Clock, Ansonia, Shelf, Scrolls, Flowers, Green, c.1900, 14 In. . . . 590.00
Planter, Tapestry Terrace, Flowers, Ormolu, Cherub Handles, Gilt Metal, 15 x 20 In. . . . *illus* 800.00
Plate, Mill Scene, Blue, White, Shaped Rim, 9 ½ In. . . . 20.00
Punch Bowl, Blue, White, Footed, 9 ¼ x 17 In. . . . 59.00
Stein, Baseball, Game In Progress, Painted, Metal Lid, c.1900, 9 In. . . . 3525.00
Urn, Cover, Flowers, Ivory, Lavender, Pedestal, Handles, 15 In. . . . 400.00
Vase, Flowers, Blue Ground, 3 Handles, Marked, DI 2666, 10 ¾ In. . . . 185.00
Vase, Flowers, Gilt Rim, 15 ½ In. . . . 225.00
Vase, Flowers, Light Blue Ground, Cobalt Blue Base, Hand Painted, Signed, 15 In. . . . 250.00
Vase, Flowers, Multicolored, Round, 5 In. . . . 110.00
Vase, Fruit, Flowers, Green Ground, Signed, M.D. Dickmann, 13 ½ x 9 ¼ In. . . . 200.00

ROYAL COPENHAGEN porcelain and pottery have been made in Denmark since 1775. The Christmas plate series started in 1908. The figurines with pale blue and gray glazes have remained popular in this century and are still being made. Many other old and new style porcelains are made today.

Bowl, Flowers, Blue, White, Reticulated, Square, 9 x 9 In. . . . 100.00
Bowl, Medieval Face Center, Mottled Glaze, Marked, Jais Nielsen, 3 x 5 In. . . . 225.00
Bowl, Tenera, Blue, White, Marked, 4 x 7 ¾ In. . . . 135.00
Compote, Flora Danica, Flower, White Ground, Sawtooth Gilt Edge, 5 x 8 In. . . . 805.00
Dish, Golden Clover, 4 In. . . . 45.00
Dish, Refineria Belot, Cuba, Marked . . . 125.00
Dish, Standard Oil Refineries, Craquelure, 1950, 7 In. . . . 125.00
Figurine, 2 Girls, Holding Hands, No. 1316, 7 ½ In. . . . 75.00
Figurine, Bear, Playing, Mottled Glaze, 4 x 6 ½ In. . . . 45.00
Figurine, Boy, Gray Pants, Girl, 9 In. . . . 425.00
Figurine, Boy, On Rock, No. 1659, Marked, 8 x 5 In. . . . 105.00
Figurine, Boy, Playing Accordion, Marked, 4 ½ x 2 In. . . . 45.00
Figurine, Boy, Whittling, Marked, 7 ½ x 3 In. . . . 60.00
Figurine, Boy, With Sow, Marked, 7 ¼ x 7 ½ In. . . . 250.00
Figurine, Boy & Girl, Standing, No. 1761, 8 ¼ x In. . . . 411.00
Figurine, Bricklayer, No. 4377, 9 ⅞ In. . . . 90.00
Figurine, Dog, Airedale, White, Black Spots, 6 ½ x 8 ½ In. . . . 90.00
Figurine, Dog, Collie, Seated, 7 ¼ In. . . . 236.00
Figurine, Dog, Dachshund, Seated, No. 3140, Marked, NMX, 4 In. . . . 60.00
Figurine, Dog, Pointer, No. 1452, 10 In. . . . 125.00
Figurine, Dog, Scottie, Gray, 4 x 5 In. . . . 80.00
Figurine, Dog, Sealyham, Seated, White, 3 ½ In. . . . 25.00
Figurine, Dog, Terrier, No. 3170, 3 ⅛ x 4 In. . . . 55.00
Figurine, Dog, With Slipper, 3 ½ In. . . . 60.00
Figurine, Dutch Boy & Girl, Holding Staff, 8 In. . . . 180.00
Figurine, Faun & Goat, No. 737, 8 ¼ In. . . . 250.00
Figurine, Faun & Parrot, No. 752, 2nd Edition, 7 In. . . . 250.00
Figurine, Faun & Squirrel, No. 456, 8 ¾ In. . . . 200.00
Figurine, Girl & Calf, No. 779, 6 ½ In. . . . 150.00
Figurine, Goat, Reclining, 6 x 11 In. . . . 85.00
Figurine, Hippopotamus, 6 ½ x 16 In. . . . 854.00
Figurine, Lion, Reclining, 6 ½ x 14 In. . . . 300.00
Figurine, Man, 2 Cows, No. 1858, Signed, 9 ½ x 7 ¼ In. . . . 175.00
Figurine, Man, Sitting On Goat, 7 x 6 In. . . . 120.00
Figurine, Man, With Gun, Dog, 9 In. . . . 300.00
Figurine, Mermaid, No. 12459, Signed, 10 ¼ In. . . . 125.00
Figurine, Nude Woman, No. 4431, 9 x 6 In. . . . 85.00
Figurine, Owl, White, No. 113, 3 ½ In. . . . 25.00
Figurine, Pheasant, No. 2143, 11 ½ In. . . . 125.00

Royal Bonn, Clock, Ansonia, Flowers, Turquoise, Signed, c.1900, 15 ½ In.
$531.00

Royal Bonn, Planter, Tapestry Terrace, Flowers, Ormolu, Cherub Handles, Gilt Metal, 15 x 20 In.
$800.00

TIP

Worried about where to hang a picture? Put a small dot of toothpaste on the top corners of the frame and press the frame against the wall so the toothpaste leaves a mark. If the position looks okay, then pound in the hook and wipe off the toothpaste. Don't do this if the wall is papered.

As always, the edited listings in *Kovels' Antiques & Collectibles Price Guide 2010* aren't available on any website, but readers should visit Kovels.com for information on trends, tips, reproductions, marks, old prices, and more!

R

Royal Copenhagen, Vase, Bottle Form, Concentric Arches, Green, Brown Glaze, Axel Salto, 10 In.
$5750.00

Royal Copenhagen, Vase, Fruiting, Brown, Cream Glaze, Axel Salto, 9 x 6 ½ In.
$9600.00

Royal Copenhagen, Egg, Imari, Stand, 5 ½ In.
$292.00

Figurine, Pig & Farmer, 7 ½ x 8 In. 225.00
Figurine, Polar Bear, Roaring, No. 502, 13 In. 140.00
Figurine, Polar Bear Cubs, Playing, No. 1107, 5 ½ In. 70.00
Figurine, Princess & Hans Clodhopper, Woman & Man, On Sofa, 9 x 9 In. 960.00
Figurine, Puppies, White, Gray Spots, 6 In. 60.00
Figurine, Shepherd & Sheep, 8 In. 150.00
Figurine, Squirrel, 2 ½ In.. .... 80.00
Figurine, Wolf & Cubs, 4 x 5 ½ In. 170.00
Figurine, Woman Knitting, No. 1317, 9 x 5 ½ In. 118.00
Group, Sonderjylland, 2 Women, Man, Marked, 13 In. 3800.00
Mother's Day Plate, Cocker Spaniel Pups, 1969 .... 50.00
Plate, Blue, Fluted, Half Lace, 8 ¾ In. 88.00
Plate, Flora Danica, Flowers, Sawtooth Gilt Edge, 7 ¾ In.. .... 460.00
Sauceboat, Flora Danica, Oval, Integral, Numbered, 6 x 10 In. 1920.00
Tureen, Platter, Flora Danica, Oval, Crabstock Handles, 14 In.. .... 2607.00
Vase, Black & White Squares, Gold, No. 3043678, Signed, Lin Utzon, 10 x 7 In.. .... 130.00
Vase, Bottle Form, Concentric Arches, Green, Brown Glaze, Axel Salto, 10 In. .... *illus* 5750.00
Vase, Bud, Blue, Celadon Flambe Glaze, Axel Salto, 10 ½ x 4 ½ In. 3900.00
Vase, Bud, Cylindrical, Blue, Olive Sung Glaze, Axel Salto, 8 ¼ x 3 ¾ In. 3240.00
Vase, Dandelions, No. 175235, Purple, Marked, 3 x 9 In.. .... 90.00
Vase, Diana & Acteon, Red, Green, Jais Neilsen, c.1926, 40 In. 27500.00
Vase, Fruiting, Brown, Cream Glaze, Axel Salto, 9 x 6 ½ In. .... *illus* 9600.00
Vase, Lake Scene, Swans, Leaves, Marked, 8897 St. Ussig, 13 ½ In.. .... 819.00
Vase, Sea Gulls, Blue, White, Gilt Rim, Signed, 5 ½ x 3 In. 40.00
Vase, Wisteria, Butterflies, Marked, c.189712 ¾ In. 115.00
Wine Cooler, Flora Danica, Applied Flowers, Gilt Handles, Marked, 6 ½ x 10 ⅝ In. 3000.00

ROYAL COPLEY china was made by the Spaulding China Company of Sebring, Ohio, from 1939 to 1960. The figural planters and the small figurines, especially those with Art Deco designs, are of great collector interest.

Bank, Pig, Pink, Blue, Gold Trim, 4 ⅝ In.. .... 32.00
Figurine, Cat, Black & White, Pink Bow, 8 In. 35.00
Planter, Cocker Spaniel, Tan, Brown, 8 In. .... 32.00 to 45.00
Vase, Bud, Parrot, c.1940, 5 x 3 ¾ In. 17.00
Wall Pocket, Country Scene, Green Border, 8 ½ In. Diam. 11.00
Wall Pocket, Girl, Leaning On Fence Post, 6 ¼ In. 21.00
Wall Pocket, Pirate, Face, Embossed, 8 ½ x 6 In. 95.00

ROYAL CROWN DERBY Company, Ltd., was established in England in 1890. There is a complex family tree that includes the Derby, Crown Derby, and Royal Crown Derby porcelains. The Royal Crown Derby mark includes the name and a crown. The words *Made in England* were used after 1921. The company is now a part of Royal Doulton Tableware Ltd.

Bowl, Gold Aves, 6-Sided, 4 ½ x 11 In.. .... 150.00
Box, Cover, Imari, c.1918, 2 ½ In., Pair. 372.00
Cup & Saucer, Derby Posies, Surrey 52.00
Cup & Saucer, Imari 74.00
Decanter, Night Watchman, Kingsware Dewar's, 8 In. 96.00
Dish, Imari, Gilt, Scroll Handles, Square, No. 8731, c.1925, 10 ½ In.. .... 180.00
Egg, Imari, Stand, 5 ½ In. .... *illus* 292.00
Figurine, Cat, Gold Seal, 5 In. .... *illus* 150.00
Figurine, Rabbit, Box. 59.00
Gnome, The Auctioneer, c.1920. .... 400.00
Paperweight, Chipmunk, Leaves, Red, Blue, Gilt, Marked, 1986-97, 4 In.. .... 77.00
Paperweight, Crab, Red, Blue Flowers, Gilt, 1988-91, 1 x 4 ½ In. 88.00
Paperweight, Dolphin, Wave, Blue, Gilt, Marked, 1987-93, 3 ¾ x 6 ½ In.. .... 88.00
Paperweight, Frog, Blue, Red, Gilt, 1998, 3 In. 95.00
Paperweight, Penguin, Blue, Red, Gilt, Marked, 1981-92, 5 ¼ In.. .... 110.00
Paperweight, Pig, Red Flowers, Blue, Gilt, 1999, 2 ½ x 5 In. 88.00
Paperweight, Seal, Red Flowers, Blue, Gilt, 1983-873 x 5 In. 110.00
Paperweight, Walrus, Flowers, Red, Blue, Gilt, Marked, 1987-91, 4 x 5 In. 88.00
Pitcher, Imari, 5 ½ In.. .... 296.00
Pitcher, Rooster, Red, Yellow, Black, Art Deco, 7 ¼ In.. .... 185.00
Plate, Bread & Butter, Derby Posies, Scalloped, Gilt Trim, Surrey, 6 ¼ In. 35.00
Plate, Dinner, Derby Posies, Surrey, 10 ⅝ In. 55.00
Plate, Dinner, Green Flowers, Gilt, Scalloped, 10 ⅜ In. 45.00
Plate, Dinner, Imari, 10 In., 12 Piece 1638.00

Plate, Luncheon, Green Flowers, Gilt, Scalloped, 8 ¼ In. 35.00
Plate, Luncheon, Partridges, Gilt, Ruffled Rim, 9 In. 125.00
Plate, Partridge, Green Border, Gold Rope Trim, 8 ¼ In. 62.00
Platter, Flowers, Geometrics, Black, Red, White, c.1937, 10 ⅞ In. 230.00
Tureen, Cover, Blue Bands, Marked, Early 1800s, 10 x 13 In. 325.00
Tureen, Underplate, Red Bird, Scroll Handles, Gilt Trim, 7 ½ x 12 In. 731.00
Vase, Flowers, Pink, Gilt, Ruffled Rim, 1890s, 8 In. 70.00

ROYAL DOULTON is the name used on Doulton and Company pottery made from 1902 to the present. Doulton and Company of England was founded in 1853. Pieces made before 1902 are listed in this book under Doulton. Royal Doulton collectors search for the out-of-production figurines, character jugs, vases, and series wares. Some vases and animal figurines were made with a special red glaze called flambe. Sung and Chang glazed pieces are rare. The multicolored glaze is very thick and looks as if it were dropped on the clay. In 2005 Royal Doulton was acquired by the Waterford Wedgwood Group, which was bought by KPS Capital Partners of New York in 2009 and became part of WWRD Holdings.

Animal, Comic Bear, Titanian, HN 270, 1922-36, 5 In. 1185.00
Animal, Dog, Cocker Spaniel, HN 1188, 1937-69, 3 ½ In. 53.00
Animal, Dog, Cocker Spaniel, Lying In Basket, HN 2585, 1941-85, 2 In. 25.00
Animal, Dog, Cocker Spaniel With Pheasant, HN 1028, 1931-85, 5 ¼ In. 324.00
Animal, Dog, Cocker Spaniel With Pheasant, HN 1029, 1931-68, 3 ½ In. 50.00
Animal, Dog, Cocker Spaniel With Pheasant, HN 1138, 1937-85, 5 ¼ In. 255.00
Animal, Dog, Labrador, Black, Box, DA 145 .... 39.00
Animal, Dog, Rough Haired Terrier, HN 1007, 1931-55, 7 ½ In. 74.00
Animal, Elephant, Flambe, 8 In. 86.00
Animal, Fox, In Hunting Dress, HN 100, 1913-42, 6 In. 1778.00
Animal, Fox, Seated, Flambe, HN 102, 1913-62, 9 ¼ In. 652.00
Animal, Fox, Seated, Flambe, HN 130, 1913-62, 9 ¼ In. .... *illus* 460.00
Animal, Fox, Seated, Flambe, HN 147B, 1918-46, 4 ½ In., Pair 173.00
Animal, Goat, Jumping, HN 1182, 1937-42, 6 ¾ In. 96.00
Animal, Hare, Crouching, HN 273, 2 In. 2844.00
Animal, Palomino Moonlight, DA 35B, 1989-96, 11 In. 84.00
Animal, Peahen, Flambe, HN 247, 1921-C.1946, 4 In. 288.00
Animal, Penguin, Flambe, 6 In. .... *illus* 201.00
Animal, Penguins, Blue Glaze, HN 133, Variation, 6 In. 770.00
Animal, Penguins, Brown & White, HN 133, 1913-46, 6 In. 830.00
Animal, Rabbits, Brown Patches, HN 209, 1920-C.1946, 3 ½ In. 1067.00
Animal, Salmon, Leaping, Flambe, 11 ¾ In. 563.00
Animal, Salmon, Leaping, Flambe, HN 666, 1940-50, 12 ¼ In. 889.00
Animal, Tiger, Seated, HN 912, Charles Noke, 1927-40, 6 ¼ In. 1304.00
Animal, Tiger, Stalking, Flambe, HN 2646, 1950-96, 13 ½ In. 770.00
Animal, Tiger On A Rock, HN 876, Charles Noke, 1924-46, 9 In. 1659.00
Box, Flambe, Footed, Cover, 2 ⅞ In. 259.00

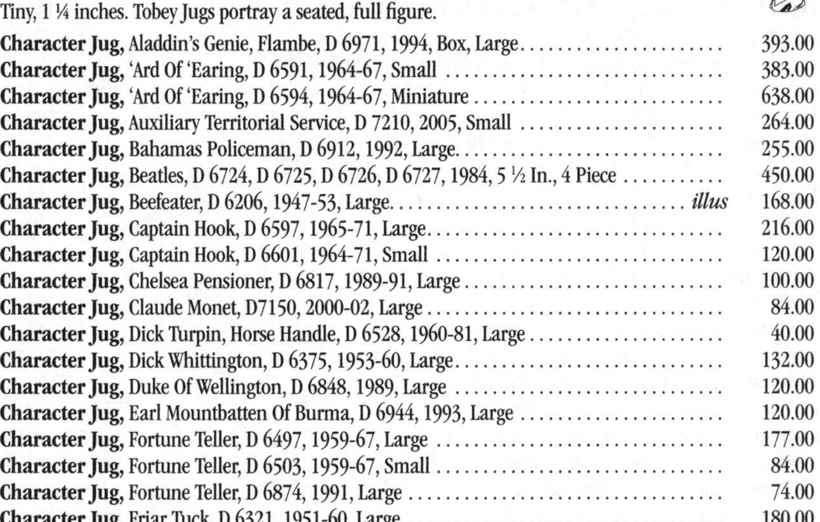

Royal Doulton Character Jugs depict the head and shoulders of the subject. They are made in four sizes: Large, 5 ¼ to 7 inches; Small, 3 ¼ to 4 inches; Miniature, 2 ¼ to 2 ½ inches; and Tiny, 1 ¼ inches. Tobey Jugs portray a seated, full figure.

Character Jug, Aladdin's Genie, Flambe, D 6971, 1994, Box, Large 393.00
Character Jug, 'Ard Of 'Earing, D 6591, 1964-67, Small 383.00
Character Jug, 'Ard Of 'Earing, D 6594, 1964-67, Miniature 638.00
Character Jug, Auxiliary Territorial Service, D 7210, 2005, Small 264.00
Character Jug, Bahamas Policeman, D 6912, 1992, Large 255.00
Character Jug, Beatles, D 6724, D 6725, D 6726, D 6727, 1984, 5 ½ In., 4 Piece 450.00
Character Jug, Beefeater, D 6206, 1947-53, Large .... *illus* 168.00
Character Jug, Captain Hook, D 6597, 1965-71, Large 216.00
Character Jug, Captain Hook, D 6601, 1964-71, Small 120.00
Character Jug, Chelsea Pensioner, D 6817, 1989-91, Large 100.00
Character Jug, Claude Monet, D7150, 2000-02, Large 84.00
Character Jug, Dick Turpin, Horse Handle, D 6528, 1960-81, Large 40.00
Character Jug, Dick Whittington, D 6375, 1953-60, Large 132.00
Character Jug, Duke Of Wellington, D 6848, 1989, Large 120.00
Character Jug, Earl Mountbatten Of Burma, D 6944, 1993, Large 120.00
Character Jug, Fortune Teller, D 6497, 1959-67, Large 177.00
Character Jug, Fortune Teller, D 6503, 1959-67, Small 84.00
Character Jug, Fortune Teller, D 6874, 1991, Large 74.00
Character Jug, Friar Tuck, D 6321, 1951-60, Large 180.00

Royal Crown Derby, Figurine, Cat, Gold Seal, 5 In.
$150.00

Royal Doulton, Animal, Fox, Seated, Flambe, HN 130, 1913-62, 9 ¼ In.
$460.00

Royal Doulton, Animal, Penguin, Flambe, 6 In.
$201.00

Royal Doulton, Character Jug, Beefeater, D 6206, 1947-53, Large
$168.00

Royal Doulton, Character Jug, Golfer, D 6623, Large
$40.00

Royal Doulton, Character Jug, Gondolier, D 6589, 1964-69, Large
$276.00

Royal Doulton, Character Jug, Granny, D 5521, Large
$105.00

Character Jug, Gardener, Red, D 6630, 1971, Large ... 1810.00
Character Jug, Gladiator, D 6553, 1961-67, Small ... 113.00
Character Jug, Gladiator, D 6556, 1961-67, Miniature ... 144.00
Character Jug, Golfer, D 6623, Large ... *illus* 40.00
Character Jug, Gondolier, D 6589, 1964-69, Large ... *illus* 276.00
Character Jug, Gondolier, D 6592, 1964-69, Small ... 144.00
Character Jug, Granny, D 5521, Large ... *illus* 105.00
Character Jug, Great Britain's Britannia, D 7179 ... 53.00
Character Jug, Guardsman, D 6771, 1987-99, Small ... 264.00
Character Jug, Gulliver, D 6563, 1962-67, Small ... 160.00
Character Jug, Jane Seymour, D 6646, Large ... 59.00
Character Jug, Jockey, D 6625, 1971-75, Large ... 98.00
Character Jug, King Cole, Yellow Crown, D 6036, 1938-39, Large ... 4693.00
Character Jug, Leprechaun, D6847, 1990-96, Large ... 1080.00
Character Jug, Lord Nelson, D 6336, Large ... 380.00
Character Jug, Mad Hatter, D 6598, Large ... 70.00
Character Jug, Mae West, D 6688, 1983-86, Large ... 144.00
Character Jug, Mrs. Claus, D 7242, 1992, Box, Miniature ... 85.00 to 96.00
Character Jug, Musical, Auld Mac, D 5889, 1938-39, 6 ¼ In. ... 330.00
Character Jug, Musical, Old Charley, D 5858, 1938-39, 5 ½ In. ... 390.00
Character Jug, Musical, Paddy, D 5887, 1938-39, 7 In. ... 270.00
Character Jug, Musical, Tony Weller, D 5888, 1937-39, 6 ½ In. ... 510.00
Character Jug, Nelson, D 6963, 1994-95, Small ... 138.00
Character Jug, North American Indian, D 6611, 1967-91, Large ... 100.00
Character Jug, Old Charley, D 5527, Small ... 72.00
Character Jug, Punch & Judy Man, D 6593, 1964-69, Small ... 120.00
Character Jug, Quasimodo, D 7108, 1998, Large ... 108.00
Character Jug, Queen Victoria, D 6788, 1988, Large ... 85.00
Character Jug, Queen Victoria, D 6913, 1992, Small ... 144.00
Character Jug, Regency Beau, D 6562, 1962-67, Small ... 204.00
Character Jug, Ringmaster, D 6863, 1990, Large ... 132.00
Character Jug, Sairey Gamp, D 6789, 1986, Small ... 55.00
Character Jug, Santa Claus, D 7123, Christmas Tree, Handle, 1998, Large ... 132.00
Character Jug, Santa Claus, D 7244, Miniature ... 48.00
Character Jug, Santa With Snowman, D 7238, Box, Large ... 85.00
Character Jug, Sir Stanley Matthews, D 7161, 2000, Small ... 74.00
Character Jug, Squire, D 6319, Medium ... 72.00
Character Jug, St. George, D 6621, 1968-75, Small ... 74.00
Character Jug, Touchstone, D 5613, 1936-60, Large ... 96.00 to 113.00
Character Jug, Ugly Duchess, D 6603, 1965-73, Small ... 84.00 to 138.00
Character Jug, Viking, D 6496, 1959-75, Large ... 96.00
Character Jug, Wilbur Wright, D 7179, 2003, Large ... 192.00
Character Jug, Winston Churchill, D 6907, 1992, Large ... 125.00
Character Jug, Winston Churchill, Union Jack Handle, D 6907, 1992, Large ... 2128.00
Character Teapot, Cowboy & Indian, 2-Sided, D 7176, Box, 7 In. ... 53.00
Charger, Gleaners, 15 ⅜ In. ... 165.00
Cruet Set, Man, Woman, Votes For Women, D 7066, Toil For Men, D7067, 2 Piece ... 144.00
Cup & Saucer, Arabesque, Blue & White, 6 In. ... 20.00
Dish, Flambe, Bird Medallion, Mottled, Cloud Border, c.1900, 14 ¾ In. ... 1304.00
Figurine, Afternoon Tea, HN 1747, 1935-82, 5 ¾ In. ... *illus* 156.00
Figurine, Anna, HN 2802, 1976-82, 5 ¾ In. ... 109.00
Figurine, Annette, HN 1550, 1933-49, 6 ¼ In. ... 204.00
Figurine, Anthea, HN 1527, 1932-40, 6 ½ In. ... 228.00
Figurine, Antoinette, HN 2326, 1967-79, 6 ¼ In. ... 29.00
Figurine, Aperitif, HN 2998, 1988, 12 ½ In. ... 60.00
Figurine, Ascot HN 3471, 1994, 8 ½ In. ... 120.00
Figurine, At Ease, HN 2473, 1973-79, 6 In. ... 77.00
Figurine, Auctioneer, HN 2988, 1986, 8 ½ In. ... 100.00
Figurine, Autumn Breezes, HN 1934, 1940-97, 8 In. ... 95.00
Figurine, Autumn Breezes, HN 2147, 1955-71, 7 ½ In. ... 144.00
Figurine, Balloon Lady, HN 2935, 1984-Present, 8 In. ... 75.00
Figurine, Balloon Man, HN 1954, 1940-Present, 7 ½ In. ... 75.00 to 140.00
Figurine, Balloon Seller, HN 583, 1923-49, 9 In. ... 426.00
Figurine, Bedtime Story, HN 2059, 1950-96, 4 ¾ In. ... 79.00
Figurine, Belle, HN 2340, 1968-88, 5 In. ... 25.00
Figurine, Belle O' The Ball, HN 1997, 1947-79, 6 In. ... *illus* 108.00

Figurine, Biddy Penny Farthing, HN 1843, 1938-Present, 9 In. 75.00 to 205.00
Figurine, Bluebeard, HN 2105, 1953-92, 11 In. 160.00
Figurine, Bunnykins, Bedtime, DB 63, 1987, 3 ¼ In. 120.00
Figurine, Bunnykins, Betsey Ross, DB 313, Box, 2004 32.00
Figurine, Bunnykins, Clown, DB 129, 250, 1992, 4 ¼ In. 396.00
Figurine, Bunnykins, Collector, DB 54, 1987, 4 ¼ In. 264.00
Figurine, Bunnykins, Day Trip, Box, DB 260, 3 ½ In. 79.00
Figurine, Bunnykins, Dodgem Car, DB 249, 2001 43.00
Figurine, Bunnykins, Goalkeeper, DB 120, Box, 1991, 4 ½ In. 360.00
Figurine, Bunnykins, Magician, DB 159, 1998, 4 ½ In. 72.00
Figurine, Bunnykins, Milkman, DB 125, 1992, 4 ½ In. 211.00
Figurine, Bunnykins, Mr. Bunnybeat Strumming, DB 16, 1982-85, 4 ½ In. 64.00
Figurine, Bunnykins, Mr. Bunnykins Autumn Days, DB 5, 1972-82, 4 In. 36.00
Figurine, Bunnykins, Santa, DB 62, Ornament, 1987, 3 ¾ In. 300.00
Figurine, Bunnykins, Sydney, DB 195, 1999, Box, 5 In. 55.00
Figurine, Bunnykins, Tally Ho, DB 78, 1988, 4 In. 132.00
Figurine, Bunnykins, Trick Or Treat, DB 162, 1995, 4 ½ In. 336.00
Figurine, Bunnykins, Welsh Lady, DB 172, 1997, 5 In. 96.00
Figurine, Bunnykins, Wizard, DB 168, 1997, 5 In. 120.00
Figurine, Buttercup, HN 2309, 1964-97, 7 In. 55.00 to 94.00
Figurine, Captain, HN 2260, 1965-82, 9 ½ In. 100.00
Figurine, Cellist, HN 2226, 1960-67, 8 In. 192.00
Figurine, Charley's Aunt, HN 35, 1913-36, 7 In. 404.00
Figurine, Charmian, HN 1569, 1933-40, 6 ½ In. 175.00
Figurine, Cherie, HN 2341, 1966-92, 5 ½ In. 125.00
Figurine, Cheryl, HN 3253, 1989-94, 7 ½ In. *illus* 154.00
Figurine, China Repairer, HN 2943, 1982-88, 6 ¾ In. 149.00
Figurine, Christmas Celebrations, HN 4721, 2004-05, Box, 6 ¾ In. 59.00
Figurine, Clarissa, HN 2345, 1968-81, 7 ½ In. 50.00
Figurine, Clock Maker, HN 2279, 1961-75, 7 In. 168.00
Figurine, Country Veterinarian, HN 4650, 2004-Present, 9 In. 107.00
Figurine, Curtsey, HN 334, 1918-36, 11 In. 962.00
Figurine, Day Dreams, HN 1731, 1935-96, 5 ¾ In. *illus* 117.00
Figurine, Debbie, HN 2400, 1983-95, 6 In. 25.00
Figurine, Debut, HN 3046, 1985-89, 12 ½ In. 99.00
Figurine, Delight, HN 1772, 1936-67, 7 In. 160.00
Figurine, Do You Wonder Where Fairies Are, HN 1544, 1933-49, 5 In. 187.00
Figurine, Doctor, HN 2858, 1979-92, 7 ½ In. 100.00
Figurine, Elaine, HN 3214, 1988, 98, 4 In. 32.00
Figurine, Elegance, HN 2264, 1961-85, 7 ¼ In. 65.00
Figurine, Elyse, HN 2429, 1972-95, 5 ¾ In. 82.00
Figurine, England, HN 3627, 1996-98, 8 In. 120.00
Figurine, Fair Lady, HN 2193, 1963-96, 7 ½ In. 59.00 to 94.00
Figurine, Family Album, HN 2321, 1966-73, 6 ¾ In. 234.00
Figurine, Fleur, HN 2368, 1968-95, 7 ½ In. *illus* 69.00
Figurine, Flower Seller's Children, HN 1342, 1929-93, 8 In. 168.00 to 293.00
Figurine, Foaming Quart, HN 2162, 1955-92, 5 ½ In. 75.00
Figurine, Gay Morning, HN 2135, 1954-67, 7 In. 85.00
Figurine, Good Friends, HN 2783, 1985-90, 8 ½ In. 100.00
Figurine, Goody Two Shoes, HN 2037, 1949-89, 5 In. 47.00
Figurine, Gossips, HN 2025, 1949-67, 5 ½ In. 180.00
Figurine, Grace, HN 2318, 7 ¾ In. 94.00
Figurine, Granny's Shawl, HN 1647, 1934-49, 5 ¾ In. 96.00
Figurine, Gypsy Dance, HN 2230, 1959-71, 7 In. 96.00
Figurine, H.R.H. Prince Of Wales, HN 2883, Lady Diana Spencer, HN 2885, 8 In., Pair. 780.00
Figurine, Harmony, HN 2824, 1978-84, 8 In. 66.00
Figurine, Heart To Heart, HN 2276, 1961-71, 5 ½ In. 192.00 to 240.00
Figurine, Helmsman, HN 2499, 1974-86, 9 In. 100.00
Figurine, Honey, HN 1909, 1939-49, 7 In. 234.00
Figurine, Isadora, HN 2938, 1986-92, 8 In. 77.00
Figurine, Janine, HN 2461, 1971-95, 7 ½ In. 22.00
Figurine, Jersey Milkmaid, HN 2057, 1950-59, 6 ½ In. 127.00
Figurine, Jester, HN 2016, 1949-97, 10 In. 94.00 to 125.00
Figurine, Judge, HN 2443, 1972-76, 6 ¾ In. 100.00
Figurine, Judge, HN 4412, 2002-Present, Box, 7 In. 96.00
Figurine, Judith, HN 2089, 1952-59, 7 In. 127.00

Royal Doulton, Figurine, Afternoon Tea, HN 1747, 1935-82, 5 ¾ In.
$156.00

Royal Doulton, Figurine, Belle O' The Ball, HN 1997, 1947-79, 6 In.
$108.00

Royal Doulton, Figurine, Cheryl, HN 3253, 1989-94, 7 ½ In.
$154.00

Figurine, Day Dreams, HN 1731, 1935-96, 5 ¾ In.
$117.00

R

Royal Doulton, Figurine, Fleur, HN 2368, 1968-95, 7 ½ In.
$69.00

Royal Doulton, Figurine, Pope John Paul II, HN 4477, 2005, 7 In.
$99.00

Royal Doulton, Figurine, Romance, HN 2430, 1972-81, 5 ¼ In.
$57.00

Royal Doulton, Figurine, Skater, HN 2117, 1953-71, 7 ¼ In.
$144.00

Figurine, Karen, HN 2388, 1982-99, 8 In. 35.00 to 60.00
Figurine, Kathleen, HN 3100, 1986, 7 In. 82.00
Figurine, Ko-Ko, HN 1286, 1938-49, 5 In. 533.00
Figurine, Lady April, HN 1958, 1940-59, 7 In. 138.00
Figurine, Lady Charmain, HN 1949, 1940-75, 8 In. 100.00
Figurine, Laird, HN 2361, 1969-2001, 8 In. 132.00
Figurine, Lavinia, HN 1955, 1940-79, 5 In. 30.00
Figurine, Little Boy Blue, HN 2062, 1950-73, 5 ½ In. 84.00
Figurine, Lobster Man, HN 2317, 1964-94, 7 ½ In. 50.00
Figurine, Louise, HN 2869, 1979-86, 6 In. 149.00
Figurine, Love Letter, HN 2149, 1958-76, 8 In. 330.00
Figurine, Lucy, HN 2863, 1980-84, 6 In. 149.00
Figurine, Lydia, HN 1908, 1939-9, 4 In. 70.00
Figurine, Lynne, HN 2329, 1971-96, 7 In. 59.00 to 94.00
Figurine, Mary, HN 3375, 1992, 8 ½ In. 127.00 to 138.00
Figurine, Mary Queen Of Scots, HN 3142, 1989, 9 In. 276.00
Figurine, Mask Seller, HN 210, 1953-95, 8 ½ In. 77.00 to 100.00
Figurine, Master Sweep, HN 2205, 1957-62, 8 ½ In. 380.00
Figurine, Memories, HN 2030, 1949-59, 6 In. 205.00
Figurine, Midinette, HN 2090, 1952-65, 7 In. 132.00
Figurine, Moor, HN 3926, 1999, 17 ½ In. 1020.00
Figurine, Moor, HN 4646, 2005, 10 ½ In. 298.00
Figurine, Nanny, HN 2221, 1958-91, 6 In. 99.00 to 129.00
Figurine, Newsboy, HN 2244, 1959-65, 8 ½ In. 192.00
Figurine, Nina, HN 2347, 1969-76, 7 ½ In. 40.00 to 55.00
Figurine, Old Balloon Seller, HN 1315, 1929-78, 7 ½ In. 127.00
Figurine, Old King, HN 2134, 1954-92, 10 ½ In. 323.00
Figurine, Pearly Boy, HN 2035, 1949-59, 5 ¼ In. 553.00
Figurine, Penelope, HN 1901, 1939-75, 7 In. 176.00
Figurine, Pied Piper, HN 2102, 1953-76, 9 In. 293.00
Figurine, Pied Piper, HN 2102, Variation, 8 ¾ In. 1185.00
Figurine, Piper, HN 2907, 1980-92, 8 In. 165.00
Figurine, Pope John Paul II, HN 4477, 2005, 7 In. *illus* 99.00
Figurine, Potter, HN 1493, 1932-92, 7 In. 90.00
Figurine, Pretty Polly, HN 2768, 1984-86, 6 ½ In. 75.00
Figurine, Prized Possessions, HN 2942, 1982, 6 ½ In. 234.00
Figurine, Promenade, HN 2076, 1951-53, 8 In. 1140.00
Figurine, Rag Doll Seller, HN 2944, 1983-95, 7 ½ In. 100.00
Figurine, Reverie, HN 2306, 1964-81, 6 ½ In. 96.00 to 121.00
Figurine, Rhapsody, HN 2267, 1961-73, 6 ¾ In. 64.00
Figurine, Robin Hood, HN 2773, 1985-90, 8 In. 100.00
Figurine, Romance, HN 2430, 1972-81, 5 ¼ In. *illus* 57.00
Figurine, Roseanna, HN 1926, 1940-59, 8 In. 175.00
Figurine, Rowena, HN 2077, 1951-55, 7 ½ In. 60.00
Figurine, Royal Canadian Mounted Police, HN 2547, 1973, 8 In. 202.00
Figurine, Royal Governers Cook, HN 2223, 1958-81, 6 ¾ In. 211.00
Figurine, Royal Governors Cook, HN 2233, 1960-83, 6 In. 190.00
Figurine, Shepherd, HN 1975, 1945-75, 8 ½ In. 78.00
Figurine, Silks & Ribbons, HN 2017, 1949-2001, 6 In. 75.00
Figurine, Sir Isaac Newton, HN 5051, 2007-08, 12 In. 157.00
Figurine, Sir Winston Churchill, White Suit, HN 3057, 1985-Present, Box, 10 ½ In. 149.00
Figurine, Skater, HN 2117, 1953-71, 7 ¼ In. *illus* 144.00
Figurine, Soiree, HN 2312, 1967-84, 7 ½ In. 25.00
Figurine, Song Of The Sea, HN 2729, 1982-91, 7 In. 146.00
Figurine, Spring Flowers, HN 1807, 1937-59, 7 In. 234.00
Figurine, Spring Morning, HN 1922, 1940-73, 7 ½ In. 74.00
Figurine, Summer Breeze, HN 3724, 1995-98, 8 In. 70.00
Figurine, Sweet & Twenty, HN 1298, 5 ¾ In. 120.00 to 149.00
Figurine, Sweet & Twenty, HN 1589, 1933-49, 3 ½ In. 205.00
Figurine, Swimmer, HN 4246, 2000, 7 ¼ In. 127.00
Figurine, Tailor, HN 2174, 1956-59, 5 In. 682.00
Figurine, Teatime, HN 2255, 1972-95, 7 ¼ In. 77.00
Figurine, Tess, HN 2865, 1978-83, 5 ¾ In. 149.00
Figurine, Thank You, HN 2732, 1982-86, 8 ¼ In. 50.00
Figurine, Thanks Doc, HN 2731, 1975-90, 8 ½ In. 100.00
Figurine, The Lamp Seller, Flambe, HN 3278, 1990-95, 9 In. 576.00

Figurine, The Wizard, Flambe, HN 3121, 1990-95, 10 In. 180.00
Figurine, To Bed, HN 1806, 1937-49, 6 In. 113.00
Figurine, Top O' The Hill, Green, HN 1833, 1937-71, 7 In. 79.00
Figurine, Top O' The Hill, Red, HN 1834, 1934-2004, 7 In. 40.00
Figurine, Tuppence A Bag, HN 2320, 1968-95, 5 ½ In. 75.00
Figurine, Veronica, M 64, 1934-49, 4 ½ In. 96.00
Figurine, Wardrobe Mistress, HN 2145, 1954-67, 5 ¾ In. 426.00
Figurine, Wayfarers, HN 2362, 1970-76, 5 ½ In. 84.00
Figurine, Winnie The Pooh, Eeyore Loses His Tail, WP 15, Box 63.00
Figurine, Winnie The Pooh, Summer's Day Picnic, WP 21, Box 49.00
Figurine, Winsome, HN 2220, 1960-85, 8 In. 25.00
Figurine, Winter's Day, HN 3769, 1996-67, 7 ¾ In. 74.00
Figurine, Wintertime, HN 3060, 1985, 8 ½ In. 74.00
Figurine, Wintertime, HN 3622, 1995-96, 8 ½ In. .... 168.00 to 204.00
Figurine, Young Love, HN 2735, 1975-90, 10 In. 156.00
Figurine, Young Miss Nightingale, HN 2010, 1948-53, 9 ½ In. 450.00
Figurine, Yum-Yum, HN 1287, 1928-36, 5 In. 533.00
Flask, Queensware, Pied Piper, Landscape, Loop Handle, Marked, c.1900, 8 ⅝ In. 1304.00
Jardiniere, Molded Flowers & Scrolls, Stoneware, Marked, 7 ¾ In. .... *illus* 82.00
Jug, Dickens Dream, Figures In Relief, Enameled, Figural Handle, 1933, 10 ½ In. 1896.00
Jug, Pied Piper, 1934, 10 ½ In. 1422.00
Pitcher, Landscape, Water, City, Mountains, Blue Transfer, 7 ⅜ In. 154.00
Pitcher, Mr. Squeers, Dickens, 6 ¾ In. .... *illus* 89.00
Plate, Bird, Scalloped Rim, Gold Trim, Joseph Hancock, 9 In., 12 Piece 805.00
Plate, Bookworm, Series Ware, D 3089, 10 In. 360.00
Plate, Bunnykins, Hoopla, 8 ½ In. 16.00
Plate, Charles Dickens, Series Ware, D 6306, 10 ½ In. 25.00
Plate, Flamingo, Tropical Flowers, Gold Trim, 10 ½ In. 60.00
Plate, Gibson Girl, Miss Babbles, Black & White, Blue Border, 10 ½ In. 250.00
Plate, Gibson Girl, Seaside, Bathing Suit, Yellow, Gilt Detail, Scalloped Edge, Limoges, 9 In. 35.00
Plate, Gibson Girl, She Decides To Die, Black & White, Blue Border, 10 ½ In. 175.00
Plate, Gibson Girl, She Finds Some Consolation, Black & White, Blue Border, 10 ½ In. 939.00
Plate, Hunting Scene, Leslie Johnson, 9 In. 211.00
Plate, Lady In Garden, Hand Painted, Gilt Trim, Leslie Johnson, 10 ½ In. 596.00
Plate, Monks, Blessing Fish On Table 70.00
Plate, Roxbury, Green & Gold, Red, 8 ¾ In. 34.00
Plate, Sailing Ship, D 3560, 10 ½ In. 40.00
Plate, Sairey Gamp, 8 ½ In. 29.00
Plate, Squire, Series Ware, D 6284, 10 ½ In. 15.00
Platter, Geneva, Blue, White, Oval, c.1875, 13 ½ x 17 In. 75.00
Punch Bowl, Coaching Scenes, Footed, 8 x 14 In. 300.00
Vase, Blue Children, Girls Playing With Doll, Cobalt Blue, 2 Handles, 4 ¾ In. 450.00
Vase, Blue Flambe, Pink Stylized Roses, 5 ½ In. 32.00
Vase, Brown, Black, Silver, Textured Base, 3 Handles, 6 ¾ In. 293.00
Vase, Cobalt Blue, Gold Trim, Painted, 10 ¾ In. 192.00
Vase, Cover, Raised White Flowers, Gray, Blue, Bulbous, Lambeth, Signed, 11 In. 230.00
Vase, Figural, Mallard Drake, Reeds, c.1945, 7 ¼ In. 295.00
Vase, Flambe, Man On Horse, Woodcut, Bulbous, Elongated Neck, 10 In. 96.00
Vase, Flambe, Sung Landscape, Woodcut, Bulbous, Tapered, 14 In. 240.00
Vase, Fox Hunt Scene, Rouge Flambe, Woodcut, 8 ½ In. .... *illus* 220.00
Vase, Grape Clusters, Blue, 7 ⅝ In. 104.00
Vase, Grapevines, Stoneware, Multicolored Glazes, 14 ⅛ In., Pair 920.00
Vase, Horses, Landscape, Stoneware, Marked, c.1875, 8 In. 2015.00
Vase, Morrison, Women Holding Garlands, Marked, 8 x 7 In. 250.00
Vase, Sung, Multicolored Veining, Marked, 6 ¼ In. 690.00
Vase, Titanian, Wisteria, Green, Yellow, Black, Purple, Blue Ground, Gold Trim, 11 In. 805.00
Wall Mask, Jester, 11 In. 596.00
Wall Plaque, Sweet Anne, HN 1654 .... 240.00

ROYAL DUX is the more common name for the Duxer Porzellanmanufaktur, which was founded by E. Eichler in Dux, Bohemia (now Duchov, Czech Republic), in 1860. By the turn of the century, the firm specialized in porcelain statuary and busts of Art Nouveau–style maidens, large porcelain figures, and ornate vases with three-dimensional figures climbing on the sides. The firm is still in business.

Figurine, Bird, No. 399, Signed, 6 x 7 In. 35.00

Royal Doulton, Jardiniere, Molded Flowers & Scrolls, Stoneware, Marked, 7 ¾ In.
$82.00

Royal Doulton, Pitcher, Mr. Squeers, Dickens, 6 ¾ In.
$89.00

Royal Doulton, Vase, Fox Hunt Scene, Rouge Flambe, Woodcut, 8 ½ In.
$220.00

R

Royal Dux, Group, 2 Seminude Females, On Conch Shells, 1900-18, 14 x 12 In. $750.00

Royal Flemish, Ewer, Raised Panels, Scrolls, Shield, Rope Twist Handle, 9 In. $4795.00

TIP
Every few years, check the hooks that are holding your paintings on the wall. Eventually, heavy pictures will loosen the nail and hook and the painting will fall. Also check the wire holding the picture.

Figurine, Dog, Borzoi, Reclining, Marked, c.1930, 12 ¼ In. . . . 125.00
Figurine, Dolphin, Tail Dancing On Wave, Green Triangle Mark, 14 In., Pair. . . . 175.00
Figurine, Gratiosus Jesulus Pragensis, Burgundy, White, Gilt, 5 ¾ x 4 In. . . . 44.00
Figurine, Polar Bear, 10 ½ In.. . . . 146.00
Figurine, Stalking Lioness, Late 1800s, Signed, 22 In.. . . . 995.00
Figurine, Woman, Snake Charmer, 1950s, 9 ¼ x 6 ½ x 3 ⅞ In. . . . 510.00
Figurine, Woman With Seashells, Art Nouveau, 15 In. . . . 800.00
Group, 2 Hunting Dogs, 8 x 10 In. . . . 30.00
Group, 2 Nomads, Camel, Pink Triangle Mark. . . . 1100.00
Group, 2 Seminude Females, On Conch Shells, 1900-18, 14 x 12 In. . . . *illus* 750.00
Group, Child, Kneeling, Dog, Seated, Oval Base, 7 x 9 ¼ x 5 ¼ In. . . . 88.00
Planter, Figural, Boy & Girl, Blossoms, Black, White, Marked, No. 991, 7 x 9 In. . . . 325.00
Wall Pocket, Mallard Duck, 15 ½ In. . . . 58.00

ROYAL FLEMISH glass was made during the late 1880s in New Bedford, Massachusetts, by the Mt. Washington Glass Works. It is a colored satin glass decorated with dark colors and raised gold designs. The glass was patented in 1894. It was supposed to resemble stained glass windows.

Ewer, Gold Panels, Raised, Scrolls, Stippled Ground, Rope Twist Handle, 9 In. . . . 4888.00
Ewer, Gold Scrolls, Red Circles, Shields, Twisted Handle, Bulbous, 9 In.. . . . 5175.00
Ewer, Raised Panels, Scrolls, Shield, Rope Twist Handle, 9 In. . . . *illus* 4795.00
Jar, Cover, Butterflies, Gold & Amethyst Daisies, Scrolls, 5 ¾ x 4 In. . . . *illus* 1955.00
Lamp, Kerosene, Banquet, Globular Shade, Footed, Stick Shape, Font, 32 In. . . . 14900.00
Lamp, Kerosene, Banquet, Griffin, Gold, Scrollwork, Olive Green, Gray, 25 x 29 ½ In. . . . 1725.00
Vase, Amethyst Scrolls, Violets, 2 Handles, Signed, 6 In.. . . . 1333.00
Vase, Ducks, Gold Sun, Stars, Pastel Triangles, Scrolls, Bulbous, 16 In. . . . 4025.00
Vase, Griffin, Earthtone Panels, Scroll Overlay, 4 In. . . . 863.00
Vase, Lions, Coins, Griffins, Blue, Red, Purple, Bulbous, 2 Handles, 14 In.. . . . 3680.00
Vase, Long Amethyst Scroll Neck, 3 Griffin Cameos, Blue, Tans, 12 In.. . . . 2875.00
Vase, Scrolls, Raised Blue Panel, Peacock, Blue Jewels, Bulbous, 13 In. . . . 5750.00

ROYAL HAEGER, *see Haeger category.*

ROYAL HICKMAN designed pottery, glass, silver, aluminum, furniture, lamps, and other items. From 1938 to 1944 and again from the 1950s to 1969, he worked for Haeger Potteries. Mr. Hickman operated his own pottery in Tampa, Florida, during the 1940s. He moved to California and worked for Vernon Potteries. The last years of his life he lived in Guadalajara, Mexico, and continued designing for Royal Haeger. Pieces made in his pottery listed here are marked *Royal Hickman* or *Hickman*.

Bowl, Amoeba Free-Form, Chartreuse, Honey Glaze, 3 x 12 x 16 In.. . . . 128.00
Bowl, Amoeba Free-Form, Gray Glaze, 3 x 7 x 13 In. . . . 100.00
Bowl, Flower, Terraceware, Burgundy Crystal Glaze, 9 x 3 ½ In.. . . . 128.00
Bowl, Seashell Shape, Wave, Chartreuse Glaze, 14 x 7 In. . . . 128.00
Dish, Amoeba Free-Form, Chartreuse Glaze, 3 x 7 x 13 In. . . . 100.00
Dish, Heart Free-Form, Burgundy Red Glaze, 9 x 7 In. . . . 128.00
Dish, Heart Shape, Burgundy, Aqua Crystalline & White Glaze, 3 ½ x 6 In. . . . 100.00
Dish, Lovebirds On Pond, Green, 10 x 9 x 4 In. . . . 48.00
Figurine, Giraffe, Black Glaze, Rock Shape Base, 13 x 6 ¼ x 4 ¼ In.. . . . 115.00
Lamp, Fawn, Pink, White Drip Glaze, 13 x 6 In., Pair . . . 188.00
Lamp Base, Black Greyhound, 12 x 4 x 10 In. . . . 498.00
Oil Jar, Terraceware, Blue Crystal Glaze, 8 x 7 In. . . . 198.00
Planter, Console, Salmon, Crystal Drip, Openwork Filigree Brass Caddy, 13 x 4 In. . . . 48.00
Planter, Ebony, White Cascade, Blue & Brown, Crystal Glaze, 4 ½ x 9 In. . . . 128.00
Plate, Chartreuse Glaze, 14 ¼ In. . . . 298.00
Vase, Bow, Iridescent Green, 11 In. . . . 68.00
Vase, Bow, Ocean Blue Glaze, 11 In. . . . 68.00
Vase, Console, Swan, Cloudy Blue, 8 ¾ x 3 ¼ In., Pair. . . . 100.00
Vase, Console, Swan, Mauve Agate, 8 ½ x 6 ¼ In., Pair . . . 120.00
Vase, Ebony, White Cascade, Blue & Brown, Crystal Glaze, 8 ¼ x 15 ½ In. . . . 148.00
Vase, Fish On Wave, Iridescent Green Agate, 10 In. . . . 148.00
Vase, Free-Form, Ocean Blue, Sky Blue Glaze, 8 In. . . . 100.00
Vase, Leaf, Stylized, Mauve Agate, Embossed, Retro, 12 ½ x 5 In. . . . 65.00
Vase, Organic Leaf Shape, Brown, Chartreuse Glaze, 8 In. . . . 98.00
Vase, Russet, Tan Layered Glaze, 11 ½ x 6 In.. . . . 168.00
Vase, Swan, Mauve Agate, 5 x 4 In. . . . 28.00

ROYAL NYMPHENBURG is the modern name for the Nymphenburg porcelain factory, which was established at Neudeck-ob-der-Au, Germany, in 1753 and moved to Nymphenburg in 1761. The company is still in existence. Marks include a checkered shield topped by a crown, a crowned CT with the year, and a contemporary shield mark on reproductions of eighteenth-century porcelain.

Bowl, Shell Form, Flowers, Marked, Crowned CT, 1800s, 7 ½ In. .... *illus* 325.00
Charger, Flowers, Gilt Rim, 13 In.. .... 100.00
Figurine, Cockatoos, 11 ½ In.. .... 800.00
Figurine, Salon Scene, Woman, Stylist, Angel, Dog, 10 ½ In. 700.00
Plate, Flower Bouquets, Openwork, Scrolled Border, Blue Mark, 8 In., 12 Piece 748.00

ROYAL OAK *pieces are listed in the Northwood category by that pattern name.*

ROYAL RUDOLSTADT, *see Rudolstadt category.*

ROYAL VIENNA, *see Beehive category.*

ROYAL WORCESTER is a name used by collectors. Worcester porcelains were made in Worcester, England, from about 1751. The firm went through many different periods and name changes. It became the Worcester Royal Porcelain Company, Ltd., in 1862. Today collectors call the porcelains made after 1862 "Royal Worcester." In 1976, the firm merged with W. T. Copeland to become Royal Worcester Spode. Some early products of the factory are listed under Worcester.

Biscuit Jar, Flowers, Branches, Gray, Brown, c.1889, 7 In. 465.00
Bowl, Flowers, 3 Sections, Handles, 10 ¾ In. 50.00
Bowl, Fruit, Leaves, Multicolored, Hand Painted, Byron Cox, 11 In. .... 263.00 to 270.00
Candlestick, Corinthian Top, Fluted Column, Square Base, Gilt, c.1885, 8 In., Pair......... 50.00
Candlestick, Square Base, 10 ¼ In. 25.00
Casserole, Cover, Blue Willow, Elephant Handles, Footed, 10 x 17 x 9 In. 175.00
Casserole, Cover, Fruits, Vegetables, Painted, Handles, 4 x 10 In.. .... 50.00
Charger, Couple, Under Tree, Sterling Silver Rim, 11 ¾ In. 110.00
Coffeepot, Fruit, Leaves, Multicolored, Hand Painted, Richard Poole, 10 In. 293.00
Cup, Demitasse, Pink Roses, 1 ½ In.. .... 10.00
Cup & Saucer, Demitasse, Cows Grazing, 3 ¾ In. 518.00
Cup & Saucer, Demitasse, Raised Gold, Yellow Ground, Marked. .... 30.00 to 50.00
Cup & Saucer, Flowers 80.00
Cup & Saucer, Padua, Black, Flower & Urn Border. 144.00
Dish, Leaf Shape, Roses, 9 ¼ In. 50.00
Ewer, Birds, Night Time Water Scene, Handles, 11 In. 130.00
Ewer, Flowers, Gold Vine Handle, 5 ¼ In. 70.00
Ewer, Flowers, Ivory, Ribs, Twig Handle & Spout, 8.5. .... 200.00
Ewer, Flowers & Butterflies, Gold Bamboo Handle, Marked, 10 In., Pair 250.00
Ewer, Moorish, Coffeepot Form, Leaf Scroll, Gilt, Reticulated Handle, 13 ½ In.. .... 1126.00
Ewer, Pink Flowers, Handles, 7 ¼ In. 100.00
Figurine, American Goldfinch, Purple Thistle, Dorothy Doughty, 7 ½ In., Pair 2040.00
Figurine, American Pintail Male, Bisque, 12 x 14 In. 263.00
Figurine, American Redstart, Hemlock Branch, Dorothy Doughty, 9 ¼ In., Pair 660.00
Figurine, Baltimore Oriole, Tulip Branch, Dorothy Doughty, 9 ½ In., Pair 1200.00
Figurine, Bather Surprised, Seminude Woman, Tree Trunk, No. 486, c.1875, 25 In. 948.00
Figurine, Blue Bird, Apple Tree Branch, Dorothy Doughty, 10 ½ In., Pair 660.00
Figurine, Blue Gray Gnatcatcher, Dogwood Branch, Dorothy Doughty, 11 ½ In., Pair....... 3360.00
Figurine, Bobwhite Quail, With Chicks, Dorothy Doughty, 6 ⅛ In., Pair 9000.00
Figurine, Boy With Parakeet, No. 3087, F.G. Doughty, 6 In.. .... 66.00
Figurine, Cerulean Warbler, Maple Branch, Dorothy Doughty, 9 ½ In., Pair. 480.00
Figurine, Dog, Terrier, 2 ¾ x 3 In.. .... 164.00
Figurine, Downy Woodpecker, Pecan Tree, Dorothy Doughty, 11 In., Pair. 1200.00
Figurine, Elf Owl, Saguaro Cactus, Dorothy Doughty, 11 ½ In. 600.00
Figurine, First Dance, No. 3629, F.G. Doughty, 7 ½ x 4 In. 64.00
Figurine, Fox, Seated, Head Turned, 7 ¼ In. 225.00
Figurine, Golden Crown Kinglets, Pine Branches, Dorothy Doughty, 7 ¾ In., Pair 480.00
Figurine, Indigo Bunting, Blackberry Branch, Dorothy Doughty, 9 In., Pair. 2400.00
Figurine, Indigo Bunting, Male, Plum Branch, Dorothy Doughty, 9 In. 1920.00
Figurine, Jersey Bull, No. 3776B, Bisque, 6 ½ x 11 In.. .... 819.00
Figurine, Lark Sparrow, Twin Pod, Red Gila, Dorothy Doughty, 6 ⅛ In. 360.00
Figurine, Mallard Male, Bisque, 9 x 15 In.. .... 351.00
Figurine, March, Girl Walking In Wind, No. 3454, 6 In.. .... 60.00 to 77.00
Figurine, Mexican Feijoa Blossoms, Lady Bugs, Dorothy Doughty, 11 In., Pair. 720.00

Royal Flemish, Jar, Cover, Butterflies, Gold & Amethyst Daisies, Scrolls, 5 ¾ x 4 In.
$1955.00

Royal Nymphenburg, Bowl, Shell Form, Flowers, Marked, Crowned CT, 1800s, 7 ½ In.
$325.00

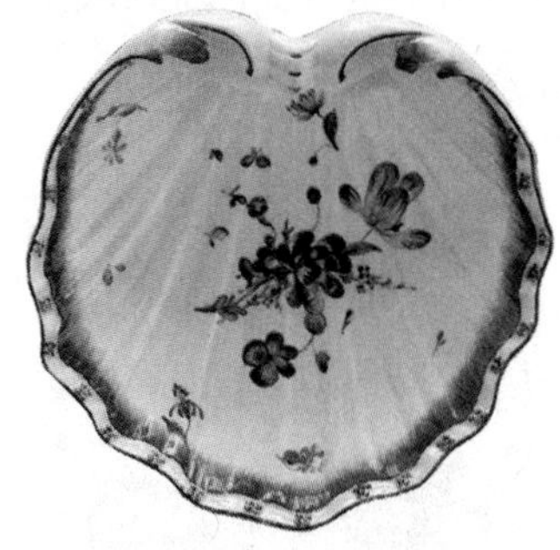

Royal Worcester, Figurine, Rachel, F.G. Doughty, Factory Mark, 6 ¾ In.
$75.00

R

Royal Worcester, Figurine, Women, Bearing Urns, Marked, 1867, 31 In., Pair
$1430.00

Royal Worcester, Urn, Highland Cattle, Hand Painted, J. Stinton, c.1914, 14 ½ In., Pair
$10800.00

Royal Worcester, Vase, Blue, Vine Encrusted, Cherub, Brown Matte, Snail Handles, 11 In.
$600.00

Figurine, Mockingbird, Peach Blossom Branch, Dorothy Doughty, 10 ¾ In., Pair 660.00
Figurine, Mountain Bluebirds, Sweet Bay Branch, Dorothy Doughty, 9 ½ In., Pair 2040.00
Figurine, Myrtle Warbler, Cherry Blossom, Dorothy Doughty, 9 In., Pair 1560.00
Figurine, Napoleon Bonaparte, White Horse, Military Attire, Bisque, 14 In. 1872.00
Figurine, Nightingale, No. 3337, 3 ¼ In. 40.00
Figurine, November, Girl Feeding Pigeons, No. 3418, 7 ½ In. 50.00
Figurine, Orange Blossom, Butterflies, Dorothy Doughty, 7 ½ In., Pair 780.00
Figurine, Phoebe, Flame Vine, Dorothy Doughty, 10 ½ In., Pair 1320.00
Figurine, Picnic, 2 Women, Food, 6 In. 702.00
Figurine, Rachel, F.G. Doughty, Factory Mark, 6 ¾ In. .... *illus* 75.00
Figurine, Scarlet Tanager, Leafy Branches, Dorothy Doughty, 12 In., Pair 510.00
Figurine, Sparrow, Hawk, Bullfinch, Bisque, 17 x 14 In. 439.00
Figurine, Vermilion Flycatcher, Pussy Willow, Dorothy Doughty, 9 ¾ In., Pair 1560.00
Figurine, Washington, Prancing Gray Horse, Military Attire, Bisque, 16 In. 1755.00
Figurine, Water Carrier, Woman, Vase On Head, In Hand, c.1893, 32 In. 948.00
Figurine, Women, Bearing Urns, Marked, 1867, 31 In., Pair .... *illus* 1430.00
Figurine, Yellow Headed Blackbirds, Spiderwort Flower, Dorothy Doughty, 12 In., Pair 3120.00
Lamp, Flowers, Butterfly, Beige, Brown, Pink, Cream Base, Blue, 10 ¼ In. 480.00
Pitcher, Flower Boughs, Gold Pinstripe, 1885, 9 In. 120.00
Pitcher, Lizard, Bamboo, Purple Mark, 6 In. 200.00
Pitcher, Roses, Round, 3 ½ In. 80.00
Pitcher, Thistle, Flowers, Gilt, 9 x 6 x 4 ½ In. 170.00
Pitcher, Wading Bird, Full Moon, Gold Trim, Long Spout, c.1885, 8 ¼ In. 207.00
Planter, Pink Roses, Leaves, Gilt, No. 2558, E. Spilsbury, 1916, 7 In. 340.00
Plate, Green, Blue, Yellow, 9 In. 35.00
Toby Jug, Man, Standing, Red Pants, Tricornered Hat, 6 In. 24.00
Tureen, Cover, Elephant Handles, Flow Blue, 12 In. 71.00
Urn, Cover, Flowers, Cobalt Blue Ground, Gilt, Handles, Square Base, 12 ½ In. 1600.00
Urn, Cows, Landscape, Lion Mask Handles, Signed, H. Davis, 12 ¾ In. 4560.00
Urn, Highland Cattle, Hand Painted, J. Stinton, c.1914, 14 ½ In., Pair .... *illus* 10800.00
Vase, Blue, Pink, Ivory Ground, Gilt, Reticulated, Stamped, 19th Century, 6 In. 400.00
Vase, Blue, Vine Encrusted, Cherub, Brown Matte, Snail Handles, 11 In. .... *illus* 600.00
Vase, Blue Wisteria, Gold Outline, Dragon Handles, 11 ½ In. 575.00
Vase, Cherub, Playing Flute On Stump, Figural, 5 ½ In. 275.00
Vase, Cottage Landscape, Enamel, Birds, Gilt Rim, Handles, Foot, c.1906, 11 ¾ In. 3555.00
Vase, Flowers, Scroll Handles, Gilt Detail, 19th Century, 14 In. 234.00
Vase, Gilt, Reticulated, Bulbous, Handles, Signed, George Owen, 1907, 5 ¼ In. 17250.00
Vase, Highland Cattle, 2 Handles, James Stinton, c.1830, 12 ½ In. 9375.00
Vase, Lid, Flowers, Leaves, 2 Dragon Handles, Dragon Base, No. 2090, 27 In. 5313.00
Vase, Lighthouse, Gilt, Dolphin Head Handles, c.1890, 18 In. 2832.00
Vase, Majolica Nautilus, Shell, Coral Pedestal, Marked, 1800s, 9 In. 1062.00
Vase, Nautilus, Mounted Lizard, White, Gilt, Marked, 9 In., Pair 2185.00
Vase, Nautilus, Shell, Pedestal, 8 ½ In. 200.00
Vase, Owl On Branch, Handles, Gilt, No. 1034, c.1890, 11 In. 420.00
Vase, Pink Flowers, Bowling Pin Form, Handles, 6 ½ In. 80.00
Vase, Pink Flowers, Gold Highlights, Pedestal, Handles, 12 In. 275.00
Vase, Roses, Pink, Yellow, 5 In. 90.00
Vase, Thistle, Gold Highlights, Pedestal, Handles, 8 ¼ In. 175.00
Vase, Trumpet Form, Flower Mold, Pedestal, 6 ¼ In. 80.00
Vase, Tusk Form, Flowers, Antler Style Handle, Marked, 11 In. 250.00
Whistle, Dog Head, Brown, White, c.1900, 1 ¾ In. 325.00

ROYCROFT products were made by the Roycrofter community of East Aurora, New York, in the late nineteenth and early twentieth centuries. The community was founded by Elbert Hubbard, famous philosopher, writer, and artist. The workshops owned by the community made furniture, metalware, leatherwork, embroidery, and jewelry. A printshop produced many signs, books, and the magazines that promoted the sayings of Elbert Hubbard. Furniture by the Roycroft community is listed in the Furniture category.

Bookends, Copper, Hammered, Braided Oval Border, Impressed Mark, 5 x 3 ½ In. 270.00
Bookends, Flower In Relief With Hammered Ground, Marked, 5 ⅝ In. 155.00
Bowl, Copper, Hammered, Folded Rim, Impressed Mark, 6 x 3 In. 120.00
Bowl, Copper, Hammered, Tooled Flowers, 8 In. 259.00
Bracelet, Sterling Silver, Tooled Flower Center, Impressed, Orb Mark, 2 ¼ In. 660.00
Candlestick, Copper, Hammered, Brass Finish, Impressed Mark, 8 In., Pair 410.00
Candlestick, Copper, Hammered, Cup On Scroll, Disc Base, Mark, 4 In., Pair 178.00
Candlestick, Copper, Hammered, Double Stick, Square Base, Patina, 7 ¾ In., Pair 600.00

Candlestick, Copper, Hammered, Patina, Impressed Mark, 7 ¾ In., Pair . . . . *illus* 600.00
Chafing Dish, Copper, Hammered, Burner, Tray, Orb & Cross Mark, 10 x 13 In. . . . . *illus* 1440.00
Cigarette Box, Copper, Hammered, Brass Washed Pull, Handles, Dogwood, Verdigris, 2 x 10 x 5 In. 2400.00
Coffeepot, Copper, Hammered, Silver Wash, Mahogany Handle, 9 ½ x 4 ½ In. 3120.00
Desk Set, Hammered, Bronze, Pen Tray, Box, 2 Inkwells, Patina, Stamped 77.00
Fernery, Copper, Dogwood, Incised, Embossed, 3 Ball Feet, Marked, 4 x 7 In. 1800.00
Kettle, Copper, Hammered, Patina, 3 Applied Feet, Handle, Marked, 4 ½ In. 420.00
Lamp, Copper, Hammered, Brass Washed, Aurene Shade, Steuben, 14 ¾ x 7 In. 4500.00
Lamp, Copper, Hammered, Mica Helmet Shade, 14 ½ x 7 ¼ In. 2640.00
Lamp, Copper, Hammered, Mica Shade, Impressed Mark, 10 x 15 In. 2520.00
Letter Opener, Copper, Hammered, Curled Handle, 8 In. 99.00
Magazine Stand, Canted, Gallery Top, Carved Orb & Cross, 37 ½ x 17 ¾ x 15 ¾ In. 4200.00
Plate, Copper, Hammered, Tooled, 10 In. 374.00
Telephone, Copper, Hammered, Bakelite, 12 x 5 In. 2640.00
Tray, Copper, Hammered, 8-Sided, Handles, 10 x 12 In. . . . . 230.00 to 330.00
Tray, Copper, Hammered, Patina, Oval, Tooled Design, Handles, Marked, 21 ½ x 10 In.. . . . . . 1200.00
Tray, Copper, Hammered, Patina, Tooled, Oval, Handles, Marked, 10 x 21 ½ In. 1200.00
Tray, Copper, Hammered, Signed, 5 ¾ In. Diam. 130.00
Vase, Bud, Copper, Hammered, Leaves, Buttressed Handles, 7 ½ In. 3360.00
Vase, Copper, Ali Baba, Bottle Form, 16 x 9 In. . . . . 1920.00 to 2880.00
Vase, Copper, Hammered, 4 Silver Squares, Wood Grain Ground, 8 ¼ x 4 ½ In. 4800.00
Vase, Copper, Hammered, 4 Tooled Designs, Folded Lip, Patina, 9 In.. 720.00
Vase, Copper, Hammered, American Beauty, Patina, Impressed, 6 x 12 In.. . . . . 900.00
Vase, Copper, Hammered, Brass Patina, Tapered, 3 x 6 In. 90.00
Vase, Copper, Hammered, Cylindrical, 21 x 7 ½ In. 5700.00
Vase, Copper, Hammered, Cylindrical, Bulbous, 11 ¾ x 5 ½ In. 3120.00
Vase, Copper, Hammered, Flower Form, Green Cluthra Glass, 6 x 3 ½ In. 2280.00
Vase, Copper, Hammered, Nickel Plated, Impressed Mark, 4 x 3 In. 215.00
Vase, Copper, Hammered, Silver Overlay, 6 ¼ x 3 In. 4800.00
Vase, Copper, Hammered, Silver Overlay, Cylindrical, 6 ¼ x 3 In. 1920.00
Vase, Copper, Hammered, Tapered, Flared Rim, 4 ⅝ In. 155.00

ROZANE, *see Roseville category.*

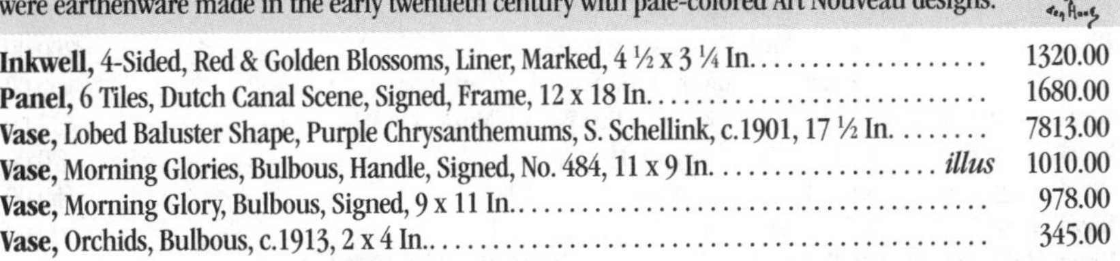

ROZENBURG worked at The Hague, Holland, from 1890 to 1914. The most important pieces were earthenware made in the early twentieth century with pale-colored Art Nouveau designs.

Inkwell, 4-Sided, Red & Golden Blossoms, Liner, Marked, 4 ½ x 3 ¼ In. 1320.00
Panel, 6 Tiles, Dutch Canal Scene, Signed, Frame, 12 x 18 In. 1680.00
Vase, Lobed Baluster Shape, Purple Chrysanthemums, S. Schellink, c.1901, 17 ½ In. 7813.00
Vase, Morning Glories, Bulbous, Handle, Signed, No. 484, 11 x 9 In. . . . . *illus* 1010.00
Vase, Morning Glory, Bulbous, Signed, 9 x 11 In.. . . . . 978.00
Vase, Orchids, Bulbous, c.1913, 2 x 4 In.. . . . . 345.00

RRP, or RRP Roseville, is the mark used by the firm of Robinson-Ransbottom. It is not a mark of the more famous Roseville Pottery. The Ransbottom brothers started a pottery in 1900 in Ironspot, Ohio. In 1920, they merged with the Robinson Clay Product Company of Akron, Ohio, to become Robinson-Ransbottom. The factory is still working.

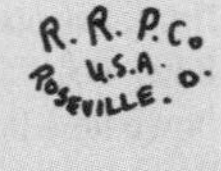

Birdbath, Frog, c.1956, 10 ¼ x 7 In. 120.00
Bowl, Pasta, Rustic Line, 1940-1951, 14 ½ x 3 In. 73.00
Bowl, Pet Feeder, Kitty, Stoneware, Brown Lettering, 6 x 3 In. 32.00
Bowl, Stoneware, 4 ½ In. 6.00
Bowl, Utility, White, Blue Horizontal Stripes 18.00
Cookie Jar, Oscar, Yellow, Red, Green Hat Cover 77.00
Crock, Cover, Spongeware, Wheat, Ivory & Blue, 1980s, 3 ¾ x 4 ½ In. 36.00
Crock, Painted, Daisy, 4 x 6 ¼ In. 45.00
Crock, Stoneware, Wood Cover, Painted, Girls, Ducks, Tulips, 2 Qt., 6 ¼ x 5 ¾ In. 34.00
Crock, Yellow Round, Blue Mottling, 4 ½ x 3 ¼ In. 10.00
Figurine, Huck Finn Fishing, 12 ¼ In. . . . . *illus* 22.00
Jardiniere, Pedestal, Drip Glaze, Relief Flowers, Marked, 8 x 10 In.. 150.00
Jardiniere, Pedestal, Majolica Glaze, Green, Brown, Raised Flowers, Sun, 10 x 23 In., Pair . . 104.00
Jardiniere, Stylized Flowers, White, Brown, Blue Ground, 8 x 9 In. 28.00
Jardiniere, White Matte, Sun & Moon, 1948-70s, 7 x 8 In. 65.00
Oil Jar, Burgundy, 15 ½ In. 295.00
Urn, Burgundy Glossy Glaze, Impressed Mark, 14 ½ x 8 ½ In. 46.00
Vase, Green Matte Glaze, Flower, 8 ½ x 5 ½ In.. . . . . 245.00
Vase, Orange, Cream Drip Glaze, Rolled Rim, 26 In., Pair. 288.00

Roycroft, Candlestick, Copper, Hammered, Patina, Impressed Mark, 7 ¾ In., Pair
$600.00

Roycroft, Chafing Dish, Copper, Hammered, Burner, Tray, Orb & Cross Mark, 10 x 13 In.
$1440.00

Rozenburg, Vase, Morning Glories, Bulbous, Handle, Signed, No. 484, 11 x 9 In.
$1010.00

RRP, Figurine, Huck Finn Fishing, 12 ¼ In.
$22.00

R

RS Prussia, Butter, Cover, Sunflower Mold, Original Liner, Satin, 4 ½ x 7 ¾ In.
$525.00

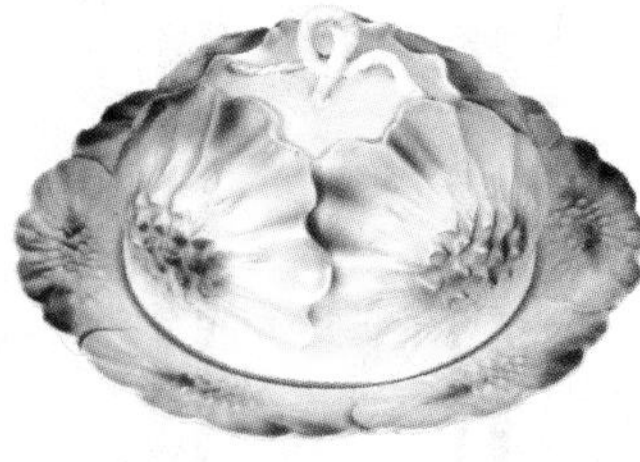

RS Prussia, Cake Plate, Gibson Girl, Satin Ground, Handles, 11 ½ In.
$1900.00

RS Prussia, Pitcher, Carnation Mold, Flowers, Gold Stencil Highlights, 8 ¾ In.
$2150.00

RS Prussia, Tankard, Carnation Mold, Poppies, Satin, 8 ¾ In.
$375.00

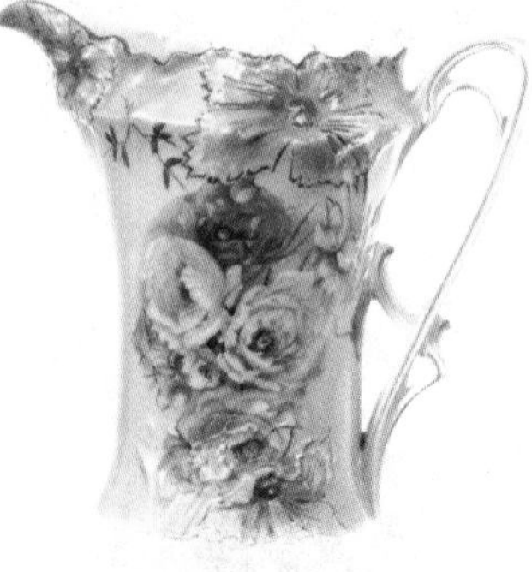

Vase, Victoria Glaze, Cornflower Blue, Mottled White, Loop Handles, c.1940, 18 In. 189.00

RS GERMANY is part of the wording in marks used by the Tillowitz, Germany, factory of Reinhold Schlegelmilch from 1914 until about 1945. The porcelain was sold decorated and undecorated. The Schlegelmilch families made porcelains marked in many ways. See also ES Germany, RS Poland, RS Prussia, RS Silesia, RS Suhl, and RS Tillowitz.

Bowl, Fruit, Flowers, Leaves, Purple, Hand Painted, c.1900, 10 ½ In. 70.00
Bowl, Pink, White Tulips, Gold Leaves, 1900s, 8 ½ x 4 In. 60.00
Bowl, Poppy, Wisteria Blossoms, 3-Footed, 5 ¼ x 2 ½ In. 25.00
Cake Plate, Gold, Peach, Green Flowers, Gold Edge 80.00
Cake Plate, Roses, 9 ⅛ In. 24.00
Candy Dish, Pink, Orange, White Roses, Handles, c.1910, 6 ⅝ x 5 In. 75.00
Creamer, Hydrangea Blooms, 4 x 5 ½ In. 57.00
Creamer, Molded Relief Details, Handle, Violet, Blue Flowers, 1910-20 .... 50.00
Dresser Box, Rose, Bowtie Shape, 9 In. 72.00
Hatpin Holder, Porcelain, Pink Peonies, 4 ½ x 2 ½ In. 145.00
Jam Pot Set, Lid, Saucer, Daffodils, Pussy Willows, 3 x 3 ½ & 5 ⅜ In. 60.00
Plate, Art Nouveau Flowers, 10 ½ In. 250.00
Relish, Rose, Blues, Greens Yellows, Cutwork Handles, 9 x 4 In. 42.00
Sugar, Lilies, Green Leaves, Cream, Tan, Brown Ground, 3 ⅜ x 4 ½ In. 25.00
Teapot, White Roses, Early 1900s, 6 ¼ x 3 ¾ In. 20.00
Toothpick, Peach, Pink Roses, Lavender, Blue Leaves, 3 Handles 55.00
Tray, 2 Pheasants By Wooded Stream, 11 ½ x 7 In. 425.00

RS POLAND (German) is a mark used by the Reinhold Schlegelmilch factory at Tillowitz from about 1946 to 1956. After 1956, the factory made porcelain marked *PT Poland.* This is one of many of the RS marks used. See also ES Germany, RS Germany, RS Prussia, RS Silesia, RS Suhl, and RS Tillowitz.

Plate, Cake, Cream To Shaded Green, 3 Flower Sprays, Red Mark, 6 ½ In., 5 Piece 150.00
Vase, House, Man With Sheep, Gold Handles & Rim, Wreath Mark, 9 ½ In. 580.00

RS PRUSSIA appears in several marks used on porcelain before 1917. Reinhold Schlegelmilch started his porcelain works in Suhl, Germany, in 1869. See also ES Germany, RS Germany, RS Poland, RS Silesia, RS Suhl, and RS Tillowitz.

Biscuit Jar, Cover, Swan, Bluebird, Handles, 5 x 9 In. 200.00
Bowl, Flora, Diana The Huntress, Flowers, Gold Stencil, Tiffany Border, 10 In. 300.00
Bowl, Flower, Gold Highlight Border, Flowers, Red Wreath Mark, 3 ¼ x 10 ½ In. 33.00
Bowl, Fruit, Flower Border, Scalloped Edge, c.1900, 2 ¾ x 10 ½ In. 70.00
Bowl, Honeycomb, Green & Blue, Flowers, 10 ¾ In. 160.00
Bowl, Masted Schooner, 10 ¾ In. 300.00
Bowl, Mold, Honeycomb, Green, Blue, Flowers, Scalloped Rim, Gilt, 10 ¾ In. 160.00
Bowl, Parrots, 10 In. 3400.00
Bowl, Red, White Roses Growing Out Of Urn, Marked, c.1900, 8 In. 236.00
Bowl, Rose Design, Scalloped Edge, c.1920, 3 x 10 In. 205.00
Bowl, Roses, Cobalt Blue Domes, Gold Highlight, 10 In. 325.00
Bowl, White Flowers, Leaves, Gilt Edge, Early 20th Century, 10 In. 146.00
Butter, Cover, Sunflower Mold, Original Liner, Satin, 4 ½ x 7 ¾ In. .... *illus* 525.00
Cake Plate, Cupid, Roses, Scalloped Rim, Cutout Handles, 9 ¾ In. 25.00
Cake Plate, Gazelles, 2 Handles, 9 ½ In. 4200.00
Cake Plate, Gibson Girl, Satin Ground, Handles, 11 ½ In. .... *illus* 1900.00
Cake Plate, Iris Mold, Poppies, Gold Stenciled Highlights, 10 ¼ In. 750.00
Cake Plate, Roses, Blue & Green Border, c.1910, 10 In. 23.00
Chocolate Pot, 6-Footed, Flowers, Gold, Beaded, 10 ¼ In. 165.00
Chocolate Pot, Flowers, Satin, Gilt, Double Handle, 9 ½ x 7 In. 70.00
Chocolate Pot, White To Green, Flowers, Lid, 8 ½ In. 70.00
Cracker Jar, Swan, Red Wreath Mark, 6 ½ x 6 ½ In. 165.00
Ewer, Yellow Roses, Leaves, Red Wreath Mark, 8 ¼ In. 99.00
Hatpin Holder, Porcelain, White & Green Flowers, 4 ½ In. 50.00
Jar, Steeple Mold, Castle Scene, Cottage Scene, 2 Handles, Underplate, 5 ½ In. 800.00
Mustard, Bird Of Paradise, 2 ¾ In. 1600.00
Pitcher, Carnation Mold, Flowers, Gold Stencil Highlights, 8 ¾ In. .... *illus* 2150.00
Pitcher, White Embossed Flowers, Rose, Red Wreath Mark, 13 ⅜ In. 275.00
Plate, Flower, Gold Border, Red Wreath Mark, 8 ¾ In. 55.00
Sugar & Creamer, Carnation Mold, Roses, Satin, 5 In. 175.00

Tankard, Carnation Mold, Poppies, Satin, 8 ¾ In. *illus* 375.00
Tankard, Icicle Mold, Barnyard Animals, Pheasant, 14 In. 1450.00
Tankard, Lily Mold, Madame LeBrun Portrait, 15 In. 3000.00
Tray, Swan, Oval, Icicle, Red Wreath, Handles, 1 ½ x 12 ¼ x 6 In. 187.00
Vase, Summer Season Keyhold Portrait, 2 Handles, 9 In. 1250.00

RS SILESIA appears on porcelain made at the Reinhold Schlegelmilch factory in Tillowitz, Germany, from the 1920s to the 1940s. The Schlegelmilch families made porcelains marked in many ways. See also ES Germany, RS Germany, RS Poland, RS Prussia, RS Suhl, and RS Tillowitz.

Candlestick, 3 Panels, Fruit, Gold Frames, Marble Finish, Cream Ground, Dwarf, Pair 60.00
Tray, Roses & Elaborate Designs, Ivory Ground, 6 ¼ In. 75.00

RS SUHL is a mark used by the Reinhold Schlegelmilch factory in Suhl, Germany, between 1900 and 1917. The Schlegelmilch families made porcelains in many places. See also ES Germany, RS Germany, RS Poland, RS Prussia, RS Silesia, and RS Tillowitz.

Bowl, Melon Eaters, Red Ground, Crimp Mold, 7 ⅜ In. 399.00
Vase, 3 Graces By River, Gold Border, Handles, 8 In. *illus* 600.00
Vase, Melon Eaters, Green Ground, Red Border, Bowling Pin Shape, 7 In. 180.00

RS TILLOWITZ was marked on porcelain by the Reinhold Schlegelmilch factory at Tillowitz from the 1920s to the 1940s. Table services and ornamental pieces were made. See also ES Germany, RS Germany, RS Poland, RS Prussia, RS Silesia, and RS Suhl.

Bowl, White Lilies, Green Ground, Gold Traces, Blue Tillowitz Mark, 9 ¼ In. 125.00
Cheese Server, Pink Wild Roses, Gold Trim, Signed 145.00
Salt Set, 2 Salts, Open Handled Plate, Gold Trim, Green & Gold Leaves, 6 ½ In., 3 Piece 75.00
Sugar & Creamer, White Lily, Angled Open Handles, Steeple Lid, Inkstamp, c.1918 55.00

RUBINA is a glassware that shades from red to clear. It was first made by George Duncan and Sons of Pittsburgh, Pennsylvania, about 1885. This coloring was used on many types of glassware. The pressed glass patterns of Royal Ivy and Royal Oak are listed under Northwood.

Pitcher, Crackle Glass, Star Shaped Rim, Applied Reed Handle, Pontil, 1875, 8 ½ In. *illus* 198.00
Pitcher, Satin, Hobbs, Brockunier, c.1880s, 8 In. 375.00

RUBINA VERDE is a Victorian glassware that was shaded from red to green. It was first made by Hobbs, Brockunier and Company of Wheeling, West Virginia, about 1890.

Basket, Rose Bowl, Handle, Enameled Flowers, 7 ¼ In. 175.00
Pitcher, Ball Shape, Flower Blossoms, 7 ¼ In. 400.00
Tumble-Up, Coin Spot, 8 In., 2 Piece 90.00
Tureen, Cover, Ribbed, 4-Footed, Applied Handle, Green Melon Finial, 9 In. 115.00
Vase, Melon Ribbed, Pillow Shape, Flowers, 6 ½ In. 160.00

RUBY GLASS is the dark red color of a ruby, the precious gemstone. It was a popular Victorian color that never went completely out of style. The glass was shaped by many different processes to make many different types of ruby glass. There was a revival of interest in the 1940s when modern-shaped ruby table glassware became fashionable. Sometimes the red color is added to clear glass by a process called flashing or staining. Flashed glass is clear glass dipped in a colored glass, then pressed or cut. Stained glass has color painted on a clear glass. Then it is refired so the stain fuses with the glass. Pieces of glass colored in this way are indicated by the word *stained* in the description. Related items may be found in other categories, such as Cranberry Glass, Pressed Glass, and Souvenir.

Bowl, Knob, Cover, Handle, 7 x 7 ½ x 5 ½ In. 40.00
Compote, Scalloped Rim, 6 ½ x 9 In. 59.00

RUDOLSTADT was a faience factory in the Thuringia region of Germany from 1720 to about 1791. In 1854, Ernst Bohne began working in the area. From about 1887 to 1918, the New York and Rudolstadt Pottery made decorated porcelain marked with the RW and crown familiar to collectors. This porcelain was imported by Lewis Straus and Sons of New York, which later became Nathan Straus and Sons. The word *Royal* was included in their import mark. Collectors often call it "Royal Rudolstadt." Most pieces found today were made in the late nineteenth or early twentieth century. Additional pieces may be listed in the Kewpie category.

Ewer, Handles, Pink, White Blossoms, Oval, 10 ½ In. 130.00
Figurine, Couple, Period Attire, Ernest Bohne Sons, Germany, c.1940, 13 x 9 In. 176.00

RS Suhl, Vase, 3 Graces By River, Gold Border, Handles, 8 In.
$600.00

Rubina, Pitcher, Crackle Glass, Star Shaped Rim, Applied Reed Handle, Pontil, 1875, 8 ½ In.
$198.00

TIP
Never store an old painting on canvas flat and face up on a floor. The paint may crack at the stretcher. A dog may step on it. Store upright.

As always, the edited listings in *Kovels' Antiques & Collectibles Price Guide 2010* aren't available on any website, but readers should visit Kovels.com for information on trends, tips, reproductions, marks, old prices, and more!

R

Rug, Chinese, Vases, Bouquets, Blue Ground, 9 Ft. x 11 Ft. 5 In. $220.00

Rug, Drugget, Geometrics, Orange, Green, Oatmeal Ground, G. Stickley, 4 Ft. 2 In. x 4 Ft. $650.00

Rug, Heriz, 3 Central Medallions, Red Ground, Blue Border, 3 Ft. 3 In. x 4 Ft. 5 In. $715.00

TIP

It is better for a rug to be cleaned by a carpet sweeper than a vacuum cleaner. If a vacuum cleaner must be used, be sure it is on low suction power.

RUGS have been used in the American home since the seventeenth century. The oriental rug of that time was often used on a table, not on the floor. Rag rugs, hooked rugs, and braided rugs were made by housewives from scraps of material. American Indian rugs are listed in the Indian category.

Afshar, Ivory Field, Repeated Tree Designs, Blue & Olive Detail, 3 Ft. 10 In. x 4 Ft. 5 In. 575.00
Afshar, Shiraz, Southern Persia, 1910-30, 5 Ft. 8 In. x 4 Ft. 5 In. 690.00
Agra, Flower Vases, Olive Field, Purple & Olive Borders, Turkey, 8 Ft. 9 In. x 11 Ft. 10 In. 1495.00
Anatolian Kilim, Serrated Diamonds, Ivory Field, 4 Ft. 6 In. x 11 Ft. 9 In. 575.00
Angelis, Rose Field, Blue & Green Rows, Crenellated Border, 5 Ft. x 3 In. x 3 Ft. 4 In. 180.00
Ardebil, Flower, Arches, Red, Blue, Ivory, Lattice Border, 8 Ft. 9 In. x 5 Ft. 6 In. 403.00
Bakhtiari, Red Field, Ivory Border, 10 Ft. 4 In. x 11 Ft. 1 In. 1150.00
Bakhtiari, Tree Designs, Blue Field, Ivory Border, Flowers, 3 Ft. 5 In. x 3 Ft. 11 In. 1380.00
Baku, Medallions, Urns, Pink, Green, Terra-Cotta, Blue, Red Latticework, 5 Ft. 11 In. x 3 Ft. 11 In. 1495.00
Beluch, Red, Brown Field, Flowering Trees, Geometric Border, 10 Ft. 6 In. x 5 Ft. 10 In. 460.00
Bidjar, Center Cartouche, Burgundy Field, Olive & Blue Highlights, 3 Ft. 6 In. x 4 Ft. 7 In. . . . 805.00
Bidjar, Flower Medallion, Blue, Ivory, Pink, Vining, Red Field, Persia, 15 Ft. 8 In. x 10 Ft. 5 In. 1093.00
Bidjar, Herati Design, Blue Spandrels, Salmon Red Ground & Border, c.1940, 4 Ft. 4 In. x 6 Ft. 823.00
Bidjar, Red Medallion, Navy Ground, Multiple Borders, c.1920, 7 x 5 Ft. 2574.00
Bidjar, Serrated Diamonds, Red Field, 3 Ft. 11 In. x 6 Ft. 5 In. 863.00
Bokhara, Geometric Design, Red, Green, c.1970, 10 Ft. x 2 Ft. 7 In. 360.00
Bokhara, Indigo, Red Gull Rows, Red Field, Lattice, Tooth Border, Afghanistan, 9 Ft. 3 In. x 8 Ft. 3 In. 633.00
Bokhara, Prayer, Medallions, Mosques, Minerettes, Beige Field, 5 Ft. 10 In. x 3 Ft. 5 In. 690.00
Bokhara, Ivory, Stylized Gull, Butterfly, Red, Black, Ivory, Border, Persia, 6 Ft. 8 In. x 4 Ft. 7 In. . 180.00
Caucasian, Cross Medallion, Blue Field, Flower & Comb Design, 3 Ft. 6 In. x 5 Ft. 1725.00
Caucasian, Flower Design, c.1970, 8 Ft. 9 In. x 6 Ft. 4 In. 660.00
Caucasian, Geometric, Ivory Field, Scattered Birds, 5 Ft. 3 In. x 3 Ft. 7 In. 431.00
Caucasian, Pink, Orange, Blue Green, Ivory, Turkey, 11 Ft. 4 In. x 5 Ft. 518.00
Chain Stitched, 32 Square Panels, Alternating Birds & Flowers, 1900s, 8 Ft. x 15 Ft. 2 In. . . . 978.00
Chinese, Art Deco, Flowers, Fowl, Pink, Green, Blue, Yellow, Red, c.1930, 5 Ft. 3 In. x 3 Ft. . . . 360.00
Chinese, Art Deco, Flowers, Pagoda, Blue Field, Butterflies, Early 1900s, 8 Ft. 11 In. x 11 Ft. 6 In. 201.00
Chinese, Art Deco, House, Flowers, Purple Field, Yellow Border, 4 Ft. 11 In. x 3 Ft. 3 ½ In. . . . 300.00
Chinese, Art Deco, Multicolored Flowers, Red Field, c.1930, 4 Ft. 9 In. x 2 Ft. 5 In. 270.00
Chinese, Nichols, Blue Design, Tan Ground, 11 x 15 Ft. 411.00
Chinese, Sculpted Flower, Center, Corner, Blue Field, 9 Ft. 8 In. x 11 Ft. 4 In. 288.00
Chinese, Tan Center, Flower Border, Blue, Red, Green, Gold, c.1930, 6 Ft. 11 In. x 4 Ft. 1080.00
Chinese, Vases, Bouquets, Blue Ground, 9 Ft. x 11 Ft. 5 In. . . . . . . *illus* 220.00
Dagestan, Kufic Border, Horses, Birds, Tribal Women, 12 Ft. 7 In. x 5 Ft. 6900.00
Deragzine, Salmon Field, Rust Border, 2 Ft. 3 In. x 3 Ft. 4 In. 88.00
Dorochsh, Flower Medallions, Salmon Field, Multicolored Borders, 8 Ft. 8 In. x 6 Ft. 7 In. . . . 2875.00
Drugget, Geometrics, Orange, Green, Oatmeal Ground, G. Stickley, 4 Ft. 2 In. x 4 Ft. . . . *illus* 650.00
Erivan, Ivory, Green Medallion, Ivory & Red Field, 4 Ft. 2 In. x 5 Ft. 8 In. 575.00
Ferahan Sarouk, Blue, Black Ground, Detailed Borders, 10 Ft. 11 In. x 14 Ft. 2 In. 11500.00
Feti, Mauve Field, Vinery, Celery Border, Chinese, c.1920, 11 Ft. 6 In. x 8 Ft. 11 In. 480.00
Flowers, Leaves, Red, Gold, Blue, Contemporary, 13 Ft. 10 In. x 13 Ft. 6 In. 1080.00
Frank Lloyd Wright, Cream Reserve, Geometric Design, Schumacher, 11 Ft. 8 In. x 8 Ft. 3 In. 780.00
Gendje, South Central Caucus, Mid 19th Century, 7 Ft. x 4 Ft. 2 In. 770.00
Hamadan, Blue Abrash Ground, Border, 3 Ft. 8 In. x 6 Ft. 118.00
Hamadan, Blue Spandrels, Rust Ground, Brown Border, c.1925, 3 Ft. 7 In. x 5 Ft. 7 In. 705.00
Hamadan, Center Diamond, Salmon Field, Serrated Borders, 4 Ft. 9 In. x 6 Ft. 10 In. 633.00
Hamadan, Center Medallion, Navy Ground, Multiple Borders, c.1915, 6 Ft. 5 In. x 4 Ft. 6 In. . 205.00
Hamadan, Center Medallion, Pendants, Beige Field, Scattered Bird Corners, 3 Ft. 9 In. x 6 Ft. 805.00
Hamadan, Center Medallion, Pendants, Salmon Field, Ivory Borders, 4 Ft. 3 In. x 6 Ft. 5 In. . 431.00
Hamadan, Curvilinear Design, Blue & Black Field, Ivory & Blue Accents, 4 Ft. x 5 Ft. 5 In. . . . 460.00
Hamadan, Ivory Center, Medallion Red Ground, c.1930, Runner, 14 Ft. x 3 Ft. 6 In. 234.00
Hamadan, Pole Medallion, Blue Black, Red Field, Turquoise Geometric, 11 Ft. 9 In. x 8 Ft. 8 In. 431.00
Hamadan, Repeating Floral, Blue & Black Field, Barber Pole Border, 4 Ft. 1 In. x 6 Ft. 9 In. . . 489.00
Hamadan, Repeating Stylized Pattern, Red Field, c.1950, Runner, 10 Ft. x 3 Ft. 1 In. 480.00
Hamadan, Sarouk, Burgundy Field, 3 Ft. 6 In. x 4 Ft. 9 In. 201.00
Herati, Multicolored, Flowers, Indigo Field, Borders, c.1930, 5 Ft. 4 In. x 10 Ft. 5 In. 1320.00
Heriz, 3 Central Medallions, Red Ground, Blue Border, 3 Ft. 3 In. x 4 Ft. 5 In. . . . . . . *illus* 715.00
Heriz, Arabesque Medallion, Turquoise Spandrels, Flowers, Vines, Border, 10 Ft. 10 In. x 7 Ft. 6 In. 2645.00
Heriz, Blue Center Medallion, Salmon Field, 7 Ft. 9 In. x 10 Ft. 11 In. 1380.00
Heriz, Center Medallion, Burgundy Field, Ivory Field, Corner Work, 12 Ft. 2 In. x 20 Ft. 6 In. . 1955.00
Heriz, Center Medallion, Salmon Field, Outside Ivory Field, 9 Ft. 10 In. x 12 Ft. 8 In. 1610.00
Heriz, Flowers, Salmon Field, c.1900, 8 Ft. 7 In. x 11 Ft. 6 In. 3410.00
Heriz, Geometric Lattice, Vining, Rose Ground, Sawtooth Edge, 10 Ft. 1 In. x 7 Ft. 6 In. 1150.00

Heriz, Geometric Medallion, Indigo, Red, Ivory Spandrels, Border, 7 Ft. 8 In. x 11 Ft. 1 In. . . . 1020.00
Heriz, Geometric Medallion, Red, Olive, Indigo, Red Field, Ivory Spandrels, 9 x 11 Ft. 1200.00
Heriz, Indigo Medallion, Red Field, Spandrels, Persia, Early 1900s, 11 Ft. 7 In. x 8 Ft. 6 In. . . . 345.00
Heriz, Ivory Ground, Salmon Spandrels, Black Border, 10 Ft. 8 In. x 14 Ft. 9 In. 4700.00
Heriz, Lobed Medallions, Red Field, Multicolored, Geometric, Spandrels, 10 Ft. x 6 Ft. 11 In. . 2358.00
Heriz, Medallions, Latticework, Ivory Field, Mid 1900s, 11 Ft. 6 In. x 8 Ft. 10 In. 920.00
Heriz, Navy, Red Ground & Border, Ivory Spandrels, c.1920, 10 Ft. 6 In. x 13 Ft. 4 In. 8813.00
Heriz, Red Field, 7 Multicolored Medallions, Blue & Green Guard Border, Persia, 11 x 3 Ft. . . 960.00
Heriz, Red Field, Geometric Latticework, Persia, c.1900, 10 Ft. 3 In. x 7 Ft. 1840.00
Heriz, Red Fields, Allover Stylized Flowers, c.1900, 2 Ft. 3 In. x 4 Ft. 7 In. 353.00
Heriz, Salmon Field, Blue Medallion, Spandrels, Turtle Border, c.1920, 9 Ft. 10 In. x 7 Ft. 2 In. 1025.00
Hooked, 2 Black Cats, Wool, Rayon, Cotton Ground, c.1910, 25 x 55 In. 1058.00
Hooked, 2 Cats, Potted Flowers, Loop Border, Wool, Burlap, c.1900, 18 x 33 In. 764.00
Hooked, 2 Deer, Flowers, Vining, Gold, Brown, Red, Orange, Borders, Runner, 25 x 70 In. 1750.00
Hooked, 2 Kittens, Salmon Features, Striated Ground, Wool, Cotton, 35 x 18 In. 805.00
Hooked, 2 Reindeer In Center, Flowers & Oak Leaves, Red Border, Wool, 1800, 31 x 64 In. . . . 2100.00
Hooked, 3 Bears, Carrying Porridge, Red, Brown, Black Border, Early 20th Century, 28 x 43 In. 1400.00
Hooked, American Flag, Multicolored, 1898, 25 x 40 In. 2574.00
Hooked, Beaver, Crouched On Mound, Tree Limb, Gray, Tan, Beige, Green, c.1900, 41 x 23 In. 2415.00
Hooked, Bird On Potted Tulip, Red Border, Canvas, 17 x 16 ½ In. . . . . *illus* 660.00
Hooked, Birds, Heart, Tulips, Arched Top, Multicolored, Burlap, Pa., 25 x 31 In. . . . . *illus* 358.00
Hooked, Black Leopard, Oversized Flowers, Yarn, Burlap, Mid 20th Century, 36 x 60 In. 58.00
Hooked, Black Rooster, White Fence, Felted Wool, Stocking Knit, Burlap, 24 x 34 In. 159.00
Hooked, Blue Heron, Cattails, Flower Heads, Tassels, Green, Beige, Blue, Pink, 42 x 17 ½ In. . 1323.00
Hooked, Blue Oak Leaf Corners, Initials A.M., Square Border, Early 1900s, 25 ½ x 29 ½ In. . . 556.00
Hooked, Cheshire Cat, Big Grin, Big Blue Eyes, Gray Ground, 1948, 28 x 18 In. 615.00
Hooked, Chicken, American Flag, Blue Ground, Ribbons, Flags, Burlap, 13 x 18 In. 66.00
Hooked, Cornucopia, Filled With Flowers, Fruit, Brown, Pastels, 26 x 32 In. 690.00
Hooked, Deer, Recumbent, Butterfly, Blue, Brown, Green, c.1920, 25 x 42 In. 330.00
Hooked, Dog, On Checkered Carpet, Black & White Border, 38 x 24 In. 288.00
Hooked, Drum, Federal Shield, Red, White, Blue, 36 x 24 In. 50.00
Hooked, Eagle, Spread Wings, Holding Flag, Frame, Wool, Burlap, 1920s, 23 ½ In. 1410.00
Hooked, Flower, Black, Red, White, 27 x 40 In. 345.00
Hooked, Flowers, Central Tulip, Multicolored, Mottled Border, Burlap, Frame, 25 x 40 In. . . . 165.00
Hooked, Flowers, Trees, White, Blue, Red, Sawtooth Border, Wool, Frame, c.1920, 40 x 34 In. . 1126.00
Hooked, Flying Geese, Landscape, Multicolored, Burlap, Frame, 18 ½ x 35 ½ In. 209.00
Hooked, Garden Of Eden, Adam & Eve, Snake, Apple Trees, Eastern Pa., 27 x 56 In. 3163.00
Hooked, General George Washington, With His Horse, Cherry Tree, Beige, 36 x 48 In. 1920.00
Hooked, Geometric, Diamonds, Multicolored, Blue Bar Border, Burlap, 38 x 25 In. 198.00
Hooked, Geometric, Quilt Pattern, Log Cabin, Red Squares, Burlap, 45 x 30 In. 323.00
Hooked, Girl, Pink, Watering Flowers, Burlap, Mid 1900s, 31 x 18 ½ In. 173.00
Hooked, Goose, Chicken, Farm Scene, Multicolored, Burlap, Frame, 20 x 25 ¼ In. 176.00
Hooked, Grenfell, Missionary, Eskimo, Ship, Sled Dogs, Aqua Ground, 19 x 26 In. 3450.00
Hooked, Grenfell, North Star, Fishing Symbols, Dogs, Sled, 1900s, 25 x 20 In. 1010.00
Hooked, Grenfell, Polar Bear, Blue, Green, White, 7 ¾ x 10 ½ In. 183.00
Hooked, Heron, Wading, Pond, Cattails, Water Lilies, White, Green, Red, Frame, 30 x 55 In. . . 889.00
Hooked, Horse Head, Bridled, Yellow Band, Flowers, Wool, Cotton, Velvet, Burlap, 23 x 34 In. . 259.00
Hooked, House, Flowers, Beige, Red, Blue, Geometric Border, Cotton, Frame, c.1900, 31 x 40 In. 711.00
Hooked, Hunt Scene, Man On Horse, Dogs, Raccoon In Tree, Multicolored, 1890s, 51 x 27 In. 660.00
Hooked, Kennebunkport Country Store, 29 x 47 In. 2588.00
Hooked, Landscape, House, Barn, Wool, Burlap, c.1938, 29 x 48 In. 235.00
Hooked, Lion, Orange, White, Brown, Pink, 18 x 30 In. 1650.00
Hooked, Log Cabin, Black Border, Wool, Burlap, Mid 1800s, 25 ½ x 45 In. 230.00
Hooked, Man, Woman, Take Oh! Take Those Lips Away, Wool, Cotton, Frame, 1900s, 33 x 50 In. 1304.00
Hooked, Man & 3 Dogs, Houses, Mountains, Brown, Black & Gray, 1930, 14 x 17 In. 605.00
Hooked, Man On Snow Shoes, Gun, Pack, Arctic Scene, Black Border, 10 ¾ x 8 ¼ In. 187.00
Hooked, Moose, Multicolored Yarn, Brick Border, Burlap, c.1940, 24 x 40 In. 303.00
Hooked, Nautical, Ship In Full Sail, Rope & Wheel Border, Wool, Burlap, 30 x 32 ½ In. 115.00
Hooked, Navajo Style, Zebras, Multiple Borders, Wool, Burlap, Early 1900s, 40 x 71 In. 588.00
Hooked, Oatmeal Ground, Brown, 4 Orbs, Clamshell Border, Wool, Burlap, 1920s, 19 x 28 In. 2450.00
Hooked, Pig Pulling Wagon, Ye Boston Baked Beans, Early 20th Century, 30 x 53 ½ In. 1520.00
Hooked, Potted Flowers, Leaves, Multicolored, Scalloped Border, Burlap, 48 x 26 In. 99.00
Hooked, Red & Yellow Flowers, White Leaves, Black Ground, Early 1900s, 34 x 48 In. 50.00
Hooked, Rooster, Sunflower, Lamb, Cow, 21 Squares, Wool, Burlap, c.1930, 61 x 29 In. 880.00
Hooked, Rosebuds, Flowers, Multicolored, Frame, 29 ½ x 44 ½ In. 132.00
Hooked, Roses, Multicolored, Geometric Borders, Braided Edges, Burlap, 30 x 45 In. 66.00

Rug Quality
Oriental rugs are graded for quality by dealers. In most cases the quality is determined by the knot count over a measured distance on the width of a rug. A 90 line count for a Chinese rug means if 1 foot of the width is marked off there will be 90 knots. Pakistani rugs have quality measured by counting knots on 1 inch of the width and 1 inch of the length, so it might be 16/18.

Rug, Hooked, Bird On Potted Tulip, Red Border, Canvas, 17 x 16 ½ In.
$660.00

Rug, Hooked, Birds, Heart, Tulips, Arched Top, Multicolored, Burlap, Pa., 25 x 31 In.
$358.00

Rug, Hooked, Swan, In Water, Lily Pad Corners, Early 1900s, 26 x 31 In.
$100.00

R

Rug, Kazar, Prayer, Medallion, Salmon Field, Stepped Diagonal Border, 3 Ft. 9 In. x 4 Ft. 4 In.
$1760.00

Rug, Shirvan, Hook Design, Ivory Field, Late 19th Century, 3 Ft. 2 In. x 4 Ft. 10 In.
$770.00

Rug, Shirvan, Prayer, Diamonds, Ivory Field, Geometric Border, Late 1800s, 3 x 5 Ft.
$1040.00

Hooked, Squirrel, Wool, Cotton, Frame, 1900s, 20 ¾ x 42 In. . . . 504.00
Hooked, Swan, In Water, Lily Pad Corners, Early 1900s, 26 x 31 In. . . . *illus* 100.00
Hooked, Swan, In Water, Lily Pads, Multicolored, Burlap, Frame, 31 x 40 In. . . . 121.00
Hooked, Verse, Don't Spit In The Well, Oak Leaves, Acorns, 23 x 37 ½ In. . . . 485.00
Hooked, Vignettes, Birds, Plants, Earth Tones, Black Border, 51 x 60 In. . . . 173.00
Hooked, Willow Pattern, Blue & White, c.1930, 28 ¼ x 47 In. . . . 2500.00
Karabaugh, 3 Borders, Orange, Blue Ground, 3 Ft. 4 In. x 3 Ft. 4 In. . . . 382.00
Karabaugh, Red Field, Multicolored Geometric, Bakhshaish Border, c.1930, 6 Ft. 2 In. x 4 Ft. 4 In. 345.00
Karabaugh, Salmon Medallions, Dark Blue Ground, Ivory Border, c.1925, 3 Ft. 9 In. x 6 Ft. . 470.00
Karaja, 3 Eagle Medallions, Red Field, Tan Border, c.1930, 7 Ft. x 4 Ft. 5 In. . . . 345.00
Karaja, 5 Medallions, Blue Highlights, Salmon Field, Runner, 3 Ft. 3 In. x 10 Ft. 3 In. . . . 863.00
Karaja, Crab Medallions, Geometric, Red Field, Blue, Black Border, 13 Ft. 2 In. x 4 Ft. 9 In. . . 1265.00
Karaja, Medallions, Claret Red Field, Multicolored, Geometric, Runner, 8 Ft. 8 In. x 3 Ft. 2 In. 546.00
Kayseri, Star & Flower Medallion, Blue Field, Ivory, Flower Border, 4 Ft. 3 In. x 5 Ft. 8 In. . . . 431.00
Kazak, 3 Medallions, Blue, Brown, Red, Ivory, Multiple Borders, c.1910, 5 Ft. 5 In. x 3 Ft. . . . 878.00
Kazak, 3 Serrated Diamond Pendants, Pink, Blue, Brown, 1800s, 4 Ft. 5 In. x 6 Ft. 6 In. . . . 1840.00
Kazak, 6 Medallions, Green Field, Red Border, c.1915, 10 Ft. 5 In. x 3 Ft. 7 In. . . . 644.00
Kazak, Flowers, Geometric, Red Ground, Blue Border, c.1910, 7 Ft. 1 In. x 4 Ft. 5 In. . . . 510.00
Kazak, Geometric Diamonds, Multicolored, 2 Stepped Borders, 3 Ft. 8 In. x 10 Ft. 4 In. . . . 1840.00
Kazak, Medallions, Blue Field, Scattered Quadrupeds, Ivory Border, 7 Ft. x 4 Ft. 2 In. . . . 1035.00
Kazak, Red, Orange, Green, Wool, c.1910, 2 Ft. 7 In. x 3 Ft. 10 In. . . . 178.00
Kazak, Ruby Medallion, Indigo, Cherry Dovetail, Geometric Borders, 5 Ft. 2 In. x 8 Ft. 9 In. . . 720.00
Kazar, Prayer, Medallion, Salmon Field, Stepped Diagonal Border, 3 Ft. 9 In. x 4 Ft. 4 In. . . . *illus* 1760.00
Kerman, Floral Urns, Burgundy, 11 Ft. 9 In. x 17 Ft. 8 In. . . . 1763.00
Kerman, Flower & Leaf Medallions, Trellis, Ivory Field, Flower Border, 11 x 8 Ft. . . . 11500.00
Kerman, Flowers, Blue Field, Rose & Olive Borders, 11 Ft. 8 In. x 15 Ft. 4 In. . . . 6900.00
Kerman, Medallion, Spandrels, Petals, Red Field, Lozenge Border, 11 x 16 Ft. . . . 7050.00
Kerman, Repeating Floral, Ivory Field, 5 Ft. 10 In. x 8 Ft. 6 In. . . . 1495.00
Keshan, Flower Filled Vase, Red Field, Indigo Flower Border, c.1920, 5 Ft. 3 In. x 3 Ft. 4 In. . . 1380.00
Khorasan, Lotus Blossoms, Leafy Vinery, Multicolored, Ivory Field, 13 Ft. 7 In. x 9 Ft. 11 In. . 2070.00
Khorasan, Persian, Vase, Peacocks, Tree, Vines, Early 20th Century, 4 Ft. 3 In. x 7 Ft. 2 In. . . . 575.00
Kilim, Joined Panels, Geometric, Red, Brown, Blue, Iran, Runner, 9 Ft. 3 In. x 2 Ft. 2 In. . . . 230.00
Kuba, Red, Blue, Ivory Medallions, Black Field, Multicolored Borders, Late 1800s, 6 Ft. 10 In. x 4 Ft. 2588.00
Kurdish, Geometric Design, Multicolored, Tan Field, Runner, c.1940, 6 Ft. 10 In. x 3 Ft. . . . 720.00
Kurdish, Rust Spandrels, Blue Field, Multiple Borders, 4 Ft. 5 In. x 6 Ft. 1 In. . . . 235.00
Kurdish, Stylized Design, Red Field, Blue, Beige, Yellow Border, Runner, c.1960, 8 Ft. 11 In. x 3 Ft. 270.00
Lilihan, Flower Latticework, Rose Pink Border, Midnight Blue Field, 6 Ft. 4 In. x 5 Ft. 5 In. . . 1265.00
Lilihan, Flowers, Red, Blue, Green, Gold, c.1920, 4 Ft. 10 ½ In. x 3 Ft. 7 ½ In. . . . 450.00
Luristan, Multicolored, Dark Blue Field, Ivory Border, 3 Ft. 10 In. x 7 Ft. 11 In. . . . 823.00
Mahal, Medallion, Latticework, Flower, Madder Red Field, 10 Ft. 10 In. x 7 Ft. 11 In. . . . 1725.00
Malayer, Ivory Medallion, Blue Floral Field, Red Floral Border, 10 Ft. 4 In. x 12 Ft. . . . 1528.00
Malayer, Repeating Design, Pumpkin Field, Blue Border, 3 Ft. 4 In. x 6 Ft. 3 In. . . . 575.00
Mashad, Center Medallion, Red Field, Magenta Detail, 10 Ft. 5 In. x 15 Ft. 9 In. . . . 403.00
Maslaghan, Red Field, Dark Blue Spandrels, White Border, 4 Ft. 1 In. x 6 Ft. 5 In. . . . 441.00
Mohajransk, Flowers, Maroon Field, c.1920, 6 Ft. 5 ½ In. x 4 Ft. 4 In. . . . 300.00
Patchwork, Applique, Dog, Pup, Silhouette, Beige Field, Hearts, Symbols, 2 Ft. 7 In. x 4 Ft. 6 In. 805.00
Penny, Circles, Teardrops, Yellow, Green, Brown, White, Oval, 51 x 34 In. . . . 275.00
Penny, Embroidery Thread, Ticking, 5 Rows Of Overlapping Petals, Wool, c.1885, 22 x 42 In. 470.00
Perpetual, Flowers, Geometric Shapes, c.1920, 4 Ft. x 2 Ft. 11 ½ In. . . . 450.00
Persian, Medallions, Ivory, Blue Green, Gold, Red Field, Flower Border, 10 Ft. 10 In. x 8 Ft. 3 In. 589.00
Persian, Prayer, Moses, Aaron, Kotel, 12 Tribe Symbols, 3 Ft. 2 In. x 3 Ft. 11 In. . . . 504.00
Persian, Stylized Flowers, Red Field, Blue Border, c.1930, Runner, 17 Ft. x 3 Ft. 3 In. . . . 1560.00
Quashkai, 3 Ivory Medallions, Blue Field, Flowers, Hook Borders, 4 Ft. 3 In. x 6 Ft. 10 In. . . . 1380.00
Saraban, Flowers, Geometric Shapes, Red, Blue, Brown, c.1950, 5 Ft. 8 ½ In. x 3 Ft. 11 In. . . 270.00
Sarouk, Blue, Ivory, Brown Flowers, Red Field, Blue Floral Border, c.1920, 6 Ft. 9 In. x 4 Ft. . . 805.00
Sarouk, Burgundy Field, Blue Border, 8 Ft. 9 In. x 12 Ft. . . . 588.00
Sarouk, Center Medallion, Blue & Ivory Details, Brick Red Field, 3 Ft. 4 In. x 4 Ft. 9 In. . . . 575.00
Sarouk, Flower Sprays, Red Reserve, Leaf Border, Blue Reserve, 8 Ft. 10 In. x 10 Ft. 2 In. . . . 3120.00
Sarouk, Indigo, Mustard, Flower Sprays, Cranberry Field, c.1920, 10 Ft. 6 In. x 13 Ft. 4 In. . . 3900.00
Sarouk, Indigo Flowers, Medallion, Wine Field, Scrolling, c.1900, 17 Ft. 8 In. x 12 Ft. . . . 8338.00
Sarouk, Ivory Field, Red Border, 9 Ft. 3 In. x 12 Ft. 2 In. . . . 2115.00
Sarouk, Prayer, Flowers, Spandrels, Buff Field, Flower Border, c.1900, 6 Ft. 8 In. x 4 Ft. 3 In. . 5175.00
Sarouk, Stylized Indigo Vining, Red Field, Flower Border, c.1920, 6 Ft. 10 In. x 4 Ft. 2 In. . . . 150.00
Sarouk, Vases, Flowers, Dark Blue Field, 3 Ft. 4 In. x 4 Ft. 8 In. . . . 1150.00
Serapi, Blue Medallion, Mustard Field, Red Corners, Navy Border, c.1910, 18 x 11 Ft. . . . 19890.00
Serapi, Center Medallion, Ivory Field, Late 19th Century, 8 Ft. 8 In. x 11 Ft. 1 In. . . . 3680.00

Serapi, Mustard, Sand Medallion, Ivory Spandrels, Terra-Cotta Field, 8 Ft. 1 In. x 10 Ft. 3 In.. 1560.00
Serrated Medallions, Flowers, Birds, Red Field, 5 Ft. x 11 Ft. 10 In. 83.00
Shiraz, 2 Figures, Horse, Rider, Corn, Orange Field, 4 Ft. 4 In. x 6 Ft. 7 In. 460.00
Shiraz, 7 Serrated Diamonds, Blue Field, Geometric, Runner, 3 Ft. 5 In. x 12 Ft. 1 In. 1035.00
Shiraz, Diamond Medallion, Geometric, Red Field, Mid 1900s, 9 Ft. 10 In. x 6 Ft. 6 In. 978.00
Shiraz, Geometric Designs, Red Field, Mid 1900s, 10 Ft. x 7 Ft. 4 In. 690.00
Shiraz, Grape Center Medallion, Red Field, Green Border, Late 1900s, 5 Ft. x 3 Ft. 3 In. 460.00
Shirvan, 2 Medallions, Navy Blue Field, Ivory Border, Early 20th Century, 5 Ft. x 3 Ft. 8 In. 1170.00
Shirvan, 3 Octagonal Medallions, Blue Field, Star Borders, 3 Ft. x 4 Ft. 11 In. 4140.00
Shirvan, Hook Design, Ivory Field, Late 19th Century, 3 Ft. 2 In. x 4 Ft. 10 In. *illus* 770.00
Shirvan, Multicolored Octagons, Blue Field, Ivory Border, Late 1800s, 6 Ft. 2 In. x 3 Ft. 4 In. 1140.00
Shirvan, Prayer, Diamonds, Ivory Field, Geometric Border, Late 1800s, 3 x 5 Ft. *illus* 1040.00
Shirvan, Prayer, Flower Lattice, Blue Arch, Ivory Field, Borders, c.1890, 4 Ft. 11 In. x 4 Ft. 2 In. 420.00
Shirvan, Prayer, Repeat Design, Ivory Field, Multiple Borders, Late 1800s, 6 Ft. x 2 Ft. 7 In. 7020.00
Sultanabad, Palmette, Lattice, Cinnabar, Indigo, Black, c.1910, 11 Ft. x 14 Ft. 10 In. 2640.00
Tabriz, Center Medallion, Ivory Field, Corner Work, Silk Inlay, 8 Ft. x 11 Ft. 10 In. 4600.00
Tabriz, Figures Hunting, Ivory Field, Cobalt Blue Border, c.1915, 6 Ft. x 4 Ft. 6 In. 1755.00
Tabriz, Geometric Flower, Red Field, Flowerhead Border, 3 Ft. 10 In. x 2 Ft. 8 In., Pair 805.00
Tabriz, Medallion, Turquoise Lotus, Urns, Flowers, Beige Field, c.1950, 19 Ft. x 10 Ft. 7 In. 920.00
Tabriz, Scalloped Medallion, Burgundy Field, Blue, Ivory Detail, Silk, 6 Ft. 4 In. x 6 Ft. 4 In. 3910.00
Turkish, Blue Center Medallion, Pendants, Salmon Field, c.1913, 5 Ft. x 7 Ft. 5 In. 1380.00
Turkish, Stylized Flowers, Shapes, Red Field, c.1970, 6 Ft. 7 In. x 3 Ft. 3 ½ In. 330.00
Turkoman, Geometric Design, Red, Gold, Blue, 3 Ft. 10 In. x 2 Ft. 8 In. 780.00
Turkoman, Salmon, White, Dark Blue, 3 Ft. 1 In. x 5 Ft. 1 In. 59.00
Velvet, Embroidered, Appliqued Heart, Animals, Vine, Tree, Sun, 1887, 18 x 18 In. 15495.00
Vernon Panton, Geometrics, Black, Natural, Wool, 7 Ft. 9 In. x 5 Ft. 2 In. *illus* 650.00
William Morris, Geometric Flowers, Blue, Gray, Buff, Slate Field, 6 Ft. x 9 Ft. 1 In. 510.00
William Morris, Geometric Flowers, Ivory Field, 8 Ft. 4 In. x 10 Ft. 1 In. 840.00
William Morris, Pods, Acanthus Leaves, Red, Celadon, Black Field, Border, 9 Ft. x 11 Ft. 10 In. 900.00
William Morris, Poppy Pod, Vines, Cherry, Celadon, Ocher Field, 9 Ft. 6 In. x 12 Ft. 3 In. 780.00
Wool, Arts & Crafts, Floral Bind, Scotland, 7 x 5 Ft. *illus* 960.00
Wool, Hand Knotted, Geometric, Beige, Fringe, France, c.1930, 8 Ft. 6 ½ In. x 5 Ft. 6 In. 8125.00
Wool, Wittrup Botnia Rya, Circles, Orange, Olive, Rust, Denmark, 9 Ft. x 5 Ft. 8 In. *illus* 330.00

RUMRILL Pottery was designed by George Rumrill of Little Rock, Arkansas. From 1933 to 1938, it was produced by the Red Wing Pottery of Red Wing, Minnesota. In January 1938, production was transferred to the Shawnee Pottery in Zanesville, Ohio. It was moved again in December of 1938 to Florence Pottery Company in Mt. Gilead, Ohio, where Rumrill ware continued to be manufactured until the pottery burned in 1941. It was then produced by Gonder Ceramic Arts in South Zanesville until early 1943.

RumRill

Jardiniere, Rose, Green Matte Glaze, Marked, No. 174, 6 x 8 In. 60.00
Jug, Ball, Green Matte Glaze, Marked, Rumrill 50, 6 ¼ x 8 In. *illus* 33.00
Vase, Swirl Tan Exterior, Blue, Green Interior, Jug Handles, Marked, No. 644, 7 x 6 In. 70.00

RUSKIN is a British art pottery of the twentieth century. The Ruskin Pottery was started by William Howson Taylor, and his name was used as the mark until about 1899. The factory, at West Smethwick, Birmingham, England, stopped making new pieces in 1933 but continued to glaze and sell the remaining wares until 1935. The art pottery is noted for its exceptional glazes.

RUSKIN POTTERY WEST SMETHWICK

Candlestick, Yellow Luster Glaze, Marked, No. 1917, 6 ½ x 4 ½ In. 120.00
Pin, Disc, Ceramic, Mottled Purple & Blue, Silver Ring Rim, c.1910, 1 ⅜ In. 125.00
Pin, Pewter, Mottled Green Cabochon, Bezel Set, C Clasp, Hand Wrought, c.1905 55.00
Vase, Shouldered, Yellow Luster Glaze, Marked, 9 ½ x 5 In. 240.00

RUSSEL WRIGHT designed dinnerwares in modern shapes for many companies. Iroquois China Company, Harker China Company, Steubenville Pottery, and Justin Tharaud and Sons made dishes marked *Russel Wright*. The Steubenville wares, first made in 1938, are the most common today. Wright was a designer of domestic and industrial wares, including furniture, aluminum, radios, interiors, and glassware. Dinnerwares and other pieces by Wright are listed here. For more prices, go to Kovels.com.

Russel Wright MFG. BY STEUBENVILLE

American Modern, Bowl, Salad, Cedar Green, 8 In. 95.00
American Modern, Bowl, Salad, Granite Gray, 8 In. 95.00
American Modern, Bowl, Salad, Seafoam Green, 8 In. 125.00
American Modern, Bowl, Vegetable, Divided, Chartreuse 150.00
American Modern, Celery Dish, Chartreuse 50.00
American Modern, Celery Dish, Coral, 13 ½ In. 22.00

Rug, Vernon Panton, Geometrics, Black, Natural, Wool, 7 Ft. 9 In. x 5 Ft. 2 In.
$650.00

Rug, Wool, Arts & Crafts, Floral Bind, Scotland, 7 x 5 Ft.
$960.00

Rug, Wool, Wittrup Botnia Rya, Circles, Orange, Olive, Rust, Denmark, 9 Ft. x 5 Ft. 8 In.
$330.00

R

Rumrill, Jug, Ball, Green Matte Glaze, Marked, Rumrill 50, 6 ¼ x 8 In.
$33.00

Russel Wright, Oceana, Bowl, Starfish, Wood, Signed, 13 ½ In.
$1200.00

Sabino, Box, Flowers, Opalescent, Signed, 2 ½ x 2 ⅝ In.
$66.00

R

TIP

Attractive acid-free boxes to store photographs are available in many stores. Dozens of looks are available, from pseudo leather to boxes covered with maps or flowers.

American Modern, Celery Dish, Granite Gray 40.00
American Modern, Creamer, Black Chutney 20.00
American Modern, Cup & Saucer, Chartreuse 7.00
American Modern, Cup & Saucer, Sugar White 35.00
American Modern, Dish, Pickle, Chartreuse. 25.00
American Modern, Gravy Boat, Chartreuse, 10 ½ In. 19.00
American Modern, Gravy Boat, Gray Blue 15.00
American Modern, Pitcher, Coral, 10 ⅞ In. 85.00
American Modern, Plate, Bread & Butter, Granite Gray, 6 ¼ In. 5.50
American Modern, Plate, Dinner, Chartreuse, 10 In. 15.00
American Modern, Plate, Dinner, Granite Gray, 10 In. 9.00
American Modern, Plate, Hostess, Cup Holder, Black Chutney, 10 x 11 ¾ In. 115.00
American Modern, Plate, Hostess, Cup Holder, Cedar Green, 10 x 11 ¾ In. 185.00
American Modern, Plate, Hostess, Cup Holder, Granite Gray, 10 x 11 ¾ In. 115.00
American Modern, Plate, Salad, Bean Brown, 8 In. 21.00
American Modern, Plate, Salad, Granite Gray, 8 In. 9.00
American Modern, Platter, Square, Granite Gray, 13 In. 28.00
American Modern, Platter, Square, Seafoam, 13 In. 60.00
American Modern, Salt & Pepper, Black Chutney 25.00
American Modern, Salt & Pepper, Coral, 2 In. 25.00
American Modern, Saltshaker, Cedar Green. 45.00
American Modern, Soup, Lug, Coral, 7 In. 13.00
American Modern, Teapot, Coral 115.00
Chrome, Cocktail Ball & Saucer, Hors D'Oeuvre, 3 Sections, Chase 75.00
Chrome, Corn Set, Cobalt Blue, Pitcher, Sugar Shaker, Salt, Tray, Chase, 1930s, 4 Piece 295.00
Eclipse, Ice Bucket, Glass, Turquoise & Gold, Rimmed, 6 ½ x 4 ½ In. 45.00
Eclipse, Tumbler, Whiskey, Turquoise & Gold, 2 ⅛ In. 32.00
Eclipse, Tumbler, Zombie, 7 In., 4 Piece 95.00
Iroquois Casual, Bowl, Cereal, Ice Blue, 5 In. 12.00
Iroquois Casual, Bowl, Cereal, Nutmeg Brown, 5 In. 15.00
Iroquois Casual, Bowl, Cereal, Ripe Apricot, 5 In. 12.00
Iroquois Casual, Bowl, Gumbo, Ripe Apricot 60.00
Iroquois Casual, Bowl, Vegetable, Divided, Cover, Round, Oyster, 10 ¼ In. 75.00
Iroquois Casual, Bowl, Vegetable, Open, Ripe Apricot 35.00
Iroquois Casual, Creamer, Charcoal, Stacking 35.00
Iroquois Casual, Cup, Lemon Yellow. 8.00
Iroquois Casual, Cup & Saucer, Charcoal. 25.00
Iroquois Casual, Cup & Saucer, Nutmeg Brown 15.00
Iroquois Casual, Cup & Saucer, Ripe Apricot 15.00
Iroquois Casual, Plate, Bread & Butter, Ripe Apricot, 6 ½ In. 18.00
Iroquois Casual, Plate, Bread & Butter, Sugar White, 6 ½ In. 6.00
Iroquois Casual, Plate, Dinner, Lemon Yellow, 10 In. 20.00
Iroquois Casual, Plate, Dinner, Nutmeg Brown, 10 In. 14.00
Iroquois Casual, Plate, Dinner, Ripe Apricot, 10 In. 15.00
Iroquois Casual, Plate, Dinner, Sugar White, 10 In. 10.00
Iroquois Casual, Platter, Nutmeg Brown, 12 ¾ In. 30.00
Iroquois Casual, Platter, Nutmeg Brown, 14 ½ In. 40.00
Iroquois Casual, Platter, Pink Sherbet, Oval. 15.00
Iroquois Casual, Platter, Sugar White, 12 ¾ In. 30.00
Iroquois Casual, Saucepan, Cantaloupe, 4 x 7 ½ In. 250.00
Iroquois Casual, Saucer, Lemon Yellow 4.00
Iroquois Casual, Saucer, Ripe Apricot, 6 In. 5.00
Iroquois Casual, Sugar, Stacking, Ripe Apricot 25.00
Iroquois Casual, Teapot, Sugar White. 199.00
Lamp, Black, Pottery, Lucite, 27 ½ x 7 ½ In. 40.00
Oceana, Bowl, Starfish, Wood, Signed, 13 ½ In. . . . . *illus* 1200.00

SABINO glass was made in the 1920s and 1930s in Paris, France. Founded by Marius-Ernest Sabino (1878–1961), the firm was noted for Art Deco lamps, vases, figurines, and animals in clear, colored, and opalescent glass. Production stopped during World War II but resumed in the 1960s with the manufacture of nude figurines and small opalescent glass animals. Pieces made in recent years are a slightly different color and can be recognized. Only vintage pieces are listed here.

Sabino France

Box, Flowers, Opalescent, Signed, 2 ½ x 2 ⅝ In. . . . . *illus* 66.00
Figurine, 5 Birds, Branch, Opalescent, Signed, Late 1920s, 7 ½ x 7 ¾ In. 800.00
Figurine, Dragonfly, Opalescent Body, Iridescent Wings, 1920s, 6 x 5 In. 205.00
Figurine, Elephants, Mother & Baby, Opalescent, Signed, c.1928, 8 x 10 In. 1200.00

Figurine, Gazelle, Opalescent, Signed, 1920s, 4 x 6 ¼ In. 200.00
Figurine, Heron Stork, Opalescent, Base, Signed, 7 ½ x 1 ¾ In. 220.00
Figurine, Hesitation, Cloth Draped, Signed, c.1929, 8 ¾ In. 275.00
Figurine, L'Espagnole, Woman, Ruffled Dress, Tambourine, Opalescent, Signed, 1930, 11 In. 2000.00
Figurine, L'Idole, Woman, Legs Crossed, Opalescent, Signed, c.1928, 6 ¼ In. 600.00
Figurine, Panthers, Opalescent, Signed, c.1928, 6 x 8 In. 1000.00
Figurine, Rooster, Opalescent, Signed, c.1928, 7 ½ In. 325.00
Figurine, Storks, Standing, Resting, Opalescent, Signed, c.1928, 6 ½ In. 375.00
Figurine, Woman & Doves, Opalescent, Signed, c.1929, 6 In. .... 293.00 to 325.00
Plate, King Henry IV, Maria De Medicis, Clear Geometric Rim, Opalescent Center, 1970, 8 In . 88.00
Vase, La Danse, Dancing Ladies, Opalescent, Incised Mark, c.1929, 13 ¾ In. 2300.00
Vase, La Danse & Colombes, Birds, Nudes, Opalescent, Incised Mark, c.1930, 9 x 6 In. 600.00
Vase, Nymph, Nude Females, Opalescent, Incised Mark, c.1928, 7 ½ x 9 In. 1700.00

Salopian

SALOPIAN ware was made by the Caughley factory of England during the eighteenth century. The early pieces were blue and white with some colored decorations. Another ware referred to as Salopian is a late nineteenth-century tableware decorated with color transfers.

Cup & Saucer, 2 Classical Figures, Butterfly Border, Handleless, c.1825 .... 205.00
Cup & Saucer, Acorns, Handleless, c.1825 .... *illus* 234.00
Cup Plate, Elephant & Palace, Chinoiserie, c.1825, 5 ½ In. 117.00
Pitcher, Asian Figure, Pagoda, Flowers, Chinoiserie, c.1825, 6 ½ In. 244.00
Punch Pot, Chinoiserie, c.1825, 11 ½ In. 1287.00
Sugar, Cover, Chinoiserie, Lion Finial, c.1825 .... 322.00
Teapot, 2 Lovers, Landscape, Transfer, c.1825, 12 ¼ In. 176.00
Teapot, Boy & Cow, Transfer, c.1825, 4 ½ In. .... *illus* 351.00
Teapot, Boy & Cow, Transfer, c.1825, 10 ½ In. 936.00
Teapot, Cottage, Landscape, Transfer, c.1825, 10 ¾ In. 410.00
Waste Bowl, Family, Pastoral Landscape, c.1825, 3 ¼ x 6 ¼ In. 263.00

SALT AND PEPPER SHAKERS in matched sets were first used in the nineteenth century. Collectors are primarily interested in figural examples made after World War I. Huggers are pairs of shakers that appear to embrace each other. Many salt and pepper shakers are listed in other categories and can be located through the index at the back of this book.

Aunt Jemima, Yellow Shirt, Red Skirt, F & F Mold & Die Works, 5 ¼ In. 30.00
Bakelite, Marbled, Chrome Feet, Round, 1 ⅞ In. 110.00
Binoculars, Joan Of Arc Portrait, Marked, Porcelaine De France, c.1965, 3 ⅛ In. 24.00
Blue & White Lids, Ball Mason-USA 18.00
Bonzo The Dog, Japan 65.00
Bride & Groom, Cast Aluminum, Painted, Cork Stopper, 3 ½ In. 12.00
Cattails, Script Lettering, White, Black, Red, Tipp City, 2 ¾ In. 50.00
Dean Martin & Jerry Lewis, Guess Who, Pottery, Napco, 3 ¼ In. 560.00
Delphite Blue, Basket Weave, Jeannette, 6 In. 42.00
Eskimos Kissing, On Bench, White, Yellow, Ceramic, Wood, c.1965, 4 ½ x 4 In. 26.00
Gay Fad, Outlined Fruit, Frosted, 3 ¾ In. 28.00
Kromex, Aluminum, Black Top, c.1960, 4 In. 18.00
Mammy, Butler, Ceramic, Japan, 5 In. 17.00
New York, Pink, Gilt Bands, Etched, Glass, Plastic Lid, 3 ½ x 1 ½ In. 40.00
Nodder, Chickens, Flowers, Porcelain, 4 ¼ x 3 In. 22.00
Nodder, Indian Man & Woman, Flirting, Teepee Base, Fire, Hatchet, Porcelain, 4 In. 33.00
Old Milwaukee, c.1971, 3 In. 5.00
Piel's Beer Brother, Bert & Harry, Ceramic, 1960s 215.00
Polar Bear & Penguin, Sterling Silver, David Andersen 170.00
Postman, Letterbox, British Royal Mail 35.00
Rabbit, Nodders, Hand Painted, Ceramic, 3 ½ x 3 In. 60.00
Rabbit, On Tree Stump, 1950-60 .... 25.00
Red, Ivory, Plastic, Melmac, Lustro Ware, 2 In. 6.00
Salty & Peppy, Cook Attire, White, Ceramic, Pearl China Co., 7 ½ In. 35.00
Spoon & Fork, Fork Ran Away With The Spoon, Green Legs, Japan, c.1900, 5 x 2 In. 60.00
Tappan Chefs, Blue, Yellow, Roman Arch, 3 ¾ x 2 ¼ In. 55.00
Telephone, Handset Shaker, Japan .... *illus* 28.00
Ultramarine, Jennyware 71.00
Uncle Sam, White, Red & Blue Top Hats, Glass 43.00
Vegetable Men, Py Miyao, 2 ¾ In. .... *illus* 50.00
Watkins Brand, Vanilla, Black Pepper, Plastic Stopper, 3 ½ & 2 ½ In. 15.00
West Bend, Copper Aluminum, Black Plastic Top, Insert, Box, c.1960, 4 In. 40.00
Woman's Head, Wide-Eyed, Open Mouth, Japan, 1950s, 1 ¾ x 1 ½ In. 38.00

Salopian, Cup & Saucer, Acorns, Handleless, c.1825
$234.00

Salopian, Teapot, Boy & Cow, Transfer, c.1825, 4 ½ In.
$351.00

Salt & Pepper, Telephone, Handset Shaker, Japan
$28.00

Salt & Pepper, Vegetable Men, Py Miyao, 2 ¾ In.
$50.00

TIP

Don't ever take your rings off and put them on the edge of the sink when you wash your hands. They can fall into the sink and down the drain or be forgotten and left behind.

TIP
Samplers stitched with silk are usually more valuable than those stitched with wool. Alphabets and pictures are more popular with buyers than religious messages.

Sampler, 4 Alphabets, Numbers, Verse, Green, White, Peach, S.T. Easton, 1835, 22 x 15 ¾ In.
$1210.00

Sampler, Alphabet, Gray Cats, Skirted Women, Willow Trees, Clarissa Crowell, 16 x 10 ½ In.
$1116.00

TIP
Do not store potpourri or other sachets with fabrics. The oil can harm fabric.

SALT GLAZE has a grayish white surface with a texture like an orange peel. It is a method of decoration that has been used since the eighteenth century. Salt-glazed pieces are still being made.

Churn, Impressed, Closed Handles, Van Loon & Boyden, c.1850, 2 Gal. 115.00
Crock, Brown Glaze, Handles, 13 ¼ x 15 ¼ In. 45.00
Jug, Batter, Tulip, Wreath, Tin Lid, Wood Handle, Evan R. Jones Pottery, c.1880, 10 In. 265.00
Plate, Reticulated, Scalloped Rim, 11 In. 351.00
Stein, Figural, Bearded Gentleman, Hands On Belly, Hinged, 13 ½ In. 288.00
Teapot, Melon Shape, Pewter Cover, Embossed, 10 x 6 x 6 In. 328.00

SAMPLERS were made in America from the early 1700s. The best examples were made from 1790 to 1840. Long, narrow samplers are usually older than square ones. Early samplers just had stitching or alphabets. The later examples had numerals, borders, and pictorial decorations. Those with mottoes are mid-Victorian. A revival of interest in the 1930s produced simpler samplers, usually with mottoes.

ABCDE

2 Alphabets, Flower, Birds, Chair, Bottles, Hanna Martins, 1830, Frame, 20 ¾ x 19 ¾ In. 440.00
2 Alphabets, Potted Flowers, Bird, Gilt Wood Frame, 22 ¼ x 21 ¼ In. 110.00
3 Alphabets, House, Leaf, Elizabeth Bousher, 1828, Frame, 17 ¾ x 12 ¾ In. 495.00
4 Alphabets, Numbers, Verse, Green, White, Peach, S.T. Easton, 1835, 22 x 15 ¾ In. . . . . *illus* 1210.00
4 Alphabets, Verse, Religious, Flowers, E. Robinson, Aged 8 Years, 1886, 14 x 19 ¼ In. 358.00
Adam & Eve, Flower Border, Margaret Stanley, 1821, 12 x 17 In. 590.00
Alphabet, 11 Lines, Syche Rue, November 1788, Wood Frame, 9 ¾ x 6 ¾ In. 431.00
Alphabet, Anne Marie Pearson, Fontstown, Kildare, 1884, Wool On Cotton, Frame, 10 ½ x 16 In. 59.00
Alphabet, Auguste Tescharek, 1881, Cross-Stich, Frame, 16 x 13 In. 190.00
Alphabet, Bird, Tree, Dog, Peacock, Jane Duncan, Age 13, 1844, Silk On Wool, 20 x 20 In. 880.00
Alphabet, Blue Bands, HMS.JB, 1847, Silk On Linen, Gilt Frame, 12 x 10 In. 323.00
Alphabet, Blue House, Vine Border, Susan Tyson, 1850s, Silk On Linen, Frame, 18 x 17 In. 702.00
Alphabet, Buildings, Pine Trees, Rhoda Brainerd, 1826, Silk On Linen, 18 x 16 ¾ In. 6169.00
Alphabet, Butterflies, Plants, Basket Of Fruit, Elizabeth Dean, Age 7, Silk, Linen, 14 x 19 In. . 352.00
Alphabet, Catherine A. Lowman, Frame, 1828, 8 x 11 In. 288.00
Alphabet, Dorcas G. Babcock, 10 Years, Rhode Island, c.1826, Silk On Linen, Frame, 17 x 21 In. 1175.00
Alphabet, Elizabeth Mary Kline, Aged 9, Eaton, Preble County, 1831, Frame, 19 x 14 ½ In. 823.00
Alphabet, Eunice P. Wyman, Middlesex County, 1824, Silk On Linen, Frame, 13 x 16 In. 940.00
Alphabet, Flower Border, Silk On Linen, 1839, 15 x 18 ¼ In. 6756.00
Alphabet, Flowers, Anna Smedely, 16 Years Old, 1810, Frame, 16 ¼ x 13 In. 2185.00
Alphabet, Flowers, Butterflies, AMF, 1858, 20 x 23 In. 224.00
Alphabet, Flowers, Elizabeth Wesler, 1844, Silk On Linen, Frame, 15 x 10 In. 353.00
Alphabet, Flowers, Mary Ainslie, Aged 9, 1870, Wool On Scrim, 21 ½ x 17 ¼ In. 259.00
Alphabet, Frances Elizabeth Davenport, 1822, Silk On Linen, 17 x 12 In. 293.00
Alphabet, Gray Cats, Skirted Women, Willow Trees, Clarissa Crowell, 16 x 10 ½ In. . . . . *illus* 1116.00
Alphabet, House, Margaret Wilson, 1838, Silk On Linen, 14 ¼ x 19 ¾ In. 345.00
Alphabet, Houses, Flowers, Trees, Sheep, Marie Noyes, Age 7, Mass., 1809, 17 x 17 In. 948.00
Alphabet, Joyce Beacon, Suffolk, England, Frame, 26 ¾ x 9 In. 940.00
Alphabet, Mary Ann Warren, Feb. 23, 1816, 7 Years, Silk, 16 x 16 In. 2450.00
Alphabet, Number, Religious, Susan Hasbrook, Aged 11, Silk On Linen, 1830, 18 x 21 In. 1292.00
Alphabet, Numbers, Angel Charlson, October 20, 1814, 12 ½ x 13 ¾ In. 293.00
Alphabet, Numbers, Basket Of Fruit, Birds, Shrubs, Tree, Adaline Taylor, 18 ½ x 19 In. 6463.00
Alphabet, Numbers, Cross-Stitch, 1813, 17 x 18 In. 1035.00
Alphabet, Numbers, Figures, Flower Baskets, Trees, House, England, 1835, Frame, 12 In. 410.00
Alphabet, Numbers, Flowerpots, Castle, Vine Border, Wool, Linen, Frame, c.1799, 16 ½ x 14 In. 259.00
Alphabet, Numbers, Flowers, Trees, Birds, Deer, Sarah Mullmer, c.1796, 14 ½ x 12 ¾ In. 575.00
Alphabet, Numbers, Nancy C Kelly, Born May 22, 1796, Silk On Linen, 20 In. 646.00
Alphabet, Numbers, Rebekah A. Baker, Charlestown, 15, 1812, Frame, 15 ½ x 15 ½ In. 936.00
Alphabet, Numbers, Verse, Birds, Flowers, Mary Joy, 1788, Frame, 16 x 9 ¾ In. 644.00
Alphabet, Numbers, Verse, Flower & 8-Point Star Border, c.1804, 17 x 20 In. 881.00
Alphabet, Numbers, Verse, Flowers, Vines, Animals Surrounding Frame, 12 x 13 In. 472.00
Alphabet, Numbers, Verse, Mary Ann Taylor, 1838, Silk On Linen, 18 x 17 In. 235.00
Alphabet, Polly Campbell, Age 10, Putney, Vermont, 1800, Silk On Linen, Frame, 11 x 15 In. . 5053.00
Alphabet, Trees, Birds, Flower Border, Anne Johnson, Age 7 Years, 1796, Frame, 14 x 11 In. . . 250.00
Alphabet, Urns Of Flowers, Peacocks, Birds, Cathren Kennedy, Silk, Linen, 16 x 11 In. 323.00
Alphabet, Verse, Ann Warner, Aged 12, 1828, Frame, 16 x 7 ½ In. 201.00
Alphabet, Verse, Berries, Louisa Bendall, Age 13, Silk On Wool, Frame, 15 x 18 In. 323.00
Alphabet, Verse, Flower Bouquet, Crewel Work, Frame, 1823, 23 x 20 In. 2750.00
Alphabet, Verse, Mary Murrell, Born 1715, Silk On Linen, England, 17 x 8 ¾ In. 1708.00
Alphabet, Verse, Schoolhouse, Silk On Linen, Frame, 19th Century, 12 x 16 In. 330.00
Alphabet, Verse, Tree, Animals, Flower Border, Linen, Frame, 19th Century, 13 x 15 In. 796.00
Alphabet, Vines, Dog, Silk On Linen, Frame, 5 x 8 In. 590.00

S

Alphabets, Numbers, Verse, Ann Scott Gleason, Silk On Linen, 21 x 17 In. 763.00
Animals, Scenes, Sarah Hill, March 14, 1823, 13 x 15 ½ In. 413.00
Anna Staddard, 9th Year, Friday March Second, 1798, Silk On Linen, 13 x 11 In. 705.00
Basket, Vines, Birds, Trees, Flower Basket, Nancy W. Shackford, 1809, Silk On Linen, 12 x 14 In. 1880.00
Brick Building, Flower, Sarah Camden, 11 Years, February 18, 1847, Frame, 14 x 23 In. 1035.00
Brick Building, Lion Crest, Initials, 1830, Silk On Linen, Frame, 17 ½ x 17 ½ In. 1093.00
Emma Whitehouse At Mrs. Horne's Seminary, Landscape, Girl, 1843, Frame, 20 x 24 In. . 1872.00
Family Record, Phebe A Balard, 11th Year, 1822, 17 x 19 In. 840.00
Family Register, Alphabet, Sarah Kimball, 1827, Frame, 17 x 16 ½ In. 1380.00
Flower Bouquet, Vine Border, Silk, Frame, 8 ¾ x 9 In. 1534.00
Flower Sprays, Leaping Stag, Vine Border, Frame, Ann Hoggard, Late 1700s, 16 x 13 In. 915.00
Flowers, Birds, Silk On Linen, Frame, 11 ¼ x 16 ½ In. 265.00
Flowers, Dogs, Bird, Strawberry Vine Border, Wool On Linen, Frame, 23 x 25 In. 324.00
Flowers, Leaves, Scenic, Elizabeth Sowden, Aged 12, 1833, 18 ½ x 17 ½ In. 330.00
Flowers, Verse, Arcaded Borders, Matilda Ann Charles, 1833, Silk On Wool, Frame, 20 x 16 In. . 176.00
Flowers, Verse, Betsey Ann Burnet, Aged 11, 1827, Silk On Wool, Frame, 16 ½ x 17 In. 529.00
Flowers, Verse, Prayer, Louisa Hazell, Aged 13 Years, 1875, 26 x 25 In. 590.00
Genealogy, Numbers, Coat Of Arms, August, 1821, Silk On Linen, 16 x 17 In. 1175.00
Hearts, Birds, Peacock, Caroline Street, 1832, Silk On Linen, Frame, 18 ½ x 9 ½ In. 470.00
House, Trees, Potted Flowers, Trellis, Poems, Massamar Family, 1832, 19 ½ x 19 In. 3575.00
Manor House, Chenille Lawn, Helen Dicks, Age 10, 1798, Silk On Wool, Frame, 25 x 29 In. . . 1645.00
Map, Sarah Beech, 1829, Silk On Linen, Frame, 25 x 23 In. 575.00
Memorial, Tombstone, For Mary Conant, By Sister Huldah, Age 12, Silk On Linen, 20 x 16 In. 575.00
Memorial, Willow, Tombstone, William Briggs, Age 11, Mass., c.1828, Silk On Linen, 19 x 19 In. 3525.00
Mourning, Memory Of John Atkinson, Died Ma 14, 1885, Frame, 33 x 30 In. . . . . *illus* 165.00
Numbers, Wrought By Euginia Spear, Ninth Year, Quaker, Silk On Linen, 1822, 17 x 12 In. . . 470.00
Potted Flowers, Tulip Vine Border, Agnes Turnbull, 1803, Painted Gauze, Frame, 10 x 8 In. . 3042.00
Scenic, Scottish, Marion Robertson, Aged 13, Aug. 1834, Silk On Wool, Frame, 22 x 17 In. . . . 2703.00
Town Scene, Church, Houses, Trees, Animals, Birds, A.C. Boyer, 1839, 17 x 19 ½ In. 7150.00
Verse, Adam & Eve, An Orphans Gift, Angels, Birds, Silk On Wool Gauze, Frame, 19 x 18 In. . . 529.00
Verse, Adam & Eve, Birds, Flowers, Eliz. Summers, 1808, Ogee Frame, 17 x 17 In. 1610.00
Verse, Adam & Eve, Flower Border, Margaret Stanley, 1821, 17 x 12 In. . . . . *illus* 590.00
Verse, Alphabet, Flower Vines, Hannah Baker, March 3, 1809, Silk On Wool, Frame, 14 x 14 In. 646.00
Verse, Alphabet, Flowering Vines, Harriet Atwood Brooks, Age 11, Silk On Linen, 19 x 18 In. . . 999.00
Verse, Alphabet, House, Mary Jones, Age 12, Shropshire, 1821, Silk On Wool, 19 x 13 In. 823.00
Verse, Alphabet, Lucinda Parsons, Silk On Linen, Burl Walnut Frame, 10 x 14 In. 1485.00
Verse, Alphabet, Numbers, Sarah Ann Huff, 1831, Wool On Linen, Frame, 20 x 23 In. 460.00
Verse, Alphabet, Vine, Oval, Sarah Waters, England, Silk On Wool, Frame, 18 ½ x 16 ½ In. . . . 705.00
Verse, Alphabets, Flower Urns, Pine Trees, Keziah Jeffs, Aged 12, 1821, 13 x 12 In. 2300.00
Verse, Alphabets, Martha Frost, Age 6, January 28, 1769, Silk On Linen, Frame, 8 ½ x 8 In. . . 588.00
Verse, Alphabets, Sawtooth Border, Mary Bowman, Age 12, 1830, Silk On Linen, 19 x 18 In. . . 460.00
Verse, Alphabets, Strawberry, Vine Border, 1795, Silk On Linen, Frame, 11 x 18 ½ In. 206.00
Verse, Cherubs, House, Stags, Trees, Vine Border, Sarah Sheldrake, Age 13, 1836, 18 x 20 In. . 764.00
Verse, Church, Graveyard, Mary Ann Latham, 1828, 13 ¾ x 15 ¾ In. 633.00
Verse, Doves, Butterflies, Flowers, 2 Houses, Anna Wilfong, 1825, Frame, 16 x 17 ½ In. 644.00
Verse, Elisabeth Brown Woodaman, Halifax National School, 1822, Silk On Linen, 21 x 11 In. 646.00
Verse, Elizabeth Macbeth, Aged 12 Years, 1819, 13 x 16 In. 561.00
Verse, Elizabeth Richardson, 8 Years, New York, January 29, 1829, Silk On Linen, 20 x 21 In. . 633.00
Verse, Flower Band, Elizabeth Flockhart, 1760, Silk On Wool, Frame, 14 x 15 In. 1380.00
Verse, Flower Border, Plants, Dogs, Crowns, Hearts, Ann White, 1833, 16 x 17 ½ In. 403.00
Verse, Flowers, Birds, Ann Parkinson, 1803, England, Frame, 20 ½ x 22 ½ In. 2340.00
Verse, House, Ann Richardson, Silk On Linen, 23 ½ x 18 ½ In. 805.00
Verse, House, Crowns, Angels, Baskets, Mary Drummond, July 1830, 19 ½ x 12 ½ In. 1840.00
Verse, House, Flowers, Birds, M. Cathrine Metchger, 1863, Frame, 14 ½ x 15 In. 550.00
Verse, House, Rachel Skiles, Age 14, Lancaster County, 1806, Silk On Linen, Frame, 14 x 14 In. 1410.00
Verse, House, Red, Sheep, Grapevine, Mary Ann Crowe, Dauphin, Pa., 1836, 25 x 21 In. 16100.00
Verse, Mary Palmer, Aged 10, 1785, Silk On Wool, 19 ¾ x 14 ½ In. 403.00
Verse, Peacocks, Sarah Kingston, Aged 7, 1818, Frame, 12 x 15 ½ In. 475.00
Verse, Religious, Flower Wreath Border, Mary Ann Hyatt, 1833, Silk On Gauze, Frame, 17 x 15 In. 352.00
Verse, Scenes, Mary Ellingworth, 1798, 19 x 23 ½ In. 944.00
Verse, Trees, Animals, Strawberry, Vine, Hannah Harvey, Linen, Frame, 11 ¼ x 12 In. 690.00

SAMSON and Company, a French firm specializing in the reproduction of collectible wares of many countries and periods, was founded in Paris in the early nineteenth century. Chelsea, Meissen, Famille Verte, and Chinese Export porcelain are some of the wares that have been reproduced by the company. The firm uses a variety of marks on the reproductions. It is still in operation.

Box, Globular, Lid, Rose Finial, Oval Cartouches, Purple Net, Early 1900s, 5 ½ In., Pair 460.00

Sampler, Mourning, Memory Of John Atkinson, Died Ma 14, 1885, Frame, 33 x 30 In.
$165.00

Sampler, Verse, Adam & Eve, Flower Border, Margaret Stanley, 1821, 17 x 12 In.
$590.00

TIP

The embroidery on linens and dresses should be raised. Iron properly or it will flatten. Put the embroidery face down on a soft towel, then press.

As always, the edited listings in *Kovels' Antiques & Collectibles Price Guide 2010* aren't available on any website, but readers should visit Kovels.com for information on trends, tips, reproductions, marks, old prices, and more!

Samson, Box, Hinged Lid, Flowers, Farm, Veuve Perrin Of Marseilles, c.1840, 2 x 3 ½ In.
$330.00

Samson, Box, Purple Net, Oval Cartouches, Rose Finial, Marked, Late 19th Century, 5 ½ In., Pair
$440.00

Sandwich Glass, Basket, Fruit, Fiery Opalescent, Openwork, 32-Point Rim, 8 x 8 ⅜ In.
$17800.00

TIP

Wear rubber gloves when handling bleaching materials, strong solvents, or other harsh chemicals.

Box, Hinged Lid, Flowers, Farm, Veuve Perrin Of Marseilles, c.1840, 2 x 3 ½ In. . . . . *illus* 330.00
Box, Purple Net, Oval Cartouches, Rose Finial, Marked, Late 19th Century, 5 ½ In., Pair *illus* 440.00
Figurine, Dog, Pug, Female, Male, Collar, Gilt Spheres, Blue Ribbon, 1890s, 4 In., Pair. 750.00
Figurine, Man, Holding Grape, Leaning On Tree Trunk, Blue Crossed Sword Mark, 11 In. . . . 125.00
Group, 2 Cherubs Attending Lady, Gilt & Painted Enamel Designs, Marked, c.1885, 9 ¼ In. . . 385.00
Lamp, 2-Light, Flowers, Armorial, 25 In., Pair 250.00

SANDWICH GLASS is any of the myriad types of glass made by the Boston and Sandwich Glass Works in Sandwich, Massachusetts, between 1825 and 1888. It is often very difficult to be sure whether a piece was really made at the Sandwich factory because so many types were made there and similar pieces were made at other glass factories. Additional pieces may be listed under Pressed Glass and in related categories.

Basket, Fruit, Fiery Opalescent, Openwork, 32-Point Rim, 8 x 8 ⅜ In. . . . . *illus* 17800.00
Candlestick, Acanthus, Opaque Blue Socket, Clambroth Base, c.1865, 11 In. 374.00
Candlestick, Blown Ring, Beehive Domed Foot, 1813-35, 9 x 2 In. . . . . *illus* 16500.00
Candlestick, Crucifix, Citron Green, Hexagonal Base, 1840-80, 11 ½ In. 1430.00
Candlestick, Crucifix, Jade Green, Hexagonal Base, 11 x 5 In. . . . . *illus* 6215.00
Candlestick, Dolphin, Amber, Hexagonal Base, 1850-70, 6 ¾ x 4 ¼ In. . . . . *illus* 1430.00
Candlestick, Dolphin, Canary Yellow, Hexagonal Socket, Base, 6 ¾ In., Pair . . . . *illus* 295.00
Candlestick, Dolphin, Yellow-Green, Double Step Base, 9 ⅞ In. *illus* 362.00
Candlestick, Hexagonal, Yellow, c.1840, 10 ¾ In. 226.00
Candlestick, Loop & Petal, Blue, Wafer, c.1850, 6 ¾ In., Pair. 424.00
Candlestick, Loop & Petal, Electric Blue, 7 In., Pair 1430.00
Candlestick, Petal, Blue, Hexagonal Base, Wafer, 7 ¼ In.. . . . . 311.00
Cologne, Opaque White Cut To Green, 7-Point Lip, Hollow Stopper, 1850-70, 9 ¾ In. 2010.00
Cologne, Sapphire Blue, Flared Mouth, Stopper, 14 ¾ In.. . . . . 1725.00
Compote, Loop & Leaf, Amethyst, Gauffered Rim, 1850-70, 6 x 7 ⅜ In. . . . . *illus* 12100.00
Cup & Saucer, Lacy, Diamond Scroll & Lily, Toy, c.1845, 1 ⅛ In.. . . . . 84.00
Cup Plate, Fiery Opalescent, Floral Band, Plain Rim, c.1835, 3 ⅝ In.. . . . . 170.00
Cup Plate, Hearts & Arrow Lyre Band, Medium Blue, Scalloped Rim, c.1835, 3 ½ In. . . . *illus* 102.00
Cup Plate, Waffle Star, 15 Scallops, Small Dots, c.1835, 3 ½ In.. . . . . 57.00
Dish, Cover, Figural, Melon, Blue, 11-Rib Base, 1850, 5 ½ x 4 In.. . . . . 1100.00
Eggcup, Loop, Firery Opalescent, Rayed Base, 3 ½ In.. . . . . 180.00
Goblet, Morning Glory, Clear, Flint, 6 In. . . . . *illus* 66.00
Lamp, Fluid, Heart & Punty Pattern, Double Camphene Burners, 11 In.. . . . . 165.00
Lamp, Fluid, White, Lions On Plinth, 7 ¼ In.. . . . . 275.00
Lamp, Fluid, White Cut To Amethyst, Double Marble Base, 1800s, 12 ½ In., Pair 1210.00
Lamp, Kerosene, Opalescent, Gilt, Applied Glass Ring Hanger, c.1850, 8 In. 136.00
Lamp, Kerosene, Quatrefoil, Punty, Marble Base, c.1860, 16 In.. . . . . 3600.00
Lamp, Kerosene, Winter Cottage Scene, Brass Foot, c.1870-90, 16 In. 311.00
Lamp, Oil, Clear, Cranberry Shade, Bronze Stem, Marble Base, c.1875, 12 In.. . . . . 590.00
Lamp, Oil, Cobalt Blue, 10 In.. . . . . 1430.00
Lamp, Whale Oil, Applied Handle, Pewter Collar, Burner, c.1875, 3 In. 147.00
Lamp, Whale Oil, Blown, 12 Flutes, Peg, c.1825, 4 In.. . . . . 72.00
Lamp, Whale Oil, Peacock Blue, 6-Panel Front, 1840-60, 10 ¼ x 3 ⅛ In. 3102.00
Lamp, Whale Oil, Sapphire Blue, Elongated Loop, 1840-60, 3 x 2 ½ In. . . . . *illus* 1870.00
Lamp, Whale Oil, Translucent Starch Blue, 1840-60, 10 ⅛ x 3 In., Pair . . . . *illus* 2320.00
Lamp, Whale Oil, Tulip & Columnar, Blue Alabaster, c.1850, 12 ½ x 4 ¼ In.. . . . . 565.00
Mug, Fine Rib With Band, Amethyst, Molded Handle, Toy, c.1875, 1 ¾ In. 254.00
Paperweight, 2 Blueberries, Central Stem, Concave Base, c.1875, 1 ¾ In. 1140.00
Paperweight, 5 Purple Plums, Green Leaves, Clear Ground, 2 ¾ In.. . . . . 420.00
Paperweight, Dahlia, Cobalt Blue, Goldstone Petals, Cane Center, 1 ¾ x 3 ¼ In.. . . . . 3672.00
Paperweight, Pear Bouquet, Red, Stem, Leaves, 2 ⅞ x 1 ⅞ In.. . . . . 720.00
Paperweight, Poinsettia, Blue Petals, Leaves, Stem, Clear Ground, 2 ¼ In. . . . . . . 690.00 to 750.00
Paperweight, Poinsettia, Millefiori Cane, Blue & Red Petals, Jasper Ground, 2 ¾ In. 720.00
Paperweight, Weed Flower, Millefiori Cane, 6 Blue Petals, Yellow Dots, 2 ½ In.. . . . . 1200.00
Perfume Bottle, Blown Molded, Ribbed, Green, Stopper, c.1860, 5 In. 158.00
Pitcher, Champagne, Overshot, Ice Bladder, Triangular Rim, Rope Handle, c.1885, 11 In. . . . 120.00
Pitcher, Overshot, Blue, Bulbous, Pontil, Applied Amber Reeded Handle, c.1880, 8 In.. . . . . . . 390.00
Puff Box, Hobnail, Clambroth, Applied Green Stem Finial, c.1860, 5 ¼ x 3 In.. . . . . 254.00
Salt, Eagle, Empire Sofa Shape, 4 Scrolled Feet, c.1840, 2 x 2 ⅝ In.. . . . . 452.00
Salt, Eagle & Ship, Leafy Chain Rim, c.1840, 1 ⅞ In.. . . . . 509.00
Salt, Lafayette Steamboat, Pale Blue, Opalescent, Marked, c.1840, 1 ⅝ x 3 ⅝ In. 1320.00
Salt, Lyre, Medium Blue, 4 Scrolled Feet, c.1840, 1 ⅞ x 2 ⅛ In. 1080.00
Salt, Strawberry Diamond, Salt, Purple Blue, Scallop & Point Rim, c.1835, 1 ⅞ x 2 ⅛ In.. . . . . 158.00
Shelf Support, Translucent Blue, Sanded, Column, 1850-65, 6 ½ In. . . . . *illus* 1100.00
Sugar, Cover, Acanthus, Lacy, Fiery Opalescent, Scalloped Foot, 1835-50, 5 ½ In. . . . . . *illus* 465.00

Sandwich Glass, Candlestick, Blown Ring, Beehive Domed Foot, 1813-35, 9 x 2 In.
$16500.00

Sandwich Glass, Candlestick, Dolphin, Canary Yellow, Hexagonal Socket, Base, 6 ¾ In., Pair
$295.00

Sandwich Glass, Cup Plate, Hearts & Arrow Lyre Band, Medium Blue, Scalloped Rim, c.1835, 3 ½ In.
$102.00

Sandwich Glass, Candlestick, Crucifix, Jade Green, Hexagonal Base, 11 x 5 In.
$6215.00

Sandwich Glass, Candlestick, Dolphin, Yellow-Green, Double Step Base, 9 ⅞ In.
$362.00

Sandwich Glass, Goblet, Morning Glory, Clear, Flint, 6 In.
$66.00

Sandwich Glass, Candlestick, Dolphin, Amber, Hexagonal Base, 1850-70, 6 ¾ x 4 ¼ In.
$1430.00

Sandwich Glass, Compote, Loop & Leaf, Amethyst, Gauffered Rim, 1850-70, 6 x 7 ⅜ In.
$12100.00

Glass Patterns

The early 1840s were the time of pressed glass table settings. Early patterns were simple, with heavy loops or ribbed effects. The 1870s brought more elaborate naturalistic patterns. Clear and frosted patterns with figures were in style during the 1870s. Overall patterns that were slightly geometric in feeling were in style by 1880, and patterns such as Daisy and Button and Hobnail came into vogue. Colored pressed glass patterns became popular after the Civil War.

Sandwich Glass, Lamp, Whale Oil, Sapphire Blue, Elongated Loop, 1840-60, 3 x 2 ½ In.
$1870.00

Sandwich Glass, Lamp, Whale Oil, Translucent Starch Blue, 1840-60, 10 ⅛ x 3 In., Pair
$2320.00

TIP

Don't put a runner or a vase on your wooden table if it is in sunlight. Eventually the finish will fade around the ornaments and leave a shadow of the items on the wood.

Sandwich Glass, Shelf Support, Translucent Blue, Sanded, Column, 1850-65, 6 ½ In.
$1100.00

Sandwich Glass, Sugar, Cover, Acanthus, Lacy, Fiery Opalescent, Scalloped Foot, 1835-50, 5 ½ In.
$465.00

Sandwich Glass, Vase, Elongated Loop, Fiery Opalescent, Bisecting Lines, 1840-70, 4 ¾ In.
$132.00

Sandwich Glass, Vase, Loop, Emerald Green, 7-Flute Rim, 9 ¼ x 3 ⅜ In.
$3300.00

Sandwich Glass, Vase, Loop, Sapphire Blue, Flared Rim, 1840-60, 11 ¼ In., Pair
$6050.00

Sandwich Glass, Vase, Three Printie Block, Amethyst, Flared Rim, 1845-60, 10 x 5 ⅛ In.
$2420.00

Sugar, Cover, Cobalt Blue, Octagonal, Paneled, 1860-80, 5 ½ In. 633.00
Toothpick, Cover, Basket, Alabaster, Pressed, Ribbed Finial, Handles, c.1850, 3 ⅞ x 2 ¼ In. .. 102.00
Toothpick, Cover, Basket, Jade Green, Ribbed Knop Finial, 1850-70, 3 ⅞ In. 1430.00
Toothpick, Cover, Jade Green, Cover, c.1850, 3 In. 1469.00
Tumbler, Fine Rib With Band, Jade Green, Toy, c.1875, 1 ¾ In. 311.00
Tumbler, Lemonade, Blue, Green, Ribbed, Thick Rim Band, 1 ¾ x 1 ¾ In. 396.00
Vase, Elongated Loop, Fiery Opalescent, Bisecting Lines, 1840-70, 4 ¾ In. .... *illus* 132.00
Vase, Loop, Emerald Green, 7-Flute Rim, 9 ¼ x 3 ⅜ In. .... *illus* 3300.00
Vase, Loop, Emerald Green, c.1840, 9 ¼ In. 3390.00
Vase, Loop, Sapphire Blue, Flared Rim, 1840-60, 11 ¼ In., Pair .... *illus* 6050.00
Vase, Opal, Red, Blue Loops, Pontil, Ruffled Rim, 1876, 8 In., Pair 9605.00
Vase, Printie, Lines, Amethyst, Petal Rim, 9 In. 935.00
Vase, Sandwich Tulip, Green, Panels, c.1845, 10 In. 14690.00
Vase, Three Printie Block, Amethyst, Flared Rim, 1845-60, 10 x 5 ⅛ In. .... *illus* 2420.00
Vase, Trumpet, Amethyst, Cupped, 9 In., Pair 863.00
Vase, Trumpet, Swirling Smoky Amethyst, Pontil, 1840-60, 13 In., Pair .... *illus* 2200.00
Vase, Trumpet, Three Printie Block, Canary Yellow, Scalloped Rim, Footed, 12 In., Pair 1100.00
Vase, Tulip, Canary Yellow, Scalloped Rim, 1840-60, 10 ¼ x 5 In. .... *illus* 660.00
Vase, Tulip, Emerald Green, Red Amber Striations, 8-Sided Base, 1845-65, 10 In. 3600.00
Vial, Medicine, Aquamarine, Pontil, Rack, 1830-40, 5 ⅛ In., 12 Piece .... *illus* 99.00
Whimsy, Darning Ball, Blown, Mottled Opal & Cobalt Blue, Teal, Rose, Amber, 6 In. ..... *illus* 120.00
Wine, Horn Of Plenty, 12 Piece 1315.00
Witch's Ball, Deep Red, Pontil Mark, 1850, 4 ½ In. 410.00
Witch's Ball, Red & Green Splotches, Plaster Lining, Pontil, c.1875, 5 In. 452.00

SARREGUEMINES is the name of a French town that is used as part of a china mark. Utzschneider and Company, a porcelain factory, made ceramics in Sarreguemines, Lorraine, France, from about 1775. Transfer-printed wares and majolica were made in the nineteenth century. The nineteenth-century pieces, most often found today, usually have colorful transfer-printed decorations showing peasants in local costumes.

Bank, Tuba Player, White Outfit, Black Shoes, Marked, 6 In. 380.00
Basket, Potpourri, Morning Glories, Reticulated Border, Footed, 5 x 10 ¼ In. 259.00
Compote, Majolica, Dolphin Base, 10 x 12 ½ In. 460.00
Dessert Set, Pansies, Platter, Plates, 11 ½ & 8 In., 10 Piece 58.00
Dish, Corncob Shape, Yellow, Green, Majolica, 13 In., Pair 234.00
Dish, Mulberry, Wireware Basket, 1800s, 5 ¾ & 9 ¾ In. 30.00
Oyster Plate, 6 Wells, Dark Green, 10 In. 23.00
Oyster Plate, 6 Wells, Gray Green, 9 ½ In. 12.00
Oyster Plate, Shell & Seaweed, Green, Textured, Majolica, 9 ¼ In. 46.00
Pitcher, Figural, Admiral, Blue Collar, Majolica, 7 In. 115.00
Pitcher, Figural, Bulldog, Majolica, 6 ½ In. 748.00
Pitcher, Figural, Judge, Majolica, 6 ½ In. 115.00
Pitcher, Figural, Lion, Majolica, 7 In. 1093.00
Pitcher, Figural, Woman With Bonnet, Majolica, 7 In. 316.00
Pitcher, Green Leaves, Blue Ground, Footed, Majolica, c.1900, 11 ½ In. 50.00
Plate, Children Playing, Embossed, Scalloped, Pink Floral Border, 8 ½ In. 125.00
Plate, Couple Baking, Embossed, Scalloped, Pink Floral Border, 8 ½ In. 125.00
Plate, Seafood, Fish Shape, 9 ½ In., 8 Piece 29.00
Plate, Strawberries, Turquoise, Majolica, 8 In. 127.00
Plate, Transfer Figural Scenes, 8 ¾ In., 7 Piece 60.00
Tray, Fish, Dark Green, Majolica, 21 In. 58.00
Tureen, Fruit Covered, 7 ½ In. 58.00
Tureen, Grapevines, Attached Underplate, 7 x 7 ½ In. 403.00
Vase, 4 Handles, Crystalline Glaze, 5 ⅝ In. 518.00
Vase, Bulbous, Olive Green Crystalline Glaze, 10 ¼ In. 288.00
Vase, Woman, Fruit, Flowers, Blue, Yellow, Gold, Faience, Signed, 14 x 7 In. 120.00
Wall Pocket, Basket Weave, Blackberries, Trellis Back, 8 ½ In. 104.00

SASCHA BRASTOFF made decorative accessories, ceramics, enamels on copper, and plastics of his own design. He headed a factory, Sascha Brastoff of California, Inc., in West Los Angeles, from 1953 until about 1973. He died in 1993. Pieces signed with the signature *Sascha Brastoff* were his work and are the most expensive. Other pieces marked *Sascha B.* or with a stamped mark were made by others in his company.

Box, Cover, Abstract Fish, Gold, Blue, Signed, Rooster Mark, 5 x 8 In. 135.00
Candy Dish, Cover, Seated Figure, Turban, Mottled Gray Matte Glaze, Signed, 5 ¾ In. 149.00

Sandwich Glass, Vase, Trumpet, Swirling Smoky Amethyst, Pontil, 1840-60, 13 In., Pair
$2200.00

Sandwich Glass, Vase, Tulip, Canary Yellow, Scalloped Rim, 1840-60, 10 ¼ x 5 In.
$660.00

Sandwich Glass, Vial, Medicine, Aquamarine, Pontil, Rack, 1830-40, 5 ⅛ In., 12 Piece
$99.00

Sandwich Glass, Whimsy, Darning Ball, Blown, Mottled Opal & Cobalt Blue, Teal, Rose, Amber, 6 In.
$120.00

S

Plate, Green Ground, Blue Flowers, Enamel, Copper, 12 In. 58.00
Tobacco Jar, Cover, Figural, Pipe, Houses, Signed, 8 In. 125.00
Vase, Blue, Horse, Brown, White, Signed, California USA, 9 ¾ x 8 In. 70.00

SATIN GLASS is a late nineteenth-century art glass. It has a dull finish that is caused by hydrofluoric acid vapor treatment. Satin glass was made in many colors and sometimes has applied decorations. Satin glass is also listed by factory name, such as Webb, or in the Mother-of-Pearl category in this book.

Biscuit Jar, Pink, Diamond Quilted, Metal Lid, Handle, c.1870, 9 x 6 In. 146.00
Biscuit Jar, Pink, Enamel Leaves, Flowers, Berries, Metal Lid, Handle, 8 ½ In. 180.00
Candlestick, Figural, Woman Kneeling, Cachepot Base, Pink, 1930s, 6 In., Pair .. 235.00 to 310.00
Cologne, White Stylized Flowers, Leaves, Silver Screw Cap, 5 In. 403.00
Perfume Bottle, Aqua, Sterling Silver Lid, c.1890, 4 x 3 In. 351.00
Perfume Bottle, Pink, Diamond Quilted, Gilt Metal Ormolu Collar & Lid, 4 In. 500.00
Powder Jar, Lovebirds, Green, Embossed Flowers, L.E. Smith 95.00
Rose Bowl, Blue, Lavender Flowers, Enameled, Crimped Rim, Round, 4 In. 50.00
Rose Bowl, Enameled Flowers, Green Swirls, White Interior, Cupped Rim, 5 ½ In. 1210.00

SATSUMA is a Japanese pottery with a distinctive creamy beige crackled glaze. Most of the pieces were decorated with blue, red, green, orange, or gold. Almost all Satsuma found today was made after 1860, especially during the Meiji Period, 1868–1912. During World War I, Americans could not buy undecorated European porcelains. Women who liked to make hand-painted porcelains at home began to decorate plain Satsuma. These pieces are known today as "American Satsuma."

Bottle, Women, Applied Twisted Dragons, 6 ⅔ In., Pair 350.00
Bowl, Daily Scenes Vignette Interior, Center Gold Phoenix, 19th Century, 5 ¼ x 12 In. 1287.00
Bowl, Mountains, Faces, Round, Cream, Gold Ground, 3 x 7 In. 468.00
Box, Cover, River Landscape, Pottery, Round, Signed, 20th Century, 3 ¾ In. 75.00
Censor, Foo Dog Finial, Footed, Handles, Late 19th Century, 10 ½ In. 325.00
Charger, Figures, Multicolored, Japan, c.1960, 16 In. 380.00
Dish, Beachside Scene, People With Boat, Multicolored, Gilt, 15 In. 490.00
Dish, Immortal With Attendant, Cloud Border, Enamel, Gilt Relief, Japan, 1900s, 8 ½ In. 250.00
Ewer, 100 Buddhist Saints, Dragon Spout, Handle, 19th Century, Japan, 7 In. .... 474.00 to 1007.00
Jar, Cover, Figures, Scene, Footed, 3 ¾ x 3 ½ In. 1880.00
Jar, Landscape, Tapered, Birds, Gold Outline, 7 ½ In., Pair 90.00
Oyster Plate, 6 Wells, Birds, Fish, Flowers, 9 In. 863.00
Plate, Birds By Tree, Gold Scalloped Rim, Signed, 9 ⅞ In. 100.00
Tea Caddy, Cover, Earthenware, Japan, Early 20th Century, 5 ½ x 4 In. 82.00
Tea Caddy, Earthenware, Hexagonal Shape, Man Finial, c.1880-1900, 6 ¼ x 3 ¼ In. 1762.00
Tea Set, Dragons, Immortals, Japan, Signature Cartouches, c.1900, 9 Piece 353.00
Teapot, Flowers, 6-Sided, 3-Footed, 11 x 12 In. 1700.00
Temple Jar, Lid, Separate Base, Mask Feet, Foo Dog Handle, Finials, 30 In. 264.00
Urn, Cover, Scene, Figures, Earthenware, Footed, 3 ¼ x 3 In. 1057.00
Urn, Flower Cart Design, Wood Stand, 14 In. 2800.00
Urn, Men, Women, Houses, Multicolored, Earthenware, Japan, 25 x 19 In. 468.00
Vase, Birds, Flowers, Seals, Molded Basketry, 19th Century, 18 In. 1007.00
Vase, Bulbous, Flowers, Multicolored, Earthenware, 7 ¼ x 3 ½ In. 998.00
Vase, Conifer, Prunus, Willow, Blue, Gilt, 4-Sided, Sekizan Mark, 1890, 5 In., Pair ...... *illus* 700.00
Vase, Immortals, Earthenware, Painted, Japan, Early 20th Century, 15 In. 266.00
Vase, Kinkozan, Cloisonne, Open Shape Cartouches, Gilt, Scenic, Late 1800s, 11 ¾ In. 374.00
Vase, Mille Fleurs, Multicolored, Gold Ground, Gilt Rim, Japan, Early 1900s, 4 ⅜ In., Pair ... 345.00
Vase, Quadrilateral, Multicolored, Gilt, Roundels, Navy Ground, Japan, 4 ¾ In., Pair 805.00
Vase, Roses On Neck, Japanese Figures, River, Bridge, S. Kinkozan, c.1900, 12 In. 1404.00
Vase, Samurai Warriors, Figural, Foo Dog Base, 10 In. 550.00
Vase, White Flower, Blue Ground, 24 In. 4000.00
Vase, Wooded Scene, Gilt, White Ground, c.1875, 5 In. 117.00
Vase, Mounted On Recumbent Elephant, Wooden Base, Hododa, c.1900, 3 ⅝ In., Pair 1840.00

SATURDAY EVENING GIRLS, *see Paul Revere Pottery category.*

SCALES have been made to weigh everything from babies to gold. Collectors search for all types. Most popular are small gold dust scales and special grocery scales.

Balance, Brass, Cast Iron, Gold Painted Details, Round & Square Pans, 54 x 53 In. 230.00
Balance, Brass, Iron Base, Victorian, 19th Century, 45 x 35 In. 585.00

Satsuma, Vase, Conifer, Prunus, Willow, Blue, Gilt, 4-Sided, Sekizan Mark, 1890, 5 In., Pair
$700.00

Scale, Balance, Dayton, Painted, 28 In.
$800.00

Scale, Computing, Angldile Automatic Computing, 1904, 21 x 29 In.
$1000.00

Scale, Jockey, Chair, Edwardian, Mahogany, Iron, No. 1308, Avery, 1900, 38 In.
$10000.00

Balance, Brass, Molded Collar, 19th Century, 63 x 41 In. 5000.00
Balance, Brass, Weights, Stamped, Corssen, Germany, c.1856, 2 In., 7 Piece........ 70.00
Balance, Dayton, Painted, 28 In. .... *illus* 800.00
Balance, Degrave & Co., Brass, London, 22 ¾ x 15 x 12 In. 350.00
Candy, E.J. Hoadley, Brass, Iron, Signed, Hartford, Conn., 8 In. 110.00
Candy, National Store Specialty Co., Cast Iron, Green, 10 ½ x 10 ½ In........ 248.00
Candy, Pennsylvania, Shield, Red, White, Blue, 10 x 9 In........ 500.00
Candy, Red, Enamel, Pennsylvania, 22 ½ x 20 In........ 95.00
Candy, Wrigley's, Green Paint, 5 x 9 In. 523.00
Computing, Angldile Automatic Computing, 1904, 21 x 29 In. .... *illus* 1000.00
Desk, Brass & Walnut, Single Drawer, 2 Weights, England, 1900s, 1 & 2 Oz., 11 In. 89.00
Jockey, Chair, Edwardian, Mahogany, Iron, No. 1308, Avery, 1900, 38 In. .... *illus* 10000.00
Jockey, Chair, Edwardian, Oak, Leather, Painted Cast Iron, Padded, c.1900, 38 In........ 12250.00
Micrometer, Brass Pan, Marble, 10 Lb., 15 x 21 In........ 201.00
Micrometer, Dodge Co., Yonkers, N.Y., Nickel Plated Cast Iron, Marble, c.1903, 13 x 15 In..... 385.00
Micrometer, Dodge Scale Company, Cast Iron, Marble, Pat.1903, 2 x 12 In........ 590.00
Milk, Chatillon, 10 In. 15.00
Milk, Chatillon, 14 In. 25.00
Weighing, American Family Scale, Black, Gold, 1898-1909, 24 Lb., 9 ½ In. 38.00
Weighing, American Scale Mfg., Character Readings, Your Wate & Fate, 52 In. 44.00
Weighing, Aylmer Pump & Scale, Dairy, Iron, Brass, Signed, Ontario, 3 Discs 170.00
Weighing, Caille Bros., George Washington, Cast Iron, Copper, Penny, 76 x 23 x 27 In........ 9000.00
Weighing, Chicago Seale Co., Slide, Doctor's, Painted, Metal, 59 ½ In. 22.00
Weighing, Computing, Standard, Red, Gilt, Glass, Detroit, Mich., 35 In........ 550.00
Weighing, Countertop, Cast Iron, Brass, Nickel, Troemner, Philadelphia, 12 In........ 287.00
Weighing, Enterprise, White Paint, 20 Lb. Capacity, 18 In........ 195.00
Weighing, Gram, Weights, Accessories, Case, c.1900, 7 x 12 ½ In. 117.00
Weighing, Hanging, Salter, Brass, Bracket, 8 ¼ In. Diam........ 30.00
Weighing, N. Custer, Hanging, Iron, Stamped, 47 In. 122.00
Weighing, Salter, Brass, Round, Britain, 10 In. 43.00
Weighing, Toledo, No Springs, Highest Weight, 81 ½ In........ 110.00
Weighing, Watling Scale Co., Coin-Operated, Answers Questions, Mirror, 1950s, 61 x 26 In.... 1100.00
Weighing, Wrigley's Spearmint Pepsin Gum, Painted, Embossed, Brass, Metal, 7 ¾ x 10 In.... 943.00

SCHAFER & VATER, makers of small ceramic items, are best known for their amusing figurals. The factory was located in Volkstedt-Rudolstadt, Germany, from 1890 to 1962. Some pieces are marked with the crown and R mark, but many are unmarked.

Bottle, Figural, Rabbit, Porcelain, Marked, 9 ½ In. 552.00
Bottle, Man, Wine Bottles, Music Box, Impressed, Prohibition, 1920, 11 ½ In. 330.00
Figurine, Cook, 5 In. 184.00
Figurine, Woman With Basket, Marked, 4 ¾ In. 104.00

SCHNEIDER Glassworks was founded in 1917 at Epinay-sur-Seine, France, by Charles and Ernest Schneider. Art glass was made between 1917 and 1930. The company still produces clear crystal glass. See also the Le Verre Français category.

Charger, Brown, Etched, 14 In........ 400.00
Lamp, Mushroom Shade, Rose, Blue Frosted Ground, 3 Applied Punts, Cameo, Metal Base, 5 x 5 In. 1150.00
Vase, Clear, Frosted, Drip, Bullet Form, Signed, c.1930, 12 In........ 500.00
Vase, Clear, Yellow Enamel Stripes, Bottle Shape, Elongated Neck, 16 In........ 359.00
Vase, Fluted, Orange, Purple Saucer Foot, Iron Leaf, Berry Frame, 16 In. 690.00
Vase, Mottled Orange, Brown, Bulbous, Flared Rim, Footed, 15 In. 588.00
Vase, Mottled Purple Shaded To Pink, Cupped Rim, Signed, c.1925, 14 ½ In. .... *illus* 600.00
Vase, Mottled Yellow, Amethyst, Orange, Cameo, 9 ½ x 11 In. .... *illus* 1680.00
Vase, Orange, Mottled Purple, Bulbous, Footed, Signed, c.1920, 18 ¼ In........ 1000.00
Vase, Red Orange, Round, Signed, c.1920, 13 In........ 925.00
Vase, Rose, Amethyst, Yellow Splashes, Handles, Bulbous, c.1925, 8 ¾ In........ 598.00
Vase, Stick, Vertical Yellow Stripe, Bulbous, Base, 17 In. 190.00
Vase, Yellow Over Sapphire Blue, Iron Frame, 9 ¾ In........ *illus* 1035.00

SCIENTIFIC INSTRUMENTS of all kinds are included in this category. Other categories such as Barometer, Binoculars, Dental, Medical, Nautical, and Thermometer may also price scientific apparatus.

Alidade, 2 Fluid Levels, Telescope, Eyepiece, Calibrated, 10 In........ 259.00
Anemometer, Hot Air Balloon Wind Meter, J. Casartelli, Box, 1880s 82.00
Artillery Theodolite, No. 51/703, France, 6 In........ 310.00

Schneider, Vase, Mottled Purple Shaded To Pink, Cupped Rim, Signed, c.1925, 14 ½ In.
$600.00

Schneider, Vase, Mottled Yellow, Amethyst, Orange, Cameo, 9 ½ x 11 In.
$1680.00

Schneider, Vase, Yellow Over Sapphire Blue, Iron Frame, 9 ¾ In.
$1035.00

TIP

To remove the odor in a closed chest or trunk, try spreading cat litter on the inside. Close the drawer or lid for several days. Repeat until the odor seems gone. Then wash the inside and let it dry.

S

Scientific Instrument, Telescope, On Compass, T.S. Randolph, 7-In. Telescope
$650.00

Scientific Instrument, Transit, Engineer's, Gurley, Double Vernier, No. 11342, 13 ¾ In.
$600.00

Scrimshaw, Crossed Swords, Swordfish Bill, Patriotic Symbols, Wood Handle, Paint, 1800s, 34 In.
$3450.00

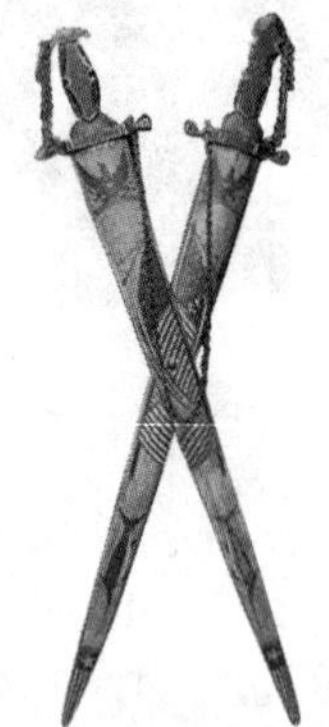

TIP
Vintage watches should be cleaned regularly, probably once a year.

Barograph, James Hicks, London, Oak Case, Glass Cover, Drawer, 9 x 16 In. 764.00
Brass, Ebonized Sheath, 3-Footed Stand, 19th Century, 15 x 30 ½ In. 750.00
Chronometer, Marine, Chas. Frodsham, Silvered Dial, Rosewood Box, 7 x 6 ½ In. 4140.00
Compass, Spencer & Co., London, Brass, Case, 3 ¼ In. 183.00
Compass, Surveyor's, Brass, Joseph M. Wightman, c.1845, 14 ½ x 6 In. 690.00
Compass, Surveyor's, Thos. Whitney Maker, 3 Spirit Levels, Needle, 6 x 13 ¾ In. 860.00
Computer, Mits Altair 8800, 1st Personal Computer, 1975 . . . . 3563.00
Distance Meter, Lee & Son, Portsmouth, Celluloid, Brass, Case, 3 ½ x 5 ½ In. 201.00
Drafting Set, Brass Protractor, Ebony & Bone Rules, Fishkin Case, 6 ½ In. 385.00
Graphoscope, Burl Veneer, Late 19th Century 500.00
Level, Farm, No. 2, Bostrom-Brady Mfg. Co., Carrying Case, 11 ½ In. 119.00
Magnifying Glass, Beveled Glass Handle, 14 In. 50.00
Microscope, Bausch & Lomb, Black & Nickel, Case, Accessories, 15 In. 381.00
Microscope, Bausch & Lomb, Brass, Early 20th Century, 14 ½ In. 61.00
Microscope, Bausch & Lomb, Brass, Painted Base, Cherry Case, 10 ½ In. 264.00
Microscope, Brass, Germany, Black Paint, Marked Shutz, Wood Case, 12 In. 235.00
Microscope, Compound, Bausch & Lomb, Brass, Patd. October 3, 1876 . . . . 830.00
Microscope, Compound, Brass, Rack & Pinion Coarse Focusing, Case, 11 In. 237.00
Microscope, Dissecting, Swift & Sons, London, Brass, Fitted Case, 13 ½ In. 1007.00
Microscope, E. Leitz, Wetzlar, No. 61258, Brass, Lacquered, Case, 13 In. 207.00
Microscope, Optometrist's, D.V. Brown, Brass, Lenses, Fitted Case, 11 ¼ In. 264.00
Microscope, Spencer, Black & Nickel, Box, Accessories, 14 ¾ In. 118.00
Microscope, Unitron, Metallurgical, Electric, Case, 14 ½ In. 118.00
Microscope, Wood Case, Brass Bail Pull, Diamond, 12 ½ x 13 ½ In. 275.00
Printing Press, Jobbing Platen Press, No. 4, London, 1890, 38 x 19 In. 240.00
Shoe X-Ray Fluoroscopic Equipment, Pedoskop, 3 Peep Shafts, 1925, 60 In. 2634.00
Spyglass, Reverse Tapered, 1 In., 24-In. Mahogany Tube 1067.00
Telescope, Bardou, Paris, Brass, Engraved, 2 Eyepieces, Tripod Base, 36 In. 711.00
Telescope, Bardou & Son, Brass, Wood Case, Signed, 19th Century, 50 In. 650.00
Telescope, Brass, Mahogany, Collapsible Tripod Base, 19th Century, 13 In. . . . . . . 600.00 to 732.00
Telescope, Brass, Oak, Tripod, 37 In. 321.00
Telescope, Brass, Wood Tripod, 20th Century, 39 In. 425.00
Telescope, France, Brass, 5-Draw, 37 ½ In. 316.00
Telescope, Library, Dollond, Tripod, 43-In. Mahogany Tube, 2 ¾ In. 3555.00
Telescope, On Compass, T.S. Randolph, 7-In. Telescope . . . . *illus* 650.00
Telescope, Refracting, Case, Tripod, Lenses, 58 In. 5750.00
Telescope, Refracting, Dacremont Ingeur Opticien, Brass, Tripod Mount, 45 In. 593.00
Telescope, Tabletop, Brass Scope, Tripod, Leather Wrapped, 12 ½ In. 690.00
Telescope, W. Ottoway, Orion Works, Brass, Mahogany Case, c.1935, 64 x 26 In. 1680.00
Thatcher's Calculator, Brass Mounted, Wood Drum, Patent 1932, 7 x 25 In. 518.00
Theodolite, Construction, Kern, No. KO-S, Fitted Case, Manual, 10 In. 259.00
Theodolite, Vernier, Weather, Brass Telescope, Vertical Scale, Case, 7 ¼ In. 385.00
Theodolite, Vernier, Weather Balloon, Telescope, Silvered Scale, Magnifier, Case, 9 In. 385.00
Transit, Engineer's, Gurley, Double Vernier, No. 11342, 13 ¾ In. *illus* 600.00
Transit, Exploration, Keuffel & Esser, Seagmuller Solar Attachment, 12 In. 805.00
Transit, Explorer, Gurley, Telescope, Case, Plumb Bob, Shield, Tripod, 11 x 8 ½ In. 2070.00
Transit, Keuffel & Esser, New York, Wood Case, 16 ½ x 13 In. 235.00
Transit Level, Dietzgen, Brass Fittings, Dovetailed Box, Marked, 16 In. 441.00
Wye Level, Scope, Young & Sons, c.1870, 16 ½ In. 518.00

SCRIMSHAW is bone or ivory or whale's teeth carved by sailors and others for entertainment during the sailing-ship days. Some scrimshaw was carved as early as 1800. There are modern scrimshanders making pieces today on bone, ivory, or plastic. Other pieces may be found in the Ivory and Nautical categories.

Box, Lid, Mahogany, Panbone, Engraved Eagle, House, Animals, Flowers, Oval, c.1850, 3 x 6 In. 1778.00
Busk, Bone, Incised Design, Hearts, Sunbursts, Flower, Urn, Building, Lyre, 1800s, 14 In. 316.00
Cane, Whale Ivory, Turk's Head Knot, Whale Bone Shaft, Baleen Spacers, c.1800, 33 ½ In. . . . 411.00
Corset Busk, Designs, 18th Century, 14 ½ x 2 In. 550.00
Cribbage Board, Seals, Birds, Inuit, Custom Stand, 24 In. 115.00
Cribbage Board, Walrus Tusk, Screw Cap, 4 Pegs, Engraved, c.1935, 10 In. 633.00
Cribbage Board, Walrus Tusk, Wooden Walrus Head, Inuit, c.1900, 9 In. 176.00
Crossed Swords, Swordfish Bill, Patriotic Symbols, Wood Handle, Paint, 1800s, 34 In. . . *illus* 3450.00
Letter Opener, Woman's Head Handle, Ship, Eagle, Flag, Liberty Dana, Patagonia, 19 In. . . . 2420.00
Pie Crimper, Whale Bone, Turned Handle, 7 ½ In. 316.00
Pie Crimper, Whale Ivory, Relief Carved, 19th Century, 10 x 2 In. 2250.00
Pie Crimper, Whale Ivory, Serpent Form, 19th Century, 7 x 2 ¾ In. 900.00

Pie Crimper, Whale Ivory, Wood Inlaid Grip, 4-Tine Fork, 19th Century, 8 In. 330.00
Spoon, Bone, Patriotic Shield, Lincoln Name, 1860, 4 ¾ In. 1314.00
Tooth, Whale, Pirate On Ship With Cannon, c.1800, 5 ¾ In. 764.00
Tusk, Carved, Inuit, 6 In. 351.00
Tusk, Whale Hunt Scene, Barque Hecla Ship, Silver End Cap Mount, c.1945, 16 In. 590.00
Walrus Tusk, 3 Figures, Eagle, Spread Wing, Late 1800s, 21 ¼ In. 1100.00
Walrus Tusk, Northwest Territory, 6 ½ In. 146.00
Whale's Tooth, Battle, USS Constitution & Guerriere, Woman Holding Book, 6 In. 2990.00
Whale's Tooth, Engraved Ship, Star, Bird, American Symbols, Text, 1800s, 6 In. 2133.00
Whale's Tooth, Figure, Standing, Coat-Of-Arms, Laurel Leaves, Imperial Robed, 6 In. 1610.00
Whale's Tooth, Harbor Scene, 8 ½ In. 3450.00
Whale's Tooth, Jack Tar, Free Trade, Sailors' Rights, Ship, W. Gilpin, c.1835, 6 x 3 In. 98500.00
Whale's Tooth, Portraits Of Young Women, Signed J.F. Bailey, c.1882, 4 In. 230.00
Whale's Tooth, Sailors, Whales, Harpoons, Ship, Signed M.S., Madagascar, 1864, 6 In. 6250.00
Whale's Tooth, Whaling Scene, 6 ½ In. 863.00
Whale's Tooth, Woman, Elegantly Dressed, Multicolored Base, 7 In. 12870.00
Yarn Swift, Sewing Stand, Mahogany, Whalebone, 2 Drawers, c.1850, 25 In. 14220.00

SEG, *see Paul Revere Pottery category.*

SEVRES porcelain has been made in Sevres, France, since 1769. Many copies of the famous ware have been made. The name originally referred to the works of the Royal Porcelain factory. The name now includes any of the wares made in the town of Sevres, France. The entwined lines with a center letter used as the mark is one of the most forged marks in antiques. Be very careful to identify Sevres by quality, not just by mark.

Bowl, Shell, Painted Cartouche, Musicians, Lovers, Blue Border, Birds, Gilt, c.1770, 9 In., Pair 805.00
Bulb Planter, Man & Woman, Blue, Gilt, Hand Painted Insert, Footed, 9 In. 250.00
Bust, Madame De Pompadour, Ruffled Blouse, Bisque, 31 ½ In. 2489.00
Centerpiece, Gilt Bronze, Pedestal, Porcelain, A. Daret, c.1875, 15 ½ x 15 In. 3510.00
Chamber Pot, Handle, Green Ground, Color Flower Panel, Gilt Flowers, Rim, Oval, 1781, 9 In. 8125.00
Charger, Court Ladies Of Louis XVI Surrounding The King, 19th Century, 23 In. 3290.00
Coffeepot, Gilt Banding, Napoleonic Crest, Berry Finial, 9 ¼ In. 323.00
Compote, People In Garden, Flower Cartouches, Flowers, Scrolls, Blue, Gilt, 10 x 13 In. 1100.00
Cordial Set, Cut Glass Stem, Vertical Blades, Multi-Cut Diamond, 4 ¼ x 1 ¼ In., 6 Piece 195.00
Creamer, Portrait Reserve, Mme. Elisabeth, 3 ¾ x 4 In. 41.00
Cup, Lid, Stand, Garlands, Flowers, Scallops, Twig Knop, Gilt, Green, Pink, Mark 9375.00
Cup, Lid, Stand, Painted Flower Filled Vases, Garlands, Scroll Handles, Gilt, c.1780, 10 In. 10625.00
Cup, Tea, Saucer, Green Ground, Crested Bird, Branch, Gilt Scrolls, Edge, Aloncle, c.1761, 5 In. 8750.00
Cup & Saucer, Birds Amid Green Leafy Designs, Gilt Trim, Blue Marks, c.1815, 5 ¼ In. 12690.00
Dresser Box, Cherubs, Bombe, Silver Overlay, Gilt, 6-Footed, Marked, 1846, 4 x 8 In. .... *illus* 1210.00
Dresser Box, Figures, In Bar, Yellow, Gilt, Oval, Marked, Late 19th Century, 5 ½ x 14 In. 800.00
Dresser Box, Flambe Red, Brass, Red Velvet Liner, 3 ½ x 6 ¾ In. 50.00
Ewer, Blue, Gold, Bird, Flowers, Man's Face Handle, c.1880, 16 x 7 In. 550.00
Figurine, Dog, Pinscher, Seated, Biscuit Porcelain, 1906, 14 ¾ x 11 ¼ In. 551.00
Figurine, Duck, Pottery, 6 In. 30.00
Figurine, Lovers, Flower Basket, White, Marked, 8 ½ In. 175.00
Figurine, Madame Pompadour, 10 ½ x 8 In. 375.00
Figurine, Woman, Holding Club, Leopard Headdress, Flower Skirt, Marked, 16 In. 990.00
Garniture Set, 2 Urns, Lids, Footed Centerpiece, Pastoral Cameos, Gold Rim, c.1950, 14 x 22 In. 4680.00
Group, La Fete Du Chateau, Lovers, Flower Filled Urn, Biscuit, c.1770, 8 In. 3750.00
Inkstand, Pansies, Boat Form, Gilt Ring Handles, Quill Holes, c.1910, 5 ⅛ In. 70.00
Inkwell, Cobalt Blue, Bronze Mounts, Bird Finial, Marked, MP Sevres, 3 ¼ x 4 ¾ In. 232.00
Inkwell, Earthenware, Ormolu Mounted, Cobalt Blue Mottled Glaze, Beaded Lid, 5 In. 267.00
Lamp, Cobalt, Gilt, Brass Mounts, Fleur-De-Lis Finial, Shade, Marked, 5 In., Pair 748.00
Mantel Set, Clock, 2 Urns, Enamel, Porcelain, Gilt, Blue, Flowers, Ornate, 16 & 11 In. 936.00
Mug, Milk, Rose Pompadour, Pink Ribbons, Flowers, Gilt Edge, Mereaud, c.1758, 5 In. 28125.00
Pedestal, Gilt Bronze & Onyx, Henrion, 42 x 11 x 11 In. 5265.00
Plaque, 2 Women, Girl, Dog, In Garden, 18th Century, 9 x 10 ½ In. 1000.00
Plaque, Women, Cupid, Velvet Matte, Silver Gilt Frame, Taxile Doat, 1881, 3 x 4 ½ In., Pair .. 840.00
Plate, Cabinet, Cobalt Blue, Jeweled, Gilt Profile Medallion, Laural, 9 ½ In. .... *illus* 652.00
Plate, Chateau De Chaumont, Cobalt Blue & Gilt Border, Empire Mark, 1804-14, 9 ½ In. 840.00
Plate, Dinner, Bleu Celeste Border, Floral Reserves, Courting Couple, Gilt, c.1837, 9 ½ In. ... 480.00
Plate, Napoleon Crest, Garlands, Putti, Pink, Gilt, Mark, Shadowbox Frame, 12 x 12 In., Pair 230.00
Plate, Napoleon Family Medallion Portraits, Green, Gilt, Signed, c.1815, 9 In., 12 Piece 12500.00
Plate, Portrait, Marie Antoinette, Cobalt Blue & Gilt Border, Signed Rou, 1771, 10 In. 275.00
Plate, Portrait, Marie Levzinska, Signed, Debrie, 9 ¼ In. 90.00

TIP

To easily remove wax that has dripped on a candlestick, put the candlestick in the freezer for about an hour. The wax will flake off.

Sevres, Dresser Box, Cherubs, Bombe, Silver Overlay, Gilt, 6-Footed, Marked, 1846, 4 x 8 In.
$1210.00

Sevres, Plate, Cabinet, Cobalt Blue, Jeweled, Gilt Profile Medallion, Laural, 9 ½ In.
$652.00

Sevres, Urn, Cover, Louis XVI Style, Flowers, Rose & White Ground, Gilt, 1890s, 14 ¾ In., Pair
$2100.00

Sewer Tile, Figure, Dog, Seated, Tooled Eyelashes, Ears, Early 1900s, 9 ½ In.
$118.00

Sewing, Box, Rosette Pincushion, Drawer, Painted, Softwood, 7 ¼ x 6 ¼ x 6 In.
$176.00

Sewing, Cabinet, Spool, Oak, 4 Drawers, Brass Pulls, c.1900, 14 x 23 x 14 In.
$315.00

TIP
Put a piece of cardboard between the back of the plate and the wire plate holder to keep the back from scratching.

Plate, Royal Blue Banded, c.1868, 9 ½ In., 6 Piece 960.00
Plate, Victorian Couple, Chateau Des Tuileriers, Flowers, Marked, 9 ½ In. 77.00
Plate, White Ground, Flower Sprays, Sprigs, Scrolls, Blue, Gilt Rim, c.1760, 10 In., 17 Piece.. 8125.00
Punch Bowl, Orange, Black, Gilt Border, France, 14 ¼ In. 266.00
Tray, Round Flower Center, Radiating Circles, Pierced Rim, Blue, Red, White, Gilt, c.1766, 7 In. 17500.00
Tureen, Vegetable, Cover, Berry Finial, Ironstone, Pearson, 11 In. 125.00
Urn, Courting Couple, Hand Painted, Blue, Gilt, Brass Base, Signed, A. Cora, 19 In. 250.00
Urn, Cover, Couple Walking, Enamel, Gold, Green Base, C. Rochette, c.1900, 18 x 5 In. 2047.00
Urn, Cover, Louis XVI Style, Flowers, Rose & White Ground, Gilt, 1890s, 14 ¾ In., Pair .. *illus* 2100.00
Urn, Dore Bronze, Cover, Woman Sitting In Garden, 17 ½ In. 2340.00
Urn, Lid, Hand Painted Pastoral Scene, Ormolu Base, Gilt, Signed Jocelyn, France, c.1890, 38 In. 4830.00
Urn, Lid, Painted, Floral Bouquets, Blue Ground, Gilt, Bronze Mounts, 1900s, 13 ¼ In., Pair . 805.00
Urn, Mantel, Blue Mottled Glaze, Dome Lid, Maiden, Cherub, Loop Handles, 14 In., Pair. 1659.00
Urn, Parisian Landmarks, Gold, Blue, Bolted, 2 Handles, c.1975, 13 In., Pair 708.00
Vase, Cobalt Blue, Medallion Scene, Fired Gold, c.1900, 18 x 7 In. 1989.00
Vase, Gold & Cream Crystals, Feathered Crystalline Ground, c.1900, 14 ½ In. 1920.00
Vase, Lid, Gilt Bronze Mounted, Painted, Courtesans, Landscape, c.1895, 34 In. 8125.00
Vase, Military Scene, Green, White, Gold, Cover, Square Base, 1804, 18 In. 600.00
Vase, Pink, Teal Stylized Flowers, Avocado Green, Art Nouveau, 11 ½ In. 767.00

SEWER TILE figures were made by workers at the sewer tile and pipe factories in the Ohio area during the late nineteenth and early twentieth centuries. Figurines, small vases, and cemetery vases were favored. Often the finished vase was a piece of the original pipe with added decorations and markings. All types of sewer tile work are now considered folk art by collectors.

Birdhouse, Tooled Bark Texture, Curved Roof, c.1900, 8 In. 176.00
Bust, William Howard Taft, Painted, Early 20th Century, 10 ¾ In. 2808.00
Chicken Waterer, Cylindrical, c.1900, 12 x 12 In. 235.00
Crock, Lid, 10 Gal. 50.00
Figure, Dog, Collie, Standing. 1250.00
Figure, Dog, Seated, Flat Head, Ohio, Early 20th Century, 9 ½ In. 230.00
Figure, Dog, Seated, Tooled Eyelashes, Ears, Early 1900s, 9 ½ In. .... *illus* 118.00
Figure, Dog, Spaniel, Oval Base, 7 ¾ In. 235.00
Figure, Dog, Spaniel, Salt Glazed Red Clay, Ohio, Late 19th Century, 10 ½ x 8 In. 230.00
Figure, Dog, Spaniel, Seated, 19th Century, 7 ¼ In. .... 300.00 to 800.00
Figure, Dog, Spaniel, Seated, Tooled Collar, Eyelashes, Early 20th Century, 10 In. 115.00
Figure, Elephant, Ohio, Early 1900s, 11 ½ x 14 ¼ In. 4700.00
Figure, Football, Signed EJE, Tuscarawas County, Ohio, Early 20th Century, 9 ½ In. 345.00
Figure, Lion, Carved, 6 x 10 x 5 In. 80.00
Figure, Lion, Lying Down, Plinth, Tooled, Swords, Signed, 6 ¾ x 9 In. 748.00
Figure, Lion, Lying Down, Scalloped Base, Ohio, Early 1900s, 9 x 6 In., Pair 235.00
Figure, Raccoon, Molded, Scratch Carved Initials, Early 20th Century, 15 ¼ In. 173.00
Planter, Tree Trunk Shape, c.1922, 13 In. 264.00
Sculpture, Man's Face, 4 x 4 x 4 In. 110.00
Umbrella Stand, Tree Bark Decoration, 26 In. 135.00

SEWING equipment of all types is collected, from sewing birds that held the cloth to tape measures, needle books, and old wooden spools. Sewing machines are included here. Needlework pictures are listed in the Picture category.

Basket, Wallpaper, Stripes, Pincushion, Swing Handle, 19th Century, 7 ¾ x 7 In. 990.00
Bench, Victorian, Lift Top, 16 x 20 x 12 In., Pair 201.00
Bench, Victorian, Lift Top, 18 x 21 x 10 In. 130.00
Bird, Brass, Tatting Shuttle, Cloth Pincushion, 5 In., 2 Piece 201.00
Box, Birch, Mahogany, Bone Ebony Inlay Heart, Hinged Lid, Early1800s, 5 ½ x 9 In. 1896.00
Box, Biscuit, Figural, Mother & Child, Embossed Base, 8 ½ x 7 ¼ In. 140.00
Box, Burl, Mother-Of-Pearl Inlay, Fitted Interior, Velvet Lining, 6 ½ x 12 In. 840.00
Box, Burl, Tunbridge Marquetry, 12 Compartments, Lift-Out Tray, 5 x 13 x 9 In. 1200.00
Box, Fabric Lift Lid, Printed Design, Sam Looked At The Fat Boy, 6-Sided, Inscribed, 3 ½ In. .. 497.00
Box, Fruitwood, Bone Inlay, Drop Flap, Compartments, 6 ¼ x 14 x 10 ¼ In. 780.00
Box, Hardwood, Sandalwood, Sadeli Mosaic, Sarcophagus, Anglo-Indian, 4 ½ x 13 In. 201.00
Box, Lacquerware, Carved Dragon, Head, Feet, Chinese, Mid 19th Century, 6 x 14 x 11 In. 75.00
Box, Leather, Brass Mount, 4 Drawers, Compartments, English Rose, 9 ¼ x 8 x 6 ½ In. 2880.00
Box, Mahogany, Hearts, Inlay, Pincushion Top, Square, Initials, M.C. 2645.00
Box, Paneled, Black Lacquer, Gilt, Figural Scene, Lift-Out Tray, Chinese Export, 14 x 10 x 6 In. 646.00
Box, Paper Board, Wallpaper, Printed, Gray Ground, Oval, Pincushion, 3 x 8 ½ x 5 ¼ In. 77.00
Box, Parcel Gilt, Black Lacquer, Pierced Grilles, Spools, Awls, Pincushion, 6 x 15 x 11 In. 1560.00

Box, Rosette Pincushion, Drawer, Painted, Softwood, 7 ¼ x 6 ¼ x 6 In. . . . . *illus* 176.00
Box, Softwood, Nail Construction, Flat Lid, Drawer, Wood Pull, 5 ⅞ x 9 x 5 ¾ In. 385.00
Box, Softwood, Raised Paneled, Dovetailed, 6-Compartment Shelf, 6 ¾ x 11 ½ In. 1870.00
Box, Thread, Clark Tartanware, Photo On Lid, Spools, Needle Bin, England, 1800s, 3 x 4 In. . . 374.00
Box, Tunbridge, Marquetry Bands, Escutcheon, c.1899, 4 ¾ x 9 ¾ In. 81.00
Box, Veneers, Slope Lid, Silver Latch, Interior Compartments, Tools, England, c.1825, 4 x 3 In. 2489.00
Box, Wallpaper, Pincushion Lid, Swag Design, Mid 19th Century, 4 ¼ x 8 ¾ In. 1320.00
Box, Wood, Lift Out Tray, Bone Grilles, Awls, Floss Winder, Spools, Paw Feet, Chinese, 5 x 12 In. 1320.00
Box, Wood, Marquetry, Divided Interior, 4 x 10 x 6 In. 30.00
Box, Wood, Windmill Marquetry, 4 x 8 x 5 ½ In. 60.00
Buttonhole Cutter, Iron, Wood Holster, Mid 18th Century, Pair 644.00
Cabinet, Martha Washington, Mahogany, 3 Drawers, 4-Footed, Oval, 27 x 29 x 14 In. 25.00
Cabinet, Needle, Walnut, A. Shrimpton & Son, c.1900, 7 x 18 In. 288.00
Cabinet, Spool, see also the Advertising category under Cabinet, Spool.
Cabinet, Spool, Oak, 4 Drawers, Brass Pulls, c.1900, 14 x 23 x 14 In. . . . . *illus* 315.00
Cabinet, Spool, Walnut, 3 Drawers, Slide-Out Shelves, Curved Glass, c.1890, 18 x 21 In. 2500.00
Caddy, Pine, 2 Drawers, Tiered Spool Holders, Carved Birds, Painted Red, 11 In. 1293.00
Caddy, Pine, Maple Veneer, Dovetailed Drawer, Wire Spool Posts, c.1875, 5 x 5 x 7 In. 499.00
Caddy, Wood, Drawer, 7 Wire Spool Spindles, Pincushion, Turned Feet, 6 ½ x 5 In. 80.00
Case, Leather Over Tin, Silk Lining, Pockets, Shadowbox Frame, c.1800, 14 x 16 In. 118.00
Clamp, Rosewood, 7 x 1 ¾ x 1 ¾ In. 25.00
Darner, Wood, Black, c.1950, 5 ½ In. 12.00
Darner, Wood, Metal Head, c.1900 . . . . 20.00
Distaff, Wood, Chipped, Pierce Carved, 31 ½ In. 201.00
Machine, E. Howe, France, c.1880 . . . . 542.00
Machine, H. Dermant, Hand Operated, Shuttle, Odense, Denmark 1859.00
Machine, La Merveilleuse, Embroidery, France, c.1890. . . . . 879.00
Machine, Louis Beckh, Cast Iron, Black, Gold Flowers, Booklet, Oak Carrying Case, c.1869, 9 In. 563.00
Machine, Moiter, Shaw & Clark, Chain Stitch, c.1865 . . . . 1038.00
Machine, Muller, Model 16, Treadle, Cover, Gold Flowers, Cast Iron, Wood, Germany, 36 In. . . 1540.00
Machine, Schroder, Hand Operated, Germany, 1873 . . . . 1065.00
Machine, Singer, No. 20, Electric, Child's, 7 In. 138.00
Needle Book, Rocket, c.1955, 6 ½ x 3 ¾ In. 12.00
Needle Book, Sewing Susan, c.1955, 5 ¾ x 3 ½ In. 12.00
Needle Book, Sweetheart, c.1960, 5 x 3 ½ In. 12.00
Needle Book, Woolworth Building, c.1955, 5 x 3 In. 8.00
Needle Case, Fish Shape, Brass, 1 x 3 ¼ In. 11.00
Needle Case, Fish Shape, Wood, Hollow, Multicolored, Gouged Highlight, 4 ⅝ In. 303.00
Needle Case, Heart Form, Flowers, Cloth, Pincushion, Felt, 3 x 2 ¾ x 1 In. . . . . *illus* 400.00
Needle Case, Silver, Chain, Attached Acorn Shape Vinaigrette, 5 ½ x ¼ In. 289.00
Needle Dispenser, Boye, Needle Shuttles, Bobbins, Tin, Rotates, Round, 3 ⅜ x 16 In. 33.00
Niddy Noddy, Wood, Round, T-Shape Terminals, Pegged Mortised Joints, 17 ½ x 14 ½ In. . . . 22.00
Pattern, Cabbage Patch Doll, Cabbage Patch Kids, No. 6661, c.1984. 29.00
Pattern, Doll, Tiny Tears, McCall's, No. 2349, c.1959, 9-In. Doll. 30.00
Pattern, Doll Clothes, Teen Wardrobe, McCall's, No. 2580, 11 ½-In. Doll 35.00
Pincushion, Beaded, Velvet, Embroidered Flower, Leaves, Victorian, 6 ½ x 6 ½ In. 30.00
Pincushion, Cast Iron Blackamoor Figure Holding Cushion, Brass Drawer, 4 ¾ In. 235.00
Pincushion, Dog, Patchwork, Blue Eyes, I.W. Rice & Co., 7 In. 18.00
Pincushion, Duck, Painted, Softwood, Scissor Holder, Stuffed Wings, 6 x 7 x 4 In. . . . . . *illus* 165.00
Pincushion, Embroidered, Red, Tan, Brown Diamonds, 6-Sided Mirror Panels, 19th Century 380.00
Pincushion, Fish, Thimble Mouth, Glass Eye, Red & Black Highlights, Fabric Cover. 1170.00
Pincushion, Indian With Bow, Teepee, Drawnwork On Silk, Silk Cord, Early 1800s. 819.00
Pincushion, Needle Sharpener, Measuring Tape, Tomato Shape, c.1950, 2 ¾ In. 25.00
Pincushion, Pillow Form, Silk, Pin Design Of Tulip, 07 SC, Embroidered, Pa., 5 ½ In. 585.00
Pincushion, Spade Shape, Beaded, Velvet, Embroidered Flowers, Victorian, 11 x 9 ½ In. 30.00
Pincushion, Victorian, Needlepoint, Glass Base, 6 x 4 In. 165.00
Pincushion Dolls are listed in their own category.
Pinking Shears, Kleen Cut, Black Handles, Box, c.1958, 7 ½ In. 10.00
Pins, Steel, Pack, Banner, c.1970. . . . . 2.00
Scissors, Sterling Silver, Beaded Rope, Horizontal Reeding, 3 ⅝ In. 125.00
Sewing Machine, Moldacot, Nickeled Brass, Closed Handwheel, c.1890, 7 ½ In. 426.00
Sock Darner, Wooden, Black Lacquer, Needle & Thread Storage In Ball, 1920s, 7 In. 15.00
Spool Cabinets are listed here or in the Advertising category under Cabinet, Spool.
Spool Holder, 2 Tiers, Pincushion Top, Footed, Cast Iron, Black Paint, 8 ½ x 5 In. . . . . . *illus* 99.00
Spool Stand, Brown Paint, Red & Yellow Pinstriping, Wood Carving, 19th Century, 13 x 14 In. 1053.00
Swift, Wood, Bone, 26 In. 700.00
Tape Measure, Fish, Brass, Figural, 1 ½ x 2 ¼ In. 77.00

Sewing, Needle Case, Heart Form, Flowers, Cloth, Pincushion, Felt, 3 x 2 ¾ x 1 In.
$400.00

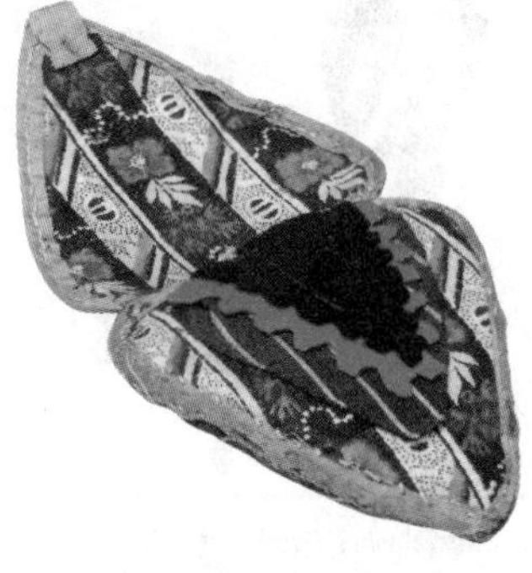

Sewing, Pincushion, Duck, Painted, Softwood, Scissor Holder, Stuffed Wings, 6 x 7 x 4 In.
$165.00

Sewing, Spool Holder, 2 Tiers, Pincushion Top, Footed, Cast Iron, Black Paint, 8 ½ x 5 In.
$99.00

Sewing, Wool Winder, Wood
$64.00

Shaker, Basket, Oval, Slats, Metal Band, Wire, Wood Handle, Patina, 1890, Ky., 9 x 15 x 10 In.
$275.00

Shaker, Basket, Wood, Bale Handle, 15 x 13 ½ In.
$225.00

S

Scuttle Mug
A scuttle mug is made in the shape of a Victorian coal scuttle. The mug has a "pouch" in the front that holds a brush.

Tape Measure, Ring Of Roses On Top & Side, Green, Pink, Celluloid, 1 In. 17.00
Tape Measure, Straw Hat, Most Hats Cover The Head, Brass, Nickel Plated, 2 x 2 ½ In. 44.00
Thimble, 14K Gold 60.00 to 80.00
Thimble, Bone China, Cottage, Garden, Painted, Gold Trim, c.1970, 1 In. 18.00
Thimble, Butterfly, Blue, Spring Flowers, Porcelain, 1 In. 9.00
Thread Holder, Ivory, Wood, 2 Tiers, Footed, Early 1800s. 660.00
Thread Pocket, Roll-Up, 3 Pockets, Flower Print Cloth, Red Cloth Loop, 15 x 4 ¾ In. 550.00
Thread Puller, Eagle Form, Iron, Pa., Early 19th Century, 3 ¾ In. 4400.00
Tower, Maple, Hand Carved, 11 In. 100.00
Vinaigrette, Compendium Shape, Sterling Silver, Thistle, Cotton Spool, Wax Holder, 4 In. 971.00
Vinaigrette, Etui, Sterling Silver, Egg Shape, Tape Measure, Pin Holder, England, 1870, 2 In. 2048.00
Wool Winder, Wood *illus* 64.00
Zipper, Orchid, Talon, c.1970, 22 In. 1.88
Zipper, Pink, Talon, c.1970, 7 In. 1.88

SHAKER items are characterized by simplicity, functionalism, and orderliness. There were many Shaker communities in America from the eighteenth century to the present day. The religious order made furniture, small wooden pieces, and packaged medicines, herbs, and jellies to sell to "outsiders." Other useful objects were made for use by members of the community. Shaker furniture is listed in this book in the Furniture category.

Band Box, Oval Lap Joints, Red Ocher Paint, 3 x 7 ½ In. 176.00
Basket, Black Ash, Rounded Square, Cross Wrapped Rim, Late 19th Century, 13 ¼ In. 215.00
Basket, Oval, Slats, Metal Band, Wire, Wood Handle, Patina, 1890, Ky., 9 x 15 x 10 In. *illus* 275.00
Basket, Wood, Bale Handle, 15 x 13 ½ In. *illus* 225.00
Bonnet, Woven, Natural & Brown, Splint, Pleated Back, Sewn Binding, 10 In. 288.00
Box, 2-Finger, Oval, Lid, Copper Tacks, Early 20th Century, 2 ½ x 3 ¾ In. 863.00
Box, 2-Finger, Oval, Lid, Copper Tacks, Early 20th Century, 5 x 7 ½ In. 489.00
Box, 2-Finger, Oval, Maple, Pine, Copper Paint, Red Paint, c.1890, 3 x 8 In. 1293.00
Box, 2-Finger, Oval, Maple, Pine, Copper Tacks, c.1890, 3 x 6 In. 353.00
Box, 2-Finger, Oval, Tin & Wood Pins, 2 ¼ x 5 ¼ In. 259.00
Box, 3-Finger, Oval, Copper Tacks, Pine Top, Maple Sides, Blue, Green Paint, c.1850, 3 x 7 In. 356.00
Box, 3-Finger, Oval, Copper Tacks, Pine Top, Maple Sides, Green Paint, c.1890, 2 x 7 In. 474.00
Box, 3-Finger, Oval, Copper Tacks, Pine Top, Maple Sides, Natural Finish, c.1935, 3 x 7 In. 770.00
Box, 3-Finger, Oval, Copper Tacks, Red Paint, 4 ½ x 12 ½ x 8 ¾ In. 120.00
Box, 3-Finger, Oval, Lid, Copper Tacks, Early 20th Century, 8 ¾ x 11 ½ In. 805.00
Box, 3-Finger, Oval, Lid, Copper Tacks, Green & Brown Paint, 9 x 3 ½ In. 546.00
Box, 3-Finger, Oval, Lid, Mahogany Stain, Copper Tacks, 7 ¼ x 10 ⅜ In. 489.00
Box, 3-Finger, Oval, Maple, Pine, Copper Tacks, c.1890, 6 x 13 In. 881.00
Box, 3-Finger, Oval, Salmon Paint, 8 ½ x 11 ½ In. 891.00
Box, 4-Finger, Oval, Copper Tacks, Pine Top, Maple Sides, Green Paint, c.1890, 5 x 12 In. 711.00
Box, 4-Finger, Oval, Copper Tacks, Pine Top, Maple Sides, Red Paint, c.1890, 4 x 10 In. 1067.00
Box, 4-Finger, Oval, Lid, Copper Tacks, Early 20th Century, 9 ½ x 13 ½ In. 575.00
Box, 4-Finger, Sewing, Copper Tacks, Pine Lid, Maple Sides, Handle, Silk Lining, c.1900, 8 x 8 In. 178.00
Box, Oval, Cover, Varnished, Flowers, Copper Tacks, 7 In. 265.00
Box, Oval, Wood, Red Paint, 3 ¼ x 7 ⅝ x 5 ⅛ In. 6875.00
Box, Pantry, Pine, Birch, Maple, Printed Label, Sam'l Hersey, Mass., c.1860, 3 x 6 In. 510.00
Box, Rolling Wood, Iron Tongs, Pine, Oak, Dovetailed, 2 Rollers, 16 x 18 In., Tongs, c.1870, 22 In. 830.00
Bucket, Wood, Open Slats, Bale, 14 x 15 In. 248.00
Bucket, Wood, Vertical Slats, Bale, 11 x 9 In. 275.00
Drying Rack, Mortised Construction, New Hampshire, 27 ½ x 38 In. 230.00
Measure, Lapped Seam, Copper Tacks, Yellow Paint, Turned Handle, 1800s, 7 x 9 In. 345.00
Rug Beater, Bentwood, 40 In. 29.00
Swift, Maple, Table Clamp, Late 19th Century, 18 ½ x 24 ½ In. *illus* 690.00

SHAVING MUGS were popular from 1860 to 1900. Many types were made, including occupational mugs featuring pictures of men's jobs. There were scuttle mugs, silver-plated mugs, glass-lined mugs, and others.

Boy & Dog, Girl, Relief, Panels, Creamware, 19th Century, 4 ½ x 5 ¾ In. 70.00
Fraternal, B.O.P.E. Elks, Clock Face, 3 ⅞ In. 44.00
Fraternal, Masonic Emblem, E.C. Bowdish, 3 ½ In. 22.00
Fraternal, Masonic Emblem, Flower, John F. Willimann, 3 ¾ In. 33.00
Occupational, 2 House Painters, C. L. Patterson, France 1300.00
Occupational, 2 Race Cars, Grandstand, W. Greenfield 1500.00
Occupational, African Americans, Playing Pool, S.C. Hunson 1200.00
Occupational, Bakers, Lester C. Sterner, Gilt, 3 ½ In. 220.00

Occupational, Barber, Pole, C.H. Phelps, 3 ¾ In. 1800.00
Occupational, Barbershop, 3 Barbers, 5 Customers, Andrew Bradford, 3 ½ In. 2200.00
Occupational, Bartender, 2 Toasting Patrons, Leroy Jones, 3 ¾ In. 230.00
Occupational, Bicyclist, Riding High Wheeler, P.J. Laubach, 3 ½ In. 600.00
Occupational, Bird Hunter, Shotgun, 2 Bird Dogs, Grant Norton, Gilt Trim, 3 ½ In. 270.00
Occupational, Blacksmith, Holding Hammer, Baxter Hamilton, 3 ⅝ In. 75.00
Occupational, Blacksmith, K.C. Decatur, Gilt, Marked, Limoges, 3 ½ In. 195.00
Occupational, Blacksmith's Tools, M.J. Dougham, 3 ⅜ In. 22.00
Occupational, Bricklayer, Building Wall, N. Matthews, 3 ½ In. 460.00
Occupational, Butcher, Bull's Head, Crossed Knives, R. Edwards, 3 ⅝ In. 75.00
Occupational, Butcher, Wearing Top Hat, Bull, J. Fernel, Gilt, 3 ½ In. 270.00
Occupational, Caboose, Frank Vincent, Gilt, 3 ½ In. 165.00
Occupational, Carpenter, Joseph Gill, T & V Limoges, 3 ¾ In. 316.00
Occupational, Carpenter, Siding House, S.W. Stowe, 3 ½ In. 1300.00
Occupational, Cowboy, Roping Steer, Chas. M. Kealey, c.1885, 3 ⅝ In. 1035.00
Occupational, Delivery Driver, F.M. Dorcoiv, 3 ⅝ In. 207.00
Occupational, Duck Hunter, Harry Bishop, Gilt, Marked, Limoges, 3 ½ In. 470.00
Occupational, Farmer, 2 Horses, Plow, John Stoffel, Gilt, Koken Stamp, 3 ¾ In. 230.00
Occupational, Farmer, 2 White Horses, Plow, Farmhouse, C.H. Parke, Gilt, 3 ¾ In. 300.00
Occupational, Farmer, Horse Drawn Plow, A.T. Butterwick, 3 ½ In. 300.00
Occupational, Farmer, Plowing Field, M. Cleveland, T. V & D., 3 ¾ In. 316.00
Occupational, Ferrier, Shoeing Horse, John Graney, 3 ⅝ In. 125.00
Occupational, Firemen, Hook & Ladder Truck, Newton J. Buck, Limoges, 3 ½ In. 750.00
Occupational, Fisherman, On Rock, C.D. Fisher, 3 ½ In. 325.00
Occupational, Grocer, Sam Gurtz, Carr China, 4 In. .... *illus* 120.00
Occupational, Harness Maker, At Workbench, J.J. Lenton, 3 ½ In. 250.00
Occupational, Horse, Jockey, Cart, Geo. B. Wells, 3 ⅝ In. 250.00
Occupational, Horse Drawn Ice Wagon, Glen Willow, J.R. Hinkel, 3 ⅝ In. 550.00
Occupational, Horse Trainer, 3 Men Gait Training Horse, H.F. Rientordts, 4 In. 1300.00
Occupational, Horseman, Sulky, Driver, 3 ¾ In. 77.00
Occupational, Knitting Loom, William Day, 3 ½ In. 489.00
Occupational, Livery Stable, Horse Head, F.H. Lee, Porcelain, T & V France, 4 In. 230.00
Occupational, Log Wagon, Driver, 2 Horse Team, O.H. Hill, Gilt, 3 ½ In. 1440.00
Occupational, Man, 2 Horse Buggy, F.W. Keller, 3 ⅞ In. 110.00
Occupational, Man, Installing Iron Fence, O.R. Schellenberger, Limoges, 3 ½ In. 4000.00
Occupational, Man, Painting Brick Wall, On Scaffold, Gilt, R.G. Koch, 3 ⅝ In. 900.00
Occupational, Map, State Of Maine, Porcelain, 3 In. 60.00
Occupational, Milliner, Stanley Gruber, 4 In. .... *illus* 210.00
Occupational, Mortar & Pestle, J.G. Jennings, Stamped, R.W., Minneapolis, 3 ½ In. 232.00
Occupational, Policeman, H.D. Lewis, 3 ⅝ In. 225.00
Occupational, Singer Sewing Machine, G.A. Ziemendorf, 4 In. 790.00
Occupational, Slaughterhouse, Man Butchering Cow, A.W. Aldrich, 3 ½ In. 125.00
Occupational, Steam Tractor, Pulling Cars, J.C. Osgood, c.1885 .... 2070.00
Occupational, Trolley Car, George Carson, 3 ¾ In. 633.00
Occupational, Woman, Being Fitted For Shoes, Chas. Lowenthal, 3 ½ In. 250.00
Patriotic, Eagle & Flag, Bavaria, 4 In. 115.00
Patriotic, Foe Patriotic, Martin A. Dodd, T & V, Limoges, 3 ½ In. 115.00
Stallions, Black, White, George Batche, 3 ¾ In. 55.00
Swagged Drapery, Flower, T.J. Lang, 3 ¾ In. 11.00
Swagged Drapery, Hanging Pot, Flowers, Fred Aldrich, 3 ⅝ In. 77.00

SHAWNEE POTTERY was started in Zanesville, Ohio, in 1937. The company made vases, novelty ware, flowerpots, planters, lamps, and cookie jars. Three dinnerware lines were made: Corn, Lobster Ware, and Valencia (a solid color line). White Corn pattern utility pieces were made in 1945. Corn King was made from 1946 to 1954; Corn Queen, with darker green leaves and lighter colored corn, from 1954 to 1961. Shawnee produced pottery for George Rumrill during the late 1930s. The company closed in 1961.

Shawnee USA

Bowl, Corn King, c.1950, 6 In. 50.00
Bowl, Shell Form, Pink, 4 ½ x 7 ¾ In. 24.00
Casserole, Cover, Corn King, 11 In. 75.00
Cookie Jar, Clover Bud Smiley, Marked, 11 ½ In. 173.00
Cookie Jar, Dutch Boy, Blue Scarf 88.00
Cookie Jar, Puss 'N Boots, Red Bow, 10 In. 83.00
Cookie Jar, Sailor Boy, Jack Tar, Black Scarf, Blue Suit 35.00
Cookie Jar, Smiley Pig, Green Scarf, Shamrocks, 11 In. 249.00
Cookie Jar, Smiley Pig, Red Scarf, 1940s, 11 In. 39.00

Shaker, Swift, Maple, Table Clamp, Late 19th Century, 18 ½ x 24 ½ In.
$690.00

Shaving Mug, Occupational, Grocer, Sam Gurtz, Carr China, 4 In.
$120.00

Shaving Mug, Occupational, Milliner, Stanley Gruber, 4 In.
$210.00

TIP
Look behind all hanging pictures once a year to be sure there are no insect nests, dust, or loose wires.

Shawnee Pottery, Doves, Glossy Green, Marked, No. 829, 8 ¾ In.
$15.00

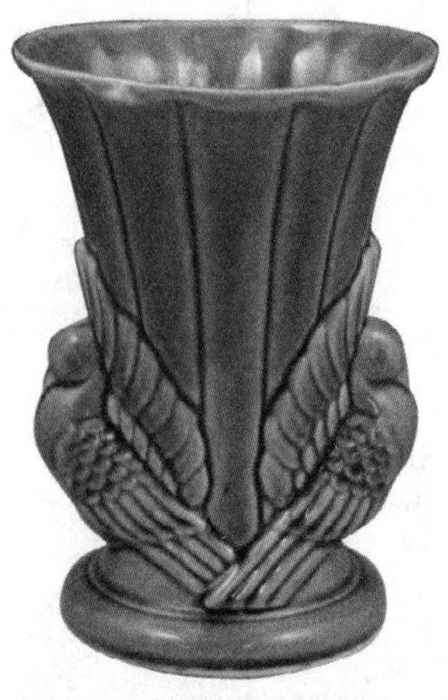

Corn Holder, Corn King, 8 ½ In., Pair 190.00
Creamer, Corn King, 1950, 12 Oz 35.00
Creamer, Puss 'N Boots, 4 ½ In. 20.00
Figurine, Chinese Boy, Hat, 5 In. 20.00
Figurine, Chinese Girl, 5 In. 20.00
Flowerpot, White, Green Saucer, Marked, 3 ½ x 5 In. 20.00
Pitcher, Bo-Peep, Blue Bonnet, Yellow Dress, Signed, 7 ½ In. 215.00
Pitcher, Green, Porpoise Handle, Marked, 8 x 6 ½ In. 95.00
Pitcher, Rooster, Tail Feathers Form Handle, 7 ½ x 10 In. 90.00
Planter, Dog, With Shoe, 4 x 4 ½ In. 20.00
Planter, Green, White Splatter, 13 ½ x 5 In. 20.00
Planter, Saucer, Basket Weave, Maroon, 5 ¼ x 5 ½ In. 10.00
Salt & Pepper, Corn King, 5 ¼ In. 40.00
Salt & Pepper, Dutch Boy & Girl, Blue, Yellow, F.W. Woolworth, c.1950, 5 In. 45.00
Salt & Pepper, Muggsy, Large 245.00
Salt & Pepper, Owl, 3 In. 33.00
Salt & Pepper, Smiley & Winnie Pig, Pink Handkerchief, Blue Collar, 3 In. 80.00
Sugar, Corn King, White, 3 ½ In. 10.00
Teapot, Corn King, No. 65, Individual 250.00
Teapot, Granny Ann, Purple & Green Apron, 8 ½ x 8 In. 44.00
Teapot, Tom, The Piper's Son, 7 In. 74.00
Vase, Bud, Tulip, 5 In. 14.00
Vase, Doves, Glossy Green, Marked, No. 829, 8 ¾ In. .... *illus* 15.00
Vase, Fan, Marked, USA 1264, 1950s, 4 In. 16.00
Wall Pocket, Blue Birds On Roof 19.00

SHEARWATER pottery is a family business started by Mr. and Mrs. G.W. Anderson, Sr., and their three sons. The local Ocean Springs, Mississippi, clays were used to make the wares in the 1930s. The company is still in business.

Bowl, Mallard Ducks, Waves, Sgraffito, 1900s, 10 In. 4406.00
Mug, Fish, Green Glaze, Finger Pots, Walter Anderson, 4 x 5 ¼ In. 470.00
Mug, Stylized Frog, Blue & White Underglaze, c.1960, 4 In. 2350.00
Plate, Stylized Fish, Blue, Black, Ocher Underglaze, White Slip Ground, c.1950, 8 In. 3231.00
Sculpture, 3 Fish, Marked, Anderson, Ink Stamp, 7 ¾ In. .... *illus* 355.00
Vase, Bulbous, Pinched Neck, Coastal Landscape, James Anderson, c.1984, 6 In. 1410.00
Vase, Swirl Design, Cobalt Blue, Impressed Mark, 5 ⅞ In. .... *illus* 978.00
Vase, Wave Design, Green Glaze, Peter Anderson, c.1940, 6 ¼ In. 705.00

Shearwater, Sculpture, 3 Fish, Marked, Anderson, Ink Stamp, 7 ¾ In.
$355.00

SHEET MUSIC from the past centuries is now collected. The favorites are examples with covers featuring artistic or historic pictures. Early sheet music covers were lithographed, but by the 1900s photographic reproductions were used. The early music was larger than more recent sheets, and you must watch out for examples that were trimmed to fit in a twentieth-century piano bench.

All American Girl Collegiate Fox Trot Song, 9 x 12 In. 10.00
Ancient Honorable Artillery Co. March, Pikeman, Sousa Signed, c.1924, 12 x 9 In. 708.00
Buttons & Bows, Picture Of Jane Russell & Bob Hope, 1958 .... 10.00 to 12.00
Carolina Mammy, 1922 .... 30.00
Dixie, By Frederic Lorin, 1904 .... 9.00
Dreaming At Twilight, Woman In Pajamas Sitting On Rock With Daisies, 1910 .... 12.00
Grand March, General McClellan, Horse, Color, T. Sinclair, Phil., Frame, 14 x 18 In. 311.00
Havin' A Wonderful Time, Wish You Were Here, Bob Hope, Lucille Ball, 1949, 4 Sheet 210.00
High Cost Of Living, Introduced By Emma Caru, 1914 .... 8.00
How It Lies, Sonny Burke, Doris Day On Cover, 1941 .... 11.00
Just A Girl That Men Forget, Ballads, 1923 .... 11.00
Keep Fire A Burning, Jerome H. Remick & Co., 1912, 10 ½ x 13 ½ In. 7.00
Ladies Man, Dapper-Dan From Dixie Lane, Eddie Cantor 16.00
Love To Sleep In Mammy's Arms, Cover Art, 1920s 9.00
Marines Hymn, From Movie To The Shores Of Tripoli, John Payne, 1932 .... 12.00
My New York, Eddie Cantor & Jimmy Walker, 1927 .... 50.00
Napoleon's Last Charge, By E.T. Paull, 1910 .... 30.00
Now It Can Be Told, Irving Berlin, Ragtime Band, 1938 .... 14.00
Now's The Time To Fall In Love, Eddie Cantor, 8 Pages 8.00
Okay Toots, Eddie Cantor 8.00
Piano Solo, Convent Bells, By Henry Bollman, 1930s 12.00
Porgy & Bess, Cast Signed, Sidney Poitier, Sammy Davis Jr., 1959, 4 Pages 125.00

Shearwater, Vase, Swirl Design, Cobalt Blue, Impressed Mark, 5 ⅞ In.
$978.00

Put Another Nickel In, Music, Music, Music, Carmen Cavallaro, 1950 .... 12.50
Song Dedicated To Your Mother & Mine, Eddie Cantor 9.00
Temple Cup Two-Step March, N.Y. Giants Dedication, J. Cavanagh, 1894, 4 x 6 In......... 1528.00
These Grand United States, Catherine Scanlon-Pier, 1915 .... 40.00
West Side Story, Natalie Wood Signed, c.1957-61, 4 Pages.............................. 173.00
When It's Darkness On The Delta, 1932.. 12.00

SHEFFIELD *items are listed in the Silver Plate and Silver-English categories.*

SHELLEY first appeared on English ceramics about 1912. The Foley China Works started in England in 1860. Joseph Ball Shelley joined the company in 1862 and became a partner in 1872. Percy Shelley joined the firm in 1881. The company went through a series of name changes and in 1910 the then Foley China Company became Shelley China. In 1929 it became Shelley Potteries. The company was acquired in 1966 by Allied English Potteries, then merged with the Doulton group in 1971. The name Shelley was put into use again in 1980. A trio is the name for a cup, saucer, and cake plate set.

Coffeepot, Polkadot, Turquoise, Dainty, 6 ½ In.. .... 388.00
Cup & Saucer, Cappers Rose, Low Oleander 128.00
Cup & Saucer, Harebell, Low Oleander 118.00
Cup & Saucer, Plum & Apple, Blue, Gainsborough....................................... 88.00
Cup & Saucer, Polkadot, Turquoise, Dainty.. 228.00
Cup & Saucer, Pompadour, Gainsborough 108.00
Cup & Saucer, Primrose, Pale Green Trim, Dainty 118.00
Cup & Saucer, Tapestry Chintz, Yellow, Lincoln 228.00
Cup & Saucer, Trees On A Hill With Leaves, Orange Handle, Regent...................... 108.00
Dish, Muffin, Cover, Polkadot, Turquoise, Dainty, 4 ½ x 8 ¼ In......................... 158.00
Eggcup, Polkadot, Turquoise, Dainty, 2 In.. 88.00
Plate, Salad, Polkadot, Turquoise, Dainty, 8 ⅛ In....................................... 88.00
Trio, Blue, Dainty, Cup, Saucer, Luncheon Plate, Back Stamp, 3 Piece.................. 160.00

SHIRLEY TEMPLE, the famous movie star, was born in 1928. She made her first movie in 1932. Thousands of items picturing Shirley have been and still are being made. Shirley Temple dolls were first made in 1934 by Ideal Toy Company. Millions of Shirley Temple cobalt blue glass dishes were made by Hazel Atlas Glass Company and U.S. Glass Company from 1934 to 1942. They were given away as premiums for Wheaties and Bisquick. A bowl, mug, and pitcher were made as a breakfast set. Some pieces were decorated with the picture of a very young Shirley, others used a picture of Shirley in her 1936 Captain January costume. Although collectors refer to a cobalt creamer, it is actually the 4 ½-inch-high milk pitcher from the breakfast set. Many of these items are being reproduced today.

Book, Child Star, Leather Cover Edition, Signed By Shirley, 1988....................... 99.00
Bowl, Blue Glass, Scalloped Edge, 6 ½ In.. .... 18.00
Bowl, Cereal, Ritz Blue... 70.00
Doll, Composition, Blue & White Dress & Hat, Stand, Ideal, 13 In....................... 165.00
Doll, Composition, Brown Sleep Eyes, Lashes, Mohair Curls, Ideal, c.1930, 18 In.......... 468.00
Doll, Composition, Flirty Eyes, Blond Mohair Curls, 1930s, 26 In. 121.00
Doll, Composition, Jointed, Mohair Wig, Fur Coat, Hat, Ideal, Box, 1935, 18 In......... *illus* 4025.00
Doll, Composition, Jointed, Open Mouth, 6 Teeth, Ideal, 18 In........................... 303.00
Doll, Composition, Jointed, Sleep Eyes, Plaid Dress, Celluloid Button, 1930s, 16 In.......... 355.00
Doll, Composition, Polka Dot Dress, No. 2020, Blue Box, Ideal, 18 In................. *illus* 295.00
Doll, Composition, Sleep Hazel Eyes, Mohair Wig, Blue & White Dress, 1930s, 18 In......... 148.00
Doll, Composition, Tagged White & Black Dress, Matching Hat, Ideal, 13 In. 173.00
Doll, Hazel Sleep Eyes, Blond Mohair Wig, Cowboy Outfit, Ideal, 1937, 10 In............... 1985.00
Doll, Pink Dress, Ideal, Box, 12 In. 187.00
Doll, Poor Little Rich Girl, Blue Coat, Ideal, Box, 12 In. 44.00
Doll, Vinyl, Sleep Eyes, Fabric, Purse, c.1958, 12 In.. .... 278.00
Doll, Vinyl, Sleep Eyes, Necklace, Handbag, Ideal, 1958-59, 12 In....................... 278.00
Doll, Vinyl, White Dress, Red Dots & Bow, Box, 1973, 16 In. 22.00
Doll Carriage, Canopy, Rattan, Shirley Portraits, Iron, Wood, 1935, 34 In. 100.00
Doll Carriage, Rattan, Lithographed Portraits, Iron Frame, Wood Wheels, c.1935, 34 In.. .... 110.00
Lobby Card, Dimples, 1936, 17 x 14 In.. 320.00
Mechanical Pencil, Blue, 4 In.. .... 12.00
Movie Poster, Captain January, 20th Century Fox, 1936, Full Sheet, 27 x 41 In. 990.00
Movie Poster, Curly Top, 20th Century Fox, 1935, Full Sheet, 41 x 27 In................. 3850.00
Mug, Blue, 6 Oz., 3 ¾ In. 55.00
Paper Doll Book, 3 Dolls, Clothes, Dover, Uncut, 1986, 12 ¼ x 9 ¼ In., 16 Pages 12.50
Paper Doll Book, Dolls & Dresses, No. 2112, Saalfield Publishing, Uncut, 9 x 12 In......... 110.00

Shirley Temple, Doll, Composition, Jointed, Mohair Wig, Fur Coat, Hat, Ideal, Box, 1935, 18 In.
$4025.00

Shirley Temple, Doll, Composition, Polka Dot Dress, No. 2020, Blue Box, Ideal, 18 In.
$295.00

Shirley Temple, Pitcher, Milk, Cobalt Blue, 1938
$22.00

Silver Deposit, Cologne, Cranberry, Flowers, Metal Overlay, Marked, 8 ⅝ In.
$990.00

Silver Deposit, Vase, Green Glass, Urn Form, Flared Rim, Marked, 7 ¾ x 3 ¾ In.
$550.00

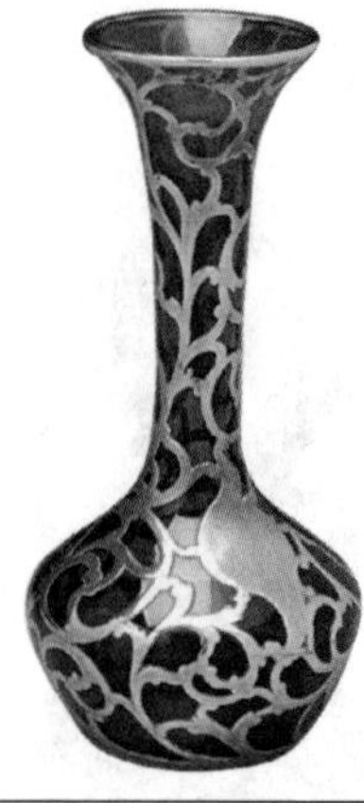

Silver Flatware Sterling, Acorn, Sugar Nippers, Georg Jensen, c.1950, 4 In.
$70.00

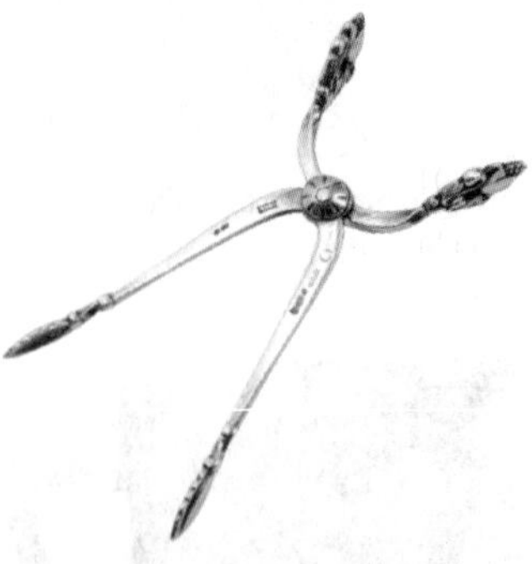

TIP

Always repair dented silver. Repeated cleaning of a piece with a dent can eventually lead to a hole.

Pin, My Friend Shirley Temple, Pink Rim 10.00
Pitcher, Milk, Cobalt Blue, 1938 . . . . . *illus* 22.00
Pitcher, Ritz Blue, 12 Oz., 4 ½ In. 45.00
Record, Little Miss Wonderful, Movie Sound Track, LP 1.00

SILVER DEPOSIT glass was first made during the late nineteenth century. Solid sterling silver is applied to the glass by a chemical method so that a cutout design of silver metal appears against a clear or colored glass. It is sometimes called silver overlay.

Cologne, Cranberry, Flowers, Metal Overlay, Marked, 8 ⅝ In. . . . . . *illus* 990.00
Decanter, Cranberry Glass, Iris, Overlay, Scroll Reserve, c.1900, 9 ⅞ In. 1715.00
Decanter, Glass, Green Cut To Clear, Oval, Flower Overlay, Steeple Stopper, 8 In. 175.00
Jar, Glass, Silver Overlay, Blue Favrile Style, Double Gourd, 7 ½ In. 4740.00
Paperweight, Cube, Glass, Floral Silver Overlay, Monogram CRH, c.1900, 2 In. 448.00
Pitcher, Cut Glass, Flower Basket Medallions, 9 ¾ In. 110.00
Vase, Cobalt Blue Glass, Blue Iridescent, Cypriot Texture, Applied Freeform Foot, 7 ¾ In. 115.00
Vase, Cobalt Blue Glass, Footed, Tiffany & Co., 18 x 6 ¾ In. 3500.00
Vase, Cobalt Blue Glass, Textured, Scroll Overlay, 5 ¼ In. 465.00
Vase, Cranberry Glass, Flower Overlay, Medallion, 8 In. 711.00
Vase, Green Glass, Flower Overlay, Bulbous, Flared, c.1910, 14 In. 504.00
Vase, Green Glass, Flower Overlay, Bulbous, Flared, Metal Base Rim, Marked, c.1900, 10 In. . . . 1541.00
Vase, Green Glass, Flower Overlay, Hourglass Shape, Wide Base, c.1910, 6 In. 1007.00
Vase, Green Glass, Flower Overlay, Tapered, Flared, Marked, 1900s, 14 In. 1185.00
Vase, Green Glass, Urn Form, Flared Rim, Marked, 7 ¾ x 3 ¾ In. . . . . . *illus* 550.00
Vase, Trumpet, Green Glass, Footed, Flower Overlay, Medallion, c.1910, 8 In. 652.00

SILVER FLATWARE includes many of the current and out-of-production silver and silver-plated flatware patterns made in the past eighty years. Other silver is listed under Silver-American, Silver-English, etc. Most silver flatware sets that are missing a few pieces can be completed through the help of one of the many silver matching services listed on our website, Kovels.com.

SILVER FLATWARE PLATED

Godetia, Jelly Server, Image Of Horse Drawn Buggy, Wm. Rogers & Sons, 2 x 7 In. 85.00
Vintage, Grapes, Chocolate Spoon, 1847 Rogers Bros., 4 ¼ In., 6 Piece 360.00

SILVER FLATWARE STERLING

Acorn, Bar Set, Bottle Opener, Tongs, Beaded, Oval, Georg Jensen, 6.5, 4 ½ In. 593.00
Acorn, Carving Set, Fork, Knife, Stainless Steel, Georg Jensen, 12.5, 13 9/16 In. 296.00
Acorn, Cheese Scoop, Georg Jensen, Mid 20th Century, 7 In. 240.00
Acorn, Ice Tongs, Georg Jensen, c.1950, 6 In. 175.00
Acorn, Pie Server, Georg Jensen, 9 ¼ In. 375.00
Acorn, Sugar Nippers, Georg Jensen, c.1950, 4 In. . . . . . *illus* 70.00
Arabesque, Gravy Ladle, S Monogram Terminal, Whiting Co., c.1875, 7 In. 179.00
Bridal Rose, Asparagus Server, Pierced, Alvin, Co, c.1903, 10 In. 263.00
Buttercup, Ladle, Gorham, c.1930, 11 In. 146.00
Buttercup, Strawberry Fork, Gorham, 4 ⅝ In., 8 Piece 440.00
Cactus, Cake Server, Georg Jensen, 8 ¾ In. 598.00
Cactus, Carving Set, Knife, Fork, Georg Jensen, 2 Piece. 190.00
Cactus, Ice Tongs, G. Albertus, Copenhagen, G. Jensen, c.1930, 6 In. 418.00
Cactus, Pie Server, Georg Jensen, 1930, 10 In. . . . . . 237.00 to 410.00
Cactus, Stuffing Spoon, Georg Jensen, 11 ¼ In. 130.00
Cat Tails, Cream Ladle, Gilt, Wm. Durgin Co., New Hampshire, c.1898, 5 In. 329.00
Chateau Rose, Butter Pick, Alvin, c.1940, 5 ¾ In. 85.00
Chrysanthemum, Fork, Monogram, Gorham, 6 ¾ In., 4 Piece 110.00
Cluny, Knife, Floral Engraved Blade, Repousse Handle, Gorham, c.1883, 11 In. 568.00
Corinthian, Ladle, Monogram, Gorham, 10 ½ In. 230.00
Cromwell, Strawberry Fork, Durgin, 5 In. 42.00
Dessert Set, Neoclassical, Enamel, Gilt, J. Tostrup, Norway, Case, 14 Piece . . . . . *illus* 355.00
Diamond, Spoon, Monogram, George W. Shiebler, 8 ½ In. 78.00
Eglantine, Salad Servers, Gilt Bowl, Tines, Gorham Mfg. Co., c.1870, 9 In., 2 Piece 657.00
Florence Nightingale, Soup Ladle, Alvin, 1920, 10 ½ In. 500.00
Francis I, Dinner Set, 7 Place Setting, Reed & Barton, 80 Piece 4095.00
Gadroonette, Teaspoon, Manchester, 5 ½ In. 25.00
Georgian, Ice Tongs, Towle, 1898, 7 In. 175.00
Grande Baroque, Cheese Grater, Wallace, 9 ¼ In. 263.00
Grape, Bonbon Spoon, Pierced Bowl, Dominick & Haff, c.1895, 5 In. 120.00

Grape, Macaroni Server, Gilt Vine Bowl, Dominick & Haff, c.1895, 10 In. 1315.00
Grecian, Slice, Scalloped Handle, Gorham, c.1861, 10 In. 179.00
Hindostanee, Waffle Server, Scrolled, Shaped Bowl, Gorham, c.1870, 9 In. 478.00
Hizen, Serving Spoon, Chased Terminal Flowers, Gorham, c.1880, 7 In. 657.00
Imperial Chrysanthemum, Serving Spoon, Monogram, Gorham, 7 ½ In. 36.00
Indian, Macaroni Server, Shaped Wing Blade, Whiting Co., c.1880, 11 In. 657.00
Iris, Ice Cream Spoon Set, Shaped, Gilt Bowl, Gorham, c.1870, 6 ½ In., 4 Piece 538.00
Iris, Sugar Tongs, Gilt Blades, Gorham Mfg., R.I., c.1870, 5 In. 418.00
Japanese, Butter Knife, Mum Terminal, Bamboo, Bird Ground, Gorham, c.1871, 7 In. 287.00
Japanese, Butter Knife, Pagoda Terminal, Birds, Flower Gilt Blade, c.1871, 8 In. 388.00 to 508.00
Japanese, Cheese Knife, Etched Gilt, Gorham, c.1871, 8 In. 388.00
Japanese, Cheese Knife, Pagoda, Engraved, 4-Tine Blade, Gorham, c.1871, 8 In. *illus* 717.00
Japanese, Cream Ladle, Gilt Bowl, Gorham, c.1871, 6 In. 508.00
Japanese, Ice Cream Spade, Peacock Finial, Engraved Gilt Blade, Gorham, c.1871, 8 In. 1315.00
Japanese, Ice Tongs, Flowers, Birds, Bamboo, Gilt Claws, Gorham, c.1871, 6 In. 598.00
Jenny Lind, Cake Knife, Leaf Handle, A. Coles & Co., c.1855, 11 In. 239.00
King George, Serving Spoon, Gorham, 8 ½ In., 6 Piece 384.00
La Marquise, Fish Serving Set, Pierced Blades, Reed & Barton, c.1895, 12 In., 2 Piece 956.00
Lancaster, Ice Cream Fork, Gorham, 5 ⅜ In., 12 Piece 480.00
Laurel, Ladle, Frank Smith, 5 In. 55.00
Les Six Fleurs, Serving Spoon, Shaped Bowl, Reed & Barton, 11 In. 478.00
Lily, Seafood Fork, Embossed, Whiting, 6 In. 92.00
Lily Of The Valley, Server, Georg Jensen, 1915-27, 8 In. 175.00
Lotus, Macaroni Server, Shaped Tines, Gilt, Fluted Bowl, Whiting, c.1865, 9 In. 717.00
Marie, Tea Strainer, Wallace, 7 In. 78.00
Marion, Spoon, Wendell, 5 In. 24.00
Mazarin, Ladle, Monogram, Dominick & Haff, 6 ½ In. 65.00
Medallion, Server, Pierced Bowl, Duhme & Co., Cinn., c.1865, 9 In. 1076.00
Medallion, Serving Spoon, Minerva Portrait, Gilt Fluted Bowl, Gorham, c.1864, 9 In. *illus* 448.00
Medallion, Soup Ladle, Gorham, c.1864, 14 In. 574.00
Medici, Sugar Spoon, Gorham, c.1880, 8 ⅝ In. 82.00
Morning Glory, Butter Knife, S Monogram, Gorham, c.1865, 8 In. 896.00
Newport Shell, Ladle, Frank Smith, 5 In. 65.00
Nuremberg, Teaspoon, Five O'Clock, Gilt, Gorham, c.1884, 5 In., 12 299.00
Old English, Strawberry Fork, Towle, 5 In., Pair *illus* 120.00
Overture, Cocktail Fork, 6 In., 12 Piece 146.00
Persian, Macaroni Server, Engraved Gilt Bowl, Gorham, c.1870, 10 In. 586.00
Repousse, Demitasse Spoon, Embossed Floral, Kirk, 4 ⅜ In., 12 Piece 390.00
Repousse, Hot Cake Server, Round Blade, S. Kirk & Son, Baltimore, c.1875, 9 In. *illus* 120.00
Repousse, Oyster Fork, Embossed Floral, Kirk, 5 ⅜ In., 11 Piece 580.00
Repousse, Serving Spoon, Kirk, 9 In. 201.00
Rustic, Serving Spoon, Monogram, Towle, 7 ¾ In. 110.00
Saxon Stag, Crumber, Flower Engraved Blade, Gorham, c.1855, 12 In. 1315.00
Sphinx, Gravy Ladle, Gilt Bowl, Gorham, c.1869, 8 In. 478.00
Sphinx, Serving Spoon, Gilt Bowl, Terminal, Gorham Mfg. Co., c.1869, 6 In. 418.00
Stieff Rose, Berry Spoon, Embossed Fruit, Kirk, 5 In. 88.00
Strasbourg, Serving Spoon, B Monogram, Gorham, c.1897, 12 In. 191.00
Stratford, Teaspoon, Simpson, Hall, Miller & Co., c.1902, 5 ¾ In., 6 Piece 70.00
Sunflower, Ice Cream Spoon Set, Terminal, Gilt Bowl, Vanderslice, c.1870, 5 In., 6 Piece 568.00
Tyrolean, Spoon, Whiting, 5 ⅜ In. 30.00
Versailles, Asparagus Fork, Gorham, c.1888, 9 In. 311.00
Versailles, Fish Fork, Gilt Wash Tines, Gorham, 8 ⅝ In. 176.00
Violet, Teaspoon, Whiting, 6 In. 36.00
Virginia, Teaspoon, Beaded, Gorham, 5 ½ In. 22.00

SILVER PLATE is not solid silver. It is a ware made of a metal, such as nickel or copper, that is covered with a thin coating of silver. The letters *EPNS* are often found on American and English silver-plated wares. *Sheffield* is a term with two meanings. Sometimes it refers to sterling silver made in the town of Sheffield, England. Sometimes it refers to an old form of plated silver.

Bacon Dish, Roll Top, Footed, Fitted Tray, Sheffield, c.1880, 8 ½ x 13 x 10 In. 147.00
Basket, Octagonal, Rose Rim & Feet, Swing Handle, Dolphin Terminals, Sheffield, 4 In. 324.00
Biscuit Box, Cover, Footed, Sheffield, Roberts & Belk, Late 19th Century, 8 x 7 In. 71.00
Biscuit Box, Cylindrical Body, Chased Fern, Hinged Cover, Ball Feet, c.1890, 7 x 7 In. 122.00
Biscuit Jar, Victorian, Classical Figures Frieze, Face Finial, 1800s, 10 In. 265.00
Biscuit Warmer, Shell Shape, Handle, Footed, England, c.1900, 10 x 8 ¼ In. 176.00
Bottle Opener, G. Greggio, Italy, c.1970, 6 In. 49.00

Silver Flatware Sterling, Dessert Set, Neoclassical, Enamel, Gilt, J. Tostrup, Norway, Case, 14 Piece
$355.00

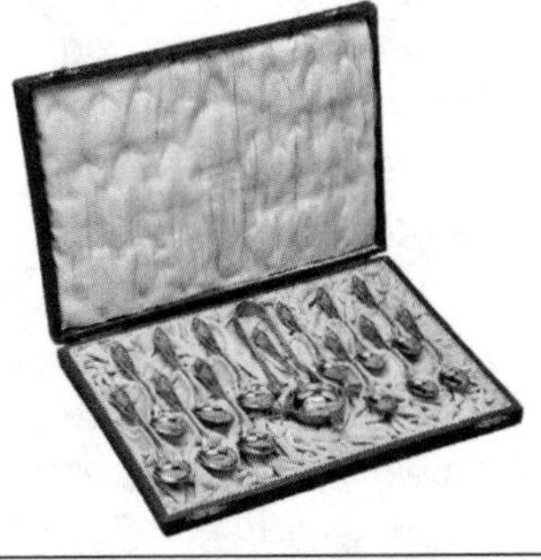

Silver Flatware Sterling, Japanese, Cheese Knife, Pagoda Terminal, Engraved, 4-Tine Blade, Gorham, c.1871, 8 In.
$717.00

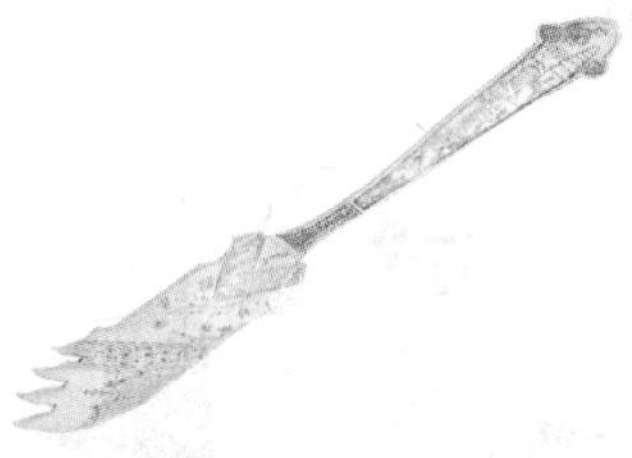

Silver Flatware Sterling, Medallion, Serving Spoon, Minerva Portrait, Gilt Fluted Bowl, Gorham, c.1864, 9 In.
$448.00

Silver Flatware Sterling, Repousse, Hot Cake Server, Round Blade, S. Kirk & Son, Baltimore, c.1875, 9 In.
$120.00

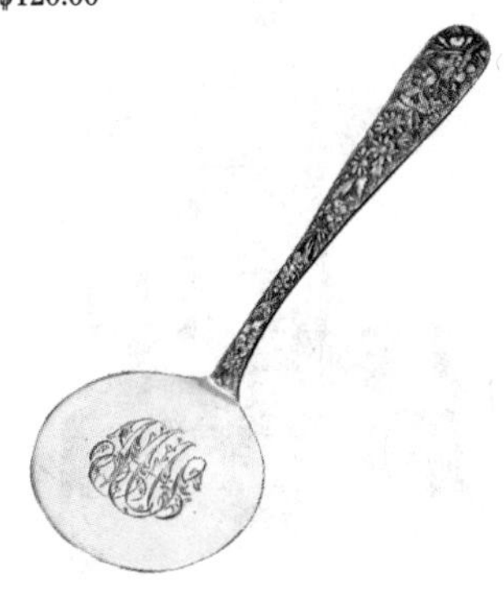

TIP
Do not have old monograms removed from silver. It lowers the value. If it bothers you to have an old initial, don't buy the piece. We like to tell people it belonged to a great aunt with that initial.

Silver Plate, Cheese Dish, Leaves, Marked, William Harrison, England, 1880s, 7 x 8 ½ x 7 In.
$195.00

Silver Plate, Epergne, 4 Scroll Arms, Cut Glass, Family Crest, 1890s, 15 ½ x 21 In.
$1210.00

Silver Plate, Ice Water Stand, Aesthetic Movement, Gilt, Simpson, Hall, Miller, 1887, 22 x 17 In.
$4800.00

Bowl, Center, Egg, Dart Border, 3 Crane Supports, 3 Flower Feet, c.1945, 9 x 8 In. 259.00
Bowl, Cranberry Glass, Stand, Reed & Barton, 2 Handles, 3-Footed, c.1875, 12 In. 292.00
Bowl, Fruit, Footed, Floral Trimmed Rim, Oneida, 1970s, 10 ½ x 4 ½ In. 40.00
Bowl, Vegetable, Neoclassical, Cover, Bird, Acanthus, Scroll Handles, 7 x 14 In., Pair 823.00
Box, Rectangular, Tapered Feet, Relief Hunting Scenes, 3 ½ x 6 In. 374.00
Butter, Cover, Cow Finial, Flowers, Ram's Head Legs, Knife, 7 ¼ x 7 In. 323.00
Cake Basket, Meriden Brittannia, Reticulated, c.1930, 8 In. 94.00
Cake Basket, Renaissance, c.1800 .... 323.00
Cake Knife, Engraved, Lillie, Monogram, 11 ¼ In. 275.00
Candelabra are listed in the Candelabrum category.
Candlesnuffer, Sheffield, 19th Century, c.1850, 7 ½ In. 81.00
Candlesticks are listed in their own category.
Card Receiver, Peacock Form, c.1890 .... 45.00
Card Tray, Crab Center, Bird On Corner, Crimped & Rolled Rim, Pairpoint, 6 ½ In. 80.00
Carving Set, Beaded Handles, Towle, Velvet Lined Box, 14 x 10 ½ In. 24.00
Castor Tongs, Rosettes, Bird Talon Grippers, 6 In. 135.00
Centerpiece, 4 Griffin Arms, Orange Tipped Glass Inserts, c.1895, 17 In. 546.00
Centerpiece, Mirror, Rococo, Mermaid Supports, Oval, Paris, c.1905, 27 In. 17500.00
Chafing Dish, Warming Stand, Sheraton, 11 x 21 In., Pair 293.00
Champagne, Bucket, Repousse, Handles, Inscribed, Sheffield, 10 x 9 In., Pair 1521.00
Champagne Bucket, Stand, Top Hat Shape, Cane Shape Stand, 32 In. 270.00
Cheese Dish, Leaves, Marked, William Harrison, England, 1880s, 7 x 8 ½ x 7 In. ...... *illus* 195.00
Coffee Urn, Hepplewhite Style, Ivory Spigot, Scrolled Handles, 24 x 12 In. 410.00
Coffeepot, Gadroon, Angular Handle, England, 14 x 9 ½ In. 293.00
Coffeepot, Monticello, Eagle Finial On Lid, Victorian, 11 In. 657.00
Cold Drink Dispenser, Eagle Handles, Polar Bear, Icicles, c.1890. .... 3500.00
Coupe, Normandie, Large Balls On Stem, Luc Lanel, France, c.1933, 4 x 13 ¾ In., Pair 11250.00
Cover, Meat, Leafy Handle, Sheffield, c.1800, 10 x 15 ¼ In. 144.00
Cover, Meat, Oval, Scroll & Shell Border, Crest, Crestwick, Sheffield, 1835, 7 x 12 x 10 In. 863.00
Creamer, Quadruple Plate, Aesthetic, West Silver Co., Applied Feet, Engraved, 5 In. 59.00
Crumber, Tray, Art Nouveau Figure, Tufts, 11 ¾ x 3 & 7 ¾ x 7 In. 575.00
Dish, Cover, Rectangular, Interior Tray, Matthew Boulton, Sheffield, c.1775, 7 x 15 In. 316.00
Dish, Entree, Scrolled Hinged Lid, Ivory, Top, Handles, J.E. & S. Ltd., England, c.1880, 15 x 10 In. 316.00
Dish Cover, Shaped Sides, Leaf Decorated Handle, Family Crest, Sheffield, c.1830, 14 In. 240.00
Egg Set, 2 Eggcups, Salt Dip, Pepper, Stand, 2 Spoons, Knickerbocker, 11 In. 30.00
Epergne, 2 Hanging Glass Vases, Stag On Base, Meriden Co., c.1890, 9 x 13 In. 175.00
Epergne, 4 Scroll Arms, Cut Glass, Family Crest, 1890s, 15 ½ x 21 In. .... *illus* 1210.00
Epergne, Caryatid Supports, Removable Arms, Etched Glass Bowls, 15 x 22 In. 2056.00
Epergne, Cut Glass Bowl, 4 Scroll Candle Arms, Hounds Heads Post, England, c.1885, 27 x 19 In. 460.00
Epergne, Etched Trumpet Vase, 3 Griffins On Base, England, c.1885, 15 In. 431.00
Epergne, Rogaska Crystal, Reed & Barton, 15 x 16 In. 1989.00
Ewer, Neoclassical, Figures, Garlands, 24 In. 878.00
Eyeglass Case, Flowers, Gorham 100.00
Fish Service, Celluloid Handles, Wood Case, George V, c.1919, 7 ½ To 8 ¾ In., 24 Piece 215.00
Goblet, Carved Coconut, 1824, 6 ½ x 4 In. 175.00
Grape Scissors, Grasoli, Germany, 6 ⅛ x 2 In. 135.00
Group, Desert Oasis, Palm Trees, Camel, Rider, Waterfall, England, 35 In. 2640.00
Hobo Knife, Doghead Emblem, Fork Is Bottle Opener, Union Cutlery, 1907, 9 In. 365.00
Hot Water Urn, Oval, Pedestal Base, Opaline Glass Handles, Sheffield, 15 ½ x 12 In. 206.00
Hot Water Urn, Reeded, Masque Ring Handles, Ball Feet, Sheffield, Regency, 17 ½ In. 1003.00
Ice Bucket, Cover, Rope Twist Feet, Draped Cast Tassels, Plastic Liner, 10 ½ In. 413.00
Ice Water Stand, Aesthetic Movement, Gilt, Simpson, Hall, Miller, 1887, 22 x 17 In. ... *illus* 4800.00
Jewelry Box, Porcelain Cover, Pink & White, Blue Flowers, Pairpoint, 3 x 4 In. 150.00
Kettle, Leaf, Scroll, Crest, Ivory Inserts, Pierced Stand, R. Dismore, England, c.1850, 18 In. .. 717.00
Knife Rest, Running Squirrel, Marked, Wilcox Silver Plate Co. 58.00
Knife Set, Steel, Blunt Blades, Ivory Handles, Monogram, Case, 9 ¾ In., 12 Piece 510.00
Ladle, Punch, Cut Glass Handle, Pairpoint. 100.00
Lazy Susan, Shell Shape Dishes, Sheffield, Early 20th Century, 9 ½ In. 159.00
Match Safe, Acorns, Leaves, Stars, Moon, Marked, Pairpoint, 2 ⅝ x 1 In. 50.00
Meat Server, Dome, Footed Well, Tree Hot Water Base, Leafy Handle, 1900s, 15 x 25 In. 1438.00
Mirror, Round Head, Cutout Stem, Female Nude Handle, Hagenauer, Austrian, 5 x 12 In. ... 960.00
Monstrance, Sunburst, Gilt Rays, Bell Base, Saints, Cross, Putti, Chased, F. Freres, c.1875, 29 In. 4248.00
Muffineer, Etched, Beaded, Pindar Bros., England, 6 ¼ In. 250.00
Napkin Rings are listed in their own category.
Pill Box, Sailboats, On Lake, Flowers, 2 ⅛ x 1 ⅛ In. 125.00
Pitcher, 2 Goblets, Stand With Handles, Victorian, 22 In. 263.00
Plaque, Pompeian Lady At Her Toilette, Leonard Morel-Ladeuil, c.1876, 20 ¼ In. 230.00

Plate Set, Service, Chippendale Style, Flaring Border, Gadroon Rim, 11 In., 12 Piece 657.00
Plateau, Footed, Scalloped, Scrolling, Flowers, Old Sheffield, Early 1800s, 21 x 21 In........ 1150.00
Plateau, Mirror, Oval, Elizabethan Style Strapwork, Putti, c.1860, 39 In. 16250.00
Plateau, Oval, Cast Frame, Fruit, Mirrored, Victorian, 25 ½ x 21 In. 270.00
Plateau, Shell Border, Rococo Engraving, Coat Of Arms, Georgian, 1900s, 22 ½ In. 1528.00
Platter, Lobster Serving, Oval Tray, Cast Lobster, On Brass, Italy, 33 x 18 In. 3738.00
Salad Servers, Floral Repousse Handles, Italy, 10-In. Fork, 9 ½-In. Spoon. 20.00
Salver, Shell Border, Piecrust Rim, Footed, Sheffield, 22 ⅜ In. 1762.00
Sauce Spoon, E. Viners, Sheffield, c.1912, 5 In. 47.00
Sculpture, Hunting Dog, Gucci, 8 ½ In. 295.00
Server, Dome Cover, Revolving, Oval, Lion & Paw Legs, Beaded Border, 8 x 13 In. 345.00
Server, Dome Top, Animals, Garlands, 2 Interior Plates, J. Dixon, England, c.1875, 9 x 14 In. 345.00
Server, Etched Dome, Oval, Revolving, Flowers, Leaves, 2 Interior Trays, c.1895, 9 x 13 In.... 431.00
Server, Ivy Dome, Revolving, Flower, Shell, 2 Interior Trays, Marked, England, c.1890, 10 x 16 In. 633.00
Serving Dish, Victorian, Revolving Cover, 8 x 14 x 10 In. 380.00
Serving Set, Fish, Ivory Handles, Knife, Fork, Case, 9 ¼ & 12 ½ In. 450.00
Souffle Dish, Dome Lid, Gadroon, Ivory Finial, Scroll Handles, 6 ½ x 10 In., Pair. 2070.00
Souvenir, see souvenir category.
Spoon Warmer, Shell Form, Hinged Lid, James Dixon & Sons, 4 ½ x 7 In. .... *illus* 605.00
Spoon Warmer, Shell Shape, Rocky Base, Shells, 5 ½ x 6 ½ In. 201.00
Spooner, Ruby Glass Insert, Victorian, c.1890, 8 ½ x 8 In. 358.00
Stein, Relief, Art Nouveau, W.M.F., 3 Liter, 16 In. 1840.00
Sugar, Cover, Eagle, Openwork Over Blue Opaque Liner, 1820s, 7 x 6 ½ In. 5079.00
Tankard, Victorian, Rococo, Embossed, Masked Spout, Mid 1900s, 8 ¾ In. 206.00
Tantalus, Sheffield, 3 Crystal Decanters, Matching Stoppers, c.1800, 14 ¾ In. 403.00
Tea & Coffee Set, Dimension, J. Prip, Black Handles, Reed & Barton, 5 Piece, 1960s, 8 In.... 1080.00
Tea Set, Art Nouveau Style, Pairpoint, 3 Piece 468.00
Teapot, Relief Bird, Leaves, Meriden Silver Plate Co., c.1875, 7 In. 94.00
Teapot, Wood Knob, Handle, Vertical Ribs, I. Karasz, Paye & Baker, c.1928, 5 In. 1920.00
Toast Rack, 6 Slots, Ring Handle, Bun Feet, England 35.00
Tray, Fruit & Flower Rim, Handle, Scroll Engraved, Oval, Paw Feet, 29 x 17 ½ In. 201.00
Tray, Grapevine Border, 14 x 24 In. 175.00
Tray, Hand Chased, Double Handles, Sheffield, 19 x 28 In. 146.00
Tray, On Stand, Turtleback, Pierced, 4 Reeded Legs, Top Shape Feet, c.1910, 23 x 24 In. 2880.00
Tray, Oval, Chased, Vacant Reserve, Handles, Victorian, 19th Century, 31 x 20 In. 294.00
Tray, Oval, Raised Rim, Cut Out Handle, Gorham, 24 In. 70.00
Tray, Oval, Reticulated Gallery, Integral Handles, Gadroon Rim, George VI, 24 x 18 In....... 840.00
Tray, Pierced Gallery, Ellis-Barker, Sheffield, c.1940, 13 ¾ x 20 ¼ In. 263.00
Tray, Pierced Rim, Openwork Handles, Bun Feet, Engraved Leaves, 24 x 18 In. 307.00
Tray, Round, English, Engraved Scrolls, 12 ¼ In. 58.00
Tray, Rounded Rectangular, Handles, 27 x 16 In. 82.00
Tray, Scalloped Oval, 2 Scroll Handle, Scroll & Leaf Engraving, 1900, 29 x 21 In. 201.00
Tray, Scroll Handles, Key Border, Beaded, Oval, Rogers, Smith & Co., c.1865, 31 x 19 In...... 960.00
Tray, Tooled Rosettes, Swags, Beaded Rim, Coat Of Arms, Oval, Sheffield, Georgian, 32 x 20 In. 472.00
Tureen, Round, Wild Turkey Finial, Stag Handles, 2 Panels Forest Animals, 16 x 16 In. 805.00
Tureen, Serving, Revolving, Mounted, Garlands, Sheffield, 9 In. 32.00
Tureen, Soup, Scroll Handles, Gadroon Border, Paw Feet, Sheffield, 10 x 15 In. 1527.00
Urn, Round, Gadroon, Blossom Finial, Bun Feet, 1890s, 16 ½ x 13 In. .... *illus* 880.00
Urn, Square Base, Sheffield, 19th Century, 20 ½ In. 205.00
Vase, Basket Shape, Meriden Brittannia, c.1930, 6 In. 88.00
Vase, Etched, Daalerop, Dutch, 8 In. 35.00
Warming Dish, Shaped Dish, Dome Top, Gadroon Borders, Sheffield, 7 ¾ x 14 In. 230.00
Warming Stand, Lion Finial, Gadroon Border, Turned Handles, Footed, Cover, 18 x 23 In.... 1292.00
Water Stand, Kettle, 3 Cups, Indian, Ornate Fretwork, Gilt, Conn., 1887, 23 x 17 In. 5060.00
Wine Coaster, Mahogany Center, Sheffield, Early 19th Century, 8 x 2 ½ In., Pair 374.00
Wine Cooler, Campagna Shape, Gadroon Borders, Handles, 9 ½ x 9 ½ In, Pair. 705.00
Wine Cooler, Campagna Shape, Leaf Bands, Handles, Georgian, 10 x 10 ¾ In., Pair. 360.00
Wine Cooler, Embossed Leaves, Gadroon Rim, Silver On Copper, c.1800, 11 In., Pair 3068.00
Wine Cooler, Fluted Rim, Applied Grapes, Leaves, Stems, Sheffield, 12 ½ x 11 In. 690.00
Wine Cooler, Gadroon Waist, Foot, Lion's Head Handles, 1900s, 11 ½ In., Pair 598.00
Wine Cooler, Steamboat Form, 3 Supports, Removable Liner, 14 ½ x 6 ¾ In. 2280.00
Wine Cooler, Urn Shape, Twig Handles, Leaf, Mounts, Ruby Glass, c.1890, 11 x 11 In., Pair.. 2645.00
Wine Ewer, Flower Finial, Hinged Lid, Sheffield, c.1900, 14 In. 236.00
Wine Funnel, Ribbed, Smooth Hook, Gilt Interior, c.1810, 7 In. .... *illus* 448.00
Wine Funnel, Sheffield, c.1780, 5 In. 115.00

SILVER, SHEFFIELD, *see Silver Plate; Silver-English categories.*

Silver Plate, Spoon Warmer, Shell Form, Hinged Lid, James Dixon & Sons, 4 ½ x 7 In.
$605.00

Silver Plate, Urn, Round, Gadroon, Blossom Finial, Bun Feet, 1890s, 16 ½ x 13 In.
$880.00

Silver Plate, Wine Funnel, Ribbed, Smooth Hook, Gilt Interior, c.1810, 7 In.
$448.00

TIP

Repainting your front door or kitchen cabinets? Don't put brass hardware back on the doors for at least a week. Paint fumes hasten discoloration.

Silver-American, Berry Spoon, Flower, Fruit Repousse, Crimped, S. Kirk & Son Sterling, 9 In.
$250.00

Silver-American, Bowl, 8-Sided, Tapered, Marked, Randahl Shop, 1900s, 7 ¼ In.
$175.00

Silver-American, Bowl, Flared, Footed, Marked, Arthur Stone, 5 ¼ x 9 ½ In.
$1010.00

Silver-American, Bowl, Monteith, Asian Landscape, Repousse, Coin, Marked, S. Kirk, 7 x 10 In.
$5200.00

SILVER-AMERICAN. American silver is listed here. Coin and sterling silver are included. Most of the sterling silver listed in this book is subdivided by country. There are also other pieces of silver and silver plate listed under special categories, such as Candelabrum, Napkin Ring, Silver Flatware, Silver Plate, Silver-Sterling, and Tiffany Silver. For information about makers and marks, see *Kovels' American Silver Marks: 1650 to the Present.*

Asparagus Fork, Cornucopia Pattern, Shiebler, c.1900, 10 In.. . . . . 478.00
Aspic Server, Hammered, Shaped, Elongated, KVL Monogram, Kalo, c.1900, 12 In. 207.00
Baby Cup, Dancing Woman, J.E. Caldwell & Co., c.1850, 4 In. 292.00
Baby Cup, Engraved Flowers, Applied Draped Child, Gorham, c.1800, 5 x 5 In. 1075.00
Baby Food Pusher, Wm. Rogers & Son, 4 In. 20.00
Baby Spoon, Ivory Handle, Engraved, Ollie, N.Y., c.1800, 4 ¾ x ⅞ In. 190.00
Basket, Chased Flowers, Knot Twist Handle, Signed, Wood & Hughes, 5 ½ x 4 In.. . . . . 225.00
Basket, Cutout Design, Frank Smith Silver Co., 1909, 7 ½ x 7 In. 60.00
Basket, Cutwork, Whiting, Monogram, 10 ⅛ x 7 ¾ In. 675.00
Basket, Hammered, Shaped Handle, Waisted Rectangle Body, 4 Ball Feet, Lebolt, 9 x 4 In. . . . 533.00
Basket, Openwork Floral Sides, Handle, Glass Liner, Frog, Gorham, c.1909, 14 x 10 In.. . . . . 1093.00
Basket, Oval, Scallop Border, Hinged Handle, Pedestal, c.1863, 9 ¾ x 12 ¼ In.. . . . . 5520.00
Basket, Oval, Swing Handle, Cut Scrolls, Gilt Interior, Coin, A. Coles, c.1850.7 x 5 In. 598.00
Basket, Rococo, Round, Leaves & Flowers, Landscapes, Swing Handle, c.1852, 9 In. 490.00
Basket, Swing Handle, Footed, Engraved Rim, Side Lion Knobs, Gorham, c.1869, 6 x 9 In.. . . 717.00
Basket, Swing Handle, Scallop Rim, Lobed Foot, 10 x 12 In.. . . . . 1673.00
Beaker, Barrel Shape, Incised Bands, Baltimore, c.1810, 3 ¼ In., Pair 1140.00
Beaker, Tapered, Cone Shape, Reeded Base Rim, Monogram, Coin, c.1795, 3 In. 326.00
Beaker, Tapered Cylinder, Reeded Rim, Engraved, Coin, R. & W. Wilson, Penn., c.1830, 4 In. . 356.00
Belt, Textured Disks, Gilt, Cartier, c.1970, 30 In.. . . . . 2160.00
Berry Bowl, Fruit Repousse Undulating Rim, Monogram MLS, Gorham, 1902, 11 In. 448.00
Berry Bowl, Lobed, Pierced Cast Strawberry, Leaf Rim, New York, c.1900, 9 In. 353.00
Berry Bowl, Wavy Strawberry Repousse Border, Woodside Sterling, c.1900, 10 In.. . . . . 239.00
Berry Spoon, Apollo, Gilt Flower Repousse Bowl, Nude Terminal, Wendt, c.1870, 9 In.. . . . . 418.00
Berry Spoon, Engraved Bowl, Stem, Lotus Capital, Bust Terminal, c.1870, 9 In. 538.00
Berry Spoon, Flower, Fruit Repousse, Crimped, S. Kirk & Son Sterling, 9 In. . . . . *illus* 250.00
Berry Spoon, Hammered & Applied Pattern, Applied Mounts, c.1880, 9 In. 1374.00
Berry Spoon, Lobed, Fluted Bowl, Whiting, New York, c.1901, 10 In. 96.00
Berry Spoon, Loop Finial, Engraved Warrior, Chased Fruit, Gilt Bowl, Coin, c.1865, 8 In.. . . 478.00
Berry Spoon, Medallion Pattern, Gilt, Shaped Bowl, Engraved Strawberries, c.1862, 9 In. . . . 598.00
Berry Spoon, Vermeil, c.1875, 9 In. 175.00
Binoculars, Chased Yachts, Steel, Gorham Mfg. Co., R.I., c.1880, 5 In. 1195.00
Bonbon, Francis I, Reed & Barton, c.1907, 2 x 8 In. 263.00
Bonbon Spoon, Pierced, Flower Repousse Bowl, Whiting, Late 1800s, 7 ½ In. 472.00
Bonbon Spoon, Pierced Bowl, Scroll Handle, G. Shiebler Co., c.1890, 6 In. 215.00
Bonbon Spoon, Pierced Stem, Bowl, Scrolls, Leaves, Gorham, c.1900, 10 x 5 In.. . . . . 338.00
Bonbon Spoon, Reticulated, Alvin, 4 ½ In. 55.00
Bowl, 6 Silver Petals, Gold Bead, Chased Leaf Center, Mark, A. Stone, 12 x 2 In. 17775.00
Bowl, 8-Sided, Tapered, Marked, Randahl Shop, 1900s, 7 ¼ In. . . . . *illus* 175.00
Bowl, Art Nouveau, Repousse Rim, Flowers, Bud Veins, Gorham, 5 ½ In. 395.00
Bowl, Center, Banded, Footed, International Silver Co., c.1924, 5 x 10 In. 448.00
Bowl, Center, Oval, Openwork Border, Flowers, Swag, Dominick & Haff, 5 ½ x 15 In.. . . . . 1265.00
Bowl, Chased, Embossed Rim, Trefoil, Scrolls, Bands, Footed, Stone, c.1929, 6 x 8 In. 1126.00
Bowl, Chased Bud, Vine, Stepped, Round Foot, A. Stone, c.1925, 2 x 5 In. 3911.00
Bowl, Child's, Applied Children, Flutes, Leaves, Gilt, Whiting Co., Mass., c.1885, 3 x 5 In. . . . 896.00
Bowl, Cylindrical, Gadroon, Acanthus, Ivory Handles, 7 x 11 In., Pair. 3360.00
Bowl, Decorated Rim, Wallace, 10 In. 144.00
Bowl, Double Handle, Hand Wrought, Kalo, No. 277, 11 x 2 In. 1080.00
Bowl, Embossed Garlands, Rococo Scroll Edge, Footed, 4 ¾ x 11 x 17 ½ In. 2880.00
Bowl, Empire, Bead Border, Coin, A. Warner, Baltimore, c.1845, 2 x 10 In. 1093.00
Bowl, Flared, Footed, Marked, Arthur Stone, 5 ¼ x 9 ½ In. . . . . *illus* 1010.00
Bowl, Flared Lobed Sides, Reticulated Border, Oval, c.1900. . . . . 587.00
Bowl, Fruit, Danish Design, Allan Adler, 1950s, 12 ¼ In. 1320.00
Bowl, Fruit, Floral Repousse, Folded Rim, Signed, S. Kirk & Son, 2 ½ x 12 x 8 In. 350.00
Bowl, Fruit, Repousse Scrolls, Footed, Coin, Ball, Black & Co., 1851-76, 7 x 11 In. 1300.00
Bowl, Hammered, Flower Repousse, Wavy Lip, Gilt Interior, c.1880, 2 x 5 In. 717.00
Bowl, Hammered, Scalloped Edge, Arts & Crafts, 1 ¾ x 5 In. 148.00
Bowl, Hammered, Undulating Sides, 3 Turtle Feet, Wood & Hughes, c.1890, 2 x 5 In. 1434.00
Bowl, Hammered, Wavy Lip, Applied Insect, Snake, Bat, Flower, Shiebler, c.1880, 3 x 4 In. . . . 956.00
Bowl, Hammered Interior, Cutout Handle, Lebolt, No. 192, 7 In. 210.00
Bowl, Hand Hammered, Attached Underplate, Kalo, 2 x 7 ¾ In. 450.00
Bowl, Hand Wrought, Impressed Mark, Kalo, 2 x 4 In. 300.00

Bowl, Honeycomb Pattern, 2 Handles, Wood & Hughes, N.Y., c.1880, 11 In. 717.00
Bowl, Lobed Rim, Foot, Kalo, 12 5/8 In. 2160.00
Bowl, Lobed Sides, Reticulated Rim, Oak Leaves, Acorns, Gorham, c.1903, 14 In. 1800.00
Bowl, Monteith, Asian Landscape, Repousse, Coin, Marked, S. Kirk, 7 x 10 In. . . . . *illus* 5200.00
Bowl, Octagonal, Reticulated, Scrolls, Shells, J.E. Caldwell, c.1900, 4 x 10 In. 657.00
Bowl, Olive, Hammered, Chased, Stems, Leaves, Gorham, 1886, 2 x 6 In. 1016.00
Bowl, Oval, 2 Applied Lobsters, Upturned Sides, Footed, c.1860, 4 x 7 In. 1434.00
Bowl, Oval, Lobed Shape, Kalo Workshop, c.1916, 2 x 9 In. 415.00
Bowl, Oyster Shape, Beaded, Wood & Hughes, c.1880, 7 x 4 In. 598.00
Bowl, Oyster Shape, Folded Handle, Wood & Hughes, c.1880, 7 x 4 In. 526.00
Bowl, Paul Revere Style, Monogram, c.1930, 3 1/4 x 7 1/4 In. 147.00
Bowl, Reeded Foot, S. Kirk & Son, 1900s, 4 x 9 In. 881.00
Bowl, Revere Style, Gorham, 5 1/4 x 10 1/4 In. 345.00
Bowl, Rope Twist Border, Pedestal Base, Coin, Mitchell & Tyler, 3 x 7 1/2 In. 375.00
Bowl, Round, Embossed Lilies, Flared Rim, Art Nouveau, 11 1/2 x 2 In. 411.00
Bowl, Round, Flared Wave Rim, Chased Flowers, Rounded Feet, Martele, 7 1/4 In. 2645.00
Bowl, Rounded Octagonal, Tapered Sides, Randahl Shop, Chicago, 1 3/4 x 4 1/4 In. 201.00
Bowl, Scalloped Rim, Circular Foot, 8 5/8 In. 652.00
Bowl, Scrolling Morning Glories, Vines, Art Nouveau, 12 In. 546.00
Bowl, Vegetable, English Flute Pattern, 1900s, 10 5/8 In. 150.00
Bowl, Vegetable, Francis I, Reed & Barton, c.1907, 11 1/2 In. 600.00
Bowl, Vegetable, Francis I, Undulating Rim, Reed & Barton, c.1907, 11 In. 776.00
Bowl, Vegetable, Lid, Handle, 4 Arch Rim, Bust, Scrolls, Plants, Sharp, c.1870, 6 x 13 In. 2390.00
Bowl, Vegetable, Repousse, Signed, S. Kirk & Son, 2 1/2 x 11 3/4 x 8 In. 400.00
Bowl, Wave Rim, Flowers, Footed, Gorham, Marked, Martele, 7 1/4 In. . . . . *illus* 2300.00
Bowl, Wm. B. Durgin, Caldwell & Co., Late 19th Century, 8 1/2 x 11 In. 293.00
Bowl & Plate, Noah's Ark, Sterling, Gold Wash, Gorham 750.00
Bread Tray, Lobed, Undulating Rim, Repousse Scroll, Flowers, Gorham, 1917, 14 In. 1434.00
Bread Tray, Rolled Rim, Repousse Cherries, Leaves, Wallace & Sons, Conn., 11 In. 155.00
Buckwheat Server, Medallion, Flower Scalloped Blade, Wood & Hughes, c.1865, 8 In. 777.00
Buckwheat Server, Twisted Stem, Flower Terminal, Bowl, Polhamus, c.1870, 10 In. 382.00
Butter, Cover, Francis I, Repousse Rim, Fruit, Scrolled, Reed & Barton, 3 1/2 In. 374.00
Butter, Mixed Metals, Hammered, Bamboo, Prunus, Crane, Carp, Butterfly, 4, 2 1/2 In. 2640.00
Butter Knife, Diamond, Engraved Monogram, George Shiebler, 7 1/4 In. 64.00
Butter Knife, Fiddle Handle, Charleston, Coin, Inscribed, J. Ewan, 8 In. . . . . *illus* 465.00
Butter Knife, Fiddle Handle, Rounded Fins, Coin, Hallmarks, 8 In. 430.00
Butter Knife, Fiddle Handle, Rounded Fins, Inscribed, South Carolina, 8 In. 489.00
Butter Knife, Flowers, Scrolls, Scale, Coin, Mitchell & Tyler, 1855, 6 1/2 In. . . . . *illus* 27.00
Butter Pick, Monogram, J.W. Cusack, 5 3/4 In. 88.00
Butter Tub, Dome Top, Cow Finial, Presentation, Capt. T. Hall, N.y., c.1863, 7 x 6 In. 6900.00
Buttonhook, Twist Stem, Hammered, Notched Terminal, c.1880, 7 In. 90.00
Cake Basket, Pierced, Engraved, Swing Handle, Footed, c.1920, 14 x 11 x 9 In. 4200.00
Cake Knife, Basket Weave Stem, Flower Blade, Hebbard & Moore, c.1850, 12 In. 765.00
Cake Knife, Twisted Stem, Shaped Loop Terminal, Warrior Medallion Blade, c.1862, 11 In. . . 478.00
Cake Plate, Pedestal Foot, Scrolls, Fruit, Galt & Bros., Inc., Wash. D.C., c.1915, 12 In. 748.00
Candelabra are listed in the Candelabrum category.
Candlesticks are listed in their own category.
Candy Dish, Wide Rim, 6 Lines, Wheelock, 9 In. 200.00
Cann, Cup, Pear Shape, Leaf Molded Lyre Form Handle, Scrolled, 5 11/16 In. 2500.00
Cann, Cup, Tapered, Cylindrical, Bands, Scrolling Handle, Monogram, 3 1/2 In. 3068.00
Carafe, Cut Glass, Engraved R, Gorham, c.1897, 8 1/2 In. 147.00
Card Case, Engraved, Chain, Spring Ring, Crystal Palace, N.Y., c.1850, 3 5/8 x 2 1/4 In. 300.00
Case, Wine Bottle, Rococo Scroll, Flower, Twisted Branch Handle, c.1900, 10 In. 2040.00
Cheese Scoop, Fiddle & Thread Handle, Rounded Fins, Marked, Charleston, 7 1/2 In. 403.00
Cheese Scoop, Onslow, Marked, A. Stone, c.1910, 9 In. 533.00
Chocolate Pot, Mum Repousse, Gilt, Mermod & Jaccard, c.1900, 7 In. 1673.00
Cigar Vase, Mermaids, Waves, Leaves, 4 Dolphin Feet, Gorham, Martele, 1902, 4 In. 5625.00
Cigarette Case, Monogram, Reed & Barton. 47.00
Cocktail Shaker, Top, LLP Monogram, Manchester Silver Co., 10 In. 329.00
Coffee Set, Coffeepot, Teapot, Sugar, Creamer, Tray, Chester, Gorham, c.1907 . . . . 863.00
Coffee Set, Fruit, Leaves, Wavy Feet, Martele, Gorham, 1899, 4 Piece 16250.00
Coffee Set, Octagon Shape, Flowers, Swags, International Co., 4 Piece 633.00
Coffee Set, RKH Monogram, Gorham, 10 In., 4 Piece 329.00
Coffeepot, Queen Anne Style, Leaf Capped Handle, Watson, 20th Century, 9 1/8 In. 75.00
Compote, Fruit, Flat, Circular Urn Shape, C Handles, Putti, 7 7/8 x 7 In. 1750.00
Compote, Gadroon, Knop Stem, Dome Foot, Leaves, 8 x 10 1/2 In., Pair 1920.00
Compote, Hand Hammered Bowl, Raised Round Foot, Asheville, North Carolina, 4 x 8 In. . . . 415.00

Silver-American, Bowl, Wave Rim, Flowers, Footed, Gorham, Marked, Martele, 7 1/4 In.
$2300.00

Silver-American, Butter Knife, Fiddle Handle, Charleston, Coin, Inscribed, J. Ewan, 8 In.
$465.00

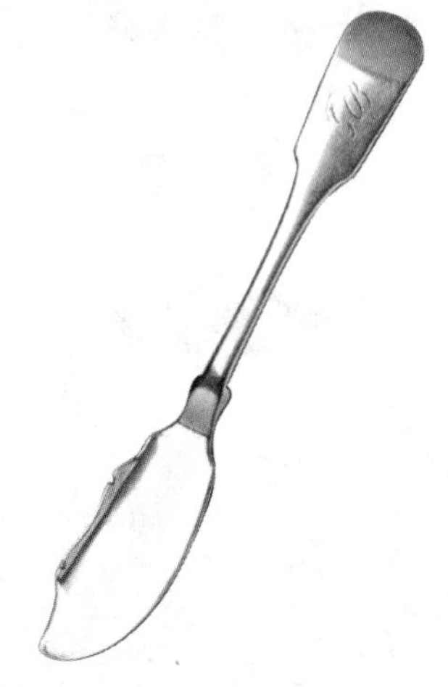

Silver-American, Butter Knife, Flowers, Scrolls, Scale, Coin, Mitchell & Tyler, 1855, 6 1/2 In.
$27.00

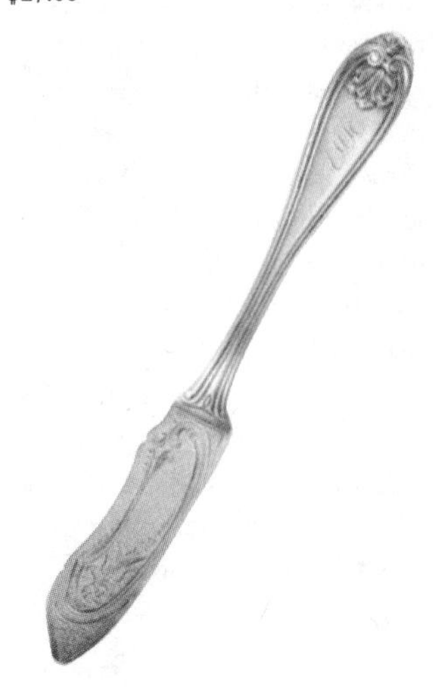

Silver-American, Cup, Grapes, Vines, Coin, Marked, H. Hudson, Louisville, 3 ¾ x 3 In., Pair
$1650.00

Silver-American, Cup, Ram's Heads, Flowers, Repousse, Coin, Marked, S. Kirk & Son, 8 ¼ In.
$495.00

Grapefruit Spoons
"I wish they had a left-handed grapefruit spoon," said the lefty struggling to loosen the sections from the grapefruit half she was eating for breakfast. The comment made us wonder. A grapefruit spoon looks like a pointed teaspoon with serrated edges on the bowl. A right-handed spoon has serrated edges on one side—the wrong side for a person eating with the left hand. We checked. The grapefruit or citrus spoon was introduced in the 1890s. It was silver or silver plated. The bowl was pointed but not serrated, so it was good for right- and left-handed diners. The serrated spoon was a twentieth century improvement.

Compote, Openwork Poppy Borders, Monogram, Woodside Sterling Co., 5 x 9 In. 403.00
Compote, Repousse, Footed, Signed, S. Kirk & Son, 3 ¼ x 6 ½ In., Pair 750.00
Compote, Repousse, Steiff, Early 20th Century, 3 ½ x 7 ¼ In. 351.00
Compote, Repousse Rim, S. Kirk & Sons, 3 ¼ x 4 ¼ In. 1495.00
Compote, Wide, Shallow Bowl, Long, Flared Stem, Lebolt, c.1920, 6 x 10 In. 385.00
Cream Ladle, Shaped Bowl, Roger, Lunt & Bowlen Co., c.1905, 5 In. 39.00
Cream Ladle, Sphinx, Gilt Bowl, Gorham, c.1869, 7 In. 311.00
Creamer, Baluster, Repousse Chased Oak Leaf, Beaded Lip, Thumbpiece, c.1851, 5 In. 960.00
Creamer, Embossed, Boats, Grapes, Ribbed Handles, A.E. Warner, Md., 1800s, 5 ¾ In. 2252.00
Creamer, Federal, Pear Shape, Gadroon Rims, Serpentine Handle, c.1780, 4 ¼ In. 415.00
Creamer, Pear Shape, Scalloped Rim, Dome Top, Twig & Leaf Handle, 7 x 7 ½ In. 3910.00
Creamer, Pear Shape, Scroll Handle, 3 Shell Feet, EB Mark, Coin, c.1730, 5 In. 1185.00
Creamer, Round, Pierced Rim, Base, Mask Spout, S-Handle, Gorham, c.1871, 4 x 6 In. 239.00
Cup, Chased Renaissance Figures Band, Flower Rim, Gilt Interior, Gorham, 1890, 3 x 5 In. 478.00
Cup, Child, Gold Interior, Fisher, 1950s, 3 In. 47.00
Cup, Child's, Hammered, Flower, Bird, Insect, Branch Repousse, Shiebler, c.1890, 3 In. 388.00
Cup, Daffodil Repousse, Gorham, 1870, 5 In., Pair 2032.00
Cup, Fluted, Repousse Flowers, Twist Handle, Whiting, c.1890, 3 x 5 In. 263.00
Cup, Grapes, Vines, Coin, Marked, H. Hudson, Louisville, 3 ¾ x 3 In., Pair .... *illus* 1650.00
Cup, Ram's Heads, Flowers, Repousse, Coin, Marked, S. Kirk & Son, 8 ¼ In. .... *illus* 495.00
Decanter, Overlay, Rounded Shape, Clear Glass, Scroll Handle, Stopper, 8 x 6 In. 805.00
Demitasse Spoon, Federal, Hand & Crane, 5 ⅜ In., 3 Piece 99.00
Dish, Cover, Floral Repousse, Scroll, Coin, Bailey & Co., 4 ¼ x 9 In. 400.00
Dish, Flower Rim, Etched Glass Insert, S. Kirk & Son Inc., c.1925, 6 ¼ In. 82.00
Dish, Leaf Form, Handle, Reed & Barton, 1937, 11 ¼ In. 248.00
Dish, Scalloped Edges, Old Newbury Crafters, 11 In. 175.00
Dish, Scalloped Rim, Stone Associates, 1900s, 6 In. 410.00
Dish, Swan, Gorham, 20th Century, 6 x 8 In. 1057.00
Dresser Set, Enameled, Mirror, Cut Glass Powder Jar, Brushes, 19th Century, 4 Piece 403.00
Dresser Set, Mirror, Brush, File, Shoehorn, Hook, William B. Kerr, 10 ¼ In., 5 Piece 72.00
Dresser Set, Mirror, Comb Frame, Brush, R. Wallace & Sons 72.00
Dresser Set, Raised Flowers, Gorham, Box, c.1890, 10 Piece 450.00
Eggcup, Gilt Interior, Monogram, c.1850, 2 x 2 In. 21.00
Ewer, Applied Flourishes To Handle, Coin, Philadelphia, c.1839, 13 In. 823.00
Ewer, Baluster, Scroll Handle, Flared Lip, Flower Repousse, Coin, Bogert, c.1850, 13 In. 1315.00
Ewer, Egg Shape, Narrow Neck, Flaring Spout, Pedestal, Grapes, Leaves, c.1900, 14 In. 2467.00
Ewer, Flared Spout, Pierced Handle, Flower Engraved Body, Coin, c.1860, 9 In. 382.00
Figurine, Dog, Poodle, S. Kirk & Son, 2 In. 60.00
Fish Knife, Twisted Stem, Gilt Serrated Blade, Dominick & Haff, N.Y., c.1870, 8 In., 8 Piece 179.00
Fish Server, Chased & Engraved Handle, Coin, James Watts, c.1835-50, 12 In. 100.00
Fish Server, Olive Pattern, Openwork Handle, Coin, Marked, J.E. Spear, 11 ¾ In. 325.00
Fish Slice, Shaped Blade, Carp, Cranes, Flowers, Whiting Co., Mass., 1881, 11 In. 657.00
Flask, Basket Weave, Plain Base, Glass Liner, Twist Cap, Engraved Brandy, c.1900, 7 In. 956.00
Flask, Bowed, Etched Birds, Water, Grass, Screw Cap, Gorham, c.1880, 6 x 4 In. 956.00
Flask, Fish Shape, Chain, Repousse Flowers, Screw Cap, CA Monogram, c.1890, 7 In. 717.00
Flask, Gilt, Repousse Oranges, Leaves, Cushion Shape, Inscribed, Gorham, 1882, 7 In. 3884.00
Flask, Moon Face, Woman, Flowing Hair, Night, Wind, Smoke, Unger Bros., 4 In. 593.00
Flask, Teardrop Shape, Chased Flowers, Plants, Gorham, 1890, 5 In. 263.00
Fork, 4 Tines, Acanthus Terminal, Woods & Hughes, 8 In., 12 Piece 478.00
Fork, Fiddle & Thread Handles, Monogram, 8 In., 5 Piece 201.00
Fork, Seafood, Twisted Stem, Gilt, Multicolored Enamel Handle, c.1880, 4 In., 3 Piece 102.00
Fruit Set, Mother-Of-Pearl Handle, Wood Presentation Box, 1800s, 16 In., 12 Piece 120.00
Gilt Shell Bowl, Twisted Stem, Whiting Mfg. Co., Mass., 6 In. 60.00
Goblet, Flared Rims, Chicago Silver Co., c.1950, 7 In., 12 Piece 1150.00
Goblet, Inverted Bell Shape, Applied Rim, Round Foot, Coin, Ball, Tompkins & Black, 1839, 5 In. 235.00
Goblet, Stepped Base, Repousse Grapevine, Eoff & Shepherd, c.1865, 7 x 4 In., Pair 1016.00
Goblet, Urn Shape, Engraved, Flowers, Scroll, Monogram, Schofield, 6 ¾ In., 8 Piece 2760.00
Grape Scissors, Female Figure Handles, Steel Blade, 1893, 7 In. 179.00
Grape Scissors, Grape Handle, Repousse, Signed, S. Kirk & Son, 6 ¾ In. 400.00
Grapefruit Spoon, Gilt Bowl, Whiting Mfg., Mass., c.1893, 5 In., 6 Piece 120.00
Gravy Boat, Helmet Form, Ring Foot, Scroll Handle, Coin, Hayden & Co, 2 x 6 x 3 In. 750.00
Gravy Boat, Underplate, Windsor Castle Pattern, Wallace & Co. 160.00
Gravy Ladle, Beaded Stem, Classical Bust Terminal, Gilt Bowl, Coin, 7 In. 478.00
Gravy Ladle, Square Stem, Warrior Terminal, Gilt Bowl, Coin, Coles & Co., c.1860, 9 In. 574.00
Hair Comb, Colonial Pineapple, 7 Thistles, Coin, Marked, E.W. 160.00
Hand Mirror, Broadway & Co., c.1985, 14 In. 176.00
Hot Water Urn, Melon Finial, Lobed Neck, Picturesque Vignette, c.1850, 14 In. 10575.00

Hot Water Urn, Scalloped Corners, Oval, Scroll Base, 4 Ball Feet, Edward Ball, 14 In. 489.00
Ice Bucket, Barrel Shape, Pierced Irremovable Tray, Round, Moore, c.1860, 7 x 11 In. 7768.00
Ice Cream Knife, Engraved Leaves Blade, Basket Weave, Flower Stem, c.1865, 10 In. 568.00
Ice Cream Server, Sunflower Terminal, Gilt Bowl, Vanderslice & Co., c.1870, 9 In. 538.00
Ice Cream Slice, Bric A Brac, Shaped Flower Blade, Gorham, c.1875, 10 In. 1016.00
Ice Cream Slice, Classical Woman On Twisted Stem, Coin, c.1850, 10 In. 385.00
Ice Cream Slice, Engraved Flowers, Curved Stem, Shaped, Gilt Blade, c.1890, 11 In. 478.00
Ice Cream Slice, Grapes, Ball Handle, Engraved, C, Signed, H. Richardson, 10 ¼ In. 215.00
Ice Cream Slice, Ivory Handles, Gilt Shaped Blade, Whiting, c.1890, 12 In. 837.00
Ice Cream Slice, Mayflower, Cow, Fruit Baskets, Engraved Blade, c.1870, 10 In. 508.00
Ice Cream Slice, Shaped Blade, Engraved Flowers, Gorham, c.1880, 10 In. 657.00
Jewelry Box, Hinged Lid, Repousse Flowers, Cherubs, Swags, Gorham, 1890, 2 x 9 In. 2390.00
Jug, Hot Water, Spherical, Cylindrical Neck, Thistles, Fruit, Acanthus Scrolls, 9 x 6 ½ In. 3120.00
Julep Cup, Beaded Foot, Rim, Flower Repousse Cartouche, c.1850, 3 ⅜ In. 259.00
Julep Cup, Coin, H. Hudson, J. Dolfinger, Kentucky, 4 In. 1657.00
Julep Cup, Inscribed, M. Scearce, Kent., c.1964, 4 x 3 In., 4 Piece 956.00
Julep Cup, Molded Lip, Applied Foot, Coin, Marked, Hudson & Dolfinger, 3 ¾ In. 1057.00
Julep Cup, Reeded Border, J. Akin, Kentucky, 1850s, 3 ½ x 3 In., Pair 1610.00
Julep Cup, Tapered, Applied Beaded Detail, Coin, Marked, Kitts, 1850, 4 In. 940.00
Julep Cup, Tapered, Applied Beading, Coin, John Kitts, c.1850, 4 In. 881.00
Julep Cup, Tapered, Coin, Marked, T. Emond, 3 ¼ In. 3200.00
Julep Cup, Tapered Cylindrical Form, Applied Beading, Coin, Marked, J. Kitts & Co., 1860, 3 ¾ In. 881.00
Kettle, Stand, Repousse Base, Rim, Lid, Crossed Handle, Kirk, Baltimore, c.1885, 15 In. 3884.00
Ladle, Bright Cut, Engraved Handles, Twist Stems, Monogram, Coin, 7 ½ In., Pair 345.00
Ladle, Coin, Marked, W.H. Calhoun, Nashville, c.1845-50, 12 ½ In. 2800.00
Ladle, Cream, Chased Leaves, Bowl, Twisted Leaves Stem, Towle, Mass., c.1900, 6 In. 239.00
Ladle, Downturned Handle, Marked, J. Anthony, Penn., c.1810, 13 In. 863.00
Ladle, Downturned Tipt Back, Fiddle Handle, Rounded Fins, Charleston, 13 In. 633.00
Ladle, Downturned Tipt Back, Fiddle Handle, Rounded Fins, Monogram, 13 In. 920.00
Ladle, Female Figure Terminal, Gilt Bowl, Leaf Rim, Wood & Hughes, c.1870, 7 In. 448.00
Ladle, Fiddle & Thread Handle, Coin, Marked, J. Conning, Mobile, 12 ¾ In. 650.00
Ladle, Fiddle Handle, Oval Bowl, Coin, Marked, Stauffer & Harley, 13 In. 200.00
Ladle, Fiddle Handle, Shell Bowl, B. Barton, Virginia, Coin, 10 In. 518.00
Ladle, Leaves, Branch Stem, Floral Shape Gilt Bowl, Redlich & Co., N.Y., c.1895, 7 In. 311.00
Ladle, Oval, Downturned Handle, Round Bowl, Monogram, Marked, 12 ¾ In. 2185.00
Ladle, Oval Bowl, Fiddle & Thread Handle, Coin, Marked, David Kinsey, c.1840, 13 ½ In. 176.00
Ladle, Oval Bowl, Fiddle Handle, Marked, Sterling, Duhme & Co., 13 In. 175.00
Ladle, Oval Handle, Bowl, Coin, Geo. Riggs, Georgetown, D.C., 13 ½ In. 748.00
Ladle, Reeded Rim, Chased Cartouche Medallion, Leaves, Wood Handle, 15 In. 83.00
Ladle, Round Bowl, Strawberry Handle Decoration, Monogram, 11 ¾ In. 173.00
Ladle, Scalloped Shell Bowl, Beaded, Anthemion, Coin, G.B. Sharp, 9 ½ In. 150.00
Ladle, Shell Bowl, Fiddle Handle, Coin, Marked, B. Barton, 10 ¼ In. .... *illus* 495.00
Ladle, Sickle & Wheat Design, Fiddle Handle, Coin, Marked, J. Ewan, 13 In. .... *illus* 1100.00
Lemonade Stirrer, Reed & Barton, c.1893, 13 In. 131.00
Letter Opener, Chased Seawood, Shells, Crab, G.W. Shiebler, c.1890, 11 ⅜ In. 1440.00
Letter Opener, Chased Waves, Homeric Gold Cameo, Shiebler, c.1890, 12 In. 1554.00
Letter Opener, Rectangular Ivory Blade, Silver Pumpkin Overlay, 2 Opals, 1900s, 11 In. 296.00
Letter Opener, Saxon Stag, Stag Head Finial, Monogram JMB, Gorham, 1913, 6 In. 287.00
Loving Cup, Hizen, Fluted, Engraved Sea Life, Chased, Gorham, c.1885, 7 x 8 In. 11353.00
Loving Cup, Yale, Dated 1909, Dominick & Haff, 10 x 10 In. 2530.00
Macaroni Server, Foliage Stem, Terminal, Shaped Blade, 11-Tine, Boston, 10 In. 448.00
Mirror, Vanity, Heart Shape, Floral, Bird Repousse, Dominick & Haff, c.1890, 14 x 11 In. 538.00
Muffineer, Hallmarks, T. Kirkpatrick & Co., Signed, Gorham, 6 ½ In. 150.00
Muffineer, Repousse, Signed, Schofield, 5 In. 750.00
Mug, Cylinder, Scroll Handle, Beaded Rim, Flowers, Fruit, Coin, J. & W. Moir, c.1850, 4 In. 178.00
Mug, Handle, Repousse Top Flower Edge, Coin, Gorham, 3 ¼ In. 240.00
Mug, Pear Shape, Leaf, Serpentine Handle, Coin, Lewis & Smith, Philadelphia, c.1825, 4 In. . 1185.00
Mug, Reeded Borders, S-Scroll Handle, Coin 900.00
Mug, Round, Flared Rim, Acanthus & Scroll, Coin, J.H. Connor, 4 ½ x 4 ½ In. 288.00
Mug, Round, Hourglass Sides, Arabesque, Gilt Interior, Gorham, 3 ½ x 4 ½ In. 316.00
Mug, Shaped Sides, Square C Handle, Coin, Bigelow & Bros., 4 x 5 In. 144.00
Napkin Clip, Horse Shape, Paye & Baker Mfg., Mass., c.1920, 3 x 2 In. 84.00
Napkin Rings are listed in their own category.
Nut Dish, 3 Repousse Bowls, Handle, S. Kirk & Son, Maryland, c.1945, 4 x 6 In. 311.00
Nut Dish, Kirk, Trifid Feet, Repousse, Baltimore, Early 1900s, 3 x 6 ½ In., Pair 300.00
Nut Scoop, Gilt, R. Blackinton & Co., c.1900, 4 In. 227.00
Nut Scoop, Pierced Star Bowl, Gilt, Towle, c.1900, 5 In. 96.00

TIP
Candle drippings can be removed from fabric or furniture with the help of ice cubes. Rub the wax with the ice until the wax hardens. Scrape off the hard wax with a credit card or stiff cardboard. If some wax remains, put a blotter over it, and then iron with a cool iron.

Silver-American, Ladle, Shell Bowl, Fiddle Handle, Coin, Marked, B. Barton, 10 ¼ In.
$495.00

Silver-American, Ladle, Sickle & Wheat Design, Fiddle Handle, Coin, Marked, J. Ewan, 13 In.
$1100.00

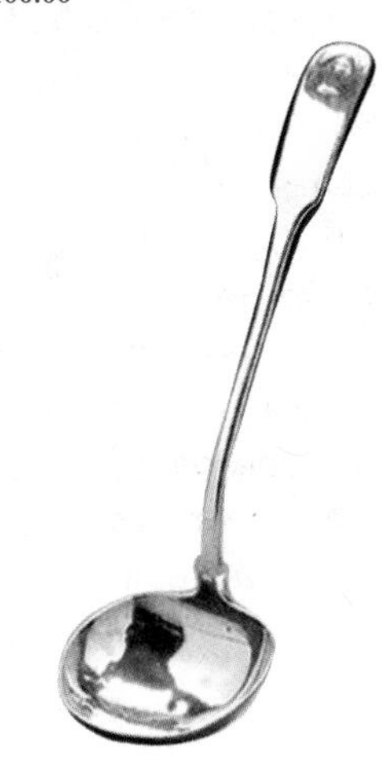

S

Silver-American, Pitcher, Bigelow, Kennard & Co., 13 In.
$915.00

Silver-American, Pitcher, Grapes, Acorns, Coin, Marked, Clark & Co., Georgia, 8 x 6 In.
$2400.00

TIP
Real tortoiseshell smells like burning hair when it is held over a match. Plastic smells like burning plastic. Because you have to remove a piece of the shell to hold it over a match, this is not a very useful test.

Nut Spoon, Banded Stem, Squirrel Terminal, Fluted Bowl, Gorham, c.1870, 11 In. 896.00
Olive Spoon, Twig Stem, Leaf, Olive Terminal, Pierced Bowl, Gorham, c.1870, 6 In. 598.00
Pancake Lifter, Leaf Handle, Engraved Blade, Coin, Hemingway & Stevens, 8 ½ In. 403.00
Pie Server, Pierced Bowl, Unger Bros., N.J., c.1890, 7 In. 179.00
Pie Server, Scroll Blade, Twisted, Beaded Handle, A. Coles & Co., N.Y., c.1855, 10 In. 191.00
Pin, Corsage, Homeric Pattern, 2 Profiles, G. Shiebler & Co., N.Y., c.1885, 5 In. 239.00
Pin Tray, Rectangle, Embossed Waves, Fish, Crab, Gorham, 1884, 4 In., Pair 717.00
Pitcher, Bigelow, Kennard & Co., 13 In. .... *illus* 915.00
Pitcher, Bulbous, Wide Spout, Applied Handle, Gyllenberg & Swanson, c.1930, 7 In. 444.00
Pitcher, Chased Tropical Scene, Man, Inscribed, G. Stewart, Kentucky, c.1845, 5 x 5 In. 3107.00
Pitcher, Floral Repousse, Footed, Steiff, 14 ½ In. 4212.00
Pitcher, Flowers, Ram Head Handle, Brackett, Crosby & Brown, Mass., c.1860, 8 In. 717.00
Pitcher, Flowers, Repousse, Marked, No. 1396, Shiebler, 7 ¼ In. 600.00
Pitcher, Flowers & Scale, Pear Form, Pad Feet, Coin, Bailey & Co., 4 x 2 ¾ In. 325.00
Pitcher, Grapes, Acorns, Coin, Marked, Clark & Co., Georgia, 8 x 6 In. .... *illus* 2400.00
Pitcher, Grapevine Handle, Beaded Rim, Shells, Scrolls, Coin, Wm. Gale & Son, 1851, 12 In. 1778.00
Pitcher, Hammered, Copper Fruit, Branches, Gilt, Gorham, 1879, 8 In. 15625.00
Pitcher, Hand Wrought, Monogram M, Impressed, Kalo, No. 12, 6 ½ x 8 In. 1200.00
Pitcher, Lid, Acorn Finial, Reeded Handle, N. Taylor & Co., N.Y., c.1825, 11 In. 3851.00
Pitcher, Lobed Body, 4 Ornate Feet, Ball, Tompkins & Black, N.Y., c.1845, 10 In. 1315.00
Pitcher, Paneled Pear Shape, S-Scroll Handle, Footed, Marked, W.G. & S., 5 x 6 In. 431.00
Pitcher, Pear Shape, Raised Foot Rim, Anthemion Border, Scroll Handle, Coin, 1837, 28 Oz. 1150.00
Pitcher, Pear Shape, Scroll Handle, Footed, Flower & Scroll Repousse, 6 x 6 In. 575.00
Pitcher, Scroll Handle, Grape, Acorn Design, Marked, Clark & Co., c.1850, 8 x 6 x 5 In. 2530.00
Pitcher, Scroll Handle, Reeding, Stepped Foot, Fisher, 11 ¼ In. 570.00
Pitcher, Undertray, Classical, Paneled, Monogram, Gorham, c.1928, 8 ¼ & 10 ¾ In. 499.00
Pitcher, Water, Allover Flower Repousse, Whiting Co., c.1880, 7 x 8 In., Pair 3585.00
Pitcher, Water, Baluster, Bands, Scroll Handle, Thumbpiece, c.1837, 9 ⅝ In. 764.00
Pitcher, Water, Baluster, Water Leaves, Monogram, Spreading Foot, c.1839, 11 In. 1715.00
Pitcher, Water, Chased Seaweed, Shells, Whiting Co., New York, c.1880, 7 In. 16250.00
Pitcher, Water, Collar, Foot Ring, Circular Geometric Band, 9 ¼ x 7 ½ In. 4800.00
Pitcher, Water, Globular, Cylindrical Neck, Olive Branch, Gorham, c.1882, 7 In. 857.00
Pitcher, Water, Hand Chased, Wreath, Frank M. Whiting, 10 x 9 ½ In. 775.00
Pitcher, Water, Oval, Spread Foot, Elongated Handle, Black, Starr & Frost, 13 In. 1652.00
Pitcher, Water, Pear Shape, Scroll Border, Theodore Starr, 9 x 9 In. 518.00
Pitcher, Water, Repousse, Chased Flowers, S. Kirk & Sons, Baltimore, c.1930, 8 x 8 In. 2390.00
Pitcher, Water, Scroll Handle, Trumpet Foot, Fisher, c.1900, 10 In. 533.00
Pitcher, Water, Urn Shape, Chased Swags, Bell Drops, Squared Handle, c.1920, 11 x 9 In. 1135.00
Plate, Ice Cream, Scalloped Rim, Repousse Flowers, Martele, Gorham, c.1909, 7 In. 2868.00
Plate, Sandwich, Francis I, Reed & Barton, c.1907, 12 In. 478.00
Platter, Banded, S. Kirk & Son, Baltimore, c.1945, 11 In. 120.00
Platter, Well & Tree, International, 20 ¼ In. 960.00
Porringer, Child's, Bunny Repousse Handle, Hammered, Kalo Shop, c.1920, 2 x 6 In. 657.00
Porringer, Crown Cresting Handle, Peter David, Phila., c.1750, 4 ⅝ In. 1150.00
Porringer, Keyhole Handle, Domed Bowl, Engraved, Boston, c.1720, 6 In. 3081.00
Porringer, Pierced Handle, Monogram, Marked, John Potwine, c.1740, 8 In. 2703.00
Porringer, Pierced Scroll Handle, Monogram, Coin, Daniel Rogers, Mass., 1753, 8 In. 3081.00
Porringer, Pierced Scroll Handle, Round, Engraved, A. Stone, c.1919, 7 In. 563.00
Porringer, Round Bulbous Bowl, Pierced Cast Handle, HR Initials, Boston, 5 In. 2133.00
Portfolio, Flower, Scroll Overlay, Center MB Monogram, Gorham, c.1890, 13 x 10 In. 837.00
Pudding Spoon, 14th Century, Shreve, San Francisco, c.1915, 10 In. 1434.00
Pudding Spoon, Cattail, Butterfly Terminal, Leaf Bowl, Coin, c.1865, 10 In. 538.00
Punch Bowl, Ellmore, c.1940, 12 x 6 In. 468.00
Punch Bowl, Footed, Bulbous Bowl, Lobed Rim, Applied Scrolling, Mauser, 6 x 15 In. 1912.00
Punch Bowl, Ladle, Bacchus Mounts, Putti, Fruit, Gorham, 1886, 17 In., 14 In. 10000.00
Punch Bowl, Spiral Gadroons, Cabochon Strings, 8 ¼ x 13 ½ In. 2640.00
Punch Bowl, Tray & Ladle, Beaded Rim, 8 Enameled Bars, Old Newbury Crafters, 10, 19, 12 In. 8295.00
Punch Ladle, Beaded Rim, Coin, Marked, E.A. Tyler, N.O., 12 ½ In. .... *illus* 250.00
Punch Ladle, Egyptian Revival, Whiting Mfg. Co., c.1880, 13 In. 123.00
Punch Ladle, George Washington Medallion, Coin, Newell Harding, 14 In. 550.00
Punch Ladle, Gilt Bowl, Classical Warrior Medallion, Wendt & Co., c.1862, 14 In. 837.00
Punch Ladle, Medallion Head, Signed, Wood & Hughes, 8 ¼ In. 325.00
Punch Ladle, Oval Bowl, Threaded Handle, MW Monogram, Coin, Ohio, c.1840, 14 In. 176.00
Relish Tray, Rimmed, Etched, Divided, Mid 20th Century, Wallace, 1 ½ x 14 In. 234.00
Salad Servers, Flared Repousse Bowl, Lily Terminal, Gorham, c.1870, 11 In., 2 Piece 2629.00
Salad Servers, Martele Texture, Carved Wood Handles, 12 ¼ In. 259.00
Salad Servers, Sterling, Plastic, Ponti, Reed & Barton, c.1958, 13 In. .... *illus* 960.00
Salt, Beaded Rim, Banded Scroll & Flower Decorations, 4-Footed, c.1850, Pair 777.00

Salt, Castor, Blue Glass Insert, Lion Headed Paw Feet, Amston, 4 ¾ In. 360.00
Salt, Half Eggshell Shape, Gilt Interior, Wheat Base, Gorham, c.1865, 2 x 3 In., Pair 1554.00
Salt, Master, Kettle Shape, Repousse Shell, Flowers, Scroll Feet, c.1935, 2 x 3 In., Pair 478.00
Salt, Master, Mermaids, Seated Among Leaves, c.1900, 4 ½ In., 2 Piece 960.00
Salt, Master, Monogram, Hallmarks, Gorham, c.1900, 1 ½ x 2 ⅝ In. 68.00
Salt, Octagonal, Stylized Flowers, Scroll Feet, c.1850, 1 ⅞ In., Pair 956.00
Salt, Open, Oval, Cast Butterfly, Twig, Berry Handle, Gorham, c.1860, 2 x 4 In., 2 Piece...... 777.00
Salver, Chippendale, Shell Rim, 3 Hoof Feet, Abercrombie, Newport, c.1742, 6 ⅝ In. 1955.00
Salver, Round, Winged Paw Feet, Repousse Floral Border, S. Kirk & Son, 9 ½ In. 748.00
Sandwich Tray, Trianon, Classical Rim, International, 14 ½ In.. .... 588.00
Sauceboat, Helmet Shape, Greek Key Rim, Scroll Handle, Moore, c.1854, 6 x 8 In., Pair..... 1434.00
Sauceboat, Square Handle, Stepped Foot, Beaded Rim, Wendt, c.1863, 5 x 10 In. 777.00
Server, Handwrought, Todd & Cosio, Chicago, 10 ½ In. 204.00
Server, Mug Shape, Hinged Lid, Pierced Designs, Bud, Vine, Glass Liner, A. Stone, c.1910, 3 In. 1185.00
Serving Dish, Lid, Oval, Cow Finial, Greek Key Rim, Ball, Black & Co., c.1870, 6 x 12 In..... 2988.00
Serving Dish, Lid, Oval, Greek Key Rim, Bead Border, Moore, 1854, 6 x 11 In., Pair 3346.00
Serving Fork, Oval Handle, Heart Pierced Bowl, 4 Tines, 1 Wide Tine, 14 In. 531.00
Serving Fork, Palm Beach, Engraved Frond Handle, Gorham, c.1890, 9 In.. .... 263.00
Serving Scoop, Flowers & Scrolls On Handle, J.E. Caldwell, c.1875, 10 In. 153.00
Serving Scoop, Octagon Shaft, Cube, Spike Terminal, Scroll Gilt Bowl, c.1863, 10 In. 896.00
Serving Set, Leaf Decoration, Whiting, 9 ¾ In., 2 Piece 390.00
Serving Spoon, Banded Reed Stem, Lily Terminal, Gilt Bowl, c.1870, 11 In. 538.00
Serving Spoon, Beaded, Gilt Bowl, Medallion Handle, Woods & Co., N.Y., c.1865, 9 In....... 418.00
Serving Spoon, Classical Bust Terminal, Gilt Bowl, Leaves, c.1860, 9 In. 508.00
Serving Spoon, Cruciform To Cat Tail Terminal, Gilt Bowl, c.1870, 9 In. 311.00
Serving Spoon, Gold Wash, Velvet Box, Shiebler, 10 ½ x 3 ¾ In. 695.00
Serving Spoon, Ivy & Scroll, Oval Bowl, Flowers, Button Back, Theodore Starr, 13 In. 259.00
Serving Spoon, Leaf Stem, Rose Bloom Terminal, Whiting Mfg. Co., Mass., c.1880, 9 In..... 335.00
Serving Spoon, Riding Crop Terminal, Shaped Bowl, Gorham, c.1880, 12 In. 717.00
Serving Spoon, Shaped Handle, Initials, Jas. Barnes, Kentucky, c.1850, 9 In., 3 Piece....... 203.00
Serving Tongs, Ribbon Pattern, Shaped, Pierced Blades, Wendt & Co., c.1870, 12 In. 896.00
Shaker, Chased Flower, Applied Metal Flower, Bug, Bird, Dominick, 1880, 3 x 2 In., Pair..... 1195.00
Shoehorn, Repousse, Signed, S. Kirk & Son, 6 ½ x 2 In. 35.00
Soup Ladle, Banded Stem, Homeric Bust Finial, Bowl Applied Stag, Coin, c.1875, 14 In.. .... 1076.00
Soup Ladle, Federal, Plain Back, Tipped Stem, Coin, J. Lownes, Philadelphia, c.1790, 14 In. . 326.00
Spectacles, Original Oval Lenses In Frames, Telescoping Temples, Coin, 1830s, 5 In. 710.00
Spoon, Gilt Bowl, Twist Stem, Pharaoh Terminal, Jaccard Co., St. Louis, c.1880, 6 In., 6 Piece 598.00
Spoon, Long Handle, Pierced, Chased Bowl, Marked, A. Stone, c.1909 .... 267.00
Spoon, Mandolin Form, Intertwined Ribbon, G. Shiebler Co., c.1890, 8 In.. .... 287.00
Spoon, Muddler, Hand Hammered, Shaped Bowl, Kalo Shop, c.1910, 14 In.. .... 239.00
Spoon, Serving, Stamped H 86, Gorham, c.1875, 9 In. 351.00
Spoon, Set, Palm Beach, Shaped Bowl, Gilt Palm Frond, Gorham, c.1890, 6 In. 143.00
Spoon, Spear, Olive & Branch Handle, Gilt, No. 267, Marked, Gorham, 11 ¾ In. 520.00
Stamp Box, Flared, Repousse Indian Head Lid, Gilt Interior, Unger Bros., c.1890, 1 x 3 In.. .. 1852.00
Sugar, 6-Point Stars, Eagle, Lobed Sides, Stepped Pedestal, Cover, c.1851, 8 In. 705.00
Sugar & Creamer, Crane, Bamboo Bands, Handles, c.1880, 3 In., 2 Piece 908.00
Sugar & Creamer, Fairfax, Gorham, 4 x 7 ¾ & 3 ½ x 6 ½ In. 143.00
Sugar & Creamer, Flowers, Stieff, c.1932, 4 & 4 ¼ In. 837.00
Sugar Basket, Boat Shape, Swing Handle, Greek Key Rims, Gilt, Moore, c.1860, 7 x 5 In..... 478.00
Sugar Spoon, Etched Floral, Scalloped Bowl, J.B. & S.M. Knowles, 6 In. 68.00
Sugar Spoon, Fiddle Handle, Shell Bowl, Coin, W. Carrington & Co., c.1865, 6 ½ In. 288.00
Sugar Tongs, Bright Cut, Acorn Terminals, Coin, 5 ½ In.. .... 143.00
Sugar Tongs, Oval Terminals, Coin, Signed, I. Yates, 5 ½ In. 66.00
Sugar Tongs, Scroll Handles, Shell Tips, Engraved, Boston, c.1830 .... 3851.00
Syrup, Hammered, Octagon, Lid, Plate, Initials, Lebolt & Co., c.1915, 5 In.. .... 1434.00
Tablespoon, Christopher Burr, Rhode Island, c.1815, 9 ½ In., Pair 173.00
Tablespoon, Fiddle Back, E. Wiggers, Tennessee, c.1855, 8 In. 225.00
Tankard, Lid, Engraved, Scroll Handle, Step Base, R. Van Dyke, N.Y., c.1750, 7 In. 26290.00
Tankard, Tapered, Cylindrical, Dome Lid, Bell Finial, TD, Boston, c.1755, 8 ¼ In. 9945.00
Tazza, Reticulated Flower Medallions, Footed, Theodore B. Starr, c.1920, 9 In.. .... 225.00
Tazza, Reticulated Scroll Border, Monogram, T. Starr, c.1910, 3 x 9 In. 299.00
Tazza, Round, Beaded Border, Stepped Foot, Wm. Gale & Son, 3 ½ x 5 ½ In.. .... 201.00
Tea & Coffee Set, Ornate, Chased, Cat Head Spouts, S. Kirk, c.1920, 7 Piece. 31250.00
Tea Caddy, Lid, Cast Fleur-De-Lis, Wm. Linker, Penn., c.1908, 5 In. 263.00
Tea Caddy, Lid, Squat Ginger Jar Shape, Chrysanthemum Pattern, c.1900, 4 In. 1016.00
Tea Caddy, Old Newbury Crafters, Mass., c.1920, 3 x 3 In. 191.00
Tea Caddy, Oval, Dome Top, Atlantic Yacht Club, Gorham, 5 ½ x 3 ½ In. 748.00
Tea Caddy, Shell, Gilt Bowl, Portrait Terminal, Geo. Shiebler & Co., N.Y., c.1880, 3 In. 508.00

TIP
Keep a piece of white chalk in the drawer with your sterling or plated silver. It retards moisture and slows tarnishing.

Silver-American, Punch Ladle, Beaded Rim, Coin, Marked, E.A. Tyler, N.O., 12 ½ In.
$250.00

Silver-American, Salad Servers, Sterling, Plastic, Ponti, Reed & Barton, c.1958, 13 In.
$960.00

S

TIP
You can clean your silver with a paste of baking soda and water. Rub it on, rinse, wipe.

Silver-American, Tea Strainer, Repousse, Marked, S. Kirk & Son Co., 3 x 6 ½ In.
$140.00

Silver-American, Waffle Lifter, Leaf, Engraved, Coin, Hemingway & Stevens, Case, 1890s, 8 ½ In.
$385.00

Silver-American, Waste Bowl, Flared Rim, Reeded Stem, Coin, G. Boyce, New York, c.1814, 5 x 8 In.
$444.00

Tea Set, Chased Ivy Pattern, E. Moore, c.1865, 10 x 9 In., 3 Piece. . . . 3227.00
Tea Set, Georgian Rose, Reed & Barton, Mid 1900s, 5 Piece 1035.00
Tea Set, Rococo Style, Repousse Flowers, S. Kirk & Son, c.1830, 8 ½ In. 5280.00
Tea Strainer, Pierced, Deep Bowl, Curvilinear Design, Bailey, Banks, & Biddle, 8 In. 207.00
Tea Strainer, Pierced Bowl, Loop Handle, c.1880, 6 In. 90.00
Tea Strainer, Repousse, Marked, S. Kirk & Son Co., 3 x 6 ½ In. . . . . *illus* 140.00
Tea Strainer, Scalloped, Pierced, Whiting Mfg., c.1900, 1 x 6 In. 90.00
Teapot, Gadroon & Beaded Border, Animal Head Spout, Bird Finial, c.1817, 9 In. 1899.00
Teapot, Lid, Flower Finial, Leaves, Coin, W.W. Hannah, New York, c.1840, 10 In. 444.00
Teapot, Lid, Urn Finial, Leaf Fruitwood Handle, Coin, J. Musgrave, Philadelphia, c.1795, 12 In. 2726.00
Teapot, Wood Handle, Finial, Hinged Lid, Monogram, Gorham, 10 ¾ In. 228.00
Teaspoon, Beaded Border, Engraved Emilie Starke, Wood & Hughes, 6 ⅛ In., 6 Piece 110.00
Teaspoon, Quatrefoil, Arch Handle, Gilt Bowl, Wm. Gale & Son, N.Y., 1850, 6 In, 4 Piece 717.00
Tongs, Fiddle Handle, Oval Terminals, Coin, Marked, J. Ewan, 7 In.. . . . . 300.00
Tongs, Fiddle Handle, Starburst Terminals, No. Carolina, c.1830, 6 In. 633.00
Tongs, Figural Medallions, Pierced Blade, Bird Claw Terminal, c.1865, 13 In. 1912.00
Tongs, Shell, Scroll, Claw End Terminals, Monogram, Whiting, 4 ¾ In. 11.00
Tongs, Talon Form Tongs, Coin, Marked, Jones, Ball & Poor, 19th Century, 5 ¾ In. 90.00
Toothpick Holder, Chrysanthemum Pattern, Shiebler & Co., c.1900, 2 x 2 In.. . . . . 658.00
Tray, 2 Handles, Flower & Leaf Flared Rim, 1900s, 28 ¾ x 17 ½ In. 3062.00
Tray, Banded Border, Flowers, Engraved, Round, Coin, W. Carrington & Co., c.1865, 9 In. 1840.00
Tray, Beaded Rim, Engraved, Coin, Marked, Hayden & Gregg, 7 ¼ In. Diam. 500.00
Tray, Dominick & Haff, Oval, Stylized Border, Early 20th Century, 18 In.. . . . . 649.00
Tray, Floral Repousse Border, Signed, R. Wallace & Son, 10 ¾ x 16 In. 400.00
Tray, Hammered, Undulating Lip, Engraved Flowers, Insect, Shiebler, c.1890, 2 x 8 In. 1195.00
Tray, Handles, Scalloped Rim, Flowers, Garlands, Gorham, c.1953, 18 x 26 In.. . . . . 3218.00
Tray, Handwrought, Round, Lobed, Marked, Felix Novick, Chicago, 6 In. 267.00
Tray, Leaves, Scroll Feet, Oval, Coin, J.E. Spear & Co., 16 ¼ x 12 In. 3600.00
Tray, Oval, Greek Key Rim, Beaded Border, Leaves, Scrolls, 4-Footed, Moore, 13 In. 1434.00
Tray, Oval, Poppy Repousse, Wallace, c.1900, 12 x 7 In.. . . . . 167.00
Tray, Oval, Scroll Edge, SCP Monogram, Gorham, 1948, 2 x 26 In. 2629.00
Tray, Raised, Scalloped Edge, 13 ¾ In. 230.00
Tray, Round, Chippendale, Gorham, Mid 20th Century, 12 In. 410.00
Tray, Round, Etruscan, 1919, 14 In. 590.00
Tray, Round, Pentafoil Rim, Kalo Shop, Chicago, 9 ¾ In. 748.00
Tray, Round, Pinched Pie Crust Rim, Pennsylvania, Marked, Joel Hewes, 7 In. 356.00
Tray, Round, Scalloped Rim, Center Embossed Scrolls, Flowers, Birks, 13 In. 293.00
Tray, Scalloped, Bead Rim, Gorham, 9 x 13 In. 263.00
Tray, Seville, Monogram, Towle, Mid 20th Century, 19 ¼ x 15 ¼ In. 633.00
Tureen, Cover, Regency, Bulbous, Handles, Rounded, Paw Feet, 6 x 4 ¾ x 8 ¾ In. 4800.00
Urn, Gothic Revival, Devil Handles, Scrolls, Leaves, Bead Border, Footed, 18 In. 3680.00
Vase, Art Nouveau, Urn Shape, Scroll Handles, Pedestal Base, Gorham, 9 ½ x 9 In. 259.00
Vase, Arts & Crafts, Trumpet Shape, Hammered, Lebolt & Co., 7 ¼ x 3 ½ In.. . . . . 316.00
Vase, Baluster, Iris Repousse, Shaped, Pierced Rim, T. Starr, c.1900, 15 In. 3884.00
Vase, Hammered, Inverted Lip, Monogram, C. Friedell, Cal., c.1920, 16 In. 2868.00
Vase, Mermaid, Plant Swirls, Undulating Rim, 4 Dolphin Feet, Gorham, 1909, 4 In. 5378.00
Vase, Round Foot, Flared, Petal Rim, Watson, 9 ⅛ In. 354.00
Vinaigrette, Boar's Tusk, Chain, Sun Face, Scrolls On Tusk, Clip, Coin, 1800s, 5 x 3 In. 575.00
Vinaigrette, Horn Shape, Chased Birds, Scrolls, Flowers, Blue Stone Tip, Gorham, 3 In. 473.00
Waffle Lifter, Leaf, Engraved, Coin, Hemingway & Stevens, Case, 1890s, 8 ½ In. . . . . *illus* 385.00
Waste Bowl, Flared Rim, Reeded Stem, Coin, G. Boyce, New York, c.1814, 5 x 8 In. . . . . *illus* 444.00
Wine Coaster, Embossed Flowers, Scrolls, Wood Base, Gorham, 1895, 7 x 5 In., Pair 1126.00
Wine Coaster, Flowers, Shells, Glass, Reed & Barton, c.1907, 7 In. 120.00
Zipper Pull, Cast Ball, Claw Terminal, 1870, 9 In.. . . . . 478.00

SILVER-ARGENTINEAN

Wine Cooler, Neoclassical, Vignettes, Swags, Greek Key Design, 10 In. 403.00

SILVER-AUSTRIAN

Basket, Scalloped Border, Bail Handle, Schiffer, 6 x 8 ¼ In. 690.00
Box, Gilt Interior, Wood Liner, Dividers, c.1922, 3 ¼ x 13 ¼ In. 748.00
Box, Hinged, Smooth Lid, Ribbed Base, Applied Scroll Feet, c.1900, 4 In.. . . . . 351.00
Cup, Nautilus, Mermaid, Dolphins, Triton, F. Bruder, Vienna, c.1890, 23 In. 33750.00
Dish, Entree, Round, Ring Handles, Acanthus Finial, c.1816, 3 ¼ x 7 In., Pair 3910.00
Figure, Enamel, Piper, Hermann Boehm, c.1880, 10 ¼ In. 9375.00
Pitcher, Gilt Interior, Palms, Beading, Ebony Handle, Biedermeier, 1828, 7 x 5 In.. . . . . 956.00
Punch Ladle, Ivory Handle, Carved, Openwork Grapes, Strainer Lid, 16 ½ In. 230.00
Stand, Holds Bottle, 12 Glasses, Floral Repousse, 19th Century, 14 In.. . . . . 900.00
Teapot, Spherical, Flat, Gadroon Bands, Biedermeier, 1830, 4 ½ x 5 ½ x 9 In. 300.00

Tray, Reeded Border, Monogram, Ignaz Binder, 16 ¼ x 10 ¾ In. 2070.00
Vase, Cornucopia, Enamel, Rudolf Linke, c.1890, 13 In. 8750.00
Vase, Etched Shell Crystal Bowl, Satyr, Dolphin Stem, Enamel, Gilt, c.1880, 9 In. 47800.00

SILVER-AUSTRO-HUNGARIAN
Lacemaking Set, Tools, Black, White Alpine Scene, Wood Case, 8 In. 237.00
Ladle, Engraved, Heraldic Device, Coronet Over Raven, Turk, 13 In. 1265.00
Lobster Pick, Oval, Reeded, Monogram, Marked, 5 ½ In., 22 Piece 1725.00
Pot, Lid, Reeded, Acanthus Finial, Marked, AT, 4 ¾ x 10 x 9 In. .... *illus* 1200.00
Sauceboat, Underplate, Double Spout, Scalloped, 5 ½ x 9 In., 4 Piece 4600.00

SILVER-CAMBODIAN
Box, Cover, Figural, Pumpkin, Flowers, Hand Hammered, Early 20th Century, 8 ¾ x 10 In. 1100.00
Dish, Cover, Figural, Elephant, Hand Hammered, Early 20th Century, 10 x 10 x 5 In. 1100.00

SILVER-CANADIAN
Tray, Round, Raised Rippled Edge, Birks, 12 In. 380.00

SILVER-CHINESE
Box, Cover, Enameled, Stylized Taotie Mask & Bird, 6 ¾ In. 826.00
Flask, Gilt, Repousse, Winged Mythical Beast, C-Shape Handle, 7 ½ x 5 ¼ In. 7670.00
Goblet, Presentation, Shanghai Tobacco Co., Chinese Export, c.1908 .... 920.00
Salt Cellar, 2 Porters Carrying Chair, Spoon, Shaker, Jar, Liner, Hong Kong, 9 ½ In. 175.00
Sugar, Cover, Floral Repousse, Mums, Dragon Heads, 1800s, 4 ¾ In. .... *illus* 330.00
Tea & Coffee Set, Early 20th Century, 10 ½-In. Coffeepot, 7 Piece .... *illus* 2860.00

SILVER-CONTINENTAL
Basket, Oval, Repousse, Reticulated Border, Swags, Putti, Dolphins, 17 x 14 ½ In. 717.00
Box, Oval, Bacchic Scene, Impressed 925, 11 ¾ In. 1320.00
Centerpiece, Swan, Jeweled Green Eyes, c.1890, 18 In. 708.00
Decanter, Octagonal, Intaglio Cut, Silver Mounts, Cupids, Garland, 10 In. 201.00
Ewer, Baluster Shape, Spreading Foot, Body, Continuous Flower Band, 12 ½ In. 359.00
Fruit Set, Floral Handle, c.1910, Knives 9 In., Forks 7 In., 12 Piece 1380.00
Hoof Spoon, 18th Century, 7 In. 409.00
Jug, Claret, Baluster Shape, Flowers, Scrolls, Putti Finial, c.1890, 14 In. 7500.00
Salt & Pepper, Bonnet Caps, Flared Bases, Repousse, 3 ¾ In. 104.00
Tea Caddy, Repousse, Square, Pull Off Lid, Figural, 5 ¼ In. 329.00
Tray, Round, Scalloped Rim, Sterling, Germany, 20th Century, 11 In. 100.00
Tray, Scrolling Grapevine, Battle, Horse Soldiers, Swords, Spears, 18 In. 1955.00
Vinaigrette, Jester's Ball Shape, Threaded Post For Twist Opening, 1 ½ In. 189.00

SILVER-CZECHOSLOVAKIAN
Cocktail Shaker, Tumblers, 4 ½ x 9 In., 4 Piece 598.00

SILVER-DANISH
Bowl, Berry & Leaf Stem, Georg Jensen, 1940s, 4 ⅛ x 4 ½ In. .... *illus* 500.00
Bowl, Center, Hammered, Fish Wave Band, Oval, A. Dragsted, c.1919, 14 x 6 In. 4444.00
Bowl, Flared Lobes, Scalloped Beaded Rim, 3 Ball Feet, Flowers, D. Anderson, 6 x 12 In. 593.00
Bowl, No. 700, Trumpet Shape, Embossed, Acorns, Leaves Base Rim, c.1933, 4 x 7 In. 1778.00
Bowl, Oval, Melon Shape, Hammered, Openwork Leaf Feet, 3 x 5 ½ In., Pair 460.00
Bowl, Rounded, Triangle Shape, Marked, A. Dragsted, 1900s, 4 x 10 In. 385.00
Cheese Scoop, Signed, Georg Jensen, 7 In. 110.00
Coffee Set, Coffeepot, Sugar, Creamer, 4-Sided, Roif Fritiof 440.00
Compote, Footed, Marked, Dessin, 17B, Rohde, Georg Jensen, 5 ¼ x 5 ¾ In. 750.00
Creamer, Cow Shape, Flip Lid, Red Glass Eyes, Collar, Bell, Marked, Late 1800s, 3 x 5 In. 1820.00
Creamer, Cow Shape, Hinged Lid, Fly On Back, Red Glass Eyes, Collar, Bell, 4 x 6 ½ In. 920.00
Cruet Set, Sterling, Threaded Neck, Cork Stopper, F. Hingelberg, 7 ¼ x 2 In., 2 Piece 3000.00
Demitasse Set, Blossom, Lid, Hammered, Ivory Handle, Georg Jensen, 6 In., 3 Piece 3851.00
Fork & Spoon, Sterling, Dolphin Decoration, Frigast, 7 ⅝ In. 120.00
Plate, Acorn Pattern, J. Rohde, Jensen, 1915, 6 In., 8 Piece 3304.00
Serving Set, Acorn, Fork, Spoon, Georg Jensen, Mid 20th Century, 8 In., 2 Piece 660.00
Shoe Horn, Lined Handle, H. Neilsen, Georg Jensen, 4 In. 380.00
Spoon, Demitasse, Dansk Guldindustri, c.1948-58, 4 In., 6 Piece 117.00
Tea Set, Teapot, Creamer, Sugar, Cover, Ebony Handles, Finials, Beadwork, G. Jensen, 6 x 4 In. 4740.00
Tray, Royal Danish, Applied Handles, 13 In. 322.00

SILVER-DUTCH
Belt Buckle, Oval, Reticulated, Embossed Flowers, Steel Teeth, c.1841, 4 ½ In. 59.00
Bowl, Scalloped Rim, Embossed Flowers, Openwork, C-Scroll Handles, c.1790, 9 In. 1185.00
Bowl, Shaped Rim, Scrolled, Footed, c.1900, 4 In. 191.00
Box, Cover, Flower Trees, Round, 1 ¾ x 4 In. 125.00
Box, Cover, Hinges, Rectangular, Continental, 19th Century, 1 x 2 x 1 ⅛ In. 146.00

Silver-Austro-Hungarian, Pot, Lid, Reeded, Acanthus Finial, Marked, AT, 4 ¾ x 10 x 9 In.
$1200.00

Silver-Chinese, Sugar, Cover, Floral Repousse, Mums, Dragon Heads, 1800s, 4 ¾ In.
$330.00

Silver-Chinese, Tea & Coffee Set, Early 20th Century, 10 ½-In. Coffeepot, 7 Piece
$2860.00

Silver-Danish, Bowl, Berry & Leaf Stem, Georg Jensen, 1940s, 4 ⅛ x 4 ½ In.
$500.00

TIP
Never drain silver on a rubber mat. It will tarnish faster.

TIP
If you must wash silver in a dishwasher, use very little detergent and remove the silver before the drying cycle.

Chatelaine Clip, Pierced, Engraved Flowers, Loop, 2 Chain Links, Oblong, c.1875, 4 In. 71.00
Fish Knife, Openwork Casting, Figures In Trees, 3-Masted Sailing Ship, 15 In. 118.00
Salt, Sedan Chair Style, 2 ¼ x 3 ¾ In. 322.00
Salt & Pepper, Bird Form, 3 x 6 ¼ In. 585.00
Tea Strainer, Pierced Bowl, Dutch Scenes, Flowers, Windmill Handle, 7 In. 132.00

SILVER-EGYPTIAN

Box, Hinged, Oval, Footed, c.1946, 5 x 10 In. 468.00

SILVER-ENGLISH. English sterling silver is marked with a series of four or five small hallmarks. The standing lion mark is the most commonly seen sterling quality mark. The other marks indicate the city of origin, the maker, and the year of manufacture. These dates can be verified in many good books on silver.

Basket, Chased Shells, Leaves, Acanthus Border, Hinged Handle, George III, 11 ½ In. 2040.00
Basket, Cobalt Blue Glass Insert, Ann Chesterman, George III, 1776, 5 ¾ In. 1521.00
Basket, Pedestal Base, Blue Glass Liner, Swing Handle, George III, 1774, 7 In. 660.00
Basket, Sugar, Navette Form, Ribbon, Leaf Band, Swing Handle, 4 x 4 x 5 ¾ In. 1800.00
Basket, Sugar, Neoclassical, Gilt Interior, Swing Handle, George III, 4 ¼ In. 264.00
Basket, Sugar, Pedestal Foot, Ruby Glass Liner, Swing Handle, George III, 5 ¾ In. 1416.00
Basket, Sweetmeat, Beaded, Hester Bateman, 1 ½ x 6 In. ..... *illus* 2010.00
Basket, Sweetmeat, Oval, Reticulated, Embossed, Swing Handle, George III, 6 x 5 In. 720.00
Basket, Sweetmeat, Reticulated Sides, Swing Handle, George III, 6 ¼ In. 705.00
Bowl, Engraved Flowers, Garlands, J. Deakin & Sons, c.1899, 2 x 4 In., Pair 70.00
Bowl, Footed, Round, Montieth Style Rim, Engraved Scroll & Flowers, 6 x 9 ¼ In. 690.00
Bowl, Half Reeded, Applied Scrolled Rim, Pedestal, 1910, 8 x 10 In. 960.00
Bowl, Monteith, Gadroon Bands, Swag, Ribbons, R & S Garrard, 1886, 8 x 12 In. ..... *illus* 4600.00
Bowl, Openwork Sides, Flowers, Scroll Border, Footed, Marked, c.1900, 3 ½ x 7 ¼ In. 431.00
Bowl, Oval, Leaf Swag, Openwork Sides, Footed, Maker's Marked, c.1895, 6 x 12 ¼ In. 863.00
Bowl, Pedestal Foot, Flower Trails, Matte Ground, Applied Flowers 5520.00
Bowl, Service, Regency, Engraved Rim, Baronet's Crest, Griffin, George III, 9 ¾ In. 2160.00
Bowl, T. Wallis, Scalloped Rim, Reeding To Base, London, George III, 10 x 7 In. 1195.00
Bowl, T. Webb, Flower Etched Glass, Silver Rim, England, Tiffany & Co., c.1890, 6 In. 478.00
Box, Camel Finial, Scrolls, Lions, Shield, God Grant Grace, 1897, 3 x 4 In. 633.00
Box, Cymric, Enamel, Stamped, L & C, Anchor, Lion, 1 ¾ x 2 In. ..... *illus* 1080.00
Box, Tea, Scrolls, Geometrics, Oval, N. Bloom & Sons, 1941, 5 x 5 x 3 ½ In. 475.00
Brandy Warmer, Chased Armorial, Treen Handle, George III, c.1795 ..... 413.00
Caddy Shovel, Fig Design, Rectangular Handle, c.1826, 3 ½ In. 230.00
Cake Basket, Engraved Shield, 4 Moon Over Crescent, George III, c.1796, 5 In. 1528.00
Cake Basket, Repousse Flower Panels, Embossed, Sterling, S.C.Y. Co., 12 ½ In. 1400.00
Candelabra are listed in the Candelabrum category.
Candlesticks are listed in their own category.
Cann, Cup, Flared Chased Pastoral Scene, Scroll Handle, 1796, 5 x 3 In. 896.00
Card Case, Engraved, Chatsworth House, 1874 ..... 7525.00
Card Tray, Scalloped Rim, Footed, George III, 1787, 5 ½ x 7 ⅛ In. 585.00
Castor, Baluster Shape, Pierced Diaper, George III, 7 x 2 ½ In. 450.00
Castor, Baluster Shape, Pierced Spiraling, George III, 7 ¼ x 2 ½ In. 450.00
Castor, Baluster Shape, Pierced Top, John & Daniel Welby, London, 1921, 8 In. 265.00
Castor, Paneled Urn Shape, Monogram, Marked, Chester, c.1935, 8 ¼ In. 201.00
Castor, Pierced Dome Top, Hester Bateman, 1779, 2 ½ x 1 ¼ In. ..... *illus* 945.00
Centerpiece, Eagle Handles, Scalloped Rim, Pierced Scrolls, Leaves, Oval, c.1905, 6 x 12 In. 1076.00
Chocolate Pot, Flared Cylindrical, Swan's Neck Spout, Queen Anne, 10 ¼ In. 9775.00
Christening Mug, Baluster, George II, c.1731, 3 In. 324.00
Coffeepot, Baluster, Scroll & Flower Repousse, Raffia Handle, George III, c.1764, 9 In. 1116.00
Coffeepot, Dome Lid, Repousse Flower, Scrolled Handle, George III, 13 ¼ In. 1121.00
Coffeepot, Lighthouse Shape, Scrolled Wooden Handle, Crest, 1920s, 7 ½ In., Pair 633.00
Coffeepot, Lighthouse Shape, Serpentine Fruitwood Handle, London, 1734, 8 In. 1896.00
Coffeepot, Oval Armorial, Scrolled Border, Wood Handle, Queen Anne, 11 In. 3600.00
Compote, Gothic, Openwork, Fox, Scrolls, Marked, London, 1849, 10 x 11 In., Pair 5060.00
Creamer, Flower Repousse Band, Swirling Gadroon Waist, Victorian, 1888, 3 ¾ In. 207.00
Creamer, Lobed Body, 2 Handles, Engraved Designs, Bateman, George III, 1795, 7 In. 770.00
Creamer, Repousse Figures, Flowers, Table, E. Farrell, George IV, 4 x 6 In. 2340.00
Cruet Stand, Condiment Holders, Mustard Pots, Pineapple Cut, George III, 11 In. 1680.00
Cruet Stand, Shell Feet, 5-Panel Cut Bottles, Coasters, Mustard Pot, 8 ½ In. 1080.00
Cup, Flared, Gilt Interior, Oval Cartouche, Hester Bateman, c.1788, 3 ¾ In. 2875.00
Cup, Prize For Ploughing, Handles, Footed, H. Bateman, George III, 1789, 5 ½ In. 1521.00
Cup, Urn Shape, Double Scroll Handles, Stepped Foot, Dome Lid, George II, 12 In. 1725.00
Cup, Urn Shape, S-Scroll, Handles, Acanthus Leaf Thumbpiece, c.1917, 7 ¼ x 9 ½ In. 546.00
Demitasse Spoon, Philip Ashberry & Sons, 4 ½ In., 5 Piece 78.00

Silver-English, Basket, Sweetmeat, Beaded, Hester Bateman, 1 ½ x 6 In. $2010.00

Silver-English, Bowl, Monteith, Gadroon Bands, Swag, Ribbons, R & S Garrard, 1886, 8 x 12 In. $4600.00

Silver-English, Box, Cymric, Enamel, Stamped, L & C, Anchor, Lion, 1 ¾ x 2 In. $1080.00

S

Dish Cover, Lobed, Royal Armorial, George III, 1801, 10 In. 2040.00
Dish Cross, Adjustable Sliding Supports, London, George III, 1790, 11 x 4 In. 1225.00
Dish Set, Boat Shape, Oval Pedestal Foot, Bateman, George III, c.1800, 5 x 3 In., 6 Piece 2124.00
Egg Stand, R. Hennell, 6 Woven Cups, Basket, Handle, England, c.1854, 6 x 9 x 6 In. 2629.00
Epergne, 4-Light, Crystal Bowl, Paw Feet, Flowers, Gadroon, 14 x 23 In. 2185.00
Epergne, Grapevine Post, 3 Branch Arms, Top Glass Bowl, Grapes, Marked, 1871, 24 x 16 In. . 2530.00
Ewer, Baluster Shape, Engraved Scroll Sunburst, Garland, Gilt Lid, Interior, c.1875, 14 In. . . . 1135.00
Ewer, Baluster Shape, Spreading Foot, Flowers, Fruit, Victorian, c.1845, 12 ½ In. 1121.00
Ewer, Wine, Mask Spout, Female Handle, Scrolls, Flowers, J.S. Hunt, 1850, 12 x 7 x 5 In. 2760.00
Ewer, Wine, S-Handle, Scroll Terminal, Flower-Form Finial, George III, 1781, 12 In. 1800.00
Fish Serving Set, Carved Ivory, Dolphins, Serpent, c.1848, 10 & 14 In. 1150.00
Fish Serving Set, Fork, Slice, Ivory Handle, Shell, Branches, 10 & 12 ½ In., 2 Piece 4320.00
Fish Serving Set, Slice & Fork, Victorian, George Adams, London, c.1858, 12 In. 234.00
Fish Slice, Gills On Shaped Blade, London, c.1822, 12 In. 179.00
Fork, Romanov Russia Crest, Paul Storr, England, c.1816, 8 In., 6 Piece 518.00
Frame, Arts & Crafts, Horon & Alldy, Birmingham, England, c.1903, 7 In. 351.00
Frame, Hammered, Double Panel, Enamel, Marked, William Hutton, Sheffield, 3 x 4 ½ In. . . 430.00
Fruit Ladle, Repousse Horn Of Plenty Handle, Engraved Fruit Branch, 8 ⅝ In. 92.00
Goblet, Bell Shape Bowl, Gold Wash, Beaded Band, Base, Chas. Wright, 1771, 7 In., Pair. 1778.00
Hot Water Urn, Beaded Handles, Ivory Spigot, Coat Of Arms, Oval, London, George III, 1783 2832.00
Inkstand, Central Chamber, Handle, Inkwells, 1858, 10 ½ x 7 ¼ In. 1200.00
Inkstand, Pen Trays, Diamond Cut Inkwells, Wafer Box, Taper Stick, 5 x 10 In. 940.00
Inkwell, Plate, Neoclassical Style, Taper Stick, Cobalt Blue, George III, 8 ½ In. 144.00
Inkwell, Police Helmet, Cut Glass, Wood Base, Victorian, 1889, 7 In. 2160.00
Jug, Claret, Glass, Etched, Frosted Flower Swags, C-Scroll Cartouche, Victorian, 10 ½ In. 2478.00
Jug, Spring Lid, Lion Finial, Grape Motif, Loop Handle, Collar, Victorian, 13 In. 1140.00
Knife, Gilt, Carved Coral Handle, Royal Victorian, 1841-59, 7 ¼ In. 1800.00
Knife Set, Decorated Pistol Handle, George II, c.1760, 10 ½ In., 8 Piece 1150.00
Knife Set, Pistol Handle, Engraved Crests, George III, 10 In., 6 Piece 676.00
Ladle, Beaded Rim, Twist Whalebone Handle, c.1800, 13 ¼ In. 117.00
Ladle, Beveled, Pointed Shoulders, Fiddle Shape, George IV, 1821-22, 13 ⅜ In. 210.00
Ladle, Curved Handle, Stamped, DF, London, c.1926, 12 ½ In. 225.00
Ladle, Rococo, Shell Form Bowl, Scroll Terminal, Case, George III, Pair, 7 In. 360.00
Ladle, Shell Form Bowl, George II, 1754, 13 In. 1170.00
Ladle Set, Toddy, Part Twist Handles, Thistle Terminals, 1840, 3 Piece 397.00
Letter Opener, Hollow Handle, Scroll Decoration, Presentation, c.1882, 12 ½ In. 345.00
Loving Cup, 2 Handles, Engraved, Footed, Scroll, Leaf, William IV, 7 x 5 In., Pair 8625.00
Loving Cup, Scroll Handles, Pedestal, Peter & Ann Bateman, c.1791, 6 x 7 ¼ In. 360.00
Mug, Rebecca Eames, Edward Barnard, George IV, 1827, 3 ¼ In. 878.00
Mustard Pot, Hinged Lid, Crest, Cobalt Glass Liner, George III, c.1800, 4 In. 234.00
Mustard Pot, Oval, Lid, Urn Finial, Glass Liner, Chas. Chesterman, London, c.1796, 4 x 4 In. 448.00
Napkin Rings are listed in their own category.
Nutmeg Grater, Melon Shape, Repousse Fruit, Birmingham, 1 ¼ x 1 ¾ In. 2415.00
Nutmeg Grater, Melon Shape, Repousse Fruit, Marked, Ada, 1853, 1 x 4 In. . . . . . *illus* 2100.00
Nutmeg Grater, Rounded, Hinged, Reeded, Swirl Design, George III, c.1818, 1 ¾ In. 2990.00
Pen Tray, Gadroon Edges, Cast Shell Ends, Candleholder, 2 Glass Inkwells, c.1894, 11 In. . . . 1195.00
Pie Server, Bone Handle, Chased Flower Border, 1904, Edwared VI, 12 In. 227.00
Pitcher, Claret, Lid, Flower Finial, Slender Neck, Oval Body, Chased Flowers, 1860, 14 In. 1185.00
Pitcher, Milk, Reeded, Ball Finial, Wood Handle, Marked, 2737, 1894, 7 In. 250.00
Plate, 8-Sided, Gadroon Border, Elizabeth Godfrey, George II, 1748, 9 ⅛ In. 1053.00
Plate, Gadroon Rim, Elizabeth Godfrey, George II, 1747, 9 ½ In. 519.00
Plate, Round, Gadroon Border, Family Crest, c.1827, George IV, 10 In., Pair 1150.00
Plate, Soup, Gadroon Border, Crest, George IV, c.1826, 11 ¼ In. 674.00
Plate Set, Tudor Rose, Gadroon Border, George II, 9 ½ In., 12 Piece 5100.00
Plateau Mirror, Sheffield, Coat-Of-Arms, 1886-87, 13 ¾ x 26 ½ In. 4329.00
Platter, Armorial, Oval, Serpentine Border, Gadroon Rim, Avian, Geroge III, 9 In. 767.00
Presentation Cup, Handles, Inscription, Wood Base, George V, c.1917, 8 In. 885.00
Punch Bowl, Armada, 2 Ring Handles, Winged Creatures, Sheffield, 1897, 14 In. 4375.00
Punch Bowl, Hemispherical, Cavetto Band, Rim, Scroll Handles, 8 x 13 x 19 In. 5520.00
Punch Bowl, Molded Rim, Foot, London, George, c.1728, 8 ¼ x 11 ⅝ In. 9600.00
Punch Ladle, Coin Bowl, Wood Handle, George III, c.1765, 13 ½ In. 270.00
Punch Ladle, Shell Tip, John Walton, Newcastle, 13 ½ In. 351.00
Quaich, Porringer Shape, Oval Handles, Crosshatch Engraving, Hammered, c.1725, 4 In. . . . 296.00
Salt, 3 Stepped Feet, Gadroon Rim, D. Mills, George III, 1761, 1 x 3 In., Pair 299.00
Salt, Lion Paw Feet, Applied Winged Cartouche, Gilt Interior, W. Fountain, 2 x 4 In., Pair. . . *illus* 837.00
Salt, Boat Shape, Pedestal, London, George III, c.1806, 2 ½ x 3 ½ In. 263.00
Salt, Cobalt Blue Glass Liner, Bateman, England, c.1785, 3 ¼ In., 2 Pair. 460.00
Salt, Engraved Crest, 3 Cast Paw Feet, George III, c.1815, 2 ½ In., Pair 837.00

TIP
Do not display or store silver on shelves painted with latex paint. It encourages tarnish.

Silver-English, Castor, Pierced Dome Top, Hester Bateman, 1779, 2 ½ x 1 ¼ In.
$945.00

Silver-English, Nutmeg Grater, Melon Shape, Repousse Fruit, Marked, Ada, 1853, 1 x 4 In.
$2100.00

TIP
Never wash silver and stainless steel together, not even in a dishwasher.

As always, the edited listings in *Kovels' Antiques & Collectibles Price Guide 2010* aren't available on any website, but readers should visit Kovels.com for information on trends, tips, reproductions, marks, old prices, and more!

Silver-English, Salt, Lion Paw Feet, Applied Winged Cartouche, Gilt Interior, W. Fountain, 2 x 4 In., Pair
$837.00

Silver-English, Spoon, Apostle, St. Peter, Fig Shape, James I, c.1606, 7 In.
$5750.00

Silver-English, Tea Caddy, Lid, Leaf Finial, Shield Engraved Sides, M. Plummer, c.1786, 6 x 4 In.
$2032.00

TIP

Remove egg stains from silver by rubbing the piece with salt, then washing it in dishwashing liquid. Rinse well or the salt will add stains.

Salt, Fluted, Banded Rim, Oval Base, 2 Handles, George III, 3 ¼ x 5 ⅞ In., 6 Piece.......... 4183.00
Salt, Neoclassical, Blue Glass Liners, Oval, Claw Feet, George III, 3 ¼ In., Pair............ 540.00
Salt, Oval, Openwork, 4 Ball & Claw Feet, Swag & Shield, Glass Liner, 2 x 3 ½ In. 460.00
Salt, Reeded Rim, Repousse Flowers, Trifid Feet, London, 1840, Pair.................... 415.00
Salt, Round, 3-Footed, George II, c.1741, 1 ¾ x 3 In., Pair 497.00
Salt, Round, 3-Footed, London, George II, c.1755, 1 ¾ x 2 ½ In. 293.00
Salt, Star Cut Base, Blue Glass Liner, Oval, George III, 1769, 3 ¼ In., Pair................ 720.00
Salt Set, Tapered Sides, Rams Head, Ring Drop Handles, George III, 2 x 4 In., 3 Piece....... 1150.00
Salver, 3 Paw Feet, Shell & Scroll Border, Crest, Engraved, George III, 7 ¼ In. 748.00
Salver, Chippendale Rim, 3 Ball & Claw Feet, George VI, 14 In......................... 1200.00
Salver, Leaf, Shell Border, Engraved Flower Rococo Scrolls, George III, 17 In. 4560.00
Salver, Neoclassical, Splayed Pierced Border, Armorials, George II, 14 In................. 2400.00
Salver, Reticulated Rim, Laurel Swags, 3-Footed, George III, 16 ¾ In.................... 4800.00
Salver, Scalloped Edge, London, 1862, 10 In.. 351.00
Salver, Shell, Scroll Border, 3-Footed, Marked, London, George II, 1775, 7 In. 633.00
Salver, Shell Border, Scroll Feet, Dorothy Mills, George II, 1752, 12 ⅝ In................. 3978.00
Salver, Shell Rim, Dorothy Sarbitt, George II, 1754, 7 ½ In............................ 1638.00
Sauceboat, 3 Hoof Feet, C-Scroll Handle, George II, 5 ½ x 7 ½ In. 1840.00
Sauceboat, Footed, Gadroon Border, Scrolled Handle, George III, 1765, 8 ½ In., Pair....... 2400.00
Sauceboat, Isaac Cockson, Newcastle-On-Tyne, George II, c.1754, 6 x 2 ¾ In.............. 489.00
Saucepan, Baluster Shape, Wooden Side Handle, George II, c.1731, 4 x 7 In................ 489.00
Saucepan, Cylindrical, Handle, Wood Turning, George I, 9 ½ x 2 ¾ In. 1955.00
Saucepan, Wood Handle, George II, c.1731, 2 x 5 In. 265.00
Serving Dish, Lid, Serpent Finial, Gadroon Borders, Marked, London, 6 x 12 x 8 In......... 4830.00
Skewer, Family Crest, William Eley & William Fearn, Early 1800s, 13 & 12 In., 2 Piece...... 374.00
Skewer, Meat, Chased Armorial, George III, 9 ¼ In. 142.00
Spoon, Apostle, Maker's Mark, Punch Engraved Initials, Charles I, 7 ⅜ In................. 940.00
Spoon, Apostle, St. Peter, Fig Shape, James I, c.1606, 7 In. .... *illus* 5750.00
Spoon, Apostle, St. Simon The Zealot, Fig Shape, c.1658, 6 ¾ In........................ 6325.00
Stuffing Spoon, Fiddle Pattern, William IV, c.1835, 12 In., Pair 418.00
Sugar, E. Farrell, 2 Handles, Horse, Man, Flowers, Chased, c.1822, 5 x 7 In. 1989.00
Sugar Tongs, Exeter, 5 ¾ In.. 144.00
Tablespoon, Engraved, Hedgehogs On Handle, George III, c.1784, 6 ½ In., 9 Piece......... 353.00
Tablespoon, Trifid, Shaped Reserve, William & Mary, c.1690, 7 ⅞ In., Pair 1410.00
Tankard, Applied Girdle, Domed, Flower Scrolls, George II, c.1752, 6 ⅞ In. 1762.00
Tankard, Bulbous, Molded Foot, Leafy Scroll Handle, H. Bateman, ½ Pt., 3 ¾ In. 780.00
Tankard, Heart Shape, George I, 1722, 4 ¼ In. 840.00
Tankard, Newcastle, Engraved Flowers, George II, 1733, 4 In.......................... 288.00
Tea & Coffee Set, Hot Water Kettle, Stand, Gadroon, Edward VII, 5 Piece 568.00
Tea Caddy, Lid, Leaf Finial, Shield Engraved Sides, M. Plummer, c.1786, 6 x 4 In....... *illus* 2032.00
Tea Urn, Square Base, Paw Feet, Ivory Spout, Smith & Sharp, George III, 20 x 11 In. 3200.00
Teapot, 4-Footed, Greek Key, Flower Band, Crispin Fuller, London, George III, 1804, 7 In..... 598.00
Teapot, 8-Sided, Wood Handle, Frances Purton, George III, 1790, 5 ¼ x 10 In.............. 2106.00
Teapot, Bullet Shape, Engraved, Cover, Applied Foot, George II, c.1736, 4 ⅞ In............ 1762.00
Teapot, Flower Finial, Gooseneck Spout, 4-Footed, Marked CL, c.1840, 8 ¾ In............. 650.00
Teapot, Gadroon Rim, Ribbed Body, Footed, George III, 1814, 9 ¾ In.................... 1053.00
Teapot, Hinged Lid, Melon Shape, Chased Leaves, Ivory Insulators, c.1824, 5 x 12 In........ 1673.00
Teapot, Neoclassical, Engraved Flowers, Geometric Border, George II, 5 ½ In. 1298.00
Teapot, Oval Body, Greek Key Border, Scroll Lid, Wood Finial, Handle, 1864, 6 x 11 In. 431.00
Toast Rack, Scrolls, 4-Footed, Marked, JE, 1852, 6 ¼ x 7 ¼ x 4 ¾ In. .... *illus* 575.00
Toast Rack, Victorian, Reily & Storer, 1842, 7 ½ In. 780.00
Toasted Cheese Dish, Gadroon Rim, Shell Corners, George III, 1809, 12 x 9 ¾ In.......... 3978.00
Toothpick, Flared Rim, Tapered Bowl, Shell Form Legs, 3 Hoof Feet, 2 ¾ In. 25.00
Tray, Engraved, Oval, Reeded Handles, Reticulated Gallery, 1890s, 26 x 17 In. 420.00
Tray, Gadroon Border, Family Crest, Marked, George III, c.1770, 12 In................... 1265.00
Tray, Plate, Armorial, Stamped Anchor, Lion Rampant, Bell, George III, 29 ½ In............ 510.00
Tray, Rectangular, Gadroon, Leafy Shell, Handles, 29 ⅜ x 19 ¼ In. 3360.00
Tray, Scalloped Rim, Gadroon Border, 4 Pad Feet, Barker Brothers, c.1911, 10 ½ In......... 460.00
Tray, Shell, Scroll Border, 3-Footed, Crest, Ebenezer Coker, George III, 1700, 15 In. 3450.00
Tureen, Cover, Round, Looped Handles, Stepped Base, Reeded Rim, 6 x 8 In., Pair 1195.00
Tureen, Cover, Scroll Feet, Handles, Acanthus, Gadroon Border, 5 ½ In., Pair.............. 3525.00
Tureen, Cover, Step Footed, 2 Handles, Gadroon Edge, Fruit Knop, 12 x 10 In............. 1265.00
Tureen, Oval, Lobed, Wavy Rim, 2 Flower Handles, 4-Footed, Coat Of Arms, 1835, 7 x 17 In.. . 4780.00
Tureen, Sauce, Oval, Lid, Armorial, Lion Feet, T. Robbins, c.1812, 7 x 9 In., 2 Piece......... 8365.00
Tureen, Sauce, Shell & Gadroon Rim, Acanthus Handles, Crest, c.1812, 3 x 8 In............ 367.00
Vinaigrette, 6 Lobes With Agate Stones, Hinged Lid, Birmingham, 1857, 1 ¼ In............ 604.00
Vinaigrette, Battleship Victory, Lord Nelson, Trafalgar, 1805, Birmingham, 1 ¼ In. 1995.00

Vinaigrette, Book Shape, Engine Turned, Oval Agate On Cover, Floral Grill, 1823, 1 ½ In. 499.00
Vinaigrette, Book Shape, Pierced Shell, Grill, Taylor & Perry, Birmingham, c.1810, 1 In. 448.00
Vinaigrette, Christmas Cracker Shape, Sydney & Co., Birmingham, 1910, 4 x ¾ In. 630.00
Vinaigrette, Combination Lock, Barrel Form, Marked MW, 1879, 1 ¼ x 1 ¼ In. 1103.00
Vinaigrette, Cornucopia Shape, Swirled, Chased Fruit Screw Lid, 1878, London, 3 In. 551.00
Vinaigrette, Engraved Leaves, Diamond Grill, M. Linwood, Birmingham, c.1811, 1 In. 131.00
Vinaigrette, Hunting Horn Shape, Chased Birds, Swirls, S. Mordan, London, 4 In. 761.00
Vinaigrette, Poppy Shape, Pierced Flower Top Cover, London, 1893, 3 ¼ In. 2205.00
Vinaigrette, Sairey Gamp's Head, Lift-Off Cover, London, 1882, 1 ¾ In. 1313.00
Vinaigrette, Top Engraved Maze Pattern, M. Linwood, Birmingham, c.1806, 1 In. 167.00
Waiter, Chippendale Rim, 3-Sided Scroll, Pad Feet, George VI, 10 In. 600.00
Waiter, Raised Scallop Rim, 3 Scrolled Legs, Pad Feet, George II, 6 x 1 In. 2875.00
Wine, Funnel, Grapevine, Flowers, C-Scroll, Gilt, Emes & Barnard, 1808, 5 In. .... *illus* 700.00
Wine Coaster, Lobed Sides, Hardwood Base, Ornate Rim, Regency, c.1825, 6 ½ In., Pair 2937.00
Wine Cooler, Urn Shape, 2 Open Handles, Engraved, Scrolls, Birds, Fruit, c.1865, 12 In., Pair 1896.00
Wine Funnel, Round, Reeded Borders, Tapering Spout, Crest, George III, 4 ¾ In. 460.00

SILVER-FRENCH

Asparagus Server, Pierced, Triangular Blade, Hollow Cast Handle, Engraved, c.1900, 10 In.. 352.00
Box, Monogram, G. Keller, 2 x 6 ¾ x 3 ½ In. 325.00
Brandy Warmer, Flared Rim, Gilt Interior, Reeded Ribbon Border, 2 ½ x 9 ½ In. 489.00
Cake Lifter, Wood Handle, c.1810, 13 ½ In. 325.00
Centerpiece, Art Nouveau, Scalloped, Flowers, Footed, Gilt Bronze Liner, H. Ruolz, c.1890, 17 In. 2596.00
Chalice, Bell Shape, Knopped Stem, Scrollwork, 13 In. 470.00
Chalice, Wheat, Grapes, Christ Life Scenes Panels, 1800s, 9 In. 1298.00
Chocolate Pot, Baluster Shape, Flower Finial, Monogram, Marked, 10 ¼ In. 1998.00
Creamer, Oval Shape, Applied Foot, Bands, Rosettes, Ebonized Handle, 6 In. 764.00
Decanter, Cap, Engraved Glass, Chevroned Fluting, Flower Swags, 7 x 3 ¼ In. 300.00
Dish, Entree, Round, Guilloche Border, Floral Finial, Tapered, Odiot, 2 ½ x 7 In. 1840.00
Knife Set, Silver Blade, Aventurine Handle, Jean Puiforcat, 1930s, 9 In., 12 Piece 8750.00
Lighter, Ribs, Monogram, Cartier, 5 x ½ In. 325.00
Tea & Coffee Set, Octagonal Form, Panels, Alphonse Debain, c.1900, 4 Piece 2160.00
Tea Caddy, Oval, Scalloped, Festoon & Ribbon, Marked, L. Lapan, 1890s, 5 x 4 In. 575.00

SILVER-GERMAN

Basket, Art Nouveau, Crystal Liner, 7 x 6 In. 175.00
Basket, Reticulated, Swags, Gilt Interior, Glass Insert, Swing Handle, 6 x 8 ½ In. 649.00
Bowl, Cover, Repousse, Albert Lenz, c.1930, 8 x 10 ½ In. 351.00
Bowl, Flower Repousse Border, Rim, Foot, Glass Liner, Handles .... *illus* 495.00
Bowl, Repousse, J.D. Schleibner Sohne, Early 20th Century, 6 ¾ In. 94.00
Bowl, Scroll, Shell Rim, 4-Footed, Glass, Stainless Liner, c.1960, 12 In. 388.00
Box, Heart Shape, c.1900-20, 2 ⅜ x 2 ⅜ In. 409.00
Box, Lid, Repousse, Garden Drinking Scene, Oval, c.1900, 5 In. 147.00
Casket, Wedding, Hinged Cover, Bun Feet, Cobalt Blue Glass Liner, 5 x 4 ½ x 3 ¼ In. 1035.00
Centerpiece, Basket, Scalloped Rim, Ram Rings, Swagged Base, c.1900, 12 x 13 In. 1553.00
Coffeepot, Round Foot, Acanthus Border, Bulbous Body, Leaf Band, 8 ½ In. 598.00
Cup, Nautilus, Medieval War Scenes, Hercules, Lion Finial, Enamels, c.1890, 18 In. 23750.00
Dessert Set, Jugendstil, Gilt Bowls, Embossed Poppy Decoration, 5 ¼ To 9 In. 359.00
Dish, Sweetmeat, Boat Bowl, Gilt Interior, Dolphin Stem, Scroll Base, Marked, 5 x 6 In. 1093.00
Fish Set, Knife & Fork, Dolphin Handles, c.1890, 12-In. Knife, 10-In. Fork 489.00
Goblet, Ribbed, Pedestal Base, Munich, 1833, 12 In. 585.00
Ice Cream Scoop, Mayer, Rectangular Bowl, Wood Handle, 12 In. 165.00
Jardiniere, Copper Liner, Handles, Oval, Paw Feet, c.1875, 15 ⅞ In. 490.00
Platter, Oval, Applied Scrolling Border, Early 20th Century, 22 x 14 In. 508.00
Platter, Round, Stepped Flared Border, Hammered, 17 In. 448.00
Punch Bowl Set, Glass Insert, Pedestal Base, 9 x 14 ½ In., 24 Cups 2900.00
Ship Model, Seashell Wheels, Mermaids, Tritons, 3 Masts, c.1890, 24 In. 15000.00
Tankard, Nativity Scene, Gilt, 19th Century, 9 ½ In. .... *illus* 2928.00
Tea & Coffee Service, Rococo, Koerner & Proebl, Berlin, c.1887, 4 Piece 960.00
Tea Service, Rococo, Repousse, Coffeepot, Teapot, Creamer, After 1880, 9 In. 960.00
Tea Set, Repousse, Sterling, T.H. Strube & Sohn, 4 Piece. 1320.00
Tea Set, Rokoko Rose, Rose Finial, Border, Scroll Handle, Heidelberg, 9 ¼ In., 5 Piece 546.00

SILVER-HUNGARIAN

Wedding Cup, Figural, Woman Holding Up Cup, c.1900, 3 x 2 ¼ In. 205.00

SILVER-INDIAN

Bowl, Chased Leaf Designs, 20th Century, 8 ⅝ In. 155.00
Bowl, Hand Raised, Repousse Rim Band, c.1900, 2 ½ x 4 ¾ In., 6 Piece 230.00
Box, Ivory, 18 Painted Ovals, Places, Moguls, Women, Indian Co. Sch., 1800s, 4 x 4 In. 2760.00

TIP
Don't use the popular aluminum-foil-and-baking-soda system to clean antique silver. It leaves the silver with an undesirable tin-looking color.

Silver-English, Toast Rack, Scrolls, 4-Footed, Marked, JE, 1852, 6 ¼ x 7 ¼ x 4 ¾ In.
$575.00

Silver-English, Wine, Funnel, Grapevine, Flowers, C-Scroll, Gilt, Emes & Barnard, 1808, 5 In.
$700.00

Silver-German, Bowl, Flower Repousse Border, Rim, Foot, Glass Liner, Handles
$495.00

S

Silver-German, Tankard, Nativity Scene, Gilt, 19th Century, 9 ½ In.
$2928.00

Silver-Italian, Bowl, Garland, Fruit, Hammered, Repousse, Stamped, Buccellati, 10 x 22 In.
$16520.00

Silver-Mexican, Salad Set, Eagle, Intaglio Hallmark, Hector Aguilar, c.1948-55, 8 ¾ In.
$770.00

TIP

When cleaning silver, use plastic or cotton gloves, not rubber. Rubber makes silver tarnish faster.

Box, Shield, Brass Elephant, Presentation Plaque, c.1924, 2 ¾ x 8 In. 345.00
Cigarette Case, Etched Map Of Indonesia, 3 x 5 In. 59.00
Teapot, Scrolling Leaves, c.1800, 6 ¼ In. 413.00

SILVER-IRISH
Bowl, 3-Footed, Daniel Egan, c.1788, 3 x 5 ¼ In. 351.00
Chocolate Pot, Dome Lid, Wood Handle, Snake Spout, Dublin, 1759, 9 In. 8295.00
Coffeepot, Lid, Ivory Handle, Gadroon, Engraved Shield, Crest, George III, 12 In. 3290.00
Creamer, Bulbous, Ribbed, Banded, Applied Handle, Paw Feet, Jas. Fry, Dublin, 1815, 4 x 6 In. 382.00
Cup, 2 Handles, Armorial Shield, Conch Shell Terminals, George III, 1773, 6 ¾ In. 2040.00
Plate, Footed, Winged Griffin, Baronet's Chevron, George II, c.1732, 7 ¼ In. 4500.00
Punch Ladle, Keating & Flood, Early 19th Century, 13 ½ In. 375.00
Sauceboat, Leaves, Scroll Handle, Beaded Rim, Carden Terry, c.1770, 6 ¼ In. 1800.00
Soup Ladle, Bright Cut Pattern, Gilded Shell Bowl, c.1818, 13 ¾ In. 660.00
Stuffing Spoon, Michael Keaton, Dublin, 1780, 11 In. 410.00

SILVER-ITALIAN
Bowl, Garland, Fruit, Hammered, Repousse, Stamped, Buccellati, 10 x 22 In. *illus* 16520.00
Figurine, Baby Birds, Thin Strips Of Feathers, Sterling, Buccellati, 4 x 3 ½ In. 325.00
Figurine, Corpus Of Christ, Closed Eyes, Chased Hair, Beard, Hollow Back, 8 In. 17700.00
Figurine, Elephant, Seated, Agate Base, Sterling, Cartier, 2 x 4 x 2 ½ In. 200.00
Figurine, Monkey, Seated, Right Hand Over Ear, Buccellati, Rome, c.1950, 4 x 4 In. 3800.00
Lighter, Artichoke Head Form, 3 ½ In. 250.00
Pickle Fork, 2 Prong, Fleur-De-Lis Terminal, 3 ½ In. 15.00
Plate Set, Serving Dish, Round, Plates, Molded Shell, Scroll Border, 13 & 8 In., 7 Piece 6900.00
Sterling, Ladle, Palm Beach, Oval Bowl, Spout, Buccellati, 12 ½ In. 345.00
Sugar & Creamer, Bulbous Gadrooned Body, Footed, Scroll Handle, Peruzzi, c.1940 270.00
Tea & Coffee Set, Baroque, Vercelli, Teapot, Coffeepot, Sugar, Creamer, 4 Piece. 2280.00
Tureen, Cover, Lobed, Pedestal, Scroll, Shell, Handles, Vine Finial, 10 x 15 ½ In. 2040.00

SILVER-JAPANESE
Bowl, Double Wall, Chased, Embossed Iris, Stylized Water, Oval, 1900s, 8 In. 889.00
Bowl, Enamel Iris, Engraved Waterlines, Openwork Foot, 1900s, 4 x 7 In. 3200.00
Bowl, Oval, 4 Characters, 2-Walled Vase, Dragons, Late 19th Century, 9 ¼ In. 2844.00
Box, Flowers, Inset, Mixed Metal Bust Of Woman, 2 ½ x 2 ½ In. 652.00
Box, Round, 3 Monkeys, Engraved, 2 ½ In. 711.00
Container, Cover, 3-Footed, Silver Liner, Leafy Vines, Wisteria Pods, 5 In. 1265.00
Figurine, Crayfish, 3 Flower Form Supports, 4 ½ In. 708.00
Vase, Enamel Decorated, Signed, 1868-1912, 7 ½ In. 468.00

SILVER-MEXICAN
Ashtray, Art Deco, Wood Base, Carved, Lafayette, 3 x 7 In. 295.00
Bowl, Flower Form, Trumpet Foot, c.1950, 6 In. 89.00
Bowl, Hammered, Incised Lines, 3 Loop Handles, W. Spratling, c.1940, 8 ¾ x 3 In. 2040.00
Bowl, Ruffled Edge, Footed, Marked, R.J.L., 11 ½ In. 225.00
Box, Hinged Lid, Turtle Form, Abalone, Marked, Taxco Alpaca, 3 x 9 ½ x 7 ½ In. 150.00
Bucket, Scalloped Edge, Rope Handles, Marked, R.J.L., 6 In. 325.00
Chocolate Pot, Hinged Cover, Wood Handle, William Spratling, 6 ¼ In. 748.00
Coffeepot, Hinged Cover, Jaguar Finial, Wood Handle, William Spratling, 8 ¾ In. 2070.00
Cordial Set, Deep Bowl, Slender Stem, Round Foot, R. Lopez, c.1950, 8 Piece 178.00
Dish, Leaf Shape, Stem Handle, J.L. Reves, 1950s, 8 In. 234.00
Goblet, Footed, Chased Petals, Hammered, 1940s, 4 In., 12 Piece. 590.00
Jigger, William Spratling, c.1956-64, 4 ½ In. 322.00
Pitcher, C. Zurita, c.1950, 10 In. 380.00
Pitcher, Toucan, Turquoise, Taxco, 6 In. 100.00
Pitcher, Water, Ribbed, Circular Foot, C-Scroll Handle, Oval, c.1960, 13 ½ In. 472.00
Plate, Embossed Mayan Calendar, Jaguars, Birds, Warriors, Sanborns, c.1950, 10 x 16 In. 178.00
Punch Set, Leafy Rim, Bowl, Ladle, Tray, 12 Cups, 7 ¾ x 13 In., 15 Piece 2574.00
Salad Set, Eagle, Intaglio Hallmark, Hector Aguilar, c.1948-55, 8 ¾ In. *illus* 770.00
Sauceboat, 3-Footed, Lopez, Taxco, 2 x 6 ½ x 3 ½ In. 44.00
Sugar & Creamer, Cover, Vertical Flutes, Scroll Handles, Circular Feet, 4 ¼ In. 173.00
Sugar & Creamer, Round, Wide Spout, Scroll Handle, Sanborns, Mexico City, 3 In. 119.00
Tea & Coffee Set, Coffeepot, Teapot, Sugar, Creamer, Waste Bawl, Tray, Lobed, 6 Piece 2242.00
Teapot, Bowl, Melon Lobed, Flower Finial, Footed, Leaf Rim, Handles, 4 ¼ In. 863.00
Teapot, Hinged Cover, Jaguar Finial, Wood Handle, William Spratling, 6 ⅝ In. 1840.00
Teapot, Wood Handle, 8 ½ In. 403.00
Tongs, Leaf Shape, Beaded Handle, AEM Mark, 11 In. 178.00
Tray, Canape, Divided Beaded Handles, Applied Leaves, Oval, c.1950, 16 In. 178.00
Tray, Castillo, Turquoise, Oval, 14 ¼ In. 527.00

Tray, Decorated Edges, Handles, 18 ⅛ In. 840.00
Tray, Oval, Marked, Hecho En Mexico, R. Lopez, 15 ⅝ x 26 ¼ In. 605.00
Tray, Oval, Scrollwork Rim, Handles, 25 ¼ x 16 ½ In. 805.00
Tray, Recessed Border, Shell, Berry, Rope-Like, Ortega, 30 ¾ x 17 ¼ In. 2070.00
Tureen, Tray, Lobed, Mosaics, Turquoise, Castillo, Taxco, 1950s, 15 In. .... *illus* 1000.00

SILVER-NORWEGIAN

Compote, Green Enamel Center, Filigree Scrolled Rim, 1901, 2 x 8 In. 1315.00
Tea Set, Bulbous Shape, Curved Feet, Ebony Finials, D. Anderson, 7 In., 4 Piece 1422.00

SILVER-PERSIAN

Box, Flowers, Leaves, 19th Century, 2 ¼ x 8 In. 660.00

SILVER-PERUVIAN

Bowl, Hammered, Stylized Leaf Shape, Kohler Mark, 11 In, 2 Piece 267.00
Box, Lid, Hinged, Sloped Sides, Face Latch, Engraved Inca Figures, Symbols, 5 In. 148.00
Hand Forged, Applied Pre-Columbian Design, Wood Interior, 4 In. 120.00
Ice Bucket, Swing Handle, Drain, 12 x 7 In. 526.00
Vase, Globular, Pinched Neck, c.1950, 6 x 5 ½ In. 205.00

SILVER-POLISH

Box, Sugar, Rocaille Design, Beaded Lid, Ball Feet, 1857, 3 ½ x 6 ¼ x 5 In. .... *illus* 1760.00
Tumbler, Impressed, International Coins, Cylindrical, Early 1900s, 7 ½ In. 359.00

SILVER-PORTUGUESE

Dish, Cover, Scroll Rim, Round, Marked, Portugal 660.00
Tea Set, Teapot, Coffeepot, Sugar, Cover, Creamer, Tray, 16 ¼ x 25 ½ In. 1600.00
Tray, Octagonal, Openwork Grape & Vine Border, Footed, 2 ¼ x 16 In. 920.00
Tray, Prata 90, Bead Edge, 2 Handles, Wolff, 13 x 19 In. 585.00
Tray, Scalloped Border, Deer, Handles, Openwork Feet, Open Gallery, 21 x 16 In. 1840.00

SILVER-RUSSIAN. Russian silver is marked with the Cyrillic, or Russian, alphabet. The numbers 84, 88, or 91 indicate the silver content. Russian silver may be higher or lower than sterling standard. Other marks indicate maker, assayer, or city of manufacture. Many pieces of silver made in Russia are decorated with enamel. Faberge pieces are listed in their own category.

Basket, Openwork Sides, 2 Trays, Hinged Handle, A. Yashinov, 1800s, 11 x 12 In. 12650.00
Basket, Woven Mold, Oval, Flowers, Wheat, Insects, Twisted Handle, P. Akimov, 6 x 6 In. 4444.00
Beaker, Gilt, Cloisonne Enamel, Flared, Flowers, P.A. Ovchinnikov, Moscow, c.1912, 2 In. 2629.00
Beaker, Niello, Scenic Reserves, 2 ¾ x 3 In. 895.00
Beaker, Scrolled Leafy Vines, Diamond Forms, Peasant Woman, 3 In. 1840.00
Beaker, Tapestry Design, Scrolling Leaves, Flowers, Stippled Ground, 2 ⅛ In. 288.00
Beaker Set, Hunting, Stag Head Cup, Wood, Velvet Lined Case, 1900s, 3 In., 6 Piece 1652.00
Belt, Sections Held By Leather Straps, 1 x 25 ½ In. 400.00
Box, Cloisonne Enamel, Lid, Multicolored, Crown Finial, 3-Footed, Moscow, c.1890, 2 In. 311.00
Box, Gilt, Enamel, Hinged, Scalloped Edge, 3 ½ In. 409.00
Box, Hammered Finish, Flowers, Ball Feet, 4 ¾ x 6 ¼ x 4 In. 1200.00
Box, Lid, Round, Basket Weave, Metal Flowers, Insect, Khlebnikov, c.1890, 4 x 4 In. 418.00
Box, Trunk Shape, Domed, Hinged Handles, Bracket Feet, c.1889, 3 ¼ x 5 ¾ In. 431.00
Card Case, Scrolling Vines, Thumb Lift, Pink Ruby Stone, Monogram 316.00
Cigarette Box, Cover, Amethyst, Man On Horseback, Carrying Flag, 1908-17, 5 In. 593.00
Cigarette Case, 2 Mountaineers, Stone Clasp, Stamped, AMIO522, 4 x 3 In. 800.00
Cigarette Case, Applied Gold Charms, Moscow, c.1880, 3 ¾ In. .... *illus* 1650.00
Cigarette Case, Enameled Lid, Birds, Flowers, Berries, Wirework Spiral, c.1912, 4 In. 8295.00
Cigarette Case, Engraved Flowers, Gilt Interior, Monogram, 4 x 3 In. 196.00
Cigarette Case, Etched Kremlin View, Ruby Latch, Gilt Interior, Moscow, c.1936, 4 In. 215.00
Cigarette Case, Kremlin Cartouche, Engraved Silver Gilt, Niello, 1892, 4 x 3 In. 1076.00
Cigarette Case, Monogram, Sapphire Blue Cabochon Fastener, 4 ½ x 3 In. 173.00
Cigarette Case, Radiant Gadroon, Cabochon Sapphire Thumb Piece, Nicholas II, c.1910 ... 660.00
Cigarette Case, Repousse 2-Headed Imperial Eagle, Stamp, 4 In. 2360.00
Cigarette Case, Scrolls, Flowers, Enamel Covering, Blue, White, Red, c.1900, 4 In. 2726.00
Cigarette Case, Woods, Village, Stone Set Enamel, Wood Case, H.T. Mark, c.1910, 4 x 3 In. ... 8295.00
Compote, Enamel, Blue Ground, Spade Shapes, Late 19th Century, 4 ¼ In. 1638.00
Creamer, 4 Leafy Feet, Applied Ivy Rim, C-Scroll Branch Handle, 1859, 4 ¾ In. 384.00
Creamer, Bulbous Body, Gilt Interior, Shaped Oval Foot, C-Scroll Handle, 4 ¾ In. 239.00
Creamer, Engraved, Climbing Rose Vine, Gold Wash Interior, 3 In. 230.00
Creamer, Engraved Flowers, Footed, 4 In. 316.00
Cup, Enamel, Silver Gilt, Flowers, Glass Liner, Soviet Era, 4 ¼ In. 115.00
Cup, Griffins, Wreaths, Gilt Interior, Marked, Faberge, 2 x 2 ¼ In. .... *illus* 5500.00

TIP

When cleaning silver, be careful of pieces like candlesticks or hollow knife handles that could hold the remains of chemical cleaner. Use a polish that is made to be used dry and wiped off.

Silver-Mexican, Tureen, Tray, Lobed, Mosaics, Turquoise, Castillo, Taxco, 1950s, 15 In.
$1000.00

Silver-Polish, Box, Sugar, Rocaille Design, Beaded Lid, Ball Feet, 1857, 3 ½ x 6 ¼ x 5 In.
$1760.00

Silver-Russian, Cigarette Case, Applied Gold Charms, Moscow, c.1880, 3 ¾ In.
$1650.00

SILVER-RUSSIAN

Silver-Russian, Cup, Griffins, Wreaths, Gilt Interior, Marked, Faberge, 2 x 2 ¼ In. $5500.00

Silver-Russian, Kovsh, Scroll & Flower Repousse, Marked, 1886, 1 ¾ x 5 ½ x 3 In. $550.00

Silver-Russian, Tea Strainer, Gilt, Enamel, Scroll Filigree, Blue, White, G.G. Klingert, Moscow, 1892, 6 In. $717.00

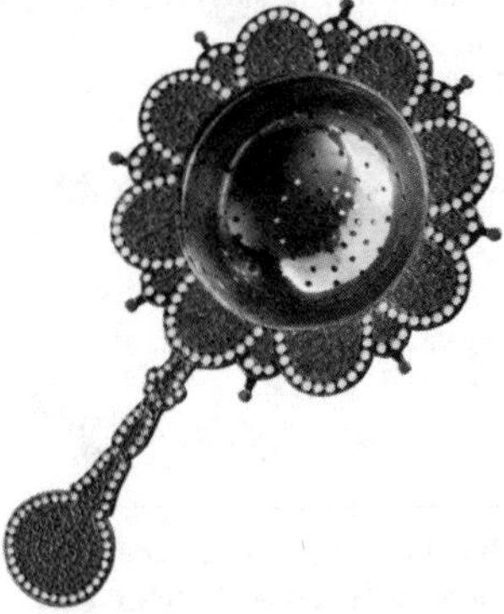

TIP

If polishing a wooden-handled copper or silver teapot, be sure to cover the wood so it is not stained by the metal polish.

Cup, Vodka, Allover Repousse Flower, Eagle, 1756, 3 ½ In. 1062.00
Cup, Vodka, Chased Border, Cartouches Centering Flowers, 1871, 2 ¾ In. 201.00
Cup, Vodka, Chased Flower, 3 In. 179.00
Cup, Vodka, Flowers, Leaves, Marked 84, 19th Century, 3 ½ In.. .... 25.00
Cup, Vodka, Scenic Medallions, Diamond Patterned Ground, Flower Border, 3 In. 269.00
Cup & Saucer, Demitasse, St. George Slaying Dragon, c.1894, 3 ¼ x 5 ½ In. 750.00
Cup & Saucer, Gilt, Scrolls, Flowers, St. Petersburg, 1855, 3 x 5 In.. .... 1534.00
Egg, Chickens, Enamel, Silver, Dolphin Stand, Hallmark, 4 In.. .... 950.00
Egg, Flowers, Dots, Enamel, Gilt, Jeweled Lid, Stand, Hallmark, c.1910, 3 ½ In. 950.00
Egg, Flowers, Leaves, Enamel, Marked, Pavel Ovchinikov, 4 x 2 ⅜ In. 1025.00
Egg, Gilt, Enamel, Multicolor, 4 x 2 ¾ In. 1872.00
Egg, Gold, Enamel, 7 Cabochon Rubies, 5 ½ x 4 In.. .... 4680.00
Egg, Hinged Lid, 3 Scroll Feet, Eagle On Lid, Stamped, 1891, 4 ¾ In. 1600.00
Egg, Multicolored Swans, Enamel, Hoof Legs, Marked, Pavel Ovchinikov, 3 ⅝ In.. .... 1025.00
Ewer, Round, Slender Neck, C-Scroll Handle, Chased, Flowers, c.1841, 13 ¾ In.. .... 2478.00
Figurine, Nude Woman, Marble Base, 3 ⅞ In. 325.00
Helmet Cup, Imperial Regiment Style, 3 x 2 ½ In. 877.00
Honey Cup, Barrel Form, Scroll Handle, Alexandra, 1894, 2 ½ x 2 ¾ In. 450.00
Knife Set, Knives, Forks, Neoclassical Style, Oak Case, Moscow, c.1910, 6 In., 24 Piece 7080.00
Kovsh, Enamel, Stamped, Double-Headed Eagle, 84, 3 ½ x 6 ½ In. 2750.00
Kovsh, Gilt, Enamel, Scrolls, Flowers, M. Semenova, Moscow, c.1912, 3 In.. .... 1652.00
Kovsh, Plain Body, Chased Edge Band, Geometric Handle, c.1900, 5 x 2 In. 944.00
Kovsh, Scroll & Flower Repousse, Marked, 1886, 1 ¾ x 5 ½ x 3 In. .... *illus* 550.00
Ladle, Enameled, Gold Washed Bowl, Jeweled, Gilded, Medallion, c.1858, 17 ½ In.. .... 2300.00
Ladle, Gilt Bowl, Neoclassical Handle, Monogram, 13 In. 142.00
Ladle, Round Bowl, Fiddle Handle, Pointed Fins, 1896-1908, 12 ¼ In. 173.00
Ladle, Turned Round Bowl, Engraved Handle, Vining, c.1854, 11 ½ In.. .... 173.00
Opium Pipe, Cobalt Blue, Turquoise, Flowers, 2 ¾ In. 374.00
Pill Box, Gilt, Cloisonne Enamel, Flowers, Leaves, Stone Insert On Lid, c.1912, 2 In. 1912.00
Pitcher, Beading, Banding, Scroll Handle, Moscow, 1893, 10 In. 2868.00
Ring Holder, 2 Shells, Ball Feet, Handle, Marked, 6 x 5 ⅛ x 2 ½ In. 650.00
Salt, Basket Weave Bowl, Gilt Spoons, Wooden Box, c.1888, 13 Piece 5676.00
Salt, Chased Side, Scalloped Rim, 4 Ball Feet, St. Petersburg, 1839, 4 In., 2 Piece 649.00
Salt, Cloisonne Enamel, Textured Ground, Flowers, c.1899, 1 x 2 In.. .... 335.00
Salt, Embossed Swans, Scrolls, Beaded Rim, Ball Feet, 1896-1908, 2 ⅛ In. 1778.00
Scent Case, Filigree, Loop, 1875, 1 ⅜ x 1 ⅞ In. 230.00
Sculpture, Pig, 3 ½ In. 800.00
Serving Spoon, Mikhail H. Kilpeleinen, St. Petersburg, 1846, 8 In.. .... 49.00
Spoon, Gilt, Cloisonne Enamel Bowl, Twist Handle, V.S. Agafonov, Moscow, 1886, 8 In. 598.00
Spoon, Gold Wash Bowl, Flowers, 7 ½ In. 2875.00
Strainer Ladle, Enameled Stem, Tapered, Beaded Bowl, Monogram, c.1912, 6 ¾ In. 1896.00
Sugar Scoop, Enamel Handle, c.1950, 3 ¾ In. 146.00
Sugar Shovel, Cloisonne, Turquoise Backdrop, Multicolored Medallion, 4 ¼ In.. .... 546.00
Sugar Tongs, Eagle Claw Ends, St. Petersburg, 5 ½ In.. .... 225.00
Tankard, Floral Repousse, Gilt Interior, Ball Feet, 5 ¼ In. 7200.00
Tankard, Morozov, Raised Relief, Warriors, 16 x 10 In.. .... 8190.00
Tea Holder, Glass, Oak Leaf Wreath, Applied Leaf Handle, Monogram, 1935, 3 In., Pair 177.00
Tea Strainer, Gilt, Enamel, Scroll Filigree, Blue, G.G. Klingert, Moscow, 1892, 6 In. .... *illus* 717.00
Teapot, Gourd Shape, Vine Finial, Branch Handle, Leaf Border, c.1860, 5 ¼ In. 1770.00
Teaspoon Set, Silver Gilt, A. Yashinov, St. Petersburg, 5 In., 12 Piece 234.00
Tray, 2 Handles, Serpentine Border, Shell, Scroll, c.1842, 24 x 15 In. 3107.00
Tray, Cloisonne, 8 Sections, Flowers, Leaves, Multicolored, Marked, 4 ½ In. 1265.00
Vodka Set, Carafe, Tray, Beakers, Engraved, Cattails, Lilies, 1900, 7 Piece .... *illus* 1700.00

SILVER-SCOTTISH

Ewer, C-Shape Handle, c.1883, 12 ½ In. 2106.00
Ladle, Downturned Fiddle Handle, Pointed Fins, Oval Bowl, Marked, 13 ¼ In. 288.00
Spoon, Strawberry, WRJ Monogram, Victorian, c.1842, 9 In., Pair 201.00
Tea Set, Figures, Paw Feet, 14-In. Kettle On Stand, 1876, 6 Piece .... *illus* 1750.00
Vinaigrette, Barrel Shape, Agate Staves, Bezel-Set Spangle Glass Finial, 3 In. 3413.00
Vinaigrette, Book Shape, Mother-Of-Pearl Sides, Etched Flowers, Thistle Grill, 2 In. 341.00
Vinaigrette, Bottle Shape, 6 Sides, Agate Inlay, Cushion Cover, Citrine, 2 ¼ In. 1155.00
Vinaigrette, Sporran Shape, Applied Stones & Thistle, Chain & Loop, 3 In. 1680.00
Vinaigrette, Thistle Form, Marked, EHS, c.1875, 3 ¾ x 2 In. 4400.00
Vinaigrette, Thistle Shape, Chased, Stippled, Hinged Cover, Chain & Loop, 2 In. 1523.00

SILVER-SPANISH

Basin, 6-Lobed, Deep Slope Sides, Ring Handles, 18th Century, 2 ¼ x 11 In. 600.00

SILVER-STERLING. Sterling silver is made with 925 parts silver out of 1,000 parts of metal. The word *sterling* is a quality guarantee used in the United States after about 1860. The word was used much earlier in England and Ireland. Pieces listed here are not identified by country. Other pieces of sterling quality silver are listed under Silver-American, Silver-English, etc.

Berry Spoon, Repousse Decoration, Stamped, 9 In. 48.00
Bowl, Beaded, Oval, Leaf Border, Marked, 3 ⅛ x 8 ⅛ In. 345.00
Bowl, Classical, 4-Footed, Monogram, 19th Century, 5 ⅝ x 3 ⅛ In. 295.00
Bowl, Conforming Foot, Scroll & Flower Repousse, Monogram, c.1908, 3 ¾ x 9 In. 863.00
Bowl, Embossed Pineapple, Shaped Rim, Scrolls, 3 ⅛ x 12 ½ In. 1320.00
Bowl, Oval, Floral Repousse Border, Marked, Monogram, 1 ½ x 12 ½ In. 489.00
Box, Hammered, Landscape, Enamel, 1 ¾ x 3 ½ In. 1560.00
Box, Silver Crest, Bronze, Applied Octagonal Design, Wood Liner, 6 14 x 1 ½ In. 230.00
Butter Chip, Puffed Rim, Flowers, Leaves, Scrolled Edge, 5 ⅝ x 3 ½ In., Pair 115.00
Candelabra are listed in the Candelabrum category.
Candlesnuffer, Wood Handle, Marked, Cartier, 10 In. 20.00
Candlesticks are listed in their own category.
Card Case, Hinged Top, Incised Flowers, Center Medallion, Monogram, 3 ⅝ In. 216.00
Card Case, Scroll Border, Trinity Church 1175.00
Castor, Gilded, Pierced, Lobed, Engraved Monogram, c.1890, 5 ½ In., Pair 480.00
Centerpiece, 3-Branch Grape, Leaves Post, 3 Baskets, Scroll Base, Marked, 21 x 13 In. 5520.00
Cigarette Box, Cylindrical, Hermes, 3 x 2 ½ In. 440.00
Cigarette Case, 14K Gold & Brass Stripes, Marked, 3 x 4 In. 50.00
Cigarette Case, Blue Enamel, Marked, 2 ½ x 3 ¼ In. 475.00
Cigarette Case, Flowers, Woman's Face, Art Nouveau, Engraved, 3 ½ x 3 ¼ In. 140.00
Cocktail Shaker, Hand Beaten, c.1930, 12 In. 351.00
Cocktail Shaker, Royal Danish, International, Scroll Finial, 8 Cups 764.00
Compote, Footed, Hammered, Notched Bowl, 5 In. 780.00
Cover, Vanity Jar, Monogram, Floral, Scrolled, 3 x 2 ⅜ In. 210.00
Cream Jug, Inverted Pear Shape, Round Pedestal Foot, Beaded Rim, c.1782, 5 In. 240.00
Decanter, Stopper, Overlay Clear Glass, Marked, Alvin, Early 1900s, 9 ½ In. 690.00
Decanter, Urn Shape, Holly & Flowers, Stopper, Inscription, 10 ½ x 5 ¼ In. 748.00
Decanter Set, Sea Serpent, Twisted Rams Horn, Holds 6 Goblets, Marked, 16 In. 690.00
Dessert Fork, Silver Gilt, Grape Cluster Handle, Vining, 7 ½ In., 12 Piece 540.00
Dish, Flower, Leaf, Ruffled Edge, Pedestal, 5 ¼ x 7 ¾ In. 55.00
Dish, Sweetmeat, Shell Bowl, Dolphin Post, Wave Base, Marked, c.1890, 7 x 8 In., Pair 1495.00
Dresser Set, Brush, Comb, Art Deco, Box, 1920s 60.00
Figurine, Bulldog, Seated, Detailed, Leather Collar, 5 ¼ In. 1800.00
Fish Knife, Fork, Floral Repousse, Pierced, Engraved Scimitar Blade, 12 In. 206.00
Fish Serving Set, Repousse Handle, Pierced, Scrolling, Monogram, 12 In., 2 Piece 236.00
Flask, Chrysanthemum, 6 ¼ In. 750.00
Grape Scissors, Figural Grapes & Vines 70.00
Ice Cream Knife, Vine With Berry Handle, Engraved Gilt, Case, c.1875, 11 ⅜ In. 276.00
Jug, Claret, Cut Glass, Fluted, Oculus Banding, Gadroon Handle, 13 ½ x 6 In. 1920.00
Kettle, Hot Water, Dome Lid, Leaf Finial, Short Handles, Laurel Branches, c.1875, 16 In. 1778.00
Letter Holder, Rectangular, Arched Dividers, Scroll Borders, 6 x 8 In. .... *illus* 748.00
Mirror, Dressing, Upright, Green Velvet Lining, Scrolling Strapwork, 14 x 11 In. 478.00
Mug, Flower, Scroll, Child's, 2 ½ In. 11.00
Napkin Rings are listed in their own category.
Perfume Burner, Repousse, Egg Shape, Chain, Flower Decoration, 3 x 2 ¼ In. .... *illus* 288.00
Pie Server, Ivy, Victorian, 9 ½ In. 180.00
Pitcher, Baluster Shape, Ear Handle, Gadroon Rim, c.1910, 7 In. 504.00
Pitcher, Danish Style, Pear Shape, Scroll Handle, Ring Base, Marked, 8 ¾ x 6 ¾ In. 374.00
Pitcher, Water, Helmet Shape, Square Handle, Marks, S Monogram, c.1910, 9 x 9 In. 748.00
Plateau, Mirrored, Round, Scrolling Anthemion Border, 15 ½ In. 767.00
Purse, Art Nouveau, Rectangular, Scroll & Leaf, Blue Glass Clasp, 5 x 2 ½ In. 259.00
Rattle, Baby, Round, Marked, 3 In. 20.00
Salad Spoon & Fork, Cartier, 11 In. 146.00
Spoon, Egyptian Goddess Handle, Enamel Ship Scene 110.00
Spoon, Enamel Bowl, 3 Boys In Front Of Watermelon 1550.00
Spoon, Little Miss Muffet, Hallmark 30.00
Spoon, Souvenir, are listed in the Souvenir category.
String Jar, Art Nouveau, Signed, Shiebler, 3 ¾ x 3 ½ In. 250.00
Sugar & Creamer, Beaded Rims, Gilt Interior, Marked, Sterling 100.00
Tape Measure, Leafy Design, Round, 1 ¼ In. 85.00
Tea Infuser, Stand, Teapot Shape, Early 1900s, 3 ⅜ x 1 ¾ In. 275.00
Tea Set, Round, Urn Shape, Acanthus Bud Finials, Chased, Monogram, 5 Piece 1035.00
Tea Set, Urn Finial, Scroll Handles, Rose Decorated Feet, 20th Century, 4 Piece 920.00

TIP

Empty your silver saltshaker after every party to avoid corrosion.

Silver-Russian, Vodka Set, Carafe, Tray, Beakers, Engraved, Cattails, Lilies, 1900, 7 Piece
$1700.00

Silver-Scottish, Tea Set, Figures, Paw Feet, 14-In. Kettle On Stand, 1876, 6 Piece
$1750.00

Silver-Sterling, Letter Holder, Rectangular, Arched Dividers, Scroll Borders, 6 x 8 In.
$748.00

Silver-Sterling, Perfume Burner, Repousse, Egg Shape, Chain, Flower Decoration, 3 x 2 ¼ In.
$288.00

SILVER-STERLING

Silver-Sterling, Trophy, Steeplechase, Egg & Dart Border, Hillsboro Hounds, 1960s, 18 In.
$3335.00

Sinclaire, Vase, Fan, Amber, Ribbed, Engraved Flowers, Signed, 10 ⅝ x 9 In.
$58.00

Slag Glass, Purple, Paperweight, Obelisk, Hollow, Ribs, Prism Edge, 1890s, 7 ¾ x 3 ¾ In.
$82.00

Slag Glass, Turquoise, Spooner, 3 Flying Swans, Challinor, Taylor & Co., 1890s, 4 ½ x 3 ½ In.
$89.00

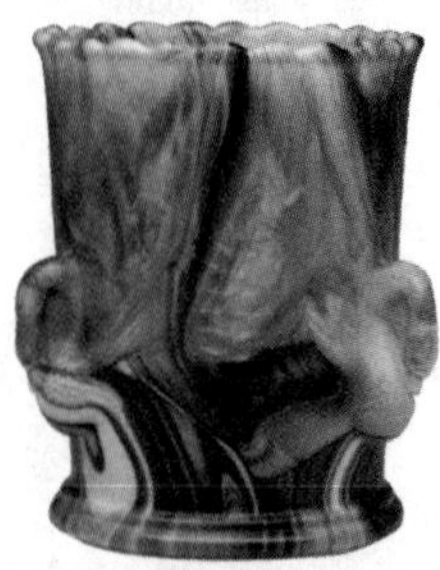

Teapot, Embossed Flowers, Leaves, Scrolls, Slender, Marked, A8271, 9 ½ In. 475.00
Teapot, Engraved, Rococo Scrolls, Acanthus, Gooseneck Spout, 6 ½ x 5 In. 720.00
Toddy Ladle, Round Bowl, Twisted Whalebone Handle, Thistle Ferrule, c.1861, 7 In. 120.00
Tray, Fish, Oval, Laurel Wreath Border, Handles, 31 ½ x 12 ¾ In. 2760.00
Tray, Footed, Round, Scroll Border, Strawberry Decoration, 8 ½ In., Pair 805.00
Tray, Medallion, Rolled Border, Horse Race Trophy, c.1870, 17 ½ x 13 ¾ In. 2185.00
Tray, Oblong, Art Deco, Monogram, c.1928, 26 In. 999.00
Trophy, Steeplechase, Egg & Dart Border, Hillsboro Hounds, 1960s, 18 In. . . . . *illus* 3335.00
Vase, Overlay, Green Glass, Baluster Shape, Flowers, Scrolls, Monogram, 10 In. 1495.00
Vase, Overlay, Green Glass, Urn Shape, Flared Top, Scroll Overlay, 7 ¾ x 3 ¾ In. 633.00
Vase, Trumpet Shape, Fluting, Applied Shell & Scrolls, Dome Foot, 10 x 5 In., Pair 2400.00
Vinaigrette, Artillery Shell Shape, Gold Washed, Red Enamel Stripe, 1900, 3 ¾ In. 761.00
Vinaigrette, Bagpipes Shape, Pierced Abalone Sides, Hinged, 1860, ¾ In. 210.00
Vinaigrette, Book Shape, Engraved, Blue & White Agate Cover, Hinged, 1 x ¾ In. 1103.00
Vinaigrette, Curling Stone Shape, Hinged, Gilt Grill, 1 In. 368.00
Vinaigrette, Figural, Bearded Asian Man's Head, Lift-Off Cover, 3 ¼ x 1 ¾ In. 473.00
Vinaigrette, Flower Bouquet, Chased, Domed, Dolphin Handle Screws Off, 2 In. 263.00
Vinaigrette, Flower Shape, 8 Chased Petals, Stem, Removable Front & Back, 4 In. 147.00
Vinaigrette, Heart-Shaped Padlock, Engraved, Hinged, Bright Cut Grill, 1818, 2 In. 788.00
Vinaigrette, Orb Shape, Concentric Rings, Screw Top, Footed, 1 ¼ x ¾ In. 230.00
Vinaigrette, Spinning Top Shape, Rings, Pointed Spindle, 1 ¼ In. 1050.00
Vinaigrette, Teapot Shape, Swing Handle, Swirl Cover, c.1800, 2 ¼ x 2 In. 315.00
Yo-Yo, LSM Co., 3 In. 75.00

SILVER-SWEDISH

Beaker, Cone Shape, Gold Interior, Embossed Rim, Uddevallea, c.1787, 7 In. 1304.00
Tankard, Hinged Lid, Grapes, Vines, 3 Ball Feet, 1933, 6 ¾ In. 360.00
Tea Set, Tray, Teapot, Creamer, Sugar, Covered Bowl, Jacob Angman, 19 ¼ In. 1560.00
Vinaigrette, Standing Heart Shape, Crown On Top, Footed, 2 ¾ In. 126.00

SILVER-SWISS

Eggcup, Ostrich, Lid, Putti, Violin, Leaves, Gilt Mounts, Lucerne, c.1890, 18 In. 23750.00

SILVER-SYRIAN

Tray, Copper, Brass, Scrolls, c.1900, 38 In. 819.00

SINCLAIRE cut glass was made by H.P. Sinclaire and Company of Corning, New York, between 1904 and 1929. He cut glass made at other factories until 1920. Pieces were made of crystal as well as amber, blue, green, or ruby glass. Only a small percentage of Sinclaire glass is marked with the S in a wreath.

Banana Boat, Engraved Pear & Vintage, Signed, 4 x 11 In. 220.00
Bowl, Snowflake & Holly, Hobstar Cut Wafer Base, Signed, 5 x 10 In. 1800.00
Clock, Dresser, Intaglio, Gothic Arch, 5 In. 173.00
Compote, Etched, 8 ½ x 7 In. 173.00
Plate, Laurel, Engraved, Clear, 8 In., 4 Piece 58.00
Rum Pot, Engraved Flowers, 5 x 8 ½ In. 605.00
Tray, Engraved, 8 ¼ x 17 ¾ In. 5290.00
Tumbler, Whiskey, Queens Pattern, 2 ½ In. 165.00
Urn, Cover, Intaglio, Ribbon Tied Flower Garlands, Rolled Rim, 12 ½ x 7 In. 374.00
Vase, Blue, Intaglio Floral, Silver Banded, Rolled Rim, 7 ½ x 6 ¼ In. 297.00
Vase, Diamonds & Silver Threads, Engraved, Tapered, Crosshatch, Grapes, 15 ½ x 7 In. 690.00
Vase, Fan, Amber, Ribbed, Engraved Flowers, Signed, 10 ⅝ x 9 In. . . . . *illus* 58.00
Vase, Fan, Cut Medallion, Leafy Frame, Optic Ribbed, Footed, 9 In. 58.00
Vase, Flared Neck, Scalloped Edge, 12 In. 805.00
Vase, Flip, Turquoise, Engraved Flowers, 8 ¼ x 5 ¾ In. 175.00
Vase, Intaglio, Signed, 12 In. 144.00

SKIING, *see Sports category.*

SLAG GLASS resembles a marble cake. It can be streaked with different colors. There were many types made from about 1880. Caramel slag is the incorrect name for Chocolate glass. Pink slag was an American product made by Harry Bastow and Thomas E.A. Dugan at Indiana, Pennsylvania, about 1900. Purple and blue slag were made in American and English factories in the 1880s. Red slag is a very late Victorian and twentieth-century glass. Other colors are known but are of less importance to the collector. New versions of chocolate glass and colored slag glass are being made.

Caramel Slag is listed in the Imperial Glass category.
Orange, Ashtray, Lighter Recess, Yellow, Onyx, Vidrio Products, Ill., 5 ⅞ x 3 ⅞ In. 45.00

Sleepy Eye, Bowl, Butter, Blue, Gray, Indian, Teepees, Stoneware, Early 1900s, 5 In.
$560.00

Sleepy Eye, Sign, Sleepy Eye Flour, Indian, Tin Lithograph, Self-Framed, 18 x 13 ⅜ In.
$3540.00

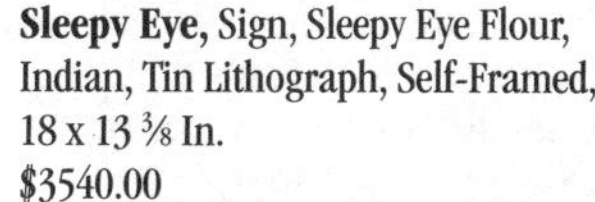

Sleepy Eye, Sugar, Blue, Gray, Indian, Early 1900s, 3 ⅛ In.
$502.00

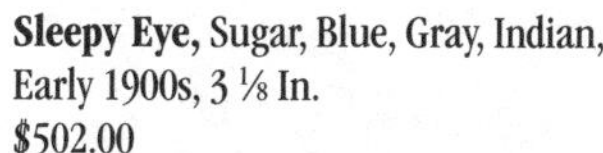

Sleepy Eye, Crock, Salt, Blue, Gray, Indian, Stoneware, Early 1900s, 4 In.
$502.00

Sleepy Eye, Stein, Blue, Gray, Indian, Stoneware, Early 1900s, 7 ⅝ In.
$413.00

Sleepy Eye, Vase, Blue, Gray, Indian, Cattails, Cylindrical, Early 1900s, 9 In.
$225.00

Sleepy Eye, Pitcher, Blue, White, Indian, Teepee, Tree, Monmouth WSCO, Diamond Stamp, 6 ½ In.
$100.00

Sleepy Eye, Stein, Brown, Indian, Early 1900s, 7 ⅝ In.
$295.00

TIP

Look for a sunken hole on the inside of a Sleepy Eye pitcher where the handle is attached. This indicates a reproduction. Old pitchers are smooth. Reproductions of Sleepy Eye pitchers weigh less than old ones.

TIP

Put together a "flea market transportation kit." Start with a large shopping bag to carry small items or a collapsible shopping cart if you think you'll need it. Include packing materials like newspapers, bubble wrap, boxes, or old blankets. Diapers and plastic-lined bedding pads are good for wrapping breakables. Carry a rope or bungee cords to hold items on top of the car or to secure an open trunk. Don't forget a screwdriver, hammer, and rust-loosening oil in case you have to dismantle a bed or table to fit it in your car. Take a tape measure to check the size of a chair against the size of your car's open door and storage space. We have seen people trying to force a chair into a trunk or backseat by twisting it in every direction.

Pink, Punch Bowl Set, Inverted Feather & Fan, Dugan, 14-In. Bowl, 7 Piece. 4025.00
Pink, Toothpick, Inverted Fan & Feather, 2 ⅝ In. . . . . 259.00 to 750.00
Pink, Tumbler, Inverted Feather & Fan, Dugan, 4 In., 4 Piece 518.00
Purple, Cruet, Stopper, 1970s, 7 In.. . . . . 80.00
Purple, Paperweight, Obelisk, Hollow, Ribs, Prism Edge, 1890s, 7 ¾ x 3 ¾ In. . . . . *illus* 82.00
Turquoise, Spooner, 3 Flying Swans, Challinor, Taylor & Co., 1890s, 4 ½ x 3 ½ In. . . . . . *illus* 89.00

SLEEPY EYE collectors look for anything bearing the image of the nineteenth-century Indian chief with the drooping eyelid. The Sleepy Eye Milling Co., Sleepy Eye, Minnesota, used his portrait in advertising from 1883 to 1921. It offered many premiums, including stoneware and pottery steins, crocks, bowls, mugs, and pitchers, all decorated with the famous profile of the Indian. The popular pottery was made by Western Stoneware, Weir Pottery Company, and other companies long after the flour mill went out of business in 1921. Reproductions of the pitchers are being made today. The original pitchers came in only five sizes: 4 inches, 5 ¼ inches, 6 ½ inches, 8 inches, and 9 inches. The Sleepy Eye image was also used by companies unrelated to the flour mill.

Bowl, Butter, Blue, Gray, Indian, Teepees, Stoneware, Early 1900s, 5 In. . . . . *illus* 560.00
Crock, Salt, Blue, Gray, Indian, Stoneware, Early 1900s, 4 In. . . . . *illus* 502.00
Fan, Sleepy Eye Mills, Barrett Merc. Co. & Buster Brown Shoes, Cardboard, Wood Handle 49.00
Mug, Blue, White, Indian, Campfire, W In Maple Leaf Mark, 5 ½ In. 121.00
Mug, Blue, White, Indian, Campfire, WSCo. Monmouth, Ill., 4 ⅝ In. 187.00
Mug, Indian, Teepees, 4 ⅜ In., 6 Piece 944.00
Pitcher, Blue, White, Indian, Teepee, Tree, Monmouth WSCO, Diamond Stamp, 6 ½ In. . *illus* 100.00
Pitcher, Blue, White, Indian, Teepees, Campfire, 8 ½ In.. . . . . 125.00
Postcard, Sleepy Eye Milling, Indians Around Flour Barrel, Horse, 1900s. 10.00
Sign, Sleepy Eye Flour, Indian, Tin Lithograph, Self-Framed, 18 x 13 ⅜ In. . . . . *illus* 3540.00
Sign, Sleepy Eye Flour, Indian, Tin Over Cardboard, 19 x 14 ¼ In. 1300.00
Stein, Blue, Gray, Indian, Stoneware, Early 1900s, 7 ⅝ In. . . . . *illus* 413.00
Stein, Brown, Indian, Early 1900s, 7 ⅝ In. . . . . *illus* 295.00
Stein, Cobalt Blue, Indian, Campfire, Indian On Handle, 8 x 4 ½ In.. 925.00
Sugar, Blue, Gray, Indian, Early 1900s, 3 ⅛ In. . . . . *illus* 502.00
Vase, Blue, Gray, Cattail, Dragonfly, Frog, Cylindrical, Impressed O, 8 ½ In. 225.00
Vase, Blue, Gray, Cattail, Dragonfly, Frog, Cylindrical, Impressed W, 8 ½ In. 225.00
Vase, Blue, Gray, Indian, Cattails, Cylindrical, Early 1900s, 9 In. *illus* 225.00
Vase, Blue, Gray, Indian, Stoneware, 8 ¾ In., Pair 708.00
Vase, Blue, White, Cattail, Cylindrical, 9 In. 770.00
Vase, Blue, White, Cattail, Indian, Cylindrical, Impressed W, 8 ½ In. 80.00

SLOT MACHINES *are included in the Coin-Operated Machine category.*

SMITH BROTHERS glass was made after 1878. Alfred and Harry Smith had worked for the Mt. Washington Glass Company in New Bedford, Massachusetts, for seven years before going into their own shop. They made many pieces with enamel decoration.

Smith Bros. Co.

Biscuit Jar, Red Flowers, Melon Ribbed, Rope Twist Handle, 1890, 6 In. . . . . *illus* 132.00
Biscuit Jar, Wisteria, Square, Rounded Edges, Enameled, 6 ½ x 5 ¾ In. 1250.00
Bookends, Bird, Blue, 8 ½ In. 45.00
Bowl, Cream Ground, Blue, Purple Pansies, Mauve Medallions, Melon Ribbed, 9 In. 288.00
Bowl, Melon Ribbed, Green Fern, 4 In. 58.00
Cologne, Diagonal Ribs, Opaque, Gold Highlights, Mums, Pink, Purple, 5 ¼ In. 201.00
Console, Moon & Star, Ruby, Footed, 10 x 4 ¾ In. 65.00
Vase, Milk Glass, Blue Painted Birds, Leaves, Silver Holder, 11 In. 150.00
Vase, Opal, Enameled Bird, Flowers, Ormolu Stand, 15 In. . . . . *illus* 480.00

SNOW BABIES, made from bisque and spattered with glitter sand, were first manufactured in 1864 by Hertwig and Company of Thuringia. Other German and Japanese companies copied the Hertwig designs. Originally, Snow Babies were made of candy and used as Christmas decorations. There are also Snow Babies tablewares made by Royal Bayreuth. Copies of the small Snow Babies figurines are being made today and a line called "Snowbabies" was introduced by Department 56 in 1987.

Doll, Bisque Shoulder Head, Molded Hood, Painted Features, Cloth, 1910, 10 In. 518.00
Doll, Bisque Shoulder Head, Molded Snow Hood, c.1910, 10 In. 518.00
Figure, Baby In Igloo, Santa On Top, 2 ¼ In.. . . . . 175.00
Figure, Baby In Red Snowsuit, On Sled, Pulled By Polar Bear, Scarf, 1 ½ In. 220.00
Figure, Boy, Girl, Yellow Mittens, Standing On Mound, 4 ¼ In., Pair 1200.00
Figure, Boy, On Mound, Holding Pot Of Orange Flowers, 4 In. 900.00
Figure, Mama, Pushing Twins In Red Sled Buggy, 2 ¼ In. 365.00

Smith Brothers, Biscuit Jar, Red Flowers, Melon Ribbed, Rope Twist Handle, 1890, 6 In. $132.00

Figure, Scottie, Playing Soccer, 2 In. 320.00

SNUFF BOTTLES *are listed in the Bottle category.*

SNUFFBOXES held snuff. Taking snuff was popular long before cigarettes became available. The gentleman or lady would take a small pinch of the ground tobacco or snuff in the fingers, then sniff it and sneeze. Snuffboxes were made of many materials, including gold, silver, enameled metal, and wood. Most snuffboxes date from the late eighteenth or early nineteenth centuries.

Amboyna Burl Wood, Figural, Tortoise Lined, Chinese, c.1800, 4 In. 1170.00
Brass, Hinged Lid, Sun, Moon, 2 Clocks, Mechanical Lock, Late 1700s, 3 ½ In. Diam. 761.00
Carved Horn, Stopper, Bottle Shape, 19th Century, 4 ½ In. 263.00
Enamel, Coastal Scene, Inlayed Blue, Red Border, Scrolled Silver Gilt Clip, 1900s, 3 x 2 In. 1062.00
Enamel, Trophies Of The Hunt, Flowers, Ribbed Base, England, c.1770 1850.00
Gilt Brass Mounted, Carnelian, Oval, Russia, Late 19th Century, 2 ¼ In. 150.00
Horn, Carved, Emperor Napoleon, Standing, 3 ⅛ x 1 ¾ In. 210.00
Horn, Napoleonic, Black, Hinged Lid, Pressed Battle Scene, c.1796, 4 In. 360.00
Horn, Soldiers, Pinwheel, Flowers, Inscribed, L. Bourgueu, 19th Century, 2 ½ In. Diam. 500.00
Iron, Dome, Hinged, Oval, 1 x 3 x 2 ½ In. 77.00
Ivory, Lid Inset With Parian Dog, Tortoiseshell Lining, Round, 1800s, 3 ¼ In. 294.00
Lignum Vitae, Mother-Of-Pearl Inlay, Carved Bottom & Top, Round, 1800s, 3 ¾ In. 118.00
Papier-Mache, Oval, Black, Silver Inlay, 3 ⅜ x 2 ¼ In. 150.00
Porcelain, Cockerel's Head, Yellow Feathered Head, Ormolu Hinged Lid, France, 1800s, 4 x 2 In. 375.00
Silver, Continental, Elliptical, Lid, Chain, c.1825, 2 ½ x 2 In. 60.00
Silver, Crossed Bands, Engraved Village Scene, Monogram, Moscow, c.1895, 3 In. 120.00
Silver, Enamel, Hinged Lid, Flowers, Scrolls, Blue, Red, M. Semenova, Russia, c.1970, 3 In. 590.00
Silver, Flowers, Etched Ground, Chain Link Border, Gilt Interior, England, c.1880, 1 In. 239.00
Silver, George III, Hinged Lids, 2-Sided, Gold Interior, England, 1808, 3 In. 237.00
Silver, Hand Chased, Flowers, Austria, c.1850, 1 x 1 ½ x 3 ½ In. 322.00
Silver, Lid, Urns, Swags, Blue Enamel Reeding, Leather Case, Octagon, Continental, c.1800, 2 In. 474.00
Silver, Round, Catherine The Great Medallion Lid, Russia, c.1925, 3 In. 1888.00
Silver, Shell Form, Gadroon, Gilt Interior, London, c.1725, 3 In. 388.00
Spruce Gum, Pegged, Carved, 19th Century, 3 ⅜ x 2 ¼ In. 425.00
Sterling Silver, Cartouche, Gilt Wash Lined, Matthew Linwood, Birmingham, 1804, Pocket 100.00
Sterling Silver, Engraved, Family Crest, Motto, Hinged Lid, James Keating, Dublin, c.1785, ⅝ x 3 In. 500.00
Tole, America Liberty & Free Trade, Pitcher, Wheat, Black Ground, Oval, 3 ½ x 6 In. 1521.00
Tortoiseshell, Hinged, Horn Base, 2 ¾ x ¾ In. 185.00
Tortoiseshell, Ivory Mount, Round, Woman's Portrait, Blue Dress, c.1809, 3 ⅜ In. 326.00
Tortoiseshell, Pique Gold Inlay, c.1800, 2 ⅛ x 1 ⅜ x ¾ In. 350.00
Veneered, Silver Monogram, Oblong, c.1820, 2 ⅝ x 2 ⅞ x ⅝ In. 495.00
Walnut, Bellow Shape, Applied Brass Pin, Heart, My Only Love, Slide Lid, 4 x 2 In. 303.00
Wood, Black Lacquer, Image Of Defense Of New Orleans, c.1812, 3 ¼ In. Diam. 850.00 to 1100.00
Wood, Black Lacquer, New Orleans Defense Print On Lid, c.1812, 3 In. 1298.00

SOAPSTONE is a mineral that was used for foot warmers or griddles because of its heat-retaining properties. Soapstone was carved into figurines and bowls in many countries in the nineteenth and twentieth centuries. Most of the soapstone seen today is from China or Japan. It is still being carved in the old styles.

Brush Pot, Horse, Under Pine Tree, Relief Carved, Pierced Base, Asia, 6 In. 46.00
Censer, Qilin Form, Chinese, 20th Century, 7 ½ In. 177.00
Figurine, Boulder, Carved Figures, Pine Trees, Green To Brown, Chinese, 6 In. 478.00
Figurine, Foo Dog, Chinese, 4 ½ In., Pair. 236.00
Figurine, Goddess Of Mercy, Standing, Holding Scepter, Chinese, 19th Century, 19 In. 2252.00
Figurine, Kwan Yin, Holding Flowering Staff, Deer, Wood Stand, 20 ½ In. 330.00
Figurine, Lohan, Seated, At Ease, Holding Ruyi Scepter, Chinese, 3 ½ x 4 ¼ In. 1652.00
Figurine, Men Under Pine Tree, Mountain Landscape, Chinese, 6 ½ x 7 In. 944.00
Figurine, Mountain, Village, Pine Trees, Pierced Base, Chinese, 20th Century, 7 x 12 In. 125.00
Figurine, Phoenix, Flowering Chrysanthemums, Carved, Chinese, 7 ½ In. 30.00
Figurine, Seal, 3 Foo Dogs, Carved, Chinese, Late 18th Century, 4 ¾ x 3 ¼ x 3 ¼ In. 420.00
Figurine, Seal, 3 Foo Dogs Finial, Chinese, 5 ½ In. 354.00
Figurine, Seal, 3 Writhing Dragons, Pearl, Chinese, 5 x 3 ¼ In. 590.00
Figurine, Seal, Carved Dragon Finial, Square Base, Red, Chinese, c.1800, 5 In. 478.00
Figurine, Seal, Chih Lung, Strap Handle, Chinese, 18th Century, 1 ½ In. *illus* 119.00
Figurine, Seal, Dragon Finial, Chinese, 5 In. 418.00
Figurine, Seal, Foo Dog, Ling Chih In Mouth, Amber, Yellow, Chinese, 19th Century, 3 ¼ In. 119.00

Smith Brothers, Vase, Opal, Enameled Bird, Flowers, Ormolu Stand, 15 In.
$480.00

Soapstone, Figurine, Seal, Chih Lung, Strap Handle, Chinese, 18th Century, 1 ½ In.
$119.00

TIP
Soapstone (steatite) is a very soft mineral. To clean carvings, wash with soapy water and a soft brush. To improve the sheen, rub with jewelers' rouge. Don't use a harsh abrasive.

Soft Paste, Tureen, Flower Bands, Attached Underplate, 1830s, 6 In.
$235.00

Souvenir, Spoon, Monte Carlo, Gambling, Sterling Silver, Enamel, 5 In.
$250.00

Souvenir, Spoon, Venezia, Brass, Silver, Griffin Top
$75.00

Souvenir, Tray, Pacific Fleet, Admiral Sperry & Evans Bust, Stippled Rim, Gilt, 1908, 8 x 11 In.
$260.00

Figurine, Seal, Foo Dog Finial, Square Base, Burnt Orange, Chinese, 5 In. . . . 299.00
Figurine, Seal, Lotus Frond, Green, Calligraphy, Carved, Chinese, Late 1800s, 8 ⅝ x 1 ⅜ In . . . 176.00
Figurine, Seal, Mythical Beast Finial, Chinese, 20th Century, 5 In. . . . 177.00
Figurine, Seal, Reclining Chih Lung, Cash Coin, Dark Tan, Chinese, 19th Century, 2 x 2 In. . . 267.00
Figurine, Seal, Top, Foo Dog, Chinese, 19th Century, 2 ¾ In. . . . 119.00
Figurine, Wise Man, Carved, 2-Tone, Chinese, Late 19th Century, 19 In. . . . 90.00
Figurine, Woman, Mounted As Lamp, Chinese, 20 In. . . . 88.00
Figurine, Woman, On Dragon Head, Wearing Robes, High Chignon, Chinese, 19 In. . . . 1062.00
Shoe Warmers, Foot Shape, New England, Early 19th Century, Child's . . . 595.00
Vase, Woman, 2 Children, Making Offering, Chinese, 18th Century, 5 In. . . . 1304.00

SOFT PASTE is a name for a type of pottery. Although it looks very much like porcelain, it is a chemically different material. Most of the soft-paste wares were made in the early nineteenth century. Other pieces may be listed under Gaudy Dutch or Leeds.

Bowl, Pink Border, Raised Leaves, c.1780, 8 ½ In. . . . 35.00
Cup & Saucer, Queen's Rose, Creamware, c.1815 . . . 101.00
Tureen, Flower Bands, Attached Underplate, 1830s, 6 In. . . . *illus* 235.00
Vase, Flowers, Cords, Tassels, Coral Offshoots, Fan Top, Enamel, Gold, Japan, c.1900, 10 In. . . 50.00

SOUVENIRS of a trip—what could be more fun? Our ancestors enjoyed the same thing and souvenirs were made for almost every location. Most of the souvenir pottery and porcelain pieces of the nineteenth century were made in England or Germany, even if the picture showed a North American scene. In the twentieth century, the souvenir china business seems to have gone to the manufacturers in Japan, Taiwan, Hong Kong, England, and America. Another popular souvenir item is the souvenir spoon, made of sterling or silver plate. These are usually made in the country pictured on the spoon. Related pieces may be found in the Coronation and World's Fair categories.

Ashtray, Bedpan Shape, Atlantic City, N.J., 5 In. . . . 20.00
Ashtray, Mt. Rainier National Park, 12 Cigarette Rests, Salem China, 7 ¾ In. . . . 10.00
Ashtray, Olympics, Glass, Ich Rufe Die Jugend Der Welt, 1936, 4 ½ x 4 ½ In. . . . 127.00
Ashtray, Pine Bluff, Arkansas, Fire-King, Anchor Hocking, 4 In. . . . 7.50
Booklet, Philadelphia, 1908, 8 ½ x 6 ¼ In., 24 Pages . . . 12.00
Button, No. 9 Fishermen's Wharf, San Francisco, Fisherman Caricature, 1 ¼ In. . . . 52.00
Button, Omaha Expo Medal Award, 1898, Palacine Oil, Gasoline, 1 ¼ In. . . . 145.00
Button, Trans-Mississippi Expo, 1898, Photograph, Omaha, Bird's-Eye View, 1 ½ In. . . . 76.00
Canteen, Grand Army Of The Republic, Embossed, Bust, 2 ¼ In. Diam. . . . 22.00
Cigar Holder, Eagle, Crossed Cannons, Balls, White, Gold, Pottery, 7 x 25 In. . . . 508.00
Cup & Saucer, Olympics, 1936, Porcelain, Crown Over M Mark, 4 In. . . . 253.00
Dish, Sequoia National Park, Woodland Creatures, Faux Wood, 7 ½ x 6 In. . . . 12.00
Dish, Utah, Strawberries, Flowers, Scalloped Edge, Treasure Craft, 1960s, 5 In. . . . 13.00
Fan, Heroes Of Spanish American War, 1900s. . . . 420.00
Glass, Clear, 1876 Centennial, 7 In. . . . 90.00
Handkerchief, 1876 Philadelphia Centennial Exhibition, 24 ½ x 27 ½ In. . . . 253.00
Lap Robe, Spanish-American War, Rough Riders, Color, 60 x 45 In. . . . 335.00
Letter Opener, T. Roosevelt, Rough Rider Handle, Sterling Silver, 7 ¼ In. . . . 478.00
Mug, Gettysburg, Historic Scenes, Yellow, Federal Glass . . . 6.50
Pin, Olympiad Equestrian, 1936 Olympics . . . 110.00
Pin, Sioux City Flower Festival & Business Expo, Pansy, 1899, 1 ¾ In. . . . 168.00
Pitcher, Fundy National Park, Canada, Royal Winton, 4 x 5 In. . . . 25.00
Plate, Chicago Skyline, Blue, White, 9 In. . . . 20.00
Plate, Daytona Beach, Flow Blue, 10 In. . . . 20.00
Plate, Dinner, Pennsylvania, Golden Shell, Gay Fad, 1970s. . . . 12.00
Plate, Exposition Music Hall, Pittsburgh, c.1910, 5 ⅜ In. . . . 45.00
Plate, Gibson Girl, Waynesboro, Pa., Sesquicentennial, 1797-1947, 9 In. . . . 22.00
Plate, Nautilus, Yosemite National Park, ½ Dome, Eggshell, Homer Laughlin, 9 ⅞ In. . . . 13.00
Plate, Yellowstone National Park, 6 Scenes, Staffordshire Transfer, Adams, 7 ½ In. . . . 15.00
Salt & Pepper, New York, Etched, Pink & Gilt Bands, Plastic Lid, 3 ½ x 1 ½ In. . . . 50.00
Spoon, Baseball, Sterling Silver, c.1909, 1 ⅛ x 5 ¼ In. . . . 125.00
Spoon, Demitasse, Lincoln Life Scenes, Enamel, Case, Albert Dechasle Co., Mo., 6 Piece . . . 598.00
Spoon, Liberty Head 1 Dollar 1923 Coin, Statue Of Liberty Handle, Sterling, Gorham, 5 In. . . 325.00
Spoon, Maryland, Round Bowl, Sterling Silver, Gorham, 5 In. . . . 110.00
Spoon, Massachusetts, Paul Revere Bowl, Sterling Silver, Gorham, 5 ¼ In. . . . 170.00
Spoon, Monte Carlo, Gambling, Sterling Silver, Enamel, 5 In. . . . *illus* 250.00
Spoon, Mosquee De Sophie, Enamel, Crescent Handle, Ottoman, Sterling Silver, Scheid . . . 70.00
Spoon, Port Said, Ship, Egyptian Goddess Handle, Sterling Silver, Enamel . . . 110.00
Spoon, Savannah, Ga., City Hall, Obelisk Handle, Sterling Silver, Gorham, 5 In. . . . 300.00
Spoon, Sterling, Manilla, Life Buoy & Anchor Handle, Market Scene, 4 ½ In. . . . 150.00

S

Spoon, Venezia, Brass, Silver, Griffin Top . . . *illus* 75.00
Stein, Statue Of Liberty, Stroh's, 100th Anniversary, Limited Edition, c.1986. . . 50.00
Tray, Pacific Fleet, Admiral Sperry & Evans Bust, Stippled Rim, Gilt, 1908, 8 x 11 In. . . . *illus* 260.00
Tumbler, Pocono Mountains, Hazel Atlas. . . 5.00
Vase, Mardi Gras, Black Glass, Silver Overlay, 8-Sided, Marked, Rex, 1917, 6 In. . . . *illus* 60.00
War Club, Indian, Great Lakes, Wood, Carved, Painted, Early 20th Century, 26 ½ In. . . . 439.00

SPANGLE GLASS is multicolored glass made from odds and ends of colored glass rods. It includes metallic flakes of mica covered with gold, silver, nickel, or copper. Spangle glass is usually cased with a thin layer of clear glass over the multicolored layer. Similar glass is listed in the Vasa Murrhina category.

Vase, Amber, White Lining, Silver Mica Fleck Seaweed, Applied Enamel Flowers, 9 In., Pair. . . 288.00

SPANISH LACE *is listed in the Opalescent category as Opaline Brocade.*

SPATTERWARE and spongeware are terms that have changed in meaning in recent years, causing much confusion for collectors. Some say that *spatterware* is the term used by Americans, *sponged ware* or *spongeware* by the English. Spatterware is creamware or soft paste dinnerware decorated with colored spatter designs. The earliest pieces were made in the late eighteenth century, but most of the spatterware found today was made from about 1800 to 1850. Early spatterware was made in the Staffordshire district of England for sale in America. Collectors also use the word *spatterware* to refer to kitchen crockery with added spatter made in America during the late nineteenth and early twentieth centuries. Spongeware is very similar to spatterware in appearance. Designs were applied to ceramics by daubing the color on with a sponge or cloth. Many collectors do not differentiate between spongeware and spatterware and use the names interchangeably. Modern pottery is being made to resemble old spongeware, but careful examination will show it is new.

Bowl, Bull's-Eye, Rainbow, Red, Blue, 10 ½ In. . . . 2340.00
Bowl, Red & Blue Squares, Green Splotches, 19th Century, 4 x 8 ¾ In. . . . 176.00
Bowl, Thistle, Red, Green Leaves, Blue Border, 9 ½ In. . . . 234.00
Bowl, Thistle, Red, Green Leaves, Red Border, 10 ½ In. . . . 761.00
Bowl, Tulip, Blue, White, Red, Purple Border, 10 ¼ In. . . . 500.00
Bowl, Tulip, Blue, White, Red, Purple Border, 19th Century, 10 ¼ In.. . . . 176.00
Bowl, Vegetable, Blue Sponge, 11 In.. . . . 288.00
Bowl, Vegetable, Cover, Rainbow, Blue, Purple, 7 ½ In. . . . 4446.00
Chamber Pot, Lid, Rainbow, Black, Blue, Red, Green, Yellow, 8 ¾ In. . . . 1287.00
Chop Plate, Virginia, Stick Spatter, Cobalt Blue Rim, Flowers, 10 ½ In. . . . 45.00
Creamer, Blue, Black Rainbow Spatter, Loop Handle, Bulbous, 4 In.. . . . 550.00
Creamer, Blue, Red, Blue, Red Spatter, Bulbous, 3 ⅝ In.. . . . 110.00
Creamer, Morning Glory, Blue Flower, Green Leaves, Bulbous, Loop Handle, 4 ¾ In.. . . . 140.00
Creamer, Open Flower, Blue, 4 In. . . . 115.00
Creamer, Peafowl, Blue, Yellow, Green, Red Spatter, Bulbous, 3 ½ In. . . . 110.00
Creamer, Peafowl, Red, 4 In. . . . 173.00
Creamer, Pineapple, Red, Green, Blue Spatter, 3 ½ x 3 In.. . . . 1650.00 to 2574.00
Creamer, Primrose, Red Bud, Green Leaf, Blue Spatter, Bulbous, 4 In. . . . 303.00
Creamer, Purple, Tree, Helmet Shape, Shaped Handle, Embossed Leaf, 4 ½ In. . . . 330.00
Creamer, Rainbow, Red, Green, Paneled, 4 ½ In. . . . *illus* 2200.00
Creamer, Red & Green Rainbow, Helmet Shape, Serpentine, 5 x 5 ½ In.. . . . 248.00
Creamer, Rose, Green, Red, Bulbous, Black, Brown Spatter, 3 ½ In. . . . 220.00
Creamer, Rose, Red, Green, Purple Spatter, 5 In.. . . . 143.00
Creamer, Rose, Red, Green Leaves, 2-Sided, Red, Blue Rainbow Spatter, 4 ⅛ In. . . . 358.00
Creamer, Rose, Red, Green Leaves, Black & Brown Ground, 3 ½ In. . . . *illus* 220.00
Creamer, Rose, Red Rose, Green Leaves, Blue Spatter, 4 ½ In. . . . 66.00
Creamer, Thistle, Red, Green Leaves, Yellow Spatter, 3 ½ In. . . . 7605.00
Creamer, Tulip, Red, Green Leaf, Blue Spatter To Rim, Helmet Form, 4 ⅜ In.. . . . 154.00
Creamer, Tulip, Red, Yellow Ground, 4 ¾ In. . . . 351.00
Cup, Drape, Rainbow, Red, Yellow, Green, Handleless, 19th Century. . . . 1170.00
Cup, Tulip, Red, Yellow, Sprigs, Green Leaf, Purple, Blue Rainbow Spatter, Handleless . . . 22.00
Cup & Saucer, American Shield, Blue, Red Spatter, Handleless, 19th Century . . . 2574.00
Cup & Saucer, Bird, Blue, Yellow, Red, Green Spatter . . . 702.00
Cup & Saucer, Blue, Red, Green Line, Handleless, 2 ⅝ x 4 & 5 ⅞ In.. . . . 500.00
Cup & Saucer, Brown Spatter, Bulbous, Handleless, Child's, 1 ⅞ x 2 ⅞ & 4 ½ In. . . . 22.00
Cup & Saucer, Bull's-Eye, Black & Purple Rainbow Spatter, Handleless, Child's. . . . 143.00
Cup & Saucer, Bull's-Eye, Blue, Purple Spatter, 1 ¾ x 2 ⅝ & 4 ½ In.. . . . 99.00
Cup & Saucer, Bull's-Eye, Rainbow, Purple, Black, Handleless, 2 & 4 ½ In. . . . 209.00
Cup & Saucer, Bull's-Eye, Rainbow, Red, Green, Handleless, 2 x 3 & 4 ½ In.. . . . 143.00 to 275.00
Cup & Saucer, Bull's-Eye, Red, Blue Spatter, 2 ⅜ x 4 & 6 In. . . . 121.00
Cup & Saucer, Castle, Red, Flared Rim, Handleless . . . *illus* 110.00

Souvenir, Vase, Mardi Gras, Black Glass, Silver Overlay, 8-Sided, Marked, Rex, 1917, 6 In.
$60.00

Spatterware, Creamer, Rainbow, Red, Green, Paneled, 4 ½ In.
$2200.00

Spatterware, Creamer, Rose, Red, Green Leaves, Black & Brown Ground, 3 ½ In.
$220.00

TIP
Cheesecloth is a good polishing cloth.

Spatterware, Cup & Saucer, Castle, Red, Flared Rim, Handleless
$110.00

Spatterware, Cup & Saucer, Clovers, Red & Green, Handleless, Child's
$1600.00

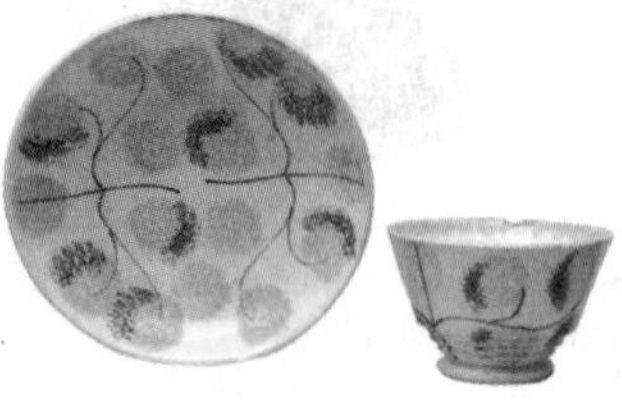

Spatterware, Cup & Saucer, Rainbow, Light Blue, Dark Blue, Handleless, Child's
$880.00

Spatterware, Plate, Dahlia, Red, Blue Flower, Green Sprigs, Purple Ground, Paneled, 8 ¼ In.
$350.00

Spatterware, Plate, Peafowl, Blue, Yellow, Red, Blue Spatter, Paneled, 9 ⅜ In.
$1900.00

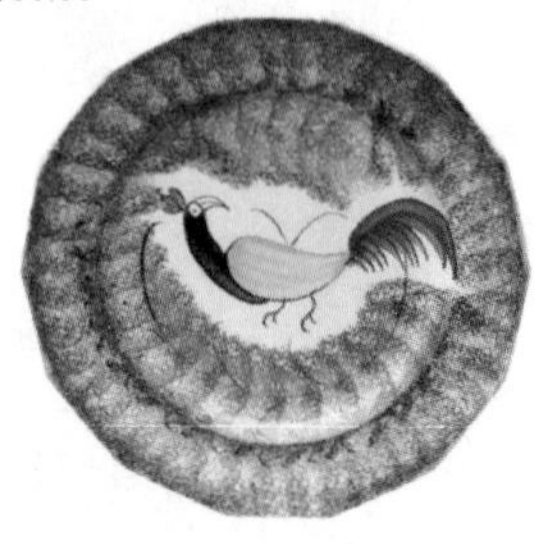

Cup & Saucer, Clover, Green, Red, Handleless 1521.00
Cup & Saucer, Clovers, Red & Green, Handleless, Child's .... *illus* 1600.00
Cup & Saucer, Cluster Of Buds, Red, Green, Blue Spatter, 2 ½ x 3 ⅞ x 5 ⅞ In. 44.00
Cup & Saucer, Cluster Of Buds, Red, Green, Blue Spatter Ground, 2 ½ & 4 ⅛ In.. .... 160.00
Cup & Saucer, Cockscomb, Thistle, Red, Green, Yellow Spatter, Handleless 330.00
Cup & Saucer, Dahlia, Red, Blue, Yellow Border, Handleless 4914.00
Cup & Saucer, Dahlia, Red, White, Blue, Handleless 322.00
Cup & Saucer, Deer, Black Transfer, Red Sponged, Handleless, 2 ½ x 4 & 5 ⅝ In. 330.00
Cup & Saucer, Deer, Red Sponge, Handleless, 2 ⅝ x 4 & 5 ¾ In. 850.00
Cup & Saucer, Dove, On Branch, Blue, Tan, Green Leaves, Blue Spatter, Handleless 880.00
Cup & Saucer, Dove, Purple, Yellow & Blue, Handleless, 2 ½ x 3 ⅞ & 5 ⅞ In.. .... 935.00
Cup & Saucer, Drape, Blue Spatter, Handle, Child's 121.00
Cup & Saucer, Drape, Red & Yellow Christmas Balls, Green Border, Handleless 936.00
Cup & Saucer, Festoon, Yellow, Red, Green, Handleless, 1 ¾ x 3 & 4 ⅝ In. 3080.00
Cup & Saucer, Flower, Blue, Yellow, 6 In. 2070.00
Cup & Saucer, Fort, Blue Spatter, Handleless, Child's, 1 ¾ x 3 ⅛ & 4 ⅜ In.. .... 209.00
Cup & Saucer, Fort, Olive Green, Brown, Handleless .... 439.00 to 644.00
Cup & Saucer, Holly Berry, Blue Spatter, 1 ¾ x 3 & 4 ½ In. 99.00
Cup & Saucer, House, Blue, Red, Yellow, Blue Spatter 303.00
Cup & Saucer, House, Blue, Red, Yellow, Red Spatter, Handleless, 2 ⅜ x 4 & 5 ¾ In. 385.00
Cup & Saucer, Parrot, Blue, Brown, Blue Border, Handleless 2223.00
Cup & Saucer, Parrot, Red, Handleless 205.00
Cup & Saucer, Parrot On Branch, Red, Green, Handleless, 2 ½ x 3 ⅞ & 5 ⅝ In.. .... 154.00
Cup & Saucer, Peafowl, Blue, Red, Yellow & Green, Handleless, 2 ½ x 4 ¼ & 6 In.. .... 66.00
Cup & Saucer, Peafowl, Blue, Yellow, Green, Red Spatter, 2 ½ x 4 & 3 In. 121.00
Cup & Saucer, Peafowl, Blue, Yellow, Green, Red Spatter Ground, Handleless 150.00
Cup & Saucer, Peafowl, Blue, Yellow, Red, Blue & Red Border, Handleless 819.00
Cup & Saucer, Peafowl, Blue, Yellow, Red, Green Spatter, Handleless, 2 ½ x 3 ⅞ In. 198.00
Cup & Saucer, Peafowl, Blue, Yellow, Red, Green Spatter, Handleless, 2 ¼ x 4 & 5 ¾ In. 143.00
Cup & Saucer, Peafowl, Blue, Yellow, Red, Handleless, 2 ½ x 4 & 5 ½ In. 176.00
Cup & Saucer, Peafowl, Blue, Yellow, Red, Purple & Red Border, Handleless 439.00
Cup & Saucer, Peafowl, Blue Sponge, Handleless, 2 ⅝ x 3 ⅞ & 5 ¾ In.. .... 990.00
Cup & Saucer, Peafowl, On Branch, Red, Green, Blue, Red Spatter, 2 ½ x 3 & 6 In.. .... 468.00
Cup & Saucer, Peafowl, Red, 6 In. 259.00
Cup & Saucer, Peafowl, Red, Blue, Yellow, Handleless, 2 ½ x 3 ⅞ & 6 In. 187.00
Cup & Saucer, Peafowl, Red, Blue, Yellow, Handleless, 2 ⅝ x 3 ¾ & 5 ¾ In. 220.00
Cup & Saucer, Peafowl, Red, Branch, Handleless, 2 ⅜ x 4 & 6 In. 220.00
Cup & Saucer, Peafowl, Teal, Blue, Yellow, Red, Handleless, 2 ⅜ x 4 & 5 ¾ In.. .... 187.00
Cup & Saucer, Plaid, Red, Blue, Green, Handleless 3042.00
Cup & Saucer, Rainbow, Black, Purple, Handleless 234.00
Cup & Saucer, Rainbow, Light Blue, Dark Blue, Handleless, Child's .... *illus* 880.00
Cup & Saucer, Rainbow, Red, Yellow, Spatter, Handleless, Child's 220.00
Cup & Saucer, Rooster, Purple Rim, Handleless, Early 19th Century 118.00
Cup & Saucer, Rooster, Yellow, Blue, Red, Blue Border, Handleless .... 322.00 to 644.00
Cup & Saucer, Rose, Blue Green Leaves, Red Spatter, Handleless 121.00
Cup & Saucer, Rose, Red, Black, Brown Spatter, Handleless, Child's, 1 ¾ x 2 ⅝ & 4 In. 132.00
Cup & Saucer, Rose, Red & Green, 2 ¾ x 4 & 5 ½ In. 88.00
Cup & Saucer, Schoolhouse, Blue, Red, Yellow, Handleless, 2 ½ x 4 & 5 ¾ In. 2090.00
Cup & Saucer, Schoolhouse, Landscape, Red, Yellow, Blue Spatter, Handle, Child's 143.00
Cup & Saucer, Schoolhouse, Red, Brown, Green Rim, Handleless 1170.00
Cup & Saucer, Shed, Red, Blue Roof, Red Border, Handleless 2106.00
Cup & Saucer, Spotted Bird, Red, Yellow, Blue, Green, Blue Border, Handleless 12870.00
Cup & Saucer, Spray, Red & Blue Flower, Blue, Green Leaves, 2 x 3 ¼ & 4 ⅝ In. 330.00
Cup & Saucer, Star, Blue, Red, Green, Red Border, Handleless 293.00
Cup & Saucer, Star, Red, Yellow, Green, Blue Border, Handleless 234.00
Cup & Saucer, Stick, Blue & Green, Star, Handleless, 2 ½ x 3 ⅞ & 5 ⅞ In. 330.00
Cup & Saucer, Sunflower, Rainbow, Red, Blue, Handleless 1112.00
Cup & Saucer, Thistle, Blue, 6 In.. .... 173.00
Cup & Saucer, Thistle, Red, Green Leaves, Yellow Border, Handleless .... 293.00 to 527.00
Cup & Saucer, Thistle, Red Flower, Green Leave, 2 ½ x 4 & 5 ⅞ In.. .... 413.00
Cup & Saucer, Thistle, Red Flower, Green Leaves, Red, Green Rainbow Spatter 220.00
Cup & Saucer, Thistle, Red Flower, Green Leaves, Yellow Spatter, 2 12 x 4 & 5 ⅞ In. 700.00
Cup & Saucer, Thistle, Yellow, 6 In. 1150.00
Cup & Saucer, Tree, Green, Blue Border, Handleless 1708.00
Cup & Saucer, Tree, Green, Blue Border, Handleless, 2 ¾ x 4 & 5 ⅞ In. 385.00
Cup & Saucer, Tree, Purple Spatter, Handleless, Child's, 1 ¾ x 2 ¾ & 4 ⅛ In.. .... 880.00
Cup & Saucer, Tulip, Blue, Red, Leaves, Red Spatter, Handleless, 2 ⅝ x 3 ⅞ & 6 In. 413.00
Cup & Saucer, Tulip, Red, Yellow Tipped, Leaves, Blue Sponge, 2 ¾ x 4 & 5 ⅝ In. 77.00

Cup & Saucer, Tulip, Yellow, Blue Flower, Red Buds, Green Leaves, 2 ⅝ x 4 In. 650.00
Cup & Saucer, Yellow Spatter, Handleless, 2 ⅜ x 3 ¾ & 5 ¾ In. 66.00
Cup Plate, Peafowl, Blue, Green, Red, Blue Border, 5 In. 366.00
Cup Plate, Peafowl, Blue, Green, Red, Red Border, 19th Century, 5 In. 176.00
Dish, Peafowl, Green, Red, Blue Spatter, 5 In., 4 Piece 468.00
Dish, Peafowl, Red, Tan, Green, Blue, Red Spatter, 5 ¼ In. 413.00
Jar, Blue, White, Circle Pattern, Bulbous, Flared Rim, 19th Century, 11 ½ In. 878.00
Mug, Strawberry, X Pattern, Green, Rose Pink, Blue Spatter, Child's, 2 ¾ x 2 ⅝ In. 187.00
Pepper Pot, Blue, White, 19th Century, 4 ¾ In. 293.00
Pitcher, Fort, Green, Blue Ground, 19th Century, 12 ¼ In. 225.00
Pitcher, Mulberry, Blue Vertical Bands, 11 In. 633.00
Pitcher, Rainbow, Yellow, Black, Blue, Red, Green, 19th Century, 8 ½ In. 4680.00
Pitcher, Scalloped Rim, Red, Blue, Green Stripes, Handle, c.1830, 8 In. 688.00
Pitcher, Tulip, Red, Rainbow, Purple, Black, 8 ¾ In. 2808.00
Pitcher, Water, Primrose, Purple Flower, Bud, Green Leaves, Red Spatter, 10 In. 1650.00
Pitcher & Bowl, Rainbow, Red, Blue, 12-In. Pitcher 2808.00
Plate, 3 Roses, Red, Green Leaves, Blue Spatter Banding, 9 ¼ In. 66.00
Plate, 6-Point Star, Yellow, Red, Green, Blue Spatter, 8 ¾ In. 165.00
Plate, Acorn, Red, Paneled, Brown Acorns, Teal Stems, Green Leaves, 8 ½ In. 523.00
Plate, Acorn, Teal, Light Green Leaves, Purple Spatter, 9 ¼ In. 3250.00
Plate, Arabian Scene, Brown, Green Spatter, 9 ½ In. 88.00
Plate, Blue, Pomegranate Center, Early 19th Century, 8 ½ In. 115.00
Plate, Bull's-Eye, Rainbow, Purple & Red, 8 ¼ In. 935.00
Plate, Bull's-Eye, Rainbow, Red, Black, 8 ½ In. 8775.00
Plate, Castle, Toddy, Blue Spatter, 5 In. 176.00
Plate, Columbine, Green, 8 In., Pair 175.00
Plate, Cut Star, Green, Diamond Band, John Moses & Co., 9 ¼ In. 25.00
Plate, Dahlia, Rainbow, Blue, Red, 8 ¼ In. 1287.00
Plate, Dahlia, Red, Blue Flower, Green Sprigs, Purple Ground, Paneled, 8 ¼ In. .... *illus* 350.00
Plate, Flowers, Bud, Green & Blue Spatter, Creamware, 7 ¼ In. 143.00
Plate, Holly Berry, Red, Green, Black Banding, Purple Spatter, 9 ½ In. 55.00
Plate, Line, Purple, Red, Blue Green, 9 ⅜ In. 8800.00
Plate, Peafowl, Blue, Green, Red Spatter, 7 ½ In. 154.00
Plate, Peafowl, Blue, Red, Red Spatter, 7 ½ In. 198.00
Plate, Peafowl, Blue, Yellow, Red, Blue Spatter, Paneled, 9 ⅜ In. .... *illus* 1900.00
Plate, Peafowl, Blue, Yellow, Red, Green Spatter, 7 ¾ In. 170.00
Plate, Peafowl, Blue, Yellow, Red, Incised Feather Edge, Blue Spatter, 6 ⅜ In. 275.00
Plate, Peafowl, Green, 9 In. 345.00
Plate, Peafowl, Green, Red, Blue Spatter, 9 ½ In. 275.00
Plate, Peafowl, On Branch, Red, Blue, Yellow, Green, 9 ½ In. 110.00
Plate, Peafowl, On Branch, Red, Green, Blue, Red Spatter, 8 ½ In. 440.00
Plate, Peafowl, Purple, Green, Yellow, Red Spatter, 6 ¼ In. 143.00
Plate, Peafowl, Red, Blue, Green, Red Spatter, 9 ½ In. 220.00
Plate, Peafowl, Red, Yellow, Green, Blue Border, 9 ¾ In. 234.00
Plate, Peafowl, Red, Yellow, Green, Blue Spatter, 9 ¾ In. .... *illus* 250.00
Plate, Peafowl, Zigzag, Green Spatter, 7 ½ In. 1500.00
Plate, Rabbitware, Red, Blue, Green Flower Border, 9 ¼ In. .... *illus* 250.00
Plate, Rainbow, Purple, Black, 8 ¼ In. 1755.00
Plate, Rainbow, Red & Blue, Crisscross Center, 12 ¼ x 15 ¾ In. 275.00
Plate, Red, Black, Green, Bands, 9 In. 75.00
Plate, Red Flower, Green Leaves, Yellow Cockscomb, Paneled, 9 ⅞ In. .... *illus* 3000.00
Plate, Rose, Green, Red, Blue Spatter, 6 ¼ In. 55.00
Plate, Rose, Red, Blue, Blue Buds, Green Leaves, Paneled, 8 ¾ In. 55.00
Plate, Rose, Red, Blue Bud, Green Leaves, Blue Border, Paneled, 8 ½ In. 209.00
Plate, Rose, Red, Green Leaves, Blue Spatter, 6 ⅜ In. 99.00
Plate, Rose, Red, Green Leaves, Blue Spatter, Paneled, 10 ¾ In. 66.00
Plate, Rose, Yellow, 8 In. 805.00
Plate, Schoolhouse, Blue, Red, Yellow, Green, Black Foreground, 8 ½ In. 358.00
Plate, Schoolhouse, Red, Brown Ground, Green Trees, Blue Spatter, 9 ½ In. 2750.00
Plate, Schoolhouse, Red, Green Trees, 6 ¾ In. 900.00
Plate, Schoolhouse, Red, Green Trees & Ground, 6 ¾ In. 990.00
Plate, Soup, Umbrella Flower, Red, Blue, Green, Blue Leaves, 10 ½ In. 413.00
Plate, Star, 6-Point, Red, Green, Blue, Blue Border, 8 ¼ In. 176.00
Plate, Star, Blue, 9 ½ In. 144.00
Plate, Sunburst, 6-Point, Red, Green, Blue Spatter, Paneled, 9 ½ In. 176.00
Plate, Sunburst, Blue Spatter, 7 ⅜ In. 88.00
Plate, Thistle, Red, Green, Yellow Border, 8 ¾ In. 2223.00
Plate, Toddy, Peafowl, Blue, Yellow, Green, Red Spatter Ground, 5 In. 44.00

Spatterware, Plate, Peafowl, Red, Yellow, Green, Blue Spatter, 9 ¾ In.
$250.00

Spatterware, Plate, Rabbitware, Red, Blue, Green Flower Border, 9 ¼ In.
$250.00

Spatterware, Plate, Red Flower, Green Leaves, Yellow Cockscomb, Paneled, 9 ⅞ In.
$3000.00

TIP

If your old lampshade fabric wears out, keep the metal frame. It can be recovered. New shades are not the same size or shape as the old ones, and an old lamp will look out of proportion with the wrong shade.

SPATTERWARE

Spatterware, Platter, Rabbitware, Stick Spatter, Rabbit & Frog Border, Oval, 10 x 14 ½ In.
$556.00

Spatterware, Platter, Rainbow, Red, Blue, Crisscross Center, 12 ¼ x 15 ¾ In.
$250.00

Spatterware, Relish, Tulip, Blue, Red, Green Leaves, Blue Ground, Ribs, 8 ¾ x 4 ⅜ In.
$1540.00

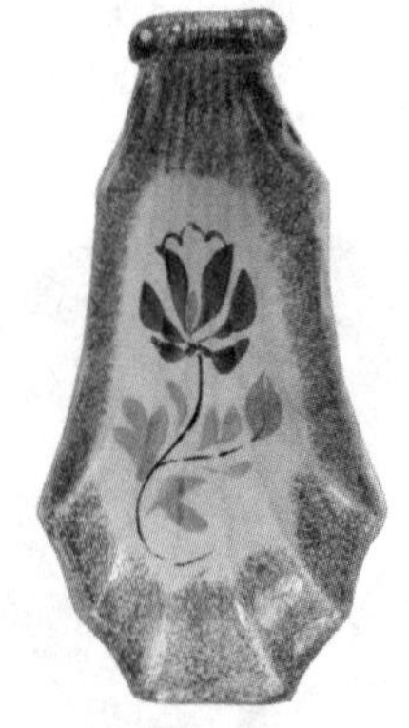

Spatterware, Sugar, Cover, Acorns, Leaves, Brown, Teal, Green, Blue, 4 ⅜ x 5 ½ In.
$650.00

Plate, Toddy, Tulip, Red, Blue, White Flower, Green Leaves, Blue Spatter, 5 ⅛ In. 55.00
Plate, Tree, Purple Spatter, 8 In. 1045.00
Plate, Tulip, Blue, Red Flower, Green Leaves, Paneled, 8 ¼ In. 900.00
Plate, Tulip, Blue, White Red, Rainbow, Purple, Black, 7 In. 2074.00
Plate, Tulip, Green, Yellow, Red, Blue Sponge, 8 ¾ In. 132.00
Plate, Tulip, Open, Red, Yellow Spatter, 8 ½ In. 4095.00
Plate, Tulip, Red, Blue, Red Springs, Green Leaves, Blue Spatter, 9 ⅜ In. 770.00
Plate, Tulip, Red, Purple, Yellow, Green Stem, Leaves, 7 ⅝ In. 413.00
Plate, Tulip, Red, White, Blue, Rainbow, Red, Green, 8-Sided, 10 ¾ x 13 ¾ In. 4680.00
Platter, Bull's-Eye, Blue, 13 In. 167.00
Platter, Hex Sign, Blue, Stenciled, Blue Spatter, 13 x 9 ¾ In. 248.00
Platter, Rabbitware, Stick Spatter, Rabbit & Frog Border, Oval, 10 x 14 ½ In. . . . . *illus* 556.00
Platter, Rainbow, Red, Blue, Crisscross Center, 12 ¼ x 15 ¾ In. . . . . *illus* 250.00
Pot, Cover, Fort, Blue Spatter, Handle, 8 ¾ In. 263.00
Pot, Yellow, Green, Basket Form, Late 1800s, 10 ¼ In. 260.00
Relish, Tulip, Blue, Red, Green Leaves, Blue Ground, Ribs, 8 ¾ x 4 ⅜ In. . . . . *illus* 1540.00
Sauce, Blue, Fort, Yellow, Red, Brown, Green Trees, 5 ¼ In. 303.00
Sauce, Peafowl, Blue Green, Red, Blue Spatter, 5 In. 154.00
Sauce Bowl Set, Peafowl, Blue, Yellow, Green, Red Spatter, 5 ¾ In., 3 Piece. 66.00
Saucer, Peafowl, Green, 6 In. 29.00
Saucer, Rose, Brown, 6 In. 35.00
Sugar, Cover, Acorns, Leaves, Brown, Teal, Green, Blue, 4 ⅜ x 5 ½ In. . . . . *illus* 650.00
Sugar, Cover, Finial, Red Spatter, Octagonal Paneled, Handles, 7 x 5 ¼ In. 110.00
Sugar, Cover, Fort, Blue Spatter, 4 ¾ x 5 In. 132.00
Sugar, Cover, Peafowl, Blue, Yellow, Red, Green Spatter, 3 ⅜ x 3 ⅜ In. 110.00
Sugar, Cover, Rainbow, Red, Blue, Green, 4 ¼ In. 293.00
Sugar, Cover, Red Buds, Green Leaves, Blue & Green Ground, 4 ¾ x 4 ½ In. . . . . *illus* 121.00
Sugar, Cover, Rooster, Yellow, 4 ½ In. 3510.00
Sugar, Cover, Rose, Green, Red, Blue Spatter, 4 ¼ x 4 ¼ In. 66.00
Sugar, Cover, Rose, Green, Red, Brown Spatter, 4 ⅜ x 4 ½ In. 66.00
Sugar, Cover, Vine & Berry, Red, Green Spatter, 5 ¼ In. 3978.00
Teapot, Cover, House, Blue, Red, Yellow, Red Foreground, Red Spatter, 5 ¼ x 6 ¼ In. 77.00
Teapot, Lone Star, Blue, Red, Blue Spatter, 5 x 9 ½ In. 121.00
Teapot, Parrot, Red, 7 In. 3042.00
Teapot, Rainbow, 3-Petal Flower, Red, Green, 6 In. 1200.00
Teapot, Rainbow, 5 Colors, 10 In. 8050.00
Teapot, Rainbow, Red & Green, Squat Body, Shaped Handle, 7 x 10 ½ In. 935.00
Teapot, Schoolhouse, Red, Yellow, Green, Brown, Blue Ground, 6 In. . . . . *illus* 14300.00
Teapot, Star, Red, Blue Border, 6 ¾ In. 205.00
Teapot, Thistle, Rainbow, Red, Green, 4 ¼ In. 497.00
Toddy Plate, Peafowl, Blue, Green, Red, Red Border, 4 In. 468.00
Toddy Plate, Red & Blue Rainbow, Paneled, Crisscross Center, 6 ½ In. 523.00
Waste Bowl, Peafowl, Red, Yellow, Green, Blue Spatter, 3 x 5 ⅝ In. 22.00
Waste Bowl, Star, Blue, Red Rim, 2 ¾ x 5 In. 59.00

SPELTER is a synonym for a zinc alloy. Figurines, candlesticks, and other pieces were made of spelter and given a bronze or painted finish. The metal has been used since about the 1860s to make statues, tablewares, and lamps that resemble bronze. Spelter is soft and breaks easily. To test for spelter, scratch the base of the piece. Bronze is solid; spelter will show a silvery scratch.

Bust, Napoleon, Military Dress, Gilded, Square Socle, Marble Base, c.1915, 17 In. 385.00
Sculpture, Arab Figure On Horse, Signed, Guillemin, 19th Century, 32 x 24 In. 1600.00
Sculpture, Cupid With Bow, Patina, Auguste Moreau, Stamped, VICI, France, 12 In. 425.00
Sculpture, Diana, Holding Bow, Wood Base, Patina, Early 20th Century, 18 ⅛ In. 400.00
Sculpture, Distress, Woman Standing, Waving, Brown Patina, Marked, Mestais, France, 20 In. 90.00
Sculpture, Fawn, Lying Down, Marble Base, c.1930, 5 x 8 In. 47.00
Sculpture, Lioness, On Rock, Stamped, T. Cartier, 24 In. 500.00
Sculpture, Man, Sowing Seeds, Plaque, Psalm 126:6, Signed, F. Milliot, 1899, 40 x 14 x 15 In. 550.00
Sculpture, Man, With Sword, Marble Base, Signed, Hip Noreay, 1900, 28 ½ x 9 ½ x 7 ½ In. . . 330.00
Sculpture, Nude Female, Seated, Plinth, Marked, Kathodian Works, 1910-16, 9 ½ x 5 In. . . . 150.00
Sculpture, Penelope, c.1880, 12 In. 410.00

SPINNING WHEELS in the corner have been symbols of earlier times for the past 100 years. Although spinning wheels date back to medieval days, the ones found today are rarely more than 200 years old. Because the style of the spinning wheel changed very little, it is often impossible to place an exact date on a wheel.

Castle, Maple, Oak, Baluster & Ring Turnings, Pa., c.1780, 48 In. 1170.00
Chip Carved, Branded, K. Leier, Child's, 29 x 28 In. 200.00

S

Maple, Carding Paddles, 19th Century, 37 In. 212.00
Maple, Chestnut, Daniel Danner, Manheim, Pa., 1860-70, 51 x 28 x 14 In. 2200.00
Mixed Woods, Turned, 19th Century, 36 In. .... *illus* 212.00
Mustard Paint, Stenciled, O. Dion, Quebec, Canada. 121.00
Oak, Flower Stamps, Marked, IH 1831 .... 95.00
Vertical Form, c.1890, 40 In. 518.00

SPODE pottery, porcelain, and bone china were made by the Stoke-on-Trent factory of England founded by Josiah Spode about 1770. The firm became Copeland and Garrett from 1833 to 1847, then W.T. Copeland or W.T. Copeland and Sons until 1976. It then became Royal Worcester Spode Ltd. The word *Spode* appears on many pieces made by the factories. Most collectors include all the wares under the more familiar name of Spode. Porcelains are listed in this book by the name that appears on the piece. Related pieces may be listed under Copeland, Copeland Spode, and Royal Worcester.

SPODE Stone-China

Bowl, Blue Transferware, Ring Foot, Castle, c.1800, 5 ½ x 12 ⅜ In. 265.00
Cup & Saucer, Colonel, White, Green Floral & Leaf, Gold Line Trim, 1 ¼ x 2 ½ In. 20.00
Dish, Fruit, Shell Shape, 6 x 6 ¼ In. 12.50
Gravy Boat, Cover, Underplate, Pinecone Finial, Handles, Ironstone, 4 ¼ x 7 ¾ x 4 In. 40.00
Plate, Blue Tower, Blue Transferware, Flower Border, Scalloped Blank, 10 ⅝ In. 44.00
Plate, Imperial Plate Of Persia, Red, Blue Center Crest, Blue, Gold, Border, 1971 .... 322.00
Sugar & Creamer, Strawberry Ripe, Hammersley, 1 ½ x 3 & 1 ¾ x 4 ⅛ In. 40.00
Teapot, Strawberry Ripe, Hammersley, 4 ½ x 6 ¼ In. 60.00
Tureen, Lid, Plate, Indian Tree Transfer, Multicolored, c.1800, 11 x 13 In. 403.00

SPORTS equipment, sporting goods, brochures, and related items are listed here. Items are listed by sport. Other categories of interest are Bicycle, Card, Fishing, Sword, Toy, and Trap. Kentucky Derby glasses are listed in the Decorated Tumblers category.

Archery, Arrow Sheath, Leather, Strap, 20 ½ x 7 ½ In. 25.00
Auto Racing, Budweiser Racing Jumpsuit, Kenny Bernstein, Red, Slogans, 1990. .... 660.00
Baseball, Apron, Cleveland Indians, World Series, 1948, Red Felt Chief Wahoo, Nona Lou Co. 3450.00
Baseball, Ball, Autographed, A.L., N.L. All Stars Teams, 1936 .... 1560.00
Baseball, Ball, Autographed, Babe Ruth, 1932. .... 5377.00
Baseball, Ball, Autographed, Babe Ruth, Blue Ink 9600.00
Baseball, Ball, Autographed, Babe Ruth, c.1918 .... 3346.00
Baseball, Ball, Autographed, Boston Red Sox, World Champs, 1915, With Babe Ruth 14100.00
Baseball, Ball, Autographed, Cleveland Indians, 1948 World Champions 1553.00
Baseball, Ball, Autographed, Cy Young, c.1920 .... 5676.00
Baseball, Ball, Autographed, Gerald Ford. 300.00
Baseball, Ball, Autographed, Joe DiMaggio .... 780.00 to 960.00
Baseball, Ball, Autographed, Lou Gehrig, Black Ink, 1927 .... 21600.00
Baseball, Ball, Autographed, Mickey Mantle, c.1980 .... 1792.00
Baseball, Ball, Autographed, New York Giants, 1935. .... 1016.00
Baseball, Ball, Autographed, Pete Rose, I'm Sorry I Bet On Baseball. 360.00
Baseball, Ball, Autographed, Roberto Clemente, 1970 .... 1998.00
Baseball, Ball, Autographed, Roger Maris 600.00
Baseball, Ball, Autographed, Tris Speaker 2280.00
Baseball, Ball, Autographed, Tris Speaker, 1955 .... 6600.00
Baseball, Ball, Autographed, Washington Senators, 1927. .... 5079.00
Baseball, Ball, Lemon Peel, Dark Brown, 1850-60s. 845.00
Baseball, Ball, Roberto Clemente, 3000th Hit, 1972 .... 5975.00
Baseball, Ball, Wilson Pacific Coast, Box, 1950s, 10 Balls. 800.00
Baseball, Ball Throwing Machine, c.1900 .... 275.00
Baseball, Banner, 1961 World Series, Cincinnati Reds & New York Yankees, 9 x 17 In. 147.00
Baseball, Bat, Autographed, Babe Ruth, 1930s 21510.00
Baseball, Bat, Autographed, Bill Mazeroski, All Star, Adirondack, 1950. .... 4200.00
Baseball, Bat, Autographed, Eddie Murray, Louisville Slugger, 1986-89 .... 1080.00
Baseball, Bat, Autographed, Jim Bottomley, 1921-1931 .... 9600.00
Baseball, Bat, Autographed, Joe DiMaggio, 1941. .... 1314.00
Baseball, Bat, Autographed, Ted Williams, 500 Home Run Club 600.00
Baseball, Bat, Autographed, Wade Boggs, Louisville Slugger, 1983-85. .... 390.00
Baseball, Bat, George Babe Ruth, Store Model, 1961-64. .... 787.00
Baseball, Bat, George Brett, Game Used, Louisville Slugger, 1990 .... 840.00
Baseball, Bat, Jackie Robinson, Louisville Slugger, Store Model, 1947, 31 ½ In. 70.00
Baseball, Bat, Jimmie Foxx, Lathe, Game Used. 330.00
Baseball, Bat, Joe DiMaggio, Game Used, 1951 All Star Edition, H. & B., c.1958, 36 In. 33600.00

Spatterware, Sugar, Cover, Red Buds, Green Leaves, Blue & Green Ground, 4 ¾ x 4 ½ In.
$121.00

Spatterware, Teapot, Schoolhouse, Red, Yellow, Green, Brown, Blue Ground, 6 In.
$14300.00

Spinning Wheel, Mixed Woods, Turned, 19th Century, 36 In.
$212.00

As always, the edited listings in *Kovels' Antiques & Collectibles Price Guide 2010* aren't available on any website, but readers should visit Kovels.com for information on trends, tips, reproductions, marks, old prices, and more!

TIP

Store your sports card albums flat, not upright. This prevents the cards from getting bent or damaged. Check the cards periodically to be sure that the pages are not sticking together. If you notice any problems, replace the pages.

Sports, Baseball, Button, Ty Cobb, Detroit Tigers, Sweet Caporal, P-2
$480.00

Sports, Baseball, Figure, Ty Cobb, Hartland, Box, 1990
$227.00

TIP

The best way to dust books is with a vacuum cleaner brush attachment.

Baseball, Bat, Johnny Bench, Game Used, Louisville Slugger, 1977-79 .... 960.00
Baseball, Bat, Lou Gehrig, New York Yankees, 40 Series, Store Model, 1925-30.......... 535.00
Baseball, Bat, Mel Ott, 40 Series, Store Model, c.1940.......... 241.00
Baseball, Bat, Roy Campanella, Game Used, World Series, 1951 .... 8962.00
Baseball, Bat, Ty Cobb, 40 Series Store Model, 1925-30 .... 1127.00
Baseball, Blanket, Ty Cobb, Felt, American Tobacco Co., c.1914, 5 x 5 In.......... 235.00
Baseball, Blanket, Ty Cobb, White Infield, Green, Blue, B 18, 5 In. Square 570.00
Baseball, Booklet, How To Hit, Rogers Hornsby, Autographed, 1945.......... 960.00
Baseball, Box, Cereal, All-Pro, Roger Maris, Ralston Purina, c.1968, 9 x 6 In. 1058.00
Baseball, Box, Sweatshirt, Dizzy & Paul Dean, c.1934, 15 ½ x 10 ½ x 8 In.. .... 705.00
Baseball, Button, Babe Ruth, Quaker Oats Baseball Club, 1938.......... 480.00
Baseball, Button, Babe Ruth Club, B On Cap, Jordan Marsh, 1 In.. .... 575.00
Baseball, Button, Philadelphia Athletics, Clean Sweep, Oct. 1911 .... 400.00
Baseball, Button, Ty Cobb, Detroit Tigers, Sweet Caporal, P-2 .... *illus* 480.00
Baseball, Button, Ty Cobb, Ornate Frame, 1915 .... 23900.00
Baseball, Candy Container, Jackie Robinson, Figural, Hard Plastic, Early 1950s, 4 ¾ In.. .... 230.00
Baseball, Cap, Autographed, Gene Woodling, New York Yankees, Game Used, 1949-1954 .... 300.00
Baseball, Cap, Autographed, Rickey Henderson, New York Yankees, Game Used, 1985-1989 .. 400.00
Baseball, Cap, Autographed, Ted Williams, Boston Red Sox, Pro Model.......... 350.00
Baseball, Catcher's Mitt, Salesman's Sample, 1887, 6 ½ x 1 In.......... 365.00
Baseball, Clock, Babe Ruth Bust, Desk, Electric, 2 Balls, Abbotwares Co., c.1948, 10 In. 3819.00
Baseball, Cuff Links, Joe Pignatano, New York Mets, World Champions, 1969 .... 600.00
Baseball, Display, Topps Baseball Cards, Five Cent, 1953 .... 180.00
Baseball, Dumbbell, Autographed, Babe Ruth, Wood, 1925 .... 3231.00
Baseball, Figure, Babe Ruth Carnival Prize, 1930s.......... 300.00
Baseball, Figure, Ty Cobb, Hartland, Box, 1990 .... *illus* 227.00
Baseball, Glove, Autographed, Joe DiMaggio, Hutch, c.1950.......... 350.00
Baseball, Glove, Bobby Thomson, Store Model, Wrapper, Pictorial Band, 1950s.......... 170.00
Baseball, Glove, Button Back, Reach, c.1890.......... 776.00
Baseball, Glove, Dixie Walker, Store Model, 1940s.......... 39.00
Baseball, Glove, Fielder, Buckskin, Pennant Brand, c.1920s.......... 780.00
Baseball, Glove, Mickey Mantle Pictures, Model MM8, 1954-57, Box, 8 x 8 x 6 In.......... 2115.00
Baseball, Handprint, Hugh Casey, Autographed, c.1936 .... 168.00
Baseball, Home Plate, Shea Stadium Framed, c.1960.......... 634.00
Baseball, Jacket, Warm Up, Boston Red Sox, Chenille Sock Patch, Patriotic Cuffs, 1940s.......... 478.00
Baseball, Jacket, Warm Up, Hawk Taylor, Milwaukee Braves, Tomahawk Logo, Size 46 .... 717.00
Baseball, Jersey, Alex Rodriguez, Seattle Mariners, Rookie, Game Used, 1994.......... 11404.00
Baseball, Jersey, Autographed, Bobo Newsom, Brooklyn Dodgers, Flannel, Game Used, c.1943. 6436.00
Baseball, Jersey, Autographed, Hank Aaron, Atlanta Braves, Game Used, 1972 .... 29375.00
Baseball, Jersey, Autographed, Joe DiMaggio, Game Used, 1980s 2390.00
Baseball, Jersey, Autographed, Joe DiMaggio, Game Used, 1990.......... 7523.00
Baseball, Jersey, Cleveland Indians, Flannel, No. 40, 1958 .... 787.00
Baseball, Jersey, Hank Edwards, Cleveland Indians, Red, White, Game Used, 1947.......... 3819.00
Baseball, Jersey, Pittsburgh Federal League, Green, White Stripes, 1913 .... 11750.00
Baseball, Jersey, Ted Williams, Boston Red Sox, Flannel, 1960.......... 36720.00
Baseball, Menu, Autographed, Babe Ruth, Toots Shor Restaurant, 1946, N.Y.......... 4406.00
Baseball, Movie, Babe Comes Home, Foldover, 1927, 5 ½ x 3 ½ In., 2 Pages.......... 940.00
Baseball, Nodder, Boy, Chicago, White Sox, c.1960, 6 ½ In. 201.00
Baseball, Nodder, Cleveland Indian, Chief Wahoo, 1961.......... 303.00
Baseball, Nodder, Detroit Tiger, c.1961.......... 187.00
Baseball, Nodder, Mickey Mantle, New York Yankees Uniform, c.1960, 7 In.......... *illus* 597.00
Baseball, Nodder, Phillie, Philadelphia On Base, Raised Letters, 1968, 6 In.......... 99.00
Baseball, Nodder, Roberto Clemente, Pittsburgh Pirates, 1962.......... 1792.00
Baseball, Pennant, 1921 World Series, New York Yankees, 26 ¼ In.. .... 13200.00
Baseball, Pennant, 1939 Baseball Centennial, Felt, 8 ½ x 3 ¾ In.......... 65.00
Baseball, Pennant, Miller Huggins, Ferguson Bakery, Felt, BF2, 1916 .... 9000.00
Baseball, Photograph, Babe Ruth, Yankee, F. Mendelsohn, c.1920.......... 2880.00
Baseball, Photograph, Chicago American Giants, Negro League, c.1914, 17 x 7 In.......... 35350.00
Baseball, Photograph, Chicago White Sox, World War I, News Service, 1917 .... 170.00
Baseball, Photograph, Cleveland Americans, Dog, Fatima Cigarettes, Frame, 1913, 19 x 27 In. 9600.00
Baseball, Photograph, Connie Mack, Autographed.......... 510.00
Baseball, Photograph, Connie Mack, Harry Davis, c.1915 .... 144.00
Baseball, Photograph, General Abner Doubleday, , Mathew Brady, c.1865.......... 705.00
Baseball, Photograph, J. Honus Wagner, Autographed, With Bats, Frame, 1940s, 14 x 13 In. . 1175.00
Baseball, Photograph, Jackie Robinson, Dodgers Uniform, Autographed, Frame, 19 x 21 In. . 1920.00
Baseball, Photograph, Joe DiMaggio, Autographed.......... 420.00
Baseball, Photograph, Joe Jackson, At Bat, Standard Biscuit No. 87, 1916.......... 3300.00
Baseball, Photograph, Lou Gehrig, Autographed, Black & White, 1938, 9 x 7 ⅛ In.......... 8400.00

Baseball, Photograph, Mickey Cochrane, Catcher, 1933 .... 510.00
Baseball, Photograph, Mickey Mantle, Batting, A. Rickerby, c.1962, 11 x 14 In. 150.00
Baseball, Photograph, New York Yankees, Team Autographed, 1962, 11 x 14 In. 6572.00
Baseball, Photograph, Roger Maris, Autographed 600.00
Baseball, Photograph, Satchel Paige, Autographed, 1955 .... 960.00
Baseball, Photograph, Satchel Paige, Cleveland Indian, c.1948 .... 300.00
Baseball, Photograph, Thurman Munson, Autographed, c.1970, 4 x 5 In. 1293.00
Baseball, Photograph, Tony Lazzeri, 1927 .... 840.00
Baseball, Photograph, Walter Johnson, Hung In Griffith Stadium, 20 x 35 In. 6000.00
Baseball, Planter, Jackie Robinson Souvenir, Inarco, 1950s, 4 x 5 ½ In. .... 110.00 to 365.00
Baseball, Pocketknife, 1915 World Series, Red Sox, Phillies Players, Celluloid, 3 In. 2115.00
Baseball, Postcard, Photograph, John Wanamaker, World Series Souvenir, 1911 .... 275.00
Baseball, Postcard, Photograph, Rogers Hornsby, Eastern Exhibit Supply Co., 1922 .... 180.00
Baseball, Postcard, Photograph, Walter Johnson, Idaho Minor League, 1907, 3 x 5 In. 2640.00
Baseball, Press Pin, 1913 World Series, Phil. Athletics, Medal, Ribbon, Logos, Blue, 5 In. 12925.00
Baseball, Press Pin, 1920 World Series, Brooklyn Dodgers, Metal, Red Enamel, ¾ In. 1292.00
Baseball, Press Pin, 1942 World Series, St. Louis Cardinals 2031.00
Baseball, Press Pin, 1948 World Series, Boston Braves, Man, Headdress 275.00
Baseball, Program, 1903 World Series, Game 2, 8 x 5 ⅜ In. 96000.00
Baseball, Program, 1907 World Series, Chicago Cubs, 16 Pages 3346.00
Baseball, Program, 1910 World Series, Philadelphia, 54 Pages 17925.00
Baseball, Program, 1911 World Series, Philadelphia Athletics, N.Y. Giants 600.00
Baseball, Program, 1930 World Series, Babe Ruth & John McGraw Autographs 2031.00
Baseball, Program, 1935 All-Star Game, Cleveland Stadium, Umpire Making Call 650.00
Baseball, Program, 1937 All-Star Game, Washington, D.C., FDR Throwing Ball 250.00
Baseball, Program, Dinner, Phil. Athletics, 1913 Championship Team, Autographed 11750.00
Baseball, Program, N.Y. Giants Vs. Boston Braves, Babe Ruth Autograph, 1945 .... 2350.00
Baseball, Program, Yankee Stadium Opening Day, April 18, 1923 .... 3884.00
Baseball, Ring, 1992 World Series, Toronto Blue Jays, Diamonds, Gold, Tiffany & Co., Size 9 ½ 8400.00
Baseball, Ring, Gabby Street, 1931 World Series Championship 21510.00
Baseball, Ring, Jerry Grote, Los Angeles Dodgers, World Series, 1981 .... 13800.00
Baseball, Ring, Joe Collins, New York Yankees, 1953 World Championship 31070.00
Baseball, Ring, N.Y. Yankees, 1939 World Series Champions, 14K Gold, Dieges & Clust, Size 8 ½ In. 21600.00
Baseball, Ring, New York Yankees, Team Of The Century, Hall Of Fame, 2000 .... 6433.00
Baseball, Score Keeper, Babe Ruth, Celluloid, Leather Strap, 1 ¾ In. .... *illus* 106.00
Baseball, Seat, Cleveland Municipal Stadium 132.00
Baseball, Seat, Comiskey Park, Green Paint 140.00
Baseball, Seat, Ebbets Field, Slat Back, Wood, Iron, Mounted, Plaque, 1913-57, 33 In. 2050.00
Baseball, Seat, Polo Grounds, Wood, Iron, Figural Sides, N.Y. Giants Logo, Polo Grounds, 1911-63 .... 1398.00
Baseball, Seat, Wood, Iron, Flat Slat, No. 3, 1923-73 .... 1693.00
Baseball, Seat, Yankee Stadium, Blue, 1923-73 .... 2270.00
Baseball, Seat, Yankee Stadium, No. 24, 1923-73 .... 1613.00
Baseball, Speaker, Ebbets Field, Public Address, 26 x 25 ½ In. 323.00
Baseball, Trophy, 2004 World Series, Pennants, Baseballs, Sterling, Tiffany, 30 Lbs., 24 In. 31200.00
Baseball, Trophy, Christy Mathewson's Best Season, 1908 .... 9600.00
Baseball, Trophy, Gold Glove, Jim Piersall, Golden Ball, Glove, Plaque, 1961, 16 x 7 In. 5100.00
Baseball, Vending Machine, Baseball Cards, Gumball, 1950s 475.00
Baseball, Watch, Pocket, Batsman, Rockford Open Face, 14K Gold, 1895 .... 1135.00
Baseball, Wristwatch, Dizzy Dean, Metal Link Band, Image Of Dizzy Pitching, 1935 .... 955.00
Baseball, Wristwatch, Mantle, Maris, Mays, Green, White Face, Red Box, 1964, 6 x 4 In. 470.00
Basketball, Autographed, Michael Jordon, Spaulding 500.00
Basketball, Ball, ABA Game, 1975-76 .... 2031.00
Basketball, Ball, Autographed, Michael Jordon, Wilson, 1990s 896.00
Basketball, Ball, Autographed, Philadelphia 76ers, 11 Signatures, 1984-85 .... 360.00
Basketball, Ball, Autographed, Wilt Chamberlain, 1978 .... 1920.00
Basketball, Contract, Pete Maravich, New Orleans Jazz, 1974 .... 4481.00
Basketball, Jacket, Leather, San Antonio Spurs, NBA Championship, 1999 .... 300.00
Basketball, Jersey, Kareem Abdul-Jabbar, Los Angeles Lakers, Game Used, c.1979-80 .... 11405.00
Basketball, Jersey, Lebron James, Rookie, Cleveland Cavaliers, Game Used, 2003-04 .... 4182.00
Basketball, Jersey, Roy Hinson, Philadelphia 76ers, Game Used, 1986-87 .... 198.00
Basketball, Plaque, Hakeem Olajuwon, NBA Blocked Shot Award, 1990-91 .... 1680.00
Basketball, Poster, Harlem Globetrotters, Wilt Chamberlain, 1958, 14 x 22 In. 1075.00
Basketball, Sneakers, Lebron James, Cleveland Cavaliers, Game Used 1596.00
Basketball, Watch, Michael Jordan, Chicago Bulls Championship, 1991-92 .... 726.00
Billiards, Balls, Albany Billiard Ball, Co., 16, 2 ¾ In., Box 58.00
Bowling, Ball, Skull, Ebonite, Lavender, Resin, No. 93J0021, 1990s 300.00
Boxing, Ashtray, Joe Louis, Figural, Brown Bomber, Chalkware, 1940s 620.00
Boxing, Book, Pugilistica, 3 Volumes 240.00

Sports, Baseball, Nodder, Mickey Mantle, New York Yankees Uniform, c.1960, 7 In.
$597.00

Sports, Baseball, Score Keeper, Babe Ruth, Celluloid, Leather Strap, 1 ¾ In.
$106.00

Autograph Hunting Tips

- Mail requests for coaches and everyday players.
- Call the team's community relations department about signing events.
- Read the sports section of your local newspaper to find out what teams are playing in your hometown.
- Go to minor league games.
- Go early and stay late at games.
- Pay attention to radio and TV announcements of special events where players will appear.
- Go to spring training games.

Sports, Croquet Set, Wood, Ivory, Ceramic, 8 Wickets, Mallets, Balls, Stand, 1890
$300.00

Sports, Football, Helmet, Yale University, Leather, Sheepskin, 1910s
$360.00

Sports, Hockey, Program, Autographed, Toronto Maple Leafs, 17 Signatures, 1946-47
$897.00

Boxing, Full Ticket, Cassius Clay Vs. Sonny Liston, 1964 .... 5079.00
Boxing, Gloves, Autographed, Muhammad Ali 1501.00
Boxing, Gloves, Jack Dempsey, Leather, Signed, 1940, Child's Size 805.00
Boxing, Poster, Ali-Frazier Madison Square Garden Fight, Black, Yellow, 1971, 28 x 22 In. 4406.00
Boxing, Program, Muhammad Ali & Joe Frazier, Autographed, 3/8/1971 .... 1024.00
Boxing, Robe, Training, Muhammad Ali, c.1975 .... 1195.00
Boxing, Serial Movie Slide, Jack Dempsey, Daredevil Jack, Glass Slide, 3 x 4 In. 115.00
Boxing, Ticket, Jack Dempsey-Jess Willard Fight, 1919 .... 420.00
Croquet Set, Wood, Ivory, Ceramic, 8 Wickets, Mallets, Balls, Stand, 1890 .... *illus* 300.00
Cycling, Medal, Bicycle Race, 5-Mile, Nickel Silver, Gold Flash, C.J. Schoening, Oak Park, 1 ½ x 3 In. 78.00
Diving, Helmet, Copper, Brass, 18 x 16 In. 144.00
Football, Ball, Autographed, Cleveland Browns World Champions, 1955 .... 1702.00
Football, Ball, Autographed, Walter Payton 600.00
Football, Button, Leatherhead Player, Kicking Football, Nickel Plated, Engraved, 2 Parts 115.00
Football, Helmet, Arrow Design, J.C. Higgins, 1930s 780.00
Football, Helmet, Autographed, New York Jets, 1968 .... 836.00
Football, Helmet, Aviator, Cotton Batting, Leather, c.1900 .... 1680.00
Football, Helmet, Four Spoke, Leather, Wool Felt, Reach Co., 1890 .... 3600.00
Football, Helmet, Leather, Dog Ears, c.1910 .... 180.00
Football, Helmet, Leather, Rain Cap, Spalding, 1900s 1920.00
Football, Helmet, Peyton Manning, Indianapolis Colts, 2000 .... 4834.00
Football, Helmet, Yale University, Leather, Sheepskin, 1910s .... *illus* 360.00
Football, Jersey, Autographed, John Mackey, Baltimore Colts, c.1970 .... 12545.00
Football, Jersey, Brett Favre, Atlanta Falcons, Rookie, 1991 .... 3300.00
Football, Jersey, Carleton College, Navy Blue, 6 Leather Inserts, 1910 .... 2280.00
Football, Jersey, John Brodie, San Francisco 49ers, 1960s 1800.00
Football, Jersey, Orange Bowl, Long Sleeves, 1949 .... 180.00
Football, Nodder, Pittsburgh Steeler, Plaster 77.00
Football, Nodder, Texas A & M Aggie, Late 1950s 133.00
Football, Nose Guard, Morrill's, 1890s 325.00
Football, Nose Guard, Victor Special, Batwing Style, Original Strap, 1898 .... 600.00
Football, Pants, Reeded, Worn, Wright & Ditson, c.1900 .... 100.00
Football, Pendant, San Francisco 49ers, Super Bowl Champions, 1981 .... 401.00
Football, Pennant, Carlisle Indian School, Red, Yellow Lettering, c.1910 .... 170.00
Football, Program, Michigan, Pennsylvania, Cheerleader, 1911 .... 900.00
Football, Program, Rose Bowl, 1931 .... 478.00
Football, Shin Guards, Reeded, Leather, Reach, c.1910 .... 300.00
Football, Shoulder Pads, Quilted, c.1900 .... 2040.00
Football, Sweater, High School Referee, Black, White Stripes, Insignia, c.1925 .... 140.00
Football, Sweater, Letterman's, John Niemiec, Notre Dame, Navy Blue, 3 Stripes, 1928 .... 780.00
Football, Sweater, Notre Dame, Dick Hendricks, Size 46, c.1955 .... 325.00
Football, Tobacco Premuim, Blanket, Harvard, Player, Geometric Border, Oversized Felt, 1910s 300.00
Football, Uniform, Vest, Pants, Cap, Pads, Canvas, Used, c.1890 .... 7200.00
Football, Usher Hat, Notre Dame, c.1948 .... 140.00
Golf, Bag, Autographed, Jack Nicklaus, Tournament, 1972 .... 5677.00
Golf, Bag, Autographed Twice, Jack Nicklaus, Green, White, McGregor 4800.00
Golf, Bag, Gucci, 1970s, 46 x 13 In. 400.00
Golf, Ball, Feather, 3 Leather Panels, c.1855 .... 2400.00
Golf, Ball, Gutta Percha, Hand Hammered, Brown, c.1870 .... 900.00
Golf, Ball, Gutta Percha, Hand Hammered, Carved Lines, c.1870 .... 540.00
Golf, Ball, Gutta Percha, Hand Hammered, Scored Lines, Red, Brown, c.1870 .... 840.00
Golf, Ball, Gutta Percha, Line Cut, Black 510.00
Golf, Ball, Wonder Ball, Rubber Core, Worthington Golf Ball Co., c.1920 .... 390.00
Golf, Contract, Arnold Palmer, ABC Network, Signed, 1963 .... 420.00
Golf, Flag, Autographed, Tiger Woods, Masters, U.S. Map, Yellow, 14 x 19 In. 1800.00
Golf, Jacket, Masters Tournament, Augusta National Golf Club, Green 3884.00
Golf, Program, Autographed, Jack Nicklaus, U.S.G.A. Amateur Championship, 1961 .... 660.00
Golf, Shirt, Autographed, Tiger Woods, 2006 Masters Tournament, Red, Nike Polo 43000.00
Hockey, Cuff Links, Boston Bruins, Monogram, 1926 .... 657.00
Hockey, Nodder, Baltimore Clippers, Bearded Man, Blue Hat, Magnet Base, Japan, 6 In. 80.00
Hockey, Program, Autographed, Toronto Maple Leafs, 17 Signatures, 1946-47 .... *illus* 897.00
Hockey, Seat, Olympia Stadium 480.00
Hockey, Stick, Autographed, Montreal Canadiens, 1953-54 .... 508.00
Hockey, Stick, Bobby Orr, Game Used, Victoriaville Pro, c.1970 .... 836.00
Hunting, Cartridge Box, Liberty Cartridge Co., 12 Gauge 3205.00
Hunting, Cartridge Box, Peters Trap Load, Pumpkin Box, 12 Gauge 2492.00
Hunting, Cartridge Box, Western New Chief Squirrel Hunter 1542.00

Hunting, Clay Target, Geo. Ligowsky, Cardboard Tab, 5 ½ In. 134.00
Hunting, Clay Target, Geo. Ligowsky, Clay Tab, Pat Sep. 7, 1880, 23 Oz., 5 In. 112.00
Hunting, Crow Call, Wood, 1930-40, 5 In. 20.00
Hunting, Crow Call, Wood, Metal Collar, Charles Ditto, Keithsburg, Ill., 3 ½ In. 28.00
Hunting, Duck Call, Checkered Panel, Brass Banded, 5 In. 115.00
Hunting, Game Call, Walnut, Brass Band, Buddy Drake, Tenn., Box, 5 In. 429.00
Hunting, Target Thrower, Felt Cup Liner, Bogardus, 32 ⅜ x 11 ½ In. 2912.00
Hunting, Target Thrower, Metal, 2-Prong Winding Handle, France, c.1890, 9 ½ In. 364.00
Hunting, Tin, DuPont Eagle Gun Powder Duck Shooting Powder, 1 Lb. 210.00
Pool, Ball Rack, Wood, Mechanical Dispenser, Brunswick Balke Collender, 35 x 18 x 7 In. 1210.00
Pool, Cue Balls, Bakelite, Set Of 16 Balls, Original Box 115.00
Pool, Cue Cabinet, Cherry, Mahogany, Carved Rosettes, Shelves, 77 x 46 ½ x 10 In. 8050.00
Pool, Cue Rack, Oak, 9 Cue Sticks, Brunswick, 68 x 31 ½ In. 410.00
Pool, Cue Rack, Oak, Quartersawn, Brunswick Balke Collender, 66 x 35 ½ x 5 In. 1750.00
Pool, Table, Bumper, Slate, Wood, 1960s, 31 x 50 x 34 In. 80.00
Riding, Bridle, Horsehair, Indian Designs, By Montana Correctional Prisoners, Shelby, 32 In. 588.00
Rugby, Nodder, Balmain Tigers, Australia, 1960s 120.00
Skating, Ice Skates, Wrought Iron, Wood, Slots, Curled Front, Pa., 1800s, 5 ½ x 13 x 2 In. *illus* 275.00
Snowshoes, Bentwood, Rawhide 90.00
Snowshoes, Woven, Color Tassels, 19 x 27 In. 489.00
Tennis, Racket, Autographed, Martina Navratilova, Bosworth, 2006 Match 3600.00
Tennis, Racket, Winchester, W4, Precision Model, As Good As The Gun, 9 x 27 In. 55.00
Track, Shoes, Carl Lewis, Seoul Summer Olympics, Used, Autographed, 1988 780.00

STAFFORDSHIRE, England, has been a district making pottery and porcelain since the 1700s. Hundreds of kilns are still working in the area. Thousands of types of pottery and porcelain have been made in the many factories that worked and still work in the area. Some of the most famous factories have been listed separately, such as Adams, Davenport, Ridgway, Rowland & Marsellus, Royal Doulton, Royal Worcester, Spode, Wedgwood, and others. Some Staffordshire pieces are listed under categories like Fairing, Flow Blue, Mulberry, Shaving Mug, etc.

Bank, Cottage, White, Yellow, Marked 10.00
Bowl, Fruit, Blue Transfer, 3-Lobed Cutout, Pedestal, 13 x 5 In. 600.00
Bowl, Vegetable, Blue, Virginia State Arms, Flowers, 10 ½ x 12 ½ In. 1150.00
Bowl, Vegetable, Cover, Bothwell Castle, Clydesdale, Blue, Adams, 6 x 12 In. *illus* 225.00
Bowl, Vegetable, Cover, General Lafayette, Landing, Blue, White, 19th Century, Clews, 6 x 12 In. 1989.00
Bowl, Waterfront, Steamships, Sailboats, Flag, Soldiers, Blue, 1 ½ x 8 ¾ In. 300.00
Bust, Wesley, Religious Leader On Plinth, Hand Colored, 19th Century, 11 In. 176.00
Bust, William Shakespeare, Painted, Faux Marble Base, 9 x 7 In. 130.00
Cake Plate, Sprig, Red, Green, Blue, 9 In. 25.00
Coffeepot, Lafayette At Franklin's Tomb, Blue, 19th Century, 11 ½ In. 1159.00
Coffeepot, Purple Transfer, Beehive Finial, Embossed Handle, 12 x 11 In. 500.00
Compote, Fruit & Flowers, Dark Blue, Hicks Meigh & Co., c.1825, 4 ½ x 11 In. 431.00
Creamer, Fern, Light Purple, Alcock, 6 ½ x 4 ½ In. 49.00
Creamer, Geometric, Yellow Luster, Black, Transfer, 3 ¼ In. 25.00
Creamer, Queen's Rose, Helmet Shape, Vine Border, Embossed, 4 ¾ In. 154.00
Cup, Woman, Leaf, Flower Border, Red, Handleless, 2 ⅜ x 3 ⅞ In., 6 Piece 11.00
Cup & Saucer, Dahlia, Pink Luster, Handleless, 2 ½ x 5 ½ In. 45.00
Cup & Saucer, Field Flower Sprig, 4 x 6 In. 45.00
Cup & Saucer, Flower, Leaves, Handleless *illus* 110.00
Cup & Saucer, Mother & Child, Black Transfer, Pink Luster, Handleless, 2 ½ x 5 ½ In. 45.00
Cup & Saucer, Queen's Rose, 2 ¾ x 5 ½ In. 45.00
Cup & Saucer, Rebecca At Well, Flowers, Shells, Handleless, 2 ½ x 4 & 5 ¾ In. 99.00
Cup & Saucer, Sower, Red, 2 ½ x 3 ¾ & 5 ⅞ In. 66.00
Cup & Saucer, Sprig, 12-Sided, Green & Purple, 3 ¾ x 5 ¾ In. 48.00
Cup & Saucer, Sprigs, Painted, 3 x 5 ½ In. 35.00
Cup & Saucer, Thistle, Pink Luster 75.00
Cup & Saucer, Tree & Cone, c.1830 70.00
Cup & Saucer, Wadsworth Tower, Blue, 2 ½ x 3 ¾ & 5 ¾ In. 248.00
Cup Plate, Figures, Animals, Water, Building, Blue, White, Transfer, Luster Rim, Clews, 3 ⅞ In. 45.00
Dinnerware, Old Chelsea, Plate, Dinner, W.H. Grindley, 10 In., 12 Piece 88.00
Dish, Green Glaze, Open Twig Handle, 18th Century, 7 ½ In., Pair 1126.00
Dish, Hen, On Nest, Cover, Multicolored, 7 ½ x 9 x 7 ¼ In. 425.00
Dish, Hen, On Nest, Cover, Multicolored, 9 ½ x 13 x 8 ¼ In. 165.00
Dish, Hen On Nest Cover, Brown, Red, Yellow, Green, Black, 9 ½ x 13 x 8 ¼ In. *illus* 165.00
Figurine, Abraham Lincoln, White Horse, Green Cape, 15 In. 1554.00
Figurine, Dog, Dalmatian, Cobalt Blue Base, c.1850, 7 ½ In., Pair 431.00
Figurine, Dog, Dalmatian, Seated, Blue Base, Mid 1800s, 7 ¼ In., Pair 1116.00

Sports, Skating, Ice Skates, Wrought Iron, Wood, Slots, Curled Front, Pa., 1800s, 5 ½ x 13 x 2 In.
$275.00

Staffordshire, Bowl, Vegetable, Cover, Bothwell Castle, Clydesdale, Blue, Adams, 6 x 12 In.
$225.00

Staffordshire, Cup & Saucer, Flower, Leaves, Handleless
$110.00

Staffordshire, Dish, Hen On Nest Cover, Brown, Red, Yellow, Green, Black, 9 ½ x 13 x 8 ¼ In.
$165.00

TIP

Pennant collections can be ruined by moths. Store your pennants in moth-proof containers.

Staffordshire, Figurine, Dog, Spaniel, Painted, 19th Century, 9 In., Pair
$525.00

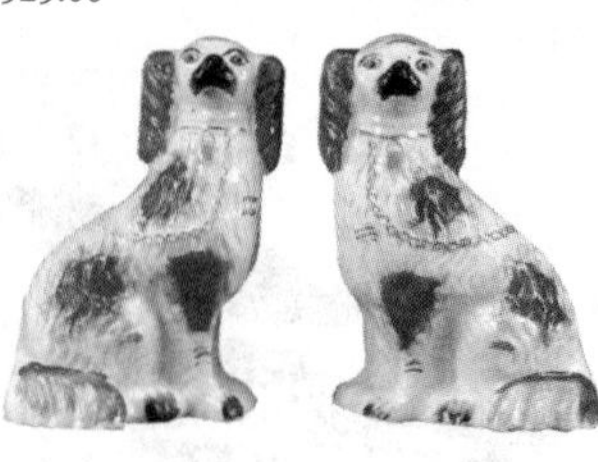

Staffordshire, Figurine, Milkmaid, Churn, Spaniel, c.1800, 9 x 6 ½ In.
$356.00

Staffordshire, Flask, Potato Form, Red, White, Blue Leaves, Green Top, 1835, 7 In.
$351.00

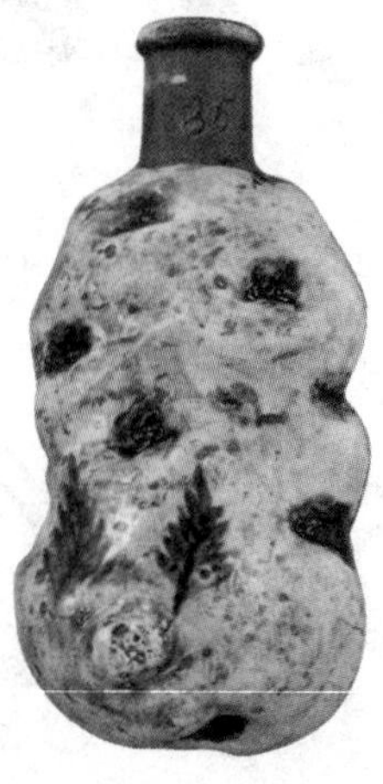

Staffordshire, Gravy Boat, Bridge, Cottage Scene, Flower Border, 3 ½ x 5 ¾ x 2 ⅜ In.
$22.00

Figurine, Dog, Hand Painted Face, c.1850, 13 In., Pair 352.00
Figurine, Dog, Pug, Black Face, Tan & White Body, 6 ½ x 7 In. 175.00
Figurine, Dog, Red Spots, Free Standing Front Legs, c.1950, 9 ½ In., Pair 352.00
Figurine, Dog, Sitting, White, Black Spots, 10 ½ In., Pair 351.00
Figurine, Dog, Spaniel, Free Front Leg, Flat Back, 8 In. 195.00
Figurine, Dog, Spaniel, Mauve & Gilt Highlights, 11 In. 140.00
Figurine, Dog, Spaniel, Painted, 19th Century, 9 In., Pair *illus* 525.00
Figurine, Dog, Spaniel, Seated, Red, White, 1800s, 8 In., Pair 205.00
Figurine, Dog, Spaniel, Sitting, Collar & Leash, c.1850, 9 In., Pair 234.00
Figurine, Dog, Spaniel, White, Gilt Patches, Highlighted Fur, Chain, 1800s, 15 In., Pair 533.00
Figurine, Dog, Stylized, Lying Down, Black, Orange, Green, 1 ⅞ x 2 ¼ x 1 ¼ In. 11.00
Figurine, Dog, Whippet, White Base, Mid 19th Century, 13 In., Pair 1840.00
Figurine, Garibaldi, Leaning On Column, Inscribed, 19 ½ x 10 In. 176.00
Figurine, Girl Sitting On Dog, 8 ½ In. 350.00
Figurine, Hunter, 19th Century, 16 In. 117.00
Figurine, Jeremiah, Standing, Plinth, Early 19th Century, 11 In. 575.00
Figurine, King Charles Spaniel, Seated, White, Late 19th Century, 12 ½ x 10 In. 82.00
Figurine, Lady On Goat, 4 ¾ x 4 In. 55.00
Figurine, Lion, 10 x 13 In., Pair 150.00
Figurine, Lion, Lying Down, Brown, Late 19th Century, 9 x 11 ½ In. 105.00
Figurine, Lion Slayer, 17 In. 225.00
Figurine, Man, Holding Handkerchief, White Outfit, Black Hair, Gilt, 15 In. 800.00
Figurine, Milkmaid, Churn, Spaniel, c.1800, 9 x 6 ½ In. *illus* 356.00
Figurine, Milkmaid & Cow, Hand Painted, 7 ¼ x 8 ¾ In. 413.00
Figurine, Napoleon, 19th Century, 12 x 6 ½ In. 263.00
Figurine, Napoleon, Military Uniform, Seated On Cannon, Titled, c.1875, 16 In. 148.00
Figurine, Return From Egypt, 19th Century, 9 ½ In. 575.00
Figurine, Rooster, Red & Black Face, Gilt Accents, c.1875, 12 ¼ In., Pair 3172.00
Figurine, Sailor, Blue Shirt, Yellow Hat, Smoking Pipe, Mid 1800s, 12 In. 259.00
Figurine, Woman, Leaning Against Post, c.1820, 9 ½ In. 41.00
Flask, Potato Form, Red, White, Blue Leaves, Green Top, 1835, 7 In. *illus* 351.00
Gravy Boat, Bridge, Cottage Scene, Flower Border, 3 ½ x 5 ¾ x 2 ⅜ In. *illus* 22.00
Gravy Boat, Sprig, Footed, 7 ¼ In. 48.00
Group, Arbor Couple, Children, 13 In. 225.00
Group, Arbor Couple, Courting, 4 ½ In. 75.00
Group, Biblical, Jesus, Mary, Martha, Lazarus, 1800s, 8 In. 3910.00
Group, Gentleman & Lady, 12 ¾ x 9 In. 88.00
Group, Greyhound, Seated, Rabbit In Mouth, Late 19th Century, 9 ½ In. 175.00
Group, Greyhound & Rabbit, Late 19th Century, 12 ¼ In. 200.00
Group, Greyhounds, Beige, Gray, Late 19th Century, 11 In. 325.00
Group, Jesus, Woman Of Samaria, Early 19th Century, 8 In. 3400.00
Group, Man, Seated Woman, Rabbit, 7 x 5 In. 40.00
Group, Man, Woman, Dog, 10 ¼ In. 50.00
Group, Marriage Act, Couple, Parson, Tree, Verse, 19th Century, 6 ¾ In. 1500.00
Group, Samuel Anointing David, c.1820, 9 ½ In. 1800.00
Group, The Prodigal Returns, c.1880, 13 ½ In. 117.00
Group, Tithe Pig, 3 Figures, 19th Century, 5 ½ In. 545.00
Group, Water Buffalo, Boy, Lead Glazed, Enameled, c.1760, 8 In. 16250.00
Jug, Eagle, Shield, Banner, Flower, Blue & White Transfer, c.1820, 8 In. 1422.00
Mug, Eagle, Spread Wing, Child's, 2 ½ In. 77.00
Mug, Welsh Costumes, Black Transfer, 3 In. 25.00
Pitcher, Abbey, Blue Transfer, Enoch Wood, 10 ⅔ In. 250.00
Pitcher, Lafayette, Franklin's Tomb, Blue, Enoch Wood, c.1825, 6 ½ In. 360.00
Pitcher, Pink Luster, 5 ½ In. 86.00
Pitcher & Basin, State Names, Banners, Flower Panels, Blue, 9 & 12 In. 3750.00
Pitcher & Bowl, Palestine Pattern, Blue, White, 11 ¾ In. 380.00
Plaque, Religious, Prepare To Meet Thy God, Yellow Luster, 8 ½ x 7 ½ In. 400.00
Plate, Acorns, Leaves, White Salt Glaze, Veined Ground, Scalloped Rim, 9 ½ In. 1007.00
Plate, America & Independence, Romantic Scenes, Blue, Transfer, Clews, c.1834, 8 In. 424.00
Plate, Asian Scenery, Purple Transfer, 10 In. 125.00
Plate, Asian Scenery, Red Transfer, Jackson, 9 In. 99.00
Plate, Bakers Falls, Hudson River, Brown Transfer, Clews, 9 In. 75.00
Plate, Cambridge, Hammersley, Flow Blue, 10 ¾ In. 25.00
Plate, Canova, Black & Purple, T. Mayer, 9 ¼ In. 200.00
Plate, Canova, Purple Transfer, Mayer, 7 ¼ In. 85.00
Plate, Canovian, Purple Transfer, Clews, 7 In. 125.00
Plate, Capitol, Washington, Scalloped & Gadrooned Edge, Blue, 10 ¼ In. 248.00
Plate, City Hall, Blue, 10 In. 110.00

Plate, City Hall, New York, Blue Transfer, 9 7/8 In. 154.00
Plate, Cologne, Pink Transfer, Stevenson, 9 3/4 In. 125.00
Plate, Cookie, Sprig, Green & Purple, 10-Sided, 9 In. 48.00
Plate, Dinner, Haddon, Mulberry, 9 1/2 In. 75.00
Plate, Dinner, Italian Villas, Brown Transfer, 10 1/2 In. 150.00
Plate, Dot, Coat Of Arms, Star, Leaf Medallions, White Slat Glaze, Scalloped, 9 1/8 In. 5036.00
Plate, English Cities, Hereford, Blue Transfer, Enoch Wood, 10 1/2 In. 140.00
Plate, European Scenery, Red Transfer, Enoch Wood, 9 1/4 In. 125.00
Plate, Fair Mount, Near Philadelphia, Blue, 10 1/4 In. 358.00
Plate, Falls Of Killarney, Blue Transfer, Hackwood, 6 1/2 In. 75.00
Plate, Fishkill, Hudson River, Brown Transfer, Clews, 10 1/2 In. 225.00
Plate, Frolics Of Youth, Prattware Style, Flowers, Fruit Border, Child's, 6 3/4 In. 33.00
Plate, Gem, Purple Transfer, Mayer, 6 1/2 In. 75.00
Plate, Gipsy, Blue Transfer, 9 1/4 In. 125.00
Plate, Gipsy, Brown Transfer, 7 1/4 In. 85.00
Plate, Hartford, Connecticut, Red Transfer, Jacksons, 10 1/4 In. 225.00
Plate, Hartford, Connecticut, Red Transfer, Scalloped Rim, 19th Century, 10 1/2 In. 527.00
Plate, Indian Temple, Red, 10 1/4 In. 44.00
Plate, Italia, Blue Transfer, 10 1/4 In. 95.00
Plate, Japanese, Pink Transfer, Alcock, 9 1/2 In. 125.00
Plate, Kingsweston, Glouscestershire, Blue Transfer, 9 In. 225.00
Plate, Landing Of Gen. Lafayette, Blue, Clews, 10 1/8 In. *illus* 300.00
Plate, Lozere, Blue Transfer, E. Challinor, 7 1/2 In. 75.00
Plate, Meadow, Cows, Sheep, Shell, Fruit, Flower Border, Blue Transfer, 9 In. 165.00
Plate, Mesina, Blue Transfer, Wood & Challinor, 9 In. 125.00
Plate, Millennium, Purple Transfer, 10 1/2 In. *illus* 176.00
Plate, Millennium, Scalloped Edge, Brown Transfer, 9 In. 250.00
Plate, Monterey, Pink Transfer, Joseph Heath, 9 1/2 In. 95.00
Plate, Motto, George's Fate, Blue Transfer, Child's, 5 In. 85.00
Plate, Ontario Lake Scenery, Blue Transfer, 9 In. 95.00
Plate, Palestine, Blue Transfer, 8 1/2 In. 150.00
Plate, Palestine, Blue Transfer, Stevenson, 6 3/4 In. 125.00
Plate, Pantheon, Red Transfer, 9 1/2 In. 95.00
Plate, Paradise, Blue Transfer, Clobbered, 8 1/2 In. 55.00
Plate, Parisian, Blue Transfer, Phillips, 10 1/2 In. 125.00
Plate, Priory, Blue Transfer, Challinor, 8 1/2 In. 125.00
Plate, Priory, Blue Transfer, John Alcock, 9 1/2 In. 125.00
Plate, Rabbits Playing Tennis, 13 In. 2800.00
Plate, Rhone Scenery, Blue Transfer, Mayer, 9 1/2 In. 125.00
Plate, Richard Jordan's House, Red Transfer, 10 1/4 In. 644.00
Plate, Sicilian, Blue Transfer, 9 1/2 In. 125.00
Plate, Sicilian Beauties, Blue Transfer, Clews, 10 1/2 In. 39.00
Plate, Sicilian Flowers, Pink Transfer, 9 In. 105.00
Plate, Soup, Hudson River, Blue Transfer, Clews, 10 In. 175.00
Plate, Soup, Pompeii, Brown Transfer, Alcock, 9 In. 125.00
Plate, Soup, President's House, Washington, Black, 10 1/2 In. *illus* 88.00
Plate, Soup, Shanghae, Flow Blue, Furnival, 9 In. 49.00
Plate, Soup, Shield, Blue Transfer, 10 1/2 In. 125.00
Plate, Star, Black Transfer, Purple, Black, Yellow Luster, 10 1/2 In. 75.00
Plate, Stevens Mansion, 7 3/4 In. 132.00
Plate, Tuscan Rose, Black Transfer, Clews, 6 3/4 In. 95.00
Plate, Tuscany, Pink Transfer, 9 In. 75.00
Plate, Villain Regent's Park, Blue, White, 8 1/2 In. 60.00
Plate, Virginia, Red Flower, Blue, Green Leaves, Red Banded Edge, 9 1/4 In. 25.00
Plate, Winchester College, Purple Transfer, 6 1/2 In. 25.00
Platter, Asiatic Pheasant, Blue Transfer, 12 x 9 1/2 In. 75.00
Platter, Blantyre, Blue Transfer, Alcock, 16 x 12 In. 250.00
Platter, Blue Feather Edge, Octagonal, 15 1/2 x 11 1/2 In. 50.00
Platter, Castle, Blue Transfer, 19 x 14 In. 500.00
Platter, Coburg, Blue Transfer, Challinor, 15 1/2 x 12 In. 275.00
Platter, Dromedary, Blue Transfer, J. Riley, 18 1/4 x 14 In. 700.00
Platter, Equestrian Scene, Mansion, c.1870, 15 x 30 In. 351.00
Platter, Fruit, Flower Border, Blue Transfer, Oval, c.1810, 12 x 15 In. 356.00
Platter, Gipsy, Blue Transfer, Octagonal, 13 x 10 In. 300.00
Platter, Kent, Blue Transfer, Swinnerton, 15 1/2 x 11 3/4 In. 75.00
Platter, Landing Of General Lafayette, Blue, White, Clews, 19th Century, 11 3/4 In. *illus* 2223.00
Platter, Marino, Pink Transfer, T. Phillips, 16 x 12 In. 375.00
Platter, Nankin Jar, Blue Transfer, Flowers & Vase, 15 x 11 In. 125.00

Staffordshire, Plate, Landing Of Gen. Lafayette, Blue, Clews, 10 1/8 In.
$300.00

Staffordshire, Plate, Millennium, Purple Transfer, 10 1/2 In.
$176.00

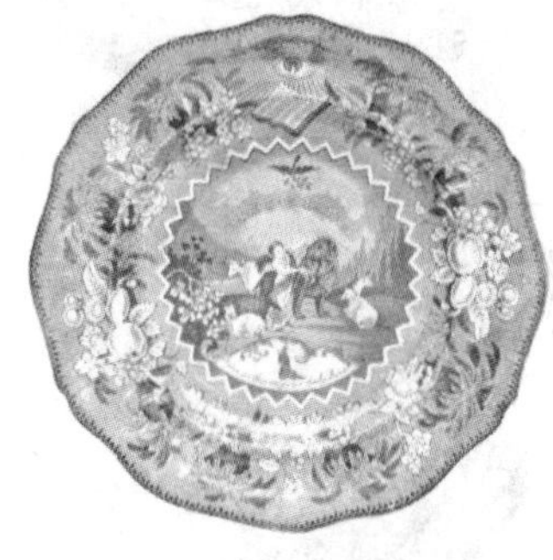

Staffordshire, Plate, Soup, President's House, Washington, Black, 10 1/2 In.
$88.00

Staffordshire, Platter, Landing Of General Lafayette, Blue, White, Clews, 19th Century, 11 3/4 In.
$2223.00

Staffordshire, Teapot, Cover, Pagodas, White Salt Glaze, Crabstock Handle, Twig Finial, 4 ¾ In.
$533.00

Staffordshire, Teapot, Strawberry, Queen's Rose, Shaped Handle, 6 ¾ In.
$495.00

Stangl, Bird, Key West Quail Dove, No. 3454, Marked, 8 ¾ In.
$121.00

Stangl, Bird, Pheasant Hen, No. 3491, Marked, 5 ⅞ x 11 ¼ In.
$66.00

Platter, Netley Abbey, Well & Tree, Blue Transfer, 18 ½ x 15 In. 350.00
Platter, Rhone Scenery, Light Blue, 8-Sided, Marked, T.J. Maier, 1800s, 14 x 18 In. 99.00
Platter, Romantic Design, Ruins, Cow Herds, Medium Blue, 15 ¼ x 21 In. 264.00
Platter, Roselle, Blue Transfer, J. Meir, 15 x 11 ½ In. 295.00
Platter, Spanish Beauties, Blue Transfer, Deakin & Sons, 15 ½ x 12 ¼ In. 400.00
Platter, Udina, Blue Transfer, Octagonal, Clementson, 15 ¾ x 12 ½ In. 400.00
Platter, Unique, Blue Transfer, Zigzag Edge, 13 ½ x 11 ½ In. 95.00
Platter, Villager, Blue Transfer, Embossed, 17 x 14 ½ In. 425.00
Platter, Whiteware, Blue Feather Edge, Octagonal, 17 x 13 In. 185.00
Sauceboat, Parisian, Blue Transfer, G. Phillips, 9 x 5 In. 95.00
Saucer, Scroll Fond, Brown Transfer, 4 In. 75.00
Spill Vase, Ram, Stand, Leaves, Flowers, 1800s, 5 ½ In. 164.00
Sugar, Andrew Johnson Personal Pattern, 7 ¾ In. 239.00
Sugar, Cover, Oak Leaf, Embossed, Red Flowers, Black Oak Leaf, 7 ½ x 6 In. 75.00
Sugar, Cover, Sprig, Octagonal, Loop Handles, Finial, 8 x 6 In. 50.00
Sugar, Girl, With Flowers, Blue Transfer, Clews, 7 x 4 ½ In. 55.00
Sugar, Strawberry, Queen's Rose, Scrolled Handles, Leaf Embossed Feet, 6 ¼ In. 550.00
Sugar Cover, Pink Luster, 5 x 2 ¾ In. 25.00
Syrup, Dog Form, Pewter Top, c.1890, 9 In. 275.00
Teapot, Cover, Mansion, White Salt Glaze, Serpent Molded Spout, c.1760, 4 ⅞ In. 3318.00
Teapot, Cover, Oriental Scene, Brown Transfer, Buildings, Landscape, 12 ½ In. 44.00
Teapot, Cover, Pagodas, White Salt Glaze, Crabstock Handle, Twig Finial, 4 ¾ In. ...... *illus* 533.00
Teapot, Cover, Serpent, Putto Head Masks, White Salt Glaze, Rectangular, 6 In. 1778.00
Teapot, Cover, Serpent Handle, Flower Finial, Footed, 11 ¾ x 7 In. 50.00
Teapot, Cover, White Salt Glaze, Pink Ground, Globular, Crabstock Handle, 5 In. 5036.00
Teapot, Parisian, Brown Transfer, Octagonal, 10 ½ x 6 In. 300.00
Teapot, Pewter Cover, Scroddled, Brown, Yellow Luster, 9 x 7 In. 95.00
Teapot, Pink Luster, 7 In. 144.00
Teapot, Queen's Rose, 11 x 7 In. 125.00
Teapot, Ribs, Beading, Duck Finial, Basalt, Chetham & Wooley, c.1800, 6 x 4 In. 80.00
Teapot, Sprig, Octagonal, 10 ½ x 8 In. 95.00
Teapot, Strawberry, Queen's Rose, Shaped Handle, 6 ¾ In. .... *illus* 495.00
Teapot, White, Salt Glaze, Globular Form, 3-Footed, c.1765, 4 ½ In. 936.00
Toby Jugs are listed in their own category.
Toddy Plate, Corinth, Blue Transfer, 10-Sided, 4 ½ In. 75.00
Toddy Plate, Venus, Blue Transfer, Ironstone, Podmore Walker, 5 ¼ In. 55.00
Trivet, General, Officers On Horseback, Battlefield, Blue, 19th Century, 9 x 12 In. 549.00
Tureen, Gracefield Queens County, Trees, Homes, Blue, 13 x 14 In. 330.00
Tureen, Vegetable, Verona, Blue Transfer, Footed, 10 x 6 ½ In. 225.00
Urn, Mantel, Flowers, Scrolls, Navy, Gold, White, 11 In., Pair 322.00
Vase, Figural, 2 Girls, c.1840, 10 ½ In. 117.00
Vase, Flowers, Leaves, Gilt, Blue, Rose, 18 x 11 In., Pair 643.00
Vase, Greyhound & Rabbit, Figural, 10 ½ In. 80.00
Vase, Little Red Riding Hood, 19th Century, 10 ½ In., Pair 470.00

STANGL Pottery traces its history back to the Fulper Pottery of New Jersey. In 1910, Johann Martin Stangl started working at Fulper. He left to work at Haeger Pottery from 1915 to 1920. Stangl returned to Fulper Pottery in 1920, became president in 1926, and changed the company name to Stangl Pottery in 1929. Stangl acquired the firm in 1930. The pottery is known for dinnerware and a line of bird figurines. Martin Stangl died in 1972 and the pottery was sold to Frank Wheaton, Jr., of Wheaton Industries. Production continued until 1978, when Pfaltzgraff Pottery purchased the right to the Stangl trademark and the remaining inventory was liquidated. A single bird figurine is identified by a number. Figurines made up of two birds are identified by a number followed by the letter *D* indicating Double.

STANGL

Ashtray, Duck, Flying, No. 3820, 8 In. 90.00
Bird, Bird Of Paradise, No. 3408, 5 In. 80.00
Bird, Blue Headed Vireo, No. 3448, 4 In. 60.00
Bird, Blue Jay With Leaf, No. 3716, Marked, 10 ½ In. 154.00
Bird, Cardinal, On Stump, No. 3444, 6 ½ In. .... 75.00 to 100.00
Bird, Chickadees Group, No. 3581, 5 ¾ x 8 ¼ In. 175.00
Bird, Cockatoo, Green, Yellow, Blue, No. 3580, 9 In. 125.00
Bird, Cockatoo, No. 3564, 12 In. 225.00
Bird, Cockatoos, Double, No. 3405D, 10 In. 125.00
Bird, Hen, Yellow, No. 3446, Incised, 7 ½ In. 100.00
Bird, Hummingbird Group, No. 3599D, 8 ¾ In. 175.00
Bird, Key West Quail Dove, No. 3454, Marked, 8 ¾ In. .... *illus* 121.00
Bird, Parakeets, Blue, Double, No. 3582D, Marked, 7 In. .... 125.00 to 200.00

Bird, Pheasant Hen, No. 3491, Marked, 5 ⅞ x 11 ¼ In. .... *illus* 66.00
Bird, Quail, No. 3458, 7 ⅜ In. 125.00
Bird, White-Crowned Pigeons, Double, No. 3518D 400.00
Fruit & Flowers, Bowl, Fruit, 5 ½ In. 12.00
Fruit & Flowers, Creamer 17.00
Fruit & Flowers, Cup 6.00
Fruit & Flowers, Plate, Dinner, 10 In. 8.00
Fruit & Flowers, Tidbit Tray, Center Handle 13.00
Garden Flower, Jug, Pink Flower, White Ground, Yellow Rim, 2 ½ In. 8.50
Golden Blossom, Cup 8.00
Golden Blossom, Pitcher, Brown Trim, Yellow, c.1964, Qt., 5 In. 48.00
Golden Blossom, Pitcher, c.1968, 5 In. 18.00
Golden Blossom, Plate, Dinner, 10 In. 12.00
Golden Blossom, Plate, Salad, 8 In. 6.50
Golden Harvest, Chop Plate, 12 In. 30.00
Golden Harvest, Cup & Saucer 12.00
Golden Harvest, Plate, Dinner, 10 ¼ In. 10.00
Golden Harvest, Platter, Kidney Shape, 14 In. 25.00
Golden Harvest, Skillet, Open Pan, 1950s, 6 ¾ In. 18.00
Lamp, Wig Head, Woman, Brown Short Hair, Brown Eyes, Electric, Paper Label, 22 In. 160.00
Pitcher & Mug, Franklin D. Roosevelt, Happy Days Are Here Again, Caricature, 1934 .... 950.00
Town & Country, Pitcher, Brown, Signed, 11 In. 30.00
Vase, Phoenician, Brushed Gold, Kay Hackett, c.1962, 9 ½ In. 75.00
Wig Stand, Woman, Blond, Label, 15 In. 110.00
Wig Stand, Woman, Brown Short Hair, Pottery, 15 In. 225.00

STAR TREK AND STAR WARS collectibles are included here. The original *Star Trek* television series ran from 1966 through 1969. The series spawned an animated TV series, three TV sequels, and a TV prequel. The first *Star Trek* movie was released in 1979 and ten others followed, the most recent in 2009. The movie *Star Wars* opened in 1977. Sequels were released in 1980 and 1983; prequels in 1999, 2002, and 2005. Other science fiction and fantasy collectibles can be found under Batman, Buck Rogers, Captain Marvel, Flash Gordon, Movie, Superman, and Toy.

STAR TREK

Display, Hanging USS Enterprise, Cardboard, 1991 Paramount Pictures, 16 x 32 In. 86.00
Lunch Box, Metal, Thermos, Aladdin, c.1968 .... 735.00
Lunch Box, Motion Picture, Metal, 1977 .... 49.00
Model Kit, Galileo Seven Shuttlecraft, Plastic, Box, AMT, 1966 .... 55.00
Model Kit, USS Enterprise, Box, Ertl, 1983 .... 30.00
Photograph, Television Show Cast, Signed By Members, Color, c.1969, 8 x 10 In. 550.00
Pin, Insignia, Round, Punched Elongated Star, Silvertone Metal, 1960s, 1 ½ In. 10.00
Poster, Motion Picture, Starship Enterprise, David Kimble, 1979 .... 10.00
Poster, Motion Picture, There Is No Comparison, 1979, 27 x 41 In. .... *illus* 44.00
Tumbler, Mr. Spock, Taco Bell, 1984, 5 ½ In. 5.00

STAR WARS

Clock, Quartz, Talking Alarm, Bradley Time, Hong Kong, 1984, 9 In. 53.00
Comic Book, Return Of The Jedi, No. 4, Marvel 8.00
Cookie Jar, R2-D2, Roman Ceramics, 1979 .... 72.00 to 88.00
Figure, Bobba Fett, Box, Kenner, 1980, 12 In. 749.00
Figure, Darth Vader, Light Saber, Kenner, 1977, 4 In. 8.00
Figure, General Lando Calrissian, Weapon, Kenner, 1984, 4 In. 57.00
Figure, Han Solo, Box, 12 In. .... *illus* 288.00
Figure, IG-88, Bounty Hunter, Empire Strikes Back, Posable, Kenner, Box, 1980, 15 In. 403.00
Figure, IG-88, Bounty Hunter, On Card, Kenner, 1982, 3 ¾ In. 82.00
Figure, Imperial Gunner, Weapon, Kenner, 3 In. 50.00
Figure, Jawa, Box, Meccano, 1977 .... 90.00
Figure, Jawa, Posable, Cloth Cape, On Empire Card, 2 In. 230.00
Figure, Princess Leia, Box, Meccano, 1977, 12 In. 240.00
Figure, Princess Leia, Posable, On Empire Card, 3 ½ In. 174.00
Figure, R2-D2, Plastic, Die Cast Metal, Box, Japan, c.1978, 4 ¼ In. 115.00
Helmet, Storm Trooper, White Plastic, 1970s 21.00
Lunch Box, Return Of The Jedi, Metal, Thermos, 1983 .... 75.00
Mask, Yoda, Latex, Nose & Mouth, Eyes, Lucafilm Ltd., 1980, Adult Size 100.00
Model Kit, Star Destroyer, Box, Ertl, 1980 .... 31.00
Playset, Death Star Space Station, Box, Kenner, 1977 .... 53.00
Playset, Jabba The Hutt, Plastic, Box, Kenner, 1983 .... 60.00
Poster, Empire Strikes Back, Saga Continues, 1980, 36 x 14 In. .... *illus* 575.00

Star Trek, Poster, Motion Picture, The Human Adventure Is Just Beginning, 1979, 27 x 41 In.
$44.00

Star Wars, Figure, Hans Solo, Box, 12 In.
$288.00

Star Wars, Poster, Empire Strikes Back, Saga Continues, 1980, 36 x 14 In.
$575.00

S

Stein, Character, Kaiser Wilhelm I, Ivory, Tan, Musterschutz, Early 1900s, 7 ¾ In., ½ Liter
$770.00

Stein, Character, Monk, Pottery, Inlaid Lid, ½ Liter
$150.00

High-Priced Copper
A Roycroft copper stein made and marked by Karl Kipp sold for a record $66,000. Roycroft steins are rare, and this one, made by the community's top coppersmith, was in the Arts & Crafts style. It was made of hammered copper with pierced nickel silver bands and four jade cabochons. It sold for $25 in 1911, a very high price for that time, so few were sold.

Poster, Star Wars, Long Time Ago In A Galaxy Far Far Away, 20th Century Fox, 1977, 27 x 41 In. 425.00
Poster, Star Wars, Luke, Han Solo, Leia Shooting, 20th Century Fox, 1977, 27 x 41 In. 550.00
Poster, Star Wars Is Back, 1982, 30 x 40 In. 195.00
Toy, Land Speeder, Die Cast Metal, Palitoy, Box, 1977 ...... 240.00
Toy, Millennium Falcon, Die Cast Metal, Box, Palitoy, 1979 ...... 299.00
Toy, Millennium Falcon, Return Of The Jedi, Plastic, Meccano, Box, 1983 ...... 180.00
Toy, R2-D2, Radio Controlled, Plastic, Battery Operated, Kenner, Box, 1978, 11 x 11 In. 158.00
Toy, Tie Fighter, Die Cast Metal, Box, Original Packaging, Palitoy, 1977 ...... 195.00
Toy, Y-Wing Fighter, Die Cast Metal, Box, Palitoy, 1979 ...... 225.00
Wristwatch, C-3PO & R2-D2 On Face, Gold Metal, Plastic Case, Bradley, 1977 ...... 253.00

STEINS have been used by beer and ale drinkers for over 500 years. They have been made of ivory, porcelain, stoneware, faience, silver, pewter, wood, or glass in sizes up to nine gallons. Although some were made by Mettlach, Meissen, Capo-di-Monte, and other famous factories, most were made by less important German potteries. The words *Geschutz* or *Musterschutz* on a stein are the German words for "patented" or "registered design" not company names. Steins are still being made in the old styles. Lithophane steins may be found in the Lithophane category.

Character, Alligator, Inlaid Lid, E. Bohne & Sohne, ¼ Liter 391.00
Character, Alligator, Inlaid Lid, Porcelain, E. Bohne & Sohne, ½ Liter 633.00
Character, Alligator, Wraparound Stein, Porcelain, E. Bohne Sohne, ⅓ Liter 460.00
Character, Bismarck, Porcelain, Marked, Germany, c.1950, ½ Liter 161.00
Character, Bismarck Radish, Porcelain, Marked, Musterschutz, Schierholz, ½ In. 404.00
Character, Cat, Pottery, Pottery Lid, ½ Liter 138.00
Character, Devil, Inlaid Lid, Porcelain, Marked E. Bohne & Sohne, ½ Liter 431.00
Character, Devil, Pottery, Pottery Lid, ½ Liter 173.00
Character, Devil & Skull, 2-Sided, Porcelain, E. Bohne & Sohne, ¼ Liter 403.00
Character, Dog, Green Hat, Glasses, Pipe, Porcelain, Musterschutz, Schierholz, ½ Liter 299.00
Character, Dog, Porcelain, Marked, Musterschutz, Schierholz, ½ Liter 242.00
Character, Fireman, Pottery, Marked, ½ Liter 173.00
Character, Football, Harvard, Pottery, Pottery Lid, ½ Liter 265.00
Character, Fox, Green Hat, Feather, Porcelain, Marked, Musterschutz, Schierholz, ½ Liter ... 920.00
Character, Frauenkirche Tower, Stoneware, Blue Salt Glaze, ¼ Liter 138.00
Character, Gen. Von Moltke, Enamel, Ivory, Tan, Pewter Thumb Rest, Musterschutz, ½ Liter, 6 ½ In. 770.00
Character, Hops Lady, Porcelain Lid, Marked, Musterschutz, Schierholz, ½ Liter 253.00
Character, Hunter Fox, Pottery, Pottery Lid, ½ Liter 115.00
Character, Hunter Rabbit, Inlaid Lid, Porcelain, R.P.M., ½ Liter 128.00
Character, Indian, Headdress, Porcelain, E. Bohne & Sohne, ⅓ Liter 300.00
Character, Kaiser Wilhelm I, Ivory, Tan, Musterschutz, Early 1900s, 7 ¾ In., ½ Liter ... *illus* 770.00
Character, Lawn Tennis, Etched, Pottery, Pewter Lid, 1914, ½ Liter 374.00
Character, Man, Pottery, Majolica Glaze, ½ Liter 403.00
Character, Man, Shooting, Pottery, Pewter Lid, Schiessleistung April 26, 1895, ½ Liter 150.00
Character, Monk, Pottery, Inlaid Lid, ½ Liter ...... *illus* 150.00
Character, Monkey, Pottery, Pottery Lid, ½ Liter 150.00
Character, Monkey, With Fish, Stoneware, Pottery Inlaid Lid, 1 Liter 431.00
Character, Munich Child, Stoneware, Inlaid Lid, Marked, J. Reinemann, Munchen, ¼ Liter. . 489.00
Character, Pierrot, Mime, Marked, Musterschutz, 8 ¾ In. 2825.00
Character, Pig, Singing, Porcelain, Marked, Musterschutz, ½ Liter 403.00
Character, Rich Man, Pottery, Inlaid Lid, Marked, ½ Liter 161.00
Character, Richard Wagner, Porcelain, Inlaid Lid, Marked, E. Bohne & Sohne, ½ Liter 518.00
Character, Rooster, Porcelain, Marked, Musterschutz, Schierholz, ½ Liter 128.00
Character, Schoolteacher, Porcelain, Lid, Musterschutz, Schierholz, ½ Liter 2185.00
Character, Skull, Porcelain, Inlaid Ring, E. Bohne & Sohne, ½ Liter 265.00
Character, Skull, Porcelain, Schierholtz, ½ Liter 518.00
Character, Skull & Devil, Porcelain, Inlaid Lid, E. Bohne & Sohne, ¼ Liter 270.00
Character, Student, Porcelain, Inlaid Lid, Marked, Bruder Tannhauser, Munchen, ½ Liter .. 1380.00
Character, Tower, Stoneware, Pewter Lid, Marked, ½ Liter 374.00
Character, Umbrella Men, Porcelain, Silver Plated Lid, ½ Liter 322.00
Character, Uncle Sam, Porcelain, Marked, Musterschutz, Schierholz, ½ Liter 159.00
Character, Wilhelm I, Porcelain, Marked, Musterschutz, Schierholz, ½ Liter 891.00
Character, Wilhelm II, Porcelain, Marked, Musterschutz, ½ Liter 3105.00
Character, Woman, Porcelain, Lid, Musterschutz, Schierholz, ½ Liter 460.00
Faience, Flowers, Hand Painted, Creamware, Pewter Lid, c.1820, 8 In. 403.00
Fresh Water Fishing, Hinged Lid, Avon, 8 ½ x 6 In. 15.00
Glass, Blown, Clear, Applied Amber Prunts, Engraved, Pewter Lid, ½ Liter 173.00
Glass, Blown, Cranberry, Ribbed, Pewter Overlay, Inlaid Lid, ½ Liter 213.00
Glass, Blown, Fireman, Bronze Inlaid Lid, Fireman Thumblift, ½ Liter 145.00

S

Glass, Blown, Green Opaline, Gilt Mounts, Inlaid Lid, c.1850, ½ Liter 1150.00
Glass, Blown, Pink, Threading, Pewter Base, Lid, ½ Liter 138.00
Glass, Blown, Pink Cased, Inlaid Lid, Handle, ½ Liter 115.00
Glass, Blown, Pink To Clear, Threading, Pewter Base, Lid, ½ Liter 138.00
Glass, Blown, Red On Clear Overlay, Inlaid Lid, c.1880, 3 Liter 1380.00
Glass, Blown, Ruby, Cut, Rounded Facets, Gilt, Inlaid Lid, c.1840, ½ Liter 518.00
Glass, Blown, Ruby Flashed, Wheel-Engraved, Inlaid Glass Lid, c.1870, ½ Liter 161.00
Mettlach steins are listed in the Mettlach category.
Occupational, Bergmann, Porcelain, Transfer, Enamel, Pewter Lid, ½ Liter 301.00
Occupational, Blacksmith, Porcelain, Transfer, Enamel, Pewter Lid, Wurzburg, 1913, ½ Liter 276.00
Occupational, Cooper, Porcelain, Transfer, Enamel, Pewter Lid, ½ Liter 299.00
Occupational, Glaser, Porcelain, Transfer, Enamel, Pewter Lid, Glaser-Meister, 1898, ½ Liter 403.00
Occupational, Kraftwagenfuhrer, Porcelain, Transfer, Enamel, Pewter Lid, 1936, ½ Liter 891.00
Occupational, Kufer, Porcelain, Transfer, Enamel, Pewter Lid, ½ Liter 357.00
Occupational, Maler, Painter, Stoneware, Transfer, Enamel, Pewter Lid, Lion Thumblift, ½ Liter 265.00
Occupational, Maurer, Porcelain, Transfer, Enamel, Pewter Lid, ½ Liter 345.00
Occupational, Schreiner, Porcelain, Transfer, Enamel, Pewter Lid, ½ Liter 196.00
Occupational, Senner, Alpine Dairyman, Pewter Lid, Sennerei I, Allgauer Alpen, ½ Liter 518.00
Pewter, Apostle Figures, Leaf Border, Brown Medallion, Germany, 6 In.. .... 948.00
Pewter, Deer, Engraved, c.1820, 1 Liter 161.00
Pewter, Impressed, Enamel Accents, Blue, Gray, Pewter Lid, Wicker Handle, Liberty & Co., 5 x 6 In. 180.00
Porcelain, Faust's Own, Hand Painted, Inlaid Lid, ½ Liter 219.00
Porcelain, Waterfall Scene, Transfer, Pewter Lid, ¼ Liter 127.00
Porcelain, Windmills, Hand Painted, ½ Liter 196.00
Pottery, Angel, Paschal Lamb, Relief, Pewter Base, Lid, Creussen, c.1880, ½ Liter, 7 In. 482.00
Pottery, Anti-Semitic Scenes, Relief, Inlaid Lid, Musterschutz, Jacob Gref, ½ Liter 1495.00
Pottery, Birch Tree, Stag, Figural Pottery Lid, 2 ½ Liter 115.00
Pottery, Chess Game At Tavern, Pewter, Figural Inlaid Lid, ½ Liter 138.00
Regimental, Roster, 1 Comp., Bayr., Fuss Artl. Regt. Nr. 1neu-Ulm, Porcelain, 1902-04, ½ Liter 489.00
Regimental, Roster, 2 Comp., Inft., Regt. Nr. 145, Metz, Porcelain, 1908-10, ½ Liter 311.00
Regimental, Roster, 5 Comp., Inft. Regt. Nr. 166, Hanau, Porcelain, 1902-04, ½ Liter 322.00
Regimental, Roster, 12 Comp., Bayr., Inft. Regt. Nr. 14, Nurnberg, Porcelain, 1909, ½ Liter .. 661.00
Regimental, Roster, Eagle Thumbprint, Ketteniss, Glass, 1903-06, ½ Liter, 10 In. 1495.00
Regimental, Roster, Eagle Thumbprint, R. Schroder, Pottery, 1907-09, ½ Liter, 12 In. 1380.00
Regimental, Roster, F. Ziegele, Wren Thumblift, Porcelain, 1904-06, ½ Liter, 10 In. 345.00
Regimental, Roster, R. Hoffmann, Eagle Thumbprint, Porcelain, 1905-07, ½ Liter, 12 In. 334.00
Silver On Copper, Coin Design, Relief, Crown Finial, c.1880, 1 ½ Liter 1006.00
Stoneware, Bicycle, Transfer, Enamel, Pewter Lid, Radfahr-Blub Nord West, 1908, ½ Liter 230.00
Stoneware, Dancing Gnomes, Relief, Empire Theatre, Blue Glaze, Pewter Lid, Whites, Utica, 1 Liter 184.00
Stoneware, R. Riemerschmid, Blue Salt Glaze, Threading, Pewter Lid, 1769, 2 Liter 1208.00
Stoneware, Revolutionary War Scene, Blue Pewter Lid, White's, New York, 11 In. 299.00
Stoneware, Woman, Blue Glaze, Pewter Lid, White's, Utica, New York, ½ Liter 161.00
Third Reich, Eagle Carrying Swastika, Pottery, Pewter Lid With Relief Helmet, ½ Liter 690.00
Third Reich, Labor Co. Insignia, Brown, Stoneware, Wood Lid, ½ Liter 201.00
Third Reich, Nazi Flag, 3 Soldiers, Pulverberg, Coburg, Pottery, Pewter Lid, ½ Liter 345.00
Third Reich, Soldier, Swastika Relief Helmet, Cannon, Text, Pottery, Pewter Lid, ½ Liter 299.00
Third Reich, Soldiers With Binoculars, Regensburg Scene, Porcelain, Pewter Lid, ½ Liter 403.00
Tin, Flowers, Blue Manganese Trees, Pewter Rim, Cover, Germany, 7 ⅜ In. .... *illus* 250.00
Tin, Flowers, Leaves, Multicolored Glaze, Pewter Foot Rim, Hinged Lid, Thumb Rest, 8 In. 207.00

STEREO CARDS that were made for stereoscope viewers became popular after 1840. Two almost identical pictures were mounted on a stiff cardboard backing so that, when viewed through a stereoscope, a three-dimensional picture could be seen. Value is determined by maker and by subject. These cards were made in quantity through the 1930s.

A Hurried Toilet, No. 83, Griffith & Griffith 8.00
A Light Lunch, No. 76, Griffith & Griffith 7.00
Beautiful Upper Falls, Yellowstone Park, H.C. White Co., North Bennington, Vt., 1904 .... 75.00
Bliss Very Much Disturbed, No. 88, Griffith & Griffith 8.00
Bunker Hill Monument, Boston Harbor, c.1930 .... 35.00
Camel & Baby, Sphinx, Pyramid 18.00
Gems Of German Life, Kendrick & Co. 5.00
Getting Ready For The Masquerade, Color 9.00
Girl, 12 Puppies, Keystone, c.1907 .... 18.00
Grand Canyon, H.C. White Co., North Bennington, Vt., 1906 .... 100.00
Her Guardian Angel, No. 619, Keystone 24.00
Homecoming Soldier, Fathers Holding Newborns, World War II 16.00

Stein Catalog Definitions

Definitions used by Stein collectors and dealers—

Enamel: painted decoration, usually on glass

Gasthaus: a bar or inn that serves food

Mkd.: marked

P.U.G: print under glaze, similar to a transfer

Tang: the pewter part from the hinge to the lid

Stein, Tin, Flowers, Blue Manganese Trees, Pewter Rim, Cover, Germany, 7 ⅜ In.
$250.00

TIP

Buy a paint-by-number kit to get an inexpensive assortment of paint colors to use for touch-ups and restorations for paintings and furniture.

Stereoscope, Brewster-Type, Mahogany, Brass Label, Unis France
$77.00

Steuben, Bottle, Toilet Water, Oriental Orchid, Opalescent Ribs, Flower Stopper, 4 ¾ In.
$660.00

Steuben, Bowl, Amethyst, Swirled Center, Everted Rolled Rim, Signed, 12 In.
$140.00

Steuben, Bowl, Centerpiece, Flower Frog, Asian Woman, Rosaline, Calcite, 10 x 12 In.
$1380.00

TIP
Wooden drawers and cardboard boxes contain acids and resins that can harm textiles.

House, Woman On Porch, Child & Man Near Fence 28.00
Indian Mothers & Their Babies, Norman A. Forsyth, 1906 ..... 100.00
Jackson Square, New Orleans, No. 33936, Keystone 22.00
Japanese Women Feeding Silkworms 5.00
King Of The Beasts In Captivity, Keystone 16.00
Monk At Table, Rat On Floor 5.00
NYC Castle Garden, Battery Park, c.1904-20 ..... 25.00
Oft In The Stilly Night, No. 77, Griffith & Griffith 6.00
Playing Rainstorm On Momma's Parlor Carpet, American Stereoscope Co., 1897 ..... 8.00
Rosin On The Docks, No. 13722, Keystone 32.00
Snake Chiefs, Indians, Standing In Front Of Teepee, O.C. Smith, N.Y., c.1860 ..... 500.00
Stolen Sweets, No. 84, Griffith & Griffith 7.00
Victorian Ghost Parlor, Only A Dream, Keystone, c.1898 ..... 6.00
William Harrison, Captain Of Great Eastern, At Lifeboat, London Stereoscopic Co. 400.00
World's Fair Grand Fountain, 1904 ..... 5.00

STEREOSCOPES were used for viewing stereo cards. The hand viewer was invented by Oliver Wendell Holmes, although more complicated table models were used before his was produced in 1859. Do not confuse the stereoscope with the stereopticon, a magic lantern that used glass slides.

A. Mattey, Unis, Walnut, Scenes, Unis France, c.1930 ..... 4900.00
Black Ebony, Folding, France, c.1890 ..... 595.00
Brewster-Type, Mahogany, Brass Label, Unis France ..... *illus* 77.00
Burl Walnut, Ebony, Tulip, Mahogany, Inlay 1125.00
Burl Walnut Veneer, France, c.1880 ..... 1250.00
Dark Burl Wood, Inlay, Table Top Model 2400.00
Etched Face, Wood Handles, 12 In., 10 Cards 138.00
Keystone, Eye Doctor's, Arizona Dept. Of Corrections 650.00
Le Taxiphote, Wood, c.1900, 19 ½ x 11 In. 425.00
Metal, Adjustable Stand, 11 ½ In., 9 Cards 250.00
Tiger Maple, Hinged Handle, c.1875, 12 ¾ In. 50.00
Underwood & Underwood, N.Y., Wood, Tin, Hand Stamped Design, Folding Handle, 1901 ..... 30.00
Underwood & Underwood, Patented June 11, 1901 ..... 35.00
Underwood & Underwood, Vatican, Pope, Palaces, Box, 48 Piece 53.00
Underwood & Underwood, Walnut, June 11, 1901, 10 Cards 125.00
Verascope, Mahogany, c.1910, 4 ¼ x 1 ¾ In. 150.00
Verascope, Mahogany, Unis France, c.1910 ..... 150.00
Wood, Painted Flowers, Black Lacquered Ground, France, c.1860 ..... 613.00

STERLING SILVER, *see Silver-Sterling category.*

STEUBEN glass was made at the Steuben Glass Works of Corning, New York. The factory, founded by Frederick Carder and T.G. Hawkes, Sr., was purchased by the Corning Glass Company. In 2008 Steuben became Steuben Glass LLC, part of the Schottenstein Luxury Group, a division of Schottenstein Stores Corp. Corning holds an equity stake in Steuben. Many types of art glass were made at Steuben. The firm is still making exceptional quality glass but it is clear, modern-style glass. Additional pieces may be found in the Aurene, Cluthra, and Perfume Bottle categories.

Basket, Clear, Pinched, Twisted Rosa Handle, Signed, 5 ½ In. 230.00
Bottle, Mouth Wash, Oriental Orchid, Flower Stopper, c.1926 ..... 3105.00
Bottle, Toilet Water, Amber, Rectangular, Flower Stopper, 5 ¼ In. 575.00
Bottle, Toilet Water, Oriental Orchid, Opalescent Ribs, Flower Stopper, 4 ¾ In. ..... *illus* 660.00
Bowl, Acid Cutback, Chinese Pattern, Blue Jade, Over Flint White, 10 In. 1208.00
Bowl, Acid Cutback, Chinese Pattern, Rosaline, Over Alabaster, c.1920, 10 In. 1067.00
Bowl, Acid Cutback, Oriental Symbol, Flowers, Green To Alabaster, 13 In. 1400.00
Bowl, Amber, Swirls, Cone Shape, 10 In. 115.00
Bowl, Amethyst, Swirled Center, Everted Rolled Rim, Signed, 12 In. ..... *illus* 140.00
Bowl, Amethyst, Swirls, Footed, Flared Rolled Rim, Signed, 12 In. 144.00
Bowl, Centerpiece, Cintra Orange, Blue Ring Handles, Rim, Base, 9 In. 1840.00
Bowl, Centerpiece, Clear, Oval, Free-Form Foot, Signed, 10 In. 431.00
Bowl, Centerpiece, Flower Frog, Asian Woman, Rosaline, Calcite, 10 x 12 In. ..... *illus* 1380.00
Bowl, Centerpiece, Gold Calcite, Rolled Flared Rim, 14 In. 1150.00
Bowl, Centerpiece, Grotesque, Clear, c.1930, 5 x 5 x 9 In. 176.00
Bowl, Centerpiece, Pink Swirl, 5 ¼ x 14 In. ..... *illus* 1755.00
Bowl, Cintra Yellow, Flattened Rim, Rosa Ball Feet, 12 In. 1035.00
Bowl, Clear, Eagle & Globe, Engraved, Box, 10 ¾ x 9 ¾ In. 12870.00

Bowl, Clear, Elongated, Signed, 11 ¼ In. 200.00
Bowl, Clear, Oblong, Applied Feet, 5 x 9 In. 146.00
Bowl, Clear, Scroll Feet, 7 ¼ x 9 ¼ In. 468.00
Bowl, Clear, Swan, Box, c.1985, 8 In. 25740.00
Bowl, Clear, Tranquility, Footed, 5 x 13 In. 614.00
Bowl, Clear, Transportation, Engraved, c.1942, 6 ¼ x 7 ½ In. 4388.00
Bowl, Clear, Trillium, 9 In. 88.00
Bowl, Clear, Wide Lip, Leaf Base, 8 x 12 In. 213.00
Bowl, Cyprian, Applied Blue Rim, Footed, 3 x 4 In. 173.00
Bowl, Floret, Clear, 3 ¼ x 7 ¾ In. 105.00
Bowl, Grotesque, Clear, Scalloped Edge, 7 x 8 ½ x 13 In. 351.00
Bowl, Opaque Yellow Center, Flared Rim, 14 x 4 In. 201.00
Bowl, Plum Jade, Oriental Medallions, Oval, Flared Rim, 8 ½ In. 2300.00
Bowl, Underplate, Amber, Grapes, Engraved, c.1930, 5 x 6 ⅞ In. 293.00
Bowl, Underplate, Green To Clear, Leafy Stemmed Thistles, 6 In. 489.00
Candlestick, Amethyst, Topaz, Lobbed Stem, 12 In, Pair. 1150.00
Candlestick, Blue, Clear, c.1925, 10 In. *illus* 351.00
Candlestick, Blue, Ribbed Baluster, 10 In. 283.00
Candlestick, Calcite, Twist Stem, Footed, Gold Aurene Edge, 10 In. 805.00
Candlestick, Celeste Blue, Amber, Optic Ribbed, Rolled Edge, 12 In., Pair. 690.00
Candlestick, Clear, Bud Shape Cup, Bubble Stem, Beaded Bobeche, Signed, 4 ¾ In., Pair. 180.00
Candlestick, Clear, Leafy Teardrop, 8 ½ In., Pair. 526.00
Candlestick, Clear, Random Bubbles, Applied Amethyst Threading, 4 ½ In. 115.00
Candlestick, Gold Ruby Cups, Clear, Cone Shape Foot, Twist Stems, 6 In., Pair 288.00
Chandelier, 4-Light, Arts & Crafts, Bronze, 35 x 22 ½ In. 4500.00
Chandelier, 5-Light, White, Gold, Green Pulled-Wave Shades, Metal Ribbed Bowl, Hardware, 33 In. 1680.00
Cocktail Mixer, Black Threading, c.1920, 10 ¼ In. 1053.00
Cologne, Oriental Orchid, Opalescent Stripes, Band, Flower Petal Stopper, 5 ½ In. 2300.00
Cologne, Topaz, Melon Ribbed, French Blue Foot, Lip Wrap, 3 ½ In. 575.00
Compote, Amethyst To Clear, Fruit, Apple Core Stem, Engraved, 8 x 8 ½ In. 175.00
Compote, Blue Jade, Flared Rim, Cone Shape Foot, 12 In. 4600.00
Compote, Bristol Yellow, Optic Swirl, Signed, 7 In. 288.00
Compote, Calcite, Gold Aurene Interior, Knopped Stem, 8 In. 403.00
Compote, Clear, Controlled Bubbles, Green Thread, Scalloped Rim, Teardrop Stem, 5 ⅝ x 8 In. 288.00
Compote, French Blue, Hollow Stem, Swirled Wafer Foot, 6 ¾ x 6 ¾ In. 150.00
Compote, Gold Calcite, Flared Rim, 8 x 10 In. 489.00
Compote, Green, Spiral Threaded Bowl, Bubble Stem, Signed, 7 x 7 In., Pair 225.00
Compote, Mirror Black, Flared Foot, Wide Cupped Rim, 12 In. 1205.00
Compote, Pink, Diamond Optic, Opalescent Foot, Stem, 6 In. 920.00
Console Set, Amber, Celeste Blue, c.1925, 3 Piece 877.00
Console Set, Green, c.1925, 3 Piece 644.00
Cordial, Calcite, Gold Interior, 4 ½ In. 259.00
Decanter, Clear, Moon Stopper, 4 Rings, 1942, 10 x 7 ¼ In. 570.00
Decanter, Clear, Ship's, 10 ¼ In. 205.00
Decanter, Clear, Stopper, Eagle, 1973, 10 ⅜ x 5 ½ In. 360.00
Figurine, Apple, 4 ½ In. 292.00
Figurine, Apple Of Eden, 18K Gold Stem, Leaf & Worm, 6 x 3 In. 1638.00 to 1755.00
Figurine, Butterfly, 18K Gold Mounts, Box, 2 ½ In. 1521.00
Figurine, Dolphin, Clear, 5 ¼ x 9 In. *illus* 400.00
Figurine, Eagle, Spread Wings, Clear, 3 ¼ In. 117.00 to 322.00
Figurine, Elephant, Raised Trunk, Clear, Signed, 8 In. 474.00
Figurine, Hand Cooler, Dog, Signed, Lloyd Atkins, 3 ⅜ x 2 In. 200.00
Figurine, Koala, Clear, 8 In. 819.00
Figurine, Mouse & Cheese, James Houston, 1975, 3 ⅞ In. 2574.00
Figurine, Mushroom, Clear, 18K Gold Butterfly, 3 ½ x 3 ¾ In. 1287.00
Figurine, Owl, Clear, Donald Pollard, 5 In. 330.00 to 410.00
Figurine, Pheasants, Ringneck, Clear, 6 ½ x 13 ½ In., Pair 1265.00
Figurine, Porpoise, Clear, 5 x 9 In. 351.00
Figurine, Seahorse, 6 x 7 In. 1053.00
Figurine, Swan, Clear, Allover Gold, Ruby Threading, 7 In. 633.00
Finger Bowl, Underplate, Vaseline, Grapes, Engraved, Signed, 2 ¾ x 7 In. 250.00
Flower Frog, Asian Woman, Flowers, Emerald Green, 9 In. 518.00
Flower Frog, Asian Woman, Flowers, Moonstone, 9 In. 863.00
Flower Frog, Fish In Coral, Celeste Blue, 2 Tiers, 2 ¼ In. 546.00
Flower Frog, Kneeling Nude Woman, Clear, Silver Base, 8 In. 920.00
Flower Frog, Quan Yin, Pomona Green, 9 In. *illus* 1840.00
Flower Frog, Yellow, 2-Tier, 16 Looped Holders, 11 ½ In. 690.00

Steuben, Bowl, Centerpiece, Pink Swirl, 5 ¼ x 14 In.
$1755.00

Steuben, Candlestick, Blue, Clear, c.1925, 10 In.
$351.00

Steuben, Figurine, Dolphin, Clear, 5 ¼ x 9 In.
$400.00

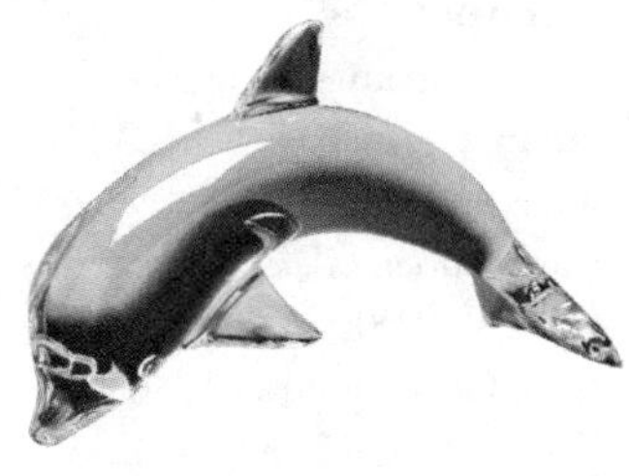

Steuben, Flower Frog, Quan Yin, Pomona Green, 9 In.
$1840.00

Steuben, Plaque, Kneeling Woman, Amber, 9 In.
$1150.00

Steuben, Sculpture, Stars & Stripes, Clear, 4 x 4 In.
$1404.00

Steuben Glass

The company that makes Steuben glass has changed its name many times. It was Steuben Glass Works (1903–1918); Steuben Division, Corning Glass Works (1918–1933); Steuben Glass Inc. (1933–1958); Steuben Glass, Division of Corning Glass Works (1958–1989); and Steuben Glass Division of Corning Inc. (1989–2008). On July 23, 2008, Steuben was sold to Schottenstein Stores Corp., which will operate it as Steuben Glass LLC. Manufacturing in Corning, New York will continue.

S

Ginger Jar, Cover, White Hearts, Vines, Shaded Platinum Blue, Transparent Maize Knop, 9 In. 3600.00
Goblet, Opal, Cintra Stem, Block Signed, 6 In., Pair 230.00
Goblet, Rosaline, Alabaster, Engraved, c.1920, 8 ½ In., 16 Piece 23400.00
Goblet Set, Selenium Red, Cut Facets, 6 In., 8 Piece 719.00
Lamp, Acid Cutback, Acanthus, Rosa Leaves, Green Cintra, 4-Footed Metal Base, 27 In. 1955.00
Lamp, Acid Cutback, Green Texture, Gold Aurene Drips, Metal Stem, Base, Oval, 23 In. 2013.00
Lamp, Acid Cutback, Indian, Mirror Black, Green, Metal Flower Base, 26 In. 1495.00
Lamp, Cone, Blue Mottled, Green, Gold, Amethyst, Urn Shape, 26 In. 2588.00
Lamp, Kerosene, Demonic Masks, Tangled Vines, Hoofed Tripod Base, 14 ½ In. 518.00
Lamp, Luminor, Leaping Gazelle, Wave, Clear, Frosted, Cage Shape Pillar, Prisms, 14 ½ x 10 ½ In. 720.00
Lamp, Pulled Heart, Vine, Gold Opal Shade, Curved Metal Shaft, Base, 12 In. 523.00
Lamp, Torchere, Moss Agate Shade, Green, Amber, Red, Brass Base, Twisted Riser, 9 x 2 In., Pair. 12650.00
Lamp Base, Acid Cutback, Flowers, Rose Quartz, 31 In. 3278.00
Lamp Base, Green Jade, Applied Alabaster Ornament, 24 In. 288.00
Lamp Base, Green Jade, Stick, Bulbous Shape, Alabaster Swirled Neck, 11 ½ In. 144.00
Mug, Green Jade, Alabaster, 6 In., 6 Piece 644.00
Paperweight, Cane Twist, 3 ¼ In. 146.00
Paperweight, Excalibur, Clear, Silver Sword Letter Opener, James Houston, Box, 4 ½ In. 550.00
Paperweight, Seashell, 3 ½ In. 205.00
Perfume Bottle, Green Jade, Fig Shape, Flame Stopper, Dabber, 4 ⅝ In. 375.00
Perfume Bottle, Oriental Poppy, Opalescent Ribbing, White Satin Stopper, 10 In. 4800.00
Perfume Bottle, Pomona Green, Footed, Teardrop Stopper, 6 ½ In. 500.00
Pitcher, Footed, Scroll Handle, 8 ½ In. 380.00
Pitcher, Green Jade, Alabaster, 9 ½ x 8 In. 1521.00
Pitcher, Rosaline, Alabaster Handle, Diamond Point Pattern, 6 ½ In. 360.00
Plaque, Kneeling Woman, Amber, 9 In. .... *illus.* 1150.00
Plate, Alabaster, Swirled, 10 ⅞ In., 12 Piece 3803.00
Plate, Blue, 8 ½ In. 518.00
Plate, Clear, Gold Ruby Flower Garland Border, 9 In. 345.00
Plate, Clear, Grouse, Engraved, 1940s, 10 In. 259.00
Plate, Clear, Snowy Owl, Engraved, Signed, c.1946, 10 In. 500.00
Plate, Mirror Black, Signed, 8 ½ In., Pair 920.00
Plate, Oriental Jade, Swirled Stripes, Opalescent, 9 In. 460.00
Plate, Rosaline, Engraved, c.1920, 8 ⅜ In., 16 Piece 5850.00
Plate, Selenium Red, 9 In. 575.00
Platter, Ivrene, Optic Ribbed, Scalloped Rim, 15 In. 345.00
Powder Jar, Cover, Blue, Oval, 4 In. 1725.00
Puff Box, Cover, French Blue, Optic Ribbed, Bulbous, Diamond Finial, 6 In. 460.00
Salt, Gold Calcite, Footed, 1 ¾ In., Pair 230.00
Sculpture, Arctic Fisherman, James Houston, 6 ½ In. 3510.00
Sculpture, Castle Of Dreams, Clear, 6 x 10 x 5 ½ In. .... 1989.00 to 3510.00
Sculpture, Cathedral, Clear, 15 In. 7020.00
Sculpture, Cupola With Golden Whale, Clear, James Houston, 8 In. 3510.00
Sculpture, Excalibur, James Houston, 8 In. 1053.00
Sculpture, Ice Hunter In Kayak, 6 In. 3510.00
Sculpture, New Colossus, Script, Clear, 9 In. 1521.00
Sculpture, Nosegay, Clear, Engraved, 6 ¾ x 6 ½ In. 5265.00
Sculpture, Pyramidon, Clear, 7 ½ x 4 In. 1521.00
Sculpture, Shooting Star, Clear, c.1986, 5 In. 878.00
Sculpture, Stars & Stripes, Clear, 4 x 4 In. .... *illus* 1404.00
Shade, Calcite, Gold Aurene Feathers, Pulled Hooked Borders, Ruffled Rims, 5 ¼ In., Pair ... 403.00
Shade, Calcite, Gold Wave, Gold Iridescent Interior, 12 In. 2875.00
Shade, Calcite, Green Pulled Loop, 4 ¾ x 5 In. 173.00
Shade, Calcite, Pulled Leaves, Vines, Gold, Green, 5 x 4 In. 180.00
Shade, Gold Calcite, Ribbed, Scalloped Rim, 11 In., 4 Piece 403.00
Shade, Trumpet, Calcite, Gold Hooked Feather Design, 6 ½ In. 345.00
Sherbet, Underplate, Rosaline, Alabaster, 6 In. 173.00
Sherbet, Underplate, Yellow Jade, 4 In. 345.00
Sugar, Creamer, Clear, Scroll Handles, 4 x 5 In. 176.00
Sugar & Creamer, Clear, Scrolling Handles, Irene Benton, c.1943, 5 ¼ In. 156.00
Tazza, Flemish Blue, 3 ½ In. 144.00
Tile, Cruise Liner Ventilation Grate, Bristol Yellow, Fleur-De-Lis, Wheel, 10 In. 1610.00
Tumbler, Lemonade, Topaz, Celeste Blue Handle, Footed, 6 In. 167.00
Urn, Clear, Trail Driver, Engraved, Box, 10 x 10 In. 10530.00
Urn, Cover, Clear, The Sciences, Engraved, c.1943, 11 ¾ x 5 In. 1521.00
Urn, Cover, Valor Cup, Engraved, 15 x 11 In. 1120.00
Vase, Acid Cutback, Acanthus, Rose Quartz, 10 ½ In. 2588.00
Vase, Acid Cutback, Center Lily, Leaves, Green Jade, 9 x 6 In. 633.00

Vase, Acid Cutback, Dragon, Green Jade, Alabaster, 10 In. 2185.00
Vase, Acid Cutback, Flowers, Leaves, Green Jade Over Yellow Jade, 7 ¾ In. 2875.00
Vase, Acid Cutback, Flowers, Rosaline Over Alabaster, Oval, Ball, 7 In. 2013.00
Vase, Acid Cutback, Flowers, Stems, Green Jade, Alabaster, c.1910, 9 In. 885.00
Vase, Acid Cutback, Grapevine, Leaves, Stems, Grape Clusters, Alabaster, 14 In. 1265.00
Vase, Acid Cutback, Japanese Pattern, Green Jade, Alabaster, 7 x 8 In. 920.00
Vase, Acid Cutback, Matzu, Green, Gingko Branches, Clouds, Oval, 7 In. 550.00
Vase, Acid Cutback, Pussy Willows, Alabaster, Mirror Black, Stalactite Border, 6 In. *illus* 1395.00
Vase, Acid Cutback, Sculptured, Green Jade Over Alabaster, 10 In. 1610.00
Vase, Acid Cutback, Valeria, Art Deco Flowers, Alabaster, 9 ½ In. 1150.00
Vase, Acid Cutback, Yellow, Sculptured, Green Jade, 8 In. *illus* 2300.00
Vase, Amethyst, Ribbed, Footed, 10 In. 288.00
Vase, Blue, Swirled, Bulbous, Flared Rim, 6 ¾ x 5 ½ In. 850.00
Vase, Blue Calcite, 5 x 6 In. 748.00
Vase, Blue Jade, Bulbous, Flared Rim, 6 ½ x 7 In. 4025.00
Vase, Bristol Yellow, Footed, Fluted, Ruffled Rim, Signed, 1900s, 9 ⅛ In. 239.00
Vase, Bud, Clear, Teardrop, 8 In. 146.00
Vase, Calcite, Gold Interior, 8 ½ In. 288.00
Vase, Calcite, Ruffled Edge, Gold Interior, 5 In. 230.00
Vase, Clear, Bubbles, Applied Blue Threading, 7 ¾ In. 120.00
Vase, Clear, Envy, 7 ¼ x 4 ¾ In. 995.00
Vase, Cornucopia, Green Jade, Flower Swag, Engraved, Ruffled Rim, 8 ½ In. 546.00
Vase, Fan, Amber, Blue Foot, c.1920, 11 x 9 In. 761.00
Vase, Fan, Amber, Optic Ribbed, Engraved Flowers, Pomona Green Foot, 11 In. 288.00
Vase, Fan, Bristol Yellow, Optic Ribbed, Footed, 8 ¼ In. 86.00
Vase, Fan, Honey Amber, Pomona Green Foot, Signed, 8 ½ In. 375.00
Vase, Fan, Ivrene, Cone Shape Foot, 9 In. 225.00
Vase, Fan, Spanish Green, Controlled Bubbles, Threading, 8 ½ In. 115.00
Vase, Flower Form, Ivrene, Tricornered Rim, 12 x 5 ¼ In. 700.00
Vase, French Blue, Urn Shape, Footed, Ring Handles, Signed, 10 In. 1064.00
Vase, Green, Urn Shape, Signed, 5 In. 403.00
Vase, Green Jade, Alabaster, Footed, c.1920, 9 x 4 ¾ In. 527.00
Vase, Green Jade, Alabaster Handles, Flared, Rolled Rim, 10 In. 1380.00
Vase, Green Jade, Bulbous, Flared Mouth, 4 Alabaster Handles, 10 In. 1150.00
Vase, Green Jade, Signed, 6 ¾ In. 403.00
Vase, Grotesque, Amethyst To Clear, Fan Shape, 9 ¼ In. 267.00
Vase, Grotesque, Blue, Square, Rim, c.1930, 6 ¾ In. 600.00
Vase, Grotesque, Clear, Ribbed, Footed, Wavy Rim, 7 In. 144.00
Vase, Grotesque, Jade, Alabaster, 9 x 12 ½ In. 1404.00
Vase, Ivory, c.1920, 10 ¼ x 9 In. 633.00 to 936.00
Vase, Ivory, Swirled, Clear Bubbles, Bulbous, Flared, 8 In. 990.00
Vase, Ivrene, Pink & Blue Highlights, Ribbed, 5 In. 150.00
Vase, Lily, 3-Flower, Ivrene, c.1930, 12 ½ In. 2106.00
Vase, Oriental Jade, Green, Amber Opalescent Stripes, Oval, 7 In. 2013.00
Vase, Oriental Poppy, Pink Opalescent Stripes, Oval, 7 In. 3565.00
Vase, Rosaline, Alabaster, Footed, 7 x 5 ¾ In. 1170.00
Vase, Rosaline, Urn Shape, Alabaster Foot, 5 In. 489.00
Vase, Ruby, Footed, Flared Rim, Diamond Optic, Clear Ring Handles, 10 In. 575.00
Vase, Silveria, Diamond Optic, 7 In. 460.00
Vase, Teardrop, Bubble, Signed, David Hills, c.1949, 8 In. 315.00
Vase, Topaz, Gingko Branch Silver Overlay, Footed, Flower Form, Urn Shape, 5 In. 201.00
Vase, Tree Trunk, 3-Prong, Amber, 6 In. *illus* 410.00
Vase, Tree Trunk, 3-Prong, Clear, Signed, 6 ¼ In. 269.00
Vase, Trumpet, Calcite, Ruffled Rim, Blue Aurene Interior, 10 In. 1265.00
Vase, Trumpet, Celeste Blue, Optic Ribbed, Scalloped Rim, 10 In. 259.00
Vase, Trumpet, Light Blue Jade, Footed, Flared Rim, 8 In. 1150.00
Vase, Trumpet, Pomona Green, Footed, Twist Optic, Tricornered Rim, 8 In. 230.00
Vase, Tyrian, Gold Iridescence, Pulled Leaf, Vine, Green, Purple Ground, 10 In. 25000.00
Vase, Wisteria, Wide Optic Ribs, Flared Rim, 6 ½ In. 403.00
Verre De Soie, Bowl, Centerpiece, 2 ¾ x 9 ¾ In. 410.00
Wine, Blue, Reeded, c.1920, 8 ½ In., 10 Piece. 2340.00
Wine Cooler, Clear, Square Base, Scroll Handles, 12 ¾ x 9 ¾ In., Pair 1287.00

STEVENGRAPHS are woven pictures made like fancy ribbons. They were manufactured by Thomas Stevens of Coventry, England, and became popular in 1862. Most are marked *Woven in silk by Thomas Stevens* or were mounted on a cardboard that tells the story of the Stevengraph. Other similar ribbon pictures have been made in England and Germany.

Steuben, Vase, Acid Cutback, Pussy Willows, Alabaster, Mirror Black, Stalactite Border, 6 In.
$1395.00

Steuben, Vase, Acid Cutback, Yellow, Sculptured, Green Jade, 8 In.
$2300.00

Steuben, Vase, Tree Trunk, 3-Prong, Amber, 6 In.
$410.00

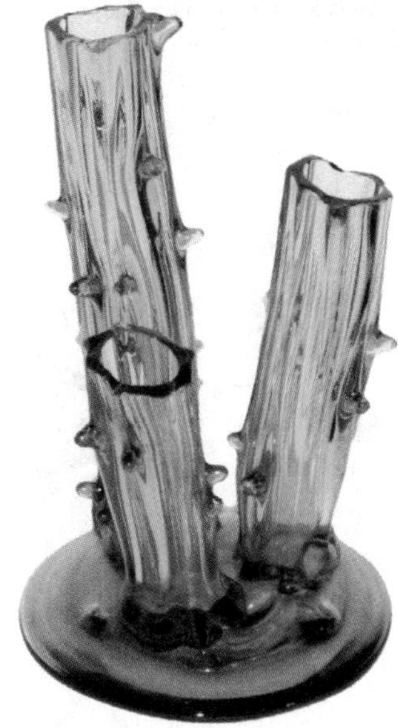

S

Stevens & Williams, Bowl, White Flowers, Leaves, Red Satin, Cameo, 5 In.
$425.00

Stevens & Williams, Bowl, Yellow, Red Pulled Waves, Pink Interior, Oval, John Northwood, 9 In.
$945.00

Stevens & Williams, Jar, Cover, Pumpkin Shape, Pink Jade, 7 ½ In.
$88.00

Stevens & Williams, Vase, Bud, Thorny Branches, Blue Satin, c.1800, 7 ½ In., Pair
$215.00

Bookmark, George Washington, Flag, Centennial 1876, 9 ½ x 2 In. 365.00
Picture, Are You Ready?, Oxford's Boating Team, Silk, Mat, Frame, 9 x 6 ½ In. 525.00
Picture, Call To The Rescue, Silk, Mat, Frame, 8 ¾ x 5 ¾ In. 575.00
Picture, Declaration Of Independence, Silk, Velvet Mat, Frame, 8 ¾ x 4 ⅜ In. 225.00
Picture, Dick Turpin's Last Ride On His Bonny Black Bess, On Board, c.1879 .... 230.00
Picture, General Pershing's Troops, Eagle, Shield, LaFayette Nous Voici, Frame, 7 ½ x 6 In. 115.00
Picture, The Last Lap, Bicycle Race, Silk, c.1879, 8 x 5 ½ In. 595.00
Picture, The Start, The Finish, Horses, Silk, Mat, Frame, 1880s, 6 ⅛ x 9 In., Pair 1400.00

STEVENS & WILLIAMS of Stourbridge, England, made many types of glass, including layered, etched, cameo, and art glass, between the 1830s and 1930s. Some pieces are signed *S & W.* Many pieces are decorated with flowers, leaves, and other designs based on nature.

Bowl, Green Cut To Clear, Rococo, Sterling Silver Rim, 8 In. 500.00
Bowl, Ruby Red & Coral, Clear Cased, Pulled Waves, 9 In. 546.00
Bowl, White Flowers, Leaves, Red Satin, Cameo, 5 In. .... *illus* 425.00
Bowl, Yellow, Red Pulled Waves, Pink Interior, Oval, John Northwood, 9 In. .... *illus* 945.00
Decanter, Amethyst Cut To Clear, Flowers, Sterling Silver Collar, 4-Sided, 11 ½ In. 1200.00
Jar, Cover, Pumpkin Shape, Pink Jade, 7 ½ In. .... *illus* 88.00
Lamp, Oil, Pompeian Swirl, Red, Green, Oval, 11 In. 489.00
Mug, Amberina, Applied Amber Flowers, Handle, Thorny Feet, Optic Ribbed, 5 In. 144.00
Salt, Raspberry Satin, Metal, Ruffled Rim, Rigaree Collar, 3 ½ In. 575.00
Vase, Amethyst, White, Vines, Beetles, Cameo, Egg Shape, 1885, 6 In. 948.00
Vase, Blue Cased, White, Thorny Handles, 5 x 4 In., Pair 265.00
Vase, Bud, Thorny Branches, Blue Satin, c.1800, 7 ½ In., Pair .... *illus* 215.00
Vase, Peachblow, Mat-Su-No-Ke Stems, Crimped Scalloped Rim, Oval, 9 In. 259.00
Vase, Pompeian Swirl, Amber, Red, Blue, White Interior, Bulbous, Pinched Waist, 16 In. 1265.00
Vase, Pompeian Swirl, Green, Footed, 5 ¾ In. 110.00
Vase, Pompeian Swirl, Mother-Of-Pearl, Vine Of Flowers, 6 ¾ In. 633.00
Vase, Rainbow Swirl, Frosted Ribbon Handles, Base, 9 ¾ In. 350.00
Vase, Swirl, Bulbous, Pink Shaded To Amber, Gold Branch, 3 ½ In. 86.00
Vase, Trumpet, Cranberry, Green Ribs, Gorham Sterling Silver Base, c.1920, 13 In. 1180.00

STIEGEL TYPE glass is listed here. It is almost impossible to be sure a piece was actually made by Stiegel, so the knowing collector refers to this glass as "Stiegel type." Henry William Stiegel, a colorful immigrant to the colonies, started his first factory in Pennsylvania in 1763. He remained in business until 1774. Glassware was made in a style popular in Europe at that time and was similar to the glass of many other makers. It was made of clear or colored glass and was decorated with enamel colors, mold blown designs, or etching.

Bottle, Clear, Enameled, Flowers, Bird, Pewter Screw Cap, Pontil, 5 ½ In. .... *illus* 275.00
Bottle, Clear, Multicolored Leaf, Flowers, Bird, Pewter Screw Cap, 5 ¾ x 2 ½ In. 176.00
Bottle, Cordial, Clear, Multicolored Leaf, Tulip, Rim Stopper, Pontil, 6 x 2 ½ In. 143.00
Cologne, Clear, Enameled Flower, Woman, Pewter Screw Cap, Pontil, 5 ⅜ In. 110.00
Creamer, Cobalt Blue, Diamond Quilted, Footed, c.1750, 4 In. 2223.00
Creamer, Emerald Green, Diamond Quilted, Footed, c.1780, 3 ½ In. 2223.00
Goblet, Clear, Tapered, Spiral Cotton Stem, Footed, Pontil, c.1770, 7 ⅛ x 3 ½ In. 440.00
Mug, Clear, Gold Enameled, Drape, Swag Leaf, C-Shape Handle, Pontil, 5 ¾ x 4 ½ In. 11.00
Salt, Clear, Ribbed, Footed, Pontil, 3 x 2 ½ In. 88.00
Salt, Cobalt Blue, Ribbed, Flared Foot, Pontil, 2 ¾ x 2 ⅝ In. .... *illus* 132.00
Salt, Diamond Quilted, Cobalt Blue, Flared Foot, Pontil, 3 ⅛ x 2 ⅝ In. 198.00
Sugar, Cover, Diamond Quilted, Cobalt Blue, Twisted Flame Finial, c.1800, 6 ¼ In. 2808.00
Sugar, Diamond Quilted, Cobalt Blue, c.1770, 2 ¾ In. 915.00
Tumbler, Clear, Enameled, Bird, Leaves, Broken Pontil, 3 In. .... *illus* 358.00
Tumbler, Clear, Enameled, Multicolored Draped Flowers, 3 ⅞ x 3 In. 468.00
Tumbler, Flip, Clear, Enameled, Coat Of Arms, Birds, Horse, Riders, 3 ¾ x 2 ¼ In. 77.00
Tumbler, Flip, Clear, Enameled, Heart, Lovebirds, Sunburst Border, 4 ½ x 3 ⅝ In. 187.00
Tumbler, Flip, Clear, Enameled, Multicolored Flowers, Birds, Tapered, 4 ½ x 4 In. 248.00
Tumbler, Flip, Clear, Enameled, Wheel Engraved, Bird, Yellow & Red Circle, Flower, 6 In. 198.00
Tumbler, Flip, Clear, Engraved, Crosshatched Flower, Pontil, 4 x 3 ⅜ In. 132.00
Tumbler, Flip, Clear, Engraved, Flowers In Basket, Tapered, 4 x 3 ⅜ In. 248.00
Tumbler, Flip, Clear, Engraved, Tulip, 6 x 4 ⅝ In. 286.00
Tumbler, Flip, Clear, Engraved, Wriggled Border, Tapered, 4 ⅞ x 4 In. 165.00
Tumbler, Flip, Clear, Paneled, Enameled Tulip, Flowers, Broken Pontil, 4 ¼ x 3 ½ In. 88.00
Tumbler, Flip, Smoke, Engraved, Tulip, Urn, Pontil, 5 ¼ x 3 ⅜ In. 176.00
Wine, Clear, Diamond Quilted, Cone Shape, Baluster, Spiral Bubble Stem, Footed, 6 ¼ x 2 ⅞ In. 550.00
Wine, Clear, Twisted, Flat Footed, Spiraling, Pontil, c.1760, 6 ½ x 3 ⅛ In. 110.00

STONE includes those articles made of stones, coral, shells, and some other natural materials not listed elsewhere in this book. Micro mosaics, (small decorative designs made by setting pieces of stone into a pattern), urns, vases, and other pieces made of natural stone are listed here. Stoneware is pottery and is listed in the Stoneware category. Alabaster, Jade, Malachite, Marble, and Soapstone are in their own categories.

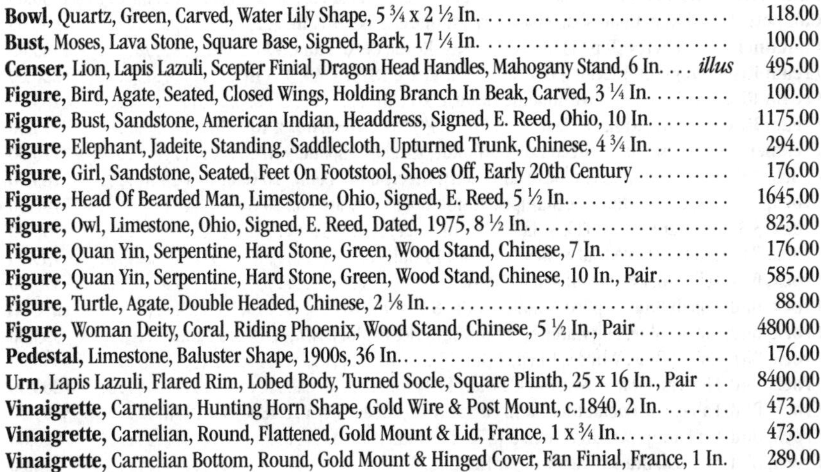

Bowl, Quartz, Green, Carved, Water Lily Shape, 5 ¾ x 2 ½ In. 118.00
Bust, Moses, Lava Stone, Square Base, Signed, Bark, 17 ¼ In. 100.00
Censer, Lion, Lapis Lazuli, Scepter Finial, Dragon Head Handles, Mahogany Stand, 6 In. .... *illus* 495.00
Figure, Bird, Agate, Seated, Closed Wings, Holding Branch In Beak, Carved, 3 ¼ In. 100.00
Figure, Bust, Sandstone, American Indian, Headdress, Signed, E. Reed, Ohio, 10 In. 1175.00
Figure, Elephant, Jadeite, Standing, Saddlecloth, Upturned Trunk, Chinese, 4 ¾ In. 294.00
Figure, Girl, Sandstone, Seated, Feet On Footstool, Shoes Off, Early 20th Century 176.00
Figure, Head Of Bearded Man, Limestone, Ohio, Signed, E. Reed, 5 ½ In. 1645.00
Figure, Owl, Limestone, Ohio, Signed, E. Reed, Dated, 1975, 8 ½ In. 823.00
Figure, Quan Yin, Serpentine, Hard Stone, Green, Wood Stand, Chinese, 7 In. 176.00
Figure, Quan Yin, Serpentine, Hard Stone, Green, Wood Stand, Chinese, 10 In., Pair 585.00
Figure, Turtle, Agate, Double Headed, Chinese, 2 ⅛ In. 88.00
Figure, Woman Deity, Coral, Riding Phoenix, Wood Stand, Chinese, 5 ½ In., Pair 4800.00
Pedestal, Limestone, Baluster Shape, 1900s, 36 In. 176.00
Urn, Lapis Lazuli, Flared Rim, Lobed Body, Turned Socle, Square Plinth, 25 x 16 In., Pair 8400.00
Vinaigrette, Carnelian, Hunting Horn Shape, Gold Wire & Post Mount, c.1840, 2 In. 473.00
Vinaigrette, Carnelian, Round, Flattened, Gold Mount & Lid, France, 1 x ¾ In. 473.00
Vinaigrette, Carnelian Bottom, Round, Gold Mount & Hinged Cover, Fan Finial, France, 1 In. 289.00

STONEWARE is a coarse, glazed, and fired potter's ceramic that is used to make crocks, jugs, bowls, etc. It is often decorated with cobalt blue decorations. In the nineteenth and early twentieth centuries, potters often decorated crocks with blue numbers indicating the size of the container. A *2* meant 2 gallons. Stoneware is still being made. American stoneware is listed here.

Bank, Blue Design, Garland, No. 4, Bulbous, Jug Form, 5 ⅛ x 4 ¼ In. 11000.00
Bank, Double Spire Finial, Mustard Slip Script, Mangense Glaze, S. Steer, England, 1855, 8 In. 390.00
Basket, Groove Center, Raised Edges, Dark Cinnamon, c.1980, 9 In. 33.00
Batter Jug, Cobalt Blue, Impressed, JM Harris, Easton, Pa., 1800s, 12 ½ In. .... *illus* 585.00
Batter Jug, Cobalt Blue, Tin Spout, Cover, Bail Handle, T.G. Daub, Easton, Pa., Gal., 9 In. 1287.00
Batter Jug, Wire Bail Handle, Wood Hand Grip, Gal., 8 ½ x 9 ½ In. 176.00
Bean Pot, Cover, Handle, Embossed, Boston Home Of The Bean, White's, Utica, 7 ½ x 8 In. .. 230.00
Bean Pot, Dark Brown Alkaline Glaze, Handle, Lid Ledge, 7 ½ In. 440.00
Bean Pot, Double Grape, Thin Alkaline Glaze, Edwin Meaders, 1970s, 8 x 7 In. 550.00
Bird, On Stump, Cleater Meaders, 6 ¾ In. 92.00
Bird Feeder, Jug Form, Cobalt Blue Top, Incribed, 1864 March 20th, 2 ½ In. 12870.00
Birdhouse, Clear, Crush Glass Glaze, Brown, Cream Swirl, Perch, Hanging Hole, 8 ¼ In. 275.00
Birdhouse, Gray & Cream Swirl, Pierced Perch Hole, Finial, c.1980, 8 ⅜ In. 165.00
Birdhouse, Sine Wave, Finial, c.1980, 9 ¾ In. 33.00
Bottle, B. Whitcombe Sarsaparilla Beer, Salt Glaze, c.1855, 10 In. 250.00
Bottle, Beer, Salt Glaze Gray, Cobalt Blue Slip Lettering, JC, 10 ¼ In. 130.00
Bottle, Beer, Salt Glaze Tan, Brown Glaze, John Lynch, 10 ⅛ In. 160.00
Bottle, No. 3, Lines, Signed, Claude Conover, 1970s, 14 x 12 In. 3600.00
Bottle, Wine, Pear Shape, Trumpet Mouth, Celadon, Tan Colored Glaze, 10 ½ In. 237.00
Bowl, Clabber, Handle, Cobalt Blue Band & Base, c.1900, 5 ½ In. 400.00
Bowl, Lotus, Satin Gloss, Chinese White, Medallions, Finger Contortions, 2 ⅛ x 5 ¼ In. 248.00
Bowl, Spherical Cutout, Signed, Jane Parshall, 5 ¼ x 7 ½ In. 100.00
Bust, John Locke, Cylindrical, Raised, Waisted Black Basalt Plinth, Turner White, 10 In. 1422.00
Cake Crock, Flower, Leaf Banding, Cobalt Blue, Round, Ear Handles, 8 x 13 In. 209.00
Cake Stand, Alkaline Glaze, Pedestal Base, Stamped, BB Craig, 3 ½ x 8 ½ In. 1300.00
Candlestick, Chamber, Satin Gloss, Blue Lead Glaze, Oval Handle, Tapered, 2 ½ In. 110.00
Charger, Abstract, Gray, Indigo, Signed, Robert Arneson, 12 ½ In. 2160.00
Chicken Feeder, Band, Cobalt Blue, Rim, 19th Century, 5 ¾ In. 1112.00
Chicken Feeder, Tulip, Cobalt Blue, Thos. Haig, 975 N. 2nd St., Phila., 1800s, 9 In. .... *illus* 1112.00
Churn, Cobalt Blue, Handles, 17 x 8 ¾ In. 5175.00
Churn, Eagle, Stenciled Cobalt, Applied Double Handles, c.1850, 16 ½ In. 1175.00
Churn, Flaring Rim, 2 Handles, Wide Base, H. Hancock, Cover, c.1875, 12 ¾ In. 220.00
Churn, Flowers, Cobalt Blue, W. Roberts, Binghampton, N.Y., c.1865, 5 Gal., 18 ½ In. 200.00
Churn, Freehand Brushed Bands, Vining Leaves, 6, Applied Handle, 1800s, 16 ¼ In. 1610.00
Churn, Freehand Flowers, Cobalt Blue, Stencil, Hamilton & Jones, c.1870, 15 x 24 In. 1725.00
Churn, Handle, Cobalt Blue Letters, J & E Wood, 5, Maysville, Ky., c.1890, 17 x 9 In. 5175.00
Churn, Leaf, Cobalt Blue, White's, Utica, 5 Gal. 288.00
Churn, Lug Handles, Oval, Salt Glaze, S. Purdy, Ohio, 19 In. 235.00

Stiegel Type, Bottle, Clear, Enameled, Flowers, Bird, Pewter Screw Cap, Pontil, 5 ½ In.
$275.00

Stiegel Type, Salt, Cobalt Blue, Ribbed, Flared Foot, Pontil, 2 ¾ x 2 ⅝ In.
$132.00

Stiegel Type, Tumbler, Clear, Enameled, Bird, Leaves, Broken Pontil, 3 In.
$358.00

Stone, Censer, Lion, Lapis Lazuli, Scepter Finial, Dragon Head Handles, Mahogany Stand, 6 In.
$495.00

S

Stoneware, Batter Jug, Cobalt Blue, Impressed, JM Harris, Easton, Pa., 1800s, 12 ½ In.
$585.00

Stoneware, Chicken Feeder, Tulip, Cobalt Blue, Thos. Haig, 975 N. 2nd St., Phila., 1800s, 9 In.
$1112.00

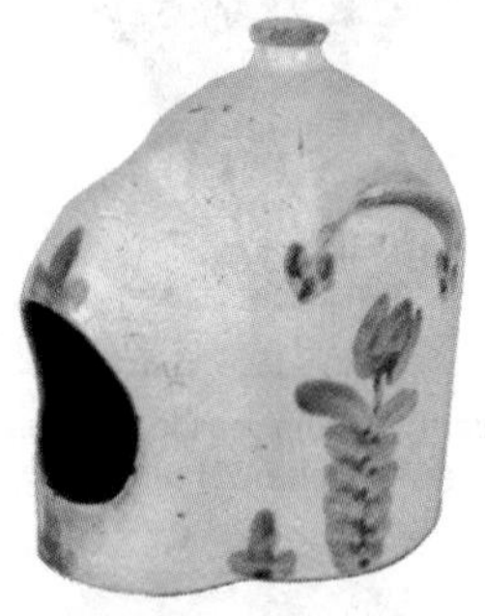

Stoneware, Crock, Butter, Flowers, Leaves, Cobalt Blue, 19th Century, 6 x 10 ¼ In.
$577.00

Stoneware, Crock, Cake, Flowers, Leaves, Blue, Incised Band, Applied Handles, 4 ½ x 8 In.
$275.00

Churn, Mechanical, Jas. Hamilton Manufacturing, Penn., 4 Gal., 35 In. 2970.00
Churn, Olive Alkaline Glaze, Handles, 18 ¼ In. 121.00
Churn, Olive Green Alkaline Glaze, Vertical Strap Handles, 5 Gal., 18 x 7 ½ In. 748.00
Churn, Parrot, Branch, Cobalt Blue, Lug Handles, F.B. Norton, Mass., 4 Gal., c.1890, 17 In. 889.00
Churn, Parrot, Branch, Cobalt Blue, Lug Handles, F.B. Norton Co., 3 Gal., c.1880, 15 In. 1778.00
Churn, Red Wing Salt Glaze, 3 Gal. 1050.00
Compote, Fluted Rim, Cone Shape Base, Cream Glaze, 5 ⅝ x 9 ¼ In. 66.00
Container, Pewter Screw Top Lid, Raised Molded Roses, Bead, Band, 4 ¾ x 3 In. 132.00
Cream Riser, Frogskin Interior, J.D. Craven, Marked, c.1875, 7 ½ x 9 ¼ In. 220.00
Cream Riser, Satin Glass, Olive Alkaline Glaze, 8 x 11 In. 183.00
Cream Riser, Sloping Rim, Marked, Reed Creek, PO NC, c.1850, 6 ⅛ x 10 ¾ In. 715.00
Creamer, Clear Glass Glaze, Green Collar, Handle, Extended Spout, 9 In. 110.00
Crock, 2 Handles, Hamilton & Jones Star Pottery, Greensboro, Penn., 20 Gal., 16 x 26 In. 165.00
Crock, 2 Leaves, Cobalt Blue, 20, Stamped Minnesota Stoneware Co., 20 Gal. 7700.00
Crock, 3 Swans, Gardner, c.1875, 5 Gal., 12 ½ In. 150.00
Crock, Bail Handle, Maple Leaf & Western Oval, 15 Gal. 135.00
Crock, Bardwell's Root Beer, Salt Glaze, 10 In. 575.00
Crock, Bird, Cobalt Blue, Applied Handles, 6 Qt., 8 ¼ x 9 ¼ In. 250.00
Crock, Bird, Cobalt Blue, Lug Handles, 4 Gal., Satterlee & Mory, N.Y., c.1870, 12 In. 593.00
Crock, Bird, Cobalt Blue, White's, Utica, 4 Gal. 546.00
Crock, Bird, Flowers, Edmands, c.1865, 2 Gal., 11 ¾ In. 1200.00
Crock, Bird, Foliage, 2, Cobalt Blue, W.H. Farrar & Co., Geddes, N.Y., c.1860, 9 x 10 In. 3055.00
Crock, Bird, On Stump, Wright & Son, c.1870, 1 ½ Gal., 8 ¼ In. 850.00
Crock, Bird, Stylized, Branch, Applied Ear Handles, 9 ¾ In. 413.00
Crock, Butter, Flowers, Leaves, Cobalt Blue, 19th Century, 6 x 10 ¼ In. .... *illus* 577.00
Crock, Butter, Oval Top Handles, Slope Shape, J. Jordan, c.1875, 7 ½ x 6 ¼ In. 303.00
Crock, Cake, Antler Design, Blue Slip, Jacob Caire & Co., c.1850, Gal., 8 In. 385.00
Crock, Cake, Flat Rim, Stylized Banding, Blue, 4 ⅛ x 7 ¼ In. 220.00
Crock, Cake, Flowers, Leaves, Applied Handles, Incised Bands, 4 ½ x 8 ½ In. 275.00
Crock, Cake, Flowers, Leaves, Blue, Incised Band, Applied Handles, 4 ½ x 8 In. .... *illus* 275.00
Crock, Cake, Leaves, Cobalt Blue, Applied Handles, Cover, c.1850, 12 x 7 In. 558.00
Crock, Cat, Standing, P.H. Webster, c.1870, 2 Gal., 9 ½ In. 13750.00
Crock, Cobalt Blue, Oval, Handles, Wm. E. Warner, 11 In. 6518.00
Crock, Cobalt Blue, Stenciled Maker, D.C. Rankin, Newark, Ohio, c.1885, 11 x 11 In. 499.00
Crock, Cobalt Blue, Stenciled Maker, Ironton Pottery, Ohio, c.1885, 12 x 12 In. 720.00
Crock, Cobalt Blue, Storers-Keystone Mustard & Pickle Works, Applied Ears, 2 Gal. 135.00
Crock, Cobalt Blue Clover, Impressed Star, 2 In Circle, Applied Handles, 12 In. 288.00
Crock, Cobalt Blue Decoration, Applied Handles, Boughner, Greensboro, 15 In. 1058.00
Crock, Cobalt Blue Design, Applied Handles, Stenciled, Upton Stuckey, c.1875, 15 In. 705.00
Crock, Cobalt Blue Design, Jas. Hamilton, 9 ½ In. 248.00
Crock, Cobalt Blue Designs, Incised Lines, Applied Open Handles, c.1850, 10 ½ In. 205.00
Crock, Cow, 3, Salt Glaze, Incised, Blue Highlighted, Gardiner Stoneware, 11 ¾ In. 431.00
Crock, Deer, Palm Tree, Hubbell & Cheseboro, c.1870, 5 Gal., 12 ½ In. 12650.00
Crock, Deer, Trees, Fort Edward, 6 Gal., 13 ¾ In. 6000.00
Crock, Dinosaur, Fulper Bros., c.1880, 2 Gal., 9 In. 14300.00
Crock, Eagle, Cobalt Blue, Bulbous, Round Rim, Ear Handle, 13 x 9 In. 303.00
Crock, Elephant Ear, Union Oval, 15 Gal. 2600.00
Crock, Feathers, Lines, Cobalt Blue, Lug Handles, 10 Gal., W. Va., c.1870, 19 x 12 In. 4600.00
Crock, Flattened Rim, Salt Glaze, Incised, M. David, Tenn., 8 ¾ In. 173.00
Crock, Flower, 3, Cobalt Blue, Handles, Wm. Rowley, c.1880, 10 In. 374.00
Crock, Flower, Blue, Salt Glaze, Albany Slip, Gruber & Martin Grocers, 7 x 9 In. .... *illus* 1320.00
Crock, Flower, Blue Slip, Flat Tim, Incised Banding, D.P. Shenfelder, 7 ¼ x 8 In. 440.00
Crock, Flower, Butterfly, Cobalt Blue, N.A. White & Son, Utica, N.Y., 3 Gal., 10 x 11 In. 176.00
Crock, Flower, Cobalt Blue, Applied Handles, C.E. Pharis Co., 10 ¼ In. 519.00
Crock, Flower, Double, Cobalt Blue, 8 x 9 ¾ In. 132.00
Crock, Flower, Leaf, Cobalt Blue, 3 Gal., 10 x 11 ½ In. 220.00
Crock, Flower, Open Handles, c.1810, 2 Gal., 11 In. 1705.00
Crock, Flower, Stylized, Cobalt Blue, ¼ x 10 ¼ In. 165.00
Crock, Flower & Leaf Band, Cobalt Blue, 5 x 10 In. 143.00
Crock, Flowers, Cobalt Blue, H. Lourdes Maker, Petersburg, Va., Lug Handles, 2 Gal., 13 In. 4945.00
Crock, Flowers, Cobalt Blue, Impressed, Cowden & Wilcox, 1800s, 2 Gal., 8 ¾ In. 380.00
Crock, Flowers, Cobalt Blue, Lug Handles, Nicolos & Boynton, Ver., c.1856, 10 In. 267.00
Crock, Flowers, Cobalt Blue, N. Clark Jr., Athens, N.Y., 1800s, 2 Gal., 9 ½ x 10 In. 322.00
Crock, Freehand, Flage, 6, Cobalt Blue, 2 Applied Handles, Mid 1800s, 13 ¾ In. 3105.00
Crock, H.F. Behren Grocer, 2217 & 2219 Market Street, Tab Handles, 3 Gal., 13 ¾ In. 176.00
Crock, Hamilton & Jones, Blue, 1880s, 6 ¾ x 8 In. 225.00
Crock, Hamilton & Jones, Gray, Tab Handles, 8 Gal., 20 x 12 In. 925.00
Crock, Heinz's, Chow Chow, Paper Label, Bail Handle, 9 ½ x 10 In. 150.00

Crock, Indian, Mohawk, Hold Him, Cobalt Blue, C.W. Baun, N.Y., c.1885, 11 In. 23500.00
Crock, Ironton Pottery, 3, Brown, Cobalt Blue, Tab Handles, 1880-90, 12 x 11 ½ In. 660.00
Crock, J. Weaver, Cobalt Blue Leaves, Lug Handles, Beaver, Penn., 3 Gal., 12 ¾ In. 418.00
Crock, James Hamilton & Co., Greensboro, Pa., Cobalt Blue, 6 Gal., 16 x 9 ½ In. 1280.00
Crock, Leaf, 3, Cobalt Blue, Oval, Handles, J.F. Brayton & Co., Utica, 12 ½ In. 235.00
Crock, Leaf Banding, Blue, Straight-Sided, Flat Rim, Rounded Shoulder, 6 ⅞ x 5 In. 165.00
Crock, Leaf Design, Blue, Cylindrical, Flat Rim, 9 x 6 In. 165.00
Crock, Lid, Pecking Chicken, Corn On Ground, 5, 14 In. 518.00
Crock, Marriage, Flowers, Initials, Cobalt Blue, May 16, 1869, 6 Gal., 14 ¼ x 12 In. 336.00
Crock, Parrot, Leaves, Cobalt Blue, F.B. Norton & Co., 4 Gal., 11 ½ x 12 In. 275.00
Crock, Salt Glaze, Cobalt Blue, Cedar Falls, 6 Gal., 13 ¾ In. 3304.00
Crock, Sprig Banding, Stylized, Blue, Bulbous, Flat Rim, 7 x 4 ½ In. 220.00
Crock, Spring Design, Blue Slip, Handle, James Morgan, Jr., c.1790, 3 Gal., 12 ½ In. 3740.00
Crock, Trumpeter Flower, 3, Cobalt Blue, J. Burger Jr., Rochester, N.Y., 11 ½ x 10 In. 230.00
Crock, Tulip, Cobalt Blue, Applied Handles, E.A. Montrell, Olean, N.Y., 11 In. 558.00
Crock, Tulips, Cobalt Blue, Applied Handles, c.1875, 12 In. 176.00
Crock, Tulips, Cross, Stylized Blue, Flared Rim, Bulbous, 7 ½ x 6 ½ In. 330.00
Crock, Tulips, Drooping, Ruffled, Cobalt Blue, 6 Gal, 13 x 13 ½ In. 294.00
Crock, Tulips, Lines, Cobalt Blue, Handles, Oval, 12 In. 588.00
Crock, Vining Tulips, Cobalt Blue, Applied Handles, c.1875, 12 ½ In. 323.00
Crock, Willow Tree, Rounded Shoulder, Flared Rim, Ear Handles, Cobalt Blue, 2 Gal. 1760.00
Crock, Wreath, 2, Cobalt Blue, Applied Handles, Burger & Lang, 9 ¼ In. 411.00
Cup, Gold, Ceracron, Ammerland, 8 Oz. 3.50
Ewer, Phoenix Top, Dragon Handle, Rosettes, Green, Straw Glaze, Chinese, 16 In. 1067.00
Figurine, Cat, Smiling, Coiled Tail, Dark Eyes, Black Spots, Clear Lead Glaze, 5 ¾ x 8 In. 1155.00
Figurine, Catfish, Frogskin, Applied Fins & Whiskers, W. Boyce Yow, c.1980, 9 ½ In. 248.00
Figurine, Dog, Spaniel, Collar, Chain, Cobalt Blue, 11 ½ In. 1528.00
Figurine, Dog, Spaniel, Stepped Base, Detailed Fur, Cobalt Blue, c.1800s, 10 ¼ In. 1762.00
Figurine, Elephant, Brown Glaze, 1, Signed, Flossie Meaders, 13 In. 400.00
Figurine, Night Watchman, Parson, Oval Base, Turner White, c.1800, 8 ¼ In. 1267.00
Figurine, Owl, Bristol Glaze, Cobalt Blue, Signed, Arie Meaders, 7 In. 8000.00
Figurine, Pigeon, Carved, Molded, Inscribed, W. Smith, c.1890, 8 In. 644.00
Figurine, Rooster, Alkaline Green Glaze, Edwin Meaders, c.1986, 14 ½ In. 1500.00
Figurine, Rooster, Brown Glaze, Signed, Reggie Meaders, 13 In. . . . . *illus* 550.00
Figurine, Rooster, Cobalt Blue Glaze, Edwin Nub Meaders, 8/1/1985, 5 ¾ x 8 ½ In. . . . . . *illus* 525.00
Figurine, Rooster, Green Ash Glaze, Signed, David Meaders, 18 In. 325.00
Figurine, Rooster, Olive Glossy Glaze, Billy Henson, 13 In. 748.00
Figurine, Squirrel, Seated, Nut In Paws, Black Brown, c.1990, 3 ¼ In. 66.00
Figurine, Wild Boar, Brown Glaze, 3, Signed, Reggie Meaders, 13 In. 275.00
Flask, Bellflower, Stems, Cobalt Blue, Flattened Oval, Applied Lip, c.1840, 7 x 5 In. 1058.00
Flask, Pig, Incised, Cobalt Blue Splotches, 19th Century, 3 ½ x 8 ½ In. 37440.00
Flowerpot, 5 Peepers Over Rim, Hilton Pottery Co., c.1920, 5 ¾ In. 33.00
Flowerpot, Sunflower, Blue, Crimped Collar, Applied, c.1860, 8 ¾ x 10 ⅝ In. 9000.00
Jar, 2 Handles, Celadon Alkaline Glaze, Oval, c.1850, 16 x 12 In. 3600.00
Jar, Applied Handles, Albany Slip Glaze, Brown Pottery, Arden, Mid 1900s, 33 In. 460.00
Jar, Baluster Shape, Brown Drip Glaze, Green & Beige Drip Overglaze, 30 In. 480.00
Jar, Brown Matte Glaze, 19th Century, Chinese, 13 In. 210.00
Jar, Canning, Salt Glaze, Incised Shoulder, Flat Style Rim, Orange Peel Texture, 6 In. 825.00
Jar, Canning, Salt Glaze, Overall Orange Peel, 7 ½ In. 1265.00
Jar, Cobalt Blue, Daubs On Neck, Handles, I.M. Mead, Mogadore, Ohio, c.1850, 4 Gal., 13 In. . 206.00
Jar, Cobalt Blue, Oval, Lug Handles, Galleried Rim, D. Fisk, Mogadore, Ohio, c.1830, Gal., 10 In. 294.00
Jar, Cobalt Blue, Straight Rim, Lug Handles, Salt Glaze, U. Kendall, Ohio, c.1840, 3 Gal., 14 In. 588.00
Jar, Cover, Brown Glaze, Inscribed Sugar, Bulbous, Rounded Rim, 9 ¼ x 7 In. 770.00
Jar, Demuth's Snuff, Cover, H. Cowden, Rounded Shoulder, Applied Handles, 12 x 9 In. 248.00
Jar, Dome Cover, Morning Glories, Leaves, Vine, Glossy White Feldspathic Glaze, 8 In. 55.00
Jar, Edgefield, Lug Handles, Slipped Loop Decoration, Olive Glaze, 15 ½ In. 1610.00
Jar, Flower In Circle Design, Gray, Olive Green Glaze, Chinese, 1800s, 9 In. 960.00
Jar, Flowers, Cobalt Blue, Sloped, Reidinger & Caire, N.Y., c.1870, 4 Gal., 18 In. 235.00
Jar, Flowers, Cobalt Blue, Straight-Sided, Lug Handles, W. Smith, New York, c.1840, 14 In. . . . 300.00
Jar, Glossy, Salt Glaze, Rust Brown, Gray, Lug Handles, 12 In. 385.00
Jar, Glossy Olive Alkaline Glaze, Flared, Flange Base, Drools, Drips, 12 ½ In. 605.00
Jar, Glossy Olive Alkaline Glaze, Handle, Saddle Bulbous Rim, 15 ¼ x 37 In. 715.00
Jar, Handles, Slope Shoulder, c.1840, 14 ¾ In. 880.00
Jar, Knoxville, Tenn. Shoulder Stamp, Half Crescent Mark, William Grindstaff, c.1890, 8 In. . . 1237.00
Jar, Leaf, Blue Banded, Cylindrical, 6 ¾ x 5 In. 198.00
Jar, Leaves, Cylindrical, Flat Rim, 1 Gal., 10 ½ x 7 In. 187.00
Jar, Olive, Double Dipped Alkaline Glaze, Rutile Glaze, Flared Rim, Lid Ledge, 8 ⅜ In. 165.00
Jar, Olive Alkaline Glaze, Lug Handles, Flat Style Rim, 13 x 36 In. 660.00

Stoneware, Crock, Flower, Blue, Salt Glaze, Albany Slip, Gruber & Martin Grocers, 7 x 9 In.
$1320.00

Stoneware, Figurine, Rooster, Brown Glaze, Signed, Reggie Meaders, 13 In.
$550.00

Stoneware, Figurine, Rooster, Cobalt Blue Glaze, Edwin Nub Meaders, 8/1/1985, 5 ¾ x 8 ½ In.
$525.00

TIP

Chrome should be cleaned with a mild chrome cleaner, not an abrasive.

S

Stoneware, Jardiniere Stand, Tree, Vines, Branches, Bird, Nest, Blue, White, RH, 27 x 20 In.
$110.00

Stoneware, Jug, Face, Alkaline Glaze, Ceramic Eyes, Stone Teeth, Marked, L. Meaders, 10 In.
$1380.00

Stoneware, Jug, Face, Blue Swirl, Broken China Teeth, Stamped, B.B. Craig, Vale, N.C., 7 ¾ In.
$220.00

S

Jar, Olive Shiny Runny Glaze, Brown Slip Loop Band, Edgefield, 15 In. 3335.00
Jar, Olive Streaked Alkaline Glaze, Roll Rim, Groove, Bulbous, No Handle, 9 ¼ In. 4620.00
Jar, Open Mouth, Bulbous, Tapered, Flat Lip Rim, Chinese, 25 In. 240.00
Jar, Oval, Charlestown, Lug Handles, Impressed Heart, c.1820, 10 ½ In. 660.00
Jar, Oval, Edgefield, 2 Lug Handles, Runny & Mottled Glaze, 9, 1800s, 16 ¾ In. 1725.00
Jar, Oval, Flared Rim, Strap Handle, Olive Glaze, Edgefield, 19th Century, 15 x 8 In. 1093.00
Jar, Oval, Handles, Olive Runny & Mottled Glaze, Edgefield, 15 In. 1380.00
Jar, Oval, Lug Handles, Flared Rim, Green & Brown Glossy Glaze, Seagrove, 15 ¾ In. 431.00
Jar, Persian, 4 Looped Handles, Orange & Olive, Spotted, Applied Roping, c.1920, 19 In. 4620.00
Jar, Round, Rounded Rim, Interior Lid Rim, Blue Stencil, Parkersburg, 8 x 5 In. 77.00
Jar, Runny Drip Glaze, Impressed Initials, Kim Ellington, 19 ½ In. 546.00
Jar, Rust Brown, Olive Streaked Clay Slip, Handles, Stenciled, Albany Slip Glaze, 11 In. 4620.00
Jar, Salt Glaze, Handles, Cylindrical, Sloping Shoulder, Flat Rim, 15 In. 990.00
Jar, Toasting Scene, Black Couple, Glossy Feldspathic Glaze, Gray, Ear Handles, 13 In. 605.00
Jar, Wavy Line, Cobalt Blue, Salt Glaze, Samuel Booker/Louisville, Ky., c.1800, 2 Gal., 12 In. 2990.00
Jar, Wax Seal, Salt Glaze, Brown Glaze, Dark Blue Transfer, 9 ¾ In. 80.00
Jardiniere, Pedestal, Blue, White, Dragon Head Handles, England, 39 ⅝ In. 288.00
Jardiniere Stand, Tree, Vines, Branches, Bird, Nest, Blue, White, RH, 27 x 20 In. *illus* 110.00
Jug, Bellarmine, Brown Glaze, Bearded Face, Handle, 7 In. 896.00
Jug, Bird, Cobalt Blue, Applied Strap Handle, White's, Utica, 2, Late 1800s, 14 In. 382.00
Jug, Bird, Cobalt Blue, Brady & Ryan, 14 In. 316.00
Jug, Bird, Cobalt Blue, Impressed, White's, Utica, 3 Gal., 16 In. 400.00
Jug, Bird, Geddes, c.1850, 3 Gal., 16 In. 3750.00
Jug, Bird, On Branch, Cobalt Blue, Applied Handle, Label, 13 In. 441.00
Jug, Bird, On Perch, Cobalt Blue, Flat Trim, C-Shape Handle, 14 ¼ x 9 In. 275.00
Jug, Bird, Stylized Tail, Cobalt Blue, Strap Handle, White's, Utica, 3, 14 In. 470.00
Jug, Blue Slip Decoration, E. Thayer, 1800s, 18 In. 35.00
Jug, Brown & Cream, Black Stencil, Plymouth, Vt., Stenciled, Urn Shape, c.1880, ½ Pt. 79.00
Jug, Brown Albany Glaze, Handle, J.G. Freeman, Wilkes Barre, Penn, 9 ¼ In. 70.00
Jug, Brown Glaze, Handle, Bullet Head, Cowden & Wilcox, 7 ¼ In. 40.00
Jug, Brown Glaze, Lamort & Golay, Tryon, N.C., 9 In. 515.00
Jug, Clear Feldspathic Glaze, Cinnamon, Milk Swirls, Flat Style Handle, 8 ¾ In. 110.00
Jug, Cobalt Blue, Applied Handle, R.T. Williams, New Geneva, Late 1800s, 14 ½ In. 264.00
Jug, Cobalt Blue, Cream, Handle, Geo. Lockett & Sons, Brooklyn, 9 ⅜ In. 70.00
Jug, Cobalt Blue, Marked, F.H. Cowden, Harrisburg, 19th Century, 2 Gal., 13 In. 244.00
Jug, Devil's Face, Olive, Alkaline Glaze, John Meaders, c.1996, 10 ½ In. 4290.00
Jug, Devil's Face, Olive Brown Glaze, 6 Horns, Flat Top Handles, Earthenware, 20 In. 990.00
Jug, Dogs, Rabbits, Fence, Trees, Mountains, Blue, Embossed, Qt. 159.00
Jug, Double Face, Cleater Meaders Jr. & Sr., 10 ¼ In. 366.00
Jug, Double Flower, Cobalt Blue, Semi-Oval, Double Handle, c.1850-60, 18 ½ In. 1200.00
Jug, Eagle, Banner, Cobalt Blue, Applied Handle, Wm. E. Warner, Troy, N.Y., 9 ½ In. 1645.00
Jug, Face, 2-Sided, Ash Glaze, Inset Stone Teeth, Lanier Meaders, 8 ½ In. 4112.00
Jug, Face, Albany Slip, Quartz Teeth, Bulging Eyes, Lanier Meaders, 1970, 9 ½ In. 1400.00
Jug, Face, Alkaline Glaze, Ceramic Eyes, Stone Teeth, Marked, L. Meaders, 10 In. *illus* 1380.00
Jug, Face, B.B. Craig, Blue Swirl Body, China Teeth, Signed, Vale, N.C., 8 In. 230.00
Jug, Face, Blue Swirl, Broken China Teeth, Stamped, B.B. Craig, Vale, N.C., 7 ¾ In. *illus* 220.00
Jug, Face, Brown Glaze, Rock Teeth, Signed, Lanier Meaders, 10 In. 1200.00
Jug, Face, China Teeth, Ash Glaze, Signed, B.B. Craig, 5 Gal., 21 In. 1600.00
Jug, Face, China Teeth, Tobacco Spit Glaze, Green Drip, Lanier Meaders, 1960s, 8 In. 5800.00
Jug, Face, Clear, Feldspathic Glaze, Gray, White Swirl, B.B. Craig, 3 ½ In. 715.00
Jug, Face, Devil, Brown Glaze, Red Eyes, Handles, Ruby Meaders, 1999, 8 ½ In. 250.00
Jug, Face, Devil, Tobacco Spit Glaze, A.G. Meaders, 11 In. 550.00
Jug, Face, Glossy Olive, Crush Glass Glaze, Weep Eye, China Teeth, Rutile Drools, 6 In. 1045.00
Jug, Face, Handle, Broken China Teeth, Swirl Body, Incised, B.B. Craig, 13 ½ In. 345.00
Jug, Face, Lead Glaze, Orange, Yellow, Green, Black, Brown Drippings, 7 ¼ In. 385.00
Jug, Face, Mrs. Freckle Face, Brown Glazed, Flossie Meaders, 10 ½ In. 250.00
Jug, Face, Olive Alkaline Glaze, Flat Style Handles, Glass Melts, Zombie Eye, 19 ½ In. 770.00
Jug, Face, Olive Alkaline Glaze, White Clay Teeth, Eyes, Incised Eyebrows, Handles, 19 ¾ In. 440.00
Jug, Face, Rock Teeth, Green Alkaline Glaze, Signed, Lanier Meaders, 1960s, 8 In. 2300.00
Jug, Face, Rock Teeth, Wide Smile, Lanier Meaders, 1970s, 9 In. 4290.00
Jug, Face, Runny Olive Glaze, Ceramic Teeth, Signed, Lanier Meaders, 9 ½ In. *illus* 1210.00
Jug, Face, Satin Gloss, Black Albany Slip Glaze, Handle, Teeth, Blue Eyes, 10 In. 44.00
Jug, Face, Satin Gloss, Olive Brown Albany Slip, Gravel Eyes, Teeth, Shaped Ears, 6 In. 10450.00
Jug, Face, Satin Gloss Glaze, Double, China Teeth, Protruding Eye Lids, Pierced Pupils, 8 In. 330.00
Jug, Face, Satin Gloss Olive Glaze, Round Eyes, Pierced Pupils, Oval Handle, 3 ⅜ In. 110.00
Jug, Face, Streaked Olive Alkaline Glaze, Melts, Mustache, White Eyes, Teeth, 18 ½ In. 825.00

Jug, Face, Vampire, Triangular Plate Teeth, Pointy Ears, Ash Glaze, B.B. Craig, 16 In. 800.00
Jug, Face, Weeping Eye, Medium Olive, 2 Handles, 6 ¼ In. 1650.00
Jug, Flower, Blue, Flat Rim, Applied Handle, J. M. Harris, 2 Gal., 13 x 8 In. 121.00
Jug, Flower, Blue, Flat Rim, C-Shape Handle, Cowden & Wilcox, 4 Gal., 17 ¾ x 11 In. 605.00
Jug, Flower, Poppy Style, Oval, Cobalt Blue, Leaf, 2 Gal., 14 ½ In. 2200.00
Jug, Flower X, Blue, Rounded Shoulder, Strap Handle, J. M. Harris, 13 ½ x 8 ¼ In. 176.00
Jug, Flowers, Blue, Rounded Shoulder, Flat Rim, Strap Handle, T.G. Daub, 11 ¼ x 7 In. 220.00
Jug, Flowers, Blue Slip, Bulbous, Applied Handle, D.P. Shenfelder, 2 x 14 x 10 In. 468.00
Jug, Flowers, Brown & Cream, A.C. Kerr & Co., Buffalo N.Y., Qt. 59.00
Jug, Glossy Rutile Drippings, Black, Brown Alkaline Clay Slip Glaze, Handle, 12 ⅜ In. 660.00
Jug, Grape Cluster, Leaf, Blue Brushwork, Flat Rim, Bulbous, Cowden, 26 x 10 ½ In. 1650.00
Jug, Hayes & Co., Wholesale Dealers, Manchester, N.H., Ottoman Brothers, 2 Gal. 403.00
Jug, Incised Face, Closed Lips, Blue Eyes, Flat Handle, c.1990, 9 ¼ In. 275.00
Jug, J.W. Deakin Brewers, Bolton, Screw Top, 2-Tone, Marked, 1935, 11 In. 70.00
Jug, Jas. Hamilton & Co., Greensboro, Pa., Cobalt Blue, 2 Gal., 14 In. 650.00
Jug, John Hay Banner, Cobalt Blue, 2 Ring Incised Neck, N.Y., c.1870, 2 Gal., 14 In. 510.00
Jug, Leaves, Cobalt Blue, Impressed, A.J. Butler Mfg., New Brunswick, N.J., 12 In., 3 Gal. 300.00
Jug, Man-In-The-Moon, Impressed, Cowden, Harrisburg, 10 ½ In. 468.00
Jug, Men & Women Figures, Blue, Embossed, Parker Rye, Qt. 195.00
Jug, Olive Alkaline Glaze, Earth Tones, Handle, Streaking, 8 In. 165.00
Jug, Olive Alkaline Glaze, Handle, 2 Grooves, Bulbous Rim, Raised Ridge, 14 In. 5500.00
Jug, Olive Alkaline Glaze, Handles, Streaking, Flared, Bevel Rim, 15 ½ x 36 In. 990.00
Jug, Olive Streaked Alkaline Glaze, Bulbous, Handle, 13 ⅛ x 33 In. 1265.00
Jug, Oval, Incised Leaves, Cobalt Blue Detail, Tooled Neck Rings, Early 1800s, 11 In. 259.00
Jug, Oval, Salt Glaze, Daniel Goodale, 11 In. 345.00
Jug, Paddletail, Cobalt Blue, N.A. White & Son, N.Y., 19th Century, 2 Gal., 14 ¼ In. 380.00
Jug, Rattlesnake, Alkaline Glaze, Marked, Michael Crocker, 13 In. .... *illus* 920.00
Jug, Rounded Shoulder, Flat Rim, C-Shape Handle, Wm. Becker, Gal., 11 x 7 ¼ In. 55.00
Jug, Salt Glaze, 2 Bands, Horizontal Lines, Overall, Orange Peel, Arch Drip, 7 ⅜ In. 4290.00
Jug, Salt Glaze, Blue Floral Spray, Applied Handle, Ballard & Brothers, 3 Gal., 16 In. 460.00
Jug, Salt Glaze, Cobalt Blue Decoration, Follin & Fougeaud, Charleston, 2 Gal., 12 ¾ In. 2530.00
Jug, Salt Glaze, Glossy To Matte Glaze, Gray, Tan, Brown, Looping Handle, 15 ⅛ In. 523.00
Jug, Salt Glaze, Handle, Brown Body, Fly Ash, Drippings, 8 In. 44.00
Jug, Salt Glaze, Handle, Gray, White Swirl, Orange Peel Overall, Strong Rim, 7 In. 99.00
Jug, Salt Glaze, Oval, Handle, Overall Orange Peel, 10 x 24 In. 5060.00
Jug, Salt Glaze, Oval, Orange Peel, Fly Ash, Melt To Shoulder, Round Handle, 9 ½ x 28 In. 2310.00
Jug, Salt Lake City Liquor, Brown, White, 8 ½ x 5 ¾ In. 275.00
Jug, Sand, Glossy, Clear Crush Glass Glaze, Square, Flat Top Handle, 3 ¼ In. 55.00
Jug, Scratch, Satin Glass, Brown Albany Slip Glaze, Flat Style Handle, 4 ⅞ In. 110.00
Jug, Slip Decorated, Oval, Westerwald, Leaves, Flowers, Incised Neck, 13 ½ In. 230.00
Jug, Snowflake, Cobalt Blue, F.H. Cowden, Harrisburg, 2 Gal. 345.00
Jug, Songbird, On Branch, Cobalt Blue, Upturned Head, Handle, 13 ¼ In. 529.00
Jug, Spray, Cobalt Blue, Applied Handle, Welding & Belding, Ont., 5, 19 In. 118.00
Jug, Strawberry Planter, Hanging Hole, c.1900, 8 ¾ In. 22.00
Jug, Stylized Blue Flower Spray, Applied Handle, Ballard & Bros., 3 Gal. 690.00
Jug, Tapering Bottom, Bulbous Shoulder, Drippings, c.1835, 11 ⅛ In. 2310.00
Jug, Tin Lid, Flower, Cobalt Blue, Wire Bail Handle, 8 ½ In. 413.00
Jug, West Troy Pottery, Cobalt Blue, Salt Glaze, Handle, 11 ⅜ In., Gal. 184.00
Jug, Whiteway's Devon Cyder, 2-Tone, 2 Gal. 40.00
Jug, Wine, Blossom, Blue Slip, Gray, Wood Stopper, Incised, No. 3, 13 x 7 In. 185.00
Jug, Wreath, Cobalt Blue, Fort Edward Pottery, c.1858, Applied Handle, 10 ¾ In. 558.00
Jug, Wreath, Cobalt Blue Tulip, N.A. White & Son, Utica, Mid 1800s, 15 ½ In. 529.00
Keg, Glossy, Clear Crush Glass Glaze, Gray, White Swirls, Spout, 4 ¾ In. 770.00
Lamp, Jug, Cobalt Blue Bird, On Branch, Applied Handle, White's, Utica, 10 In. 441.00
Match Holder, Cobalt Blue, Flower, Diamond, Cone Shape, Coiled Rope, 2 ¾ x 3 ¾ In. 110.00
Milk Pan, Leaf Sprig Band, Blue Sprig, Flat Rim, Pour Spout, 4 ¼ x 9 ½ In. 330.00
Mug, Cobalt Blue, Flower Sprays, John G. Slocker, Reading, Pa., 1895, 3 ¼ In. 7020.00
Mug, Cobalt Blue, Flower Sprays, Striped Handle, E.E. Hipple, 19th Century, 4 In. 1170.00
Mug, Cover, Leaf Thumb Hold, C-Shape Handle, Cylindrical, White Glaze, 9 ¼ x 4 In. 44.00
Oyster Jug, Worthington & Carrell, Black Stencil, c.1880, Qt. 89.00
Pillow, Chinese, Glazed, Cobalt Blue Decoration, 12 In. 225.00
Pillow, Chinese, Multicolored Dragon, Geometric Design, Applied Frog Spout, 19 x 15 In. 150.00
Pitcher, Applied Dogwood, Catawba Valley, Hilton, Mid 1900s, 6 ¼ In. 526.00
Pitcher, Clear, Crush Glass Glaze, Gray, White Swirl, Thumb Pressed End, 10 In. 220.00
Pitcher, Clear Feldspathic Glaze, Gray, Cream Swirl, Clay Pupils, China Teeth, Handle, 8 ⅜ In. 77.00
Pitcher, Cobalt Blue Flower, Oval, Incised, Applied Ribbed Handle, c.1825, 14 In. 646.00

Jug, Face, Runny Olive Glaze, Ceramic Teeth, Signed, Lanier Meaders, 9 ½ In.
$1210.00

Stoneware, Jug, Rattlesnake, Alkaline Glaze, Marked, Michael Crocker, 13 In.
$920.00

TIP

Be careful about putting antique china or glass in the dishwasher. Glass will sometimes crack from the heat. Porcelains with gold overglaze decoration often lose the gold. Damaged or crazed glaze will sometimes pop off the plates in large pieces.

Stoneware, Pitcher, Cobalt Blue Flowers, Pa., 19th Century, 8 ¾ In.
$3510.00

Stoneware, Rolling Pin, Blazier & Kimble, Blue Letters, Brown Bands, Wood, 8 In.
$413.00

Stoneware, Soap Dish, Brown Mottled Glaze, Flared Rim, Footed, 2 ¾ x 5 ½ In.
$50.00

Stoneware, Water Cooler, Cobalt Blue Leaf Band, Incised Band, Applied Handles, 11 ¾ x 9 In.
$400.00

Pitcher, Cobalt Blue Flowers, Impressed, D. Albright, Ohio, c.1870, 2 Gal., 12 In. 3738.00
Pitcher, Cobalt Blue Flowers, Pa., 19th Century, 8 ¾ In. *illus* 3510.00
Pitcher, Daubed Cobalt Blue Designs, Strap Handle, Initials GT, c.1850, 11 In. 764.00
Pitcher, Fish Shape, White Clay, Brown & Blue Glaze, 10 In. 646.00
Pitcher, Flowers, Cobalt Blue, Flared Rim, Pour Spout, C-Shape Handle, Bulbous, 7 ¼ x 5 In. 440.00
Pitcher, Glossy, Cream Swirl, Clear Crush Glass Glaze, Cord Style Handle, 11 ⅝ In. 275.00
Pitcher, Glossy Olive Alkaline Glaze, Groove Top Handle, c.1950s, 9 In. 220.00
Pitcher, Glossy Olive Alkaline Glaze, Icon Shape, Groove Top, Flared Neck, 10 ¼ In. 330.00
Pitcher, Orange & Green Mottled Glaze, Applied Flowers, Leaves, Handle, 9 ¼ In. 173.00
Pitcher, Rust, Brown Red Glaze, 2 Parts, 2 Wavy Lines, Oval Top Handle, 3 In. 220.00
Pitcher, Salt Glaze, Handle, Clay Slip, Olive Brown, Interior, Rim, Overall Orange Peel, 9 ½ In. 110.00
Pitcher, Small Spout, Cobalt Blue Ring By Shoulder, 2 Gal., 13 ½ In. 920.00
Planter, Applied Molded Designs, Cherry Branches, Rosettes, Salt Glaze, 16 x 21 ½ In. 4406.00
Planter, Rooster, Brown Glaze, John Meaders, c.1980, 4 ½ In. 225.00
Planter, Strawberry, Unglazed, 4 Holes, Horizontal Line, 15 ¾ In. 165.00
Plate, Birds, Incised, Mottled Green Ground, Signed, Martz, 10 x 6 In. 75.00
Plate, Winter Scene, Marked, Catawba River Pottery, Marion, N.C., 1992, 8 In. 99.00
Pot, Grapes, Brown, Purple, Signed, Edwin Meaders, 1986, 6 ½ In. 1300.00
Rolling Pin, Blazier & Kimble, Blue Letters, Brown Bands, Wood, 8 In. *illus* 413.00
Rooster, Alkaline Glaze, Marked, Edwin Meaders, EM, 25 ¾ In. 1750.00
Rundlet, Geometric, Flowers, Footed, Filling Hole, Spigot, Cobalt Blue, 9 x 8 ½ In. 198.00
Sculpture, Hare Basket, Chrome Slip Glaze, Ken Ferguson, 22 x 16 In. 1200.00
Soap Dish, Brown Mottled Glaze, Flared Rim, Footed, 2 ¾ x 5 ½ In. *illus* 50.00
Sugar & Creamer, Lid, Brown, Signed, Lanier Meaders, Early 1970 165.00
Tankard, Pewter Lid, Cobalt Blue Bands, F. Heyde, 6 x 3 ½ In. 805.00
Teapot, Dogwood Blossoms, Earthy Brown, Hilton, Signed, c.1940, 6 x 8 ¼ In. 880.00
Tureen, Soup, Dome Lid, Satin Glossy Gray, Feldspathic Glaze, Flowers, Leaves, Vine, 7 ½ In. 44.00
Vase, Black Ankle Glaze, Double Cord Style Loop Handles, 6 In. 330.00
Vase, Brocade & Flower Head Decoration, Japan, 20 In. 620.00
Vase, Brown Glaze, Etched, Signed, Claude Conover, 13 ½ x 10 x 10 In. 8400.00
Vase, Clear Feldspathic Glaze, Swirls, 4 Handles, 4 Colors, 17 ¼ In. 303.00
Vase, Cobalt Blue, Manganese Splotches, Salt Glaze, Flute Top, Brown, Black Drips, 5 ½ In. 193.00
Vase, Cover, Gray, Brown Drip Glaze, Ken Ferguson, Signed, 24 x 12 In. 3000.00
Vase, Elongated Neck, Brown, Blue Glaze, Salt Glaze, 22 x 8 ½ In. 1080.00
Vase, Flowers, Cobalt Blue, Butterfly, Bristol Glaze, Arie Meaders, 18 In. 3000.00
Vase, Glossy White Feldspathic Glaze, Morning Glories, Vine, Leaves, 8 ½ In. 55.00
Vase, Gray, 2 Handles, Splayed Foot, Baluster, Wood Stand, 6 ½ x 8 ¼ x 7 ½ In. 480.00
Vase, Hunting Scene, Acid Etched, Salt Glazed, 1885, 7 ¼ x 4 ½ In. 3600.00
Vase, Oval, Flared Rim, Blue Drip & Foamy Glaze, Mid 1900s, 22 ½ In. 1035.00
Vase, Parrots, Butterfly, Branch, Salt Glaze, Acid Etched, 1885, 7 ¼ x 5 ½ In. 3600.00
Vase, Stippled, Garlands, Salt Glaze, 5 Handles, S. Frackleton, 4 ½ x 5 ¼ In. 3600.00
Vase, Textured White Glaze, Geometric Design, 13 x 10 In. 1560.00
Water Cooler, 4 Peacocks, Picket Fence, Pine Trees, Tinsmith Collar, 6 Gal., 17 In. 12075.00
Water Cooler, Birch Leaf, Blue Ink, Straight-Sided, 2 Gal. 2700.00
Water Cooler, Blue, 2 Birds, Flowers, L. & B.G. Chace Somerset, Incised, 1890, 16 In. 5500.00
Water Cooler, Cobalt Blue, Branching Clover, Lug Handles, Baltimore, c.1850, 4 Gal., 14 In. 830.00
Water Cooler, Cobalt Blue Leaf Band, Incised Band, Applied Handles, 11 ¾ x 9 In. *illus* 400.00
Water Cooler, Cobalt Blue Man's Profile, 6 Gal. 9945.00
Water Cooler, Eagle Pottery, Jas Hamilton Manufacturing, Penn., 10 Gal., 15 x 20 In. 1770.00
Water Cooler, Rachel At The Well, Blue, Gray, 15 In. 1800.00
Water Cooler, Wells & Richards, Reading, Berks Co., Pa., Blue, 1800s, 19 In. *illus* 13470.00
Wine, Flared Mouth, Layered Shoulder, Manganese Underglaze, Korea, 11 ½ In. 533.00

STORE fixtures, cases, cutters, and other items that have no advertising as part of the decoration are listed here. Most items found in an old store are listed in the Advertising category in this book.

Bag Rack, Twisted Wire, Stringholder, F.M. Thorpe Co., Missouri, 30 x 10 x 11 In. *illus* 143.00
Beer Tap, 3 Spigots, Marble & Brass, From The Driskill Hotel, 1900s. 1795.00
Bin, Grain, Softwood, Red Paint, Slant Front, 2 Inside Compartments, 34 x 44 In. 495.00
Bin, Softwood, Square, Slant Lid, Painted, White, Orange, Black 9, 30 x 18 In. 468.00
Broom Holder, Black Boy, Red Coat, Painted, Cast Iron, Signed, 1894 200.00
Cabinet, Needle, Walnut, 2 Drawers, 1880s, 15 ¼ In. 225.00
Cabinet, Seed, 18 Drawers, Glass Top, Cubbies, Oak, 52 x 52 In. 3450.00
Cabinet, Tariff, Counter, Pine, 2 Pattern Glass Doors, 18 Compartments, Stencil, 36 x 44 In. 690.00
Candy Show Jar, Century Sample, Ground Neck, Stopper, 8-Sided Base, 16 In. 385.00
Candy Show Jar, Dakota Globe, c.1900, 16 In. 165.00

Candy Show Jar, Touraine, Ground Neck, Vented Stopper, c.1900, 19 In. 330.00
Case, Bean Counter, Oak, 18 Drawers, 90 x 34 In. 1898.00
Case, Display, Curved Glass, 2 Sliding Back Doors, Chrome Over Wood, 60 x 26 x 13 In. 402.00
Case, Display, Curved Glass, 3 Mirrored Back Doors, Chrome Over Wood, 68 x 26 x 14 In..... 402.00
Case, Display, Curved Glass, Nickel Frame, 25 x 33 In.. .... 385.00
Case, Display, Maple, Fitted With Glass, Peg Construction, Glass Shelf, c.1800, 28 x 26 x 19 In. 529.00
Case, Display, Nickel Plated, Sliding Doors, Mirrored Lower, Curved Glass Front, 35 x 36 In... 1093.00
Case, Display, Sliding Back Doors, 3 Shelves, 34 ½ x 21 ½ x 41 ½ In. 172.00
Case, Display, Steeple Top, Curved Glass, Nickel Plated, Sliding Doors, Mirrored, 41 x 30 In... 1495.00
Case, Display, Walnut, Double Tower, Nickel Corners, Montreal Showcase Co., 71 x 35 In..... 6050.00
Case, Display, Wood, Glass, Pat. May 14, 1889, Crystal Case Co., Alliance, Ohio, 25 x 35 In.... 1100.00
Cigar Cutter, Huntsman, Lantern, Match Holder, Ashtray, Steel, 20th Century, 38 In. 660.00
Cigar Cutter, Lighter, Elephant, Iron, Painted, Milk Glass Globe, Depress Trunk, 10 ½ In. 1495.00
Clothes Stand, Brass, Scrolling Leaf Cast Iron Base, France, c.1900, 73 x 18 In., Pair....... 885.00
Coffee Grinders are listed in their own category.
Counter, Marble Top, Wood Base, One Flat End, 116 x 36 In. 275.00
Display, Hat, Wood, 24 ¼ x 5 ¾ In. 10.00
Display, Ice Cream Cone, White, Pink, Tan, Papier-Mache, 21 In. 70.00
Display, Ice Cream Sundae, Green Cup, Hot Fudge, Cherry, Whipped Cream, 45 In.......... 880.00
Display, Magician, Philadelphia Novelty, Magic Shop, Clothing, Head, Arms Move, 40 In..... 345.00
Display, Pipe, Brown, Black, White, 36 In. 295.00
Display, Rooster, Scalloped Tray, Painted, Zinc, 19th Century, 18 ½ In. .... *illus* 501.00
Display, Sugar Cone, Glass, Metal, 14 In. 286.00
Display, Umbrella, Oak, Hinged Curved Glass Top, Wood Grillwork, Bead Board, 48 x 37 In.. 863.00
Display, Ungvarsky Fur Co., Metal, Glass Doors, 28 In. 115.00
Glass Dome, Wood Base, Velvet Interior, c.1890, 18 x 12 In.. .... 275.00
Ice Cream Cone Holder, Glass Cylinder, Metal Insert, Lid, 14 ½ In. 358.00
Jar, Counter, Green Aqua, Square, 9 In.. .... 149.00
Jar, Show Globe, Green, Metal Stand, c.1930, 24 In. .... *illus* 350.00
Jar, Straw, Aqua Blue, Ribbed, Mushroom Lid, 11 ½ In.. .... 523.00
Jar, Straw, Pressed, Clear Glass, Quilting, Bull's-Eyes, Metal Insert & Lid, 11 ½ In. 165.00
Jar, Straw, Pressed Square Clear Glass, Flared Base, c.1900, 9 ¾ In. 110.00
Jar, Straw, Ribbed, Pressed, Flared Metal Base, Mushroom Top, Finial, c.1918, 12 In.......... 138.00
Mannequin, Man, Handlebar Mustache, Painted, Papier-Mache, Plaster, c.1890, 40 In. 1870.00
Mannequin, Toddler, Molded Hair, Jointed, Metal Stand, 33 In. 193.00
Mannequin, Warner Bros. Corset Co., Doll Head, E. Heybach, No. 302, 25 In.. .... 440.00
Paper Cutter, Oak, Metal, 1890-1910, 5 x 22 In. 25.00
Rack, Haberdasher's, Mahogany, Brass, Glass, 2 Tiers, Brass Hooks, France, c.1900, 56 x 21 In. 646.00
Sack Rack, Country Store, Metal, Holds 10 Sizes, c.1900, 31 x 9 In. 193.00
Sign, Boot, Iron, Old Paint, 2 Mounts, Late 19th Century, 24 ½ x 29 ½ In. .... *illus* 357.00
Sign, Boot, Red, Black, Pine, Carved, Iron Ring Hanger, 19 x 4 x 10 ½ In.. .... 198.00
Sign, Boot, Spurs, Figural, Hammered, Copper, Inscribed, Regal, Early 1900s, 43 In.......... 1100.00
Sign, Boot Shape, Carved Wood, Gilt, c.1890, 26 In.. .... 1541.00
Sign, Butcher, Bull's Head Shape, Molded Zinc, Gilt Surface, 15 x 12 In. 2070.00
Sign, Caduceus, Cast Iron, 30 x 25 ½ In. 75.00
Sign, Eyeglasses, Eyes, Banner, Gold Paint, Iron, Metal, 2-Sided, Late 1800s, 41 In. 2450.00
Sign, Eyeglasses, Eyes, Cast Iron, Wood, 30 In. 800.00
Sign, Figural, Pointing Finger, Sheet Metal, Painted, Plywood Back, 46 x 19 In.. .... 360.00
Sign, Fish, Carved, Yellow, Black, Iridescent Glass Eyes, Wooden Brackets, 17 x 61 In. 294.00
Sign, Fishmonger, Pressed Metal, Applied Fins, Hanging Holes, 22 x 8 In. 1320.00
Sign, Folding Razor, Open Position, Wood, Original Paint, c.1800, 26 ½ In. 450.00
Sign, Gilt Eagle, 2-Sided, Penn., Early19th Century, 44 x 25 In. 1495.00
Sign, Haberdasher, Stovepipe Hat Form, Red, Gold Paint, Tin, Early 1800s, 6 ½ x 12 In. 1100.00
Sign, Hamburger, Bun Open, Embossed, Tin, c.1950-60, 38 x 51 In. 403.00
Sign, Hand Sewn, Man Sewing Shoes, Brass, Oval, 18 In. 895.00
Sign, Hanger, Boot Form, Wrought Iron Ring Hanger, Black, Red, Brown, 19 x 4 x 10 ½ In... 198.00
Sign, Heart Shape, Tin, Punched, Chain, Iron Hanging Bracket, 1800s, 35 x 33 In. 690.00
Sign, Horse Head, Zinc, c.1880, 18 x 16 x 15 In. 770.00
Sign, Jeweler, Zinc Pocket Watch, Painted, 1800s, 41 x 29 In. 920.00
Sign, Key, Winding, Iron, 35 ½ In. 125.00
Sign, Key Shape, Iron, Multicolored Paint Layers, Late 1800s, 22 ½ x 13 In. 588.00
Sign, Key Shape, Metal, Multicolored Paint Layers, Late 1800s, 32 ½ In. 823.00
Sign, Key Shape, Sheet Iron, Multicolored Paint Layers, Late 1800s, 34 In. 294.00
Sign, Mortar & Pestle, Figural, Brass, Early 20th Century, 35 In. 2000.00
Sign, Mortar & Pestle, Figural, Tin, Stamped, W.T. Co., c.1900, 25 In. 650.00
Sign, Mortar & Pestle Shape, Wood, Carved, Gilt Over Black, 13 In. 881.00

Stoneware, Water Cooler, Wells & Richards, Reading, Berks Co., Pa., Blue, 1800s, 19 In.
$13470.00

Store, Bag Rack, Twisted Wire, Stringholder, F.M. Thorpe Co., Missouri, 30 x 10 x 11 In.
$143.00

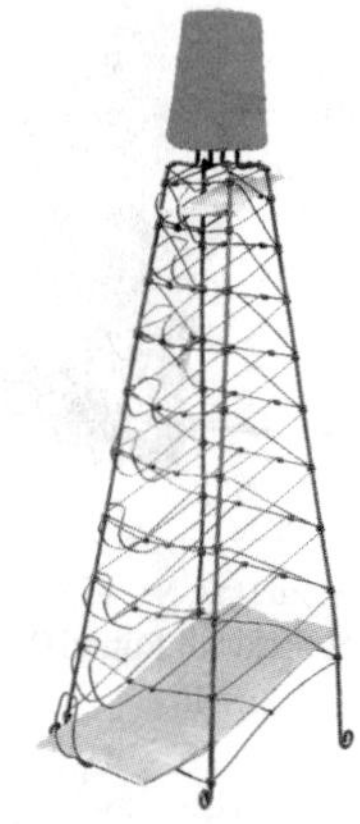

Store, Display, Rooster, Scalloped Tray, Painted, Zinc, 19th Century, 18 ½ In.
$501.00

TIP

Always roll a rag rug for storage with the right side on the outside. This puts less stress on the backing.

S

Store, Jar, Show Globe, Green, Metal Stand, c.1930, 24 In.
$350.00

Store, Sign, Boot, Iron, Old Paint, 2 Mounts, Late 19th Century, 24 ½ x 29 ½ In.
$357.00

Stove, Crawford Oak, No. 15, Base Burner, Beckwith Round Oak Crown, 64 x 27 x 27 In.
$2900.00

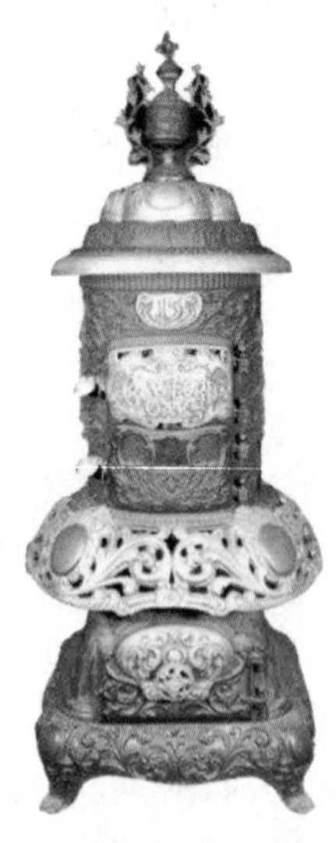

Sign, Padlock Shape, Tin, Iron, Painted Salmon, Movable Keeper, 13 In. 881.00
Sign, Pencil, Red, Wood, 36 ¼ x 1 ¾ In. 187.00
Sign, Pig, Wood, Carved, Painted, c.1900, 19 x 32 In. 350.00
Sign, Pipe Shape, Pine, End Painted Black, Early 1900s, 27 In. 588.00
Sign, Pocket Billiards, Balls In Rack, Metal, Glass, Reverse Painted, Electric, 21 x 8 In. 1800.00
Sign, Pocket Watch, Watches, Roman Numerals, Cast Metal, 2-Sided, Late 1800s, 41 In. 400.00
Sign, Pocket Watch, Wood, Painted, 19th Century, 24 ½ In. 644.00
Sign, Pocket Watch, Zinc, Painted Black Dial, c.1875, 23 In. Diam. 764.00
Sign, Post Office, Painted, Red White & Blue, Wooden, East Thetford, Vermont, 25 ½ x 57 ½ In. 248.00
Sign, Pretzel, Painted, Wood, Iron Bracket, 15 In. 220.00
Sign, Pretzel, Scrolls, Wood, Iron, c.1900, 44 x 42 ½ In. 950.00
Sign, Sale Time, Wood, Painted, 25 ½ x 34 ½ In. 25.00
Sign, Shoe, Woman's, High Button, Carved Wood, Metal Top, c.1900, 13 ¼ In. 705.00
Sign, Tobacco Pipe, Figural, Wood, Tin, Cardboard, 47 x 16 In. 90.00
Sign, Top Hat, Painted, Orange, Black, Tin, Mid 19th Century, 8 ¾ x 10 ½ In. 1100.00
Sign, Toys & Dolls, Tin, Cardboard, 27 x 6 In. 780.00
Soda Fountain Dispenser, The Innovation, Marble Base, Stained Glass Shade, 39 In. 4950.00
Strawholder, No Touch, Sanitized, Pat'd 1917 135.00
Stringholder, Beehive Form, Lignum-Vitae, Threaded Base, Treen, 19th Century, 5 x 5 ½ In. 220.00
Stringholder, Wood, Cast Iron, Pat. March, 1841, N.C. Byram, Boston, 10 x 6 In. 193.00
Tobacco Cutter, Fowler Co., Waterloo, Iowa, Nickel Plated, Cast Iron, 1914, 9 x 15 In. 110.00
Tobacco Cutter, Griswold, No. 2500, Iron 125.00
Tobacco Cutter, Haas, Baruch & Co., Los Angeles, 16 In. 120.00
Tobacco Cutter, Master Workman, Cast, Mounting, 2 x 12 ½ In. 201.00
Tobacco Cutter, P.J. Sorg Co., Arrow, Feather, Cast Iron, Nickel Plated, 8 x 18 ½ In. 245.00
Tobacco Cutter, Spearhead, Red, 4 ½ x 17 In. 66.00
Tobacco Cutter, Stone-Ordean Wells Co., Cast Iron, Name Plate 165.00

STOVES have been used in America for heating since the eighteenth century and for cooking since the nineteenth century. Most types of wood, coal, gas, kerosene, and even some electric stoves are collected.

Crawford Oak, No. 15, Base Burner, Beckwith Round Oak Crown, 64 x 27 x 27 In. *illus* 2900.00
Diadem, No. 22, Cast Iron, Nickel Silver Plated, 2 Door, M.L. Filley, Troy, N.Y., 30 x 18 In. 1150.00
Isabella Furnace, Cast Iron, 19th Century, 20 x 24 In. 325.00
Parlor, Green, Porcelain, 25 x 18 x 14 In. *illus* 350.00
Parlor, Riverside, Cast Iron, Nickel Plated, Rock Island Stove Co., 72 x 29 In. 770.00
Parlor, Round, Oak, Doe-Wah-Jack Finial, Cast Iron, Patent 1909, 75 x 27 In. 1100.00
Parlor, White Paint, Cast Iron, Cylindrical, Footed, 31 x 14 In. 100.00
Stove Plate, 6-Petal Rosette Center, Iron, Square, 1870, 25 x 25 In. 1430.00
Stove Plate, Depicting Oil Miracle, Arches, Garland, Drape, German Text, Iron, 1700s, 27 x 21 In. 275.00

STRETCH GLASS is named for the strange stretch marks in the glass. It was made by many glass companies in the United States from about 1900 to the 1920s. It is iridescent. Most American stretch glass is molded; most European pieces are blown and may have a pontil mark.

Candy Jar, Cover, Paneled, Celeste Blue 30.00
Cigarette Holder, Wheel Carved Flower, Marigold 165.00
Console Bowl, Rolled Edge, Celeste Blue 10.00
Sherbet, Laurel Leaves, Celeste Blue 30.00
Vase, Flared, Red, 5 In. 60.00

SULPHIDES are cameos of unglazed white porcelain encased in transparent glass. The technique was patented in 1819 in France and has been used ever since for paperweights, decanters, tumblers, marbles, and other type of glassware. Paperweights and Marbles are listed in their own categories.

Jar, Cover, George IV Bust, Footed, Aspley Pellat, c.1820, 8 ½ In. 2574.00

SUMIDA is a Japanese pottery that was made from about 1895 to 1941. Pieces are usually everyday objects—vases, jardinieres, bowls, teapots, and decorative tiles. Most pieces have a very heavy orange-red, blue, brown, black, green, purple, or off-white glaze, with raised three-dimensional figures as decorations. The unglazed part is painted red, green, black, or orange. Sumida is sometimes mistakenly called *Sumida gawa*, but true Sumida gawa is a softer pottery made in the early 1800s.

Bowl, Fish Shape, Karp & Pond, 1900, 10 x 4 In. *illus* 220.00
Tankard, Dragons, 15 x 8 In. *illus* 431.00

SUNBONNET BABIES were first introduced in 1900 in the book *The Sunbonnet Babies*. The stories were by Eulalie Osgood Grover, illustrated by Bertha Corbett. The children's faces were completely hidden by the sunbonnets. The children had been pictured in black and white before this time, but the color pictures in the book were immediately successful. The Royal Bayreuth China Company made a full line of children's dishes decorated with the Sunbonnet Babies. Some Sunbonnet Babies plates have been reproduced, but are clearly marked.

Plate, Friday, Sweeping, 7 In. 30.00
Plate, Girls, Doing Housework, Child's, 6 In. 98.00
Plate, Playing Catch, 7 In. 225.00
Plate, Round Dance, 7 In. 225.00
Plate, Saturday, Baking, 7 ¼ In. 175.00
Plate, Sunday, Fishing, 7 ¼ In. 199.00
Plate, Swinging, 7 In. 225.00
Plate, Thursday, Scrubbing, 7 ¼ In. 199.00
Postcard, Valentine's Day, Two Is Company, 1910 .... 14.00
Sugar, Girls, Doing Housework 175.00

SUNDERLAND luster is a name given to a special type of pink luster made by Leeds, Newcastle, and other English firms during the nineteenth century. The luster glaze is metallic and glossy and appears to have bubbles in it. Other pieces of luster are listed in the Luster category.

Bowl, English Ships, Sailor's Farewell, Pink Luster, Robert Burns, c.1800, 5 ½ x 11 In. 750.00
Bowl, Ship Caroline, 1800s, 4 x 10 In. 468.00
Canister, City, Black Transfer, Purple, 19th Century, 8 In. 100.00
Figurine, Cat, Seated, Pink, Green Eyes, c.1825, 9 ¾ In. 1645.00
Jug, West View Of Iron Bridge, Masonic, 7 In. 518.00
Pitcher, Masonic Emblems, Bridge, Verse, Pink Luster, 7 ½ In. .... *illus* 225.00
Pitcher, Woman, Followed By Page, Pink, Green, c.1825, 6 ½ In. 59.00
Plaque, Thou God See'st Me, Pink, 9 x 8 In. 400.00

SUPERMAN was created by two seventeen-year-olds in 1938. The first issue of *Action* comics had the strip. Superman remains popular and became the hero of a radio show in 1940, cartoons in the 1940s, a television series, and several major movies.

Bank, Mechanical, Dime Register, Superman Breaking Out Of Chains, Tin, 2 ½ In. 164.00
Cake Decorations, Superman With Buildings, Wilton, 1978, 6 Piece 16.00
Cards, Wax Box, Unopened, Topps, 1966 .... 1700.00
Comic Book, No. 30, Superman, Lois Lane, Clark Kent, DC Comics 875.00
Cookie Jar, Superman Breaking Out Of Chains, Warner Bros., 1997, 12 x 9 ¼ In. 65.00
Cookie Jar, Superman In Phone Booth, California Originals, 1978 .... 405.00
Costume, Cape, Adventures Of Superman, Geo. Reeves, Red, Cotton, 1950s, 53 x 55 In. 32313.00
Display, Prop, Kryptonite, Box, 10 ¼ x 13 ¼ x 10 ¼ In. 253.00
Doll, Superman, Wood, Composition, Jointed, Painted, Cloth, Ideal, 13 In. 605.00
Figure, Chalk, Painted, Blue, Red, Mica, Molded, 15 ½ In. 201.00
Figure, Christopher Reeve, As Superman, Mego, 1978, 12 ½ In. 40.00
Figure, Superman, Yellow, Green, Chalkware, Carnival, 15 In. 86.00
Game, Calling Superman, News Reporting, Transogram Co., 1954 .... 90.00
Game, Radio Quiz Master, Premium, Return Envelope, 9 ½ x 10 In. 115.00
Hand Puppet, Cloth Body, Ideal, 1965, 9 ½ x 16 In. 65.00
Jigsaw Puzzle, Superman Over The City, 1940, 16 x 20 In., 500 Piece 495.00
Jigsaw Puzzle, Superman Springs Into Action, 1940, 16 x 20 In., 500 Piece 395.00
Lobby Card, Superman II, Christopher Reeve, Signed, 11 x 14 In. 173.00
Lunch Box, Clark Kent In News Office, Superman Flying, Metal, Thermos, 1978 .... 43.00
Movie Viewer, Plastic, Sealed, Acme, 2 Films, 1955, 5 x 6 ½ In. 195.00
Ornament, Clark Kent Changes To Superman, Phone Booth, Light & Motion, Hallmark, 1995 22.00
Ornament, Lunch Box, Metal, Hallmark Keepsake, Box, 1998, 2 ¼ x 3 ¼ In. 18.00
Overnight Bag, Blue, Yellow, Red, Vinyl, Handles, 7 ½ x 12 In. 85.00
Pencil Box, Superman, Pencil, Ruler, 2 Erasers, 8 ¼ In. 57.50
Pin, Superman, Sunday Mail Comics Club, Black, Red, Australia, 1940s, 1 In. 345.00
Poster, Breaking Kryptonite Chains, Linen Mount, 40 ¼ x 26 ¾ In. 115.00
Ring, Secret Compartment Initial, Defense Club Milk Program, Ostby & Barton, Premium .. 3500.00
Ring, Superman, Standing, Glass Top, Adjustable, Yellow Ground 44.00
Ring, Superman Breaking Out Of Chains, Contest Prize, DC Comics, 1940 .... 6555.00
Stringholder, Superman, Painted, Plaster, c.1950, 7 ½ x 6 x 3 In. .... *illus* 863.00
Toy, Kryptonite Rock, Booklet, Box 22.00
Toy, Superman & Airplane, Rollover, Tin, Windup, Marx, Box, 6-In. Wingspan 2376.00
Toy, Supermobile, Red Fists, Corgi, Box, 1979, 6 ¾ x 4 In. 63.00

Stove, Parlor, Green, Porcelain, 25 x 18 x 14 In.
$350.00

Sumida, Bowl, Fish Shape, Karp & Pond, 1900, 10 x 4 In.
$220.00

Sumida, Tankard, Dragons, 15 x 8 In.
$431.00

Sunderland, Pitcher, Masonic Emblems, Bridge, Verse, Pink Luster, 7 ½ In.
$225.00

Superman, Stringholder, Superman, Painted, Plaster, c.1950, 7 ½ x 6 x 3 In. $863.00

Superman, Toy, Tank, Rollover, Tin Lithograph, Windup, c.1940, 3 ⅞ In. $306.00

Swastika Keramos, Vase, Green Leaves, Gold Iridescent, Handles, Marked, 7 ¾ In. $330.00

Swastika Keramos, Vase, Iris, Ruby Red, Gold Ground, Bulbous Neck, Footed, 6 ⅝ In. $184.00

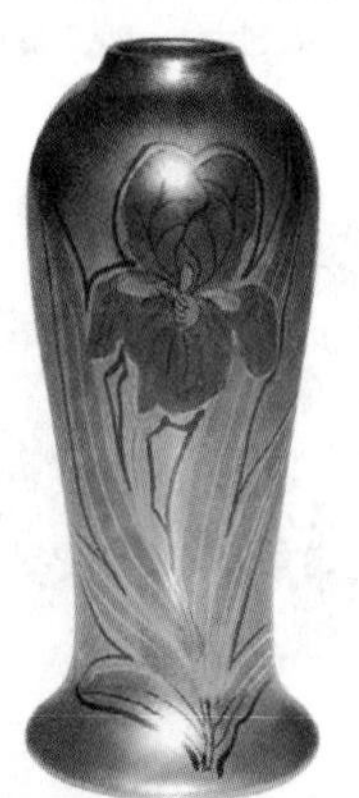

Toy, Tank, Rollover, Tin Lithograph, Windup, c.1940, 3 ⅞ In. .... *illus* 306.00
Tumbler, Superman Caped Wonder To The Rescue, Pepsi-Cola, 1978, 5 ½ In. 10.00
Wallet, Vinyl, Brushed Felt Cape, Certificate, National Comics Pub., 1958, 4 ½ In. 135.00
Wristwatch, S-Shield, Supertime, New Haven Clock Co., c.1950, Box 1531.00
Wristwatch, Superman, Hands On Hips, New Haven Watch, Box, 1940, 4 x 7 In. 460.00
Wristwatch, Superman, Rectangular, New Haven Clock Co., Box, 1940 .... 1581.00
Wristwatch, Superman Spins Around Watch, Plastic Case, Hinged Lid, 3 x 5 ¾ In. 343.00

SUSIE COOPER began as a designer in 1925 working for the English firm A.E. Gray & Company. In 1932 she formed Susie Cooper Pottery, Ltd. In 1950 it became Susie Cooper China, Ltd., and the company made china and earthenware. In 1966 it was acquired by Josiah Wedgwood & Sons, Ltd. The name Susie Cooper appears with the company names on many pieces of ceramics.

Chop Plate, Endon, 8 ¾ In. 48.00
Cup & Saucer, Endon, 1932-64, 2 ¾ & 5 ¾ In. 38.00
Plate, Bread & Butter, Endon, 6 ¾ In. 20.00
Plate, Salad, Fruit Center, Blue Border, 1930s, 8 ¾ In., 12 Piece 200.00
Soup, Dish, Saucer, Endon, Handles, 2 x 4 ¾ & 6 ½ In. 68.00

SWANKYSWIGS are small drinking glasses. In 1933, the Kraft Food Company began to market cheese spreads in these decorated, reusable glass tumblers. They were discontinued from 1941 to 1946, then made again from 1947 to 1958. Then plain glasses were used for most of the cheese, although a few special decorated Swankyswigs have been made since that time. For more prices, go to Kovels.com.

Antique No. 1, Orange, 3 ¾ In. 8.00
Antique No.1, Black, 3 ¾ In. 5.00
Cornflower No. 2, Blue, 3 ¼ In. 23.00
Cornflower No. 2, Red, 3 ¼ In. 23.00
Cornflower No. 2, Red, 4 In. 8.00
Daisy, Red & White, 3 ¼ In. 23.00
Forget-Me-Not, Blue, 3 ½ In. .... 8.00 to 15.00
Forget-Me-Not, Red, 3 ½ In. 8.00
Kiddie Kup, Bear, Blue, 3 ¾ In. 6.00
Kiddie Kup, Bear, Blue, 4 ½ In. 25.00
Kiddie Kup, Bird & Elephant, Red, 3 ¼ In. 22.00
Kiddie Kup, Cat & Rabbit, Green, 3 ¼ In. 23.00
Kiddie Kup, Deer, Brown, 4 In. 8.00
Kiddie Kup, Dog & Rooster, Orange, 3 ¼ In. 22.00
Kiddie Kup, Duck & Horse, Black, 3 ¼ In. 23.00
Kiddie Kup, Elephant, Red, 4 In. 8.00
Kiddie Kup, Rooster, Orange, 3 ¾ In. 8.00
Tulip, Blue, 3 ½ In. 20.00
Tulip, Green, 3 ½ In. 8.00
Tulip, Red, 3 ½ In. 8.00

SWASTIKA KERAMOS is a line of art pottery made from 1906 to 1908 by the Owen China Company of Minerva, Ohio. Many pieces were made with an iridescent glaze.

Tankard, Cosmos, Maroon Leaves, Gold Ground, 10 ¼ In. 207.00
Vase, Baby Blackbirds, On Branch, Red Flowers, Tapered, 8 ½ In. 138.00
Vase, Branches, Green Leaves, Bell Shape, Rolled Rim, 15 ¾ x 11 In. 604.00
Vase, Cosmos, Maroon, Green Leaves, Gold Ground, Tapered, Handle, 10 ¼ In. 207.00
Vase, Flower, Maroon, Green Stem, Leaves, Gold Iridescent, Bulbous Neck, 8 In. 242.00
Vase, Flowers, Gold Iridescent Ground, Wafer Mark, 7 ⅞ In. 245.00
Vase, Gold Iridescent, Coralene, Green Accents, Incised Bands, Handles, 8 In. 173.00
Vase, Green Leaves, Gold Iridescent, Handles, Marked, 7 ¾ In. .... *illus* 330.00
Vase, Iris, Ruby Red, Gold Ground, Bulbous Neck, Footed, 6 ⅝ In. .... *illus* 184.00
Vase, Speckled Gold Glaze, Coralene Handle, Mark 706E, 8 x 7 In. 295.00

SWORDS of all types that are of interest to collectors are listed here. The military dress sword with elaborate handle is probably the most wanted. A *tsuba* is a hand guard fitted to a Japanese sword between the handle and the blade. Be sure to display swords in a safe way, out of reach of children.

Artillery, Brass Guard, Leather & Brass Wrapped Handle, Scabbard, Ames, 1862, 32 In. 1600.00
Bayonet, Rifle Saber, Navy, Brass Handle, Leather Scabbard, Merrill, 1862, 25 ½-In. Blade ... 1000.00
Broad, Scotland Regimental, Leather Covered Grip, c.1820, 31 ½ In. 3600.00

Cavalry, Brass Bow & Pommel, Wrapped Handle, Marked, MS, Ames, 1850, 36 In. 1300.00
Cavalry, Officer, England, Wilkinson, Chased Design On Guard, Royal Emblem. 525.00
Cavalry, Officers, England, Iron Hilt, Stirrup Guard, Cross Guard, Ebony Grip, c.1780, 30 ½ In. 850.00
Cavalry, U.S., Trooper, Iron Hilt, Leather Covered Grip, c.1808, 24 In. 1450.00
Chinese, Boxer Period, 29 In. 2970.00
Cutlass, Naval, Revolutionary War, Iron Hilt, Scalloped Shell Guard, Wood Grip, c.1750, 26 In. 1550.00
Cutlass, Navy, Leather & Brass Wire Handle, Leather Copper Riveted Scabbard, 26 In. 950.00
Diplomatic, Japan, Gilt Bronze, Paulownia Crest, Phoenix Finial, 33 In. 711.00
Dress, Officer's, Engraved Blade, Gilt Mounts, c.1863 . . . . 296.00
Foot Artillery, Eagle Head, c.1820, 38 In.. . . . . 440.00
Foot Officer's, Eagle Head, Handle, Signed F.W. Widmann, Philadelphia, Engraved Blade, 39 In. 440.00
Foot Officer's, Eagle Head, Non Regulation Model 1821, 35 In.. . . . . 165.00
Foot Officer's, Engraved Blade, Wire Wrapped Shagreen Handle, 37 In. 863.00
Hanger, Brass Hilt, Acorn Terminals, Fluted Pommel Cap, Wood Grip, Colonial, c.1700, 22 In. 850.00
Hanger, France, Infantry, French Revolution, Curved Fullered Blade, Ribbed Grip, Brass Hilt, 25 In. 775.00
Hanger, U.S., Silver Hilt, American, Lion Pommel, c.1765, 32 In.. . . . . 2145.00
Infantry, Eagle Head, c.1818, 34 In.. . . . . 550.00
Infantry, Officer's, Eagle Head, c.1820, 38 In. 715.00
Katana, Japan, Irregular Patterns, Signed, Kane-Tomo, 26 ⅛ In.. . . . . 1652.00
Katana, Japan, Wood Scabbard, 28 ½ In. . . . . *illus* 359.00
Metal Scabbard, Shagreen Handle, 20th Century, Japan, 27 ¼ In. 900.00
Musician's, Saber, Brass Handle, Leather Scabbard, Roby, 1864, 28 In.. . . . . 325.00
Navy, U.S., Gold, Engraved, Dolphin Hilt, Acorns, Leaves, Scabbard, 38 In. 595.00
Portuguese, Silver Hilt, Inscribed Blade, c.1790, 38 In. 880.00
Saber, Cavalry, Brass Bow, Wrapped Handle, Scabbard, Marked, 1847, 35 ½ In. 500.00
Saber, Cavalry, Wood Handle, Leather Grips, Brass Wire, Scabbard, Horstmann, 32 In. . . *illus* 750.00
Shamshis, Curved, Single Edge, Gilt, Steel Guard, Ivory Grip, Persia, 1700s, 39 ½ In. . . . *illus* 8050.00
Split Guard, American, Eagle Head, c.1790, 33 In. 550.00
Steel Blade, Bird Form Silver Hilt, Persia, 33 ½ In.. . . . . 770.00
Swordfish Bill, Wood Handle, Old Red Paint, New England, Early 20th Century, 42 ⅜ In. . . . 144.00
Wakizashi, Japan, Dragon, Leather Guard, Shakudo Mounts Inlaid Gold, 21 ½ In. 5036.00
Wakizashi, Japan, Fighting Samurai, Boat, Bridges, 17th Century, 18 ⅜ In.. . . . . 2242.00
Wakizashi, Japan, Fullers, 3 Mekugi, 22 In.. . . . . 3851.00
Wakizashi, Japan, Scabbard, Carved Inscriptions, 1860, 18 In. 1121.00
Yataghan, Afghanistan, Scabbard, Silver Plated Handle, Repousse Flower, 20th Century, 27 In. 472.00

SYRACUSE is a trademark used by the Onondaga Pottery of Syracuse, New York. The company was established in 1871. It is still working. The name became the Syracuse China Company in 1966. It is known for fine dinnerware and restaurant china.

SYRACUSE China

America, Platter, Suzanne Federal Shape, 14 In. 40.00
Baroque, Cup & Saucer 22.00
Baroque, Plate, Bread & Butter, 7 ⅜ In. 11.00
Baroque, Soup, Cream, Handles, 6 ⅞ In. 18.00
Bird Series, Cup, Flora, Fauna, Rust, Blue, Blue, 6 Oz. 5.00
Bridal Rose, Cup & Saucer 13.50
Bridal Rose, Plate, Dinner, 10 ½ In.. . . . . 23.00
Captain's Table, Bowl, Cereal, 7 In. 7.99
Captain's Table, Cup & Saucer. 8.99
Captain's Table, Plate, Dinner, 9 ¾ In. 9.99
Captain's Table, Plate, Salad, 7 ¼ In. 5.99
Charm, Cup & Saucer 18.50
Charm, Plate, Bread & Butter, 6 ¼ In. 9.25
Charm, Plate, Salad, 8 In. 14.00
Concord Rose, Creamer, 4 ⅛ In. 14.99
Concord Rose, Plate, Bread & Butter, 6 ¼ In. 6.99
Concord Rose, Sugar, Cover, 3 ¾ In. 14.99
Coralbel, Bowl, Fruit, 5 In. 11.00
Coralbel, Bowl, Vegetable, Cover. 75.00
Coralbel, Creamer 15.00
Coralbel, Cup & Saucer. 21.00
Coralbel, Plate, Bread & Butter, 6 ¼ In.. . . . . 5.00 to 11.00
Coralbel, Plate, Dinner, 9 ¾ In.. . . . . 21.00
Coralbel, Plate, Salad, 8 In.. . . . . 12.00
Coralbel, Soup, Cream, Saucer. 21.00
Coralbel, Sugar, Cover 25.00
Coventry, Cup & Saucer, 2 ⅜ In. 20.00

Sword, Katana, Japan, Wood Scabbard, 28 ½ In. $359.00

Sword, Saber, Cavalry, Wood Handle, Leather Grips, Brass Wire, Scabbard, Horstmann, 32 In. $750.00

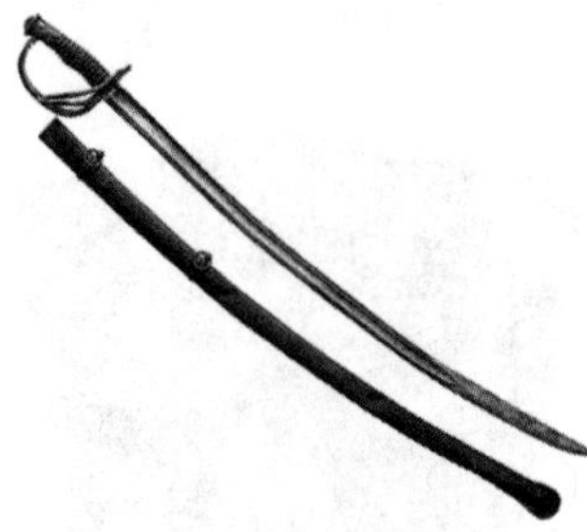

Sword, Shamshis, Curved, Single Edge, Gilt, Steel Guard, Ivory Grip, Persia, 1700s, 39 ½ In. $8050.00

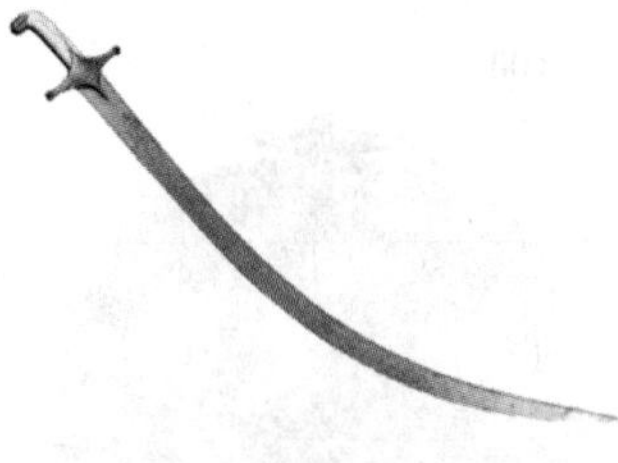

TIP

To clean an old coffee grinder, grind white rice through the mill. When the rice appears to be clean, the grinder is clean enough to use.

Tea Caddy, Bone, England, c.1800, 4 ¾ x 4 ½ In.
$1476.00

Tea Caddy, Burl, Coffin Shape, String Inlay, Brass Feet, Britain, 1800s, 6 x 7 x 4 In.
$300.00

Tea Caddy, Fruitwood, Melon Shape, Green, Brown Stained Segments, Handle, Eng., c.1825, 5 In.
$9480.00

Tea Caddy, Lacquer, Blue Lapis, Steel Mounts, George III, c.1800, 8 In.
$945.00

Debutant, Creamer, 2 ¼ In. 22.00
Debutant, Plate, Salad, 8 In. 16.00
Debutant, Sugar, Cover, 3 ¼ In. 25.00
Dogwood, Cake Server, Open Handle, 10 ½ In. 68.00
Finesse, Plate, Salad, Carefree Line 9.00
Indian Tree, Saucer, Orange Flowers, 4 Piece 25.00
Monticello, Bowl, Vegetable, 9 In. 8.00
Selma, Bowl, Fruit, 5 In. 9.50
Selma, Cup & Saucer, Footed Cup 23.00
Sherwood, Gravy Boat, Underplate 30.00
Sherwood, Plate, 8 ¾ In. 10.00
Victoria, Cup & Saucer 25.00
Victoria, Gravy Boat, Attached Underplate, 9 In. 69.00
Victoria, Plate, Bread & Butter, 6 ¼ In. 6.60
Vintage, Bowl, Vegetable, Divided, Carefree Line, 10 x 8 ½ In. 14.00
Vintage, Butter, Cover, Carefree Line 16.00
Vintage, Creamer, Carefree Line 8.00
Vintage, Plate, Dinner, Carefree Line, 10 In. 9.00
Webster, Bowl, Dessert, 1966, 5 ¾ In. 10.00
Webster, Cup & Saucer, 1966 .... 28.00
Woodbine, Butter, Cover 20.00
Woodbine, Plate, Dinner, 10 ¼ In. 10.00
Woodbine, Plate, Salad, 8 ⅛ In. 8.00
Woodbine, Salt & Pepper 15.00
Woodbine, Sugar 9.00

TAPESTRY, PORCELAIN, *see Rose Tapestry category.*

TEA CADDY is the name for a small box made to hold tea leaves. In the eighteenth century, tea was very expensive and it was stored under lock and key. The first tea caddies were made with locks. By the nineteenth century, tea was more plentiful and the tea caddy was larger. Often there were two sections, one for green tea, one for black tea.

Amboyna, Coffin Shape, 2 Lidded Compartments, Ring Handles, Regency, 6 x 9 In. 1080.00
Black Lacquer, Gilt, Incised, Landscape, 5 ½ x 11 In. 1680.00
Black Lacquer, Gilt, Incised, Landscape, 5 x 9 ½ In. 1440.00
Black Lacquer, Scenic, Paktong Lidded Compartment, 6 x 11 In. 930.00
Bone, England, c.1800, 4 ¾ x 4 ½ In. .... *illus* 1476.00
Brass, Applied Beaded Flowers, c.1800, 5 ¼ In. 1755.00
Burl, Coffin Shape, String Inlay, Brass Feet, Britain, 1800s, 6 x 7 x 4 In. .... *illus* 300.00
Burl Veneer, Dome Lid, Brass Hardware, 2 Compartments, England, 1800s, 8 x 4 In. 293.00
Burl Walnut, Inlay, Glass Bowl, England, 19th Century, 6 ¼ x 12 x 6 ¾ In. 439.00
Burl Walnut, Tunbridgeware, Parquetry Surround, Fitted Interior, c.1850, 5 ¾ x 9 ½ In. 720.00
Burled Yew, Boxwood, Coffin Shape, Compartments, Ball Feet, 6 x 7 ½ x 4 ½ In. 840.00
Cover, Ivory Veneer, Tortoiseshell Trim, 10-Sides, Early 19th Century, 4 x 4 ¼ In. 353.00
Cover, Rosewood, Ivory, 2 Compartments, Brass Lion Head Handles, 5 x 8 x 4 ¼ In. 281.00
Creamware, Painted, Asian Relief Decoration, England, 4 ½ In. 420.00
Dome Top, Walnut, Brass Straps, Georgian, c.1880, 7 x 9 x 5 In. 750.00
Fruitwood, Apple Shape, Foil Interior, c.1890, 4 In. 863.00
Fruitwood, Apple Shape, Foil Liner, England, 5 x 4 ½ In. 250.00
Fruitwood, Barber Pole & Burl Banded Inlay, Stars, Britain, 1790s, 4 x 4 x 4 In. 650.00
Fruitwood, Bone Inlaid, Carved, George V, 6 ½ x 5 In. 360.00
Fruitwood, Carved, Apple Shape, Stem, Lock, Foil Lining, Hinged, Painted Green, 5 ¾ In. 3055.00
Fruitwood, Carved, Bone Inlaid, Stained, England, 4 ½ x 3 ½ In. 318.00
Fruitwood, Carved, Pear Shape, Stem, Lock, Foil Lining, Hinged, Early 1800s, 6 ¼ In. 1645.00
Fruitwood, Iron Escutcheon, Britain, Early 19th Century, 7 In. 173.00
Fruitwood, Melon Shape, Green, Brown Stained Segments, Handle, Eng., c.1825, 5 In. .... *illus* 9480.00
Fruitwood, Pear Shape, Foil Liner, England, George III Style, 7 x 4 ½ In. 275.00
Fruitwood, Pear Shape, Ivory Escutcheon, 7 In. .... 300.00 to 385.00
Georgian, Hourglass Shape, 2 Oval Reserves, Inlaid Satinwood, Seashells, c.1815, 7 x 12 In. 1440.00
Ivory, Inlaid Tortoise, Ivory, Silver Mounts, Georgian, 1700s, 4 In. 3776.00
Kingwood, Rosewood Marquetry, Inlaid Brass Plaque, France, 19th Century, 5 x 9 ½ In. 295.00
Lacquer, Black, Circular, Chinese, 6 ½ x 6 ½ In. 1020.00
Lacquer, Black, Gilt, Figures, Interior 2 Pewter Boxes, Fan Shape, Chinese, 5 x 15 In. 2070.00
Lacquer, Blue Lapis, Steel Mounts, George III, c.1800, 8 In. .... *illus* 945.00
Lacquer, Red, Gilt Designs, Exotic Birds, Pewter Insert, Ivory Knob, Chinese, 1800s, 7 x 5 In. 470.00
Mahogany, 8-Sided, Double Compartment, Georgian, 5 x 7 ¼ x 4 In. 450.00

Mahogany, Apple, Fluted Decoration, Ivory Escutcheon, George III, 5 ¾ x 4 ½ In.......... 240.00
Mahogany, Bombe Form, Fitted Interior, Chippendale Style, 8 ½ x 12 x 6 In.............. 200.00
Mahogany, Brass Ball, Claw Feet, Chippendale, c.1880, 7 x 9 x 6 In..................... 440.00
Mahogany, Carved, Coffin Shape, 2 Compartments, William IV, 8 x 17 x 8 ¾ In........... 1440.00
Mahogany, Coffin Shape, Bun Brass Feet, Regency, c.1830, 5 x 8 In..................... 354.00
Mahogany, Cube Shape, Inlaid Holly Wood, Mahogany Inlay, 4 x 4 x 4 In................. 660.00
Mahogany, Federal, Early 19th Century, 8 x 11 ½ In.................................... 263.00
Mahogany, Herringbone & Banded Inlay, Round Patera, 1790s, 5 ½ x 4 x 4 In............ 600.00
Mahogany, House, Dog, Flowers Needlepoint Under Glass, Inlays, England, 1800s, 7 x 9 In... 460.00
Mahogany, Inlaid, Cover, Hinged, Deer, Acorn, Conch Shell, 5 x 7 ½ x 4 ¼ In............. 531.00
Mahogany, Inlaid Compass Star, Hinged Lid, 3-Dividers, England, c.1800, 6 x 12 In. 474.00
Mahogany, Inlay, Canted Corners, Chamfered, Late 18th Century, 5 ½ x 4 ½ x 4 In......... 350.00
Mahogany, Ivory, Ring Handles, Button Feet, English Regency, 1800s, 7 x 12 In........... 300.00
Mahogany, Oval Panel, Herringbone Inlay, Fitted, George III, c.1800, 4 ½ x 8 ½ In......... 359.00
Mahogany, Scrolled Sideboard Shape, Lid, 2 Compartments, England, 1800s, 12 x 20 In..... 575.00
Mahogany, Tassel Key, 7 ½ x 6 ¼ x 12 In. 117.00
Mahogany Inlay, Seashells, Georgian, 4 ¾ x 4 ½ x 3 ½ In., Pair....................... 1560.00
Mixed Wood, Girl With Bird, Dog, Brass Hinges, Box Lock, 4 ¾ x 8 x 5 In................ 187.00
Mother-Of-Pearl, Inlaid Tortoiseshell, Ivory, 2 Compartments, 5 ¼ x 7 ½ x 4 ½ In......... 3120.00
Oak, Barrel Form, Porcelain Liner, Chrome, England, 6 x 4 ½ In......................... 35.00
Papier-Mache, Abalone, Victorian, Painted, Bouquets, Late 1800s, 4 ¼ x 6 ⅜ In. .... *illus* 356.00
Papier-Mache, Ebonized, Multicolored, Gilt, Aesthetic, Late 1800s, 5 ¼ x 8 ¾ In........... 345.00
Papier-Mache, Flowers, Gilt Scrolls, Mother-Of-Pearl Inlay, Lid, Pedestal, c.1850, 30 x 16 In. 324.00
Papier-Mache, Mother-Of-Pearl Floral Inlays, 2 Interior Boxes, Well, Gilt, c.1850, 15 x 9 In.. 501.00
Pewter, Incised Figure, Flowers, Continental, Signed, 7 In.............................. 20.00
Porcelain, Flattened, Rounded Shoulders, Famille Verte, Garden Scene, 5 ¾ In............ 270.00
Porcelain, Flowers, Burgundy, Gilt, Dog Stopper, 5 ½ In................................ 190.00
Rosewood, Bombe, Brass Inlay, 3 Compartments, William IV, 7 ½ x 13 x 6 ½ In............ 1140.00
Rosewood, Coffin Shape, Ball Feet, Lidded Wells, Regency, 7 ¾ x 9 ¼ In.................. 889.00
Rosewood, Coffin Shape, England, c.1830, 7 ½ x 13 ¼ In................................ 351.00
Rosewood, Marquetry, Compartments, Burlwood Cover, Ring Handle, 6 x 10 ½ x 5 ½ In..... 1320.00
Rosewood, Mother-Of-Pearl Inlay, Hinged Lid, Coffin Shape, Regency, 6 ½ x 8 x 5 In. 575.00
Rosewood Veneer, Divided Interior, Handle, c.1831, 6 x 9 x 4 In........................ 240.00
Rosewood Veneer, Mother-Of-Pearl Flower Inlay, Bun Feet, Ring Handles, 1800s, 8 x 6 In... 529.00
Satinwood, Marquetry, Medallion, 2 Compartments, 5 ½ x 8 ½ x 5 In..................... 2640.00
Satinwood, Shell Inlay, Interior Compartment, George III, Early 1800s, 3 ¾ x 6 In......... 472.00
Silver Plate, Finial, Hinged Lid, Chased & Etched Flowers, Geometric, 6 ¼ In.............. 240.00
Sterling Silver, Flower Repousse, Round, Ritter & Sullivan, Baltimore, c.1900, 4 x 3 In. 1265.00
Sterling Silver, Repousse, Flower Heads, Marked, Gorham, 1913, 3 ¼ In. 425.00
Stoneware, Pewter, Cylindrical, Honey Gold Glaze, Acanthus Leaves, Germany, 8 ¾ In. 413.00
Tole, Slant Hinged Lid, Painted Flowers, Scrolls, Multicolored, 19 x 18 x 19 In. 259.00
Tortoiseshell, Blond, Bombe Shape, 2 Compartments, Bone Grips, 5 ½ x 6 ¾ x 4 In........ 4080.00
Tortoiseshell, Bone, Domed Lid, 4 Bun Feet, Edwardian, c.1915, 3 ¼ x 4 x 3 In........... 1320.00
Tortoiseshell, Bowfront, 2 Compartments, Velvet Lined, Bone Feet, 5 ½ x 7 ¾ x 5 In........ 6900.00
Tortoiseshell, Cantered Corners, Silver, Ivory Inlay Banding, George III, 1700s, 4 x 8 In..... 2950.00
Tortoiseshell, Mother-Of-Pearl, Ivory, Octagonal, Georgian, Silver Mounted, c.1780, 4 x 4 In. 6300.00
Tortoiseshell, Nickel Silver Inlaid, 2 Compartments, England, 4 ¾ x 7 ¼ x 4 ¼ In. 2400.00
Tortoiseshell, Serpentine Front, George III, 5 ¼ In.................................... 1989.00
Tortoiseshell, Silver Gilt, Gold, Flowers, Birds, 2 Interior Canisters, Italy, 5 x 9 In. ..... *illus* 5313.00
Tortoiseshell, Silver Inlaid, Serpentine Front, Edwardian, 7 ¼ x 10 ¼ x 5 ¾ In............ 4080.00
Tortoiseshell, Silver Mounted, Lidded, Ivory Pull, 3 ¾ x 4 ½ In......................... 840.00
Walnut, Maple, Dome Top, Turned Finial, Vertical Bands, Regency, 8 x 5 ⅝ In. 900.00
Walnut, Rope Twist Inlaid, Compartments, Brass Mounted, Georgian, 6 x 10 x 6 In......... 1560.00
Wood, Apple Shape, Golden Orange, Black Stem, George III, c.1780, 6 In.................. 2629.00
Wood, Pear Shape, Original Hinge, Lock, George III, 7 In.............................. 3410.00

TEA LEAF IRONSTONE dishes are named for their decorations. There was a superstition that it was lucky if a whole tea leaf unfolded at the bottom of your cup. This idea was translated into the pattern of dishes known as "tea leaf." By 1850 at least twelve English factories were making this pattern, and by the 1870s it was a popular pattern in many countries. The tea leaf was always a luster glaze on early wares, although now some pieces are made with a brown tea leaf. There are many variations of tea leaf designs, such as Teaberry, Pepper Leaf, and Gold Leaf. The designs were used on many different white ironstone shapes, such as Bamboo, Lily of the Valley, Empress, and Cumbow.

Basin, Round, Alfred Meakin, 15 x 5 In.. 45.00
Bowl, Vegetable, Cover, Alfred Meakin, 7 x 9 ½ In....................................... 25.00

Tea Caddy, Papier-Mache, Abalone, Victorian, Painted, Bouquets, Late 1800s, 4 ¼ x 6 ⅜ In.
$356.00

Tea Caddy, Tortoiseshell, Silver Gilt, Gold, Painted Flowers, Birds, 2 Interior Canisters, Italy, 5 x 9 In.
$5313.0

TIP

To date an antique chair, look under the seat frame. Eighteenth-century chairs were braced with a thin piece of wood across the front corners of the seat. Later chairs were braced with a solid block of wood screwed into each corner.

Teco, Urn, 4 Handles, Charcoal, Green Matte Glaze, Stamped, 11 ¾ x 4 ½ In.
$3240.00

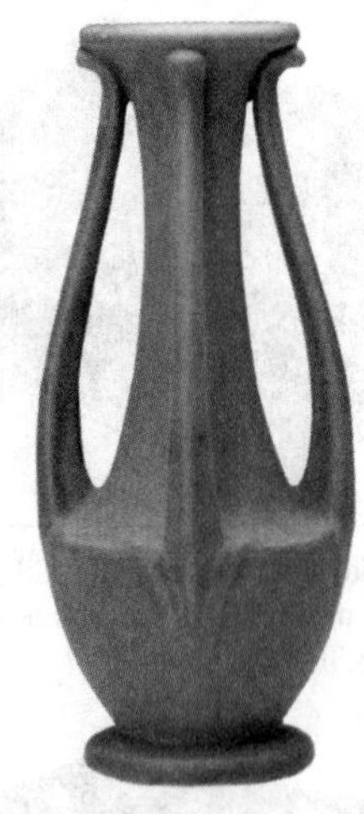

Teco, Vase, No. 167, Green Matte Glaze, 16 ½ x 11 In.
$14200.00

Teddy Bear Stuffing
Early teddy bears were stuffed with excelsior, straw, or kapok. Modern bears are stuffed with polyester, nylon, or plastic. Boot-button eyes were used before World War I, glass eyes beginning in the 1920s, and plastic eyes and noses since the 1950s.

T

Butter Pat, Scalloped Edge, c.1860, 2 ¾ x 2 ¾ In. . . . 28.00
Coffeepot, Alfred Meakin . . . 75.00
Coffeepot, Shaped, Mellor Taylor, Late 1880s, 8 ½ In. . . . 186.00
Creamer, Angled Handle, 6 x 4 ½ In. . . . 30.00
Gravy Boat, 7 ¾ x 4 In. . . . 65.00
Pitcher, 1870s, 9 In. . . . 197.00
Pitcher, Powell Bishop, Late 1800s, 8 ½ In. . . . 168.00
Plate, Alfred Meakin, 1875-1896, 9 ¾ In. . . . 27.00
Plate, Alfred Meakin, Royal Ironstone, 1800s, 8 ½ In. . . . 25.00
Plate, Anthony Shaw, Mid 1800s, 9 In. . . . 45.00
Plate, Royalstone China, 7 ½ In. . . . 14.00
Platter, Alfred Meakin, 13 x 17 ½ In. . . . 60.00
Platter, Alfred Meakin, 16 x 11 ½ In. . . . 52.00
Platter, Oval, Anthony Shaw, Mid 1800s, 15 In. . . . 175.00
Platter, Rectangular, Rounded Corners, 8 ¾ x 12 In. . . . 24.00
Soap Dish, Alfred Meakin, Royal Ironstone, 5 ¾ x 4 In. . . . 6.00
Tea Set, Teapot, Cover, Sugar, Creamer, Alfred Meakin, 3 Piece . . . 140.00
Toothbrush Holder, Interior Drain Holes, Arthur J. Wilkinson, 5 In. . . . 70.00

TECO is the mark used on the art pottery line made by the American Terra Cotta and Ceramic Company of Terra Cotta and Chicago, Illinois. The company was an offshoot of the firm founded by William D. Gates in 1881. The Teco line was first made in 1885 but was not sold commercially until 1902. It continued in production until 1922. Over 500 designs were made in a variety of colors, shapes, and glazes. The company closed in 1930.

TECO

Bookends, Gnomes, Green, Brown Matte Glaze, 9 In. . . . 823.00
Bowl, Flared, 4-Footed, Green Matte Glaze, Ivory, H. Smith, Marked, 12 x 6 In. . . . 4200.00
Bowl, Lobed, Charcoal Green Matte Glaze, 3 x 8 In. . . . 1195.00
Jardiniere, No. 253, Lobed, Green Matte Glaze, Marked, 4 ½ x 8 ½ In. . . . 960.00
Tray, Raised Rim, Green Matte Glaze, William Gates, 10 x 14 In. . . . 690.00
Urn, 4 Handles, Charcoal, Green Matte Glaze, Stamped, 11 ¾ x 4 ½ In. . . . *illus* 3240.00
Vase, 2 Buttressed Handles, Tapered, Green Matte Glaze, 11 ¼ x 5 In. . . . 2880.00
Vase, 2 Handles, Carmel Brown Glaze, 6 ¾ In. . . . 795.00
Vase, 2 Looping Handles, Oval, Squat, 5 ½ x 8 ½ In. . . . 5700.00
Vase, 2 Looping Handles, Squat, Oval, Green Matte Glaze, Stamped, 5 ½ x 8 ½ In. . . . 1600.00
Vase, 4 Buttressed Handles, Charcoal, Green Matte Glaze, Stamped, 11 ¾ x 4 ½ In. . . . 2700.00
Vase, 4 Buttressed Handles, Gourd Shape, Green Matte Glaze, 6 ½ x 5 ¼ In. . . . 3000.00
Vase, Beaker Shape, Green Matte Glaze, Double Stamped, 9 ¾ x 5 ½ In. . . . 1995.00
Vase, Blades Of Grass, Green Matte Glaze, 11 ½ x 4 ½ In. . . . 4800.00
Vase, Buttress Shape, Brown Matte Glaze, 7 x 4 In. . . . 895.00
Vase, Buttresses, Feathered Green Matte Glaze, 9 x 3 ¾ In. . . . 10800.00
Vase, Dimpled Base, Charcoal, Matte Green Glaze, 5 x 4 In. . . . 425.00
Vase, Double Handles, Green Matte Glaze, William Gates, 4 x 8 ½ In. . . . 1035.00
Vase, Flower Form Rim, 4-Footed, Bottle Shape, Green Matte Glaze, 13 ½ x 7 ½ In. . . . 2160.00
Vase, Handles, Green Matte Glaze, 7 x 4 In. . . . 1095.00
Vase, No. 116, Squat, Blob Shape, Footed Base, Green Matte Glaze, F. Albert, 8 x 16 In. . . . 3600.00
Vase, No. 119, 4 Handles, Marked, Green Matte Glaze, 13 ½ x 10 In. . . . 22000.00
Vase, No. 145, Bulbous, Flared, Ribbed Neck, Green Matte Glaze, 17 x 7 In. . . . 9000.00
Vase, No. 167, Green Matte Glaze, 16 ½ x 11 In. . . . *illus* 14200.00
Vase, No. 216, Green Matte Glaze, Bulbous, Stamped, 3 ½ x 4 In. . . . 525.00
Vase, No. 252, Prairie School, Horizontal & Vertical Lines, Green Matte Glaze, 12 In. . . . 3750.00
Vase, No. 262, Spherical Top, 4-Footed, Green Matte Glaze, 18 ½ In. . . . 5400.00
Vase, No. 266, Double Handle, Winged Shape, Green Matte Glaze, W.B. Mundie, 5 x 11 In. . . . 2400.00
Vase, No. 283, 2 Handles, Mahogany Brown, High Glaze, 9 x 5 In. . . . 1375.00
Vase, No. 347, Arts & Craft Shape, Green Matte Glaze, W.D. Gates, 7 x 3 In. . . . 895.00
Vase, No. 402, 2 Handles, Caramel Brown Glaze, 7 x 5 In. . . . 795.00
Vase, No. 402A, Double Buttress Shape, Green Matte Glaze, 7 x 5 In. . . . 660.00
Vase, No. 404, Buttress Shape, Gray Matte Glaze, Wm. Gates, 8 x 3 In. . . . 1095.00
Vase, No. 404, Buttressed, Brown Matte Glaze, W.D. Gates, 7 ¼ x 3 ¼ In. . . . 1095.00
Vase, Oval, Squat, 2 Looping Handles, 5 ½ x 8 ½ In. . . . 1920.00
Vase, Pompeian, Shouldered, Green Matte Glaze, Charcoal Highlights, Marked, 165, 8 x 4 In. . . . 720.00
Vase, Squat, Bulbous, Green Matte Glaze, Marked, 3 ¾ In. . . . 130.00
Vase, Squatty, Brown, 5 ¾ In. . . . 895.00
Vase, Tapered, 4-Sided, 4 Open Handles On Top, Green Matte Glaze, Fritz Albert, 14 In. . . . 16750.00
Vase, Tulip, Buttressed, Charcoal, Green Matte Glaze, 11 ¾ x 5 ½ In. . . . 8400.00
Vase, Tulip Shape, Green Matte Glaze, Charcoal Highlights, F. Moreau, 5 ½ x 12 In. . . . 4800.00
Vase, Tulips, Overlapping Leaves, Green Matte Glaze, William Dodd, 11 In. . . . 4190.00

TEDDY BEARS were named for a president of the United States. The first teddy bear was a cuddly toy said to be inspired by a hunting trip made by Teddy Roosevelt in 1902. Morris and Rose Michtom started selling their stuffed bears as "teddy bears" and the name stayed. The Michtoms founded the Ideal Novelty and Toy Company. The German version of the teddy bear was made about the same time by the Steiff Company. There are many types of teddy bears and all are collected. The old ones are being reproduced. Other bears are listed in the Toy section.

Brown, Stitched Nose, Mouth & Claws, Shoebutton Eyes, Germany, 22 In. 1150.00
Cotton, Jointed, 1901 Fire Dept. Ribbon, 26 In. 35.00
Hermann, Squeaker, Mohair, Jointed, Stitched Mouth, Nose, Germany, 10 x 11 ½ In. 275.00
Mohair, Brown, Embroidered Nose, Mouth, Swivel Head, Humpback, Elongated, Jointed, 14 In. 2500.00
Mohair, Golden, Protruding Snout, Swivel Head, Humpback, Elongated, Jointed, 20 In. 2700.00
Mohair, Golden, Swivel Head, Pointy Snout, Glass Eyes, Elongated Arms, Paw Pads, 21 In.... 2100.00
Mohair, Jointed, Bowtie, 23 In. 35.00
Mohair, Jointed, Rough Pads, Plastic Eyes, 12 In. 23.00
Mohair, Jointed, Shoebutton Eyes, 16 In. 40.00
Mohair, Jointed, Swivel Head, Stitched Nose & Mouth, Felt Pads, Glass Eyes, 16 In. 660.00
Mohair, Straw Stuffed, Jointed, Googly Eyes, Squeaker, Sailor Suit, Germany, 14 In. 440.00
Schuco, Mohair, Green, Stitched, Nose, Mouth, Jointed, Glass Eyes, 1930, 5 ½ In. 403.00
Schuco, Yes-No, Mohair, Stitched Nose, Jointed, Glass Eyes, Germany, 1950, 8 In. .... *illus* 230.00
Steiff, Blond, Felt Pads, Movable Limbs, Shoebutton Eyes, Blank Button, 12 In. 1920.00
Steiff, Center Seam, Hump On Back, Shoebutton Eyes, 15 In. 2040.00
Steiff, Chocolate, Hump On Back, Shoebutton Eyes, 9 In. 1560.00
Steiff, Cinnamon, Stitched Nose, Mouth & Claws, Shoebutton Eyes, c.1906, 16 In. 4312.00
Steiff, Growler, Brown, Metal Ear Clip, Sound Box, Wheels, 22 x 32 x 13 In. 880.00
Steiff, Growler, Cone, Golden, Long Arms, Humped Back, Paw Pads, Pre 1914, 20 In. 4800.00
Steiff, Mohair, Apricot, Stitched Nose, Felt Pads, Jointed Limbs, Glass Eyes, 1920s, 12 In...... 1320.00
Steiff, Mohair, Beige, Stitched Nose, Mouth, Jointed, Glass Eyes, 1930, 6 In. 144.00
Steiff, Mohair, Beige, Stitched Nose, Mouth, Shoebutton Eyes, Ear Button, 1910, 16 In....... 1725.00
Steiff, Mohair, Beige, Stitched Nose & Mouth, Shoebutton Eyes, 3 ½ In. 287.00
Steiff, Mohair, Blond, Embroidered, Swivel Joints, Button Eyes, Excelsior Stuffing, 13 In. 1896.00
Steiff, Mohair, Blond, Stitched Nose, Claws, Button Eyes, Excelsior Stuffing, 16 In. 2252.00
Steiff, Mohair, Brown, Swivel Head, Stitched Ears, Hip Jointed, Paw Pads, 15 In. 300.00
Steiff, Mohair, Carmel, Embroidered, Jointed, Amber Glass Eyes, Button In Ear, 9 In. 80.00
Steiff, Mohair, Golden, Curly, Stitched, Button Eyes, Excelsior Stuffing, 27 In. 7110.00
Steiff, Mohair, Golden, Jointed, Shoebutton Eyes, Button In Ear, 1910, 16 In. 5616.00
Steiff, Mohair, Golden, Stitched Nose, Mouth, Glass Eyes, 1920, 5 In. .... *illus* 230.00
Steiff, Mohair, Golden, Stitched Nose, Mouth, Glass Eyes, Ear Button, 1925, 20 In. 2588.00
Steiff, Mohair, Golden, Stitched Nose, Mouth & Claws, Swivel Joints, Glass Eyes, c.1950, 13 In. 86.00
Steiff, Mohair, Golden, Swivel Joints, Stitched Nose, Mouth & Claws, 8 In. 575.00
Steiff, Mohair, Gray, Golden, Mounted On Wheel Base, Leather Collar, Pull Toy, 23 In. 1500.00
Steiff, Mohair, Jointed, Clown Hat, Glass Eyes, c.1926, 10 In. 4025.00
Steiff, Mohair, Stitched Mouth, Nose & Claws, Shoebutton Eyes, c.1935, 29 ½ In. 12650.00
Steiff, Mohair, Stitched Nose, Mouth & Claws, Glass Eyes, 8 In. 517.00
Steiff, Mohair, Swivel Head, Stitched Features, Felt Pads, Claws, Jointed, Glass Eyes, 9 In. 575.00
Steiff, Mohair, White, Jointed, Stitched Nose, Glass Eyes, Ear Button, 1950s, 3 ½ In. 288.00
Steiff, Mohair, White, Stitched Nose, Shoebutton Eyes, Blank Button, 1910, 10 In. 1840.00
Steiff, Mohair, White, Swivel Joints, Excelsior Stuffing, 10 In. 2963.00
Steiff, Mohair, Yellow, Embroidered, Jointed, Black Steel Eyes, Ear Button, 1905, 16 In....... 2200.00
Steiff, Off-White, Jointed, Shoebutton Eyes, Iron Ear Button, 1904, 9 In. 1600.00
Steiff, Somersault, Mohair, Beige, Shoebutton Eyes, Mechanical Movement, c.1909, 12 In.... 5462.00
Steiff, Squeaker, Blond, Humpback, Jointed, Shoebutton Eyes, Button In Ear, 12 In. 580.00
Steiff, Squeaker, Mohair, Brown, On Bicycle, 4-Wheels, 9 In. 1870.00
Steiff, Squeaker, Mohair, Brown, On Cart, Wood Wheels, 9 In. .... *illus* 1955.00
Steiff, Squeaker, Mohair, Stitched Mouth, Nose & Claws, Shoebutton Eyes, c.1935, 17 In. 7475.00
Steiff, White, Stitched Nose & Mouth, Swivel Neck, Arms & Legs, Shoebutton Eyes, 3 ¾ In.... 259.00

TELEPHONES are wanted by collectors if the phones are old enough or unusual enough. The first telephone may have been made in Havana, Cuba, in 1849, but it was not patented. The first publicly demonstrated phone was used in Frankfurt, Germany, in 1860. The phone made by Alexander Graham Bell was shown at the Centennial Exhibition in Philadelphia in 1876, but it was not until 1877 that the first private phones were installed. Collectors today want all types of old phones, phone parts, and advertising. Even recent figural phones are popular.

American Telephone & Telegraph, Candlestick, Courtesy Box, Key, 8 x 12 In. 358.00
Baird Paystation, Craycraft-Leich Fiddleback Cabinet, Cast Iron Slot, c.1901 .... 1150.00
Bell Telephone Mfg. Co., Wall Mount, Oak, 28 x 7 In. 173.00

Teddy Bear, Schuco, Yes-No, Mohair, Stitched Nose, Jointed, Glass Eyes, Germany, 1950, 8 In.
$230.00

Teddy Bear, Steiff, Mohair, Golden, Stitched Nose, Mouth, Glass Eyes, 1920, 5 In.
$230.00

Teddy Bear, Steiff, Squeaker, Mohair, Brown, On Cart, Wood Wheels, 9 In.
$1955.00

Glass Eyes for Teddy

Glass eyes were first used on teddy bears in 1921. Black boot buttons were used before that.

T

TIP
The old cord on a vintage phone adds value. Green cords are best. Other old forms are twisted cords, brown cords, or patterned cords called rattlesnakes.

Booth, Portable, Mahogany Cabinet, American Electric Co, Chicago, Ill., 14 x 45 In.. . . . . 2065.00
Candlestick, Additional Earphone, Wood Case, France, 14 In. 558.00
Candlestick, Potbelly Upright Desk Stand, Chicago, c.1905 . . . . 690.00
Chicago Telephone Supply Co., Wall, Oak, Beveled Glass, 31 x 12 In.. . . . . 259.00
English House, 1 Button, Cord, Harp Stand, Wood Base, British Manufacture, c.1900 . . . . . . 270.00
GPO, Wall, No. 121, Wood, 2 Alarm Clocks, England . . . . *illus* 215.00
Intercom, Wall, 10 Lines, Handset, L. M. Ericsson, Sweden, c.1900 . . . . 542.00
Kellogg, Wall, Shelf, Oak Case, 23 x 9 In. 374.00
Kellogg, Wall Set, Oak, Fiddleback Cabinet, Pencil Holder, c.1899 . . . . 175.00
LM Ericson, Desk Set, Walnut Base, 10 Station Intercom, PTT Transreceiver, c.1910. . . . . 1093.00
Montgomery Ward & Co., Wall, 20 x 8 ¾ In. . . . . *illus* 101.00
Pay Station, Metal, Wall Mount, 5 Cents For Dial Tone, 17 x 8 In.. . . . . 259.00
Plaque, New Jersey Bell Telephone Company, Bell, Brass, 21 x 16 ½ In.. . . . . 300.00
Sign, American Telephone & Telegraph Co., Porcelain, 2-Sided Flange, 17 x 12 In. 354.00
Sign, Bell Telephone, Public, New England, Blue, White, Porcelain, Enamel, 5 x 19 In. 55.00
Sign, Bell Telephone Booths, Local, Long Distance Telephones, Blue, White, 19 x 87 In. 600.00
Sign, Government Telephones, Saskatchewan, Green, Yellow, Red, White, Flange, 20 In. 300.00
Sign, Independent Public Telephone, Blue, White, Flange, 11 x 11 In.. . . . . 200.00
Sign, Inter Mountain Public Telephone Company, Blue, White, Yellow, Flange, 11 In. 100.00
Sign, Local & Trunk Telephone, Telegrams May Be Telephoned, Blue, White 100.00
Sign, Ontario Northland Telegraphs Communications, Black, White, Flange, 12 x 18 In. 400.00
Sign, Pacific Bell, Light-Up, Black, White, Red, Flange, Metal, 5 x 22 x 4 ½ In. 150.00
Sign, Pay Here, Candlestick Phone Image, Tin, Curved, Wood, 7 x 34 In.. . . . . 360.00
Sign, Southwestern Bell Telephone Co., Bell System, Blue, White, Flange, 12 x 11 In. 250.00
Sign, Telephone, Arrow, Bell, Blue, White, 10 x 30 In. 200.00
Sign, Telephone, Arrow, Bell, Blue, White, Hanging Bracket, 20 x 40 In. 400.00
Sign, Western Union Telegraph Building, Blue, White, Frame, 39 x 33 In.. . . . . 200.00
Sign, You May Telephone From Here, Blue, White, 9 x 22 In. 250.00
Skeleton, No. 37723, Handset Right Angle To Base, Cast Iron, Nickel Plated, c.1908 . . . . 1278.00
Stromberg Carlson, Candlestick, Oil Can Base, Gold Electrode Ball Transmitter, c.1898 . . . . 1380.00
Stromberg Carlson, Model 1243, Black, Metal Outer Case, 1940s 168.00
Switchboard, American Bell Telephone, Oak Cabinet, Chair, Pat.1892, 23 x 50 In. 1485.00
Switchboard, Oak, c.1915-30, 64 x 25 ½ In. 1955.00
Switchboard, Wood, Metal, c.1900, 56 x 24 In. 201.00
Thomson-Houston, Candlestick, No. 45260, Metal Handset, Horn, Extra Earphone, France . 144.00
Wall Set, Oak, 2-Box Cabinet, Top Mounted Transmitter, Steer Horn Hook, Chicago, c.1899. . 173.00
Western Electric, Candlestick, Pay, Key, c.1904 . . . . *illus* 531.00
Western Electric, Cradle, Model 202 Cabinet, 5 Cent, Push Button Dial Lock, c.1929. . . . . . . 1610.00
Western Electric, No. 102, Black, Ringer Box Modified For Phone Jack, c.1925-29 . . . . 405.00
Western Electric, Wall, Wood, Oak Crank, 1907, 23 x 9 x 12 In. 294.00

Telephone, GPO, Wall, No. 121, Wood, 2 Alarm Clocks, England
$215.00

Telephone, Montgomery Ward & Co., Wall, 20 x 8 ¾ In.
$101.00

Telephone, Western Electric, Candlestick, Pay, Key, c.1904
$531.00

TELEVISION sets are twentieth-century collectibles. Although the first television transmission took place in England in 1925, collectors find few sets that pre-date 1946. The first sets had only five channels, but by 1949 the additional UHF channels were included. The first color television set became available in 1951.

DuMont, Fold Back Cabinet Doors, Rabbit Ears, c.1950, 24 x 37 In. 1150.00
Experimental Television Set, 15 Pictures Per Second, Documentation, Germany, c.1930. . . 7987.00
Motorola, 9T1, 8-In. Round Black & White Screen, Bakelite Cabinet, c.1948, 17 x 10 In. 1265.00
Philco, Model 4654, Predicta, Barber Pole, Pedestal, 1959, 25 x 12 x 12 ½ In. 2520.00
Philco, Model 4710, Predicta, Penthouse, Swiveling Stem, Chrome Plated, 1950s 720.00
Philco, Predicta, Separate Screen & Wood Console, c.1957, 25 x 49 In.. . . . . 2530.00
Philco, Predicta Princess, Futuristic, Tilt & Swivel Screen, c.1959, 24 ½ x 23 In. 1725.00
Zenith, Porthole Console, c.1949, 23 x 35 ½ In.. . . . . 1610.00

TEPLITZ refers to art pottery manufactured by a number of companies in the Teplitz-Turn area of Bohemia during the late nineteenth and early twentieth centuries. Two of these companies were the Alexandra Works and The Amphora Porcelain Works, run by Reissner, Stellmacher, and Kessel. Ernst Wahliss, connected with the RS & K wares, started his own factory after 1900.

Bust, Woman, Smiling, Lace Collars, Edwardian Clothing, Hat, Gilt, 16 ½ In.. . . . . 690.00
Ewer, Flowers, Pink Cream Ground, c.1865, 9 ¼ In. 35.00
Ewer, Gres Bijou, Amphora, 7 ¾ x 6 ½ In. 1200.00
Figurine, Girl Drinking From Fountain, Amphora, 13 ¾ In. 750.00
Figurine, Maiden, Holding Flower Basket, Marked, 21 In. 175.00
Figurine, Man, Holding Jug, Austria, Early 20th Century, 11 ½ x 4 In. 259.00

Figurine, Man & Lute, Signed, 22 In. 100.00
Figurine, Putti Sitting On Goat, 2 Empty Baskets, Amphora, Austria, Large 638.00
Pitcher, Water, Blue Flowers, Cream Ground, Fish Scale Top, 9 ¾ In. 125.00
Teapot, Urn Form, Dragon Handle, Dolphin Finial, Marked, Stellmacher, 1890s, 9 In. . . *illus* 118.00
Vase, 4 Lotus Tendrils Handles, Art Nouveau, Amphora, 19 In. 1440.00
Vase, Birch Trees, Painted, Paul Dachsel, 8 ¾ x 5 ¾ In. 1560.00
Vase, Blue & Mother-Of-Pearl Flowers, Gilt Lady Bugs, Amphora, Daschel, 13 In. . . . . . . *illus* 10200.00
Vase, Bottle Shape, Incised, Glazed Owl, Blue, Green, Orange, Amphora, c.1910, 15 ½ In. 590.00
Vase, Bottle Shape, Stylized Trees, Purple, Gold, Amphora, 6 ½ In. 300.00
Vase, Bulbous, Green Matte Glaze, 4 Handles, Rim Signed, 7 x 11 In. 750.00
Vase, Cherries, Yellow, Green, Red, Brown, Amphora, 4 In. 100.00
Vase, Cobalt Blue, Gold Scrolls, Green Reticulated Center, Handles, Marked, Amphora, 19 In. . 300.00
Vase, Farm Design, Blue, Green, Brown, White Glaze, Marked, Amphora, 18 ½ In. 1093.00
Vase, Holly, Green, 4 ½ In. 85.00
Vase, Maidens, Water, Lilies, Stamped, Amphora, Red RSTK Mark, 6 ¾ x 8 In. . . . . *illus* 1200.00
Vase, Pitcher Shape, Handle, Brown, Green, Blue Matte Glaze, Marked, Amphora, 6 ½ x 5 ½ In. 720.00
Vase, Pitcher Shape, Handle, Flowers, Multicolored, Marked, Ernst Wahliss, Amphora, 11 ¾ x 8 In. 510.00
Vase, Pitcher Shape, Nude On Handle, Enamel, Pink, Green, Marked, Ernst Wahliss, Amphora, 13 x 5 In. 900.00
Vase, Sovereign Of The Night, Woman, Inset Turquoise, Quartz, Amphora, 6 x 8 In. 18000.00

TERRA-COTTA is a special type of pottery. It ranges from pale orange to dark reddish-brown in color. The color comes from the clay, which is fired but not always glazed in the finished piece.

Bust, Alexander The Great, Arles, France, c.1800, 27 In. 1000.00
Bust, Art Nouveau, Nude Female, Floral Garland, Signed, 28 x 10 In. 2070.00
Bust, Dionysus, Reclining, Greece, 4 In. 863.00
Bust, Girl, Faux Bronze Patina, Signed, R. Bertelli, Italy, Early 20th Century, 12 In. 245.00
Bust, Man, Triangular Eyes, Headdress, Nok, Nigeria, c.1920, 10 x 7 In. 239.00
Bust, Young Man, Late 19th Century, 17 ½ x 10 ½ In. . . . . *illus* 2937.00
Bust, Young Woman, 18th-Century Clothing, Marble Socle, Continental, 1800s, 17 In. 2478.00
Cachepot, Neoclassical, Paneled, White Paint, France, Early 1900s, 12 x 13 ½ In., Pair 240.00
Charger, Arab On Horseback, Painted, Signed, Johann Maresch, 19th Century, 15 ¼ In. 75.00
Cheese Dome, Underplate, Provincial, Southern France, 5 ¼ x 7 ¼ In. 120.00
Cigar & Match Holder, Dog, Glass Eyes, No. 2243, 9 x 9 ¼ In. 50.00
Crock, Storage, Provincial, Glazed, France, 20th Century, 6 x 6 In. 72.00
Draining Plate, Glazed, 2 ¼ x 10 ¼ In. 84.00
Figurine, Angel, Semi Reclining, Spread Wings, Drapes, Paint Trace, 24 x 22 In., Pair 1150.00
Figurine, Blackamoor, Glazed, Standing, Holding Out Hands, Plinth Base, 41 x 9 ¼ In. 1293.00
Figurine, Bust, Sculpted Hair, White Clay Eyes, China Teeth, Adam's Apple, 12 ¾ In. 880.00
Figurine, Chinese Man, Seated, Pillow, Green, Red, Brown, c.1830, 22 x 15 In. 11875.00
Figurine, Clown, Wrestling, Gustel Morton, 21 ½ In. 805.00
Figurine, Dachshund, Glass Eye, 13 x 11 In. 431.00
Figurine, Deer, Reclining, Glass Eyes, Removable Antlers, c.1900, 19 x 19 x 10 In. 940.00
Figurine, Dog, Whippet, On Cushion, 26 x 17 x 9 In., Pair 450.00
Figurine, Dragon, Coiled Shape, Chinese, 2 x 2 ½ In. 146.00
Figurine, Eagle, On Rocks, Early 20th Century, 22 In. 100.00
Figurine, Falstaff, No. 6424, Marked, J.M., 15 ½ In. 265.00
Figurine, Foo Dog, Temple Guard, Relic, Chinese, 2 x 3 In. 234.00
Figurine, Girl, Painted, c.1880, 25 x 9 ½ x 9 In. 385.00
Figurine, Gnome Shoemaker, 5 ½ In. 92.00
Figurine, Lion, Crouching, Plinth, c.1900, 22 x 15 In., Pair 5175.00
Figurine, Lion, Reclining, Glazed, Italy, c.1950-55, 43 x 15 In., Pair 4780.00
Figurine, Man On Pole, 2-Piece, Christine Federighi, 47 x 10 x 9 In. 720.00
Figurine, Mother & Children, France, c.1820, 13 In. 805.00
Figurine, Owl, On Book, Majolica Glaze, Marked, B.B. 1466, 4 ½ In. 115.00
Figurine, Pauper Boy, Lighting Cigarette, c.1880, 30 x 9 x 7 ¼ In. 605.00
Figurine, Pig Chef, Wearing Apron, Scarf, Hat, 24 ½ In. 55.00
Figurine, Sphinx, Marble Style Base, 18-19th Century, 26 x 38 ½ x 19 In. 500.00
Figurine, Venus, Standing, High Square Base, 9 ¾ In. 978.00
Figurine, Warrior On Horseback, Chinese, 14 ¼ x 11 In. 175.00
Figurine, Young Woman, Carrying Basket On Shoulder, Province, Haniroff, 1800s, 26 In. . . . 518.00
Garden Seat, Elephant, Enamel, 23 ¼ In. 82.00
Head, Dancer, Jean-Baptiste Carpeaux, c.1860, 9 ½ In. 2000.00
Humidor, Black Man Smoking Pipe, On Bale, Marked, J.M. 3510, Austria, 8 In. 250.00
Humidor, Black Woman, Sitting In Chair, Holding Pug, Marked, J.M. 3511, Austria, 8 In. 275.00
Jar, Storage, Rounded Lip Rim, Ribs, Baluster Form, Chinese, 44 In. 540.00

Teplitz, Teapot, Urn Form, Dragon Handle, Dolphin Finial, Marked, Stellmacher, 1890s, 9 In.
$118.00

Teplitz, Vase, Blue & Mother-Of-Pearl Flowers, Gilt Lady Bugs, Amphora, Daschel, 13 In.
$10200.00

Teplitz, Vase, Maidens, Water, Lilies, Stamped, Amphora, Red RSTK Mark, 6 ¾ x 8 In.
$1200.00

T

TIP

Do not store papers near heaters, radiators, furnaces, stoves, lamps, television sets, VCRs, or any other heat-producing device.

Terra-Cotta, Bust, Young Man, Late 19th Century, 17 ½ x 10 ½ In. $2937.00

Terra-Cotta, Sculpture, Deport Pour L'Ecole, Mother, Children, France, c.1890, 20 ½ In. $550.00

TIP

It can be hard to thread a needle, especially with the old pure cotton thread that should be used for repairing old fabric. Put hairspray on the end of the thread to stiffen it.

Jug, Handle, 2 Spouts, Glazed, France, 8 ½ In. 96.00
Jug, Long Neck, Black Glaze, Globular, Handle, 3 ½ In. 288.00
Jug, Oil, Leaning, Footed, Globular, Handle, Funnel Type Rim, c.1400 B.C., 5 ½ In. 259.00
Lamp, Square, Lion's Masks, 17 ½ In., Pair 460.00
Panel, Woman's Head, Swags, c.1925, 36 x 20 In., 3 Piece 900.00
Planter, Cherubs, W.D. Gates, Shape No. G21, 8-Sided, 13 x 14 In., Pair 1080.00
Planter, Demilune, Embossed Flower Swag, 20 x 19 ¾ x 9 In. 50.00
Planter, Glazed White, Relief Bows, Fruit Swags, 20 x 27 In., Pair 690.00
Plaque, Landscape, Mountain, Castle, 11 x 15 In., Pair 431.00
Plaque, Landscape, Sunrise, 11 ½ x 6 ½ In. 207.00
Plaque, Woman, Holding Pitcher, Shield Form, Relief, 19 ¾ x 16 ¾ In. 207.00
Plaque Set, Neoclassical Style, Oval, 4 Different Heads, 16 ½ x 14 In., 4 Piece 1410.00
Pot, Confit, Ocher Glaze, Molded Lip, Handles, Early 1900s, 8 x 6 ½ In. 210.00
Sculpture, Deport Pour L'Ecole, Mother, Children, France, c.1890, 20 ½ In. . . . . . *illus* 550.00
Sculpture, Nude, Seated Woman, Head Down, Mary Adams Winter, c.1910, 15 x 15 In. 720.00
Sculpture, Nude, Seated Woman, Head Turned, Mary Adams Winter, c.1910, 14 x 11 In. 660.00
Teapot, Tree Trunk Design, Signed, 2 ⅛ x 5 ½ In. 35.00
Umbrella Jar, Dragon Motif, Chinese, 24 x 8 ½ In. 117.00
Urn, Loose Ring Handles, 29 x 18 In. 70.00

TEXTILES listed here include many types of printed fabrics and table and household linens. Some other textiles will be found under Clothing, Coverlet, Rug, Quilt, etc.

Altar Cloth, Cross, Silver Thread, Burgundy Velvet, Vine Border, Russia, 16 x 17 In. 546.00
Bag, Silver Dollar, U.S. Mint, Carson City, Nevada, 1878-93, Frame 2350.00
Banner, Motto, Symbols, Lily, Heart, Scales, Purity, Charity, Honesty, 20 x 22 In., 3 Piece 58.00
Banner, Theater, Uncle Tom's Cabin, Gold Velvet, Green Felt, Metal Rod, Tassel, 30 x 32 In. 205.00
Bed Cover, Cotton, Checked Red & White Plaid, String Ties, Child's, 38 x 28 ½ In. 110.00
Bell Pull, Flowers, Leaves, Needlepoint, Brass, 62 In. 25.00
Bell Pull, Tapestry, Flowers, Red, Yellow, O. Kessler & Co., Vienna, Austria, 57 ¼ In. 20.00
Belt, Embroidered, Louisiana Officers, Metallic, Pelican Below Banner, Late 1800s, 38 In. 575.00
Blanket, Wool, Red, Trapper Point, Black Stripe, Eaton, Early1900s, 76 x 58 In. 300.00
Christmas Hanging, Santa Claus, Vignettes, Toys, Flag, Sled, Oriental Print Works, 17 x 23 In. 127.00
Comforter, Centennial, George Washington Portrait, Liberty Bell, 13 Colonies, Cotton 1675.00
Curtain Door, Peacocks, Flowers, Wool, 72 x 62 In. . . . . . *illus* 900.00
Curtains, Wool, Maroon With Pink Flower, Satin Stitched, 1912, 26 x 56 In., Pair 290.00
Doily, Crochet, Pineapple, White Cotton, Oblong, 12 In. 4.00
Duvet, Chintz, One Piece, Cutout Bottom, c.1800, 124 x 112 In. 4500.00
Fabric, Silk Damask, Seta Pura, Gold Tone Wreath, Olive Green Ground, Italy, 25 x 3 Ft. 690.00
Flag, American, 13 Stars, Sesquicentennial, Wool, 1932, 57 x 57 In. 610.00
Flag, American, 37 Stars, Hand Stitched, Silk, Painted Stars, Mounted, 1867-1877, 12 ½ x 8 ¼ In. 460.00
Flag, American, 44 Stars, Frame, c.1895 . . . . . . 265.00
Flag, American, 45 Stars, 120 x 63 In. 66.00
Flag, American, 46 Stars, Frame, c.1910 . . . . . . 265.00
Flag, Nazi, 33 x 24 In. 132.00
Flag, U.S. Naval, Hand Sewn, Linen, Canvas, Hemp Roping, 35 Stars, 83 x 130 In. 660.00
Fragment, Chintz, Armor, Weapons, Flowers, Gilt Frame, Early 1800s, 14 ½ x 16 ½ In. 86.00
Handkerchief, Violons Celebres, 6 Musicians, France, Late 19th Century, 27 x 29 In. 497.00
Horse Blanket, Wool, Suede, Brown, Apple Green, 4 Brass Eyelets, Hermes, 60 x 58 In. 652.00
Lace, Blue Linen Backing, Map Of England & Wales, 18th Century, 8 x 9 In. 1180.00
Needlework, Embroidered, Eagle, Flags, Silk, Metallic, Red, Frame, Early 1900s, 23 x 20 In. . . *illus* 315.00
Needlework, Embroidered, Geometric, Multicolored, New York Sites, Round, Frame, 22 ¼ In. 495.00
Needlework, Embroidered, Mass. State Seal, Silk, Frame, Blue, Black, Label, Japan, c.1900, 25 x 30 In. 2252.00
Needlework, Embroidered, Silk, Lovers, Pastoral Landscape, Cottage, c.1805, 22 x 24 ½ In. . . 8190.00
Needlework, Embroidered, Silk, Tiger, Snow Scene, Chinese, 13 ⅝ x 23 ¾ In., Pair 70.00
Needlework, Panel, Empire, Brown, Cream, Red, France, c.1810, 44 x 36 In. 5000.00
Panel, Brocade, Dragon, Chasing Celestial Pearl, Chinese, 18th Century, 29 ½ x 20 In. 1422.00
Panel, Crewelwork, Wool, Linen, Flowers, Fruit, Mary Balentine, Mass., 1700s.11 ½ x 81 In. . . 5036.00
Panel, Embroidered, 2 Women, Child In Garden, Chinese, 19th Century, 21 x 15 In. 178.00
Panel, Embroidered, Ducks In Glade, Silk, Taupe, Mat, Frame, Glazed, France, 23 x 28 In. 1020.00
Panel, Embroidered, Owl On Branch, Frame, Glazed, Japan, 19th Century, 29 ½ x 24 In. 356.00
Panel, Embroidered, Roosters, Hens, Chicks, Plants, Frame, Chinese, 49 x 14 ½ In., Pair 504.00
Panel, Embroidered, Silk, 100 Birds In Garden, Frame, Glaze, Chinese, 29 x 21 ½ In. 2844.00
Panel, Embroidered, Silk, Dragons, Flowers, Dark Blue Ground, Oval, Chinese, 49 x 38 In. . . 1126.00
Panel, Embroidered, Silk, Phoenix, Flowers, 20th Century, Chinese, 67 x 36 In. 356.00
Panel, Embroidered, Silk, Red, Satin Stitch, Flowering Branches, Bats, Chinese, 83 x 36 In. . . 155.00
Panel, Tapestry, Country House Park, Swans, Roses, Multicolored, 72 x 48 In. 2160.00

Panel, Woven, Center Dragon, 4 Others, Silk, Gilt Frame, 47 ½ x 44 ½ In. 411.00
Pillow, Tapestry, Aubusson, Boy, Girl, Tassel Fringe, Multicolored, 18 ½ x 15 In., Pair 780.00
Pillow Case, Piecework, Cotton Prints, Star Pattern, Sawtooth Border, Tie Closure, 21 x 25 In., Pair 235.00
Placemat, Napkins, Ladybug, Plastic, Cloth, Vera, 1960s, 8 Piece. 15.00
Pot Holder, Chevrons, Navy Blue, White, Blue Border, 7 In. 7.50
Pot Holder, Chevrons, Pink, Blue, 7 In., Pair. 12.00
Pot Holder, Chevrons, Variegated Green Border, 7 ½ In. 8.00
Pot Holder, Round, Green, White, 18 Lobe. 7.50
Pot Holder, Square, Pink & Yellow Rose, 6 In., Pair 15.00
Pot Holder, White Squares, Red Border, 6 x 4 In. 7.50
Sachet, Linen, Lavender Buds, Crochet Trim, 8 In. 26.00
Sachet, Linen, Lavender Buds, Crochet Trim, Satin Ribbons, 6 x 3 ½ In. 30.00
Saddle Cover, Cream, Blue Flower Border, Red Field, Multicolored, 40 x 37 In. 1725.00
Scarf, Gulliver's Travels, Paramount Pictures, 1930s, 18 x 20 In. 75.00
Sculpture, Pear Shape, Yellow, Orange Velvet, Paneled, Applied Wicker Stem, 5 x 3 In. 358.00
Seat Cover, Red Silk, Metallic & Silk Embroidery, Flowers, Birds, Gilt Frame, 26 x 24 In. 294.00
Seat Cover, Tapestry, Bear, Attacked By Dogs & Men On Horseback, 1700s, 15 x 20 In. 173.00
Silk, Embroidered, Figures, Houses, Flowers, Multicolored, Chinese, 57 x 29 In. 760.00
Table Runner, Homespun, Checked, Blue & White, 57 x 19 In. 66.00
Table Scarf, Embroidered, Metallic Threads, Red Fabric, Yellow Border, 18th Century, 33 x 33 In. 360.00
Table Scarf, Embroidered, Metallic Threads, Sewn On Red Fabric, 32 x 33 In. 465.00
Tablecloth, Crochet, Ecru, 64 x 80 In. 39.00
Tablecloth, Drawn Thread Flower, Embroidered, 1920s, 40 x 32 In. 75.00
Tablecloth, Drawn Thread Pattern, Double Border, 1920s, 34 x 34 In. 85.00
Tablecloth, Flower Basket, Bird, Flower Vines, Crewelwork, E. Clarke, 1850, 43 x 42 In. 1112.00
Tablecloth, Irish Linen, Circular Pattern Cutwork, 1920s, 49 x 49 In. 112.00
Tablecloth, Irish Linen, Crochet Border, Embroidered, Early 1900s, 36 x 36 In. 85.00
Tablecloth, Irish Linen, Madeira, Embroidered, Cutwork, Grapes, Vines, 50 x 50 In. 120.00
Tablecloth, Linen, Bobbin Lace, Scalloped Border, Embroidered, 36 x 36 In. 98.00
Tablecloth, Linen, Fillet Lace, White Work, Embroidered, Oriental Symbols, 36 x 36 In. 115.00
Tablecloth, Linen, Floral Crochet Border, Early 1900s, 40 x 40 In. 98.00
Tablecloth, Linen, Homespun, Checked Brown & White, 52 x 33 ½ In. 248.00
Tablecloth, Linen, Lace, Floral Crochet Border, White Work Embroidery, 46 x 46 In. 165.00
Tablecloth, Linen, Lace, Ladder Work Border, Fillet Lace Inserts, Early 1900s, 44 x 44 In. 60.00
Tablecloth, Linen, White Work, Embroidered, Floral Corners, Early 1900s, 42 x 42 In. 148.00
Tablecloth, Linen, White Work, Embroidery, Crochet Border, Floral Corners, 42 x 45 In. 112.00
Tablecloth, Napkins, Ecru Linen, Lace Trim, 1920s, 50 x 50 & 12 x 12 In., 5 Piece 125.00
Tapestry, Aubusson Style, Royal Arms Of France, Mars, Athena, Seated Around Globe, 90 x 60 In. 2640.00
Tapestry, Brussel Style, Wool, Lovers, Landscape, Castle, Leaf Border, 88 x 61 In. 830.00
Tapestry, Embroidered, Black Reserve, Bessarabia, 19th Century, 64 x 50 In. 900.00
Tapestry, Family Crest, 2 Lions, Beige, Tan, Red Ground, Frame, 18th Century, 30 x 27 ¾ In. . 250.00
Tapestry, Flowers, Red Border, Hanging Rod, Giltwood Finials, Silk Tassels, 102 x 55 In. 2160.00
Tapestry, Landscape, Columns, Urns, Salmon Ground, c.1860, 65 x 53 In. 1725.00
Tapestry, Mythological Scenes, Pink, Ground, 8 Panels, Frame, Chinese, 40 ¾ x 10 In. 1778.00
Tapestry, New World Vista, Loja Saarinen Style, Hand Loomed Wool, Fringe, 57 x 58 In. 177.00
Tapestry, Still Life, Hand Woven, Signed, 20th Century, 49 x 59 In. 295.00
Tapestry, Sun, Red, Blue, Golden Ground, Alexander Calder, 1974, 4 x 6 In. 6000.00
Tapestry, Verdure, Woodland Scene, Flower Border, 1700s, 80 x 84 In. 4025.00
Tea Cozy, Mama Katzenjammer, Felt, Swivel Head, Shoebutton Eyes, Steiff, 1910, 16 In. 290.00
Throw, Peruvian Alpaca, Woven Stripes, Natural Brown, Beige, Cream, 1900s, 73 x 56 In. . . . 47.00
Towel, Cotton, Flowerpots, Birds, Blue, Red Needlework, 1828, 68 ½ x 24 ½ In. 385.00
Towel, Needlework, Green, Red, Cotton, Flowers, Geometrics, c.1821, 46 x 17 In. 154.00
Towel, Show, Blue & Orange Bands, Fringe, Victorian. 65.00
Towel, Show, Blue Shaded, Fringe, Victorian 65.00
Towel, Show, Christopher Columbus, 1492, Turkey Red, Victorian. 65.00
Towel, Show, Cross-Stitch, Peacocks, Flowerpots, Figures, Barbara Marky, 1800s, 63 In. 1872.00
Towel, Show, Dina Hauts, Cross-Stitch, Figures, Stylized Trees, 62 In. 2223.00
Towel, Show, Fleur-De-Lis, Ribbon, Turkey Red, Victorian 85.00
Towel, Show, Gentleman, Long-Tailed Coat, Peaked Hat, Embroidered, c.1836, 52 x 17 In. . . . 645.00
Towel, Show, Geometrics, Fringe, Turkey Red, Victorian 55.00
Towel, Show, Silk, On Linen, Crewelwork, Birds, Tulips, Flowerpots, 19th Century, 56 In. 3744.00
Towel, Show, Wool, On Linen, Fanny Hess, Crewelwork, Tulip Trees, Flowerpots, Birds, 1843. . 8190.00
Tray Cloth, Embroidered, Pulled Thread Border, White Work, Crochet Edge, 24 x 28 In. 60.00
Tray Cloth, Linen, Crochet Border, 1920s, 24 x 19 In. 60.00
Wall Hanging, Silk, Eagle, American Shield, Flag, Metallic Thread, Frame, Late 1800s, 24 In. 323.00
Wall Hanging, Wool, 8 Stylized Fish, Alternating Directions, Brown Triangles, 45 x 27 In. . . . 288.00

Textile, Curtain Door, Peacocks, Flowers, Wool, 72 x 62 In.
$900.00

Textile, Needlework, Embroidered, Eagle, Flags, Silk, Metallic, Red, Frame, Early 1900s, 23 x 20 In.
$315.00

Vintage Printed Cloth

Vintage printed tablecloths and dish towels from the 1940s and 1950s are being faked and reproduced today. Copycats have several differences. Vintage tablecloths have one selvage edge that shows. New ones are hemmed on four sides. Old fabrics are "overprinted," each color printed over the last one. Old fabric is "oxidized," so not as white as new textiles.

As always, the edited listings in *Kovels' Antiques & Collectibles Price Guide 2010* aren't available on any website, but readers should visit Kovels.com for information on trends, tips, reproductions, marks, old prices, and more!

T

Thermometer, Belfast Root Beer, Like You Haven't Tasted In Years, Metal, 1950, 27 x 8 In.
$275.00

Thermometer, Ex-Lax, Chocolated Laxative, Porcelain, 1930-40, 36 x 8 In.
$190.00

TIP

If you store paper ephemera like trade cards or labels in notebooks or photo albums, be sure to open the albums several times a year to let the air circulate.

THERMOMETER is a name that comes from the Greek word for heat. The thermometer was invented in 1731 to measure the temperature of either water or air. All kinds of thermometers are collected, but those with advertising messages are the most popular.

7Up, First Against Thirst, White Ground, 12 1 ¼ In. . . . 134.00
7Up, Ohio Thermometer Co., 12 x 4 ¼ In. . . . 123.00
Alka-Seltzer, Metal, Glass, Round, c.1950, 12 In. . . . 403.00
American Brakeblock, Yellow, Metal, Dog, 1950s, 5 ¾ x 20 In. . . . 179.00
Auburn Cord, 4 Cars, White, 39 x 9 In. . . . 490.00
B.B. Snavely's Grain, On Tray, Couple In Field, 5 ¾ In. . . . 60.00
Baxter Rendering Service, Yellow Paint, Wood, Iowa, 12 ¾ In. . . . 40.00
Bearded Man Faces, Bronze, Slate Base, Victorian, 10 ¼ In. . . . 100.00
Belfast Root Beer, Like You Haven't Tasted In Years, Metal, 1950, 27 x 8 In. . . . *illus* 275.00
Borden's Ice Cream, Tin, Cow's Head In Flower, c.1950, 27 x 8 ½ In. . . . 230.00
Bubble Up, Tune Up, Drink Up, Yellow, Green, c.1940, 21 x 9 In. . . . 400.00
Calotabs For Biliousness, Torpidity, Painted, Wood, 15 ¼ In. . . . 20.00
Calumet Baking Powder, Best By Test, Kewpie, Wood, 22 x 6 In. . . . 389.00
Carnation City, Alliance, Ohio, Embossed Enameled, 8 x 24 In. . . . 308.00
Carter's White Lead Paint, All Weather, Porcelain, 1920-30, 27 x 7 In. . . . 225.00
Clark Bar, Wood, Yellow Ground, c.1930, 5 ½ x 21 In. . . . 288.00
Cloverdale Soft Drinks, Bottle Cap Logo, T.W. O'Connell & Co., Chicago, 1950s . . . 450.00
Cloverdale Soft Drinks, Metal, Glass, Round, 12 In. . . . 58.00
Dad's Diet Root Beer, Yellow, White, Black, Trim, Late 1950, 27 x 7 In. . . . 171.00
Deep Sea, c.1900, 15 In. . . . 58.00
Double Cola, Make It A Double Or Nothing, White, Red, Tin, 1950s . . . 26.00
Dr Pepper, At 10, 2 & 4, Bottle, Green, Yellow, Red, Black, 1930s, 17 x 5 ½ In. . . . 700.00 to 800.00
Dr Pepper, Drink A Bite To Eat, Bottle, Clock, Diecut, Tin, 13 ¾ x 4 ¾ In. . . . 350.00
Dr Pepper, Hot Or Cold, Pepper Up At 10, 2 & 4, Tin, 12 ¼ In. . . . 70.00
Dr Pepper, When Hungry, Bottle, Yellow, Red, Black, 1930s, 25 ½ x 10 In. . . . 250.00
Drink Double Cola, You'll Like It Better, Tin, Embossed, Red & White, 5 x 17 In. . . . 78.00
Ex-Lax, Chocolated Laxative, Porcelain, 1930-40, 36 x 8 In. . . . *illus* 190.00
Figural, Woman, Spelter, Gold Patina, Marble Base, Art Nouveau, 8 In. . . . 90.00
Fly Piper Cub, Glass & Metal, Round, 1950s, 12 In. . . . 805.00
Frostie Root Beer, Drink Frostie, A Real Taste, Bottle, Red, White, Blue, Tin, 36 In. . . . 150.00
Frostie Root Beer, The Smooth One, Red, White, Blue Brown, Marked, 12 ¼ In. Diam. . . . 80.00
Gall Cure Horse Collars, J.W. Murray, Wood, Tin Lithograph, 10 ⅝ x 3 In. . . . 350.00
Ganong's Chocolates, Porcelain, 1920-30, 39 In. . . . *illus* 173.00
Gilbey's Please, London Dry Gin, Copper Case, 1930s, 9 In. . . . 179.00
Herr & Co., Lancaster, Pa., Wood, 15 ¼ In. . . . 25.00
Hick's Capudine Liquid, Stomach & Rheumatism, Yellow, Black, Wood, 21 In. . . . 45.00
Hill & Hill Kentucky Whiskey, White, Red, Patina, 15 In. . . . 25.00
Hills Bros. Coffee, Turkish Man Drinking, Mug, Porcelain, 21 x 9 In. . . . 605.00
Hills Bros. Tea & Coffee, Porcelain, Red, Yellow, White, c.1930, 9 x 21 In. . . . 690.00
Hires Root Beer, Bottle, Brown, Red, White, Tin, 28 ½ In. . . . 100.00
International Marine Paints, Interlux, Man Holding Can, Metal, Glass, Pam, c.1940, 12 In. 403.00
Jests, Laughing Jester, Blue, Red, Yellow, Porcelain, 1930-40, 36 x 8 In. . . . 632.00
Ken-L-Ration, For Best Results, Feed Your Dog, Tin, c.1950, 27 x 7 In. . . . 230.00
Ken-L-Ration Dog Food, Tin, Yellow Ground, Image Of Can, 1950s, 11 x 9 In. . . . 350.00
King, America's Premium Blend Whiskey, 12 In. . . . 130.00
L & M Cigarettes, Check Today's Change, Tin Lithograph, 13 ¼ x 5 ¾ In. . . . 90.00
La Fendrich Cigar, Always A Cool Smoke, Red, Yellow, Tin, c.1940, 26 x 10 In. . . . 450.00
Land O' Lakes, Indian Maiden, Metal, 27 In. . . . 55.00
Lash's Bitters, For Constipation, Painted, Wood, c.1900-20, 21 x 5 ½ In. . . . 210.00
Lash's Bitters, Homer's Ginger & Brandy For Diarrhoea, Wood, 21 In. . . . 275.00
Mail Pouch, Treat Yourself To The Best, Blue, White, Yellow, Porcelain, 38 ½ x 8 In. . . . 198.00
Mail Pouch, Treat Yourself To The Best, Blue, Yellow, White, Porcelain, 1930s, 27 In. . . . 287.00
Mail Pouch Tobacco, Treat Yourself To The Best, Blue, Yellow, Porcelain, 39 x 8 In. . . . 231.00
Martin-Senour Paints, Goes Farther, Orange, Black, Porcelain, 1920-30, 39 x 8 In. . . . 275.00
Moxie, Man In White Pointing Finger, Tin, c.1940-50, 25 x 10 In. . . . 403.00
Mythological Woman With Globe, Cast Metal, Marble Base, c.1900, 8 In. . . . 55.00
Nature's Remedy, Come In, If You Get It Here It's Good, Blue, White, Porcelain, 27 In. . . . 130.00
Negretti & Zambra, London, Centigrade, c.1910, 37 x 5 x 3 In. . . . 643.00
Northwind & Devil, Generad Felt Products Inc., Marked, Taylor, 6 ¾ In. . . . 60.00
Oven, Stoneware, Stand, Early 20th Century, 9 ¼ In. . . . 100.00
Pabst Blue Ribbon, Tin, Man On Skis, c.1960, 15 x 14 In. . . . 115.00
Pennsy Supply Fueloil, Red, White, Blue, Tin, 36 x 8 ½ In. . . . 230.00
Penway's Bakery, Tin, 38 ½ In. . . . 50.00

Peters Shoes, Diamond Brand, Blue, Yellow, Porcelain, c.1920-30, 19 x 6 In. 275.00
Peters Weatherbird Shoes, Porcelain, c.1920-30, 27 x 7 In. 275.00
Prestone Anti-Freeze, Magnetic Film, Tin, 1930s 53.00
Ramon's Brownie Pills, Real Laxative, Kidneys, Boy, Yellow, Metal, 20 ½ In. 345.00
Ramon's Brownie Pills, Real Laxative, Kidneys, Pink Pills, Green, Red, Yellow Ground, Tin, 21 In. 1840.00
Red Crown Gasoline, Power, Service, Economy, Polarine, Red, White, Blue, 21 x 5 In. 2300.00
Red Goose Shoes, Finest & Best, Porcelain, 1920-30, 27 x 7 In. 748.00
Remington Cutlery, Blue, Yellow, White, Porcelain, 1930-40, 39 In. 275.00
Royal Crown Cola, Red, White, Tin 70.00
Rugby Temprite Jackets, Glass, Metal, Pam, 12 In. 150.00
Sauer's Pure Vanilla Extract, Black, White, Wood, Die Cut, c.1920, 22 x 8 In. 805.00
Spine, Gilt, Metal, 10 ¼ x 4 In. 154.00
Squirt Bottle, c.1940, Tin, Round, 9 In. 460.00
Sterling Salt, Service & Research, Glass, Metal, Pam, c.1940, 12 In. 125.00
Sunbeam Bread, Let's Be Friends, Metal, Glass, 1950s, 12 In. Diam. 402.00
Sword, Oak, Brass Trim, Hanging, c.1900, 18 In. 55.00
Vess, All Your Favorite Flavors, Boy, Bottle 450.00
Webber Lumber Co., Red, White, c.1930 .... 30.00

TIFFANY is a name that appears on items made by Louis Comfort Tiffany, the American glass designer who worked from about 1879 to 1933. His work included iridescent glass, Art Nouveau styles of design, and original contemporary styles. He was also noted for stained glass windows, unusual lamps, bronze work, pottery, and silver. Other types of Tiffany are listed under Tiffany Glass, Tiffany Gold, Tiffany Pottery, or Tiffany Silver. The famous Tiffany lamps are listed in this section. Tiffany jewelry is listed in the Jewelry and Wristwatch categories. Some Tiffany Studio desk sets have matching clocks. They are listed here. Clocks made by Tiffany & Co. are listed in the Clock category. Reproductions of some types of Tiffany are being made.

Louis C. Tiffany

Andirons, Brass, Urn Shape Top, Double Ring, Leaf Carved Base, 30 In. 690.00
Ashtray, Band, 2 Rests, Gold Dore, Rectangle, c.1905, 5 x 5 In. 208.00
Bill File, Bookmark, Bronze, Gold Dore, Round, 7 ½ In. 2000.00
Bill File, Pine Needle, Green Slag Glass, Bronze, Round, 7 ½ In. 1500.00
Blotter, Abalone, Bronze, Gold Dore, 5 ¾ x 2 ¾ In. 650.00
Blotter, American Indian, Bronze, Dark Patina, 3 x 5 ½ In. 350.00
Blotter, Pine Needle, Green Slag Glass, Bronze, Dark Patina 650.00
Blotter, Pine Needle, Slag Glass, Bronze, 5 In. 296.00
Blotter Ends, Art Deco, Blue Enameled Squares, Multicolored Accents, 19 In. 1553.00
Blotter Ends, Byzantine, Faceted Jewels, Turquoise Cabochons, Bronze, Gold Dore, 12 In., Pair 1320.00
Blotter Ends, Grapevine, Dark Patina, 19 x 2 In., Pair 650.00
Blotter Ends, Ninth Century, Green & Blue Jewels, 12 In., Pair 1150.00
Blotter Ends, Ninth Century, Green & Blue Jewels, Bronze, 19 In., Pair 2645.00
Blotter Ends, Pine Needle, Bronze, Signed No. 999, 19 In., Pair 201.00
Blotter Ends, Zodiac, Bronze, 3 ½ x 3 ½ In., 4 Piece 259.00
Book Rack, Grape Vine, Slag Glass, Bronze, c.1910, 6 x 6 x 14 In. 2633.00
Book Rack, Grapevine, Green Slag, Bronze, Green Brown Patina, Adjustable, 14 x 6 In. 2300.00
Book Rack, Pine Needle, Green Slag Glass, Bronze, Adjustable, 6 x 5 ¼ In. 3500.00
Bookends, Art Deco, Blue Enameled Squares, Multicolored Accents, Signed, 5 ¼ x 5 In. 3450.00
Bookends, Graduate, Bronze, Gold Dore, Signed 1500.00
Bookends, Zodiac, Bronze, Gold Dore, 6 x 4 ¾ In. 805.00
Bowl, Bronze, Gold Dore, Patina, 9 In. 230.00
Bowl, Bronze, Mother-Of-Pearl Border, Monogram, Signed, 1 ½ x 9 In. 165.00
Bowl, Copper, Crimped Rim, Applied Insects, Square, c.1905, 12 In. 4148.00
Box, Abalone, Bronze, Gold Dore, 3 ½ x 7 In. .... *illus* 5020.00
Box, Abalone, Bronze, Gold Dore, Cedar Lined, c.1900, 7 x 4 In. 5428.00
Box, Glove, Grapevine, Green Slag Glass, Bronze, Dark Patina, 3 x 13 ¼ x 4 ¼ In. 4500.00
Box, Grapevine, Green Slag Glass, Bronze, Beaded, Ball Feet, 4 ½ x 3 In. 850.00
Box, Hinged Cover, Jewelry, Raised Posts, Arches, Bronze, Ball Feet, 8 x 3 ¾ x 3 In. 4000.00
Box, Hinged Cover, Zodiac, Bronze, Dark Patina, Cedar Lining, 2 ½ x 6 x 6 ½ In. 3000.00
Box, Pine Needle, Green Slag Glass, Bronze, 2 ¼ x 4 x 7 In. 550.00
Box, Pine Needle, Green Slag Glass, Bronze, 4 x 6 In. 780.00
Box, Pine Needle, Green Slag Glass, Bronze, 5 x 2 In. 600.00
Box, Pine Needle, Green Slag Glass, Dore, Ball Feet, Metal Insert, 1 ⅜ x 4 ⅛ x 2 5/16 In. 474.00
Box, Venetian, Bronze, Gold Dore, 2 ⅝ x 6 ⅛ x 5 ⅝ In. 2252.00
Box, Zodiac, Bronze, Patina, Signed, 2 ½ x 6 ½ In. 870.00
Calendar, American Indian, Perpetual, Bronze, Dark Patina, Easel Back, 6 x 7 ½ In. 1500.00
Calendar, Bookmark, Perpetual, Bronze, Gold Dore, Easel Back, 6 x 5 ½ In. 2000.00
Calendar, Grapevine, Green Slag Glass, Bronze, Dark Patina, 1 ½ x 4 ½ x 3 ½ In. 1500.00

Thermometer, Ganong's Chocolates, Porcelain, 1920-30, 39 In.
$173.00

Tiffany, Box, Abalone, Bronze, Gold Dore, 3 ½ x 7 In.
$5020.00

Elongated Pennies

Elongated pennies were first made at the World's Columbian Exposition in Chicago in 1893, and they are still being made for tourists at places like the Empire State Building and Niagara Falls.

A penny is placed in a machine and rolled out so that words or images are impressed on the finished oval-shaped piece. The Lord's Prayer, important events and places, presidents' faces, and famous people have been honored by the elongated coins. Pennies, nickels, dimes, quarters, half-dollars, silver dollars, and foreign coins have been used. The date of the coin can often be seen on the finished piece. There are collectors and collector clubs for elongated coins as well as for the machines that made them.

T

Tiffany, Candlestick, Bronze, Gold Dore, Embossed Flames, Stamped, 9 ¼ x 6 ¾ In., Pair
$4800.00

Tiffany, Candlestick, Green Glass Cup, 3-Legged, Snuffer, Bronze, Patina, Signed, 10 x 5 In.
$4800.00

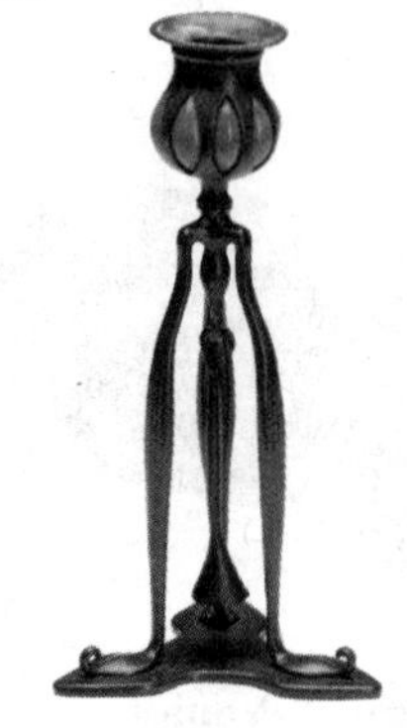

Tiffany, Centerpiece, Mosaic, Overlapping Leaves, Bronze, Gold Dore, Signed, 16 x 24 In.
$57500.00

Tiffany, Desk Set, Venetian, Frame, Letter Holder, Box, Inkwell, Blotter Ends, Signed, 6 Piece
$1800.00

Candelabrum, 3-Light, Bulbous Cups, Prong Supports, Chained Snuffer, 14 In. 4025.00
Candelabrum, 4-Light, Bronze, Bobeche, Snuffer, Oval Base, 15 x 14 In. 7500.00
Candelabrum, 4-Light, Stick Body, Bronze, Dark Patina, Oval Base, 15 x 14 In. 7500.00
Candle Lamp, Bronze, Green Tulip Pulled Feather Shade, Ribbed Stick Stem, 21 In., Pair ... 2185.00
Candle Lamp, Bronze, Root Base, Jeweled, Tulip Shade, Green Pulled Feather, Platinum, 17 In. 5750.00
Candle Lamp, Green, Ruffled & Stretched Shade, Blue Iridescent, Twisted Base, 12 In. 2645.00
Candle Lamp, Kerosene, Font, Gold, Green, Pink, Pulled Feathers, Shade, Signed, 13 x 8 In. . 1920.00
Candle Lamp, King Tut Iridescent Ruffled Shade, Bamboo Bronze Stem, Signed, Stamped, 17 In.. 8050.00
Candle Lamp, Pulled Feather Shade, Bronze, Queen Anne's Lace, Base, Signed, 20 In. 1100.00
Candlestick, 2-Light, Bronze, Gold Dore, Fleur-De-Lis Foot, Snuffer, 9 In. 3163.00
Candlestick, 3-Light, Cobra, Bronze, Gold Dore, Diamond Shape Pad Foot, 8 In.. .... 2013.00
Candlestick, Bronze, Bobeche, Brown Patina, 4-Footed, 11 In., Pair 2300.00
Candlestick, Bronze, Gold Dore, 3-Legged, 3 Ball Feet, Signed, 9 In., Pair 1840.00
Candlestick, Bronze, Gold Dore, Embossed Flames, Stamped, 9 ¼ x 6 ¾ In., Pair ...... *illus* 4800.00
Candlestick, Bronze, Gold Dore, Paw Feet, c.1920, 11 In., Pair 2400.00
Candlestick, Bronze, Gold Dore, Ribbed Saucer Foot, Bulbous, Curving, 8 ½ In. 2280.00
Candlestick, Bronze, Medallion, Green Mottled, Yellow Enamel, Round Foot, 9 In., Pair 3450.00
Candlestick, Cat's Paw, Bronze, Curving Legs, Reticulated Cup, Glass Insert, 10 ¼ In. 3163.00
Candlestick, Cobra, Bronze, Green Brown Patina, 7 ½ In., Pair 3450.00
Candlestick, Cobra, Bronze, Green Brown Patina, Green Jewels, Pulled Feather, 12 In. 5750.00
Candlestick, Green Glass Cup, 3-Legged, Snuffer, Bronze, Patina, Signed, 10 x 5 In. .... *illus* 4800.00
Candlestick, Patinated Cobra, Bronze, Green Glass Cup, Leaf Base, c.1900, 9 In. 2607.00
Candlestick, Purple, Blue Jewels Rim Cup, 3-Leg Base, Curled Feet, Hanging Snuffer, Bronze, 10 In. 4600.00
Candlestick, Saxifrage, Bronze, c.1905, 18 In.. .... 23750.00
Candlestick, Zodiac, Square Top, 8-Sided Base, Bronze, Patina, c.1920, 5 ¾ In., Pair 1900.00
Canister, Sailboat, Bronze, Gold Dore, 3 ½ x 3 In.. .... 450.00
Centerpiece, Mosaic, Overlapping Leaves, Bronze, Gold Dore, Signed, 16 x 24 In. ..... *illus* 57500.00
Chandelier, Green Turtleback Tile Shade, Bronze Chain, Favrile, c.1910, 44 x 25 In. 74500.00
Cigar Box, Adam, Red Enameled, Bronze, 5 x 3 ½ In.. .... 3450.00
Cigar Box, Art Deco, Blue Enameled Squares, Multicolored Accents, Bronze, 6 ¼ x 2 ¼ In.. .. 2875.00
Cigarette Box, Grapevine, Double Beading, Green Slag Glass, Bronze, 7 x 4 In. 1438.00
Cigarette Box, Pine Needle, Dore Bronze, Carmel, Slag Glass, c.1905, 2 x 6 In. 356.00
Clip, Art Deco, Blue Enameled Squares, Multicolored Accents, Bronze, 3 ½ x 3 ½ In. 2588.00
Clip, Bronze, Zodiac Pattern, Original Patina, Signed, 3 ¾ x 2 ¼ In. 118.00
Clock, Art Deco, Blue Enameled Squares, Bronze, Gold Dore, Signed, 5 ½ x 5 ½ In. 8050.00
Clock, Art Deco, Red Enameled Squares, Bronze, Gold Dore, Signed, 5 ½ x 5 ½ In. 7475.00
Clock, Chinese Pattern, Cathedral Shape, Bronze, Gold Dore, Signed, 5 ½ In.. .... 4600.00
Clock, Venetian, Ermine Border, Brass, c.1920, 3 ¼ x 4 x 4 In. 2000.00
Compote, Bronze, Enamel, Flower Border, Roundels, Geometric, 10 x 5 x 3 In. 1500.00
Desk Set, Pine Needle, Box, Hinged Cover, Inkwell, Penholder, 3 Piece 570.00
Desk Set, Shell & Ribbon, Flowers, Bowl, Tray, Letter Opener, 3 Piece 431.00
Desk Set, Venetian, Frame, Letter Holder, Box, Inkwell, Blotter Ends, Signed, 6 Piece ... *illus* 1800.00
Door Knob, Scrolls, Bronze, c.1915, 2 ¼ In., 4 Piece .... *illus* 550.00
Fireplace Surround, Mottled Orange, Glass Tiles, Favrile, Oak Mantle, c.1911, 30 x 35 In. .. 31250.00
Flower Frog, 2 Tiers, Gold, Iridescent, Loop Holders, Favrile, 4 In. 805.00
Frame, Abalone, Bronze, Patina, Signed, 6 x 6 ½ In.. .... 1440.00
Frame, Abalone, Incised Lines, Bronze, 7 x 6 In. 1680.00
Frame, Art Deco, Blue Enameled Squares, Multicolored Accents, Signed, 7 x 5 In. 4025.00
Frame, Chinese Pattern, Bronze, Gold Dore, Signed, 9 x 6 ¾ In. .... *illus* 2040.00
Frame, Graduate, Easel Back, 3 ½ x 2 In.. .... 750.00
Frame, Grapevine, Carmel Slag Glass, Bronze, Gold Dore, Signed, 7 x 6 ½ In. .... *illus* 1320.00
Frame, Grapevine, Green Slag Glass, Bronze, Beaded Edge, c.1920, 9 ½ x 8 In.... 2800.00 to 3600.00
Frame, Grapevine, Slag Glass, Bronze, Beaded Edge, 14 x 12 In. 4888.00
Frame, Indian, No. 1187, Bronze, Geometric, Face Designs, c.1900, 8 x 6 In. 5900.00
Frame, Ninth Century, Green & Blue Jewels, Easel Back, 4 ¾ x 6 In. 2415.00
Frame, Pine Needle, Caramel Slag Glass, Bronze, Signed, 4 ¼ In. 720.00
Frame, Pine Needle, Green, Blue Slag Glass, Bronze, Patina, Signed, 9 ¼ x 7 ½ In. 3600.00
Frame, Pine Needle, Green Slag Glass, Bronze, Easel Back, 8 x 10 In. 4000.00
Frame, Pine Needle, Green Slag Glass, Green Brown Patina, 4 ½ x 3 ½ In.. .... 518.00
Frame, Pine Needle, Slag Glass, Oval Opening, Bronze, 10 x 8 In. 3738.00
Frame, Zodiac, Bronze, Dark Patina, Easel Back, 7 x 8 In. 2500.00
Goblet, Bronze, Gold Dore, Thistle, Inscribed, December 9, 1907, 7 ½ In. 880.00
Inkstand, Ninth Century, Green & Blue Jewels, Bronze, Glass Insert, 4 x 3 In. 2760.00
Inkwell, Art Deco, Blue Enameled Squares, Multicolored Accents, Bronze, 3 ½ x 2 ½ In.. .... 2588.00
Inkwell, Hinged Cover, Abalone, Octagonal, Bronze, 3 ½ x 3 ½ x 3 ½ In. 850.00
Inkwell, Hinged Cover, American Indian, Bronze, Dark Patina, Glass Insert, 3 x 5 ½ In. 950.00
Inkwell, Hinged Cover, Bookmark, Octagonal, Bronze, Gold Dore, Glass Insert, 2 ½ x 4 In. .. 1200.00
Inkwell, Hinged Cover, Bookmark, Square, Bronze, Gold Dore, Glass Insert, 2 ½ x 3 In. 750.00

Inkwell, Hinged Cover, Grapevine, Green Slag Glass, Bronze, 3 In. 3000.00
Inkwell, Hinged Cover, Heraldic, Green Enamel, Silver Shield, 3 ½ x 3 In. 3500.00
Inkwell, Hinged Cover, Louis XVI, Bronze, Leaf Swag, Leaf Feet, 3 x 4 x 2 ¾ In. 1200.00
Inkwell, Nautical, Dolphin Footed, Glass Insert, 2 ½ x 5 In. 3450.00
Inkwell, Pine Needle, Bronze, Dipping Insert, Signed, 3 ½ x 4 ¼ In. 480.00
Inkwell, Pine Needle, Double Beaded Edge, Green Slag, Glass, Bronze, 4 In.. . . . . 460.00
Inkwell, Pine Needle, Green Slag Glass, Bronze, Brown Patina, 3 ¼ In.. . . . . 575.00
Inkwell, Pine Needle, Green Slag Glass, Bronze, Glass Insert, Square, 3 ½ x 4 In. 950.00
Inkwell, Pine Needle, Slag Glass, Bronze, Patina, Square, 4 x 4 In. 356.00
Inkwell, Pond Lily, Fish In Water, Blue Glass Insert, 7 ½ x 3 ½ In.. . . . . 10925.00
Inkwell, Spanish Pattern, Gargoyles, Birds, Medallions, Bronze, Gold Dore, 5 x 4 x 4 ¼ In. . . 3400.00
Inkwell, Venetian, 2 Wells, Bronze, Gold Dore, 5 ¼ x 3 In. 1955.00
Inkwell, Zodiac, Bronze, Gold Dore, Signed, 2 x 4 In. 240.00
Inkwell, Zodiac, Bronze, Patina, Glass Insert, Signed, 3 ½ x 6 ½ In. 530.00
Lamp, 3-Light, Bronze, Tulip Shades, Favrile, 12 ¾ In.. . . . . 7500.00
Lamp, 3-Lily, Fluted Bronze Base, Patina, Favrile, Signed, 306, 17 x 9 In. . . . . *illus* 9000.00
Lamp, 3-Lily, Green Pulled Feather Shades, Bronze Base, Adjustable, 22 In. 3600.00
Lamp, 3-Lily, Iridescent Orange Shaded To White Shades, Ruffled Rims, 13 ½ In. 5462.00
Lamp, 12-Lily, Favrile, Shades, Bronze Base, Stem, c.1910, 21 In.. . . . . 50000.00
Lamp, Abalone Shade, Adjustable Bronze Leaf Base, Signed, 9 x 12 In. 12000.00
Lamp, Abalone Shade, Bronze Base, 5 x 9 In.. . . . . 3900.00
Lamp, Acorn, Shade, Bronze Base, 18 ½ x 16 In. 8400.00
Lamp, Acorn, Shade, Green, Gold, Bronze, Branch Base, Patina, Marked, 23 x 16 In.. . . . . 10650.00
Lamp, Acorn, Shade, Pottery Base, 16 In.. . . . . 14000.00
Lamp, Art Deco, Iridescent Shade, Blue Mottled Enamel, Bronze Square Base, 7 x 14 In.. . . . . 14375.00
Lamp, Bell Shade, Green Pulled Feather, Bronze Harp, Fluted Pedestal Foot, 13 In. 2400.00
Lamp, Blue Zipper Shade, Bronze Base, Gold Dore, Blue Enamel, 14 In.. . . . . 4400.00
Lamp, Brass Mesh Shade, Bronze, Signed, 27 In.. . . . . 2500.00
Lamp, Chinese Tyler, Green, Yellow, Tile Shade, Bronze Swan Neck Base, 34 In. 41400.00
Lamp, Colonial, Mottled Geometric Tiles, Turquoise, Green, Yellow, Bronze, 16 x 21 In. 9200.00
Lamp, Counter-Balance, Blue, Gold Glass Shade, Bronze Base, c.1910, 55 In.. . . . . 43750.00
Lamp, Counter-Balance, Gold Iridescent Shade, Green Wave, Bronze, 7 x 55 In.. . . . . 7475.00
Lamp, Counter-Balance, Green, Gold Damascene Waves Shade, Bronze Curved Arm, 17 In. . . 11258.00
Lamp, Counter-Balance, Green Damascene Waves Shade, Bronze Base, 8 x 15 In. 10200.00
Lamp, Counter-Balance, Turtleback Tile, Blue Damascene Shade, Bronze Base, Signed, 15 In. 32775.00
Lamp, Counter-Balance, Yellow Damascene Shade, Bronze Base, 17 x 14 In. 6600.00
Lamp, Daffodil Shade, Green, Yellow, Blue Shade, Bronze Base, c.1910, 25 x 20 In. 62500.00
Lamp, Damascene Ribbed Shade, Green, Platinum, Blue Waves, 3-Arm, Bronze Base, 15 In. . 9000.00
Lamp, Damascene Shade, Gold Iridescent, Green Ground, Kerosene, 7 x 12 ½ In. 9600.00
Lamp, Damascene Shade, Iridescent Green, Harp, Arm, Adjustable, Bronze, Gold Dore Base, 18 In. 4200.00
Lamp, Damascene Waves Shade, Green, Gold, Platinum Blue Highlights, 3-Arm, Bronze Base, 20 In. 6613.00
Lamp, Geometric Shade, Adjustable, Green, Yellow, Orange, Bronze Base, c.1908, 29 x 19 In.. 46875.00
Lamp, Geometric Yellow Panel Shade, Signed, 25 In. 8050.00
Lamp, Gold, Leaded Glass Shade, Bronze, Gold Dore, Base, c.1910, 21 ½ x 16 In.. . . . . 27500.00
Lamp, Gold Amber Shade, Blue & Purple Iridescent, White Lining, Bronze Base, 56 x 9 In.. . . 6490.00
Lamp, Gold Linenfold Shade, 3-Sided Brass Base, 16 In.. . . . . 7500.00
Lamp, Gold Shade, Rainbow Iridescence, White Lining, 3-Arm Brass Base, 7 In. 4200.00
Lamp, Gold Wave Shade, Iridescent, Bronze, Column, Base, Signed, 55 In.. . . . . 12075.00
Lamp, Grapevine Bullet Shade, Bronze, Carmel Slag Glass, Gold Dore, Adjustable, 8 In.. . . . . . 3600.00
Lamp, Green Tile Shade, Bulbous, Oil Font Bronze Base, 14 x 19 In.. 6518.00
Lamp, Green Tile Shade, Caramel Slag Glass, Green Acorn Band, Bronze Stick Base, 22 In. . . 17250.00
Lamp, Green Tile Shade, Yellow, Orange, Pomegranate Band, Urn Base, 20 In. 16100.00
Lamp, Hanging, Cream Shade, Bronze, Gold Dore, Ceiling Plate, Rod, 3 Chains, 33 In.. . . . . . . 2370.00
Lamp, Hanging, Geometric Shade, Gold Iridescent, Caramel Slag, Bent Panel, 10 ½ In.. . . . . . 5750.00
Lamp, Hanging, Gold Iridescent Hooked Feather Shade, Ribbed, Bronze, Chains, 24 In.. . . . . . 7188.00
Lamp, King Tut Gold, Green Pink Shade, Adjustable Bronze Base, Metal Collar, 19 In. . . 2160.00 to 6900.00
Lamp, Leaf & Vine Shade, Green, Yellow, Bronze Base, Patina, 64 x 20 In.. . . . . 48500.00
Lamp, Lemon Leaf Shade, Green Tiles, Yellow Leaf Band, Bronze Base, Signed, 26 In.. . . . . . . 17250.00
Lamp, Linenfold Shade, Amber Tiles, Abalone Finial, Ribbed Dore Base, No. 617, 17 In. 6900.00
Lamp, Mosiac Domed Shade, Caramel, Green Slag Glass, Stylized Flowers, Scrolls, 24, 18 ¾ In. 2133.00
Lamp, Mosque Shade, Pulled Green Feather, Ivory Opalescent, Bronze, Gold Dore, Wood, 8 ½ In. 5500.00
Lamp, Nautilus Shell Shade, Bronze Base, c.1910, 13 ½ In.. . . . . 6900.00 to 8125.00
Lamp, Nautilus Shell Shade, Silvered Bronze, Mermaid Base, c.1900, 17 In.. . . . . 37500.00
Lamp, Oak Leaf Shade, Green & Brown, Bronze Base, Twisted, Signed, 18 x 7 In.. . . . . 55812.00
Lamp, Octagonal Shade, Gold Flower Panels, Blue Iridescence, Bronze Urn Base, 14 In.. . . . . . 2990.00
Lamp, Parasol Shade, Bronze, Green Patina, Chain Fringe, White Glass Balls, 17 x 10 In.. . . . 5925.00
Lamp, Parasol Shade, Green Leaded Glass, Pottery Base, Handles, Brown, c.1910, 24 x 24 In.. 35000.00

c.1915, 2 ¾ ...
$550.00

Tiffany, Frame, Chinese Pattern, Bronze, Gold Dore, Signed, 9 x 6 ¾ In.
$2040.00

Tiffany, Frame, Grapevine, Carmel Slag Glass, Bronze, Gold Dore, Signed, 7 x 6 ½ In.
$1320.00

Tiffany, Lamp, 3-Lily, Fluted Bronze Base, Patina, Favrile, Signed, 306, 17 x 9 In.
$9000.00

[illegible]iano, 3-Lily, Gold Iridescent Shades, Ribbed, 8 ½ In. 7475.00
[illegible]mp, Pomegranate Shade, Leaded Glass, Pine Needle Bronze Base, Patina, 22 x 16 In. 16000.00
Lamp, Pulled Feather Shade, Fluted Bronze Base, Harp Arm, Rotating, Favrile, 12 x 9 In. . . . *illus* 6600.00
Lamp, Pulled Gold On White Shade, Bronze Harp Frame, 9 x 12 In. 4800.00
Lamp, Scarab Shade, Green, Purple, Harp Arm, Bronze Base, Patina, Signed, 9 x 6 In. . . . . *illus* 20400.00
Lamp, Spanish Pattern, Bronze, Patina, Signed, 643, 14 x 11 In. . . . . *illus* 9600.00
Lamp, Student, Maroon Domed Shade, Brass, Rope & Bead, c.1880, 23 ½ In. 4230.00
Lamp, Tile Shade, Green, Rust, Bronze Base, c.1910, 28 ½ x 22 In. 25000.00
Lamp, Turtleback Shade, Bronze Urn Base, c.1905, 23 In. 40625.00
Lamp, White, Green, Gold, Favrile Shade, Bronze, 3-Footed Base, Signed, 57 x 12 In. 12000.00
Lamp, Yellow Pulled Feather Tiles, Textured Jewels, Grecian Urn Base, 23 In. 10925.00
Lamp Base, 3-Arm, Colonial, Bronze, Brown Patina, Pedestal, 20 In. . . . . 3163.00 to 3600.00
Lamp Base, 3-Arm Spider, Bullet Shape, 4 Ribbed Legs, Paw Feet, Green Patina, 13 In. 4025.00
Lamp Base, Bronze, Green Patina, 5 Spade Feet, Signed, 58 In. 3393.00
Lamp Base, Counter-Balance, 5 Legs, Lily Pad Feet, Bronze, Brown Patina, 52 In. 5175.00
Letter Holder, Bookmark, Bronze, Gold Dore, Monogram, 6 x 4 In. 690.00
Letter Holder, Pine Needle, Green, White Slag Glass, Bronze, c.1905, 6 x 10 In. . . 593.00 to 652.00
Letter Opener, Pine Needle, Green Slag Glass, Bronze, Signed, 9 In. 300.00
Letter Rack, Abalone, 2 Sections, Bronze, Gold Dore, Marked 1500.00
Letter Rack, Art Deco, Blue Enamel Squares, Multicolor Accents, Signed, 6 x 4 In. . . . . . *illus* 3163.00
Letter Rack, Bookmark, 2 Sections, Bronze, Gold Dore, 5 ½ x 9 ¼ x 2 ¼ In. 1500.00
Letter Rack, Bronze, 2 Sections, Iridescent Abalone Discs, Leaf, Line, Gold Dore 1500.00
Letter Rack, Grapevine, 2 Sections, Green Slag Glass, Bronze, 12 ½ x 3 ½ x 8 ¾ In. 700.00 to 1000.00
Letter Rack, Grapevine, 2 Sections, Green Slag Glass, Bronze, Dark Patina, 6 x 10 In. 1500.00 to 2000.00
Lipstick Case, Enamel, Nephrite, Chinoiserie Design, Rose Cut Diamonds, Mirror, c.1930 . . . 37552.00
Magnifying Glass, Abalone, Bronze, c.1920, 8 ¾ In. 900.00
Magnifying Glass, American Indian, Bronze, Gold Dore, 8 ½ In. 1500.00
Magnifying Glass, Grapevine, Bronze, Gold Dore, 8 In. 1800.00
Magnifying Glass, Iridescent Abalone Disc, Bronze, Gold Dore, 8 ¾ In. 2000.00
Magnifying Glass, Venetian, Bronze, 9 In. 1500.00
Magnifying Glass, Venetian, Bronze, Gold Dore, 4 x 9 In. 1900.00
Magnifying Glass, Zodiac, Bronze, Gold Dore, Signed, 1619, 9 x 4 In. . . . . *illus* 600.00
Match Holder, Grapevine, Cream Slag Glass, Bronze, Round, c.1906, 4 In. 296.00
Match Holder, Venetian, Bronze, Gold Dore, Signed, 5 x 3 ½ In. 200.00
Match Holder, Venetian, Red, Black, Bronze, Gold Dore, c.1920, 3 ¾ In. 375.00
Matchbox Holder, Venetian, Bronze, Gold Dore, 3 ¾ x 5 ¼ In. 633.00
Mirror, Grapevine, Amber Slag Glass, Bronze, Curved Handle, Bevel Edge, 11 In. 2500.00
Music Box, Zodiac, Singing Bird, Enamel, Blue, Gold Borders, 2 x 4 In. . . . . *illus* 8625.00
Note Pad Holder, Bookmark, Bronze, Gold Dore, 4 ½ x 7 ½ In. . . . . 625.00 to 950.00
Note Pad Holder, Heraldic, Burgundy, Signed, c.1920, 7 ½ x 4 ⅝ In. 1300.00
Paper Clip, American Indian, Bronze, Dark Patina, 2 ¾ x 4 In. 650.00
Paper Clip, Bookmark, Raised Leaf, Bronze, Gold Dore, 2 ½ x 3 ¼ In. 750.00
Paper Clip, Grapevine, Carmel Slag Glass, Bronze, Gold Dore, c.1920, 2 ½ x 3 ¾ In. 225.00
Paper Clip, Grapevine, Green Slag Glass, Bronze, Dark Patina, 2 ½ x 3 ¼ In. . . . . 350.00 to 650.00
Paper Clip, Venetian, Gold Finish, c.1920, 2 ¾ x 3 ⅜ In. 400.00
Paper Rack, Art Deco, Blue Enameled Squares, Multicolored Accents, 2 Tiers, 5 x 9 ¼ In. . . . 3738.00
Paper Rack, Bookmark, Red Enamel, Bronze, Gold Dore, 9 ¼ x 5 ⅜ In. 748.00
Paper Rack, Zodiac, Bronze, Gold Dore, 2 Tier, 6 x 9 ½ In. 575.00
Paperweight, Bulldog, Resting, Bronze, Gold Dore, 2 ¼ In. 720.00
Paperweight, Dore, Glass, 4 Triangles, Central Green Stone, Rectangle, c.1906, 2 x 4 In. 1007.00
Paperweight, Grapevine, Green Slag Glass, Knob Handle, Bronze, 3 ½ In. 650.00
Paperweight, Lioness, Bronze, Signed, 5 In. . . . . 600.00 to 770.00
Paperweight, Ninth Century, Green Jewel, Gold Dore, 4 x 2 ¼ In. 2300.00
Paperweight, Shando, Retriever, Dog's Head, Bronze, Brown Patina, 3 x 2 In. 2760.00
Paperweight, Turtleback Tile, Bronze Mount, Footed, 6 x 5 In. 2750.00
Paperweight, Venetian, Bronze, Gold Dore, ¾ x 4 ¼ x 2 ½ In. 2500.00
Pen, Art Deco, Blue Enameled Squares, Bronze, Gold Dore, 7 ¼ In. 2875.00
Pen Brush, Bookmark, Bronze, Gold Dore, Signed 750.00
Pen Tip Cleaner, Pine Needle Pattern, Bulbous, Flared Lip, Metal, No. 982, c.1910, 2 ½ In. . . 205.00
Pen Tray, American Indian, Bronze, Black Patina, Red Highlights, 11 x 4 In. . . . . 288.00 to 450.00
Pen Tray, Art Deco, Blue Enameled Squares, Multicolored Accents, Bronze, 9 x 3 In. 1610.00
Pen Tray, Grapevine, Green Slag Glass, Bronze, Dark Patina, 4-Footed, 9 ½ x 3 ½ x ¾ In. . . . 550.00
Pen Tray, Mosaic, Inlaid Blue Glass, Swirled, Bronze, 8 In. 9200.00
Pen Tray, Ninth Century, Green & Blue Jewels, Bronze, 9 ½ x 3 ½ In. . . . . 805.00 to 900.00
Pen Tray, Venetian, Bronze, Gold Dore, c.1920, 3 ¾ x 10 In. 300.00
Pen Wipe, Art Deco, Blue Enameled Squares, Multicolored Accents, Bronze, Pedestal, 3 x 3 In. 2875.00
Pen Wipe, Pine Needle, Slag Glass, Bronze, 2 x 2 ½ In. 450.00

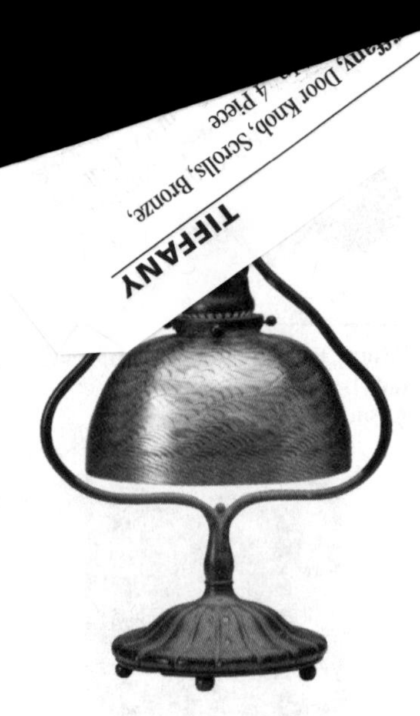

Tiffany, Lamp, Scarab Shade, Green, Purple, Harp Arm, Bronze Base, Patina, Signed, 9 x 6 In.
$20400.00

Tiffany, Lamp, Spanish Pattern, Bronze, Patina, Signed, 643, 14 x 11 In.
$9600.00

Penholder, Grapevine, Green Slag Glass, Bronze, Dark Patina, 4 x 5 In.................. 2500.00
Penholder, Pine Needle, Green Slag Glass, Bronze, 5 ¼ x 4 In. 600.00
Planter, Bowl, 3 Leaves On Triangular Column, 3 Paw Feet, Bronze, 27 In. 5925.00
Planter, Geometrics, Bronze, Gold Dore, Liner, 2 ½ x 8 ½ In............................ 750.00
Planter, Grapevine, Carmel Slag Glass, Bronze, c.1920, 11 In. Diam. 1250.00
Plate, Bronze, Gold Dore, 8 ⅞ In. 92.00
Postage Scale, Art Deco, Blue Enameled Squares, Multicolored Accents, Ball Feet, Bronze, 4 ⅛ In. 4025.00
Postage Scale, Bookmark, Raised Leaves, Emblem, Gold Dore, 3 x 1 ½ x 3 ¼ In. 2500.00
Postage Scale, Grapevine, Green Slag Glass, Bronze, Dark Patina, 3 x 2 x 3 In. . . 1150.00 to 2000.00
Postage Scale, Pine Needle, Caramel Slag Glass, Bronze, Signed, c.1910, 3 In. 900.00
Postage Scale, Pine Needle, Green Slag Glass, Bronze, Dark Patina, 3 x 2 x 3 In. 2000.00
Postage Scale, Venetian, Bronze, Gold Dore, 3 ½ In. 2415.00
Powder Box, Hinged Cover, Bronze, Round, Favrile, Signed, 4 ¼ In....................... 3000.00
Powder Box, Hinged Cover, Gold Iridescent, Bronze, Round, Favrile, 1 ¾ x 4 ¼ In.......... 3000.00
Radiator Cap, Openwork Design, Bronze, Brown Patina, 4 In. 920.00
Ring, Egyptian Hieroglyphics, Scarab, Favrile, 18K Gold, Size 6 ½....................... 382.00
Rocker Blotter, Art Deco, Blue Enameled Squares, Multicolored Accents, Bronze, 6 x 2 ¼ In. 1495.00
Rocker Blotter, Ninth Century, Green & Blue Jewels, Bronze, 5 ½ In.................... 1150.00
Shade, Brass, Pierced, Patinated, Green Slag Glass, 3 ½ x 6 ⅜ In. 345.00
Smoking Stand, Artichoke, Overlapping Stylized Leaves, Catch Tray, Bronze, 25 In......... 2013.00
Stamp Box, Abalone, Bronze.. 750.00
Stamp Box, American Indian, Bronze, Black Patina, Red Highlights, 3 x 5 In.. .... 748.00
Stamp Box, Art Deco, Blue Enameled, Multicolored Accents, 2 ½ x 2 In......... 1553.00 to 2016.00
Stamp Box, Chinese Pattern, 3 Sections, Bronze, Dark Brown Patina, 1920, 2 ⅝ x 5 ½ x 3 ½ In. 900.00
Stamp Box, Chinese Pattern, Bronze, Dark Patina, 8-Sided, 2 ½ x 5 ½ x 3 ½ In........... 1200.00
Stamp Box, Grapevine, Caramel Slag Glass, Bronze, Liner, Signed, No. 801, 1 ½ x 4 ¼ In.... 360.00
Stamp Box, Pine Needle, Green Slag Glass, Bronze, Ball Feet, 1 ¾ x 4 ⅜ x 3 ¼ In.. .... 444.00
Stamp Box, Venetian, Hinged Cover, Bronze, Gold Dore, 3 ¼ x 4 ¾ x 2 ½ In. 750.00
Tazza, Enameled, Gold Iridescent, Heart Shape, Bronze, Gold Dore, Favrile, 6 ½ x 7 In. 3500.00
Tazza, Pale Striated Bowl, Flared Rim, Bronze, Gold Dore, Signed No. 172, 6 x 4 In. 431.00
Tea Screen, 3 Sections, Multicolored Glass, Bronze Ball Feet, Swirl Patina, 4 x 7 In......... 4500.00
Thermometer, Pine Needle, Green Slag Glass, Bronze, Dark Patina, Easel Back, 8 x 4 In. 2200.00 to 3500.00
Thermometer, Venetian Pattern, Easel Back, Raised Minks, Bronze, 8 ¼ x 4 In. 3000.00
Tray, Abalone, Bronze, Gold Dore, Raised Border, 12 In. 1200.00
Tray, Bird Of Paradise, Bronze, Enameled, Multicolored, Raised Rim, 8 In. Diam. 3000.00
Tray, Enameled, Oval, Bronze, Gold Dore, 10 x 5 ½ In. 1500.00
Tray, Grapevine, Green Slag, Bronze, 3 ½ x 4 x 4 In. 550.00
Vase, Bud, Enameled, Green, Gold, Blue Iridescent, Bronze, Gold Dore, Favrile, 13 In........ 1800.00
Vase, Bulbous, Flared Lip, Circular Foot, Bronze, Gold Dore, 6 ¼ In. 889.00
Vase, Fluted, Bronze, Gold Dore, Favrile, c.1910, 12 In................................... 1638.00
Vinaigrette, Bell Shape, Hinged Base, Gilt Interior Grill, Silver, 1 ¼ In. 1680.00
Window, Fruit Bowl, Grape Vines, Leaded Glass, Column, Metal Frame, Hooks, 29 x 31 In.... 16100.00

TIFFANY GLASS

Ball, Stained & Leaded Glass, Blue Iridescent Panels, Ring For Hanging, 3 In. 690.00
Bowl, Amethyst, Ribbed, Oval, Scalloped Rim, 10 In.. .... 863.00
Bowl, Blue Favrile, Iridescent Rim, 1 ¾ x 5 ¾ In. 825.00
Bowl, Blue Iridescent, Ribbed, Wide Flared Rim, Favrile, 4 x 12 In. 770.00
Bowl, Blue Iridescent, Rolled Rim, Short Foot, Favrile, 1925, 9 ⅞ In.. .... 250.00
Bowl, Blue To Yellow Iridescent, Favrile, 3 x 7 In. 940.00
Bowl, Centerpiece, Blue, Gold Iridescent, Blue Edge, 3 Shell Feet, Favrile, 2 ½ In. 2500.00
Bowl, Centerpiece, Blue Iridescent, Footed, Favrile, 3 x 11 ¼ In.. .... 3000.00
Bowl, Centerpiece, Blue Iridescent, Ruffled & Cupped Edge, Favrile, Signed, 2 x 9 In. 1500.00
Bowl, Centerpiece, Blue Iridescent, Ruffled Edge, Ribbed, Favrile, Signed, 9 x 2 In. 1500.00
Bowl, Centerpiece, Flower Frog, Gold, Favrile, c.1917, 2 ½ x 13 In. 1755.00
Bowl, Centerpiece, Gold, Ribbed, Scalloped Rim, Favrile, Signed, 10 In. 748.00
Bowl, Centerpiece, Pastel Green, Opalescent, Ribs, Applied Green Foot, 6 x 11 In.. .... 1610.00
Bowl, Centerpiece, Peacock Blue, Footed, Favrile, 11 ½ x 5 x 3 In........................ 3000.00
Bowl, Flower Frog, Blue, Platinum Highlights, Favrile, 3 ¼ In. 540.00
Bowl, Flower Frog, Blue Iridescent, 6 Lily Pads, 2-Tier Holder, Favrile, 11 ½ In., 2 Piece 4500.00
Bowl, Flower Frog, Blue Iridescent, Pulled Leaf & Vine, Favrile, Signed, 5 x 10 In....... *illus.* 2400.00
Bowl, Flower Frog, Iridescent Peacock Blue, Undulating Rim, Favrile, 3 ¾ x 9 ⅞ In......... 2390.00
Bowl, Gold, Scalloped Rim, Favrile, c.1915, 2 x 6 In...................................... 351.00
Bowl, Gold Iridescent, Blue Highlights, Vertical Ribbing, Scalloped Rim, 4 ½ x 1 ¾ In....... 480.00
Bowl, Gold Iridescent, Pink & Green Highlights, Footed, Ruffled Rim, 6 In. 1150.00
Bowl, Gold Iridescent, Platinum Highlights, Ruffled Edge, Ribbed, 4 ¾ In.. .... 230.00
Bowl, Gold Iridescent, Ribbed, Scalloped Edge, c.1893, 2 ½ x 6 ½ In............ 1527.00 to 1880.00
Bowl, Gold Iridescent, Round, Undulating Rim, Engraved Leaves, Vines, Favrile, 7 In.. .... 474.00

Ti... Blue Enamel...
Signed, 6 x 4 In.
$3163.00

Tiffany, Magnigying Glass, Zodiac, Bronze, Gold Dore, Signed, 1619, 9 x 4 In.
$600.00

Tiffany, Music Box, Zodiac, Singing Bird, Enamel, Blue, Gold Borders, 2 x 4 In.
$8625.00

Tiffany Glass, Bowl, Flower Frog, Blue Iridescent, Pulled Leaf & Vine, Favrile, Signed, 5 x 10 In.
$2400.00

TIP
Store crystal stemware rim side up on the shelf.

T

…Tiffany, Letter Rack, Art Deco, …Squares, Multicolor Accents,

TIFFANY GLASS

…1 ½ …g on how far … All the rest are …nce.

1863 ....3¢
1885 ....2¢
1917 ....3¢
1919 ....2¢
1932 ....3¢
1958 ....4¢
1963 ....5¢
1968 ....6¢
1971 ....8¢
1974 ....10¢
1975 ....13¢
1978 ....15¢
March 1981 ....18¢
November 1981 ....20¢
1985 ....22¢
1988 ....24¢
1991 ....29¢
1995 ....32¢
1999 ....33¢
2000 ....34¢
2002 ....37¢
2006 ....39¢
2007 ....41¢
2008 ....42¢
2009 ....44¢

Tiffany Glass, Vase, Agate, Amber, Umber, Emerald, 4 Dimples, Favrile, Signed, 3 In.
$4800.00

…aglio, Ribbed Opalescent, Gold Iridescent Foot, Blue Rim, Favrile, 6 In. 2645.00
…dlestick, Gold, Applied Inverted Saucer Ribbed Foot, Favrile, 12 In., Pair 2875.00
Candlestick, Gold, Favrile, c.1893, 4 ½ In., Pair 3803.00
Candlestick, Gold, Favrile, c.1910, 12 In., Pair 3510.00
Candlestick, Red, Tulip Cup, Pastel, Opalescent Ribs, Blue, Green Stem, Stripe Base, 16 In. ... 6613.00
Chalice, Gold Iridescent, Baluster Stem, Favrile, 6 ¼ x 4 In. 2150.00
Compote, Amber Opalescent Stem, Green Leaf Bowl, Favrile, Signed, 6 In. 1006.00
Compote, Blue, Grape Leaf Intaglio Band, Low, Favrile, 8 In. 2070.00
Compote, Blue, Rim, White Opaque Bowl, Pedestal, Favrile, c.1919, 4 x 8 ¾ In. 1638.00
Compote, Blue Iridescent, Boat Shape, Favrile, c.1893, 5 ½ x 10 In. 1880.00
Compote, Blue Iridescent, Ribbed, Footed, Favrile, Signed, 6 x 4 ½ In. 2500.00
Compote, Brass, Flared Rim, c.1920, 4 ¼ x 6 ½ In. 1170.00
Compote, Diamond Quilted, Pink Highlights, Saucer Foot, 8 ¼ x 3 ½ In. 805.00
Compote, Flower Form, Blue Iridescent, Stretched & Ruffled Rim, 4 ⅜ In. 2250.00
Compote, Gold, Etched Vines, Favrile, c.1893, 4 x 5 ¾ In., Pair 3218.00
Compote, Gold, Flower Shape, Ruffled Edge, Favrile, c.1918, 5 ¼ x 6 ½ In. 3218.00
Compote, Gold Iridescent, Flared, Long Stem, Favrile, c.1910, 6 In. 474.00
Compote, Gold Iridescent, Green, Favrile, 6 ½ In. 920.00
Compote, Gold Iridescent, Shaped Stem, Round Foot, Favrile, c.1910, 4 x 8 In. 8295.00
Compote, Intaglio, Gold Iridescent, Favrile, 4 ½ x 5 ½ In. 2200.00
Compote, Intaglio, Leaf, Vine, Gold Iridescent, Pedestal, Favrile, 2 ¾ x 4 ½ In. 2200.00
Compote, Morning Glory, Paperweight, Opalescent, Favrile, c.1921, 7 ½ x 7 ½ In., Pair 25740.00
Compote, Pastel, Opalescent, Pulled Feather, Rolled Yellow Rim, 7 ½ In. 1150.00
Compote, Pink Pastel, Opalescent Diamonds, Stretched Rim, Favrile, 2 ½ x 8 In. 1500.00
Cordial, Gold, Fluted, Leaves, 4 ⅝ In. 259.00
Cordial, Gold Iridescent, White Pulled Design, Signed, c.1908, 5 In. 237.00
Creamer, Blue, Pinched Waist, Applied Handle, Favrile, Signed, 4 In. 690.00
Cruet, Gold Iridescent, Favrile, c.1893, 6 In. 1292.00
Dish, Agate, Tan, Brown, Blue, Yellow, Green, Scalloped Rim, Favrile, 6 In. 170.00
Dish, Gold Iridescent, Undulating Rim, Circular Foot, Pontil, Favrile, 3 ⅞ x 7 ½ In. 593.00
Dish, Salt, Gold Iridescent, Rolled Rim, Applied Foot, Engraved, 5 In. 575.00
Dish, Sweetmeat, Gold Iridescent, Undulating Rim, Favrile, 4 In. 356.00
Finger Bowl, Gold Iridescent, Scalloped Edge, 2 x 4 ¾ In. 352.00
Finger Bowl, Underplate, Gold, Pig Tail Prunts, Favrile, Signed, 6 In. 460.00
Finger Bowl, Underplate, Gold Iridescent, Lobed, Ribbed, Favrile, 6 ¾ In. 504.00
Finger Bowl, Underplate, Gold Iridescent, Pink & Platinum Highlights, Favrile, 6 In. 288.00
Goblet, Gold Iridescent, Blue & Purple Highlights, 6 In., 4 Piece 1840.00
Goblet, Gold Iridescent, Footed, c.1925, 5 ¼ In. 413.00
Goblet, Gold Iridescent, Shaped Stem, Favrile, 7 ¹⁄₁₆ In. 296.00
Goblet, Gold Iridescent, Twist Stem, 7 In. 1035.00
Goblet, Pastel, Rose, Lavender, Pulled White Opalescent Design, Signed, 8 In. 1680.00
Hurricane Shade, Green Pulled Feather, Gold Iridescent, White Ribbing, 7 ½ In. 4025.00
Jar, Cover, Gold Iridescent, Rounded, Sunburst Knob, Favrile, 7 ½ In. 2000.00
Lamp, Green Favrile Shade, Stem, Base, Platinum Pulled Feathers, Blue Highlights, 18 In. .. 5750.00
Lamp, Perfume Burner, Gold, Etched Leaves, Branches, Favrile, Signed, 10 In. 1035.00
Lamp Base, Green Leaf, Vine, White Flowers, Gold Iridescent Ground, Favrile, 17 ½ In. 4313.00
Loving Cup, Gold Iridescent, Green Leaf, Vine, 3 Handles, Favrile, 5 x 3 ¼ In. 2200.00
Loving Cup, Gold Iridescent, Leaf & Vine, 3 Applied Handles, Favrile, 5 In. 2200.00
Medallion, Eagle & Liberty Bell, Gold Iridescent, Blue, Purple, Favrile, 1918, 2 ¾ In. 1500.00
Perfume Bottle, Gold Iridescent, Platinum Highlights, Oriental Hat Shape Stopper, 4 ¼ In. . 2016.00
Plate, Gold Iridescent, Pink & Green Highlights, Ruffled Rim, Favrile, 6 In. 345.00
Plate, Turquoise Pastel, Opalescent Optic, c.1920, 11 In. 585.00
Rondel, Gold Iridescent, Red, Green Bands, Black Mat, Frame, 12 In. 633.00
Salt, Blue, Gold, Scalloped Rim, 4-Footed, 1 ¼ In. 288.00
Salt, Blue Favrile, Amethyst, Ruffles Edge, Signed, 2 ¼ In. 316.00
Salt, Blue Iridescent, Flared, Pulled Feet, Favrile, 2 ¼ In. 593.00
Salt, Gold Iridescent, 4-Footed, Favrile, 1 ½ x 2 ¼ In. 235.00
Salt, Gold Iridescent, Blue Interior, Favrile, 1 x 1 ¾ In. 300.00
Salt, Gold Iridescent, Fluted Rim, Favrile, Signed, 3 In. 150.00
Salt, Gold Iridescent, Ruffled Edge, Favrile, 1 x 2 ½ In. 200.00
Shade, Bell Shape, Pulled Feather, Translucent Green, Gold Trim, Oyster Ground, 2 x 5 In. .. 2530.00
Shade, Bell Shape, White Matte Ground, Gold Iridescent Pulled Chain, Signed, 5 x 4 In. 270.00
Shade, Butterscotch Pulled Feather, White Ground, Ruffled Edge, 5 ¼ In., 6 Piece 6900.00
Shade, Emerald Green Translucent Body, Raised Wave, Iridescent, 5 In. 1668.00
Shade, Flared, Ribbed, Scalloped Rim, Gold, Favrile, 2 x 5 In. 863.00
Shade, Green, Yellow, Iridescent Swirls, Favrile, 7 x 4 In. 850.00
Shade, Green Linenfold, For Candle Lamp, c.1913, 4 x 5 ½ In. 633.00
Shade, Lily, Green Pulled Feather, White Ribbed Ground, 4 ¼ In. 3105.00

Shade, Lily, Opalescent Ribs, Green, Yellow Fluted Rim, Blue Iridescent Feather, Signed, 5 In. 2040.00
Shade, Lily, Opalescent Tan Ribs, Green, Amber Ground, Gold, Pink Highlights, 4 In. 2040.00
Shade, Lily, Red, Green, Gold, Green, Gold Iridescent Interior, Favrile, Signed, 4 In. 1955.00
Shade, Pulled Feather, Iridescent Orange Ground, Brown Pulled Feather, 5 In. 1035.00
Shade, Red Murano, Pink Wave, White Ground, Ribbed, 5 ¼ In. 2300.00
Shade, Tulip, Ribbed, Iridescent Blue, Purple Highlights, Signed, 5 In. 2588.00
Sherbet, Gold, Grapes, Leaves Band, Favrile, Signed, 3 In. 403.00
Sherbet, Gold Favrile, Applied Stem, Ruffled Rim, Pink Highlights, 2 ¾ x 4 In. 270.00
Sherbet, Gold Iridescent, Applied Foot, Stem, Engraved, 6 In. 403.00
Tazza, Leaves, Green Luster, Favrile, 6 ½ In. 1020.00
Tile, Stylized 4 Leaf Clover, Gold, Green, 3 ⅞ In. 356.00
Toothpick, Blue, Gold, Ribbed, Tugged, Pulled Pigtails, 2 In. 230.00
Toothpick, Gold Iridescent, Pinched Sides, c.1910, 2 In., Pair 356.00
Tumbler, Pink, Pinched Waist, Label, 5 ½ In. 575.00
Vase, 5 Green Pulled Feathers, Ruffled, Domed Foot, 11 In. 5333.00
Vase, Agate, Amber, Umber, Emerald, 4 Dimples, Favrile, Signed, 3 In. *illus* 4800.00
Vase, Amber Foot, Green Pulled Leaves, Iridescent Peach Stretched Ruffled Rim, 15 In. 5980.00
Vase, Blue, Black Top & Base, Egyptian Shape, Favrile, 5 ¾ In. 3800.00
Vase, Blue, Flared Rim, Tapered, Bulbous, Indented Sides, Favrile, 4 ½ In. 948.00
Vase, Blue, Tulip Shape, Ribbed, Undulating Rim, Footed, Favrile, Signed, 9 ½ In. 2243.00
Vase, Blue Iridescent, Bulbous, Tapered, Ribbed, Signed, c.1910, 7 In. 1422.00
Vase, Blue Iridescent, Green Gold Shoulder & Neck, Favrile, 6 ½ In. 1320.00
Vase, Blue Iridescent, Platinum Highlights, Favrile, Signed, 5 ¾ In. 748.00
Vase, Blue Iridescent, Purple To Turquoise, Green, Oval, Ribbed, Favrile, 4 ¾ In. 2478.00
Vase, Bronze, 4 Sided, Buttresses, Dragon, 12 x 7 In. 3240.00
Vase, Bud, Blue, Bulbous, Narrow Neck, Favrile, c.1910, 6 In. 3510.00
Vase, Bud, Gold, Ruffled Edge, Footed, Favrile, c.1906, 4 x 4 ½ In. 761.00
Vase, Bud, Gold Iridescent, Favrile, 10 In. 900.00
Vase, Bud, Gold Iridescent, Pedestal Base, Favrile, Signed, 12 ½ In. 550.00
Vase, Bud, Opal To Green, Iridescent, Feather, Favrile, Signed, 2 ¾ In. *illus* 1320.00
Vase, Bud, Pulled Green Heart, Gold, Favrile, 6 x 3 ¼ In. 1920.00
Vase, Cabinet, Pinch Sided, Teal, Blue, Gold Iridescent, 3 In. 805.00
Vase, Compote, White, Turquoise Stripe, Favrile, Signed, 7 x 7 In. 1080.00
Vase, Corona, Green Iridescent, Gold Hooked Feathers, Oval, 6 In. 3220.00
Vase, Crackle, Gold Iridescent, Multicolored Detail, Favrile, 8 In. 4025.00
Vase, Cranberry Swirl, 8 ½ In. 80.00
Vase, Elongated Neck, Square Shoulder, Platinum To Cobalt, Favrile, Signed, 6 In. 920.00
Vase, Flower Shape, Applied Gold Iridescent Foot, White Pulled Feather, Gold Ground, 8 ¼ In. 1323.00
Vase, Flower Shape, Gold, Favrile, c.1913, 13 In. 3510.00
Vase, Flower Shape, Gold, Green & White Hearts & Vines, Favrile, Signed, c.1910, 12 In. 5750.00
Vase, Flower Shape, Gold, Ribbed, Favrile, Signed, 10 ¼ In. 1980.00
Vase, Flower Shape, Gold Iridescent, 5-Sided, Flared Rim, Stretched Edge, 4 In. 1800.00
Vase, Flower Shape, Gold Iridescent, Favrile, 15 In. 3738.00
Vase, Flower Shape, Gold Iridescent, Green Pulled Leaf, Saucer Foot, 11 In. 10925.00
Vase, Flower Shape, Gold Iridescent, Scalloped Rim, Favrile, Signed, 6 ½ In. 4000.00
Vase, Flower Shape, Green Iridescent Pulled Feather, White Opalescent, 10 ½ In. 3738.00
Vase, Flower Shape, Green Pulled Feather, Applied Gold Iridescent Foot, 11 ¾ In. 3450.00
Vase, Flower Shape, Green Pulled Feather, Ruffled Rim, Favrile, Signed, 12 In. 978.00
Vase, Flower Shape, Green Pulled Feather, White Ground, Gold Applied Foot, 5 ½ x 7 In. 1725.00
Vase, Flower Shape, Green Pulled Feather, White Ground, Rolled Edge, 9 ½ In. 6325.00
Vase, Flower Shape, Opal, Green Pulled Leaves, Footed, Signed, 4 ½ In. *illus* 978.00
Vase, Flower Shape, Opalescent Pulled Feather, Amber, Green Stem, 13 In. 11000.00
Vase, Flower Shape, Pulled Feather, Brown Red, Gold Iridescent Ground, Saucer Foot, 11 In. 5750.00
Vase, Flower Shape, Pulled Green Feather, Opal, Favrile, Signed, c.1900, 13 In. 748.00
Vase, Flower Shape, Pulled Loops, Green Pulled Feather, 12 In. 1440.00
Vase, Flower Shape, Ribbed Body, Rolled Rim, Marked, 5 ¾ In. 920.00
Vase, Flower Shape, White, Iridescent Gold Pulled Feather, Ribbed Amber Foot, 13 ¾ In. 4600.00
Vase, Glass, Gold Iridescent, 2 Handles, Favrile, c.1910, 8 In. 652.00
Vase, Gold, Barrel Ribbed, 8 Prunts, Amethyst Highlights, Favrile, c.1911, 3 In. 431.00
Vase, Gold, Barrel Shape, Opal, Pulled Feathers, Favrile, 2 ½ In. 748.00
Vase, Gold, Optic Ribs, Footed, Favrile, Signed, 2 In. 460.00
Vase, Gold, Ribbed, Embossed Bronze Base, Favrile, Signed, 11 In. 1610.00
Vase, Gold, Ribbed, Free Form, Flared Scalloped Rim, Favrile, Signed, 3 ¼ In. 805.00
Vase, Gold, Silver Iridescent, Double Gourd, Favrile, Signed, 1 ½ x 2 In. *illus* 435.00
Vase, Gold, Stylized Broad Leaves, Stems, Favrile, c.1918, 12 In. 16965.00
Vase, Gold, Wide Ribs, Ruffled Edge, Button Pontil, Favrile, 3 ½ x 5 ½ In. 800.00
Vase, Gold Iridescent, Ball Shape, Pinched Border, Favrile, 6 In. 885.00
Vase, Gold Iridescent, Cameo Relief, Green Vines, Signed, Favrile, 9 ¾ In. 1900.00

Tiffany Glass, Vase, Bud, Opal To Green, Iridescent, Feather, Favrile, Signed, 2 ¾ In.
$1320.00

Tiffany Glass, Vase, Flower Shape, Opal, Green Pulled Leaves, Footed, Signed, 4 ½ In.
$978.00

Tiffany Glass, Vase, Gold, Silver Iridescent, Double Gourd, Favrile, Signed, 1 ½ x 2 In.
$435.00

What's a Tiffany?
The description "Tiffany lamp" is often used today for any old or new lamp with a stained glass shade or even a colored glass shade. True Tiffany lamps have stained glass or other art glass shades and are almost all marked "Tiffany Studios" or, on the iridescent glass shades, "Favrile." Tiffany made over 500 lampshade designs.

Tiffany Glass, Vase, Green Iridescent, Gold Feather Plume, Opal Cased, Cupped Rim, Favrile, 6 ½ In.
$7100.00

Tiffany Glass, Vase, Green Pulled Feather, Orange Ground, Signed, 6 ½ x 3 ½ In.
$3600.00

Tiffany Pottery, Vase, Incised Ribs, Buff, Forest Green Glaze, Signed, 6 In.
$2000.00

Vase, Gold Iridescent, Flared Rim, Tapered, Favrile, 7 In. 593.00
Vase, Gold Iridescent, Green Heart-Shape Leaves, Vines, Round, Favrile, 2 ½ x 3 In. 2200.00
Vase, Gold Iridescent, Pinched Sides, Stick Neck, Favrile, 1910, 7 ½ In. 300.00
Vase, Gold Iridescent, Ribbed, Flared, Scalloped, Applied Foot, 12 In. 2280.00
Vase, Gold Iridescent, Twisted Prints, Bottle Shape, Favrile, Marked, 6 ½ x 3 In. 2500.00
Vase, Gold Iridescent, Undulating Rim, c.1910, 13 In. 1067.00
Vase, Gold Iridescent, White Neck, Wide Shoulders, Favrile, c.1910, 10 In. 4148.00
Vase, Gold Pulled Feather, Bronze, Gold Dore Base, Flared, Favrile, 14 ½ In. 2040.00
Vase, Green Iridescent, Gold Feather Plume, Opal Cased, Cupped Rim, Favrile, 6 ½ In. ... *illus* 7100.00
Vase, Green Pulled Feather, Opalescent Ground, Flared Rim, Favrile, 11 In. 3680.00
Vase, Green Pulled Feather, Orange Ground, Signed, 6 ½ x 3 ½ In. .... *illus* 3600.00
Vase, Hooked Feather, Iridescent Cobalt Blue, Urn Shape, Favrile, 5 In. 2875.00
Vase, Intaglio Carved, Green Leaves, Gold Ground, Favrile, Marked, 6 ½ In. 3910.00
Vase, Iridescent Gold, Burnished Magenta, 2 In. 230.00
Vase, Jack-In-The-Pulpit, Elephant Ear Face, Scalloped Rim, Footed, Ribbed, 12 ½ In. 5463.00
Vase, Jack-In-The-Pulpit, Gold Iridescent, Onionskin, Signed, 16 ¼ x 8 ½ In. 14000.00
Vase, Jack-In-The-Pulpit, Gold Iridescent, Stretched Rim, Rounded Foot, 14 In. 6325.00
Vase, Paperweight, Flowers, Gold Stems, Orange, Favrile, c.1905, 8 In. 10000.00
Vase, Paperweight, Millefiore, Multicolored, Favrile, c.1910, 4 ½ In. 1500.00
Vase, Pastel, White Opalescent Rim, Ribs, Yellow Interior, Clear Foot, 10 In. 1380.00
Vase, Peacock, Pulled, Swirled, Blue, Purple, Gold, Favrile, c.1895, 12 In. 53125.00
Vase, Pink Opalescent, Footed, Favrile, Signed, 13 ¾ In. 1200.00
Vase, Platinum Iridescent, Hooked, Purple Ground, Yellow Neck, 9 ¼ In. 8625.00
Vase, Pulled Leaf, Green, Orange, Favrile, c.1897, 11 In. 17500.00
Vase, Ruby & Gold, Favrile, 9 In. 2358.00
Vase, Stick, Gold, Green Leaves, Favrile, 1918, 10 In. 1175.00
Vase, Stick, White, Iridescent Cream, Favrile, c.1893, 10 In. 1410.00
Vase, Tel El Amarna, Red, Applied Decorated Collar, Favrile, Signed, 6 In. 5750.00
Vase, Trumpet, Gold Iridescent, 5 Green Pulled Leaves, Favrile, 10 In. 1668.00
Vase, Trumpet, Gold Iridescent, Pulled Feather, Round Metal Base, 15 In. 1778.00
Vase, Trumpet, Green, Opalescent, Metal Base, Favrile, c.1900, 14 ⅜ In. 1880.00
Vase, Trumpet, Green, Opalescent, Pulled Leaf, Favrile, Signed, 6 In. 900.00
Vase, Trumpet, Green Heart Vine, Gold Iridescent, Signed, 10 In. 1700.00
Vase, Trumpet, Green Leaf, Vine, Gold Iridescent, Signed, 15 In. 2300.00
Vase, Trumpet, Purple, Opalescent Stripes, Footed, Favrile, Signed, 12 In. 2013.00
Vase, Trumpet, Purple, Pink Opalescent Stripes, Favrile, c.1921, 10 In. 1035.00
Vase, Trumpet, Yellow To Green, Gold Interior, Favrile, 11 ¾ x 3 ½ In. 900.00
Vase, Tulip Shape, Blue Iridescent, Ribbed, Undulating Rim, Favrile, Signed, 9 ½ In. 1500.00
Vase, Turquoise, White Stripe, Fluted, Bronze Base, Signed, 11 x 4 In. 960.00
Whiskey Set, Blue Iridescent, Threading, Marked, 10 Piece 2070.00

TIFFANY GOLD

Cigar Cutter, 14K, Signed, 2 In. 250.00
Cigarette Case, Hinged Lid, Inscribed, Jan. 25, 1947, 14K, 5 In. 1900.00
Compact, Floral Engraved Borders, Wreath, Monogram, Mirror, 14K, 1 ½ In. 374.00

TIFFANY POTTERY

Vase, Carved Leaves, Bronze Clad, Flared, Patina, Signed, 6 x 7 In. 9100.00
Vase, Green Matte Glaze, Bronze Rim, Long Neck, Bulbous Base, 6 In. 2185.00
Vase, Incised Ribs, Buff, Forest Green Glaze, Signed, 6 In. .... *illus* 2000.00
Vase, Leaves, Sculpted, Brown Glaze, Aqua Interior, 4 ½ In. .... *illus* 1500.00

TIFFANY SILVER

Asparagus Dish, Underplate, Reeded Rim, Scroll Feet, c.1907, 12 ⅜ In. 2015.00
Asparagus Tongs, Colonial, Pierced Blade, Engraved, c.1895, 7 ½ In. 478.00
Basket, Reticulated, Pierced, Engraved Vines, Swing Handle, Sterling, c.1902, 11 In. 6518.00
Basket, Round, Scalloped Leafy Edge, Openwork, Border, Bail Handle, 11 x 12 In. 2070.00
Basket, Swing Handle, Footed, 8 In. 600.00
Bell, Dinner, Sterling, 2 ½ In. 150.00
Berry Spoon, Blackberry Pattern, Monogram, 1902-1944, 9 ½ In. 345.00
Berry Spoon, Strawberry Pattern, Monogram, ACR, c.1870, 10 In. 388.00
Berry Spoon, Winthrop, Fitted Box, 1909, 7 ¾ In. 117.00
Bottle, Toilet Water, Cylindrical, Repousse, Flower, Pierced Top, c.1881, 3 In. 418.00
Bowl, Art Deco Tomato, Pumpkin Band, c.1940, 9 In. 1673.00
Bowl, Centerpiece, 3 Tiers, Trumpet Shape Bowls, 3-Footed, c.1956-61, 17 x 11 In. 960.00
Bowl, Centerpiece, Art Nouveau, Initials, Anniversary Date, 11 In. 863.00
Bowl, Centerpiece, Chrysanthemum, Flared, Flower & Scroll Rim, Splayed Mum Feet, c.1895, 19 In. 16250.00
Bowl, Centerpiece, Chrysanthemum, Flared, Scalloped Flower Rim, 8 Flower Feet, c.1885, 15 In. 8750.00
Bowl, Centerpiece, Flowers, Acanthus Cartouches, Gilt Brass, Flared Sides, 14 In. 5629.00

Bowl, Centerpiece, Flowers, Fruit, Embossed, Pierced, Claw Feet, New York, c.1895, 22 In. 23750.00
Bowl, Centerpiece, Hexagonal, Vertical Flutes, Applied Foot, c.1937, 3 ½ x 9 In. 2937.00
Bowl, Centerpiece, Repousse, Gilt Interior, Grapevine Handles, Sterling, c.1876, 9 ¼ In. 4130.00
Bowl, Chased Shell & C-Scroll, Flared Rim, John Moore, 12 In. 1200.00
Bowl, Decorated Bands, Domed Foot, Sterling, 5 ⅝ In. 330.00
Bowl, Etched Squirrels, Oak Leaves, c.1909, 2 x 5 In. 478.00
Bowl, Flared, Footed, Bordered Panels, Flowers, 4 ¼ x 9 In. 1495.00
Bowl, Flared, Scrolled Rim, Footed, 1875, 3 x 8 In. 508.00
Bowl, Fruit, Footed, c.1950, 9 ¼ In. 570.00
Bowl, Fruit, Leaf Border, 1 ½ x 6 ½ In. 110.00
Bowl, Gilt, Scalloped Rim, Marked, 5 ¼ x 5 ½ In. .... *illus* 431.00
Bowl, Inlaid, Leaves, Monogram, c.1910, 3 x 8 In. 4422.00
Bowl, Leaf Pattern, Shaped Edge, Bin, Cartouche, c.1921, 3 x 17 In. 1793.00
Bowl, Oval, Lobed Border, Monogram, c.1884, 9 ¾ In. 649.00
Bowl, Round, Flared Rim, Footed Ring Base, Reproduction, c.1950, 4 x 9 In. 805.00
Bowl, Round Stylized Ribbon Handles, Sterling, Monogram, Marked, 1 ¾ x 12 In. 633.00
Bowl, Shaped & Scrolled Rim, Monogram, 10 In. 234.00
Bowl, Smooth, Flared, Footed, c.1920, 4 x 9 In. 351.00
Bowl, Stepped Base, Sterling, 7 ¼ In. 450.00
Bowl, Vegetable, Fluted, Acanthus Scrolls & Shells, Square, Ball & Claw Feet, 9 ¼ In. 1185.00
Box, Ivory, Nude With Angel, Carved, 2 x 7 x 3 ½ In. 2400.00
Box, Sea Life, Enamel, Sterling, Italy, 1930-40, 4 ½ x 10 ½ x 7 ½ In. 4000.00
Bread Basket, Oval, Undulating Rim, Chased Shells & Scrolls, c.1895, 15 In., Pair 8750.00
Brush Holder, Gilt Exterior, Marked, 6 In. 80.00
Cake Knife, Engraved Pattern, Shaped Blade, Chased Handle, c.1790, 13 In. 657.00
Cake Knife, Lap Over Edge Pattern, Ducks In Flight Blade, c.1880, 10 In. 1195.00
Cake Stand, Chrysanthemum, 1890s, 6 ½ In. 660.00
Candelabrum, 7-Light, Chrysanthemum, Pair 67850.00
Candlestick, Fluted, Stems, Leaves, Square Base, Paw Feet, c.1875, 8 ⅞ In., Pair 237.00
Candlestick, Leaves, Putti, Ribbons, Animals, 4 Paw Feet, c.1885, 10 In., Pair 8750.00
Candlestick, St. Dunstan, Molded Clover Banded Base, c.1910, 9 In., 4 Piece 6250.00
Carving Set, Renaissance, Monogram, 1907-1938, 11 To 14 In., 3 Piece 978.00
Cheese Scoop, Stilton, Olympian, Gilt Bowl, Monogram, c.1876, 7 In. 418.00
Cigarette Box, Square, Chased, Engraved, Sterling, Gilt Interior, c.1876, 3 x 3 In. 224.00
Coffee Set, Banded, Scrolled Rims, Monogram, c.1895, 8 In., 4 Piece 1912.00
Coffee Set, Sugar, Creamer, Octagonal, Tray, Strap Handles, Sterling, 4 Piece 960.00
Compote, Flared Foot, Sterling, Monogram, Marked, 1907-1947, 5 ¼ x 10 ½ In. 748.00
Compote, Medallions, Classical Style, Greek Key Rim, Sterling, 5 x 11 In. 1725.00
Compote, Pedestal Base, Stepped Borders, Marked, 3 x 9 In., Pair 1840.00
Compote, Repousse Flower Medallions, 8 ¾ In. 748.00
Creamer, Applied Copper Plants, Insects, Square Shape, Flared Base, c.1877, 4 In. 8963.00
Dessert Fork Set, Lap Over Edge, 2-Tine, Hammered, Applied Metals, Gilt, 7 In., 18 Piece 598.00
Dish, Entree, Cover, Wave Edge, Square, Gadrooned, Crest, Flower Knop, c.1889, 5 x 8 In. 2151.00
Dish, Gilt, Openwork Round Border, Ball Feet, 1907-1947, 1 ½ x 6 In. 403.00
Dish, Leaf Shape, Pierced Handle, Late 1950s, 10 ⅝ In. 200.00
Dish, Leaf Shaped Rim, Round Base, Sterling, 1950s, 9 ⅜ In. 175.00
Dish, Oval, Wave Rim, Husk Handles, Lid, Bud Finial, Sterling, c.1907, Monogram, 10 In. 2607.00
Dish, Shell Shape, 6 x 6 In. 293.00
Dish, Sterling, Tri-Leaf Shape, Heart Shaped Handle, Marked, c.1960, 2 ½ x 9 ½ In. 374.00
Dresser Set, Sterling, Monogram, 6 Piece 585.00
Egg Plate, Renaissance, Pierced Bowl, c.1905, 91 In. 837.00
Ewer, Chased, Mythological Figures In Relief, Scroll Handle, c.1895, 24 In. 11875.00
Figurine, Clown, With Hoops & Balls, Enamel, 4 ¼ x 2 ¼ In. 1053.00
Figurine, Tiger On Circus Ball, Enamel, 3 x 3 ¾ In. 2106.00
Fish Knife Set, English King Pattern, Sterling, 7 ¾ In., 6 Piece 236.00
Fish Server, English King Pattern, c.1885, 11 In. 538.00
Fish Server, Vine, Repousse Grapes, c.1872, 10 In. 388.00
Fish Slice, Daisy, Vermeil, c.1900, 12 ¼ In. .... *illus* 205.00
Fish Slice, Vine, Repousse Grapes, c.1872, 13 In. 347.00
Flask, Hammered, Chased, Applied Fish, Plant, Crab On Lid, Gilt, Monogram, c.1880, 8 In. 9560.00
Flask, Hammered, Screw Lid, Monogram, c.1917, 6 In. 239.00
Flask, Repousse Flowers, Cylindrical, Sterling, Marked, Late 19th Century, 7 In. 1600.00
Flask, Round, Monogram, 5 ½ In. 500.00
Fork, Dessert, Alvan T. Fuller Service, c.1918, 7 In., 4 Piece 239.00
Fork, Dinner, William K. Vanderbilt Pattern, c.1884, 8 In., Pair 598.00
Fork, Flowers, Gold Washed Bowl, Monogram, Sterling, Signed, 9 ½ In. 440.00
Fork, Fruit, Chased Handle Edge, c.1895, 6 In., 4 Piece 84.00
Fork, Japanese Pattern, Signed, 7 ¼ In., 6 Piece 935.00

Tiffany Pottery, Vase, Leaves, Sculpted, Brown Glaze, Aqua Interior, 4 ½ In.
$1500.00

Tiffany Silver, Bowl, Gilt, Scalloped Rim, Marked, 5 ¼ x 5 ½ In.
$431.00

Tiffany Silver, Fish Slice, Daisy, Vermeil, c.1900, 12 ¼ In.
$205.00

TIP

Sterling silver is a solid metal that is at least 925 parts pure silver out of 1,000. Silver plate is made of a metal like copper or nickel or Britannia with a thin coating of silver. Sometimes the coating wears off and the base metal shows.

Tiffany Silver, Ladle, Olympian, Hebe The Cup Bearer, Sterling, Marked, 1869-91, 10 ¾ In.
$863.00

Tiffany Silver, Mug, Acanthus Leaves, Flowers, Scroll Handle, Rebecca Comstock, 3 ¾ In.
$990.00

Tiffany Silver, Salad Set, Tomato, Gilt Bowls, Marked, 1907-47, 9 ⅞ In., 2 Piece
$605.00

Fork, Salad, Dancing Indian, Marked, 9 ¼ In. 2100.00
Frame, Arched Top, Sterling, c.1930, 9 ¾ x 7 In. 650.00
Grape Scissors, Cast Flowers, Pierced Banded Handle, N.Y., c.1870, 6 In. 239.00
Grape Scissors, Persian Pattern, Pierced Handle, Gilt, c.1872, 7 In. 1912.00
Grape Scissors, Rococo, 6 ¼ In. 120.00
Ice Bowl, Hammered, Engraved Flowers, Leaves, Gilt, c.1877, 5 x 7 In. 1912.00
Ice Cream Server, Chased Frog, Lily Pad Handle, 12 ½ In. 239.00
Ice Cream Server, Flowers, Sterling, Gold Washed Bowl, Monogram, Signed, 11 ½ In. 440.00
Ice Cream Server, Italian Pattern, Textured Blade, Monogram Tip, c.1870, 12 In. 418.00
Ice Cream Server, Japanese Pattern, Monogram, c.1871, 10 In. 765.00
Ice Cream Slice, Richelieu Pattern, Gilt Shaped Blade, c.1892, 12 In. 508.00
Ice Tongs, Castilian Pattern, Pierced Bowls, c.1929, 7 In. 448.00
Jug, Cream, Hammered, Tapered, Reeded Handle, 1878, 4 x 3 In. 359.00
Ladle, Olympian, Hebe The Cup Bearer, Sterling, Marked, 1869-91, 10 ¾ In. . . . . *illus* 863.00
Ladle, Oyster, Vine, Fluted Shaped Bowl, c.1872, 11 In. 1315.00
Ladle, Soup, Audubon, Signed, 13 In. 525.00
Ladle, Soup, Faneuil, 1910, 11 In. 351.00
Ladle, Soup, Vine, Repousse Tomatoes, Monogram, c.1872, 12 In. 1315.00
Meat Fork, Vine, Grape Leaves, c.1872, 9 In. 191.00
Melon Fork, Lap Over Edge, Handles, Monogram, c.1905, 8 In., 10 Piece 4183.00
Muffineer, Paneled, Baluster Shape, Lobed Foot, Sterling, Portugal, 7 ½ In. 173.00
Mug, Acanthus Leaves, Flowers, Scroll Handle, Rebecca Comstock, 3 ¾ In. . . . . *illus* 990.00
Mug, Flared Base, Sterling, Baby's, 2 ⅜ x 2 ⅛ In. 265.00
Nut Pick, Chased Stem, Branch, Squirrel, Nut Terminal, Gilt, c.1870, 5 In., Pair 1076.00
Nut Pick, Twisted, Figural Handle, c.1890, 5 In. 167.00
Nut Scoop, Colonial, Pierced Gilt Bowl, c.1895, 6 In. 131.00
Oil Can, Cap, Sterling, Signed, 4 x 2 ¼ In. 80.00
Phone Dialer, Sterling, Marked, 3 In. 300.00
Pie Server, Vine, Repousse Grapes, Monogram, c.1872, 11 In. 538.00
Pie Server, Wave Edge, Stainless Steel Blade, Monogram, 10 ⅜ In. 300.00
Pitcher, Chased Flowers, Cylindrical Neck, Fluted Base, c.1870, 7 x 8 In. 3107.00
Pitcher, Egg Shape, Cylindrical Neck, Flat Leaf Ear Handle, Sterling, c.1875, 7 ¾ In. 1896.00
Pitcher, Japanese Scene, Rectangular, Gilt, Copper, Niello, E. Moore, 1875, 9 In. 32500.00
Pitcher, Water, Art Nouveau Leaves, 4 Pod Feet, c.1910, 6 Pt. 2250.00
Pitcher, Water, Urn Shape, Flared Spout, D-Shape Handle, c.1911, 9 In. 1135.00
Pitcher, Water, Vase Form, Reeded Rim, Angular Handle, 1907-38, 9 ⅜ In. 1541.00
Pitcher, Water, Wave Decoration Bands, Sterling, 1907-1947, 7 ¼ In. 2185.00
Plate, Round, Blue Enamel Border, Interior Ring, Footed, Sterling, 10 ½ In. 1093.00
Platter, Chrysanthemum, Flower, Oval, Leaves On Rim, Engraved, c.1904, 20 In. 4375.00
Platter, Round, c.1928, 10 In. 388.00
Porringer, Cover, Hammered, Shaped Wave Edge, Pierced Handle, c.1879, 4 x 7 In. 896.00
Porringer, Gilt Interior, S-Scroll Handles, c.1970, 2 x 6 In. 239.00
Porringer, Sterling, Monogram, 6 ¼ In. 135.00
Punch Ladle, Sterling, Bone Handle, 15 x 2 ¾ In. 795.00
Rattle, 3 Rings, 3 ¾ In. 82.00
Rose Jar, Hammered, 2 Turtles In Grass, Gilt, Frog Finial, Sterling, Signed, 7 In. 10450.00
Salad Set, Colonial, Gilt Bowls, Marked, c.1930s, 10 In., 2 Piece 633.00
Salad Set, St. Dunstan, Gilt Bowls, c.1930s, 9 ¾ In., 2 Piece 374.00
Salad Set, Tomato, Gilt Bowls, Marked, 1907-47, 9 ⅞ In., 2 Piece . . . . . *illus* 605.00
Salt, Oil Lamp Shape, Applied Palmette, Braided Rim, Stepped Foot, c.1869, 3 x 4 In., Pair . . . 717.00
Salt Spoon, Tripod Shape, Gilt Bowl, Lion's Head Ring Mounts, Paw Feet, c.1900, 3 In. 2151.00
Salver, George II Style, Chippendale Rim, 3 Pad Feet, Storage Bag, 14 In. 1680.00
Salver, Round, 3 Ball & Claw Feet, Moore, c.1864, 10 In. 570.00
Sandwich Tong, Flemish Pattern, Pierced Blades, Monogram, c.1911, 5 In. 418.00
Serving Dish, Hammered, Undulating Rim, F Monogram, Oval, c.1880, 2 x 10 In., Pair 1315.00
Serving Spoon, Olympian, 9 ¾ In. 191.00
Serving Spoon, Vine, Repousse Grapes, Shaped Pierced Bowl, c.1872, 9 In., Pair 1554.00
Soup, Engraved Rim, Squirrel, Nut, 1886, 9 ¾ In., Pair 448.00
Spoon, Serving, Teardrop Shape, Buffalo Head, Figural Tip, Indian, Monogram, c.1885, 8 In. 2489.00
Spoon Set, Hammered, Gilt Bowls, Monogram, c.1878, 5 In., 12 Piece 6573.00
Spoon Set, Ice Cream, Vine, Gourd Shaped Bowl, Repousse, c.1872, 6 In., 9 Piece 717.00
Stuffing Spoon, Vine, Repousse Grapes, Monogram, c.1872, 11 In. 777.00
Sugar, Cover, 4 x 7 In. 146.00
Sugar Tongs, Atlantis, Gilt Talon Ends, c.1899, 5 In. 131.00
Tablespoon, Japanese Pattern, Signed, 8 ¾ In., 6 Piece 935.00
Tazza, Repousse Flowers, Square, Gilt Center, Raised Flared Stem, c.1875, 4 x 7 In., Pair 2868.00
Tea & Coffee Set, Engraved Scrolls, Lattice, Bellflowers, 8 Piece 9000.00
Tea Ball, Sterling, Marked 180.00

Tea Caddy, Gadrooned Shoulder, Scroll Cover, c.1895, 4 In. 529.00
Tea Caddy, Hammered, Pinecones & Branches, Japanese Beetle On Cover, Gilt, c.1880, 6 In. .. 8750.00
Tea Caddy, Monogram, Sterling, 4 1/8 x 2 In. 425.00
Tea Set, Chrysanthemum, Sterling, c.1902, 6 Piece 28750.00
Teapot, Flowers, Oval, Beaded Edge, Rose Finial, Monogram, 6 x 6 1/2 In. .... *illus* 3500.00
Teapot, Oval, Dome Lid, Rose Finial, Beaded Border, Coin Silver, 6 1/4 x 6 1/2 In. 3680.00
Teaspoon, Japanese Pattern, Signed, 6 In., 6 Piece 605.00
Toast Rack, 7 Loop Dividers, Vine Handle, Sandal Feet, Sterling, 6 1/4 x 5 1/2 In. 1265.00
Toothpick, Cover, Glass Liner 150.00
Toothpick, Floral Repousse 120.00
Tray, Chrysanthemum, Leafy Center, Floral Border, c.1880, 14 In. 2629.00
Tray, Egyptian, Chased, 3-Footed, Sterling, J.C. Moore, 10 In. 6800.00
Tray, Elliptical, Scroll Border, c.1890, 15 7/8 x 12 1/4 In.. .... 2937.00
Tray, Engraved, Oval, Reeded Rim, Engraved, Paneled Feet, Handles, c.1915, 22 x 14 In.. .... 1470.00
Tray, Hammered, Rectangular, Rolled Rim, Flowers, Insects, Gilt, c.1880, 17 x 12 In. 10755.00
Tray, Heart Shape, Leaf Scroll Handle 200.00
Tray, Persian Pattern, Sterling, c.1872, 13 In. 878.00
Tray, Reticulated Rim, Marked, 13 3/4 In. Diam. 1800.00
Tray, Round, Flower Medallion Rim, Center Monogram, Boggert & Co., c.1867, 7 In. 388.00
Tray, Round, Gadrooned Edge, c.1956, 10 3/4 In.. .... 352.00
Tray, Rounded Rectangular, Stepped Border, Scroll Handles, Monogram, 16 1/2 In.. .... 4140.00
Tray, Square, Sterling, Signed, 9 In. 650.00
Tray, Tree Shape, 12-Sided Well, Reeded Border, 14 1/2 x 20 In. 1650.00
Trophy, Bowl, Firestone Skeet Club, Akron, Ohio, Sterling, c.1942, 11 1/8 In. 1080.00
Tureen, Gadroon Stem, Ogee Domed Foot, Lion Masque Ring Handles, 13 x 9 1/2 In. 5520.00
Tureen, Hammered, Splayed Loop Handles, Domed Cover, Ring Finial, c.1879, 8 x 11 In. 1793.00
Tureen, Oval, Geometric & Beaded, Handles, Scrolls, Leaves, Lid, Sterling, c.1854, 12 x 16 In. 8295.00
Tureen, Repousse Flowers, Gadrooned Band, Oval, 3 Handles, c.1875, 11 x 14 In. 7170.00
Vanity Bottle, Oval, Cap, Inner Cover, Engraved Monogram, c.1900, 4 1/4 In. 390.00
Vase, Repousse Flowers, Sterling, 1873-1891, 7 1/2 In. 527.00
Vase, Tapered, Fluted Band Of Husk Swags, Reeded Rim, Classical Revival, c.1907, 16 In. 3318.00
Vase, Trumpet Shape, Fluted, Openwork Shell & Scroll Rim, c.1935, 15 In., Pair 8750.00
Walking Stick, Hammered, 2 Applied Beetles, Copper, 14K Gold, Marked, 36 1/2 In. 2500.00
Warming Dish, Hinged Cover, Urn Finial, Gadroon Border, Marked, 5 x 9 1/2 x 12 In. 2200.00
Wine Cooler, 3 Ear Handles, Figures & Cherubs, 3 Paw Feet, Acanthus, 1905, 9 In. 4740.00
Wine Taster, Sterling, 4 1/2 x 3 In. 69.00

TIFFIN Glass Company of Tiffin, Ohio, was a subsidiary of the United States Glass Co. of Pittsburgh, Pennsylvania, in 1892. The U.S. Glass Co. went bankrupt in 1963, and the Tiffin plant employees purchased the building and the inventory. They continued running it from 1963 to 1966, when it was sold to Continental Can Company. In 1969, it was sold to Interpace, and in 1980, it was closed. The black satin glass, made from 1923 to 1926, and the stemware of the last twenty years are the best-known products.

Arcadian, Plate, Bread & Butter, Pink, 6 In.. .... 7.00
Arcadian, Plate, Salad, Pink, 8 In. 12.00
Basket, Amberina, Satin, Handle, 6 In.. .... 71.00
Basket, Emerald Green, Satin, 6 In. 62.00
Basket, Favor, Blue, 3 1/2 x 3 3/4 In.. .... 30.00
Basket, Green, Handle, 11 In. 65.00
Chipperfield, Tray, Dresser, Powder Jar Insert, Cover, Green 135.00
Dancing Girl, Powder Box, Aqua Blue Satin, 8 1/2 In. .... *illus* 22.00
Eve, Dresser Box, Pink Glass, Nude Woman, 6 3/4 x 3 1/2 In. 65.00
Flanders, Plate, Pink, 8 In. 32.00
Fontaine, Sundae, Twilight, 6 In. 95.00
No. 315, Candlestick, Amberina, 9 x 3 In., Pair .... *illus* 95.00
No. 15179, Candy Jar, Cover, Green Satin, 7 1/2 In. 75.00
Palm Beach, Creamer, Milk Glass, 4 x 4 1/2 In.. .... 25.00
Palm Beach, Nappy, Milk Glass, 5 1/4 In.. .... 23.00
Rambling Rose, Pitcher, Cover, Amber, 9 In. .... *illus* 60.00

TILES have been used in most countries of the world as a sturdy building material for floors, roofs, fireplace surrounds, and surface toppings. The cuerda seca (dry cord) technique of decoration uses a greasy pigment to separate different glaze colors during firing. In cuenca (raised line) decorated tiles, the design is impressed, leaving ridges that separate the glaze colors. Many of the American tiles are listed in this book under the factory name.

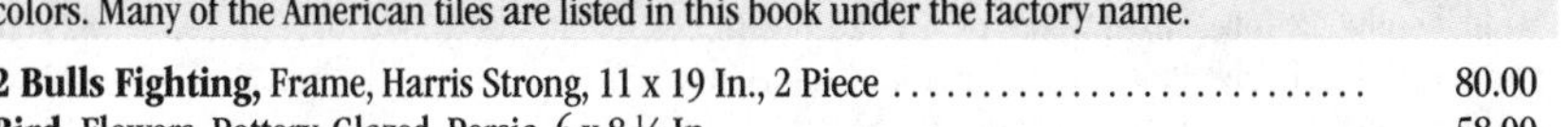

2 Bulls Fighting, Frame, Harris Strong, 11 x 19 In., 2 Piece 80.00
Bird, Flowers, Pottery, Glazed, Persia, 6 x 8 1/2 In.. .... 58.00

Tiffany Silver, Teapot, Flowers, Oval, Beaded Edge, Rose Finial, Monogram, 6 x 6 1/2 In.
$3500.00

Tiffin, Dancing Girl, Powder Box, Aqua Blue Satin, 8 1/2 In.
$22.00

Tiffin, No. 315, Candlestick, Amberina, 9 x 3 In., Pair
$95.00

Tiffin, Rambling Rose, Pitcher, Cover, Amber, 9 In.
$60.00

T

Tile, Cityscape, Multicolored, Rosewood Board, Harris Strong, 24 x 48 In.
$120.00

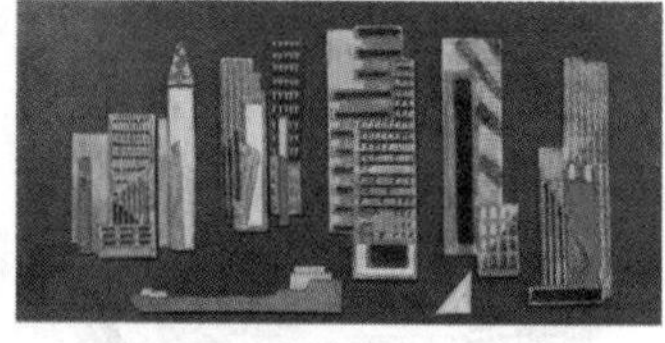

Tile, Galleon, Multicolored, Stamped, Flint Faience Tile Co., 9 In.
$960.00

Tile, Mardi Gras Clown, Harris Strong, 12 In.
$187.00

Tile, Puss 'N Boots, Cuenca, De Porceleyne Fles, 8 ½ In.
$1440.00

Birds, On Red Flowering Branches, Gilt, Eastlake, 1870, 6 In. 220.00
Birds, Perched On Frame, 6 x 6 In. 92.00
Boy Reading Book, Classical Head, Low, Frame, c.1882, 6 ¼ x 6 ¼ In., Pair 633.00
Cherubs, Frolicking, Dark Brown Glaze, 6 x 12 ⅛ In. 296.00
Children, Mauve Glaze, 8 ¹⁄₁₆ x 6 In. 444.00
Cityscape, Multicolored, Rosewood Board, Harris Strong, 24 x 48 In. .... *illus* 120.00
Dandelions, Faience, Frame, 5 x 5 In. 863.00
Dogs, Olive Green Glaze, Triangle Within Triangle, 6-In. Square, 2 Piece 178.00
Falconer, On Horseback, Pottery, Glazed, Persia, 8 x 6 In. 69.00
Farmer Planting Seeds, Signed, 12 ¼ x 6 In. 960.00
Flowers, Chocolate Brown, 6 x 6 In. 59.00
Frieze, Goldfish, Waves, Orange, Pink, Blue, Oak Arts & Crafts Frame, 13 x 18 In., 2 Piece ... 420.00
Galleon, Multicolored, Stamped, Flint Faience Tile Co., 9 In. .... *illus* 960.00
Geishas, Frame, Harris Strong, 24 In., 3 Piece 50.00
Geometric Pattern, Mounted, Rosewood, Frame, 36 x 11 In. 390.00
Lamplighter, Cobalt Blue, Blue Crystalline Glaze, 8 ¾ x 8 ¾ In. 230.00
Landscape, Green Glaze, Brown Glaze, Triangle, 6 x 12 In., 2 Piece 652.00
Limoges, Landscape, Green, Purple, Brown, Marked, Tress-Mann & Vogt, Frame, 17 x 14 In. . 480.00
Lizard, Landscape, Multicolored, Carved, Painted, Multicolored, Frame, 12 ¼ x 3 ¾ In. 450.00
Man, Teal Glaze, Wood Frame, Stand, Lord Salisbury, 9 ¾ x 8 In. 59.00
Mardi Gras Clown, Harris Strong, 12 In. .... *illus* 187.00
Mosaic, Egyptian Boat, Multicolored, Frame, E. Ackerman, ERA Industries, 49 x 13 In. 1020.00
Mosaic, Roman Aqueduct, Frame, 36 x 24 In. 600.00
Mother, Child, Blue Glaze, 18 x 6 In., 3 Piece 237.00
Musicians, Mauve, Marbled, Blue Glaze, 18 x 6 In., 2 Piece 830.00
Nautical Scene, Mounted, Rosewood, 9 x 36 In. 180.00
Portrait, Abraham Lincoln, Round, Frame, c.1916 .... 131.00
Portrait, Wm. McKinley, Frame, 6 x 6 In. 131.00
Puss 'N Boots, Cuenca, De Porceleyne Fles, 8 ½ In. .... *illus* 1440.00
Ship, Brown, Blue, Green, California Faience, 5 ½ In. 360.00
Sparrow, Parrot, Painted, Multicolored, Blue Corners, Delft Type, 5 ¼ x 5 ¼ In., Pair 88.00
Street Scene, Frame, Harris Strong, 26 In., 4 Piece 80.00
White Horse, Sid Dickens, 8 x 6 In. 40.00
Woman, Classical Style Dress, Olive Green Glaze, 13 ⅛ x 10 In. 652.00
Woman, With Jug, Green Glaze, 12 x 6 In. 237.00
Woman's Profile, High Collar Dress, Pearls, Bonnet, Green Gloss Glaze, 8 x 8 In. 150.00
Women, Classical, Leaf Border, Green Glaze, 12 x 6 In., 2 Piece 504.00
Women, Dancing, Mauve, Marbled, Blue Glaze, 18 ¼ x 6 In., 2 Piece 889.00
Women, Portraits, Figures, Glazed, Round, J. & J. G. Low Tileworks, 6 In., 5 Piece 385.00
Women, With Parasols, Blue Glaze, 18 ¼ x 6 ⅛ In. 474.00

TINWARE containers for household use have been made in America since the seventeenth century. The first tin utensils were brought from Europe, but by 1798, tin plate was imported and local tinsmiths made the wares. Painted tin is called tole and is listed separately. Some tin kitchen items may be found listed under Kitchen. The lithographed tin containers used to hold food and tobacco are listed in the Advertising category under Tin.

Bird, Cut, Multicolored, Goldfinch, Oriole, Blue Jay, Cardinal, Penn., 8 ½ In., 4 Piece 198.00
Coffeepot, Dome Lid, Punched Flower Bouquets, Brass Finial, c.1830, 11 ¼ In. 4700.00
Coffeepot, Pierced, Wriggle Work, Flowers, Applied Spout & Handle, Pa., c.1825, 14 In. 2820.00
Lamp, Oil, Wick Holder, Capped Fill Hole, Reservoir, Footed, 6 ¾ x 4 ¼ x 4 ½ In. 358.00
Megaphone, Red, Black, Yellow, Cream Interior, Cone Shape, Strap Handle, 33 x 11 In. 350.00 to 385.00
Mold, Candle, 6 Tube, Handle, 19th Century, 10 ¾ x 4 x 3 ¾ In. .... 10.00 to 40.00
Mold, Candle, 6 Tube, Shaped Handle, Copper 395.00
Mold, Candle, 6 Tube, Tapered, Applied Handle, 4 ½ x 3 x 3 ¼ In. 750.00
Mold, Candle, 6 Tube, Wire Hanger Ring, 4 ½ x 3 x 3 ¼ In. 825.00
Mold, Candle, 8 Tube, Applied C-Shape Handle, Wire Ring, 9 x 6 x 5 In. .... *illus* 40.00
Mold, Candle, 12 Tube, Crimped, Flared, T-Shape Holder, Wood, 16 x 15 x 6 In. 325.00
Mold, Candle, 12 Tube, Crimped Flared Tops, Softwood, 16 x 15 x 6 In. 358.00
Mold, Candle, 12 Tube, C-Shape Handle, 9 ¼ x 8 ½ x 5 ¼ In. 55.00
Mold, Candle, 12 Tube, C-Shape Handle, Strap, 6 x 7 ¾ x 4 ¾ In. .... 250.00 to 275.00
Mold, Candle, 12 Tube, C-Shape Handle, Wire Hanger, 10 ¾ x 7 ½ x 3 ½ In. 44.00
Mold, Candle, 12 Tube, Handles, 19th Century, 11 x 10 x 3 In. 110.00
Mold, Candle, 12 Tube, Rectangular Fill Top, Base, Applied Reeded Handle, 10 ½ x 7 ⅝ In. .. 55.00
Mold, Candle, 18 Tube, Mixed Wood, 15 ¼ x 22 x 6 ¾ In. 825.00
Mold, Candle, 24 Tube, Pine Frame, Mid 19th Century, 6 ½ x 22 In. 999.00
Mold, Candle, 24 Tube, Softwood Case, 11 x 12 ½ x 7 ¼ In. 1210.00

Mold, Candle, 24 Tube, Wood, Painted, Cutout Bracket Feet, 11 x 12 ½ x 7 ¼ In. 1100.00
Mold, Candle, 36 Tube, Bench Type, Red Paint, Wood, 12 x 11 In. 1093.00
Mold, Candle, 36 Tube, Wood, Late 19th Century, 10 x 30 ½ In. 322.00
Plate, H.R.H. Duke Of Edinburgh, Portland, 1950s, 10 In. 23.00
Rattle, Hammer Shape, New England, 19th Century, 14 ½ In. 144.00
Sconce, Shield Shape, Mosaic, Reflector, Mirrors, Scallop Drip Tray, 15 x 11 In., Pair 77.00
Teapot, Round Cover, Flower, Teal Blue, Oval, C-Shape Handle, Ring, 2 ¼ x 4 ½ In. 303.00
Tray, Sunburst, Pressed, Leaf, Gadrooned Border, Shell Corners, Gilt, 14 ¼ x 11 ¼ In. 11.00

TOBACCO CUTTERS *may be listed in either the Advertising or Store categories.*

TOBACCO JAR collectors search for those made in odd shapes and colors. Because tobacco needs special conditions of humidity and air, it has been stored in special containers since the eighteenth century.

Barrel, Jade Green, Pewter Lid, Furled Tobacco Leaf Top, 4 ½ x 3 ½ In. 375.00
Bismarck, Terra-Cotta, Marked B.B. 154, 10 ¾ In. 949.00
Black Boy On Barrel, Terra-Cotta, Marked 3461, 7 In. 345.00
Chinese Man, Glass Eyes, Real Hair, Composition, c.1890, 7 ½ In. 440.00
Dog, Glass Eyes, Terra-Cotta, Marked, B.B., 8 ½ In. 311.00
Eastern Woman, Head, White Headscarf, Dark Skin, Porcelain, 5 In. 50.00
Female Bust, Majolica, Headband, Flower Over Each Ear, Painted, Porcelain, 7 x 6 In. 75.00
Hunter With Target, Terra-Cotta, Marked B.B. 392, 12 In. 748.00
Indian Chief Busts, Cast Bronze, Hammered Copper, 7 x 5 ¼ In. 13225.00
Lid, Relief Molded Scenes Of Merriment, Salt Glaze, Stoneware, 4 ¾ In. 15.00
Man With Newspaper, Terra-Cotta, Marked, B.B., 8 ¾ In. 518.00
Monk, Terra-Cotta, Marked 8116, 10 ¼ In. 431.00
Mountain Climber, Terra-Cotta, Marked J.M. 3705, 11 ½ In. 546.00
North African Man, Terra-Cotta, Marked, F.W., 8 In. 403.00
Pheasants, Black Matte, Brass Accents, Fielding's Crown Devon, England, 6 In. 3895.00
Pirate, Terra-Cotta, Marked B.B. 158, 11 ½ In. 633.00
Pug & Doghouse, Figural, Brown Glaze, Box Shape, Terra-Cotta, Marked, 6 ⅝ x 8 ¼ In. 395.00
Sailor Head, Pipe In Mouth, Hat, Painted, Porcelain, 5 In. 50.00
Woman With Flowers, Terra-Cotta, Marked, B.B., 10 ½ In. 518.00

TOBY JUG is the name of a very special form of pitcher. It is shaped like the full figure of a man or woman. A pitcher that shows just the top half of a person is not correctly called a toby. More examples of toby jugs can be found under Royal Doulton and other factory names.

Man, Head Turned, Yellow Pants, Tricornered Pants, 9 ½ In. 96.00
Man, Holding Cane, Lead Glaze, 13 ¾ In. .... *illus* 1540.00
Man, Seated, 18th Century Attire, Lancastor Sandland, Charrington Toby Ales, Staffordshire, 9 In. 132.00
Man, Tricornered Hat, Hoare & Co. Ale In A Bottle, Staffordshire, 9 In. 120.00
Monk, Beige Robe, Foley Faince, 8 ½ In. 94.00
Sailor, Seated, Holding Glass, Green Coat, Blue Pants, Staffordshire, 1800s, 11 ½ In. 600.00
Seated Figure, Holding Jug, Wood Style, Staffordshire, Late 1700s, 9 ¾ In. 1896.00
Tit Bits, Man Reading Newspaper, Ault England, Staffordshire, 9 ½ In. 149.00

TOLE is painted tin. It is sometimes called *japanned ware, pontypool,* or *toleware*. Most nineteenth-century tole is painted with an orange-red or black background and multicolored decorations. Many recent versions of toleware are made and sold. Related items may be listed in the Tinware category.

Bowl, Centerpiece, Flowers, Leaves, Multicolored, 6 ¼ x 11 ⅛ x 20 ¼ In. 88.00
Bowl, Fruit, Convex Sides, Japanned Black, Gilt Stencil, 3 x 11 In. 154.00
Bowl, Fruit, Scrolls, Black Ground, Handles, 19th Century, 3 ½ x 14 ¼ x 18 ¼ In. 275.00
Bowl, Lotus Flowers, Multicolored, Daher, c.1971, 10 ¼ In. 15.00
Box, Document, Bellflowers, Black Ground, Wire Handle, Hasp, 6 ½ x 3 ¼ In. 3995.00
Box, Document, Bird, Red Flowers, Black Ground, 19th Century, 6 ½ x 9 ¼ In. 16380.00
Box, Document, Dome Lid, Flower, Black Japanned, Brass Pull, Hasp, 6 ½ x 9 ½ In. 385.00
Box, Document, Dome Lid, Flower, Japanned, Wire Ring Pull, 4 ¾ x 8 x 3 ½ In. 440.00
Box, Document, Dome Lid, Flowers, Black Japanned, 4 ½ x 8 ½ x 4 In. 121.00
Box, Document, Dome Lid, Flowers, Japanned Ground, Wire Ring Pull, 6 ½ x 9 ½ In. 605.00
Box, Document, Dome Lid, Flowers, Medallion, Handle, 19th Century, 11 ¼ x 11 ¾ In. 175.00
Box, Document, Dome Lid, Flowers, White Band, Yellow Scrolls, 9 ½ x 6 ¼ In. 118.00
Box, Document, Dome Lid, Flowers, Yellow Scrolls, Japanned, 9 x 4 ½ In. 646.00
Box, Document, Dome Lid, Japanned, Wire Handle, Upson Workshop, 7 x 3 ½ In. 235.00
Box, Document, Dome Lid, Painted Swags, Flowers, Japanned, c.1840, 8 x 4 In. 1410.00

Tinware, Mold, Candle, 8 Tube, Applied C-Shape Handle, Wire Ring, 9 x 6 x 5 In.
$40.00

Toby Jug, Man, Holding Cane, Lead Glaze, 13 ¾ In.
$1540.00

Tole, Bread Box, Flowers, Fruit, Brown Ground, 8 x 12 x 7 In.
$50.00

TIP

Old, clean cloth diapers are ideal for cleaning metal: very soft and lint free.

Tole, Canister, Slant Lid, Flowers, Scrolls, Black Ground, Hinged Lid, 19 x 18 x 18 ½ In.
$45.00

Tole, Creamer, Flowers, Red Ground, Tapered Sides, 4 x 3 In.
$200.00

Tole, Sifter, Buds, Leaves, Red, Green, Yellow Ground, Applied Handle, 4 ¾ x 3 ⅜ In.
$187.00

TIP
Never put metal in the microwave. It will cause arcing, which can damage the oven and burn the dishes.

Box, Document, Dome Lid, Red, Yellow, Pink, White, Blue, c.1825, 10 x 6 x 7 In. 588.00
Box, Document, Dome Lid, Red & Yellow Swags, Black Ground, Ring Handle, 9 ½ x 5 In. 118.00
Box, Document, Dome Lid, Red Border, Swags, Japanned, Wire Handle, Hasp, 10 x 5 In. 1058.00
Box, Document, Dome Lid, Red Flowers, Japanned Ground, Wire Handle, Hasp, 8 x 4 In. 470.00
Box, Document, Dome Lid, Red Ground, Swags, White Band, Wire Handle, Hasp, c.1840, 8 x 4 In. 176.00
Box, Document, Dome Lid, Stenciled Fruit, Yellow, Mary Ann Bishop, May 18th, 1838, 6 x 9 In. 702.00
Box, Document, Dome Lid, Stylized Flowers, Red, Black Japanned, Pull, 4 ½ x 9 In.. . . . . 55.00
Box, Document, Dome Lid, White Band, Flowers, Wire Handle, Hasp, 4 ¾ x 3 ¾ In. 235.00
Box, Document, Dome Lid, White Bands, Red Flowers, Buds, Wire Handle, 8 x 4 In. 940.00
Box, Document, Flat Lid, Blue Leaves, Black Ground, Wire Handle, Hasp, 8 ¾ x 5 ¾ In. 2585.00
Box, Document, Flower, Red, Yellow, Black Ground, 19th Century, 4 ¾ x 8 ½ In. 7200.00
Box, Document, Leaves, Buds, Eggs, Multicolor, Brass Bail Handle, 8 x 13 ½ In.. . . . . 881.00
Box, Document, Leaves, Flowers, Zachariah Stevens, 9 x 5 In. 9775.00
Box, Document, Painted Flowers, White Border, Yellow Swags, Black Ground, 9 ½ x 6 In. 2585.00
Box, Document, Red & Yellow Swags, Black Ground, 19th Century, 6 ¼ x 9 ¾ In. 5500.00
Box, Document, Red Flowers, Green Leaves, Black Ground, Handle, 19th Century, 5 ½ x 9 In. 375.00
Box, Dome Lid, Fruit & Leaf Border, Inscribed, James Nichols, 1800s, 3 ¾ x 7 In. 234.00
Box, Flower, Heart, Black Ground, Rounded, Belt Loop, Pierced Lid, 3 ½ x 3 In. 646.00
Box, Hat, Faux Wood Grain, Handle, 11 x 14 In.. . . . . 77.00
Box, Potpourri, Cover, Brass Stand, 7 x 6 ¼ In. 117.00
Bread Box, Flowers, Fruit, Brown Ground, 8 x 12 x 7 In. . . . . *illus* 50.00
Candleholder, Red Ground, Stripes, Shell Shape Push-Up, Snuffer Cap, 3 ¾ x 6 ¾ In. 382.00
Canister, Black, Red Flowers, Conch Shell, Oval, Wire Handle, Hasp, c.1842, 7 x 5 In. 411.00
Canister, Coffee, 3 Hinged Lids, Painted, Gilt, Wood Base, 12 ¾ x 26 ½ x 13 ¾ In. 800.00
Canister, Flowers, Black Ground, Oval, Handle, Hasp, Divided Interior, 12 ¼ x 8 ½ In. 8225.00
Canister, Slant Lid, Flowers, Scrolls, Black Ground, Hinged Lid, 19 x 18 x 18 ½ In. . . . . *illus* 45.00
Canister, Starburst Design Lid, Tulips, White Band, Wire Handle, Hasp, 8 ½ x 9 In. 499.00
Coal Scuttle, Woodland Scene, Reverse Painted, Cartouche Form, Gilt, Glass, 19 ½ In.. . . . . . 600.00
Coffeepot, Cover, Wrigglework, American Flag, Eagle, Vine, Snake, Brass Finial, 9 ¾ In.. . . . . 17625.00
Coffeepot, Domed Lid, Flower Medallions, Japanned, Gooseneck Spout, Brass Finial, c.1800, 10 In. 3290.00
Coffeepot, Domed Lid, Gooseneck, Brass Finial, Hinged, C-Shape Handle, 10 ½ x 6 ½ In.. . . . 11.00
Coffeepot, Domed Lid, Yellow & Red Flower, Yellow Swags, Black Ground, Mid 1800s, 11 In. . 3600.00
Coffeepot, Flower Medallions, Black Ground, Strap Handle, c.1845, 8 ¼ In.. . . . . 382.00
Coffeepot, Flowers, Blue Medallions, Black Ground, Gooseneck Spout, Brass Finial, 10 ¼ In.. 1293.00
Coffeepot, Flowers, Red, Orange, Yellow, Green, Black Ground, 19th Century, 8 In. 585.00
Coffeepot, Flowers, Yellow, Ivory, Red Ground, Gooseneck Spout, 19th Century, 10 In. 23400.00
Coffeepot, Fruit, Flowers, Black Japanned, Gooseneck Spout, Strap Handle, 10 ¼ In. 1998.00
Coffeepot, Green, Yellow Flowers, Red Ground, Gooseneck Spout, Strap Handle, 1800s, 10 In. 3200.00
Coffeepot, Hooked Spout, Black Ground, Yellow, Red Flowers, c.1820, 11 In. 2133.00
Coffeepot, Japanned Ground, Striated Design, Red Flower, Side Spout, c.1819, 8 ½ In. 1998.00
Coffeepot, Punched, Tulip Design, Gooseneck Spout, Brass Finial, Strap Handle, 1800s, 11 In. 999.00
Coffeepot, Red & Yellow Flowers, Black Ground, 19th Century, 10 ½ In.. . . . . 2100.00
Coffeepot, Red Flowers, Black Ground, Japanned, Lighthouse Shape, c.1830, 11 In. 705.00
Coffeepot, Red Flowers, Yellow Designs, Black Ground, Applied Handle, 1800s, 11 ½ In.. . . . . 1645.00
Coffeepot, Red Ground, Flowers, Multicolored, c.1800, 8 ¾ In. 4700.00
Coffeepot, Tray, Tulips, Blue Leaves, White, Side Spout, Strap Handle, 10 ½ & 6 x 9 In.. . . . . . 176.00
Coffeepot, Wriggle Work, 2 Birds, Tulip, Star, Flowers, Penn., 19th Century, 11 ½ In. 2420.00
Coffeepot, Yellow Bird, Flower Branch, Black Ground, 19th Century, 11 In. 3978.00
Coffeepot, Yellow Fruit, Ivory Bands, Black Ground, 19th Century, 20 ¾ In.. . . . . 3300.00
Container, Lid, Red Poppies, Black Ground, Rounded Corners, c.1835, 8 ½ x 9 In. 2233.00
Creamer, Flowers, Leaves, Black Ground, 4 ¾ In. 353.00
Creamer, Flowers, Red Ground, Tapered Sides, 4 x 3 In. . . . . *illus* 200.00
Creamer, Spout, Japanned, Stylized Flower, Swag, C-Shape Handle, 3 ¾ x 3 In. 303.00
Flour Bin, Slant Lid, Flowers, Gilt, Footed, Figural Handle, 23 x 11 ¾ x 8 ¾ In. 80.00
Hat Box, Flowers, Black Ground, St. Omers, Elmira, N.Y., 14 x 17 In.. 305.00
Inkwell, Flowers, Red Ground, Double, Inserts, 4 Penholders, 2 ¾ x 7 x 3 In.. . . . . 200.00
Map Case, Armorial, Painted, Inscribed, Regardes Mon Droit, c.1800, 31 In. 117.00
Match Safe, Crimped Crest, Smoked White Band, Hanging, c.1800, 7 ½ In. 176.00
Mug, Flowers, Red, Yellow, Black Ground, 19th Century, 4 ¼ In.. . . . . 1760.00
Mug, Round, Japanned Black, Multicolor Flowered Banding, C-Shape Handle, 5 ¾ x 4 In. . . . 413.00
Pail, Dome Lid, Orange, Gold Stencil, Bands, Wire Bail Handle, 5 x 6 ½ In. 44.00
Pitcher, Red & Yellow Border, Black Ground, Strap Handle, 19th Century, 7 ¾ In. 588.00
Planter, Gilt, Multicolor, Mustard Ground, Metal Liner, 19th Century, 7 ½ In., Pair. 748.00
Powder Flask, Hunting Dogs, Gilt Border, c.1830, 8 In. 235.00
Sander, Trailing Flowers, Japanned, Mid 19th Century, 2 ⅝ In. 1116.00
Sconce, Printed Flower Bud, Crimped Crest, Pan, 7 ½ In.. . . . . 382.00

Sifter, Buds, Leaves, Red, Green, Yellow Ground, Applied Handle, 4 ¾ x 3 ⅜ In. .... *illus* 187.00
Spice Box, 6 Interior Compartments, Flowers, Black Ground, Hexagonal, 1800s, 7 x 10 In. .. 403.00
Sugar, Cover, Blue, Yellow, Japanned, Philadelphia, c.1840, 3 ¾ In. 881.00
Sugar, Cover, White Band, Leaf Designs, Red Ground, Conn., c.1846, 3 ¾ In. 294.00
Syrup, Flowers, Red, Green, Yellow, Black Ground, 19th Century, 4 In. 1320.00
Syrup, Fruit, Swags, Red Ground, c.1800, 4 In. 881.00
Syrup, Red Flower, Black Ground, 19th Century, 4 ½ In. 25.00
Syrup, Scrolling, Red Ground, Bloomfield, Conn., c.1846, 3 ¾ In. 529.00
Tea Caddy, Ball Shape, Flowers, Banded Shoulder, Japanned, c.1800, 8 In. 118.00
Tea Caddy, Fruit, Flower Branch, Black Ground, Mid 1800s, 8 ½ In. 294.00
Tea Caddy, Multicolor Flowers, Red Ground, c.1800, 5 In. 353.00
Teapot, Flowers, White, Green, Yellow, Black Ground, Buckley Workshop, 5 ¼ In. 646.00
Teapot, Red, Yellow, Tassel Border, Japanned, c.1800, 5 ¼ In. 588.00
Tray, 2 Women At Fence, Flower Ground, Banded, Stencil, 17 ¼ x 12 ¼ In. 44.00
Tray, Apple, Red, Yellow, Green, Floral Border, c.1825, 8 x 13 x 3 In. 176.00
Tray, Apple, Roses, Yellow, Red, Japanned, c.1800, 12 x 12 x 2 ¾ In. 353.00
Tray, Asian City, Figures, Lakeside, Gilt, Black, Stand, 19 ¾ x 33 x 26 In. 2400.00
Tray, Bird, Red, Yellow, Green, Scalloped Rim, 28 ½ x 21 ½ In. 100.00
Tray, Birds, Fountain, Flowers, Scalloped Rim, Black Ground, Gilt, 13 ¼ x 16 ¾ In. .... *illus* 225.00
Tray, Birds, Water Fountain, Flowers, Multicolored, Scalloped Edges, 16 ¾ x 13 In. 11.00
Tray, Black, Japanned, Multicolored Flowers, 8-Sided, 1840s, 12 ¼ x 8 ½ In. 1540.00
Tray, Black & Gold, Abalone Shell Floral Inlay, Brass Handle, 1800s, 9 In. 146.00
Tray, Black Ground, Open Fretwork, Beaded Tapered Sides, Iron Handles, 18 ½ x 27 ½ In. 330.00
Tray, Bread, Asphaltum Ground, Multicolored, Oblong, Arched Sides, 2 x 13 ½ x 7 In. 44.00
Tray, Bread, Flower, Black, Red, Green, c.1850, 7 x 14 In. 115.00
Tray, Bread, Flower, Black Japanned, Arched Ends, 2 x 13 x 7 ½ In. 77.00
Tray, Bread, Flower Band, Black Japanned, Square, Arched Rounded Top, 2 ½ x 12 ½ In. 550.00
Tray, Bread, Flowers, Black Ground, 19th Century, 6 ¾ In. 880.00
Tray, Bread, Flowers, Black Japanned, Tapered, Oval, 3 ½ x 13 ½ x 8 In. 88.00
Tray, Bread, Flowers, Red, Yellow, Black Ground, Oval, Handles, 19th Century, 4 x 13 ¾ In. .. 510.00
Tray, Bread, Red, Yellow, Leaves, Japanned, Cutout Handles, 8 x 13 ½ x 3 ¾ In. 353.00
Tray, Bread, Red Circles, Green Leaves, Yellow Rim, 19th Century, 12 ½ In. 175.00
Tray, Cherries, Japanned, Oblong, Thin End Bands, Cherries, 7 ¾ x 14 In. 353.00
Tray, Cherries, White Band, Black Ground, 8-Sided, Mid 1800s, 8 ¾ x 12 ½ In. 235.00
Tray, Crystallized Center, Painted Swags, 8-Sided, Penn., Late 1800s, 9 x 12 ½ In. 2703.00
Tray, Dogs, Leaf Border, Black Ground, 19 ½ In. 25.00
Tray, Eagle, Fruit, Flowers, Black Ground, Handles, 19 x 26 ¼ In. 660.00
Tray, Flower Spray Border, Butterflies, Scalloped Edge, 29 x 21 In. 748.00
Tray, Flowers, Fruit, Vegetables, Black Ground, Oval, 11 x 16 ¼ In. 20.00
Tray, Flowers, Yellow Ground, 8-Sided, 19th Century, 17 x 24 ¼ In. 764.00
Tray, Gilt, Birds, Fountain, Flowers, Black Ground, Scalloped Edge, 13 ¼ x 16 ¾ In. 248.00
Tray, Gilt Rim, Flowers, Scalloped Edge, 19th Century, 24 x 31 In. 234.00
Tray, Harbor Scene, Gilt Vines, Red Ground, Cutout Handles, Oval, 1900, 25 In. .... *illus* 470.00
Tray, Horse, Rider, Hounds, Red, Stenciled, Metallic, Leaves, 22 ½ x 27 ½ In. 176.00
Tray, Horseman, Rearing Horse, Fruit & Loop Border, Cutout Handles, 16 ⅝ x 22 In. 70.00
Tray, Hunt Scene, Heart Shape Cutout Handles, Early 1800s, 22 x 30 In. 150.00
Tray, Jenny Lind Portrait, Green Ground, Handles, Mid 19th Century, 14 ½ x 19 ½ In. 1287.00
Tray, Landscape, Figures, Green Ground, Black Scrollwork, Oval, Continental, 1800s, 19 x 15 In. 323.00
Tray, Pin, Pink Rose, Green Ground, Shaped Edges, 1800s, 3 ¼ x 4 ¼ In. 382.00
Tray, Red Cherries, White Border, Black Ground, Mid 1800s, 8 ¾ x 12 ¾ In. 264.00
Tray, Swags, Red Border, Japanned, 8-Sided, c.1800, 6 ¼ x 9 In. 176.00
Tray, White Band, Flowers, 8 ¾ x 12 ½ In. 176.00
Urn, Cover, Gilt Vines, Flowers, Loop Handles, Early 19th Century, 8 ½ x 11 ¼ In., Pair...... 805.00
Vase, Red, Classical Landscape, Oval Pendent, Metal Lining, Continental, 1800s, 9 ½ In., Pair. 5938.00
Whistle, Bird, Rooster & Bird, Cut Out Silhouette, Painted, Vermont, 2 ¾ In. 176.00

TOM MIX was born in 1880 and died in 1940. He was the hero of over 100 silent movies from 1910 to 1929, and 25 sound films from 1929 to 1935. There was a Ralston Tom Mix radio show from 1933 to 1950, but the original Tom Mix was not in the show. Tom Mix comics were published from 1942 to 1953.

Book, Tom Mix & The Hoard Of Montezuma, Big Little Book, Whitman, 1937 .... 30.00
Boots, Cowboy, Leather, 1930s, 10 ¾ x 9 ½ In. 261.00
Bracelet, Identification, Ralston Straight Shooters, Cereal Premium, Metal. 24.50
Buckle, Secret Compartment, Ralston, Premium, c.1950 .... 95.00
Button, Miracle Rider, Red, Black, White, 1935, 1 ¼ In. .... *illus* 337.00
Comic Book, Tom Mix Western, No. 1, 1988 .... 4.95
Gloves, Cowboy, Leather, 1930s 150.00

TIP
Some old locks must have the key turned twice to open.

Tole, Tray, Birds, Fountain, Flowers, Scalloped Rim, Black Ground, Gilt, 13 ¼ x 16 ¾ In.
$225.00

Tole, Tray, Harbor Scene, Gilt Vines, Red Ground, Cutout Handles, Oval, 1900, 25 In.
$470.00

Tom Mix, Button, Miracle Rider, Red, Black, White, 1935, 1 ¼ In.
$337.00

Tom Mix, Rocking Horse, Western, Painted, 25 x 40 In.
$86.00

Tom Mix, Rodeo Rope, Instructions, Box, 1928, 11 x 12 x 1 ¾ In.
$173.00

Tom Mix, Toy, Spurs, Glow-In-The-Dark, Aluminum, Ralston Purina Premium, Box, 5 In.
$58.00

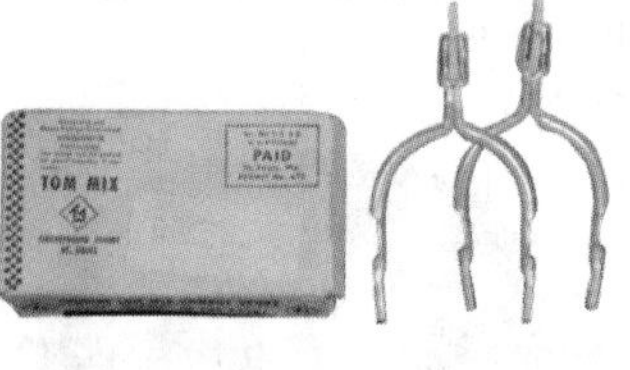

Tool, Anvil, Cast Iron, Painted, Bittersweet, 3 ¾ x 8 x 3 In.
$55.00

Tool, Cranberry Picker, Wood, Metal, Bentwood Handles, 18 x 12 x 19 In.
$330.00

Jackknife, Pearlized Handle, Ralston Premium, Ralston Straight Shooters, 1939 .... 31.00
Poster, Huntington, Friday July 10, Yellow, Green, Red, 1930s, 21 x 28 In.. .... 144.00
Poster, Movie, Speed Maniac, Museum Mount, 28 x 41 In. 354.00
Ring, TM Initials, Gold, Box. 50.00
Rocking Horse, Western, Painted, 25 x 40 In. .... *illus* 86.00
Rodeo Rope, Instructions, Box, 1928, 11 x 12 x 1 ¾ In. .... *illus* 173.00
Song Book, Western Songs, M.M. Cole Publishing Co., Chicago, 64 Pages, 1935 .... 47.00
Telescope, Ralston Straight Shooters, Cardboard Mailing Tube, 1937, 2 ½ x 1 ¼ In. 140.00
Toy, Horse, Rocking, Tom Mix, Wood, Painted, 25 x 40 In. 85.00
Toy, Spurs, Glow-In-The-Dark, Aluminum, Ralston Purina Premium, Box, 5 In. ...... *illus* 58.00
Wagon, Big Six Circus & Wild West Show, Wood, Cast Iron, 17 x 7 In. 605.00

TOOLS of all sorts are listed here, but most are related to industry. Other tools may be found listed under Iron, Kitchen, Tinware, and Wooden.

Anvil, Cast Iron, Painted, Bittersweet, 3 ¾ x 8 x 3 In. .... *illus* 55.00
Bench, Cobbler, Softwood, Leather Work Area, Drawer, 20 x 51 x 21 ½ In. 55.00
Bench, Harness Maker's, Wood, Blue Paint, 19th Century 125.00
Book Press, Georgian, Mahogany, Beech Spiral, Drawer, 1800s, 66 x 32 In. 1093.00
Book Press, Oak, Elm, Tall Frame, Screw, Drawer, Tapered Legs, England, 18th Century, 54 ½ In. 2070.00
Card Cutter, No. 455, Will & Frinck, Copper, Steel, Brass Ivory Handle, San Francisco, 9 x 6 In. 3575.00
Chest, Machinist's, Oak, 10 ½ x 14 x 8 In. 88.00
Chest, Machinist's, Oak, Gerstner & Sones, Dayton, Ohio, 13 x 16 In. 330.00
Cigar Press, 4 Molds, Wood, Iron, Holds, 30 x 28 In.. .... 275.00
Cigar Sizer, Metal, Wood Base, Patent July 16, 1901, 7 ½ x 16 In. 495.00
Combination, 2 Tine Fork, Triangular Spatula, Iron, Square Shaft, 14 ½ In.. .... 22.00
Corn Crib, Salesman's Sample, Wood, 10-Sided Oilcloth Roof, Painted, 20 x 22 In. 330.00
Corn Planter, Check Row, Patent Model, J.A. Clearwater, Copper, Zinc & Wood, 1880, 7 x 13 In. 4950.00
Corn Planter, Red, Acmeline Mfg. Co., Mich., 33 In. 66.00
Cranberry Picker, Wood, Metal, Bentwood Handles, 18 x 12 x 19 In. .... *illus* 330.00
Dust Pan, 3-Sided, Handle, H. D. Levengood, Reading, Pa., 28 In. 70.00
Guillotine, Hardwood, Metal, Patina, Blade Weighs 40 Lbs., c.1920, 101 x 47 x 40 In.. .... 26290.00
Guillotine, Wood & Metal, Prisoner's Art, Devil's Island, 1928, Miniature, 14 In. 598.00
Harvester, Cranberry, Red Paint, 17 x 10 ½ x 11 In. 50.00
Hasp, Tulip Terminal, Iron, Pa., Late 18th Century, 14 In. 440.00
Hatchel, Beech, Central Flax Comb, Oblong Board, Cut Out Handles, 1800s, 27 In. 646.00
Hay Fork, Wood, Carved, 3 Tines, 16 ¾ x 4 ½ In.. .... 30.00
Hay Hook, Metal, Wood Handle, Painted Red, 11 In. 16.00
Head, Iron, Belt, Brass Inlay, Early 19th Century, 5 ½ In. 995.00
Hod, Grape, Metal, Painted, Handles, Tapered Cone Shape, Flat Back, Flange Bottom, 28 x 24 In. 316.00
Jack, Wagon, Conestoga, Marked, 1815 .... 244.00
Mallet, Wood, Wire & Wood Handle, c.1950, 21 ¼ x 6 In. 21.00
Measure, Cast Iron, Wiley & Russell Mfg. Co., Mass., 12 ½ In. .... *illus* 33.00
Oiler, DeLaval Patent, 1915, 3 ¼ In. 18.00
Padlock, Key, Metal, Strong Box 30.00
Padlock, Old Yale, Brass, 2 Keys 6.00
Pitchfork, 3-Prong, Hardwood, Incised, 62 ½ x 14 ¼ In. .... *illus* 99.00
Pitchfork, 4 Tines, Wood, 62 In. 25.00
Plane, Fishing Rod Maker, Wood, Folding, Atkin & Son Angled Blade, 10 ½ In. 58.00
Plane, Jointer, L. Bailey Series c.1857, 21 ½ In. 18700.00
Plane, Plow, Ohio Tool Co., Ebony Ivory Tips, Rosewood Wheel & Stem 29150.00
Plane, Smoothing, O.R. Chaplin, No. ½, Nickel Plated, Red Orange Japanned 28600.00
Plow, S.L. Allen & Co., Planet Jr., No. 119, Pa., 1919, 53 In. 405.00
Press, Grape, Wood, Iron, Turnscrew, Slats, Iron Crank Wheel, 20th Century, 51 In. 561.00
Pulley, Wood, c.1950, 10 ¾ x 3 ¾ In. 21.00
Pump, Etter, No. 7, Little Giant, Iron, 60 In. 75.00
Punch, Sterling Silver Handle, 5 ½ In. 40.00
Rake, Aluminum, Orange, c.1960, 10 ½ In. 12.50
Rake, Hay, 9 Tines, Chestnut, Hickory, Pa., 84 In. 250.00
Rake, Wood Handle, c.1960, 16 In. 12.00
Ripsaw, Disston & Sons, Etching, Extra Large Teeth, 29 In. 143.00
Rope Maker, Hawkeye Mfg. Co., Painted, Metal, Wood, 8 ½ In. .... *illus* 250.00
Rule, Folding, Stanley, No. 68, Collapsing, 24 In. 18.00
Ruler, Mathematical, Early Style Numbers, Brass, c.1700, 12 In. 325.00
Scissors, Winchester No, 9056-7 ½, Full Nickel Blade, Black Handles 45.00
Screwdriver, H.R. Eby, Tooled, Geometrics, Sawtooth Ferrule, Marked, c.1850, 20 ⅝ In. 1755.00
Screwdriver, Stanley, No. 2703, Phillips Head, No. 3. .... 25.00
Separator, Cream, DeLaval, Electric, Countertop, 1920-30, 25 In. .... *illus* 115.00

Shovel, Aluminum, Green, c.1960, 11 ½ In. 14.00
Solder Iron, Stand, Iron, Wood Handle, 6 x 15 In. 121.00
Spade, Blubber, Iron, Martha's Vineyard Provenance, 19th Century, 16 ½ x 4 In. 275.00
Square, Carpenter's, Iron, Initials, Penn., c.1797, 24 In. 676.00
Steam Boiler, Salesman's Sample, Schaffer & Budenberg, Germany, Wood, Metal, 14 x 8 In. 1100.00
Swift, Double, Ivory Inlays, Ebony Pole, Wood Case, 25 In. 235.00
Tape Loom, Pine, c.1800, 35 In. 499.00
Tongs, Pipe, Iron, Late 18th Century, 16 In. 263.00
Tool Caddy, Galvanized Metal, c.1980, 9 x 7 ½ In. 18.00
Tractor Seat, Iron, Walter A. Wood, 17 x 16 In. 40.00
Trammel, Iron, Saw Tooth, Hooked, Knobbed Ends, Ratchet Release, 32 In. 66.00
Trammel, Iron, Tulip Finials, 19th Century, 6 In. 1989.00
Trammel, Wrought Iron, Sawtooth, Hooked, Knobbed Ends, Articulated Release, 32 In. *illus* 60.00
Trencher, Pumpkin, 20 In. 690.00
Wagon Hitch Plate, Oblong, V-Shaped Arms, Flame Form Terminals, Iron, 16 x 12 ½ In. 22.00
Well Pump, Manchester Hardware Co., Red, Gold Stencil, 81 x 6 In. 950.00
Wheelbarrow, Blue Paint, Star, Wood, Metal Wheel, 19th Century 375.00
Wheelbarrow, Pine, Red Paint, Wood Wheel, Buch, Mountville, 24 In. 110.00
Wheelbarrow, Wood, Red Paint, Buch Mfg. Co., Elizabethtown, Pa., 26 x 67 x 24 In. 187.00

TOOTHBRUSH HOLDERS were part of every bowl and pitcher set in the late nineteenth century. Most were oblong covered dishes. About 1920, manufacturers started to make children's toothbrush holders shaped like animals or cartoon characters. A few modern toothbrush holders are still being made.

3 Bears, Standing, With Bowls, Hole, On Back Of Bear, Imperial China, Japan, 4 x 4 ½ In. 131.00
3 Little Pigs, Pottery, Painted, c.1930, 4 x 4 In. 95.00
Cowboy, Next To Cactus, Brushes Fit Into Holsters & Top Of Hat, Tray For Toothpaste, 5 ½ In. 148.00
Cowboy, Right Holster Holds Toothbrush, Left Holds Toothpaste, Ceramic, 5 ⅛ In. 224.00
Davenport, View In Geneva, Blue Transfer, Lid, 2 Rests, Groove For Brush, 7 ⅞ x 1 ¾ In. 220.00
Girl, Pink Hat, Blue Dress, Celluloid, Box, 6 ¾ x 3 ¾ In. 30.00
Girl, Yellow Dress, Blue Trim, Pink Hat, Celluloid, Original Box, 6 ¾ x 3 ¾ In. 25.00
Kayo, Wall Hanger, Japan, 1930s, 5 In. 225.00
Listerine, Pro.phy.lac.tic, Skeezix, Tin Lithograph, Die Cut, 3 x 6 In. 146.00
Little Dutch Boy, Lavender Pants, Red Hat & Bowtie, Wooden Shoes, 5 In. 95.00
Metal, Nickel Finish, Embossed Tooth Brushes, Scrolls, Wall Mount, Pat. 1904, 5 In. 195.00
Nursery Rhymes, Ceramic, Center Pedestal Holds Brush, Decal, 3 In. 72.00
Old King Cole, Hole For Toothbrush, Feet Hold Toothpaste, Wall Mount, Japan, 5 ¼ In. 113.00
Peter, Peter, Pumpkin Eater, Pottery, Japan, 4 ⅞ x 2 ⅞ x 2 ⅜ In. 95.00
RS Germany, Pink Roses, Green Mark, Germany, c.1900, 3 ¾ x 3 ¾ In. 175.00
Skippy, Bisque, Figural, 6 In. 185.00
Skippy, Painted, Bisque, 5 ½ In. 185.00
Skippy, Shorts, Coat, Hat, Bisque, Marked Percy Crosby, Made In Japan, 1930s, 5 ½ In. 60.00
Toby Tortoise, Boxing Gloves, Maw Of London, Marked, 1936, 4 In. *illus* 348.00

TOOTHPICK HOLDERS are sometimes called *toothpicks* by collectors. The variously shaped containers used to hold small wooden toothpicks are made of glass, china, or metal. Most of the toothpick holders are Victorian. Additional items may be found in other categories, such as Bisque, Silver Plate, Slag Glass, etc.

Banded Portland 18.00
Bead & Scroll 45.00
Beaded Ovals In Sand 135.00
Connecticut, Engraved 50.00 to 65.00
Cranberry Opalescent, Silver Plated Leaf Shape Frame, 2 ½ x 3 ¾ In. 375.00
Custard Glass, Parker & Davis Portraits, Flags, Eagle, 2 ¾ In. 287.00
Daisy, Clear & Button 35.00
Daisy & Button, Gypsy Kettle, 2 ⅛ x 3 In. 13.00
Deep File 45.00
Delaware 40.00
Diamond Quilted, Crimped, Ruffled Rim, Yellow, Glossy 345.00
Diamond Spearhead, Vaseline Opalescent, 2 ⅜ In. 125.00
Double Circle, Blue 150.00
Double Circle, Green 145.00
Double Ring Panel 40.00
Eureka, Ruby Stain 125.00
Fig Mold, Opal 400.00
Figural, Birds In Eggshell 35.00
Figural, Bootie, Blue 30.00

Tool, Measure, Cast Iron, Wiley & Russell Mfg. Co., Mass., 12 ½ In.
$33.00

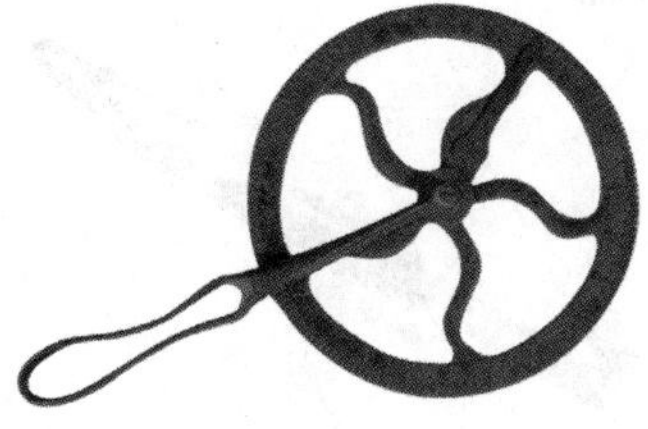

Tool, Pitchfork, 3-Prong, Hardwood, Incised, 62 ½ x 14 ¼ In.
$99.00

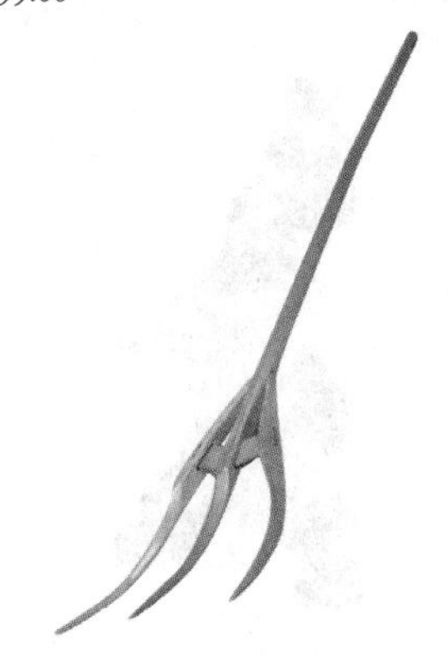

Tool, Rope Maker, Hawkeye Mfg. Co., Painted, Metal, Wood, 8 ½ In.
$250.00

Tool, Separator, Cream, DeLaval, Electric, Countertop, 1920-30, 25 In.
$115.00

T

Tool, Trammel, Wrought Iron, Sawtooth, Hooked, Knobbed Ends, Articulated Release, 32 In.
$60.00

Toothbrush Holder, Toby Tortoise, Boxing Gloves, Maw Of London, Marked, 1936, 4 In.
$348.00

Toothpick Holder, Figural, Hand With Torch, Blue, Rayed Base, 1890s, 4 x 1 ¾ In.
$105.00

Tortoiseshell, Cigarette Case
$106.00

Figural, Boy, Sunflower 240.00
Figural, Buttons, Blue 55.00
Figural, Chick, On Tree Branch, Embossed Berry Egg, Pinecone, Milk Glass, 3 ¼ x 3 ½ In.... 11.00
Figural, Double Shoe, Amber 100.00
Figural, Early Bird, Amber........ 65.00
Figural, Egg, Blue Satin, Crimped Top On 45 Degree Angle, Amber Foot........ 195.00
Figural, Goat 185.00
Figural, Hand With Torch, Blue, Rayed Base, 1890s, 4 x 1 ¾ In. .... *illus* 105.00
Figural, Indian Chief........ 55.00
Figural, Man With Hat........ 70.00
Figural, Prayer Lady, Cold Paint........ 15.00
Figural, Snake On Stump, Blue........ 45.00
Figural, Squirrel, Horn 250.00
Four Rabbits, Opal 100.00
Georgia Gem, Gold Trim........ 30.00
Hand, Flowers, Amber 60.00
Harvard, Custard Glass, Souvenir Of St. Augustine, Florida........ 50.00
Klondike, Gold Stain, 2 ⅜ x 1 ¾ In........ 650.00
Ladder With Diamonds........ 35.00
Moon & Stars, Amberina, Flat Base, L.E. Smith 7.00
Moon & Stars, Amberina, Scalloped Base, L.E. Smith........ 8.00
New Hampshire, Maiden's Blush Stain........ 15.00
New Jersey, Gold Trim........ 50.00
Opalescent Rib, 2 In. 99.00
Oval Star 15.00
Paddlewheel & Star........ 35.00
Paddlewheel & Star, Gold Trim........ 35.00
Palm Leaf, Blue Satin 95.00
Palm Leaf, Pink........ 85.00
Parallel Greek Key........ 425.00
Parrot With Top Hat, Milk Glass........ 45.00
Pearls & Shells, Milk Glass........ 40.00
Pineapple & Fan........ 13.00
Plastic, Woodpecker On Branch, Yellow, 4 ¼ In........ 15.00
Porcelain, Batwing Handles, Bridge & Lake Scene, Nippon 129.00
Porcelain, Elk Head, Royal Bayreuth........ 299.00
Porcelain, Peasant With Donkey, Royal Bayreuth........ 279.00
Priscilla 25.00
Prism 40.00
Ring & Beads, Amethyst, Souvenir Of Milwaukee, Wis......... 50.00
Salisia, Handles, Marked, R.S. Tillowitz 12.00
Scroll, Fan, Feet, Scroll, Gold Trim 30.00
Shoshone, 2 ½ In........ 20.00
Six Point, Scalloped........ 40.00
Star Base Swirl........ 75.00
Stars & Bars........ 100.00
Stars & Bars, Amber 115.00
Sunk Daisy........ 35.00
Swirl & Dot, Cranberry Opalescent, 2 ½ In......... 100.00
Tacoma, 2 In........ 25.00
Thumbprint, Souvenir, Flowers, Niagara Falls 25.00
Truncated Cube, Ruby Stain 20.00
Union, Ruby Stain, 2 ¼ In. 135.00
Windows, Blue Opalescent 75.00
Zipper Slash, Ruby Stain 10.00
Zippered, Diamond Star 20.00
Zippered, Swirl & Diamond........ 30.00

TORQUAY

TORQUAY is the name given to ceramics by several potteries working near Torquay, England, from 1870 until 1962. Until about 1900, the potteries used local red clay to make classical-style art pottery vases and figurines. Then they turned to making souvenir wares. Items were dipped in colored slip and decorated with painted slip and sgraffito designs. They often had mottoes or proverbs, and scenes of cottages, ships, birds, or flowers. The Scandy design was a symmetrical arrangement of brushstrokes and spots done in colored slips. Potteries included Watcombe Pottery (1870–1962); Torquay Terra-Cotta Company (1875–1905); Aller Vale (1881–1924); Torquay Pottery (1908–1940); and Longpark (1883–1957).

Creamer, Parrot, In Tree, Blue Ground, Legend, Elp Yerzel Tu Cram, 3 ¾ In........ 41.00

Dish, Ship, Commemorative, 1620 Mayflower 1957, Blue, Oval, 6 x 5 In. 15.00
Eggcup, Rooster, Motto, New Laid Egg, 2 ½ In. 35.00
Jug, 3 Pouring Spouts, 3 Angled Handles, Motto, Success Comes Not, 6 ⅛ In. 115.00
Jug, Cottage Scene, Motto, To Say Well Is Good, Handle, Watcombe, 5 In. 55.00
Jug, Milk, Cottage Scene, Motto, Little Duties Left Undone, 4 ¼ In. 150.00
Perfume Bottle, Wicker Wrapped, Handle, Bermuda Violets By Lowends Pateman, 4 ½ In. . . 28.00
Spooner Basket, Pigeon Blood, Silver Plate Rim, Handle, Victorian, 7 In. 450.00

TORTOISESHELL is the shell of the tortoise. It has been used as inlay and to make small decorative objects since the seventeenth century. Some species of tortoise are now on the endangered species list, and old or new objects made from these shells cannot be sold legally.

Box, Bombe Form, Handle, Ormolu Mounts, France, 1800s, 9 x 12 x 10 In. 3910.00
Box, Carved, Court Scene, Riverscape, Chinese, 3 ¾ In. 575.00
Box, Lid, Regency, Shaped Front, Corners, Bun Feet, c.1830, 3 x 4 In. 590.00
Box, Metal, Ivory Borders, Fabric Interiors, 1800s, 10 x 7 In. 978.00
Card Case, c.1860, 4 ¼ x 3 In. 144.00
Cigarette Case . . . . illus 106.00
Desk Set, Brass Inlay, Trim, Ormolu Feet, 2 Glass Inkwells, Covered Well, 14 x 8 In. 345.00
Etui, Victorian, Hinged Top Opening, Fitted Interior, 19th Century, 4 x 2 ½ In. 570.00
Hair Comb, c.1833, 5 x 6 In. 77.00
Jewelry Box, Green, Silver Inlays, 3 Monograms, Interior Compartments, 1800s, 7 x 5 In. . . . 4140.00
Lorgnette, c.1890, 7 In. 81.00
Perfume Case, 3 Interior Bottles, Silver Caps, Ivory Edging, 1800s, 3 x 5 x 2 In. 2185.00
Snuffbox, Horn, 19th Century, 3 ¼ In. 115.00
Tea Caddy, Corner Columns, Brass Feet, 2 Lidded Compartments, England, c.1865, 6 x 7 In. . 3910.00
Tea Caddy, Fluted, Ball Feet, 2 Lidded Interior Compartments, England, 1800s, 5 x 7 ½ In. . . 2415.00
Tea Caddy, Fluted Front Panel, Metal Inlays, 2 Interior Compartments, 1800s, 5 x 7 In. 2530.00
Tea Caddy, Tapered, 2 Lidded Interior Compartments, Canister, England, c.1825, 7 x 11 In. . . 2185.00

TOY collectors have special clubs, magazines, and shows. Toys are designed to entice children, and today they have attracted new interest among adults who are still children at heart. All types of toys are collected. Tin toys, iron toys, battery operated toys, and many others are collected by specialists. Dolls, Games, Teddy Bears, and Bicycles are listed in their own categories. Other toys may be found under company or celebrity names.

2 Black Men Boxing, Painted, Wood, Cloth, Cast Iron, Windup, Ives, Box, 11 In. 10450.00
2 Black Women Dancing, Painted, Wood, Cloth, Windup, Ives, 9 ½ In. 520.00
3 Piece Jazz Band, Black Men, Drum, Cymbals, Cardboard, Wood, Steinfeld Products, 9 ½ In. 40.00
Acrobat, 3 Cutout Silhouettes, Spin, Wood, Pinned Joints, String, Spacers, 13 ½ x 14 ¼ In. . . 176.00
Acrobat, Boy, Green Hat, Red Shirt, Celluloid, Metal, Windup, 11 ½ In. 55.00
Acrobat, Chinese, Wood, Jointed, Cloth Outfit, Schoenhut, 8 ½ In. 201.00
Acrobat, Gent, Porcelain Head, Painted, Wood Jointed, Barbell, Schoenhut, 7 In. . . . . . *illus* 356.00
Acrobat, Lola, Lady Marvel, Celluloid, Metal, Windup, Prewar Japan, Box, 11 In. 138.00
Acrobatic Marvel Monkey, Tin Lithograph, Windup, Marx, 13 ½ In. 165.00
Aerial Defense Set, 7 Airplanes, No. 05051, Die Cast, Tootsietoy, Box . . . . *illus* 385.00
Aero Swing, Musical, Tin Lithograph, Windup, Chein, 10 x 19 In. 275.00
Aero Swing, Musical, Tin Lithograph, Windup, Chein, Box, 10 x 19 In. 465.00
Airplane, 4 Propellers, Metal, Windup, U.S. Zone, Germany, 10 In. 95.00
Airplane, A.F. Line Air Service, Pressed Steel, Windup, No. 555, American Flyer, 19 In. . . *illus* 2750.00
Airplane, Air Mail, Rider, Red, Silver, Decals, Keystone, 1930s, 24-In. Wingspan. 650.00
Airplane, Air Mail, Sit-N-Ride, Painted, Pressed Steel, Wood, Keystone, c.1935, 24 In. . . . *illus* 1093.00
Airplane, Air Mail, Yellow, Cast Iron, Kenton, 7 ¾ In. 700.00
Airplane, Airford, Red, Cast Iron, Hubley, 1929, 4 In. 27.00
Airplane, Airways Express, World Tours, Tin, Windup, Girard, 13 x 13 In. 88.00
Airplane, American Airlines Flagship, NC 5000, No. 170, Fisher-Price, 1941, 14 x 20 In. 650.00
Airplane, Biplane, Pilot, In Crepe Paper Coat, Lithograph, Penny Toy, Meier, 3 In. 690.00
Airplane, Catapult, Hanger, 3 Monocoupes, Flag, Pressed Steel, Buddy L, 20 In. 690.00
Airplane, Dagwood's Solo Flight, Tin, Windup, Marx, 1935 . . . . 850.00
Airplane, DC-7 American Airlines, Douglas Lights, Tin, Battery Operated, Linemar, Box, 19 ½ In. 419.00
Airplane, DC-7C American Airlines, Prop Turns, Lights, Passengers, Door Opens, 23 ½ In. . . . 791.00
Airplane, DC-7C American Airlines, Prop Turns, Lights, Tin, Battery Operated, Linemar, c.1958, 19 In. 150.00
Airplane, Dual Cock Pit, Decals, Pressed Steel, Steelcraft, 17 In. 460.00
Airplane, Electra, Lights, Tin, Plastic, Japan, Box, 16 ½ In. 275.00
Airplane, Empire Express, Monocoupe, Tin Lithograph, Painted, 18 In. 173.00
Airplane, Gerard, Windup, c.1930, 8 In. 175.00
Airplane, Green, Red Wings, Little Jim Playthings, Keystone, 24-In. Wingspan . . . . *illus* 1980.00
Airplane, Jet, Atomic, Tin, Friction, Plastic Canopy, Rubber Nose Cone, Japan, 10 ½ In. 316.00

Toy, Acrobat, Gent, Porcelain Head, Painted, Wood Jointed, Barbell, Schoenhut, 7 In.
$356.00

Toy, Aerial Defense Set, 7 Airplanes, No. 05051, Die Cast, Tootsietoy, Box
$385.00

Toy, Airplane, A.F. Line Air Service, Pressed Steel, Windup, No. 555, American Flyer, 19 In.
$2750.00

Toy, Airplane, Air Mail, Sit-N-Ride, Painted, Pressed Steel, Wood, Keystone, c.1935, 24 In.
$1093.00

Toy, Airplane, Green, Red Wings, Little Jim Playthings, Keystone, 24-In. Wingspan
$1980.00

T

Lego
"Lego" comes from the Danish expression *leg godt*, meaning "play well." Later the company learned the Latin word *lego* can be translated to mean "I put together."

Toy, Airplane, Sparking, U.S. Army, No. 712, Tin, Windup, Marx, Box, 8 In. $460.00

Toy, Airport Set, 2 Planes, Hangar, Die Cast, Tootsietoy, Box, 6 x 6 In. $288.00

Toy, Baby, Buttercup, Crawls, Painted, Tin, Windup, Germany, 7 In. $575.00

Airplane, Lindy, Gray, Red Letters, Cast Iron, Hubley, 10-In. Wingspan ... 1265.00
Airplane, Lindy, Tailwheel Gear, Prop Turns, Blue, Gold, Cast Iron, Hubley, 10 In. ... 920.00
Airplane, Lockheed Sirius, Tin, Windup, Prewar Japan, 10 In. ... 403.00
Airplane, Mail, Green Fuselage, Yellow Tail, Pressed Steel, Steelcraft, 22 ½ In. ... 403.00
Airplane, Monocoupe, Black Fuselage, Orange Wing, Decal, Arcade, 10 ½ In. ... 1093.00
Airplane, Monoplane, NR 1600, Airman, Propellers Turn, Tin, Windup, Japan, 7-In. Wingspan 181.00
Airplane, Pan Am Strato Clipper, Propellers Turn, Friction, Alps, 14 In. ... 115.00
Airplane, Pilot, Wings Flap, Propellers Turn, Embossed, Tin Lithograph, Windup, 9 ¾ In. ... 990.00
Airplane, Pilots, 3 Motors, Aluminum Wings, Cast Iron, Hubley, 16 ¾ In. ... 1725.00
Airplane, Plastic, Blue, Red, Yellow, Nosco, c.1954, 9 In. ... 85.00
Airplane, Pontoon, Navy, Prop, Aqua, Linemar, Box, 13-In. Wingspan ... 452.00
Airplane, Pressed Steel, 1930s, 14-In. Wingspan ... 145.00
Airplane, Pressed Steel, Wyandotte, 18 In. ... 86.00
Airplane, Pursuit, Red, Nickel Wings, 5-In. Wingspan ... 275.00
Airplane, Rapid Fire, Tri-Motor, Red, Yellow, Pressed Steel, Keystone, c.1927, 24 In. ... 633.00
Airplane, Seaplane, Tin Lithograph, Windup, Chein, Box, 7 ½ In. ... 300.00
Airplane, Sky Hawk Control Tower, 2 Airplanes, Tin Lithograph, Windup, Marx, Box ... 150.00
Airplane, Sparking, U.S. Army, No. 712, Tin, Windup, Marx, Box, 8 In. ... *illus* 460.00
Airplane, Spiral, 2 Planes, Wood, Spring Support, Penny Toy, Einfalt, 6 ½ In. ... 460.00
Airplane, Spirit Of St. Louis, Lindy, Cast Iron, Pull Toy, Hubley, 13-In. Wingspan ... 3450.00
Airplane, Stork, Fiesler Fi 156, 2-Tone Green, Luftwaffe Marks, Copy Of German Plane ... 719.00
Airplane, Tin, Copper, Windup, Marx, 18 In. ... 245.00
Airplane, U.S. Air Force, Military Transport C-124, Vehicles, Props Spin, Lights, Tin, Japan, 20 In. 625.00
Airplane, Whiz Sky Fighter, Tin, Windup, Girard, 9 x 7 In. ... 690.00
Airplane Set, 5 Jets, Die Cast, No. 5698, Tootsietoy, Box ... 150.00
Airport, 2 Airplanes, Tin Lithograph, Windup, Ohio Art, Box ... 110.00
Airport, Semi-Trailer, Red, Green, Yellow, Doepke, c.1955, 26 In. ... 225.00
Airport Set, 2 Planes, Hangar, Die Cast, Tootsietoy, Box, 6 x 6 In. ... *illus* 288.00
Airship, Pressed Steel, Marked, Akron, 25 In. ... 708.00
Ajax Warrior, Holds Club, Somersaults, Tin, Windup, Lehmann, 7 In. ... 1035.00
Alabama Coon Jigger, Tin, Windup, Germany, 1912, 10 ½ In. ... 440.00
Alligator, Chasing Bee, Mouth Opens, Tail Swivels, Tin, Windup, S & E Co., Japan, 11 ½ In. ... 125.00
Alligator, Green, Wood, Jointed, Glass Eyes, Leather Feet, Schoenhut, 12 ½ In. ... 115.00
Alligator, Native Rider, Tin, Windup, 14 ¾ In. ... 125.00
Alligator, Walks, Mouth Opens & Closes, Tin, 15 In. ... 37.00
Ambulance, Blue Cross, Rear Opening, Decal, Painted, Steel, Canvas Sides, Keystone, 27 ½ In. 652.00
Ambulance, Chevrolet, Hub Caps, Tin, Friction, Japan, 1957, 9 ½ In. ... 145.00
Ambulance, Chevrolet, Tin, Friction, Japan, 1958, 8 ½ In. ... 125.00
Ambulance, Military, Driver, Soldier On Stretcher, Windup, Tipp & Co., Germany, 1930s ... 595.00
Ambulance, No. 14C1, Matchbox, Box ... 230.00
Ambulance, Pressed Steel, Marusan, Japan, 13 In. ... 127.00
Ambulance, Pressed Steel, U.S.A., 1930, 11 In. ... 175.00
Ambulance, Red Cross, Nash Rambler, Tin, Friction, Japan, 11 In. ... 450.00
Ambulance, Van, Tin, Friction, Box, Chinese, 10 In. ... 75.00
Ambulance, White, Wyandotte, 11 In. ... 125.00 to 250.00
Ambulance, Yellow, Pressed Steel, Buddy L, 27 ½ In. ... 702.00
American Airlines Flagship, No. 170, Fisher-Price, c.1941, 14 x 20 In. ... 748.00
American Football Player, Throws Football, Cloth, Composition, Windup, Frankonia, Box . 45.00
Amos 'N' Andy, Andy, Waddles, Stationary Eyes, Tin, Windup, Marx, 1930, 11 In. ... 660.00
Amos 'N' Andy, Andy, Walker, Eyes Move, Tin Lithograph, Marx, 11 In. ... 316.00
Amos 'N' Andy, Walker, Swinging Arms, Tin Lithograph, Windup, Marx, Box, 11 In. ... 2185.00
Amusement Park, Rides, Figures, Plastic, Wood, No. 932, Fisher-Price, Box, 1963, 14 x 18 In. 500.00
Andy Gump, Driver, Red & Green Car, No. 348, Cast Iron, Arcade, 7 In. ... 1100.00
Anxious Bride & Rad Cycle, Tin, Windup, Lehmann, Germany, 9 In. ... 1840.00
Arnold Monkey, On Tricycle, Tin Lithograph, Windup, U.S. Zone, Germany, 3 ½ In. ... 66.00
Art Finegan, On Cart, Luggage, Tin Lithograph, Windup, Unique Art, 14 In. ... 66.00
Astronaut, X-70, Walks, Moves Arms, Head, Plastic, Windup, 6 ½ In. ... 226.00
Baby, Buttercup, Crawls, Painted, Tin, Windup, Germany, 7 In. ... *illus* 575.00
Baby, Girl, Crawling, Painted, Cast Iron, Ives, 5 In. ... 220.00
Baby Quieter, Man On Couch, Bell, Painted, Cast Iron, Pull Toy, J. & E. Stevens, 1890s, 7 ½ In. 1080.00
Balancing, Wood, Black, Figure Holding Balance Beam, On Pedestal, Multicolored, 10 In. ... 144.00
Balking Mule, Yellow Outfit, Painted, Tin Lithograph, Lehmann, Box, 7 ¼ In. ... 489.00
Balky Mule, Clown Driver, Tin Lithograph, Clockwork, Lehmann, Box, 8 In. ... *illus* 440.00
Ball, Animals, Canvas, Painted, 5 In. ... 575.00
Ball, Canvas, Painted, Black & White, 4 ½ In. ... 316.00
Ball, Canvas, Painted, Green, Yellow, Blue, 4 In. ... 575.00
Ball, Canvas, Painted, Red, White, Blue, 4 ½ In. ... 316.00

Ball, Leatherette, Green, Yellow, Red Stitching, 3 ½ In. 403.00
Ball, Mouse, Seated, Velveteen, 5 In. 288.00
Ballerina, Dances, Moving Picture, Sand Activated, 6 x 7 x 6 In. 385.00
Ballerina, Ratchet Bar, Tin Lithograph, Marx, Box, 6 In. 220.00
Balloon Vendor, Vinyl, Cloth, Hard Rubber, Tin Lithograph, Battery Operated, 4 x 4 x 10 ½ In. 201.00
Band, Bullfrog Serenaders, 10 Frogs, Painted, 22 x 24 x 10 In. 1045.00
Band Master, Drum, Cymbals, Molded & Painted, Hat & Uniform, Schoenhut, 8 ½ In. 1610.00
Banjo Player, Blond, Vibrates, Head & Arms Move, Tin, Windup, Linemar, Box, 5 ¼ In. 906.00
Barnacle Bill, Sailor Outfit, Walker, Tin Lithograph, Windup, Chein, 6 In. 173.00
Barney Google, Black Hat, Painted Face, Felt Jacket, Wood, Jointed, Schoenhut, 7 ½ In. 58.00
Bartender, Shakes Drink, Smoking Ears, Rubber, Cloth, Tin, Battery Operated, Rosko, Box, 12 In. 27.00
Bartender, Whistler, Pours Drinks, Head Moves, Carved, Wood, Windup, 13 ½ In. 1955.00
Bear, Cashier, Cloth, Tin, Battery Operated, Moderne Toys, Japan, Box, 7 In. 176.00
Bear, Golfer, Tin, Windup, Box, 7 In. 425.00
Bear, Golfer, Tin Lithograph, Windup, T.P.S. Japan, Box, 4 ¼ In. 132.00
Bear, Grandma, Picnic, Mixed Material, Battery Operated, Alps, 9 In. 250.00
Bear, Maxwell Coffee Loving, Pours Coffee, Battery Operated, Nomura, Box, 10 In. 360.00
Bear, Peanut Vendor, Walker, Smokes, Makes Noise, Battery Operated, Box, Japan, 9 In. 230.00
Bear, Picnic, Tin, Plush, Battery Operated, Alps, Box, 9 ½ In. 150.00
Bear, Polar, Fishing, Tin, Fabric, Plush, Battery Operated, Alps, Box, 10 In. 395.00
Bear, Poll Parrot Shoes, Wood, Yellow, Red, Wheels, Pull Toy, 5 ¾ In. 44.00
Bear, Ride-On, Fur, Rubber Wheels, Steiff, Mid 20th Century, 18 x 23 In. 153.00
Bear, Sneezing, Tin, Plush, Battery Operated, Linemar, Box, 9 In. 325.00
Bear, Walker, Fur, Windup, Occupied Japan, 5 In. 16.00
Bear, Yes-No, Golden Mohair, Stitched Mouth, Nose, Metal Glasses, Tail Lever, Schuco, 1920s, 5 In. 288.00
Bear, Yes-No, White Mohair, Jointed, Red Ribbon, Tail Twists, U.S. Zone, Germany, 13 ½ In. ... 201.00
Bears are also listed in the Teddy Bear category.
Bed, Doll's, Dolly Dearie, Verse On Headboard, Toys On Footboard, Painted, Iron, 20 x 28 In. .. 330.00
Bed, Doll's, Iron, Painted, Marked, Chicago Art Bed Co., 28 In. 225.00
Bed, Doll's, Renaissance Revival, Rosewood, Marquetry, 18 x 11 In. 115.00
Bed, Doll's, Wood, Turned Spool Posts, Rope Bottom, Feather Mattress, c.1885, 18 x 10 In. 58.00
Bedroom Set, Doll's, Red, Victorian Woman On Headboard, Paper Litho, 1900s, 20-In. Bed, 6 Piece. 115.00
Beetle, Flaps Wings, Tin Lithograph, Windup, Lehmann, Germany, 3 ¾ In. 489.00
Bell Ringer, Holding Brass Bells, Pull Toy, Germany, 14 In. 2133.00
Bell Toy, Girl, On Sleigh, Doll, Hands In Muff, Cast Iron, Pull Toy, Daisy, 8 ¼ In. 575.00
Bell Toy, Gong, Kneeling Figure, Flag, Cast Iron, Tin, Pull Toy, c.1880, 6 In. .... *illus* 13800.00
Bell Toy, Gong, Wild Mule Jack, Painted, Cast Iron, Pull Toy, 8 In. .... *illus* 1150.00
Bell Toy, Harold Lloyd, Eyes, Glasses Move, Tin Lithograph, Distler, 6 ½ In. 195.00
Bell Toy, Horse & Driver, Red Jacket, Brown Horse, Cast Iron, Watrous Mfg., 1905, 8 In. 390.00
Bell Toy, Rough Riders, 2 Figures, Center Bell, Cast Iron, Watrous, c.1884, 6 ½ In. 460.00
Betty The Dancing Doll, Tin, Windup, Lindstrom, Box, 8 In. 207.00
Bicycles that are large enough to ride are listed in their own category.
Billiard Player, Shoots Pool, Tin, Windup, Kico Co., Germany, 1920s, 6 In. 350.00
Bird, Head Turns, Wings Flap, Tail Bobs, Tin, Windup, Germany, 4 ¾ In. 80.00
Bird, In Cage, Tin, Windup, Germany, 8 ½ In. 230.00
Bird, On Branch, Chirps, Moves, Painted, Windup, Germany, 7 In. 575.00
Bird, Pip-Squeak, Attached Feather Tail, Bellows, Painted, Papier-Mache, 5 ½ In. 118.00
Bison, Wood, Jointed, Cloth Mane, Glass Eyes, Leather Ears, Tail, Schoenhut, 8 In. 144.00
Black, 2 Dancing Boys, Worn Clothing, Oak Base, Windup, Key, 6 x 10 In. 944.00
Black, Alabama Coon Jigger, Tombo, Green & Yellow Jacket, Strauss, Box, 10 In. 509.00
Black, Dapper Dan Carter's Coon Jigger, Red & White Checkered Jacket, Box, c.1922, 10 In. ... 565.00
Black, Marionette, Man, Paper, Composition, Wood Arms, Legs, Carved Hands, Feet, 45 x 19 In. 44.00
Black, Porter, Tin Lithograph, Windup, Distler, 7 ½ In. 489.00
Black Child, Pushes Baby Carriage, Hinged Legs, Composition, Pull Toy, 1930s, 9 x 11 In. ... 431.00
Black Man, In Rocker, Embossed, Tin Lithograph, Penny Toy, Germany, 2 In. 375.00
Black Man, Riding Log, Hand Lowers To Ring Bell, Pull Toy, 5 ½ x 6 ¼ In. 345.00
Blacksmith Bear, Heats Up Horseshoe, Eyes Light, Bell Rings, Battery Operated, Box, Japan, 9 In. 282.00
Blimp, Los Angeles, Green Paint, Gold Fins, Nickel Plated Wheels, Cast Iron, Kenton, 7 ½ In. .. 403.00
Blimp, Pony, Blue, Nickel Wheels, Kenton, 5 ½ In. 450.00
Blinky The Clown, Drum, Walks, Eyes Light, Remote Contol, Battery Operated, Amico, Box, 13 In. 204.00
Blinky The Clown, Xylophone, Walks, Eyes Light, Remote, Battery Operated, Amico, Box, 13 In. 204.00
Blocks, ABC, Pictures, Graduated, Paper Lithograph, Wood, 2 ⅞ To 3 ⅜ In., 5 Piece 110.00
Blocks, Alphabet, Wood, Stamped, Multicolored, Victorian, 8 x 9 ⅜ In. 575.00
Blocks, Eagle, Richters, Wood, 3 Colors, Pat. March 1900, Box, 10 ¼ x 8 In. 198.00
Blocks, Fire Engines, Horse Drawn, Paper Lithograph, Cardboard, Box, 9 To 12 ½ In. 1495.00
Blocks, Letters, Bittersweet, Cream, Painted, Wood, Slide Lid Box, 1 x 6 x 6 In. .... *illus* 385.00
Blocks, Wood, Letters, Painted Bittersweet, Cream, Wood Slide Lid Box, 1 ¼ x 6 In. 385.00

Toy, Balky Mule, Clown Driver, Tin Lithograph, Clockwork, Lehmann, Box, 8 In.
$440.00

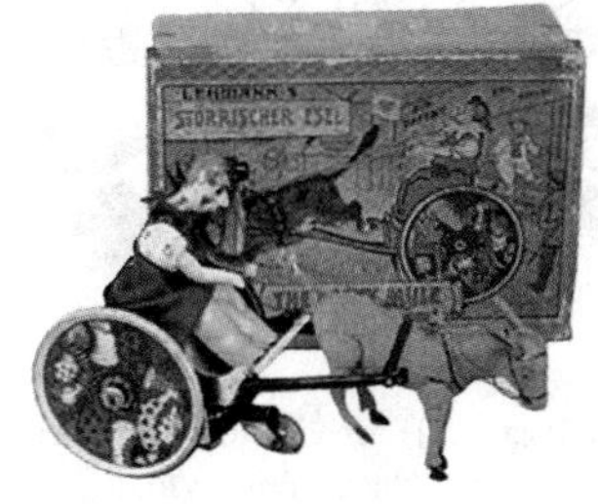

Toy, Bell Toy, Gong, Kneeling Figure, Flag, Cast Iron, Tin, Pull Toy, c.1880, 6 In.
$13800.00

Toy, Bell Toy, Gong, Wild Mule Jack, Painted, Cast Iron, Pull Toy, 8 In.
$1150.00

TIP

To remove an unwanted gummed price sticker, try heating it with a hair dryer. The glue will melt a bit, and it will be easier to peel off the sticker.

As always, the edited listings in *Kovels' Antiques & Collectibles Price Guide 2010* aren't available on any website, but readers should visit Kovels.com for information on trends, tips, reproductions, marks, old prices, and more!

Toy, Blocks, Letters, Bittersweet, Cream, Painted, Wood, Slide Lid Box, 1 x 6 x 6 In.
$385.00

Toy, Boat, PT 21, Wood, Battery Operated, Marked, Tmy. Eductio, Box, 18 In.
$395.00

Toy, Boy, On Tricycle, Heinie Irish Mail, Tin, Windup, Germany, 6 In.
$300.00

TIP

If you have a battery-operated 1940s toy such as "Smoking Grandpa," you might want to replenish the smoke-maker when it wears out. Just put a few drops of sewing machine oil into the smoking tube. An electric spark in the toy causes the oil to smoke, and allows the toy to seem to puff on a cigarette, pipe, or cigar.

Boat, 2 Passengers, Painted, Tin, Lead, Penny Toy, Meier, 4 ¾ In. . . . 405.00
Boat, Battleship, Gray, 2-Tone Hull, Brown Deck, Turrets, Masts, 3 Stacks, Bing, 28 In. . . . 6325.00
Boat, Cabin Cruiser, Railed Deck, 2 Stacks, Painted, Tin Lithograph, Windup, Bing, 13 ½ In. . . 2185.00
Boat, Cannon, Fires Caps, Turns, Windup, Kasuga, Bing, 19 In. . . . 2588.00
Boat, Cannon, Searchlight, Tin Lithograph, Steam, 9 ½ In. . . . 77.00
Boat, Liberty Liner, Wood, Blue Hull, Tin Lithograph Cabin, Wire Railed Sides, 27 In. . . . 3163.00
Boat, Luxury Liner, Tin, Friction, Marx, U.S.A., 14 ½ In. . . . 195.00
Boat, Ocean Liner, Black Hull, White Cabin, Tin, Windup, Tucher & Walther, Germany, 24 In. 374.00
Boat, Ocean Liner, Red, White, Tin, Germany, Marked, BW, Bing, 13 In. . . . 1430.00
Boat, Ocean Liner, Red & Blue Hull, White Deck, Lifeboats, 2 Stacks, Windup, Arnold, 13 In. . 374.00
Boat, Ocean Liner, Tin Lithograph, Penny Toy, Fischer, 4 ½ In. . . . 135.00
Boat, Peggy Jane Motorboat, Yellow, Red, White, Blue, Tin, Windup, Chein, 14 In. . . . 55.00
Boat, PT 21, Wood, Battery Operated, Marked, Tmy. Eductio, Box, 18 In. . . . *illus* 395.00
Boat, Riverboat, Puritan, Painted, Cast Iron, Wilkins, 10 ½ In. . . . 495.00
Boat, Rowboat, 3 Men, Rocking Action, Embossed, Tin Lithograph, Penny Toy, Meier, 3 ½ In. 825.00
Boat, Sidewheeler, Puritan, Painted, Cast Iron, Wilkiens, 10 ½ In. . . . 275.00
Boat, Speedboat, Bowman, White, Red, Open Deck, Steam Boiler, Wood Hull, Box, 18 ½ In. . . 805.00
Boat, Speedboat, Dragon, Tin, Japan, 8 In. . . . 95.00
Boat, Speedboat, Red Hull, White Deck, Pressed Steel, Windup, Stand, Lionel, 16 ¼ In. . . . 258.00
Boat, Steamboat, Paddlewheel, Wilkins, 6 In. . . . 250.00
Boat, Steamship, Blue, White, Tin Lithograph, Windup, Schuco, Box, 12 ½ In. . . . 180.00
Boat, Steamship, Double Paddlewheel, City Of Baltimore, Windup, 19th Century, 42 In. . . . 4600.00
Boat, Wood, Motor, Oars, Windup, Wood Stand, 21 In. . . . 288.00
Bowling Set, 2 Balls, 8 Turned Pins, Painted, Bittersweet, Orange, Black, Wood, 10-In. Pins . 275.00
Boxcar, Budweiser, Bing Miniature Railway System, Tin, 7 In. . . . 2550.00
Boxers, Red & Blue Trunks, Celluloid, Tin, Windup, Japan, Box, 8 In. . . . 220.00
Boxing, Rap & Tap, Tin, Windup, Unique Art, 5 ½ In. . . . 150.00
Boy, Big Head, Butterfly, Head Sways, Mouth & Eyes Change, Celluloid, Tin, Windup, 9 ½ In. . 770.00
Boy, Feeding Chicken, Tin, Windup, Toyodo & Co., Japan, Prewar, 7 In. . . . 460.00
Boy, Feeding Dog, Embossed, Tin Lithograph, Lever, Penny Toy, Meier, 3 ¾ In. . . . 189.00
Boy, In Bed, Musical, Windup, Boy Sits Up, Mechanical, Heubach, 9 ½ x 6 ½ In. . . . 1035.00
Boy, On Donkey, Celluloid, Tin, Windup, 7 ½ In. . . . 80.00
Boy, On Rocker, Embossed, Tin Lithograph, Penny Toy, Meier, 2 ½ In. . . . 295.00
Boy, On Scooter, Celluloid, Tin, Windup, Japan, 7 ½ In. . . . 450.00
Boy, On Sled, Celluloid, Tin, Japan, 3 ¼ In. . . . 66.00
Boy, On Sled, Cloth, Tin, Windup, Japan, 3 ½ x 6 ½ In. . . . 80.00
Boy, On Sled, Hill Climber, Painted, Pressed Steel, 9 In. . . . 220.00
Boy, On Stick Horse, Celluloid, Windup, Japan, Box, 7 ½ In. . . . 300.00
Boy, On Tricycle, Bisque Head, Painted, Carton Body, Wood Arms, Vichy, c.1860, 8 In. . . . 2100.00
Boy, On Tricycle, Heinie Irish Mail, Tin, Windup, Germany, 6 In. . . . *illus* 300.00
Boy, Playing Violin, Green Hat, Schuco, 5 ½ In. . . . 110.00
Boy, Riding Scooter, 3-Wheel, Tin Lithograph, Windup, Fischer, 7 In. . . . 690.00
Bubbles Washing Bear, Moves Back & Forth, Battery Operated, Yonezawa, Box, 8 In. . . . 186.00
Bucky Burro, Wood, Plastic Ears, No. 166, Fisher-Price, c.1955, 12 ½ In. . . . 403.00
Buffalo, Glass Eyes, Brown Paint, Wood, Jointed, Leather Horns, Rope Tail, Schoenhut, 8 In. . 316.00
Buffalo, Painted Eyes, Schoenhut, 7 In. . . . 295.00 to 350.00
Bugle Boy, On Horse, Embossed, Tin Lithograph, Penny Toy, Meier, 3 In. . . . 475.00
Bugs Bunny, Stuffed, Pressed Canvas Face, Gray, Red, Holding Carrot, M & H Novelty, 22 In. . 144.00
Building Set, Grid & Panel, Kenner, Box, 13 ½ x 17 ½ In. . . . 15.00
Bulldog, Painted Eyes, Wood Jointed, Leather Tail, Ears, Collar, Schoenhut, 5 ½ In. . . . 1380.00
Bulldog, Papier-Mache, Flocked, Horsehair Collar, Chain, Wheels, c.1885, 19 In. . . . 1725.00
Bulldozer, Driver, Piston Action, Lights, Battery Operated, Friction, Box, Japan, 7 ½ In. . . . 150.00
Bulldozer, Driver, Red, Tractor, Diesel, Rubber Treads, Cast Iron, Arcade, 8 In. . . . 978.00
Bulldozer, Metal, Hubley, c.1950, 10 ½ In. . . . 135.00
Bulldozer, Yellow, No. 2012, Doepke, c.1953, 15 In. . . . 395.00
Burger Chef, Dog Sways Back & Forth, Oven Lights, Battery Operated, Yonezawa, Box, 11 In. 135.00
Burro, Glass Eyes, Wood, Jointed, Painted, Gray, White, Rope Tail, Schoenhut, 6 ½ In. . . . 115.00
Bus, All State Express, Rubber Roof, Warning Lights, Modern Toys, Japan, 1950s, 8 ½ In. . . . 150.00
Bus, Army, Tin, Friction, Japan, c.1950, 8 ½ In. . . . 120.00
Bus, Atlanta Coach Company, Arcade, 12 In. . . . 1700.00
Bus, Blue, Red, Pressed Steel, Cor-Cor, 1926, 24 In. . . . 395.00
Bus, Blue, White Rubber Tires, Barclay, 3 In. . . . 65.00
Bus, Circus, Tin, Battery Operated, Japan, c.1950, 15 In. . . . 295.00
Bus, Coast To Coast, Packard Front Cab, Blue, Pressed Steel, Keystone, c.1938, 32 In. . . . 1840.00
Bus, Coast To Coast, Painted, Cast Iron, Hubley, 10 In. . . . 200.00
Bus, D.C. Transit, Air Conditioned, Japan, 17 In. . . . 195.00
Bus, Double-Decker, Arcade, c.1926, 13 ½ In. . . . 2250.00

Bus, Double-Decker, Buying British National Service, Tin, Windup, Wells, 7 x 3 ½ In. 77.00
Bus, Double-Decker, Drink Ovaltine, Painted, Tin, Windup, Minic, 7 ¼ In. 135.00
Bus, Double-Decker, Driver, Green, Yellow, Cast Iron, Kenton, 8 In. .... *illus* 1045.00
Bus, Double-Decker, Green, Gold Trim, Arcade, c.1940, 8 In. 750.00
Bus, Double-Decker, Mobil Gas, Tin, Friction, Japan, c.1950, 8 In. 95.00
Bus, Double-Decker, Nickel Plated Driver, Rubber Tires, Cast Iron, Arcade, 8 In.. .... 460.00
Bus, Double-Decker, Painted, Barclay B 34, 4 In. 85.00
Bus, Double-Decker, Spiral Staircase, Brown, Yellow, Tin, Windup, Lehmann, 8 In. 2588.00
Bus, Double-Decker, Tin Lithoroute, Ads, Wells-Brimtoy, 1950s 75.00
Bus, Double-Decker, World Service, Thanks For Buying British, Windup, 6 ¾ In. 90.00
Bus, Driver, Spare Tire, Bumper, Headlights, Tin, Windup, Girard, 14 In.. .... 403.00
Bus, Green, White Rubber Tires, Barclay, 3 In. 65.00
Bus, Greyhound, Pressed Steel, Rubber Tires, Windup, Buddy L, c.1938, 16 In. ... 173.00 to 345.00
Bus, Greyhound, Scenic Cruiser, Tootsietoy, Box, 7 In.. .... 225.00
Bus, Ice Cream, Tin, Friction, Japan, 1950s, 9 In.. .... 195.00
Bus, Jackie Gleason, 8 Characters, Blue, Red, White, Tin Lithograph, Push 'N' Go, Wolverine, 14 In. 405.00
Bus, Jitney, Green, Yellow, Driver, Tin Lithograph, Windup, Strauss, 9 ¼ In. 1495.00
Bus, Junior, Yellow, Red, Green, Curtains, Tin Lithograph, Windup, Chein, 10 In.. .... 403.00
Bus, Lake Shoreline, Fageol, Arcade, 12 In. 2000.00
Bus, Molic, Bisquit Tin Lithograph, G. DeAndreis Et Cie, France, 12 In. 460.00
Bus, Nite Coach, Pickwick, Blue, Orange Stripe, Cast Silver Wheels, Cast Iron, Kenton, 11 In.. 1035.00
Bus, No Driver, Green, Gold, Cast Iron, Arcade, 6 In. .... *illus* 518.00
Bus, Robot, No. 300, Red, Yellow, Tin Lithograph, Windup, Woodhaven, 14 In. 165.00
Bus, Royal Blue Line, Hercules, Gray, Red Hood, Black Running Boards, Chein, c.1927, 18 In. 1610.00
Bus, Royal Bus Line, Tin, Windup, Marx, 10 In. 460.00
Bus, School, Tin, Friction, Japan, 1950s, 9 In. 175.00
Bus, Space Robots, Astronauts, Rockets, Spaceships, Tin, Friction, Usagiya, Miura, 15 In. 524.00
Bus, Turnabout, Headlights, Battery Operated, Japan, Box, 14 In. 345.00
Bus, Twin Coach, Cast Iron, Kenton, 8 ½ In. 250.00
Bus, Wayne School, Orange, Black Trim, Red Interior, Wheels, Black Tires, 1961-64, 2 Piece . 150.00
Bus Terminal, Greyhound, Buses, Waiting Room, Tin Lithograph, Marx, 16 ½ In. ...... *illus* 660.00
Busy Bridge, Tin Lithograph, Windup, Marx, 24 In. 160.00
Butcher Shop, 3-Sided, Counter, Accessories, Painted, Gray, Blue Trim, France, 10 x 20 In... 920.00
Butter & Egg Man, Tin Lithograph, Louis Marx & Co., c.1930, 7 ¾ In.. .... 480.00
Buttercup & Spareribs, Pull Toy, Tin Lithograph, Nifty, 7 ½ In.. .... 440.00
Button, Official Green Hornet Agent, Greenway Prod., ABC TV Logo, 1966, 4 In. 50.00
Cable Car, No. 303, Tin, Windup, Technofix, Germany, Box, 5 ¾ x 18 ½ x 8 In. 210.00
Calliope, Driver, Musician, Cast Iron, Kenton, 9 In.. .... 1250.00
Calypso Joe, Drummer, Moves Back & Forth, Tin, Windup, T.P.S., Box, 5 ½ In.. .... 328.00
Calypso Joe, Walker, Eyes Light-Up, Plays Drum, Battery Operated, Linemar, Box, 11 In. 418.00
Camel, Stuffed, Steiff, Germany, 23 x 29 x 8 In. 70.00
Camera, On Tripod, Gold, Red, Simulated Negative, Penny Toy, Germany, 4 ¼ In. 690.00
Cannon, Big-Bang Celebrations, Painted, Cast Iron, Conestoga Corp., Box, 9 In. 82.00
Cannon, Red Wheels, Painted, Cast Iron, 5 In.. .... 27.00
Cannon, Swamp Angel, Cast Iron, Kenton, 5 ½ In. 66.00
Cannon, Young American, Rapid Fire, Painted Black, Red Spoke Wheels, Cast Iron, c.1907, 15 In. 230.00
Canoe, Li'l Abner & Lonesome Polecat, Plastic, Windup, Ideal, Box, 1951 .... 485.00
Canteen, Mobile, Refreshment, Cream, Blue, Matchbox, 1959 .... 633.00
Cap Gun, Al Capone, Mini, Playset, 1940s, 10 ½ In.. .... 95.00
Cap Gun, Bulldog, Cast Iron, 6 In. 20.00
Cap Gun, Flat Pan, Cast Iron, Late 19th Century, 3 ¼ In. 40.00
Cap Gun, Flowers, Scrolls, Cast Iron, Late 19th Century, 5 In. 70.00
Cap Gun, Grit, Cast Iron, Pat. Mar. 22, 1887, 3 ¼ In.. .... 60.00
Cap Gun, Leather Holster, Cast Iron, 3 ¾ In. 38.00
Cap Gun, Lightning Express, Cast Iron, Kenton, 5 In. 143.00
Cap Gun, Monkey & Coconut, Painted, Cast Iron, Stevens, 4 ½ In. .... *illus* 715.00
Captain Video, Vehicle Set, 4 Supersonic Spaceships, Lido Toy Co., Box, 6 x 8 In. 350.00
Car, 3 Wheels, Driver, Rubber Tires, Painted, Tin, Spring Windup, Germany, 5 In. 1540.00
Car, Andy Gump, Red, Green, White Trim, Cast Iron, Nickel, Arcade, c.1923, 7 In. 1093.00
Car, Armored, Cannon, Distler, Germany, Penny Toy 325.00
Car, Armored, Spoke Wheels, Painted, Pressed Steel, Friction, Dayton, c.1911, 10 ½ In. 259.00
Car, Armored, Tin Lithograph, Windup, Japan, c.1950, 4 In. 115.00
Car, Army, Driver, Tin, Windup, England, c.1940, 14 In. 395.00
Car, Aston Martin, Driver, White, 20, No. 110, Dinky Toys, Box 140.00
Car, Atom, White Helmeted Driver, Green, Chrome Trim, Yonezawa, 16 In. 2825.00
Car, Auto Dump, Red, Black, Tilted Body, Pressed Steel, Cast Iron, Structo, 18 In.. .... 460.00
Car, Beatnik Bandit, Purple, Redline, Matchbox, 1968. .... 35.00

Battery-operated Toys
Battery-operated toys were possible after C and D batteries became easily available after World War II. Many of the toys were made in Japan after the war, often using tin from discarded American drink cans left by soldiers.

Toy, Bus, Double-Decker, Driver, Green, Yellow, Cast Iron, Kenton, 8 In.
$1045.00

Toy, Bus, No Driver, Green, Gold, Cast Iron, Arcade, 6 In.
$518.00

Toy, Bus Terminal, Greyhound, Buses, Waiting Room, Tin Lithograph, Marx, 16 ½ In.
$660.00

Toy, Cap Gun, Monkey & Coconut, Painted, Cast Iron, Stevens, 4 ½ In.
$715.00

Toy, Car, Buick, Deluxe Sedan, Driver, Cast Iron, Nickel Plated, Arcade, 1927, 8 In.
$4950.00

Toy, Car, Cadillac, Coupe, 1929 Model, Driver, Luggage Rack, Windup, Marx, 12 ½ In.
$550.00

Toy, Car, Chrysler, Airflow, Rose, Cast Iron, Hubley, Box, 7 ¾ In.
$3162.00

Toy, Car, Coupe, Pressed Steel, Friction, Dayton, c.1925, 13 In.
$345.00

TIP

Light your yard so that some of the lights face the garage door and light up the entrances to the house. Put the lights high enough to be out of easy reach.

Car, BMW, Isetta, Red, White, Tin, Friction, Japan, 6 ½ In. . . . 185.00
Car, Bouncing Benny, Safety Car, Metal, Wood Wheels, Pull Toy, Marx, 7 In. . . . 175.00
Car, Buick, Deluxe Sedan, Driver, Cast Iron, Nickel Plated, Arcade, 1927, 8 In. . . . *illus* 4950.00
Car, Buick, Tin, Friction, Bandai, Japan, c.1958, 8 ½ In. . . . 175.00
Car, Cabrio Super, Driver, Red, Convertible, Tin Plated, Friction, Kellerman, Box, 9 In. . . . 575.00
Car, Cadillac, Coupe, 1929 Model, Driver, Luggage Rack, Windup, Marx, 12 ½ In. . . . *illus* 550.00
Car, Cadillac, Coupe DeVille, Steerable Wheels, Battery Operated, K Co., Japan, 1955, 7 ½ In. . . . 75.00
Car, Cadillac, Electricmobile, 1950 Model, Lights, Blue, Battery Operated, Box, Japan, 13 In. . . . 3738.00
Car, Cadillac, Jet Black, Red Upholstery, Friction, 1950s, 11 In. . . . 95.00
Car, Cadillac, Police, Japan, 1962, 25 In. . . . 295.00
Car, Cadillac, Tin, Friction, Dandai, Japan, Box, c.1960, 11 In. . . . 403.00
Car, Cadillac, Tin, Friction, Japan, 1950s, 9 ½ In. . . . 245.00
Car, Champion Racer, 301, Engine Noise, Battery Operated, Modern Toys, Japan, Box, 1960s, 18 In. . . . 460.00
Car, Chevrolet, Corvette, Hardtop, White, Red Interior, Friction, 1953, 10 In. . . . 95.00
Car, Chevrolet, Coupe, 1920s Model, Driver, License Plate, Spare Tire, Gray, Cast Iron, Arcade, 8 In. . . . 863.00
Car, Chevrolet, Coupe, 1929 Model, Arcade, 8 ¼ In. . . . 900.00
Car, Chevrolet, Coupe, 1930s Model, Enameled, Black & Gray, Arcade, 8 ½ In. . . . 546.00
Car, Chevrolet, Impala, Blue, White Top, No. 57B3, Matchbox, Box . . . 120.00
Car, Chevrolet, LaSalle Land Cruiser, Red, Wyandotte, c.1936, 15 In. . . . 395.00
Car, Chevrolet, Red, Japan, Box, 13 In. . . . 395.00
Car, Chevrolet, Sedan, Blue, Tan, No. 6024, Tootsietoy . . . 30.00
Car, Chevrolet, Sedan, Double Stripe, c.1930, 8 ¼ In. . . . 1250.00
Car, Chevrolet, Sedan, Stripe, Arcade, c.1929 . . . 1050.00
Car, Chevrolet, Tin, Friction, Japan, 1956, 10 In. . . . 175.00
Car, Chevrolet, Tin, Windup, Occupied Japan, 1948, 5 In. . . . 55.00
Car, Chrysler, Airflow, Rose, Cast Iron, Hubley, Box, 7 ¾ In. . . . *illus* 3162.00
Car, Chrysler, Coupe, Convertible, Driver, Tin, Friction, Japan, 1954, 10 In. . . . 475.00
Car, Chrysler, Tin, Friction, Japan, 1954, 12 In. . . . 375.00
Car, Circus, Driver, Tin, Windup, 1950s, 3 In. . . . 120.00
Car, Circus, Metal, Windup, 1930s, 7 In. . . . 95.00
Car, Citroen, DS-19, Tin, Friction, Plastic Windshields, Bandai, Box, Japan, 12 In. . . . 403.00
Car, Citroen, Tin, Friction, Japan, 1950s, 8 ¼ In. . . . 195.00
Car, Citroen 2 GV, Noise, Tin, Friction, Japan, 1950, 8 ½ In. . . . 195.00
Car, Coast To Coast, Green, Windup, Marx, 6 In. . . . 175.00
Car, Convertible, Celluloid Windshield, Tin Lithograph, Windup, Lehmann, 9 ½ In. . . . 1035.00
Car, Coo Coo, Tin Lithograph, Plastic, Windup, Marx, 8 ½ In. . . . 195.00
Car, Corvair, Hub Caps, Tin, Friction, Japan, 1958, 9 In. . . . 175.00
Car, Corvette 8, Racing, Orange, Red, White, Tin, Friction, Bandai, Box, 1962 . . . 325.00
Car, Coupe, Black, Die Cast, Tin Lithograph Chassis, Kiddie Toy, Hubley, 5 ½ In. . . . 65.00
Car, Coupe, Blue, Red, Lights, Rubber Tires, Electric, Marx, Box, 14 In. . . . 4888.00
Car, Coupe, Blue, Silver, Dummy Lights, Grille, Bumper, Tin Lithograph, 12 In. . . . 374.00
Car, Coupe, Convertible, Tin, Friction, Japan, 1950s, 10 In. . . . 475.00
Car, Coupe, Convertible, Tin, Friction, San Francisco, Japan, 1950s, 6 ½ In. . . . 95.00
Car, Coupe, Driver, Light Blue, Black Roof, Spoked Rims, Cast Iron, Arcade, 8 ½ In. . . . 2875.00
Car, Coupe, Green, Yellow, White, Cast Iron, Hubley, 5 In. . . . 275.00
Car, Coupe, Headlights, Rubber Tires, Pressed Steel, Battery Operated, Girard, 14 In. . . . 230.00
Car, Coupe, Nickel Driver, Red, Gold Trim Lights, Cast Iron, Hubley, 9 In. . . . 1265.00
Car, Coupe, Pressed Steel, Friction, Dayton, c.1925, 13 In. . . . *illus* 345.00
Car, Coupe, Red, Black, Tin, Windup, Chad Valley, Box, 10 In. . . . 88.00
Car, Coupe, Red, Tin Rumble Seat, Nickel Spoke Wheels, Cast Iron, Arcade, 6 In. . . . 713.00
Car, Coupe, Red, Yellow, Sun Rubber, 4 In. . . . 35.00
Car, Coupe, Reversible, Blue, Rubber Bumpers, Tin, Windup, Marx, 16 In. . . . 460.00
Car, Coupe, Rumble Seat, Green, Arcade, 6 In. . . . 300.00
Car, Coupe, Ubilda, Metal Kit, England, 1930s, 9 In. . . . 375.00
Car, Crazy, Rodeo Joe, Unique Art, 1950s, 15 In. . . . 195.00
Car, Dan Dipsy, Crazy, Head Bobs, Tin, Windup, Marx, Box, 6 In. . . . 237.00
Car, Delivery, City Meat Market, Tin, Windup, Courtland, USA, 1948, 7 In. . . . 75.00
Car, DeSoto, Painted, Kingsbury, 12 In. . . . 250.00
Car, Detailed Coach, Driver, Bench Seat, Windup, Lehmann, Germany, 5 In. . . . 503.00
Car, Dizzie Lizzie, Sedan, Leaping, Windup, Strauss, 8 In. . . . 350.00
Car, Dodge 'Em, Red, 2 Figures, Rubber Surround, Tin Plate Bumper, Buffalo Toys, 10 In. . . . 690.00
Car, Dora Dipsy, Crazy, Head Bobs, Tin, Windup, Marx, Box, 6 In. . . . 238.00
Car, Driver, Red, Green, Yellow, Tin, Windup, Chein, c.1928, 9 In. . . . 316.00
Car, Edsel, Tin, Friction, Japan, 13 ½ In. . . . 125.00
Car, Electromobile, Lights, Battery Operated, Japan, 1950s, 8 ½ In. . . . 145.00
Car, Ferrari, Racer, Driver, Blue, No. 234, Dinky Toys, Box . . . 100.00
Car, Ferrari, Tin, Friction, Bandai, Japan, c.1950, 8 ½ In. . . . 95.00

Car, Fiat, Red, Luggage On Roof, No. 56B3, Matchbox, Box 60.00
Car, Fiat 600, Tin, Friction, Japan, 1950s, 7 In. 145.00
Car, Fire Chief, Electric Lights, Red, Yellow Stenciling, Pressed Steel, Windup, Marx, 15 In. . . . 460.00
Car, Fire Chief, Red, White, Courtland, Box, 7 In. 165.00
Car, Fire Chief, Siren, Battery Operated Headlights, Pressed Steel, Hoge, Box, 14 In. . . . . . *illus* 1380.00
Car, Fire Department, Pressed Steel, Self-Winding Zephyr Motor, Wyandotte, 13 In. 805.00
Car, Flivver, Driver's Head Spins, Tin, Windup, Marx, Box, 1926, 7 In. 904.00
Car, Ford, 2-Tone, Gold Plated Trim, Tin, Friction, Occupied Japan, 1949, 4 In. 70.00
Car, Ford, Convertible, 1957 Model, Crank Top, Tin, Friction, 10 ½ In. 295.00
Car, Ford, Coupe, 1934 Model, Rumble Seat, Yellow, Cast Iron, Nickel Grille, Arcade, 6 ½ In. . . 1150.00
Car, Ford, Coupe, Tin, Friction, Japan, 1957, 12 In. 295.00
Car, Ford, Coupe, Tin, Friction, Japan, 7 In. 75.00
Car, Ford, Fairlane, 1958 Model, Japan, 10 In. 195.00
Car, Ford, Fairlane, Station Wagon, Standard Fresh Coffee, Black, Yellow Roof, Bandai, c.1955, 12 In. 863.00
Car, Ford, Lotus, Lights, Battery Operated, Japan, c.1960, 15 ½ In. 175.00
Car, Ford, Model T, Coupe, Black, Gold Stripe, Arcade, 6 ½ In. 650.00
Car, Ford, Model T, Coupe, Driver, Black, High Top, Tulip Body, Arcade, 6 ½ In. 425.00
Car, Ford, Model T, Coupe, Driver, Gray, Nickel Wheels, Kilgore, 6 ½ In. 500.00
Car, Ford, Model T, Coupe, Yellow, Nickel Wheels, A.C. Williams, 5 In. 325.00
Car, Ford, Model T, Driver, Black, Simulated Soft Top, Windup, c.1920, 6 ½ In. 978.00
Car, Ford, Model T, Go-Kart Style, Vinyl Seat, Spoke Wheels, Metal, 1960-70, 72 x 34 x 36 In. . 920.00
Car, Ford, Model T, Touring, Arcade, 6 ½ In. 450.00
Car, Ford, Open Top, Tin, Crank, Friction, Japan, 1959, 10 ½ In. 275.00
Car, Ford, Police, Undercover, Lights, Japan, 1954, 10 ½ In. 145.00
Car, Ford, Rambler, 1960 Model, Maroon & White, Friction, Bandai, Japan, 11 In. 86.00
Car, Ford, Ranchero, 1957 Model, Tin Lithograph, Friction, Bandai, Japan, 11 ½ In. 173.00
Car, Ford, Roadster, 1935 Model, Blue, White Top, Nickel Grille, Box, 4 ¾ In. 295.00
Car, Ford, Sedan, 1940 Model, Delivery Ambulance, Nutmeg, 9 In. 135.00
Car, Ford, Sedan, Fordson, Painted, Cast Iron, Arcade, 1927, 6 ½ In. 77.00
Car, Ford, SW, Back Door Opens, Japan, 1957, 7 ½ In. 110.00
Car, Ford, Thunderbird, Blue, Classic 57, Matchbox 99.00
Car, Ford, Thunderbird, Convertible, Battery Operated, TM, Japan, 1956, 11 In. 135.00
Car, Ford, Thunderbird, Dual Landau Arms, Red, Cream, Friction, 1963, 10 ¾ In. 95.00
Car, Ford, Tin, Friction, Japan, 1954, 10 In. 245.00
Car, Ford, Woody S.W., Tin, Friction, Japan, 1958, 8 In. 275.00
Car, Giant King Racer, Driver, No. 711, Tin, Windup, Marx, 12 ½ In. 628.00
Car, Graham, Blue Streak, Hood Ornament, Tin, Windup, 11 ½ In. 1695.00
Car, Green Hornet, Black Beauty, Die Cast, Corgi, 1966, 5 In. 363.00
Car, Hairy Hauler, Yellow, Redline, Matchbox, 1971 . . . . 25.00
Car, Hi-Way Henry, Wash Line, Stove, Tin, Windup, Oscar Hitt, Germany, 9 In. . . . . *illus* 2300.00
Car, Hot Rod, Flat Head, V8 Motor, Tin, Friction, Japan, 9 In. 175.00
Car, Hudson, Plastic, c.1949, 12 In. 748.00
Car, Jaguar, Blue, Japan, 9 ½ In. 185.00
Car, Jaguar, Red, XK-140, No. 32A3, Matchbox, Box 50.00
Car, Jaguar, Tin, Friction, Cragstan, Japan, 8 ½ In. 95.00
Car, Jaguar, XK 120, No. 157, Dinky Toys, 1950s 115.00
Car, Jaguar, XK-120, Doepke, 1955, 18 In. 425.00
Car, Jet Racer, J.T.T., Open Wheel, Lithograph, Paper Label, TN, Japan, Box, 12 In. 690.00
Car, Jolly Joe, Army, Big Headed Man, Machine Gun, Tin Lithograph, Windup, Marx, 5 ¾ In. . 207.00
Car, Kit, Lightronic Solar Cell, Battery Operated, Plastic, c.1964, 11 In. 125.00
Car, Lamborghini, Miura, Doors Open, Yellow, No. 33C1, Matchbox, Box 230.00
Car, Leaping Lena, Driver, Tin, Windup, Marx, 7 In. 71.00
Car, Limousine, Burnett, Driver, Blue, Black Roof, Tin Lithograph, Windup, 8 In. 431.00
Car, Limousine, Doors Open, Turn Signals, Green, Black, Tin, Windup, Bing, 1920s, 11 In. . . . 1322.00
Car, Limousine, Driver, Glass Windows, Tin Lithograph, Windup, Carette, c.1914, 14 In. 2875.00
Car, Limousine, Driver, Gray, Black, Tin Lithograph, Fisher, 8 In. 165.00
Car, Limousine, Driver, Hessmobile, Green, Orange Trim, Tin Lithograph, 7 ¾ In. 690.00
Car, Limousine, Driver, Orange, Friction, Clark, 6 ½ x 13 ¼ x 4 In. 330.00
Car, Limousine, Driver, Red, Black, Gold Highlights, Tin Lithograph, Carette, 5 ½ x 9 In. 1870.00
Car, Limousine, Driver, Wearing Eagle Band, Tin Lithograph, Windup, Karl Bub, Germany, 14 In. 1610.00
Car, Limousine, Driver, Windup, Karl Bub, 1920s, 11 In. 1150.00
Car, Limousine, Glass Windows, Headlights, Lamps, Tin Tires, 15 In. 1265.00
Car, Limousine, Green, Brake Lever, Disc Wheels, Tin Lithograph, Windup, Tippco, 10 In. 633.00
Car, Limousine, Orange, Tin, Windup, Mettoy, 9 In. 99.00
Car, Limousine, Red, Black Fenders, Graphic Passengers, Windup, Chad Valley, 9 In. 518.00
Car, Limousine, Yellow, Black Roof, Electric Lights, Tin Lithograph, Distler, 9 ¾ In. 1495.00
Car, Limping Lizzie, Tin Lithograph, Windup, Marx, Box, 7 In. 374.00

TIP
Wear cotton gloves when cleaning any type of metal. Oils in the skin will leave a mark.

Toy, Car, Fire Chief, Siren, Battery Operated Headlights, Pressed Steel, Hoge, Box, 14 In.
$1380.00

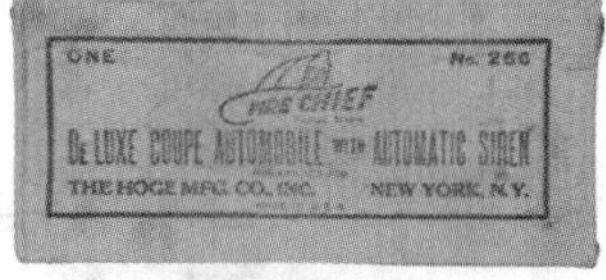

Toy, Car, Hi-Way Henry, Wash Line, Stove, Tin, Windup, Oscar Hitt, Germany, 9 In.
$2300.00

Toy, Car, Milton Berle, Tin Lithograph, White Hat, Windup, Marx, Box, 6 In.
$420.00

Toy, Car, OHO, Driver, Tin Lithograph, Clockwork, Lehmann, 4 In.
$330.00

Toy, Car, Police, Siren, No. 1, First Precinct, Pressed Steel, Battery Operated, Marx, 14 In.
$518.00

TIP

Restoration of an old dollhouse should be restrained. Wash it, repair the structural problems, repaint as little as possible, and redecorate with appropriate old wallpaper fabrics and paint colors.

Toy. Car, Station Wagon, No. 234, Cardboard Insert, Fisher-Price, Box, c.1960, 13 In.
$288.00

Car, Lincoln, 1956 Model, Barking Dog, Red, Friction, Ichiko, 7 ½ In. 185.00
Car, Lincoln, Coupe, 1954 Model, Dog Comes Out Window, Tin, Friction, Japan, 8 In. 145.00
Car, Magnette, Mark III, Convertible, Blue, Light Blue, Tin Lithograph, Wrapper, Bandai, 8 ½ In. 625.00
Car, Mercedes-Benz, Sedan, Tin, Friction, Japan, 8 ¼ In. 110.00
Car, Mercedes-Benz 300SL, Tin, Friction, Cragstan, Japan, 8 ½ In. 145.00
Car, Messerschmitt, TG5000, Convertible, 4-Wheel Tiger, Tin, Friction, Bandai, Box, 8 In. 356.00
Car, MG, 1500, Marmande, Spyder, Red, Convertible, Resin, 3 ¼ In. 800.00
Car, MG, TD, Sports, Cream, Metal Wheels, Matchbox, 1956 . . . . . 45.00
Car, MG, Ventura, Racer, Painted, Red, Yellow, Tin, Wood, Windup, Box 5100.00
Car, MGA, Convertible, Red, Gearshift, Tin Lithograph, Battery Operated, Bandai, Box, 8 ½ In. 1300.00
Car, Milton Berle, Red Hat, Tin Lithograph, Plastic, Windup, Marx, 6 In. 220.00
Car, Milton Berle, Tin Lithograph, White Hat, Windup, Marx, Box, 6 In. . . . . *illus* 420.00
Car, Monkey Driver, Graphics, Railed Seating, Tin Lithograph, Windup, Distler, 6 In. 978.00 to 1725.00
Car, Monorail, Gyroscope, Tin Lithograph, Friction, Label, Lehmann, Box, 10 In. 2185.00
Car, Nash, Tin, Friction, Japan, c.1950, 8 In. 110.00
Car, OHO, Driver, Tin Lithograph, Clockwork, Lehmann, 4 In. . . . . *illus* 330.00
Car, Old Time, Tin, Windup, Marx, U.S.A., 1930s, 7 In. 375.00
Car, Oldsmobile, Highway Patrol, Sound Lights, Tin, Battery Operated, Japan, 10 In. 145.00
Car, Oldsmobile, Roadster, Tan, Red, No. 6301, Tootsietoy 20.00
Car, Opel, Tin, Battery Operated, Japan, 1950s, 10 ½ In. 120.00
Car, Open, Driver, Blue, Red Interior, Tin Lithograph, Flywheel, Fischer, 5 ½ In. 863.00
Car, Open Tourer, 4 Seats, Painted, White, Red Stripes, Embossed, Tin, Windup, Bing, c.1910 . 1380.00
Car, Open Tourer, Green, Tin Lithograph, Nickel Plated Grille, Delage, 13 ¼ In. 1380.00
Car, Packard, Convertible, Driver, Green, No. 132, Dinky Toys, Box, 4 In. 60.00
Car, Packard, Fire Chief, Coupe, Die Cast, Tin Lithograph Chassis, Hubley, 1948, 5 ½ In. 165.00
Car, Packard, Sedan, Green, Gray, Tin Lithograph Chassis, Kiddie Toy, Hubley, 5 ½ In. 110.00
Car, Packard, Sedan, No. 180, Cream, Red Roof, Dinky Toys, Box, 1958 . . . . . 150.00
Car, Packard, Speedster, CC, Red, Turner, c.1925, 26 In. 570.00
Car, Peter Rabbit, Eccentric, Crazy Action, Head Spins, Tin, Plastic, Windup, Marx, 1950, 5 ½ In. 593.00
Car, Pierce-Arrow, Brooklyn Models, No. 1, Box, 1933 . . . . . 100.00
Car, Pierce-Arrow, Sedan, Cast Iron, Arcade, 7 In. 980.00
Car, Piggy's, Driver, Tin, Friction, 1950s, 6 In. 95.00
Car, Plymouth, 4 Door, Hardtop, 2-Tone Green, Tin, Friction, Japan, Box, c.1956, 8 In. 835.00
Car, Plymouth, Station Wagon, 1954 Model, White, Metal, Friction, 7 ¾ In. 33.00
Car, Police, Mercury, Tin, Friction, Yonezawa, Japan, c.1958, 11 ½ In. 395.00
Car, Police, Oldsmobile, Tin, Battery Operated Light, Friction, Japan, 1960, 12 ½ In. 175.00
Car, Police, Siren, No. 1, First Precinct, Pressed Steel, Battery Operated, Marx, 14 In. . . . *illus* 518.00
Car, Police, Sound, Lights, Tin, Battery Operated, Japan, 12 ½ In. 145.00
Car, Police Patrol, Blue, Gold, 4 Policemen, Kenton, 9 ¾ In. 1500.00
Car, Police Squad, Siren, Embossed Trunk Wheel, Tin Lithograph, Wells, 14 In. 1035.00
Car, Pontiac, Convertible, Purple, No. 39B1, Matchbox, Box 140.00
Car, Pontiac, Safari, Station Wagon, Blue, Gray, No. 895, Tootsietoy, Box 370.00
Car, Porsche, Electromatic 7500, Convertible, Rubber Tires, Battery Operated, Distler, 10 In. . 288.00
Car, Racing, 2 Drivers, No. 12, Tin, Windup, Marx, 16 In. 327.00
Car, Racing, Auburn Rubber, Open Wheeled, Red, Silver, c.1930, 10 ½ In. 60.00
Car, Racing, Black, Silver Driver, Gold Spoke Wheels, Cast Iron, A.C. Williams, 7 ½ In. 374.00
Car, Racing, Blue, White, Tin, Windup, Marx, 1950s, 13 In. 375.00
Car, Racing, Buick, Smokes, Tin, Battery Operated, Cragstan, Japan, 12 In. 275.00
Car, Racing, Champion, No. 98, Driver, Tin, Friction, Yonezawa, Box, 18 In. 6842.00
Car, Racing, Champion, Tin, Friction, Japan, ATC, 1950s, 8 ½ In. 225.00
Car, Racing, Connaught, No. 236, Green, Dinky Toys, Box 180.00
Car, Racing, Crank, Dummy Light, Fuel Tank, Painted, Pressed Steel, Republic, c.1921, 10 ½ In. 575.00
Car, Racing, Driver, Bluebird, Tin Lithograph, Windup, 6 In. 88.00
Car, Racing, Driver, Boattail, Tin, Fischer, Germany, 4 ½ In. 115.00
Car, Racing, Driver, Bubble Top, Green, Triang-Minic, 4 ¾ In. 85.00
Car, Racing, Driver, Embossed, Tin Lithograph, Penny Toy, Meier, 3 ½ In. 110.00
Car, Racing, Driver, No. 3, Red, Yellow, Tin Lithograph, Windup, Marx, 13 In. 135.00
Car, Racing, Driver, No. 22, Red, Cast Iron, Hubley, 7 ¼ In. 44.00
Car, Racing, Driver, Red, Aluminum Rear, Cast Iron, Nickel Plated, Hubley, 9 ½ In. 948.00
Car, Racing, Driver, Red, Yellow, Tin, Windup, Germany, 6 ½ In. 187.00
Car, Racing, Driver, Silver Dash Decal, Tin, Windup, Lever Operated, Buffalo Toys, 14 In. 633.00
Car, Racing, Driver, Tin, Plastic, Rubber, Friction, Marx, 1950, 16 In. 238.00
Car, Racing, Driver, Tin, Windup, Marx, 1920s, 12 ½ In. 375.00
Car, Racing, Driver, Yellow, No. 6, Cast Iron, Nickel Pistons, Hubley, 4 ¾ In. 200.00
Car, Racing, Driver, Yellow, Tin Lithograph, Windup, Strauss, 7 In. 230.00
Car, Racing, Jet, Driver, Japan, Box, c.1950, 12 In. 850.00
Car, Racing, Metal, Windup, Japan, c.1950, 4 In., Pair 55.00

Car, Racing, No. 3, Red, Plastic, Pyro, 4 In. 20.00
Car, Racing, No. 8, Tin, Friction, Lupor, 1950s, 7 In. 145.00
Car, Racing, No. 11, Green, Plastic, Windup, Marx, c.1950, 6 In. 110.00
Car, Racing, No. 22, Silver, Green, Tin Lithograph, Windup, Tippco, 16 In. 2588.00
Car, Racing, No. 629, Orange, Hubley, 6 ¾ In. 425.00
Car, Racing, No. 2330D, Red, Silver, Cast Iron, Rubber, Hubley, 7 ½ In. 27.00
Car, Racing, Pistons Pump, Cast Iron, Hubley, 1930s. 116.00
Car, Racing, Red, Black, Tin, Windup, Marx, 1950s, 13 In. 325.00
Car, Racing, Red, Cast Iron, Walker Stewart, c.1920, 5 ½ In. 250.00
Car, Racing, Red Devil, Budwill, Tin, Windup, 8 In. 95.00
Car, Racing, Speed Demon, Rubber Tires, Vindex, c.1929, 11 In. 1850.00
Car, Racing, Speed Racer, Driver, No. 3, Marx, Box, 1950, 6 ¼ In. 441.00
Car, Racing, Speedster, Green, Friction, Wyandotte, c.1938, 10 In. 375.00 to 650.00
Car, Racing, Studio, Silver, Schuco, Box, 5 In. 27.00
Car, Racing, Super Sonic, No. 36, Tin, Friction, Modern Toys, Japan, Box, 9 In. 540.00
Car, Racing, Thunderbird 8, Gold, Red, White, Tin, Friction, Bandai, Box, 1961 265.00
Car, Racing, Tin, Friction, Japan, c.1950, 8 In. 145.00
Car, Racing, Tin Lithograph, Built-In Key, Windup, Marx, 1930s, 5 In. 288.00
Car, Racing, Tin Lithograph, Windup, Marx, 5 In. 174.00
Car, Racing Set, Red & Blue Car, 10 Curved Tracks, Key, Box. 180.00
Car, Racing Set, Track, Pressed Steel Open Racers, Electric, Lionel, c.1916, 8 In. 3163.00
Car, Rambler, Tin, Friction, Japan, 1950s, 8 In. 75.00
Car, Reo, Coupe, Gray, Red, Arcade, 9 In. 3500.00
Car, Roadster, Driver, Red, Weight Driven, Scheible, 13 In. 220.00
Car, Roadster, Flivver, Black, Red Wheels, Decal, Buddy L, 1925, 11 In. 625.00
Car, Roadster, Hercules, Rumble Seat, Running Boards, Luggage Rack, Chein, c.1927, 18 In. 1495.00
Car, Roadster, Orange, Metal Masters, 1938, 7 In. 50.00
Car, Roadster, Red, Tin Lithograph, Bing, Box, 6 ½ In. 1950.00
Car, Roadster, Rubber Tires, Electric Headlights, Pressed Steel, Windup, Kingsbury, 13 In. 2588.00
Car, Roadster, Steel, Red Chassis, Lights, Rubber Tires, Battery Operated, Kingsbury, 12 ½ In. 415.00
Car, Roadster, Uncle Walt, Green, Red, Die Cast Metal, Tootsietoy, 3 ¼ In. 110.00 to 160.00
Car, Roadster, Woman Driver, Black, Simulated Soft Top, Tin, Windup, Bing, 6 ½ In. 518.00
Car, Roadster, Yellow, Green, Red, Kilgore, 5 In. 275.00
Car, Runabout, Red, Yellow Spoke Wheels, Tiller, Cast Iron, Kenton, 6 ½ In. 230.00
Car, Safety Car, Bouncing Benny, Pull Toy, Marx, 1930s, 6 In. 225.00
Car, Sand Crab, Magenta, Redline, Matchbox, 1970. 132.00
Car, Sedan, 2 Door, Model A, Green, Gold Stripe, Cast Iron, Nickel Plate, Arcade, 6 ½ In. 575.00
Car, Sedan, Center Door, Black, Spoke Wheels, Tin, Windup, Bing, 8 ½ In. 518.00
Car, Sedan, Coil Spring Drive, Tin Lithograph, Windup, Lehmann, 5 ½ In. 316.00
Car, Sedan, Dark Blue, Cast Iron, Sharon, 5 In. 575.00
Car, Sedan, Driver, Black, Tin, Windup, Strauss, 7 In. 55.00
Car, Sedan, Green, Passengers, Applied Bumpers, Tin Lithograph, Friction, Japan, c.1954, 7 In. 115.00
Car, Sedan, Painted Red, Nickel Plated Grille, Tin, Windup, Occupied Japan, 5 ¾ In. 115.00
Car, Sedan, Red, Black Roof, Driver, Tin Lithograph, Windup, Lehmann, 9 ½ In. 805.00
Car, Sedan, Terraplane, No. 20, Orange, Black Bumpers, Trickel Toy, Box, 4 ½ In. 80.00
Car, Sedan, Tin, Windup, England, 1930s, 9 ½ In. 295.00
Car, Service, Green, Metal Wheels, Nickel Plated Hook, Cast Iron, Hubley, 1 ⅞ x 5 x 1 ⅞ In. 66.00
Car, Skeeter Bug, Women Passengers, Tin, Windup, Lindstrom, Box, 9 In. 978.00
Car, Space, Driver, Turns, Blows Stream Of Air, Tin, Battery Operated, Yonezawa, 9 ½ In. 1695.00
Car, Space Patrol, Astronaut Moves Gun, Tin, Battery Operated, Nomura, Box, 9 ½ In. 1356.00
Car, Space Patrol, Convertible, Astronaut, Lights, Tin, Battery Operated, Nomura, c.1963, 13 In. 2938.00
Car, Space Robot, Driver, Lighted Popcorn Popper, Tin, Battery Operated, Masudaya, c.1955, 7 In. 3221.00
Car, Sports, Gray, Blue Fenders, Rubber Tires, Metal, Windup, Germany, c.1950, 9 ¾ In. 178.00
Car, Star Brand Shoes, Tin Lithograph, Open, Driver, 8 ¼ In. 374.00
Car, Station Wagon, Edsel, Tin, Friction, Japan, 10 ½ In. 375.00
Car, Station Wagon, No. 234, Cardboard Insert, Fisher-Price, Box, c.1960, 13 In. *illus* 288.00
Car, Station Wagon, Woody, Tailgate, Maroon, Tan, Metal Masters, c.1948, 9 In. 165.00
Car, Studebaker, No. 24Y, Die Cast, Dinky Toys, Box *illus* 259.00
Car, Studebaker, Roadster, Red, Hubley, 7 In. 500.00
Car, Stutz, Roadster, Cream, Red Frame, Fenders, Brass Bumpers, Grill, Cast Iron, Kilgore, 10 In. 1265.00
Car, Tiller, Boy Driver, Chasing Dog, Windup, Germany, 7 ½ In. 1380.00
Car, Tom & Jerry, Red, Battery Operated, Modern Toys, Japan, Box. 220.00
Car, Torpedo, Gold, Red Stripe, Driver, Tin Lithograph, Fischer, Germany, 6 ½ In. 374.00
Car, Touring, Chauffeur, Woman, Movable Arms, Cast Iron, Kenton, 9 In. 775.00
Car, Touring, Convertible, Driver, Tin Lithograph, Penny Toy, Initials, GF, 2 x 6 In. 440.00
Car, Touring, Driver, Open, Brown, Gold Highlights, Tin Lithograph, Windup, Fischer, 8 In. 1495.00
Car, Touring, Facing Seating, Gold Trim, Cast Iron, Pressed Steel, Friction, 11 In. 374.00

Toy, Car, Studebaker, No. 24Y, Die Cast, Dinky Toys, Box
$259.00

Toy, Carriage, Horseless, 2 Figures, Wood, Tin, Cast Iron, Clark, 1899, 11 In.
$690.00

TIP

"Lead rot" is a disease of lead soldiers and other lead toys. Gray dust forms on the soldier and eventually the toy will disintegrate. It is not contagious but it often appears on a group of soldiers stored together because it is caused by oxidation brought on by the environment. It seems to appear if lead items are stored in new wooden cases (use metal cases). Old wooden cases that are sealed with latex paint seem safe.

T

Toy, Cart, Stock Boy Driver, 3 Wheels, Tin Lithograph, Clockwork, Germany, 4 ½ In.
$895.00

Toy, Cat, Felix, Riding Scooter, Orange, Tin, Windup, Pat Sullivan, c.1922, 7 ¼ In.
$575.00

Toy, Cat, Green Eyes, Wood, Jointed, Painted, Gray, White, Schoenhut, 5 In.
$863.00

Toy, Cat, Guarding Caged Mouse, Painted, Clockwork, Germany, 10 In.
$660.00

TIP
To loosen a rusted metal part on a toy, try soaking it in cola.

Car, Touring, Woman Driver, Black, Simulated Soft Top, Tin, Windup, Bing, 6 ½ In. 518.00
Car, Town Car, Embossed, Tin Lithograph, Penny Toy, Marked, MS, Japan, 3 ¼ In. 110.00
Car, Toytown Estate Auto, Driver, Red, Simulated Wood Sides, Wyandotte, 20 In. 405.00
Car, Trailer, Green Car, Red Trailer, No. 1491R, Cast Iron, Arcade, 12 In. 880.00
Car, Turbo-Jet, Red, Yellow, Ideal, Box, 11 In. 175.00
Car, Tut-Tut, Driver, Steers, Toots Horn, Tin, Windup, Lehmann, Box, 7 x 6 ½ In. 2520.00
Car, Uncle Wiggily, Marx, Box, 7 In. 1150.00
Car, Volkswagen, Beetle, Blue, Battery Operated, Japan, Box, 9 ½ In. 165.00
Car, Volkswagen, Beetle, Tin, Friction, Alps, Japan, Box, 8 ½ In. 85.00
Car, Volkswagen, Porsche 914, Blue, Red, Black Hood, 1975 30.00
Car, Whoopee, Cowboy Driver, Laughing Cows On Wheels, Tin Lithograph, Marx, 8 ¾ In. 288.00
Car, Whoopee, Crazy, Driver's Head Spins, Tin, Windup, Marx, Box, 1930, 7 In. 1130.00
Car, Whoopee, Suitcase, Flappers, Tin Lithograph, Plastic, Windup, Marx, Box, 8 In. 515.00
Car, With Camper, Red, Silver, Picnic Table, Graphics, Tin, Box, Japan, 16 ½ In. 431.00
Car, Wonder, Driver, Yellow Plastic Roadster, Battery Operated, Box, Irwin Corp, 16 In. 633.00
Car, Woody, Pressed Steel, Wyandotte, c.1940, 13 In. 175.00
Car, Wrecker, Cast Iron, Hubley, 5 ½ In. 190.00
Car, Yell-O-Taxi, Orange, Black, Driver, Tin Lithograph, Windup, Strauss, 7 ¾ In. 518.00
Car, Yellow, Blue Top, Tin, Windup, U.S.A., c.1930, 9 In. 225.00
Car, Zodiac, Convertible, Driver, Pink, No. 39A4, Matchbox, Box 120.00
Car & Trailer, Pressed Steel, Windup, Kingsbury, 1937, 21 In. 230.00
Car Set, Car, Stake Side Truck, Tow Truck, Dump Truck, No. 3440, Arcade, Box 3500.00
Carnival Ride, Tin Lithograph, Windup, West Germany, 8 ½ In. 259.00
Carnival Roundabout, Passengers In Seats, Wires, Windup, Germany, 1900, 14 In. 650.00
Carousel, 3 Horses, Riders, Canopy Top, Painted, Windup, Gunthermann, 14 ½ In. 690.00
Carousel, 4 Flying Boats, Muller & Kaderer, Germany, 17 In. 1500.00
Carousel, 5 Horses, 2 Swing-Out Planes, Tin Lithograph, Lever Action, Wolverine, c.1945, 12 In. 119.00
Carousel, Animals, Tin Lithograph, Windup, Japan, Box, 8 In. 69.00
Carousel, Bicycle Race, 6 Figures, Embossed, Tin Lithograph, Penny Toy, Meier, 2 ½ In. 330.00
Carousel, Embossed, Tin Lithograph, Penny Toy, Meier, 2 ¾ In. 187.00
Carousel, Tin, Crank, Wyandotte, 4 ½ In. 195.00
Carousel, Tin, Dual Action, Suspended Gondolas, Bing, Germany, 11 ½ In. 690.00
Carousel, Tin, Tower, Canopy, Gondolas, Horses, Figures, Windup Driven, Germany, 18 In. 2185.00
Carousel, Tin Lithograph, Girl On Ostrich, Boy & Girl In Gondola, Boy On Horse, Bing, 10 In. 316.00
Carriage, 3 Wheels, Driver, 2 Passengers, Dog, Tin, Windup, Lehmann, 5 ¾ In. 1955.00
Carriage, Baby, Pink & Blue, Baby, Plastic, Wannatoy, 1950s, 3 ⅝ x 4 ½ x 1 ¾ In. 20.00
Carriage, Baby, Yellow & Pink, Metal, Marked, Made In USA, 4 ½ x 5 In. 68.00
Carriage, Barouche, Driver, Black, Spoke Wheels, Cast Iron, Pratt & Letchworth, 1890s, 18 In. 3738.00
Carriage, Doll's, Baby Pull, Wicker, Wood Seat, Spoke Wheels, 32 x 23 In. 35.00
Carriage, Doll's, Blue, Spoke Wheels, Fringed Sun Shade, 28 ½ In. 563.00
Carriage, Doll's, Ellis Style, Wood, Red Paint, Folding Canvas, Wood Handle, 31 In. 86.00
Carriage, Doll's, Leather Seats, Canopy, Wood Spoke Wheels, Original Paint, Stenciling, 38 x 26 In. 440.00
Carriage, Doll's, Scrolled Wicker, Tight Weave, Metal Wheels, Stenciled Green Metal, 26 x 34 In. 86.00
Carriage, Doll's, Silver, Metal, Filigree, Spoked Wheels, Curved Foot, Detachable Sunshade, 6 In. 300.00
Carriage, Doll's, Tin, Lace Covered Hood, Bisque Baby, Wire Jointed, 2 ⅝ In. 237.00
Carriage, Doll's, Victorian, Fringe Top, Upholstered, 27 x 34 In. 546.00
Carriage, Doll's, Wicker, Metal Frame, Gray Paint, Convertible Hood, c.1930, 31 ½ In. 24.00
Carriage, Horse Drawn, Cart, Wool, Germany, c.1910, 25 In. 345.00
Carriage, Horseless, 2 Figures, Wood, Tin, Cast Iron, Clark, 1899, 11 In. *illus* 690.00
Carriage, Horseless, Driver, Articulated Passenger, Tin Lithograph, Graphics, 5 In. 3162.00
Carriage, Horseless, Hillclimber, Tin, Cast Iron Wheels, Mechanical, 5 ¼ x 8 x 3 ½ In. 55.00
Carriage, Phaeton, Painted Black, Curved Fenders, Cast Iron, Pratt & Letchworth, c.1883, 16 In. 575.00
Carriage & Stable, Horse Drawn, Lead Wheels, Tin, 1910 500.00
Cart, 3 Wheels, Baker, Chimney Sweep, Tin, Lehmann, 5 x 5 In. 2405.00
Cart, 3 Wheels, Black Man, Dressed As Clown, Lantern, Tin, Windup, Lehmann, 4 ½ x 4 ½ In. 805.00
Cart, Black Horse, Woman Passenger, Cast Iron, 9 ½ In. 201.00
Cart, Doctor's, Bench Seat, Backrest, Red Spoke Wheels, Brown Horse, Cast Iron, Wilkins, 10 In. 633.00
Cart, Easter, Rabbit, Pressed Steel Cart, Tin Lithograph, Pull Toy, c.1930, 10 ½ In. 268.00
Cart, Goose Drawn, Black Driver, Butcher Barrel, Windup, 9 ½ In. 2185.00
Cart, Horse Drawn, Black Horse, Pleasure, Red, Yellow Spoke Wheels, Cast Iron, Hubley, 10 In. 86.00
Cart, Horse Drawn, Dray, Wood Floor, Pratt & Letchworth, 1885, 10 In. 595.00
Cart, Horse Drawn, Driver, Brown, Spoke Wheels, Cast Iron, 9 ½ In. 173.00
Cart, Horse Drawn, Pressed Steel, Converse, 19 In. 115.00
Cart, Horse Drawn, Slide Panel, Spoke Wheels, Multicolored, Leather Tack, 7 ¾ x 18 In. 88.00
Cart, Horse Drawn, Wolf Express Wagon, Tin, Chein, 11 In. 136.00
Cart, Horse Drawn, Wood, Painted, Stenciled, Leather, Cloth, 22 In. 259.00
Cart, Man-Dar-In, 2 Chinese Men, Pulling Cart, Sedan Type Chair, Tin, Windup, 7 x 5 ½ In. 2300.00

Cart, Mule Drawn, Driver, Head Moves, Rubber Neck, Cast Iron, Kenton, 6 In. 316.00
Cart, Mule Drawn, Driver, Tin, Windup, Marx, c.1950, 10 In. 195.00
Cart, Ostrich Drawn, Zulu, Mail Slot, Tin, Windup, Lehmann, 7 In.. . . . . 805.00
Cart, Ostrich Drawn, Zulu, Mail Slot, Tin, Windup, Lehmann, Box, 7 In.. . . . . 5750.00
Cart, Stock Boy Driver, 3 Wheels, Tin Lithograph, Clockwork, Germany, 4 ½ In. . . . . *illus* 895.00
Case, Display, Painted, Wood, Glass, Gottschalk, 20 In. 330.00
Cash Register, Red, Decal, Tom Thumb, 1950s, 7½ In. 40.00
Casper The Friendly Ghost, Hops Up & Down, Head Bobs, Tin, Windup, Linemar, 5 In. 460.00
Castle, Soldier, Painted, Tin, Steam & Chain Driven, 14 In. 1600.00
Castle, Towers, Drawbridge, Ramp, Faux Stone, Painted, Wood, Moritz Gottschalk, 17 x 19 In. 403.00
Castle Fort, Wood, Cork, Painted, Draw Bridge, Flag, Winding Trail, 30 x 29 In. 320.00
Castle Fort, Wood, Painted, 16 x 36 In. 340.00
Cat, Cloth, Straw Stuffed, Button Eyes, Rag Ball, Black & White Fabric, Late 1800s, 6 ½ In.. . . 805.00
Cat, Cloth, Stuffed, Seated, Gray, Stitched Mouth, Nose, Toes, Collar, Amish, 10 In.. . . . . 936.00
Cat, Drinking, Licking, Battery Operated, TN, Japan, Box, 10 In. 170.00
Cat, Felix, Riding Scooter, Orange, Tin, Windup, Pat Sullivan, c.1922, 7 ¼ In. . . . . *illus* 575.00
Cat, Felix, Sparkler, Nifty, 5 In.. . . . . 200.00
Cat, Green Eyes, Wood, Jointed, Painted, Gray, White, Schoenhut, 5 In. . . . . *illus* 863.00
Cat, Guarding Caged Mouse, Painted, Clockwork, Germany, 10 In. . . . . *illus* 660.00
Cat, Nina, Pursuing Mouse, Lehmann, 11 In.. . . . . 920.00
Cat, Pink Bow, Ears, Jointed, Celluloid, Japan, 5 x 2 In.. . . . . 70.00
Cat, Playing Violin, Black, White, Celluloid, Japan, 5 ¾ x 2 In.. . . . . 132.00
Cat, Tabby, Pip-Squeak, Papier-Mache, Flocked, Painted, Bellows, 3 ⅞ In.. . . . . 441.00
Cat, White, Walker, Turns Head, Alps, 6 x 6 In.. . . . . 10.00
Cat & Dog, Embossed, Tin Lithograph, Lever, Penny Toy, Meier, 2 ½ In. 110.00
Cavalryman, Mounted On Horse, Wags Tail, Cannon, Tin, Windup, T.P.S., Box, 6 In.. . . . . 260.00
Cement Mixer, Jaeger, Blue, Yellow, Nickel Plated, Cast Iron, Kenton, c.1935, 7 In. . . . . . *illus* 375.00
Cement Mixer, No. 2002, Yellow, Black, Doepke, c.1947, 15 In. 225.00
Cement Mixer, Turbine, Yellow, Tonka, 1970, 14 In.. . . . . 110.00
Chariot, Horse Drawn, 1880s, 7 ½ In.. . . . . 375.00
Charleston Trio, Tin, Windup, Marx, 1920s, 9 In.. . . . . 300.00
Charlie Weaver, Bartender, Battery Operated, 11 In. 35.00
Chest, Bombay, Bulbous, Inlay, Marble Top, Cast Highlights, 2 Drawers, 14 x 16 In.. . . . . 201.00
Chicken, Laying Egg, Marbles, Tin Lithograph, Baldwin Mfg. Co., c.1950, 5 ½ x 5 In. 144.00
Child, On Tricycle, Celluloid, Tin, Windup, Japan, 2 ¾ In.. . . . . 30.00
Chimpanzee, Somersaults, Ginger Mohair, Glass Eyes, Felt Face, Button In Ear, Steiff, c.1910, 9 In. 652.00
Church, Cathedral Form, Tin Lithograph, Windup, Chein, 9 ¼ In. 75.00
Church Altar, Priest, Accessories, 19th Century, 29 In.. . . . . 431.00
Circus, Humpty Dumpty, Animals, Clowns, Props, Schoenhut, Box, 15 x 23 In. . . . . *illus* 345.00
Circus, Humpty Dumpty, Canvas Tent, Animals, Ringmaster, Schoenhut, Box, c.1922, 24 x 18 In. 1440.00
Circus Boy, Head Moves, Rings Bell, Tin Lithograph, Joustra, France, Box, 6 In. 110.00
Circus Parade, Elephant Pulls 3 Clowns, Tin, Windup, T.P.S., Box, 13 ½ In.. . . . . 163.00
Clicker, Alligator, Tail Wags, Mouth Opens, Squeeze Toy, Gely, Germany, 10 ¾ In. 175.00
Climbing Linesman, Man Climbs Pole, Head Light, Tin, Battery Operated, T.P.S., Box, 24 In. 768.00
Clown, Ball Blowing, Waves Arms, Battery Operated, Nomura, Box, 11 In. 192.00
Clown, Bozo, Capital Clown, Squeeze Me, Painted, Rubber, 1950s, 8 ½ In. 20.00
Clown, Cap Bomb Set, Painted, Cast Iron, Kilgore, Box, 12 Piece . . . . *illus* 2875.00
Clown, Car, Unique Artie, Jo Jo, Crazy, Tin, Battery Operated, Box, 7 x 9 ½ In.. . . . . 360.00
Clown, Chasing Donkey, Embossed, Tin Lithograph, Penny Toy, Meier, 3 ¾ In.. . . . . 220.00
Clown, Circus, On Motorcycle, T.T. Japan, Box, 6 In. 213.00
Clown, Circus, Roller Skating, Tin, Cloth, Windup, T.P.S., Box, 6 In. 275.00
Clown, Circus Cyclist, Pedals, Bell Rings, Tin, Windup, T.P.S., 6 ½ In. 350.00
Clown, Claps Cymbals, Painted, Bisque Head, Blue Glass Eyes, Germany, 12 ¼ In.. . . . . 144.00
Clown, Drummer, Beats Drum, Shakes Head, Japan, Box, 9 In. 135.00
Clown, Handstand, Red & White Stripe Pants, Tin, Windup, J. Chein, 5 In. 60.00
Clown, Handstand, Tin Lithograph, Windup, 7 In.. . . . . 805.00
Clown, Happy Fiddler, With Violin, Head Moves, Battery Operated, Alps, Box, 10 In.. . . . . 204.00
Clown, Hopsa, Raises Baby Mouse, Chenille Legs, Felt Skirt, Box, Schuco, 4 ¼ In. 173.00
Clown, In Barrel, Embossed, Tin Lithograph, Penny Toy, Stock & Co., Germany, 2 ½ In.. . . . . 110.00
Clown, In Box, Pop-Up, Wiggles Nose, Porcelain, Lithograph, Inscribed, 6 In. 127.00
Clown, Lion Jumps Through Flaming Hoop, Tin, Windup, T.P.S., Box, 5 ½ In. 186.00
Clown, Magic Man, Battery Operated, Remote, Marusan, Box, 12 In.. 295.00
Clown, Magician, Lifts Hat, Rabbit Appears, Cloth, Tin, Windup, Japan, 6 ¾ In. . . 110.00 to 275.00
Clown, Monkey, Whirligig, Celluloid, Waving Top Hat, Wheeled Platform, 9 ¼ In.. . . . . 92.00
Clown, On Donkey, Wheeled Platform, Windup, Gunthermann, 10 In. 1093.00
Clown, On Scooter, Tin Lithograph, Windup, Tippco, 5 ¾ In.. . . . . 920.00
Clown, Playing Banjo, Celluloid, Tin, Lead, Cloth, Windup, 11 ½ In.. . . . . 275.00

Toy, Cement Mixer, Jaeger, Blue, Yellow, Nickel Plated, Cast Iron, Kenton, c.1935, 7 In.
$375.00

Toy, Circus, Humpty Dumpty, Animals, Clowns, Props, Schoenhut, Box, 15 x 23 In.
$345.00

Toy, Clown, Cap Bomb Set, Painted, Cast Iron, Kilgore, Box, 12 Piece
$2875.00

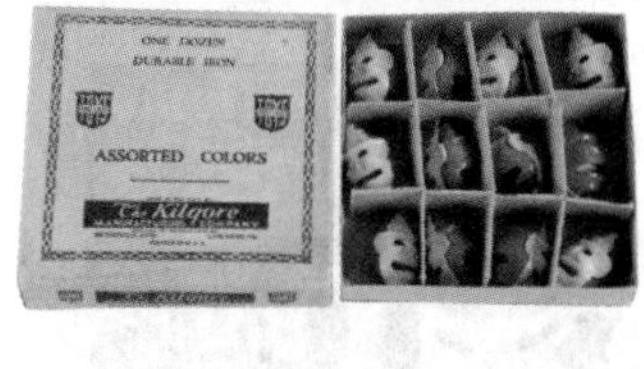

Toy, Clown, Rolly, Tin, Composition, Cloth, Felt, Windup, Schuco, Box, 9 In.
$260.00

Toy, Clown, Roly Poly, Swivel Head, Schoenhut, 14 In.
$550.00

Toy, Clown, Spinning Star, Painted, Tin, Clockwork, Gunthermann, 9 ¼ In.
$795.00

Toy, Colonel Hap Hazard, Tin, Plastic, Battery Operated, Marx, Box, 1968, 12 In.
$863.00

Toy, Combine, John Deere, Driver, Painted, Cast Iron, Vindex, 11 x 14 In.
$6900.00

Clown, Playing Bass Drum, Painted Tin Head, Lithograph, Cloth Outfit, Windup, 6 ¼ In. 489.00
Clown, Playing Bell, Painted, Tin, Windup, Gunthermann, 7 In. 978.00
Clown, Playing Cello, Painted, Tin, Windup, Germany, 9 In. 2200.00
Clown, Playing Violin, Cloth, Tin, Windup, 8 ½ In. 200.00
Clown, Propeller, On Cart, Tin, Painted, Windup, Germany, 5 ⅛ In. 748.00
Clown, Punching, Painted, Composition Head, Hands, Cloth Outfit, Windup, Germany, 9 In. 288.00
Clown, Riding Pig, Painted, Tin, Windup, Germany, c.1920, 4 ¼ In. 506.00
Clown, Rocking Horse, Felt Suit, Painted, Wood Rocket, Composition, Windup, 7 ¼ In. 259.00
Clown, Rolly, Tin, Composition, Cloth, Felt, Windup, Schuco, Box, 9 In. .... *illus* 260.00
Clown, Roly Poly, Composition, Schoenhut, c.1920, 5 ½ In. 175.00
Clown, Roly Poly, Swivel Head, Schoenhut, 14 In. .... *illus* 550.00
Clown, Seated, Outfit, Glass Eyes, Papier-Mache, Wood, Lever Action, Stand, 14 In. 1265.00
Clown, Seesaw, Center Wheel Balance, Tin Lithograph, Windup, Distler, 11 ½ In. 1150.00
Clown, Skippy, Unicyclist, Cloth, Tin Lithograph, Windup, T.P.S., Box, 6 In. .... 92.00 to 175.00
Clown, Sommersaults, Red, Green, Yellow, Celluloid, Windup, Japan, 7 x 4 In. 60.00
Clown, Spinning Star, Painted, Tin, Clockwork, Gunthermann, 9 ¼ In. .... *illus* 795.00
Clown, Twirling Cane, Tin, Cloth, Windup, Japan, 9 In. 135.00
Clown Chariot, Horse Drawn, Painted, Cast Iron, Hubley, 10 In. 350.00
Coach, Fageol Safety, Nickel Plated Driver, Blue, Cast Wheels, Cast Iron, Arcade, 12 In. 173.00
Coast Defense, Airplane Circles, Tin Lithograph, Windup, Marx, Box, 9 In. .... 1045.00 to 3850.00
Coaster Boy, No. 140, Pull Toy, Fisher-Price, 1941 .... 120.00
Colonel Hap Hazard, Tin, Plastic, Battery Operated, Marx, Box, 1968, 12 In. .... *illus* 863.00
Colorforms, Family Affair, Kit No. 515, Sealed Box, c.1970, 8 x 12 In. 86.00
Combine, Case, Painted, Embossed Letters, Cast Iron, Vindex, 13 ½ In. 3738.00
Combine, John Deere, Driver, Painted, Cast Iron, Vindex, 11 x 14 In. .... *illus* 6900.00
Combine, Terra-Cotta Red, Yellow, Rubber Tires, Die Cast, Reuhl, 11 In. 230.00
Construction Set, Army Raiders Victory Unit, Built-Rite, No. 50 .... 275.00
Construction Set, Bethlehem Manger, Built-Rite, No. 19 .... 33.00
Construction Set, Garage & Salesroom, Built-Rite, No. 15, Sealed 219.00
Construction Set, Railroad Accessory & Scenic Set, Built-Rite, No. 212 .... 220.00
Construction Set, Service Station, Station Wagon, Sedan, Built-Rite, No. 17 .... 187.00
Construction Set, Toy Village, Built-Rite, No. 245 .... 143.00
Cookware Set, Copper, Mammy, New In Box, Italy, 1970s, 12 Piece 70.00
Cottage, Garage, Tin Lithograph, Electric, Marx, 16 ½ In. 201.00
Cottontail Cart, No. 525, Fisher-Price, c.1940, 12 In. 259.00
Cow & Milkmaid, Leather Horned Cow, Composition Mask Faced Maid, Schoenhut, 8 & 9 In. 780.00
Cowboy, Shooting, Eyes Shift, Twists At Waist, Tin, Technofix, Germany, 1940, 9 In. 165.00
Cowboy, Tin, Windup, Cragstan, Japan, Box, 1950s, 6 ½ In. 120.00
Cowboy Set, Dennis The Menace, Guns, Holsters, Card, Milner Leather Products 88.00
Cradle, Doll's, Bassinet Style, Cast Iron, Splayed Legs, Tassels, Early 1900s, 39 x 60 In. 86.00
Cradle, Doll's, Hood, Multicolored, Flowers, Butterflies, c.1950, 10 x 18 In. 117.00
Cradle, Doll's, Pine, Red, Painted Flowers, c.1900, 18 ¾ x 11 In. 352.00
Cradle, Doll's, Poplar, Blue, White, Salmon, Pinwheels, Compass Artist, c.1800, 8 x 16 In. 37440.00
Cradle, Doll's, Swinging, Boat Shape, Ribbed Bentwood, Cast Iron Wheels, Stencil, 1800s, 15 x 27 In. 523.00
Cradle, Doll's, Wood, Rocker Legs, Enclosed Headboard, 37 In. 57.00
Cradle, Doll's, Wood, Slat Board, Painted, Red, Spindle Sides, Decals, Black Striping, 21 In. 58.00
Cradle, Doll's, Wood, Tole Decorated, Oak Grain Finish, Mid 1800s, 17 In. 86.00
Crane, Magno Crane, Electro Magnetic, Red, Green, Roberts c.1950, 18 In. 150.00
Crawler, Caterpillar, Driver, Chains Around Wheels, Arcade, 5 ½ In. 650.00
Croquette Wicket, Figural, Boy, Holds Arms At Sides, Painted, Cast Iron, c.1900, 17 ¾ In. 345.00
Cycle, Police, Rider, Rubber Tires, Champion, 7 ¼ In. 950.00
Cyclist, Echo, Tin Lithograph, Windup, Lehmann, Early 1900s, 8 ⅜ In. 1430.00
Cyclist, Gay 90's, Pedals, Bell Rings, Tin, Windup, T.P.S., Box, 7 In. 288.00
Cyclist, Kiddy, Tin Lithograph, Windup, Unique Art, 8 ½ In. 127.00
Dagwood, Solo Flight Airplane, Crazy Action, Tin Lithograph, Marx, c.1935, 11 ½ In. 622.00 to 850.00
Dagwood, The Driver, Crazy Action, Head Spins, Tin, Windup, Marx, 1941, 8 ½ In. 989.00
Dagwood, Walker, Painted, Celluloid, Windup, Occupied Japan, 6 ¼ In. 135.00
Dancers, Black, Checkered Coats, Dance On Box, Windup, 1920s 285.00
Dancing Black, Girls, Skirts, Hats, Tin, Windup, Key, Wood Stand, 6 x 10 In. 1770.00
Dancing Black, Man, Musicians, Dog, Sand Activated, Frederick Dotter, Dec. 25. 1865, 7 x 9 In. 770.00
Dancing Black, Man, Sand Activated, 6 ¼ x 4 ¼ In. 470.00
Dancing Couple, Celluloid, Windup, Occupied Japan, 1948, 5 In. 75.00
Dancing Couple, Tin Lithograph, Lever, Penny Toy, Meier, 2 ¾ In. 550.00
Dancing Mouse, With Baby, Baby Is Raised & Lowered, Schuco, 4 ½ In. 86.00
Dancing Sam, Black, Tin Lithograph, Windup, S & E, Japan, 8 ½ In. 195.00
Dancing Sam, Tin Lithograph, Windup, A.H.I. Japan, Box, 9 In. 198.00
Dandy Jim, Dancing Clown, Circus Tent, Tin Lithograph, Windup, Unique Art, 1922, 13 x 5 In. 540.00

Daredevil, Open Seat Cart, Zebra Drawn, Tin Lithograph, Windup, Lehmann, 7 In. 546.00
Deer, Cloth, Stuffed, Button Eyes, Iron Wheels, Pull Toy, 6 ½ In. 497.00
Delivery Boy, Pushing Cart, Red Disc Wheels, Tin, Windup, Martin, 7 In.. .... 552.00
Dentist Bear, Crying Baby Bear, Drill Lights, Battery Operated, Suzuki & Edwards, Box, 10 In. 802.00
Derby Horse Race, Horses Move, Bell Chimes, Tin Lithograph, Windup, Japan, 7 ¼ In. 195.00
Desk, Davenport, Lift Top, Letter Slots, Drawers, 3 Drawers, Footed Base, 10 x 5 ½ In. 431.00
Desk, Doll's, Tambour, Victorian, Glazed Cupboard, Rococo Ormolu Mounts, 11 x 9 In. 460.00
Dining Table, Mahogany, 4 Leaves, 1920-50, 25 ½ x 14 In. 58.00
Diorama, Bakery, Wizard's Workbench Case, Fully Stocked, Bisque Figures, 10 x 12 In. 173.00
Diorama, Bedroom, Wizard's Workbench, Textiles, Phonograph, Spinning Wheel, 1900s, 33 x 10 In. 230.00
Diorama, Bridal Shop, Bisque Doll, Gown, China Display Heads, Accessories, Germany, 23 x 10 In. 633.00
Diorama, Circus, Figures, Animals, Tents, Move In Circle, Motorized, Early 1900s, 31 x 49 In. 750.00
Diorama, Ice Cream Parlor, Coca-Cola, Pepsi-Cola, Miniatures, 18 x 42 x 15 In.. .... 550.00
Dirigible Ride, Baskets, Flags, Painted, Tin, Steam Driven, 10 In.. .... 1900.00
Ditcher, Buckeye, Nickel Plate, Orange, Green, Cast Iron, Kenton, 9 In. .... *illus* 1100.00
Doctor Moon, Head Turns Side To Side As Advances, Tin, Plastic, Windup, Box, 7 In. 791.00
Dog, Brown, White, Mohair, Glass Eyes, Cast Iron Wheels, Button In Ear, Steiff, 9 ¾ x 8 In.... 220.00
Dog, Bulldog, Composition, Wood, Cloth, Glass Eyes, Wheels, c.1880, 8 x 7 ¾ In. 275.00
Dog, Chasing Cat, Cat Circles House, Celluloid, Tin, Windup, Japan, 3 In. 220.00
Dog, Cloth, Stuffed, Black, White Spots, Glass Eye, Amish, 6 ¾ x 8 ½ In. 644.00
Dog, Dachshund, Plush, Fur, Wood Wheels, Yellow Tag, Button, Pull Toy, Steiff, 12 In.. .... 100.00
Dog, Mohair, 4 Wood Wheels, Pull Toy, Early 20th Century, 10 x 12 In. 115.00
Dog, Scottie, Guide Dog, Tin Lithograph, Windup, Marx, Box, 12 In. 220.00
Dog, Seated, Pip-Squeak, Papier-Mache, Painted, Bellows, Early 20th Century, 6 ½ In. 59.00
Dog, St. Bernard, Shuffles, Tin, Windup, 6 In. 780.00
Dog, Tyras, Tin, Windup, Lehmann, Box, 7 In. .... *illus* 3100.00
Dog, White, Black Spots, Red Collar, Papier-Mache, Germany, 7 x 6 In. 22.00
Doghouse, Dog, Music, Tin, Crank, Ohio Art, c.1950. .... 75.00
Dollhouse, 2 Rooms, Kitchen Box, Stove, Pantry, Table, Chairs, 37 x 16 ¼ x 17 In. 2645.00
Dollhouse, 2 Story, 2 Rooms, 2 Porches, Wooden Bricks, Shutters, Amish, Pa., c.1895, 32 x 39 In. 575.00
Dollhouse, 2 Story, 2 Rooms, Lithographed Facade, Gottschalk, 16 ¼ x 7 ¼ In.. .... 575.00
Dollhouse, 2 Story, 4 Rooms, Georgian, Glazed Windows, Fan Light, Curtains, Stairs, 31 x 20 In. 863.00
Dollhouse, 2 Story, 4 Rooms, Hallways, Wallpaper, Hinged Front, 33 x 38 x 16 ½ In.. .... 2588.00
Dollhouse, 2 Story, 4 Rooms, Stained Glass, 2 Chimneys, Electrified, 49 x 48 x 21 ½ In...... 1150.00
Dollhouse, 2 Story, 6 Rooms, Flat Roof, Bay Windows, Staircases, Fireplace, 45 x 34 x 18 In.. 2300.00
Dollhouse, 2 Story, 8 Rooms, Clapboard, Porches, Widows Walk, Electrified, c.1910, 39 x 37 In. 575.00
Dollhouse, 2 Story, 8 Rooms, Cranberry Cove, 2 Staircases, Pam Throop, c.1984, 56 x 35 In.. 1840.00
Dollhouse, 2 Story, 10 Rooms, Gambrel Roof, Shingles, Cream, Black, c.1880, 40 x 59 x 25 In. 8625.00
Dollhouse, 2 Story, Attic, Paper, Double Windows, Brick Chimneys, c. Hacker, 24 x 21 x 11 In. 1700.00
Dollhouse, 2 Story, Cottage, Side Access, Porch, Gottschalk, 1920s, 13 ½ x 9 In. 345.00
Dollhouse, 2 Story, Farmhouse, Queen Anne Style, Furniture, Accessories, 27 x 26 In. 805.00
Dollhouse, 2 Story, Mediterranean Villa, Wood, Roof Tiles, Paned Windows, Porch, 25 x 22 x 16 In. 1700.00
Dollhouse, 2 Story, Paper On Wood, Balcony, Gottschalk, 1890, 15 x 10 In. .... *illus* 825.00
Dollhouse, 2 Story, Side Entrance, Porch, Slanted Roof, Balcony, 2 Chimneys, 21 x 14 x 8 In. 1900.00
Dollhouse, 2 Story, Stone Lithograph, Cutout Windows, Front Steps, Bliss, 12 ½ x 7 In. 690.00
Dollhouse, 2 Story, Town House, Paper On Wood, Drapes, Gottschalk, 22 In. 2750.00
Dollhouse, 2 Story, Wood, Stone, Brick, 2-Pane Windows, Hinged Sides, 22 x 13 x 17 In. 850.00
Dollhouse, 2 Story, Wood, Wallpaper, Tin Lattice, CR. Bliss, 19 ½ x 12 ½ x 8 In. .... *illus* 940.00
Dollhouse, 3 Story, 4 Rooms, 2 Hallways, Porches, Balconies, Basement, 45 x 44 x 24 In.. .... 6900.00
Dollhouse, 3 Story, Red Roof, Dormer, Flower Boxes, Gable, Staircase, 36 x 28 x 28 In.. ..... 4025.00
Dollhouse, 4 Rooms, Attic, Balcony, No. 5609, Gottschalk, 1915, 32 x 28 x 15 In. ...... *illus* 3850.00
Dollhouse, 4 Rooms, Mystery, White & Black, Shingles, Attic Door, F.A.O. Schwarz, 1897..... 2870.00
Dollhouse, 4 Rooms, Victorian Style, Furniture, Accessories, Gottschalk, c.1910, 40 x 27 In. . 431.00
Dollhouse, 4 Rooms, Villa, Early 20th Century Style, Bowfront, Christian Hacker, 28 x 18 In. 3163.00
Dollhouse, 4 Story, 6 Rooms, Painted Brownstone, Pine, Hinged Front, 58 x 43 x 23 In...... 3737.00
Dollhouse, 4 Story, Victorian Style, Bay Windows, Balconies, Tower, 80 ½ x 28 ½ x 30 In. ... 2415.00
Dollhouse, 5 Rooms, Dutch Baroque Style, Lift Lid Roof, Hinged Front, Electrified, 34 x 35 In. 142.00
Dollhouse, 6 Rooms, Colonial Revival, Porches, Softwood Floors, Wallpapers, c.1930, 53 x 20 In. 633.00
Dollhouse, 6 Rooms, Red Roof, Cardboard, No. 5193, Moritz Gottschalk, 1912, 40 x 38 In. .. 7500.00
Dollhouse, Bungalow, Wood Frame, Embossed Faux Tile Lift Roof, Schoenhut, 18 x 14 In. .. 144.00
Dollhouse, Cardboard Lithograph, No. 36, Unpunched, Built-Rite, Box, 27 Piece 90.00
Dollhouse, Cardboard Lithograph, Unpunched, Built-Rite, Box, 44 Piece Furniture 230.00
Dollhouse, Cottage, Wood, Pressed Shingle Roof, Porch, Shutters, Hinged Sides, 9 x 11 x 10 In. 650.00
Dollhouse, Germantown Georgian, Architectural Details, Dormers, Portico, c.1860, 30 x 29 In. 2300.00
Dollhouse, Kitchen, Wood, Table, Stove, Cutting Board, Copperware, 29 x 16 x 15 In.. .... 2600.00
Dollhouse, Porch, Red Roof, Green Door, Shutters, Painted, Wood, Cardboard, Schoenhut, 16 In. 80.00
Dollhouse, Shop, Boulangerie Patisserie, Plastic Windows, c.1950s, 18 x 13 In. .... *illus* 485.00

Toy, Ditcher, Buckeye, Nickel Plate, Orange, Green, Cast Iron, Kenton, 9 In.
$1100.00

Toy, Dog, Tyras, Tin, Windup, Lehmann, Box, 7 In.
$3100.00

Toy, Dollhouse, 2 Story, Paper On Wood, Balcony, Gottschalk, 1890, 15 x 10 In.
$825.00

Toy, Dollhouse, 2 Story, Wood, Wallpaper, Tin Lattice, CR. Bliss, 19 ½ x 12 ½ x 8 In.
$940.00

T

Toy, Dollhouse, 4 Rooms, Attic, Balcony, No. 5609, Gottschalk, 1915, 32 x 28 x 15 In.
$3850.00

Toy, Dollhouse, Shop, Boulangerie Patisserie, Plastic Windows, c.1950s, 18 x 13 In.
$485.00

Toy, Dollhouse Furniture, Bedroom, Painted, Wood, Schoenhut, 6 Piece
$495.00

Toy, Dollhouse Furniture, Parlor Set, Animal & Bug Lithograph, 8 Piece
$710.00

Dollhouse, Shop, Drawers, Counter, Tins, Mahogany Stained, Germany, 1890, 15 x 28 x 12 In. 1955.00
Dollhouse, Wood, Curved Front, Lithographed, Bricks, Stained Glass, 22 x 13 x 9 In. 600.00
Dollhouse, Wood, Stone, Brick, 3-Pane Windows, Porch, Railing, Steps, Hinged Sides, 17 x 22 x 16 In. 750.00
Dollhouse, Wood, Tin, Multicolored, Hinged Front, Door, Wallpapered, 19 x 12 ½ x 8 ½ In. 935.00
Dollhouse Accessories, Food Items, Gateleg Dining Table, Germany, 3 In. 431.00
Dollhouse Furniture, Armoire, Renaissance Revival Style, Rosewood Veneer, 10 x 6 In. 316.00
Dollhouse Furniture, Baby Carriage, Pink & Blue, Acme Thomas Ind., 1 ¾ In. 10.00
Dollhouse Furniture, Bedroom, Painted, Wood, Schoenhut, 6 Piece *illus* 495.00
Dollhouse Furniture, Bench, Wood, Shaped Graining, Curved Arms, Painted Black, 27 x 22 In. 700.00
Dollhouse Furniture, Birdcage, Parrot On Perch, Painted, Lead, Tin, 2 ½ In. 44.00
Dollhouse Furniture, Carpet Sweeper, Gold Paint, Pot Metal, Germany 52.00
Dollhouse Furniture, Cradle, Lattice Cutouts, Red, Green, Cast Iron, 2 ½ x 3 In. 40.00
Dollhouse Furniture, Desk, Tulipwood, Ebonized, Gilt Metal, 11 3/16 x 9 ¾ x 6 ¾ In. 1304.00
Dollhouse Furniture, Dresser, Pine, Brass Pull, 3 Drawers, Scrollwork Mirror, 12 In. 46.00
Dollhouse Furniture, Fainting Couch, Fabric, Oak, 18 In. 40.00
Dollhouse Furniture, French Kitchen Cookware, Pots, Pans, Ladles, Sieves, 2 To 4 In., 15 Piece 86.00
Dollhouse Furniture, Grand Piano, Wood, Strombecker, 1930. 14.00
Dollhouse Furniture, Kitchen, Victorian, Utensil Rack, Bench, Table, 7 ¾ x 4 ¼ In. 86.00
Dollhouse Furniture, Parlor Set, Animal & Bug Lithograph, 8 Piece *illus* 710.00
Dollhouse Furniture, Stove, Eagle, Cookware, Nickel Plated, Cast Iron, Hubley, 15 In. 88.00
Dollhouse Furniture, Washbowl, Pitcher, China, Flower Pattern, Wood Stand, Painted. 316.00
Dolls are listed in their own category.
Donkey, Glass Eyes, Saddle, Wheeled Base, Stuffed, Pull Toy, 16 In. 115.00
Donkey, Gray, White, Black, Fur, Stuffed, Button In Ear, Steiff, 21 x 22 x 9 ½ In. 385.00
Donkey, Red Felt Blanket, Wood Jointed, Glass Eyes, Rope Tail, Schoenhut, 9 ¼ In. 173.00
Donkey, Wheels, Tin Lithograph, Penny Toy, Meier & Frank Co., Germany, c.1910, 2 ½ In. 450.00
Dottie The Driver, Head Bobs, Plastic, Tin, Windup, Marx, Box, 4 ¾ x 6 ¾ In. 275.00
Drum, American Eagle, Tin, Wood Drumsticks, 7 x 12 In. 30.00
Drum, Pressed Oak, Soldiers, Tension Twine, Leather Heads, c.1900, 8 x 6 ¼ In. 323.00
Drum Set, Hercules Jazz Band, Clown, Chein, 1930 95.00
Drummer, Black Boy, Blue Jacket, Red & White Pants, Celluloid, Windup, 7 ½ In. 300.00
Drummer, Jazz, Hits Cymbals, Tin, Windup, Marx, 8 ½ In. 660.00
Drummer, Marching Band, Tin Lithograph, Windup, Chein, 9 In. 55.00
Drummer, Nazi Uniform, Helmet, Beats Drum, Moves, Windup, Schuco, Germany, 1930s, 9 In. 660.00
Drummer, Parade, Tin Lithograph, Flywheel Mechanism, Rossignol, France, 3 ⅜ In. *illus* 660.00
Drummer Boy, Celluloid, Cloth Outfit, Holds Drum, Windup, 10 In. 115.00
Drummer Boy, Let The Drummer Boy Play, While You Swing & Sway, Tin, Windup, Marx, 8 ½ In. 650.00
Dry Sink, Drawer Over 2 Doors, Yellow Paint, Brown Trim, Porcelain Knobs, 15 x 22 In. 240.00
Duck, Green, Red, Metal, Pull Toy, 6 x 8 In. 132.00
Duck, Popcorn Vendor, Pushes Cart, Tin Lithograph, Battery Operated, TN, Box. 230.00
Duck, Waddler, Holding Bell, Iron, 4 Wheels, Gong Bell Mfg., East Hampton, Conn., c.1893 2800.00
Duck, Wood, No. 148, Pull Toy, Fisher-Price, 7 ¾ x 11 ½ x 9 ¼ In. 140.00
Duck Amphibious Taxi, Monkey Driver, Squirrel Passengers, Tin, Windup, Box, 6 ½ In. 795.00
Duck Set, Baby Ducks Trailing, Tin, Windup, USA, Wyandotte, 1930s, 14 In. 110.00
Dump Cart, Flivver, Open Dump Body Tilts, Painted, Black, Pressed Steel, Buddy L, 11 In. 748.00
Dunkie Donut Head, Hasbro, Box, 1969 70.00
Elephant, Bubble Blowing, Battery Operated, Yonezawa, Box, 7 In. 100.00
Elephant, Circus Barker, Rings Bell, Waves, Celluloid, Tin, Windup, 10 In. 350.00
Elephant, Composition, Pull Toy, c.1940, 12 In. 75.00
Elephant, Drummer, Cloth, Windup, Japan, Box 45.00
Elephant, Trainer, Platform, Spoke Wheels, Tin, Pull Toy, Althof Bergman, c.1880, 9 x 6 In. 2070.00
Elephant, Windy, Juggling Umbrella In Trunk, Plush, Tin, Battery Operated, TN, Japan, Box. 75.00
Elephant, Wood, Glass Eyes, Painted Gray, Cloth Blanket, Schoenhut, 8 In. 201.00
Elves, Hammering Anvil, Penny Toy, Germany, 3 ½ In. 95.00
Engine Kit, Rotary, Mazda Wankel, Parts In Sealed Bag, Battery Operated, Japan, 1971 75.00
Erector Set, No. 7 ½, Wood Box, A.C. Gilbert, 10 x 22 In. *illus* 345.00
Erector Set, No. 8 ½, Giant Ferris Wheel, A.C. Gilbert 33.00
Erector Set, No. 10 ½, Builds Merry-Go-Round Parachute Jump, A.C. Gilbert, Box, 22 x 13 In. 295.00
Erector Set, No. 12 ½, Walking Giant, Remote Control, A.C. Gilbert 33.00
Erector Set, White Truck, Wood Box, Brass Fittings, 7 ½ In. 303.00
Farm, Modern Stock, Cardboard Lithograph, Unpunched, Wards, Built-Rite, Box 160.00
Farm Animal Set, Composition, Rooster, Chickens, Ducks, Turkeys, Birds, 1 ⅞ To 2 ½ In. 154.00
Ferris Wheel, 6 Cars, Tin, Windup, Chein, 16 In. 405.00
Ferris Wheel, 6 Passengers In Chairs, Tin Lithograph, Windup, Marked, Germany, 14 ½ In. 460.00
Ferris Wheel, 8 Open Seats, Figures, Bing, Germany, 13 ½ In. 517.00
Ferris Wheel, Hercules, Tin Lithograph, Windup, Chein, Box, 16 ½ In. 300.00 to 385.00
Ferris Wheel, Nifty, Tin Lithograph, Windup, Chein, 16 ½ In. 405.00

Ferris Wheel, Painted, Tin Lithograph, Steam Driven, 13 In.. 1800.00
Field Glasses, Tom Corbett, Space Cadet, Decals, Steel, Plastic, Strap, Box, 1950s, 5 ¼ In. 198.00
Figure, Captain America, Mego Superheroes, Box *illus* 345.00
Figure, Green Goblin, Mego Superheroes, Box *illus* 575.00
Figure, Peddler, Wizard's Workbench, Wood, Black Cape, Glass Encased, Accessories, 11 x 10 In. 690.00
Figure, Six Million Dollar Man, Test Flight Suit, Kenner, 1975, 12 In. 259.00
Figure, Wizard Of Oz, Tin Woodsman, Cloth Body, Mego, Box, c.1974, 15 In. 86.00
Figure, World's Greatest Superheroes, Amazing Spiderman, Mego, 1977, 12 ½ In.. 110.00
Filling Station, Oil, Gas, Red, Blue, Tin Lithograph, Brightlight, Marx, 1940s, 9 ¼ In. *illus* 220.00
Fire Department Set, No. 30, 3 Vehicles, Motorcycle, Accessories, Painted, Hubley, Box 489.00
Fire Department Set, No. 5211, Trucks, Tools, Ladders, Badge, Hats, Die Cast, Tootsietoy, Box 210.00
Fire House, Alarm, 2 Fire Trucks, Tin, Marx, 17 x 11 In. 895.00
Fire Pumper, Driver, Pull Cord, Tin, Windup, Kingsbury, 9 In.. 403.00
Fire Pumper, Driver, Red, Black, Gold, Tin, Friction, Modern Toys, Japan, c.1950, 9 In. 85.00
Fire Pumper, Fireman, Cast Iron, Metal Hubcaps, Spoke Wheels, Rubber Tires, Matchbox, 1920s, 5 In. 33.00
Fire Pumper, Fireman, Cast Iron, Metal Wheels, Matchbox, 1920s, 5 ½ In. 69.00
Fire Pumper, Fireman, Cast Iron, Metal Wheels, Rubber Tires, Hat, Matchbox, 1920s, 7 ½ In. 44.00
Fire Pumper, Ladders, Driver, Red, Nickel, Hubley 4500.00
Fire Pumper, Ladders, Open Cab, Pressed Steel, Hillclimber Motor, c.1920, 25 In.. 440.00
Fire Pumper, Nickel Plated, White Rubber Tires, Wood Hubcaps, Hubley, 1930s, 4 ¾ In. 45.00
Fire Pumper, Pressed Steel, Kingsbury, c.1936, 18 In., 2 Piece 748.00
Fire Pumper, Pressed Steel, Rubber Wheels, Turner, c.1926, 20 In. 460.00
Fire Pumper, Red, Silver, Wood Wheels, Cast Iron, Hubley, 1930s, 5 In. 75.00
Fire Pumper, Red, Silver Trim, Cast Iron, Rubber Tires, Hubley, 11 In.. 173.00
Fire Pumper, Removable Driver, Cast Iron, Nickel Plated, Ideal, Late 1800s, 15 In.. 575.00
Fire Pumper, T.F.D., No. 5, Red, No. 950, Tonka, 17 In.. 195.00
Fire Truck, 6 Men, Tin, Windup, Prewar Germany, 14 In.. 375.00
Fire Truck, Aerial Ladder, 3 Parts, Pulley Wheel Guides, Buddy L, 1920s, 55 ½ In.. 390.00
Fire Truck, Chemical, Drivers, Ladder, Nickel Grille, Ladder Hoist, Hubley, 13 In. 1200.00
Fire Truck, Chemical, Pressed Steel, Painted, Spoke Wheels, Schieble, c.1913, 12 In. 1610.00
Fire Truck, Driver, Red, Gold, Pressed Steel, Tin, Friction, Schieble, c.1913, 12 ¼ In. *illus* 395.00
Fire Truck, Hillclimber, Tin, Wood, Wheels, Painted, Mechanical, 9 x 14 x 3 ½ In. 165.00
Fire Truck, Hook & Ladder, Pressed Steel, Buddy L, c.1926, 24 In. 460.00
Fire Truck, Hook & Ladder, Pressed Steel, Steelcraft, c.1926, 26 In.. 633.00
Fire Truck, Hook & Ladder, Pressed Steel, Structo, 18 In. 201.00
Fire Truck, Hose, Green, Gold, Rubber Tires, Kenton, 7 In.. 575.00
Fire Truck, Kiddies Oh-Boy, Orange Boiler, Red Open Cab, Fenders, Chassis, Bell, 23 In.. 403.00
Fire Truck, Ladder, 5 Firemen, Nickel Bumpers, Tin Lithograph, Windup, Penny Toy, 4 ¼ In. 431.00
Fire Truck, Ladder, Battery Operated, Japan, c.1950, 13 In. 145.00
Fire Truck, Ladder, Bell, Hose Reel, Pressed Steel, Keystone, c.1927, 29 In.. 690.00
Fire Truck, Ladder, Red, Black Frame, Nickel Lights, Bumper, Cast Iron, Hubley, 10 ½ In. 863.00
Fire Truck, Ladder, Red, Silver, Nickel Plated, Rubber Wheels, Hubley, 1 ¾ x 5 x 2 In.. 88.00
Fire Truck, Ladder, Red, Spoke Wheels, Driver, Hose Reel, Cast Iron, Kenton, 22 In. 920.00
Fire Truck, Ladder, Rubber Tires, Cast Iron, Matchbox, 1920, 7 ½ In.. 39.00
Fire Truck, Ladder, Yellow, Green, Red, Pressed Steel, Dayton, c.1910, 19 ½ In. 575.00
Fire Truck, L-Mack, Aerial Ladder, Pressed Steel, Smith-Miller, 27 In.. 575.00
Fire Truck, Pumper, Pressed Steel, Live Water Pumper Model, Structo, c.1926, 22 In. 748.00
Fire Truck, Red, No. 9C4, Matchbox, Box 100.00
Fire Truck, White Rubber Wheels, Red, Silver, Cast Iron, Hubley, 2 x 4 ⅞ x 1 ¾ In. 33.00
Fire Wagon, 2 Horses, Removable Driver, Hose Reel, Cast Iron, 6 ¼ x 17 ½ x 3 ¾ In. 413.00
Fire Wagon, Hook & Ladder, 2 Horses, 2 Firemen, Yellow, Phoenix, 1880s, 16 In.. 1195.00
Fire Wagon, Hook & Ladder, 2 Horses, Drivers, 3 Wood Ladders, Gong Bell, 1908, 31 In.. 2200.00
Fire Wagon, Hook & Ladder, Articulating Horses, Driver, Gong Bell, Hubley, 1910, 24 In. 700.00
Fire Wagon, Hook & Ladder, Articulating Horses, Firemen, Gong Bell, Dent, c.1905, 26 In.. 950.00
Fire Wagon, Hook & Ladder, Horses, Carriage, Wagon, Spoke Wheels, Hubley, 16 In.. 95.00
Fire Wagon, Hook & Ladder, Horses, Gong Bell, Jones & Bixler, 1908, 31 In.. 2495.00
Fire Wagon, Ladder, 2 Black & 1 White Horse, Red, Yellow, Open Frame, Cast Iron, Kenton, 16 In. 115.00
Fire Wagon, Patrol, Driver, 6 Firemen, Open Bench Seat, Railed Sides, Cast Iron, Ives, 18 In.. 1265.00
Fire Wagon, Pumper, 2 Horses, Painted, Cast Iron, Ives, c.1890, 7 x 18 x 4 In. 800.00
Fire Wagon, Pumper, 3 Horses, Driver, Harris, 1903, 15 In. 595.00
Fire Wagon, Pumper, Horse, Driver, Nickel, Bronze Frame, Hubley, 1910, 21 In. 2200.00
Fire Wagon, Pumper, Horse Drawn, Fireman, Hubley, c.1915, 4 ½ In. 325.00
Fire Wagon, Pumper, No. 10, Articulating Horses, Gong Bell, Nickel Pumper, 1910, 21 In. 1900.00
Fireman, Climbing, Tin Lithograph, Windup, Marx, 22 In. 160.00
Flintstones, Barney, Rubbles Wreck, Tin, Vinyl Head, Hanna-Barbera Prod., Marx, c.1962, 7 ¼ In. 153.00
Flintstones, Dinosaur, Dino, Steiff, 12 In. 468.00
Flintstones, Flivver, Fred Driver, Tin & Plastic, Remote Control, Battery Operated, Marx, 7 In. 518.00

Toy, Drummer, Parade, Tin Lithograph, Flywheel Mechanism, Rossignol, France, 3 ⅜ In.
$660.00

Toy, Erector Set, No. 7 ½, Wood Box, A.C. Gilbert, 10 x 22 In.
$345.00

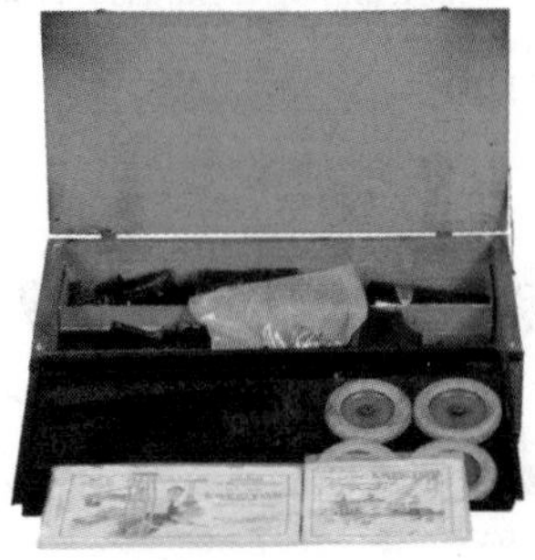

Toy, Figure, Captain America, Mego Superheroes, Box
$345.00

TIP
Battery-operated toys should be run regularly to keep the parts working. Remove batteries before storing the toy.

Toy, Figure, Green Goblin, Mego Superheroes, Box
$575.00

Toy, Filling Station, Oil, Gas, Red, Blue, Tin Lithograph, Brightlight, Marx, 1940s, 9 ¼ In.
$220.00

Toy, Fire Truck, Driver, Red, Gold, Pressed Steel, Tin, Friction, Schieble, c.1913, 12 ¼ In.
$395.00

Toy, G.I. Joe, Kung Fu Grip, Talks, Hair, Beard, Rifle, Dog Tags, Hasbro, No. 7290, Box, 1974
$176.00

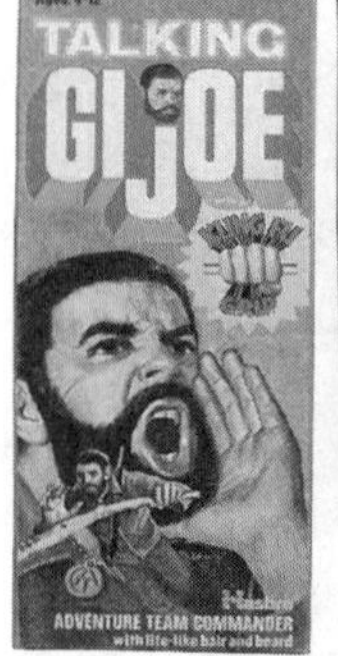

Flintstones, Fred, On Tricycle, Linemar, 4 In. 150.00
Flintstones, Fred, Riding Dino, Battery Operated, Fur Covered, Linemar, 18 In. 345.00
Flintstones, Wilma, On Tricycle, Linemar, Box, 4 In. 295.00
Flower Shop, Cloth Awning, 2 Shelves, Flower Bunches, Wood Frame, 19 x 18 In. 115.00
Flower Vendor, Black, Pink Dress, Hand Painted, Tin, Windup, Germany, 8 In. 830.00
Flying Hollander, Painted, Tin, Lead, Penny Toy, Meier, 3 ¼ In. 275.00
Flying Saucer, Bump & Go, Light Blinks, Tin, Plastic, Battery Operated, 8 In. .... 73.00 to 198.00
Flyman Robot, SY, Tin, Windup, Japan, Box, 11 In. 490.00
Fork Lift, Metal, Tin, Friction, Battery Operated, 1950s, 9 In. 95.00
Fortress, Drawbridges, Towers, Turrets, Moritz Gottschalk, 22 x 22 In. 489.00
Fox The Magician, Tin, Fabric, Plush, Windup, Nomura, Japan, Box, 7 In. 350.00
Foxy Grandpa, Roly Poly, Papier-Mache, Early 1900s, 9 ½ In. 450.00
Frankenstein, Bends, Tin, Vinyl, Battery Operated Remote, Nomura, Marx, Box, c.1963, 12 ½ In. 1413.00
Frankenstein, Walker, Moves Arms, Tin, Plastic, Windup, Marx, Box, c.1963, 5 ½ In. 583.00
Fruit Juice Counter, Girl, Tin, Cloth, Vinyl, Battery Operated, IGB, Japan, Box, 7 ½ In. 165.00
Fruit Vendor, Black Man, Seated, Cloth, Tin, Windup, Martin French, 7 ½ In. 440.00
Frying Pan, Cast Iron, Kenton, 3 ½ In. 45.00
Fun Slate, Three Stooges, Moe, Curly & Larry, Norman Maurer Production, 1959, 8 x 13 In. 175.00
Funny Face, Facial Expressions Change, Wobbles, Tin, Windup, Marx, c.1924, 11 In. 599.00
G.I. Joe, Deep Sea Diver, Hasbro, 1965, 12 In. 175.00
G.I. Joe, German Storm Trooper, No. 8100, Hasbro, 1966, 12 In. 195.00
G.I. Joe, Jeep, Tin Lithograph, Windup, Unique Art Mfg. Co., 7 In. 239.00
G.I. Joe, Kung Fu Grip, Talks, Hair, Beard, Rifle, Dog Tags, Hasbro, No. 7290, Box, 1974 . *illus* 176.00
G.I. Joe, Scarface, Blond Hair, Marine Manual, Shoes, Belt, Pat. Pending 275.00
G.I. Joe & Jouncing Jeep, Tin, Windup, Unique Art, Box, 1950, 7 In. 295.00
Gabby Goose, Articulated, Without Hat, No. 120, Fisher-Price, c.1936, 9 In. 316.00
Gallop Cowboy, Jumps, Zebra Pulled Cart, Windup, 1954 .... 350.00
Games are listed in their own category.
Garage, Racing Car, Green Sedan, Children Silhouettes, Lehmann, 6 ½ x 4 ½ In. 1610.00
Garage, Stable, 2 Story, Scalloped Edge Shingles, 3 Doors, Painted, Wood, 27 x 18 In. 201.00
Gas Pump, Hulco Stop & Go Sign, Pressed Steel, Wyandotte, 9 In. 460.00
Gas Pump, Metal, U.S.A., 1930s, 7 ½ In. 175.00
Gas Station, Car, Tin, England, 9 ½ In. 245.00
Gas Station, Embossed, Painted, Paper Over Tin, Gibbs, 9 x 15 In. 77.00
Gas Station, Mobile, Racing Car, Tin, Penny Toy, Japan 150.00
Gas Station, Texaco, Cars, Pumps, Equipment, Buddy L, Box, 24 ½ x 15 ¾ x 2 ¾ In. 326.00
Gas Station Garage, Gas Pump, Red, Yellow, Tin Lithograph, Penny Toy, Germany, 2 x 4 In. 90.00
Gazebo, Railing, Red & White Canopy, Swing, Flower Boxes, Tin, Doll Sized, Marklin, 20 x 11 In. 12650.00
Geese, Pecking, Embossed, Tin Lithograph, Penny Toy, Germany, 2 In. 165.00
George The Drummer Boy, Tin Lithograph, Windup, Marx, Box, 9 In. .... 110.00 to 250.00
Gerty The Galloping Goose, Walker, Tin Lithograph, Windup, Unique Art, 1930s, 9 In. 44.00
Gino Neapolitan Balloon Blower, Battery Operated, Rosko Toy, Tomiyama, Japan, Box 100.00
Girl, Bouncing Ball, Tin Lithograph, Windup, T.P.S., Japan, 5 In. 40.00
Girl, In Highchair, Converts To Table, Tin Lithograph, Penny Toy, Meier, 2 ¾ In. 250.00
Girl, In Stroller, Embossed, Tin Lithograph, Penny Toy, 3 In. 135.00
Girl, On Sled, Metal, Plastic, Windup, Box, 4 In. 29.00
Girl, On Swing, Boy Rings Bell, Celluloid, Tin, Windup, 7 ½ In. 1650.00
Girl, On Swing, Embossed, Tin Lithograph, Penny Toy, Distler, 2 ¾ In. 135.00
Girl Skipping Rope, Tin, Windup, Japan, 1950s, 12 ½ In. 145.00
Gnome, Feeding Parrot, Embossed, Tin Lithograph, Penny Toy, Meier, 4 ¼ In. 187.00
Gnome, On Egg, With Rabbit, Penny Toy, 3 ⅜ In. 850.00
Gnome, Yes-No, Jointed, Felt, Mohair, Schuco, 9 In. 138.00
Gnomes, At Anvil, Embossed, Tin Lithograph, Lever, Penny Toy, Meier, 4 In. 187.00
Going To The Fair, Woman In Promenade Chair, Porter, Flywheel, Tin Lithograph, 5 x 6 ½ In. 2300.00
Golden Goose, Tin Lithograph, Windup, Marx, Box, 9 In. 110.00
Gondola, 4 Passengers, Musical, Painted, Tin, Germany, 11 ⅜ In. 652.00
Goose, Nodding, Windup, Marx, 1924, 6 In. 75.00
Goose, Riding, Red Goose Shoes, Wood, Steel Disc Wheels, Rubber Tires, 1920 .... 2000.00
Gorilla, Walker, Roars, Fur, Battery Operated, TN, Japan, Box, 7 ½ In. 132.00
Grader, Caterpillar, Yellow, Motor, Plastic, Box, 1950s, 12 In. 175.00
Grader, Yellow, No. 2006, Doepke, c.1949, 26 In. 275.00
Grain Elevator, Green, Pressed Steel, B. Greene, 14 x 18 In. 354.00
Granny Doodle & Family, Wood, Pull Toy, No. 101, Fisher-Price, 1933, 9 ½ In. 450.00
Grasshopper, Clicks, Green, Painted, Cast Iron, Aluminum, Rubber, Pull Toy, Hubley, 10 In. 550.00
Grasshopper, Daddy Long Legs, Green, Cast Iron, Hubley, Box, 9 In. .... *illus* 1725.00
Gravel Crusher, Instructions, Reuhl Pitmaster, c.1950, Box 1300.00
Great Garloo, Bends, Picks Up Objects, Plastic, Battery Operated, Remote Control, Marx, 24 In. 390.00

Grocery Store, Toy Town, Wood, Accessories, 21 In. 195.00
Grocery Store, Wood, Green Walls, Linoleum Floor, Germany, 17 ¾ x 29 x 13 In. 237.00
Guitar, Civil War Centennial, Painted, Wood, Plastic, American Toys, Jefferson Co., Box, 30 In. 10.00
Gun, BB, Daisy Eagle, Pouch, Holder, Strap, Box, c.1957 .... 1430.00
Gun, BB, Pistol, Daisy Targeteer, 2 Tubes Of Shot, Tarey, Box, 1939, 4 ½ In. 345.00
Gun, Colt 45, 6 Cartridges, Die Cast, Hubley, Box, 13 In. 275.00
Gun, Ray, Signal, Get Smart, Agent 86 Sticker, Plastic, Battery Operated, Copyright NBC, 1966, 7 In. 790.00
Gun, Ray, Tin, Friction, Sparking Action, Japan, 1960s, 5 In. 22.00
Gun, Rifle Pistol, Steve McQueen, Wanted Dead Or Alive, Marx, 1960, 7 ½ x 3 ¾ In. 80.00
Gun, Space, Sparks, Tin Lithograph, Japan, Marked, San, Box, 1950s, 3 ½ x 3 ½ In. 220.00
Gun & Holster Set, Wild Bill Hickok, Jingles, Die Cast, Leather, 12 Bullets, Box, 9 In. .. *illus* 518.00
Gunboat, Gray, White, Red Trimmed Stacks, Tin, Windup, Fleischmann, 9 ¼ In. 1093.00
Gymnast, Man, Painted, Composition, Cloth, Wood, Windup, Pat'd By Will Hubbel, 1875, 8 In. 1760.00
Gyro Cycle, Boy On Bicycle, Metal, Celluloid, Cloth, Triang, Box, 9 In. .... 127.00 to 213.00
Ham & Sam, Minstrel Team, Tin, Windup, F. Strauss Corp., 7 x 7 In. .... 452.00 to 605.00
Hamburger Chef, Tin Lithograph, Battery Operated, G.B.C., Japan, Box 110.00
Happy Band Trio, Plush Animals, Battery Operated, Modern Toys, Japan, Box, 11 In. 380.00 to 550.00
Happy Hippo, Native On Back, Moves In Circle, Gray, Tin, Windup, T.P.S., Box, 6 In. 791.00
Happy Hooligan, Head Pops Out Of Ball, Papier-Mache, Tin Wheels, 3 ½ x 4 In. 55.00
Happy Hooligan, Roly Poly, Yellow, Red, Germany, 5 ½ In. .... *illus* 115.00
Happy Hooligan, Walker, Tin, Windup, Chein, Box, 1932, 6 In. .... *illus* 720.00
Happy Skaters, Bear, Tin, Windup, T.P.S., Box, 6 ¼ In. 536.00
Harlequin, Girl Boy Ballet Dancers, Moving Picture, Sand Activated, Triple Action, 10 x 8 In. 330.00
Harold Lloyd, Bell Ringer, Squeeze, Face Changes Expressions, Germany, 1930s 350.00
Hat, Texaco Fire Chief, Microphone, Battery Operated, Hard Plastic, Box, 1960s, 8 ¼ x 8 ¼ In. 173.00
Hay Fork, Wood, 3 Prongs, Support Stretchers, 16 ¾ x 4 ½ In. 33.00
Hay Loader, John Deere, Cast Iron, Chain Driven, Embossed, Vindex, 9 x 8 In. 2070.00
Hearse, Painted, Spoked Hubs, Rubber Tires, Cast Iron, Motorcade Toys, 10 In. 690.00
Helicopter, HUP-2, Navy, U.S. Air Force Marking, Tin, Friction, 10 In. 147.00
Helicopter, Piston, Tin, Friction, Japan, 11 In. 95.00
Helmet, Fire Chief, Texaco, Red, Plastic, 1960s, 9 x 14 ½ In. 55.00
Hen, Pip-Squeak, Papier-Mache, Painted, Hinged Wings, Bellows, 3 ¾ In. 176.00
Hen, With Wicker Basket, Pressed Cardboard, Wood Platform, Wheels, Multicolored, 9 ¾ In. . 58.00
Henry, With Elephant, Native Rider, Celluloid, Windup, Japan, Box, 8 ½ In. 880.00
Henry, With His Brother, Celluloid, Tin, Windup, Repro Box, 6 ½ In. 440.00
Henry, With Swan Cart, Celluloid, Tin, Windup, 6 x 7 In. 770.00
Hey-Hey Chicken Snatcher, Black Man, Chicken, Tin, Windup, Louis Marx & Co., 8 In. 542.00 to 770.00
High Jinks At The Circus, Clown, Nose Lights, Chimp, Battery Operated, Alps, Box, 10 In. .. 186.00
Hippopotamus, Painted Brown, Leather Tail, Ears, Wood Jointed, Painted Eyes, Schoenhut, 9 ¼ In. 86.00
Hobbyhorse, Carved, Wood, Multicolored, Horsehair Mane, Tail, 50 In. 201.00
Hobbyhorse, Glider, Leather Tack, Horsehair Mane & Tail, Carved Wood, Gray Paint, c.1900, 45 In. 646.00
Hobbyhorse, Painted, White, Gray, Black, Spots, Saddle, Horsehair Mane, Tail, 1900, 37 x 45 In. 995.00
Hobbyhorse, Painted, White, Green Saddle, Flowers, Horsehair Tail, 1900, 37 x 60 In. 322.00
Hobbyhorse, Rawhide & Leather Tack, Leather Saddle, Glass Eyes, Wood Frame, c.1850, 62 In. 588.00
Holster Belt, Lash LaRue, Leather, Embossed Lettering, Flowers, 17 Bullets, 41 In. 1440.00
Home Run King, Batter Swings, Tin, Windup, Selrite Products, 6 ½ In. 360.00
Honeymoon Express, Train, Tunnel, Bridge, Tin Lithograph, Windup, Marx, Box, 9 In. 201.00
Hoop, Stick, Pinstriped, Wood, Late 1800s, 33 In. 110.00
Hoopy The Fishing Duck, 3 Tin Fish, Plush, Battery Operated, Alps, Box 200.00
Hoosier Cabinet, Pine, 2 Parts, 4 Drawers, 2 Glass Doors, Pullout Cutting Boards, 32 x 19 In. 180.00
Hopping Elroy, Jetsons, Tin, Windup, Hanna-Barbera, Marx, Japan, Box, 1963, 4 In. 402.00
Hopping George, Jetsons, Tin, Windup, Hanna-Barbera, Marx, Japan, 1963, 4 In. 518.00
Hopping Goose, Tin Lithograph, Windup, Unique Art, 9 ½ In. 80.00
Horn, Carousel, Embossed, Tin Lithograph, Penny Toy, France, 4 ½ In. 85.00
Horn, Carousel, Embossed, Tin Lithograph, Penny Toy, Kico, Germany, 4 In. 110.00
Horn, Monkey, Embossed, Tin Lithograph, Penny Toy, Germany, 4 ½ In. 85.00
Horn, Spirit Painted, Penny Toy, Germany, 9 In. 35.00
Horse, Annie Oakley Rider, Rearing Tan Horse, Gun, Hat, Plastic, Hartland, 9 In. 144.00
Horse, Brown, White, Fur, Pull Toy, Steiff, 27 x 22 In. 200.00
Horse, Buffalo Bill Rider, Plastic, Rearing Brown Horse, Hartland, 9 In. 144.00
Horse, Cheyenne Rider, Semi Rearing Pinto, Knife, Gun, Hat, Plastic, Hartland, 9 In. 144.00
Horse, Chief Thunder Cloud Rider, Rearing Palamino, Spear, Head Dress, Plastic, Hartland, 9 In. 86.00
Horse, Composition, Horsehair, Cloth Reins, Plastic Hooves, 8 ½ x 11 ½ In. 22.00
Horse, General Custer Rider, Rearing Tan Horse, Gun, Hat, Plastic, Hartland, 9 In. 115.00
Horse, General Washington Rider, Plastic, Walking White Horse, Sword, Hat, Hartland, 9 In. . 86.00
Horse, Hide Covered, Wheeled Platform, Leather Saddle, Cast Iron Wheels, Painted, 37 In. .. 690.00
Horse, On Platform, Felt Covered, Hollow, Composition, Glass Eyes, Tin Wheels, Pull Toy, 11 ½ In. 403.00

Toy, Grasshopper, Daddy Long Legs, Green, Cast Iron, Hubley, Box, 9 In.
$1725.00

Toy, Gun & Holster Set, Wild Bill Hickok, Jingles, Die Cast, Leather, 12 Bullets, Box, 9 In.
$518.00

Toy, Happy Hooligan, Roly Poly, Yellow, Red, Germany, 5 ½ In.
$115.00

Toy, Happy Hooligan, Walker, Tin, Windup, Chein, Box, 1932, 6 In.
$720.00

T

Toy, Jack-In-The-Box, Chicken, Composition, Paper Over Wood, 4 x 3 ¾ In.
$200.00

Toy, Kangaroo, Painted Eyes, Wood Jointed, Schoenhut, 7 ¼ x 8 In.
$275.00

Toy, Kitty Kat, Tin, Wood, Lever Activated, Marx, Box, 8 In.
$201.00

TIP
Rusted toys have very low value.

Horse, Papier-Mache, Pull Toy, Germany, 7 In. 125.00
Horse, Pedal, Mobo Bronco, Painted Metal, On Wheels, 20th Century, 30 In. 58.00
Horse, Race, Tin, Friction, Japan, 1950s, 5 In. 75.00
Horse, Rifleman Rider, Walking Brown Horse, Rifle, Hat, Plastic, Hartland, 9 In. 144.00
Horse, Rocking, Brown & Black Paint, Carved, Laminated Wood, c.1900, 29 x 40 In. 206.00
Horse, Rocking, Hide Cover, Flowing Mane, Tail, Wood Snout, Hooves, Leather Saddle, 39 x 30 In. 345.00
Horse, Rocking, Horsehide Cover, Wood, Glass Eyes, Open Mouth, Leather Saddle, 28 x 14 In. 489.00
Horse, Rocking, Painted, Wood, Glass Eye, Leather Saddle, Spring Action, c.1890, 18 x 29 In.. 167.00
Horse, Rocking, White, Green, Red Rocker, Carved, Original Paint, 32 In. 220.00
Horse, Rocking, Wood, Masonite, Red, Black, Spring Platform, 34 In. 115.00
Horse, Rocking, Wood, Painted, Horsehair Mane, Tail, Smoke Design, Late 1800s, 28 x 46 In. 750.00
Horse, Wunderflitz, Dappled Gray Paint, Saddle, Wheeled Base, Schoenhut, 27 x 24 In. 10925.00
Horse & Driver, Racing Cycle, Composition, Germany, 1930s 225.00
Horse & Jockey, Tin, Germany, 5 In. 100.00
Horse & Rider, Composition, Tin Lithograph, Windup, Kohler, Germany, 4 In. 69.00
Horse & Wagon, Dairy, Tin, Windup, Marx, 1930s, 10 ½ In. 175.00
Horse & Wagon, Hay, Pull Toy, Wood Lithograph, 25 In. 165.00
Horse Race, Embossed, Tin Lithograph, Penny Toy, Germany, 3 ¼ In. 187.00
Hot Mammy, No. 810, Windup, Fisher-Price, Box, 7 In. 1380.00
Hot Mammy, Walker, Cast Iron Feet, Windup, No. 810, Fisher-Price, Box, 7 In. 1380.00
House, Front Porch, Woods, Fruit Crate, Brick Pattern Paper, 20 ¾ x 17 ¾ x 25 In. 99.00
House, Wood, Stucco, Glass Windows, Shutters, Tin Spouting, Chimney, 25 x 29 x 23 In. 935.00
Howitzer & Tractor, Gift Set, Green, No. 695, Dinky Toys, Box 500.00
Humphrey Mobile, Humphrey, Shack On Tricycle, Smokestack, Tin, Windup, 9 In. 489.00 to 644.00
Hungry Cat, Fish In Bowl, Battery Operated, Linemar, Box, 8 ½ In. 625.00
Hurdy Gurdy, Monkey, Wood, Rubber, Metal, 14 In. 86.00
I.C.B.M Launching Station, 2-Stage Rocket, Tin, Friction, Crank, Horikawa, 8 In. 848.00
Ice Cream Cart, Penguin, Gong Bell, Paper Over Wood, Disc Wheels, Bells, 8 ¾ In. 288.00
Ice Cream Cart, Tin, Windup, Courtland Ice, U.S.A., 1948, 6 ½ In. 395.00
Ice Cream Scooter, Windup, Scooter, U.S.A., 1948, 7 In. 375.00
Ice Cream Table Set, Wire Chairs, Wood Seats, Round Table, 17 In. 144.00
Indian, Riding Snake, Pink, White, Celluloid, Windup, 18 In. 90.00
Iron, Dover, Dolly, Green Handle, 3 ½ In. 22.00
Jackie The Hornpipe Dancer, Sailor Figure, On Boat Deck, Tin Lithograph, Strauss, 8 ½ In. 863.00
Jack-In-The-Box, Chicken, Composition, Paper Over Wood, 4 x 3 ¾ In. .... *illus* 200.00
Jack-In-The-Box, Chimney Sweep, Painted, Composition, Wood, 6 In. 110.00
Jack-In-The-Box, Devil's Head, Painted, Embossed, Carved, Wood, Ribbon, 8 ½ In. 135.00
Jail, 2 Story, Wood, Paper Lithograph, Cells, Germany, 20 x 21 In. 259.00
Jazzbo Jim, Dances On Roof, Tin, Windup, Unique Art, 1921, 9 x 5 x 3 In. .... 275.00 to 546.00
Jazzbo Jim, Plaid Jacket, Pants, Plays Violin, Dances, Strauss, Box, c.1921, 10 In. 311.00
Jeep, Fire Patrol, Friction, TN Co., Japan, Box, 7 In. 95.00
Jeep, Flying, Spinners, Tin, Friction, Asahitoy, 8 In. 153.00
Jenny The Mule, Driver, Wagon, Tin, Windup, Strauss, 1930s, 10 In. 295.00
Jet Helmet, Steve Canyon, Ideal, Box, 1959 .... 125.00
Jetrail Express, 12 Rods, Tin, Windup, Northrup Products, Box, 11 In. 70.00
Jigger, Dapper Dan, Dances, Windup, Marx, 10 In. 690.00
Jigger, Stands On Planking, Dances, Holds Flag, Windup, Lehmann, Box, 10 ½ In. 863.00
Jigger, Tombo, Dances On Box, 10 In. 575.00
Jiggling Jim, High Stepping Dancer, Top Hat, Stars On Pants, Dances, Lever, England. 250.00
Jockey, On Horse, Painted, Cast Iron, Metal Holder, Wood Rod, Pull Toy, 1930s. 20.00
Joe Penner, Carrying Duck, Suitcase, Tin Lithograph, Marx, 8 ½ In. 350.00
Joe Penner, Wanna Buy A Duck, Windup, Marx, 8 ½ In. 138.00
Johnny Tremain, Revolutionary War Playset, 3 British Sets, No. 3402, Marx, Box, 20 ½ In... 2070.00
Jolly Black Joe, Drum, Moving Head, Eyes, Celluloid, Windup, 7 In. 316.00
Jumping Jalopy, 4 Riders, Tin, Windup, Marx, Box, 6 ¾ In. 694.00
Jumping Rocket, Rider Hops, Arms Move, Tin, Windup, Yonezawa, Box, c.1965, 6 In. 565.00
Jungle Trio, Elephant Blows Whistle, Monkeys, Battery Operated, Linemar, Box, 7 ½ In. 566.00
Kangaroo, Joey, Beige Fur, Excelsior Stuffing, Embroidered, Steiff, 6 ¼ & 16 ½ In. 563.00
Kangaroo, Joey In Pouch, Glass Eyes, Mama's Head Swivels, Steiff, 1950s, 19 In. 115.00
Kangaroo, Painted Eyes, Wood Jointed, Schoenhut, 7 ¼ x 8 In. .... *illus* 275.00
Kitchen, 5 Walls, Stove, Plate Shelf, Utensils, Accessories, 19th Century, 15 x 32 In. 1955.00
Kitchen, Cast Iron Furniture, Accessories, Arcade, 20 In. 690.00
Kitchen Set, Maid, Appliances, Pots & Pans, No. 16041, Marklin, Box. 260.00
Kitchenware, Tin, Pots & Pans, Lids, George Brown American, Miniature, c.1870, 10 Piece.. 115.00
Kite, Green Hornet, Roalex, 1966, 36 x 6 In. 395.00
Kitty Kat, Tin, Wood, Lever Activated, Marx, Box, 8 In. .... *illus* 201.00
Knockout Champs, Boxers, Ring, Celluloid, Windup, Marx. 450.00

Komical Kop, Beat It, Driver's Head Spins, Tin, Windup, Marx, Box, 1930, 7 In. 904.00
Krampus, Painted, Composition, Crepe Body, Cardboard, Squeak, Stamped, Germany, 9 In.. . 245.00
Lady Pup, Tending Her Garden, Pup Waters Flowers, Battery Operated, Tomiyama, Box, 8 In. 310.00
Ladybug, Painted, Tin Lithograph, Windup, Gunthermann, Germany, c.1920, 7 ½ In. 287.00
Lamb, Glass Eyes, Composition Head, Platform, Pull Toy, 9 ¾ In. 690.00
Landing Of Columbus, Ship, Bell, Gold Paint, Cast Iron, Pull Toy, Gong Mfg. Co., 1892, 7 In. 600.00
Li'l Abner Dogpatch Band, Tin Litho, Windup, Unique Art, Box, c.1945, 8 x 9 In. ..... *illus* 440.00
Lion, Magic Action Circus, Stands, Roars, Battery Operated, Rock Valley Toys, Box, 10 In..... 220.00
Lion, Plush, Growls, Mechanical, Marx, Box, 8 In.. .... 150.00
Lion, Wood, Jointed, Cloth Mane, Glass Eyes, Rope Tail, Leather Ears, Schoenhut, 7 In....... 259.00
Lion Tamer, Wood Jointed, Composition Head, Leather Boots, Red Fez, Schoenhut, 8 In. 144.00
Little Shoemaker, Tin, Cloth, Windup, Alps, Box, 6 In.. .... 70.00
Loop The Loop, Spins, Rings Bell, Wolverine, 1930s, 19 In. 880.00
Lunch Basket, Spaceship, Space Graphic, Decoware, 1950, 7 ½ x 5 x 4 In. 94.00
Maggie & Jiggs, On Cart, Tin Lithograph, Windup, Nifty, 7 In. 990.00
Maggie & Jiggs, On Platform, Umbrella, Cane, Tin Lithograph, Windup, c.1924, 7 In. 1150.00
Magic Man, Walks, Smokes Pipe, Battery Operated, Remote, Marusan, Box, 12 In. 204.00
Magic Slate, Munsters, Cardboard Backed Slate, Stylus, c.1965, 9 x 14 In. 345.00
Magician, Happy-Go-Lucky, Bobo, Tin, Windup, Nomura, Box, 8 ½ In.. .... 500.00
Make-Up Bear, Pink, In Rocker, Battery Operated, Modern Toys, Box 360.00
Mama Kangaroo, Playful Baby, Jumps, Tin, Windup, T.P.S., Box, 6 In. 170.00
Mambo Elephant Drummer, Pink, Battery Operated, Box, Alps, Japan, 1960s 10.00
Mammy, Sweeps, Dances, Tin, Windup, Lindstrom, Box, 8 In. 305.00
Man, Dancing On Drum, Tin, Windup, Japan, 8 ½ In.. .... 70.00
Man, In Boat, Standing, Flag On Bow, Green Hull, Penny Toy, Meier, Germany, 4 ½ In. 546.00
Man, On 3-Wheel Cart, Tin, Windup, Germany, 7 x 4 ½ In.. .... 195.00
Man, On Elephant, In Howdah, Legs Lift, Umbrella, Windup, Gunthermann, Germany, 8 ¼ In. 1380.00
Man, Pedaling Airship, Painted, Pole Balance Support, Windup, Muller & Kadeder, 18 In. ... 2300.00
Man, Seated, Swing, Pine, Gesso, Painted, Pull Toy, 19th Century, 8 In. 823.00
Man, Shooting Pool, Ball Automatically Returns, Windup, Gunthermann, c.1900, 11 In. 975.00
Man, Walking 2 Pigs, Windup, Martin, France, 8 In. .... *illus* 4100.00
Man, With Spinning Wheel, Embossed, Tin Lithograph, Lever, Distler, 5 ½ In. 715.00
Man, Zebra Pulling Cart, Tin, Windup, Lehmann, Na-Nu Toy, 7 In. .... *illus* 385.00
Man From Mars, Advances, Raises, Lowers Arms, Plastic, Windup, Irwin, 11 ½ In.. .... 272.00
Manure Spreader, John Deere, Vindex, c.1928, 9 ¼ In. 1000.00
Marionette Theater, Ballerina, Clown, Celluloid, Tin Lithograph, Windup, Box, Japan, 9 ½ In. 400.00
Market Woman, Pushing Cart, Goose Flaps Wings, Painted, Tin, Windup, Germany, 8 In.... 1430.00
Martin The Drunkard, Tin, Cloth, Windup, France, c.1915, 8 In. 288.00
Marvelous Mike Robot Tractor, Electromagnetic, Battery Operated, Saunders, Box, 16 In. . 403.00
Mary & Her Lamb, Celluloid, Tin, Windup, 6 ¾ In. 245.00
Mary & Lamb, Composition Head, Wood, Jointed, Glass Eyes, Schoenhut, 8 ½ In. ..... *illus* 330.00
Masuyama, Asian Woman, Rickshaw, Parasol, Tin Lithograph, Windup, Lehmann, 6 ¾ In.. . 1955.00
Mechanic's Tools & Parts, Biplane, Metal Plates, Original Paint, 1900s, 7 x 16 In. 206.00
Mego Man, Red Face, Walks, Moves Arms, Legs, Bell Rings, Tin, Windup, Yoneya, 6 ¾ In..... 294.00
Mego Man, Silver Face, Walks, Sparking Eyes, Tin, Windup, Yoneya, 6 ¾ In. 582.00
Merry-Go-Round, 4 Horses, Riders, Painted, Tin, Germany, 12 In. 340.00
Merry-Go-Round, Men, Pigs, Horses, Tin, Windup, Marked, Germany SG, 8 In. .... *illus* 747.00
Merry-Go-Round, Playland, Bell Rings, 5 Horses, 5 Swans, Tin Lithograph, Windup, Chein, 11 In. 275.00
Merrymakers Band, Mice, Tin Lithograph, Windup, Marx, 9 In. 770.00
Mexicali Pete, Plays Drum, Battery Operated, Alps, Box, 12 In. 175.00
Mickey Mantle Automatic Batting Machine, Tin, Mechanical, K Corp., Box, Japan, c.1960, 7 In. 940.00
Minstrel, Arm Strums, White Dress, Blue Apron, Painted, Tin, Germany, 8 In. 1540.00
Miss Friday, Typist, Tin, Vinyl, Cloth, Battery Operated, Box, Japan, 8 ½ In. 220.00
Model Kit, Car, Duesenberg, Town Car, Model SJ, Metal, Hubley, Box, 1950s 50.00
Model Kit, Car, Duesenberg Straight 8, Metal, Hubley, 1975, 13 x 7 In. 73.00
Model Kit, Truck, Delivery, Model I, Metal, Hubley, 1912, 10 ¼ x 7 In.. .... 60.00
Model Kit, UFO From The Invaders, No. 813, Aurora, Box, 1968, 135 x 7 In.. .... 25.00
Monkey, Basketball Player, Tin, Windup, T.P.S. Japan, Box, 99 In. 165.00
Monkey, Bellman, Yes-No, Mohair, Jointed Arms & Legs, Felt Suit, Schuco, 1920s, 11 x 6 ¾ In. 100.00
Monkey, Climbing, Embossed, Tin Lithograph, Penny Toy, Distler, 6 ¾ In. 110.00
Monkey, Cobbler, Hammers, Fur, Glass Eyes, Papier-Mache, Windup, Descamp, 12 In. 465.00
Monkey, Cymbals, Fur, Glass Eyes, Red Cap, Windup, 5 ½ x 3 In.. .... 11.00
Monkey, Dressed, Felt Cloth, Molded Head, Articulated Legs, Mouth, Mechanical, 8 ¼ x 5 In.. 44.00
Monkey, In Palm Tree, Tin, Windup, Emporium, 17 ½ In. 50.00
Monkey, Jocko, Ear Tag, No. 5350½, Steiff, 18 ½ In.. .... 355.00
Monkey, Mohair, White, Plush Face, Paws, Plastic Eyes, Excelsior Stuffing, Steiff, 12 ½ In.... 178.00
Monkey, On Tricycle, Painted, Tin, Windup, U.S. Zone, Germany, 4 x 3 ½ In. 40.00

Toy, Li'l Abner Dogpatch Band, Tin Litho, Windup, Unique Art, Box, c.1945, 8 x 9 In.
$440.00

Toy, Man, Walking 2 Pigs, Windup, Martin, France, 8 In.
$4100.00

Toy, Man, Zebra Pulling Cart, Tin, Windup, Lehmann, Na-Nu Toy, 7 In.
$385.00

Toy, Mary & Lamb, Composition Head, Wood, Jointed, Glass Eyes, Schoenhut, 8 ½ In.
$330.00

T

Toy, Merry-Go-Round, Men, Pigs, Horses, Tin, Windup, Marked, Germany SG, 8 In.
$747.00

Toy, Motorcycle, Policeman, No. 3, Tin, Windup, Marx, 8 In.
$230.00

Toy, Motorcycle, Rider, Green, Tin Lithograph, Clockwork, Arnold, Germany, 7 ½ In.
$2200.00

Toy, Motorcycle, Speed Boy Delivery, Tin, Windup, Marx, 9 In.
$518.00

Monkey, On Tricycle, Stuffed Monkey, Felt Suit, Schuco, Germany, 9 ½ In. 345.00
Monkey, Performing, Sand Activated, France, 10 x 8 ¼ In. 220.00
Monkey, Playing Cymbals, Tin, Cloth, 10 In. 27.00
Monkey, Rock & Roll, Plays Guitar, Sways, Sings, Battery Operated, Alps, Box, 13 In. 186.00
Monkey, Yes-No, Red Jacket, Hat, Fur, Straw Stuffed, 10 In. 55.00
Monocoupe, Painted, Orange, Blue Striping, Electric Lights, Tin Lithograph, Distler, 16 In. . . 518.00
Monocoupe, Rookie Pilot, Graphics, Tin Lithograph, Windup, Marx, Box, 8 In. . . 330.00 to 489.00
Monoplane, Go-Round, Tin Lithograph, Trestle Based Pole, Bing, Germany, 12 In. 575.00
Moon Astronaut, Walks, Raises, Lowers Space Gun, Fires, Tin, Windup, Daiya, 9 In. 2260.00
Moon Explorer, Antenna Rotates, Lights, Cameraman, Tin, Battery Operated, Yonezawa, 8 In. 2260.00
Moon Man 001, Walker, Head Turns, Plastic, Battery Operated, Hong Kong, Box, 6 In. 175.00
Moon Mullins, Handcar, Kayo, Tin Lithograph, Windup, Marx, 6 In. 330.00
Moon Mullins, Handcar, Kayo, Tin Lithograph, Windup, Track Wheels, Marx, 6 In. 230.00
Moon Mullins, Handcar, Kayo, Track, Tin, Steel, Windup, Marx, Box, 11 x 6 ½ In. 600.00
Moon Mullins, Handcar, Painted, Tin, Windup, 6 ½ x 6 ¼ x 2 ½ In. 225.00
Moon Mullins, Handcar, Track, Windup, Marx, Box, 1930s, 7 In. 450.00
Motor Coach, Driver, Red, Black, Tin Lithograph, Windup, Lehmann, 6 In. 805.00
Motorcycle, Clown Acrobat, Comes Off Seat, Tin Lithograph, Windup, 6 In. 490.00
Motorcycle, Cop, Sidecar Rider, Red, Blue, Hubley, 4 In. 250.00
Motorcycle, Delivery, Driver, Light-Up, Tin, Windup, Battery Operated, Marx, Box, 1932, 9 ½ In. 2825.00
Motorcycle, Driver, Harley Jr, Cast Iron, Metal Wheels, Hubley, 5 In. 300.00
Motorcycle, Driver, Motodrill 1006, Tin Lithograph, Windup, Schuco, Box, 5 In. 330.00
Motorcycle, Driver, Tin, Friction, Japan, c.1950, 8 In. 95.00
Motorcycle, Driver, Triumph, Tin Lithograph, Penny Toy, Germany, 2 ½ In. 550.00
Motorcycle, Driver, Windup, Marx, c.1930, 9 In. 345.00
Motorcycle, Fix-All, Red, Marx, Box, 12 ½ In. 475.00
Motorcycle, Harley-Davidson, Driver, Red, Cast Iron, Hubley, 6 In. 325.00
Motorcycle, Harley-Davidson, Rider, Red, Twin Headlights, Hubley, 6 ½ In. 550.00
Motorcycle, Harley-Davidson, Sidecar, Driver, Passenger, Green, Cast Iron, 5 ½ x 9 x 5 In. . . . 475.00
Motorcycle, Honda, Policeman, On & Off Seat, Tin, Battery Operated, 11 ½ In. 425.00
Motorcycle, Ice Cream, Red, White, Yellow, Blue, Plastic, Wyandotte, c.1950, 4 ½ In. 65.00
Motorcycle, Kico, Driver, Long Handle Bars, Tin Lithograph, c.1910, 8 In. 5175.00
Motorcycle, Mystic, Policeman, Black Hair, Blue Uniform, Tin, Windup, Marx, Box, 4 ¼ In. . 282.00
Motorcycle, No. 1006, Driver, Graphics, Tin Lithograph, Windup, Schuco, 5 In. 575.00
Motorcycle, Parcel Post, Harley-Davidson, Driver, Cast Iron, Hubley, 9 ½ In. 2300.00
Motorcycle, Patrol Cop Blows Whistle, Light Flashes, Box, Japan, 10 In. 345.00
Motorcycle, Police, White Rubber Wheels, Cast Iron, Hubley, 3 x 5 In. 99.00
Motorcycle, Police Rider, Electric Headlight, Rubber Tires, Cast Iron, Hubley, 6 In. 230.00
Motorcycle, Police Squad, No. 3, Siren, Plastic Windshield, Windup, Marx, Box, 9 In. 863.00
Motorcycle, Police Squad, Sidecar, Siren, Tin Lithograph, Windup, Marx, 8 ½ In. 230.00
Motorcycle, Policeman, Champion, Cast Iron, 7 In. 195.00
Motorcycle, Policeman, No. 3, Tin, Windup, Marx, 8 In. . . . . *illus* 230.00
Motorcycle, Policeman, Sidecar, Blue Paint, Cast Iron, Hubley, 4 In. 88.00
Motorcycle, Rider, Blue, Cast Iron, Champion, 4 ½ x 7 ½ In. 176.00
Motorcycle, Rider, Green, Tin Lithograph, Clockwork, Arnold, Germany, 7 ½ In. . . . . . . *illus* 2200.00
Motorcycle, Rookie Cop, Tips Over, Tin, Windup, Marx, Box, 1933, 8 In. 694.00
Motorcycle, Sidecar, Driver, Air Mail, Indian Decal, Cast Iron, Hubley, 9 ½ In. 4025.00
Motorcycle, Sidecar, Driver, Black Passenger, Windup, Paya, 11 In. 4715.00
Motorcycle, Sidecar, Driver, Hubley, 9 In. 500.00
Motorcycle, Sidecar, Driver, Woman, Indian Decal, Cast Iron, Hubley, 9 ¼ In. 3163.00
Motorcycle, Sidecar, Red, Cast Iron, Label, Hubley, 4 x 8 ½ x 4 ¼ In. 200.00
Motorcycle, Sidecar, Smitty, Driver, Passenger, Yellow, Red, Black, No. 5103, Tootsietoy 310.00
Motorcycle, Sparking Siren Police Squad, Sidecar, Marx, Box, 1949, 8 ½ In. 660.00
Motorcycle, Sparkling Soldier, Tin, Windup, Marx, Box, 1940, 8 In. 695.00
Motorcycle, Speed Boy Delivery, Tin, Windup, Marx, 9 In. . . . . *illus* 518.00
Motorcycle, Sunbeam, Sidecar, 2 Speeds, Head, Tail Lights, Tin, Battery Operated, 9 ¼ In. . . . 1102.00
Motorcycle, Tricky, Policeman, Tin, Windup, Marx, Box, 4 ¼ In. 283.00
Motorcycle, Windup, Penny Toy, Germany, 3 ⅝ In. 395.00
Motorcycle Cop, Chasing Car, Tin, Windup, Germany, Box 450.00
Mr. Butts, Cigarette Boy, Tin, Vinyl, Cloth, Windup, Alps, Japan, Box, 9 In. 330.00
Mr. Dan, Hotdog Eating Man, Tin Lithograph, Windup, 7 In. 10.00
Mr. Fox, Magician, Disappearing Rabbit, Red Base, Battery Operated, Cragstan Toys, Box. . . . 460.00
Mr. Fox, Magician, Head Turns, Battery Operated, Yonezawa, Box, 9 ½ In. 305.00
Musicians, 3 Black Figures, Painted, Drummer, Cymbalist, Bass Fiddler, On Base, Windup, 9 In. 2875.00
Nanny, With Child, Walker, Wheeled High Chair, Die Cut Feet, Penny Toy, Meier, 3 ¼ In. 546.00
NASA Space Station, Battery Operated, Japan, 11 In. . . . . *illus* 460.00
Naughty Boy, Man, Blue, White, Tin, Windup, Lehmann, Germany, 6 In. . . . . *illus* 830.00

New Century Cycle, Tin Lithograph, Umbrella, Birds, Flowers, Crank Driven, Lehmann, 5 ½ In. 748.00
New Century Cycle, Tin Lithograph, Umbrella, Driver Waves Hat, Windup, Lehmann, 5 In. . 1955.00
New York Buildings, Train, Overhead Plane, Tin, Windup, Die Cut, Lithographed, Marx, 1930s, 9 In. 374.00
Noah's Ark, 18 Animals, Iron Wheels, Flat Bottom 1500.00
Noah's Ark, 21 Animals, Wood, Painted, Paper Lithograph, Germany, 4 ¼ x 9 ½ x 3 In. 220.00
Noah's Ark, 22 Animals, Pine, Painted, Decal Ends, Germany, Early 1900s, 15 x 8 In. 382.00
Noah's Ark, 26 Carved Animals, 2 People, Wood, Painted, Hinged Roof, Full Hull Base, 22 In. 546.00
Noah's Ark, 108 Animals, Softwood, Slide Panel Side, Multicolored, 19 ½ x 4 ½ In. 880.00
Noah's Ark, Animal Figures, Wood, Sliding Doors, Pigeonholes, People, 1900s, 33 x 12 x 38 In. 1380.00
Noah's Ark, Painted, Wood Grain, Simulated Windows, Animals, Roof Opens, c.1900, 4 x 24 In. 2300.00
Noisemaker, Child In Barrel, Yellow, Green, Celluloid, 7 ¼ x 4 In. 33.00
Nu-Nu, Chinese Porter, Pulling Tea Chest, Painted, Tin Lithograph, Windup, Lehmann, 5 In. 805.00
Nutty Nibs, Mouth Opens, Catches Nuts, Eyes & Arms Move, Battery Operated, Box 550.00
Oh-My Jigger, Box Stage, Tin Lithograph, Windup, Lehmann, 10 In. 546.00
Old Jalopy, Special Delivery Male, 4 Men, Tin Lithograph, Windup, Marx, Box, 6 In. 220.00
Old Time Truck, 7 Colors, Tin, Friction, Japan 75.00
Optical Mirror, 12 Cards, Wood, Metal, 4 In. 1380.00
Organ Grinder, Girl Musician, Bisque Head, Bear, Paper Lithograph, Plays Music, 15 In. . . . 1495.00
Paddlewheel Boat, Adirondack, Painted, Cast Iron, Wilkins Co., 15 In. 950.00
Paddy, Riding Blanketed Pig, Cloth, Lehmann, Box, 6 x 5 ¾ In. 2040.00
Paddy, Riding Pig, Gyrates, Rides Pig, Windup, Lehmann, 1907, 6 x 6 ¼ In. 1165.00
Pail, 3 Eagles With Shields, Shovel, Ohio Art, 6 In. 125.00
Pail, Beach Scene, Graphics, Tin Lithograph, Canada, 5 ½ In. 230.00
Pail, Children On Carnival Rides, Blue, White, Handle, Tin Lithograph, J. Chein, 6 In. 40.00
Pail, Tropical Birds, Flowers, Purple Ground, Handle, Ohio Art 5.00
Pail, Who's Afraid Of The Big Bad Wolf, Three Little Pigs, Tin Lithograph, Ohio Art, 1934, 4 ¼ In. 759.00
Paint By Numbers, Green Hornet, Stardust, Touch Of Velvet Art, Hasbro, 1966, 14 x 11 In. . . 171.00
Pango-Pango, African Dancer, Vibrates, Head Moves Back & Forth, Tin, Windup, T.P.S., Box, 6 In. 305.00
Panorama, Drug Store, Metal, Wolverine, 1930s, 15 x 12 In. 275.00
Parrot, On Swing, Mohair, Bell, Windup, Germany, 11 In. 230.00
Parrot, Pip-Squeak, Painted, Wire Legs, Bellows, Early 20th Century, 5 In. 59.00
Peace Corps Man, Tin Lithograph, Windup, Mego Corp., Box, 7 In. 190.00
Pedal Car, Airplane, Wood, Metal, Painted, Steering Wheel, Rubber Pedals, Propeller, 21 x 39 In. 978.00
Pedal Car, Austin, Pressed Steel, Rubber Tires, Trunk & Hood Open, Electric Lights, 56 In. . . . 2070.00
Pedal Car, Austin J40, Headlights, Lift Hood, Trunk, Brake, 21 x 58 x 27 In. 2750.00
Pedal Car, Austin Pathfinder, 3-Spoke Wheel, Horn Button, Paper Gauges, Green 14750.00
Pedal Car, Buick, Station Wagon, Steel, Wood, Spoke, Disk Wheels, Rubber Tires, 1930s, 48 In. 770.00
Pedal Car, Cadillac, License Tag 1741, Framed Windshield, Dash Decals, Steelcraft, 36 x 20 In. 1200.00
Pedal Car, Champion, Jet Flow Drive, Blue, White, Pressed Steel, Murray, 34 In. . . . . *illus* 475.00
Pedal Car, Chrysler, Burgundy, Chrome Trim, Murray, 19 x 37 x 15 In. . . . . 1700.00 to 1955.00
Pedal Car, Chrysler, Pressed Steel, Full Fender, Steelcraft, 40 In. 920.00
Pedal Car, Circus Monkey Race Car, Carnival Electric Track, Pressed Steel, c.1930, 30 In. . . . 1265.00
Pedal Car, Dodge, Pressed Steel, Tan, Green, American National, 34 In. . . . . *illus* 1210.00
Pedal Car, Fire Chiefs, Pressed Steel, Red, Black, High Bonnet, Bell, Gendron, 47 In. 2185.00
Pedal Car, Fire Engine, Red Paint, Yellow Stripe, Ladder, c.1900, 68 In. 3744.00
Pedal Car, Fire Truck, Fire Dept. Ladder, 45 In. 115.00
Pedal Car, Fire Truck, Hood Mounted Bell, Flashing Red Light, Ladders, Chrome Trim, 46 x 24 In. 748.00
Pedal Car, Fire Truck, Ladders, Back Steering Wheel, Running Boards, Coney Island, 60 x 24 x 30 In. 3990.00
Pedal Car, Fire Truck, Ladders, Rubber Hose, Bell, Flashing Light, Pressed Steel, 45 In. 259.00
Pedal Car, Irish Mail Hand, Wood Seat, 42 In. 345.00
Pedal Car, LaSalle, Painted Green, Gold, White, Black Fenders, American National, 45 In. . . . 8050.00
Pedal Car, LaSalle, Speedster, Skippy, Pressed Steel, Blue, Gray, Gendron, 45 In. 1495.00
Pedal Car, Lincoln, Greyhound Hood Ornament, Pressed Steel, Spare Tire, Fenders, Bumpers, 52 In. 1035.00
Pedal Car, Metal Body, Wood Radiator, Leather Seat, Adjustable, 29 x 51 In. 1430.00
Pedal Car, Morgan, Roadster, Fiberglass, White, Leather Seat, Headlights, 15 x 48 x 19 In. . . . 1500.00
Pedal Car, Nash, Red, Blue, Yellow, Tin, Wood, c.1910, 24 x 45 ½ x 28 In. 2420.00
Pedal Car, Phaeton, 2-Seater, Black, Red, White, 29 x 63 x 21 In. 1900.00
Pedal Car, Pontiac, Pressed Steel, Red, Cream, Hood Ornament, c.1925, 48 In. 1495.00
Pedal Car, Pontiac, Station Wagon, Chrome Trim, Wood, Murray, 1948-50, 20 x 43 x 13 In. . . 1300.00
Pedal Car, Retro Style, Orange, Chrome Trim, Upholstered Seat, 38 x 18 x 18 In. 288.00
Pedal Car, Roadster, Pressed Steel, Gendron, c.1929, 42 In. 1840.00
Pedal Car, Supersonic Jet, Silver, Red Trim, Murray, 46 x 24 x 25 In. 920.00
Pedal Car, Tanker Truck, Texaco, Covered Cab, Metal Rear Tank, Red, Green, White Letters, 75 x 38 In. 1495.00
Pedal Car, Taxi, New York Checker, Yellow, 36 x 35 x 15 ½ In. 80.00
Pedal Car, Tow Truck, Wire Spokes, Rubber Tires, Richfield, 58 x 22 x 24 In. 364.00
Penguin, Walker, Tin, Windup, J. Chein, 3 ⅞ In. 40.00
Pete The Pup, Composition Head, Wood, Jointed, Painted, Label, 1930, 11 ½ In. 173.00

Toy, NASA Space Station, Battery Operated, Japan, 11 In.
$460.00

Toy, Naughty Boy, Man, Blue, White, Tin, Windup, Lehmann, Germany, 6 In.
$830.00

Toy, Pedal Car, Champion, Jet Flow Drive, Blue, White, Pressed Steel, Murray, 34 In.
$475.00

Toy, Pedal Car, Dodge, Pressed Steel, Tan, Green, American National, 34 In.
$1210.00

Smokey the Bear
Smokey Bear was created to talk about fire prevention in 1944.

T

Toy, Plastic Man, Red, Arms Move, Shoots Gun, Irwin, Mars Toy, 10 In.
$260.00

Toy, Red The Iceman, Walker, Carries Ice Block, Tin, Windup, Marx, Box, 9 In.
$5175.00

Toy, Ringmaster, Wood, Jointed, Painted, Clothes, Schoenhut, 8 In.
$135.00

Peter Rabbit, Cloth Tag, Pants, Glass Eyes, Brass Ear Button, Steiff, 11 In.. 115.00
Photographer, Boy, Tin, Battery Operated, Japan, 8 In. 143.00
Photographer, Posing Man, Waves, Tips Hat, Embossed, Tin Lithograph, Nickel Toy, 5 ¾ In.. 990.00
Piano, Green, Schoenhut, 8 ⅜ x 11 x 9 In. 29.00 to 40.00
Pierrot Monkey Cycle, Battery Operated, Modern Toys, Japan, 1960s, 5 x 8 ½ In.. 350.00
Pig, Walker, Pigskin Over Papier-Mache, Windup, France, 11 In. 1870.00
Plastic Man, Red, Arms Move, Shoots Gun, Irwin, Mars Toy, 10 In. *illus* 260.00
Plow, 3-Bottom, Case, Cast Iron, Embossed Lettering, Vindex, 10 ¼ In. 1840.00
Plow, Man, Horse, No. 142F, Postwar, Britain, Box 266.00
Policeman, Pop-Up, Composition Lithograph, Germany, 7 In.. 173.00
Pony Race, 2 Horses, Red & Yellow Disc Base, Tin Lithograph, 7 In. 50.00
Pool Player, Billiards Table, Painted, Tin Lithograph, Windup, Gunthermann, 8 In.. 633.00
Pool Player, Embossed, Tin Lithograph, Penny Toy, Kellerman, 2 ½ In. 110.00
Pool Players, Ranger, Steel, Black & White Balls, Tin, Windup, 14 In. 201.00
Popcorn Vendor, Bear Sways, Umbrella Turns, Battery Operated, Suzuki & Edwards, Box, 9 In. 254.00
Porky Pig, Parasol Spins, Tin Lithograph, Windup, Marx, 1939, 9 In. 210.00 to 275.00
Porter, Baggage, Tin Lithograph, Windup, Great Britain, 12 In.. 80.00
Porter, Black, Carrying Suitcases, Red Cap, Tin, Windup, Marx, 1930s, 8 ¼ In.... 460.00 to 575.00
Porter, Pushes Dolly With Trunk, Tin Lithograph, Windup, Lehmann, 8 In.. 1150.00
Porter, Pushing Black Man, Embossed, Tin Lithograph, Penny Toy, Germany, 2 ½ In.. 385.00
Porter, Pushing Cart, Tin Lithograph, Windup, Strauss, 6 ½ In. 184.00
Pot, Lid, O Handle, Wagner, 4 ¾ In.. 30.00
Power Shovel, Ruston Bucyrus, Red, Yellow, Matchbox, Box 120.00
Powerful Katrinka, Jimmy In Wheelbarrow, Lithograph, Windup, Germany, 1920s, 5 In. 920.00 to 1320.00
Powerful Katrinka, Rolls Wheelbarrow & Lifts Jimmy In Air, Tin, Windup, Nifty, 1925, 6 ½ In. 1200.00
Pretty Village, Buildings, People, Stands, Paper Grounds Layout, McLoughlin, Box, 11 In. .. 58.00
Pullman, Felt Bead, Curtains, Glassine Windows, Embossed, Tin, Playskool, 11 ½ x 9 In.... 110.00
Pumpkin-Head, Walker, Cloth, Metal, Composition, Mechanical, Windup, Germany, 8 In.... 661.00
Puppet, Black Boy, Wood, Carved, Hinged Mouth, Cloth Body, Horse Hair, Painted, c.1900, 22 In. 165.00
Purse, Girl From U.N.C.L.E., Vinyl, Shoulder Strap, Ideal, c.1967, 7 x 9 In. 288.00
Puss In Boots, Cat, Celluloid, Jointed, Painted, Germany, 5 x 2 In. 93.00
Queen Of The Campus, 4 College Men Riding In Car, Tin Lithograph, Windup, Marx, 5 ¾ In. 119.00
Rabbit, Gold Fur, Charcoal Gray Ear Tips, Button Eyes, Squeaker, Steiff, 1940s, 10 In. 259.00
Rabbit, In Cabbage, Head Raises, Wiggles Ears, Windup, Battery Operated, Descamp, 8 ½ In. 935.00
Rabbit, On Bike, Haji, Japan, Box, 5 In. 70.00
Rabbit, On Tricycle, Balloon, Tin Lithograph, Celluloid, Windup, Marx, 3 ½ x 4 In. 28.00
Rabbit, Standing On Egg, Pulled By Rooster, Windup, Lehmann, Box, 7 In. 6325.00
Rabbit, Woodland, Resting Position, Ear Button, Shoebutton Eyes, Steiff, 1920s, 9 In.. 259.00
Rabbits, On Rabbit, Embossed, Tin Lithograph, Penny Toy, Meier, 2 ¾ In. 440.00
Ram, White, Gray, Celluloid, Irwin Toy Co., 7 ½ x 9 ½ In.. 40.00
Range Rider, Tin Lithograph, Windup, Marx, Box, 10 ½ In. 175.00
Rattle, Child's Face, Blue Eyes, Rosy Cheeks, Brown Curl, Chime, Celluloid, Japan. 44.00
Rattle, Girl, Pink Dress, Chimes, Painted, Celluloid, Paper Label, 8 ½ x 2 ¾ In. 44.00
Rattle, Man-In-Moon Face, Round, On Stick, Pink, White, Celluloid, 8 ½ x 2 ¾ In. 17.00
Rattle, Pig, Plastic, Yellow, c.1950 14.00
Red The Iceman, Walker, Carries Ice Block, Tin, Windup, Marx, Box, 9 In. *illus* 5175.00
Reindeer, Painted, Tin, Brown, Gold, Clicker On Axle, Pull Toy, 8 ¼ In. 259.00
Reindeer, White, Felt, Cast Antlers, Glass Eyes, Nodder, Windup, Germany, 11 x 12 In.. 2320.00
Reindeer, Wood, Jointed, Glass Eyes, Leather Ears, Antlers, Tail, Schoenhut, 7 In. 144.00
Rhino, Wood, Jointed, Carved, Painted Eyes, Schoenhut, 9 In. 173.00
Rickshaw, Coolie Pulling Chinese Woman Rider, Tin, Windup, Lehmann, 7 In.. 1438.00
Rickshaw, Woman, Holding Fan, Tin, French Martin, Flywheel, 8 In. 1955.00
Rifle, Tom Corbett Space Cadet, 1507-A, Box, 10 In. 316.00
Ring, Green Hornet, Blue Plastic, Flicker, Image Of Hornet Running With Gun, 1966 15.00
Ring, Power Green Lantern, Silver Metal, Enameled Symbol, Box & Case, 1998, Size 6 115.00
Ringmaster, Wood, Jointed, Painted, Clothes, Schoenhut, 8 In. *illus* 135.00
Road Roller, Bump & Go, Engine Lights, Tin, Plastic, Battery Operated, Dalya, 9 In.. 3221.00
Road Roller, Tin, Windup, Marx, Box, 8 In.. 518.00
Road Scraper, Driver, Green, Black, Cast Iron, Kenton, 6 In. 33.00
Robot, Acrobat, Walks, Adjustable Moving Arms, Legs, Plastic, Battery Operated, 9 ½ In. 170.00
Robot, Action Planet, Olive, Gray, Metal Claw Hands, Sparking Head, Tin, Windup, Yoshiya, 8 In. 362.00
Robot, Answer Game, Adding Machine, Tin, Box, Japan, 1963, 14 In. 805.00 to 1859.00
Robot, Astro Scout, Tin, Friction, Crank Operated, Box, c.1963, 9 ¼ In.. 13560.00
Robot, Astroman, Helmet, Tin, Windup, Nomura, Box, c.1960, 10 ¼ In. 9605.00
Robot, Atom, Small Skirt, Friction, Crank Operated, K.O., Japan, 6 In. *illus* 230.00
Robot, Atomic Man, Tin Lithograph, 12 In. 50.00
Robot, Big Lou, Darts, Rockets, Whistle, Grenade, Plastic, Battery Operated, Marx, c.1965, 38 In. 1808.00

Robot, Buzzer, Bump & Go, Eyes Light-Up, Dome, Tin, Yonezawa, Box, c.1957, 10 ½ In. 3560.00
Robot, Chief Robotman, Silver Gray, K.O. Japan, Box, 11 ¾ In. 3390.00
Robot, Deep Sea, Walker, Arms Swing, Gun Tip, Springs, Tin, Windup, Naito Shoten, 7 ¾ In. . 1526.00
Robot, Diamond Planet, Sound, Tin, Windup, Yonezawa, Box, c.1962, 10 ¼ In. 50850.00
Robot, Directional, Tin, Battery Operated, Yonezawa, Japan, 11 In. . . . . *illus* 460.00
Robot, Gear Robot, Walker, Eyes Light Up, Moving Eyes, Tin, Plastic, Japan, 14 In. 460.00
Robot, Hook, Free Hanging Arms, Tin Lithograph, Friction, Wacko, Japan, c.1955, 7 In. 1304.00
Robot, Jupiter, Remote, Battery Operated, Japan, 7 In. 13560.00
Robot, Jupiter, Walker, Head Lights, Chest Gears Turn, Tin, Plastic, Windup, Suzuki, 4 ¼ In. . 735.00
Robot, Lavender, Nonstop, Tin, Battery Operated, Japan, 15 In. 690.00
Robot, Lilliput, Shuffles, Spikes, Arms Swing, Claw Hands, Tin, Windup, KT/CK, 6 ¼ In. 6478.00
Robot, Lost In Space, Motorized, Plastic, c.1966, 12 ½ In. 600.00
Robot, Mechanical Brain, Walks, Hands Light, Battery Operated, Tin, Windup, 8 ¾ In. 1074.00
Robot, Mechanized, Battery Operated, Osaka, Japan, Box, 1990s, 13 In. . . . . *illus* 403.00
Robot, Mighty, Walker, Flexes Arms, Plastic, Tin, Windup, Yonezawa, Box, c.1865, 10 ¼ In.. . . 2882.00
Robot, Mighty 8, Tin, Battery Operated, Masudaya, Box, c.1955, 12 In. 14973.00
Robot, Mighty Robot, Sparks In Chest Panel, Tin, Windup, Noguchi, Box, 5 ⅓ In. 141.00
Robot, Mr. Atomic, Blue, Battery Operated, Japan, Cragstan, Box, c.1960 . . . . 17876.00
Robot, Mr. Baby Robot, Swinging, Mouth Moves, Flag, Plastic, Tin, Windup, Yonezawa, Box, 11 In. 322.00
Robot, Mr. Hustler, Astronaut, Horikawa, Box, Japan, 11 In. 520.00
Robot, Mr. Robot, Bell Rings, Radar Screen, Plastic, Tin, Windup, Yonezawa, Box, 6 ¾ In. . . . 520.00
Robot, Mr. Robot, Head Lights, Spins, Plastic, Chrome Chest Plate, Tin, Battery Operated, Box, 11 In. 367.00
Robot, Mr. Robot, Red, Cragstan, Box, Japan 819.00
Robot, Mr. Robot The Mechanical Brain, Japan, Battery Operated, 11 In. 3842.00
Robot, Mr. Zerox, Japan, 8 ½ In. 147.00
Robot, Planet, Walker, Head Lights, Rubber Hands, Tin, Battery Operated, Remote, Box, 9 In. 684.00
Robot, Radar, Tin, Plastic, Windup, Topolino, Box, c.1968, 11 In. 14125.00
Robot, Robby, Space Patrol, Bump & Go, Lights, Tin, Battery Operated, Nomura, Box, 12 ¾ In. 763.00
Robot, Robby, Walker, Sparks, Boy's Face Inside Helmet, Tin, Windup, Yonezawa, c.1958, 8 ¼ In. 3560.00
Robot, Rotate-O-Matic, Super Astronaut, Plastic Feet, Japan 79.00
Robot, Sky, Walker, Light Blinks, Chest Wheels Turn, Plastic, Battery Operated, Box, 8 ¾ In.. . 123.00
Robot, Space, Waddles, Ears Flap, Mouth Opens, Closes, Tin, Windup, Yoshiya, Box, 7 ½ In. . . 525.00
Robot, Space Commando, Walker, Arm Swings, Helmet, Tin, Windup, Nomura, Box, 7 ½ In. . 1808.00
Robot, Space Explorer, Battery Operated, Box, Japan. 1017.00
Robot, Space Scout, Walker, Radiation Counter, Tin, Friction, Crank, Yonezawa, 10 ½ In.. . . . 6498.00
Robot, Space Trooper, Black, Walker, Antenna Turns, Tin, Crank, Yoshiya, 6 ½ In.. . . . . 791.00
Robot, Space Trooper, Red, Walker, Antenna Turns, Tin, Crank, Yoshiya, 6 ½ In. 678.00
Robot, Space Trooper, Walker, Light-Up, Battery Operated, Yoshiya, Japan, c.1955, 6 ½ In. . . . 403.00
Robot, Spaceship X-8, Blue & Red, Tada, Japan, Box 1865.00
Robot, Sparky Robot, Tin Lithograph, Windup, K.O., Box, 7 ¾ In. 350.00
Robot, Swinging Baby, Yellow, Tin, Windup, Yonezawa 750.00
Robot, Swinging Baby Robot, M, Tin, Windup, Japan, 12 In. 495.00
Robot, Target, Dart Gun, Sound, Lights, Tin, Battery Operated, Masudaya, Box, c.1955, 15 In. 16385.00
Robot, Target, Gun, Darts, Box, Japan 9605.00
Robot, Torpedo, Crank Operated, Prop Turns, Tin, Friction, Marusan, Box, c.1950s, 12 ¼ In. . 802.00
Robot, Tremendous Mike, Tin, Windup, Antenna, Aoshin, Box, c.1960, 10 ½ In.. . . . . 25425.00
Robot, Tricycle, Space Graphics, Rider, Tin, Plastic, Windup, Suzuki, 4 ¼ In. 876.00
Robot, Tulip Head, Walker, Neck, Head Light, Camera, Tin, Plastic, Windup, Nomura, 1960 . . 2384.00
Robot, Venus Robot, Walks, Plastic, Tin Face, Chest Panels, Yoshiya, Box, 5 ½ In. 153.00
Robot, Walker, Arms Move, Eyes Light, Tin, Battery Operated, Remote, Linemar, c.1958, 7 ½ In. 531.00
Robot, Walker, Eyes, Ear, Dome Lights Flash, Plastic, Battery Operated, 8 ½ In. 428.00
Robot, Walker, Pistons Move, Spin, Gold, Black Legs, Tin, Battery Operated, Remote, 8 ½ In. . 1526.00
Robot, Winky, Walker, Oxygen Meter, Tin, Windup, Yonezawa, c.1958, 9 ¼ In. 2938.00
Robot, X-27 Explorer, Sound, Tin, Friction, Crank, Yonezawa, Box, c.1963, 10 In. 12995.00
Robot, Z Tank, Tin, Plastic, Battery Operated, Japan, Box, 10 In. 460.00
Robot, Zoomer, Sparks, George G. Wagner, Tin, Windup, TN, Japan, 8 In. 345.00
Robot, Zoomer, Walker, Head Lights, Tin, Battery Operated, Nomura, Box, c.1955, 9 ½ In. . . . 934.00
Robot 7, Tin, Windup, Japan, 6 ¾ In. 181.00
Rocket, Atomic, Tin, Friction, Push Down Lever, Masudaya, 6 ¾ In. 1085.00
Rocket, Pull String, Tin, Windup, Marusan, Box, 8 ½ In. 3108.00
Rocket, X-2 Space Rocket, Advances, Sparks, Tin, Friction, Masudaya, 7 ½ In. 237.00
Rocket Fighter, Tin Lithograph, Windup, Marx, 12 In.. . . . . 150.00
Rocket Missile, Rubber Nose Cone, Tin, Friction, Japan, Box, c.1950, 13 ¾ In. 333.00
Rocket Racer, Driver, Tin, Windup, Marx, 16 In.. . . . . 551.00
Rocket Ship, Tom Corbet, Space Cadet, Tin Lithograph, Windup, Marx, 12 In. 550.00
Roller Coaster, Coney Island, Graphics, Tower Trestles, Tin Lithograph, Windup, Goso, 43 In. 748.00
Roller Coaster, Tin Lithograph, Windup, Chein, Box, 19 In. 165.00

Toy, Robot, Atom, Small Skirt, Friction, Crank Operated, K.O., Japan, 6 In.
$230.00

Toy, Robot, Directional, Tin, Battery Operated, Yonezawa, Japan, 11 In.
$460.00

Toy, Robot, Mechanized, Battery Operated, Osaka, Japan, Box, 1990s, 13 In.
$403.00

Slinky
The original Slinkys had sharp ends. Modern Slinkys with crimped ends are safer.

Toy, Roly Poly, Happy Hooligan, Yellow Outfit, Red Hat, Germany, 5 ½ In.
$110.00

Toy, Sewing Machine, Treadle, Tin Lithograph, Penny Toy, Meier, c.1910, 3 In.
$125.00

Toy, Skittles Set, Chickens, Wood Wheels, Papier- Mache, Germany, 6 ½ x 14 In., 10 Piece
$2070.00

Roller Skates, Winchester Model No. 30, Windup, Box. . . . 80.00
Rollo-Chair, Walking The Boardwalk, Porter Pushing Cart, Tin Lithograph, Windup, 8 In. . . 1150.00
Roly Poly, Black Man, Red Vest, White Top Hat, Painted, Composition, Schoenhut, 11 ¼ In.. . 1610.00
Roly Poly, Black Man, Yellow Shirt, Orange Tie, Pants, Papier-Mache, Chimes, 9 ¾ In.. . . . 405.00
Roly Poly, Clown, Green, Beige, Schoenhut, 9 ½ In. . . . 86.00
Roly Poly, Clown, Red, Yellow, Blue, Green, Musical, Germany, 15 In. . . . 195.00
Roly Poly, Foxy Grandpa, Blue Outfit, Painted, Papier-Mache, Schoenhut, 10 In. . . . 275.00
Roly Poly, Happy Hooligan, Yellow Outfit, Red Hat, Germany, 5 ½ In. . . . *illus* 110.00
Rooster Cart, No. 469, Fisher-Price, 10 In. . . . 403.00
Roosters, Fighting, Spring, Tin, Windup, Wheels, Japan, 6 In. . . . 88.00
Roosters, Pecking, Embossed, Tin Lithograph, Lever, Penny Toy, Meier, 3 ¾ In. . . . 245.00
Roundabout, Green, Red Canopy, Tin Lithograph, Windup, Penny Toy, Germany, 4 In. . . . 173.00
Royal Cub, Mama Bear Pushes Carriage, Baby Cries, Battery Operated, Japan, Box, 8 In. . . . 170.00
Runabout, Hill Climbing, Fold Down Top, Cast Figures, Cast Iron, Electric, c.1902, 6 ¼ In. . . 920.00
Sailboat, On Wheels, Embossed, Tin Lithograph, Penny Toy, Meier, 3 ¼ In. . . . 495.00
Sailor, Wobbles, Windup, From The H.M.S. Dreadnought, Lehmann, 7 ½ In. . . . 633.00
Sailor With Paper Bellows Accordion, Egely, Germany, 6 In.. . . . 295.00
Sam, City Gardner, Plastic, Tin Lithograph, Windup, Marx, Box, 8 In. . . . 220.00 to 350.00
Sam The Shaving Man, Face Lights, Shaves, Battery Operated, Plaything, Box, 12 In.. . . . 282.00
Sammy Wong, Tea Totaler, Tin Lithograph, Battery Operated, Rosko Toys, Box. . . . 484.00
Samurai Warrior, Ferdinand Martin, Fierce Expression, Holds Sabers, Windup, 7 ¼ In. . . . 3163.00
Sand, 2 Dancers, Paper Lithograph, Sand Activated, England, 8 x 6 In.. . . . 365.00
Sand Loader, Driver, Red, Yellow, Green, Cast Iron, Arcade, 8 ½ In.. . . . 1093.00
Sand Loader, Driver, Red Body, Green Spoke Wheels, Yellow Scoop, Cast Iron, Arcade, 8 ½ In. 1093.00
Saxophone Player, Tin Lithograph, Distler, 6 ¼ In. . . . 88.00
Scissor Sharpener, Tin Lithograph, Windup, Arnold, 6 ½ In. . . . 86.00
Scooter, King, Rider, Tin, Friction, Yonezawa, 9 In. . . . 638.00
Scooter, Skippy Racer, Pressed Steel, Red Paint, Foot Brake, 1920s, 44 x 32 In. . . . 510.00
Scraper, No. 2011, Doepke, c.1951, 29 In. . . . 275.00
Sea Lion, Wood Ball, Horse Hair Bristle Whiskers, Schoenhut, 3-In. Ball, 8 ½-In. Seal . . . 403.00
Seal, Playing Drums, Painted, Tin Lithograph, Windup, Gunthermann, 5 ½ x 5 ½ In. . . . 489.00
Secretary, Miss Friday, Typist, Bell Rings, Tin, Vinyl, Battery Operated, c.1958, 7 ½ x 8 ½ In. . 309.00
Seesaw, Boy, Girl, Painted, Tin, Wood, Cloth, Windup, Ives, 18 ½ In. . . . 5120.00
Seesaw, Gibbs, 14 ¼ In. . . . 70.00
Seesaw, Rocking R Ranch, Metal, Windup, Cortland, c.1948, 17 ½ In. . . . 195.00
Service Station, Oil Cart, Stake Truck, Light-Up Gas Pumps, Tin Lithograph, Marx, 13 In. . . 330.00
Service Station, Painted, Embossed, Tin Lithograph, Wood, Gibbs, 7 In. . . . 275.00
Sewing Machine, Black, Steel, Bird Transfer, Table Clamp, Box, Germany, c.1920, 7 In.. . . . 154.00
Sewing Machine, Flowers, Stenciled, Tin, Cast Iron, Hand Operated, Germany, 5 ½ x 6 x 2 In. 100.00
Sewing Machine, Sew Master, Red, Instructions, Kayanee, Box, 7 ½ x 4 In. . . . 17.00
Sewing Machine, Treadle, Tin Lithograph, Penny Toy, Meier, c.1910, 3 In. . . . *illus* 125.00
Sheep, Wood, Composition, Cotton Cover, Platform, Metal Wheels, 8 ¾ x 7 ¼ In.. . . . 60.00
Shooting Gallery, Gorilla, Eyes Light Up, Roars, Raises Arms, Battery Operated, Box, 9 In. . . 288.00
Shop, German, Oak Stained, Mirrored Sides, Drawers, Compartments, Counter, c.1890, 29 x 12 In. 3163.00
Shop, Millinery, 19th-Century Style, Shelves, Drawers, Accessories, Robert Bernhard, 22 x 10 In. 345.00
Shutterbug, Boy With Camera, Walker, Tin, Rubber, Battery Operated, Nomura, Box, 8 ¾ In. 537.00
Sibyl, Fortune Teller, Tube Holder, Answer Book, Composition, Cloth, Carved, 10 ½ In. . . . 403.00
Skating Chef, Tin Lithograph, Windup, T.P.S., 6 In. . . . 110.00
Ski Jumper, No. B50, Metal, Wolverine, c.1950, 24 In. . . . 195.00
Ski Jumper, Wheeled Platform, Box, Schoenhut, 26 In. . . . 316.00
Skip The Rope Animals, Tin, Windup, Japan, 1950s, 8 In. . . . 120.00
Skippy The Tricky Cyclist, Tin, Windup, T.P.S. Japan, Box, 5 ½ In.. . . . 135.00
Skittles Set, Camel, Nodder, 9 Arabs, Papier-Mache, Wheels, Wood, Pull Toy, Germany, 19 In. 11000.00
Skittles Set, Chickens, Wood Wheels, Papier- Mache, Germany, 6 ½ x 14 In., 10 Piece . . *illus* 2070.00
Skittles Set, Dogs, Papier-Mache, Metal Wheels, 8 x 17 In., 8 Piece. . . . 2588.00
Skittles Set, Frogs, Papier-Mache, Metal Wheels, Germany, Marked, 6 x 18 In., 8 Piece. . . . 17825.00
Skittles Set, Indians, Papier-Mache, Wood Wheels, 23 x 9 In., 10 Piece. . . . 4025.00
Skittles Set, Rabbits, Papier-Mache, Metal Wheels, Marked, Germany, 19 In., 10 Piece . . . 8625.00
Skittles Set, Roosters, Papier-Mache, Wood Balls, Metal Wheels, Germany, 14 In., 6 Piece . . . 2185.00
Sky Rangers, Zeppelin, Monocoupe, Circle Tower, Tin Lithograph, Unique Art, Box, 9 x 10 In. 144.00
Skybird Flyer, Control Tower, Airplane, Tin Lithograph, Windup, Marx, Box, 9 In. . . . 195.00
Sled, Chief, Wood, Red, Iron Runners, Inscribed EAC, 1910, 10 ½ x 36 ½ In. . . . 119.00
Sled, Doll's, Wood, Painted, Cat In Canoe, Iron Runners, 16 x 4 In. . . . 708.00
Sled, Doll's, Wood, Painted, Stenciled, c.1910, 16 In. . . . 173.00
Sled, Flexible Flyer, Painted, Early 20th Century, 44 In.. . . . 12.00
Sled, Flowers, Red, Green, Iron Runners, Swan Pulls, 41 x 17 In.. . . . 424.00
Sled, Machine Age Styling, Original Grips, Duralite Racer, 1950s, 48 In. . . . 207.00

Sled, Painted, Flowers, Curled Runners, Wood, 19th Century, 28 x 12 In. 190.00
Sled, Painted, Pond, Fisherman Scene, Iron Runners, Salesman's Sample, 16 x 6 In. 791.00
Sled, Wood, 3 Center Slats, Curved Runner, Signed, Davos, Switzerland, 1883 .... 50.00
Sled, Wood, Bird, Flowers, Metal, Marked, B. Mill's Co., Berlin, N.Y., 19th Century, Child's 322.00
Sled, Wood, Orange, Roses, Metal Runners, Paper Label, Deposit Mfg. Co., N.Y., c.1910, 28 In. 205.00
Sled, Wood, Painted, Elk Scene, Metal Runners, Removable Seat, No. 52, Paris Mfg., Me., 31 In. 230.00
Sled, Wood, Painted, Flowers, Greek Key Border, Side Rails, Iron Runners, c.1880, 42 In. 1955.00
Sled, Wood, Painted, Green, Flowers, Albert, 19th Century, 20 x 36 In.. .... 75.00
Sled, Wood, Red Paint, Metal Runners, Stamped, Paris Mfg. Co., Maine, Late 1800s, 40 In.... 380.00
Sled, Wood, Swan Terminals, Plank Seat, Iron Runners, Child's, 18 x 40 x 16 In.. .... 715.00
Sled, Wooden, Iditarod Dog, Salesman's Sample, 17 x 4 In. 295.00
Sleigh, Horse Drawn, Bell Ringer, Embossed, Painted, Spoke Wheels, 12 ½ In. 201.00
Sleigh, Horse Drawn, Griffon Head, Cast Iron, Early 1900s, 15 ¼ In. 676.00
Sleigh, Open, White Horse, Green, Yellow, Figure, Cast Iron, Dent, c.1911, 15 ½ In. 1380.00
Sleigh, Painted Scene, Red, Iron Runner, Paper Label, 36 In.. .... 1150.00
Smitty Scooter, Boy Riding Scooter, Tin Lithograph, Windup, Marx, 8 In. .... *illus* 1210.00
Snake, In Box, Wood, Painted, Pa., 19th Century, 3 x 3 ¾ In. 878.00
Snake Charmer, Man, Plays Flute, Cobra Rises, Basket, Battery Operated, Linemar, Box, 8 In. 475.00
Snowplow, Red, White, No. 16C1, Matchbox, Box 140.00
Solar Rocket, Sparking Action, Lauches Spinning Disc, Plastic, Marx, Box, 1950s, 12 In.. .... 86.00
Soldier, Babes In Toyland, Walks, Plays Drum, Tin, Windup, Linemar, Box, 1961, 6 In.. .... 282.00
Soldier, Crawling Doughboy, Tin, Windup, Marx, 7 ½ In. 220.00
Soldier Set, Argentine Infantry, No. 216, Britains, Postwar, 8 Piece 295.00
Soldier Set, Band Of Royal Marines, No. 1291, Britains, Postwar, 12 Piece 295.00
Soldier Set, Bodyguards, Emperor Of Ethiopia, No. 1424, Britains, 8 Piece. 165.00
Soldier Set, British Machine Gunners, Sitting, Lying, Britains, Box, Postwar, 9 Piece 201.00
Soldier Set, Cape Town Highlanders, No. 1901, Britains, Box, 8 Piece. 110.00
Soldier Set, Century Knights, Armor Foot, Mounted, Britains, Postwar, 9 Piece 153.00
Soldier Set, Coldstream Guards Band, Metal, No. 37, Britains, Postwar, 17 Piece. 177.00
Soldier Set, Confederate Cavalry, Officer, No. 9286, Britains, Postwar, 4 Piece 212.00
Soldier Set, Ethiopian Tribesmen, No. 1425, Britains, Postwar, Roan Box, 8 Piece. 266.00
Soldier Set, French Matelots, Officer, No. 143, Britains, 1948-49, 8 Piece 560.00
Soldier Set, Kings African Rifles, No. 225, Britains, Postwar, 8 Piece 142.00
Soldier Set, Papal Swiss Guards, Officer, Britains, Postwar, 9 Piece 236.00
Soldier Set, Republic Of Ireland Infantry, Battle Dress, No. 1603, Britains, Box, 8 Piece 110.00
Soldier Set, Royal Navy, Officer, No. 2080, Britains, Box, Postwar, 8 Piece. 212.00
Soldiers Of Fortune, 8 Figures, Tin Lithograph, Marx, Box, 6 x 8 In.. .... 135.00
Space Capsule, No. 6, Front Lights Up, Makes Noise, Battery Operated, MT, Japan, 10 In. 345.00
Space Capsule, Stop & Go, Doors Open, TV Screen, Tin, Plastic, Battery Operated, 9 ¼ In.... 96.00
Space Fighter, Walker, Stops, Doors Open, Fires Guns, Tin, Plastic, Battery Operated, 9 ¼ In. 170.00
Space Station, Lights Blink, Gears Move, Dish Turns, Tin, Battery Operated, Horikawa, Box, 11 In. 2825.00
Space Station, Refuel, Antenna, Lights, Rotates, Tin, Battery Operated, Waco, Box, 1960s, 15 In. 4068.00
Space Tank, Rex Mars, Patrol, Turret Gun, Figure, Antenna, Tin, Windup, Marx, Box, 10 In.. 458.00
Space Vehicle, Bubble Cockpit, Tin Lithograph, Battery Operated, Box, 8 In. 316.00
Spaceman, Shuffles, Arms Move, Helmet Lights, Tin, Battery Operated, Remote, Masudaya, 9 In. 650.00
Spaceship, Lights, Tin, Battery Operated, Japan, c.1950, 8 In. 225.00
Spaceship, X-7 Space Explorer, Plastic, Battery Operated, 8 In. .... *illus* 58.00
Sparkler, Amos 'N' Andy, Amos, Squeeze, Sparks In Glass Eyes, 1930s 660.00
Sparkler, Swami Magician, Tin Lithograph, Distler, 4 ½ In. 165.00
Speedball, Oak, Compartments, 24 Metal Labels, 9 x 10 x 1 ½ In. 134.00
Speedball, Oak, Sloped Glass Front, Quill Styles, Sliding Door, 5 x 9 x 15 In. 235.00
Spelling Board, Alphabet, Wood, Yellow, Red, 8-Sided, Universal, Pat. Feb. 16, 1886, 13 ½ In. 88.00
Spic & Span, Black Man Plays Snare Drum, Cymbals, Violin & Dances, c.1924, 10 In. 1582.00
Squirrel, Book, Eyes Move, Tin, Windup, Mikuni, 4 ¾ In.. .... 50.00
Squirrel, Ginger Mohair, Black Shoebutton Eyes, Embroidered Features, Steiff, c.1913, 7 In.. 296.00
Squirt Gun, Luger, Plastic, Park's, Box, 1950, 7 In. 50.00
Stable, 3 Story, Wood, Paper Lithograph, Elevator, Accessories, Moritz Gottschalk, 27 x 25 In. 920.00
Stable, Wood, Hinged Door, Tin Fence, 5 Animals, CR. Bliss, 18 x 12 x 8 In. .... *illus* 770.00
Steam Pumper, Driver, Red, Gold, Nickel Bumper, Kenton, 12 In.. .... 425.00
Steam Roller, Ride 'em, No. 6, Red, Gray, Keystone, c.1930, 20 In. 225.00
Steam Shovel, Nickel Plated Scoop, Red, Cast Iron, Hubley, 2 ¼ x 4 ½ x 1 ¼ In. 22.00
Steam Shovel, Painted, Pressed Steel, Buddy L, 1930s, 20 ½ In. 110.00
Steam Shovel, Pressed Steel, Open Housing, Red Corrugated Roof, Keystone, 18 ½ In.. .... 173.00
Store, Upstairs Gallery, Wood, Porcelain Labels, Germany, 29 In.. .... 604.00
Stove, Buck's Jr., Nickel Plated Cast Iron, St. Louis, c.1889, 20 In. 164.00
Stove, Buck's Jr. No. 4, Cast Iron, Nickel Plated Trim, Buck's Stove & Range Co., 23 In. 127.00
Stove, Cast Iron, A.C. Williams, c.1936, 3 ¼ In. 35.00

Toy, Smitty Scooter, Boy Riding Scooter, Tin Lithograph, Windup, Marx, 8 In.
$1210.00

Toy, Spaceship, X-7 Space Explorer, Plastic, Battery Operated, 8 In.
$58.00

Toy, Stable, Wood, Hinged Door, Tin Fence, 5 Animals, CR. Bliss, 18 x 12 x 8 In.
$770.00

T

Toy, Stove, Royal, Nickel Plated, 2 Side Shelves, Cover Plates, 15 In. $1050.00

Toy, Tango Dancers, Painted, Tin, Clockwork, Gunthermann, Box, 8 In. $4888.00

Toy, Tank, Bulldog, Monkey Division, Soldiers, Plastic, Metal, Windup, Remco, Box, 16 In. $144.00

TIP
Reproduction cast-iron toys and banks are heavier and thicker than the originals.

Stove, Cast Iron, Blue Enamel, Nickel Chrome, Claw Legs, Salesman's Sample, 18 x 12 x 8 In. 4000.00
Stove, Cast Iron, Kenton, Child's, 5 x 8 In. 144.00
Stove, Cotton Plant Jr. Cast Iron Cook, Working Model, Copper Finish, c.1880, 12 ½ In. 920.00
Stove, Crescent, Cast Iron, 11 ¾ x 13 x 6 ½ In. 33.00
Stove, Dolly's Favorite, Child's Cook Stove, Gold, Blue Paint, Cast Iron, Piqua, Ohio, 20 x 30 In. 2640.00
Stove, Eagle, Cast Iron, 10 x 11 x 6 In. 55.00
Stove, Eagle, Cast Iron, Nickel Plated, No. 879, Hubley, c.1920, 22 In. 230.00
Stove, Eagle, Iron, Scrolls, Vines, Painted, Impressed, 14 ¼ x 16 In. 176.00
Stove, Eagle, Silver Paint, Cast Iron, 12 ½ x 13 x 6 In. 66.00
Stove, Empire, Electric, 2 Burners, Nickel Plated Front, Metalware Corp., Child's 58.00
Stove, Empire, Electric, No. B27, Marked, Empire Metal Ware Corp., Wisc., 15 x 14 ½ x 7 In. 60.00
Stove, Empire, Tin, Green, Black, Electric, 20 In. 225.00
Stove, Empire, Tin, Green, Yellow, Electric, 9 x 11 In. 95.00
Stove, Jewel Range Jr., Cast Iron, Detroit, Works, 19 In. 460.00
Stove, Karr Range Co., Child's Stove, Blue Speckled Enamel, Belleville, Ill., 14 x 21 In. 1320.00
Stove, Little Lady, Tin, Green, Cream, Electric, 1920s 95.00
Stove, Model Range, Nickel Plate, Cast Iron, Accessories, Kenton Hardware, 26 x 11 x 21 In. 2160.00
Stove, Mt. Joy, Penn., Cast Iron Potbelly, Gray, 14 In. 92.00
Stove, Oak, Cast Iron, Kenton, 7 In. 25.00
Stove, Orr Painter & Co., Lilly Cast Iron, 12 In. 288.00
Stove, Orr Painter Co., Sunshine Cast Iron Cabin, c.1890, 13 In. 489.00
Stove, Philadelphia Stove Works, Little Fanny Cast Iron, 12 In. 58.00
Stove, Queen, Cast Iron, Nickel, Child's, 12 x 16 In. 1093.00
Stove, Quick Meal No. 407-16, Cast Iron Burners, c.1910, 27 x 17 In. 2310.00
Stove, Recovery Range Co., Brass, Metal, Child's, 12 x 8 x 26 In. 1725.00
Stove, Rival, Cast Iron, J. & E. Stevens, c.1895, 15 In. 58.00
Stove, Royal, Black Paint, Cast Iron, 8 x 8 ½ x 5 ½ In. 22.00
Stove, Royal, Cast Iron, 2 Copper Pots, Kenton, c.1910, 12 In. 25.00
Stove, Royal, Cast Iron, 6 ⅝ x 12 x 6 ½ In. 22.00
Stove, Royal, Nickel Plated, 2 Side Shelves, Cover Plates, 15 In. *illus* 1050.00
Stove, Tin Lithograph, Embossed Cookware, Germany, 7 In. 127.00
Stove, Triumph, Cast Iron, No. 941, Kenton Hardware, 13 In. 40.00
Stove, Venus, Green Paint, Cast Iron, 4 ½ x 4 x 4 ½ In. 44.00
Stove, Wood, Alert, Cast Iron, Tin, Nickel Trim, Marked 409, 38 In. 345.00
Street Musician, Ferdinand Martin, Painted, Felt Suit, Tin Lithograph, Windup, France, 9 In. 3163.00
Street Sweeper, Driver, Tin Lithograph, Windup, Ny-Lint, c.1950, 8 In. 172.00
Street Sweeper, Orange, Lever Operated Brushes, Tin, Friction, Japan, c.1960, 7 ¾ In. 175.00
Streetcar, White Horse, Red, Yellow, Consolidated Street RR, Cast Iron, Wilkins, 14 ½ In. 978.00
Stroller, Doll's, Metal, Chrome Trim, Landau Bars, Storage Compartment, 25 x 37 x 48 In. 460.00
Stroller, Doll's, Metal, Tin Litho Seat, Wood Handle, Practical Pig, Pluto, c.1934, 8 x 11 x 18 In. 575.00
Stroller, Doll's, Wicker, White Paint, Rolled Arms, Metal Frame, Sun Shade, c.1920, 32 In. 148.00
Strutting Sam, Black Man, Dances On Tub, Tin, Battery Operated, Japan 250.00
Submarine, Painted, Gray, Deck Railing, Tin, Fleischmann, 7 In. 201.00
Submarine, Painted, Tin, Windup, Bing, 10 In. 280.00
Submarine, Tin Lithograph, Windup, Wolverine, 13 In. 165.00
Super Susie, Bear Cashier, Lights, Bell Rings, Battery Operated, Linemar, Box, 8 In. 587.00
Swan, Painted, Celluloid, Horlave, 7 ½ x 5 In. 11.00
Sweeper, Bissel's Midget, Wood, Stenciled, c.1900, 28 x 7 x 5 In. 75.00
Sweeping Katinka, Tin, Windup, Lindstrom Co., Box, 1930s, 8 In. 450.00
Sweeping Mammy, Black Woman, Tin Lithograph, Windup, Lindstrom, Box, 8 In. 269.00
Swimming Pool, Detachable Bath, Diving House, Hand Enameled, Tin, Germany, c.1905, 17 In. 230.00
Switchboard Operator, Switchboard Lights, Tin, Vinyl, Battery Operated, Linemar, Box, 8 In. 621.00
Switchboard Operator, Tin Lithograph, Battery Operated, Linemar, 7 In. 90.00
Table, Mahogany, Inlay, Hinged Top, W.C. Collins, c.1836, 10 ½ In. 58.00
Tailspin Tabby, Pop-Up Kritter, Red, Black, Wood, Fisher-Price, 1930s 5.00
Tango Dancers, Painted, Tin, Clockwork, Gunthermann, Box, 8 In. *illus* 4888.00
Tank, Bulldog, Monkey Division, Soldiers, Plastic, Metal, Windup, Remco, Box, 16 In. *illus* 144.00
Tank, Combat, Bump & Go, Plastic, Battery Operated, 6 Actions, Tano Kogyo Co., Japan, 11 In. 141.00
Tank, Rapid Fire, Battery Operated, Japan, Daisy, 8 In. 75.00
Tank, Rollover, No. 3, Wood Wheels, Tin Lithograph, Windup, Marx, 7 ¾ In. 65.00
Tank, Rollover, No. 5, Wood Wheels, Tin Lithograph, Windup, Marx, 4 In. 45.00
Tank, Soldier Pops Up, Yellow, Black, Tin, Windup, Marx, 10 In. 130.00
Taxi, American Yellow Cab, Driver, Orange, Black, Tin Lithograph, Windup, Gundka, 7 In. 431.00
Taxi, Amos 'N' Andy, Fresh Air, Driver, Dog, Passenger, Tin Lithograph, Windup, 8 In. 425.00 to 650.00
Taxi, Checker, Tin, Windup, Courtland, 1948 110.00
Taxi, Driver, Red, Tin Lithograph, Clockwork, Germany, c.1910, 7 ½ In. *illus* 495.00
Taxi, Driver, Yellow, Black, Cast Iron, Copper Electroplate, Arcade, 8 In. *illus* 8250.00

Taxi, Driver, Yellow, Cast Iron, Hubley, 8 ½ In. 295.00
Taxi, Flat Top, Orange, Black, Arcade, 8 ½ In. 1750.00
Taxi, Ford, Yellow, 1947-48 Model, Pot Metal, Master Caster 425.00
Taxi, Graham, Green, Black, Tootsietoy 90.00
Taxi, Green & Black Checker, Driver, White Wheels, Checker Decal, Cast Iron, 8 In. 489.00
Taxi, Green Cab Co., 9 In. 1250.00
Taxi, Hansom Cab, Horse Drawn, Driver, Blue, Woman Passenger, Kenton, 16 In. 230.00
Taxi, Limousine, Yellow, Flat Top, Arcade, 8 ½ In. 4250.00
Taxi, Lincoln Zephyr, Yellow, Hubley, 8 In. 1500.00
Taxi, Mercedes Benz, License Plate, Hood Ornament, Tin Lithograph, Bandai, Box, 1960s, 10 In. 173.00
Taxi, Metal, Push Down, Wolverine, c.1940, 13 In. 225.00
Taxi, Mystery, Red, White, Tin, Wolverine, Box, 13 In. 350.00
Taxi, Oldsmobile, 1960 Model, Red, Yellow, Tin, Friction, Nomura, Box, 8 ¾ In. 685.00
Taxi, Red Top, Painted Driver, Arcade, 8 In. 1500.00
Taxi, Red Top, White Body, Black Hood, Running Boards, Stencil, Cast Iron, Arcade, 8 In. 690.00
Taxi, Trailer, Chicago World's Fair, Greyhound Lines, Cast Iron, 10 ½ In. 325.00
Taxi, Tricky, On Busy Street, Tin Lithograph, Windup, Box, 10 In. 99.00
Taxi, Tricky, Red, White, Tin, Windup, Marx, 4 ½ In. 50.00
Taxi, Yellow, Driver, Cast Iron, Arcade, 7 ¾ In. 650.00
Taxi, Yellow, Driver, No. 2, Arcade, c.1923, 8 In. 750.00
Taxi, Yellow, Driver, Orange, Black, No. 361, Tin Lithograph, Windup, 3 x 7 In. 70.00
Taxi, Yellow Cab, Dent, 4 ½ In. 350.00
Taxi, Yellow Cab, Driver, No. 311, Orange, Black, Cast Iron, Arcade, 9 ½ In. 1000.00
Taxi, Yellow Cab, No. 1, Arcade, 1930s, 9 In. 1000.00
Taxi, Yellow Cab, No. 3, Arcade, 5 In. 750.00 to 1500.00
Tea Set, Gingham Dog & Calico Cat, Tin, Art By Fern Bisel Peat, Ohio Art, 1930, 15 Piece 500.00
Teakettle, Wire Handle, Cast Iron, Kenton, 5 ½ In. 55.00
Teapot, Griswold, No. 576, Colonial Design, Cast Iron, Erie, Penn., 5 x 5 In. 660.00
Teddy Bear, Skipping Rope, Mohair, Clothes, Wood Legs, Metal Swing, Windup, Germany, 12 In. 173.00
Teddy Bear Parade, Band Leader, Bear Plays Drum, Wood, No. 195, Fisher-Price, 14 In. 1200.00
Teddy Bears are also listed in the Teddy Bear category.
Teddy Roosevelt, On Horse, Bells, Pull Toy, Wood, Bronze, Mechanical, 6 x 6 In. 657.00
Teddy The Artist, Bear At Desk, Pencil, Tin Lithograph, Battery Operated, Box, Japan, 9 In. 259.00
Telephone, Hello, Toy Voice Phone, Red, Gong Bell Manufacturing Co., Box 22.00
Telephone Bear, Cloth, Tin, Battery Operated, Linemar, Box, 7 ¼ In. 132.00
Telephone Bear, Winking Eyes, Head Nods, Battery Operated, Nomura, Box, 8 In. 238.00
Television Spaceman, Walker, Lights, Tin, Plastic, Battery Operated, Japan, 15 In. 316.00
Thresher, John Deere, Vindex, c.1929, 15 In. 1950.00
Thresher, McCormick Deering, Cast Iron, Arcade, 10 In. 93.00
Tick & Tack, Flip On Bars, Tin Lithograph, Marx, Box, 17 In. 88.00
Tillicum Convoy Set, Milton Bradley, Box, 1940s 300.00
Tippy Canoe, Indian, Tin, Windup, No. 27, Strauss, 9 In. 350.00
Toaster, Sunni Miss, Green, Yellow, Little Girl Graphic, Aluminum, Ohio Art, 7 ½ x 5 In. 18.00
Tom Corbet Space Academy, Plastic Spaceship, Metal Buildings, Marx, Box, 14 x 22 In. 1093.00
Tom Corbett, Space Cadet, Spaceship, Sparks, Boing Noise, Tin, Rockhill Prod., Marx, 12 In. 525.00
Tom Corbett, Space Pistol, Clicker, Dark Blue, Rockhill, Marx, Box, 10 In. 390.00
Tom Corbett, Space Pistol, Clicker, Light Blue, Rockhill, Marx, 10 In. 164.00
Tombo, Alabama Coon Jigger, Dances On Box, Windup, Straus, 1918, 10 ¼ In. 495.00
Toonerville Trolley, Cracker Jack Size, 1 ¾ In. 450.00
Toonerville Trolley, Tin Lithograph, Windup, Fontaine Fox, c.1922, 7 In. *illus* 355.00
Top, Clown, Chein, 7 In. 16.00
Tortoise, Walker, Tin, Windup, Occupied Japan, Box, 4 ¾ In. 33.00
Town Dairy Horse & Wagon, Tin, Windup, Marx, c.1930, 10 In. 195.00
Tractor, Allis-Chalmers, Folk Art, Metal, Wood, c.1940, 14 x 22 In. 193.00
Tractor, Bulldozer, Scoop, Headlight, Tin, Battery Operated, Remote Control, 1950s, 8 ½ In. 125.00
Tractor, Construction, Hauling, Tin Lithograph, Key, c.1950, 14 In. 266.00
Tractor, Driver, Army, Tan, Red Wheels, No. 4634, Tootsietoy 180.00
Tractor, Driver, Auburn Rubber, Molinered, Silver, c.1930, 8 In. 75.00
Tractor, Driver, Bates, Steel Mule, Painted, Embossed, Cast Iron, Vindex, c.1929, 6 In. 3450.00
Tractor, Driver, Cast Iron, Vindex, c.1928, 7 ¼ In. 650.00
Tractor, Driver, Caterpillar, Cast Iron, Steel Traction Tread, Arcade, Box, 7 In. 805.00 to 978.00
Tractor, Driver, Caterpillar, Metal Treads, Painted, Cast Iron, Arcade, 6 ½ In. *illus* 460.00
Tractor, Driver, Caterpillar, Yellow, Metal Rollers, Matchbox, 1959 35.00
Tractor, Driver, Fordson, Cast Iron, Arcade, 3 In. 30.00
Tractor, Driver, John Deere, Cast Iron, Vindex, c.1928, 6 ½ In. 800.00
Tractor, Driver, John Deere D, Cast Iron, Vindex, c.1928, 7 In. 2875.00
Tractor, Driver, McCormick Deering, Gray, Red Spoke Wheels, Cast Iron, Arcade, 7 In. 345.00

Toy, Taxi, Driver, Red, Tin Lithograph, Clockwork, Germany, c.1910, 7 ½ In.
$495.00

Toy, Taxi, Driver, Yellow, Black, Cast Iron, Copper Electroplate, Arcade, 8 In.
$8250.00

Toy, Toonerville Trolley, Tin Lithograph, Windup, Fontaine Fox, c.1922, 7 In.
$355.00

Toy, Tractor, Driver, Caterpillar, Metal Treads, Painted, Cast Iron, Arcade, 6 ½ In.
$460.00

As always, the edited listings in *Kovels' Antiques & Collectibles Price Guide 2010* aren't available on any website, but readers should visit Kovels.com for information on trends, tips, reproductions, marks, old prices, and more!

TIP

You can clean copper with lemon juice and salt or with Worcestershire sauce.

Toy, Train Car, Lionel, Locomotive, No. 42, Black, Red, Standard Gauge
$259.00

Toy, Train Set, American Flyer, Frontiersman, No. 20550, Franklin Passenger, Box, S Gauge
$115.00

Toy, Train Set, American Flyer, Viking Set, Cast Iron, Tin, Clockwork, Box, 1927
$375.00

Tractor, Driver, Oliver, Red Paint, Cast Iron, Arcade, 5 ¼ In. 22.00
Tractor, Driver, Red, Nickel Plated, Rubber Tires, Arcade, 5 ½ In. 325.00
Tractor, Driver, Rubber Wheels, No. 128F, Britains, Box, Postwar 649.00
Tractor, Driver, Spud, Metal Wheels, Britains, No. 127F. 266.00
Tractor, Driver, Trac-Tractor, Cast Iron, Nickel Plated, Rubber, Arcade, 1941, 7 ½ In. 850.00
Tractor, Dump Trailer, Allis-Chalmers, Arcade, 12 ½ In. 175.00
Tractor, Dump Trailer, Allis-Chalmers, Red & Green, Arcade, 13 In. 450.00
Tractor, Fordson Farm, Red, Tootsietoy, 5 In. 110.00
Tractor, Huber Star, Red, Black, Tootsietoy, 3 In. 195.00
Tractor, International Harvester, Turbo Model, Red, White, 9 ½ In. 35.00
Tractor, Minneapolis Moline, Prairie Gold Rush, 1984, 9 ½ In. 10.00
Tractor, Rodeo Joe, Cowboy, Tin Lithograph, Windup, Unique Art, Box, 7 In. 405.00
Tractor, Scraper, Caterpillar, Yellow, Plastic, Revell Toy, Box, c.1950, 12 In. 200.00
Tractor, Shovel, Hatra, Yellow Cab, Hubs, Orange Shovel, Matchbox, 1965 . . . . . 800.00
Tractor, Wagon, Bottom Dumper, Caterpillar, Yellow, Plastic, Revell Toy, Box, c.1950, 12 In. . . 185.00
Traffic Cop, Arms Swing Out, With Stop Circles, Tin Lithograph, Cast Iron, 1930s, 8 In. 139.00
Traffic Signal, Gray, Yellow, Red, Cast Base, Electric Light, Cast Iron, Arcade, 6 In. 690.00
Trailer, House, Removable Roof, Aluminum, Plastic, Wood, Cloth, Smith-Miller, Box, 26 In. . 715.00
Trailer, Motor Transit, 2 Cars, Pressed Steel, Marx, Mid 1930s, 23 In. 460.00
Trailer, Roamer, Red, Rubber Tires, No. 1044, Tootsietoy 210.00
Train, Cocoa Puffs, Windup, Tin Lithograph, Linemar, Built-In Key, 1 ½ x 12 In. 115.00
Train, Jetson Express, Engine & 3 Cars, Tin Lithograph, Windup, Marx, Box, 12 In. 402.00
Train, Jetson Express, George, Jane, Rosie, Elroy, Astro, Judy, Tin, Windup, 12 In. 200.00
Train Accessory, America Flyer, Trestle Bridge, Red, Wire Supports, Wide Gauge, Wood, 27 In. 115.00
Train Accessory, American Flyer, District School, No. 50, Box, c.1953-54, 7 x 5 ½ x 7 In. 485.00
Train Accessory, American Flyer, Station, Hyde Park, No. 90, c.1925-33, 4 x 6 x 3 ½ In. 95.00
Train Accessory, Bing, Steam Accessories, Blacksmith, Tools, Sifting Chute, Painted, 5 x 5 In. 173.00
Train Accessory, Bing, Telegraph Station, Painted, Lithograph, 11 x 6 x 10 In. 805.00
Train Accessory, Depot, Glendale, Metal, Marx, 1930s, 13 In. 195.00
Train Accessory, Ives, Crossing Gate, Gate House, Railed Ends, Tin Lithograph, c.1910, 22 In. 1495.00
Train Accessory, Ives, Union Station, Station, Glass Dome, Graphics, Tin Lithograph, 22 In. . 1093.00
Train Accessory, Lionel, 115 Station, Red, Window, Doors, Lights, Pressed Steel, Box, 14 x 8 ½ In. 316.00
Train Accessory, Lionel, Hells Gate Bridge, Silver, Green 200.00
Train Accessory, Lionel, Oil Derrick, No. 455, c.1950-54, 14 ¼ x 5 ¾ x 9 ¾ In. 165.00
Train Accessory, Lionel, Tunnel, Mountain, Bungalows, Tin, 33 x 22 ½ In. 840.00
Train Accessory, Marklin, Crossing Gate, 2 Gates, Painted, Hand Crank, O Gauge, 7 ½ x 10 ½ In. 2750.00
Train Accessory, Marklin, Freight Station, Painted, Embossed Walls, Ramp, Germany, 18 x 19 In. 2300.00
Train Accessory, Marklin, Telegraph Pole, Painted, Cast Iron, 10 In. 77.00
Train Accessory, Marklin, Trestle, Bridge, Blue, Attachable Approaches, Shrubbery, 1 Gauge, 48 In. 230.00
Train Accessory, Marklin, Tunnel, Lighthouse, Textured, Painted, Tin, O Gauge, 8 x 12 In. . . 135.00
Train Accessory, Marx, Railroad Station, Automatic Gate, Accessories, Electric, Glendale, Box 525.00
Train Accessory, Marx, Railroad Station, Metal, Glendale, 14 In. 225.00
Train Accessory, Scenic Set, Built-Rite, No. 212, Cardboard Lithograph, Unpunched, Box . . . 200.00
Train Accessory, Schoenhut, Railroad Station, Painted, Wood, Celluloid, Embossed Paper, 17 In. 248.00
Train Car, Bing, Locomotive, Box Cab, Maroon, Gray Roof, Yellow Trim, Electric, O Gauge, 8 ½ In. 489.00
Train Car, Bing, Postal Telegraph Van Coach, Painted Brown, Black, Olive Green, 1 Gauge, 18 In. 489.00
Train Car, Buddy L, Auto Transport Flat Car, Pressed Steel, 30 In. 288.00
Train Car, Buddy L, Boxcar, Pressed Steel, c.1928, 22 In. 460.00
Train Car, Buddy L, Caboose, Pressed Steel, c.1928, 22 In. 575.00
Train Car, Buddy L, Coal, Pressed Steel, c.1928, 22 In. 345.00
Train Car, Buddy L, Engine, Tender, 5 Straight Tracks, 9 Curved Tracks, 44 In. 633.00
Train Car, Buddy L, Locomotive, Tender, Pressed Steel, c.1928, 44 In. 920.00
Train Car, Caboose, B & O, No. 2110, Voltamp, Gold Stamp Lettered Cupola, 10 ¼ In. 1150.00
Train Car, Fleischman, Steam Engine, Horizontal Boiler, Simulated Brickwork, 11 ¼ In. 201.00
Train Car, Freight, Lionel, Penn Steam, No. 2020, 1949 . . . . . 595.00
Train Car, Handcar, Windup, Painted Figures, Germany, 5 In. 431.00
Train Car, Hull & Stafford, Locomotive, Cast Iron Spoke Wheels, Bell, Tin, Windup, 8 ¾ In. . . 259.00
Train Car, Ives, Locomotive, Black, Red Trim, Silver, Cast Iron, Electric, O Gauge, 9 ¼ In. . . . 201.00
Train Car, Ives, Locomotive, Painted, Die Cut, Cow Catcher, Cast Iron, Tin, Windup, c.1876, 18 In. 8625.00
Train Car, Ives, Locomotive, Tender, No. 20, Cast Iron, Tin Lithograph, Windup, O Gauge, 13 In. 288.00
Train Car, Ives, Locomotive, Wide Gauge 3242, Maroon, Steel Body, Cast Iron Frame, 12 In. . 403.00
Train Car, Lionel, AEC Switcher, No. 57, Reproduction Box, c.1959-60, 7 ½ x 2 ½ x 3 ½ In. . . 690.00
Train Car, Lionel, Freight, Diesel Switcher, No. 622, 1949. . . . . 595.00
Train Car, Lionel, Gondola, No. 812, 2 Barrels, Box, c.1931-34, 10 ½ x 2 ½ x 2 In. 135.00
Train Car, Lionel, Locomotive, No. 42, Black, Red, Standard Gauge . . . . . *illus* 259.00
Train Car, Lionel, Locomotive, No. 54, Brass Standard Gauge, Cast Wheels, Bells, Electric, 15 ½ In. 2300.00

Train Car, Lionel, Locomotive, No. 392E, Gray, Box. 400.00
Train Car, Lionel, Pres. McKinley Observation Car, No. 2521, Box, 1960s, 15 x 2 ½ x 3 ½ In. 185.00
Train Car, Lionel, Pullman Car, No. 2534, Silver Bluff, Hex Head Screws, c.1952-59 205.00
Train Car, Lionel, Searchlight Car, Type II, No. 2620, c.1940, 8 x 2 x 3 ¾ In. 120.00
Train Car, Locomotive, Dribbler, Schoenner Gauge 4, Nickeled Boiler, Frame, Copper Cab, 7 In. 978.00
Train Car, Marklin, Boxcar, Heinz 57 Varieties, Graphic Pickle, Tomato Ketchup, 1 Gauge, 11 In. 2875.00
Train Car, Marklin, Caboose, Coal Stove, Brakeman's Cab, Figure, O Gauge, 7 In. 1725.00
Train Car, Osceola, Locomotive, Painted, Pine, Brass, Copper, Steel, c.1900, 23 x 33 In. 16250.00
Train Car, Steam Engine, Folk Design, Mixed Woods, Metal, Original Paint, 1900s, 27 In. 646.00
Train Car, Triang, Locomotive, Puff Puff, Rider, England, 1950s, 18 In. 135.00
Train Set, American Flyer, Frontiersman, No. 20550, Franklin Passenger, Box, S Gauge *illus* 115.00
Train Set, American Flyer, Viking Set, Cast Iron, Tin, Clockwork, Box, 1927 *illus* 375.00
Train Set, Bing, Locomotive, 3 Cars, Passenger, 4-4-0, Cast Iron, Electric, 1 Gauge, 12 ½ In. 1035.00
Train Set, Bing, Mercury, Locomotive, 2 Dining Cars, Tender, Windup, Box, O Gauge, 11 ¼ In. 2875.00
Train Set, Buddy L, Engine, Tender, Boxcar, Gondola, Caboose, Tracks, 8-Ft. Track 1610.00
Train Set, Buddy L, Industrial Railroad, Decals, c.1929 633.00
Train Set, Carette, Steam, Nickel Plated Boiler, Parlor & Baggage Cars, 1 Gauge, 6 ½ In. 748.00
Train Set, Dent, No. 711, Steam Locomotive, 3 Passenger Cars, Toyland's Treasure Chest, Box 115.00
Train Set, Freight, Cast Metal, Engine, Tender, Caboose, Signal, Electric, Box, 25 ⅞ In. 356.00
Train Set, Hafner, Locomotive, Black, Red Tender, 3 Coaches, Tin Lithograph, Windup, Box, c.1920 288.00
Train Set, Lionel, Comet, Blue, Tender, 2 Pullmans, 712 Observation, O Gauge, 11 ½ In. 863.00
Train Set, Lionel, No. 11440, 0-27, Box *illus* 173.00
Train Set, Lionel, No. 11530, Diesel Freight, Box, O Gauge *illus* 288.00
Train Set, Lionel, Passengers, 309 Pullman, 310 Baggage, 312 Observation, Standard Gauge, 13 In. 748.00
Train Set, Marklin, 0-4-0, Locomotive, Green, Red, Baggage, 2 Coaches, Windup, 1 Gauge, 4 ½ In. 3450.00
Train Set, Marklin, Freight, Tanker, Hopper, Dump, Lumber, Tracks, Electric, OO Gauge, Box 504.00
Train Set, Marklin, Locomotive, Coal, Passenger, Box Car, Tracks, Wood Case, O Gauge, Box, 18 In. 4266.00
Train Set, Sankei, Locomotive, Exploration, 3 Cars, Battery Operated, Box, 21 ½ In. 3503.00
Train Set, Steelcraft, Locomotive, Tender, Pressed Steel, 20th Century Limited, 5 Piece 748.00
Train Set, Tootsietoy, Freight, Locomotive, 8 Cars, Caboose, No. 5600, Box, 3 To 5 In. 575.00
Tricyclist, Boy, Painted, Cast Iron, 5 In. 330.00
Tricyclist, Man, Cast Iron, Ideal, 4 In. 66.00
Trolley, Grand Central Depot, Merriam Mfg., c.1880, 13 In. 595.00
Trolley, Green, Yellow Stripes, Tin, Windup, Gunthermann, 10 In. 135.00
Trolley, Hillclimber, Painted, Spoke Wheels, Cast Iron, Pressed Steel, c.1897, 14 ½ In. 259.00
Trolley, No. 100, Painted, Blue, Yellow, Nickel Frame, Steel, Lionel, 10 ½ In. *illus* 2588.00
Trolley, Painted, Pressed Steel, Converse, 16 In. 210.00
Trolley, Red, White, Tin, Windup, Gunthermann, Box, 12 In. 770.00
Trombone Player, Black Hair, Vibrates, Head & Arms Move, Tin, Windup, Linemar, Box, 5 ¼ In. 560.00
Trombone Player, Blond, Vibrates, Head & Arms Move, Tin, Windup, Linemar, Box, 5 ¼ In. 706.00
Truck, ABC Freight, Tin, Friction, Japan, 1950s, 11 ½ In., 2 Piece 120.00
Truck, Aerial Ladder, Yellow, Red, Pressed Steel, Keystone, Box, 24 In. 259.00
Truck, American Express, Kiddies Oh-Boy, Open Cab, Painted, Green, Pressed Steel, 22 In. 2070.00
Truck, American National Circus, Blue Streak Toledo, Pressed Steel, 26 In. 2875.00
Truck, Arctic Ice Cream, Cast Iron, Embossed Letters, Kilgore, 8 In. 374.00
Truck, Army, Hercules, C-Cab, Canvas Canopy Cover, Khaki Color, Chein, 19 ½ In. 690.00
Truck, Army, L. Tan Jr., Yellow, Canvas, Rubber Wheels, Pressed Steel, Steelcraft, c.1927, 28 In. 805.00
Truck, Artillery, Movable Gun, Wood Shells, Windup, Wilkins, c.1917, 11 In. 665.00
Truck, Baby Dump, Yellow, Harvester, 10 ½ In. 1750.00
Truck, Baby Stationary Bed, Red, Cast Iron, Arcade, 10 In. 633.00
Truck, Baggage, Sit-N-Ride, Headlight, Painted, Pressed Steel, Buddy L, c.1934, 26 In. *illus* 1093.00
Truck, Bell Telephone, Hubley, 4 In. 350.00
Truck, Bell Telephone, Olive Green, Nickel Plated Spoke Wheels, Cast Iron, Hubley, 4 In. 230.00
Truck, Bell Telephone, White Rubber Wheels, Green, Cast Iron, Hubley, 2 x 3 ¾ x 2 In. 220.00
Truck, Black, Green, Red, Pressed Steel, Buddy L, 25 In. 2574.00
Truck, Blue, Tin Lithograph, Friction, Box, 1950s, 10 ¼ In. 285.00
Truck, Bread, Panel, International Hathaway, Cast Iron, Driver, Rubber Tires, Arcade, 9 ½ In. 805.00
Truck, Bump & Dump, Driver, Plastic, Saunders, Box, 1950s, 10 ½ In. 145.00
Truck, Camper, Dodge, Tin, Friction, Japan, 1950s, 7 ½ In. 95.00
Truck, Car Carrier, 3 Austin Cars, Green Cab, Trailer, White Rubber Tires, Cast Iron, Arcade, 14 In. 575.00
Truck, Car Carrier, 3 Cars, Tin, Japan, 1950s, 8 In. 145.00
Truck, Car Carrier, 3 Austin Cars, Trailer, White Rubber Tires, Cast Iron, Arcade, 14 In. *illus* 575.00
Truck, Car Carrier, 3 Racers, Blue Tractor, Green Trailer, Red Disc Wheels, Tin Plated, Marx, 12 In. 546.00
Truck, Car Carrier, 4 Model A Cars, Green, Red, Nickel Plated Wheels, Cast Iron, Arcade, 24 1/2 In. 1150.00
Truck, Car Carrier, 4 Sedans, Yellow, Red, Allied, 9 ½ In. 125.00
Truck, Car Carrier, 6 Chevy Cars, Double Wide Ramp, Tin, Friction, Linemar, Japan, 16 In. 78.00

Toy, Train Set, Lionel, No. 11440, 0-27, Box
$173.00

Toy, Train Set, Lionel, No. 11530, Diesel Freight, Box, O Gauge
$288.00

Toy, Trolley, No. 100, Painted, Blue, Yellow, Nickel Frame, Steel, Lionel, 10 ½ In.
$2588.00

Toy, Truck, Baggage, Sit-N-Ride, Headlight, Painted, Pressed Steel, Buddy L, c.1934, 26 In.
$1093.00

TIP

Don't store old paint rags. They may ignite spontaneously.

TIP
Stainless steel and aluminum can be cleaned with silver polish.

Toy, Truck, Car Carrier, 3 Austin Cars, Green Cab, Trailer, White Rubber Tires, Cast Iron, Arcade, 14 In.
$575.00

Toy, Truck, Dump, Contractor's, Pressed Steel, Motor Driven, Kingsbury, 9 In.
$345.00

Toy, Truck, Dump, GMC, L. Boycraft Decal, Hand Lift Dump, Pressed Steel, Steelcraft, 23 In.
$144.00

Toy, Truck, Dump, Hydraulic, Blue, White, Pressed Steel, Buddy L, Box, c.1938, 26 In.
$2200.00

Truck, Car Carrier, Blue, No. A2A1, Matchbox, Box 80.00
Truck, Car Carrier, Mack, Bulldog, 3 1928 Buicks, Tootsietoy 250.00
Truck, Cattle Hauler, Structo, 1955, 22 In. 95.00
Truck, CBC Television, Tin, Friction, Japan, 6 In. 115.00
Truck, Cement Mixer, Emmets, Pressed Steel, Lithograph, c.1928, 20 In. 403.00
Truck, Cement Mixer, Kenton, Green, Cast Iron, Nickel Plated, Jaeger, 9 In. 1093.00
Truck, Chevrolet, Corvair, Pickup, Japan, 1959, 8 ½ In. 195.00
Truck, Circus, Horse, Pressed Steel, Triang, England, 1940s, 23 In. 375.00
Truck, Circus, Pressed Steel, American National, c.1927, 26 In. 1265.00
Truck, Coal, Pressed Steel, Buddy L, c.1926, 26 In. 575.00
Truck, Coal & Ice, Painted, Green, Enclosed Cab, Stencil, Pressed Steel, Friction, 13 ¼ In. . . . 1265.00
Truck, Construction, Painted, Green Cab, Black Fenders, Pressed Steel, Sturditoy, 26 ½ In. . . . 690.00
Truck, Contractor's, Yellow, Buddy L, 1961, 14 In. 55.00
Truck, Crane, Mack, Hercules, C-Cab, Painted, Green, Red, Black, Chein, c.1930 . . . . . 690.00
Truck, Crank Lift, Closed Cab, Pressed Steel, Keystone, c.1920, 27 In. 413.00
Truck, Dairy, Borden's, No. 745, Fisher-Price 395.00
Truck, Dairy, Hercules, Blue & Red, Open Body, Balloon Wheels, Tin Lithograph, Chein, 19 In. 748.00
Truck, Dairy, Wood Steering Handle, Decals, Pressed Steel, Keystone, c.1930, 26 In. 1265.00
Truck, Delivery, Borden's, Yellow Wood Roof, Tin Lithograph, 13 ½ In. 1003.00
Truck, Delivery, Brown Van Body, Rear Doors Open, Tin Lithograph, Gundka, 5 ½ In. 920.00
Truck, Delivery, Hathaway's Bread & Cake, Painted, Arcade, 1932, 9 ¼ In. 1210.00
Truck, Delivery, Horse Drawn, Painted, Milk Carriers, Bottles, Spoke Wheels, Sheffield Farms, 23 In. 550.00
Truck, Delivery, Mazda, 3 Wheels, Rubber Tires, Tin Lithograph, Friction, Bandai, 1950s, 8 ½ In. 345.00
Truck, Delivery, Mensa, Driver, 3 Wheels, Tin, Lehmann, Box, 5 ½ x 2 ¾ In. 1800.00
Truck, Delivery, Red, Hillclimber, 11 In. 88.00
Truck, Delivery, Stake, Victor Co., Painted, Stenciled, Wood, 15 In. 2070.00
Truck, Driver, Embossed, Tin Lithograph, Penny Toy, Meier, 3 ¼ In. 135.00
Truck, Dump, 3-Axle, Red, Silver, Hubley, 1938, 7 ½ In. 450.00
Truck, Dump, Bottom, Orange, No. 2009, Doepke, c.1950, 27 In. 175.00
Truck, Dump, Cement Mixer, Dark Yellow, Tonka, 1968, 19 In. 75.00
Truck, Dump, Chevrolet, Crank Operated, Mirror, Tin, Friction, 1954, 12 In. 283.00
Truck, Dump, Contractor's, Pressed Steel, Motor Driven, Kingsbury, 9 In. . . . . . *illus* 345.00
Truck, Dump, Electric Lights, Wyandotte, 10 In. 195.00
Truck, Dump, GMC, Big Fat, Tin, Friction, Japan, 14 ½ In. 245.00
Truck, Dump, GMC, L. Boycraft Decal, Hand Lift Dump, Pressed Steel, Steelcraft, 23 In. . *illus* 144.00
Truck, Dump, GMC, Tipper, Yellow Cab, Red Matchbox, 1968 . . . . . 969.00
Truck, Dump, Green & Red, Decals, Rubber Tires, International, Arcade, c.1931, 10 ¾ In. . . . 3500.00
Truck, Dump, High Lift, Windup, Structo, 1951, 12 ½ In. 95.00
Truck, Dump, Hydraulic, Blue, White, Pressed Steel, Buddy L, Box, c.1938, 26 In. . . . . . *illus* 2200.00
Truck, Dump, Hydraulic, Orange, Ny-Lint, 1956, 24 In. 150.00
Truck, Dump, Hydraulic, Yellow, Bronze, Structo, 1961, 18 In. 55.00
Truck, Dump, International Harvester, Driver, Red, Cast Iron, Arcade, 4 ¼ x 10 ¾ x 3 ¼ In. . . 350.00
Truck, Dump, Packard, Lift Lever, Closed Cab, Pressed Steel, Keystone, c.1920, 27 In. 330.00
Truck, Dump, Pressed Steel, Painted, Yellow, Enclosed Cab, Open Body, Electric, c.1934, 20 In. 173.00
Truck, Dump, Pressed Steel, Sturditoy, c.1926, 33 In. 1265.00
Truck, Dump, Red, Black Cab, Pressed Steel, Buddy L, 20 In. 345.00
Truck, Dump, Red, Orange, Marx, 5 ¾ In. 185.00
Truck, Dump, Red & Green, Pressed Steel, Wyandotte, 21 In. 365.00
Truck, Dump, Red & Silver, Black Rubber Tires, Cast Iron, Arcade, 11 In. 316.00
Truck, Dump, Renault Stella, Green, Yellow, Tin Lithograph, Rossignol, 1936, 15 ½ In. 1725.00
Truck, Dump, Rose, Blue, Cast Iron, Kilgore, 4 In. 195.00
Truck, Dump, Scoop, Gray, Red, Rubber Tires, Pressed Steel, Marx, c.1950, 20 ½ In. 535.00
Truck, Dump, Shovel, Contractor's & Builders, Barrow, Green, Yellow, Marx, c.1938, 10 ½ In. 375.00
Truck, Dump, Tin, Windup, Bing, 10 ½ In. 700.00
Truck, Dump, Tin, Windup, Marx, 1920s, 11 In. 225.00
Truck, Dump, Winch Lift, Open Cab, Pressed Steel, Buddy L, c.1920, 25 In. 468.00
Truck, Dump, Woolridge, Bottom, Yellow, No. 2000, Doepke, 1946, 25 In. 225.00
Truck, Emergency, Moon, Van Body, Painted, Stenciled, Pressed Steel, Neff, 12 ½ In. 1035.00
Truck, Emergency, Red, Decals, Ladders, Rubber Tires, Buddy L, Box, 12 ½ In. 119.00
Truck, Emergency Rescue, Courtland, Box, 12 ½ In. 260.00
Truck, First Prize Frankfurters, Battery Operated Headlights, Metalcraft, 13 In. 6325.00
Truck, Flat Bed, Hot Rod, Structo, 1950s 95.00
Truck, Flat Bed, Tin, Friction, Bandai, Japan, c.1950, 18 In. 225.00
Truck, Flat Bed, U.S. Army, Smith-Miller 1200.00
Truck, Ford, Canopy Express, Marx, 1958, 15 ½ In. 375.00
Truck, Ford, Flower Delivery, Bandaum 5675.00
Truck, Ford, Log, Orange, Hubley, Box, 9 ¼ In. 225.00

Truck, Ford, Pickup, 1958, Bandai, Japan, 8 In. 145.00
Truck, Freightliner, Chippewa Motor, White, 2 Trailers, Rear Doors Open, Tin, Japan, 21 In. 147.00
Truck, Freightliner, Eastern Express, White, Air Deflector, Tin, Friction, Japan, 15 ½ In. 125.00
Truck, Freightliner, International Transport Inc., White, 2 Trailers, Tin, Friction, Japan, 21 In. 175.00
Truck, Freightliner, Raymond Motor Transportation, 2 Trailers, Doors Open, Japan, 1980, 21 In. 124.00
Truck, Freightliner, Yale, White Air Deflector, Doors Open, Tin, Friction, Japan, 15 ½ In. 130.00
Truck, Fuel, Rubber Wheels, Red, Silver, Cast Iron, Hubley, 1 ½ x 5 ½ x 1 ¾ In. 77.00
Truck, Gilbert City Meat Market, Tin, Windup, Courtland, 7 In. 110.00
Truck, GMC, U.S. Army Rocket, Japan, 1950s, 10 In. 275.00
Truck, Graham Commercial Tire, Die Cast, Orange, Brown, Tootsietoy, 4 In. 250.00
Truck, Graham Dairy, Die Cast, Cream, Black, Tootsietoy, 4 In. 145.00
Truck, Grocery, Orange, Rubber Tires, Metal, Toy Town, 11 In. 325.00
Truck, Grocery, Polar Ice Co., Red, Yellow Stake Body, Pressed Steel, Marx, 14 In. 288.00
Truck, Guided Missile Carrier, No. 2800, Ny-Lint, Box, 15 ½ In. 30.00
Truck, Hathaway's Bakery, Arcade, c.1932, 9 ½ In. 1300.00
Truck, Hauler, Machinery Shovel, Orange, Wyandotte, 1950, 26 In. 95.00
Truck, Heinz Pickle, Headlights, Pressed Steel, Metalcraft, 12 In. 201.00
Truck, Huckster, Pressed Steel, Buddy L, c.1927, 14 In. 2875.00
Truck, Ice, Blue Paint, Cast Iron, Arcade, 3 x 6 ½ In. 75.00
Truck, Ice, Enclosed Cab, Painted, Black, Yellow, Disc Wheels, Pressed Steel, Buddy L, 25 ½ In. 1610.00
Truck, Ice, Kiddies Oh-Boy, Painted, Green, Open Cab, Open Bed, Decal, Pressed Steel, 19 ¼ In. 403.00
Truck, Ice, Studebaker, Ice & Tongs, Red, Arcade, 7 In. 500.00
Truck, Ice Cream, Good Humor, White, Blue, Black Wall Wheels, Clear Windows, Matchbox, 1983 13.00
Truck, Ice Cream, Howard Johnson, Tin, Friction, 1950s, 8 ¼ In. 195.00
Truck, Ice Cream, Metal, Windup, Cortland, U.S.A., c.1948, 9 In. 195.00
Truck, International, Orange, Cream, Tailgate, Pressed Steel, Tru-Scale, 1955, 14 ½ In. 475.00
Truck, Jet Fuel, Texaco, Box, 23 In. 325.00
Truck, Jordan Marsh Co., Green, Gray, Black Rubber Tires, Pressed Steel, 19 In. *illus* 1610.00
Truck, Katz Drug Store, Cat, Red, Black, White, Tin, Friction, Japan, 4 ½ x 10 In. 245.00
Truck, Ladder, Aerial, Red, Pressed Steel, Buddy L, 34 In. 700.00
Truck, Ladder, Driver, Silver, Red, Hubley, 5 In. 250.00
Truck, Ladder, Drivers, Spoke Wheels, Cast, Embossed Eagles, Open Frame, 15 In. 518.00
Truck, Ladder, Hydraulic, Pressed Steel, Hand Crank Operated Platform, Buddy L, c.1926, 39 In. 575.00
Truck, Ladder, Oh Boy, Pressed Steel, c.1926, 17 In. 1035.00
Truck, Ladder, Painted, Nickel Plated Body Runners, Decals, Pressed Steel, Structo, 32 ½ In. 86.00
Truck, Ladder, Silver, Red, Hubley, 5 In. 150.00
Truck, Lammerts Moving Van, Black Enamel, Cast Iron, 13 ½ In. 2160.00
Truck, Livestock, Trailer, Tin, Friction, Japan, 9 In. 95.00
Truck, Log, Semi-Trailer, Pressed Steel, Smith-Miller, 37 In., 2 Piece 575.00
Truck, Log, Semi-Trailer, Red, White, Courtland, Box, 12 In. 165.00
Truck, Lumber, Lumber Pieces, Pressed Steel, Buddy L, c.1926, 25 In. 575.00
Truck, Lyons Maid Ice Cream Shop, Man, Blue, No. 47B1, Matchbox, Box. 800.00
Truck, Mack, Animal, Tootsietoy, c.1931 150.00
Truck, Mack, Anti-Aircraft Gun, Tootsietoy, c.1931 125.00
Truck, Mack, Hollywood Film Ad, Red, Die Cast, Electric Spot Light, Decal, Smith-Miller, 18 In. 690.00
Truck, Mack, Panama Digger, Painted, Green, Nickel Cast Iron, Hubley, 13 In. 1495.00
Truck, Mail, Mack, U.S. Airmail, Red, Olive, Tootsietoy, 3 In. 195.00
Truck, Menagerie, Lion Tamers, Lions, Seesaw, Ball, Tin, Friction, Japan, 10 In. 150.00
Truck, Milk, Cow Decal, Green Windows, Bottles, Matchbox 39.00
Truck, Milk, Mack, 4 Cans, Red, Arcade, 12 In. 3250.00
Truck, Milk, Mack, Nickel Driver, 1929, 11 In. 1300.00
Truck, Milk, Open Sides, No. 21C7, Matchbox, Box 600.00
Truck, Moving Van, Allied, Tin, Friction, Japan, 1950s, 13 In. 175.00
Truck, Moving Van, Bekins, Pressed Steel, Smith-Miller, 28 In. 1100.00
Truck, Moving Van, Driver, Tan, Red Hood, Stripe, Rubber Tires, Red Hubs, Cast Iron, Arcade, 13 In. 2588.00
Truck, Moving Van, Express Line, Pressed Steel, Buddy L, 1920s, 25 In. *illus* 460.00
Truck, Moving Van, Green, Disc Wheels, Tin Lithograph, Windup, Chein, 8 ¼ In. 489.00
Truck, Moving Van, Green, Yellow, Red, Tin Lithograph, J. Chein & Co., 3 ¾ x 7 ½ x 2 ¾ In. 275.00
Truck, Moving Van, No. 204, Green, Black, Red, Buddy L, c.1924, 24 In. 995.00
Truck, Moving Van, Pressed Steel, Structo, Box, c.1927, 16 In. 805.00
Truck, Moving Van, Prime Mover, Yellow, No. 15A1, Matchbox, Box 900.00
Truck, Mr. Porter, Figure, Metal, Windup, England, 1940s, 12 In. 275.00
Truck, Overland Circus, Painted, Kenton, 7 In. 775.00
Truck, Patrol, Driver, Blue, Red Spoke Wheels, Bench Seat, Cast Iron, Hubley, 7 ½ In. 345.00
Truck, Pickfords, Removers & Storers, Green, No. 46, Matchbox, Box 60.00
Truck, Pickup, Flivver, Pressed Steel, Buddy L, 12 In. 403.00
Truck, Pickup, Flivver, Roadster, c.1920, 13 In. 550.00

Toy, Truck, Jordan Marsh Co., Green, Gray, Black Rubber Tires, Pressed Steel, 19 In.
$1610.00

TIP
If the batteries in a battery toy have corroded, remove them and rub an emery board or 0000 steel wool on the contact points. Then put new batteries in the toy and it should work.

Toy, Truck, Moving Van, Express Line, Pressed Steel, Buddy L, 1920s, 25 In.
$460.00

TIP
Metal polish paste or cream cleans better than polish-impregnated cloth if you have a very tarnished piece. Cloths are good for small metal parts with little tarnish.

TIP
Use silicone, not soap, on the bottom of drawers that stick.

Toy, Truck, Sonny Cannon, Silver, Pressed Steel, c.1926, 25 In.
$259.00

Toy, Truck, Tanker, Black, Green, No Doors, Disc Wheels, Pressed Steel, Buddy L, 24 ½ In.
$1210.00

Toy, Truck, Tanker, Richfield Oil, Celluloid Windshield, Decals, Pressed Steel, c.1925
$1150.00

TIP
Phillips screws were introduced in the 1920s, a good clue to dating furniture with original Phillips screws. But remember, sometimes old screws have been replaced with newer ones.

T

Truck, Pickup, Gray, Freidag, 7 ½ In. . . . 1600.00
Truck, Pickup, Jeep, Red, No. 71B1, Matchbox, Box. . . . 130.00
Truck, Pickup, Red, Silver, Die Cast, Tin Lithograph Chassis, Kiddie Toy, Hubley, 5 ½ In. . . . 75.00
Truck, Pickup, Silver, Die Cast, Tin Lithograph Chassis, Kiddie Toy, Hubley, 5 ½ In. . . . 65.00
Truck, Postal, Royal Mail, Red, Black, Driver, Tin Lithograph, Windup, Brimtoy, 11 ½ In. . . . 2875.00
Truck, Railway Express, Open Cab, Black, Green, Screen Side Van, Pressed Steel, Sturditoy, 26 In. . 2185.00
Truck, Railway Express, Pressed Steel, Buddy L, 26 In. . . . 518.00
Truck, Railway Express, Rubber Wheels, Green, Cast Iron, Hubley, 2 ¼ x 3 ¾ x 2 In. . . . 143.00
Truck, Red Ball Express, Tin, Friction, Japan, 1950s, 14 In. . . . 145.00
Truck, Red Star, Driver, Green, White, Red, Tin Lithograph, Windup, Strauss Co., 3 ½ x 8 x 4 In. 300.00
Truck, Red Star, Tin Lithograph, Windup, Strauss Co., 3 ½ x 8 x 4 In. . . . 330.00
Truck, Refuse, Hood Opens, Rear Operates, Trash Can, Pressed Steel, Structo, 21 In. . . . 325.00
Truck, Refuse Collector, Silver, No. 38A4, Matchbox, Box . . . 140.00
Truck, Rescue Squad Fire Dept., White, Red, Tonka, 1956, 12 In. . . . 275.00
Truck, Schrafft's Candies, Tin, Friction, Japan, 1950, 8 ½ In. . . . 95.00
Truck, Searchlight, Red, White, Smith-Miller, 1953, 26 In. . . . 850.00
Truck, Semi-Trailer, Drop Down Tailgate, Orange, Black, Wood, Buddy L, 27 In. . . . 695.00
Truck, Semi-Trailer, Express, Lindstrom American Railway, 16 In. . . . 750.00
Truck, Semi-Trailer, Horse Van, Tin, Friction, 9 In. . . . 95.00
Truck, Semi-Trailer, Jupiter Rocket, Tin, Friction, Momoya, Box, 13 & 8 In., 2 Piece . . . 2938.00
Truck, Semi-Trailer, People Mover, World's Fair, Blue, Cast Iron, Rubber Tires, Kenton, 10 ½ In. 1610.00
Truck, Semi-Trailer, Red, No. 20A6, Matchbox, Box. . . . 380.00
Truck, Semi-Trailer, Red, Silver, Hubley, 7 ½ In. . . . 375.00
Truck, Semi-Trailer, Rubber Tires, Cast Iron, 5 ½ In. . . . 115.00
Truck, Semi-Trailer, Safeway, Freightliner, White, Tin, Friction, Box, Japan, 15 ½ In. . . . 136.00
Truck, Semi-Trailer, Safeway, White, Tin, Shudi Shoji, Box, c.1964, 16 ½ In. . . . 145.00
Truck, Service, Hillclimber, Painted, Pressed Steel, Schieble, c.1927, 17 ⅝ In. . . . 403.00
Truck, Shovel, Green, Red, Hubley, 8 ½ In. . . . 650.00
Truck, Shovel, Green, Red, Hubley, 10 ½ In. . . . 950.00
Truck, Side Dump, Red, Green, Wyandotte, 20 In. . . . 250.00
Truck, Sonny Cannon, Silver, Pressed Steel, c.1926, 25 In. . . . *illus* 259.00
Truck, Stake, 5 Ton, Green, Red, Gold Highlights, Crates, Barrels, Cast Iron, Hubley, 17 In. . . . 1955.00
Truck, Stake, Blue, Cast Iron, A.C. Williams, 4 ½ In. . . . 110.00
Truck, Stake, Driver, Chain Drive, Penny Toy, Meier, c.1910, 3 In. . . . 69.00
Truck, Stake, Green, Rubber Wheels, Cast Iron, 1 ½ x 5 x 1 ½ In. . . . 88.00
Truck, Stake, Mack, Bulldog, Orange, Hubley, 5 ¾ In. . . . 275.00
Truck, Stake, Mack, Hercules, Lithograph, Balloon Wheels, Nickel Plated, Chein, 18 ½ In. . . . 690.00
Truck, Stake, Mack, Red, Champion, White Rubber Tires, Blue Hubs, Cast Iron, 7 ½ In. . . . 201.00
Truck, Stake, Marcrest Dairy, White Paint, Marx, 1941, 14 In. . . . 130.00
Truck, Stake, Pressed Steel, Push, Marx, Box, 12 ½ In. . . . 173.00
Truck, Stake, Red, Black, Rubber Tires, Pressed Steel, Cor-Cor, c.1929, 23 ½ In. . . . 935.00
Truck, Stake, Red, Coaster Version, Pressed Steel, Dayton, c.1928, 16 ½ In. . . . 535.00
Truck, Stake, Shell Motor Oil, Red & Yellow, 8 Oil Drums, Metalcraft . . . 1500.00
Truck, Stake, Sunshine Biscuits, Enclosed Cab, Pressed Steel, Metalcraft, 11 ¾ In. . . . 288.00
Truck, Steam Shovel, General, Red, Green, White Rubber Tires, Cast Iron, Hubley, 10 In. . . . 288.00
Truck, Steam Shovel, Painted Red, Nickel Shovel, White Rubber Tires, Cast Iron, 8 In. . . . 288.00
Truck, Steam Wagon, Mamod, Bank Of America, 13 ½ In. . . . 201.00
Truck, Store, Painted, Pressed Steel, Wyandotte, 13 In. . . . 201.00
Truck, Studebaker, Green, Tin, 12 In. . . . 50.00
Truck, Tanker, Black, Green, No Doors, Disc Wheels, Pressed Steel, Buddy L, 24 ½ In. . . . *illus* 1210.00
Truck, Tanker, Black Cab, Green Tank, Aluminum Disc Wheels, Buddy L, 25 In. . . . 863.00
Truck, Tanker, Gas & Oil, Champion Red, 8 In. . . . 650.00
Truck, Tanker, Gas & Oil, Driver, Green, Gold Trim, Silver Wheels, Cast Iron, Kenton, 10 In. . . 1150.00
Truck, Tanker, Gas & Oil, Driver, Red, Kenton, 7 ¼ In. . . . 650.00
Truck, Tanker, Gasoline, Mobil, Trailer, Pegasus Emblem, Tin, Friction, 13 In. . . . 210.00
Truck, Tanker, GM Mobilgas, Red, Hoses, Nozzles, Smith-Miller, 1949, 22 In. . . . 400.00
Truck, Tanker, Hercules Oil Co., Chein, 19 In. . . . 2895.00
Truck, Tanker, International Oil, Tin, Windup, Great Britain, c.1940, 8 ½ In. . . . 175.00
Truck, Tanker, Oil, Non Pareil, Red, Blue, Yellow, Tin Lithograph, 10 In. . . . 345.00
Truck, Tanker, Oil, Pressed Steel, Sturditoy, c.1926, 33 In., 2 Piece. . . . 2300.00
Truck, Tanker, Painted, Tin, West Germany, 13 ½ In. . . . 167.00
Truck, Tanker, Red, Black, Pressed Steel, Steelcraft, c.1927, 26 In. . . . 460.00
Truck, Tanker, Red, Green, Cast Iron, 5 ½ In. . . . 17.00
Truck, Tanker, Richfield Oil, Celluloid Windshield, Decals, Pressed Steel, c.1925 . . . *illus* 1150.00
Truck, Tanker, Shell, Pressed Steel, England, c.1950, 13 In. . . . 375.00
Truck, Tanker, Sinclair, Green, Marx, 1930s, 11 In. . . . 125.00
Truck, Tanker, Standard, Red, Silver, Rubber Tires, Tootsietoy, c.1938, 5 ⅔ In. . . . 95.00

Truck, Tin, Windup, Courtland, USA, 1948, 12 In. 145.00
Truck, Tow, Boom, Nickel Plated Grille, Cast Iron, Hubley, 8 In. 201.00
Truck, Tow, Cities Service, Green, White, Tools, Marx, 1950s, 21 In. 225.00
Truck, Tow, Driver, Metal, Windup, France, 1950s, 11 In. 375.00
Truck, Tow, Ford, Model A, Red, Green, Nickeled Wheels, Arcade, 8 In. 350.00
Truck, Tow, Girard, Pull, Bell Clapper, Pressed Steel, 10 In. 633.00
Truck, Tow, Graham, Die Cast, Cream, Black, Tootsietoy, 4 In. 160.00
Truck, Tow, Green, Nickel Plated Hook, Arm, Rubber Tires, Cast Iron, Hubley, 5 ½ x 1 ¾ In. 44.00
Truck, Tow, Hercules, Open Cab, Black, Open Body, Chein, c.1925, 17 ½ In. 403.00
Truck, Tow, Mack, Painted Red, Green, Weaver Crane, Railed Open Body, Cast Iron, Arcade, 12 In. 978.00
Truck, Tow, Model A, Red, Green Weaver Boom, Nickel Plate, Cast Iron, Arcade, 11 In. 288.00
Truck, Tow, Open Cab, Pressed Steel, Keystone, c.1920, 26 In. 770.00
Truck, Tow, Pressed Steel, Triang, England, 1940's, 18 In. 395.00 to 475.00
Truck, Tow, Red, Black, France, Dinky Toys, Box 330.00
Truck, Tow, Red, Green Paint, Cast Iron, Arcade, 11 ½ In. 688.00
Truck, Tow, Sit-N-Ride, Electric Lights, Pressed Steel, Buddy L, c.1934, 27 In. *illus* 1100.00
Truck, U.S. Army, Green, Metal, Cloth, Keystone, 26 In. 395.00
Truck, U.S. Army, Open Cab, Decals, Canvas Top, Balloon Tires, 1920s, 26 In. 533.00
Truck, U.S. Mail, Black, Red, Green, Keystone, 1926, 27 In. 1450.00
Truck, U.S.A. Army, No. D-105, Canvas Top, Tin, Windup, Marx, c.1930, 10 ½ In. 282.00
Truck, Walter's Toffee, Plastic, Tin Lithograph, Friction, Great Britain, 1950s, 9 In. 104.00
Truck, Waste Mangement, Roll Back, Plastic, Duncan, Box, 17 ½ In. 115.00
Truck, Water Sprinkler, Tin Lithograph, Windup, Strauss *illus* 550.00
Truck, Wonder Bread, White, Black, Black Wall Wheels, Clear Windows, Matchbox, 1980s 6.00
Truck, Wrecker, Goodrich Tire, Red & White, Metalcraft 1250.00
Truck, Yellow, Orange, No. 482, Bedford, Dinky Toys, Box 160.00
Trunk, Doll's, Dome Top, Leatherette Covered, Wood Strips, Metal Straps, 10 x 16 x 10 In. 95.00
Tut-Tut, Man, Driver With Horn, Windup, Lehmann, 1903 650.00
Twirly Whirly Rocket Ride, Tin, Battery Operated, Alps, Box, 12 In. 450.00
Typewriter, Tom Thumb, President, Western Stamping 25th Anniversary, Case, 5 x 11 ½ In. 10.00
Typist, Head, Arms Moves, Tin, Windup, Japan, 1950s 145.00
Van, Delivery, Driver, International, Blue, Yellow Stripe, Decal, Cast Iron, Arcade, 1932, 9 ½ In. 345.00
Van Brunt Seed Drill, John Deere, Gold Trim, Spoke Wheels, Cast Iron, Vindex, 9 ¾ In. 3450.00
Velocipede, Boy Driver, Painted, Tin, Windup, Germany, 5 In. 880.00
View-Master, Black, Sawyers, Bakelite, c.1945 75.00
Village, Row Houses, Building, Painted, Multicolored, Wood, 1 ⅝-In. Each 345.00
Violinist, Blond, Vibrates, Head & Arms Move, Tin, Windup, Linemar, Box, 5 ¼ In. 384.00
Violinist, Hands, Flannel Coat, Black, White Trousers, Tin, Windup, Martin, 7 ⅝ In. 2015.00
Volkswagen, Van, Television Broadcasting, Tin, Battery Operated, Box, Japan, 7 ½ In. 375.00
Wagon, 2 Horses, Black Driver, Cast Iron, Hubley, 15 In. 295.00
Wagon, Art Deco, Blue, Wood Wheels, Pressed Steel, Wyandotte, c.1938, 4 In. 85.00
Wagon, Auto Wagon, Painted, Wood, Wicker Basket, Gears, Pat. 1917, 45 In. *illus* 6600.00
Wagon, Bakery, Wheeled Horse, Wood, Wool, Schoenhut, Germany, 27 In. 1840.00
Wagon, Bentwood Back, Spoked Iron Wheels, Oak, Huntley Hill Stockton, 15 x 30 In. 288.00
Wagon, Bentwood Wheels, Tin Hubcaps, Wood, S. Paris, Maine, 1890s 45.00
Wagon, Circus, Bell, Piano Plays, No. 156, Pull Toy, Fisher-Price, c.1942, 12 In. 345.00
Wagon, Circus, Cage, White Horses, Red, Stenciled Marquee, Schoenhut, 10 In. 1955.00
Wagon, Circus, Overland, Cage, Lion, Horses, Yellow Chassis, Cast Iron, Kenton, 14 ¼ In. 296.00
Wagon, Circus, Overland, Cage, Polar Bear, White Horses, Red, Cast Iron, Kenton, 14 In. 345.00
Wagon, Circus, Overland, Driver, 6 Bandsmen, White Horses, Cast Iron, Kenton, 15 ½ In. 518.00
Wagon, Circus, Royal Circus, 2 Horses, Cage, Bear, Yellow Spoke Wheels, Hubley, 12 In. 144.00
Wagon, Circus, Royal Circus, 2 Horses, Driver, Cage, Lions, Red Wheels, Cast Iron, Hubley, 12 ½ In. 288.00
Wagon, Circus, Royal Circus, 2 Horses, Driver, Calliope, Blue, Cast Iron, Hubley, 12 ½ In. 805.00
Wagon, Coal & Wood, Black Horse, Driver, Green, Stenciled, Spoke Wheels, Cast Iron, Harris, 12 In. 460.00
Wagon, Conestoga, 2 Horses, Driver, Red, Yellow Wheels, Cast Iron, Kenton, 13 ½ In. 144.00
Wagon, Delivery, Borden's Farm Products, Black & White Horse, 1930s, 20 x 9 x 5 In. 135.00
Wagon, Dray, 2 Horses, Open Stake Body, Red, Yellow Wheels, Cast Iron, Wilkins, 21 In. 403.00
Wagon, Dray, 2 Wheel, Wood Bed Flooring, Painted Black, Green, Pratt & Letchworth, 10 ½ In. 316.00
Wagon, Dray, Horse Drawn, Wood Floor, Pratt & Letchworth, 10 In. 595.00
Wagon, Dump, Contractors, Arcade, 1908, 14 In. 550.00
Wagon, Fantasy Land, Beetle Pulls Leaf Cart, Squirrels, Monkey, Tin, Windup, T.P.S., Box, 12 In. 163.00
Wagon, Green, Spoke Wheels, Wood, Sheet Metal, Iron, c.1880, 14 ½ x 32 x 14 ½ In. 70.00
Wagon, Greyhound De Luxe, Blue, Yellow, Pressed Steel, 40 In. *illus* 300.00
Wagon, Hay, Oxen, Slanted Stake Side, Standing Figure, Spoke Wheels, Cast Iron, Hubley, 14 In. 748.00
Wagon, Horse Drawn, Driver, Milk, Borden's, Metal, Wood, Milk Carrier, Bottle, 20 In. 345.00
Wagon, Huckster, Driver, Rubber Tires, Spoke Wheels, Cast Iron, Motorcade Toys, 8 ¼ In. 288.00
Wagon, Ice, 2 Horses, Red Paint, Yellow Roof, Embossed, Cast Iron, Hubley, 15 In. 690.00

Toy, Truck, Tow, Sit-N-Ride, Electric Lights, Pressed Steel, Buddy L, c.1934, 27 In.
$1100.00

Toy, Truck, Water Sprinkler, Tin Lithograph, Windup, Strauss
$550.00

Toy, Wagon, Auto Wagon, Painted, Wood, Wicker Basket, Gears, Pat. 1917, 45 In.
$6600.00

Toy, Wagon, Greyhound De Luxe, Blue, Yellow, Pressed Steel, 40 In.
$300.00

T

Lincoln Logs

Lincoln Logs were invented by John Lloyd Wright, son of the famous architect Frank Lloyd Wright.

Toy, Wagon, National Uneeda Biscuit, Green Wood Roof, Tin Lithograph, 9 ½ In.
$266.00

Toy, Zeppelin, Silver, Tri-Motor, Decals, Pressed Steel, Steelcraft, 30 In.
$518.00

Toy, Zilotone, Clown Plays Xylophone, Tin, Windup, Wolverine, 1920s
$425.00

Tupperware
Tupperware, the plastic bowls with the "burping lids," was first sold in stores in 1946. In 1951 the famous Tupperware parties started. Housewives sold the plastic items from home. Sales went up and women were able to earn a living selling a product from home. The company was sold in 1958. Other companies made similar items after 1984, when the patent expired. Some of the early patented pieces are so well designed they are in museum collections.

Wagon, Kansas City Journal Post, Wood, c.1900, 14 ½ x 36 x 15 ½ In. 220.00
Wagon, Little Teddy, Wood, Bartholomew Products, 11 x 44 x 9 ⅓ In. 176.00
Wagon, Mail, 2 Horses, Lithograph, Spoke Wheels, Blue Bench, Converse, 17 In. 863.00
Wagon, Man Leading Horse, 4 Wheels, Britains, Prewar, Box 201.00
Wagon, Milk, Black Horse, Embossed, White, Red, Cast Iron, Kenton, 13 In. 115.00
Wagon, Milk, Borden's Rich Toys, Wood Roof, Wheels, Glass Bottles, Tin Lithograph, 18 ½ In. 288.00
Wagon, Milk, Horse Drawn, Borden's, Driver, Bottle Rack, Stenciled Wood, Tin Lithograph, 18 ½ In. 187.00
Wagon, Milk, Horse Drawn, Borden's Farm Products, Bottles, 1920s, 20 In. 303.00
Wagon, Milk, Horse Drawn, Borden's Milk & Cream, Wood, Metal, Pull Toy, c.1930, 20 In. 523.00
Wagon, Milk, Horse Drawn, Gallop Motion, Painted, Wood, Sheffield, 22 In. 403.00
Wagon, Milk, Horse Drawn, Sheffield Farms, 6 Glass Bottles, Carrier, 21 In. 1750.00
Wagon, Milk, Horse Drawn, Tin, Windup, Marx, 1930s, 10 In. 275.00
Wagon, National Uneeda Biscuit, Green Wood Roof, Tin Lithograph, 9 ½ In. .... *illus* 266.00
Wagon, Ranch, Ford, Custom, Tailgate, Rear Window, Tin, Friction, Bandai, Japan, 1956 .... 295.00
Wagon, Red, Green, Yellow, Dreadnought Farm Wagon, Plexiglas Cover, c.1895, 30 x 75 In. .. 1495.00
Wagon, Red, White Tires, Black Fender Skirts, Steel, Wyandotte Toy Co., 2 ½ x 8 ½ x 2 In. 40.00
Wallet, Green Hornet, Vinyl, Standard Plastic Products, Inc., 1966, 4 x 3 In. 139.00
Washer, Doll Clothes, Wood, Metal, Salesman's Sample, 6 x 8 In. 300.00
Washing Machine, Wood, Cast Iron, 18 In. 150.00
Washing Machine, Wood, Iron, Columbia, c.1895, 20 In. 161.00
Washing Machine, Wringer, Folding, Stenciled, Painted, 17 In. 138.00
Washing Machine, Wringer, Wood, Stenciled, Painted, 14 In. 161.00
Washtub, Wringer, Tin Lithograph, 6 In. 16.00
Watermelon Boy Chased By Dog, Cloth, Celluloid, Windup, 5 ½ In. 495.00
Wee Little Baby Bear, Eyes Light, Head Moves, Battery Operated, Alps, Box, 10 In. 350.00
Western Set, Ride-Em Cowboy Boots, Maverick Gun, Spurs, Belt, Handcuffs, Holster, 1920s .. 200.00
Wheelbarrow, Original Paint, Stenciling, Wood, 18 x 26 x 48 In. 440.00
Wheelbarrow, Red Paint, Wood, c.1900, 28 In. 183.00
Whirly Tinker, Pull Toy, Tinkertoys, 7 x 2 In. 33.00
Whistle, Dancing Poodle, Embossed, Tin Lithograph, Penny Toy, France, 4 ¼ In. 99.00
Whistle, Monkey, At Grinding Wheel, Spins, Embossed, Tin Lithograph, Penny Toy, 4 ½ In. .. 99.00
Whistle, Xylophone, Animals, Flowers, Baseball Players, Tin Lithograph, Japan, 3 ¼ In. 108.00
Wild Mule Jack, Indian, On Mule, Tail Moves, Early 1900s, 9 In. 470.00
Wild West Bucking Bronco, Brown Horse, Painted, Tin Lithograph, Windup, Lehmann, 6 ¼ In. 489.00
Willy The Walking Car, Head Light-Up, Japan, 1950s, 9 In. 120.00
Windmill, Iron, Painted, Wood, Tin, No. 2., Arcade, Box, 26 In. 110.00
Windmill, Man, Donkey, Painted, Tin Lithograph, Steam Driven, 10 In. 425.00
Windmill, Sand Driven, Tin Lithograph, 9 In. 18.00
Woman & Cat, Painted, Tin, Windup, Germany, 9 ½ In. 250.00
Woodchopper, Moving Picture, Sand Activated, Germany, 6 ½ x 5 In. 82.00
Word Speller, Tin, Wood, Foxy Toys, 9 ¾ In. Diam. 55.00
Xylophone Player, Celluloid, Hard Plastic, Tin, Windup, 6 In. 55.00
Xylophone Player, Celluloid, Tin, Occupied Japan, 5 ¾ In. 50.00
Yo-Yo, Amazing Spiderman Magic Motion, Duncan, Package, Flicker Ring, 1978 .... 20.00
Yo-Yo, Blue, Gold, Plastic, Display, Duncan Professional, Box, 1970s 50.00
Yo-Yo, Spiderman, Magic Motion, Vari-Vue Images, Clear, Plastic Package 20.00
Zeppelin, Graf, Wheels, Painted, Decals, Pressed Steel, Steelcraft, 25 ½ In. 440.00
Zeppelin, Graf Jr., Windup, Strauss Co., 1930s, 10 In. 275.00
Zeppelin, Painted, Cast Iron, 4 ¾ In. 33.00
Zeppelin, Silver, Tri-Motor, Decals, Pressed Steel, Steelcraft, 30 In. .... *illus* 518.00
Zeppelin, Tin, Windup, Strauss, 10 In. 165.00
Zeppelin, Zep, Silver, Dent, 5 In. 125.00
Zeppelin Ride, 3 Zeppelins, Tin, Windup, Prewar, Germany, 11 In. 800.00
Zig Zag, Black Man, White Man, Driving Big Wheel, Windup, Lehmann, 1910, 5 ½ In. 1275.00
Zilotone, Clown Plays Xylophone, Tin, Windup, Wolverine, 1920s .... *illus* 425.00
Zoo Set, Paper Lithograph, Tiny Town, J.W. Spear & Son, Box, 16 x 25 In. 316.00

TRAMP ART is a form of folk art made since the Civil War. It is usually made from chip-carved cigar boxes. Examples range from small boxes and picture frames to full-sized pieces of furniture.

Basket, Chip Carved, Open Slats, Purple Silk Lining, Rich. Bohleber, 1910, 9 ½ x 11 In. 441.00
Bird Tree, Chip Carved, 4 Birds, Pine, Mirror, Painted, 23 ½ x 15 x 9 ½ In. .... *illus* 275.00
Birdcage, Carved Wood, Crown-Of-Thorns Pattern, Hinged Door, 1885, 13 In. 200.00
Box, 2 Drawers, Footed, Handle, c.1925, 10 x 10 x 7 In. 135.00
Box, Hinged Lid, Church Form, B, J, Heart, Brown Paint, Blue, Green, 15 x 13 x 8 In. 810.00
Box, Hinged Lid, Geometrics, Hearts, Footed, Mirror, 7 ¾ x 13 ½ x 8 ¾ In. .... *illus* 132.00

Box, Hinged Lid, Metal Handle, Carved Wood, Red Inlay, 1901, 11 x 15 In. 117.00
Box, Lid, Rhomboid Shape, Applied Decorations, Brown Over Gray Paint, 7 ½ x 11 In. 58.00
Box, Sewing, Lid, Exterior Photos Of Women, Sewing Tools, Interior Tray, 8 x 7 In. 330.00
Box, Shaking Hands, Stylized Tulips, Applied Design, 5 ½ x 8 In. 100.00
Box, Velvet Liner, Mirror, Footed, 7 x 11 x 6 In. 110.00
Church, White, 33 In. 150.00
Desk, Crate Wood, 2 Parts, Glass Doors, Drawers, Side Doors, Child's, 62 x 38 x 25 ½ In. 605.00
Dresser Box, 9 Layers, Hinged Lid, Pedestal Base, Early 20th Century, 8 x 10 x 8 In. 275.00
Frame, Chip Carved, Multitier, Blocks, Arches, Corner Blocks, 1914, 38 ½ x 43 ½ In. 248.00
Frame, Chip Carved, Multitier, Diamond, 19 ¼ x 14 ¾ In. 33.00
Frame, Hearts Rosettes, Stars, Alligatored Varnish, c.1900, 20 ¾ x 25 ¼ In. 352.00
Frame, Pediment, Carving, c.1890, 27 x 29 In. 180.00
Frame, Rosette Pattern, 4 Divided Interior Openings, 13 ½ x 11 In. . . . . *illus* 66.00
Frame, Tic-Tac-Toe Board Form, 6 Layers, Patina, 16 x 14 ½ In. 45.00
Jewelry Box, Lift Lid, Pedestal Base, 5 x 7 ½ In. 115.00
Mirror, Carved Wood, c.1900, 22 ¼ x 16 ¾ In. 1250.00
Mirror, Chip Carved, 5-Point Star Frame, c.1920, 14 x 15 In. 1422.00
Mirror, Chip Carved, Geometric, Mirror Segments, c.1900, 22 x 18 In. 652.00
Mirror, Flowers, 5 Layers, Early 20th Century, 21 x 16 In. 170.00
Mirror, Red, White, Blue, c.1900, 22 x 14 In. 889.00
Pincushion, Thread Dispenser, 3-Footed, c.1900, 12 x 6 x 6 In. 165.00
Table, Center, Oak, Half Diamond Carved Border, 26 ¼ x 33 In. 2750.00
Wall Pocket, Comb Box, Applied Comb, Vines, Hearts, c.1900, 16 ¾ x 11 In. 489.00
Wall Pocket, Wood, Carved, Painted, Shaped Backboard, Kissing Birds, 18 x 13 In. 880.00
Watch Safe, Town Hall Form, Bell, Stars, Yellow Paint, 23 x 15 ½ In. 176.00

TRAPS for animals may be handmade. One of the most unusual is the mousetrap made so that when the mouse entered the trap, it was hit on the head with a mallet. Other traps were commercially manufactured and often are marked with the name of the manufacturer. Many traps were designed to be as humane as possible, and they would trap the live animal so it could be released in the woods.

Animal, Newhouse, Oneida Community, Double Spring, 27 In. 115.00
Animal, Triumph High Grip 415-X, Double Springs, 24 In. 173.00
Bear, No. 5, Double Springs, Newhouse, Kenwood, N.Y., 34 In. 582.00
Bear, Oneida Newhouse, No. 5, 34 In. 11.00
Frog, Metal, Signed, S.W. Evans & Son, Frankfurt, Pa., 1877, 4 ½ In. 300.00
Minnow, Tarred Wire, Hinged Lid, Ring, c.1900, 15 x 9 In. 75.00
Mouse, Glass, Wiggington Mouse Exterminator, Wood Base, Winchester, Va., 6 ½ x 7 In. 30.00
Queen Bee, Wood Frame, Rectangular, Tin Strip, 12 x 5 In. 50.00

TREEN, *see Wooden category.*

TRENCH ART is a form of folk art made by soldiers. Metal casings from bullets and mortar shells were cut and decorated to form useful objects, such as vases.

Humidor, Artillery Shell, Brass, Marked, Eagle, Spread Wings, Swastika, 6 ½ x 4 In. 55.00
Shell, Miss Liberty, 14 x 3 In., Pair 55.00
Vase, American Flag, Anchor, Stars, 18 ¾ x 4 In. 44.00
Vase, Statue Of Liberty, 12 ⅛ x 3 In. 22.00
Vase, Statue Of Liberty, 14 x 3 ½ In. 27.00

TRIVETS are now used to hold hot dishes. Most trivets of the late nineteenth and early twentieth centuries were made to hold hot irons. Iron or brass reproductions are being made of many of the old styles.

Brass, Colonial Revival, George Washington, Bust, 2 x 9 ½ In. 48.00
Brass, Double Heart, Punched, Marked, A & E, 8 x 3 ⅝ In. 45.00
Brass, George Washington, Virginia Metalcrafters 12.00
Brass, Heart Cutout, 3 Mortised Legs, Bun Feet, 9 ⅛ x 4 ¼ In. 65.00
Brass, Iron, Turned Wood Handle, 19th Century, 12 In. 23.00
Brass, Lion, Crown, Coat Of Arms, Temple Quam Ecta, 4-Footed, England 1200.00
Brass, Open Heart Shape, Heart Shape Cutout Center, 3-Footed, 9 ¼ x 5 ¼ In. 75.00
Brass, Scroll Design, Claw Foot, 3 x 9 ⅛ x 7 ½ In. 33.00
Brass, Stylized Cotton Blossom, Turned Feet, White Brass, Newcomb College, c.1925, 5 ¼ In. . 734.00
Brass, Stylized Leaves, F Center, Turned Feet, White Brass, Newcomb College, c.1925, 12 In. . . 1293.00
Bronze, Jenny Lind, 8 ⅞ x 4 ½ In. 44.00
Bronze, Jenny Lind, Figure, Scrolls 40.00

Tramp Art, Bird Tree, Chip Carved, 4 Birds, Pine, Mirror, Painted, 23 ½ x 15 x 9 ½ In.
$275.00

Tramp Art, Box, Hinged Lid, Geometrics, Hearts, Footed, Mirror, 7 ¾ x 13 ½ x 8 ¾ In.
$132.00

Tramp Art, Frame, Rosette Pattern, 4 Divided Interior Openings, 13 ½ x 11 In.
$66.00

T

TIP

Never store tortoiseshell combs or pins in plastic bags. The lack of air will cause the shell to crack or fade.

Trivet, Sandstone, Heart, Tree, Duck, 19th Century, 9 x 7 ¼ In.
$1287.00

Trivet, Wrought Iron, 3-Footed, Stamped, T, 7 ¼ x 14 x 6 ½ In.
$66.00

Trivet, Wrought Iron, Adjustable Pan Handle, Twisted, Black Paint, 14 ½ x 22 x 9 In.
$132.00

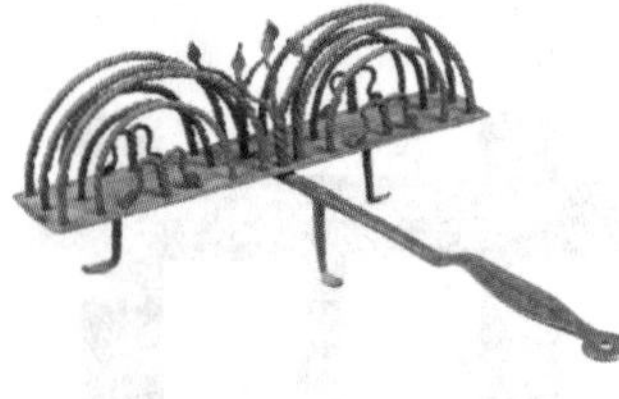

Trunk, Louis Vuitton, Damier Canvas, Strap, Squat Wheels, c.1900, 20 x 23 x 16 In.
$17150.00

Bronze, Jenny Lind, Loop Handle 44.00
Cast Iron, 5-Footed, Round, 5 In. 88.00
Cast Iron, Cinderella Stoves 22.00
Cast Iron, Heart, Long Handle, 10 ½ In. 22.00
Cast Iron, Heart Center, Heart Handle, 1800s, 11 In.. . . . . 61.00
Cast Iron, Heart Cutouts, Tripod Base, 10 In.. . . . . 176.00
Cast Iron, Hearts, Flower, Good Luck For Us All. 138.00
Cast Iron, Jenny Lind, Portrait, Square, 4 ¾ In. 77.00
Cast Iron, Nickel Finish, Cinderella Stoves Never Fail, 4-Leaf Clover, c.1890, 5 ⅜ x 4 ¾ In.. . . . 22.00
Cast Iron, OM Co., Grid, Monogram Center, Square, 3 ⅛ In. 33.00
Cast Iron, Open Flower Design, Child's, 3 ⅛ In.. . . . . 209.00
Cast Iron, Running Wheel, Hex Designs, Crosshatched Handle, Pa., 1800s, 10 ¼ In.. . . . . 27.00
Cast Iron, U.S., Nickel Finish, 5 5/16 x 4 11/16 In.. . . . . 22.00
Cast Iron, Wolf, Girl, c.1914, 11 ⅜ x 6 ⅜ In. 72.00
Griswold, No. 7, Cast Iron, Round 25.00
Griswold, No. 8, Cast Iron, Round 7.00
Iron, 4-Footed, Handle, 4 x 12 x 17 ½ In. 50.00
Iron, Double Point, I Want U, Comfort Iron, Strause Gas Iron Co., Phila., Pa. 11.00
Iron, Handle, 3-Footed, Wrought Iron, 7 ¼ x 14 x 6 ½ In. 66.00
Iron, M In Center, Handle, LM Co., 4 ¼ In. 165.00
Iron, Sunshine's Home, Iron Stand, New York 17.00
Iron, Tulip Form, Brass Inlay, 3-Footed, SM 1824 J6, Pa., 9 In. 11000.00
Pottery, 6 Points, Stylized Grape, Purple, Tan, Yellow Ground, 1916, ⅝ x 6 In.. . . . . 46.00
Sandstone, Heart, Tree, Duck, 19th Century, 9 x 7 ¼ In. . . . . *illus* 1287.00
Silver Plate Over Copper, Cloverleaf, Late 1800s, 4 ¼ x 7 ½ In.. . . . . 40.00
Wrought Iron, 3-Footed, Stamped, T, 7 ¼ x 14 x 6 ½ In. . . . . *illus* 66.00
Wrought Iron, Adjustable Pan Handle, Twisted, Black Paint, 14 ½ x 22 x 9 In. . . . . *illus* 132.00

TRUNKS of many types were made. The nineteenth-century sea chest was often handmade of unpainted wood. Brass-fitted camphorwood chests were brought back from the Orient. Leather-covered trunks were popular from the late eighteenth to mid-nineteenth centuries. By 1895, trunks were covered with canvas or decorated sheet metal. Embossed metal coverings were used from 1870 to 1910. By 1925, trunks were covered with vulcanized fiber or undecorated metal. Suitcases are listed here.

Blue Green Paint, Nailed Construction, Mary Sweeney, Boston, Mid 1800s, 14 ½ x 25 In.. . . . 940.00
Brass Tack, Geometric Designs, Hinged Top, 19th Century, 16 x 40 x 19 In. 118.00
Campaign Chest, Brass Bound, Yorkshire House, 21 x 42 In. 518.00
Dome Top, Pine, Blue Black Paint, 10 x 17 x 11 In. 50.00
Dome Top, Pine, Dovetailed, Iron Fittings, Cedar Lined, 20 x 37 ½ x 19 In. 153.00
Dome Top, Pine, Iron Strapping, Handles, Multicolored Fisheye, 15 x 25 x 18 In. 3163.00
Dome Top, Poplar, Painted, Red, Yellow Pinstriping, Flowers, Pa., Mid 1800s, 14 x 24 In.. . . . . 878.00
Dome Top, Soft Wood, Painted Urn & Flower Designs, 1800s, 27 x 14 ½ x 13 In. 352.00
E.P. Brainard & Co., Leather, Brass Tacks & Handles, c.1875, 10 x 20 x 11 In.. . . . . 441.00
Humpback, Wood, Victorian, 24 x 32 x 19 In. 110.00
Iberian Hardwood, Brass Bound, Tooled Leather, Domed, Hinged, Nailhead, c.1800, 19 x 31 In. 235.00
Immigrant's, Sponge Painted, Dovetailed, 20 ½ x 35 x 20 ½ In. 225.00
Leather, Brass Tacks, Iron Lock, Tremont Row, Boston, Salesman's Sample, 3 ¾ x 8 ¼ In.. . . . 316.00
Leather, Red, Gilt Designs, 2 Brass Plates, 4 Bronze Handles, Stand, Chinese, c.1890, 32 x 59 In. 690.00
Louis Vuitton, Damier Canvas, Strap, Squat Wheels, c.1900, 20 x 23 x 16 In. . . . . *illus* 17150.00
Louis Vuitton, Steamer, Monogram, 20th Century, 21 ½ x 29 ½ x 19 In. 8260.00
Louis Vuitton, Steamer, No. 81839, Canvas, Leather, Wood, 21 ½ x 24 x 15 In. 8250.00
Louis Vuitton, Suitcase, 16 ½ x 24 x 6 ⅞ In. 700.00
Louis Vuitton, Suitcase, 18 ½ x 27 ¾ x 8 ¾ In.. . . . . 550.00
Louis Vuitton, Suitcase, 19 ½ x 29 ¾ x 8 ½ In.. . . . . 600.00
Louis Vuitton, Suitcase, Chocolate Leather, LV Logo, Original Tag, 7 x 28 x 18 ½ In.. . . . . 850.00
Louis Vuitton, Suitcase, Hard Sides, 31 ½ x 20 ¾ x 7 In. 1200.00
Louis Vuitton, Suitcase, Hard Sides, 32 x 20 x 9 In. 1045.00
Louis Vuitton, Suitcase, Leather, Signature Logo, Soft Case, Zip Top, 13 ¼ x 18 ¾ In.. . . . . 717.00
Louis Vuitton, Tray, 22 ½ x 35 ½ x 21 In. 7930.00
Papier-Mache, Trees, Birds, Red Ground, Asian, 20th Century, 13 ½ x 22 x 13 ½ In.. . . . . 88.00
Pine, Dovetailed, Iron Straps, Lift Handles, Flowers, c.1800, 23 ½ x 15 ¼ x 11 ¾ In. 705.00
Pine, Hinged Top, Bracket Feet, Grain Painting, 19th Century, 14 x 25 x 14 In. 531.00
Red Leather, Gilt, 100 Boys, Brass Lock Plate, Handle, Chinese, 12 x 30 In. 201.00
Samsonite Streamline, Suitcase, Hanger Inside, Saddle Tan, Brass, 1950s, 24 x 19 x 7 In.. . . 95.00
Steamer, Buffalo Hide, Painted, Buckle Straps, Metal Corners, Nail Trim, 27 x 10 x 24 In.. . . . 118.00
Steamer, Goyard, Early 20th Century, France, 22 ½ x 31 ½ In. 1912.00

Steamer, Humpback, Wood Straps, 26 x 34 x 23 In. 40.00
Tack, Army, Fitted Interior, Stenciled Name, Brass Mounted, France, Early 1900s, 25 x 33 In. . 230.00
Yew, Bracket Feet, Hinged, c.1800, 12 x 29 x 17 In. 206.00

TUTHILL Cut Glass Company of Middletown, New York, worked from 1902 to 1923. Of special interest are the finely cut pieces of stemware and tableware.

Basket, Handle, 9 x 7 x 6 ½ In. 975.00
Celery Dish, Vintage Pattern, Marked, 10 ¾ In.. .... 400.00
Plate, Intaglio, Geometric, 8 In. 325.00
Vase, Flower Shape, Engraved Daisies, Serpentine Stem, Flower Wreath, 12 ¼ In. 104.00

TYPEWRITER collectors divide typewriters into two main classifications: the index machine, which has a pointer and a dial for letter selection, and the keyboard machine, most commonly seen today. The first successful typewriter was made by Sholes & Glidden in 1874.

Barlock, No. 6, Serial No. 35482, Desk Model. 1064.00
Blickensderfer, No. 5, Keyboard & Letter Wheel, Dovetailed Wooden Case, 12 x 9 In. 345.00
Blickensderfer, No. 5, Serial No. 14985, Wood Case, Carrying Case, Portable. 168.00
Blickensderfer, No. 9, No. 187344, Wood Case, c.1908, Portable 168.00
Columbia, Shift, 4 Row Full Keyboard, Tin Cover, 1904 .... 1394.00
Corona, No. 3, Serial No. 321246, Folding, Case Finger Rest, Tools, Portable 28.00
Crandall, Serial No. 6083, Desk Model, Mother-Of-Pearl Flower Inlay. 6160.00
Fisher Book Typewriting Co., Bookkeepers Rail, 1896 .... 349.00
Granville Automatic, 2 Carriage Release Levers, No. 5937, 1896 .... *illus* 3689.00
Hammond, Multiplex, Serial No. 186039, Case Base Only 135.00
Hammond, Multiplex, Type Sleeve, Foreign Language Machine, 4-Shift, 1913. .... 465.00
Hammond, Serial No. 111109, Round, Ideal Key Layout, Greek, Wooden Base, Portable. 224.00
International, Double Keyboard, L. Crandall, Full Keyboard, No. 3738, 1889 .... 10071.00
Lambert, No. 3541, Wood Case, 1886 .... 1704.00
Maskelyne No. 3, Grasshopper Mechanism, London, 1893 .... 2790.00
Mignon AEG Stylus Indicator, Serial No. 199936, Case, Germany, c.1915, Portable 123.00
Odell, No. 2, Linier Index, Capitals, Lower Case, Numbers, c.1889 .... 308.00
Odell, No. 4, Nickel Plated 1007.00
Oliver, No. 1, 1st Model, Nickel Plate, No. 288, 1896 .... 7437.00
Philadelphia Typewriting Co, No. 69, Typewheel Machine, Travis Patent, 1896. .... 5888.00
Rem-Blick, No. K581448, Case, Remington Typewriter Co., Blickensderfer Style, Portable ... 168.00
Remington, No. 5, U.S. Army, Tape Printer, 1941, Portable .... *illus* 697.00
Remington Rand, Original Prototype, 1970. .... 108.00
Sholes & Glidden, No. 3972, 1873 .... 6817.00
Yost, No. 1, Serial No. 2042, Full Keyboard, Wood Case, Label, c.1887 .... 560.00

UHL pottery was made in Evansville, Indiana, in 1854. The pottery moved to Huntingburg, Indiana, in 1908. Stoneware and glazed pottery were made until the mid-1940s.

Casserole, Cover, Prairie Green Glaze, Handles, 9 In. Diam.. .... 21.00
Jug, Blue, Handle, Cork Stopper, Marked, 3 ½ In.. .... 15.00
Mug, Blue Exterior, White Interior, 1930s, 3 ½ In.. .... 56.00
Pitcher, Band Of Leaves, Grapes & Leaves, Trellis Design Ground, Brown, 7 In. 75.00
Pitcher, Barrel Design, Green & Brown Spatter, 5 ¼ x 5 ¾ In. 46.00
Pitcher, Creme De Coffee, Narrow Neck, Bulbous Body, Raspberry Glaze, Angled Handle, 5 ½ In. 14.00
Vase, Blue, Tapered, White Interior, 1930s, 9 ½ In.. .... 53.00

UMBRELLA collectors like rain or shine. The first known umbrella was owned by King Louis XIII of France in 1637. The earliest umbrellas were sunshades, not designed to be used in the rain. The umbrella was embellished and redesigned many times. In 1852, the fluted steel rib style was developed and it has remained the most useful style.

12K Gold Handle, Ball End, Engraved Name, R.K. & Co. Balto., 12-In. Handle, 1890s 100.00
Bakelite Handle, Molded, Black Nylon, Case, 1940-50s, 32 In. 59.00
Cane Handle, Wire Frame, Sterling Silver Scrolled Fitting, Hallmark, London 1912, 36 ½ In. 86.00
Gold Handle, Netting, Hand Loop, Black Nylon, Case, 1940-50s, 24 ¾ In.. .... 49.00
Gold Handle, Scrolled Leaf & Fringe Design, Mother-Of-Pearl Center, Late 1800s 265.00
Leather Handle, Cherry Smiling Faces, Brass Hardware, Bag, Louis Vuitton 875.00
Parasol, Bamboo Handle, Linen, Eyelet & Embroidered Design, c.1910, 38 ½ In. 85.00
Parasol, Wood & Paper, Pinwheel Design, 2-Tone Blue, Japan, 1940s, 26 In. 50.00
Plastic Knob Handle, Clear Yellow, Black Swirling, Mourning, c.1930, 22 In.. .... 28.00

Typewriter, Granville Automatic, 2 Carriage Release Levers, No. 5937, 1896
$3689.00

Typewriter, Remington, No. 5, U.S. Army, Tape Printer, 1941, Portable
$697.00

TIP

Musty odors in trunks seem to be a constant problem. Try this system. Fill the trunk with wrinkled, crushed newspaper, close the lid for a week, remove and replace the papers. Repeat the process until the musty odor is gone. This system also helps with car interiors for tobacco odors, musty books if kept in a closed paper bag, and suitcases.

Vallerysthal, Dish, Cover, Figural, Alligator, Painted, Early 1900s, 3 ½ x 12 ⅛ In.
$735.00

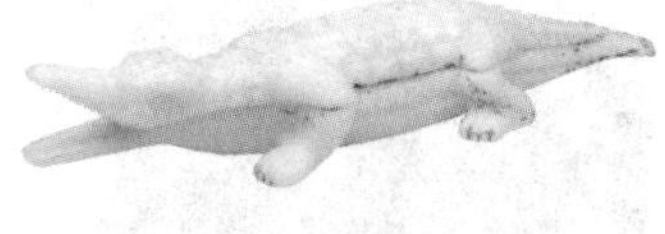

Vallerysthal, Dish, Cover, Figural, Dromedary Camel, Opaque Caramel, 1910, 4 ¼ x 3 x 8 ½ In.
$390.00

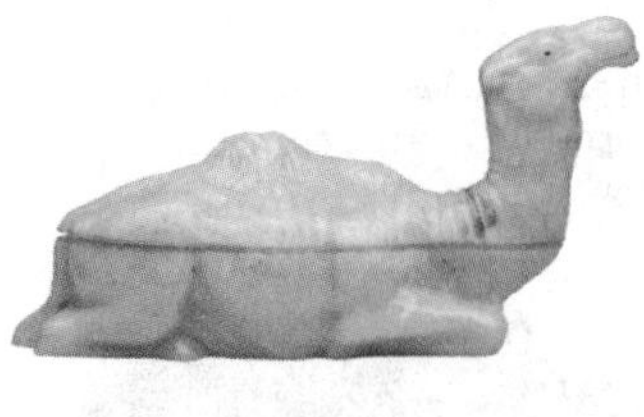

Vallerysthal, Dish, Rabbit Cover, Lop Eared, Green, Vaseline, 1900s, 3 ¼ x 2 ⅜ x 6 In.
$65.00

Vallerysthal, Vase, Leaves & Flowers, Pink, Orange, Gold Enameled, Squat, Cameo, 5 ½ x 4 ¾ In.
$2280.00

U

TIP

Milk glass will yellow with repeated washings in a dishwasher.

Wood & Sterling Handle, Engraved, Button Closure, Marked, 33 ½ In. . . . 85.00
Wood Handle, Nylon, Red, White & Blue American Flag, Made In USA, 46 In. Diam. . . . 27.00

UNION PORCELAIN WORKS was established at Greenpoint, New York, in 1848 by Charles Cartlidge. The company went through a series of ownership changes and finally closed in the early 1900s. The company made a fine quality white porcelain that was often decorated in clear, bright colors.

UNION PORCELAIN WORKS GREENPOINT N.Y.

Creamer, White, Eagles Head Handle, 3 In. . . . 75.00
Match Holder, Plant System Railroad, Striker, 2 ½ In. . . . 335.00
Oyster Plate, 4 Shell Shape Wells, Shells, Seaweed, Lobster Claw, 8 ½ In. . . . 345.00
Oyster Plate, 6 Wells, Raised Crab Between 2 Wells, 1880s, 9 ½ In. . . . 850.00
Oyster Plate, Fruits Of The Sea, White Multicolored, 1880s, 10 x 9 In., Pair . . . 420.00
Pitcher, King Gambrinus, Uncle Sam, Animal Handle, Spout, Blue, White, 1870s, 10 In. . . . 3240.00
Vase, Jack-In-The-Pulpit, Held By Frog, Lobed Base, c.1877, 5 ¾ In. . . . 1840.00

UNIVERSITY CITY POTTERY of University, Missouri, worked from 1909 to 1915. Well-known artists, including Taxile Doat, Adelaide Alsop Robineau, and Frederick Hurten Rhead, worked there.

Bowl, Band Of Green Squirrels, Green Ground, Incised, 2 ¼ x 6 In. . . . 3900.00

UNIVERSITY OF NORTH DAKOTA, *see North Dakota School of Mines category.*

VAL ST. LAMBERT Cristalleries of Belgium was founded by Messieurs Kemlin and Lelievre in 1825. The company is still in operation. All types of table glassware and decorative glassware have been made. Pieces are often decorated with cut designs.

Val St. Lambert

Biscuit Jar, Cranberry, Blossoms, Vines, Brass Lid & Bail, 7 In. . . . 600.00
Bottle, Intaglio Gilt Flowers, Polychrome, Alcohol Medallion, Stopper, 5 In. . . . 98.00
Candleholder, 2-Light, Clear Cut, 8 x 3 ¾ In. . . . 165.00
Compote, Pillar & Star Burst, Pedestal, Signed, 8 x 10 In., Pair . . . 130.00
Decanter, Apricot Cut To Clear, Pedestal, Hob Button, Stopper, 12 ¾ In. . . . 300.00
Paperweight, Dog Bone, Clear, Signed, 7 In. . . . 50.00
Paperweight, Iceberg, Silvery Cubes, 3 x 3 ¾ x 2 ¼ In. . . . 75.00
Perfume Bottle, Vaseline Cut To Clear, Flowers, Leaves, 7 In. . . . 200.00
Tumbler, Dancing Figures, Gilt Intaglio, Cranberry Cut To Clear Border, 6 ¾ In., 5 Piece . . . 805.00
Vase, Clear Cut Panel, 8-Sided, 6 x 3 In. . . . 65.00
Vase, Cranberry Flowers, Leaf Background, Cameo, 5 ½ In. . . . 300.00
Vase, Grapevine, Iridized, Pinched Waist, 11 ½ x 4 ¾ In. . . . 3360.00
Vase, Purple Cut To Clear, Panels, Pointed Bands, Signed, 6 ½ x 8 In. . . . 425.00
Vase, Red Flowers, Frosted Ground, Cameo, 11 In. . . . 600.00
Vase, Ruby To Clear, Honeycomb Wreath Collar, Wide Fans, 6 ¼ In. . . . 127.00

VALLERYSTHAL Glassworks was founded in 1836 in Lorraine, France. In 1854, the firm became Klenglin et Cie. It made table and decorative glass, opaline, cameo, and art glass. A line of covered, pressed glass animal dishes was made in the nineteenth century. The firm is still working.

Vallerysthal

Box, Automobile, Cover, Milk Glass, 4 ⅞ x 3 ¼ x 5 ½ In. . . . 65.00
Dish, Cover, Figural, Alligator, Painted, Early 1900s, 3 ½ x 12 ⅛ In. . . . *illus* 735.00
Dish, Cover, Figural, Dromedary Camel, Opaque Caramel, 1910, 4 ¼ x 3 x 8 ½ In. . . . *illus* 390.00
Dish, Cover, Figural, Dromedary Camel, Opaque Ivory, c.1980, 7 ½ In. . . . 510.00
Dish, Cover, Figural, Swan, 6 x 5 ½ In. . . . 40.00
Dish, Fly On Walnut Cover, Milk Glass, Marked, 4 x 4 In. . . . 218.00
Dish, Frog Cover, Milk Glass, Embossed, 3 ¾ In. . . . 156.00
Dish, Rabbit Cover, Lop Eared, Green, Vaseline, 1900s, 3 ¼ x 2 ⅜ x 6 In. . . . *illus* 65.00
Dish, Squirrel On Acorn Cover, Blue Milk Glass, 5 In. . . . 100.00
Paperweight, Dog, St. Bernard, Milk Glass, Rib Edge, Marked, 3 ⅜ In. . . . 610.00
Salt, Master, Figural, Duck, Milk Glass . . . 29.00
Vase, Deep Red Daffodils, Frosted Pale Green Ground, Cameo, 12 In. . . . 2125.00
Vase, Enameled, Flowers, Green Frosted Ground, 13 In. . . . 2760.00
Vase, Leaves, Cattails, Dragonflies, Gold Enameled, Cameo, 13 ¾ In., Pair . . . 1045.00
Vase, Leaves & Flowers, Pink, Orange, Gold Enameled, Squat, Cameo, 5 ½ x 4 ¾ In. . . . *illus* 2280.00
Vase, Morning Glories, Deep Amethyst, Pale Green Frosted Ground, Cameo, 9 ¾ In. . . . 2040.00
Vase, Pink, Orange, Frosted, Gold Enameled Ground Flowers, Leaves, Cameo, 5 ½ x 4 ¾ In. . . . 2280.00
Vase, Pink Etched Flowers, 6 x 1 ½ In. . . . 150.00

VAN BRIGGLE pottery was started by Artus Van Briggle in Colorado Springs, Colorado, after 1901. Van Briggle had been a decorator at Rookwood Pottery of Cincinnati, Ohio. He died in 1904 and his wife took over managing the pottery. The wares usually had modeled relief decorations and a soft, dull glaze. The pottery is still working and still making some of the original designs.

Bowl, Cast Design, Mulberry Matte Glaze, c.1916, 3 ¼ In. 316.00
Bowl, Centerpiece, Lotus, Raised Leaf Form Rim, Blue, Green Crackle Glaze, 5 x 6 In. 125.00
Bowl, Centerpiece, Tulip, Leaf, Blue, Green Crackle Glaze, Signed, 3 x 8 x 5 In. 125.00
Bowl, Flower Form, Signed, Colorado Springs, 5 In. 100.00
Bowl, Philodendron Leaf, Blue, Green Crackle Glaze, 4 x 4 ½ In. 125.00
Chamberstick, Maroon & Blue Matte Glaze, Marked, 1915-20, 5 x 5 ½ In. . . . . *illus* 240.00
Dish, Hopi Maiden, Dress, Braids, Grinding Corn, Blue, Green Crackle Glaze, 6 x 6 In. 163.00
Dish, Lotus, 5-Leaf Petals On Round Base, Blue, Green Crackle Glaze, Signed, 3 x 5 ½ In. 125.00
Dish, Turtle, Brown & Green Glaze, Cover, Anna Van Briggle, 6 ¾ In. 66.00
Ewer, Stylized, Mauve Glaze, Signed, 12 In. 144.00
Figurine, Lion, Seated, Brown, 10 In. 325.00
Figurine, Rabbit, Turquoise Matte Glaze, Marked, 4 x 3 In. 39.00
Flower Frog, Bowl, Green Matte Glaze, 3 x 6 In. 88.00
Flower Frog, Minidan Maiden Overlooking Pound, Marked, 10 x 15 In. 515.00
Jardiniere, Morning Glories, Red, Yellow Glaze, c.1905, 6 ½ x 8 In. 1200.00
Lamp Base, Persian Rose, Maiden Holding Vase, Marked, 1940s, 10 ¼ In. 110.00
Planter, Shell Shape, 9 x 5 In. 55.00
Plate, Mermaid, Dark Blue, 11 In. 100.00
Tile, Bird, On Branch, Blue, Cuenca, 6 In. Square 3240.00
Tile, Tree, Mountainous Landscape, Cuenca, 12 ¼ In. Square 14400.00
Tray, Mermaid, Pink, Blue, Marked, Colo Spgs, 10 ½ In. 80.00
Vase, 2 Climbing Bears On Rim, Persian Rose Glaze, Bottle Shape, 15 ¾ x 5 ¼ In. 5700.00
Vase, 3-Headed Indian, Mulberry Glaze, c.1925, 10 ½ In. 345.00
Vase, Applied American Indian Heads, Rose, Gray, 5 x 11 In. 295.00
Vase, Blue Matte Glaze, Arrowhead Plant, 5 ¼ x 1 In. 345.00
Vase, Crushed Rim, Maple Leaves, Squat, c.1902, 2 ¾ In. 259.00
Vase, Daffodils, Mountain Craig Brown Glaze, c.1920, 9 ¼ In. 900.00
Vase, Daffodils, Turquoise, 9 ½ In. 82.00
Vase, Daisies, Eggplant & Teal Feathered Glaze, 2 Handles, c.1903, 9 ¾ In. 3360.00
Vase, Despondency, Blue, Green Matte Glaze, Marked, 1940s, 16 ½ x 4 In. . . . . *illus* 1010.00
Vase, Flower, Leaves, Green Matte Glaze, Curdled, c.1906, 9 ½ x 3 ¾ In. 2280.00
Vase, Flower, Maroon Matte Glaze, Double Gourd Shape, Mark, c.1904, 9 ½ x 4 In. 1560.00
Vase, Flowers, Green Matte Glaze, Bulbous, Incised Mark, 1907-12, 5 x 4 In. 240.00
Vase, Flowers, Leaves, Feather Green To Blue Glaze, 1903, 14 x 5 ½ In. 8400.00
Vase, Geese, Green Matte Glaze, c.1902, 6 ¼ In. 8400.00
Vase, Indian Maiden At Edge Of Pond, Flower Frog With Frog On Top, 10 x 15 In. 515.00
Vase, Irises, Mulberry Glaze, 2 Handles, 12 ¼ In. 259.00
Vase, Lady Of The Lily, Persian Rose Glaze, 1920s, 10 ½ x 11 ½ In. . . . . *illus* 2160.00
Vase, Leaves, Blue Over Blue Matte Glaze, 1916, 4 ⅜ In. 288.00
Vase, Leaves, Brown, Blue Matte Glaze, Marked, 9 x 10 In. 600.00
Vase, Leaves, Mulberry Glaze, 2 Handles, Marked, 8 ½ In. 288.00
Vase, Leaves, Purple & Green Glaze, Squat, c.1906, 1 ½ x 5 ¼ In. 1020.00
Vase, Limp Flowers, Mustard Glaze, Tapered, Short Neck, Marked, 1903, 5 In. 2133.00
Vase, Lorelei, Blue & White, 10 ¾ In. 176.00
Vase, Molded Leaves, Maroon & Blue Glaze, 2 Handles, Marked, c.1924, 13 x 6 ½ In. 270.00
Vase, Mulberry Matte Glaze, Squat, 1920s, 4 x 8 In. 230.00
Vase, Poppies & Pods, Blue Matte, Green Highlights, 1902, 8 x 4 In. 16900.00
Vase, Purple Matte Glaze, Squat, Small Neck, Signed, c.1905, 4 x 6 In. 480.00
Vase, Spiderwort, Red Textured Matte Glaze, Bulbous, 1906, 5 x 4 In. 1500.00
Vase, Stylized Flower, Blue, Green Matte Glaze, Tapered Shape, 6 x 12 In. 450.00
Vase, Stylized Flowers, Crystalline Blue Green Matte Glaze, Marked, 9 ⅞ In. 1610.00
Vase, Swirling Leaves, Mulberry, Green Matte Glaze, c.1910, 5 x 4 In. 495.00
Vase, Tulip, Red, Purple, 3 ½ In. 47.00
Vase, Tulips, Red, Brown Glaze, Oval, 14 In. 3360.00
Vase, Turquoise Matte Glaze, 1913, 7 In. 575.00
Vase, Wreath Of Leaves, Violet To Pink Glaze, 4 x 7 ½ In. 50.00

VASA MURRHINA is the name of a glassware made by the Vasa Murrhina Art Glass Company of Sandwich, Massachusetts, about 1884. The glassware was transparent and was embedded with small pieces of colored glass and metallic flakes. The mica flakes were coated with silver, gold, copper, or nickel. Some of the pieces were cased. The same type of glass was made in England. Collectors often confuse Vasa Murrhina glass with aventurine, spatter, or spangle glass. There is uncertainty about what actually was made by the Vasa Murrhina factory. Related pieces may be listed under Spangle Glass.

Van Briggle, Chamberstick, Maroon & Blue Matte Glaze, Marked, 1915-20, 5 x 5 ½ In.
$240.00

Van Briggle, Vase, Despondency, Blue, Green Matte Glaze, Marked, 1940s, 16 ½ x 4 In.
$1010.00

Van Briggle, Vase, Lady Of The Lily, Persian Rose Glaze, 1920s, 10 ½ x 11 ½ In.
$2160.00

Verlys, Bowl, Birds & Bees, 12 In.
$160.00

Verlys, Bowl, Rose, Frosted, 5 ¼ In.
$175.00

Verlys, Vase, Gems, Opalescent, 1930, 6 x 7 In.
$263.00

TIP
If you find a clock with a complete, original paper label, add 35 percent to the value.

Creamer, Yellow, Clear Handle, 3 ¼ x 2 ¼ In. 75.00
Tumbler, Baby Thumbprint, 2 ¾ x 3 ½ In. 125.00
Vase, Autumn Orange, Ribbed, Fluted, 14 In. 325.00
Vase, Autumn Orange, Silver Fleck, 8 x 4 ½ In. 75.00
Vase, Gold On White, Blue, Green, 8 ½ x 6 In. 65.00
Vase, Metallic Flakes, Cased, 9 ¼ x 3 ⅛ In. 325.00
Vase, Multicolored, Satin, Footed, 7 ⅝ x 3 ⅞ In. 245.00

VASELINE GLASS is a greenish-yellow glassware resembling petroleum jelly. Pressed glass of the 1870s was often made of vaseline-colored glass. Some vaseline glass is still being made in old and new styles. Additional pieces of vaseline glass may also be listed under Pressed Glass in this book.

Ashtray, Daisy, 1920s, 5 ¼ In. 35.00
Basket, Frosted, Beaded Edge, Applied Handle, 6 x 4 ¾ In. 95.00
Bowl, Basket Weave, 5 ½ x 2 ½ In. 21.00
Bowl, Opalescent, Star & Arch, 3 x 6 ½ In. 60.00
Box, Cover, Heart Shape, Arrow Finial, 6 x 2 ¼ In. 65.00
Butter, Cover, Croesus, Knob Finial, 3-Footed, 7 ½ x 5 ½ In. 68.00
Cake Stand, 12 In. 75.00
Champagne, 5 ½ In. 60.00
Dish, Hands, Flower On Wrist, 5 In. 12.00
Figurine, Slipper, Pointed Toe 45.00
Goblet, c.1920, 6 ½ x 3 ½ In. 95.00
Match Holder, Daisy & Button, c.1875, 2 ¼ In. 59.00
Platter, Scalloped Edge, c.1920, 20 x 14 ½ In. 795.00
Relish, 5 x 7 x 2 In. 38.00
Salt, Hobnail, Opalescent, 1 ¾ In. 10.00
Toothpick, Boot Shape 65.00
Vase, Hobnail, Fan Shape, 1940-50s, 11 x 7 ½ x 3 In. 285.00
Water Set, Bulbous Pitcher, 7 Piece 795.00

VENETIAN GLASS, *see Glass-Venetian category.*

VENINI GLASS *is listed in the Glass-Venetian category.*

VERLYS glass was made in Rouen, France, by the Société Holophane Français, a company that started in 1920. It was made in Newark, Ohio, from 1935 to 1951. The art glass is either blown or molded. The American glass is signed with a diamond-point-scratched name, but the French pieces are marked with a molded signature. The designs resemble those used by Lalique.

Verlys

Bowl, Birds & Bees, 12 In. .... *illus* 160.00
Bowl, Kingfisher, Signed, 13 ½ In. 160.00
Bowl, Rose, Frosted, 5 ¼ In. .... *illus* 175.00
Bowl, Water Lily, 13 In. 234.00
Vase, Gems, Opalescent, 1930, 6 x 7 In. .... *illus* 263.00

VERNON KILNS was the name used by Vernon Potteries, Ltd. The company, which started in 1931 in Vernon, California, made dinnerware and figurines until it went out of business in 1958. The molds were bought by Metlox, which continued to make some patterns. Collectors search for the brightly colored dinnerware and the pieces designed by Rockwell Kent, Walt Disney, and Don Blanding. For more prices, go to kovels.com.

Vernon

Barkwood, Cup & Saucer, Jumbo, 4 ¼ In. & 6 ¾ In. 32.00
Barkwood, Dish, Divided, San Marino Shape, 11 ½ x 6 ½ In. 30.00
Beverly, Plate, Luncheon, Melinda Shape, 1940s, 9 ½ In. 15.00
Casual, Plate, San Marino Shape, Dawn Pink, 10 ¼ In. 10.00
Casual, Saucer, San Marino Shape, Dawn Pink, 6 In. 2.00
Figurine, Fantasia Sprite, White, Hand On Head Looking Into Distance, 1940, 5 In. 205.00
Gingham, Bowl, Cereal, Deep 20.00
Gingham, Butter Chip, Green & Yellow, 2 ½ In. 25.00
Gingham, Cup & Saucer, Green & Yellow, Large 47.00
Gingham, Pitcher, Green & Yellow, ½ Pt., 5 In. 33.00
Gingham, Salt & Pepper, Green & Yellow 20.00
Gingham, Salt & Pepper, Montecito Shape 20.00
Heyday, Cup & Saucer 10.00
Hibiscus, Bowl, Chowder, Lug Handles 24.00
Homespun, Chop Plate, Green, Yellow & Cinnamon, 12 In. 18.00
Homespun, Serving Bowl, Montecito Shape, Rimmed, 9 x 2 ⅜ In. 21.00

Linda, Cup & Saucer 25.00
May Flower, Sugar, No Cover, 3 ¼ In. 19.00
Monterey, Sugar, Cover, 5 In. 9.00
Organdie, Bowl, Vegetable, Brown & Yellow, 9 In. 35.00
Organdie, Cup & Saucer 10.00
Organdie, Plate, Dinner, 9 ½ In. 18.50
Organdie, Saucer, 6 ½ In. 5.00
Raffia, Butter, Cover 35.00
Raffia, Plate, Dinner, 10 ⅛ In. 10.00
Tam O'Shanter, Cup & Saucer, Rust, Chartreuse & Dark Green 12.00
Texas, Plate, Blue & White, Attractions, 10 ½ In. 15.00
Tickled Pink, Chop Plate, 13 In. 35.00

VERRE DE SOIE glass was first made by Frederick Carder at the Steuben Glass Works from about 1905 to 1930. It is an iridescent glass of soft white or very, very pale green. The name means "glass of silk," and it does resemble silk. Other factories have made verre de soie, and some of the English examples were made of different colors. Verre de soie is an art glass and is not related to the iridescent, pressed, white carnival glass mistakenly called by its name. Related pieces may be found in the Steuben category.

Basket, Helmet, Loop Handle, Raspberry Prunts, Steuben, 12 In. 345.00
Bowl, Engraved Garland, Applied Rosaline Lip, Steuben, 12 In. 660.00
Bowl, Footed, Flared, Steuben, 5 x 11 ¾ In. 497.00
Bowl, Iridescent, Scalloped Rim, Steuben, 5 x 8 ½ In. 173.00
Loving Cup, Blue Threading, Handles, Steuben, Early 1900s, 6 In. .... *illus* 132.00
Perfume Bottle, Black Stopper, Steuben, 4 ¾ In. 230.00
Perfume Bottle, Melon Ribbed, Elongated Neck, Teardrop Stopper, 7 In. 403.00
Perfume Bottle, Melon Ribbed, Green Jade Teardrop Stopper, Steuben, 4 ½ In. 345.00
Perfume Bottle, Melon Ribbed, Rose DuBarry Stopper, Steuben, 4 ½ In. 374.00
Perfume Bottle, Optic Ribbed, Footed, Celeste Blue Stopper, Steuben, 10 In. 345.00
Perfume Bottle, Oval, Celeste Blue Stopper, Steuben, 3 ½ In. 230.00
Shade, Helmet Shape, Blue Threading, 10 In. 460.00
Sherbet, Oriental Poppy Wafer Stem, 7 In., 6 Piece 1553.00
Vase, Applique Plums, Bohemian, c.1910, 9 In. .... *illus* 180.00
Vase, Green Threading, Steuben, 7 ½ x 5 ¼ In. 1053.00
Vase, Hawkes Etched, Steuben, 10 In. 185.00

VIENNA, *see Beehive category.*

VIENNA ART PLATES PAT. FEB. 21 '05 1905

VIENNA ART plates are round metal serving trays produced at the turn of the century. The designs, copied from Royal Vienna porcelain plates, usually featured a portrait of a woman encircled by a wide, ornate border. Many were used as advertising or promotional items and were produced in Coshocton, Ohio, by J. F. Meeks Tuscarora Advertising Co. and H.D. Beach's Standard Advertising Co.

Plate, Dr Pepper King Of Beverages, Free From Caffeine, Woman, 1900s, 10 ¼ In. 1200.00
Plate, Victorian Girl, Gold, Wood, Frame, c.1910, 16 ½ In. .... *illus* 225.00
Plate, Woman Holding Vase Of Flowers, Gold & Green Border, Tin, 10 ⅛ In. 30.00
Plate, Woman With Cupid, Flower Border, Tin, Signed, 10 ⅛ In. 10.00
Plate, Woman With Flowers, Butterfly, Flower Border, Signed, 10 ⅛ In. 20.00

V.&B.

VILLEROY & BOCH Pottery of Mettlach was founded in 1836. The firm made many types of wares, including the famous Mettlach steins. Collectors can be confused because although Villeroy & Boch made most of its pieces in the city of Mettlach, Germany, the company also had factories in other locations. The dating code impressed on the bottom of most pieces makes it possible to determine the age of the piece. Additional items, including steins and earthenware pieces marked with the famous castle mark or the word *Mettlach*, may be found in the Mettlach category.

Charger, Basel, Switzerland, Scene, 12 ⅛ In. 80.00
Charger, Heidelberg Hillside Ruins, 12 ⅛ In. 80.00
Charger, Konigsberger Schilofs, 20th Century, 18 In. 205.00
Dessert Set, Violets, Reticulated Border, Compote, Plates, 9 & 6 ½ In., 7 Piece 81.00
Globular, Geometric Patterns, Brown Matte, 4 ¾ In. 115.00
Plaque, African Man & Woman, Hand Painted Relief, Dresden, 20 ½ In., Pair 5405.00
Plaque, Mediterranean Women, Hand Painted Relief, Dresden, 22 In., Pair 6038.00
Platter, Dresden, Flow Blue, c.1915, 14 ½ x 20 ¼ In. 27.00
Vase, Flora, Frosted, Clear, Wavy Rim, Box, 10 In. 25.00
Vase, Stylized Flowers, Light Green Ground, 14 ⅞ In. 1035.00

Verre De Soie, Loving Cup, Blue Threading, Handles, Steuben, Early 1900s, 6 In.
$132.00

Verre De Soie, Vase, Applique Plums, Bohemian, c.1910, 9 In.
$180.00

Vienna Art, Plate, Victorian Girl, Gold, Wood, Frame, c.1910, 16 ½ In.
$225.00

Volkmar, Vase, Blue Trillium, Swirling Leaves, Brown & Green Ground, Shouldered, 8 ¼ In.
$2040.00

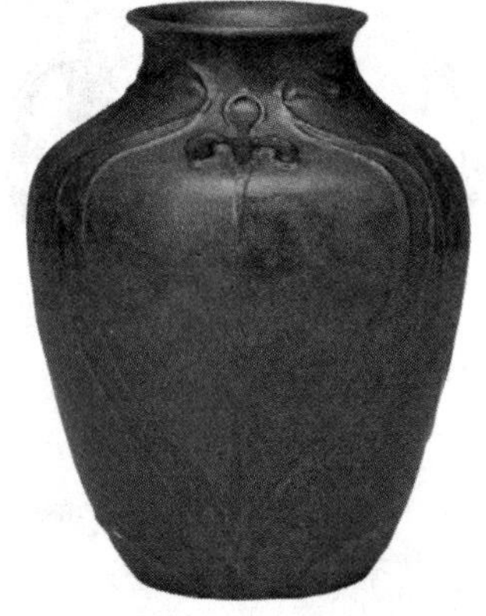

Walrath, Bowl, Applied Center, Kneeling Woman, Green, Brown Matte Glaze, 8 x 7 In.
$420.00

Walrath, Vase, Red Lilies, Green Leaves & Ground, Incised, 7 ½ x 4 In.
$5100.00

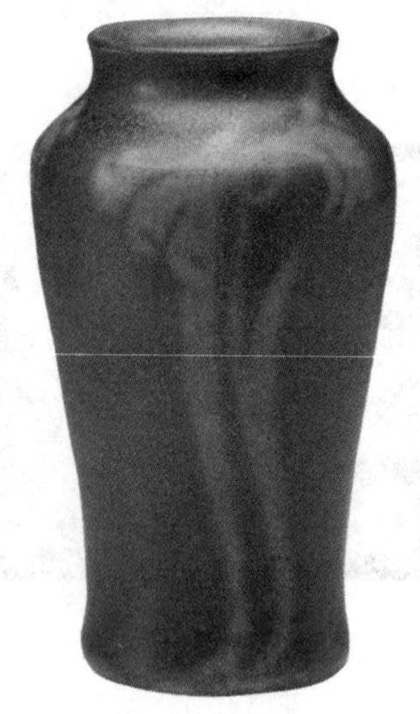

VOLKMAR pottery was made by Charles Volkmar of New York from 1879 to about 1911. He was associated with several firms, including the Volkmar Ceramic Company, Volkmar and Cory, and Charles Volkmar and Son. He was hired by Durant Kilns of Bedford Village, New York, in 1910 to oversee production. Volkmar bought the business and after 1930 only the Volkmar name was used as a mark. Volkmar had been a painter, and his designs often look like oil paintings drawn on pottery.

Tile, Duck, Male, Female, Landscape, Signed, Stamped, 12 x 8 In. 415.00
Vase, Blue Trillium, Swirling Leaves, Brown & Green Ground, Shouldered, 8 ¼ In. . . . . . *illus* 2040.00

VOLKSTEDT was a soft-paste porcelain factory started in 1760 by Georg Heinrich Macheleid at Volkstedt, Thuringia. Volkstedt-Rudolstadt was a porcelain factory started at Volkstedt-Rudolstadt by Beyer and Bock in 1890. Most pieces seen in shops today are from the later factory.

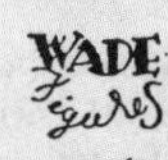

Figurine, 3 Musicians Instruments, 1700s Attire, c.1930, 9 x 10 In.. . . . . 234.00
Figurine, Amazon On Horseback, Nude, Holding Shield & Sword, Marked, 1900s, 20 In.. . . . . 830.00
Figurine, Flower Vendor, On Tree Form Base, c.1890, 8 In. 410.00
Group, Diana Huntress, 2 Attendants, Putti, Game, Rookery Base, Marked, 1800s, 24 In. 1062.00

WADE pottery is made by the Wade Group of Potteries started in 1810 near Burslem, England. Several potteries merged to become George Wade & Son, Ltd. early in the twentieth century, and other potteries have been added through the years. The best-known Wade pieces are the small figurines given away with Red Rose Tea and other promotional items. The Disney figures are listed in this book in the Disneyana category.

Figurine, Farm Cart Horse, c.1974, 2 ¾ x 3 In. 35.00
Pin Tray, Angel Fish, Aqua, c.1960, 4 x 3 ⅛ In. 20.00
Saber Tooth Tiger, Christmas Cracker Premium, c.1965, 1 ⅝ In. 30.00
Tray, Double-Decker Bus, Player's Navy Cut, Green, Red Metal Bus, No. 5, c.1975, 6 x 3 ½ In.. 35.00
Trinket Box, Treasure Chest, c.1961, 3 ½ x 2 In. 65.00
Vase, Flower, Yellow, Leaves, Green Ground, Ireland, 6 ½ In.. . . . . 40.00
Vase, Posey, Viking Ship, Brown, Blue, c.1965, 7 ⅜ x 1 ⅞ In. . . . . 50.00 to 58.00
Whimsey, North American Animals, Grizzly Bear, c.1958, 1 ⅞ In. 75.00

WAHPETON POTTERY, *see Rosemeade category.*

WALL POCKETS were popular in the 1930s. They were made by many American and European factories. Glass, pottery, porcelain, majolica, chalkware, and metal wall pockets can be found in many fanciful shapes.

Bird, Majolica Style, Brown, Multicolored Glaze, Japan, 6 ¾ In.. . . . . 40.00
Curly Maple, Carved Rosette Design, 1800s, 11 x 9 In. 881.00
Parrot On Perch, Figural, Majolica, Yellow, Bretby, 12 ½ In. 518.00
Wood, Rack, Black Paint, Cherries, Leaves, 15 x 10 ½ x 3 In. 38.00

WALRATH was a potter who worked in New York City; Rochester, New York; and at the Newcomb Pottery in New Orleans, Louisiana. Frederick Walrath died in 1920. Pieces listed here are from his Rochester period.

Bowl, Applied Center, Kneeling Woman, Green, Brown Matte Glaze, 8 x 7 In. . . . . *illus* 420.00
Figurine, Woman, Nude, Prone, High Glaze, Caramel, Inscribed, 1912, 5 ½ In. 266.00
Vase, Bulbous, Blue, Tan Painted Flowers, Brown Matte Glaze, 4 x 4 In. 1440.00
Vase, Green Pine Boughs, Yellow, Blue Sky, Green Matte Ground, 8 ¼ x 4 ½ In. 5700.00
Vase, Red Lilies, Green Leaves & Ground, Incised, 7 ½ x 4 In. . . . . *illus* 5100.00

WALT DISNEY, *see Disneyana category.*

WALTER, *see A. Walter category.*

WARWICK china was made in Wheeling, West Virginia, in a pottery working from 1887 to 1951. Many pieces were made with hand painted or decal decorations. The most familiar Warwick has a shaded brown background. The name *Warwick* is part of the mark and sometimes the mysterious word *IOGA* is also included.

IOGA

Celery Dish, Pansy, Flow Blue, c.1900, 5 ¼ x 12 ¼ In. 24.00
Pitcher, Gibson Girl Transfer, Tan, Marked, Ioga, 5 ½ x 5 ¼ In.. . . . . 33.00
Pitcher, Warwick Pansy, Flow Blue, c.1900, 5 ¾ In.. . . . . 59.00
Platter, Warwick Pansy, Flow Blue, c.1900, 8 ¼ x 12 ¼ In. 11.80
Vase, Poinsettia, Scalloped, Flared Rim, c.1940, 11 ½ In. 12.00

V

WATCH pockets held the pocket watch that was important in Victorian times because it was not until World War I that the wristwatch was used. All types of watches are collected: silver, gold, or plated. Watches are listed here by company name or by style. Wristwatches are a separate category.

A. Von Loehr, Patent Perpetual Wind, Power Indicator, Silver, Enamel, Steel Crescent, c.1880 956.00
Agassiz, Gold Split Second Chronograph, 4 Body, Enamel, Spade Hands, Register, Signed, c.1895 2151.00
Alexander Johnstone, Verge, London, c.1830, Pocket 359.00
Ansonia Clock Co., Rose Gold, c.1888, Pocket 155.00
Ball Watch Co., Open Face, Crest On Back, 21 Jewel 225.00
Baume & Mercier, Diamond, 14K Yellow Gold, Woven Band, 7 In. 1035.00
Bonheur, Exposed Balance, Blue, White Gold Face, c.1895, Pocket 507.00
Bourquin, Center Seconds, Pouzait Escapement, 3 Body, Clear Front, Back, Signed, c.1790 7768.00
Bullingford, Open Face, Verge Fusee, London, c.1835, Pocket 359.00
Burlington, 21 Jeel, Art Deco, 1920s, Pocket 150.00
Captain's, Double Dial, Roman Numerals, Gilt Reverse Dial, Porcelain, c.1890 1195.00
Cartier, Pasha Chronograph, 37 Jewel, Stainless Steel, Rotating Bezel, Arabic Numerals 5258.00
Cartier, Sapphire Set Crown, Water Resistant, 18K White Gold 4402.00
Colomby, 18K Gold, Multicolored Mother, Child, Flowers, Cherubs, Paste Stones 4780.00
Cross Shape, 3-Body, Pierced Covers, Sides, Religious Images, Birds, Flowers, Silver, 1800s 2390.00
Daniel & Thomas Grignion, Gold Verge Fusee, 20K, Enamel, Pierced Cock, Mask, London, c.1750 2988.00
Dietrich Gruen, Platinum Rim Diamonds, Black Enamel Edge, 19 Rubies, c.1920, Pocket 1434.00
Ditisheim, Multicolored, 2 Women, Enamel, Pearls, 14K Gold Floral Pin, Red Stone, 16 Jewel, c.1915 598.00
Ditisheim, Platinum Dial, Diamond Mounts, 18 Jewel, Leather Holder, Signed, c.1915 2271.00
Elgin, Black Enamel Leaf, Landscape Covers, 18K Gold, Scalloped Rim, 7 Jewel, c.1879, Pocket 1434.00
Elgin, Fancy Face, 14K Gold, 15 Jewel, No. 26958486 220.00
Elgin, Father Time, 21 Jewel, Silver, c.1909, Pocket *illus* 237.00
Elgin, Father Time, White Gold, 21 Jewel, c.1917, Pocket 239.00
Elgin, Flower, Monogram, Mahogany Hinged Lid, Velour, Box, 14K Gold, Pocket 275.00
Elgin, Flowers, Leaf, 7 Jewel, 14K Gold, Pocket, 2 x 1 ½ In. 132.00
Elgin, Hunting Case, 14K Gold, Round Ivory Tone Dial, Leaf Designs, Pocket, Size 0 415.00
Elgin, Hunting Case, Tricolor, Gold, Embossed Flowers, Green Stones, c.1888 1016.00
Elgin, Incised Flower, Bird, Woman's, Pocket, 2 x 1 ⅜ In. 121.00
Elgin, Locomotive Case, Nickel, Rose Gold, c.1890, Pocket 90.00
Elgin, Lord, Open Face, 14K Gold, 21 Jewel, Inscribed, Buick Motor Division 25 Years 400.00
Elgin, Monogramed Case, Diamond, 14K, Woman's, Pocket, 1 ¾ x 1 ¼ In. 165.00
Elgin, Open Face, 14K Gold, Enamel Dial, c.1893, Pocket 633.00
Freres, Oval Diamond, Black Enamel Accents, 18K, Gold Covette, 18 Jewel, c.1875 478.00
George Lafond, Calculating, 4-Disc Adder, Decadic Transmission, Swiss, 1899 3408.00
Green Satin Enamel, Fleur-De-Lis Pin, 14K, Marked, AW, Swiss, 1 ⅜-In. Watch *illus* 250.00
Hamilton, 21 Jewel, Double Roller Movement, 10K Gold Filled Case, c.1930, Pocket, 2 In. 144.00
Hamilton, Ball Grade 999 B, Official Railroad Standard, c.1930, Pocket 717.00
Hamilton, Baseball, Game In Progress Scene, Gold, 1902, Pocket, 2 In. 705.00
Hamilton, Bell Shape, 17 Jewel, 2 Tone Dial, 14K White Gold Filled, 2 ⅛ x 1 ¾ In. 55.00
Hamilton, Lapel, Open Face, Monogram, Flower, Woman's, 1 ⅜ x 1 ⅛ In. 44.00
Hampden, Pink, White Face, c.1908, Pocket 191.00
Hampden, Railroad, Hunting Case, 14K Gold, Pocket, c.1882 698.00
Hampden, Railway, c.1883, Pocket 113.00
Howard, Open Face, White Enamel Dial, 14K Gold, c.1915, Pocket 978.00
Hunting Case, Diamond, Ruby, Seed Pearl, Enamel, Swiss, c.1910 3585.00
Hunting Case, Illinois, Flower & Leaf Design, 18K Gold, c.1877, Pocket 920.00
Hunting Case, Silver, Moon Phase Calendar, 15 Jewel, Silver, Chased Flowers, Leaves, Swiss, c.1905 598.00
Illinois, Silver Hunting Case, Sailboat, Fisherman Scene, 23 Jewel, Interstate, c.1911, Pocket 1793.00
Illinois Washington Watch Co., Senate, Locomotive Case, c.1911, Pocket 114.00
J. Falise, Gothic Revival, Cover, Silver, Pierced Hunt Scenes, Cock, Oval, 3 Body, c.1840 2749.00
J. Smith, Verge Fusee, Repousse Case, Solomon's Court, Bow Dial, Silver, Signed, London, c.1767 1793.00
James Payne, Gold, Pair Case Fusee, 18K Leaf, Cock, Rabbit Snail, London, c.1820 1673.00
Jas. Allan, 18K Yellow Gold, Black Enamel Case, Enameled Face, Charleston, Pocket, 2 ¼ In. 546.00
John Moncas, Open Face, Lever Fusee, c.1840, Pocket 478.00
Josephson, Sterling Silver Case, Outer Cherub, Scroll, Flowers Repousse Verge, London, c.1775 2032.00
Jules Jurgensen, 5 Minute Repeater, Ribbon Script Monogram, 30 Jewel, c.1885 2629.00
Jules Jurgensen, Blue Enamel Bezel, 21 Jewel, 18K, Gold Deco, Copenhagen, c.1923 1315.00
Jules Jurgensen, Hunting Case, Repeater, 18K, Diamonds, 32 Jewel, Tiffany, c.1890 *illus* 4780.00
Jules Jurgensen, Open Face, 18K Gold, White Dial, Pocket 3851.00
Kelbert, Nickel Case, 17 Jewel, 2 Men, Cattle, Flowers, Swiss Movement, Pocket, 2 ¾ x 2 In. 66.00
Keystone, Hunting Case, 17 Jewel, Arabic Numbers, Engraved Birds, c.1888, Size 18 196.00
Liverpool, Key Wind, Silver, Hunting Case, Rampant Lion, Pocket 460.00
Lohengrin, Niello, Gold, Airplanes, c.1910, Pocket 418.00

Watch. Elgin, Father Time, 21 Jewel, Silver, c.1909, Pocket
$237.00

Watch, Green Satin Enamel, Fleur-De-Lis Pin, 14K, Marked, AW, Swiss, 1 ⅜-In. Watch
$250.00

Watch, Jules Jurgensen, Hunting Case, Repeater, 18K, Diamonds, 32 Jewel, Tiffany, c.1890
$4780.0

As always, the edited listings in *Kovels' Antiques & Collectibles Price Guide 2010* aren't available on any website, but readers should visit Kovels.com for information on trends, tips, reproductions, marks, old prices, and more!

New Owner
Tiffany Watch Company is now owned by Swatch Group, maker of Swatch watches.

Watch, Omega, Art Deco, Aztec Style Design, Soldiers On Back, 15 Jewel, Pocket, 2 ⅛ x 1 ⅝ In.
$575.00

Watch, Waltham, 14K, 17 Jewel, Marked, John B Stetson Co., Engraved, Box, 1904, 2 In.
$518.00

TIP
Replace broken or scratched watch crystals immediately. The crack may let moisture get to the works, and soon your watch will not tell time accurately.

Lohengrin, Niello, Gold, Silver, Hunt Scene, Alvarez, 15 Jewel, Swiss, c.1905 .... 538.00
Longines, Lapel, Fleur-De-Lis Pin, Diamond Filigree, Enamel, Platinum, 14K Gold, Woman's, c.1910 1554.00
Longines, Neillo, Hunting Case, Rose Gold Black Enamel Ground, Iris, c.1915, Pocket...... 335.00
Longines, Niello, Doctor's, Rose Gold Case, Flowers, c.1905, Pocket..................... 608.00
Longines, Pendant, 14K Gold, Blue Enamel, White Trim, 15 Jewel, Neck Chain, Woman's, c.1915 1195.00
Longines, Pendant, Black Enamel, 18Kgold, Diamonds, Black Ribbon, 17 Jewel, Woman's, c.1910 2270.00
Longines, Silver Tandem Wind, Alarm, Opens To Night Table Stand, 15 Ruby, c.1905, Pocket 1315.00
Louis Mathile, Lapel, Woman's, Gold, Blue Enamel, Pin, c.1870........................ 418.00
Mio, Niello, Gold, Silver, Automobile Race Scene, 11 Jewel, Swiss, c.1905................. 538.00
Monard, Quarter Hour Repeater, Pink 18K Gold, Ruby Jewels In Screw, Signed, c.1895...... 3884.00
Moon Phase Calendar, Gilt Filigree Hands, 11 Jewel, No. 3984, c.1900, 2 ⅝ In. 1195.00
Movado, Hunting Case, Engine Turned, White Face, Luminous Numbers, Hands, 1 5/16 x 1 ⅞ In. 1140.00
Movado Golf, Ivory Tone Dial, Date Aperture, Manual Wind, Tiffany & Co. 474.00
New Era, Incised Flower, Plaque Case, Key Wind, Coil Silver Case, Pocket, 3 x 2 ⅛ In........ 88.00
New Era, Incised Leaf, Star, Central Plaque, Horse, Jumping, Pocket, 3 x 2 ⅛ In............ 44.00
New York Standard, Gold, Scalloped Edge, Flowers, c.1905, Pocket.................... 155.00
Niello, Gold, Woman, Horse, Cart, Man, Top Hat, Open Face Dial, 11 Jewel, Swiss, c.1905 .... 598.00
Niello, Hunting Case, Hunter, Dog, Hare, Cyclist, Pocket............................ 296.00
Omega, Art Deco, Aztec Style Design, Soldiers On Back, 15 Jewel, Pocket, 2 ⅛ x 1 ⅝ In... *illus* 575.00
Onoto, Niello, Rose Gold, Woman, Flowers, c.1910, Pocket........................... 227.00
Open Face, Key Wind, 18K Yellow Gold Rose, White & Green Gold, Flowers, 2 ¼ In.......... 764.00
Paris, Open Face, Roman Numerals, Push Pendant, Pocket.......................... 1955.00
Patek Philippe, 18K Gold, Dial No. 61970, Box, 15 Jewel, Woman's, c.1883, Pocket......... 1195.00
Patek Philippe, Gold Chronometro Gondolo, 20 Jewel, 18K, Painted Enamel, c.1914....... 4183.00
Patek Philippe, Lapel, Woman's, Blue Enamel, Diamonds, Flower Spray, 18K Gold, c.1870 .. 2629.00
Paul Flato, Lapel, Mexican Gold Peso, Coat Of Arms, Hook, Woman's, Signed, 2 ¼ x 1 ¾ In. . 1920.00
Perret & Fils, Minute Repeater, Perpetual Calendar, Moon Phase, 18K Gold, c.1890........ 33460.00
Pin, Bow Shape, 10K Yellow Gold, England 58.00
R. Trap, Verge Fusee, Pair Case, Blue Spade Hands, Fleur-De-Lis, Scroll, Silver, London, c.1750 1793.00
Rockford, Open Face, Chain, Flower, Leaf Border, Engraved Case, 2 ¾ x 2 In. 55.00
Rockford, Silver, Deer On Case, c.1887, Pocket 203.00
Rolex, Bracelet, 18K Gold, Diamond, Square Ivory Tone Dial, 17 Jewel, c.1960, 5 ½ In....... 1007.00
Rosselet, Hunting Case, 18K Gold Detent Chronometer, Cap Jewels On Escape, Signed, c.1870 3884.00
S. Thomas Jr. & Bros., Double Case, 14K Yellow Gold, Pocket, 3 x 2 In.................. 2415.00
Samson, Silver, Verge, Champleve Dial, Fleur-De-Lis, Rose Gold Spade Hands, London, c.1790 2151.00
Samuel Berry, 20K Gold Case, Pillars, Pierced Cock, Mask, Signed, London, c.1731 .... 5079.00
Silver, Enamel, Bull's-Eye Crystal, Battle Scene, Inscription, London, 1803 .... 16590.00
Silver, Open Face, Musical Instruments, Fern Leaves, Enamel, c.1885.................. 4183.00
Silver Repousee, Pair Case, Scenic, Forest, Figures, Chatelaine, c.1780 .... 1793.00
South Bend, Narry's Special, c.1904, Pocket...................................... 102.00
Swiss, Gold, Skeleton, Bull, Toreador Enamel Scene, 15 Jewel, c.1885, Pocket 1315.00
Swiss, Gold Chronograph, Register, 18K Yellow Gold, Blue Spade Hands, 18 Jewel, c.1905.... 1076.00
Swiss, Gold Hunter, 8 Diamonds, 14K Gold, Multicolored Flowers, Horse, Rose, 17 Jewel, c.1890 5378.00
Swiss, Minute Repeater, 18K Rose Gold, 32 Jewel, Case No. 180011, Signed, c.1890 .... 3585.00
Swiss, Minute Repeater, Gold Demi-Hunting Case, 18K Yellow Gold, Blue Enamel Chapters, c.1890 2689.00
Swiss, Minute Repeating, Split Second Chronograph, Register, 18K Yellow Gold, 32 Jewel, c.1900 5975.00
Swiss, Moon Phase, Calendar, Black Rim, c.1880, Pocket............................ 837.00
Swiss, Platinum, Silver Dial, Nickel Bridge, 17 Jewel, c.1930 .... 1793.00
Swiss, Quarter Hour Repeater, Silver, Black Niello Case, Blank Rose Gold Crest, 17 Jewel, c.1905 . 1793.00
Swiss, Quarter Hour Repeater Skeleton Dial, Sunburst Pattern, 18K Gold, Blue, Black, c.1790 4481.00
Tavannes, Buttonhole, Black Surround, Wood Trim, Small Central Face, c.1905, Pocket 90.00
Tiffany & Co., Split Seconds Chronograph, 18K Gold, Enamel, 20 Jewel, c.1880 .... 2151.00
Tiffany & Co., White Gold, 18K, 18 Jewel, Friction Ruby Jewels, c.1925.................. 1195.00
Ulysse Nardin, 17 Jewel Movement, Hinged, Arabic Numerals, Chain, c.1915 .... 1075.00
Ulysse Nardin, Enamel, Gold, Art Deco, 18K Gold, Engraved Roses, Black Numerals, 16 Jewel, c.1925 1315.00
Union Horlogere, Golden Spring Cover, Stamped Case, Swiss, Pocket 399.00
Vacheron & Constantin, 14K Gold, Black Enamel Leaf, Scroll, 17 Jewel, c.1905, Pocket 1793.00
Vacheron & Constantin, 18K Gold, Double Hinged Back, 17 Jewel, c.1907 .... 2032.00
Vacheron & Constantin, Hunting Case, Silvertone Dial, 18K Gold, Pocket 2489.00
Vacheron & Constantin, Hunting Case Tiger, Serpent Cover, 15 Jewel, c.1910, Pocket...... 3346.00
Vacheron & Constantin, Pendant, 14K, Open Face, Pink & White Enamel Dial, Woman's, 1 ½ In. 920.00
Valere Paris, Multicolored Enamel Fountain, Monument Scene, Brass Gilt, c.1790......... 1793.00
Verge Escapement, William Craig, No. 246, Silvered Case, England.................. 144.00
W. Kipling, Oignon, Owner's Names, Dates, Verge Fusee, Chain, Silver, London, c.1700...... 5676.00
W.E. Huguenin, Open Face, Horse, Rider, Rose Cut Diamond Fence, 18K Gold, c.1895 ...... 4481.00
Waltham, 14K, 17 Jewel, Marked, John B Stetson Co., Engraved, Box, 1904, 2 In. ...... *illus* 518.00
Waltham, 23 Jewel, Star Case, Rolled Gold Plate Case, Pocket, 2 ⅜ x 1 ⅞ In. 303.00
Waltham, Flower, Picture Frame, Pocket, 1 ⅞ x 1 ⅜ In.............................. 44.00

Waltham, Hunting Case, 14K Gold, Ivory Tone Dial, 15 Jewel Movement, Size 0, Pocket 237.00
Waltham, Hunting Case, Enamel Dial, Sundial Second Hand, Engraved, 14K Gold, 1 ¼ In. . . 264.00
Waltham, Lapel, Hunting Case, Pin, Circle, Swirls, Stones, Enamel, Woman's, c.1901 . . . . 1076.00
Waltham, Open Face, Engraved, Pink Gold, c.1902, Pocket 167.00
Waltham, P.S. Bartlett, Blue, Pink Dial, c.1888, Pocket. 155.00
Waltham, Railroad, Incised Steam Engine, Marked, Illinois Watch Case Co., 2 ⅜ In. . . . *illus* 55.00
Waltham, Sterling, Blue, White Dial, c.1906, Pocket. 335.00
Waltham, Vanguard, 23 Jewel, 10K Gold, Arabic Numbers, Size 16, c.1921, Pocket 805.00
Waltham, Wm. Ellery, Key Wind, Coin Silver Hunting Case, American Watch Co., c.1865, Pocket 717.00
Waterbury Watch Co., Portrait, Horace Greeley, 1891, 2 In. 2031.00
Windmills, Quarter Repeating, Pierced Pinchbeck Case, Ruby Pendant, 20K, Signed, London, c.1725 6573.00

WATCH FOBS were worn on watch chains. They were popular during Victorian times and after. Many styles, especially advertising designs, are still made today.

Anheuser-Busch, Michelob, Budweiser, Letter A, Eagle, Brass, 2 x 1 ½ In. 66.00
Art Deco, Inkwell Shape, 14K Rose Gold, Leather Stopper, Open Side Panel, c.1930. . . . . *illus* 1016.00
Art Nouveau, 14K Gold, Fiend, Patinated Face, Red Stones For Eyes & Mouth 889.00
Avery, Teeth Talk, Bulldog, Bared Teeth, Silvered Brass, 1 ¾ In. 171.00
Dr Pepper, Silvered Brass, Billiken Good Luck Character, 1908, 2 In. 86.00
J.I. Case Threshing Machine Co., Silvered Brass, 1 ⅞ In.. . . . . 75.00
Lehigh Valley Railroad, Red & Black Enamel, Silvery Ground. 10.00
Mesh, Gold Metal, Victorian. 32.00
Oakland 5 Cent Cigar, Mansion, Celluloid, Fiberboard, Early 1900s, 1 ¼ In. . . . . *illus* 126.00

WATERFORD type glass resembles the famous glass made from 1783 to 1851 in the Waterford Glass Works in Ireland. It is a clear glass that was often decorated by cutting. Modern glass is being made again in Waterford, Ireland, and is marketed under the name Waterford. Waterford merged with Wedgwood in 1986 to form the Waterford Wedgwood Group. Most Waterford Wedgwood assets were bought by KPS Capital Partners of New York in 2009 and became part of WWRD Holdings.

Biscuit Jar, Cover, Lismore, Acid Signed, 6 ⅜ x 4 ⅝ In. 225.00
Bowl, Centerpiece, Glenbrook, 10 In. 145.00
Bowl, Penrose, 5 ¼ x 7 ¾ In., Pair 88.00
Brandy Snifter, Lismore, Stamped, Acid Etched Logo, c.1980, 10 Oz. 95.00
Candlestick, 6-Sided Stem, 6-Panel Base, Flower Shaped Top, Etched Mark, 10 In., Pair 99.00
Claret, Lismore, 5 ¾ In., 12 Piece 293.00
Clock, Desk, Signed, Label, 6 ¾ x 2 ½ In. 115.00
Clock, Round, 8-Sided, Cut, 2 ¾ In. 105.00
Decanter, Brookside, Stopper, 10 x 4 In.. . . . . 90.00
Decanter, Colleen, Ball Stopper, 1968, 10 ¾ In.. . . . . 245.00
Decanter, Lismore, Ball Stopper, 1957, 10 ¾ In. 242.00
Decanter, Lismore, Stopper, 13 In. . . . . *illus* 117.00
Goblet, Tramore, Stem, Trumpet Shape, Etched Name, 5 ½ In. 70.00
Paperweight, American Flag, Signed, 4 ½ In.. . . . . 20.00
Paperweight, Penguin, Signed, 4 ¾ x 2 In.. . . . . 45.00
Paperweight, Rose, Etched Name, 3 ½ x 1 ½ In.. . . . . 125.00
Pitcher, Crisscross Cutting, Vertical Lines Cut Into Top & Bottom, 7 ½ In. 150.00
Pitcher, Milk, Star Cut, 7 ½ In. 95.00
Razor, Glass Handle, Box, 3 x 1 ½ In. 105.00
Rose Bowl, Glandore, 6 In. 90.00
Salt & Pepper, Colleen, Cone Shape Screw Tops, 3 ¾ In. 95.00
Shaving Brush, Glass Handle, Signed, Box, 4 x 2 In. 45.00
Sherbet, Sheila, Paneled Stem, 4 ¾ x 4 In. 35.00
Sherry, Colleen, Stem, 4 ¼ In.. . . . . 50.00
Sugar & Creamer, Lismore, 3 ¼-In. Sugar, 4 ½-In. Creamer 129.00
Vase, Cut Crystal, Pedestal Base, Scalloped Edge, 21st Century, 10 ⅛ x 6 ½ In. 59.00
Vase, Cut Glass, 4 ¼ x 2 ½ In. 40.00
Vase, Hand Cut, 9 In. . . . . 175.00 to 263.00
Vase, Limited Edition, 1980s, 4 ¼ x 2 ½ In. 40.00
Vase, Lismore, Crystal, Flared, Footed, 8 ½ x 5 In. 180.00
Vase, Maritana, Flared Lip, Signed, Jim O'Leary, 13 x 9 In. . . . . *illus* 409.00
Vase, Marquis, 16-Point Star, Alternating Points & Drapes 88.00
Vase, Penrose, 8 ½ x 5 In., Pair 263.00
Wine, Lismore, Signed, 7 ½ In. 58.00
Wine, Maeve, 3 x 8 In., 12 Piece 410.00
Wine Set, Decanter, Lid, 6 Wineglasses, 7 Piece 322.00

Watch, Waltham, Railroad, Incised Steam Engine, Marked, Illinois Watch Case Co., 2 ⅜ In.
$55.00

Watch Fob, Art Deco, Inkwell Shape, 14K Rose Gold, Leather Stopper, Open Side Panel, c.1930
$1016.00

Watchfob, Oakland 5 Cent Cigar, Mansion, Celluloid, Fiberboard, Early 1900s, 1 ¼ In.
$126.00

TIP

Install large windows in your house—burglars avoid shattering them because of noise.

Waterford, Decanter, Lismore, Stopper, 13 In.
$117.00

Waterford, Vase, Maritana, Flared Lip, Signed, Jim O'Leary, 13 x 9 In.
$409.00

Watt, Apple, Bowl, Salad, Cover, No. 73
$75.00

Watt, Apple, Cookie Jar, No. 503
$210.00

WATT family members bought the Globe pottery of Crooksville, Ohio, in 1922. They made pottery mixing bowls and tableware of the type made by Globe. In 1935 they changed the production and made the pieces with the freehand decorations that are popular with collectors today. Apple, Starflower, Rooster, Tulip, and Autumn Foliage are the best-known patterns. Pansy, also called Rio Rose, was the earliest pattern. Apple, the most popular pattern, can be dated from the leaves. Originally, the apples had three leaves; after 1958 two leaves were used. The plant closed in 1965. For more information, see *Kovels' Depression Glass & Dinnerware Price List.*

Advertising, Bowl, Burchinal, Iowa, Dutch Tulip, Ribbed, No. 5 .... 185.00
Advertising, Kitch-N-Queen, Bowl, Inter-State Lumber, No. 5 .... 40.00
Advertising, Plate, Dinner, Coon's Corner, Oxford Jct., No. 29 .... 350.00
Apple, Baker, Cover, No. 54 .... 225.00
Apple, Baker, Cover, No. 66 .... 125.00
Apple, Baker, Cover, No. 115 .... 115.00
Apple, Baker, No. 95 .... 55.00
Apple, Bean Pot, No. 76 .... 35.00 to 60.00
Apple, Bean Pot, No. 502 .... 900.00
Apple, Bowl, 2-Leaf, No. 5 .... 75.00
Apple, Bowl, 2-Leaf, No. 7 .... 25.00
Apple, Bowl, 2-Leaf, No. 8 .... 75.00
Apple, Bowl, 2-Leaf, No. 55 .... 45.00
Apple, Bowl, Grease Jar, Cover, No. 1 .... 60.00 to 105.00
Apple, Bowl, Plate, Dinner, No. 29 .... 300.00
Apple, Bowl, Ribbed, No. 6 .... 23.00
Apple, Bowl, Salad, No. 73 .... *illus* 75.00
Apple, Bowl, Soup, Flat, Green Band, No. 44 .... 110.00
Apple, Bowl, Spaghetti, Slant Sided, No. 39 .... 70.00 to 165.00
Apple, Canister, 2-Leaf Cover, No. 84 .... 425.00
Apple, Casserole, Cover, No. 2/48 .... 255.00
Apple, Casserole, Cover, No. 3/19 .... 195.00
Apple, Casserole, Cover, Tab Handles, No. 18 .... 100.00
Apple, Cheese Crock, Cover, No. 80 .... 20.00
Apple, Chop Plate, No. 49 .... 205.00
Apple, Coffee Carafe, Knob Cover, No. 115 .... 2100.00 to 4000.00
Apple, Cookie Jar, No. 21 .... 175.00
Apple, Cookie Jar, No. 503 .... *illus* 210.00
Apple, Creamer, 2-Leaf, No. 62 .... 135.00
Apple, Mixing Bowl, 2-Leaf, No. 64 .... 74.00
Apple, Mixing Bowl, 3-Leaf, No. 8 .... 94.00
Apple, Mixing Bowl, No. 61 .... 105.00
Apple, Mixing Bowl, No. 63 .... 70.00
Apple, Mixing Bowl, No. 64 .... 110.00
Apple, Mug, No. 121 .... 115.00
Apple, Pitcher, 2-Leaf, No. 15 .... 140.00
Apple, Pitcher, 2-Leaf, No. 16 .... 140.00
Apple, Pitcher, 3-Leaf, No. 15 .... 45.00 to 60.00
Apple, Pitcher, 3-Leaf, No. 16 .... 60.00
Apple, Platter, No. 31 .... 95.00
Apple, Salt & Pepper, No. 117 & 118 .... 130.00
Apple, Teapot, No. 505 .... 4700.00
Autumn Foliage, Bowl, No. 5 .... 13.00 to 57.00
Autumn Foliage, Creamer, No. 62 .... 235.00
Autumn Foliage, Pie Plate, Advertising, B & B Co-Op Oil Co., Waverly, Iowa, 9 In. 115.00
Autumn Foliage, Pitcher, No. 15 .... 30.00
Autumn Foliage, Pitcher, No. 16 .... 65.00
Basket Weave, Bean Pot, Brown, No. 76, Oven Ware, 10 In. 17.00
Basket Weave, Mixing Bowl, Blue, No. 5 .... 20.00
Brown-Banded, Creamer, No. 62 .... 525.00
Brown-Banded, Sugar, Cover, No. 98 .... 200.00
Brownstone, Bowl, Green, No. 5 .... 5.00
Brownstone, Creamer, Blue, No. 62 .... 265.00
Brownstone, Cup, Bean, Blue, No. 75 .... 5.00
Brownstone, Pitcher, Blue, No. 15 .... 105.00
Butterfly, Bowl, No. 5 .... 775.00
Butterfly, Ice Bucket, No. 59 .... 475.00
Butterfly, Pitcher, No. 16 .... 375.00
Cherry, Bowl, No. 54 .... 105.00
Cherry, Pitcher, No. 15 .... 175.00

Cherry, Pitcher, No. 16 .... 85.00
Cherry, Salt, No. 45 .... 45.00
Corn Row, Pitcher, Rose, No. 15 .... 40.00
Cross-Hatch Pansy, Bowl, No. 6 .... 100.00
Cross-Hatch Pansy, Bowl, No. 7 .... 90.00
Cross-Hatch Pansy, Bowl, No. 8 .... 75.00
Cross-Hatch Pansy, Bowl, No. 9 .... 85.00
Cross-Hatch Pansy, Pie Plate, No. 33 .... 20.00
Cross-Hatch Pansy, Platter, No. 31 .... 135.00
Diamonds, Bowl, Brown, 4 ½ In. 28.00
Double Apple, Bowl, Ribbed, No. 05 .... 75.00
Double Apple, Bowl, Ribbed, No. 06 .... 105.00
Double Apple, Creamer, No. 15 .... 66.00
Double Apple, Creamer, No. 62 .... 66.00
Dutch Tulip, Bowl, Rimmed, No. 05 .... 115.00
Dutch Tulip, Pitcher, No. 16 .... 180.00
Dutch Tulip, Pitcher, No. 62 .... 175.00
Dutch Tulip, Salt, Barrel, No. 45 .... 283.00
Eagle, Bowl, Ribbed, No. 5 .... 200.00
Kolor Kraft, Bowl, Lip, Shoulder, Blue, No. 6 .... 20.00
Kolor Kraft, Bowl, Lip, Shoulder, Gray, No. 8 .... 15.00
Kolor Kraft, Bowl, Lip, Shoulder, Rose, No. 7 .... 15.00 to 18.00
Kolor Kraft, Bowl, Lip, Shoulder, Turquoise, No. 8 .... 18.00
Kolor Kraft, Bowl, Shoulder, White, No. 5 .... 13.00
Morning Glory, Cookie Jar, Embossed Flowers, Lattice, 1958, 10 ¾ In. .... *illus* 338.00
Morning Glory, Quilted, Bowl, No. 5 .... 45.00
Old Pansy, Platter, No. 31 .... 50.00
Pansy, Bowl, Cut-Leaf, No. 4 .... 13.00
Pansy, Bowl, Cut-Leaf, No. 5 .... 13.00
Pansy, Bowl, Raised, No. 5 .... 85.00
Pansy, Cup & Saucer, Cut-Leaf, Jumbo 80.00
Pansy, Pitcher, Cut-Leaf, No. 15 .... 195.00
Pansy, Plate, Dinner, Cut-Leaf 70.00
Pansy, Plate, Spaghetti, Cut-Leaf 12.00
Pedeeco, Bean Cups, 4 In., 3 Piece 11.00
Rio Rose, see Pansy
Rooster, Baker, Tab Handles, No. 85 .... *illus* 716.00
Rooster, Creamer, No. 62 .... 175.00
Rooster, Pitcher, No. 15 .... 165.00 to 175.00
Rooster, Pitcher, No. 16 .... 195.00
Starflower, Bowl, Open, No. 52 .... 18.00
Starflower, Bowl, Rimmed, No. 5 .... 35.00
Starflower, Bowl, Spaghetti, No. 39 .... 75.00
Starflower, Creamer, No. 62 .... 305.00
Starflower, Mug, No. 121 .... 225.00
Starflower, Pitcher, No. 15 .... 85.00
Starflower, Pitcher, No. 16 .... 70.00
Starflower, Pitcher, No. 17 .... 90.00
Starflower, Sugar, 2 Handles, No. 35 .... 525.00
Starflower, Tumbler, Round-Sided, No. 56 .... 110.00
Starflower, Tumbler, Slant-Sided, No. 56 .... 200.00
Teardrop, Creamer, No. 62 .... 300.00
Teardrop, Pitcher, No. 15 .... 15.00 to 74.00
Teardrop, Pitcher, No. 16 .... 105.00
Tulip, Bowl, Salad, No. 73 .... 300.00
Tulip, Pitcher, No. 15 .... 475.00
Tulip, Pitcher, No. 16 .... 115.00
White Daisy, Bowl, No. 5 .... 165.00

WAVE CREST glass is an opaque white glassware manufactured by the Pairpoint Manufacturing Company of New Bedford, Massachusetts, and some French factories. It was decorated by the C.F. Monroe Company of Meriden, Connecticut. The glass was painted in pastel colors and decorated with flowers. The name Wave Crest was used after 1898.

WAVE CREST WARE

Biscuit Jar, Blue & Cream, Pink Flowers, Silver Plate Cover & Bail, 6 ½ In. 60.00
Biscuit Jar, Egg Crate Mold, Pink Flowers, Yellow Ground, Metal Cover, Handle, 5 x 8 In. 138.00
Biscuit Jar, Pansies, Metal Cover & Bail, 8 ½ x 6 In. .... *illus* 165.00
Biscuit Jar, Pink, Purple Flower Panels, Raised Scrolls, Silver Plate Collar, Handle, Cover, 10 In. 90.00

Watt, Morning Glory, Cookie Jar, Embossed Flowers, Lattice, 1958, 10 ¾ In.
$338.00

Watt, Rooster, Baker, Tab Handles, No. 85
$716.00

Wave Crest, Biscuit Jar, Pansies, Metal Cover & Bail, 8 ½ x 6 In.
$165.00

TIP

An old Staffordshire or majolica pitcher has a small hole inside where the handle meets the body. A new pitcher will not have this hole but will often have a large hole in the base.

Wave Crest, Dresser Box, Puffy Mold, Blue, White, Round, 7 x 4 In.
$354.00

Wave Crest, Humidor, Enameled Brass, Cigars, Purple, Marked, 6 ¾ x 6 ¾ In.
$275.00

Wave Crest, Humidor, Swirl Mold, Flowers, Metal Cover & Clasp, 5 x 7 In.
$248.00

Wave Crest, Vase, Flowers, Metal Base, Wings, Marked, 12 x 9 ½ x 6 In.
$250.00

Biscuit Jar, Swirl Mold, White, Flowers, Silver Plate Cover & Bail, 7 In.. . . . . 210.00
Biscuit Jar, White & Yellow, Scroll, Square, Pink Flowers, Silver Plate Cover & Bail, 7 In. 100.00
Biscuit Jar, Yellow, Purple Flowers, Yellow Ground, Metal Cover & Bail, 5 x 8 In.. . . . . 177.00
Box, Baroque, Shell, Mold, Pink & Blue Flowers, Hinged Cover, Marked, 3 x 5 ¼ In.. . . . . 150.00
Box, Collars & Cuffs, Egg Crate Mold, Flowers, Mauve Lettering, Brass Band, 6 ½ x 6 In. 518.00
Box, Glove, Cobalt Blue, Enameled Flowers, Blown-Out Cover, Blue Satin Lining, 9 ¾ x 4 In. . 3220.00
Box, Pink Rose, Yellow, 4-Footed Metal Base, Signed, 9 ½ In. 748.00
Card Holder, Scroll Mold, Pink Flowers, White Ground, Signed, 2 ½ x 4 In.. . . . . 70.00
Cigar Box, Egg Crate Mold, Gold Lettering, Flowers, 7 x 5 In.. . . . . 440.00
Cigar Holder, Match Holders At Sides, Blue Flowers, Cream Ground, Metal Frame, 4 x 8 In.. . 460.00
Cracker Barrel, Raspberry, Daisies, Gold Letters, Gilt Metal Bail, Rim, 7 ½ In. 2875.00
Dish, Swirl Mold, Gold Ormolu Rim & Handles, Flowers, 5 ½ In.. . . . . 80.00
Dish, Swirl Mold, White, Flowers, Brass Rim & Handles, Marked, 5 ½ In. 260.00
Dresser Box, Blue Flowers, Yellow Ground, Rectangle, 7 x 3 In. 55.00
Dresser Box, Glass, 3 Sitting Ladies, Hinged, C. F. Monroe Co., 3 ½ x 6 In.. . . . . 292.00
Dresser Box, Green Daisy, Blue Ground, Satin Lining, Round, 6 x 5 In.. . . . . 330.00
Dresser Box, Helmschmied Swirl Mold, Blue Flowers, Oval, 6 ½ In.. . . . . 259.00
Dresser Box, Helmschmied Swirl Mold, Flowers, Round, 7 In.. . . . . 300.00
Dresser Box, Pink Flowers, Round, Lining, Marked, 3 ¾ x 6 In. 185.00
Dresser Box, Puffy Mold, Blue, White, Round, 7 x 4 In.. . . . . *illus* 354.00
Dresser Box, Swirl Mold, Yellow Daisy Mum, Round, 6 x 5 In.. . . . . 177.00
Dresser Box, Swirl Mold, Yellow Tones, Pink Flowers, Gilt Metal Feet, 6 x 7 In. 175.00
Ewer, Gilt Spout, Handle & Base, Yellow Body, Flowers, Pedestal, 13 In.. . . . . 75.00
Fernery, Egg Crate Mold, Cream, Blue Flowers, 3 ¼ x 6 ½ In.. . . . . 50.00 to 92.00
Humidor, Enameled Brass, Cigars, Purple, Marked, 6 ¾ x 6 ¾ In. . . . . *illus* 275.00
Humidor, Pink Flowers, Marked, 6 ¼ In.. . . . . 400.00
Humidor, Swirl Mold, Flowers, Metal Cover & Clasp, 5 x 7 In. . . . . *illus* 248.00
Jewelry Box, Puff & Scroll Mold, Cream, Cherubs, Oval Hinged Cover, 4 In.. . . . . 120.00
Lamp, Kerosene, Barn Scene, 11 In.. . . . . 150.00
Letter Holder, Egg Crate Mold, Pink, White, Fern, Brass Rim, 4 x 5 ¾ In.. . . . . 200.00
Match Holder, Scrolls, Flowers, Enameled, Metal Frame, 4 x 4 ¼ In.. . . . . 50.00
Napkin Holder, Clovers, Footed, Marked, 7 In. 325.00
Napkin Holder, Clovers, Ormolu, Footed, 6 In.. . . . . 125.00
Pin Dish, Blown Out, White, Flowers, Metal Cover, Marked, 4 ¼ x 1 ¾ In.. . . . . 60.00
Pin Dish, Blue Flowers, White Ground, Round, 3 ½ In. 50.00
Pin Tray, Light Blue, Flowers, 4 In.. . . . . 50.00
Planter, Scroll Mold, Cartouche, Flowers, Marked, 6 x 3 In.. . . . . 180.00
Powder Jar, Bird Perched On Branch, Flowers, 4 ½ x 7 x 7 In.. . . . . 345.00
Powder Pot, Flowers, Metal Rim, Handles, 1 ½ x 4 ½ In.. . . . . 10.00
Trinket Box, Pink Flowers, Embossed Ruffles, Mirror In Cover, Marked, 4 ¾ x 4 In. 125.00
Urn, Courting Couple, Flowers, Melon Rib Bed, Lion Masks, Spelter Top, Base, 15 ¼ In., Pair . 200.00
Vase, Flowers, Metal Base, Handles, Marked, 10 x 12 In.. . . . . 295.00
Vase, Flowers, Metal Base, Wings, Marked, 12 x 9 ½ x 6 In. . . . . *illus* 250.00
Vase, Green, White, Flowers, Border Trim, Marked, 4 ¼ In.. . . . . 70.00
Vase, Pink Daisies, Plum Ground, Metal Base, Wings, Top, 10 x 12 In.. 1045.00
Vase, Pink Flowers, Pale Green Ground, Metal Base, Rim, Wings, 7 x 6 In. 354.00
Vase, Scroll Mold, Blue & White, Pink Flowers, 9 ¼ In.. . . . . 100.00
Vase, White Flowers, Ground, Long Neck, Metal Rim, Footed Base, Wings, 3 x 10 In. 118.00
Whiskbroom Holder, Blue, Scrolling Ormolu, Wall Mount, Oval, c.1890, 10 In.. . . . . 885.00

WEATHER VANES were used in seventeenth-century Boston. The direction of the wind was an indication of coming weather, important to the seafaring and farming communities. By the mid-nineteenth century, commercial weather vanes were made of metal. Today's collectors often consider weather vanes to be examples of folk art, even though they may not have been handmade.

Arrow, Banner, Wood, Iron, Zinc, Paint, Gilt, Late 1800s, 18 x 68 In.. . . . . 3851.00
Arrow & Globe, Copper, Gold Gilt, Metal Stand, 57 In.. . . . . 805.00
Buccaneer, Copper, Directionals, Wood Base, 19th Century, 32 x 19 In. 200.00
Car, Roadster, Sheet Metal, Hood Ornament, Black Alligatored, 29 ¾ x 17 ½ In.. . . . . 294.00
Codfish, Copper, Wood Base, Late 19th Century, 5 ½ x 18 In.. . . . . 2200.00
Colonel Sanders, KFC, Painted, Metal, 2-Sided, 1950-60, 5 x 3 Ft. . . . . *illus* 288.00
Cow, Bullet Holes, Board Mounted, Milk Glass Lightning Ball, c.1900, 21 x 9 ½ In. 575.00
Cow, Copper, Cast Zinc Horns, Verdigris Patina, Gilt, c.1880, 19 In. 9988.00
Cow, Name, 2-Directional Arrow, Copper, Iron, Sheet Metal, Cone Stand, c.1925, 34 x 32 In.. . 333.00
Deer, Running, Tin, Hollow, Directionals, 37 In.. . . . . 234.00
Dragon, Flying, Cutout, Silhouette, Sheet Metal, Hollow Post, 34 x 19 In.. . . . . 633.00
Eagle, Ball, Copper, Verdigris, Metal Stand, 21 x 24 In.. . . . . 3240.00

W

Eagle, Copper, Full-Bodied, Spread Wings, Green Verdigris, 18 x 20 In. 288.00
Eagle, Full-Bodied, Copper, Zinc, Perched On Ball, Directional, c.1925, 29 ½ In. 1410.00
Eagle, Spread Wings, Arrow, Ball, Molded Copper, Gilt, Verdigris, 22 x 31 In. 1896.00
Eagle, Spread Wings, Copper, Directionals, Cupola, 53 x 22 In. 650.00
Eagle, Spread Wings, Copper, Gilt, Directional, Early 20th Century, 28 x 17 In. 1500.00
Eagle, Spread Wings, Open Beak, Ball, Arrow, Copper, Zinc, 28 x 38 In. 3450.00
Fire Horn, Copper, Ball, Shaft, Stand, 1800s, 28 x 51 In. 3555.00
Fish, Sheet Metal, Gold Paint, Stand, 20th Century, 33 ¾ In. 881.00
Fox, Running, Pierced Eye, Sheet Iron, 10 ½ x 38 In. 1150.00
Game Cock, Arched Head, Copper, 28 ½ x 17 In. 3738.00
Goose, In Flight, Figural, Copper, Directionals, 20 x 29 In. 300.00
Horse, Blackhawk, Copper, Full-Bodied, Zinc Ears, Verdigris, Gilding, 26 x 17 In. 4600.00
Horse, Jockey, Copper, Full-Bodied, 18 ½ x 32 x 4 ¾ In. 4025.00
Horse, Jockey, Copper, Gilt, 32 In. 10350.00
Horse, Jumping In Hoop, Full-Bodied, Copper, Cast Zinc Head, Verdigris, 23 x 31 In. 21150.00
Horse, Leaping, Full-Bodied, Cutout Eyes, Copper, 1895, 25 In. 1525.00
Horse, Lexington, Molded Sheet Copper, Cast Iron, Mass., c.1890, 27 x 33 In. 14950.00
Horse, Prancing, Full-Bodied, Bannerette, Gilt, 23 ½ x 21 ½ In. 403.00
Horse, Racing, Cutout, Sheet Metal, Modern Stand, Blackhawk, c.1890, 19 x 26 In. 470.00
Horse, Running, Copper, 17 x 32 In. 825.00
Horse, Running, Copper, Gilt, Steel Base, Late 19th Century, 13 x 25 x 1 ¾ In. 550.00
Horse, Running, Copper, Molded, Harris & Co., Mass., 1880s, 20 x 26 In. 3081.00
Horse, Running, Copper, White Paint, Directionals, Late 1800s, 18 x 31 In. 2000.00
Horse, Running, Copper, Zinc, Arrow Mount, c.1875, 18 x 47 In. 7500.00
Horse, Running, Copper, Zinc, Gilt, Iron Base, Late 19th Century, 16 x 30 x 2 ¾ In. 800.00
Horse, Running, Copper, Zinc, Green, Stand, J.W. Frske Co., N.Y., c.1890, 19 x 34 In. 6325.00
Horse, Running, Cutout, Bronze, Arrow Directional, Metal Base, c.1900, 54 In. 764.00
Horse, Running, Cutout, Silhouette, Sheet Metal, Black Paint Over Red, 21 x 28 In. 352.00
Horse, Running, Embossed Tail, Mane, Jewell & Co., Mass., c.1875, 11 x 25 In. 7705.00
Horse, Running, Full-Bodied, Copper, Cast Zinc Head, Black Overpaint, c.1875, 19 x 28 In. 5581.00
Horse, Running, Full-Bodied, Copper, Verdigris Patina, Late 1800s, 12 ½ x 24 In. 705.00
Horse, Running, Light Green, Patina, Zinc Head, Wood Support, 1890s, 10 x 15 In. 1400.00
Horse, Running, Yellow, Patchen, c.1880, 20 ½ x 44 In. 2340.00
Horse, Running, Zinc, White Paint, Directionals, Steel Pipe Stand, 38 x 31 In. 250.00
Horse, Standing, Perked Ears, Cropped Tail, Sheet Iron, Painted, Black, White, 54 x 32 In. 460.00
Horse, Sulky, Copper, Wood Plinth, 37 In. 413.00
Horse, Sulky, St. Julien, Copper, Cast Iron, 22 x 39 In. 46800.00
Horse, Trotting, Blue Milk Glass Lightning Ball, Board Mount, c.1900, 35 In. 143.00
Horse, Trotting, Copper, Metal Stand, 4 Bullet Holes, 28 x 18 In. 1380.00
Horse, Trotting, Copper, Verdigris, Zinc Head, 19 ½ x 39 ½ In. 2300.00
Horse, Trotting, On Sulky, Copper, Full-Bodied, Mottled, Verdigris, 18 ½ x 35 In. 1035.00
Horse, Trotting, Zinc Head, Copper Body, Green Patina, Directionals, 30 In. 2000.00
Horse, Walking, Tail Up, Sheet Iron, White Paint, 19 x 27 In. 375.00
Horse & Sulky, Copper, 30 In. 489.00
Indian, Standing, Bow & Arrow, Iron, Directional, Green Paint, 44 x 46 In. .... *illus* 978.00
Indian, Standing In Canoe, Holding Spear, Metal, Wood Post, Painted, 55 ½ In. 2600.00
Miss Liberty, Holding Flag, Arm Outstretched, Copper, 69 x 53 In. 58500.00
Pig, Full-Bodied, Copper, Applied Verdigris Patina, Late 1900s, 17 x 28 In. .... *illus* 823.00
Pig, Verdigris, Gilt, Cast Zinc Tail, 19th Century, 19 x 37 In. 14000.00
Putti, Dancing, Iron, Multicolored, 25 In. 1680.00
Ram, Molded Copper, 28 In. 49000.00
Rooster, Cast Iron, Copper Tail, Paint, Rochester Ironworks, 1800s, 32 x 34 In. 13000.00
Rooster, Cast Iron, Sheet Metal, c.1880, 31 x 34 ½ In. 6900.00
Rooster, Copper, Metal Stand, Washburne & Co., New York, c.1920, 23 x 19 In. 3450.00
Rooster, Crowing, Cutout Tail, Copper, Patina, Post, 35 In. 1880.00
Rooster, Cutout Wood, White, Mustard Paint, c.1900, 25 x 20 In. 326.00
Rooster, Embossed Feathers, Half-Body, Copper, Arrow, 19th Century, 29 ½ In. 200.00
Rooster, Embossed Tail, Cut Sheet, Copper, Metal Stand, J.W. Friske, 32 x 24 In. 14950.00
Rooster, Milk Glass Lightning Ball, Board Mount, c.1900, 32 In. 575.00
Rooster, Outstretched Wings, Arrow, Molded Copper, Mounted, 1800s, 23 x 22 In. 7703.00
Rooster, Pine, Copper, Painted, 30 x 34 In. 2070.00
Rooster, Sheet Iron, 19th Century, 23 x 23 In. 1760.00
Rooster, Sheet Iron, Directionals, 36 x 60 In. .... *illus* 1094.00
Rooster, Sheet Metal, Iron Tripod Base, 20th Century, 64 In. 360.00
Rooster, Swell-Bodied, Copper, Yellow & Verdigris, Late 19th Century, 26 In. 3400.00
Rooster, Zinc, Crimped Copper Tail, Legs, Base, A.J. Howard & Co., c.1875, 24 In. 7931.00
Sailing Ship, Wood, c.1900, 39 x 27 In. 646.00
Sea Captain, Wood Peg Leg, Telescope, Sheet Metal, 1930s, 28 x 17 In. 395.00

Weather Vane, Colonel Sanders, KFC, Painted, Metal, 2-Sided, 1950-60, 5 x 3 Ft.
$288.00

Weather Vane, Indian, Standing, Bow & Arrow, Iron, Directional, Green Paint, 44 x 46 In.
$978.00

Weather Vane, Pig, Full-Bodied, Copper, Applied Verdigris Patina, Late 1900s, 17 x 28 In.
$823.00

Weather Vane, Rooster, Sheet Iron, Directionals, 36 x 60 In.
$1094.00

Weather Vane, Stag, Leaping, Copper Molded, Gilt, Rod, Stand, Late 1800s, 29 x 24 In.
$7703.00

Webb, Jar, Potpourri, Pierced Cover, Pink Flowers, Green Vines, Gold Scrolls, Opal, 1890s, 6 In.
$330.00

Webb, Nut Dish, Alexandrite, Handkerchief Shape, Ruffled Rim, 2 In.
$945.00

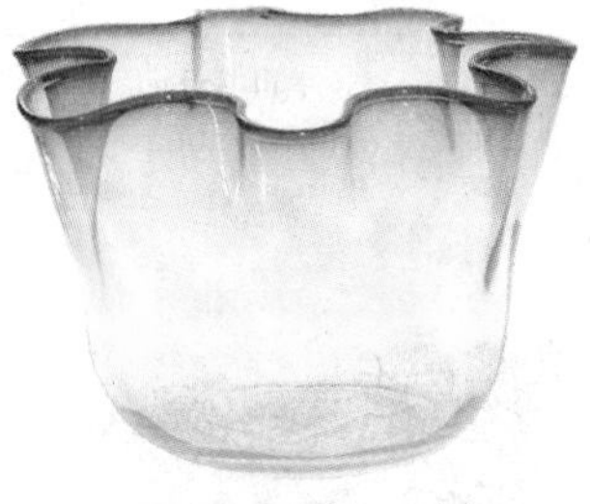

Webb, Vase, Rose, Flowers, Frosted Foot, Scroll Handles, 4 ¼ x 3 In.
$1800.00

Sheep, Iron, Zinc, 21 ¼ In. 850.00
Ship, Wood, Painted, Copper Sails, 20th Century, 28 x 23 In. 316.00
Snake, Tongue Out, Hand-Forged Metal, Black Paint, 1900s, 11 x 32 ½ In. 10000.00
Soldier, Holding Rifle, Black, Sheet Iron, Late 19th Century, 33 ¾ In. 1989.00
Stag, Leaping, Applied Zinc Head, Antlers, 30 In. 9200.00
Stag, Leaping, Copper Gilt, Zinc Head, Connecticut, 30 In. 9200.00
Stag, Leaping, Copper Molded, Gilt, Rod, Stand, Late 1800s, 29 x 24 In. .... *illus* 7703.00
Touring Car, Pierced, Cutout, Gilt Sheet Copper, Brass Rod, c.1900, 11 x 24 In. 5925.00
Winged Corncob, Dekalb, Tin Lithograph, 23 In. 40.00

WEBB glass was made by Thomas Webb & Sons of Ambelcot, England. Many types of art and cameo glass were made by them during the Victorian era. Production ceased by 1991 and the factory was demolished in 1995. Webb Burmese and Webb Peachblow are special colored glasswares of the Victorian era. They are listed at the end of this section. Glassware that is not Burmese or Peachblow is included here.

Webb

Bottle, Scent, Frosted, White Over Pink Vine, Morning Glories, Butterfly, Oval, 6 ½ In. 1668.00
Bride's Bowl, Pigeon Blood, Ruffled Rim, Silver Plate Frame, Scrolling, 11 x 9 ¾ In. 161.00
Bride's Bowl, Pink, Melon Ribbed, Herringbone, Yellow Cased, Ruffled Rim, 5 x 10 In. 2115.00
Bride's Bowl, Pink Herringbone, Flowers, Yellow Cased, Ruffled Rim, 4 ½ x 10 In. 1116.00
Celery Vase, Blue, White Blossoms, Satin Ruffled Rim, Handles, Metal Caddy, 8 In. 345.00
Compote, Amethyst, Undulating Waves, Flared Spreading Rim, Signed, 9 In. .... 86.00 to 100.00
Dish, Sweatmeat, Butterflies, Rose, Round, Cameo, Metal Rim, Handle, Lid, 5 In. 1200.00
Ewer, Satin, Amber Rigaree Collar, Faceted Stopper, Egg Shape, 10 In. 230.00
Jar, Potpourri, Pierced Cover, Pink Flowers, Green Vines, Gold Scrolls, Opal, 1890s, 6 In. *illus* 330.00
Lamp, Oil, Red Cameo Satin Glass, White Ivy Shade, Flowered Base, Signed, 8 In. 8050.00
Lamp Base, Cascading Gingko Branches, Butterflies, Oval, Cameo, 5 ½ In. 374.00
Muffineer, Pink Mother-Of-Pearl, Yellow Coralene Seaweed, Silver Plate Lid, 4 In. 460.00
Nut Dish, Alexandrite, Handkerchief Shape, Ruffled Rim, 2 In. .... *illus* 945.00
Perfume Bottle, Cream, Gold Enameled, Brown, Green Palm, Bamboo, Bulbous Stick, 6 ½ In. 201.00
Perfume Bottle, Intaglio, White, Yellow Backing, Flowers, Spider Reverse, 1 ⅞ In. 3278.00
Perfume Bottle, Tree Bark, Intertwined Chinese Rampant Dragon, Leaves, Oval, Cameo, 5 In. 230.00
Perfume Bottle, White Flowers, Ruby Ground, Cameo Leaves, Gold Plate Lid, 4 ½ In. 4600.00
Pitcher, Egret, In Marsh, Blown, Engraved, Ruffled Top, Blown Handle, 9 x 5 In. 425.00
Vase, Cased Yellow, Red Over White Vines, Bulbous Bottle Shape, Cameo, 3 In. 1035.00
Vase, Cobalt Blue, Birds, Signed, 5 ½ In. 40.00
Vase, Cranberry, White Flowers, Leaves, Bulbous, Cameo, 1900, 5 ¼ In. 2000.00
Vase, Flowers, Brown & Ivory, Cameo, Signed, 6 ¼ In. 550.00
Vase, Flowers, Leaves, Yellow, Red, White, Slender Neck, Cameo, 8 ½ x 4 In. 3600.00
Vase, Flowers, Red, White, Footed, Scroll Handles, Cameo, 4 ½ In. 1000.00
Vase, Flowers, White Over Citron, Tall Neck, Gourd Shape, Cameo, 12 ¼ x 5 In. 1200.00
Vase, Green, Gold Stemmed Flowers, Insects, Lemon Yellow Cased, Satin, Footed, Urn Shape, 12 In. 86.00
Vase, Leaf Vines, Pink, White, Cameo, 7 ¼ In. 700.00
Vase, Maroon Grouped, Gold Bird & Branch, Cameo, 8 ½ In. 160.00
Vase, Morning Glories, Butterfly, Citron, Cameo, 5 ½ In. 1150.00
Vase, Red, White Butterfly, Morning Glory, Leaves, Citron Ground, Shouldered, Cameo, 6 In. . 4025.00
Vase, Rose, Flowers, Frosted Foot, Scroll Handles, 4 ¼ x 3 In. .... *illus* 1800.00
Vase, Stick, Flowers, Leaves, Bee, Butterflies, Citron, Bulbous Base, Cameo, 13 In. 5248.00
Vase, Stick, Green Satin, Bird, Fern, Signed, 10 ¼ In. 175.00
Vase, Stick, Red, Birds, Flowers, Gold Enameled, White Interior, Bulbous Base, 9 ½ In. 140.00
Vase, Stick, White Over Red, Cascading Stem, Butterfly, Flared Rim, Bulbous Base, 5 In. 1380.00
Vase, White Cascading Flower, Butterfly, Oval, Rose Ground, Cameo, 2 In. 920.00
Vase, White Flowers, Butterflies, Blue Ground, Cameo, 9 In. 2040.00
Vase, White Leaves, Red Ground, Cameo, 4 ¼ In. 150.00
Vase, White Over Red Leafy Fuchsia, Butterfly, Yellow, 5 ¼ In. .... *illus* 1400.00
Vase, Yellow, Bird, Blossom, Handles, Pedestal, 8 ¼ In. 70.00
Vase, Yellow, Cascading Morning Glories, Butterflies, Cameo, 6 ½ In. 805.00
Whimsy, Mushroom, Optic Ribbed, Amber, Fuchsia, Blue, 3 In. 1725.00

WEBB BURMESE is a colored Victorian glass made by Thomas Webb & Sons of Stourbridge, England, from 1886.

Biscuit Jar, Red Primrose, Green Stem, Satin, Egg Shape, 7 In. 288.00
Condiment Set, Enameled Butterflies, Flowers, Caddy, 7 In. 1265.00
Fairy Lamp, 4 In. 180.00
Fairy Lamp, Acid Domed Shade, Upturned Ruffles Base, Signed, 6 x 7 In. 403.00
Fairy Lamp, Clarke Insert, 5 ½ In. 518.00
Fairy Lamp, Double Clear Insert, Footed, Signed, 6 In. 2300.00
Fairy Lamp, Ruffled Foot, S Clarke Insert, 6 In. 575.00

Lamp, Oil, Peach, Pink, Yellow, Enamel Branch, Bird Base, 9 In. 2300.00
Rose, Bowl, Prunus, Hexagonal Mouth, 4 In. 125.00
Tumbler, Whiskey, Barrel Shape, Enameled, 2 ⅝ In. 1639.00
Vase, Applied Leaf, Crimped Rim, 2 ½ In. 345.00
Vase, Bud, Star Shape, Flared Rim, Footed, 4 In. 100.00
Vase, Bulbous, Star Shape Rim, Red Flowering Branch, 3 In. 259.00
Vase, Enameled Red Raspberries, Footed, Egg Shape, Cupped, 3 ½ In. 316.00
Vase, Gold, Orange Leaves, Red Enameled Border, Bulbous, 12 In. 2130.00
Vase, Hawthorne, Ruffled Rim, 3-Footed Metal Stand, 7 ½ In. 259.00
Vase, Lavender Blue Flowers, 3 In. 173.00
Vase, Lavender Flowers, Leaves, Egg Shape, Piecrust Base, 4 In. 374.00
Vase, Prunus Blossoms, Ruffled Edge, Footed, 4 In., Pair 374.00
Vase, Ribbed, Tricornered, 6 In. 230.00
Vase, Rose Bowl, Enameled Hawthorne, Flared Rim, 3 In. 201.00
Vase, Stick, Cascading Green Leaves, Signed, 8 In. 403.00

WEBB PEACHBLOW is a colored Victorian glass made by Thomas Webb & Sons of Stourbridge, England, from 1885.

Biscuit Jar, Gingko Flowers, Oval, Moorish Lid, 7 ½ In. 604.00
Biscuit Jar, Song Birds On Branches, Oval, 6 In. 175.00
Bride's Basket, Green, Quilted, Multicolored Flowers, Butterflies, 13 In. 472.00
Vase, Double Gourd, Seaweed Coralene, Signed, 7 In. 282.00
Vase, Hobnail, Ruffled Edge, Amber Petal Feet, Satin, 6 In. 200.00

WEDGWOOD, one of the world's most successful potteries, was founded by Josiah Wedgwood, who was considered a cripple by his brother and was forbidden to work at the family business. The pottery was established in England in 1759. A large variety of wares has been made, including the well-known jasperware, basalt, creamware, and even a limited amount of porcelain. There are two kinds of jasperware. One is made from two colors of clay, the other is made from one color of clay with a color dip to create the contrast in design. In 1986 Wedgwood and Waterford Crystal merged to form the Waterford Wedgwood Group. Most Waterford Wedgwood assets were bought by KPS Capital Partners of New York in 2009 and became part of WWRD Holdings. Some manufacturing will be transferred to Germany, Indonesia, and Slovakia. Other Wedgwood pieces may be listed under Flow Blue, Majolica, Tea Leaf Ironstone, or in other porcelain categories.

WEDGWOOD

Ashtray, Jasperware, Blue, Muses Watering Pegasus, Grapevine Border, 4 ½ In. 36.00
Ashtray, Queen's Ware, Jasperware, Blue, Raised White Leaf Edge, 3 ⅝ In. 12.00
Barber Bottle, Cover, Jasperware, White Ground, Lilac, Green, Late 1800s, 10 In. 2350.00
Basket, Majolica, Putti, Oval, Bamboo Edge Base, c.1876, 14 ½ In. 5200.00
Biscuit Barrel, Cover, Jasper Dip, Yellow, Tapered Foot, Applied Black Muses, 5 ½ In. 356.00
Biscuit Barrel, Jasperware, Blue, Handle, Silver Plate Lid, 5 ½ x 5 ¼ In. 111.00
Biscuit Barrel, Jasperware, Classical Figures, Dark Blue, Silver Plate Lid, Handle, 6 In. 53.00
Biscuit Barrel, Jasperware, Dark Blue, Classical Figures, Marked, 9 x 7 In. 190.00
Biscuit Barrel, Jasperware, Moss Green, 19th Century, 8 x 5 In. 176.00
Biscuit Jar, Jasper Dip, Blue, Sacrifice Figures, Silver Plated Fittings, Handle, 9 In. 358.00
Biscuit Jar, Jasperware, Blue, Silver Plate Frame, c.1880, 6 x 5 ½ In. 117.00
Biscuit Jar, Pale Blue, White, Sacrifice To Hymen, Hinged Lid, Marked, 1895, 7 ¾ In. 150.00
Biscuit Jar, Stand, Jasper Dip, Blue, Applied White Classical Figures, Acorns, 8 ⅜ In. 178.00
Bough Pot, Jasperware, Blue, Man Between Urns, Paneled, Paw Feet, 8 ½ In. 652.00
Bowl, Argenta, Grape Leaf, Wicker, Oval, 11 ½ In. 104.00
Bowl, Basalt, Engine Turned Ribs, Black, c.1800, 2 ¾ x 5 In. 210.00
Bowl, Black Basalt, Vertical Turned Fluting, Impressed, c.1779, 7 ⅜ In. 593.00
Bowl, Butterflies, Yellow Luster Ground, Gold, Orange, Red, 9 In. 360.00
Bowl, Centerpiece, Jasperware, Blue, 19th Century, 3 ½ x 8 In. 176.00
Bowl, Centerpiece, Jasperware, Moss Green, 20th Century, 5 x 8 ½ In. 88.00
Bowl, Cover, Queen's Ware, Orange, Scrolled Bands, Flowers, Scalloped, c.1879, 11 ¾ In. 1659.00
Bowl, Daventry Luster, Oriental Design, Thorns, Landscape, Red, Yellow Ground, 8 ¼ In. 948.00
Bowl, Dragon, Luster, Mottled Blue Exterior, Pale Blue Interior, 8-Sided, 1920, 9 In. 326.00
Bowl, Dragon, Luster Melba, Brown Mottled To Green, Gilt Dragons, Red Inside, 7 ¾ In. 593.00
Bowl, Fairyland Luster, Boxing Match, Gilt, 8-Sided, 5 x 11 ½ In. .... *illus* 5400.00
Bowl, Fairyland Luster, Daventry, Nizami Pattern, Signed, 5 x 13 In. .... *illus* 32775.00
Bowl, Fairyland Luster, Daventry, Oriental Design, Medallion, Mottled Orange, Red, 6 ½ In. 770.00
Bowl, Fairyland Luster, Iridescent Blue & Purple Interior, Gilt, 8-Sided, 3 x 4 ¾ In. 288.00
Bowl, Fairyland Luster, Leapfrogging Elves, Z4968, c.1920, 2 ½ x 4 ¾ In. 1638.00
Bowl, Fairyland Luster, Warriors, Animals, Swags, Lanterns, Black, Gold, Yellow, 9 ¾ In. 1067.00
Bowl, Gold Dragon, Blue Ground, Turquoise Interior Luster, Dragons, 9 In. 403.00
Bowl, Imperial, Fairyland Luster, Poplar Tree, Midnight, Buildings, Bridges, 9 ¼ In. 3795.00
Bowl, Imperial, Fairyland Luster, Willow, Leaf Border, Violet Flowers, 10 In. 3163.00

Wedgwood
The real Wedgwood company run by Josiah Wedgwood is spelled WEDGWOOD. Another English company took advantage of the name by using the mark WEDGEWOOD.

Webb, Vase, White Over Red Leafy Fuchsia, Butterfly, Yellow, 5 ¼ In.
$1400.00

Wedgwood, Bowl, Fairyland Luster, Boxing Match, Gilt, 8-Sided, 5 x 11 ½ In.
$5400.00

Wedgwood, Bowl, Fairyland Luster, Daventry, Nizami Pattern, Signed, 5 x 13 In.
$32775.00

TIP
To remove stains from a glass vase, fill it with a mixture of ammonia and water and let it stand for a few hours.

Wedgwood, Box, Butterfly Luster, Gold Highlights, Orange Interior, Signed, 4 In.
$920.00

Wedgwood, Bust, Mercury, Black Basalt, Impressed, Late 19th Century, 18 In.
$4800.00

Wedgwood, Bust, Rousseau, Black Basalt, Impressed, Wedgwood, Bentley, 6 ½ In.
$770.00

Bowl, Jasper Dip, Black, Dancing Hours, Applied White Classical Figures, Acanthus, 10 ¼ In.. 652.00
Bowl, Jasper Dip, Yellow, Footed, Bulbous, Applied Black Classical Figures, 6 ½ In. 2370.00
Bowl, Jasperware, Blue, Children, Textured Ground, Footed, Polished Interior, 6 ½ In. 4740.00
Bowl, Jasperware, Blue, The Dancing Hours, 1950s, 4 x 10 In. 585.00
Bowl, Jasperware, Green, Footed, 9 In. 32.00
Bowl, Luster, Gilt Birds, Blue Mottled Ground, Orange Mottled Interior, 2 ⅞ x 5 ¾ In. 575.00
Bowl, Potpourri, Jasperware, Blue, 19th Century, 4 In., Pair 439.00
Bowl, Salad, Argenta, Lincoln, Silver Rim, 10 In.. 104.00
Bowl, Salad, Jasperware, Raised Classical Figures, Silver Rim, Fork, Spoon, 4 ½ In.. 120.00
Bowl, Vegetable, Floral Pattern, Mark, 9 ½ x 6 ¾ In. 65.00
Box, Biscuit, Jasperware, Blue Reserve, Silver Plate Cover, 6 ½ In. 204.00
Box, Butterfly Luster, Gold Highlights, Orange Interior, Signed, 4 In. *illus* 920.00
Box, Butterfly Luster, In Flight, Multicolored, Gold, Orange Interior, 4 In.. 575.00
Box, Heart Form, Teal, White Design, 1 ½ x 2 ½ In.. 33.00
Box, Star Form, White Design, Terra-Cotta, 1 ⅜ x 3 ½ In. 33.00
Bucket, Jasperware, Lavender, Classical Figures, Silver Plate Lid, Footed, 7 ½ In.. 330.00
Buckle, Classical Figure, Jasperware, Dark Blue, Steel, Oval, Medallion, 2 ½ x 3 ⅛ In. 948.00
Bust, Mercury, Black Basalt, Impressed, Late 19th Century, 18 In. *illus* 4800.00
Bust, Napoleon, Black Basalt, Tapered Plinth, Flags, Cannons, 19th Century, 8 In.. 474.00
Bust, Rousseau, Black Basalt, Impressed, Wedgwood, Bentley, 6 ½ In. *illus* 770.00
Bust, Rousseau, Black Basalt, Waisted Round Socle, Mark, 1800s, 6 ⅛ In. 415.00
Bust, Sir Isaac Newton, Black Basalt, Waisted Round Socle, Mark, Early 1900s, 9 ¼ In.. 356.00
Candleholder, Black Basalt, Athena, Instrument, Scroll, Pedestal Foot, 5 ¾ In. 60.00
Candleholder, Black Basalt, Nike & Athena, Pedestal Foot, c.1840, 5 In.. 60.00
Candleholder, Black Basalt, Psyche Wounded & Bound By Cupids, c.1840, 5 In. 70.00
Candlestick, Jasper Dip, Lilac, Applied White Classical Medallions, Festoons, 6 In., Pair 1659.00
Candlestick, Jasperware, Blue, Classical Females, Cornucopia, Pedestal, 10 ⅜ In., Pair 2370.00
Candy Box, Jasperware, Blue, Queen's Silver Jubilee, Scalloped Edge, 5 x 2 In.. 65.00
Charger, Bouquet, Flow Blue, Marked, 1846, 16 ½ In. 175.00
Charger, Majolica, Nude Woman On Sea Serpent, Bird On Dolphins, Flowers, 1871, 15 ¼ In.. 444.00
Charger, Marsden Art Ware, Leaves, Flower Branches, Flower Border, c.1884, 16 ¼ In. 563.00
Charger, Queen's Ware, Animals, Black Ground, Purple Panels, Marked, 12 In. *illus* 2200.00
Charger, Queen's Ware, Persian Design, Blue, Green, Enameled, Millicent Taplin, 21 ¾ In. 3911.00
Charger, Silver Luster, Shallow Center, Dark Blue Wash, Enamel Trim, Louise Powell, 16 In.. 3200.00
Charger, Wellesley Bullfinch, Fruit Embossed Border, 10 ¾ In. 75.00
Cheese Keeper, Argenta, Birds & Fans, 3 Rectangular Feet, 9 x 9 In. 633.00
Cheese Keeper, Jasperware, Blue, White, Women Figures, c.1895, 8 x 12 In.. 439.00
Cheese Keeper, Jasperware, c.1900, 7 x 12 ½ In.. 205.00
Cheese Keeper, Jasperware, Green, Women c.1895, 6 x 9 In. 410.00
Cheese Keeper, Majolica, Primrose, Brown, Tan Basket Weave Bottom, 10 In. 633.00
Chess Piece, King, Jasperware, White, Circular Plinth, Impressed, 4 ⅛ In. 593.00
Chess Piece, Queen, Caneware, Circular Plinth, 19th Century, 4 In. 2370.00
Chocolate Pot, Cover, Jasper Dip, Yellow, Classical Relief, 3 ¼ In. 4444.00
Clock, Wall, Jasper Dip, Green, Flower Swags, Lion Masks, Dancers, 12 ¾ x 17 In. 2489.00
Compote, Dragon Luster, Footed, Flared, Mottled Red, 8 In. 1380.00
Compote, Lavender Ground, White Garland, Goat Head Design, 3 ¼ x 6 In. 50.00
Crater Urn, Cover, Caneware, Applied Rosso Antico Relief, Vining, Leaves, 13 In.. 652.00
Creamer, Argenta, Bird & Fan, 3 ½ In. 58.00
Creamer, Black Basalt, Shamrock, Thistle, Rose, Harp, Leaves, 1860, 4 ¾ x 5 In.. 60.00
Creamer, Phoebe, Flow Blue, c.1906, 5 In. 11.80
Creamer, Sugar, Cover, Jasperware, Lilac, Classical Figurines, 1800s, 4 In. 351.00
Creamer, Terra-Cotta, Prunus, Oval, Applied White Relief, 19th Century, 6 ¼ In.. 563.00
Cup, Cann, Saucer, Jasperware, Green, White Ribbon, Swags, Lavender Putti, 5 ½ In. 1020.00
Cup & Saucer, Black Basalt, Psyche & Cupid, 3 Graces, c.1840 85.00
Cup & Saucer, Black Basalt, Warrior, Athena, 3 Graces, Early 20th Century 70.00
Cup & Saucer, Chinese Baroque, Green Transfer, 5 ½ x 4 ½ In.. 49.00
Cup & Saucer, Jasper Dip, Lilac, Classical Putti, Striping, Acanthus Leaf Border, 5 ⅛ In. 1778.00
Dish, Bread & Butter, Wellesley, 7 In.. 15.00
Dish, Ice Cream, Lincoln, Cobalt Blue, 6 In. 58.00
Dish, Jasperware, Blue, Diamond Shape, Grecian Woman, 4 ½ x 5 ½ In. 19.00
Dish, Mother, Child, Man, Lessor Type, Yellow Glaze, Scalloped, Multicolored, 12 ⅜ In. 415.00
Dish, Pickle, Cobalt Blue, Wheat Handles, Oval, 9 In. 161.00
Dish, Queen's Ware, Jasperware, Blue, Raised White Man's Bust, 4 ⅜ In.. 18.00
Dish, Shell Shape, Kutani Crane, 6 x 5 ½ In. 23.00
Drum Base, Jasper Dip, Blue, Applied White Classical Figurines, Bands, 4 In., Pair 948.00
Ewer, Black Basalt, Wine & Water, Satyr, Triton, Fluted Stem, Square Base, 16 In., Pair 6250.00
Ewer, Jasperware, Black, Wine, Water, Applied White Relief, Triton, Seated, Satyr, 16 In., Pair. 3318.00
Ewer, Rosso Antico, Silver Overlay, Orange Base, 1800s, 12 x 5 ½ In. 585.00

Figurine, Bulldog, Black, Glass Eyes, Marked, 2 ½ x 5 In.. 300.00
Figurine, Cupid, Black Basalt, Seated On Rocky Base, Early 20th Century, 8 ¼ In.. 237.00
Figurine, Cupid & Psyche, Black Basalt, Seated On Free-Form Base, 1800s, 8 ½ In.. 948.00
Figurine, Faun, With Flute, Black Basalt, Standing Figure, Leaning On Tree, 1800s, 17 In.. 1896.00
Figurine, Water Carrier, Woman, Holding Vase, Circular Plinth, Bone China, 9 ¼ In. 533.00
Flask, Pilgrim, Terra-Cotta Glaze, Cane, Ivory, Leaf Panels, c.1880, 7 In.. 415.00
Incense Burner, Cover, Jasperware, Black, White, Dolphin, Leaves, Swags, 5 In. 1067.00
Infuser, Drab Ware, Blue Grapevines, Pierced Lids, Marked, c.1820, 12 ¾ In. *illus* 1650.00
Jar, Canopic, Primrose & Terra-Cotta, Yellow, Red, Pharaoh, Symbols, 10 x 5 In. 1287.00
Jar, Cover, Hummingbird Luster, Cylindrical, Mottled Green, Multicolored, 10 In. 690.00
Jar, Lid, Sir Walter Raleigh, Seek New Worlds, Blue, White, Gold Letters, 4 ¾ x 3 ½ In.. 60.00
Jardiniere, Classical Figures, Flower Drapery, White, Blue Ground, Marked, 9 x 10 In. 500.00
Jardiniere, Jasper Dip, Black, White Classical Figures, Laurel, Acanthus Leaf, 10 ¼ In. 415.00
Jardiniere, Jasper Dip, Crimson, White Relief Muses, Festoons, Lion Masks, 9 x 10 ¼ In. 948.00
Jardiniere, Jasper Dip, Yellow, Applied Black Classical Relief, Acanthus, 6 In., 2 Piece 770.00
Jardiniere, Jasperware, Green, Pink Accents, Swags, Figures, c.1895, 7 x 8 In. 234.00
Jardiniere, Jasperware, Olive Green, Muses, Garlands, Lion's Head Masks, 8 ⅛ In. 420.00
Jardiniere, Majolica, Simulated Tree Bark Ground, Leafy Relief, c.1882, 7 ⅛ In. 563.00
Jardiniere, Pearlware, Washed Green, Brown Ground, Shield Shape, C. Dresser, 7 ½ In. 11258.00
Jelly Mold Cone, Pearlware, Multicolored Flower Swags, Wedge Shape, 5 x 8 ⅝ In.. 1126.00
Jug, Black Basalt, Gilded, Helmet Shape, Bacchanalian Boys, Banded, Late 1700s, 5 ¼ In. 2252.00
Jug, Flowers, Leaves, Brown, Yellow Glaze, Sterling Silver Rim, Spout, Harry Barnard, 15 In. 652.00
Jug, Jasper Dip, Blue, Grass, Leaf, c.1863, 7 ¾ In.. 830.00
Jug, Jasper Dip, Blue, Oenochoe, Oval, Applied White Classical Relief Figures, 14 In. 4148.00
Jug, Jasper Dip, Crimson, Figures, Fruiting Grapevines, Rope Twist Handle, c.1920, 6 ½ In. 385.00
Jug, Jasper Dip, Yellow, Applied Black Classical Relief, Floral Bands, Etruscan, 7 ⅜ In.. 889.00
Jug, Jasperware, Embossed Hunt Scene, Blue, Marked, 1850s, 6 In. 385.00
Jug, Milk, Caneware, Bacchanalian Boys, Bamboo Handle, Neck, c.1785, 5 ½ In. 2726.00
Jug, Milk, Cover, Diceware, Jasperware, Tricolor, Yellow Quatrefoils, 4 In. 3081.00
Loving Cup, Jasperware, Blue, 2 Handles, Swags, Lattices, c.1895, 4 ½ x 6 ½ In. 205.00
Match Striker, Cobalt Blue, Brown Mottle, 3 ½ In.. 46.00
Medallion, Jasperware, Black, George Washington, White Bust, Self-Framed, Bert Bentley, 4 ⅛ In. 1659.00
Medallion, Jasperware, Black, Mrs. Cecil Wedgwood, White Bust, Self-Framed, c.1940, 4 x 5 In. 336.00
Medallion, Jasperware, Black, Phoebe Wedgwood, White Bust, Oval, Self-Framed, c.1940, 4 x 5 In. 356.00
Medallion, Jasperware, Blue, Nelson, Oval, Applied White Relief, Inscribed, 1900s, 13 x 14 In. 326.00
Medallion, Jasperware, White, Slave, Oval, Verse, Applied Black Jasper Figure, 1 x 1 ⅛ In. 2133.00
Mug, Jasperware, Green, George Washington, Ben Franklin, 1800s, 5 ¼ In. 264.00
Mustard Jar, Lavender, Classic Scene, Silver Plated Lid & Bail, 5 In. 175.00
Oyster Plate, 6 Wells, Fish Heads, 7 ¼ In. 403.00
Patch Box, Round, Green, Classic Decor, Marked, 1 ½ In. 80.00
Pen Tray, Jasperware, Teal Green, Shell Center, 6 ¼ x 3 ½ In. 58.00
Pie Dish, Cover, Caneware, Game, Molded, Hare Finial, Insert, c.1865, 8 ¼ In. *illus* 295.00
Pitcher, Ben Franklin, Washington Cameos, Raised White Vines, Blue Ground, 6 ½ In.. 275.00
Pitcher, Jasperware, Green, Pink Accents, Classical Figures, c.1895, 7 ¼ In. 205.00
Planter, Jasperware, Blue, Washington, Franklin, Lafayette, 19th Century, 6 ½ x 7 In.. 263.00
Plaque, Black Basalt, Death Of Roman Warrior, Gilded Wood Frame, 10 ⅝ x 19 ¼ In. 6518.00
Plaque, Dancing Maidens, Jasperware, Green, White, Gilt Frame, Signed, 6 x 18 In. 275.00
Plaque, Jasper Dip, Black, Applied White Jasperware, Choice Of Hercules, Frame, 10 x 2 ¼ In. 1422.00
Plaque, Jasper Dip, Black, Applied White Relief, Discovery Of Achilles, Frame, 12 x 27 In.. 326.00
Plaque, Jasper Dip, Black, Applied White Relief, Playing Putti, Frame, 10 x 15 In. 2133.00
Plaque, Jasperware, Black, Applied Dancing Hours, Oval, Frame, 13 ½ x 16 In., Pair 235.00 to 356.00
Plaque, Jasperware, Green, Adults, Children, Frame, 1800s, 6 x 10 In.. 234.00
Plaque, Jasperware, Green, Blue, Women Figures, 1800s, 2 In.. 234.00
Plaque, Woman Holding Wreath, Oval, Marked, Frame, 4 In.. 60.00
Plate, Birds At Fountain, Exotic Birds, Flow Blue, 8 In., 2 Piece 24.00
Plate, Black Basalt, Crocodiles, Gilt, 4 ½ In. 44.00
Plate, Blue & Gold Trim, Peacock, Porcelain, 10 ¼ In., 12 Piece 420.00
Plate, Christmas, Jasperware, Blue, Winchester Cathedral, c.1989, 7 ¼ In. 65.00
Plate, Cobalt Ground, Gilt Flowers Allover, Bone China, 10 ¾ In., 12 Piece 1434.00
Plate, Countryside, Blue & White, Bridge Landscape Design, 10 In. 10.00
Plate, Dinner, Floral Center, Gold Rim, 11 In., 8 Piece 70.00
Plate, Green Sunflower, 8 ½ In.. 45.00
Plate, Ivanhoe, Flow Blue, c.1910, 10 ¼ In. 35.00
Plate, My Memories Collection, Mary Vickers, c.1983, 8 In.. 35.00
Plate, Scalloped Rim, Gilt, Ivory Flowers, Crimson Ground, 11 In., 12 Piece. 840.00
Plate, Service, University Of Maine, Blue & White, Bough Border, 10 ¼ In., 8 Piece 345.00
Plate, Water Lily, Flow Blue, England, 10 In. 130.00
Platter, Alternating Birds & Fans, Cobalt Blue, Turquoise, Majolica, Oval, 13 ½ In. 431.00

Wedgwood, Charger, Queen's Ware, Animals, Black Ground, Purple Panels, Marked, 12 In.
$2200.00

Wedgwood, Infuser, Drab Ware, Blue Grapevines, Pierced Lids, Marked, c.1820, 12 ¾ In.
$1650.00

Wedgwood, Pie Dish, Cover, Caneware, Game, Molded, Hare Finial, Insert, c.1865, 8 ¼ In.
$295.00

TIP

Put a wide-angle viewer in a solid outside door so you can see who is there before opening the door.

Wedgwood, Pot, Malfrey, Fairyland Luster, Candelmas, 6 Panels, Signed, 9 ½ x 11 In.
$32775.00

Wedgwood, Sugar, Cover, Rosso Antico, Black Relief, Sybil Finial, Marked, 4 ⅝ In.
$770.00

Weller, Cameo Jewel, Vase, Beethoven Portrait, Lyre, Marked, 11 ½ x 5 ½ In.
$198.00

TIP

If you have a smelly tin, try filling it with fragrant peppermint tea for a few weeks. When you empty it, the tin will still smell, but like peppermint.

Platter, Argenta, Chrysanthemum Panels, Oval, Scalloped, 13 ½ In. 115.00
Platter, Chapoo, Flow Blue, 8-Sided, 16 In. 198.00
Platter, Columbia, Blue Transfer, 10 ¼ x 7 ½ In. 200.00
Platter, Fish, Gray, Green, Black, Yellow, Scalloped Rim, Majolica, 1890s, 13 x 26 In. 2400.00
Platter, Fishbowl, Flower Baskets, Flower Border, Impressed Ridges, Oval, 14 In. 90.00
Platter, Yale College & State House, Blue, 1932, 16 x 20 ¼ In. 250.00
Pot, Malfrey, Fairyland Luster, Candelmas, 6 Panels, Signed, 9 ½ x 11 In. .... *illus* 32775.00
Potpourri, Cover, Jasper Dip, Yellow, Handles, Applied Blue Relief, Acanthus, 2 ½ In. 1422.00
Potpourri, Pierced Cover, Jasperware, White, Laurel Swags, 3 Dolphin Feet, Gilt, 3 ¾ In. 948.00
Potpourri, Vase, Caneware, Bird, In Flower Garden, Globular, Loop Handles, c.1820, 7 ¾ In. 563.00
Potpourri, Vase, Cover, White Biscuit, Shield Shape, Pierced, Impressed, 9 ⅛ In., Pair 504.00
Punch Bowl, Fairyland Luster, Elves & Bell Branch, Woman In Flowing Gown, 9 ¼ x 5 In. 5750.00
Salad Set, Jasper Dip, Yellow, Applied Black Relief, Festoons, Lion Mask, Ring, 11 ¼ In. 1067.00
Salt, Fairyland Luster, Nizami, Deer Grazing, Landscape, Triangle Border, c.1920, 3 In. 4740.00
Spill Vase, Jasper Dip, Yellow, Applied Black Classical Figures, Band, 6 ½ In., Pair 770.00
Sugar, Cover, Jasper Dip, Crimson, Handles, Applied White Classical Relief, 4 ½ In. 504.00
Sugar, Cover, Rosso Antico, Black Relief, Sybil Finial, Marked, 4 ⅝ In. .... *illus* 770.00
Syrup Jug, Rosso Antico, Club Shape, Multicolor Enamel Flowers, Pewter Lid, 6 ¾ In. 356.00
Tankard, Figures, Grapes, Blue, White, Marked, 7 ½ In. 90.00
Tea Set, Jasper Dip, Yellow, Applied Black Classical Relief, c.1930, 3 Piece 2133.00
Tea Set, Jasperware, Crimson, White, 3 Piece 760.00
Teapot, Cover, Rosso Antico, Silver Overlay, Pear Shape, Rouletted Rim, Foot, 7 In. 415.00
Teapot, Cream, Embossed Ribs, Dots, 5 ¼ x 7 In. 103.00
Teapot, Rosso Antico, Black Reserves, Classical Figures, 6 ½ x 5 ½ x 10 In. 1140.00
Teapot, Terra-Cotta, Multicolored Flowers, 6 ½ In. 200.00
Tile, Blue Transferware, Flower, Leaf & Scroll, 6 x 6 In. 80.00
Tobacco Jar, Cover, Jasper Dip, Black, Applied White Stylized Egyptian Motif, 6 ¼ In. 296.00
Tray, Ice Cream, Ivanhoe, Blue Transfer, Molded Icicle Border, c.1883, 16 In. 474.00
Tray, Jewel, Majolica, Cherub Pulling Net, Multicolored, 8 In. 444.00
Tray, Mottled Geranium Leaf, 8 ¾ In. 81.00
Tray, Vase, Jasperware, Classical, Raised, Flowers, 6 In. 800.00
Urn, 2 Handles, Jasperware, Deep Blue, White, Figures, Garlands, c.1895, 15 x 7 In. 878.00
Urn, 2 Handles, Jasperware, Green, Purple, White, c.1800, 8 x 5 In. 351.00
Urn, 2 Handles, Lid, Jasperware, Dancing Hours, Light Blue, 1800s, 8 ½ In. 702.00
Urn, 2 Handles, Pedestal, Dancing Women, Marked, Cover, 8 ½ In. 350.00
Urn, Black, White Pinstripe, Man's Face, Square Base, Ram's Horns, Lid, 8 In., Pair 750.00
Urn, Cameo, Basket, Light Blue, White Flowers, Scrolls, Handles, Cover, 11 In., Pair 1700.00
Urn, Jasperware, Blue, 2 Handles, 20th Century, Cover, 12 x 6 In. 380.00
Urn, Jasperware, Blue, Late 19th Century, 8 ½ x 6 ¾ In. 526.00
Urn, Jasperware, Green, Dancing Figures, Oak Leaves, Acorns, 9 ¼ In. 480.00
Urn, Lid, Jasperware, Lilac, Classical Figures, Garlands, c.1950, 12 x 7 In. 702.00
Vase, Altar, Jasperware, Blue, 2 Handles, Flower Medallion, Trophies, Swags, 4 ¾ In. 4740.00
Vase, Basalt, Vines, Buckles, Black, Flared, Scalloped Rim, Footed, c.1860-70, 10 In. 75.00
Vase, Black, White Pinstripes, Women Holding Hands, Footed, Cover, 9 ½ In. 450.00
Vase, Bowling Pin Shape, Cream, Bronze, Bird, Flowers, 7 ¾ In. 100.00
Vase, Bud, Firbolgs Luster, Gilded Black Figures, Blue Green Ground, 5 ¼ In. 474.00
Vase, Bud, Jasperware, Blue, White Bas-Relief, c.1972, 5 In. 40.00
Vase, Cover, Jasper Dip, Black, Applied White Relief, Torches, Leaf Borders, 6 ½ In. 711.00
Vase, Cover, Jasper Dip, Black, Turned Body, Applied White Drapery Band, 10 In. 711.00
Vase, Cover, Jasper Dip, Crimson, Classical Relief, Bottle Shape, c.1920, 8 In. 3081.00
Vase, Cover, Jasperware, Black, Applied White Relief, Upturned Handles, 15 In. 593.00
Vase, Cover, Jasperware, Blue, Apollo & 9 Muses, Acanthus Leaf Border, 7 ¾ In. 5333.00
Vase, Cover, Queen's Ware, Crimson Yellow Figures, Landscape, Bacchus Heads, Emile Lessore, 16 In. 593.00
Vase, Dragon, Luster, Blue Ground, Cloud Bands, Ki-Rin Gilt, c.1925, 16 ½ In. 805.00
Vase, Dragon, Luster, Blue Mottled Ground, Multicolored, c.1920, 12 ½ In., Pair 1422.00
Vase, Fairyland Luster, Butterfly Woman, Black Ground, Mother-Of-Pearl, 9 ½ In. 6325.00
Vase, Fairyland Luster, Castle On A Road, Maroon Bridge, Figures, Stairway, 7 ½ In. 7475.00
Vase, Fairyland Luster, Cover, Rainbow, Coral, Bronze, Butterfly Woman, 9 In. 3450.00
Vase, Fairyland Luster, Imps On A Bridge, Trees, Green Roc Bird, Black Fairy, 10 ¼ In. 9488.00
Vase, Gilt Lacquered, Jasperware, Bicolor, Brass Masks, Pomegranates Finial, 11 ½ In., Pair 7500.00
Vase, Grid, Jasperware, Classical Scenes, Blue, 7 In. 53.00
Vase, Hummingbird, Luster, Mottled Orange, c.1920, 8 In. 593.00
Vase, Hummingbird Luster, Bulbous, Blue Stick, 6 Birds In Flight, Gold Rims, 8 In. 575.00
Vase, Jasper Dip, Black, Applied White Relief, Bacchanalian Boys, Swags, 14 In. 5333.00
Vase, Jasper Dip, Dark Blue, Classical Figures, Phrygian Cap, 10 In. 2133.00
Vase, Jasperwae, Blue, White, Muses, Allegorical Figures, 6 In. 65.00
Vase, Jasperware, Black, Cream, Men, Women, Cherub, Handles, Marked, 6 ½ In. 175.00
Vase, Jasperware, Black, Portland, White Classical Relief, Figure In Phrygian Cap, 10 In. 2133.00

Vase, Jasperware, Lilac, Portland, 19th Century, 6 ¼ In. 761.00
Vase, Lindsay Ware, Butterfly, 2 Handles, c.1901, 9 ¼ In. 1541.00
Vase, Lindsay Ware, Butterfly, Multicolored Enamels, c.1901, 7 ⅝ In. 1778.00
Vase, Pedestal, Light Blue, Mythological Scenes, Marked, 5 ¼ In. 100.00
Vase, Stoneware, Drab Ground, Blue Enamel Bands, Yellow Striping, 10 ¼ In. 296.00
Vase, Tricolor, Jasper, Lilac Ground, Applied White & Green Leaves, 7 ¾ In. 237.00

WELLER pottery was first made in 1872 in Fultonham, Ohio. The firm moved to Zanesville, Ohio, in 1882. Artwares were introduced in 1893. Hundreds of lines of pottery were produced, including Louwelsa, Eocean, Dickens Ware, and Sicardo, before the pottery closed in 1948.

LOUWELSA WELLER

Ansonia, Vase, Ribs, Brown & Red Matte Glaze, 3 Handles, 5 ½ x 10 ¼ In. 173.00
Art Nouveau, Umbrella Stand, Seashells, Dragon, 4-Sided, 24 In. 575.00
Art Nouveau, Vase, Bud, Etna Glaze, Chicks & Egg, 7 In. 518.00
Aurelian, Ewer, Currant, 8 ½ In. 207.00
Aurelian, Jardiniere, Pedestal, Nasturtium, 38 In. 805.00
Aurelian, Vase, Flowers, Yellow Brown, Green, 12 In. 748.00
Aurelian, Vase, Gladiolas, Red, Yellow, 17 In. 3220.00
Aurelian, Vase, Iris, Brown Glaze, Bulbous, C. Dibowski, 8 x 11 In. 1265.00
Aurelian, Vase, Nasturtiums, 5 In. 184.00
Aurelian, Vase, Virginia Creeper, 4 Lobes, 11 In. 403.00
Aurora, Vase, Daisies, Blue, Cream Ground, 5 ¼ In. 546.00
Aurora, Vase, Flowers, Long Stems, Blue Ground, 8 In. 720.00
Baldin, Umbrella Stand, 22 ½ In. 1950.00
Bedford Matte, Umbrella Stand, Green, Impressed, 20 ¼ In. 605.00
Blue Ware, Vase, Classical Women, 11 In. 295.00
Blue Ware, Vase, Rose, Embossed, Scrolling Panels, Footed, 9 ¾ In. 502.00
Bookends, Mayan Faces, 6 ¾ In. 288.00
Brighton, Box, Woman, Flower Dress, Marked, 7 ½ In. 75.00
Brighton, Figurine, Parrot On Perch, 7 ⅞ In. 374.00
Brighton, Figurine, Pheasant, Green, Yellow, 11 x 7 In. 200.00
Brighton, Flower, Frog, Kingfisher, Multicolored, Marked, 8 ⅝ In. 207.00
Brighton, Flower Frog, Geese, 6 x 8 In. 100.00
Brighton, Wall Pocket, Kingfisher In Tree, Gray, Green, 11 ½ In. 374.00
Burnt Wood, Vase, Incised Flowers, Bulbous, 6 In. 70.00
Cameo Jewel, Vase, Beethoven Portrait, Lyre, Marked, 11 ½ x 5 ½ In. .... *illus* 198.00
Claywood, Jardiniere, Pedestal, Fish, Paneled, 25 In. 770.00
Claywood, Vase, Grapevines, Panels, Marked, 16 In. 535.00
Coppertone, Bowl, Applied Frog, Fish On Sides, Green, 5 x 10 In. 425.00
Coppertone, Bowl, Frog, Lotus Blossom, Marked, 3 ¾ x 4 ¼ In. .... *illus* 187.00
Coppertone, Bowl, Frog On Rim, Elongated, Marked, 5 ¼ x 9 ½ In. 431.00
Coppertone, Bud Vase, Frog, Holding Grasses, 3 ½ x 9 In. 489.00
Coppertone, Candlestick, Lily Pad, Green, Marked, 5 In., Pair 175.00
Coppertone, Candlestick, Turtle, Lotus Blossom, Marked, 3 ¼ In. 230.00
Coppertone, Candlestick, Turtle, Water Lilies, 5 x 3 ¼ In., Pair 460.00
Coppertone, Figurine, Frog, 2 ¼ x 2 ¾ In. .... *illus* 198.00
Coppertone, Figurine, Frog, Holding Lotus Blossom Bowl, 3 ¾ x 5 In. .... 184.00 to 196.00
Coppertone, Figurine, Frog, Playing, Banjo, Marked, 7 ½ In. 1955.00
Coppertone, Flower Frog, Form Of Piled Rocks, 2 ½ x 5 In. 127.00
Coppertone, Paperweight, Turtle, Marked, 1 ¾ x 5 In. 288.00
Coppertone, Vase, 2 Frogs Perched At Rim, No. 27, Marked, 8 x 9 In. 880.00
Coppertone, Vase, Green, Brown, Handles, 7 x 9 In. 295.00
Coppertone, Vase, Handles, 14 ¾ In. 780.00
Coppertone, Vase, Oil Jar Shape, Turned Rib, Flared Mouth, Handles, 25 ¾ In. 575.00
Copra, Vase, Flowers, Attached Loop Handles, Flared, 7 ⅞ In. 69.00
DeDonatis, Vase, Brown, White, Signed, FDD, 9 In. .... *illus* 800.00
Dickens Ware, Ewer, Mr. Weller Dispelling Me Feverish Remains, Pickwick Papers, 11 ½ In. .. 403.00
Dickens Ware, Humidor, Irishman, 7 x 6 ½ In. .... 173.00 to 403.00
Dickens Ware, Jardiniere, Autumn Leaves, Blue Glaze, Gold Interior, 8 x 12 In. 316.00
Dickens Ware, Jug, 2 Men Playing Checkers, 4 ¾ In. 288.00
Dickens Ware, Jug, Bridge, Mt. Vernon Bridge Co., 5 ⅞ In. 288.00
Dickens Ware, Mug, Yellow Butterflies, Brown Ground, 4 ⅝ In. 184.00
Dickens Ware, Pitcher, Fish Swimming, Blue To Green Ground, Edwin L. Pickens, 11 ⅜ In. .. 420.00
Dickens Ware, Tobacco Jar, Turk, 7 ½ In. 450.00
Dickens Ware, Vase, American Indian, Headress, Blackheart, Handles, 10 In. 690.00
Dickens Ware, Vase, Canterbury Pilgrimage, Pinched Neck, 18 In. 3120.00
Dickens Ware, Vase, Cavalier, Claude Leffler, 17 ¾ In. 1035.00

TIP
Don't store fabrics in cedar chests, cardboard boxes, or plastic. The fabrics will yellow and may mildew. Use archival boxes.

Weller, Coppertone, Bowl, Frog, Lotus Blossom, Marked, 3 ¾ x 4 ¼ In.
$187.00

Weller, Coppertone, Figurine, Frog, 2 ¼ x 2 ¾ In.
$198.00

Weller, DeDonatis, Vase, Brown, White, Signed, FDD, 9 In.
$800.00

Weller, Dickens Ware, Vase, Inn Scene, Marked, Signed, JH, 14 ½ In.
$1320.00

Weller, Garden Ornament, Dog, Terrier, 11 ¼ In.
$2000.00

Weller, Hobart, Wall Pocket, Maiden, Blue Green Glaze, 12 x 7 ¼ In.
$655.00

Dickens Ware, Vase, Cavalier, Painted, Incised, 10 ½ x 6 ¼ In. 173.00
Dickens Ware, Vase, Christopher Columbus, Clergymen On Island, Marked, 11 ⅜ In. 805.00
Dickens Ware, Vase, Fish, Triangular, 3 Handles, Signed, E. Roberts, 4 ¾ x 6 ¼ In. 345.00
Dickens Ware, Vase, Inn Scene, Marked, Signed, JH, 14 ½ In. .... *illus* 1320.00
Dickens Ware, Vase, Man Golfer, Caddy, Carved, Matte Glaze, Signed K.W., 9 ½ In. 1725.00
Dickens Ware, Vase, Native American, Fox Tail, Double Handles, 5 x 6 In. 374.00
Dickens Ware, Vase, Woman Playing Lyre, 10 ⅝ In. 345.00
Eocean, Jardiniere, Jonquils, 3-Footed, 12 ¼ In. 345.00
Eocean, Oil Lamp, Flowers, Pink, Yellow, Green, Signed, Hester Pillsbury, 18 In. 300.00
Eocean, Vase, Berries, Blossoms, Signed, L.M., 10 In. 115.00
Eocean, Vase, Cherries, Shouldered, 10 ½ In. 575.00
Eocean, Vase, Daisies, Narrow Neck, Signed, L.J.B, 13 ¾ In. 1300.00
Eocean, Vase, Dog Portrait, Handles, Signed, E. Blake, 5 ½ x 5 ½ In. 920.00
Eocean, Vase, Flowers, Dark To Light Green, Tapered, 12 In. 518.00
Eocean, Vase, Irises, Maroon, Pink, White, 17 In. 2530.00
Eocean, Vase, Nasturtium, Blue & Pink, Leaves, Gray Ground, Globular, 7 ½ In. 316.00
Eocean, Vase, Poppy, 10 ½ x 4 ½ In. 1265.00
Eocean, Vase, Rose, Dogwood Blossoms, 4 ½ In. 207.00
Eocean, Vase, Roses, Multicolored, 16 ⅛ In. 575.00
Eocean, Vase, Trumpet, Open Rose Design, 10 ⅝ x 5 ⅝ In. 176.00
Etna, Pitcher, Flowers, Hand Painted, Marked, Weller Etna, 6 x 3 ¾ In. 145.00
Etna, Vase, Purple Flowers, Bulbous, Flared Rim, High Relief, 4 ¾ x 4 ¾ In. 90.00
Figurine, Dog, Pop Eye, 4 In. .... 115.00 to 300.00
Figurine, Dog, Scottie, Matte Glaze, 4 ⅞ In. .... 5060.00 to 5175.00
Figurine, Dog, Spaniel, 10 ½ In. 2530.00
Figurine, Rooster, 9 x 10 In. 1700.00
Flemish, Jardiniere, Pedestal, Parrots, Ring Handles, Marked 1150.00
Flemish, Umbrella Stand, Tree, Fruit, 22 ½ In. 489.00
Flemish, Vase, Plum, Marked, 12 In. 350.00
Flower Frog, Boy & Goose, 9 In. 150.00
Flower Frog, Kingfisher, 6 ¼ In. 138.00
Flower Frog, Nude, Hand On Head, Green Matte Glaze, 6 In. 90.00
Forest, Jardiniere, Pedestal, 29 ¾ In. 1093.00
Garden Ornament, Dog, Terrier, 11 ¼ In. .... *illus* 2000.00
Garden Ornament, Dog, Scottie, Black, White, 11 In. 550.00
Garden Ornament, Squirrel, Marked, Late 1920s, 11 ¾ In. .... 950.00 to 1380.00
Glendale, Vase, Baluster, 12 x 5 In. 380.00
Glendale, Vase, Bird, Cattails, Body Of Water, 6 In. 403.00
Glendale, Wall Pocket, Nest Of Baby Birds, Mother Bird In Tree, 12 ½ In. 230.00
Graystone, Fountain, Fish, Jumping Out Of Water, Lily Pads, Brass Holder, 21 In., 2 Piece 633.00
Hobart, Figurine, Maiden, Light Blue Green Glaze, 12 x 7 ¼ In. 655.00
Hobart, Flower Frog, Duck & Girl, Marked, 5 ¼ In. 230.00
Hobart, Wall Pocket, Maiden, Blue Green Glaze, 12 x 7 ¼ In. .... *illus* 655.00
Hudson, Vase, Cabin, Pine Trees, Snow Covered Landscape, 9 ¼ In. 3220.00
Hudson, Vase, Crocus, Yellow Ground, 6 In. 374.00
Hudson, Vase, Dogwood, White Blooming, 6 ¾ In. 358.00
Hudson, Vase, Flowers, Raised, Pink To Blue Ground, 5 x 13 ¼ In. 575.00
Hudson, Vase, Forget-Me-Nots, Cylindrical, Flared Rim, 7 ½ In. 288.00
Hudson, Vase, Hollyhocks, Pink, White, Signed, 11 ½ In. 1200.00
Hudson, Vase, Irises, Blue Ground, 15 x 7 ½ In. 2100.00
Hudson, Vase, Morning Glory, Pink, Green, Blue Matte Glaze, Signed, Kennedy, 8 In. 288.00
Hudson, Vase, Open Rose, Blue, Pink, Marked, Pillsbury, 5 ½ x 5 ½ In. .... *illus* 385.00
Hudson, Vase, Passion Flower, Buds, Vines, 9 ⅝ In. 1380.00
Hudson, Vase, Sailboat, Oval, Signed, 8 ¾ In. 1320.00
Hunter, Vase, Fish, Incised Waves, Handles, 4 ¼ In. 173.00
Incense Burner, Foxy Grandpa, 5 In. 200.00
Ivory, Vase, Garland, Flared Base & Rim, 14 ½ In. 92.00
Jap Birdimal, Vase, Flying Goose, White Slip, Teal Ground, 4 ¼ In. 275.00
Jap Birdimal, Vase, Viking Ship, Blue-Green Seas, Pillow, Marked, 4 ¾ x 5 ⅛ In. 300.00
Jardiniere, 4 Large Leaves, Green Matte Glaze, 9 x 11 In. 1920.00
Jardiniere, Pedestal, Cattail Panels, Trees, Kingfisher, 31 ¼ In. 1320.00
Jewelry Box, Mermaid, Fish, Round, Head Finial, Footed, 4 ¼ In. 1035.00
Knifewood, Jardiniere, Pedestal, Daisies, Butterflies, 32 ¼ x 12 ½ In. 1610.00
Knifewood, Vase, Birds, Yellow, 5 ½ In. 80.00
Knifewood, Wall Pocket, Daisies, Brown Ground, 5 ½ In. 92.00
Lamar, Vase, Trees, Castle, River, 14 ⅞ In. 690.00
LaSa, Vase, Elk In Forest, Clouds, Marked, 13 ⅜ In. 2990.00
LaSa, Vase, Landscape, Cylindrical, Signed, 9 In. 300.00

LaSa, Vase, Tree, Lake, Hill, Clouds, Metallic Glaze, 3 ⅝ In. 690.00
LaSa, Vase, Trees, Mountains, River, 9 ⅛ In. 460.00
LaSa, Vase, Tropical Landscape, Green, Blue, 9 In. 546.00
Lavonia, Vase, Wheat, Embossed, Lavender To Green, 11 ¾ In. 161.00
Louwelsa, Ewer, Yellow Daffodil, 4 In. 127.00
Louwelsa, Mug, Spaniel, 6 ¾ In. 196.00
Louwelsa, Mug, Wrens On Branches, 6 ⅝ In. 546.00
Louwelsa, Tankard, Blackberries, 17 ½ In. 184.00
Louwelsa, Tankard, Native American Indian, 10 ⅞ In. 978.00
Louwelsa, Tankard, Portrait Of A Cleric, 12 ½ In. 207.00
Louwelsa, Vase, 4 Baby Chicks, Pecking In Hay, 15 In. 690.00
Louwelsa, Vase, Carnations, Pillow, Signed, E.R., 7 ¼ x 8 In. 245.00
Louwelsa, Vase, Dog Portrait, Bulbous, 10 ½ In. 805.00
Louwelsa, Vase, Flowers, Brown Shaded To Green To Amber Ground, Signed, 10 In. 173.00
Louwelsa, Vase, Jonquil, Blue Ground, 11 ½ In. 460.00
Louwelsa, Vase, Poppies, Blue, 8 ½ In. 805.00
Louwelsa, Vase, Spider Mum, Blue, 7 In. 633.00
Louwelsa, Vase, Swallows, Squat, 6 In. 863.00
Louwelsa, Vase, Wading Stork, 22 ⅜ In. 805.00
Louwelsa, Vase, Yellow Buttercup Spray, Elizabeth Ayers, 9 ¼ In. 178.00
Mammy, Cookie Jar, Holding Watermelon, 11 In. .... 935.00 to 1100.00
Mammy, Creamer, White, Brown, 4 In. 200.00
Mammy, Mixing Bowl, Handle, 5 x 12 In. 250.00
Mammy, Sugar, Cover, Mammy Head Handles, Watermelon Finial, 3 x 7 In. 250.00
Mammy, Syrup, 7 In. 250.00
Mammy, Teapot, Figural, White, Brown, 8 x 9 In. 175.00
Marvo, Vase, Matte Green, Tapered, Marked, 9 In. 145.00
Muskota, Figurine, Cats, On Fence, 7 ½ In. 230.00
Muskota, Figurine, Fisher Boy, Pant Leg Rolled Up, Hands Together, 19 ¼ In. 1380.00
Muskota, Fish Bowl Stand, Boy Fishing, Sitting On Tree Trunk, 12 x 10 In. .... 125.00 to 460.00
Muskota, Flower Frog, Buff & Green Glaze, 4 ¼ x 4 ½ x 3 ½ In. 150.00
Muskota, Flower Frog, Crab, Pink, Green, 6 In. 100.00
Muskota, Flower Frog, Figurine With Nude & Swan, 7 ⅛ x 7 ½ In. 385.00
Muskota, Flower Frog, Mushroom, Yellow, Green, 6 In. 100.00
Muskota, Flower Frog, Starfish, 6 In. 259.00
Muskota, Vase, Cat, Tree Trunk Bud Vase, Vaseline Glass Bowl, 10 ½ x 10 ½ In. .... *illus* 1800.00
Muskota, Vase, Kneeling Woman, Green, Brown, Cream Matte Glaze, 8 x 7 In. 475.00
Novelty Line, Ashtray, Red Fox, 3 ⅛ x 7 ½ In. 288.00
Paragon, Vase, Golden Yellow, Bulbous, 10 In. 150.00
Pearl, Vase, Yellow, Blue, Marked, 5 ¼ x 4 ¾ In. .... *illus* 258.00
Perfecto, Jardiniere, Pedestal, Stork, Palm Tree, 33 In. .... 1093.00 to 4255.00
Perfecto, Umbrella Stand, Stork, Palm Fronds, Pastels, Marked, 23 In. 3450.00
Perfecto, Vase, Grape Clusters, Lavender Ground, 15 ½ In. 780.00
Planter, Log, Mottled Green & Brown, Center Handle, Footed, 4 ¼ x 9 ½ In. 50.00
Racene, Vase, Flowers, Blue, Hand Painted, Signed, NP, 9 In. .... 288.00 to 400.00
Rosemont, Jardiniere, Bluebirds, Pink Blossoms, 7 ⅜ In. 259.00
Rosemont, Planter, Bluebirds, On Blossoms, Gathered Neck, 7 In. 288.00
Sabrinian, Vase, Shell, Purple, Green, Pink, Handles, 11 x 6 In. 176.00
Selma, Basket, Hanging, Hunting Dogs, Thistle, 4 ¼ x 9 ½ In. 460.00
Selma, Bowl, Swans, Cattails, Marked, 3 ¼ In. 316.00
Sicardo, Dish, Iridescent Amethyst, Shamrock, Matching Lid, Signed, 5 In. 288.00
Sicardo, Vase, Berries, Leaves Green, Red Iridescent, Squat, 4 ½ In. 345.00
Sicardo, Vase, Blossoms, Purple Luster Ground, Handles, 9 x 7 In. 2520.00
Sicardo, Vase, Bronze Ground, Green Iridescent Highlights, Signed, 8 x 9 In. 1900.00
Sicardo, Vase, Cyclamen, Nodding, 8 ¾ In. 489.00
Sicardo, Vase, Daisies, Purple Ground, 4 Lobes, Handles, 7 ½ x 8 ½ In. 2400.00
Sicardo, Vase, Daisy & Dots, Twist Body, Signed, 4 ½ In. 288.00
Sicardo, Vase, Flowers, Metallic Iridescent, Signed, 16 In. 1955.00
Sicardo, Vase, Iridescent, Fat Shape, Green Highlights, Bronze Ground, Signed, 8 x 9 In. 1900.00
Sicardo, Vase, Iridescent Green Scrolls, Signed, 7 In. 891.00
Sicardo, Vase, Peacock, Signed, 9 ¼ In. 1500.00
Sicardo, Vase, Snails, Gold, Green, Purple, Iridescent Swirled Ground, 12 ½ x 4 ¾ In. 6000.00
Sicardo, Vase, Twist, Lobes, Signed, 11 ⅝ In. 1200.00
Silvertone, Candleholder, 3 In., Pair 90.00
Silvertone, Vase, Butterfly, Large Flowers, 12 x 9 In. 205.00
Silvertone, Vase, Irises, Multicolored, Flared Rim, 5 ½ In. 184.00
Silvertone, Vase, Poppies, Pinched Neck, Marled, 11 ¼ In. 316.00
Tobacco Jar, Student, Terra-Cotta, Marked J.M., 3654, 8 ¼ In. 690.00

Weller, Hudson, Vase, Open Rose, Blue, Pink, Marked, Pillsbury, 5 ½ x 5 ½ In.
$385.00

Weller, Muskota, Vase, Cat, Tree Trunk Bud Vase, Vaseline Glass Bowl, 10 ½ x 10 ½ In.
$1800.00

Weller, Pearl, Vase, Yellow, Blue, Marked, 5 ¼ x 4 ¾ In.
$258.00

TIP

If you have an old piano, beware of moths. They sometimes infest the interior fabrics.

Westmoreland Glass, Chas West Lattice, Dish, Mayonnaise, Ladle, Dark Violet, Black, 1920s, 4 In.
$85.00

Westmoreland Glass, Doric, Compote, Dark Blue Mist, 4 ⅞ In.
$38.00

Westmoreland Glass, Doric, Console Set, Laurel Green, Bowl, Candlesticks, 1960s, 3 piece
$75.00

Westmoreland Glass, Lotus, Salt, Green, 1930s
$25.00

Wisteria, Vase, Blue & Brown, Foil Label, Double Handles, 6 ½ x 10 ¼ In. . . . 1495.00
Woodcraft, Bowl, Squirrels In Oak Tree, 3-Footed, 3 ¼ x 6 ¼ In. . . . 115.00
Woodcraft, Planter, Wooded Scene, 6 x 16 ½ In. . . . 978.00
Woodcraft, Vase, 3 Branch, Buttresses, Chalice Shape, 9 ⅛ In. . . . 161.00
Woodcraft, Vase, Owl, Squirrel, 17 ⅝ In. . . . 518.00
Woodcraft, Wall Pocket, Bluebird, 10 x 11 In. . . . 1610.00
Woodcraft, Wall Pocket, Squirrel, At Foot Of Tree, 8 ¾ In. . . . 115.00
Woodcraft, Wall Pocket, Squirrel, Forest, Signed, 9 ½ In. . . . 240.00
Woodcraft, Wall Pocket, Squirrel With Nut, Oak Leaves, Acorns, 9 ½ In. . . . 115.00
Xenia, Vase, Roses, Scottish Red, Maroon, Blue, Gray Ground, 4 ⅛ x 8 ⅛ In. . . . 1093.00

WESTMOROLAND GLASS was made by the Westmoreland Glass Company of Grapeville, Pennsylvania, from 1890 to 1984. The company made clear and colored glass of many varieties, such as milk glass, pressed glass, and slag glass.

Animal, Dish, Cat Cover, Oblong Lacy Base, Blue Glass Eyes, Foil Label, 6 ½ x 8 In. . . . 150.00
Animal, Dish, Lion On Basket, Milk Glass, Glass Eyes, 8 x 6 In. . . . 135.00
Animal, Dish, Love Bird Cover, Milk Glass, 6 ½ x 5 ¼ In. . . . 95.00
Animal, Dish, Robin, On Nest Cover, Golden Sunset, 6 ¼ In. . . . 58.00
Beaded Edge, Plate, Dinner, Plum, 10 ½ In. . . . 45.00
Beaded Edge, Tumbler, Fruits, Footed . . . 18.00
Blue Mist, Trinket Box, Satin Glass, 3 ½ x 2 ½ In. . . . 20.00
Brown Mist, Basket, Painted Flowers, 4 ⅝ x 2 ¾ In. . . . 35.00
Chas West Lattice, Dish, Mayonnaise, Ladle, Dark Violet, Black, 1920s, 4 In. . . . *illus* 85.00
Crystal Mist, Fairy Lamp, 6 ¼ x 4 In., 2 Piece . . . 30.00
Della Robbia, Bowl, Ruby Flashed, Belled, Footed, 12 In. . . . 125.00
Della Robbia, Candy Dish, Cover, Scalloped Edge, Footed, 7 In. . . . 105.00
Della Robbia, Torte Plate, 14 In. . . . 75.00
Doric, Compote, Dark Blue Mist, 4 ⅞ In. . . . *illus* 38.00
Doric, Console Set, Laurel Green, Bowl, Candlesticks, 1960s, 3 piece . . . *illus* 75.00
English Hobnail, Berry Bowl, Ice Blue, 4 ½ In. . . . 28.00
English Hobnail, Bonbon, Handle, Hexagonal, 6 In. . . . 15.00
English Hobnail, Candleholder, Ice Blue, 3 ½ In., Pair . . . 20.00
English Hobnail, Candlestick, Green, Round, 3 ½ In. . . . 22.00
English Hobnail, Candlestick, Green, Square, 5 ¾ In. . . . 35.00
English Hobnail, Coaster . . . 8.00
English Hobnail, Cologne Bottle, Stopper, Green . . . 50.00
English Hobnail, Cologne Bottle, Stopper, Ice Blue . . . 50.00
English Hobnail, Console, Amber, Rolled Edge, 11 In. . . . 30.00
English Hobnail, Cordial, 1 Oz., 3 ¼ In. . . . 15.00
English Hobnail, Cordial, 1 Oz., 3 ⅜ In. . . . 8.00 to 10.00
English Hobnail, Creamer, Crystal Hexagonal Foot . . . 10.00
English Hobnail, Creamer, Green, Square Footed. . . . 55.00
English Hobnail, Cup, After Dinner . . . 15.00
English Hobnail, Cup & Saucer, Ice Blue . . . 24.00
English Hobnail, Dinner, Plate, Amber, 10 ½ In. . . . 18.00
English Hobnail, Dresser Bottle, Ice Blue, Wide Mouth, Stopper . . . 100.00
English Hobnail, Goblet, Ice Blue, 9 Oz., 6 ½ In. . . . 30.00
English Hobnail, Lamp, Hurricane . . . 36.00
English Hobnail, Nappy, Amber, Square, 6 In. . . . 11.00
English Hobnail, Plate, Dinner, Ice Blue, 10 ½ In. . . . 62.00
English Hobnail, Plate, Ice Blue, 8 ½ In. . . . 20.00
English Hobnail, Plate, Luncheon, 8 In. . . . 10.00 to 12.50
English Hobnail, Plate, Luncheon, Amber, 8 In. . . . 15.00
English Hobnail, Plate, Luncheon, Pink, 8 In. . . . 12.00
English Hobnail, Plate, Sherbet, 6 ½ In. . . . 6.00
English Hobnail, Plate, Sherbet, Ice Blue, 5 ½ In. . . . 10.00
English Hobnail, Salt, Green, Footed, 2 In. . . . 14.00
English Hobnail, Salt, Hexagonal Foot . . . 8.00
English Hobnail, Salt, Spoon Rest, Pink, Footed, 2 In. . . . 15.00
English Hobnail, Salver, Green, 13 ½ In. . . . 60.00
English Hobnail, Sandwich Server, Center Handle, 8 In. . . . 15.00
English Hobnail, Sherbet, Ice Blue, 4 ⅞ In. . . . 20.00
English Hobnail, Sugar, Hexagonal Foot. . . . 10.00
English Hobnail, Tumbler, Iced Tea, Ice Blue, 10 Oz., 5 In. . . . 28.00
English Hobnail, Tumbler, Iced Tea, Square Foot, 11 Oz. . . . 12.00
English Hobnail, Tumbler, Juice, Footed, 5 Oz. . . . 9.00
English Hobnail, Wine, 2 Oz., 4 ½ In. . . . 9.00
Figurine, Bull Dog, Amber, Leather Collar, 7 x 4 ½ x 6 In. . . . 59.00

Figurine, Bull Dog, Black, Leather Collar, 7 x 4 ¼ x 6 In. 70.00
Figurine, Owl, Blue Mist, Rhinestone Eyes, 3 ½ In. 18.00
Forget-Me-Not, Plate, Milk Glass, Pierced Rim, 8 ½ In. 25.00
Lily Of The Valley, Vase, Milk Glass, 6 x 5 ½ In. 40.00
Lotus, Salt, Green, 1930s .... *illus* 25.00
No. 1042, Candlestick, Cranberry, 9 ¼ x 5 ¼ In. 30.00
Paneled Grape, Basket, Milk Glass, Split Handle, 6 ½ In.. .... 22.00
Paneled Grape, Candy Dish, Dogwood, Almond, 3-Footed, 7 ¾ x 3 ⅜ In. 45.00
Paneled Grape, Celery Vase, Milk Glass, Ruffled Edge, 5 ¾ x 4 ¼ In. 34.00
Paneled Grape, Creamer, Milk Glass, 5 ½ In. 25.00
Paneled Grape, Cruet, Milk Glass, 4 ⅞ In.. .... 25.00
Paneled Grape, Gravy Boat, Underplate, Milk Glass, 8 In. 65.00
Paneled Grape, Pitcher, Milk Glass, 24 Oz., 8 ¼ x 4 In. 30.00
Paneled Grape, Planter, Window Box, Milk Glass, 8 ½ x 3 In. 28.00
Paneled Grape, Plate, Dinner, 10 ½ In. 48.00
Paneled Grape, Plate, Salad, 8 ½ In. 24.00
Paneled Grape, Sherbet, 5 Oz., 3 ½ In. 35.00
Paneled Grape, Sugar, Spoon Holder, Open Lace Edge, Milk Glass 95.00
Paneled Grape, Vase, Bud, Milk Glass, 6 x 3 ½ In. 23.00
Paneled Grape, Vase, Milk Glass, 9 ½ In.. .... 36.00
Paneled Grape, Vase, Milk Glass, Footed, 3 ½ In. 28.00
Roses & Bows, Basket, Paneled Grape, Milk Glass, 6 ½ x 4 In.. .... 30.00
Roses & Bows, Basket, Pansy, White Milk, 4 ¾ x 3 ⅝ In.. .... 30.00
Roses & Bows, Candy Box, Heart Shape, Milk Glass, Signed, L. Plues, 6 x 2 ½ In. 250.00
Roses & Bows, Wedding Bowl, Cover, Milk Glass, 8 x 4 In. 68.00
Sawtooth, Compote, Golden Sunset, Footed, c.1950, 8 ¾ x 11 In. .... *illus* 50.00
Slag Glass, Red, Dish, Sleigh, 9 ¼ In. 45.00
Swirl & Ball, Candy Box, Milk Glass, 7 ¼ x 5 In. 25.00
Wedding Bowl, Cover, Ruby Stain, 10 In. .... *illus* 55.00

WHEATLEY Pottery was established in 1880. Thomas J. Wheatley had worked in Cincinnati, Ohio, with the founders of the art pottery movement, including M. Louise McLaughlin of the Rookwood Pottery. Wheatley Pottery was purchased by the Cambridge Tile Manufacturing Company in 1927.

Tile, Rampant Lion, Green Matte Glaze, 8 In. 288.00
Vase, Barbotine, Cornflowers, Daisies, Mottled Cream & Brown Glaze, Baluster, 1880, 12 In.. .... 165.00
Vase, Daisies, Wheat, Mottled Tan & Brown Glaze, Marked, IR, 12 In. 220.00
Vase, Flowers, Green & Brown Glaze, Square, Signed, 1880, 9 x 7 ¼ In. .... *illus* 160.00
Vase, Mottled Green Matte Glaze, 8 x 14 In. 780.00
Vase, Mottled Green Matte Glaze, Marked, 10 x 7 In. 495.00
Vase, Native American Style, Squat, Green Matte Glaze, 4 ¼ x 7 In. 518.00
Vase, Raised Leaves, Buds, Blue Matte Glaze, Broad Form, 7 ½ x 10 In. .... *illus* 1920.00

WHEELING Pottery Company of Wheeling, West Virginia, worked from 1879 to about 1923. The firm went through a number of mergers and name changes during that time. Pottery, semiporcelain, artware, and sanitary wares were made.

Bone Dish, LaBelle, Flow Blue, c.1900 .... 201.00
Pitcher, Cherubs, Gold, Flow Blue, 8 In. 124.00
Vase, Peachblow, Shouldered, Mahogany Rim Color, Butter Cream Base, 6 ¾ x 6 In. 1250.00
Vase, Peachblow, Shouldered, White Interior, 4 ½ x 4 ½ In. 1050.00

WHIELDON was an English potter who worked alone and with Josiah Wedgwood in eighteenth-century England. Whieldon made many pieces in natural shapes, like cauliflowers or cabbages, and is almost always unmarked. Do not confuse it with F. Winkle & Co., which made a dinnerware pattern called *Whieldon*.

Plate, Multicolored, Rust, Green, 10 In. 173.00

WILLETS Manufacturing Company of Trenton, New Jersey, began work in 1879. The company made belleek in the late 1880s and 1890s in shapes similar to those used by the Irish Belleek factory. It stopped working about 1912. A variety of marks were used, all including the name Willets.

Bowl, Dark Pink Roses, Parcel Gilt, Scalloped Rim, Handles, 3 ¾ x 8 ¼ In.. .... 90.00
Compote, Pink Roses, Parcel Gilt, Handles, Belleek, 5 x 8 ¼ In. 90.00
Cup & Saucer, Shell, Iridescent Pearl, Gold Handle, Trim, Belleek, 4 ½ x 3 ⅝ In. 65.00
Mug, Blackberries, Purple, White Ground, Green Leaves, c.1909, 5 ⅛ In.. .... 195.00

Westmoreland Glass, Sawtooth, Compote, Golden Sunset, Footed, c.1950, 8 ¾ x 11 In.
$50.00

Westmoreland Glass, Wedding Bowl, Cover, Ruby Stain, 10 In.
$55.00

Wheatley, Vase, Flowers, Green & Brown Glaze, Square, Signed, 1880, 9 x 7 ¼ In.
$160.00

Wheatley, Vase, Raised Leaves, Buds, Blue Matte Glaze, Broad Form, 7 ½ x 10 In.
$1920.00

W

Window, Leaded, Farm Landscape, Arts & Crafts, 35 x 28 In.
$3360.00

Window, Stained, Multicolored, Wizards Den, Pinball Emporium, c.1980, 22 x 36 In., 2 Piece
$176.00

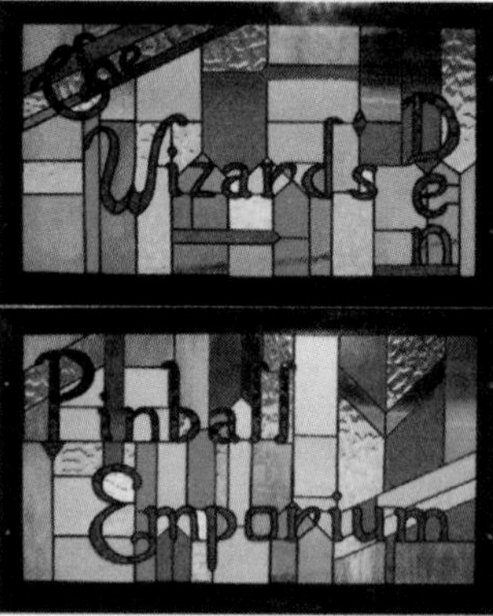

TIP
Scrape your fingernail across the scratch on the glass on your mirror. If it catches, the scratch is too deep to be polished out at home. It requires professional work.

Mug, Grape Clusters, Multicolored Ground, Belleek, 4 ¼ x 3 In. 108.00
Mug, Lavender Ground, White Snails, Belleek, c.1909, 5 ¼ In. 265.00
Pitcher, Water, Green Ground, Pink Blossoms, c.1910, 5 In. 100.00
Plate, Pink Rose, Lilac Blossom, Belleek, c.1909, 8 ½ In. 165.00
Tankard, Gooseberries, Molded Vine, Signed, Blake, c.1909, 12 In. 1200.00
Vase, Cylindrical, Gray, Blue, White Roses, 9 ½ In. 125.00
Vase, Flowers, Purple, White Ground, Belleek, 12 x 3 ¾ In. 275.00
Vase, Rose, Pink & White, Green Leaves, Thorns, Belleek, 9 ¾ x 4 ½ In. 795.00

WILLOW pattern has been made in England since 1780. The pattern has been copied by factories in many countries, including Germany, Japan, and the United States. It is still being made. Willow was named for a pattern that pictures a bridge, birds, willow trees, and a Chinese landscape. Most pieces are blue and white.

Bowl, Vegetable, Pink, Royal China, 9 In. 22.00
Bowl, Vegetable, Royal China, 10 ⅛ In. 7.50
Creamer, Pink, Royal China 20.00
Creamer, Royal China 12.00
Cup, Churchill, England, 2 ¾ In. 8.95
Cup & Saucer, Johnson Brothers, Staffordshire 18.95
Grill Plate, 3 Sections, Japan, 10 ⅞ In. 9.50
Pitcher & Bowl, Japan, 10 & 13 In. 37.50
Plate, Dinner, Johnson Brothers, Staffordshire, 10 ⅛ In. 25.00
Plate, Luncheon, Stamped, U.S., 7 ½ In. 9.50
Platter, Blue Transfer, 16 x 12 ¼ In. 200.00
Saucer, Japan, 6 In. 4.00
Tureen, Johnson Brothers, Handles, Cover, c.1925, 9 x 16 In. 58.00

WINDOW glass that was stained and beveled was popular for houses during the late nineteenth and early twentieth centuries. The old windows became popular with collectors in the 1970s; today, old and new examples are seen.

Arched, White Paint, 4 Panes, 29 ¾ x 47 ½ x 6 In. 70.00
Beveled, 3 Sections, Geometric, Aluminum Frame, 38 x 47 In. 300.00
Leaded, Beveled, Jeweled, Central Cartouche, 31 ½ x 36 In. 230.00
Leaded, Farm Landscape, Arts & Crafts, 35 x 28 In. .... *illus* 3360.00
Leaded, Painted Pink Morning Glories, Enamel Decorated, 40 x 64 In. 4600.00
Leaded, Stained, 7-Sided, Stylized Orange Flower, Entwined Arms, Purple Blue, 24 In. 150.00
Leaded, Stained, Flower Bouquet, Handles, Beveled Diamonds, 52 ½ x 34 In. 2151.00
Leaded, Stained Glass, Frame, c.1970, 42 x 62 In. 460.00
Leaded, Stained Glass, Lion Head, Wood Frame, 1880s, 34 ½ x 25 ½ In. 748.00
Leaded, Stained, Shield, Wood Frame, 24 ½ In., Pair 230.00
Leaded, Woman With Basket Of Flowers, Multicolored, 60 x 15 In. 660.00
Stained, Art Deco, Geometric, Red, Green, Frame, 31 x 17 ¾ In. 168.00
Stained, Art Deco Style, Blue, Red, Amber Jewels, 26 x 27 In. 259.00
Stained, Christ, Pontius Pilate, Crucifixion, Arched, Colored, England, 44 x 26 In. 780.00
Stained, Daum, 4 Seasons, Iridescent Prisms, Geometric Borders, Jeweled, 31 x 31 In. 546.00
Stained, Deer, Antler Jewels, Corner Bull's-Eyes, Yellow, Green, 26 x 38 In. 316.00
Stained, Flower Prairie Design, Green, Red, Opalescent, Caramel, 24 x 34 In. 770.00
Stained, Flower Vase, Scale Borders, Wood Frame, Painted, Early 1900s, 41 x 29 In. 259.00
Stained, Flowers, Jewels, Beveled Center, 34 x 22 In. 440.00
Stained, Frank Lloyd Wright, Nakoma, Painted, Gold, Impressed, 1942, 12 x 4 In. 3360.00
Stained, Interlocking Circle Center, Striated, Green, Blue, Round, Frame, c.1900, 36 x 40 In. 7110.00
Stained, Jeweled, Wood Frame, 19th Century, 24 x 24 In., Pair 1080.00
Stained, Multicolored, Flowers, Scrolls, Jewels, Wood Frame, Tenn., c.1881, 59 x 40 In. 844.00
Stained, Multicolored, Wizards Den, Pinball Emporium, c.1980, 22 x 36 In., 2 Piece ... *illus* 176.00
Stained, Oval B. Franklin Portrait, Red, Brown, 18 Clear Panes, c.1850, 23 x 30 In. 1003.00
Stained, Owl & Bird Medallions, Red & Blue Jewels, 32 x 32 In. 1430.00
Stained, Painted, Landscape, Castles, Wood Frame, 19th Century, 28 x 24 ½ In., Pair 1440.00
Stained, Woodshed, Grape Clusters, Vines, Tools, 20th Century, 44 x 58 In. 600.00
Transom, Leaded, 4 Bull's-Eyes, Turquoise, Flowerhead, Panels, Multicolored, 22 x 93 In. 345.00
Transom, Leaded, Beveled, Coffee Marbleized, C-Scrolls, Green, Panels, 18 x 62 In. 288.00
Transom, Leaded, Scrolling Leaf Tips, Ribbed Frosted, Smoky Quartz Panels, 19 x 52 In. 230.00

WOOD CARVINGS and wooden pieces are listed separately in this book. Many of the wood carvings are figurines or statues. There are also wooden pieces found in other categories, such as Kitchen.

Abraham Lincoln, W.H. Jones, Feb. 12, 1948, 7 ½ In. 165.00

Alligator, Black, Green, Red, Yellow, Pa., 19th Century, 13 ¼ In. 10530.00
American Eagle, Turned Head, Raised Wings, 1920s, 18 x 2 In. 978.00
Angel, Carrying Chalice, Germany, 1800s, 32 In. 2360.00
Angel, Gesso, Carved, Continental, 26 In., Pair. 2000.00
Angel, Oak, Neo-Gothic, Eucharistic Host, Cup, Germany, c.1850, 14 In. 502.00
Angel, Oak, Outstretched Arms, Scroll, Psalm 95 Text, 19 x 38 In. 4720.00
Angel Wings, Pine, Articulated Feathers, Gilt, Late 1800s, 16 x 61 In., Pair 1955.00
Animated Figures, Gaming, Around Table, Oriental, Mid 20th Century, 12 x 8 In. 180.00
Archangel, Oak, St. Michael, Slaying Satan, Germany, 1800s, 35 In. 3776.00
Backpack, Lid, Mythological Figures, Sepik River, New Guinea, c.1910, 25 x 14 In. 478.00
Band Organ Figure, Woman, Green, Yellow, Gilt, Plinth, France, c.1880s, 41 ½ In. 14220.00
Bear, Softwood, Carved, Painted Black, Maryland, 3 ¾ In. 154.00
Bird, Brass Stand, Hagenauer, Marked, WHW, 11 ½ x 11 In. 375.00
Bird, Senufo, Large Beak, Knob, Multicolored, Red, Blue, Stand, Ivory Coast, 16 x 8 In. 418.00
Bird, Thrush, Carved, Painted, Gesso, Wire Legs, Robert Hogg, 4 ⅜ x 5 ¾ In. 143.00
Bishop, Pine, Multicolored, Parcel Gilt, Spain, 23 x 6 ¾ x 6 ¾ In. 600.00
Bowl, Treen, Oval, 19th Century, 4 x 28 ½ x 14 ½ In. 936.00
Bowl, Treen, Yellow, New England, 19th Century, 3 x 11 In. 410.00
Boy, Buffalo, Inlaid Teeth, Eyes, Tree Carved Base, Boulders, Chinese, 10 ½ x 13 In. 1020.00
Brushpot, Bamboo, Berries, Leaves, Cloud Collar, Chinese, 1800s, 5 x 3 ½ x 3 In. 600.00
Brushpot, Zitan Wood, Fitted Base, 8 Immortals, 19th Century, 10 ½ x 9 ½ In. 3910.00
Buddha, 2 Attendants Posed, Lotus Throne, Flames, Gilt, Blue Hair, Japan, 1800s, 14 x 8 In. 1495.00
Buddha, Carved, Siam, Base, 6 x 4 In. 82.00
Buddha, Giltwood, Base, 13 ¾ In. 643.00
Buddha, Lacquered, Lotus Plinth, Sanghati, Rows Of Curls, Japan, 20 In. 354.00
Buddha, Lizard, Disks, Stand, 20th Century, 10 In. 250.00
Buddha, Lotus Position, 4 Ft. 165.00
Buddha, Robed, Headdress, Necklace, On Rocky Plinth, 40 In. 1200.00
Buddha, Robed, Standing, Lotus Base, Cloud Carved Crest, Chinese, 19th Century, 20 In. 440.00
Buddha, Seated, Lacquered, Gilt, Burma, 28 In. 944.00
Buddha, Seated Cross-Legged On Dog, Robed, Crown, 29 ½ In. 900.00
Buddha, Standing, Lacquered, 17 In. 237.00
Buddhist Monk, Standing, Multicolored, Chinese, 15 ½ In. 415.00
Bust, African American Man, Rough Carved Features, Ohio, c.1900, 19 ¾ In. 294.00
Bust, Dog, Pug, Glass Marble Eyes, c.1910, 4 In. 425.00
Bust, Quan Yin, High Chignon, Leafy Diadem, Multicolored, Stand, Chinese, 21 In. 2124.00
Bust, Monkey Head, Grinning, Multicolored, Dayak, Indonesia, c.1910, 13 x 10 In. 598.00
Bust, Woman, Ebonized, Parcel Gilt, Mahogany Base, Cube, 10 ¾ x 4 ⅜ In. 420.00
Butler, Hand Raised, Painted, 19th Century, 25 ½ In. 1100.00
Camel, Mahogany, Horsehair Tail, Joseph Gregory, 11 ¼ x 12 ¼ In. 644.00
Canada Goose, Gray, Tan, Black, Signed B.J., 12 x 24 In. 293.00
Cat, Bamboo, Japan, 12 In. 325.00
Cat, Carousel, Brass Pole, Wood Platform, Gustav Dentzel, 42 x 50 In. 2880.00
Cat, White, Black, Claws, Folded Tail, 7 ¾ In. 55.00
Cherub, Gilt, Continental, c.1900, 12 x 8 In. 168.00
Cherub, With Horn, Walnut, 19th Century, 18 ½ In. 150.00
Christ's Face, Crown Of Thorns, Shrine, Germany, 19th Century, 17 In. *illus* 121.00
Clown, Holding Hat, Wearing Suit, Multicolored, 20th Century, 77 In. 3600.00
Coat Hook, Cat & Mouse, Signed F. Zelezny, 1921, 11 x 7 In., Pair 776.00
Coat Of Arms, Royal, Victorian, Parcel Gilt, Multicolored, 19th Century, 53 x 49 In. 8125.00
Coat Of Arms, Title Plaque, Double Headed Crowned Eagle, Shield Shape, 61 x 54 In. *illus* 6518.00
Corpus, French Ivory, Black Lacquer Cross, Red Velvet, Giltwood Frame, 20 x 11 In. 1800.00
Crow, Painted, Applied Eyes, 10 x 16 ¾ In. 358.00
Crucifix, Oak, Gothic Design, Linden Corpus, Deep Folds, 32 x 19 In. 708.00
Doll Head, Burl, Drilled Holes, Patina, 19th Century, 4 ¼ In. 3643.00
Eagle, Folk Art, Spread Wings, Multicolored, Daniel Strawser, 11 x 18 ½ In. 147.00
Eagle, In Full Flight, Pine, Gilt, 34 x 15 In. 345.00
Eagle, On Rectangular Base, Drawer, Joseph Gregory, 21 x 24 In. 1989.00
Eagle, On Rock Base, 20 ½ In. 200.00
Eagle, Original Paint, Varnish, Wilhelm Schimmel, Pennsylvania, c.1850, 5 In. 10340.00
Eagle, Raised Wings, On Globe, Square Plinth, Signed, Chapman, 43 In. 2360.00
Eagle, Raised Wings, Perched On Rock Base, Pine, Glass Eyes, Sam Blye, 1811, 28 x 37 In. 5000.00
Eagle, Shield, Arrows, Cypress, Weathered, Vermont, c.1900, 14 x 46 In. *illus* 481.00
Eagle, Spread Wings, Carved, Gilt, 1800s, 9 x 44 In. 3851.00
Eagle, Spread Wings, Facing Left, Holding Leaves, 29 In. 250.00
Eagle, Spread Wings, Holding 3 Arrows, Painted, Yellow Beak, 1800s, 17 In. 575.00
Eagle, Spread Wings, On Base, Signed, Alf Stahli, 14 ¼ In. 250.00
Eagle, Spread Wings, Openwork Talons, Pine, Gilt, Gesso Base, 1900s, 21 In. 2300.00

TIP
Never use olive oil to treat a wooden bowl. It will turn rancid. If you used an olive oil–based salad dressing in the bowl at a meal, be sure to rinse the bowl.

Wood Carving, Christ's Face, Crown Of Thorns, Shrine, Germany, 19th Century, 17 In.
$121.00

Wood Carving, Coat Of Arms, Title Plaque, Double Headed Crowned Eagle, Shield Shape, 61 x 54 In.
$6518.00

Wood Carving, Eagle, Shield, Arrows, Cypress, Weathered, Vermont, c.1900, 14 x 46 In.
$481.00

Wood Carving, Madonna, Child, Neo-Gothic, Long Hair, Deep Robe Folds, c.1850, 19 In.
$1298.00

Wood Carving, Milliner's Model, Jointed Limbs, Painted, Continental, c.1830, 13 In.
$748.00

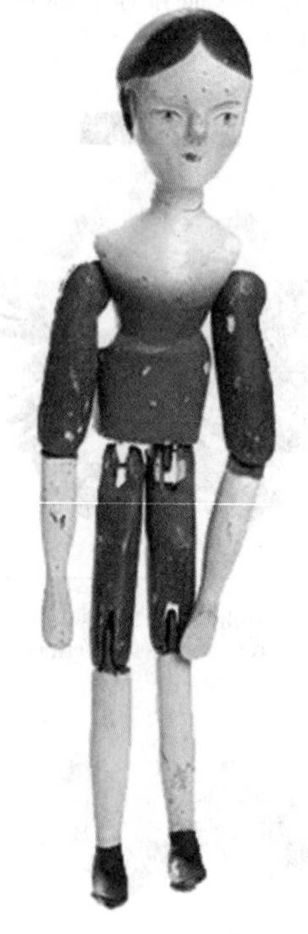

Eagle, Standing On Pedestal, Painted, Softwood, Multicolored, 5 ¾ x 8 ¼ In. 165.00
Eagle, Wings Held High, Dark Finish, Marked, Alf, Stahli, 14 ¼ In. 299.00
Eaglet, Standing, Black, Red, Yellow, Pine, Wilhelm Schimmel, 4 In. 14040.00
Elephant, Carrying Log, Walnut, Wood Base, 12 x 4 25.00
Elephant, Mahogany, Bone Tusks & Eyes, 10 ½ x 9 In. 95.00
Engraving, Wildflower, Field, Warren Mack, Frame, c.1940, 7 x 10 In. 300.00
French Cavalier, Holding Torch, c.1880, 73 x 28 x 17 In. 8625.00
Frog, Teak, Painted Eyes, 1 x 2 In., Pair 65.00
Furniture Legs, Dog Head, Walnut, c.1890, 12 x 5 In. 237.00
Glove Form, Pine, Movable Thumbs, Daniel Hays, Late 1800s, 11 ½ x 11 In., Pair 1200.00
Gnome, Black Forest, Gnome With Pick, Linden Wood, Brienz, Swiss, c.1900, 23 In. 2300.00
Goddess Of Mercy, Gilded, 19th Century, 7 In. 2133.00
Griffin, Seated, Ebonized, Art Deco, 1900s, 29 In., Pair 354.00
Guanyin, Knotted & Sashed Dhoti, Standing On Lotus Throne, Paint Trace, 48 In. 489.00
Guanyin, Multicolored, Chinese, 12 ½ In., Pair 299.00
Guanyin, Wearing Long Robes, Beaded Jewelry, Paint Traces, Chinese, 67 In. 1770.00
Hat Rack, Ibex, Oak Leaves, Black Forest, 18 x 27 In. 850.00
Head, Wig Maker's Model, Stylized Facial Features, 10 In. 411.00
Horse, Galloping, Black, White Feet, Horsehair, Mane, Tail, Joseph Gregory, 11 x 11 In. 1989.00
Horse, Pinto, Harry O. Cochran, 8 ½ In. 201.00
Horse, White, Glass Eyes, Horsehair Mane, Tail, Joseph Gregory, c.1940, 22 x 20 In. 4446.00
Horse & Buggy, White, Black, Red, Joseph Gregory, 15 ½ x 19 ¼ In. 878.00
Horse's Head, Multicolored, Wood Plinth, England, c.1900, 21 ¼ x 16 ½ In. 518.00
Humidor, Boar's Head, Elm, Bone, Hinged Jaw, Leaf Scroll Feet, Late 1800s, 25 x 14 In. 14688.00
Hunting Dog, Duck In Mouth, Painted, Noah Weiss, 22 In. 3010.00
Indian & Bear, Folk Art, Early 20th Century, 14 x 13 In. 316.00
Indian Princess, Cigar Store, Multicolored Dress, Feathered Headdress, 67 In. 7475.00
Junkyard Dog, White, Black, Red, Painted, Isaac Smith, 14 ½ x 22 ½ x 13 ½ In. 1100.00
Knight's Head, Painted, Brass Helmet, Early 20th Century, 16 ½ In. 441.00
Lion, Poplar, Pine Base, 9 ¼ x 20 In. 990.00
Lion, Lying Down, Mane, Snarling, Open Mouth, 28 x 60 In. 1610.00
Lion, Roaring, Ebonized Base, Folk Art, 20th Century, 22 x 12 x 6 ¾ In. 240.00
Lioness, Painted, Teeth, Horsehair Whiskers, Glass Eyes, J. Gregory, 12 x 17 In. 5382.00
Liu Hai, Standing, Hardwood Base, 18th, 19th Century, 9 In. 4740.00
Loon Mother With Chick, Egg, Raised Wings, Wendell Gilley, 9 x 6 In. 1680.00
Louis XVI, Multicolored, Gris-De-Trianon Painted, Molded Frame, 49 x 46 In. 4560.00
Madonna, Child, Cross, Crown, Ball, Multicolored, Germany, 1900s, 26 In. 3304.00
Madonna, Child, Deeply Carved Folds, Flowing Hair, Germany, c.1800, 28 In. 3068.00
Madonna, Child, Neo-Gothic, Long Hair, Deep Robe Folds, c.1850, 19 In. *illus* 1298.00
Male Hunter, Mahogany, Vase On Head, 12 x 37 In. 450.00
Man, Articulated, Pine, France, 19th Century, 31 ½ In. 3510.00
Man, Dancing, Articulated, Wearing Top Hat, Tails, High Boots, 9 ½ In. 1093.00
Man, Multicolored, Gilt, Germany, 60 In. 1195.00
Man, On Water Buffalo, Bone Teeth, Stand, 20th Century, 9 ¾ In. 150.00
Man, Pantaloons, Beret, Jointed Limbs, 17 ¼ In. 2233.00
Man With Lantern, c.1890, 43 x 18 ½ x 9 In. 1778.00
Mary, Jesus, Blessing, Detailed Robes, Multicolored, Gilt, Germany, 69 In. 9735.00
Milliner's Model, Jointed Limbs, Painted, Continental, c.1830, 13 In. *illus* 748.00
Monk, Hands Clasped In Prayer, Wall Mounted, Continental, c.1920, 13 x 4 In. 205.00
Ornament, Cross, Leaves, Flowers, Gilded, Italy, 40 x 14 In. 82.00
Panel, Buddhist Figure, Intaglio, Closed Eyes, Mudra Hands, Lotus Plinth, 46 x 23 In. 288.00
Panel, Flowers, Chinese, 21 ½ x 30 In. 295.00
Panel, Gilt, Li Tieh Kuai Instructing Pupil, Chinese, 18th Century, 17 x 23 In. 269.00
Panel, Gilt, Octagonal, Carved Openwork, Qilin, Phoenix Bird, Clouds, Chinese, 31 In. 295.00
Panel, Indian, Teakwood, Vining, Reticulated, Pagoda Shape Niche, 14 x 9 ½ In. 12.00
Panel, Oak, Angels, Flowers, Putti, Bible Scenes, J. Sowinski, c.1920, 62 In. 1298.00
Panel, St. Michael, Sword, Armor, Gilt, Donald De Lue, c.1942, 45 In. 18750.00
Panel, Walnut, Demilune Shape, Intaglio Castle Scene, 18th Century, 10 ½ x 39 In. 460.00
Parrot, Painted, Tack Eyes, Wire Legs, Stand, 11 ½ In. 813.00
Pig, Standing, Long Snout, Open Mouth, Pointed Teeth, Painted, 19 x 39 In. 1140.00
Plaque, Deer & Bird, Satchel, Rifle, Oak Leaf, Acorn, Black Forest, c.1870, 36 x 21 In. 1760.00
Plaque, Eagle, Banner, Text, Pine, Multicolored, Paint, Gilt, c.1950, 28 x 10 In. 2074.00
Plaque, Eagle, On Hanging Fruit, Glass Eye, Oak, Wall Mount, 18 ½ In. *illus* 330.00
Plaque, Eagle, Spread Wings, On Branch, Pine, 19th Century, 16 x 27 ½ In. 936.00
Plaque, Eagle's Head, Banner In Beak, Incised Feathers, 7 x 12 ½ x 3 ¾ In. 805.00
Plaque, Indian, Profile, Holding 3 Cigars, Painted, 1910, 37 In. 400.00
Plaque, Pyrography, Italian Courtyard, Pierrefonds Chateau, 9 ½ x 11 In., 2 Piece 100.00
Rabbit, Brown, Pine, Inserted Ears, Front Legs, Felt Marked, 5 x 11 In. 77.00

Renaissance Man, Making Toast, On Carved Pedestal, Folk Art Style, 72 In. 2300.00
Rooster, Orange, Yellow, Brown, Green, 19th Century, 5 ½ In. 2340.00
Rooster, Red, Back, Yellow, Green, Pine, 7 x 5 In. 1750.00
Rooster, Red, Yellow, Green, Hollow, Lift Top Compartment, J. Gregory, 22 x 18 In. 4680.00
Rooster, Red, Yellow, Green, Leather Comb, Joseph Gregory, 21 x 17 ½ In. 9360.00
Rooster, Schimmel Style, Painted, Multicolored, 3 ¾ x 3 ¾ In. 66.00
Roundel, Playing Putti, Satyr, Walnut, Brown Patina, France, 28 In., Pair 3600.00
Sailor, Dewy Boy, Whirligig, Stand, Painted, Nantucket, 1890-1910, 15 ¼ In. 1422.00
Saint, With Book, Standing, Continental, 37 In. 1180.00
Sandpiper, Applied Beak, Tack Eyes, Wire Leg, Cedar Base, Ayer, 3 ¾ x 6 In. 33.00
Santo, Angel, Outstretched Arms, Paint Over Gesso, 19th Century, 14 ½ In. 235.00
Santo, Martyr, Woman, In Flames, Clasped Hands, Spanish Colonial, 9 ½ In. 236.00
Santo, Spanish Colonial, Carved, Painted, 19th Century, Glass Eyes, 19 In. 561.00
Sculpture, Head Of Don Quixote, 12 x 7 x 14 In. 468.00
Shelf, Antlers, Black Forest, 16 x 13 In. 460.00
Shepherd, Holding Reed Pipes, 1800s, 42 In. 2115.00
Snow Goose, Pine, White Paint, Glass Eyes, Mid 20th Century, 10 ½ x 20 In. 499.00
Snowy Owl, Tupelo Wood, Glass Eyes, Painted, Frank Finney, 24 ¼ In. 1955.00
Soldier, Cherrywood, Germany, 19th Century, 32 ½ In. 351.00
Songbird, On Branch, Gray Paint, 20th Century, 5 ½ In. 58.00
Souls In Purgatory, 8 People, Painted, c.1860, 27 x 65 ½ x 11 ½ In. 5600.00
Spirit House, Teak, Collapses, Base, 15 In. 35.00
Squirrel, Holding Nut, Walnut, 13 In. 1210.00
St. Francis, Kneeling On Swirl Design, Painted, 19th Century, 35 In. 550.00
St. Martin Of Torres, Hat, Flowing Robes, Hair, Horse, Reins, Multicolored, Stand, 40 ½ In. . 3540.00
St. Paul, Gothic Style, Bearded, Nimbus, Holding Sword, Hand Over Heart, 61 In. 3840.00
Stag, Lying Down, Long Antlers, Pine, 15 In. 527.00
Stag, Standing, Antlers, Brown, Ivory, Black, John Reber, Late 19th Century, 15 ½ In. 4212.00
Statue, Protecting Offspring From Eagle, Black Forest, 9 ½ In. 325.00
Stork, White, Red, Black, Joseph Gregory, 18 ½ x 16 ½ In. 3744.00
Tiger, Painted, Yellow, Orange, Black, Glass Eye, Red Plinth, Chinese, 1800s, 14 x 14 In. 748.00
Trencher, Poplar, Salmon Paint, Pa., 5 x 15 x 26 In. 650.00
Turkey, Yellow, Beige, Gray, Joseph Gregory, 26 x 15 In. 7020.00
Uncle Sam, Outstretched Arms, Cutout, Painted, c.1940, 69 ½ In. 316.00
Urn, Lehnware, Lid, Painted, Leaves, Flowers, 5 In. 920.00
Urn, Neoclassical, Painted, Gilt Bronze Mount, Faux Malachite Base, 24 x 12 In., Pair 1763.00
Vase, Baluster Shape, Hollowed From Tree Trunk, Blond, Brown Mottled, 38 x 7 In. 600.00
Vase, Walnut, Flared Rim, Overlapping Tapered Leaves, Stippled, M. Holzapfel, 1989, 12 In. . . 1541.00
Virgin Mary, Child, Globe, Multicolored, Gilt, Germany, 1800s, 33 In. 944.00
Virgin Mary, Child, Long Hair, Deep Folds, Multicolored, Gilt, Germany, 1800s, 29 In. 1416.00
Virgin Mary, Child, Spanish Colonial, Gilded, Multicolored, 1800s, 18 ½ In. 478.00
Virgin Mary, On Snake Encircled Sphere, Flowing Robes, Multicolored, 18 ½ In. 660.00
Warrior, Standing, Gold Leaf, Chinese, 54 x 18 In. 352.00
Water Bearer, Ironwood, Africa, 13 In. 12.00
Whimsy Spectacle, Pine, Arched Top, Blue Glass Opening, 4 ¾ x 2 ⅜ In. 55.00
Whip Hook, Hunter Form, Black Forest, 12 ½ In. 400.00
Wolf's Head, Black Forest, 15 In. 1112.00
Woman, Ceremonial, Multicolored, Red, White, Hemba Tribe, Congo, 22 x 5 In. 215.00
Woman, Indian, Holding Flowers, Flowing Robes, Painted, Full-Bodied, 67 In. 4600.00
Woman, Nodding Head, Folk Art, 11 In. 230.00
Woman, Organ Figure, Painted, Italy, 41 ½ In. 14220.00
Wood Duck Drake, Sits On Driftwood, Tiger Maple & Glass Case, 10 x 8 x 11 In. 173.00

WOODEN wares were used in all parts of the home. Wood was used for many containers and tools. Small wooden pieces are called treenware in England, but the term *woodenware* is more common in the United States. Additional pieces may be found in the Advertising, Kitchen, and Tool categories.

Baby Walker, Windsor, Caster Wheels, Square, 19th Century . . . . *illus* 500.00
Barn, Animals, Early Red Robin, 13 x 11 In. 138.00
Barrel, 3 Staves, 19th Century, 32 x 19 In. 117.00
Barrel, Storage, Cover, 18th Century, 9 In. 425.00
Bathtub, Oak, Copper Lined, 25 x 68 x 27 In. 427.00
Berry Bucket, Lid, Lehnware, c.1870 . . . . 30000.00
Blackamoor, Scroll Base Plinths, Seminude, Helmet, Rock, 98 & 99 In., Pair 28600.00
Blue Heron, Blue Paint, Overvarnish, 20th Century, 36 x 24 In. 431.00
Bowl, Ash Burl, Early 19th Century, 8 x 19 ½ In. 3510.00
Bowl, Ash Burl, Old Varnish Over Yellow Paint, c.1800, 16 In. 1760.00

Wood Carving, Plaque, Eagle, On Hanging Fruit, Glass Eye, Oak, Wall Mount, 18 ½ In.
$330.00

Wooden, Baby Walker, Windsor, Caster Wheels, Square, 19th Century
$500.00

TIP

It's O.K. to repair tools with obviously broken parts. Tighten screws and lightly wash wood and metal to remove built-up dirt if you don't want to do a major restoration. But don't coat the wood or metal with wax, varnish, oil, or other coatings that won't wash off.

As always, the edited listings in *Kovels' Antiques & Collectibles Price Guide 2010* aren't available on any website, but readers should visit Kovels.com for information on trends, tips, reproductions, marks, old prices, and more!

Wooden, Bowl, Cover, Burl, Turned Foot, Inset Finial, 19th Century, 4 ½ x 4 ¾ In.
$300.00

Wooden, Cheese Trolley, Regency, Mahogany, Leather Casters, 7 x 18 In.
$633.00

Wooden, Cup, Saffron, Cover, Pansies, Strawberries, Footed, Lehnware, 4 ½ x 2 ⅝ In.
$800.00

Wooden, Firkin, Cover, Pine, Salmon Orange, Black, Metal Bands, N.E., 11 x 12 In.
$440.00

Bowl, Ash Burl, Turned, New England, c.1815, 4 ¼ x 11 ¼ In. 2468.00
Bowl, Ash Burl, Turned Lid, c.1780, 5 x 8 In. 17775.00
Bowl, Ash Burl, Upswept Handles, Cutout Holds, Oval, c.1790, 9 x 20 x 15 In. 21250.00
Bowl, Burl, Cover, Turned, Finial, 19th Century, 4 ⅛ x 2 ½ In. 1955.00
Bowl, Burl, Cover, Turned, Footed, Inset Finial, 4 ½ x 4 ¾ In. 353.00
Bowl, Burl, Hanging Hole, c.1800, 16 ¼ x 5 ½ In. 3055.00
Bowl, Burl, Oval, Dark Patina, 14 x 18 In. 3878.00
Bowl, Burl, Patina, 19th Century, 11 ½ x 13 ½ In. 1528.00
Bowl, Burl, Raised Rim, 19th Century, 11 ½ In. 1175.00
Bowl, Burl, Turned, Footed, Brown Patina, 19th Century, 5 ¼ x 1 ¾ In. 1495.00
Bowl, Cover, Blue Paint, Footed, Treen, Early 1800s, 10 x 13 ½ In. 3744.00
Bowl, Cover, Burl, Turned Foot, Inset Finial, 19th Century, 4 ½ x 4 ¾ In. .... *illus* 300.00
Bowl, Fruit, Treen, Waxed, 5 x 13 ⅜ In. 180.00
Bowl, Lid, Treen, Ash, Globular, 1800s, 5 x 6 ⅜ In. 550.00
Bowl, Maple, Red Painted Exterior, 19th Century, 6 ¾ x 2 ½ In. 646.00
Bowl, Maple, Treen, New England, 19th Century, 7 x 20 ½ In. 205.00
Bowl, Maple, Turned, One Piece, c.1975, 6 ½ x 16 ¼ In. 150.00
Bowl, Maple Burl, Cheese, Hand Hewn, Open Flange, c.1770, 7 x 18 In. 960.00
Bowl, Poplar, Turned, Round, Rim, Green Paint, 4 ½ x 14 ¾ In. 385.00
Bowl, Tiger Maple, Patina, 15 In. 695.00
Bowl, Treen, Blue Paint, 19th Century, 2 ½ x 6 ¾ In. 439.00
Bowl, Treen, Carved, Tooled, Curved Sides, Flat Bottom, 4 ½ x 17 ¾ In. 121.00
Bowl, Turned, Painted Interior, Lake Scene, Pier, Red Exterior, 17 x 5 In. 235.00
Bowl, Turned, Painted Putty, 16 In. 403.00
Bowl, Walnut, Free-Form Shape, Signed, Rude Osoinik, 10 x 3 In. 390.00
Bowl, Walnut, Lathe Turned, 1860s 50.00
Bucket, Dry Measure, Softwood, White, Smoke Painted, Metal Bands, 6 ¾ x 9 ¼ In. 935.00
Bucket, Kerosene, Staved, Wire Bail Handle, Turned Handle, Metal Spout, 13 ½ x 13 In. 99.00
Bucket, Lid, Staved, Iron Straps, Flowers, Vines, Salmon Ground, Joseph Lehn, 8 ½ In. 1287.00
Bucket, Pine, Stave Construction, Painted Red Flowers, Birds, Bail Handle, c.1920, 5 ½ In. 588.00
Bucket, Round, Teak, Swivel Handle, Copper Fasteners, Denmark, 16 x 18 In. 150.00
Bucket, Sap, Tapered, Drilled, 3 Staves, 13 x 13 In. 46.00
Bucket, Sugar, Cover, Flower Vine, Salmon Ground, Painted, Joseph Lehn, 9 In. 1320.00
Bucket, Sugar, Cover, Grained, Painted, Iron Bands, Flower Vines, 7 ½ x 8 ½ In. 4375.00
Bucket, Sugar, Cover, Lehnware, 9 In. 117.00
Bucket, Sugar, Cover, Lehnware, Oak Staves, Metal Bands, Salmon, Vining, 9 x 7 In. 1210.00
Bucket, Sugar, Dark Blue Paint, Bail Handle, Metal Bands, 13 x 13 ¼ In. 95.00
Bucket, Sugar, Pine, Stave Construction, Blue Paint, Bentwood Swing Handle, c.1850, 10 x 11 In. 264.00
Bucket, Sugar, Softwood Lid, Wood Pull, Flower Banding, 9 ½ x 8 ¼ In. 1210.00
Bucket, Sugar, Stave Construction, Wood Bands, Bentwood Swing Handle, 12 x 13 In. 500.00
Bucket, Sugar, Staved, Wire Bail Handle, Finger Bands, Late 1800s, 6 ¾ x 6 ½ In. 441.00
Canteen, Bull's-Eye, Butternut, Wool Cover, Marked NG NY, Porter & Booth Phila. 500.00
Canteen, Butternut, Wool Cover, Cotton Sling, U.S., 1858 .... 400.00
Canteen, Cotton Strap, Oval, Metal Hoops, Blue, Green Paint, c.1830, 7 x 3 In. 974.00
Cash Box, Lift Top, Tray, Drawer, Dovetail, Cut Nail, Cherry, Poplar, 9 x 14 In. 431.00
Cellarette, Walnut, Fishtail Hinges, Handles, Pa., Late 18th Century, 14 x 14 ½ In. 8190.00
Cheese Trolley, Regency, Mahogany, Leather Casters, 7 x 18 In. .... *illus* 633.00
Chopping Bowl, Green Painted, 22 x 12 In. 575.00
Clothes Tree, Softwood, Green Paint, 32 Dowel Hangers, 2 Part Base, Va., 72 ½ In. 550.00
Clothes Tree, Softwood, Painted Green, Octagonal Post, 32 Dowel Hangers, 73 x 17 In. 605.00
Clothing Hanger, Softwood, Painted Blue, Beaded Edges, 17 Mushroom Pegs, 3 ½ x 139 In. 605.00
Compote, Burl Wood, Footed, Turned Stem, Molded Base, 7 ¾ x 6 ¾ In. 110.00
Compote, Flared Rim, Maple, Peaseware, c.1890, 5 x 7 In. 330.00
Compote, Turned, Softwood, Footed Base, Treen, 5 ½ x 13 ¼ In. 110.00
Container, Cover, Turned, Original Vinegar Decoration, Red Brown On Mustard, 1800s, 4 ¾ In. 529.00
Container, Saffron, Salmon Ground, Pansy, Footed, Finial, Lehnware, 4 ½ x 2 ⅝ In. 880.00
Cup, Saffron, Cover, Pansies, Strawberries, Footed, Lehnware, 4 ½ x 2 ⅝ In. .... *illus* 800.00
Dice Shaker, Mahogany, Corset Form, Bone Dice, 18th Century 225.00
Dish, Burl, Outside Rim, Dark Patina, Turned, 19th Century, 10 ½ x 2 In. 2820.00
Dish, Soinn & Kni, Laminated, Clamshell, Tapio Wirkkala, c.1954, 10 x 9 In. 6300.00
Dummy Board, Trompe L'Oeil, Gentleman, Maidservant, 40 x 12 In., Pair 16250.00
Easel, Artist's, Pine, Adjustable, 100 In. 322.00
Easel, Carved, Pierced, Serpents, Peacocks, Iron Hook & Eye, c.1910, 75 In. 646.00
Eggcup, Red & Blue, Flowers, Salmon Ground, Lehnware, 2 ¾ In. 646.00
Firkin, Blue Paint, Handle, Signed, W. Cissy, 10 x 9 ½ In. 385.00
Firkin, Cover, Pine, Salmon Orange, Black, Metal Bands, N.E., 11 x 12 In. .... *illus* 440.00
Firkin, Cover, Softwood, Green, Tongue & Groove Staves, Handle, Pa., 10 x 19 In. 605.00
Firkin, Joe Jones, American Flag, Painted, Bail Handle, 1921, 7 In. 1450.00

Firkin, Old Green Paint, Swing Handle, 19th Century, 12 ½ In.	761.00
Firkin, Pine, Oak, Handle, Signed, E.F. Lane & Son, 19th Century, 16 ½ x 12 In.	50.00
Firkin, Softwood, Bittersweet Orange, Bail Handle, Cover, 11 x 12 ¼ In.	770.00
Firkin, Softwood, Brown Paint, Oval, Bentwood Handle, Illegible Names, 14 ½ x 16 In.	3250.00
Firkin, Softwood, Cover, Painted Orange, Wood Finial, Wire Bail Swing Handle, 7 ¼ x 7 In.	110.00
Firkin, Softwood, Cover, Tongue & Groove Staves, Bentwood Swing Handle, 14 x 15 In.	2310.00
Firkin, Softwood, Painted Blue, Lap Joint Bands, Bentwood Handle, 11 ½ x 12 In.	715.00
Firkin, Softwood, Staves, Tapered Lap Joint, Bentwood Handle, 12 x 12 ½ In.	495.00
Firkin, Tongue & Groove, Powder Blue, Bentwood Handle, New England, 12 x 12 ½ In.	950.00
Foot Warmer, Mahogany, Handle, Initials, EB, 7 x 9 ½ In.	175.00
Hair Receiver, Burl, Footed Globular Shape, Maple, Screw Lid, 1800s, 4 x 3 ¼ In.	240.00
Hairpin Machine, Flat Board, Hinged Handles, Screws, 2 ½ x 9 ½ x 5 ½ In.	44.00
Hat Mold, 6 ½ x 12 In.	60.00
Humidor, Walnut, Lift Top, Grapes, Vines, 5 Inner Tiers, Lion Finial, 9 x 9 x 8 In. *illus*	460.00
Jar, Cover, Decoupage Flower Sprays, Red, Green, Yellow, Black, Joseph Lehn, 5 ¼ In.	410.00
Jar, Cover, Turned, Fan Shape, Red Brown Vinegar Graining Over Mustard, 4 x 4 ¼ In.	411.00
Jar, Lid, Cherry, Incised Ring, Carved Knob, 19th Century, 6 ¾ In.	230.00
Jar, Lid, Poplar, Footed, Red Orange Over Yellow Vinegar, Treen, 6 ½ In.	1880.00
Jardiniere, Provincial, Round, Twisted Border, 27 x 30 In.	330.00
Keg, Rum, Incised Banding, Caulked Ends, Bung Hole, 4 x 4 In.	99.00
Keg, Rum, Swigger, Stave Sides, Applied Ends, Metal Bands, 6 12 x 4 ¼ x 2 ¾ In.	77.00
Keg, Rum, Wood Stave Sides, Applied Ends, Spout, Wicker Banding, 8 x 5 x 3 In.	275.00
Keg, Turned, Barrel, Incised Banding, Caulked Wood Ends, Bung Hole, 2 ¼ x 2 ½ In.	66.00
Lap Board, Softwood, Applied Ends, Molded Wood Lip, Ogee Cut Ends, Penn., 25 x 37 In.	66.00
Lap Desk, Inlaid, Rosewood, Brass Mounted, Leather Flap, Sections, Tray, 6 x 20 x 11 In.	1920.00
Letter Writing Sander, Incised Lines, Treen, 3 x 3 In.	70.00
Model, Spiral Staircase, Mahogany, Balusters, Supports, Base, England, 41 ½ In.	9000.00
Mold, Cigar, Carved, Makes 10 Cigars, America, Early 1900s, 4 x 11 ¾ x 2 ½ In.	59.00
Mug, Cylindrical, Side Handle, Treen, 5 ¼ x 3 ⅝ In.	165.00
Necessaire De Voyage, Victorian, Brass Mounted, Burled Walnut, Bottles, 15 ½ x 8 In.	826.00
Noisemaker, Oak Base, Wood Crank Handle, Roller, Raised Squares, 20 ½ x 16 In.	187.00
Obelisk, Beechwood, Stepped, Black, Square, Pedestal Base, 16 ½ x 3 ½ In.	840.00
Peat Bucket, Regency, Ebonized, Mixed Woods, Tapered, Gilt Metal Liner, 14 x 12 In.	960.00
Piggin, Painted, 19th Century, 5 ¾ In.	936.00
Piggin, Pine Iron Banding, 12 In.	403.00
Piggin, Rose Head, Oak Staves, Riveted Bands, Patina, 13 ½ x 12 In.	80.00
Piggin, Softwood, Green, Elongated Handle, Tapered Lap Joint, Metal Band, 10 x 8 In.	225.00
Piggin, Softwood, Staves, Wood Bands, Pegged, Lollipop Handle, Peter Hersey, 10 x 8 In.	385.00
Piggin, Wood Staves, Lap Joint, Metal Band, Green, White Interior, 10 ½ x 8 In. *illus*	248.00
Puzzle, Sculpture, Stained, Late 19th Century, England, 17 ¼ x 11 ¼ In., 6 Piece	313.00
Saffron Cup, Flowers, Leaves, Red, Green, Black, Salmon Ground, Joseph Lehn, 4 ¾ In.	380.00
Salad Bowl, Walnut, Layered, 3-Leg Teak Base, 30 x 18 In.	188.00
Shelf, Bracket, Oak, Woman's Face, 19th Century, 20 x 22 In.	1440.00
Stocking Dryer, Leg Form, Softwood, Patina, Child's, 20 x 3 ¾ In.	99.00
Stringholder, Oval Medallions, Harbor, Boats, Stores, Beach Scene, Treen, 3 ¾ x 4 In.	50.00
Stringholder, Rosewood, Turned, Patina, Treen, 5 ¼ x 4 ½ In.	132.00
Sugar Pail, Birch, Maple, Lid, Handle, 10 x 10 In.	117.00
Tankard, Hinged Lid, Barrel Shape, Leaves, Acorns, Ferns, Flowers, Antler Finial, 15 In.	431.00
Towel Holder, Flat Back Board, Stamped Compass, Round Roller, Painted, 4 x 19 In.	88.00
Tray, Apple, Poplar, Brown, Scalloped Base, 19th Century, 3 ¾ x 11 In.	585.00
Tray, Bone Inlaid, Ebony, France, c.1930, 2 ½ x 19 ¾ x 11 ½ In.	438.00
Tray, Cherry, Dovetailed, Heart Cutout, 1800s, 6 ½ x 15 In.	411.00
Tray, Cutlery, Oak, Scalloped, England, c.1790, 13 x 3 In., Pair	411.00
Tray, Knife, Cherry, Pine, 2 Lift Lids, Scrolled Divider, Cutout Handle, 1800s, 13 x 13 x 11 In.	470.00
Tray, Lacquer, Brown, Eileen Gray, c.1922, 22 x 1 ½ In.	11875.00
Tray, Mahogany, Marquetry, Brass Bound, Oval, Ogee Rims, Brass, Leaf Border, Dutch, 21 ⅝ In.	889.00
Tray, Poplar, Yellow & Green Pinstriping, Red Ground, 19th Century, 3 x 10 x 7 In.	1755.00
Tray, Softwood, Painted Green, Kidney Bean Shape Handholds, 27 x 14 In.	330.00
Tray, Treen, Turned, Tapered Sides, Flat Rim, 2 ¾ x 20 ½ In.	248.00
Trencher, Birch, Painted, Blue Gray Paint, 1800s, 4 ¾ x 13 ¾ In.	646.00
Trolley, Double-Decker, Transports Urbains, Cast Iron, Wire, Paint, France, 15 x 30 In.	345.00
Urn, Cover, Turned, Maple, Peaseware, c.1865, 8 x 4 In.	575.00
Vase, Tassels, Metal, Painted Parchment, Birds, Red, c. Bugatti, Italy, c.1900, 18 In., Pair	10000.00
Vase, Turned Maple, Peaseware, c.1870, 8 x 7 In.	403.00
Watch Hutch, Cherry, Scalloped Crest, Heart Cutout, Round Glass, Pa., c.1800, 8 ½ In.	14040.00
Watch Hutch, Walnut, Tombstone, Line Inlay, c.1800, 8 x 5 ½ In.	1521.00
Watch Safe, Mahogany, Hanging, Pennsylvania, Early 19th Century, 12 ½ In.	644.00
Wig Stand, Turned, Old Green Paint, Late 18th Century, 7 ½ In.	1989.00

Wooden, Humidor, Walnut, Lift Top, Grapes, Vines, 5 Inner Tiers, Lion Finial, 9 x 9 x 8 In.
$460.00

Wooden, Piggin, Wood Staves, Lap Joint, Metal Band, Green, White Interior, 10 ½ x 8 In.
$248.00

Worcester, Bowl, Chamberlain, Caucasian Rhododendron, Garter Crest, Inscribed, 1870s, 12 ¾ In.
$748.00

TIP

Do not starch and fold old fabrics. It will cause the fibers to break.

Worcester, Lamp, Flowers, Beige, Brown, Pink, Blue Butterfly, Cream Base, 10 ¼ In.
$480.00

World War, Patch, 8th Air Force Bomb Wing, Felt, 7 ½ In.
$385.00

World's Fair, Bowl, 1893, Chicago, Boat Shape, Santa Maria, Embossed, Libbey, 2 ¼ x 6 ½ In.
$249.00

TIP

Never polish Trench art pieces made of brass shell casings. Collectors prefer the dark-colored metal.

WORCESTER porcelains were made in Worcester, England, from 1751. The firm went through many name changes and eventually, in 1862, became The Royal Worcester Porcelain Company Ltd. Collectors often refer to Dr. Wall, Barr, Flight, and other names that indicate time periods or artists at the factory. It became part of Royal Worcester Spode Ltd. in 1976. Related pieces may be found in the Royal Worcester category.

Basket, Pine Cone Pattern, 2 Handles, Pierced Sides, Applied Flowers, 4 x 8 x 7 In. 590.00
Biscuit Jar, Silver Plate Lid & Bail, Pineapple Pattern, 6 ½ In. 175.00
Bough Pot, Flowerpots, Covers, Stands, Chamberlain, Imari Palette, c.1810, 6 Piece 6875.00
Bowl, Chamberlain, Caucasian Rhododendron, Garter Crest, Inscribed, 1870s, 12 ¾ In. *illus* 748.00
Dish, Scalloped, Gilt Decoration, Painted Crown, Barr, Flight & Barr, 8 In., Pair 720.00
Jar, Dresser, Reticulated Leaf Scrolled Sides, Dome Lid, George Grainger, 6 ¼ In. 356.00
Lamp, Flowers, Beige, Brown, Pink, Blue Butterfly, Cream Base, 10 ¼ In. .... *illus* 480.00
Pitcher, Bouquets, Leaves, Mask Spout, c.1770, 11 ¼ In. 590.00
Plate, Blind Earl Pattern, Branch, Flower, Leaves, Scalloped Rim, c.1800, 7 ½ In. 550.00
Plate, Iron Red, Green, Cobalt Blue, Gilt, Flight, Barr & Barr, c.1810, 8 ¼ In., 4 Piece 748.00
Serving Dish, Imari, Gilded Gadroon Border, Flight, Barr & Barr, 12 x 9 In., Pair 720.00

WORLD WAR I and World War II souvenirs are collected today. Be careful not to store anything that includes live ammunition. Your local police will tell you how to dispose of the explosives. See also Sword and Trench Art.

WORLD WAR I

Pinback, 1 Country, 1 Flag, Celluloid, Multicolored, Kunstadper Co., Chicago, 1 In. 112.00
Poster, Buy Bonds To Your Utmost, Frame, Lend The Way They Fight, 41 x 27 In. 75.00
Poster, For Victory, Buy More Bonds, 4th Liberty Loan, 56 x 36 In. 420.00
Poster, I Want You For The U.S. Army, Uncle Sam, James Montgomery Flagg, 40 ½ x 30 In. ... 5500.00
Poster, Liberty Bond, Ring It Again, Ketterlinus, Philadelphia, c.1917, 30 x 20 In. 325.00
Poster, Navy Needs You, Lithograph, Hewitt Co., J.S. McLaughlin, c.1917, 14 x 22 In. 67.00
Poster, Public Warning, Sr. Joseph Canston, London, Airships, Planes, Frame, c.1915, 23 x 36 In. 86.00
Poster, Recruitment, Tell That To The Marines, Angry Man, J. Montgomery, 1918, 30 x 40 In. 320.00
Poster, U.S. Marines Want You, Red, White, Blue Ground, Marine In Uniform, 21 x 28 In. ... 476.00
Poster, Victory Liberty, Sure We'll Finish The Job, Beneker, c.1918, 38 x 26 In. 472.00
Poster, Victory Liberty Loan, For Home & Country, Alfred Everett, Frame, 30 x 20 In. 80.00
Poster, War Bonds, Liberty Loan, Flag, Statue Of Liberty, E. DeLand, 1917, 20 x 30 In. 390.00
Poster, War Bonds, Liberty Loan, Uncle Sam, Symbols, D. Grosebeck, 1917, 20 x 30 In. 360.00
Sign, Light Consumes Coal, Save Light, Save Coal, Clarence Phillips, 1918, 27 ¾ x 20 ½ In. .. 9600.00

WORLD WAR II

Arm Band, Auschwitz Nazi Concentration Camp, 13 In. 138.00
Arm Band, Birkenau Concentration Camp, 16 In. 88.00
Clock, Submarine, Seth Thomas, Black Bakelite Case, Key, 11 In. 201.00
Coat, Concentration Camp, Jewish, Star Of David, ID No., KAPO Arm Band. 468.00
Doll, Parachute Trooper, Raggy Doodle, Booklet, Prager & Reuben, Box 90.00
Flag, Nazi, Multipiece, Stitched, German, 30 x 50 In. 155.00
Helmet, German, Luftwaffe, Single Decal, Stamped ET 64, Size 56 .... 850.00
Patch, 8th Air Force Bomb Wing, Felt, 7 ½ In. .... *illus* 385.00
Poster, Don't Talk About Troop Movements, 40 x 28 In. 98.00
Poster, Free Labor Will Win, Man, Flag, 40 x 28 In. 121.00
Poster, One Leak Can Sink A Ship, Charles Mather, 41 ¾ x 26 ¼ In. 3600.00
Poster, PT Boat Attack, Give Us Lumber For More PTs, 1943, 40 x 28 ½ In. 360.00
Poster, Uncle Sam, Stay Neutral, Keep Us Out Of War, Cardboard, c.1939, 10 ¼ x 6 ½ In. 123.00
Poster, United We Are Strong, United We Will Win, 1943, Frame, 42 ¾ x 59 In. 300.00
Poster, War Bonds, Don't Let The Shadow Touch Them, 1940s, Frame, 35 x 47 In. 450.00
Poster, We Have Just Begun To Fight, Soldier, Black, White, Red, 40 x 28 In. 98.00
Poster, Your Scrap Brought It Down, Keep Scrapping, Zudor, 40 x 28 ½ In. 1080.00

WORLD'S FAIR souvenirs from all of the fairs are collected. The first fair was the Great Exhibition of 1851 in London. Some other important exhibitions and fairs include Philadelphia, 1876 (Centennial); Chicago, 1893 (World's Columbian); Buffalo, 1901 (Pan-American); St. Louis, 1904 (Louisiana Purchase); Portland, 1905 (Lewis & Clark Centennial Exposition); San Francisco, 1915 (Panama-Pacific); Philadelphia, 1926 (Sesquicentennial); Chicago, 1933 (Century of Progress); Cleveland, 1936 (Great Lakes); San Francisco, 1939 (Golden Gate International); New York, 1939 (World of Tomorrow); Seattle, 1962 (Century 21); New York, 1964; Montreal, 1967; New Orleans, 1984; Tsukuba, Japan, 1985; Vancouver, Canada, 1986; Brisbane, Australia, 1988; Seville, Spain, 1992; Genoa, Italy, 1992; Seoul, South Korea, 1993; Lisbon, Portugal, 1998; Hanover, Germany, 2000; and Aichi, Japan, 2005. Memorabilia of fairs include directories, pictures, fabrics, ceramics, etc. Memorabilia from other similar celebrations may be listed in the Souvenir category.

Item	Price
Ashtray, 1933, Chicago, Century Of Progress, Plymouth Dodge De Soto, 3 x 3 In.	14.00
Badge, 1904, St. Louis, Brass, Embossed, Suspended Missouri Mule, ¾ In.	92.00
Bank, 1893, Chicago, Christopher Columbus, Indian Chief, J. & E. Stevens, 1883	775.00
Bank, 1934, Chicago, Buildings, Tin, American Can Co., 3 ½ x 2 In.	5.00
Bank, 1934, Chicago, Libby's, Fruit, Tin, American Can Co., 3 ½ x 2 In.	22.00
Bookends, 1933, Chicago, Mayor Anton Cermak, Painted, Plaster, 7 ½ In.	99.00
Bookmark, 1904, St. Louis, Celluloid, Scruggs Vandervoort Barney Dry Goods	102.00
Bowl, 1893, Chicago, Boat Shape, Santa Maria, Embossed, Libbey, 2 ¼ x 6 ½ In. *illus*	249.00
Bus, 1933, Chicago, Greyhound Line, Painted, White, Blue, Cast Iron, Arcade, 11 ½ In.	144.00
Button, 1901, Pan-American, Globe, Uncle Sam, Woman's Head, 2 ⅛ In.	920.00
Corkscrew, 1893, Columbia Exposition, Chicago, Risque Figure, 3 In.	411.00
Creamer, 1901, Pan-American, Green To Clear, 5 In.	47.00
Darning Ball, 1893, Chicago, Blown Glass, Pink To White, Pontil, Peachblow, 5 In.	240.00
Diorama, 1939, New York, World Of Tomorrow, Folding Landscape, 6 ½ x 25 In.	115.00
Fan, 1893, Chicago, Landscape, Paper, Wood, 12 ½ In.	11.00
Figure, 1939, New York, Trylon & Perisphere, Plaster, Embossed, 7 ½ x 12 In.	316.00
Figure, 1962, Seattle, Blackamoor, Holding Basket, Nodder, Moving Eyes, Electrified, 40 In.	1725.00
Figure, 1962, Seattle, Chef, Boater Hat, Head Moves, Electrified, 25 In.	431.00
Figure, 1962, Seattle, Chinese Man, Seated, Braid, Head Moves, Electrified, 20 In.	719.00
Figure, 1962, Seattle, Clown, Holding Frog, Head Moves, Electrified, 24 In.	374.00
Figure, 1962, Seattle, Photographer, Working Flashbulb, Camera, Nodder, Electrified, 23 In.	748.00
Figure, 1962, Seattle, Scotsman, Head Moves, Native Attire, Electrified, 17 ½ In.	719.00
Flask, 1893, Chicago, Potato, Milk Glass, Brown Paint, Ground Lip, Screw Cap, 4 ⅞ In. *illus*	156.00
Globe, 1867, Paris Exposition, Terrestrial, Stand, Prize Medal, Marked, Schedler, 3 In.	800.00
Lamp, 1939, New York, Frosted, Trylon & Perisphere, 3 ½ x 5 In.	253.00
Lamp, Oil, 1901, Buffalo, Milk Glass, Western Hemisphere, Transfer, Nutmeg Burner, 8 ¾ In.	288.00
Mechanical Pencil, 1939, New York, Fair Buildings, Brass Clip, Cardboard Box, 6 In.	86.00
Medal, 1876, Philadelphia, Centennial Exhibition, Faimount Park, Case, 2 In.	168.00
Medal Set, 1876, Philadelphia International Exhibition, Wood, Carved, 6 Piece	1053.00
Menu Set, 1939, New York, Polish Pavilion, Polish Scene Covers, 5 ½ x 8 ½ In.	173.00
Mug, 1904, St. Louis, Cascade Gardens, Stoneware, Pewter Lid, ½ Liter, 7 x 5 In.	77.00
Mug, 1904, St. Louis, Machinery Building, Barrel Shape, 3 x 2 ¾ In.	72.00
Mug, 1904, St. Louis, Palace Of Liberal Arts, Hinged Lid, 4 ¼ x 3 ½ In.	55.00
Mug, 1904, St. Louis, Palace Of Varied Industries, Liberal Arts, Electricity, 6 x 2 ½ In.	27.00
Napkin Ring, 1939, New York, Catalin, Trylon, Perisphere, 5 In., Pair	215.00
New York, 1939, Pin, Trylon & Perisphere, Star, Plastic, Die Cut, 1939, 2 ¼ x 2 ½ In.	75.00
Paperweight, 1939, New York, Trylon & Perisphere, Syroco Wood, 2 ¼ x 4 In.	75.00
Parasol, 1933, Chicago, Bamboo, Paper, 29 ½ In.	420.00
Pen & Pencil Set, 1939, New York, Stratford, Orange, Blue, Pearl Finish, Box, 5 In.	173.00
Perfume Bottle, 1904, St. Louis, Clear, Stopper, Cyclamen, 5 In.	489.00
Pitcher, 1939, New York, George Washington, Homer Laughlin, 4 1/2 In. *illus*	30.00
Plate, 1876, Philadelphia, Centennial, Geo. Washington, White, Gold Trim, 9 In.	335.00
Plate, 1904, St. Louis, Louisiana Purchase, Missouri Horticulture, Ohio China Co., 8 ¾ In.	38.00
Plate, 1904, St. Louis, Palace Of Varied Industries, Green Rim, Gilt, 7 ½ In., Pair	39.00
Plate, 1905, Portland, Lewis, Clark Expedition Centennial, Scenes, Staffordshire, 10 In.	96.00
Pocketknife, 1904, St. Louis, Movable Loop, 2 ⅜ In.	86.00
Poster, 1964, New York, Unisphere, Bob Peak, 11 x 16 In.	75.00
Poster, 1964, New York, Unisphere, Bob Peak, 42 x 28 In.	99.00
Purse, 1939, New York, Beaded, 5 In. *illus*	150.00
Razor, 1893, Columbia Exposition, Columbian Expo., Straight, Black Plastic Handle, Case, 6 ¾ In.	50.00
Ribbon, 1905, Portland, Lewis & Clark Exposition, Blue, Purple Ribbon, 2 ½ x 7 ⅜ In.	144.00
Salt & Pepper, 1904, St. Louis, Louisiana Purchase, Eagle, Crest, Gray	11.00
Saltshaker, 1893, Chicago, Egg Shape, Flat Side, White, Mt. Washington, 1890, 1 ¾ In. *illus*	136.00
Sugar, 1893, Chicago, Sunflower Shape, Handles, Libbey, 2 ¾ x 3 ½ x 5 In. *illus*	23.00
Tape Measure, 1904, Louisiana Purchase, Festival Hall, Cascades, 1 ¾ In.	86.00
Tin, 1904, St. Louis, Festall Hall Coffee, Cascade Gardens, 3 Lb., 10 x 5 ¼ In.	845.00
Tip Tray, 1904, St. Louis, Have Some Junket, 4 ¾ In.	413.00
Token, 1939, New York, Brass, Trylon & Perisphere, Empire State Building, 1 In.	10.00
Toy, 1939, New York, Greyhound, Tractor Train, Arcade	750.00
Tray, 1964, New York, Peace Through Understanding, Black, 10 ½ In.	5.00
Tumbler, 1964, New York, Red, Blue, Frosted, Pool Of Industry, 6 ½ In.	22.00
Tumbler Set, 1964, New York, Various Images, Colors, Box, 8 x 14 In., 8 Piece *illus*	139.00
Vase, 1876, Philadelphia, Centennial, Eagle, Patriotic Symbols, Glass, Frosted, Gold Trim, 9 ¼ In.	478.00
Watch, 1982, Knoxville, Timex, Fair Logo, Plastic Case, Man's, 3 ½ In.	115.00

World's Fair, Flask, 1893, Chicago, Potato, Milk Glass, Brown Paint, Ground Lip, Screw Cap, 4 ⅞ In.
$156.00

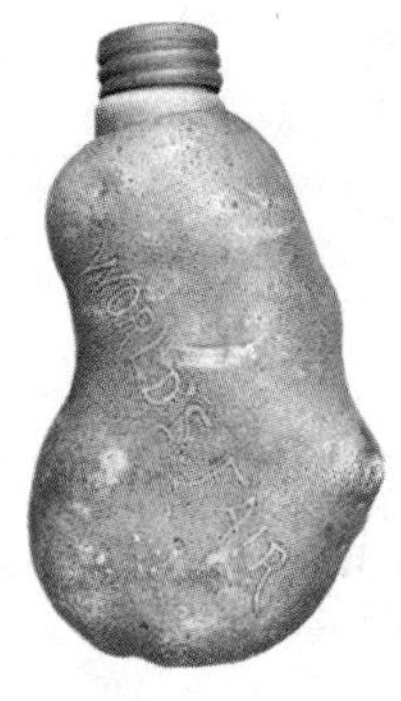

World's Fair, Pitcher, 1939, New York, George Washington, Homer Laughlin, 4 ½ In.
$30.00

World's Fair, Purse, 1939, New York, Beaded, 5 In.
$150.00

World's Fair, Saltshaker, 1893, Chicago, Egg Shape, Flat Side, White, Mt. Washington, 1890, 1 ¾ In.
$136.00

World's Fair, Sugar, 1893, Chicago, Sunflower Shape, Handles, Libbey, 2 ¾ x 3 ½ x 5 In.
$23.00

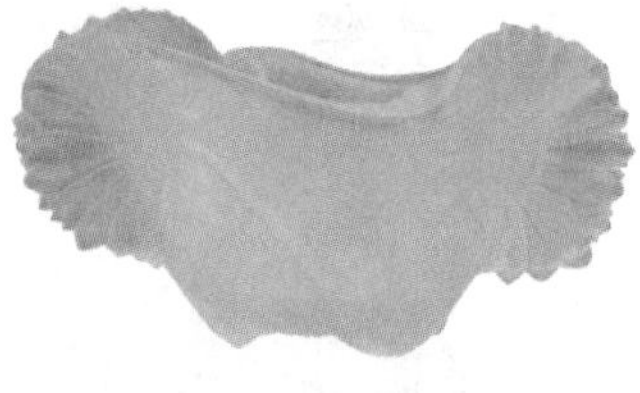

World's Fair, Tumbler Set, 1964, New York, Various Images, Colors, Box, 8 x 14 In., 8 Piece
$139.00

Wristwatches

Early wristwatches were hand-wound. In the early 1950s miniature batteries were invented. The first electric wristwatches were sold in 1957. Miniaturization made the first quartz watches possible in the late 1960s.

Wristwatch, Audemars Piguet, 18K Gold, 51 Jewels, Tachymeter, 1 ½ In.
$7000.00

WPA is the abbreviation for Works Progress Administration, a program created by executive order in 1935 to provide jobs for millions of unemployed Americans. Artists were hired to create murals, paintings, drawings, and sculptures for public buildings. Pieces are marked WPA and may have the artist's name on them.

Book, Baseball In Old Chicago, 64 Pages, 1939, 9 x 6 In. 115.00
Figurine, Little Jack Horner, Ceramic, Inscribed WPA Ohio, Edris Eckhardt, 1936, 4 ¼ In. 920.00
Painting, Laborer, Indian Pot On Back, Watercolor, Signed, 1930s, 16 x 12 In. 104.00
Painting, Loggers, Tempera On Board, 31 x 23 ½ In. 863.00
Painting, Mountain Family, Heads Down, Gouache, Jerome Burstyn, 12 x 9 In. 920.00
Poster, See America, Welcome To Montana, Indians, Mountains, Lithograph, 28 x 22 In. 575.00
Sculpture, Embracing Couple, Wood, Albert Wein, 39 x 10 x 11 In. 5060.00
Sculpture, Man, With Mallet, Wheel, Wood, 11 x 5 x 3 In. 115.00
Sculpture, Monkey Man, Elongated Limbs, Plaster, A.F. Trank, 1931, 20 In. 403.00
Vase, Pottery, Green, Incised Vertical Lines, Bulbous, Flared Rim, Clivia Calder, Mich., 4 In. 92.00

WRISTWATCHES came into use during World War I. Wristwatches are listed here by manufacturer or as advertising or character watches. Wristwatches may also be listed in other categories. Pocket watches are listed in the Watch category.

14K White Gold, Square Diamonds, Ruby, Arched Links, 6 ⅝ In. 1304.00
Audemars Piguet, 18K Gold, 51 Jewels, Tachymeter, 1 ½ In. .... *illus* 7000.00
Baume Mercier, 2 Time Zone, 18K Gold, Black Lizard Band, 17 Jewel, c.1960 .... 1195.00
Breitling Chronomat, Stainless Steel, 18K Yellow Gold, Black Dial, Leather Band 1150.00
Breitling Chronomat Date, Stainless Steel, 18K Yellow Gold, Blue Dial, Leather Band 1554.00
Bulgari, Tubogas, Woman's, Black Dial, Diamond, Baton Numberals, Gold Bracelet 3606.00
Bulgari, Woman's, Cuff, 18K, Quartz Movement 5500.00
Bulova, 17 Jewel, Square, Leather Band, 1930s 30.00
Bulova, Woman's, 21 Jewel, 14K White Gold Case, Band, 6 In. 403.00
Bulova, Woman's, Pink Gold Diamond, Ruby Face, Black Narrow Band, c.1940 .... 167.00
Cartier, 18K Gold, White Dial, Roman Numerals, 17 Jewel, Leather Strap, 19 x 18 In. 2489.00
Cartier, Stainless Steel Slide Cover, Square Dial, Back Wind Movement. 1896.00
Character, Big Bird, Sesame Street, Metal, Vinyl, Bradley, Box, 1977, 1 x 5 ½ In. .... *illus* 139.00
Character, Bugs Bunny, Glow In The Dark Hands, Rexall Drugstore Exclusive, 1951 .... 230.00
Character, Felix The Cat, Sheffield, Leather Band, c.1971 .... 633.00
Character, Skippy, Bowtie, Black Vinyl Bank, Stainless Stain, Rega Industries, Israel, c.1972 . 38.00
Character, Woodstock, Armitron, Leather Band, Box, c.1980 .... 69.00
Character, Woody Woodpecker, Webster Watch Co., Leather Band, c.1970 .... 345.00
Charlton & Co., Art Nouveau, Platinum, Diamond, Onyx, London .... *illus* 650.00
Chaumet, Woman's, Stainless Steel, Roman Numerals, Double Quartz. 1315.00
Chopard, Woman's, Gold, Black Band, c.1970 .... 657.00
Corum, 20 Dollar Liberty Gold Coin, 6 Jewel Quartz, Sapphire Crystal, 18K Gold, Band. 4362.00
Ebel, 14K Gold, Diamond, Manual Wind, 17 Jewel, 6 ⅛ In. 770.00
Ebel, Black Enamel Dial, Hausmann & Co., 17 Jewel, 18K Yellow Gold Band, 7 In. 748.00
Eberhard, 18K, Single Button Chronograph, Link Band, Signed, 18 Jewel, c.1910 .... 1673.00
Elgin, 18K Gold Anniversary Model, Black Lizard Band, 21 Jewel, c.1950 .... 1554.00
Eliot, Sculptural Bracelet, Black Face, Round, Windup 165.00
Gruen, 14K Gold, Diamond, Silvertone Dial, 17 Jewel, Gold Mesh Strap 563.00
Hamilton, Automatic Pacer, Black Leather Band, 17 Jewel, Asymmetric, c.1960. .... 1554.00
Hamilton, Piping Rock Gold, 14K, Hinged Lugs, Crocodile Band, 19 Jewel, c.1937. .... 896.00
Hamilton, Platinum Diamond Dial, Stainless Steel Band, 19 Jewel, c.1940 .... 3227.00
Hamilton, Woman's, Platinum, 38 Single Cut Diamonds, Barrel Shape Case, Black Cord Band 1135.00
Hamilton, Woman's, Platinum, Diamond Melee, Baguettes, Flexible Band. 5760.00
International Watch Co., 18K Gold Case, Black Alligator Band, 17 Jewel, c.1960. .... 836.99
Jaeger LeCoultre, Stainless Steel, Automatic Memovox Alarm, 17 Jewel, c.1960 .... 538.00
LeCoultre, 17 Jewel, Stepped Bezel, Manual Wind, Lizard Strap, 18K Gold 1912.00
LeCoultre, 18K Gold, Black Crocodile Band, Octagon Face, 15 Jewel, c.1970, 2 Piece 598.00
LeCoultre, Automatic Memovox Alarm, Flex Steel Band, 17 Jewel, c.1960. .... 956.00
LeCoultre, Stainless Steel, Master Mariner, 17 Jewel, c.1960. .... 657.00
LeCoultre, Woman's, 9K Gold Back Wind, Rolled Gold Plated Band, 15 Jewel, 6 ½ In. 359.00
LeCoultre, Woman's, 18K White Gold Integral Bracelet, 17 Jewel, c.1970, 6 ⅝ In. 507.00
Longines, Gold Diamond Dial, Hooded Lug, Crocodile Band, 17 Jewel, c.1940 .... 1195.00
Longines, White Gold, Lug Diamond Dial, Black Leather Band, 17 Jewel, c.1955 .... 1315.00
Mary Marvel, Chromed Metal Case, Green Band, Glow In Dark Numbers, Box... 345.00 to 518.00
Mauboussin, Art Deco, Platinum, Diamond, Quartz Movement, Black Cord Strap 504.00
Movado, 14K Gold, Serpentine Link Band, 17 Jewel, Tiffany & Co, c.1930, 7 In. 956.00
Movado, 14K Gold Art Deco, 17 Jewel, Padded Alligator Band, c.1930 .... 956.00

Movado, Museum Sport, Black Face, Sapphire, Steel Band, Case 300.00
Omega, 18K Rose Gold, Black Crocodile Calf Band, 17 Jewel, c.1960 .... 3585.00
Omega, Double Hinged Back, Leather Band, 11 Jewel, c.1905 .... 359.00
Omega, Stainless Steel Seamster 600, 17 Jewel, Black Leather Band, c.1960 .... 717.00
Omega, Woman's, Oval Case, Silver Dial, Mesh Bracelet, 14K Yellow Gold, 6 ½ In. 443.00
Patek Philippe, 18K Gold, Black Lizard Band, Teardrop Lugs, 18 Jewel, c.1962 .... 4183.00
Patek Philippe, 18K Gold, Silvertone Dial, Arabic Numerals, 18 Jewel 7110.00
Patek Philippe, Silver Dial, Abstract Numbers, Black Band, 18K Gold Case 11500.00
Patek Philippe, Woman's, Silver Face, 14K Gold Band, 8 ¾ In. 3335.00
Piaget, 18K Gold, Basket Weave Dial, Baton Numerals, Manual Wind, 7 ⅛ In. 2726.00
Piaget, Woman's, 18K Yellow Gold Mesh, Malachite Dial, Diamond, Oval Case, 7 In. 3107.00
Piaget, Woman's, Gold, Oval, Diamond Surround, 18K Gold Woven Link Band 5410.00
Piguet, 18K Gold, Brick Link Band, 20 Jewel, c.1944, 7 ¼ In. 3107.00
Piguet, Lapis Lazuli, Integral Bracelet, 18K White Gold Bracelet, Cartier, c.1970 .... 3107.00
Platinum, Diamond, Silvertone Metal Dial, Manual Wind, 17 Jewel, 14K White Gold 1422.00
Rolex, 14K Oyster Link Band, Date, Diamond, Blue Marker Dial, 27 Jewel, c.1985 .... 3227.00
Rolex, GMT No. 1675, Steel Oyster Band, Red, Blue Bezel Dial, 26 Jewel, c.1971 .... 3585.00
Rolex, Perpetual, 18K Gold Oyster Link Band, Beveled Face, 26 Jewel, c.1968 .... 3884.00
Rolex, Roger Moore, Submarine, Steel Oyster Link Band, No. 5523, 26 Jewel, c.1962 .... 3346.00
Rolex, Stainless Steel Case, Gold Arrow Markers, 17 Jewel, Tan Pigskin Band, c.1930 .... 717.00
Rolex, Steel Oyster Band, Perpetual Date, No. 1500, 26 Jewel, c.1968 .... 1075.00
Rolex, Woman's, Cellini, Mesh Band, Oval Face, 18K Gold, Case, 6 ¼ In. 1100.00
Rolex, Woman's, Diamond, Lugs, Enameled Hands, 18K White Gold, c.1970, 6 ⅝ In. 3585.00
Stainless Steel, White Guilloche Dial, Roman Numerals, Automatic 1126.00
Swiss, Woman's, 14K Gold, Diamonds, Leaf, Braided Rope Band, 17 Jewel, c.1930, 6 ⅜ In. 837.00
Swiss, Woman's, Diamonds, Platinum, Side Leaf Engraving, Black Band, c.1920 .... 956.00
Sylvester, Time Setters, Blue Vinyl Band, c.1971 .... 139.00
Tabbah, Woman's, Diamond, Sapphire, Hinged Lugs, Roman Numeral, 18K Gold 1912.00
Tiffany, Stainless Steel, Rectangular Case, White Enamel Dial, Flexible Strap, Box 856.00
Vacheron & Constantin, Silver Face, 18K Yellow Gold, Leather Band, 9 In. 3910.00
Waltham, Gold Filled Hunting Case, Emblems, Flowers, c.1902 .... 215.00

YELLOWWARE is a heavy earthenware made of a yellowish clay. It varies in color from light yellow to orange-yellow. Many nineteenth- and twentieth-century kitchen bowls and jugs were made of yellowware. It was made in England and in the United States. Another form of pottery that is sometimes classed as yellowware is listed in this book in the Mocha category.

Bowl, Blue Bands, 10 In. 30.00
Bowl, Pink & Aqua Bands, Watt, 7 x 14 In. 55.00
Bowl, White Band, 6 ½ x 12 ¾ In. 260.00
Bread Pan, Loaf, Yellow Clay, Manganese Glaze, Yellow Slip, 19th Century, 10 x 11 In. 2530.00
Canister, Cover, Finial, Cylindrical, Fluted Sides, Rockingham Glaze, 9 x 8 ¾ In. 22.00
Canister, Cover, Leaf Decoration, Handle, Cylindrical, Rockingham Glaze, 8 ½ x 7 In. 22.00
Canister, Molded Handle, White Band, Blue Seaweed Design, 8 In. 165.00
Crock, Cover, White Bands, 6 x 3 ¾ In. 200.00
Cup & Saucer, Grape, Banding, Fluted Sides, Rockingham Glaze, 1 ¼ & 2 ⅝ In. 44.00
Doorstop, Comforter Spaniel, Yellow, Tan, Seated, Flower, Shell, 10 x 7 In. 575.00
Figurine, Dog, Spaniel, Seated, Curled Tail, Cobalt Blue, c.1880, 10 x 8 In. 1840.00
Figurine, Dog, Spaniel, Seated, Gold Locket, Red Collar, Oval Base, 1850s, 13 x 10 In. 546.00
Figurine, Dog, Spaniel, Seated, Ocher, Flowers On Base, Teal Glaze, Ohio, c.1860, 14 x 12 In. 2185.00
Figurine, Dog, Spaniel, Seated, Rockingham Glaze, 9 ¾ In. 142.00
Figurine, Lion, Reclining, Rectangular Base, Rockingham Glaze, 4 x 9 ¼ x 3 In. 176.00
Figurine, Lion, Reclining, Rockingham Glaze, Inscribed, 1882, 4 x 9 x 3 In. 160.00
Flask, Boot, Rockingham Glaze, 6 ½ x 7 ¼ x 2 ¼ In. 99.00
Flask, Man, Holding Mug, Rockingham Glaze, Stamped, 8 ¾ x 4 ¾ x 3 In. .... *illus* 132.00
Milk Pan, 14 In. 120.00
Mixing Bowl, 3 White Center Lines, 4 ½ x 10 ½ In. 45.00
Mixing Bowl, Brown & White Bands, 5 ⅜ x 11 ½ In. 25.00
Mixing Bowl, Brown & White Bands, 6 ¾ x 14 In. 75.00
Mold, Food, Rabbit, Oval, 4 x 8 ¼ x 5 ¼ In. 200.00
Mug, Cover, Reed Handle, Brown Wavy Lines, c.1885, 6 In. 563.00
Mug, Slip Decorated, Brown Dots, c.1775, 2 In. 5333.00
Pie Plate, Marked, Blue Stamp, 2 x 11 ¼ In. 150.00
Pie Plate, RRP, Robinson Ransbottom, 2 x 10 In. 100.00
Pie Plate, Scalloped Rim, Fluted, Rockingham Glaze, 1 ¼ x 8 In. 77.00
Pipe Bowl, Boot Shape, Brown Glaze, 2 x 1 ½ In. 55.00
Pitcher, Diamond Pattern, Bulbous, Rockingham Glaze, 6 ½ x 4 ¼ In. 44.00

Wristwatch, Character, Big Bird, Sesame Street, Metal, Vinyl, Bradley, Box, 1977, 1 x 5 ½ In.
$139.00

Wristwatch, Charlton & Co., Art Nouveau, Platinum, Diamond, Onyx, London
$650.00

Yellowware, Flask, Man, Holding Mug, Rockingham Glaze, Stamped, 8 ¾ x 4 ¾ x 3 In.
$132.00

TIP
Never use commercial window cleaner on a stained glass window. It could remove the color or damage the lead.

Yellowware, Tieback, Curtain, Mushroom, Pointed Rim, Rockingham Glaze, 4 ½ x 4 In.
$33.00

Zanesville, Vase, Clovers, Standard Glaze, Marked, La Moro, 8 ¾ In.
$55.00

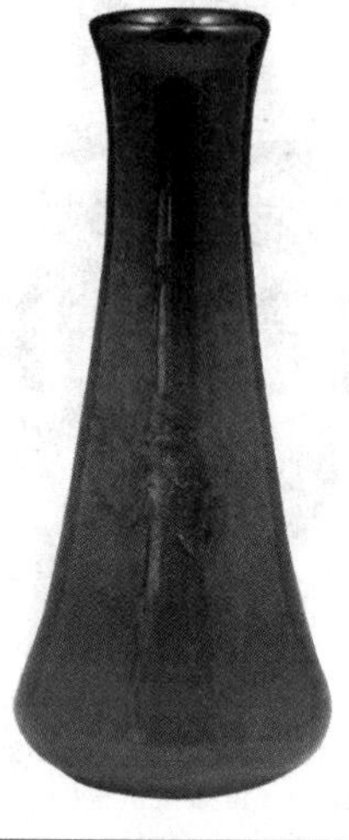

Zsolnay, Pitcher, Pelican Form, Eosin Glaze, 5 Churches Medallion, 9 ½ x 4 ½ In.
$3900.00

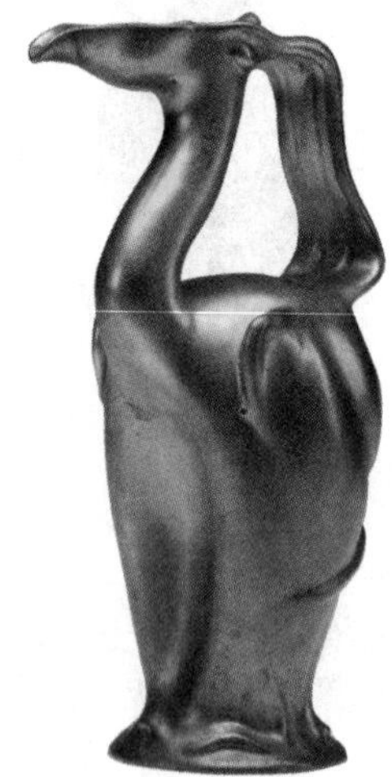

Pitcher, Stripes & Blue Seaweed In Tree Form On White Band, c.1870, 8 ¾ In. 1175.00
Rolling Pin, Wood Handles, 3 x 15 In.. .... 250.00 to 325.00
Tieback, Curtain, Mushroom, Pointed Rim, Rockingham Glaze, 4 ½ x 4 In. .... *illus* 33.00
Toby Jug, Man, Opening Snuffbox, Rockingham Glaze, 10 ½ x 4 ¼ x 6 ½ In. 33.00
Toby Jug, Man, Wearing Tricorn Hat, Rockingham Glaze, Applied Handle, 6 In. 44.00

ZANE Pottery was founded in 1921 by Adam Reed and Harry McClelland in South Zanesville, Ohio, at the old Peters and Reed Building. Zane pottery is very similar to Peters and Reed pottery, but it is usually marked. The factory was sold in 1941 to Lawton Gonder.

ZANE WARE MADE IN U.S.A.

Vase, Shouldered, Tapered, Brown & Gray Drip Glaze, 5 x 11 ¼ In. 316.00

ZANESVILLE Art Pottery was founded in 1900 by David Schmidt in Zanesville, Ohio. The firm made faience umbrella stands, jardinieres, and pedestals. The company closed in 1962. Many pieces are marked with just the words *La Moro*.

LA MORO

Bowl, Clover Band, Green Matte Glaze, Marked EL, 3 x 5 In.. .... 195.00
Jardiniere, Geometric Design, Green Matte Glaze, Marked, 5 x 7 In. 195.00
Vase, Blue, Green Drip Glaze, Lavender Ground, Marked, 9 x 6 In.. .... 95.00
Vase, Clovers, Standard Glaze, Marked, La Moro, 8 ¾ In. .... *illus* 55.00
Vase, Double Handle, Glossy Aqua Glaze, Stamped, 7 x 6 In.. .... 100.00
Vase, Leaf, Thick Maroon Matte Glaze, Incised, 8 In. 185.00
Vase, Lobed, Plum Glaze, Marked, 9 x 6 In. 95.00
Vase, Single Flower, Dark Blue Glaze, 9 x 5 In.. .... 125.00

ZSOLNAY pottery was made in Hungary after 1853 and was characterized by Persian, Art Nouveau, or Hungarian motifs. A series of new Zsolnay figurines with green-gold luster finish is available in many shops today. Early Zsolnay was not marked, but by 1878 the tower trademark was used.

ZSOLNAY PÉCS 5 TJM

Ewer, Red, Leaves, Vines, Leaf Form Handle, Blue Flowers On Shoulder, Neck, 11 In. 6900.00
Figurine, Chicken, Eosin Glaze, Art Deco, Signed, Zsolnay, Hungary, 8 ⅛ In. 150.00
Figurine, Man, Seated, Hand Painted, 13 x 6 x 9 In. 176.00
Figurine, Seminude Woman, Seated, Marked, 9 x 6 x 3 In. 165.00
Figurine, Woman, Seated, 11 x 7 x 10 ½ In. 94.00
Jug, Botanical, Stopper, 7 ¾ In. 460.00
Pitcher, Dancing Muses, Eosin Glaze, Art Nouveau, 14 In. 16800.00
Pitcher, Pelican Form, Eosin Glaze, 5 Churches Medallion, 9 ½ x 4 ½ In. .... *illus* 3900.00
Pitcher, Reticulated Dragon Handle, Blue Eosin Glaze, 10 In. 1800.00
Pitcher, Woman, Kneeling, Eosin Glaze, Lusterware, Marked, 7 x 4 In. 132.00
Vase, 3-D Nudes & Waves, Red Glaze, c.1900, 6 In.. .... 1380.00
Vase, Baluster, Birds, Persian Design, Luster, 8 ¾ In. 2400.00
Vase, Blue Green Iridescent, Ribs, Dimples, Marked, 7 ½ x 5 In.. .... 820.00
Vase, Bowling Pin Form, Multicolored, Iridescent, Marked, 9 x 2 ¼ In. 822.00
Vase, Cone Shape, Man & Dog Watching Sheep, 5 In. 1725.00
Vase, Eosin Iridescent, Ribs, Signed, 3 x 4 ½ In.. .... 80.00
Vase, Japonesque, Earthenware, Gilt Enamel, Flowering Trees, Leaf Lambrequin Borders, 14 In. 770.00
Vase, Luster Blue, Green Glaze, Burgundy, 8 Handles, 5 Medallions, 7 ½ x 5 ¼ In. 9600.00
Vase, Purple, Pink, Red Glaze, 8 Twisted Buttresses, 5 Church Medallions, 8 x 5 ½ In. 7200.00
Vase, Tapered, Snail Handles, Mottled, Majolica Glaze, 8 ¼ In.. .... 3000.00
Vase, Turquoise, Shriveled Glaze, 2 Handles, Reticulated, Marked, 12 In. 118.00

INDEX

This index is computer-generated, making it as complete and accurate as possible. References in uppercase type are category listings. Those in lowercase letters refer to additional pages where pieces can be found. There is also an internal cross-referencing system used in the main part of the book, so if you look for a Kewpie doll in the Doll category, you will be told it is in its own category. There is additional information at the end of many paragraphs about where to find prices of pieces similar to yours.

A

A. WALTER 1
ABC 1, 514, 721
ABINGDON 1
ADAMS 1–2, 339, 444, 485, 598, 660, 669
Admiral Dewey 146, 159, 227, 444
ADVERTISING 2–26, 114, 141–142, 221, 226, 244, 516, 523, 576, 580, 764
Airplane 11, 20, 23, 89, 110, 136, 159, 452–453, 455, 689, 719–720, 730, 739, 742
AKRO AGATE 26–27
ALABASTER 27–28, 143, 437, 440, 445, 447, 577, 625, 678
Album 126, 544, 575, 605
Almanac 553
ALUMINUM 8, 28, 91, 114, 136, 153–154, 157–158, 160, 234, 258–259, 290, 304, 339, 347, 415, 422–429, 439, 507, 524, 572, 577–579, 619, 716–717, 720, 746, 778
Amber, see Jewelry
AMBER GLASS 28–29, 233, 524, 539, 448, 495, 695
AMBERINA 29–30, 40, 61, 109, 246, 249, 267, 355–356, 432, 445, 452, 516, 680, 711, 718
Ambrotype 531
AMERICAN ENCAUSTIC TILING CO. 29
AMETHYST GLASS 6, 29, 108
Amos 'n' Andy 60, 720, 743–744
Amphora, see Teplitz
Andiron, see Fireplace; see also 30, 60, 98, 253–255, 701
ANIMAL TROPHY 30
ANIMATION ART 30
ANNA POTTERY 30
Apothecary 12, 75, 86, 102, 264, 439, 476
Apple Peeler, see Kitchen, Peeler, Apple
ARABIA 30–31
ARC-EN-CIEL 31
ARCHITECTURAL 31–34, 113, 143, 347, 414, 731
AREQUIPA POTTERY 34
Argy-Rousseau, see G. Argy-Rousseau
ARITA 34
ART DECO 34, 37, 43, 61, 63, 99, 105–106, 133, 138, 142–143, 145, 151, 159, 162, 178–179, 186, 234, 256, 268, 271–273, 276, 280–281, 289–290, 314, 316, 319, 323–327, 333–334, 341, 352–353, 362, 368, 383, 401, 403, 405, 412, 418–419, 432, 435, 437–438, 447–449, 472, 474, 490, 504, 525, 556, 571–572, 577, 587–588, 590–591, 614, 652, 656, 701–705, 708, 751, 761–763, 778, 780, 786, 788
Art Glass, see Glass-Art
ART NOUVEAU 34–35, 48, 54, 64, 91, 98, 101, 106–108, 146, 179, 242, 254, 264, 271, 307–309, 323–324, 326, 353, 360, 362, 368, 372, 378, 383, 404, 406, 415, 417, 429–430, 436, 438, 448, 451, 453–454, 468–469, 472–473, 519, 525, 534, 550, 554–556, 579, 608, 612, 638–640, 646, 651, 655, 697, 708, 710, 763, 777, 786, 788
Art Pottery, see Pottery-Art
ARTS & CRAFTS 33, 35, 64, 86, 93, 107, 142, 148, 164, 253, 257, 271–274, 277, 280, 289–290, 297, 302–303, 305, 307, 309, 313–316, 318–319, 322–324, 333, 335, 340–341, 394, 410, 414, 436–439, 444, 448, 474, 556, 617, 646, 649, 677, 778
Ashtray 2, 26, 36, 40, 60, 92, 94, 104, 116, 153, 163, 194, 197–198, 206, 209, 211, 221, 241, 245, 248, 250–251, 265, 268, 378, 395, 432, 453, 461, 466, 471, 481, 494, 503, 506, 538, 548–549, 556, 581, 587, 595, 598, 652, 656, 660, 667, 672, 687, 701, 758, 769, 775, 785
Atomizer 35, 40, 68, 104, 164, 178, 182, 342, 352, 434, 452, 457, 524
Aunt Jemima 42, 60, 161, 473, 619
AURENE 35–36, 677–678
Austria, see Royal Dux; Porcelain
AUTO 36–39, 114, 728
AUTUMN LEAF 39, 237
Avon, see Bottle, Avon
AZALEA 39–40, 184, 213, 262

B

Babe Ruth 10–11, 26, 114, 126, 157, 345, 665–667
BACCARAT 40–41
Backbar 31, 84
BADGE 36, 41, 91, 99, 114, 139, 407, 458, 488, 508, 538, 548, 578, 785
Banana Boat 118, 122, 170, 248, 481, 561, 656
BANK 11, 13, 42–46, 53, 56, 91, 98, 101–103, 106, 113–114, 127, 153, 164
BANKO 46–47, 212, 221, 381–382, 419, 454, 461–462, 473, 625, 669, 681, 689, 785–786
Banner 3, 12, 64, 96, 101, 130–132, 139, 142, 159, 162, 512, 518, 538, 599
BARBER 47, 212, 381–382, 419, 454, 461–462, 473, 625, 669, 681, 689, 785–786
BAROMETER 47–48, 144, 212, 381–382, 496
BASALT 2, 48–50, 406, 672, 769–772
Baseball, see Card, Baseball; Sports
BASKET 29, 48–50, 55, 92, 94, 113, 116–117, 128, 130, 152, 164, 167–170, 179, 199, 202, 204, 221, 235, 238, 242–243, 245–249, 256, 263, 270, 355, 373–376, 379, 382, 386–389, 421, 457, 462–463, 466, 473, 479, 482, 487, 498–499, 621–622, 625, 630, 632, 637, 640, 646–648, 651, 653, 681, 696, 708–709, 711, 719, 737, 752, 755, 758–759, 769, 775–777, 784
BATCHELDER 50
Bathtub 31
BATMAN 50–51, 345, 460, 545
BATTERSEA 51, 86, 109, 539
BAUER 51–52
BAVARIA 15, 52, 116, 506, 552, 595, 600, 633
Bayonet 429
Beaded Bag, see Purse
BEATLES 52–53, 488, 603
Bed Warmer 92
BEEHIVE 42, 53–55, 65, 72, 75, 108, 143, 146–147, 149, 189, 221, 238, 240, 269, 280, 354, 371, 373, 436, 513, 581, 597, 609, 622–623, 669, 688
Beer 2–3, 5–22, 25–26, 54, 65, 69–70, 83, 85–86, 92, 141–142, 153
Beer Bottle, see Bottle, Beer
BEER CAN 54
BELL 22, 36, 42–43, 54–55, 58, 64, 92, 110–111, 127, 134, 136, 143, 145–146, 158, 170, 223, 225–226, 245–249, 252, 255, 265, 354, 364, 372, 380, 445, 482, 496, 503, 533, 538, 549, 575, 577–578, 582, 647, 650, 673, 696, 698, 706, 708, 720–721, 729–730, 732–734, 736–737, 739, 746, 751, 753
BELLEEK 55, 777–778
Belt Buckle 3, 92, 647
BENNINGTON 56, 545
BERLIN 2, 56, 398, 418, 431, 585, 651
BESWICK 56–58, 222
BETTY BOOP 58
BICYCLE 50, 58, 69, 76, 129, 198, 224, 264, 531, 549, 665, 668, 675, 680, 695, 728, 735
BING & GRONDAHL 58–59
BINOCULARS 59, 65, 139, 224, 233, 525, 619, 627, 640, 675
BIRDCAGE 59, 237, 260, 264, 278–279, 317, 326, 331, 334, 336, 338–339, 505, 732, 752
Biscuit Barrel 462
Biscuit Jar 351–352, 376, 494, 512, 550, 587, 609, 612, 626, 637, 658, 756, 763, 765–766, 768–769, 784

BISQUE 2, 59–60, 62, 75, 78, 101, 110, 135–136, 141, 161, 221–224, 226–229, 231–232, 361, 378, 400, 419–421, 441, 443, 450, 471, 478, 502–503, 505–506, 508, 533, 537, 543, 546, 548, 551, 586–587, 595–596, 598, 609–610, 629, 658, 717, 722, 728–729, 731, 739
BLACK 3, 8–9, 12, 14, 23, 37, 42–45, 57, 60–61, 127, 136, 161, 166, 233, 346, 360, 512, 514–516, 531, 535, 544, 582, 589, 719, 721, 730, 732, 734–736, 738, 740–744, 751–752
BLACK AMETHYST 61, 121, 203, 352, 358, 387, 434, 516
Blanket 666, 668, 698, 732
BLENKO 61
Blown Glass, see Glass-Blown
Blue Glass, see Cobalt Blue
Blue Onion, Onion
Blue Willow, see Willow
BOCH FRERES 61–62, 464
BOEHM 62–63, 347, 451, 646
BONE 57, 63–64, 82, 86–88, 90, 112, 130, 133, 139, 140, 164, 285, 309, 346, 368, 389, 417, 451, 497–498, 521, 628–629, 631, 692–693, 756, 780
Book 212, 221–222, 242, 258, 261, 270, 287, 313, 352, 380, 383–384, 395–396, 400–402, 512, 514–515, 520, 533–534, 537, 539, 547, 560–561, 587–589, 629, 631, 635, 651, 654, 656, 667, 673, 689, 697, 701, 712, 715–716, 742–743, 755, 781, 786
BOOKENDS 1, 22, 63–64, 91, 166, 178, 268, 270, 357, 372–373, 395, 432, 454, 519, 587, 597–598, 610, 658, 694, 701, 773, 785
BOOKMARK 64, 243, 372, 537, 539, 680, 701–702, 704–705, 785
BOSSONS 64, 484–485
Boston & Sandwich Co., see Lutz; Sandwich Glass
BOTTLE 3, 7–8, 11–21, 26, 29–30, 34–36, 39, 41–43, 50, 54, 56, 60–61, 65–85, 100, 104–106, 130, 132, 136, 141, 153–155, 160, 170, 172–173, 178–179, 180, 183, 186, 191, 196, 198, 208, 221, 232, 236, 238, 240–242, 244, 247, 249, 264, 270, 272, 279, 308, 318–319, 352–353, 356–357, 361, 370, 373, 376, 379–380, 389, 400–401, 406–407, 417, 422, 434, 452, 454, 462, 466–467, 470, 476, 481, 483, 486–487, 489, 497, 500–501, 504, 506, 509, 516, 518, 520, 522–526, 528, 539, 550–553, 556, 572, 577, 582–583, 590, 602, 611, 622, 626–627, 641, 646, 654, 659, 676, 678, 680–681, 694, 697, 700–701, 706, 708, 711, 713, 719, 751–752, 756–757, 759, 768–769, 772, 776, 785
BOTTLE CAP 14–16, 18, 85, 141–142, 153, 156, 523–524, 700
BOTTLE OPENER 60, 85–86, 153–154, 636–638
Bow 382
BOX 86–91
Box 3–5, 28, 32, 40, 46, 51, 60–61, 94, 113, 126–127, 129–130, 138, 149, 157, 160, 162–163, 166–171, 174–175, 179–180, 182, 184, 187, 221–223, 241, 243–244, 252, 255, 257, 261, 264, 343, 345, 352–353, 355, 358, 362, 371–372, 380–381, 383, 389, 392, 400, 402–403, 417, 419–420, 424, 430, 432–434, 450, 453–454, 465–468, 470, 481–482, 484, 486, 491–492, 494, 496, 503, 505, 507, 521, 524, 527–528, 537–539, 543–544, 546, 548, 551–552, 587, 600, 602–603, 611–612, 618, 621–622, 625–626, 628, 630–632, 637–638, 643, 645–648, 651–655, 673, 678, 689, 701–702, 704–705, 709, 713–714, 719, 752–753, 756, 758, 760, 766, 770–771, 773, 782
BOY SCOUT 43, 91
BRADLEY & HUBBARD 63–64, 91–92, 108, 143, 162, 234–236, 254, 321, 396, 436, 439
BRASS 3, 5–6, 8, 11, 19, 28, 32–33, 35–38, 41, 47–49, 51, 54–55, 59, 63–64, 75, 78, 82, 85–93, 95, 99–101, 106–110, 112–114, 123, 127, 138–139, 142–152, 156, 159, 162–163, 165, 167, 183, 186–187, 221, 223, 225–226, 235–236, 244, 253–256, 258–261, 265, 270–272, 274, 276–279, 281–282, 285–286, 288, 290–298, 302–316, 318–319, 321–325, 328, 330–334, 336–338, 340–341, 346, 349, 355, 358, 365–366, 368, 387, 391–395, 402, 405, 407–409, 412–413, 417, 420–421, 423–430, 436–441, 443–449, 451–453, 455, 458–461, 467, 471–473, 476, 480, 491–494, 496–498, 505, 507–508, 513, 517–519, 521–522, 525, 530–531, 533–535, 538–544, 546–548, 550–552, 559, 562, 565, 571–572, 578, 600, 608, 610–611, 622, 626–632, 639, 652, 655–656, 659–661, 668–669, 676, 678, 686–687, 690–693, 696, 698, 701–706, 708, 712–716, 719, 721, 727, 732, 740, 744, 746–747, 753–756, 762–763, 766, 768, 772, 774, 779–780, 783, 785
Brastoff, see Sascha Brastoff category
Bread Plate, see various silver categories, porcelain factories, and pressed glass patterns; see also 462
Bread Tray 476, 641
BRIDE'S BASKET 93, 489, 512, 769
Bride's Bowl 100, 500, 520, 768
BRISTOL 9, 55, 84, 94, 102, 123, 164, 213, 286, 441, 460–461, 489, 493, 677–679, 683, 686
Britannia, see Pewter category
BRONZE 28, 31–33, 42, 53–54, 60–61, 63–64, 88, 94–98, 105–109, 112, 114, 123, 129, 131, 138, 143–147, 149–150, 158–159, 166–167, 171, 176, 180, 221, 235, 242, 254–256, 259–260, 272–274, 276, 277–280, 286, 294, 297–298, 302–306, 309–310, 312–313, 316, 320–322, 324, 328, 330–331, 333–337, 340–341, 343, 347–349, 353, 355–356, 364–366, 372–373, 385, 394–395, 400, 417–419, 430, 436–448, 451–452, 455, 458, 461, 466–469, 471–472, 490, 496–497, 499, 504, 513, 516, 543–545, 550, 552–553, 572, 578, 594, 611, 622, 629–630, 651, 655, 664, 674, 677, 691, 697, 700–705, 707–708, 713, 733, 745, 748, 753–754, 767, 772, 775, 781
Broom 539
BROWNIES 4, 16–17, 25, 98
Brush McCoy, see Brush and related pieces in McCoy; see also 99, 161, 473
BRUSH POTTERY 98
Bucket 180, 252–253, 255, 259, 272, 322, 347, 360–361, 402, 471, 495–496, 632, 638, 642, 652–653, 764, 770, 781–783
Buckle 647, 715, 754, 770
BUCK ROGERS 98–99
BUFFALO POTTERY 99, 106
BUFFALO POTTERY DELDARE 99
Buggy 633, 636, 658
Bugle 722
Bugs Bunny 30, 722, 786
Bunnykins, see Royal Doulton
BURMESE GLASS 99–100
BUSTER BROWN 7, 13, 101, 658
Butter Chip 369, 379, 462, 575, 578, 595, 655
Butter Mold, see Kitchen, Mold, Butter; see also 422, 582
BUTTON 53, 60, 101, 139, 539–543, 660, 666, 688, 695, 715, 723, 729, 731, 756, 785
BUTTONHOOK 101–102, 641
BYBEE POTTERY 102

C

Cabinet 476, 478, 491–492, 504
Cake Set 28
Cake Stand 138, 171
CALENDAR 99, 102–103, 134, 143–146, 153, 165, 221, 241, 394, 514, 537, 543, 578, 652, 701, 761–762
CALENDAR PLATE 99, 103
CAMARK POTTERY 103–104
CAMBRIDGE GLASS 104–105
CAMBRIDGE POTTERY 105
CAMEO GLASS 105–106, 179, 180–182, 186, 343–344, 417, 449–450, 489–490, 521, 524, 585, 680, 756, 768
Camera 11, 110
Campaign, see Political
CAMPBELL KIDS 106
CAMPHOR GLASS 106, 188, 405, 412, 439
CANDELABRUM 104, 106–108, 162, 166, 171, 207, 237, 376, 383, 556, 587, 638, 640–641, 648, 655, 702, 709
Candlesnuffer 92, 638
CANDLESTICK 2, 28–29, 35, 40, 52–53, 61, 92, 99, 104–105, 108–110, 119, 130, 139, 143, 153, 160, 167, 171, 189, 191, 194–197, 199–201, 203–204, 206–207, 236, 238, 245–249, 257, 265–266, 269, 357, 364, 366, 372–378, 385–386, 400, 417–418, 420, 432, 444, 449, 452, 457, 462, 478, 489, 499, 507, 510–513, 544, 556, 560, 562, 564–565, 572–573, 587, 594, 596–599, 609–611, 613, 617, 622–623, 626, 677, 681, 695–696, 702, 706, 709, 711, 763, 770, 773, 776–777
Candlewick, see Imperial Glass

CANDY CONTAINER 110–112, 134, 421, 455, 666
CANE 112, 354, 496, 628
Canoe 13, 171, 352, 389, 496
Canteen 139, 389, 496
CANTON CHINA 113
Cap Gun 351–352, 380
CAPO-DI-MONTE 113
CAPTAIN MARVEL 113–114
CAPTAIN MIDNIGHT 114
Car 13–14, 16–17, 23, 25, 37, 39, 43, 50, 53, 111, 114, 116, 129, 136, 155–156, 167, 453, 455, 460
Carafe 423–433, 452, 641, 654, 764
Caramel Slag, see Imperial Glass
CARD 4, 9, 50, 53, 61, 87, 113–116, 129, 157, 167, 221, 223, 261, 324–325, 480, 488–489, 514–515, 531, 543, 599–600, 635, 665, 673, 689, 730
Card Case 400, 521, 641, 648, 653, 655, 719
CARLSBAD 116
CARLTON WARE 116
CARNIVAL GLASS 116–122, 186, 244, 368
CAROUSEL 122–123, 137, 214, 221, 224, 456, 728, 735, 779
CARRIAGE 9, 17–18, 50, 122–123, 123, 136, 143, 146, 149, 432, 477, 515, 551, 635, 721, 727–728, 732–733, 742, 755
Carte De Visite 531
CASH REGISTER 8, 43–44, 123, 153, 729
Casserole 39, 52, 162, 195, 202, 205, 214, 217–218, 250–252, 257, 269, 363, 378, 423–424, 431, 450–451, 473, 480, 580–581, 586, 609, 633, 755, 764
CASTOR JAR 123–125
CASTOR SET 125
Catalog 5, 258, 432, 514
CAUGHLEY 125
CAULDON 125–126
Cel, see Animation Art; see also 30, 222
CELADON 82, 126, 130, 186, 216, 319, 366, 403–404, 410, 587, 602, 617, 681, 683
CELLULOID 5, 10–11, 13–16, 18, 22, 37, 39, 58, 64, 86, 98, 101, 110, 126–127, 129, 134–135, 164, 166, 223–225, 227–228, 253, 258–259, 269, 364, 368, 406, 408–409, 412, 429, 441, 472–473, 491, 503, 522–524, 537–544, 546–549, 571, 579, 628, 632, 635, 638, 667, 717, 719, 722, 724, 729–732, 734–737, 739–740, 744, 746, 750, 752, 763, 784–785
CERAMIC ARTS STUDIO 127, 371
Chalice 173, 176, 357, 388, 486, 508, 513, 528, 536, 651, 706, 776, 779
CHALKWARE 7–9, 19, 22, 127–129, 135, 384, 439, 502–503, 667, 689
Chamber Pot 236, 262, 272, 528, 597, 629, 661
Chamberstick 99, 130, 757
Charger 5, 34, 36, 53, 61, 130, 149–150, 178, 187, 215, 268, 360, 371, 384, 417, 433, 453–454, 462, 471, 473, 482, 484, 528, 548, 550, 556–557, 582, 587, 594–595, 600, 604, 609, 626–627, 629, 681, 697, 759, 770
CHARLIE CHAPLIN 129
CHARLIE McCARTHY 129
CHELSEA 129, 133, 143, 149, 153, 165, 496, 503, 550, 603
CHELSEA GRAPE 130
Cherry Pitter 423
CHINESE EXPORT 130–133, 244, 278, 280, 349, 497, 621, 630, 647
CHINTZ 133–134, 242, 265, 475, 496, 503, 547, 635, 698
CHOCOLATE GLASS 134, 245–246, 249, 361
Chocolate Pot 130, 257, 351, 493, 502, 612, 641, 648, 651–652, 770
Chocolate Set 369, 454
Chopper 424
CHRISTMAS 23, 58–59, 110, 134–136, 161, 237, 241, 268, 346, 352, 380, 407, 412–413, 450, 488–489, 514, 516, 524, 533, 543, 553, 574, 580, 587, 595, 599, 601, 604–605, 651, 658, 662, 698, 760, 771
Christmas, Plate, see also Collector Plate
CHRISTMAS TREE 135–137
CHROME 5–6, 31, 37, 39, 47, 58, 64, 85, 91, 105, 138, 142–145, 158–160, 225, 247–248, 267, 272, 290, 299, 303, 309, 313–314, 323, 325–327, 330, 335, 345, 413, 423, 425, 429–430, 437–441, 452–453, 488, 496, 507, 524, 544, 556, 572, 577–578, 618–619, 683, 686–687, 693, 696, 723, 739, 741, 744
Churn 264, 423, 620, 670, 681–682
Cigar Cutter 5, 92, 157, 380, 396, 453, 496, 543, 687, 708
CIGAR STORE FIGURE 138
CINNABAR 82, 138, 315, 385, 617
CIVIL WAR 28, 41, 125, 153, 156, 167, 514, 531, 561–562, 735, 752
CKAW, see Dedham
CLAMBROTH 139–141, 425, 428, 444, 447, 467, 481, 489, 622
CLARICE CLIFF 139
CLEWELL 141
CLIFTON POTTERY 141
CLOCK 1, 13, 22, 25, 46, 58, 65, 91, 95, 141–149, 153–154, 180, 182, 222, 269, 360, 417, 420–421, 433, 477, 480, 484, 496, 500, 520, 523, 543, 560, 569, 575–577, 588, 601, 605, 629, 632, 637, 656, 666, 673, 690, 700–702, 761, 763, 770, 784
CLOISONNE 82, 98, 112, 143–147, 149–151, 384, 404, 407, 409, 445, 458, 626, 653–654
CLOTHING 10, 13, 61, 102–103, 129, 134, 151–153, 381, 401, 469, 515, 687, 696–698, 721, 782
CLUTHRA 152, 240, 611
COALBROOKDALE 152
COALPORT 152–153, 394
Coaster 5, 58, 173, 197, 206, 210–211, 241, 375, 377, 535, 537, 639, 646, 651, 730, 741, 750, 776
COBALT BLUE 153
COCA-COLA 122, 153–156
Cocktail Shaker 138, 198, 207, 209, 238, 371, 373, 641, 647, 655
COFFEE MILL 156, 423
Coffeepot 92, 138, 163, 215, 250–252, 257, 262, 267–268, 270, 350, 361, 363, 397, 423, 449–451, 477, 500, 503, 507, 521, 528, 550, 595, 609, 611, 629, 635, 638, 641, 647–648, 651–653, 669, 694, 712, 714
Coffee Set 138, 503, 639, 641, 645, 647, 650–652, 709–710
COIN-OPERATED MACHINE 156–159
Cologne 35, 65, 67–68, 173, 180, 247, 249, 376, 386, 500, 524–525, 560, 622, 626, 636, 658, 671, 677, 680, 776
Comb 46, 87, 127, 264, 285, 288, 491–493, 575, 582, 614, 642, 655, 716, 719, 753, 781
COMIC ART 159, 521
COMMEMORATIVE 159, 719
COMPACT 160, 165, 560, 572, 579, 708
Compass 87–88, 90–91, 112–113, 261, 269, 276, 286, 321, 332, 367, 425, 455, 467, 496–498, 505, 575, 582, 628, 693, 730
Condiment Set 29, 100, 165, 173, 247, 249, 423, 768
Console Set 211, 248, 357, 362, 386, 677, 776
CONSOLIDATED LAMP AND GLASS COMPANY 160–161, 446
Contemporary Glass, see Glass-Contemporary
COOKBOOK 161
Cookie Cutter 423–424
COOKIE JAR 1, 39, 51, 60, 98, 161–162, 173, 191, 201, 205–206, 214, 222, 371, 379, 381–382, 473–474, 479, 520, 536–537, 548, 570, 580, 597–598, 611, 633, 673, 689, 764–765, 773
COORS 161–162
COPELAND 162, 464, 510, 518, 544, 609
COPELAND SPODE 162
COPPER 12–13, 16, 31–32, 35, 37, 41–42, 44, 49, 52, 54, 60, 64, 66–67, 82, 89–90, 92, 94, 98, 109, 123, 126, 130, 138, 141–144, 148, 150, 157, 160, 162–164, 166, 196, 221, 231, 241–242, 254–256, 259, 262–264, 270, 273, 287, 296, 302–303, 307, 309–310, 312, 316, 319, 323, 328, 333, 341, 347, 349, 351, 357–358, 359–360, 361, 365–366, 368, 383–384, 387, 389, 395–396, 398, 408–409, 412, 414, 417, 424–429, 436–446, 448, 453–454, 457, 460, 467, 471–472, 497, 512, 516, 521, 530, 544–545, 550, 552, 557–559, 583, 610–611, 619, 626–627, 632, 639, 644, 651, 656, 668, 674–675, 687, 691, 700–701, 709–713, 716, 720, 730, 744–745, 747, 754, 766–768, 781–782
Copper Luster, see Luster, Copper
CORALENE 93–94, 164, 404, 441, 448, 486, 502–503, 509, 690, 768, 769
CORKSCREW 76, 85, 153, 164, 255, 785
Cornucopia 1, 27, 48, 52, 69, 87, 97–98, 101, 108–109, 148, 247, 249, 310–311, 320, 356, 371, 382, 426, 474, 485, 571, 576, 597, 615, 640, 647, 651, 679, 770

CORONATION 164–165, 189, 193, 204, 208, 232, 547
COSMOS 165
COVERLET 165–166, 288
COWAN POTTERY 166
CRACKER JACK 25, 114, 166–167, 745
CRACKLE GLASS 167, 366, 459, 613
CRANBERRY GLASS 55, 164, 167, 245–246, 470, 486–487, 525, 613, 636, 638
CREAMWARE 100, 167–168, 441, 455–456, 483, 596–597, 632, 660, 663, 674, 692
CREDIT CARD 168
Crock 5, 56, 253, 318, 580, 581–583, 611, 620, 630, 658, 681–683, 697, 764, 787
CROWN MILANO 168
Crown Tuscan, see Cambridge
CRUET 29, 105, 117, 164, 168, 170, 173, 180, 194, 238, 355, 371, 373–378, 385, 461, 486, 489, 507, 520, 537, 560–561, 563, 588, 604, 647–648, 658, 706, 777
CT GERMANY 168
Cuff Links 407, 668
Cupboard 31, 274, 276–278, 297, 299–301, 304, 316, 342, 731
CUP PLATE 169, 519, 619, 622–623, 663, 669
CURRIER & IVES 169–170, 195, 214, 367
Cuspidor 5, 91, 126, 131, 179, 354, 396, 431, 452, 463, 487, 578, 580–581, 583, 586
CUSTARD GLASS 170, 461, 547, 579, 717–718
CUT GLASS 65, 84, 100, 106–109, 125, 145, 168, 170–178, 221, 243, 269, 357, 370, 394–395, 436–438, 440–441, 443–444, 446–448, 452, 460–461, 524–525, 595, 629, 636, 638, 641–642, 649, 655, 755, 763
CUT VELVET 177
CYBIS 178
CZECHOSLOVAKIA GLASS 97, 106, 136, 178–179, 242, 421, 466–467, 524, 552, 571
CZECHOSLOVAKIA POTTERY 179

D

Dagger 147, 390, 430
Daguerreotype 530–531
DANIEL BOONE 179, 229
D'ARGENTAL 179
Darner 631
DAUM 179–182, 778
DAVENPORT 182, 302, 453, 620, 669, 717, 731
DAVY CROCKETT 182
Decoder 114
DE VEZ 182–183
Decoder 508
DECORATED TUMBLER 183
DECOY 183–184
DEDHAM 184–186
DEGENHART 186
DEGUE 186
DELATTE 186
Deldare, see Buffalo Pottery Deldare
DELFT 83, 163, 187, 237, 243, 255, 269–270, 371, 455, 480, 513, 712
DENTAL 187–188
DEPRESSION GLASS 188–211, 425
DERBY 153, 211–212, 262–263
Desk 54, 87, 95, 132, 144–145, 149, 163, 221, 273, 281–282, 302–304, 308, 310, 319, 365, 416, 438, 496–497, 530, 572, 611, 627, 666, 696, 702–703, 719, 731–732, 745, 753, 755
Desk Set 95, 163, 221, 463, 528, 611, 625, 636, 651, 759
DICK TRACY 159, 212, 228
Dickens Ware, see Weller
DINNERWARE 212–220, 669
DIONNE QUINTUPLETS 220
Dipper 163, 424, 497, 528
DIRK VAN ERP 221
DISNEYANA 221–225
Dispenser 5–6, 22, 84, 154, 157, 159, 236, 377, 380, 453, 511, 523–524, 528, 539, 631, 638, 669, 688, 753
Doctor, see Dental; Medical
DOLL 15, 53, 58–60, 91, 101, 106–107, 123, 129, 134, 154, 158, 165, 167, 182, 212, 221–222, 226–233, 243, 270, 352, 363, 378, 380–381, 390, 393, 419, 421, 450, 458, 498, 515–516, 520, 531, 536–537, 543, 548, 551, 600, 606–607, 631, 635, 658, 687, 689, 721, 728, 730–731, 734, 742, 744, 751–752, 779, 784
DOLL CLOTHES 232–233
Dollhouse 731–732
Donald Duck, see Disneyana; also 3, 159, 221–225, 233
Doorknob 32
Doorknocker 32, 408
Door Push 8, 154, 523
DOORSTOP 36, 222, 233–237, 270, 421, 548, 586, 787
DORCHESTER POTTERY 236
DOULTON 212, 236–238, 269, 347, 352
Dr Pepper 2–3, 5–6, 8, 10–11, 14, 25–26, 82, 136, 141, 244, 472, 516, 576, 700, 763
DRESDEN 52, 103, 107, 110–111, 135–137, 147, 149, 214, 237–238, 239, 241, 310, 545, 552, 575, 759
Dresser Box 40, 53, 127, 167–168, 355, 420, 454, 494, 503, 600, 612, 629, 711, 753, 766
Dresser Set 29, 127, 179, 400, 500, 511, 642, 655, 709
Drum 8, 53, 72, 91, 128, 139, 142, 164, 176, 223, 388, 390, 393, 437, 441, 450, 464, 491–492, 505–506, 553, 565, 615, 628, 719, 721, 723, 729–730, 732, 736–737, 743, 745, 770
DUNCAN & MILLER 238
DURAND 238–241
DURANT KILNS 240–241

E

Earrings 24, 226, 229, 231, 233, 371–372, 380, 390
Eggcup 133, 162, 252, 367, 369, 380, 463, 475, 482, 555, 560, 622, 635, 642, 656, 719, 782
ELFINWARE 241
ELVIS PRESLEY 240–241, 488
ENAMEL 11–20, 23–24, 29, 34–38, 41, 47, 53–54, 56, 61–62, 64–65, 68, 71–72, 75–76, 81–82, 84–85, 87–88, 90, 92, 95, 98, 101, 107, 109, 116, 126, 131, 143, 145–147, 149, 153–155, 160, 167, 174, 182, 187, 223, 236–237, 241–243, 256–257, 264, 269, 272, 282, 311, 314, 321–323, 326, 328, 333, 338, 347–349, 355–356, 359, 366, 368, 383–384, 395, 405–410, 412–416, 418, 420–421, 423–425, 427–431, 433–434, 437, 439–440, 441, 443, 445–446, 450–451, 453–455, 459, 461, 466, 472–473, 480–481, 483, 486–487, 502, 507, 518–519, 521–523, 525–526, 538–539, 547, 552–553, 556, 571–572, 578, 610, 622, 626–627, 629–630, 636–637, 642, 646–649, 652–656, 659–661, 667, 674–675, 696–697, 702–705, 709–710, 744, 749, 761–763, 769–770, 772–773, 778, 786–788
Epergne 40, 100, 104, 167, 174, 246–248, 353, 355, 363, 457, 572, 638, 649
ERICKSON 242
ERPHILA 242
ES GERMANY 242
ESKIMO 65, 141, 226, 242–243, 615
ETLING 243
Extinguisher 253

F

FABERGE 242–243, 344, 378, 402, 451, 489, 653–654
FAIENCE 52, 95, 243–244, 361, 416, 459, 480, 556–557, 575, 589–590, 625, 674, 712
FAIRING 244
Fairyland Luster, see Wedgwood
FAN 8, 13, 16, 22–23, 32–33, 36, 41, 47, 61, 86, 89, 103, 118, 120–121, 127, 134, 148–149, 154, 161–162, 166, 170–177, 207, 221, 236, 244–247, 249, 254, 256, 258, 269, 279, 285, 293, 295–296, 303–304, 307, 323, 326, 328, 339, 348, 358, 370–371, 376, 379–380, 384, 399–402, 417, 438, 446, 452, 455, 457, 462, 464–467, 470, 474, 481, 489, 491, 495, 498–500, 503, 527, 543, 555, 561–562, 575–576, 591, 596–599, 634, 656, 658, 660, 679, 681, 692, 718, 731, 740, 758, 770, 783, 785
Federzeichnung, see Loetz
Fence 25, 59, 64, 112, 125, 136, 177, 187, 378, 384, 462, 472, 482, 546, 569, 602, 615, 633, 676, 684, 686, 715, 743, 762, 775
FENTON 56, 99, 118, 134, 170, 244–250
Fernery 120, 168, 246, 305, 454, 494, 502, 611, 766
FIESTA 250–252
Figurehead 264, 400
Finch, see Kay Finch
FINDLAY ONYX AND FLORADINE 252
Fireback 256
FIREFIGHTING 252–253

FIREGLOW 253
FIREPLACE 9, 30, 32, 93, 187, 236, 253–257, 702, 731
First Aid 91, 414
FISCHER 257, 722, 726–727
FISHING 15–20, 22, 30, 59, 83, 102, 113, 182–183, 185, 258–261, 343, 400, 402, 514, 611, 615, 665, 674, 689, 716, 721, 735
Flag, see Textile, Flag
Flagon 528
FLASH GORDON 261
Flashlight 14, 51, 91, 99, 548
Flask 56, 67, 69–71, 85, 100, 126, 142, 355, 435, 463, 473, 494, 499, 519, 543, 551–553, 559, 576, 583, 607, 642, 647, 655, 670, 683, 709, 714, 771, 785, 787
FLORENCE CERAMICS 261
FLOW BLUE 1–2, 11, 42, 126, 182, 237, 261–264, 269, 351, 397–398, 431, 545, 550, 585, 610, 660, 669–671, 759–760, 769–772, 777
Flower Frog 35, 103–105, 166, 174, 377, 379, 433, 435, 527, 555, 583, 588, 597–598, 676–677, 702, 705–706, 757, 773–775
Flowerpot 1–2, 27, 51, 52, 174, 210, 469, 474, 583, 597, 634, 683
Flue Cover 424, 543
FOLK ART 184, 188, 224, 254, 264–265, 295, 534, 745, 779–781
Football, see Card, Football; Sports
FOOT WARMER 92, 236, 265, 528, 586, 783
Fortune Teller 157, 603, 742
FOSTORIA 265–267, 429
Foval, see Fry
Frame, Picture, see Furniture, Frame
FRANCISCAN 267–268
FRANKART 268
FRANKOMA POTTERY 268–269
FRATERNAL 269, 632
Fruit Jar 3, 71–72, 581
FRY GLASS 269
FULPER 270, 672, 682
Funnel 17, 37, 72, 254, 344, 354, 428, 639, 651, 698
FURNITURE 15, 34–35, 148, 221, 267, 269–342, 349, 632, 731–732, 736, 780

G

G. ARGY-ROUSSEAU 342
GALLE 243, 307–308, 321, 324, 331, 342–344
GALLE POTTERY 344
GAME 8, 11, 18, 23, 51, 60, 91, 98, 115, 157, 167, 182, 198, 212, 215, 222, 226, 330–332, 344–347, 380, 394, 432, 455, 463, 466, 472, 480, 488, 495, 508, 515, 559, 568, 601, 665–669, 675, 689, 740, 760–761, 767, 771
GAME PLATE 347
GARDEN FURNISHINGS 347–350
GARDNER 350, 682, 742
GAUDY DUTCH 350–351
GAUDY IRONSTONE 351
GAUDY WELSH 351
GEISHA GIRL 351
GENE AUTRY 351–352
GIBSON GIRL 101, 103, 229, 352, 410, 553, 607, 612, 660, 760
GILLINDER 352
Ginger Jar 113, 116, 138, 238, 245, 439–440, 454, 484, 525, 551, 588, 645, 678
Girandole 143, 311, 355
GIRL SCOUT 352
GLASS-ART 352–353
GLASS-BLOWN 353–355
GLASS-BOHEMIAN 355
GLASS-CONTEMPORARY 355–357
Glass-Cut, see Cut Glass
Glass-Depression, see Depression Glass
GLASS-MIDCENTURY 357
GLASS-VENETIAN 357–359
GLASSES 359
GLIDDEN 359, 755
GOEBEL 359
GOLDSCHEIDER 359–360
GONDER 360
GOOFUS GLASS 360, 446
GOUDA 360
Gramophone 15, 19, 530
GRANITEWARE 360–361, 421, 427
Grater 424, 636, 649
GREENTOWN 133–134, 361
Grill Plate 51–52, 188, 192, 194, 197, 201–204, 207–208, 218–219, 269, 778
GRUEBY 340, 361–362
Gumball 157, 222, 667
Gun, see Toy
GUNDERSON 362
GUSTAVSBERG 362
GUTTA-PERCHA 147, 362, 467

H

HAEGER 362–363, 453
Hair Receiver 174, 431, 494, 502, 595, 783
Half-Doll, see Pincushion Doll
HALL CHINA 6, 39, 363–364, 471
HALLOWEEN 53, 114, 235, 364, 495
HAMPSHIRE 216, 364, 556–557
HANDEL 364–366
Handkerchief 11, 151, 182, 221–222, 245, 248, 295, 304, 329, 357, 482, 494, 571, 634, 660, 670, 698, 768
HARKER 366–367
HARLEQUIN 367–368
Harmonica 167, 458, 492, 599
Hat 8–12, 15, 21, 23, 25, 29, 38, 42–43, 45, 47, 51, 55, 60, 64, 83, 85–86, 88, 92, 96–98, 101, 106, 110–111, 113, 117, 120, 129, 134–136, 138, 144, 151–152, 155, 161, 163, 170, 182, 206, 212, 222, 225–226, 228–229, 231–237, 245–249, 253, 258, 264–265, 287, 307, 345, 352, 354, 359–360, 365, 368, 371–372, 379–381, 388, 390, 396, 401–402, 412, 419–423, 450, 454, 458, 460–461, 463, 471–474, 479, 485, 494–495, 497, 503, 506, 509, 512, 515–517, 523–524, 530–531, 536–538, 541–542, 544, 546–547, 550, 552, 554, 568, 578, 592, 600, 610–611, 619, 632–635, 638, 668, 670, 674, 687–688, 695–697, 699, 706, 713–714, 717–719, 721–722, 726, 729, 733–736, 738–740, 742, 762, 779–781, 783, 785, 788
HATPIN 120, 368, 408, 502
HATPIN HOLDER 120, 368, 600, 612
HAVILAND 368–370, 509–510
HAWKES 370–371, 759
HEAD VASE 127, 371, 380–381, 432, 450
HEDI SCHOOP 372
HEINTZ ART 372–373
HEISEY 373–378
Herend, see Fischer
HEUBACH 378
HIGBEE 378–379
Historic Blue, see factory names, such as Adams, Ridgway, and Staffordshire
HOBNAIL 379
HOLLY AMBER 379
HOLT-HOWARD 379–380
Honey Pot 55, 133, 222, 475
HOPALONG CASSIDY 380
HORN 112, 243, 341, 347, 380–381, 389–390, 393–395, 409–410, 429–430, 559, 659, 719
HOWARD PIERCE 381
HOWDY DOODY 381–382
HULL 382
Humidor 2, 46–47, 60, 98, 141, 166, 174, 308, 365, 372, 463, 469, 478, 485, 503, 577, 697, 753, 766, 773, 780, 783
HUMMEL 382–383
HUTSCHENREUTHER 383

I

Ice Bucket 28, 41, 104–105, 174, 180, 189, 199, 248, 618, 638, 642, 653, 764
ICON 383–384
IMARI 212, 261, 349–351, 384–385, 398, 505, 602, 784
IMPERIAL GLASS 385–387
Incense Burner 95, 126, 131, 150, 404, 551, 771, 774
INDIAN 3–4, 6, 8–9, 11, 13, 17–20, 22–23, 25–26, 31, 37–38, 43–44, 48, 54, 66–67, 76, 90, 97, 103, 125–128, 138–139, 141, 152, 157–158, 167, 178, 182, 216, 234, 254, 257–258, 264, 346, 371, 378, 381, 386–394, 396, 665, 692
INDIAN TREE 394
INKSTAND 91, 394, 519, 586, 629, 649, 702
INKWELL 1, 150, 221, 308, 344, 394–395, 417, 421, 433–434, 463, 478, 500, 503, 588, 611, 629, 649, 702–703, 714, 763
Inro 498
INSULATOR 395
Irish Belleek, see Belleek
IRON 395–396
Iron 425, 736
Ironing Board 519
IRONSTONE 2, 182, 262, 394, 397–400, 487, 694
ISPANKY 400

IVORY 63, 82, 88–89, 91–92, 95–96, 107, 112, 127, 139, 164, 166, 243–244, 286, 345–346, 393, 400–402, 410, 424, 428, 430, 451–452, 491, 498–499, 505, 512, 528, 535–536, 547–548

J

JACKFIELD 402–403
JACK-IN-THE-PULPIT 403
JADE 82–83, 88, 101, 126, 243–244, 315, 403–406, 410, 415, 451
Jadeite 188, 195–196, 200, 209–210, 406
JAPANESE CORALENE 404
Japanese Woodblock Print, see Print, Japanese
JASPERWARE 2, 404–405, 420–421, 769–773
JEWELRY 12–13, 28, 88, 103, 174, 195, 277, 403, 405–416, 419–420, 432, 452, 494, 517, 551, 638, 643, 701, 719, 753, 766, 774
Jigsaw Puzzle 9, 99, 212, 261, 345–346, 458, 689
JOHN ROGERS 416
JOSEF ORIGINALS 134, 416–417
JUDAICA 417–418
JUGTOWN 418
JUKEBOX 418–419

K

KATE GREENAWAY 137, 419, 520
KAY FINCH 419–420
Kayserzinn, see Pewter
KELVA 420
KEMPLE 420
KENTON HILLS 420
KEW BLAS 420
KEWPIES 420–421
Key 3, 5, 17, 25, 45, 49, 60, 87, 89–90, 111–112, 119–120, 123, 142–143, 147, 149, 154, 157–159, 171, 173–176, 180, 225, 273, 281, 297, 315, 325–326, 339, 365, 367–371, 374–375, 381, 394, 396, 400, 408, 417–419, 439, 446, 453, 491–493, 508, 519, 523, 525, 530, 561, 565, 567, 578, 600, 639, 645–646, 650, 672, 687, 693, 695–696, 709, 716, 718, 721, 727, 730, 743, 745–746, 755, 761–763, 784
King's Rose, see Soft Paste
KITCHEN 421–429, 731–732, 736
KNIFE 88, 138–140, 182, 189, 200, 223, 243, 254, 255, 391, 425, 429–430, 458, 495, 544–545, 555, 636–639, 641–643, 648–649, 651, 654–655, 709, 735, 783
Knowles, Taylor, Knowles, see KTK
Korean Ware, see Sumida
KOSTA 430
KPM 430–431
KTK 431
KU KLUX KLAN 431
KUTANI 431–432

L

L.G. WRIGHT 432
Label 1, 3–6, 9, 18, 21–25, 34, 43, 46–48, 54, 61, 65–66, 68, 71–72, 75–77, 81, 83–86, 90, 98, 103, 125, 129, 135, 139, 145, 148–149, 151, 153–154, 156, 182, 221, 240–241, 260–261, 273, 282, 285, 305, 307–308, 312, 320, 326, 328, 332–333, 335, 337, 340, 342, 344, 353, 357–358, 360–361, 382, 398, 421, 427, 432, 437, 439, 450, 459, 469, 476, 478, 480, 484, 493, 497, 506, 519–520, 524–525, 530, 534, 543–544, 547, 556–557, 587, 596, 598–599, 632, 673, 676, 682, 684, 698, 707, 725–726, 738–740, 743, 755, 763, 776
LACQUER 60, 82, 87–88, 108–109, 225, 244, 274, 276–278, 280, 294, 305–306, 311, 315, 319, 322, 324, 327, 330, 334, 336, 408, 413, 432, 438, 517, 577, 630–631, 659, 692–693, 779, 783
Lady Head Vase, see Head Vase
LALIQUE 34, 36, 160, 406, 410, 413, 432–436
LAMP 7, 9, 27–28, 31, 35–36, 40–41, 60, 91–92, 94, 100, 105, 108–109, 135, 138, 150, 154, 160, 165, 167, 173–174, 180, 182, 186–188, 221, 223, 238, 245, 247–248, 257, 264, 270, 318, 342–343, 349, 358, 362, 364–366, 372–374, 379–381, 384, 395–396, 425, 430, 432, 434, 436–449, 452–453, 455, 457–458, 469, 474, 482, 484, 487, 490–491, 493–494, 500, 504, 509, 513–514, 528–530, 544, 548, 551, 554, 560–561, 565, 572, 578, 584, 588, 594, 597–598, 606, 608, 610–611, 618, 622, 624, 627, 629, 660, 673, 678, 680, 685, 698, 702–704, 706, 710, 712, 757, 766, 768–769, 774, 776, 784–785
LAMPSHADE 447–448
LANTERN 26, 77, 110, 135, 225, 349, 364, 366, 396, 402, 438–439, 448–449, 497–498, 544, 549, 551, 578, 687, 728, 740, 780
Lazy Susan 125, 188, 308, 333, 581, 638
LE VERRE FRANCAIS 449
LEATHER 4, 47, 49, 55, 58–59, 64, 87–90, 91, 94, 101, 112, 114, 122, 139–141, 145, 149, 151–152, 168, 184, 188, 212, 225, 227–228, 231, 243, 252–253, 255–256, 258, 260–261, 264–265, 269, 274, 276, 278–290, 296, 298, 302–303, 305, 307–309, 312, 314–315, 317–320, 323–326, 330–338, 340, 342, 388, 406, 412, 430, 449, 470, 476, 488, 507, 519, 559, 571–572, 600, 630–631, 635, 653, 665, 667–668, 690–691, 715, 728, 730, 735, 754–755, 787
LEEDS 449
LEFTON 450
LEGRAS 450
Lemonade Set 29
LENOX 18, 23, 55, 114, 450–451
LETTER OPENER 9, 60, 243, 421, 451–452, 537, 611, 628, 643, 649, 660, 678, 702, 704
LIBBEY 452
Light Bulb 7, 14
LIGHTER 5, 37, 60, 452–453, 505, 544, 651–652, 656, 687
LIGHTNING ROD AND LIGHTNING ROD BALL 453
Li'l Abner 723, 737
LIMOGES 160, 347, 453–454, 510, 588, 712
Lincoln 1, 17, 43, 64, 77, 95, 99, 112, 299, 314, 316, 352, 416, 423, 436, 444, 486, 518, 531, 538–539, 541, 543–547, 554, 562, 588, 592, 629, 635, 660, 669, 712, 726, 739, 745, 770, 778
LINDBERGH 454–455
LITHOPHANE 430, 455
LIVERPOOL 455–456
LLADRO 456–457
Lock 19, 32, 60, 86–90, 264, 291, 294, 296, 348, 388, 396, 446, 476, 514, 572, 578, 651, 659, 692–693, 696, 754
LOCKE ART 457
LOETZ 457, 459, 461
LONE RANGER 458
LONGWY 458
LONHUDA 459
LOSANTI 459
LOTUS WARE 459
Loving Cup 53, 120, 480, 521, 588, 643, 649, 706, 759, 771
LOW 459
LOWESTOFT 459
Loy-Nel-Art, see McCoy
LUNCH BOX 10–11, 53, 179, 223, 352, 380–381, 459–460, 530, 600, 673, 689
LUNEVILLE 145, 460, 465
LUSTER 26–27, 31, 54, 120, 168, 186, 212, 238, 240, 371, 398, 460, 769–772
Luster, Fairyland, see Wedgwood
Luster, Sunderland, see Sunderland
Luster, Tea Leaf, see Tea Leaf Ironstone
LUSTRES 460–461
LUTZ 461

M

MAASTRICHT 461
MacIntyre, see Moorcroft
Magnifying Glass 105, 402–403, 521, 628, 704
Mailbox 33, 81, 111, 521
MAIZE 17, 387, 461
MAJOLICA 236, 460–466, 471–472, 509–510, 610–611, 625, 674, 697, 713, 760, 769–772
MALACHITE 179, 324, 355, 394, 408, 414, 451, 466–467, 525
MAP 18, 28, 183, 456, 467, 621, 633
MARBLE 51, 346, 467–468
MARBLE CARVING 468–469
MARBLHEAD 469–470
Marionette 91, 223, 229, 381, 721, 737
MARTIN BROTHERS 470
MARY GREGORY 470
Masher 427
Mask 10, 31–33, 54, 58, 64–65, 82, 93, 95, 98, 108, 126–127, 129, 132, 135, 143, 146, 149, 163, 168, 176, 227, 229, 232, 256, 272, 282–283, 285, 297, 302–303, 310, 312, 324, 327, 339, 348–349, 351, 364, 381, 390–391, 395, 400, 402–404, 410, 439, 444–445, 457–458, 463, 466,

469, 472, 498, 521, 537, 550, 552, 555, 594, 606–607, 610, 626, 642, 647, 649, 673, 730, 761–762, 772, 784
Masonic, see Fraternal
MASON'S IRONSTONE 470–471
MASSIER 471
MATCH HOLDER 11, 101, 167, 211, 378, 419, 425, 471–472, 502, 588, 685, 696, 704, 756, 758, 766
MATCH SAFE 425, 472–473, 544, 638, 714
MATT MORGAN 473
Mayonnaise Set 105
McCOY 473–475
McKEE 134, 425, 475, 579
Measure 37, 93, 426, 528, 631–632, 655, 716, 782, 785
Mechanical Bank, see Bank, Mechanical
MEDICAL 9, 11, 75, 476
MEISSEN 147, 476–478, 506–507, 550
Melodeon 492
MERCURY GLASS 448, 478
MERRIMAC 478
METLOX 478–480
METTLACH 480–481, 675
Mickey Mouse 30, 42, 221–225
Microscope 212, 628
MILK GLASS 10, 60–61, 63, 65, 67–68, 72, 75, 82, 111, 135, 164, 192, 202, 245–249, 265, 308, 352–354, 379–380, 395, 408, 420–421, 424–428, 444, 446, 448, 453, 481–482, 489, 493–494, 516, 522, 525, 543, 579, 658, 711, 718, 756, 767, 777
MILLEFIORI 36, 41, 353, 395, 439, 482, 516–517, 622
Minnie Mouse 30, 134, 221–225
MINTON 463, 465, 467, 473, 482–483, 510
Mirror 7, 10, 12, 15, 18, 31, 33, 35, 60, 87–88, 92, 95, 101, 103, 127, 142, 144, 145, 149, 154, 158–160, 225–226, 255, 264, 270–271, 274, 276–277, 293, 295, 297, 302, 304–305, 307, 309–313, 315–316, 318–319, 323, 327–329, 335–337, 341, 389, 434, 447, 449, 477–478, 480, 494, 498, 521, 524, 533, 544, 571–572, 577, 627, 631, 638, 642–643, 649, 655, 677–679, 704, 708, 732, 739, 748, 752–753, 766
MOCHA 483
Mold 10, 56, 101, 135, 163, 269, 364, 397, 421–422, 426–427, 429, 582, 584, 771, 787
MONMOUTH 484
Mont Joye, see Mt. Joye
MOORCROFT 484–485
MORGANTOWN GLASS WORKS 485
MORIAGE 485–486
Mortar & Pestle 4, 12, 76, 188, 426–427 476, 633, 687
MOSAIC TILE CO. 486
MOSER 486–487
MOSS ROSE 487
Mother-of-Pearl 82, 89, 244, 256, 308, 335, 346, 368, 408, 413, 441, 448, 507–508, 517, 521, 571, 680, 693, 788
MOTHER-OF-PEARL GLASS 487
MOTORCYCLE 11, 488, 549, 729, 738
Mount Washington, see Mt. Washington
MOVIE 129, 212, 223, 352, 488–489, 515, 576, 634–636, 666, 668–669, 716
Moxie 5, 10–11, 14, 17, 25, 700
MT. JOYE 105, 489
MT. WASHINGTON 489, 520, 570
MUD FIGURE 489–490
MULBERRY 245–246, 263, 351, 490, 625, 663, 757
MULLER FRERES 490
Muffineer 461, 483, 638, 643, 710, 768
MUNCIE 490–491
Murano, see Glass-Venetian
MUSIC 43–45, 53, 60, 88, 96, 142, 154, 223, 241, 277, 322, 383, 419, 455, 491-493, 546, 634, 731
MUSTACHE CUP 493
Mustard 1, 29, 34, 71, 82, 89, 100, 125, 127, 133–134, 166, 173, 177, 181, 250–251, 265, 268, 270, 289, 308, 345, 362, 374–377, 385, 412, 469, 482, 489, 504, 519, 522, 553, 574–575, 583, 589, 612, 616–617, 648–649, 665, 681–682, 714, 757, 767, 771, 782–783
MZ AUSTRIA 493

N

NAILSEA 441, 443, 493–494
NAKARA 494
NANKING 494–495
NAPKIN RING 419, 495–496, 503, 544, 638, 643, 649, 655, 785
Nappy 35, 52, 119, 174–175, 219, 249–252, 267, 269, 371, 374–375, 377, 379, 386, 432, 452, 500, 503, 565, 586, 711, 776
NASH 496, 726, 739
NAUTICAL 217, 496–498, 534, 615, 703, 712
NETSUKE 498–499
NEW HALL 499–500
NEW MARTINSVILLE 29, 445, 499
NEWCOMB 500–501
Nickelodeon 492, 493
NILOAK 501
NIPPON 501–502
NODDER 10, 47, 53, 58, 60, 128, 223, 502–503, 505, 508, 521, 544, 551, 619, 666, 668–669, 742
NORITAKE 503
NORSE 503, 556
NORTH DAKOTA SCHOOL OF MINES 504
NORTHWOOD 504
Nu-Art, see Imperial
NUTCRACKER 60, 504–505, 537
Nutting 569–570

O

OCCUPIED JAPAN 505, 517, 529
OFFICE TECHNOLOGY 505–506
OHR 506
Ojime 498
OLD IVORY 506
Old Paris, see Paris
Old Sleepy eye, see Sleepy Eye
ONION PATTERN 506–507
OPALESCENT GLASS 433, 440, 507
OPALINE 38, 357, 366, 443, 457, 461, 507, 675
OPERA GLASSES 111, 507–508
Organ 44–45, 86, 224, 235, 323, 491–493, 779, 781
Organ Grinder 224, 235, 739
Ornament 53, 98, 129, 134, 136–137, 380, 521, 605, 689
ORPHAN ANNIE 508
ORREFORS 508
OTT & BREWER 508
OVERBECK 508–509
OWENS 509
OYSTER PLATE 116, 350, 509–510, 576, 625–626, 756, 771

P

PADEN CITY 510–512
Pail 3, 8, 10–11, 111, 135, 163, 223, 352, 537, 543–544, 567, 584, 590, 714, 739, 783
PAINTING 90, 148, 243, 512, 633, 754, 786
PAIRPOINT 88, 100, 110, 489, 495, 512–514, 638–639
Palmer Cox, Brownies, see Brownies
PAPER 9, 12–13, 15–16, 18–19, 58, 139, 151, 225, 315, 431, 467, 469, 512, 514–515, 531, 534, 539–544, 546, 554–555, 568, 570, 578, 721, 731, 755
Paper Clip 704
PAPER DOLL 106, 515–516, 600, 635
PAPERWEIGHT 1, 40–41, 56, 98, 180, 226–228, 232, 245, 342, 355, 357–358, 395–396, 404, 430, 434, 455, 459, 513–514, 516–517, 525, 537–538, 578, 589, 602, 622, 636, 656, 658, 678, 704, 706, 708, 756, 763, 773, 785
PAPIER-MACHE 7, 8, 11, 87, 89, 101, 110–111, 134–136, 226–229, 231–232, 256, 287, 308, 332, 335–336, 339, 364, 476, 503, 517, 521, 534, 537, 544, 547, 659, 687, 693, 721–722, 729–731, 734–737, 740, 742, 754
Parasol, see Umbrella
PARIAN 231, 508, 518, 539, 585, 659
PARIS 399, 467, 518, 551, 554, 762
Parrish 570
PATE-DE-VERRE 180–181, 518–519
PATENT MODEL 506, 519, 716
PATE-SUR-PATE 367, 519, 551
PAUL REVERE POTTERY 519–520
PEACHBLOW 355, 362, 445, 520, 680, 777
PEANUTS 159, 520–521, 537–538
PEARL 12, 54, 82, 86–89, 91, 94, 96–97, 101, 120, 126–127, 130–131, 142, 144–145, 160–161, 166, 205, 346, 368, 371–372, 389, 398–399, 405, 407–410, 412–416, 419, 429–430, 432, 439, 441, 443, 445–446, 450, 487, 491–492, 498–499, 507–508, 517, 519, 521–522, 534, 552, 571–572, 579, 594, 619, 626, 630, 642, 654, 659, 680, 693, 697–698, 701, 755, 761, 768, 772, 775, 777, 785
PEARLWARE 351, 455, 483, 521, 771

PEKING GLASS 82, 521–522
PELOTON 522
PEN 7, 21, 53, 87, 380, 421, 520, 522–523, 537, 704, 785
PENCIL 30, 89, 99, 129, 223, 271, 304, 406–407, 470, 514–515, 522–523, 534, 568, 635, 688–689, 696, 745, 785
PENNSBURY 63, 523
PEPSI-COLA 51, 83, 183, 523–524, 690, 731
Perfume 35, 41, 65, 81, 105–106, 152, 159–160, 178–180, 241, 356, 407, 434, 452, 467, 487, 500, 511, 524, 572, 622, 626, 655, 676, 678, 706, 719, 756, 759, 768, 785
PERFUME BOTTLE 524–527
PETERS & REED 527
Petrus Regout, see Maastricht
PEWABIC POTTERY 527
PEWTER 29, 107, 109, 137, 145, 147, 187, 242, 269, 311, 421, 447, 466, 491, 495–496, 525, 527–529, 617, 620, 672, 674–675, 682, 686, 693, 713
PHOENIX BIRD 325, 529, 595
PHOENIX GLASS 529
PHONOGRAPH NEEDLE CASE 530
PHONOGRAPH 19, 506, 530–531
Photograph 431, 530, 660, 666–667, 673
PHOTOGRAPHY 530–533
Piano 35, 44–45, 111, 225–226, 237, 261, 273, 308, 324, 366, 378, 381, 440, 477, 491–493, 513, 533, 543, 570, 634, 704, 732, 740, 751
PIANO BABY 533
PICKARD 533
PICTURE 11, 24, 53, 56, 101, 153, 161, 241, 345–346, 402, 489, 516, 533–535, 539, 544, 762
Picture Frame, Furniture, Frame
Pierce, see Howard Pierce
PIGEON FORGE 535
PILKINGTON 535
PILLIN 535–536
Pillow 53, 60–61, 96, 98, 131, 161, 180–181, 223, 281, 344, 363, 392, 440, 459, 469, 477, 483, 488, 491, 509, 529, 533, 590–593, 598, 613, 631, 685, 697, 699, 774–775
Pin 11, 16, 37, 45, 90–91, 115, 135, 137, 175–177, 212, 227, 269, 290, 345–346, 367, 380–381, 392, 405–406, 408, 410, 412–415, 417, 431, 458, 482, 486, 493–494, 508, 521, 523, 535, 540, 543–544, 546, 548, 555, 589, 610, 613, 617, 631–632, 635, 644, 659–660, 667, 673, 689, 715, 760–763, 766, 772, 785, 788
Pinball 51, 157–158, 167, 778
Pincushion 11, 86, 228, 231, 363, 536, 630–631, 753
PINCUSHION DOLL 536
PIPE 8, 24, 46, 89, 111, 360, 392, 400, 430, 454, 463, 468, 472, 489, 536, 544, 548–549, 575–576, 586, 626, 654, 670, 674, 687–688, 697, 717, 737
PISGAH FOREST 536–537
Pistol 99, 159, 261, 351, 396, 453, 553, 649, 735, 745
Plane 8, 20, 455, 523, 541, 716, 720, 739
PLANTERS PEANUTS 537
PLASTIC 515, 522–524, 537, 549, 571–572, 578–579, 599, 619, 644, 673, 689, 718, 720, 725, 730, 734–735, 740–741, 743, 745, 751, 755
PLATED AMBERINA 537–538
PLIQUE-A-JOUR 538
POLITICAL 112, 538–547
POMONA 263, 548, 677–679
POOLE POTTERY 548–549
POPEYE 14, 512, 548–549, 554–555
PORCELAIN 2, 4, 6–7, 9–21, 31, 34, 36–39, 45, 47–48, 51, 53, 55–56, 60, 65, 68, 71, 76, 81–83, 86, 88, 90, 94–95, 97–98, 101, 107, 109, 113, 126, 132, 141, 143, 145–147, 149, 152, 154–155, 157, 159–162, 164–165, 179, 214, 222, 228, 231, 285, 294, 322, 326–327, 341, 349–350, 368, 382–383, 394–396, 414, 417–418, 421, 425–426, 428, 430, 437, 439–441, 443, 446–447, 455, 459–461, 471–472, 476, 478, 493, 499, 503, 505–507, 510, 523, 525–526, 535–536, 547–553, 555, 579, 590, 592, 600, 609, 612, 619, 627, 629, 632–633, 638, 659–660, 674–675, 688–689, 692–693, 696, 700–701, 713, 718–719, 729, 732, 743, 756, 761, 771, 784
Porringer 339, 528, 575, 585, 644, 649, 710
POSTCARD 60, 101, 114, 221, 243, 352, 421, 431, 455, 545, 549, 553–555, 658, 667, 689
POSTER 37, 53, 58, 60, 91, 99, 139, 182, 223, 272, 352, 380, 418, 458, 488–489, 509, 544–546, 548, 554–555, 567, 635, 667–668, 673–674, 689, 716, 784–786
POTLID 555
POTTERY 33, 55, 68, 90, 99, 161, 222, 261–264, 345, 348, 359–360, 364–366, 382, 388–390, 392–395, 398–399, 402, 472, 503, 516, 555–556, 579, 618, 629, 674–675, 683, 685–686, 711–712, 717, 754, 786
POTTERY-ART 556–557
POTTERY-CONTEMPORARY 557
POTTERY-MIDCENTURY 557–559
POWDER FLASK AND POWDER HORN 559
PRATT 559–560
PRESSED GLASS 109, 352, 560–567
PRINT 216, 352, 437, 531, 546, 567–570
Projector 136, 223, 497, 531
Puppet 6, 51, 129, 182, 231–232, 381, 458, 689, 740
PURINGTON POTTERY 570–571
PURSE 22, 49–50, 52, 134, 223, 233, 241, 351, 454, 571–572, 655, 740, 785
Puzzle 9, 51, 60, 86, 99, 212, 261, 264, 345–346, 380, 398, 458, 506, 585, 689, 783

Q
QUEZAL 572–574
QUILT 314, 574, 615
QUIMPER 575–576

R
RADFORD 576
RADIO 15, 19, 37–38, 46, 51, 53, 114, 129, 142, 154, 223, 261, 380, 440–441, 482, 523, 546, 555, 576–578, 589, 674, 689
RAILROAD 10, 13, 30, 33, 70, 72, 92, 523, 553–554, 578, 600, 730, 746–747, 756, 761, 763
Rattle 55, 92, 98, 224–225, 388–390, 392, 400, 499, 655, 710, 713, 740
Razor 7, 24, 545–546, 578–579, 687, 763, 785
REAMER 579
RECORD 13, 53, 114, 127, 139, 231, 233, 241, 380–381, 579–580, 636
RED WING 580–582
REDWARE 394, 426, 582–585
Regina 360, 491–492, 512
Regout, see Maastricht
Retablo 264
Revolver 68
RICHARD 585
RIDGWAY 585
Ring Tree 41, 368
RIVIERA 586
ROBLIN 586
ROCKINGHAM 56, 586, 787–788
Rogers, see John Rogers
Rolling Pin 11, 135, 366–367, 428, 494, 580, 686, 788
ROOKWOOD 365, 395, 491, 586–594
RORSTRAND 594
Rosaline, see Steuben
ROSE CANTON 594
ROSE MANDARIN 594
ROSE MEDALLION 594
Rose O'Neill, see Kewpie
ROSE TAPESTRY 595, 600
ROSEMEADE 595
ROSENTHAL 595–596
ROSEVILLE 596–599
ROWLAND & MARSELLUS 599
ROY ROGERS 598–600
ROYAL BAYREUTH 595, 600, 658, 689, 718
ROYAL BONN 600
ROYAL COPENHAGEN 601–602
ROYAL COPLEY 602
ROYAL CROWN DERBY 602–603
ROYAL DOULTON 212, 236, 269, 347, 352, 603–607
ROYAL DUX 607–608
ROYAL FLEMISH 608
ROYAL HICKMAN 608
Royal Haeger, see Haeger
Royal Ivy, see Northwood, Royal Ivy
ROYAL NYMPHENBURG 609
Royal Rudolstadt, see Rudolstadt
Royal Vienna, see Beehive
ROYAL WORCESTER 609–610
ROYCROFT 273–275, 279, 287, 296, 303, 309, 312–314, 319–320, 610–611
Rozane, see Roseville
ROZENBURG 611
RRP 161, 611–612, 787
RS GERMANY 612, 717

RS POLAND 612
RS PRUSSIA 612–613
RS SILESIA 613
RS SUHL 613
RS TILLOWITZ 613
RUBINA 440, 504, 613
RUBINA VERDE 613
RUBY GLASS 93, 446–447, 613, 639, 648
RUDOLSTADT 613
RUG 30, 223, 233, 243, 392, 614–617
Ruler 11, 113, 383, 689, 716
RUMRILL 617
RUSKIN 617
RUSSEL WRIGHT 617–618

S

SABINO 447, 618–619
Sadiron 395
Sailor's Valentine 497
SALOPIAN 619
SALT AND PEPPER SHAKER 11, 40, 51–52, 60, 100, 105–106, 127, 162, 165, 175, 186, 189, 193–194, 196–198, 200, 205, 207–209, 211, 213–215, 219, 220, 223, 245, 247–249, 251–252, 266–269, 359, 363, 367, 376, 380, 386, 417, 419, 428, 450, 475, 479, 481, 483, 489, 500, 503, 505, 520, 529, 537, 570–571, 576, 580, 595, 618–619, 634, 647–648, 660, 692, 758, 763–764, 785
SALT GLAZE 30, 83–84, 98, 418, 545, 580, 620, 670, 672, 674, 675, 681–686, 713
Saltshaker 52, 191, 199, 201–203, 205, 210–211, 219–220, 382, 461, 475, 479, 482, 489, 537, 618, 785
Samovar 92, 95
SAMPLER 391, 574, 620–621
SAMSON 621–622, 762
SANDWICH GLASS 65, 109, 153, 525, 622–625
Santa Claus 45–46, 111, 134–137, 154–155, 224, 254, 346, 379, 420, 426, 524, 604, 698
SARREGUEMINES 510, 625
SASCHA BRASTOFF 625–626
SATIN GLASS 168, 183, 394, 443–446, 461, 626, 682, 685, 768, 776
SATSUMA 88, 626
Saturday Evening Girls, see Paul Revere Pottery
SCALE 45, 64, 159, 212, 392, 429, 516, 546, 626–627, 705
SCHAFER & VATER 627
Scarf 24, 53–54, 60, 90, 152, 166, 228, 372, 381, 452, 463, 472–474, 479, 503, 519, 633, 658, 697, 699
SCHNEIDER 627
SCIENTIFIC INSTRUMENT 627–628
Scissors 47, 410, 477, 516, 546, 582, 631, 638, 642, 655, 710, 716
Scoop 8, 63, 114–115, 133, 150, 221, 271, 393, 422, 428, 636, 641, 643, 645, 647, 651, 654, 709–710, 742–743, 745, 748
Screen 58, 11, 13, 32, 35, 126, 141, 150, 154–155, 160, 221, 223, 231, 256, 315, 351, 404, 428, 498, 696, 705, 741, 743, 750
SCRIMSHAW 30, 112, 242–243, 308, 493, 496, 559, 628–629
SEG, see Paul Revere Pottery
SEVRES 1, 88, 90, 109, 147, 437, 440, 519, 550–552, 556–557, 629–630
SEWER TILE 630
SEWING 20, 45, 50, 223, 337, 432, 539, 629, 630–633, 687, 742, 753
SHAKER 58, 273, 279, 287, 301, 314, 323, 337, 632
SHAVING MUG 352, 482, 632–633
SHAWNEE POTTERY 633–634
SHEARWATER 634
SHEET MUSIC 43, 60, 154, 169, 223, 241–242, 455, 488, 495, 546, 634–635
Sheffield, see Silver Plate; Silver-English
SHELLEY 133, 165, 444, 635
SHIRLEY TEMPLE 488, 635–636
Shotgun 18, 102, 633
Shriner, see Fraternal
Sideboard 318–319, 693
Sign 10–21, 36–39, 47, 51, 60, 85, 101, 106, 123, 139, 142, 154–155, 222–223, 359, 379–380, 396, 458, 476, 497, 524, 537, 547, 578, 598, 658, 664, 687–688, 696, 734, 784
Silent Butler 28
Silhouette 18, 109, 221, 273, 352, 455, 469, 515, 529, 534, 569, 598, 616, 715, 766–767
SILVER DEPOSIT 636
SILVER FLATWARE 636–637
SILVER PLATE 93, 100–101, 106–108, 110, 123, 125, 134, 147, 160, 168, 174–175, 177, 384, 394–395, 417, 419, 430, 437, 440, 445–447, 451, 473, 493, 495–496, 507, 513, 520, 525, 543, 550, 571–572, 637–639, 693, 717, 719, 754, 784
Silver, Sheffield, see Silver Plate; Silver-English
SILVER-AMERICAN 639–646
SILVER-ARGENTINEAN 646
SILVER-AUSTRIAN 646–647
SILVER-AUSTRO-HUNGARIAN 647
SILVER-CAMBODIAN 647
SILVER-CANADIAN 647
SILVER-CHINESE 647
SILVER-CONTINENTAL 647
SILVER-CANADIAN 647
SILVER-CZECHOSLOVAKIAN 647
SILVER-DANISH 647
SILVER-DUTCH 647–648
SILVER-EGYPTIAN 648
SILVER-ENGLISH 648–651
SILVER-FRENCH 651
SILVER-GERMAN 651
SILVER-HUNGARIAN 651
SILVER-INDIAN 651
SILVER-IRISH 652
SILVER-ITALIAN 652
SILVER-JAPANESE 652
SILVER-MEXICAN 652–653
SILVER-NORWEGIAN 653
SILVER-PERSIAN 653
SILVER-PERUVIAN 653
SILVER-POLISH 653
SILVER-PORTUGUESE 653
SILVER-RUSSIAN 653–654
SILVER-SCOTTISH 654
SILVER-SPANISH 654
SILVER-STERLING 655–656
SILVER-SWEDISH 656
SILVER-SWISS 656
SILVER-SYRIAN 656
SINCLAIRE 656
Singing Bird 492, 704
Skiing, see Sports
Slag, Caramel, see Imperial Glass
SLAG GLASS 4, 35, 91–92, 365–366, 436–440, 442, 448, 453, 656–658, 701–705, 717, 777
Sled 7, 111, 135–137, 223, 495, 519, 521, 578, 615, 658, 698, 722, 734, 742–743
SLEEPY EYE 657–658
Sleigh 12, 55, 93, 111, 123, 135–137, 144, 272, 302, 451, 531, 721, 743, 777
Slot Machine, see Coin-Operated Machine
SMITH BROTHERS 658
Smoking Set 502
Smoking Stand 138, 705
SNOW BABIES 658–659
Snuff Bottle, see Bottle, Snuff
SNUFFBOX 51, 159, 547, 659, 719, 788
Soap 3–4, 8, 21–22, 25, 39, 53, 221
Soap Dish 399, 417, 450, 490, 686, 694
SOAPSTONE 83, 243, 659–660
Soda Fountain 6, 26, 71, 688
SOFT PASTE 660
SOUVENIR 233, 376, 472, 525, 535, 560, 660–661, 718
SPANGLE GLASS 661
Sparkler 549, 729, 743
SPATTERWARE 661–664
SPELTER 41, 63–64, 108, 145, 395, 453, 523, 537, 664, 700
Spice Box 428–429, 715
SPINNING WHEEL 9, 236, 664–665, 731, 737
SPODE 394, 552, 665
Spoon 63, 82, 91, 100, 106, 125, 129, 139, 150, 165–166, 213, 218, 221, 242–243, 247, 259, 285, 309, 329, 366–367, 372, 374, 385, 387, 393, 402, 417, 425, 429, 465–466, 482, 538, 547, 557, 578, 619, 629, 636–637, 639–640, 642–645, 647–648, 650, 652, 654–655, 660–661, 708, 710, 770, 776
Spooner 29, 100, 119, 176, 246, 252, 373, 379, 487, 560, 562, 565, 639, 658, 719
Spoon Holder 777
SPORTS 1, 5, 229, 258, 352, 452, 515, 559, 665–669, 787
Sprinkler 61, 349, 751
STAFFORDSHIRE 169, 215, 217, 262, 368, 379, 394–395, 397–400, 482, 490, 499, 660–661, 669–672, 713, 765, 778, 785
STANGL 465, 672–673
STAR TREK AND STAR WARS 673–674
STEIN 9, 54, 60, 98, 113, 159, 163, 474, 479–481, 620, 639, 657–658, 661, 674–675
Stein, Mettlach, see Mettlach, Stein

Stencil 4, 7, 41, 85, 89, 258–259, 285, 289, 314, 322, 486, 534, 551, 612, 681, 684–686, 713–715, 717, 730, 745–748
STEREO CARD 675–676
STEREOSCOPE 676
Sterling Silver, see Silver-Sterling
STEUBEN 35–36, 116, 152–153, 572, 611, 676–679, 759
STEVENGRAPH 679–680
STEVENS & WILLIAMS 443, 680
Stickpin 21, 352, 416, 547
STIEGEL TYPE 680
Still 42, 512, 534, 569, 699
STONE 27, 33, 83, 92, 131, 263–264, 336, 345, 347–349, 367, 389, 392, 400, 403, 408–409, 413, 415, 418, 466, 581, 681, 732
STONEWARE 11, 20, 236–237, 474, 580, 607, 611, 674, 681–686, 700, 773
STORE 3, 7, 9–12, 102–103, 123, 142, 531, 615, 686–688, 735, 739, 749–750, 780
STOVE 688
Stretch Glass 249, 387, 504, 688
SULPHIDE 41, 468, 517, 688
SUMIDA 688
SUNBONNET BABIES 689
SUNDERLAND 338, 689
Sundial 349, 763
SUPERMAN 673, 689–690
SUSIE COOPER 690
SWANKYSWIG 690
SWASTIKA KERAMOS 690
Sweeper 223–225, 424, 732, 744
SWORD 9, 95, 139, 243, 269, 400, 402–404, 430–431, 477, 515, 542, 569, 628, 664, 690–691, 701, 780
Symphonion 45, 148, 491–493
SYRACUSE 691–692

T
Tapestry, Porcelain, see Rose Tapestry
TEA CADDY 237, 626, 645, 647, 650–651, 692–693, 711, 715, 719
TEA LEAF IRONSTONE 693–694
TECO 694
TEDDY BEAR 4, 46, 161, 233, 241, 421, 533, 542, 695, 745
TELEPHONE 111, 155, 223, 228, 261, 322–323, 521, 611, 619, 695–696, 745, 747
Telescope 112, 498, 547, 627, 628, 716, 767
Television 15, 103, 380, 441, 673, 696, 745, 748, 751
TEPLITZ 696–697
TERRA-COTTA 31–33, 60, 166, 349, 360, 391, 481, 590, 697–698, 713, 718, 730, 770–772, 775
TEXTILE 546–547, 698–699
THERMOMETER 47–48, 92, 155, 522, 524, 627, 700–701, 705
Thermos 34, 46, 53, 179, 223, 352, 380, 459, 460, 520–521, 548, 600, 673, 689
Thimble 39, 548, 631–632
TIFFANY 116, 148–149, 176, 347, 352, 364, 394, 413, 437, 488, 636, 640, 648, 667, 701–711, 761–762, 786, 787
TIFFIN 711
TILE 29, 33, 50, 61, 166, 187, 225, 360–361, 380, 418, 459, 469, 476, 483, 486, 520, 527, 547, 589–590, 678, 703–704, 707, 711–712, 757, 760, 772, 777
Tintype 531, 533, 538, 547
TINWARE 712–713
Toaster 154, 429, 745
Toast Rack 133–134, 548, 639, 650, 711
Tobacco Cutter 25, 688
TOBACCO JAR 2, 56, 61, 159, 187, 366, 466, 527, 590, 600, 626, 713, 772–773, 775
TOBY JUG 56–58, 83, 547, 610, 713, 788
Toilet 9–10, 16, 68, 362, 493, 675–676, 708
TOLE 339, 659, 693, 713–715
TOM MIX 715–716
Tongs 28, 125, 150, 162, 253, 396, 429, 632, 636–638, 645–646, 650, 652, 654, 708, 710, 717, 749
TOOL 90, 92, 425, 716–717
TOOTHBRUSH HOLDER 182, 223, 399, 694, 717–718
TOOTHPICK HOLDER 717–718
Torchere 93, 108, 446–447, 678, 718
TORQUAY 718–719
TORTOISESHELL 33, 88, 90, 312–313, 357, 359, 413, 437, 449, 452, 507, 521, 556, 659, 692–693, 718–719
Towel 95, 231, 342, 429, 699, 783
TOY 51, 53, 61, 98–99, 101, 114, 129, 135, 155, 166–167, 179, 182, 212, 223–226, 232, 244, 261, 344, 364, 376, 379–382, 455, 458, 508, 524, 548–549, 564–566, 600, 622, 625, 665, 674, 689–690, 695, 716, 719–752, 785
Tractor Seat 717
Trade Stimulator 135, 158
Train 17, 23, 143, 147–149, 154, 169, 223–224, 406, 474, 512, 539, 546, 578, 735, 739, 746–747, 785
TRAMP ART 752–753
TRAP 259, 753
Tray 1, 5–6, 8, 25–26, 28–29, 31, 34–35, 44, 49, 51, 61, 87–92, 95, 98, 101, 104–106, 108, 110, 113, 119–121, 125, 127, 133, 138, 150, 155–156, 159, 164, 171, 173, 176, 186, 192, 194–195, 197, 199–201, 207, 209–210, 221, 238, 241–242, 246–247, 251–252, 257, 264–265, 268, 307–308, 323–324, 329, 331–332, 334–339, 341, 345, 352–353, 359, 372–376, 379, 382, 385–386, 388, 393–395, 399, 403–404, 417, 420–421, 424, 432, 436, 446–447, 452–453, 459, 461, 463, 465–466, 471, 476, 478–479, 481–482, 486, 493–494, 500, 502, 507, 511, 514, 517, 519, 523–524, 529, 536, 547, 551, 556–557, 559, 560–562, 576, 583, 589–590, 594, 600, 611–613, 618, 625, 630–631, 637–639, 641–642, 644–650, 652–654, 656, 661, 673, 687, 694, 699–700, 702, 704–705, 709, 711, 713–715, 717, 753–754, 757, 760, 766, 771–772, 782–783, 785
Treen, see Wooden
TRENCH ART 753
TRIVET 31, 92, 164, 186, 225, 269, 362, 380, 424, 429, 474, 500, 507, 576, 590, 672, 753–754
Truck 17, 38, 77, 155, 167, 223, 225, 448, 516, 524, 549, 633, 728, 732–733, 737, 739, 742, 747–751
TRUNK 39, 139, 225, 547, 740, 751, 754–755
T-Shirt 600
TUTHILL 173, 176, 755
TYPEWRITER 751, 755

U
UHL 755
UMBRELLA 59, 72,75, 93, 98, 132, 135, 164, 235–236, 307, 341, 380, 385, 402, 466, 472–474, 505, 516, 556, 597–598, 630, 663, 674, 687, 698, 737, 740, 755–756, 773–775
Umbrella Stand 93, 98, 132, 164, 307, 341, 385, 466, 473–474, 556, 597–598, 630, 773–775
Uncle Sam 5, 25, 45–46, 114, 137, 158, 236, 265, 346, 541, 543, 619, 674, 756, 781, 784–785
Uniform 91, 106, 111, 139, 151, 154, 233, 512, 518, 538, 666, 668, 670, 721, 732, 738, 784
UNION PORCELAIN WORKS 510, 756
UNIVERSITY CITY 756

V
VAL ST. LAMBERT 756
Valentine 115, 129, 497, 543, 567, 689
VALLERYSTHAL 756
VAN BRIGGLE 757
VASA MURRHINA 249, 757–758
VASELINE GLASS 758
Venetian Glass, see Glass-Venetian
Vienna, see Beehive
VERLYS 377, 758
VERNON KILNS 222, 758–759
VERRE DE SOIE 679, 759
VIENNA ART 759
VILLEROY & BOCH 759
Violin 53, 68, 113, 222, 226, 348, 453, 493, 589, 656, 722, 729–730, 736, 743
VOLKMAR 760
VOLKSTEDT 149, 760

W
WADE 99, 222, 472, 665, 760
Waffle Iron 429
Wagon 1, 15–16, 18, 25, 42, 55, 77, 87, 90, 111, 135, 143, 224, 269, 333, 381, 460, 472, 531, 542, 546, 549, 575, 600, 615, 633, 716–717, 725–728, 730, 733, 736, 739, 745–746, 750–752
Wahpeton Pottery, see Rosemeade
Wallace Nutting photographs are listed under Print, Nutting. His reproduction furniture is listed under Furniture
Wallpaper 18, 86–90, 515, 630–631, 731
WALL POCKET 1, 31, 47, 50, 104, 164, 186, 264, 351, 382, 393, 466, 471, 475,

478, 503, 505, 535, 576, 582, 585, 594, 596–600, 602, 608, 625, 634, 753, 760, 773–774, 776
WALRATH 760
Walt Disney, see Disneyana
Walter, see A. Walter
WARWICK 255, 378, 760
Wash Board 429
Washbowl 56, 182, 454, 732
Washing Machine 164, 225, 752
Washstand 341–342
Washtub 479, 752
WATCH 14, 19, 21, 25, 93, 95, 99, 112, 142, 167, 225, 352, 395, 547, 560, 667, 687–688, 753, 761–763, 783, 785–786
WATCH FOB 225, 547, 763
Watch Holder 95
WATERFORD 211, 763
Watering Can 93, 225, 241–242, 350, 471, 505, 528, 549
WATT 86, 148, 764–765, 787
WAVE CREST 494, 765–766
WEATHER VANE 13, 142, 766–768
WEBB 768
WEBB BURMESE 768–769
WEBB PEACHBLOW 769
WEDGWOOD 397–398, 490, 769–773
WELLER 773–776
WESTMORELAND 445, 776–777
Whale's Tooth 629
WHEATLEY 777
Wheelbarrow 55, 137, 361, 456, 717, 740, 752
WHEELING 777
WHIELDON 777
Whirligig 37, 84, 155, 224, 264–265, 582, 729, 781
Whiskbroom 39, 536, 766
Whistle 7, 21, 91–92, 129, 547, 555, 578, 585, 610, 715, 736, 738, 740, 752
WILLETS 777–778
WILLOW 351, 393, 483, 521, 599, 609, 616, 778
Windmill Weight 396
WINDOW 778
Windup 346, 364, 380–381, 492, 508, 530, 548–549, 689–690, 719–752, 786
Wine Set 119, 121, 386, 500, 763
WOOD CARVING 158, 264, 778–781
WOODEN 89, 111, 136–137, 155, 184, 259, 264, 346, 482, 528, 626, 628, 631, 648, 650, 743, 781–783
WORCESTER 784
WORLD WAR I & II 91, 521, 547, 675, 784
WORLD'S FAIR 25, 91, 159, 198, 269, 660, 676, 745, 750, 784–785
WPA 786
Wrench 488
WRISTWATCH 53, 114, 212, 225, 352, 382, 458, 508, 521, 537, 600, 667, 674, 690, 761, 786–787

Y

YELLOWWARE 31, 395, 483, 586, 787–788

Z

ZANE 788
ZANESVILLE 69, 71, 168, 788
ZSOLNAY 788

Picture Credits

Alderfer Auction Co.: 107, 113–115, 152, 169, 220, 226–230, 233, 237, 245, 250–252, 269, 313, 337, 390, 407–408, 413–416, 420, 430–431, 456, 536, 539, 569, 576–577, 635, 666, 689, 732, 734, 762
Auction Team Koln: 123, 497, 505, 532, 696, 755
Bertoia Auctions: 7, 17, 110–111, 129, 134, 136–137, 157, 222, 224, 233–235, 350, 452, 549, 719, 721–723, 726, 728, 730–734, 736–738, 740, 744–747, 750–751
Brunk Auctions: 2, 31, 40, 55, 88, 90, 95, 97–98, 107–108, 130–132, 140, 144, 146–147, 149–150, 163, 181, 187, 239, 256–257, 270, 273, 276, 279–282, 287–289, 291–293, 295–296, 298–302, 304–306, 312, 314, 316–317, 320–321, 328– 330, 333–334, 338–339, 342, 345, 348, 350, 366, 384–385, 388, 391, 393, 395, 399, 401, 406, 409–415, 430–432, 434, 437, 439, 448, 460, 464, 467, 477– 479, 492, 496, 513, 518, 521–522, 526, 529, 533–534, 556, 568, 594, 602, 610, 614, 616, 622, 626, 628–629, 636–644, 646–651, 654–656, 668, 677, 681, 683–685, 688–689, 691–692, 699, 707, 709–711, 714, 762, 766–767, 770, 781–783, 786
Belhorn Auction Services: 1, 29, 51, 62, 103, 167, 185, 270–271, 362–363, 382–383, 419, 473–475, 491, 508–509, 519, 527, 532–533, 535–537, 556–558, 581, 590–591, 593, 596–599, 611, 618, 634, 672, 690, 712, 772–775, 777, 788
Conestoga Auction Co.: 2, 3, 19, 32, 49–50, 54, 86–87, 89–90, 108–110, 113, 127–128, 151, 153, 156, 166, 168–169, 183, 185, 255– 256, 258, 262, 265, 273, 279, 291, 293–294, 296, 300–301, 304, 309, 313–314, 321, 337, 347, 349, 388, 396, 421–422, 424–429, 442, 446, 449, 472, 483–484, 491, 496, 512, 515, 528–529, 534, 555, 574, 582–586, 615, 620, 630–632, 661–665, 669–672, 681–682, 684, 686–687, 713–718, 722, 731, 736, 743, 753–754, 761, 763, 782–783, 787–788
Cincinnati Art Galleries: 61–62, 186, 240–241, 343, 450, 459, 485, 504, 585, 587–594, 627, 690
Cowan's Auctions: 28, 30, 53, 56, 68, 99, 182, 254, 264, 275, 304–305, 311, 318, 387, 389, 392, 398, 460, 476, 484, 507, 517, 531–532, 540, 543, 628, 633, 676, 691, 718, 759, 779–780
Copake Auction: 58
DuMouchelles: 30, 36, 40, 82, 96, 132–133, 353, 400, 432, 451, 477, 550, 571, 578, 602, 604–606, 636, 677–679, 698, 709, 758, 764, 778
Early Auction Co.: 29, 57, 100, 106, 164, 168, 173, 239, 270, 358, 440, 449, 456–457, 513–514, 520, 539, 573, 659, 676–680, 708, 768–769, 770
Eastbourne Auction: 57, 141, 153, 606–609

Garth's Auctions: 47–48, 55, 59, 63, 91, 163, 269, 272, 275–276, 278, 281, 285, 291–292, 300, 307–309, 322–324, 327–328, 336, 338, 377, 393, 398, 401–402, 499, 516, 528, 535, 540, 606, 608, 620, 630, 660, 767, 782
Green Valley Auctions & Jeffrey S. Evans: 60, 112, 133, 140, 167, 170, 352–356, 379, 394, 411, 443–446, 448, 461, 471, 481–482, 489, 507, 560–567, 622–625, 656, 660, 718, 756, 764, 784–786
Glass Works Auctions: 65–81, 83–85, 253, 394–395, 425, 581, 785
Heritage Auction Galleries: 41, 53, 108, 115–116, 308, 352, 356, 458, 488, 498–499, 516, 539, 542–547, 637, 639, 650, 654, 666–668, 673, 761, 763
Hake's Americana & Collectibles: 51, 53, 58, 114, 212, 521, 539–542, 544–546, 690, 715–718, 763, 787
Jackson's International Auctioneers: 35, 54, 83, 88, 93, 95, 99, 105, 108–109, 117–122, 124, 126, 138, 140, 142–144, 146, 149–151, 165, 179–182, 238, 242–243, 255, 284, 286, 290, 294, 297, 303, 305–307, 312–313, 316–317, 319, 321, 325, 329, 331, 340, 342, 348, 350, 356–357, 360, 362, 366, 378, 383–384, 388, 390–391, 394, 405, 408–409, 411, 416, 423, 431, 436–442, 444–445, 447–448, 454, 463, 465–466, 468–469, 472, 480, 485–486, 490–493, 502–503, 517, 520, 522–523, 530–531, 535, 537, 551, 553, 578, 601, 606–607, 621, 630, 647, 652–653, 655, 657–658, 665, 667, 670, 680, 686–687, 692, 697–698, 701, 708–709, 715, 752, 759, 768, 779–780, 784
James D. Julia Auctioneers: 29, 36, 100, 135, 148, 161, 164, 353, 379, 434–437, 442, 445–446, 452, 455, 486–487, 489, 494, 514, 517, 573, 609, 676, 679, 702, 705, 769, 772, 784
Lang's Sporting Collectables: 30, 183, 258–261
Leland Little Auctions: 107, 112, 140, 142, 274–275, 277, 282, 285, 299, 319, 322, 453, 533–534, 621–622, 640–641, 645, 647–648, 651–653
Monsen & Baer: 178–179, 525–526
Morphy Auctions: 1, 3–16, 18–26, 33, 37–39, 42, 44–45, 51, 54, 63–64, 101, 109, 111, 114, 116, 119, 122–123, 126, 129, 136–137, 139, 143, 154–155, 157–158, 179, 221–225, 228–229, 231–232, 235–237, 264, 269, 307, 345, 347, 364, 380, 396, 405, 408–409, 411, 418–419, 428, 441, 455, 458, 468, 471, 495, 523–524,–538, 548–549, 554–555, 575–576, 599, 635, 673, 695, 700–701, 703, 713, 715–717, 719–727, 729–731, 733–752, 767, 785
Noel Barrett Antiques & Auctions: 212, 261, 723
Neal Auction Co.: 32, 89, 94, 96, 126–127, 172, 244, 272, 274, 278, 280, 284, 297, 301, 306, 309, 311, 315–316, 323–324, 329, 410–411, 460, 469, 482, 515, 518, 526, 550–551, 571, 595, 609, 626, 651, 653, 655, 661, 683, 754, 787
Richard Opfer Auctioneering: 40, 128, 135, 362, 364, 381, 494, 504, 559, 579, 600, 603
Pook & Pook: 41, 48–49, 56, 86, 88, 90, 110–111, 128, 139, 143, 145, 148, 163, 166, 168, 187, 239, 253, 264–265, 275, 290, 293, 300, 302, 306, 319, 337, 346, 351, 380, 397, 401, 407, 421, 423–424, 427, 429, 483, 503, 515, 574–575, 584, 615, 619, 632, 644, 652, 664, 670–671, 682, 686–687, 692, 696, 754, 767, 781
Rago Arts & Auction Center/Sollo Rago Modern Auctions: 1, 34– 35, 60, 92, 96, 106, 112, 148, 150, 162, 180, 185, 221, 240, 242, 254, 270–271, 277, 283, 285–286, 294, 299, 303, 306–307, 310, 312, 315, 318, 320–321, 330, 333, 341–343, 345, 361, 365–366, 414, 433–435, 438–439, 441–443, 457, 469–470, 490, 496, 501, 506, 509, 519, 529, 557–558, 568, 586–587, 591–594, 602, 610–611, 617, 627, 648, 694, 697, 699, 702–706, 708, 712, 756–757, 760, 768–769, 775, 778, 788
Ruby Lane: 7, 27–28, 52, 61, 104–105, 125, 127, 133, 137, 152, 160–161, 165, 182, 186, 188–221, 230–231, 233, 239, 242, 246–250, 262–263, 266–268, 360–361, 363, 367–370, 374–378, 385–386, 398–399, 406, 411, 417, 450, 475, 493, 500, 511–512, 521, 553, 571–572, 579–580, 595, 604, 619, 635, 711, 758, 764–765, 776–777, 785–786
Rich Penn Auctions: 4–5, 15, 26, 72, 79, 85, 124, 129, 158, 162, 325, 395, 397, 426–428, 453–454, 476, 523, 538, 576, 599, 626, 633, 657, 688, 700, 717, 759, 766
RSL Auction Co.: 42–46
Stein Auction Co.: 674
Skinner: 27, 56, 82, 94, 96–98, 105–106, 141, 149, 153, 159–160, 170, 179, 184, 226, 238, 241, 244, 257, 325, 327, 334, 346, 357, 400, 402–404, 413, 416–417, 430, 451, 454, 456, 460, 477, 480, 483, 486, 490, 498–499, 508, 518, 521, 552, 559, 603, 617, 629, 636, 646, 659, 670, 672, 674–675, 693, 713, 768, 770–772, 779
Sotheby's: 211, 284, 286, 295, 335, 692–693
Showtime Auction Services: 2, 4–5, 10, 16, 25, 31, 37, 41, 47, 54, 91, 101–103, 124–126, 223, 244, 381, 397, 418, 425, 471–473, 494, 524, 536, 626, 632, 688–689, 696, 765–766
Strawser Auctions: 98, 162, 250, 462–466, 510
Treadway Gallery: 1, 28, 35–36, 99, 103, 107, 141, 145, 151, 162, 181, 241, 271, 274–275, 279–280, 283, 287–290, 303, 306, 310, 313, 315–316, 318–320, 322–323, 326–328, 331–332, 340, 343–344, 358–359, 365, 372–373, 385, 392, 406, 412, 415–416, 435, 440, 457–458, 479, 501–502, 504, 508, 553, 558, 570, 587–588, 590, 611, 614, 617–618, 627, 640, 645, 694, 705, 707, 712, 757, 760, 777
Tom Harris Auctions: 29, 39, 53, 59, 63, 93–94, 117–121, 124, 134, 232, 245, 247, 360, 363–364, 371, 383, 466, 613, 618, 656, 716–717
Woody Auction Co.: 40, 117, 167, 171–177, 272, 357, 370–371, 450, 452, 464, 486–489, 510, 513–514, 525, 601, 612–613, 660

Kovels' Antiques & Collectibles Price Guide 2010

America's bestselling antiques annual is new every year with ACTUAL prices recorded during the year—*never* estimates. It lists more prices than any other guide on the market, and organizes them for easy pricing and collecting on the go. Use the price guide as a companion to the website and the iPhone application—no pricing information is ever repeated and the guide is a quick reference with thousands of color photographs so you can see what collectors are buying.

Kovels' price guides give collectors the insider's edge!

For more than 50 years, Kovels' price guides, newsletters, syndicated columns, TV shows, and website have been <u>the</u> ultimate sources for reliable information about antiques & collectibles— go to Kovels.com to learn more

The Kovels' iPhone App

The Kovels' iPhone App is another great way to explore the world of antiques and collectibles. While the website provides history and context and *Kovels' Antiques & Collectibles Price Guide 2010* contains organized, actual prices from the past year, the Kovels' App allows access to the latest information from the Kovels and puts expert Kovels advice at your fingertips anywhere you happen to be—whether at an estate sale, an auction, or the local antiques shop.

Visit Kovels.com or Apple's App store to download your Kovels App for the iPhone or iTouch today and put the expertise of Kovels in the palm of your hand.